Official 2014 National Football League
Record & Fact Book

NATIONAL FOOTBALL LEAGUE
345 Park Avenue, New York, N.Y. 10154 (212) 450-2000. NFL Internet Address: http://www.NFL.com

Printed in the United States of America.

A National Football League Book.

Compiled by the NFL Communications Department and Seymour Siwoff, Elias Sports Bureau.
Statistics by Elias Sports Bureau.

Edited by Jon Zimmer and Brenden Lee, NFL Communications Department, and Matt Marini. Layout by William Tham.
Cover photo: Quarterback Russell Wilson of the Super Bowl XLVIII champion Seattle Seahawks.
Cover photography by AP Images. Design by NFL Creative.

Time
HOME ENTERTAINMENT

Time Home Entertainment Inc.
1271 Avenue of the Americas, New York, N.Y. 10020
Manufactured in the United States of America.
First printing, July 2014.
10 9 8 7 6 5 4 3 2 1

TABLE OF CONTENTS

TABLE OF CONTENTS

All times local. Dates and times subject to change.
Nationally televised games indicated by network in parentheses.

Sunday, August 3	NFL/Hall of Fame Game at Canton, Ohio		
	New York Giants _____ vs. Buffalo _____	(NBC) 8:00

PRESEASON/WEEK 1

Thursday, August 7	Indianapolis _____ at New York Jets _____	7:00
	San Francisco _____ at Baltimore _____	7:30
	New England _____ at Washington _____	7:30
	Cincinnati _____ at Kansas City _____	7:00
	Seattle _____ at Denver _____	7:00
	Dallas _____ at San Diego _____	7:00
Friday, August 8	Miami _____ at Atlanta _____	7:00
	Buffalo _____ at Carolina _____	7:30
	Tampa Bay _____ at Jacksonville _____	7:30
	Philadelphia _____ at Chicago _____	7:00
	Oakland _____ at Minnesota _____	7:00
	New Orleans _____ at St. Louis _____	7:00
Saturday, August 9	Cleveland _____ at Detroit _____	7:30
	Pittsburgh _____ at New York Giants _____	7:30
	Green Bay _____ at Tennessee _____	7:00
	Houston _____ at Arizona _____	5:30

PRESEASON/WEEK 2

Thursday, August 14	Jacksonville _____ at Chicago _____	(ESPN) 7:00
Friday, August 15	Philadelphia _____ at New England _____	7:30
	Tennessee _____ at New Orleans _____	7:00
	Detroit _____ at Oakland _____	7:00
	San Diego _____ at Seattle _____	7:00
Saturday, August 16	Green Bay _____ at St. Louis _____	3:00
	New York Jets _____ at Cincinnati _____	7:00
	Baltimore _____ at Dallas _____	6:00
	New York Giants _____ at Indianapolis _____	7:00
	Buffalo _____ at Pittsburgh _____	7:30
	Miami _____ at Tampa Bay _____	7:30
	Atlanta _____ at Houston _____	7:00
	Arizona _____ at Minnesota _____	7:30
Sunday, August 17	Denver _____ at San Francisco _____	1:00
	Kansas City _____ at Carolina _____	(FOX) 8:00
Monday, August 18	Cleveland _____ at Washington _____	(ESPN) 8:00

PRESEASON/WEEK 3

Thursday, August 21	Pittsburgh _____ at Philadelphia _____	7:30
Friday, August 22	Oakland _____ at Green Bay _____	(CBS) 7:00
	Jacksonville _____ at Detroit _____	7:30
	Carolina _____ at New England _____	7:30
	New York Giants _____ at New York Jets _____	7:30
	Chicago _____ at Seattle _____	7:00
Saturday, August 23	New Orleans _____ at Indianapolis _____	(CBS) 8:00
	Tampa Bay _____ at Buffalo _____	4:30
	Dallas _____ at Miami _____	7:00
	Tennessee _____ at Atlanta _____	7:00
	Washington _____ at Baltimore _____	7:30
	St. Louis _____ at Cleveland _____	8:00
	Minnesota _____ at Kansas City _____	7:00
	Houston _____ at Denver _____	7:00
Sunday, August 24	San Diego _____ at San Francisco _____	(FOX) 1:00
	Cincinnati _____ at Arizona _____	(NBC) 5:00

PRESEASON/WEEK 4

Thursday, August 28

Atlanta _____ at Jacksonville _____	6:00
Detroit _____ at Buffalo _____	7:00
Indianapolis _____ at Cincinnati _____	7:00
Kansas City _____ at Green Bay _____	6:00
St. Louis _____ at Miami _____	7:00
New York Jets _____ at Philadelphia _____	7:00
New England _____ at New York Giants _____	7:30
Carolina _____ at Pittsburgh _____	7:30
Washington _____ at Tampa Bay _____	7:30
Chicago _____ at Cleveland _____	8:00
Denver _____ at Dallas _____	7:00
San Francisco _____ at Houston _____	7:00
Baltimore _____ at New Orleans _____	7:00
Minnesota _____ at Tennessee _____	7:00
Seattle _____ at Oakland _____	7:00
Arizona _____ at San Diego _____	7:00

KICKOFF 2014 NFL

KICKOFF WEEKEND

Thursday, September 4
Sunday, September 7
FOX-TV National Weekend

Green Bay _____ at Seattle _____	(NBC) 5:30
New Orleans _____ at Atlanta _____	1:00
Cincinnati _____ at Baltimore _____	1:00
Buffalo _____ at Chicago _____	12:00
Washington _____ at Houston _____	12:00
Tennessee _____ at Kansas City _____	12:00
New England _____ at Miami _____	1:00
Oakland _____ at New York Jets _____	1:00
Jacksonville _____ at Philadelphia _____	1:00
Cleveland _____ at Pittsburgh _____	1:00
Minnesota _____ at St. Louis _____	12:00
San Francisco _____ at Dallas _____	3:25
Carolina _____ at Tampa Bay _____	4:25
Indianapolis _____ at Denver _____	(NBC) 6:30

Monday, September 8

New York Giants _____ at Detroit _____	(ESPN) 7:10
San Diego _____ at Arizona _____	(ESPN) 7:20

SECOND WEEK

Thursday, September 11
Sunday, September 14
CBS-TV National Weekend

Pittsburgh _____ at Baltimore _____	(CBS) 8:25
Miami _____ at Buffalo _____	1:00
Detroit _____ at Carolina _____	1:00
Atlanta _____ at Cincinnati _____	1:00
New Orleans _____ at Cleveland _____	1:00
New England _____ at Minnesota _____	12:00
Arizona _____ at New York Giants _____	1:00
Dallas _____ at Tennessee _____	12:00
Jacksonville _____ at Washington _____	1:00
Seattle _____ at San Diego _____	1:05
St. Louis _____ at Tampa Bay _____	4:05
Kansas City _____ at Denver _____	2:25
New York Jets _____ at Green Bay _____	3:25
Houston _____ at Oakland _____	1:25
Chicago _____ at San Francisco _____	(NBC) 5:30

Monday, September 15 Philadelphia _____ at Indianapolis _____ (ESPN) 8:30

THIRD WEEK

Thursday, September 18
Sunday, September 21
CBS-TV National Weekend

Tampa Bay _____ at Atlanta _____	(CBS) 8:25
San Diego _____ at Buffalo _____	1:00
Tennessee _____ at Cincinnati _____	1:00
Baltimore _____ at Cleveland _____	1:00
Green Bay _____ at Detroit _____	1:00
Indianapolis _____ at Jacksonville _____	1:00
Oakland _____ at New England _____	1:00
Minnesota _____ at New Orleans _____	12:00
Houston _____ at New York Giants _____	1:00
Washington _____ at Philadelphia _____	1:00
Dallas _____ at St. Louis _____	12:00
San Francisco _____ at Arizona _____	1:05
Kansas City _____ at Miami _____	4:25
Denver _____ at Seattle _____	1:25
Pittsburgh _____ at Carolina _____	(NBC) 8:30

Monday, September 22 Chicago _____ at New York Jets _____ (ESPN) 8:30

FOURTH WEEK
Open Date: Arizona, Cincinnati,
Cleveland, Denver,
St. Louis, Seattle

Thursday, September 25	New York Giants _____ at Washington _____	(CBS)	8:25
Sunday, September 28	Carolina _____ at Baltimore _____		1:00
FOX-TV National Weekend	Green Bay _____ at Chicago _____		12:00
	Buffalo _____ at Houston _____		12:00
	Tennessee _____ at Indianapolis _____		1:00
	Detroit _____ at New York Jets _____		1:00
	Miami _____ at Oakland (London) _____		6:00
	Tampa Bay _____ at Pittsburgh _____		1:00
	Jacksonville _____ at San Diego _____		1:05
	Atlanta _____ at Minnesota _____		3:25
	Philadelphia _____ at San Francisco _____		1:25
	New Orleans _____ at Dallas _____	(NBC)	7:30
Monday, September 29	New England _____ at Kansas City _____	(ESPN)	7:30

FIFTH WEEK
Open Date: Miami, Oakland

Thursday, October 2	Minnesota _____ at Green Bay _____	(CBS)	7:25
Sunday, October 5	Chicago _____ at Carolina _____		1:00
CBS-TV National Weekend	Houston _____ at Dallas _____		12:00
	Buffalo _____ at Detroit _____		1:00
	Baltimore _____ at Indianapolis _____		1:00
	Pittsburgh _____ at Jacksonville _____		1:00
	Tampa Bay _____ at New Orleans _____		12:00
	Atlanta _____ at New York Giants _____		1:00
	St. Louis _____ at Philadelphia _____		1:00
	Cleveland _____ at Tennessee _____		12:00
	Arizona _____ at Denver _____		2:05
	New York Jets _____ at San Diego _____		1:25
	Kansas City _____ at San Francisco _____		1:25
	Cincinnati _____ at New England _____	(NBC)	*8:30
Monday, October 6	Seattle _____ at Washington _____	(ESPN)	8:30

Sunday Night Games In Weeks 5-16 Subject to Change

SIXTH WEEK
Open Date: Kansas City, New Orleans

Thursday, October 9	Indianapolis _____ at Houston _____	(CBS)	7:25
Sunday, October 12	Chicago _____ at Atlanta _____		1:00
FOX-TV National Weekend	New England _____ at Buffalo _____		1:00
	Carolina _____ at Cincinnati _____		1:00
	Pittsburgh _____ at Cleveland _____		1:00
	Green Bay _____ at Miami _____		1:00
	Detroit _____ at Minnesota _____		12:00
	Denver _____ at New York Jets _____		1:00
	Baltimore _____ at Tampa Bay _____		1:00
	Jacksonville _____ at Tennessee _____		12:00
	San Diego _____ at Oakland _____		1:05
	Washington _____ at Arizona _____		1:25
	Dallas _____ at Seattle _____		1:25
	New York Giants _____ at Philadelphia _____	(NBC)	*8:30
Monday, October 13	San Francisco _____ at St. Louis _____	(ESPN)	7:30

Sunday Night Games In Weeks 5-16 Subject to Change

SEVENTH WEEK
Open Date: Philadelphia, Tampa Bay

Thursday, October 16	New York Jets _____ at New England _____	(CBS)	8:25
Sunday, October 19	Atlanta _____ at Baltimore _____		1:00
FOX-TV National Weekend	Minnesota _____ at Buffalo _____		1:00
	Miami _____ at Chicago _____		12:00
	New Orleans _____ at Detroit _____		1:00
	Carolina _____ at Green Bay _____		12:00
	Cincinnati _____ at Indianapolis _____		1:00
	Cleveland _____ at Jacksonville _____		1:00
	Seattle _____ at St. Louis _____		12:00
	Tennessee _____ at Washington _____		1:00
	Kansas City _____ at San Diego _____		1:05
	New York Giants _____ at Dallas _____		3:25
	Arizona _____ at Oakland _____		1:25
	San Francisco _____ at Denver _____	(NBC)	*6:30
Monday, October 20	Houston _____ at Pittsburgh _____	(ESPN)	8:30

Sunday Night Games In Weeks 5-16 Subject to Change

EIGHTH WEEK
Open Date: New York Giants,
San Francisco

Thursday, October 23	San Diego _____ at Denver _____	(CBS) 6:25
Sunday, October 26	Detroit _____ at Atlanta (London) _____	1:30
CBS-TV National Weekend	Seattle _____ at Carolina _____	1:00
	Baltimore _____ at Cincinnati _____	1:00
	Miami _____ at Jacksonville _____	1:00
	St. Louis _____ at Kansas City _____	12:00
	Chicago _____ at New England _____	1:00
	Buffalo _____ at New York Jets _____	1:00
	Minnesota _____ at Tampa Bay _____	1:00
	Houston _____ at Tennessee _____	12:00
	Philadelphia _____ at Arizona _____	1:05
	Oakland _____ at Cleveland _____	4:25
	Indianapolis _____ at Pittsburgh _____	4:25
	Green Bay _____ at New Orleans _____	(NBC) *7:30
Monday, October 27	Washington _____ at Dallas _____	(ESPN) 7:30

Sunday Night Games In Weeks 5-16 Subject to Change

NINTH WEEK
Open Date: Atlanta, Buffalo, Chicago,
Detroit, Green Bay, Tennessee

Thursday, October 30	New Orleans _____ at Carolina _____	(NFLN) 8:25
Sunday, November 2	Jacksonville _____ at Cincinnati _____	1:00
CBS-TV National Weekend	Tampa Bay _____ at Cleveland _____	1:00
	Arizona _____ at Dallas _____	12:00
	Philadelphia _____ at Houston _____	12:00
	New York Jets _____ at Kansas City _____	12:00
	San Diego _____ at Miami _____	1:00
	Washington _____ at Minnesota _____	12:00
	St. Louis _____ at San Francisco _____	1:05
	Denver _____ at New England _____	4:25
	Oakland _____ at Seattle _____	1:25
	Baltimore _____ at Pittsburgh _____	(NBC) *8:30
Monday, November 3	Indianapolis _____ at New York Giants _____	(ESPN) 8:30

Sunday Night Games In Weeks 5-16 Subject to Change

TENTH WEEK
Open Date: Houston, Indianapolis,
Minnesota, New England,
San Diego, Washington

Thursday, November 6	Cleveland _____ at Cincinnati _____	(NFLN) 8:25
Sunday, November 9	Tennessee _____ at Baltimore _____	1:00
FOX-TV National Weekend	Kansas City _____ at Buffalo _____	1:00
	Miami _____ at Detroit _____	1:00
	Dallas _____ at Jacksonville (London) _____	6:00
	San Francisco _____ at New Orleans _____	12:00
	Pittsburgh _____ at New York Jets _____	1:00
	Atlanta _____ at Tampa Bay _____	1:00
	Denver _____ at Oakland _____	1:05
	St. Louis _____ at Arizona _____	2:25
	New York Giants _____ at Seattle _____	1:25
	Chicago _____ at Green Bay _____	(NBC) *7:30
Monday, November 10	Carolina _____ at Philadelphia _____	(ESPN) 8:30

Sunday Night Games In Weeks 5-16 Subject to Change

ELEVENTH WEEK
Open Date: Baltimore, Dallas,
Jacksonville, New York Jets

Thursday, November 13	Buffalo _____ at Miami _____	(NFLN) 8:25
Sunday, November 16	Atlanta _____ at Carolina _____	1:00
FOX-TV National Weekend	Minnesota _____ at Chicago _____	12:00
	Houston _____ at Cleveland _____	1:00
	Philadelphia _____ at Green Bay _____	12:00
	Seattle _____ at Kansas City _____	12:00
	Cincinnati _____ at New Orleans _____	12:00
	San Francisco _____ at New York Giants _____	1:00
	Denver _____ at St. Louis _____	12:00
	Tampa Bay _____ at Washington _____	1:00
	Oakland _____ at San Diego _____	1:05
	Detroit _____ at Arizona _____	2:25
	New England _____ at Indianapolis _____	(NBC) *8:30
Monday, November 17	Pittsburgh _____ at Tennessee _____	(ESPN) 7:30

Sunday Night Games In Weeks 5-16 Subject to Change

TWELFTH WEEK
Open Date: Carolina, Pittsburgh

Thursday, November 20	Kansas City _____ at Oakland _____	(NFLN) 5:25
Sunday, November 23	Cleveland _____ at Atlanta _____	1:00
CBS-TV National Weekend	New York Jets _____ at Buffalo _____	1:00
	Tampa Bay _____ at Chicago _____	12:00
	Cincinnati _____ at Houston _____	12:00
	Jacksonville _____ at Indianapolis _____	1:00
	Green Bay _____ at Minnesota _____	12:00
	Detroit _____ at New England _____	1:00
	Tennessee _____ at Philadelphia _____	1:00
	St. Louis _____ at San Diego _____	1:05
	Arizona _____ at Seattle _____	1:05
	Miami _____ at Denver _____	2:25
	Washington _____ at San Francisco _____	1:25
	Dallas _____ at New York Giants _____	(NBC) *8:30
Monday, November 24	Baltimore _____ at New Orleans _____	(ESPN) 7:30

Sunday Night Games In Weeks 5-16 Subject to Change

NFL THANKSGIVING 2014

Thursday, November 27	Chicago _____ at Detroit _____	(CBS) 12:30
	Philadelphia _____ at Dallas _____	(FOX) 3:30
	Seattle _____ at San Francisco _____	(NFLN) 5:30
Sunday, November 30	San Diego _____ at Baltimore _____	1:00
CBS-TV National Weekend	Cleveland _____ at Buffalo _____	1:00
	Tennessee _____ at Houston _____	12:00
	Washington _____ at Indianapolis _____	1:00
	New York Giants _____ at Jacksonville _____	1:00
	Carolina _____ at Minnesota _____	12:00
	New Orleans _____ at Pittsburgh _____	1:00
	Oakland _____ at St. Louis _____	12:00
	Cincinnati _____ at Tampa Bay _____	1:00
	Arizona _____ at Atlanta _____	4:05
	New England _____ at Green Bay _____	3:25
	Denver _____ at Kansas City _____	(NBC) *7:30
Monday, December 1	Miami _____ at New York Jets _____	(ESPN) 8:30

THIRTEENTH WEEK

Sunday Night Games In Weeks 5-16 Subject to Change

FOURTEENTH WEEK

Thursday, December 4	Dallas _____ at Chicago _____	(NFLN) 7:25
Sunday, December 7	Pittsburgh _____ at Cincinnati _____	1:00
FOX-TV National Weekend	Indianapolis _____ at Cleveland _____	1:00
	Tampa Bay _____ at Detroit _____	1:00
	Houston _____ at Jacksonville _____	1:00
	Baltimore _____ at Miami _____	1:00
	New York Jets _____ at Minnesota _____	12:00
	Carolina _____ at New Orleans _____	12:00
	New York Giants _____ at Tennessee _____	12:00
	St. Louis _____ at Washington _____	1:00
	Kansas City _____ at Arizona _____	2:05
	Buffalo _____ at Denver _____	2:05
	San Francisco _____ at Oakland _____	1:25
	Seattle _____ at Philadelphia _____	4:25
	New England _____ at San Diego _____	(NBC) *5:30
Monday, December 8	Atlanta _____ at Green Bay _____	(ESPN) 7:30

Sunday Night Games In Weeks 5-16 Subject to Change

WEEK 15

Thursday, December 11	Arizona _____ at St. Louis _____	(NFLN) 7:25
Sunday, December 14	Pittsburgh _____ at Atlanta _____	1:00
FOX-TV National Weekend	Jacksonville _____ at Baltimore _____	1:00
	Green Bay _____ at Buffalo _____	1:00
	Tampa Bay _____ at Carolina _____	1:00
	Cincinnati _____ at Cleveland _____	1:00
	Minnesota _____ at Detroit _____	1:00
	Houston _____ at Indianapolis _____	1:00
	Oakland _____ at Kansas City _____	12:00
	Miami _____ at New England _____	1:00
	Washington _____ at New York Giants _____	1:00
	Denver _____ at San Diego _____	1:05
	New York Jets _____ at Tennessee _____	3:05
	San Francisco _____ at Seattle _____	1:25
	Dallas _____ at Philadelphia _____	(NBC) *8:30
Monday, December 15	New Orleans _____ at Chicago _____	(ESPN) 7:30

Sunday Night Games In Weeks 5-16 Subject to Change

SIXTEENTH WEEK

Thursday, December 18	Tennessee _____ at Jacksonville _____	(NFLN) 8:25
Saturday, December 20	San Diego _____ at San Francisco _____	**TBD
	Philadelphia _____ at Washington _____	**TBD
Sunday, December 21	Cleveland _____ at Carolina _____	1:00
CBS-TV National Weekend	Detroit _____ at Chicago _____	12:00
	Baltimore _____ at Houston _____	12:00
	Minnesota _____ at Miami _____	1:00
	Atlanta _____ at New Orleans _____	12:00
	New England _____ at New York Jets _____	1:00
	Kansas City _____ at Pittsburgh _____	1:00
	Green Bay _____ at Tampa Bay _____	1:00
	New York Giants _____ at St. Louis _____	3:05
	Indianapolis _____ at Dallas _____	3:25
	Buffalo _____ at Oakland _____	1:25
	Seattle _____ at Arizona _____	(NBC) *6:30
Monday, December 22	Denver _____ at Cincinnati _____	(ESPN) 8:30

*Sunday Night Games In Weeks 5-16 Subject to Change
** In Week 16, NFL Network (4:30 PM ET) and CBS (8:15 PM ET) will combine for a Saturday doubleheader. The kickoff times for each of the games – Philadelphia at Washington and San Diego at San Francisco – will be determined at a later date.

WEEK 17

Sunday, December 28	Carolina _____ at Atlanta _____	1:00
CBS & FOX-TV National Weekend	Cleveland _____ at Baltimore _____	1:00
	Detroit _____ at Green Bay _____	12:00
	Jacksonville _____ at Houston _____	12:00
	San Diego _____ at Kansas City _____	12:00
	New York Jets _____ at Miami _____	1:00
	Chicago _____ at Minnesota _____	12:00
	Buffalo _____ at New England _____	1:00
	Philadelphia _____ at New York Giants _____	1:00
	Cincinnati _____ at Pittsburgh _____	1:00
	New Orleans _____ at Tampa Bay _____	1:00
	Indianapolis _____ at Tennessee _____	12:00
	Dallas _____ at Washington _____	1:00
	Oakland _____ at Denver _____	2:25
	Arizona _____ at San Francisco _____	1:25
	St. Louis _____ at Seattle _____	1:25

*Sunday Night Game In Week 17 TBD

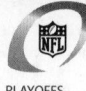

PLAYOFFS

Wild Card Playoff Games
Site Priorities
Two Wild Card teams (division non-champions with best two records) from each conference and the division champions with the third and fourth-best record in each conference will enter the first round of the playoffs. The division champion with the third-best record will play host to the Wild Card team with the second-best record. The division champion with the fourth-best record will play host to the Wild Card team with the best record. There are no restrictions on intra-division games.

Saturday, January 3, 2015 American Football Conference

_____ at _____

National Football Conference

_____ at _____

Sunday, January 4, 2015 American Football Conference

_____ at _____

National Football Conference

_____ at _____

Divisional Playoff Games
Site Priorities
In each conference, the two division champions with the highest won-lost-tied percentage during the regular season will play host to the Wild Card winners. The division champion with the best record in each conference is assured of playing the lowest seeded Wild Card survivor. There are no restrictions on intra-division games.

Saturday, January 10, 2015 American Football Conference

_____ at _____

National Football Conference

_____ at _____

Sunday, January 11, 2015 American Football Conference

_____ at _____

National Football Conference

_____ at _____

Championship Games
Site Priorities for
Championship Games
The home teams will be the surviving playoff winners with the highest seeds. A Wild Card team cannot play host unless two Wild Card teams are in the game, in which case the Wild Card team that was seeded highest in the first round of the playoffs will be the home team.

Sunday, January 18, 2015 American Football Conference

_____ at _____

National Football Conference

_____ at _____

Pro Bowl

Sunday, January 25, 2015 Pro Bowl at University of Phoenix Stadium, Glendale, Arizona

_____ vs. _____

Super Bowl XLIX

Sunday, February 1, 2015 Super Bowl XLIX at University of Phoenix Stadium, Glendale, Arizona

_____ vs. _____

2014 NATIONALLY TELEVISED GAMES
All times ET

Thursday, Sept. 4	Green Bay at Seattle (NBC)	8:30
Sunday, Sept. 7	Indianapolis at Denver (NBC)	8:30
Monday, Sept. 8	N.Y. Giants at Detroit (ESPN)	7:10
	San Diego at Arizona (ESPN)	10:20
Thursday, Sept. 11	Pittsburgh at Baltimore (CBS)	8:25
Sunday, Sept. 14	Chicago at San Francisco (NBC)	8:30
Monday, Sept. 15	Philadelphia at Indianapolis (ESPN)	8:30
Thursday, Sept. 18	Tampa Bay at Atlanta (CBS)	8:25
Sunday, Sept. 21	Pittsburgh at Carolina (NBC)	8:30
Monday, Sept. 22	Chicago at N.Y. Jets (ESPN)	8:30
Thursday, Sept. 25	N.Y. Giants at Washington (CBS)	8:25
Sunday, Sept. 28	New Orleans at Dallas (NBC)	8:30
Monday, Sept. 29	New England at Kansas City (ESPN)	8:30
Thursday, Oct. 2	Minnesota at Green Bay (CBS)	8:25
Sunday, Oct. 5	Cincinnati at New England (NBC)*	8:30
Monday, Oct. 6	Seattle at Washington (ESPN)	8:30
Thursday, Oct. 9	Indianapolis at Houston (CBS)	8:25
Sunday, Oct. 12	N.Y. Giants at Philadelphia (NBC)*	8:30
Monday, Oct. 13	San Francisco at St. Louis (ESPN)	8:30
Thursday, Oct. 16	N.Y. Jets at New England (CBS)	8:25
Sunday, Oct. 19	San Francisco at Denver (NBC)*	8:30
Monday, Oct. 20	Houston at Pittsburgh (ESPN)	8:30
Thursday, Oct. 23	San Diego at Denver (CBS)	8:25
Sunday, Oct. 26	Green Bay at New Orleans (NBC)*	8:30
Monday, Oct. 27	Washington at Dallas (ESPN)	8:40
Thursday, Oct. 30	New Orleans at Carolina (NFL Network)	8:25
Sunday, Nov. 2	Baltimore at Pittsburgh (NBC)*	8:30
Monday, Nov. 3	Indianapolis at N.Y. Giants (ESPN)	8:30
Thursday, Nov. 6	Cleveland at Cincinnati (NFL Network)	8:25
Sunday, Nov. 9	Chicago at Green Bay (NBC)*	8:30
Monday, Nov. 10	Carolina at Philadelphia (ESPN)	8:30
Thursday, Nov. 13	Buffalo at Miami (NFL Network)	8:25
Sunday, Nov. 16	New England at Indianapolis (NBC)*	8:30
Monday, Nov. 17	Pittsburgh at Tennessee (ESPN)	8:30
Thursday, Nov. 20	Kansas City at Oakland (NFL Network)	8:25
Sunday, Nov. 23	Dallas at N.Y. Giants (NBC)*	8:30
Monday, Nov. 24	Baltimore at New Orleans (ESPN)	8:30
Thursday, Nov. 27	Chicago at Detroit (CBS)	12:30
	Philadelphia at Dallas (FOX)	4:30
	Seattle at San Francisco (NBC)	8:30
Sunday, Nov. 30	Denver at Kansas City (NBC)*	8:30
Monday, Dec. 1	Miami at N.Y. Jets (ESPN)	8:30
Thursday, Dec. 4	Dallas at Chicago (NFL Network)	8:25
Sunday, Dec. 7	New England at San Diego (NBC)*	8:30
Monday, Dec. 8	Atlanta at Green Bay (ESPN)	8:30
Thursday, Dec. 11	Arizona at St. Louis (NFL Network)	8:25
Sunday, Dec. 14	Dallas at Philadelphia (NBC)*	8:30
Monday, Dec. 15	New Orleans at Chicago (ESPN)	8:30
Thursday, Dec. 18	Tennessee at Jacksonville (ESPN)	8:25
Saturday, Dec. 20	San Diego at San Francisco (TBD)**	TBD
	Philadelphia at Washington (TBD)**	TBD
Sunday, Dec. 21	Seattle at Arizona (NBC)*	8:30
Monday, Dec. 22	Denver at Cincinnati (ESPN)	8:30
Sunday, Dec. 28	To be determined (NBC)*	8:30

The NFL again will utilize "flexible scheduling" in 2014.

Flexible scheduling moves will be announced at least 12 days before games in Weeks 5-16. In Week 17, the flexible scheduling move will be announced at least six days before the game. Flexible scheduling will ensure quality matchups on Sunday night in those weeks and give "surprise" teams a chance to play their way on to primetime.

** In Week 16, NFL Network (4:30 PM ET) and CBS (8:15 PM ET) will combine for a Saturday doubleheader. The kickoff times for each of the games – Philadelphia at Washington and San Diego at San Francisco – will be determined at a later date.

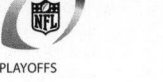

PLAYOFFS

POSTSEASON GAMES

Saturday, January 3 and Sunday, January 4	AFC and NFC Wild Card Playoffs (CBS, ESPN, FOX and NBC)
Saturday, January 10 and Sunday, January 11	AFC and NFC Divisional Playoffs (CBS, FOX, and NBC)
Sunday, January 18	AFC and NFC Championship Games (CBS and FOX)
Sunday, January 25	Pro Bowl in Arizona (ESPN)
Sunday, February 1	Super Bowl XLIX in Arizona (NBC)

SUPER BOWL XLIX

2014

Mid-July	Preseason training camps open. Clubs not permitted to open official preseason camp earlier than July 5. Veteran players cannot be required to report earlier than 15 days prior to club's first preseason game.
July 15	Deadline at 4 P.M., New York time, for any club that designated a Franchise Player to sign such player to a multi-year contract or extension. After this date, the player may sign only a one-year contract with the designating club for the 2014 season, and such contract cannot be extended until after the Club's last regular season game.
July 22	Signing period ends at 4 P.M., New York time, for Transition Players with outstanding tenders. After this date and through 4 P.M., New York time, on the Tuesday after the 10th regular season weekend, Old Club has exclusive negotiating rights to these players.
July 22#	Signing period ends at 4 P.M., New York time, for Unrestricted Free Agents to whom a June 1 tender was made by Old Club. After this date and through 4 P.M., New York time, on the Tuesday after the 10th regular season weekend, Old Club has exclusive negotiating rights to these players.
	#or the first scheduled day of the first NFL training camp, whichever is later.
August 1-3	Hall of Fame Weekend.
August 3	Pro Football Hall of Fame Game, Canton, Ohio: New York Giants vs. Buffalo
August 5	Deadline for players under contract to report to earn a season of free-agency credit.
August 5	If a Drafted Rookie has not signed with his club by this date, he may not be traded to any other club in 2014.
August 7-10	First Preseason Weekend.
August 9-13	Deadline for club to provide written notice to certain unsigned players and the NFLPA of its intent to place them on the Exempt List if they fail to report no later than one day prior to the club's second preseason game. Any player who fails to report prior to the deadline will be ineligible to play or receive compensation for at least three games (preseason or regular season) from the time that he reports.
August 26	Roster cut-down to maximum of 75 players on Active List by 4 P.M., New York time.
August 27	All tryouts on this date and for the remainder of the season must be reported to the League office.
August 30	Roster cut-down to maximum of 53 players on Active/Inactive List by 6 P.M., New York time. Clubs may dress minimum of 43 and maximum of 46 players for each regular-season and postseason game.
August 30	Simultaneously with the cut-down to 53, clubs that have players in the categories of Active/Physically Unable to Perform or Active/Non-Football Injury or Illness must take one of the following options: Place player on Reserve/Physically Unable to Perform or Reserve/Non-Football Injury or Illness, whichever is applicable; ask waivers; terminate; trade; or continue to count him on Active List.
August 31	After 12 noon, New York time, clubs may establish a Practice Squad of eight players by signing free agents who do not have an accrued season of free-agency credit or who were on the 46-player Active List for less than nine regular-season games during their only Accrued Season(s). A player cannot participate on the Practice Squad for more than three seasons.
September 2	After 4 P.M., New York time, a club is permitted to place a player on Reserve/Injured as "Designated for Return."
September 3	All clubs are required to file a personnel (injury) report with their conference information manager by 4:00 P.M., New York time. Reports are to be filed every Wednesday, Thursday and Friday before a regular-season game by 4:00 P.M., New York time (or as soon as possible after the completion of practice). An update must also be reported if there is any change in a player's condition after Friday.
September 4, 7-8	Regular Season opens.
September 5, 8-9	Beginning on these dates vested veterans terminated from the Active List or Inactive List (and from Reserve/Injured if the player is placed on Reserve/Injured after the beginning of the regular season) are entitled to receive, after the end of the regular-season schedule, Termination Pay pursuant to the terms of the CBA.
September 23	Priority on multiple waiver claims is now based on the current season's standing.
October 14	Beginning the day after the conclusion of the sixth regular-season weekend and continuing through the day after the conclusion of the ninth regular-season weekend, clubs are permitted to begin practicing players on Reserve/Physically Unable to Perform and Reserve/Non-Football Injury or Illness for a period not to exceed 21 days. Players may be activated during the 21-day practice period or until 4 P.M., New York time, on the day after the conclusion of the 21-day period.
October 28	All trading ends at 4 P.M., New York time.
October 29	Players with at least four previous pension-credited seasons are subject to the waiver system for the remainder of the regular season and postseason.

November 11	Signing period ends at 4 P.M., New York time, for Franchise Players who are eligible to receive Offer Sheets.
November 11	Deadline for clubs to sign by 4 P.M., New York time, their unsigned Franchise and Transition Players, including Franchise Players who were eligible to receive Offer Sheets until this date. If still unsigned after this date, such players are prohibited from playing in NFL in 2014.
November 11	Deadline for clubs to sign by 4 P.M., New York time, their Unrestricted Free Agents to whom June 1 tender was made. If still unsigned after this date, such players are prohibited from playing in NFL in 2014.
November 11	Deadline for clubs to sign by 4 P.M., New York time, their Restricted Free Agents to whom June 1 tender was made. If such players remain unsigned, they are prohibited from playing in NFL in 2014.
November 11	Deadline for clubs to sign Drafted players by 4 P.M., New York time. If such players remain unsigned, they are prohibited from playing in NFL in 2014.
November 28	Deadline for reinstatement of players in Reserve List categories of Retired, Did Not Report, and Exclusive Rights, and of players who were placed on Reserve/Left Squad in a previous season.
December 26	Deadline for waiver requests in 2014, except for "special waiver requests," which have a 10-day claiming period, with termination or assignment delayed until after the Super Bowl.
December 29	Clubs may begin signing free-agent players for the 2015 season.

2015

January 3-4	Wild Card Playoff Games.
January 10-11	Divisional Playoff Games.
January 18	AFC and NFC Championship Games.
January 25	Pro Bowl, Glendale, Arizona.
February 1	Super Bowl XLIX, University of Phoenix Stadium, Glendale, Arizona.

2016

February 7	Super Bowl L, Levi's® Stadium, San Francisco.

2017

February 5	Super Bowl LI, Reliant Stadium, Houston.

2018

February 4*	Super Bowl LII, New Vikings Stadium, Minnesota.

*Tentative date

The NFL is online to provide fans and media quick and easy access to all the latest professional football information.

NFL.COM—(http://NFL.com)
NFL.com, the league's year-round home page on the Internet, provides NFL information during the regular season, postseason, and offseason, including:

NEWS/STATS: Up-to-the-minute NFL news and analysis, plus game previews, injury reports, and player and team stats.

GAMEDAY COVERAGE: Live game coverage with instant highlights, play-by-play, scores, and statistics, including graphical drive charts and comprehensive scoreboard that reloads automatically with the latest information.

VIDEO HIGHLIGHTS: The site showcases instant game highlights, NFL Films video highlights of the previous week's games as well as upcoming matchups. Video also supports feature stories and team highlight clips from every game last season. In addition, exclusive NFL Network programming is featured as well as original video content.

SUBSCRIPTION PRODUCTS: Three premium video products, NFL Preseason Live, NFL Game Rewind & NFL Game Pass, that enable fans in the United States and around the world to watch games online, on demand and in HD with DVR controls. New for 2014, NFL Now (http://now.nfl.com/) is a personalized video service providing fans with the NFL news, analysis and highlights they want across their Internet-connected devices.

NFL MOBILE PRODUCTS: A suite of mobile products including the premium product NFL Mobile from Verizon (http://verizoninsider.com/nfl) that delivers live *Thursday Night Football, Sunday Night Football, Monday Night Football* and NFL RedZone to fans on the go.

NFL.COM/ESPANOL POWERED BY UNIVISION— (http://NFL.univision.com/)
The official Spanish-language site of the NFL provides in depth information on teams and players, and offers highlights of every NFL game in Spanish. The site includes Hispanic player diaries, live radio broadcasts, up-to-date stats, fantasy football, and more.

NFLEVOLUTION.COM—(http://nflevolution.com)
The site outlines the ways the NFL is addressing player health and safety issues. It houses information on the partnerships, programs and initiatives the NFL supports to protect the health of current and former NFL players and to promote safe play and healthy lifestyles at all levels of football and other sports. The site provides information to promote health and safety at all playing levels, including partnerships with USA Football and the Centers for Disease Control and Prevention.

NFLFLAG.COM—(http://nflflag.com)
NFLFLAG.com focuses on the NFL FLAG Program, which is also part of NFL PLAY 60. Boys and girls ages 5-17 nationwide have the opportunity to display their skills in a non-contact environment by playing against their peers in five-on-five flag football games. Our website is a resource for league organizers, coaches, parents and youth organizations who want to start or find a local NFL FLAG league in their area as well as promote a positive experience for their youth participants.

NFLRUSH.COM—(http://www.NFLRUSH.com)
NFLRUSH.com, which is targeted to kids 6-15, is the official kids' website of the NFL, offering unique customizable content, games, fantasy football for kids, contests, videos, fun daily features on NFL players and information on the NFL's Youth Football programs. NFLRUSH.com also features fun and interactive fitness information as part of the NFL PLAY 60 campaign, which encourages kids to be active for 60 minutes a day. The NFLRUSH ZONE, a role playing game, is an immersive virtual world where kids are able to create avatars, join their favorite team, play games, chat, watch the NFL RUSH ZONE animated series and compete with friends in safe and fun environment.

USAFOOTBALL.COM—(http://usafootball.com)
USA Football is an independent, non-profit organization which is leading the growth and development of youth, high school and international amateur football. USA Football helps youth and amateur football organizations keep the sport fun, safe, and accessible by offering resources focused on coaching education, league enhancement, officiating development and health and safety awareness. The organization also serves as the designated United States representatives to the International Federation of American Football. Based Indianapolis, USA Football was endowed by the NFL and NFLPA in 2002.

NFL.COM/COMMUNITY—(http://www.nfl.com/community)
This site is dedicated to the community service initiatives of the National Football League and the 32 member clubs. It provides news, history and informative links relating to the NFL's three primary service themes: reversing childhood obesity trends (NFL PLAY 60), the global fight against breast cancer (A Crucial Catch), and honoring the Veterans and men and women of the US Armed Forces (Salute to Service). The NFL also takes pride in recognizing the philanthropic efforts of its players, coaches and staff through the annual presentations of the Walter Payton NFL Man of the Year, Salute to Service, and NFL Teacher of the Year awards.

PROFOOTBALLHOF.COM—(http://profootballhof.com)
Profootballhof.com is the official site of the Pro Football Hall of Fame in Canton, Ohio. In addition to a complete visitor's guide to the Hall, the site features bios, stories and Q & A's with Hall of Fame inductees, a detailed archive of football history, and information on appearances by members of the Hall.

OFFICIAL NFL TEAM SITES
In addition to a dedicated area on NFL.com, all 32 teams have their own Websites, which have separate URLs, and are linked from NFL.com.

Arizona Cardinals (www.azcardinals.com)
Atlanta Falcons (www.atlantafalcons.com)
Baltimore Ravens (www.baltimoreravens.com)
Buffalo Bills (www.buffalobills.com)
Carolina Panthers (www.panthers.com)
Chicago Bears (www.chicagobears.com)
Cincinnati Bengals (www.bengals.com)
Cleveland Browns (www.clevelandbrowns.com)
Dallas Cowboys (www.dallascowboys.com)
Denver Broncos (www.denverbroncos.com)
Detroit Lions (www.detroitlions.com)
Green Bay Packers (www.packers.com)
Houston Texans (www.houstontexans.com)
Indianapolis Colts (www.colts.com)
Jacksonville Jaguars (www.jaguars.com)
Kansas City Chiefs (www.kcchiefs.com)
Miami Dolphins (www.miamidolphins.com)
Minnesota Vikings (www.vikings.com)
New England Patriots (www.patriots.com)
New Orleans Saints (www.neworleanssaints.com)
New York Giants (www.giants.com)
New York Jets (www.newyorkjets.com)
Oakland Raiders (www.raiders.com)
Philadelphia Eagles (www.philadelphiaeagles.com)
Pittsburgh Steelers (www.steelers.com)
St. Louis Rams (www.stlouisrams.com)
San Diego Chargers (www.chargers.com)
San Francisco 49ers (www.49ers.com)
Seattle Seahawks (www.seahawks.com)
Tampa Bay Buccaneers (www.buccaneers.com)
Tennessee Titans (www.titansonline.com)
Washington Redskins (www.redskins.com)

NFL Network provides fans with a network to call their own. Seven days a week, 24 hours a day, 365 days a year, fans turn to NFL Network to receive information and insight straight from the field, team headquarters, league offices and everywhere the NFL is making news.

NFL Network gives fans unprecedented year-round inside access to all NFL events, including the Super Bowl, Playoffs, regular season, preseason, Pro Bowl, Pro Football Hall of Fame induction weekend, NFL Draft, Scouting Combine, Senior Bowl, league meetings, minicamps and training camps.

This season marks the inaugural partnership between NFL Network and CBS Sports in broadcasting *Thursday Night Football*. Featuring the most marquee matchups ever on Thursday night, including 14 divisional rivalries, the 16-game *Thursday Night Football* schedule kicks off on September 11 with the Steelers vs. Ravens in Baltimore and ends with a Week 16 Saturday doubleheader on December 20. The full slate of 16 regular-season *Thursday Night Football* games will be produced by CBS with its broadcasters and production team, including **Jim Nantz** and **Phil Simms**.

In addition, NFL Network is the only place on television for fans to view NFL games outside their initial live airings. From original broadcast versions of past Super Bowls, in-week replays of current games, original network telecasts of classic NFL regular season and postseason games, to every preseason game — NFL Network is truly the year-round destination for football fans. NFL Network is currently in more than 72 million homes and has carriage agreements with each of the country's largest television providers. If your provider doesn't currently offer NFL Network, please call (866) NFL-NETWORK.

For fans on the go, all NFL Network programming can also be streamed live on the NFL Mobile from Verizon app (NFL.com/mobile), the NFL app delivered on XBOX from Microsoft, and through Watch NFL Network (NFL.com/watch), with participating cable and satellite providers. For more information, log on to NFL.com/nflnetwork. NFL.com is the exclusive internet home of NFL Network.

KEY PROGRAMMING

LIVE PRIMETIME GAMES
Thursday Night Football on CBS and NFL Network kicks off Week 2 with the Steelers vs. Ravens on September 11 in Baltimore. The 2014 *Thursday Night Football* schedule will feature games from Weeks 2-8 and Week 16 (Saturday) broadcast on CBS that also will be simulcast on NFL Network. The *Thursday Night Football* schedule in Weeks 9-12 and Weeks 14-16 will be televised on NFL Network, and will be simulcast on over-the-air stations in the primary markets of the participating teams.

NFL TOTAL ACCESS
NFL Network's signature show is the football show of record. *NFL Total Access* is uniquely structured to see the game through the participants' eyes, airing at 8:00 PM ET Monday through Saturday. Covering all 32 teams, *NFL Total Access* features interviews with players, coaches and other key league personnel.

NFL AM
Wake up to the NFL on NFL Network with *NFL AM* Monday through Friday at 6:00 AM ET. The four-hour show discusses and debates all of the NFL news, and features guests from around the league.

NFL GameDay First
NFL GameDay First returns this season, kicking off at 7:00 AM ET each Sunday, providing the first look at the day's NFL action.

NFL GAMEDAY MORNING
NFL GameDay Morning is the most comprehensive pregame show on the air Sundays at 9:00 AM ET during the regular season and playoffs, providing fans with the news and notes, as well as live reports from around the league.

NFL GAMEDAY HIGHLIGHTS
Following the late afternoon games, *NFL GameDay Highlights* analyzes the events of the day with highlights from all completed games, expert commentary, on-field interviews and postgame press conferences.

NFL GAMEDAY FINAL
After each Sunday's final game, *NFL GameDay Final* delivers comprehensive coverage of the day's action at 11:30 PM ET. The 90-minute show features highlights, post-game press conferences, on-field interviews, analysis and more in wrapping up each NFL Sunday.

NFL REPLAY
NFL games will be re-aired with the original television announcers and cameras. This offering features the most exciting games each week in an abbreviated format (eliminating halftime and other non-critical elements), and includes enhancements to each broadcast such as additional camera angles, sideline sound and postgame interviews.

PLAYBOOK
NFL Network uses the "all 22" game film watched each week by coaches and players to present football's ultimate chalkboard show. *Playbook*, produced at NFL Films, offers 60-minute strategy sessions with NFL Network analysts, who focus on each week's key matchups and discuss technique and game planning with coaches and players.

THE TOP 100: PLAYERS OF 2014
The Top 100 is the annual series which sparks wide debate each offseason on NFL Network. Current players vote for their peers to compile a list of the top 100 playmakers today, counting down from 100 to 1 with 10 players featured in each episode.

AMERICA'S GAME
The Emmy Award-winning original series continues its profiles of Super Bowl champions with the 2013 Seattle Seahawks.

A FOOTBALL LIFE
The three-time Emmy-nominated *A Football Life* biography series returns for a fourth season on NFL Network. The NFL Films-produced series offers a look inside the untold stories of NFL icons.

NFL's TOP 10
Putting a fresh twist on the countdown genre, *NFL's Top 10* is a fast-paced series that provides an irreverent look at some of the most intriguing subjects in the NFL, creating and debating a top ten list for each category. Each 60-minute episode counts down from No. 10 to the top ranking in each category.

SOUND FX
The sounds of the game that only NFL Films can capture – with exclusive on-field and sideline microphone access – will be featured on the Emmy award-winning *Sound FX.*

PRESEASON GAMES
NFL Network is the only place on television where fans can view all 65 NFL preseason games in high-definition.

Log on to www.NFL.com/NFLnetwork for more information on NFL Network.

SCHEDULING FORMULA

The NFL expanded to 32 teams in 2002 with the addition of the Houston Texans. In addition, the NFL realigned for the first time since 1970—into eight divisions of four teams each—and the scheduling formula that was introduced guarantees for the first time that all teams play each other on a regular, rotating basis. Although the number of teams has increased to 32, the number of playoff teams remains the same at 12.

Under the NFL scheduling formula, every team within a division plays 16 games as follows:

- Home and away against its three division opponents (6 games).
- The four teams from another division within its conference on a rotating three-year cycle (4 games).
- The four teams from a division in the other conference on a rotating four-year cycle (4 games).
- Two intraconference games based on the prior year's standings (2 games). These games will match a first-place team against the first-place teams in the two same-conference divisions the team is not scheduled to play that season. The second-place, third-place, and fourth-place teams in a conference will be matched in the same way each year.

The schedule format takes each team through a cycle of games—home and away—against every other team in the league. From 2002-2009, every team played every other team at least twice—once home and once away. After the 2008 season, a decision was made to continue with the same rotation in 2010 and beyond.

In determining how to begin the divisional rotation in 2002, the displacement of teams from their old divisions in the new alignment was taken into account. Preference was given to scheduling games with former division rivals and other regional opponents for clubs realigned from otherwise intact divisions.

FUTURE SCHEDULING ROTATION

		2014	2015
AFC EAST	Intraconference	AFCW	AFCS
	Interconference	NFCN	NFCE
AFC NORTH	Intraconference	AFCS	AFCW
	Interconference	NFCS	NFCW
AFC SOUTH	Intraconference	AFCN	AFCE
	Interconference	NFCE	NFCS
AFC WEST	Intraconference	AFCE	AFCN
	Interconference	NFCW	NFCN
NFC EAST	Intraconference	NFCW	NFCS
	Interconference	AFCS	AFCE
NFC NORTH	Intraconference	NFCS	NFCW
	Interconference	AFCE	AFCW
NFC SOUTH	Intraconference	NFCN	NFCE
	Interconference	AFCN	AFCS
NFC WEST	Intraconference	NFCE	NFCN
	Interconference	AFCW	AFCN

AFC EAST NON-DIVISIONAL OPPONENTS 2014

	BUFFALO		MIAMI		NEW ENGLAND		N.Y. JETS	
	Home	Away	Home	Away	Home	Away	Home	Away
Intraconference by Division	KC	DEN	KC	DEN	DEN	KC	DEN	KC
	SD	OAK	SD	OAK	OAK	SD	OAK	SD
Interconference by Division	GB	CHI	GB	CHI	CHI	GB	CHI	GB
	MINN	DET	MINN	DET	DET	MINN	DET	MINN
Intraconference by Position	AFCN	AFCS	AFCN	AFCS	AFCN	AFCS	AFCN	AFCS

AFC EAST NON-DIVISIONAL OPPONENTS 2015

	BUFFALO		MIAMI		NEW ENGLAND		N.Y. JETS	
	Home	Away	Home	Away	Home	Away	Home	Away
Intraconference by Division	HOU	JAX	HOU	JAX	JAX	HOU	JAX	HOU
	IND	TENN	IND	TENN	TENN	IND	TENN	IND
Interconference by Division	DALL	PHIL	DALL	PHIL	PHIL	DALL	PHIL	DALL
	NYG	WASH	NYG	WASH	WASH	NYG	WASH	NYG
Intraconference by Position	AFCN	AFCW	AFCN	AFCW	AFCN	AFCW	AFCN	AFCW

AFC NORTH NON-DIVISIONAL OPPONENTS 2014

	BALTIMORE		CINCINNATI		CLEVELAND		PITTSBURGH	
	Home	Away	Home	Away	Home	Away	Home	Away
Intraconference by Division	JAX	HOU	JAX	HOU	HOU	JAX	HOU	JAX
	TENN	IND	TENN	IND	IND	TENN	IND	TENN
Interconference by Division	ATL	NO	ATL	NO	NO	ATL	NO	ATL
	CAR	TB	CAR	TB	TB	CAR	TB	CAR
Intraconference by Position	AFCW	AFCE	AFCW	AFCE	AFCW	AFCE	AFCW	AFCE

AFC NORTH NON-DIVISIONAL OPPONENTS 2015

	BALTIMORE		CINCINNATI		CLEVELAND		PITTSBURGH	
	Home	Away	Home	Away	Home	Away	Home	Away
Intraconference by Division	KC	DEN	KC	DEN	DEN	KC	DEN	KC
	SD	OAK	SD	OAK	OAK	SD	OAK	SD
Interconference by Division	STL	ARZ	STL	ARZ	ARZ	STL	ARZ	STL
	SEA	SF	SEA	SF	SF	SEA	SF	SEA
Intraconference by Position	AFCS	AFCE	AFCS	AFCE	AFCS	AFCE	AFCS	AFCE

AFC SOUTH NON-DIVISIONAL OPPONENTS 2014

	HOUSTON		INDIANAPOLIS		JACKSONVILLE		TENNESSEE	
	Home	Away	Home	Away	Home	Away	Home	Away
Intraconference by Division	BALT	CLE	BALT	CLE	CLE	BALT	CLE	BALT
	CIN	PITT	CIN	PITT	PITT	CIN	PITT	CIN
Interconference by Division	PHIL	DALL	PHIL	DALL	DALL	PHIL	DALL	PHIL
	WASH	NYG	WASH	NYG	NYG	WASH	NYG	WASH
Intraconference by Position	AFCE	AFCW	AFCE	AFCW	AFCE	AFCW	AFCE	AFCW

AFC SOUTH NON-DIVISIONAL OPPONENTS 2015

	HOUSTON		INDIANAPOLIS		JACKSONVILLE		TENNESSEE	
	Home	Away	Home	Away	Home	Away	Home	Away
Intraconference by Division	NE	BUFF	NE	BUFF	BUFF	NE	BUFF	NE
	NYJ	MIA	NYJ	MIA	MIA	NYJ	MIA	NYJ
Interconference by Division	NO	ATL	NO	ATL	ATL	NO	ATL	NO
	TB	CAR	TB	CAR	CAR	TB	CAR	TB
Intraconference by Position	AFCW	AFCN	AFCW	AFCN	AFCW	AFCN	AFCW	AFCN

AFC WEST NON-DIVISIONAL OPPONENTS 2014

	DENVER		KANSAS CITY		OAKLAND		SAN DIEGO	
	Home	Away	Home	Away	Home	Away	Home	Away
Intraconference by Division	BUFF	NE	NE	BUFF	BUFF	NE	NE	BUFF
	MIA	NYJ	NYJ	MIA	MIA	NYJ	NYJ	MIA
Interconference by Division	ARIZ	STL	STL	ARIZ	ARIZ	STL	STL	ARIZ
	SF	SEA	SEA	SF	SF	SEA	SEA	SF
Intraconference by Position	AFCS	AFCN	AFCS	AFCN	AFCS	AFCN	AFCS	AFCN

AFC WEST NON-DIVISIONAL OPPONENTS 2015

	DENVER		KANSAS CITY		OAKLAND		SAN DIEGO	
	Home	Away	Home	Away	Home	Away	Home	Away
Intraconference by Division	BALT	CLE	CLE	BALT	BALT	CLE	CLE	BALT
	CIN	PITT	PITT	CIN	CIN	PITT	PITT	CIN
Interconference by Division	GB	CHI	CHi	GB	GB	CHI	CHI	GB
	MINN	DET	DET	MINN	MINN	DET	DET	MINN
Intraconference by Position	AFCE	AFCS	AFCE	AFCS	AFCE	AFCS	AFCE	AFCS

NFC EAST NON-DIVISIONAL OPPONENTS 2014

	DALLAS Home	DALLAS Away	N.Y. GIANTS Home	N.Y. GIANTS Away	PHILADELPHIA Home	PHILADELPHIA Away	WASHINGTON Home	WASHINGTON Away
Intraconference by Division	ARIZ	STL	ARIZ	STL	STL	ARIZ	STL	ARIZ
	SF	SEA	SF	SEA	SEA	SF	SEA	SF
Interconference by Division	HOU	JAX	HOU	JAX	JAX	HOU	JAX	HOU
	IND	TENN	IND	TENN	TENN	IND	TENN	IND
Intraconference by Position	NFCS	NFCN	NFCS	NFCN	NFCS	NFCN	NFCS	NFCN

NFC EAST NON-DIVISIONAL OPPONENTS 2015

	DALLAS Home	DALLAS Away	N.Y. GIANTS Home	N.Y. GIANTS Away	PHILADELPHIA Home	PHILADELPHIA Away	WASHINGTON Home	WASHINGTON Away
Intraconference by Division	ATL	NO	ATL	NO	NO	ATL	NO	ATL
	CAR	TB	CAR	TB	TB	CAR	TB	CAR
Interconference by Division	NE	BUFF	NE	BUFF	BUFF	NE	BUFF	NE
	NYJ	MIA	NYJ	MIA	MIA	NYJ	MIA	NYJ
Intraconference by Position	NFCW	NFCN	NFCW	NFCN	NFCW	NFCN	NFCW	NFCN

NFC NORTH NON-DIVISIONAL OPPONENTS 2014

	CHICAGO Home	CHICAGO Away	DETROIT Home	DETROIT Away	GREEN BAY Home	GREEN BAY Away	MINNESOTA Home	MINNESOTA Away
Intraconference by Division	NO	ATL	NO	ATL	ATL	NO	ATL	NO
	TB	CAR	TB	CAR	CAR	TB	CAR	TB
Interconference by Division	BUFF	NE	BUFF	NE	NE	BUFF	NE	BUFF
	MIA	NYJ	MIA	NYJ	NYJ	MIA	NYJ	MIA
Intraconference by Position	NFCE	NFCW	NFCE	NFCW	NFCE	NFCW	NFCE	NFCW

NFC NORTH NON-DIVISIONAL OPPONENTS 2015

	CHICAGO Home	CHICAGO Away	DETROIT Home	DETROIT Away	GREEN BAY Home	GREEN BAY Away	MINNESOTA Home	MINNESOTA Away
Intraconference by Division	ARIZ	STL	ARIZ	STL	STL	ARIZ	STL	ARIZ
	SF	SEA	SF	SEA	SEA	SF	SEA	SF
Interconference by Division	DEN	KC	DEN	KC	KC	DEN	KC	DEN
	OAK	SD	OAK	SD	SD	OAK	SD	OAK
Intraconference by Position	NFCE	NFCS	NFCE	NFCS	NFCE	NFCS	NFCE	NFCS

NFC SOUTH NON-DIVISIONAL OPPONENTS 2014

	ATLANTA		CAROLINA		NEW ORLEANS		TAMPA BAY	
	Home	Away	Home	Away	Home	Away	Home	Away
Intraconference by Division	CHI	GB	CHI	GB	GB	CHI	GB	CHI
	DET	MINN	DET	MINN	MINN	DET	MINN	DET
Interconference by Division	CLE	BALT	CLE	BALT	BALT	CLE	BALT	CLE
	PITT	CIN	PITT	CIN	CIN	PITT	CIN	PITT
Intraconference by Position	NFCW	NFCE	NFCW	NFCE	NFCW	NFCE	NFCW	NFCE

NFC SOUTH NON-DIVISIONAL OPPONENTS 2015

	ATLANTA		CAROLINA		NEW ORLEANS		TAMPA BAY	
	Home	Away	Home	Away	Home	Away	Home	Away
Intraconference by Division	PHIL	DALL	PHIL	DALL	DALL	PHIL	DALL	PHIL
	WASH	NYG	WASH	NYG	NYG	WASH	NYG	WASH
Interconference by Division	HOU	JAX	HOU	JAX	JAX	HOU	JAX	HOU
	IND	TENN	IND	TENN	TENN	IND	TENN	IND
Intraconference by Position	NFCN	NFCW	NFCN	NFCW	NFCN	NFCW	NFCN	NFCW

NFC WEST NON-DIVISIONAL OPPONENTS 2014

	ARIZONA		ST. LOUIS		SAN FRANCISCO		SEATTLE	
	Home	Away	Home	Away	Home	Away	Home	Away
Intraconference by Division	PHIL	DALL	DALL	PHIL	PHIL	DALL	DALL	PHIL
	WASH	NYG	NYG	WASH	WASH	NYG	NYG	WASH
Interconference by Division	KC	DEN	DEN	KC	KC	DEN	DEN	KC
	SD	OAK	OAK	SD	SD	OAK	OAK	SD
Intraconference by Position	NFCN	NFCS	NFCN	NFCS	NFCN	NFCS	NFCN	NFCS

NFC WEST NON-DIVISIONAL OPPONENTS 2015

	ARIZONA		ST. LOUIS		SAN FRANCISCO		SEATTLE	
	Home	Away	Home	Away	Home	Away	Home	Away
Intraconference by Division	GB	CHI	CHI	GB	GB	CHI	CHI	GB
	MINN	DET	DET	MINN	MINN	DET	DET	MINN
Interconference by Division	BALT	CLE	CLE	BALT	BALT	CLE	CLE	BALT
	CIN	PITT	PITT	CIN	CIN	PITT	PITT	CIN
Intraconference by Position	NFCS	NFCE	NFCS	NFCE	NFCS	NFCE	NFCS	NFCE

TOP ACTIVE PASSERS
1,000 or more attempts

		Yrs.	Att.	Comp.	Pct. Comp.	Yards	TD	Pct. TD	Had Int.	Pct. Int.	Ratings Pts.
1.	Aaron Rodgers	9	2,955	1,945	65.8	24,197	188	6.4	52	1.8	104.9
2.	Peyton Manning	15	8,452	5,532	65.5	64,964	491	5.8	219	2.6	97.2
3.	Philip Rivers	10	4,108	2,646	64.4	32,369	221	5.4	104	2.5	96.0
4.	Tony Romo	10	3,775	2,439	64.6	29,565	208	5.5	101	2.7	95.8
5.	Tom Brady	14	6,586	4,178	63.4	49,149	359	5.5	134	2.0	95.7
6.	Drew Brees	13	6,799	4,481	65.9	51,081	363	5.3	177	2.6	95.3
7.	Ben Roethlisberger	10	4,346	2,749	63.3	34,105	219	5.0	122	2.8	92.6
8.	Matt Ryan	6	3,288	2,093	63.7	23,472	153	4.7	77	2.3	90.6
9.	Matt Schaub	10	3,181	2,035	64.0	24,254	130	4.1	84	2.6	89.8
10.	Cam Newton	3	1,475	882	59.8	11,299	64	4.3	42	2.8	86.4
11.	Carson Palmer	10	4,682	2,930	62.6	33,739	213	4.5	152	3.2	85.9
12.	David Garrard	9	2,281	1,406	61.6	16,003	89	3.9	54	2.4	85.8
13.	Andy Dalton	3	1,630	992	60.9	11,360	80	4.9	49	3.0	85.7
14.	Jay Cutler	8	3,310	2,020	61.0	23,937	155	4.7	112	3.4	84.6
15.	Joe Flacco	6	3,103	1,869	60.2	21,545	121	3.9	78	2.5	83.7
16.	Matthew Stafford	5	2,497	1,485	59.5	17,457	109	4.4	73	2.9	83.1
17.	Matt Hasselbeck	15	5,030	3,036	60.4	34,647	201	4.0	148	2.9	82.1
18.	Jason Campbell	8	2,499	1,508	60.3	16,697	87	3.5	60	2.4	81.8
19.	Andrew Luck	2	1,197	682	57.0	8,196	46	3.8	27	2.3	81.5
20.	Eli Manning	10	5,008	2,929	58.5	35,345	229	4.6	171	3.4	81.2
21.	Alex Smith	8	2,685	1,598	59.5	17,593	104	3.9	70	2.6	81.0
22.	Michael Vick	11	3,030	1,703	56.2	21,489	128	4.2	85	2.8	80.9
23.	Matt Cassel	9	2,298	1,356	59.0	15,302	93	4.0	66	2.9	80.5
24.	Kyle Orton	8	2,265	1,326	58.5	15,019	83	3.7	59	2.6	79.9
25.	Sam Bradford	4	1,760	1,032	58.6	11,065	59	3.4	38	2.2	79.3

TOP ACTIVE SCORERS
(number in parentheses represents 2-point conversions scored)

		Yrs.	TD	FG	PAT	TP
1.	Adam Vinatieri	18	0	448	660(1)	2,006
2.	David Akers	16	0	386	563	1,721
3.	Sebastian Janikowski	14	0	345	454	1,489
4.	Jay Feely	13	1	329	444	1,437
5.	Phil Dawson	15	1	337	394	1,411
6.	Rian Lindell	14	0	306	432	1,350
7.	Matt Bryant	12	0	257	363	1,134
8.	Shayne Graham	13	0	247	375	1,116
9.	Josh Brown	11	0	254	341	1,103
10.	Rob Bironas	9	0	239	315	1,032
11.	Robbie Gould	9	0	234	323	1,025
12.	Stephen Gostkowski	8	0	208	399	1,023
13.	Josh Scobee	10	0	215	294	939
14.	Lawrence Tynes	9	0	190	357	927
15.	Mason Crosby	7	0	185	348	903
16.	Shaun Suisham	9	0	182	229	775
17.	Nick Folk	7	0	167	269	770
18.	Billy Cundiff	10	0	160	249	729
19.	Mike Nugent	9	0	164	234	726
20.	Matt Prater	7	0	142	260	686
21.	Dan Carpenter	6	0	160	186	666
22.	Adrian Peterson	7	91	0	0(1)	548
23.	Larry Fitzgerald	10	87	0	0(1)	524
24.	Antonio Gates	11	87	0	0	522
25.	Ryan Succop	5	0	119	160	517

TOP ACTIVE SCORERS (TOUCHDOWNS)

		Yrs.	Rush	Rec.	Ret.	Tot.
1.	Adrian Peterson	7	86	5	0	91
2.	Larry Fitzgerald	10	0	87	0	87
	Antonio Gates	11	0	87	0	87
4.	Maurice Jones-Drew	8	68	11	2	81
5.	Reggie Wayne	13	0	80	0	80
6.	Steve Smith	13	2	67	6	75
7.	Frank Gore	9	60	10	1	71
	Steven Jackson	10	62	9	0	71
9.	Willis McGahee	10	65	5	0	70
10.	Santana Moss	13	0	66	3	69
11.	Calvin Johnson	7	1	66	0	67
12.	Anquan Boldin	11	1	65	0	66
13.	Plaxico Burress	11	0	64	0	64
14.	Marques Colston	8	0	63	0	63
	Marshawn Lynch	7	58	5	0	63
16.	Andre Johnson	11	0	61	0	61
17.	Chris Johnson	6	50	8	0	58
18.	Greg Jennings	8	0	57	0	57
	Brandon Marshall	8	0	57	0	57
20.	Reggie Bush	8	33	18	4	55
	Roddy White	9	0	55	0	55
22.	Dallas Clark	11	0	53	0	53
	Vernon Davis	8	0	53	0	53
	DeAngelo Williams	8	46	7	0	53
25.	Arian Foster	5	45	7	0	52
	Vincent Jackson	9	0	52	0	52
	Jason Witten	11	0	52	0	52

TOP ACTIVE RUSHERS

	Yrs.	Att.	Yards	TD
1. Steven Jackson	10	2,553	10,681	62
2. Adrian Peterson	7	2,033	10,115	86
3. Frank Gore	9	2,187	9,967	60
4. Willis McGahee	10	2,095	8,474	65
5. Maurice Jones-Drew	8	1,804	8,071	68
6. Chris Johnson	6	1,742	7,965	50
7. Marshawn Lynch	7	1,753	7,389	58
8. Matt Forté	6	1,551	6,666	35
9. DeAngelo Williams	8	1,370	6,627	46
10. Ray Rice	6	1,430	6,180	37
11. Michael Vick	11	827	5,857	36
12. Jamaal Charles	6	1,043	5,823	29
13. LeSean McCoy	5	1,149	5,473	39
14. Ronnie Brown	9	1,261	5,328	38
15. Reggie Bush	8	1,190	5,168	33
16. Fred Jackson	7	1,138	5,121	28
17. Arian Foster	5	1,131	5,063	45
18. Ahmad Bradshaw	7	962	4,418	34
19. Jonathan Stewart	6	866	4,016	27
20. BenJarvus Green-Ellis	6	1,008	3,914	42
21. Ryan Mathews	4	849	3,731	20
22. Shonn Greene	5	899	3,718	22
23. Darren McFadden	6	883	3,713	23
24. Pierre Thomas	7	773	3,523	26
25. Knowshon Moreno	5	845	3,468	26

TOP ACTIVE PASS RECEIVERS

	Yrs.	No.	Yards	TD
1. Reggie Wayne	13	1,006	13,566	80
2. Andre Johnson	11	927	12,661	61
3. Jason Witten	11	879	9,799	52
4. Anquan Boldin	11	857	11,344	65
5. Larry Fitzgerald	10	846	11,367	87
6. Wes Welker	10	841	9,358	48
7. Steve Smith	13	836	12,197	67
8. Santana Moss	13	722	10,167	66
9. Antonio Gates	11	719	9,193	87
10. Brandon Marshall	8	712	9,050	57
11. Roddy White	9	685	9,436	55
12. Marques Colston	8	607	8,337	63
13. Calvin Johnson	7	572	9,328	66
14. Plaxico Burress	11	553	8,499	64
15. Deion Branch	11	518	6,644	39
16. Dallas Clark	11	505	5,665	53
17. Greg Jennings	8	493	7,341	57
18. Dwayne Bowe	7	472	6,401	44
19. Kellen Winslow	9	469	5,236	25
20. Heath Miller	9	466	5,273	40
21. Nate Burleson	11	457	5,630	39
22. Steve Jackson	10	440	3,515	9
23. Jerricho Cotchery	10	437	5,558	30
24. Reggie Bush	8	426	3,236	18
25. Vincent Jackson	9	422	7,362	52

TOP ACTIVE SCRIMMAGE YARDS LEADERS

	Yrs.	Rush	Rec	Total	TD
1. Steven Jackson	10	10,681	3,515	14,196	71
2. Reggie Wayne	13	0	13,566	13,566	80
3. Frank Gore	9	9,967	2,772	12,739	70
4. Andre Johnson	11	54	12,661	12,715	61
5. Steve Smith	13	387	12,197	12,584	69
6. Adrian Peterson	7	10,115	1,697	11,812	91
7. Anquan Boldin	11	225	11,344	11,569	66
8. Larry Fitzgerald	10	63	11,367	11,430	87
9. Maurice Jones-Drew	8	8,071	2,873	10,944	79
10. Santana Moss	13	287	10,167	10,454	66
11. Chris Johnson	6	7,965	2,003	9,968	58
12. Willis McGahee	10	8,474	1,339	9,813	70
13. Jason Witten	11	0	9,799	9,799	52
14. Matt Forté	6	6,666	2,919	9,585	47
15. Wes Welker	10	151	9,358	9,509	48
16. Calvin Johnson	7	167	9,328	9,495	67
17. Roddy White	9	19	9,436	9,455	55
18. Ray Rice	6	6,180	3,034	9,214	43
19. Antonio Gates	11	0	9,193	9,193	87
20. Brandon Marshall	8	118	9,050	9,168	57
21. Marshawn Lynch	7	7,389	1,532	8,921	63
22. Plaxico Burress	11	7	8,499	8,492	64
23. Reggie Bush	8	5,168	3,236	8,404	51
24. Marques Colston	8	7	8,337	8,344	63
25. DeAngelo Williams	8	6,627	1,577	8,204	53

TOP ACTIVE INTERCEPTORS

	Yrs.	No.	Yards	TD
1. Ed Reed	12	64	1,590	7
2. Charles Woodson	16	56	909	11
3. Champ Bailey	15	52	464	4
4. Asante Samuel	11	51	728	6
5. DeAngelo Hall	10	43	838	5
6. Terence Newman	11	36	353	3
Charles Tillman	11	36	675	8
8. Troy Polamalu	11	32	398	3
9. Rashean Mathis	11	30	512	3
10. Antonio Cromartie	8	28	480	3
11. Adrian Wilson	12	27	508	2
12. Tramon Williams	7	25	421	1
13. Leon Hall	7	23	245	2
Johnathan Joseph	8	23	420	4
Antrel Rolle	9	23	494	4
Aqib Talib	6	23	348	4
17. Jairus Byrd	5	22	409	2
Michael Griffin	7	22	287	1
19. Quentin Jammer	12	21	210	1
Darrelle Revis	7	21	367	3
21. Drayton Florence	11	20	273	3
Tim Jennings	8	20	279	3
Richard Sherman	3	20	227	2
Corey Webster	9	20	226	1
25. Dominique Rodgers-Cromartie	6	19	409	5

TOP ACTIVE PUNT RETURNERS
40 or more punt returns

	Yrs.	No.	Yards	Avg.	TD
1. Julian Edelman	5	107	1,317	12.3	3
2. Devin Hester	8	264	3,241	12.3	13
3. Dexter McCluster	4	79	959	12.1	3
4. Dwayne Harris	3	57	690	12.1	2
5. Golden Tate	4	68	787	11.6	0
6. Leodis McKelvin	6	71	817	11.5	3
7. Marc Mariani	2	73	819	11.2	2
8. Ted Ginn	7	156	1,741	11.2	3
9. Josh Cribbs	9	203	2,250	11.1	3
10. Santana Moss	13	130	1,398	10.8	3
11. Eddie Royal	6	100	1,072	10.7	2
12. T.Y. Hilton	2	43	459	10.7	1
13. Domenik Hixon	6	56	597	10.7	1
14. Danny Amendola	5	90	947	10.5	0
15. Jeremy Kerley	3	61	640	10.5	1
16. Eric Weems	7	78	815	10.4	1
17. Patrick Peterson	3	128	1,323	10.3	4
18. Marcus Sherels	4	87	899	10.3	2
19. Davone Bess	6	119	1,215	10.2	0
20. Jacoby Jones	7	235	2,398	10.2	4
21. Randall Cobb	3	60	610	10.2	2
22. Adam Jones	7	128	1,296	10.1	5
23. Leon Washington	8	174	1,746	10.0	0
24. Keshawn Martin	2	61	612	10.0	1
25. Wes Welker	10	251	2,487	9.9	0

TOP ACTIVE KICKOFF RETURNERS
40 or more kickoff returns

	Yrs.	No.	Yards	Avg.	TD
1. Cordarrelle Patterson	1	43	1,393	32.4	2
2. Joe McKnight	3	76	2,205	29.0	2
3. Percy Harvin	5	115	3,241	28.2	5
4. David Reed	4	63	1,740	27.6	1
5. Dwayne Harris	3	47	1,298	27.6	0
6. Quintin Demps	6	96	2,630	27.4	2
7. Trindon Holliday	3	49	1,327	27.1	2
8. Danieal Manning	8	116	3,103	26.8	1
9. Jacoby Jones	7	133	3,549	26.7	4
10. David Wilson	2	66	1,755	26.6	1
11. Leodis McKelvin	6	91	2,407	26.5	1
12. Randall Cobb	3	73	1,915	26.2	1
13. Leon Washington	8	261	6,815	26.1	8
14. Maurice Jones-Drew	8	79	2,054	26.0	2
15. Chris Rainey	2	45	1,166	25.9	0
16. Josh Cribbs	9	407	10,505	25.8	8
17. Brad Smith	8	111	2,852	25.7	4
18. Deji Karim	4	91	2,332	25.6	1
19. Antonio Brown	4	45	1,150	25.6	1
20. Darren Sproles	8	328	8,296	25.3	2
21. Keshawn Martin	2	67	1,688	25.2	0
22. Brandon Tate	5	154	3,870	25.1	2
23. Jacoby Ford	3	75	1,874	25.0	4
24. LaRod Stephens-Howling	5	164	4,092	25.0	3
25. Clyde Gates	3	48	1,196	24.9	0

TOP ACTIVE PUNTERS
50 or more punts

	Yrs.	No.	Avg.	LG
1. Marquette King	1	84	48.9	66
2. Shane Lechler	14	1,102	47.6	80
3. Sam Martin	1	72	47.2	72
4. Thomas Morstead	5	296	47.1	70
5. Brandon Fields	7	536	46.8	74
6. Bryan Anger	2	186	46.7	73
7. Andy Lee	10	869	46.1	82
8. Johnny Hekker	2	160	46.0	68
9. Ryan Allen	1	76	45.9	65
10. Britton Colquitt	4	319	45.8	67
11. Pat McAfee	5	366	45.6	66
12. Ryan Quigley	1	72	45.5	67
13. Donnie Jones	10	818	45.5	80
14. Matt Bosher	3	198	45.5	63
15. Brad Nortman	2	146	45.3	72
16. Mat McBriar	10	589	45.1	75
17. Mike Scifres	11	629	45.1	71
18. Dustin Colquitt	9	744	44.9	81
19. Chris Jones	3	99	44.8	62
20. Sam Koch	8	648	44.8	74
21. Brett Kern	6	432	44.8	71
22. Jon Ryan	8	622	44.8	77
23. Robert Malone	4	157	44.5	84
24. Steve Weatherford	8	594	44.4	68
25. Tim Masthay	4	260	44.3	71

TOP ACTIVE QUARTERBACK SACKERS

	Yrs.	No.
1. John Abraham	14	133.5
2. Jared Allen	10	128.5
3. Julius Peppers	12	118.5
4. DeMarcus Ware	9	117.0
5. Robert Mathis	11	111.0
6. Dwight Freeney	12	108.0
7. Terrell Suggs	11	94.5
8. Osi Umenyiora	10	82.5
9. Justin Smith	13	82.0
10. Andre Carter	13	80.5
11. Shaun Phillips	10	79.5
12. Trent Cole	9	79.0
13. Mario Williams	8	76.5
14. Tamba Hali	8	73.5
15. Elvis Dumervil	7	73.0
16. Will Smith	9	67.5
17. James Harrison	11	66.0
18. Jason Babin	10	62.5
19. Justin Tuck	9	60.5
20. Kevin Williams	11	60.0
21. Chris Clemons	9	58.0
22. LaMarr Woodley	7	57.0
23. Charles Johnson	7	54.0
24. Calvin Pace	11	52.0
25. Cameron Wake	5	51.5
Kamerion Wimbley	8	51.5

The **Chicago Bears** need three victories to become the first team in NFL history with 750 total victories. Chicago's all-time record is 747-552-42.

The **Green Bay Packers** need two regular-season victories to become the second team in NFL history with 700 regular-season victories. The Packers (698-537-37) would join Chicago (730-534-42) as the only teams to accomplish the feat.

The **Washington Redskins** need 12 victories to reach 600 total victories. Washington's all-time record is 588-564-27.

The **Dallas Cowboys** need three victories to reach 500 total victories. Dallas' all-time record is 497-373-6.

The **Indianapolis Colts** need five victories to reach 500 total victories. Indianapolis' all-time record is 495-442-7.

The **Buffalo Bills** need 10 victories to reach 400 total victories. Buffalo's all-time record is 390-451-8.

The **Tennessee Titans** need one regular-season victory to reach 400 regular-season victories. Tennessee's all-time regular-season record is 399-415-6.

Bill Belichick, New England, needs 12 victories to surpass Curly Lambeau (229) for fourth place all-time in career victories. In 19 seasons, Belichick has 218 career victories.

Tom Coughlin, New York Giants, needs 14 victories to surpass Paul Brown (170), Joe Gibbs (171), Mike Holmgren (174), Mike Shanahan (178) and Bill Parcells (183) for 10th place all-time in career victories. In 18 seasons, Coughlin has 170 career victories.

Marvin Lewis, Cincinnati, needs 10 victories to reach 100 career victories. In 11 seasons, Lewis has 90 career victories.

Peyton Manning, Denver, needs 18 touchdown passes to surpass Brett Favre (508) for the most all-time. In 16 seasons, Manning has 491 touchdown passes.

Manning needs 5,036 passing yards to join Brett Favre (71,838) as the only players with 70,000 career passing yards. In 16 seasons, Manning has 64,964 passing yards.

Manning needs two 400-yard passing games to surpass Dan Marino (13) for the most all-time (see Brees note). In 16 seasons, Manning has 12 400-yard passing games.

Manning can increase his NFL record total of 300-yard passing games. In 16 seasons, Manning has 84 300-yard passing games (see Brees note).

Manning needs 4,000 passing yards to become the first player in NFL history with 14 4,000-yard seasons. Manning is the only quarterback to accomplish the feat in 13 seasons.

Manning can increase his NFL record total of four-touchdown passing games. In 16 seasons, Manning has 31 games with four or more touchdown passes (see Brees note).

Manning can become the first player to lead the league in touchdown passes five times in his career. Manning is currently tied with Drew Brees, Len Dawson, Brett Favre, Johnny Unitas and Steve Young (4) for the most such seasons in NFL history (see Brees note).

Manning has led the league in passing yards three times in his career and can join Drew Brees (4), Dan Fouts (4), Johnny Unitas (4), Sammy Baugh (4), Dan Marino (5) and Sonny Jugensen (5) as the only players to lead the league in passing yards at least four times.

Manning has led the league in completions four times in his career and can join Sammy Baugh (5) and Dan Marino (6) as the only players to lead the league in completions at least five times.

Manning has led the league in pass attempts three times in his career and can join Sammy Baugh (4), Johnny Unitas (4), George Blanda (4) and Dan Marino (5) as the only players to lead the league in attempts at least four times.

Drew Brees, New Orleans, needs 4,000 passing yards to join Peyton Manning (13) as the only players in NFL history with at least nine 4,000-yard passing seasons. In 13 seasons, Brees has eight 4,000-yard passing seasons.

Brees needs four 400-yard passing games to surpass Peyton Manning (12) and Dan Marino (13) for the most all-time (see Manning note). In 13 seasons, Brees has 10 400-yard passing games.

Brees needs 37 touchdown passes to join Dan Marino (420), Peyton Manning (491) and Brett Favre (508) as the only players with 400 career touchdown passes (see Brady and Manning notes). In 13 seasons, Brees has 363 touchdown passes.

Brees can extend his NFL record streak of consecutive seasons with at least 30 touchdown passes. Brees has passed for at least 30 touchdowns in each of the past six seasons.

Brees has 25 games with four or more touchdown passes and needs seven such games to surpass Peyton Manning (31) for the most all-time (see Manning note).

Brees needs to pass for 300 yards in seven games to surpass Peyton Manning (84) for the most 300-yard passing games in NFL history (see Manning note). In 13 seasons, Brees has 78 300-yard passing games.

Brees needs 395 passing yards to surpass John Elway (51,475) for fourth place all-time (see Brady note). In 13 seasons, Brees has 51,081 passing yards.

Brees can become the first player to lead the league in touchdown passes five times in his career. Brees is currently tied with Len Dawson, Brett Favre, Peyton Manning, Johnny Unitas and Steve Young (4) for the most such seasons in NFL history (see Manning note).

Brees has led the league in passing yards four times in his career and can tie Sonny Jurgensen and Dan Marino (5) for the most seasons leading the league in passing yards.

Tom Brady, New England, has led the league in touchdown passes three times in his career and can tie Drew Brees, Len Dawson, Brett Favre, Peyton Manning, Johnny Unitas and Steve Young (4) for the most seasons leading the league in touchdown passes (see Brees and Manning notes).

Brady needs five touchdown passes to surpass Drew Brees (363) for fourth place all-time and needs 41 touchdown passes to join Dan Marino (420), Peyton Manning (491) and Brett Favre (508) as the only players with 400 career TDs (see Brees and Manning notes). In 14 seasons, Brady has 359 touchdown passes.

Brady needs 2,327 passing yards to surpass Warren Moon (49,325), Drew Brees (51,081) and John Elway (51,475) for fourth place all-time (see Brees note). In 14 seasons, Brady has 49,149 passing yards.

Brady needs 4,000 passing yards to join Drew Brees (8) and Peyton Manning (13) as the only players in NFL history with at least seven 4,000-yard passing seasons. In 14 seasons, Brady has six 4,000-yard passing seasons.

Brady needs four 300-yard passing games to surpass Brett Favre (62) and Dan Marino (63) for third place all-time. In 14 seasons, Brady has 59 300-yard passing games.

Philip Rivers, San Diego, has led the league in average yards per pass three times in his career and can join Steve Young (5) and Sid Luckman (7) as the only players in NFL history to do so in at least four seasons.

Adrian Peterson, Minnesota, needs 10 rushing touchdowns to join Emmitt Smith (8) and LaDainian Tomlinson (9) as the only players in NFL history to rush for 10 touchdowns in at least eight different seasons.

Peterson has five 200-yard rushing games in his career. Peterson needs two 200-yard games to surpass Tiki Barber (5) and O.J. Simpson (6) for the most all-time.

Peterson needs 14 rushing touchdowns to become the ninth player in NFL history with 100 rushing touchdowns. In seven seasons, Peterson has 86 rushing touchdowns.

Steven Jackson, Atlanta, needs 1,000 rushing yards to join Curtis Martin (10), Barry Sanders (10), Walter Payton and Emmitt Smith (11) as the only players in NFL history to rush for 1,000 yards in at least nine different seasons. In 10 seasons,

Jackson has rushed for 1,000 yards eight times.

Reggie Wayne, Indianapolis, needs 97 receptions to surpass Isaac Bruce (1,024), Terrell Owens (1,078), Tim Brown (1,094), Cris Carter (1,101) and Marvin Harrison (1,102) for third place all-time. In 13 seasons, Wayne has 1,006 receptions.

Wayne needs 1,369 receiving yards to surpass Henry Ellard (13,777), Cris Carter (13,899), James Lofton (14,004), Marvin Harrison (14,580) and Tim Brown (14,934) for sixth place all-time. In 13 seasons, Wayne has 13,566 receiving yards.

Wayne needs 100 receptions to join Andre Johnson, Brandon Marshall and Wes Welker (5) as the only players in NFL history with five 100-catch seasons. In 13 seasons, Wayne has four 100-catch seasons.

Wayne needs 1,000 receiving yards to join Terrell Owens (9), Jimmy Smith (9), Tim Brown (9), Randy Moss (10) and Jerry Rice (14) as the only players in NFL history with at least nine 1,000-yard receiving seasons. In 13 seasons, Wayne has eight 1,000-yard receiving seasons.

Calvin Johnson, Detroit, needs one 200-yard receiving game to surpass Lance Alworth (5) for the most all-time. In seven seasons, Johnson has five 200-yard receiving games.

Johnson needs 1,500 receiving yards to join Andre Johnson (3), Marvin Harrison (3) and Jerry Rice (4) as the only players with at least three such seasons in NFL history (see A. Johnson note). In seven seasons, Johnson has two 1,500-yard receiving seasons.

Wes Welker, Denver, needs 100 receptions to become the first player in NFL history with six 100-catch seasons (see A. Johnson and Marshall notes). Welker, Andre Johnson and Brandon Marshall are the only players with five 100-reception seasons.

Welker has led the league in receptions three times and can join Lionel Taylor (5) and Don Hutson (8) as the only players to lead the league in receptions at least four times.

Andre Johnson, Houston, needs 1,500 receiving yards to join Jerry Rice (4) as the only players with four 1,500-yard seasons. In 11 seasons, Johnson has three 1,500-yard receiving seasons.

Johnson needs two 100-yard receiving games to surpass Don Maynard (50) and Terrell Owens (51) for fourth-place all-time. In 11 seasons, Johnson has 50 100-yard receiving games.

Johnson needs 100 receptions to become the first player in NFL history with six 100-catch seasons (see Marshall and Welker notes). Johnson, Brandon Marshall and Wes Welker are the only players with five 100-reception seasons.

Johnson needs 73 receptions to become the 10th player in NFL history with 1,000 catches. In 11 seasons, Johnson has 927 receptions.

Brandon Marshall, Chicago, needs 100 receptions to become the first player in NFL history with six 100-catch seasons (see A. Johnson and Welker notes). Marshall, Andre Johnson and Wes Welker are the only players with five 100-reception seasons.

Jason Witten, Dallas, needs 262 receiving yards to surpass Shannon Sharpe (10,060) for second place all-time amongst tight ends (see Gates note). In 11 seasons, Witten has 9,799 receiving yards.

Antonio Gates, San Diego, needs 868 receiving yards to surpass Jason Witten (9,799) and Shannon Sharpe (10,060) for second place all-time amongst tight ends (see Witten note). In 11 seasons, Gates has 9,193 receiving yards.

Ed Reed is the all-time leader in interception-return yards and can add to his NFL record. In 12 seasons, Reed has 1,590 interception-return yards.

Reed needs eight interceptions to surpass Ken Riley (65), Dick "Night Train" Lane (68) and Rod Woodson (71) for third place all-time. In 12 seasons, Reed has 64 interceptions.

Charles Woodson, Oakland, needs two interception-return touchdowns to surpass Rod Woodson (12) for the most all-time. In 16 seasons, Woodson has 11 interception-return touchdowns.

Jared Allen, Chicago, has led the league in sacks twice in his career and can become the first player to lead the league three times since the sack became an official statistic in 1982 (see Ware note).

Allen needs 10 sacks to join John Randle (8) and Reggie White (9) as the only players with 10 sacks in at least eight consecutive seasons since 1982. Allen has accomplished the feat in each of the past seven seasons.

Allen needs 13.5 sacks to surpass Leslie O'Neal (132.5), Lawrence Taylor (132.5), John Abraham (133.5), Richard Dent (137.5), John Randle (137.5), Jason Taylor (139.5) and Michael Strahan (141.5) for fifth place since the sack became an official statistic in 1982. In 10 seasons, Allen has 128.5 sacks.

Allen needs one safety to surpass Ted Hendricks and Doug English (4) for the most all-time. In 10 seasons, Allen has four safeties.

John Abraham, Arizona, needs 8.5 sacks to surpass Richard Dent (137.5), John Randle (137.5), Jason Taylor (139.5) and Michael Strahan (141.5) for fifth place since the sack became an official statistic in 1982. In 14 seasons, Abraham has 133.5 sacks.

DeMarcus Ware, Denver, has led the league in sacks twice in his career and can become the first player to lead the league three times since the sack became an official statistic in 1982 (see Allen note).

Devin Hester, Atlanta, needs one return touchdown to surpass Deion Sanders (19) for the most all-time. In eight seasons, Hester has 19 return touchdowns (13 punt return, five kickoff return and one missed field goal return).

Adam Vinatieri, Indianapolis, needs 145 points to surpass John Carney (2,062) and Jason Hanson (2,150) for third place all-time. In 18 seasons, Vinatieri has 2,006 points.

Vinatieri needs 100 points to become the only player in NFL history to score 100 points in 17 different seasons. Vinatieri and Jason Elam are the only players to accomplish the feat 16 times.

Sebastian Janikowski, Oakland, needs eight 50-yard field goals to surpass Jason Hanson (52) for the most all-time. In 14 seasons, Janikowski has 45 50-yard field goals.

Joshua Cribbs is tied with Leon Washington (8) for the most kickoff-return touchdowns in NFL history and needs one to attain sole possession of first place (see Washington note).

Cribbs needs 1,443 kick-return yards to surpass Allen Rossum (11,947) for second place all-time. In nine seasons, Cribbs has 10,505 kick-return yards.

Leon Washington, Tennessee, is tied with Joshua Cribbs (8) for the most kickoff-return touchdowns in NFL history and needs one to attain sole possession of first place (see Cribbs note).

ACTIVE COACHES' CAREER RECORDS (Order Based on Career Victories)
Start of 2014 Season

Coach	Team(s)	Yrs.	Regular Season				Postseason			Career			
			Won	Lost	Tied	Pct.	Won	Lost	Pct.	Won	Lost	Tied	Pct.
Bill Belichick	Cleveland Browns, New England Patriots	19	199	105	0	.655	19	9	.679	218	114	0	.657
Tom Coughlin	Jacksonville Jaguars, New York Giants	18	158	130	0	.549	12	7	.632	170	137	0	.554
Jeff Fisher	Houston/Tennessee Oilers, Tennessee Titans,												
	St. Louis Rams	19	156	137	1	.532	5	6	.455	161	143	1	.530
Andy Reid	Philadelphia Eagles, Kansas City Chiefs	15	141	98	1	.590	10	10	.500	151	108	1	.583
John Fox	Carolina Panthers, Denver Broncos	12	107	85	0	.557	8	6	.571	115	91	0	.513
Marvin Lewis	Cincinnati Bengals	11	90	85	1	.514	0	5	.000	90	90	1	.500
Mike McCarthy	Green Bay Packers	8	82	45	1	.645	6	5	.545	86	50	1	.631
Lovie Smith	Chicago Bears, Tampa Bay Buccaneers	9	81	63	0	.563	3	3	.500	84	66	0	.560
Sean Payton	New Orleans Saints	8	73	39	0	.652	6	4	.600	79	43	0	.648
Pete Carroll	New York Jets, New England Patriots,	8	71	57	0	.555	6	4	.600	77	61	0	.558
	Seattle Seahawks												
Mike Tomlin	Pittsburgh Steelers	7	71	41	0	.634	5	3	.625	76	44	0	.633
John Harbaugh	Baltimore Ravens	6	62	34	0	.646	9	4	.692	71	38	0	.651
Mike Smith	Atlanta Falcons	6	60	36	0	.625	1	4	.200	61	40	0	.604
Ken Whisenhunt	Arizona Cardinals, Tennessee Titans	6	45	51	0	.469	4	2	.667	49	53	0	.480
Rex Ryan	New York Jets	5	42	38	0	.525	4	2	.667	46	40	0	.535
Jim Harbaugh	San Francisco 49ers	3	36	11	1	.760	5	3	.625	41	14	1	.741
Jason Garrett	Dallas Cowboys	4	29	27	0	.518	0	0	---	29	27	0	.518
Jim Caldwell	Indianapolis Colts, Detroit Lions	3	26	22	0	.542	2	2	.500	28	24	0	.538
Ron Rivera	Carolina Panthers	3	25	23	0	.521	0	1	.000	25	24	0	.510
Chuck Pagano	Indianapolis Colts	2	22	10	0	.688	1	2	.333	23	12	0	.657
Joe Philbin	Miami Dolphins	2	15	17	0	.469	0	0	---	15	17	0	.469
Bruce Arians	Arizona Cardinals	1	10	6	0	.625	0	0	---	10	6	0	.625
Chip Kelly	Philadelphia Eagles	1	10	6	0	.625	0	1	.000	10	7	0	.588
Mike McCoy	San Diego Chargers	1	9	7	0	.563	1	1	.500	10	8	0	.556
Marc Trestman	Chicago Bears	1	8	8	0	.500	0	0	---	8	8	0	.500
Dennis Allen	Oakland Raiders	2	8	24	0	.250	0	0	---	8	24	0	.250
Doug Marrone	Buffalo Bills	1	6	10	0	.375	0	0	---	6	10	0	.375
Gus Bradley	Jacksonville Jaguars	1	4	12	0	.250	0	0	---	4	12	0	.250
Jay Gruden	Washington Redskins	0	0	0	0	---	0	0	---	0	0	0	---
Bill O'Brien	Houston Texans	0	0	0	0	---	0	0	---	0	0	0	---
Mike Pettine	Cleveland Browns	0	0	0	0	---	0	0	---	0	0	0	---
Mike Zimmer	Minnesota Vikings	0	0	0	0	---	0	0	---	0	0	0	---

COACHES WITH 100 CAREER VICTORIES (Order Based on Career Victories)
Start of 2014 Season

Coach	Team(s)	Yrs.	Regular Season				Postseason			Career			
			Won	Lost	Tied	Pct.	Won	Lost	Pct.	Won	Lost	Tied	Pct.
1. Don Shula	Baltimore Colts, Miami Dolphins	33	328	156	6	.677	19	17	.528	347	173	6	.666
2. George Halas	Chicago Bears	40	318	148	31	.682	6	3	.667	324	151	31	.682
3. Tom Landry	Dallas Cowboys	29	250	162	6	.607	20	16	.556	270	178	6	.603
4. Earl (Curly) Lambeau	Green Bay Packers, Chicago Cardinals, Washington Redskins	33	226	132	22	.631	3	2	.600	229	134	22	.631
5. **Bill Belichick**	Cleveland Browns, New England Patriots	19	199	105	0	.655	19	9	.679	218	114	0	.657
6. Chuck Noll	Pittsburgh Steelers	23	193	148	1	.566	16	8	.667	209	156	1	.572
7. Marty Schottenheimer	Cleveland Browns, Kansas City Chiefs, Washington Redskins, San Diego Chargers	21	200	126	1	.613	5	13	.278	205	139	1	.596
8. Dan Reeves	Denver Broncos, New York Giants, Atlanta Falcons	23	190	165	2	.535	11	9	.550	201	174	2	.536
9. Chuck Knox	Los Angeles Rams, Buffalo Bills, Seattle Seahawks	22	186	147	1	.558	7	11	.389	193	158	1	.550
10. Bill Parcells	New York Giants, New England Patriots, New York Jets, Dallas Cowboys	19	172	130	1	.569	11	8	.579	183	138	1	.570
11. Mike Shanahan	Los Angeles Raiders, Denver Broncos, Washington Redskins	20	170	138	0	.552	8	6	.571	178	144	0	.553
12. Mike Holmgren	Green Bay Packers, Seattle Seahawks	17	161	111	0	.592	13	11	.542	174	122	0	.588
13. Joe Gibbs	Washington Redskins	16	154	94	0	.621	17	7	.708	171	101	0	.629
14. Paul Brown	Cleveland Browns, Cincinnati Bengals	21	166	100	6	.624	4	8	.333	170	108	6	.612
15. **Tom Coughlin**	Jacksonville Jaguars, New York Giants	18	158	130	0	.549	12	7	.632	170	137	0	.554
16. Bud Grant	Minnesota Vikings	18	158	96	5	.621	10	12	.455	168	108	5	.608
17. Bill Cowher	Pittsburgh Steelers	15	149	90	1	.623	12	9	.571	161	99	1	.619
Jeff Fisher	Houston/Tennessee Oilers, Tennessee Titans, St. Louis Rams	19	156	137	1	.532	5	6	.455	161	143	1	.530
19. Marv Levy	Kansas City Chiefs, Buffalo Bills	17	143	112	0	.561	11	8	.579	154	120	0	.562
20. Steve Owen	New York Giants	23	151	100	17	.602	2	8	.200	153	108	17	.586
21. **Andy Reid**	Philadelphia Eagles, Kansas City Chiefs	15	141	98	1	.590	10	10	.500	151	108	1	.583
22. Tony Dungy	Tampa Bay Buccaneers, Indianapolis Colts	13	139	69	0	.668	9	10	.474	148	79	0	.652
23. Hank Stram	Kansas City Chiefs, New Orleans Saints	17	131	97	10	.574	5	3	.625	136	100	10	.576
24. Weeb Ewbank	Baltimore Colts, New York Jets	20	130	129	7	.502	4	1	.800	134	130	7	.508
25. Mike Ditka	Chicago Bears, New Orleans Saints	14	121	95	0	.560	6	6	.500	127	101	0	.557
26. Dick Vermeil	Philadelphia Eagles, St. Louis Rams, Kansas City Chiefs	15	120	109	0	.524	6	5	.545	126	114	0	.525
27. Jim Mora	New Orleans Saints, Indianapolis Colts	15	125	106	0	.541	0	6	.000	125	112	0	.527
28. George Seifert	San Francisco 49ers, Carolina Panthers	11	114	62	0	.648	10	5	.667	124	67	0	.649
29. Sid Gillman	Los Angeles Rams, Los Angeles-San Diego Chargers, Houston Oilers	18	122	99	7	.552	1	5	.167	123	104	7	.542
30. George Allen	Los Angeles Rams, Washington Redskins	12	116	47	5	.712	2	7	.222	118	54	5	.686
Norv Turner	Washington Redskins, Oakland Raiders, San Diego Chargers	15	114	122	1	.483	4	4	.500	118	126	1	.484
32. Dennis Green	Minnesota Vikings, Arizona Cardinals	13	113	94	0	.546	4	8	.333	117	102	0	.534
33. **John Fox**	Carolina Panthers, Denver Broncos	12	107	85	0	.557	8	6	.571	115	91	0	.513
34. Don Coryell	St. Louis Cardinals, San Diego Chargers	14	111	83	1	.572	3	6	.333	114	89	1	.561
35. John Madden	Oakland Raiders	10	103	32	7	.759	9	7	.563	112	39	7	.739
36. Ray (Buddy) Parker	Chicago Cardinals, Detroit Lions, Pittsburgh Steelers	15	104	75	9	.581	3	1	.750	107	76	9	.585
37. Vince Lombardi	Green Bay Packers, Washington Redskins	10	96	34	6	.739	9	1	.900	105	35	6	.750
Tom Flores	Oakland-Los Angeles Raiders, Seattle Seahawks	12	97	87	0	.527	8	3	.727	105	90	0	.538
39. Bill Walsh	San Francisco 49ers	10	92	59	1	.609	10	4	.714	102	63	1	.617
40. Jon Gruden	Oakland Raiders, Tampa Bay Buccaneers	11	95	81	0	.540	5	4	.556	100	85	0	.541

Active coaches in bold.
From 1920-71, tie games were not included in winning percentage.

DRAFT LIST FOR 2014

79th Annual NFL Draft, May 8-10, 2014
+Denotes Compensatory Selection
#Denotes Underclassman Selection

ARIZONA CARDINALS
1. Deone Bucannon—27, DB, Washington State,
      from NEW ORLEANS
2.# Troy Niklas—52, TE, Notre Dame
3. Kareem Martin—84, DE, North Carolina
      John Brown—91, WR, Pittsburg State,
      from NEW ORLEANS
4. Logan Thomas—120, QB, Virginia Tech
5. Ed Stinson—160, DE, Alabama
6. Walter Powell—196, WR, Murray State

ATLANTA FALCONS
1. Jake Matthews—6, T, Texas A&M
2. Ra'Shede Hageman—37, DE, Minnesota
3. Dezmen Southward—68, DB, Wisconsin
4.# Devonta Freeman—103, RB, Florida State
  + Prince Shembo—139, LB, Notre Dame
5. Ricardo Allen—147, DB, Purdue
      Marquis Spurill—168, LB, Syracuse, from CAROLINA
      through MINNESOTA
7#+Yawin Smallwood—253, LB, Connecticut
  + Tyler Starr—255, LB, South Dakota

BALTIMORE RAVENS
1. C.J. Mosley—17, LB, Alabama
2.# Timmy Jernigan—48, DT, Florida State
3. Terrence Brooks—79, DB, Florida State
  + Crockett Gilmore—99, TE, Colorado State
4.+ Brent Urban—134, DE, Virginia
  + Lorenzo Taliaferro—138, RB, Coastal Carolina
5.+ John Urschel—175, C, Penn State
6. Keith Wenning—194, QB, Ball State
7. Michael Campanaro—218, WR, Wake Forest,
      from CLEVELAND

BUFFALO BILLS
1.# Sammy Watkins—4, WR, Clemson, from CLEVELAND
2.# Cyrus Kouandijo—44, T, Alabama, from ST. LOUIS
3. Preston Brown—73, LB, Louisville
4. Ross Cockrell—109, DB, Duke
5. Cyril Richardson—153, G, Baylor, from ST. LOUIS
7. Randell Johnson—221, LB, Florida Atlantic,
      from TAMPA BAY
      Seantrel Henderson—237, T, Miami, from PHILADELPHIA

CAROLINA PANTHERS
1.# Kelvin Benjamin—28, WR, Florida State
2.# Kony Ealy—60, DE, Missouri
3.# Trai Turner—92, G, Louisiana State
4. Tre Boston—128, DB, North Carolina
5. Bené Benwikere—148, DB, San Jose State,
      from MINNESOTA
6. Tyler Gaffney—204, RB, Stanford

CHICAGO BEARS
1. Kyle Fuller—14, DB, Virginia Tech
2.# Ego Ferguson—51, DT, Louisiana State
3. Will Sutton—82, DT, Arizona State
4.# Ka'Deem Carey—117, RB, Arizona
      Brock Vereen—131, DB, Minnesota, from DENVER
6. David Fales—183, QB, San Jose State, from TAMPA BAY
      Pat O'Donnell—191, P, Miami
7. Charles Leno—246, T, Boise State

CINCINNATI BENGALS
1. Darqueze Dennard—24, DB, Michigan State
2.# Jeremy Hill—55, RB, Louisiana State
3. Will Clarke—88, DE, West Virginia
4.# Russell Bodine—111, C, North Carolina,
      from DETROIT through SEATTLE
5. A.J. McCarron—164, QB, Alabama
6.+ Marquis Flowers—212, LB, Arizona
7. James Wright—239, WR, Louisiana State
  + Lavelle Westbrooks—252, DB, Georgia Southern

CLEVELAND BROWNS
1. Justin Gilbert—8, DB, Oklahoma State, from MINNESOTA
  # Johnny Manziel—22, QB, Texas A&M, from PHILADELPHIA
2. Joel Bitonio—35, G, Nevada
3. Christian Kirksey—71, LB, Iowa
  # Terrance West—94, RB, Towson, from SAN FRANCISCO
4. Pierre Desir—127, DB, Lindenwood, from INDIANAPOLIS

DALLAS COWBOYS
1. Zack Martin—16, G, Notre Dame
2.# Demarcus Lawrence—34, DE, Boise State,
      from WASHINGTON
4. Anthony Hitchens—119, LB, Iowa
5. Devin Street—146, WR, Pittsburgh,
      from OAKLAND through SEATTLE and DETROIT
7. Ben Gardner—231, DE, Stanford
      Will Smith—238, LB, Texas Tech, from KANSAS CITY
  + Ahmad Dixon—248, DB, Baylor
  + Ken Bishop—251, DT, Northern Illinois
  #+ Terrance Mitchell—254, DB, Oregon

DENVER BRONCOS
1.# Bradley Roby—31, DB, Ohio State
2.# Cody Latimer—56, WR, Indiana,
      from KANSAS CITY through SAN FRANCISCO
3. Michael Schofield—95, T, Michigan
5. Lamin Barrow—156, LB, Louisiana State, from CHICAGO
6. Matt Paradis—207, C, Boise State
7. Corey Nelson—242, LB, Oklahoma,
      from NEW ORLEANS through SAN FRANCISCO

DETROIT LIONS
1.# Eric Ebron—10, TE, North Carolina
2. Kyle Van Noy—40, LB, Brigham Young,
      from MINNESOTA through SEATTLE
3. Travis Swanson—76, C, Arkansas
4.+ Nevin Lawson—133, DB, Utah State
  + Larry Webster—136, DE, Bloomsburg
5. Caraun Reid—158, DT, Princeton, from DALLAS
6. T.J. Jones—189, WR, Notre Dame
7. Nate Freese—229, K, Boston College,
      from CHICAGO through DALLAS

GREEN BAY PACKERS
1.# Ha Ha Clinton-Dix—21, DB, Alabama
2.# Davante Adams—53, WR, Fresno State
3. Khyri Thornton—85, DE, Southern Mississippi
#+Richard Rodgers—98, TE, California
4. Carl Bradford—121, LB, Arizona State
5. Corey Lindsey—161, C, Ohio State
+ Jared Abbrederis—176, WR, Wisconsin
6. Demetri Goodson—197, DB, Baylor
7. Jeff Janis—236, WR, Saginaw Valley State

HOUSTON TEXANS
1.# Jadeveon Clowney—1, DE, South Carolina
2.# Xavier Su'a-Filo—33, G, UCLA
3. C.J. Fiedorowicz—65, TE, Iowa
Louis Nix—83, NT, Notre Dame, from PITTSBURGH
    through CLEVELAND and PHILADELPHIA
4.+Tom Savage—135, QB, Pittsburgh
6.# Jeoffrey Pagan—177, DE, Alabama
Alfred Blue—181, RB, Louisiana State, from OAKLAND
+ Jay Prosch—211, RB, Auburn
7. Andre Hal—216, DB, Vanderbilt
+ Lonnie Ballentine—256, DB, Memphis

INDIANAPOLIS COLTS
2. Jack Mewhort—59, G, Ohio State
3.# Donte Moncrief—90, WR, Mississippi
5. Jonathan Newsome—166, LB, Ball State
6. Andrew Jackson—203, LB, Western Kentucky
7. Ulrick John—232, T, Georgia State, from BALTIMORE

JACKSONVILLE JAGUARS
1.# Blake Bortles—3, QB, Central Florida
2.# Marqise Lee—39, WR, Southern California
Allen Robinson—61, WR, Penn State,
    from SAN FRANCISCO
3. Brandon Linder—93, G, Miami, from NEW ENGLAND
4. Aaron Colvin—114, DB, Oklahoma, from BALTIMORE
5. Telvin Smith—144, LB, Florida State
Chris Smith—159, DE, Arkansas, from BALTIMORE
6. Luke Bowanko—205, C, Virginia, from SAN FRANCISCO
7.# Storm Johnson—222, RB, Central Florida

KANSAS CITY CHIEFS
1. Dee Ford—23, DE, Auburn
3. Phillip Gaines—87, DB, Rice
4.# De'Anthony Thomas—124, RB, Oregon
5. Aaron Murray—163, QB, Georgia
6. Zach Fulton—193, G, Tennessee, from DALLAS
7. Laurent Duvernay-Tardif—200, T, McGill

MIAMI DOLPHINS
1. Ja'Wuan Jones—19, T, Tennessee
2.# Jarvis Landry—63, WR, Louisiana State,
    from DENVER through SAN FRANCISCO
3. Billy Turner—67, T, North Dakota State
4. Walt Aikens—125, DB, Liberty, from SAN DIEGO
5. Arthur Lynch—155, TE, Georgia
Jordan Tripp—171, LB, Montana
    from DENVER through SAN FRANCISCO
6. Matt Hazel—190, WR, Coastal Carolina
7. Terrence Fede—234, DE, Marist

MINNESOTA VIKINGS
1. Anthony Barr—9, LB, UCLA,
    from BUFFALO through CLEVELAND
Teddy Bridgewater—32, QB, Louisville, from SEATTLE
3.# Scott Crichton—72, DE, Oregon State
Jerick McKinnon—96, RB, Georgia Southern,
    from SEATTLE
5.# David Yankey—145, G, Stanford, from CLEVELAND
6. Antone Exum—182, DB, Virginia Tech, from ATLANTA
Kendall James—184, DB, Maine
7. Shamar Stephen—220, NT, Connecticut, from ATLANTA
Brandon Watts—223, LB, Georgia Tech
Jabari Price—225, DB, North Carolina,
    from NEW YORK GIANTS through CAROLINA

NEW ENGLAND PATRIOTS
1. Dominique Easley—29, DE, Florida
2. Jimmy Garoppolo—62, QB, Eastern Illinois
4. Bryan Stork—105, C, Florida State, from JACKSONVILLE
James White—130, RB, Wisconsin
#+Cameron Fleming—140, T, Stanford
6. Jon Halapio—179, G, Florida, from JACKSONVILLE
Zach Moore—198, DE, Concordia, St. Paul
    from PHILADELPHIA
Jemea Thomas—206, DB, Georgia Tech
7. Jeremy Gallon—244, WR, Michigan

NEW ORLEANS SAINTS
1.# Brandin Cooks—20, WR, Oregon State, from ARIZONA
2. Stanley Jean-Baptiste—58, DB, Nebraska
4.# Khairi Fortt—126, LB, California
5.# Vinnie Sunseri—167, DB, Alabama
Ronald Powell—169, LB, Florida,
    from NEW ENGLAND through PHILADELPHIA
6. Tavon Rooks—202, T, Kansas State

NEW YORK GIANTS
1.# Odell Beckham—12, WR, Louisiana State
2. Weston Richburg—43, C, Colorado State
3. Jay Bromley—74, DT, Syracuse
4. Andre Williams—113, RB, Boston College
5. Nat Berhe—152, DB, San Diego State
+ Devon Kennard—174, LB, Southern California
6. Bennett Jackson—187, DB, Notre Dame

DRAFT LIST FOR 2014

NEW YORK JETS
1.# Calvin Pryor—18, DB, Louisville
2.# Jace Amaro—49, TE, Texas Tech
3. Dexter McDougle—80, DB, Maryland
4. Jalen Saunders—104, WR, Oklahoma, from TAMPA BAY
    Shaquelle Evans—115, WR, UCLA
    + Dakota Dozier—137, G, Furman
5. Jeremiah George—154, LB, Iowa State
6. Brandon Dixon—195, DB, Northwest Missouri State
    + Quincy Enunwa—209, WR, Nebraska
    + IK Enemkpali—210, LB, Louisiana Tech
    + Tajh Boyd—213, QB, Clemson
7. Trevor Reilly—233, LB, Utah

OAKLAND RAIDERS
1. Khalil Mack—5, LB, Buffalo
2. Derek Carr—36, QB, Fresno State
3. Gabe Jackson—81, G, Mississippi State, from MIAMI
4. Justin Ellis—107, DT, Louisiana Tech
    Keith McGill—116, DB, Utah, from MIAMI
7. T.J. Carrie—219, DB, Ohio
    Shelby Harris—235, DE, Illinois State, from ARIZONA
    # Jonathan Dowling—247, DB, Western Kentucky,
        from SEATTLE

PHILADELPHIA EAGLES
1. Marcus Smith—26, LB, Louisville,
        from INDIANAPOLIS through CLEVELAND
2. Jordan Matthews—42, WR, Vanderbilt, from TENNESSEE
3. Josh Huff—86, WR, Oregon
4. Jaylen Watkins—101, DB, Florida, from HOUSTON
5. Taylor Hart—141, DE, Oregon, from HOUSTON
    # Ed Reynolds—162, DB, Stanford
7. Beau Allen—224, DT, Wisconsin, from BUFFALO

PITTSBURGH STEELERS
1.# Ryan Shazier—15, LB, Ohio State
2.# Stephon Tuitt—46, DE, Notre Dame
3.+ Dri Archer—97, RB, Kent State
4.# Martavis Bryant—118, WR, Clemson
5. Shaquille Richardson—157, DB, Arizona
    + Wesley Johnson—173, T, Vanderbilt
6. Jordan Zumwalt—192, LB, UCLA
    + Daniel McCullers—215, DE, Tennessee
7. Rob Blanchflower—230, TE, Massachusetts

ST. LOUIS RAMS
1.# Greg Robinson—2, T, Auburn, from WASHINGTON
    Aaron Donald—13, DT, Pittsburgh
2. Lamarcus Joyner—41, DB, Florida State, from BUFFALO
3.# Tre Mason—75, RB, Auburn
4. Maurice Alexander—110, DB, Utah State
6. E.J. Gaines—188, DB, Missouri
    + Garrett Gilbert—214, QB, Southern Methodist
7. Mitchell Van Dyk—226, T, Portland State
    Christian Bryant—241, DB, Ohio State, from INDIANAPOLIS
    + Michael Sam—249, DE, Missouri
    + Demetrius Rhaney—250, C, Tennessee State

SAN DIEGO CHARGERS
1. Jason Verrett—25, DB, Texas Christian
2. Jeremiah Attaochu—50, LB, Georgia Tech, from MIAMI
3. Chris Watt—89, G, Notre Dame
5. Ryan Carrethers—165, DT, Arkansas State
6. Marion Grice—201, RB, Arizona State
7. Tevin Reese—240, WR, Baylor

SAN FRANCISCO 49ERS
1. Jimmie Ward—30, DB, Northern Illinois
2. Carlos Hyde—57, RB, Ohio State,
        from SAN DIEGO through MIAMI
3.# Marcus Martin—70, C, Southern California,   .
        from JACKSONVILLE
    Chris Borland—77, LB, Wisconsin, from TENNESSEE
    + Brandon Thomas—100, G, Clemson
4.# Bruce Ellington—106, WR, South Carolina,
        from CLEVELAND
    Dontae Johnson—129, DB, North Carolina State
5.# Aaron Lynch—150, LB, South Florida,
        from DETROIT through JACKSONVILLE
    Keith Reaser—170, DB, Florida Atlantic
6. Kenneth Acker—180, DB, Southern Methodist,
        from CLEVELAND
7. Kaleb Ramsey—243, DE, Boston College, from CAROLINA
    Trey Millard—245, RB, Oklahoma

SEATTLE SEAHAWKS
2.# Paul Richardson—45, WR, Colorado, from DETROIT
    Justin Britt—64, T, Missouri
4. Cassius Marsh—108, DE, UCLA, from MINNESOTA
    Kevin Norwood—123, WR, Alabama, from CINCINNATI
    Kevin Pierre-Louis—132, LB, Boston College
5. Jimmy Staten—172, DT, Middle Tennessee
6. Garrett Scott—199, T, Marshall, from CINCINNATI
    Eric Pinkins—208, DB, San Diego State
7. Kiero Small—227, RB, Arkansas, from DETROIT

TAMPA BAY BUCCANEERS
1.# Mike Evans—7, WR, Texas A&M
2.# Austin Seferian-Jenkins—38, TE, Washington
3. Charles Sims—69, RB, West Virginia
5. Kadeem Edwards—143, G, Tennessee State
    Kevin Pamphile—149, T, Purdue, from BUFFALO
6. Robert Herron—185, WR, Wyoming, from BUFFALO

TENNESSEE TITANS
1. Taylor Lewan—11, T, Michigan
2.# Bishop Sankey—54, RB, Washington,
        from PHILADELPHIA
4. DaQuan Jones—112, DT, Penn State
    Marqueston Huff—122, DB, Wyoming,
        from PHILADELPHIA
5. Avery Williamson—151, LB, Kentucky
6. Zach Mettenberger—178, QB, Louisiana State,
        from WASHINGTON

WASHINGTON REDSKINS
2. Trent Murphy—47, LB, Stanford, from DALLAS
3. Morgan Moses—66, T, Virginia
    Spencer Long—78, G, Nebraska, from DALLAS
4.# Bashaud Breeland—102, DB, Clemson
5. Ryan Grant—142, WR, Tulane
6.# Lache Seastrunk—186, RB, Baylor, from TENNESSEE
7. Ted Bolser—217, TE, Indiana
    Zach Hocker—228, K, Arkansas, from TENNESSEE

NUMBER OF PLAYERS DRAFTED—2014

BY POSITION:

Defensive Backs 53
Linebackers 37
Wide Receivers 33
Defensive Ends 25
Running Backs 22
Tackles..19
Guards...16
Quarterbacks 14
Defensive Tackles..............................12
Centers 10
Tight Ends..10
Kicker 2
Nose Tackles.......................................2
Punters 1

BY COLLEGE:

Louisiana State 9
Alabama 8
Notre Dame..8
Florida State 7
Ohio State 6
Stanford..6
Baylor 5
Clemson 5
North Carolina......................................5
UCLA 5
Wisconsin 5
Arkansas...4
Auburn 4
Boston College 4
Florida...4
Louisville...4
Missouri 4
Oklahoma..4
Oregon 4
Arizona 3
Arizona State..3
Boise State...3
Georgia Tech 3
Iowa 3
Miami 3
Michigan 3
Nebraska...3
Penn State 3
Pittsburgh 3
Southern California...............................3
Tennessee...3
Texas A&M..3
Vanderbilt..3
Virginia..3
Virginia Tech 3
Ball State 2
California 2
Central Florida 2
Coastal Carolina 2
Colorado State 2
Connecticut...2
Florida Atlantic 2
Fresno State 2
Georgia 2
Georgia Southern 2
Indiana 2
Louisiana Tech 2
Minnesota 2
Northern Illinois....................................2
Oregon State 2
Purdue 2

San Diego State 2
San Jose State 2
South Carolina......................................2
Southern Methodist 2
Syracuse...2
Tennessee State 2
Texas Tech 2
Utah..2
Utah State 2
Washington 2
West Virginia 2
Western Kentucky 2
Wyoming 2
Arkansas State 1
Bloomsburg 1
Brigham Young 1
Buffalo 1
Colorado 1
Concordia, St. Paul 1
Duke 1
Eastern Illinois......................................1
Furman..1
Georgia State 1
Illinois State 1
Iowa State...1
Kansas State 1
Kent State 1
Kentucky...1
Liberty 1
Lindenwood 1
Maine..1
Marist 1
Marshall 1
Maryland 1
Massachusetts......................................1
McGill 1
Memphis 1
Michigan State 1
Middle Tennessee.................................1
Mississippi 1
Mississippi State 1
Montana..1
Murray State 1
Nevada..1
North Carolina State.............................1
North Dakota State...............................1
Northwest Missouri State 1
Ohio..1
Oklahoma State....................................1
Pittsburg State 1
Portland State.......................................1
Princeton 1
Rice 1
Saginaw Valley State 1
South Dakota 1
South Florida...1
Southern Mississippi 1
Texas Christian 1
Towson 1
Tulane 1
Wake Forest 1
Washington State 1

BY CONFERENCE:

Southeastern......................................49
Atlantic Coast......................................42
Pacific 12...34
Big Ten...30
Big 12...17
Mountain West.....................................16
American Athletic 12
Conference USA....................................9
Independent 9
Mid-American 8
Ohio Valley..4
Sun Belt 4
Big South 3
Mid-America Intercollegiate Athletic........3
Missouri Valley Football.........................3
Southern 3
Big Sky 2
Colonial Athletic 2
Great Lakes Intercollegiate Athletic 1
Ivy 1
Northern Sun 1
Pennsylvania State Athletic......................1
Pioneer Football 1
Quebec Student Sports Foundation.........1

UNDERCLASSMEN IN THE DRAFT

Year	D1-FBS	Drafted	In Top 10
1990	28	18	5
1991	23	19	1
1992	30	21	5
1993	34	24	5
1994	31	25	6
1995	33	22	2
1996	24	16	4
1997	34	25	6
1998	32	19	3
1999	31	22	5
2000	26	20	4
2001	35	27	5
2002	38	26	2
2003	47	32	5
2004	43	35	5
2005	51	37	4
2006	52	33	6
2007	40	29	5
2008	53	39	4
2009	46	41	5
2010	53	46	5
2011	56	43	8
2012	65	44	8
2013	73	52	3
2014	98	61	6

The NFL uses a system of Instant Replay Review to aid officiating. The following procedures will be used:

Coaches' Challenge: In each game, a team will be permitted two challenges that will initiate Instant Replay reviews. The head coach will initiate a challenge by throwing a red flag onto the field of play before the next legal snap or kick. Each challenge will require the use of a team timeout. If a challenge is upheld, the timeout will be restored. A challenge will only be restored if a team is successful on both of its challenges, in which case it shall be awarded a third challenge. No challenges will be recognized from a team that has exhausted its timeouts.

Note 1: If there is a foul that delays the next snap, the team committing that foul will no longer be able to challenge the previous ruling. A team may challenge any reviewable play except when the on-field ruling is a score for either team, an interception, a fumble or backward pass that is recovered by an opponent or goes out of bounds through an opponent's end zone, or a muffed scrimmage kick recovered by the kicking team. A team is also prohibited from challenging any ruling after the two-minute warning of each half, and throughout any overtime period.

Replay Official's Request for Review: After all scoring plays, interceptions, fumbles and backward passes that are recovered by an opponent or go out of bounds through an opponent's end zone, muffed scrimmage kicks recovered by the kicking team, after the two-minute warning of each half and throughout any overtime period, any Replay Review will be initiated by a Replay Official from a Replay Booth comparable to the location of the coaches' booth or Press Box. There is no limit to the number of Replay Reviews that may be initiated by the Replay Official. His ability to initiate a review will be unrelated to the number of timeouts that either team has remaining, and no timeout will be charged for any review initiated by the Replay Official. The Replay Official must initiate a review before the ball is next legally put in play.

Review by Referee: All Replay Reviews will be conducted by the Referee on a field-level monitor after consultation with the covering official(s), prior to review. During the review, the Referee will consult with designated members of the Officiating department at the NFL office. A decision will be reversed only when the Referee has indisputable visual evidence available to him that warrants the change. All reviewable aspects of the play may be examined and are subject to reversal, even if not identified in a coach's challenge or if not the specific reason for a Replay Official's request for review.

Time Limit: Each review will be a maximum of 60 seconds in length, timed from when the Referee begins his review of the play at the field-level monitor.

Reviewable Plays: The Replay System will cover the following play situations only:

A. Plays involving possession, including:
 1. Whether a pass was complete, incomplete, intercepted in the field of play, at sideline, goal line, end zone, and end line.
 2. Whether a loose ball was recovered in the field of play, at sideline, goal line, end zone, and end line.
 3. Whether a player (passer) fumbled or threw a pass.
 4. Whether a pass has been thrown forward or backward.
 5. Whether there has been an illegal forward handoff.
 6. Whether a runner fumbled or was down by contact.

B. Plays involving touching, including:
 1. Whether a forward pass has been touched by any player.
 2. Whether a runner is down by defensive contact.
 3. Whether a loose ball has been touched by a player.
 4. Whether the ball has touched a pylon.
 5. Whether a kick has been touched.
 6. Whether a loose ball in play has struck a video board, guide wire, sky cam, or any other object.

C. Plays governed by the goal line, including:
 1. Scoring plays, including the ball breaking the plane of the goal line.
  a. Whether a field goal or PAT attempt has crossed below or above the crossbar, inside or outside the uprights when it is lower than the top of the uprights, or has touched anything.
 2. Whether there has been a touchback, when the on-field ruling involves a runner's momentum.

D. Plays governed by the sidelines, including:
 1. Whether a runner/receiver is in or out of bounds.
 2. Whether a loose ball touches a boundary line or anything on or outside such line.

E. Plays governed by the end lines, including:
 1. Whether a runner/receiver is in or out of bounds.
 2. Whether a loose ball is in or out of bounds.

F. Plays governed by the line of scrimmage, including:
 1. Whether a forward pass has been thrown from beyond or behind the line of scrimmage.
 2. Whether a forward pass has been thrown from behind the line of scrimmage after the ball has been beyond the line.

G. Other.
 1. The position of the ball with respect to a first down.
 2. Whether more than 11 players were on the field at the snap.

Note 1: *If an on-field ruling of a dead ball (down by contact, out of bounds, or incomplete forward pass) is changed, the ball belongs to the recovering player at the spot of the recovery, and any advance is nullified. If the ball goes out of bounds in an end zone, the result of the play will be either a touchback or a safety.*

Note 2: *If the on-field ruling is a dead ball, any recovery must occur in the continuing action following the loss of possession.*

Note 3: *If the Referee does not have indisputable visual evidence as to which player recovered the loose ball, or that the ball went out of bounds, the ruling on the field will stand.*

Non-reviewable plays include, but are not limited to:
1. Status of the play or game clock.
2. Proper down.
3. Penalty administration, including the spot of a foul.
4. Runner ruled down by defensive contact or out of bounds (not involving fumbles or the line to gain).
5. The position of the ball not relating to first down or goal line.
6. Field-goal or Try attempts that cross above either upright without touching anything.
7. Inadvertent/Erroneous Whistle.
8. Quarterback "spike" to kill clock.

INSTANT REPLAY HISTORY

From 1986-1991, a limited system of Instant Replay was used on a year-by-year basis. Replay also was experimented with during the 1996 and 1998 preseasons. For the 1999 season, the NFL introduced a system of Referee Replay Review to aid officiating. That system was extended on a one-year basis for the 2000 season and then approved for the next three years through 2003. The system was extended on a five-year basis in March 2004 and was later installed permanently in March 2007.

Following are the results of the different systems:

REGULAR SEASON, 1986-1991

Year	Games	Plays Closely Reviewed	Reversals
1986	224	374	38
1987	210	490	57
1988	224	537	53
1989	224	492	65
1990	224	504	73
1991	224	570	90
TOTAL	1,330	2,967	376

PRESEASON, 1996, 1998

Year	Games	Challenges	Reversals
1996	10	13	3
1998	10	10	3
TOTAL	20	23	6

REGULAR SEASON, 1999-2013

Year	Games	Total Replay Reviews	Challenges	Reversals
1999	248	195	133	57
2000	248	247	179	84
2001	248	258	191	89
2002	256	294	208	94
2003	256	255	184	66
2004	256	283	233	88
2005	256	295	223	92
2006	256	311	237	107
2007	256	327	250	122
2008	256	315	229	117
2009	256	328	228	126
2010	256	361	252	133
2011	256	390	209	172
2012	256	435	157	170
2013	256	423	183	185
TOTAL	3,816	4,717	3,096	1,702

The following procedures will be used to break standings ties for postseason playoffs and to determine regular-season schedules. Note: Tie games count as one-half win and one-half loss for both clubs.

TO BREAK A TIE WITHIN A DIVISION

If, at the end of the regular season, two or more clubs in the same division finish with the best won-lost-tied percentage, the following steps will be taken until a champion is determined:

TWO CLUBS

1. Head-to-head (best won-lost-tied percentage in games between the clubs.)

2. Best won-lost-tied percentage in games played within the division.

3. Best won-lost-tied percentage in common games.

4. Best won-lost-tied percentage in games played within the conference.

5. Strength of victory in all games.

6. Strength of schedule in all games.

7. Best combined ranking among conference teams in points scored and points allowed in all games.

8. Best combined ranking among all teams in points scored and points allowed in all games.

9. Best net points in common games.

10. Best net points in all games.

11. Best net touchdowns in all games.

12. Coin toss.

THREE OR MORE CLUBS

(Note: If two clubs remain tied after one or more clubs are eliminated during any step, tie-breaker re-starts at Step One of two-club format. If three clubs remain tied after a fourth club is eliminated during any step, tie-breaker re-starts at Step One of three-club format.)

1. Head-to-head (best won-lost-tied percentage in games among the clubs.)

2. Best won-lost-tied percentage in games played within the division.

3. Best won-lost-tied percentage in common games.

4. Best won-lost-tied percentage in games played within the conference.

5. Strength of victory in all games.

6. Strength of schedule in all games.

7. Best combined ranking among conference teams in points scored and points allowed in all games.

8. Best combined ranking among all teams in points scored and points allowed in all games.

9. Best net points in common games.

10. Best net points in all games.

11. Best net touchdowns in all games.

12. Coin toss.

TO BREAK A TIE FOR THE WILD-CARD TEAM

If necessary to break ties to determine the two Wild Card clubs from each conference, the following steps will be taken:

A. If all the tied clubs are from the same division, apply division tie-breaker.

B. If the tied clubs are from different divisions, apply the following steps:

TWO CLUBS

1. Head-to-head, if applicable.

2. Best won-lost-tied percentage in the games played within the conference.

3. Best won-lost-tied percentage in common games, minimum of four.

4. Strength of victory in all games.

5. Strength of schedule in all games.

6. Best combined ranking among conference teams in points scored and points allowed in all games.

7. Best combined ranking among all teams in points scored and points allowed in all games.

8. Best net points in conference games.

9. Best net points in all games.

10. Best net touchdowns in all games.

11. Coin toss.

THREE OR MORE CLUBS

(Note: If two clubs remain tied after one or more clubs are eliminated during any step, tie-breaker re-starts at Step One of two-club format. If three clubs remain tied after a fourth club is eliminated during any step, tie-breaker re-starts at Step Two of three-club format.)

1. Apply division tie-breaker to eliminate all but highest ranked club in each division prior to proceeding to step two. The original seeding within a division upon application of the division tie-breaker remains the same for all subsequent applications of the procedure that are necessary to identify the two Wild Card participants.

2. Head-to-head sweep (apply only if one has defeated each of the others or one club has lost to each of the others.)

3. Best won-lost-tied percentage in games played within the conference.

4. Best won-lost-tied percentage in common games, minimum of four.

5. Strength of victory in all games.

6. Strength of schedule in all games.

7. Best combined ranking among conference teams in points scored and points allowed in all games.

8. Best combined ranking among all teams in points scored and points allowed in all games.

9. Best net points in conference games.

10. Best net points in all games.

11. Best net touchdowns in all games.

12. Coin toss.

When the first Wild Card Team has been identified, the procedure is repeated to name the second Wild Card (i.e., eliminate all but the highest ranked club in each division prior to proceeding to step two). In situations where three teams from the same division are involved in the procedure, the original seeding of the teams remains the same for subsequent applications of the tie-breaker if the top-ranked team in that division qualifies for a Wild Card berth.

OTHER TIE-BREAKING PROCEDURES

1. Only one club advances to the playoffs in any tie-breaking step. Remaining tied clubs revert to the first step of the applicable division or Wild Card tie-breakers. As an example, if two clubs remain tied in any tie-breaker step after all other clubs have been eliminated, the procedure reverts to Step 1 of the two-club format to determine the winner. When one club wins the tie-breaker, all other clubs revert to Step 1 of the applicable two-club or three-club format.

2. In comparing records against common opponents among tied teams, the best won-lost-tied percentage is the deciding factor since teams may have played an unequal number of games.

3. To determine home-field priority among division-titlists, apply Wild Card tie-breakers.

4. To determine home-field priority for Wild Card qualifiers, apply division tie-breakers (if teams are from the same division) or Wild Card tie-breakers (if teams are from different divisions).

5. To determine the best combined ranking among conference teams in points scored and points allowed, add a team's position in the two categories, and the lowest score wins. For example, if Team A is first in points scored and second in points allowed, its combined ranking is "3." If Team B is third in points scored and first in points allowed, its combined ranking is "4." Team A then wins the tiebreaker. If two teams are tied for a position, both teams are awarded the ranking as if they held it solely. For example, if Team A and Team B are tied for first in points scored, each team is assigned a ranking of "1" in that category, and if Team C is third, its ranking will still be "3."

TIE-BREAKING PROCEDURE FOR SELECTION MEETING

1. Clubs not participating in the playoffs shall select in the first through 20th positions in reverse standings order.

2. The Super Bowl winner is last and Super Bowl loser is next-to-last.

3. The losers of the Conference Championship games shall select 29th and 30th based on won-lost-tied percentage.

4. The losers of the Divisional playoff games shall select 25th through 28th based on won-lost-tied percentage.

5. The losers of the Wild Card games shall select 21st through 24th based on won-lost-tied percentage.

If ties exist in any grouping except (2) above, such ties shall be broken by strength-of-schedule. If any ties cannot be broken by strength-of-schedule, the divisional or conference tie-breakers, if applicable, shall be applied. Any ties that still exist shall be broken by a coin flip.

WAIVERS

The waiver system is a procedure by which player contracts or NFL rights to players are made available by a club to other clubs in the League. During the procedure, the 31 other clubs either file claims to obtain the players or waive the opportunity to do so—thus the term "waiver." Claiming clubs are assigned players on a priority based on the inverse of won-and-lost standing. The claiming period is 24 hours from the first business day after the Super Bowl through the conclusion of the regular season. If a player passes through waivers unclaimed, he becomes a free agent. All waivers are no recall and no withdrawal. Under the Collective Bargaining Agreement, from the beginning of the waiver system each year through the trading deadline, any veteran who has acquired four years of pension credit is not subject to the waiver system if the club desires to release him. After the trading deadline, such players are subject to the waiver system.

ACTIVE/INACTIVE LIST

The Active/Inactive List is the principal status for players participating for a club. It consists of all players under contract who are eligible for preseason, regular-season, and postseason games. Teams are permitted to open training camp with no more than 90 players under contract and thereafter must meet two mandatory roster reductions prior to the season opener. Teams will be permitted an Active List of 46 players and an Inactive List of seven players for each regular-season and postseason game. Teams also are permitted to establish Practice Squads of up to eight players who are eligible to participate in practice, but these players remain free agents and are eligible to sign with any other team in the league.

August 26....................Roster reduction to 75 players
August 30....................Roster reduction to 53 players
August 31....................Teams establish a Practice Squad of up to eight players

In addition to the squad limits described above, the overall roster limit of 90 players remains in effect throughout the regular season and postseason. The overall limit is applicable to players on a team's Active, Inactive, and certain Exempt Lists, players on the Practice Squad, and players on the Reserve List as Injured, Physically Unable to Perform, Non-Football Illness/Injury, and Suspended by Club.

RESERVE LIST

The Reserve List is a status for players who, for reasons of injury, retirement, military service, or other circumstances, are not immediately available for participation with a club. Except for one player who must be Designated for Return, players on Reserve/Injured are not eligible to practice or return to the Active/Inactive List in the same season that they are placed on Reserve. Players in the category of Reserve/Retired, Reserve/Did Not Report, Reserve/Exclusive Rights, and players who were placed in the category of Reserve/Left Squad in a previous season may not be reinstated during the period from 30 days before the end of the regular season through the postseason.

ANNUAL ACTIVE PLAYER LIMITS

NFL

Year(s)	Limit
2011-14	46
1991-2010	45**
1985-90	45
1983-84	49
1982	45†-49
1978-81	45
1975-77	43
1974	47
1964-73	40
1963	37
1961-62	36
1960	38
1959	36
1957-58	35
1951-56	33
1949-50	32
1948	35
1947	35*-34
1945-46	33
1943-44	28
1940-42	33
1938-39	30
1936-37	25
1935	24
1930-34	20
1926-29	18
1925	16

** 45 plus a third quarterback
† 45 for first two games
* 35 for first three games

AFL

Year(s)	Limit
1966-69	40
1965	38
1964	34
1962-63	33
1960-61	35

NFL FREE AGENCY MOVEMENT

The following chart details veteran free agents who signed with new teams:

	Unrestricted	Restricted	Transition	Franchise	TOTALS
1993	108	8	4	1	121
1994	121	7	4	0	132
1995	171	6	2	0	179
1996	100	4	2	0	106
1997	86	2	2	0	90
1998	112	4	1	2	119
1999	115	2	1	0	118
2000	107	4	0	0	111
2001	93	4	0	0	97
2002	130	1	0	0	131
2003	111	5	1	0	117
2004	124	1	1	0	126
2005	104	3	0	0	107
2006	149	4	1	0	154
2007	126	4	0	0	130
2008	132	3	0	0	135
2009	128	0	0	0	128
2010	51	1	0	0	52
2011	163	0	0	0	163
2012	143	0	0	0	143
2013	165	0	0	0	165

The AFC

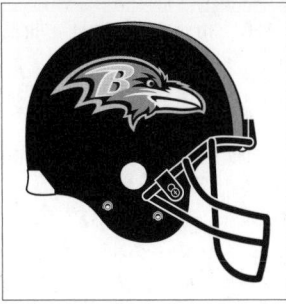

**American Football Conference
North Division
Team Colors:** Black, Purple, and Metallic
Gold
**1 Winning Drive
Owings Mills, Maryland 21117
Telephone:** (410) 701-4000

2014 SCHEDULE
PRESEASON
Aug. 7   **San Francisco** 7:30
Aug. 16 at Dallas.............................7:00
Aug. 23 **Washington** 7:30
Aug. 28 at New Orleans..................8:00

REGULAR SEASON
Sep. 7   **Cincinnati** 1:00
Sep. 11 **Pittsburgh** (Thu) 8:25
Sep. 21 at Cleveland 1:00
Sep. 28 **Carolina** 1:00
Oct. 5   at Indianapolis 1:00
Oct. 12 at Tampa Bay 1:00
Oct. 19 **Atlanta** 1:00
Oct. 26 at Cincinnati 1:00
Nov. 2   at Pittsburgh *8:30
Nov. 9   **Tennessee** 1:00
Nov. 16 BYE
Nov. 24 at New Orleans (Mon) 8:30
Nov. 30 **San Diego** 1:00
Dec. 7   at Miami 1:00
Dec. 14 **Jacksonville** 1:00
Dec. 21 at Houston 1:00
Dec. 28 **Cleveland** 1:00
*All times ET; Sunday night games in
   Weeks 5-16 subject to change

Stadium: M&T Bank Stadium
               (opened in 1998)
               • **Capacity:** 71,008
               1101 Russell Street
               Baltimore, Maryland 21230
Playing Surface: Sportexe Momentum
Training Camp: 1 Winning Drive
               Owings Mills, MD 21117

M&T BANK STADIUM

CLUB OFFICIALS
Owner: Steve Bisciotti
President: Dick Cass
General Manager & Executive Vice
   President: Ozzie Newsome
Assistant General Manager: Eric DeCosta
Senior Vice President/Public and
   Community Relations: Kevin Byrne
Senior Vice President of Football
   Administration: Pat Moriarty
Vice President, Digital Media:
   Michelle Andres
Vice President, Strategic Partnerships
   and Sales: Ed Burchell
Vice President, Operations: Bob Eller
Vice President and Chief Financial
   Officer: Jeff Goering
Vice President, Information Technology:
   Bill Jankowski
Vice President, Ticket Sales and
   Operations: Baker Koppelman
Vice President, Corporate Sales and
   Business Development: Kevin Rochlitz
Vice President, Stadium Operations:
   Roy Sommerhof
Director of Pro Personnel:
   Vincent Newsome
Director of College Scouting: Joe Hortiz
Senior Personnel Assistant:
   George Kokinis
Director of Player Development:
   Harry Swayne
Senior Advisor of Player Development:
   O.J. Brigance
Assistant Director of Pro Personnel:
   Chad Alexander
National Scout: Joe Douglas
Scouts: Mark Azevedo, David Blackburn,
   Ian Cunningham, Jack Glowik,
   Milt Hendrickson, Andy Weidl,
   Lonnie Young
Director of Football Administration and
   Executive Assistant to the GM:
   Jessica Markison
Director of Football Analytics: Sandy Weil
Equipment Manager: William Sheridan
Head Athletic Trainer: Mark Smith
Senior Director of Premium
   Services/Suites: Theresa Abato
Senior Director of Finance: Jim Coller
Senior Director of Football Video
   Operations: Jon Dube
Senior Director of Fields & Grounds/Head
   Groundskeeper: Don Follett
Senior Director of Information
   Technology: Nick Fusee
Senior Director of Human Resources:
   Elizabeth Jackson
Senior Director of Security:
   Darren Sanders
Senior Director of Public Relations:
   Chad Steele
Director of Football Video Operations:
   Mark Bienvenu
Director of Community Relations:
   Heather Darney
Director of Special Events and Special
   Assistant to the President: Lisa Dixon
Director of Marketing: Brad Downs
Director of Retail: Chris Inouye
Director of Finance: Reba Koppelman
Director of Broadcasting: Jay O'Brien
Director of Sales: Keith Weldon
Assistant Director of Public Relations:
   Patrick Gleason

COACHING HISTORY
(172-136-1)
Records include postseason games
1996-98   Ted Marchibroda 16-31-1
1999-2007 Brian Billick................85-67-0
2008-2013 John Harbaugh 71-38-0

PAID ATTENDANCE
Home 556,609   Away 525,560
Total 1,082,169
Single-game home record,
   71,547 (1/15/12)
Single-season home record, 557,835
   (2012)

2014 DRAFT CHOICES
Round	Name	Pos.	College
1	C.J. Mosley	LB	Alabama
2	Timmy Jernigan	DT	Florida St.
3	Terrence Brooks	S	Florida St.
	Crockett Gillmore	TE	Colorado St.
4	Brent Urban	DE	Virginia
	Lorenzo Taliaferro	RB	Coastal Carolina
5	John Urschel	C	Penn St.
6	Keith Wenning	QB	Ball St.
7	Michael Campanaro	WR	Wake Forest

BALTIMORE RAVENS

2013 TEAM RECORD
PRESEASON (2-2)

Date	Result	Opponent
08/08	W 44-16	at Tampa Bay
08/15	W 27-23	Atlanta
08/22	L 27-34	Carolina
08/29	L 21-24	at St. Louis

REGULAR SEASON (8-8)

Date	Result	Opponent
09/05	L 27-49	at Denver
09/15	W 14-6	Cleveland
09/22	W 30-9	Houston
09/29	L 20-23	at Buffalo
10/06	W 26-23	at Miami
10/13	L 17-19	Green Bay
10/20	L 16-19	at Pittsburgh
11/03	L 18-24	at Cleveland
11/10	W 20-17	Cincinnati (OT)
11/17	L 20-23	at Chicago (OT)
11/24	W 19-3	New York Jets
11/28	W 22-20	Pittsburgh
12/08	W 29-26	Minnesota
12/16	W 18-16	at Detroit
12/22	L 7-41	New England
12/29	L 17-34	at Cincinnati
(OT) Overtime		

SCORE BY PERIODS

Ravens	59	79	64	115	3 —	320
Opponents	63	89	63	134	3 —	352

2013 TEAM STATISTICS

	Ravens	Opp.
Total First Downs	295	284
Rushing	68	79
Passing	189	176
Penalty	38	29
3rd Down: Made/Att	92/253	78/233
3rd Down Pct.	36.4	33.5
4th Down: Made/Att	6/16	8/14
4th Down Pct.	37.5	57.1
Possession Avg.	29:51	30:09
Total Net Yards	4918	5368
Avg. Per Game	307.4	335.5
Total Plays	1090	1032
Avg. Per Play	4.5	5.2
Net Yards Rushing	1328	1687
Avg. Per Game	83.0	105.4
Total Rushes	423	440
Net Yards Passing	3590	3681
Avg. Per Game	224.4	230.1
Sacked/Yards Lost	48/324	40/257
Gross Yards	3914	3938
Att./Completions	619/363	552/314
Completion Pct.	58.6	56.9
Had Intercepted	23	16
Punts/Average	91/45.5	98/45.8
Net Punting Avg.	91/38.9	98/37.5
Penalties/Yards	112/942	126/1196
Fumbles/Ball Lost	15/6	21/8
Touchdowns	29	37
Rushing	7	7
Passing	19	25
Returns	3	5

2013 INDIVIDUAL STATISTICS

PASSING

	Att.	Comp.	Yds.	Pct.	TD	Int.	Tkld.	Rate
Flacco	614	362	3912	59.0	19	22	48/324	73.1
Taylor	5	1	2	20.0	0	1	0/0	0.0
Ravens	619	363	3914	58.6	19	23	48/324	72.0
Opponents	552	314	3938	56.9	25	16	40/257	82.2

SCORING

	TD R	TD P	TD Rt	PAT	FG	Saf	PTS
Tucker	0	0	0	26/26	38/41	0	140
M. Brown	0	7	0	0/0	0/0	0	44
Rice	4	0	0	0/0	0/0	0	26
T. Smith	0	4	0	0/0	0/0	0	26
Clark	0	3	0	0/0	0/0	0	18
J. Jones	0	2	1	0/0	0/0	0	18
Pierce	2	0	0	0/0	0/0	0	12
Dickson	0	1	0	0/0	0/0	0	6
Doss	0	0	1	0/0	0/0	0	6
Flacco	1	0	0	0/0	0/0	0	6
Leach	0	1	0	0/0	0/0	0	6
Pitta	0	1	0	0/0	0/0	0	6
D. Smith	0	0	1	0/0	0/0	0	6
Ravens	7	19	3	26/26	38/41	0	320
Opponents	7	25	5	34/34	32/35	0	352

2-Pt Conversions: M. Brown, Rice, T. Smith.
Ravens 3-3, Opponents 0-3.

RUSHING

	No.	Yds	Avg	LG	TD
Rice	214	660	3.1	47	4
Pierce	152	436	2.9	28	2
Flacco	27	131	4.9	22	1
Taylor	8	64	8.0	25	0
Leach	11	23	2.1	6	0
Scott	4	14	3.5	9	0
Draughn	4	2	0.5	3	0
J. Jones	2	0	0.0	4	0
M. Brown	1	-2	-2.0	-2	0
Ravens	423	1328	3.1	47	7
Opponents	440	1687	3.8	43	7

RECEIVING

	No.	Yds	Avg	LG	TD
T. Smith	65	1128	17.4	74	4
Rice	58	321	5.5	22	0
M. Brown	49	524	10.7	59	7
J. Jones	37	455	12.3	66t	2
Clark	31	343	11.1	45	3
Dickson	25	273	10.9	43	1
Pitta	20	169	8.5	18	1
Pierce	20	104	5.2	15	0
Doss	19	305	16.1	63	0
Stokley	13	115	8.8	18	0
Leach	11	47	4.3	12	1
D. Thompson	10	96	9.6	33	0
Bajema	2	18	9.0	18	0
Scott	2	10	5.0	8	0
Taylor	1	6	6.0	6	0
Ravens	363	3914	10.8	74	19
Opponents	314	3938	12.5	79t	25

INTERCEPTIONS

	No.	Yds	Avg	LG	TD
Graham	4	28	7.0	28	0
Ihedigbo	3	54	18.0	37	0
D. Smith	3	41	13.7	37t	1
Webb	2	19	9.5	19	0
J. Smith	2	0	0.0	0	0
Elam	1	18	18.0	18	0
Tyson	1	0	0.0	0	0
Ravens	16	160	10.0	37t	1
Opponents	23	219	9.5	74t	4

PUNTING

	No.	Yds.	Avg.	In 20	LG
Koch	90	4138	46.0	27	69
Ravens	91	4138	45.5	27	69
Opponents	98	4484	45.8	34	67

PUNT RETURNS

	Ret	FC	Yds	Avg	LG	TD
Doss	23	7	359	15.6	82t	1
J. Jones	19	2	237	12.5	37	0
Webb	1	7	13	13.0	13	0
Ravens	43	16	609	14.2	82t	1
Opponents	46	14	419	9.1	27	0

KICKOFF RETURNS

	No.	Yds	Avg	LG	TD
J. Jones	31	892	28.8	77t	1
D. Thompson	7	201	28.7	47	0
Draughn	2	53	26.5	31	0
Juszczyk	2	17	8.5	9	0
Dickson	1	0	0.0	0	0
Leach	1	0	0.0	0	0
Ravens	44	1163	26.4	77t	1
Opponents	38	873	23.0	44	0

FIELD GOALS

	1-19	20-29	30-39	40-49	50+
Tucker	0/0	10/10	12/13	10/11	6/7
Ravens	0/0	10/10	12/13	10/11	6/7
Opponents	0/0	11/11	10/10	9/11	2/3

SACKS

	No.
Suggs	10.0
Dumervil	9.5
D. Smith	5.0
A. Jones	4.0
Canty	2.0
McPhee	2.0
Tyson	2.0
Ngata	1.5
Upshaw	1.5
Graham	1.0
B. Williams	1.0
A. Brown	0.5
Ravens	40.0
Opponents	48.0

RECORD HOLDERS
INDIVIDUAL RECORDS—CAREER

Category	Name	Performance
Rushing (Yds.)	Jamal Lewis, 2000-06	7,801
Passing (Yds.)	Joe Flacco, 2008-2013	21,545
Passing (TDs)	Joe Flacco, 2008-2013	121
Receiving (No.)	Derrick Mason, 2005-2010	471
Receiving (Yds.)	Derrick Mason, 2005-2010	5,777
Interceptions	Ed Reed, 2002-2012	61
Punting (Avg.)	Sam Koch, 2006-2013	44.8
Punt Return (Avg.)	Jermaine Lewis, 1996-2001	11.8
Kickoff Return (Avg.)	Corey Harris, 1998-2001	24.0
Field Goals	Matt Stover, 1996-2008	354
Touchdowns (Tot.)	Jamal Lewis, 2000-06	47
Points	Matt Stover, 1996-2008	1,464
*Sacks	Terrell Suggs, 2003-2013	94.5

INDIVIDUAL RECORDS—SINGLE SEASON

Category	Name	Performance
Rushing (Yds.)	Jamal Lewis, 2003	2,066
Passing (Yds.)	Vinny Testaverde, 1996	4,177
Passing (TDs)	Vinny Testaverde, 1996	33
Receiving (No.)	Derrick Mason, 2007	103
Receiving (Yds.)	Michael Jackson, 1996	1,201
Interceptions	Ed Reed, 2004, 2008	9
Punting (Avg.)	Sam Koch, 2012	47.1
Punt Return (Avg.)	Jermaine Lewis, 2000	16.1
Kickoff Return (Avg.)	Jacoby Jones, 2012	30.7
Field Goals	Justin Tucker, 2013	38
Touchdowns (Tot.)	Ray Rice, 2011	15
Points	Justin Tucker, 2013	140
*Sacks	Peter Boulware, 2001	15.0

INDIVIDUAL RECORDS—SINGLE GAME

Category	Name	Performance
Rushing (Yds.)	Jamal Lewis, 9-14-03	295
Passing (Yds.)	Vinny Testaverde, 10-27-96	429
Passing (TDs)	Tony Banks, 9-10-00	5
Receiving (No.)	Priest Holmes, 10-11-98	13
Receiving (Yds.)	Qadry Ismail, 12-12-99	268
Interceptions	Many times	2
	Last time by Corey Graham, 11-24-13	
Field Goals	Justin Tucker, 12-16-13	6
Touchdowns (Tot.)	Marcus Robinson, 11-23-03	4
Points	Marcus Robinson, 11-23-03	24
*Sacks	Michael McCrary, 11-8-98	4.0
	Peter Boulware, 1-7-02	4.0

*Sacks became an official statistic in 1982.

BALTIMORE RAVENS

2014 VETERAN ROSTER

No.	Name	Pos.	Ht.	Wt.	Birthdate	NFL Exp.	College	Hometown	How Acq.	'13 Games/ Starts
11	Aiken, Kamar	WR	6-2	215	5/30/89	2	Central Florida	Hollywood, Fla.	FA-'13	0*
59	Brown, Arthur	ILB	6-0	235	6/17/90	2	Kansas State	Wichita, Kan.	D2-'13	14/0
23	Brown, Chykie	CB	5-11	190	12/26/86	4	Texas	Houston, Texas	D5a-'11	16/0
14	Brown, Marlon	WR	6-5	205	4/22/91	2	Georgia	Memphis, Tenn.	FA-'13	14/12
31	Brown, Omar	S	5-11	195	6/6/88	3	Marshall	Moncks Corner, S.C.	FA-'12	1/0
56	Bynes, Josh	ILB	6-1	240	8/24/89	3	Auburn	Lauderdale Lakes, Fla.	FA-'11	15/6
99	Canty, Chris	DE	6-7	317	11/10/82	10	Virginia	Charlotte, N.C.	FA-'13	15/13
87	# Clark, Dallas	TE	6-3	252	6/12/79	11	Iowa	Livermore, Iowa	UFA(TB)-'13	12/0
62	Cody, Terrence	NT	6-4	340	6/28/88	5	Alabama	Fort Myers, Fla.	D2b-'10	12/1
46	Cox, Morgan	LS	6-4	241	4/26/86	5	Tennessee	Collierville, Tenn.	FA-'10	16/0
81	Daniels, Owen	TE	6-3	249	11/9/82	9	Wisconsin	Naperville, Ill.	FA-'14	5/5*
58	Dumervil, Elvis	OLB	5-11	260	1/19/84	9	Louisville	Miami, Fla.	FA-'13	15/3
26	Elam, Matt	S	5-10	210	9/21/91	2	Florida	West Palm Beach, Fla.	D1-'13	16/15
5	Flacco, Joe	QB	6-6	245	1/16/85	7	Delaware	Audubon, N.J.	D1-'08	16/16
29	Forsett, Justin	RB	5-8	194	10/14/85	7	California	Lakeland, Fla.	FA-'14	9/0*
66	Gradkowski, Gino	G/C	6-3	300	11/5/88	3	Delaware	Pittsburgh, Pa.	D4a-'12	16/16
54	Hamilton, Adrian	OLB	6-3	255	11/29/87	3	Prairie View A&M	Dallas, Texas	FA-'12	0*
25	Jackson, Asa	CB/RS	5-10	182	12/2/89	3	Cal Poly	Sacramento, Calif.	D5-'12	4/0
77	Jensen, Ryan	G/C	6-4	318	5/27/91	2	Colorado State-Pueblo	Fort Morgan, Colo.	D6b-'13	0*
12	Jones, Jacoby	WR/RS	6-2	215	7/11/84	8	Lane	New Orleans, La.	FA-'12	12/9
44	Juszczyk, Kyle	FB	6-1	245	4/23/91	2	Harvard	Medina, Ohio	D4b-'13	16/0
4	Koch, Sam	P	6-1	218	8/13/82	9	Nebraska	Seward, Neb.	D6a-'06	16/0
41	Levine, Anthony	S	5-11	203	3/27/87	3	Tennessee State	Winston Salem, N.C.	FA-'12	16/0
95	Lewis-Moore, Kapron	DE	6-4	310	1/24/90	2	Notre Dame	Weatherford, Texas	D6a-'13	0*
50	McClellan, Albert	ILB	6-2	245	6/4/86	4	Marshall	Lakeland, Fla.	FA-'10	15/0
90	McPhee, Pernell	OLB	6-3	280	12/17/88	4	Mississippi State	Pahokee, Fla.	D5b-'11	16/0
13	Mellette, Aaron	WR	6-2	217	12/28/89	2	Elon	Sanford, N.C.	D7a-'13	0*
36	Miles, Jeromy	S	6-2	214	7/20/87	5	Massachusetts	Sicklerville, N.J.	FA-'13	12/0
60	t-Monroe, Eugene	T	6-5	306	4/18/87	6	Virginia	Plainfield, N.J.	T(Jax)-'13	15/15*
92	Ngata, Haloti	NT	6-4	340	1/21/84	9	Oregon	Salt Lake City, Utah	D1-'06	15/15
72	Osemele, Kelechi	G/T	6-5	330	6/24/89	3	Iowa State	Houston, Texas	D2b-'12	7/7
30	Pierce, Bernard	RB	6-0	218	5/10/91	3	Temple	Ardmore, Pa.	D3-'12	16/1
88	Pitta, Dennis	TE	6-4	245	6/29/85	5	Brigham Young	Moorpark, Calif.	D4-'10	4/1
67	Rackley, Will	G	6-3	310	10/11/89	4	Lehigh	Riverdale, Ga.	FA-'14	11/11*
76	Reid, Jah	G/T	6-7	340	7/21/88	4	Central Florida	Haines City, Fla.	D3-'11	10/0
27	Rice, Ray	RB	5-8	212	1/22/87	7	Rutgers	New Rochelle, N.Y.	D2-'08	15/15
34	# Scott, Bernard	RB	5-10	195	2/10/84	5	Abilene Christian	Wichita Falls, Texas	FA-'13	2/0
68	Shipley, A.Q.	G/C	6-1	309	5/22/86	4	Penn State	Moon Township, Pa.	T(Ind)-'13	16/9
94	Simon, John	OLB	6-1	257	10/14/90	2	Ohio State	Youngstown, Ohio	D4a-'13	7/0
51	Smith, Daryl	ILB	6-2	248	3/14/82	11	Georgia Tech	Albany, Ga.	UFA(Jax)-'13	16/16
22	Smith, Jimmy	CB	6-2	200	7/26/88	4	Colorado	Colton, Calif.	D1-'11	16/16
89	Smith, Sr., Steve	WR	5-9	185	5/12/79	14	Utah	Los Angeles, Calif.	FA-'14	15/15*
82	Smith, Torrey	WR	6-0	205	1/26/89	4	Maryland	Falmouth, Va.	D2-'11	16/16
65	Stephens, Reggie	C	6-3	325	8/28/87	2	Iowa State	Rowlett, Texas	FA-'12	0*
24	Stewart, Darian	S	5-11	214	8/4/88	5	South Carolina	Huntsville, Ala.	UFA(StL)-'14	14/6*
80	# Stokley, Brandon	WR	6-0	194	6/23/76	15	Louisiana-Lafayette	Lafayette, La.	UFA(Den)-'13	6/0
55	Suggs, Terrell	OLB	6-3	260	10/11/82	12	Arizona State	Chandler, Ariz.	D1a-'03	16/16
2	Taylor, Tyrod	QB	6-1	215	8/3/89	4	Virginia Tech	Hampton, Va.	D6-'11	3/0
83	Thompson, Deonte	WR/RS	6-0	203	2/14/89	3	Florida	Belle Glade, Fla.	FA-'12	7/0
28	Trawick, Brynden	S	6-2	215	10/23/89	2	Troy	Marietta, Ga.	FA-'13	8/0
9	Tucker, Justin	K	6-0	180	11/21/89	3	Texas	Austin, Texas	FA-'12	16/0
93	Tyson, DeAngelo	DE	6-2	315	4/12/89	3	Georgia	Statesboro, Ga.	D7-'12	13/0
91	Upshaw, Courtney	OLB	6-2	272	12/13/89	3	Alabama	Eufaula, Ala.	D2a-'12	16/13
71	Wagner, Rick	G/T	6-6	310	10/21/89	2	Wisconsin	West Allis, Wis.	D5-'13	16/2
21	Webb, Lardarius	CB/RS	5-10	182	10/12/85	6	Nicholls State	Opelika, Ala.	D3-'09	16/16
98	Williams, Brandon	DT	6-1	335	2/21/89	2	Missouri Southern St.	Kirkwood, Miss.	D3-'13	7/0
15	Williams, LaQuan	WR	6-0	195	6/27/88	3	Maryland	Baltimore, Md.	FA-'14	0*
35	Wood, Cierre	RB	5-11	215	2/21/91	2	Notre Dame	Oxnard, Calif.	FA-'14	3/0*
73	Yanda, Marshal	G/T	6-3	305	9/15/84	8	Iowa	Anamosa, Iowa	D3b-'07	16/16
53	t-Zuttah, Jeremy	G/C	6-4	308	6/1/86	7	Rutgers	Edison, N.J.	T(TB)-'14	16/16*

* Aiken last active with New England in '12; Daniels played 5 games with Houston in '13; Forsett played 9 games with Jacksonville; Hamilton missed '13 season because of injury; Jensen missed '13 season because of injury; Lewis-Moore missed '13 season because of injury; Mellette missed '13 season because of injury; Monroe played 4 games with Jacksonville and 11 games with Baltimore; Rackley played 11 games with Jacksonville; Smith, Sr. played 15 games with Carolina; Stephens last on active roster with Cincinnati in '10; Stewart played 14 games with St. Louis; L. Williams last active with Baltimore in '12; Wood played 3 games with Houston; Zuttah played 16 games with Tampa Bay.

t- Ravens traded for Monroe (Jax), Zuttah (TB).

\# Unrestriced free agent; subject to developments.

Traded—T Bryant McKinnie (5 games in '13) to Miami.

Players lost through free agency (7): TE Ed Dickson (Car; 16 games), WR Tandon Doss (Jax; 15), CB Corey Graham (Buff; 16), S James Ihedigbo (Det; 16), DT Arthur Jones (Ind; 14), ILB Jameel McClain (NYG; 10), T Michael Oher (Tenn; 16).

Also played with Ravens in '13—TE Billy Bajema (6 games), RB Shaun Draughn (3), S Michael Huff (7), LB Robert James (1), FB Vonta Leach (16), DE Marcus Spears (5).

FIRST-YEAR ROSTER

Name	Pos.	Ht.	Wt.	Birthdate	College	Hometown	How Acq.
Boyd, Xavius	LB	6-2	239	2/7/91	Western Kentucky	St. Petersburg, Fla.	FA
Brooks, Terrence	S	5-11	200	3/2/91	Florida State	Dunnellon, Fla.	D3a
Brown, Levi	DT	6-2	310	5/12/91	Temple	Bethlehem, Pa.	FA
Butler, Jeremy	WR	6-2	224	4/22/91	Tennessee-Martin	Sarasota, Fla.	FA
Campanaro, Michael	WR	5-9	192	1/25/91	Wake Forest	Clarksville, Md.	D7
Chapas, Shaun (1)	RB	6-2	244	5/2/88	Georgia	St. Augustine, Fla.	FA
Davis, Jace	WR	6-1	206	8/22/91	Northern Colorado	Denver, Colo.	FA
Gillmore, Crockett	TE	6-6	260	11/16/91	Colorado State	Bushland, Texas	D3b
Graham, Parker	T	6-7	308	2/14/91	Oklahoma State	Webb City, Mo.	FA
Hopkins, Derrick	DT	6-0	321	12/16/91	Virginia Tech	Highland Springs, Va.	FA
Hurst, James	T	6-5	296	12/17/91	North Carolina	Plainfield, Ind.	FA
Jacobs, Tramain	CB	5-11	182	5/20/92	Texas A&M	Covington, La.	FA
Jernigan, Timmy	DT	6-2	300	9/24/92	Florida State	Lake City, Fla.	D2
Jones, Ryan	LB	6-4	245	3/21/91	Montana Tech	Reno, Nev.	FA
Leone, Richie	P	6-3	211	3/10/92	Houston	Roswell, Ga.	FA
Meder, Jamie	DT	6-2	304	4/12/91	Ashland	Parma Heights, Ohio	FA
Mims, David (1)	T	6-8	350	5/18/88	Virginia Union	Charlotte, N.C.	FA
Moody, Dexter	S	6-1	213	8/14/91	Albany State	Twin City, Ga.	FA
Mosley, C.J.	LB	6-2	235	6/19/92	Alabama	Mobile, Ala.	D1
Olatoye, Deji	CB	6-1	198	7/20/91	North Carolina A&T	Cleveland, Ohio	FA
Orr, Zachary	LB	6-0	237	6/9/92	North Texas	DeSoto, Texas	FA
Overbay, Nathan (1)	TE	6-5	270	1/4/87	Eastern Washington	Lakewood, Wa.	FA
Pataiali'i, A.J.	DT	6-3	307	9/13/90	Utah State	West Valley City, Utah	FA
Patterson, Avery	CB	5-8	191	3/21/91	Oregon	Pittsburg, Calif.	FA
Seamster, Sammy	CB	6-0	200	2/5/91	Middle Tennessee State	Ooltewah, Tenn.	FA
Sheppard, Gerrard (1)	WR	6-2	215	11/16/90	Towson	Baltimore, Md.	FA
Stephens, Nick (1)	QB	6-3	221	5/19/87	Tarleton State	Flower Mound, Texas	FA
Supernaw, Phillip (1)	TE	6-5	248	1/30/90	Ouachita Baptist	Katy, Texas	FA
Taliaferro, Lorenzo	RB	6-0	230	12/23/91	Coastal Carolina	Yorktown, Va.	D4b
Urban, Brent	DE	6-7	298	5/5/91	Virginia	Mississauga, Canada	D4a
Urschel, John	G/C	6-3	313	6/24/91	Penn State	Buffalo, N.Y.	D5
Van Sloten, Brett	T	6-5	301	11/2/90	Iowa	Decorah, Iowa	FA
Wenning, Keith	QB	6-3	218	2/14/91	Ball State	Coldwater, Ohio	D6

The term NFL Rookie is defined as a player who is in his first season of professional football and has not been on the roster of another professional football team for any regular-season or postseason games. A Rookie is designated by an "R" on NFL rosters. Players who have been active in another professional football league or players who have NFL experience, including either preseason training camp or being on an Active List or Inactive List, or on Reserve/Injured or Physically Unable to Perform for fewer than six regular-season games, are termed NFL First-Year Players. An NFL First-Year Player is designated by a "1" on NFL rosters. Thereafter, a player is credited with an additional year of experience for each season in which he accumulates six games on the Active List or Inactive List, or on Reserve/Injured or Reserve/Physically Unable to Perform.

Log on to www.baltimoreravens.com for an up-to-date roster.

COACHING STAFF

Head Coach,
John Harbaugh

Pro Career: Super Bowl-winning head coach John Harbaugh enters his seventh season at the helm in Baltimore. Harbaugh has been historically good, with his teams earning the playoffs in five of his first six seasons, including the initial five (2008-2012). Impressively, he is also the only head coach in NFL history (since 1970 merger) to win a playoff game in each of his first four and five years. Prior to an 8-8 campaign in 2013, Baltimore won the AFC North for a second-straight season in 2012 by posting a 10-6 record (14-6 overall) and capturing the franchise's second Super Bowl championship. The Ravens topped the Colts at home in the Wild Card round and followed that up by earning a Divisional Round victory over top-seeded Denver before advancing to Super Bowl XLVII with a win in the AFC Championship Game at New England. In the Super Bowl in New Orleans, the Ravens bested the NFC champion San Francisco 49ers by a final of 34-31. In 2011, Baltimore won the AFC North by producing its second-straight 12-4 record, also going undefeated at home for the first time in team history. In 2010, after compiling a 12-4 regular season mark, the Ravens captured a Wild Card win at Kansas City. During the 2009 campaign, Harbaugh's Ravens posted a 9-7 regular season record prior to earning a Wild Card victory at New England. In his initial season with the team (2008), Harbaugh led Baltimore to an 11-5 record and a berth in the AFC Championship Game. Baltimore set an NFL record that season for most total wins (13) by a team with both a rookie head coach and a rookie starting quarterback (Joe Flacco). Harbaugh spent his first 10 NFL seasons (1998-2007) with the Philadelphia Eagles. He was the team's secondary coach in 2007, after nine seasons as its special teams coordinator. He was voted the 2001 NFL's Special Teams Coach of the Year by his coaching peers. Career record: 71-38.

Background: Played defensive back at Miami (Ohio) from 1980-83, earned degree in political science. Coached collegiately at Western Michigan (1984-86), Pittsburgh (1987), Morehead State (1988), Cincinnati (1989-1996), and Indiana (1997).

Personal: Born in Perrysburg, Ohio on September 23, 1962, Harbaugh and his wife, Ingrid, have a daughter, Alison. Son of longtime college coach Jack, and his brother, Jim, the current 49ers head coach, played for the Ravens in 1998. John's brother-in-law, Tom Crean, Indiana University's basketball coach, is married to his sister, Joani.

ASSISTANT COACHES

Juney Barnett, asst. strength and conditioning; born January 11, 1979, Philadelphia. Defensive back Bloomsburg 1997-2000. No pro playing experience. College coach: Bloomsburg 2001, Army 2005, Kansas 2012. Pro coach: Baltimore Ravens 2003-05, Minnesota Vikings, 2006-2011, re-joined Ravens in 2012.

Clarence Brooks, defensive line; born May 20, 1951, New York, N.Y. Guard Massachusetts 1970-73. No pro playing experience. College coach: Massachusetts 1976-1980, Syracuse 1981-89, Arizona 1990-92. Pro coach: Chicago Bears 1993-98, Cleveland Browns 1999, Miami Dolphins 2000-04, joined Ravens in 2005.

Randy Brown, kicking consultant; born July 30, 1967, Marlton, N.J. Kicker Catawba 1985-88. No pro playing experience. College coach: Catawba 1989, Tennessee-Chattanooga 2003. Pro coach: Chicago Bears 1998-2000, Philadelphia Eagles 2004-05, joined Ravens in 2008.

Juan Castillo, run game coordinator; born October 8, 1959, Port Isabel, Texas. Linebacker Texas A&I 1978-1980. No pro playing experience. College coach: Texas A&M-Kingsville 1982-85, 1990-94. Pro coach: Philadelphia Eagles: 1995-2012, joined Ravens in 2013.

Billy DeLorbe, cross-training specialist; born October 23, 1979, San Francisco, Calif. Attended St. Mary's College (Md.), Towson. No college or pro playing experience. Pro coach: Joined Ravens in 2014.

Rick Dennison, quarterbacks; born June 22, 1958, Kalispell, Mont. Tight end Colorado State 1976-79. Pro linebacker Denver Broncos 1982-1990. Pro coach: Denver Broncos 1995-2009, Houston Texans 2010-13, joined Ravens in 2014.

Bobby Engram, wide receivers; born January 7, 1973, Camden, S.C. Wide receiver Penn State 1992-95. Pro wide receiver Chicago Bears 1996-2000, Seattle Seahawks 2001-08, Kansas City Chiefs 2009. College coach: Pittsburgh 2012-13. Pro coach: San Francisco 49ers 2011, joined Ravens in 2014.

Thomas Hammock, running backs; born July 7, 1981, Jersey City, N.J. Running back Northern Illinois 1999-2002. No pro playing experience. College coach: Wisconsin 2003-04, Northern Illinois 2005-06, Minnesota 2007-2010, Wisconsin 2011-13. Pro coach: Joined Ravens in 2014.

Chris Hewitt, asst. special teams; born July 22, 1974, Kingston, Jamaica. Defensive back Cincinnati 1993-96. Pro defensive back New Orleans Saints 1999-2000. College coach: Notre Dame 2003, Rutgers 2004-2011. Pro coach: Joined Ravens in 2012.

Gary Kubiak, offensive coordinator; born August 15, 1961, Houston, Texas. Quarterback Texas A&M 1979-1982. Pro quarterback Denver Broncos 1983-1991. College coach: Texas A&M 1992-93. Pro coach: San Francisco 49ers 1994, Denver Broncos 1995-2005, Houston Texans 2006-2013 (head coach), joined Ravens in 2014.

Don Martindale, inside linebackers; born May 19, 1963, Dayton, Ohio. Linebacker Defiance College 1981-84. College coach: Defiance 1986-87, Notre Dame 1994-95, Cincinnati 1996-98, Western Illinois 1999, Western Kentucky 2001-03. Pro coach: Oakland Raiders 2004-08, Denver Broncos 2009-2010, joined Ravens in 2012.

Ted Monachino, linebackers; born October 15, 1966, Council Bluffs, Iowa. Defensive lineman Missouri 1988-1990. No pro playing experience. College coach: Texas Christian 1996-97, James Madison 1998, Southwest Missouri State 1999, Boise State 2000, Arizona State 2001-05. Pro coach: Jacksonville Jaguars 2006-09, joined Ravens in 2010.

Brian Pariani, tight ends; born July 2, 1965, San Francisco, Calif. Attended UCLA. No college or pro playing experience. College coach: UCLA 1989, Syracuse 2005. Pro coach: San Francisco 49ers 1991-94, Denver Broncos 1995-2004, Houston Texans 2006-2013, joined Ravens in 2014.

Dean Pees, defensive coordinator; born September 4, 1949, Dunkirk, Ohio. Attended Bowling Green State. No college or pro playing experience. College coach: Findlay 1979-1982, Miami (Ohio) 1983-86, Naval Academy 1987-89, Toledo 1990-93, Notre Dame 1994, Michigan State 1995-97, Kent State 1998-2003. Pro coach: New England Patriots 2004-09, joined Ravens in 2010.

Bob Rogucki, strength and conditioning; born September 27, 1953, Clarksburg, W.Va. No college or pro playing experience. College coach: Penn State 1981, Weber State 1982, Army 1983-89. Pro coach: Arizona Cardinals 1990-2003, Jacksonville Jaguars 2004, Philadelphia Eagles 2006-07, joined Ravens in 2008.

Jerry Rosburg, special teams coordinator/asst. head coach; born November 24, 1955, Fairmont, Minn. Linebacker North Dakota State 1974-77. No pro playing experience. College coach: Northern Michigan 1981-86, Western Michigan 1987-1991, Cincinnati 1992-95, Minnesota 1996, Boston College 1997-98, Notre Dame 1999-2000. Pro coach: Cleveland Browns 2001-06, Atlanta Falcons 2007, joined Ravens in 2008.

Steve Spagnuolo, senior defensive assistant; born December 21, 1959, Whitinsville, Mass. Wide Receiver Springfield 1978-1981. No pro playing experience. College coach: Massachusetts 1982-83, Lafayette (Pa.) 1984-86, Connecticut 1987-1991, Maine 1993-94, Rutgers 1994-95, Bowling Green 1996-97. Pro coach: Barcelona Dragons (WLAF) 1992, Frankfurt Galaxy (NFL Europe) 1998, Philadelphia Eagles 1999-2006, New York Giants 2007-08, St. Louis Rams 2009-2011 (head coach), New Orleans Saints 2012, joined Ravens in 2013.

Craig Ver Steeg, senior offensive assistant; born September 11, 1960, Inglewood, Calif. No college or pro playing experience. College coach: Southern California 1984-85, Utah 1986-89, Cincinnati 1990-93, Harvard 1994-95, Illinois 1998-2000, Utah 2001-02, Rutgers 2003-07. Pro coach: Chicago Bears 1996-97, joined Ravens in 2008.

Todd Washington, asst. offensive line; born July 19, 1976, Nassawadox, Va. Guard/center Virginia Tech 1993-97. Pro guard/center Tampa Bay 1998-2002, Houston 2003-05. College coach: San Diego 2007-09. Pro coach: Hartford Colonials (UFL) 2010, joined Ravens in 2011.

Matt Weiss, defensive assistant; born March 1, 1983, New Haven, Conn. Punter Vanderbilt 2001-02. No pro playing experience. College coach: Stanford 2008. Pro coach: Joined Ravens in 2009.

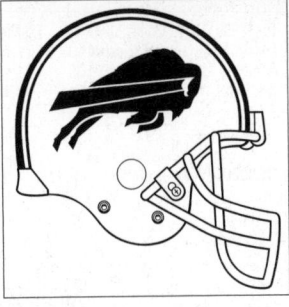

**American Football Conference
East Division**
Team Colors: Royal, Red, White and
Navy
One Bills Drive
Orchard Park, New York 14127-2296
Telephone: (716) 648-1800

2014 SCHEDULE
PRESEASON
Aug. 3   vs. N.Y. Giants (Canton)......8:00
Aug. 8   at Carolina.........................7:30
Aug. 16 at Pittsburgh 7:30
Aug. 23 **Tampa Bay**......................4:30
Aug. 28 **Detroit** 7:00

REGULAR SEASON
Sep. 7   at Chicago 1:00
Sep. 14 **Miami** 1:00
Sep. 21 **San Diego** 1:00
Sep. 28 at Houston 1:00
Oct. 5   at Detroit 1:00
Oct. 12 **New England** 1:00
Oct. 19 **Minnesota** 1:00
Oct. 26 at New York Jets 1:00
Nov. 2   BYE
Nov. 9   **Kansas City** 1:00
Nov. 13 at Miami (Thu).................8:25
Nov. 23 **New York Jets** 1:00
Nov. 30 **Cleveland** 1:00
Dec. 7   at Denver 4:05
Dec. 14 **Green Bay** 1:00
Dec. 21 at Oakland 4:25
Dec. 28 at New England 1:00
All times ET
Stadium: Ralph Wilson Stadium
(opened in 1973)
• **Capacity:** 72,169
One Bills Drive
Orchard Park, New York
14127-2296
Playing Surface: A-Turf Titan
Training Camp: St. John Fisher College
Rochester, N.Y. 14618

RALPH WILSON STADIUM

CLUB OFFICIALS
Controlling Owner: Mary Wilson
Founding Owner: Ralph Wilson, Jr. 1959-
2014
President and Chief Executive Officer:
Russ Brandon
Chief Financial Officer:
Jeffrey C. Littmann
General Manager: Doug Whaley
Special Assistant: Buddy Nix
Executive Vice President of Strategic
Planning: Mary Owen
Chief Marketing Officer: Marc Honan
Chief Revenue Officer: Bruce Popko
Chief Administrative Officer: Dave Wheat
Senior Vice President of
Communications: Scott Berchtold
Senior Vice President of Government
Relations and External Affairs:
Bill Munson
Senior Vice President of Football
Administration: Jim Overdorf
Vice President of Community Relations:
Gretchen Geitter
Vice President of Information
Technology: Dan Evans
Vice President Event Operations and
Guest Experience: Andy Major
Consultant: Christy Wilson Hofmann
Director of Player Personnel Jim Monos
Director of Pro Personnel: Tom Gibbons
Director of College Scouting:
Kelvin Fisher
Senior Director of Security: Chris Clark
Senior Director of Stadium Operations:
Matt Hunter
Director of Player Programs:
Paul Lancaster
Controller: Josh Dziurlikowski
Director of Equipment Operations:
Jeff Mazurek
Assistant Equipment Managers:
Randy Ribbeck, Spencer Haws
Head Certified Athletic Trainer:
Bud Carpenter
Certified Athletic Trainers: Chris Fischetti,
Shone Gipson, Greg McMillen
Video Director: Greg Estes
Assistant Video Director: Wes Burnard
Video Assistants: Dexter Carlo,
Casey Weidl
Scouts: Chuck Cook, Brian Fisher,
Matt Hand, Pete Harris (BLESTO),
Shawn Heinlen, CJ Leak,
Doug Majeski, Darrell Moody,
Tom Roth, (emeritus) David G. Smith,
(emeritus) David W. Smith

COACHING HISTORY
(390-451-8)
Records include postseason games
1960-61	Buster Ramsey	11-16-1
1962-65	Lou Saban	38-18-3
1966-68	Joe Collier*	13-17-1
1968	Harvey Johnson	1-10-1
1969-1970	John Rauch	7-20-1
1971	Harvey Johnson	1-13-0
1972-76	Lou Saban**	32-29-1
1976-77	Jim Ringo	3-20-0
1978-1982	Chuck Knox	38-38-0
1983-85	Kay Stephenson***	10-26-0
1985-86	Hank Bullough****	4-17-0
1986-1997	Marv Levy	123-78-0
1998-2000	Wade Phillips	29-21-0
2001-03	Gregg Williams	17-31-0
2004-05	Mike Mularkey	14-18-0
2006-09	Dick Jauron#	24-33-0
2009	Perry Fewell	3-4-0
2010-12	Chan Gailey	16-32-0
2013	Doug Marrone	6-10-0

*Released after two games in 1968
**Resigned after five games in 1976
***Released after four games in 1985
****Released after nine games in 1986
\#Released after nine games in 2009

PAID ATTENDANCE
Home 479,994   Away 494,809
Total 974,803
Single-game home record,
80,368 (10/4/92)
Single-season home record,
635,889 (1991)

2014 DRAFT CHOICES
Round	Name	Pos.	College
1	Sammy Watkins	WR	Clemson
2	Cyrus Kouandjio	T	Alabama
3	Preston Brown	LB	Louisville
4	Ross Cockrell	DB	Duke
5	Cyril Richardson	G	Baylor
7	Randell Johnson	LB	Florida Atlantic
	Seantrel Henderson	T	Miami

2013 TEAM RECORD
PRESEASON (2-2)

Date	Result	Opponent
08/11	W 44-20	at Indianapolis
08/16	W 20-16	Minnesota
08/24	L 7-30	at Washington
08/29	L 13-35	Detroit

REGULAR SEASON (6-10)

Date	Result	Opponent
09/08	L 21-23	New England
09/15	W 24-23	Carolina
09/22	L 20-27	at New York Jets
09/29	W 23-20	Baltimore
10/03	L 24-37	at Cleveland
10/13	L 24-27	Cincinnati (OT)
10/20	W 23-21	at Miami
10/27	L 17-35	at New Orleans
11/03	L 13-23	Kansas City
11/10	L 10-23	at Pittsburgh
11/17	W 37-14	New York Jets
12/01	L 31-34	Atlanta (OT)
12/08	L 6-27	at Tampa Bay
12/15	W 27-20	at Jacksonville
12/22	W 19-0	Miami
12/29	L 20-34	at New England

(OT) Overtime

SCORE BY PERIODS

Bills	73	103	75	88	0	—	339
Opponents	64	133	82	103	6	—	388

2013 TEAM STATISTICS

	Bills	Opp.
Total First Downs	301	308
Rushing	113	98
Passing	149	170
Penalty	39	40
3rd Down: Made/Att	83/244	91/245
3rd Down Pct.	34.0	37.1
4th Down: Made/Att	4/14	4/10
4th Down Pct.	28.6	40.0
Possession Avg.	28:23	31:37
Total Net Yards	5410	5334
Avg. Per Game	338.1	333.4
Total Plays	1116	1089
Avg. Per Play	4.8	4.9
Net Yards Rushing	2307	2063
Avg. Per Game	144.2	128.9
Total Rushes	546	471
Net Yards Passing	3103	3271
Avg. Per Game	193.9	204.4
Sacked/Yards Lost	48/270	57/395
Gross Yards	3373	3666
Att./Completions	522/299	561/310
Completion Pct.	57.3	55.3
Had Intercepted	15	23
Punts/Average	96/43.0	94/45.5
Net Punting Avg.	96/36.1	94/41.0
Penalties/Yards	110/952	108/931
Fumbles/Ball Lost	32/12	21/7
Touchdowns	34	42
Rushing	15	10
Passing	16	28
Returns	3	4

2013 INDIVIDUAL STATISTICS

PASSING	Att.	Comp.	Yds.	Pct.	TD	Int.	Tkld.	Rate
Manuel	306	180	1972	58.8	11	9	28/159	77.7
Lewis	157	93	1092	59.2	4	3	18/100	81.0
Tuel	59	26	309	44.1	1	3	2/11	45.1
Bills	522	299	3373	57.3	16	15	48/270	75.0
Opponents	561	310	3666	55.3	28	23	57/395	74.9

SCORING	TD R	TD P	TD Rt	PAT	FG	Saf	PTS
Carpenter	0	0	0	32/32	33/36	0	131
Jackson	9	1	0	0/0	0/0	0	60
Johnson	0	3	0	0/0	0/0	0	20
Woods	0	3	0	0/0	0/0	0	20
Goodwin	0	3	0	0/0	0/0	0	18
Chandler	0	2	0	0/0	0/0	0	12
Graham	0	2	0	0/0	0/0	0	12
Manuel	2	0	0	0/0	0/0	0	12
Searcy	0	0	2	0/0	0/0	0	12
Spiller	2	0	0	0/0	0/0	0	12
Summers	1	1	0	0/0	0/0	0	12
Gragg	0	1	0	0/0	0/0	0	6
Lewis	1	0	0	0/0	0/0	0	6
Robey	0	0	1	0/0	0/0	0	6
Bills	15	16	3	32/32	33/36	0	339
Opponents	10	28	4	41/41	31/36	0	388

2-Pt Conversions: Johnson, Woods.
Bills 2-2, Opponents 1-1.

RUSHING	No.	Yds	Avg	LG	TD
Spiller	202	933	4.6	77	2
Jackson	206	890	4.3	59	9
Manuel	53	186	3.5	19	2
Choice	35	126	3.6	20	0
Lewis	24	52	2.2	8	1
Summers	12	46	3.8	16	1
Tuel	3	17	5.7	14	0
Woods	2	16	8.0	13	0
Graham	4	14	3.5	14	0
Goodwin	3	13	4.3	17	0
Johnson	1	10	10.0	10	0
Wingo	1	4	4.0	4	0
Bills	546	2307	4.2	77	15
Opponents	471	2063	4.4	80t	10

RECEIVING	No.	Yds	Avg	LG	TD
Chandler	53	655	12.4	33t	2
Johnson	52	597	11.5	45	3
Jackson	47	387	8.2	37	1
Woods	40	587	14.7	57	3
Spiller	33	185	5.6	27	0
Graham	23	361	15.7	47	2
Goodwin	17	283	16.6	59t	3
Hogan	10	83	8.3	16	0
Summers	7	79	11.3	34	1
L. Smith	5	78	15.6	28	0
Gragg	5	53	10.6	28	1
Choice	4	10	2.5	5	0
Easley	2	13	6.5	9	0
Wingo	1	2	2.0	2	0
Bills	299	3373	11.3	59t	16
Opponents	310	3666	11.8	74	28

INTERCEPTIONS	No.	Yds	Avg	LG	TD
Byrd	4	85	21.3	57	0
Leonhard	4	72	18.0	41	0
A. Williams	4	43	10.8	34	0
Alonso	4	38	9.5	32	0
Gilmore	2	0	0.0	0	0
Searcy	1	32	32.0	32t	1
Robey	1	19	19.0	19t	1
Lawson	1	0	0.0	0	0
McKelvin	1	0	0.0	0	0
Rogers	1	0	0.0	0	0
Bills	23	289	12.6	57	2
Opponents	15	298	19.9	100t	2

PUNTING	No.	Yds.	Avg.	In 20	LG
Moorman	61	2511	41.2	16	62
S. Powell	35	1613	46.1	10	66
Bills	96	4124	43.0	26	66
Opponents	94	4274	45.5	39	74

PUNT RETURNS	Ret	FC	Yds	Avg	LG	TD
McKelvin	32	13	180	5.6	21	0
Leonhard	7	9	63	9.0	25	0
Bills	39	22	243	6.2	25	0
Opponents	45	22	477	10.6	79t	1

KICKOFF RETURNS	No.	Yds	Avg	LG	TD
Goodwin	16	351	21.9	28	0
Easley	4	83	20.8	28	0
Graham	1	19	19.0	19	0
Woods	1	9	9.0	9	0
Ross	1	7	7.0	7	0
Bills	23	469	20.4	28	0
Opponents	48	1122	23.4	83	0

FIELD GOALS	1-19	20-29	30-39	40-49	50+
Carpenter	0/0	13/13	6/6	10/11	4/6
Bills	0/0	13/13	6/6	10/11	4/6
Opponents	0/0	7/7	14/16	8/10	2/3

SACKS	No.
M. Williams	13.0
K. Williams	10.5
Hughes	10.0
Dareus	7.5
Lawson	4.0
Searcy	3.5
Robey	3.0
Alonso	2.0
Bryant	1.0
Byrd	1.0
Charles	1.0
Westerman	0.5
Bills	57.0
Opponents	48.0

RECORD HOLDERS
INDIVIDUAL RECORDS—CAREER

Category	Name	Performance
Rushing (Yds.)	Thurman Thomas, 1988-1999	11,938
Passing (Yds.)	Jim Kelly, 1986-1996	35,467
Passing (TDs)	Jim Kelly, 1986-1996	237
Receiving (No.)	Andre Reed, 1985-1999	941
Receiving (Yds.)	Andre Reed, 1985-1999	13,095
Interceptions	George (Butch) Byrd, 1964-1970	40
Punting (Avg.)	Brian Moorman, 2001-2013	43.7
Punt Return (Avg.)	C.J. Spiller, 2010-13	12.1
Kickoff Return (Avg.)	O.J. Simpson, 1969-1977	30.0
Field Goals	Steve Christie, 1992-2000	234
Touchdowns (Tot.)	Andre Reed, 1985-1999	87
	Thurman Thomas, 1988-1999	87
Points	Steve Christie, 1992-2000	1,011
*Sacks	Bruce Smith, 1985-1999	**171.0

INDIVIDUAL RECORDS—SINGLE SEASON

Category	Name	Performance
Rushing (Yds.)	O.J. Simpson, 1973	2,003
Passing (Yds.)	Drew Bledsoe, 2002	4,359
Passing (TDs)	Jim Kelly, 1991	33
Receiving (No.)	Eric Moulds, 2002	100
Receiving (Yds.)	Eric Moulds, 1998	1,368
Interceptions	Billy Atkins, 1961	10
	Tom Janik, 1967	10
Punting (Avg.)	Brian Moorman, 2011	48.2
Punt Return (Avg.)	Leodis McKelvin, 2012	18.7
Kickoff Return (Avg.)	Terrence McGee, 2005	30.2
Field Goals	Steve Christie, 1998	33
	Dan Carpenter, 2013	33
Touchdowns (Tot.)	O.J. Simpson, 1975	23
Points	Steve Christie, 1998	140
*Sacks	Bruce Smith, 1990	19.0

INDIVIDUAL RECORDS—SINGLE GAME

Category	Name	Performance
Rushing (Yds.)	O.J. Simpson, 11-25-76	273
Passing (Yds.)	Drew Bledsoe, 9-15-02	463
Passing (TDs)	Jim Kelly, 9-8-91	6
Receiving (No.)	Andre Reed, 11-20-94	15
Receiving (Yds.)	Lee Evans, 11-19-06	265
Interceptions	Many times	3
	Last time by Nate Clements, 10-20-02	
Field Goals	Steve Christie, 10-20-96	6
Touchdowns (Tot.)	Cookie Gilchrist, 12-8-63	5
Points	Cookie Gilchrist, 12-8-63	30
*Sacks	Mario Williams, 9-15-13	4.5

*Sacks became an official statistic in 1982.
**NFL Record

2014 VETERAN ROSTER

No.	Name	Pos.	Ht.	Wt.	Birthdate	NFL Exp.	College	Hometown	How Acq.	'13 Games/Starts
50	Alonso, Kiko	LB	6-3	238	8/14/90	2	Oregon	Los Gatos, Calif.	D2b-'13	16/16
62	Asper, Mark	G	6-7	325	11/8/85	2	Oregon	Idaho Falls, Idaho	FA-'13	6/0
86	Barden, Ramses	WR	6-6	224	1/1/86	5	Cal-Poly	Altadena, Calif.	FA-'14	0*
53	Bradham, Nigel	OLB	6-2	241	9/4/89	3	Florida State	Crawfordville, Fla.	D4a-'12	16/2
90	Branch, Alan	DL	6-6	325	12/29/84	8	Michigan	Rio Rancho, N.M.	UFA(Sea)-'13	16/13
33	Brooks, Ron	CB	5-10	190	10/16/88	3	Louisiana State	Irving, Texas	D4b-'12	11/0
35 t-	Brown, Bryce	RB	6-0	220	5/14/91	3	Kansas State	Wichita, Kan.	T(Phil)-'14	16/1*
97	Bryant, Corbin	DT	6-4	300	1/4/88	2	Northwestern	Chicago, Ill.	FA-'12	15/2
30	Butler, Mario	DB	6-1	187	10/20/88	2	Georgia Tech	Jacksonville, Fla.	FA-'13	0*
2	Carpenter, Dan	K	6-2	228	11/25/85	7	Montana	Helena, Mont.	FA-'13	16/0
80	Caussin, Mike	TE	6-5	243	2/26/87	4	James Madison	Springfield, Va.	FA-'10	0*
84	Chandler, Scott	TE	6-7	260	7/23/85	8	Iowa	Bedford, Texas	W(Dall)-'10	16/7
96	Charles, Stefan	DT	6-5	323	6/9/88	2	Regina	Toronto, Ontario, Canada	FA-'13	8/0
99	Dareus, Marcell	DT	6-3	331	3/13/90	4	Alabama	Huffman, Ala.	D1-'11	16/14
26	Dixon, Anthony	RB	6-1	233	9/24/87	5	Mississippi State	Jackson, Miss.	UFA(SF)-'14	16/1*
6	Dixon, Dennis	QB	6-3	215	1/11/85	5	Oregon	Oakland, Calif.	FA-'13	0*
81	Easley, Marcus	WR	6-2	217	11/2/87	4	Connecticut	Stratford, Conn.	D4-'10	16/0
18	Elliott, Kevin	WR	6-3	205	12/21/88	2	Florida A&M	Orlando, Fla.	FA-'12	0*
24	Gilmore, Stephon	CB	6-1	190	9/19/90	3	South Carolina	Rock Hill, S.C.	D1-'12	11/9
77	Glenn, Cordy	LT	6-6	345	9/18/89	3	Georgia	Riverdale, Ga.	D2-'12	16/16
88	Goodwin, Marquise	WR	5-9	179	11/19/90	2	Texas	Garland, Texas	D3-'13	12/1
89	Gragg, Chris	TE	6-3	244	6/30/90	2	Arkansas	Warren, Ark.	D7-'13	9/1
20	Graham, Corey	DB	6-0	196	7/25/85	8	New Hampshire	Buffalo, N.Y.	UFA(Balt)-'14	16/5*
11	Graham, T.J.	WR	5-11	188	7/27/89	3	North Carolina State	Raleigh, N.C.	D3-'12	16/6
75	Hairston, Chris	RT	6-6	330	4/26/89	3	Clemson	Winston-Salem, N.C.	D4b-'11	0*
15	Hogan, Chris	WR	6-1	220	10/24/88	2	Monmouth	Ramapo, N.J.	FA-'12	16/0
55	Hughes, Jerry	DE	6-2	254	8/13/88	5	Texas Christian	Sugar Land, Texas	T(Ind)-'13	16/1
22	Jackson, Fred	RB	6-1	216	2/20/81	8	Coe College	Fort Worth, Texas	FA-'06	16/6
91	Lawson, Manny	DE	6-5	240	7/13/84	9	North Carolina State	Goldsboro, N.C.	UFA(Cin)-'13	15/15
59	Legursky, Doug	G	6-1	315	6/9/86	6	Marshall	Beckley, W.Va.	FA-'13	12/11
9	Lewis, Thad	QB	6-2	219	11/19/87	4	Duke	Opa-Locka, Fla.	FA-'13	6/5
3	Manuel, EJ	QB	6-4	237	3/19/90	2	Florida State	Virginia Beach, Va.	D1-'13	10/10
21	McKelvin, Leodis	CB	5-10	185	9/4/85	7	Troy	Waycross, Ga.	D1-'08	15/13
36	Meeks, Jonathan	DB	6-0	209	11/8/89	2	Clemson	Rock Hill, S.C.	D5-'13	8/0
82	Moeaki, Tony	TE	6-3	252	6/8/87	5	Iowa	Wheaton, Ill.	FA-'13	2/0
8	Moorman, Brian	P	6-0	174	2/5/76	14	Pittsburg State	Sedgwick, Kan.	FA-'13	11/0
79	Pears, Erik	RT	6-8	316	6/25/82	9	Colorado State	Price, Utah	FA-'10	16/16
57	Powell, Ty	LB	6-2	249	4/27/88	2	Harding	Marina, Calif.	FA-'13	5/0
56	Rivers, Keith	LB	6-2	235	5/5/86	6	Southern California	Lake Mary, Fla.	UFA(NYG)-'14	16/8*
37	Robey, Nickell	CB	5-8	165	1/17/92	2	Southern California	Frostproof, Fla.	FA-'13	16/2
48	Rodriguez, Evan	FB	6-2	239	9/21/88	3	Temple	North Bergen, N.J.	FA-'13	7/0
65	Sanborn, Garrison	LS	6-1	240	7/31/85	6	Florida State	Tampa, Fla.	FA-'09	16/0
25	Searcy, Da'Norris	FS	5-11	216	11/16/88	4	North Carolina	Decatur, Ga.	D4a-'11	16/7
85	Smith, Lee	TE	6-6	265	11/21/87	4	Marshall	Powell, Tenn.	W(NE)-'11	16/14
51	Spikes, Brandon	LB	6-2	255	9/3/87	5	Florida	Shelby, N.C.	UFA(NE)-'14	16/11*
28	Spiller, C.J.	RB	5-11	200	8/5/87	5	Clemson	Lake Butler, Fla.	D1-'10	15/10
38	Summers, Frank	FB	5-9	248	9/6/85	2	Nevada-Las Vegas	Oakland, Calif.	FA-'13	15/9
7	Tuel, Jeff	QB	6-3	221	2/12/91	2	Washington State	Fresno, Calif.	FA-'13	2/1
64	'Unga, J.J.	G	6-5	320	1/5/87	2	Midwestern State	Rochester, Calif.	FA-'13	3/0
60	Urbik, Kraig	G	6-5	324	9/23/85	6	Wisconsin	Hudson, Wisc.	W(Pitt)-'10	16/16
23	Williams, Aaron	SS	6-0	199	4/23/90	4	Texas	Round Rock, Texas	D2-'11	14/14
74	Williams, Chris	OL	6-6	320	8/26/85	7	Vanderbilt	Baton Rouge, La.	UFA(StL)-'14	16/16*
27	Williams, Duke	FS	5-11	201	10/15/90	2	Nevada	Reno, Nev.	D4-'13	16/0
95	Williams, Kyle	DT	6-1	303	6/10/83	9	Louisiana State	Ruston, La.	D5a-'06	16/16
94	Williams, Mario	DE	6-6	292	1/31/85	9	North Carolina State	Richlands, N.C.	UFA(Hou)-'12	16/16
19 t-	Williams, Mike	WR	6-2	212	5/18/87	5	Syracuse	Buffalo, N.Y.	T(TB)-'14	6/5*
70	Wood, Eric	C	6-4	310	3/18/86	6	Louisville	Cincinnati, Ohio	D1b-'09	16/16
10	Woods, Robert	WR	6-0	190	4/10/92	2	Southern California	Carson, Calif.	D2a-'13	14/14
92	Wynn, Jarius	DE	6-3	285	8/29/86	6	Georgia	Augusta, Ga.	FA-'14	15/2*

* Barden did not play in '13; Brown played 16 games with Philadelphia in '13; Butler last active with Dallas in '12; Caussin missed the '13 season because of injury; A. Dixon played 16 games with San Francisco; D. Dixon last active with Pittsburgh in '10; Elliott missed '13 season because of injury; Graham played 16 games with Baltimore in '13; Hairston last active with Buffalo in '12; Rivers played 16 games with the New York Giants; Spikes played 16 games with New England; C. Williams played 16 games with St. Louis; Mike Williams played six games with Tampa Bay; Wynn played five games with San Diego and 10 games with Dallas.

Traded—WR Steve Johnson (12 games in '13) to San Francisco.

t- Bills traded for Brown (Phil), M. Williams (TB).

Players lost through free agency (2): FS Jairus Byrd (NO; 11 games in '13), DE Alex Carrington (StL; 3).

Also played with Bills in '13—CB Johnny Adams (4 games), OL Colin Brown (6), CB Brandon Burton (5), RB Tashard Choice (12), LB Marcus Dowtin (5), DB Jim Leonhard (16), LB Arthur Moats (16), P Shawn Powell (5), CB Justin Rogers (5), DL Jay Ross (5), OL Thomas Welch (16), LB Jamaal Westerman (12), T Sam Young (4).

FIRST-YEAR ROSTER

Name	Pos.	Ht.	Wt.	Birthdate	College	Hometown	How Acq.
Brim, Derek	DB	6-0	199	12/31/91	Buffalo	Buffalo, N.Y.	FA
Broomfield, Deon	DB	6-0	206	8/3/91	Iowa State	Palm Bay, Fla.	FA
Brown, Preston	LB	6-1	251	10/27/92	Louisville	Cincinnati, Ohio	D3
Carter, Michael	DB	5-11	189	4/22/91	Minnesota	Pompano Beach, Fla.	FA
Cockrell, Ross	CB	6-0	190	8/6/91	Duke	Waxhaw, N.C.	D4
Colling, Randy	OG	6-5	320	5/10/90	Gannon	Arcade, N.Y.	FA
Coughman, Edawn (1)	OT	6-4	313	7/21/88	Shaw	East Point, Ga.	FA-'13
Dombrowski, Jake	P	6-1	190	3/18/91	Harvard	Gaylord, Mich.	FA
Gaines, Jimmy	LB	6-3	240	5/11/93	Miami	Getzville, N.Y.	FA
Harley, Jajuan	FS	6-1	213	1/17/91	Middle Tennessee	Tallahassee, Fla.	FA
Henderson, Seantrel	OL	6-7	331	1/21/92	Miami	St. Paul, Minn.	D7b
Holley, Caleb	WR	6-2	200	12/26/90	East Central (Okla.)	Anchorage, Alaska	FA
Hopkins, Dustin (1)	K	6-2	193	10/1/90	Florida State	Houston, Texas	D6-'13
Igbinosun, Ikponmwosa (1)	DE	6-3	286	9/10/90	Southern Connecticut State	Rahway, N.J.	FA-'13
Jacobs, Damien	DT	6-3	284	7/22/91	Florida	Gibson, La.	FA
Johnson, Bryan	DE	6-4	250	8/13/88	West Texas A&M	Bellport, N.Y,	FA
Johnson, Randell	LB	6-4	245	3/23/91	Florida Atlantic	Miami, Fla.	D7a
Kitchens, Darrin	LB	6-2	229	11/2/91	Florida	Homestead, Fla.	FA
Kouandjio, Cyrus	OT	6-7	322	7/21/93	Alabama	Hyattsville, Md.	D2
Ladler, Kenny	DB	6-0	207	6/23/92	Vanderbilt	Stone Mountain, Ga.	FA
McClain, Antoine (1)	OG	6-5	336	12/6/89	Clemson	Anniston, Ala.	W(Oak)-'13
Richardson, Cyril	OL	6-5	343	12/27/90	Baylor	Fort Worth, Texas	D5
Robinson, Darius	DB	5-10	175	11/17/91	Clemson	College Park, Ga.	FA
Roberson, Cordell (1)	WR	6-4	205	12/3/90	Stephen F. Austin	Jefferson, Texas	FA-'13
Smith, Brandon (1)	DB	6-1	205	2/23/87	Arizona State	Bakersfield, Calif.	FA-'13
Smith, Jacquies (1)	LB	6-2	260	3/18/90	Missouri	Dallas, Texas	FA-'13
Summers, Chris	WR	6-5	215	7/10/89	Liberty	Jacksonville, Fla.	FA
Watkins, Sammy	WR	6-1	211	6/14/93	Clemson	Fort Myers, Fla.	D1
Way, Colby	DT	6-4	293	7/7/91	Buffalo	State College, Pa.	FA
Williams, Nathan	LB	6-3	249	10/16/89	Ohio State	Washington C.H., Ohio	FA
Wingo, Ronnie (1)	RB	6-3	231	2/18/91	Arkansas	St. Louis, Mo.	FA-'13

The term NFL Rookie is defined as a player who is in his first season of professional football and has not been on the roster of another professional football team for any regular-season or postseason games. A Rookie is designated by an "R" on NFL rosters. Players who have been active in another professional football league or players who have NFL experience, including either preseason training camp or being on an Active List or Inactive List, or on Reserve/Injured or Reserve/Physically Unable to Perform for fewer than six regular-season games, are termed NFL First-Year Players. An NFL First-Year Player is designated by a "1" on NFL rosters. Thereafter, a player is credited with an additional year of experience for each season in which he accumulates six games on the Active List or Inactive List, or on Reserve/Injured or Reserve/Physically Unable to Perform.

Log on to www.buffalobills.com for an up-to-date roster.

COACHING STAFF
Head Coach,
Doug Marrone

Pro Career: Marrone was named Buffalo's 16th head coach on January 7, 2013. He enters his ninth season in the NFL coaching ranks and second as a head coach after leading Buffalo to a 6-10 mark in 2013. Marrone spent the previous four years as the head coach of his alma mater's football program at Syracuse University from 2009-2012. Prior to his Syracuse tenure, Marrone spent seven years in the NFL. From 2006-08 he served as the offensive coordinator of the New Orleans Saints. From 2002-05 he was the offensive line coach of the New York Jets. Before arriving in New York, Marrone coached the tight ends and tackles at Tennessee in 2001. He spent the 2000 season at Georgia as the program's offensive line coach after spending the previous five years at Georgia Tech. In 1995, Marrone was the director of football operations before coaching the tight ends in 1996 and offensive line from 1997-99. Marrone's coaching career began in 1992 at Cortland (N.Y.) State as the school's tight ends coach before stints as the offensive line coach at the U.S. Coast Guard Academy (1993) and Northeastern University in 1994. He was drafted in the sixth round of the 1986 NFL draft by the Los Angeles Raiders and played two years in the NFL, first with the Miami Dolphins in 1987 and with the Saints in 1989. He also had playing stints with Pittsburgh, Dallas and Minnesota before closing his career with the NFLE London Monarchs (1991-92). Career record: 6-10.

Background: Marrone was a three-year letterman (1983-85) at Syracuse as an offensive lineman. He earned a degree in liberal arts from Syracuse in 1991.

Personal: Born July 25, 1964, Bronx, N.Y. He and wife, Helen, have two daughters, Madeline and Anne, and a son, Mack.

ASSISTANT COACHES

Greg Adkins, tight ends; born March 25, 1968, Cross Lanes, W. Va. Offensive line Marshall 1986-89. No pro playing experience. College coach: Marshall 1991-95, Georgia 1996-2000, Troy 2001-02, Tennessee 2003-08, Syracuse 2009-2012. Pro coach: Joined Bills in 2013.

Kurt Anderson, offensive quality control; born August 8, 1978, Glenview, Ill. Offensive line Michigan 1997-2001. No pro playing experience. College coach: Indiana State 2005, Michigan 2006-07, Eastern Michigan 2008-2012. Pro coach: Joined Bills in 2013.

John Anselmo, special teams assistant; born September 23, 1949, Freeport, N.Y. Quarterback Cortland State 1968-1970. No pro playing experience. College coach: Nassau (N.Y.) C.C. 1977-1994, 1999-2008, Georgia Tech 1995-98, Syracuse 2009-2012. Pro coach: Joined Bills in 2013.

Thad Bogardus, defensive quality control; born April 10, 1989, Redding, Conn.

Attended Elon. No college or pro playing experience. College coach: Ball State 2012-13. Pro coach: Joined Bills in 2014.

Samson Brown, asst. defensive backs; born January 11, 1980, Bronx, N.Y. Free safety Albany 1999-2002. No pro playing experience. College coach: Siena 2003, RPI 2004-05, Hofstra 2006, Albany 2007-09. Pro coach: New York Jets 2010-11, joined Bills in 2013.

Stephen Brown, asst. to the head coach; born May 3, 1987, Charlotte, N.C. Attended Tennessee. No college or pro playing experience. College coach: Syracuse 2009-2012. Pro coach: joined Bills in 2013.

Eric Ciano, head strength and conditioning; born August 8, 1973, Waltham, Mass. Offensive line Springfield (Mass.) College 1993-97. No pro playing experience. College coach: Tennessee 1997-99, Louisiana Tech 2000-02, Tennessee 2002-04, Georgia Tech 2005-09. Pro coach: Joined Bills in 2010.

Danny Crossman, special teams coordinator; born January 17, 1967, El Paso, Texas. Defensive back Pittsburgh Kansas 1985, Pittsburgh 1987-89. Pro defensive back Washington Redskins 1990, Detroit Lions 1991-92. College coach: U.S. Coast Guard Academy 1993, Western Kentucky 1994-96, Central Florida 1997-98, Georgia Tech 1999-2001, Michigan State 2002. Pro coach: Carolina Panthers 2003-09, Detroit Lions 2010-12, joined Bills in 2013.

Todd Downing, quarterbacks; born July 22, 1980, Eden Prairie, Minn. Attended Minnesota. No college or pro playing experience. Pro coach: Minnesota Vikings 2003-05, St. Louis Rams 2006-08, Detroit Lions 2009-2013, joined Bills in 2013.

Nathaniel Hackett, offensive coordinator; born December 19, 1979, Fullerton, Calif. Linebacker/long snapper U.C. Davis 1999-2002. No pro playing experience. College coach: U.C. Davis 2003, Stanford 2003-05, Syracuse 2010-12. Pro coach: Tampa Bay Buccaneers 2006-07, Buffalo Bills 2008-09, re-joined Bills in 2013.

Donnie Henderson, defensive backs; born May 17, 1957, Baltimore, Md. Defensive back Utah State 1978-79. No pro playing experience. College coach: Utah State 1983-88, Idaho 1989, California 1990-91, Arizona State 1992-97, Houston 1998, Southern 2011, Syracuse 2012. Pro coach: Baltimore Ravens 1999-2003, New York Jets 2004-05, Detroit Lions 2006, Jacksonville Jaguars 2008, California Redwoods (UFL) 2009, Arizona Cardinals 2010, joined Bills in 2013.

Jim Hostler, senior offensive assistant; born November 11, 1966, Pittsburgh, Pa. Defensive back Indiana (Pa.) 1986-19. No pro playing experience. College coach: Indiana (Pa.) 1990-92, 1994-99, Juniata (Pa.) 1993. Pro coach: Kansas City Chiefs 2000, New Orleans Saints 2001-02, New York Jets 2003-04, San Francisco 49ers 2005-07, Baltimore Ravens 2008-2013, joined Bills in 2014.

Pepper Johnson, defensive line; born July

29, 1964, Detroit, Mich. Linebacker Ohio State 1982-85. Pro linebacker New York Giants 1986-1992, Cleveland Browns 1993-95, Detroit Lions 1996, New York Jets 1997-98. Pro coach: New England Patriots 2001-2013, joined Bills in 2014.

Hal Luther, asst. strength and conditioning; born March 24, 1974, Dolgeville, N.Y. Quarterback Springfield (Mass.) College 1992-95. No pro playing experience. College coach: Western Michigan 1996, Wisconsin-LaCrosse 1996-97, North Carolina State 1998-2000, Syracuse 2000-2012. Pro coach: Joined Bills in 2013.

Rob Moore, wide receivers; born September 27, 1968, Hempstead, N.Y. Wide receiver Syracuse 1986-1990. Pro wide receiver New York Jets 1990-94, Arizona Cardinals 1995-2001. College coach: Phoenix (Ariz.) J.C. 2009, Syracuse 2010-13. Pro coach: Joined Bills in 2014.

Pat Morris, offensive line; born April 7, 1954, Cleveland, Ohio. Offensive lineman Southern California 1972-75. No pro playing experience. College coach: Southern California 1976-77, 1983-86, Northern Arizona 1978, Minnesota 1979-1982, Michigan State 1987-1994, Stanford 1995-96. Pro coach: San Francisco 49ers 1997-2003, Detroit Lions 2004-05, Minnesota Vikings 2006-2010, Tampa Bay Buccaneers 2011, joined Bills in 2013.

Fred Pagac, linebackers; born April 26, 1952, Richeyville, Pa. Tight end Ohio State 1971-73. Pro tight end Chicago Bears 1974, Tampa Bay Buccaneers 1976. College coach: Ohio State 1978-2000. Pro coach: Oakland Raiders 2001-03, Kansas City Chiefs 2004-05, Minnesota Vikings 2006-2013, joined Bills in 2014.

Jason Rebrovich, asst. defensive line; born March 15, 1978, Clarence, N.Y. Defensive line Alfred State 1996-97, Cortland 1998-99. No pro playing experience. College coach: Cortland 2001-04, 2008-2010, Ferris State 2005-07, Syracuse 2011-12. Pro coach: Joined Bills in 2013.

Jim Schwartz, defensive coordinator; born June 2, 1966, Baltimore, Md. Linebacker Georgetown 1985-88. No pro playing experience. College coach: Maryland 1989, Minnesota 1990, North Carolina Central 1991, Colgate 1992. Pro coach: Baltimore Ravens 1996-98, Tennessee Titans 1999-2008, Detroit Lions 2009-2013 (head coach), joined Bills in 2014.

Jason Vrable, offensive quality control; born January 23, 1985, South Park, Pa. Quarterback Marietta College 2004-06. No pro playing experience. College coach: Marietta 2007, Robert Morris 2008, Syracuse 2009-2010, Charleston 2011-12. Pro coach: Joined Bills in 2013.

Tyrone Wheatley, running backs; born January 19, 1972, Inkster, Mich. Running back Michigan 1991-94. Pro running back New York Giants 1995-98, Oakland Raiders 1999-2004. College coach: Ohio Northern 2008, Eastern Michigan 2009, Syracuse 2010-12. Pro coach: Joined Bills in 2013.

**American Football Conference
North Division**
Team Colors: Black, Orange, and White
One Paul Brown Stadium
Cincinnati, Ohio 45202-3492
Telephone: (513) 621-3550
Ticket Office (513) 621-TDTD (8383)

2014 SCHEDULE
PRESEASON
Aug. 7	at Kansas City	8:00
Aug. 16	**New York Jets**	7:00
Aug. 24	at Arizona	8:00
Aug. 28	**Indianapolis**	7:00

REGULAR SEASON
Sep. 7	at Baltimore	1:00
Sep. 14	**Atlanta**	1:00
Sep. 21	**Tennessee**	1:00
Sep. 28	BYE	
Oct. 5	at New England	*8:30
Oct. 12	**Carolina**	1:00
Oct. 19	at Indianapolis	1:00
Oct. 26	**Baltimore**	1:00
Nov. 2	**Jacksonville**	1:00
Nov. 6	**Cleveland** (Thu)	8:25
Nov. 16	at New Orleans	1:00
Nov. 23	at Houston	1:00
Nov. 30	at Tampa Bay	1:00
Dec. 7	**Pittsburgh**	1:00
Dec. 14	at Cleveland	1:00
Dec. 22	**Denver** (Mon)	8:30
Dec. 28	at Pittsburgh	1:00

All times ET; Sunday night games in Weeks 5-16 subject to change
Stadium: Paul Brown Stadium
(opened in 2000)
• **Capacity:** 65,515
One Paul Brown Stadium
Cincinnati, Ohio 45202-3492
Playing Surface: Synthetic
Training Camp: Paul Brown Stadium
Cincinnati, Ohio 45202

PAUL BROWN STADIUM

CLUB OFFICIALS
President: Mike Brown
Senior Vice President: Pete Brown
Executive Vice President: Katie Blackburn
Vice President: Paul Brown
Vice President: Troy Blackburn
Business Manager: Bill Connelly
Chief Financial Officer: Bill Scanlon
Director of Business Development:
Bob Bedinghaus
Managing Director of Paul Brown
Stadium: Eric Brown
Directors of Technology: Michael Kayes,
Jo Ann Ralstin
Bengals.com Editor: Geoff Hobson
Director of Security: Rusty Guy
Director of Sales and Public Affairs:
Jeff Berding
Director of Corporate Sales, Marketing
and Broadcasting: Brian Sells
Ticket Manager: Tim Kelly
Director of Player Relations: Eric Ball
Director of Player Personnel: Duke Tobin
Public Relations Director: Jack Brennan
Athletic Trainer: Paul Sparling
Equipment Manager: Jeff Brickner
Video Director: Travis Brammer

COACHING HISTORY
(321-402-2)
Records include postseason games
1968-1975	Paul Brown	55-59-1
1976-78	Bill Johnson*	18-15-0
1978-79	Homer Rice	8-19-0
1980-83	Forrest Gregg	34-27-0
1984-1991	Sam Wyche	64-68-0
1992-96	Dave Shula**	19-52-0
1996-2000	Bruce Coslet***	21-39-0
2000-02	Dick LeBeau	12-33-0
2003-2013	Marvin Lewis	90-90-1

* Resigned after five games in 1978
** Released after seven games in 1996
*** Resigned after three games in 2000

PAID ATTENDANCE
Home 483,792   Away 499,195
Total 982,987
Single-game home record,
66,188 (10/28/07)
Single-season home record, 516,154
(2006)

2014 DRAFT CHOICES
Round	Name	Pos.	College
1	Darqueze Dennard	DB	Michigan St.
2	Jeremy Hill	RB	Louisiana St.
3	Will Clarke	DE	West Virginia
4	Russell Bodine	C	North Carolina
5	A.J. McCarron	QB	Alabama
6	Marquis Flowers	LB	Arizona
7	James Wright	WR	Louisiana St.
	Lavelle Westbrooks	DB	Georgia Southern

2013 TEAM RECORD
PRESEASON (3-1)

Date	Result	Opponent
08/08	W 34-10	at Atlanta
08/17	W 27-19	Tennessee
08/24	L 18-24	at Dallas
08/29	W 27-10	Indianapolis

REGULAR SEASON (11-5)

Date	Result	Opponent
09/08	L 21-24	at Chicago
09/16	W 20-10	Pittsburgh
09/22	W 34-30	Green Bay
09/29	L 6-17	at Cleveland
10/06	W 13-6	New England
10/13	W 27-24	at Buffalo (OT)
10/20	W 27-24	at Detroit
10/27	W 49-9	New York Jets
10/31	L 20-22	at Miami (OT)
11/10	L 17-20	at Baltimore (OT)
11/17	W 41-20	Cleveland
12/01	W 17-10	at San Diego
12/08	W 42-28	Indianapolis
12/15	L 20-30	at Pittsburgh
12/22	W 42-14	Minnesota
12/29	W 34-17	Baltimore

POSTSEASON (0-1)

Date	Result	Opponent
01/05	L 10-27	San Diego

(OT) Overtime

SCORE BY PERIODS

Bengals	87	123	103	114	3 —	430
Opponents	88	71	83	58	5 —	305

2013 TEAM STATISTICS

	Bengals	Opp.
Total First Downs	330	282
Rushing	101	72
Passing	205	178
Penalty	24	32
3rd Down: Made/Att	92/225	74/225
3rd Down Pct.	40.9	32.9
4th Down: Made/Att	12/21	5/16
4th Down Pct.	57.1	31.3
Possession Avg.	31:58	28:02
Total Net Yards	5891	4888
Avg. Per Game	368.2	305.5
Total Plays	1097	1042
Avg. Per Play	5.4	4.7
Net Yards Rushing	1755	1544
Avg. Per Game	109.7	96.5
Total Rushes	481	385
Net Yards Passing	4136	3344
Avg. Per Game	258.5	209.0
Sacked/Yards Lost	29/182	43/279
Gross Yards	4318	3623
Att./Completions	587/364	614/362
Completion Pct.	62.0	59.0
Had Intercepted	20	20
Punts/Average	75/44.4	90/44.3
Net Punting Avg.	75/39.9	90/39.3
Penalties/Yards	102/1000	69/692
Fumbles/Ball Lost	20/10	16/11
Touchdowns	54	32
Rushing	14	6
Passing	33	22
Returns	7	4

2013 INDIVIDUAL STATISTICS

PASSING

	Att.	Comp.	Yds.	Pct.	TD	Int.	Tkld.	Rate
Dalton	586	363	4293	61.9	33	20	29/182	88.8
Sanu	1	1	25	100.0	0	0	0/0	118.8
Bengals	587	364	4318	62.0	33	20	29/182	89.0
Opponents	614	362	3623	59.0	22	20	43/279	74.2

SCORING

	TD R	TD P	TD Rt	PAT	FG	Saf	PTS
Nugent	0	0	0	52/53	18/22	0	106
Green	0	11	0	0/0	0/0	0	66
M. Jones	0	10	0	0/0	0/0	0	60
Bernard	5	3	0	0/0	0/0	0	48
Green-Ellis	7	0	0	0/0	0/0	0	42
Gresham	0	4	0	0/0	0/0	0	24
Dalton	2	0	0	0/0	0/0	0	12
Eifert	0	2	0	0/0	0/0	0	12
Sanu	0	2	0	0/0	0/0	0	12
Burfict	0	0	1	0/0	0/0	0	6
Crocker	0	0	1	0/0	0/0	0	6
Dye	0	0	1	0/0	0/0	0	6
A. Jones	0	0	1	0/0	0/0	0	6
Kirkpatrick	0	0	1	0/0	0/0	0	6
Newman	0	0	1	0/0	0/0	0	6
Rey	0	0	1	0/0	0/0	0	6
Al. Smith	0	1	0	0/0	0/0	0	6
Bengals	14	33	7	52/53	18/22	0	430
Opponents	6	22	4	31/31	26/31	1	305

2-Pt Conversions: Bengals 0-1, Opponents 1-1.

RUSHING

	No.	Yds	Avg	LG	TD
Green-Ellis	220	756	3.4	25	7
Bernard	170	695	4.1	35t	5
Dalton	61	183	3.0	12	2
M. Jones	8	65	8.1	34	0
J. Johnson	7	20	2.9	10	0
Peerman	8	17	2.1	5	0
Sanu	4	16	4.0	9	0
Hawkins	2	3	1.5	6	0
Huber	1	0	0.0	0	0
Bengals	481	1755	3.6	35t	14
Opponents	385	1544	4.0	51	6

RECEIVING

	No.	Yds	Avg	LG	TD
Green	98	1426	14.6	82t	11
Bernard	56	514	9.2	41	3
M. Jones	51	712	14.0	45	10
Sanu	47	455	9.7	32	2
Gresham	46	458	10.0	30	4
Eifert	39	445	11.4	61	2
Hawkins	12	199	16.6	50	0
Sanzenbacher	6	61	10.2	23	0
Green-Ellis	4	22	5.5	10	0
Al. Smith	3	12	4.0	7	1
Charles	1	8	8.0	8	0
Tate	1	6	6.0	6	0
Bengals	364	4318	11.9	82t	33
Opponents	362	3623	10.0	74t	22

INTERCEPTIONS

	No.	Yds	Avg	LG	TD
A. Jones	3	60	20.0	60t	1
Kirkpatrick	3	21	7.0	21t	1
Crocker	2	41	20.5	32t	1
Rey	2	29	14.5	25t	1
Newman	2	8	4.0	9	0
Nelson	2	0	0.0	0	0
Maualuga	1	14	14.0	14	0
Burfict	1	12	12.0	12	0
Harrison	1	9	9.0	9	0
M. Johnson	1	7	7.0	7	0
Hall	1	0	0.0	0	0
Iloka	1	-1	-1.0	-1	0
Bengals	20	200	10.0	60t	4
Opponents	20	369	18.5	94t	2

PUNTING

	No.	Yds.	Avg.	In 20	LG
Huber	66	2982	45.2	24	75
Powell	7	268	38.3	3	52
Nugent	2	80	40.0	0	43
Bengals	75	3330	44.4	27	75
Opponents	90	3984	44.3	37	65

PUNT RETURNS

	Ret	FC	Yds	Avg	LG	TD
Tate	36	16	336	9.3	43	0
A. Jones	11	0	88	8.0	27	0
Bengals	47	16	424	9.0	43	0
Opponents	27	22	254	9.4	67t	1

KICKOFF RETURNS

	No.	Yds	Avg	LG	TD
Tate	35	914	26.1	71	0
Peerman	4	66	16.5	26	0
Bengals	39	980	25.1	71	0
Opponents	52	1219	23.4	48	0

FIELD GOALS

	1-19	20-29	30-39	40-49	50+
Nugent	0/0	2/2	6/7	7/9	3/4
Bengals	0/0	2/2	6/7	7/9	3/4
Opponents	2/2	6/6	5/8	9/11	4/4

SACKS

	No.
Dunlap	7.5
Gilberry	7.5
Atkins	6.0
Rey	4.0
M. Johnson	3.5
Burfict	3.0
Peko	3.0
Harrison	2.0
Crocker	1.5
Thompson	1.5
Kirkpatrick	1.0
Maualuga	1.0
Nelson	1.0
Hunt	0.5
Bengals	43.0
Opponents	29.0

RECORD HOLDERS
INDIVIDUAL RECORDS—CAREER

Category	Name	Performance
Rushing (Yds.)	Corey Dillon, 1997-2003	8,061
Passing (Yds.)	Ken Anderson, 1971-1986	32,838
Passing (TDs)	Ken Anderson, 1971-1986	197
Receiving (No.)	Chad Johnson, 2001-2010	751
Receiving (Yds.)	Chad Johnson, 2001-2010	10,783
Interceptions	Ken Riley, 1969-1983	65
Punting (Avg.)	Kevin Huber, 2009-2013	44.2
Punt Return (Avg.)	Quan Cosby, 2009-2010	10.0
Kickoff Return (Avg.)	Brandon Tate, 2011-13	24.8
Field Goals	Jim Breech, 1980-1992	225
Touchdowns (Tot.)	Pete Johnson, 1977-1983	70
Points	Jim Breech, 1980-1992	1,151
*Sacks	Eddie Edwards, 1977-1988	47.5

INDIVIDUAL RECORDS—SINGLE SEASON

Category	Name	Performance
Rushing (Yds.)	Rudi Johnson, 2005	1,458
Passing (Yds.)	Andy Dalton, 2013	4,293
Passing (TDs)	Andy Dalton, 2013	33
Receiving (No.)	T.J. Houshmandzadeh, 2007	112
Receiving (Yds.)	Chad Johnson, 2007	1,440
Interceptions	Deltha O'Neal, 2005	10
Punting (Avg.)	Kevin Huber, 2012	46.6
Punt Return (Avg.)	Lemar Parrish, 1974	18.8
Kickoff Return (Avg.)	Tremain Mack, 1999	27.1
Field Goals	Mike Nugent, 2011	33
Touchdowns (Tot.)	Carl Pickens, 1995	17
Points	Mike Nugent, 2011	132
*Sacks	Eddie Edwards, 1983	13.0

INDIVIDUAL RECORDS—SINGLE GAME

Category	Name	Performance
Rushing (Yds.)	Corey Dillon, 10-22-00	278
Passing (Yds.)	Boomer Esiason, 10-7-90	490
Passing (TDs)	Carson Palmer, 9-16-07	6
Receiving (No.)	Carl Pickens, 10-11-98	13
Receiving (Yds.)	Chad Johnson, 11-12-06	260
Interceptions	Many times	3
	Last time by Leon Hall, 12-21-08	
Field Goals	Shayne Graham, 11-11-07	7
Touchdowns (Tot.)	Larry Kinnebrew, 10-28-84	4
	Corey Dillon, 12-4-97	4
	Marvin Jones, 10-27-13	4
Points	Larry Kinnebrew, 10-28-84	24
	Corey Dillon, 12-4-97	24
	Marvin Jones, 10-27-13	24
*Sacks	Antwan Odom, 9-20-09	5.0

Sacks became an official statistic in 1982.

2014 VETERAN ROSTER

No.	Name	Pos.	Ht.	Wt.	Birthdate	NFL Exp.	College	Hometown	How Acq.	'13 Games/ Starts
97	Atkins, Geno	DT	6-1	303	3/28/88	5	Georgia	Pembroke Pines, Fla.	D4a-'10	9/9
25	Bernard, Giovani	HB	5-9	208	11/22/91	2	North Carolina	Boca Raton, Fla.	D2a'-13	16/0
90	Bilukidi, Christo	DT	6-5	320	12/13/89	3	Georgia State	Ottawa, Ontario, Canada	FA-'13	2/0
63	Black, Larry	DT	6-2	312	12/1/89	2	Indiana	Cincinnati, Ohio	FA-'13	0*
53	#Boley, Michael	LB	6-3	230	8/24/82	10	Southern Mississippi	Elkmont, Ala.	FA-'13	10/1
65	Boling, Clint	G	6-5	311	5/9/89	4	Georgia	Alpharetta, Ga.	D4-'11	12/12
83	Brock, Kevin	TE	6-5	249	4/9/86	2	Rutgers	Hackensack, N.J.	FA-'13	4/0*
55	Burfict, Vontaze	LB	6-1	255	9/24/90	3	Arizona State	Corona, Calif.	FA-'12	16/16
33	Burkhead, Rex	HB	5-10	218	7/2/90	2	Nebraska	Plano, Texas	D6a-'13	1/0
31	Burton, Brandon	CB	5-11	185	7/31/89	4	Utah	Houston, Texas	FA-'14	5/0*
17	Campbell, Jason	QB	6-5	230	12/31/81	10	Auburn	Laurel, Miss.	FA-'14	9/8*
80	Charles, Orson	H-B	6-3	245	1/27/91	3	Georgia	Tampa, Fla.	D4-'12	13/0
4	Conley, T.J.	P	6-3	215	8/29/85	2	Idaho	Walla Walla, Wash.	FA-'14	0*
32	#Crocker, Chris	S	5-11	197	3/9/80	12	Marshall	Chesapeake, Va.	FA-'13	12/3
14	Dalton, Andy	QB	6-2	220	10/29/87	4	Texas Christian	Katy, Texas	D2-'11	16/16
51	DiManche, Jayson	LB	6-1	240	9/22/90	2	Southern Illinois	Hamilton, N.J.	FA-'13	16/0
96	Dunlap, Carlos	DE	6-6	280	2/28/89	5	Florida	North Charleston, S.C.	D2-'10	16/15
85	Eifert, Tyler	TE	6-6	250	9/8/90	2	Notre Dame	Fort Wayne, Ind.	D1-'13	15/15
91	Geathers, Robert	DE	6-3	280	8/11/83	11	Georgia	Georgetown, S.C.	D4b-'04	2/0
95	Gilberry, Wallace	DE	6-2	275	12/5/84	7	Alabama	Bay Minette, Ala.	FA-'12	16/2
18	Green, A.J.	WR	6-4	207	7/31/88	4	Georgia	Summerville, S.C.	D1-'11	16/16
42	Green-Ellis, BenJarvus	HB	5-11	220	7/2/85	7	Mississippi	New Orleans, La.	UFA(NE)-'12	16/16
84	Gresham, Jermaine	TE	6-5	260	6/16/88	5	Oklahoma	Ardmore, Okla.	D1-'10	14/14
29	Hall, Leon	CB	5-11	195	12/9/84	8	Michigan	Vista, Calif.	D1-'07	5/5
46	Harris, Clark	LS	6-5	245	7/10/84	6	Rutgers	Manahawkin, N.J.	FA-'09	16/0
72	Hawkinson, Tanner	G	6-5	300	5/14/90	2	Kansas	McPherson, Kan.	D5-'13	1/0
10	Huber, Kevin	P	6-1	212	7/16/85	6	Cincinnati	Cincinnati, Ohio	D5-'09	14/0
99	Hunt, Margus	DE	6-8	280	7/14/87	2	Southern Methodist	Karksi-Nuia, Estonia	D2b-'13	10/0
43	Iloka, George	S	6-4	217	6/20/90	3	Boise State	Houston, Texas	D5c-'12	16/16
49	Joiner, Brandon	LB	6-3	240	4/27/89	2	Arkansas State	Killeen, Texas	FA-'12	0*
24	Jones, Adam	CB	5-10	180	9/30/83	8	West Virginia	Atlanta, Ga.	FA-'10	16/13
82	Jones, Marvin	WR	6-2	195	3/12/90	3	California	Fontana, Calif.	D5b-'12	16/3
27	Kirkpatrick, Dre	CB	6-2	185	10/26/89	3	Alabama	Gadsden, Ala.	D1a-'12	14/3
59	Lamur, Emmanuel	LB	6-4	240	6/8/89	3	Kansas State	West Palm Beach, Fla.	FA-'12	0*
37	Lewis-Harris, Chris	CB	5-10	180	2/11/89	2	Tennessee-Chattanooga	Smyrna, Ga.	FA-'12	6/0
38	Manning, Danieal	S	5-11	212	8/9/82	9	Abilene Christian	Corsicana, Texas	FA-'14	6/6*
58	Maualuga, Rey	LB	6-2	255	1/20/87	6	Southern California	Eureka, Calif.	D2-'09	13/13
26	Mays, Taylor	S	6-3	220	2/7/88	5	Southern California	Seattle, Wash.	T(SF)-'11	8/1
3	#Mesko, Zoltan	P	6-5	225	3/6/86	5	Michigan	Twinsburg, Ohio	FA-'13	7/0*
69	Minter, Zach	DT	6-1	297	11/6/90	2	Montana State	Glendale, Ariz.	FA-'14	2/0*
92	Moch, Dontay	DE	6-2	255	7/19/88	2	Nevada	Phoenix, Ariz.	W(Ariz)-'14	4/0*
70	Montgomery, Sam	DE	6-3	262	5/25/90	2	Louisiana State	Greenwood, S.C.	FA-'14	0*
20	Nelson, Reggie	S	5-11	210	9/21/83	8	Florida	Melbourne, Fla.	T(Jax)-'10	15/15
74	Newhouse, Marshall	T	6-4	319	9/29/88	5	Texas Christian	Dallas, Texas	UFA(GB)-'14	15/2*
23	Newman, Terence	CB	5-10	192	9/4/78	12	Kansas State	Salina, Kan.	FA-'12	13/13
2	Nugent, Mike	K	5-10	190	3/2/82	10	Ohio State	Centerville, Ohio	FA-'10	16/0
79	Nwagbuo, Ogemdi	DT	6-5	312	12/24/85	4	Michigan State	Spring Valley, Calif.	FA-'13	0*
30	Peerman, Cedric	HB	5-10	211	10/10/86	5	Virginia	Gladys, Va.	W(Det)-'10	16/0
94	Peko, Domata	DT	6-3	322	11/27/84	9	Michigan State	Pago Pago, American Samoa	D4-'06	16/16
67	Pollak, Mike	G	6-3	300	2/16/85	7	Arizona State	Chandler, Ariz.	UFA(Car)-'13	8/5
56	Porter, Sean	LB	6-1	237	1/12/91	2	Texas A&M	Schertz, Texas	D4-'13	0*
57	Rey, Vincent	LB	6-0	250	9/6/87	4	Duke	Far Rockaway, N.Y.	FA-'10	16/3
66	Robinson, Trevor	C	6-5	300	5/16/90	3	Notre Dame	Elkhorn, Neb.	FA-'12	6/0
74	#Roland, Dennis	T	6-9	315	3/10/83	7	Georgia	Bolivar, Mo.	FA-'13	5/0
12	Sanu, Mohamed	WR	6-2	210	8/22/89	3	Rutgers	South Brunswick, N.J.	D3a-'12	16/14
11	Sanzenbacher, Dane	WR	5-11	184	10/13/88	4	Ohio State	Toledo, Ohio	W(Chi)-'12	10/1
50	Schaffer, J.K.	LB	6-0	232	6/10/90	2	Cincinnati	Cincinnati, Ohio	FA-'12	9/0
81	#Smith, Alex	TE	6-4	250	5/22/82	10	Stanford	Denver, Colo.	UFA(Cle)-'13	16/1
71	Smith, Andre	T	6-4	335	1/25/87	6	Alabama	Birmingham, Ala.	D1-'09	16/15
28	Stanford, R.J.	CB	5-10	190	5/6/88	4	Utah	Chino, Calif.	FA-'14	13/0*
75	Still, Devon	DT	6-5	320	7/11/89	3	Penn State	Wilmington, Del.	D2-'12	10/0
19	Tate, Brandon	WR	6-1	195	10/5/87	6	North Carolina	Burlington, N.C.	W(NE)-'11	16/0
98	Thompson, Brandon	DT	6-2	325	10/19/88	3	Clemson	Thomasville, Ga.	D3b-'12	16/7
88	Whalen, Ryan	WR	6-1	200	7/26/89	4	Stanford	Alamo, Calif.	D6-'11	4/0
77	Whitworth, Andrew	G	6-7	335	12/12/81	9	Louisiana State	West Monroe, La.	D2-'06	14/14
36	Williams, Shawn	S	6-0	211	5/13/91	2	Georgia	Damascus, Ga.	D3-'13	16/0
68	Zeitler, Kevin	G	6-4	315	3/8/90	3	Wisconsin	Waukesha, Wis.	D1b-'12	12/11

* Black missed '13 season because of injury; Brock played four games with Kansas City in '13; Burton played five games with Buffalo; Campbell played nine games with Cleveland; Conley last active with the New York Jets in '11; Joiner missed '13 season because of injury; Lamur missed '13 season because of injury; Manning played six games with Houston; Mesko played seven games with Pittsburgh and one postseason game with Cincinnati; Minter played two games with Chicago; Moch played four games with Arizona; Montgomery was on Houston's roster for seven games but did not play; Newhouse played 15 games for Green Bay; Nwagbuo was not on an NFL roster during the regular season and was inactive for one postseason game with the Bengals; Porter missed '13 season because of injury; Stanford played 13 games with Miami.

\# Unrestricted Free Agent; subject to developments.

Players lost through free agency (4): T Anthony Collins (TB; 15 games), CB Brandon Ghee (SD; 10), WR Andrew Hawkins (Cle; 8), DE Michael Johnson (TB; 15).

Also played with Bengals in '13—C Kyle Cook (16 games), S Tony Dye (1), LB James Harrison (15), QB Josh Johnson (2), CB Curtis Marsh (2), S Jeromy Miles (1), P Sean Powell (2).

FIRST-YEAR ROSTER

Name	Pos.	Ht.	Wt.	Birthdate	College	Hometown	How Acq.
Bodine, Russell	C	6-3	310	6/30/92	North Carolina	Scottsville, Va.	D4
Clarke, Will	DE	6-6	271	5/4/91	West Virginia	Pittsburgh, Pa.	D3
Davidson, James	LB	6-3	242	11/1/90	Texas-El Paso	Huntsville, Texas	FA
Dennard, Darqueze	CB	5-11	200	10/10/91	Michigan State	Dry Branch, Ga.	D1
Feigt, Curtis	T	6-6	307	11/23/89	West Virginia	Berlin, Germany	FA
Flowers, Marquis	LB	6-3	235	2/16/92	Arizona	Phoenix, Ariz.	D6
France, Dan	T/G	6-5	300	4/1/91	Michigan State	North Royalton, Ohio	FA
Hamilton, Cobi (1)	WR	6-2	205	11/13/90	Arkansas	Texarkana, Texas	D6b-'13
Hewitt, Ryan	TE/FB	6-4	246	1/24/91	Stanford	Denver, Colo.	FA
Hill, Jeremy	HB	6-1	233	10/20/92	Louisiana State	Baton Rouge, La.	D2
Hopkins, Trey	G	6-3	307	7/6/92	Texas	Houston, Texas	FA
Johnson, T.J. (1)	C	6-4	310	7/17/90	South Carolina	Aynor, S.C.	D7b-'13
King, David (1)	DE	6-4	285	12/27/89	Oklahoma	Houston, Texas	FA-'13
Lewis, Isaiah	S	5-10	211	10/30/91	Michigan State	Indianapolis, Ind.	FA
Lockett, Colin	WR	5-11	188	4/5/91	San Diego State	Diamond Bar, Calif.	FA
McCalebb, Onterio (1)	CB	5-10	170	8/10/89	Auburn	Fort Meade, Fla.	FA-'13
McCarron, A.J.	QB	6-3	220	9/13/90	Alabama	Mobile, Ala.	D5
Neutz, Alex	WR	6-3	214	3/2/91	Buffalo	Grand Island, N.Y.	FA
Scott, Jeff	HB	5-7	165	1/26/91	Mississippi	Miami, Fla.	FA
Scott, Matt	QB	6-3	212	11/9/90	Arizona	Corona, Calif.	W(Jax)
Sharp, Quinn	K	6-1	189	11/12/89	Oklahoma State	Mansfield, Texas	FA
Taylor, Bruce (1)	LB	6-1	245	12/31/89	Virginia Tech	Riceboro, Ga.	FA'-'13
Westbrooks, Lavelle	CB	6-0	186	1/12/92	Georgia Southern	Riverdale, Ga.	D7b
Whitlock, Nikita	FB	5-10	251	5/16/91	Wake Forest	Wylie, Texas	FA
Wilder, James Jr.	HB	6-3	232	4/14/92	Florida State	Tampa, Fla.	FA
Wright, James	WR	6-1	201	12/31/91	Louisiana State	Buras, La.	D7a

The term NFL Rookie is defined as a player who is in his first season of professional football and has not been on the roster of another professional football team for any regular-season or postseason games. A Rookie is designated by an "R" on NFL rosters. Players who have been active in another professional football league or players who have NFL experience, including either preseason training camp or being on an Active List or Inactive List, or on Reserve/Injured or Reserve/Physically Unable to Perform for fewer than six regular-season games, are termed NFL First-Year Players. An NFL First-Year Player is designated by a "1" on NFL rosters. Thereafter, a player is credited with an additional year of experience for each season in which he accumulates six games on the Active List or Inactive List, or on Reserve/Injured or Reserve/Physically Unable to Perform.

Log on to www.bengals.com for an up-to-date roster.

COACHING STAFF

Head Coach,
Marvin Lewis

Pro Career: Marvin Lewis in 2014 extends his Bengals-record head coaching tenure to 12 seasons. He has led the team to the postseason in four of the last five years, including three straight. The Bengals are one of only five NFL teams to be in the playoffs every year since 2011, and they are one of only six clubs to qualify as many as four times in five years. In total, Lewis has coached five Bengals playoff teams, a franchise record. Lewis opens 2013 with 90 career victories, 26 more than any other Bengals' coach (Sam Wyche 64). The Bengals went 11-5 in the 2013 regular season and won the AFC North Division championship by two games over Baltimore and Pittsburgh. Lewis' 2012 Bengals achieved a rare NFL feat, becoming only the ninth of 131 teams from 1990-2012 to rise from a 3-5 start to the playoffs. In 2011, Lewis guided a young squad with new stars that posted a 9-7 mark to reach the playoffs. He was the consensus choice as NFL Coach of the Year in 2009, when the Bengals won the AFC North title while sweeping all six division games. The Bengals were AFC North champions under Lewis also in 2005. Lewis was named the ninth head coach in Bengals history on January 14, 2003. In 2002, Lewis was Washington Redskins defensive coordinator and assistant head coach. He spent six seasons (1996-2001) as defensive coordinator with the Baltimore Ravens, a tenure that included a Super Bowl victory in the 2000 season. In 2000, Lewis' defense set the NFL record for fewest points allowed in a 16-game campaign (165), and the unit has been widely considered as one of the best NFL defenses of all time. Prior to Baltimore, Lewis spent four seasons (1992-95) as the Pittsburgh Steelers' linebackers coach. Career record: 90-90-1.

Background: Earned All-Big Sky Conference honors as a linebacker at Idaho State (1978-1980), and saw action at quarterback and free safety. Received his bachelor's degree in physical education and Master's degree in athletic administration. Inducted into Idaho State's Hall of Fame in 2001. Began his coaching career at Idaho State (1981-84), winning an NCAA Division I-AA championship in 1981. Was also the linebackers coach at Long Beach State (1985-86), New Mexico (1987-89), and Pittsburgh (1990-91).

Personal: Born September 23, 1958, McDonald, Pa. Lewis and his wife, Peggy, have two children—Whitney and Marcus.

ASSISTANT COACHES

Paul Alexander, asst. head coach/offensive line; born February 12, 1960, Rochester, N.Y. Tackle Cortland State 1979-1981. No pro playing experience. College coach: Penn State 1982-84, Michigan 1985-86, Central Michigan

1987-1991. Pro coach: New York Jets 1992-93, joined Bengals in 1994.

Brian Braswell, offensive assistant/quality control; born May 26, 1982, College Park, Ga. Center and tackle Hampton 2000-04. No pro playing experience. College coach: Morehouse College 2005-2013. Pro coach: Joined Bengals in 2014.

Matt Burke, linebackers; born March 25, 1976, Hudson, Mass. Safety Dartmouth 1994-97. No pro playing experience. College coach: Boston College 2000-02, Harvard 2003. Pro coach: Tennessee Titans 2006-08, Detroit Lions 2009-2013, joined Bengals in 2014.

Mark Carrier, defensive backs; born April 28, 1968, Lake Charles, La. Defensive back Southern California 1987-89. Pro defensive back Chicago Bears 1990-96, Detroit Lions 1997-99, Washington Redskins 2000. College coach: Arizona State 2004-05. Pro coach: Baltimore Ravens 2006-09, New York Jets 2010-11, joined Bengals in 2012.

Kyle Caskey, running backs; born Dec. 7, 1978, Daingerfield, Texas. Tight end Texas A&M 1997-98. No pro playing experience. College coach: Louisiana-Monroe 2004-05, Indiana State 2006-08, Mississippi 2009. Pro coach: Joined Bengals in 2010.

Brayden Coombs, asst. special teams/quality control; born Oct. 24, 1986, Cincinnati, Ohio. Wide receiver-defensive back Miami (Ohio) 2005-09. No pro playing experience. Pro coach: Joined Bengals in 2012.

Jeff Friday, asst. strength and conditioning; born Oct. 11, 1966, Milwaukee, Wisc. Attended Wisconsin-Milwaukee. No college or pro playing experience. College coach: Illinois State 1990-91, Northwestern 1992-95. Pro coach: Minnesota Vikings 1996-98, Baltimore Ravens 1999-2007, joined Bengals in 2010.

Paul Guenther, defensive coordinator; born Nov. 22, 1971, Richboro, Pa. Linebacker Ursinus College 1990-93. No pro playing experience. College coach: Western Maryland 1994-95, Ursinus College 1996, 1997-2001 (head coach 1997-2001), Jacksonville 1997. Pro coach: Washington Redskins 2002-03, joined Bengals in 2005.

Jay Hayes, defensive line; born March 3, 1960, South Fayette, Pa. Defensive end Idaho 1978-1981. Pro defensive end/linebacker Michigan Panthers (USFL) 1984, Memphis Showboats (USFL) 1985. College coach: Notre Dame 1988-1991, California 1992-94, Wisconsin 1995-98. Pro coach: Pittsburgh Steelers 1999-2001, Minnesota Vikings 2002, joined Bengals in 2003.

Jonathan Hayes, tight ends; born Aug. 11, 1962, South Fayette, Pa. Linebacker/tight end Iowa 1981-84. Pro tight end Kansas City Chiefs 1985-1993, Pittsburgh Steelers 1994-96. College coach: Oklahoma 1999-2002. Pro coach:

Joined Bengals in 2003.

Hue Jackson, offensive coordinator; born Oct. 22, 1965, Los Angeles, Calif. Quarterback Pacific 1985-86. No pro playing experience. College coach: Pacific 1987-89, Cal State-Fullerton 1990-91, Arizona State 1992-95, California 1996, Southern California 1997-2000. Pro coach: London Monarchs (WFL) 1991, Washington Redskins 2001-03, Cincinnati Bengals 2004-06, Atlanta Falcons 2007, Baltimore Ravens 2008-09, Oakland Raiders 2010-11 (head coach 2011), re-joined Bengals in 2012.

Vance Joseph, defensive backs; born September 20, 1972, Marrero, La. Defensive back Colorado 1990-94. Pro defensive back New York Jets 1995, Indianapolis Colts 1996. College coach: Colorado 1999-2001, 2002-03, Wyoming 2002, Bowling Green State 2004. Pro coach: San Francisco 49ers 2005-2010, Houston Texans 2011-13, joined Bengals in 2014.

Marcus Lewis, defensive assistant/quality control; born March 28, 1990, Albuquerque, N.M. Linebacker Indiana State 2008-2011. No pro playing experience. Pro coach: Joined Bengals in 2014.

David Lippincott, asst. linebackers/quality control; born July 6, 1977, Cincinnati, Ohio. Attended Dayton. No college or pro playing experience. College coach: Bluffton 2000-02, Minnesota 2003-04, Richmond 2005-07. Pro coach: Joined Bengals in 2011.

Chip Morton, strength and conditioning; born November 27, 1962, Hamden, Conn. Attended North Carolina. No college or pro playing experience. College coach: Ohio State 1985-86, Penn State 1987-1991. Pro coach: San Diego Chargers 1992-94, Carolina Panthers 1995-98, Baltimore Ravens 1999-2001, Washington Redskins 2002, joined Bengals in 2003.

Darrin Simmons, special teams coordinator; born April 9, 1973, Elkhart, Kan. Punter Kansas 1993-95. No pro playing experience. College coach: Kansas 1996, Minnesota 1997. Pro coach: Baltimore Ravens 1998, Carolina Panthers 1999-2002, joined Bengals in 2003.

James Urban, wide receivers; born Dec. 1, 1973, Mechanicsburg, Pa. Wide receiver Washington and Lee 1993-96. No pro playing experience. College coach: Clarion 1997-98, Pennsylvania 1999-2003. Pro coach: Philadelphia Eagles 2004-10, joined Bengals in 2011.

Ken Zampese, quarterbacks; born July 19, 1967, Santa Maria, Calif. Wide receiver San Diego 1985-88. No pro playing experience. College coach: San Diego 1989, Southern California 1990-91, Northern Arizona 1992-95, Miami (Ohio) 1996-97. Pro coach: Philadelphia Eagles 1998, Green Bay Packers 1999, St. Louis Rams 2000-02, joined Bengals in 2003.

American Football Conference
North Division
Team Colors: Brown, Orange, and White
76 Lou Groza Blvd.
Berea, Ohio 44017
Telephone: (440) 891-5000

2014 SCHEDULE
PRESEASON
Aug. 9	at Detroit	7:30
Aug. 18	at Washington	8:00
Aug. 23	**St. Louis**	8:00
Aug. 28	**Chicago**	8:00

REGULAR SEASON
Sep. 7	at Pittsburgh	1:00
Sep. 14	**New Orleans**	1:00
Sep. 21	**Baltimore**	1:00
Sep. 28	BYE	
Oct. 5	at Tennessee	1:00
Oct. 12	**Pittsburgh**	1:00
Oct. 19	at Jacksonville	1:00
Oct. 26	**Oakland**	4:25
Nov. 2	**Tampa Bay**	1:00
Nov. 6	at Cincinnati (Thu)	8:25
Nov. 16	**Houston**	1:00
Nov. 23	at Atlanta	1:00
Nov. 30	at Buffalo	1:00
Dec. 7	**Indianapolis**	1:00
Dec. 14	**Cincinnati**	1:00
Dec. 21	at Carolina	1:00
Dec. 28	at Baltimore	1:00

All times ET
Stadium: FirstEnergy Stadium (opened in 1999)
 • **Capacity:** 68,000
 100 Alfred Lerner Way
 Cleveland, Ohio 44114
Playing Surface: Grass
Headquarters/Training Camp:
 76 Lou Groza Boulevard
 Berea, Ohio 44017

FIRSTENERGY STADIUM

CLUB OFFICIALS
Owner: Jimmy Haslam
General Manager: Ray Farmer
President: Alec Scheiner
Executive Vice President, General
 Counsel: Sashi Brown
Executive Vice President, Chief Revenue
 Officer: Brent Stehlik
Executive Vice President:
 Bryan Wiedmeier
Chief Financial Officer: David A. Jenkins
Special Advisor: Jim Brown
Senior Advisor and Special Counsel:
 Fred Nance
Vice President, Stadium Operations:
 Troy Brown
Vice President, Football Operations:
 Phil Dangerfield
Vice President, Ticket Sales and Service:
 John Davis
Vice President, Fan Experience and
 Marketing: Kevin Griffin
Vice President, Cleveland Browns
 Foundation: Renee Harvey
Chief Human Resource Officer:
 Mike Nikolaus
Senior Director, Corporate Partnerships:
 Brett Reynolds
Director, Video: Chad Bogard
Director, Information Technology:
 Brandon Covert
Director, Premium & Suite Sales and
 Service: Nick Frasco
Director, Communications: Zak Gilbert
Director, Content & Production:
 Andy Hecht
Director, Corporate Partnership
 Activation: Bridget Huzicka
Director, Football Research and Player
 Personnel Assistant: Ken Kovash
Director, Creative Services:
 George Muller
Director, Player Engagement:
 Jamil Northcutt
Director, Fan Experience and Special
 Events: Carlos Oseguera
Director, Legal Affairs: Megan Rogers
Director, Finance: Gregory Rush
Director, Player Personnel: Jon Sandusky
Director, Ticket Operations: John Schulze
Director, Season and Group Ticket Sales:
 Bob Sivik
Director, Community Relations:
 Jenner Tekancic
Director, Corporate Partnerships:
 Matt Webb
Head Athletic Trainer: Joe Sheehan
Head Equipment Manager: Brad Melland
Head Groundskeeper: Chris Powell
Senior Editor: Vic Carucci

COACHING HISTORY
(462-449-10)
Records include postseason games
1950-1962	Paul Brown	115-49-5
1963-1970	Blanton Collier	79-38-2
1971-74	Nick Skorich	30-26-2
1975-77	Forrest Gregg*	18-23-0
1977	Dick Modzelewski	0-1-0
1978-1984	Sam Rutigliano**	47-52-0
1984-88	Marty Schottenheimer	46-31-0
1989-1990	Bud Carson***	12-14-1
1990	Jim Shofner	1-6-0
1991-95	Bill Belichick	37-45-0
1999-2000	Chris Palmer	5-27-0
2001-04	Butch Davis****	24-36-0
2004	Terry Robiskie	1-4-0
2005-08	Romeo Crennel	24-40-0
2009-2010	Eric Mangini	10-22-0
2011-12	Pat Shurmur	9-23-0
2013	Rob Chudzinski	4-12-0

 *Resigned after 13 games in 1977
 **Released after eight games in 1984
 ***Released after nine games in 1990
 ****Resigned after 11 games in 2004

PAID ATTENDANCE
Home 550,815   Away 537,028
Total 1,087,843
Single-game home record,
 85,073 (9/21/70)
Single-season home record, 620,496
 (1980)

2014 DRAFT CHOICES
Round	Name	Pos.	College
1	Justin Gilbert	DB	Oklahoma St.
	Johnny Manziel	QB	Texas A&M
2	Joel Bitonio	OL	Nevada
3	Christian Kirksey	LB	Iowa
	Terrance West	RB	Towson
4	Pierre Desir	DB	Lindenwood

CLEVELAND BROWNS

2013 TEAM RECORD
PRESEASON (3-1)

Date	Result	Opponent
08/08	W 27-19	St. Louis
08/15	W 24-6	Detroit
08/24	L 6-27	at Indianapolis
08/29	W 18-16	at Chicago

REGULAR SEASON (4-12)

Date	Result	Opponent
09/08	L 10-23	Miami
09/15	L 6-14	at Baltimore
09/22	W 31-27	at Minnesota
09/29	W 17-6	Cincinnati
10/03	W 37-24	Buffalo
10/13	L 17-31	Detroit
10/20	L 13-31	at Green Bay
10/27	L 17-23	at Kansas City
11/03	W 24-18	Baltimore
11/17	L 20-41	at Cincinnati
11/24	L 11-27	Pittsburgh
12/01	L 28-32	Jacksonville
12/08	L 26-27	at New England
12/15	L 31-38	Chicago
12/22	L 13-24	at New York Jets
12/29	L 7-20	at Pittsburgh

SCORE BY PERIODS

Browns	56	105	71	76	0 —	308
Opponents	67	121	73	145	0 —	406

2013 TEAM STATISTICS

	Browns	Opp.
Total First Downs	301	328
Rushing	77	103
Passing	200	197
Penalty	24	28
3rd Down: Made/Att	83/237	109/244
3rd Down Pct.	35.0	44.7
4th Down: Made/Att	14/31	4/9
4th Down Pct.	45.2	44.4
Possession Avg.	28:41	31:19
Total Net Yards	5423	5319
Avg. Per Game	338.9	332.4
Total Plays	1078	1107
Avg. Per Play	5.0	4.8
Net Yards Rushing	1383	1781
Avg. Per Game	86.4	111.3
Total Rushes	348	462
Net Yards Passing	4040	3538
Avg. Per Game	252.5	221.1
Sacked/Yards Lost	49/332	40/185
Gross Yards	4372	3723
Att./Completions	681/379	605/363
Completion Pct.	55.7	60.0
Had Intercepted	20	14
Punts/Average	86/43.2	88/43.7
Net Punting Avg.	86/37.6	88/37.6
Penalties/Yards	104/920	95/745
Fumbles/Ball Lost	17/9	13/7
Touchdowns	35	46
Rushing	4	13
Passing	26	29
Returns	5	4

2013 INDIVIDUAL STATISTICS

PASSING

PASSING	Att.	Comp.	Yds.	Pct.	TD	Int.	Tkld.	Rate
Campbell	317	180	2015	56.8	11	8	16/97	76.9
Weeden	267	141	1731	52.8	9	9	27/180	70.3
Hoyer	96	57	615	59.4	5	3	6/48	82.6
Lanning	1	1	11	100.0	1	0	0/0	152.1
Browns	681	379	4372	55.7	26	20	49/325	75.7
Opponents	605	363	3723	60.0	29	14	40/185	84.1

SCORING

SCORING	TD R	TD P	TD Rt	PAT	FG	Saf	PTS
Cundiff	0	0	0	32/32	21/26	0	95
Gordon	0	9	0	0/0	0/0	0	54
Cameron	0	7	0	0/0	0/0	0	42
Bess	0	2	0	0/0	0/0	0	14
Baker	2	0	0	0/0	0/0	0	12
Barnidge	0	2	0	0/0	0/0	0	12
Little	0	2	0	0/0	0/0	0	12
McGahee	2	0	0	0/0	0/0	0	12
Ogbonnaya	0	2	0	0/0	0/0	0	12
Ward	0	0	2	0/0	0/0	0	12
Whittaker	0	2	0	0/0	0/0	0	12
Benjamin	0	0	1	0/0	0/0	0	6
Gipson	0	0	1	0/0	0/0	0	6
Haden	0	0	1	0/0	0/0	0	6
Lanning	0	0	0	1/1	0/0	0	1
Browns	4	26	5	33/33	21/26	0	308
Opponents	13	29	4	43/43	27/32	1	406

2-Pt Conversions: Bess.
Browns 1-2, Opponents 2-3.

RUSHING

RUSHING	No.	Yds	Avg	LG	TD
McGahee	138	377	2.7	16	2
Ogbonnaya	49	240	4.9	43	0
Baker	43	171	4.0	20	2
Campbell	14	107	7.6	21	0
Richardson	31	105	3.4	10	0
Gordon	5	88	17.6	34	0
Whittaker	28	79	2.8	11	0
Benjamin	1	45	45.0	45	0
Weeden	12	44	3.7	11	0
Gray	6	43	7.2	18	0
Aubrey	1	34	34.0	34	0
Rainey	13	34	2.6	7	0
Hoyer	6	16	2.7	11	0
A. Edwards	1	0	0.0	0	0
Browns	348	1383	4.0	45	4
Opponents	462	1781	3.9	54t	13

RECEIVING

RECEIVING	No.	Yds	Avg	LG	TD
Gordon	87	1646	18.9	95t	9
Cameron	80	917	11.5	53	7
Ogbonnaya	48	343	7.1	17	2
Bess	42	362	8.6	20t	2
Little	41	465	11.3	47	2
Whittaker	21	155	7.4	35t	2
Barnidge	13	127	9.8	40t	2
Cooper	9	60	6.7	16	0
Baker	8	57	7.1	16	0
McGahee	8	20	2.5	9	0
Richardson	7	51	7.3	18	0
Benjamin	5	105	21.0	39	0
Rainey	4	19	4.8	15	0
Tyms	2	12	6.0	6	0
Gray	2	8	4.0	6	0
Gurley	1	15	15.0	15	0
A. Edwards	1	10	10.0	10	0
Browns	379	4372	11.5	95t	26
Opponents	363	3723	10.3	50	29

INTERCEPTIONS

INTERCEPTIONS	No.	Yds	Avg	LG	TD
Gipson	5	143	28.6	44t	1
Haden	4	57	14.3	29t	1
Ward	2	57	28.5	44t	1
Robertson	1	12	12.0	12	0
Skrine	1	5	5.0	5	0
Jackson	1	0	0.0	0	0
Browns	14	274	19.6	44t	3
Opponents	20	206	10.3	43t	2

PUNTING

PUNTING	No.	Yds.	Avg.	In 20	LG
Lanning	84	3679	43.8	28	59
Cundiff	1	34	34.0	0	34
Browns	86	3713	43.2	28	59
Opponents	88	3849	43.7	32	66

PUNT RETURNS

PUNT RETURNS	Ret	FC	Yds	Avg	LG	TD
Benjamin	22	7	257	11.7	79t	1
Poyer	8	7	114	14.3	38	0
Bess	4	14	19	4.8	11	0
A. Edwards	4	0	28	7.0	12	0
Browns	38	28	418	11.0	79t	1
Opponents	38	25	357	9.4	36	0

KICKOFF RETURNS

KICKOFF RETURNS	No.	Yds	Avg	LG	TD
Whittaker	23	482	21.0	56	0
Little	7	151	21.6	30	0
Rainey	6	147	24.5	33	0
Benjamin	3	146	48.7	86	0
McFadden	1	5	5.0	5	0
Browns	40	931	23.3	86	0
Opponents	27	612	22.7	40	0

FIELD GOALS

FIELD GOALS	1-19	20-29	30-39	40-49	50+
Cundiff	0/0	7/7	5/6	7/9	2/4
Browns	0/0	7/7	5/6	7/9	2/4
Opponents	0/0	5/5	9/9	9/11	4/7

SACKS

SACKS	No.
Sheard	5.5
Mingo	5.0
Kruger	4.5
D. Bryant	3.5
Robertson	3.0
Owens	2.5
A. Bryant	2.0
Groves	2.0
Rubin	2.0
Taylor	2.0
Winn	2.0
Jackson	1.5
Ward	1.5
Hughes	1.0
Posey	1.0
Skrine	1.0
Browns	40.0
Opponents	49.0

RECORD HOLDERS
INDIVIDUAL RECORDS—CAREER

Category	Name	Performance
Rushing (Yds.)	Jim Brown, 1957-1965	12,312
Passing (Yds.)	Brian Sipe, 1974-1983	23,713
Passing (TDs)	Brian Sipe, 1974-1983	154
Receiving (No.)	Ozzie Newsome, 1978-1990	662
Receiving (Yds.)	Ozzie Newsome, 1978-1990	7,980
Interceptions	Thom Darden, 1972-74, 1976-1981	45
Punting (Avg.)	Dave Zastudil, 2006-2010	44.1
Punt Return (Avg.)	Greg Pruitt, 1973-1981	11.8
Kickoff Return (Avg.)	Greg Pruitt, 1973-1981	26.3
Field Goals	Phil Dawson, 1999-2012	305
Touchdowns (Tot.)	Jim Brown, 1957-1965	126
Points	Lou Groza, 1950-59, 1961-67	1,349
*Sacks	Clay Matthews, 1978-1993	62.0

INDIVIDUAL RECORDS—SINGLE SEASON

Category	Name	Performance
Rushing (Yds.)	Jim Brown, 1963	1,863
Passing (Yds.)	Brian Sipe, 1980	4,132
Passing (TDs)	Brian Sipe, 1980	30
Receiving (No.)	Ozzie Newsome, 1983	89
	Ozzie Newsome, 1984	89
	Kellen Winslow, 2006	89
Receiving (Yds.)	Josh Gordon, 2013	1,646
Interceptions	Thom Darden, 1978	10
	Anthony Henry, 2001	10
Punting (Avg.)	Gary Collins, 1965	46.7
Punt Return (Avg.)	Leroy Kelly, 1965	15.6
Kickoff Return (Avg.)	Billy Lefear, 1975	31.7
Field Goals	Phil Dawson, 2008	30
Touchdowns (Tot.)	Jim Brown, 1965	21
Points	Jim Brown, 1965	126
*Sacks	Reggie Camp, 1984	14.0

INDIVIDUAL RECORDS—SINGLE GAME

Category	Name	Performance
Rushing (Yds.)	Jerome Harrison, 12-20-09	286
Passing (Yds.)	Brian Sipe, 10-25-81	444
Passing (TDs)	Frank Ryan, 12-12-64	5
	Bill Nelsen, 11-2-69	5
	Brian Sipe, 10-7-79	5
	Kelly Holcomb, 11-28-04	5
	Derek Anderson, 9-16-07	5
Receiving (No.)	Ozzie Newsome, 10-14-84	14
	Josh Gordon, 11-24-13	14
Receiving (Yds.)	Josh Gordon, 12-1-13	261
Interceptions	Many times	3
	Last time by Anthony Henry, 11-18-01	
Field Goals	Phil Dawson, 11-5-06	6
Touchdowns (Tot.)	Dub Jones, 11-25-51	**6
Points	Dub Jones, 11-25-51	36
*Sacks	Andra Davis, 11-9-03	4.0

*Sacks became an official statistic in 1982.
**NFL Record

2014 VETERAN ROSTER

No.	Name	Pos.	Ht.	Wt.	Birthdate	NFL Exp.	College	Hometown	How Acq.	'13 Games/ Starts
40	Adams, Royce	DB	5-10	190	5/3/88	2	Purdue	South Euclid, Ohio	FA-'14	0*
86	Armstrong, Anthony	WR	5-10	185	3/29/83	4	West Texas A&M	Carrollton, Texas	FA-'14	0*
37	Aubrey, Josh	DB	5-10	207	4/9/91	2	Stephen F. Austin	Tyler, Texas	FA-'13	6/0
19	Austin, Miles	WR	6-2	215	6/30/84	9	Monmouth	Garfield, N.J.	FA-'14	11/8*
24	Bademosi, Johnson	DB	6-0	200	7/23/90	3	Stanford	Silver Springs, Md.	FA-'12	16/0
82	Barnidge, Gary	TE	6-6	250	9/22/85	7	Louisville	Middleburg, Fla.	UFA(Car)-'13	16/12
10	Bennett, Earl	WR	5-11	209	3/23/87	7	Vanderbilt	Birmingham, Ala.	FA-'14	15/3*
80	Benjamin, Travis	WR	5-10	175	12/29/89	3	Miami	Belle Glade, Fla.	D4a-'12	8/3
95	Bryant, Armonty	DL	6-4	265	5/20/90	2	East Central	Wichita Falls, Texas	D7a-'13	12/0
92	Bryant, Desmond	DL	6-6	310	12/15/85	6	Harvard	Elizabethtown, N.C.	UFA(Oak)-'13	12/12
13	Burleson, Nate	WR	6-0	198	8/19/81	12	Nevada	Seattle, Wash.	FA-'14	9/8*
84	Cameron, Jordan	TE	6-5	249	8/7/88	4	Southern California	Newbury Park, Calif.	D4a-'11	15/14
59	Carder, Tank	LB	6-2	235	1/18/89	3	Texas Christian	Sweeny, Texas	W(Buff)-'12	15/1
8	Cundiff, Billy	K	6-1	212	3/30/80	9	Drake	Harlan, Iowa	FA-'13	16/0
56	Dansby, Karlos	LB	6-3	251	11/3/81	11	Auburn	Birmingham, Ala.	UFA(Ariz)-'14	16/16*
96	Diles, Zac	LB	6-0	245	6/11/85	8	Kansas State	Abilene, Texas	FA-'14	2/0*
81	Dray, Jim	TE	6-5	255	12/31/86	5	Stanford	Paramus N.J.	UFA(Ariz)-'14	16/15*
50	Eubanks, Darius	LB	6-2	222	7/12/91	2	Georgia Southern	Thomson, Ga.	FA-'13	9/1
70	Faulk, Chris	OL	6-6	317	1/21/90	2	Louisiana State	Slidell, La.	FA-'13	0*
78	Fragel, Reid	OL	6-8	308	2/22/91	2	Ohio State	Grosse Pointe, Mich.	FA-'13	0*
65	Gilkey, Garrett	OL	6-6	315	7/9/90	2	Chadron State	Sandwich, Ill.	D7b-'13	6/1
39	Gipson, Tashaun	DB	5-11	205	8/7/90	3	Wyoming	Dallas, Texas	FA-'12	16/15
12	Gordon, Josh	WR	6-3	225	4/13/91	3	Baylor	Houston, Texas	D2(Supp)-'12	14/14
57	Grant, Larry	LB	6-1	251	2/16/85	5	Ohio State	San Diego, Calif.	FA-'14	2/0*
47	Gray, MarQueis	TE	6-4	242	11/7/89	2	Minnesota	Indianapolis, Ind.	W(SF)-'13	12/2
77	Greco, John	OL	6-4	318	3/24/85	7	Toledo	Youngstown, Ohio	T(StL)-'11	14/14
54	Groves, Quentin	LB	6-3	265	7/5/84	7	Auburn	Greenville, Miss.	UFA(Ariz)-'13	5/0
23	Haden, Joe	DB	5-11	195	4/14/89	5	Florida	Fort Washington, Md.	D1-'10	15/15
16	Hawkins, Andrew	WR	5-7	180	3/10/86	4	Toledo	Johnstown, Pa.	RFA(Cin)-'14	8/0*
41	Heath, T.J.	DB	6-0	190	9/11/87	2	Jacksonville State	Alexandria, Ala.	FA-'14	0*
6	Hoyer, Brian	QB	6-2	215	10/13/85	6	Michigan State	North Olmsted, Ohio	FA-'13	3/3
93	Hughes, John	DL	6-2	320	4/27/89	3	Cincinnati	Gahanna, Ohio	D3-'12	15/2
11	Johnson, Charles	WR	6-2	215	2/27/89	2	Grand Valley State	Elsmere, Ky.	FA-'13	0*
67	Kitchen, Ishmaa'ily	DL	6-1	330	8/24/88	3	Kent State	Youngstown, Ohio	W(Balt)-'12	13/0
99	Kruger, Paul	LB	6-4	270	2/15/86	6	Utah	Orem, Utah	UFA(Balt)-'13	16/16
5	Lanning, Spencer	P	5-11	200	5/21/88	2	South Carolina	Rock Hill, S.C.	FA-'13	16/0
28	Lewis, Dion	RB	5-8	195	9/27/90	4	Pittsburgh	Albany, N.Y.	T(Phil)-'13	0*
55	Mack, Alex	OL	6-4	311	11/19/85	6	California	Santa Barbara, Calif.	D1-'09	16/16
49	Magee, Brandon	LB	5-11	235	10/22/90	2	Arizona State	Corona, Calif.	W(Dall)-'13	8/0
52	Martin, Eric	LB	6-2	250	7/21/91	2	Nebraska	Moreno Valley, Calif.	W(NO)-'13	16/0
29	McFadden, Leon	DB	5-10	190	10/26/90	2	San Diego State	Bellflower, Calif.	D3-'13	16/2
26	#McGahee, Willis	RB	6-0	235	10/21/81	11	Miami	Miami, Fla.	FA-'13	12/6
74	McQuistan, Paul	OL	6-6	315	4/30/83	9	Weber State	San Diego, Calif.	UFA(Sea)-'14	16/14*
63	Milton, Keavon	OL	6-4	293	6/23/90	2	Louisiana-Monroe	Canton, Texas	W(NO)-'13	8/0
51	Mingo, Barkevious	LB	6-4	240	10/4/90	2	Louisiana State	West Monroe, La.	D1-'13	15/3
25	Ogbonnaya, Chris	FB	6-0	225	5/20/86	5	Texas	Houston, Texas	FA-'11	16/7
62	Pinkston, Jason	OL	6-4	310	9/5/87	4	Pittsburgh	Pittsburgh, Pa.	D5b-'11	3/2
33	Poyer, Jordan	DB	6-0	191	4/25/91	2	Oregon State	Astoria, Ore.	W(Phil)-'13	9/0
53	Robertson, Craig	LB	6-1	234	2/11/88	3	North Texas	Stafford, Texas	FA-'11	14/14
71	Rubin, Ahtyba	DL	6-2	325	7/25/86	7	Iowa State	Pensacola, Fla.	D6a-'08	14/14
72	Schwartz, Mitchell	OL	6-5	320	6/8/89	3	California	Pacific Palisades, Calif.	D2-'12	16/16
97	Sheard, Jabaal	LB	6-3	264	5/10/89	4	Pittsburgh	Hollywood, Hills, Fla.	D2a-'11	13/13
22	Skrine, Buster	DB	5-9	185	4/26/89	4	Chattanooga	Woodstock, Ga.	D5a-'11	16/15
44	Tate, Ben	RB	5-10	220	8/21/88	5	Auburn	Sallsbury, Md.	UFA(Hou)-'14	14/7*
98	Taylor, Phil	DL	6-3	335	4/7/88	4	Baylor	Clinton, Md.	D1-'11	15/15
4	Thigpen, Tyler	QB	6-1	216	4/14/84	7	Coastal Carolina	Winnsboro, S.C.	FA-'14	0*
73	Thomas, Joe	OL	6-6	312	12/4/84	8	Wisconsin	Brookfield, Wis.	D1a-'07	16/16
34	Trufant, Isaiah	DB	5-7	170	12/9/82	4	Eastern Washington	Tacoma, Wash.	FA-'14	16/16*
64	Wallace, Martin	OL	6-6	305	4/22/90	2	Temple	New York, N.Y.	FA-'13	1/0
31	Whitner, Donte	DB	5-10	208	7/24/85	9	Ohio State	Cleveland, Ohio	UFA(SF)-'14	16/16*
90	Winn, Billy	DL	6-4	300	4/15/89	3	Boise State	Las Vegas, Nev.	D6b-'12	11/3
57	Yount, Christian	LS	6-1	250	7/8/88	4	UCLA	Coto de Caza, Calif.	FA-'11	16/0

* Adams last active with N.Y. Jets in '12; Armstrong last active with Dallas in '12; Austin played 11 games with Dallas in '13; Bennett played 15 games with Chicago; Burleson played 9 games with Detroit; Dansby played 16 games with Arizona; Diles played two games with Tennessee; Dray played 16 games with Arizona; Faulk missed '13 season because of injury; Fragel did not play in one game, inactive for seven games; Grant played two games with Chicago; Hawkins playes eight games with Cincinnati; Heath last active with Jacksonville in '11; Johnson inactive for one game; Lewis missed '13 season because of injury; McQuistan played 16 games with Seattle; Tate played 14 games with Houston; Thigpen last active with Buffalo in '12; Trufant played 16 games with the New York Jets; Whitner played 16 games with San Francisco.

\# Unrestricted Free Agent, subject to developments.

Traded—RB Trent Richardson (2 games in '13) to Indianapolis.

Players lost through Free Agency (3): OL Oniel Cousins (TB; 16 games in '13), OL Shawn Lauvao (Wash; 11), DB T.J. Ward (Den; 16).

Also played with Browns in '13 —WR Davone Bess (14 games), OL Rashad Butler (9), QB Jason Campbell (9), WR Josh Cooper (5), WR Armanti Edwards (2), WR Tori Gurley (3), LB Paul Hazel (13), LB D'Qwell Jackson (16), WR Greg Little (16), DB Chris Owens (12), RB Bobby Rainey (6), DE Brian Sanford (1), TE Andre Smith (2), WR Brian Tyms (7), QB Brandon Weeden (8), RB Fozzy Whittaker (11).

FIRST-YEAR ROSTER

Name	Pos.	Ht.	Wt.	Birthdate	College	Hometown	How Acq.
Agnew, Ray	FB	5-10	247	2/26/91	Southern Illinois	Chesterfield, Mo.	FA
Baker, Edwin (1)	RB	5-8	210	6/1/91	Michigan State	Highland Park, Mich.	FA-'13
Barnett, Calvin	DL	6-2	317	10/7/91	Oklahoma State	Tulsa, Okla.	FA
Bitonio, Joel	OL	6-4	305	10/11/91	Nevada	Long Beach, Calif.	D2
Brooks, Jourdan (1)	RB	6-0	237	8/22/88	Morgan State	Germantown, Md.	FA
Cook, Darwin	DB	5-11	195	7/17/91	West Virginia	Cleveland, Ohio	FA
Crowell, Isaiah	RB	5-11	225	1/8/93	Alabama State	Columbus, Ga.	FA
Desir, Pierre	DB	6-2	206	9/8/90	Lindenwood	St. Peter's, Mo.	D4
Gabriel, Taylor	WR	5-8	167	2/17/91	Abilene Christian	Mesquite, Texas	FA
Gilbert, Justin	DB	6-0	202	11/7/91	Oklahoma State	Huntsville, Texas	D1a
Harris, Randall	OL	6-3	296	11/19/91	Towson	Lanham, Md.	FA
Henderson, Cam (1)	DL	6-4	270	6/2/90	Central Florida	Birmingham, Ala.	FA
Jones, Chandler	WR	5-9	185	11/28/91	San Jose State	Torrance, Calif.	FA
Kirksey, Christian	LB	6-2	235	8/31/92	Iowa	St. Louis, Mo.	D3a
Krause, Jonathan	WR	5-11	190	1/18/92	Vanderbilt	Snellville, Ga.	FA
Manziel, Johnny	QB	6-0	210	12/6/92	Texas A&M	Kerrville, Texas	D1b
McDaniel, Jacobbi	DL	6-0	293	10/8/89	Florida State	Greenville, Fla.	FA
Nelson, Robert	DB	5-9	175	2/16/90	Arizona State	Lakeland, Fla.	FA
Oboh, James	TE	6-4	250	8/22/91	Towson	Olney, Md.	FA
Posey, Julian (1)	DB	5-10	190	7/17/88	Ohio	Cincinnati, Ohio	FA-'13
Shaw, Connor	QB	6-1	210	9/19/91	South Carolina	Flowery Branch, Ga.	FA
Shaw, Kenny	WR	5-11	180	1/15/92	Florida State	Orlando, Fla.	FA
Slaughter, Jamoris (1)	DB	6-0	195	12/22/89	Notre Dame	Stone Mountain, Ga.	D6-'13
Snead, Willie	WR	5-11	195	10/17/92	Ball State	Belle Grade, Fla.	FA
Staples, Justin (1)	LB	6-4	245	12/10/89	Illinois	Berea, Ohio	FA
Vernon, Conner (1)	WR	6-0	200	8/18/90	Duke	Miami, Fla.	FA
Warren, Jeremiah (1)	OL	6-3	325	9/20/87	South Florida	Panama City, Fla.	FA
West, Terrance	RB	5-10	225	1/28/91	Towson	Baltimore, Md.	D3b
Williams, K'Waun	DB	5-9	183	7/12/91	Pittsburgh	Paterson, N.J.	FA

The term NFL Rookie is defined as a player who is in his first season of professional football and has not been on the roster of another professional football team for any regular-season or postseason games. A Rookie is designated by an "R" on NFL rosters. Players who have been active in another professional football league or players who have NFL experience, including either preseason training camp or being on an Active List or Inactive List, or on Reserve/Injured or Reserve/Physically Unable to Perform for fewer than six regular-season games, are termed NFL First-Year Players. An NFL First-Year Player is designated by a "1" on NFL rosters. Thereafter, a player is credited with an additional year of experience for each season in which he accumulates six games on the Active List or Inactive List, or on Reserve/Injured or Reserve/Physically Unable to Perform.

Log on to www.clevelandbrowns.com for an up-to-date roster.

COACHING STAFF

Head Coach,
Mike Pettine

Pro Career: Mike Pettine was named the 15th full-time head coach in Browns history on January 23, 2014. Pettine joined the Browns after spending 2013 as the defensive coordinator for the Buffalo Bills and the 2009-2012 seasons as the defensive coordinator for the New York Jets. Pettine has helped his units to a top 10 finish in total defense in all five of his seasons as a defensive coordinator. During his season in Buffalo, Pettine implemented an aggressive defense that set a franchise record with 57 sacks, second-most in the NFL in 2013 after finishing tied for 18th in the league with 36 in 2012. Buffalo was the only team to have three players record double-digits sacks. Under Pettine, the Bills defense finished 10th (333.4) in the NFL in total defense, after finishing 22nd (362.9) in 2012. Buffalo also led the NFL in opponent completion percentage (55.3), finished second in interceptions (23), third in opponent quarterback rating (74.9), fourth in passing defense (204.4), sixth in yards per play (4.90) and tied for sixth in takeaways (30). During his four years with New York, the Jets defense over those combined seasons ranked first in the NFL in opposing quarterback rating (71.0), completion percentage (52.6) and passing yards per game (186.3). Prior to joining the Jets, Pettine spent seven years (2002-08) with the Baltimore Ravens. Prior to joining the NFL ranks, Pettine was the head coach at North Penn High School in Towamencin, Pa., from 1997-2001 and at William Tennent High School in Warminster, Pa. from 1995-96. He also spent two seasons (1993-94) on the college level, serving as a defensive graduate assistant at Pittsburgh. Pettine began his coaching career as an assistant for his father at Central Bucks West High School in Doylestown, Pa. from 1988-1992. Career record: 0-0.

Background: Was a two-year letterman as a free safety at Virginia, where he graduated with a degree in economics. His father, Mike, Sr., was the head coach for 33 years at Central Bucks West High School in Doylestown, Pa., where Pettine played under his father and earned all-state honors as a quarterback and defensive back. Mike Sr., retired in 1999 as the winningest coach in Pennsylvania high school football history with a career mark of 326-32-4.

Personal: Born September 25, 1966 in Doylestown, Pa. He has two daughters, Megan and Katie, and one son, Ryan.

ASSISTANT COACHES

Brian Angelichio, tight ends; born December 27, 1972, Ilion, N.Y. Linebacker St. Lawrence 1991-95. No pro playing experience. College coach: SUNY-Brockport 1995, Ithaca 1996-2005, Pittsburgh 2006-2010, Rutgers 2011. Pro coach: Tampa Bay Buccaneers 2012-13, joined Browns in 2014.

Bobby Babich, asst. defensive backs; born July 30, 1983, Tulsa, Okla. Cornerback North Dakota State 2002-05. No pro playing experience. College coach: Kent State 2006, Eastern Illinois 2007-10. Pro coach: Carolina Panthers

2011-12, joined Browns in 2013.

George DeLeone, asst. offensive line; born May 9, 1948, New Haven, Conn. No college or pro playing experience. College coach: Southern Connecticut 1970-79 (head coach 1976-79), Rutgers 1980-83, Holy Cross 1984, Syracuse 1985-1996, 1998-2004, Mississippi 2005, Temple 2006-07, Connecticut 2011-13. Pro coach: San Diego Chargers 1997, Miami Dolphins 2008-2010, joined Browns in 2014.

Chuck Driesbach, linebackers; born August 9, 1952, Doylestown, Pa. Wide receiver Villanova 1972-74. No pro playing experience. College coach: Kansas State 1976-1983, Wake Forest 1984-86, East Carolina 1987-88, Mississippi 1989, 2002-04, Cornell 1990-92, Pittsburgh 1993-96, Western Michigan 1997-2000, Texas Christian 2001, Michigan State 2005-06, Rice 2007-2011. Pro coach: Buffalo Bills 2013, joined Browns in 2014.

Brian Fleury, asst. linebackers; born January 22, 1980, Germantown, Md. Quarterback Maryland 1998, Towson 1999-2002. No pro playing experience. College coach: Maryland 2003-04, Sacred Heart 2005-08, Towson 2009-2012. Pro coach: Buffalo Bills 2013, joined Browns in 2014.

Aaron Glenn, asst. defensive backs; born July 16, 1972, Humble, Texas. Defensive back Navarro College 1990-91, Texas A&M 1992-93. Pro defensive back New York Jets 1994-2001, Houston Texans 2002-04, Dallas Cowboys 2005-06, New Orleans Saints 2008. Pro coach: Joined Browns in 2014.

Jeff Hafley, secondary; born April 4, 1979, Montvale, N.J. Wide receiver Siena 1997-2000. No pro playing experience. College coach: Worcester Polytechnic 2001, Albany 2002-05, Pittsburgh 2006-2010, Rutgers 2011. Pro coach: Tampa Bay Buccaneers 2012-13, joined Browns in 2014.

Richard Hightower, offensive quality control; born September 15, 1980, Houston, Texas. Wide receiver/defensive back Texas 1998-2002. No pro playing experience. College coach: Minnesota 2009. Pro coach: Houston Texans 2006-08, Washington Redskins 2010-13, joined Browns in 2014.

Derik Keyes, asst. strength and conditioning; born September 29, 1985, Laurel, Miss. Safety Louisiana-Lafayette 2005-08. No pro playing experience. College coach Louisiana-Lafayette 2009, 2011, South Alabama 2010. Pro coach: Houston Texans 2012, joined Browns in 2013.

Dowell Loggains, quarterbacks; born October 1, 1980, Newport, Ark. Quarterback Arkansas 2000-04. No pro playing experience. Pro coach: Dallas Cowboys 2005, Tennessee Titans 2006-2013, joined Browns in 2014.

Mike McDaniel, wide receivers; born March 6, 1983, Greeley, Colo. Wide receiver Yale 2001-04. No pro playing experience. Pro coach: Denver Broncos 2005, Houston Texans 2006-08, California Redwoods (UFL) 2009, Sacramento Mountain Lions (UFL) 2011, Washington Redskins 2011-13, joined Browns in 2014.

Shawn Mennenga, special teams assistant; born January 8, 1971, Melbourne, Iowa. Defensive back Missouri 1992. No pro playing experience. College coach: Southwest Baptist

1994-96, Western Kentucky 1997, Hutchinson (Kan.) C.C. 1998-2000, Culver-Stockton 2001-04 (head coach 2002-04), Fort Hays State 2005-08, South Dakota State 2009-2010. Pro coach: Joined Browns in 2011.

Andy Moeller, offensive line; June 15, 1964, Grand Rapids, Mich. Linebacker Michigan 1983-86. No pro playing experience. College coach: Indiana 1987, Army 1988-1993, Missouri 1994-99, Michigan 2000-07. Pro coach: Baltimore Ravens 2008-2013, joined Browns in 2014.

Wilbert Montgomery, running backs; born September 16, 1954, Greenville, Miss. Running back Abilene Christian 1973-76. Pro running back Philadelphia Eagles 1977-1984, Detroit Lions 1985. Pro coach: St. Louis Rams 1997-2005, Detroit Lions 2006-07, Baltimore Ravens 2008-2013, joined Browns in 2014.

Jim O'Neil, defensive coordinator; born August 26, 1978, Philadelphia, Pa. Defensive end Towson 1997-2000. No pro playing experience. College coach: Albany 2001, Pennsylvania 2002, Northwestern 2003-04, Towson 2005, Eastern Michigan 2006-08. Pro coach: New York Jets 2009-2012, Buffalo Bills 2013, joined Browns in 2014.

Paul Ricci, strength and conditioning; born November 15, 1969, Washington Township, N.J. Offensive lineman Penn State 1988-89. No pro playing experience. College coach: Maryland 2008-2010, Texas Tech 2011. Pro coach: Arizona Cardinals 1996-97, Baltimore Ravens 1999-2007, New York Jets 2012-13, joined Browns in 2014.

Kyle Shanahan, offensive coordinator; born December 14, 1979, Minneapolis, Minn. Wide receiver Duke 1998-99, Texas 2000-02. No pro playing experience. College coach: UCLA 2003. Pro coach: Tampa Bay Buccaneers 2004-05, Houston Texans 2006-09, Washington Redskins 2010-13, joined Browns in 2014.

Chris Tabor, special teams coordinator; born March 4, 1971, St. Joseph, Mo. Quarterback Benedictine College 1989-1992. No pro playing experience. College coach: Hutchinson (Kan.) C.C. 1994, Central Methodist 1995-96, Missouri 1997-2000, Culver-Stockton 2001 (head coach), Utah State 2002-05, Western Michigan 2006-07. Pro coach: Chicago Bears 2008-2010, joined Browns in 2011.

Tony Tuioti, defensive quality control; born February 9, 1977, Tustin, Calif. Defensive line Hawaii 1996-99, No pro playing experience. College coach: Hawaii 2000-01, 2008-2013. Pro coach: Joined Browns in 2014.

Anthony Weaver, defensive line; born July 28, 1980, Saratoga Springs, N.Y. Defensive end Notre Dame 1998-2001. Pro defensive line Baltimore Ravens 2002-05, Houston Texans 2006-08. College coach: Florida 2010, North Texas 2011. Pro coach: New York Jets 2012, Buffalo Bills 2013, joined Browns in 2014.

Mike Wolf, asst. strength and conditioning; born May 15, 1965, Allentown, Pa. Center Penn State 1983-87. No pro playing experience. College coach: Vanderbilt 1988-89, Lehigh 1990, Penn State 1991. Pro coach: Minnesota Vikings 1992-94, Philadelphia Eagles 1995-2010, joined Browns in 2014.

DENVER BRONCOS

American Football Conference
West Division
Team Colors: Orange, Broncos Navy
Blue, and White
13655 Broncos Parkway
Englewood, Colorado 80112
Telephone: (303) 649-9000

2014 SCHEDULE
PRESEASON
Aug. 7 **Seattle**............................7:00
Aug. 17 at San Francisco 2:00
Aug. 23 **Houston**..........................7:00
Aug. 28 at Dallas...........................6:00

REGULAR SEASON
Sep. 7 **Indianapolis** 6:30
Sep. 14 **Kansas City** 2:25
Sep. 21 at Seattle 2:25
Sep. 28 BYE.....................................
Oct. 5 **Arizona** 2:05
Oct. 12 at New York Jets 11:00a
Oct. 19 **San Francisco** *6:30
Oct. 23 **San Diego** (Thu) 6:25
Nov. 2 at New England 2:25
Nov. 9 at Oakland 2:05
Nov. 16 at St. Louis 11:00a
Nov. 23 **Miami** 2:25
Nov. 30 at Kansas City *6:30
Dec. 7 **Buffalo** 2:05
Dec. 14 at San Diego 2:05
Dec. 22 at Cincinnati (Mon)..........6:30
Dec. 28 **Oakland** 2:25
*All times MT; Sunday night games in
Weeks 5-16 subject to change
Stadium: Sports Authority Field at Mile
High (opened in 2001)
• **Capacity:** 76,125
1701 Bryant Street
Denver, Colorado 80204
Playing Surface: DD Grassmaster
Training Camp: 13655 Broncos Parkway
Englewood, Colorado
80112

SPORTS AUTHORITY FIELD AT MILE HIGH

CLUB OFFICIALS
Owner and CEO: Pat Bowlen
President: Joe Ellis
Executive VP of Football Operations/GM:
John Elway
Head Coach: John Fox
FOOTBALL STAFF
Director of Player Personnel: Matt Russell
Director of Pro Personnel: Tom Heckert
Director of Football Administration:
Mike Sullivan
Head Athletic Trainer: Steve Antonopulos
BUSINESS STAFF
General Counsel/Executive Vice
President: Rich Slivka
Senior Vice President of Business
Development: Mac Freeman
CFO: Justin Webster
Vice President of Operations:
Chip Conway
Vice President of Community
Development: Cindy Kellogg
Executive Director of Media Relations:
Patrick Smyth
Executive Director of Ticket Operations
and Administration: Kirk Dyer
STADIUM MANAGEMENT COMPANY
Stadium General Manager: Andy Gorchov

COACHING HISTORY
(452-396-10)
Records include postseason games
1960-61 Frank Filchock...............7-20-1
1962-64 Jack Faulkner* 9-22-1
1964-66 Mac Speedie** 6-19-1
1966 Ray Malavasi 4-8-0
1967-1971 Lou Saban*** 20-42-3
1971 Jerry Smith 2-3-0
1972-76 John Ralston.............34-33-3
1977-1980 Robert (Red) Miller......42-25-0
1981-1992 Dan Reeves...............117-79-1
1993-94 Wade Phillips 16-17-0
1995-2008 Mike Shanahan 146-91-0
2009-2010 Josh McDaniels**** ..11-17-0
2010 Eric Studesville...............1-3-0
2011-13 John Fox 37-17-0
*Released after four games in 1964
**Resigned after two games in 1966
***Resigned after nine games in 1971
****Released after 12 games in 2010

PAID ATTENDANCE
Home 602,515   Away 563,865
Total 1,166,380
Single-game home record,
77,160 (11/9/09)
Single-season home record, 601,635
(2012)

2014 DRAFT CHOICES
Round	Name	Pos.	College
1	Bradley Roby	DB	Ohio St.
2	Cody Latimer	WR	Indiana
3	Michael Schofield	T	Michigan
5	Lamin Barrow	LB	Louisiana St.
6	Matt Paradis	C	Boise St.
7	Corey Nelson	LB	Oklahoma

DENVER BRONCOS

2013 TEAM RECORD
PRESEASON (2-2)

Date	Result	Opponent
08/08	W 10-6	at San Francisco
08/17	L 10-40	at Seattle
08/24	W 27-26	St. Louis
08/29	L 24-32	Arizona

REGULAR SEASON (13-3)

Date	Result	Opponent
09/05	W 49-27	Baltimore
09/15	W 41-23	at New York Giants
09/23	W 37-21	Oakland
09/29	W 52-20	Philadelphia
10/06	W 51-48	at Dallas
10/13	W 35-19	Jacksonville
10/20	L 33-39	at Indianapolis
10/27	W 45-21	Washington
11/10	W 28-20	at San Diego
11/17	W 27-17	Kansas City
11/24	L 31-34	at New England (OT)
12/01	W 35-28	at Kansas City
12/08	W 51-28	Tennessee
12/12	L 20-27	San Diego
12/22	W 37-13	at Houston
12/29	W 34-14	at Oakland

POSTSEASON (2-1)

Date	Result	Opponent
01/12	W 24-17	San Diego
01/19	W 26-16	New England
02/02	L 8-43	Seattle @ E. Rutherford
(OT) Overtime		

SCORE BY PERIODS

Broncos	130	158	135	183	0	—	606
Opponents	64	128	104	100	3	—	399

2013 TEAM STATISTICS

	Broncos	Opp.
Total First Downs	435	339
Rushing	107	90
Passing	293	208
Penalty	35	41
3rd Down: Made/Att	95/205	83/218
3rd Down Pct.	46.3	38.1
4th Down: Made/Att	8/9	4/15
4th Down Pct.	88.9	26.7
Possession Avg.	30:06	29:54
Total Net Yards	7317	5696
Avg. Per Game	457.3	356.0
Total Plays	1156	1074
Avg. Per Play	6.3	5.3
Net Yards Rushing	1873	1626
Avg. Per Game	117.1	101.6
Total Rushes	461	420
Net Yards Passing	5444	4070
Avg. Per Game	340.3	254.4
Sacked/Yards Lost	20/128	41/290
Gross Yards	5572	4360
Att./Completions	675/461	613/357
Completion Pct.	68.3	58.2
Had Intercepted	10	17
Punts/Average	66/43.8	89/46.1
Net Punting Avg.	66/38.8	89/40.4
Penalties/Yards	117/1000	97/807
Fumbles/Ball Lost	27/16	25/9
Touchdowns	76	47
Rushing	16	15
Passing	55	29
Returns	5	3

2013 INDIVIDUAL STATISTICS

PASSING

	Att.	Comp.	Yds.	Pct.	TD	Int.	Tkld.	Rate
Manning	659	450	5477	68.3	55	10	18/120	115.1
Osweiler	16	11	95	68.8	0	0	2/8	84.1
Broncos	675	461	5572	68.3	55	10	20/128	114.4
Opponents	613	357	4360	58.2	29	17	41/290	84.5

SCORING

	TD R	TD P	TD Rt	PAT	FG	Saf	PTS
Prater	0	0	0	75/75	25/26	0	150
D. Thomas	0	14	0	0/0	0/0	0	84
Moreno	10	3	0	0/0	0/0	0	78
J. Thomas	0	12	0	0/0	0/0	0	72
Decker	0	11	0	0/0	0/0	0	66
Welker	0	10	0	0/0	0/0	0	60
Ball	4	0	0	0/0	0/0	0	24
Caldwell	0	3	0	0/0	0/0	0	18
Holliday	0	0	2	0/0	0/0	0	12
Dreessen	0	1	0	0/0	0/0	0	6
Hillman	1	0	0	0/0	0/0	0	6
Johnson	0	0	1	0/0	0/0	0	6
Manning	1	0	0	0/0	0/0	0	6
Miller	0	0	1	0/0	0/0	0	6
Rodgers-Cromartie	0	0	1	0/0	0/0	0	6
Tamme	0	1	0	0/0	0/0	0	6
Broncos	16	55	5	75/75	25/26	0	606
Opponents	15	29	3	44/44	23/26	1	399

2-Pt Conversions: Broncos 0-1, Opponents 1-3.

RUSHING

	No.	Yds	Avg	LG	TD
Moreno	241	1038	4.3	31	10
Ball	120	559	4.7	45	4
Hillman	55	218	4.0	19	1
Anderson	7	38	5.4	11	0
Bruton	1	35	35.0	35	0
Caldwell	1	7	7.0	7	0
Holliday	1	7	7.0	7	0
Osweiler	3	2	0.7	4	0
Manning	32	-31	-1.0	1t	1
Broncos	461	1873	4.1	45	16
Opponents	420	1626	3.9	35	15

RECEIVING

	No.	Yds	Avg	LG	TD
D. Thomas	92	1430	15.5	78t	14
Decker	87	1288	14.8	61	11
Welker	73	778	10.7	33	10
J. Thomas	65	788	12.1	74t	12
Moreno	60	548	9.1	35t	3
Tamme	20	184	9.2	15	1
Ball	20	145	7.3	31	0
Caldwell	16	200	12.5	36	3
Hillman	12	119	9.9	19	0
Green	9	45	5.0	10	0
Dreessen	7	47	6.7	14	1
Broncos	461	5572	12.1	78t	55
Opponents	357	4360	12.2	82t	29

INTERCEPTIONS

	No.	Yds	Avg	LG	TD
Rodgers-Cromartie	3	75	25.0	75t	1
Trevathan	3	29	9.7	29	0
Harris	3	1	0.3	1	0
R. Moore	2	18	9.0	18	0
Webster	1	10	10.0	10	0
Adams	1	3	3.0	3	0
Phillips	1	3	3.0	3	0
Knighton	1	2	2.0	2	0
T. Carter	1	0	0.0	0	0
Woodyard	1	0	0.0	0	0
Broncos	17	141	8.3	75t	1
Opponents	10	131	13.1	59t	2

PUNTING

	No.	Yds.	Avg.	In 20	LG
Colquitt	65	2893	44.5	23	60
Broncos	66	2893	43.8	23	60
Opponents	89	4100	46.1	32	66

PUNT RETURNS

	Ret	FC	Yds	Avg	LG	TD
Holliday	32	11	271	8.5	81t	1
Welker	10	2	70	7.0	27	0
T. Carter	1	0	0	0.0	0	0
Decker	1	2	2	2.0	2	0
Broncos	44	15	343	7.8	81t	1
Opponents	28	25	274	9.8	51	0

KICKOFF RETURNS

	No.	Yds	Avg	LG	TD
Holliday	28	775	27.7	105t	1
Caldwell	6	141	23.5	34	0
Bolden	2	44	22.0	25	0
Unrein	1	8	8.0	8	0
Jackson	1	6	6.0	6	0
Tamme	1	0	0.0	0	0
Broncos	39	974	25.0	105t	1
Opponents	32	936	29.3	108t	1

FIELD GOALS

	1-19	20-29	30-39	40-49	50+
Prater	2/2	4/4	5/5	8/8	6/7
Broncos	2/2	4/4	5/5	8/8	6/7
Opponents	0/0	6/6	9/10	6/8	2/2

SACKS

	No.
Phillips	10.0
Jackson	6.0
Ayers	5.5
Miller	5.0
Wolfe	4.0
Knighton	3.0
Trevathan	2.0
Williams	2.0
Woodyard	1.5
Irving	1.0
Vickerson	1.0
Broncos	41.0
Opponents	20.0

RECORD HOLDERS
INDIVIDUAL RECORDS—CAREER

Category	Name	Performance
Rushing (Yds.)	Terrell Davis, 1995-2002	7,607
Passing (Yds.)	John Elway, 1983-1998	51,475
Passing (TDs)	John Elway, 1983-1998	300
Receiving (No.)	Rod Smith, 1995-2007	849
Receiving (Yds.)	Rod Smith, 1995-2007	11,389
Interceptions	Steve Foley, 1976-1986	44
Punting (Avg.)	Britton Colquitt, 2009-2013	45.8
Punt Return (Avg.)	Darrien Gordon, 1997-98	12.5
Kickoff Return (Avg.)	Abner Haynes, 1965-66	26.3
Field Goals	Jason Elam, 1993-2007	395
Touchdowns (Tot.)	Rod Smith, 1995-2007	71
Points	Jason Elam, 1993-2007	1,786
*Sacks	Simon Fletcher, 1985-1995	97.5

INDIVIDUAL RECORDS—SINGLE SEASON

Category	Name	Performance
Rushing (Yds.)	Terrell Davis, 1998	2,008
Passing (Yds.)	Peyton Manning, 2013	5,477
Passing (TDs)	Peyton Manning, 2013	55
Receiving (No.)	Rod Smith, 2001	113
Receiving (Yds.)	Rod Smith, 2000	1,602
Interceptions	Goose Gonsoulin, 1960	11
Punting (Avg.)	Britton Colquitt, 2011	47.4
Punt Return (Avg.)	Floyd Little, 1967	16.9
Kickoff Return (Avg.)	Bill Thompson, 1969	28.5
Field Goals	Jason Elam, 1995, 2001	31
Touchdowns (Tot.)	Terrell Davis, 1998	23
Points	Matt Prater, 2013	150
*Sacks	Von Miller, 2012	18.5

INDIVIDUAL RECORDS—SINGLE GAME

Category	Name	Performance
Rushing (Yds.)	Mike Anderson, 12-3-00	251
Passing (Yds.)	Jake Plummer, 10-31-04	499
Passing (TDs)	Peyton Manning, 9-5-13	**7
Receiving (No.)	Brandon Marshall, 12-13-09	**21
Receiving (Yds.)	Shannon Sharpe, 10-20-02	214
Interceptions	Goose Gonsoulin, 9-18-60	**4
	Willie Brown, 11-15-64	**4
	Deltha O'Neal, 10-7-01	**4
Field Goals	Gene Mingo, 10-6-63	5
	Rich Karlis, 11-20-83	5
	Jason Elam, 9-3-95, 10-13-02	5
Touchdowns (Tot.)	Clinton Portis, 12-7-03	5
Points	Clinton Portis, 12-7-03	30
*Sacks	Karl Mecklenburg, 9-15-85, 12-1-85	4.0
	Simon Fletcher, 11-4-90	4.0
	Elvis Dumervil, 9-20-09	4.0

*Sacks became an official statistic in 1982.
**NFL Record

2014 VETERAN ROSTER

No.	Name	Pos.	Ht.	Wt.	Birthdate	NFL Exp.	College	Hometown	How Acq.	'13 Games/ Starts
20	#Adams, Mike	S	5-11	200	3/24/81	10	Delaware	Wayne, N.J.	UFA(Cle)-'12	16/7
22	Anderson, C.J.	RB	5-8	224	2/10/91	2	California	Vallejo, Calif.	FA-'13	5/0
28	Ball, Montee	RB	5-10	215	12/5/90	2	Wisconsin	Wentzville, Mo.	D2-'13	16/0
31	Bolden, Omar	S	5-10	195	12/20/88	3	Arizona State	Ontario, Calif.	D4a-'12	16/1
55	#Bradley, Stewart	LB	6-4	258	11/2/83	7	Nebraska	Salt Lake City	FA-'12	0*
46	Brewer, Aaron	LS	6-5	230	7/5/90	3	San Diego State	Fullerton, Calif.	FA-'12	16/0
30	Bruton, David	S	6-2	217	7/23/87	6	Notre Dame	Miamisburg, Ohio	D4a-'09	16/0
12	Caldwell, Andre	WR	6-0	200	4/15/85	7	Florida	Tampa, Fla.	UFA(Cin)-'12	16/2
38	Carter, Quinton	S	6-1	200	7/20/88	4	Oklahoma	Las Vegas, Nev.	D4a-'11	0*
32	Carter, Tony	CB	5-9	175	5/24/86	5	Florida State	Jacksonville, Fla.	FA-'11	12/2
51	Chaney, Jamar	LB	6-0	242	10/11/86	5	Mississippi State	Fort Pierce, Fla.	FA-'14	1/0*
78	Clady, Ryan	T	6-6	315	9/6/86	7	Boise State	Rialto, Calif.	D1-'08	2/2
75	Clark, Chris	T	6-5	305	10/1/85	6	Southern Mississippi	New Orleans, La.	W(Minn)-'10	16/14
34	#Cole, Marquice	CB	5-10	195	11/13/83	5	Northwestern	Hillcrest, Ill.	FA-'14	13/0*
4	Colquitt, Britton	P	6-3	205	3/20/85	6	Tennessee	Knoxville, Tenn.	FA-'09	16/0
72	Davis, Hall	DE	6-4	270	3/2/87	3	Louisiana-Lafayette	Baton Rouge, La.	FA-'13	0*
81	Dreessen, Joel	TE	6-4	245	7/26/82	9	Colorado State	Fort Morgan, Colo.	UFA(Hou)-'12	13/0
2	Dysert, Zac	QB	6-3	221	2/8/90	2	Miami (Ohio)	Ada, Ohio	D7-'13	0*
74	Franklin, Orlando	T	6-7	320	12/16/87	4	Miami	Delray Beach, Fla.	D2b-'11	15/15
91	Fua, Sione	DT	6-1	310	6/15/88	4	Stanford	Encino, Calif.	FA-'13	5/0*
85	Green, Virgil	TE	6-5	255	8/3/88	4	Nevada	Tulare, Calif.	D7a-'11	16/3
37	Hagg, Eric	S	6-1	205	9/15/89	3	Nebraska	Peoria, Ariz.	FA-'14	0*
69	Harewood, Ramon	T	6-6	330	2/3/87	4	Morehouse	St. Michael, Barbados	FA-'14	0*
25	Harris Jr., Chris	CB	5-10	199	6/18/89	3	Kansas	Bixby, Okla.	FA-'11	16/15
23	Hillman, Ronnie	RB	5-10	195	9/14/91	3	San Diego State	La Habra, Calif.	D3-'12	10/0
29	#Huff, Michael	S	6-0	211	3/6/83	8	Texas	Irving, Texas	FA-'13	10/1*
27	Ihenacho, Duke	S	6-1	207	6/16/89	2	San Jose State	Carson, Calif.	FA-'12	15/14
56	Irving, Nate	LB	6-1	245	7/12/88	4	North Carolina State	Teachey, N.C.	D3-'11	15/4
97	Jackson, Malik	DE	6-5	293	1/11/90	3	Tennessee	Van Nuys, Calif.	D5-'12	16/5
23	#Jammer, Quentin	CB	6-0	204	6/19/79	12	Texas	Angleton, Texas	UFA(SD)-'13	11/1
53	Johnson, Steven	LB	6-1	237	3/28/88	3	Kansas	Wallingford, Pa.	FA-'12	16/0
77	Justice, Winston	T	6-6	317	9/14/84	8	Southern California	Long Beach, Calif.	FA-'13	4/0
98	Knighton, Terrance	DT	6-3	335	7/4/86	6	Temple	Windsor, Conn.	UFA(Jax)-'13	16/16
82	Konz, Jameson	TE	6-3	234	7/2/86	3	Kent State	Canton, Ohio	FA-'14	0*
51	#Lenon, Paris	LB	6-2	240	11/26/77	12	Richmond	Lynchburg, Va.	FA-'13	14/6
18	Manning, Peyton	QB	6-5	230	3/24/76	17	Tennessee	New Orleans, La.	FA-'12	16/16
54	Marshall, Brandon	LB	6-1	250	9/10/89	2	Nevada	Las Vegas, Nev.	FA-'13	1/0
55	McCray, Lerentee	LB	6-3	249	8/26/90	2	Florida	Dunnellon, Fla.	FA-'13	0*
73	Miller, Ryan	OL	6-7	320	7/6/89	2	Colorado	Littleton, Colo.	FA-'14	0*
58	Miller, Von	LB	6-3	250	3/26/89	4	Texas A&M	DeSoto, Texas	D1-'11	9/9
29	Mitchell, Charles	S	5-11	205	9/13/89	2	Mississippi State	Lyon, Miss.	FA-'14	0*
64	Montgomery, Will	C	6-3	304	2/13/83	9	Virginia Tech	Clifton, Va.	FA-'14	16/16*
26	Moore, Rahim	S	6-1	195	2/11/90	4	UCLA	Los Angeles, Calif.	D2a-'11	10/10
86	Morrah, Cameron	TE	6-3	251	3/18/87	4	California	Pomona , Calif.	FA-'14	0*
45	Murphy, Jerome	CB	6-0	200	1/13/87	4	South Florida	Elizabeth, N.J.	FA-'14	11/0*
11	Norwood, Jordan	WR	5-11	180	9/28/86	5	Penn State	State College, Pa.	FA-'14	0*
17	Osweiler, Gerg	QB	6-8	240	11/22/90	3	Arizona State	Kalispell, Mont.	D2b-'12	4/0
13	Palmer, Nathan	WR	5-11	198	4/14/89	2	Northern Illinois	Elkhart, Ind.	FA-'13	0*
5	Prater, Matt	K	5-10	195	8/10/84	8	Central Florida	Estero, Fla.	FA-'07	16/0
66	Ramirez, Manny	C	6-3	320	2/13/83	8	Texas Tech	Houston, Texas	FA-'11	16/16
10	Sanders, Emmanuel	WR	5-11	180	3/17/87	5	Southern Methodist	Bellville, Texas	UFA-'14	16/10
93	Smith, Quanterus	DE	6-5	255	11/26/89	2	Western Kentucky	Loganville, Ga.	D5a-'13	0*
21	Talib, Aqib	CB	6-1	205	2/13/86	7	Kansas	Richardson, Texas	UFA(NE)-'14	13/13*
84	Tamme, Jacob	TE	6-3	230	3/15/85	7	Kentucky	Danville, Ky.	UFA(Ind)-'12	16/1
88	Thomas, Demaryius	WR	6-3	229	12/25/87	5	Georgia Tech	Montrose, Ga.	D1a-'10	16/16
80	Thomas, Julius	TE	6-5	250	6/27/88	4	Portland State	Stockton, Calif.	D4b-'11	14/14
59	Trevathan, Danny	LB	6-1	240	3/24/90	3	Kentucky	Leesburg, Fla.	D6-'12	16/16
96	Unrein, Mitch	DT	6-4	306	3/25/87	3	Wyoming	Eaton, Colo.	FA-'10	16/1
60	#Vallos, Steve	C	6-3	310	12/28/83	6	Wake Forest	Boardman, Ohio	FA-'13	15/0
65	Vasquez, Louis	G	6-5	335	4/11/87	6	Texas Tech	Corsicana, Texas	UFA(SD)-'13	16/16
99	Vickerson, Kevin	DT	6-5	328	1/8/83	9	Michigan State	Detroit, Mich.	FA-'10	11/11
43	Ward, T.J.	S	5-10	200	12/12/86	5	Oregon	Concord, Calif.	UFA(Cle)-'14	16/16*
94	Ware, DeMarcus	DE	6-4	258	7/31/82	10	Troy	Auburn, Ala.	FA-'14	13/13*
36	Webster, Kayvon	CB	5-11	190	2/1/91	2	South Florida	Opa-locka, Fla.	D3-'13	14/2
83	Welker, Wes	WR	5-9	185	5/1/81	11	Texas Tech	Oklahoma City, Okla.	UFA(NE)-'13	13/13
92	Williams, Sylvester	DT	6-2	313	11/21/88	2	North Carolina	Jefferson City, Mo.	D1-'13	13/4
95	Wolfe, Derek	DE	6-5	285	2/24/90	3	Cincinnati	Lisbon, Ohio	D2a-'12	11/11

* Bradley missed '13 season because of injury; Q. Carter missed '12 season because of injury; Chaney played one game with Atlanta; Cole played 13 games with New England; Davis last active with Cleveland in '12: Dysert inactive 16 games; Fua played three games with Carolina and two games with Denver; Hagg last played with Cleveland in '12; Harewood last played with Baltimore in '12; Huff played seven games with Baltimore and there games with Denver; Konz last active with Seattle in '11: McCray was placed on Injured Reserve on 8/31/13 after signing as an undrafted free agent on 4/30/13; R. Miller last active with Cleveland in '12: Montgomery played 16 games with Washington; Morrah last active with Seattle in '11; Murphy played 11 games with Washington; Norwood last active with Cleveland in '12; Palmer last active with Indianapolis in '12; Smith missed '13 season because of injury; Talib played 13 games with New England; Ward played 16 games with Cleveland; Ware played 13 games with Dallas.

\# Unrestricted free agent; subject to developments.

Players lost through free agency (7): DE Robert Ayers (NYG; 15 games in '13), G Zane Beadles (Jax; 16), WR Eric Decker (NYJ; 16), RB Knowshon Moreno (Mia; 16), DE Shaun Phillips (Tenn; 16), CB Dominique Rodgers-Cromartie (Den; 15), LB Wesley Woodyard (Tenn; 14).

Also played with Broncos in '13—KR Trindon Holiday (15 games), LB Adrian Robinson (6).

FIRST-YEAR ROSTER

Name	Pos.	Ht.	Wt.	Birthdate	College	Hometown	How Acq.
Anunike, Kenny	DE	6-5	260	5/22/90	Duke	Galena, Ohio	FA
Barrett, Shaquil	LB	6-2	250	11/17/92	Colorado State	Baltimore, Md.	FA
Barrow, Lamin	LB	6-1	237	11/29/90	Louisiana State	Marrero, La.	D5
Bibbs, Kapri	RB	5-11	203	1/10/93	Colorado State	Plainfield, Ill.	FA
Boyett, John (1)	S	5-10	203	12/20/89	Oregon	Napa, Calif.	FA-'13
Burse, Isaiah	WR	5-10	187	12/8/91	Fresno State	Modesto, Calif.	FA
Clark, Steven	P	6-5	230	7/20/91	Auburn	Kansas City, Mo.	FA
Clay, Brennan	RB	5-11	201	12/20/91	Oklahoma	San Diego, Calif.	FA
Cobble, Mister	DT	6-0	338	6/26/91	Kentucky	Louisville, Ky.	FA
Cornick, Paul (1)	T	6-6	310	3/15/89	North Dakota State	Orono, Minn.	FA-'12
Fort, L.J. (1)	LB	6-0	230	1/3/90	Northern Iowa	Granite City, Ill.	FA
Fowler, Bennie	WR	6-1	212	6/10/91	Michigan State	Bloomfield, Mich.	FA
Garland, Ben (1)	G	6-5	308	4/6/88	Air Force	Grand Junction, Colo.	FA-'10
Hardin, Greg	WR	5-11	177	10/30/89	North Dakota	Bellevue, Neb.	FA
Harris, Jerrell (1)	LB	6-3	242	7/8/89	Alabama	Gadsden, Ala.	FA
Latimer, Cody	WR	6-2	215	10/10/92	Indiana	Dayton, Ohio	D2
Latta, Greg	DE	6-5	260	12/27/91	Purdue	La Quina, Calif.	FA
Nelson, Corey	LB	6-1	226	4/22/92	Oklahoma	Dallas, Texas	D7
Painter, Vinston (1)	T	6-6	309	10/11/89	Virginia Tech	Norfolk, Va.	D6-'13
Paradis, Matt	C	6-3	300	10/12/89	Boise State	Council, Idaho	D6
Renner, Bryn	QB	6-3	225	1/22/90	North Carolina	West Springfield, Va.	FA
Robinson, Gerell (1)	TE	6-4	220	10/13/89	Arizona State	Chandler, Ariz.	FA-'13
Roby, Bradley	CB	5-11	194	5/1/92	Ohio State	Suwanee, Ga.	D1
Schofield, Michael	OL	6-6	301	11/15/90	Michigan	Orland Park, Ill.	D3
Sterling, Aslam	T	6-5	315	8/20/92	Kansas	Springfield Garden, N.Y.	FA
Sullen, Jordan	CB	6-0	200	6/25/90	Tulane	New Orleans, La.	FA
Thompson, Juwan	RB	5-11	225	5/13/92	Duke	Fairburn, Ga.	FA
Williams, Jerodis (1)	RB	5-10	203	3/30/91	Furman	Milton, Fla.	FA
Wilson, Greg (1)	WR	6-0	185	9/14/90	Fordham	Danville, Calif.	FA
Youboty, John (1)	DE	6-4	258	2/25/90	Temple	Houston, Texas	FA-'13
Young, Louis	CB	6-1	196	10/9/91	Georgia Tech	Washington, D.C.	FA

The term NFL Rookie is defined as a player who is in his first season of professional football and has not been on the roster of another professional football team for any regular-season or postseason games. A Rookie is designated by an "R" on NFL rosters. Players who have been active in another professional football league or players who have NFL experience, including either preseason training camp or being on an Active List or Inactive List, or on Reserve/Injured or Reserve/Physically Unable to Perform for fewer than six regular-season games, are termed NFL First-Year Players. An NFL First-Year Player is designated by a "1" on NFL rosters. Thereafter, a player is credited with an additional year of experience for each season in which he accumulates six games on the Active List or Inactive List, or on Reserve/Injured or Reserve/Physically Unable to Perform.

Log on to www.denverbroncos.com for an up-to-date roster.

COACHING STAFF
Head Coach,
John Fox

Pro Career: John Fox was named the 14th head coach in Denver Broncos history on January 13, 2011. He joined the Broncos after spending the previous nine seasons (2002-2010) as the head coach of the Carolina Panthers. In 24 NFL seasons, he has appeared in two Super Bowls and three conference championship games as a head coach or coordinator. He compiled a 73-71 (.507) regular-season record with the Panthers that included three 11-win campaigns, two NFC South Division titles and three playoff appearances. Carolina went 5-3 in the postseason under Fox, appearing in two NFC Championship Games and one Super Bowl (XXXVIII in 2003). Registered four postseason road victories. Prior to coaching the Panthers, Fox was the defensive coordinator for the N.Y. Giants (1997-2001). In 2000, Fox helped the Giants reach Super Bowl XXXV, including posting the first shutout in a conference title game since 1986. Before joining the Giants, was a Rams' consultant (1996), defensive coordinator for the Raiders (1994-95), defensive backs coach for the Chargers (1992-93) and Steelers (1989-1991), and secondary coach for the USFL's Los Angeles Express (1985). Career record: 115-91.

Background: Defensive back at San Diego State (1976-77). Coached at San Diego State (1978), U.S. International (1979) Boise State (1980), Long Beach State (1981), Utah (1982), Kansas (1983), Iowa State (1984), and Pittsburgh (1986-88). Received bachelor's degree in physical education and earned a teaching credential from San Diego State.

Personal: Born February 8, 1955, in Virginia Beach, Va. He and his wife, Robin, have four children—Mathew, Mark, Cody, and Halle.

ASSISTANT COACHES

Clancy Barone, tight ends; born July 26, 1963, San Andreas, Calif. Offensive lineman Cal State-Sacramento 1981-82, Nevada 1985-86. No pro playing experience. College coach: American River (Calif.) J.C. 1987-89, Cal State-Sacramento 1990-92, Texas A&M 1993, Eastern Illinois 1994-96, Wyoming 1997-99, Houston 2000-02, Texas State 2003. Pro coach: Atlanta Falcons 2004-06, San Diego Chargers 2007-08, joined Broncos in 2009.

Chris Beake, quality control defense; born September 10, 1972, Kansas City, Mo. Quarterback Air Force 1991-92. No pro playing experience. College coach Air Force 1994. Pro coach San Francisco 49ers 1999-2003, 2010, Atlanta Falcons 2004-06, Seattle Seahawks 2008-09, Cleveland Browns 2011-12, joined Broncos in 2013.

Brian Callahan, offensive assistant; born June 10, 1984, Champaign, Ill. Quarterback UCLA 2002-06. No pro playing experience. College coach: UCLA 2006-07. Pro coach: Joined Broncos in 2010.

James Cregg, asst. offensive line; born August 18, 1973, Syracuse, N.Y. Offensive line Colorado State 1992-95. No pro playing experience. College coach: Colorado State: 1996-99, Colgate 2000-03, Idaho 2004-06, Tennessee 2009, Southern California 2010-13. Pro coach: Oakland Raiders 2007-08,joined Broncos in 2014.

Jack Del Rio, defensive coordinator; born April 4, 1963, Castro Valley, Calif. Linebacker Southern California 1981-84. Pro linebacker New Orleans Saints 1985-86, Kansas City Chiefs 1987-88, Dallas Cowboys 1989-1991, Minnesota Vikings 1992-95. Pro coach: New Orleans Saints 1997-98, Baltimore Ravens 1999-2001, Carolina Panthers 2002, Jacksonville Jaguars 2003-2011 (head coach), joined Broncos in 2012.

Mike Eubanks, asst. strength and conditioning; born December 31, 1980, Kansas City, Kan. Defensive back Wisconsin-Eau Claire. No pro playing experience. Pro coach: Jacksonville 2009-2011, joined Broncos in 2012.

Sam Garnes, asst. secondary; born July 12, 1974, Bronx, N.Y. Safety Cincinnati 1992-96. Pro safety N.Y. Giants 1997-2001, N.Y. Jets 2002-03. Pro coach: Cologne Centurions (NFL Europe) 2006, Las Vegas Locomotives (UFL) 2009, Carolina Panthers 2010, joined Broncos in 2011.

Adam Gase, offensive coordinator; born March 29, 1978, Ypsilanti, Mich. Attended Michigan State. No college or pro playing experience. College coach: Louisiana State 2000-02. Pro coach: Detroit Lions 2003-07, San Francisco 49ers 2008, joined Broncos in 2009.

Jason George, asst. strength and conditioning; born October 3, 1968, Winnipeg, Manitoba, Canada. Safety Manitoba 1991-92. No pro playing experience. College coach: Kansas 1997-98, Fordham 1998-2008. Pro coach: Jacksonville 2009-2011, joined Broncos in 2012.

Bo Hardegree, offensive quality control; born July 5, 1984, Jackson, Tenn. Quarterback Tennessee 2003-06. No pro playing experience. College coach: Duke 2008-2010, Louisiana State 2011-13. Pro coach: Joined Broncos in 2014.

Greg Knapp, quarterbacks; born March 3, 1963, Seal Beach, Calif. Quarterback Sacramento State 1982-85. No pro playing experience. College coach: Sacramento State 1986-1994. Pro coach: San Francisco 49ers 1995-2003, Atlanta Falcons 2004-06, Oakland Raiders 2007-08, Seattle Seahawks 2009, Houston Texans 2010-11, Oakland Raiders 2012, joined Broncos in 2013.

Anthony Lomando, asst. strength and conditioning; born October 4, 1982, Katy, Tex. Cal Poly State University-San Luis Obispo. No college or pro playing experience. Pro coach: Jacksonville 2009-2011; joined Broncos in 2012.

Dave Magazu, offensive line; born June 10, 1957, Taunton, Mass. Defensive tackle Springfield College 1976-79. No pro playing experience. College coach: Ithaca 1980, Western Michigan 1981, Eastern Michigan 1982, Michigan 1983, Northern Illinois 1984,

Ball State 1985-86, Navy 1987-89, Indiana State 1990-91, Colorado State 1992-94, Kentucky 1995-96, Memphis 1997-98, Boston College 1999-2002. Pro coach: Carolina Panthers 2003-10, joined Broncos in 2011.

Luke Richesson, strength and conditioning; born April 29, 1974, Kansas City, Mo. Defensive back Kansas 1992-96. No pro playing experience. College coach: Wyoming 1998, Arizona State 1999-2000. Pro coach: Jacksonville 2009-2011, joined Broncos in 2012.

Jay Rodgers, defensive line; born August 29, 1976, St. Paul, Minn. Quarterback Indiana 1996-98, Missouri State 1999. No pro playing experience. College coach: Missouri State 2004, Stephen F. Austin 2005-06, Iowa State 2007-08. Pro coach: Joined Broncos in 2009.

Jeff Rodgers, special teams coordinator; born January 12, 1978, St. Paul, Minn. Linebacker North Texas 1996-99. College coach: Arizona 2001-02, Kansas State 2008. Pro coach: San Francisco 49ers 2003-07, Carolina Panthers 2009-2010, joined Broncos in 2011.

Richard Smith, linebackers; born October 17, 1955, Los Angeles, Calif. Offensive lineman Rio Hondo (Calif.) J.C. 1975-76, Fresno State 1977-78. College coach: Rio Hondo (Calif.) J.C. 1979-1980, Cal State-Fullerton 1981-83, California 1984-86, Arizona 1987. Pro coach: Houston Oilers 1988-1992, Denver Broncos 1993-96, San Francisco 49ers 1997-2002, Detroit Lions 2003-04, Miami Dolphins 2005, Houston Texans 2006-08, Carolina Panthers 2009-2010, re-joined Broncos 2011.

Eric Studesville, running backs; born May 29, 1967, Madison, Wisc. Defensive back Wisconsin-Whitewater 1985-88. No pro playing experience. College coach: Wingate 1994, Kent State 1995-96. Pro coach: Chicago Bears 1997-2000, New York Giants 2001-03, Buffalo Bills 2004-2009, joined Broncos in 2010 (interim head coach, four games in 2010).

Derius Swinton, asst. special teams; born April 26, 1985, Newport News, VA. Safety Hampton 2003-06. No pro playing experience. College coach: Tennessee 2007-08. Pro coach: St. Louis Rams 2009-2011, Kansas City Chiefs 2012, joined Broncos in 2013.

Tyke Tolbert, wide receivers; born September 15, 1967, Conroe, Texas. Wide receiver Louisiana State 1988-1990. No pro playing experience. College coach: Louisiana State 1994, Ohio 1995, Northeast Louisiana 1995-97, Auburn 1998, Louisiana-Lafayette 1999-2001, Florida 2002. Pro coach: Arizona Cardinals 2003, Buffalo Bills 2004-09, Carolina Panthers 2010, joined Broncos in 2011.

Corey Undlin, secondary; born June 29, 1971, St. Cloud, Minn. Defensive back California Lutheran 1990-94. No pro playing experience. College coach: California Lutheran 1998-2001, Fresno State 2002-03. Pro coach: New England Patriots 2004, Cleveland Browns 2005-08, Jacksonville Jaguars 2009-2011, joined Broncos in 2012.

**American Football Conference
South Division
Team Colors:** Deep Steel Blue, Battle
Red, and Liberty White
Two NRG Park
Houston, Texas 77054
Telephone: (832) 667-2000

2014 SCHEDULE
PRESEASON
Aug. 9   at Arizona...........................7:30
Aug. 16 **Atlanta**...............................7:00
Aug. 23 at Denver...........................8:00
Aug. 28 **San Francisco** 7:00

REGULAR SEASON
Sep. 7   **Washington** 12:00
Sep. 14 at Oakland 3:25
Sep. 21 at New York Giants 12:00
Sep. 28 **Buffalo** 12:00
Oct. 5   at Dallas 12:00
Oct. 9   **Indianapolis** (Thu) 7:25
Oct. 20 at Pittsburgh (Mon) 7:30
Oct. 26 at Tennessee 12:00
Nov. 2   **Philadelphia** 12:00
Nov. 9   BYE
Nov. 16 at Cleveland 12:00
Nov. 23 **Cincinnati** 12:00
Nov. 30 **Tennessee** 12:00
Dec. 7   at Jacksonville 12:00
Dec. 14 at Indianapolis 12:00
Dec. 21 **Baltimore** 12:00
Dec. 28 **Jacksonville** 12:00
All times CT

Stadium: NRG Stadium
(opened in 2002)
• **Capacity:** 71,054
Houston, Texas 77054
Playing Surface: Grass
Training Camp: Houston Methodist
Training Center

NRG STADIUM

CLUB OFFICIALS
Chairman and CEO: Robert C. McNair
Vice Chairman and COO: D. Cal McNair
General Manager/Executive Vice
President of Football Operations:
Rick Smith
President: Jamey Rootes
Senior Vice President, Treasurer and
CFO: Scott Schwinger
Executive Vice President, General
Counsel and CAO: Suzie Thomas
Senior Vice President, Ticketing and
Event Management: John Schriever
Vice President, Corporate Development:
Greg Grissom
Vice President and Chief Accounting
Officer: Marilan Logan
Vice President, Football Administration:
Chris Olsen
Vice President, Finance: Greg Watson
Vice President, Information Technology:
Jeff Schmitz
Vice President, Football Operations:
Doug West
Director of Football Operations:
Jason Lowrey
Director of Security: Emmett Baylor
Director of Football Information Systems:
Russell Joyner
Director of Player Engagement:
Sean Washington
Director of College Scouting:
Mike Maccagnan
Director of Pro Personnel: Brian Gaine
Asst. Director of Pro Personnel:
Larry Wright
Senior Personnel Advisor: Bobby Grier
National College Scouts: Jon Carr,
Ed Lambert
College Scouts: Bob Beers,
Ryan Cavanaugh, Rob Kisiel,
Mike Martin, Bob Merritt, Nathan Trott
Player Personnel Scout: Mozique McCurtis
Director of Sports Medicine/Head Athletic
Trainer: Geoff Kaplan
Coordinator of Rehabilitation/Assistant
Athletic Trainer: Roland Ramirez
Assistant Athletic Trainer:
A.J. Van Valkenburgh
Director of Equipment Services:
Jay Brunetti
Equipment Services Assistants:
Mike Parson, Christian Snell
Director of Video Operations: Joe Malota
Assistant Director of Video Operations:
Tim Brog
Video Operations Asst.: Gresham Oliver
Sr. Director of Communications:
Kevin Cooper
Controller and Sr. Director of Risk
Management: Jan Kelly
Associate General Counsel and Sr.
Director: Greg Kondritz
Sr. Director of Treasury: Jon Southern
Sr. Director of Human Resources:
Glenda Morrison
Sr. Director of Event Operations and
Guest Services: Diane Crossey
Sr. Director of Marketing:
Jennifer Davenport
Sr. Director of Premium Seating:
Brian Varnadoe
Director of Ticketing and Event Sales:
Derek Beeman
Director of Luxury Suite Service:
Shari Rainey
Director of Ticket Services: Trey Young
Director of Accounting: Tamala Croasmun

COACHING HISTORY
(81-115-0)
2002-05   Dom Capers.................18-46-0
2006-2013 Gary Kubiak* 63-66-0
2013   Wade Phillips 0-3-0
* Released after 13 games in 2013

PAID ATTENDANCE
Home 559,989   Away 496,057
Total 1,056,046
Single-game home record,
71,778 (11/3/13)
Single-season home record,
560,395 (2012)

2014 DRAFT CHOICES

Round	Name	Pos.	College
1	Jadeveon Clowney	OLB	South Carolina
2	Xavier Su'a-Filo	G	UCLA
3	C.J. Fiedorowicz	TE	Iowa
	Louis Nix III	NT	Notre Dame
4	Tom Savage	QB	Pittsburgh
6	Jeoffrey Pagan	DE	Alabama
	Alfred Blue	RB	Louisiana St.
	Jay Prosch	RB	Auburn
7	Andre Hal	DB	Vanderbilt
	Lonnie Ballentine	DB	Memphis

2013 TEAM RECORD
PRESEASON (3-1)

Date	Result	Opponent
08/09	W 27-13	at Minnesota
08/17	W 24-17	Miami
08/25	L 23-31	New Orleans
08/29	W 24-6	at Dallas

REGULAR SEASON (2-14)

Date	Result	Opponent
09/09	W 31-28	at San Diego
09/15	W 30-24	Tennessee (OT)
09/22	L 9-30	at Baltimore
09/29	L 20-23	Seattle (OT)
10/06	L 3-34	at San Francisco
10/13	L 13-38	St. Louis
10/20	L 16-17	at Kansas City
11/03	L 24-27	Indianapolis
11/10	L 24-27	at Arizona
11/17	L 23-28	Oakland
11/24	L 6-13	Jacksonville
12/01	L 31-34	New England
12/05	L 20-27	at Jacksonville
12/15	L 3-25	at Indianapolis
12/22	L 13-37	Denver
12/29	L 10-16	at Tennessee

(OT) Overtime

SCORE BY PERIODS

Texans	64	93	53	60	6 —	276
Opponents	97	113	106	109	3 —	428

2013 TEAM STATISTICS

	Texans	Opp.
Total First Downs	307	282
Rushing	90	88
Passing	198	158
Penalty	19	36
3rd Down: Made/Att	83/231	75/217
3rd Down Pct.	35.9	34.6
4th Down: Made/Att	6/17	3/8
4th Down Pct.	35.3	37.5
Possession Avg.	31:00	29:00
Total Net Yards	5556	5081
Avg. Per Game	347.3	317.6
Total Plays	1089	970
Avg. Per Play	5.1	5.2
Net Yards Rushing	1743	1958
Avg. Per Game	108.9	122.4
Total Rushes	414	454
Net Yards Passing	3813	3123
Avg. Per Game	238.3	195.2
Sacked/Yards Lost	42/370	32/187
Gross Yards	4183	3310
Att./Completions	633/371	484/287
Completion Pct.	58.6	59.3
Had Intercepted	22	7
Punts/Average	88/47.6	91/45.7
Net Punting Avg.	88/40.0	91/40.2
Penalties/Yards	112/1138	103/809
Fumbles/Ball Lost	21/9	15/4
Touchdowns	28	48
Rushing	7	11
Passing	19	29
Returns	2	8

2013 INDIVIDUAL STATISTICS

PASSING

PASSING	Att.	Comp.	Yds.	Pct.	TD	Int.	Tkld.	Rate
Schaub	358	219	2310	61.2	10	14	21/162	73.0
Keenum	253	137	1760	54.2	9	6	19/201	78.2
Yates	22	15	113	68.2	0	2	2/7	42.4
Texans	633	371	4183	58.6	19	22	42/370	74.0
Opponents	484	287	3310	59.3	29	7	32/187	93.9

SCORING

SCORING	TD R	TD P	TD Rt	PAT	FG	Saf	PTS
Bullock	0	0	0	26/26	26/35	0	104
G. Graham	0	5	0	0/0	0/0	0	30
A. Johnson	0	5	0	0/0	0/0	0	30
Tate	4	0	0	0/0	0/0	0	24
Daniels	0	3	0	0/0	0/0	0	18
Martin	0	2	1	0/0	0/0	0	18
Foster	1	1	0	0/0	0/0	0	14
Hopkins	0	2	0	0/0	0/0	0	12
Cushing	0	0	1	0/0	0/0	0	6
Griffin	0	1	0	0/0	0/0	0	6
Grimes	1	0	0	0/0	0/0	0	6
Keenum	1	0	0	0/0	0/0	0	6
Mays	0	0	0	0/0	0/0	1	2
Texans	7	19	2	26/26	26/35	1	276
Opponents	11	29	8	46/46	30/35	1	428

2-Pt Conversions: Foster.
Texans 1-1, Opponents 1-2.

RUSHING

RUSHING	No.	Yds	Avg	LG	TD
Tate	181	771	4.3	60	4
Foster	121	542	4.5	23	1
D. Johnson	49	183	3.7	29	0
Grimes	21	73	3.5	12	1
Keenum	14	72	5.1	22	1
Karim	12	51	4.3	14	0
Schaub	5	24	4.8	7	0
Wood	3	9	3.0	5	0
R. Graham	4	8	2.0	4	0
Keo	1	8	8.0	8	0
G. Jones	2	2	1.0	4	0
Yates	1	0	0.0	0	0
Texans	414	1743	4.2	60	7
Opponents	454	1958	4.3	80t	11

RECEIVING

RECEIVING	No.	Yds	Avg	LG	TD
A. Johnson	109	1407	12.9	62t	5
Hopkins	52	802	15.4	66	2
G. Graham	49	545	11.1	42t	5
Tate	34	140	4.1	10	0
Daniels	24	252	10.5	28	3
Martin	22	253	11.5	32	2
Foster	22	183	8.3	41	1
Griffin	19	244	12.8	40	1
Posey	15	155	10.3	42	0
D. Johnson	8	46	5.8	14	0
Grimes	6	76	12.7	31	0
G. Jones	5	34	6.8	19	0
Jean	4	35	8.8	11	0
R. Graham	1	12	12.0	12	0
Karim	1	-1	-1.0	-1	0
Texans	371	4183	11.3	66	19
Opponents	287	3310	11.5	64t	29

INTERCEPTIONS

INTERCEPTIONS	No.	Yds	Avg	LG	TD
Joseph	3	64	21.3	32	0
Cushing	1	18	18.0	18t	1
Keo	1	4	4.0	4	0
McCain	1	0	0.0	0	0
Swearinger	1	0	0.0	0	0
Texans	7	86	12.3	32	1
Opponents	22	357	16.2	98t	5

PUNTING

PUNTING	No.	Yds.	Avg.	In 20	LG
Lechler	88	4189	47.6	34	65
Texans	88	4189	47.6	34	65
Opponents	91	4161	45.7	31	64

PUNT RETURNS

PUNT RETURNS	Ret	FC	Yds	Avg	LG	TD
Martin	39	21	345	8.8	87t	1
Keo	3	0	15	5.0	9	0
Texans	42	21	360	8.6	87t	1
Opponents	43	23	530	12.3	82t	1

KICKOFF RETURNS

KICKOFF RETURNS	No.	Yds	Avg	LG	TD
Martin	36	947	26.3	50	0
D. Johnson	6	151	25.2	32	0
Karim	5	104	20.8	31	0
Wood	1	20	20.0	20	0
Manning	1	18	18.0	18	0
G. Jones	1	17	17.0	17	0
Crick	1	0	0.0	0	0
Texans	51	1257	24.6	50	0
Opponents	39	1004	25.7	57	0

FIELD GOALS

FIELD GOALS	1-19	20-29	30-39	40-49	50+
Bullock	1/1	7/7	5/5	12/17	1/5
Texans	1/1	7/7	5/5	12/17	1/5
Opponents	0/0	5/5	10/10	11/14	4/6

SACKS

SACKS	No.
Watt	10.5
Mercilus	7.0
A. Smith	5.0
B. Reed	3.0
Cushing	1.5
Mitchell	1.5
Manning	1.0
Mays	1.0
(group)	1.0
Tarpinian	0.5
Texans	32.0
Opponents	42.0

RECORD HOLDERS
INDIVIDUAL RECORDS—CAREER

Category	Name	Performance
Rushing (Yds.)	Arian Foster, 2009-2013	5,063
Passing (Yds.)	Matt Schaub, 2007-2013	23,221
Passing (TDs)	Matt Schaub, 2007-2013	124
Receiving (No.)	Andre Johnson, 2003-2013	927
Receiving (Yds.)	Andre Johnson, 2003-2013	12,661
Interceptions	Dunta Robinson, 2004-09	13
Punting (Avg.)	Matt Turk, 2007-2011	42.3
Punt Return (Avg.)	Jacoby Jones, 2007-2011	10.2
Kickoff Return (Avg.)	André Davis, 2007-09	25.4
Field Goals	Kris Brown, 2002-09	172
Touchdowns (Tot.)	Andre Johnson, 2003-2013	61
Points	Kris Brown, 2002-09	767
*Sacks	Mario Williams, 2006-2011	53.0

INDIVIDUAL RECORDS—SINGLE SEASON

Category	Name	Performance
Rushing (Yds.)	Arian Foster, 2010	1,616
Passing (Yds.)	Matt Schaub, 2009	4,770
Passing (TDs)	Matt Schaub, 2009	29
Receiving (No.)	Andre Johnson, 2008	115
Receiving (Yds.)	Andre Johnson, 2012	1,598
Interceptions	Marcus Coleman, 2003	7
Punting (Avg.)	Shane Lechler, 2013	47.6
Punt Return (Avg.)	Keshawn Martin, 2012	12.1
Kickoff Return (Avg.)	André Davis, 2007	30.3
Field Goals	Neil Rackers, 2011	32
Touchdowns (Tot.)	Arian Foster, 2010	18
Points	Shayne Graham, 2012	138
*Sacks	J.J. Watt, 2012	20.5

INDIVIDUAL RECORDS—SINGLE GAME

Category	Name	Performance
Rushing (Yds.)	Arian Foster, 9-12-10	231
Passing (Yds.)	Matt Schaub, 11-18-12	527
Passing (TDs)	Matt Schaub, 11-18-12	5
Receiving (No.)	Andre Johnson, 11-18-12	14
Receiving (Yds.)	Andre Johnson, 11-18-12	273
Interceptions	Glover Quin, 10-28-10	3
Field Goals	Kris Brown, 9-7-03, 12-4-05, 10-7-07	5
Touchdowns (Tot.)	Ryan Moats, 11-1-09	3
	Arian Foster, 9-12-10, 10-23-11	3
	Andre Johnson, 11-3-13	3
	Ben Tate, 12-1-13	3
Points	Ryan Moats, 11-1-09	18
	Arian Foster, 9-12-10, 10-23-11	18
*Sacks	Connor Barwin, 11-27-11	4.0

Sacks became an official statistic in 1982.

2014 VETERAN ROSTER

No.	Name	Pos.	Ht.	Wt.	Birthdate	NFL Exp.	College	Hometown	How Acq.	'13 Games/ Starts
16	Bonner, Alan	WR	5-10	191	11/5/90	2	Jacksonville State	Newnan, Ga.	D6b-'13	0*
34	Bouye, A.J.	CB	6-0	191	8/16/91	2	Central Florida	Tucker, Ga.	FA-'13	6/0
79	Brooks, Brandon	G	6-5	335	8/19/89	3	Miami (Ohio)	Milwaukee, Wisc.	D3b-'12	15/15
33	Brown, Andre	RB	6-0	227	12/15/86	6	North Carolina State	Greenville, N.C.	UFA(NYG)-'14	8/8*
76	Brown, Duane	T	6-4	303	8/30/85	7	Virginia Tech	Richmond, Va.	D1-'08	14/14
4	Bullock, Randy	K	5-9	206	12/16/89	3	Texas A&M	Klein, Texas	D5-'12	16/0
20	Clemons, Chris	S	6-1	215	9/15/85	6	Clemson	Arcadia, Fla.	UFA(Mia)-'14	16/16*
93	Crick, Jared	DE	6-4	285	8/21/89	3	Nebraska	Cozad, Neb.	D4c-'12	16/1
56	Cushing, Brian	LB	6-3	249	1/24/87	6	Southern California	Park Ridge, N.J.	D1-'09	7/7
14	Fitzpatrick, Ryan	QB	6-2	223	11/24/82	10	Harvard	Gilbert, Ariz.	FA-'14	11/9*
23	Foster, Arian	RB	6-1	227	8/24/86	6	Tennessee	San Diego, Calif.	FA-'09	8/8
88	Graham, Garrett	TE	6-3	243	8/4/86	5	Wisconsin	Brick, N.J.	D4b-'10	13/11
84	Griffin, Ryan	TE	6-6	254	1/11/90	2	Connecticut	Londonderry, N.H.	D6d-'13	15/8
41	Grimes, Jonathan	RB	5-10	209	12/21/89	3	William & Mary	Willingboro, N.J.	FA-'13	2/1
26	Harris, Brandon	CB	5-10	189	1/24/90	4	Miami	Miami, Fla.	D2b-'11	16/0
68	#Harris, Ryan	T	6-5	302	3/11/85	7	Notre Dame	Minneapolis, Minn.	W(Den)-'12	16/3
51	Hazel, Paul	LB	6-5	227	5/4/90	2	Western Michigan	Miami, Fla.	W(Cle)-'13	13/0*
10	Hopkins, DeAndre	WR	6-1	218	6/6/92	2	Clemson	Central, S.C.	D1-'13	16/16
25	Jackson, Kareem	CB	5-10	188	4/10/88	5	Alabama	Macon, Ga.	D1-'10	14/14
96	Jamison, Tim	DE	6-3	287	2/26/86	6	Michigan	Harvey, Ill.	FA-'09	5/0
80	Johnson, Andre	WR	6-3	230	7/11/81	12	Miami	Miami, Fla.	D1-'03	16/16
28	Johnson, Dennis	RB	5-7	193	2/24/90	2	Arkansas	Texarkana, Ark.	FA-'13	8/1
60	Jones, Ben	G/C	6-3	308	7/2/89	3	Georgia	Centreville, Ala.	D4a-'12	16/1
33	#Jones, Greg	FB	6-1	251	5/9/81	11	Florida State	Columbia, S.C.	UFA(Jax)-'13	16/5
24	Joseph, Johnathan	CB	5-11	188	4/16/84	9	South Carolina	Rock Hill, S.C.	UFA(Cin)-'11	15/15
39	#Karim, Deji	RB	5-8	209	11/18/86	5	Southern Illinois	Memphis, Tenn.	FA-'13	7/0
7	Keenum, Case	QB	6-1	205	2/12/88	2	Houston	Abilene, Texas	FA-'13	8/8*
31	Keo, Shiloh	S	5-11	208	12/17/87	4	Idaho	Everett, Wash.	D5a-'11	16/11
9	Lechler, Shane	P	6-2	237	8/7/76	15	Texas A&M	East Bernard, Texas	UFA(Oak)-'13	16/0
15	Lemon, Alec	WR	6-1	203	7/1/91	2	Syracuse	Crofton, Md.	FA-'13	0*
21	Lewis, Kendrick	S	6-0	198	6/16/88	5	Mississippi	New Orleans, La.	UFA(KC)-'14	16/15*
43	Mack, Elbert	CB	5-10	175	7/14/86	7	Troy	Wichita, Kansas	FA-'13	8/0
82	Martin, Keshawn	WR	5-11	194	3/15/90	3	Michigan State	Inkster, Mich.	D4b-'12	16/1
94	Mathews, Ricardo	NT	6-3	300	7/30/87	5	Cincinnati	Jacksonville, Fla.	UFA(Ind)-'14	16/1*
59	Mercilus, Whitney	LB	6-4	258	7/21/90	3	Illinois	Akron, Ohio	D1-'12	16/16
54	Mohamed, Mike	LB	6-3	238	3/11/88	3	California	Brawley, Calif.	FA-'13	8/0
55	Myers, Chris	C	6-4	286	9/15/81	10	Miam	Miami, Fla.	T(Den)-'08	16/16
75	Newton, Derek	T	6-6	313	11/16/87	4	Arkansas State	Utica, Miss.	D7a-'11	16/16
35	Pleasant, Eddie	S	5-10	210	12/17/88	2	Oregon	Compton, Calif.	FA-'12	16/1
11	Posey, DeVier	WR	6-1	210	3/15/90	3	Ohio State	Cincinnati, Ohio	D3a-'12	14/0
86	Potter, Zach	TE	6-7	269	5/4/86	4	Nebraska	Omaha, Neb.	FA-'14	0*
95	Powe, Jerrell	NT	6-2	331	3/15/87	4	Mississippi	Waynesboro, Miss.	FA-'14	2/1*
77	Quessenberry, David	G	6-5	306	8/24/90	2	San Jose State	La Jolla, Calif.	D6a-'13	0*
58	Reed, Brooks	LB	6-3	254	2/28/87	4	Arizona	Tucson, Ariz.	D2a-'11	16/16
91	Sapp, Ricky	LB	6-4	252	11/14/86	4	Clemson	Bamberg, S.C.	W(NYJ)-'13	10/0*
47	Smelley, Brad	FB	6-2	235	4/20/89	2	Alabama	Tuscaloosa, Ala.	FA-'13	2/0
74	#Smith, Wade	G	6-4	295	4/26/81	12	Memphis	Dallas, Texas	UFA(KC)-'10	16/16
29	Starling, Jawanza	S	6-1	206	6/21/91	2	Southern California	Tallahassee, Fla.	FA-'13	2/0
36	Swearinger, D.J.	S	5-10	208	9/1/91	2	South Carolina	Greenwood, S.C.	D2-'13	16/10
52	Tarpinian, Jeff	LB	6-3	240	10/16/87	4	Iowa	Omaha, Neb.	FA-'13	8/3
89	Thomas, Mike	WR	5-8	198	6/4/87	6	Arizona	DeSoto, Texas	FA-'13	0*
57	Tuggle, Justin	LB	6-3	249	1/4/90	2	Kansas State	Alpharetta, Ga.	FA-'13	15/1
27	Victorian, Josh	CB	5-10	190	7/10/88	2	Louisiana Tech	Metairie, La.	FA-'13	8/0
99	Watt, J.J.	DE	6-5	289	3/22/89	4	Wisconsin	Pewaukee, Wisc.	D1-'11	16/16
46	Weeks, Jon	LS	5-10	246	2/17/86	5	Baylor	Bethpage, N.Y.	FA-'10	16/0
67	White, Cody	G	6-3	303	7/1/88	3	Illinois State	Columbus, Ohio	FA-'12	1/0
73	Williams, Brennan	T	6-6	310	2/5/91	2	North Carolina	West Roxbury, Mass.	D3a-'13	0*
50	Williams, Trevardo	LB	6-1	236	12/31/90	2	Connecticut	Bridgeport, Conn.	D4-'13	0*
13	Yates, T.J.	QB	6-4	217	5/28/87	4	North Carolina	Marietta, Ga.	D5b-'11	3/0

* Bonner missed '13 season because of injury; Brown played eight games with the New York Giants in '13; Clemons played 16 games with Miami; Fitzpatrick played 11 games with Tennessee; Hazel played 13 games with Cleveland; Lemon missed '13 season because of injury; Lewis played 16 games with Kansas City; Mathews played 16 games with Indianapolis; Potter last active with Jacksonville in '12; Powe played two games with Kansas City; Quessenberry missed '13 season because of injury; Sapp played five games with the New York Jets and five games with Houston; Thomas last active with Detroit in '12; B. Williams missed '13 season because of injury; T. Williams missed '13 season because of injury.

Unrestriced Free Agent; subject to developments.

Traded—QB Matt Schaub (16 games in '13) to Oakland.

Players lost through free agency (6): T Andrew Gardner (Phil; 3 games in '13), LB Joe Mays (KC; 14), NT Earl Mitchell (Mia; 16), LB Darryl Sharpton (Wash; 15), DE Antonio Smith (Oak; 15), RB Ben Tate (Cle; 14).

Also played with Texans in '13—LB Bryan Braman (16 games), TE Jake Byrne (7), TE Owen Daniels (5), LB Tim Dobbins (3), LB Tavares Gooden (1), RB Ray Graham (1), WR Lestar Jean (13), LB Willie Jefferson (6), S Danieal Manning (6), CB Brice McCain (16), NT Terrell McClain (16), S Ed Reed (7), CB Justin Rogers (1), LB D.J. Smith (1), RB Chad Spann (1), TE Phillip Supernaw (1), RB Cierre Wood (3).

FIRST-YEAR ROSTER

Name	Pos.	Ht.	Wt.	Birthdate	College	Hometown	How Acq.
Ankrah, Jason	OLB	6-3	262	2/26/91	Nebraska	Gaithersburg, Md.	FA
Ballentine, Lonnie	S	6-3	215	4/23/93	Memphis	Memphis, Tenn.	D7b
Bester, Lacoltan	WR	6-3	208	11/12/91	Oklahoma	Scooba, Miss.	FA
Blue, Alfred	RB	6-2	223	4/21/91	Louisiana State	Boutte, La.	D6b
Boffeli, Conor	G/C	6-4	304	8/29/91	Iowa	West Des Moines, Iowa	W(Minn)
Boswell, Chris	K	6-2	185	3/16/91	Rice	Keller, Texas	FA
Brown, Austin	NT	6-2	295	9/14/91	Miami (Ohio)	Woodbridge, Va.	FA
Browner, Keith (1)	DE	6-4	288	4/7/88	California	Los Angeles, Calif.	FA-'12
Bullough, Max	ILB	6-3	249	2/11/92	Michigan State	Traverse City, Mich.	FA
Clowney, Jadeveon	OLB	6-5	266	2/14/93	South Carolina	Rock Hill, S.C.	D1
Coyle, Chris	TE	6-4	243	3/25/91	Arizona State	Westlake Village, Calif.	FA
Cruse, Andy (1)	WR	6-3	216	1/13/90	Miami (Ohio)	Cincinnati, Ohio	FA-'13
Denham, Anthony	TE	6-4	235	7/21/91	Utah	Monterey Park, Calif.	FA
Dima, Anthony	T	6-6	295	10/21/90	Massachusetts	Centereach, N.Y.	W(Cle)
Feiler, Matt	T	6-6	330	7/7/92	Bloomsburg	Strasburg, Pa.	FA
Ferentz, James	C	6-2	285	6/5/89	Iowa	Iowa City, Iowa	FA
Fiedorowicz, C.J.	TE	6-5	265	10/22/91	Iowa	Johnsburg, Ill.	D3a
Forsch, Kevin	G	6-3	307	2/2/91	Houston	Tomball, Texas	FA
Grosz, Sullivan	DE	6-4	295	2/13/91	Cal Poly	Fresno, Calif.	FA
Hal, Andre	CB	5-10	188	5/30/92	Vanderbilt	Port Allen, La.	D7a
Kupper, Alex (1)	G	6-3	305	2/14/90	Louisville	Louisville, Ky.	FA-'13
Labhart, Travis	WR	5-9	182	1/20/91	Texas A&M	Whitesboro, Texas	FA
Lloyd, Terrance	OLB	6-3	238	9/9/90	Baylor	Houston, Texas	FA
McAllister, Chris	OLB	6-2	255	3/3/91	Baylor	Converse, Texas	FA
McClung, Anthony	WR	6-0	177	9/9/91	Cincinnati	Indianapolis, Ind.	FA
Nix III, Louis	NT	6-2	331	7/31/91	Notre Dame	Jacksonville, Fla.	D3b
Nwachukwu, EZ (1)	WR	5-11	198	12/15/90	Texas A&M	Allen, Texas	FA-'13
Opurum, Toben (1)	FB	6-1	250	11/18/90	Kansas	Richardson, Texas	FA-'13
Pagan, Jeoffrey	DE	6-3	310	6/10/93	Alabama	Asheville, N.C.	D6a
Prosch, Jay	FB	6-1	256	8/21/92	Auburn	Mobile, Ala.	D6c
Savage, Tom	QB	6-4	228	4/26/90	Pittsburgh	Springfield, Pa.	D4
Su'a-Filo, Xavier	G	6-4	307	1/1/91	UCLA	American Fork, Utah	D2
Warmsley, Julius	DE	6-2	296	5/16/90	Tulane	Baton Rouge, La.	FA
Williams, Marcus	CB	5-11	196	3/24/91	North Dakota State	Minneapolis, Minn.	FA
Witzmann, Bryan	T	6-7	311	6/16/90	South Dakota State	Houlton, Wisc.	FA
Young, Chris	ILB	6-0	252	1/9/92	Arizona State	Seattle, Wash.	FA

The term NFL Rookie is defined as a player who is in his first season of professional football and has not been on the roster of another professional football team for any regular-season or postseason games. A Rookie is designated by an "R" on NFL rosters. Players who have been active in another professional football league or players who have NFL experience, including either preseason training camp or being on an Active List or Inactive List, or on Reserve/Injured or Reserve/Physically Unable to Perform for fewer than six regular-season games, are termed NFL First-Year Players. An NFL First-Year Player is designated by a "1" on NFL rosters. Thereafter, a player is credited with an additional year of experience for each season in which he accumulates six games on the Active List or Inactive List, or on Reserve/Injured or Reserve/Physically Unable to Perform.

Log on to www.houstontexans.com for an up-to-date roster.

HOUSTON TEXANS

COACHING STAFF
Head Coach,
Bill O'Brien

Pro Career: Bill O'Brien was named the third head coach in Houston Texans franchise history on Friday, Jan. 3, 2014. The 44-year old brings 21 years of collegiate and NFL coaching experience with him to Houston. O'Brien was head coach at Penn State from 2012-13 and led the storied program through one of the greatest periods of strife any major college program has endured, garnering national and conference coach-of-the-year awards in the process. Penn State won eight of its final 10 games to finish the 2011 season with an 8-4 record. O'Brien, who also served as offensive coordinator, won more games than any other first-year head coach in the program's previous 125 seasons and was named the Bear Bryant, Maxwell Football Club and ESPN National Coach of the Year, as well as the Big Ten Coach of the Year by media and coaches. The following season, PSU posted a 7-5 record and had 12 student-athletes earn all-conference recognition. From 2007-2011, O'Brien helped lead the New England Patriots to a pair of Super Bowl berths, rising from offensive assistant his first season to wide receivers coach in 2008 and then quarterbacks coach from 2009-10 prior to his promotion to offensive coordinator/quarterbacks coach in 2011. That season, the Patriots ranked third in the NFL in scoring, second in total offense and advanced to Super Bowl XLVI with O'Brien coordinating the offense. Began his coaching career at Brown in 1993 as tight ends coach before coaching inside linebackers in 1994. He joined the Georgia Tech staff in 1995 and was promoted to running backs coach in 1998, when the Yellow Jackets won the 1998 Atlantic Coast Conference title and Gator Bowl against Notre Dame. He became the offensive coordinator and quarterbacks coach in 2001, and then assistant head coach in 2002. He coached running backs at Maryland from 2003-04 before serving as offensive coordinator and quarterbacks coach at Duke from 2005-06. Career record: 0-0.

Background: O'Brien grew up in Andover, Mass. and graduated from St. John's Preparatory School in Danvers. He played linebacker and defensive end at Brown from 1990-92 and graduated with a double concentration in political science and organizational behavioral management.

Personal: Born on October 23, 1969 in Dorchester, Mass. He and his wife, Colleen, have two sons: Jack, 11, and Michael, 8.

ASSISTANT COACHES
Jim Bernhardt, director of football research; born March 26, 1956, New York, N.Y. Linebacker Hofstra 1974-76. No pro playing experience. College coach: Georgia 1980-81, Hofstra 1988-89, Brown 1990-93, Central Florida 2004-07, Penn State 2012-13. Pro coach: Joined Texans in 2014.
John Butler, secondary; born April 3, 1973,

Abbington, Pa. Defensive back Catholic University 1991-94. No pro playing experience. College coach: Catholic University 1995-96, Texas 1997-98, Midwestern State 1999-2000, Texas State 2001-02, Harvard 2003-06, Minnesota 2007-10, South Carolina 2011, Penn State 2012-13. Pro coach: Joined Texans in 2014.
Doug Colman, asst. special teams; born June 4, 1973, Ventnor, N.J. Linebacker Nebraska 1991-95. Pro linebacker New York Giants 1996-98, Tennessee Titans 1999, Cleveland Browns 2000. College coach: Nebraska 2008-09, Tulane 2010-11, Coastal Carolina 2012-13. Pro coach: Amsterdam (NFLE) 2007, joined Texans in 2014.
Romeo Crennel, defensive coordinator; born June 18, 1947, Lynchburg, Va. Defensive lineman/offensive tackle Western Kentucky 1966-69. No pro playing experience. College coach: Western Kentucky 1970-74, Texas Tech 1975-77, Mississippi 1978-79, Georgia Tech 1980. Pro coach: New York Giants 1981-1992, New England Patriots 1993-96, 2001-04, New York Jets 1997-99, Cleveland Browns 2000, 2005-08 (head coach 2005-08), Kansas City Chiefs 2010-12 (interim head coach, final three games 2011, head coach 2012), joined Texans in 2014.
Paul Dunn, offensive line; born July 7, 1960, Philadelphia, Pa. Offensive lineman Pittsburgh 1978-1982. No pro playing experience. College coach: Pittsburgh 1983, 2005-07, Penn State 1984-85, Edinboro 1986-88, Rutgers 1989, Maine 1990-93, Cincinnati 1994-95, Vanderbilt 1996-97, Kansas State 1998-2002. Pro coach: Atlanta Falcons 2008-2013, joined Texans in 2014.
Craig Fitzgerald, head strength and conditioning; born September 15, 1972, Philadelphia, Pa. Tight end Maryland 1992-96. No pro playing experience. College coach: Catholic University 1997-98, Arizona State 1999, Maryland 2000-05, Harvard 2005-09, South Carolina 2009-2011, Penn State 2012-13. Pro coach: Joined Texans in 2014.
George Godsey, quarterbacks; born January 1, 1979, Tampa, Fla. Quarterback Georgia Tech 1998-2001. Pro quarterback Tampa Bay Storm (AFL) 2003. College coach: Central Florida 2004-2010. Pro coach: New England Patriots 2011-13, joined Texans in 2014.
Sean Hayes, asst. strength and conditioning; born August 11, 1986, Merritt Island, Fla. Linebacker Harvard 2005-09. Pro linebacker/coach L'Hospitalet Pioneers (European Football League) 2010. College coach: Jacksonville University 2010-11, Penn State 2012-13. Pro coach: Joined Texans in 2014.
Stan Hixon, wide receivers; born July 24, 1957, Lakeland, Fla. Wide receiver Iowa State 1975-78. No pro playing experience. College coach: Morehead State 1980-82, Appalachian State 1983-88, South Carolina 1989-1992, Wake Forest 1993-94, Georgia Tech 1995-99, Louisiana State 2000-03, Penn State 2012-13. Pro coach: Washington Redskins 2004-09, Buffalo Bills 2010-11, joined Texans in 2014.

Tim Kelly, offensive quality control; born August 17, 1986, Chicago Heights, Ill. Defensive tackle Eastern Illinois 2004-07. No pro playing experience. College coach: Illinois Wesleyan 2008-09, Minnesota State-Moorehead 2010, Ball State 2011, Penn State 2012-13. Pro coach: Joined Texans in 2014.
Bill Kollar, defensive line; born November 27, 1952, Warren, Ohio. Defensive end Montana State 1971-73. Pro defensive end Cincinnati Bengals 1974-76, Tampa Bay Buccaneers 1977-1981. College coach: Illinois 1985-87, Purdue 1988-89. Pro coach: Tampa Bay Buccaneers 1984, Atlanta Falcons 1990-2000, St. Louis Rams 2001-05, Buffalo Bills 2006-08, joined Texans in 2009.
Will Lawing, defensive quality control; born November 27, 1985, Boone, N.C. Wide receiver North Carolina 2004-07. No pro playing experience. College coach: Juniata 2009-2012, Penn State 2013. Pro coach: Joined Texans in 2014.
Bob Ligashesky, special teams coordinator; born June 2, 1962, Pittsburgh, Pa. Defensive back Indiana (Pa.) 1982-84. No pro playing experience. Pro coach: Jacksonville Jaguars 2004, St. Louis Rams 2005-06, Pittsburgh Steelers 2007-09, Denver Broncos 2010, Oakland Raiders 2011, Tampa Bay Buccaneers 2012, joined Texans in 2013.
Charles London, running backs; born August 12, 1975, Dunwoody, Ga. Running back Duke 1994-96. No pro playing experience. College coach: Duke 2004-06, Penn State 2012-13. Pro coach: Chicago Bears 2007-09, Tennessee Titans 2011, joined Texans in 2014.
Anthony Midget, asst. secondary; born February 22, 1978, Clewiston, Fla. Cornerback Virginia Tech 1996-99. No pro playing experience. College coach: Virginia Tech 2007, Georgia State 2008-2012, Penn State 2013. Pro coach: Joined Texans in 2014.
John Perry, tight ends; born June 4, 1969, Lawrence, Mass. Wide receiver New Hampshire 1988-1992. No pro playing experience. College coach: Northeastern 1993, Brown 1994-96, New Hampshire 1997-98, 2007, Dartmouth 1999-2004, Georgetown 2005, Hofstra 2006, Merrimack 2008-2012 (head coach), Delaware 2013. Pro coach: Joined Texans in 2014.
Anthony Pleasant, asst. strength and conditioning; born January 27, 1968, Century, Fla. Defensive end Tennessee State 1987-89. Pro defensive end Cleveland Browns 1990-95, Baltimore Ravens 1996, Atlanta Falcons 1997, New York Jets 1998-99, San Francisco 49ers 2000, New England Patriots 2001-03. Pro coach: Kansas City Chiefs 2010-12, joined Texans in 2014.
Mike Vrabel, linebackers; born August 14, 1975, Akron, Ohio. Defensive end Ohio State 1993-96. Pro linebacker Pittsburgh Steelers 1997-2001, New England Patriots 2001-08, Kansas City Chiefs 2009-2010. College coach: Ohio State 2011-13. Pro coach: Joined Texans in 2014.

American Football Conference
South Division
Team Colors: Royal Blue and White
P.O. Box 535000
Indianapolis, Indiana 46253
Telephone: (317) 297-2658

2014 SCHEDULE
PRESEASON

Aug. 7	at New York Jets	7:00
Aug. 16	**New York Giants**	7:00
Aug. 23	**New Orleans**	8:00
Aug. 28	at Cincinnati	7:00

REGULAR SEASON

Sep. 7	at Denver	8:30
Sep. 15	**Philadelphia** (Mon)	8:30
Sep. 21	at Jacksonville	1:00
Sep. 28	**Tennessee**	1:00
Oct. 5	**Baltimore**	1:00
Oct. 9	at Houston (Thu)	8:25
Oct. 19	**Cincinnati**	1:00
Oct. 26	at Pittsburgh	4:25
Nov. 3	at New York Giants (Mon)	8:30
Nov. 9	BYE	
Nov. 16	**New England**	*8:30
Nov. 23	**Jacksonville**	1:00
Nov. 30	**Washington**	1:00
Dec. 7	at Cleveland	1:00
Dec. 14	**Houston**	1:00
Dec. 21	at Dallas	4:25
Dec. 28	at Tennessee	1:00

*All times ET; Sunday night games in
Weeks 5-16 subject to change*

Stadium: Lucas Oil Stadium (opened in
2008) • **Capacity:** 63,000
500 South Capitol Avenue
Indianapolis, Indiana 46225
Playing Surface: FieldTurf
Training Camp: Anderson University
1100 East Fifth Street
Anderson, IN 46012

LUCAS OIL STADIUM

CLUB OFFICIALS
Owner and CEO: James Irsay
Vice Chair/Owner: Carlie Irsay-Gordon
Vice Chair/Owner: Casey Foyt
Vice Chair/Owner: Kalen Irsay
General Manager: Ryan Grigson
Head Coach: Chuck Pagano
Chief Operating Officer: Pete Ward
Senior Vice President of Sponsorship
Sales: Jay Souers
Vice President-Finance: Kurt Humphrey
Vice President-Ticket Operations/Guest
Services: Larry Hall
Senior Director of Communications:
Avis Roper
Vice President of Sponsorship Sales:
Matt Godbout
Vice President of Premium Seating and
Ticket Sales: Greg Hylton
Vice President and General Counsel:
Dan Emerson
Vice President of Football Operations:
Jimmy Raye
Director of Football Administration:
Mike Bluem
Associate Director of Pro Personnel:
Kevin Rogers
Vice President of Equipment Operations:
Jon Scott
Video Director: Erik Kunttu
Head Athletic Trainer: Dave Hammer
Director of Rehabilitation: Erin Barill
Assistant Equipment Managers:
Mike Mays, Sean Sullivan,
Brian Seabrooks
Assistant Trainers: Dave Walston,
Kyle Davis, Kellen Norris
Assistant Video Director: John Starliper

COACHING HISTORY
Baltimore 1953-1983
(495-442-7)
Records include postseason games

1953	Keith Molesworth	3-9-0
1954-1962	Weeb Ewbank	61-52-1
1963-69	Don Shula	73-26-4
1970-72	Don McCafferty*	26-11-1
1972	John Sandusky	4-5-0
1973-74	Howard Schnellenberger**	4-13-0
1974	Joe Thomas	2-9-0
1975-79	Ted Marchibroda	41-36-0
1980-81	Mike McCormack	9-23-0
1982-84	Frank Kush***	11-28-1
1984	Hal Hunter	0-1-0
1985-86	Rod Dowhower****	5-24-0
1986-1991	Ron Meyer#	36-36-0
1991	Rick Venturi	1-10-0
1992-95	Ted Marchibroda	32-35-0
1996-97	Lindy Infante	12-21-0
1998-2001	Jim Mora	32-34-0
2002-08	Tony Dungy	92-33-0
2009-2011	Jim Caldwell	28-24-0
2012-13	Chuck Pagano	23-12-0

*Released after five games in 1972
**Released after three games in 1974
***Resigned after 15 games in 1984
****Released after 13 games in 1986
#Released after five games in 1991

PAID ATTENDANCE
Home 511,798   Away 494,618
Total 1,006,416
Single-game home record,
67,650 (1/24/10)
Single-season home record,
520,687 (2010)

2014 DRAFT CHOICES

Round	Name	Pos.	College
2	Jack Mewhort	G	Ohio St.
3	Donte Moncrief	WR	Mississippi
5	Jonathan Newsome	LB	Ball St.
6	Andrew Jackson	LB	Western Kentucky
7	Ulrick John	T	Georgia St.

INDIANAPOLIS COLTS

2013 TEAM RECORD
PRESEASON (2-2)

Date	Result	Opponent
08/11	L 20-44	Buffalo
08/18	W 20-12	at New York Giants
08/24	W 27-6	Cleveland
08/29	L 10-27	at Cincinnati

REGULAR SEASON (11-5)

Date	Result	Opponent
09/08	W 21-17	Oakland
09/15	L 20-24	Miami
09/22	W 27-7	at San Francisco
09/29	W 37-3	at Jacksonville
10/06	W 34-28	Seattle
10/14	L 9-19	at San Diego
10/20	W 39-33	Denver
11/03	W 27-24	at Houston
11/10	L 8-38	St. Louis
11/14	W 30-27	at Tennessee
11/24	L 11-40	at Arizona
12/01	W 22-14	Tennessee
12/08	L 28-42	at Cincinnati
12/15	W 25-3	Houston
12/22	W 23-7	at Kansas City
12/29	W 30-10	Jacksonville

POSTSEASON (1-1)

Date	Result	Opponent
01/04	W 45-44	Kansas City
01/11	L 22-43	at New England

SCORE BY PERIODS

Colts	70	117	106	98	0 —	391
Opponents	102	102	66	66	0 —	336

2013 TEAM STATISTICS

	Colts	Opp.
Total First Downs	318	319
Rushing	88	101
Passing	191	191
Penalty	39	27
3rd Down: Made/Att	80/213	79/210
3rd Down Pct.	37.6	37.6
4th Down: Made/Att	3/10	10/19
4th Down Pct.	30.0	52.6
Possession Avg.	29:41	30:19
Total Net Yards	5468	5713
Avg. Per Game	341.8	357.1
Total Plays	1023	1026
Avg. Per Play	5.3	5.6
Net Yards Rushing	1743	2002
Avg. Per Game	108.9	125.1
Total Rushes	409	448
Net Yards Passing	3725	3711
Avg. Per Game	232.8	231.9
Sacked/Yards Lost	32/227	42/248
Gross Yards	3952	3959
Att./Completions	582/350	536/324
Completion Pct.	60.1	60.4
Had Intercepted	10	15
Punts/Average	77/45.4	75/45.6
Net Punting Avg.	77/38.5	75/39.7
Penalties/Yards	66/576	112/990
Fumbles/Ball Lost	14/4	26/12
Touchdowns	40	38
Rushing	15	14
Passing	23	21
Returns	2	3

2013 INDIVIDUAL STATISTICS

PASSING

	Att.	Comp.	Yds.	Pct.	TD	Int.	Tkld.	Rate
Luck	570	343	3822	60.2	23	9	32/227	87.0
Hasselbeck	12	7	130	58.3	0	1	0/0	61.1
Colts	582	350	3952	60.1	23	10	32/227	86.5
Opponents	536	324	3959	60.4	21	15	42/248	84.6

SCORING

	TD R	TD P	TD Rt	PAT	FG	Saf	PTS
Vinatieri	0	0	0	34/34	35/40	0	139
D. Brown	6	2	0	0/0	0/0	0	48
Hilton	0	5	0	0/0	0/0	0	30
Fleener	0	4	0	0/0	0/0	0	28
Luck	4	0	0	0/0	0/0	0	24
Richardson	3	1	0	0/0	0/0	0	24
Wayne	0	2	0	0/0	0/0	0	14
Bradshaw	2	0	0	0/0	0/0	0	12
Brazill	0	2	0	0/0	0/0	0	12
Rogers	0	2	0	0/0	0/0	0	12
Whalen	0	2	0	0/0	0/0	0	12
Heyward-Bey	0	1	0	0/0	0/0	0	8
D. Allen	0	1	0	0/0	0/0	0	6
Butler	0	0	1	0/0	0/0	0	6
Havili	0	1	0	0/0	0/0	0	6
Howell	0	0	1	0/0	0/0	0	6
Mathis	0	0	0	0/0	0/0	1	2
Redding	0	0	0	0/0	0/0	1	2
Colts	15	23	2	34/34	35/40	2	391
Opponents	14	21	3	37/37	23/30	1	336

2-Pt Conversions: Fleener 2, Heyward-Bey,
Wayne. Colts 4-6, Opponents 0-1.

RUSHING

	No.	Yds	Avg	LG	TD
D. Brown	102	537	5.3	51t	6
Richardson	157	458	2.9	22	3
Luck	63	377	6.0	29	4
Bradshaw	41	186	4.5	27	2
Choice	11	44	4.0	8	0
Ballard	13	63	4.8	12	0
Herron	5	33	6.6	22	0
Heyward-Bey	3	26	8.7	30	0
Havili	7	7	1.0	4	0
Hilton	2	6	3.0	3	0
Wayne	1	5	5.0	5	0
Lynch	1	3	3.0	3	0
Rogers	1	0	0.0	0	0
Hasselbeck	2	-2	-1.0	-1	0
Colts	409	1743	4.3	51t	15
Opponents	448	2002	4.5	56	14

RECEIVING

	No.	Yds	Avg	LG	TD
Hilton	82	1083	13.2	73t	5
Fleener	52	608	11.7	44	4
Wayne	38	503	13.2	35	2
Heyward-Bey	29	309	10.7	27	1
Richardson	28	265	9.5	24	1
D. Brown	27	214	7.9	33t	2
Whalen	24	259	10.8	25	2
Havili	18	128	7.1	20t	1
Rogers	14	192	13.7	69t	2
Brazill	12	161	13.4	29t	2
Bradshaw	7	42	6.0	14	0
Doyle	5	19	3.8	8	0
Saunders	4	46	11.5	18	0
Jones	2	34	17.0	21	0
Herron	1	57	57.0	57	0
D. Allen	1	20	20.0	20t	1
R. Hughes	1	6	6.0	6	0
Choice	1	5	5.0	5	0
Cunningham	1	4	4.0	4	0
Reed	1	2	2.0	2	0
Satele	1	0	0.0	0	0
Ballard	1	-5	-5.0	-5	0
Colts	350	3952	11.3	73t	23
Opponents	324	3959	12.2	81t	21

INTERCEPTIONS

	No.	Yds	Avg	LG	TD
Butler	4	79	19.8	41t	1
Vaughn	3	9	3.0	8	0
Bethea	2	48	24.0	46	0
Freeman	2	13	6.5	13	0
Toler	1	26	26.0	26	0
Gordy	1	7	7.0	7	0
Angerer	1	4	4.0	4	0
Davis	1	0	0.0	0	0
Colts	15	186	12.4	46	1
Opponents	10	91	9.1	32	1

PUNTING

	No.	Yds.	Avg.	In 20	LG
McAfee	76	3499	46.0	27	65
Colts	77	3499	45.4	27	65
Opponents	75	3423	45.6	24	70

PUNT RETURNS

	Ret	FC	Yds	Avg	LG	TD
Hilton	17	12	159	9.4	34	0
Whalen	8	7	104	13.0	51	0
Rainey	4	4	29	7.3	18	0
Brazill	3	2	25	8.3	17	0
Butler	1	0	9	9.0	9	0
Colts	33	25	326	9.9	51	0
Opponents	29	17	396	13.7	98t	1

KICKOFF RETURNS

	No.	Yds	Avg	LG	TD
Reed	24	590	24.6	39	0
Rainey	6	131	21.8	27	0
Vaughn	5	142	28.4	33	0
Brazill	3	57	19.0	21	0
Choice	1	28	28.0	28	0
Williams	1	28	28.0	28	0
Whalen	1	22	22.0	22	0
Herron	1	13	13.0	13	0
Adongo	1	0	0.0	0	0
Colts	43	1011	23.5	39	0
Opponents	43	1085	25.2	56	0

FIELD GOALS

	1-19	20-29	30-39	40-49	50+
Vinatieri	0/0	6/6	10/11	15/17	4/6
Colts	0/0	6/6	10/11	15/17	4/6
Opponents	0/0	3/4	9/9	7/12	4/5

SACKS

	No.
Mathis	19.5
Freeman	5.5
Redding	4.5
Walden	3.0
Jean Francois	2.5
Werner	2.5
Moala	1.5
Bethea	1.0
Sheppard	1.0
Angerer	0.5
Mathews	0.5
Colts	42.0
Opponents	32.0

RECORD HOLDERS
INDIVIDUAL RECORDS—CAREER

Category	Name	Performance
Rushing (Yds.)	Edgerrin James, 1999-2005	9,226
Passing (Yds.)	Peyton Manning, 1998-2010	54,828
Passing (TDs)	Peyton Manning, 1998-2010	399
Receiving (No.)	Marvin Harrison, 1996-2008	1,102
Receiving (Yds.)	Marvin Harrison, 1996-2008	14,580
Interceptions	Bob Boyd, 1960-68	57
Punting (Avg.)	Pat McAfee, 2009-2013	45.6
Punt Return (Avg.)	Ron Gardin, 1970-71	13.5
Kickoff Return (Avg.)	Jim Duncan, 1969-1971	32.6
Field Goals	Mike Vanderjagt, 1998-2005	217
Touchdowns (Tot.)	Marvin Harrison, 1996-2008	128
Points	Mike Vanderjagt, 1998-2005	995
*Sacks	Robert Mathis, 2003-2013	111.0

INDIVIDUAL RECORDS—SINGLE SEASON

Category	Name	Performance
Rushing (Yds.)	Edgerrin James, 2000	1,709
Passing (Yds.)	Peyton Manning, 2010	4,700
Passing (TDs)	Peyton Manning, 2004	49
Receiving (No.)	Marvin Harrison, 2002	**143
Receiving (Yds.)	Marvin Harrison, 2002	1,722
Interceptions	Tom Keane, 1953	11
Punting (Avg.)	Pat McAfee, 2012	48.2
Punt Return (Avg.)	T.J. Rushing, 2007	13.1
Kickoff Return (Avg.)	Jim Duncan, 1970	35.4
Field Goals	Mike Vanderjagt, 2003	37
Touchdowns (Tot.)	Lenny Moore, 1964	20
Points	Mike Vanderjagt, 2003	157
*Sacks	Robert Mathis, 2013	19.5

INDIVIDUAL RECORDS—SINGLE GAME

Category	Name	Performance
Rushing (Yds.)	Edgerrin James, 10-15-00	219
Passing (Yds.)	Peyton Manning, 10-31-04	472
Passing (TDs)	Peyton Manning, 9-28-03, 11-25-04	6
Receiving (No.)	Reggie Wayne, 10-3-10	15
Receiving (Yds.)	Raymond Berry, 11-10-57	224
Interceptions	Many times	3
	Last time by Mike Prior, 12-20-92	
Field Goals	Many times	5
	Last time by Adam Vinatieri, 12-1-13	
Touchdowns (Tot.)	Many times	4
	Last time by Joseph Addai, 11-26-06	
Points	Many times	24
	Last time by Joseph Addai, 11-26-06	
*Sacks	Johnie Cooks, 11-25-84	4.5

*Sacks became an official statistic in 1982.
**NFL Record

2014 VETERAN ROSTER

No.	Name	Pos.	Ht.	Wt.	Birthdate	NFL Exp.	College	Hometown	How Acq.	'13 Games/ Starts
83	Allen, Dwayne	TE	6-3	265	2/24/90	3	Clemson	Fayetteville, N.C.	D3-'12	1/1
32	Anderson, Colt	S	5-10	194	10/25/85	5	Montana	Butte, Mont.	FA-'14	14/0*
65	Austin, Thomas	C	6-4	310	11/14/86	3	Clemson	Camden, S.C.	FA-'13	1/0
33	Ballard, Vick	RB	5-10	224	7/16/90	3	Mississippi State	Pascagoula, Miss.	D5-'12	1/1
44	Bradshaw, Ahmad	RB	5-10	217	3/19/86	8	Marshall	Bluefield, Va.	FA-'13	3/2
15	Brazill, LaVon	WR	5-11	200	3/15/89	3	Ohio	Lantana, Fla.	D6-'12	10/0
38	Brown, Sergio	S	6-2	218	5/22/88	5	Notre Dame	Maywood, Ill.	W(NE)-'12	14/0
20	Butler, Darius	CB	5-10	188	3/18/86	6	Connecticut	Tamarac, Fla.	W-'12	16/7
74	Castonzo, Anthony	T	6-7	311	8/9/88	4	Boston College	Hawthorn Woods, Ill.	D1-'11	16/16
96	Chapman, Josh	NT	6-0	341	6/10/90	3	Alabama	Hoover, Ala.	D5-'12	13/0
78	Cherilus, Gosder	T	6-7	316	6/28/84	7	Boston College	Somerville, Mass.	UFA(Det)-'13	16/16
21	Davis, Vontae	CB	5-11	204	5/27/88	6	Illinois	Washington, D.C.	T(Mia)-'12	16/16
84	Doyle, Jack	TE	6-6	258	5/5/90	2	Western Kentucky	Indianapolis, Ind.	W(Tenn)-'13	15/4
80	Fleener, Coby	TE	6-6	251	9/20/88	3	Stanford	Lemont, Ill.	D2-'12	16/12
50	Freeman, Jerrell	ILB	6-0	240	5/1/86	3	Mary Hardin-Baylor	Waco, Texas	FA-'12	16/16
27	Gordy, Josh	CB	5-11	196	2/9/87	4	Central Michigan	Warthen, Ga.	T(StL)-'12	12/0
49	Harvey, Mario	ILB	6-0	264	8/10/87	3	Marshall	Forsyth, Ga.	FA-'12	12/0
8	Hasselbeck, Matt	QB	6-4	235	9/25/75	16	Boston College	Norfolk, Mass.	FA-'13	3/0
39	Havili, Stanley	FB	6-0	243	11/14/87	3	Southern California	Salt Lake City, Utah	T(Phil)-'13	13/8
36	Herron, Daniel	RB	5-10	212	3/21/89	2	Ohio State	Warren, Ohio	FA-'13	6/0
55	Hickman, Justin	OLB	6-2	249	7/20/85	3	UCLA	Glendale, Ariz.	FA-'12	0*
13	Hilton, T.Y.	WR	5-9	178	11/14/89	3	Florida International	Miami, Fla.	D3-'12	16/10
62	Holmes, Khaled	C/G	6-3	319	1/19/90	2	Southern California	Santa Ana, Calif.	D4-'13	3/0
26	Howell, Delano	S	5-11	197	11/17/89	3	Stanford	Newhall, Calif.	FA-'12	6/3
94	Hughes, Montori	DT	6-4	349	8/25/90	2	Tennessee-Martin	Murfreesboro, Tenn.	D5-'13	4/0
52	Jackson, D'Qwell	ILB	6-0	240	9/26/83	9	Maryland	Largo, Fla.	FA-'14	16/16*
99	Jean Francois, Ricky	DT	6-3	297	11/23/86	6	Louisiana State	Miami, Fla.	UFA(SF)-'13	10/10
59	Johnson, Cam	OLB	6-3	268	5/24/90	2	Virginia	Washington, D.C.	T(SF)-'13	12/0
97	Jones, Arthur	DE	6-3	315	6/3/86	5	Syracuse	Rochester, N.Y.	UFA(Balt)-'14	14/13*
30	Landry, LaRon	S	6-0	226	10/14/84	8	Louisiana State	Metairie, La.	UFA(NYJ)-'13	12/12
60	Louis, Lance	G	6-3	320	4/24/85	5	San Diego State	New Orleans, La.	FA-'14	0*
12	Luck, Andrew	QB	6-4	240	9/12/89	3	Stanford	Houston, Texas	D1-'12	16/16
42	Lynch, Corey	S	6-0	210	5/7/85	7	Appalachian State	Cape Coral, Fla.	FA-'13	8/0*
98	Mathis, Robert	OLB	6-2	246	2/26/81	12	Alabama A&M	Atlanta, Ga.	D5-'03	16/16
1	McAfee, Pat	P	6-1	233	5/2/87	6	West Virginia	Plum, Pa.	D7-'09	16/0
95	Moala, Fili	DE	6-4	308	6/23/85	6	Southern California	Buena Park, Calif.	D2-'09	16/6
48	Morgan, Aaron	LB	6-4	250	12/30/88	4	Louisiana-Monroe	New Orleans, La.	FA-'14	0*
14	Nicks, Hakeem	WR	6-1	208	1/14/88	6	North Carolina	Charlotte, N.C.	UFA(NYG)-'14	15/15*
71	Nixon, Xavier	T	6-6	314	9/17/90	2	Florida	Fayetteville, N.C.	FA-'13	4/1
45	Overton, Matt	LS	6-1	242	7/6/85	3	Western Washington	Tracy, Calif.	FA-'12	16/0
61	Pendleton, Jeris	DT	6-2	334	11/7/83	2	Ashland	Chicago, Ill.	FA-'13	1/0
25	Rainey, Chris	RB	5-9	180	3/2/88	3	Florida	Lakeland, Fla.	FA-'13	2/0
90	Redding, Cory	DE	6-4	318	11/15/80	12	Texas	Houston, Texas	UFA(Balt)-'12	15/15
76	Reitz, Joe	G	6-7	323	8/24/85	4	Western Michigan	Fishers, Ind.	FA-'10	14/3
34 t-	Richardson, Trent	RB	5-9	225	7/10/90	3	Alabama	Pensacola, Fla.	T(Cle)-'13	16/10*
16	Rogers, Da'Rick	WR	6-3	215	6/18/91	2	Tennessee Tech	Atlanta, Ga.	FA-'13	5/3
47	Saunders, Weslye	TE	6-5	261	1/16/89	4	South Carolina	Durham, N.C.	FA-'13	6/1
53	Sheppard, Kelvin	ILB	6-2	256	1/2/88	4	Louisiana State	Stone Mountain, Ga.	T(Buff)-'13	15/7
35	Sims, David	S	5-10	210	10/20/86	2	Iowa State	Gainesville, Fla.	FA-'14	0*
58	Studebaker, Andy	OLB	6-3	248	9/16/85	7	Wheaton	Congerville, Ill.	FA-'13	11/0
66	Thomas, Donald	G	6-4	308	9/25/85	7	Connecticut	West Haven, Conn.	UFA(NE)-'13	2/2
69	Thornton, Hugh	G	6-3	334	6/28/91	2	Illinois	Oberlin, Ohio	D3-'13	14/12
28	Toler, Greg	CB	6-0	190	1/2/85	6	St. Paul's	Washington, D.C.	UFA(Ariz)-'13	9/7
4	Vinatieri, Adam	K	6-0	208	12/28/72	19	South Dakota State	Rapid City, S.D.	UFA(NE)-'06	15/0
93	Walden, Erik	OLB	6-2	250	8/21/85	7	Middle Tennessee St.	Dublin, Ga.	UFA(GB)-'13	15/15
87	Wayne, Reggie	WR	6-0	200	11/17/78	14	Miami	New Orleans, La.	D1-'01	7/7
92	Werner, Bjoern	OLB	6-3	260	8/30/90	2	Florida State	Berlin, Germany	D1-'13	13/1
17	Whalen, Griff	WR	5-11	198	3/1/90	3	Stanford	Sylvania, Ohio	FA-'12	9/3

* Anderson played 14 games with Philadelphia in '13; Hickman missed '13 season because of injury; Jackson played 16 games with Cleveland; Jones played 14 games with Baltimore; Louis last active with Chicago in '12; Lynch played three games with Tennessee and five games with Indianapolis; Morgan last active with Tampa Bay in '12; Nicks played 15 games with the New York Giants; Richardson played two games with Cleveland; Richardson played two games with Cleveland and 14 games with Indianapolis; Sims last active with Philadelphia in '12.

t- Colts traded for Richardson (Cle).

Players lost through free agency (9): S Antoine Bethea (SF; 16 games), RB Donald Brown (SD; 16), ILB Kavell Conner (SD; 10), NT Aubrayo Franklin (Ind; 16), WR Darrius Heyward-Bey (Pitt; 16), T Jeff Linkenbach (KC; 12), DT Ricardo Mathews (Hou; 16), G Mike McGlynn (Wash; 15), CB Cassius Vaughn (Det; 16).

Also played with Colts in '13—ILB Pat Angerer (11 games), S Larry Asante (5), CB Jalil Brown (5), RB Tashard Choice (3), TE Justice Cunningham (1), DE Lawrence Guy (2), FB Robert Hughes (1), TE Dominique Jones (6), WR David Reed (7), C Samson Satele (13), RB Kerwynn Williams (1), Joe Young (4).

FIRST-YEAR ROSTER

Name	Pos.	Ht.	Wt.	Birthdate	College	Hometown	How Acq.
Adongo, Daniel (1)	OLB	6-5	257	10/12/89	Pretoria (South Africa)	Nairobi, Kenya	FA-'13
Breckner, Jack	T	6-9	320	5/13/88	Gustavus Adolphus	Wayzata, Minn.	FA
Burley, Marcus (1)	CB	5-10	185	7/16/90	Delaware	Richmond, Va.	FA
Cox, Qua	CB	6-0	185	4/28/91	Jackson State	Tuskegee, Ala.	FA
Hall, Marcus	G	6-5	315	3/9/90	Ohio State	Cleveland, Ohio	FA
Harnish, Chandler (1)	QB	6-2	222	7/28/88	Northern Illinois	Bluffton, Ind.	D7-'12
Harrison, Jonotthan	C	6-4	299	8/25/91	Florida	Groveland, Fla.	FA
Hoover, Tyler	DE	6-7	290	1/28/90	Michigan State	Novi, Mich.	FA
Jackson, Andrew	ILB	6-1	254	3/16/92	Western Kentucky	Lakeland, Fla.	D6
Jackson, Kameron	CB	5-9	175	10/31/93	California	Long Beach, Calif.	FA
John, Ulrick	T	6-5	288	5/20/92	Georgia State	Hinesville, Ga.	D7
Kerr, Zach	NT	6-2	310	8/29/90	Delaware	Gaithersburg, Md.	FA
Lankford, Ryan	WR	5-11	163	12/9/91	Illinois	Jacksonville, Fla.	FA
Lenz, Josh (1)	WR	6-0	194	9/22/90	Iowa State	Dubuque, Iowa	FA-'13
Lobato, Seth	QB	6-6	223	12/5/90	Northern Colorado	Eaton, Colo.	FA
Lyn, Keon	CB	6-1	190	3/5/92	Syracuse	Miramar, Fla.	FA
McDonald, Dewey	S	6-0	220	6/10/90	California (PA)	Ranson, W.Va.	FA
McNary, Josh (1)	ILB	6-0	251	4/10/88	Army	Houston, Texas	FA-'13
Mewhort, Jack	T/G	6-6	309	9/30/91	Ohio State	Toledo, Ohio	D2
Moncrief, Donte	WR	6-2	221	8/6/93	Mississippi	Raleigh, Miss.	D3
Muamba, Henoc	LB	6-0	238	2/23/89	St. Francis Xavier	Kinshasa, Dem. Rep. of the Congo	FA
Newsome, Jonathan	DE	6-3	236	1/22/91	Ball State	Cleveland, Ohio	D5
Obukwelu, Nnamdi	DE	6-3	275	4/13/91	Harvard	Brockton, Mass.	FA
Parkey, Cody	K	6-0	190	2/19/92	Auburn	Jupiter, Fla.	FA
Price, Sheldon (1)	CB	6-2	186	3/26/91	UCLA	Chino Hills, Calif.	FA-'13
Purifoy, Loucheiz	CB	6-1	189	12/16/92	Florida	Pensacola, Fla.	FA
Swoope, Erik	TE	6-5	220	5/8/92	Miami	Lake Elsinore, Calif.	FA
Thomas, Eric	WR	6-1	209	11/11/91	Troy	Shreveport, La.	FA
Tipton, Zurlon	RB	6-0	221	4/27/90	Central Michigan	Detroit, Mich.	FA
Walker, Josh	G	6-5	323	6/2/91	Middle Tennessee State	Spring City, Tenn.	FA
Washington, Tony	WR	5-11	200	10/18/90	Appalachian State	High Point, N.C.	FA
White, Cameron	FB	6-2	251	7/15/90	Hillsdale College	Grand Rapids, Mich.	FA

The term NFL Rookie is defined as a player who is in his first season of professional football and has not been on the roster of another professional football team for any regular-season or postseason games. A Rookie is designated by an "R" on NFL rosters. Players who have been active in another professional football league or players who have NFL experience, including either preseason training camp or being on an Active List or Inactive List, or on Reserve/Injured or Reserve/Physically Unable to Perform for fewer than six regular-season games, are termed NFL First-Year Players. An NFL First-Year Player is designated by a "1" on NFL rosters. Thereafter, a player is credited with an additional year of experience for each season in which he accumulates six games on the Active List or Inactive List, or on Reserve/Injured or Reserve/Physically Unable to Perform.

Log on to www.colts.com for an up-to-date roster.

COACHING STAFF

Head Coach,
Chuck Pagano

Pro Career: Named head coach of the Indianapolis Colts on January 25, 2012. In two seasons as head coach of the Indianapolis Colts, Chuck Pagano has led the team to back-to-back 11-5 regular season records and playoff berths each year. The success culminated with an AFC South Division Championship in 2013 preceding an AFC Wild Card Playoff victory against the Kansas City Chiefs in a game that marked the second-largest comeback in NFL postseason history. Pagano became the first head coach in team history and the eighth in NFL annals to lead a team to 11 wins in each of his first two seasons. He has coached 32 games without losing consecutive contests, which is the second-longest streak for a Colts head coach and the longest streak to start a career in franchise history. In 2013, Indianapolis recorded a perfect 6-0 division record for the first time since 2009 and claimed its eighth division title since 2002. In 2013, Indianapolis placed 17 players on Injured Reserve, including six starters, and witnessed an NFL-high 73 different players take at least one snap with the team. In 2012, the Colts overcame the loss of Pagano to acute promyelocytic leukemia for 12 games and responded with seven fourth quarter or overtime game-winning drives en route to an 11-5 campaign. Previously spent four seasons with the Baltimore Ravens, the last (2011) as the team's defensive coordinator. Pagano also served as the defensive backs coach of the Oakland Raiders (2005-06) and the secondary coach of the Cleveland Browns (2001-04). Career record: 23-12.

Background: Pagano was a safety at Wyoming from 1980-83. Coached collegiately at Southern California (1984-85), Miami (1986), Boise State (1987-88), East Carolina (1989), Nevada-Las Vegas (1990-91), East Carolina (1992-94), Miami (1995-2000), North Carolina (2007).

Personal: Born in Boulder, Colo. on October 2, 1960. He and wife, Tina, have three daughters: Tara, Taylor, Tori. His brother, John, is the San Diego Chargers' defensive coordinator.

ASSISTANT COACHES

Roy Anderson, safeties; born October 5, 1979, Tallahassee, Fla. Quarterback Howard 1997-2001. No pro playing experience. Pro coach: Baltimore Ravens 2009-2011, joined Colts in 2012.

Tim Berbenich, offensive assistant; born December 19, 1979, Huntington, N.Y. Wide receiver Hamilton College 1999-2002. No pro playing experience. Pro coach: New York Jets 2002-2005, Tampa Bay Buccaneers 2006-2011, joined Colts in 2013.

Brant Boyer, asst. special teams; born June 27, 1971, Ogden, Utah. Linebacker Arizona 1992-94. Pro linebacker Miami Dolphins 1994, Jacksonville Jaguars 1995-2000, Cleveland Browns 2001-03. Pro coach: Joined Colts in 2012.

Clyde Christensen, quarterbacks; born January 28, 1956, Covina, Calif. Quarterback Fresno City College 1975, North Carolina 1976-78. No pro playing experience. College coach: Mississippi 1979, East Tennessee State 1980-82, Temple 1983-85, East Carolina 1986-88, Holy Cross 1989-1990, South Carolina 1991, Maryland 1992-93, Clemson 1994-95. Pro coach: Tampa Bay Buccaneers 1996-2001, joined Colts in 2002.

Rob Chudzinski, special asst. to the head coach; born May 12, 1968, Toledo, Ohio. Tight end Miami 1986-1990. No pro playing experience. College coach: Miami 1994-2003. Pro coach: Cleveland Browns 2004, 2007-08, 2013 (head coach 2013), San Diego Chargers 2005-06, 2009-2010, Carolina Panthers 2011-12, joined Colts in 2014.

Gary Emanuel, defensive line; born October 30, 1958, New London, Conn. Offensive lineman Westchester (N.Y.) C.C. 1976-78, Plymouth State 1979-1980. No pro playing experience. College coach: Plymouth State 1981-84, West Chester 1985-86, Massachusetts 1986-88, Dartmouth 1988-1990, Syracuse 1991-93, Washington State 1994-96, Purdue 1997-2004, San Jose State 2007, Rutgers 2008-09, Purdue 2010-11. Pro coach: San Francisco 49ers 2005-06, joined Colts in 2012.

Jeff FitzGerald, linebackers; born April 18, 1960, Burbank, Calif. Linebacker Oregon State 1980. No pro playing experience. College coach: Cincinnati 1985, Alabama 1986-89, San Diego State 1994-97. Pro coach: Tampa Bay Buccaneers 1990-93, Washington Redskins 1998-99, Arizona Cardinals 2000-03, Baltimore Ravens 2004-07, Cincinnati Bengals 2008-2011, joined Colts in 2012.

Joe Gilbert, offensive line; born January 22, 1965, Horseheads, N.Y. Offensive lineman Hamilton University 1984-87. No pro playing experience. College coach: Albany 1987-88, Pennsylvania 1989-1990, Northeastern 1991-93, Maine 1994-99, Mansfield 2000 (head coach), Toledo 2001-03, Central Florida 2004-06, Toledo 2007, Houston 2008, Illinois 2009-2011. Pro coach: Joined Colts in 2012.

Mike Gillhamer, secondary; born February 20, 1956, Oakland, Calif. Defensive back Carroll College 1972, Wenatchee (Wash.) J.C. 1973, Humboldt State 1974-75. No pro playing experience. College coach: College of the Sequoias 1979-1983, Weber State 1984, Utah 1985-89, San Jose State 1990-93, Nevada 1994-95, Oregon 2001-02, Louisville 2003, Illinois 2011. Pro coach: New York Giants 1997-2000, Carolina Panthers 2004-2010, joined Colts in 2012.

Frank Giufre, offensive quality control; born April 5, 1977, Canastota, N.Y. Offensive lineman Syracuse 1995-99. No pro playing experience. College coach: Miami 2001-03, Sacred Heart 2004-06, Maine 2007-2011. Pro coach: Joined Colts in 2012.

Pep Hamilton, offensive coordinator; born September 19, 1974, Charlotte, N.C. Quarterback Howard 1993-96. No pro playing experience. College coach: Howard 1997-2001, Stanford 2010-12. Pro coach: Kansas City Chiefs 2000, Washington Redskins 2001, Baltimore Ravens 2002, New York Jets 2003-05, San Francisco 49ers 2006, Chicago Bears 2007-09, joined Colts in 2013.

Richard Howell, asst. strength & conditioning; born February 19, 1972, Bladenboro, N.C. Quarterback Davidson 1990-93. No pro playing experience. College coach: Davidson 1994-98, North Carolina 1998-99, joined Colts in 2000.

Hal Hunter, asst. offensive line; born July 8, 1959, Canonsburg, Pa. Linebacker Northwestern 1978. No pro playing experience. College coach: William & Mary 1982, Pittsburgh 1983-84, Columbia 1985, Indiana (Pa.) 1986, Akron 1987-1990, Vanderbilt 1991-94, Louisiana State 1995-99, Indiana 2000-01, North Carolina 2002-05. Pro coach: San Diego Chargers 2006-2012, joined Colts in 2013.

Greg Manusky, defensive coordinator; born August 12, 1966, Wilkes-Barre, Pa. Linebacker Colgate 1983-87. Pro linebacker Washington Redskins 1988-1990, Minnesota Vikings 1991-93, Kansas City Chiefs 1994-99. Pro coach: Washington Redskins 2001, San Diego Chargers 2002-06, San Francisco 49ers 2007-2010, San Diego Chargers 2011, joined Colts in 2012.

Roger Marandino, strength & conditioning; born February 19, 1971, Elmer, N.J. No college or pro playing experience. College coach: Connecticut 1993-95, Brown 1995-2011. Pro coach: Philadelphia Eagles 2011, joined Colts in 2012.

Tom McMahon, special teams coordinator; Helena, Mont. Carroll College 1988-1991. No pro playing experience. College coach: Carroll College 1992, 1994, Utah State 1995-2005, Louisville 2006. Pro coach: Atlanta Falcons 2007-08, St. Louis Rams 2009-2011, Kansas City Chiefs 2012, joined Colts in 2013.

Alfredo Roberts, tight ends; born March 17, 1965, Fort Lauderdale, Fla. Tight end Miami 1983-87. Pro tight end Kansas City Chiefs 1988-1990, Dallas Cowboys 1991-93. College coach: Florida Atlantic 1999-2002. Pro coach: Jacksonville Jaguars 2003-06, Cleveland Browns 2007-08, Tampa Bay Buccaneers 2009-2011, joined Colts in 2012.

David Walker, running backs; born December 4, 1969, Rochester, N.Y. Running back Syracuse 1989-1992. No pro playing experience. College coach: Syracuse 1995-2004, Pittsburgh 2005-2010. Pro coach: Joined Colts in 2011.

Brad White, asst. linebackers; born August 13, 1982, Concord, Mass. Linebacker Georgia 2000, Wake Forest 2002-04. No pro playing experience. College coach: Wake Forest 2007-08, Murray State 2009, Air Force 2010-11. Pro coach: Joined Colts in 2012.

Charlie Williams, wide receivers; born January 31, 1958, Torrance, Calif. Defensive back Colorado State 1978-79. No pro playing experience. College coach: Long Beach City College 1984, New Mexico 1986-87, Texas Christian 1991, Minnesota 1992, Miami 1993-95, South Carolina 2003, Arizona 2004-06, North Carolina 2007-2011. Pro coach: Tampa Bay Buccaneers 1996-2001, joined Colts in 2012.

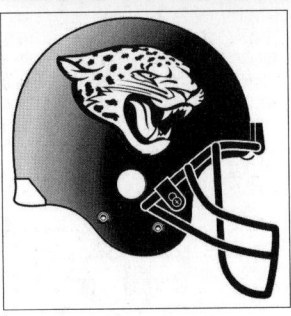

American Football Conference
South Division
Team Colors: Teal, Black, and Gold
EverBank Field
One EverBank Field Drive
Jacksonville, Florida 32202
Telephone: (904) 633-6000

2014 SCHEDULE
PRESEASON
Aug. 8   **Tampa Bay**........................7:30
Aug. 14   at Chicago.........................8:00
Aug. 22   at Detroit...........................7:30
Aug. 28   **Atlanta**..............................6:00

REGULAR SEASON
Sep. 7   at Philadelphia 1:00
Sep. 14   at Washington 1:00
Sep. 21   **Indianapolis** 1:00
Sep. 28   at San Diego 4:05
Oct. 5   **Pittsburgh** 1:00
Oct. 12   at Tennessee 1:00
Oct. 19   **Cleveland** 1:00
Oct. 26   **Miami** 1:00
Nov. 2   at Cincinnati 1:00
Nov. 9   **Dallas** (London).................1:00
Nov. 16   BYE
Nov. 23   at Indianapolis 1:00
Nov. 30   **New York Giants**................1:00
Dec. 7   **Houston** 1:00
Dec. 14   at Baltimore 1:00
Dec. 18   **Tennessee** (Thu)................8:25
Dec. 28   at Houston 1:00
All times ET
Stadium: EverBank Field
   (opened in 1995)
   •**Capacity:** 67,297
   One EverBank Field Drive
   Jacksonville, Florida 32202
Playing Surface: Grass
Training Camp: EverBank Field
   One EverBank Field Drive
   Jacksonville, Florida 32202

EVERBANK FIELD

CLUB OFFICIALS
Owner: Shahid Khan
President: Mark Lamping
General Manager: David Caldwell
Senior Vice President, Communications:
   Dan Edwards
Senior Vice President, Fan Engagement:
   Hussain Naqi
Senior Vice President, Corporate
   Partnerships: Scott Massey
Senior Vice President, Ticket Sales:
   Chad Johnson
Vice President and General Counsel:
   Megha Parekh
Vice President, Finance and Planning;
   Kelly Flanagan
President, Jaguars Foundation:
   Peter Racine

Assistant Director, Player Personnel:
   Andy Dengler
Director, College Scouting: Kyle O'Brien
Assistant Director, College Scouting:
   Paul Roell
Eastern Regional Scout: Mark Ellenz
College Scouts: Jason DesJarlais,
   Jarrod Highberger, Marty Miller,
   Tim Mingey, Brian Simmons
BLESTO Scout: Jared Kirksey
Director of Pro Personnel: Chris Polian
Pro Scout: Chris Driggers
Scouting Assistants: Kevin Mashak,
   Antonio Robinson
Executive Assistant, Player Personnel:
   Dana DesJarlais

Senior Vice President, Football
   Technology & Analytics: Tony Khan
Director, Football Research: Daniel Adler
Director, Team Security: Skip Richardson
Director, Football Administration:
   Tim Walsh
Director, Player Development:
   Marcus Pollard
Director, Football Logistics & Facilities:
   Hamzah Ahmad
Head Athletic Trainer: Scott Trulock
Director, Football Technology:
   Mike Perkins
Equipment Manager: Jimmy Luck

Director, Public Relations: Ryan Robinson
Public Relations Coordinator:
   Tad Dickman
Manager, Communications: Katie Vaughn
Vice President, Corporate Sales:
   Mike DeMartino
Controller: Debye Whelchel
Director, Information Technology:
   Mike Webb
Director, Marketing: Genya Adesso
Director, Ticket Sales: Sean Flood
Director, Ticket Operations & Service:
   Tim Bishko
Director, Game Events/Production: Kurt
   Wisenbaugh
Director, Guest Services: Angie Nix
Director, Partner Relations: Anne Boccuzzi
Director, Finance & Funding Development,
   Foundation: Janet Burnside
Director, Financial Planning and Analysis:
   Maureen Brown

COACHING HISTORY
(149-166-0)
Records include postseason games
1995-2002   Tom Coughlin.............72-64-0
2003-2011   Jack Del Rio*...........69-73-0
2011   Mel Tucker....................2-3-0
2012   Mike Mularkey 2-14-0
2013   Gus Bradley.................4-12-0
   *Released after 11 games in 2011

PAID ATTENDANCE
Home 399,819   Away 504,120
Total 903,939
Single-game home record,
   74,143 (12/28/98), EverBank Field
   83,559 (10/27/13), Wembley Stadium
Single-season home record,
   561,472 (1998)

2014 DRAFT CHOICES
Round	Name	Pos.	College
1	Blake Bortles	QB	Central Florida
2	Marqise Lee	WR	Southern California
	Allen Robinson	WR	Penn St.
3	Brandon Linder	G	Miami
4	Aaron Colvin	DB	Oklahoma
5	Telvin Smith	LB	Florida St.
	Chris Smith	DE	Arkansas
6	Luke Bowanko	C	Virginia
7	Storm Johnson	RB	Central Florida

JACKSONVILLE JAGUARS

2013 TEAM RECORD
PRESEASON (1-3)

Date	Result		Opponent
08/09	L	3-27	Miami
08/17	L	13-37	at New York Jets
08/24	L	24-31	Philadelphia
08/29	W	20-16	at Atlanta

REGULAR SEASON (4-12)

Date	Result		Opponent
09/08	L	2-28	Kansas City
09/15	L	9-19	at Oakland
09/22	L	17-45	at Seattle
09/29	L	3-37	Indianapolis
10/06	L	20-34	at St. Louis
10/13	L	19-35	at Denver
10/20	L	6-24	San Diego
10/27	L	10-42	San Francisco
11/10	W	29-27	at Tennessee
11/17	L	14-27	Arizona
11/24	W	13-6	at Houston
12/01	W	32-28	at Cleveland
12/05	W	27-20	Houston
12/15	L	20-27	Buffalo
12/22	L	16-20	Tennessee
12/29	L	10-30	at Indianapolis

SCORE BY PERIODS

Jaguars	70	66	50	61	0	—	247
Opponents	107	139	102	101	0	—	449

2013 TEAM STATISTICS

	Jaguars	Opp.
Total First Downs	271	353
Rushing	71	121
Passing	176	200
Penalty	24	32
3rd Down: Made/Att	70/225	96/226
3rd Down Pct.	31.1	42.5
4th Down: Made/Att	13/30	9/12
4th Down Pct.	43.3	75.0
Possession Avg.	27:22	32:38
Total Net Yards	4701	6070
Avg. Per Game	293.8	379.4
Total Plays	1020	1089
Avg. Per Play	4.6	5.6
Net Yards Rushing	1260	2108
Avg. Per Game	78.8	131.8
Total Rushes	378	507
Net Yards Passing	3441	3962
Avg. Per Game	215.1	247.6
Sacked/Yards Lost	50/310	31/225
Gross Yards	3751	4187
Att./Completions	592/349	551/354
Completion Pct.	59.0	64.2
Had Intercepted	21	11
Punts/Average	95/45.7	76/43.0
Net Punting Avg.	95/40.5	76/39.3
Penalties/Yards	96/797	87/729
Fumbles/Ball Lost	18/6	27/10
Touchdowns	25	53
Rushing	7	20
Passing	16	29
Returns	2	4

2013 INDIVIDUAL STATISTICS

PASSING

	Att.	Comp.	Yds.	Pct.	TD	Int.	Tkld.	Rate
Henne	503	305	3241	60.6	13	14	38/243	76.5
Gabbert	86	42	481	48.8	1	7	12/67	36.0
Jones-Drew	1	1	8	100.0	1	0	0/0	139.6
Robinson	1	0	0	0.0	0	0	0/0	39.6
Sanders	1	1	21	100.0	1	0	0/0	158.3
Jaguars	592	349	3751	59.0	16	21	50/310	71.8
Opponents	551	354	4187	64.2	29	11	31/225	96.5

SCORING

	TD R	TD P	TD Rt	PAT	FG	Saf	PTS
Scobee	0	0	0	22/23	23/25	0	91
Jones-Drew	5	0	0	0/0	0/0	0	30
M. Lewis	0	4	0	0/0	0/0	0	24
Shorts	0	3	0	0/0	0/0	0	18
Todman	2	1	0	0/0	0/0	0	18
Brown	0	2	0	0/0	0/0	0	12
Harbor	0	2	0	0/0	0/0	0	12
J. Blackmon	0	1	0	0/0	0/0	0	6
W. Blackmon	0	0	1	0/0	0/0	0	6
Noble	0	1	0	0/0	0/0	0	6
Posluszny	0	0	1	0/0	0/0	0	6
Sanders	0	1	0	0/0	0/0	0	6
Taylor	0	1	0	0/0	0/0	0	6
J. Thomas	0	0	0	0/0	0/0	1	2
Jaguars	7	16	2	22/23	23/25	3	247
Opponents	20	29	4	53/53	26/29	0	449

2-Pt Conversions: Jaguars 0-2, Opponents 0-0

RUSHING

	No.	Yds	Avg	LG	TD
Jones-Drew	234	803	3.4	48	5
Todman	76	256	3.4	33	2
Henne	27	77	2.9	14	0
Robinson	20	66	3.3	24	0
Gabbert	9	32	3.6	7	0
Forsett	6	31	5.2	10	0
Sanders	2	4	2.0	4	0
Ta'ufo'ou	1	1	1.0	1	0
Anger	1	0	0.0	0	0
J. Blackmon	1	-1	-1.0	-1	0
Burton	1	-9	-9.0	-9	0
Jaguars	378	1260	3.3	48	7
Opponents	507	2108	4.2	50	20

RECEIVING

	No.	Yds	Avg	LG	TD
Shorts	66	777	11.8	59	3
Sanders	51	484	9.5	51	1
Jones-Drew	43	314	7.3	17	0
Brown	32	446	13.9	43	2
J. Blackmon	29	415	14.3	67t	1
M. Lewis	25	359	14.4	41	4
Harbor	24	292	12.2	31	2
Taylor	19	189	9.9	17	1
Forsett	15	82	5.5	14	0
Todman	14	116	8.3	30	1
Ta'ufo'ou	10	40	4.0	11	0
Burton	8	76	9.5	22	0
Reisner	5	40	8.0	16	0
Ebert	3	18	6.0	8	0
Noble	2	63	31.5	62t	1
L. Thomas	2	31	15.5	18	0
Meester	1	9	9.0	9	0
Jaguars	349	3751	10.7	67t	16
Opponents	354	4187	11.8	95t	29

PUNTING

	No.	Yds.	Avg.	In 20	LG
Anger	95	4338	45.7	31	61
Jaguars	95	4338	45.7	31	61
Opponents	76	3268	43.0	19	65

INTERCEPTIONS

	No.	Yds	Avg	LG	TD
Posluszny	2	69	34.5	59t	1
Hayes	2	39	19.5	28	0
Gratz	2	20	10.0	17	0
Ball	2	8	4.0	8	0
Cyprien	1	27	27.0	27	0
Davis	1	8	8.0	8	0
W. Blackmon	1	1	1.0	1	0
Jaguars	11	172	15.6	59t	1
Opponents	21	355	16.9	82t	3

PUNT RETURNS

	Ret	FC	Yds	Avg	LG	TD
Sanders	25	16	140	5.6	17	0
W. Blackmon	5	5	2	0.4	5	0
Jaguars	30	21	142	4.7	17	0
Opponents	47	22	330	7.0	38	0

KICKOFF RETURNS

	No.	Yds	Avg	LG	TD
Todman	26	712	27.4	59	0
Burton	4	99	24.8	32	0
Robinson	4	88	22.0	27	0
Sanders	3	75	25.0	31	0
Taylor	2	60	30.0	43	0
Forsett	1	21	21.0	21	0
Ta'ufo'ou	1	5	5.0	5	0
Jaguars	41	1060	25.9	59	0
Opponents	25	509	20.4	47	0

FIELD GOALS

	1-19	20-29	30-39	40-49	50+
Scobee	0/0	3/3	12/12	4/5	4/5
Jaguars	0/0	3/3	12/12	4/5	4/5
Opponents	0/0	10/10	9/10	6/6	1/3

SACKS

	No.
Babin	7.5
Branch	6.0
Marks	4.0
Posluszny	3.0
Mincey	2.0
Alualu	1.5
Allen	1.0
W. Blackmon	1.0
Cyprien	1.0
Davis	1.0
Guy	1.0
Hayes	1.0
Deaderick	0.5
Jones	0.5
Jaguars	31.0
Opponents	50.0

RECORD HOLDERS
INDIVIDUAL RECORDS—CAREER

Category	Name	Performance
Rushing (Yds.)	Fred Taylor, 1998-2008	11,271
Passing (Yds.)	Mark Brunell, 1995-2003	25,698
Passing (TDs)	Mark Brunell, 1995-2003	144
Receiving (No.)	Jimmy Smith, 1995-2005	862
Receiving (Yds.)	Jimmy Smith, 1995-2005	12,287
Interceptions	Rashean Mathis, 2003-2012	30
Punting (Avg.)	Bryan Anger, 2012-13	46.7
Punt Return (Avg.)	Bobby Shaw, 2002	12.4
Kickoff Return (Avg.)	Maurice Jones-Drew, 2006-2013	26.0
Field Goals	Josh Scobee, 2004-2013	215
Touchdowns (Tot.)	Maurice Jones-Drew, 2006-2013	81
Points	Josh Scobee, 2004-2013	939
*Sacks	Tony Brackens, 1996-2003	55.0

INDIVIDUAL RECORDS—SINGLE SEASON

Category	Name	Performance
Rushing (Yds.)	Maurice Jones-Drew, 2011	1,606
Passing (Yds.)	Mark Brunell, 1996	4,367
Passing (TDs)	David Garrard, 2010	23
Receiving (No.)	Jimmy Smith, 1999	116
Receiving (Yds.)	Jimmy Smith, 1999	1,636
Interceptions	Rashean Mathis, 2006	8
Punting (Avg.)	Bryan Anger, 2012	47.8
Punt Return (Avg.)	Reggie Barlow, 1998	12.9
Kickoff Return (Avg.)	Maurice Jones-Drew, 2006	27.7
Field Goals	Mike Hollis, 1997, 1999	31
Touchdowns (Tot.)	Fred Taylor, 1998	17
Points	Mike Hollis, 1997	134
*Sacks	Tony Brackens, 1999	12.0

INDIVIDUAL RECORDS—SINGLE GAME

Category	Name	Performance
Rushing (Yds.)	Fred Taylor, 11-19-00	234
Passing (Yds.)	Mark Brunell, 9-22-96	432
Passing (TDs)	Mark Brunell, 11-29-98	4
	Quinn Gray, 12-30-07	4
	David Garrard, 10-31-10	4
	Chad Henne, 11-18-12	4
Receiving (No.)	Keenan McCardell, 10-20-96	16
Receiving (Yds.)	Jimmy Smith, 9-10-00	291
Interceptions	Many times	2
	Last time by Derek Cox, 10-31-10	
Field Goals	Mike Hollis, 12-1-96, 11-30-97, 9-10-00	5
	Josh Scobee, 11-25-07, 10-10-10	5
Touchdowns (Tot.)	James Stewart, 10-12-97	5
Points	James Stewart, 10-12-97	30
*Sacks	Kelvin Pritchett, 10-5-97	3.0
	John Henderson, 10-6-02	3.0
	Paul Spicer, 9-25-05	3.0

Sacks became an official statistic in 1982.

2014 VETERAN ROSTER

No.	Name	Pos.	Ht.	Wt.	Birthdate	NFL Exp.	College	Hometown	How Acq.	'13 Games/ Starts
93	Alualu, Tyson	DE	6-3	295	5/12/87	5	California	Honolulu, Hawaii	D1-'10	16/16
19	Anger, Bryan	P	6-3	202	10/6/88	3	California	Camarillo, Calif.	D3-'12	16/0
58	Babin, Jason	DE	6-3	267	5/24/80	11	Western Michigan	Paw Paw, Mich.	W(Phil)-'12	16/16
23	Ball, Alan	DE	6-2	197	3/29/85	7	Illinois	Detroit, Mich.	UFA(Hou)-'13	15/15
68	Beadles, Zane	G	6-4	305	11/19/86	5	Utah	Casper, Wyoming	UFA(Den)-'14	16/16*
24	Blackmon, Will	CB	6-0	204	10/27/84	8	Boston College	Providence, R.I.	UFA(Sea)-'13	15/8
78	Bradfield, Cameron	OL	6-4	308	9/14/87	4	Grand Valley State	Grand Rapids, Mich.	FA-'11	15/11
43	Bradford, Allen	LB	5-11	235	8/31/88	3	Southern California	San Bernardino, Calif.	W(NYG)-'14	9/0*
90	Branch, Andre	DE	6-5	265	7/14/89	3	Clemson	Richmond, Va.	D2-'12	16/0
60	Brewster, Mike	G/C	6-4	305	7/27/89	3	Ohio State	Orlando, Fla.	FA-'12	14/3
12	Brown, Mike	WR	5-10	200	2/9/89	2	Liberty	Charlottesville, Va.	FA-'12	11/6
79	Bryant, Red	DE	6-4	323	4/18/84	7	Texas A&M	Jasper, Texas	UFA(Sea)-'14	15/15*
91	Clemons, Chris	DE	6-3	254	10/30/81	11	Georgia	Griffin, Ga.	UFA(Sea)-'14	14/11*
37	Cyprien, Johnathan	S	6-0	217	7/29/90	2	Florida International	N. Miami Beach, Fla.	D2-'13	15/15
59	Davis, Ryan	DE	6-2	260	2/24/89	2	Bethune-Cookman	Tampa, Fla.	FA-'13	7/0
17	Doss, Tandon	WR	6-2	205	9/22/89	4	Indiana	Indianapolis, Ind.	FA-'14	15/2*
26	Evans, Josh	S	6-0	205	6/5/91	2	Florida	Irvington, N.J.	D6-'13	15/11
33	Ewing, Bradie	FB	5-11	243	12/26/89	3	Wisconsin	Richland Center, Wisc.	W(Atl)-'14	2/2*
29	Fleming, Jamell	CB	5-11	206	5/5/89	3	Oklahoma	Arlington, Texas	W(Ariz)-'13	8/0
21	Gerhart, Toby	RB	6-0	231	3/28/87	5	Stanford	Norco, Calif.	UFA(Minn)-'14	14/0*
27	Gratz, Dwayne	CB	5-11	201	3/8/90	2	Connecticut	Piscataway, N.J.	D3-'13	10/8
22	Guy, Winston	S	6-1	218	4/23/90	3	Kentucky	Lexington, Ky.	W(Sea)-'13	14/2
86	Harbor, Clay	TE	6-3	255	7/2/87	5	Missouri State	Libertyville, Ill.	W(Phil)-'13	16/7
31	Harris, Jeremy	CB	6-2	185	4/26/91	2	New Mexico State	Dorsey, Calif.	D7a-'13	0*
20	Harris, Mike	CB	5-10	188	1/5/89	3	Florida State	Miami, Fla.	D6-'12	16/2
55	Hayes, Geno	LB	6-1	226	8/10/87	7	Florida State	Greenville, Fla.	UFA(Chi)-'13	14/14
7	Henne, Chad	QB	6-3	230	7/2/85	7	Michigan	Wyomissing, Pa.	UFA(Mia)-'12	15/13
92	Hood, Ziggy	DT	6-3	300	2/16/87	6	Missouri	Amarillo, Texas	UFA(Pitt)-'14	16/7*
76	Joeckel, Luke	OT	6-6	306	11/6/91	2	Texas A&M	Arlington, Texas	D1-'13	5/5
95	Jones, Abry	DT	6-4	312	9/8/91	2	Georgia	Warner Robins, Ga.	FA-'13	8/0
89	Lewis, Marcedes	TE	6-6	272	5/19/84	9	UCLA	Long Beach, Calif.	D1-'06	11/11
61	Lewis, Patrick	C	6-1	311	1/30/91	2	Texas A&M	Reserve, Louis.	PS(Cle)-'13	0*
53	Lotulelei, John	LB	5-11	233	12/4/91	2	Nevada-Las Vegas	Kihei, Hawaii	W(Sea) -'13	12/2
72	Love, DeMarcus	OT	6-4	315	3/7/88	3	Arkansas	Lancaster, Texas	FA-'13	0*
99	Marks, Sen'Derrick	DT	6-2	294	2/23/87	6	Auburn	Mobile, Ala.	UFA(Tenn)-'13	16/16
25	Martin, Sherrod	S	6-1	200	10/12/84	5	Troy	Griffin, Ga.	FA-'14	0*
66	McClendon, Jacques	G	6-3	324	12/10/87	3	Tennesse	Cleveland, Tenn.	W(Atl)-'13	5/2
35	McCray, Demetrius	CB	6-0	185	5/11/91	2	Appalachian State	Covington, Ga.	D7b-'13	16/1
97	Miller, Roy	DT	6-2	310	7/9/87	6	Texas	Killeen, Texas	UFA(TB)-'13	14/14
64	Nowak, Drew	G	6-3	300	3/7/90	2	Western Michigan	Green Bay, Wisc.	FA-'12	2/0
67	Pasztor, Austin	G	6-7	308	11/26/90	2	Virginia	Tillsonburg, Ontario	FA-'12	15/12
51	Posluszny, Paul	LB	6-2	242	10/10/84	8	Penn State	Aliquippa, Pa.	UFA(Buff)-'11	15/15
42	Prosinski, Chris	S	6-1	208	4/28/87	4	Wyoming	Buffalo, Wyo.	D4b-'11	16/1
56	Reynolds, LaRoy	LB	6-1	243	11/3/90	2	Virginia	Norfolk, Va.	FA-'13	12/0
94	Rivers, Gerald	DE	6-5	258	6/22/90	2	Mississippi	Ellenwood, Ga.	W(StL)-'13	2/0*
16	Robinson, Denard	WR	6-0	197	9/22/90	2	Michigan	Deerfield Beach, Fla.	D5-'13	16/0
18	Sanders, Ace	WR/PR	5-7	178	11/11/91	2	South Carolina	Bradenton, Fla.	D4-'13	15/4
10	Scobee, Josh	K	6-1	210	6/23/82	11	Louisiana Tech	Longview, Texas	D5a-'04	16/0
84	Shorts III, Cecil	WR	6-0	202	12/22/87	4	Mount Union	Cleveland, Ohio	D4a-'11	13/13
62	Stankiewitch, Matt	C	6-4	305	2/8/90	2	Penn State	Pottsville, Penn.	FA-'14	0*
2	Stanzi, Ricky	QB	6-4	228	9/3/87	4	Iowa	Mentor, Iowa	W(KC) -'13	0*
54	Stupar, Nate	LB	6-2	240	3/14/88	2	Penn State	State College, Penn.	W(SF)-'13	12/0*
45	Ta'ufo'ou, Will	FB	5-11	247	6/19/86	3	California	San Carlos, Calif.	FA-'12	16/7
13	Taylor, Kerry	WR	6-0	200	2/20/89	2	Arizona State	Chandler, Ariz.	PS(Ariz)-'13	10/0*
52	Thomas, J.T.	LB	6-1	236	8/15/88	4	West Virginia	Ft. Lauderdale, Fla.	W(Chi)-'13	15/2
46	Tinker, Carson	LS	6-0	233	11/15/89	2	Alabama	Murfreesboro, Tenn.	FA-'13	16/0
30	Todman, Jordan	RB	5-10	198	2/24/90	2	Connecticut	North Darmouth, Mass.	PS(Minn)-'12	16/2
57	Watson, Dekoda	LB	6-2	240	3/3/88	5	Florida State	Aiken, S.C.	UFA(TB)-'14	15/3*
36	Young, Joe	S	6-0	204	6/2/88	3	Rutgers	Germantown, Md.	FA-'14	4/0*
74	Young, Sam	OT	6-8	316	6/24/87	5	Notre Dame	Coral Springs, Fla.	W(Buff)-'13	15/0*

* Beadles played 16 games with Denver in '13; Bradford played nine games with the New York Giants; Bryant played 15 games with Seattle; Clemons played 14 games with Seattle; Doss played 15 games with Baltimore; Ewing played two games with Atlanta; Gerhart played 14 games with Minnesota; J. Harris missed the '13 season because of injury; Hood played 16 games with Pittsburgh; P. Lewis inactive two games; Love inactive three games; Martin was not on an NFL roster in '13; Rivers played two games with St. Louis; Stankiewitch was not on NFL roster in '13; Stanzi did not play in four games and inactive 11 games; Stupar played five games with San Francisco and seven games with Jacksonville; Taylor played three games with Arizona and seven games with Jacksonville; Watson played 15 games with Tampa Bay; J. Young played four games for Indianapolis; S. Young played four games with Buffalo and 11 games with Jacksonville.

Traded—QB Blaine Gabbert (three games in '13) to San Francisco, T Eugene Monroe (4) to Baltimore.

Retired—C Brad Meester, 14-year center, 16 games in '13.

Players lost through free agency (2): RB Maurice Jones-Drew (Oak; 15 games in '13), WR Taylor Price (Sea; 0).

Also played with Jaguars in '13—LB Russell Allen (14 games), WR Justin Blackmon (4), Stephen Burton (4), DT Brandon Deaderick (13), WR Jeremy Ebert (5), RB Justin Forsett (9), Kyle Knox (4), Kyle Love (1), S Dwight Lowery (3), DT Jordan Miller (2), DT Drake Nevis (1), TE Danny Noble (8), G Uche Nwaneri (16), WR Tobias Palmer (1), G/C Will Rackley (11), TE Allen Reisner (5), TE D.J. Williams (7), WR Stephen Williams (2).

FIRST-YEAR ROSTER

Name	Pos.	Ht.	Wt.	Birthdate	College	Hometown	How Acq.
Barden, Brandon (1)	TE	6-4	253	3/15/89	Vanderbilt	Lincolnton, Ga.	FA-'13
Blankenship, Beau	RB	5-9	206	8/13/90	Ohio	Norman, Okla.	FA
Bortles, Blake	QB	6-5	230	12/16/91	Central Florida	Oviedo, Fla.	D1
Bowanko, Luke	C	6-6	300	6/13/91	Virginia	Clifton, Va.	D6
Bumphis, Chad (1)	WR	5-10	202	10/18/89	Mississippi State	Tupelo, Miss.	FA-'13
Cobb, Terrance	RB	5-11	220	4/18/90	Cumberland (KY)	Knoxville, Tenn.	FA
Coleman, DeAndre	DT	6-3	255	1/27/91	California	Seattle, Wash.	FA
Colvin, Aaron	CB	6-0	186	10/2/91	Oklahoma	Tulsa, Okla.	D4
Copeland, Damian	WR	6-1	182	10/17/90	Louisville	Bradenton, Fla.	FA
Gillette, Trevor	LS	6-3	240	5/28/92	Rice	Austin, Texas	FA
Havili-Heimuli, Ricky	DT	6-4	314	9/18/91	Oregon	Glendale, Utah	FA
Hurns, Allen	WR	6-3	195	11/12/91	Miami	Miami, Fla.	FA
Jensen, Marcel	TE	6-6	270	2/12/90	Fresno State	Fairfield, Calif.	FA
Johnson, Storm	RB	6-0	216	7/10/92	Central Florida	Loganville, Ga.	D7
Jordan, Reggie	TE	6-3	240	7/3/91	Missouri-Western State	Hazelwood, Mo.	FA
Junior, Jerome	SS	6-1	207	9/8/90	Winston State-Salem	Baltimore, Md.	FA
Lee, Marqise	WR	6-0	192	11/25/91	Southern California	Inglewood, Calif.	D2
Linder, Brandon	G	6-5	311	1/25/92	Miami	Southwest Ranches, Fla.	D3
Loston, Craig	S	6-2	209	12/21/89	Louisiana State	Houston, Texas	FA
Miller, Jordan (1)	DT	6-1	316	2/1/88	Southern University	Marlboro, Md.	FA-'13
Morris, Stephen	QB	6-2	218	8/27/92	Miami	Miami, Fla.	FA
Reynolds, Rashaad	CB	5-11	187	2/2/91	Oregon State	Pacoima, Calif.	FA
Robinson, Allen	WR	6-3	210	8/24/93	Penn State	Southfield, Mich.	D2a
Shatley, Tyler	G	6-3	300	5/5/91	Clemson	Icard, N.C.	FA
Smith, Chris	DE	6-1	266	2/11/92	Arkansas	Mount Ulla, N.C.	D5
Smith, Telvin	LB	6-3	218	4/11/91	Florida State	Valdosta, Ga.	D5a
Thomas, Lamaar (1)	WR	6-0	185	4/23/90	New Mexico	Ft. Washington, Md.	FA-'13
Tialavea, D.J.	TE	6-4	260	7/27/91	Utah State	West Jordan, Utah	FA
Wells, Josh	OT	6-6	310	2/14/91	James Madison	Mechanicsville, Va.	FA
Whitfield, Marcus	LB	6-3	250	12/15/90	Maryland	Germantown, Md.	FA

The term NFL Rookie is defined as a player who is in his first season of professional football and has not been on the roster of another professional football team for any regular-season or postseason games. A Rookie is designated by an "R" on NFL rosters. Players who have been active in another professional football league or players who have NFL experience, including either preseason training camp or being on an Active List or Inactive List, or on Reserve/Injured or Reserve/Physically Unable to Perform for fewer than six regular-season games, are termed NFL First-Year Players. An NFL First-Year Player is designated by a "1" on NFL rosters. Thereafter, a player is credited with an additional year of experience for each season in which he accumulates six games on the Active List or Inactive List, or on Reserve/Injured or Reserve/Physically Unable to Perform.

Log on to www.jaguars.com for an up-to-date roster.

COACHING STAFF

Head Coach,
Gus Bradley

Pro Career: Gus Bradley was named the fifth head coach in Jacksonville Jaguars history on January 17, 2013. Bradley spent the previous four seasons (2009-12) with the Seattle Seahawks as defensive coordinator and played an important role in the club advancing to the postseason twice. Under Bradley's direction in 2012, the Seahawks led the NFL by allowing a franchise-record low 15.3 points per game despite playing with the third-youngest defensive starting unit in the league. He joined Seattle after spending three years (2006-08) with the Tampa Bay Buccaneers, serving the last two as linebackers coach after one season as their defensive quality control coach. Prior to Tampa Bay, Bradley spent 10 seasons (1996-2005) as an assistant coach at North Dakota State. He was the head coach at Fort Lewis College for four months (December 1995-March 1996) and was defensive coordinator/linebackers coach at Fort Lewis for four seasons (1992-1995). Prior to Fort Lewis, he was a graduate assistant coach at NDSU for two seasons (1990-1991). Career record: 4-12.

Background: Four-year letterman at North Dakota State (1984-1988), where he was a free safety and punter, a four-time academic All-North Central Conference selection and a member of the 1988 national championship football team. He earned his bachelor's degrees in business administration (1989) and physical education (1990) from North Dakota State as well as a master's degree in athletic administration from NDSU in 1992.

Personal: Born July 5, 1966 in Zumbrota, Minnesota. He and his wife, Michaela, have four children, Carter, Anna, Eli and Ella.

ASSISTANT COACHES

Bob Babich, defensive coordinator; born February 20, 1961, Aliquippa, Pa. Linebacker Mesa (Colo.) C.C. 1979-1980, Tulsa 1981-82. No pro playing experience. College coach: Tulsa 1984-87, 1990, Wisconsin 1988-89, Bowling Green 1991, East Carolina 1992-93, Pittsburgh 1994-96, North Dakota State 1997-2002 (head coach). Pro coach: St. Louis Rams 2003, Chicago Bears 2004-2012, joined Jaguars in 2013.

Luke Butkus, asst. offensive line coach; born June 26, 1979, Steger, Ill. Center Illinois 1998-2001. Pro center Chicago Bears 2002, San Diego Chargers 2002, Rhein Fire (NFL Europe) 2003, Cologne Centurions (NFL Europe) 2004. College coach: Oregon 2005-06, Illinois 2012. Pro coach: Chicago Bears 2007-09, Seattle Seahawks 2010-11, joined Jaguars in 2013.

Jedd Fisch, offensive coordinator; born May 5, 1976, Livingston, N.J. No college or pro playing experience. College coach: Florida 1999-2000, Minnesota 2009, Miami 2011-12. Pro coach: New Jersey Red Dogs (Arena League) 1998, Houston Texans 2001-03, Baltimore Ravens 2004-07, Denver Broncos 2008, Seattle Seahawks 2010, joined Jaguars in 2013.

Alex Hampton, strength assistant; born March 23, 1989, Hobart, Tasmania, Australia. Attended Deakin University. No college or pro playing experience. College coach: Florida State 2012. Pro coach: Joined Jaguars in 2013.

Scottie Hazelton, asst. linebackers; born December 19, 1973, Hackettstown, N.J. Linebacker Fort Lewis 1992-94. No pro playing experience. College coach: Fort Lewis 1996-99, North Dakota State 2000-01, 2007-2011, St. Olaf 2002-03, Missouri Southern State 2004-05, Michigan Tech 2006, Southern California 2012, Nevada 2013. Pro coach: Joined Jaguars in 2014.

Jess Langvardt, strength assistant; born September 28, 1982, North Platte, Neb. No pro playing experience. College coach: Sterling College 2005-09, 2012, Memphis 2009-2011, Tulane 2012. Pro coach: Joined Jaguars in 2013.

Mike Mallory, special teams coordinator; born Nov. 16, 1962, Bowling Green, Ohio. Linebacker Michigan 1982-85. No pro playing experience. College coach: Indiana 1986-87, Kent State 1988-1990, Eastern Illinois 1991-92, Rhode Island 1993-95, Northern Illinois 1996-99, Maryland 2000, Illinois 2001-05, Kansas 2006, Louisville 2007. Pro coach: New Orleans Saints 2008-2012, joined Jaguars in 2013.

Ron Middleton, tight ends/asst. special teams; born July 17, 1965, Atmore, Ala. Tight end Auburn 1982-85. Pro tight end Atlanta Falcons 1986-87, Washington Redskins 1988, 1990-93, Cleveland Browns 1989, Los Angeles Rams 1994, San Diego Chargers 1995. College coach: Troy 1997-98, Mississippi 1999-2003, Alabama 2007, Duke 2008-2012. Pro coach: Tampa Bay Buccaneers 2004-06, joined Jaguars in 2013.

Tom Myslinski, strength and conditioning; born December 7, 1968, Rome, N.Y. Guard Tennessee 1989-1991. Pro guard Washington Redskins 1992, Buffalo Bills 1993, Chicago Bears 1993-94, Jacksonville Jaguars 1995, Pittsburgh Steelers 1996-97, 2000, Indianapolis Colts 1998, Dallas Cowboys 1999. College coach: Robert Morris 2005-06, Memphis 2010, North Carolina 2011. Pro coach: Cleveland Browns 2003-04, 2007-09, joined Jaguars in 2012.

Terry Richardson, running backs; born October 8, 1971, Ft. Lauderdale, Fla. Running back Syracuse 1990-93. Pro running back Cincinnati Bengals 1994, Philadelphia Eagles 1995, Kansas City Chiefs 1996, Pittsburgh Steelers 1996-97. College coach: Connecticut 1999-2010, Miami 2011-12. Pro coach: Joined Jaguars in 2013.

Mike Rutenberg, asst. defensive backs; born October 29, 1981, Washington, D.C. Attended Cornell. No college or pro playing experience. College coach: UCLA 2006-08, New Mexico State 2009-2012. Pro coach: Washington Redskins 2003-05, joined Jaguars in 2013.

Robert Saleh, linebackers; born January 31, 1979, Dearborn, Mich. Tight end Northern Michigan 1997-2000. No pro playing experience. College coach: Michigan State 2002-03, Central Michigan 2004, Georgia 2005. Pro coach: Houston Texans 2005-2010, Seattle Seahawks 2011-13, joined Jaguars in 2014.

Frank Scelfo, quarterbacks; born February 9, 1959, Abbeville, La. Attended Northeast Louisiana. No college or pro playing experience. College coach: Tulane 1996-2006, Louisiana Tech 2007-09, Arizona 2010-11. Pro coach: Joined Jaguars in 2013.

Cedric Scott, asst. strength and conditioning; born October 19, 1977, Gulfport, Miss. Defensive end Southern Mississippi 2000. Pro defensive end New York Giants 2001, Cleveland Browns 2002. College coach: Southern Mississippi 2009-2011. Pro coach: Joined Jaguars in 2012.

Dan Shamash, defensive quality control; born December 20, 1985, New York, N.Y. Linebacker Carnegie-Mellon 2004-07. No pro playing experience. College coach: Columbia 2008. Pro coach: New York Jets 2008, Cleveland Browns 2009-2010, Tampa Bay Buccaneers 2012-13, joined Jaguars in 2014.

Matthew Smiley, asst. special teams; born October 2, 1978, Danville, Ill. Wide receiver Illinois 1997-98. No pro playing experience. College coach: Dartmouth 2005-06, Eureka College 2007-08 (interim head coach 2008), Eastern Illinois 2009-2011, Charleston Southern 2012. Pro coach: Joined Jaguars in 2013.

Tony Sorrentino, offensive quality control; born June 28, 1983, Belleville, N.J. Wide receiver The College of New Jersey 2001-04. No pro playing experience. College coach: The College of New Jersey 2006-07, 2012, Minnesota 2009-2010, Miami 2011. Pro coach: Joined Jaguars in 2013.

Jerry Sullivan, wide receivers; born July 13, 1944, Miami, Fla. Quarterback Florida State 1963-64. No pro playing experience. College coach: Kansas State 1971-72, Texas Tech 1973-75, South Carolina 1976-1982, Indiana 1983, Louisiana State 1984-1990, Ohio State 1991. Pro coach: San Diego Chargers 1992-96, Detroit Lions 1997-2000, Arizona Cardinals 2001-03, Miami Dolphins 2004, San Francisco 49ers 2005-2010, joined Jaguars in 2012.

DeWayne Walker, defensive backs; born December 3, 1960, Los Angeles, Calif. Defensive back Pasadena City (Calif.) C.C. 1978-79, Minnesota 1980-81. Pro defensive back Edmonton Eskimos (CFL) 1982, Arizona Outlaws (USFL) 1983, Oakland Invaders (USFL) 1984. College coach: Mt. San Antonio (Calif.) J.C. 1988-1992, Utah State 1993, Brigham Young 1994, Oklahoma State 1995, California 1996-97, Southern California 2001, UCLA 2006-08, New Mexico State 2009-2012 (head coach). Pro coach: New England Patriots 1998-2000, New York Giants 2002-03, Washington Redskins 2004-05, joined Jaguars in 2013.

Todd Wash, defensive line; born July 19, 1968, Miles City, Mont. Linebacker North Dakota State 1988-1991. No pro playing experience. College coach: Fort Lewis College 1996-99 (head coach 1997-99), Nebraska-Kearney 2000-01, North Dakota State 2002-03, 2005-06, Missouri Southern State 2004. Pro coach: Tampa Bay Buccaneers 2006-2010, Seattle Seahawks 2011-12, joined Jaguars in 2013.

George Yarno, offensive line; born August 12, 1957, Spokane, Wash. Offensive line Washington State 1975-78. Pro offensive line Tampa Bay Buccaneers 1979-1983, 1985-87, Denver Gold (USFL) 1984-85, Atlanta Falcons 1988, Houston Oilers 1989, Green Bay Packers 1990. College coach: Louisiana State 2001-02, Washington State 2003-07. Pro coach: Tampa Bay Buccaneers 2008, Detroit Lions 2009-12, joined Jaguars in 2013.

**American Football Conference
West Division
Team Colors:** Red, Gold, and White
**One Arrowhead Drive
Kansas City, Missouri 64129
Telephone:** (816) 920-9300

2014 SCHEDULE
PRESEASON
Aug. 7   **Cincinnati** 7:00
Aug. 17 at Carolina..........................7:00
Aug. 23 **Minnesota** 7:00
Aug. 28 at Green Bay 6:00

REGULAR SEASON
Sep. 7   **Tennessee** 12:00
Sep. 14 at Denver 3:25
Sep. 21 at Miami 3:25
Sep. 29 **New England** (Mon)...........7:30
Oct. 5   at San Francisco 3:25
Oct. 12 BYE
Oct. 19 at San Diego 3:05
Oct. 26 **St. Louis** 12:00
Nov. 2   **New York Jets** 12:00
Nov. 9   at Buffalo 12:00
Nov. 16 **Seattle** 12:00
Nov. 20 at Oakland (Thu)................7:25
Nov. 30 **Denver** *7:30
Dec. 7   at Arizona 3:05
Dec. 14 **Oakland** 12:00
Dec. 21 at Pittsburgh 12:00
Dec. 28 **San Diego** 12:00
*All times CT; Sunday night games in
  Weeks 5-16 subject to change

Stadium: Arrowhead Stadium
  (opened in 1972,
  fully renovated in 2010)
  •**Capacity:** 76,416
  One Arrowhead Drive
  Kansas City, Missouri 64129
Playing Surface: Grass
Training Camp: Missouri Western St. Univ.
  St. Joseph, Missouri 64507

ARROWHEAD STADIUM

CLUB OFFICIALS
Chairman & CEO: Clark Hunt
Head Coach: Andy Reid
General Manager: John Dorsey
President: Mark Donovan
Director of Player Personnel:
  Chris Ballard
Director of Pro Scouting: Will Lewis
Director of College Scouting:
  Marvin Allen
Director of Football Administration:
  Trip MacCracken
Chief Financial Officer: Dan Crumb
Senior Vice President of Business
  Operations: Bill Chapin
Vice President of Communications:
  Ted Crews
Vice President of Business Development:
  Tyler Epp
Vice President of Administration:
  Kirsten Krug
Vice President of Stadium Operations:
  David Young
Director of Ticket Operations:
  Dave Felsen
Director of Facilities: Brandon Hamilton
Director of Chiefs Cheerleaders:
  Stephanie Judah
Director of Ticket Sales: Tyler Kirby
Director of Sales: Shawn Long
Director of Fan Experience: Jayne Martin
Director of Production: Jodain Massad
Director of Corporate Partnerships:
  Adam Rossbach
Director of Foundation and Development:
  Anne Scharf
Director of Marketing and Event
  Acquisition: Jeremy Slavens
Director of Event Operations: Ryan Smith
Director of Special Events: Gary Spani
Director of Information Technology:
  Bob Stirton
Director of Digital Media and Strategy:
  Jeremy Zimmer
Equipment Manager: Allen Wright
Assistant Equipment Managers:
  Chris Shropshire, Kyle Crumbaugh,
  Jimmy White
Head Athletic Trainer: Rick Burkholder
Assistant Athletic Trainers: Aaron
  Borgmann, Evan Craft, David Glover,
  Nick Potter
Director of Video Operations: Pat Brazil
Assistant Director of Video Operations:
  Ken Radino
Video Assistants: Colin Clark,
  Josh Schmidt
Football Operations Coordinator:
  Mitch Reynolds
Team Security Manager: Brian Shafar

COACHING HISTORY
**Dallas Texans 1960-62
(423-408-12)**
Records include postseason games

1960-1974	Hank Stram	129-79-10
1975-77	Paul Wiggin*	11-24-0
1977	Tom Bettis	1-6-0
1978-1982	Marv Levy	31-42-0
1983-86	John Mackovic	30-35-0
1987-88	Frank Gansz	8-22-1
1989-1998	Marty Schottenheimer	...104-65-1
1999-2000	Gunther Cunningham	16-16-0
2001-05	Dick Vermeil	44-37-0
2006-08	Herm Edwards	15-34-0
2009-2011	Todd Haley**	19-26-0
2011-12	Romeo Crennel	4-15-0
2013	Andy Reid	11-6-0

*Released after seven games in 1977
**Released after 13 games in 2011

PAID ATTENDANCE
Home 585,995   Away 504,711
Total 1,090,706
Single-game home record,
  *82,893 (10/2/00)
Single-season home record,
  629,569 (1999)
*Arrowhead Stadium attendance: 78,502
  Kauffman Stadium attendance: 4,391

2014 DRAFT CHOICES
Round	Name	Pos.	College
1	Dee Ford	LB	Auburn
3	Phillip Gaines	DB	Rice
4	De'Anthony Thomas	RB	Oregon
5	Aaron Murray	QB	Georgia
6	Zach Fulton	G	Tennessee
	Laurent Duvernay-Tardif	T	McGill

2013 TEAM RECORD

PRESEASON (2-2)

Date	Result	Opponent
08/09	L 13-17	at New Orleans
08/16	L 13-15	San Francisco
08/24	W 26-20	OTat Pittsburgh
08/29	W 30-8	Green Bay

REGULAR SEASON (11-5)

Date	Result	Opponent
09/08	W 28-2	at Jacksonville
09/15	W 17-16	Dallas
09/19	W 26-16	at Philadelphia
09/29	W 31-7	New York Giants
10/06	W 26-17	at Tennessee
10/13	W 24-7	Oakland
10/20	W 17-16	Houston
10/27	W 23-17	Cleveland
11/03	W 23-13	at Buffalo
11/17	L 17-27	at Denver
11/24	L 38-41	San Diego
12/01	L 28-35	Denver
12/08	W 45-10	at Washington
12/15	W 56-31	at Oakland
12/22	L 7-23	Indianapolis
12/29	L 24-27	at San Diego (OT)

POSTSEASON (0-1)

Date	Result	Opponent
01/04	L 44-45	at Indianapolis

(OT) Overtime

SCORE BY PERIODS

Chiefs	124	133	65	108	0 —	430
Opponents	51	106	91	54	3 —	305

2013 TEAM STATISTICS

	Chiefs	Opp.
Total First Downs	323	303
Rushing	110	88
Passing	179	189
Penalty	34	26
3rd Down: Made/Att	74/213	78/229
3rd Down Pct.	34.7	34.1
4th Down: Made/Att	4/11	9/18
4th Down Pct.	36.4	50.0
Possession Avg.	30:43	29:17
Total Net Yards	5396	5885
Avg. Per Game	337.3	367.8
Total Plays	1029	1067
Avg. Per Play	5.2	5.5
Net Yards Rushing	2056	1923
Avg. Per Game	128.5	120.2
Total Rushes	442	428
Net Yards Passing	3340	3962
Avg. Per Game	208.8	247.6
Sacked/Yards Lost	41/221	47/309
Gross Yards	3561	4271
Att./Completions	546/333	592/334
Completion Pct.	61.0	56.4
Had Intercepted	8	21
Punts/Average	89/45.3	87/46.6
Net Punting Avg.	89/39.9	87/37.7
Penalties/Yards	101/774	112/852
Fumbles/Ball Lost	21/10	22/15
Touchdowns	52	34
Rushing	17	9
Passing	24	25
Returns	11	0

2013 INDIVIDUAL STATISTICS

PASSING

PASSING	Att.	Comp.	Yds.	Pct.	TD	Int.	Tkld.	Rate
A. Smith	508	308	3313	60.6	23	7	39/210	89.1
Daniel	38	25	248	65.8	1	1	2/11	81.9
Chiefs	546	333	3561	61.0	24	8	41/221	88.6
Opponents	592	334	4271	56.4	25	21	47/309	78.5

SCORING

SCORING	TD R	TD P	TD Rt	PAT	FG	Saf	PTS
Succop	0	0	0	52/52	22/28	0	118
Charles	12	7	0	0/0	0/0	0	114
Bowe	0	5	0	0/0	0/0	0	30
Davis	4	0	1	0/0	0/0	0	30
McCluster	0	2	2	0/0	0/0	0	24
Fasano	0	3	0	0/0	0/0	0	18
Avery	0	2	0	0/0	0/0	0	12
Berry	0	0	2	0/0	0/0	0	12
Hali	0	0	2	0/0	0/0	0	12
Hemingway	0	2	0	0/0	0/0	0	12
McGrath	0	2	0	0/0	0/0	0	12
Abdullah	0	0	1	0/0	0/0	0	6
Cooper	0	0	1	0/0	0/0	0	6
Demps	0	0	1	0/0	0/0	0	6
Sherman	0	1	0	0/0	0/0	0	6
A. Smith	1	0	0	0/0	0/0	0	6
S. Smith	0	0	1	0/0	0/0	0	6
Chiefs	17	24	11	52/52	22/28	0	430
Opponents	9	25	0	33/33	22/28	1	305

2-Pt Conversions: Chiefs 0-0, Opponents 0-1.

RUSHING

RUSHING	No.	Yds	Avg	LG	TD
Charles	259	1287	5.0	46	12
A. Smith	76	431	5.7	26	1
Davis	70	242	3.5	20	4
Daniel	14	52	3.7	29	0
Gray	9	24	2.7	9	0
Avery	2	6	3.0	4	0
Jenkins	2	6	3.0	5	0
McCluster	8	5	0.6	5	0
Sherman	2	3	1.5	2	0
Chiefs	442	2056	4.7	46	17
Opponents	428	1923	4.5	61	9

RECEIVING

RECEIVING	No.	Yds	Avg	LG	TD
Charles	70	693	9.9	71t	7
Bowe	57	673	11.8	34t	5
McCluster	53	511	9.6	43	2
Avery	40	596	14.9	51	2
McGrath	26	302	11.6	25	2
Fasano	23	200	8.7	20	3
Sherman	18	155	8.6	26	1
Hemingway	13	125	9.6	24	2
Davis	11	75	6.8	17	0
Jenkins	8	130	16.3	48	0
Gray	7	46	6.6	18	0
Brock	3	36	12.0	25	0
Hall	2	20	10.0	11	0
Gordon	1	3	3.0	3	0
A. Smith	1	-4	-4.0	-4	0
Chiefs	333	3561	10.7	71t	24
Opponents	334	4271	12.8	77	25

INTERCEPTIONS

INTERCEPTIONS	No.	Yds	Avg	LG	TD
Demps	4	61	15.3	35	0
Berry	3	134	44.7	49	2
Cooper	3	32	10.7	20	0
S. Smith	2	96	48.0	100t	1
D. Johnson	2	44	22.0	41	0
Parker	2	29	14.5	15	0
Abdullah	1	44	44.0	44t	1
Flowers	1	32	32.0	32	0
Hali	1	10	10.0	10t	1
Zombo	1	5	5.0	5	0
Lewis	1	1	1.0	1	0
Chiefs	21	488	23.2	100t	5
Opponents	8	21	2.6	17	0

PUNTING

PUNTING	No.	Yds.	Avg.	In 20	LG
Colquitt	87	4005	46.0	35	65
Succop	1	29	29.0	0	29
Chiefs	89	4034	45.3	35	65
Opponents	87	4052	46.6	25	64

PUNT RETURNS

PUNT RETURNS	Ret	FC	Yds	Avg	LG	TD
McCluster	58	11	686	11.8	89t	2
Hall	1	0	9	9.0	9	0
Chiefs	59	11	695	11.8	89t	2
Opponents	38	19	246	6.5	27	0

KICKOFF RETURNS

KICKOFF RETURNS	No.	Yds	Avg	LG	TD
Demps	33	992	30.1	95t	1
Davis	10	321	32.1	108t	1
McCluster	1	3	3.0	3	0
Chiefs	44	1316	29.9	108t	2
Opponents	43	1048	24.4	39	0

FIELD GOALS

FIELD GOALS	1-19	20-29	30-39	40-49	50+
Succop	0/0	6/6	9/10	6/8	1/4
Chiefs	0/0	6/6	9/10	6/8	1/4
Opponents	0/0	5/5	8/10	5/7	4/6

SACKS

SACKS	No.
Hali	11.0
Houston	11.0
D. Johnson	4.5
Poe	4.5
T. Jackson	4.0
Berry	3.5
Zombo	2.0
Bailey	1.0
Catapano	1.0
Flowers	1.0
J. Johnson	1.0
Parker	1.0
Powe	1.0
Abdullah	0.5
Chiefs	47.0
Opponents	41.0

RECORD HOLDERS
INDIVIDUAL RECORDS—CAREER

Category	Name	Performance
Rushing (Yds.)	Priest Holmes, 2001-07	6,070
Passing (Yds.)	Len Dawson, 1962-1975	28,507
Passing (TDs)	Len Dawson, 1962-1975	237
Receiving (No.)	Tony Gonzalez, 1997-2008	916
Receiving (Yds.)	Tony Gonzalez, 1997-2008	10,940
Interceptions	Emmitt Thomas, 1966-1978	58
Punting (Avg.)	Dustin Colquitt, 2005-2013	44.9
Punt Return (Avg.)	Dexter McCluster, 2010-13	12.1
Kickoff Return (Avg.)	Noland Smith, 1967-69	26.8
Field Goals	Nick Lowery, 1980-1993	329
Touchdowns (Tot.)	Priest Holmes, 2001-07	83
Points	Nick Lowery, 1980-1993	1,466
*Sacks	Derrick Thomas, 1989-1999	126.5

INDIVIDUAL RECORDS—SINGLE SEASON

Category	Name	Performance
Rushing (Yds.)	Larry Johnson, 2006	1,789
Passing (Yds.)	Trent Green, 2004	4,591
Passing (TDs)	Len Dawson, 1964	30
Receiving (No.)	Tony Gonzalez, 2004	102
Receiving (Yds.)	Derrick Alexander, 2000	1,391
Interceptions	Emmitt Thomas, 1974	12
Punting (Avg.)	Dustin Colquitt, 2012	46.8
Punt Return (Avg.)	Dante Hall, 2003	16.3
Kickoff Return (Avg.)	Quintin Demps, 2013	30.1
Field Goals	Nick Lowery, 1990	34
Touchdowns (Tot.)	Priest Holmes, 2003	27
Points	Priest Holmes, 2003	162
*Sacks	Derrick Thomas, 1990	20.0

INDIVIDUAL RECORDS—SINGLE GAME

Category	Name	Performance
Rushing (Yds.)	Jamaal Charles, 1-3-10	259
Passing (Yds.)	Elvis Grbac, 11-5-00	504
Passing (TDs)	Len Dawson, 11-1-64	6
Receiving (No.)	Tony Gonzalez, 1-2-05	14
Receiving (Yds.)	Stephone Paige, 12-22-85	309
Interceptions	Bobby Ply, 12-16-62	**4
	Bobby Hunt, 10-4-64	**4
	Deron Cherry, 9-29-85	**4
Field Goals	Ryan Succop, 9-23-12	6
Touchdowns (Tot.)	Abner Haynes, 11-26-61	5
	Jamaal Charles, 12-15-13	5
Points	Abner Haynes, 11-26-61	30
	Jamaal Charles, 12-15-13	30
*Sacks	Derrick Thomas, 11-11-90	**7.0

*Sacks became an official statistic in 1982.
**NFL Record

2014 VETERAN ROSTER

No.	Name	Pos.	Ht.	Wt.	Birthdate	NFL Exp.	College	Hometown	How Acq.	'13 Games/ Starts
39	Abdullah, Husain	S	6-0	204	7/27/85	6	Washington State	Pomona, Calif.	FA-'13	16/2
71	Allen, Jeff	G	6-4	306	1/8/90	3	Illinois	Chicago, Ill.	D2-'12	15/14
17	Avery, Donnie	WR	5-11	200	6/12/84	7	Houston	Houston, Texas	UFA(Ind)-'13	16/14
97	Bailey, Allen	DL	6-3	288	3/25/89	4	Miami	Sapelo Island, Ga.	D3b-'11	15/3
29	Berry, Eric	S	6-0	211	12/29/88	5	Tennessee	Fairburn, Ga.	D1-'10	15/15
82	Bowe, Dwayne	WR	6-2	221	9/21/84	8	Louisiana State	Miami, Fla.	D1-'07	15/15
9	Bray, Tyler	QB	6-6	215	12/27/91	2	Tennessee	Kingsburg, Calif.	FA-'13	0*
77	Catapano, Mike	DE	6-4	270	8/17/90	2	Princeton	Bayville, N.Y.	D7-'13	15/0
25	Charles, Jamaal	RB	5-11	199	12/27/86	7	Texas	Port Arthur, Texas	D3a-'08	15/15
2	Colquitt, Dustin	P	6-3	210	5/6/82	10	Tennessee	Knoxville, Tenn.	D3-'05	16/0
26	Commings, Sanders	S	6-0	223	3/8/90	2	Georgia	Augusta, Ga.	D5-'13	2/0
31	Cooper, Marcus	CB	6-2	192	2/1/90	2	Rutgers	Hartford, Conn.	W(SF)-'13	16/6
98	Cudjo, Jermelle	DT	6-2	304	9/28/86	4	Central Oklahoma	Lawton, Okla.	FA-'14	13/0*
10	Daniel, Chase	QB	6-0	225	10/7/86	6	Missouri	Southlake, Texas	UFA(NO)-'13	5/1
34	Davis, Knile	RB	5-10	227	10/5/91	2	Arkansas	Missouri City, Texas	D3b-'13	16/1
70	DeVito, Mike	DL	6-3	305	6/10/84	8	Maine	Wellfleet, Mass.	UFA(NYJ)-'13	14/13
80	Fasano, Anthony	TE	6-4	255	4/20/84	9	Notre Dame	Verona, N.J.	UFA(Tenn)-'13	9/9
72	Fisher, Eric	T	6-7	306	1/5/91	2	Central Michigan	Rochester, Mich.	D1-'13	14/13
24	Flowers, Brandon	CB	5-9	187	2/18/86	7	Virginia Tech	Delray Beach, Fla.	D2-'08	13/13
43	Gafford, Thomas	LS	6-2	250	1/29/83	7	Houston	Friendswood, Texas	FA-'13	16/0
81	Gordon, Richard	TE	6-4	265	6/7/87	4	Miami	Miami, Fla.	FA-'13	2/0
32	Gray, Cyrus	RB	5-10	206	11/18/89	3	Texas A&M	DeSoto, Texas	D6-'12	16/0
91	Hali, Tamba	LB	6-3	275	11/3/83	9	Penn State	Teaneck, N.J.	D1-'06	15/15
88	Hemingway, Junior	WR	6-1	225	12/27/88	2	Michigan	Conway, S.C.	D7b-'12	16/2
65	Henry, Ricky	G	6-4	310	7/27/87	3	Nebraska	Omaha, Neb.	W(NO)-'13	0*
50	Houston, Justin	LB	6-3	258	1/12/89	4	Georgia	Statesboro, Ga.	D3a-'11	11/11
96	Howard, Jaye	DT	6-3	301	12/20/88	3	Florida	Apopka, Fla.	W(Sea)-'13	3/1
67	Hudson, Otis	G	6-5	330	7/19/86	2	Eastern Illinois	Barrington, Ill.	FA-'14	0*
61	Hudson, Rodney	C	6-2	299	7/12/89	4	Florida State	Mobile, Ala.	D2-'11	16/15
15	Jenkins, A.J.	WR	6-0	200	9/8/89	3	Illinois	Jacksonville, Fla.	T(SF)-'13	16/1
56	Johnson, Derrick	LB	6-3	242	11/22/82	10	Texas	Waco, Texas	D1-'05	15/15
52	Johnson, James-Michael	LB	6-1	240	8/20/89	3	Nevada	Fairfield, Calif.	W(Cle)-'13	16/1
57	Johnson, Nico	LB	6-2	249	6/19/90	2	Alabama	Andulusia, Ala.	D4-'13	6/1
75	Johnson, Rishaw	G	6-3	313	2/24/89	2	California (Pa.)	Hammond, La.	FA-'13	3/1
87	Kelce, Travis	TE	6-5	260	10/5/89	2	Cincinnati	Cleveland Heights, Ohio	D3a-'13	1/0
59	Kelly, Colin	OL	6-5	298	12/29/89	2	Oregon State	Kelso, Wash.	FA-'13	0*
64	Kush, Eric	C	6-4	313	9/9/89	2	California (Pa.)	Bridgeville, Pa.	D6a-'13	3/1
74	Linkenbach, Jeff	T	6-6	325	6/9/87	5	Cincinnati	Sandusky, Ohio	UFA(Ind)-'14	12/5*
94	Love, Kyle	DT	6-1	315	11/18/86	4	Mississippi State	Fairburn, Ga.	FA-'14	1/0
95	Martin, Josh	LB/DE	6-3	245	11/7/91	2	Columbia	Aurora, Colo.	FA-'13	5/1
53	Mays, Joe	LB	5-11	244	7/6/85	7	North Dakota State	Chicago, Ill.	UFA(Hou)-'14	14/13*
84	McGrath, Sean	TE	6-5	247	12/3/87	2	Henderson State	Mundelein, Ill.	W(Sea)-'13	16/9
30	McKnight, Joe	RB	5-11	205	7/6/85	4	Southern California	River Ridge, La.	FA-'14	0*
34	McMillian, Jerron	S	5-11	203	4/2/89	3	Maine	Hillside, N.J.	FA-'14	12/2*
54	Moses, Dezman	LB	6-2	249	1/4/89	3	Tulane	Willingboro, N.J.	W(GB)-'13	13/0
20	Owens, Chris	CB	5-9	180	12/1/86	6	San Jose State	Los Angeles, Calif.	UFA-'14	13/2*
38	Parker, Ron	CB	6-0	206	8/17/87	4	Newberry	St. Helena Island, S.C.	W(Sea)-'13	16/1
92	Poe, Dontari	DT	6-3	346	8/18/90	3	Memphis	Memphis, Tenn.	D1-'12	15/15
22	Rutland, Kevin	CB	6-0	193	4/2/88	3	Missouri	Houston, Texas	FA-'14	0*
42	Sherman, Anthony	FB	5-10	242	12/11/88	4	Connecticut	North Attleborough, Mass.	T(Ariz)-'13	16/8
11	Smith, Alex	QB	6-4	217	5/7/84	10	Utah	La Mesa, Calif.	T(SF)-'13	15/15
21	Smith, Sean	CB	6-3	218	7/14/87	6	Utah	Pasadena, Calif.	UFA(Mia)-'13	16/15
79	Stephenson, Donald	OL	6-6	312	9/30/88	3	Oklahoma	Blue Springs, Mo.	D3-'12	16/7
6	Succop, Ryan	K	6-2	218	9/19/86	6	South Carolina	Hickory, N.C.	D7c-'09	16/0
40	Van Dyke, DeMarcus	CB	6-1	187	1/17/89	4	Miami	Miami, Fla.	FA-'14	2/0*
99	Walker, Vance	DE	6-2	305	4/26/87	6	Georgia Tech	Fort Mill, S.C.	UFA(Oak)-'14	15/15*
69	Watkins, Rokevious	OL	6-3	338	5/31/86	3	South Carolina	Fairburn, Ga.	FA-'13	3/1
68	Webb, J'Marcus	T	6-7	333	8/8/88	5	West Texas A&M	Mesquite, Texas	FA-'14	8/1*
19	Williams, Kyle	WR	5-10	186	7/19/88	6	Arizona State	Scottsdale, Ariz.	FA-'14	1/0
51	Zombo, Frank	LB	6-3	254	3/5/87	5	Central Michigan	Sterling Heights, Mich.	FA-'14	16/5

* Bray did not play in one game and inactive 15 games; Cudjo played 13 games with St. Louis in '13; Henry missed '13 season because of injury; Hudson was last active with Cincinnati in '12; Kelly missed '13 season because of injury; Linkenbach played 12 games with Indianapolis; Mays played 14 games with Houston; McKnight last active with N.Y. Jets in '12; McMillian played 12 games with Green Bay; Owens played 12 games with Cleveland and one game with Miami; Rutland last active with Jacksonville in '12; Van Dyke played two games with Pittsburgh in '13; Walker played 15 games with Oakland; Webb played eight games with Minnesota.

Players lost through free agency (8): T Branden Albert (Mia; 12 games in '13), G Jon Asamoah (Atl; 14), S Quintin Demps (NYG; 16), DE Tyson Jackson (Atl; 15), LB Akeem Jordan (Wash; 16), S Kendrick Lewis (Hou; 16), WR Dexter McCluster (Tenn; 15), G/T Geoff Schwartz (NYG; 16).

Also played with Chiefs in '13—TE Kevin Brock (4 games), WR Chad Hall (9), TE Dominique Jones (2), S Bradley McDougald (1), DT Jerrell Powe (2), CB Dunta Robinson (8), DT Anthony Toribio (8).

FIRST-YEAR ROSTER

Name	Pos.	Ht.	Wt.	Birthdate	College	Hometown	How Acq.
Alecxih, Chas (1)	DL	6-3	304	2/10/89	Pittsburgh	Columbia, Pa.	FA
Baker, Chris	FB	6-2	228	7/13/91	Idaho	Deerfield Beach, Fla.	FA
Bronson, Malcolm (1)	S	5-11	192	5/11/90	McNeese State	Jasper, Texas	FA
Broussard, Risean (1)	DT	6-2	278	9/8/91	Hinds Junior College	Lake Charles, La.	FA
Campbell, Jordan (1)	FB	5-11	240	6/29/88	New Mexico-Highlands	Corona, Calif.	FA
Dressler, Weston (1)	WR	5-7	179	6/14/85	North Dakota	Bismarck, N.D.	FA
Duvernay-Tardif, Laurent	OL	6-5	321	2/11/91	McGill	Montreal, Quebec	D6b
Ford, Dee	LB	6-2	252	3/19/91	Auburn	Odenville, Ala.	D1
Fulton, Zach	G	6-5	316	9/23/91	Tennessee	Homewood, Ill.	D6a
Furr, DeRon	LB	6-3	230	9/27/89	Fort Valley State	Columbus, Ga.	FA
Gaines, Phillip	CB	6-0	193	4/4/91	Rice	Converse, Texas	D3
Gottschalk, Ben	C	6-5	293	2/15/92	Southern Methodist	Sherman Oaks, Calif.	FA
Hamilton, Dominique (1)	DL	6-5	315	1/18/89	Missouri	El Paso, Texas	FA
Hammond Jr., Frankie (1)	WR	6-1	184	2/17/90	Florida	Hallandale Beach, Fla.	FA
Harris, Demetrius (1)	TE	6-7	230	7/29/91	UW-Milwaukee	Jacksonville, Ark.	FA
Highsmith, Alonzo (1)	LB	6-0	240	11/21/89	Arkansas	Missouri City, Texas	FA
Jackson, Jerrell (1)	WR	6-0	192	2/6/90	Missouri	Houston, Texas	FA
Johnson, Ben	LB	6-2	235	5/7/91	Tennessee-Martin	Primm Springs, Tenn.	FA
Kearney, Vernon (1)	CB	6-2	185	1/31/89	Lane	Bradenton, Fla.	FA
McKee, Ryan (1)	T	6-6	308	11/4/86	Southern Mississippi	Spanish Fort, Ala.	FA
Murray, Aaron	QB	6-1	207	11/10/90	Georgia	Tampa, Fla.	D5
Santos, Cairo	K	5-8	160	11/12/91	Tulane	St. Augustine, Fla.	FA
Schwenke, Kona	DL	6-4	297	5/11/92	Notre Dame	Hauula, Hawaii	FA
Sorensen, Daniel	S	6-2	208	3/5/90	Brigham Young	Colton, Calif.	FA
Surgent, Darryl	WR	6-0	195	5/13/92	Louisiana-Lafayette	Alexandria, La.	FA
Thomas, De'Anthony	RB/WR	5-8	176	1/5/93	Oregon	Los Angeles, Calif.	D4
Van Dyke, David	CB	6-0	185	3/6/91	Tennessee State	Miami, Fla.	FA
West, Charcandrick	RB	5-10	205	6/2/91	Abilene Christian	Springhill, La.	FA
Williams, Fred (1)	WR	6-0	190	4/15/88	St. Cloud State	Milwaukee, Wis.	FA
Wilson, Albert	WR	5-9	200	7/12/92	Georgia State	Port St. Lucie, Fla.	FA

The term NFL Rookie is defined as a player who is in his first season of professional football and has not been on the roster of another professional football team for any regular-season or postseason games. A Rookie is designated by an "R" on NFL rosters. Players who have been active in another professional football league or players who have NFL experience, including either preseason training camp or being on an Active List or Inactive List, or on Reserve/Injured or Reserve/Physically Unable to Perform for fewer than six regular-season games, are termed NFL First-Year Players. An NFL First-Year Player is designated by a "1" on NFL rosters. Thereafter, a player is credited with an additional year of experience for each season in which he accumulates six games on the Active List or Inactive List, or on Reserve/Injured or Reserve/Physically Unable to Perform.

Log on to www.kcchiefs.com for an up-to-date roster.

COACHING STAFF
Head Coach,
Andy Reid

Pro Career: Andy Reid was named the 13th head coach in Kansas City Chiefs history on January 7, 2013. He is entering his 23rd season in the National Football League and his 16th season as an NFL head coach in 2014. In his first season in Kansas City in 2013, Reid helped orchestrate the franchise's best single-season turnaround as the Chiefs won 11 games and made the playoffs after going 2-14 the previous season. Prior to joining the Chiefs, Reid served as the head coach of the Philadelphia Eagles for 14 years (1999-2012), earning NFL Coach of the Year honors three times. Reid compiled the best win total (140) and playoff victory total (10) in Philadelphia Eagles history. He captured six division titles and five trips to the NFC Championship Game. During his tenure in Philadelphia, only New England (9) earned more divisional playoff round appearances than Philadelphia (7). In his 22-year NFL coaching career, Reid's teams have made the playoffs 16 times (19-15 record). He has coached in the Super Bowl three times and the NFC Championship Game nine times. Reid was an assistant coach with Green Bay (1992-98) under Mike Holmgren. With Green Bay, Reid helped the Packers earn a Super Bowl XXXI victory over New England. Career record: 151-108-1.

Background: Coached at Brigham Young (1982), San Francisco State (1983-85) Northern Arizona (1986), Texas-El Paso (1987-88) and Missouri (1989-1991). Reid was an offensive tackle and guard on three BYU Cougar Holiday Bowl teams. Reid graduated with a bachelor's degree in physical education. He also received a master's degree in professional leadership in physical education and athletics.

Personal: Born March 19, 1958 in Los Angeles, Calif. Reid and his wife Tammy have five children—Britt, Crosby, Drew Ann, Spencer, and the late Garrett.

ASSISTANT COACHES

Eric Bieniemy, running backs; born August 15, 1969, New Orleans, La. Running back Colorado 1987-1990. Pro running back San Diego 1991-94, Cincinnati Bengals 1995-98, Philadelphia Eagles 1999. College coach: Colorado 2001-02, UCLA 2003-05, Colorado 2009-2012. Pro coach: Minnesota Vikings 2006-2010, joined Chiefs in 2013.

Tommy Brasher, defensive line; born Dec. 30, 1940, El Dorado, Ark. Linebacker Arkansas 1962-63. No pro playing experience. College coach: Arkansas 1970, Virginia Tech 1971, Northeast Louisiana 1974, 1976, Southern Methodist 1977-1981. Pro coach: Shreveport Steamer (WFL) 1975, New England Patriots 1982-84, Philadelphia Eagles 1985, Atlanta Falcons 1986-89, Tampa Bay Buccaneers 1990, Seattle Seahawks 1992-98, Philadelphia Eagles 1999-2005, 2012, joined Chiefs in 2013.

Brad Childress, spread game analyst/special projects; born June 27, 1956, Aurora, Ill. Quarterback/wide receiver Eastern Illinois 1975. No pro playing experience. College coach: Illinois 1978-1984, Northern Arizona 1986-89, Utah 1990, Wisconsin 1991-98. Pro coach:

Indianapolis Colts 1985, Philadelphia Eagles 1999-2005, Minnesota Vikings 2006-2010 (head coach), Cleveland Browns 2012, joined Chiefs in 2013.

Eugene Chung, asst. offensive line; born June 14, 1969, Prince George's County, Md. Offensive lineman Virginia Tech 1988-1991. Pro offensive lineman New England Patriots 1992-94, Jacksonville Jaguars 1995, Indianapolis Colts 1997. Pro coach: Philadelphia Eagles 2010-12, joined Chiefs in 2013.

Travis Crittenden, asst. strength and conditioning; born April 6, 1981, Wichita Falls, Texas. Tackle Fork Union Military Academy 1999, Virginia Military Institute 2000-03. No pro playing experience. Pro coach: Philadelphia Eagles 2012, joined Chiefs in 2013.

David Culley, asst. head coach/wide receivers; born September 17, 1955, Sparta, Tenn. Quarterback Vanderbilt 1973-77. No pro playing experience. College coach: Austin Peay 1978, Vanderbilt 1979-1981, Middle Tennessee State 1982, Tennessee-Chattanooga 1983, Western Kentucky 1984, Southwestern Louisiana 1985-88, Texas-El Paso 1989-1990, Texas A&M 1991-93. Pro coach: Tampa Bay Buccaneers 1994-95, Pittsburgh Steelers 1996-98, Philadelphia Eagles 1999-2012, joined Chiefs in 2013.

Mark DeLeone, defensive quality control; born June 30, 1987, Syracuse, N.Y. Attended Iowa. No college or pro playing experience. College coach: Florida 2010, Temple 2011. Pro coach: New York Jets 2012, joined Chiefs in 2013.

Gary Gibbs, linebackers; born August 13, 1952, Beaumont, Texas. Linebacker Oklahoma 1972-74. No pro playing experience. College coach: Oklahoma 1975-1994 (head coach 1989-1994), Georgia 2000, Louisiana State 2001. Pro coach: Dallas Cowboys 2002-04, New Orleans Saints 2006-08, joined Chiefs in 2009.

Al Harris, defensive assistant/secondary; born December 7, 1974, Pompano Beach, Fla. Cornerback Trinity Valley (Texas) C.C. 1993-94, Texas A&M-Kingsville 1995-96. Pro cornerback Tampa Bay Buccaneers 1997, Philadelphia Eagles 1998-2002, Green Bay Packers 2003-09, Miami Dolphins 2010, St. Louis Rams 2011. Pro coach: Miami Dolphins 2012, joined Chiefs in 2013.

Andy Heck, offensive line; born January 1, 1967, Fargo, N.D. Tackle Notre Dame 1985-88. Pro tackle Seattle Seahawks 1989-1993, Chicago Bears 1994-98, Washington Redskins 1999-2000. College coach: Virginia 2001-03. Pro coach: Jacksonville Jaguars 2004-12, joined Chiefs in 2013.

Corey Matthaei, offensive quality control; born February 1, 1985, Fircrest, Wash. Offensive lineman Willamette 2003-06. No pro playing experience. College coach: Willamette 2007. Pro coach: Philadelphia Eagles 2008-2012, joined Chiefs in 2013.

Tom Melvin, tight ends; born October 1, 1961, Redwood City, Calif. Offensive lineman San Francisco State 1982-83. No pro playing experience. College coach: San Francisco State 1984-85, Northern Arizona 1986-87, California-Santa Barbara 1988-1990, Occidental College 1991-98. Pro coach: Philadelphia Eagles 1999-2012,

joined Chiefs in 2013.

Matt Nagy, quarterbacks; born April 24, 1978, Plainfield, N.J. Quarterback Delaware 1996-2000. Pro quarterback New York Dragons (AFL) 2002, Carolina Cobras (AFL) 2004, Georgia Force (AFL) 2005-06, Columbus Destroyers (AFL) 2007-08. Pro coach: Philadelphia Eagles 2011-12, joined Chiefs in 2013.

Brock Olivo, asst. special teams coach; born June 24, 1976, St. Louis, Mo. Running back Missouri 1994-97. Pro running back Detroit Lions 1998-2001, S.S. Lazio Marines (IFL) 2002. College coach: Coastal Carolina 2012-13. Pro coach: Joined Chiefs in 2014.

Doug Pederson, offensive coordinator; born January 31, 1968, Bellingham, Wash. Quarterback Louisiana-Monroe 1987-1990. Pro quarterback Miami Dolphins 1993-95, Green Bay Packers 1995-98, 2001-04, Philadelphia Eagles 1999, Cleveland Browns 2000. Pro coach: Philadelphia Eagles 2009-2012, joined Chiefs in 2013.

Britt Reid, defensive quality control; born April 28, 1985, San Francisco, Calif. Attended Temple. No college or pro playing experience. College coach: Temple 2012. Pro coach: Joined Chiefs in 2013.

Barry Rubin, strength and conditioning; born June 25, 1957, Monroe, La. Running back/punter Louisiana State 1976-77, tight end/punter Northwestern (La.) State 1978-1980. No pro playing experience. College coach: Northeast Louisiana 1981-83, 1987-1990, 1994, Louisiana State 1984-85. Pro coach: Green Bay Packers 1995-2005, Philadelphia Eagles 2008-2012, joined Chiefs in 2013.

Brent Salazar, asst. strength and conditioning; born May 22, 1980, Denver, Colo. Attended New Mexico. No college or pro playing experience. College coach: New Mexico 2002-03, Nevada-Las Vegas 2005, Pacific 2006. Pro coach: Joined Chiefs in 2007.

Bob Sutton, defensive coordinator; born January 28, 1951, Ypsilanti, Mich. Attended Eastern Michigan. No college or pro playing experience. College coach: Michigan 1972-73, Syracuse 1974, Western Michigan 1975-76, 1980-81, Illinois 1977-79, North Carolina State 1982, Army 1983-1999 (head coach 1991-99). Pro coach: New York Jets 2000-2012, joined Chiefs in 2013.

Emmitt Thomas, defensive backs; born June 3, 1943, Angleton, Texas. Quarterback/wide receiver Bishop (Texas) College 1963-65. Pro defensive back Kansas City Chiefs 1966-1978. Inducted into Pro Football Hall of Fame 2008. College coach: Central Missouri State 1979-1980. Pro coach: St. Louis Cardinals 1981-85, Washington Redskins 1986-1994, Philadelphia Eagles 1995-98, Green Bay Packers 1999, Minnesota Vikings 2000-01, Atlanta Falcons 2002-09 (interim head coach 2007), re-joined Chiefs in 2010.

Dave Toub, special teams coordinator; born June 1, 1962, Ossining, N.Y. Offensive lineman Springfield College 1980-81, Texas-El Paso 1983-84. No pro playing experience. College coach: Texas El-Paso 1987-89, Missouri 1989-2000. Pro coach: Philadelphia Eagles 2001-03, Chicago Bears 2004-2012, joined Chiefs in 2013.

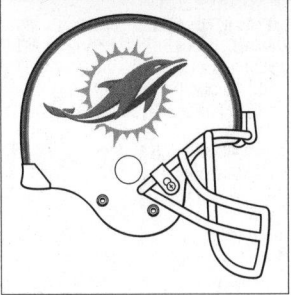

**American Football Conference
East Division**
Team Colors: Aqua, Orange, White, and
    Blue
7500 S.W. 30th Street
Davie, Florida 33314
Telephone: (954) 452-7000

2014 SCHEDULE
PRESEASON
Aug. 8	at Atlanta	7:00
Aug. 16	at Tampa Bay	7:30
Aug. 23	**Dallas**	7:00
Aug. 28	**St. Louis**	7:00

REGULAR SEASON
Sep. 7	**New England**	1:00
Sep. 14	at Buffalo	1:00
Sep. 21	**Kansas City**	4:25
Sep. 28	at Oakland (London)	1:00
Oct. 5	BYE	
Oct. 12	**Green Bay**	1:00
Oct. 19	at Chicago	1:00
Oct. 26	at Jacksonville	1:00
Nov. 2	**San Diego**	1:00
Nov. 9	at Detroit	1:00
Nov. 13	**Buffalo** (Thu)	8:25
Nov. 23	at Denver	4:25
Dec. 1	at New York Jets (Mon)	8:30
Dec. 7	**Baltimore**	1:00
Dec. 14	at New England	1:00
Dec. 21	**Minnesota**	1:00
Dec. 28	**New York Jets**	1:00

* All times ET

Stadium: Sun Life Stadium
    (opened in 1987)
    •**Capacity:** 75,192
    2269 Dan Marino Blvd.
    Miami Gardens, Florida 33056
Playing Surface: Grass (PAT)
Training Camp: Doctors Hospital Training
    Facility Nova Southeastern Univ.
    7500 S.W. 30th Street
    Davie, Florida 33314

SUN LIFE STADIUM

CLUB OFFICIALS
Chairman of the Board/Managing General
    Partner: Stephen M. Ross
Vice-Chairman/Partner: Jorge Perez
Vice-Chairman: Donald F. Shula
Vice-Chairman: Matt Higgins
President and Chief Executive Officer:
    Tom Garfinkel
General Manager: Dennis Hickey
Executive Vice President of Football
    Administration: Dawn Aponte
Senior Vice President of Operations-Sun
    Life Stadium: Todd Boyan
Senior Vice President of Human
    Resources: Dan Caspersen
Senior Vice President-Chief Financial
    Officer: Chris Clements
Senior Vice President of Operations-
    Davie: Bill Galante
Senior Vice President-Chief Technology
    Officer: Tery Howard
Senior Vice President-Chief Marketing
    Officer: Claudia Lezcano
Senior Vice President/Special Projects
    and Alumni Relations: Nat Moore
Senior Vice President-Chief Revenue
    Officer: Jeremy Walls
Vice President of Ticket Sales and
    Service: Nick Forro
Vice President of Historical Affairs:
    Harvey Greene
Vice President of Communications:
    Jason Jenkins
Vice President of Corporate Partnerships
    and Integrated Media: Bob Lynch
Vice President of Sun Life Stadium
    Events: George Torres
Assistant General Manager: Eric Stokes
Director of Player Personnel: Joe Schoen
Director of College Scouting: Chris Grier
Director of Pro Personnel: Anthony Hunt
Assistant Director of Pro Scouting:
    Chris Shea
Manager of Football Administration:
    Ryan Herman
Head Athletic Trainer: Ryan Grove
Equipment Manager: Joe Cimino
Video Director: Bob Hack
Director of Player Engagement:
    Kaleb Thornhill
Director of Team Security:
    Stuart Weinstein
Director of Team Operations: Scott Bullis
General Counsel: Adam Zissman
Director of Miami Dolphins Cheerleaders:
    Emily Snow
Senior Director of Communications:
    Fitz Ollison
Senior Director of Community Affairs and
    Miami Dolphins Foundation:
    Twan Russell
Managing Director, Content and Creative:
    Surf Melendez
Director of Creative Services and
    Photography: Jon Willey
Senior Director of Security: Joe Cicini
Senior Director of Digital and Print Media:
    Scott Stone
Senior Director of Entertainment and
    Brand Impact: Dorie Grogan
Senior Director of Finance: Betsy Christy
Director of Financial Reporting and
    Planning: Jeremy Campos
Director of Government and Community
    Affairs: Leslie Nixon
Senior Director of Programming and
    Production: Jeff Griffith

COACHING HISTORY
(435-337-4)
Records include postseason games
1966-69	George Wilson	15-39-2
1970-1995	Don Shula	274-147-2
1996-99	Jimmy Johnson	38-31-0
2000-04	Dave Wannstedt*	43-33-0
2004	Jim Bates	3-4-0
2005-06	Nick Saban	15-17-0
2007	Cam Cameron	1-15-0
2008-2011	Tony Sparano**	29-33-0
2011	Todd Bowles	2-1-0
2012-13	Joe Philbin	15-17-0

    *Resigned after nine games in 2004
    **Released after 13 games in 2011

PAID ATTENDANCE
Home 505,903   Away 519,091
Total 1,024,994
Single-game home record,
    75,283 (10/27/96)
Single-season home record, 592,161
    (1999)

2014 DRAFT CHOICES
Round	Name	Pos.	College
1	Ja'Wuan James	T	Tennessee
2	Jarvis Landry	WR	Louisiana St.
3	Bill Turner	T	North Dakota St.
4	Walt Aikens	DB	Liberty
5	Arthur Lynch	TE	Georgia
	Jordan Tripp	LB	Montana
6	Matt Hazel	WR	Coastal Carolina
7	Terrence Fede	DE	Marist

2013 TEAM RECORD
PRESEASON (2-3)

Date	Result		Opponent
08/04	L	20-24	at Dallas
08/09	W	27-3	at Jacksonville
08/17	L	17-24	at Houston
08/24	L	16-17	Tampa Bay
08/29	W	24-21	New Orleans

REGULAR SEASON (8-8)

Date	Result		Opponent
09/08	W	23-10	at Cleveland
09/15	W	24-20	at Indianapolis
09/22	W	27-23	Atlanta
09/30	L	17-38	at New Orleans
10/06	L	23-26	Baltimore
10/20	L	21-23	Buffalo
10/27	L	17-27	at New England
10/31	W	22-20	Cincinnati (OT)
11/11	L	19-22	at Tampa Bay
11/17	W	20-16	San Diego
11/24	L	16-20	Carolina
12/01	W	23-3	at New York Jets
12/08	W	34-28	at Pittsburgh
12/15	W	24-20	New England
12/22	L	0-19	at Buffalo
12/29	L	7-20	New York Jets

(OT) Overtime

SCORE BY PERIODS

Dolphins	43	117	88	67	2	—	317
Opponents	67	92	88	88	0	—	335

2013 TEAM STATISTICS

	Dolphins	Opp.
Total First Downs	278	327
Rushing	61	114
Passing	205	192
Penalty	12	21
3rd Down: Made/Att	76/217	91/238
3rd Down Pct.	35.0	38.2
4th Down: Made/Att	3/12	8/15
4th Down Pct.	25.0	53.3
Possession Avg.	28:27	31:33
Total Net Yards	5007	5750
Avg. Per Game	312.9	359.4
Total Plays	1001	1106
Avg. Per Play	5.0	5.2
Net Yards Rushing	1440	1998
Avg. Per Game	90.0	124.9
Total Rushes	349	484
Net Yards Passing	3567	3752
Avg. Per Game	222.9	234.5
Sacked/Yards Lost	58/399	42/272
Gross Yards	3966	4024
Att./Completions	594/357	580/344
Completion Pct.	60.1	59.3
Had Intercepted	19	18
Punts/Average	85/48.8	78/43.7
Net Punting Avg.	85/42.4	78/38.7
Penalties/Yards	70/598	95/748
Fumbles/Ball Lost	16/7	14/6
Touchdowns	34	33
Rushing	8	14
Passing	24	17
Returns	2	2

2013 INDIVIDUAL STATISTICS

PASSING	Att.	Comp.	Yds.	Pct.	TD	Int.	Tkld.	Rate
Tannehill	588	355	3913	60.4	24	17	58/399	81.7
Mat. Moore	6	2	53	33.3	0	2	0/0	27.1
Dolphins	594	357	3966	60.1	24	19	58/399	80.1
Opponents	580	344	4024	59.3	17	18	42/272	77.3

SCORING	TD R	TD P	TD Rt	PAT	FG	Saf	PTS
Sturgis	0	0	0	33/33	26/34	0	111
Clay	1	6	0	0/0	0/0	0	42
Dan. Thomas	4	2	0	0/0	0/0	0	36
Wallace	0	5	0	0/0	0/0	0	30
Hartline	0	4	0	0/0	0/0	0	24
Gibson	0	3	0	0/0	0/0	0	18
Matthews	0	2	0	0/0	0/0	0	12
L. Miller	2	0	0	0/0	0/0	0	12
Grimes	0	0	1	0/0	0/0	0	6
R. Jones	0	0	1	0/0	0/0	0	6
Sims	0	1	0	0/0	0/0	0	6
Tannehill	1	0	0	0/0	0/0	0	6
Thigpen	0	1	0	0/0	0/0	0	6
Wake	0	0	0	0/0	0/0	1	2
Dolphins	8	24	2	33/33	26/34	1	317
Opponents	14	17	2	33/33	34/40	1	335

2-Pt Conversions: Dolphins 0-1, Opponents 0-0.

RUSHING	No.	Yds	Avg	LG	TD
L. Miller	177	709	4.0	49	2
Dan. Thomas	109	406	3.7	55	4
Tannehill	40	238	6.0	48	1
Wallace	3	33	11.0	13	0
Gillislee	6	21	3.5	6	0
Thigpen	6	18	3.0	9	0
Clay	7	15	2.1	13	1
Fields	1	0	0.0	0	0
Dolphins	349	1440	4.1	55	8
Opponents	484	1998	4.1	51	14

RECEIVING	No.	Yds	Avg	LG	TD
Hartline	76	1016	13.4	50	4
Wallace	73	930	12.7	57	5
Clay	69	759	11.0	67	6
Matthews	41	448	10.9	29	2
Gibson	30	326	10.9	46	3
L. Miller	26	170	6.5	22	0
Dan. Thomas	15	63	4.2	16	2
Thigpen	8	97	12.1	50	1
Egnew	7	69	9.9	14	0
Mar. Moore	6	56	9.3	13	0
Sims	6	32	5.3	8	1
Dolphins	357	3966	11.1	67	24
Opponents	344	4024	11.7	67	17

INTERCEPTIONS	No.	Yds	Avg	LG	TD
Grimes	4	102	25.5	94t	1
Patterson	4	7	1.8	3	0
Carroll	3	24	8.0	24	0
Ellerbe	2	25	12.5	16	0
Wilson	2	21	10.5	23	0
R. Jones	1	25	25.0	25t	1
Clemons	1	0	0.0	0	0
M. Thomas	1	0	0.0	0	0
Dolphins	18	204	11.3	94t	2
Opponents	19	165	8.7	29	2

PUNTING	No.	Yds.	Avg.	In 20	LG
Fields	85	4150	48.8	33	74
Dolphins	85	4150	48.8	33	74
Opponents	78	3406	43.7	22	72

PUNT RETURNS	Ret	FC	Yds	Avg	LG	TD
Thigpen	34	20	264	7.8	34	0
Dolphins	34	20	264	7.8	34	0
Opponents	42	13	407	9.7	52	0

KICKOFF RETURNS	No.	Yds	Avg	LG	TD
Thigpen	39	870	22.3	50	0
Clay	2	23	11.5	15	0
Spitler	1	0	0.0	0	0
Dolphins	42	893	21.3	50	0
Opponents	36	826	22.9	47	0

FIELD GOALS	1-19	20-29	30-39	40-49	50+
Sturgis	1/1	4/4	10/12	8/10	3/7
Dolphins	1/1	4/4	10/12	8/10	3/7
Opponents	0/0	14/14	10/13	5/7	5/6

SACKS	No.
Vernon	11.5
Wake	8.5
Odrick	4.5
Starks	4.0
Shelby	2.5
Carroll	2.0
Jordan	2.0
Misi	2.0
R. Jones	1.5
Ellerbe	1.0
Patterson	1.0
Soliai	1.0
Wheeler	0.5
Dolphins	42.0
Opponents	58.0

RECORD HOLDERS
INDIVIDUAL RECORDS—CAREER

Category	Name	Performance
Rushing (Yds.)	Larry Csonka, 1968-1974, 1979	6,737
Passing (Yds.)	Dan Marino, 1983-1999	61,361
Passing (TDs)	Dan Marino, 1983-1999	420
Receiving (No.)	Mark Clayton, 1983-1992	550
Receiving (Yds.)	Mark Duper, 1982-1992	8,869
Interceptions	Jake Scott, 1970-75	35
Punting (Avg.)	Brandon Fields, 2007-2013	46.8
Punt Return (Avg.)	Jeff Ogden, 2000-01	13.7
Kickoff Return (Avg.)	Mercury Morris, 1969-1975	26.5
Field Goals	Olindo Mare, 1997-2006	245
Touchdowns (Tot.)	Mark Clayton, 1983-1992	82
Points	Olindo Mare, 1997-2006	1,048
*Sacks	Jason Taylor, 1997-2007, 2009, 2011	131.0

INDIVIDUAL RECORDS—SINGLE SEASON

Category	Name	Performance
Rushing (Yds.)	Ricky Williams, 2002	1,853
Passing (Yds.)	Dan Marino, 1984	5,084
Passing (TDs)	Dan Marino, 1984	48
Receiving (No.)	O.J. McDuffie, 1998	90
Receiving (Yds.)	Mark Clayton, 1984	1,389
Interceptions	Dick Westmoreland, 1967	10
Punting (Avg.)	Brandon Fields, 2012	50.2
Punt Return (Avg.)	Jeff Ogden, 2000	17.0
Kickoff Return (Avg.)	Duriel Harris, 1976	32.9
Field Goals	Olindo Mare, 1999	39
Touchdowns (Tot.)	Mark Clayton, 1984	18
Points	Olindo Mare, 1999	144
*Sacks	Jason Taylor, 2002	18.5

INDIVIDUAL RECORDS—SINGLE GAME

Category	Name	Performance
Rushing (Yds.)	Ricky Williams, 12-1-02	228
Passing (Yds.)	Dan Marino, 10-23-88	521
Passing (TDs)	Bob Griese, 11-24-77	6
	Dan Marino, 9-21-86	6
Receiving (No.)	Chris Chambers, 12-4-05	15
Receiving (Yds.)	Brian Hartline, 9-30-12	253
Interceptions	Dick Anderson, 12-3-73	**4
Field Goals	Olindo Mare, 10-17-99	6
Touchdowns (Tot.)	Paul Warfield, 12-15-73	4
	Mark Ingram, 11-27-94	4
	Ronnie Brown, 9-21-08	4
Points	Paul Warfield, 12-15-73	24
	Mark Ingram, 11-27-94	24
	Ronnie Brown, 9-21-08	24
*Sacks	Cameron Wake, 9-30-12	4.5

*Sacks became an official statistic in 1982.
**NFL Record

2014 VETERAN ROSTER

No.	Name	Pos.	Ht.	Wt.	Birthdate	NFL Exp.	College	Hometown	How Acq.	'13 Games/ Starts
71	Albert, Branden	T	6-5	316	11/4/84	7	Virginia	Glen Burnie, Md.	UFA(KC)-'14	13/13*
66	Arkin, David	OL	6-5	310	10/7/87	3	Missouri State	Wichita, Kan.	FA-'13	1/0
19	Binns, Armon	WR	6-3	211	9/8/89	3	Cincinnati	Pasadena, Calif.	W(Cin)-'12	0*
65	Brenner, Sam	C	6-2	310	4/27/90	2	Utah	Oceanside, Calif.	FA-'13	7/4
30	Brown, Jalil	CB	6-1	204	10/17/87	4	Colorado	Phoenix, Ariz.	W(Ind)-'13	0*
42	Clay, Charles	TE	6-3	255	2/13/89	4	Tulsa	Little Rock, Ark.	D6-'11	16/15
15	Cone, Kevin	WR	6-2	216	3/20/88	3	Georgia Tech	Atlanta, Ga.	FA-'14	16/0*
29	Davis, Will	CB	5-11	190	5/8/90	2	Utah State	Spokane, Wash.	D3b-'13	5/0
25	Delmas, Louis	S	5-11	202	4/12/87	6	Western Michigan	North Miami Beach, Fla.	FA-'14	16/15*
92	Denney, John	LS	6-5	255	12/13/78	10	Brigham Young	Thornton, Colo.	FA-'05	16/0
7	Devlin, Pat	QB	6-3	225	4/12/88	4	Delaware	Exton, Pa.	FA-'11	0*
84	Egnew, Michael	TE	6-5	262	11/1/89	3	Missouri	Plainview, Texas	D3b-'12	16/5
59	Ellerbe, Dannell	LB	6-1	245	11/29/85	6	Georgia	Rockingham, N.C.	UFA(Balt)-'13	15/15
2	Fields, Brandon	P	6-5	249	5/21/84	8	Michigan State	Toledo, Ohio	D7b-'07	16/0
24	Finnegan, Cortland	CB	5-10	179	2/22/84	9	Samford	Milton, Fla.	FA-'14	7/5*
74	Fox, Jason	T	6-6	314	5/2/88	5	Miami	Fort Worth, Texas	UFA(Det)-'14	8/3*
96	Francis, AJ	DT	6-5	316	5/7/90	2	Maryland	Severn, Md.	FA-'13	0*
56	Freeny, Jonathan	LB	6-2	250	6/15/89	3	Rutgers	Margate, Fla.	FA-'12	16/0
75	Garner, Nate	G	6-7	320	1/18/85	7	Arkansas	Roland, Ark.	W(NYJ)-'08	16/6
10	Gibson, Brandon	WR	6-0	207	8/13/87	6	Washington State	Puyallup, Wash.	UFA(StL)-'13	7/3
23	Gillislee, Mike	RB	5-11	213	11/1/90	2	Florida	DeLand, Fla.	D5a-'13	3/0
21	Grimes, Brent	CB	5-10	190	7/19/83	8	Shippensburg	Philadelphia, Pa.	UFA(Atl)-'13	16/16
82	Hartline, Brian	WR	6-2	199	11/22/86	6	Ohio State	North Canton, Ohio	D4-'09	16/15
53	Jenkins, Jelani	LB	6-0	243	3/13/92	2	Florida	Olney, Md.	D4a-'13	16/0
36	Jones, Don	S	5-11	200	5/14/90	2	Arkansas State	Town Creek, Ala.	D7-'13	16/0
20	Jones, Reshad	S	6-1	215	2/25/88	5	Georgia	Atlanta, Ga.	D5b-'10	16/16
95	Jordan, Dion	DE	6-6	260	3/5/90	2	Oregon	Chandler, Ariz.	D1-'13	16/0
44	Kovacs, Jordan	S	5-10	210	6/12/90	2	Michigan	Curtice, Ohio	FA-'13	9/0
18	Matthews, Rishard	WR	6-0	210	10/12/89	3	Nevada	Santa Ana, Calif.	D7b-'12	16/5
86	Miller, Kyle	TE	6-5	262	4/18/88	2	Mount Union	Elida, Ohio	FA-'14	0*
26	Miller, Lamar	RB	5-10	216	4/25/91	3	Miami	Miami, Fla.	D4b-'12	16/15
55	Misi, Koa	LB	6-3	254	1/17/87	5	Utah	Santa Rosa, Calif.	D2-'10	15/12
90	Mitchell, Earl	DT	6-3	300	9/25/87	5	Arizona	Houston, Texas	UFA(Hou)-'14	16/14*
8	Moore, Matt	QB	6-3	216	8/9/84	8	Oregon State	Newhall, Calif.	UFA(Car)-'11	1/0
28	Moreno, Knowshon	RB	5-11	220	7/16/87	6	Georgia	Middletown, N.J.	UFA(Den)-'14	19/18*
98	Odrick, Jared	DT	6-5	302	12/31/87	5	Penn State	Lebanon County, Pa.	D1-'10	16/5
51	Pouncey, Mike	C	6-5	305	7/24/89	4	Florida	Lakeland, Fla.	D1-'11	14/14
79	Shelby, Derrick	DE	6-2	280	3/4/89	3	Utah	Houston, Texas	FA-'12	16/1
80	Sims, Dion	TE	6-4	265	2/18/91	2	Michigan State	Detroit, Mich.	D4b-'13	15/5
64	Smith, Shelley	G	6-4	312	5/21/87	5	Colorado State	Phoenix, Ariz.	UFA(StL)-'14	14/2*
94	Starks, Randy	DT	6-3	305	12/14/83	11	Maryland	Waldorf, Md.	UFA(Tenn)-'08	16/14
9	Sturgis, Caleb	K	5-9	190	8/9/89	2	Florida	St. Augustine, Fla.	D5b-'13	16/0
17	Tannehill, Ryan	QB	6-4	222	7/27/88	3	Texas A&M	Big Spring, Texas	D1-'12	16/16
22	Taylor, Jamar	CB	5-10	195	9/29/90	2	Boise State	San Diego, Calif.	D2-'13	9/0
34	Thigpen, Marcus	RB	5-9	195	5/15/86	3	Indiana	Detroit, Mich.	FA-'12	16/0
70	Thomas, Dallas	G	6-5	315	10/30/89	2	Tennessee	Baton Rouge, La.	D3a-'13	6/0
33	Thomas, Daniel	RB	6-1	235	10/29/87	4	Kansas State	Hilliard, Fla.	D2-'11	15/1
31	Thomas, Michael	S	5-11	196	3/17/89	2	Stanford	Houston, Texas	FA-'13	3/0
93	Trusnik, Jason	LB	6-4	252	6/6/84	8	Ohio Northern	Macedonia, Ohio	UFA(Cle)-'11	16/2
50	Vernon, Olivier	DE	6-2	268	10/7/90	3	Miami	Miami, Fla.	D3a-'12	16/14
91	Wake, Cameron	DE	6-3	258	1/30/82	6	Penn State	Hyattsville, Md.	FA-'09	15/15
11	Wallace, Mike	WR	6-0	195	8/1/86	6	Mississippi	New Orleans, La.	UFA(Pitt)-'13	16/16
52	Wheeler, Philip	LB	6-2	240	12/12/84	7	Georgia Tech	Columbus, Ga.	UFA(Oak)-'13	16/16
1	Williams, Damian	WR	6-1	193	5/26/88	5	Southern California	Springdale, Ark.	UFA(Tenn)-'14	10/1*
81	Williams, Stephen	WR	6-5	208	6/29/86	4	Toledo	Levelland , Texas	FA-'14	6/0*
27	Wilson, Jimmy	S	5-11	205	7/30/86	4	Montana	San Diego, Calif.	D7b-'11	16/3

* Albert played 13 games with Kansas City in '13; Binns missed '13 season because of injury; Brown inactive two games; Cone played 16 games with Atlanta; Delmas played 16 games with Detroit; Devlin inactive 16 games; Finnegan played 7 games with St. Louis; Fox played eight games with Detroit; Francis inactive five games; K. Miller inactive six games with Miami in '12; Mitchell played 16 games with Houston; Moreno played 16 games with Denver; Smith played 14 games with St. Louis; D. Williams played 10 games with Tennessee; S. Williams played 2 games with Jacksonville and 4 games with Seattle.

Traded (1) —T Jonathan Martin (7 games in '13) to San Francisco.

Players lost through free agency (5): CB Nolan Carroll (Phil; 16 games in '13), S Chris Clemons (Hou; 16), G John Jerry (NYG; 16), CB Christopher Owens (KC; 1), DT Paul Soliai (Atl; 15).

Also played with Dolphins in '13— DT Isaako Aaitui (4 games), DT Marvin Austin (2), CB D.J. Campbell (4), T Tyson Clabo (15), FB Tyler Clutts (4), G Richie Incognito (8), LB Josh Kaddu (1), DT Vaughn Martin (3), S Kelcie McCray (4), T Bryant McKinnie (10), WR Marlon Moore (8), CB Dimitri Patterson (6), WR Ryan Spadola (1), LB Austin Spitler (12), CB R.J. Stanford (13), G Danny Watkins (1), T Will Yeatman (8).

FIRST-YEAR ROSTER

Name	Pos.	Ht.	Wt.	Birthdate	College	Hometown	How Acq.
Aaitui, Isaako (1)	DT	6-4	315	1/25/87	Nevada-Las Vegas	Pago Pago, American Samoa	FA
Aikens, Walt	DB	6-1	209	6/19/91	Liberty	Charlotte, N.C.	D4
Belue, Deion	DB	5-11	182	9/3/92	Alabama	Tuscumbia, Ala.	FA
Clarke, Steven	DB	5-10	189	4/19/91	Vanderbilt	Lauderdale Lakes, Fla.	FA
Darkwa, Orleans	RB	6-0	210	2/28/92	Tulane	Nashville, Tenn.	FA
Edwards, Tariq	LB	6-2	235	5/1/91	Virginia Tech	Cheraw, S.C.	FA
Fede, Terrence	DE	6-4	277	11/19/91	Marist	Nyack, N.Y.	D7
Finkenberg, Evan	OL	6-4	300	10/4/90	Arizona State	Coto De Caza, Calif.	FA
Hazel, Matt	WR	6-1	198	1/23/92	Coastal Carolina	North Agusta, S.C.	D6
Hoskins, Harold	TE	6-2	253	12/19/91	Marshall	Gainesville, Fla.	FA
Hurd, David	OL	6-6	308	10/20/90	Arkansas	West Monroe, La.	FA
James, Ja'Wuan	OL	6-6	311	6/3/92	Tennessee	Suwannee, Ga.	D1
Jensen, Brock	QB	6-3	223	9/19/90	North Dakota State	Waupaca, Wisc.	FA
Johnson, Anthony	DT	6-2	308	1/24/93	Louisiana State	New Orleans, La.	FA
Johnson, Derrell	LB	6-2	257	3/27/90	East Carolina	Baltimore, Md.	FA
Johnson, Kamal	DT	6-3	305	12/9/91	Temple	Willingboro, N.J.	FA
Landry, Jarvis	WR	5-11	205	11/28/92	Louisiana State	Lutcher, La.	D2
Larsen, Tyler	OL	6-4	313	7/8/91	Utah State	Salt Lake City, Utah	FA
Lynch, Arthur	TE	6-5	258	6/17/90	Georgia	Dartmouth, Mass	D5
Marshall, Cameron	RB	5-9	217	10/14/91	Arizona State	San Jose, Calif.	FA
McCain, Chris	LB	6-5	224	11/21/91	California	Greensboro, N.C.	FA
Mims, Tevin	DE	6-4	260	1/23/91	South Florida	Round Rock, Texas	FA
Ogbuehi, Emmanuel	TE/FB	6-3	250	8/17/90	Georgia State	Buford, Ga.	FA
Ola, Michael	T	6-3	278	4/19/88	Hampton	Riverside, Calif.	FA
Smith, Garrison	DT	6-1	294	10/9/91	Georgia	Atlanta, Ga.	FA
Spadola, Ryan (1)	WR	6-1	201	2/15/91	Lehigh	Freehold, N.J.	FA
Thompson, Marcus	LB	6-1	250	10/9/90	Rutgers	Oakland Park, Fla.	FA
Tripp, Jordan	LB	6-3	234	4/30/91	Montana	Missoula, Mont.	D5b
Turner, Billy	OL	6-5	315	10/17/91	North Dakota State	Shoreview, Minn.	D3
Wallace, Davonte	OL	6-3	308	12/21/91	New Mexico State	El Paso, Texas	FA
Williams, Damien	RB	5-11	222	4/3/92	Oklahoma	San Diego, Calif.	FA
Wilson, Andrew	LB	6-3	239	2/7/91	Missouri	Peculiar, Mo.	FA
Wooten, Rantavious	WR	5-9	178	9/26/89	Georgia	Belle Glade, Fla.	FA
Wright, Demetrius	DB	6-0	203	12/19/91	Southern California	Corona, Calif.	FA

The term NFL Rookie is defined as a player who is in his first season of professional football and has not been on the roster of another professional football team for any regular-season or postseason games. A Rookie is designated by an "R" on NFL rosters. Players who have been active in another professional football league or players who have NFL experience, including either preseason training camp or being on an Active List or Inactive List, or on Reserve/Injured or Reserve/Physically Unable to Perform for fewer than six regular-season games, are termed NFL First-Year Players. An NFL First-Year Player is designated by a "1" on NFL rosters. Thereafter, a player is credited with an additional year of experience for each season in which he accumulates six games on the Active List or Inactive List, or on Reserve/Injured or Reserve/Physically Unable to Perform.

Log on to www.miamidolphins.com for an up-to-date roster.

COACHING STAFF

Head Coach,
Joe Philbin

Pro Career: Became the ninth coach in Dolphins history on January 20, 2012. Philbin joined Miami after serving as the offensive coordinator with the Green Bay Packers from 2007-2011. During that era, his offense ranked in the top 10 in points scored and total yards every season. In five seasons at the helm of the Packers' prolific offense, the team scored 2,263 points (third in the NFL during that span). In 2011, the Packers set franchise records for victories (15), points (560), and total yards (6,357). The 560 points ranked second in NFL history. In 2008-09, the Packers became the first team in league annals to have a 4,000-yard passer (Aaron Rodgers), a 1,200-yard rusher (Ryan Grant) and two 1,000-yard receivers (Greg Jennings, Donald Driver) in consecutive seasons. Philbin joined the Packers in 2003 as an assistant offensive line coach. He served as the tight ends/assistant offensive line coach from 2004-05 and offensive line coach in 2006. Career record: 15-17.
Background: Philbin played one year at Washington & Jefferson, where he earned his degree in sociology. He has coached collegiately at Tulane (1984-85), Worcester Polytechnic Institute (1986-87), Allegheny (1990-93), Ohio (1994), Northeastern (1995-96), Harvard (1997-98) and Iowa (1999-2002).
Personal: Born July 2, 1961 in Springfield, Mass. He and his wife Diane have six children Matthew, John, Kevin, Tim, Colleen and a deceased son, Michael.

ASSISTANT COACHES

Blue Adams, asst. defensive backs; born October 15, 1979, Miami, Fla. Defensive back Cincinnati 1998-2003. Pro defensive back New York Giants/Jacksonville Jaguars 2003, Rhein Fire 2004, Tampa Bay Buccaneers 2005-06, Cincinnati Bengals 2007. College coach: Purdue 2010, Northern Iowa 2011. Pro coach: Joined Dolphins in 2012.
Lou Anarumo, defensive backs; born August 18, 1966, Staten Island, N.Y. Attended Wagner. No college or pro playing experience. College coach: U.S. Merchant Marine Academy 1989-1990, 1992-94, Wagner 1990, Syracuse 1990-91, Harvard 1995-2000, Marshall 2001-03, Purdue 2004-2011. Pro coach: Joined Dolphins in 2012.
John Benton, offensive line; born December 13, 1963, Los Angeles, Calif. Offensive lineman Colorado State 1986-1990. No pro playing experience. College coach: California University (Pa.) 1990-94, Colorado State 1996-2003. Pro coach: St. Louis Rams 2004-05, Houston Texans 2006-2013, joined Dolphins in 2014.
Jack Bicknell Jr., assistant offensive line; born February 7, 1963, North Plainfield, N.J. Center Boston College 1981-1985. No

pro playing experience. College coach: Boston College 1985-86, 2007-08, New Hampshire 1987-1996, Louisiana Tech 1997-2006. Pro coach: New York Giants 2009-2011, Kansas City Chiefs 2012, Pittsburgh Steelers 2013, joined Dolphins in 2014.
Charlie Bullen, asst. defensive line; born September 28, 1984, Palatine, Ill. Attended Iowa. No college or pro playing experience. College coach: Iowa 2007-2011. Pro coach: Joined Dolphins in 2012.
Jeff Burris, defensive assistant; born June 6, 1972, Rock Hill, S.C. Defensive back Notre Dame 1990-93. Pro defensive back Buffalo Bills 1994-97, Indianapolis Colts 1998-2001, Cincinnati Bengals 2002-03. College coach: Massachusetts 2012. Pro coach: Sacramento Mountain Lions (UFL) 2011, joined Dolphins in 2013.
Dan Campbell, tight ends; born April 13, 1976, Clifton, Texas. Tight end Texas A&M 1994-98. Pro tight end New York Giants 1999-2002, Dallas Cowboys 2003-05, Detroit Lions 2006-08, New Orleans Saints 2009. Pro coach: Joined Dolphins in 2010.
David Corrao, asst. linebackers; born June 11, 1974, Mission Viejo, Calif. Running back San Diego 1992. No pro playing experience. College coach: Syracuse 2000-03, Northeastern 2004, Mississippi 2005-07. Pro coach: Joined Dolphins in 2008.
Kevin Coyle, defensive coordinator: born January 14, 1956, Staten Island, N.Y. Defensive back Massachusetts 1975-77. No pro playing experience. College coach: Cincinnati 1978-79, Arkansas 1980, U.S. Merchant Marine Academy 1981, Holy Cross 1982-1990, Syracuse 1991-93, Maryland 1994-96, Fresno State 1997-2000. Pro coach: Cincinnati Bengals 2001-2010. Pro coach: Joined Dolphins in 2012.
Mark Duffner, linebackers; born July 19, 1953, Annandale, Va. Defensive lineman William & Mary 1972-74. No pro playing experience. College coach: Ohio State 1975-76, Cincinnati 1977-1980, Holy Cross 1981-1991 (head coach 1986-1991), Maryland 1992-1996 (head coach). Pro coach: Cincinnati Bengals 1997-2002, Green Bay Packers 2003-05, Jacksonville Jaguars 2006-2013, joined Dolphins in 2014.
Ben Johnson, asst. quarterbacks; born May 11, 1986, Charleston, S.C. Quarterback North Carolina 2004-08. No pro playing experience. College coach: Boston College 2010-11. Pro coach: Joined Dolphins in 2012.
Darren Krein, head strength & conditioning; born July 7, 1971, Aurora, Colo. Linebacker/defensive end Miami 1989-1993. Pro linebacker San Diego Chargers 1994, Barcelona Dragons (NFLE) 1996. Pro coach: Seattle Seahawks 1997-98, 2002-09, joined Dolphins in 2011.
Bill Lazor, offensive coordinator; born June 14, 1972, Scranton, Pa. Quarterback Cornell 1990-93. No pro playing experience. College coach: Cornell 1994-2000,

Buffalo 2001-02, Virginia 2010-12. Pro coach: Atlanta Falcons 2003, Washington Redskins 2004-07, Seattle Seahawks 2008-09, Philadelphia Eagles 2013, joined Dolphins in 2014.
Marwan Maalouf, asst. special teams; born November 26, 1976, Strongsville, Ohio. Guard Baldwin-Wallace 1997-99. No pro playing experience. College coach: Baldwin-Wallace 2000, Fordham 2001, Rutgers 2002-03. Pro coach: Cleveland Browns 2004-06, Baltimore Ravens 2008-2011, Indianapolis Colts 2012, joined Dolphins in 2013.
Phil McGeoghan, asst. wide receivers, July 8, 1979 in Springfield, Mass. Wide receiver Maine 1998-2000. Pro wide receiver Denver 2001. College coach: Maine 2007, Naval Academy Prep 2008, South Florida 2009-2011. Pro coach: Joined Dolphins in 2012.
Jeff Nixon, running backs; born October 16, 1974, Rochester, Pa. Running back West Virginia 1993-94, Penn State 1996. No pro playing experience. College coach: Penn State 1997, Princeton 1998, Shippensburg 1999-2002, Tennessee-Chattanooga 2003-05, Temple 2006. Pro coach: Philadelphia Eagles 2007-2010, joined Dolphins in 2011.
Ken O'Keefe, wide receivers; born August 18, 1953, Milford, Conn. No pro playing experience. College coach: New Haven 1976-77, Allegheny 1986-1997, Fordham 1998, Iowa 1999-2011. Pro coach: Joined Dolphins in 2012.
Dave Puloka, asst. strength and conditioning; born January 12, 1979, Arlington, Mass. Linebacker Holy Cross 1997-2000. No pro playing experience. College coach: Stevens Institute of Technology 2005, Virginia 2006. Pro coach: Atlanta Falcons 2007, joined Dolphins in 2008.
Darren Rizzi, special teams coordinator; born July 21, 1970, Hillsdale, N.J. Tight end Rhode Island 1988-1991. College coach: Rhode Island 1992, Colgate 1993, New Haven 1993-97, Northeastern 1998, New Haven 1999-2001 (head coach), Rutgers 2002-07, Rhode Island 2008 (head coach). Pro coach: Joined Dolphins in 2009.
Kacy Rodgers, defensive line; born June 24, 1969, Humboldt, Tenn. Linebacker/defensive end Tennessee 1988-1991. Pro linebacker Shreveport Pirates (CFL) 1994. College coach: Tennessee-Martin 1994-97, Louisiana-Monroe 1998, Middle Tennessee State 1999-2001, Arkansas 2002. Pro coach: Dallas Cowboys 2003-07, joined Dolphins in 2008.
Zac Taylor, quarterbacks; born May 10, 1983, Norman Okla. Quarterback Nebraska 2005-06. Pro quarterback Tampa Bay Buccaneers 2007. College coach: Texas A&M 2011. Pro coach: Joined Dolphins in 2012.

**American Football Conference
East Division**
Team Colors: Blue, Red, Silver, and White
Gillette Stadium
One Patriot Place
Foxborough, Massachusetts 02035
Telephone: (508) 543-8200

2014 SCHEDULE
PRESEASON
Aug. 7   at Washington 7:30
Aug. 15   **Philadelphia** 7:30
Aug. 22   **Carolina**............................7:30
Aug. 28   at New York Giants 7:30

REGULAR SEASON
Sep. 7   at Miami 1:00
Sep. 14   at Minnesota 1:00
Sep. 21   **Oakland** 1:00
Sep. 29   at Kansas City (Mon).........8:30
Oct. 5   **Cincinnati** *8:30
Oct. 12   at Buffalo 1:00
Oct. 16   **New York Jets** (Thu).........8:25
Oct. 26   **Chicago** 1:00
Nov. 2   **Denver** 4:25
Nov. 9   BYE
Nov. 16   at Indianapolis *8:30
Nov. 23   **Detroit** 1:00
Nov. 30   at Green Bay 4:25
Dec. 7   at San Diego *8:30
Dec. 14   **Miami** 1:00
Dec. 21   at New York Jets 1:00
Dec. 28   **Buffalo** 1:00
*All times ET; Sunday night games in
   Weeks 5-16 subject to change
Stadium: Gillette Stadium
   (opened in 2002)
   •**Capacity:** 68,756
   One Patriot Place
   Foxborough, Massachusetts 02035
Playing Surface: FieldTurf
Training Camp: Gillette Stadium
                  Foxborough, MA 02035

GILLETTE STADIUM

CLUB OFFICIALS
Chairman & CEO: Robert K. Kraft
President: Jonathan A. Kraft
President of New England Patriots
   Charitable Foundation: Josh Kraft
Director of Player Development:
   Kevin Anderson
Vice President of Human Resources:
   Robin Boudreau
Chief Operating Officer of TeamOps
   Security: Mark Briggs
Equipment Manager: Dave Schoenfeld
Director of Player Personnel:
   Nick Caserio
Vice President of Information
   Technology: Pat Curley
Video Director: Jimmy Dee
Senior Vice President of Marketing and
   Brand Development: Jennifer Ferron
Vice President of Customer Marketing
   and Strategy: Jessica Gelman
Vice President, The Kraft Group and Club
   Counsel, the New England Patriots:
   Robyn Glaser
Vice President of Media and Community
   Relations: Stacey James
Publisher and Vice President of Content:
   Fred Kirsch
Vice President of Corporate Sales:
   Murray Kohl
Assistant to the Coaching Staff:
   Michael Lombardi
Associate Director of Football Operations:
   Michelle Martini
Director of Research: Richard Miller
Vice President of Stadium Business
   Development and External Affairs:
   Dan Murphy
Director of Football / Head Coach
   Administration: Berj Najarian
Senior Vice President of Finance,
   Administration and Operation:
   James Nolan
Vice President of Corporate
   Relationships: David Pearlstein
Senior Executive Producer of Broadcast
   Production: Matt Smith
Director of Cheerleaders: Tracy Sormanti
Executive Director of Community Affairs:
   Andre Tippett
Senior Director of Marketing Services
   and Operations: Gail Titus
Head Athletic Trainer: Jim Whalen
Vice President of Food and Beverage:
   David Wheeler
Vice President of Finance: Jim Wilson
Executive Director of The Hall at Patriot
   Place presented by Raytheon:
   Bryan Morry
Executive Director of Sales: Brian Oates

COACHING HISTORY
Boston 1960-1970
(463-391-9)
Records include postseason games
1960-61   Lou Saban*....................7-12-0
1961-68   Mike Holovak 53-47-9
1969-1970   Clive Rush**..................5-16-0
1970-72   John Mazur*** 9-21-0
1972   Phil Bengtson 1-4-0
1973-78   Chuck Fairbanks**** 46-41-0
1978   Hank Bullough-Ron Erhardt# ...0-1-0
1979-1981   Ron Erhardt 21-27-0
1982-84   Ron Meyer## 18-16-0
1984-89   Raymond Berry 51-41-0
1990   Rod Rust.........................1-15-0
1991-92   Dick MacPherson 8-24-0
1993-96   Bill Parcells 34-34-0
1997-99   Pete Carroll 28-23-0
2000-2013 Bill Belichick...............181-69-0
      *Released after five games in 1961
   **Released after seven games in 1970
  ***Resigned after nine games in 1972
****Suspended for final regular-season game in 1978
      #Co-coaches
   ##Released after eight games in 1984

PAID ATTENDANCE
Home 535,811   Away 557,491
Total 1,093,302
Single-game home record,
   71,768 (11/30/08)
Single-season home record,
   579,182 (2007)

2014 DRAFT CHOICES
Round	Name	Pos.	College
1	Dominique Easley	DE	Florida
2	Jimmy Garoppolo	QB	Eastern Illinois
4	Bryan Stork	C	Florida St.
	James White	RB	Wisconsin
	Cameron Fleming	T	Stanford
6	Jon Halapio	G	Florida
	Zach Moore	DE	Concordia-St. Paul
	Jemea Thomas	DB	Georgia Tech
7	Jeremy Gallon	WR	Michigan

2013 TEAM RECORD
PRESEASON (3-1)

Date	Result	Opponent
08/09	W 31-22	at Philadelphia
08/16	W 25-21	Tampa Bay
08/22	L 9-40	at Detroit
08/29	W 28-20	New York Giants

REGULAR SEASON (12-4)

Date	Result	Opponent
09/08	W 23-21	at Buffalo
09/12	W 13-10	New York Jets
09/22	W 23-3	Tampa Bay
09/29	W 30-23	at Atlanta
10/06	L 6-13	at Cincinnati
10/13	W 30-27	New Orleans
10/20	L 27-30	at New York Jets (OT)
10/27	W 27-17	Miami
11/03	W 55-31	Pittsburgh
11/18	L 20-24	at Carolina
11/24	W 34-31	Denver (OT)
12/01	W 34-31	at Houston
12/08	W 27-26	Cleveland
12/15	L 20-24	at Miami
12/22	W 41-7	at Baltimore
12/29	W 34-20	Buffalo

POSTSEASON (1-1)

Date	Result	Opponent
01/11	W 43-22	Indianapolis
01/19	L 16-26	at Denver

(OT) Overtime

SCORE BY PERIODS

Patriots	74	104	85	178	3	—	444
Opponents	70	74	95	96	3	—	338

2013 TEAM STATISTICS

	Patriots	Opp.
Total First Downs	378	338
Rushing	110	110
Passing	225	208
Penalty	43	20
3rd Down: Made/Att	83/221	98/232
3rd Down Pct.	37.6	42.2
4th Down: Made/Att	7/15	4/21
4th Down Pct.	46.7	19.0
Possession Avg.	29:38	30:22
Total Net Yards	6152	5969
Avg. Per Game	384.5	373.1
Total Plays	1138	1118
Avg. Per Play	5.4	5.3
Net Yards Rushing	2065	2145
Avg. Per Game	129.1	134.1
Total Rushes	470	481
Net Yards Passing	4087	3824
Avg. Per Game	255.4	239.0
Sacked/Yards Lost	40/256	48/313
Gross Yards	4343	4137
Att./Completions	628/380	589/336
Completion Pct.	60.5	57.0
Had Intercepted	11	17
Punts/Average	77/45.8	80/44.5
Net Punting Avg.	77/39.8	80/39.2
Penalties/Yards	69/625	110/951
Fumbles/Ball Lost	24/9	21/12
Touchdowns	47	39
Rushing	19	11
Passing	25	25
Returns	3	3

2013 INDIVIDUAL STATISTICS

PASSING

	Att.	Comp.	Yds.	Pct.	TD	Int.	Tkld.	Rate
Brady	628	380	4343	60.5	25	11	40/256	87.3
Patriots	628	380	4343	60.5	25	11	40/256	87.3
Opponents	589	336	4137	57.0	25	17	48/313	81.0

SCORING

	TD R	TD P	TD Rt	PAT	FG	Saf	PTS
Gostkowski	0	0	0	44/44	38/41	0	158
Blount	7	0	0	0/0	0/0	0	42
Ridley	7	0	0	0/0	0/0	0	42
Edelman	0	6	0	0/0	0/0	0	40
Dobson	0	4	0	0/0	0/0	0	24
Gronkowski	0	4	0	0/0	0/0	0	24
Thompkins	0	4	0	0/0	0/0	0	24
Vereen	1	3	0	0/0	0/0	0	24
Bolden	3	0	0	0/0	0/0	0	18
Amendola	0	2	0	0/0	0/0	0	12
Develin	1	0	0	0/0	0/0	0	6
Hoomanawanui	0	1	0	0/0	0/0	0	6
Cha. Jones	0	0	1	0/0	0/0	0	6
Mulligan	0	1	0	0/0	0/0	0	6
Ryan	0	0	1	0/0	0/0	0	6
T. Wilson	0	0	1	0/0	0/0	0	6
Patriots	19	25	3	44/44	38/41	0	444
Opponents	11	25	3	38/38	22/27	0	338

2-Pt Conversions: Edelman 2.
Patriots 2-3, Opponents 0-1.

RUSHING

	No.	Yds	Avg	LG	TD
Ridley	178	773	4.3	29	7
Blount	153	772	5.0	47t	7
Bolden	55	271	4.9	46	3
Vereen	44	208	4.7	21	1
Brady	32	18	0.6	11	0
Edelman	2	11	5.5	7	0
Develin	4	10	2.5	4	1
Amendola	1	1	1.0	1	0
Washington	1	1	1.0	1	0
Patriots	470	2065	4.4	47t	19
Opponents	481	2145	4.5	34	11

RECEIVING

	No.	Yds	Avg	LG	TD
Edelman	105	1056	10.1	44	6
Amendola	54	633	11.7	57	2
Vereen	47	427	9.1	50	3
Gronkowski	39	592	15.2	50	4
Dobson	37	519	14.0	81t	4
Thompkins	32	466	14.6	49	4
Bolden	21	152	7.2	18	0
Hoomanawanui	12	136	11.3	19	1
Ridley	10	62	6.2	24	0
Boyce	9	121	13.4	30	0
Collie	6	63	10.5	19	0
Develin	4	62	15.5	31	0
Blount	2	38	19.0	32	0
Mulligan	2	16	8.0	15	1
Patriots	380	4343	11.4	81t	25
Opponents	336	4137	12.3	80t	25

PUNTING

	No.	Yds.	Avg.	In 20	LG
Allen	76	3491	45.9	29	65
Brady	1	32	32.0	0	32
Patriots	77	3523	45.8	29	65
Opponents	80	3559	44.5	28	64

INTERCEPTIONS

	No.	Yds	Avg	LG	TD
Ryan	5	82	16.4	79t	1
Talib	4	12	3.0	14	0
Harmon	2	44	22.0	42	0
T. Wilson	1	74	74.0	74t	1
Arrington	1	5	5.0	5	0
Spikes	1	3	3.0	3	0
Cole	1	0	0.0	0	0
Dennard	1	0	0.0	0	0
McCourty	1	0	0.0	0	0
Patriots	17	220	12.9	79t	2
Opponents	11	56	5.1	31	1

PUNT RETURNS

	Ret	FC	Yds	Avg	LG	TD
Edelman	35	23	374	10.7	43	0
Amendola	1	0	13	13.0	13	0
Patriots	36	23	387	10.8	43	0
Opponents	29	14	221	7.6	24	0

KICKOFF RETURNS

	No.	Yds	Avg	LG	TD
Blount	17	494	29.1	83	0
Boyce	9	214	23.8	41	0
McCourty	7	132	18.9	27	0
Vereen	3	66	22.0	24	0
Slater	2	10	5.0	10	0
Washington	1	19	19.0	19	0
Patriots	39	935	24.0	83	0
Opponents	32	664	20.8	50	0

FIELD GOALS

	1-19	20-29	30-39	40-49	50+
Gostkowski	1/1	8/8	13/13	11/13	5/6
Patriots	1/1	8/8	13/13	11/13	5/6
Opponents	0/0	4/4	10/13	5/6	3/4

SACKS

	No.
Cha. Jones	11.5
Ninkovich	8.0
Chr. Jones	6.0
Siliga	3.0
Kelly	2.5
Arrington	2.0
Buchanan	2.0
Carter	2.0
Fletcher	2.0
Vellano	2.0
Mayo	1.5
Ryan	1.5
Gregory	1.0
Hightower	1.0
Sopoaga	1.0
(group)	1.0
Patriots	48.0
Opponents	40.0

RECORD HOLDERS
INDIVIDUAL RECORDS—CAREER

Category	Name	Performance
Rushing (Yds.)	Sam Cunningham, 1973-79, 1981-82	5,453
Passing (Yds.)	Tom Brady, 2000-2013	49,149
Passing (TDs)	Tom Brady, 2000-2013	359
Receiving (No.)	Wes Welker, 2007-2012	672
Receiving (Yds.)	Stanley Morgan, 1977-1989	10,352
Interceptions	Raymond Clayborn, 1977-1989	36
	Ty Law, 1995-2004	36
Punting (Avg.)	Tom Tupa, 1996-98	44.7
Punt Return (Avg.)	Julian Edelman, 2009-2013	12.3
Kickoff Return (Avg.)	Ellis Hobbs, 2005-08	27.7
Field Goals	Adam Vinatieri, 1996-2005	263
Touchdowns (Tot.)	Stanley Morgan, 1977-1989	68
Points	Adam Vinatieri, 1996-2005	1,158
*Sacks	Andre Tippett, 1982-1993	100.0

INDIVIDUAL RECORDS—SINGLE SEASON

Category	Name	Performance
Rushing (Yds.)	Corey Dillon, 2004	1,635
Passing (Yds.)	Tom Brady, 2011	5,235
Passing (TDs)	Tom Brady, 2007	50
Receiving (No.)	Wes Welker, 2009	123
Receiving (Yds.)	Wes Welker, 2011	1,569
Interceptions	Ron Hall, 1964	11
Punting (Avg.)	Zoltan Mesko, 2011	46.5
Punt Return (Avg.)	Julian Edelman, 2012	15.5
Kickoff Return (Avg.)	Raymond Clayborn, 1977	31.0
Field Goals	Stephen Gostkowski, 2013	38
Touchdowns (Tot.)	Randy Moss, 2007	23
Points	Stephen Gostkowski, 2013	158
*Sacks	Andre Tippett, 1984	18.5

INDIVIDUAL RECORDS—SINGLE GAME

Category	Name	Performance
Rushing (Yds.)	Tony Collins, 9-18-83	212
Passing (Yds.)	Tom Brady, 9-12-11	517
Passing (TDs)	Tom Brady, 10-21-07, 10-18-09	6
Receiving (No.)	Troy Brown, 9-22-02	16
	Wes Welker, 9-25-11	16
Receiving (Yds.)	Wes Welker, 9-25-11	217
Interceptions	Many times	3
	Last time by Leigh Bodden 11-22-09	
Field Goals	Gino Cappelletti, 10-4-64	6
Touchdowns (Tot.)	Randy Moss, 11-18-07	4
Points	Gino Cappelletti, 12-18-65	28
*Sacks	Andre Carter, 11-13-11	4.0

*Sacks became an official statistic in 1982.
**NFL Record

2014 VETERAN ROSTER

No.	Name	Pos.	Ht.	Wt.	Birthdate	NFL Exp.	College	Hometown	How Acq.	'13 Games/ Starts
48	Aiken, Danny	LS	6-4	255	8/28/88	4	Virginia	Roanoke, Va.	W(Buff)-'11	16/0
6	Allen, Ryan	P	6-2	215	2/28/90	2	Louisiana Tech	Salem, Ore.	FA-'13	16/0
80	Amendola, Danny	WR	5-11	195	11/2/85	6	Texas Tech	The Woodlands, Texas	UFA(StL)-'13	12/6
25	Arrington, Kyle	CB	5-10	190	8/12/86	6	Hofstra	Accokeek, Md.	FA-'09	16/12
64	Barker, Chris	OL	6-2	310	8/3/90	2	Nevada	Etiwanda, Calif.	W(Mia)-'13	4/0
58	Beauharnais, Steve	LB	6-2	230	5/2/90	2	Rutgers	Saddle Brook, N.J.	D7b-'13	2/0
92	Bequette, Jake	DE	6-5	265	2/21/89	3	Arkansas	Little Rock, Ark.	D3-'12	5/0
38	Bolden, Brandon	RB	5-11	220	1/26/90	3	Mississippi	Baton Rouge, La.	FA-'12	12/2
82	Boyce, Josh	WR	5-11	205	5/6/91	2	Texas Christian	Copperas Cove, Texas	D4a-'13	9/3
12	Brady, Tom	QB	6-4	225	8/3/77	15	Michigan	San Mateo, Calif.	D6b-'00	16/16
39	Browner, Brandon	CB	6-4	221	8/2/84	5	Oregon State	Sylmar, Calif.	UFA(Sea)-'14	8/8*
99	Buchanan, Michael	DL	6-6	255	1/24/91	2	Illinois	Homewood, Ill.	D7a-'13	15/0
61	Cannon, Marcus	OL	6-5	335	5/6/88	4	Texas Christian	Odessa, Texas	D5a-'11	14/6
96	#Carter, Andre	DE	6-4	260	5/12/79	14	California	San Jose, Calif.	FA-'13	9/0
23	Chung, Patrick	S	5-11	210	8/19/87	6	Oregon	Racho Cucamonga, Calif.	FA-'14	12/10*
10	#Collie, Austin	WR	6-0	204	11/11/85	6	Brigham Young	El Dorado Hills, Calif.	FA-'13	7/1
91	Collins, Jamie	LB	6-3	250	10/20/89	2	Southern Mississippi	McCall Creek, Miss.	D2a-'13	16/8
63	Connolly, Dan	OL	6-4	305	9/2/82	9	Southeast Missouri St.	St. Louis, Mo.	FA-'08	16/16
37	Dennard, Alfonzo	CB	5-10	200	9/9/89	3	Nebraska	Rochelle, Ga.	D7a-'12	13/9
46	Develin, James	FB	6-3	255	7/23/88	2	Brown	Gilbertsville, Pa.	FA-'12	16/6
17	Dobson, Aaron	WR	6-3	200	7/23/91	2	Marshall	Dunbar, W.Va.	D2b-'13	12/9
43	Ebner, Nate	DB	6-0	210	12/14/88	3	Ohio State	Dublin, Ohio	D6-'12	15/0
11	Edelman, Julian	WR	5-10	200	5/22/86	6	Kent State	Redwood City, Calif.	D7a-'09	16/11
44	Fleming, Darius	LB	6-2	255	7/19/89	3	Notre Dame	Chicago, Ill.	FA-'14	0*
98	Forston, Marcus	DL	6-3	305	9/28/89	2	Miami	Miami, Fla.	FA-'12	3/0
3	Gostkowski, Stephen	K	6-1	215	1/28/84	9	Memphis	Madison, Miss.	D4b-'06	16/0
87	Gronkowski, Rob	TE	6-6	265	5/14/89	5	Arizona	Pittsburgh, Pa.	D2a-'10	7/6
30	Harmon, Duron	DB	6-1	205	1/24/91	2	Rutgers	Magnolia, Del.	D3b-'13	15/3
54	Hightower, Dont'a	LB	6-3	270	3/12/90	3	Alabama	Lewisburg, Tenn.	D1b-'12	16/14
47	Hoomanawanui, Michael	TE	6-4	260	7/4/88	5	Illinois	Bloomington, Ill.	FA-'12	13/10
52	Hull, Josh	LB	6-3	245	5/21/87	5	Penn State	State College, Pa.	FA-'14	11/0*
95	Jones, Chandler	DE	6-5	265	2/27/90	3	Syracuse	Endicott, N.Y.	D1a-'12	16/16
94	Jones, Chris	DT	6-1	309	7/12/90	2	Bowling Green	Brownsburg, Ind.	W(TB)-'13	13/11
93	Kelly, Tommy	DL	6-6	310	12/27/80	11	Mississippi State	Jackson, Miss.	FA-'13	5/5
67	Kline, Josh	OL	6-3	295	12/29/89	2	Kent State	Mason, Ohio	FA-'13	7/1
19	LaFell, Brandon	WR	6-2	210	11/4/86	5	Louisiana State	Houston, Texas	UFA(Car)-'14	16/16
15	Mallett, Ryan	QB	6-6	245	6/5/88	4	Arkansas	Texarkana, Texas	D3b-'11	0*
70	Mankins, Logan	G	6-4	308	3/10/82	10	Fresno State	Catheys Valley, Calif.	D1-'05	16/16
51	Mayo, Jerod	LB	6-1	250	2/23/86	7	Tennessee	Hampton, Va.	D1-'08	6/6
32	McCourty, Devin	DB	5-10	195	8/13/87	5	Rutgers	Montvale, N.J.	D1-'10	15/15
50	Ninkovich, Rob	DE	6-2	260	2/1/84	9	Purdue	Blue Island, Ill.	FA-'09	16/16
24	Revis, Darrelle	CB	5-11	198	7/14/85	8	Pittsburgh	Aliquippa, Penn.	FA-'14	16/16*
22	Ridley, Stevan	RB	5-11	220	1/27/89	4	Louisiana State	Natchez, Miss.	D3a-'11	14/6
26	Ryan, Logan	CB	5-11	195	2/9/91	2	Rutgers	Voorhees, N.J.	D3a-'13	16/7
96	Siliga, Sealver	DT	6-2	325	4/26/90	3	Utah	West Jordan, Utah	FA-'13	5/4
18	Slater, Matthew	WR	6-0	210	9/9/85	7	UCLA	Anaheim, Calif.	D5-'08	12/0
90	Smith, Will	DE	603	282	7/4/81	11	Ohio State	Utica, N.Y.	FA-'14	0*
77	Solder, Nate	T	6-8	320	4/12/88	4	Colorado	Buena Vista, Colo.	D1-'11	15/15
74	#Svitek, Will	OL	6-6	310	1/8/82	9	Stanford	Newbury Park, Calif.	FA-'13	13/2
85	Thompkins, Kenbrell	WR	6-1	195	7/29/88	2	Cincinnati	Miami, Fla.	FA-'13	12/8
72	Vellano, Joe	DL	6-2	300	10/30/88	2	Maryland	Rexford, N.Y.	FA-'13	16/8
34	Vereen, Shane	RB	5-10	205	5/2/89	4	California	Valencia, Calif.	D2b-'11	8/1
76	Vollmer, Sebastian	T	6-8	320	7/10/84	6	Houston	Kaarst, Germany	D2d-'09	8/8
62	Wendell, Ryan	OL	6-2	300	3/4/86	6	Fresno State	Pomona, Calif.	FA-'08	16/16
59	White, Chris	LB	6-3	238	1/15/89	4	Mississippi State	Vancleave, Miss.	W(Det)-'13	16/0
75	Wilfork, Vince	DL	6-2	325	11/4/81	11	Miami	Boynton Beach, Fla.	D1a-'04	4/4
45	Williams, D.J.	TE	6-2	245	9/10/88	4	Arkansas	Little Rock, Ark.	FA-'13	9/1*
27	Wilson, Tavon	DB	6-0	215	3/19/90	3	Illinois	Washington, D.C.	D2-'12	13/0

* Browner played eight games with Seattle in '13; Chung played 12 games with Philadelphia; Fleming missed '13 season because of injury with San Francisco; Hull played 11 games with Washington; Mallett did not play in 16 games; Smith missed '13 season because of injury with New Orleans; Williams played seven games with Jacksonville and two with New England.

\# Unrestriced Free Agent; subject to developments.

Players lost through free agency (5): RB LeGarrette Blount (Pitt; 16 games in '13), LB Dane Fletcher (TB: 15), TE Matthew Mulligan (Chi; 15), LB Brandon Spikes (Buff; 16); CB Aqib Talib (Den; 13).

Also played with Patriots in '13—CB Marquice Cole (13 games), LB Ja'Gared Davis (1), S Kanorris Davis (3), DB Justin Green (2), S Steve Gregory (14), DT Andre Neblett (1), DT Isaac Sopoaga (6), TE Zach Sudfeld (3), RB Leon Washington (2).

FIRST-YEAR ROSTER

Name	Pos.	Ht.	Wt.	Birthdate	College	Hometown	How Acq.
Armstead, Armond (1)	DL	6-5	305	8/3/90	Southern California	Elk Grove, Calif.	FA-'13
Butler, Malcolm	CB	5-11	180	3/2/90	West Alabama	Vicksburg, Miss.	FA
Cave, Braxston (1)	OL	6-3	305	7/29/89	Notre Dame	Mishawaka, Ind.	FA-'13
Davis, Ja'Gared (1)	LB	6-0	238	9/11/90	Southern Methodist	Crockett, Texas	W(Hou)-'13
Davis, Kanorris (1)	S	5-10	207	1/21/90	Troy	Perry, Ga.	FA-'13
Devey, Jordan (1)	T	6-6	317	1/11/88	Memphis	American Fork, Utah	FA-'13
Dunn, Reggie (1)	WR	5-9	178	1/5/89	Utah	Compton, Calif.	FA-'13
Easley, Dominique	DL	6-2	288	4/28/92	Florida	Staten Island, N.Y.	D1
Finch, Roy	RB	5-7	167	10/1/91	Oklahoma	Niceville, Fla.	FA
Fleming, Cameron	OL	6-6	318	9/3/92	Stanford	Houston, Texas	D4c
Gallon, Jeremy	WR	5-8	184	2/9/90	Michigan	Apopka, Fla.	D7
Garoppolo, Jimmy	QB	6-2	226	11/2/91	Eastern Illinois	Arlington, Ill.	D2
Gary, Shamiel	S	6-0	210	2/31/90	Oklahoma State	Tulsa, Okla.	FA
Gordon, Cameron	LB	6-3	237	6/5/91	Michigan	Detroit, Mich.	FA
Gray, Jonas (1)	RB	5-10	225	6/27/90	Notre Dame	Pontiac, Mich.	FA
Green, Justin (1)	DB	5-11	195	2/26/91	Illiinois	Louisville, Ky.	FA-'13
Halapio, Jon	OL	6-2	320	6/23/91	Florida	St. Petersburg, Fla.	D6a
Harrison, Mark (1)	WR	6-3	230	12/11/90	Rutgers	Stratford, Conn.	FA-'13
Hawkins, Travis	DB	5-10	195	2/18/91	Delaware	Rockville, Md.	FA
Houston, Stephen	RB	6-0	230	10/28/91	Indiana	Little Rock, Ark.	FA
Johnson, Derrick	WR	5-11	190	7/6/91	Maine	Hemstead, N.Y.	FA
Jones, Justin	TE	6-8	277	9/25/91	East Carolina	Conyers, Ga.	FA
Mattes, R.J. (1)	OL	6-6	315	4/29/90	North Carolina State	Concord, N.C.	FA-'13
McCuller, Taylor	LB	6-2	240	10/31/89	West Texas A&M	Red Oaks, Texas	FA
Moore, Zach	DL	6-6	285	9/5/90	Concordia-St. Paul	Chicago, Ill.	D6b
Ott, Tyler	LS	6-3	245	2/28/92	Harvard	Tulsa, Okla.	FA
Skinner, Deontae	LB	6-2	250	12/18/90	Mississippi State	Macon, Miss.	FA
Stork, Bryan	OL	6-4	300	11/15/90	Florida State	Vero Beach, Fla.	D4a
Swanson, Daxton (1)	DB	5-11	191	3/21/91	Sam Houston State	Waco, Texas	FA
Thomas, Jemea	DB	5-10	195	4/7/90	Georgia Tech	Queensland, Ga.	D6c
Tuipulotu, L.T.	DL	6-1	305	8/3/90	Utah	Euless, Texas	FA
Watson, Asa	TE	6-3	237	8/2/90	North Carolina State	Rock Hill, S.C.	FA
White, James	RB	5-10	195	2/3/92	Wisconsin	Ft. Lauderdale, Fla.	D4b

The term NFL Rookie is defined as a player who is in his first season of professional football and has not been on the roster of another professional football team for any regular-season or postseason games. A Rookie is designated by an "R" on NFL rosters. Players who have been active in another professional football league or players who have NFL experience, including either preseason training camp or being on an Active List or Inactive List, or on Reserve/Injured or Reserve/Physically Unable to Perform for fewer than six regular-season games, are termed NFL First-Year Players. An NFL First-Year Player is designated by a "1" on NFL rosters. Thereafter, a player is credited with an additional year of experience for each season in which he accumulates six games on the Active List or Inactive List, or on Reserve/Injured or Reserve/Physically Unable to Perform.

Log on to www.patriots.com for an up-to-date roster.

COACHING STAFF

Head Coach,
Bill Belichick

Pro Career: Bill Belichick is in his 40th season as an NFL coach and is the only head coach in NFL history to win three Super Bowl titles in a four-year span. Belichick leads all active head coaches and is currently ranked fifth on the NFL's all-time list with 218 total victories. He is the eighth NFL coach to reach 200 career wins. Hired by Chairman and CEO Robert Kraft on Jan. 27, 2000, Belichick is in his 15th season as New England's head coach. Through 14 seasons, Belichick has delivered three Super Bowl championships, five conference titles, 11 division crowns and 18 playoff victories, while posting an overall record of 181-69. Belichick directed the Patriots to victories in Super Bowls XXXVI (2001), XXXVIII (2003) and XXXIX (2004), and in 2007 he became the first NFL head coach to guide his team to a 16-0 regular season. Only one coach (Pittsburgh's Chuck Noll, 4) has won more Super Bowls than Belichick, and his three Super Bowl titles tie Washington's Joe Gibbs and San Francisco's Bill Walsh for second place on the NFL's all-time list. Belichick has led the Patriots to a winning record in each of the last 13 seasons. The only other NFL coach to have 10 consecutive winning seasons with one team since the 1970 merger was Tom Landry, who led the Dallas Cowboys to 16 consecutive winning seasons (1970-1985). Belichick's 13 winning consecutive winning seasons are third all-time, behind 20 by Landry (1966-1985) and 14 by Curly Lambeau with Green Bay (1934-1947). In 2013, Belichick guided the Patriots to a 12-4 record, a division title and his eighth AFC Championship game appearance. Belichick's eight conference championships are the second-most by an NFL head coach. Landry led Dallas to 10 conference championships. Belichick helped the Patriots become the first franchise in NFL history to score 500 or more points in four seasons (2007-589, 2010-518, 2011-513 and 2012-557). St. Louis is the only other team to have done it three times. Belichick is the first head coach in NFL history to lead a team to three straight 500-point seasons. Belichick is the only head coach in NFL history to win at least 13 regular-season games in five separate seasons. Belichick's Patriots teams own the all-time NFL records for consecutive victories, including the postseason (21 from 2003-04) and consecutive playoff victories (10 from 2001-05). Belichick's 19 postseason wins are tied with Don Shula for second all-time, behind Tom Landry (20). Over a 100-game span from 2003-08, he directed the Patriots to an 82-18 record – the best record for any 100-game span in NFL history. Belichick (.657) has the third highest winning percentage among coaches with at least 150 wins, trailing only Hall of Famers George Halas (.682) and Don

Shula (.667). Belichick's recent accomplishments are the latest triumphs in a career during which he has helped produce five Super Bowl titles, eight conference championships and 18 division titles since entering the NFL in 1975. He won his first two Super Bowls as the defensive coordinator for the New York Giants in 1986 and 1990 before claiming three Super Bowl championships with the Patriots. George Seifert is the only other man to have won multiple Super Bowls as a head coach and as an assistant coach. Belichick launched his coaching career in 1975 with the Baltimore Colts and continued as an assistant coach with Detroit (1976-77), Denver (1978), the Giants (1979-1990), New England (1996, as a key contributor to the Patriots' first Super Bowl appearance in 10 years), and the New York Jets (1997-99). In 1991, Belichick was named head coach of Cleveland, becoming the NFL's youngest head coach (38). By 1994, Belichick's Browns advanced to the postseason's second round. Career record: 218-114.

Background: Belichick was a center/tight end at Wesleyan 1971-74.

Personal: Born April 16, 1952, Nashville, Tenn.

ASSISTANT COACHES

Josh Boyer, cornerbacks; born January 21, 1977, Heath, Ohio. Wide receiver/defensive back Muskingum College 1996-99. No pro playing experience. College coach: King's College (Pa.) 2000, Dayton 2001, Kent State 2002-03, Bryant University 2004, South Dakota School of Mines and Technology 2005. Pro coach: Joined Patriots in 2006.

Moses Cabrera, asst. strength and conditioning; born August 20, 1978, Deming, N.M. Oral Roberts 1996-2000. No pro playing experience. College coach: Fresno State 2004-09, Colorado 2010. Pro coach: Joined Patriots in 2010.

Brian Daboll, offensive assistant; born April 4, 1975, Welland, Ont., Canada. Safety Rochester 1995-97. No pro playing experience. College coach: William & Mary 1997, Michigan State 1998-99. Pro coach: New England Patriots 2000-06, New York Jets 2007-08, Cleveland Browns 2009-2010, Miami Dolphins 2011, Kansas City Chiefs 2012, re-joined Patriots in 2013.

Brendan Daly, defensive assistant; born September 10, 1975, Springfield, Ill. Tight end Drake 1993-96. No pro playing experience. College coach: Drake 1998, Villanova 1999, 2005, Maryland 2000, Oklahoma State 2001-03, Illinois State 2004. Pro coach: Minnesota Vikings 2006-08, 2012-13, St. Louis Rams 2009-2011, joined Patriots in 2014.

Dave DeGuglielmo, offensive line; born July 15, 1968, Cambridge, Mass. Offensive line Boston University 1987-1990. No pro playing experience. College coach; Boston College 1991-92, Boston University 1993-96, Connecticut 1997-98, South Carolina

1999-2003. Pro coach: New York Giants 2004-08, Miami Dolphins 2009-2011, New York Jets 2012, joined Patriots in 2014.

Ivan Fears, running backs; born November 15, 1954, Portsmouth, Va. Running back William & Mary 1973-75. No pro playing experience. College coach: William & Mary 1977-79, Syracuse 1980-1990. Pro coach: New England Patriots 1991-92, Chicago Bears 1993-98, re-joined Patriots in 1999.

Brian Flores, safeties; born February 24, 1981, Brooklyn, N.Y. Linebacker Boston College 1999-2003. No pro playing experience. Pro coach: Joined Patriots in 2008.

Patrick Graham, defensive line; born January 24, 1979, Des Plaines, Ill. Defensive line Yale 1997-2001. College coach: Wagner College 2002-03, Richmond 2004-06, Notre Dame 2007-08. Pro coach: Joined Patriots in 2009.

Joe Judge, asst. special teams; born December 31, 1981, Philadelphia, Pa. Running back Mississippi State 2000-04. No pro playing experience. College coach: 2005-07 Mississippi State, Birmingham-Southern 2008, Alabama 2009-11. Pro coach: Joined Patriots in 2012.

Josh McDaniels, offensive coordinator/quarterbacks; born April 22, 1976, Canton, Ohio. No pro playing experience. College coach: Michigan State 1999-2000. Pro coach: New England Patriots 2001-2008, Denver Broncos, 2009-2010 (head coach), St. Louis Rams 2011, re-joined Patriots in 2012.

Harold Nash, strength and conditioning; born May 5, 1970, New Orleans, La. Defensive back Louisiana-Lafayette 1988-1993. Pro defensive back Shreveport Pirates (CFL) 1994-95, Montreal Alouettes (CFL) 1996-99, Winnipeg Blue Bombers (CFL) 1999-2003, Edmonton Eskimos (CFL) 2004. Pro coach: Joined Patriots in 2005.

Scott O'Brien, special teams; born June 25, 1957, Superior, Wisc. Linebacker Wisconsin-Superior 1975-78. No pro playing experience. College coach: Wisconsin-Superior 1980-82, Nevada-Las Vegas 1983-85, Rice 1986, Pittsburgh 1987-1990. Pro coach: Cleveland Browns 1991-95, Baltimore Ravens 1996-98, Carolina Panthers 1999-2004, Miami Dolphins 2005-06, Denver Broncos 2007-08, joined Patriots in 2009.

Chad O'Shea, receivers; born December 18, 1972, Houston, Texas. Quarterback Marshall 1991-93, Houston 1994-95. No pro playing experience. College coach: Houston 1996-99, Southern Mississippi 2000-02. Pro coach: Kansas City Chiefs 2003-05, Minnesota Vikings 2006-08, joined Patriots in 2009.

Matt Patricia, defensive coordinator; born September 13, 1974, Sherrill, N.Y. Center-guard Rensselaer 1992-96. No pro playing experience. College coach: Rensselaer 1996, Amherst 1999-2000, Syracuse 2001-03. Pro coach: Joined Patriots in 2004.

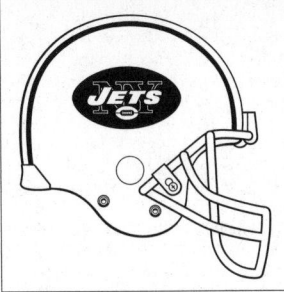

**American Football Conference
East Division
Team Colors:** Green and White
**1 Jets Drive
Florham Park, New Jersey 07932
Telephone (973) 549-4800**

2014 SCHEDULE
PRESEASON
Aug. 7	**Indianapolis**	7:00
Aug. 16	at Cincinnati	7:00
Aug. 22	**New York Giants**	7:30
Aug. 28	at Philadelphia	7:00

REGULAR SEASON
Sep. 7	**Oakland**	1:00
Sep. 14	at Green Bay	4:25
Sep. 22	**Chicago** (Mon)	8:30
Sep. 28	**Detroit**	1:00
Oct. 5	at San Diego	4:25
Oct. 12	**Denver**	1:00
Oct. 16	at New England (Thu)	8:25
Oct. 26	**Buffalo**	1:00
Nov. 2	at Kansas City	1:00
Nov. 9	**Pittsburgh**	1:00
Nov. 16	BYE	
Nov. 23	at Buffalo	1:00
Dec. 1	**Miami** (Mon)	8:30
Dec. 7	at Minnesota	1:00
Dec. 14	at Tennessee	4:05
Dec. 21	**New England**	1:00
Dec. 28	at Miami	1:00
All times ET

Stadium: MetLife Stadium
 (opened in 2010)
 •**Capacity:** 82,500
 East Rutherford, New Jersey
 07073
Playing Surface: FieldTurf
Training Camp: SUNY Cortland
 Cortland, New York 13045

METLIFE STADIUM

CLUB OFFICIALS
Chairman and CEO: Robert Wood
 Johnson IV
President: Neil Glat
General Manager: John Idzik
Chief Financial Officer: Brian Friedman
S.V.P., Corporate Sponsorship: Ian Lasher
S.V.P., Marketing and Fan Engagement:
 Seth Rabinowitz
S.V.P., Consumer & Premium Sales and
 Services: Rob Sullivan
V.P., Premium Partnerships, Sales and
 Services: Roberto Beltramini
V.P., Business & Legal Affairs:
 Hymie Elhai
V.P., Business Development & Ventures:
 Jeff Fernandez
V.P., Security and Facility Operations:
 Robert Mastroddi
V.P., IT: Tom Murphy
Senior Director, College Scouting:
 Terry Bradway
Director, College Scouting: Jeff Bauer
Coordinator, College Scouting:
 Dan Zbojovsky
Area Scouts: David Hinson,
 Cole Hufnagel, Jay Mandolesi,
 Christopher Prescott
NFS College Scout: Rick Courtright
Director, Pro Personnel: Brendan Prophett
Assistant Director, Pro Personnel:
 Matt Bazirgan
Assistant, Pro Personnel: Greg Nejmeh
Senior Director, Football Administration:
 Rod Graves
Manager, Football Administration:
 Jacqueline Davidson
Administrative Assistant to Player
 Personnel: Christina Salvemini
Senior Director, Athletic Training:
 John Mellody
Assistant Athletic Trainers: Josh Koch,
 Dave Zuffelato
Senior Director, Partnership and Media
 Sales: Tracy Belmear
Senior Director, Content: Jessica Ciccone
Senior Director, Consumer Sales &
 Service: Larry Fitzpatrick
Senior Director, Football Operations:
 Clay Hampton
Senior Director, Ticket Operations:
 Jeff Hecker
Senior Director, Corporate Sponsorships:
 Jennifer Linn
Senior Director, Human Resources &
 Administration: Jessica Mandler
Senior Director, Events & Game
 Operations: Brian Mulligan
Senior Director, Merchandise &
 Concessions: Chris Pierce
Senior Director, Media Relations:
 Bruce Speight
Director, Equipment: Gus Granneman
Manager, Equipment: Vito Contento
Assistant Manager, Equipment:
 Jim Gallione
Assistant, Equipment: Brendan Burger
Director, Community Relations:
 Jesse Linder
Director, Player Development: David Szott
Director, Video: Tim Tubito

COACHING HISTORY
**New York Titans 1960-62
(385-452-8)**
Records include postseason games
1960-61	Sammy Baugh	14-14-0
1962	Clyde (Bulldog) Turner	5-9-0
1963-1973	Weeb Ewbank	73-78-6
1974-75	Charley Winner*	9-14-0
1975	Ken Shipp	1-4-0
1976	Lou Holtz**	3-10-0
1976	Mike Holovak	0-1-0
1977-1982	Walt Michaels	41-49-1
1983-89	Joe Walton	54-59-1
1990-93	Bruce Coslet	26-39-0
1994	Pete Carroll	6-10-0
1995-96	Rich Kotite	4-28-0
1997-99	Bill Parcells	30-20-0
2000	Al Groh	9-7-0
2001-05	Herman Edwards	41-44-0
2006-08	Eric Mangini	23-26-0
2009-2013	Rex Ryan	46-40-0
*Released after nine games in 1975
**Resigned after 13 games in 1976

PAID ATTENDANCE
Home 552,896   Away 533,406
Total 1,086,302
Single-game home record,
 79,572 (11/19/06)
Single-season home record,
 628,773 (2002)

2014 DRAFT CHOICES
Round	Name	Pos.	College
1	Calvin Pryor	DB	Louisville
2	Jace Amaro	TE	Texas Tech
3	Dexter McDougle	DB	Maryland
4	Jalen Saunders	WR	Oklahoma
	Shaquelle Evans	WR	UCLA
	Dakota Dozier	G	Furman
5	Jeremiah George	LB	Iowa St.
6	Brandon Dixon	DB	NW Missouri St.
	Quincy Enunwa	WR	Nebraska
	Ikemefuna Enemkpali	LB	Louisiana Tech
	Tajh Boyd	QB	Clemson
7	Trevor Reilly	LB	Utah

NEW YORK JETS

2013 TEAM RECORD
PRESEASON (1-3)

Date	Result	Opponent
08/09	L 17-26	at Detroit
08/17	W 37-13	Jacksonville
08/24	W 24-21	at New York Giants (OT)
08/29	W 27-20	Philadelphia

REGULAR SEASON (8-8)

Date	Result	Opponent
09/08	W 18-17	Tampa Bay
09/12	L 10-13	at New England
09/22	W 27-20	Buffalo
09/29	L 13-38	at Tennessee
10/07	W 30-28	at Atlanta
10/13	L 6-19	Pittsburgh
10/20	W 30-27	New England (OT)
10/27	L 9-49	at Cincinnati
11/03	W 26-20	New Orleans
11/17	L 14-37	at Buffalo
11/24	L 3-19	at Baltimore
12/01	L 3-23	Miami
12/08	W 37-27	Oakland
12/15	L 20-30	at Carolina
12/22	W 24-13	Cleveland
12/29	W 20-7	at Miami

(OT) Overtime

SCORE BY PERIODS

Jets	44	106	63	74	3	—	290
Opponents	71	136	89	91	0	—	387

2013 TEAM STATISTICS

	Jets	Opp.
Total First Downs	280	293
Rushing	105	68
Passing	154	198
Penalty	21	27
3rd Down: Made/Att	90/231	85/231
3rd Down Pct.	39.0	36.8
4th Down: Made/Att	1/8	7/18
4th Down Pct.	12.5	38.9
Possession Avg.	29:55	30:05
Total Net Yards	5090	5359
Avg. Per Game	318.1	334.9
Total Plays	1020	1048
Avg. Per Play	5.0	5.1
Net Yards Rushing	2158	1412
Avg. Per Game	134.9	88.3
Total Rushes	493	421
Net Yards Passing	2932	3947
Avg. Per Game	183.3	246.7
Sacked/Yards Lost	47/338	41/242
Gross Yards	3270	4189
Att./Completions	480/266	586/345
Completion Pct.	55.4	58.9
Had Intercepted	22	13
Punts/Average	89/45.1	82/44.9
Net Punting Avg.	89/38.5	82/39.0
Penalties/Yards	108/837	92/833
Fumbles/Ball Lost	15/7	18/2
Touchdowns	27	41
Rushing	12	9
Passing	13	26
Returns	2	6

2013 INDIVIDUAL STATISTICS

PASSING

	Att.	Comp.	Yds.	Pct.	TD	Int.	Tkld.	Rate
Smith	443	247	3046	55.8	12	21	43/315	66.5
Simms	31	16	156	51.6	1	1	4/23	63.4
Cribbs	3	2	38	66.7	0	0	0/0	109.7
Powell	1	1	30	100.0	0	0	0/0	118.8
Bush	1	0	0	0.0	0	0	0/0	39.6
Kerley	1	0	0	0.0	0	0	0/0	39.6
Jets	480	266	3270	55.4	13	22	47/338	66.6
Opponents	586	345	4189	58.9	26	13	41/242	86.5

SCORING

	TD R	TD P	TD Rt	PAT	FG	Saf	PTS
Folk	0	0	0	27/27	33/36	0	126
Smith	6	0	0	0/0	0/0	0	36
Cumberland	0	4	0	0/0	0/0	0	24
Ivory	3	0	0	0/0	0/0	0	18
Kerley	0	3	0	0/0	0/0	0	18
Allen	0	0	2	0/0	0/0	0	12
Nelson	0	2	0	0/0	0/0	0	12
Richardson	2	0	0	0/0	0/0	0	12
Winslow	0	2	0	0/0	0/0	0	12
Hill	0	1	0	0/0	0/0	0	6
Holmes	0	1	0	0/0	0/0	0	6
Powell	1	0	0	0/0	0/0	0	6
Jets	12	13	2	27/27	33/36	1	290
Opponents	9	26	6	40/40	33/37	0	387

2-Pt Conversions: Jets 0-0, Opponents 1-1.

RUSHING

	No.	Yds	Avg	LG	TD
Ivory	182	833	4.6	69	3
Powell	176	697	4.0	39	1
Smith	72	366	5.1	32	6
Bohanon	17	62	3.6	8	0
Goodson	7	61	8.7	26	0
Cribbs	13	55	4.2	9	0
Simms	5	37	7.4	22	0
Green	11	35	3.2	9	0
Kerley	4	11	2.8	8	0
Richardson	4	4	1.0	1t	2
Hakim	2	-3	-1.5	9	0
Jets	493	2158	4.4	69	12
Opponents	421	1412	3.4	63t	9

RECEIVING

	No.	Yds	Avg	LG	TD
Kerley	43	523	12.2	26	3
Nelson	36	423	11.8	31	2
Powell	36	272	7.6	36	0
Winslow	31	388	12.5	34	2
Cumberland	26	398	15.3	47	4
Hill	24	342	14.3	51t	1
Holmes	23	456	19.8	69t	1
Gates	12	122	10.2	34	0
Bohanon	11	69	6.3	21	0
Salas	8	143	17.9	44	0
Sudfeld	5	63	12.6	25	0
Goodson	2	19	9.5	10	0
Ivory	2	10	5.0	12	0
Green	2	8	4.0	7	0
Cribbs	2	6	3.0	5	0
Smith	1	13	13.0	13	0
Obomanu	1	8	8.0	8	0
Reuland	1	7	7.0	7	0
Jets	266	3270	12.3	69t	13
Opponents	345	4189	12.1	77t	26

PUNTING

	No.	Yds.	Avg.	In 20	LG
Quigley	72	3278	45.5	21	67
Malone	16	740	46.3	3	84
Jets	89	4018	45.1	24	84
Opponents	82	3679	44.9	30	66

INTERCEPTIONS

	No.	Yds	Avg	LG	TD
Reed	3	49	16.3	25	0
Milliner	3	31	10.3	19	0
Cromartie	3	20	6.7	20	0
Landry	1	38	38.0	38	0
Allen	1	23	23.0	23t	1
Wilkerson	1	6	6.0	6	0
D. Davis	1	0	0.0	0	0
Jets	13	167	12.8	38	1
Opponents	22	411	18.7	79t	5

PUNT RETURNS

	Ret	FC	Yds	Avg	LG	TD
Reynaud	0	2	0	—	—	0
Kerley	13	5	115	8.8	24	0
Cribbs	8	1	96	12.0	21	0
Wilson	4	4	13	3.3	6	0
Jets	25	12	224	9.0	24	0
Opponents	43	21	488	11.3	38	0

KICKOFF RETURNS

	No.	Yds	Avg	LG	TD
Cribbs	20	490	24.5	42	0
Reynaud	3	75	25.0	27	0
Gates	9	209	23.2	36	0
Cromartie	6	164	27.3	41	0
Douzable	2	20	10.0	10	0
Green	1	22	22.0	22	0
Kerley	1	19	19.0	19	0
Bohanon	1	15	15.0	15	0
T. Davis	1	7	7.0	7	0
Bellore	1	0	0.0	0	0
Jets	45	1021	22.7	42	0
Opponents	42	938	22.3	71	0

FIELD GOALS

	1-19	20-29	30-39	40-49	50+
Folk	0/0	8/8	10/11	12/14	3/3
Jets	0/0	8/8	10/11	12/14	3/3
Opponents	1/1	8/8	10/10	12/15	2/3

SACKS

	No.
Wilkerson	10.5
Pace	10.0
Coples	4.5
Richardson	3.5
A. Barnes	2.0
Harris	2.0
McIntyre	2.0
Douzable	1.5
Allen	1.0
D. Davis	1.0
Harrison	1.0
Landry	1.0
(group)	1.0
Jets	41.0
Opponents	47.0

RECORD HOLDERS

INDIVIDUAL RECORDS—CAREER

Category	Name	Performance
Rushing (Yds.)	Curtis Martin, 1998-2005	10,302
Passing (Yds.)	Joe Namath, 1965-1976	27,057
Passing (TDs)	Joe Namath, 1965-1976	170
Receiving (No.)	Don Maynard, 1960-1972	627
Receiving (Yds.)	Don Maynard, 1960-1972	11,732
Interceptions	Bill Baird, 1963-69	34
Punting (Avg.)	Ben Graham, 2005-08	43.7
Punt Return (Avg.)	Dick Christy, 1961-63	16.2
Kickoff Return (Avg.)	Joe McKnight, 2010-12	29.0
Field Goals	Pat Leahy, 1974-1991	304
Touchdowns (Tot.)	Don Maynard, 1960-1972	88
Points	Pat Leahy, 1974-1991	1,470
*Sacks	Mark Gastineau, 1979-1988	74.0

INDIVIDUAL RECORDS—SINGLE SEASON

Category	Name	Performance
Rushing (Yds.)	Curtis Martin, 2004	1,697
Passing (Yds.)	Joe Namath, 1967	4,007
Passing (TDs)	Vinny Testaverde, 1998	29
Receiving (No.)	Al Toon, 1988	93
Receiving (Yds.)	Don Maynard, 1967	1,434
Interceptions	Dainard Paulson, 1964	12
Punting (Avg.)	Robert Malone, 2012	45.8
Punt Return (Avg.)	Dick Christy, 1961	21.3
Kickoff Return (Avg.)	Joe McKnight, 2011	31.6
Field Goals	Jim Turner, 1968	34
Touchdowns (Tot.)	Thomas Jones, 2008	15
Points	Jim Turner, 1968	145
*Sacks	Mark Gastineau, 1984	22.0

INDIVIDUAL RECORDS—SINGLE GAME

Category	Name	Performance
Rushing (Yds.)	Thomas Jones, 10-18-09	210
Passing (Yds.)	Joe Namath, 9-24-72	496
Passing (TDs)	Joe Namath, 9-24-72	6
	Brett Favre, 9-28-08	6
Receiving (No.)	Clark Gaines, 9-21-80	17
Receiving (Yds.)	Don Maynard, 11-17-68	228
Interceptions	Many times	3
	Last time by Ty Law, 1-1-06	
Field Goals	Jim Turner, 11-3-68	6
	Bobby Howfield, 12-3-72	6
Touchdowns (Tot.)	Wesley Walker, 9-21-86	4
Points	Wesley Walker, 9-21-86	24
*Sacks	Mark Gastineau, 11-6-83, 9-2-84	4.0
	John Abraham, 11-4-01	4.0

*Sacks became an official statistic in 1982.

2014 VETERAN ROSTER

No.	Name	Pos.	Ht.	Wt.	Birthdate	NFL Exp.	College	Hometown	How Acq.	'13 Games/ Starts
75	Aboushi, Oday	OL	6-5	308	6/5/91	2	Virginia	Brooklyn, N.Y.	D5-'13	0*
39	Allen, Antonio	S	6-1	210	6/5/91	3	South Carolina	Ocala, Fla.	D7a-'12	16/9
95	Barnes, Antwan	LB	6-1	251	10/19/84	8	Florida International	Miami, Fla.	UFA(SD)-'13	5/0
54	Bellore, Nick	LB	6-1	250	5/12/89	4	Central Michigan	Whitefish Bay, Wisc.	FA-'11	16/0
#Berry, Aaron		CB	5-11	180	6/25/88	5	Pittsburgh	Harrisburg, Pa.	FA-'12	0*
40	Bohanon, Tommy	FB	6-1	247	9/10/90	2	Wake Forest	North Fort Myers, Fla.	D7-'13	16/8
32	Bush, Josh	S	5-11	205	3/6/89	3	Wake Forest	Lexington, N.C.	D6a-'12	16/0
18	Campbell, Michael	WR	6-2	205	8/12/89	2	Temple	Edison, N.J.	FA-'13	4/0
65	Campbell, Will	G	6-4	311	7/6/91	2	Michigan	Detroit, Mich.	D6-'13	0*
66	Colon, Willie	G	6-3	315	4/9/83	9	Hofstra	Bronx, N.Y.	FA-'13	16/16
98	Coples, Quinton	LB	6-6	290	6/22/90	3	North Carolina	Kinston, N.C.	D1-'12	14/13
#Cribbs, Josh		WR	6-1	192	6/9/83	10	Kent State	Washington, D.C.	FA-'13	6/0
85	Cumberland, Jeff	TE	6-4	260	5/2/87	5	Illinois	Columbus, Ohio	FA-'10	15/12
55	Cunningham, Jermaine	LB	6-3	255	4/24/88	5	Florida	Stone Mountain, Ga.	FA-'13	2/0
56	Davis, Demario	LB	6-2	239	1/11/89	3	Arkansas State	Brandon, Miss.	D3-'12	16/16
58	Davis, Troy	LB	6-2	251	1/6/91	2	Central Florida	Queens, N.Y.	FA-'13	4/0
87	Decker, Eric	WR	6-3	214	3/15/87	5	Minnesota	Cold Spring, Minn.	UFA(Den)-'14	16/16*
78	Douzable, Leger	DL	6-4	284	5/31/86	7	Central Florida	Tampa, Fla.	FA-'13	16/0
34	Dowling, Ras-I	CB	6-1	210	5/9/88	3	Virginia	Chesapeake, Va.	FA-'13	0*
59	Edds, A.J.	LB	6-4	256	9/18/87	4	Iowa	Marion, Ind.	FA-'14	0*
93	Ellis, Kenrick	DT	6-4	346	12/10/87	4	Hampton	Greenacres, Fla.	D3-'11	16/1
60	Ferguson, D'Brickashaw	T	6-6	310	12/10/83	9	Virginia	Freeport, N.Y.	D1a-'06	16/16
2	Folk, Nick	K	6-1	222	11/5/84	8	Arizona	Hollywood, Calif.	FA-'10	16/0
19	Ford, Jacoby	WR	5-9	190	7/27/87	5	Clemson	West Palm Beach, Fla.	UFA(Oak)-'14	14/1*
#Garrard, David		QB	6-1	239	2/14/78	11	East Carolina	East Orange, N.J.	FA-'13	0*
10	Gates, Clyde	WR	6-0	197	6/13/86	4	Abilene Christian	Vernon, Texas	W(Mia)-'12	6/2
68	Giacomini, Breno	OL	6-7	318	9/27/85	7	Louisville	Cambridge, Mass.	UFA(Sea)-'14	9/9*
23	Goodson, Mike	RB	6-0	210	5/23/87	6	Texas A&M	Klein, Texas	UFA(Oak)-'13	2/0
25	Green, Alex	RB	6-2	220	6/23/88	4	Hawaii	Portland, Ore.	W(GB)-'13	13/0
15	Hakim, Saalim	WR	5-11	188	2/1/90	2	Palomar College	Atlanta, Ga.	FA-'13	3/0
38	Hardin, Brandon	S	6-3	217	10/30/89	2	Oregon State	Kealakekua, Hawaii	FA-'13	0*
52	Harris, David	LB	6-2	250	1/21/84	8	Michigan	Grand Rapids, Mich.	D2-'07	16/16
94	Harrison, Damon	DL	6-4	350	11/29/88	3	William Penn	Lake Charles, La.	FA-'12	16/16
84	Hill, Stephen	WR	6-4	215	4/25/91	3	Georgia Tech	Lithonia, Ga.	D2-'12	12/11
#Hilliard, Lex		FB	5-11	235	7/30/84	6	Montana	Kalispell, Mont.	FA-'12	0*
71	Ijalana, Ben	T	6-4	322	8/6/89	4	Villanova	North Brunswick, N.J.	W(Ind)-'13	0*
33	Ivory, Chris	RB	6-0	222	3/22/88	5	Tiffin	Longview, Texas	T(NO)-'13	15/6
37	Jarrett, Jaiquawn	S	6-0	196	9/21/89	3	Temple	Brooklyn, N.Y.	FA-'12	16/2
21	Johnson, Chris	RB	5-11	203	9/23/85	7	East Carolina	Orlando, Fla.	FA-'14	16/16*
11	Kerley, Jeremy	WR	5-9	188	11/8/88	4	Texas Christian	Hutto, Texas	D5-'11	12/8
26	Landry, Dawan	S	6-1	212	12/30/82	9	Georgia Tech	Ama, La.	FA-'13	16/16
31	Lankster, Ellis	CB	5-9	190	6/3/86	5	West Virginia	Whistler, Ala.	FA-'10	15/0
74	Mangold, Nick	C	6-4	307	1/13/84	9	Ohio State	Centerville, Ohio	D1b-'06	16/16
#Mauga, Josh		LB	6-1	245	6/20/87	5	Nevada	Fallon, Nev.	FA-'09	0*
50	McIntyre, Garrett	LB	6-3	255	11/26/84	4	Fresno State	South Lake Tahoe, Calif.	FA-'11	13/3
27	Milliner, Dee	CB	6-0	201	9/14/91	2	Alabama	Millbrook, Ala.	D1a-'13	13/12
86	Nelson, David	WR	6-5	215	11/7/86	5	Florida	Wichita Falls, Texas	FA-'13	12/6
97	Pace, Calvin	LB	6-4	265	10/28/80	12	Wake Forest	Douglasville, Ga.	UFA(Ariz)-'08	16/16
22	Patrick, Johnny	CB	5-11	190	8/17/88	4	Louisville	Deland, Fla.	W(SD)-'14	13/4*
24	Patterson, Dimitri	CB	6-0	200	6/18/83	9	Tuskegee	Miami, Fla.	FA-'14	6/4*
29	Powell, Bilal	RB	5-10	204	10/27/88	4	Louisville	Lakeland, Fla.	D4-'11	16/11
46	Purdum, Tanner	LS	6-3	270	8/15/84	5	Baker	Waco, Texas	FA-'10	16/0
4	Quigley, Ryan	P	6-3	188	1/26/90	2	Boston College	Little River, S.C.	FA-'13	14/0
#Reed, Ed		S	5-11	205	9/11/78	13	Miami	St. Rose, La.	FA-'13	14/10*
#Reynaud, Darius		RB	5-9	208	12/29/84	6	West Virginia	Luling, La.	FA-'13	2/0
35	Richardson, Daryl	RB	5-10	204	4/12/90	3	Abilene Christian	Jacksonville, Fla.	W(StL)-'14	8/3*
91	Richardson, Sheldon	DL	6-3	294	11/29/90	2	Missouri	St. Louis, Mo.	D1b-'13	16/15
17	Salas, Greg	WR	6-2	210	8/25/88	4	Hawaii	Chino, Cal.	FA-'13	8/0
72	Schlauderaff, Caleb	G	6-4	302	11/7/87	4	Utah	Shelton, Wash.	T(GB)-'11	6/0
5	Simms, Matt	QB	6-3	210	9/27/88	2	Tennessee	Franklin Lakes, N.J.	FA-'12	3/0
7	Smith, Geno	QB	6-3	221	10/10/90	2	West Virginia	Miami, Fla.	D2-'13	16/16
44	Sudfeld, Zach	TE	6-7	260	4/17/89	2	Nevada	Santa Cruz, Calif.	W(NE)-'13	11/2
1	Vick, Michael	QB	6-0	215	6/26/80	14	Virginia Tech	Newport News, Va.	UFA(Phil)-'14	7/6*
30	Walls, Darrin	CB	6-0	190	6/20/88	4	Notre Dame	Pittsburgh, Pa.	FA-'12	16/3
96	Wilkerson, Muhammad	DL	6-4	315	10/22/89	4	Temple	Linden, N.J.	D1-'11	16/16
20	Wilson, Kyle	CB	5-10	190	9/8/87	5	Boise State	Piscataway, N.J.	D1-'10	16/1

2014 VETERAN ROSTER

No.	Name	Pos.	Ht.	Wt.	Birthdate	NFL Exp.	College	Hometown	How Acq.	'13 Games/ Starts
	#Winslow, Kellen	TE	6-4	240	7/21/83	10	Miami	San Diego, Calif.	FA-'13	12/3
67	Winters, Brian	G	6-4	320	7/16/91	2	Kent State	Hudson, Ohio	D3-'13	16/12
76	Zusevics, Markus	OL	6-5	300	4/25/89	3	Iowa	Arlington Heights, Ill.	FA-'14	0*

* Aboushi inactive for 16 games; Berry missed '13 season because of injury; Campbell inactive for 16 games; Decker played 16 games with Denver in '13; Dowling last active with New England in '12; Edds last active with New England in '11; Ford played 14 games with Oakland; Garrard inactive for 9 games; Giacomini played nine games with Seattle; Hardin missed '13 season because of injury; Hilliard missed '13 season because of injury; Ijalana inactive for 16 games; Johnson played 16 games with Tennessee; Mauga missed '13 season because of injury; Patrick played 13 games with San Diego; Patterson played six games with Miami; Reed played seven games with Houston and seven games with the Jets; D. Richardson played eight games with St. Louis; Vick played seven games with Philadelphia; Zusevics missed '13 season because of injury.

\# Unrestriced Free Agent; subject to developments.

Players lost through free agency (2): OL Vladimir Ducasse (Minn; 16 games in '13), T Austin Howard (Oak; 16).

Also played with Jets in '13—CB Antonio Cromartie (16 games), WR Santonio Holmes (11), P Robert Malone (2), S Rontez Miles (1), WR Ben Obomanu (3), TE Konrad Reuland (10), LB Ricky Sapp (5), LB Scott Solomon (1), WR Ryan Spadola (3), CB Isaiah Trufant (16).

FIRST-YEAR ROSTER

Name	Pos.	Ht.	Wt.	Birthdate	College	Hometown	How Acq.
Amaro, Jace	TE	6-5	265	6/26/92	Texas Tech	San Antonio, Texas	D2
Anderson, Colin (1)	TE	6-4	240	11/21/89	Furman	Dallas, Texas	FA-'13
Barnes, T.J. (1)	NT	6-7	364	6/14/90	Georgia Tech	Enterprise, Ala.	FA-'13
Boyd, Tajh	QB	6-1	222	9/25/90	Clemson	Hampton, Va.	D6d
Divitto, Steele	LB	6-2	237	10/24/91	Boston College	Ridgefield, Conn.	FA
Dixon, Brandon	CB	5-11	203	4/26/90	Northwest Missouri State	Pompano Beach, Fla.	D6a
Dozier, Dakota	OL	6-4	313	4/30/91	Furman	West Columbia, S.C.	D4c
Enemkpali, Ikemefuna	LB	6-1	261	7/3/91	Louisiana Tech	Pflugerville, Texas	D6c
Enunwa, Quincy	WR	6-2	225	5/31/92	Nebraska	Moreno Valley, Calif.	D6b
Evans, Shaquelle	WR	6-1	213	3/7/91	UCLA	Inglewood, Calif.	D4b
Finau, Tevita (1)	DT	6-5	288	1/13/86	Utah	Lahaina, Hawaii	FA-'12
Ford, Patrick (1)	OL	6-6	305	4/11/90	New Mexico	Richmond, Ky.	FA-'13
Freeman, Dalton (1)	C	6-5	291	6/18/90	Clemson	Pelion, S.C.	FA-'13
Fugger, Tim (1)	LB	6-4	250	7/1/89	Vanderbilt	Oak Brook, Ill.	FA-'13
George, Jeremiah	LB	5-11	234	1/24/92	Iowa State	Clearwater, Fla.	D5
Grady, Anthony	DE	6-7	289	8/6/90	Missouri State	Texarkana, Ark.	FA
Hyder, Kerry	DL	6-2	280	5/2/91	Texas Tech	Austin, Texas	FA
McDougle, Dexter	CB	5-10	195	4/8/91	Maryland	Falmouth, Va.	D3
Miles, Rontez (1)	S	6-0	203	11/25/88	California (Pa.)	Braddock, Pa.	FA-'13
Miller, Terrence	TE	6-4	234	1/16/92	Arizona	Moreno Valley, Conn.	FA
Pantale, Chris (1)	TE	6-5	254	3/22/90	Boston College	Wayne, N.J.	FA-'13
Pryor, Calvin	S	5-11	207	7/2/92	Louisville	Port St. Joe, Fla.	D1
Qvale, Brent	T	6-7	315	3/11/91	Nebraska	Williston, N.D.	FA
Reeves, Jeremy (1)	DB	5-7	176	9/15/89	Iowa State	Allen, Texas	D7
Reilly, Trevor	LB	6-5	245	1/17/88	Utah	Valley Center, Calif.	D7
Rose, Lowell (1)	CB	6-1	192	3/11/90	Tulsa	Los Angeles, Calif.	FA-'13
Saunders, Jalen	WR	5-9	165	9/30/92	Oklahoma	Elk Grove, Calif.	D4a
Thompson, Zach	DL	6-5	265	1/18/91	Wake Forest	Ashburn, Va.	FA
Young, Chad	FB	5-10	240	7/29/91	San Diego State	La Verne, Calif.	FA

The term NFL Rookie is defined as a player who is in his first season of professional football and has not been on the roster of another professional football team for any regular-season or postseason games. A Rookie is designated by an "R" on NFL rosters. Players who have been active in another professional football league or players who have NFL experience, including either preseason training camp or being on an Active List or Inactive List, or on Reserve/Injured or Reserve/Physically Unable to Perform for fewer than six regular-season games, are termed NFL First-Year Players. An NFL First-Year Player is designated by a "1" on NFL rosters. Thereafter, a player is credited with an additional year of experience for each season in which he accumulates six games on the Active List or Inactive List, or on Reserve/Injured or Reserve/Physically Unable to Perform.

Log on to www.newyorkjets.com for an up-to-date roster.

COACHING STAFF
Head Coach,
Rex Ryan

Pro Career: Named the 15th full-time head coach of the New York Jets on January 19, 2009. Ranks as the third-longest tenured head coach in franchise history. Since Ryan became the head coach, club ranks second in the NFL in total defense (302.8) and first in passing defense (198.4). During his five years with the franchise, Ryan has tutored 15 Pro Bowl selections. He has also had five defensive position coaches matriculate into coordinators or head coaches at the NFL and NCAA levels (Mike Pettine, Head Coach, Cleveland Browns; Jim O'Neil, Defensive Coordinator, Cleveland Browns; Bob Sutton, Defensive Coordinator, Kansas City Chiefs; Dennis Thurman, Defensive Coordinator, New York Jets; Brian VanGorder, Defensive Coordinator, Notre Dame). In 2013, Ryan guided the Jets to eight victories with rookie quarterback Geno Smith under center, becoming the only head coach in the Super Bowl era to win eight-or-more games with a rookie quarterback in two different seasons. Ryan led New York to the AFC Championship game in 2009 as a first-time head coach, notching nine regular-season and two playoff wins behind rookie quarterback Mark Sanchez. In 2010, directed team to 11-5 record and became second coach in NFL history to guide club to the conference championship game in his first two seasons after inheriting a team that did not reach the playoffs the year prior to him becoming head coach. Ryan spent 10 seasons (1999-2008) with the Baltimore Ravens. Ravens allowed fewest points in NFL history for 16-game season (165) in 2000 en route to winning Super Bowl XXV. Began NFL career with Arizona under his father, Buddy Ryan, as coach for defensive line (1994) and linebackers (1995). Career record: 46-40.

Background: Coached at Eastern Kentucky (1987-88), New Mexico Highlands (1989), Morehead State (1990-93), Cincinnati (1996-97) and Oklahoma (1998). Played defensive end at Southwestern Oklahoma State with his twin brother, Rob, who is the New Orleans defensive coordinator. Earned his bachelor's and master's degree in physical education at Eastern Kentucky.

Personal: Born December 13, 1963, Ardmore, Okla. Ryan and his wife Michelle have two sons, Payton and Seth.

ASSISTANT COACHES

Louie Aguiar, asst. special teams; born June 30, 1966, Livermore, Calif. Punter Chabot (Calif.) College, punter/kicker Utah State 1987-88. Pro punter Barcelona Dragons (WLAF) 1991, New York Jets 1991-93, Kansas City Chiefs 1994-98, Green Bay Packers 1999, Chicago Bears 2000. Pro coach: Joined Jets in 2013.

Bobby April III, linebackers; born August 15, 1981, Tucson, Ariz. Attended Louisiana-Lafayette. No college or pro playing experience. College coach: Tulane 2005-06, Portland State 2007-09, Nicholls State 2010.

Pro coach: Philadelphia Eagles 2011-12, joined Jets in 2013.

Mike Devlin, offensive line; born November 16, 1969, Blacksburg, Va. Offensive line Iowa 1989-1992. Pro offensive lineman Buffalo Bills 1993-95, Arizona Cardinals 1996-99. College coach: Toledo 2004-05. Pro coach: Arizona Cardinals 2000-03, joined Jets in 2006.

Karl Dunbar, defensive line; born May 18, 1967, Plaisance, La. Defensive lineman Louisiana State 1986-89. Pro defensive lineman Pittsburgh Steelers 1990, New Orleans Saints 1992-93, Arizona Cardinals 1994-95. College coaching: Nicholls State 1998-99, Louisiana State 2000-01, Oklahoma State 2002-03. Pro coach: Chicago Bears 2004, Louisiana State 2005, Minnesota Vikings 2006-2011, joined Jets in 2012.

Justus Galac, head strength and conditioning; born August 15, 1980, Cattaraugus, N.Y. Nose tackle SUNY Brockport 1998-2001. No pro playing experience. College coach: SUNY Brockport 2002, Dickenson College 2003-04, Villanova 2005-11. Pro coach: Joined Jets in 2012.

Steve Hagen, tight ends; born September 15, 1961, Forest City, Iowa. Wide receiver Cal Lutheran 1979-1983. No pro playing experience. College coach: Illinois 1984, Kansas 1985-86, Northern Arizona 1987-88, Notre Dame 1989-1990, Kent State 1991, Nevada 1992-93, Nevada-Las Vegas 1994-95, Wartburg 1996, San Jose State 1997-98, California 1999-2000, Fresno State 2006, North Carolina 2007-08. Pro coach: Cleveland Browns 2001-04, 2009-12, joined Jets in 2013.

Ron Heller, asst. offensive line; born August 25, 1962, East Meadow, N.Y. Offensive tackle Penn State 1980-83. Pro offensive tackle Tampa Bay Buccaneers 1984-87, Philadelphia Eagles 1988-92, Miami Dolphins 1993-95. Pro coach: Amsterdam Admirals (NFLE) 2004, 2006-07, Toronto Argonauts (CFL) 2009, Jacksonville Jaguars 2010-11, Omaha Knighthawks (UFL) 2012, joined Jets in 2013.

Sanjay Lal, wide receivers; born July 23, 1969, London, England. Wide receiver UCLA 1989, Washington 1990-93. Pro receiver St. Louis Rams 1998, Scottish Claymores (NFLE) 1999. College coach: Los Medanos (Calif.) College 2003, St. Mary's College 2004, California 2005-06. Pro coach: Oakland Raiders 2007-2011, joined Jets in 2012.

David Lee, quarterbacks; born July 2, 1953, Cape Girardeau, Mo. Quarterback Vanderbilt 1971-74. No pro playing experience. College coach: Tennessee-Martin 1975-76, Vanderbilt 1977, Mississippi 1978-1982, 2011, New Mexico 1983, Arkansas 1984-88, 2001-02, 2007, Texas-El Paso 1989-1993 (head coach), Rice 1994-2000. Pro coach: Dallas Cowboys 2003-06, Miami Dolphins 2008-2010, Buffalo Bills 2012, joined Jets in 2013.

Anthony Lynn, asst. head coach/running backs; born December 21, 1968, McKinney, Texas. Running back Texas Tech 1987-1991. Pro running back Denver Broncos 1993, 1997-99, San Francisco 49ers 1995-96. Pro coach: Denver Broncos 2000-02, Jacksonville Jaguars 2003-04, Dallas Cowboys 2005-06, Cleveland

Browns 2007-08, joined Jets in 2009.

Tim McDonald, defensive backs; born January 6, 1965, Fresno, Calif. Defensive back Southern California 1983-86. Pro defensive back St. Louis/Phoenix Cardinals 1987-1992, San Francisco 49ers 1993-99. College coach: Fresno State 2012. Pro coach: Joined Jets in 2013.

Thomas McGaughey, special teams coordinator; born May 8, 1973, Chicago, Ill. Safety Houston 1991-95. Pro safety Philadelphia Eagles 1996, Barcelona Dragons (NFLE) 1997. College coach: Houston 1997, 2003-04, Louisiana State 2011-12. Pro coach: Scottish Claymores (NFLE) 2002, Kansas City Chiefs 2002, Denver Broncos 2005-06, New York Giants 2007-2010, joined Jets in 2014.

Aaron McLaurin, asst. strength and conditioning; born February 27, 1984, Buffalo, N.Y. Attended Hampton. No college or pro playing experience. College coach: Michigan State 2008-2010, Colgate 2011. Pro coach: Minnesota Vikings 2012, joined Jets in 2014.

Marty Mornhinweg, offensive coordinator; born March 29, 1962, Edmond, Okla. Quarterback Montana 1981-84. Pro quarterback Denver Dynamite (AFL) 1987. College coach: Montana 1985, Texas-El Paso 1986-87, Northern Arizona 1988, 1994, Southeast Missouri State 1989-1990, Missouri 1991-93. Pro coach: Green Bay Packers 1995-96, San Francisco 49ers 1997-2000, Detroit Lions 2001-02 (head coach), Philadelphia Eagles 2003-2012, joined Jets in 2013.

Jason Oszvart, asst. strength and conditioning; born December 24, 1988, Robinsville, N.J. Attended East Stroudsburg. No college or pro playing experience. Pro coach: Joined Jets in 2013.

Brian Smith, asst. defensive backs; born July 15, 1979, Wilmington, Del. Defensive back Massachusetts 1997-2000. No pro playing experience. College coach: Massachusetts 2004-06. Pro coach: Joined Jets in 2007.

Tony Sparano Jr., offensive assistant; born October 22 1986, Colleyville, Texas. Defensive end Albany 2006-08. No pro playing experience. Pro coach: Hartford Colonials (UFL) 2010, Miami Dolphins 2011, joined Jets in 2012.

Dennis Thurman, defensive coordinator; born April 13, 1956, Los Angeles, Calif. Defensive back Southern California 1974-77. Pro defensive back Dallas Cowboys 1978-1985, St. Louis Cardinals 1986. College coach: Southern California 1993-2000. Pro coach: Phoenix Cardinals 1988-89, Ohio Glory (WLAF) 1992, Baltimore Ravens 2002-07, joined Jets in 2009.

Jeff Weeks, defensive assistant: defensive line/linebackers; born May 30, 1962, Denver, Colo. Wide receiver Southwest Oklahoma State 1982-84, Northwest Oklahoma State 1995. No pro playing experience. College coach: Western Kentucky 1987-88, Morehead State 1990-91, Phoenix (Ariz.) C.C. 1996, Oklahoma 1999, Fort Scott (Kan.) C.C. 2001-04, Southeast Oklahoma State 2005, Texas A&M-Kingsville 2006. Pro coach: Oakland Raiders 2008, New York Jets 2009-2011, re-joined Jets in 2013.

**American Football Conference
West Division**
Team Colors: Silver and Black
1220 Harbor Bay Parkway
Alameda, California 94502
Telephone: (510) 864-5000

2014 SCHEDULE
PRESEASON
Aug. 8   at Minnesota 5:00
Aug. 15 **Detroit**.............................7:00
Aug. 22 at Green Bay......................5:00
Aug. 28 **Seattle**..............................7:00

REGULAR SEASON
Sep. 7   at New York Jets 10:00a
Sep. 14 **Houston** 1:25
Sep. 21 at New England 10:00a
Sep. 28 **Miami** (London) 10:00a
Oct. 5   BYE
Oct. 12 **San Diego** 1:05
Oct. 19 **Arizona** 1:25
Oct. 26 at Cleveland 1:25
Nov. 2   at Seattle 1:05
Nov. 9   **Denver** 1:05
Nov. 16 at San Diego 1:05
Nov. 20 **Kansas City** (Thu) 5:25
Nov. 30 at St. Louis 10:00a
Dec. 7   **San Francisco** 1:25
Dec. 14 at Kansas City 10:00a
Dec. 21 **Buffalo** 1:25
Dec. 28 at Denver 1:25
All times PT

Stadium: O.co Coliseum
         (opened in 1966)
         •**Capacity:** 53,286
         7000 Coliseum Way
         Oakland, CA 94621-1917
Playing Surface: Grass
Training Camp: Napa Valley Marriott
                Napa, California 94558

O.CO COLISEUM

CLUB OFFICIALS
Owner: Mark Davis
General Manager: Reggie McKenzie
Director – Football Administration:
   Tom Delaney
Director – Player Personnel:
   Joey Clinkscales
Director – College Scouting:
   Shaun Herock
Scouting Coordinator: Teddy Atlas
Pro Scouts: Von Hutchins,
   Dane Vandernat
College Scouts: Calvin Branch, Zack
   Crockett, Brad Kaplan, Mickey Marvin,
   David McCloughan, Raleigh McKenzie,
   Trey Scott
Head Athletic Trainer: H. Rod Martin
Team Orthopedist: Dr. Warren King
Equipment Manager: Bob Romanski
Director - Video Operations: Dave Nash
Assistant to Head Coach: Tom Jones
Director – Media Relations: Will Kiss
Director – Player Engagement:
   Lamonte Winston
Director – Team Security: Fred Formosa
Director – Team Travel: Pete Caracciolo
Legal: Dan Ventrelle
Finance: Marc Badain, Tom Blanda
Tickets, Suites & Premium Seats:
   Mark Shearer
Community: Rosie Bone
Sponsorships: Airikuh Anderson
Public Affairs: Mike Taylor
Internet: Jerry Knaak
Broadcasting: Vittorio DeBartolo,
   Brad Phinney
Technology: Matthew Pasco

COACHING HISTORY
Oakland 1960-1981
Los Angeles 1982-1994
(459-393-11)
Records include postseason games
1960-61   Eddie Erdelatz* 6-10-0
1961-62   Marty Feldman**.....2-15-0
1962   Red Conkright.................1-8-0
1963-65   Al Davis 23-16-3
1966-68   John Rauch 35-10-1
1969-1978   John Madden...........112-39-7
1979-1987   Tom Flores.............91-56-0
1988-89   Mike Shanahan*** 8-12-0
1989-1994   Art Shell....................56-41-0
1995-96   Mike White...............15-17-0
1997   Joe Bugel....................4-12-0
1998-2001   Jon Gruden..............40-28-0
2002-03   Bill Callahan 17-18-0
2004-05   Norv Turner.................9-23-0
2006   Art Shell....................2-14-0
2007-08   Lane Kiffin**** 5-15-0
2008-2010   Tom Cable.................17-27-0
2011   Hue Jackson..................8-8-0
2012-13   Dennis Allen...............8-24-0
     * Released after two games in 1961
    ** Released after five games in 1962
   *** Released after four games in 1989
  **** Released after four games in 2008

PAID ATTENDANCE
Home 383,635   Away 576,197
Total 959,832
Single-game home record,
   62,660 (11/3/02)
Single-season home record,
   471,151 (2002)

2014 DRAFT CHOICES

Round	Name	Pos.	College
1	Khalil Mack	LB	Buffalo
2	Derek Carr	QB	Fresno St.
3	Gabe Jackson	G	Mississippi St.
4	Justin Ellis	DT	Louisiana Tech
	Keith McGill	DB	Utah
7	T.J. Carrie	DB	Ohio
	Shelby Harris	DE	Illinois St.
	Jonathan Dowling	DB	Western Kentucky

2013 TEAM RECORD
PRESEASON (1-3)

Date	Result	Opponent
08/09	W 19-17	Dallas
08/16	L 20-28	at New Orleans
08/23	L 26-34	Chicago
08/29	L 6-22	at Seattle

REGULAR SEASON (4-12)

Date	Result	Opponent
09/08	L 17-21	at Indianapolis
09/15	W 19-9	Jacksonville
09/23	L 21-37	at Denver
09/29	L 14-24	Washington
10/06	W 27-17	San Diego
10/13	L 7-24	at Kansas City
10/27	W 21-18	Pittsburgh
11/03	L 20-49	Philadelphia
11/10	L 20-24	at New York Giants
11/17	W 28-23	at Houston
11/24	L 19-23	Tennessee
11/28	L 24-31	at Dallas
12/08	L 27-37	at New York Jets
12/15	L 31-56	Kansas City
12/22	L 13-26	at San Diego
12/29	L 14-34	Denver

SCORE BY PERIODS

Raiders	89	98	68	67	0	—	322
Opponents	89	150	96	118	0	—	453

2013 TEAM STATISTICS

	Raiders	Opp.
Total First Downs	275	330
Rushing	90	100
Passing	168	202
Penalty	17	28
3rd Down: Made/Att	78/223	91/211
3rd Down Pct.	35.0	43.1
4th Down: Made/Att	7/12	2/6
4th Down Pct.	58.3	33.3
Possession Avg.	29:54	30:06
Total Net Yards	5340	5819
Avg. Per Game	333.8	363.7
Total Plays	1000	1029
Avg. Per Play	5.3	5.7
Net Yards Rushing	2000	1727
Avg. Per Game	125.0	107.9
Total Rushes	437	442
Net Yards Passing	3340	4092
Avg. Per Game	208.8	255.8
Sacked/Yards Lost	44/289	38/260
Gross Yards	3629	4352
Att./Completions	519/298	549/374
Completion Pct.	57.4	68.1
Had Intercepted	20	9
Punts/Average	86/47.8	77/41.7
Net Punting Avg.	86/40.1	77/37.0
Penalties/Yards	116/912	87/686
Fumbles/Ball Lost	27/11	26/13
Touchdowns	37	54
Rushing	16	15
Passing	17	33
Returns	4	6

2013 INDIVIDUAL STATISTICS

PASSING

	Att.	Comp.	Yds.	Pct.	TD	Int.	Tkld.	Rate
Pryor	272	156	1798	57.4	7	11	31/203	69.1
McGloin	211	118	1547	55.9	8	8	6/53	76.1
Flynn	34	22	246	64.7	1	1	7/33	83.7
D. McFadden	1	1	16	100.0	1	0	0/0	158.3
Reece	1	1	22	100.0	0	0	0/0	118.8
Raiders	519	298	3629	57.4	17	20	44/289	73.9
Opponents	549	374	4352	68.1	33	9	38/260	105.1

SCORING

	TD R	TD P	TD Rt	PAT	FG	Saf	PTS
Janikowski	0	0	0	37/37	21/30	0	100
Jennings	6	0	0	0/0	0/0	0	36
D. McFadden	5	0	0	0/0	0/0	0	30
D. Moore	0	5	0	0/0	0/0	0	30
Reece	2	2	0	0/0	0/0	0	24
Rivera	0	4	0	0/0	0/0	0	24
Streater	0	4	0	0/0	0/0	0	24
Pryor	2	0	0	0/0	0/0	0	12
Stewart	1	0	1	0/0	0/0	0	12
Holmes	0	1	0	0/0	0/0	0	6
G. Jenkins	0	0	1	0/0	0/0	0	6
Kasa	0	1	0	0/0	0/0	0	6
Porter	0	0	1	0/0	0/0	0	6
Woodson	0	0	1	0/0	0/0	0	6
Raiders	16	17	4	37/37	21/30	0	322
Opponents	15	33	6	52/52	25/28	0	453

2-Pt Conversions: Raiders 0-0, Opponents 1-2

RUSHING

	No.	Yds	Avg	LG	TD
Jennings	163	733	4.5	80t	6
Pryor	83	576	6.9	93t	2
D. McFadden	114	379	3.3	30	5
Reece	46	218	4.7	63t	2
McGloin	11	27	2.5	20	0
Jones	5	23	4.6	19	0
Streater	2	17	8.5	9	0
Ford	5	15	3.0	4	0
Olawale	3	6	2.0	4	0
Flynn	3	4	1.3	2	0
Stewart	2	2	1.0	2t	1
Raiders	437	2000	4.6	93t	16
Opponents	442	1727	3.9	45	15

RECEIVING

	No.	Yds	Avg	LG	TD
Streater	60	888	14.8	66	4
D. Moore	46	695	15.1	73t	5
Rivera	38	407	10.7	37	4
Jennings	36	292	8.1	24	0
Reece	32	331	10.3	45	2
Holmes	25	431	17.2	40	1
D. McFadden	17	108	6.4	16	0
Ford	13	99	7.6	22	0
Butler	9	103	11.4	29	0
Olawale	7	63	9.0	25	0
Mastrud	6	88	14.7	41	0
Criner	3	32	10.7	20	0
Jones	2	55	27.5	52	0
Stewart	2	6	3.0	5	0
Chekwa	1	22	22.0	22	0
Kasa	1	9	9.0	9t	1
Raiders	298	3629	12.2	73t	17
Opponents	374	4352	11.6	71t	33

INTERCEPTIONS

	No.	Yds	Avg	LG	TD
Porter	2	44	22.0	43t	1
M. Jenkins	2	0	0.0	0	0
Young	1	26	26.0	26	0
Woodson	1	13	13.0	13	0
Ke. Burnett	1	0	0.0	0	0
Hayden	1	0	0.0	0	0
Roach	1	0	0.0	0	0
Raiders	9	83	9.2	43t	1
Opponents	20	375	18.8	65	3

PUNTING

	No.	Yds.	Avg.	In 20	LG
King	84	4107	48.9	23	66
Raiders	86	4107	47.8	23	66
Opponents	77	3214	41.7	24	65

PUNT RETURNS

	Ret	FC	Yds	Avg	LG	TD
Ford	9	8	77	8.6	14	0
P. Adams	8	8	59	7.4	30	0
G. Jenkins	6	3	49	8.2	14	0
Crawford	1	0	-1	-1.0	-1	0
Young	1	0	0	0.0	0	0
Hayden	0	0	22	—	22	0
Raiders	25	19	206	8.2	30	0
Opponents	42	11	438	10.4	87t	1

KICKOFF RETURNS

	No.	Yds	Avg	LG	TD
Jones	26	623	24.0	41	0
Ford	11	253	23.0	30	0
G. Jenkins	10	221	22.1	29	0
Stewart	5	95	19.0	28	0
Olawale	1	6	6.0	6	0
Rivera	1	3	3.0	3	0
Raiders	54	1201	22.2	41	0
Opponents	30	613	20.4	50	0

FIELD GOALS

	1-19	20-29	30-39	40-49	50+
Janikowski	0/0	6/6	4/6	8/11	3/7
Raiders	0/0	6/6	4/6	8/11	3/7
Opponents	1/1	9/9	6/9	5/5	4/4

SACKS

	No.
Houston	6.0
Roach	5.5
S. Moore	4.5
Hunter	3.0
Walker	3.0
Ke. Burnett	2.5
Young	2.5
Ross	2.0
Sims	2.0
Woodson	2.0
Porter	1.5
Bilukidi	1.0
Branch	1.0
Muir	1.0
McGee	0.5
Raiders	38.0
Opponents	44.0

RECORD HOLDERS
INDIVIDUAL RECORDS—CAREER

Category	Name	Performance
Rushing (Yds.)	Marcus Allen, 1982-1992	8,545
Passing (Yds.)	Ken Stabler, 1970-79	19,078
Passing (TDs)	Ken Stabler, 1970-79	150
Receiving (No.)	Tim Brown, 1988-2003	1,070
Receiving (Yds.)	Tim Brown, 1988-2003	14,734
Interceptions	Willie Brown, 1967-1978	39
	Lester Hayes, 1977-1986	39
Punting (Avg.)	Shane Lechler, 2000-2012	**47.5
Punt Return (Avg.)	Claude Gibson, 1963-65	12.6
Kickoff Return (Avg.)	Jack Larscheid, 1960-61	28.4
Field Goals	Sebastian Janikowski, 2000-2013	345
Touchdowns (Tot.)	Tim Brown, 1988-2003	104
Points	Sebastian Janikowski, 2000-2013	1,489
*Sacks	Greg Townsend, 1983-1993, 1997	107.5

INDIVIDUAL RECORDS—SINGLE SEASON

Category	Name	Performance
Rushing (Yds.)	Marcus Allen, 1985	1,759
Passing (Yds.)	Rich Gannon, 2002	4,689
Passing (TDs)	Daryle Lamonica, 1969	34
Receiving (No.)	Tim Brown 1997	104
Receiving (Yds.)	Tim Brown, 1997	1,408
Interceptions	Lester Hayes, 1980	13
Punting (Avg.)	Shane Lechler, 2009	51.1
Punt Return (Avg.)	Claude Gibson, 1964	14.4
Kickoff Return (Avg.)	Harold Hart, 1975	30.5
Field Goals	Jeff Jaeger, 1993	35
Touchdowns (Tot.)	Marcus Allen, 1984	18
Points	Sebastian Janikowski, 2010	142
*Sacks	Derrick Burgess, 2005	16.0

INDIVIDUAL RECORDS—SINGLE GAME

Category	Name	Performance
Rushing (Yds.)	Napoleon Kaufman, 10-19-97	227
Passing (Yds.)	Cotton Davidson, 10-25-64	427
Passing (TDs)	Tom Flores, 12-22-63	6
	Daryle Lamonica, 10-19-69	6
Receiving (No.)	Tim Brown, 12-21-97	14
	Brandon Myers, 12-2-12	14
Receiving (Yds.)	Art Powell, 12-22-63	247
Interceptions	Many times	3
	Last time by Rod Woodson, 9-29-02	
Field Goals	Sebastian Janikowski, 11-27-11	6
Touchdowns (Tot.)	Art Powell, 12-22-63	4
	Marcus Allen, 9-24-84	4
	Harvey Williams, 11-16-97	4
	Darren McFadden, 10-24-10	4
Points	Art Powell, 12-22-63	24
	Marcus Allen, 9-24-84	24
	Harvey Williams, 11-16-97	24
	Darren McFadden, 10-24-10	24
*Sacks	Howie Long, 10-2-83	5.0

*Sacks became an official statistic in 1982.
**NFL Record

2014 VETERAN ROSTER

No.	Name	Pos.	Ht.	Wt.	Birthdate	NFL Exp.	College	Hometown	How Acq.	'13 Games/ Starts
86	Ausberry, David	TE	6-4	250	9/25/87	4	Southern California	Lemoore, Calif.	D7-'11	0*
69	Barnes, Khalif	T/G	6-6	320	4/21/82	10	Washington	Spring Valley, Calif.	UFA(Jax)-'09	16/16
70	Bergstrom, Tony	G	6-5	315	8/6/86	3	Utah	Salt Lake City, Utah	D3-'12	0*
67	Boothe, Kevin	G	6-5	325	7/5/83	9	Cornell	Fort Lauderdale, Fla.	UFA(NYG)-'14	16/16*
33	Branch, Tyvon	S	6-0	210	12/11/86	7	Connecticut	Cicero, N.Y.	D4-'08	2/0
23	Brown, Tarell	CB	5-11	190	1/6/85	8	Texas	Mesquite, Texas	UFA(SF)-'14	13/10*
95	Burnett, Kaelin	LB	6-4	240	9/6/89	3	Nevada	Lakewood, Calif.	FA-'12	16/0
94	Burnett, Kevin	LB	6-3	230	12/24/82	10	Tennessee	Compton, Calif.	FA-'13	16/16
56	Burris, Miles	LB	6-2	235	6/27/88	3	San Diego State	Granite Bay, Calif.	D4-'12	6/0
12	Butler, Brice	WR	6-3	210	1/29/90	2	San Diego State	Norcross, Ga.	D7a-'13	10/2
62	Carter, David	DT	6-5	300	12/10/87	3	UCLA	Los Angeles, Calif.	FA-'14	3/0*
35	Chekwa, Chimdi	CB	6-0	190	1/7/88	3	Ohio State	Clermont, Fla.	D4-'11	15/1
46	Cole, Justin	LB	6-3	240	11/22/87	4	San Jose State	Pasadena, Calif.	FA-'14	0*
59	Condo, Jon	LS	6-3	240	8/26/81	8	Maryland	Philipsburg, Pa.	FA-'06	16/0
99	Crawford, Jack	DE	6-5	275	9/7/88	3	Penn State	London, England	D5a-'12	15/0
84	Criner, Juron	WR	6-3	220	12/12/89	3	Arizona	Las Vegas, Nev.	D5b-'12	1/0
38	Dye, Tony	S	5-10	200	2/11/90	2	UCLA	San Jose, Calif.	FA-'14	1/0*
5	Edwards, Trent	QB	6-4	230	10/30/83	6	Stanford	Los Gatos, Calif.	FA-'14	0*
#Gurode, Andre	C/G	6-4	320	3/6/79	13	Colorado	Houston, Texas	FA-'13	10/4
25	Hayden, DJ	CB	5-11	190	6/27/90	2	Houston	Houston, Texas	D1-'13	8/2
18	Holmes, Andre	WR	6-4	210	6/16/88	3	Hillsdale	Elk Grove, Ill.	W(NE)-'13	10/4
77	Howard, Austin	G/T	6-7	330	3/22/87	5	Northern Iowa	Davenport, Iowa	UFA(NYJ)-'14	16/16*
#Hunter, Jason	DE	6-4	270	8/28/83	8	Appalachian State	Fayetteville, N.C.	UFA(Den)-'13	13/10
11	Janikowski, Sebastian	K	6-1	260	3/2/78	15	Florida State	Daytona Beach, Fla.	D1-'00	16/0
10	Jenkins, Greg	WR	6-1	205	8/23/89	2	Alabama State	Dade City, Fla.	FA-'13	6/0
89	Jones, James	WR	6-1	208	3/31/84	8	San Jose State	San Jose, Calif.	UFA(GB)-'14	14/14*
22	Jones, Taiwan	CB	6-0	195	7/26/88	4	Eastern Washington	Antioch, Calif.	D4b-'11	16/0
21	Jones-Drew, Maurice	RB	5-7	210	3/23/85	9	UCLA	Antioch, Calif.	UFA(Jax)-'14	15/15*
88	Kasa, Nick	TE	6-6	265	11/5/90	2	Colorado	Thornton, Colo.	D6a-'13	16/1
7	King, Marquette	P	6-0	190	10/26/88	3	Fort Valley State	Macon, Ga.	FA-'12	16/0
63	Mady, Lamar	G	6-2	315	12/13/90	2	Youngstown State	Topeka, Kan.	FA-'13	7/0
50	Maiava, Kaluka	LB	6-0	230	12/27/86	6	Southern California	Wailuku, Hawaii	UFA(Cle)-'13	9/1
#Mastrud, Jeron	TE	6-5	255	12/17/87	5	Kansas State	Beaverton, Ore.	FA-'13	16/12
73	McCants, Matt	T	6-6	315	8/18/89	2	Alabama Birmingham	Mobile, Ala.	UFA(Mia)-'13	13/3
20	McFadden, Darren	RB	6-1	218	8/27/87	7	Arkansas	North Little Rock, Ark.	D1-'08	10/7
92	McGee, Stacy	DT	6-3	310	1/17/90	2	Oklahoma	Muskogee, Okla.	D6d-'13	15/5
14	McGloin, Matt	QB	6-1	210	12/2/89	2	Penn State	Scranton, Pa.	FA-'13	7/6
17	Moore, Denarius	WR	6-0	190	12/9/88	4	Tennessee	Tatum, Texas	D5-'11	13/10
55	Moore, Sio	LB	6-1	240	5/2/90	2	Connecticut	Cary, N.C.	D3-'13	15/11
#Muir, Daniel	DT	6-2	322	9/12/83	7	Kent State	Lanham, Md.	FA-'13	10/1
28	Murray, Latavius	RB	6-3	225	1/18/90	2	Central Florida	Nedrow, N.Y.	D6b-'13	0*
76	Nix, Lucas	G	6-5	325	9/28/89	3	Pittsburgh	Jefferson Hills, Pa.	FA-'12	14/10
49	Olawale, Jamize	FB/RB	6-1	235	4/17/89	2	North Texas	Long Beach, Calif.	FA-'12	16/1
#Pashos, Tony	T	6-6	325	8/3/80	11	Illinois	Palos Heights, Ill.	FA-'13	12/12
72	Penn, Donald	T	6-4	340	4/27/83	9	Utah State	Playa del Rey, Calif.	FA-'14	16/16*
45	Reece, Marcel	FB	6-1	250	6/23/85	5	Washington	Inglewood, Calif.	FA-'08	16/15
81	Rivera, Mychal	TE	6-3	245	9/8/90	2	Tennessee	Valencia, Calif.	D6c-'13	16/3
53	Roach, Nick	LB	6-1	235	6/16/85	8	Northwestern	Milwaukee, Wisc.	UFA(Chi)-'13	16/16
58	Robinson, Ryan	DE	6-4	255	12/9/90	2	Oklahoma State	Buford, Ga.	FA-'13	11/0
27	Rogers, Carlos	CB	6-0	195	7/2/81	10	Auburn	Augusta, Ga.	FA-'14	16/16*
29	Ross, Brandian	S	6-1	190	9/28/89	3	Youngstown State	Meadowbrook, Va.	FA-'12	16/13
8	t-Schaub, Matt	QB	6-6	235	6/25/81	11	Virginia	West Chester, Pa.	T(Hou)-'14	10/8*
74	Shaw, Jarrod	OL	6-4	315	1/7/88	2	Tennessee	Lafayette, La.	FA-'14	0*
30	Sheets, Kory	RB	5-11	208	3/31/85	3	Purdue	Manchester, Conn.	FA-'14	0*
90	Sims, Pat	DT	6-2	310	11/29/85	6	Auburn	Ft. Lauderdale, Fla.	UFA(Cin)-'13	16/16
97	Smith, Antonio	DL	6-3	290	10/21/81	10	Oklahoma State	Oklahoma City, Okla.	UFA(Hou)-'14	15/15*
32	Stewart, Jeremy	RB	5-11	215	2/17/89	3	Stanford	Baton Rouge, La.	FA-'14	13/0
80	Streater, Rod	WR	6-3	195	2/9/88	3	Temple	Burlington, N.J.	FA-'12	16/14
31	Thorpe, Neiko	CB	6-1	200	2/1/90	2	Auburn	Tucker, Ga.	FA-'14	0*
64	Troup, Torell	DT	6-3	320	6/23/88	4	Central Florida	Conyers, Ga.	FA-'14	0*
91	Tuck, Justin	DE	6-5	265	3/29/83	10	Notre Dame	Kellyton, Ala.	UFA(NYG)-'14	16/15*
71	Watson, Menelik	T	6-5	315	12/22/88	2	Florida State	Manchester, England	D2-'13	5/3
98	Wilson, C.J.	DL	6-3	300	3/30/87	5	East Carolina	Pinetown, N.C.	UFA(GB)-'14	8/0*
61	Wisniewski, Stefen	C/G	6-3	315	3/22/89	4	Penn State	Pittsburgh, Pa.	D2-'11	14/14
57	Woodley, LaMarr	DE	6-2	265	11/3/84	8	Michigan	Saginaw, Mich.	FA-'14	11/11*
24	Woodson, Charles	S	6-1	210	10/7/76	17	Michigan	Fremont, Ohio	FA-'13	16/16
26	Young, Usama	S	5-11	195	5/8/85	8	Kent State	Largo, Md.	FA-'13	12/1

* Ausberry missed '13 season because of injury; Bergstrom missed '13 season because of injury; Carter played three games with Dallas in '13; Cole last active with St. Louis in '12; Dye played one game with Cincinnati; Edwards last active with Philadelphia in '12; Howard played 16 games with the New York Jets; J. Jones played 14 games with Green Bay; Jones-Drew played 15 games with Jacksonville; Murray missed '13 season because of injury; Penn played 16 games with Tampa Bay; Rogers played 16 games with San Francisco; Shaw inactive eight games with Cleveland in '12; Sheets last active with Miami in '09; Smith played 15 games with Houston; Thorpe last active with Kansas City in '12; Troup last active with Buffalo in '11; Wilson played eight games with Green Bay; Woodley played 11 games with Pittsburgh.

\# Unrestricted Free Agent; subject to developments.

t- Raiders traded for Schaub (Hou).

Traded—QB Terrelle Pryor (11 games in '13) to Seattle.

Players lost through free agency (7): DB Phillip Adams (Sea; 16 games in '13), DE Lamarr Houston (16: Chi), DB Mike Jenkins (TB; 15), RB Rashad Jennings (15; NYG), DB Tracy Porter (Wash; 16), T Jared Veldheer (Ariz; 15), DT Vance Walker (KC; 15).

Also played with Raiders in '13—DT Christo Bilukidi (5 games), G Mike Brisiel (15), CB Chance Casey (2), T Jack Cornell (1), QB Matt Flynn (2), WR Jacoby Ford (14), S Shelton Johnson (4), DE Ricky Lumpkin (1), LB Marshall McFadden (4), DE Brian Sanford (5), DE Martez Wilson (3).

FIRST-YEAR ROSTER

Name	Pos.	Ht.	Wt.	Birthdate	College	Hometown	How Acq.
Adams, Johnny (1)	CB	5-11	180	6/9/89	Michigan State	Des Plaines, Ill.	FA-'13
Atkinson III, George	RB	6-1	218	11/29/92	Notre Dame	Stockton, Calif.	FA
Beltre, Frank (1)	LB	6-2	240	1/28/91	Towson	Randolph, N.J.	FA
Carr, Derek	QB	6-3	214	3/28/91	Fresno State	Bakersfield, Calif.	D2
Carrie, T.J.	CB	6-0	204	7/28/90	Ohio	Antioch, Calif.	D7a
Casey, Chance (1)	CB	5-11	190	3/11/91	Baylor	Crosby, Texas	FA-'13
Coles, D.J.	WR	6-3	225	9/29/89	Virginia Tech	Maidens, Va.	FA
Cornell, Jack (1)	T	6-5	300	6/4/89	Illinois	Quincy, Ill.	FA-'13
Davis, Mike	WR	6-0	189	5/11/92	Texas	Dallas, Texas	FA
Dowling, Jonathan	S	6-3	190	12/8/91	Western Kentucky	Bradenton, Fla.	D7c
Ellis, Justin	DT	6-2	334	12/27/90	Louisiana Tech	Monroe, La.	D4a
Fields, Carlos	LB	6-1	238	10/3/90	Winston-Salem State	Henderson, N.C.	FA
Green, Jared (1)	WR	6-1	185	4/1/89	Southern	Vienna, Va.	FA-'13
Grigsby, Noel	WR	5-10	185	10/2/91	San Jose State	Los Angeles, Calif.	FA
Harper, Eric (1)	LB	6-3	240	10/29/87	Grambling State	Marrero, La.	FA-'13
Harris, Shelby	DE	6-2	288	8/11/91	Illinois State	Milwaukee, Wisc.	D7b
Jackson, Gabe	G	6-3	336	7/12/91	Mississippi State	Liberty, Miss.	D3
Johnson, Shelton (1)	S	6-0	195	7/16/90	Wisconsin	Carrollton, Texas	FA-'13
Kistler, Dan	T	6-7	315	3/30/91	Montana	Seattle, Wash.	FA
Ladson, Erle	T	6-6	346	11/27/91	Delaware	Bronx, N.Y.	FA
Leonhardt, Brian (1)	TE	6-5	255	4/2/90	Bemidji State	Blaine, Minn.	FA-'13
Lumpkin, Ricky (1)	DE	6-4	300	9/7/88	Kentucky	Mount Holly, N.J.	FA-'13
Mack, Khalil	LB	6-3	252	2/22/91	Buffalo	Fort Pierce, Fla.	D1
McCoy, Chris (1)	DE	6-3	260	11/25/86	Middle Tennessee State	Villa Rica, Ga.	FA-'13
McFadden, Marshall (1)	LB	6-1	235	8/4/86	South Carolina State	Lamar, S.C.	FA-'13
McGill, Keith	CB	6-3	211	3/9/89	Utah	La Mirada, Calif.	D4b
Murphy, Jake	TE	6-4	249	9/21/89	Utah	Alpine, Utah	FA
Roberts, Seth	WR	6-2	196	2/22/91	West Alabama	Tallahassee, Fla.	FA
Simonson, Scott	TE	6-5	249	4/13/92	Assumption	Red Bank, N.J.	FA
Williams, Karl	FB	6-0	244	7/17/90	Utah	Layton, Utah	FA
Zychlinski, Daniel	P	6-2	215	4/17/90	Stanford	Tampa, Fla.	FA

The term NFL Rookie is defined as a player who is in his first season of professional football and has not been on the roster of another professional football team for any regular-season or postseason games. A Rookie is designated by an "R" on NFL rosters. Players who have been active in another professional football league or players who have NFL experience, including either preseason training camp or being on an Active List or Inactive List, or on Reserve/Injured or Reserve/Physically Unable to Perform for fewer than six regular-season games, are termed NFL First-Year Players. An NFL First-Year Player is designated by a "1" on NFL rosters. Thereafter, a player is credited with an additional year of experience for each season in which he accumulates six games on the Active List or Inactive List, or on Reserve/Injured or Reserve/Physically Unable to Perform.

Log on to www.raiders.com for an up-to-date roster.

COACHING STAFF
Head Coach,
Dennis Allen

Pro Career: Dennis Allen is in his third season as head coach of the Oakland Raiders. At age 41, Allen is the youngest current head coach in the NFL. Allen has 18 years of coaching experience, including 10 as an NFL assistant. In 2013, the Raiders ranked sixth in the league in yards per rush (4.6), improving 21 places in the NFL rankings. On defense, the Silver and Black recorded 38 sacks, 13 more than 2012, and tied for second in the NFL with 15 different players getting to the quarterback. Prior to coming to Oakland, Allen was an assistant coach for teams that captured a division title four times—Denver, 2011; New Orleans, 2009, 2006; Atlanta, 2004—and qualified for the postseason in two other seasons—2010 and 2002. Allen was the NFL's second-youngest defensive coordinator when hired by the Denver Broncos in 2011. He coordinated a defense that helped the Broncos win the AFC West and post a wild card victory. Allen was an assistant coach for five seasons with the New Orleans Saints (2006-2010). He tutored a secondary that played a key role in helping the Saints to their first Super Bowl victory (XLIV). His unit accounted for an NFL-high six interception returns for touchdowns en route to team championship. Allen's first NFL coaching position was as a defensive assistant for the Atlanta Falcons (2002-05). Career record: 8-24.

Background: Allen coached at Texas A&M (1996-99) and Tulsa (2000-01). He was a four-year letterman as a safety at Texas A&M, earning both honorable mention and second team All-Southwest Conference honors during his collegiate career. Allen was signed as an undrafted free agent by the Buffalo Bills in 1996.

Personal: Born September 22, 1972, in Atlanta, Ga. Allen and his wife, Alisson, have a son, Garrison, and a daughter, Layla. His father, Grady, played as a linebacker for the Atlanta Falcons from 1968-1972.

ASSISTANT COACHES

Bobby April, special teams coordinator; born April 15, 1953, New Orleans, La. Linebacker Nicholls State 1972-76. College coach: Southern Miss 1978, Tulane 1979, Arizona 1980-86, Southern California 1987-1990, Ohio State 1990. Pro coach: Atlanta Falcons 1991-93, Pittsburgh Steelers 1994-95, New Orleans Saints 1996-99, St. Louis Rams 2001-03, Buffalo Bills 2004-09, Philadelphia Eagles 2010-12, joined Raiders in 2013.

Chris Boniol, asst. special teams; born December 9, 1971, Alexandria, La. Kicker Louisiana Tech 1991-93. Pro kicker Dallas Cowboys 1994-96, Philadelphia Eagles 1997-98, Chicago Bears 1999. Pro coach: Dallas Cowboys 2010-13, joined Raiders

in 2014.

John DeFilippo, quarterbacks; born April 12, 1978, Youngstown, Ohio. Quarterback James Madison 1996-1999. College coach: Fordham 2000, Notre Dame 2001-02, Columbia 2003-04, San Jose State 2010-11. Pro coach: New York Giants 2005-06, Oakland Raiders 2007-08, New York Jets 2009, re-joined Raiders in 2012.

Ted Gilmore, wide receivers; born March 21, 1967, Wichita, Kan. Receiver Butler County (Kan.) Community College 1986-87, Wyoming 1988-89. No pro playing experience. College coach: Wyoming 1994-98, Kansas 1999, Houston 2000, Purdue 2001-02, Colorado 2003-04, Nebraska 2005-10, Southern California 2011. Pro coach: Joined Raiders in 2012.

John Grieco, strength and conditioning; born October 7, 1972, Greensburg, Pa. No pro playing experience. College coach: Florida 1995-2003, East Carolina 2004-05, Nevada-Las Vegas 2006-09, Louisiana-Monroe 2010-11. Pro coach: Joined Raiders in 2012.

Justin Griffith, quality control-offense; born July 21, 1980, Magee, Miss. Running back Mississippi State 1999-2002. Pro running back Atlanta Falcons 2003-06, Oakland Raiders 2007-08, Seattle Seahawks 2009. Pro coach: Seattle Seahawks 2011, joined Raiders in 2012.

Mark Hutson, tight ends; born August 29, 1966, Fort Smith, Ark. Offensive line Oklahoma 1984-87. No pro playing experience. College coach: Oklahoma 1990-92, Murray State 1993-97, Boise State 1997, Arkansas 1998-99, Tulsa 2000-02, Eastern Illinois 2003-2006 (interim head coach 2006), Tulane 2007-2011 (interim head coach 2011). Pro coach: Joined Raiders in 2012.

Greg Olson, offensive coordinator; born March 1, 1961, Richland, Wash. Quarterback Spokane Falls (Wash.) J.C. 1981-82, Central Washington 1983-84. College coach: Washington State 1987-89, Central Washington 1990-93, Idaho 1994-96, Purdue 1997-2000, 2002. Pro coach: San Francisco 49ers 2001, Chicago Bears 2003, Detroit Lions 2004-05, St. Louis Rams 2006-07, Tampa Bay Buccaneers 2008-2011, Jacksonville Jaguars 2012, joined Raiders in 2013.

Marcus Robertson, asst. defensive backs; born October 2, 1969, Pasadena, Calif. Safety Iowa State 1989-91. Pro safety Houston/Tennessee Oilers/Tennessee Titans 1991-2000, Seattle Seahawks 2001-02. Pro coach: Tennessee Titans 2007-2011, Detroit Lions 2012-13, joined Raiders in 2014.

Bob Sanders, linebackers; born December 5, 1953, Jacksonville, N.C. Defensive player Davidson College 1972-75. College coach: Georgia Tech 1978, East Carolina 1980-82, Richmond 1983-84, Duke 1985-88, Duke 1989, Florida 1990-2000. Pro coach: Miami Dolphins 2001-2004, Green Bay Packers 2005-08, Buffalo Bills 2009-

2012, joined Raiders in 2013.

Eric Sanders, quality control-defense; born August 2, 1983, Poughkeepsie, N.Y. No pro playing experience. College coach: UC Davis 2006, 2008-09, Utah State 2007. Pro coach: Joined Raiders in 2010.

Al Saunders, senior offensive assistant; born February 1, 1947, London, England. Defensive back San Jose State 1966-68. No pro playing experience. College coach: Southern California 1970-71, Missouri 1972, Utah State 1973-75, California 1976-1981, Tennessee 1982. Pro coach: San Diego Chargers 1983-88 (head coach 1986-88), Kansas City Chiefs 1989-1998, St. Louis Rams 1999-2000, Kansas City Chiefs 2001-05, Washington Redskins 2006-07, St. Louis Rams 2008, Baltimore Ravens, 2009-2010, joined Raiders in 2011.

Kelly Skipper, running backs; born July 25, 1967, Brawley, Calif. Running back Fresno State 1985-88. No pro playing experience. College coach: Fresno State 1989-1997, UCLA 1998-2002, Washington State 2003-06. Pro coach: Joined Raiders in 2007.

Tony Sparano, asst. head coach/offensive line; born Oct. 7, 1961, West Haven, Conn. Center New Haven 1984-87. College coach: Boston University 1988-1993, New Haven 1994-98. Pro coach: Cleveland Browns 1999-2000, Washington Redskins 2001, Jacksonville Jaguars 2002, Dallas Cowboys 2003-07, Miami Dolphins 2008-2011 (head coach), New York Jets 2012, joined Raiders in 2013.

Vernon Stephens, asst. strength and conditioning; born November 30, 1974, Jacksonville, Fla. No pro playing experience. College coach: North Florida 1999-2003, Colorado 2003-07. Pro coach: San Diego Chargers 2007-2013, joined Raiders in 2014.

Jason Tarver, defensive coordinator; born August 28, 1974, Palo Alto, Calif. No pro playing experience. College coach: UCLA 1998-2000, Stanford 2011. Pro coach: San Francisco 49ers 2001-2010, joined Raiders in 2012.

Terrell Williams, defensive line; born June 19, 1974, Los Angeles, Calif. Nose guard East Carolina 1995-96. No pro playing experience. College coach: Fort Scott (Kan.) C.C. 1998, North Carolina A&T 1999-2001, Youngstown State 2002-2003, Akron 2004-2005, Purdue 2006-2009, Texas A&M 2010-11. Pro coach: Joined Raiders in 2012.

Joe Woods, defensive backs, born June 25, 1970, North Vandergrift, Pa. Defensive back Illinois State 1988-1991. No pro playing experience. College coach: Muskingum 1992, Eastern Michigan 1993, Northwestern State 1994, Grand Valley State 1994-96, Kent State 1997, Hofstra 1998-2000, Western Michigan 2001. Pro coach: Tampa Bay Buccaneers 2004-05, Minnesota Vikings 2006-2013, joined Raiders in 2012.

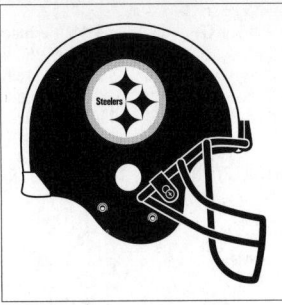

American Football Conference
North Division
Team Colors: Black and Gold
3400 South Water Street
Pittsburgh, Pennsylvania 15203
Telephone: (412) 432-7800

2014 SCHEDULE
PRESEASON
Aug. 9   at New York Giants 7:30
Aug. 16   **Buffalo**..............................7:30
Aug. 21   at Philadelphia 7:30
Aug. 28   **Carolina**............................7:30

REGULAR SEASON
Sep. 7   **Cleveland** 1:00
Sep. 11   at Baltimore (Thu) 8:25
Sep. 21   at Carolina 8:30
Sep. 28   **Tampa Bay** 1:00
Oct. 5   at Jacksonville 1:00
Oct. 12   at Cleveland 1:00
Oct. 20   **Houston** (Mon)..................8:30
Oct. 26   **Indianapolis** 4:25
Nov. 2   **Baltimore** *8:30
Nov. 9   at New York Jets 1:00
Nov. 17   at Tennessee (Mon)............8:30
Nov. 23   BYE
Nov. 30   **New Orleans** 1:00
Dec. 7   at Cincinnati 1:00
Dec. 14   at Atlanta 1:00
Dec. 21   **Kansas City** 1:00
Dec. 28   **Cincinnati** 1:00
*All times ET; Sunday night games in
    Weeks 5-16 subject to change
Stadium: Heinz Field (opened in 2001)
    •**Capacity:** 65,500
    100 Art Rooney Avenue
    Pittsburgh, Pennsylvania 15212
Playing Surface: Natural Grass
Training Camp: St. Vincent College
                Latrobe, PA 15650

HEINZ FIELD

CLUB OFFICIALS
Chairman: Daniel M. Rooney
President: Arthur J. Rooney II
Vice President: Arthur J. Rooney Jr.
Administration Advisor: Charles H. Noll
Director of Planning & Development:
    Mark Hart
Director of Finance: Bob Tyler
Director of Football and Business
    Administration: Omar Khan
General Manager: Kevin Colbert
College Scouting Coordinator:
    Phil Kreidler
Pro Scouting Coordinator: Brandon Hunt
Head Athletic Trainer: John Norwig
Director of Media and Marketing:
    Tony Quatrini
Communications Coordinator:
    Burt Lauten
Director of Stadium Management:
    Jim Sacco
Video/Facilities Coordinator:
    Bob McCartney
HR Manager: Katrina Smith
Ticket Manager: Ben Lentz

COACHING HISTORY
Pittsburgh Pirates 1933-39
(607-554-21)
Records include postseason games
1933   Forrest (Jap) Douds 3-6-2
1934   Luby DiMelio 2-10-0
1935-36   Joe Bach.......................10-14-0
1937-39   Johnny (Blood) McNally* ..6-19-0
1939-1940 Walt Kiesling 3-13-3
1941   Bert Bell** 0-2-0
           Aldo (Buff) Donelli*** 0-5-0
1941-44   Walt Kiesling**** 13-20-2
1945   Jim Leonard 2-8-0
1946-47   Jock Sutherland............13-10-1
1948-1951 Johnny Michelosen 20-26-2
1952-53   Joe Bach.......................11-13-0
1954-56   Walt Kiesling 14-22-0
1957-1964 Raymond (Buddy) Parker .51-47-6
1965   Mike Nixon 2-12-0
1966-68   Bill Austin......................11-28-3
1969-1991 Chuck Noll 209-156-1
1992-2006 Bill Cowher 161-99-1
2007-2013 Mike Tomlin..................76-44-0
    *Released after three games in 1939
    **Resigned after two games in 1941
    ***Released after five games in 1941
    ****Co-coach with Earle (Greasy) Neale in
        Philadelphia-Pittsburgh merger in 1943 and
        with Phil Handler in Chicago Cardinals-
        Pittsburgh merger in 1944

PAID ATTENDANCE
Home 510,394   Away 556,492
Total 1,066,886
Single-game home record,
    66,662 (1/23/11)
Single-season home record,
    517,599 (2009)

2014 DRAFT CHOICES
Round	Name	Pos.	College
1	Ryan Shazier	LB	Ohio St.
2	Stephon Tuitt	DE	Notre Dame
3	Dri Archer	RB/WR	Kent St.
4	Martavis Bryant	WR	Clemson
5	Shaquille Richardson	CB	Arizona
	Wesley Johnson	OL	Vanderbilt
6	Jordan Zumwalt	LB	UCLA
	Daniel McCullers	DL	Tennessee
7	Rob Blanchflower	TE	Massachusetts

2013 TEAM RECORD
PRESEASON (0-4)

Date	Result		Opponent
08/10	L	13-18	New York Giants
08/19	L	13-24	at Washington
08/24	L	20-26	Kansas City (OT)
08/29	L	10-25	at Carolina

REGULAR SEASON (8-8)

Date	Result		Opponent
09/08	L	9-16	Tennessee
09/16	L	10-20	at Cincinnati
09/22	L	23-40	Chicago
09/29	L	27-34	at Minnesota
10/13	W	19-6	at New York Jets
10/20	W	19-16	Baltimore
10/27	L	18-21	at Oakland
11/03	L	31-55	at New England
11/10	W	23-10	Buffalo
11/17	W	37-27	Detroit
11/24	W	27-11	at Cleveland
11/28	L	20-22	at Baltimore
12/08	L	28-34	Miami
12/15	W	30-20	Cincinnati
12/22	W	38-31	at Green Bay
12/29	W	20-7	Cleveland

(OT) Overtime

SCORE BY PERIODS

Steelers	78	87	106	108	0 —	379
Opponents	84	108	57	121	0 —	370

2013 TEAM STATISTICS

	Steelers	Opp.
Total First Downs	312	303
Rushing	81	106
Passing	207	174
Penalty	24	23
3rd Down: Made/Att	82/216	91/230
3rd Down Pct.	38.0	39.6
4th Down: Made/Att	9/15	9/20
4th Down Pct.	60.0	45.0
Possession Avg.	30:53	29:07
Total Net Yards	5400	5395
Avg. Per Game	337.5	337.2
Total Plays	1023	1036
Avg. Per Play	5.3	5.2
Net Yards Rushing	1383	1849
Avg. Per Game	86.4	115.6
Total Rushes	394	433
Net Yards Passing	4017	3546
Avg. Per Game	251.1	221.6
Sacked/Yards Lost	43/289	34/205
Gross Yards	4306	3751
Att./Completions	586/377	569/329
Completion Pct.	64.3	57.8
Had Intercepted	14	10
Punts/Average	76/41.1	79/43.0
Net Punting Avg.	76/35.7	79/35.8
Penalties/Yards	80/677	92/798
Fumbles/Ball Lost	16/10	21/10
Touchdowns	41	41
Rushing	9	18
Passing	28	21
Returns	4	2

2013 INDIVIDUAL STATISTICS

PASSING

	Att.	Comp.	Yds.	Pct.	TD	Int.	Tkld.	Rate
Roethlisberger	584	375	4261	64.2	28	14	42/282	92.0
A. Brown	1	1	15	100.0	0	0	1/7	118.8
McBriar	1	1	30	100.0	0	0	0/0	118.8
Steelers	586	377	4306	64.3	28	14	43/289	92.3
Opponents	569	329	3751	57.8	21	10	34/198	82.7

SCORING

	TD R	TD P	TD Rt	PAT	FG	Saf	PTS
Suisham	0	0	0	39/39	30/32	0	129
Cotchery	0	10	0	0/0	0/0	0	60
A. Brown	0	8	1	0/0	0/0	0	54
Bell	8	0	0	0/0	0/0	0	48
Sanders	0	6	0	0/0	0/0	0	38
C. Allen	0	0	1	0/0	0/0	0	6
Gay	0	0	1	0/0	0/0	0	6
W. Johnson	0	1	0	0/0	0/0	0	6
Miller	0	1	0	0/0	0/0	0	6
Moye	0	1	0	0/0	0/0	0	6
Polamalu	0	0	1	0/0	0/0	0	6
Roethlisberger	1	0	0	0/0	0/0	0	6
Spaeth	0	1	0	0/0	0/0	0	6
Steelers	9	28	4	39/39	30/32	1	379
Opponents	18	21	2	38/38	28/31	0	370

2-Pt Conversions: Sanders.
Steelers 1-2, Opponents 1-2.

RUSHING

	No.	Yds	Avg	LG	TD
Bell	244	860	3.5	43	8
Dwyer	49	197	4.0	30	0
F. Jones	48	184	3.8	14	0
Roethlisberger	27	99	3.7	19	1
Sanders	1	25	25.0	25	0
Stephens-Howling	6	19	3.2	5	0
Redman	10	12	1.2	8	0
A. Brown	7	4	0.6	10	0
Cotchery	1	-5	-5.0	-5	0
Suisham	1	-12	-12.0	-12	0
Steelers	394	1383	3.5	43	9
Opponents	433	1849	4.3	93t	18

RECEIVING

	No.	Yds	Avg	LG	TD
A. Brown	110	1499	13.6	56	8
Sanders	67	740	11.0	55t	6
Miller	58	593	10.2	31	1
Cotchery	46	602	13.1	36	10
Bell	45	399	8.9	43	0
F. Jones	9	63	7.0	15	0
Dwyer	8	64	8.0	23	0
W. Johnson	8	41	5.1	9	1
Paulson	6	102	17.0	34	0
Wheaton	6	64	10.7	21	0
D. Johnson	4	70	17.5	32	0
Redman	4	14	3.5	7	0
Moye	2	20	10.0	19	1
Stephens-Howling	2	11	5.5	7	0
Spaeth	1	11	11.0	11t	1
Palmer	1	8	8.0	8	0
Roethlisberger	0	5	—	5	0
Steelers	377	4306	11.4	67	28
Opponents	329	3751	11.4	81t	21

INTERCEPTIONS

	No.	Yds	Avg	LG	TD
Clark	2	50	25.0	37	0
C. Allen	2	43	21.5	40t	1
Polamalu	2	36	18.0	19t	1
Timmons	2	26	13.0	23	0
W. Allen	1	27	27.0	27	0
Gay	1	21	21.0	21t	1
Steelers	10	203	20.3	40t	3
Opponents	14	170	12.1	57	1

PUNTING

	No.	Yds.	Avg.	In 20	LG
McBriar	40	1652	41.3	13	70
Mesko	34	1445	42.5	3	65
Roethlisberger	1	28	28.0	1	28
Steelers	76	3125	41.1	17	70
Opponents	79	3397	43.0	22	61

PUNT RETURNS

	Ret	FC	Yds	Avg	LG	TD
A. Brown	32	23	409	12.8	67t	1
Steelers	32	23	409	12.8	67t	1
Opponents	35	16	313	8.9	43	0

KICKOFF RETURNS

	No.	Yds	Avg	LG	TD
F. Jones	23	510	22.2	42	0
Sanders	10	268	26.8	46	0
Dwyer	4	90	22.5	27	0
Wheaton	2	37	18.5	25	0
Stephens-Howling	1	25	25.0	25	0
A. Brown	1	16	16.0	16	0
Heyward	1	11	11.0	11	0
Palmer	1	5	5.0	5	0
Steelers	43	962	22.4	46	0
Opponents	55	1225	22.3	73	0

FIELD GOALS

	1-19	20-29	30-39	40-49	50+
Suisham	0/0	9/9	13/15	8/8	0/0
Steelers	0/0	9/9	13/15	8/8	0/0
Opponents	1/1	8/8	10/10	8/10	1/2

SACKS

	No.
Worilds	8.0
Heyward	5.0
Woodley	5.0
Keisel	4.0
Hood	3.0
Timmons	3.0
Polamalu	2.0
Woods	2.0
Gay	1.0
J. Jones	1.0
Steelers	34.0
Opponents	43.0

RECORD HOLDERS
INDIVIDUAL RECORDS—CAREER

Category	Name	Performance
Rushing (Yds.)	Franco Harris, 1972-1983	11,950
Passing (Yds.)	Ben Roethlisberger, 2004-2013	34,105
Passing (TDs)	Ben Roethlisberger, 2004-2013	219
Receiving (No.)	Hines Ward, 1998-2011	1,000
Receiving (Yds.)	Hines Ward, 1998-2011	12,083
Interceptions	Mel Blount, 1970-1983	57
Punting (Avg.)	Bobby Joe Green, 1960-61	45.7
Punt Return (Avg.)	Bobby Gage, 1949-1950	14.9
Kickoff Return (Avg.)	Lynn Chandnois, 1950-56	29.6
Field Goals	Gary Anderson, 1982-1994	309
Touchdowns (Tot.)	Franco Harris, 1972-1983	100
Points	Gary Anderson, 1982-1994	1,343
*Sacks	Jason Gildon, 1994-2003	77.0

INDIVIDUAL RECORDS—SINGLE SEASON

Category	Name	Performance
Rushing (Yds.)	Barry Foster, 1992	1,690
Passing (Yds.)	Ben Roethlisberger, 2009	4,328
Passing (TDs)	Ben Roethlisberger, 2007	32
Receiving (No.)	Hines Ward, 2002	112
Receiving (Yds.)	Antonio Brown, 2013	1,499
Interceptions	Mel Blount, 1975	11
Punting (Avg.)	Bobby Joe Green, 1961	47.0
Punt Return (Avg.)	Bobby Gage, 1949	16.0
Kickoff Return (Avg.)	Lynn Chandnois, 1952	35.2
Field Goals	Norm Johnson, 1995	34
Touchdowns (Tot.)	Willie Parker, 2006	16
Points	Norm Johnson, 1995	141
*Sacks	James Harrison, 2008	16.0

INDIVIDUAL RECORDS—SINGLE GAME

Category	Name	Performance
Rushing (Yds.)	Willie Parker, 12-7-06	223
Passing (Yds.)	Ben Roethlisberger, 12-20-09	503
Passing (TDs)	Terry Bradshaw, 11-15-81	5
	Mark Malone, 9-8-85	5
	Ben Roethlisberger, 11-5-07, 10-9-11	5
Receiving (No.)	Courtney Hawkins, 11-1-98	14
Receiving (Yds.)	Plaxico Burress, 11-10-02	253
Interceptions	Jack Butler, 12-13-53	**4
Field Goals	Gary Anderson, 10-23-88	6
	Jeff Reed, 12-1-02	6
Touchdowns (Tot.)	Ray Mathews, 10-17-54	4
	Roy Jefferson, 11-3-68	4
Points	Ray Mathews, 10-17-54	24
	Roy Jefferson, 11-3-68	24
*Sacks	Chad Brown, 10-13-96	4.5

*Sacks became an official statistic in 1982.
**NFL Record

2014 VETERAN ROSTER

No.	Name	Pos.	Ht.	Wt.	Birthdate	NFL Exp.	College	Hometown	How Acq.	'13 Games/ Starts
76	Adams, Mike	T	6-7	323	3/10/90	3	Ohio State	Farrell, Pa.	D2-'12	15/10
28	Allen, Cortez	CB	6-1	196	10/29/88	4	The Citadel	Ocala, Fla.	D4-'11	14/8
20	Allen, Will	S	6-1	200	6/17/82	11	Ohio State	Dayton, Ohio	FA-'13	17/2*
68	Beachum, Kelvin	G	6-3	303	6/8/89	3	Southern Methodist	Mexia, Texas	D7d-'12	15/12
26	Bell, Le'Veon	RB	6-1	244	2/18/92	2	Michigan State	Reynoldsburg, Ohio	D2-'13	13/13
41	Blake, Antwon	CB	5-9	198	8/8/90	3	Texas-El Paso	Houston, Texas	W(Jax)-'13	14/0
27	Blount, LeGarrette	RB	6-0	250	12/5/86	5	Oregon	Madison, Fla.	UFA(NE)-'14	16/7*
84	Brown, Antonio	WR	5-10	186	7/10/88	5	Central Michigan	Miami, Fla.	D6b-'10	16/14
#Burress, Plaxico		WR	6-5	232	8/12/77	13	Michigan State	Norfolk, Va.	FA-'12	0*
54	Carter, Chris	LB	6-1	248	4/6/89	4	Fresno State	Fontana, Calif.	D5-'11	13/1
66	DeCastro, David	G	6-5	316	1/11/90	3	Stanford	Bellevue, Wash.	D1-'12	15/15
64	Embernate, Nik	G	6-4	304	11/3/90	2	San Diego State	Yucaipa, Calif	FA-'13	0*
92	Fangupo, Hebron	DT	6-0	324	7/19/85	2	Brigham Young	Orange County, Calif.	W(Sea)-'12	4/0
73	Foster, Ramon	G	6-6	325	1/7/86	6	Tennessee	Henning, Tenn.	FA-'09	15/15
57	Garvin, Terence	LB	6-3	221	1/1/91	2	West Virginia	Baltimore, Md.	FA-'13	15/1
22	Gay, William	CB	5-10	190	1/1/85	8	Louisville	Tallahassee, Fla.	FA-'13	16/11
77	Gilbert, Marcus	T	6-6	330	2/15/88	4	Florida	Fort Lauderdale, Fla.	D2-'11	16/16
21	Golden, Robert	S	5-11	202	9/13/90	3	Arizona	Fresno, Calif.	FA-'12	16/0
5	Gradkowski, Bruce	QB	6-1	220	1/27/83	9	Toledo	Pittsburgh, Pa.	UFA(Cin)-'13	0*
39	Green, Isaiah	CB	5-10	180	8/10/89	2	Fresno State	Los Angeles, Calif.	FA-'12	3/0
97	Heyward, Cameron	DE	6-5	288	5/6/89	4	Ohio State	Pittsburgh, Pa.	D1-'11	16/13
85	Heyward-Bey, Darrius	WR	6-2	219	2/26/87	6	Maryland	Silver Spring, Md.	UFA(Ind)-'14	16/11*
46	Johnson, Will	FB	6-2	238	11/14/89	3	West Virginia	Dayton, Ohio	FA-'12	15/5
#Jones, Felix		RB	5-10	215	5/8/87	7	Arkansas	Tulsa, Okla.	T(Phil)-'13	16/2
95	Jones, Jarvis	LB	6-2	245	10/13/89	2	Georgia	Richland, Ga.	D1-'13	14/8
3	Jones, Landry	QB	6-3	221	4/4/89	2	Oklahoma	Artesia, N.M.	D4b-'13	0*
#Keisel, Brett		DE	6-5	285	9/19/78	13	Brigham Young	Greybull, Wyo.	D7b-'02	12/12
#McBriar, Mat		P	6-0	227	7/8/79	11	Hawaii	Melbourne, Victoria	FA-'13	9/0
25	McCain, Brice	CB	5-9	187	12/10/86	6	Utah	Terrell, Texas	FA-'14	16/4*
90	McLendon, Steve	NT	6-4	320	1/3/86	5	Troy	Ozark, Ala.	FA-'09	14/10
83	Miller, Heath	TE	6-5	256	10/22/82	10	Virginia	Swords Creek, Va.	D1-'05	14/14
23	Mitchell, Mike	S	6-0	210	6/10/87	6	Ohio	Fort Thomas, Ky.	UFA(Car)-'14	15/14*
55	Moats, Arthur	LB	6-2	250	3/14/88	5	James Madison	Portsmouth, Va.	UFA(Buff)-'14	16/12*
16	Moore, Lance	WR	5-9	190	8/31/83	9	Toledo	Columbus, Ohio	FA-'14	13/5*
14	Moye, Derek	WR	6-5	210	8/12/88	2	Penn State	Rochester, Pa.	FA-'12	7/0
82	Palmer, Michael	TE	6-5	252	1/18/88	5	Clemson	Stone Mountain, Ga.	W(Sea)-'13	16/0
81	Paulson, David	TE	6-4	246	2/22/89	3	Oregon	Auburn, Wash.	D7b-'12	16/4
4	Podlesh, Adam	P	5-11	200	8/11/83	8	Maryland	Pittsford, N.Y.	FA-'14	16/0*
43	Polamalu, Troy	S	5-10	207	4/19/81	12	Southern California	Santa Ana, Calif.	D1-'03	16/16
38	Poole, Tauren	RB	5-10	210	10/19/89	2	Tennessee	Toccoa, Ga.	FA-'14	0*
53	Pouncey, Maurkice	C	6-4	304	7/24/89	5	Florida	Lakeland, Fla.	D1-'10	1/1
7	Roethlisberger, Ben	QB	6-5	241	3/2/82	11	Miami (Ohio)	Cory Rawson, Ohio	D1-'04	16/16
71	Snow, David	C/G	6-4	303	11/9/89	2	Texas	Longview, Texas	FA-'13	0*
49	So'oto, Vic	LB	6-3	263	8/6/87	3	Brigham Young	Oceanside, Calif.	FA-'14	1/0*
87	Spaeth, Matt	TE	6-7	260	11/24/83	8	Minnesota	St. Michael, Minn.	FA-'13	4/2
51	Spence, Sean	LB	5-11	231	6/7/90	3	Miami	Miami, Fla.	D3-'12	0*
#Stephens-Howling, LaRod		RB	5-7	185	4/26/87	6	Pittsburgh	Johnstown, Pa.	UFA(Ariz)-'13	1/0
6	Suisham, Shaun	K	6-0	200	12/29/81	10	Bowling Green	Wallaceburg, Ontario	FA-'10	16/0
#Sylvester, Stevenson		LB	6-2	231	7/18/88	5	Utah	Las Vegas, Nev.	FA-'13	9/1
24	Taylor, Ike	CB	6-2	195	5/5/80	12	Louisiana-Lafayette	Gretna, La.	D4-'03	16/16
96	Thomas, Cam	DT	6-4	330	12/12/86	5	North Carolina	Cheraw, S.C.	UFA(SD)-'14	16/10*
29	Thomas, Shamarko	S	5-9	217	2/23/91	2	Syracuse	Virginia Beach, Va.	D4a-'13	14/2
94	Timmons, Lawrence	LB	6-1	234	5/14/86	8	Florida State	Florence, S.C.	D1-'07	16/16
#Velasco, Fernando		C/G	6-4	312	2/22/85	5	Georgia	Wrens, Ga.	FA-'13	11/11
35	Ventrone, Ross	S	5-8	195	9/27/86	2	Villanova	Bridgeville, Pa.	FA-'13	0*
72	Wallace, Cody	C/G	6-4	300	11/26/84	5	Texas A&M	Cuero, Texas	FA-'13	9/4
60	Warren, Greg	LS	6-3	252	10/18/81	10	North Carolina	Goldsboro, N.C.	FA-'05	16/0
#Westerman, Jamaal		LB	6-3	255	2/21/85	6	Rutgers	Brooklyn, N.Y.	FA-'13	13/0*
11	Wheaton, Markus	WR	5-11	182	2/7/91	2	Oregon State	Chandler, Ariz.	D3-'13	12/1
78	Whimper, Guy	T	6-5	315	5/21/83	9	East Carolina	Honolulu, Hawaii	FA-'13	11/2
91	Williams, Nick	DE	6-4	309	2/21/90	2	Samford	Birmingham, Ala.	D7b-'13	0*
98	Williams, Vince	LB	6-1	250	12/27/89	2	Florida State	Davenport, Fla.	D6b-'13	15/11
48	Wilson, Kion	LB	6-0	230	10/24/86	4	South Florida	Jacksonville, Fla.	FA-'13	7/2
93	Worilds, Jason	LB	6-2	262	3/3/88	5	Virginia Tech	Carteret, N.J.	D2-'10	15/11

* W. Allen played five games with Dallas and 12 games with Pittsburgh in '13; Blount played 16 games with New England; Burress missed '13 season because of injury; Embernate missed '13 season because of injury; Gradkowski did not play in 16 games; Heyward-Bey played 16 games with Indianapolis; L. Jones inactive 16 games; McCain played 16 games with Houston; Mitchell played 15 games with Carolina; Moats played 16 games with Buffalo; Moore played 13 games with New Orleans; Podlesh played 16 games with Chicago; Poole missed '12 season because of injury with Carolina; Snow last active with Buffalo in '12; So'oto played one game with Arizona; Spence missed '13 sesaon because of injury; C. Thomas played 16 games with San Diego; Ventrone last active with New England in '11; Westerman played 12 games with Buffalo and one game with Pittsburgh; N. Williams missed '13 season because of injury.

Players lost through free agency (8): S Ryan Clark (Wash; 16 games in '13), WR Jerricho Cotchery (Car; 16), RB Jonathan Dwyer (Ariz; 15), DE Ziggy Hood (Jax; 16), TE/FB David Johnson (SD; 5), C Eric Olsen (Tenn; 0), WR Emmanuel Sanders (Den; 16), DL Al Woods (Tenn; 16).

Also played with Steelers in '13—DE Brian Arnfelt (2 games), CB Curtis Brown (7), S DaMon Cromartie-Smith (4), LB Larry Foote (1), P Zoltan Mesko (7), RB Isaac Redman (3), CB DeMarcus Van Dyke (2), LB LaMarr Woodley (11).

FIRST-YEAR ROSTER

Name	Pos.	Ht.	Wt.	Birthdate	College	Hometown	How Acq.
Alexander, Alvester (1)	RB	5-11	213	10/17/90	Wyoming	Houston, Texas	FA-'13
Archer, Dri	RB/WR	5-8	173	8/9/91	Kent State	Laurel, Fla.	D3
Arnfelt, Brian (1)	DE	6-4	298	10/11/89	Northwestern	Lake Elmo, Minn.	FA-'13
Blanchflower, Rob	TE	6-4	256	6/8/90	Massachusetts	Leominster, Mass.	D7
Brown, Justin (1)	WR	6-3	209	3/10/91	Oklahoma	Wilmington, Del.	D6a-'13
Browning, Bryant (1)	G	6-4	325	6/26/88	Ohio State	Cleveland, Ohio	FA-'13
Bryant, Martavis	WR	6-4	211	12/20/91	Clemson	Calhoun Falls, S.C.	D4
Coale, Danny (1)	WR	6-0	187	6/27/88	Virginia Tech	Lexington, Va.	FA
Collins, Jasper (1)	WR	5-11	190	11/28/91	Mount Union	Geneva, N.Y.	FA
Dangerfield, Jordan (1)	S	5-11	200	12/25/90	Towson	Elmont, N.Y.	FA
Davis, Bryce (1)	LS	6-3	245	6/6/89	Central Oklahoma	Duncan, Okla.	FA
Elkins, Chris	OL	6-4	300	6/24/92	Youngstown State	Beaver Falls, Pa.	FA
Hemer, Ethan	DE	6-6	285	3/30/91	Wisconsin	Medford, Wisc.	FA
Hubbard, Chris (1)	G	6-4	286	4/23/91	Alabama-Birmingham	Columbus, Ga.	FA-'13
Ike, Kaycee	T	6-5	293	7/23/91	Alabama-Birmingham	Norcross, Ga.	FA
Johnson, Wesley	OL	6-5	297	1/9/91	Vanderbilt	Nashville, Tenn.	D5b
Jones, Howard	LB	6-4	238	2/10/90	Shepherd	Woodbridge, Va.	FA
Kay, Brendon	QB	6-4	228	12/29/89	Cincinnati	Marine City, Mich.	FA
Lapuaho, Al (1)	DT	6-2	301	8/4/91	Utah State	West Valley City, Utah	FA
Mauro, Josh	DE	6-6	282	2/17/91	Stanford	St. Albans, England	FA
Maysonet, Miguel (1)	RB	5-10	210	12/13/89	Stony Brook	Bayamon, Puerto Rico	FA
McCullers, Daniel	DL	6-7	352	8/11/92	Tennessee	Raleigh, N.C.	D6b
Molls, Dan (1)	LB	6-0	238	2/12/91	Toledo	North Royalton, Ohio	FA
Moore, Kashif (1)	WR	5-9	180	11/21/88	Connecticut	Burlington, N.J.	FA-'13
Philon, Roy	DT	6-3	291	3/26/91	Louisville	Lexington, Ky.	FA
Richardson, Shaquille	CB	6-0	194	3/21/92	Arizona	Carson, Calif.	D5a
Sampson, Lanear (1)	WR	5-11	205	7/17/90	Baylor	Dallas, Texas	FA
Shazier, Ryan	LB	6-1	237	9/6/92	Ohio State	Fort Lauderdale, Fla	D1
Simmons, Will	G	6-5	342	1/31/91	East Carolina	Ahoskie, N.C.	FA
Smith, Devin (1)	CB	5-11	186	8/8/90	Wisconsin	Coppell, Texas	FA
Tuitt, Stephon	DE	6-5	303	5/23/93	Notre Dame	Miami, Fla.	D2
Waters, Eric	TE	6-5	245	7/29/91	Missouri	Mansfield, Texas	FA
Wing, Brad (1)	P	6-3	205	1/27/91	Louisiana State	Melbourne, Australia	FA
Zumwalt, Jordan	LB	6-4	235	10/13/91	UCLA	LaHabra, Calif.	D6a

The term NFL Rookie is defined as a player who is in his first season of professional football and has not been on the roster of another professional football team for any regular-season or postseason games. A Rookie is designated by an "R" on NFL rosters. Players who have been active in another professional football league or players who have NFL experience, including either preseason training camp or being on an Active List or Inactive List, or on Reserve/Injured or Reserve/Physically Unable to Perform for fewer than six regular-season games, are termed NFL First-Year Players. An NFL First-Year Player is designated by a "1" on NFL rosters. Thereafter, a player is credited with an additional year of experience for each season in which he accumulates six games on the Active List or Inactive List, or on Reserve/Injured or Reserve/Physically Unable to Perform.

Log on to www.steelers.com for an up-to-date roster.

COACHING STAFF

Head Coach,
Mike Tomlin

Pro Career: Named the sixteenth head coach in Steelers history when he replaced Bill Cowher on January 22, 2007. Became the youngest coach (36 years, 323 days) in NFL history to win a Super Bowl when the Steelers defeated the Arizona Cardinals, 27-23, in Super Bowl XLIII on February 1, 2009. Tomlin reached the playoffs four times in his first five seasons and he is the only coach in Steelers' history to win division titles each of his first two seasons. In 2010 Tomlin's club won its third division title in in a four-year span. In 2008, Tomlin directed the Steelers to a 12-4 record, winning his second-consecutive AFC North title. That season culminated with a Super Bowl triumph, making Tomlin one of only seven coaches in league history to win a Super Bowl within his first two seasons as an NFL head coach. In his first season, Tomlin guided the Steelers to a 10-6 record and their first AFC North title since 2004. Tomlin was the Minnesota Vikings defensive coordinator in 2006 after spending the previous five seasons (2001-05) as defensive backs coach for the Tampa Bay Buccaneers. Tomlin coached one of the top defensive back-fields in the NFL for the Buccaneers, culminating with its performance in Super Bowl XXXVII. The secondary recorded four interceptions, returning two for touchdowns to help Tampa Bay capture the franchise's first Super Bowl title. Tomlin served two seasons as the defensive backs coach at the University of Cincinnati (1999-2000) before going to Tampa Bay. Prior to joining the Cincinnati staff, Tomlin had a short stint on the coaching staff at Tennessee-Martin and then spent two seasons at Arkansas State. He spent the 1996 season as a graduate assistant at Memphis. Tomlin began his coaching career in 1995 as wide receivers coach at Virginia Military Institute. Career record: 76-44.

Background: Was a three-year starter at wide receiver at William & Mary (1990-94) and finished his career with 101 receptions for 2,046 yards and a school-record 20 touchdown receptions. A first-team All-Yankee Conference selection in 1994, he established a school record with a 20.2 yards per catch average. Tomlin was a teammate of current Viking Pro Bowl safety Darren Sharper at William and Mary. Graduated in 1994 with a degree in sociology.

Personal: Born in Hampton, Va., on March 15, 1972. He and his wife, Kiya, have two sons, Dino and Mason, and a daughter Harlyn Quinn.

ASSISTANT COACHES

Keith Butler, linebackers; born May 16, 1956, Anniston, Ala. Linebacker Memphis 1974-77. Pro linebacker Seattle Seahawks 1978-1987. College coach: Memphis 1990-97, Arkansas State 1998. Pro coach: Cleveland Browns 1999-2002, joined Steelers in 2003.

James Daniel, tight ends; born January 17, 1953, Wetumpka, Ala. Guard Alabama State 1970-73. No pro playing experience. College coach: Auburn 1981-1992. Pro coach: New York Giants 1993-96, Atlanta Falcons 1997-2003, joined Steelers in 2004.

Randy Fichtner, quarterbacks; born November 7, 1963, Cleveland, Ohio. Defensive back Purdue 1982-85. No pro playing experience. College coach: Michigan 1986-87, Southern California 1988, Nevada-Las Vegas 1989, Memphis 1990-93, Purdue 1994-96, Arkansas State 1997-2000, Memphis 2001-06. Pro coach: Joined Steelers in 2007.

Todd Haley, offensive coordinator; February 28, 1967, Atlanta, Ga. No college or pro playing experience. Pro coach: New York Jets 1997-2000, Chicago Bears 2001-03, Dallas Cowboys 2004-06, Arizona Cardinals 2007-08, Kansas City Chiefs 2009-2011, joined Steelers in 2012.

Carnell Lake, defensive backs; born July 15, 1967, Salt Lake City, Utah. Outside linebacker UCLA 1985-1988. Pro defensive back Pittsburgh Steelers 1989-1998, Jacksonville Jaguars 1999-2000, Baltimore Ravens 2001. College coach: UCLA 2009. Pro coach: Joined Steelers in 2011.

Dick LeBeau, defensive coordinator; born September 9, 1937, London, Ohio. Defensive back Ohio State 1955-58. Pro cornerback Detroit Lions 1959-1972. Pro coach: Philadelphia Eagles 1973-75, Green Bay Packers 1976-79, Cincinnati Bengals 1980-1991, 1997-2002 (head coach 2000-02), Pittsburgh Steelers 1992-96, Buffalo Bills 2003, re-joined Steelers in 2004.

Richard Mann, wide receivers; born April 20, 1947, Aliquippa, Pa. Tight end Arizona State 1966-68. No pro playing experience. College coach: Arizona State 1974-79, Louisville 1980-81. Pro coach: Baltimore/Indianapolis Colts 1982-84, Cleveland Browns 1985-1993, New York Jets 1994-1996, Baltimore Ravens 1997-98, Kansas City Chiefs 1999-2000, Washington Redskins 2001, Tampa Bay Buccaneers 2002-09, joined Steelers in 2013.

John Mitchell, asst. head coach/defensive line; born October 14, 1951, Mobile, Ala. Defensive end Eastern Arizona J.C. 1969-1970, Alabama 1971-72. No pro playing experience. College coach: Alabama 1973-76, Arkansas 1977-1982, Temple 1986, Louisiana State 1987-1990. Pro coach: Birmingham Stallions (USFL) 1983-85, Cleveland Browns 1991-93, joined Steelers in 1994.

Mike Munchak, offensive line; born March 5, 1960, Scranton, Pa. Guard Penn State 1979-1981. Pro guard Houston Oilers 1982-1993. Inducted into Pro Football Hall of Fame 2001. Pro coach: Houston Oilers/Tennessee Oilers/Tennessee Titans 1994-2013 (head coach 2011-13), joined Steelers in 2014.

James Saxon, running backs; born March 23, 1966, Beaufort, S.C. Running back American River (Calif.) C.C. 1984-85, San Jose State 1986-87. Pro running back Kansas City Chiefs 1988-1991, Miami Dolphins 1992-94, Philadelphia Eagles 1995. College coach: Rutgers 1997-98, Menlo 1999. Pro coach: Buffalo Bills 2000, Kansas City Chiefs 2001-07, Miami Dolphins 2008-2010, Minnesota Vikings 2011-13, joined Steelers in 2014.

Danny Smith, special teams; born September 7, 1953, Pittsburgh, Pa. Defensive back Edinboro State 1971-75. No pro playing experience. College coach: Edinboro State 1976, Clemson 1979, William & Mary 1980-83, The Citadel 1984-86, Georgia Tech 1987-1994. Pro coach: Philadelphia Eagles 1995-98, Detroit Lions 1999-2000, Buffalo Bills 2001-03, Washington Redskins 2004-2012, joined Steelers in 2013.

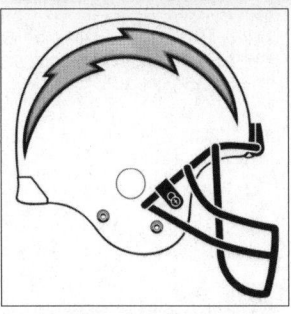

American Football Conference
West Division
Team Colors: Navy Blue, Powder Blue,
White, and Gold
P.O. Box 609609
San Diego, California 92160-9609
Telephone: (858) 874-4500

2014 SCHEDULE
PRESEASON
Aug. 7 **Dallas** 7:00
Aug. 15 at Seattle................................7:00
Aug. 24 at San Francisco.................1:00
Aug. 28 **Arizona** 7:00

REGULAR SEASON
Sep. 8 at Arizona (Mon) 7:20
Sep. 14 **Seattle** 1:05
Sep. 21 at Buffalo 10:00a
Sep. 28 **Jacksonville** 1:05
Oct. 5 **New York Jets** 1:25
Oct. 12 at Oakland 1:05
Oct. 19 **Kansas City** 1:05
Oct. 23 at Denver (Thu) 5:25
Nov. 2 at Miami 10:00a
Nov. 9 BYE
Nov. 16 **Oakland** 1:05
Nov. 23 **St. Louis** 1:05
Nov. 30 at Baltimore 10:00a
Dec. 7 **New England** *5:30
Dec. 14 **Denver** 1:05
Dec. 20 at San Francisco (Sat).........TBD
Dec. 28 at Kansas City 10:00a
*All times PT; Sunday night games in
Weeks 5-16 subject to change*

Stadium: Qualcomm Stadium
(opened in 1967)
•**Capacity:** 70,000 (app.)
9449 Friars Road
San Diego, California 92108
Playing Surface: Grass
Training Camp: Chargers Park
4020 Murphy Canyon Rd.
San Diego, CA 92123

QUALCOMM STADIUM

CLUB OFFICIALS
Owner: Alex G. Spanos
Chairman of the Board-President:
Dean A. Spanos
Executive Vice President:
Michael A. Spanos
Executive Vice President-Chief Executive
Officer: A.G. Spanos
Executive Vice President of Football
Operations: John Spanos
General Manager: Tom Telesco
Executive Vice President of Football
Administration-Player Finance:
Ed McGuire
Executive Vice President-Chief Financial
Officer: Jeanne M. Bonk
Senior Vice President-Chief Marketing
Officer: Ken Derrett
Director of Player Personnel:
JoJo Wooden
Director of Pro Scouting:
Dennis Abraham
Director of College Scouting: Kevin Kelly
Senior Executive: Randy Mueller
Head Athletic Trainer: James Collins
Director of Video Operations:
Brian Duddy
Equipment Manager: Bob Wick
Director of Player Development:
Arthur Hightower
Vice President of Marketing Partnerships:
Dennis O'Leary
Senior Director of Ticket Sales and
Service: Todd Poulsen
Director of Business Operations:
John Hinek
Director of Public Relations: Bill Johnston
Director of Public Affairs &
Corporate/Community Relations:
Kimberley Layton
Director of Digital Media: Nicoletta Ruhl
Director of Security: Bill Stetson
Director of Stadium/Game Operations &
Events: Sean O'Connor
Controller: Marsha Wells
Director of Ticket Operations:
Michael L. Dougherty

COACHING HISTORY
Los Angeles 1960
(419-418-11)
Records include postseason games
1960-69   Sid Gillman* 83-51-6
1969-1970 Charlie Waller 9-7-3
1971   Sid Gillman** 4-6-0
1971-73   Harland Svare*** 7-17-2
1973   Ron Waller.....................1-5-0
1974-78   Tommy Prothro**** ...21-39-0
1978-1986 Don Coryell# 72-60-0
1986-88   Al Saunders 17-22-0
1989-1991 Dan Henning...............16-32-0
1992-96   Bobby Ross...............50-36-0
1997-98   Kevin Gilbride## 6-16-0
1998   June Jones....................3-7-0
1999-2001 Mike Riley..................14-34-0
2002-06   Marty Schottenheimer.47-35-0
2007-2012 Norv Turner 59-43-0
2013   Mike McCoy 10-8-0
*Retired after nine games in 1969
**Resigned after 10 games in 1971
***Resigned after eight games in 1973
****Resigned after four games in 1978
#Resigned after eight games in 1986
##Released after six games in 1998

PAID ATTENDANCE
Home 514,035   Away 497,711
Total 1,011,746
Single-game home record,
69,288 (11/7/99)
Single-season home record,
547,937 (2005)

2014 DRAFT CHOICES
Round	Name	Pos.	College
1	Jason Verrett	DB	Texas Christian
2	Jeremiah Attaochu	LB	Georgia Tech
3	Chris Watt	G	Notre Dame
5	Ryan Carrethers	DT	Arkansas St.
6	Marion Grice	RB	Arizona St.
7	Tevin Reese	WR	Baylor

2013 TEAM RECORD

PRESEASON (1-3)

Date	Result		Opponent
08/08	L	10-31	Seattle
08/15	L	28-33	at Chicago
08/24	W	24-7	at Arizona
08/29	L	6-41	San Francisco

REGULAR SEASON (9-7)

Date	Result		Opponent
09/09	L	28-31	Houston
09/15	W	33-30	at Philadelphia
09/22	L	17-20	at Tennessee
09/29	W	30-21	Dallas
10/06	L	17-27	at Oakland
10/14	W	19-9	Indianapolis
10/20	W	24-6	at Jacksonville
11/03	L	24-30	at Washington (OT)
11/10	L	20-28	Denver
11/17	L	16-20	at Miami
11/24	W	41-38	at Kansas City
12/01	L	10-17	Cincinnati
12/08	W	37-14	New York Giants
12/12	W	27-20	at Denver
12/22	W	26-13	Oakland
12/29	W	27-24	Kansas City (OT)

(OT) Overtime

POSTSEASON (1-1)

Date	Result		Opponent
01/05	W	27-10	at Cincinnati
01/12	L	17-24	at Denver

SCORE BY PERIODS

Chargers	61	132	85	115	3	—	396
Opponents	68	106	79	89	6	—	348

2013 TEAM STATISTICS

	Chargers	Opp.
Total First Downs	373	327
Rushing	104	98
Passing	230	208
Penalty	39	21
3rd Down: Made/Att	101/206	70/180
3rd Down Pct.	49.0	38.9
4th Down: Made/Att	5/6	6/13
4th Down Pct.	83.3	46.2
Possession Avg.	32:59	27:01
Total Net Yards	6293	5864
Avg. Per Game	393.3	366.5
Total Plays	1060	959
Avg. Per Play	5.9	6.1
Net Yards Rushing	1965	1725
Avg. Per Game	122.8	107.8
Total Rushes	486	376
Net Yards Passing	4328	4139
Avg. Per Game	270.5	258.7
Sacked/Yards Lost	30/150	35/248
Gross Yards	4478	4387
Att./Completions	544/378	548/364
Completion Pct.	69.5	66.4
Had Intercepted	11	11
Punts/Average	56/43.2	65/47.0
Net Punting Avg.	56/40.0	65/42.9
Penalties/Yards	95/765	100/850
Fumbles/Ball Lost	14/10	15/6
Touchdowns	42	40
Rushing	9	14
Passing	32	23
Returns	1	3

2013 INDIVIDUAL STATISTICS

PASSING

	Att.	Comp.	Yds.	Pct.	TD	Int.	Tkld.	Rate
Rivers	544	378	4478	69.5	32	11	30/150	105.5
Chargers	544	378	4478	69.5	32	11	30/150	105.5
Opponents	548	364	4387	66.4	23	11	35/248	96.4

SCORING

	TD R	TD P	TD Rt	PAT	FG	Saf	PTS
Novak	0	0	0	42/42	34/37	0	144
Allen	0	8	0	0/0	0/0	0	48
Royal	0	8	0	0/0	0/0	0	48
Woodhead	2	6	0	0/0	0/0	0	48
Mathews	6	1	0	0/0	0/0	0	42
Gates	0	4	0	0/0	0/0	0	24
Green	0	3	0	0/0	0/0	0	18
Ajirotutu	0	1	0	0/0	0/0	0	6
R. Brown	1	0	0	0/0	0/0	0	6
V. Brown	0	1	0	0/0	0/0	0	6
Lissemore	0	0	1	0/0	0/0	0	6
Chargers	9	32	1	42/42	34/37	0	396
Opponents	14	23	3	39/39	23/30	0	348

2-Pt Conversions: Chargers 0-0, Opponents 0-0

RUSHING

	No.	Yds	Avg	LG	TD
Mathews	285	1255	4.4	51	6
Woodhead	106	429	4.0	14	2
R. Brown	45	157	3.5	13	1
Rivers	28	72	2.6	18	0
McClain	11	32	2.9	7	0
Royal	3	21	7.0	15	0
Weddle	2	4	2.0	2	0
Whitehurst	6	-5	-0.8	0	0
Chargers	486	1965	4.0	51	9
Opponents	376	1725	4.6	46	14

RECEIVING

	No.	Yds	Avg	LG	TD
Gates	77	872	11.3	56t	4
Woodhead	76	605	8.0	39	6
Allen	71	1046	14.7	43t	8
Royal	47	631	13.4	54	8
V. Brown	41	472	11.5	51	1
Mathews	26	189	7.3	17	1
Green	17	376	22.1	60t	3
R. Brown	8	60	7.5	15	0
Floyd	6	149	24.8	47	0
Phillips	4	30	7.5	13	0
Ajirotutu	3	64	21.3	26t	1
McClain	2	-7	-3.5	7	0
Rivers	0	-9	—	-9	0
Chargers	378	4478	11.8	60t	32
Opponents	364	4387	12.1	74t	23

INTERCEPTIONS

	No.	Yds	Avg	LG	TD
Gilchrist	2	43	21.5	26	0
Weddle	2	21	10.5	21	0
Wright	1	41	41.0	41	0
D. Butler	1	30	30.0	30	0
Keiser	1	6	6.0	6	0
Cox	1	2	2.0	2	0
Lissemore	1	0	0.0	0t	1
Patrick	1	0	0.0	0	0
Thomas	1	0	0.0	0	0
Chargers	11	143	13.0	41	1
Opponents	11	146	13.3	52t	2

PUNTING

	No.	Yds.	Avg.	In 20	LG
Scifres	56	2417	43.2	30	61
Chargers	56	2417	43.2	30	61
Opponents	65	3054	47.0	20	75

PUNT RETURNS

	Ret	FC	Yds	Avg	LG	TD
Allen	15	13	125	8.3	28	0
Royal	7	7	41	5.9	12	0
Chargers	22	20	166	7.5	28	0
Opponents	19	19	158	8.3	38	0

KICKOFF RETURNS

	No.	Yds	Avg	LG	TD
Woodhead	12	262	21.8	37	0
Hawkins	8	176	22.0	27	0
Whittaker	6	156	26.0	42	0
R. Brown	6	113	18.8	28	0
Chargers	32	707	22.1	42	0
Opponents	73	1797	24.6	46	0

FIELD GOALS

	1-19	20-29	30-39	40-49	50+
Novak	1/1	9/9	13/16	9/9	2/2
Chargers	1/1	9/9	13/16	9/9	2/2
Opponents	0/0	6/7	6/6	8/11	3/6

SACKS

	No.
Liuget	5.5
Reyes	5.0
Keiser	4.5
Ja. Johnson	3.0
Walker	3.0
English	2.5
Lissemore	2.0
Patrick	1.5
Addae	1.0
Gilchrist	1.0
Ingram	1.0
Weddle	1.0
T. Williams	1.0
Wynn	1.0
(group)	1.0
D. Butler	0.5
Freeney	0.5
Chargers	35.0
Opponents	30.0

RECORD HOLDERS
INDIVIDUAL RECORDS—CAREER

Category	Name	Performance
Rushing (Yds.)	LaDainian Tomlinson, 2001-09	12,490
Passing (Yds.)	Dan Fouts, 1973-1987	43,040
Passing (TDs)	Dan Fouts, 1973-1987	254
Receiving (No.)	Antonio Gates, 2003-2013	719
Receiving (Yds.)	Lance Alworth, 1962-1970	9,584
Interceptions	Gill Byrd, 1983-1992	42
Punting (Avg.)	Mike Scifres, 2003-2013	45.1
Punt Return (Avg.)	Darrien Gordon, 1993-96	13.7
Kickoff Return (Avg.)	Leslie (Speedy) Duncan, 1964-1970	25.3
Field Goals	John Carney, 1990-2000	261
Touchdowns (Tot.)	LaDainian Tomlinson, 2001-09	153
Points	John Carney, 1990-2000	1,076
*Sacks	Leslie O'Neal, 1986-1995	105.5

INDIVIDUAL RECORDS—SINGLE SEASON

Category	Name	Performance
Rushing (Yds.)	LaDainian Tomlinson, 2006	1,815
Passing (Yds.)	Dan Fouts, 1981	4,802
Passing (TDs)	Philip Rivers, 2008	34
Receiving (No.)	LaDainian Tomlinson, 2003	100
Receiving (Yds.)	Lance Alworth, 1965	1,602
Interceptions	Antonio Cromartie, 2007	10
Punting (Avg.)	Mike Scifres, 2012	48.3
Punt Return (Avg.)	Leslie (Speedy) Duncan, 1965	15.5
Kickoff Return (Avg.)	Keith Lincoln, 1962	28.4
Field Goals	John Carney, 1994	34
	Nick Novak, 2013	34
Touchdowns (Tot.)	LaDainian Tomlinson, 2006	**31
Points	LaDainian Tomlinson, 2006	**186
*Sacks	Leslie O'Neal, 1992	17.0
	Shawne Merriman, 2006	17.0

INDIVIDUAL RECORDS—SINGLE GAME

Category	Name	Performance
Rushing (Yds.)	LaDainian Tomlinson, 12-28-03	243
Passing (Yds.)	Philip Rivers, 9-26-10	455
Passing (TDs)	Dan Fouts, 11-22-81	6
Receiving (No.)	Kellen Winslow, 10-7-84	15
Receiving (Yds.)	Wes Chandler, 12-20-82	260
Interceptions	Many times	3
	Last time by Antonio Cromartie, 11-11-07	
Field Goals	John Carney, 9-5-93, 9-18-93	6
	Greg Davis, 10-5-97	6
Touchdowns (Tot.)	Kellen Winslow, 11-22-81	5
Points	Kellen Winslow, 11-22-81	30
*Sacks	Leslie O'Neal, 11-16-86	5.0

*Sacks became an official statistic in 1982.
**NFL Record

2014 VETERAN ROSTER

No.	Name	Pos.	Ht.	Wt.	Birthdate	NFL Exp.	College	Hometown	How Acq.	'13 Games/ Starts
37	Addae, Jahleel	S	5-10	195	1/24/90	2	Central Michigan	Valrico, Fla.	FA-'13	16/2
16	Ajirotutu, Seyi	WR	6-3	215	6/12/87	5	Fresno State	El Dorado Hills, Calif.	FA-'13	14/0
13	Allen, Keenan	WR	6-2	211	4/27/92	2	California	Greensboro, N.C.	D3-'13	15/14
67	Becton, Nick	T	6-6	323	2/11/90	2	Virginia Tech	Wilmington, N.C.	FA-'13	1/0
34	Brown, Donald	RB	5-10	207	4/11/87	6	Connecticut	Red Bank, N.J.	UFA(Ind)-'14	16/5*
86	Brown, Vincent	WR	5-11	190	1/25/89	4	San Diego State	Rancho Cucamonga, Calif.	D3a-'11	16/12
20	Butler, Crezdon	CB	6-1	191	5/26/87	5	Clemson	Asheville, N.C.	FA-'13	12/0
56	Butler, Donald	ILB	6-1	242	10/17/88	5	Washington	Fair Oaks, Calif.	D3-'10	13/12
81	Byrne, Jake	TE	6-4	258	1/24/90	2	Wisconsin	Rogers, Ark.	FA-'13	8/0*
66	Clary, Jeromey	G-T	6-6	320	11/5/83	8	Kansas State	Mansfield, Tex.	D6a-'06	15/15
10	Clemens, Kellen	QB	6-2	220	6/6/83	9	Oregon	Burns, Ore.	UFA(StL)-'14	10/9*
53	Conner, Kavell	ILB	6-0	245	2/23/87	5	Clemson	Midlothian, Va.	UFA(Ind)-'14	10/0*
77	Dunlap, King	T	6-9	330	9/14/85	7	Auburn	Brentwood, Tenn.	UFA(Phil)-'13	11/11
51	English, Larry	OLB	6-2	255	1/22/86	6	Northern Illinois	Aurora, Ill.	D1-'09	9/5
80	Floyd, Malcom	WR	6-5	225	9/8/81	9	Wyoming	Sacramento, Calif.	FA-'04	2/2
76	Fluker, D.J.	T	6-5	339	3/13/91	2	Alabama	Foley, Ala.	D1-'13	15/15
93	Freeney, Dwight	OLB	6-1	268	2/19/80	13	Syracuse	Bloomfield, Conn.	UFA(Ind)-'13	4/4
59	Gachkar, Andrew	ILB	6-3	240	11/4/88	4	Missouri	Overland Park, Kan.	D7-'11	16/3
85	Gates, Antonio	TE	6-4	255	6/18/80	12	Kent State	Detroit, Mich.	FA-'03	16/15
95	Geathers, Kwame	DT	6-6	335	10/4/90	2	Georgia	Georgetown, S.C.	FA-'13	7/0
41	Ghee, Brandon	CB	6-0	200	6/6/87	5	Wake Forest	Fayetteville, N.C.	UFA(Cin)-'14	10/0*
38	Gilchrist, Marcus	SS	5-10	198	12/8/88	4	Clemson	High Point, N.C.	D2a-'11	16/16
89	Green, Ladarius	TE	6-6	240	5/29/90	3	Louisiana-Lafayette	Pensacola, Fla.	D4-'12	16/10
71	Guy, Lawrence	DE	6-4	318	3/17/90	4	Arizona State	Las Vegas, Nev.	W(Ind)-'13	12/0*
61	Hardwick, Nick	C	6-4	305	9/2/81	11	Purdue	Indianapolis, Ind.	D3b-'04	16/16
79	Harris, Mike	T	6-5	318	12/5/88	3	UCLA	Duarte, Calif.	FA-'12	5/3
54	Ingram, Melvin	OLB	6-2	265	4/26/89	3	South Carolina	Rockingham, N.C.	D1-'12	4/1
88	Johnson, David	TE	6-2	260	8/26/87	6	Arkansas State	Pine Bluff, Ark.	UFA(Pitt)-'14	5/2*
96	Johnson, Jarret	OLB	6-3	260	8/14/81	12	Alabama	Chiefland, Fla.	UFA(Balt)-'12	11/9
90	Keiser, Thomas	OLB	6-4	260	3/28/89	4	Stanford	Wexford, Pa.	FA-'13	12/3
98	Lissemore, Sean	DT	6-3	303	9/11/87	5	William & Mary	Dumont, N.J.	T(Dall)-'13	15/2
94	Liuget, Corey	DE	6-2	300	3/11/90	4	Illinois	Miami, Fla.	D1-'11	16/16
31	Marshall, Richard	CB	5-11	198	12/12/84	9	Fresno State	Los Angeles, Calif.	FA-'13	16/6
24	Mathews, Ryan	RB	6-0	220	10/10/87	5	Fresno State	Bakersfield, Calif.	D1-'10	16/14
62	McDonald, Nick	C	6-4	305	6/27/87	4	Grand Valley State	Sterling Hills, Mich.	FA-'14	0*
57	Mouton, Jonas	ILB	6-2	240	3/17/88	4	Michigan	Los Angeles, Calif.	D2b-'11	0*
9	Novak, Nick	K	6-0	198	8/21/81	7	Maryland	Charlottesville, Va.	FA-'12	16/0
74	Ohrnberger, Rich	C-G	6-2	300	2/14/86	6	Penn State	East Meadow, N.Y.	UFA(Ariz)-'13	13/1
83	Phillips, John	TE	6-5	251	6/11/87	6	Virginia	Hot Springs, Va.	UFA(Dall)-'13	15/6
91	Reyes, Kendall	DE	6-4	300	9/26/89	3	Connecticut	Nashua, N.H.	D2-'12	16/16
78	Rinehart, Chad	G	6-5	321	5/4/85	7	Northern Iowa	Boone, Iowa	UFA(Buff)-'13	11/10
17	Rivers, Philip	QB	6-5	228	12/8/81	11	North Carolina State	Athens, Ala.	T(NYG)-'04	16/16
11	Royal, Eddie	WR-KR	5-10	185	5/21/86	7	Virginia Tech	Chantilly, Va.	UFA(Den)-'12	15/3
5	Scifres, Mike	P	6-2	215	10/8/80	12	Western Illinois	Destrehan, La.	D5-'03	16/0
69	Smith, Willie	T	6-5	310	11/13/86	4	East Carolina	Kenly, N.C.	FA-'13	1/0
4	Sorensen, Brad	QB	6-5	230	3/13/88	2	Southern Utah	Colton, Calif.	D7-'13	0*
25	Stuckey, Darrell	S	5-11	212	6/16/87	5	Kansas	Kansas City, Kan.	D4-'10	16/0
28	Taylor, Brandon	SS	5-11	205	1/29/90	3	Louisiana State	Franklinton, La.	D3-'12	0*
50	Te'o, Manti	ILB	6-1	241	1/26/91	2	Notre Dame	Laie, Hawaii	D2-'13	13/13
63	Troutman, Johnnie	G	6-4	330	11/11/87	2	Penn State	Brown Mills, N.J.	D5-'12	14/9
52	Walker, Reggie	LB	6-0	244	12/15/86	6	Kansas State	Sacramento, Calif.	FA-'13	16/6
32	Weddle, Eric	FS	5-11	200	1/4/85	8	Utah	Alta Loma, Calif.	D2-'07	16/16
72	Wiggins, Kenny	T	6-6	314	8/8/88	2	Fresno State	Elk Grove, Calif.	FA-'13	0*
23	Williams, Steve	CB	5-10	185	3/7/91	2	California	Dallas, Tex.	D5-'13	0*
58	Williams, Tourek	OLB	6-4	262	5/9/91	2	Florida International	Miami, Fla.	D6-'13	13/6
47	Windt, Mike	LS	6-1	237	5/29/86	5	Cincinnati	Cincinnati, Ohio	FA-'10	16/0
39	Woodhead, Danny	RB	5-8	200	1/25/85	7	Chadron State	North Platte, Neb.	UFA(NE)-'13	16/2
29	Wright, Shareece	CB	5-11	182	4/8/87	4	Southern California	Colton, Calif.	D3b-'11	13/13

* Brown played 16 games with Indianapolis in '13; Byrne played seven games with Houston and one game with San Diego; Clemens played 10 games with St. Louis; Conner played 10 games with Indianapolis; Ghee played 10 games with Cincinnati; Guy played two games with Indianapolis and 10 games with San Diego; D. Johnson played five games with Pittsburgh; McDonald last active with New England in '12; Mouton missed '13 season because of injury; Sorensen inactive 16 games; Taylor inactive 16 games; Wiggins did not play in three games and inactive four games; S. Williams missed '13 season because of injury.

\# Unrestriced Free Agent; subject to developments.

Players lost through free agency (3): WR Lavelle Hawkins (TB; 4 games in '13), DT Cam Thomas (Pitt; 16), QB Charlie Whitehurst (Tenn; 2).

Also played with Chargers in '13—LB Bront Bird (16 games), RB Ronnie Brown (16), CB Derek Cox (16), LB Terrell Manning (1), FB Le'Ron McClain (16), CB Johnny Patrick (13), T Mike Remmers (1), LB Adrian Robinson (2), G/T Stephen Schilling (7), RB Fozzy Whittaker (3), DE Jarius Wynn (5).

FIRST-YEAR ROSTER

Name	Pos.	Ht.	Wt.	Birthdate	College	Hometown	How Acq.
Adams, D.J.	RB	5-9	199	9/27/90	Portland State	Norcross, Ga.	FA
Allen. Torrence	WR	6-0	183	3/31/91	West Texas A&M	Meridian, Tex.	FA
Attaochu, Jerry	OLB	6-3	252	1/17/93	Georgia Tech	Washington, D.C.	D2
Boren, Zack (1)	FB	6-0	255	5/13/91	Ohio State	Pickerington, Ohio	FA
Carrethers, Ryan	DT	6-1	333	2/26/91	Arkansas State	Nashville, Tenn.	D5
Chancellor, Brelan	WR	5-8	188	8/6/92	North Texas	Copperas Cove, Texas	FA
Cromartie, Marcus (1)	CB	6-0	195	12/3/90	Wisconsin	Mansfield, Texas	FA-'13
Darby, Alden	S	5-10	192	6/22/92	Arizona State	Long Beach, Calif.	FA
Davis, Chris	CB	5-10	201	11/4/90	Auburn	Birmingham, Ala.	FA
Ducre, Greg	CB	5-10	183	1/22/92	Washington	Los Angeles, Calif.	FA
Flacco, Mike	TE	6-5	251	1/17/87	New Haven	Deptford Township, N.J.	FA
Grice, Marion	RB	6-0	208	7/19/92	Arizona State	Houston, Texas	D6
Hatfield, Micah	WR	6-1	182	8/10/89	Oregon State	Lake Oswego, Ore.	FA
Herndon, Javontee	WR	6-0	194	6/29/91	Arkansas	Jacksonville, Fla.	FA
Inman, Dontrelle (1)	WR	6-3	200	1/31/89	Virginia	Batesburg, S.C.	FA
Johnson, D.J.	G	6-4	295	2/10/91	New Mexico	Baton Rouge, La.	FA
Jones, Brandon (1)	CB	6-1	190	11/2/89	Rutgers	Atco, N.J.	FA-'13
Law, Cordarro (1)	DE	6-1	255	10/15/88	Southern Mississippi	York, Ala.	FA
Oliver, Brendan	RB	5-8	208	5/7/91	Buffalo	Miami, Fla.	FA
Otten, Ryan (1)	TE	6-6	241	4/7/90	San Jose State	Loomis, Calif.	FA-'13
Palepoi, Tenny	DE	6-1	298	12/19/90	Utah	Salt Lake City, Utah	FA
Reese, Tevin	WR	5-10	170	1/2/91	Baylor	Temple, Texas	D7
Scafe, Damik (1)	DE	6-2	300	4/26/88	Boston College	Windsor, Conn.	FA-'11
Scioneaux, Alvin	ILB	6-2	232	5/2/91	Wofford	Garyville, La.	FA
Sirles, Jeremiah	T	6-6	315	8/8/91	Nebraska	Lakewood, Colo.	FA
Tenpenny, Chase	P	6-3	252	8/6/91	Nevada	Oskaloosa, Kan.	FA
Tjong-A-Tjoe, Ricky	DE	6-2	309	4/4/90	Boise State	Boise, Idaho	FA
Underwood, Colton	OLB	6-3	254	1/26/92	Ilinois State	Washington, Ill.	FA
Verrett, Jason	CB	5-10	178	6/18/91	Texas Christian	Fairfield, Calif.	D1
Watt, Chris	G	6-2	311	8/17/90	Notre Dame	Glen Ellyn, Ill.	D3
Watts, Craig	G	6-4	335	6/20/91	West Texas A&M	Killeen, Texas	FA
Williams, Kerwynn (1)	RB	5-8	198	6/9/91	Utah State	Las Vegas, Nev.	FA-'13

The term NFL Rookie is defined as a player who is in his first season of professional football and has not been on the roster of another professional football team for any regular-season or postseason games. A Rookie is designated by an "R" on NFL rosters. Players who have been active in another professional football league or players who have NFL experience, including either preseason training camp or being on an Active List or Inactive List, or on Reserve/Injured or Reserve/Physically Unable to Perform for fewer than six regular-season games, are termed NFL First-Year Players. An NFL First-Year Player is designated by a "1" on NFL rosters. Thereafter, a player is credited with an additional year of experience for each season in which he accumulates six games on the Active List or Inactive List, or on Reserve/Injured or Reserve/Physically Unable to Perform.

Log on to www.chargers.com for an up-to-date roster.

SAN DIEGO CHARGERS

COACHING STAFF
Head Coach,
Mike McCoy
Pro Career: Hired January 15, 2013, as the 15th head coach in team history, Mike McCoy led the Chargers to the playoffs in his first season. At the time of his hiring, McCoy, then 41, was the second-youngest active head coach in the NFL and the second-youngest in team history. The Bolts went 9-7 under McCoy and won four consecutive and five of their last six to close out the regular season. McCoy then led the Chargers to a Wild Card Playoff win in Cincinnati for the franchise's first playoff victory since the 2008 season. The Chargers' playoff appearance in 2013 marked the organization's first since 2009 and McCoy joined Sid Gillman (1960), Don Coryell (1979), Bobby Ross (1992), and Norv Turner (2007) as the only rookie coaches in team history to lead the Bolts to the playoffs in their first season. Then with the team's win over the Bengals, McCoy became only the third head coach (Ross and Turner) to win his first playoff game. McCoy spent the 2009-2012 seasons in Denver. He began his coaching career as an offensive assistant with Carolina in 2000, serving additionally as wide receivers coach (2001), quarterbacks coach (2002-08) and passing game coordinator (2007-08). The Panthers reached the playoffs three times, with two NFC Championship Game appearances and a berth in Super Bowl XXXVIII (2003), during McCoy's tenure on the staff. Career record: 10-8.
Background: McCoy played quarterback at Long Beach State and Utah before signing with the Denver Broncos. He spent his rookie season on the practice squad in Green Bay and then had stops with NFL Europe's Amsterdam Admirals, San Francisco 49ers and the Philadelphia Eagles before concluding his playing career with the Canadian Football League's Calgary Stampeders in 1999.
Personal: Born in San Francisco, April 1, 1972. McCoy and his wife, Kellie, have a daughter, Liv, and a son, Luke.

ASSISTANT COACHES
Craig Aukerman, asst. special teams; born November 22, 1976, McComb, Ohio. Defensive back/wide receiver Findlay 1995-98. No pro playing experience. College coach: Findlay 2000, Miami (Ohio) 2001-02, 2005-08, Western Kentucky 2003-04, Kent State 2009. Pro coach: Denver Broncos 2010, Jacksonville Jaguars 2011-12, joined Chargers in 2013.
Joe Barry, linebackers; born July 5, 1970, Murphysboro, Ill. Linebacker Michigan 1989-1990, Southern California 1991-93. No pro playing experience. College coach: Southern California 1995, 2010-11, Northern Arizona 1996-98, Nevada-Las Vegas 1999. Pro coach: San Francisco 49ers 2000, Tampa Bay Buccaneers 2001-06, 2009, Detroit Lions 2007-08, joined Chargers in 2012.
Joe D'Alessandris, offensive line; born April, 29, 1954, Aliquippa, Pa. Guard Western Carolina 1972-76. No pro playing experience.

College coach: Western Carolina 1977-78, Livingston 1979-1983, Memphis 1984-85, Tennessee-Chattanooga 1986-89, Samford 1993, Texas A&M 1994, Pittsburgh 1996, Duke 1997-2001, Georgia Tech 2002-07. Pro coach: Ottawa Rough Riders (CFL) 1990, Birmingham Fire (WLAF) 1991-92, Memphis (AFL) 1995, Kansas City Chiefs 2008-09, Buffalo Bills 2010-12, joined Chargers in 2013.
Andrew Dees, asst. offensive line; born December 1, 1969, Babylon, N.Y. Offensive line/tight end Syracuse 1988-1991. Pro offensive line Cincinnati Bengals 1992, Seattle Seahawks 1993. College coach: Wagner 1997, Stony Brook 1998-2000, Buffalo 2001-05, Temple 2006-2010, Massachusetts 2011. Pro coach: Buffalo Bills 2012, joined Chargers in 2013.
Fred Graves, wide receivers; born March 2, 1950, Los Angeles, Calif. Halfback/split end Utah 1969-1971. No pro playing experience. College coach: Northeast Missouri State 1975-76, Western Illinois 1977-78, New Mexico State 1979-1981, Utah 1982-2000. Pro coach: Buffalo Bills 2001-03, Cleveland Browns 2004, Detroit Lions 2005, Tennessee Titans 2007-2010, Carolina Panthers 2011-12, joined Chargers in 2013.
Chad Grimm, quality control-defense; born May 18, 1985, Fairfax, Va. Linebacker Virginia Tech 2003-06. No pro playing experience. Pro coach: Arizona 2009-2012, joined Chargers in 2013.
Don Johnson, defensive line; born November 3, 1954, Newark, N.J. Linebacker Jersey City State 1973-76. College coach: Jersey City State 1984-85. Riverside (Calif.) C.C. 1987-1990, Cal State-Fullerton 1991-92, Nevada 1995-98, UCLA 1999-2004. Pro coach: Chicago Bears 2005-06, Oakland Raiders 2007-08, joined Chargers in 2009.
Kent Johnston, strength and conditioning; born February 21, 1966, Mexia, Texas. Defensive back Stephen F. Austin 1974- 77. No pro playing experience. College coach: Northwestern Louisiana 1981, Alabama 1985-86, 2004-05. Pro coach: Tampa Bay Buccaneers 1987-1991, Green Bay Packers 1992-98, Seattle Seahawks 1999-2003, Cleveland Browns 2010-12, joined Chargers in 2013.
Bobby King, asst. linebackers; born June 29, 1978, Louisville, Ky. Defensive lineman Texas-El Paso 1998-2000. No pro playing experience. College coach: Texas-El Paso 2002-03, West Texas A&M 2005, 2008-09, Baylor 2006-07. Pro coach: Dallas Cowboys 2010, Houston Texans 2011-13, joined Chargers in 2014.
Rick Lyle, asst. strength and conditioning; born February 26, 1971, Monroe, La. Defensive lineman Missouri 1989-1993. Pro defensive lineman Cleveland Browns 1994-95, Baltimore Ravens 1996, New York Jets 1997-2001, New England Patriots 2002-03. Pro coach: New York Jets 2006-08, Cleveland Browns 2009-2012, joined Chargers in 2013.
Pete Metzelaars, tight ends; born May 24, 1960, Three Rivers, Mich. Tight end Wabash College 1978-1981. Pro tight end Seattle Seahawks 1982-84, Buffalo Bills 1985-1994, Carolina Panthers 1995, Detroit Lions 1996-

97. College coach: Wingate 2003. Pro coach: Barcelona Dragons (NFLE) 2003, Indianapolis Colts 2004-2011, Buffalo Bills 2012, joined Chargers in 2014.
Ron Milus, secondary; born November, 25, 1963, Tacoma, Wash. Cornerback Washington 1982-85. College coach: Washington 1991-98, Texas A&M 1999. Pro coach: Denver Broncos 2000-02, 2011-12, Arizona Cardinals 2003, New York Giants 2004-05, St. Louis Rams 2006-08, Carolina Panthers 2009-2010, joined Chargers in 2013.
John Pagano, defensive coordinator; born March 30, 1967, Boulder, Colo. Linebacker Mesa State College 1985-88. No pro playing experience. College coach: Mesa State College 1989, Nevada-Las Vegas 1990-91, Louisiana Tech 1994, Mississippi 1995. Pro coach: New Orleans Saints 1996-97, Indianapolis Colts 1998-2001, joined Chargers in 2002.
Frank Reich, offensive coordinator; born December 4, 1961, Freeport, N.Y. Quarterback Maryland 1981-84. Pro quarterback Buffalo Bills 1985-1994, Carolina Panthers 1995, New York Jets 1996, Detroit Lions 1997-98. Pro coach: Indianapolis Colts 2008-2011, Arizona Cardinals 2012, joined Chargers in 2013.
Nick Sirianni, quarterbacks; born June 15, 1981, Jamestown, N.Y. Wide receiver Mount Union 2000-03. No pro playing experience. College coach: Mount Union 2004-05, Indiana (Pa.) 2006-08. Pro coach: Kansas City 2009-2012, joined Chargers in 2013.
Kevin Spencer, special teams coordinator; born November 2, 1953, Queens, N.Y. Outside linebacker Springfield College 1971. No pro playing experience. College coach: SUNY-Cortland 1975-76, Cornell 1979-1980, Ithaca 1981-86, Wesleyan 1987-1991. Pro coach: Cleveland Browns 1991-94, Oakland Raiders 1995-97, Indianapolis Colts 1998-2001, Pittsburgh Steelers 2002-06, Arizona Cardinals 2007-12, joined Chargers in 2013.
Shane Steichen, quality control-offense; born May 11, 1985, Sacramento, Calif. Quarterback Nevada-Las Vegas 2003-06. No pro playing experience. College coach: Nevada-Las Vegas 2007-0, Louisville 2010. Pro coach: San Diego Chargers 2011-12, Cleveland Browns 2013, re-joined Chargers in 2014.
Greg Williams, asst. secondary; born March 12, 1976, Chicago, Ill. Wide receiver/defensive back North Carolina 1994-97. Pro defensive back Amsterdam Admirals (NFL Europe) 1999-2000, San Francisco Demons (XFL) 2001, Indiana Firebirds (AFL) 2001-03, Chicago Rush (AFL) 2004. College coach: Arizona State 2003, College of DuPage 2004-05, Arkansas Tech 2006-07, Pittsburgh 2008. Pro coach: Joined Chargers in 2009.
Ollie Wilson, running backs; born March 3, 1951, Worcester, Mass. Wide receiver Springfield 1971-73. No pro playing experience. College coach: Springfield 1975, Northeastern 1976-1982, California 1983-1990. Pro coach: Atlanta Falcons 1991-96, 2002-07, San Diego Chargers 1997-2001, re-joined Chargers in 2008.

American Football Conference
South Division
Team Colors: Navy, Titans Blue, Red,
Silver
460 Great Circle Road
Nashville, Tennessee 37228
Telephone: (615) 565-4000

2014 SCHEDULE
PRESEASON
Aug. 9   **Green Bay**..........................7:00
Aug. 15 at New Orleans 7:00
Aug. 23 at Atlanta 6:00
Aug. 28 **Minnesota**......... .... 7:00

REGULAR SEASON
Sep. 7   at Kansas City 12:00
Sep. 14 **Dallas** 12:00
Sep. 21 at Cincinnati 12:00
Sep. 28 at Indianapolis 12:00
Oct. 5   **Cleveland** 12:00
Oct. 12 **Jacksonville** 12:00
Oct. 19 at Washington 12:00
Oct. 26 **Houston** 12:00
Nov. 2   BYE
Nov. 9   at Baltimore 12:00
Nov. 17 **Pittsburgh** (Mon) 7:30
Nov. 23 at Philadelphia 12:00
Nov. 30 at Houston 12:00
Dec. 7   **New York Giants** 12:00
Dec. 14 **New York Jets** 3:05
Dec. 18 at Jacksonville (Thu) 7:25
Dec. 28 **Indianapolis** 12:00
All times CT

Stadium: LP Field (opened in 1999)
    • **Capacity:** 69,143
      One Titans Way
      Nashville, Tennessee 37213
Playing Surface: Natural Grass
Training Camp: Saint Thomas Sports Park
      460 Great Circle Road
      Nashville, TN 37228

CLUB OFFICIALS
President/CEO: Thomas Smith
Co-Chairman: Susie Adams Smith
Co-Chairman: Amy Adams Hunt
Executive V.P. of Administration/Facilities:
    Don MacLachlan
Executive V.P./General Manager:
    Ruston Webster
Senior Vice President/General Counsel:
    Elza Bullock
Vice President/Player Personnel:
    Lake Dawson
Vice President/CFO: Jenneen Kaufman
Vice President/Football Administration:
    Vincent Marino
Vice President/Marketing:
    Ralph Ockenfels
Vice President/Business Operations and
    Sales: Stuart Spears

Director of Player Development: TBA
Equipment Manager: Paul Noska
Asst. Equipment Manager: Joey Barranco
Video Director: Anthony Pastrana
Asst. Video Director: Craig Patterson
Director of Sports Medicine:
    Todd Toriscelli
Asst. Athletic Trainers: Don Moseley,
    Casey Carter
Director of College Scouting:
    Blake Beddingfield
Asst. Dir. of Football Admin./Pro Scout:
    Dennis Polian
Pro Scout: James Kirkland
College Scouts: Phil Neri, Tim Ruskell,
    Jon Salge, Richard Shelton,
    Marv Sunderland, Brandon Taylor,
    Mike Yowarsky
Combine Scout: Dale Thompson
Scouting Consultant: C.O. Brocato

Director of Security: Jim Arts
Director of Media Relations:
    Robbie Bohren
Senior Director of Ticketing:
    Marty Collins
Director of Information Systems:
    Russ Hudson
Alumni Relations Coordinator: Bob Hyde
Director of Internet
    Operations/Publications: Gary Glenn
Director of Broadcasting: Mike Keith
Director of Cheerleading: Stacie Kinder
Director of Marketing: Brad McClanahan
General Manager of LP Field: Walter
    Overton
Head Groundskeeper: Terry Porch
Director of Community Relations:
    Tina Tuggle
Director of Suite Sales and Services:
    Bill Wainwright

COACHING HISTORY
Houston 1960-1996
(413-434-6)
Records include postseason games
1960-61   Lou Rymkus* 12-7-1
1961   Wally Lemm 10-0-0
1962-63   Frank (Pop) Ivy ...17-12-0
1964   Sammy Baugh..............4-10-0
1965   Hugh Taylor 4-10-0
1966-1970 Wally Lemm 28-40-4
1971   Ed Hughes.....................4-9-1
1972-73   Bill Peterson** 1-18-0
1973-74   Sid Gillman..................8-15-0
1975-1980 O.A. (Bum) Phillips 59-38-0
1981-83   Ed Biles***..................8-23-0
1983   Chuck Studley 2-8-0
1984-85   Hugh Campbell****.. ...8-22-0
1985-89   Jerry Glanville..............35-35-0
1990-94   Jack Pardee#.............44-35-0
1994-2010 Jeff Fisher................147-126-0
2011-13   Mike Munchak ...22-26-0
    *Released after five games in 1961
   **Released after five games in 1973
  ***Resigned after six games in 1983
****Released after 14 games in 1985
    #Released after 10 games in 1994

PAID ATTENDANCE
Home 516,424   Away 481,068
Total 997,492
Single-game home record,
    69,149, many times (last: 12/18/05)
Single-season home record,
    553,192 (2005)

2014 DRAFT CHOICES

Round	Name	Pos.	College
1	Taylor Lewan	T	Michigan
2	Bishop Sankey	RB	Washington
4	DaQuan Jones	DT	Penn St.
	Marqueston Huff	DB	Wyoming
5	Avery Williamson	LB	Kentucky
6	Zach Mettenberger	QB	Louisiana St.

TENNESSEE TITANS

2013 TEAM RECORD
PRESEASON (1-3)

Date	Result	Opponent
08/08	L 21-22	Washington
08/17	L 19-27	at Cincinnati
08/24	W 27-16	Atlanta
08/29	L 23-24	at Minnesota

REGULAR SEASON (7-9)

Date	Result	Opponent
09/08	W 16-9	at Pittsburgh
09/15	L 24-30	at Houston (OT)
09/22	W 20-17	San Diego
09/29	W 38-13	New York Jets
10/06	L 17-26	Kansas City
10/13	L 13-20	at Seattle
10/20	L 17-31	San Francisco
11/03	W 28-21	at St. Louis
11/10	L 27-29	Jacksonville
11/14	L 27-30	Indianapolis
11/24	W 23-19	at Oakland
12/01	L 14-22	at Indianapolis
12/08	L 28-51	at Denver
12/15	L 34-37	Arizona (OT)
12/22	W 20-16	at Jacksonville
12/29	W 16-10	Houston
(OT) Overtime		

SCORE BY PERIODS

Titans	71	77	65	149	0	—	362
Opponents	76	83	88	125	9	—	381

2013 TEAM STATISTICS

	Titans	Opp.
Total First Downs	311	329
Rushing	103	108
Passing	172	191
Penalty	36	30
3rd Down: Made/Att	94/227	69/201
3rd Down Pct.	41.4	34.3
4th Down: Made/Att	11/17	7/11
4th Down Pct.	64.7	63.6
Possession Avg.	30:00	30:00
Total Net Yards	5390	5407
Avg. Per Game	336.9	337.9
Total Plays	1032	1027
Avg. Per Play	5.2	5.3
Net Yards Rushing	1894	1795
Avg. Per Game	118.4	112.2
Total Rushes	462	446
Net Yards Passing	3496	3612
Avg. Per Game	218.5	225.8
Sacked/Yards Lost	37/214	36/227
Gross Yards	3710	3839
Att./Completions	533/328	545/344
Completion Pct.	61.5	63.1
Had Intercepted	16	13
Punts/Average	79/42.9	76/45.0
Net Punting Avg.	79/39.7	76/40.0
Penalties/Yards	101/900	95/779
Fumbles/Ball Lost	27/9	24/12
Touchdowns	41	40
Rushing	16	21
Passing	22	15
Returns	3	4

2013 INDIVIDUAL STATISTICS

PASSING	Att.	Comp.	Yds.	Pct.	TD	Int.	Tkld.	Rate
Fitzpatrick	350	217	2454	62.0	14	12	21/109	82.0
Locker	183	111	1256	60.7	8	4	16/105	86.7
Titans	533	328	3710	61.5	22	16	37/214	83.6
Opponents	545	344	3839	63.1	15	13	36/227	83.3

SCORING	TD R	TD P	TD Rt	PAT	FG	Saf	PTS
Bironas	0	0	0	41/41	25/29	0	116
C. Johnson	6	4	0	0/0	0/0	0	60
Walker	0	6	0	0/0	0/0	0	36
Greene	4	0	0	0/0	0/0	0	24
Hunter	0	4	0	0/0	0/0	0	24
Fitzpatrick	3	0	0	0/0	0/0	0	18
N. Washington	0	3	0	0/0	0/0	0	18
Locker	2	0	0	0/0	0/0	0	12
Preston	0	2	0	0/0	0/0	0	12
Wright	0	2	0	0/0	0/0	0	12
Battle	1	0	0	0/0	0/0	0	6
Klug	0	0	1	0/0	0/0	0	6
McCourty	0	0	1	0/0	0/0	0	6
Thompson	0	1	0	0/0	0/0	0	6
Verner	0	0	1	0/0	0/0	0	6
Titans	16	22	3	41/41	25/29	0	362
Opponents	21	15	4	37/38	32/39	3	381

2-Pt Conversions: Titans 0-0, Opponents 1-1.

RUSHING	No.	Yds	Avg	LG	TD
C. Johnson	279	1077	3.9	30t	6
Greene	77	295	3.8	29	4
Fitzpatrick	43	225	5.2	26	3
Locker	24	155	6.5	39	2
Battle	36	142	3.9	37	1
Kern	2	0	0.0	0	0
Reynaud	1	0	0.0	0	0
Titans	462	1894	4.1	39	16
Opponents	446	1795	4.0	60	21

RECEIVING	No.	Yds	Avg	LG	TD
Wright	94	1079	11.5	45	2
Walker	60	571	9.5	33	6
N. Washington	58	919	15.8	77t	3
C. Johnson	42	345	8.2	66t	4
Hunter	18	354	19.7	57	4
Williams	15	178	11.9	32	0
Britt	11	96	8.7	15	0
Greene	6	39	6.5	28	0
Mooney	6	32	5.3	22	0
Preston	5	37	7.4	10t	2
Battle	4	36	9.0	24	0
Thompson	3	13	4.3	9t	1
Stevens	2	5	2.5	6	0
Shiancoe	2	2	1.0	3	0
Reynaud	1	4	4.0	4	0
Fitzpatrick	1	0	0.0	0	0
Titans	328	3710	11.3	77t	22
Opponents	344	3839	11.2	55	15

INTERCEPTIONS	No.	Yds	Avg	LG	TD
Verner	5	68	13.6	34	1
Pollard	3	36	12.0	32	0
Ayers	1	5	5.0	5	0
Brown	1	3	3.0	3	0
McCarthy	1	1	1.0	1	0
Griffin	1	0	0.0	0	0
G. Wilson	1	0	0.0	0	0
Titans	13	113	8.7	34	1
Opponents	16	132	8.3	35	1

PUNTING	No.	Yds.	Avg.	In 20	LG
Kern	78	3386	43.4	32	63
Titans	79	3386	42.9	32	63
Opponents	76	3422	45.0	28	61

PUNT RETURNS	Ret	FC	Yds	Avg	LG	TD
Reynaud	18	8	135	7.5	35	0
L. Washington	6	9	78	13.0	33	0
Williams	4	3	12	3.0	8	0
Wylie	2	0	4	2.0	4	0
Verner	1	0	11	11.0	11	0
Titans	31	20	240	7.7	35	0
Opponents	35	25	210	6.0	24	0

KICKOFF RETURNS	No.	Yds	Avg	LG	TD
L. Washington	16	481	30.1	95	0
Reynaud	15	355	23.7	40	0
Williams	5	123	24.6	37	0
Wylie	5	94	18.8	23	0
Battle	1	26	26.0	26	0
Verner	1	17	17.0	17	0
Bailey	1	0	0.0	0	0
Titans	44	1096	24.9	95	0
Opponents	45	1099	24.4	46	0

FIELD GOALS	1-19	20-29	30-39	40-49	50+
Bironas	0/0	10/10	8/9	5/7	2/3
Titans	0/0	10/10	8/9	5/7	2/3
Opponents	2/2	6/6	6/8	15/18	3/5

SACKS	No.
Casey	10.5
Morgan	6.0
Brown	4.0
Pitoitua	4.0
A. Johnson	3.0
Wimbley	3.0
Klug	2.0
Ayers	1.0
Fokou	1.0
Mi. Martin	1.0
Pollard	0.5
Titans	36.0
Opponents	37.0

RECORD HOLDERS
INDIVIDUAL RECORDS—CAREER
Category Name Performance

Rushing (Yds.)	Eddie George, 1996-2003	10,009
Passing (Yds.)	Warren Moon, 1984-1993	33,685
Passing (TDs)	Warren Moon, 1984-1993	196
Receiving (No.)	Ernest Givins, 1986-1994	542
Receiving (Yds.)	Ernest Givins, 1986-1994	7,935
Interceptions	Jim Norton, 1960-68	45
Punting (Avg.)	Brett Kern, 2009-2013	44.4
Punt Return (Avg.)	Billy Johnson, 1974-1980	13.2
Kickoff Return (Avg.)	Bobby Jancik, 1962-67	26.5
Field Goals	Al Del Greco, 1991-2000	246
Touchdowns (Tot.)	Eddie George, 1996-2003	74
Points	Al Del Greco, 1991-2000	1,060
*Sacks	Ray Childress, 1985-1995	75.5

INDIVIDUAL RECORDS—SINGLE SEASON
Category Name Performance

Rushing (Yds.)	Chris Johnson, 2009	2,006
Passing (Yds.)	Warren Moon, 1991	4,690
Passing (TDs)	George Blanda, 1961	36
Receiving (No.)	Charley Hennigan, 1964	101
Receiving (Yds.)	Charley Hennigan, 1961	1,746
Interceptions	Fred Glick, 1963	12
	Mike Reinfeldt, 1979	12
Punting (Avg.)	Brett Kern, 2012	47.6
Punt Return (Avg.)	Billy Johnson, 1977	15.4
Kickoff Return (Avg.)	Ken Hall, 1960	31.3
Field Goals	Al Del Greco, 1998	36
Touchdowns (Tot.)	Earl Campbell, 1979	19
Points	Al Del Greco, 1998	136
*Sacks	William Fuller, 1991	15.0

INDIVIDUAL RECORDS—SINGLE GAME
Category Name Performance

Rushing (Yds.)	Chris Johnson, 11-1-09	228
Passing (Yds.)	Warren Moon, 12-16-90	527
Passing (TDs)	George Blanda, 11-19-61	**7
Receiving (No.)	Charley Hennigan, 10-13-61	13
	Haywood Jeffires, 10-13-91	13
	Drew Bennett, 12-19-04	13
Receiving (Yds.)	Charley Hennigan, 10-13-61	272
Interceptions	Many times	3
	Last time by Keith Bulluck, 9-24-07	
Field Goals	Rob Bironas, 10-21-07	**8
Touchdowns (Tot.)	Billy Cannon, 12-10-61	5
Points	Billy Cannon, 12-10-61	30
*Sacks	William Fuller, 11-28-93	4.0

Sacks became an official statistic in 1982.
**NFL Record*

2014 VETERAN ROSTER

No.	Name	Pos.	Ht.	Wt.	Birthdate	NFL Exp.	College	Hometown	How Acq.	'13 Games/ Starts
56	Ayers, Akeem	LB	6-3	253	7/10/89	4	UCLA	Los Angeles, Calif.	D2-'11	16/14
57	Bailey, Patrick	LB	6-4	243	11/19/85	7	Duke	Elmendorf, Texas	W(Pitt)-'10	13/0
44	Battle, Jackie	RB	6-2	240	10/1/83	7	Houston	Houston, Texas	FA-'13	16/0
48	Brinkley, Beau	LS	6-4	248	1/25/90	3	Missouri	Kearney, Mo.	FA-'12	16/0
55	Brown, Zach	LB	6-1	248	10/23/89	3	North Carolina	Estill, S.C.	D2-'12	16/13
37	Campbell, Tommie	CB	6-3	198	9/19/87	4	California (Pa.)	Aliquippa, Pa.	D7b-'11	8/0
99	Casey, Jurrell	DT	6-1	305	12/5/89	4	Southern California	Long Beach, Calif.	D3-'11	15/14
79	Dixon, Marcus	DE	6-4	295	9/16/84	3	Hampton	Rome, Ga.	FA-'14	0*
98	Edwards, Lavar	DE	6-4	278	4/29/90	2	Louisiana State	Baton Rouge, La.	D5-'13	7/1
53	Fokou, Moise	LB	6-1	243	8/28/85	6	Maryland	Cameroon, Africa	UFA(Ind)-'13	12/12
50	Gooden, Zaviar	LB	6-1	231	8/31/90	2	Missouri	Pflugerville, Texas	D3b-'13	9/1
23	Greene, Shonn	RB	5-11	233	8/21/85	6	Iowa	Sicklerville, N.J.	UFA(NYJ)-'13	11/0
33	Griffin, Michael	S	6-0	215	1/4/85	8	Texas	Austin, Texas	D1-'07	14/14
94	Hill, Sammie	DT	6-4	328	11/8/86	6	Stillman	West Blocton, Ala.	UFA(Det)-'13	13/10
15	Hunter, Justin	WR	6-4	203	5/20/91	2	Tennessee	Virginia Beach Va.	D2-'13	14/0
90	Johnson, Antonio	DT	6-3	328	12/8/84	8	Mississippi State	Leland, Miss.	UFA(Ind)-'13	16/6
6	Kern, Brett	P	6-2	214	2/17/86	7	Toledo	Grand Island, N.Y.	W(Den)-'09	16/0
97	Klug, Karl	DE/DT	6-3	278	3/31/88	4	Iowa	Caledonia, Minn.	D5-'11	16/3
67	Levitre, Andy	G	6-2	303	5/15/86	6	Oregon State	Santa Cruz, Calif.	UFA(Buff)-'13	16/16
10	Locker, Jake	QB	6-3	223	6/15/88	4	Washington	Ferndale, Wash.	D1-'11	7/7
83	Mariani, Marc	WR	6-1	187	5/2/87	5	Montana	Havre, Mont.	D7a-'10	0*
93	Martin, Mike	DT	6-1	298	9/1/90	3	Michigan	Detroit, Mich.	D3-'12	13/1
61	#Matthews, Kevin	C/G	6-3	302	2/4/87	3	Texas A&M	Houston, Texas	FA-'10	0*
52	McCarthy, Colin	LB	6-1	243	5/30/88	4	Miami	Tampa, Fla.	D4a-'11	16/5
22	McCluster, Dexter	RB	5-8	170	8/25/88	5	Mississippi	Largo, Fla.	UFA(KC)-'14	15/6*
30	McCourty, Jason	CB	6-0	193	8/13/87	6	Rutgers	Montvale, N.J.	D6a-'09	16/16
42	Mooney, Collin	FB	5-10	238	4/3/86	2	Army	Katy, Texas	FA-'12	12/4
91	Morgan, Derrick	DE	6-3	271	1/6/89	5	Georgia Tech	Coatesville, Pa.	D1-'10	15/14
72	Oher, Michael	T	6-4	315	5/28/86	6	Mississippi	Memphis, Tenn.	UFA(Balt)-'14	16/16*
66	Olsen, Eric	G/C	6-3	305	6/16/88	3	Notre Dame	Staten Island, N.Y.	UFA(Pitt)-'14	0*
66	#Otto, Mike	T	6-5	308	7/24/83	7	Purdue	Kokomo, Ind.	D7-'07	15/2
32	Pellerin, Micah	DB	6-0	192	11/23/88	2	Hampton	Metairie, La.	W(Dall)-'13	3/0
58	Phillips, Shaun	LB	6-3	255	5/13/81	11	Purdue	Willingboro, N.J.	UFA(Den)-'14	16/12*
92	Pitoitua, Ropati	DE	6-8	298	4/6/85	5	Washington State	Lakewood, Wash.	UFA(KC)-'13	16/13
31	Pollard, Bernard	S	6-1	226	12/23/84	9	Purdue	Fort Wayne, Ind.	FA-'13	16/16
14	Preston, Michael	WR	6-5	213	6/1/89	4	Heidelberg	Euclid, Ohio	FA-'11	7/0
17	Robiskie, Brian	WR	6-4	212	12/3/87	6	Ohio State	Cleveland, Ohio	FA-'13	1/0*
71	Roos, Michael	T	6-7	313	10/5/82	10	Eastern Washington	Vancouver, Wash.	D2-'05	16/16
62	Schwenke, Brian	C	6-3	318	3/22/91	2	California	Oceanside, Calif.	D4-'13	9/9
24	Sensabaugh, Coty	CB	5-11	187	11/15/88	3	Clemson	Kingsport, Tenn.	D4-'12	14/3
11	#Smith, Rusty	QB	6-5	223	1/28/87	5	Florida Atlantic	Jacksonville, Fla.	D6a-'10	0*
60	Spencer, Chris	G/C	6-3	308	3/28/82	10	Mississippi	Flora, Miss.	UFA(Chi)-'13	16/1
39	Stafford, Daimion	S	6-1	218	2/18/91	2	Nebraska	Norco, Calif.	D7-'13	16/0
88	Stevens, Craig	TE	6-3	263	9/1/84	7	California	San Pedro, Calif.	D3-'08	15/14
68	Stingily, Byron	T	6-5	318	9/9/88	4	Louisville	Country Club Hills, Ill.	D6-'11	5/2
84	Thompson, Taylor	TE	6-6	268	10/19/89	3	Southern Methodist	Prosper, Texas	D5-'12	16/3
59	#Turner, Rob	C/G	6-4	308	8/20/84	7	New Mexico	Austin, Texas	UFA(StL)-'13	6/6
82	Walker, Delanie	TE	6-0	248	8/12/84	9	Central Missouri	Pomona, Calif.	UFA(SF)-'13	15/11
70	Warmack, Chance	G	6-2	323	9/14/91	2	Alabama	Atlanta, Ga.	D1-'13	16/16
29	Washington, Leon	RB	5-8	192	8/29/82	9	Florida State	Jacksonville, Fla.	FA-'13	5/0
85	Washington, Nate	WR	6-1	183	8/28/83	10	Tiffin	Toledo, Ohio	UFA(Pitt)-'09	16/15
12	Whitehurst, Charlie	QB	6-5	226	8/6/82	9	Clemson	Duluth, Ga.	UFA(SD)-'14	2/0*
21	Wilson, George	S	6-0	210	3/14/81	9	Arkansas	Paducah, Ky.	FA-'13	16/3
95	Wimbley, Kamerion	DE	6-4	258	10/13/83	9	Florida State	Wichita, Kansas	FA-'12	16/1
96	Woods, Al	DE	6-4	307	3/25/87	5	Louisiana State	Jennings, La.	UFA(Pitt)-'14	16/2*
59	Woodyard, Wesley	LB	6-0	233	7/21/86	7	Kentucky	LaGrange, Ga.	UFA(Den)-'14	14/10*
25	Wreh-Wilson, Blidi	CB	6-1	198	12/5/89	2	Connecticut	Edinboro, Pa.	D3a-'13	13/0
13	Wright, Kendall	WR	5-10	191	11/12/89	3	Baylor	Pittsburg, Texas	D1-'12	16/12

* Dixon last active with New York Jets in '12; Mariani missed '13 season because of injury; Matthews inactive for five games and did not play one game; McCluster played 15 games with Kansas City; Oher played 16 games with Baltimore; Olsen did not play four games with Pittsburgh; Phillips played 16 games with Denver; Robiskie played one game with Atlanta; Smith inactive three games and did not play nine games; Whitehurst played two games with San Diego; Woods played 16 games with Pittsburgh; Woodyard played 14 games with Denver.

\# Unrestricted free agent; subject to developments.

Players lost through free agency (3): WR Kenny Britt (StL; 12 games in '13), CB Alterraun Verner (TB; 16), WR Damian Williams (Mia; 10).

Also played with Titans in '13—K Rob Bironas (16 games), DE Keyunta Dawson (2), LB Zac Diles (2), QB Ryan Fitzpatrick (11), RB Chris Johnson (16), FB Quinn Johnson (4), S Corey Lynch (3), RB Darius Reynaud (7), S Shann Schillinger (1), TE Visanthe Shiancoe (1), T David Stewart (12), WR Devon Wylie (2).

FIRST-YEAR ROSTER

Name	Pos.	Ht.	Wt.	Birthdate	College	Hometown	How Acq.
Adams, Jeff (1)	T	6-7	305	9/6/89	Columbia	Berwyn, Ill.	FA-'13
Anderson, Ri'Shard	CB	5-11	194	4/3/91	Syracuse	Miramar, Fla.	FA
Andrews, Antonio	RB	5-10	225	8/17/92	Western Kentucky	Fort Campbell, Ky.	FA
Anunoby, Chigbo (1)	DL	6-4	324	1/4/89	Morehouse	Jefferson City, Mo.	FA-'13
Bonani, Maikon (1)	K	5-10	183	1/29/89	South Florida	Matáo, Brazil	FA
Bryant, Lamont (1)	WR	6-5	225	1/6/88	Morgan State	Newport News, Va.	FA
Coons, Travis	K	6-1	194	2/6/92	Washington	Alta Loma, Calif.	FA
Copeland, Brandon (1)	LB	6-3	260	7/2/91	Pennsylvania	Sykesville, Md.	FA-'13
Gayle, James	LB	6-4	259	2/15/91	Virginia Tech	Hampton, Va.	FA
Gilbert, David	LB	6-4	254	10/31/91	Miami	Coral Springs, Fla.	FA
Hinds, David (1)	LB	6-0	235	2/25/90	Florida Atlantic	Miami, Fla.	FA
Horn, Tyler (1)	G/C	6-4	305	3/1/89	Miami	Memphis, Tenn.	FA-'13
Horton, Julian	WR	6-1	205	12/12/91	Arkansas	Norcross, Ga.	FA
Huff, Marqueston	DB	5-11	196	4/6/92	Wyoming	Texarkana, Texas	D4b
Ikard, Gabe	C	6-4	304	9/26/90	Oklahoma	Oklahoma City, Okla.	FA
James, Waymon	RB	5-8	203	1/24/91	Texas Christian	Sherman, Texas	FA
Jones, DaQuan	DL	6-4	322	12/17/91	Penn State	Johnson City, N.Y.	D4a
Lewan, Taylor	T	6-7	309	7/22/91	Michigan	Cave Creek, Ariz.	D1
McCray, Justin	G	6-3	321	5/31/92	Central Florida	Miami, Fla.	FA
Merisma, Viondy	G/T	6-2	294	6/20/91	American International	Waltham, Mass.	FA
Mettenberger, Zach	QB	6-5	224	7/16/91	Louisiana State	Watkinsville, Ga.	D6
Poehls, Will	T	6-8	334	11/27/91	Montana	Chandler, Ariz.	FA
Reynolds, Jaz	WR	6-2	201	2/26/91	Oklahoma	Houston, Texas	FA
Sankey, Bishop	RB	5-10	209	9/15/92	Washington	Wadsworth, Ohio	D2
Schepler, Jason (1)	TE	6-2	274	2/6/90	Northern Illinois	Woodstock, Ill.	FA
Schiltz, Adam (1)	TE	6-4	256	6/27/90	Emporia State	Ponca City, Okla.	FA-'13
Smith, Hakeem	S	6-0	194	11/9/89	Louisville	Jonesboro, Ga.	FA
Stewart, Josh	WR	5-10	178	10/22/92	Oklahoma State	Denton, Texas	FA
Walker, Derel	WR	6-1	188	6/29/91	Texas A&M	Hillsboro, Texas	FA
Willard, Jonathan (1)	LB	6-2	231	1/10/90	Clemson	Loris, S.C.	FA-'13
Williams, Isaiah (1)	WR	6-2	201	1/30/87	Maryland	Montclair, N.J.	FA
Williamson, Avery	LB	6-1	246	3/9/92	Kentucky	Milan, Tenn.	D5
Wilson, Tyler (1)	QB	6-2	215	8/16/89	Arkansas	Fort Smith, Ark.	FA-'13
Wooten, Khalid (1)	CB	5-11	212	2/19/90	Nevada	Rialto, Calif.	D6-'13
Wright, David	TE	6-4	251	3/21/91	Westminster	Solon, Ohio	FA
Wright, Winston	CB	5-10	190	3/16/91	South Dakota State	Lee's Summit, Mo.	FA

The term NFL Rookie is defined as a player who is in his first season of professional football and has not been on the roster of another professional football team for any regular-season or postseason games. A Rookie is designated by an "R" on NFL rosters. Players who have been active in another professional football league or players who have NFL experience, including either preseason training camp or being on an Active List or Inactive List, or on Reserve/Injured or Reserve/Physically Unable to Perform for fewer than six regular-season games, are termed NFL First-Year Players. An NFL First-Year Player is designated by a "1" on NFL rosters. Thereafter, a player is credited with an additional year of experience for each season in which he accumulates six games on the Active List or Inactive List, or on Reserve/Injured or Reserve/Physically Unable to Perform.

Log on to www.titansonline.com for an up-to-date roster.

COACHING STAFF

Head Coach,
Ken Whisenhunt

Pro Career: Whisenhunt became the 17th head coach in franchise history on Jan. 13, 2014. He arrived with 17 seasons of NFL coaching experience, including six years (2007-2012) as head coach of the Arizona Cardinals. In 2013, Whisenhunt served as offensive coordinator for the San Diego Chargers, and his unit ranked fifth in the NFL in total offense, first in third-down conversions and fourth in passing offense. For his efforts, Whisenhunt was named Professional Football Writers of America's 2013 Assistant Coach of the Year. He became a head coach for the first time when hired by Arizona in 2007 and won a franchise-record 49 games with the Cardinals. In 2008 (9-7 record) and 2009 (10-6), he led the club to back-to-back NFC West titles. The 2008 team fielded the fourth best offense in the NFL, set a team record with 427 points, won the franchise's first NFC Championship, and clinched the club's first Super Bowl berth. Prior to joining the Cardinals, Whisenhunt spent the previous six seasons as an assistant with the Pittsburgh Steelers, the first three as tight ends coach and the last three as offensive coordinator. Whisenhunt became offensive coordinator in 2004 and helped rookie quarterback Ben Roethlisberger set an NFL record with wins in his first 13 career starts. In 2005, the Steelers defeated the Seattle Seahawks in Super Bowl XL. Whisenhunt also coached at the pro level with the New York Jets (tight ends, 2000), Cleveland Browns (special teams, 1999) and Baltimore Ravens (tight ends, 1997-98). Career record: 49-53.

Background: After walking on at Georgia Tech, played four seasons primarily as a tight end and H-back. As a senior in 1984, he was a consensus All-ACC and honorable mention All-America selection. He earned a degree in civil engineering. Selected in the 12th round of the 1985 NFL Draft by the Atlanta Falcons and went on to play 74 games (37 starts) in nine NFL seasons with the Falcons (1985-88), Washington Redskins (1989-1990), and New York Jets (1991-93). Began his coaching career in the collegiate ranks with two seasons at Vanderbilt (1995-96).

Personal: Born February 28, 1962 in Atlanta, Ga., and raised in Augusta, Ga. He and his wife, Alice, have two children—Kenneth, Jr. and Mary Ashley.

ASSISTANT COACHES

Bob Bostad, offensive line; born September 7, 1966, Pardeeville, Wisc. Linebacker Wisconsin-Stevens Point 1986-89. No pro playing experience. College coach: Wisconsin-Stevens Point 1990-91, Minnesota 1992-94, Cal State-Northridge 1995-96, San Jose State 1997-98, New Mexico 1999-2005, Wisconsin 2006-2011. Pro coach: Tampa Bay Buccaneers 2012-13, joined Titans in 2014.

Steve Brown, asst. secondary; born March 20, 1960, Sacramento, Calif. Defensive back Oregon 1978-1982. Pro cornerback Houston

Oilers 1983-1990. College coach: Kentucky 2003-2011. Pro coach: St. Louis Rams 1995-2000, joined Titans in 2012.

Louie Cioffi, secondary; born September 21, 1973, Queens, N.Y. Attended State University of New York at Stony Brook. No college or pro playing experience. College coach: C.W. Post 1995-96. Pro coach: New York Jets 1993-94, Cincinnati Bengals 1997-2010, Arizona Cardinals 2011-12, Cleveland Browns 2013, joined Titans in 2014.

Sylvester Croom, running backs; born September 25, 1954, Tuscaloosa, Ala. Linebacker/tight end/center Alabama 1971-74. Pro center New Orleans Saints 1975. College coach: Alabama 1976-1986, Mississippi State 2004-08 (head coach). Pro coach: Tampa Bay Buccaneers 1987-1990, Indianapolis Colts 1991, San Diego Chargers 1992-96, Detroit Lions 1997-2000, Green Bay Packers 2001-03, St. Louis Rams 2009-2011, Jacksonville Jaguars 2012, joined Titans in 2013.

Nick Eason, asst. defensive line; born May 29, 1980, Lyons, Ga. Defensive lineman Clemson 1998-2002. Pro defensive tackle Denver Broncos 2003, Cleveland Browns 2004-06, Pittsburgh Steelers 2007-2010, Arizona Cardinals 2011-12. Pro coach Cleveland Browns 2013, joined Titans in 2014.

Steve Hoffman, asst. special teams; born September 8, 1958, Camden, N.J. Quarterback/ wide receiver/ running back/ kicker/ punter Dickinson College 1976-79. Pro punter Washington Federals (USFL) 1983. College coach: Miami 1985-88. Pro coach: Dallas Cowboys 1989-2004, Atlanta Falcons 2006, Miami Dolphins 2007-08, Kansas City Chiefs 2009-2011, Oakland Raiders 2012, joined Titans in 2013.

Ray Horton, defensive coordinator; born April 12, 1960, Tacoma, Wash. Cornerback Washington 1979-1982. Pro cornerback Cincinnati Bengals 1983-88, Dallas Cowboys 1989-1992. Pro coach: Washington Redskins 1994-96, Cincinnati Bengals 1997-2001, Detroit Lions 2002-03, Pittsburgh Steelers 2004-2010, Arizona Cardinals 2011-12, Cleveland Browns 2013, joined Titans in 2014.

Shawn Jefferson, wide receivers; born February 22, 1969, Jacksonville, Fla. Wide receiver Central Florida 1988-1990. Pro wide receiver San Diego Chargers 1991-95, New England Patriots 1996-99, Atlanta Falcons 2000-02, Detroit Lions 2003. Pro coach: Detroit Lions 2005-2012, joined Titans in 2013.

Nate Kaczor, special teams; born April 8, 1967, Scott City, Kan. Center Utah State 1987-89. No pro playing experience. College coach: Utah State 1991-99, Nebraska-Kearney 2000-03, Idaho 2004-05, Louisiana-Monroe 2006-07. Pro coach: Jacksonville Jaguars 2008-2011, joined Titans in 2012.

Cannon Matthews, quality control coordinator – defense; born June 21, 1985, Cleveland, Ohio. Attended Ohio University. No college or pro playing experience. College coach: Kentucky Christian 2012. Pro coach: Joined

Titans in 2014.

John McNulty, quarterbacks; born May 29, 1968, Scranton, Pa. Safety Penn State 1988-1990. No pro playing experience. College coach: Michigan 1991-94, Connecticut 1995-97, Rutgers 2004-08. Pro coach: Jacksonville Jaguars 1998-2002, Dallas Cowboys 2003, Arizona Cardinals 2009-2012, Tampa Bay Buccaneers 2013, joined Titans in 2014.

Jason Michael, offensive coordinator; born October 15, 1978, Portsmouth, Ohio. Quarterback Western Kentucky 1999-2002. No pro playing experience. College coach: Tennessee 2003-04, 2008. Pro coach: Oakland Raiders 2005, New York Jets 2006-07, San Francisco 49ers 2009-2010, San Diego Chargers 2011-13, joined Titans in 2014.

Mike Mularkey, tight ends; born November 19, 1961, Ft. Lauderdale, Fla. Tight end Florida 1979-1982. Pro tight end Minnesota Vikings 1983-88, Pittsburgh Steelers 1989-1991. College coach: Concordia 1993. Pro coach: Tampa Bay Buccaneers 1994-1995, Pittsburgh Steelers 1996-2003, Buffalo Bills 2004-05 (head coach), Miami Dolphins 2006-07, Atlanta Falcons 2008-2011, Jacksonville Jaguars 2012 (head coach), joined Titans in 2014.

Kevin Patullo, asst. wide receivers; born July 14, 1981, Hillsborough, N.J. Quarterback/wide receiver South Florida 1999-2001. College coach: South Florida 2003, Arizona 2004-06. Pro coach: Kansas City Chiefs 2007-2008, Buffalo Bills 2010-12, joined Titans in 2014.

Arthur Smith, asst. tight ends; born May 27, 1982, Memphis, Tenn. Offensive lineman North Carolina 2001-05. No pro playing experience. College coach: North Carolina 2006. Pro coach: Washington Redskins 2007-08, joined Titans in 2011.

Giff Smith, defensive line; born October 23, 1968, Atlanta, Ga. Defensive end Georgia Southern 1986-1990. No pro playing experience. College coach: Arkansas 1991-93, Georgia 1994-95, Georgia Southern 1996-98, Tulane 1999-2003, Georgia Tech 2004-09. Pro coach: Buffalo Bills 2010-12, joined Titans in 2014.

Lou Spanos, linebackers; born March 27, 1971, Pittsburgh, Pa. Center Tulsa 1989-1992. No pro playing experience. College coach: UCLA 2012-13. Pro coach: Pittsburgh Steelers 1994-2009, Washington Redskins 2010-11, joined Titans in 2014.

Mike Sullivan, asst. offensive line; born December 22, 1967, Chicago, Ill. Offensive lineman Miami 1986-1990. Pro offensive lineman Dallas Cowboys 1991, Tampa Bay Buccaneers 1992-95. College coach: Miami 2000, Western Michigan 2005-06. Pro coach: Cleveland Browns 2001-04, 2007-08, 2013, San Diego Chargers 2009-2012, joined Titans in 2014.

Steve Watterson, strength & conditioning; born November 27, 1956, Newport, R.I. Attended Rhode Island. No college or pro playing experience. Pro coach: Philadelphia Eagles 1984-85, joined Titans/Oilers in 1986.

The NFC

National Football Conference
West Division
Team Colors: Cardinal Red, Black, and
White
8701 S. Hardy Drive
Tempe, Arizona 85284
Telephone: (602) 379-0101

2014 SCHEDULE
PRESEASON
Aug. 9 **Houston** 5:30
Aug. 16 at Minnesota 5:30
Aug. 24 **Cincinnati** 5:00
Aug. 28 at San Diego......................7:00

REGULAR SEASON
Sep. 8 **San Diego** (Mon) 7:20
Sep. 14 at New York Giants 10:00a
Sep. 21 **San Francisco** 1:05
Sep. 28 BYE
Oct. 5 at Denver 1:05
Oct. 12 **Washington** 1:25
Oct. 19 at Oakland 1:25
Oct. 26 **Philadelphia** 1:05
Nov. 2 at Dallas 11:00a
Nov. 9 **St. Louis** 2:25
Nov. 16 **Detroit** 2:25
Nov. 23 at Seattle 2:05
Nov. 30 at Atlanta 2:05
Dec. 7 **Kansas City** 2:05
Dec. 11 at St. Louis (Thu) 6:25
Dec. 21 **Seattle** *6:30
Dec. 28 at San Francisco 2:25
*All times MST; Sunday night games in
Weeks 5-16 subject to change
Stadium: University of Phoenix Stadium
(opened in 2006)
•**Capacity:** 65,000
1 Cardinals Drive
Glendale, Arizona 85305
Playing Surface: Grass
Training Camp: University of Phoenix Stadium
Glendale, Arizona 85305

UNIVERSITY OF PHOENIX STADIUM

CLUB OFFICIALS
Owner: William V. Bidwill
President: Michael Bidwill
General Manager: Steve Keim
Executive Vice President/Chief Operating
Officer: Ron Minegar
Vice President, Player Personnel:
Terry McDonough
Chief Financial Officer: Greg Lee
General Counsel: David Koeninger
Vice President, Media Relations:
Mark Dalton
Vice President, Marketing: Lisa Manning
Vice President, Business Development:
Steve Ryan
Vice President, Technology: Mark Feller
Vice President, Security: Rick Knight
Vice President, Stadium Operations:
John Drum
Senior Director, Player Development:
Anthony Edwards
Senior Director, Broadcasting/Executive
Producer: Tim DeLaney
Senior Director, Community Relations:
Luis Zendejas
Senior Director, Ticketing: Steve Bomar
Senior Director, Ticket Sales:
Ron Campbell
Director, Pro Scouting: Quentin Harris
Director, College Scouting: Dru Grigson
Assistant Director, Pro Scouting:
Malik Boyd
Western Regional Scout: Chris Culmer
Eastern Regional Scout: Luke Palko
Director, Football Administration:
Mike Disner
Director, Media Relations: Chris Melvin
Director, Premium Services and Guest
Relations: Cari Belanger-Maas
Director, Business Development:
Mike Iaquinta
Director, Corporate Partner Service &
Activation: Scott Coleman
Football Operations Coordinator:
Matt Caracciolo
College Scouting Coordinator:
Debbie Pollom
Scouts: Mike Boni, Zac Canty, Glen Fox,
John Mancini, John Ritcher,
Josh Scobey, Darius Vinnett
Website Manager: Darren Urban
Video Director: Rob Brakel
Video Assistant Director: Jeff Wallo
Video Assistant: Craig Norgren
Head Athletic Trainer: Tom Reed
Assistant Athletic Trainers:
Michael Blankenship, Jeff Herndon,
Chad Cook
Equipment Manager: Mark Ahlemeier
Assistant Equipment Managers:
Steve Christensen, Jeff Schwimmer

COACHING HISTORY
Chicago 1920-1959, St. Louis 1960-1987
(517-723-39)
Records include postseason games
1920-22 John (Paddy) Driscoll 17-8-4
1923-24 Arnold Horween...................13-8-1
1925-26 Norman Barry......................16-8-2
1927 Guy Chamberlin 3-7-1
1928 Fred Gillies............................1-5-0
1929 Dewey Scanlon.......................6-6-1
1930 Ernie Nevers 5-6-2
1931 LeRoy Andrews* 0-1-0
1931 Ernie Nevers 5-3-0
1932 Jack Chevigny 2-6-2
1933-34 Paul Schissler.......................6-15-1
1935-38 Milan Creighton 16-26-4
1939 Ernie Nevers 1-10-0
1940-42 Jimmy Conzelman 8-22-3
1943-45 Phil Handler** 1-29-0
1946-48 Jimmy Conzelman 27-10-0
1949 Phil Handler-Buddy Parker*** 2-4-0
1949 Raymond (Buddy) Parker.....4-1-1
1950-51 Earl (Curly) Lambeau****....7-15-0
1951 Phil Handler-Cecil Isbell# 1-1-0
1952 Joe Kuharich 4-8-0
1953-54 Joe Stydahar 3-20-1
1955-57 Ray Richards......................14-21-1
1958-1961 Frank (Pop) Ivy##...........15-31-2
1961 Chuck Drulis-Ray Prochaska-
Ray Willsey### 2-0-0
1962-65 Wally Lemm 27-26-3
1966-1970 Charley Winner 35-30-5
1971-72 Bob Hollway 8-18-2
1973-77 Don Coryell 42-29-1
1978-79 Bud Wilkinson#### 9-20-0
1979 Larry Wilson 2-1-0
1980-85 Jim Hanifan 39-50-1
1986-89 Gene Stallings@...............23-34-1
1989 Hank Kuhlmann 0-5-0
1990-93 Joe Bugel 20-44-0
1994-95 Buddy Ryan 12-20-0
1996-2000 Vince Tobin@@...............29-44-0
2000-03 Dave McGinnis 17-40-0
2004-06 Dennis Green 16-32-0
2007-2012 Ken Whisenhunt.................49-53-0
2013 Bruce Arians.....................10-6-0

* Resigned after one game in 1931
** Co-coach with Walt Kiesling in Chicago
Cardinals-Pittsburgh merger in 1944
*** Co-coaches for first six games in 1949
**** Resigned after 10 games in 1951
\# Co-coaches
\#\# Resigned after 12 games in 1961
\#\#\# Co-coaches
\#\#\#\# Released after 13 games in 1979
@ Released after 11 games in 1989
@@ Released after seven games in 2000

PAID ATTENDANCE
Home 447,968   Away 470,041
Total 918,009
Single-game home record, 73,025*
(9/19/93)
Single-season home record, 516,646 (2007)
*Team also had attendance of 103,467 for regular-
season home game at Azteca Stadium, Mexico City,
Mexico

2014 DRAFT CHOICES

Round	Name	Pos.	College
1	Deone Bucannon	DB	Washington St.
2	Troy Niklas	TE	Notre Dame
3	Kareem Martin	DE	North Carolina
	John Brown	WR	Pittsburg St.
4	Logan Thomas	QB	Virginia Tech
5	Ed Stinson	DE	Alabama
6	Walt Powell	WR	Murray St.

2013 TEAM RECORD
PRESEASON (3-1)

Date	Result	Opponent
08/09	W 17-0	at Green Bay
08/17	W 12-7	Dallas
08/24	L 7-24	San Diego
08/29	W 32-24	at Denver

REGULAR SEASON (10-6)

Date	Result	Opponent
09/08	L 24-27	at St. Louis
09/15	W 25-21	Detroit
09/22	L 7-31	at New Orleans
09/29	W 13-10	at Tampa Bay
10/06	W 22-6	Carolina
10/13	L 20-32	at San Francisco
10/17	L 22-34	Seattle
10/27	W 27-13	Atlanta
11/10	W 27-24	Houston
11/17	W 27-14	at Jacksonville
11/24	W 40-11	Indianapolis
12/01	L 21-24	at Philadelphia
12/08	W 30-10	St. Louis
12/15	W 37-34	at Tennessee (OT)
12/22	W 17-10	at Seattle
12/29	L 20-23	San Francisco

(OT) Overtime

SCORE BY PERIODS

Cardinals	49	122	93	112	3	—	379
Opponents	94	89	41	100	0	—	324

2013 TEAM STATISTICS

	Cardinals	Opp.
Total First Downs	329	309
Rushing	84	68
Passing	205	208
Penalty	40	33
3rd Down: Made/Att	74/210	78/221
3rd Down Pct.	35.2	35.3
4th Down: Made/Att	5/9	6/16
4th Down Pct.	55.6	37.5
Possession Avg.	30:51	29:09
Total Net Yards	5542	5079
Avg. Per Game	346.4	317.4
Total Plays	1037	1042
Avg. Per Play	5.3	4.9
Net Yards Rushing	1540	1351
Avg. Per Game	96.3	84.4
Total Rushes	422	370
Net Yards Passing	4002	3728
Avg. Per Game	250.1	233.0
Sacked/Yards Lost	41/289	47/337
Gross Yards	4291	4065
Att./Completions	574/363	625/367
Completion Pct.	63.2	58.7
Had Intercepted	22	20
Punts/Average	78/45.7	88/46.4
Net Punting Avg.	78/40.1	88/42.3
Penalties/Yards	97/744	111/960
Fumbles/Ball Lost	22/9	20/10
Touchdowns	41	35
Rushing	12	5
Passing	24	29
Returns	5	1

2013 INDIVIDUAL STATISTICS

PASSING

	Att.	Comp.	Yds.	Pct.	TD	Int.	Tkld.	Rate
Palmer	572	362	4274	63.3	24	22	41/289	83.9
Fitzgerald	1	0	0	0.0	0	0	0/0	39.6
Peterson	1	1	17	100.0	0	0	0/0	118.8
Cardinals	574	363	4291	63.2	24	22	41/289	83.9
Opponents	625	367	4065	58.7	29	20	47/337	80.3

SCORING

	TD R	TD P	TD Rt	PAT	FG	Saf	PTS
Feely	0	0	0	37/37	30/36	0	127
Fitzgerald	0	10	0	0/0	0/0	0	60
Mendenhall	8	0	0	0/0	0/0	0	50
Floyd	0	5	0	0/0	0/0	0	30
Ellington	3	1	0	0/0	0/0	0	24
Ballard	0	2	0	0/0	0/0	0	12
Dansby	0	0	2	0/0	0/0	0	12
Dray	0	2	0	0/0	0/0	0	12
Roberts	0	2	0	0/0	0/0	0	12
J. Brown	0	1	0	0/0	0/0	0	6
Cason	0	0	1	0/0	0/0	0	6
Housler	0	1	0	0/0	0/0	0	6
Shaughnessy	0	0	1	0/0	0/0	0	6
Smith	1	0	0	0/0	0/0	0	6
D. Williams	0	0	1	0/0	0/0	0	6
Abraham	0	0	0	0/0	0/0	1	2
Campbell	0	0	0	0/0	0/0	1	2
Cardinals	12	24	5	37/37	30/36	2	379
Opponents	5	29	1	33/33	25/32	1	324

2-Pt Conversions: Mendenhall.
Cardinals 1-4, Opponents 2-2.

RUSHING

	No.	Yds	Avg	LG	TD
Mendenhall	217	687	3.2	28	8
Ellington	118	652	5.5	80t	3
S. Taylor	36	115	3.2	15	0
Smith	18	54	3.0	21	1
Peterson	4	21	5.3	12	0
Fitzgerald	2	8	4.0	4	0
Palmer	27	3	0.1	10	0
Cardinals	422	1540	3.6	80t	12
Opponents	370	1351	3.7	56	5

RECEIVING

	No.	Yds	Avg	LG	TD
Fitzgerald	82	954	11.6	75t	10
Floyd	65	1041	16.0	91t	5
Roberts	43	471	11.0	34t	2
Housler	39	454	11.6	31	1
Ellington	39	371	9.5	38	1
Dray	26	215	8.3	18	2
Mendenhall	18	134	7.4	24	0
J. Brown	11	140	12.7	32	1
Smith	10	68	6.8	10	0
S. Taylor	8	71	8.9	29	0
Ballard	7	75	10.7	29	2
Peterson	6	54	9.0	19	0
Golden	4	136	34.0	63	0
K. Taylor	3	40	13.3	17	0
T. Williams	1	51	51.0	51	0
Sperry	1	16	16.0	16	0
Cardinals	363	4291	11.8	91t	24
Opponents	367	4065	11.1	72t	29

INTERCEPTIONS

	No.	Yds	Avg	LG	TD
Dansby	4	48	12.0	23t	2
Peterson	3	59	19.7	43	0
R. Johnson	3	35	11.7	18	0
Washington	2	49	24.5	41	0
Cason	2	36	18.0	20t	1
Mathieu	2	7	3.5	7	0
Bell	2	6	3.0	6	0
Powers	1	9	9.0	9	0
D. Williams	1	2	2.0	2t	1
Cardinals	20	251	12.6	43	4
Opponents	22	399	18.1	66t	1

PUNTING

	No.	Yds.	Avg.	In 20	LG
Zastudil	78	3566	45.7	35	60
Cardinals	78	3566	45.7	35	60
Opponents	88	4084	46.4	33	69

PUNT RETURNS

	Ret	FC	Yds	Avg	LG	TD
Peterson	33	22	198	6.0	22	0
Arenas	1	0	0	0.0	0	0
Mathieu	0	1	0	—	—	0
Cardinals	34	23	198	5.8	22	0
Opponents	36	20	321	8.9	29	0

KICKOFF RETURNS

	No.	Yds	Avg	LG	TD
Arenas	23	493	21.4	46	0
Mathieu	2	8	4.0	13	0
Ellington	1	21	21.0	21	0
Peterson	1	18	18.0	18	0
Cardinals	27	540	20.0	46	0
Opponents	54	1298	24.0	59	0

FIELD GOALS

	1-19	20-29	30-39	40-49	50+
Feely	0/0	9/11	7/8	11/12	3/5
Cardinals	0/0	9/11	7/8	11/12	3/5
Opponents	0/0	8/10	6/6	7/10	4/6

SACKS

	No.
Abraham	11.5
Campbell	9.0
Dansby	6.5
Dockett	4.5
Shaughnessy	3.0
Washington	3.0
Benard	2.5
Acho	1.0
Arenas	1.0
Bell	1.0
Mathieu	1.0
Moch	1.0
Rucker	1.0
D. Williams	1.0
Cardinals	47.0
Opponents	41.0

RECORD HOLDERS
INDIVIDUAL RECORDS—CAREER

Category	Name	Performance
Rushing (Yds.)	Ottis Anderson, 1979-1986	7,999
Passing (Yds.)	Jim Hart, 1966-1983	34,639
Passing (TDs)	Jim Hart, 1966-1983	209
Receiving (No.)	Larry Fitzgerald, 2004-2013	846
Receiving (Yds.)	Larry Fitzgerald, 2004-2013	11,367
Interceptions	Larry Wilson, 1960-1972	52
Punting (Avg.)	Dave Zastudil, 2011-13	45.9
Punt Return (Avg.)	Charley Trippi, 1947-1955	13.7
Kickoff Return (Avg.)	Ollie Matson, 1952, 1954-58	28.5
Field Goals	Jim Bakken, 1962-1978	282
Touchdowns (Tot.)	Larry Fitzgerald, 2004-2013	87
Points	Jim Bakken, 1962-1978	1,380
*Sacks	Freddie Joe Nunn, 1985-1993	66.0

INDIVIDUAL RECORDS—SINGLE SEASON

Category	Name	Performance
Rushing (Yds.)	Ottis Anderson, 1979	1,605
Passing (Yds.)	Neil Lomax, 1984	4,614
Passing (TDs)	Kurt Warner, 2008	30
Receiving (No.)	Larry Fitzgerald, 2005	103
Receiving (Yds.)	David Boston, 2001	1,598
Interceptions	Bob Nussbaumer, 1949	12
Punting (Avg.)	Ben Graham, 2009	47.0
Punt Return (Avg.)	John (Red) Cochran, 1949	20.9
Kickoff Return (Avg.)	Ollie Matson, 1958	35.5
Field Goals	Neil Rackers, 2005	40
Touchdowns (Tot.)	John David Crow, 1962	17
Points	Neil Rackers, 2005	140
*Sacks	Simeon Rice, 1999	16.5

INDIVIDUAL RECORDS—SINGLE GAME

Category	Name	Performance
Rushing (Yds.)	Beanie Wells, 11-27-11	228
Passing (Yds.)	Boomer Esiason, 11-10-96 (OT)	522
Passing (TDs)	Jim Hardy, 10-2-50	6
	Charley Johnson, 9-26-65, 11-2-69	6
Receiving (No.)	Sonny Randle, 11-4-62	16
Receiving (Yds.)	Sonny Randle, 11-4-62	256
Interceptions	Bob Nussbaumer, 11-13-49	**4
	Jerry Norton, 11-20-60, 11-26-61	**4
	Kwamie Lassiter, 12-27-98	**4
Field Goals	Jim Bakken, 9-24-67	7
Touchdowns (Tot.)	Ernie Nevers, 11-28-29	**6
Points	Ernie Nevers, 11-28-29	**40
*Sacks	Curtis Greer, 12-18-83	4.5

*Sacks became an official statistic in 1982.
**NFL Record

2014 VETERAN ROSTER

No.	Name	Pos.	Ht.	Wt.	Birthdate	NFL Exp.	College	Hometown	How Acq.	'13 Games/ Starts
55	Abraham, John	LB	6-4	263	5/6/78	15	South Carolina	Timmonsville, S.C.	FA-'13	16/13
94	Acho, Sam	LB	6-3	257	9/6/88	4	Texas	Dallas, Texas	D4-'11	3/2
97	Alexander, Lorenzo	LB	6-1	244	5/31/83	8	California	Berkeley, Calif.	UFA(Wash)-'13	3/3
86	Ballard, Jake	TE	6-6	275	12/21/87	4	Ohio State	Springboro, Ohio	FA-'13	8/3
59	Benard, Marcus	LB	6-2	260	7/26/85	5	Jackson State	Adrian, Mich.	FA-'13	12/1
28	Bethel, Justin	CB	6-0	200	6/17/90	3	Presbyterian	Blythewood, S.C.	D6a-'12	16/0
64	Blake, Philip	C/G	6-3	310	11/27/85	2	Baylor	Toronto, Ontario	FA-'13	0*
13	Brown, Jaron	WR	6-2	205	1/8/90	2	Clemson	Cheraw, S.C.	FA-'13	16/0
93	Campbell, Calais	DE	6-8	300	9/1/86	7	Miami	Aurora, Colo.	D2-'08	16/16
89	Carlson, John	TE	6-5	248	5/12/84	7	Notre Dame	Litchfield, Minn.	FA-'14	13/8*
44	Clayton, Keenan	LB	6-1	230	6/19/87	4	Oklahoma	Sulphur Springs, Tex	FA-'14	0*
61	Cooper, Jonathan	G	6-2	311	1/19/90	2	North Carolina	Wilmington, N.C.	D1-'13	0*
31	Cromartie, Antonio	CB	6-2	210	4/15/84	9	Florida State	Tallahassee, Fla.	FA-'14	16/16*
90	Dockett, Darnell	DT	6-4	290	5/27/81	11	Florida State	Burtonsville, Md.	D3-'04	16/16
20	Dwyer, Jonathan	RB	5-11	229	7/26/89	5	Georgia Tech	Marietta, Ga.	UFA(Pitt)-'14	15/0*
38	Ellington, Andre	RB	5-9	199	2/3/89	2	Clemson	Moncks Corner, S.C.	D6b-'13	15/1
74	Fanaika, Paul	G	6-5	327	4/9/86	5	Arizona State	San Mateo, Calif.	FA-'13	16/16
4	Feely, Jay	K	5-10	208	5/23/76	14	Michigan	Tampa, Fla.	UFA(NYJ)-'10	16/0
11	Fitzgerald, Larry	WR	6-3	218	8/31/83	11	Pittsburgh	Minneapolis, Minn.	D1-'04	16/16
15	Floyd, Michael	WR	6-2	220	11/27/89	3	Notre Dame	St. Paul, Minn.	D1-'12	16/16
50	Foote, Larry	LB	6-1	239	6/12/80	13	Michigan	Detroit, Mich.	FA-'14	1/1*
19	Ginn Jr., Ted	WR	5-11	185	4/12/85	8	Ohio State	Cleveland, Ohio	UFA(Car)-'14	16/2*
10	Golden, Brittan	WR	5-11	186	7/20/88	2	West Texas A&M	Denver City, Texas	FA-'13	5/0
84	Housler, Rob	TE	6-5	250	3/17/88	4	Florida Atlantic	El Paso, Texas	D3-'11	13/10
39	Hughes, Robert	RB	5-11	235	6/21/89	2	Notre Dame	Chicago, Ill.	FA-'13	1/0*
22	Jefferson, Tony	S	5-11	212	1/27/92	2	Oklahoma	Chula Vista, Calif.	FA-'13	16/2
26	Johnson, Rashad	S	5-11	204	1/2/86	6	Alabama	Sulligent, Ala.	D3-'09	13/7
62	Larsen, Ted	G/C	6-2	305	6/13/87	5	North Carolina State	Palm Harbor, Fla.	UFA(TB)-'14	16/4*
82	Leach, Mike	LS	6-2	235	10/18/76	15	William & Mary	Jefferson Township, N.J.	FA-'09	16/0
14	Lindley, Ryan	QB	6-3	232	6/22/89	3	San Diego State	Alpine, Calif.	D6b-'12	0*
70	Massie, Bobby	T	6-6	316	8/1/89	3	Mississippi	Lynchburg, Va.	D4-'12	8/0
32	Mathieu, Tyrann	S	5-9	186	5/13/92	2	Louisiana State	New Orleans, La.	D3-'13	13/11
23	McCann, Bryan	CB	5-11	185	9/29/87	5	Southern Methodist	Oklahoma City, Okla.	FA-'13	6/0
51	Minter, Kevin	LB	6-0	246	12/3/90	2	Louisiana State	Suwanee, Ga.	D2-'13	13/0
57	Okafor, Alex	LB	6-4	261	2/8/91	2	Texas	Pflugerville, Texas	D4a-'13	1/0
3	Palmer, Carson	QB	6-5	235	12/27/79	12	Southern California	Rancho Santa Margarita, Calif.	T(Oak)-'13	16/16
34	Parmele, Jalen	RB	5-11	223	12/30/85	4	Toledo	Midland, Mich.	FA-'14	0*
21	Peterson, Patrick	CB	6-1	219	7/11/90	4	Louisiana State	Pompano Beach, Fla.	D1-'11	16/16
76	Potter, Nate	T/G	6-5	295	5/16/88	3	Boise State	Boise, Idaho	D7-'12	13/0
25	Powers, Jerraud	CB	5-10	187	7/19/87	6	Auburn	Decatur, Ala.	UFA(Ind)-'13	16/16
98	Rucker, Frostee	DE	6-3	280	9/14/83	9	Southern California	Tustin, Calif.	FA-'13	16/1
63	Sendlein, Lyle	C	6-3	308	3/16/84	8	Texas	Scottsdale, Ariz.	FA-'07	16/16
91	Shaughnessy, Matt	LB	6-5	285	9/23/86	6	Wisconsin	Norwich, Conn.	UFA(Oak)-'13	16/12
79	Sowell, Bradley	T	6-7	315	6/6/89	3	Mississippi	Hernando, Miss.	W(Ind)-'13	16/12
5	Stanton, Drew	QB	6-3	243	5/7/84	8	Michigan State	Farmington Hills, Mich.	UFA(Ind)-'13	0*
66	Ta'amu, Alameda	NT	6-3	348	8/23/90	3	Washington	Kent, Wash.	W(Pitt)-'13	14/3
27	Taylor, Curtis	S	6-2	212	7/13/85	3	Louisiana State	Franklinton, La.	FA-'13	1/0
30	Taylor, Stepfan	RB	5-9	216	6/9/91	2	Stanford	Mansfield, Texas	D5-'13	16/0
47	Tracy, Adrian	LB	6-2	248	4/6/87	3	William & Mary	Fairfax, Va.	FA-'14	0*
67	Tupou, Christian	DT	6-2	300	5/7/89	2	Southern California	Sacramento, Calif.	W(SF)-'14	5/0*
68	Veldheer, Jared	T	6-8	321	6/14/87	5	Hillsdale	Grand Rapids, Mich.	UFA(Oak)-'14	5/5*
37	Walters, Anthony	S	6-1	207	9/19/88	4	Delaware	Philadelphia, Pa.	FA-'14	13/0*
58	Washington, Daryl	LB	6-2	238	10/9/86	5	Texas Christian	Irving, Texas	D2-'10	12/12
78	Watford, Earl	G	6-3	300	6/24/90	2	James Madison	Philadelphia, Pa.	D4b-'13	0*
92	Williams, Dan	NT	6-3	314	6/1/87	5	Tennessee	Memphis, Tenn.	D1-'10	14/10
16	Williams, Teddy	WR	6-1	207	7/3/88	3	Texas-San Antonio	Tyler, Texas	FA-'13	3/0
9	Zastudil, Dave	P	6-3	220	10/26/78	13	Ohio	Bay Village, Ohio	FA-'11	16/0

* Blake inactive for two games with Denver in '12; Carlson played 13 games with Minnesota in '13; Clayton last active with Oakland in '12; Cooper missed '13 season because of injury; Cromartie played 16 games with the New York Jets; Dwyer played 15 games with Pittsburgh; Foote played one game with Pittsburgh; Ginn Jr. played 16 games with Carolina; Hughes played one game with Indianapolis; Larsen played 16 games with Tampa Bay; Lindley did not play in two games and inactive for 14 games; Parmele last active with Jacksonville in '12; Stanton did not play in 16 games; Tracy last active with the New York Giants in '12; Tupou played five games with Chicago; Veldheer played five games with Oakland; Walters played 13 games with Chicago; Watford did not play in three games and inactive for 13 games.

Traded—T Levi Brown (4 games in '13) to Pittsburgh.

Players lost through free agency (5): CB Javier Arenas (Atl; 16 games in '13), CB Antone Cason (Car; 16), LB Karlos Dansby (Cle; 16), TE Jim Dray (Cle; 16), WR Andre Roberts (Wash; 16).

Also played with Cardinals in '13—S Yeremiah Bell (16 games), LB Jasper Brinkley (15), LB Kenny Demens (2), G/C Mike Gibson (16), TE D.C. Jefferson (4), RB Rashard Mendenhall (15), LB Dontay Moch (4), RB Alfonso Smith (16), LB Vic So'oto (1), TE Kory Sperry (8), DE Ronald Talley (6), WR Kerry Taylor (3), T Eric Winston (16).

FIRST-YEAR ROSTER

Name	Pos.	Ht.	Wt.	Birthdate	College	Hometown	How Acq.
Bauman, Zach	RB	5-10	200	7/24/92	Northern Arizona	Chandler, Ariz.	FA
Brandon, Cory (1)	T	6-7	324	10/5/87	Oklahoma	Corsicana, Texas	FA
Brown, John	WR	5-11	179	4/3/90	Pittsburg State	Homestead, Fla.	D3b
Brown, Jonathan	LB	6-1	230	6/22/92	Illinois	Memphis, Tenn.	FA
Bucannon, Deone	S	6-1	211	8/30/92	Washington State	Fairfield, Calif.	D1
Buckner, Dan (1)	WR	6-4	215	5/31/90	Arizona	Allen, Texas	FA-'13
Carson, Glenn	LB	6-3	235	12/5/90	Penn State	Manahawkin, N.J.	FA
Catanzaro, Chandler	K	6-3	200	2/26/91	Clemson	Greenville, S.C.	FA
Demens, Kenny (1)	LB	6-1	242	2/4/90	Michigan	Oak Park, Mich.	FA-'13
Dickson, JoJo (1)	LB	6-1	245	7/13/89	Idaho	Wailuku, Hawaii	FA
Draheim, Tom (1)	C	6-4	309	12/23/88	San Diego State	Lakeside, Calif.	FA-'13
Fells, Darren (1)	TE	6-7	281	4/22/86	UC Irvine	Fullerton, Calif.	FA-'13
Gaston, Bruce	DT	6-2	310	11/29/91	Purdue	Chicago, Ill.	FA
Hardy, Andre (1)	TE	6-6	245	3/18/87	Cal State Fullerton	San Diego, Calif.	FA
Hrapmann, Danny (1)	K	5-9	164	4/21/89	Southern Mississippi	New Orleans, La.	FA
Johnson, Christian (1)	G	6-4	325	10/17/86	Kentucky	Ft. Campbell, Ky.	FA
Johnson, Orhian (1)	S	6-3	211	10/9/89	Ohio State	Gulfport, Fla.	FA-'13
Legree, Jimmy (1)	CB	6-0	187	1/13/91	South Carolina	Beaufort, S.C.	FA
Martin, Kareem	DE	6-6	272	2/19/92	North Carolina	Roanoke Rapids, N.C.	D3a
McCloud, Anthony (1)	DT	6-2	313	8/6/89	Florida State	Thomasville, Ga.	FA-'13
Niklas, Troy	TE	6-6	270	9/18/92	Notre Dame	Fullerton, Calif.	D2
Ozier, Kevin	WR	6-2	200	12/24/90	Arizona State	San Diego, Calif.	FA
Palmer, Kelvin	T	6-4	290	10/23/90	Baylor	Dallas, Texas	FA
Pope, Kelsey	WR	6-0	202	5/8/92	Samford	Sylacauga, Ala.	FA
Powell, Walt	WR	6-0	189	11/23/91	Murray State	St. Louis, Mo.	D6
Renfrow, Justin	DT	6-6	310	11/23/89	Miami	Morrisville, Pa.	FA
Sermons, Brandon	CB	5-11	195	6/1/91	UCLA	Diamond Bar, Calif.	FA
Smith, Kevin	WR	5-11	214	12/21/91	Washington	Compton, Calif.	FA
Steen, Anthony	G/C	6-3	309	5/9/90	Alabama	Clarksdale, Miss.	FA
Stinson, Ed	DE/DT	6-4	287	2/15/90	Alabama	Homestead, Fla.	D5
Thomas, Logan	QB	6-6	250	7/1/91	Virginia Tech	Lynchburg, Va.	D4
Washington, Todd	CB	5-11	190	4/20/92	Southeastern Louisiana	Lutcher, La.	FA
Whitley, Eddie (1)	CB	6-0	191	10/26/89	Virginia Tech	Fayetteville, N.C.	FA

The term NFL Rookie is defined as a player who is in his first season of professional football and has not been on the roster of another professional football team for any regular-season or postseason games. A Rookie is designated by an "R" on NFL rosters. Players who have been active in another professional football league or players who have NFL experience, including either preseason training camp or being on an Active List or Inactive List, or on Reserve/Injured or Reserve/Physically Unable to Perform for fewer than six regular-season games, are termed NFL First-Year Players. An NFL First-Year Player is designated by a "1" on NFL rosters. Thereafter, a player is credited with an additional year of experience for each season in which he accumulates six games on the Active List or Inactive List, or on Reserve/Physically Unable to Perform.

Log on to www.azcardinals.com for an up-to-date roster.

COACHING STAFF

Head Coach,
Bruce Arians

Pro Career: Became an NFL head coach for the first time when hired by Arizona on January 17, 2013. In his first season with the Cardinals, the team finished with a 10-6 record after winning seven of its final nine games. Arizona doubled its win total from 2011 and the five-win improvement equaled the best one-season turnaround in team history. It marked the franchise's seventh double-digit win season and first since 2009. Among all-time Cardinals coaches, only Norm Barry (11 in 1925) had more wins in his first season than Arians. Came to Arizona after working as offensive coordinator for the Indianapolis Colts in 2012, while also serving 12 games as interim head coach during Chuck Pagano's absence while being treated for leukemia. Arians was selected as the 2012 NFL Coach of the Year after leading Indianapolis to a 9-3 record and helping the Colts clinch a playoff berth while tying the NFL record for most wins ever by an interim coach. Arians previously coached at the pro level with the Pittsburgh Steelers (offensive coordinator, wide receivers, 2004-2011), Cleveland Browns (offensive coordinator, 2001-03), the Colts (quarterbacks, 1998-2000), the New Orleans Saints (tight ends, 1996) and the Kansas City Chiefs (running backs, 1989-1992). Career record: 10-6.

Background: Arians played quarterback (1972-74) collegiately at Virginia Tech and was voted the team's MVP as a senior. Collegiately, he was head coach at Temple (1983-88). He also coached at Virginia Tech (1977), Mississippi State (1978-1980, 1993-95) and Alabama (1981-82, 1997).

Personal: Born October 3, 1952 in Paterson, N.J., Arians and his wife, Christine, have two children—son, Jake and daughter, Kristi Anne.

ASSISTANT COACHES

Pete Alosi, asst. strength and conditioning; born July 31, 1982, Massapequa, N.Y. Linebacker Salisbury 2000-02. No pro playing experience. Pro coach: Joined Cardinals in 2010.

James Bettcher, outside linebackers; born May 27, 1978, Lakeville, Ind. Offensive lineman St. Francis 1999-2002. No pro playing experience. College coach: St. Francis 2003-05, Bowling Green 2006, North Carolina 2007-09, Ball State 2010, New Hampshire 2011. Pro coach: Indianapolis Colts 2012, joined Cardinals in 2013.

Anthony Blevins, coaching assistant/special teams; born July 23, 1976, Birmingham, Ala. Cornerback Alabama-Birmingham 1995-98. Pro cornerback Birmingham Steeldogs (AFL2) 2000, Birmingham Thunderbolts (XFL) 2000-01. College coach: Tennessee-Martin 2008, Tennessee State 2009-2011, Alabama-Birmingham 2012. Pro coach: Joined Cardinals in 2013.

Todd Bowles, defensive coordinator; born November 18, 1963, Elizabeth, N.J. Defensive back Temple 1982-85. Pro defensive back Washington Redskins 1986-1990, 1992-93, San Francisco 49ers 1991. College coach: Morehouse College 1997, Grambling State 1998-99. Pro coach: New York Jets 2000, Cleveland Browns 2001-04, Dallas Cowboys 2005-07, Miami Dolphins 2008-2011 (interim head coach 2011), Philadelphia Eagles 2012, joined Cardinals in 2013.

Brentson Buckner, defensive line; born September 30, 1971, Charlotte, N.C. Defensive tackle Clemson 1990-93. Pro defensive tackle Pittsburgh Steelers 1994-96, Cincinnati Bengals 1997, San Francisco 49ers 1998-2000, Carolina Panthers 2001-05. Pro coach: Joined Cardinals in 2013.

Mike Caldwell, linebackers; born August 31, 1971, Oak Ridge, Tenn. Linebacker Middle Tennessee State 1989-1992. Pro linebacker Cleveland Browns 1993-95, Baltimore Ravens 1996, Arizona Cardinals 1997, Philadelphia Eagles 1998-2001, Chicago Bears 2002, Carolina Panthers 2003. Pro coach: Philadelphia Eagles 2008-2012, joined Cardinals in 2013.

Rick Christophel, tight ends; born October 27, 1952, Reading, Ohio. Quarterback Austin Peay 1971-74. No pro playing experience. College coach: Austin Peay 1975, 1979-1981, 2007-2012 (head coach 2007-2012), Southern Arkansas State 1982, Cincinnati 1983, Rice 1984-85, Vanderbilt 1986-1990, Mississippi State 1991-94, Alabama-Birmingham 1995-2001, 2004-06. Pro coach: Joined Cardinals in 2013.

David Diaz-Infante, offensive assistant; born March 31, 1964, San Jose, Calif. Offensive lineman San Jose State 1982-87. Pro guard/center San Diego Chargers 1987, Frankfurt Galaxy (WLAF) 1991-92, Sacramento Gold Miners (CFL) 1993-94, Denver Broncos 1995-98, 2001, Philadelphia Eagles 1999, Las Vegas Outlaws (XFL) 2001. Pro coach: Joined Cardinals in 2013.

Darryl Drake, wide receivers; born December 11, 1956, Louisville, Ky. Wide receiver Western Kentucky 1975-78. Pro wide receiver Ottawa Rough Riders (CFL) 1981. College coach: Western Kentucky 1983-91, Georgia 1992-96, Baylor 1997, Texas 1998-2003. Pro coach: Chicago Bears 2004-2012, joined Cardinals in 2013.

Kevin Garver, offensive assistant; born July 28, 1987, Tuscaloosa, Ala. Attended Alabama. No college or pro playing experience. College coach: Alabama 2007-2012. Pro coach: Joined Cardinals in 2013.

Harold Goodwin, offensive coordinator; born November 14, 1973, Columbia S.C. Offensive lineman Michigan 1992-94. No pro playing experience. College coach: Michigan 1995-97, Eastern Michigan 1998-99, Central Michigan 2000-03. Pro coach: Chicago Bears 2004-06, Pittsburgh Steelers 2007-2011, Indianapolis Colts 2012, joined Cardinals in 2013.

Steve Heiden, asst. special teams/asst. tight ends; born September 21, 1976, Rushford, Minn. Tight end South Dakota State 1995-98. Pro tight end San Diego Chargers 1999-2001, Cleveland Browns 2002-09. College coach: Concordia University 2012. Pro coach: Joined Cardinals in 2013.

Amos Jones, special teams coordinator; born December 31, 1959, Tallahassee, Fla. Safety/running back Alabama 1978-1980. No pro playing experience. College coach: Alabama 1981-82, 1990-91, Temple 1983-88, Pittsburgh 1992, Tulane 1995-96, Cincinnati 1999-2002, James Madison 2003, Mississippi State 2004-06. Pro coach: British Columbia (CFL) 1997, Pittsburgh Steelers 2007-2012, joined Cardinals in 2013.

Roger Kingdom, asst. strength and conditioning; born August 26, 1962, Vienna, Ga. Wide receiver Pittsburgh 1981-82. No pro playing experience. College coach: California University (Pa.) 2004-2013. Pro coach: Joined Cardinals in 2014.

Freddie Kitchens, quarterbacks; born November 29, 1974, Gadsden, Ala. Quarterback Alabama 1994-97. No pro playing experience. College coach: Glenville State College 1999, Louisiana State 2000, North Texas 2001-03, Mississippi State 2004-05. Pro coach: Dallas Cowboys 2006, joined Cardinals in 2007.

Stump Mitchell, running backs; born March 15, 1959, St. Mary's Ga. Running back The Citadel 1977-1980. Pro running back St. Louis/Phoenix Cardinals 1981-89. College coach: Morgan State 1995-98 (head coach 1996-98), Southern 2010-12. Pro coach: San Antonio Rough Riders (WLAF) 1991, Seattle Seahawks 1999-2007, Washington Redskins 2008-09, joined Cardinals in 2013.

Tom Moore, asst. head coach/offense; born November 7, 1938, Owatonna, Minn. Quarterback Iowa 1957-1960. No pro playing experience. College coach: Iowa 1961-62, Dayton 1965-68, Wake Forest 1969, Georgia Tech 1970-71, Minnesota 1972-73, 1975-76. Pro coach: New York Stars (WFL) 1974, Pittsburgh Steelers 1977-1989, Minnesota Vikings 1990-93, Detroit Lions 1994-96, New Orleans Saints 1997, Indianapolis Colts 1998-2010, joined Cardinals in 2013.

Buddy Morris, strength and conditioning; born September 29, 1957, South Park, Pa. No college or pro playing experience. College coach: Pittsburgh 1980-89, 1997-2001, 2007-2010, Buffalo 2006. Pro coach: Cleveland Browns 2002-04, joined Cardinals in 2014.

Tom Pratt, pass rush specialist; born June 21, 1935, Edgerton, Wisc. Linebacker Miami 1953-56. No pro playing experience. College coach: Miami 1957-1960, Southern Mississippi 1961-62, U.S. Coast Guard Academy 1997. Pro coach: Kansas City Chiefs 1963-1977, 1989-1994, 2000, New Orleans Saints 1978-1980, Cleveland Browns 1981-88, Tampa Bay Buccaneers 1995, joined Cardinals in 2013.

Nick Rapone, defensive backs; born April 25, 1956, New Castle, Pa. Wide receiver Virginia Tech 1974-77. No pro playing experience. College coach: Pittsburgh 1980-1989, 1991-1992, East Tennessee State 1981-82, Temple 1983-88, 1999-2005, Connecticut 1995-98, Delaware 2006-2012. Pro coach: Joined Cardinals in 2013.

Kevin Ross, cornerbacks; born January 16, 1962, Camden, N.J. Defensive back Temple 1980-83. Pro defensive back Kansas City Chiefs 1984-93, 1997, Atlanta Falcons 1994-95, San Diego Chargers 1996. Pro coach: Minnesota Vikings 2003-05, San Diego Chargers 2007-08, Oakland Raiders 2010-11, joined Cardinals in 2013.

Ryan Slowik, defensive assistant/asst. def. backs; born Dec. 27, 1980, Chicago, Ill. Safety Wisconsin-Oshkosh 2002-03. No pro playing experience. College coach: Wisconsin-Oshkosh 2004. Pro coach: Denver Broncos 2005-08, joined Cardinals in 2009.

Larry Zierlein, asst. offensive line; born July 12, 1945, Norton, Kan. Linebacker/tight end Pratt (Kan.) J.C. 1967-68, linebacker Fort Hays State 1969-1970. No pro playing experience. College coach: Fort Hays State 1970-71, Houston 1978-1986, Tulane 1988-1990, 1995-96, Louisiana State 1993-94, Cincinnati 1997-2000. Pro coach: Washington (AFL) 1987, New York/New Jersey Knights (WLAF) 1991-92, Cleveland Browns 2001-04, Buffalo Bills 2006, Pittsburgh Steelers 2007-09, Hartford Colonials (UFL) 2011, joined Cardinals in 2013.

National Football Conference
South Division
Team Colors: Black, Red, Silver, and White
4400 Falcon Parkway
Flowery Branch, Georgia 30542
Telephone: (770) 965-3115

2014 SCHEDULE
PRESEASON
Aug. 8	**Miami**	7:00
Aug. 16	at Houston	8:00
Aug. 23	**Tennessee**	7:00
Aug. 28	at Jacksonville	6:00

REGULAR SEASON
Sep. 7	**New Orleans**	1:00
Sep. 14	at Cincinnati	1:00
Sep. 18	**Tampa Bay** (Thu)	8:25
Sep. 28	at Minnesota	4:25
Oct. 5	at New York Giants	1:00
Oct. 12	**Chicago**	1:00
Oct. 19	at Baltimore	1:00
Oct. 26	**Detroit** (London)	9:30a
Nov. 2	BYE	
Nov. 9	at Tampa Bay	1:00
Nov. 16	at Carolina	1:00
Nov. 23	**Cleveland**	1:00
Nov. 30	**Arizona**	4:05
Dec. 8	at Green Bay (Mon)	8:30
Dec. 14	**Pittsburgh**	1:00
Dec. 21	at New Orleans	1:00
Dec. 28	**Carolina**	1:00

All times ET

Stadium: Georgia Dome
    (opened in 1992)
    •**Capacity:** 71,228
    One Georgia Dome Drive
    Atlanta, Georgia 30313
Playing Surface: FieldTurf
Training Camp: Atlanta Falcons
    4400 Falcon Parkway
    Flowery Branch, GA 30542

GEORGIA DOME

CLUB OFFICIALS
Owner & Chairman: Arthur M. Blank
President & CEO: Rich McKay
General Manager: Thomas Dimitroff
Head Coach: Mike Smith
Director of Human Resources:
  Karen Walters
Executive Vice President of
  Administration & CFO: Greg Beadles
Senior Vice President of Sales &
  Marketing: Tim Zulawski
Vice President of Community Relations:
  Kendyl Baugh Moss
Controller/CFO Retail: Rob Geoffroy
Vice President of Football
  Communications: Reggie Roberts
Vice President of Information
  Technology: Danny Branch
Chief Marketing Officer: Jim Smith
Senior Director of Media Relations:
  Frank Kleha
Senior Director of Player Development:
  Kevin Winston
Director of Logistics and Facilities:
  Spencer Treadwell
Director of Ticket Operations:
  Mike Gilsenan
Director of Event Marketing: Roddy White
Director of Player Personnel: Steve Sabo
Director of Pro Personnel: DeJuan Polk
Director of Football Operations: Nick Polk
Associate Director of Player Personnel:
  Lionel Vital
Director of College Scouting: Steve Sabo
Eastern Regional Scout: Marvin Allen
National Scout: Mark Olson
Regional Scout: Shepley Heard
Area Scouts: Anthony Robinson,
  Michael Ross, Tokunbo Abanikanda,
  Mike Potts, Sae Woon Jo
Pro Scout: Bob Kronenberg
Scouting Assistant: Scott Sika
Director of Sports Medicine &
  Performance: Marty Lauzon
Assistant Athletic Trainer: Danny Long
Assistant Athletic Trainer: Eric Avila
Video Director: Mike Crews
Video Assistant: Phil Tieman
Equipment Manager: Brian Boigner
Director of New Media: Dan Levak
Football Communications Coordinator:
  Brian Cearns
Football Communications Coordinator:
  Matt Haley

COACHING HISTORY
(323-426-6)
Records include postseason games
1966-68	Norb Hecker*	4-26-1
1968-1974	Norm Van Brocklin**	37-49-3
1974-76	Marion Campbell***	6-19-0
1976	Pat Peppler	3-6-0
1977-1982	Leeman Bennett	47-44-0
1983-86	Dan Henning	22-41-1
1987-89	Marion Campbell****	11-32-0
1989	Jim Hanifan	0-4-0
1990-93	Jerry Glanville	28-38-0
1994-96	June Jones	19-30-0
1997-2003	Dan Reeves#	52-61-1
2003	Wade Phillips	2-1-0
2004-06	Jim Mora	27-23-0
2007	Bobby Petrino##	3-10-0
2007	Emmitt Thomas	1-2-0
2008-2013	Mike Smith	61-40-0

*Released after three games in 1968
**Released after eight games in 1974
***Released after five games in 1976
****Retired after 12 games in 1989
#Released after 13 games in 2003
##Resigned after 13 games in 2007

PAID ATTENDANCE
Home 544,959   Away 498,429
Total 1,043,388
Single-game home record,
  71,151 (10/22/06)
Single-season home record,
  553,979 (1992)

2014 DRAFT CHOICES
Round	Name	Pos.	College
1	Jake Matthews	T	Texas A&M
2	Ra'Shede Hageman	DE	Minnesota
3	Dezmen Southward	DB	Wisconsin
4	Devonta Freeman	RB	Florida St.
	Prince Shembo	LB	Notre Dame
5	Ricardo Allen	DB	Purdue
	Marquis Spruill	LB	Syracuse
7	Yawin Smallwood	LB	Connecticut
	Tyler Starr	LB	South Dakota

ATLANTA FALCONS

2013 TEAM RECORD
PRESEASON (0-4)

Date	Result		Opponent
08/08	L	10-34	Cincinnati
08/15	L	23-27	at Baltimore
08/24	L	16-27	at Tennessee
08/29	L	16-20	Jacksonville

REGULAR SEASON (4-12)

Date	Result		Opponent
09/08	L	17-23	at New Orleans
09/15	W	31-24	St. Louis
09/22	L	23-27	at Miami
09/29	L	23-30	New England
10/07	L	28-30	New York Jets
10/20	W	31-23	Tampa Bay
10/27	L	13-27	at Arizona
11/03	L	10-34	at Carolina
11/10	L	10-33	Seattle
11/17	L	28-41	at Tampa Bay
11/21	L	13-17	New Orleans
12/01	W	34-31	at Buffalo (OT)
12/08	L	21-22	at Green Bay
12/15	W	27-26	Washington
12/23	L	24-34	at San Francisco
12/29	L	20-21	Carolina

(OT) Overtime

SCORE BY PERIODS

Falcons	79	122	56	93	3	—	353
Opponents	54	169	93	127	0	—	443

2013 TEAM STATISTICS

	Falcons	Opp.
Total First Downs	330	326
Rushing	64	102
Passing	227	196
Penalty	39	28
3rd Down: Made/Att	89/207	96/209
3rd Down Pct.	43.0	45.9
4th Down: Made/Att	6/14	7/11
4th Down Pct.	42.9	63.6
Possession Avg.	30:15	29:45
Total Net Yards	5490	6070
Avg. Per Game	343.1	379.4
Total Plays	1024	1003
Avg. Per Play	5.4	6.1
Net Yards Rushing	1247	2173
Avg. Per Game	77.9	135.8
Total Rushes	321	455
Net Yards Passing	4243	3897
Avg. Per Game	265.2	243.6
Sacked/Yards Lost	44/298	32/231
Gross Yards	4541	4128
Att./Completions	659/445	516/341
Completion Pct.	67.5	66.1
Had Intercepted	17	10
Punts/Average	70/45.2	62/46.7
Net Punting Avg.	70/41.1	62/40.1
Penalties/Yards	91/788	104/885
Fumbles/Ball Lost	17/11	18/11
Touchdowns	40	49
Rushing	11	14
Passing	26	31
Returns	3	4

2013 INDIVIDUAL STATISTICS

PASSING

	Att.	Comp.	Yds.	Pct.	TD	Int.	Tkld.	Rate
Ryan	651	439	4515	67.4	26	17	44/298	89.6
Do. Davis	7	5	34	71.4	0	0	0/0	81.8
Schillinger	1	1	-8	100.0	0	0	0/0	79.2
Falcons	659	445	4541	67.5	26	17	44/298	89.5
Opponents	516	341	4128	66.1	31	10	32/231	102.4

SCORING

	TD R	TD P	TD Rt	PAT	FG	Saf	PTS
Bryant	0	0	0	39/39	24/27	0	111
Gonzalez	0	8	0	0/0	0/0	0	50
Jackson	6	1	0	0/0	0/0	0	42
Jac. Rodgers	2	2	0	0/0	0/0	0	24
Snelling	1	3	0	0/0	0/0	0	24
White	0	3	0	0/0	0/0	0	18
Dr. Davis	0	2	0	0/0	0/0	0	12
Douglas	0	2	0	0/0	0/0	0	12
J. Jones	0	2	0	0/0	0/0	0	12
A. Smith	2	0	0	0/0	0/0	0	12
Toilolo	0	2	0	0/0	0/0	0	12
DeCoud	0	0	1	0/0	0/0	0	6
D. Johnson	0	1	0	0/0	0/0	0	6
Umenyiora	0	0	1	0/0	0/0	0	6
Weatherspoon	0	0	1	0/0	0/0	0	6
Falcons	11	26	3	39/39	24/27	0	353
Opponents	14	31	4	47/47	34/35	0	443

2-Pt Conversions: Gonzalez.
Falcons 1-1, Opponents 0-2.

RUSHING

	No.	Yds	Avg	LG	TD
Jackson	157	543	3.5	50	6
Jac. Rodgers	96	332	3.5	19t	2
Snelling	44	164	3.7	17	1
A. Smith	5	145	29.0	50t	2
Ryan	17	55	3.2	17	0
J. Jones	1	7	7.0	7	0
Vaughan	1	1	1.0	1	0
Falcons	321	1247	3.9	50t	11
Opponents	455	2173	4.8	80t	14

RECEIVING

	No.	Yds	Avg	LG	TD
Douglas	85	1067	12.6	80t	2
Gonzalez	83	859	10.3	25	8
White	63	711	11.3	39t	3
Jac. Rodgers	52	341	6.6	22	2
J. Jones	41	580	14.1	81t	2
Jackson	33	191	5.8	25	1
Snelling	29	216	7.4	34	3
D. Johnson	22	210	9.5	17	1
Dr. Davis	12	216	18.0	59	2
Toilolo	11	55	5.0	12	2
DiMarco	8	49	6.1	12	0
Ewing	2	29	14.5	15	0
A. Smith	2	10	5.0	6	0
Cone	1	12	12.0	12	0
Vaughan	1	-5	-5.0	-5	0
Falcons	445	4541	10.2	81t	26
Opponents	341	4128	12.1	67	31

INTERCEPTIONS

	No.	Yds	Avg	LG	TD
Moore	3	36	12.0	19	0
Alford	2	0	0.0	0	0
Trufant	2	0	0.0	0	0
Weatherspoon	1	71	71.0	71t	1
Umenyiora	1	68	68.0	68t	1
Samuel	1	1	1.0	1	0
Falcons	10	176	17.6	71t	2
Opponents	17	215	12.6	89t	4

PUNTING

	No.	Yds.	Avg.	In 20	LG
Bosher	68	3166	46.6	26	63
Falcons	70	3166	45.2	26	63
Opponents	62	2898	46.7	19	64

PUNT RETURNS

	Ret	FC	Yds	Avg	LG	TD
McClain	19	9	193	10.2	25	0
Douglas	10	3	57	5.7	15	0
Alford	1	1	0	0.0	0	0
Falcons	30	13	250	8.3	25	0
Opponents	33	23	251	7.6	32	0

KICKOFF RETURNS

	No.	Yds	Avg	LG	TD
Jac. Rodgers	25	575	23.0	34	0
Snelling	1	23	23.0	23	0
DiMarco	1	21	21.0	21	0
A. Smith	0	40	—	40	0
Falcons	27	659	24.4	50	0
Opponents	23	571	24.8	36	0

FIELD GOALS

	1-19	20-29	30-39	40-49	50+
Bryant	0/0	9/9	7/8	5/5	3/5
Falcons	0/0	9/9	7/8	5/5	3/5
Opponents	0/0	7/7	12/12	12/12	3/4

SACKS

	No.
Umenyiora	7.5
Peters	5.0
Massaquoi	4.0
Bartu	3.5
Jerry	3.5
Moore	2.0
Worrilow	2.0
Dent	1.5
Babineaux	1.0
McClain	1.0
Nicholas	1.0
Falcons	32.0
Opponents	44.0

RECORD HOLDERS
INDIVIDUAL RECORDS—CAREER

Category	Name	Performance
Rushing (Yds.)	Gerald Riggs, 1982-88	6,631
Passing (Yds.)	Steve Bartkowski, 1975-1985	23,470
Passing (TDs)	Steve Bartkowski, 1975-1985	154
Receiving (No.)	Roddy White, 2005-2013	685
Receiving (Yds.)	Roddy White, 2005-2013	9,436
Interceptions	Rolland Lawrence, 1973-1980	39
Punting (Avg.)	Matt Bosher, 2011-13	45.5
Punt Return (Avg.)	Darrien Gordon, 2001	14.1
Kickoff Return (Avg.)	Darrick Vaughn, 2000-01	25.7
Field Goals	Morten Andersen, 1995-2000, 2006-07	184
Touchdowns (Tot.)	Michael Turner, 2008-2012	61
Points	Morten Andersen, 1995-2000, 2006-07	806
Sacks*	John Abraham, 2006-2012	68.5

INDIVIDUAL RECORDS—SINGLE SEASON

Category	Name	Performance
Rushing (Yds.)	Jamal Anderson, 1998	1,846
Passing (Yds.)	Matt Ryan, 2012	4,719
Passing (TDs)	Matt Ryan, 2012	32
Receiving (No.)	Roddy White, 2010	115
Receiving (Yds.)	Roddy White, 2010	1,389
Interceptions	Scott Case, 1988	10
Punting (Avg.)	Matt Ryan, 2012	47.5
Punt Return (Avg.)	Darrien Gordon, 2001	14.1
Kickoff Return (Avg.)	Darrick Vaughn, 2000	27.7
Field Goals	Matt Bryant, 2012	33
Touchdowns (Tot.)	Michael Turner, 2008	17
Points	Matt Bryant, 2012	143
Sacks*	John Abraham, 2008	16.5

INDIVIDUAL RECORDS—SINGLE GAME

Category	Name	Performance
Rushing (Yds.)	Michael Turner, 9-7-08	220
Passing (Yds.)	Chris Chandler, 12-23-01	431
Passing (TDs)	Wade Wilson, 12-13-92	5
Receiving (No.)	William Andrews, 11-15-81	15
Receiving (Yds.)	Roddy White, 10-11-09	210
Interceptions	Many times	2
	Last time by William Moore, 11-29-12	
Field Goals	Norm Johnson, 11-13-94	6
Touchdowns (Tot.)	T.J. Duckett, 12-12-04	4
	Michael Turner, 11-23-08	4
Points	T.J. Duckett, 12-12-04	24
	Michael Turner, 11-23-08	24
Sacks*	Chuck Smith, 10-12-97	5.0

*Sacks became an official statistic in 1982.

2014 VETERAN ROSTER

No.	Name	Pos.	Ht.	Wt.	Birthdate	NFL Exp.	College	Hometown	How Acq.	'13 Games/ Starts
23	Alford, Robert	CB	5-10	186	11/1/88	2	Southeast Louisiana	Hammond, La.	D2-'13	16/4
28	Arenas, Javier	CB	5-9	197	10/28/87	5	Alabama	Tampa, Fla.	UFA(Ariz)-'14	16/0*
75	Asamoah, Jon	G	6-4	305	7/21/88	5	Illinois	Park Forest, Ill.	UFA(KC)-'14	14/9*
95	Babineaux, Jonathan	DT	6-2	300	10/12/81	10	Iowa	Port Arthur, Texas	D2-'05	16/16
72	Baker, Sam	T	6-5	301	5/30/85	7	Southern California	Tustin, Calif.	D1b-'08	4/4
59	Bartu, Joplo	LB	6-2	230	10/3/90	2	Texas State	Waller, Texas	FA-'13	16/13
71	Biermann, Kroy	DE	6-3	255	9/12/85	7	Montana	Hardin, Mont.	D5b-'08	2/2
63	Blalock, Justin	G	6-4	326	12/20/83	8	Texas	Dallas, Texas	D2a-'07	16/16
5	Bosher, Matt	P	6-0	208	10/18/87	4	Miami	Jupiter, Fla.	D6-'11	16/0
3	Bryant, Matt	K	5-9	203	5/29/75	13	Baylor	Orange, Texas	FA-'09	16/0
68	Carimi, Gabe	OL	6-7	316	6/13/88	4	Wisconsin	Lake Forest, Ill.	FA-'14	14/3*
4	Davis, Dominique	QB	6-3	210	7/17/89	3	East Carolina	Lakeland, Fla.	FA-'12	1/0
19	Davis, Drew	WR	6-1	205	1/4/89	3	Oregon	Denver, Colo.	FA-'12	16/3
52	Dent, Akeem	LB	6-1	239	9/24/87	4	Georgia	Atlanta, Ga.	D3-'11	15/7
42	DiMarco, Patrick	FB	6-1	234	4/30/89	3	South Carolina	Altamonte Springs, Fla.	FA-'13	14/7
83	Douglas, Harry	WR	6-0	183	9/16/84	6	Louisville	Jonesboro, Ga.	D3b-'08	16/11
93	Goodman, Malliciah	DE	6-4	276	1/4/90	2	Clemson	Florence, S.C.	D4a-'13	14/1
69	Gunn, Harland	G	6-2	310	8/30/89	2	Miami	Omaha, Neb.	FA-'12	3/0
47	Harris, Josh	LS	6-1	224	4/27/89	3	Auburn	Carrollton, Ga.	FA-'12	16/0
61	Hawley, Joe	C	6-3	302	10/22/88	5	Nevada-Las Vegas	Yorba Linda, Calif.	D4-'10	16/7
17	Hester, Devin	WR	5-11	190	11/4/82	9	Miami	Riviera Beach, Fla.	UFA(Chi)-'14	16/0*
76	Holmes, Lamar	T	6-6	333	7/8/89	3	Southern Mississippi	Gastonia, N.C.	D3-'12	16/15
36	Ishmael, Kemal	S	6-0	206	5/6/91	2	Central Florida	Miami, Fla.	D7a-'13	4/0
39	Jackson, Steven	RB	6-2	240	7/22/83	11	Oregon State	Las Vegas, Nev.	FA-'13	12/12
99	Jackson, Tyson	DE	6-4	296	6/6/86	6	Louisiana State	Edgard, La.	UFA(KC)-'14	15/9*
97	Jerry, Peria	DT	6-2	295	10/23/84	6	Mississippi	Batesville, Miss.	D1-'09	16/14
13	Johnson, Darius	WR	5-10	175	2/22/91	2	Southern Methodist	Missouri City, Texas	FA-'13	10/2
79	Johnson, Mike	OL	6-6	304	4/2/87	4	Alabama	Pensacola, Fla.	D3b-'10	0*
11	Jones, Julio	WR	6-3	220	2/3/89	4	Alabama	Foley, Ala.	D1-'11	5/5
74	Jones, Terren	T	6-7	341	11/19/91	2	Alabama State	Ft. Walton Beach, Fla.	FA-'13	0*
66	Konz, Peter	C	6-5	317	12/20/89	3	Wisconsin	Neehan, Wisc.	D2-'12	16/15
20	Lowery, Dwight	S	5-11	212	1/23/86	7	San Jose State	Santa Cruz, Calif.	FA-'14	3/3*
90	Maponga, Stansly	DE	6-2	265	3/5/91	2	Texas Christian	Carrollton, Texas	D5-'13	12/0
94	Massaquoi, Jonathan	DE	6-2	264	5/18/88	3	Troy	Lawrenceville, Ga.	D5b-'12	16/4
98	Matthews, Cliff	DE	6-4	268	8/5/89	4	South Carolina	Cheraw, S.C.	D7b-'11	15/0
27	McClain, Robert	CB	5-9	195	7/22/88	5	Connecticut	Philadelphia, Pa.	FA-'12	16/6
25	Moore, William	S	6-0	221	5/18/85	5	Missouri	Hayti, Mo.	D2-'09	16/16
22	Motta, Zeke	S	6-2	215	5/14/90	2	Notre Dame	Vero Beach, Fla.	D7b-'13	10/1
86	Pascoe, Bear	TE	6-5	265	2/23/86	6	Fresno State	Porterville, Calif.	UFA(NYG)-'14	16/6*
91	Peters, Corey	DT	6-3	305	6/8/88	5	Kentucky	Louisville, Kent.	D3a-'10	15/15
12	Renfree, Sean	QB	6-5	225	4/28/90	2	Duke	Scottsdale, Ariz.	D7c-'13	0*
92	Robertson, Travian	DT	6-4	304	12/9/88	3	South Carolina	Laurinburg, N.C.	D7-'12	5/0
32	Rodgers, Jacquizz	RB	5-6	196	2/6/90	4	Oregon State	Richmond, Texas	D5-'11	15/4
2	Ryan, Matt	QB	6-4	217	5/17/85	7	Boston College	Exton, Pa.	D1a-'08	16/16
73	Schraeder, Ryan	T	6-7	300	5/4/88	2	Valdosta State	Wichita, Kan.	FA-'13	13/4
82	Shuler, Mickey	TE	6-4	247	10/9/86	4	Penn State	Enola, Pa.	FA-'13	0*
35	Smith, Antone	RB	5-9	192	9/17/85	5	Florida State	Pahokee, Fla.	FA-'09	15/0
96	Soliai, Paul	DT	6-4	345	12/30/83	8	Utah	Pago Pago, American Samoa	FA-'14	15/15*
85	Szczerba, Andrew	TE	6-6	256	7/16/88	2	Penn State	Wilmington, Del.	FA-'13	0*
80	Toilolo, Levine	TE	6-8	265	7/30/91	2	Stanford	La Mesa, Calif.	D4b-'13	16/3
21	Trufant, Desmond	CB	6-0	190	9/10/90	2	Washington	Tacoma, Wash.	D1-'13	16/16
50	Umenyiora, Osi	DE	6-3	255	11/16/81	12	Troy	London, England	FA-'13	16/13
30	Vaughan, Josh	RB	6-0	225	12/3/86	4	Richmond	Richmond, Va.	FA-'12	6/0
56	Weatherspoon, Sean	LB	6-2	244	12/29/87	5	Missouri	Jasper, Texas	D1-'10	7/7
84	White, Roddy	WR	6-0	211	11/2/81	10	Alabama-Birmingham	James Island, S.C.	D1-'05	13/13
26	Wilson, Josh	CB	5-9	188	3/11/85	8	Maryland	Upper Marlboro, Md.	UFA(Wash)-'14	16/16*
55	Worrilow, Paul	LB	6-0	230	5/1/90	2	Delaware	Wilmington, Del.	FA-'13	16/12

* Arenas played 16 games with Arizona in '13; Asamoah played 14 games with Kansas City; Carimi played 14 games with Tampa Bay; Hester played 16 games with Chicago; T. Jackson played 15 games with Kansas City; M. Johnson missed '13 season because of injury; T. Jones inactive five games; Lowery played three games with Jacksonville; Pascoe played 16 games with the New York Giants; Renfree missed '13 season because of injury; Shuler last active with Miami in '10; Soliai played 15 games with Miami; Szczerba missed '13 season because of injury; Wilson played 16 games with Washington.

Also played with Falcons in '13—LB Jamar Chaney (1 game), LB Chase Coffman (11), WR Kevin Cone (16), FB Bradie Ewing (2), CB Dominique Franks (16), LB Omar Gaither (8), TE Tony Gonzalez (16), LB Thomas Howard (2), OLB Stephen Nicholas (14), G Garrett Reynolds (15), CB Asante Samuel (11), DB Shann Schillinger (5), RB Jason Snelling (14), T Jeremy Trueblood (15),

FIRST-YEAR ROSTER

Name	Pos.	Ht.	Wt.	Birthdate	College	Hometown	How Acq.
Allen, Ricardo	CB	5-9	186	12/18/91	Purdue	Daytona Beach, Fla.	D5a
Baker, Sean (1)	S	6-0	209	11/6/88	Ball State	Youngstown, Ohio	FA-'13
Boldewijn, Geraldo	WR	6-4	220	2/14/91	Boise State	Boise, Idaho	FA
Croom, Dominique (1)	WR	6-0	190	4/26/91	Central Arkansas	Cleveland, Ala.	FA-'13
Daley, Brenden	LB	6-3	250	5/30/91	Hawaii	Moorpark, Calif.	FA
Eguae, Nosa	DE	6-3	269	8/15/91	Auburn	Mansfield, Texas	FA
Freeman, Devonta	RB	5-8	206	3/15/92	Florida State	Miami, Fla.	D4a
Glover-Wright, Devonta	CB	6-0	175	6/28/92	Utah State	Smyrna, Ga.	FA
Hageman, Ra'Shede	DE	6-6	318	8/8/90	Minnesota	Minneapolis, Minn.	D2
Hagens, Maurice	FB	5-11	250	6/28/92	Miami	Riverview, Fla.	FA
Jones, Julian	WR	6-0	202	3/26/91	Arkansas State	Memphis, Tenn.	FA
Mabin, Jordan (1)	CB	5-11	180	10/31/88	Northwestern	Northfield Center, Ohio	FA-'13
Martino, Freddie	WR	6-0	195	9/7/91	North Greenville	North, S.C.	FA
Mathews, Jeff	QB	6-4	229	8/25/91	Cornell	Camarillo, Calif.	FA
Matthews, Jake	T	6-5	309	2/11/92	Texas A&M	Missouri City, Texas	D1
May, Walker	OLB	6-5	250	9/4/90	Vanderbilt	Birmingham, Ala.	FA
McFadden, Kimario	S	5-11	197	4/13/91	South Carolina State	Riverdale, Ga.	FA
Nix, Roosevelt	FB	5-11	260	3/30/92	Kent State	Reynoldsburg, Ohio	FA
Pedersen, Jacob	TE	6-5	240	4/27/91	Wisconsin	Menominee, Mich.	FA
Reedy, Bernard	WR	5-9	175	12/31/91	Toledo	St. Petersburg, Fla.	FA
Replogle, Adam (1)	OL	6-3	294	10/10/90	Indiana	Centerville, Ohio	FA-'13
Rumph, Donte	DT	6-3	320	1/15/90	Kentucky	St. Matthews, S.C.	FA
Shembo, Prince	LB	6-0	253	12/24/91	Notre Dame	Charlotte, N.C.	D4b
Smallwood, Yawin	LB	6-4	236	12/25/91	Connecticut	Worcester, Mass.	D7a
Smith, Jacques	OLB	6-2	258	12/31/91	Tennessee	Chattanooga, Tenn.	FA
Smith, Jerome	RB	6-0	226	4/6/91	Syracuse	Bear, Del.	FA
Southward, Dezmen	S	6-2	210	10/1/91	Wisconsin	Sunrise, Fla.	D3
Spruill, Marquis	LB	6-0	224	5/14/91	Syracuse	Hillside, N.J.	D5b
Starr, Tyler	LB	6-5	250	1/25/91	South Dakota	Little Rock, Iowa	D7b
Stone, James	C	6-3	291	4/26/92	Tennessee	Nashville, Tenn.	FA
Thompson, Tramaine	WR	5-8	167	4/10/90	Kansas State	Jenks, Okla.	FA
Wozniak, Brian	TE	6-4	255	8/9/90	Wisconsin	Loveland, Ohio	FA
Yoklic, Matt	P	6-4	220	10/10/90	Pittsburgh	Gibsonia, Pa.	FA

The term NFL Rookie is defined as a player who is in his first season of professional football and has not been on the roster of another professional football team for any regular-season or postseason games. A Rookie is designated by an "R" on NFL rosters. Players who have been active in another professional football league or players who have NFL experience, including either preseason training camp or being on an Active List or Inactive List, or on Reserve/Injured or Reserve/Physically Unable to Perform for fewer than six regular-season games, are termed NFL First-Year Players. An NFL First-Year Player is designated by a "1" on NFL rosters. Thereafter, a player is credited with an additional year of experience for each season in which he accumulates six games on the Active List or Inactive List, or on Reserve/Injured or Reserve/Physically Unable to Perform.

Log on to www.atlantafalcons.com for an up-to-date roster.

COACHING STAFF

Head Coach,
Mike Smith

Pro Career: Mike Smith was named the 14th head coach in Atlanta Falcons franchise history on January 23, 2008. In six seasons with the team, he has compiled a 60-36 regular-season record, three playoff appearances and, for the first time in franchise history, four consecutive winning seasons. His .688 winning percentage is the best in team history over a three-year period (2010-12). Smith's 33 wins are easily the most victories by a Falcons head coach in his first three years on the job. Smith's club posted the NFC's top record at 13-3 in both 2010 and 2012. When Smith's charges captured the NFC South title in 2010, it was only the fourth Division crown in franchise history (and first since 2004) and the eight consecutive victories in 2010 was the second longest streak ever. In 2008, Smith guided the Falcons to an 11-5 record, marking a seven-win turnaround from the previous season. For his efforts, he was named the Associated Press and *Sporting News* NFL Coach of the Year. From 2003-07, Smith served as the defensive coordinator for the Jacksonville Jaguars following a four-year stint with the Baltimore Ravens from 1999-2002, which included the team's 2000 Super Bowl season. Prior to the NFL, Smith coached at San Diego State (1982-85), Morehead State (1986), and Tennessee Tech (1987-1998). Career record: 61-40.

Background: Played linebacker for the CFL's Winnipeg Blue Bombers (1982). He played at East Tennessee (1977-1981) and named defensive MVP twice at his position. Led team with 186 tackles as a senior.

Personal: Born November 30, 1959 in Chicago, Ill. Native of Daytona Beach, Florida. He and his wife Julie have one daughter, Logan.

ASSISTANT COACHES

Keith Armstrong, special teams coordinator; born December 15, 1963, Levittown, Pa. Running back Temple 1983-86. No pro playing experience. College coach: Temple 1987, Miami 1988, Akron 1989, Oklahoma State 1990-92, Notre Dame 1993. Pro coach: Atlanta Falcons 1994-96, Chicago Bears 1997-2000, Miami Dolphins 2001-2007, re-joined Falcons 2008.

Jonas Beauchemin, strength and conditioning assistant; born October 11, 1984, Burlington, Vt. Attended Keene State. No college or pro playing experience. Pro coach: Joined Falcons in 2009.

Gerald Brown, running backs; born September 4, 1959, Sweetwater, Tenn. Attended Memphis State. No college or pro playing experience. College coach: Tennessee Tech 1991-2000, Indiana 2002-07. Pro coach: Joined Falcons in 2008.

Mark Collins, outside linebackers; born August 30, 1975, Sault Ste. Marie, Mich. Defensive end/outside linebacker East Tennessee State 1995-98. No pro playing experience. College coach: East Tennessee State 1999-2002, Michigan 2003-04, Elon, 2005, Georgia Southern, 2006, Georgia 2007, Louisiana-Monroe 2009. Pro coach: Joined Falcons in 2010.

Bryan Cox, defensive line; born February 17, 1968, East St. Louis, Ill. Linebacker Western Illinois 1987-1990. Pro linebacker Miami Dolphins 1991-95, Chicago Bears 1996-97, New York Jets 1998-2000, New England Patriots 2001, New Orleans Saints 2002. Pro coach: New York Jets 2006-08, Cleveland Browns 2009-2010, Miami Dolphins 2011, Tampa Bay Buccaneers 2012-13, joined Falcons in 2014.

Joe Danna, defensive backs; born April 3, 1977, Midland, Mich. Attended Central Michigan. No college or pro playing experience. College coach: Michigan 1999-2000, Georgia 2001, Central Michigan 2002-05, Georgia Southern 2006, James Madison 2007. Pro coach: Atlanta Falcons 2008-09, Miami Dolphins 2010-11, re-joined Falcons in 2012.

Wade Harman, asst. offensive line; born October 1, 1963, Corydon, Iowa. Linebacker Drake 1985, Utah State 1986. No pro playing experience. College coach: Utah State 1987-1991, Pacific 1992-95, Morningside 1996. Pro coach: Minnesota Vikings 1997-98, Baltimore Ravens 1999-2013, joined Falcons in 2014.

Dirk Koetter, offensive coordinator; born February 5, 1959, Pocatello, Idaho. Quarterback Idaho State 1978-1981. No pro playing experience. College coach: San Francisco State 1985, Texas El-Paso 1986-88, Missouri 1989-1993, Boston College 1994-95, Oregon 1996-97, Boise State 1998-2000 (head coach), Arizona State 2001-06 (head coach). Pro coach: Jacksonville Jaguars 2007-2011, joined Falcons in 2012.

Tim Lewis, secondary; born December 18, 1961, Quakertown, Pa. Cornerback Pittsburgh 1979-1982. Pro cornerback Green Bay Packers 1983-86. Pro coach: Pittsburgh Steelers 1995-2003, New York Giants 2004-06, Carolina Panthers 2007-08, Seattle Seahawks 2009, joined Falcons in 2010.

A.J. Neibel, head strength and conditioning; born August 31, 1972, Cupertino, Calif. Attended Long Beach State. No college or pro playing experience. Pro coach: Oakland Raiders 2003-09, joined Falcons in 2011.

Mike Nolan, defensive coordinator; born March 7, 1965, Haverhill, Mass. Safety Oregon 1978-1980. No pro playing experience. College coach: Oregon 1981, Stanford 1982-83, Rice 1984-85, Louisiana State 1986. Pro coach: Denver Broncos 1987-1992, 2009, New York Giants 1993-96, Washington Redskins 1997-99, New York Jets 2000, Baltimore Ravens 2001-04, San Francisco 49ers 2005-08 (head coach), Miami Dolphins 2010-11, joined Falcons in 2012.

Glenn Pires, linebackers; born September 13, 1958, New Bedford, Mass. Offensive lineman Springfield College 1976-79. No pro playing experience. College coach: Dartmouth 1985-88, Syracuse 1989-1994, Michigan State 1995. Pro coach: Arizona Cardinals 1996-2000, Detroit Lions 2001-02, Miami Dolphins 2003-07, joined Falcons in 2008.

Terry Robiskie, asst. head coach/wide receivers; born November 12, 1954, New Orleans, La. Running back Louisiana State 1973-76. Pro running back Oakland Raiders 1977-79, Miami Dolphins 1980-81. Pro coach: Los Angeles Raiders 1982-1993, Washington Redskins 1994-2000 (interim head coach 2000), Cleveland Browns 2001-06 (interim head coach 2004), Miami Dolphins 2007, joined Falcons in 2008.

Chris Scelfo, tight ends; born September 30, 1963, New Iberia, La. Center Northeast Louisiana 1981-84. No pro playing experience. College coach: Northeast Louisiana 1986-87, Oklahoma 1988-89, Marshall 1990-95, Georgia 1996-98, Tulane 1998-2006. Pro coach: Joined Falcons in 2008.

Eric Sutulovich, asst. special teams; born February 28, 1974, Kansas City, Kan. Tight end Louisiana Tech 1993-95. No pro playing experience. College coach: Louisiana Tech 1997-99, Pittsburgh 2000, Kansas 2006. Pro coach: Houston Texans 2002-05, Detroit Lions 2008, joined Falcons in 2009.

Glenn Thomas, quarterbacks; born September 22, 1977, Eastland, Texas. Attended Texas Tech. No college or pro playing experience. College coach: Texas Tech 1998-2001, Midwestern State 2001-07. Pro coach: Joined Falcons in 2008.

Andrew Thacker, defensive assistant; Safety Furman 2006-09. No pro playing experience. College coach: Central Florida 2010-11, Oklahoma State 2012, Southern Mississippi 2013. Pro coach: Joined Falcons in 2014.

Mike Tice, offensive line; born February 2, 1959, Bay Shore, N.Y. Quarterback Maryland 1977-1980. Pro tight end Seattle Seahawks 1981-88, 1990-91, Washington Redskins 1989, Minnesota Vikings 1992-93, 1995. Pro coach: Minnesota Vikings 1996-2005 (head coach 2001-05), Jacksonville Jaguars 2006-09, Chicago Bears 2010-12, joined Falcons in 2014.

Andrew Weidinger, offensive assistant; born July 10, 1982, Phoenix, Ariz. Attended Arizona. No college or pro playing experience. Pro coach: Joined Falcons in 2008.

National Football Conference
South Division
Team Colors: Black, Panther Blue, and
Silver
800 South Mint Street
Charlotte, North Carolina 28202-1502
Telephone: (704) 358-7000

2014 SCHEDULE
PRESEASON
Aug. 8   **Buffalo** 7:30
Aug. 17 **Kansas City** 8:00
Aug. 22 at New England 7:30
Aug. 28 at Pittsburgh.......................7:30

REGULAR SEASON
Sep. 7   at Tampa Bay 4:25
Sep. 14 **Detroit** 1:00
Sep. 21 **Pittsburgh** 8:30
Sep. 28 at Baltimore 1:00
Oct. 5   **Chicago** 1:00
Oct. 12 at Cincinnati 1:00
Oct. 19 at Green Bay 1:00
Oct. 26 **Seattle** 1:00
Oct. 30 **New Orleans** (Thu) 8:25
Nov. 10 at Philadelphia (Mon).........8:30
Nov. 16 **Atlanta** 1:00
Nov. 23 BYE
Nov. 30 at Minnesota 1:00
Dec. 7   at New Orleans 1:00
Dec. 14 **Tampa Bay** 1:00
Dec. 21 **Cleveland** 1:00
Dec. 28 at Atlanta 1:00
All times ET

Stadium: Bank of America Stadium
(opened in 1996)
• **Capacity:** 73,778
Charlotte, North Carolina
28202-1502
Playing Surface: Grass
Training Camp: Wofford College
Spartanburg,
South Carolina 29303

BANK OF AMERICA STADIUM

CLUB OFFICIALS
Owner/Founder: Jerry Richardson
President, Panthers Football LLC:
Danny Morrison
General Manager: Dave Gettleman
General Counsel: Richard Thigpen
Chief Financial Officer: Dave Olsen
Chief Revenue Officer: Phil Youtsey
Executive Office Director: Tina Becker
Director of Finance: Mike Dudan
Controller: Kristi Coleman
Director of Human Resources:
Larry Griffin
Director of Pro Scouting: Mark Koncz
Director of College Scouting:
Don Gregory
Pro Scouts: Matt Allen, Clyde Powers,
Don Warren
College Scouts: Jeff Beathard,
Ryan Cowden, Khary Darlington,
Robert Haines, Jeff Morrow,
John Peterson, Mike Szabo
Director of Communications:
Charlie Dayton
Assistant Director of Communications:
Steven Drummond
Director of Ticketing: Chrystal Rowe
Director of Community Relations and
Cheerleader/Mascot Programs:
Riley Fields
Director of Sponsor Sales and Services:
John Berger
Director of Broadcast Administration:
Henry Thomas
Executive Producer-Television:
Greg Brannon
Executive Producer-Radio: David Langton
Director of Team Administration:
Rob Rogers
Director of Football Operations:
Brandon Beane
Video Director: Mark Hobbs
Assistant Video Director: Jeff Mueller
Head Trainer: Ryan Vermillion
Assistant Trainer: Mark Shermansky
Equipment Manager: Jackie Miles
Assistant Equipment Manager: Don Toner
Director of Security: Lance Emory
Stadium Operations Manager: Scott Paul
Director of PantherVision: Kyle Ritchie
Facility Manager: Matthew Getz
Head Groundskeeper: Tom Vaughan

COACHING HISTORY
(150-165-0)
Records include postseason games
1995-98   Dom Capers 31-35-0
1999-2001 George Seifert 16-32-0
2002-2010 John Fox....................78-74-0
2011-13   Ron Rivera.................25-24-0

PAID ATTENDANCE
Home 575,693   Away 484,756
Total 1,060,449
Single-game home record,
76,136 (12/10/95)
Single-season home record, 579,192
(2006)

2014 DRAFT CHOICES
Round	Name	Pos.	College
1	Kelvin Benjamin	WR	Florida St.
2	Kony Ealy	DE	Missouri
3	Trai Turner	G	Louisiana St.
4	Tre Boston	DB	North Carolina
5	Bene' Benwikere	DB	San Jose St.
6	Tyler Gaffney	RB	Stanford

CAROLINA PANTHERS

2013 TEAM RECORD

PRESEASON (3-1)

Date	Result	Opponent
08/09	W 24-17	Chicago
08/15	L 9-14	at Philadelphia
08/22	W 34-27	at Baltimore
08/29	W 25-10	Pittsburgh

REGULAR SEASON (12-4)

Date	Result	Opponent
09/08	L 7-12	Seattle
09/15	L 23-24	at Buffalo
09/22	W 38-0	New York Giants
10/06	L 6-22	at Arizona
10/13	W 35-10	at Minnesota
10/20	W 30-15	St. Louis
10/24	W 31-13	at Tampa Bay
11/03	W 34-10	Atlanta
11/10	W 10-9	at San Francisco
11/18	W 24-20	New England
11/24	W 20-16	at Miami
12/01	W 27-6	Tampa Bay
12/08	L 13-31	at New Orleans
12/15	W 30-20	New York Jets
12/22	W 17-13	New Orleans
12/29	W 21-20	at Atlanta

POSTSEASON (0-1)

Date	Result	Opponent
01/12	L 10-23	San Francisco

SCORE BY PERIODS

Panthers	64	115	86	101	0	—	366
Opponents	31	79	54	77	0	—	241

2013 TEAM STATISTICS

	Panthers	Opp.
Total First Downs	319	278
Rushing	122	70
Passing	169	178
Penalty	28	30
3rd Down: Made/Att	91/208	76/212
3rd Down Pct.	43.8	35.8
4th Down: Made/Att	10/13	3/11
4th Down Pct.	76.9	27.3
Possession Avg.	31:54	28:06
Total Net Yards	5069	4820
Avg. Per Game	316.8	301.3
Total Plays	999	975
Avg. Per Play	5.1	4.9
Net Yards Rushing	2026	1391
Avg. Per Game	126.6	86.9
Total Rushes	483	352
Net Yards Passing	3043	3429
Avg. Per Game	190.2	214.3
Sacked/Yards Lost	43/336	60/424
Gross Yards	3379	3853
Att./Completions	473/292	563/375
Completion Pct.	61.7	66.6
Had Intercepted	13	20
Punts/Average	70/47.8	73/45.5
Net Punting Avg.	70/41.6	73/40.6
Penalties/Yards	80/671	84/753
Fumbles/Ball Lost	12/6	17/10
Touchdowns	42	21
Rushing	14	4
Passing	24	17
Returns	4	0

2013 INDIVIDUAL STATISTICS

PASSING	Att.	Comp.	Yds.	Pct.	TD	Int.	Tkld.	Rate
Newton	473	292	3379	61.7	24	13	43/336	88.8
Panthers	473	292	3379	61.7	24	13	43/336	88.8
Opponents	563	375	3853	66.6	17	20	60/424	81.4

SCORING	TD R	TD P	TD Rt	PAT	FG	Saf	PTS
Gano	0	0	0	42/42	24/27	0	114
Tolbert	5	2	0	0/0	0/0	0	42
Newton	6	0	0	0/0	0/0	0	36
Olsen	0	6	0	0/0	0/0	0	36
Ginn	0	5	0	0/0	0/0	0	30
LaFell	0	5	0	0/0	0/0	0	30
S. Smith	0	4	0	0/0	0/0	0	24
D. Williams	3	1	0	0/0	0/0	0	24
Munnerlyn	0	0	2	0/0	0/0	0	12
Florence	0	0	1	0/0	0/0	0	6
Hixon	0	1	0	0/0	0/0	0	6
White	0	0	1	0/0	0/0	0	6
Panthers	14	24	4	42/42	24/27	0	366
Opponents	4	17	0	19/19	30/34	2	241

2-Pt Conversions: Panthers 0-0, Opponents 1-2.

RUSHING	No.	Yds	Avg	LG	TD
D. Williams	201	843	4.2	43t	3
Newton	111	585	5.3	56	6
Tolbert	101	361	3.6	22	5
Stewart	48	180	3.8	16	0
Ginn	4	29	7.3	14	0
LaFell	2	15	7.5	9	0
Barner	6	7	1.2	2	0
A. Smith	4	5	1.3	5	0
Brockel	1	1	1.0	1	0
Anderson	5	0	0.0	2	0
Panthers	483	2026	4.2	56	14
Opponents	352	1391	4.0	46	4

RECEIVING	No.	Yds	Avg	LG	TD
Olsen	73	816	11.2	31	6
S. Smith	64	745	11.6	44	4
LaFell	49	627	12.8	79t	5
Ginn	36	556	15.4	47t	5
Tolbert	27	184	6.8	18	2
D. Williams	26	333	12.8	72t	1
Hixon	7	55	7.9	14t	1
Stewart	7	44	6.3	16	0
Barner	2	7	3.5	5	0
Brockel	1	12	12.0	12	0
Panthers	292	3379	11.6	79t	24
Opponents	375	3853	10.3	73	17

INTERCEPTIONS	No.	Yds	Avg	LG	TD
Mitchell	4	63	15.8	38	0
Kuechly	4	33	8.3	30	0
Lester	3	5	1.7	5	0
Munnerlyn	2	86	43.0	45t	2
Florence	2	40	20.0	38t	1
White	2	9	4.5	8t	1
Davis	2	-2	-1.0	0	0
Thomas	1	0	0.0	0	0
Panthers	20	234	11.7	45t	4
Opponents	13	204	15.7	43	0

PUNTING	No.	Yds.	Avg.	In 20	LG
Nortman	70	3344	47.8	25	72
Panthers	70	3344	47.8	25	72
Opponents	73	3321	45.5	19	69

PUNT RETURNS	Ret	FC	Yds	Avg	LG	TD
Ginn	26	26	316	12.2	41	0
Brockel	1	0	0	0.0	0	0
Florence	1	0	0	0.0	0	0
LaFell	1	0	0	0.0	0	0
Thomas	1	0	0	0.0	0	0
Panthers	30	26	316	10.5	41	0
Opponents	36	13	335	9.3	23	0

KICKOFF RETURNS	No.	Yds	Avg	LG	TD
Ginn	25	595	23.8	38	0
Barner	2	17	8.5	17	0
Blackburn	1	0	0.0	0	0
Panthers	28	612	21.9	38	0
Opponents	18	407	22.6	34	0

FIELD GOALS	1-19	20-29	30-39	40-49	50+
Gano	0/0	9/9	4/5	5/7	6/6
Panthers	0/0	9/9	4/5	5/7	6/6
Opponents	1/1	10/10	3/4	11/13	5/6

SACKS	No.
Hardy	15.0
Johnson	11.0
Davis	4.0
Mitchell	3.5
Munnerlyn	3.5
D. Edwards	3.0
Lotulelei	3.0
Mikell	3.0
Addison	2.5
Horton	2.0
Klein	2.0
Kuechly	2.0
Short	1.5
Alexander	1.0
Cole	1.0
Godfrey	1.0
(group)	1.0
Panthers.	60.0
Opponents	43.0

RECORD HOLDERS
INDIVIDUAL RECORDS—CAREER

Category	Name	Performance
Rushing (Yds.)	DeAngelo Williams, 2006-2013	6,627
Passing (Yds.)	Jake Delhomme, 2003-09	19,258
Passing (TDs)	Jake Delhomme, 2003-09	120
Receiving (No.)	Steve Smith, 2001-2013	836
Receiving (Yds.)	Steve Smith, 2001-2013	12,197
Interceptions	Chris Gamble, 2004-2012	27
Punting (Avg.)	Todd Sauerbrun, 2001-04	45.5
Punt Return (Avg.)	Winslow Oliver, 1996-98	10.7
Kickoff Return (Avg.)	Michael Bates, 1996-2000	25.7
Field Goals	John Kasay, 1995-2010	351
Touchdowns (Tot.)	Steve Smith, 2001-2013	75
Points	John Kasay, 1995-2010	1,482
*Sacks	Julius Peppers, 2002-09	81.0

INDIVIDUAL RECORDS—SINGLE SEASON

Category	Name	Performance
Rushing (Yds.)	DeAngelo Williams, 2008	1,515
Passing (Yds.)	Steve Beuerlein, 1999	4,436
Passing (TDs)	Steve Beuerlein, 1999	36
Receiving (No.)	Steve Smith, 2005	103
Receiving (Yds.)	Steve Smith, 2005	1,563
Interceptions	Doug Evans, 2001	8
Punting (Avg.)	Brad Nortman, 2013	47.8
Punt Return (Avg.)	Ted Ginn, Jr., 2013	12.2
Kickoff Return (Avg.)	Michael Bates, 1996	30.2
Field Goals	John Kasay, 1996	37
Touchdowns (Tot.)	DeAngelo Williams, 2008	20
Points	John Kasay, 1996	145
*Sacks	Kevin Greene, 1998	15.0
	Greg Hardy, 2013	15.0

INDIVIDUAL RECORDS—SINGLE GAME

Category	Name	Performance
Rushing (Yds.)	DeAngelo Williams, 12-30-12	210
Passing (Yds.)	Cam Newton, 9-18-11	432
Passing (TDs)	Steve Beuerlein, 1-2-00	5
Receiving (No.)	Steve Smith, 11-20-05	14
Receiving (Yds.)	Steve Smith, 10-30-05	201
Interceptions	Deon Grant, 9-22-02	3
Field Goals	John Kasay, 12-5-04	6
Touchdowns (Tot.)	DeAngelo Williams, 11-30-08, 12-21-08	4
Points	DeAngelo Williams, 11-30-08, 12-21-08	24
*Sacks	Greg Hardy, 12-29-13	4.0

*Sacks became an official statistic in 1982.

2014 VETERAN ROSTER

No.	Name	Pos.	Ht.	Wt.	Birthdate	NFL Exp.	College	Hometown	How Acq.	'13 Games/ Starts
97	Addison, Mario	DE	6-3	260	9/6/87	4	Troy	Tarrant, Ala.	FA-'12	16/2
90	Alexander, Frank	DE	6-4	270	12/17/89	3	Oklahoma	Baton Rouge, La.	D4a-'12	12/3
3	Anderson, Derek	QB	6-6	240	6/15/83	10	Oregon State	Scappoose, Ore	FA-'11	4/0
81	Avant, Jason	WR	6-0	210	4/20/83	9	Michigan	Chicago, Ill.	FA-'14	16/13*
25	Barner, Kenjon	RB	5-9	190	4/28/89	2	Oregon	Sherman Oaks, Calif.	D6-'13	8/0
77	Bell, Byron	T	6-5	340	1/17/89	4	New Mexico	Greenville, Texas	FA-'11	16/14
93	Blackburn, Chase	LB	6-3	245	6/10/83	10	Akron	Marysville, Ohio	UFA(NYG)-'13	13/7
47	Brockel, Richie	TE/FB	6-1	255	7/24/86	4	Boise State	Phoenix, Ariz.	FA-'11	16/0
73	#Campbell, Bruce	T	6-6	320	5/25/88	5	Maryland	Hamden, Conn.	T(Oak)-'12	0*
20	Cason, Antoine	CB	6-1	195	7/9/86	7	Arizona	Long Beach, Calif.	UFA(Ariz.)-'14	16/0*
78	Chandler, Nate	T	6-4	310	6/1/89	3	UCLA	San Diego, Calif.	FA-'12	16/8
7	#Clausen, Jimmy	QB	6-2	210	9/21/87	5	Notre Dame	Westlake Village, Calif.	D2-'10	0*
91	Cole, Colin	DT	6-2	335	6/24/80	8	Iowa	Fort Lauderdale, Fla.	FA-'13	15/13
55	#Connor, Dan	LB	6-2	240	11/2/85	7	Penn State	Wallingford, Pa.	FA-'13	5/0
82	Cotchery, Jerricho	WR	6-1	200	6/16/82	11	North Carolina State	Birmingham, Ala.	UFA(Pitt)-'14	16/6*
58	Davis, Thomas	LB	6-1	235	3/22/83	10	Georgia	Shellman, Ga.	D1-'05	16/16
21	DeCoud, Thomas	S	6-2	190	3/19/85	7	California	Pinole, Calif.	FA-'14	15/15*
84	Dickson, Ed	TE	6-4	255	7/25/87	5	Oregon	Bellflower, Calif.	UFA(Balt)-'14	16/14*
31	Dockery, James	CB	6-1	185	11/9/88	4	Oregon State	Palm Desert, Calif.	FA-'12	5/0
92	Edwards, Dwan	DT	6-3	305	5/16/81	11	Oregon State	Columbus, Mont.	FA-'12	11/3
29	#Florence, Drayton	CB	6-0	200	12/19/80	12	Tuskegee	Ocala, Fla.	FA-'13	14/5
64	Folkerts, Brian	C	6-4	305	1/30/90	2	Washburn	Florissant, Mo.	FA-'13	10/0
9	Gano, Graham	K	6-2	200	4/9/87	5	Florida State	Cantonment, Fla.	FA-'12	16/0
61	Gaydosh, Linden	DT	6-3	315	1/4/91	2	Calgary	Peace River, Alberta, Canada	FA-'13	0*
30	Godfrey, Charles	CB	5-11	210	11/15/85	7	Iowa	Baytown, Texas	D3a-'08	2/2
50	Hall, Alex	DE	6-5	250	8/17/85	4	St. Augustine's	Glenarden, Md.	FA-'14	0*
76	Hardy, Greg	DE	6-4	290	7/28/88	5	Mississippi	Millington, Tenn.	D6a-'10	16/13
41	Harper, Roman	S	6-1	200	12/11/82	9	Alabama	Prattville, Ala.	FA-'14	9/5
84	#Hartsock, Ben	TE	6-4	265	7/5/80	11	Ohio State	Chillicothe, Ohio	FA-'11	13/2
96	Horton, Wes	DE	6-5	265	1/18/90	2	Southern California	Sherman Oaks, Calif.	FA-'13	10/0
72	Hughes, Kevin	T	6-4	315	8/6/88	2	Southeastern Louisiana	New Orleans, La.	FA-'14	0*
53	Jacobs, Ben	LB	6-4	245	4/17/88	2	Fresno State	Las Vegas, Nev.	FA-'13	0*
44	Jansen, J.J.	LS	6-2	245	1/20/86	7	Notre Dame	Phoenix, Ariz.	T(GB)-'09	16/0
80	Jefferson, D.C.	TE	6-6	255	5/7/89	2	Rutgers	Lake Hamilton, Fla.	FA-'13	4/0*
95	Johnson, Charles	DE	6-2	285	7/10/86	8	Georgia	Hawkinsville, Ga.	D3-'07	14/14
42	Jones, Colin	S	6-0	210	10/27/87	4	Texas Christian	Bridgeport, Texas	T(SF)-'12	16/0
67	Kalil, Ryan	C	6-2	300	3/29/85	8	Southern California	Corona, Calif.	D2b-'07	16/16
12	King, Tavarres	WR	6-1	190	7/14/90	2	Georgia	Mt. Airy, Ga.	W(Den)-'13	0*
56	Klein, A.J.	LB	6-1	245	7/30/91	2	Iowa State	Kimberly, Wis.	D5-'13	16/2
59	Kuechly, Luke	LB	6-3	235	4/20/91	3	Boston College	Cincinnati, Ohio	D1-'12	16/16
71	Kugbila, Edmund	G	6-4	325	9/21/90	2	Valdosta State	Lawrenceville, Ga.	D4-'13	0*
38	Lester, Robert	S	6-1	215	4/30/88	2	Alabama	Foley, Ala.	FA-'13	12/4
98	Lotulelei, Star	DT	6-2	315	12/20/89	2	Utah	South Jordan, Utah	D1-'13	16/16
85	McNeill, Mike	TE	6-4	240	3/7/88	4	Nebraska	St. Louis, Mo.	FA-'14	14/0*
15	McNutt, Marvin	WR	6-2	215	7/4/89	2	Iowa	St. Louis, Mo.	FA-' 13	1/0
26	Menzie, De'Quan	CB	5-11	200	1/1/90	2	Alabama	Columbus, Ga.	FA-'14	0*
27	#Mikell, Quintin	S	5-10	205	9/16/80	12	Boise State	New Orleans, La.	FA-' 13	14/12
73	#Nevis, Drake	DT	6-1	310	5/8/89	4	Louisiana State	Thibodaux, La.	W(Jax)-'14	12/0*
1	Newton, Cam	QB	6-5	245	5/11/89	4	Auburn	College Park, Ga.	D1-'11	16/16
24	Norman, Josh	CB	6-0	200	12/15/87	3	Coastal Carolina	Greenwood, S.C.	D5-'12	7/0
8	Nortman, Brad	P	6-2	210	9/12/89	3	Wisconsin	Brookfield, Wisc.	D6-'12	16/0
88	Olsen, Greg	TE	6-5	255	3/11/85	8	Miami	Wayne, N.J.	T(Chi)-'11	16/16
19	Pilares, Kealoha	WR	5-10	205	2/20/88	4	Hawaii	Honolulu, Hawaii	D5-'11	0*
40	Russell, Anderson	S	6-0	205	5/30/87	3	Ohio State	Atlanta, Ga.	FA-'14	0*
75	Scott, Chris	G	6-4	315	8/4/87	3	Tennessee	Hampton, Ga.	FA-'13	10/8
99	Short, Kawann	DT	6-3	310	2/2/89	2	Purdue	East Chicago, Ind.	D2-'13	16/0
66	Silatolu, Amini	G	6-4	315	9/16/88	3	Midwestern State	Tracy, Calif.	D2-'12	3/3
52	Smith, D.J.	LB	6-0	240	2/24/89	3	Appalachian State	Charlotte, N.C.	FA-'14	1/0*
28	Stewart, Jonathan	RB	5-10	235	3/21/87	7	Oregon	Lacey, Wash.	D1a-'08	6/1
22	Thomas, Josh	CB	5-11	190	5/3/89	4	Buffalo	Cedar Hills, Texas	W(Dall)-'11	13/6
35	Tolbert, Mike	FB	5-9	245	11/23/85	7	Coastal Carolina	Douglasville, Ga.	UFA(SD)-'12	16/13
11	Underwood, Tiquan	WR	6-1	185	2/17/87	6	Rutgers	Lawrenceville, N.J.	UFA(TB)-'14	12/7*
14	Webb, Joe	QB	6-4	220	11/14/86	5	Alabama-Birmingham	Birmingham, Ala.	UFA(Minn)-'14	16/1*
70	#Wharton, Travelle	G	6-4	315	5/19/81	11	South Carolina	Fountain Inn, S.C.	FA-'13	16/12
23	White, Melvin	CB	6-1	205	6/26/90	2	Louisiana-Lafayette	Freeport, Texas	FA-'13	15/10
86	Williams, Brandon	TE	6-4	250	10/12/87	2	Oregon	Blue Island, Ill.	FA-'13	9/0
34	Williams, DeAngelo	RB	5-9	215	4/25/83	9	Memphis	Wynne, Ark.	D1-'06	15/15

2014 VETERAN ROSTER (CONTINUED)

No.	Name	Pos.	Ht.	Wt.	Birthdate	NFL Exp.	College	Hometown	How Acq.	'13 Games/ Starts
65	Williams, Garry	T	6-3	315	8/20/86	6	Kentucky	Louisville, Ky.	FA-'09	1/1
54	Williams, Jason	LB	6-1	245	4/23/86	6	Western Illinois	Chicago, Ill.	FA-'13	11/0
39	Zordich, Michael	FB	6-1	240	10/29/89	2	Penn State	Youngstown, Ohio	FA-'13	0*

* Avant played 16 games with Philadelphia in '13; Campbell missed '13 season because of injury; Cason played 16 games with Arizona; Clausen missed '13 season because of injury; Cotchery played 16 games with Pittsburgh; DeCoud played 15 games with Atlanta; Dickson played 16 games with Baltimore; Gaydosh missed '13 season because of injury; Hall last active with the New York Giants in '10; Harper played nine games with New Orleans; Hughes last active with St. Louis in '11; Jacobs inactive for one game; Jefferson played four games with Arizona; King inactive 10 games; Kugbila missed '13 season because of injury; McNeill played 14 games with St. Louis; Menzie missed '12 season because of injury with Kansas City; Nevis played 11 games with Dallas and one game with Jacksonville; Pilares missed '13 season because of injury; Russell last active with Carolina in '12; Smith played one game with Houston; Underwood played 12 games with Tampa Bay; Webb played 16 games with Minnesota; Zordich missed '13 season because of injury.

\# Unrestricted Free Agent; subject to developments.

Traded—LB Jon Beason (3 games in '13) to the New York Giants.

Retired—G/C Jeff Byers (8), Jordan Gross, 11-year tackle, 16 games in '13, G/C Geoff Hangartner (8).

Players lost through free agency (6): WR Ted Ginn Jr. (Ariz; 16 games in '13), WR Domenik Hixon (Chi; 15), WR Brandon LaFell (NE; 16), S Mike Mitchell (Pitt; 15), CB Captain Munnerlyn (Minn; 16), LB Jordan Senn (Chi; 14).

Also played with Carolina in '13—T Travis Bond (2 games), WR Armanti Edwards (4), DT Sione Fua (3), CB D.J. Moore (2), RB Armond Smith (5), WR Steve Smith (15), G Travelle Wharton (16).

FIRST-YEAR ROSTER

Name	Pos.	Ht.	Wt.	Birthdate	College	Hometown	How Acq.
Allen, Denicos	LB	5-11	220	8/9/90	Michigan State	Hamilton, Ohio	FA
Benjamin, Kelvin	WR	6-5	240	2/5/91	Florida State	Belle Glade, Fla.	D1
Benwikere, Bené	CB	6-0	190	9/3/91	San Jose State	Gardena, Calif.	D5
Bersin, Brenton (1)	WR	6-3	210	5/9/90	Wofford College	Charlotte, N.C.	FA-'13
Blanchard, Matt (1)	QB	6-3	225	3/21/89	Wisconsin-Whitewater	Lake Zurich, Ill	FA-'13
Boston, Tre	S	6-1	205	6/25/92	North Carolina	Fort Myers, Fla.	D4
Boyko, Billy	LB	6-2	240	8/3/91	Lehigh	Northhampton, Pa.	FA
Brown, Philly	WR	5-11	180	12/16/91	Ohio State	Upper Darby, Pa.	FA
Byndom, Carrington	CB	6-0	180	7/7/92	Texas	Lufkin, Texas	FA
Clemons, Toney	WR	6-2	220	10/11/88	Colorado	New Kensington, Pa.	FA
Dennis, Derek	G	6-3	315	7/16/88	Temple	Pawling, N.Y.	FA
Ealy, Kony	DE	6-4	275	12/21/91	Missouri	New Madrid, Mo.	D2
Gaffney, Tyler	RB	6-0	225	4/20/91	Stanford	San Diego, Calif.	D6
Glanton, Adarius	LB	6-1	215	9/21/90	Florida Atlantic	Lakeland, Fla.	FA
Gay, Jordan	P	6-1	200	3/29/90	Centre College	Danville, Ky.	FA
Johnson, Oscar	T	6-6	340	3/1/90	Louisiana Tech	Crystal Springs, Miss.	FA
Lucas, Marcus	WR	6-4	215	3/1/92	Missouri	Liberty, Mo.	FA
McDonald, Andrew (1)	T	6-6	310	9/8/88	Indiana	Indianapolis, Ind.	FA-'13
Norwell, Andrew	G	6-6	315	10/25/91	Ohio State	Cincinnati, Ohio	FA
Presley, De'Andre (1)	WR	5-10	185	1/10/90	Appalachian State	Tampa, Fla.	FA-'13
Reaves, Darrin	RB	5-10	210	4/17/93	Alabama-Birmingham	Birmingham, Ala.	FA
Roh, Craig (1)	DE	6-4	275	1/25/91	Michigan	Scottsdale, Ariz.	FA-'13
Rowell, Shaq	DT	6-4	305	1/7/90	West Virginia	Maple Heights, Ohio	FA
Turner, Trai	G	6-3	315	6/14/93	Louisiana State	New Orleans, La.	D3
Walker, Casey (1)	DT	6-1	345	12/6/89	Oklahoma	Garland, Texas	FA-'13
Wheeler, Jared	C	6-5	320	10/3/90	Miami	Hollywood, Fla.	FA

The term NFL Rookie is defined as a player who is in his first season of professional football and has not been on the roster of another professional football team for any regular-season or postseason games. A Rookie is designated by an "R" on NFL rosters. Players who have been active in another professional football league or players who have NFL experience, including either preseason training camp or being on an Active List or Inactive List, or on Reserve/Injured or Reserve/Physically Unable to Perform for fewer than six regular-season games, are termed NFL First-Year Players. An NFL First-Year Player is designated by a "1" on NFL rosters. Thereafter, a player is credited with an additional year of experience for each season in which he accumulates six games on the Active List or Inactive List, or on Reserve/Injured or Reserve/Physically Unable to Perform.

Log on to www.panthers.com for an up-to-date roster.

CAROLINA PANTHERS

COACHING STAFF

Head Coach,
Ron Rivera

Pro Career: Became the fourth coach in Carolina Panthers history on January 11, 2011. In 2013, his third year with the Panthers, Rivera led Carolina to 12 wins, the NFC South division title and its first playoff appearance since 2008. After starting the season with a 1-3 record, the Panthers won 11 of their final 12 regular season games – including a franchise record eight-game winning streak – to secure the No. 2 seed in the NFC and a first-round bye. In recognition of that success, Rivera was named NFL Coach of the Year by the Associated Press. Carolina's record has improved every season since Rivera took over a team that went 2-14 in 2010, with the Panthers going 6-10 in his first year, 7-9 in 2012 and 12-4 in 2013. Dating back to Week 12 of the 2012 season, the Panthers have won 17 of their last 22 regular season games. Before joining the Panthers, Rivera worked with the San Diego Chargers from 2007-2010, coaching inside linebackers before taking over as defensive coordinator midway through the 2008 season. In 2010, San Diego led the NFL with an average of 271.6 total yards allowed per game and gave up a league-low 178 passing yards per game. From 2004-06, Rivera oversaw the Chicago Bears defense, guiding the unit to two top-five finishes in the league. In 2006, the Bears defense led the NFL with 44 takeaways, helping propel Chicago to an appearance in Super Bowl XLI. In 2005, the Bears went 43 consecutive quarters without allowing more than seven points – the longest streak in the NFL since 1969. Rivera was also linebackers coach for the Eagles (1999-2003) and defensive quality control coach for the Bears (1997-98). He is just the third Latino head coach in NFL history, joining Tom Flores with the Oakland Raiders (1979-1987) and Seattle Seahawks (1992-94) and Tom Fears with the New Orleans Saints (1967-1970). A second-round draft choice in 1984 by Chicago, Rivera played nine seasons with the Bears. Primarily an outside linebacker, he was a member of the Super Bowl XX championship team in 1985. Career record: 25-24.

Background: Linebacker at California (1980-83).

Personal: Born January 7, 1962 in Fort Ord, Calif. He and his wife, Stephanie, have two children—Christopher and Courtney.

ASSISTANT COACHES

Jason Benguche, asst. strength and conditioning; born April 11, 1984, Pittsfield, Mass. Offensive lineman Springfield (Mass.) College 2002-05. No pro playing experience. College coach: Massachusetts 2005 (spring), Florida State 2006-07, Georgia Tech 2008-2012. Pro coach: Joined Panthers in 2013.

Ray Brown, asst. offensive line; born December 12, 1962, Marion, Ark. Offensive lineman/tight end Arkansas State 1983-85. Pro offensive lineman St. Louis/Phoenix Cardinals 1986-88, Washington Redskins 1989-1995, 2004-05, San Francisco 49ers 1996-2001, Detroit Lions 2002-03. Pro coach: Washington Redskins 2006, Buffalo Bills 2008-09, San Francisco 49ers 2010, joined Panthers in 2011.

Bruce DeHaven, asst. special teams; born September 6, 1948, Trousdale, Kan. Attended Southwestern (Kan.) College. No college or pro playing experience. College coach: Kansas 1979-1981, New Mexico State 1982. Pro coach: New Jersey Generals (USFL) 1983, Pittsburgh Maulers (USFL) 1984, Orlando Renegades (USFL) 1985, Buffalo Bills 1987-1999, 2010-12, San Francisco 49ers 2000-02, Dallas Cowboys 2003-06, Seattle Seahawks 2007-09, joined Panthers in 2013.

Ken Dorsey, quarterbacks; born April 22, 1981, Orinda, Calif. Quarterback Miami 1999-2002. Pro quarterback San Francisco 49ers 2003-05, Cleveland Browns 2006-08, Toronto Argonauts (CFL) 2010. Pro scout: Carolina Panthers 2011-12. Pro coach: Joined Panthers in 2013.

Pete Hoener, tight ends; born June 14, 1954, Peoria, Ill. Tight end/defensive end Bradley 1969-1970. No pro playing experience. College coach: Missouri 1975-76, Illinois State 1977, Indiana State 1978-1984, Illinois 1987-88, Purdue 1989-1991, Texas Christian 1992-97, Iowa State 1998-99, Texas A&M 2000. Pro coach: St. Louis/Arizona Cardinals 1985-86, 2001-03, Chicago Bears 2004, San Francisco 49ers 2005-2010, joined Panthers in 2011.

Al Holcomb, linebackers; born October 22, 1970, Queens, N.Y. Attended West Virginia. No college or pro playing experience. College coach: Temple 1995-96, Colby College 1997, Bloomsburg 1998-2003, Kutztown 2004-05, Lafayette 2006-08. Pro coach: New York Giants 2009-2012, joined Panthers in 2013.

Joe Kenn, strength and conditioning; born October 13, 1966, Far Rockaway, N.Y. Guard Wake Forest 1987-88. No pro playing experience. College coach: Wake Forest 1991 (winter/spring), Boise State 1991-98, Utah 1999-2000, Arizona State 2001-07, Louisville 2008-09. Pro coach: Joined Panthers in 2011.

John Matsko, offensive line; born February 2, 1951, Cleveland, Ohio. Fullback Kent State 1970-72. No pro playing experience. College coach: Miami (Ohio) 1974-75, 1977, North Carolina 1978-1984, Navy 1985, Arizona 1986, Southern California 1987-1991. Pro coach: Phoenix Cardinals 1992-93, New Orleans Saints 1994-96, New York Giants 1997-98, St. Louis Rams 1999-2005, Kansas City Chiefs 2006-07, Baltimore Ravens 2008-2010, joined Panthers in 2011.

Sean McDermott, defensive coordinator; born March 21, 1974, Omaha, Neb. Safety William & Mary 1994-97. No pro playing experience. College coach: William & Mary 1998. Pro coach: Philadelphia Eagles 1999-2010, joined Panthers in 2011.

Sam Mills III, asst. defensive line; born May 20, 1978, Long Branch, N.J. Defensive back Montclair State 1997-1999. No pro playing experience. Pro coach: Joined Panthers in 2005.

Ricky Proehl, wide receivers; born March 7, 1968, Bronx, N.Y. Wide receiver Wake Forest 1986-89. Pro wide receiver Phoenix/Arizona Cardinals 1990-94, Seattle Seahawks 1995-96, Chicago Bears 1997, St. Louis Rams 1998-2002, Carolina Panthers 2003-05, Indianapolis Colts 2006. Pro coach: Joined Panthers in 2011.

John Ramsdell, senior offensive assistant; born August 16, 1954, Lafayette, Ind. Running back Springfield (Mass.) College 1972-75. No pro playing experience. College coach: San Francisco State 1976-77, Long Beach State 1978, Pacific 1979-1982, Oregon 1983-1994. Pro coach: St. Louis Rams 1995-2005, San Diego Chargers 2006-2012, joined Panthers in 2014.

Richard Rogers, special teams coordinator; born October 28, 1961, St. Louis, Mo. Linebacker California 1980-83. No pro playing experience. College coach: Diablo Valley (Calif.) C.C. 1989-94, San Jose State, 1995-1996, Portland State 1997-2000, New Mexico State 2001-2004, Holy Cross 2005-2011. Pro coach: Joined Panthers in 2012.

Mike Shula, offensive coordinator; born June 3, 1965, Baltimore, Md. Quarterback Alabama 1984-86. Pro quarterback Tampa Bay Buccaneers 1987. College coach: Alabama 2003-06 (head coach). Pro coach: Tampa Bay Buccaneers 1988-1990, 1996-99, Miami Dolphins 1991-92, 2000-02, Chicago Bears 1993-95, Jacksonville Jaguars 2007-2010, joined Panthers in 2011.

Jim Skipper, running backs; born January 23, 1949, Breaux Bridge, La. Defensive back Whittier College 1971-72. No pro playing experience. College coach: Cal Poly-Pomona 1974-76, San Jose State 1977-78, Pacific 1979, Oregon 1980-82. Pro coach: Philadelphia/Baltimore Stars (USFL) 1983-85, New Orleans Saints 1986-1995, Arizona Cardinals 1996, New York Giants 1997-2000, San Francisco Demons (XFL) 2001 (head coach), Carolina Panthers 2002-2010, Tennessee Titans 2011-12, re-joined Panthers in 2013.

Eric Washington, defensive line; born October 29, 1969, Shreveport, La. Tight end Grambling State 1989-1990. No pro playing experience. College coach: Texas A&M 1997, Ohio 2001-03, Northwestern 2004-07. Pro coach: Chicago Bears 2008-2010, joined Panthers in 2011.

Steve Wilks, secondary/passing defense coordinator; born August 8, 1969, Charlotte, N.C. Defensive back Appalachian State 1987-1991. No pro playing experience. College coach: Johnson C. Smith 1995-96, Savannah State 1997-1999, Illinois State 2000, Appalachian State 2001, East Tennessee State 2002, Bowling Green State 2003, Notre Dame 2004, Washington 2005. Pro coach: Chicago Bears 2006-2008, San Diego Chargers 2009-2011, joined Panthers in 2012.

National Football Conference
North Division
Team Colors: Navy Blue, Orange, and White
Halas Hall at Conway Park
1920 Football Drive
Lake Forest, Illinois 60045
Telephone: (847) 295-6600

2014 SCHEDULE
PRESEASON
Aug. 8 **Philadelphia** 7:00
Aug. 14 **Jacksonville**.......................7:00
Aug. 22 at Seattle 9:00
Aug. 28 at Cleveland 7:00

REGULAR SEASON
Sep. 7 **Buffalo** 12:00
Sep. 14 at San Francisco 7:30
Sep. 22 at New York Jets (Mon) 7:30
Sep. 28 **Green Bay** 12:00
Oct. 5 at Carolina 12:00
Oct. 12 at Atlanta 12:00
Oct. 19 **Miami** 12:00
Oct. 26 at New England 12:00
Nov. 2 BYE
Nov. 9 at Green Bay *7:30
Nov. 16 **Minnesota** 12:00
Nov. 23 **Tampa Bay** 12:00
Nov. 27 at Detroit (Thu) 11:30a
Dec. 4 **Dallas** (Thu).......................7:25
Dec. 15 **New Orleans** (Mon) 7:30
Dec. 21 **Detroit** 12:00
Dec. 28 at Minnesota 12:00
*All times CT; Sunday night games in
  Weeks 5-16 subject to change
Stadium: Soldier Field
      (opened in 1924)
      •**Capacity:** 61,500
      1410 S. Museum Campus Dr.
      Chicago, Illinois 60605
Playing Surface: Natural Grass
Training Camp: Olivet-Nazarene Univ.
        Bourbonnais, Illinois
        60901

SOLDIER FIELD

CLUB OFFICIALS
Chairman: George H. McCaskey
Secretary: Virginia H. McCaskey
President and CEO: Ted Phillips
General Manager: Phil Emery
Senior Director of Special Projects:
  Pat McCaskey
Senior Director of Business Development
  & Alumni Relations: Brian McCaskey
Vice President of Business
  Administration: John Bostrom
Vice President of Communications:
  Scott Hagel
Vice President of Sales & Marketing:
  Chris Hibbs
Vice President of Football Administration
  and General Counsel: Cliff Stein
Chief Financial Officer & Treasurer:
  Karen Murphy
Senior Director of Ticket Operations:
  Lee Twarling
Director of Video Services:
  Dave Hendrickson
Assistant Video Director: Dean Pope
College Video Coordinator: Dan Tuohy
Video Assistant: Jack Dowling
Head Athletic Trainer: Chris Hanks
Head Equipment Manager: Tony Medlin
Assistant Equipment Managers:
  Carl Piekarski, Travis Brown,
  Travis Knoch
Director of Pro Scouting: Kevin Turks
Director of College Scouting:
  Marty Barrett
Associate Director of Pro Scouting:
  Dwayne Joseph
Executive Scout/Asst. Director of College
  Scouting: Jeff Shiver
Senior National Scout: Mark Sadowski
National Scout: Rex Hogan
Area Scouts: Breck Ackley, Jay Muraco,
  Francis Saint-Paul, Sam Summerville,
  Zach Truty
Scout/Player Personnel: Ryan Kessenich,
  David Williams
Scouting Assistants: Bobby Macedo,
  Andre Odom
Director of Community Relations:
  Caroline Guip Schrenker
Director of Broadcasting & Scoreboard
  Operations: Greg Miller
Media Services Manager: Jim Christman
Media Relations Coordinator: Mike Corbo
Media Relations Assistant: Jared Ellerson

COACHING HISTORY
Decatur Staleys 1920,
Chicago Staleys 1921
(747-552-42)
Records include postseason games

Year	Coach	Record
1920-29	George Halas	84-31-19
1930-32	Ralph Jones	24-10-7
1933-1942	George Halas*	88-24-4
1942-45	Hunk Anderson-Luke Johnsos**	24-12-2
1946-1955	George Halas	76-43-2
1956-57	John (Paddy) Driscoll	14-10-1
1958-1967	George Halas	76-53-6
1968-1971	Jim Dooley	20-36-0
1972-74	Abe Gibron	11-30-1
1975-77	Jack Pardee	20-23-0
1978-1981	Neill Armstrong	30-35-0
1982-1992	Mike Ditka	112-68-0
1993-98	Dave Wannstedt	41-57-0
1999-2003	Dick Jauron	35-46-0
2004-2012	Lovie Smith	84-66-0
2013	Marc Trestman	8-8-0

*Retired after five games to enter U.S. Navy
**Co-coaches

PAID ATTENDANCE
Home 483,336   Away 541,926
Total 1,025,262
Single-game home record,
  66,900 (9/5/93)
Single-season home record, 527,769
  (1999)

2014 DRAFT CHOICES

Round	Name	Pos.	College
1	Kyle Fuller	DB	Virginia Tech
2	Ego Ferguson	DT	Louisiana St.
3	Will Sutton	DT	Arizona St.
4	Ka'Deem Carey	RB	Arizona
	Brock Vereen	DB	Minnesota
6	David Fales	QB	San Jose St.
	Pat O'Donnell	P	Miami
7	Charles Leno	T	Boise St.

CHICAGO BEARS

2013 TEAM RECORD
PRESEASON (2-2)

Date	Result	Opponent
08/09	L 17-24	at Carolina
08/15	W 33-28	San Diego
08/23	W 34-26	at Oakland
08/29	L 16-18	Cleveland

REGULAR SEASON (8-8)

Date	Result	Opponent
09/08	W 24-21	Cincinnati
09/15	W 31-30	Minnesota
09/22	W 40-23	at Pittsburgh
09/29	L 32-40	at Detroit
10/06	L 18-26	New Orleans
10/10	W 27-21	New York Giants
10/20	L 41-45	at Washington
11/04	W 27-20	at Green Bay
11/10	L 19-21	Detroit
11/17	W 23-20	Baltimore (OT)
11/24	L 21-42	at St. Louis
12/01	L 20-23	at Minnesota (OT)
12/09	W 45-28	Dallas
12/15	W 38-31	at Cleveland
12/22	L 11-54	at Philadelphia
12/29	L 28-33	Green Bay

(OT) Overtime

SCORE BY PERIODS

Bears	96	124	90	132	3	—	445
Opponents	112	147	97	119	3	—	478

2013 TEAM STATISTICS

	Bears	Opp.
Total First Downs	344	353
Rushing	102	147
Passing	215	184
Penalty	27	22
3rd Down: Made/Att	83/197	83/200
3rd Down Pct.	42.1	41.5
4th Down: Made/Att	8/13	12/16
4th Down Pct.	61.5	75.0
Possession Avg.	30:25	29:35
Total Net Yards	6109	6313
Avg. Per Game	381.8	394.6
Total Plays	1013	1021
Avg. Per Play	6.0	6.2
Net Yards Rushing	1828	2583
Avg. Per Game	114.3	161.4
Total Rushes	404	483
Net Yards Passing	4281	3730
Avg. Per Game	267.6	233.1
Sacked/Yards Lost	30/169	31/189
Gross Yards	4450	3919
Att./Completions	579/373	507/315
Completion Pct.	64.4	62.1
Had Intercepted	13	19
Punts/Average	69/40.0	58/44.5
Net Punting Avg.	69/37.9	58/38.4
Penalties/Yards	85/708	69/647
Fumbles/Ball Lost	21/10	25/9
Touchdowns	52	56
Rushing	13	22
Passing	32	25
Returns	7	9

2013 INDIVIDUAL STATISTICS

PASSING

	Att.	Comp.	Yds.	Pct.	TD	Int.	Tkld.	Rate
Cutler	355	224	2621	63.1	19	12	19/132	89.2
McCown	224	149	1829	66.5	13	1	11/37	109.0
Bears	579	373	4450	64.4	32	13	30/169	96.9
Opponents	507	315	3919	62.1	25	19	31/189	86.9

SCORING

	TD R	TD P	TD Rt	PAT	FG	Saf	PTS
Gould	0	0	0	45/46	26/29	0	123
Marshall	0	12	0	0/0	0/0	0	76
Forté	9	3	0	0/0	0/0	0	74
Jeffery	0	7	0	0/0	0/0	0	44
M. Bennett	0	5	0	0/0	0/0	0	30
E. Bennett	0	4	0	0/0	0/0	0	26
Bush	3	1	0	0/0	0/0	0	24
Jennings	0	0	2	0/0	0/0	0	12
Bass	0	0	1	0/0	0/0	0	6
Bowman	0	0	1	0/0	0/0	0	6
Hester	0	0	1	0/0	0/0	0	6
McCown	1	0	0	0/0	0/0	0	6
Peppers	0	0	1	0/0	0/0	0	6
Wright	0	0	1	0/0	0/0	0	6
Bears	13	32	7	45/46	26/29	0	445
Opponents	22	25	9	54/54	28/30	1	478

2-Pt Conversions: Marshall 2, E. Bennett, Forté, Jeffery. Bears 5-6, Opponents 1-2.

RUSHING

	No.	Yds	Avg	LG	TD
Forté	289	1339	4.6	55	9
Bush	63	197	3.1	40t	3
Cutler	23	118	5.1	18	0
Jeffery	16	105	6.6	38	0
McCown	13	69	5.3	20	1
Bears	404	1828	4.5	55	13
Opponents	483	2583	5.3	65t	22

RECEIVING

	No.	Yds	Avg	LG	TD
Marshall	100	1295	13.0	44	12
Jeffery	89	1421	16.0	80t	7
Forté	74	594	8.0	34	3
M. Bennett	65	759	11.7	43	5
E. Bennett	32	243	7.6	17t	4
Fiammetta	4	57	14.3	30	0
Bush	4	48	12.0	17t	1
M. Wilson	2	13	6.5	10	0
Rosario	1	13	13.0	13	0
Weems	1	8	8.0	8	0
K. Long	1	-1	-1.0	-1	0
Bears	373	4450	11.9	80t	32
Opponents	315	3919	12.4	48t	25

INTERCEPTIONS

	No.	Yds	Avg	LG	TD
Jennings	4	111	27.8	48t	2
Tillman	3	69	23.0	41	0
Bowman	3	67	22.3	43t	1
Conte	3	48	16.0	35	0
Wright	2	46	23.0	38t	1
Greene	1	49	49.0	49	0
Bass	1	24	24.0	24t	0
Peppers	1	14	14.0	14	0
Bostic	1	0	0.0	0	0
Bears	19	428	22.5	49	5
Opponents	13	225	17.3	54t	3

PUNTING

	No.	Yds.	Avg.	In 20	LG
Podlesh	68	2763	40.6	27	65
Bears	69	2763	40.0	27	65
Opponents	58	2581	44.5	16	65

PUNT RETURNS

	Ret	FC	Yds	Avg	LG	TD
Hester	18	11	256	14.2	81t	1
Weems	0	1	0	—	—	0
Bears	18	12	256	14.2	81t	1
Opponents	15	25	111	7.4	57	0

KICKOFF RETURNS

	No.	Yds	Avg	LG	TD
Hester	52	1436	27.6	80	0
Jo. Anderson	5	82	16.4	21	0
Ford	5	37	7.4	11	0
Weems	5	57	11.4	19	0
Rosario	2	10	5.0	6	0
Marshall	1	-8	-8.0	-8	0
Bears	70	1614	23.1	80	0
Opponents	47	883	18.8	105t	1

FIELD GOALS

	1-19	20-29	30-39	40-49	50+
Gould	0/0	11/11	6/7	6/7	3/4
Bears	0/0	11/11	6/7	6/7	3/4
Opponents	1/1	9/9	10/10	7/8	1/2

SACKS

	No.
Peppers	7.0
Ja. Anderson	4.0
McClellin	4.0
Briggs	3.0
Wootton	3.0
Bostic	2.0
D. Williams	2.0
Paea	1.5
Ratliff	1.5
Bass	1.0
Collins	1.0
Ozougwu	1.0
Bears	31.0
Opponents	30.0

RECORD HOLDERS
INDIVIDUAL RECORDS—CAREER

Category	Name	Performance
Rushing (Yds.)	Walter Payton, 1975-1987	16,726
Passing (Yds.)	Jay Cutler, 2009-2013	14,913
Passing (TDs)	Sid Luckman, 1939-1950	137
Receiving (No.)	Walter Payton, 1975-1987	492
Receiving (Yds.)	Johnny Morris, 1958-1967	5,059
Interceptions	Gary Fencik, 1976-1987	38
Punting (Avg.)	George Gulyanics, 1947-1952	44.5
Punt Return (Avg.)	George McAfee, 1940-1950	**12.8
Kickoff Return (Avg.)	Gale Sayers, 1965-1971	**30.6
Field Goals	Kevin Butler, 1985-1995	243
Touchdowns (Tot.)	Walter Payton, 1975-1987	125
Points	Kevin Butler, 1985-1995	1,116
*Sacks	Richard Dent, 1983-1993, 1995	124.5

INDIVIDUAL RECORDS—SINGLE SEASON

Category	Name	Performance
Rushing (Yds.)	Walter Payton, 1977	1,852
Passing (Yds.)	Erik Kramer, 1995	3,838
Passing (TDs)	Erik Kramer, 1995	29
Receiving (No.)	Brandon Marshall, 2012	118
Receiving (Yds.)	Brandon Marshall, 2012	1,508
Interceptions	Mark Carrier, 1990	10
Punting (Avg.)	Bobby Joe Green, 1963	46.5
Punt Return (Avg.)	Devin Hester, 2010	17.1
Kickoff Return (Avg.)	Gale Sayers, 1967	37.7
Field Goals	Robbie Gould, 2006	32
Touchdowns (Tot.)	Gale Sayers, 1965	22
Points	Kevin Butler, 1985	144
*Sacks	Richard Dent, 1984	17.5

INDIVIDUAL RECORDS—SINGLE GAME

Category	Name	Performance
Rushing (Yds.)	Walter Payton, 11-20-77	275
Passing (Yds.)	Johnny Lujack, 12-11-49	468
Passing (TDs)	Sid Luckman, 11-14-43	**7
Receiving (No.)	Jim Keane, 10-23-49	14
Receiving (Yds.)	Alshon Jeffery, 12-1-13	249
Interceptions	Many times	3
	Last time by Mark Carrier, 12-9-90	
Field Goals	Roger LeClerc, 12-3-61	5
	Mac Percival, 10-20-68	5
Touchdowns (Tot.)	Gale Sayers, 12-12-65	**6
Points	Gale Sayers, 12-12-65	36
*Sacks	Richard Dent, 11-4-84, 12-27-87	4.5

*Sacks became an official statistic in 1982.
**NFL Record

2014 VETERAN ROSTER

No.	Name	Pos.	Ht.	Wt.	Birthdate	NFL Exp.	College	Hometown	How Acq.	'13 Games/ Starts
69	Allen, Jared	DE	6-6	270	4/3/82	11	Idaho State	Los Gatos, Calif.	UFA(Minn)-'14	16/16*
#	Anderson, James	LB	6-2	235	9/26/83	9	Virginia Tech	Roanoke Rapids, N.C.	FA-'13	16/16
91	Bass, David	DE	6-4	256	9/11/90	2	Missouri Western St.	St. Louis, Mo.	W(Oak)-'13	12/1
83	Bennett, Martellus	TE	6-6	265	3/10/87	7	Texas A&M	Alief, Texas	UFA(NYG)-'13	16/15
60	Boggs, Taylor	G/C	6-3	285	2/20/87	2	Humboldt State	Pasedena, Calif.	FA-'13	1/0
57	Bostic, Jonathan	LB	6-1	245	5/5/91	2	Florida	Wellington, Fla.	D2-'13	16/9
55	Briggs, Lance	LB	6-1	244	11/12/80	12	Arizona	Sacramento, Calif.	D3-'03	9/9
62	Britton, Eben	G/T	6-6	308	10/14/87	6	Arizona	Burbank, Calif.	UFA(Jax)-'13	13/4
78	Brown, James	T/G	6-4	306	11/30/88	3	Troy	Magnolia, Miss.	FA-'12	0*
74	Bushrod, Jermon	T	6-5	320	8/19/84	8	Towson	Fredericksburg, Va.	UFA(NO)-'13	16/16
#	Cohen, Landon	DT	6-1	300	8/3/86	5	Ohio	Spartanburg, S.C.	FA-'13	13/3
98	Collins, Nate	DT	6-2	296	12/14/87	5	Virginia	White Plains, N.Y.	UFA(Jax)-'12	5/2
47	Conte, Chris	S	6-2	203	2/23/89	4	California	Los Angeles, Calif.	D3-'11	16/16
#	Costanzo, Blake	LB	6-1	235	4/14/84	8	Lafayette	Franklin Lakes, N.J.	UFA(SF)-'12	16/0
6	Cutler, Jay	QB	6-3	220	4/29/83	9	Vanderbilt	Santa Claus, Ind.	T(Den)-'09	11/11
64	de la Puente, Brian	C	6-3	306	5/13/85	5	California	San Clemente, Calif.	UFA(NO)-'14	16/16*
38	Draughn, Shaun	RB	6-0	205	12/7/87	2	North Carolina	Tarboro, N.C.	FA-'14	3/0*
43	Fiammetta, Tony	FB	6-0	250	8/22/86	5	Syracuse	Walkersville, Md.	FA-'13	16/7
32	Ford, Michael	RB	5-10	216	5/27/90	2	Louisiana State	Leesville, La.	FA-'13	12/0
22	Forté, Matt	RB	6-2	218	12/10/85	7	Tulane	Slidell, La.	D2-'08	16/16
53	Franklin, Jerry	LB	6-1	245	1/10/88	2	Arkansas	Marion, Ark.	FA-'12	10/0
31	Frey, Isaiah	CB	6-0	190	4/6/90	2	Nevada	Olivehurst, Calif.	D6-'12	16/6
63	Garza, Roberto	C/G	6-2	310	3/26/79	14	Texas A&M-Kingsville	Rio Hondo, Texas	UFA(Atl)-'05	16/16
9	Gould, Robbie	K	6-0	185	12/30/81	10	Penn State	Lock Haven, Pa.	FA-'05	16/0
52	Greene, Khaseem	LB	6-1	241	2/4/89	2	Rutgers	Elizabeth, N.J.	D4-'13	15/4
24	Hayden, Kelvin	CB	6-0	195	7/23/83	10	Illinois	Chicago, Ill.	UFA(Atl)-'12	0*
87	Hixon, Domenik	WR/KR	6-2	205	10/8/84	9	Akron	Neukirchen, W. Germany	UFA(Car)-'14	15/0*
99	Houston, Lamarr	DE	6-3	300	6/24/87	5	Texas	San Francisco, Calif.	UFA(Oak)-'14	16/16*
71	Idonije, Israel	DL	6-6	275	11/17/80	11	Manitoba	Brandon, Manitoba; Lagos, Nigeria	UFA(Det)-'14	15/0*
17	Jeffery, Alshon	WR	6-3	216	2/14/90	3	South Carolina	St. Matthews, S.C.	D2-'12	16/14
37	Jennings, M.D.	S	6-0	187	7/25/88	4	Arkansas State	Grenada, Miss.	UFA(GB)-'14	16/16*
26	Jennings, Tim	CB	5-8	185	12/24/83	9	Georgia	Orangeburg, S.C.	UFA(Ind)-'10	16/16
73	Lane, Austen	DE	6-6	265	11/9/87	4	Murray State	Iola, Wisc.	FA-'14	2/0*
75	Long, Kyle	G	6-6	313	12/5/88	2	Oregon	Ivy, Va.	D1-'13	16/16
65	Mannelly, Patrick	LS	6-5	265	4/18/75	17	Duke	Atlanta, Ga.	D6b-'98	14/0
15	Marshall, Brandon	WR	6-4	230	3/23/84	9	Central Florida	Pittsburgh,Pa.	T(Mia)-'12	16/16
39	Martin, Derrick	CB	5-10	198	5/16/85	9	Wyoming	Denver, Colo.	UFA(NE)-'13	7/0
50	McClellin, Shea	LB	6-3	260	8/1/89	3	Boise State	Caldwell, Idaho	D1-'12	14/10
29	McCray, Danny	S	6-1	221	3/10/88	5	Louisiana State	Houston, Texas	UFA(Dall)-'14	15/0*
27	McManis, Sherrick	CB	6-1	193	12/19/87	5	Northwestern	Peoria, Ill.	T(Hou)-'12	15/1
86	Miller, Zach	TE	6-5	236	10/4/84	5	Nebraska-Omaha	Wahoo, Neb.	FA-'13	0*
67	Mills, Jordan	T	6-5	316	12/24/90	2	Louisiana Tech	Thibodaux, La.	D5-'13	16/16
19	Morgan, Josh	WR	6-1	220	6/20/85	7	Virginia Tech	Washington D.C.	UFA(Wash)-'14	14/7*
85	Mulligan, Matthew	TE	6-4	267	1/18/85	6	Maine	Enfield, Maine	UFA(NE)-'14	15/4*
21	Mundy, Ryan	S	6-1	209	2/11/85	6	West Virginia	Wilkins Township, Pa.	UFA(NYG)-'14	16/9*
84	Onobun, Fendi	TE	6-6	260	11/17/86	3	Houston	Houston, Texas	FA-'13	0*
92	Paea, Stephen	DT	6-1	300	5/11/88	4	Oregon State	Vava'u, Tonga	D2-'11	13/10
2	Palmer, Jordan	QB	6-5	230	5/30/84	6	Texas-El Paso	Westlake Village, Calif.	UFA(Jax)-'13	0*
90	Ratliff, Jeremiah	DT	6-4	303	8/29/81	10	Auburn	Valdosta, Ga.	FA-'13	5/4
88	Rosario, Dante	TE	6-3	242	10/25/84	8	Oregon	Beaverton, Ore.	T(Dall)-'13	15/3
#	Scott, Jonathan	T	6-6	318	1/10/83	8	Texas	Dallas, Texas	FA-'12	0*
76	Scott, Trevor	DE	6-5	260	8/30/84	7	Buffalo	Potsdam, N.Y.	FA-'14	4/0*
59	Senn, Jordan	LB	5-11	225	6/11/84	7	Portland State	Beaverton, Ore.	UFA(Car)-'14	14/0*
68	Slauson, Matt	G	6-5	315	2/18/86	6	Nebraska	Colorado Springs, Colo.	UFA(NYJ)-'13	16/16
20	Steltz, Craig	S	6-1	210	5/7/86	7	Louisiana State	Metairie, La.	D4-'08	16/1
33	Tillman, Charles	CB	6-2	198	2/23/81	12	Louisiana-Lafayette	Copperas Cove, Texas	D2-'03	8/8
#	Walters, Anthony	S	6-1	207	9/19/88	4	Delaware	Philadelphia, Pa.	FA-'11	13/0
94	Washington, Cornelius	DE	6-4	265	9/10/89	2	Georgia	Hephzibah, Ga.	D6-'13	2/0
14	Weems, Eric	WR/KR	5-9	195	7/4/85	8	Bethune-Cookman	Daytona Beach, Fla.	UFA(Atl)-'12	16/0
58	Williams, D.J.	LB	6-1	242	7/20/82	11	Miami	Pittsburg, Calif.	FA-'13	6/4
25	Wilson, C.J.	CB	5-11	187	9/26/89	2	North Carolina State	Lincolnton, N.C.	FA-'13	2/0
10	Wilson, Marquess	WR	6-4	184	9/14/92	2	Washington State	Tulare, Calif.	D7-'13	10/1
97	Young, Willie	DE	6-4	251	9/19/85	5	North Carolina State	Palm Beach Gardens, Fla.	UFA(Det)-'14	16/15*

* Allen played 16 games with Minnesota in '13; Brown inactive 16 games; de la Puente played 16 games with New Orleans; Draughn played three games with Baltimore; Hayden missed '13 season because of injury; Hixon played 15 games with Carolina; Houston played 16 games with Oakland; Idonije played 15 games with Detroit; M.D. Jennings played 16 games with Green Bay; Lane played two games with Detroit; McCray played 15 games with Dallas; Miller last active with Jacksonville in '11; Morgan played 14 games with Washington; Mulligan played 15 games with New England; Mundy played 16 games with the New York Giants; Onobun last active with Jacksonville in '11; Palmer inactive 4 games, did not play 5 games; J. Scott inactive 15 games; T. Scott played four games with Tampa Bay; Senn played 14 games with Carolina; Young played 16 games with Detroit.

Players lost through free agency (6): CB Zackary Bowman (NYG; 16 games in '13), KR Devin Hester (Atl; 16), QB Josh McCown (TB; 8), DT Henry Melton (Dall; 3), DE Corey Wootton (Minn; 16); S Major Wright (TB; 15).

Also played with Bears in '13—TE Kyle Adams (1 game), WR Joe Anderson (6), WR Earl Bennett (15), RB Michael Bush (15), LS Jeremy Cain (2), S Sean Cattouse (1), LB Larry Grant (2), TE Steve Maneri (4), DT Zach Minter (2), LB Cheta Ozougwu (7), DE Julius Peppers (16), P Adam Podlesh (16), DT Tracy Robertson (1), DT Christian Tupou (5).

FIRST-YEAR ROSTER

Name	Pos.	Ht.	Wt.	Birthdate	College	Hometown	How Acq.
Bellamy, Josh (1)	WR	6-0	206	5/18/89	Louisville	St. Petersburg, Fla.	W(Wash)-'14
Booth, Cody	T	6-4	292	4/22/91	Temple	Millersville, Pa.	FA
Carey, Ka'Deem	RB	5-10	207	10/30/92	Arizona	Tuscon, Ariz.	D4a
Cattouse, Sean (1)	S	6-2	210	10/4/88	California	Chicago, Ill.	FA-'13
Dunbar, James	G	6-5	311	3/3/91	Texas Christian	New Boston, Texas	FA
Dunn, Brandon	DT	6-2	300	9/5/92	Louisville	Louisville, Ky.	FA
Fales, David	QB	6-1	228	10/4/90	San Jose State	Salinas, Calif.	D6a
Ferguson, Ego	DT	6-2	315	9/22/91	Louisiana State	Miami, Fla.	D2
Fuller, Kyle	CB	5-11	190	2/6/92	Virginia Tech	Baltimore, Md.	D1
Gaines, Rogers (1)	T	6-6	329	10/28/89	Tennessee State	Nashville, Tenn.	FA-'13
Groy, Ryan	G	6-5	320	9/30/90	Wisconsin	Middleton, Wis.	FA
Hartson, Brandon (1)	LS	6-2	238	10/3/89	Houston	Fairfield, Texas	FA-'13
Hurst, Demontre (1)	CB	5-10	183	3/24/91	Oklahoma	Lancaster, Texas	FA-'13
Johnson, Jerrod (1)	QB	6-5	251	7/27/88	Texas A&M	Houston, Texas	FA-'13
Jones, Christian	LB	6-3	240	2/18/91	Florida State	Winter Park. Fla.	FA
Lattimore, Devekeyan	LB	6-1	237	1/30/91	South Florida	Athens, Ga.	FA
Leno, Jr., Charles	T	6-3	302	10/9/91	Boise State	Oakland, Calif.	D7
Long, Joe (1)	T	6-5	304	7/27/89	Wayne State	Lapeer, Mich.	FA-'13
Lynch, Jordan	RB	6-0	220	10/3/90	Northern Illinois	Chicago, Ill.	FA
O'Donnell, Patrick	P	6-4	220	2/22/91	Miami	Lake Worth, Fla.	D6b
Patrick, Tana	LB	6-3	238	9/30/89	Alabama	Bridgeport, Ala.	FA
Pegues, Lee	DT	6-2	291	7/13/91	Eastern Carolina	Cheraw, S.C.	FA
Perry, Senorise	RB	6-0	187	9/19/91	Louisville	Summerville, Ga.	FA
Purdy, Derricus	CB	6-0	190	3/3/90	Texas Southern	Trotwood, Ohio	FA
Rempel, Chad	LS	6-2	229	5/23/82	Saskatchewan	Sherwood Park, Alberta	FA
Robertson, Tracy (1)	DE	6-4	300	9/26/89	Baylor	Houston, Texas	FA-'13
Sutton, Will	DT	6-0	303	10/3/91	Arizona State	Corona, Calif.	D3
Toliver, Terrence (1)	WR	6-5	204	5/7/88	Louisiana State	Hempstead, Texas	FA-'13
Trice, Marcus	S	5-8	193	11/8/90	North Texas	Mesquite, Texas	FA
Vereen, Brock	S	5-11	199	8/17/92	Minnesota	Valencia, Calif.	D4b
Way, Tress (1)	P	6-1	215	4/18/90	Oklahoma	Tulsa, Okla.	FA-'13
Williams, Chris (1)	WR	5-8	175	9/16/87	New Mexico State	Rio Rancho, N.M.	FA-'13
Wilson, Lawrence (1)	LB	6-1	229	11/18/89	Connecticut	Tuscaloosa, Ala.	FA-'13

The term NFL Rookie is defined as a player who is in his first season of professional football and has not been on the roster of another professional football team for any regular-season or postseason games. A Rookie is designated by an "R" on NFL rosters. Players who have been active in another professional football league or players who have NFL experience, including either preseason training camp or being on an Active List or Inactive List, or on Reserve/Injured or Reserve/Physically Unable to Perform for fewer than six regular-season games, are termed NFL First-Year Players. An NFL First-Year Player is designated by a "1" on NFL rosters. Thereafter, a player is credited with an additional year of experience for each season in which he accumulates six games on the Active List or Inactive List, or on Reserve/Injured or Reserve/Physically Unable to Perform.

Log on to www.chicagobears.com for an up-to-date roster.

COACHING STAFF

Head Coach,
Marc Trestman

Pro Career: Named the fourteenth head coach in Chicago Bears history on January 15, 2004. In its first year under Trestman, Chicago's offense gained a franchise-best 6,109 net yards. The passing offense set single-season records in gross passing yards (4,450), net passing yards (4,281), completion percentage (64.4), passing touchdowns (32) and passer rating (96.9). The Bears offense also set a franchise mark with 344 first downs and finished second in team history with 445 points. The 445 points were second most in the NFL in 2013. Prior to Chicago, spent five seasons as head coach in the Canadian Football League, Trestman led the Montreal Alouettes to back-to-back Grey Cup championships in 2009 and 2010 and was named the CFL's Coach of the Year in 2009. During his time in Montreal, Trestman compiled a 59-31 (.656) regular season record, which included four East Division titles and a 5-3 (.625) record in the playoffs. Trestman has 17 years of coaching experience in the NFL, including eight as an offensive coordinator and 13 working with quarterbacks. During his time in the NFL, Trestman helped his teams to eight playoff appearances, two conference championship games and a Super Bowl appearance (XXXVII as offensive coordinator of the Raiders). Under Trestman, Raiders quarterback Rich Gannon was named NFL MVP in 2002. Trestman oversaw the NFL's No. 1 scoring offense as offensive coordinator of the San Francisco 49ers in 1998, the No. 2 scoring offense with the Oakland Raiders in 2002 and the No. 3 scoring offense with the 49ers in 1996. Trestman also has NFL coaching experience with the Minnesota Vikings, Cleveland Browns, Detroit Lions, Arizona Cardinals and Miami Dolphins. He was also a consultant to the New Orleans Saints. Collegiately, Trestman has been a part of the coaching staffs of the Miami Hurricanes and North Carolina State. Career record: 8-8.

Background: Quarterback for University of Minnesota and Minnesota State University Moorhead. He was a college coach at Miami (1981-84) and North Carolina State (2005-06).

Personal: Born January 15, 1956 in Minneapolis, Minnesota. Trestman and wife, Cindy, have two daughters- Sarahanne and Chloe.

ASSISTANT COACHES

Jim Arthur, strength and conditioning assistant; born July 12, 1978, Cheshire, Conn. Attended Springfield (Mass.) College. No college or pro playing experience. College coach: Springfield (Mass.) College 2000, Louisiana Tech 2001, Boston College 2002. Pro coach: Joined Bears in 2005.

Andy Bischoff, tight ends; born December 8, 1972, Fargo, N.D. Offensive line South Dakota 1989-1993. No pro playing experience. Pro coach: Montreal Alouettes (CFL)

2008-2012, joined Bears in 2013.

Matt Cavanaugh, quarterbacks; born October 27, 1956, Youngstown, Ohio. Quarterback Pittsburgh 1974-77. Pro quarterback New England Patriots 1978-1982, San Francisco 49ers 1983-85, Philadelphia Eagles 1986-89, New York Giants 1990-91. College coach: Pittsburgh 1991-93, 2005-08. Pro coach: Arizona Cardinals 1994-95, San Francisco 49ers 1996, Chicago Bears 1997-98, Baltimore Ravens 1999-2004, New York Jets 2009-2012, joined Bears in 2013.

Mike Clark, strength and conditioning; born August 22, 1954, Wichita, Kan. Center Ottawa 1973-76. No pro playing experience. College coach: Kansas 1977-78, 1982, Wyoming 1981, Oregon 1983-87, Southern California 1988-89, Texas A&M 1990-2003. Pro coach: Seattle Seahawks 2004-09, Kansas City Chiefs 2010-12, joined Bears in 2013.

Joe DeCamillis, asst. head coach/special teams coordinator; born June 29, 1965, Arvada, Colo. Attended Wyoming. No college or pro playing experience. Pro coach: Denver Broncos 1988-1992, New York Giants 1993-96, Atlanta Falcons 1997-2006, Jacksonville Jaguars 2007-08, Dallas Cowboys 2009-2012, joined Bears in 2013.

Sean Desai, defensive quality control; born April 21, 1983, Shelton, Conn. Attended Boston University. No college or pro playing experience. College coach: Temple 2007-2010, Miami, 2011, Boston College 2012. Pro coach: Joined Bears in 2013.

Mike Groh, wide receivers; born December 19, 1971, Charlottesville, Va. Quarterback Virginia, 1991-95. Pro Rhein Fire (WLAF) 1997. College coach: Virginia 2001-08, Alabama 2009, 2011-12, Louisville 2010. Pro coach: New York Jets 2000, joined Bears in 2013.

Chris Harris, defensive quality control; born August 6, 1982, Little Rock, Ark. Safety Louisiana Monroe 2001-04. Pro safety Chicago Bears 2005-06, 2010-11, Carolina Panthers 2007-09, Detroit Lions 2011, Jacksonville Jaguars 2012. Pro coach: Joined Bears in 2013.

Reggie Herring, linebackers; born July 3, 1959, Myrtle Beach, S.C. Linebacker Florida State 1978-1980. No pro playing experience. College coach: Oklahoma State 1981-85, Auburn 1986-1991, Texas Christian 1992-93, Clemson 1994-2001, North Carolina State 2004, Arkansas 2005-07 (interim head coach 2007). Pro coach: Houston Texans 2002-03, 2011-13, Dallas Cowboys 2008-2010, joined Bears in 2014.

Jon Hoke, defensive backs; born January 24, 1957, Kettering, Ohio. Defensive back Ball State 1976-79. Pro defensive back Chicago Bears 1980. College coach: Bowling Green 1983-86, San Diego State 1987-88, Kent State 1989-1993, Missouri 1994-98, Florida 1999-2001. Pro coach: Houston Texans 2002-08, joined Bears in 2009.

Clint Hurtt, assistant defensive line; born November 7, 1978, Rochester, N.Y. Defensive lineman Miami 1997-2000. No pro playing

experience. College coach: Miami 2001-04, 2006-09, Florida International 2005, Louisville 2010-13. Pro coach: Joined Bears in 2014.

Aaron Kromer, offensive coordinator; born April 30, 1967, Sandusky, Ohio. Tackle Miami (Ohio) 1986-89. No pro playing experience. College coach: Miami (Ohio) 1990-98, Northwestern 1999-2000. Pro coach: Oakland Raiders 2001-04, Tampa Bay Buccaneers 2005-07, New Orleans Saints 2008-2012 (interim head coach first six games 2012), joined Bears in 2013.

Pat Meyer, offensive line; born April 5, 1972, Youngstown, Ohio. Offensive line Colorado State 1991-94. Offensive line St. Louis Stampede (AFL) 1996. College coach: Memphis 1997-1999, North Carolina State 2000-06, Colorado State 2008-2011. Pro coach: Montreal Alouettes (CFL) 2012, joined Bears in 2013.

Brendan Nugent, offensive quality control; born February 14, 1983, Port Chester, N.Y. Linebacker Catholic University of America 2001-04. No pro playing experience. College coach: Iowa 2005-06, William & Mary 2007-2011. Pro coach: Montreal Alouettes (CFL) 2012, joined Bears in 2013.

Paul Pasqualoni, defensive line; born August 16, 1949, Cheshire, Conn. Linebacker Penn State 1968-1971. College coach: Southern Connecticut State 1976-1981, Western Connecticut State 1982-86 (head coach), Syracuse 1987-2004 (head coach 1991-2004), Connecticut 2011-13 (head coach). Pro coach: Dallas Cowboys 2005-07, 2010, Miami Dolphins 2008-09, joined Bears in 2014.

Skip Peete, running backs; born January 30, 1963, Mesa, Ariz. Wide receiver Arizona 1981-82, Kansas 1984-85. Pro wide receiver New York Jets 1987. College coach: Pittsburgh 1988-1992, Michigan State 1993-94, Rutgers 1995, UCLA 1996-97. Pro coach: Oakland Raiders 1998-2006, Dallas Cowboys 2007-2012, joined Bears in 2013.

Dwayne Stukes, asst. special teams; born January 24, 1977, Portsmouth, Va. Cornerback/safety Virginia 1996-1999. Pro safety Berlin Thunder (NFL Europe) 2001-2002, Colorado Crush (AFL) 2004. Pro coach: Tampa Bay Buccaneers 2006-2011, joined Bears in 2013.

Mel Tucker, asst. head coach/defensive coordinator; born January 4, 1972, Cleveland, Ohio. Defensive back Wisconsin 1992-95. No pro playing experience. College coach: Michigan State 1997-98, Miami (Ohio) 1999, Louisiana State 2000, Ohio State 2001-04. Pro coach: Cleveland Browns 2005-08, Jacksonville Jaguars 2009-12 (interim head coach 2011), joined Bears in 2013.

Carson Walch, offensive quality control; born March 6, 1978, Milwaukee, Wisc. Running back/wide receiver Winona State 1996-99. No pro playing experience. College coach: Dakota State 2003-05, St. Thomas (Minn.) 2006, Winona State 2007-09. Pro coach: Montreal Alouettes (CFL) 2010-12, joined Bears in 2013.

National Football Conference
East Division
Team Colors: Royal Blue, Metallic Silver
Blue, and White
Cowboys Center, One Cowboys Parkway
Irving, Texas 75063
Telephone: (972) 556-9900

2014 SCHEDULE
PRESEASON
Aug. 7   at San Diego 9:00
Aug. 16 **Baltimore**...........................6:00
Aug. 23 at Miami............................7:00
Aug. 28 **Denver**..............................7:00

REGULAR SEASON
Sep. 7   **San Francisco** 3:25
Sep. 14 at Tennessee 12:00
Sep. 21 at St. Louis 12:00
Sep. 28 **New Orleans** 7:30
Oct. 5   **Houston** 12:00
Oct. 12 at Seattle 3:25
Oct. 19 **New York Giants** 3:25
Oct. 27 **Washington** (Mon) 7:30
Nov. 2   **Arizona** 12:00
Nov. 9   at Jacksonville (London)...12:00
Nov. 16 BYE
Nov. 23 at New York Giants *7:30
Nov. 27 **Philadelphia** (Thu) 3:30
Dec. 4   at Chicago (Thu) 7:25
Dec. 14 at Philadelphia *7:30
Dec. 21 **Indianapolis** 3:25
Dec. 28 at Washington 12:00
*All times CT; Sunday night games in
     Weeks 5-16 subject to change
Stadium: AT&T Stadium (opened in 2009)
  •**Capacity:** 80,000 (expandable to
  100,000 for special events)
  One AT&T Way
  Arlington, Texas 76011
Playing Surface: SoftTop Matrix Turf
Training Camp: Marriott Residence Inn
     Oxnard, California 93030

AT&T STADIUM

CLUB OFFICIALS
Owner/President/General Manager:
  Jerry Jones
Chief Operating Officer/Executive Vice
  President/Director of Player Personnel:
  Stephen Jones
Executive Vice President/VP of Brand
  Management/President Charity
  Foundation: Charlotte Anderson
Executive Vice President/Chief Sales and
  Marketing Officer: Jerry Jones Jr.
Chief Financial Officer: David Frey
Executive Vice President Business
  Operations: Chad Estis
Vice President Public Relations/
  Communications: Rich Dalrymple
Director of Corporate Communications:
  Brett Daniels
Senior Director of Community Relations
  and Alumni Affairs: Emily Robbins
Senior Director of Football
  Administration: Todd Williams
Assistant Director of Player Personnel:
  Will McClay
Director of Scouting: Tom Ciskowski
Director of Player Development:
  Bryan Wansley
Director of Information Technology:
  John Winborn
Senior Director of Brand and Media:
  Matt O'Neil
Director of Broadcasting: Scott Purcel
Internet Director: Derek Eagleton
Director of Ticket Operations:
  Ann Bihari
Head Athletic Trainer: Jim Maurer
Equipment Manager: Mike McCord
Video Director: Robert Blackwell
Cheerleader Director: Kelli Finglass

COACHING HISTORY
(497-373-6)
Records include postseason games
1960-1988 Tom Landry 270-178-6
1989-1993 Jimmy Johnson 51-37-0
1994-97   Barry Switzer 45-26-0
1998-99   Chan Gailey 18-16-0
2000-02   Dave Campo 15-33-0
2003-06   Bill Parcells 34-32-0
2007-2010 Wade Phillips* 35-24-0
2010-13   Jason Garrett 29-27-0
*Released after eight games in 2010

PAID ATTENDANCE
Home 648,683   Away 559,957
Total 1,208,640
Single-game home record,
   105,121 (9/20/09)
Single-season home record,
   648,683 (2013)

2014 DRAFT CHOICES
Round	Name	Pos.	College
1	Zack Martin	G	Notre Dame
2	Demarcus Lawrence	DE	Boise St.
4	Anthony Hitchens	LB	Iowa
5	Devin Street	WR	Pittsburgh
7	Ben Gardner	DE	Stanford
	Will Smith	LB	Texas Tech
	Ahmad Dixon	DB	Baylor
	Ken Bishop	DT	Northern Illinois
	Terrance Mitchell	DB	Oregon

2013 TEAM RECORD
PRESEASON (2-3)

Date	Result	Opponent
08/04	W 24-20	Miami (at Canton, OH)
08/09	L 17-19	at Oakland
08/17	L 7-12	at Arizona
08/24	W 24-18	Cincinnati
08/29	L 6-24	Houston

REGULAR SEASON (8-8)

Date	Result	Opponent
09/08	W 36-31	New York Giants
09/15	L 16-17	at Kansas City
09/22	W 31-7	St. Louis
09/29	L 21-30	at San Diego
10/06	L 48-51	Denver
10/13	W 31-16	Washington
10/20	W 17-3	at Philadelphia
10/27	L 30-31	at Detroit
11/03	W 27-23	Minnesota
11/10	L 17-49	at New Orleans
11/24	W 24-21	at New York Giants
11/28	W 31-24	Oakland
12/09	L 28-45	at Chicago
12/15	L 36-37	Green Bay
12/22	W 24-23	at Washington
12/29	L 22-24	Philadelphia

SCORE BY PERIODS

Cowboys	91	125	98	125	0 —	439
Opponents	67	119	108	138	0 —	432

2013 TEAM STATISTICS

	Cowboys	Opp.
Total First Downs	325	388
Rushing	80	122
Passing	213	231
Penalty	32	35
3rd Down: Made/Att	63/180	91/210
3rd Down Pct.	35.0	43.3
4th Down: Made/Att	4/6	9/18
4th Down Pct.	66.7	50.0
Possession Avg.	29:02	30:58
Total Net Yards	5458	6645
Avg. Per Game	341.1	415.3
Total Plays	957	1094
Avg. Per Play	5.7	6.1
Net Yards Rushing	1504	2056
Avg. Per Game	94.0	128.5
Total Rushes	336	437
Net Yards Passing	3954	4589
Avg. Per Game	247.1	286.8
Sacked/Yards Lost	35/272	34/246
Gross Yards	4226	4835
Att./Completions	586/375	623/403
Completion Pct.	64.0	64.7
Had Intercepted	12	15
Punts/Average	77/45.0	61/47.2
Net Punting Avg.	77/39.1	61/38.9
Penalties/Yards	102/867	112/875
Fumbles/Ball Lost	18/8	16/13
Touchdowns	51	51
Rushing	12	17
Passing	33	33
Returns	6	1

2013 INDIVIDUAL STATISTICS

PASSING

	Att.	Comp.	Yds.	Pct.	TD	Int.	Tkld.	Rate
Romo	535	342	3828	63.9	31	10	35/272	96.7
Orton	51	33	398	64.7	2	2	0/0	85.3
Cowboys	586	375	4226	64.0	33	12	35/272	95.7
Opponents	623	403	4835	64.7	33	15	34/246	96.0

SCORING

	TD R	TD P	TD Rt	PAT	FG	Saf	PTS
Bailey	0	0	0	47/47	28/30	0	131
Bryant	0	13	0	0/0	0/0	0	78
Murray	9	1	0	0/0	0/0	0	60
Witten	0	8	0	0/0	0/0	0	48
Williams	0	5	0	0/0	0/0	0	32
Harris	0	2	1	0/0	0/0	0	18
Beasley	0	2	0	0/0	0/0	0	12
Escobar	0	2	0	0/0	0/0	0	12
Randle	2	0	0	0/0	0/0	0	12
Carr	0	0	1	0/0	0/0	0	6
Church	0	0	1	0/0	0/0	0	6
Hayden	0	0	1	0/0	0/0	0	6
Heath	0	0	1	0/0	0/0	0	6
Lee	0	0	1	0/0	0/0	0	6
Tanner	1	0	0	0/0	0/0	0	6
Cowboys	12	33	6	47/47	28/30	0	439
Opponents	17	33	1	47/48	25/29	0	432

2-Pt Conversions: Williams.
Cowboys 1-4, Opponents 2-3.

RUSHING

	No.	Yds	Avg	LG	TD
Murray	217	1121	5.2	43	9
Randle	54	164	3.0	19	2
Dunbar	30	150	5.0	45	0
Romo	20	38	1.9	15	0
Tanner	9	12	1.3	9	1
Orton	1	8	8.0	8	0
Harris	1	6	6.0	6	0
Williams	3	4	1.3	5	0
Bryant	1	1	1.0	1	0
Cowboys	336	1504	4.5	45	12
Opponents	437	2056	4.7	60	17

RECEIVING

	No.	Yds	Avg	LG	TD
Bryant	93	1233	13.3	79	13
Witten	73	851	11.7	34	8
Murray	53	350	6.6	22	1
Williams	44	736	16.7	82t	5
Beasley	39	368	9.4	23	2
Mi. Austin	24	244	10.2	20	0
Hanna	12	73	6.1	21	0
Escobar	9	134	14.9	25	2
Harris	9	80	8.9	24t	2
Randle	8	61	7.6	13	0
Dunbar	7	59	8.4	17	0
Tanner	3	33	11.0	17	0
Clutts	1	4	4.0	4	0
Cowboys	375	4226	11.3	82t	33
Opponents	403	4835	12.0	87	33

INTERCEPTIONS

	No.	Yds	Avg	LG	TD
Lee	4	174	43.5	74	1
Carr	3	49	16.3	49t	1
Scandrick	2	0	0.0	0	0
Moore	1	21	21.0	21	0
Allen	1	13	13.0	13	0
Church	1	0	0.0	0	0
Claiborne	1	0	0.0	0	0
Heath	1	0	0.0	0	0
Ware	1	0	0.0	0	0
Cowboys	15	257	17.1	74	2
Opponents	12	140	11.7	91	0

PUNTING

	No.	Yds.	Avg.	In 20	LG
C. Jones	77	3467	45.0	30	62
Cowboys	77	3467	45.0	30	62
Opponents	61	2880	47.2	20	68

PUNT RETURNS

	Ret	FC	Yds	Avg	LG	TD
Harris	20	10	256	12.8	86t	1
Beasley	10	3	68	6.8	14	0
Spurlock	1	0	62	62.0	62	0
Cowboys	31	13	386	12.5	86t	1
Opponents	37	27	339	9.2	26	0

KICKOFF RETURNS

	No.	Yds	Avg	LG	TD
Harris	28	857	30.6	90	0
Williams	6	142	23.7	32	0
Spurlock	3	51	17.0	19	0
Bosworth	2	29	14.5	16	0
Dunbar	1	28	28.0	28	0
Clutts	1	12	12.0	12	0
Beasley	1	11	11.0	11	0
A. Smith	1	10	10.0	10	0
Randle	1	7	7.0	7	0
Escobar	1	0	0.0	0	0
Cowboys	45	1147	25.5	90	0
Opponents	38	791	20.8	45	0

FIELD GOALS

	1-19	20-29	30-39	40-49	50+
Bailey	2/2	2/2	8/9	10/10	6/7
Cowboys	2/2	2/2	8/9	10/10	6/7
Opponents	0/0	11/11	6/7	6/7	2/4

SACKS

	No.
Hatcher	11.0
Selvie	7.0
Ware	6.0
B. Carter	2.0
Holloman	2.0
Scandrick	2.0
Wilber	2.0
Wynn	1.0
Brown	1.0
Cowboys	34.0
Opponents	35.0

RECORD HOLDERS
INDIVIDUAL RECORDS—CAREER

Category	Name	Performance
Rushing (Yds.)	Emmitt Smith, 1990-2002	**17,162
Passing (Yds.)	Troy Aikman, 1989-2000	32,942
Passing (TDs)	Tony Romo, 2003-2013	208
Receiving (No.)	Jason Witten, 2003-2013	879
Receiving (Yds.)	Michael Irvin, 1988-1999	11,904
Interceptions	Mel Renfro, 1964-1977	52
Punting (Avg.)	Mat McBriar, 2004-2011	45.3
Punt Return (Avg.)	Deion Sanders, 1995-99	13.3
Kickoff Return (Avg.)	Mel Renfro, 1964-1977	26.4
Field Goals	Rafael Septien, 1978-1986	162
Touchdowns (Tot.)	Emmitt Smith, 1990-2002	164
Points	Emmitt Smith, 1990-2002	986
*Sacks	DeMarcus Ware, 2005-2013	117.0

INDIVIDUAL RECORDS—SINGLE SEASON

Category	Name	Performance
Rushing (Yds.)	Emmitt Smith, 1995	1,773
Passing (Yds.)	Tony Romo, 2012	4,903
Passing (TDs)	Tony Romo, 2007	36
Receiving (No.)	Michael Irvin, 1995	111
Receiving (Yds.)	Michael Irvin, 1995	1,603
Interceptions	Everson Walls, 1981	11
Punting (Avg.)	Mat McBriar, 2006	48.2
Punt Return (Avg.)	Bob Hayes, 1968	20.8
Kickoff Return (Avg.)	Dwayne Harris, 2013	30.6
Field Goals	Richie Cunningham, 1997	34
Touchdowns (Tot.)	Emmitt Smith, 1995	25
Points	Emmitt Smith, 1995	150
*Sacks	DeMarcus Ware, 2008	20.0

INDIVIDUAL RECORDS—SINGLE GAME

Category	Name	Performance
Rushing (Yds.)	DeMarco Murray, 10-23-11	253
Passing (Yds.)	Tony Romo, 10-6-13	506
Passing (TDs)	Many times	5
	Last time by Tony Romo, 10-6-13	
Receiving (No.)	Jason Witten, 10-28-12	18
Receiving (Yds.)	Miles Austin, 10-11-09	250
Interceptions	Many times	3
	Last time by Terence Newman, 12-14-03	
Field Goals	Chris Boniol, 11-18-96	7
	Billy Cundiff, 9-15-03	7
Touchdowns (Tot.)	Many times	4
	Last time by Terrell Owens, 11-18-07	
Points	Many times	24
	Last time by Terrell Owens, 11-18-07	
*Sacks	Jim Jeffcoat, 11-10-85	5.0

*Sacks became an official statistic in 1982.
**NFL Record

2014 VETERAN ROSTER

No.	Name	Pos.	Ht.	Wt.	Birthdate	NFL Exp.	College	Hometown	How Acq.	'13 Games/ Starts
5	Bailey, Dan	K	6-0	191	1/26/88	4	Oklahoma State	Mustang, Okla.	FA-'11	16/0
79	Bass, Ben	DE	6-5	294	10/12/89	3	Texas A&M	Plano, Texas	FA-'12	0*
11	Beasley, Cole	WR	5-8	180	4/26/89	3	Southern Methodist	Little Elm, Texas	FA-'12	14/3
73	Bernadeau, Mackenzy	G	6-4	333	1/3/86	7	Bentley	Waltham, Mass.	UFA(Car)-'12	16/11
88	Bryant, Dez	WR	6-2	222	11/4/88	5	Oklahoma State	Lufkin, Texas	D1-'10	16/16
80	Byrd, LaRon	WR	6-4	220	8/18/89	3	Miami	Hahnville, La.	FA-'14	0*
39	Carr, Brandon	CB	6-0	206	5/19/86	7	Grand Valley State	Flint, Mich.	UFA(KC)-'12	16/16
54	Carter, Bruce	LB	6-2	246	2/19/88	4	North Carolina	Havelock, N.C.	D2-'11	15/13
42	Church, Barry	S	6-2	218	2/11/88	5	Toledo	Pittsburgh, Pa.	FA-'10	16/16
24	Claiborne, Morris	CB	5-11	190	2/7/90	3	Louisiana State	Shreveport, La.	D1-'12	10/7
44	Clutts, Tyler	FB	6-2	254	11/9/84	4	Fresno State	Clovis, Calif.	FA-'13	4/0
98	Crawford, Tyrone	DE	6-4	284	11/22/89	3	Boise State	Windsor, Ontario	D3-'12	0*
25	Dunbar, Lance	RB	5-8	188	1/25/90	3	North Texas	Haltom City, Texas	FA-'12	9/0
52	Durant, Justin	LB	6-1	228	9/21/85	8	Hampton	Florence, S.C.	UFA(Det)-'13	10/6
89	Escobar, Gavin	TE	6-6	249	2/3/91	2	San Diego State	Orange County, Calif.	D2-'13	16/1
72	Frederick, Travis	C	6-3	311	3/18/91	2	Wisconsin	Sharon, Wisc.	D1-'13	16/16
68	Free, Doug	T	6-6	325	1/6/84	8	Northern Illinois	Manitowoc, Wisc.	D4b-'07	16/16
23	Hamilton, Jakar	S	5-11	195	10/2/89	2	South Carolina State	Johnston, S.C.	FA-'13	3/0
7	Hanie, Caleb	QB	6-2	222	9/11/85	6	Colorado State	Dallas, Texas	FA-'13	0*
84	Hanna, James	TE	6-4	250	7/14/89	3	Oklahoma	Flower Mound, Texas	D6-'12	16/8
17	Harris, Dwayne	WR	5-10	207	9/16/87	4	East Carolina	Stone Mountain, Ga.	D6-'11	13/3
96	Hayden, Nick	DT	6-4	301	2/4/86	7	Wisconsin	Hartland, Wisc.	FA-'13	16/16
38	Heath, Jeff	S	6-1	209	5/14/91	2	Saginaw Valley State	Lake Orion, Mich.	FA-'13	16/9
57	Holloman, DeVonte	LB	6-2	242	2/12/91	2	South Carolina	Charlotte, N.C.	D6-'13	9/2
37	Johnson, Matt	S	6-1	212	7/22/89	3	Eastern Washington	Olympia, Wash.	D4b-'12	0*
6	Jones, Chris	P	6-0	197	7/21/89	3	Carson Newman	Rome, Ga.	FA-'11	16/0
91	Ladouceur, Louis-Philippe	LS	6-5	259	3/13/81	10	California	Pointe-Claire, Quebec	FA-'05	16/0
53	Lawrence, Cameron	LB	6-2	234	1/20/91	2	Mississippi State	Coldwater, Miss.	FA-'13	11/0
65	Leary, Ronald	G	6-3	331	4/29/89	2	Memphis	Baton Rouge, La.	FA-'12	16/16
50	Lee, Sean	LB	6-2	234	7/22/86	5	Penn State	Pittsburgh, Pa.	D2-'10	11/11
58	Lemon, Orie	LB	6-1	242	9/9/87	4	Oklahoma State	Houston, Texas	PS(Ariz)-'13	3/0
97	McClain, Terrell	DT	6-2	293	7/20/88	4	South Florida	Pensacola, Fla.	FA-'14	16/0*
69	Melton, Henry	DT	6-3	295	10/11/86	6	Texas	Grapevine, Texas	UFA(Chi)-'14	3/3*
92	Mincey, Jeremy	DE	6-4	265	12/14/83	7	Florida	Statesboro, Ga.	UFA(Den)-'14	10/0*
26	Moore, Sterling	CB	5-10	199	2/3/90	4	Southern Methodist	Antioch, Calif.	FA-'13	5/0
29	Murray, DeMarco	RB	6-0	219	2/12/88	4	Oklahoma	Las Vegas, Nev.	D3-'11	14/14
60	Okyoe, Amobi	DT	6-2	292	6/10/87	7	Louisville	Huntsville, Ala.	FA-'14	0*
18	Orton, Kyle	QB	6-4	228	11/14/82	10	Purdue	Altoona, Iowa	UFA(KC)-'12	3/1
78	Parnell, Jermey	T	6-6	307	7/20/86	5	Mississippi	Blytheville, Ark.	FA-'10	16/1
21	Randle, Joseph	RB	6-0	198	12/29/91	2	Oklahoma State	Wichita, Kan.	D5-'13	13/2
9	Romo, Tony	QB	6-2	236	4/21/80	12	Eastern Illinois	Burlington, Wisc.	FA-'03	15/15
32	Scandrick, Orlando	CB	5-10	195	2/10/87	7	Boise State	Los Alamitos, Calif.	D5-'08	16/15
99	Selvie, George	DE	6-4	270	3/6/87	5	South Florida	Pensacola, Fla.	FA-'13	16/16
77	Smith, Tyron	T	6-5	318	12/12/90	4	Southern California	Moreno Valley, Calif.	D1-'11	16/16
93	Spencer, Anthony	DE	6-3	262	1/23/84	8	Purdue	Fort Wayne, Ind.	D1-'07	1/0
20	Webb, B.W.	CB	5-11	178	5/3/90	2	William & Mary	Newport News, Va.	D4-'13	15/0
3	Weeden, Brandon	QB	6-3	220	10/14/83	3	Oklahoma State	Edmond, Okla.	FA-'14	8/5*
75	Weems, Darrion	T	6-5	308	9/4/88	2	Oregon	Winnetka, Calif.	PS(Den)-'12	0*
51	Wilber, Kyle	LB	6-4	250	4/26/89	3	Wake Forest	Apopka, Fla.	D4a-'12	16/6
27	Wilcox, J.J.	S	6-0	217	2/14/91	2	Georgia Southern	Cairo, Ga.	D3b-'13	13/5
34	Williams, Ryan	RB	5-9	207	4/9/90	2	Virginia Tech	Manassas, Va.	FA-'14	5/3*
83	Williams, Terrance	WR	6-2	206	9/8/89	2	Baylor	Dallas, Texas	D3a-'13	16/8
56	Wilson, Martez	DE	6-4	252	9/21/88	4	Illinois	Chicago, Ill.	FA-'14	9/0
82	Witten, Jason	TE	6-6	261	5/6/82	12	Tennessee	Elizabethton, Tenn.	D3-'03	16/16

*   Bass missed '13 season because of injury; Byrd missed '13 season because of injury; Crawford missed '13 season because of injury; Hanie last active with Chicago in '11; Johnson missed '13 season because of injury; McClain played 16 games with Houston; Melton played three games with Chicago; Mincey played eight games with Jacksonville, two games with Denver; Okyoe last played in Chicago in '12; Weeden played eight games with Cleveland in '13; Weems inactive for 16 games; R. Williams played five games with Arizona.

Players lost through free agency (2): DT Jason Hatcher (Wash; 15 games in '13), Danny McCray (Chi; 15).

Also played with Cowboys in '13—S Will Allen (5 games), DT Marvin Austin (1), WR Miles Austin (11), LB Kyle Bosworth (14), DE Everette Brown (7), DT Everett Dawkins (1), DT Corvey Irvin (6), DE Edgar Jones (7), DT Jerome Long (3), DT Drake Nevis (11), S Micah Pellerin (2), TE Andre Smith (3), RB Phillip Tanner (16), DE Jason Vega (2), DE DeMarcus Ware (13).

FIRST-YEAR ROSTER

Name	Pos.	Ht.	Wt.	Birthdate	College	Hometown	How Acq.
Aladenoye, Josh	T	6-5	329	9/26/90	Illinois State	Mesquite, Texas	FA
Benford, Tim (1)	WR	5-11	193	9/7/89	Tennessee Tech	Chattanooga, Tenn.	FA
Bishop, Ken	NT	6-0	305	9/8/90	Northern Illinois	Lauderhill, Fla.	D7d
Boyd, Chris	WR	6-4	206	12/16/91	Vanderbilt	Roswell, Ga.	FA
Clarke, Brian	G	6-2	296	10/14/89	Bloomsburg	Hanover Township, Penn.	FA
Coleman, Davon	DT	6-2	297	1/11/91	Arizona State	Cleveland, Ohio	FA
Copeland, J.C.	FB	5-11	275	7/21/91	Louisiana State	LaGrange, Ga.	FA
Cureton, Andre'	G	6-5	343	7/26/91	Cincinnati	Indianapolis, Ind.	FA
Dixon, Ahmad	S	6-0	205	9/5/91	Baylor	Waco, Texas	D7c
Gardner, Ben	DE	6-4	260	4/29/91	Stanford	Mequon, Wisc.	D7a
Hitchens, Anthony	LB	6-0	240	6/10/92	Iowa	Lorain, Ohio	D4
Kreiter, Casey	LS	6-2	246	8/13/90	Iowa	DeWitt, Iowa	FA
Lawrence, DeMarcus	DE	6-3	250	4/28/92	Boise State	Aiken, S.C.	D2
Malena, Ben	RB	5-8	196	5/29/92	Texas A&M	Cedar Hill, Texas	FA
Mandell, Cody	P	6-2	214	4/7/92	Alabama	Lafayette, La.	FA
Martin, Zack	G	6-4	308	11/20/90	Notre Dame	Indianapolis, Ind.	D1
Mitchell, Terrance	CB	5-11	193	5/17/92	Oregon	Sacramento, Calif.	D7e
Morris, Darius	G	6-4	320	4/28/88	Temple	Long Branch, N.J.	FA
Najvar, Jordan	TE	6-6	256	1/8/91	Baylor	Spring, Texas	FA
Newsome, Jamar (1)	WR	6-1	201	11/5/87	Central Florida	St. Petersburg, Fla.	FA
Patmon, Tyler	CB	5-10	179	1/26/91	Oklahoma State	Round Rock, Texas	FA
Patrick, Ronald	G	6-1	318	11/1/91	South Carolina	Cocoa, Texas	FA
Phillips, Dashaun	CB	5-11	181	1/3/91	Tarleton State	Duncanville, Texas	FA
Rayford, Caesar (1)	DE	6-7	267	3/4/86	Washington	Spanaway, Wash.	FA
Sapp, Dontavis	LB	6-2	235	1/17/91	Tennessee	Valdosta, Ga.	FA
Skinner, Jocquel	CB	6-0	179	7/12/92	Bethel (Tenn.)	St. Petersburg, Fla.	FA
Smith, Keith	S	6-0	233	4/8/92	San Jose State	Covina, Calif.	FA
Smith, Ryan	S	6-0	199	5/12/92	Auburn	Cordova, Ala.	FA
Smith, Will	LB	6-2	227	1/13/92	Texas Tech	Riverside, Calif.	D7b
Street, Devin	WR	6-3	190	3/30/91	Pittsburgh	Bethlehem, Pa.	D5
Vaughan, Dustin	QB	6-5	233	1/27/91	West Texas A&M	Corpus Christi, Texas	FA
Washington, L'Damian	WR	6-4	188	5/10/91	Missouri	Shreveport, La.	FA
Wetzel, John (1)	T	6-7	315	7/18/91	Boston College	Pittsburgh, Pa.	FA
Whaley, Chris	DT	6-3	272	12/8/90	Texas	Madisonville, Texas	FA
Wilson, Evan	TE	6-6	253	2/13/92	Illinois	Woodstock, Ga.	FA
Windsor, Joe	LB	6-0	232	9/3/91	Northern Illinois	Kearney, Mo.	FA

The term NFL Rookie is defined as a player who is in his first season of professional football and has not been on the roster of another professional football team for any regular-season or postseason games. A Rookie is designated by an "R" on NFL rosters. Players who have been active in another professional football league or players who have NFL experience, including either preseason training camp or being on an Active List or Inactive List, or on Reserve/Injured or Reserve/Physically Unable to Perform for fewer than six regular-season games, are termed NFL First-Year Players. An NFL First-Year Player is designated by a "1" on NFL rosters. Thereafter, a player is credited with an additional year of experience for each season in which he accumulates six games on the Active List or Inactive List, or on Reserve/Injured or Reserve/Physically Unable to Perform.

Log on to www.dallascowboys.com for an up-to-date roster.

DALLAS COWBOYS

COACHING STAFF

Head Coach,
Jason Garrett

Pro Career: Named the eighth head coach in Dallas Cowboys history on January 5, 2011 and became the first former Cowboys player to become the team's head coach. Named the club's interim head coach at the midpoint of the 2010 season and went on to guide a Dallas team that had started the season with a 1-7 record to a 5-3 mark down the stretch. Since the 2007 season Garrett had been the Cowboys offensive coordinator, and in 2008, he was assigned the additional duties of being the club's assistant head coach. Under Garrett, the Dallas offense finished among the NFL's top-10 four times: 2012 (6th), 2010 (10th), 2009 (2nd), and 2007 (2nd). En route to winning the 2009 NFC Eastern Division title, Dallas established club records for total offensive yards (6,390), net passing yards (4,287) and pass completions (347). Dallas won the NFC East in 2007 with a team-record tying 13 victories and finished second in the NFL in scoring. Garrett was named *Pro Football Weekly's* NFL's Assistant Coach of the Year in March of 2008. Career record: 29-27.

Background: Played quarterback at Princeton (1987-88) and was named the Ivy League's Player of the Year and honorable mention All American as a senior. Played professionally in World League and Canadian Football League (both 1991) before joining Dallas (1992-99), Giants (2000-03), Buccaneers (2004) and Dolphins (also 2004). Key reserve on three Super Bowl teams with Dallas and one with the Giants. Began his coaching career as quarterbacks coach with Nick Saban's Dolphins.

Personal: Born March 28, 1966, in Abington, Pa. He and his wife Brill reside in Dallas.

ASSISTANT COACHES

Joe Baker, asst. secondary coach; born June 29, 1969, Glen Ridge, N.J. Wide receiver Princeton 1987-1990. No pro playing experience. College coach: East Stroudsburg 1991, Samford 1993, Wisconsin 1999. Pro coach: Birmingham Fire (WFL) 1992, Jacksonville Jaguars 1995-98, New Orleans Saints 2000-04, Green Bay Packers 2005, St. Louis Rams 2006, Denver Broncos 2007-08, Tampa Bay Buccaneers 2009-2011, joined Cowboys in 2012.

Rich Bisaccia, special teams coordinator; born June 3, 1960, Yonkers, N.Y. Defensive back Yankton College 1979-1982. Pro defensive back Philadelphia Stars (USFL) 1983. College coach: Wayne State 1983-87, South Carolina 1988-1993, Clemson 1994-98, Mississippi 1999-2001. Pro coach: Tampa Bay Buccaneers 2002-2010, San Diego Chargers 2011-12, joined Cowboys in 2013.

Ben Bloom, asst. defensive line/defensive ends; born October 17, 1982, Wellesley, Mass. Offensive line Tufts 2001-04. No pro playing experience. College coach: Tufts 2005-07, Harvard 2008. Pro coach: Cleveland Browns 2010, joined Cowboys in 2011.

Gary Brown, running backs; born July 1, 1969, Williamsport, Pa. Running back Penn State 1987-1990. Pro running back Houston Oilers 1991-95, San Diego Chargers 1997, New York Giants 1998-99. College coach: Lycoming 2003-05, Susquehanna 2006-07, Rutgers 2008. Pro coach: Cleveland Browns 2009-2012, joined Cowboys in 2013.

Bill Callahan, offensive coordinator/offensive line; born July 31, 1956, Chicago, Ill. Quarterback Benedictine 1975-77. No pro playing experience. College coach: Illinois 1980-86, Northern Arizona 1987-88, Southern Illinois 1989, Wisconsin 1990-94, Nebraska 2004-07 (head coach). Pro coach: Philadelphia Eagles 1995-97, Oakland Raiders 1998-2003 (head coach 2002-03), New York Jets 2008-2011, joined Cowboys in 2012.

Kevin Carberry, offensive assistant; born May 19, 1983, Chicago, Ill. Defensive end Ohio 2001-04. Pro defensive line Berlin Thunder (NFL Europe) 2006, New York Dragons (AFL) 2007, Philadelphia Soul (AFL) 2008. College coach: Kansas 2009-2011, Stephen F. Austin 2012-13. Pro coach: Joined Cowboys in 2014.

Derek Dooley, wide receivers; born June 10, 1968, Athens, Ga. Wide receiver Virginia 1987-1990. No pro playing experience. College coach: Georgia 1996, Southern Methodist 1997-99, Louisiana State 2000-04, Louisiana Tech 2007-09 (head coach), Tennessee 2010-12 (head coach). Pro coach: Miami Dolphins 2005-06, joined Cowboys in 2013.

Matt Eberflus, linebackers; born May 17, 1970, Toledo, Ohio. Linebacker Toledo 1988-1991. No pro playing experience. College coach: Toledo 1992-2000, Missouri 2001-08. Pro coach: Cleveland Browns 2009-2010, joined Cowboys in 2011.

Jerome Henderson, secondary; born August 8, 1969, Portsmouth, Va. Defensive back Clemson 1987-1990. Pro cornerback New England Patriots 1991-93, 1996, Buffalo Bills 1993-94, Philadelphia Eagles 1995, New York Jets 1997-98. Pro coach: New York Jets 2007-08, Cleveland Browns 2009-2011, joined Cowboys in 2012.

Monte Kiffin, asst. head coach/defense; born February 29, 1940, Lexington, Neb. Offensive/defensive tackle Nebraska 1959-1963. Pro defensive end Winnipeg Blue Bombers (CFL) 1965. College coach: Nebraska 1966-1976, Arkansas 1977-79, North Carolina State 1980-82 (head coach), Tennessee 2009, Southern California 2010-12. Pro coach: Green Bay Packers 1983, Buffalo Bills 1984-85, Minnesota Vikings 1986-89, 1991-94, New York Jets 1990, New Orleans Saints 1995, Tampa Buccaneers 1996-2008, joined Cowboys in 2013.

Leon Lett, asst. defensive line/defensive tackles; born October 12, 1968, Mobile, Ala. Defensive tackle Hinds (Miss.) C.C. 1987-88, Emporia State 1989-1990. Pro defensive tackle Dallas Cowboys 1991-2000, Denver Broncos 2001. College coach: Louisiana-Monroe 2009-2010. Pro coach: Joined Cowboys in 2011.

Scott Linehan, passing game coordinator; born September 17, 1963, Sunnyside, Wash. Quarterback Idaho 1982-86. No pro playing experience. College coach: Idaho 1989-1990, 1992-93, Nevada-Las Vegas 1991, Washington 1994-98, Louisville 1999-2001. Pro coach: Minnesota Vikings 2002-04, Miami Dolphins 2005, St. Louis Rams 2006-08 (head coach), Detroit Lions 2009-2013, joined Cowboys in 2014.

Rod Marinelli, defensive coordinator; born July 13, 1949, Rosemead, Calif. Offensive/defensive tackle Utah 1968, offensive tackle California Lutheran 1970-72. No pro playing experience. College coach: Utah State 1976, California 1983-1991, Arizona State 1992-94, Southern California 1995. Pro coach: Tampa Bay Buccaneers 1996-2005, Detroit Lions 2006-08 (head coach), Chicago Bears 2009-2012, joined Cowboys in 2013.

Keith O'Quinn, asst. special teams; born July 28, 1973, Pensacola, Fla. Safety North Texas 1991-96. No pro playing experience. College coach: Hardin-Simmons 2000-02, Abilene Christian 2003-04. Pro coach: Joined Cowboys in 2010.

Frank Pollack, asst. offensive line; born November 5, 1967, Camp Springs, Md. Offensive tackle/offensive guard Northern Arizona 1985-89. Pro tackle, guard San Francisco 49ers 1990-97. College coach: Northern Arizona 2005-06. Pro coach: Houston Texans 2007-2011, Oakland Raiders 2012, joined Cowboys in 2013.

Michael Pope, tight ends; born March 15, 1942, Monroe, N.C. Quarterback Lenoir-Rhyne College 1962-64. No pro playing experience. College coach: Florida State 1970-74, Texas Tech 1975-77, Mississippi 1978-1982. Pro coach: New York Giants 1983-1991, 2000-2013, Cincinnati Bengals 1992-93, New England Patriots 1994-96, Washington Redskins 1997-99, joined Cowboys in 2014.

Kyle Valero, asst. wide receivers; born April 24, 1986, Fountain Valley, Calif. Attended Florida State. No college or pro playing experience. College coach: Florida State 2008-09. Pro coach: Detroit Lions 2010-12, joined Cowboys in 2014.

Turner West, defensive assistant; born December 19, 1987, Germantown, Tenn. Wide receiver Memphis 2006-2010. No pro playing experience. College coach: Alabama-Birmingham 2011, Samford 2012, Middle Tennessee State 2012-13. Pro coach: Joined Cowboys in 2014.

Wade Wilson, quarterbacks; born February 1, 1959, Commerce, Texas. Quarterback East Texas State 1977-1980. Pro quarterback Minnesota Vikings 1981-1991, Atlanta Falcons 1992, New Orleans Saints 1993-94, Dallas Cowboys 1995-97, Oakland Raiders 1998-99. Pro coach: Dallas Cowboys 2000-02, Chicago Bears 2004-06, re-joined Cowboys in 2007.

Mike Woicik, strength and conditioning; born September 26, 1956, Baltimore. Attended Boston College. No college or pro playing experience. College coach: Springfield College 1978-1980, Syracuse 1980-89. Pro coach: Dallas Cowboys 1990-96, New Orleans Saints 1997-99, New England Patriots 2000-10, re-joined Cowboys in 2011.

National Football Conference
North Division
Team Colors: Honolulu Blue and Silver
222 Republic Drive
Allen Park, Michigan 48101
Telephone: (313) 216-4000

2014 SCHEDULE

PRESEASON

Aug. 9	**Cleveland**	7:30
Aug. 15	at Oakland	10:00
Aug. 22	**Jacksonville**	7:30
Aug. 28	at Buffalo	7:00

REGULAR SEASON

Sep. 8	**New York Giants** (Mon)	7:10
Sep. 14	at Carolina	1:00
Sep. 21	**Green Bay**	1:00
Sep. 28	at New York Jets	1:00
Oct. 5	**Buffalo**	1:00
Oct. 12	at Minnesota	1:00
Oct. 19	**New Orleans**	1:00
Oct. 26	at Atlanta (London)	9:30a
Nov. 2	BYE	
Nov. 9	**Miami**	1:00
Nov. 16	at Arizona	4:25
Nov. 23	at New England	1:00
Nov. 27	**Chicago** (Thu)	12:30
Dec. 7	**Tampa Bay**	1:00
Dec. 14	**Minnesota**	1:00
Dec. 21	at Chicago	1:00
Dec. 28	at Green Bay	1:00

All times ET

Stadium: Ford Field (opened in 2002)
 •**Capacity:** 64,500
 2000 Brush Street
 Detroit, Michigan 48226
Playing Surface: FieldTurf
Training Camp: 222 Republic Drive
 Allen Park, Michigan
 48101

FORD FIELD

CLUB OFFICIALS

Owner: Martha Firestone Ford
Vice Chairman: Bill Ford
President: Tom Lewand
Executive Vice President of Football
 Operations and General Manager:
 Martin Mayhew
Senior Personnel Executive:
 Brian Xanders
Senior Personnel Advisor: James Harris
Corporate Secretary: Dave Hempstead
Senior Vice President of
 Communications: Bill Keenist
Senior Vice President, Marketing &
 Partnerships: Elizabeth Parkinson
Senior Vice President & CFO: Luis Perez
Senior Advisor: Tom Lesnau
Vice President of Football Operations:
 Cedric Saunders
Vice President of Pro Personnel:
 Sheldon White
Director of College Scouting:
 Scott McEwen
Player Personnel: Cary Conklin,
 Chad Henry, Joe Kelleher,
 Rob Lohman, Miller McCalmon,
 Silas McKinnie, Lance Newmark,
 Charlie Sanders, Dave Sears,
 Dave Uyrus, Darren Anderson
Director of Media Relations:
 Matt Barnhart
Director of Corporate Communications:
 Ben Manges
Director of Community Relations:
 Robert Wooley
Director of Broadcasting and Production:
 Bryan Bender
Director of Ticket Operations:
 Mark Graham
Coordinator of Athletic Medicine/Athletic
 Training: Dean Kleinschmidt
Head Athletic Trainer: Kevin Bastin
Equipment Manager: Tim O'Neill
Video Director: Robert Yanagi

COACHING HISTORY

Portsmouth Spartans 1930-33
(524-631-32)
Records include postseason games

1930	Hal (Tubby) Griffen	5-6-3
1931-36	George (Potsy) Clark	49-20-6
1937-38	Earl (Dutch) Clark	14-8-0
1939	Elmer (Gus) Henderson	6-5-0
1940	George (Potsy) Clark	5-5-1
1941-42	Bill Edwards*	4-9-1
1942	John Karcis	0-8-0
1943-47	Charles (Gus) Dorais	20-31-2
1948-1950	Alvin (Bo) McMillin	12-24-0
1951-56	Raymond (Buddy) Parker	50-24-2
1957-1964	George Wilson	55-45-6
1965-66	Harry Gilmer	10-16-2
1967-1972	Joe Schmidt	43-35-7
1973	Don McCafferty	6-7-1
1974-76	Rick Forzano**	15-17-0
1976-77	Tommy Hudspeth	11-13-0
1978-1984	Monte Clark	43-63-1
1985-88	Darryl Rogers***	18-40-0
1988-1996	Wayne Fontes	67-71-0
1997-2000	Bobby Ross****	27-32-0
2000	Gary Moeller	4-3-0
2001-02	Marty Mornhinweg	5-27-0
2003-05	Steve Mariucci#	15-28-0
2005	Dick Jauron	1-4-0
2006-08	Rod Marinelli	10-38-0
2009-2013	Jim Schwartz	29-52-0

 *Released after three games in 1942
 **Resigned after four games in 1976
 ***Released after 11 games in 1988
 ****Resigned after nine games in 2000
 # Released after 11 games in 2005

PAID ATTENDANCE

Home 503,563   Away 524,188
Total 1,027,751
Single-game home record,
 80,444 (12/20/81)
Single-season home record, 644,904
 (1980)

2014 DRAFT CHOICES

Round	Name	Pos.	College
1	Eric Ebron	TE	North Carolina
2	Kyle Van Noy	LB	Brigham Young
3	Travis Swanson	C	Arkansas
4	Nevin Lawson	DB	Utah St.
	Larry Webster	DE	Bloomsburg
5	Caraun Reid	DT	Princeton
6	T.J. Jones	WR	Notre Dame
7	Nate Freese	K	Boston College

2013 TEAM RECORD

PRESEASON (3-1)

Date	Result	Opponent
08/09	W 26-17	New York Jets
08/15	L 6-24	at Cleveland
08/22	W 40-9	New England
08/29	W 35-13	at Buffalo

REGULAR SEASON (7-9)

Date	Result	Opponent
09/08	W 34-24	Minnesota
09/15	L 21-25	at Arizona
09/22	W 27-20	at Washington
09/29	W 40-32	Chicago
10/06	L 9-22	at Green Bay
10/13	W 31-17	at Cleveland
10/20	L 24-27	Cincinnati
10/27	W 31-30	Dallas
11/10	W 21-19	at Chicago
11/17	L 27-37	at Pittsburgh
11/24	L 21-24	Tampa Bay
11/28	W 40-10	Green Bay
12/08	L 20-34	at Philadelphia
12/16	L 16-18	Baltimore
12/22	L 20-23	New York Giants (OT)
12/29	L 13-14	at Minnesota

(OT) Overtime

SCORE BY PERIODS

Lions	48	136	90	121	0 —	395
Opponents	61	120	60	132	3 —	376

2013 TEAM STATISTICS

	Lions	Opp.
Total First Downs	350	290
Rushing	106	62
Passing	221	197
Penalty	23	31
3rd Down: Made/Att	95/221	64/211
3rd Down Pct.	43.0	30.3
4th Down: Made/Att	5/14	9/12
4th Down Pct.	35.7	75.0
Possession Avg.	32:07	27:53
Total Net Yards	6274	5546
Avg. Per Game	392.1	346.6
Total Plays	1102	982
Avg. Per Play	5.7	5.6
Net Yards Rushing	1792	1596
Avg. Per Game	112.0	99.8
Total Rushes	445	377
Net Yards Passing	4482	3950
Avg. Per Game	280.1	246.9
Sacked/Yards Lost	23/168	33/249
Gross Yards	4650	4199
Att./Completions	634/371	572/338
Completion Pct.	58.5	59.1
Had Intercepted	19	15
Punts/Average	73/46.6	84/44.4
Net Punting Avg.	73/40.4	84/38.8
Penalties/Yards	110/925	87/681
Fumbles/Ball Lost	28/15	19/7
Touchdowns	48	38
Rushing	15	10
Passing	29	24
Returns	4	4

2013 INDIVIDUAL STATISTICS

PASSING

	Att.	Comp.	Yds.	Pct.	TD	Int.	Tkld.	Rate
Stafford	634	371	4650	58.5	29	19	23/168	84.2
Lions	634	371	4650	58.5	29	19	23/168	84.2
Opponents	572	338	4199	59.1	24	15	33/249	85.0

SCORING

	TD R	TD P	TD Rt	PAT	FG	Saf	PTS
Akers	0	0	0	42/43	19/24	0	99
Johnson	0	12	0	0/0	0/0	0	72
Bell	8	0	0	0/0	0/0	0	50
Fauria	0	7	0	0/0	0/0	0	44
Bush	4	3	0	0/0	0/0	0	42
Ross	0	1	2	0/0	0/0	0	18
Durham	0	2	0	0/0	0/0	0	12
Pettigrew	0	2	0	0/0	0/0	0	12
Stafford	2	0	0	0/0	0/0	0	12
Fairley	0	0	1	0/0	0/0	1	8
Burleson	0	1	0	0/0	0/0	0	6
Levy	0	0	1	0/0	0/0	0	6
Ogletree	0	1	0	0/0	0/0	0	6
Riddick	1	0	0	0/0	0/0	0	6
Suh	0	0	0	0/0	0/0	1	2
Lions	15	29	4	42/43	19/24	2	395
Opponents	10	24	4	29/29	37/40	0	376

2-Pt Conversions: Bell, Fauria.
Lions 2-5, Opponents 4-9.

RUSHING

	No.	Yds	Avg	LG	TD
Bush	223	1006	4.5	39	4
Bell	166	650	3.9	20	8
Stafford	37	69	1.9	14	2
Ross	2	40	20.0	24	0
Riddick	9	25	2.8	7	1
Leshoure	2	9	4.5	5	0
Martin	2	3	1.5	3	0
Hill	2	-2	-1.0	-1	0
Burleson	2	-8	-4.0	0	0
Lions	445	1792	4.0	39	15
Opponents	377	1596	4.2	78t	10

RECEIVING

	No.	Yds	Avg	LG	TD
Johnson	84	1492	17.8	87	12
Bush	54	506	9.4	77t	3
Bell	53	547	10.3	37	0
Pettigrew	41	416	10.1	31	2
Burleson	39	461	11.8	47	1
Durham	38	490	12.9	40	2
Fauria	18	207	11.5	25	7
Ogletree	13	199	15.3	43	1
Broyles	8	85	10.6	22	0
Scheffler	7	82	11.7	22	0
Ross	5	59	11.8	19	1
Edwards	5	46	9.2	11	0
Riddick	4	26	6.5	8	0
Dickerson	2	34	17.0	26	0
Lions	371	4650	12.5	87	29
Opponents	338	4199	12.4	85t	24

INTERCEPTIONS

	No.	Yds	Avg	LG	TD
Levy	6	76	12.7	66t	1
Quin	3	57	19.0	42	0
Delmas	3	44	14.7	42	0
Houston	2	34	17.0	30	0
Tulloch	1	0	0.0	0	0
Lions	15	211	14.1	66t	1
Opponents	19	364	19.2	74	3

PUNTING

	No.	Yds.	Avg.	In 20	LG
Martin	72	3399	47.2	22	72
Lions	73	3399	46.6	22	72
Opponents	84	3733	44.4	25	70

PUNT RETURNS

	Ret	FC	Yds	Avg	LG	TD
Spurlock	22	12	145	6.6	57	0
Ross	15	15	243	16.2	58t	1
Broyles	1	2	4	4.0	4	0
Lions	38	29	392	10.3	58t	1
Opponents	32	18	250	7.8	50	0

KICKOFF RETURNS

	No.	Yds	Avg	LG	TD
Ross	15	439	29.3	98t	1
Spurlock	15	338	22.5	36	0
Dickerson	1	18	18.0	18	0
Riddick	1	12	12.0	12	0
Gandy	1	5	5.0	5	0
Bell	1	4	4.0	4	0
Lions	34	816	24.0	98t	1
Opponents	35	924	26.4	56	0

FIELD GOALS

	1-19	20-29	30-39	40-49	50+
Akers	1/1	5/5	6/8	4/7	3/3
Lions	1/1	5/5	6/8	4/7	3/3
Opponents	0/0	10/10	7/8	11/12	9/0

SACKS

	No.
Ansah	8.0
Fairley	6.0
Suh	5.5
Tulloch	3.5
Young	3.0
Taylor	2.5
Delmas	2.0
Quin	2.0
Idonije	0.5
Lions	33.0
Opponents	23.0

RECORD HOLDERS
INDIVIDUAL RECORDS—CAREER

Category	Name	Performance
Rushing (Yds.)	Barry Sanders, 1989-1998	15,269
Passing (Yds.)	Matthew Stafford, 2009-2013	17,457
Passing (TDs)	Bobby Layne, 1950-58	118
Receiving (No.)	Herman Moore, 1991-2001	670
Receiving (Yds.)	Calvin Johnson, 2007-2013	9,328
Interceptions	Dick LeBeau, 1959-1972	62
Punting (Avg.)	Yale Lary, 1952-53, 1956-1964	44.3
Punt Return (Avg.)	Jack Christiansen, 1951-58	12.8
Kickoff Return (Avg.)	Pat Studstill, 1961-67	25.7
Field Goals	Jason Hanson, 1992-2012	495
Touchdowns (Tot.)	Barry Sanders, 1989-1998	109
Points	Jason Hanson, 1992-2012	2,150
*Sacks	Robert Porcher, 1992-2003	95.5

INDIVIDUAL RECORDS—SINGLE SEASON

Category	Name	Performance
Rushing (Yds.)	Barry Sanders, 1997	2,053
Passing (Yds.)	Matthew Stafford, 2011	5,038
Passing (TDs)	Matthew Stafford, 2011	41
Receiving (No.)	Herman Moore, 1995	123
Receiving (Yds.)	Calvin Johnson, 2012	**1,964
Interceptions	Don Doll, 1950	12
	Jack Christiansen, 1953	12
Punting (Avg.)	Yale Lary, 1963	48.9
Punt Return (Avg.)	Pat Studstill, 1962	15.8
Kickoff Return (Avg.)	Mel Gray, 1994	28.4
Field Goals	Jason Hanson, 1993	34
Touchdowns (Tot.)	Barry Sanders, 1991	17
Points	Jason Hanson, 2012	134
*Sacks	Robert Porcher, 1999	15.0

INDIVIDUAL RECORDS—SINGLE GAME

Category	Name	Performance
Rushing (Yds.)	Barry Sanders, 11-13-94	237
Passing (Yds.)	Matthew Stafford, 1-1-12	520
Passing (TDs)	Gary Danielson, 12-9-78	5
	Matthew Stafford, 11-9-09, 11-20-11, 1-1-12	5
Receiving (No.)	Herman Moore, 12-4-95	14
	Calvin Johnson, 10-27-13	14
Receiving (Yds.)	Calvin Johnson, 10-27-13	329
Interceptions	Don Doll, 10-23-49	**4
Field Goals	Garo Yepremian, 11-13-66	6
	Jason Hanson, 10-17-99	6
Touchdowns (Tot.)	Dutch Clark, 10-22-34	4
	Cloyce Box, 12-3-50	4
	Barry Sanders, 11-24-91	4
Points	Dutch Clark, 10-22-34	24
	Cloyce Box, 12-3-50	24
	Barry Sanders, 11-24-91	24
*Sacks	Bill Gay, 9-4-83	5.5

*Sacks became an official statistic in 1982.
**NFL Record

2014 VETERAN ROSTER

No.	Name	Pos.	Ht.	Wt.	Birthdate	NFL Exp.	College	Hometown	How Acq.	'13 Games/ Starts
42	Abdul-Quddus, Isa	S	6-1	205	8/3/89	4	Fordham	Union, N.J.	W(NO)-'14	11/0*
94	Ansah, Ezekiel	DE	6-5	271	5/29/89	2	Brigham Young	Accra, Ghana	D1-'13	14/12
35	Bell, Joique	RB	5-11	220	8/4/86	4	Wayne State	Benton Harbor, Mich.	FA-'11	16/4
28	Bentley, Bill	CB	5-10	176	5/16/89	3	Louisiana-Lafayette	Pahokee, Fla.	D3-'12	13/5
84	Broyles, Ryan	WR	5-10	188	4/9/88	3	Oklahoma	Norman, Okla.	D2-'12	6/3
21	Bush, Reggie	RB	6-0	203	3/2/85	9	Southern California	Spring Valley, Calif.	UFA(Mia)-'13	14/14
26	Carey, Don	S	5-11	192	2/14/87	6	Norfolk State	Norfolk, Va.	FA-'11	14/3
45b	Collins, Jed	FB	6-1	255	3/3/86	4	Washington State	Mission Viejo, Calif.	FA-'14	16/8*
18	Durham, Kris	WR	6-6	216	3/17/88	4	Georgia	Calhoun, Ga.	FA-'12	16/13
83	Edwards, Patrick	WR	5-9	175	10/25/88	2	Houston	Hearne, Texas	FA-'12	4/2
98	Fairley, Nick	DT	6-4	298	1/23/88	4	Auburn	Mobile, Ala.	D1-'11	15/15
80	Fauria, Joseph	TE	6-7	255	1/16/90	2	UCLA	Encino, Calif.	FA-'13	16/2
96	Fluellen, Andre	DT	6-2	302	3/7/85	6	Florida State	Cartersville, Ga.	FA-'13	13/0
24	Gomes, DeJon	S	6-0	201	11/17/89	4	Nebraska	Union City, Calif.	W(Wash)-'13	16/0
36	Green, Jonté	CB	6-0	184	7/19/89	3	New Mexico State	St. Petersburg, Fla.	D6b-'12	9/2
33	Greenwood, Chris	CB	6-1	193	7/10/89	3	Albion	Detroit, Mich.	D5b-'12	3/0
53	Greenwood, Cory	LB	6-2	235	6/5/85	5	Concordia (Quebec)	Kingston, Ontario	W(KC)-'13	0*
78	Hilliard, Corey	T	6-6	300	4/26/85	6	Oklahoma State	New Orleans, La.	FA-'09	9/7
23	Houston, Chris	CB	5-11	178	10/18/84	8	Arkansas	Austin, Texas	T(Atl)-'10	12/12
32	Ihedigbo, James	S	6-1	214	12/3/83	8	Massachusetts	Northampton, Mass.	UFA(Balt)-'14	16/16*
81	Johnson, Calvin	WR	6-5	236	9/29/85	8	Georgia Tech	Tyrone, Ga.	D1-'07	14/14
68	Johnson, George	DE	6-4	270	12/11/87	3	Rutgers	Glassboro, N.J.	FA-'14	0*
91	Jones, Jason	DE	6-5	276	5/23/86	7	Eastern Michigan	Southfield, Mich.	UFA(Sea)-'13	3/3
25	Leshoure, Mikel	RB	6-0	233	3/30/90	4	Illinois	Champaign, Ill.	D2b-'11	3/0
54	Levy, DeAndre	LB	6-2	238	3/26/87	6	Wisconsin	Milwaukee, Wisc.	D3a-'09	16/16
50	Lewis, Travis	LB	6-2	222	1/15/88	3	Oklahoma	San Antonio, Texas	D7-'12	12/0
6	Martin, Sam	P	6-1	205	2/27/90	2	Appalachian State	Fayetteville, Ga.	D5-'13	16/0
72	Martin, Vaughn	DT	6-4	300	4/18/86	5	Western Ontario	Lucea, Jamaica	FA-'14	3/0*
31	Mathis, Rashean	CB	6-1	195	8/27/80	12	Bethune-Cookman	Jacksonville, Fla.	UFA(Jax)-'13	15/13
17	Moore, Kellen	QB	6-0	197	7/12/89	3	Boise State	Prosser, Wash.	FA-'12	0*
99	Mosley, C.J.	DT	6-2	310	8/6/83	10	Missouri	Fort Knox, Ky.	UFA(Jax)-'13	16/1
48	Muhlbach, Don	LS	6-4	265	8/17/81	11	Texas A&M	Lufkin, Texas	FA-'04	16/0
11	Ogletree, Kevin	WR	6-1	198	8/5/87	6	Virginia	Queens, N.Y.	FA-'13	12/1
8	Orlovsky, Dan	QB	6-5	230	8/18/83	10	Connecticut	Shelton, Conn.	UFA(TB)-'14	2/0*
34	Owens, Montell	RB	5-10	225	5/4/84	9	Maine	Wilmington, Del.	FA-'13	1/0
58	Palmer, Ashlee	LB	6-1	236	4/7/86	6	Mississippi	Compton, Calif.	W(Buff)-'10	16/11
87	Pettigrew, Brandon	TE	6-5	265	2/23/85	6	Oklahoma State	Tyler, Texas	D1b-'09	14/14
27	Quin, Glover	S	6-0	209	1/15/86	6	New Mexico	Summit, Miss.	UFA(Hou)-'13	16/16
51	Raiola, Dominic	C	6-1	295	12/30/78	14	Nebraska	Honolulu, Hawaii	D2a-'01	16/16
71	Reiff, Riley	T	6-6	313	12/1/88	3	Iowa	Parkston, S.D.	D1-'12	16/16
41	Riddick, Theo	RB	5-9	200	5/4/91	2	Notre Dame	Manville, N.J.	D6-'13	14/0
19	Roosevelt, Naaman	WR	6-0	200	12/24/87	3	Buffalo	Buffalo, N.Y.	FA-'14	0*
12	Ross, Jeremy	WR	6-0	215	3/16/88	2	California	Sacramento, Calif.	FA-'13	10/2
63w	Saddler-McQueen, Jimmy	DT	6-3	299	8/4/87	2	Texas A&M-Kingsville	Houston, Texas	FA-'12	0*
67	Sims, Rob	G	6-3	312	12/6/83	9	Ohio State	Macedonia, Ohio	T(Sea)-'10	16/16
30	Slay, Darius	CB	6-0	192	1/1/91	2	Mississippi State	Brunswick, Ga.	D2-'13	13/4
9	Stafford, Matthew	QB	6-3	232	2/7/88	6	Georgia	Highland Park, Texas	D1a-'09	16/16
49w	Stanford, Julian	LB	6-1	230	9/2/90	2	Wagner	Bloomfield, Conn.	FA-'13	4/0
90	Suh, Ndamukong	DT	6-4	307	1/6/87	5	Nebraska	Portland, Ore.	D1a-'10	16/16
52	Tapp, Darryl	DE	6-1	270	9/13/84	9	Virginia Tech	Portsmouth, Va.	UFA(Wash)-'14	11/0*
15	Tate, Golden	WR	5-10	202	8/2/88	5	Notre Dame	Hendersonville, Tenn.	UFA(Sea)-'14	16/13*
92	Taylor, Devin	DE	6-7	276	11/15/89	2	South Carolina	Beaufort, S.C.	D4-'13	14/2
55	Tulloch, Stephen	LB	5-11	240	1/1/85	9	North Carolina State	Miami, Fla.	UFA(Tenn)-'11	16/16
29	Vaughn, Cassius	CB	5-11	199	11/3/87	5	Mississippi	Memphis, Tenn.	UFA(Ind)-'14	16/4*
66	Waddle, LaAdrian	T	6-6	321	7/21/91	2	Texas Tech	Columbus, Texas	FA-'13	12/8
75	Warford, Larry	G	6-3	333	7/18/91	2	Kentucky	Richmond, Ky.	D3-'13	16/16
59	Whitehead, Tahir	LB	6-2	228	4/2/90	3	Temple	Newark, N.J.	D5a-'12	16/0
89	Williams, Michael	TE	6-6	270	9/8/90	2	Alabama	Reform, Ala.	D7-'13	0*

* Abdul-Quddus played 11 games with New Orleans in '13; Collins played 16 games with New Orleans; Cory Greenwood missed '13 season because of injury; Ihedigbo played 16 games with Baltimore; G. Johnson inactive four games with Minnesota; V. Martin played three games with Miami; Moore inactive 16 games; Orlovsky played two games with Tampa Bay; Roosevelt last active with Buffalo in '11; Saddler-McQueen last active with Detroit in '12; Tapp played 11 games with Washington; Tate played 16 games with Seattle; Vaughn played 16 games with Indianapolis; Williams missed '13 season because of injury.

Players lost through free agency (3): T Jason Fox (Mia; 8 games in '13), Israel Idonije (Chi; 15), DE Willie Young (Chi; 16).

Also played with Lions in '13—K David Akers (16 games), DT Justin Bannan (3), WR Nate Burleson (9), S Louis Delmas (16), TE Dorin Dickerson (5), C Dylan Gandy (15), G Leroy Harris (1), DE Austen Lane (2), LB Rocky McIntosh (16), DB Akwasi Owusu-Ansah (1), T Barry Richardson (1), TE Tony Scheffler (5), WR Micheal Spurlock (10), TE Matt Veldman (1), S John Wendling (16).

FIRST-YEAR ROSTER

Name	Pos.	Ht.	Wt.	Birthdate	College	Hometown	How Acq.
Abram, Chad	FB	6-0	229	5/22/91	Florida State	Lakeland, Fla.	FA
Austin, Rodney (1)	G	6-4	311	12/4/88	Elon	Charlotte, N.C.	FA-'12
Brown, Kourtnei (1)	DE	6-4	253	4/17/88	Clemson	Charlotte, N.C.	W(Buff)
Bullard, Alex	G	6-2	302	3/20/91	Tennessee	Franklin, Tenn.	FA
Couplin, Jerome	S	6-2	215	8/31/91	William & Mary	Upper Marlboro, Md.	FA
Dalton, A.J.	T	6-4	280	2/17/92	Robert Morris	Carrollton, Ohio	FA
Ebron, Eric	TE	6-4	250	4/10/93	North Carolina	Greensboro, N.C.	D1
Franklin, James	QB	6-2	230	7/23/91	Missouri	Corinth, Texas	FA
Freese, Nate	K	6-0	185	8/18/90	Boston College	Strongsville, Ohio	D7
Fuller, Corey (1)	WR	6-2	196	6/23/90	Virginia Tech	Baltimore, Md.	D6-'13
Hepburn, Brandon (1)	LB	6-4	235	12/6/89	Florida A&M	Pomona, N.Y.	D7-'13
Hester, Aaron (1)	CB	6-1	207	3/1/90	UCLA	Los Angeles, Calif.	FA
Hickman, Gregory	DT	6-2	280	11/23/90	Florida International	Tampa, Fla.	FA
Jackson, Justin	LB	6-1	230	8/24/91	Wake Forest	Rockingham, N.C.	FA
Jones, TJ	WR	6-0	188	7/19/92	Notre Dame	Roswell, Ga.	D6
Keyton, Darren (1)	G	6-3	305	6/15/90	Central Michigan	Traverse City, Mich.	FA
Lawson, Nevin	CB	5-9	190	4/23/91	Utah State	Lauderhill, Fla.	D4
Lucas, Cornelius	T	6-9	328	7/18/91	Kansas State	New Orleans, La.	FA
Lynn, Gabe	S	6-0	204	2/24/91	Oklahoma	Tulsa, Okla.	FA
Maxwell, Jacob	TE	6-4	240	1/4/91	Louisiana-Lafayette	Pearl River, La.	FA
Miller, Steven (1)	RB	5-7	172	3/23/91	Appalachian State	Piscataway, N.J.	FA-'13
Morrell, D.J.	G	6-6	325	8/19/91	Old Dominion	Norwalk, Conn.	FA
Peacock, Andrew	WR	5-10	190	1/14/91	Appalachian State	Durham, N.C.	FA
Proctor, Xavier (1)	DT	6-6	272	11/1/90	North Carolina Central	Ellicott City, Md.	FA-'13
Reid, Caraun	DT	6-2	305	11/23/91	Princeton	Bronx, N.Y.	D5
Seisay, Mohammed	CB	6-2	200	5/22/90	Nebraska	Springfield, Va.	FA
Shugarts, J.B. (1)	T	6-6	299	10/26/89	Ohio State	Klein, Texas	FA
Swanson, Travis	C	6-5	312	1/30/91	Arkansas	Kingwood, Texas	D3
Tavecchio, Giorgio (1)	K	5-10	182	7/16/90	California	Milan, Italy	FA
Thompson, Jordan (1)	TE	6-4	248	7/12/89	Ohio	Rockford, Ohio	FA
Van Noy, Kyle	LB	6-3	243	6/19/90	Brigham Young	Reno, Nev.	D2
Webster, Larry	DE	6-6	252	2/14/90	Bloomsburg	Hagerstown, Md.	D4

The term NFL Rookie is defined as a player who is in his first season of professional football and has not been on the roster of another professional football team for any regular-season or postseason games. A Rookie is designated by an "R" on NFL rosters. Players who have been active in another professional football league or players who have NFL experience, including either preseason training camp or being on an Active List or Inactive List, or on Reserve/Injured or Reserve/Physically Unable to Perform for fewer than six regular-season games, are termed NFL First-Year Players. An NFL First-Year Player is designated by a "1" on NFL rosters. Thereafter, a player is credited with an additional year of experience for each season in which he accumulates six games on the Active List or Inactive List, or on Reserve/Injured or Reserve/Physically Unable to Perform.

Log on to www.detroitlions.com for an up-to-date roster.

COACHING STAFF
Head Coach,
Jim Caldwell

Pro Career: Named Lions' 26th head coach on January 14, 2014. Caldwell spent previous two seasons as offensive coordinator for the Baltimore Ravens (2012-13). Originally was Ravens' quarterbacks coach. Was promoted to offensive coordinator with just three weeks to play in the 2012 season, and went on to help lead Baltimore to the AFC North crown and a win over San Francisco in Super Bowl XLVII. In the team's final seven games, including four in the postseason, the Ravens averaged 400.6 yards per game and 27.3 points per game. Caldwell coached the previous 10 seasons (2002-2011) with the Indianapolis Colts, including three as head coach (2009-2011). While there, the Colts had a nine-consecutive playoff appearances that included six AFC South titles, two Super Bowl berths (XLI and XLIV) and one Super Bowl title (XLI). Caldwell began his NFL coaching career as the Tampa Bay Buccaneers' quarterbacks coach in 2001. Career record: 28-24.

Background: Caldwell was the head coach at Wake Forest (1993-2000) and an assistant in Penn State (1986-1992), Louisville (1985), Colorado (1982-84), Northwestern (1981) and Southern Illinois (1978-1980). Was a four-year starter at defensive back at Iowa from 1973-76.

Personal: Born January 16, 1955 in Beloit, Wisc. He and his wife, Cheryl, have four children (sons Jimmy, Jermaine and Jared, and daughter Natalie). Earned a bachelor's degree in liberal arts from the University of Iowa.

ASSISTANT COACHES

Jason Arapoff, coordinator of physical development; born July 8, 1965, Weymouth, Mass. Defensive back Springfield College 1985-88. No pro playing experience. Pro coach: Washington Redskins 1992-2000, joined Lions in 2001.

Teryl Austin, defensive coordinator; born March 3, 1965, Sharon, Pa. Safety Pittsburgh 1984-87. Pro defensive back Montreal Machine (WLAF) 1991. College coach: Penn State 1991-92, Wake Forest 1993-95, Syracuse 1996-98, Michigan 1999-2002, Florida 2003. Pro coach: Seattle Seahawks 2003-06, Arizona Cardinals 2007-09, Baltimore Ravens 2011-13, joined Lions in 2014.

John Bonamego, special teams coordinator; August 14, 1963, Waynesboro, Penn. Wide receiver/safety Central Michigan 1984-87. No pro playing experience. College coach: Maine 1988-1991, Lehigh 1992, Army 1993-98. Pro coach: Green Bay Packers 2003-05, New Orleans Saints 2006-07, Miami Dolphins 2008-2010, New Orleans Saints 2011, Jacksonville Jaguars 2012, joined Lions in 2013.

Jim Bob Cooter, quarterbacks: born July 3, 1984, Huntsville, Ala. Quarterback Tennessee 2002-05. No pro playing experience. College coach: Tennessee 2007-08. Pro coach: Indianapolis Colts 2009-2011, Kansas City Chiefs 2012, Denver Broncos 2013, joined Lions in 2014.

Gunther Cunningham, senior coaching assistant; born June 19, 1946, Munich, Germany. Linebacker/placekicker Oregon 1966-68. No pro playing experience. College coach: Oregon 1969-1971, Arkansas 1972, Stanford 1973-76, California 1977-1980. Pro coach: Hamilton Tiger-Cats (CFL) 1981, Baltimore/Indianapolis Colts 1982-84, San Diego Chargers 1985-1990, L.A. Raiders 1991-94, Kansas City Chiefs 1995-2000, 2004-08 (head coach 1999-2000), Tennessee Titans 2001-03, joined Lions in 2009.

Devin Fitzsimmons, asst. special teams; born October 18, 1982, Folsom, La. Quarterback/wide receiver Bucknell 2001-05. No pro playing experience. College coach: Shaw 2005, Bucknell 2006, Kansas State 2007-08, Virginia 2009, Richmond 2010, Rutgers 2012, Delaware 2013. Pro coach: Indianapolis Colts 2011, joined Lions in 2014.

Terry Heffernan, offensive quality control; born October 12, 1980, Arlington Heights, Ill. Center Dayton 2001-03. No pro playing experience. College coach: Cumberland 2003, Louisville 2004, Michigan 2005-06, Wayne State 2007-2012. Pro coach: Joined Lions in 2013.

Bobby Johnson, asst. offensive line; born February 28, 1973, Akron, Ohio. Offensive tackle Miami (Ohio) 1992-94. No pro playing experience. College coach: Akron 1995-98, Miami (Ohio) 1999-2004, Indiana 2005-09. Pro coach: Buffalo Bills 2010-11, Jacksonville Jaguars 2012, joined Lions in 2013.

Kris Kocurek, defensive line; born November 15, 1978, Rockdale, Texas. Defensive tackle Texas Tech 1997-2000. Pro defensive tackle Seattle Seahawks 2001, Tennessee Titans 2002. College coach: Texas Tech 2003, Texas A&M-Kingsville 2004-05, Texas A&M-Commerce 2006, West Texas A&M 2007, Stephen F. Austin State 2008. Pro coach: Joined Lions in 2009.

Joe Lombardi, offensive coordinator; June 6, 1971, Seattle, Wash. Tight end Air Force 1992-94. No pro playing experience. College coach: Dayton 1996-98, Virginia Military Institute 1999, Bucknell 2000, Mercyhurst 2002-05. Pro coach: New York/New Jersey Hitmen (XFL) 2001, Atlanta Falcons 2006, New Orleans Saints 2007-2013, joined Lions in 2014.

Curtis Modkins, running backs/run game coordinator; born November 15, 1970. Running back Texas Christian 1990-92. No pro playing experience. College coach: Texas Christian 1995-97, New Mexico 1998-2001, Georgia Tech 2002-07. Pro coach: Kansas City Chiefs 2008, Arizona Cardinals 2009, Buffalo Bills 2010-12, joined Lions in 2013.

Tony Oden, defensive backs/cornerbacks; born June 30, 1973, Cleveland Heights, Ohio. Linebacker Baldwin-Wallace 1992-95. No pro playing experience. College coach: Millersville 1996, Boston College 1997, Army 1998-99, East Carolina 2000-02, Eastern Michigan 2003. Pro coach: Houston Texans 2004-05, New Orleans Saints 2006-2011, Jacksonville Jaguars 2012, Tampa Bay Buccaneers 2013, joined Lions in 2013.

Robert Prince, wide receivers; born May 8, 1965, Okinawa, Japan. Wide receiver

Humboldt State 1987-1990. No pro playing experience. College coach: Humboldt State 1989-1990, Montana State 1991, Sacramento State 1992-93, Fort Lewis College 1994-95, Portland State 1998-2000, Boise State, 2001-03, 2011-13, Colorado 2010. Pro coach: Japanese X League 1996-97, Atlanta Falcons 2004-06, Jacksonville Jaguars 2007-08, Seattle Seahawks 2009, joined Lions in 2014.

Ron Prince, asst. head coach/tight ends; born September 18, 1969, Junction City, Kan. Offensive line Appalachian State 1990-91. No pro playing experience. College coach: Dodge City (Kan.) C.C. 1992, Alabama A&M 1993, South Carolina State 1994, James Madison 1995-97, Cornell 1998-2000, Virginia 2001-05, Kansas State 2006-08, Virginia 2009, Rutgers 2013. Pro coach: Indianapolis Colts 2010-11, Jacksonville Jaguars 2012, joined Lions in 2014.

Matt Raich, defensive quality control; born August 16, 1970, Monaca, Pa. Linebacker Westminster College 1989-1992. No pro playing experience. College coach: Westminster College 1993-94, Robert Morris 1996-98, 2000-02, Glenville State 1999, Duquesne 2013. Pro coach: Pittsburgh Steelers 2003-06, Arizona Cardinals 2007-2012, joined Lions in 2014.

Ted Rath, asst. strength and conditioning; born November 22, 1983, Monroe, Mich. Linebacker Toledo 2003-06. No pro playing experience. College coach: Toledo 2007-09. Pro coach: Joined Lions in 2009.

Evan Rothstein, special projects; born April 20, 1988, Merrick, N.Y. Attended SUNY Cortland. No college or pro playing experience. College coach: SUNY Cortland 2010, Syracuse 2010-11. Pro coach: Joined Lions in 2012.

Bill Sheridan, linebackers; born January 27, 1959, Detroit, Mich. Linebacker Grand Valley State 1979-1982. No pro playing experience. College coach: Michigan 1985-86, 2002-04, Maine 1987-88, Cincinnati 1989-1991, Army 1992-97, Michigan State 1998-2000, Notre Dame 2001. Pro coach: New York Giants 2005-09, Miami Dolphins 2010-11, Tampa Bay Buccaneers 2012-13, joined Lions in 2014.

Jeremiah Washburn, offensive line; Guard Arkansas 1998-2000. No pro playing experience. College coach: Arkansas 2000-01. Pro coach: Carolina Panthers 2002, Baltimore Ravens 2003-08, joined Lions in 2009.

Jim Washburn, defensive line; born December 2, 1963, Shelby, N.C. Defensive line Gardner Webb 1970-73. No pro playing experience. College coach: Southern Methodist 1976, Lees-McRae 1977-78, Livingston 1979, New Mexico 1980-82, South Carolina 1983-88, Arkansas 1994-97, Houston 1998. Pro coach: Tennessee Titans 1999-2010, Philadelphia Eagles 2011-12, joined Lions in 2013.

Alan Williams, defensive backs/safeties; born November 4, 1969, Norfolk, Va. Running back William & Mary 1988-1991. No pro playing experience. College coach: William & Mary 1996-2000. Pro coach: Tampa Bay Buccaneers 2001, Indianapolis Colts 2002-2011, Minnesota Vikings 2012-13, joined Lions in 2014.

National Football Conference
North Division
Team Colors: Dark Green, Gold, and White
Lambeau Field Atrium
1265 Lombardi Avenue
Green Bay, Wisconsin 54304
Telephone: (920) 569-7500

2014 SCHEDULE
PRESEASON
Aug. 9   at Tennessee 7:00
Aug. 16 at St. Louis.........................3:00
Aug. 22 **Oakland** 7:00
Aug. 28 **Kansas City** 6:00

REGULAR SEASON
Sep. 4   at Seattle (Thu)...................7:30
Sep. 14 **New York Jets** 3:25
Sep. 21 at Detroit 12:00
Sep. 28 at Chicago 12:00
Oct. 2   **Minnesota** (Thu) 7:25
Oct. 12 at Miami 12:00
Oct. 19 **Carolina** 12:00
Oct. 26 at New Orleans *7:30
Nov. 2   BYE
Nov. 9   **Chicago** *7:30
Nov. 16 **Philadelphia** 12:00
Nov. 23 at Minnesota 12:00
Nov. 30 **New England** 3:25
Dec. 8   **Atlanta** (Mon) 7:30
Dec. 14 at Buffalo 12:00
Dec. 21 at Tampa Bay 12:00
Dec. 28 **Detroit** 12:00
*All times CT; Sunday night games in
   Weeks 5-16 subject to change*
Stadium: Lambeau Field (opened in 1957)
   •**Capacity:** 80,750
   1265 Lombardi Avenue
   Green Bay, Wisconsin 54304
Playing Surface: DD GrassMaster
Training Camp: St. Norbert College
                De Pere, Wisconsin 54115

LAMBEAU FIELD

CLUB OFFICIALS
President and Chief Executive Officer:
   Mark Murphy
Executive Vice President/General
   Manager/Director of Football
   Operations: Ted Thompson
Vice President of Football Administration/
   Player Finance: Russ Ball
Vice President of Finance and
   Administration: Paul Baniel
Vice President of Sales and Business
   Development: Craig Benzel
Vice President of Human Resources:
   Nicole Ledvina
Vice President and General Counsel:
   Ed Policy
Vice President of Marketing and Fan
   Engagement: Gabrielle Valdez Dow
Director of Pro Personnel: Eliot Wolf
Director of College Scouting:
   Brian Gutekunst
Director of Player Engagement:
   Rob Davis
Director of Research and Development:
   Mike Eayrs
Director of Public Relations:
   Jason Wahlers
Director of Public Affairs:
   Aaron Popkey
Assistant Director of Public Relations:
   Sarah Quick
Communications Manager: Tom Fanning
Public Relations Coordinator:
   Nathan LoCascio
Director of Ticket Operations:
   Mark Wagner
Director of Stadium Services:
   Jennifer Ark
Director of Retail Operations:
   Kate Hogan
Director of Information Technology:
   Wayne Wichlacz
Director of Facility Operations:
   Ted Eisenreich
Director of Security/Risk Management:
   Doug Collins
Director of Packers Media Group and
   Brand Engagement: Joan Malcheski
Director of Community Outreach &
   Player/Alumni Relations:
   Cathy Dworak
Senior Personnel Executive:
   Alonzo Highsmith
West Regional Scout: Sam Seale
Assistant Director of Pro Personnel:
   Tim Terry
Area Scouts: Lee Gissendaner,
   Jon-Eric Sullivan,
   John Wojciechowski,
   Richmond Williams
Pro Scouts: Chad Brinker, Glenn Cook
College Scouts: Mike Owen,
   Alonzo Dotson
College Scouting Coordinator:
   Danny Mock
Coaching Administrator: David Raih
Strength and Conditioning Assistants:
   Thadeus Jackson, Chris Gizzi
Football Administration Coordinator:
   Matt Klein
Video Director: Bob Eckberg
Head Athletic Trainer: Pepper Burruss
Equipment Manager: Gordon (Red) Batty

COACHING HISTORY
(728-556-37)
Records include postseason games
1921-1949 Earl (Curly) Lambeau .212-106-21
1950-53   Gene Ronzani* 14-31-1
1953   Hugh Devore-
            Ray (Scooter) McLean**..0-2-0
1954-57   Lisle Blackbourn...........17-31-0
1958   Ray (Scooter) McLean....1-10-1
1959-1967 Vince Lombardi..............98-30-4
1968-1970 Phil Bengtson 20-21-1
1971-74   Dan Devine...................25-28-4
1975-1983 Bart Starr 53-77-3
1984-87   Forrest Gregg 25-37-1
1988-1991 Lindy Infante................24-40-0
1992-98   Mike Holmgren 84-42-0
1999   Ray Rhodes...................8-8-0
2000-05   Mike Sherman 59-43-0
2006-2013 Mike McCarthy............88-50-1
   *Resigned after 10 games in 1953
**Co-coaches

PAID ATTENDANCE
Home 623,559   Away 552,111
Total 1,175,670
Single-game home record,
   71,213 (11/1/09)
Single-season home record,
   623,559 (2013)

2014 DRAFT CHOICES

Round	Name	Pos.	College
1	Ha Ha Clinton-Dix	DB	Alabama
2	Davante Adams	WR	Fresno St.
3	Khyri Thornton	DE	Southern Mississippi
	Richard Rodgers	TE	California
4	Carl Bradford	LB	Arizona St.
5	Corey Linsley	C	Ohio St.
	Jared Abbrederis	WR	Wisconsin
6	Demetri Goodson	DB	Baylor
7	Jeff Janis	WR	Saginaw Valley St.

2013 TEAM RECORD
PRESEASON (1-3)

Date	Result		Opponent
08/09	L	0-17	Arizona
08/17	W	19-7	at St. Louis
08/23	L	10-17	Seattle
08/29	L	8-30	at Kansas City

REGULAR SEASON (8-7-1)

Date	Result		Opponent
09/08	L	28-34	at San Francisco
09/15	W	38-20	Washington
09/22	L	30-34	at Cincinnati
10/06	W	22-9	Detroit
10/13	W	19-17	at Baltimore
10/20	W	31-13	Cleveland
10/27	W	44-31	at Minnesota
11/04	L	20-27	Chicago
11/10	L	13-27	Philadelphia
11/17	L	13-27	at New York Giants
11/24	T	26-26	Minnesota (OT)
11/28	L	10-40	at Detroit
12/08	W	22-21	Atlanta
12/15	W	37-36	at Dallas
12/22	L	31-38	Pittsburgh
12/29	W	33-28	at Chicago

(OT) Overtime

POSTSEASON (0-1)

Date	Result		Opponent
01/05	L	20-23	San Francisco

SCORE BY PERIODS

Packers	78	105	113	118	3	—	417
Opponents	79	103	115	128	3	—	428

2013 TEAM STATISTICS

	Packers	Opp.
Total First Downs	351	330
Rushing	119	116
Passing	201	190
Penalty	31	24
3rd Down: Made/Att	89/216	78/204
3rd Down Pct.	41.2	38.2
4th Down: Made/Att	9/13	10/17
4th Down Pct.	69.2	58.8
Possession Avg.	30:24	29:36
Total Net Yards	6404	5956
Avg. Per Game	400.3	372.3
Total Plays	1074	1015
Avg. Per Play	6.0	5.9
Net Yards Rushing	2136	2000
Avg. Per Game	133.5	125.0
Total Rushes	459	432
Net Yards Passing	4268	3956
Avg. Per Game	266.8	247.3
Sacked/Yards Lost	45/270	44/238
Gross Yards	4538	4194
Att./Completions	570/366	539/332
Completion Pct.	64.2	61.6
Had Intercepted	16	11
Punts/Average	64/44.6	70/42.8
Net Punting Avg.	64/39.0	70/35.6
Penalties/Yards	86/801	99/883
Fumbles/Ball Lost	19/9	18/11
Touchdowns	46	51
Rushing	17	16
Passing	25	30
Returns	4	5

2013 INDIVIDUAL STATISTICS

PASSING

	Att.	Comp.	Yds.	Pct.	TD	Int.	Tkld.	Rate
Rodgers	290	193	2536	66.6	17	6	21/117	104.9
Flynn	166	102	1146	61.4	7	4	17/102	86.1
Tolzien	90	55	717	61.1	1	5	3/26	66.8
Wallace	24	16	139	66.7	0	1	4/25	64.4
Packers	570	366	4538	64.2	25	16	45/270	91.7
Opponents	539	332	4194	61.6	30	11	44/238	95.9

SCORING

	TD R	TD P	TD Rt	PAT	FG	Saf	PTS
Crosby	0	0	0	42/42	33/37	0	141
Lacy	11	0	0	0/0	0/0	0	66
Nelson	0	8	0	0/0	0/0	0	48
Boykin	0	3	1	0/0	0/0	0	24
Cobb	0	4	0	0/0	0/0	0	24
Starks	3	1	0	0/0	0/0	0	24
Finley	0	3	0	0/0	0/0	0	18
J. Jones	0	3	0	0/0	0/0	0	18
Quarless	0	2	0	0/0	0/0	0	12
Bostick	0	1	0	0/0	0/0	0	6
Burnett	0	0	1	0/0	0/0	0	6
Franklin	1	0	0	0/0	0/0	0	6
Hyde	0	0	1	0/0	0/0	0	6
Jennings	0	0	1	0/0	0/0	0	6
Kuhn	1	0	0	0/0	0/0	0	6
Tolzien	1	0	0	0/0	0/0	0	6
Packers	17	25	4	42/42	33/37	0	417
Opponents	16	30	5	48/49	24/30	1	428

2-Pt Conversions: Packers 0-4, Opponents 0-2

RUSHING

	No.	Yds	Avg	LG	TD
Lacy	284	1178	4.1	60	11
Starks	89	493	5.5	41	3
Rodgers	30	120	4.0	18	0
Franklin	19	107	5.6	51	1
Cobb	4	78	19.5	67	0
Flynn	17	61	3.6	17	0
Tolzien	5	55	11.0	19	1
Kuhn	10	38	3.8	12	1
Jennings	1	6	6.0	6	0
Packers	459	2136	4.7	67	17
Opponents	432	2000	4.6	41	16

RECEIVING

	No.	Yds	Avg	LG	TD
Nelson	85	1314	15.5	76t	8
J. Jones	59	817	13.8	83t	3
Boykin	49	681	13.9	52	3
Lacy	35	257	7.3	34	0
Quarless	32	312	9.8	22	2
Cobb	31	433	14.0	48t	4
Finley	25	300	12.0	52	3
Kuhn	13	81	6.2	20	0
Starks	10	89	8.9	23	1
White	9	66	7.3	15	0
Bostick	7	120	17.1	26	1
R. Taylor	6	30	5.0	8	0
Franklin	4	30	7.5	10	0
Ross	1	8	8.0	8	0
Packers	366	4538	12.4	83t	25
Opponents	332	4194	12.6	67	30

INTERCEPTIONS

	No.	Yds	Avg	LG	TD
Shields	4	3	0.8	7	0
Williams	3	10	3.3	10	0
House	1	11	11.0	11	0
Hawk	1	7	7.0	7	0
Neal	1	5	5.0	5	0
Bush	1	0	0.0	0	0
Packers	11	36	3.3	11	0
Opponents	16	279	17.4	76	3

PUNTING

	No.	Yds.	Avg.	In 20	LG
Masthay	64	2854	44.6	22	62
Packers	64	2854	44.6	22	62
Opponents	70	2994	42.8	25	61

PUNT RETURNS

	Ret	FC	Yds	Avg	LG	TD
Hyde	24	14	296	12.3	93t	1
Cobb	3	5	23	7.7	16	0
Ross	2	2	20	10.0	11	0
Kuhn	1	0	0	0.0	0	0
Packers	30	21	339	11.3	93t	1
Opponents	20	19	261	13.9	49	0

KICKOFF RETURNS

	No.	Yds	Avg	LG	TD
Hyde	22	531	24.1	70	0
Ross	6	75	12.5	21	0
Franklin	4	82	20.5	26	0
Kuhn	2	40	20.0	21	0
Bell	1	22	22.0	22	0
Hill	1	19	19.0	19	0
Banjo	1	12	12.0	12	0
Cobb	1	10	10.0	10	0
Stoneburner	1	0	0.0	0	0
Packers	39	791	20.3	70	0
Opponents	61	1577	25.9	109t	1

FIELD GOALS

	1-19	20-29	30-39	40-49	50+
Crosby	1/1	13/13	8/8	6/8	5/7
Packers	1/1	13/13	8/8	6/8	5/7
Opponents	0/0	9/9	5/7	7/8	3/6

SACKS

	No.
Matthews	7.5
Daniels	6.5
Hawk	5.0
Neal	5.0
Perry	4.0
D. Jones	3.5
B. Jones	3.0
Williams	2.5
Lattimore	2.0
House	1.0
Hyde	1.0
Jennings	1.0
Jolly	1.0
Mulumba	1.0
Packers	44.0
Opponents	45.0

RECORD HOLDERS
INDIVIDUAL RECORDS—CAREER

Category	Name	Performance
Rushing (Yds.)	Ahman Green, 2000-06, 2009	8,322
Passing (Yds.)	Brett Favre, 1992-2007	**61,655
Passing (TDs)	Brett Favre, 1992-2007	**442
Receiving (No.)	Donald Driver, 1999-2012	743
Receiving (Yds.)	Donald Driver, 1999-2012	10,137
Interceptions	Bobby Dillon, 1952-59	52
Punting (Avg.)	Tim Masthay, 2010-13	44.3
Punt Return (Avg.)	Desmond Howard, 1996, 1999	13.8
Kickoff Return (Avg.)	Travis Williams, 1967-1970	26.7
Field Goals	Ryan Longwell, 1997-2005	226
Touchdowns (Tot.)	Don Hutson, 1935-1945	105
Points	Ryan Longwell, 1997-2005	1,054
*Sacks	Kabeer Gbaja-Biamila, 2000-08	74.5

INDIVIDUAL RECORDS—SINGLE SEASON

Category	Name	Performance
Rushing (Yds.)	Ahman Green, 2003	1,883
Passing (Yds.)	Aaron Rodgers, 2011	4,643
Passing (TDs)	Aaron Rodgers, 2011	45
Receiving (No.)	Sterling Sharpe, 1993	112
Receiving (Yds.)	Robert Brooks, 1995	1,497
Interceptions	Irv Comp, 1943	10
Punting (Avg.)	Tim Masthay, 2011	45.6
Punt Return (Avg.)	Billy Grimes, 1950	19.1
Kickoff Return (Avg.)	Travis Williams, 1967	**41.1
Field Goals	Chester Marcol, 1972	33
	Ryan Longwell, 2000	33
	Mason Crosby, 2013	33
Touchdowns (Tot.)	Ahman Green, 2003	20
Points	Paul Hornung, 1960	176
*Sacks	Tim Harris, 1989	19.5

INDIVIDUAL RECORDS—SINGLE GAME

Category	Name	Performance
Rushing (Yds.)	Ahman Green, 12-28-03	218
Passing (Yds.)	Matt Flynn, 1-1-12	480
	Aaron Rodgers, 9-15-13	480
Passing (TDs)	Matt Flynn, 1-1-12	6
	Aaron Rodgers, 10-14-12	6
Receiving (No.)	Don Hutson, 11-22-42	14
Receiving (Yds.)	Billy Howton, 10-21-56	257
Interceptions	Bobby Dillon, 11-26-53	**4
	Willie Buchanon, 9-24-78	**4
Field Goals	Chris Jacke, 11-11-90, 10-14-96	5
	Ryan Longwell, 9-24-00	5
	Mason Crosby, 10-6-13	5
Touchdowns (Tot.)	Paul Hornung, 12-12-65	5
Points	Paul Hornung, 10-8-61	33
*Sacks	Vonnie Holliday, 12-22-02	5.0

*Sacks became an official statistic in 1982.
**NFL Record

2014 VETERAN ROSTER

No.	Name	Pos.	Ht.	Wt.	Birthdate	NFL Exp.	College	Hometown	How Acq.	'13 Games/ Starts
69	Bakhtiari, David	T	6-4	300	9/30/91	2	Colorado	San Mateo, Calif.	D4a-'13	16/16
32	Banjo, Chris	S	5-10	207	2/26/90	2	Southern Methodist	Sugar Land, Texas	FA-'13	16/1
67	Barclay, Don	T/G	6-4	305	4/18/89	3	West Virginia	Harmony, Pa.	FA-'12	14/14
58	Barrington, Sam	LB	6-1	235	10/5/90	2	South Florida	Jacksonville, Fla.	D7b-'13	7/0
86	Bostick, Brandon	TE	6-3	250	5/3/89	2	Newberry	Florence, S.C.	FA-'12	11/0
93	Boyd, Josh	DE	6-3	310	8/3/89	2	Mississippi State	Philadelphia, Miss.	D5b-'13	9/0
11	Boykin, Jarrett	WR	6-2	218	11/4/89	3	Virginia Tech	Matthews, N.C.	FA-'12	16/8
75	Bulaga, Bryan	T	6-5	314	3/21/89	5	Iowa	Woodstock, Ill.	D1-'10	0*
42	Burnett, Morgan	S	6-1	209	1/13/89	5	Georgia Tech	College Park, Ga.	D3-'10	13/13
24	Bush, Jarrett	CB	6-0	200	5/21/84	9	Utah State	Vacaville, Calif.	W(Car)-'06	12/0
18	Cobb, Randall	WR	5-10	192	8/22/90	4	Kentucky	Alcoa, Tenn.	D2-'11	6/4
2	Crosby, Mason	K	6-1	207	9/3/84	8	Colorado	Georgetown, Texas	D6c-'07	16/0
76	Daniels, Mike	DT	6-0	300	5/5/89	3	Iowa	Blackwood, N.J.	D4a-'12	16/1
6	Dorsey, Kevin	WR	6-1	207	2/23/90	2	Maryland	Forestville, Md.	D7b-'13	0*
10	Flynn, Matt	QB	6-2	225	6/20/85	7	Louisiana State	Tyler, Texas	D7-'08	5/4
23	Franklin, Johnathan	RB	5-10	205	10/23/89	2	UCLA	Los Angeles, Calif.	D4c-'13	11/0
61	Goode, Brett	LS	6-1	255	11/2/84	7	Arkansas	Fort Smith, Ark.	FA-'08	16/0
98	Guion, Letroy	DT	6-4	315	6/21/87	7	Florida State	Starke, Fla.	FA-'14	13/13*
13	Harper, Chris	WR	6-1	228	9/10/89	2	Kansas State	Wichita, Kan.	W(SF)-'13	4/0
26	Harris, DuJuan	RB	5-8	203	9/3/88	2	Troy	Brooksville, Fla.	FA-'12	0*
50	Hawk, A.J.	LB	6-1	247	1/6/84	9	Ohio State	Centerville, Ohio	D1-'06	16/16
29	Hayward, Casey	CB	5-11	192	9/9/89	3	Vanderbilt	Perry, Ga.	D2b-'12	3/1
22	Hill, Michael	RB	5-10	210	8/14/89	2	Missouri Western State	St. Joseph, Mo.	FA-'14	8/0*
33	House, Davon	CB	6-0	195	7/10/89	4	New Mexico State	Palmdale, Calif.	D4-'11	16/5
33	Hyde, Micah	CB	6-0	197	12/31/90	2	Iowa	Fostoria, Ohio	D5a-'13	16/3
59	Jones, Brad	LB	6-3	242	4/1/86	6	Colorado	East Lansing, Mich.	D7-'09	12/12
95	Jones, Datone	DE	6-4	285	7/24/90	2	UCLA	Compton, Calif.	D1-'13	16/0
30	Kuhn, John	RB	6-0	250	9/9/82	9	Shippensburg	York, Pa.	W(Pitt)-'07	15/6
27	Lacy, Eddie	RB	5-11	230	6/2/90	2	Alabama	Geismar, La.	D2-'13	15/15
70	Lang, T.J.	G	6-4	318	9/20/87	6	Eastern Michigan	Birmingham, Mich.	D4-'09	16/16
57	Lattimore, Jamari	LB	6-2	230	10/6/88	4	Middle Tennessee State	Hialeah, Fla.	FA-'11	15/4
8	Masthay, Tim	P	6-1	200	3/16/87	5	Kentucky	Murray, Ky.	FA-'10	16/0
52	Matthews, Clay	LB	6-3	255	5/14/86	6	Southern California	Agoura Hills, Calif.	D1b-'09	11/11
55	Mulumba, Andy	LB	6-3	260	1/30/90	2	Eastern Michigan	Montreal, Quebec	FA-'13	14/3
96	Neal, Mike	LB/DE	6-3	285	6/26/87	5	Purdue	Merrillville, Ind.	D2-'10	16/10
87	Nelson, Jordy	WR	6-3	217	5/31/85	7	Kansas State	Riley, Kan.	D2a-'08	16/16
51	Palmer, Nate	LB	6-2	248	9/23/89	2	Illinois State	Chicago, Ill.	D6-'13	8/2
56	Peppers, Julius	LB/DE	6-7	287	1/18/80	13	North Carolina	Bailey, N.C.	FA-'14	16/16*
53	Perry, Nick	LB	6-3	265	4/12/90	3	Southern California	Detroit, Mich.	D1-'12	11/6
81	Quarless, Andrew	TE	6-4	252	10/6/88	5	Penn State	Uniondale, N.Y.	D5a-'10	16/10
90	Raji, B.J.	DT	6-2	337	7/11/86	6	Boston College	Washington Township, N.J.	D1a-'09	16/16
28	Richardson, Sean	S	6-2	216	1/21/90	3	Vanderbilt	Linden, Ala.	FA-'12	6/0
12	Rodgers, Aaron	QB	6-2	225	12/2/83	10	California	Chico, Calif.	D1-'05	9/9
78	Sherrod, Derek	T	6-5	321	4/23/89	4	Mississippi State	Caledonia, Miss.	D1-'11	7/0
37	Shields, Sam	CB	5-11	184	12/8/87	5	Miami	Sarasota, Fla.	FA-'10	14/14
71	Sitton, Josh	G	6-3	318	6/6/86	7	Central Florida	Pensacola, Fla.	D4b-'08	16/16
44	Starks, James	RB	6-2	218	2/25/86	5	Buffalo	Niagara Falls, N.Y.	D6-'10	13/1
85	Stoneburner, Jake	TE	6-3	249	8/4/89	2	Ohio State	Dublin, Ohio	FA-'13	9/0
65	Taylor, Lane	G	6-3	324	11/22/89	2	Oklahoma State	Arlington, Texas	FA-'13	10/0
82	Taylor, Ryan	TE	6-3	254	11/16/87	4	North Carolina	Winston-Salem, N.C.	D7a-'11	14/1
68	Tiller, Andrew	G	6-4	324	3/13/89	2	Syracuse	Central Islip, N.Y.	FA-'13	0*
16	Tolzien, Scott	QB	6-2	213	9/4/87	4	Wisconsin	Palatine, Ill.	FA-'13	3/2
73	Tretter, JC	C/G	6-4	307	2/12/91	2	Cornell	Akron, N.Y.	D4b-'13	0*
19	White, Myles	WR	6-0	182	3/30/90	2	Louisiana Tech	Livonia, Mich.	FA-'13	7/0
38	Williams, Tramon	CB	5-11	191	3/16/83	8	Louisiana Tech	Napoleonville, La.	FA-'06	16/16
99	Worthy, Jerel	DE	6-2	308	4/28/90	3	Michigan State	Huber Heights, Ohio	D2a-'12	2/0

* Bulaga missed '13 season because of injury; Dorsey missed '13 season because of injury; Guion played 13 games with Minnesota in '13; Harris missed '13 season because of injury; Hill played six games with Tampa Bay and two games with Green Bay; Peppers played 16 games with Chicago; Tiller missed '12 season with New Orleans because of injury; Tretter inactive three games.

Players lost through free agency (4): C/G Evan Dietrich-Smith (TB; 16 games), WR James Jones (Oak; 14), T Marshall Newhouse (Cin; 15), DE C.J. Wilson (Oak; 8).

Also played with Packers in '13—LB Victor Aiyewa (5 games), RB Kahlil Bell (3), TE Jermichael Finley (6), LB Robert Francois (4), S M.D. Jennings (16), DT Johnny Jolly (13), S Jerron McMillian (12), CB James Nixon (3), DT Ryan Pickett (16), WR Jeremy Ross (3), G/C Greg Van Roten (3), QB Seneca Wallace (2).

FIRST-YEAR ROSTER

Name	Pos.	Ht.	Wt.	Birthdate	College	Hometown	How Acq.
Abbrederis, Jared	WR	6-1	195	12/17/90	Wisconsin	Wautoma, Wisc.	D5b
Adams, Aaron (1)	T	6-5	303	5/16/89	Eastern Kentucky	Greenacres, Fla.	FA-'13
Adams, Davante	WR	6-1	215	12/24/92	Fresno State	Palo Alto, Calif.	D2
Aiyewa, Victor (1)	LB	6-1	237	2/4/89	Washington	Missouri City, Texas	FA-'13
Bradford, Carl	LB	6-1	252	8/15/92	Arizona State	Norco, Calif.	D4
Clay, Charles	S	5-10	204	5/15/91	Hawaii	Hilo, Hawaii	FB
Clinton-Dix, Ha Ha	S	6-1	208	12/21/92	Alabama	Orlando, Fla.	D1
Dennard, Antonio (1)	CB	5-11	189	12/20/89	Langston	Chicago, Ill.	FA-'13
Doughty, Jake	LB	6-0	234	8/17/91	Utah State	Draper, Utah	FA
Elliott, Jayrone	LB	6-3	255	11/11/91	Toledo	Cleveland, Ohio	FA
Fullington, John	T	6-5	300	5/30/91	Washington State	Belfair, Wash.	FA
Gerhart, Garth (1)	C	6-1	310	10/21/88	Arizona State	Norco, Calif.	FA-'12
Gillett, Alex (1)	WR	6-1	214	5/17/91	Eastern Michigan	Clyde, Ohio	FA-'13
Goodson, Demetri	CB	5-11	197	6/11/89	Baylor	Spring, Texas	D6
Gray, Carlos	DE	6-2	313	6/30/92	North Carolina State	Pinson, Ala.	FA
Hubbard, Adrian	LB	6-6	257	2/27/92	Alabama	Norcross, Ga.	FA
Janis, Jeff	WR	6-3	219	6/24/91	Saginaw Valley State	Tawas City, Mich.	D7
Liaina, Ina (1)	FB	6-0	250	1/3/90	San Jose State	Oxnard, Calif.	FA
Linsley, Corey	C	6-3	301	7/27/91	Ohio State	Boardman, Ohio	D5a
Lyerla, Colt	TE	6-4	247	11/13/92	Oregon	Hillsboro, Ore.	FA
McCray, Jordan	G	6-3	322	5/31/92	Central Florida	Miami, Fla.	FA
Miller, Tanner	S	6-1	211	12/15/91	Iowa	Wellman, Iowa	FA
Neal, Rajion	RB	5-11	220	3/28/92	Tennessee	Tyrone, Ga.	FA
Pennel, Mike	DT	6-4	332	5/9/91	Colorado State-Pueblo	Aurora, Colo.	FA
Perillo, Justin	TE	6-3	250	1/5/91	Maine	Wilmington, Del.	FA
Perkins, LaDarius	RB	5-7	195	9/18/90	Mississippi State	Greenville, Miss.	FA
Rettig, Chase	QB	6-2	215	9/26/91	Boston College	San Clemente, Calif.	FA
Robinson, Luther	DE	6-3	301	2/24/91	Miami	Fort Pierce, Fla.	FA
Rodgers, Richard	TE	6-4	257	1/22/92	California	Shrewsbury, Mass.	D3b
Rolle, Jumal (1)	CB	6-0	188	5/28/90	Catawba	Wilson, N.C.	FA-'13
Thomas, Joe	LB	6-1	227	5/6/91	South Carolina State	Blackville, S.C.	FA
Thornton, Khyri	DE	6-3	304	11/21/89	Southern Mississippi	Panama City, Fla.	D3a
Vujnovich, Jeremy (1)	T	6-5	300	10/12/90	Louisiana College	Belle Chasse, La.	FA
White, Ryan	CB	5-10	197	1/2/92	Auburn	Tallahassee, Fla.	FA

The term NFL Rookie is defined as a player who is in his first season of professional football and has not been on the roster of another professional football team for any regular-season or postseason games. A Rookie is designated by an "R" on NFL rosters. Players who have been active in another professional football league or players who have NFL experience, including either preseason training camp or being on an Active List or Inactive List, or on Reserve/Injured or Reserve/Physically Unable to Perform for fewer than six regular-season games, are termed NFL First-Year Players. An NFL First-Year Player is designated by a "1" on NFL rosters. Thereafter, a player is credited with an additional year of experience for each season in which he accumulates six games on the Active List or Inactive List, or on Reserve/Injured or Reserve/Physically Unable to Perform.

Log on to www.packers.com for an up-to-date roster.

COACHING STAFF
Head Coach,
Mike McCarthy

Pro Career: Named the fourteenth head coach in team history January 12, 2006. Joined Vince Lombardi and Mike Holmgren as the only coaches to guide the Packers to a Super Bowl title with a win over Pittsburgh in Super Bowl XLV. Joined Pittsburgh's Bill Cowher (2005) as the only Super Bowl-winning coaches to lead their respective teams to three road wins as the No. 6 seed in the postseason en route to a world title. Has led the Packers to playoff appearances in six of his eight seasons at the helm, and the team's five consecutive berths and six over the past seven seasons are the most by an NFC team. Has guided the club to three consecutive NFC North titles, the first time Green Bay has done so since winning three straight division crowns from 2002-04. The Packers are the only team in the NFC to win its division each of the last three seasons (2011-13) and one of only three teams to do so over that span (Denver, New England). His .637 winning percentage (including playoffs) ranks No. 4 among active NFL coaches (min. 60 games) entering 2014. Has led the Packers to 55 regular-season wins since 2009, which is tied for No. 2 in the NFL over that span. In 2011, guided the team to a franchise-record 15 wins as well as team marks for points (560), touchdowns (70) and total net yards (6,482) on the way to the NFC North title and the top seed in the conference for the first time since 1996. The offense has ranked in the top 10 in scoring and total yards in seven of his eight seasons as head coach. Was 2007 Motorola Coach of the Year. He became the first coach since Lombardi to lead Packers to a championship game in his second season. McCarthy returned to Green Bay after serving as team's quarterbacks coach in 1999. Career record: 88-50-1.

Background: Graduated with business administration degree from Baker University. Was an all-conference tight end (1985-86), helping the school to a NAIA Division II runner-up finish as a senior captain. Coached collegiately at Fort Hays State (1987-88) and Pittsburgh (1989-1992), before moving to the NFL with the Chiefs (1993-98), Packers (1999), Saints (2000-04) and 49ers (2005).

Personal: Born November 10, 1963, in Pittsburgh, Pa. Family includes wife, Jessica, and their five children.

ASSISTANT COACHES

Edgar Bennett, wide receivers; born February 15, 1969, Jacksonville, Fla. Running back Florida State 1987, 1989-1991. Pro running back Green Bay Packers 1992-96, Chicago Bears 1998-99. Pro coach: Joined Packers in 2001.

James Campen, offensive line; born June 11, 1964, Sacramento, Calif. Center Sacramento City (Calif.) J.C. 1982-83, Tulane 1984-85. Pro center New Orleans Saints 1987-88, Green Bay Packers 1989-1993. Pro coach: Joined Packers in 2004.

Dom Capers, defensive coordinator; born August 7, 1950, Cambridge, Ohio. Defensive back Mount Union 1968-1971. No pro playing experience. College coach: Kent State 1972-74, Hawaii 1975-76, San Jose State 1977, California 1978-79, Tennessee 1980-81, Ohio State 1982-83. Pro coach: Philadelphia/Baltimore Stars (USFL) 1984-85, New Orleans Saints 1986-1991, Pittsburgh Steelers 1992-94, Carolina Panthers 1995-98 (head coach), Jacksonville Jaguars 1999-2000, Houston Texans 2001-05 (head coach), Miami Dolphins 2006-07, New England Patriots 2008, joined Packers in 2009.

Tom Clements, offensive coordinator; born June 18, 1953, McKees Rocks, Pa. Quarterback Notre Dame 1972-74. Pro quarterback Ottawa Rough Riders (CFL) 1975-78, Hamilton Tiger-Cats (CFL) 1979, 1981-82, Kansas City Chiefs 1980, Winnipeg Blue Bombers (CFL) 1983-87. College coach: Notre Dame 1992-95. Pro coach: New Orleans Saints 1997-99, Kansas City Chiefs 2000, Pittsburgh Steelers 2001-03, Buffalo Bills 2004-05, joined Packers in 2006.

Jerry Fontenot, tight ends; born November 21, 1966, Lafayette, La. Guard Texas A&M 1985-88. Pro center Chicago Bears 1989-1996, New Orleans Saints 1997-2003, Cincinnati Bengals 2004. Pro coach: Joined Packers in 2006.

Sam Gash, running backs; born March 7, 1969, Henderson, N.C. Fullback Penn State 1987-1991. Pro fullback New England Patriots 1992-97, Buffalo Bills 1998-99, 2003, Baltimore Ravens 2000-02. Pro coach: New York Jets 2005-06, Detroit Lions 2007-2012, joined Packers in 2014.

Luke Getsy, offensive quality control; born February 16, 1984, Munhall, Pa. Quarterback Pittsburgh 2002-03, Akron 2005-06. No pro playing experience. College coach: Akron 2007-08, West Virginia Wesleyan 2009, Pittsburgh 2010, Indiana University (Pa.) 2011-12, Western Michigan 2013. Pro coach: Joined Packers in 2014.

Mark Lovat, strength & conditioning coordinator; born Oct. 9, 1969, Pocatello, Idaho. Attended Butler. No college or pro playing experience. Pro coach: Joined Packers in 1999.

Steve Marshall, asst. offensive line; born June 20, 1956, Hartford, Conn. Guard/tight end Louisville 1976-78. No pro playing experience. College coach: Plymouth State 1979, Tennessee 1980-81, Marshall 1982-83, Louisville 1984, Murray State 1985-86, Virginia Tech 1987-1992, Tennessee 1993-95, UCLA 1996, Texas A&M 1997, North Carolina 1998-99, Colorado 2000-01, California 2009-2010, Colorado 2011-12, New Mexico State 2014. Pro coach: Houston Texans 2002-05, Cleveland Browns 2007-08, joined Packers in 2014.

Scott McCurley, asst. linebackers; born August 1, 1980, New Castle, Pa. Linebacker Pittsburgh 1998-2002. No pro playing experience. College coach: Pittsburgh 2003-05. Pro coach: Joined Packers in 2006.

Winston Moss, asst. head coach/

linebackers; born December 24, 1965, Miami, Fla. Linebacker Miami 1983-86. Pro linebacker Tampa Bay Buccaneers 1987-1990, Los Angeles Raiders 1991-94, Seattle Seahawks 1995-97. Pro coach: Seattle Seahawks 1998, New Orleans Saints 2000-05, joined Packers in 2006.

Darren Perry, secondary-safeties; born December 29, 1968, Norfolk, Va. Safety Penn State 1989-1991. Pro safety Pittsburgh Steelers 1992-98, San Diego Chargers 1999, New Orleans Saints 2000. Pro coach: Cincinnati Bengals 2002, Pittsburgh Steelers 2003-06, Oakland Raiders 2007-08, joined Packers in 2009.

John Rushing, defensive quality control; born February 26, 1972, Merced, Calif. Defensive back Washington State 1991-94. No pro playing experience. College coach: Willamette (Ore.) 1996-97, Boise State 1998-99, Montana State 2000-02, Utah State 2003-08. Pro coach: Joined Packers in 2009.

Jason Simmons, defensive/special teams assistant; born March 30, 1976, Inglewood, Calif. Cornerback Arizona State 1994-97. Pro defensive back Pittsburgh Steelers 1998-2001, Houston Texans 2002-07. Pro coach: Joined Packers in 2011.

Shawn Slocum, special teams coordinator; born February 21, 1965, Bryan, Texas. Linebacker Texas A&M 1983-84. No pro playing experience. College coach: Texas A&M 1989, 1991-97, 2000-02, Pittsburgh 1990, Southern California 1998-99, Mississippi 2005. Pro coach: Joined Packers in 2009.

Mike Trgovac, defensive line; born February 27, 1959, Youngstown, Ohio. Defensive lineman Michigan 1977-1980. No pro playing experience. College coach: Michigan 1984-85, Ball State 1986-88, Navy 1989, Colorado State 1990-91, Notre Dame 1992-94. Pro coach: Philadelphia Eagles 1995-98, Green Bay Packers 1999, Washington Redskins 2000-01, Carolina Panthers 2002-08, rejoined Packers in 2009.

Alex Van Pelt, quarterbacks; born May 1, 1970, Pittsburgh, Pa. Quarterback Pittsburgh 1989-1992. Pro quarterback Buffalo Bills 1995-2003. College coach: Buffalo 2005. Pro coach: Frankfurt Galaxy (NFLE) 2005, Buffalo Bills 2006-09, Tampa Bay Buccaneers 2010-11, joined Packers in 2012.

Joe Whitt Jr., secondary-cornerbacks; born July 19, 1978, Auburn, Ala. Wide receiver Auburn 1997-99. No pro playing experience. College coach: Auburn 2000-01, The Citadel 2002, Louisville 2003-06. Pro coach: Atlanta Falcons 2007, joined Packers in 2008.

Ron Zook, asst. special teams; born April 28, 1954, Loudonville, Ohio. Defensive back Miami (Ohio) 1972-75. No pro playing experience. College coach: Murray State 1978-1980, Cincinnati 1981-82, Kansas 1983, Tennessee 1984-86, Virginia Tech 1987, Ohio State 1988-1990, Florida 1991-95, 2002-04 (head coach), Illinois 2005-2011 (head coach). Pro coach: Pittsburgh Steelers 1996-98, Kansas City Chiefs 1999, New Orleans Saints 2000-01, joined Packers in 2014.

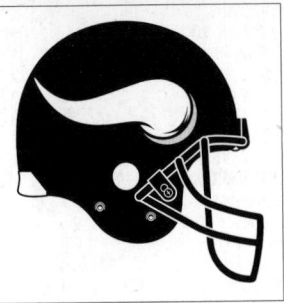

National Football Conference
North Division
Team Colors: Purple, Gold, and White
9520 Viking Drive
Eden Prairie, Minnesota 55344
Telephone: (952) 828-6500

2014 SCHEDULE
PRESEASON
Aug. 8   **Oakland** 7:00
Aug. 16   **Arizona** 7:30
Aug. 23   at Kansas City 7:00
Aug. 28   at Tennessee 7:00

REGULAR SEASON
Sep. 7   at St. Louis.......................12:00
Sep. 14   **New England** 12:00
Sep. 21   at New Orleans 12:00
Sep. 28   **Atlanta** 3:25
Oct. 2   at Green Bay (Thu) 7:25
Oct. 12   **Detroit** 12:00
Oct. 19   at Buffalo 12:00
Oct. 26   at Tampa Bay 12:00
Nov. 2   **Washington** 12:00
Nov. 9   BYE
Nov. 16   at Chicago 12:00
Nov. 23   **Green Bay** 12:00
Nov. 30   **Carolina** 12:00
Dec. 7   **New York Jets** 12:00
Dec. 14   at Detroit 12:00
Dec. 21   at Miami 12:00
Dec. 28   **Chicago** 12:00
All times CT

Stadium: TCF Bank Stadium
          (opened in 2009)
• **Capacity:** 52,000
   420 SE 23rd Avenue
   Minneapolis, Minnesota 55455
Playing Surface: Field Turf
Training Camp: Minnesota State-Mankato
            Mankato, Minnesota
            56001

TCF BANK STADIUM

CLUB OFFICIALS
Owner/Chairman: Zygi Wilf
Owner/President: Mark Wilf
Owner/Vice Chairman: Leonard Wilf
Ownership Partners: Reggie Fowler,
   Alan Landis, David Mandelbaum
General Manager: Rick Spielman
Assistant General Manager:
   George Paton
Vice President of Public Affairs/Stadium
   Development: Lester Bagley
Vice President of Football Operations:
   Rob Brzezinski
Vice President of Sales and Marketing:
   Steve LaCroix
Vice President of Finance: Steve Poppen
Vice President of Operations and Legal
   Counsel: Kevin Warren
Vice President of Strategic Planning &
   Business Initiatives: Jonathan Wilf
Director of Pro Scouting: Ryan Monnens
Director of College Scouting:
   Jamaal Stephenson
Executive Director of Communications:
   Jeff Anderson
Director of Public Relations: Bob Hagan
Executive Director of Community
   Relations: Brad Madson
Director of Information Technology:
   Cheryl Nygaard
Director of Operations/Team Travel:
   Luther Hippe
Director of Operations & Facilities:
   Chad Lundeen
Director of New Stadium Corporate
   Development: J.P. Paul
Director of Ticketing and Hospitality:
   Phil Huebner
Director of Video: Bob Marcus
Executive Director of Player
   Development/Legal: Les Pico
Director of Security: Kim Klawiter
Head Athletic Trainer: Eric Sugarman
Equipment Manager: Dennis Ryan
Director of Marketing & Business
   Development: Dannon Hulskotter
Director of Corporate Sales: Mike Slates
Director of Human Resources:
   Lisa Larson
Director of Food Service Operations:
   Geji McKinney

COACHING HISTORY
(450-392-10)
Records include postseason games
1961-66   Norm Van Brocklin 29-51-4
1967-1983 Bud Grant 161-99-5
1984   Les Steckel 3-13-0
1985   Bud Grant 7-9-0
1986-1991 Jerry Burns................55-46-0
1992-2001 Dennis Green* 101-70-0
2001-05   Mike Tice 33-34-0
2006-2010 Brad Childress** 40-37-0
2010-13   Leslie Frazier.............21-33-1
   *Resigned after 15 games in 2001
   **Released after 10 games in 2010

PAID ATTENDANCE
Home 522,147   Away 548,342
Total 1,070,489
Single-game home record,
   64,482 (11/2/03)
Single-season home record,
   522,147 (2013)

2014 DRAFT CHOICES
Round	Name	Pos.	College
1	Anthony Barr	LB	UCLA
	Teddy Bridgewater	QB	Louisville
3	Scott Crichton	DE	Oregon St.
	Jerick McKinnon	RB	Georgia Southern
5	David Yankey	G	Stanford
6	Antone Exum	DB	Virginia Tech
	Kendall James	DB	Maine
7	Shamar Stephen	NT	Connecticut
	Brandon Watts	LB	Georgia Tech
	Jabari Price	DB	North Carolina

2013 TEAM RECORD
PRESEASON (1-3)

Date	Result		Opponent
08/09	L	13-27	Houston
08/16	L	16-20	at Buffalo
08/25	L	14-34	at San Francisco
08/29	W	24-23	Tennessee

REGULAR SEASON (5-10-1)

Date	Result		Opponent
09/08	L	24-34	at Detroit
09/15	L	30-31	at Chicago
09/22	L	27-31	Cleveland
09/29	W	34-27	Pittsburgh
10/13	L	10-35	Carolina
10/21	L	7-23	at New York Giants
10/27	L	31-44	Green Bay
11/03	L	23-27	at Dallas
11/07	W	34-27	Washington
11/17	L	20-41	at Seattle
11/24	T	26-26	at Green Bay (OT)
12/01	W	23-20	Chicago (OT)
12/08	L	26-29	at Baltimore
12/15	W	48-30	Philadelphia
12/22	L	14-42	at Cincinnati
12/29	W	14-13	Detroit

(OT) Overtime

SCORE BY PERIODS

Vikings	82	108	85	110	6	—	391
Opponents	105	125	114	133	3	—	480

2013 TEAM STATISTICS

	Vikings	Opp.
Total First Downs	309	368
Rushing	106	101
Passing	173	247
Penalty	30	20
3rd Down: Made/Att	78/214	102/231
3rd Down Pct.	36.4	44.2
4th Down: Made/Att	10/19	11/18
4th Down Pct.	52.6	61.1
Possession Avg.	27:39	32:21
Total Net Yards	5508	6362
Avg. Per Game	344.3	397.6
Total Plays	1013	1132
Avg. Per Play	5.4	5.6
Net Yards Rushing	2081	1767
Avg. Per Game	130.1	110.4
Total Rushes	423	443
Net Yards Passing	3427	4595
Avg. Per Game	214.2	287.2
Sacked/Yards Lost	44/218	41/274
Gross Yards	3645	4869
Att./Completions	546/325	648/419
Completion Pct.	59.5	64.7
Had Intercepted	19	12
Punts/Average	75/44.2	77/43.2
Net Punting Avg.	75/39.2	77/37.8
Penalties/Yards	70/695	100/1003
Fumbles/Ball Lost	23/13	17/8
Touchdowns	45	57
Rushing	23	14
Passing	18	37
Returns	4	6

2013 INDIVIDUAL STATISTICS

Passing	Att.	Comp.	Yds.	Pct.	TD	Int.	Tkld.	Rate
Cassel	254	153	1807	60.2	11	9	16/85	81.6
Ponder	239	152	1648	63.6	7	9	27/119	77.9
Freeman	53	20	190	37.7	0	1	1/14	40.6
Vikings	546	325	3645	59.5	18	19	44/218	76.0
Opponents	648	419	4869	64.7	37	12	41/274	98.6

SCORING	TD R	TD P	TD Rt	PAT	FG	Saf	PTS
Walsh	0	0	0	43/44	26/30	0	121
Peterson	10	1	0	0/0	0/0	0	66
Patterson	3	4	2	0/0	0/0	0	54
Jennings	0	4	0	0/0	0/0	0	24
Ponder	4	0	0	0/0	0/0	0	24
Asiata	3	0	0	0/0	0/0	0	18
Rudolph	0	3	0	0/0	0/0	0	18
Wright	0	3	0	0/0	0/0	0	18
Gerhart	2	0	0	0/0	0/0	0	12
Carlson	0	1	0	0/0	0/0	0	6
Cassel	1	0	0	0/0	0/0	0	6
Ellison	0	1	0	0/0	0/0	0	6
Robison	0	0	1	0/0	0/0	0	6
Sherels	0	0	1	0/0	0/0	0	6
Simpson	0	1	0	0/0	0/0	0	6
Vikings	23	18	4	43/44	26/30	0	391
Opponents	14	37	6	53/53	27/29	0	480

2-Pt Conversions: Vikings 0-1, Opponents 2-4

RUSHING	No.	Yds	Avg	LG	TD
Peterson	279	1266	4.5	78t	10
Gerhart	36	283	7.9	41t	2
Asiata	44	166	3.8	39	3
Patterson	12	158	13.2	50t	3
Ponder	34	151	4.4	19t	4
Cassel	18	57	3.2	13	1
Vikings	423	2081	4.9	78t	23
Opponents	443	1767	4.0	41	14

RECEIVING	No.	Yds	Avg	LG	TD
Jennings	68	804	11.8	70t	4
Simpson	48	726	15.1	51	1
Patterson	45	469	10.4	79t	4
Carlson	32	344	10.8	30	1
Rudolph	30	313	10.4	31t	3
Peterson	29	171	5.9	22	1
Wright	26	434	16.7	42	3
Gerhart	13	88	6.8	13	0
Ford	11	133	12.1	37	0
Felton	6	37	6.2	11	0
Ellison	5	61	12.2	17	1
Jo. Webb	5	33	6.6	15	0
Asiata	5	13	2.6	8	0
Banyard	1	11	11.0	11	0
Line	1	8	8.0	8	0
Vikings	325	3645	11.2	79t	18
Opponents	419	4869	11.6	80t	37

INTERCEPTIONS	No.	Yds	Avg	LG	TD
Greenway	3	23	7.7	23	0
Henderson	2	19	9.5	10	0
H. Smith	2	4	2.0	4	0
Prater	1	30	30.0	30	0
Jefferson	1	1	1.0	1	0
Sendejo	1	1	1.0	1	0
Sherels	1	0	0.0	0	0
K. Williams	1	0	0.0	0	0
Vikings	12	78	6.5	30	0
Opponents	19	370	19.5	49	3

PUNTING	No.	Yds.	Avg.	In 20	LG
Locke	75	3316	44.2	23	65
Vikings	75	3316	44.2	23	65
Opponents	77	3325	43.2	27	69

PUNT RETURNS	Ret	FC	Yds	Avg	LG	TD
Sherels	22	27	335	15.2	86t	1
Patterson	0	1	0	—	—	0
Vikings	22	28	335	15.2	86t	1
Opponents	36	20	318	8.8	93t	1

KICKOFF RETURNS	No.	Yds	Avg	LG	TD
Patterson	43	1393	32.4	109t	2
Gerhart	7	106	15.1	20	0
Asiata	2	28	14.0	20	0
Felton	2	22	11.0	13	0
Ford	2	17	8.5	15	0
Carlson	2	13	6.5	12	0
Floyd	2	9	4.5	9	0
Jefferson	1	21	21.0	21	0
Jo. Webb	1	9	9.0	9	0
Wright	1	9	9.0	9	0
Ellison	1	7	7.0	7	0
Banyard	1	6	6.0	6	0
Mitchell	1	6	6.0	6	0
Vikings	66	1646	24.9	109t	2
Opponents	41	1113	27.1	80	1

FIELD GOALS	1-19	20-29	30-39	40-49	50+
Walsh	0/0	7/7	12/12	5/6	2/5
Vikings	0/0	7/7	12/12	5/6	2/5
Opponents	0/0	10/10	8/8	6/7	3/4

SACKS	No.
Allen	11.5
Robison	9.0
Griffen	5.5
Henderson	4.0
K. Williams	3.5
Greenway	3.0
Floyd	2.5
Cole	1.0
Guion	1.0
Vikings	41.0
Opponents	44.0

RECORD HOLDERS
INDIVIDUAL RECORDS—CAREER

Category	Name	Performance
Rushing (Yds.)	Adrian Peterson, 2007-2013	10,115
Passing (Yds.)	Fran Tarkenton, 1961-66, 1972-78	33,098
Passing (TDs)	Fran Tarkenton, 1961-66, 1972-78	239
Receiving (No.)	Cris Carter, 1990-2001	1,004
Receiving (Yds.)	Cris Carter, 1990-2001	12,383
Interceptions	Paul Krause, 1968-1979	53
Punting (Avg.)	Chris Kluwe, 2005-2012	44.4
Punt Return (Avg.)	Mewelde Moore, 2004-07	10.4
Kickoff Return (Avg.)	Percy Harvin, 2009-2012	27.9
Field Goals	Fred Cox, 1963-1977	282
Touchdowns (Tot.)	Cris Carter, 1990-2001	110
Points	Fred Cox, 1963-1977	1,365
*Sacks	John Randle, 1990-2000	114.0

INDIVIDUAL RECORDS—SINGLE SEASON

Category	Name	Performance
Rushing (Yds.)	Adrian Peterson, 2012	2,097
Passing (Yds.)	Daunte Culpepper, 2004	4,717
Passing (TDs)	Daunte Culpepper, 2004	39
Receiving (No.)	Cris Carter, 1994, 1995	122
Receiving (Yds.)	Randy Moss, 2003	1,632
Interceptions	Paul Krause, 1975	10
Punting (Avg.)	Chris Kluwe, 2008	47.6
Punt Return (Avg.)	Marcus Sherels, 2013	15.2
Kickoff Return (Avg.)	Percy Harvin, 2012	35.9
Field Goals	Gary Anderson, 1998	35
	Blair Walsh, 2012	35
Touchdowns (Tot.)	Chuck Foreman, 1975	22
Points	Gary Anderson, 1998	164
*Sacks	Jared Allen, 2011	22.0

INDIVIDUAL RECORDS—SINGLE GAME

Category	Name	Performance
Rushing (Yds.)	Adrian Peterson, 11-4-07	**296
Passing (Yds.)	Tommy Kramer, 11-2-86	490
Passing (TDs)	Joe Kapp, 9-28-69	**7
Receiving (No.)	Rickey Young, 12-16-79	15
Receiving (Yds.)	Sammy White, 11-7-76	210
Interceptions	Many Times	3
	Last time by Darren Sharper, 11-13-05	
Field Goals	Rich Karlis, 11-5-89	7
Touchdowns (Tot.)	Chuck Foreman, 12-20-75	4
	Ahmad Rashad, 9-2-79	4
Points	Chuck Foreman, 12-20-75	24
	Ahmad Rashad, 9-2-79	24
*Sacks	Randy Holloway, 9-16-84	5.0

*Sacks became an official statistic in 1982.
**NFL Record

2014 VETERAN ROSTER

No.	Name	Pos.	Ht.	Wt.	Birthdate	NFL Exp.	College	Hometown	How Acq.	'13 Games/ Starts
44	Asiata, Matt	RB	6-0	234	7/24/87	3	Utah	Santa Ana, Calif.	FA-'11	11/1
60	Baca, Jeff	G	6-3	302	1/10/90	2	UCLA	Mission Viejo, Calif.	D6-'13	4/0
91	Baker, Chase	DT	6-2	300	5/21/88	2	Boise State	Rocklin, Calif.	FA-'12	5/0
23	Banyard, Joe	RB	5-10	205	11/12/88	2	Texas-El Paso	Sweetwater, Texas	PS-'12	3/0
61	Berger, Joe	C	6-5	305	5/25/82	10	Michigan Tech	Newaygo, Mich.	FA-'11	16/2
36	Blanton, Robert	S	6-1	200	9/7/89	3	Notre Dame	Matthews, N.C.	D5-'12	16/3
54	Brinkley, Jasper	LB	6-1	252	7/12/85	6	South Carolina	Thomson, Ga.	FA-'14	15/3*
16	Cassel, Matt	QB	6-4	228	5/17/82	10	Southern California	Chatsworth, Calif.	UFA(KC)-'13	9/6
57	Cole, Audie	LB	6-5	239	6/1/89	3	North Carolina State	Monroe, Mich.	D7a-'12	13/5
20	Coleman, Kurt	S	5-11	200	7/1/88	5	Ohio State	Clayton, Ohio	FA-'14	15/0*
37	Cox, Derek	CB	6-1	195	9/22/86	6	William & Mary	Winterville, N.C.	FA-'14	16/11*
51	Dean, Larry	LB	6-0	226	8/7/88	4	Valdosta State	Tifton, Ga.	FA-'11	16/0
49	DeCicco, Dom	LB	6-3	235	9/11/88	3	Pittsburgh	Jefferson Hills, Pa.	FA-'14	0*
62	Ducasse, Vladimir	G	6-5	325	10/15/87	5	Massachusetts	Port-au-Prince, Haiti	FA-'14	16/4*
85	Ellison, Rhett	TE	6-5	250	10/3/88	3	Southern California	Portola Valley, Calif.	D4b-'12	11/6
90	Evans, Fred	DT	6-4	305	11/6/83	7	Texas St.-San Marcos	Morgan Park, Ill.	FA-'07	14/3
42	Felton, Jerome	FB	6-0	248	7/3/86	7	Furman	Madisonville, Tenn.	UFA(Ind)-'12	13/9
73	Floyd, Sharrif	DT	6-3	305	5/28/91	2	Florida	Philadelphia, Pa.	D1a-'13	16/1
86	Ford, Chase	TE	6-6	255	7/19/90	2	Miami	Corrigan, Texas	PS-'12	9/0
63	Fusco, Brandon	G	6-4	306	7/26/88	4	Slippery Rock	Cranberry Township, Pa.	D6c-'11	15/15
52	Greenway, Chad	LB	6-2	242	1/12/83	9	Iowa	Mt. Vernon, S.D.	D1-'06	16/16
97	Griffen, Everson	DE	6-3	273	12/22/87	5	Southern California	Avondale, Ariz.	D4-'10	16/0
50	Hodges, Gerald	LB	6-2	243	1/17/91	2	Penn State	Paulsboro, N.J.	D4b-'13	11/0
11	Jean, Lestar	WR	6-3	212	2/5/88	4	Florida Atlantic	Miami, Fla.	FA-'14	13/0*
15	Jennings, Greg	WR	6-0	195	9/21/83	9	Western Michigan	Kalamazoo, Mich.	UFA(GB)-'13	15/15
74	Johnson, Charlie	G	6-4	305	5/2/84	9	Oklahoma State	Sherman, Texas	UFA(Ind)-'11	15/15
92	Johnson, Tom	DT	6-3	288	8/30/84	4	Southern Mississippi	Moss Point, Miss.	FA-'14	12/0*
98	Joseph, Linval	DT	6-4	323	10/10/88	5	East Carolina	Gainesville, Fla.	FA-'14	15/15*
75	Kalil, Matt	T	6-7	308	7/6/89	3	Southern California	Corona, Calif.	D1a-'12	16/16
48	Line, Zach	FB	6-1	233	4/26/90	2	Southern Methodist	Oxford, Mich.	FA-'13	3/1
71	Loadholt, Phil	T	6-8	343	1/21/86	6	Oklahoma	Fountain, Colo.	D2-'09	15/15
18	Locke, Jeff	P	6-0	203	9/27/89	2	UCLA	Glendale, Ariz.	D5-'13	16/0
46	Loeffler, Cullen	LS	6-5	241	1/27/81	11	Texas	Ingram, Texas	FA-'04	16/0
56	Mauti, Michael	LB	6-2	243	1/19/90	2	Penn State	Mandeville, La.	D7a-'13	14/0
24	Munnerlyn, Captain	CB	5-8	195	4/10/88	6	South Carolina	Mobile, Ala.	FA-'12	16/16*
68	Murphy, Kevin	T	6-7	305	2/16/90	2	Harvard	San Clemente, Calif.	FA-'12	0*
84	Patterson, Cordarrelle	WR	6-2	220	3/17/91	2	Tennessee	Rock Hill, S.C.	D1c-'13	16/6
28	Peterson, Adrian	RB	6-1	217	3/21/85	8	Oklahoma	Palestine, Texas	D1-'07	14/14
7	Ponder, Christian	QB	6-2	229	2/25/88	4	Florida State	Colleyville, Texas	D1-'11	9/9
27	Prater, Shaun	CB	5-10	190	10/27/89	3	Iowa	Omaha, Neb.	W(Phil)-'13	8/3
79	Randall, Kheeston	DT	6-5	325	5/7/90	2	Texas	Beaumont, Texas	FA-'14	0*
41	Raymond, Mistral	S	6-1	194	9/7/87	4	South Florida	Palmetto, Fla.	D6b-'11	12/2
87	Reisner, Allen	TE	6-3	255	9/29/88	4	Iowa	Cedar Rapids, Iowa	FA-'14	5/3*
67	Remmers, Mike	T	6-5	300	4/11/89	2	Oregon State	Portland, Ore.	W(SD)-'13	1/0
29	Rhodes, Xavier	CB	6-1	210	6/19/90	2	Florida State	Miami, Fla.	D1b-'13	13/6
21	Robinson, Josh	CB	5-10	199	1/8/91	3	Central Florida	Sunrise, Fla.	D3-'12	10/10
96	Robison, Brian	DE	6-3	259	4/27/83	8	Texas	Splendora, Texas	D4-'07	16/16
82	Rudolph, Kyle	TE	6-6	258	11/9/89	4	Notre Dame	Cincinnati, Ohio	D2-'11	8/8
64	Samuda, Josh	G	6-3	315	12/23/88	2	Massachusetts	Hollywood, Fla.	FA-'14	0*
33	Sanford, Jamarca	S	5-10	200	8/27/85	6	Mississippi	Batesville, Miss.	D7-'09	13/13
34	Sendejo, Andrew	S	6-1	200	9/9/87	4	Rice	Spring Branch, Texas	FA-'11	16/10
35	Sherels, Marcus	CB	5-10	175	9/30/87	4	Minnesota	Rochester, Minn.	FA-'10	16/3
81	Simpson, Jerome	WR	6-2	189	2/4/86	7	Coastal Carolina	Reidsville, N.C.	UFA(Cin)-'12	16/8
22	Smith, Harrison	S	6-2	214	2/2/89	3	Notre Dame	Knoxville, Tenn.	D1b-'12	8/7
83	Smith, Rodney	WR	6-5	220	3/11/90	2	Florida State	Miami, Fla.	FA-'13	4/0
65	Sullivan, John	C	6-4	301	8/8/85	7	Notre Dame	Old Greenwich, Conn.	D6a-'08	16/16
94	Trattou, Justin	DE	6-4	268	8/28/88	3	Florida	Ramsey, N.J.	W(NYG)-'13	1/0
3	Walsh, Blair	K	5-10	192	1/8/90	3	Georgia	Boca Raton, Fla.	D6-'12	16/0
99	Wootton, Corey	DE	6-6	270	6/22/87	5	Northwestern	Rutherford, N.J.	FA-'14	16/15*
17	Wright, Jarius	WR	5-10	180	11/25/89	3	Arkansas	Warren, Ark.	D4a-'12	16/3

* Brinkley played 15 games with Arizona in '13; Coleman played 15 games with Philadelphia; Cox played 16 games with San Diego; DeCicco last active with Chicago in '12; Ducasse played 16 games with the New York Jets; Jean played 13 games with Houston; T. Johnson played 12 games with New Orleans; Joseph played 15 games with the New York Giants; Munnerlyn played 16 games with Carolina; Murphy did not play in one game; Randall did not play two games with Cincinnati; Reisner played five games with Jacksonville; Samuda last active with Miami in '12; Wootton played 16 games with Chicago.

Players lost through free agency (6): DE Jared Allen (Chi; 16 games in '13), CB Chris Cook (SF; 12), QB Josh Freeman (NYG; 1), RB Toby Gerhart (Jax; 14), OL J'Marcus Webb (KC; 8), WR Joe Webb (Car; 16).

Also played with Vikings in '13—LB Desmond Bishop (4 games), TE John Carlson (13), Letroy Guion (13), LB Erin Henderson (14), CB A.J. Jefferson (10), LB Marvin Mitchell (16), CB Robert Steeples (2), DT Kevin Williams (15).

FIRST-YEAR ROSTER

Name	Pos.	Ht.	Wt.	Birthdate	College	Hometown	How Acq.
Barr, Anthony	LB	6-5	255	3/18/92	UCLA	San Pedro, Calif.	D1a
Bishop, Brandan (1)	S	6-1	208	1/23/91	North Carolina State	Boca Raton, Fla.	FA-'13
Bridgewater, Teddy	QB	6-2	210	11/10/92	Louisville	Miami, Fla.	D1b
Burton, Pierce	T	6-6	305	4/16/91	Mississippi	Sacramento, Calif.	FA
Colter, Kain	WR	6-0	195	5/24/92	Northwestern	Denver, Colo.	FA
Cox, Rakim	DE	6-4	265	2/12/91	Villanova	San Diego, Calif.	FA
Crichton, Scott	DE	6-3	273	10/1/91	Oregon State	Tacoma, Wash.	D3a
Edwards, Kip (1)	CB	6-1	195	12/4/89	Missouri	Arlington, Texas	FA-'13
Exum, Antone	S	6-0	219	2/27/91	Virginia Tech	Glen Allen, Va.	D6a
Faciane, Isame	DT	6-4	302	5/11/91	Florida International	Slidell, La.	FA
Foster, Donte	WR	6-1	193	11/10/90	Ohio	Guthrie, Okla.	FA
Hall, Matt	T	6-9	326	4/24/90	Belhaven	Russellville, Ark.	FA
James, Kendall	CB	5-11	180	6/29/91	Maine	Scotch Plains, N.J.	D6b
Jorden, Kamar (1)	WR	6-3	200	5/17/89	Bowling Green	Lansdowne, Pa.	FA-'13
Kerin, Zac	C	6-5	305	8/13/91	Toledo	Lewis Center, Ohio	FA
Leonard, AC	TE	6-2	250	1/15/92	Tennessee State	Jacksonville, Fla.	FA
Lora, Erik	WR	5-10	202	3/14/91	Eastern Illinois	Miami, Fla.	FA
McKinnon, Jerick	RB	5-9	208	5/3/92	Georgia Southern	Marietta, Ga.	D3b
Nealy, Spencer (1)	DE	6-3	295	12/8/90	Texas A&M	San Antonio, Texas	FA-'13
Price, Jabari	CB	5-11	200	8/31/92	North Carolina	Pompano Beach, Fla.	D7a
Richardson, Antonio	T	6-6	330	2/24/92	Tennessee	Nashville, Tenn.	FA
Scott, Tyler	DE	6-4	250	5/6/91	Northwestern	Warren, Ohio	FA
Snyder, Jake	DE	6-4	275	4/7/91	Virginia	Glen Allen, Va.	FA
Steeples, Robert (1)	CB	6-1	195	11/27/89	Memphis	St. Louis, Mo.	FA-'13
Stephen, Shamar	DT	6-5	310	2/25/91	Connecticut	Brookville, N.Y	D7a
Thielen, Adam (1)	WR	6-2	195	8/22/90	Minnesota State-Mankato	Detroit Lakes, Minn.	FA-'13
Watts, Brandon	LB	6-2	231	1/21/91	Georgia Tech	Sandersville, Ga.	D7b
Wentworth, Austin	G	6-5	306	5/10/90	Fresno State	Rocklin, Calif.	FA
Williams, Dominique	RB	5-9	205	9/2/90	Wagner	Bridgeton, N.J.	FA
Yankey, David	G	6-6	315	1/18/92	Stanford	Roswell, Ga.	D5
Zimmer, Mike (1)	LB	6-2	239	9/23/90	Illinois State	Prospect Heights, Ill.	FA

The term NFL Rookie is defined as a player who is in his first season of professional football and has not been on the roster of another professional football team for any regular-season or postseason games. A Rookie is designated by an "R" on NFL rosters. Players who have been active in another professional football league or players who have NFL experience, including either preseason training camp or being on an Active List or Inactive List, or on Reserve/Injured or Reserve/Physically Unable to Perform for fewer than six regular-season games, are termed NFL First-Year Players. An NFL First-Year Player is designated by a "1" on NFL rosters. Thereafter, a player is credited with an additional year of experience for each season in which he accumulates six games on the Active List or Inactive List, or on Reserve/Injured or Reserve/Physically Unable to Perform.

Log on to www.vikings.com for an up-to-date roster.

COACHING STAFF

Head Coach,
Mike Zimmer

Pro Career: Named the ninth head coach in Vikings history on January 15, 2014. A veteran defensive coordinator, Zimmer enters his 21st season on an NFL sideline, the past 14 working as defensive coordinator for Cincinnati, Atlanta and Dallas. Zimmer has been a part of 11 playoff teams in his NFL tenure and teams that have won seven division titles. He coached the Cowboys defensive backs when the team won Super Bowl XXX over Pittsburgh after the 1995 season. Zimmer's arrival in Cincinnati for the 2008 season signaled a franchise turnaround on the defensive side of the ball. The Bengals notched four top-10 defensive rakings since 2008 after only cracking the NFL's top 10 once in the previous 18 seasons before Zimmer joined the team. Since 2011, the Bengals' defense ranked #2 in the NFL with 139 sacks (46.3 per season) and have allowed 18.8 points per game, ranking #4 in the NFL in points allowed. Zimmer led top-10 defenses for Dallas in both a 4-3 and 3-4 scheme, led the league in 2003 in total defense, and the team ranked in the top five of NFL scoring defense a total of six times. Under Zimmer's direction, 8 defensive players have been selected to the Pro Bowl a total of 23 times. Four different players have posted 10-plus sacks while working under Zimmer. Career record: 0-0.

Background: Played quarterback and later linebacker at Illinois State (1974-77). Coached collegiately at Missouri (1979-1980), Weber State (1981-88) and Washington State (1989-1993).

Personal: Born June 5, 1956 in Peoria, Ill. Has three children, son Adam and daughters Corri and Marki. Vikki Zimmer, Mike's wife of 27 years, passed away in Cincinnati on October 8, 2009. Zimmer earned a degree in physical education from Illinois State.

ASSISTANT COACHES

Robb Akey, asst. defensive line; born July 24, 1966, Colorado Springs, Colo. Tight end/defensive end Weber State 1984-87. No pro playing experience. College coach: Weber State 1988-1994, Northern Arizona 1995-98, Washington State 1999-2006, Idaho 2007-2012, joined Vikings in 2014.

Jeff Davidson, offensive line; born October 3, 1967, Akron, Ohio. Offensive line Ohio State 1986-89. Pro offensive lineman Denver Broncos 1990-92, New Orleans Saints 1994. Pro coach: New Orleans Saints 1995-96, New England Patriots 1997-2004, Cleveland Browns 2005-06, Carolina Panthers 2007-10, joined Vikings in 2011.

George Edwards, defensive coordinator; born January 16, 1967, Siler City, N.C. Linebacker Duke 1986-89. No pro playing experience. College coach: Florida 1991, Appalachian State 1992-95, Duke 1996, Georgia 1997. Pro coach: Dallas Cowboys 1998-2001, Washington Redskins 2002-03, Cleveland Browns 2004, Miami Dolphins 2005-09, Buffalo Bills 2010-11, Miami Dolphins 2012-13, joined Vikings in 2014.

Ryan Ficken, special teams assistant; born February 20, 1980, Aurora, Colo. Wide receiver Arizona State 1998-99. No pro playing experience. College coach: UCLA 2004-06. Pro coach: Joined Vikings in 2007.

Hank Fraley, asst. offensive line; born September 21, 1977, Gaithersburg, Md. Offensive line Robert Morris 1996-99. Pro offensive lineman Philadelphia Eagles 2000-06, Cleveland Browns 2006-09, St. Louis Rams 2010. College coach: San Diego 2012, San Jose State 2013. Pro coach: Joined Vikings in 2014.

Jonathan Gannon, asst. defensive backs/quality control; born Jan. 4, 1983, Cleveland, Ohio. Safety Louisville 2002. No pro playing experience. College coach: Louisville 2006. Pro coach: Atlanta Falcons 2007, St. Louis Rams 2009-2011, Tennessee Titans 2012-13, joined Vikings in 2014.

Jerry Gray, defensive backs; born December 16, 1962, Lubbock, Texas. Safety Texas 1981-84. Pro defensive back Los Angeles Rams 1985-1991, Houston Oilers 1992, Tampa Bay Buccaneers 1993. College coach: Southern Methodist 1995-96. Pro coach: Tennessee Oilers/Titans 1997-2000, Buffalo Bills 2001-05, Washington Redskins 2006-09, Seattle Seahawks 2010, Tennessee Titans 2011-13, joined Vikings in 2014.

Jeff Howard, defensive assistant; born January 13, 1983, Grand Island, Neb. Linebacker Eastern New Mexico 2001-04. No pro playing experience. College coach: Texas Tech 2011-12. Pro coach: Joined Vikings in 2013.

Jeff Hurd, asst. strength and conditioning; born April 24, 1958, Pomona, Calif. Attended Fort Hays State. No college or pro playing experience. College coach: Fort Hays State 1984, Delta State 1985-86, Clemson 1986-87, Western Michigan 1987-1992, Tulsa 1994. Pro coach: Kansas City Chiefs 1992-93, Jacksonville Jaguars 1995-97, Kansas City Chiefs 1998-2006, San Diego Chargers 2007-2012, joined Vikings in 2013.

Klint Kubiak, asst. wide receivers/quality control; born February 17, 1987, Houston, Texas. Defensive back Colorado State 2005-09. No pro playing experience. College coach: Texas A&M 2010-12. Pro coach: Joined Vikings in 2013.

Evan Marcus, strength and conditioning; born January 2, 1968, Union, N.J. Offensive line Ithaca 1986-89. No pro playing experience. College coach: Arizona State 1991-92, Rutgers 1993, Maryland 1994, Texas 1995-97, Louisville 1998-99, Virginia 2003-06, 2011-13. Pro coach: Atlanta Falcons 2007, Miami Dolphins 2008-10, joined Vikings in 2014.

Andre Patterson, defensive line; born June 12, 1960, Camden, Ark. Offensive line Contra Costa (Calif.) C.C. 1980, Montana 1981. No pro playing experience. College coach: Montana 1982, Weber State 1988, Western Washington 1989, Cornell 1990-91, Washington State 1992-93, Cal Poly 1994-96, Nevada-Las Vegas 2008-09, Texas-El Paso 2010-12, Florida International 2013. Pro coach: New England Patriots 1997, Minnesota Vikings 1998-99, Dallas Cowboys 2000-02, Cleveland Browns 2003-04, Denver Broncos 2005-06,

re-joined Vikings in 2014.

Drew Petzing, coaching assistant; born March 12, 1987, Rochester, N.Y. Defensive back Middlebury 2005-06. No pro playing experience. College coach: Middlebury 2007-08, Harvard 2009, Boston College 2010-11, Yale 2012. Pro coach: Cleveland Browns 2013, joined Vikings in 2014.

Mike Priefer, special teams coordinator; born August 21, 1966, Cleveland, Ohio. Quarterback/wide receiver Navy 1985-88. No pro playing experience. College coach: Navy 1994-96, Youngstown State 1997-98, Virginia Military Institute 1999, Northern Illinois 2000-01. Pro coach: Jacksonville Jaguars 2002, N.Y. Giants 2003-05, Kansas City Chiefs 2006-08, Denver Broncos 2009-10, joined Vikings in 2011.

Kevin Stefanski, tight ends; born May 8, 1982, Philadelphia, Pa. Safety Pennsylvania 2000-04. No pro playing experience. College coach: Pennsylvania 2005. Pro coach: Joined Vikings in 2006.

George Stewart, wide receivers; born December 29, 1958, Little Rock, Ark. Guard Arkansas 1977-1980. No pro playing experience. College coach: Minnesota 1984-85, Notre Dame 1986-88. Pro coach: Pittsburgh Steelers 1989-1991, Tampa Bay Buccaneers 1992-95, San Francisco 49ers 1996-2002, Atlanta Falcons 2003-06, joined Vikings in 2007.

Norv Turner, offensive coordinator; born May 17, 1952, LeJeune, N.C. Quarterback Oregon 1971-74. No pro playing experience. College coach: Oregon 1975, Southern California 1976-1984. Pro coach: Los Angeles Rams 1985-1990, Dallas Cowboys 1991-93, Washington Redskins 1994-2000 (head coach), San Diego Chargers 2001, 2007-2012 (head coach 2007-2012), Miami Dolphins 2002-03, Oakland Raiders 2004-05 (head coach), San Francisco 49ers 2006, Cleveland Browns 2013, joined Vikings in 2014.

Scott Turner, quarterbacks; born August 7, 1982, Englewood, Calif. Quarterback Nevada-Las Vegas 2002-04. No pro playing experience. College coach: Oregon State 2005, Pittsburgh 2008-2010. Pro coach: Carolina Panthers 2011-12, Cleveland Browns 2013, joined Vikings in 2014.

Kirby Wilson, running backs; born August 24, 1961, Los Angeles, Calif. Running back/wide receiver Pasadena (Calif.) C.C. 1980, Illinois 1981-82. Pro cornerback Winnipeg Blue Bombers (CFL) 1983, Toronto Argonauts (CFL) 1984. College coach: Pasadena (Calif.) C.C. 1985, Southwest (Calif.) C.C. 1986-1990, Southern Illinois 1991-92, Wyoming 1993-94, Iowa State 1995-96, Southern California 2001. Pro coach: New England Patriots 1997-99, Washington Redskins 2000, Tampa Bay Buccaneers 2002-03, Arizona Cardinals 2004-06, Pittsburgh Steelers 2007-2013, joined Vikings in 2014.

Adam Zimmer, linebackers; born January 13, 1984, Ogden, Utah. Safety Trinity 2002-05. No pro playing experience. Pro coach: New Orleans Saints 2006-09, Kansas City Chiefs 2010-12, Cincinnati Bengals 2013, joined Vikings in 2014.

National Football Conference
South Division
Team Colors: Old Gold, Black, and White
5800 Airline Drive
Metairie, Louisiana 70003
Telephone: (504) 733-0255

2014 SCHEDULE
PRESEASON

Aug. 8	at St. Louis	7:00
Aug. 15	Tennessee	7:00
Aug. 23	at Indianapolis	7:00
Aug. 28	Baltimore	7:00

REGULAR SEASON

Sep. 7	at Atlanta	12:00
Sep. 14	at Cleveland	12:00
Sep. 21	Minnesota	12:00
Sep. 28	at Dallas	7:30
Oct. 5	Tampa Bay	12:00
Oct. 12	BYE	
Oct. 19	at Detroit	12:00
Oct. 26	Green Bay	*7:30
Oct. 30	at Carolina (Thu)	7:25
Nov. 9	San Francisco	12:00
Nov. 16	Cincinnati	12:00
Nov. 24	Baltimore (Mon)	7:30
Nov. 30	at Pittsburgh	12:00
Dec. 7	Carolina	12:00
Dec. 15	at Chicago (Mon)	7:30
Dec. 21	Atlanta	12:00
Dec. 28	at Tampa Bay	12:00

*All times CT; Sunday night games in
Weeks 5-16 subject to change
Stadium: Mercedes-Benz Superdome
(opened in 1975)
•**Capacity:** 73,000
1500 Poydras Street
New Orleans, Louisiana 70112
Playing Surface: UBU Speed Series-S5-M
Training Camp: The Greenbrier
White Sulpher Springs, W.Va. 24986

MERCEDES-BENZ SUPERDOME

CLUB OFFICIALS
Owner/Chairman of the Board:
Tom Benson
Owner/Vice Chairman of the Board:
Rita Benson LeBlanc
President: Dennis Lauscha
Executive Vice President/General
Manager: Mickey Loomis
Senior Vice President of
Communications: Greg Bensel
Senior Vice President of Marketing and
Business Development: Ben Hales
Senior Vice President/Chief Financial
Officer: Ed Lang
Senior Vice President/General Counsel:
Vicky Neumeyer
Senior Vice President of Sales:
Mike Stanfield
Senior Vice President of Corporate
Partnerships: Jean-Paul Dardenne
Director of Player Personnel: Ryan Pace
Director of Football Administration:
Khai Harley
Director of Operations: James Nagaoka
Director of College Scouting:
Rick Reiprish
Director of Pro Scouting: Terry Fontenot
Pro Scout: Ryan Powell
Regional Scouts: Josh Lucas,
Dwaune Jones
Area Scouts: Brian Adams, Mike Baugh,
Ryan Hollern, Jason Mitchell,
Terry Wooden
College Scouting Coordinator:
Paul Zimmer
Combine Scout: Joey Vitt Jr.
Salary Cap Analyst/Player Personnel:
Joseph Laine
Scouting Assistants: Michael Parenton,
Casey Talley
Equipment Manager: Dan Simmons
Assistant Equipment Manager:
John Baumgartner
Equipment Assistant: Corey Gaudet
Head Athletic Trainer: Scottie B. Patton
Assistant Athletic Trainers:
Duane Brooks, Kevin Mangum
Assistant Athletic Trainer/Physical
Therapist: Beau Lowery
Video Director: Dave Desposito
Assistant Video Director: Joe Alley
Video Assistants: Justin Matthews,
Tim Youngblood
Director of Player Development:
Fred McAfee
Director of Security: Danny Lawless
Executive Director of Football
Communications: Doug Miller
Football Communications Manager:
Justin Macione
Communications Coordinator:
Matt Mendelson
Communications Coordinator:
Courtney Foret
Communications Coordinator:
Samantha McLain
Director of Photography:
Michael C. Hebert
IT Director: Jeff Huffman
Facilities Manager: Terry Ashburn
Administrative Director: Jay Romig

COACHING HISTORY
(324-409-5)
Records include postseason games

1967-70	Tom Fears*	13-34-2
1970-72	J.D. Roberts	7-25-3
1973-75	John North**	11-23-0
1975	Ernie Hefferle	1-7-0
1976-77	Hank Stram	7-21-0
1978-80	Dick Nolan***	15-29-0
1980	Dick Stanfel	1-3-0
1981-85	O.A. (Bum) Phillips****	27-42-0
1985	Wade Phillips	1-3-0
1986-96	Jim Mora#	93-78-0
1996	Rick Venturi	1-7-0
1997-99	Mike Ditka	15-33-0
2000-05	Jim Haslett	46-52-0
2006-2011	Sean Payton	67-37-0
2012	Aaron Kromer##	2-4-0
2012	Joe Vitt###	5-5-0
2013	Sean Payton	12-6-0

* Released after seven games in 1970
** Released after six games in 1975
*** Released after 12 games in 1980
**** Resigned after 12 games in 1985
\# Resigned after eight games in 1996
\#\# Interim head coach first six games in 2012
\#\#\# Interim head coach final 10 games in 2012

PAID ATTENDANCE
Home 562,763   Away 520,106
Total 1,082,869
Single-game home record,
73,085 (12/26/11)
Single-season home record,
573,876 (2008)

2014 DRAFT CHOICES

Round	Name	Pos.	College
1	Brandin Cooks	WR	Oregon St.
2	Stanley Jean-Baptiste	DB	Nebraska
4	Khairi Fortt	LB	California
5	Vinnie Sunseri	DB	Alabama
	Ronald Powell	LB	Florida
6	Tavon Rooks	T	Kansas St.

2013 TEAM RECORD
PRESEASON (3-1)

Date	Result	Opponent
08/09	W 17-13	Kansas City
08/16	W 28-20	Oakland
08/25	W 31-23	at Houston
08/29	L 21-24	at Miami

REGULAR SEASON (11-5)

Date	Result	Opponent
09/08	W 23-17	Atlanta
09/15	W 16-14	at Tampa Bay
09/22	W 31-7	Arizona
09/30	W 38-17	Miami
10/06	W 26-18	at Chicago
10/13	L 27-30	at New England
10/27	W 35-17	Buffalo
11/03	L 20-26	at New York Jets
11/10	W 49-17	Dallas
11/17	W 23-20	San Francisco
11/21	W 17-13	at Atlanta
12/02	L 7-34	at Seattle
12/08	W 31-13	Carolina
12/15	L 16-27	at St. Louis
12/22	L 13-17	at Carolina
12/29	W 42-17	Tampa Bay

POSTSEASON (1-1)

Date	Result	Opponent
01/04	W 26-24	at Philadelphia
01/11	L 15-23	at Seattle

SCORE BY PERIODS

Saints	86	155	70	103	0	—	414
Opponents	87	112	46	59	0	—	304

2013 TEAM STATISTICS

	Saints	Opp.
Total First Downs	359	274
Rushing	87	82
Passing	244	168
Penalty	28	24
3rd Down: Made/Att	97/221	69/199
3rd Down Pct.	43.9	34.7
4th Down: Made/Att	9/19	4/12
4th Down Pct.	47.4	33.3
Possession Avg.	32:41	27:19
Total Net Yards	6391	4891
Avg. Per Game	399.4	305.7
Total Plays	1079	943
Avg. Per Play	5.9	5.2
Net Yards Rushing	1473	1786
Avg. Per Game	92.1	111.6
Total Rushes	391	387
Net Yards Passing	4918	3105
Avg. Per Game	307.4	194.1
Sacked/Yards Lost	37/244	49/336
Gross Yards	5162	3441
Att./Completions	651/446	507/304
Completion Pct.	68.5	60.0
Had Intercepted	12	12
Punts/Average	61/46.9	83/46.4
Net Punting Avg.	61/42.3	83/43.4
Penalties/Yards	95/817	91/750
Fumbles/Ball Lost	12/7	15/7
Touchdowns	49	33
Rushing	10	11
Passing	39	20
Returns	0	2

2013 INDIVIDUAL STATISTICS

PASSING

	Att.	Comp.	Yds.	Pct.	TD	Int.	Tkld.	Rate
Brees	650	446	5162	68.6	39	12	37/244	104.7
McCown	1	0	0	0.0	0	0	0/0	39.6
Saints	651	446	5162	68.5	39	12	37/244	104.5
Opponents	507	304	3441	60.0	20	12	49/336	83.6

SCORING

	TD R	TD P	TD Rt	PAT	FG	Saf	PTS
Hartley	0	0	0	41/41	22/30	0	107
J. Graham	0	16	0	0/0	0/0	0	96
Colston	0	5	0	0/0	0/0	0	30
Stills	0	5	0	0/0	0/0	0	30
Thomas	2	3	0	0/0	0/0	0	30
Sproles	2	2	0	0/0	0/0	0	24
Brees	3	0	0	0/0	0/0	0	18
S. Graham	0	0	0	7/7	2/2	0	13
Meachem	0	2	0	0/0	0/0	0	12
Moore	0	2	0	0/0	0/0	0	12
Watson	0	2	0	0/0	0/0	0	12
Cadet	0	1	0	0/0	0/0	0	6
Collins	1	0	0	0/0	0/0	0	6
Hill	0	1	0	0/0	0/0	0	6
Ingram	1	0	0	0/0	0/0	0	6
K. Robinson	1	0	0	0/0	0/0	0	6
Saints	10	39	0	48/48	24/32	0	414
Opponents	11	20	2	32/32	24/28	0	304

2-Pt Conversions: Saints 0-1, Opponents 1-1.

RUSHING

	No.	Yds	Avg	LG	TD
Thomas	147	549	3.7	18	2
Ingram	78	386	4.9	34	1
K. Robinson	54	224	4.1	25	1
Sproles	53	220	4.2	38	2
Brees	35	52	1.5	16	3
Collins	15	45	3.0	12	1
Stills	3	10	3.3	4	0
Meachem	2	-1	-0.5	4	0
McCown	3	-4	-1.3	-1	0
Hill	1	-8	-8.0	-8	0
Saints	391	1473	3.8	38	10
Opponents	387	1786	4.6	52	11

RECEIVING

	No.	Yds	Avg	LG	TD
J. Graham	86	1215	14.1	56t	16
Thomas	77	513	6.7	29	3
Colston	75	943	12.6	35	5
Sproles	71	604	8.5	48	2
Moore	37	457	12.4	44t	2
Stills	32	641	20.0	76t	5
Watson	19	226	11.9	32	2
Meachem	16	324	20.3	60	2
Collins	14	54	3.9	8	0
Ingram	7	68	9.7	23	0
Hill	6	44	7.3	9	1
Toon	4	68	17.0	35	0
Cadet	2	5	2.5	3t	1
Saints	446	5162	11.6	76t	39
Opponents	304	3441	11.3	60	20

INTERCEPTIONS

	No.	Yds	Avg	LG	TD
Lewis	4	34	8.5	20	0
M. Jenkins	2	35	17.5	31	0
White	1	43	43.0	43	0
Vaccaro	1	29	29.0	29	0
Greer	1	22	22.0	22	0
Herring	1	6	6.0	6	0
Carr	1	0	0.0	0	0
Harper	1	0	0.0	0	0
Saints	12	169	14.1	43	0
Opponents	12	117	9.8	85t	1

PUNTING

	No.	Yds.	Avg.	In 20	LG
Morstead	61	2859	46.9	25	61
Saints	61	2859	46.9	25	61
Opponents	83	3853	46.4	27	60

PUNT RETURNS

	Ret	FC	Yds	Avg	LG	TD
Sproles	29	21	194	6.7	28	0
Moore	2	3	0	0.0	0	0
Cadet	1	1	0	0.0	0	0
Saints	32	25	194	6.1	28	0
Opponents	24	12	180	7.5	32	0

KICKOFF RETURNS

	No.	Yds	Avg	LG	TD
Sproles	12	255	21.3	32	0
Cadet	9	239	26.6	82	0
Thomas	1	12	12.0	12	0
Saints	22	506	23.0	82	0
Opponents	33	830	25.2	46	0

FIELD GOALS

	1-19	20-29	30-39	40-49	50+
Hartley	2/2	5/6	5/8	9/13	1/1
S. Graham	0/0	1/1	0/0	1/1	0/0
Saints	2/2	6/7	5/8	10/14	1/1
Opponents	0/0	9/9	8/8	4/6	3/5

SACKS

	No.
Jordan	12.5
Galette	12.0
Hicks	4.5
Haralson	3.5
Foster	3.0
Hawthorne	3.0
M. Jenkins	2.5
T. Johnson	2.0
Lofton	2.0
Vaccaro	1.0
Walker	1.0
Wilson	1.0
Dawson	0.5
Humber	0.5
Saints	49.0
Opponents	37.0

RECORD HOLDERS
INDIVIDUAL RECORDS—CAREER

Category	Name	Performance
Rushing (Yds.)	Deuce McAllister, 2001-09	6,096
Passing (Yds.)	Drew Brees, 2006-2013	38,733
Passing (TDs)	Drew Brees, 2006-2013	283
Receiving (No.)	Marques Colston, 2006-2013	607
Receiving (Yds.)	Marques Colston, 2006-2013	8,337
Interceptions	Dave Waymer, 1980-89	37
Punting (Avg.)	Thomas Morstead, 2009-2013	46.9
Punt Return (Avg.)	Mel Gray, 1986-88	13.4
Kickoff Return (Avg.)	Travaris Cadet, 2012-13	26.5
Field Goals	Morten Andersen, 1982-1994	302
Touchdowns (Tot.)	Marques Colston, 2006-2013	63
Points	Morten Andersen, 1982-1994	1,318
*Sacks	Rickey Jackson, 1981-1993	115.0

INDIVIDUAL RECORDS—SINGLE SEASON

Category	Name	Performance
Rushing (Yds.)	George Rogers, 1981	1,674
Passing (Yds.)	Drew Brees, 2011	5,476
Passing (TDs)	Drew Brees, 2011	46
Receiving (No.)	Jimmy Graham, 2011	99
Receiving (Yds.)	Joe Horn, 2004	1,399
Interceptions	Dave Whitsell, 1967	10
Punting (Avg.)	Thomas Morstead, 2012	50.1
Punt Return (Avg.)	Mel Gray, 1987	14.7
Kickoff Return (Avg.)	John Gilliam, 1967	30.1
Field Goals	Morten Andersen, 1985	31
	John Carney, 2002	31
Touchdowns (Tot.)	Dalton Hilliard, 1989	18
Points	John Kasay, 2011	147
*Sacks	Pat Swilling, 1991	17.0
	La'Roi Glover, 2000	17.0

INDIVIDUAL RECORDS—SINGLE GAME

Category	Name	Performance
Rushing (Yds.)	George Rogers, 9-4-83	206
Passing (Yds.)	Drew Brees, 11-19-06	510
Passing (TDs)	Billy Kilmer, 11-2-69	6
	Drew Brees, 9-13-09	6
Receiving (No.)	Tony Galbreath, 9-10-78	14
Receiving (Yds.)	Wes Chandler, 9-2-79	205
Interceptions	Tommy Myers, 9-3-78	3
	Dave Waymer, 10-6-85	3
	Reggie Sutton, 10-18-87	3
	Gene Atkins, 12-22-91	3
	Sammy Knight, 9-9-01	3
Field Goals	Many times	5
	Last time by John Carney, 9-26-04	
Touchdowns (Tot.)	Joe Horn, 12-14-03	4
	Reggie Bush, 12-3-06	4
Points	Joe Horn, 12-14-03	24
	Reggie Bush, 12-3-06	24
*Sacks	Many times	4.0
	Last time by Wayne Martin, 9-21-97	

*Sacks became an official statistic in 1982.
**NFL Record

2014 VETERAN ROSTER

No.	Name	Pos.	Ht.	Wt.	Birthdate	NFL Exp.	College	Hometown	How Acq.	'13 Games/ Starts
72	Armstead, Terron	T	6-5	304	7/23/91	2	Arkansas-Pine Bluff	Cahokia, Ill.	D3a-'13	6/2
27	Bailey, Champ	CB	6-0	192	6/22/78	16	Georgia	Folkston, Ga.	FA-'14	5/3*
9	Brees, Drew	QB	6-0	209	1/15/79	14	Purdue	Austin, Texas	UFA(SD)-'06	16/16
77	Bunkley, Brodrick	NT	6-2	306	11/23/83	9	Florida State	Tampa, Fla.	UFA(Den)-'12	12/10
25	Bush, Rafael	S	5-11	200	5/12/87	4	South Carolina State	Williston, S.C.	WAI(Den)-'12	13/6
90	Butler, Victor	OLB	6-2	245	7/29/87	6	Oregon State	Rialto, Calif.	UFA(Dall)-'13	0*
31	Byrd, Jairus	S	5-10	203	10/7/86	6	Oregon	Clayton, Mo.	UFA(Buff)-'13	11/9*
39	Cadet, Travaris	RB	6-1	210	2/1/89	3	Appalachian State	Miami, Fla.	FA-'12	13/0
12	Colston, Marques	WR	6-4	225	6/5/83	9	Hofstra	Harrisburg, Pa.	D7b-'06	15/11
55	Dawson, Keyunta	OLB	6-3	258	9/13/85	7	Texas Tech	Shreveport, La.	FA-'13	6/0
47	Drescher, Justin	LS	6-1	235	1/1/88	5	Colorado	Southlake, Texas	FA-'10	16/0
73	Evans, Jahri	G	6-4	318	8/22/83	9	Bloomsburg	Philadelphia, Pa.	D4-'06	14/14
97	Foster, Glenn	DE	6-4	285	5/31/90	2	Illinois	Chicago, Ill.	FA-'13	12/0
93	Galette, Junior	OLB	6-2	258	3/27/88	5	Stillman	Montvale, N.J.	FA-'10	16/15
80	Graham, Jimmy	TE	6-7	265	11/24/86	5	Miami	Goldsboro, N.C.	D3-'10	16/12
3	Graham, Shayne	K	6-0	210	12/9/77	15	Virginia Tech	Dublin, Va.	FA-'13	2/0
4	Griffin, Ryan	QB	6-5	206	11/17/89	2	Tulane	Westlake Village, Calif.	FA-'13	0*
66	Grubbs, Ben	G	6-3	310	3/10/84	8	Auburn	Eclectic, Ala.	UFA(Balt)-'12	16/16
98	Haralson, Parys	OLB	6-0	255	1/24/84	9	Tennessee	Madison, Miss.	T(SF)-'13	16/8
79	Harris, Bryce	T	6-6	300	1/16/89	3	Fresno State	Tulare, Calif.	FA-'12	16/1
57	Hawthorne, David	ILB	6-0	246	5/14/85	7	Texas Christian	Corsicana, Texas	UFA(Sea)-'12	16/15
76	Hicks, Akiem	DE	6-5	324	11/16/89	3	Regina	Fair Oaks, Calif.	D3-'12	16/16
89	Hill, Josh	TE	6-5	229	5/21/90	2	Idaho State	Blackfoot, Idaho	FA-'13	14/3
53	Humber, Ramon	ILB	5-11	232	8/10/87	6	North Dakota State	Brooklyn Park, Minn.	FA-'10	16/3
22	Ingram, Mark	RB	5-9	215	12/21/89	4	Alabama	Flint, Mich.	D1b-'11	11/3
92	Jenkins, John	NT	6-3	359	7/11/89	2	Georgia	Meriden, Conn.	D3b-'13	16/5
94	Jordan, Cameron	DE	6-4	287	7/10/89	4	California	Chandler, Ariz.	D1a-'11	16/16
65	Kelemete, Senio	G	6-3	300	5/10/90	2	Washington	Seattle, Wash.	FA-'13	0*
68	Lelito, Tim	C/G	6-4	315	7/21/89	2	Grand Valley State	St. Clair, Mich.	FA-'13	16/2
28	Lewis, Keenan	CB	6-1	208	5/17/86	6	Oregon State	New Orleans, La.	UFA(Pitt)-'13	16/16
50	Lofton, Curtis	ILB	6-0	241	6/2/86	7	Oklahoma	Kingfisher, Okla.	UFA(Atl)-'12	16/16
41	Lorig, Erik	FB	6-4	250	11/17/86	5	Stanford	Rolling Hills, Calif.	UFA(TB)-'14	15/9*
7	McCown, Luke	QB	6-4	217	7/12/81	11	Louisiana Tech	Jacksonville, Texas	UFA(Atl)-'13	16/0
17	Meachem, Robert	WR	6-2	215	9/28/84	8	Tennessee	Tulsa, Okla.	FA-'13	15/5
13	Morgan, Joseph	WR	6-1	184	3/23/88	3	Walsh	Canton, Ohio	FA-'11	0*
6	Morstead, Thomas	P	6-4	235	3/8/86	6	Southern Methodist	Pearland, Texas	D5-'09	16/0
99	Ozougwu, Cheta	OLB	6-2	255	11/18/88	3	Rice	Houston, Texas	FA-'14	7/0*
52	Reddick, Kevin	ILB	6-1	246	12/28/89	2	North Carolina	New Bern, N.C.	FA-'13	16/0
29	Robinson, Khiry	RB	6-0	220	12/28/89	2	West Texas A&M	Temple, Texas	FA-'13	10/6
21	Robinson, Patrick	CB	5-11	191	9/7/87	4	Florida State	Miami, Fla.	D1-'10	2/0
84	Stills, Kenny	WR	6-0	194	4/22/92	2	Oklahoma	Carlsbad, Calif.	D5-'13	16/10
64	Strief, Zach	T	6-7	320	9/22/83	9	Northwestern	Milford, Ohio	D7a-'06	15/15
38	Sweeting, Rod	CB	6-0	187	9/28/90	2	Georgia Tech	Luella, Ga.	FA-'13	9/0
23	Thomas, Pierre	RB	5-11	215	12/18/84	8	Illinois	Lansing, Ill.	FA-'07	16/9
88	Toon, Nick	WR	6-4	218	11/4/88	2	Wisconsin	Middleton, Wisc.	D4-'12	8/3
32	Vaccaro, Kenny	S	6-0	214	2/15/91	2	Texas	Early, Texas	D1-'13	14/14
30	Wade, Trevin	CB	5-10	190	8/1/89	3	Arizona	Austin, Texas	FA-'13	2/0
75	Walker, Tyrunn	DE	6-4	294	3/18/90	3	Tulsa	New Iberia, La.	FA-'12	7/0
82	Watson, Benjamin	TE	6-3	255	12/18/80	11	Georgia	Rock Hill, S.C.	UFA(Cle)-'13	15/7
60	Welch, Thomas	T	6-7	310	6/19/87	4	Vanderbilt	Brentwood, Tenn.	FA-'14	16/0*
24	White, Corey	CB	6-1	205	5/9/90	3	Samford	Dunwoody, Ga.	D5-'12	16/6

* Bailey played five games with Denver in '13; Butler missed '13 season because of injury; Byrd played 11 games with Buffalo; Griffin inactive 10 games; Kelemete last active with Arizona in '12; Lorig played 15 games with Tampa Bay; Morgan missed '13 season because of injury; Ozougwu played seven games with Chicago; Welch played 16 games with Buffalo.

Traded—RB Darren Sproles (15 games in '13) to Philadelphia.

Players lost through free agency (3): T Charles Brown (NYG; 16 games in '13), C Brian de la Puente (Chi; 16), S Malcolm Jenkins (Phil; 14).

Also played with Saints in '13—S Isa Abdul-Quddus (11 games), CB Chris Carr (11), FB Jed Collins (16), S Eric Frampton (2), CB Jabari Greer (10), S Roman Harper (9), K Garrett Hartley (14), ILB Will Herring (16), DE Tom Johnson (12), WR Lance Moore (13), OLB Jay Richardson (4), ILB Jonathan Vilma (1), OLB Martez Wilson (4).

FIRST-YEAR ROSTER

Name	Pos.	Ht.	Wt.	Birthdate	College	Hometown	How Acq.
Armstrong, Matt	C	6-2	302	5/24/90	Grand Valley State	Lansing, Mich.	FA
Ball, Marcus (1)	S	6-1	209	7/21/87	Memphis	Stone Mountain, Ga.	FA
Brooks, Derrius (1)	CB	5-10	192	5/29/88	Western Kentucky	Pine Mountain, Ga.	FA
Coleman, Brandon	WR	6-6	225	6/22/92	Rutgers	Forestville, Md.	FA
Cooks, Brandin	WR	5-10	189	9/25/93	Oregon State	Stockton, Calif.	D1
Davis, A.J. (1)	CB	6-0	183	7/6/89	Jacksonville State	Pinson, Ala.	FA-'12
Dimke, Derek (1)	K	6-0	180	4/16/90	Illinois	Rockford, Ill.	FA
Dixon, Brian	CB	6-0	195	4/26/90	Northwest Missouri State	Coconut Creek, Fla.	FA
Edebali, Kasim	OLB	6-2	253	8/17/89	Boston College	Meriden, N.H.	FA
Flanders, Tim	RB	5-9	210	9/29/91	Sam Houston State	Midwest City, Okla.	FA
Foketi, Manase (1)	T	6-5	310	9/18/90	West Texas A&M	Hesperia, Calif.	FA
Fortt, Khairi	ILB	6-2	240	3/24/92	California	Stamford, Conn.	D4
Frederick, Terrence (1)	CB	5-10	187	2/10/90	Texas A&M	Katy, Texas	FA-'13
Givens, Chris (1)	WR	6-2	203	1/28/89	Miami (Ohio)	Chillicothe, Ohio	FA-'12
Golic Jr., Mike (1)	G	6-4	300	9/28/89	Notre Dame	West Hartford, Conn.	FA
Hadley, Spencer	ILB	6-1	227	10/30/89	Brigham Young	Connell, Wash.	FA
Hamm, Je'Ron	TE	6-3	236	6/15/92	Louisiana-Monroe	Leesville, La.	FA
Hawkins, Charles (1)	WR	5-8	180	8/30/90	Southern	New Orleans, La.	FA-'13
Hull, Steve	WR	6-2	200	7/20/90	Illinois	Cincinnati, Ohio	FA
Jacobs, Nic	TE	6-5	269	10/13/91	McNeese State	Many, La.	FA
Jean-Baptiste, Stanley	CB	6-3	218	4/12/90	Nebraska	Davie, Fla.	D2
Johnson, Austin (1)	FB	6-2	240	6/16/89	Tennessee	Hickory, N.C.	FA-'13
Johnson Jr., Rufus (1)	OLB	6-5	272	8/28/90	Tarleton State	Dallas, Texas	D6-'13
Jones, Marcel (1)	T	6-7	320	9/4/88	Nebraska	Phoenix, Ariz.	D7-'12
Jones, Seantavius	WR	6-3	200	8/9/92	Valdosta State	Tucker, Ga.	FA
Kilgore, Logan	QB	6-3	206	5/24/90	Middle Tennessee State	Carmichael, Calif.	FA
Knox, Kyle (1)	OLB	6-1	220	3/10/89	Fresno State	Los Angeles, Calif.	FA-'13
McCray, Moses	NT	6-2	318	1/12/90	Akron	Tampa, Fla.	FA
Nsekhe, Ty (1)	T	6-8	325	10/27/85	Texas State	Arlington, Texas	FA
Powell, Ronald	OLB	6-3	237	5/14/91	Florida	Moreno Valley, Calif.	D5b
Rooks, Tavon	T	6-5	300	5/10/90	Kansas State	Baltimore, Md.	D6
Strozier, Derrick	RB	5-8	181	10/27/90	Tulane	Orlando, Fla.	FA
Sunseri, Vinnie	S	6-0	210	10/28/91	Alabama	Tuscaloosa, Ala.	D5a
Tanner, Andy (1)	WR	6-0	183	5/16/88	Midwestern State	Rockwall, Texas	FA-'10
Uko, George	DE	6-3	284	2/11/92	Southern California	Chino, Calif.	FA
Uzo-Diribe, Chidera	OLB	6-3	250	5/30/92	Colorado	Corona, Calif.	FA
Virgil, Lawrence	DE	6-5	290	1/20/91	Valdosta State	Quitman, Ga.	FA
Warren, Pierre	S	6-2	200	8/16/92	Jacksonville State	Deatsville, Ala.	FA
Zimmerman, Ty	S	6-1	204	6/23/90	Kansas State	Junction City, Kan.	FA

The term NFL Rookie is defined as a player who is in his first season of professional football and has not been on the roster of another professional football team for any regular-season or postseason games. A Rookie is designated by an "R" on NFL rosters. Players who have been active in another professional football league or players who have NFL experience, including either preseason training camp or being on an Active List or Inactive List, or on Reserve/Injured or Reserve/Physically Unable to Perform for fewer than six regular-season games, are termed NFL First-Year Players. An NFL First-Year Player is designated by a ".1" on NFL rosters. Thereafter, a player is credited with an additional year of experience for each season in which he accumulates six games on the Active List or Inactive List, or on Reserve/Injured or Reserve/Physically Unable to Perform.

Log on to www.neworleanssaints.com for an up-to-date roster.

COACHING STAFF

Head Coach,
Sean Payton

Pro Career: Named the fourteenth head coach in Saints history on Jan. 18, 2006 and has led the team to five playoff appearances, three NFC South titles, two NFC Championship berths and the Super Bowl XLIV title. Earned unanimous NFL Coach of the Year honors in his first season in 2006 and received the same honors from some outlets in 2009. Considered one of the NFL's brightest offensive minds, the Saints have ranked among the league's top ten offenses each season since his arrival, including finishing first in the NFL (with a league record 7,474 yards) in 2011, in addition to 2009, 2008 and 2006. With Dallas Cowboys (2003-05), served as the assistant head coach/passing game coordinator in 2005 after spending his first two seasons as assistant head coach/ quarterbacks. Coached four years with the New York Giants (1999-2002), the last three seasons as offensive coordinator, and was quarterbacks coach for the Philadelphia Eagles (1997-98). Career record: 79-43.

Background: Earned a degree in communications at Eastern Illinois, where he departed with a school-record 10,665 passing yards, then the third-highest total in NCAA Division I-AA history. A three-time All-American, Payton had brief playing stops with Chicago of the Arena League, the CFL's Ottawa Rough Riders and the Chicago Bears in 1987. Payton coached collegiately at San Diego State (1988-89, 1992-93), Indiana State (1990-91), Miami (Ohio) in 1994-95, and Illinois (1996).

Personal: Born Dec. 29, 1963 in San Mateo, Calif. and raised in Naperville, Ill.

ASSISTANT COACHES

Charles Byrd, asst. strength and conditioning; born June 24, 1981, Oxford, Ohio. Defensive back Morehead State 2001-04. Pro defensive back Las Vegas Gladiators (AFL) 2006. College coach: Miami (Ohio) 2006-07. Pro coach: Joined Saints in 2008.

Pete Carmichael, offensive coordinator; born October 6, 1971, Framingham, Mass. Attended Boston College. No college or pro playing experience. College coach: New Hampshire 1994, Louisiana Tech 1995-99. Pro coach: Cleveland Browns 2000, Washington Redskins 2001, San Diego Chargers 2002-05, joined Saints in 2006.

Andre Curtis, asst. secondary; born December 8, 1976, Beaverdam, Va. Linebacker Virginia Military Institute 1996-99. No pro playing experience. College coach: Virginia Military Institute 2000-03, Georgia Southern 2004-05. Pro coach: New York Giants 2006-08, St. Louis Rams 2009-2011, joined Saints in 2012.

Dan Dalrymple, head strength and conditioning; born Aug. 26, 1965, Cleveland, Ohio. Offensive lineman Miami (Ohio) 1983-86. No pro playing experience.

College coach: Miami (Ohio) 1987-2005. Pro coach: Joined Saints in 2006.

Henry Ellard, wide receivers; born July 21, 1961, Fresno, Calif. Wide receiver Fresno State 1979-1982. Pro wide receiver/punt returner Los Angeles Rams 1983-1993, Washington Redskins 1994-98, New England Patriots 1998. College coach: Fresno State 2000. Pro coach: St. Louis Rams 2001-08, New York Jets 2009-2011, joined Saints in 2012.

Bret Ingalls, offensive line; born Aug. 19, 1960, San Jose, Calif. Running back Wichita State 1979-1981. No pro playing experience. College coach: Idaho 1982-88, San Diego State 1989-1993, Eastern Michigan 1994, Louisville 1995-96, Northern Iowa 1997-99, Idaho 2000-03, Indiana State 2004, Miami (Ohio) 2005, Northwestern 2006-08. Pro coach: Joined Saints in 2009.

Bill Johnson, defensive line; born June 23, 1955, Monroe, La. Defensive lineman Northwestern (La.) State 1976-79. No pro playing experience. College coach: Northwestern (La.) State 1980-84, McNeese State 1985-86, Miami 1987, Louisiana Tech 1988-89, Arkansas 1990-91, 2000, Texas A&M 1992-99. Pro coach: Atlanta Falcons 2001-06, Denver Broncos 2007-08, joined Saints in 2009.

Stan Kwan, asst. special teams; born November 2, 1967, Phoenix. Attended South Mountain (Ariz.) C.C., San Diego State. No college or pro playing experience. Pro coach: San Diego Chargers 1991-96, Detroit Lions 1997-2000, Arizona Cardinals 2001-03, Detroit Lions 2004-09, Buffalo Bills 2010-12, joined Saints in 2013.

Terry Malone, tight ends; born February 26, 1960, Buffalo, N.Y. Tight end Holy Cross 1978-1982. No pro playing experience. College coach: Arizona 1983-84, Holy Cross 1985, Bowling Green 1986-1995, Boston College 1996, Michigan 1997-2005. Pro coach: Joined Saints in 2006.

Wesley McGriff, secondary; born January 23, 1968, Tifton, Ga. Linebacker Savannah State 1986-89. No pro playing experience. College coach: Savannah State 1990-94, Kentucky State 1995-99, Eastern Kentucky 2000, Kentucky 2001-02, Baylor 2003-06, Miami 2007-2010, Vanderbilt 2011, Mississippi 2012. Pro coach: Joined Saints in 2013.

Greg McMahon, special teams coordinator; born Jan. 2, 1960, Rantoul, Ill. Defensive back Eastern Illinois 1978-1981. No pro playing experience. College coach: Eastern Illinois 1982, Minnesota 1983-84, North Alabama 1985-87, Southern Illinois 1988, Valdosta State 1989, Nevada Las-Vegas 1990-91, Illinois 1992-2004, East Carolina 2005. Pro coach: Joined Saints in 2006.

Mike Neu, quarterbacks; born September 30, 1970, Indianapolis, Ind. Quarterback Ball State 1990-93. Pro quarterback Calgary Stampeders (CFL) 1995, Orlando Predators (AFL) 1996, Nashville Kats (AFL)

1997. College coach: Ball State 1994, Tulane 2012-13. Pro coach: Augusta Stallions (af2-head coach) 2000, Carolina Cobras (AFL) 2001-02 (head coach, 2002), New Orleans VooDoo (AFL-head coach) 2004-08, joined Saints in 2014.

Dan Roushar, running backs; born September 27, 1960, Clinton, Iowa. Quarterback Northern Illinois 1982-83. No pro playing experience. College coach: Northern Illinois 1984, Butler 1986-1992, Rhode Island 1993, Ball State 1994, Illinois 1995-96, Northern Illinois 1997-2002, Cincinnati 2003-06, Michigan State 2007-2012. Pro coach: Joined Saints in 2013.

Rob Ryan, defensive coordinator; born December 13, 1962, Ardmore, Okla. Linebacker Oklahoma State 1984, Southwestern Oklahoma State 1985-86. No pro playing experience. College coach: Western Kentucky 1987, Ohio State 1988, Tennessee State 1989-1993, Hutchinson (Kan.) C.C. 1996, Oklahoma State 1997-99. Pro coach: Arizona Cardinals 1994-95, New England Patriots 2000-03, Oakland Raiders 2004-08, Cleveland Browns 2009-2010, Dallas Cowboys 2011-12, joined Saints in 2013.

Carter Sheridan, offensive assistant/ wide receivers; born Nov. 20, 1977, New Orleans, La. Defensive back Florida A&M 1996-98. No pro playing experience. Pro coach: Joined Saints in 2006.

Frank Smith, offensive assistant/offensive line; born February 21, 1981, Milwaukee, Wisc. Offensive lineman Miami (Ohio) 1999-2003. No pro playing experience. College coach: Miami (Ohio) 2004-05, Butler 2006-09. Pro coach: Joined Saints in 2010.

Marcus Ungaro, defensive assistant; born October 9, 1984, Seattle. Defensive back Southwestern College 2004-05. No pro playing experience. Pro coach: Joined Saints in 2010.

Joe Vitt, asst. head coach/linebackers; born August 23, 1954, Syracuse, N.Y. Linebacker Towson State 1974-78. No pro playing experience. Pro coach: Baltimore Colts 1979-1981, Seattle Seahawks 1982-1991, Los Angeles Rams 1992-94, Philadelphia Eagles 1995-98, Green Bay Packers 1999, Kansas City Chiefs 2000-03, St. Louis Rams 2004-05 (head coach, final 11 games of 2005), joined Saints in 2006 (interim head coach, final 10 games of 2012).

Rob Wenning, strength and conditioning assistant, born December 10, 1984, Coldwater, Ohio. Offensive line/tight end Findlay (Ohio) 2003-06. No pro playing experience. College coach: Ohio State 2007, Louisiana State 2008-2009. Pro Coach: Joined Saints in 2010.

Brian Young, defensive assistant/ linebackers; born July 8, 1977, Lawton, Okla. Defensive tackle Texas El-Paso 1996-99. Pro defensive tackle St. Louis Rams 2000-03, New Orleans Saints 2004-08. Pro coach: Joined Saints in 2009.

**National Football Conference
East Division**
Team Colors: Blue, Red, and White
Quest Diagnostics Training Center
1925 Giants Drive
East Rutherford, New Jersey 07073
Telephone: (201) 935-8111

2014 SCHEDULE
PRESEASON

Aug. 3	vs. Buffalo (Canton)	8:00
Aug. 9	**Pittsburgh**	7:30
Aug. 16	at Indianapolis	7:00
Aug. 22	at New York Jets	7:30
Aug. 28	**New England**	7:30

REGULAR SEASON

Sep. 8	at Detroit (Mon)	7:10
Sep. 14	**Arizona**	1:00
Sep. 21	**Houston**	1:00
Sep. 25	at Washington (Thu)	8:25
Oct. 5	**Atlanta**	1:00
Oct. 12	at Philadelphia	*8:30
Oct. 19	at Dallas	4:25
Oct. 26	BYE	
Nov. 3	**Indianapolis** (Mon)	8:30
Nov. 9	at Seattle	4:25
Nov. 16	**San Francisco**	1:00
Nov. 23	**Dallas**	*8:30
Nov. 30	at Jacksonville	1:00
Dec. 7	at Tennessee	1:00
Dec. 14	**Washington**	1:00
Dec. 21	at St. Louis	4:05
Dec. 28	**Philadelphia**	1:00

*All times ET; Sunday night games in
Weeks 5-16 subject to change
Stadium: MetLife Stadium
(opened in 2010)
• **Capacity:** 82,500
East Rutherford, New Jersey 07073
Playing Surface: FieldTurf
Training Camp: Quest Diagnostics Training Center
1925 Giants Drive
East Rutherford, N.J. 07073

METLIFE STADIUM

CLUB OFFICIALS
President/CEO: John K. Mara
Chairman/EVP: Steve Tisch
Treasurer: Jonathan Tisch
Senior Vice President-General Manager:
Jerry Reese
Senior Vice President and Chief
Marketing Officer: Michael Stevens
Senior Vice President and General
Counsel: William J. Heller, Esq.
Senior Vice President, Player Personnel:
Chris Mara
Senior Vice President, Medical Services:
Ronnie Barnes
Senior Vice President and Chief Financial
Officer: Christine Procops
Senior Vice President, Corporate
Partnerships: John Maguire
Senior Vice President, Communications:
Pat Hanlon
Vice President, Communications:
Peter John-Baptiste
Vice President of Community Relations:
Frank Mara
Vice President of Marketing:
Rusty Hawley
Vice President of Media and
Partnerships: Dan Lynch
Vice President, Giants Entertainment:
Don Sperling
Vice President of Finance:
Steven Hamrahi
Vice President, Player Evaluation:
Marc Ross
Assistant General Manager:
Kevin Abrams
Director of Pro Player Personnel:
Ken Sternfield
Assistant Director of Pro Player
Personnel: Matt Shauger
Director of Player Development:
Charles Way
Pro Scouts: Patrick Hanscomb,
Tim McDonnell
College Scouts: Joe Collins,
Jeremiah Davis, Steve Verderosa,
Jeremy Breit, Steve Devine,
Donnie Etheridge, Ryan Jones,
Steve Malin, Chris Pettit, Chris Watts
Director of Ticketing: John Gorman
Director of Administration: Jim Phelan
Director of Community Relations:
Allison Stangeby
Director of Creative Services:
Doug Murphy
Communications Manager:
DeAndré Phillips
Assistant Head Athletic Trainer:
Steve Kennelly
Coordinator or Rehabilitation:
Byron Hansen
Physical Therapist/Assistant Athletic
Trainer: Leigh Weiss
Equipment/Locker Room Manager:
Ed Wagner, Jr.
Equipment Director: Joseph Skiba
Assistant Equipment Managers:
Ed Skiba, Tim Slaman
Video Director: Dave Maltese
Assistant Video Directors:
Carmen Pizzano, Ed Triggs,
Steve Venditti
Assistant Director of Community
Relations: Jen Conley
Vice President, Information Technology:
Justin Warren
Director of Information Technology:
Julie Glisky
Director of Client Services:
Ethan Medley

COACHING HISTORY
(685-571-33)
Records include postseason games

1925	Bob Folwell	8-4-0
1926	Joe Alexander	8-4-1
1927-28	Earl Potteiger	15-8-3
1929-1930	LeRoy Andrews*	24-5-1
1930	Benny Friedman-Steve Owen	2-0-0
1931-1953	Steve Owen	153-108-17
1954-1960	Jim Lee Howell	55-29-4
1961-68	Allie Sherman	57-54-4
1969-1973	Alex Webster	29-40-1
1974-76	Bill Arnsparger**	7-28-0
1976-78	John McVay	14-23-0
1979-1982	Ray Perkins	24-35-0
1983-1990	Bill Parcells	85-52-1
1991-92	Ray Handley	14-18-0
1993-96	Dan Reeves	32-34-0
1997-2003	Jim Fassel	60-56-1
2004-2013	Tom Coughlin	98-73-0

*Released after 15 games in 1930
**Released after seven games in 1976

PAID ATTENDANCE
Home 638,827   Away 547,737
Total 1,186,564
Single-game home record,
82,287 (1/1/12)
Single-season home record,
639,513 (2012)

2014 DRAFT CHOICES

Round	Name	Pos.	College
1	Odell Beckham, Jr.	WR	Louisiana St.
2	Weston Richburg	C	Colorado St.
3	Jay Bromley	DT	Syracuse
4	Andre Williams	RB	Boston College
5	Nat Berhe	DB	San Diego St.
	Devon Kennard	LB	Southern California
6	Bennett Jackson	DB	Notre Dame

2013 TEAM RECORD
PRESEASON (1-3)

Date	Result		Opponent
08/10	W	18-13	at Pittsburgh
08/18	L	12-20	Indianapolis
08/24	L	21-24	New York Jets (OT)
08/29	L	20-28	at New England

REGULAR SEASON (7-9)

Date	Result		Opponent
09/08	L	31-36	at Dallas
09/15	L	23-41	Denver
09/22	L	0-38	at Carolina
09/29	L	7-31	at Kansas City
10/06	L	21-36	Philadelphia
10/10	L	21-27	at Chicago
10/21	W	23-7	Minnesota
10/27	W	15-7	at Philadelphia
11/10	W	24-20	Oakland
11/17	W	27-13	Green Bay
11/24	L	21-24	Dallas
12/01	W	24-17	at Washington
12/08	L	14-37	at San Diego
12/15	L	0-23	Seattle
12/22	W	23-20	at Detroit (OT)
12/29	W	20-6	Washington

(OT) Overtime

SCORE BY PERIODS

Giants	46	90	80	75	3	—	294
Opponents	61	136	87	99	0	—	383

2013 TEAM STATISTICS

	Giants	Opp.
Total First Downs	280	327
Rushing	77	101
Passing	176	198
Penalty	27	28
3rd Down: Made/Att	69/211	93/232
3rd Down Pct.	32.7	40.1
4th Down: Made/Att	6/12	4/15
4th Down Pct.	50.0	26.7
Possession Avg.	29:03	30:57
Total Net Yards	4920	5316
Avg. Per Game	307.5	332.3
Total Plays	988	1089
Avg. Per Play	5.0	4.9
Net Yards Rushing	1332	1743
Avg. Per Game	83.3	108.9
Total Rushes	381	454
Net Yards Passing	3588	3573
Avg. Per Game	224.3	223.3
Sacked/Yards Lost	40/287	34/214
Gross Yards	3875	3787
Att./Completions	567/325	601/361
Completion Pct.	57.3	60.1
Had Intercepted	29	17
Punts/Average	91/46.9	87/43.4
Net Punting Avg.	91/38.2	87/39.4
Penalties/Yards	91/786	105/904
Fumbles/Ball Lost	26/15	25/12
Touchdowns	32	42
Rushing	11	12
Passing	18	21
Returns	3	9

2013 INDIVIDUAL STATISTICS

PASSING	Att.	Comp.	Yds.	Pct.	TD	Int.	Tkld.	Rate
Manning	551	317	3818	57.5	18	27	39/281	69.4
Painter	16	8	57	50.0	0	2	1/6	19.0
Giants	567	325	3875	57.3	18	29	40/287	67.6
Opponents	601	361	3787	60.1	21	17	34/214	78.3

SCORING	TD R	TD P	TD Rt	PAT	FG	Saf	PTS
J. Brown	0	0	0	31/31	23/26	0	100
Randle	0	6	0	0/0	0/0	0	36
Cruz	0	4	0	0/0	0/0	0	24
Jacobs	4	0	0	0/0	0/0	0	24
Myers	0	4	0	0/0	0/0	0	24
A. Brown	3	0	0	0/0	0/0	0	20
Jernigan	1	2	0	0/0	0/0	0	18
Hillis	2	0	0	0/0	0/0	0	12
Hill	0	0	1	0/0	0/0	0	6
Murphy	0	1	0	0/0	0/0	0	6
Pierre-Paul	0	0	1	0/0	0/0	0	6
Scott	0	1	0	0/0	0/0	0	6
Taylor	0	0	1	0/0	0/0	0	6
Wilson	1	0	0	0/0	0/0	0	6
Giants	11	18	3	31/31	23/26	0	294
Opponents	12	21	9	40/40	29/30	1	383

2-Pt Conversions: A. Brown.
Giants 1-1, Opponents 1-2.

RUSHING	No.	Yds	Avg	LG	TD
A. Brown	139	492	3.5	23t	3
Hillis	73	247	3.4	27	2
Jacobs	58	238	4.1	37	4
Wilson	44	146	3.3	18	1
Scott	20	73	3.7	16	0
Jernigan	2	57	28.5	49t	1
Cox	22	43	2.0	9	0
Manning	18	36	2.0	14	0
Pascoe	1	2	2.0	2	0
Weatherford	1	0	0.0	0	0
Painter	3	-2	-0.7	0	0
Giants	381	1332	3.5	49t	11
Opponents	454	1743	3.8	34	12

RECEIVING	No.	Yds	Avg	LG	TD
Cruz	73	998	13.7	70t	4
Nicks	56	896	16.0	57	0
Myers	47	522	11.1	27t	4
Randle	41	611	14.9	37t	6
Jernigan	29	329	11.3	30	2
A. Brown	20	103	5.2	14	0
Hillis	13	96	7.4	16	0
Pascoe	12	81	6.8	14	0
Scott	11	102	9.3	23t	1
Murphy	6	37	6.2	8	1
Conner	6	31	5.2	12	0
Donnell	3	31	10.3	11	0
Cox	3	12	4.0	11	0
Jacobs	2	13	6.5	8	0
Wilson	2	8	4.0	6	0
Hynoski	1	5	5.0	5	0
Giants	325	3875	11.9	70t	18
Opponents	361	3787	10.5	56	21

INTERCEPTIONS	No.	Yds	Avg	LG	TD
Rolle	6	23	3.8	25	0
Hill	2	38	19.0	38t	1
McBride	2	17	8.5	17	0
Mundy	1	91	91.0	91	0
Thomas	1	65	65.0	65	0
Pierre-Paul	1	24	24.0	24t	1
Beason	1	9	9.0	9	0
Ross	1	9	9.0	9	0
Tuck	1	-2	-2.0	-2	0
Amukamara	1	-4	-4.0	-4	0
Giants	17	270	15.9	91	2
Opponents	29	377	13.0	49t	3

PUNTING	No.	Yds.	Avg.	In 20	LG
Weatherford	91	4271	46.9	25	68
Giants	91	4271	46.9	25	68
Opponents	87	3774	43.4	34	61

PUNT RETURNS	Ret	FC	Yds	Avg	LG	TD
Randle	29	24	237	8.2	32	0
Hosley	3	1	9	3.0	8	0
James	1	0	0	0.0	0	0
McBride	1	0	0	0.0	0	0
Jernigan	0	1	0	—	—	0
Giants	34	26	246	7.2	32	0
Opponents	48	17	655	13.6	89t	3

KICKOFF RETURNS	No.	Yds	Avg	LG	TD
Cox	20	436	21.8	56	0
Jernigan	11	246	22.4	46	0
Wilson	9	222	24.7	31	0
Kuhn	1	13	13.0	13	0
Moore	1	12	12.0	12	0
Rolle	1	4	4.0	4	0
Mosley	1	0	0.0	0	0
Giants	44	933	21.2	56	0
Opponents	33	721	21.8	69	0

FIELD GOALS	1-19	20-29	30-39	40-49	50+
J. Brown	0/0	8/8	7/8	7/8	1/2
Giants	0/0	8/8	7/8	7/8	1/2
Opponents	0/0	6/6	9/9	10/10	4/5

SACKS	No.
Tuck	11.0
Kiwanuka	6.0
Jenkins	5.0
Joseph	3.0
Pierre-Paul	2.0
Rolle	2.0
Mundy	1.0
Paysinger	1.0
Rivers	1.0
Thomas	1.0
(group)	1.0
Giants	34.0
Opponents	40.0

RECORD HOLDERS
INDIVIDUAL RECORDS—CAREER

Category	Name	Performance
Rushing (Yds.)	Tiki Barber, 1997-2006	10,449
Passing (Yds.)	Eli Manning, 2004-2013	35,345
Passing (TDs)	Eli Manning, 2004-2013	229
Receiving (No.)	Amani Toomer, 1996-2008	668
Receiving (Yds.)	Amani Toomer, 1996-2008	9,497
Interceptions	Emlen Tunnell, 1948-1958	74
Punting (Avg.)	Don Chandler, 1956-1964	43.8
Punt Return (Avg.)	Ward Cuff, 1941-45	12.1
Kickoff Return (Avg.)	Rocky Thompson, 1971-73	27.2
Field Goals	Pete Gogolak, 1966-1974	126
Touchdowns (Tot.)	Frank Gifford, 1952-1964	78
Points	Pete Gogolak, 1966-1974	646
*Sacks	Michael Strahan, 1993-2007	141.5

INDIVIDUAL RECORDS—SINGLE SEASON

Category	Name	Performance
Rushing (Yds.)	Tiki Barber, 2005	1,860
Passing (Yds.)	Eli Manning, 2011	4,933
Passing (TDs)	Y.A. Tittle, 1963	36
Receiving (No.)	Steve Smith, 2009	107
Receiving (Yds.)	Victor Cruz, 2011	1,536
Interceptions	Otto Schnellbacher, 1951	11
	Jim Patton, 1958	11
Punting (Avg.)	Don Chandler, 1959	46.6
Punt Return (Avg.)	Merle Hapes, 1942	15.5
Kickoff Return (Avg.)	John Salscheider, 1949	31.6
Field Goals	Ali Haji-Sheikh, 1983	35
	Jay Feely, 2005	35
	John Carney, 2008	35
Touchdowns (Tot.)	Joe Morris, 1985	21
Points	Jay Feely, 2005	148
*Sacks	Michael Strahan, 2001	**22.5

INDIVIDUAL RECORDS—SINGLE GAME

Category	Name	Performance
Rushing (Yds.)	Tiki Barber, 12-30-06	234
Passing (Yds.)	Phil Simms, 10-13-85	513
Passing (TDs)	Y.A. Tittle, 10-28-62	**7
Receiving (No.)	Tiki Barber, 1-2-00	13
Receiving (Yds.)	Del Shofner, 10-28-62	269
Interceptions	Many times	3
	Last time by Terry Kinard, 9-20-87	
Field Goals	Joe Danelo, 10-18-81	6
Touchdowns (Tot.)	Ron Johnson, 10-2-72	4
	Earnest Gray, 9-7-80	4
	Rodney Hampton, 9-24-95	4
Points	Ron Johnson, 10-2-72	24
	Earnest Gray, 9-7-80	24
	Rodney Hampton, 9-24-95	24
*Sacks	Osi Umenyiora, 9-30-07	6.0

*Sacks became an official statistic in 1982.
**NFL Record

NEW YORK GIANTS

2014 VETERAN ROSTER

No.	Name	Pos.	Ht.	Wt.	Birthdate	NFL Exp.	College	Hometown	How Acq.	'13 Games/ Starts
89	Adams, Kris	WR	6-3	194	9/4/87	3	Texas-El Paso	Everman, Texas	FA-'13	0*
49	Adkins, Spencer	LB	5-11	236	5/16/87	4	Miami	Naples, Fla.	FA-'14	0*
20	Amukamara, Prince	CB	6-0	207	6/6/89	4	Nebraska	Glendale, Ariz.	D1-'11	16/16
91	Ayers, Robert	DE	6-3	275	9/6/85	6	Tennessee	Bennettsville, S.C.	UFA(Den)-'14	15/3*
52	t-Beason, Jon	LB	6-0	232	1/14/85	8	Miami	Miramar, Fla.	T(Car)-'13	12/11
65	Beatty, Will	T	6-6	319	3/2/85	6	Connecticut	York, Pa.	D2-'09	16/16
31	Bowman, Zack	DB	6-1	196	11/18/84	7	Nebraska	Anchorage, Alaska	UFA(Chi)-'14	16/7*
73	Brewer, James	T	6-6	330	12/23/87	4	Indiana	Indianapolis, Ind.	D4-'11	16/8
71	Brown, Charles	T	6-5	300	4/10/87	5	Southern California	Chino Hills, Calif.	UFA(NO)-'14	16/14*
3	Brown, Josh	K	6-0	202	4/29/79	12	Nebraska	Foyil, Okla.	FA-'13	16/0
27	Brown, Stevie	S	5-11	215	7/17/87	5	Michigan	Columbus, Ind.	FA-'12	0*
39	Conner, John	FB	5-11	245	6/8/87	5	Kentucky	West Chester, Ohio	FA-'13	13/7
29	Cox, Michael	RB	6-1	222	11/14/88	2	Massachusetts	Avon, Conn.	D7-'13	14/1
80	Cruz, Victor	WR	6-0	204	11/11/86	5	Massachusetts	Paterson, N.J.	FA-'10	14/12
87	Davis, Kellen	TE	6-7	265	10/11/85	7	Michigan State	Adrian, Mich.	UFA(Sea)-'14	15/4*
35	Demps, Quintin	S	5-11	208	6/29/85	7	Texas-El Paso	San Antonio, Texas	UFA(KC)-'14	16/6*
51	DeOssie, Zak	LS	6-4	249	5/24/84	8	Brown	No. Andover, Mass.	D4-'07	16/0
84	Donnell, Larry	TE	6-6	265	11/1/88	2	Grambling	Ozark, Ala.	FA-'13	16/1
85	Fells, Daniel	TE	6-4	260	9/23/83	7	California-Davis	Anaheim, Calif.	FA-'14	0*
2	Freeman, Josh	QB	6-6	240	1/13/88	6	Kansas State	Kansas City, Mo.	UFA(NYG)-'14	4/4*
79	Goodin, Stephen	G	6-6	310	8/5/88	2	Nebraska-Kearney	Hastings, Neb.	FA-'13	1/0
95	Hankins, Johnathan	DT	6-2	320	3/30/92	2	Ohio State	Detroit, Mich.	D2-'13	11/0
62	Herman, Eric	G	6-4	320	8/5/89	2	Ohio	Oregon, Ohio	D7-'13	0*
58	Herzlich, Mark	LB	6-4	246	9/1/87	4	Boston College	Conestoga, Pa.	FA-'11	16/2
25	Hill, Will	S	6-1	207	3/7/90	3	Florida	Jersey City, N.J.	FA-'12	12/10
34	Hillis, Peyton	RB	6-2	250	1/21/86	7	Arkansas	Conway, Ark.	FA-'13	7/1
15	Holliday, Trindon	WR	5-5	166	4/27/86	5	Louisiana State	Zachary, La.	FA-'14	15/0*
28	Hosley, Jayron	CB	5-10	178	9/18/90	3	Virginia Tech	Delray Beach, Fla.	D3-'12	11/1
45	Hynoski, Henry	FB	6-1	266	12/30/88	4	Pittsburgh	Catawissa, Pa.	FA-'11	3/2
37	James, Charles	CB	5-9	179	5/14/90	2	Charleston Southern	Jacksonville, Fla.	FA-'13	12/0
99	Jenkins, Cullen	DT	6-2	305	1/20/81	11	Central Michigan	Belleville, Mich.	FA-'13	16/15
23	Jennings, Rashad	RB	6-1	231	3/26/85	6	Liberty	Lynchburg, Va.	FA-'14	15/8*
12	Jernigan, Jerrel	WR	5-8	189	6/14/89	4	Troy	Eufaula, Ala.	D3-'11	15/3
77	Jerry, John	G	6-5	340	6/14/86	5	Mississippi	Batesville, Tenn.	UFA(NYG)-'14	16/16*
94	Kiwanuka, Mathias	DE	6-5	267	3/8/83	9	Boston College	Indianapolis, Ind.	D1-'06	16/10
70	Kropog, Troy	T	6-6	295	7/31/86	4	Tulane	Metairie, La.	FA-'14	0*
78	Kuhn, Markus	DT	6-4	303	5/6/86	3	North Carolina State	Weinheim, Germany	D7-'12	5/0
10	Manning, Eli	QB	6-4	218	1/3/81	11	Mississippi	New Orleans, La.	T(SD)-'04	16/16
86	Manningham, Mario	WR	5-11	183	5/25/86	7	Michigan	Warren, Ohio	FA-'14	6/3*
38	McBride, Trumaine	CB	5-9	185	9/24/85	7	Mississippi	Clarkdale, Miss.	FA-'13	15/10
53	McClain, Jameel	LB	6-1	245	7/25/85	7	Syracuse	Philadelphia, Pa.	FA-'14	10/10*
98	Moore, Damontre	DE	6-5	250	9/11/92	2	Texas A&M	Rowlett, Texas	D3-'13	15/0
75	Mosley, Brandon	G	6-5	318	12/21/88	3	Auburn	Jefferson, Ga.	D4-'12	13/1
9	Nassib, Ryan	QB	6-2	223	3/10/90	2	Syracuse	Malvern, Pa.	D4-'13	0*
17	Painter, Curtis	QB	6-4	230	6/24/85	5	Purdue	Vincennes, Ind.	FA-'13	3/0
83	Parker, Preston	WR	6-0	200	2/13/87	4	North Alabama	Delray Beach, Fla.	FA-'14	0*
93	Patterson, Mike	DT	6-1	300	9/1/83	10	Southern California	Los Alamitos, Calif.	FA-'13	16/1
54	Paysinger, Spencer	LB	6-2	236	6/28/88	4	Oregon	Beverly Hills, Calif.	FA-'11	16/10
90	Pierre-Paul, Jason	DE	6-5	278	1/1/89	5	South Florida	Deerfield Beach, Fla.	D1-'10	11/6
67	Pugh, Justin	T	6-4	301	8/15/90	2	Syracuse	Holland, Pa.	D1-'13	16/16
82	Randle, Rueben	WR	6-2	208	5/7/91	3	Louisiana State	Bastrop, La.	D2-'12	16/3
61	Reynolds, Dallas	C	6-4	320	4/23/84	3	Brigham Young	Provo, Utah	FA-'13	3/0
81	Robinson, Adrien	TE	6-4	264	9/23/88	3	Cincinnati	Indianapolis, Ind.	D4-'12	1/0
21	Rodgers-Cromartie, Dominque	CB	6-2	193	4/7/86	7	Tennessee State	Bradenton, Fla.	FA-'14	15/13*
26	Rolle, Antrel	S	6-0	206	12/16/82	10	Miami	Homestead, Fla.	FA-'10	16/16
74	Schwartz, Geoff	G	6-6	340	7/11/86	6	Oregon	Los Angeles, Calif.	FA-'14	16/7*
76	Snee, Chris	G	6-3	310	1/18/82	11	Boston College	Montrose, Pa.	D2-'04	3/3
19	Talley, Julian	WR	6-1	192	6/9/89	2	Massachusetts	Atco, N.J.	FA-'13	2/0
30	Taylor, Cooper	S	6-4	228	4/14/90	2	Richmond	Atlanta, Ga.	D5-'13	10/0
24	Thurmond, III, Walter	CB	5-11	190	8/12/87	5	Oregon	West Covina, Calif.	UFA-'14	12/3*
55	Walton, J.D.	C	6-3	305	3/24/87	5	Baylor	Allen, Texas	FA-'14	0*
5	Weatherford, Steve	P	6-2	210	12/17/82	9	Illinois	Terre Haute, Ind.	FA-'11	16/0
57	Williams, Jacquian	LB	6-3	231	7/20/88	4	South Florida	Riverview, Fla.	D6-'11	16/8
22	Wilson, David	RB	5-9	205	6/15/91	3	Virginia Tech	Danville, Va.	D1-'12	5/4

* Adams missed '13 season because of injury; Adkins last active with Atlanta in '11; Ayers played 15 games with Denver in '13; Bowman played 16 games with Chicago; C. Brown played 16 games with New Orleans; S. Brown missed '13 season because of injury with St. Louis; Davis played 15 games with Seattle; Demps played 16 games with Kansas City; Fells last active with New England in '12; Freeman played three games with Tampa Bay and one game with Minnesota; Herman inactive one game; Holiday played 15 games with Denver; Jennings played 15 games with Oakland; Jerry played 16 games with Miami; Kropog played last active with Tennessee in '12; Manningham played six games with San Francisco; McClain played 10 games with Baltimore; Nassib inactive 16 games; Parker last active with Tampa Bay in '12; Rodgers-Cromartie played 15 games with Denver; Schwartz played 16 games with Kansas City; Thurmond played 12 games with Seattle; Walton inactive six games with Denver and inactive two games with Washington.

t- Giants traded for Beason (Car).

Retired—G David Diehl, 11-year guard, 11 games in '13.

Players lost through free agency (10): C/G Kevin Boothe (Oak; 16 games in '13), RB Andre Brown (Hou; 8), DT Linval Joseph (Minn; 15), DB Ryan Mundy (Chi; 16), WR Louis Murphy (TB; 14), TE Brandon Myers (TB; 16), WR Hakeem Nicks (Ind; 15), TE Bear Pascoe (Atl; 16), LB Keith Rivers (Buff; 16), DE Justin Tuck (Oak; 16).

Also played with Giants in '13—C David Baas (3 games), LB Allen Bradford (9), LB Dan Connor (1), C Jim Cordle (11), LB Marcus Dowtin (3), RB Brandon Jacobs (7), DT Shaun Rogers (7), DB Aaron Ross (4), RB Da'Rel Scott (5), DB Terrell Thomas (16), DE Justin Trattou (5), DB Corey Webster (4).

FIRST-YEAR ROSTER

Name	Pos.	Ht.	Wt.	Birthdate	College	Hometown	How Acq.
Adams, Kendrick (1)	LB	6-5	250	11/3/88	Louisiana State	Enterprise, Ala.	FA-'13
Anderson, Justin	LB	6-2	232	1/16/91	Louisiana-Lafayette	Foley, Ala.	FA
Baker, Steven (1)	T	6-8	340	11/24/88	East Carolina	Rocky Mount, N.C.	FA-'13
Barnett, C.J.	S	6-0	201	4/21/91	Ohio State	Clayton, Ohio	FA
Beckham Jr., Odell	WR	5-11	198	11/5/92	Louisiana State	New Orleans, La.	D1
Berhe, Nat	S	6-0	194	7/6/91	San Diego State	Colton, Calif.	D5a
Bromely, Jayson	DT	6-3	310	5/28/92	Syracuse	Flushing, N.Y.	D3
Dieke, Emmanuel	DE	6-6	257	9/23/90	Georgia Tech	Clayton County, Ga.	FA
Fox, Dan	LB	6-3	233	3/17/91	Notre Dame	Cleveland, Ohio	FA
Gaskins, Kendall (1)	RB	6-1	238	11/4/90	Richmond	Woodberry Forest, Va	FA-'13
Gordon, Thomas	S	6-0	214	3/20/91	Michigan	Detroit, Mich.	FA
Harris, Marcus (1)	WR	6-1	187	8/1/89	Murray State	St. Louis, Mo.	FA-'13
Harvey, Travis	WR	6-2	185	5/18/90	Florida A&M	Inglewood, Calif.	FA
Howard, Travis (1)	CB	6-1	200	11/24/89	Ohio State	Miami, Fla.	FA-'13
Jackson, Bennett	CB	6-0	192	9/16/91	Notre Dame	Hazlet, N.J.	D6
Kennard, Devon	LB	6-3	251	6/24/91	Southern California	Phoenix, Ariz.	D5
Manumaleuna, Eathyn	DT	6-2	289	1/15/89	Brigham Young	Anchorage, Ala.	FA
McManus, Brandon	K	6-3	201	7/25/91	Temple	Hatfield, Pa.	FA
Quarles, Kelcy	DT	6-4	294	1/23/92	South Carolina	Greenwood, S.C.	FA
Richburg, Weston	C	6-3	298	7/9/91	Colorado State	Bushland, Texas	D2
Stanton, Jordan	DE	6-4	263	4/11/91	James Madison	Fairfax, Va.	FA
Weaver, Ross (1)	DB	6-1	210	1/9/87	Michigan State	Southfield, Mich.	FA-'13
Williams, Andre	RB	5-11	230	8/28/92	Boston College	Allentown, Pa.	D4
Wynn, Kerry	DE	6-5	264	2/12/91	Richmond	Louisa, Va.	FA

The term NFL Rookie is defined as a player who is in his first season of professional football and has not been on the roster of another professional football team for any regular-season or postseason games. A Rookie is designated by an "R" on NFL rosters. Players who have been active in another professional football league or players who have NFL experience, including either preseason training camp or being on an Active List or Inactive List, or on Reserve/Injured or Reserve/Physically Unable to Perform for fewer than six regular-season games, are termed NFL First-Year Players. An NFL First-Year Player is designated by a "1" on NFL rosters. Thereafter, a player is credited with an additional year of experience for each season in which he accumulates six games on the Active List or Inactive List, or on Reserve/Injured or Reserve/Physically Unable to Perform.

Log on to www.giants.com for an up-to-date roster.

COACHING STAFF
Head Coach,
Tom Coughlin

Pro Career: Was named the sixteenth head coach in Giants history on January 6, 2004. This season marks Coughlin's eleventh with the Giants and nineteenth as an NFL head coach. In 2013, Coughlin led the Giants to a 7-9 record, finishing the season winning seven of their last 10 games after starting the season 0-6. It was second losing season since joining the team. In 2012, Coughlin led the Giants to a 9-7 record and the team's third-straight winning season and eighth consecutive non-losing season. In 2011, he helmed the Giants to their second championship in four seasons with a 21-17 win against the New England Patriots in Super Bowl XLVI. He also guided the team to a 9-7 record, en route to winning an NFC East crown. In 2010, the Giants posted a record of 10-6. The Giants finished the 2009 season with an 8-8 record. In the 2008 season the Giants finished with a 12-4 record, which won the NFC East division. Coughlin directed the Giants 17-14 win over the New England Patriots in Super Bowl XLII on February 3, 2008, the third championship in the team's history. Coached the Giants to an 11-5 record, the NFC East title and the playoffs in 2005-06, his second and third seasons with the team. Coughlin previously spent eight years (1995-2002) with the Jacksonville Jaguars. Under Coughlin, the Jaguars had the most victories of any NFL expansion team in its first seven seasons. They were also the only expansion team in NFL history to advance to the playoffs four times in their first five seasons. Coughlin's team went 9-7 in 1996 and an NFL-best 14-2 in 1999, both times reaching the AFC Championship Game. Coughlin previously coached the Philadelphia Eagles (1984-85), Green Bay Packers (1986-87), and Giants (1988-1990). He was a member of the Giants' Super Bowl XXV champion coaching staff. Career record: 170-137.
Background: Served as head coach at Boston College (1991-93), and coached at Syracuse (1969, 1974-1980), Rochester Institute of Technology 1970-73 (head coach), and Boston College (1981-83). Played wingback for Syracuse (1965-67).
Personal: Born August 31, 1946, Waterloo, N.Y. Tom and his wife Judy have two daughters, Keli and Katie; two son-in-laws named Chris; two sons, Brian and Tim; two daughters-in-law, Andrea (Tim's wife) and Susie (Brian's wife); and 10 grandchildren, Emma Rose, Dylan, Shea, Cooper, Caroline, Marin, Wesley, Brennon, Clara, and Walker.

ASSISTANT COACHES

Joe Danos, performance manager/strength and conditioning assistant; born Jan. 2, 1981, New Orleans, La. No college or pro playing experience. College coach: Louisiana State 2005-06, Southern Methodist 2007-09, Florida State 2010-12. Pro coach: Joined Giants in 2013.

Perry Fewell, defensive coordinator; born September 7, 1962, Gastonia, N.C. Defensive back Lenoir-Rhyne 1981-84. No pro playing experience. College coach: North Carolina 1985-86, Army 1987, 1992-94, Kent State 1988-1991, Vanderbilt 1995-97. Pro coach: Jacksonville Jaguars 1998-2002, St. Louis Rams 2003-04, Chicago Bears 2005, Buffalo Bills 2006-09, joined Giants in 2010.
Pat Flaherty, offensive line; born April 27, 1956, Hanover, Pa. Center East Stroudsburg 1974-77. No pro playing experience. College coach: East Stroudsburg 1980-81, Penn State 1982-83, Rutgers 1984-1991, East Carolina 1992, Wake Forest 1993-98, Iowa 1999. Pro coach: Washington Redskins 2000, Chicago Bears 2001-03, joined Giants in 2004.
Kevin M. Gilbride, tight ends; born December 14, 1979, Jacksonville, Fla. Quarterback Hawaii 2000. No pro playing experience. College coach: Syracuse 2004-05, Georgetown 2006, Temple 2007-09. Pro coach: Joined Giants in 2010.
Peter Giunta, secondary/corners; born August 11, 1956, Salem, Mass. Running back/defensive back Northeastern 1974-77. No pro playing experience. College coach: Penn State 1981-83, Brown 1984-87, Lehigh 1988-1990. Pro coach: Philadelphia Eagles 1991-94, N.Y. Jets 1995-96, St. Louis Rams 1997-2000, Kansas City Chiefs 2001-2005, joined Giants in 2006.
Jim Hermann, linebackers; born December 8, 1960, Hollywood, Calif. Linebacker Michigan 1979-1982. No pro playing experience. College coach: Michigan 1983, 1986-2005. Pro coach: New York Jets 2006-2008, joined Giants in 2009.
Larry Izzo, asst. special teams; born September 26, 1974, Fort Belvoir, Va. Linebacker Rice 1992-95. Pro linebacker/special teamer Miami Dolphins 1996-2000, New England Patriots 2001-08, New York Jets 2009. Pro coach: Joined Giants in 2011.
Craig Johnson, running backs; born March 3, 1960, Rome, N.Y. No college or pro playing experience. College coach: Wyoming 1983, Arkansas 1984, Army 1985, Rutgers 1986-88, Virginia Military Institute 1989-1991, Northwestern 1992-96, Maryland 1997-99. Pro coach: Tennessee Titans 2000-2010, Minnesota Vikings 2011-13, joined Giants in 2014.
Danny Langsdorf, quarterbacks; born June 28, 1972, McMinnville, Ore. Quarterback Boise State 1991-93, Linfield 1994-95. No pro playing experience. College coach: California Lutheran 1996, Oregon State 1997-98, 2005-2013. Pro coach: Edmonton Eskimos (CFL) 1999-01, New Orleans Saints 2002-04, joined Giants in 2014.
Robbie Leonard, defensive assistant; born July 14, 1985, Moon Township, Pa., Linebacker Washington & Jefferson College 2004, North Carolina State 2005-08. No pro playing experience College coach: North Carolina State 2010-12. Pro coach: Joined

Giants in 2013.
Ben McAdoo, offensive coordinator; born July 9, 1977, Homer City, Pa. No pro playing experience. College coach: Fairfield 2000, Michigan State 2001, Pittsburgh 2003, Akron 2004, Stanford 2005. Pro coach: New Orleans Saints 2004, San Francisco 49ers 2005, Green Bay Packers 2006-2013, joined Giants in 2014.
David Merritt Sr., secondary/safeties; born September 8, 1971, Raleigh, N.C. Linebacker North Carolina State 1989-1992. Pro linebacker Miami Dolphins 1993, Arizona Cardinals 1993-96, Rhein Fire (NFLE) 1997. College coach: Chattanooga 1997, Virginia Military Institute 1998-2000. Pro coach: New York Jets 2001-2003, joined Giants in 2004.
Robert Nunn, defensive line; born June 10, 1965, Apache, Okla. Linebacker Oklahoma State 1984-87. No pro playing experience. College coach: Northeastern Oklahoma 1988, Tennessee 1989-1990, Georgia Military 1991-99. Pro coach: Miami Dolphins 2000-02, 2004, Washington Redskins 2003, Green Bay Packers 2005-08, Tampa Bay Buccaneers 2009, joined Giants in 2010.
Jerry Palmieri, strength and conditioning; born October 30, 1958, Englewood, N.J. Attended Montclair State. No college or pro playing experience. College coach: North Carolina 1982-83, Oklahoma State 1984-86, Kansas State 1987-1992, Boston College 1993-94. Pro coach: Jacksonville Jaguars 1995-2002, New Orleans Saints 2003, joined Giants in 2004.
Markus Paul, asst. strength and conditioning; born April 1, 1966, Orlando, Fla. Safety Syracuse 1984-88. Pro safety Chicago Bears 1989-1993, Tampa Bay Buccaneers 1993. Pro coach: New Orleans Saints 1998-99, New England Patriots 2000-04, New York Jets 2005-2006, joined Giants in 2007.
Tom Quinn, special teams coordinator; born January 27, 1968, Pasadena, Calif. Linebacker Arizona 1986-1990. No pro playing experience. College coach; Davidson College 1991, James Madison 1992-94, Boston 1995, Holy Cross 1996-98, San Jose State 1999-2001, Stanford 2002-05. Pro coach: Joined Giants in 2006.
Ryan Roeder, offensive assistant; born February 14, 1980, Bethlehem, Pa., Quarterback Albany 1999-2002. No pro playing experience. College coach: Holy Cross 2004, Temple 2006-08, Rhode Island 2009, Princeton 2010-12. Pro coach: Joined Giants in 2013.
Sean Ryan, tight ends; born May 1, 1972, Glenn Falls, N.Y. Defensive back Hamilton College 1994. No pro playing experience. College coach: Albany 1998-99, Colgate 2000, Boston College 2001-02, Columbia 2003-04, Harvard 2006. Pro coach: Joined Giants in 2007.
Lunda Wells, asst. offensive line; born February 10, 1983, Baker, Ala. Offensive line Southern 2003-07. No pro playing experience. College coach: Louisiana State 2008-2011. Pro coach: Joined Giants in 2012.

**National Football Conference
East Division**
Team Colors: Midnight Green, Silver, Black,
and White
NovaCare Complex
One NovaCare Way
Philadelphia, Pennsylvania 19145
Telephone: (215) 463-2500

2014 SCHEDULE
PRESEASON
Aug. 8	**at Chicago**	8:00
Aug. 15	**at New England**	7:30
Aug. 21	Pittsburgh	7:30
Aug. 28	New York Jets	7:00

REGULAR SEASON
Sep. 7	**Jacksonville**	1:00
Sep. 15	at Indianapolis (Mon)	8:30
Sep. 21	**Washington**	1:00
Sep. 28	at San Francisco	4:25
Oct. 5	**St. Louis**	1:00
Oct. 12	**New York Giants**	*8:30
Oct. 19	BYE	
Oct. 26	at Arizona	4:05
Nov. 2	at Houston	1:00
Nov. 10	**Carolina** (Mon)	8:30
Nov. 16	at Green Bay	1:00
Nov. 23	**Tennessee**	1:00
Nov. 27	at Dallas (Thu)	4:30
Dec. 7	**Seattle**	4:25
Dec. 14	**Dallas**	*8:30
Dec. 20	at Washington (Sat)	TBD
Dec. 28	at New York Giants	1:00

*All times ET; Sunday night games in
Weeks 5-16 subject to change*
Stadium: Lincoln Financial Field
(opened in 2003)
•**Capacity:** 69,144
One Lincoln Financial Field Way
Philadelphia, Pennsylvania 19148
Playing Surface: Natural Grass
Training Camp: NovaCare Complex
One NovaCare Way
Philadelphia, PA 19145

LINCOLN FINANCIAL FIELD

CLUB OFFICIALS
Chairman/Chief Executive Officer:
Jeffrey Lurie
President: Don Smolenski
Head Coach: Chip Kelly
General Manager: Howie Roseman
President, Eagles Youth Partnership,
Eagles Social Responsibility:
Christina Weiss Lurie
Chief Financial Officer: Frank Gumienny
Senior Vice President/Business:
Ari Roitman
Senior Vice President of Media and
Communications: Anne Gordon
Senior Vice President, General Counsel:
Aileen Dagrosa
Vice President of Facility Operations:
Jason Miller
Vice President of Player Personnel:
Tom Gamble
Director of College Scouting:
Anthony Patch
Vice President, Corporate Partnerships:
Molly Arbogast
Vice President of Marketing:
Brian Papson
Vice President of Human Resources:
Kristie Pappal
Vice President of Ticket and Fan
Services: Laini DeLawter
Executive Director of Eagles Youth
Partnership: Sarah Martinez-Helfman
Director of Team Security: Dom DiSandro
Director of Football Technology:
Patrick Dolan
Director of Public Relations: Derek Boyko
Director of Broadcast Production:
Chris Johnson
Director, Digital and Social Media:
Linda Thomas
Director, Client Service: Tracy Foster
Director, Premium Sales and Service:
Mat Warner
Director of Information Technology:
John Pawling
Director of Grounds: Tony Leonard
Director of Community Relations:
Julie Hirshey
Head Athletic Trainer: Chris Peduzzi
Head Equipment Manager:
Greg Delimitros

COACHING HISTORY
(550-588-26)
Records include postseason games
1933-35	Lud Wray	9-21-1
1936-1940	Bert Bell	10-44-2
1941-1950	Earle (Greasy) Neale*	66-44-5
1951	Alvin (Bo) McMillin**	2-0-0
1951	Wayne Millner	2-8-0
1952-55	Jim Trimble	25-20-3
1956-57	Hugh Devore	7-16-1
1958-1960	Lawrence (Buck) Shaw	20-16-1
1961-63	Nick Skorich	15-24-3
1964-68	Joe Kuharich	28-41-1
1969-1971	Jerry Williams***	7-22-2
1971-72	Ed Khayat	8-15-2
1973-75	Mike McCormack	16-25-1
1976-1982	Dick Vermeil	57-51-0
1983-85	Marion Campbell****	17-29-1
1985	Fred Bruney	1-0-0
1986-1990	Buddy Ryan	43-38-1
1991-94	Rich Kotite	37-29-0
1995-98	Ray Rhodes	30-36-1
1999-2012	Andy Reid	140-102-1
2013	Chip Kelly	10-7-0

*Co-coach with Walt Kiesling in Philadelphia-
Pittsburgh merger in 1943
**Retired after two games in 1951
***Released after three games in 1971
****Released after 15 games in 1985

PAID ATTENDANCE
Home 529,623   Away 562,297
Total 1,091,920
Single-game home record,
72,111 (11/1/81)
Single-season home record,
557,325 (1980)

2014 DRAFT CHOICES
Round	Name	Pos.	College
1	Marcus Smith	LB	Louisville
2	Jordan Matthews	WR	Vanderbilt
3	Josh Huff	WR	Oregon
4	Jaylen Watkins	DB	Florida
5	Taylor Hart	DE	Oregon
	Ed Reynolds	DB	Stanford
7	Beau Allen	DT	Wisconsin

2013 TEAM RECORD
PRESEASON (2-2)

Date	Result	Opponent
08/09	L 22-31	New England
08/15	W 14-9	Carolina
08/24	W 31-24	at Jacksonville
08/29	L 20-27	at New York Jets

REGULAR SEASON (10-6)

Date	Result	Opponent
09/09	W 33-27	at Washington
09/15	L 30-33	San Diego
09/19	L 16-26	Kansas City
09/29	L 20-52	at Denver
10/06	W 36-21	at New York Giants
10/13	W 31-20	at Tampa Bay
10/20	L 3-17	Dallas
10/27	L 7-15	New York Giants
11/03	W 49-20	at Oakland
11/10	W 27-13	at Green Bay
11/17	W 24-16	Washington
12/01	W 24-21	Arizona
12/08	W 34-20	Detroit
12/15	L 30-48	at Minnesota
12/22	W 54-11	Chicago
12/29	W 24-22	at Dallas

POSTSEASON (0-1)

Date	Result	Opponent
01/04	L 24-26	New Orleans

SCORE BY PERIODS

Eagles	89	121	110	122	0	— 442
Opponents	60	97	100	125	0	— 382

2013 TEAM STATISTICS

	Eagles	Opp.
Total First Downs	355	368
Rushing	133	100
Passing	197	239
Penalty	25	29
3rd Down: Made/Att	83/213	93/231
3rd Down Pct.	39.0	40.3
4th Down: Made/Att	7/14	8/20
4th Down Pct.	50.0	40.0
Possession Avg.	26:24	33:36
Total Net Yards	6676	6304
Avg. Per Game	417.3	394.0
Total Plays	1054	1150
Avg. Per Play	6.3	5.5
Net Yards Rushing	2566	1668
Avg. Per Game	160.4	104.3
Total Rushes	500	443
Net Yards Passing	4110	4636
Avg. Per Game	256.9	289.8
Sacked/Yards Lost	46/296	37/271
Gross Yards	4406	4907
Att./Completions	508/310	670/408
Completion Pct.	61.0	60.9
Had Intercepted	9	19
Punts/Average	83/44.3	74/42.5
Net Punting Avg.	83/40.5	74/39.4
Penalties/Yards	95/846	106/855
Fumbles/Ball Lost	19/10	29/12
Touchdowns	53	43
Rushing	19	12
Passing	32	25
Returns	2	6

2013 INDIVIDUAL STATISTICS

PASSING

	Att.	Comp.	Yds.	Pct.	TD	Int.	Tkld.	Rate
Foles	317	203	2891	64.0	27	2	28/173	119.2
Vick	141	77	1215	54.6	5	3	15/99	86.5
Barkley	49	30	300	61.2	0	4	3/24	44.6
Smith	1	0	0	0.0	0	0	0/0	39.6
Eagles	508	310	4406	61.0	32	9	46/296	102.7
Opponents	670	408	4907	60.9	25	19	37/271	84.0

SCORING

	TD R	TD P	TD Rt	PAT	FG	Saf	PTS
Henery	0	0	0	45/45	23/28	0	114
McCoy	9	2	0	0/0	0/0	0	66
Jackson	0	9	0	0/0	0/0	0	54
Cooper	0	8	0	0/0	0/0	0	52
Celek	0	6	0	0/0	0/0	0	36
Ertz	0	4	0	0/0	0/0	0	24
Foles	3	0	0	0/0	0/0	0	18
Polk	3	0	0	0/0	0/0	0	18
Brown	2	0	0	0/0	0/0	0	14
Avant	0	2	0	0/0	0/0	0	12
Vick	2	0	0	0/0	0/0	0	12
Boykin	0	0	1	0/0	0/0	0	6
Goode	0	0	1	0/0	0/0	0	6
Maehl	0	1	0	0/0	0/0	0	6
Cole	0	0	0	0/0	0/0	1	2
Thornton	0	0	0	0/0	0/0	1	2
Eagles	19	32	2	45/45	23/28	2	442
Opponents	12	25	6	35/36	27/32	0	382

2-Pt Conversions: Cooper 2, Brown.
Eagles 3-8, Opponents 4-7

RUSHING

	No.	Yds	Avg	LG	TD
McCoy	314	1607	5.1	57t	9
Brown	75	314	4.2	65t	2
Vick	36	306	8.5	61	2
Foles	57	221	3.9	21	3
Polk	11	98	8.9	38t	3
Cooper	0	18	—	18	0
Jackson	3	2	0.7	8	0
Smith	2	2	1.0	2	0
Barkley	2	-2	-1.0	-1	0
Eagles	500	2566	5.1	65t	19
Opponents	443	1668	3.8	35	12

RECEIVING

	No.	Yds	Avg	LG	TD
Jackson	82	1332	16.2	61t	9
McCoy	52	539	10.4	70	2
Cooper	47	835	17.8	63t	8
Avant	38	447	11.8	31	2
Ertz	36	469	13.0	38	4
Celek	32	502	15.7	42	6
Brown	8	84	10.5	35	0
Maehl	4	67	16.8	37	1
Polk	4	61	15.3	34	0
Casey	3	31	10.3	12	0
Smith	2	27	13.5	14	0
D. Johnson	2	14	7.0	8	0
Vick	0	-2	—	-2	0
Eagles	310	4406	14.2	70	32
Opponents	408	4907	12.0	66	25

PUNTING

	No.	Yds.	Avg.	In 20	LG
Jones	82	3681	44.9	33	70
Eagles	83	3681	44.3	33	70
Opponents	74	3146	42.5	29	68

PUNT RETURNS

	Ret	FC	Yds	Avg	LG	TD
Jackson	14	8	71	5.1	32	0
D. Johnson	12	12	100	8.3	21	0
Eagles	26	20	171	6.6	32	0
Opponents	28	22	223	8.0	58t	1

INTERCEPTIONS

	No.	Yds	Avg	LG	TD
Boykin	6	136	22.7	76	1
Kendricks	3	25	8.3	18	0
Williams	3	16	5.3	15	0
Ryans	2	46	23.0	36	0
Fletcher	2	30	15.0	25	0
Allen	1	43	43.0	43	0
Wolff	1	0	0.0	0	0
Barwin	1	-2	-2.0	-2	0
Eagles	19	294	15.5	76	1
Opponents	9	128	14.2	38t	1

KICKOFF RETURNS

	No.	Yds	Avg	LG	TD
D. Johnson	17	441	25.9	33	0
Boykin	9	205	22.8	41	0
Smith	4	106	26.5	47	0
Graham	2	14	7.0	14	0
Casey	1	10	10.0	10	0
Jackson	1	10	10.0	10	0
Polk	1	8	8.0	8	0
Ertz	1	0	0.0	0	0
Cooper	1	-4	-4.0	-4	0
Eagles	37	790	21.4	47	0
Opponents	52	1229	23.6	105t	2

FIELD GOALS

	1-19	20-29	30-39	40-49	50+
Henery	0/0	8/8	7/8	7/10	1/2
Eagles	0/0	8/8	7/8	7/10	1/2
Opponents	0/0	5/5	11/11	8/10	3/6

SACKS

	No.
Cole	8.0
Barwin	5.0
Curry	4.0
Kendricks	4.0
Ryans	4.0
Cox	3.0
Graham	3.0
Logan	2.0
Allen	1.0
Goode	1.0
Thornton	1.0
Williams	1.0
Eagles	37.0
Opponents	46.0

RECORD HOLDERS

INDIVIDUAL RECORDS—CAREER

Category	Name	Performance
Rushing (Yds.)	Wilbert Montgomery, 1977-1984	6,538
Passing (Yds.)	Donovan McNabb, 1999-2009	32,873
Passing (TDs)	Donovan McNabb, 1999-2009	216
Receiving (No.)	Harold Carmichael, 1971-1983	589
Receiving (Yds.)	Harold Carmichael, 1971-1983	8,978
Interceptions	Bill Bradley, 1969-1976	34
	Eric Allen, 1988-1994	34
	Brian Dawkins, 1996-2008	34
Punting (Avg.)	Joe Muha, 1946-1950	42.9
Punt Return (Avg.)	Ernie Steele, 1942-48	16.8
Kickoff Return (Avg.)	Steve Van Buren, 1944-1951	26.7
Field Goals	David Akers, 1999-2010	294
Touchdowns (Tot.)	Harold Carmichael, 1971-1983	79
Points	David Akers, 1999-2010	1,323
*Sacks	Reggie White, 1985-1992	124.0

INDIVIDUAL RECORDS—SINGLE SEASON

Category	Name	Performance
Rushing (Yds.)	LeSean McCoy, 2013	1,607
Passing (Yds.)	Donovan McNabb, 2008	3,916
Passing (TDs)	Sonny Jurgensen, 1961	32
Receiving (No.)	Brian Westbrook, 2007	90
Receiving (Yds.)	Mike Quick, 1983	1,409
Interceptions	Bill Bradley, 1971	11
Punting (Avg.)	Joe Muha, 1948	47.2
Punt Return (Avg.)	Steve Van Buren, 1944	15.3
Kickoff Return (Avg.)	Al Nelson, 1972	29.1
Field Goals	David Akers, 2008	33
Touchdowns (Tot.)	LeSean McCoy, 2011	20
Points	David Akers, 2008	144
*Sacks	Reggie White, 1987	21.0

INDIVIDUAL RECORDS—SINGLE GAME

Category	Name	Performance
Rushing (Yds.)	LeSean McCoy, 12-8-13	217
Passing (Yds.)	Donovan McNabb, 12-5-04	464
Passing (TDs)	Adrian Burk, 10-17-54	**7
	Nick Foles, 11-3-13	**7
Receiving (No.)	Don Looney, 12-1-40	14
	Brian Westbrook, 11-4-07	14
Receiving (Yds.)	Tommy McDonald, 12-10-61	237
Interceptions	Russ Craft, 9-24-50	**4
Field Goals	Tom Dempsey, 11-12-72	6
Touchdowns (Tot.)	Many times	4
	Last time by Brian Westbrook, 11-27-08	
Points	Bobby Walston, 10-17-54	25
*Sacks	Clyde Simmons, 9-15-91	4.5
	Hugh Douglas, 10-18-98	4.5

*Sacks became an official statistic in 1982.
**NFL Record

2014 VETERAN ROSTER

No.	Name	Pos.	Ht.	Wt.	Birthdate	NFL Exp.	College	Hometown	How Acq.	'13 Games/ Starts
51	Acho, Emmanuel	LB	6-2	240	11/10/90	3	Texas	Dallas, Texas	T(Cle)- '13	6/0
29	Allen, Nate	S	6-1	210	11/30/87	5	South Florida	Cape Coral, Fla.	D2-'10	16/16
93	Bair, Brandon	DE	6-6	285	11/24/84	2	Oregon	St. Anthony, Idaho	FA-'13	0*
76	Barbre, Allen	G/T	6-4	310	6/22/84	7	Missouri Southern State	Granby, Mo.	FA-'13	15/0
2	Barkley, Matt	QB	6-2	227	9/8/90	2	Southern California	Santa Ana, Calif.	D4-'13	3/0
98	Barwin, Connor	LB	6-4	264	10/15/86	6	Cincinnati	Detroit, Mich.	UFA(Hou)-'13	16/15
17	Benn, Arrelious	WR	6-2	220	9/8/88	5	Illinois	Washington, D.C.	T(TB)-'13	0*
22	Boykin, Brandon	CB	5-10	185	7/13/90	3	Georgia	Fayetteville, Ga.	D4-'12	16/2
56	Braman, Bryan	LB	6-5	241	5/4/87	4	West Texas A&M	Spokane, Wash.	FA-'14	16/0*
21	Carmichael, Roc	CB	5-10	197	9/9/88	4	Virginia Tech	Brandywine, Md.	FA-'13	13/2
23	Carroll II, Nolan	CB	6-1	205	1/18/87	5	Maryland	Green Cove Springs, Fla.	UFA(Mia)-'14	16/12*
85	Casey, James	TE	6-3	240	9/22/84	6	Rice	Azle, Texas	UFA(Hou)-'13	15/1
87	Celek, Brent	TE	6-4	255	1/25/85	8	Cincinnati	Cincinnati, Ohio	D5b-'07	16/15
58	Cole, Trent	LB	6-3	270	10/5/82	10	Cincinnati	Xenia, Ohio	D5a-'05	16/16
14	Cooper, Riley	WR	6-3	222	9/9/87	5	Florida	Clearwater, Fla.	D5b-'10	16/15
91	Cox, Fletcher	DE	6-4	300	12/13/90	3	Mississippi State	Yazoo City, Miss.	D1-'12	16/16
75	Curry, Vinny	DE	6-3	279	6/30/88	3	Marshall	Neptune, N.J.	D2b-'12	14/0
46	Dorenbos, Jon	LS	6-0	250	7/21/80	12	Texas-El Paso	Garden Grove, Calif.	FA-'06	16/0
86	Ertz, Zach	TE	6-5	250	11/10/90	2	Stanford	Danville, Calif.	D2-'13	16/3
24	Fletcher, Bradley	CB	6-0	200	6/25/86	6	Iowa	Youngstown, Ohio	UFA(StL)-'13	13/12
9	Foles, Nick	QB	6-6	243	1/20/89	3	Arizona	Austin, Texas	D3-'12	13/10
66	Gardner, Andrew	T	6-6	308	4/4/86	5	Georgia Tech	Tyrone, Ga.	UFA(Hou)-'14	3/0*
53	Goode, Najee	LB	6-0	244	6/4/89	3	West Virginia	Cleveland, Ohio	W(TB)-'13	14/1
55	Graham, Brandon	LB	6-2	265	4/3/88	5	Michigan	Detroit, Mich.	D1-'10	16/0
6	Henery, Alex	K	6-1	177	8/18/87	4	Nebraska	Omaha, Neb.	D4b-'11	16/0
79	Herremans, Todd	G/T	6-6	321	10/13/82	10	Saginaw Valley State	Ravenna, Mich.	D4b-'05	16/16
82	Igwenagu, Emil	TE	6-2	245	3/27/89	2	Massachusetts	Worcester, Mass.	FA-'12	0*
27	Jenkins, Malcolm	S	6-0	204	12/20/87	6	Ohio State	Piscataway, N.J.	UFA(NO)-'14	14/14*
13	Johnson, Damaris	WR	5-8	175	11/22/89	3	Tulsa	Destrehan, La.	FA-'12	13/0
65	Johnson, Lane	T	6-6	310	5/8/90	2	Oklahoma	Groveton, Texas	D1-'13	16/16
8	Jones, Donnie	P	6-2	221	7/5/80	11	Louisiana State	Baton Rouge, La.	UFA(Hou)-'13	16/0
49	Kaddu, Josh	LB	6-3	246	3/12/90	3	Oregon	Vacaville, Calif.	FA-'14	1/0*
62	Kelce, Jason	C	6-3	295	11/5/87	4	Cincinnati	Cleveland, Ohio	D6a-'11	16/16
67	Kelly, Dennis	T	6-8	321	1/16/90	3	Purdue	Chicago Heights, Ill.	D5-'12	0*
95	Kendricks, Mychal	LB	6-0	240	9/28/90	3	California	Fresno, Calif.	D2a-'12	15/15
54	Knott, Jake	LB	6-2	243	10/24/90	2	Iowa State	Waukee, Iowa	FA-'13	12/0
73	Kruger, Joe	DE	6-6	290	6/4/92	2	Utah	Orem, Utah	D7a-'13	0*
96	Logan, Bennie	DT	6-2	309	12/28/89	2	Louisiana State	Coushatta, La.	D3-'13	16/8
18	Maclin, Jeremy	WR	6-0	198	5/11/88	6	Missouri	Kirkwood, Mo.	D1-'09	0*
88	Maehl, Jeff	WR	6-0	184	3/16/89	2	Oregon	Paradise, Calif.	T(Hou)-'13	16/0
42	Maragos, Chris	S	5-10	200	1/6/87	5	Wisconsin	Racine, Wis.	UFA(Sea)-'14	16/0*
31	Marsh, Curtis	CB	6-1	197	3/1/88	4	Utah State	Simi Valley, Calif.	D3-'11	4/0*
69	Mathis, Evan	G	6-5	298	11/1/81	10	Alabama	Homewood, Ala.	UFA(Cin)-'11	16/16
50	Matthews, Casey	LB	6-1	245	1/16/89	4	Oregon	Westlake Village, Calif.	D4a-'11	16/1
25	McCoy, LeSean	RB	5-11	208	7/12/88	6	Pittsburgh	Harrisburg, Pa.	D2-'09	16/16
63	Molk, David	C	6-1	300	12/15/88	2	Michigan	Lemont, Ill.	FA-'14	0*
71	Peters, Jason	T	6-4	328	1/22/82	11	Arkansas	Queen City, Texas	T(Buff)-'09	16/16
52	Phillips, Jason	LB	6-1	240	2/14/86	6	Texas Christian	Waller, Texas	UFA(Car)-'13	0*
32	Polk, Chris	RB	5-11	222	12/16/89	3	Washington	Redlands, Calif.	FA-'12	15/0
59	Ryans, DeMeco	LB	6-1	247	7/28/84	9	Alabama	Bessemer, Ala.	T(Hou)-'12	16/16
3	Sanchez, Mark	QB	6-2	225	11/11/86	6	Southern California	Mission Viejo, Calif.	FA-'14	0*
16	Smith, Brad	WR	6-2	213	12/12/83	9	Missouri	Youngstown, Ohio	FA-'13	6/0
43 t-	Sproles, Darren	RB	5-6	190	6/20/83	10	Kansas State	Olathe, Kan.	T(NO)-'14	15/4*
77	Square, Damion	DE	6-2	293	2/6/89	2	Alabama	Houston, Texas	FA-'13	10/0
72	Thornton, Cedric	DE	6-4	309	6/21/88	3	Southern Arkansas	Star City, Ark.	FA-'11	16/16
64	Tobin, Matt	T	6-6	303	6/5/90	2	Iowa	Worthington, Iowa	FA-'13	1/0
39	Tucker, Matthew	RB	6-1	227	5/24/91	2	Texas Christian	Tyler, Texas	FA-'13	2/0
61	Vandervelde, Julian	C/G	6-2	300	10/7/87	3	Iowa	Davenport, Iowa	D5b-'11	14/0
26	Williams, Cary	CB	6-1	190	12/23/84	6	Washburn	Hollywood, Fla.	UFA(Balt)-'13	16/16
28	Wolff, Earl	S	5-11	210	12/15/89	2	North Carolina State	Raeford, N.C.	D5-'13	11/6

* Bair inactive for one game with Oakland in '12; Benn missed '13 season because of injury; Braman played 16 games with Houston in '13; Carroll II played 16 games with Miami; Gardner played three games with Houston; Igwenagu inactive six games; Jenkins played 14 games with New Orleans; Kaddu played one game with Miami; Kelly inactive 16 games; Kruger missed '13 season because of injury; Maclin missed '13 season because of injury; Maragos played 16 games with Seattle; Marsh played two games with Cincinnati and two with Philadelphia; Molk last active with San Diego in '12; Phillips missed '13 season because of injury; Sanchez inactive two games with the New York Jets; Sproles played 15 games with New Orleans.

t- Eagles traded for Sproles (NO).

   Traded—RB Bryce Brown (16 games in '13) to Buffalo, DT Isaac Sopoaga (8) to New England.

   Players lost through free agency (4): S Colt Anderson (Ind; 14 games in '13), S Kurt Coleman (Minn; 15), DE Clifton Geathers (Wash; 16), QB Michael Vick (NYJ; 7).

   Also played with Eagles in '13—WR Jason Avant (16 games), S Patrick Chung (12), WR B.J. Cunningham (2), CB Brandon Hughes (1), WR DeSean Jackson (16), S Keelan Johnson (2), CB Jordan Poyer (3), CB Shaun Prater (1).

FIRST-YEAR ROSTER

Name	Pos.	Ht.	Wt.	Birthdate	College	Hometown	How Acq.
Allen, Beau	DT	6-2	333	11/14/91	Wisconsin	Minnetonka, Minn.	D7
Andrews, Josh	G	6-2	311	6/21/91	Oregon State	Ontario, Calif.	FA
Annen, Blake	TE	6-4	247	5/28/91	Cincinnati	Upper Arlington, Ohio	FA
Bamiro, Michael (1)	T	6-8	340	10/9/90	Stony Brook	Brooklyn, N.Y.	FA-'13
Barton, Karim	G	6-2	313	12/13/91	Morgan State	Los Angeles, Calif.	FA
Boone, Kadron	WR	6-0	204	9/13/91	Louisiana State	Ocala, Fla.	FA
Burton, Trey	TE	6-2	224	10/29/91	Florida	Venice, Fla.	FA
Cunningham, B.J. (1)	WR	6-2	215	5/29/89	Michigan State	Westerville, Ohio	FA-'12
Fluellen, David	RB	5-11	224	1/29/92	Toledo	Lockport, N.Y.	FA
Graf, Kevin	T	6-6	309	6/17/91	Southern California	Agoura Hills, Calif.	FA
Hart, Taylor	DE	6-6	281	2/22/91	Oregon	Tualatin, Ore.	D5a
Hawkins, Donald	G	6-4	301	4/22/92	Texas	Tunica, Miss.	FA
Huff, Josh	WR	5-11	206	10/14/91	Oregon	Houston, Texas	D3
Johnson, Keelan (1)	S	5-11	209	9/26/89	Arizona State	Mesa, Ariz.	FA-'13
Josey, Henry	RB	5-8	194	9/25/91	Missouri	Angleton, Texas	FA
Keliikipi, Wade	DT	6-2	303	7/21/91	Oregon	Waianae, Hawaii	FA
Kinne, G.J. (1)	QB	6-2	218	12/1/88	Tulsa	Gilmer, Texas	FA-'13
Long, Travis (1)	LB	6-4	255	7/24/91	Washington State	Spokane, Wash.	FA-'13
Lowe, Daytawion	S	5-11	196	3/23/91	Oklahoma State	Midwest City, Okla.	FA
Matthews, Jordan	WR	6-3	212	7/16/92	Vanderbilt	Madison, Ala.	D2
Mays, Frances	DE	6-9	291	10/18/90	Florida A&M	Bemidji, Minn.	FA
Momah, Ifeanyi (1)	WR	6-7	239	10/23/89	Boston College	Elwood, N.Y.	FA-'13
Morgan, Davon (1)	DB	6-0	189	1/28/89	Virginia Tech	Richmond, Va.	FA-'13
Murphy, Will (1)	WR	6-2	200	5/15/90	Oregon	Albany, Ore.	FA-'13
Pratt, Quron	WR	5-11	195	4/25/91	Rutgers	Palmyra, N.J.	FA
Reynolds, Ed	S	6-1	207	10/18/91	Stanford	Woodberry Forest, Va.	D5b
Smith II, Marcus	LB	6-3	251	3/31/92	Louisville	Columbus, Ga.	D1
Spear, Carey	K	5-9	194	1/5/92	Vanderbilt	Mayfield Village, Ohio	FA
Villanueva, Alejandro	DE	6-9	277	9/22/88	Army	Mons, Belgium	FA
Watkins, Jaylen	DB	5-11	194	11/27/92	Florida	Cape Coral, Fla.	D4

The term NFL Rookie is defined as a player who is in his first season of professional football and has not been on the roster of another professional football team for any regular-season or postseason games. A Rookie is designated by an "R" on NFL rosters. Players who have been active in another professional football league or players who have NFL experience, including either preseason training camp or being on an Active List or Inactive List, or on Reserve/Injured or Reserve/Physically Unable to Perform for fewer than six regular-season games, are termed NFL First-Year Players. An NFL First-Year Player is designated by a "1" on NFL rosters. Thereafter, a player is credited with an additional year of experience for each season in which he accumulates six games on the Active List or Inactive List, or on Reserve/Injured or Reserve/Physically Unable to Perform.

Log on to www.philadelphiaeagles.com for an up-to-date roster.

COACHING STAFF
Head Coach,
Chip Kelly
Pro Career: Chip Kelly became the 21st head coach in franchise history on January 16, 2013. Guided Eagles to NFC Eastern Division title in first season as coach. The 2013 season was his first NFL coaching experience after 23 years of working in the college ranks. One of college football's most successful coaches, Kelly put his stamp on a new generation of offensive schemes during his four years at the helm of the University of Oregon program. In four seasons as the head coach of the Ducks, he compiled a 46-7 overall record and transformed the school into one of the nation's premiere college football destinations. Career record: 10-7.
Background: Attended the University of New Hampshire and earned a bachelor's degree in physical education in 1990. Coached at Columbia (1990-91), New Hampshire (1992, 1994-2006), Johns Hopkins (1993), Oregon (2007-12)
Personal: Born November 25, 1963, Dover, N.H.

ASSISTANT COACHES
Greg Austin, asst. offensive line; born November 19, 1984, Cypress, Texas. Guard Nebraska 2003-06. No pro playing experience. College coach: Oregon 2011-12. Pro coach: Joined Eagles in 2013.
Jerry Azzinaro, defensive line/assistant head coach; born July 11, 1958, Brooklyn, N.Y. Linebacker American International 1978-1981. No pro playing experience. College coach: American International 1982-84, 1987-1991, Westfield 1985, Western New England 1986, Massachusetts 1992-94, 1997, Boston College 1995-96, Maine 1998, Syracuse 1999-2003, Duke 2004-06, New Hampshire 2007, Marshall 2008, Oregon 2009-2012. Pro coach: Joined Eagles in 2013.
Bob Bicknell, wide receivers; November 13, 1969, Holliston, Mass. Tight end Boston College 1989-1991. No pro playing experience. College coach: Boston University 1993-97, Temple 2006. Pro coach: Frankfurt Galaxy 1998-99, Berlin Thunder 2000-03, Cologne Centurions (NFL Europe) 2004-05, Kansas City Chiefs 2007-09, Buffalo Bills 2010-12, joined Eagles in 2013.
Michael Clay, defensive quality control; born August 30, 1991, Santa Clara, Calif. Linebacker Oregon 2009-2012. No pro playing experience. Pro coach: Joined Eagles in 2014.
Bill Davis, defensive coordinator; born November 5, 1965, Youngstown, Ohio. Quarterback/wide receiver Cincinnati 1985-88. No pro playing experience. College coach: Michigan State 1990-91. Pro coach: Pittsburgh Steelers 1992-94, Carolina Panthers 1995-98, Cleveland Browns 1999, Green Bay Packers 2000,

Atlanta Falcons 2001-03, New York Giants 2004, San Francisco 49ers 2005-06, Arizona Cardinals 2007-10, Cleveland Browns 2011-12, joined Eagles in 2013.
Mike Dawson, asst. defensive line; born November 26, 1974, Secaucus, N.J. Linebacker UMass-Amherst 1994-96. No pro playing experience. College coach: UMass-Lowell 1998, Maine 1998-99, Pittsburgh 1999, New Hampshire 2000-05, Akron 2006-08, Boston College 2009-11. Pro coach: Joined Eagles in 2013.
Dave Fipp, special teams coordinator; born August 8, 1974, Albuquerque, N.M. Safety Arizona 1994-97. No pro playing experience. College coach: Holy Cross 1998-99, Arizona 2000, Cal Poly 2001-03, Nevada 2004, San Jose State 2005-07. Pro coach: San Francisco 49ers 2008-2010, Miami Dolphins 2011-12, joined Eagles in 2013.
Matthew Harper, asst. special teams; born November 26, 1984, Secaucus, N.J. Safety City College of San Francisco 2004-05, Oregon 2006-07. No pro playing experience. College coach: City College of San Francisco 2008, Oregon 2009-2012. Pro coach: Joined Eagles in 2013.
Josh Hingst, strength and conditioning; born December 29, 1978, Fremont, Neb. Attended Nebraska. No college or pro playing experience. College coach: Florida State 2003-07. Pro coach: Jacksonville Jaguars 2012, joined Eagles in 2013.
John Lovett, defensive backs; born December 1, 1950, Nyack, N.Y. Linebacker C.W. Post 1970-73. No pro playing experience. College coach: Union College 1978-1982, Brown 1983, Maine 1985-88, 1994, Cincinnati 1989-1992, Nevada-Las Vegas 1993, Maine 1994, Ole Miss 1994-98, Auburn 1999-2001, Clemson 2002-04, Bowling Green 2005-06, North Carolina 2007-08, Miami 2009-2010, Texas Tech 2012. Pro coach: New York Jets 1984, joined Eagles in 2013.
Todd Lyght, asst. defensive backs; born February 9, 1969, Kwajalein, Marshall Islands. Cornerback Notre Dame 1987-1990. Pro cornerback Los Angeles/St. Louis Rams 1991-2000, Detroit Lions 2001-02. College coach: Oregon 2011-12. Pro coach: Joined Eagles in 2013.
Bill McGovern, outside linebackers; born December 31, 1962, Teaneck, N.J. Defensive back Holy Cross 1981-84. No pro playing experience. College coach: Pennsylvania 1985, Holy Cross 1986-87, Massachusetts 1988-1990, Holy Cross 1991-92, Massachusetts 1993, Boston College 1994-96, Pittsburgh 1997-99, Boston College 2000-2012. Pro coach: Joined Eagles in 2013.
Rick Minter, inside linebackers; born October 4, 1954, Nash, Texas. Defensive end Henderson State 1973-76. No pro playing experience. College coach: Henderson State 1977, Arkansas 1978,

Louisiana Tech 1979, North Carolina State 1980-82, New Mexico State 1984, Ball State 1985-1991, Notre Dame 1992-93, Cincinnati 1994-2003, South Carolina 2004, Notre Dame 2005-07, Marshall 2008-09, Indiana State 2010, Kentucky 2011-12. Pro coach: Joined Eagles in 2013.
Bill Musgrave, quarterbacks; born November 11, 1967, Grand Junction, Colo. Quarterback Oregon 1987-1990. Pro quarterback San Francisco 49ers 1991-94, Denver Broncos 1995-96. College coach: Virginia 2001-02. Pro coach: Oakland Raiders 1997, Philadelphia Eagles 1998, Carolina Panthers 1999-2000, Jacksonville Jaguars 2003-04, Washington Redskins 2005, Atlanta Falcons 2006-2010, Minnesota Vikings 2011-13, re-joined Eagles in 2014.
Justin Peelle, asst. tight ends; born March 15, 1979, Fresno, Calif. Tight end Oregon 1997-2001. Pro tight end San Diego Chargers 2002-05, Miami Dolphins 2006-07, Atlanta Falcons 2008-2010, San Francisco 49ers 2011. Pro coach: Joined Eagles in 2013.
Pat Shurmur, offensive coordinator; born April 14, 1965, Dearborn, Mich. Center/linebacker Michigan State 1984-87. No pro playing experience. College coach: Michigan State 1988-1997, Stanford 1998. Pro coach: Philadelphia Eagles 1999-2008, St. Louis Rams 2009-2010, Cleveland Browns 2011-12 (head coach), re-joined Eagles in 2013.
Duce Staley, running backs; born February 27, 1975, Tampa, Fla. Running back South Carolina 1995-96. Pro running back Philadelphia Eagles 1997-2003, Pittsburgh Steelers 2004-06. Pro coach: Joined Eagles in 2011.
Jeff Stoutland, offensive line; born February 10, 1962, New York City, N.Y. Linebacker Southern Connecticut State. No pro playing experience. College coach: Southern Connecticut State 1984-85, 1988-1992, Syracuse 1986-87, 1997-99, Cornell 1993-96, Michigan State 2000-06, Miami 2007-2010, Alabama 2011-12. Pro coach: Joined Eagles in 2013.
Press Taylor, offensive quality control. Quarterback Butler (Kan.) C.C. 2007-08, Marshall 2009-2010. No pro playing experience. College coach: Tulsa 2011-12. Pro coach: Joined Eagles in 2013.
Ted Williams, tight ends; born November 17, 1943, Lyons, Texas. Attended Cal Poly-Pomona. No college or pro playing experience. College coach: UCLA 1980-89, Washington State 1991-93, Arizona 1994. Pro coach: Joined Eagles in 1995.

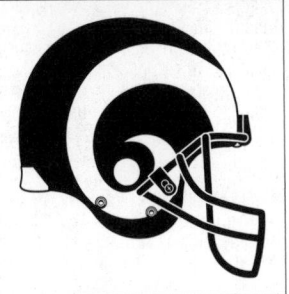

National Football Conference
West Division
Team Colors: New Century Gold, Millennium Blue, and White

One Rams Way
St. Louis, Missouri 63045
Telephone: (314) 982-7267

2014 SCHEDULE
PRESEASON
Aug. 8	**New Orleans**	7:00
Aug. 16	**Green Bay**	3:00
Aug. 23	at Cleveland	7:00
Aug. 28	at Miami	7:00

REGULAR SEASON
Sep. 7	**Minnesota**	12:00
Sep. 14	at Tampa Bay	3:05
Sep. 21	**Dallas**	12:00
Sep. 28	BYE	
Oct. 5	at Philadelphia	12:00
Oct. 13	**San Francisco** (Mon)	7:30
Oct. 19	**Seattle**	12:00
Oct. 26	at Kansas City	12:00
Nov. 2	at San Francisco	3:05
Nov. 9	at Arizona	3:25
Nov. 16	**Denver**	12:00
Nov. 23	at San Diego	3:05
Nov. 30	**Oakland**	12:00
Dec. 7	at Washington	12:00
Dec. 11	**Arizona** (Thu)	7:25
Dec. 21	**New York Giants**	3:05
Dec. 28	at Seattle	3:25
All times CT

Stadium: Edward Jones Dome
 (opened in 1995)
 •**Capacity:** 66,000
 901 N. Broadway
 St. Louis, Missouri 63101
Playing Surface: FieldTurf
Training Camp: Russell Training Center
 1 Rams Way
 St. Louis, Missouri 63045

EDWARD JONES DOME

CLUB OFFICIALS
Owner/Chairman: Stan Kroenke
Executive Vice President of Football
 Operations/Chief Operating Officer:
 Kevin Demoff
General Manager: Les Snead
Treasurer: Jeff Brewer
Vice President of Finance:
 Michael T. Naughton
VP/Legal Affairs: Todd Davis
Executive Vice President/Chief Revenue
 Officer: Bob Reif
Vice President of Broadcasting and
 Creative: Scott Brooks
Vice President of Corporate
 Communications and Civic Affairs:
 Molly Higgins
Vice President of Marketing and Brand
 Strategy: Brian Killingsworth
Vice President/Executive Services,
 Special Projects: Mike Moyneur
Vice President of Sales: Mike O'Keefe
Senior Director of Communications:
 Artis Twyman
VP/ Ticket Sales and Premium Seating:
 Jake Bye
Director of Video Operations:
 Larry Clerico
Director of Information Technology:
 Bill Consoli
Director of Special Events: Keely Fimbres
Senior Assistant: Tony Pastoors
Director of Player Engagement:
 La'Roi Glover
Director of Player Personnel:
 Taylor Morton
Director of College Scouting:
 Brad Holmes
Director of Pro Personnel: Ran Carthon
Director of Security: Steve Miller
Director of Partnership Development and
 Administration: Susan Slemmer
Director of Operations: Bruce Warwick
Director of Corporate Sales:
 Chad Watson
Director of Ticket Operations:
 Kanyon West
Head Trainer: Reggie Scott
Assistant Trainers: Byron Cunningham,
 James Lomax, Tyler Williams
Equipment Manager: Jim Lake
Assistant Equipment Managers:
 Matt Taylor, John Welby, Ben Bloomer
Senior Player Personnel Analyst:
 Rich Snead
Player Personnel Coordinator: JW Jordan
National Scouts: Lawrence McCutcheon,
 Ted Monago
Scouts: Ray Agnew, Evan Ardoin,
 Barto Danton, George Foster,
 Sean Gustus, Brian Heimerdinger,
 Steve Kazor, Brian Shields,
 Will Rodriguez, John Zernhelt
Scouting Assistant: Brian Hill,
 Billy Johnson

COACHING HISTORY
Cleveland 1937-1945,
Los Angeles 1946-1994
(546-547-21)
Records include postseason games
1937-38	Hugo Bezdek*	1-13-0
1938	Art Lewis	4-4-0
1939-1942	Earl (Dutch) Clark	16-26-2
1944	Aldo (Buff) Donelli	4-6-0
1945-46	Adam Walsh	16-5-1
1947	Bob Snyder	6-6-0
1948-49	Clark Shaughnessy	14-8-3
1950-52	Joe Stydahar**	19-9-0
1952-54	Hamp Pool	23-11-2
1955-59	Sid Gillman	28-32-1
1960-62	Bob Waterfield***	9-24-1
1962-65	Harland Svare	14-31-3
1966-1970	George Allen	49-19-4
1971-72	Tommy Prothro	14-12-2
1973-77	Chuck Knox	57-20-1
1978-1982	Ray Malavasi	43-36-0
1983-1991	John Robinson	79-74-0
1992-94	Chuck Knox	15-33-0
1995-96	Rich Brooks	13-19-0
1997-99	Dick Vermeil	25-26-0
2000-05	Mike Martz****	56-36-0
2005	Joe Vitt	4-7-0
2006-08	Scott Linehan#	11-25-0
2008	Jim Haslett	2-10-0
2009-2011	Steve Spagnuolo	10-38-0
2012-13	Jeff Fisher	14-17-1

   * Released after three games in 1938
  ** Resigned after one game in 1952
 *** Resigned after eight games in 1962
**** Took medical leave after five games in 2005
   # Released after four games in 2008

PAID ATTENDANCE
Home 438,560   Away 533,314
Total 971,874
Single-game home record,
 66,273 (12/10/00)
Single-season home record,
 520,926 (1999)

2014 DRAFT CHOICES
Round	Name	Pos.	College
1	Greg Robinson	T	Auburn
	Aaron Donald	DT	Pittsburgh
2	Lamarcus Joyner	DB	Florida St.
3	Tre Mason	RB	Auburn
4	Maurice Alexander	DB	Utah St.
6	E.J. Gaines	DB	Missouri
	Garrett Gilbert	QB	Southern Methodist
7	Mitchell Van Dyk	T	Portland St.
	Christian Bryant	DB	Ohio St.
	Michael Sam	DE	Missouri
	Demetrius Rhaney	C	Tennessee St.

2013 TEAM RECORD
PRESEASON (1-3)

Date	Result		Opponent
08/08	L	19-27	at Cleveland
08/17	L	7-19	Green Bay
08/24	L	26-27	at Denver
08/29	W	24-21	Baltimore

REGULAR SEASON (7-9)

Date	Result		Opponent
09/08	W	27-24	Arizona
09/15	L	24-31	at Atlanta
09/22	L	7-31	at Dallas
09/26	L	11-35	San Francisco
10/06	W	34-20	Jacksonville
10/13	W	38-13	at Houston
10/20	L	15-30	at Carolina
10/28	L	9-14	Seattle
11/03	L	21-28	Tennessee
11/10	W	38-8	at Indianapolis
11/24	W	42-21	Chicago
12/01	L	13-23	at San Francisco
12/08	L	10-30	at Arizona
12/15	W	27-16	New Orleans
12/22	W	23-13	Tampa Bay
12/29	L	9-27	at Seattle

SCORE BY PERIODS

Rams	67	101	80	100	0	—	348
Opponents	79	100	85	100	0	—	364

2013 TEAM STATISTICS

	Rams	Opp.
Total First Downs	282	337
Rushing	82	87
Passing	165	203
Penalty	35	47
3rd Down: Made/Att	73/212	78/201
3rd Down Pct.	34.4	38.8
4th Down: Made/Att	6/18	9/16
4th Down Pct.	33.3	56.3
Possession Avg.	29:05	30:55
Total Net Yards	4877	5520
Avg. Per Game	304.8	345.0
Total Plays	968	1014
Avg. Per Play	5.0	5.4
Net Yards Rushing	1752	1646
Avg. Per Game	109.5	102.9
Total Rushes	426	440
Net Yards Passing	3125	3874
Avg. Per Game	195.3	242.1
Sacked/Yards Lost	36/235	53/326
Gross Yards	3360	4200
Att./Completions	506/301	521/355
Completion Pct.	59.5	68.1
Had Intercepted	11	14
Punts/Average	78/46.3	74/48.6
Net Punting Avg.	78/44.2	74/42.1
Penalties/Yards	123/1009	105/978
Fumbles/Ball Lost	20/10	27/15
Touchdowns	38	44
Rushing	10	18
Passing	22	21
Returns	6	5

2013 INDIVIDUAL STATISTICS

PASSING

	Att.	Comp.	Yds.	Pct.	TD	Int.	Tkld.	Rate
Bradford	262	159	1687	60.7	14	4	15/97	90.9
Clemens	242	142	1673	58.7	8	7	21/138	78.8
Austin	1	0	0	0.0	0	0	0/0	39.6
Hekker	1	0	0	0.0	0	0	0/0	39.6
Rams	506	301	3360	59.5	22	11	36/235	84.8
Opponents	521	355	4200	68.1	21	14	53/326	94.7

SCORING

	TD R	TD P	TD Rt	PAT	FG	Saf	PTS
Zuerlein	0	0	0	34/34	26/28	0	112
Stacy	7	1	0	0/0	0/0	0	48
Austin	1	4	1	0/0	0/0	0	36
Cook	0	5	0	0/0	0/0	0	30
Kendricks	0	4	0	0/0	0/0	0	24
Pettis	0	4	0	0/0	0/0	0	24
Harkey	0	2	0	0/0	0/0	0	12
Quick	0	2	0	0/0	0/0	0	12
B. Cunningham	1	0	0	0/0	0/0	0	8
Bailey	1	0	0	0/0	0/0	0	6
Bates	0	0	1	0/0	0/0	0	6
Giordano	0	0	1	0/0	0/0	0	6
C. Long	0	0	1	0/0	0/0	0	6
Ogletree	0	0	1	0/0	0/0	0	6
R. Quinn	0	0	1	0/0	0/0	0	6
Bradford	0	0	0	0/0	0/0	0	2
Pead	0	0	0	0/0	0/0	0	2
Sims	0	0	0	0/0	0/0	1	2
Rams	10	22	6	34/34	26/28	1	348
Opponents	18	21	5	42/42	18/26	1	364

2-Pt Conversions: Bradford, B. Cunningham, Pead. Rams 3-4, Opponents 1-2.

RUSHING

	No.	Yds	Avg	LG	TD
Stacy	250	973	3.9	40t	7
B. Cunningham	47	261	5.6	56	1
Richardson	69	215	3.1	14	0
Austin	9	151	16.8	65t	1
Clemens	23	64	2.8	16	0
Bailey	2	33	16.5	27t	1
Bradford	15	31	2.1	23	0
Pead	7	21	3.0	11	0
Givens	3	8	2.7	16	0
Giordano	1	-5	-5.0	-5	0
Rams	426	1752	4.1	65t	10
Opponents	440	1646	3.7	41	18

RECEIVING

	No.	Yds	Avg	LG	TD
Cook	51	671	13.2	47	5
Austin	40	418	10.5	81t	4
Pettis	38	399	10.5	31t	4
Givens	34	569	16.7	47	0
Kendricks	32	258	8.1	21	4
Stacy	26	141	5.4	25	1
Quick	18	302	16.8	73	2
Bailey	17	226	13.3	28	0
Richardson	14	121	8.6	19	0
Harkey	13	113	8.7	31t	2
Pead	11	78	7.1	14	0
B. Cunningham	6	59	9.8	18	0
McNeill	1	5	5.0	5	0
Rams	301	3360	11.2	81t	22
Opponents	355	4200	11.8	81t	21

INTERCEPTIONS

	No.	Yds	Avg	LG	TD
Johnson	3	36	12.0	29	0
Laurinaitis	2	9	4.5	9	0
McLeod	2	2	1.0	2	0
Ogletree	1	98	98.0	98t	1
Giordano	1	82	82.0	82t	1
Witherspoon	1	20	20.0	20	0
Hayes	1	5	5.0	5	0
Jenkins	1	5	5.0	5	0
Finnegan	1	1	1.0	1	0
McDonald	1	-2	-2.0	-2	0
Rams	14	256	18.3	98t	2
Opponents	11	230	20.9	68t	5

PUNTING

	No.	Yds.	Avg.	In 20	LG
Hekker	78	3609	46.3	19	64
Rams	78	3609	46.3	19	64
Opponents	74	3597	48.6	27	68

PUNT RETURNS

	Ret	FC	Yds	Avg	LG	TD
Austin	33	11	280	8.5	98t	1
Veltung	7	0	61	8.7	15	0
Pettis	2	0	37	18.5	32	0
Reynolds	1	0	0	0.0	0	0
Rams	43	11	378	8.8	98t	1
Opponents	30	23	79	2.6	17	0

KICKOFF RETURNS

	No.	Yds	Avg	LG	TD
Austin	18	398	22.1	32	0
B. Cunningham	13	299	23.0	32	0
Pead	5	138	27.6	31	0
Barnes	1	0	0.0	0	0
Rams	37	835	22.6	32	0
Opponents	25	544	21.8	39	0

FIELD GOALS

	1-19	20-29	30-39	40-49	50+
Zuerlein	0/0	7/7	10/10	8/9	1/2
Rams	0/0	7/7	10/10	8/9	1/2
Opponents	1/1	3/5	10/12	3/3	1/5

SACKS

	No.
R. Quinn	19.0
C. Long	8.5
Brockers	5.5
Hayes	5.0
Langford	5.0
Laurinaitis	3.5
Sims	2.0
Ogletree	1.5
Conrath	1.0
Jenkins	1.0
McDonald	1.0
Rams	53.0
Opponents	36.0

RECORD HOLDERS
INDIVIDUAL RECORDS—CAREER

Category	Name	Performance
Rushing (Yds.)	Steven Jackson, 2004-2012	10,135
Passing (Yds.)	Jim Everett, 1986-1993	23,758
Passing (TDs)	Roman Gabriel, 1962-1972	154
Receiving (No.)	Isaac Bruce, 1994-2007	942
Receiving (Yds.)	Isaac Bruce, 1994-2007	14,109
Interceptions	Ed Meador, 1959-1970	46
Punting (Avg.)	Donnie Jones, 2007-2011	46.6
Punt Return (Avg.)	Az-Zahir Hakim, 1998-2001	11.4
Kickoff Return (Avg.)	Ron Brown, 1984-89, 1991	26.3
Field Goals	Jeff Wilkins, 1997-2007	265
Touchdowns (Tot.)	Marshall Faulk, 1999-2005	85
Points	Jeff Wilkins, 1997-2007	1,223
*Sacks	Leonard Little, 1998-2008	81.0

INDIVIDUAL RECORDS—SINGLE SEASON

Category	Name	Performance
Rushing (Yds.)	Eric Dickerson, 1984	**2,105
Passing (Yds.)	Kurt Warner, 2001	4,830
Passing (TDs)	Kurt Warner, 1999	41
Receiving (No.)	Isaac Bruce, 1995	119
Receiving (Yds.)	Isaac Bruce, 1995	1,781
Interceptions	Dick (Night Train) Lane, 1952	**14
Punting (Avg.)	Donnie Jones, 2008	50.0
Punt Return (Avg.)	Woodley Lewis, 1952	18.5
Kickoff Return (Avg.)	Verda (Vitamin T) Smith, 1950	33.7
Field Goals	Jeff Wilkins, 2003	39
Touchdowns (Tot.)	Marshall Faulk, 2000	26
Points	Jeff Wilkins, 2003	163
*Sacks	Robert Quinn, 2013	19.0

INDIVIDUAL RECORDS—SINGLE GAME

Category	Name	Performance
Rushing (Yds.)	Willie Ellison, 12-5-71	247
Passing (Yds.)	Norm Van Brocklin, 9-28-51	**554
Passing (TDs)	Many times	5
	Last time by Kurt Warner, 10-10-99	
Receiving (No.)	Tom Fears, 12-3-50	18
Receiving (Yds.)	Willie Anderson, 11-26-89	**336
Interceptions	Many times	3
	Last time by Keith Lyle, 12-15-96	
Field Goals	Jeff Wilkins, 9-10-06	6
Touchdowns (Tot.)	Many times	4
	Last time by Marshall Faulk, 10-20-02	
Points	Many times	24
	Last time by Marshall Faulk, 10-20-02	
*Sacks	Gary Jeter, 9-18-88	5.0

*Sacks became an official statistic in 1982.
**NFL Record

2014 VETERAN ROSTER

No.	Name	Pos.	Ht.	Wt.	Birthdate	NFL Exp.	College	Hometown	How Acq.	'13 Games/Starts
50	Armstrong, Ray Ray	LB	6-3	234	3/5/91	2	Miami	Sanford, Fla.	FA-'13	16/0
11	Austin, Tavon	WR	5-8	174	3/15/91	2	West Virginia	Baltimore, Md.	D1a-'13	13/3
12	Bailey, Stedman	WR	5-10	193	11/11/90	2	West Virginia	Miami, Fla.	D3b-'13	16/2
72	Barksdale, Joe	T	6-5	329	1/1/88	4	Louisiana State	Detroit, Mich.	W(Oak)-'12	16/13
61	Barnes, Tim	C	6-4	300	5/14/88	3	Missouri	Longwood, Mo.	FA-'11	16/4
53	Bates, Daren	LB	5-11	225	11/27/90	2	Auburn	Olive Branch, Miss.	FA-'13	15/0
8	Bradford, Sam	QB	6-4	228	11/8/87	5	Oklahoma	Oklahoma City, Okla.	D1-'10	7/7
81	Britt, Kenny	WR	6-3	223	9/18/88	6	Rutgers	Bayonne, N.J.	UFA(Tenn)-'14	12/3*
90	Brockers, Michael	DT	6-5	322	12/21/90	3	Louisiana State	Houston, Texas	D1-'12	16/16
57	Brown, Sammy	DE	6-2	254	4/17/90	2	Houston	Wiggins, Miss.	FA-'12	0*
92	Carrington, Alex	DT	6-5	301	6/19/87	5	Arkansas State	Tupelo, Miss.	UFA(Buff)-'14	3/3*
71	Conrath, Matt	DT	6-7	290	8/11/89	3	Virginia	Oak Lawn, Ill.	FA-'12	8/0
89	Cook, Jared	TE	6-5	248	4/7/87	6	South Carolina	Suwanee, Ga.	UFA(Tenn)-'13	16/13
36	Cunningham, Benny	RB	5-10	217	7/7/90	2	Middle Tennessee	Nashville, Tenn.	FA-'13	14/0
62	#Dahl, Harvey	G	6-5	306	6/24/81	7	Nevada-Reno	Fallon, Nev.	UFA(Atl)-'11	9/9
37	Daniels, Matthew	S	6-0	211	9/27/89	3	Duke	Fayetteville, Ga.	FA-'12	2/0
9	Davis, Austin	QB	6-2	221	6/2/89	2	Southern Mississippi	Collinsville, Miss.	FA-'13	0*
38	Davis, Cody	S	6-1	206	6/6/89	2	Texas Tech	Stephenville, Texas	FA-'13	12/0
58	Dunbar, Jo-Lonn	LB	6-0	235	3/13/85	7	Boston College	Syracuse, N.Y.	UFA(NO)-'12	12/10
13	Givens, Chris	WR	6-0	198	12/6/89	3	Wake Forest	Wylie, Texas	D4-'12	16/13
46	Harkey, Cory	TE	6-4	260	6/17/90	3	UCLA	Chino Hills, Calif.	FA-'12	15/10
95	Hayes, William	DE	6-3	272	5/2/85	7	Winston-Salem State	High Point, N.C.	UFA(Tenn)-'12	14/0
6	Hekker, Johnny	P	6-5	227	2/8/90	3	Oregon State	Bothell, Wash.	FA-'12	16/0
14	Hill, Shaun	QB	6-3	220	1/9/80	13	Maryland	Parsons, Kan.	UFA(Det)-'14	1/0*
27	#Giordano, Matt	S	5-11	208	10/16/82	9	California	Clovis, Calif.	UFA(Oak)-'13	16/2
21	Jenkins, Janoris	CB	5-10	193	10/29/88	3	North Alabama	Pahokee, Fla.	D2b-'12	16/16
22	Johnson, Trumaine	CB	6-2	204	1/1/90	3	Montana	Stockton, Calif.	D3-'12	16/12
67	Jones, Barrett	C/G	6-4	306	5/25/90	2	Alabama	Germantown, Tenn.	D4-'13	3/0
88	Kendricks, Lance	TE	6-3	247	1/30/88	4	Wisconsin	Milwaukee, Wisc.	D2-'11	15/13
98	Langford, Kendall	DT	6-6	295	1/27/86	7	Hampton	Petersburg, Va.	UFA(Mia)-'12	16/16
55	Laurinaitis, James	LB	6-2	247	12/3/86	6	Ohio State	Plymouth, Minn.	D2-'09	16/16
91	Long, Chris	DE	6-3	276	3/28/85	7	Virginia	Charlottesville, Va.	D1-'08	16/16
77	Long, Jake	T	6-7	319	5/9/85	7	Michigan	Lapeer, Mich.	UFA(Mia)-'13	15/15
25	McDonald, T.J.	S	6-2	219	1/26/91	2	Southern California	Fresno, Calif.	D3a-'13	10/10
32	McGee, Brandon	CB	5-11	193	12/11/90	2	Miami	Plantation, Fla.	D5a-'13	15/0
38	McLeod, Rodney	S	5-10	183	6/23/90	3	Virginia	Oxon Hill, Md.	FA-'12	16/16
44	McQuaide, Jake	LS	6-2	247	12/7/87	4	Ohio State	Cincinnati, Ohio	FA-'11	16/0
52	Ogletree, Alec	LB	6-2	242	9/25/91	2	Georgia	Newnan, Ga.	D1b-'13	16/16
24	Pead, Isaiah	RB	5-10	204	12/14/89	3	Cincinnati	Columbus, Ohio	D2c-'12	10/0
73	Person, Mike	T	6-4	299	6/17/88	4	Montana State	Glendive, Mont.	W(Sea)-'13	1/0*
18	Pettis, Austin	WR	6-3	207	2/8/88	4	Boise State	Orange, Calif.	D3-'11	16/6
33	#Pointer, Quinton	CB	5-9	194	4/16/88	2	Nevada-Las Vegas	Ft. Myers, Fla.	FA-'13	2/0
83	Quick, Brian	WR	6-3	220	6/5/89	3	Appalachian State	Columbia, S.C.	D2a-'12	16/5
3	#Quinn, Brady	QB	6-3	235	10/27/84	7	Notre Dame	Dublin, Ohio	FA-'13	0*
94	Quinn, Robert	DE	6-4	264	5/18/90	4	North Carolina	Ladson, S.C.	D1-'11	16/16
34	Reynolds, Chase	RB	6-0	200	10/22/87	2	Montana	Drummond, Mont.	FA-'11	16/0
76	Saffold, Rodger	T	6-5	332	6/6/88	5	Indiana	Bedford, Ohio	D2-'10	12/9
92	Sims, Eugene	DE	6-6	250	3/18/86	5	West Texas A&M	Mt. Olive, Miss.	D6B-'10	16/0
30	Stacy, Zac	RB	5-8	216	4/9/91	2	Vanderbilt	Centreville, Ga.	D5B-'13	14/12
70	Washington, Brandon	G	6-2	318	8/13/88	2	Miami	Miami, Fla.	FA-'12	1/0
63	Wells, Scott	C	6-2	300	1/7/81	11	Tennessee	Brentwood, Tenn.	UFA(GB)-'12	12/12
51	#Witherspoon, Will	LB	6-1	242	8/19/80	12	Georgia	Panama City, Fla.	UFA(Tenn)-'13	16/3
4	Zuerlein, Greg	K	6-0	187	12/27/87	3	Missouri Western	Lincoln, Nebr.	D6-'12	16/0

* Britt played 12 games with Tennessee in '13; Brown inactive one game; Carrington played in three games with Buffalo; A. Davis did not play nine games; Hill played one game with Detroit; Person played one game with Seattle; Quinn inactive six games with the New York Jets and inactive three games with St. Louis.

\# Unrestricted Free Agent; subject to developments.

Players lost through free agency (4): QB Kellen Clemens (SD; 10 games in '13), G/T Shelley Smith (Mia; 14), S Darian Stewart (Balt; 13), G Chris Williams (Buff; 16).

Also played with Rams in '13—DT Jermelle Cudjo (13 games), CB Cortland Finnegan (7), TE Mike McNeill (14), RB Daryl Richardson (8), T Max Starks (2).

FIRST-YEAR ROSTER

Name	Pos.	Ht.	Wt.	Birthdate	College	Hometown	How Acq.
Alexander, Maurice	S	6-1	220	2/16/91	Utah State	St. Louis, Mo.	D4
Bayer, Alex	TE	6-4	258	11/8/90	Bowling Green	Pickering, Ohio	FA
Blake, Emory (1)	WR	6-0	192	7/18/91	Auburn	Austin, Texas	FA-'13
Bond, Travis	OL	6-6	329	12/10/90	North Carolina	Windsor, N.C.	W(Car)
Brodine, Mason (1)	TE	6-7	284	2/18/88	Nebraska-Kearney	Elm Creek, Neb.	FA-'12
Bryant, Christian	S	5-9	198	3/21/92	Ohio State	Cleveland, Ohio	D7b
Bryant, Jarrid	CB	6-3	185	4/2/90	South Dakota	Corona, Calif.	FA
Cowan, Bobby	P	6-4	219	3/5/90	Idaho	Vancouver, Wash.	FA
Cunningham, Avery	S	5-11	200	1/2/91	Central Michigan	Cincinnati, Ohio	FA
Cunningham, Justice (1)	TE	6-3	258	1/14/91	South Carolina	Pageland, S.C.	FA-'13
Donald, Aaron	DT	6-1	285	5/23/91	Pittsburgh	Pittsburgh, Pa.	D1b
Franklin, Austin	WR	5-11	189	12/6/92	New Mexico	Dallas, Texas	FA
Gaines, E.J.	CB	5-10	190	2/23/92	Missouri	Independence, Mo.	D6a
Gilbert, Garrett	QB	6-4	221	7/1/91	Southern Methodist	Austin, Texas	D6b
Harlan, Deantre	DT	6-4	281	12/20/90	Bacone	Everman, Texas	FA
Harris, Jordan	WR	6-2	215	12/8/91	Bryant	Lincoln University, Fla.	FA
Hill, Aaron	LB	6-1	231	9/5/90	Minnesota	St. Charles, Mo.	FA
Hooey, Sean (1)	OL	6-9	304	7/26/90	Cincinnati	Litchfield, Mich.	FA-'13
Hus, Jorgen	LS	6-1	232	9/12/89	Regina (Canada)	Saskatoon, Saskatchewan, Canada	FA
Jones, Kadeem	FB	6-0	266	3/25/92	Western Kentucky	Dundee, Fla.	FA
Joyner, Lamarcus	DB	5-8	184	11/27/90	Florida State	Ft. Lauderdale, Fla.	D2
Mason, Tre	RB	5-8	207	8/6/93	Auburn	Palm Beach, Fla.	D3
McSurdy, Caleb (1)	LB	6-1	237	2/24/90	Montana	Boise, Idaho	FA-'13
Millard, Johnny	LB	6-2	232	6/5/91	Cal Poly State	Dublin, Calif.	FA
Moe, T.J.	WR	5-11	204	10/14/90	Missouri	O'Fallon, Mo.	FA
Reid, Greg	CB	5-8	190	9/8/90	Valdosta State	Valdosta, Ga.	FA
Rhaney, Demetrius	OL	6-2	301	6/22/92	Tennessee State	Ft. Lauderdale, Fla.	D7d
Roberson, Marcus	CB	6-0	191	10/4/92	Florida	Ft. Lauderdale, Fla.	FA
Robinson, Greg	OL	6-5	332	10/21/92	Auburn	Thibodaux, La.	D1a
Sabino, Etienne (1)	LB	6-2	247	11/13/90	Ohio State	North Miami Beach, Fla.	FA
Salimu, Abasi	T	6-5	310	4/14/90	Nicholls State	Los Angeles, Calif.	FA
Sam, Michael	DE	6-2	261	1/7/90	Missouri	Hitchcock, Texas	D7c
Sherman, Jamaine	WR	6-2	188	10/13/91	East Texas Baptist	Fort Pierce, Fla.	FA
Spencer, Diontae	WR	5-9	161	3/19/92	McNeese State	New Iberia, La.	FA
Steward, Phillip (1)	LB	6-1	235	9/7/90	Houston	Missouri City, Texas	FA
Van Dyk, Mitchell	T	6-7	299	1/2/91	Portland State	Paso Robles, Calif.	D7a
Veltung, Justin (1)	WR	5-11	182	3/30/91	Idaho	Puyallup, Wash.	FA-'13
Watts, Trey	RB	5-9	208	2/13/91	Tulsa	Fairfax, Va.	FA
Westbrooks, Ethan	DT	6-4	267	11/15/90	West Texas A&M	Oakland, Calif.	FA
Wilson, Tavarius	LB	5-11	239	8/30/90	North Alabama	Florence, Ala.	FA
Woodard, Darren (1)	CB	5-11	175	9/21/89	Texas-El Paso	Freeport, Texas	FA-'13

The term NFL Rookie is defined as a player who is in his first season of professional football and has not been on the roster of another professional football team for any regular-season or postseason games. A Rookie is designated by an "R" on NFL rosters. Players who have been active in another professional football league or players who have NFL experience, including either preseason training camp or being on an Active List or Inactive List, or on Reserve/Injured or Reserve/Physically Unable to Perform for fewer than six regular-season games, are termed NFL First-Year Players. An NFL First-Year Player is designated by a "1" on NFL rosters. Thereafter, a player is credited with an additional year of experience for each season in which he accumulates six games on the Active List or Inactive List, or on Reserve/Injured or Reserve/Physically Unable to Perform.

Log on to www.stlouisrams.com for an up-to-date roster.

ST. LOUIS RAMS

COACHING STAFF
Head Coach,
Jeff Fisher
Pro Career: Named the twenty-sixth head coach in franchise history on January 17, 2012. Fisher ranks tied for 17th on the NFL's career wins list (161, including postseason), and third among active coaches. Spent 16 full seasons as head coach of the Tennessee Titans, 11 as executive vice president. Guided the Titans to six playoff appearances, three division titles, two AFC Championship games (1999, 2002) and one Super Bowl appearance (XXXIV). Joined the Oilers'/Titans' coaching staff in 1994. He was elevated to head coach in November 1994, replacing Jack Pardee, for the season's final six games. Previously coached with Philadelphia Eagles (defensive backs, 1986-88), Los Angeles Rams (youngest defensive coordinator in NFL, 1989-1991), and San Francisco 49ers (defensive backs, 1992-93). Played with Chicago Bears (1981-85) as a defensive back and return specialist. Earned a Super Bowl ring following Chicago's Super Bowl XX victory (1985), despite spending the year on injured reserve with an ankle injury. Fisher began his post-playing career that season by assisting Buddy Ryan as the Bears' "unofficial" coach. Career record: 161-143-1.
Background: Played defensive back at Southern California.
Personal: Born February 25, 1958 in Woodland Hills, California. Has three children: sons Brandon (age 26) and Trent (age 21), and daughter Tara (age 24).

ASSISTANT COACHES
Adam Bailey, asst. strength coach; born March 30, 1976, Lindale, Texas. No college or pro playing experience. College coach: Texas 1996-97, Louisville 1998-99, Auburn 2000-01, Missouri 2002-03. Pro coach: New Orleans Saints 2004-09, joined Rams in 2010.
Rob Boras, tight ends; born Sept. 30, 1970, Glen Ellyn, Ill. Center De Pauw 1988-1991. No pro playing experience. College coach: DePauw 1992-93, Texas 1994-97, Benedictine 1998 (head coach), Nevada-Las Vegas 1999-2003. Pro coach: Chicago Bears 2004-09, Jacksonville Jaguars 2010-11, joined Rams in 2012.
Paul Boudreau, offensive line; born Dec. 30, 1949, Arlington, Mass. Guard Boston College 1970-73. No pro playing experience. Pro coach: New Orleans Saints 1987-1993, Detroit Lions 1994-96, New England Patriots 1997-98, Miami Dolphins 1999-2000, Carolina Panthers 2001-02, Jacksonville Jaguars 2003-05, St. Louis Rams 2006-07, Atlanta Falcons 2008-2011, re-joined Rams in 2012.
Paul F. Boudreau, asst. special teams; born June 2, 1975, Boston, Mass. No college or pro playing experience. College coach: Northeastern 1997-98, Cincinnati 1998-99, Brown 2000-06, Central Connecticut State 2007-08, Massachusetts Maritime 2010, Widener 2011. Pro coach: Joined Rams in 2012.
Joe Bowden, asst. linebackers; born February

25, 1970, Dallas, Texas. Linebacker Oklahoma 1988-1991. Pro linebacker Oilers/Tennessee Titans 1992-99, Dallas Cowboys 2000. College coach: Central Oklahoma 2006-08. Pro coach: Joined Rams in 2012.
Frank Bush, linebackers; born January 10, 1963, Athens, Ga. Linebacker North Carolina State 1981-1984. Pro linebacker Houston Oilers 1985-86. Pro coach: Houston Oilers 1987-1991 (scout), 1992-94, Denver Broncos 1995-2003, Arizona Cardinals 2004-06, Houston Texans 2007-2010, Tennessee Titans 2011-12, joined Rams in 2013.
Chuck Cecil, secondary; born Nov. 8, 1964, Red Bluff, Calif. Defensive back Arizona 1983-87. Pro safety Green Bay Packers 1988-1992, Phoenix Cardinals 1993, Houston Oilers 1995. Pro coach: Tennessee Titans 2001-2010, joined Rams in 2012.
Frank Cignetti, quarterbacks; born October 4, 1965, Pittsburgh, Pa. Safety Indiana Univ. (Pa.) 1985-88. No pro playing experience. College coach: Pittsburgh 1989, Indiana Univ. (Pa.) 1990-98, Fresno State 2002-05, North Carolina 2006, California 2008, Pittsburgh 2009-2010, Rutgers 2011. Pro coach: Kansas City Chiefs 1999, New Orleans Saints 2000-01, San Francisco 49ers 2007, joined Rams in 2012.
Andy Dickerson, asst. offensive line; born January 29, 1982, Wilmington, Del. Offensive lineman Tufts 1999-2002. No pro playing experience. College coach: Tufts 2003. Pro coach: New York Jets 2006-08, 2011, Cleveland Browns 2009-2010, joined Rams in 2012.
John Fassel, special teams coordinator; born January 10, 1974, Anaheim, Calif. Wide receiver/quarterback Pacific 1994-95, Weber State 1996-98. No pro playing experience. College coach: Bucknell 1999, 2001, Idaho State 2000, New Mexico Highlands 2002-03. Pro coach: Amsterdam Admirals (NFLE) 2000, Baltimore Ravens 2005-07, Oakland Raiders 2008-2011, joined Rams in 2012.
Brandon Fisher, asst. secondary, born June 16, 1987, Franklin, Tenn. Safety/linebacker Montana 2007-09. No pro playing experience. Pro coach: Detroit Lions 2011, joined Rams in 2012.
Rock Gullickson, strength; born April 11, 1955, Moorhead, Minn. Guard Moorhead State 1973-76. No pro playing experience. College coach: Moorhead State 1978, Maryville State (N.D.) 1979-1980, South Dakota State 1981, Montana State 1982-89, Rutgers 1990-92, Texas 1993-97, Louisville 1998-99. Pro coach: New Orleans Saints 2000-05, Green Bay Packers 2006-08, joined Rams in 2009.
Dave McGinnis, asst. head coach; born August 7, 1951, Independence, Kan. Defensive back Texas Christian 1970-73. No pro playing experience. College coach: Texas Christian 1973-74, 1982, Missouri 1975-77, Indiana State 1978, 1980-81, Kansas State 1983-85. Pro coach: Chicago Bears 1986-1995, Arizona Cardinals 1996-2003 (head coach 2000-03), Tennessee Titans 2004-2011, joined Rams in 2012.

Brian Schottenheimer, offensive coordinator; born October 16, 1973, Denver, Colo. Quarterback Kansas 1992, Florida 1993-96. No pro playing experience. College coach: Syracuse 1999, Southern California 2000. Pro coach: St. Louis Rams 1997, Kansas City Chiefs 1998, Washington Redskins 2001, San Diego Chargers 2002-05, New York Jets 2006-2011, joined Rams in 2012.
Ray Sherman, wide receivers; born Nov. 27, 1951, Berkeley, Calif. Wide receiver/defensive back Fresno State 1971-72. No pro playing experience. College coach: San Jose State 1974, California 1975, 1981, Michigan State 1976-77, Wake Forest 1978-1980, Purdue 1982-85, Georgia 1986-87. Pro coach: Houston Oilers 1988-89, Atlanta Falcons 1990, San Francisco 49ers 1991-93, New York Jets 1994, Minnesota Vikings 1995-97, 1999, Pittsburgh Steelers 1998, Green Bay Packers 2000-04, Tennessee Titans 2005-06, Dallas Cowboys 2007-2010, joined Rams in 2012.
Clyde Simmons, asst. defensive line; born August 4, 1964, Lanes, S.C. Defensive end Western Carolina 1982-85. Pro defensive end Philadelphia Eagles 1986-1993, Arizona Cardinals 1994-95, Jacksonville Jaguars 1996-97, Cincinnati Bengals 1998, Chicago Bears 1999-2000. Pro coach: New York Jets 2010, joined Rams in 2012.
Ben Sirmans, running backs; born October 17, 1970, East Orange, N.J. Running back Maine 1990-93. No pro playing experience. College coach: Maine 1996-99, Kent State 2000-04, Michigan State 2005-06, Boston College 2007-2011. Pro coach: Joined Rams in 2012.
Andy Sugarman, offensive quality control; born May 23, 1972, Lafayette, Calif. No college or pro playing experience. College coach: California 1991-97. Pro coach: San Francisco 49ers 1998-2002, Detroit Lions 2003-05, Atlanta Falcons 2007, joined Rams in 2012.
Mike Waufle, defensive line; born June 27, 1954, Hornell, N.Y. U.S. Marines 1972-75. Defensive lineman Bakersfield (Calif.) J.C. 1975-76, Utah State 1977-78. No pro playing experience. College coach: Alfred 1979, Utah State 1980-84, Fresno State 1985-88, UCLA 1989, Oregon State 1990-91, California 1992-97. Pro coach: Oakland Raiders 1998-2003, 2010-11, New York Giants 2004-09, joined Rams in 2012.
Gregg Williams, defensive coordinator; born July 15, 1958, Excelsior Springs, Mo. Quarterback Northeastern Missouri State 1976-79. No pro playing experience. College coach: Houston 1988-89. Pro coach: Houston Oilers/Tennessee Titans 1990-2000, Buffalo Bills 2001-03 (head coach), Washington Redskins 2004-07, Jacksonville Jaguars 2008, New Orleans Saints 2009-2011, Tennessee Titans 2013, joined Rams in 2014.
Dennard Wilson, defensive quality control; born March 31, 1982, Upper Marlboro, Md. Safety Maryland 2000-03. Pro safety Washington Redskins 2004. College coach: Maryland 2007-08. Pro coach: Joined Rams in 2012.

National Football Conference
West Division
Team Colors: 49ers Gold and 49ers Red
4949 Marie P. DeBartolo Way
Santa Clara, California 95054
Telephone: (408) 562-4949

2014 SCHEDULE
PRESEASON
Aug. 7   at Baltimore 4:30
Aug. 17 **Denver** 1:00
Aug. 24 **San Diego** 1:00
Aug. 28 at Houston..............................5:00

REGULAR SEASON
Sep. 7   at Dallas 1:25
Sep. 14 **Chicago** 5:30
Sep. 21 at Arizona 1:05
Sep. 28 **Philadelphia** 1:25
Oct. 5   **Kansas City** 1:25
Oct. 13 at St. Louis (Mon) 5:30
Oct. 19 at Denver *5:30
Oct. 26 BYE
Nov. 2   **St. Louis** 1:05
Nov. 9   at New Orleans 10:00a
Nov. 16 at New York Giants 10:00a
Nov. 23 **Washington** 1:25
Nov. 27 **Seattle** (Thu).....................5:30
Dec. 7   at Oakland 1:25
Dec. 14 at Seattle 1:25
Dec. 20 **San Diego** (Sat).................TBD
Dec. 28 **Arizona** 1:25
*All times PT; Sunday night games in
  Weeks 5-16 subject to change

Stadium: Levi's® Stadium
  (opened in 2014)
  •**Capacity:** 68,500
  Santa Clara, California 95054
Playing Surface: Natural Grass
Training Camp: SAP Performance Facility
    4949 Marie P. DeBartolo Way
    Santa Clara, CA 95054

LEVI'S® STADIUM

CLUB OFFICIALS
OWNERSHIP
Co-Chairman: Denise DeBartolo York
Co-Chairman: John York
Chief Executive Officer: Jed York
Ownership: Gideon Yu
Ownership: Mark Wan
Ownership: John M. Sobrato
MANAGEMENT
General Manager: Trent Baalke
President: Paraag Marathe
Chief Operating Officer: Al Guido
Chief Financial Officer: Cipora Herman
Chief Revenue Officer: Ethan Casson
Executive Vice President of Development:
  Larry MacNeil
Executive Vice President: Patty Inglis
Vice President of Stadium Operations:
  Jim Mercurio
Vice President of Football Affairs:
  Keena Turner
Vice President of Fan Experience:
  Jamie Brandt
Vice President of Football Operations and
Sports Medicine: Jeff Ferguson
Vice President of Finance: Scott Sabatino
Executive Producer: Robert Alberino Jr.
Vice President of Marketing: Ali Towle
Vice President of Technology:
  Dan Williams
Director of Pro Personnel: Mike Williams
Director of College Scouting:
  Matt Malaspina
Director of Football Administration &
  Analytics: Brian Hampton
Equipment Manager: Steve Urbaniak
Video Operations Manager: Mike Bracken
Director of Alumni Relations:
  Guy McIntrye
Director of Public Relations: Bob Lange
New Stadium Project Executive: Jack Hill
Director of Business Operations:
  Morrie Eisenberg
Director of Business Operations:
  Chris Giles
Director of Stadium Operations:
  Larry Minasian
Director of Engineering Operations:
  Pat Rogan
Director of Guest Services: Mike McCarroll
Director of Security: Dan Cory
Director of Facilities: Bill Howell
Sports Turf Manager/Head
  Groundskeeper: Matthew Greiner
Director of Corporate Partnerships:
  Brent Schoeb
Director of Broadcast Partnerships:
  Bob Sargent
Director of Community Relations/49ers
  Foundation: Joanne Pasternack
Director of Legal Affairs: Hannah Gordon
Director of Human Resources and
  Employment Counsel: Sean Kundu
Museum Director: Jesse Lovejoy
Director of Gameday Production and
  Broadcast Operations: Aron Kennedy

COACHING HISTORY
(530-428-14)
Records include postseason games
1950-54   Lawrence (Buck) Shaw ..33-25-2
1955   Norman (Red) Strader 4-8-0
1956-58   Frankie Albert 19-17-1
1959-1963 Howard (Red) Hickey* .27-27-1
1963-67   Jack Christiansen 26-38-3
1968-1975 Dick Nolan....................56-56-5
1976   Monte Clark....................8-6-0
1977   Ken Meyer.......................5-9-0
1978   Pete McCulley** 1-8-0
1978   Fred O'Connor 1-6-0
1979-1988 Bill Walsh 102-63-1
1989-1996 George Seifert 108-35-0
1997-2002 Steve Mariucci..............60-43-0
2003-04   Dennis Erickson 9-23-0
2005-08   Mike Nolan*** 18-37-0
2008-2010 Mike Singletary****.....19-22-0
2010   Jim Tomsula....................1-0-0
2011-13   Jim Harbaugh...............41-14-1
          * Resigned after three games in 1963
         ** Released after nine games in 1978
        *** Released after seven games in 2008
       **** Released after 15 games in 2010

PAID ATTENDANCE
Home 535,141   Away 535,306
Total 1,070,447
Single-game home record,
  69,732 (1/12/13)
Single-season home record,
  544,228 (1999)

2014 DRAFT CHOICES
Round	Name	Pos.	College
1	Jimmie Ward	DB	Northern Illinois
2	Carlos Hyde	RB	Ohio St.
3	Marcus Martin	C	Southern California
	Chris Borland	LB	Wisconsin
	Brandon Thomas	G	Clemson
4	Bruce Ellington	WR	South Carolina
	Dontae Johnson	CB	North Carolina St.
5	Aaron Lynch	LB	South Florida
	Keith Reaser	CB	Florida Atlantic
6	Kenneth Acker	CB	Southern Methodist
7	Kaleb Ramsey	DT	Boston College
	Trey Millard	FB	Oklahoma

SAN FRANCISCO 49ERS

2013 TEAM RECORD

PRESEASON (3-1)

Date	Result	Opponent
08/08	L 6-10	Denver
08/16	W 15-13	at Kansas City
08/25	W 34-14	Minnesota
08/29	W 41-6	at San Diego

REGULAR SEASON (12-4)

Date	Result	Opponent
09/08	W 34-28	Green Bay
09/15	L 3-29	at Seattle
09/22	L 7-27	Indianapolis
09/26	W 35-11	at St. Louis
10/06	W 34-3	Houston
10/13	W 32-20	Arizona
10/20	W 31-17	at Tennessee
10/27	W 42-10	at Jacksonville
11/10	L 9-10	Carolina
11/17	L 20-23	at New Orleans
11/25	W 27-6	at Washington
12/01	W 23-13	St. Louis
12/08	W 19-17	Seattle
12/15	W 33-14	at Tampa Bay
12/23	W 34-24	Atlanta
12/29	W 23-20	at Arizona

POSTSEASON (2-1)

Date	Result	Opponent
01/05	W 23-20	at Green Bay
01/12	W 23-10	at Carolina
01/19	L 17-23	at Seattle

SCORE BY PERIODS

49ers	97	121	71	117	0	—	406
Opponents	31	86	36	119	0	—	272

2013 TEAM STATISTICS

	49ers	Opp.
Total First Downs	286	284
Rushing	115	77
Passing	148	181
Penalty	23	26
3rd Down: Made/Att	77/211	76/223
3rd Down Pct.	36.5	34.1
4th Down: Made/Att	7/11	10/23
4th Down Pct.	63.6	43.5
Possession Avg.	30:35	29:26
Total Net Yards	5180	5071
Avg. Per Game	323.8	316.9
Total Plays	961	1020
Avg. Per Play	5.4	5.0
Net Yards Rushing	2201	1535
Avg. Per Game	137.6	95.9
Total Rushes	505	397
Net Yards Passing	2979	3536
Avg. Per Game	186.2	221.0
Sacked/Yards Lost	39/231	38/283
Gross Yards	3210	3819
Att./Completions	417/244	585/345
Completion Pct.	58.5	59.0
Had Intercepted	8	18
Punts/Average	79/48.2	87/44.6
Net Punting Avg.	79/41.7	87/40.1
Penalties/Yards	103/845	96/878
Fumbles/Ball Lost	20/10	21/12
Touchdowns	44	30
Rushing	18	11
Passing	21	19
Returns	5	0

2013 INDIVIDUAL STATISTICS

PASSING

	Att.	Comp.	Yds.	Pct.	TD	Int.	Tkld.	Rate
Kaepernick	416	243	3197	58.4	21	8	39/231	91.6
McCoy	1	1	13	100.0	0	0	0/0	118.8
49ers	417	244	3210	58.5	21	8	39/231	91.7
Opponents	585	345	3819	59.0	19	18	38/283	76.4

SCORING

	TD R	TD P	TD Rt	PAT	FG	Saf	PTS
Dawson	0	0	0	44/44	32/36	0	140
V. Davis	0	13	0	0/0	0/0	0	78
Gore	9	0	0	0/0	0/0	0	54
Boldin	0	7	0	0/0	0/0	0	42
Hunter	3	0	1	0/0	0/0	0	24
Kaepernick	4	0	0	0/0	0/0	0	24
Dixon	2	0	0	0/0	0/0	0	12
Bowman	0	0	1	0/0	0/0	0	6
Brock	0	0	1	0/0	0/0	0	6
Crabtree	0	1	0	0/0	0/0	0	6
Osgood	0	0	1	0/0	0/0	0	6
Skuta	0	0	1	0/0	0/0	0	6
Lemonier	0	0	0	0/0	0/0	1	2
49ers	18	21	5	44/44	32/36	1	406
Opponents	11	19	0	28/28	20/25	1	272

2-Pt Conversions: 49ers 0-0, Opponents 1-2.

RUSHING

	No.	Yds	Avg	LG	TD
Gore	276	1128	4.1	51	9
Kaepernick	92	524	5.7	28	4
Hunter	78	358	4.6	45	3
James	12	59	4.9	21	0
Dixon	28	56	2.0	9	2
Patton	1	26	26.0	26	0
K. Williams	2	23	11.5	13	0
Miller	7	13	1.9	4	0
Boldin	2	11	5.5	11	0
Moore	1	9	9.0	9	0
McCoy	6	-6	-1.0	-1	0
49ers	505	2201	4.4	51	18
Opponents	397	1535	3.9	30	11

RECEIVING

	No.	Yds	Avg	LG	TD
Boldin	85	1179	13.9	63	7
V. Davis	52	850	16.3	64t	13
Miller	25	243	9.7	43	0
Crabtree	19	284	14.9	60	1
Gore	16	141	8.8	29	0
K. Williams	12	113	9.4	16	0
Manningham	9	85	9.4	14	0
V. McDonald	8	119	14.9	25	0
Patton	3	34	11.3	29	0
Dixon	3	30	10.0	19	0
Baldwin	3	28	9.3	15	0
Celek	2	38	19.0	30	0
James	2	16	8.0	12	0
Hunter	2	13	6.5	9	0
Osgood	1	17	17.0	17	0
Staley	1	14	14.0	14	0
Moore	1	6	6.0	6	0
49ers	244	3210	13.2	64t	21
Opponents	345	3819	11.1	75t	19

INTERCEPTIONS

	No.	Yds	Avg	LG	TD
Brock	5	82	16.4	41	1
Reid	4	54	13.5	53	0
Bowman	2	93	46.5	89t	1
Rogers	2	14	7.0	11	0
Whitner	2	7	3.5	7	0
Brooks	1	22	22.0	22	0
Jerod-Eddie	1	6	6.0	6	0
Wright	1	0	0.0	0	0
49ers	18	278	15.4	89t	2
Opponents	8	117	14.6	43	0

PUNTING

	No.	Yds.	Avg.	In 20	LG
Lee	79	3804	48.2	27	62
49ers	79	3804	48.2	27	62
Opponents	87	3884	44.6	27	65

PUNT RETURNS

	Ret	FC	Yds	Avg	LG	TD
James	23	12	251	10.9	40	0
K. Williams	12	20	61	5.1	22	0
49ers	35	32	312	8.9	40	0
Opponents	38	21	330	8.7	38	0

KICKOFF RETURNS

	No.	Yds	Avg	LG	TD
James	12	321	26.8	41	0
K. Williams	7	134	19.1	35	0
Dixon	5	101	20.2	47	0
Hunter	4	81	20.3	30	0
Cox	3	82	27.3	30	0
Patton	1	7	7.0	7	0
49ers	32	726	22.7	47	0
Opponents	54	1104	20.4	82	0

FIELD GOALS

	1-19	20-29	30-39	40-49	50+
Dawson	0/0	12/13	6/6	10/11	4/6
49ers	0/0	12/13	6/6	10/11	4/6
Opponents	0/0	1/1	10/11	8/11	1/2

SACKS

	No.
Brooks	8.5
A. Smith	8.5
J. Smith	6.5
Bowman	5.0
R. McDonald	3.5
Willis	3.0
Dorsey	2.0
Lemonier	1.0
49ers	38.0
Opponents	39.0

RECORD HOLDERS
INDIVIDUAL RECORDS—CAREER

Category	Name	Performance
Rushing (Yds.)	Frank Gore, 2005-2013	9,967
Passing (Yds.)	Joe Montana, 1979-1992	35,124
Passing (TDs)	Joe Montana, 1979-1992	244
Receiving (No.)	Jerry Rice, 1985-2000	1,281
Receiving (Yds.)	Jerry Rice, 1985-2000	19,247
Interceptions	Ronnie Lott, 1981-1990	51
Punting (Avg.)	Andy Lee, 2004-2013	46.1
Punt Return (Avg.)	Ted Ginn Jr., 2010-12	11.8
Kickoff Return (Avg.)	Abe Woodson, 1958-1964	29.4
Field Goals	Ray Wersching, 1977-1987	190
Touchdowns (Tot.)	Jerry Rice, 1985-2000	187
Points	Jerry Rice, 1985-2000	1,130
*Sacks	Bryant Young, 1994-2007	89.5

INDIVIDUAL RECORDS—SINGLE SEASON

Category	Name	Performance
Rushing (Yds.)	Frank Gore, 2006	1,695
Passing (Yds.)	Jeff Garcia, 2000	4,278
Passing (TDs)	Steve Young, 1998	36
Receiving (No.)	Jerry Rice, 1995	122
Receiving (Yds.)	Jerry Rice, 1995	1,848
Interceptions	Dave Baker, 1960	10
	Ronnie Lott, 1986	10
Punting (Avg.)	Andy Lee, 2011	50.9
Punt Return (Avg.)	Jimmy Williams, 2002	16.8
Kickoff Return (Avg.)	Joe Arenas, 1953	34.4
Field Goals	David Akers, 2011	**44
Touchdowns (Tot.)	Jerry Rice, 1987	23
Points	David Akers, 2011	166
*Sacks	Aldon Smith, 2012	19.5

INDIVIDUAL RECORDS—SINGLE GAME

Category	Name	Performance
Rushing (Yds.)	Frank Gore, 11-19-06	212
Passing (Yds.)	Joe Montana, 10-14-90	476
Passing (TDs)	Joe Montana, 10-14-90	6
Receiving (No.)	Terrell Owens, 12-17-00	20
Receiving (Yds.)	Jerry Rice, 12-18-95	289
Interceptions	Dave Baker, 12-4-60	**4
Field Goals	Ray Wersching, 10-16-83	6
	Jeff Wilkins, 9-29-96	6
Touchdowns (Tot.)	Jerry Rice, 10-14-90	5
Points	Jerry Rice, 10-14-90	30
*Sacks	Fred Dean, 11-13-83	6.0

*Sacks became an official statistic in 1982.
**NFL Record

2014 VETERAN ROSTER

No.	Name	Pos.	Ht.	Wt.	Birthdate	NFL Exp.	College	Hometown	How Acq.	'13 Games/ Starts
82	Baldwin, Jon	WR	6-4	230	8/10/89	4	Pittsburgh	Aliquippa, Pa.	T(KC)-'13	7/1
24	Bethea, Antoine	S	5-11	206	7/27/84	9	Howard	Newport News, Va.	FA-'14	16/16*
5	Bethel-Thompson, McLeod	QB	6-3	230	7/3/88	3	Sacramento State	San Francisco, Calif.	W(Minn)-'13	0*
81	Boldin, Anquan	WR	6-1	220	10/3/80	12	Florida State	Pahokee, Fla.	T(Balt)-'13	16/16
75	Boone, Alex	G/T	6-8	300	5/4/87	5	Ohio State	Cleveland, Ohio	FA-'09	16/16
53	Bowman, NaVorro	LB	6-0	242	5/28/88	5	Penn State	Forestville, Md.	D3-'10	16/16
26	Brock, Tramaine	CB	5-10	197	8/20/88	5	Belhaven	Long Beach, Miss.	FA-'10	16/7
55	Brooks, Ahmad	LB	6-3	259	3/14/84	9	Virginia	Woodbridge, Va.	W(Cin)-'08	16/16
45	Campbell, D.J.	S	6-0	205	7/24/89	2	California	Las Vegas, Nev.	FA-'14	4/0*
95	Carradine, Tank	DT	6-4	273	2/18/90	2	Florida State	Cincinnati, Ohio	D2a-'13	0*
46	Carrier, Derek	TE	6-4	241	7/25/90	2	Beloit	Edgerton, Wisc.	FA-'13	5/0
88	Celek, Garrett	TE	6-5	252	5/29/88	3	Michigan State	Cincinnati, Ohio	FA-'12	12/1
22	Cook, Chris	CB	6-2	212	2/15/87	4	Virginia	Lynchburg, Va.	FA-'14	12/11*
20	Cox, Perrish	CB	6-0	190	1/10/87	3	Oklahoma State	Waco, Texas	FA-'13	11/0*
15	Crabtree, Michael	WR	6-1	214	9/14/87	6	Texas Tech	Dallas, Texas	D1-'09	5/5
29	Culliver, Chris	CB	6-0	199	8/17/88	4	South Carolina	Garner, N.C.	D3-'11	0*
43	Dahl, Craig	S	6-1	212	6/17/85	7	North Dakota State	Madison Lake, Minn.	UFA(StL)-'13	16/0
76	Davis, Anthony	T	6-5	323	10/11/89	5	Rutgers	Piscataway, N.J.	D1a-'10	16/16
85	Davis, Vernon	TE	6-3	250	1/31/84	9	Maryland	Washington, D.C.	D1a-'06	15/15
9	Dawson, Phil	K	5-11	200	1/23/75	16	Texas	Dallas, Texas	UFA(Cle)-'13	16/0
92	Dial, Quinton	DT	6-5	318	7/21/90	2	Alabama	Pinson, Ala.	D5-'13	3/0
83	Dobbs, Demarcus	TE/DT	6-2	282	11/30/87	4	Georgia	Savannah, Ga.	FA-'11	15/0
90	Dorsey, Glenn	DL	6-1	297	8/1/85	7	Louisiana State	Baton Rouge, La.	UFA(KC)-'13	16/13
2	t-Gabbert, Blaine	QB	6-4	235	10/15/89	4	Missouri	Ballwin, Mo.	T(Jax)-'14	3/3*
21	Gore, Frank	RB	5-9	217	5/14/83	10	Miami	Coral Gables, Fla.	D3a-'05	16/16
33	Hampton, Jewel	RB	5-9	210	12/23/89	2	Southern Illinois	Indianapolis, Ind.	FA-'12	0*
32	Hunter, Kendall	RB	5-7	199	9/16/88	4	Oklahoma State	Tyler, Texas	D4-'11	16/0
77	Iupati, Mike	G	6-5	331	5/12/87	5	Idaho	Anaheim, Calif.	D1b-'10	12/12
23	James, LaMichael	RB	5-9	195	10/22/89	3	Oregon	Texarkana, Texas	D2-'12	10/0
63	Jerod-Eddie, Tony	DT	6-5	301	3/29/90	3	Texas A&M	DeSoto, Texas	FA-'12	15/2
13	t-Johnson, Stevie	WR	6-2	207	7/22/86	7	Kentucky	Fairfield, Calif.	T(Buff)-'14	12/12*
7	Kaepernick, Colin	QB	6-4	230	11/3/87	4	Nevada	Turlock, Calif.	D2-'11	16/16
67	Kilgore, Daniel	G/C	6-3	308	12/18/87	4	Appalachian State	Kingsport, Tenn.	D5-'11	16/0
38	Lattimore, Marcus	RB	5-11	221	10/29/91	2	South Carolina	Duncan, S.C.	D4b-'13	0*
4	Lee, Andy	P	6-2	180	8/11/82	11	Pittsburgh	Westminster, S.C.	D6a-'04	16/0
96	Lemonier, Corey	LB	6-3	255	11/19/91	2	Auburn	Hialeah, Fla.	D3-'13	16/0
84	Lloyd, Brandon	WR	6-0	200	7/5/81	11	Illinois	Kansas City, Mo.	FA-'14	0*
78	Looney, Joe	G	6-3	315	8/31/90	3	Wake Forest	Lake Worth, Fla.	D4-'12	4/0
71	t-Martin, Jonathan	T	6-5	312	8/19/89	3	Stanford	North Hollywood, Calif.	T(Mia)-'14	7/7*
47	McDermott, Kevin	LS	6-4	234	1/12/90	2	UCLA	Nashville, Tenn.	FA-'13	16/0
91	McDonald, Ray	DT	6-3	290	9/2/84	8	Florida	Belle Glade, Fla.	D3b-'07	14/14
89	McDonald, Vance	TE	6-4	267	6/13/90	2	Rice	Winnie, Texas	D2b-'13	15/4
49	Miller, Bruce	FB	6-2	248	8/6/87	4	Central Florida	Woodstock, Ga.	D7a-'11	14/13
54	Moody, Nick	LB	6-1	236	1/29/90	2	Florida State	Philadelphia, Pa.	D6-'13	4/0
40	Morris, Darryl	CB	5-10	188	9/4/90	2	Texas State	San Antonio, Texas	FA-'13	13/0
98	Okoye, Lawrence	DL	6-6	304	10/6/91	2	No College	Croydon, England	FA-'13	0*
14	Osgood, Kassim	WR	6-5	220	5/20/80	11	San Diego State	Boston, Mass.	FA-'13	14/0
11	Patton, Quinton	WR	6-0	204	8/9/90	2	Louisiana Tech	Nashville, Tenn.	D4a-'13	6/0
10	Reed, David	WR	6-0	190	3/22/87	5	Utah	Dubuque, Iowa	FA-'14	7/0*
35	Reid, Eric	S	6-1	213	12/10/91	2	Louisiana State	Baton Rouge, La.	D1-'13	16/16
62	Seymour, Ryan	G	6-4	301	2/7/90	2	Vanderbilt	Kingsland, Ga.	FA-'13	0*
51	Skuta, Dan	LB	6-2	250	4/21/86	6	Grand Valley State	Burton, Mich.	UFA(Cin)-'13	16/8
99	Smith, Aldon	LB	6-4	265	9/25/89	4	Missouri	Raytown, Mo.	D1-'11	11/8
94	Smith, Justin	DT	6-4	285	9/30/79	14	Missouri	Jefferson City, Mo.	FA-'08	16/16
68	Snyder, Adam	G	6-6	325	1/30/82	10	Oregon	Whittier, Calif.	FA-'13	16/4
27	Spillman, C.J.	S	6-0	199	5/6/86	6	Marshall	Louisville, Ky.	W(SD)-'10	16/0
74	Staley, Joe	T	6-5	315	8/30/84	8	Central Michigan	Rockford, Mich.	D1b-'07	16/16
48	Tukuafu, Will	FB	6-4	293	1/3/84	4	Oregon	Salt Lake City, Utah	FA-'13	2/0
41	Ventrone, Bubba	S	5-10	200	10/21/82	9	Villanova	Pittsburgh, Pa.	FA-'13	16/0
57	Wilhoite, Michael	LB	6-0	240	12/7/86	3	Washburn	Topeka, Kan.	FA-'11	16/2
93	Williams, Ian	NT	6-1	305	8/31/89	4	Notre Dame	Altamonte Springs, Fla.	FA-'11	2/1
52	Willis, Patrick	LB	6-1	240	1/25/85	8	Mississippi	Bruceton, Tenn.	D1a-'07	14/14
30	Wright, Eric	CB	5-10	200	7/24/85	8	Nevada-Las Vegas	San Francisco, Calif.	FA-'13	7/0
19	Wylie, Devon	WR	5-9	187	9/2/88	3	Fresno State	Roseville, Calif.	FA-'13	2/0*

* Bethea played 16 games with Indianapolis in '13; Bethel-Thompson did not play one game and inactive three games with Minnesota, and inactive six games with San Francisco; D.J. Campbell played four games with Miami; Carradine missed '13 season because of injury; Cook played 12 games with Minnesota; Cox played two games with Seattle and nine games with San Francisco; Culliver missed '13 season because of injury; Hampton inactive five games in '12; Gabbert played three games with Jacksonville; Johnson played 12 games with Buffalo; Lattimore missed '13 season because of injury; Lloyd last active with New England in '12; Martin played seven games with Miami; Okoye missed '13 season because of injury; Reed played seven games with Indianapolis; Seymour inactive for three games; Wylie played two games with Tennessee.

t- 49ers traded for Gabbert (Jax), Johnson (Buff) and Martin (Mia).

Players lost through free agency (6): CB Tarell Brown (Oak; 13 games), RB Anthony Dixon (Buff; 16), C Jonathan Goodwin (NO; 16), WR Mario Manningham (NYG; 6), QB Colt McCoy (Wash; 4), S Donte Whitner (Cle; 16).

Also played with 49ers in '13—CB Nnamdi Asomugha (3 games), C Jonathan Goodwin (16), WR Marlon Moore (6), CB Carlos Rogers (16), LB Nate Stupar (5), WR Kyle Williams (9).

FIRST-YEAR ROSTER

Name	Pos.	Ht.	Wt.	Birthdate	College	Hometown	How Acq.
Acker, Kenneth	CB	6-0	195	2/6/92	Southern Methodist	Portland, Ore.	D6
Borland, Chris	LB	5-11	248	12/26/90	Wisconsin	Kettering, Ohio	D3b
Bykowski, Carter (1)	T	6-7	306	7/25/90	Iowa State	Eden Prairie, Minn.	D7b-'13
Cleveland, Asante	TE	6-5	260	3/21/92	Miami	Sacramento, Calif.	FA
Ellington, Bruce	WR	5-9	197	8/22/91	South Carolina	Moncks Corner, S.C.	D4a
Farrell, Dillon	G/C	6-5	303	9/7/90	New Mexico	Baton Rouge, La.	FA
Faulkner, Kory	QB	6-4	227	8/11/90	Southern Illinois	Farmington, Mo.	FA
Fonoti, Fouimalo	G	6-4	310	11/15/90	Michigan State	Lakewood, Calif.	FA
Greene, Kevin (1)	TE	6-4	255	5/14/90	Southern California	Oakland, Calif.	FA
Hyde, Carlos	RB	6-0	235	9/20/91	Ohio State	Naples, Fla.	D2
Jacobs, Chuck (1)	WR	6-0	178	5/11/90	Utah State	Richmond, Calif.	FA-'13
Johnson, Dontae	CB	6-2	200	12/1/91	North Carolina State	Pennington, N.J.	D4b
Lynch, Aaron	LB	6-6	244	3/8/93	South Florida	Cape Coral, Fla.	D5a
Martin, Marcus	C	6-3	321	11/29/93	Southern California	Los Angeles, Calif.	D3a
McCray, James	S	6-0	210	6/18/91	Catawba	Charlotte, N.C.	FA
Millard, Trey	FB	6-2	247	7/25/91	Oklahoma	Columbia, Mo.	D7b
Netter, Al (1)	G	6-6	310	7/21/89	Northwestern	Rohnert Park, Calif.	FA-'13
Purcell, Mike (1)	NT	6-3	303	4/20/91	Wyoming	Highlands Ranch, Colo.	FA-'12
Ramsey, Kaleb	DT	6-3	285	6/20/89	Boston College	Uniontown, Pa.	D7a
Reaser, Keith	CB	6-0	190	7/31/91	Florida Atlantic	Miami, Fla.	D5b
Schmidt, Colton (1)	P	5-11	225	10/27/90	UC Davis	Bakersfield, Calif.	FA
Skov, Shayne	LB	6-3	247	7/9/90	Stanford	Guadalajara, Mexico	FA
Thomas, Brandon	G	6-3	317	2/8/91	Clemson	Spartanburg, S.C.	D3c
Thomas, Chase (1)	LB	6-3	242	6/10/89	Stanford	Marietta, Ga.	FA
Ward, Jimmie	DB	5-11	193	7/18/91	Northern Illinois	Mobile, Ala.	D1

The term NFL Rookie is defined as a player who is in his first season of professional football and has not been on the roster of another professional football team for any regular-season or postseason games. A Rookie is designated by an "R" on NFL rosters. Players who have been active in another professional football league or players who have NFL experience, including either preseason training camp or being on an Active List or Inactive List, or on Reserve/Injured or Reserve/Physically Unable to Perform for fewer than six regular-season games, are termed NFL First-Year Players. An NFL First-Year Player is designated by a "1" on NFL rosters. Thereafter, a player is credited with an additional year of experience for each season in which he accumulates six games on the Active List or Inactive List, or on Reserve/Injured or Reserve/Physically Unable to Perform.

Log on to www.49ers.com for an up-to-date roster.

COACHING STAFF
Head Coach,
Jim Harbaugh
Pro Career: Named the seventeenth head coach in 49ers history on Jan. 7, 2011. In just three seasons, Harbaugh has tallied a 41-14-1 overall record (5-3 in the postseason), won two NFC West Division titles and one NFC Championship. He followed a 14-4 rookie campaign, which earned him Associated Press 2011 NFL Coach of the Year honors, with a 13-5-1 mark in 2012 and a 14-5 record in 2013. Harbaugh is just the second NFL coach to win consecutive division titles in his first two seasons after inheriting a team with a losing record. His 36 regular season wins are the second most by any coach in NFL history over their first three seasons. Harbaugh was previously the head coach at Stanford (2007-2010), where he led the Cardinal to its first BCS game appearance and victory in the Orange Bowl, in 2010. He was head coach at the University of San Diego (2004-06). Harbaugh started in the NFL as an offensive assistant with the Oakland Raiders (2002-03). His first coaching job came from his father, Jack Harbaugh, at Western Kentucky as a volunteer assistant coach. Played 15 years with the Bears (1987 first-round pick), Colts, Ravens, Chargers and Panthers. He appeared in one Pro Bowl and was placed in the Colts' Ring of Honor in 2005. Career record: 41-14-1.
Background: Harbaugh earned First-Team All-America and Big Ten Player of the Year honors as a senior at Michigan, finishing third in the Heisman Trophy balloting.
Personal: Born December 23, 1963, Toledo, Ohio. He and his wife, Sarah, have two daughters, Addison and Katherine. He also has three children, Jay, James Jr. and Grace.

ASSISTANT COACHES
Demir Boldin, offensive assistant; born June 20, 1986, Pahokee, Fla. Wide receiver Wake Forest 2005-08. Pro wide receiver Detroit Lions 2009, Toronto Argonauts (CFL) 2010-12. Pro coach: Joined 49ers in 2013.
Geep Chryst, quarterbacks; born June 25, 1962, Madison, Wisc. Linebacker Princeton 1981-84. Pro linebacker Orlando Thunder (World League) 1992. College coach: Wisconsin-Platteville 1987, Wisconsin 1988, Wyoming 1989-1990. Pro coach: Orlando Thunder (World League) 1991, Chicago Bears 1991-95, Arizona Cardinals 1996-98, San Diego Chargers 1999-2000, Arizona Cardinals 2001-03, Carolina Panthers 2006-2010, joined 49ers in 2011.
Ronald Curry, offensive assistant; born May 28, 1979, Hampton, Va. Wide receiver North Carolina 1998-2001. Pro wide receiver Oakland Raiders 2002-08. Pro coach: Joined 49ers in 2013.
Reggie Davis, offensive line; born September 3, 1976, Long Beach, Calif. Linebacker/tight end Washington 1994-98. Pro tight end San Diego Chargers 1999-2000. College coach: San Diego State 2004, UNLV 2005-07, Oregon State 2008-2010. Pro coach: Joined 49ers in 2011.
Ed Donatell, secondary; born February 4, 1957, Akron, Ohio. Defensive back Glenville (W. Va.) State 1975-78. No pro playing experience.

College coach: Kent State 1979-1980, Washington 1981-82, 2008, Pacific 1983-85, Idaho 1986-88, Cal State Fullerton 1989. Pro coach: New York Jets 1990-94, Denver Broncos 1995-99, Green Bay Packers 2000-03, Atlanta Falcons 2004-06, New York Jets 2007, Denver Broncos 2009-2010, joined 49ers in 2011.
Ejiro Evero, defensive assistant; born January 6, 1981, Colchester, England. Safety California-Davis 2000-03. No pro playing experience. College coach: California-Davis 2005-06, Redlands 2010. Pro coach: Tampa Bay Buccaneers 2007-09, joined 49ers in 2011.
Vic Fangio, defensive coordinator; born August 22, 1958, Dunmore, Pa. Attended East Stroudsburg State. No pro playing experience. College coach: North Carolina 1983, Stanford 2010. Pro coach: Philadelphia/Baltimore Stars (USFL) 1984-85, New Orleans Saints 1986-1994, Carolina Panthers 1995-98, Indianapolis Colts 1999-2001, Houston Texans 2002-05, Baltimore Ravens 2006-09, joined 49ers in 2011.
Richmond Flowers III, offensive assistant; born May 4, 1978, Birmingham, Ala. Wide receiver Duke 1996, 1998-99, Tennessee-Chattanooga 2000. Pro wide receiver Jacksonville Jaguars 2001, Dallas Cowboys 2001, Washington Redskins 2002, Barcelona Dragons (NFL Europe) 2002, Washington Redskins 2003, New York Dragons (AFL) 2004, Saskatchewan Roughriders (CFL) 2007. Pro coach: Washington Redskins 2010-13, joined 49ers in 2014.
Greg Jackson, asst. secondary; born August 20, 1966, Hialeah, Fla. College safety Louisiana State 1985-88. Pro safety New York Giants 1989-1993, Philadelphia Eagles 1994-95, New Orleans Saints 1996, San Diego Chargers 1997-2000. College coach: Idaho 2003, Louisiana-Monroe 2004-2006, Tulane 2007-09, Wisconsin 2010. Pro coach: Joined 49ers in 2011.
Jim Leavitt, linebackers; born December 5, 1956, Harlingen, Texas. No college or pro playing experience. College coach: Missouri 1978-79, Dubuque 1980-81, Morning Side 1983-87, Iowa 1988-89, Kansas State 1990-95, South Florida 1995-2009. Pro coach: Joined 49ers in 2011.
Mick Lombardi, offensive assistant; born October 1, 1988, Ocean City, NJ. No college or pro playing experience. College coach: Fordham 2009-10. Pro coach: New England Patriots 2011-2012, joined 49ers in 2013.
Eric Mangini, tight ends; born January 19, 1971, Hartford, Conn. Nose tackle Wesleyan University. Pro coach: Cleveland Browns 1995, Baltimore Ravens 1996, New York Jets 1997-99, 2006-08 (head coach 2006-08), New England Patriots 2000-05, Cleveland Browns 2009-10 (head coach), joined 49ers in 2013.
John Morton, wide receivers; born Sept. 24, 1969, Rochester Hills, Mich. Wide receiver Western Michigan 1991-92. Pro wide receiver Toronto Argonauts (CFL) 1995-96, Frankfurt Galaxy (World League) 1997. College coach: San Diego 2005, Southern California 2007-2010. Pro coach: Oakland Raiders 2002-04, New Orleans Saints 2006, joined 49ers in 2011.
Tom Rathman, running backs; born October 7, 1962, Grand Island, Neb. Running back Nebraska 1983-85. Pro running back San

Francisco 49ers 1986-1993, Los Angeles Raiders 1994. College coach: Menlo College 1996. Pro coach: San Francisco 1997-2002, Detroit Lions 2003-05, Oakland Raiders 2007-08, re-joined 49ers in 2009.
Greg Roman, offensive coordinator; born August 19, 1972, Atlantic City, N.J. Defensive line/linebacker John Carroll 1990-94. No pro playing experience. College coach: Stanford 2009-2010. Pro coach: Carolina Panthers 1995-2001, Houston Texans 2002-05, Baltimore Ravens 2006-07, joined 49ers in 2011.
Kurt Schmidt, strength, conditioning and nutrition assistant; born August 19, 1979, Elma, Iowa. Attended Wisconsin-La Crosse. No college or pro playing experience. College coach: Utah 2003-04, Louisville 2004-06, Utah State 2006-08, Arkansas 2008-12, Memphis 2012. Pro coach: Joined 49ers in 2013.
Brad Seely, asst. head coach/special teams coordinator; born September 6, 1956, Vinton, Iowa. Offensive lineman South Dakota State 1974-77. No pro playing experience. College coach: South Dakota State 1978, Colorado State 1980, Southern Methodist 1981, North Carolina State 1982, Pacific 1983, Oklahoma State 1984-88. Pro coach: Indianapolis Colts 1989-1993, New York Jets 1994, Carolina Panthers 1995-98, New England Patriots 1999-2008, Cleveland Browns 2009-2010, joined 49ers in 2011.
Tracy Smith, special teams assistant; born February 23, 1982, Beaumont, Texas. No college or pro playing experience. College coach: Utah State 2006-08. Pro coach: Cleveland Browns 2009-10, Seattle Seahawks 2011, joined 49ers in 2012.
Mike Solari, offensive line, born January 16, 1955, Daly City, Calif. Offensive lineman San Diego State 1972-75. No pro playing experience. College coach: Mira Costa (Calif.) J.C. 1978, U.S. International 1979, Boise State 1980, Cincinnati 1981-82, Kansas 1983-85, Pittsburgh 1986, Alabama 1990-91. Pro coach: Dallas Cowboys 1987-88, Phoenix Cardinals 1989, San Francisco 1992-1996, Kansas City Chiefs 1997-2007, Seattle Seahawks 2008-09, rejoined 49ers in 2010.
Kevin Tolbert, asst. strength and conditioning; born September 11, 1958, St. Albans, N.Y. Fullback Naval Academy 1978-1980. No pro playing experience. College coach: Miami 1998-2000, Michigan 2001-07, Stanford 2009-2010. Pro coach: Philadelphia Eagles 1996-97, Detroit Lions 2008, joined 49ers in 2011.
Jim Tomsula, defensive line; born April 14, 1967, Homestead, Pa. Middle Tennessee State 1985-86, Catawba College 1987-1990. No pro playing experience. College coach: Charleston Southern 1997. Pro coach: London Monarchs (NFLE) 1998, Scottish Claymores (NFLE) 1999-2003, Berlin Thunder (NFLE) 2004-05, Rhein Fire (NFLE) 2006 (head coach), joined 49ers in 2007 (interim head coach, one game, 2010).
Mark Uyeyama, head strength and conditioning; born December 2, 1975, Vancouver, B.C. Nose Guard Butte (Mont.) C.C. 1994-95, Northern State 1996-97. No pro playing experience. College coach: Arizona State 2001-03, Utah State 2004-07. Pro coach: Joined 49ers in 2008.

National Football Conference
West Division
Team Colors: Action Green, College Navy,
Wolf Grey
Virginia Mason Athletic Center
12 Seahawks Way
Renton, Washington 98056
Telephone: (425) 203-8000

2014 SCHEDULE
PRESEASON
Aug. 7   at Denver............................6:00
Aug. 15 **San Diego**.........................7:00
Aug. 22 **Chicago** 7:00
Aug. 28 at Oakland.........................7:00

REGULAR SEASON
Sep. 4   **Green Bay** (Thu) 5:30
Sep. 14 at San Diego 1:05
Sep. 21 **Denver** 1:25
Sep. 28 BYE
Oct. 6   at Washington (Mon).........5:30
Oct. 12 **Dallas** 1:25
Oct. 19 at St. Louis 10:00a
Oct. 26 at Carolina 10:00a
Nov. 2   **Oakland** 1:25
Nov. 9   **New York Giants**...............1:25
Nov. 16 at Kansas City 10:00a
Nov. 23 **Arizona** 1:05
Nov. 27 at San Francisco (Thu) 5:30
Dec. 7   at Philadelphia 1:25
Dec. 14 **San Francisco** 1:25
Dec. 21 at Arizona *5:30
Dec. 28 **St. Louis** 1:25
*All times PT; Sunday night games in
Weeks 5-16 subject to change
Stadium: CenturyLink Field
(opened in 2002)
•**Capacity:** 67,000
Playing Surface: FieldTurf
Training Camp: VMAC
Renton, WA 98056

CENTURYLINK FIELD

CLUB OFFICIALS
Chairman: Paul Allen
President: Peter McLoughlin
Executive Vice President of Football
Operations & Head Coach: Pete Carroll
Executive Vice President/
General Manager: John Schneider
CFO & VP/Finance: Karen Beckman
Chief Operating Officer: Chuck Arnold
VP/Community Relations: Mike Flood
VP/Human Resources & Administration:
Cindy Kelley
VP/Communications, Broadcasting &
Web Content: Dave Pearson
VP/Corporate Partnerships & Suites:
Amy Sprangers
VP/Technology: Chip Suttles
VP/Football Administration: Matt Thomas
Director of Pro Personnel: Trent Kirchner
Asst. Director of Pro Personnel:
Dan Morgan
Director of Team Operations: Tag Ribary
Director of College Scouting: Scott
Fitterer
Director of Health & Player Performance:
Sam Ramsden
Director of Football Video: Brad Campbell
Equipment Manager: Erik Kennedy
Football Operations Coordinator:
Matt Capurro
Team Travel: Jeremy Young
Director of Finance: Peter Fonfara
Director of Communications:
Lane Gammel
Director of Community Outreach:
Sandy Gregory
Director of Retail Operations:
Doug Orwiler
Director of Corporate Communications:
Suzanne Lavender
Director of Ticket Sales & Service:
Chris Lawrence
Director of I.T.: Sterling Monroe
Director of Digital & Emerging Media:
Kenton Olson
Director of Marketing: Jeff Richards
Director of Event Presentation & Fan
Engagement: Mark Tamar
Director of Fields & Facilities:
John Wright
Asst. Director of Broadcasting:
Brian O'Connell
Executive Producer/Seahawks Radio
Network: Matt Johnson

COACHING HISTORY
(305-315-0)
Records include postseason games
1976-1982 Jack Patera*................35-59-0
1982   Mike McCormack 4-3-0
1983-1991 Chuck Knox.................83-67-0
1992-94   Tom Flores..................14-34-0
1995-98   Dennis Erickson............31-33-0
1999-2008 Mike Holmgren 90-80-0
2009   Jim Mora......................5-11-0
2010-13   Pete Carroll.................43-28-0
*Released after two games in 1982

PAID ATTENDANCE
Home 532,926   Away 534,654
Total 1,067,580
Single-game home record,
68,681 (12/16/00)
Single-season home record,
533,657 (2007)

2014 DRAFT CHOICES
Round	Name	Pos.	College
2	Paul Richardson	WR	Colorado
	Justin Britt	T	Missouri
4	Cassius Marsh	DE	UCLA
	Kevin Norwood	WR	Alabama
	Kevin Pierre-Louis	LB	Boston College
5	Jimmy Staten	DT	Middle Tennessee
6	Garrett Scott	T	Marshall
	Eric Pinkins	DB	San Diego St.
7	Kiero Small	FB	Arkansas

SEATTLE SEAHAWKS

2013 TEAM RECORD
PRESEASON (4-0)

Date	Result	Opponent
08/08	W 31-10	at San Diego
08/17	W 40-10	Denver
08/23	W 17-10	at Green Bay
08/29	W 22-6	Oakland

REGULAR SEASON (13-3)

Date	Result	Opponent
09/08	W 12-7	at Carolina
09/15	W 29-3	San Francisco
09/22	W 45-17	Jacksonville
09/29	W 23-20	at Houston (OT)
10/06	L 28-34	at Indianapolis
10/13	W 20-13	Tennessee
10/17	W 34-22	at Arizona
10/28	W 14-9	at St. Louis
11/03	W 27-24	Tampa Bay (OT)
11/10	W 33-10	at Atlanta
11/17	W 41-20	Minnesota
12/02	W 34-7	New Orleans
12/08	L 17-19	at San Francisco
12/15	W 23-0	at New York Giants
12/22	L 10-17	Arizona
12/29	W 27-9	St. Louis

POSTSEASON (3-0)

Date	Result	Opponent
01/11	W 23-15	New Orleans
01/19	W 23-17	San Francisco
02/02	W 43-8	Denver @ E. Rutherford

(OT) Overtime

SCORE BY PERIODS

Seahawks	69	140	87	115	6 —	417
Opponents	22	108	41	60	0 —	231

2013 TEAM STATISTICS

	Seahawks	Opp.
Total First Downs	307	282
Rushing	116	83
Passing	160	156
Penalty	31	43
3rd Down: Made/Att	76/204	76/216
3rd Down Pct.	37.3	35.2
4th Down: Made/Att	6/11	4/11
4th Down Pct.	54.5	36.4
Possession Avg.	29:57	30:03
Total Net Yards	5424	4378
Avg. Per Game	339.0	273.6
Total Plays	973	990
Avg. Per Play	5.6	4.4
Net Yards Rushing	2188	1626
Avg. Per Game	136.8	101.6
Total Rushes	509	422
Net Yards Passing	3236	2752
Avg. Per Game	202.3	172.0
Sacked/Yards Lost	44/272	44/298
Gross Yards	3508	3050
Att./Completions	420/267	524/309
Completion Pct.	63.6	59.0
Had Intercepted	9	28
Punts/Average	76/41.6	82/46.1
Net Punting Avg.	76/39.2	82/38.0
Penalties/Yards	128/1183	98/879
Fumbles/Ball Lost	26/10	26/11
Touchdowns	45	22
Rushing	14	4
Passing	27	16
Returns	4	2

2013 INDIVIDUAL STATISTICS

PASSING	Att.	Comp.	Yds.	Pct.	TD	Int.	Tkld.	Rate
Wilson	407	257	3357	63.1	26	9	44/272	101.2
Jackson	13	10	151	76.9	1	0	0/0	140.2
Seahawks	420	267	3508	63.6	27	9	44/272	102.4
Opponents	524	309	3050	59.0	16	28	44/298	63.4

SCORING	TD R	TD P	TD Rt	PAT	FG	Saf	PTS
Hauschka	0	0	0	44/44	33/35	0	143
Lynch	12	2	0	0/0	0/0	0	84
Baldwin	0	5	0	0/0	0/0	0	30
Miller	0	5	0	0/0	0/0	0	30
Tate	0	5	0	0/0	0/0	0	30
Kearse	0	4	0	0/0	0/0	1	26
Rice	0	3	0	0/0	0/0	0	18
Bennett	0	0	1	0/0	0/0	0	6
Coleman	0	1	0	0/0	0/0	0	6
Davis	0	1	0	0/0	0/0	0	6
Jackson	1	0	0	0/0	0/0	0	6
Sherman	0	0	1	0/0	0/0	0	6
M. Smith	0	0	1	0/0	0/0	0	6
Thurmond	0	0	1	0/0	0/0	0	6
Willson	0	1	0	0/0	0/0	0	6
Wilson	1	0	0	0/0	0/0	0	6
Seahawks	14	27	4	44/44	33/35	2	417
Opponents	4	16	2	17/17	26/27	0	231

2-Pt Conversions: Seahawks 0-1, Opponents 2-5

RUSHING	No.	Yds	Avg	LG	TD
Lynch	301	1257	4.2	43	12
Wilson	96	539	5.6	27	1
Turbin	77	264	3.4	15	0
Michael	18	79	4.4	13	0
Tate	3	31	10.3	20	0
Ware	3	10	3.3	5	0
Baldwin	2	6	3.0	3	0
Coleman	2	3	1.5	4	0
Jackson	4	1	0.3	5t	1
Maragos	1	0	0.0	0	0
Robinson	1	0	0.0	0	0
Lockette	1	-2	-2.0	-2	0
Seahawks	509	2188	4.3	43	14
Opponents	422	1626	3.9	51	4

RECEIVING	No.	Yds	Avg	LG	TD
Tate	64	898	14.0	80t	5
Baldwin	50	778	15.6	52	5
Lynch	36	316	8.8	55	2
Miller	33	387	11.7	60	5
Kearse	22	346	15.7	43t	4
Willson	20	272	13.6	39t	1
Rice	15	231	15.4	31t	3
Coleman	8	62	7.8	12	1
Turbin	8	60	7.5	19	0
Lockette	5	82	16.4	33	0
Davis	3	32	10.7	23	1
Robinson	2	27	13.5	21	0
Harvin	1	17	17.0	17	0
Seahawks	267	3508	13.1	80t	27
Opponents	309	3050	9.9	73t	16

INTERCEPTIONS	No.	Yds	Avg	LG	TD
Sherman	8	125	15.6	58t	1
Thomas	5	9	1.8	11	0
Maxwell	4	6	1.5	6	0
Chancellor	3	78	26.0	32	0
M. Smith	2	69	34.5	37t	1
Wagner	2	9	4.5	9	0
Browner	1	49	49.0	49	0
Thurmond	1	29	29.0	29t	1
Irvin	1	8	8.0	8	0
McDonald	1	3	3.0	3	0
Seahawks	28	385	13.8	58t	3
Opponents	9	21	2.3	10	0

PUNTING	No.	Yds.	Avg.	In 20	LG
Ryan	74	3159	42.7	28	69
Seahawks	76	3159	41.6	28	69
Opponents	82	3779	46.1	22	61

PUNT RETURNS	Ret	FC	Yds	Avg	LG	TD
Tate	51	14	585	11.5	71	0
Sherman	1	0	-6	-6.0	-6	0
Seahawks	52	14	579	11.1	71	0
Opponents	21	30	82	3.9	32	0

KICKOFF RETURNS	No.	Yds	Avg	LG	TD
Kearse	13	283	21.8	40	0
Turbin	8	177	22.1	27	0
Tate	3	57	19.0	24	0
Baldwin	2	57	28.5	37	0
Lane	2	47	23.5	25	0
Harvin	1	58	58.0	58	0
Willson	1	15	15.0	15	0
Robinson	1	4	4.0	4	0
Coleman	1	0	0.0	0	0
Davis	1	0	0.0	0	0
Seahawks	33	698	21.2	58	0
Opponents	44	1056	24.0	40	0

FIELD GOALS	1-19	20-29	30-39	40-49	50+
Hauschka	0/0	10/11	9/9	11/12	3/3
Seahawks	0/0	10/11	9/9	11/12	3/3
Opponents	0/0	9/9	7/7	7/7	3/4

SACKS	No.
Bennett	8.5
Avril	8.0
McDonald	5.5
Wagner	5.0
Clemons	4.5
Irvin	2.0
McDaniel	2.0
Bryant	1.5
Hill	1.5
Wright	1.5
Schofield	1.0
M. Smith	1.0
Thurmond	1.0
(group)	1.0
Seahawks	44.0
Opponents	44.0

RECORD HOLDERS
INDIVIDUAL RECORDS—CAREER

Category	Name	Performance
Rushing (Yds.)	Shaun Alexander, 2000-07	9,429
Passing (Yds.)	Matt Hasselbeck, 2001-2010	29,434
Passing (TDs)	Dave Krieg, 1980-1991	195
Receiving (No.)	Steve Largent, 1976-1989	819
Receiving (Yds.)	Steve Largent, 1976-1989	13,089
Interceptions	Dave Brown, 1976-1986	50
Punting (Avg.)	Jon Ryan, 2008-2013	44.8
Punt Return (Avg.)	Charlie Rogers, 1999-2001	12.7
Kickoff Return (Avg.)	Leon Washington, 2010-12	26.2
Field Goals	Norm Johnson, 1982-1990	159
Touchdowns (Tot.)	Shaun Alexander, 2000-07	112
Points	Norm Johnson, 1982-1990	810
*Sacks	Jacob Green, 1980-1991	97.5

INDIVIDUAL RECORDS—SINGLE SEASON

Category	Name	Performance
Rushing (Yds.)	Shaun Alexander, 2005	1,880
Passing (Yds.)	Matt Hasselbeck, 2007	3,966
Passing (TDs)	Dave Krieg, 1984	32
Receiving (No.)	Bobby Engram, 2007	94
Receiving (Yds.)	Steve Largent, 1985	1,287
Interceptions	John Harris, 1981	10
	Kenny Easley, 1984	10
Punting (Avg.)	Jon Ryan, 2011	46.6
Punt Return (Avg.)	Charlie Rogers, 1999	14.5
Kickoff Return (Avg.)	Leon Washington, 2012	29.0
Field Goals	Todd Peterson, 1999	34
Touchdowns (Tot.)	Shaun Alexander, 2005	28
Points	Shaun Alexander, 2005	168
*Sacks	Michael Sinclair, 1998	16.5

INDIVIDUAL RECORDS—SINGLE GAME

Category	Name	Performance
Rushing (Yds.)	Shaun Alexander, 11-11-01	266
Passing (Yds.)	Matt Hasselbeck, 12-29-02	449
Passing (TDs)	Dave Krieg, 12-2-84, 9-15-85, 11-28-88	5
	Warren Moon, 10-26-97	5
	Matt Hasselbeck, 11-23-03, 9-24-06	5
Receiving (No.)	Steve Largent, 10-18-87	15
Receiving (Yds.)	Steve Largent, 10-18-87	261
Interceptions	Kenny Easley, 9-3-84	3
	Eugene Robinson, 12-6-92	3
	Darryl Williams, 9-21-97	3
	Lofa Tatupu, 12-2-07	3
	Marcus Trufant, 12-9-07	3
Field Goals	Norm Johnson, 9-20-87, 12-18-88	5
	Olindo Mare, 10-24-10, 11-14-10	5
	Todd Peterson, 9-26-99	5
	Steven Hauschka, 11-13-11	5
Touchdowns (Tot.)	Shaun Alexander, 9-29-02	5
Points	Shaun Alexander, 9-29-02	30
*Sacks	Many times	4.0
	Last time by Chris Clemons, 9-24-12	

Sacks became an official statistic in 1982.

2014 VETERAN ROSTER

No.	Name	Pos.	Ht.	Wt.	Birthdate	NFL Exp.	College	Hometown	How Acq.	'13 Games/ Starts
28	Adams, Phillip	CB	5-11	195	7/20/88	5	South Carolina State	Rock Hill, S.C.	UFA(Oak)-'14	16/2*
36	Auguste, Akeem	CB	5-10	185	10/10/89	2	South Carolina	Hollywood, Fla.	FA-'13	0*
56	Avril, Cliff	DE	6-3	260	4/8/86	7	Purdue	Green Cove Springs, Fla.	UFA(Det)-'13	15/2
78	Bailey, Alvin	T	6-3	320	8/26/91	2	Arkansas	Broken Arrow, Okla.	FA-'13	14/0
89	Baldwin, Doug	WR	5-10	189	9/21/88	4	Stanford	Gulf Breeze, Fla.	FA-'11	16/9
88	Bates, Phil	WR	6-1	220	9/20/89	3	Ohio University	Omaha, Neb.	FA-'13	0*
72	Bennett, Michael	DE	6-4	274	11/13/85	6	Texas A&M	Alief, Texas	UFA(TB)-'13	16/3
52	Boatright, Kenneth	DE	6-3	254	3/6/90	2	Southern Illinois	Bolingbrook, Ill.	FA-'13	0*
73	Bowie, Michael	T	6-4	332	9/25/91	2	Northeastern State	Tulsa, Okla.	D7d-'13	9/8
70	Brooks, Michael	DT	6-3	276	8/28/91	2	East Carolina	Roxboro, N.C.	W(Det)-'13	1/0
77	Carpenter, James	G	6-5	321	3/22/89	4	Alabama	Augusta, Ga.	D1-'11	16/10
31	Chancellor, Kam	SS	6-3	232	4/3/88	5	Virginia Tech	Norfolk, Va.	D5-'10	16/16
40	Coleman, Derrick	FB	6-0	233	10/18/90	3	UCLA	W. Los Angeles, Calif.	FA-'12	12/3
5	Daniels, B.J.	QB	5-11	217	10/24/89	2	South Florida	Tallahassee, Fla.	W(SF)-'13	0*
55	Farwell, Heath	LB	6-0	235	12/31/81	10	San Diego State	Fontana, Calif.	FA-'11	16/0
38	Fenner, Chandler	CB	6-1	189	7/6/90	3	Holy Cross	Virginia Beach, Va.	FA-'12	0*
49	Gresham, Clint	LS	6-3	240	8/24/86	5	Texas Christian	Corpus Christi, Texas	FA-'10	16/0
11	Harvin, Percy	WR	5-11	184	5/28/88	6	Florida	Virginia Beach, Va.	T(Minn)-'13	1/0
74	Hauptmann, Caylin	T	6-3	300	7/10/91	2	Florida International	Los Angeles, Calif.	PS(Cle)-'13	0*
4	Hauschka, Steven	K	6-4	210	6/29/85	7	North Carolina State	Needham, Mass.	W(Den)-'11	16/0
97	Hill, Jordan	DT	6-1	303	2/8/91	2	Penn State	Steelton, Pa.	D3-'13	4/0
51	Irvin, Bruce	LB	6-3	248	11/1/87	3	West Virginia	Atlanta, Ga.	D1-'12	12/12
7	Jackson, Tarvaris	QB	6-2	225	4/21/83	9	Alabama State	Montgomery, Ala.	FA-'13	3/0
61	Jeanpierre, Lemuel	C	6-3	301	5/19/87	5	South Carolina	Orlando, Fla.	FA-'10	16/3
32	Jefferson, A.J.	CB	6-1	190	4/4/88	5	Fresno State	Bakersfield, Calif.	FA-'14	10/0*
23	Johnson, Jeron	SS	5-10	212	6/12/88	4	Boise State	Compton, Calif.	FA-'11	7/0
15	Kearse, Jermaine	WR	6-1	209	2/6/90	3	Washington	Lakewood, Wash.	FA-'12	15/5
20	Lane, Jeremy	CB	6-0	190	7/14/90	3	Northwestern St. (La.)	Tyler, Texas	D6a-'12	15/0
83	Lockette, Ricardo	WR	6-2	211	5/21/86	4	Fort Valley State	Albany, Ga.	FA-'13	8/1
24	Lynch, Marshawn	RB	5-11	215	4/22/86	8	California	Oakland, Calif.	T(Buff)-'10	16/16
41	Maxwell, Byron	CB	6-1	207	2/23/88	4	Clemson	Charleston, S.C.	D6-'11	16/5
95	Mayowa, Benson	DE	6-3	252	8/3/91	2	Idaho	Inglewood, Calif.	FA-'13	2/0
85	McCoy, Anthony	TE	6-5	259	12/28/87	5	Southern California	Fresno, Calif.	D6-'10	0*
99	McDaniel, Tony	DT	6-7	305	1/20/85	9	Tennessee	Columbia, S.C.	UFA(Mia)-'13	16/15
92	Mebane, Brandon	DT	6-1	311	1/15/85	8	California	Los Angeles, Calif.	D3-'07	16/16
33	Michael, Christine	RB	5-10	221	11/9/90	2	Texas A&M	Beaumont, Texas	D2-'13	4/0
86	Miller, Zach	TE	6-5	255	12/11/85	8	Arizona State	Phoenix, Ariz.	UFA(Oak)-'11	14/12
57	Morgan, Mike	LB	6-3	226	1/16/88	4	Southern California	Dallas, Texas	FA-'11	16/0
76	Okung, Russell	T	6-5	310	10/7/88	5	Oklahoma State	Houston, Texas	D1a-'10	8/8
16	Price, Taylor	WR	6-1	195	10/8/87	5	Ohio University	Hilliard, Ohio	UFA(Jax)-'14	0*
2 t-	Pryor, Terrelle	QB	6-4	233	6/20/89	4	Ohio State	Jeannette, Pa.	T(Oak)-'14	11/9*
18	Rice, Sidney	WR	6-4	202	9/1/86	8	South Carolina	Gaffney, S.C.	UFA(Minn)-'11	8/6
9	Ryan, Jon	P	6-0	217	11/26/81	9	Regina	Regina, Saskatchewan, Canada	FA-'08	16/0
63	Schilling, Stephen	G	6-5	312	7/21/88	4	Michigan	Bellevue, Wash.	UFA(SD)-'14	7/0*
93	Schofield, O'Brien	DE	6-3	242	4/3/87	5	Wisconsin	Camden, S.C.	W(Ariz)-'13	15/2
98	Scruggs, Greg	DE	6-3	310	8/17/90	3	Louisville	Cincinnati, Ohio	D7b-'12	0*
35	Shead, DeShawn	CB	6-2	220	6/28/88	3	Portland State	Palmdale, Calif.	FA-'12	5/0
25	Sherman, Richard	CB	6-3	195	3/30/88	4	Stanford	Compton, Calif.	D5a-'11	16/16
94	Smith, D'Anthony	DT	6-2	300	6/9/88	5	Louisiana Tech	Leesville, La.	T(Jax)-'13	2/0
53	Smith, Malcolm	LB	6-0	226	7/5/89	4	Southern California	Northridge, Calif.	D7b-'11	15/8
64	Sweezy, J.R.	G	6-5	298	4/8/89	3	North Carolina State	Mooresville, N.C.	D7a-'12	15/15
29	Thomas, Earl	FS	5-10	202	5/7/89	5	Texas	Orange, Texas	D1b-'10	16/16
22	Turbin, Robert	RB	5-10	222	12/2/89	3	Utah State	Fremont, Calif.	D4a-'12	16/0
60	Unger, Max	C	6-5	305	4/14/86	6	Oregon	Kailua-Kona, Hawaii	D2-'09	13/13
62	Van Roten, Greg	G	6-3	303	2/26/90	3	Pennsylvania	Brooklyn, N.Y.	FA-'14	3/0*
54	Wagner, Bobby	LB	6-0	241	6/27/90	3	Utah State	Ontario, Calif.	D2-'12	14/14
19	Walters, Bryan	WR	6-0	190	11/4/87	5	Cornell	Kirkland, Wash.	FA-'12	4/1
44	Ware, Spencer	FB	5-10	229	11/23/91	2	Louisiana State	Cincinnati, Ohio	D6-'13	2/0
90	Williams, Jesse	DT	6-3	325	11/2/90	2	Alabama	Brisbane, Australia	D5a-'13	0*
82	Willson, Luke	TE	6-5	252	1/15/90	2	Rice	Lasalle, Ontario, Canada	D5c-'13	16/7
3	Wilson, Russell	QB	5-11	206	11/29/88	3	Wisconsin	Richmond, Va.	D3-'12	16/16
50	Wright, K.J.	LB	6-4	246	7/23/89	4	Mississippi State	Olive Branch, Miss.	D4a-'11	13/13

* Adams played 16 games with Oakland in '13; Boatright missed '13 season because of injury; Daniels did not play one game and inactive five games; Fenner missed '13 season because of injury; Hauptmann did not play three games and inactive 10 games; Jefferson played 10 games with Minnesota; McCoy missed '13 season because of injury; Price missed '13 season because of injury with Jacksonville; Pryor played 11 games with Oakland: Schilling played seven games with San Diego; Scruggs missed '13 season because of injury; Van Roten played three games with Green Bay; Williams missed '13 season because of injury.

t- Seahawks traded for Pryor (Oak).

Players lost through free agency (7): S Brandon Browner (NE; 8 games in '13), TE Kellen Davis (NYG; 15), T Breno Giacomini (NYJ; 9), DB Chris Maragos (Phil; 16), DT Clinton McDonald (TB; 15), OL Paul McQuistan (Cle; 16), WR Golden Tate (Det; 16).

Also played with Seahawks in '13—LB Allen Bradford (1 game), DE Red Bryant (15), DE Chris Clemons (14), CB Perrish Cox (2), LB John Lotulelei (2), T Mike Person (1), FB Michael Robinson (9), CB Walter Thurmond (12), WR Stephen Williams (4).

FIRST-YEAR ROSTER

Name	Pos.	Ht.	Wt.	Birthdate	College	Hometown	How Acq.
Allen, Rashaun	TE	6-4	250	2/25/90	Southern	Cleveland, Ohio	FA
Auguste, Akeem (1)	CB	5-10	185	10/10/89	South Carolina	Hollywood, Fla.	FA-'13
Bailey, Dion	SS	6-0	211	3/2/92	Southern California	Lakewood, Calif.	FA
Bates, Phil (1)	WR	6-1	220	9/20/89	Ohio	Omaha, Neb.	FA-'13
Britt, Justin	T	6-6	325	5/29/91	Missouri	Lebanon, Mo.	D2b
Cherrington, Dewayne (1)	DT	6-3	335	8/3/90	Mississippi State	Lawrenceville, Ga.	FA-'13
Clark, Arceto (1)	WR	5-10	180	9/29/89	Mississippi State	Tupelo, Miss.	FA-'13
Coyle, Brock	LB	6-1	243	10/12/90	Montana	Bozeman, Mont.	FA
Dixon, Chase	TE	6-5	240	5/30/91	Central Arkansas	Fort Smith, Ark.	FA
Gilliam, Garry	T	6-5	306	11/26/90	Penn State	Carlisle, Pa.	FA
Helfet, Cooper (1)	TE	6-3	239	6/2/89	Duke	Kentfield, Calif.	FA-'12
Irwin, Bronson	G	6-4	316	2/16/92	Oklahoma	Mustang, Okla.	FA
Isles, Nate	G	6-5	348	1/4/92	North Carolina A&T	Atlanta, Ga.	FA
Jeffcoat, Jackson	DE	6-3	253	12/26/91	Texas	Plano, Texas	FA
Marsh, Cassius	DE	6-4	254	7/7/92	UCLA	Simi Valley, Calif.	D4a
Matthews, Chris	WR	6-5	218	10/6/89	Kentucky	Long Beach, Calif.	FA
Norwood, Kevin	WR	6-2	199	9/23/89	Alabama	D'Iberville, Miss.	D4b
Parks, Terrance	CB	6-2	218	4/14/90	Florida State	Fairburn, Ga.	FA
Pierre-Louis, Kevin	LB	6-0	236	10/7/91	Boston College	Norwalk, Conn.	D4c
Pinkins, Eric	CB	6-3	220	4/7/91	San Diego State	Sacramento, Calif.	D6b
Price, Keith	QB	6-1	204	6/28/91	Washington	Compton, Calif.	FA
Pulu, Andru	DT	6-1	322	7/29/91	Eastern Washington	Federal Way, Wash.	FA
Richardson, Paul	WR	6-0	183	4/13/92	Colorado	Los Angeles, Calif.	D2a
Simon, Tharold (1)	CB	6-3	202	3/6/91	Louisiana State	Eunice, La.	D5b-'13
Small, Kiero	FB	5-8	247	5/1/89	Arkansas	Baltimore, Md.	D7
Smith, Jared (1)	C/G	6-4	302	3/20/90	New Hampshire	Greencastle, Pa.	D7c-'13
Staten, Jimmy	DT	6-3	311	5/4/91	Middle Tennessee	Waycross, Ga.	D5
Taylor, Mike	LB	6-2	222	10/7/89	Wisconsin	Ashwaubenon, Wisc.	FA
Toomer, Korey (1)	LB	6-2	243	12/9/88	Idaho	Las Vegas, Nev.	D5-'12

The term NFL Rookie is defined as a player who is in his first season of professional football and has not been on the roster of another professional football team for any regular-season or postseason games. A Rookie is designated by an "R" on NFL rosters. Players who have been active in another professional football league or players who have NFL experience, including either preseason training camp or being on an Active List or Inactive List, or on Reserve/Injured or Reserve/Physically Unable to Perform for fewer than six regular-season games, are termed NFL First-Year Players. An NFL First-Year Player is designated by a "1" on NFL rosters. Thereafter, a player is credited with an additional year of experience for each season in which he accumulates six games on the Active List or Inactive List, or on Reserve/Injured or Reserve/Physically Unable to Perform.

Log on to www.seahawks.com for an up-to-date roster.

SEATTLE SEAHAWKS

COACHING STAFF
Head Coach,
Pete Carroll

Pro Career: Named as Seattle's eighth head coach on January 11, 2010. Began his NFL career as defensive backs coach for the Buffalo Bills (1984) and Minnesota Vikings (1985-89), before becoming the N.Y. Jets defensive coordinator (1990-93) and head coach (1994). Spent two years as the San Francisco 49ers defensive coordinator (1995-96) before leading the New England Patriots to a 27-21 record and two playoff appearances as head coach (1997-99). Returned to the NFL after spending nine years (2001-09) as head coach at USC, where he won seven consecutive Pac-10 titles (2002-08), two national championships and led the Trojans to a 97-19 record. Career record: 77-61.

Background: Two-time All-Pacific Coast Conference safety at Pacific (1971-72). Earned degree in business administration (1973) and secondary teaching credential and master's degree in physical education (1976) from Pacific. College coach: Pacific 1974-76, 1983, Arkansas 1977, Iowa State 1978, Ohio State 1979, North Carolina State 1980-82, USC 2001-09.

Personal: Born September 15, 1951 in San Francisco, Calif. He and his wife, Glena, have three children: Brennan, Nate, Jaime, and four grandchildren.

ASSISTANT COACHES

Darrell Bevell, offensive coordinator; born January 6, 1970, Yuma, Ariz. Quarterback Northern Arizona 1989, Wisconsin 1992-95. No pro playing experience. College coach: Westmar 1996, Iowa State 1997, Connecticut 1998-99. Pro coach: Green Bay Packers 2000-05, Minnesota Vikings 2006-2010, joined Seahawks in 2011.

Kippy Brown, wide receivers; born March 6, 1955, Sweetwater, Tenn. Quarterback Memphis State 1974-77. No pro playing experience. College coach: Memphis State 1978-1980, Louisville 1982, Tennessee 1983-89, 1993-94, 2009. Pro coach: New York Jets 1990-92, Tampa Bay Buccaneers 1995, Miami Dolphins 1996-99, Green Bay Packers 2000, Houston Texans 2002-05, Detroit Lions 2006-08, joined Seahawks in 2010.

Tom Cable, asst. head coach/offensive line; born November 26, 1964, Merced, Calif. Offensive lineman Idaho 1982-86. Pro lineman Indianapolis Colts 1987. College coach: Idaho 1987-88, San Diego State 1989, Cal State-Fullerton 1990, UNLV 1991, California 1992-97, Idaho 2000-03, UCLA 2004-05. Pro coach: Atlanta Falcons 2006, Oakland Raiders 2007-10 (head coach 2008-2010), joined Seahawks in 2011.

Dave Canales, asst. quarterbacks/offensive quality control; born May 7, 1981, Carson, Calif. Wide receiver Azusa Pacific 2000-03. No pro playing experience. College coach: El Camino (Calif.) J.C. 2006-08, Southern California 2009. Pro coach: Joined Seahawks in 2010.

Chris Carlisle, head strength & conditioning; born August 7, 1962, Mason City, Iowa.

Offensive lineman North Iowa Area Community College 1980-81, Chadron (Neb.) State College 1982-83. No pro playing experience. College coach: Arkansas 1992-93, Trinity Valley (Texas) C.C. 1997, Tennessee 1998-2000, Southern California 2001-09. Pro coach: Joined Seahawks in 2010.

Nate Carroll, offensive assistant; born March 24, 1987, Edina, Minn. Attended Southern California. No college or pro playing experience. Pro coach: Joined Seahawks in 2010.

Mondray Gee, asst. strength & conditioning; born June 15, 1976, Detroit, Mich. Attended Michigan State. No college or pro playing experience. College coach: Michigan State 2000-01. Pro coach: Detroit Lions 2001-07, Green Bay Packers 2008-09, joined Seahawks in 2010.

John Glenn, quality control/defense; born July 20, 1981, Scranton, Pa. Linebacker East Stroudsburg 2002-05. No pro playing experience. College coach: Washington 2010-11. Pro coach: Joined Seahawks in 2012.

Travis Jones, defensive line; born June 6, 1972, Milledgeville, Ga. Linebacker Georgia 1991-94. Pro linebacker Baltimore Stallions (CFL) 1995. College coach: Georgia 1997, Appalachian State 1998-2000, Kansas 2001-02, Louisiana State 2003-04. Pro coach: Miami Dolphins 2005-07, New Orleans Saints 2008-2012, joined Seahawks in 2012.

Marquand Manuel, defensive assistant; born July 11, 1979, Miami, Fla. Safety Florida 1998-2001. Pro safety Cincinnati Bengals 2002-03, Seattle Seahawks 2004-05, Green Bay Packers 2006, Carolina Panthers 2007, Denver Broncos 2008, Detroit Lions 2009. Pro coach: Joined Seahawks in 2011.

Pat McPherson, tight ends; born April 15, 1969, Santa Clara, Calif. Linebacker Santa Clara 1991-92. No pro playing experience. Pro coach: San Francisco 49ers 1996, Denver Broncos 1998-2008, joined Seahawks in 2010.

Chris Morgan, asst. offensive line; born September 24 1976, Killeen, Texas. Offensive lineman Colorado 1996-99. No pro playing experience. College coach: Idaho 2003. Pro coach: Oakland Raiders 2009-2010, Washington Redskins 2011-12, joined Seahawks in 2014.

Chad Morton, special teams assistant; born April 4, 1977, Torrance, Calif. Running back Southern California 1995-99. Pro running back New Orleans Saints 2000, New York Jets 2001-02, Washington Redskins 2003-04, New York Giants 2005-06. Pro coach: Green Bay Packers 2009-2013, joined Seahawks in 2014.

Ken Norton, Jr., linebackers; born September 29, 1966, Lincoln, Ill. Linebacker UCLA 1984-87. Pro linebacker Dallas Cowboys 1988-1993, San Francisco 49ers 1994-2000. College coach: Southern California 2004-09. Pro coach: Joined Seahawks in 2010.

Dan Quinn, defensive coordinator; born September 11, 1970, Orange, N.J. Defensive lineman Salisbury State 1990-93. No pro playing experience. College coach: William & Mary 1994, Virginia Military Institute 1995, Hofstra 1997-2000, Florida 2010-11. Pro

coach: San Francisco 49ers 2001-04, Miami Dolphins 2005-06, New York Jets 2007-08, Seattle Seahawks 2009-2010, re-joined Seahawks 2013.

Kris Richard, defensive backs/cornerbacks; born October 28, 1978, Carson, Calif. Defensive back Southern California 1998-2001. Pro defensive back Seattle Seahawks 2002-04, San Francisco 49ers 2005. College coach: Southern California 2008-09. Pro coach: Joined Seahawks in 2010.

Pat Ruel, asst. offensive line; born December 5, 1950, Coral Gables, Fla. Offensive lineman Miami 1971-72. No pro playing experience. College coach: Miami 1974-76, Arkansas 1977, Washington State 1978-1981, Texas A&M 1982-84, Northern Illinois 1985-87, Kansas 1988-1996, Michigan State 1998-99, USC 2005-09. Pro coach: Detroit Lions 2000, Green Bay Packers 2001-02, Buffalo Bills 2003, New York Giants 2004, joined Seahawks in 2010.

Brian Schneider, special teams coordinator; born May 16, 1971, San Diego, Calif. Linebacker Colorado State 1989-1993. No pro playing experience. College coach: Colorado State 1994-2002, UCLA 2003-05, Iowa State 2006, Air Force 2007, Southern California 2009. Pro coach: Oakland Raiders 2007-08, joined Seahawks in 2010.

Rocky Seto, asst. defensive backs/safeties; born March 12, 1976, Arcadia, Calif. Linebacker Southern California 1997-98. No pro playing experience. College coach: Southern California 1999-2009. Pro coach: Joined Seahawks in 2010.

Carl Smith, quarterbacks; born April 26, 1948, Wasco, Calif. Quarterback Bakersfield 1966-67, defensive back Cal Poly-San Luis Obispo 1969-1970. No pro playing experience. College coach: Cal Poly-San Luis Obispo 1971, Colorado 1972-73, Southwestern Louisiana 1974-78, Lamar 1979-1981, North Carolina State 1982, Southern California 2004. Pro coach: Philadelphia/Baltimore Stars 1983-85, New Orleans Saints 1986-1996, New England Patriots 1997-99, Cleveland Browns 2001-03, 2009-2010, Jacksonville Jaguars 2005-06, joined Seahawks in 2011.

Sherman Smith, running backs; born November 1, 1954, Youngstown, Ohio. Quarterback Miami (Ohio) 1972-75. Pro running back Seattle Seahawks 1976-1982, San Diego Chargers 1983-84. College coach: Miami (Ohio) 1990-91, Illinois 1992-94. Pro coach: Houston Oilers/Tennessee Titans 1995-2007, Washington Redskins 2008-09, joined Seahawks in 2010.

Nick Sorensen, coaching assistant/special teams; born July 31, 1978, Winter Haven, Fla. Safety Virginia Tech 1997-2000. Pro safety St. Louis Rams 2001-02, Jacksonville Jaguars 2003-06, Cleveland Browns 2007-2010. Pro coach: Joined Seahawks in 2012.

Jamie Yanchar, asst. strength & conditioning; born December 29, 1963, Cleveland, Ohio. Attended Louisville. No college or pro playing experience. College coach: Southern California 1990-2009. Pro coach: Joined Seahawks in 2010.

**National Football Conference
South Division
Team Colors:** Buccaneer Red, Pewter,
Black, and Orange
**One Buccaneer Place
Tampa, Florida 33607
Telephone:** (813) 870-2700

2014 SCHEDULE
PRESEASON
Aug. 8   at Jacksonville...................7:30
Aug. 16   **Miami**...............................7:30
Aug. 23   at Buffalo..........................4:30
Aug. 28   **Washington** 7:30

REGULAR SEASON
Sep. 7   **Carolina** 4:25
Sep. 14   **St. Louis** 4:05
Sep. 18   at Atlanta (Thu) 8:25
Sep. 28   at Pittsburgh 1:00
Oct. 5   at New Orleans 1:00
Oct. 12   **Baltimore** 1:00
Oct. 19   BYE
Oct. 26   **Minnesota** 1:00
Nov. 2   at Cleveland 1:00
Nov. 9   **Atlanta** 1:00
Nov. 16   at Washington 1:00
Nov. 23   at Chicago 1:00
Nov. 30   **Cincinnati** 1:00
Dec. 7   at Detroit 1:00
Dec. 14   at Carolina 1:00
Dec. 21   **Green Bay** 1:00
Dec. 28   **New Orleans** 1:00
* All times ET

Stadium: Raymond James Stadium
        (opened in 1998)
        •**Capacity:** 65,908
        Tampa, Florida 33607
Playing Surface: Grass
Training Camp: One Buccaneer Place
        Tampa, Florida 33607

RAYMOND JAMES STADIUM

CLUB OFFICIALS
Owner/President: Malcolm Glazer
Co-Chairman: Bryan Glazer
Co-Chairman: Joel Glazer
Co-Chairman: Edward Glazer
Co-President, Glazer Family Foundation:
   Darcie Glazer-Kassewitz
General Manager: Jason Licht
Chief Operating Officer: Brian Ford
Director of Football Administration:
   Mike Greenberg
Director of Football Operations:
   Shelton Quarles
Director of Football Technology:
   Spencer Dille
Director of Player Engagement:
   Isaiah Harris
Director of Player Personnel: Jon Robinson
Director of College Scouting: Mike Biehl
Director of Pro Scouting: Scott Cohen
Director of Team Security: Henry Duran
National Scout: Rob McCartney
National Scout: Andy Speyer
Pro Scout: Steve West
College Scouts: Andre Forde, Tony
   Hardie, Brian Hudspeth, Byron Kiefer,
   Tony Kinkela, Pat Perles
Scouting Assistants: Donovan Cotton,
   Zach Grossi
Manager of Analytics: Tyler Oberly
Football Technology Specialist:
   Kingsley Osei-Asibey
Chief Financial Officer: Joe Fada
Chief Marketing Officer: Ailey Pennigroth
Chief Ticketing Officer: Ben Milsom
General Legal Counsel: David Cohen
Director of Broadcast Operations: Jeff Ryan
Director of Communications: Nelson Luis
Director of Community Relations:
   Eileen Sweeney
Director of Corporate Security and
   Facilities: Andres Trescastro
Director of Digital: Kevin Corbett
Director of Group Sales: Amy Saxon
Director of Guest/Member Relations:
   Chris Cook
Director of Human Resources:
   Kristin Houston
Director of Information Technology:
   Ed Johnston
Director of New Business Development:
   Matt Kaiser
Director of Sales: Deno Anagost
Director of Special Events and Game
   Operations: Connie Mojallal
Head Athletic Trainer: Bobby Slater
Assistant Athletic Trainer: John Ames
Assistant Athletic Trainer: Adrian Dixon
Team Sports Dietitian: Kevin Luhrs
Head Equipment Manager:
   James Sorenson
Asst. Equipment Manager: Mike Myrick
Video Director: Dave Levy
Asst. Video Director: Chris Bryan
Cheerleading Manager: Tara Battiato
Player Benefits and Alumni Program
   Manager: Jill Hobbs
Senior Business Administration Manager:
   Caleb Quaid
Senior Community Relations Manager:
   Kevin Brown
Senior Game Operations and Special
   Events Manager: Jim Mackes
Senior Luxury Suites Manager:
   Lauren Compton
Senior Public Relations Manager:
   Michael Pehanich
Senior Purchasing Manager: Brian Mathiews
Senior Team Operations Manager:
   Tim Jarocki
Senior Ticket Operations Manager:
   Amy Weber
Senior Writer: Scott Smith
Video Production Manager: Ed Bottger

COACHING HISTORY
(239-371-1)
Records include postseason games
1976-1984 John McKay.................45-91-1
1985-86   Leeman Bennett.............4-28-0
1987-1990 Ray Perkins*.................19-41-0
1990-91   Richard Williamson....4-15-0
1992-95   Sam Wyche 23-41-0
1996-2001 Tony Dungy................56-46-0
2002-08   Jon Gruden.................60-57-0
2009-2011 Raheem Morris 17-31-0
2012-13   Greg Schiano 11-21-0
*Released after 13 games in 1990

PAID ATTENDANCE
Home 420,424   Away 519,777
Total 940,201
Single-game home record,
   73,523 (12/7/97)
Single-season home record,
   545,980 (1979)

2014 DRAFT CHOICES
Round	Name	Pos.	College
1	Mike Evans	WR	Texas A&M
2	Austin Seferian-Jenkins	TE	Washington
3	Charles Sims	RB	West Virginia
5	Kadeem Edwards	G	Tennessee St.
	Kevin Pamphile	T	Purdue
6	Robert Herron	WR	Wyoming

2013 TEAM RECORD
PRESEASON (1-3)

Date	Result		Opponent
08/08	L	16-44	Baltimore
08/16	L	21-25	at New England
08/24	W	17-16	at Miami
08/29	L	12-30	Washington

REGULAR SEASON (4-12)

Date	Result		Opponent
09/08	L	17-18	at New York Jets
09/15	L	14-16	New Orleans
09/22	L	3-23	at New England
09/29	L	10-13	Arizona
10/13	L	20-31	Philadelphia
10/20	L	23-31	at Atlanta
10/24	L	13-31	Carolina
11/03	L	24-27	at Seattle (OT)
11/11	W	22-19	Miami
11/17	W	41-28	Atlanta
11/24	W	24-21	at Detroit
12/01	L	6-27	at Carolina
12/08	W	27-6	Buffalo
12/15	L	14-33	San Francisco
12/22	L	13-23	at St. Louis
12/29	L	17-42	at New Orleans

(OT) Overtime

SCORE BY PERIODS

Buccaneers	80	125	33	50	0	—	288
Opponents	64	140	76	106	3	—	389

2013 TEAM STATISTICS

	Buccaneers	Opp.
Total First Downs	269	324
Rushing	75	95
Passing	157	190
Penalty	37	39
3rd Down: Made/Att	69/221	80/204
3rd Down Pct.	31.2	39.2
4th Down: Made/Att	8/22	8/14
4th Down Pct.	36.4	57.1
Possession Avg.	29:24	30:36
Total Net Yards	4432	5568
Avg. Per Game	277.0	348.0
Total Plays	981	1020
Avg. Per Play	4.5	5.5
Net Yards Rushing	1612	1762
Avg. Per Game	100.8	110.1
Total Rushes	420	438
Net Yards Passing	2820	3806
Avg. Per Game	176.3	237.9
Sacked/Yards Lost	47/361	35/255
Gross Yards	3181	4061
Att./Completions	514/291	547/352
Completion Pct.	56.6	64.4
Had Intercepted	12	21
Punts/Average	87/44.2	68/44.1
Net Punting Avg.	87/38.3	68/39.0
Penalties/Yards	121/1136	105/1012
Fumbles/Ball Lost	18/9	18/10
Touchdowns	31	42
Rushing	6	10
Passing	22	30
Returns	3	2

2013 INDIVIDUAL STATISTICS

PASSING

	Att.	Comp.	Yds.	Pct.	TD	Int.	Tkld.	Rate
Glennon	416	247	2608	59.4	19	9	40/314	83.9
Freeman	94	43	571	45.7	2	3	7/47	59.3
Koenen	2	0	0	0.0	0	0	0/0	39.6
James	1	1	2	100.0	1	0	0/0	118.8
Rainey	1	0	0	0.0	0	0	0/0	39.6
Buccaneers	514	291	3181	56.6	22	12	47/361	79.6
Opponents	547	352	4061	64.4	30	21	35/255	88.9

SCORING

	TD R	TD P	TD Rt	PAT	FG	Saf	PTS
Lindell	0	0	0	31/31	23/29	0	100
Jackson	0	7	0	0/0	0/0	0	42
Rainey	5	1	0	0/0	0/0	0	36
Wright	0	5	0	0/0	0/0	0	30
Underwood	0	4	0	0/0	0/0	0	24
M. Foster	0	0	2	0/0	0/0	0	12
Williams	0	2	0	0/0	0/0	0	12
Crabtree	0	1	0	0/0	0/0	0	6
Johnson	0	0	1	0/0	0/0	0	6
Martin	1	0	0	0/0	0/0	0	6
Ogletree	0	1	0	0/0	0/0	0	6
Penn	0	1	0	0/0	0/0	0	6
David	0	0	0	0/0	0/0	1	2
Buccaneers	6	22	3	31/31	23/29	1	288
Opponents	10	30	2	40/40	31/32	1	389

2-Pt Conversions: Buccaneers 0-0, Opponents 1-2

RUSHING

	No.	Yds	Avg	LG	TD
Rainey	137	532	3.9	80t	5
Martin	127	456	3.6	28	1
James	60	295	4.9	24	0
Leonard	47	182	3.9	24	0
Glennon	27	37	1.4	16	0
Hill	9	23	2.6	10	0
Goldson	1	22	22.0	22	0
Freeman	5	20	4.0	13	0
Dawson	2	15	7.5	14	0
Demps	1	14	14.0	14	0
Page	2	14	7.0	19	0
Wright	1	2	2.0	2	0
Jackson	1	0	0.0	0	0
Buccaneers	420	1612	3.8	80t	6
Opponents	438	1762	4.0	56	10

RECEIVING

	No.	Yds	Avg	LG	TD
Jackson	78	1224	15.7	60	7
Wright	54	571	10.6	36	5
Leonard	29	179	6.2	19	0
Underwood	24	440	18.3	85t	4
Williams	22	216	9.8	28	2
Owusu	13	114	8.8	20	0
Martin	12	66	5.5	13	0
Lorig	11	47	4.3	20	0
Rainey	11	27	2.5	11	1
James	10	43	4.3	20	0
Ogletree	8	70	8.8	20	1
Page	4	68	17.0	30	0
Crabtree	4	21	5.3	14	1
Byham	3	38	12.7	34	0
Demps	3	21	7.0	10	0
Hill	2	23	11.5	12	0
Dawson	2	12	6.0	9	0
Penn	1	1	1.0	1t	1
Buccaneers	291	3181	10.9	85t	22
Opponents	352	4061	11.5	80t	30

INTERCEPTIONS

	No.	Yds	Avg	LG	TD
David	5	87	17.4	32	0
M. Foster	3	122	40.7	85t	2
Tandy	3	42	14.0	20	0
Banks	3	33	11.0	18	0
Barron	2	3	1.5	3	0
Revis	2	3	1.5	3	0
Johnson	1	48	48.0	48t	1
Goldson	1	0	0.0	0	0
Watson	1	0	0.0	0	0
Buccaneers	21	338	16.1	85t	3
Opponents	12	135	11.3	38	0

PUNTING

	No.	Yds.	Avg.	In 20	LG
Koenen	87	3846	44.2	19	62
Buccaneers	87	3846	44.2	19	62
Opponents	68	3002	44.1	32	84

PUNT RETURNS

	Ret	FC	Yds	Avg	LG	TD
Page	23	20	251	10.9	52	0
Dawson	1	0	17	17.0	17	0
Buccaneers	24	20	268	11.2	52	0
Opponents	35	20	393	11.2	71	0

KICKOFF RETURNS

	No.	Yds	Avg	LG	TD
Page	22	548	24.9	44	0
Demps	4	93	23.3	29	0
Dawson	3	67	22.3	25	0
Martin	1	40	40.0	40	0
Ogletree	1	25	25.0	25	0
S. Larsen	1	17	17.0	17	0
Rainey	1	15	15.0	15	0
Lorig	1	6	6.0	6	0
Buccaneers	34	811	23.9	44	0
Opponents	24	452	18.8	30	0

FIELD GOALS

	1-19	20-29	30-39	40-49	50+
Lindell	0/0	3/3	12/14	4/6	4/6
Buccaneers	0/0	3/3	12/14	4/6	4/6
Opponents	0/0	10/10	5/5	14/15	2/2

SACKS

	No.
McCoy	9.5
David	7.0
Clayborn	5.5
Barron	2.0
M. Foster	2.0
Gholston	2.0
Watson	2.0
M. Adams	1.0
Bowers	1.0
Landri	1.0
Revis	1.0
Spence	1.0
Buccaneers	35.0
Opponents	47.0

RECORD HOLDERS
INDIVIDUAL RECORDS—CAREER

Category	Name	Performance
Rushing (Yds.)	James Wilder, 1981-89	5,957
Passing (Yds.)	Vinny Testaverde, 1987-1992	14,820
Passing (TDs)	Josh Freeman, 2009-2013	80
Receiving (No.)	James Wilder, 1981-89	430
Receiving (Yds.)	Mark Carrier, 1987-1992	5,018
Interceptions	Ronde Barber, 1997-2012	47
Punting (Avg.)	Michael Koenen, 2011-13	44.8
Punt Return (Avg.)	Clifton Smith, 2008	14.1
Kickoff Return (Avg.)	Aaron Stecker, 2000-03	23.8
Field Goals	Martín Gramatica, 1999-2004	137
Touchdowns (Tot.)	Mike Alstott, 1996-2006	71
Points	Martín Gramatica, 1999-2004	592
*Sacks	Warren Sapp, 1995-2003	77.0

INDIVIDUAL RECORDS—SINGLE SEASON

Category	Name	Performance
Rushing (Yds.)	James Wilder, 1984	1,544
Passing (Yds.)	Josh Freeman, 2012	4,065
Passing (TDs)	Josh Freeman, 2012	27
Receiving (No.)	Keyshawn Johnson, 2001	106
Receiving (Yds.)	Mark Carrier, 1989	1,422
Interceptions	Ronde Barber, 2001	10
Punting (Avg.)	Josh Bidwell, 2005	45.6
Punt Return (Avg.)	Karl Williams, 1996	21.1
Kickoff Return (Avg.)	Sammie Stroughter, 2009	29.5
Field Goals	Martín Gramatica, 2002	32
	Matt Bryant, 2008	32
Touchdowns (Tot.)	James Wilder, 1984	13
Points	Matt Bryant, 2008	131
*Sacks	Warren Sapp, 2000	16.5

INDIVIDUAL RECORDS—SINGLE GAME

Category	Name	Performance
Rushing (Yds.)	Doug Martin, 11-4-12	251
Passing (Yds.)	Doug Williams, 11-16-80	486
Passing (TDs)	Steve DeBerg, 9-13-87	5
	Brad Johnson, 11-3-02	5
	Josh Freeman, 12-26-10	5
Receiving (No.)	James Wilder, 9-15-85	13
	Earnest Graham, 10-21-07	13
Receiving (Yds.)	Vincent Jackson, 10-21-12	216
Interceptions	Ronde Barber, 12-23-01, 12-4-05	3
	Aqib Talib, 9-21-08	3
Field Goals	Martín Gramatica, 12-29-02	5
Touchdowns (Tot.)	Jimmie Giles, 10-20-85	4
	Doug Martin, 11-4-12	4
Points	Jimmie Giles, 10-20-85	24
*Sacks	Marcus Jones, 10-19-00	4.0
	Simeon Rice, 10-12-03	4.0

*Sacks became an official statistic in 1982.

TAMPA BAY BUCCANEERS

2014 VETERAN ROSTER

No.	Name	Pos.	Ht.	Wt.	Birthdate	NFL Exp.	College	Hometown	How Acq.	'13 Games/ Starts
+	Adams, Kyle	TE	6-4	255	1/19/88	4	Purdue	Austin, Texas	FA-'13	6/1*
#	Adams, Michael	CB	5-8	181	6/17/85	8	Louisiana-Lafayette	Dallas, Texas	FA-'13	6/0
86	Baker, Josh	FB	6-3	244	12/25/86	2	Northwest Missouri State	Chesapeake, Va.	FA-'14	0*
27	Banks, Johnthan	CB	6-2	185	10/3/89	2	Mississippi State	Maben, Miss.	D2-'13	16/16
23	Barron, Mark	S	6-2	213	10/27/89	3	Alabama	Mobile, Ala.	D1a-'12	14/14
10	Barth, Connor	K	5-11	200	4/11/86	6	North Carolina	Wilmington, N.C.	FA-'09	0*
91	Bowers, Da'Quan	DE	6-4	288	2/23/90	4	Clemson	Bamberg, S.C.	D2-'11	13/2
+	Byham, Nate	TE	6-4	264	6/27/88	5	Pittsburgh	Franklin, Pa.	FA-'12	4/3
44	Cain, Jeremy	LS	6-1	245	3/24/80	9	Massachusetts	Boynton Beach, Fla.	FA-'14	2/0*
33	Carr, Deveron	CB	5-11	190	8/10/90	2	Arizona State	Scottsdale, Ariz.	FA-'13	9/0
52	Casillas, Jonathan	LB	6-1	227	6/3/87	6	Wisconsin	New Brunswick, N.J.	UFA(NO)-'13	12/4
94	Clayborn, Adrian	DE	6-3	280	7/6/88	4	Iowa	St. Louis, Mo.	D1-'11	16/16
73	Collins, Anthony	T	6-5	315	11/2/85	7	Kansas	Beaumont, Tex.	UFA(Cin)-'14	15/7*
75	Cousins, Oniel	G	6-4	315	6/29/84	7	Texas El-Paso	Fullerton, Calif.	UFA(Cle)-'14	16/4*
84	Crabtree, Tom	TE	6-4	245	11/4/85	5	Miami (Ohio)	Carroll, Ohio	UFA(GB)-'13	7/5
#	Cutrera, Jacob	LB	6-3	238	5/18/88	4	Louisiana State	Lafayette, La.	FA-'11	0*
54	David, Lavonte	LB	6-1	233	1/23/90	3	Nebraska	Miami, Fla.	D2-'12	16/16
18	Dawson, Skye	WR	5-9	183	12/2/90	2	Texas Christian	Mesquite, Texas	FA-'13	7/0
32	Demps, Jeff	RB	5-7	191	1/8/90	2	Florida	Okahumpka, Fla.	T(NE)-'13	2/0
62	Dietrich-Smith, Evan	C	6-2	308	7/19/86	5	Idaho State	Salinas, Calif.	UFA(GB)-'14	16/16*
69	Dotson, Demar	T	6-9	315	10/11/85	6	Southern Miss	Alexandria, La.	FA-'09	16/16
48	# Economos, Andrew	LS	6-1	250	6/24/82	9	Georgia Tech	Atlanta, Ga.	FA-'06	16/0
50	Fletcher, Dane	LB	6-2	245	9/14/86	5	Montana State	Bozeman, Mont.	UFA(NE)-'14	15/1*
59	Foster, Mason	LB	6-1	241	3/1/89	4	Washington	Seaside, Calif.	D3-'11	15/13
26	Gaitor, Anthony	CB	5-10	182	10/9/88	3	Florida International	Miami, Fla.	D7a-'11	0*
92	Gholston, William	DE	6-6	281	7/31/91	2	Michigan State	Detroit, Mich.	D4b-'13	12/2
95	# Gibson, Gary	DT	6-3	312	5/5/82	8	Rutgers	Lafayette, N.Y.	UFA(StL)-'12	13/1
58	Glaud, Ka'Lial	LB	6-2	220	11/9/90	2	Rutgers	Atco, N.J.	FA-'13	7/0
8	Glennon, Mike	QB	6-6	225	12/12/89	2	North Carolina State	Centreville, Va.	D3-'13	13/13
38	Goldson, Dashon	S	6-2	200	9/18/84	8	Washington	Carson, Calif.	UFA(SF)-'13	13/13
36	Gorrer, Danny	CB	6-0	180	6/1/86	5	Texas A&M	Port Arthur, Texas	W(Sea)-'12	7/0
15	Hawkins, Lavelle	WR	5-11	194	7/12/86	7	California	Stockton, Calif.	UFA(SD)-'14	4/0*
72	Hunter, David	DL	6-2	301	9/19/89	2	Houston	Houston, Texas	FA-'14	0*
83	Jackson, Vincent	WR	6-5	230	1/14/83	10	Northern Colorado	Colorado Springs, Colo.	UFA(SD)-'12	16/16
25	James, Mike	RB	5-10	223	4/13/91	2	Miami	Haines City, Fla.	D6-'13	8/3
24	Jenkins, Mike	CB	5-10	197	3/22/85	7	South Florida	Bradenton, Fla.	UFA(Oak)-'14	15/15*
29	Johnson, Leonard	CB	5-10	202	3/30/90	3	Iowa State	Clearwater, Fla.	FA-'12	16/8
90	Johnson, Michael	DE	6-7	270	2/7/87	6	Georgia Tech	Plantersville, Ala.	UFA(Cin)-'14	15/15*
3	Kafka, Mike	QB	6-3	225	7/25/87	3	Northwestern	Chicago, Ill.	FA-'14	0*
9	Koenen, Michael	P	5-11	198	7/13/82	10	Western Washington	Ferndale, Wash.	UFA(Atl)-'11	16/0
46	Lane, Jorvorskie	FB	5-11	258	2/4/87	2	Texas A&M	Lufkin, Texas	FA-'14	0*
51	Lansanah, Danny	LB	6-1	245	8/28/85	3	Connecticut	Harrisburg, Pa.	FA-'13	1/0
#	Leonard, Brian	RB	6-1	225	2/3/84	8	Rutgers	Gouverneur, N.Y.	UFA(Cin)-'13	16/1
4	# Lindell, Rian	K	6-3	227	1/20/77	15	Washington State	Vancouver, Wash.	FA-'13	16/0
87	Maneri, Steve	TE	6-7	280	3/20/88	4	Temple	Saddle Brook, N.J.	FA-'14	4/1*
22	Martin, Doug	RB	5-9	215	1/13/89	3	Boise State	Oakland, Calif.	D1b-'12	6/6
65	Masifilo, Matthew	DT	6-3	280	10/1/89	3	Stanford	Ewa Beach, Hawaii	FA-'12	0*
12	McCown, Josh	QB	6-4	213	7/4/79	12	Sam Houston State	Jacksonville, Texas	UFA(Chi)-'14	8/5*
93	McCoy, Gerald	DT	6-4	300	2/25/88	5	Oklahoma	Oklahoma City, Okla.	D1-'10	16/16
35	McCray, Kelcie	S	6-1	205	9/21/88	3	Arkansas State	Columbus, Ga.	W(Mia)-'13	15/0*
98	McDonald, Clinton	DT	6-2	297	1/6/87	6	Memphis	Jacksonville, Ark.	UFA(Sea)-'14	15/1*
49	McDougald, Bradley	S	6-1	209	11/15/90	2	Kansas	Dublin, Ohio	W(KC)-'13	4/0*
96	Means, Steven	DE	6-3	260	9/16/90	2	Buffalo	Buffalo, N.Y.	D5-'13	10/0
79	Meredith, Jamon	G/T	6-5	312	5/11/86	6	South Carolina	Simpsonville, S.C.	UFA(Pitt)-'12	16/8
30	Moore, D.J.	CB	5-9	190	3/22/87	6	Vanderbilt	Spartanburg, S.C.	FA-'14	2/0*
11	Murphy Jr., Louis	WR	6-2	200	5/11/87	6	Florida	St. Petersburg, Fla.	UFA(NYG)-'14	14/0*
82	Myers, Brandon	TE	6-3	256	9/4/85	6	Iowa	Prairie City, Iowa	UFA(NYG)-'14	16/14*
77	Nicks, Carl	G	6-5	349	5/14/85	7	Nebraska	Salinas, Calif.	UFA(NO)-'12	2/2
66	Omameh, Patrick	G	6-4	305	12/29/89	2	Michigan	Columbus, Ohio	FA-'13	0*
80	Owusu, Chris	WR	6-2	200	1/6/90	3	Stanford	Westlake Village, Calif.	FA-'12	9/4
17	Page, Eric	WR	5-10	180	9/23/91	2	Toledo	Toledo, Ohio	FA-'13	16/1
45	Pryor, Lonnie	FB/RB	6-0	224	2/22/90	2	Florida State	Okeechobee, Fla.	FA-'13	0*
43	Rainey, Bobby	RB	5-8	212	10/16/87	3	Western Kentucky	Griffin, Ga.	W(Cle)-'13	15/6*
89	Shepard, Russell	WR	6-1	195	9/17/90	2	Louisiana State	Houston, Texas	W(Phil)-'13	14/0
34	Smith, Michael	RB	5-9	205	8/9/88	2	Utah State	Tucson, Ariz.	D7a-'12	0*
60	Solomon, Scott	DL	6-3	262	11/5/88	3	Rice	San Antonio, Texas	FA-'13	1/0*
97	Spence, Akeem	DT	6-1	307	11/29/91	2	Illinois	Fort Walton Beach, Fla.	D4a-'13	16/14

No.	Name	Pos.	Ht.	Wt.	Birthdate	NFL Exp.	College	Hometown	How Acq.	'13 Games/ Starts
88	Stocker, Luke	TE	6-5	253	7/17/88	4	Tennessee	Berea, Ky.	D4-'11	2/2
37	Tandy, Keith	DB	5-10	205	2/12/89	3	West Virginia	Hopkinsville, Ky.	D6-'12	16/5
	#Te'o-Nesheim, Daniel	DE	6-3	263	6/12/87	5	Washington	Kameula, Hawaii	FA-'11	16/12
21	Verner, Alterraun	CB	5-10	187	12/13/88	5	UCLA	Lakewood, Calif.	UFA(Tenn)-'14	16/16*
31	Wright, Major	S	5-11	204	7/1/88	5	Florida	Miramar, Fla.	UFA(Chi)-'14	15/15*
81	Wright, Tim	TE	6-4	220	4/7/90	2	Rutgers	Wall Township, N.J.	FA-'13	16/8

* Adams played one game with Chicago and five games with Tampa Bay in '13; Baker last active with N.Y. Jets in '11; Barth missed '13 season because of injury; Cain played two games with Chicago; Collins played 15 games with Cincinnati; Cousins played 16 games with Cleveland; Cutrera missed '13 season because of injury; Dietrich-Smith played 16 games with Green Bay; Fletcher played 15 games with New England; Gaitor missed '13 season because of injury; Hawkins played four games with San Diego; Hunter inactive one game with Houston in '12; Jenkins played 15 games with Oakland; M. Johnson played 15 games with Cincinnati; Kafka last active with Philadelphia in '11; Lane last active with Miami in '12; Maneri played four games with Chicago; Masifilo inactive for two games; McCown played eight games with Chicago; McCray played four games with Miami and 11 games with Tampa Bay; McDonald played 15 games with Seattle; McDougald played one game with Kansas City and three games with Tampa Bay; Moore played two games with Carolina; Murphy Jr. played 14 games with the New York Giants; Myers played 16 games with the New York Giants; Omameh inactive for 12 games; Pryor inactive for six games; Rainey played six games with Cleveland and nine games with Tampa Bay; Smith missed '13 season because of injury; Solomon played one game with the New York Jets; Verner played 16 games with Tennessee; Wright played 15 games with Chicago.

+ Restricted Free Agent; subject to developments.

Unrestricted Free Agent; subject to developments.

Traded—WR Mike Williams (6 games in '13) to Buffalo, C/G Jeremy Zuttah (16) to Baltimore.

Players lost through free agency (6): LB Adam Hayward (Wash; 16 games in '13), G/C Ted Larsen (Ariz; 13), FB Erik Lorig (NO; 15), QB Dan Orlovsky (Det; 2), WR Tiquan Underwood (Car; 12), LB Dekoda Watson (Jax; 15).

Also played with Buccaneers in '13—S Ahmad Black (4 games), G/T Gabe Carimi (14), QB Josh Freeman (3), RB Michael Hill (6), G Davin Joseph (16), DT Derek Landri (9), WR Kevin Ogletree (4), T Donald Penn (16), CB Darrelle Revis (16), DE Trevor Scott (4).

FIRST-YEAR ROSTER

Name	Pos.	Ht.	Wt.	Birthdate	College	Hometown	How Acq.
Allen, Josh	G	6-3	315	12/30/91	Louisiana-Monroe	Cedar Hill, Texas	FA
Anthony, Marc (1)	CB	5-11	196	11/14/89	California	Chandler, Ariz.	FA-'13
Askew, Nate	LB	6-4	235	8/20/91	Texas A&M	San Antonio, Texas	FA
Burks, Aaron	WR	6-3	205	9/23/90	Boise State	Grand Prairie, Texas	FA
Cummings, Euclid	DT	6-4	275	5/6/91	Georgia Tech	Atlanta, Ga.	FA
Daniels, Jace (1)	OL	6-4	300	3/6/90	Northern Michigan	Escanaba, Mich.	FA-'13
Dawkins, Everett (1)	DT	6-2	300	6/13/90	Florida State	Spartanburg, S.C.	FA-'13
Edwards, Kadeem	G	6-4	313	1/24/91	Tennessee State	Sanford, Fla.	D5a
Evans, Mike	WR	6-5	231	8/21/93	Texas A&M	Galveston, Texas	D1
Foster, Jason (1)	G	6-3	300	10/21/88	Rhode Island	East Pittsford, Vt.	FA
Herron, Robert	WR	5-9	193	6/2/92	Wyoming	Los Angeles, Calif.	D6
Lewis, Keith	CB	6-1	190	3/28/89	Virginia-Lynchburg	Chicago, Ill.	FA
Miller, Andrew	G	6-4	296	4/24/90	Virginia Tech	Bassett, Va.	FA
Munoz, Damaso (1)	LB	5-11	219	7/10/86	Rutgers	Miami, Fla.	FA
Murray, Patrick (1)	K	5-7	160	6/22/91	Fordham	Mahwah, N.J.	FA
Pamphile, Kevin	T	6-5	315	11/27/90	Purdue	Miami, Fla.	D5b
Patchan, Matt	T	6-7	300	4/2/90	Boston College	Tampa, Fla.	FA
Patton, Solomon	WR	5-9	169	10/17/90	Florida	Mobile, Ala.	FA
Schum, Jacob (1)	P	5-11	210	1/11/89	Buffalo	Hamburg, N.Y,	FA
Seferian-Jenkins, Austin	TE	6-5	262	9/29/92	Washington	Fox Island, Wash	D2
Sims, Charles	RB	6-0	214	9/17/90	West Virginia	Houston, Texas	D3
Smith, Brett	QB	6-3	206	6/8/92	Wyoming	Salem, Ore.	FA
Sutton, Chaz	DE	6-5	263	9/7/89	South Carolina	Savannah, Ga.	FA
Swaim, Mycal	S	6-4	215	11/6/90	Eastern Michigan	Chico, Calif.	FA

The term NFL Rookie is defined as a player who is in his first season of professional football and has not been on the roster of another professional football team for any regular-season or postseason games. A Rookie is designated by an "R" on NFL rosters. Players who have been active in another professional football league or players who have NFL experience, including either preseason training camp or being on an Active List or Inactive List, or on Reserve/Injured or Reserve/Physically Unable to Perform for fewer than six regular-season games, are termed NFL First-Year Players. An NFL First-Year Player is designated by a "1" on NFL rosters. Thereafter, a player is credited with an additional year of experience for each season in which he accumulates six games on the Active List or Inactive List, or on Reserve/Injured or Reserve/Physically Unable to Perform.

Log on to www.buccaneers.com for an up-to-date roster.

TAMPA BAY BUCCANEERS

COACHING STAFF

Head Coach,
Lovie Smith

Pro Career: Named the 10th head coach in franchise history on January 2, 2014. Lovie Smith joins the Buccaneers after having spent nine seasons as the head coach of the Chicago Bears (2004-2012). During his tenure, Smith led Chicago to an 81-63 (.563) regular season record, while going 3-3 in the postseason. He led the Bears to three division titles, two NFC Championship Game appearances and the 2006 NFC title, which propelled Chicago to its first Super Bowl appearance in 21 years. Smith left Chicago ranked third all-time in coaching victories, behind only Hall of Famers George Halas and Mike Ditka. Prior to his time with Chicago, Smith spent three seasons as the defensive coordinator for the St. Louis Rams (2001-03), helping the team return to the Super Bowl in 2001. Smith began his NFL career in Tampa Bay, working on Tony Dungy's staff (1996-2000). Career record: 84-66.

Background: Played linebacker and safety at Tulsa (1976-79), earning two-time All-America and three-time All-Missouri Conference honors. Coached at Big Sandy (Texas) High School in 1980 and Cascia Hall Prep in Tulsa (1981-82). Smith then began coaching collegiately, working at Tulsa (1983-86), Wisconsin (1987), Arizona State (1988-1991), Kentucky (1992), Tennessee (1993-94) and Ohio State (1995).

Personal: Born on May 8, 1958 in Gladewater, Texas. He and his wife, MaryAnne, have three sons, Mikal, Matthew and Miles, and eight grandchildren.

ASSISTANT COACHES

Marcus Arroyo, quarterbacks; born January 23, 1980, Sacramento, Calif. Quarterback San Jose State 1998-2002. No pro playing experience. College coach: San Jose State 2003, 2005-08, Prairie View A&M 2004, Wyoming 2009-2010, California 2011-12, Southern Mississippi 2013. Pro coach: Joined Buccaneers in 2014.

Dave Borgonzi, defensive quality control; born November 19, 1982, Everett, Mass. Linebacker Amherst College 2002-05. No pro playing experience. College coach: Syracuse 2006-07, Harvard 2008-2010. Pro coach: Dallas Cowboys 2011-13, joined Buccaneers in 2014.

Gill Byrd, cornerbacks; born February 20, 1961, San Francisco, Calif. Cornerback San Jose State 1978-1982. Pro cornerback San Diego Chargers 1983-1992. Pro coach: St. Louis Rams 2003-05, Chicago Bears 2006-2012, joined Buccaneers in 2014.

Joe Cullen, defensive line; born December 15, 1967, Quincy, Mass. Defensive lineman Massachusetts 1986-89. No pro playing experience. College coach: Massachusetts 1990-91, Richmond, 1992-98, 2000, Louisiana State 1999, Memphis 2001, Indiana 2002-04, Illinois 2005, Idaho State 2009. Pro coach: Detroit Lions 2006-08, Jacksonville Jaguars 2010-12, Cleveland Browns 2013, joined Buccaneers in 2014.

Jon Embree, tight ends; born October 15, 1965, Los Angeles, Calif. Tight end Colorado

1983-86. Pro tight end Los Angeles Rams 1987-89. College coach: Colorado 1991, 1993-2002, 2011-12 (head coach), UCLA 2003-05. Pro coach: Kansas City Chiefs 2006-08, Washington Redskins 2010, Cleveland Browns 2013, joined Buccaneers in 2014.

Leslie Frazier, defensive coordinator; born April 3, 1959, Columbus, Miss. Cornerback Alcorn State 1977-1980. Pro cornerback Chicago Bears 1981-85. College coach: Trinity International 1988-1996, Illinois 1997-98. Pro coach: Philadelphia Eagles 1999-2002, Cincinnati Bengals 2003-04, Indianapolis Colts 2005-06, Minnesota Vikings 2007-2013 (head coach 2011-13), joined Buccaneers in 2014.

Andrew Hayes-Stoker, wide receivers; born January 9, 1979, Arlington, Texas. Running back Texas Christian 1999-2002. No pro playing experience. College coach: Texas A&M 2005-06, Florida International 2013. Pro coach: Chicago Bears 2006-2012, joined Buccaneers in 2014.

Dave Kennedy, head strength & conditioning coach; born November 15, 1960, Omaha, Neb. Attended Nebraska. No collegiate or pro playing experience. College coach: Nebraska, 1982-88, 2004-07, Ohio State, 1989-2001, Pittsburgh 2002-03, Texas A&M 2008-2012. Pro coach: Joined Buccaneers in 2014.

Larry Marmie, senior defensive assistant; born October 17, 1942, Barnesville, Ohio. Quarterback Eastern Kentucky 1962-65. No pro playing experience. College coach: Morehead State 1968-1971, Eastern Kentucky 1972-76, Tulsa 1977-78, North Carolina 1979-1982, Tennessee 1983-84, 1992-94, Arizona State 1985-1991 (head coach 1988-1991), UCLA 1995. Pro coach: Arizona Cardinals 1996-2003, St. Louis Rams 2004-05, Seattle Seahawks 2006-08, Las Vegas Locomotives (United Football League) 2010-12, joined Buccaneers in 2014.

Hardy Nickerson, linebackers; born September 1, 1965, Compton, Calif. Linebacker California 1983-86. Pro linebacker Pittsburgh Steelers 1987-1992, Tampa Bay Buccaneers 1993-99, Jacksonville Jaguars 2000-01, Green Bay Packers 2002. Pro coach: Chicago Bears 2007, joined Buccaneers in 2014.

Kevin O'Dea, special teams coordinator; born June 9, 1960, Williamsport, Pa. Wide receiver/defensive back Lock Haven 1984-85. No pro playing experience. College coach: Lock Haven 1986, Cornell 1987, Virginia 1988-1990, Penn State 1991-93 Pro coach: San Diego Chargers 1994-95, Tampa Bay Buccaneers 1996-2001, Detroit Lions 2002-03, Arizona Cardinals 2004-05, Chicago Bears 2006-07, 2011-12, N.Y. Jets 2008-09, Kansas City Chiefs 2013, re-joined Buccaneers in 2014.

Mike Phair, asst. defensive line; November 8, 1969, Mesa, Ariz. Cornerback Mesa (Ariz.) C.C. 1988-89, Arizona State 1990-91. No pro playing experience. College coach: Arizona State 1999-2000, Tiffin 2001. Pro coach: Seattle Seahawks 2008-2010, Chicago Bears 2011-13, joined Buccaneers in 2014.

Carlos Polk, asst. special teams; born February 22, 1977, Memphis, Tenn. Linebacker Nebraska 1997-2000. Pro linebacker San Diego Chargers

2001-07, Dallas Cowboys 2008. College coach: Grossmont (Calif.) C.C. 2009. Pro coach: San Diego Chargers 2010-12, Dallas Cowboys 2013, joined Buccaneers in 2014.

Mikal Smith, safeties; born November 16, 1976, Dallas, Texas. Safety Arizona 1995-96. No pro playing experience. College coach: Trinity International 2006-07. Pro coach: Chicago Bears 2010-12, Dallas Cowboys 2013, joined Buccaneers in 2014.

Tim Spencer, running backs; born December 10, 1960, Martins Ferry, Ohio. Running back Ohio State 1979-1982. Pro running back Chicago Blitz (USFL) 1983, Arizona Wranglers (USFL) 1984, Memphis Showboats (USFL) 1985, San Diego Chargers 1985-1990. College coach: Ohio State 1994-2003. Pro coach: Chicago Bears 2004-2012, joined Buccaneers in 2014.

Ben Steele, offensive quality control; born May 27, 1978, Denver, Colo. Tight end Fort Lewis College 1997-98, Mesa State 1999-2000. Pro tight end San Francisco 49ers 2001-02, Oakland Raiders 2002, Seattle Seahawks 2003, Minnesota Vikings 2003-04, Green Bay Packers 2004-05, Houston Texans 2006-07. College coach: Mesa State 2008, Colorado 2009-2010, California, 2011-12, UC Davis 2013. Pro coach: Joined Buccaneers in 2014.

Jeff Tedford, offensive coordinator; born November 21, 1961, Lynwood, Calif. Quarterback Cerritos (Calif.) C.C. 1979-1980, Fresno State 1981-82. Pro quarterback Hamilton Tiger-Cats (CFL) 1983-85, Calgary Stampeders (CFL) 1986, Saskatchewan Roughriders (CFL) 1987, Winnipeg Blue Bombers (CFL) 1988. College coach: Fresno State 1987-88, 1992-97, Oregon 1998-2001, California 2002-2012 (head coach). Pro coach: Calgary Stampeders (CFL) 1989-1991, joined Buccaneers in 2014.

Joe Vaughn, asst. strength and conditioning; born November 14, 1982, Del City, Okla. Center Northeastern Oklahoma 2001-02, Kansas 2003-04. No pro playing experience. College coach: Kansas 2006, 2007-2011, Oklahoma 2007. Pro coach: Joined Buccaneers in 2012.

Chad Wade, asst. strength and conditioning coach; born December, 5, 1973, Weeping Water, Neb. Offensive line Nebraska-Wesleyan 1992-94. No pro playing experience. College coach: Nebraska 1996-2013. Pro coach: Joined Buccaneers in 2014.

George Warhop, offensive line; born September 19, 1961, Riverside, Calif. Offensive line Mount San Jacinto (Calif.) J.C. 1979-1980, Cincinnati 1981-82 No pro playing experience. College coach: Cincinnati 1983, Kansas 1984-86, Vanderbilt 1987-89, New Mexico 1990, Southern Methodist 1993, Boston College 1994-95. Pro coach: London Monarchs (NFL Europe), St. Louis Rams 1996-97, Arizona Cardinals 1998-2002, Dallas Cowboys 2003-04, San Francisco 49ers 2005-08, Cleveland Browns 2009-2013, joined Buccaneers in 2014.

Matt Wiegand, asst. offensive line; born March 1, 1983. Offensive line La Verne 2004-06. No pro playing experience. College coach: Claremont-Mudd Scripps 2007, Occidental 2008, Utah 2009-2010, California 2011-12, UC Davis 2013. Pro coach: Los Angeles Avengers (AFL) 2008, joined Buccaneers in 2014.

**National Football Conference
East Division
Team Colors:** Burgundy and Gold
**Redskins Park
21300 Redskins Park Drive
Ashburn, Virginia 20147
Telephone:** (703) 726-7000

2014 SCHEDULE
PRESEASON
Aug. 7	**New England**	7:30
Aug. 18	**Cleveland**	8:00
Aug. 23	at Baltimore	7:30
Aug. 28	at Tampa Bay	7:30

REGULAR SEASON
Sep. 7	at Houston	1:00
Sep. 14	**Jacksonville**	1:00
Sep. 21	at Philadelphia	1:00
Sep. 25	**New York Giants** (Thu)	8:25
Oct. 6	**Seattle** (Mon)	8:30
Oct. 12	at Arizona	4:25
Oct. 19	**Tennessee**	1:00
Oct. 27	at Dallas (Mon)	8:30
Nov. 2	at Minnesota	1:00
Nov. 9	BYE	
Nov. 16	**Tampa Bay**	1:00
Nov. 23	at San Francisco	4:25
Nov. 30	at Indianapolis	1:00
Dec. 7	**St. Louis**	1:00
Dec. 14	at New York Giants	1:00
Dec. 20	**Philadelphia** (Sat)	TBD
Dec. 28	**Dallas**	1:00

All times ET

Stadium: FedExField (opened in 1997)
  • **Capacity:** 85,000
  1600 FedEx Way
  Landover, Maryland 20785
Playing Surface: Natural Grass
Training Camp: Bon Secours Washington
  Redskins Training Center
  Richmond, Virginia 23220

FEDEXFIELD

CLUB OFFICIALS
Owner: Daniel M. Snyder
Executive Vice President/General
  Manager: Bruce Allen
Executive Vice President/Head Coach:
  Mike Shanahan
Chief Marketing Officer: Mitch Gershman
President, Business Operations:
  Dennis Greene
Senior Vice President, Executive
  Producer of Media: Larry Michael
Senior Vice President, Stadium
  Operations: Lon Rosenberg
Senior Vice President, Chief Strategy
  Officer: Shripal Shah
Senior Vice President, Communications:
  Tony Wyllie
Vice President, Football Administration/
  General Counsel: Eric Schaffer
Vice President, Corporate Controller:
  Stephen Choi
Vice President, Sales: Jason Friedman
Vice President, Sales and Marketing:
  Nancy Hubacher
Vice President, Information Technology:
  Asheesh Kinra
Vice President, Sales and Marketing:
  Rod Nenner
Vice President, Ticket Operations:
  Jeff Ritter
Vice President, Business Operations and
  Executive Entertainment:
  John Schlieman
Vice President, Sales, Marketing and
  Strategic Alliances: Scott Shepherd
Vice President, Finance: Joe Smilari
Vice President, Administration:
  Aaron Waller
Director of Player Personnel:
  Scott Campbell
Director of Pro Personnel:
  Morocco Brown
Pro Scouts: Richard Mann II, Alex Santos
College Scouts: Tim Gribble, Kyle Smith,
  Cole Spencer, David Whittington,
  Jim Zeches
BLESTO Scout: Darryl Franklin
Director of Football Operations: Paul Kelly
Senior Executive: A.J. Smith
Director of Player Development:
  Malcolm Blacken
Executive Director, Washington Redskins
  Charitable Foundation: Jane Rodgers
Head Athletic Trainer: Larry Hess
Assistant Athletic Trainers: Elliott Jermyn,
  Eli Bisnett-Cobb, Kyle Blackman
Video Director: Mike Bracken
Video Department: Zachary Kennedy,
  Mike Adams
Equipment Manager: Brad Berlin
Assistant Equipment Manager:
  Anders Beutel, Darwin Beacham
Assistant Director of Communications:
  Daniel Sampson
Communications Manager: Ross Taylor
Corporate Communications:
  Angela Alfano

COACHING HISTORY
Boston 1932-36
(588-564-27)
Records include postseason games
1932	Lud Wray	4-4-2
1933-34	William (Lone Star) Dietz	11-11-2
1935	Eddie Casey	2-8-1
1936-1942	Ray Flaherty	56-23-3
1943	Arthur (Dutch) Bergman	7-4-1
1944-45	Dudley DeGroot	14-6-1
1946-48	Glen (Turk) Edwards	16-18-1
1949	John Whelchel*	3-3-1
1949-1951	Herman Ball**	4-16-0
1951	Dick Todd	5-4-0
1952-53	Earl (Curly) Lambeau	10-13-1
1954-58	Joe Kuharich	26-32-2
1959-1960	Mike Nixon	4-18-2
1961-65	Bill McPeak	21-46-3
1966-68	Otto Graham	17-22-3
1969	Vince Lombardi	7-5-2
1970	Bill Austin	6-8-0
1971-77	George Allen	69-35-1
1978-1980	Jack Pardee	24-24-0
1981-1992	Joe Gibbs	140-65-0
1993	Richie Petitbon	4-12-0
1994-2000	Norv Turner***	50-60-1
2000	Terry Robiskie	1-2-0
2001	Marty Schottenheimer	8-8-0
2002-03	Steve Spurrier	12-20-0
2004-07	Joe Gibbs	31-36-0
2008-09	Jim Zorn	12-20-0
2010-13	Mike Shanahan	24-41-0

  *Released after seven games in 1949
  **Released after three games in 1951
  ***Released after 13 games in 2000

PAID ATTENDANCE
Home 579,080   Away 563,316
Total 1,142,396
Single-game home record,
  90,910 (12/30/07)
Single-season home record,
  * 711,471 (2007)
NFL Record

2014 DRAFT CHOICES
Round	Name	Pos.	College
2	Trent Murphy	LB	Stanford
3	Morgan Moses	T	Virginia
	Spencer Long	G	Nebraska
4	Basahud Breeland	DB	Clemson
5	Ryan Grant	WR	Tulane
6	Lache Seastrunk	RB	Baylor
7	Ted Bolser	TE	Indiana
	Zach Hocker	K	Arkansas

2013 TEAM RECORD
PRESEASON (3-1)

Date	Result	Opponent
08/08	W 22-21	at Tennessee
08/19	W 24-13	Pittsburgh
08/24	W 30-7	Buffalo
08/29	W 30-12	at Tampa Bay

REGULAR SEASON (3-13)

Date	Result	Opponent
09/09	L 27-33	Philadelphia
09/15	L 20-38	at Green Bay
09/22	L 20-27	Detroit
09/29	W 24-14	at Oakland
10/13	L 16-31	at Dallas
10/20	W 45-41	Chicago
10/27	L 21-45	at Denver
11/03	W 30-24	San Diego (OT)
11/07	L 27-34	at Minnesota
11/17	L 16-24	at Philadelphia
11/25	L 6-27	San Francisco
12/01	L 17-24	New York Giants
12/08	L 10-45	Kansas City
12/15	L 26-27	at Atlanta
12/22	L 23-24	Dallas
12/29	L 6-20	at New York Giants

(OT) Overtime

SCORE BY PERIODS

Redskins	47	114	82	85	6	—	334
Opponents	126	141	91	120	0	—	478

2013 TEAM STATISTICS

	Redskins	Opp.
Total First Downs	329	329
Rushing	112	102
Passing	198	204
Penalty	19	23
3rd Down: Made/Att	95/235	66/194
3rd Down Pct.	40.4	34.0
4th Down: Made/Att	6/20	12/17
4th Down Pct.	30.0	70.6
Possession Avg.	30:42	29:18
Total Net Yards	5915	5665
Avg. Per Game	369.7	354.1
Total Plays	1107	993
Avg. Per Play	5.3	5.7
Net Yards Rushing	2164	1769
Avg. Per Game	135.3	110.6
Total Rushes	453	443
Net Yards Passing	3751	3896
Avg. Per Game	234.4	243.5
Sacked/Yards Lost	43/306	36/238
Gross Yards	4057	4134
Att./Completions	611/355	514/337
Completion Pct.	58.1	65.6
Had Intercepted	19	16
Punts/Average	85/41.5	74/46.4
Net Punting Avg.	85/33.8	74/41.2
Penalties/Yards	99/802	83/697
Fumbles/Ball Lost	30/15	19/10
Touchdowns	39	59
Rushing	14	23
Passing	20	29
Returns	5	7

2013 INDIVIDUAL STATISTICS

PASSING

	Att.	Comp.	Yds.	Pct.	TD	Int.	Tkld.	Rate
Griffin III	456	274	3203	60.1	16	12	38/274	82.2
Cousins	155	81	854	52.3	4	7	5/32	58.4
Redskins	611	355	4057	58.1	20	19	43/306	76.1
Opponents	514	337	4134	65.6	29	16	36/238	96.1

SCORING

	TD R	TD P	TD Rt	PAT	FG	Saf	PTS
Forbath	0	0	0	26/26	18/22	0	80
Morris	7	0	0	0/0	0/0	0	42
Garçon	0	5	0	0/0	0/0	0	30
Helu	4	0	0	0/0	0/0	0	24
Young	3	1	0	0/0	0/0	0	24
Hall	0	0	3	0/0	0/0	0	18
Hankerson	0	3	0	0/0	0/0	0	18
Paulsen	0	3	0	0/0	0/0	0	18
Reed	0	3	0	0/0	0/0	0	18
Potter	0	0	0	7/7	3/4	0	16
Moss	0	2	0	0/0	0/0	0	12
Al. Robinson	0	2	0	0/0	0/0	0	12
Amerson	0	0	1	0/0	0/0	0	6
Davis	0	1	0	0/0	0/0	0	6
Orakpo	0	0	1	0/0	0/0	0	6
Griffin III	0	0	0	0/0	0/0	0	2
N. Williams	0	0	0	0/0	0/0	0	2
Redskins	14	20	5	33/33	21/26	0	334
Opponents	23	29	7	59/59	21/25	1	478

2-Pt Conversions: Griffin III, N. Williams.
Redskins 2-5, Opponents 0-0.

RUSHING

	No.	Yds	Avg	LG	TD
Morris	276	1275	4.6	45t	7
Griffin III	86	489	5.7	26	0
Helu	62	274	4.4	24	4
Young	12	41	3.4	19	3
Moss	3	25	8.3	18	0
Garçon	2	19	9.5	10	0
Reed	1	18	18.0	18	0
Cousins	4	14	3.5	6	0
Morgan	2	13	6.5	9	0
Royster	2	0	0.0	9	0
Al. Robinson	3	-4	-1.3	9	0
Redskins	453	2164	4.8	45t	14
Opponents	443	1769	4.0	50t	23

RECEIVING

	No.	Yds	Avg	LG	TD
Garçon	113	1346	11.9	53t	5
Reed	45	499	11.1	38	3
Moss	42	452	10.8	28	2
Helu	31	251	8.1	28	0
Hankerson	30	375	12.5	29	3
Paulsen	28	267	9.5	33	3
Morgan	20	214	10.7	21	0
Al. Robinson	18	365	20.3	62	2
Morris	9	78	8.7	17	0
Davis	7	70	10.0	23t	1
Young	4	71	17.8	62t	1
Paul	4	51	12.8	25	0
N. Williams	3	15	5.0	6	0
Royster	1	3	3.0	3	0
Redskins	355	4057	11.4	62t	20
Opponents	337	4134	12.3	57	29

INTERCEPTIONS

	No.	Yds	Avg	LG	TD
Hall	4	49	12.3	26t	2
Meriweather	2	62	31.0	32	0
Amerson	2	45	22.5	45t	1
Orakpo	1	29	29.0	29t	1
Doughty	1	25	25.0	25	0
Pugh	1	16	16.0	16	0
Biggers	1	15	15.0	15	0
Jackson	1	4	4.0	4	0
Gumbs	1	2	2.0	2	0
Riley	1	0	0.0	0	0
Wilson	1	0	0.0	0	0
Redskins	16	247	15.4	45t	4
Opponents	19	214	11.3	75t	2

PUNTING

	No.	Yds.	Avg.	In 20	LG
Rocca	84	3526	42.0	26	63
Redskins	85	3526	41.5	26	63
Opponents	74	3437	46.4	29	72

PUNT RETURNS

	Ret	FC	Yds	Avg	LG	TD
Moss	18	8	130	7.2	18	0
Morgan	8	1	59	7.4	34	0
C. Thompson	7	1	36	5.1	11	0
Murphy	1	0	0	0	0	0
N. Williams	1	1	0	0.0	0	0
Redskins	35	11	225	6.4	34	0
Opponents	39	18	655	16.8	86t	3

KICKOFF RETURNS

	No.	Yds	Avg	LG	TD
Paul	20	411	20.6	39	0
Morgan	12	239	19.9	25	0
N. Williams	9	188	20.9	29	0
C. Thompson	8	160	20.0	28	0
Moss	1	15	15.0	15	0
Gettis	1	5	5.0	5	0
Redskins	51	1018	20.0	39	0
Opponents	47	1048	22.3	95t	1

FIELD GOALS

	1-19	20-29	30-39	40-49	50+
Forbath	0/0	3/4	10/10	4/6	1/2
Potter	0/0	2/2	0/0	1/1	0/1
Redskins	0/0	5/6	10/10	5/7	1/3
Opponents	2/2	6/6	7/9	5/5	1/3

SACKS

	No.
Orakpo	10.0
Kerrigan	8.5
Riley	3.0
Cofield	2.5
Fletcher	2.0
Jackson	2.0
J. Jenkins	2.0
Wilson	2.0
Baker	1.0
Meriweather	1.0
Rambo	1.0
Tapp	1.0
Redskins	36.0
Opponents	43.0

RECORD HOLDERS
INDIVIDUAL RECORDS—CAREER

Category	Name	Performance
Rushing (Yds.)	John Riggins, 1976-79, 1981-85	7,472
Passing (Yds.)	Joe Theismann, 1974-1985	25,206
Passing (TDs)	Sammy Baugh, 1937-1952	187
Receiving (No.)	Art Monk, 1980-1993	888
Receiving (Yds.)	Art Monk, 1980-1993	12,026
Interceptions	Darrell Green, 1983-2001	54
Punting (Avg.)	Sammy Baugh, 1937-1952	45.1
Punt Return (Avg.)	Johnny Williams, 1952-53	12.8
Kickoff Return (Avg.)	Bobby Mitchell, 1962-68	28.5
Field Goals	Mark Moseley, 1974-1986	263
Touchdowns (Tot.)	Charley Taylor, 1964-1977	90
Points	Mark Moseley, 1974-1986	1,206
*Sacks	Dexter Manley, 1981-89	91.0

INDIVIDUAL RECORDS—SINGLE SEASON

Category	Name	Performance
Rushing (Yds.)	Alfred Morris, 2012	1,613
Passing (Yds.)	Jay Schroeder, 1986	4,109
Passing (TDs)	Sonny Jurgensen, 1967	31
Receiving (No.)	Pierre Garçon, 2013	113
Receiving (Yds.)	Santana Moss, 2005	1,483
Interceptions	Dan Sandifer, 1948	13
Punting (Avg.)	Sammy Baugh, 1940	**51.4
Punt Return (Avg.)	Johnny Williams, 1952	15.3
Kickoff Return (Avg.)	Mike Nelms, 1981	29.7
Field Goals	Mark Moseley, 1983	33
Touchdowns (Tot.)	John Riggins, 1983	24
Points	Mark Moseley, 1983	161
*Sacks	Dexter Manley, 1986	18.5

INDIVIDUAL RECORDS—SINGLE GAME

Category	Name	Performance
Rushing (Yds.)	Gerald Riggs, 9-17-89	221
Passing (Yds.)	Brad Johnson, 12-26-99	471
Passing (TDs)	Sammy Baugh, 10-31-43, 11-23-47	6
	Mark Rypien, 11-10-91	6
Receiving (No.)	Roy Helu, 11-6-11	14
Receiving (Yds.)	Anthony Allen, 10-4-87	255
Interceptions	Sammy Baugh, 11-14-43	**4
	Dan Sandifer, 10-31-48	**4
	DeAngelo Hall, 10-24-10	**4
Field Goals	Many times	5
	Last time by Shaun Suisham, 11-4-07	
Touchdowns (Tot.)	Dick James, 12-17-61	4
	Larry Brown, 12-16-73	4
Points	Dick James, 12-17-61	24
	Larry Brown, 12-16-73	24
*Sacks	Dexter Manley, 10-2-88	4.0
	Ken Harvey, 11-23-97	4.0
	Phillip Daniels, 12-18-05	4.0
	Brian Orakpo, 12-13-09	4.0

*Sacks became an official statistic in 1982.
**NFL Record

2014 VETERAN ROSTER

No.	Name	Pos.	Ht.	Wt.	Birthdate	NFL Exp.	College	Hometown	How Acq.	'13 Games/ Starts
39	Amerson, David	CB	6-1	205	12/8/91	2	North Carolina State	Greensboro, N.C.	D2-'13	16/8
92	Baker, Chris	DL	6-2	333	10/8/87	3	Hampton	Windsor, Conn.	FA-'11	15/3
30	Biggers, E.J.	CB	6-0	185	6/13/87	6	Western Michigan	North Miami Beach, Fla.	UFA(TB)-'13	16/5
72	Bowen, Stephen	DE	6-5	310	3/28/84	9	Hofstra	Dix Hills, N.Y.	UFA(Dall)-'11	10/10
66	Chester, Chris	G	6-3	309	1/12/83	9	Oklahoma	Tustin, Calif.	UFA(Balt)-'11	16/16
25	Clark, Ryan	S	5-11	205	10/12/79	13	Louisiana State	Marrero, La.	UFA(Pitt)-'14	16/16*
96	Cofield, Barry	NT	6-4	318	3/19/84	9	Northwestern	Cleveland Heights, Ohio	UFA(NYG)-'11	16/16
68	Compton, Tom	T	6-5	308	5/10/89	2	South Dakota	Rosemount, Minn.	D6b-'12	15/0
8	Cousins, Kirk	QB	6-3	209	8/19/88	3	Michigan State	Holland, Mich.	D4a-'12	5/3
20	Crawford, Richard	CB	5-11	188	8/1/90	3	Southern Methodist	Oceanside, Calif.	D7a-'12	0*
2	Forbath, Kai	K	5-11	197	9/2/87	3	UCLA	Sherman Oaks, Calif.	FA-'12	13/0
88	Garçon, Pierre	WR	6-0	212	8/8/86	7	Mount Union	Greenacres, Fla.	UFA(Ind)-'12	16/16
94	Geathers, Clifton	DE	6-8	340	12/11/87	5	South Carolina	Hemingway, S.C.	UFA(Phil)-'14	16/1*
73	Gettis, Adam	G	6-2	292	12/9/88	3	Iowa	Frankfort, Ill.	D5-'12	13/0
64	Golston, Kedric	DL	6-4	318	5/30/83	9	Georgia	Tyrone, Ga.	D6-'06	16/8
10	Griffin III, Robert	QB	6-2	217	2/12/90	3	Baylor	Copperas Cove, Texas	D1-'12	13/13
23	Hall, DeAngelo	CB	5-10	193	11/19/83	11	Virginia Tech	Chesapeake, Va.	FA-'08	16/16
85	Hankerson, Leonard	WR	6-2	211	1/30/89	4	Miami	Fort Lauderdale, Fla.	D3-'11	10/7
97	Hatcher, Jason	DE	6-6	299	7/13/82	9	Grambling State	Jena, La.	UFA(Dall)-'14	15/15*
55	Hayward, Adam	LB	6-1	240	6/23/84	8	Portland State	Westminster, Calif.	UFA(TB)-'14	16/2*
29	Helu, Jr., Roy	RB	5-11	215	12/7/88	4	Nebraska	Danville, Calif.	D4-'11	16/0
79	Hurt, Maurice	G/T	6-3	329	11/8/87	4	Florida	Milledgeville, Ga.	D7b-'11	0*
11	Jackson, DeSean	WR	5-10	175	12/1/86	7	California	Long Beach, Calif.	FA-'14	16/16*
50	Jackson, Rob	LB	6-4	266	11/3/85	6	Kansas State	West Haven, Conn.	D7b-'08	12/1
36	Jackson, Tanard	S	6-0	193	7/21/85	5	Syracuse	Potomac, Md.	FA-'12	0*
51	Jenkins, Brandon	LB	6-2	251	2/9/90	2	Florida State	Tallahassee, Fla.	D5b-'13	5/0
99	Jenkins, Jarvis	DE	6-4	315	4/24/88	4	Clemson	Central, S.C.	D2-'11	12/5
54	Jordan, Akeem	LB	6-1	230	8/17/85	8	James Madison	Harrisonburg, Va.	UFA(KC)-'14	16/10*
73	Kearse, Frank	G	6-5	310	10/28/88	3	Alabama A&M	Savannah, Ga.	FA-'14	2/0*
91	Kerrigan, Ryan	LB	6-4	260	8/16/88	4	Purdue	Muncie, Ind.	D1-'11	16/16
47	Kimbrough, Jeremy	LB	5-11	240	5/22/91	2	Appalachian State	Ellenwood, Ga.	CFA-'13	0*
61	Kowalski, Kevin	OL	6-3	298	1/2/89	3	Toledo	Macedonia, Ohio	FA-'14	0*
77	Lauvao, Shawn	G	6-3	315	10/26/87	5	Arizona State	Honolulu, Hawaii	UFA(Cle)-'14	11/11*
67	LeRibeus, Josh	G	6-2	315	7/2/89	3	Southern Methodist	Richardson, Texas	D3-'12	0*
78	Lichtensteiger, Kory	G/C	6-2	284	3/22/85	6	Bowling Green	Convoy, Ohio	FA-'10	16/16
3	Malone, Robert	P	6-2	215	2/4/88	3	Fresno State	Riverside, Calif.	FA-'13	2/0*
16	McCoy, Colt	QB	6-1	215	9/5/86	5	Texas	Tuscola, Texas	UFA(SF)-'14	4/0*
75	McGlynn, Mike	G/C	6-4	325	3/8/85	7	Pittsburgh	Austintown, Ohio	UFA(Ind)-'14	15/14*
31	Meriweather, Brandon	S	5-11	197	1/14/84	8	Miami	Apopka, Fla.	UFA(Chi)-'12	13/13
45	Miller, Gabe	LB	6-3	261	12/5/87	2	Oregon State	Lake Oswego, Ore.	FA-'13	0*
38	Minnifield, Chase	CB	6-0	186	3/31/89	2	Virginia	Lexington, Ky.	CFA-'12	0*
46	Morris, Alfred	RB	5-10	218	12/12/88	3	Florida Atlantic	Pensacola, Fla.	D6a-'12	16/16
89	Moss, Santana	WR	5-10	189	6/1/79	14	Miami	Carol City, Fla.	T(NYJ)-'05	16/1
95	Neild, Chris	NT	6-2	325	12/1/87	4	West Virginia	Stroudsburg, Pa.	D7d-'11	8/0
40	Nelson, Kyle	LS	6-2	240	10/3/86	3	New Mexico State	Waco, Texas	FA-'13	11/0
98	Orakpo, Brian	LB	6-4	257	7/31/86	6	Texas	Houston, Texas	D1-'09	15/15
84	Paul, Niles	TE	6-1	233	8/9/89	4	Nebraska	Omaha, Neb.	D5b-'11	15/4
82	Paulsen, Logan	TE	6-5	261	2/26/87	5	UCLA	West Hills, Calif.	CFA-'10	16/14
74	Polumbus, Tyler	T	6-8	305	4/10/85	6	Colorado	Englewood, Colo.	FA-'11	16/16
22	Porter, Tracy	CB	5-11	188	8/11/86	7	Indiana	Port Allen, La.	UFA(Oak)-'14	16/16*
24	Rambo, Bacarri	S	6-0	215	6/27/90	2	Georgia	Donalsonville, Ga.	D6-'13	11/3
86	Reed, Jordan	TE	6-2	243	7/3/90	2	Florida	New London, Conn.	D3-'13	9/4
56	Riley, Jr., Perry	LB	6-0	238	5/3/88	5	Louisiana State	Stone Mountain, Ga.	D4-'10	16/16
12	Roberts, Andre	WR	5-11	195	1/9/88	5	The Citadel	Columbia, S.C.	UFA(Ariz)-'14	16/2*
40	Robinson, Adrian	LB	6-1	250	11/21/89	2	Temple	Harrisburg, Pa.	FA-'13	8/0*
15	Robinson, Aldrick	WR	5-10	181	11/24/88	3	Southern Methodist	Waxahachie, Texas	D6b-'11	16/1
52	Robinson, Keenan	LB	6-3	238	7/7/89	3	Texas	Plano, Texas	D4b-'12	0*
34	Robinson, Trenton	S	5-9	193	2/16/90	3	Michigan State	Bay City, Mich.	FA-'13	11/0
26	Royster, Evan	RB	6-1	216	11/26/87	4	Penn State	Chantilly, Va.	D6a-'11	10/0
53	Sharpton, Darryl	LB	5-11	235	1/1/88	5	Miami	Coral Gables, Fla.	UFA(Hou)-'14	15/8*
57	Sundberg, Nick	LS	6-0	251	7/29/87	5	California	Phoenix, Ariz.	FA-'10	5/0
41	Thomas, Phillip	S	6-0	210	3/1/89	2	Fresno State	Bakersfield, Calif.	D4-'13	0*
25	Thompson, Chris	RB	5-8	187	10/20/90	2	Florida State	Madison, Fla.	D5a-'13	4/0
13	Williams, Nick	WR	5-10	184	11/23/90	2	Connecticut	Princeton, N.J.	CFA-'13	5/0
71	Williams, Trent	T	6-5	325	7/19/88	5	Oklahoma	Longview, Texas	D1-'10	16/16
90	Worthington, Doug	DE	6-5	311	8/10/87	3	Ohio State	Athol Springs, N.Y.	W(TB)-'11	0*
36	Young, Darrel	FB	5-11	251	4/8/87	5	Villanova	Amityville, N.Y.	FA-'10	13/7

* Clark played 16 games with Pittsburgh in '13; Crawford missed '13 season because of injury; Geathers played 16 games with Philadelphia; Hatcher played 15 games with Dallas; Hayward played 16 games with Tampa Bay; Hurt missed '13 season because of injury; D. Jackson played 16 games with Philadelphia; T. Jackson last active with Tampa Bay in '11; Jordan played 16 games with Kansas City; Kearse played two games with Dallas; Kimbrough missed '13 season because of injury; Kowalski last active with Dallas in '12; Lauvao played 11 games with Cleveland; LeRibeus inactive for 16 games; Malone played two games with the New York Jets; McCoy played four games with San Francisco; McGlynn played 15 games with Indianapolis; Miller last active with Kansas City in '11; Minnifield inactive for five games; Porter played 16 games with Oakland; Roberts played 16 games with Arizona; A. Robinson played six games with Denver and two games with San Diego; K. Robinson missed '13 season because of injury; Sharpton played 15 games with Houston; Thomas missed '13 season because of injury; Worthington missed '13 season because of injury.

Retired—London Fletcher, 16-year linebacker, 16 games in '13.

Players lost through free agency (4): WR Josh Morgan (Chi; 15 games in '13); LB Darryl Tapp (Det; 11); C J.D. Walton (NYG; 0), CB Josh Wilson (Atl; 16).

Also played with Redskins in '13—LB Nick Barnett (14 games), WR Josh Bellamy (5), LB Will Compton (1), TE Fred Davis (10), S Reed Doughty (15), S Jose Gumbs (8), LB Josh Hull (11), LB Bryan Kehl (5), WR Lance Lewis (3), DE Phillip Merling (3), C Will Montgomery (16), CB Jerome Murphy (11), K John Potter (3), S Jordan Pugh (4), P Sav Rocca (16).

FIRST-YEAR ROSTER

Name	Pos.	Ht.	Wt.	Birthdate	College	Hometown	How Acq.
Bolser, Ted	TE	6-5	257	10/22/90	Indiana	Cincinnati, Ohio	D7a
Breeland, Bashaud	CB	5-11	197	1/30/92	Clemson	Allendale, S.C.	D4
Bridget, Jr., Courtney	CB	6-3	195	3/22/91	Hampton	Baltimore, Md.	FA
Clingan, Blake (1)	P	6-3	233	12/7/88	Central Florida	Coral Springs, Fla.	FA
Compton, Will (1)	LB	6-2	230	9/19/89	Nebraska	Bonne Terre, Mo.	FA-'13
Davis, Akeem	S	6-1	200	12/25/89	Memphis	Laurel, Miss.	FA
Doss, Lee	WR	6-1	178	4/9/91	Southern	New Orleans, La.	FA
Grant, Ryan	WR	6-0	197	12/19/90	Tulane	Beaumont, Texas	D5
Hocker, Zach	K	6-0	191	8/23/91	Arkansas	Russellville, Ark.	D7b
Hoffman, Cody	WR	6-4	210	3/13/91	Brigham Young	Crescent City, Calif.	FA
Lawrence, Rashad	WR	6-2	190	6/10/92	Northwestern	Orlando, Fla.	FA
Long, Spencer	G	6-5	320	11/8/90	Nebraska	Elkhorn, Neb.	D3b
Moses, Morgan	T	6-6	314	3/3/91	Virginia	North Chesterfield, Va.	D3a
Murphy, Trent	LB	6-5	250	12/20/90	Stanford	Phoenix, Ariz.	D2
Redd, Silas	RB	5-10	200	3/1/92	Southern California	Stamford, Conn.	FA
Ross, Rashad (1)	WR	6-0	181	2/2/90	Arizona State	Vallejo, Calif.	FA
Sailors, Blake	CB	5-10	179	5/23/91	Georgia	Watkinsville, Ga.	FA
Seastrunk, Lache	RB	5-9	210	7/29/91	Baylor	Temple, Texas	D6
Shepherd, Bryan	CB	5-10	180	3/2/91	North Dakota State	Olathe, Kan.	FA
Stevens, Tevita (1)	OL	6-1	306	7/4/87	Utah	Hemet, Calif.	FA-'13
Thomas, Robert	DL	6-3	325	2/18/91	Arkansas	Muskogee, Okla.	FA
Thompson, Peyton (1)	CB	5-11	180	9/26/90	San Jose State	Granite Bay, Calif.	FA-'13

The term NFL Rookie is defined as a player who is in his first season of professional football and has not been on the roster of another professional football team for any regular-season or postseason games. A Rookie is designated by an "R" on NFL rosters. Players who have been active in another professional football league or players who have NFL experience, including either preseason training camp or being on an Active List or Inactive List, or on Reserve/Injured or Reserve/Physically Unable to Perform for fewer than six regular-season games, are termed NFL First-Year Players. An NFL First-Year Player is designated by a "1" on NFL rosters. Thereafter, a player is credited with an additional year of experience for each season in which he accumulates six games on the Active List or Inactive List, or on Reserve/Injured or Reserve/Physically Unable to Perform.

Log on to www.redskins.com for an up-to-date roster.

COACHING STAFF

Head Coach,
Jay Gruden
Pro Career: Named the 29th head coach in franchise history on January 9, 2014. Gruden spent his previous three seasons as offensive coordinator for the Cincinnati Bengals, during which time the Bengals averaged 10 wins a season, making three consecutive playoff appearances and earning an AFC North championship in 2013. In three seasons together, Gruden helped quarterback and 2011 second-round pick Andy Dalton to a 30-18 regular season record as a starter (.625). He also spent seven seasons with the Tampa Bay Buccaneers as an offensive assistant from 2002-08, helping the team to its first league championship in Super Bowl XXXVII. Gruden is also one of the most celebrated individuals in Arena Football League history, having won six combined league championships — four as a quarterback and two as a head coach. He was named the 1992 AFL Most Valuable Player and was honored with induction into the AFL Hall of Fame in 1999. Career record: 0-0.

Background: Played quarterback for four years at Louisville from 1985-88, twice being named team MVP. Played quarterback for the Barcelona Dragons and Sacramento Surge (WLAF, 1990), the Tampa Bay Storm (AFL, 1991-96) and the Orlando Predators (AFL, 2002-03). Coached in various capacities for the University of Louisville (1989-1991), Nashville Kats (AFL, 1997), Orlando Predators (AFL, 1998-2001, 2004-08), Tampa Bay Buccaneers (2002-08), Florida Tuskers (2009-2010) and Cincinnati Bengals (2011-13).

Personal: Born on March 4, 1967 in Tiffin, Ohio. He and his wife, Sherry, have three sons — J.J., Joey and Jack.

ASSISTANT COACHES

Brian Baker, outside linebackers; born June 20, 1962, Baltimore, Md. Linebacker Maryland 1981-83. No pro playing experience. College coach: Maryland 1984-85, Army 1986, Georgia Tech 1987-1995. Pro coach: San Diego Chargers 1996, Detroit Lions 1997-2000, Minnesota Vikings 2001-05, St. Louis Rams 2006-2008, Carolina Panthers 2009-2010, Dallas Cowboys 2011-12, Cleveland Browns 2013, joined Redskins in 2014.

Bradford Banta, asst. special teams; born December 14, 1979, Baton Rouge, La. Tight end Southern California 1990-93. Pro tight end/long snapper Indianapolis Colts 1993-99, New York Jets 2000, Detroit Lions 2001-03, Buffalo Bills 2004. College coach: Tennessee-Chattanooga 2007. Pro coach: Detroit Lions 2008-2013, joined Redskins in 2014.

Jacob Burney, defensive line; born January 24, 1959, Chattanooga, Tenn. Defensive tackle Tennessee-Chattanooga 1977-1980. No pro playing experience. College coach: New Mexico 1983-86, Tulsa 1987, Mississippi State 1988, Wisconsin 1989, UCLA 1990-92, Tennessee 1993. Pro coach: Cleveland Browns/Baltimore Ravens 1994-98, Carolina Panthers 1999-2001, Denver Broncos 2002-08, joined Redskins in 2010.

Chad Englehart, asst. strength and conditioning; born June 5, 1981, New Orleans, La. Attended Southeastern Louisiana. No college or pro playing experience. College coach: New Orleans 2006. Pro coach: Florida Tuskers (UFL) 2009, joined Redskins in 2010.

Chris Foerster, offensive line; born October 12, 1961, Milwaukee, Wisc. Center Colorado State 1979-1982. No pro playing experience. College coach: Colorado State 1983-87, Stanford 1988-1991, Minnesota 1992. Pro coach: Minnesota Vikings 1993-95, Tampa Bay Buccaneers 1996-2001, Indianapolis Colts 2002-03, Miami Dolphins 2004, Baltimore Ravens 2005-07, San Francisco 49ers 2008-09, joined Redskins in 2010.

Jim Haslett, defensive coordinator; born December 9, 1955, Pittsburgh, Pa. Defensive end Indiana (Pa.) 1975-78. Pro linebacker Buffalo Bills 1979-1986, N.Y. Jets 1987. College coach: Buffalo 1988-1990. Pro coach: Sacramento Surge (NFLE) 1991-92, Los Angeles Raiders 1993-94, New Orleans Saints 1995-96, Pittsburgh Steelers 1997-99, New Orleans Saints 2000-05 (head coach), St. Louis Rams 2006-08 (head coach 2008), Florida Tuskers (UFL head coach 2009), joined Redskins in 2010.

Ike Hilliard, wide receivers; born April 5, 1976, Patterson, La. Wide receiver Florida 1994-96. Pro wide receiver New York Giants 1997-2004, Tampa Bay Buccaneers 2005-08. Pro coach: Florida Tuskers (UFL) 2009-2010, Miami Dolphins 2011, Washington Redskins 2012, Buffalo Bills 2013, re-joined Redskins in 2014.

Randy Jordan, running backs; born June 6, 1970, Henderson, N.C. Running back North Carolina 1989-1992. Pro running back Los Angeles/Oakland Raiders 1993, 1998-2002, Jacksonville Jaguars 1995-97. College coach: Nebraska 2004-07, Texas A&M 2008-2011, North Carolina 2012-13. Pro coach: Oakland Raiders 2003, joined Redskins in 2014.

Ben Kotwica, special teams coordinator; born December 8, 1974, Tinley Park, Ill. Linebacker Army 1993-96. No pro playing experience. Pro coach: New York Jets 2007-13, joined Redskins in 2014.

Sean McVay, offensive coordinator; born January 24, 1986, Marietta, Ga. Wide receiver Miami (Ohio) 2004-07. No pro playing experience. Pro coach: Tampa Bay Buccaneers 2008, Florida Tuskers (UFL) 2009, joined Redskins in 2010 (promoted to offensive coordinator in 2014).

Raheem Morris, defensive backs; born September 3, 1976, Irvington, N.J. Safety Hofstra 1994-97. No pro playing experience. College coach: Hofstra 1998, 2000-01, Cornell 1999, Kansas State 2006. Pro coach: Tampa Bay Buccaneers 2002-05, 2007-2011 (head coach 2009-2011), joined Redskins in 2012.

Kirk Olivadotti, inside linebackers; born January 1, 1974, Wilmington, Del. Wide receiver Purdue 1992-96. No pro playing experience. College coach: Marine Maritime Academy 1997, Indiana State 1998-99, Georgia 2011-13. Pro coach: Washington Redskins 2000-2010, re-joined Redskins in 2014.

Jake Peetz, offensive quality control; born April 5, 1983, O'Neill, Neb. Defensive back Nebraska 2003-05. No pro playing experience. College coach: Santa Barbara (Calif.) C.C. 2006, UCLA 2007. Pro coach: Jacksonville Jaguars 2012, joined Redskins in 2014.

Wes Phillips, tight ends; born February 17, 1979, Houston, Texas. Quarterback Texas-El Paso 1997-2001. Pro quarterback San Diego Riptide (AFL2) 2002-03. College coach: Texas-El Paso 2003, West Texas A&M 2004-05, Baylor 2006. Pro coach: Dallas Cowboys 2007-2013, joined Redskins in 2014.

Aubrey Pleasant, defensive quality control; born August 20, 1986; Safety Wisconsin 2005-08. No pro playing experience. College coach: Michigan 2011-12. Pro coach: Joined Redskins in 2013.

Ray Wright, strength and conditioning; born December 30, 1971, Fort Worth, Texas. Running back/wide receiver Duke 1990-95. No pro playing experience. College coach: Cornell 2000, Maryland 2001. Pro coach: Houston Texans 2002-09, joined Washington in 2010.

2013 Season in Review

2013 TRADES (since May 1)

Running back **Anthony Sherman** from Arizona to Kansas City for defensive back **Javier Arenas**. (5/1)

Center **A.Q. Shipley** from Indianapolis to Baltimore for an unannounced future selection (2014 seventh round, T **Ulrick John**). (5/9)

Tackle **Gabe Carimi** from Chicago to Tampa Bay for an unannounced future selection (2014 sixth round, QB **David Fales**). (6/10)

Defensive back **Eric Wright** from Tampa Bay to San Francisco for an unannounced future selection. (7/19)

Wide receiver **Jeff Maehl** from Houston to Philadelphia for tackle **Nate Menkin**. (8/13)

Wide receiver **Jon Baldwin** from Kansas City to San Francisco for wide receiver **A.J. Jenkins**. (8/19)

Defensive end **Brian Sanford** from Cleveland to Seattle for guard **John Moffitt**. (8/20)

Defensive tackle **Sealver Siliga** from Denver to Seattle for running back **Delone Carter**. (8/21)

Running back **Felix Jones** from Philadelphia to Pittsburgh for linebacker **Adrian Robinson**. (8/23)

Linebacker **Chris White** from Buffalo to Detroit for quarterback **Thaddeus Lewis**. (8/26)

Linebacker **Parys Haralson** from San Francisco to New Orleans for an unannounced selection. (8/27)

Defensive tackle **D'Anthony Smith** from Jacksonville to Seattle for an unannounced selection. (8/31)

Linebacker **Edgar Jones** and a Chiefs' unannounced future selection (2014 seventh round, LB **Will Smith**) from Kansas City to Dallas for Cowboys' unannounced future selection (2014 sixth round, G **Zach Fulton**). (9/1)

Defensive tackle **Sean Lissemore** from Dallas to San Diego for an unannounced selection. (9/1)

Tight end **Dante Rosario** from Dallas to Chicago for an unannounced future selection. (9/1)

Linebacker **Cam Johnson** from San Francisco to Indianapolis for an unannounced future selection. (9/2)

Linebacker **Caesar Rayford** from Indianapolis to Dallas for an unannounced selection. (9/3)

Running back **Trent Richardson** from Cleveland to Indianapolis for an unannounced future selections (2014 first round selection, pick #26 traded to Philadelphia, and 2014 fourth round, DB

Pierre Desir). (9/19)

Tackle **Levi Brown** and a Cardinals' unannounced future selection from Arizona to Pittsburgh for an unannounced future selection. (10/3)

Tackle **Eugene Monroe** from Jacksonville to Baltimore for an unannounced future selection (2014 fifth round, DE **Chris Smith**). (10/3)

Linebacker **Jon Beason** from Carolina to the New York Giants for an unannounced future selection. (10/4)

Tackle **Bryant McKinnie** from Baltimore to Miami for an unannounced future selection. (10/21)

Defensive tackle **Isaac Sopoaga** and an Eagles' unannounced future selection from Philadelphia to New England for an unannounced future selection (DE **Zach Moore**). (10/29)

Draft choice number is listed if club later traded the pick.

2014 TRADES

Quarterback **Blaine Gabbert** from San Francisco to Jacksonville for an unannounced selection (2014 sixth round, C **Luke Bowanko**). (3/11)

Tackle **Jonathan Martin** from Miami to San Francisco for an unannounced selection. (3/11)

Running back **Darren Sproles** from New Orleans to Philadelphia for an unannounced selection. (3/13)

Quarterback **Matt Schaub** from Houston to Oakland for an unannounced selection (2014 sixth round, RB **Alfred Blue**). (3/24)

Center **Jeremy Zuttah** from Tampa Bay to Baltimore for an unannounced selection. (3/24)

Wide receiver **Mike Williams** from Tampa Bay to Buffalo for the Bills' 2014 sixth-round selection (WR **Robert Herron**). (4/4)

Quarterback **Terrelle Pryor** from Oakland to Seattle for the Seahawks' 2014 seventh-round selection (DB **Jonathan Dowling**). (4/22)

Cleveland trades 2014 first-round selection (WR **Sammy Watkins**) from Cleveland to Buffalo for the Browns' 2014 first-round selection (#9), 2015 first-round selection and 2015 fourth-round selection. (5/8)

Minnesota trades 2014 first-round selection (DB **Justin Gilbert**) from Minnesota to Cleveland for the Bills' 2014 first-round selection (LB **Anthony Barr**) and the Vikings' 2014 fifth-round selection (G **David Yankey**). (5/8)

Arizona trades 2014 first-round selec-

tion (WR **Brandin Cooks**) from Arizona to New Orleans for the Saints' 2014 first-round selection (DB **Deone Bucannon**) and 2014 third-round selection (WR **John Brown**). (5/8)

Philadelphia trades 2014 first-round selection (QB **Johnny Manziel**) from Philadelphia to Cleveland for the Colts' 2014 first-round selection (LB **Marcus Smith**) and the Steelers' 2014 third-round selection (#83). (5/8)

Seattle trades 2014 first-round selection (QB **Teddy Bridgewater**) from Seattle to Minnesota for the Vikings' 2014 second-round selection (#40) and fourth-round selection (DE **Cassius Marsh**). (5/8)

Wide receiver **Steve Johnson** from Buffalo to San Francisco for the 49ers' 2015 fourth-round selection. (5/9)

Washington trades Redskins' 2014 second-round selection (DE **Demarcus Lawrence**) from Washington to Dallas for the Cowboys' 2014 second-round selection (LB **Trent Murphy**) and third-round selections (G **Spencer Long**). (5/9)

Seattle trades Vikings' 2014 second-round selection (LB **Kyle Van Noy**) and Raiders' 2014 fifth-round selection (#146) from Seattle to Detroit for the Lions' 2014 second-round selection (WR **Paul Richardson**), 2014 fourth-round selection (#111), and 2014 seventh-round selection (RB **Kiero Small**). (5/9)

Buffalo trades Bills' 2014 second-round selection (DB **Lamarcus Joyner**) from Buffalo to St. Louis for the Rams' 2014 second-round selection (T **Cyrus Kouandjio**) and 2014 fifth-round selection (G **Cyril Richardson**). (5/9)

Tennessee trades 2014 second-round selection (WR **Jordan Matthews**) from Tennessee to Philadelphia for the Eagles' 2014 second-round selection (RB **Bishop Sankey**) and 2014 fourth-round selection (DB **Marqueston Huff**). (5/9)

Miami trades 2014 second-round selection (LB **Jeremiah Attaochu**) from Miami to San Diego for the Chargers' 2014 second-round selection (#57) and 2014 fourth-round selection (DB **Walt Aikens**). (5/9)

San Francisco trades the Chiefs' 2014 second-round selection (WR **Cody Latimer**) and the Saints' 2014 seventh-round selection (LB **Corey Nelson**) from San Francisco to Denver for the Broncos' 2014 second-round selection (#63), 2014 fifth-round selection (#171), and 2015 fourth-round selection. (5/9)

Miami trades Chargers' 2014 second-round selection (RB **Carlos Hyde**) from Miami to San Francisco for the Broncos' 2014 second-round selection (WR **Jarvis Landry**) and Broncos' 2014 fifth-round selection (LB **Jordan Tripp**). (5/9)

San Francisco trades 49ers' second-round selection (WR **Allen Robinson**) from San Francisco to Jacksonville for Jaguars' 2014 third-round selection (C **Marcus Martin**) and Lions' fifth-round selection (LB **Aaron Lynch**). (5/9)

Oakland trades Raiders' 2014 third-round selection (T **Billy Turner**) from Oakland to Miami for Dolphins' 2014 third-round selection (G **Gabe Jackson**) and Dolphins' 2014 fourth-round selection (DB **Keith McGill**). (5/9)

Philadelphia trades Steelers' 2014 third-round selection (NT **Louis Nix III**) from Philadelphia to Houston for Texans' 2014 fourth-round selection (DB **Jaylen Watkins**) and Texans' 2014 fifth-round selection (DE **Taylor Hart**). (5/9)

New England trades Patriots' 2014 third-round selection (G **Brandon Linder**) from New England to Jacksonville for Jaguars' 2014 fourth-round selection (C **Bryan Stork**) and Jaguars' 2014 sixth-round selection (G **Jon Halapio**). (5/9)

San Francisco trades 49ers' 2014 third-round selection (RB **Terrance West**) from San Francisco to Cleveland for Browns' 2014 fourth-round selection (WR **Bruce Ellington**) and Browns' 2014 sixth-round selection (DB **Kenneth Acker**). (5/9)

Seattle trades Lions' 2014 fourth-round selection (C **Russell Bodine**) from Seattle to Cincinnati for Bengals' 2014 fourth-round selection (WR **Kevin Norwood**) and Bengals' 2014 sixth-round selection (T **Garrett Scott**). (5/10)

Running back **Bryce Brown** and Eagles' 2014 seventh-round selection (T **Seantrel Henderson**) from Philadelphia to Buffalo for Bills' 2014 seventh-round selection (DT **Beau Allen**) and 49ers' 2015 fourth-round selection. (5/10)

Denver trades Broncos' 2014 fourth-round selection (DB **Brock Vereen**) and Broncos' 2014 seventh-round selection (T **Charles Leno**) from Denver to Chicago for Bears' 2014 fifth-round selection (LB **Lamin Barrow**) and Bears' 2015 fifth-round selection. (5/10)

Detroit trades Raiders' 2014 fifth-round selection (WR **Devin Street**) from Detroit to Dallas for Cowboys' 2014 fifth-round selection (DT **Caraun Reid**) and Bears' 2014 seventh-round selection (K **Nate Freese**). (5/10)

Minnesota trades Vikings' 2014 fifth-round selection (DB **Bené Benwikere**) from Minnesota to Carolina for Panthers' 2014 fifth-round selection (LB **Marquis Spruill**) and Giants' 2014 seventh-round selection (DB **Jabari Price**). (5/10)

Buffalo trades Bills' 2014 fifth-round selection (T **Kevin Pamphile**) from Buffalo to Tampa Bay for Buccaneers' 2014 seventh-round selection (LB **Randell Johnson**) and Buccaneers' 2015 fifth-round selection. (5/10)

Minnesota trades Panthers' 2014 fifth-round selection (LB **Marquis Spruill**) from Minnesota to Atlanta for Falcons' 2014 sixth-round selection (DB **Antone Exum**) and Falcons' 2014 seventh-round selection (NT **Shamar Stephen**). (5/10)

Washington trades Redskins' 2014 sixth-round selection (QB **Zach Mettenberger**) from Washington to Tennessee for Titans' 2014 sixth-round selection (RB **Lache Seastrunk**) and Titans' 2014 seventh-round selection (K **Zach Hocker**). (5/10)

Cleveland trades Browns' 2014 seventh-round selection (WR **Michael Campanaro**) from Cleveland to Baltimore for Ravens' 2015 sixth-round selection. (5/10)

Draft choice number is listed if club later traded the pick.

PRESEASON STANDINGS
AMERICAN FOOTBALL CONFERENCE

East Division

	W	L	T	Pct.	Pts.	OP
New York Jets	3	1	0	.750	105	80
New England	3	1	0	.750	93	103
Buffalo	2	2	0	.500	84	101
Miami	2	3	0	.400	104	89

North Division

	W	L	T	Pct.	Pts.	OP
Cincinnati	3	1	0	.750	106	63
Cleveland	3	1	0	.750	75	68
Baltimore	2	2	0	.500	119	97
Pittsburgh	0	4	0	.000	56	93

South Division

	W	L	T	Pct.	Pts.	OP
Houston	3	1	0	.750	98	67
Indianapolis	2	2	0	.500	77	89
Jacksonville	1	3	0	.250	60	111
Tennessee	1	3	0	.250	90	89

West Division

	W	L	T	Pct.	Pts.	OP
Denver	2	2	0	.500	71	104
Kansas City	2	2	0	.500	82	60
Oakland	1	3	0	.250	71	101
San Diego	1	3	0	.250	68	112

AFC PRESEASON RECORDS—TEAM BY TEAM

East Division

BUFFALO (2-2)

44	at Indianapolis	20
20	Minnesota	16
7	at Washington	30
13	Detroit	35
84		101

MIAMI (2-3)

20	vs. Dallas (a)	24
27	at Jacksonville	3
17	at Houston	24
16	Tampa Bay	17
24	New Orleans	21
104		89

NEW ENGLAND (3-1)

31	at Philadelphia	22
25	Tampa Bay	21
9	at Detroit	40
28	New York Giants	20
93		103

NEW YORK JETS (3-1)

17	at Detroit	26
37	Jacksonville	13
24	at New York Giants	21
27	Philadelphia	20
105		80

North Division

BALTIMORE (2-2)

44	at Tampa Bay	16
27	Atlanta	23
27	Carolina	34
21	at St. Louis	24
119		97

CINCINNATI (3-1)

34	at Atlanta	10
27	Tennessee	19
18	at Dallas	24
27	Indianapolis	10
106		63

CLEVELAND (3-1)

27	St. Louis	19
24	Detroit	6
6	at Indianapolis	27
18	at Chicago	16
75		68

PITTSBURGH (0-4)

13	New York Giants	18
13	at Washington	24
20	Kansas City	26
10	at Carolina	25
56		93

South Division

HOUSTON (3-1)

27	at Minnesota	13
24	Miami	17
23	New Orleans	31
24	at Dallas	6
98		67

INDIANAPOLIS (2-2)

20	Buffalo	44
20	at New York Giants	12
27	Cleveland	6
10	at Cincinnati	27
77		89

JACKSONVILLE (1-3)

3	Miami	27
13	at New York Jets	37
24	Philadelphia	31
20	at Atlanta	16
60		111

TENNESSEE (1-3)

21	Washington	22
19	at Cincinnati	27
27	Atlanta	16
23	at Minnesota	24
90		89

West Division

DENVER (2-2)

10	at San Francisco	6
10	at Seattle	40
27	St. Louis	26
24	Arizona	32
71		104

KANSAS CITY (2-2)

13	at New Orleans	17
13	San Francisco	15
26	at Pittsburgh	20
30	Green Bay	8
82		60

OAKLAND (1-3)

19	Dallas	17
20	at New Orleans	28
26	Chicago	34
6	at Seattle	22
71		101

SAN DIEGO (1-3)

10	Seattle	31
28	at Chicago	33
24	at Arizona	7
6	San Francisco	41
68		112

NFC PRESEASON RECORDS—TEAM BY TEAM

East Division
DALLAS (2-3)

24	vs. Miami (a)	20
17	at Oakland	19
7	at Arizona	12
24	Cincinnati	18
6	Houston	24
78		93

NEW YORK GIANTS (1-3)

18	at Pittsburgh	13
12	Indianapolis	20
21	New York Jets	24
20	at New England	28
71		85

PHILADELPHIA (2-2)

22	New England	31
14	Carolina	9
31	at Jacksonville	24
20	at New York Jets	27
87		91

WASHINGTON (4-0)

22	at Tennessee	21
24	Pittsburgh	13
30	Buffalo	7
30	at Tampa Bay	12
106		53

North Division
CHICAGO (2-2)

17	at Carolina	24
33	San Diego	28
34	at Oakland	26
16	Cleveland	18
100		96

DETROIT (3-1)

26	New York Jets	17
6	at Cleveland	24
40	New England	9
35	at Buffalo	13
107		63

GREEN BAY (1-3)

0	Arizona	17
19	at St. Louis	7
10	Seattle	17
8	at Kansas City	30
37		71

MINNESOTA (1-3)

13	Houston	27
16	at Buffalo	20
14	at San Francisco	34
24	Houston	23
67		104

South Division
ATLANTA (0-4)

10	Cincinnati	34
23	at Baltimore	27
16	at Tennessee	27
16	Jacksonville	20
65		108

CAROLINA (3-1)

24	Chicago	17
9	at Philadelphia	14
34	at Baltimore	27
25	Pittsburgh	10
92		68

NEW ORLEANS (3-1)

17	Kansas City	13
28	Oakland	20
31	at Houston	23
21	at Miami	24
97		80

TAMPA BAY (1-3)

16	Baltimore	44
21	at New England	25
17	at Miami	16
12	Washington	30
66		115

West Division
ARIZONA (3-1)

17	at Green Bay	0
12	Dallas	7
7	San Diego	24
32	at Denver	24
68		55

ST. LOUIS (1-3)

19	at Cleveland	27
7	Green Bay	19
26	at Denver	27
24	Baltimore	21
76		94

SAN FRANCISCO (3-1)

6	Denver	10
15	at Kansas City	13
34	Minnesota	14
41	at San Diego	6
96		43

SEATTLE (4-0)

31	at San Diego	10
40	Denver	10
17	at Green Bay	10
22	Oakland	6
110		36

PRESEASON STANDINGS
NATIONAL FOOTBALL CONFERENCE
East Division

	W	L	T	Pct.	Pts.	OP
Washington	4	0	0	1.000	106	53
Philadelphia	2	2	0	.500	87	91
Dallas	2	3	0	.400	78	93
New York Giants	1	3	0	.250	71	85

North Division

	W	L	T	Pct.	Pts.	OP
Detroit	3	1	0	.750	107	63
Chicago	2	2	0	.500	100	96
Green Bay	1	3	0	.250	37	71
Minnesota	1	3	0	.250	67	104

South Division

	W	L	T	Pct.	Pts.	OP
Carolina	3	1	0	.750	92	68
New Orleans	3	1	0	.750	97	80
Tampa Bay	1	3	0	.250	66	115
Atlanta	0	4	0	.000	65	108

West Division

	W	L	T	Pct.	Pts.	OP
Seattle	4	0	0	1.000	110	36
Arizona	3	1	0	.750	68	55
San Francisco	3	1	0	.750	96	43
St. Louis	1	3	0	.250	76	94

(a) Pro Football Hall of Fame Game, Canton, OH

AMERICAN FOOTBALL CONFERENCE

BALTIMORE RAVENS (8-8)
27	at Broncos	49
14	Browns	6
30	Texans	9
20	at Bills	23
26	at Dolphins	23
17	Packers	19
16	at Steelers	19
18	at Browns	24
20	Bengals	17
20	at Bears	23
19	Jets	3
22	Steelers	20
29	Vikings	26
18	at Lions	16
7	Patriots	41
17	at Bengals	34
320		**352**

BUFFALO BILLS (6-10)
21	Patriots	23
24	Panthers	23
20	at Jets	27
23	Ravens	20
24	at Browns	37
24	Bengals	27
23	at Dolphins	21
17	at Saints	35
13	Chiefs	23
10	at Steelers	23
37	Jets	14
31	Falcons	34
6	at Buccaneers	27
27	at Jaguars	20
19	Dolphins	0
20	at Patriots	34
339		**388**

CINCINNATI BENGALS (11-5)
21	at Bears	24
20	Steelers	10
34	Packers	30
6	at Browns	17
13	Patriots	6
27	at Bills	24
27	at Lions	24
49	Jets	9
20	at Dolphins	22
17	at Ravens	20
41	Browns	20
17	at Chargers	10
42	Colts	28
20	at Steelers	30
42	Vikings	14
34	Ravens	17
430		**305**

CLEVELAND BROWNS (4-12)
10	Dolphins	23
6	at Ravens	14
31	at Vikings	27
17	Bengals	6
37	Bills	24
17	Lions	31
13	at Packers	31
17	at Chiefs	23
24	Ravens	18
20	at Bengals	41
11	Steelers	27
28	Jaguars	32
26	at Patriots	27
31	Bears	38
13	at Jets	24
7	at Steelers	20
308		**406**

DENVER BRONCOS (13-3)
49	Ravens	27
41	at Giants	23
37	Raiders	21
52	Eagles	20
51	at Cowboys	48
35	Jaguars	19
33	at Colts	39
45	Redskins	21
28	at Chargers	20
27	Chiefs	17
31	at Patriots	34
35	at Chiefs	28
51	Titans	28
20	Chargers	27
37	at Texans	13
34	at Raiders	14
606		**399**

HOUSTON TEXANS (2-14)
31	at Chargers	28
30	Titans	24
9	at Ravens	30
20	Seahawks	23
3	at 49ers	34
13	Rams	38
16	at Chiefs	17
24	Colts	27
24	at Cardinals	27
23	Raiders	28
6	Jaguars	13
31	Patriots	34
20	at Jaguars	27
3	at Colts	25
13	Broncos	37
10	at Titans	16
276		**428**

INDIANAPOLIS COLTS (11-5)
21	Raiders	17
20	Dolphins	24
27	at 49ers	7
37	at Jaguars	3
34	Seahawks	28
9	at Chargers	19
39	Broncos	33
27	at Texans	24
8	Rams	38
30	at Titans	27
11	at Cardinals	40
22	Titans	14
28	at Bengals	42
25	Texans	3
23	at Chiefs	7
30	Jaguars	10
391		**336**

JACKSONVILLE JAGUARS (4-12)
2	Chiefs	28
9	at Raiders	19
17	at Seahawks	45
3	Colts	37
20	at Rams	34
19	at Broncos	35
6	Chargers	24
10	49ers	42
29	at Titans	27
14	Cardinals	27
13	at Texans	6
32	at Browns	28
27	Texans	20
20	Bills	27
16	Titans	20
10	at Colts	30
247		**449**

KANSAS CITY CHIEFS (11-5)
28	at Jaguars	2
17	Cowboys	16
26	at Eagles	16
31	Giants	7
26	at Titans	17
24	Raiders	7
17	Texans	16
23	Browns	17
23	at Bills	13
17	at Broncos	27
38	Chargers	41
28	Broncos	35
45	at Redskins	10
56	at Raiders	31
7	Colts	23
24	at Chargers	27
430		**305**

MIAMI DOLPHINS (8-8)
23	at Browns	10
24	at Colts	20
27	Falcons	23
17	at Saints	38
23	Ravens	26
21	Bills	23
17	at Patriots	27
22	Bengals	20
19	at Buccaneers	22
20	Chargers	16
16	Panthers	20
23	at Jets	3
34	at Steelers	28
24	Patriots	20
0	at Bills	19
7	Jets	20
317		**335**

NEW ENGLAND PATRIOTS (12-4)
23	at Bills	21
13	Jets	10
23	Buccaneers	3
30	at Falcons	23
6	at Bengals	13
30	Saints	27
27	at Jets	30
27	Dolphins	17
55	Steelers	31
20	at Panthers	24
34	Broncos	31
34	at Texans	31
27	Browns	26
20	at Dolphins	24
41	at Ravens	7
34	Bills	20
444		**338**

NEW YORK JETS (8-8)
18	Buccaneers	17
10	at Patriots	13
27	Bills	20
13	at Titans	38
30	at Falcons	28
6	Steelers	19
30	Patriots	27
9	at Bengals	49
26	Saints	20
14	at Bills	37
3	at Ravens	19
3	Dolphins	23
37	Raiders	27
20	at Panthers	30
24	Browns	13
20	at Dolphins	7
290		**387**

OAKLAND RAIDERS (4-12)
17	at Colts	21
19	Jaguars	9
21	at Broncos	37
14	Redskins	24
27	Chargers	17
7	at Chiefs	24
21	Steelers	18
20	Eagles	49
28	at Giants	24
28	at Texans	23
19	Titans	23
24	at Cowboys	31
27	at Jets	37
31	Chiefs	56
13	at Chargers	26
14	Broncos	34
322		**453**

PITTSBURGH STEELERS (8-8)
9	Titans	16
10	at Bengals	20
23	Bears	40
27	at Vikings	34
19	at Jets	6
19	Ravens	16
18	at Raiders	21
31	at Patriots	55
23	Bills	10
37	Lions	27
27	at Browns	11
20	at Ravens	22
28	Dolphins	34
30	Bengals	20
38	at Packers	31
20	Browns	7
379		**370**

SAN DIEGO CHARGERS (9-7)
28	Texans	31
33	at Eagles	30
17	at Titans	20
30	Cowboys	21
17	at Raiders	27
19	Colts	9
24	at Jaguars	6
24	at Redskins	30
20	Broncos	28
16	at Dolphins	20
41	at Chiefs	38
10	Bengals	17
37	Giants	14
27	at Broncos	20
26	Raiders	13
27	Chiefs	24
396		**348**

TENNESSEE TITANS (7-9)
16	at Steelers	9
24	at Texans	30
20	Chargers	17
38	Jets	13
17	Chiefs	26
13	at Seahawks	20
17	49ers	31
28	at Rams	21
27	Jaguars	29
27	Colts	30
23	at Raiders	19
14	at Colts	22
28	at Broncos	51
34	Cardinals	37
20	at Jaguars	16
16	Texans	10
362		**381**

NATIONAL FOOTBALL CONFERENCE

ARIZONA CARDINALS (10-6)

24	at Rams	27
25	Lions	21
7	at Saints	31
13	at Buccaneers	10
22	Panthers	6
20	at 49ers	32
22	Seahawks	34
27	Falcons	13
27	Texans	24
27	at Jaguars	14
40	Colts	11
21	at Eagles	24
30	Rams	10
37	at Titans	34
17	at Seahawks	10
20	49ers	23
379		**324**

ATLANTA FALCONS (4-12)

17	at Saints	23
31	Rams	24
23	at Dolphins	27
23	Patriots	30
28	Jets	30
31	Buccaneers	23
13	at Cardinals	27
10	at Panthers	34
10	Seahawks	33
28	at Buccaneers	41
13	Saints	17
34	at Bills	31
21	at Packers	22
27	Redskins	26
24	at 49ers	34
20	Panthers	21
353		**443**

CAROLINA PANTHERS (12-4)

7	Seahawks	12
23	at Bills	24
38	Giants	0
6	at Cardinals	22
35	at Vikings	10
30	Rams	15
31	at Buccaneers	13
34	Falcons	10
10	at 49ers	9
24	Patriots	20
20	at Dolphins	16
27	Buccaneers	6
13	at Saints	31
30	Jets	20
17	Saints	13
21	at Falcons	20
366		**241**

CHICAGO BEARS (8-8)

24	Bengals	21
31	Vikings	30
40	at Steelers	23
32	at Lions	40
18	Saints	26
27	Giants	21
41	at Redskins	45
27	at Packers	20
19	Lions	21
23	Ravens	20
21	at Rams	42
20	at Vikings	23
45	Cowboys	28
38	at Browns	31
11	at Eagles	54
28	Packers	33
445		**478**

DALLAS COWBOYS (8-8)

36	Giants	31
16	at Chiefs	17
31	Rams	7
21	at Chargers	30
48	Broncos	51
31	Redskins	16
17	at Eagles	3
30	at Lions	31
27	Vikings	23
17	at Saints	49
24	at Giants	21
31	Raiders	24
28	at Bears	45
36	Packers	37
24	at Redskins	23
22	Eagles	24
439		**432**

DETROIT LIONS (7-9)

34	Vikings	24
21	at Cardinals	25
27	at Redskins	20
40	Bears	32
9	at Packers	22
31	at Browns	17
24	Bengals	27
31	Cowboys	30
21	at Bears	19
27	at Steelers	37
21	Buccaneers	24
40	Packers	10
20	at Eagles	34
16	Ravens	18
20	Giants	23
13	at Vikings	14
395		**376**

GREEN BAY PACKERS (8-7-1)

28	at 49ers	34
38	Redskins	20
30	at Bengals	34
22	Lions	9
19	at Ravens	17
31	Browns	13
44	at Vikings	31
20	Bears	27
13	Eagles	27
13	at Giants	27
26	Vikings	26
10	at Lions	40
22	Falcons	21
37	at Cowboys	36
31	Steelers	38
33	at Bears	28
417		**428**

MINNESOTA VIKINGS (5-10-1)

24	at Lions	34
30	at Bears	31
27	Browns	31
34	Steelers	27
10	Panthers	35
7	at Giants	23
31	Packers	44
23	at Cowboys	27
34	Redskins	27
20	at Seahawks	41
26	at Packers	26
23	Bears	20
26	at Ravens	29
48	Eagles	30
14	at Bengals	42
14	Lions	13
391		**480**

NEW ORLEANS SAINTS (11-5)

23	Falcons	17
16	at Buccaneers	14
31	Cardinals	7
38	Dolphins	17
26	at Bears	18
27	at Patriots	30
35	Bills	17
20	at Jets	26
49	Cowboys	17
23	49ers	20
17	at Falcons	13
7	at Seahawks	34
31	Panthers	13
16	at Rams	27
13	at Panthers	17
42	Buccaneers	17
414		**304**

NEW YORK GIANTS (7-9)

31	at Cowboys	36
23	Broncos	41
0	at Panthers	38
7	at Chiefs	31
21	Eagles	36
21	at Bears	27
23	Vikings	7
15	at Eagles	7
24	Raiders	20
27	Packers	13
21	Cowboys	24
24	at Redskins	17
14	at Chargers	37
0	Seahawks	23
23	at Lions	20
20	Redskins	6
294		**383**

PHILADELPHIA EAGLES (10-6)

33	at Redskins	27
30	Chargers	33
16	Chiefs	26
20	at Broncos	52
36	at Giants	21
31	at Buccaneers	20
3	Cowboys	17
7	Giants	15
49	at Raiders	20
27	at Packers	13
24	Redskins	16
24	Cardinals	21
34	Lions	20
30	at Vikings	48
54	Bears	11
24	at Cowboys	22
442		**382**

ST. LOUIS RAMS (7-9)

27	Cardinals	24
24	at Falcons	31
7	at Cowboys	31
11	49ers	35
34	Jaguars	20
38	at Texans	13
15	at Panthers	30
9	Seahawks	14
21	Titans	28
38	at Colts	8
42	Bears	21
13	at 49ers	23
10	at Cardinals	30
27	Saints	16
23	Buccaneers	13
9	at Seahawks	27
348		**364**

SAN FRANCISCO 49ERS (12-4)

34	Packers	28
3	at Seahawks	29
7	Colts	27
35	at Rams	11
34	Texans	3
32	Cardinals	20
31	at Titans	17
42	at Jaguars	10
9	Panthers	10
20	at Saints	23
27	at Redskins	6
23	Rams	13
19	Seahawks	17
33	at Buccaneers	14
34	Falcons	24
23	at Cardinals	20
406		**272**

SEATTLE SEAHAWKS (13-3)

12	at Panthers	7
29	49ers	3
45	Jaguars	17
23	at Texans	20
28	at Colts	34
20	Titans	13
34	at Cardinals	22
14	at Rams	9
27	Buccaneers	24
33	at Falcons	10
41	Vikings	20
34	Saints	7
17	at 49ers	19
23	at Giants	0
10	Cardinals	17
27	Rams	9
417		**231**

TAMPA BAY BUCCANEERS (4-12)

17	at Jets	18
14	Saints	16
3	at Patriots	23
10	Cardinals	13
20	Eagles	31
23	at Falcons	31
13	Panthers	31
24	at Seahawks	27
22	Dolphins	19
41	Falcons	28
24	at Lions	21
6	at Panthers	27
27	Bills	6
14	49ers	33
13	at Rams	23
17	at Saints	42
288		**389**

WASHINGTON REDSKINS (3-13)

27	Eagles	33
20	at Packers	38
20	Lions	27
24	at Raiders	14
16	at Cowboys	31
45	Bears	41
21	at Broncos	45
30	Chargers	24
27	at Vikings	34
16	at Eagles	24
6	49ers	27
17	Giants	24
10	Chiefs	45
26	at Falcons	27
23	Cowboys	24
6	at Giants	20
334		**478**

FINAL STANDINGS

AMERICAN FOOTBALL CONFERENCE

East Division	W	L	T	Pct.	Pts.	OP
* New England	12	4	0	.750	444	338
New York Jets	8	8	0	.500	290	387
Miami	8	8	0	.500	317	335
Buffalo	6	10	0	.375	339	388

North Division	W	L	T	Pct.	Pts.	OP
* Cincinnati	11	5	0	.688	430	305
Pittsburgh	8	8	0	.500	379	370
Baltimore	8	8	0	.500	320	352
Cleveland	4	12	0	.250	308	406

South Division	W	L	T	Pct.	Pts.	OP
* Indianapolis	11	5	0	.688	391	336
Tennessee	7	9	0	.438	362	381
Jacksonville	4	12	0	.250	247	449
Houston	2	14	0	.125	276	428

West Division	W	L	T	Pct.	Pts.	OP
* Denver	13	3	0	.813	606	399
# Kansas City	11	5	0	.688	430	305
# San Diego	9	7	0	.563	396	348
Oakland	4	12	0	.250	322	453

NATIONAL FOOTBALL CONFERENCE

East Division	W	L	T	Pct.	Pts.	OP
* Philadelphia	10	6	0	.625	442	382
Dallas	8	8	0	.500	439	432
New York Giants	7	9	0	.438	294	383
Washington	3	13	0	.188	334	478

North Division	W	L	T	Pct.	Pts.	OP
* Green Bay	8	7	1	.531	417	428
Chicago	8	8	0	.500	445	478
Detroit	7	9	0	.438	395	376
Minnesota	5	10	1	.344	391	480

South Division	W	L	T	Pct.	Pts.	OP
* Carolina	12	4	0	.438	366	241
# New Orleans	11	5	0	.438	414	304
Atlanta	4	12	0	.813	353	443
Tampa Bay	4	12	0	.438	288	389

West Division	W	L	T	Pct.	Pts.	OP
* Seattle	13	3	0	.813	417	231
# San Francisco	12	4	0	.750	406	272
Arizona	10	6	0	.625	379	324
St. Louis	7	9	0	.438	348	364

* *Division champion*
# *Wild Card team*

Cincinnati finished ahead of Indianapolis based on head-to-head victory. New York Jets finished ahead of Miami based on better division record (3-3 to Dolphins' 2-4). Pittsburgh finished ahead of Baltimore based on better division record (4-2 to Ravens' 3-3). Atlanta finished ahead of Tampa Bay based on better conference record (3-9 to Buccaneers' 2-10).

WILD CARD PLAYOFFS

AFC
INDIANAPOLIS 45, Kansas City 44
San Diego 27, CINCINNATI 10
NFC
New Orleans 26, PHILADELPHIA 24
San Francisco 23, GREEN BAY 20

DIVISIONAL PLAYOFFS

AFC
NEW ENGLAND 43, Indianapolis 22
DENVER 24, San Diego 17
NFC
SEATTLE 23, New Orleans 15
San Francisco 23, CAROLINA 10

CHAMPIONSHIP GAMES

AFC
DENVER 26, New England 16
NFC
SEATTLE 23, San Francisco 17

2014 PRO BOWL

Team Rice 22, Team Sanders 21
at Aloha Stadium, Honolulu, Hawaii

SUPER BOWL XLVIII

SEATTLE (NFC) 43, Denver (AFC) 8
MetLife Stadium, New York-New Jersey

Home teams in playoff games are indicated in CAPS.

FIRST WEEK STANDINGS
American Football Conference

East Division	W	L	T	Pct.	Pts.	OP
New England	1	0	0	1.000	23	21
Miami	1	0	0	1.000	23	10
New York Jets	1	0	0	1.000	18	17
Buffalo	0	1	0	.000	21	23
North Division	**W**	**L**	**T**	**Pct.**	**Pts.**	**OP**
Cincinnati	0	1	0	.000	21	24
Pittsburgh	0	1	0	.000	9	16
Baltimore	0	1	0	.000	27	49
Cleveland	0	1	0	.000	10	23
South Division	**W**	**L**	**T**	**Pct.**	**Pts.**	**OP**
Indianapolis	1	0	0	1.000	21	17
Houston	1	0	0	1.000	31	28
Tennessee	1	0	0	1.000	16	9
Jacksonville	0	1	0	.000	2	28
West Division	**W**	**L**	**T**	**Pct.**	**Pts.**	**OP**
Kansas City	1	0	0	1.000	28	2
Denver	1	0	0	1.000	49	27
San Diego	0	1	0	.000	28	31
Oakland	0	1	0	.000	17	21

National Football Conference

East Division	W	L	T	Pct.	Pts.	OP
Philadelphia	1	0	0	1.000	33	27
Dallas	1	0	0	1.000	36	31
Washington	0	1	0	.000	27	33
New York Giants	0	1	0	.000	31	36
North Division	**W**	**L**	**T**	**Pct.**	**Pts.**	**OP**
Detroit	1	0	0	1.000	34	24
Chicago	1	0	0	1.000	24	21
Green Bay	0	1	0	.000	28	34
Minnesota	0	1	0	.000	24	34
South Division	**W**	**L**	**T**	**Pct.**	**Pts.**	**OP**
New Orleans	1	0	0	1.000	23	17
Tampa Bay	0	1	0	.000	17	18
Carolina	0	1	0	.000	7	12
Atlanta	0	1	0	.000	17	23
West Division	**W**	**L**	**T**	**Pct.**	**Pts.**	**OP**
St. Louis	1	0	0	1.000	27	24
San Francisco	1	0	0	1.000	34	28
Seattle	1	0	0	1.000	12	7
Arizona	0	1	0	.000	24	27

SECOND WEEK STANDINGS
American Football Conference

East Division	W	L	T	Pct.	Pts.	OP
New England	2	0	0	1.000	36	31
Miami	2	0	0	1.000	47	30
New York Jets	1	1	0	.500	28	30
Buffalo	1	1	0	.500	45	46
North Division	**W**	**L**	**T**	**Pct.**	**Pts.**	**OP**
Cincinnati	1	1	0	.500	41	34
Baltimore	1	1	0	.500	41	55
Cleveland	0	2	0	.000	16	37
Pittsburgh	0	2	0	.000	19	36
South Division	**W**	**L**	**T**	**Pct.**	**Pts.**	**OP**
Houston	2	0	0	1.000	61	52
Indianapolis	1	1	0	.500	41	41
Tennessee	1	1	0	.500	40	39
Jacksonville	0	2	0	.000	11	47
West Division	**W**	**L**	**T**	**Pct.**	**Pts.**	**OP**
Kansas City	2	0	0	1.000	45	18
Denver	2	0	0	1.000	90	50
Oakland	1	1	0	.500	36	30
San Diego	1	1	0	.500	61	61

National Football Conference

East Division	W	L	T	Pct.	Pts.	OP
Dallas	1	1	0	.500	52	48
Philadelphia	1	1	0	.500	63	60
New York Giants	0	2	0	.000	54	77
Washington	0	2	0	.000	47	71
North Division	**W**	**L**	**T**	**Pct.**	**Pts.**	**OP**
Chicago	2	0	0	1.000	55	51
Detroit	1	1	0	.500	55	49
Green Bay	1	1	0	.500	66	54
Minnesota	0	2	0	.000	54	65
South Division	**W**	**L**	**T**	**Pct.**	**Pts.**	**OP**
New Orleans	2	0	0	1.000	39	31
Atlanta	1	1	0	.500	48	47
Carolina	0	2	0	.000	30	36
Tampa Bay	0	2	0	.000	31	34
West Division	**W**	**L**	**T**	**Pct.**	**Pts.**	**OP**
Seattle	2	0	0	1.000	41	10
St. Louis	1	1	0	.500	51	55
San Francisco	1	1	0	.500	37	57
Arizona	1	1	0	.500	49	48

THIRD WEEK STANDINGS
American Football Conference

East Division	W	L	T	Pct.	Pts.	OP
New England	3	0	0	1.000	59	34
Miami	3	0	0	1.000	74	53
New York Jets	2	1	0	.667	55	50
Buffalo	1	2	0	.333	65	73
North Division	**W**	**L**	**T**	**Pct.**	**Pts.**	**OP**
Cincinnati	2	1	0	.667	75	64
Baltimore	2	1	0	.667	71	64
Cleveland	1	2	0	.333	47	64
Pittsburgh	0	3	0	.000	42	76
South Division	**W**	**L**	**T**	**Pct.**	**Pts.**	**OP**
Houston	2	1	0	.667	70	82
Indianapolis	2	1	0	.667	68	48
Tennessee	2	1	0	.667	60	56
Jacksonville	0	3	0	.000	28	92
West Division	**W**	**L**	**T**	**Pct.**	**Pts.**	**OP**
Denver	3	0	0	1.000	127	71
Kansas City	3	0	0	1.000	71	34
San Diego	1	2	0	.333	78	81
Oakland	1	2	0	.333	57	67

National Football Conference

East Division	W	L	T	Pct.	Pts.	OP
Dallas	2	1	0	.667	83	55
Philadelphia	1	2	0	.333	79	86
New York Giants	0	3	0	.000	54	115
Washington	0	3	0	.000	67	98
North Division	**W**	**L**	**T**	**Pct.**	**Pts.**	**OP**
Chicago	3	0	0	1.000	95	74
Detroit	2	1	0	.667	82	69
Green Bay	1	2	0	.333	96	88
Minnesota	0	3	0	.000	81	96
South Division	**W**	**L**	**T**	**Pct.**	**Pts.**	**OP**
New Orleans	3	0	0	1.000	70	38
Carolina	1	2	0	.333	68	36
Atlanta	1	2	0	.333	71	74
Tampa Bay	0	3	0	.000	34	57
West Division	**W**	**L**	**T**	**Pct.**	**Pts.**	**OP**
Seattle	3	0	0	1.000	86	27
St. Louis	1	2	0	.333	58	86
San Francisco	1	2	0	.333	44	84
Arizona	1	2	0	.333	56	79

WEEK 1 RESULTS
Thursday, September 5
DENVER 49, Baltimore 27

Sunday, September 8
New England 23, BUFFALO 21
Seattle 12, CAROLINA 7
CHICAGO 24, Cincinnati 21
Miami 23, CLEVELAND 10
DETROIT 34, Minnesota 24
INDIANAPOLIS 21, Oakland 17
Kansas City 28, JACKSONVILLE 2
NEW ORLEANS 23, Atlanta 17
NEW YORK JETS 18, Tampa Bay 17
Tennessee 16, PITTSBURGH 9
ST. LOUIS 27, Arizona 24
SAN FRANCISCO 34, Green Bay 28
DALLAS 36, New York Giants 31

Monday, September 9
Philadelphia 33, WASHINGTON 27
Houston 31, SAN DIEGO 28

*In the 2013 Week By Week section,
home teams are indicated by
ALL CAPS.*

**For game recaps, box scores, and
video highlights, please visit
www.NFL.com/scores.*

WEEK 2 RESULTS
Thursday, September 12
NEW ENGLAND 13, New York Jets 10

Sunday, September 15
ATLANTA 31, St. Louis 24
BALTIMORE 14, Cleveland 6
BUFFALO 24, Carolina 23
CHICAGO 31, Minnesota 30
GREEN BAY 38, Washington 20
HOUSTON 30, Tennessee 24 (OT)
Miami 24, INDIANAPOLIS 20
KANSAS CITY 17, Dallas 16
San Diego 33, PHILADELPHIA 30
ARIZONA 25, Detroit 21
New Orleans 16, TAMPA BAY 14
Denver 41, NEW YORK GIANTS 23
OAKLAND 19, Jacksonville 9
SEATTLE 29, San Francisco 3

Monday, September 16
CINCINNATI 20, Pittsburgh 10

WEEK 3 RESULTS
Thursday, September 19
Kansas City 26, PHILADELPHIA 16

Sunday, September 22
BALTIMORE 30, Houston 9
CAROLINA 38, New York Giants 0
CINCINNATI 34, Green Bay 30
DALLAS 31, St. Louis 7
Cleveland 31, MINNESOTA 27
NEW ENGLAND 23, Tampa Bay 3
NEW ORLEANS 31, Arizona 7
TENNESSEE 20, San Diego 17
Detroit 27, WASHINGTON 20
MIAMI 27, Atlanta 23
NEW YORK JETS 27, Buffalo 20
Indianapolis 27, SAN FRANCISCO 7
SEATTLE 45, Jacksonville 17
Chicago 40, PITTSBURGH 23

Monday, September 23
DENVER 37, Oakland 21

FOURTH WEEK STANDINGS
American Football Conference

East Division	W	L	T	Pct.	Pts.	OP
New England	4	0	0	1.000	89	57
Miami	3	1	0	.750	91	91
New York Jets	2	2	0	.500	68	88
Buffalo	2	2	0	.500	88	93

North Division	W	L	T	Pct.	Pts.	OP
Baltimore	2	2	0	.500	118	90
Cleveland	2	2	0	.500	64	70
Cincinnati	2	2	0	.500	91	119
Pittsburgh	0	4	0	.000	69	110

South Division	W	L	T	Pct.	Pts.	OP
Indianapolis	3	1	0	.750	105	51
Tennessee	3	1	0	.667	98	69
Houston	2	2	0	.500	90	105
Jacksonville	0	4	0	.000	31	129

West Division	W	L	T	Pct.	Pts.	OP
Denver	4	0	0	1.000	179	91
Kansas City	4	0	0	1.000	102	41
San Diego	2	2	0	.500	108	102
Oakland	1	3	0	.250	71	91

National Football Conference

East Division	W	L	T	Pct.	Pts.	OP
Dallas	2	2	0	.500	104	85
Philadelphia	1	3	0	.250	99	138
Washington	1	3	0	.250	91	112
New York Giants	0	4	0	.000	61	146

North Division	W	L	T	Pct.	Pts.	OP
Detroit	3	1	0	.750	122	101
Chicago	3	1	0	.750	127	114
Green Bay	1	2	0	.333	96	88
Minnesota	1	3	0	.250	115	123

South Division	W	L	T	Pct.	Pts.	OP
New Orleans	4	0	0	1.000	108	55
Carolina	1	2	0	.333	68	36
Atlanta	1	3	0	.250	94	104
Tampa Bay	0	4	0	.000	44	70

West Division	W	L	T	Pct.	Pts.	OP
Seattle	4	0	0	1.000	109	47
San Francisco	2	2	0	.500	79	95
Arizona	2	2	0	.500	69	89
St. Louis	1	3	0	.250	69	121

WEEK 4 RESULTS
Thursday, September 26
San Francisco 35, ST. LOUIS 11

Sunday, September 29
BUFFALO 23, Baltimore 20
CLEVELAND 17, Cincinnati 6
DETROIT 40, Chicago 32
Seattle 23, HOUSTON 20 (OT)
Indianapolis 37, JACKSONVILLE 3
KANSAS CITY 31, New York Giants 7
MINNESOTA 34, Pittsburgh 27 (London)
Arizona 13, TAMPA BAY 10
TENNESSEE 38, New York Jets 13
DENVER 52, Philadelphia 20
Washington 24, OAKLAND 14
SAN DIEGO 30, Dallas 21
New England 30, ATLANTA 23

Monday, September 30
NEW ORLEANS 38, Miami 17

Byes: Carolina, Green Bay

FIFTH WEEK STANDINGS
American Football Conference

East Division	W	L	T	Pct.	Pts.	OP
New England	4	1	0	.800	95	70
Miami	3	2	0	.600	114	117
New York Jets	3	2	0	.600	98	116
Buffalo	2	3	0	.400	112	130

North Division	W	L	T	Pct.	Pts.	OP
Baltimore	3	2	0	.600	117	110
Cleveland	3	2	0	.600	101	94
Cincinnati	3	2	0	.600	94	87
Pittsburgh	0	4	0	.000	69	110

South Division	W	L	T	Pct.	Pts.	OP
Indianapolis	4	1	0	.800	139	79
Tennessee	3	2	0	.600	115	95
Houston	2	3	0	.400	93	139
Jacksonville	0	5	0	.000	51	163

West Division	W	L	T	Pct.	Pts.	OP
Denver	5	0	0	1.000	230	139
Kansas City	5	0	0	1.000	128	58
Oakland	2	3	0	.400	98	108
San Diego	2	3	0	.400	125	129

National Football Conference

East Division	W	L	T	Pct.	Pts.	OP
Philadelphia	2	3	0	.400	135	159
Dallas	2	3	0	.400	152	136
Washington	1	3	0	.250	91	112
New York Giants	0	5	0	.000	82	182

North Division	W	L	T	Pct.	Pts.	OP
Detroit	3	2	0	.600	131	123
Chicago	3	2	0	.600	145	140
Green Bay	2	2	0	.500	118	97
Minnesota	1	3	0	.250	115	123

South Division	W	L	T	Pct.	Pts.	OP
New Orleans	5	0	0	1.000	134	73
Carolina	1	3	0	.250	74	58
Atlanta	1	4	0	.200	122	134
Tampa Bay	0	4	0	.000	44	70

West Division	W	L	T	Pct.	Pts.	OP
Seattle	4	1	0	.800	137	81
San Francisco	3	2	0	.600	113	98
Arizona	3	2	0	.600	91	95
St. Louis	2	3	0	.400	103	141

WEEK 5 RESULTS
Thursday, October 3
CLEVELAND 37, Buffalo 24

Sunday, October 6
New Orleans 26, CHICAGO 18
CINCINNATI 13, New England 6
GREEN BAY 22, Detroit 9
INDIANAPOLIS 34, Seattle 28
Baltimore 26, MIAMI 23
Philadelphia 36, NEW YORK GIANTS 21
ST. LOUIS 34, Jacksonville 20
Kansas City 26, TENNESSEE 17
ARIZONA 22, Carolina 6
Denver 51, DALLAS 48
SAN FRANCISCO 34, Houston 3
OAKLAND 27, San Diego 17

Monday, October 7
New York Jets 30, ATLANTA 28

Byes: Minnesota, Pittsburgh,
Tampa Bay, Washington

SIXTH WEEK STANDINGS
American Football Conference

East Division	W	L	T	Pct.	Pts.	OP
New England	5	1	0	.833	125	97
Miami	3	2	0	.600	114	117
New York Jets	3	3	0	.500	104	135
Buffalo	2	4	0	.333	136	157

North Division	W	L	T	Pct.	Pts.	OP
Cincinnati	4	2	0	.667	121	111
Baltimore	3	3	0	.500	134	129
Cleveland	3	3	0	.500	118	125
Pittsburgh	1	4	0	.200	88	116

South Division	W	L	T	Pct.	Pts.	OP
Indianapolis	4	2	0	.667	148	98
Tennessee	3	3	0	.500	128	115
Houston	2	4	0	.333	106	177
Jacksonville	0	6	0	.000	70	198

West Division	W	L	T	Pct.	Pts.	OP
Kansas City	6	0	0	1.000	152	65
Denver	6	0	0	1.000	265	158
San Diego	3	3	0	.500	144	138
Oakland	2	4	0	.333	105	132

National Football Conference

East Division	W	L	T	Pct.	Pts.	OP
Dallas	3	3	0	.500	183	152
Philadelphia	3	3	0	.500	166	179
Washington	1	4	0	.200	107	143
New York Giants	0	6	0	.000	103	209

North Division	W	L	T	Pct.	Pts.	OP
Detroit	4	2	0	.667	162	140
Chicago	4	2	0	.667	172	161
Green Bay	3	2	0	.600	137	114
Minnesota	1	4	0	.200	125	158

South Division	W	L	T	Pct.	Pts.	OP
New Orleans	5	1	0	.833	161	103
Carolina	2	3	0	.400	109	68
Atlanta	1	4	0	.200	122	134
Tampa Bay	0	5	0	.000	64	101

West Division	W	L	T	Pct.	Pts.	OP
Seattle	5	1	0	.833	157	94
San Francisco	4	2	0	.667	145	118
St. Louis	3	3	0	.500	141	154
Arizona	3	3	0	.500	111	127

WEEK 6 RESULTS
Thursday, October 10
CHICAGO 27, New York Giants 21

Sunday, October 13
Green Bay 19, BALTIMORE 17
Cincinnati 27, BUFFALO 24 (OT)
Detroit 31, CLEVELAND 17
St. Louis 38, HOUSTON 13
KANSAS CITY 24, Oakland 7
Carolina 35, MINNESOTA 10
Pittsburgh 19, NEW YORK JETS 6
Philadelphia 31, TAMPA BAY 20
DENVER 35, Jacksonville 19
SEATTLE 20, Tennessee 13
NEW ENGLAND 30, New Orleans 27
SAN FRANCISCO 32, Arizona 20
DALLAS 31, Washington 16

Monday, October 14
SAN DIEGO 19, Indianapolis 9

Byes: Atlanta, Miami

SEVENTH WEEK STANDINGS
American Football Conference

East Division	W	L	T	Pct.	Pts.	OP
New England	5	2	0	.714	152	127
New York Jets	4	3	0	.571	134	162
Miami	3	3	0	.500	135	140
Buffalo	3	4	0	.429	159	178
North Division	**W**	**L**	**T**	**Pct.**	**Pts.**	**OP**
Cincinnati	5	2	0	.714	148	135
Baltimore	3	4	0	.429	150	148
Cleveland	3	4	0	.429	131	156
Pittsburgh	2	4	0	.333	107	132
South Division	**W**	**L**	**T**	**Pct.**	**Pts.**	**OP**
Indianapolis	5	2	0	.714	187	131
Tennessee	3	4	0	.429	145	146
Houston	2	5	0	.286	122	194
Jacksonville	0	7	0	.000	76	222
West Division	**W**	**L**	**T**	**Pct.**	**Pts.**	**OP**
Kansas City	7	0	0	1.000	169	81
Denver	6	1	0	.857	298	193
San Diego	4	3	0	.571	168	144
Oakland	2	4	0	.333	105	132

National Football Conference

East Division	W	L	T	Pct.	Pts.	OP
Dallas	4	3	0	.571	200	155
Philadelphia	3	4	0	.429	169	196
Washington	2	4	0	.333	152	184
New York Giants	1	6	0	.143	126	216
North Division	**W**	**L**	**T**	**Pct.**	**Pts.**	**OP**
Green Bay	4	2	0	.667	168	127
Detroit	4	3	0	.571	186	167
Chicago	4	3	0	.571	213	206
Minnesota	1	5	0	.167	132	181
South Division	**W**	**L**	**T**	**Pct.**	**Pts.**	**OP**
New Orleans	5	1	0	.833	161	103
Carolina	3	3	0	.500	139	83
Atlanta	2	4	0	.333	153	157
Tampa Bay	0	6	0	.000	87	132
West Division	**W**	**L**	**T**	**Pct.**	**Pts.**	**OP**
Seattle	6	1	0	.857	191	116
San Francisco	5	2	0	.714	176	135
St. Louis	3	4	0	.429	156	184
Arizona	3	4	0	.429	133	161

WEEK 7 RESULTS
Thursday, October 17
Seattle 34, ARIZONA 22

Sunday, October 20
ATLANTA 31, Tampa Bay 23
CAROLINA 30, St. Louis 15
Cincinnati 27, DETROIT 24
San Diego 24, JACKSONVILLE 6
KANSAS CITY 17, Houston 16
Buffalo 23, MIAMI 21
NEW YORK JETS 30, New England 27 (OT)
Dallas 17, PHILADELPHIA 3
WASHINGTON 45, Chicago 41
San Francisco 31, TENNESSEE 17
GREEN BAY 31, Cleveland 13
PITTSBURGH 19, Baltimore 16
INDIANAPOLIS 39, Denver 33

Monday, October 21
NEW YORK GIANTS 23, Minnesota 7

Byes: New Orleans, Oakland

EIGHTH WEEK STANDINGS
American Football Conference

East Division	W	L	T	Pct.	Pts.	OP
New England	6	2	0	.750	179	144
New York Jets	4	4	0	.500	143	211
Miami	3	4	0	.429	152	167
Buffalo	3	5	0	.375	176	213
North Division	**W**	**L**	**T**	**Pct.**	**Pts.**	**OP**
Cincinnati	6	2	0	.750	197	144
Baltimore	3	4	0	.429	150	148
Cleveland	3	5	0	.375	148	179
Pittsburgh	2	5	0	.286	125	153
South Division	**W**	**L**	**T**	**Pct.**	**Pts.**	**OP**
Indianapolis	5	2	0	.714	187	131
Tennessee	3	4	0	.429	145	146
Houston	2	5	0	.286	122	194
Jacksonville	0	8	0	.000	86	264
West Division	**W**	**L**	**T**	**Pct.**	**Pts.**	**OP**
Kansas City	8	0	0	1.000	192	98
Denver	7	1	0	.875	343	218
San Diego	4	3	0	.571	168	144
Oakland	3	4	0	.429	126	150

National Football Conference

East Division	W	L	T	Pct.	Pts.	OP
Dallas	4	4	0	.500	230	186
Philadelphia	3	5	0	.375	176	211
Washington	2	5	0	.286	173	229
New York Giants	2	6	0	.250	141	223
North Division	**W**	**L**	**T**	**Pct.**	**Pts.**	**OP**
Green Bay	5	2	0	.714	212	158
Detroit	5	3	0	.625	217	197
Chicago	4	3	0	.571	213	206
Minnesota	1	6	0	.143	163	225
South Division	**W**	**L**	**T**	**Pct.**	**Pts.**	**OP**
New Orleans	6	1	0	.833	196	210
Carolina	4	3	0	.500	170	96
Atlanta	2	5	0	.333	166	184
Tampa Bay	0	7	0	.000	100	163
West Division	**W**	**L**	**T**	**Pct.**	**Pts.**	**OP**
Seattle	7	1	0	.857	205	125
San Francisco	6	2	0	.714	218	145
Arizona	4	4	0	.429	160	174
St. Louis	3	5	0	.429	165	198

WEEK 8 RESULTS
Thursday, October 24
Carolina 31, TAMPA BAY 13

Sunday, October 27
DETROIT 31, Dallas 30
San Francisco 42, JACKSONVILLE 10
(London)
KANSAS CITY 23, Cleveland 17
NEW ENGLAND 27, Miami 17
NEW ORLEANS 35, Buffalo 17
New York Giants 15, PHILADELPHIA 7
OAKLAND 21, Pittsburgh 18
CINCINNATI 49, New York Jets 9
ARIZONA 27, Atlanta 13
DENVER 45, Washington 21
Green Bay 44, MINNESOTA 31

Monday, October 28
Seattle 14, ST. LOUIS 9

Byes: Baltimore, Chicago, Houston, Indianapolis, San Diego, Tennessee

NINTH WEEK STANDINGS
American Football Conference

East Division	W	L	T	Pct.	Pts.	OP
New England	7	2	0	.778	234	175
New York Jets	5	4	0	.556	169	231
Miami	4	4	0	.500	174	187
Buffalo	3	6	0	.333	189	236
North Division	**W**	**L**	**T**	**Pct.**	**Pts.**	**OP**
Cincinnati	6	3	0	.667	217	166
Cleveland	4	5	0	.444	172	197
Baltimore	3	5	0	.375	168	172
Pittsburgh	2	6	0	.250	156	208
South Division	**W**	**L**	**T**	**Pct.**	**Pts.**	**OP**
Indianapolis	6	2	0	.750	214	155
Tennessee	4	4	0	.500	173	167
Houston	2	6	0	.250	146	221
Jacksonville	0	8	0	.000	86	264
West Division	**W**	**L**	**T**	**Pct.**	**Pts.**	**OP**
Kansas City	9	0	0	1.000	215	111
Denver	7	1	0	.875	343	218
San Diego	4	4	0	.500	192	174
Oakland	3	5	0	.375	146	199

National Football Conference

East Division	W	L	T	Pct.	Pts.	OP
Dallas	5	4	0	.556	257	209
Philadelphia	4	5	0	.444	225	231
Washington	3	5	0	.375	203	253
New York Giants	2	6	0	.250	141	223
North Division	**W**	**L**	**T**	**Pct.**	**Pts.**	**OP**
Detroit	5	3	0	.625	217	197
Chicago	5	3	0	.625	240	226
Green Bay	5	3	0	.625	232	185
Minnesota	1	7	0	.125	186	252
South Division	**W**	**L**	**T**	**Pct.**	**Pts.**	**OP**
New Orleans	6	2	0	.750	216	146
Carolina	5	3	0	.625	204	106
Atlanta	2	6	0	.250	176	218
Tampa Bay	0	8	0	.000	124	190
West Division	**W**	**L**	**T**	**Pct.**	**Pts.**	**OP**
Seattle	8	1	0	.889	232	149
San Francisco	6	2	0	.750	218	145
Arizona	4	4	0	.500	160	174
St. Louis	3	6	0	.333	186	226

WEEK 9 RESULTS
Thursday, October 31
MIAMI 22, Cincinnati 20 (OT)

Sunday, November 3
Kansas City 23, BUFFALO 13
CAROLINA 34, Atlanta 10
DALLAS 27, Minnesota 23
NEW YORK JETS 26, New Orleans 20
Tennessee 28, ST. LOUIS 21
WASHINGTON 30, San Diego 24 (OT)
Philadelphia 49, OAKLAND 20
SEATTLE 27, Tampa Bay 24 (OT)
CLEVELAND 24, Baltimore 18
NEW ENGLAND 55, Pittsburgh 31
Indianapolis 27, HOUSTON 24

Monday, November 4
Chicago 27, GREEN BAY 20

Byes: Arizona, Denver, Detroit, Jacksonville, New York Giants, San Francisco

TENTH WEEK STANDINGS
American Football Conference

East Division	W	L	T	Pct.	Pts.	OP
New England	7	2	0	.778	234	175
New York Jets	5	4	0	.556	169	231
Miami	4	5	0	.444	193	209
Buffalo	3	7	0	.300	199	259

North Division	W	L	T	Pct.	Pts.	OP
Cincinnati	6	4	0	.600	234	186
Cleveland	4	5	0	.444	172	197
Baltimore	4	5	0	.444	188	189
Pittsburgh	3	6	0	.333	179	218

South Division	W	L	T	Pct.	Pts.	OP
Indianapolis	6	3	0	.667	222	193
Tennessee	4	5	0	.444	200	196
Houston	2	7	0	.222	170	248
Jacksonville	1	8	0	.111	115	291

West Division	W	L	T	Pct.	Pts.	OP
Kansas City	9	0	0	1.000	215	111
Denver	8	1	0	.889	371	238
San Diego	4	5	0	.444	212	202
Oakland	3	6	0	.333	166	223

National Football Conference

East Division	W	L	T	Pct.	Pts.	OP
Dallas	5	5	0	.500	274	258
Philadelphia	5	5	0	.500	252	244
New York Giants	3	6	0	.333	165	243
Washington	3	6	0	.333	230	287

North Division	W	L	T	Pct.	Pts.	OP
Detroit	6	3	0	.667	238	216
Chicago	5	4	0	.556	259	247
Green Bay	5	4	0	.556	245	212
Minnesota	2	7	0	.222	220	279

South Division	W	L	T	Pct.	Pts.	OP
New Orleans	7	2	0	.778	265	163
Carolina	6	3	0	.667	214	115
Atlanta	2	7	0	.222	186	251
Tampa Bay	1	8	0	.111	146	209

West Division	W	L	T	Pct.	Pts.	OP
Seattle	9	1	0	.900	265	159
San Francisco	6	3	0	.667	227	155
Arizona	5	4	0	.556	187	198
St. Louis	4	6	0	.400	224	234

WEEK 10 RESULTS

Thursday, November 7
MINNESOTA 34, Washington 27

Sunday, November 10
Seattle 33, ATLANTA 10
BALTIMORE 20, Cincinnati 17 (OT)
Detroit 21, CHICAGO 19
Philadelphia 27, GREEN BAY 13
St. Louis 38, INDIANAPOLIS 8
NEW YORK GIANTS 24, Oakland 20
PITTSBURGH 23, Buffalo 10
Jacksonville 29, TENNESSEE 27
Carolina 10, SAN FRANCISCO 9
ARIZONA 27, Houston 24
Denver 28, SAN DIEGO 20
NEW ORLEANS 49, Dallas 17

Monday, November 11
TAMPA BAY 22, Miami 19

Byes: Cleveland, Kansas City
New England, New York Jets

ELEVENTH WEEK STANDINGS
American Football Conference

East Division	W	L	T	Pct.	Pts.	OP
New England	7	3	0	.700	254	199
New York Jets	5	5	0	.500	183	268
Miami	5	5	0	.500	213	225
Buffalo	4	7	0	.364	236	273

North Division	W	L	T	Pct.	Pts.	OP
Cincinnati	7	4	0	.636	275	206
Pittsburgh	4	6	0	.400	216	245
Baltimore	4	6	0	.400	208	212
Cleveland	4	6	0	.400	192	238

South Division	W	L	T	Pct.	Pts.	OP
Indianapolis	7	3	0	.700	252	220
Tennessee	4	6	0	.400	227	226
Houston	2	8	0	.200	193	276
Jacksonville	1	9	0	.100	129	318

West Division	W	L	T	Pct.	Pts.	OP
Denver	9	1	0	.900	398	255
Kansas City	9	1	0	.900	232	138
Oakland	4	6	0	.400	194	246
San Diego	4	6	0	.400	228	222

National Football Conference

East Division	W	L	T	Pct.	Pts.	OP
Philadelphia	6	5	0	.545	276	260
Dallas	5	5	0	.500	274	258
New York Giants	4	6	0	.400	192	256
Washington	3	7	0	.300	246	311

North Division	W	L	T	Pct.	Pts.	OP
Detroit	6	4	0	.600	265	253
Chicago	6	4	0	.600	282	267
Green Bay	5	5	0	.500	258	239
Minnesota	2	8	0	.200	240	320

South Division	W	L	T	Pct.	Pts.	OP
New Orleans	8	2	0	.800	288	183
Carolina	7	3	0	.700	238	135
Tampa Bay	2	8	0	.200	187	237
Atlanta	2	8	0	.200	214	292

West Division	W	L	T	Pct.	Pts.	OP
Seattle	10	1	0	.909	306	179
San Francisco	6	4	0	.600	247	178
Arizona	6	4	0	.600	214	212
St. Louis	4	6	0	.400	224	234

WEEK 11 RESULTS

Thursday, November 14
Indianapolis 30, TENNESSEE 27

Sunday, November 17
BUFFALO 37, New York Jets 14
CHICAGO 23, Baltimore 20 (OT)
CINCINNATI 41, Cleveland 20
Oakland 28, HOUSTON 23
Arizona 27, JACKSONVILLE 14
MIAMI 20, San Diego 16
PHILADELPHIA 24, Washington 16
PITTSBURGH 37, Detroit 27
TAMPA BAY 41, Atlanta 28
NEW YORK GIANTS 27, Green Bay 13
NEW ORLEANS 23, San Francisco 20
SEATTLE 41, Minnesota 20
DENVER 27, Kansas City 17

Monday, November 18
CAROLINA 24, New England 20

Byes: Dallas, St. Louis

TWELFTH WEEK STANDINGS
American Football Conference

East Division	W	L	T	Pct.	Pts.	OP
New England	8	3	0	.727	288	230
New York Jets	5	6	0	.455	186	287
Miami	5	6	0	.455	229	245
Buffalo	4	7	0	.364	236	273

North Division	W	L	T	Pct.	Pts.	OP
Cincinnati	7	4	0	.636	275	206
Pittsburgh	5	6	0	.455	243	256
Baltimore	5	6	0	.455	227	215
Cleveland	4	7	0	.364	203	265

South Division	W	L	T	Pct.	Pts.	OP
Indianapolis	7	4	0	.636	263	260
Tennessee	5	6	0	.455	250	245
Jacksonville	2	9	0	.182	142	324
Houston	2	9	0	.182	199	289

West Division	W	L	T	Pct.	Pts.	OP
Denver	9	2	0	.818	429	289
Kansas City	9	2	0	.818	270	179
San Diego	5	6	0	.455	269	260
Oakland	4	7	0	.364	213	269

National Football Conference

East Division	W	L	T	Pct.	Pts.	OP
Dallas	6	5	0	.545	298	279
Philadelphia	6	5	0	.545	276	260
New York Giants	4	7	0	.364	213	280
Washington	3	8	0	.273	252	338

North Division	W	L	T	Pct.	Pts.	OP
Detroit	6	5	0	.545	286	277
Chicago	6	5	0	.545	303	309
Green Bay	5	5	1	.500	284	265
Minnesota	2	8	1	.227	266	346

South Division	W	L	T	Pct.	Pts.	OP
New Orleans	9	2	0	.818	305	196
Carolina	8	3	0	.727	258	151
Tampa Bay	3	8	0	.273	211	258
Atlanta	2	9	0	.182	227	309

West Division	W	L	T	Pct.	Pts.	OP
Seattle	10	1	0	.909	306	179
San Francisco	7	4	0	.636	274	184
Arizona	7	4	0	.636	254	223
St. Louis	5	6	0	.455	266	255

WEEK 12 RESULTS

Thursday, November 21
New Orleans 17, ATLANTA 13

Sunday, November 24
BALTIMORE 19, New York Jets 3
Pittsburgh 27, CLEVELAND 11
Tampa Bay 24, DETROIT 21
Minnesota 26, GREEN BAY 26 (OT-tie)
Jacksonville 13, HOUSTON 6
San Diego 41, KANSAS CITY 38
Carolina 20, MIAMI 16
ST. LOUIS 42, Chicago 21
ARIZONA 40, Indianapolis 11
Tennessee 23, OAKLAND 19
Dallas 24, NEW YORK GIANTS 21
NEW ENGLAND 34, Denver 31 (OT)

Monday, November 25
San Francisco 27, WASHINGTON 6

Byes: Buffalo, Cincinnati,
Philadelphia, Seattle

THIRTEENTH WEEK STANDINGS
American Football Conference

East Division	W	L	T	Pct.	Pts.	OP
New England	9	3	0	.750	322	261
Miami	6	6	0	.500	252	248
New York Jets	5	7	0	.417	189	310
Buffalo	4	8	0	.333	267	307

North Division	W	L	T	Pct.	Pts.	OP
Cincinnati	8	4	0	.667	292	216
Baltimore	6	6	0	.500	249	235
Pittsburgh	5	7	0	.417	263	278
Cleveland	4	8	0	.333	231	297

South Division	W	L	T	Pct.	Pts.	OP
Indianapolis	8	4	0	.667	285	274
Tennessee	5	7	0	.417	264	267
Jacksonville	3	9	0	.250	174	352
Houston	2	10	0	.167	230	323

West Division	W	L	T	Pct.	Pts.	OP
Denver	10	2	0	.833	464	317
Kansas City	9	3	0	.750	298	214
San Diego	5	7	0	.417	279	277
Oakland	4	8	0	.333	237	300

National Football Conference

East Division	W	L	T	Pct.	Pts.	OP
Dallas	7	5	0	.545	329	303
Philadelphia	7	5	0	.545	300	281
New York Giants	5	7	0	.364	237	297
Washington	3	9	0	.273	269	362

North Division	W	L	T	Pct.	Pts.	OP
Detroit	7	5	0	.583	326	287
Chicago	6	6	0	.500	323	332
Green Bay	5	6	1	.458	294	305
Minnesota	3	8	1	.292	289	366

South Division	W	L	T	Pct.	Pts.	OP
New Orleans	9	3	0	.818	312	230
Carolina	9	3	0	.727	285	157
Tampa Bay	3	9	0	.273	217	285
Atlanta	3	9	0	.182	261	340

West Division	W	L	T	Pct.	Pts.	OP
Seattle#	11	1	0	.917	340	186
San Francisco	8	4	0	.667	297	197
Arizona	7	5	0	.583	275	247
St. Louis	5	7	0	.417	279	278

#Clinched playoff berth

WEEK 13 RESULTS
Thursday, November 28
DETROIT 40, Green Bay 10
DALLAS 31, Oakland 24
BALTIMORE 22, Pittsburgh 20

Sunday, December 1
CAROLINA 27, Tampa Bay 6
Jacksonville 32, CLEVELAND 28
New England 34, HOUSTON 31
INDIANAPOLIS 22, Tennessee 14
MINNESOTA 23, Chicago 20 (OT)
Miami 23, NEW YORK JETS 3
PHILADELPHIA 24, Arizona 21
Atlanta 34, BUFFALO 31 (OT) (Toronto)
SAN FRANCISCO 23, St. Louis 13
Cincinnati 17, SAN DIEGO 10
New York Giants 24, WASHINGTON 17
Denver 35, KANSAS CITY 28

Monday, December 2
SEATTLE 34, New Orleans 7

FOURTEENTH WEEK STANDINGS
American Football Conference

East Division	W	L	T	Pct.	Pts.	OP
New England	10	3	0	.769	349	287
Miami	7	6	0	.538	286	276
New York Jets	6	7	0	.462	226	337
Buffalo	4	9	0	.308	273	334

North Division	W	L	T	Pct.	Pts.	OP
Cincinnati	9	4	0	.692	334	244
Baltimore	7	6	0	.538	278	261
Pittsburgh	5	8	0	.385	291	312
Cleveland	4	9	0	.308	257	324

South Division	W	L	T	Pct.	Pts.	OP
Indianapolis*	8	5	0	.615	313	316
Tennessee	5	8	0	.385	292	318
Jacksonville	4	9	0	.308	201	372
Houston	2	11	0	.154	250	350

West Division	W	L	T	Pct.	Pts.	OP
Denver#	11	2	0	.846	515	345
Kansas City	10	3	0	.769	343	224
San Diego	6	7	0	.462	316	291
Oakland	4	9	0	.308	264	337

National Football Conference

East Division	W	L	T	Pct.	Pts.	OP
Philadelphia	8	5	0	.615	334	301
Dallas	7	6	0	.538	357	348
New York Giants	5	8	0	.385	251	334
Washington	3	10	0	.231	279	407

North Division	W	L	T	Pct.	Pts.	OP
Detroit	7	6	0	.538	346	321
Chicago	7	6	0	.538	368	360
Green Bay	6	6	1	.500	316	326
Minnesota	3	9	1	.269	315	395

South Division	W	L	T	Pct.	Pts.	OP
New Orleans	10	3	0	.769	343	243
Carolina	9	4	0	.692	298	188
Tampa Bay	4	9	0	.308	244	291
Atlanta	3	10	0	.231	282	362

West Division	W	L	T	Pct.	Pts.	OP
Seattle#	11	2	0	.846	357	205
San Francisco	9	4	0	.692	316	214
Arizona	8	5	0	.615	305	257
St. Louis	5	8	0	.385	289	308

*Clinched division title
#Clinched playoff berth

WEEK 14 RESULTS
Thursday, December 5
JACKSONVILLE 27, Houston 20

Sunday, December 8
BALTIMORE 29, Minnesota 26
CINCINNATI 42, Indianapolis 28
GREEN BAY 22, Atlanta 21
NEW ENGLAND 27, Cleveland 26
NEW YORK JETS 37, Oakland 27
PHILADELPHIA 34, Detroit 20
Miami 34, PITTSBURGH 28
TAMPA BAY 27, Buffalo 6
Kansas City 45, WASHINGTON 10
DENVER 51, Tennessee 28
ARIZONA 30, St. Louis 10
SAN DIEGO 37, New York Giants 14
SAN FRANCISCO 19, Seattle 17
NEW ORLEANS 31, Carolina 13

Monday, December 9
CHICAGO 45, Dallas 28

FIFTEENTH WEEK STANDINGS
American Football Conference

East Division	W	L	T	Pct.	Pts.	OP
New England	10	4	0	.714	369	311
Miami	8	6	0	.571	310	296
New York Jets	6	8	0	.429	246	367
Buffalo	5	9	0	.357	300	354

North Division	W	L	T	Pct.	Pts.	OP
Cincinnati	9	5	0	.643	354	274
Baltimore	8	6	0	.571	296	277
Pittsburgh	6	8	0	.429	321	332
Cleveland	4	10	0	.286	288	362

South Division	W	L	T	Pct.	Pts.	OP
Indianapolis*	9	5	0	.643	338	319
Tennessee	5	9	0	.357	326	355
Jacksonville	4	10	0	.286	221	399
Houston	2	12	0	.143	253	375

West Division	W	L	T	Pct.	Pts.	OP
Denver#	11	3	0	.768	535	372
Kansas City#	11	3	0	.786	399	255
San Diego	7	7	0	.500	343	311
Oakland	4	10	0	.286	295	393

National Football Conference

East Division	W	L	T	Pct.	Pts.	OP
Philadelphia	8	6	0	.571	334	301
Dallas	7	7	0	.500	357	348
New York Giants	5	9	0	.357	251	334
Washington	3	11	0	.214	279	407

North Division	W	L	T	Pct.	Pts.	OP
Chicago	8	6	0	.571	406	391
Green Bay	7	6	1	.536	353	362
Detroit	7	7	0	.500	362	339
Minnesota	4	9	1	.321	363	425

South Division	W	L	T	Pct.	Pts.	OP
New Orleans	10	4	0	.714	359	270
Carolina	10	4	0	.714	328	208
Tampa Bay	4	10	0	.286	258	324
Atlanta	4	10	0	.286	309	388

West Division	W	L	T	Pct.	Pts.	OP
Seattle#	12	2	0	.857	380	205
San Francisco	10	4	0	.714	349	228
Arizona	9	5	0	.643	342	291
St. Louis	6	8	0	.429	316	324

*Clinched division title
#Clinched playoff berth

WEEK 15 RESULTS
Thursday, December 12
San Diego 27, DENVER 20

Sunday, December 15
ATLANTA 27, Washington 26
Chicago 38, CLEVELAND 31
INDIANAPOLIS 25, Houston 3
Buffalo 27, JACKSONVILLE 20
MIAMI 24, New England 20
MINNESOTA 48, Philadelphia 30
Seattle 23, NEW YORK GIANTS 0
ST. LOUIS 27, New Orleans 16
San Francisco 33, TAMPA BAY 14
Arizona 37, TENNESSEE 34 (OT)
CAROLINA 30, New York Jets 20
Kansas City 56, OAKLAND 31
Green Bay 37, DALLAS 36
PITTSBURGH 30, Cincinnati 20

Monday, December 16
Baltimore 18, DETROIT 16

SIXTEENTH WEEK STANDINGS
American Football Conference

East Division	W	L	T	Pct.	Pts.	OP
New England*	11	4	0	.733	410	318
Miami	8	7	0	.533	310	315
New York Jets	7	8	0	.467	270	380
Buffalo	6	9	0	.400	319	354

North Division	W	L	T	Pct.	Pts.	OP
Cincinnati*	10	5	0	.667	396	288
Baltimore	8	7	0	.533	303	318
Pittsburgh	7	8	0	.467	359	363
Cleveland	4	11	0	.267	301	386

South Division	W	L	T	Pct.	Pts.	OP
Indianapolis*	10	5	0	.667	361	326
Tennessee	6	9	0	.400	346	371
Jacksonville	4	11	0	.267	237	419
Houston	2	13	0	.133	266	412

West Division	W	L	T	Pct.	Pts.	OP
Denver*	12	3	0	.800	572	385
Kansas City#	11	4	0	.733	406	278
San Diego	8	7	0	.533	369	324
Oakland	4	11	0	.267	308	419

National Football Conference

East Division	W	L	T	Pct.	Pts.	OP
Philadelphia	9	6	0	.600	418	360
Dallas	8	7	0	.533	417	408
New York Giants	6	9	0	.400	274	377
Washington	3	12	0	.200	328	458

North Division	W	L	T	Pct.	Pts.	OP
Chicago	8	7	0	.533	417	445
Green Bay	7	7	1	.500	384	400
Detroit	7	8	0	.467	382	362
Minnesota	4	10	1	.300	377	467

South Division	W	L	T	Pct.	Pts.	OP
Carolina#	11	4	0	.733	345	221
New Orleans	10	5	0	.667	372	287
Atlanta	4	11	0	.267	333	422
Tampa Bay	4	11	0	.267	271	347

West Division	W	L	T	Pct.	Pts.	OP
Seattle#	12	3	0	.800	390	222
San Francisco#	11	4	0	.733	383	252
Arizona	10	5	0	.667	359	301
St. Louis	7	8	0	.467	339	337

*Clinched division title
#Clinched playoff berth

WEEK 16 RESULTS
Sunday, December 22
BUFFALO 19, Miami 0
CAROLINA 17, New Orleans 13
CINCINNATI 42, Minnesota 14
Denver 37, HOUSTON 13
Tennessee 20, JACKSONVILLE 16
Indianapolis 23, KANSAS CITY 7
NEW YORK JETS 24, Cleveland 13
ST. LOUIS 23, Tampa Bay 13
Dallas 24, WASHINGTON 23
New York Giants 23, DETROIT 20 (OT)
Arizona 17, SEATTLE 10
New England 41, BALTIMORE 7
Pittsburgh 38, GREEN BAY 31
SAN DIEGO 26, Oakland 13
PHILADELPHIA 54, Chicago 11

Monday, December 23
SAN FRANCISCO 34, Atlanta 24

SEVENTEENTH WEEK STANDINGS
American Football Conference

East Division	W	L	T	Pct.	Pts.	OP
New England*	12	4	0	.750	444	338
New York Jets	8	8	0	.500	290	387
Miami	8	8	0	.500	317	335
Buffalo	6	10	0	.375	339	388

North Division	W	L	T	Pct.	Pts.	OP
Cincinnati*	11	5	0	.688	430	305
Pittsburgh	8	8	0	.500	379	370
Baltimore	8	8	0	.500	320	352
Cleveland	4	12	0	.250	308	406

South Division	W	L	T	Pct.	Pts.	OP
Indianapolis*	11	5	0	.688	391	336
Tennessee	7	9	0	.438	362	381
Jacksonville	4	12	0	.250	247	449
Houston	2	14	0	.125	276	428

West Division	W	L	T	Pct.	Pts.	OP
Denver*	13	3	0	.813	606	399
Kansas City#	11	5	0	.688	430	305
San Diego#	9	7	0	.563	396	348
Oakland	4	12	0	.250	322	453

National Football Conference

East Division	W	L	T	Pct.	Pts.	OP
Philadelphia*	10	6	0	.625	442	382
Dallas	8	8	0	.500	439	432
New York Giants	7	9	0	.438	294	383
Washington	3	13	0	.188	334	478

North Division	W	L	T	Pct.	Pts.	OP
Green Bay*	8	7	1	.531	417	428
Chicago	8	8	0	.500	445	478
Detroit	7	9	0	.438	395	376
Minnesota	5	10	1	.344	391	480

South Division	W	L	T	Pct.	Pts.	OP
Carolina*	12	4	0	.750	366	241
New Orleans#	11	5	0	.688	414	304
Atlanta	4	12	0	.250	353	443
Tampa Bay	4	12	0	.250	288	389

West Division	W	L	T	Pct.	Pts.	OP
Seattle*	13	3	0	.813	417	231
San Francisco#	12	4	0	.750	406	272
Arizona	10	6	0	.625	379	324
St. Louis	7	9	0	.438	348	364

*Clinched division title
#Clinched wild-card berth

WEEK 17 RESULTS
Sunday, December 29
Carolina 21, ATLANTA 20
CINCINNATI 34, Baltimore 17
INDIANAPOLIS 30, Jacksonville 10
New York Jets 20, MIAMI 7
MINNESOTA 14, Detroit 13
NEW ORLEANS 42, Tampa Bay 17
NEW YORK GIANTS 20, Washington 6
PITTSBURGH 20, Cleveland 7
TENNESSEE 16, Houston 10
San Francisco 23, ARIZONA 20
Green Bay 33, CHICAGO 28
NEW ENGLAND 34, Buffalo 20
Denver 34, OAKLAND 14
SAN DIEGO 27, Kansas City 24 (OT)
SEATTLE 27, St. Louis 9
Philadelphia 24, DALLAS 22

2013 NFL PAID ATTENDANCE BREAKDOWN

Games	Attendance	Average
NFL Preseason Total		
65	3,673,827	56,520
NFL Regular-Season Total		
256	16,837,676	65,772
NFL Postseason Total		
12	822,651	68,554
NFL All Games		
333	21,334,154	64,067

1.1-MILLION CLUB
During the 2013 season, five teams drew more than 1.1 million paid attendance home and away during the regular season. The Dallas Cowboys led the NFL in regular-season paid attendance (1,208,640). The Cowboys also led the league in home paid attendance (648,683).

Team	Total Paid Home Attendance	Total Paid Visiting Attendance	Total Paid Cumulative Attendance
Dallas	648,683	559,957	1,208,640
New York Giants	638,827	547,737	1,186,564
Green Bay	623,559	552,111	1,175,670
Denver	602,515	563,865	1,166,380
Washington	579,080	563,316	1,142,396

For complete year-by-year attendance records, see pages 541-542.

2013 AFC PLAYERS OF THE WEEK

	Offense	Defense	Special Teams
Week 1	QB Peyton Manning, Denver	LB Justin Houston, Kansas City	K Nick Folk, New York Jets
Week 2	QB Philip Rivers, San Diego	DE Mario Williams, Buffalo	PR-WR Trindon Holliday, Denver
Week 3	QB Peyton Manning, Denver	LB Justin Houston, Kansas City	P Spencer Lanning, Cleveland
Week 4	QB Philip Rivers, San Diego	CB Alterraun Verner, Tennessee	PR Dexter McCluster, Kansas City
Week 5	QB Geno Smith, New York Jets	S Charles Woodson, Oakland	PR Travis Benjamin, Cleveland
Week 6	QB Andy Dalton, Cincinnati	LB Tamba Hali, Kansas City	K Nick Novak, San Diego
Week 7	QB Andrew Luck, Indianapolis	DE Mario Williams, Buffalo	K Shaun Suisham, Pittsburgh
Week 8	WR Marvin Jones, Cincinnati	CB Dominque Rodgers-Cromartie, Denver	K Ryan Succop, Kansas City
Week 9	QB Jason Campbell, Cleveland	DE Cameron Wake, Miami	K Nick Folk, New York Jets
Week 10	WR Demaryius Thomas, Denver	LB Paul Posluszny, Jacksonville	K Justin Tucker, Baltimore
Week 11	QB Ben Roethlisberger, Pittsburgh	LB Vontaze Burfict, Cincinnati	K Adam Vinatieri, Indianapolis
Week 12	QB Tom Brady, New England	S Troy Polamalu, Pittsburgh	K Justin Tucker, Baltimore
Week 13	WR Eric Decker, Denver	DE Olivier Vernon, Miami	P Kevin Huber, Cincinnati
Week 14	QB Andy Dalton, Cincinnati	LB Tamba Hali Kansas City	K Matt Prater, Denver
Week 15	RB Jamaal Charles, Kansas City	S Michael Thomas, Miami	K Justin Tucker, Baltimore
Week 16	QB Peyton Manning, Denver	LB Jerrell Freeman, Indianapolis	K Nick Novak, San Diego
Week 17	RB LeGarrette Blount, New England	CB Dee Milliner, New York Jets	K Adam Vinatieri, Indianapolis

2013 AFC PLAYERS OF THE MONTH

	Offense	Defense	Special Teams
September	QB Peyton Manning, Denver	LB Justin Houston, Kansas City	KR Trindon Holliday, Denver
October	QB Andy Dalton, Cincinnati	LB Robert Mathis, Indianapolis	K Stephen Gostkowski, New England
November	QB Ben Roethlisberger, Pittsburgh	DE Chandler Jones, New England	K Justin Tucker, Baltimore
December	QB Peyton Manning, Denver	LB Robert Mathis, Indianapolis	PR Dexter McCluster, Kansas City

2013 NFC PLAYERS OF THE WEEK

	Offense	Defense	Special Teams
Week 1	WR Anquan Boldin, San Francisco	DE Robert Quinn, St. Louis	WR-PR Dwayne Harris, Dallas
Week 2	QB Aaron Rodgers, Green Bay	CB Richard Sherman, Seattle	KR-PR Devin Hester, Chicago
Week 3	TE Jimmy Graham, New Orleans	DE Greg Hardy, Carolina	P Sam Martin, Detroit
Week 4	QB Drew Brees, New Orleans	CB Patrick Peterson, Arizona	K Steve Hauschka, Seattle
Week 5	WR DeSean Jackson, Philadelphia	CB Tramaine Brock, San Francisco	K Mason Crosby, Green Bay
Week 6	QB Nick Foles, Philadelphia	LB Thomas Davis, Carolina	WR-PR Dwayne Harris, Dallas
Week 7	QB Matt Ryan, Atlanta	LB Sean Lee, Dallas	P Andy Lee, San Francisco
Week 8	WR Calvin Johnson, Detroit	CB Terrell Thomas, New York Giants	KR Cordarrelle Patterson, Minnesota
Week 9	QB Nick Foles, Philadelphia	DE Shea McClellin, Chicago	PR Golden Tate, Seattle
Week 10	QB Drew Brees, New Orleans	LB Luke Kuechly, Carolina	PR-KR Tavon Austin, St. Louis
Week 11	RB Bobby Rainey, Tampa Bay	DE Jason Pierre-Paul, New York Giants	P Donnie Jones, Philadelphia
Week 12	QB Carson Palmer, Arizona	LB Lavonte David, Tampa Bay	K Blair Walsh, Minnesota
Week 13	QB Russell Wilson, Seattle	DE Justin Tuck, New York Giants	P Donnie Jones, Philadelphia
Week 14	QB Josh McCown, Chicago	LB John Abraham, Arizona	K Phil Dawson, San Francisco
Week 15	RB Eddie Lacy, Green Bay	CB Richard Sherman, Seattle	K Jay Feely, Arizona
Week 16	RB LeSean McCoy, Philadelphia	LB Luke Kuechly, Carolina	K Josh Brown, New York Giants
Week 17	QB Drew Brees, New Orleans	DE Greg Hardy, Carolina	K Phil Dawson, San Francisco

2013 NFC PLAYERS OF THE MONTH

	Offense	Defense	Special Teams
September	TE Jimmy Graham, New Orleans	CB Richard Sherman, Seattle	KR Cordarrelle Patterson, Minnesota
October	WR Calvin Johnson, Detroit	LB Sean Lee, Dallas	K Mason Crosby, Green Bay
November	QB Nick Foles, Philadelphia	LB Thomas Davis, Carolina	PR-KR-WR Tavon Austin, St. Louis
December	RB LeSean McCoy, Philadelphia	LB NaVorro Bowman, San Francisco	P Brad Nortman, Carolina

2013 NFL ROOKIES OF THE MONTH

	Offense (College)		Defense (College)
September	WR DeAndre Hopkins, Houston (Clemson)	LB	Kiko Alonso, Buffalo (Oregon)
October	RB Eddie Lacy, Green Bay (Alabama)	S	Tyrann Mathieu, Arizona (Louisiana State)
November	QB Mike Glennon, Tampa Bay (North Carolina State)	DT	Sheldon Richardson, New York Jets (Missouri)
December	WR Cordarrelle Patterson, Minnesota (Tennessee)	CB	Dee Milliner, New York Jets (Alabama)

2013 PRO FOOTBALL AWARDS

ASSOCIATED PRESS
Most Valuable Player	Peyton Manning
Offensive Player of the Year	Peyton Manning
Defensive Player of the Year	Luke Kuechly
Offensive Rookie of the Year	Eddie Lacy
Defensive Rookie of the Year	Sheldon Richardson
Coach of the Year	Ron Rivera
Comeback Player of the Year	Philip Rivers

THE SPORTING NEWS
Offensive Player of the Year	Peyton Manning
Defensive Player of the Year	Luke Kuechly
Rookie of the Year	Keenan Allen
Coach of the Year	Ron Rivera
Coordinator of the Year	Sean McDermott
Executive of the Year	Ryan Grigson
Comeback Player of the Year	Darrelle Revis

PRO FOOTBALL WEEKLY/PFWA
Most Valuable Player	Peyton Manning
Offensive Player of the Year	Peyton Manning
Defensive Player of the Year	Robert Quinn
Rookie of the Year	Eddie Lacy
Offensive Rookie of the Year	Keenan Allen
Defensive Rookie of the Year	Kiko Alonso
Comeback Player of the Year	Philip Rivers
Most Improved Player	Alshon Jeffery
Coach of the Year	Ron Rivera
Assistant Coach of the Year	Ken Whisenhunt
Executive of the Year	John Dorsey

SPORTS ILLUSTRATED
Most Valuable Player	Peyton Manning
Offensive Player of the Year	Peyton Manning
Defensive Player of the Year	J.J. Watt
Offensive Rookie of the Year	Keenan Allen
Defensive Rookie of the Year	Sheldon Richardson
Coaches of the Year	Andy Reid
	Ron Rivera

MAXWELL CLUB AWARDS
Player of the Year (Bert Bell Trophy)	Peyton Manning
Coach of the Year	Chip Kelly

WALTER PAYTON/ NFL MAN OF THE YEAR
Man of the Year	Charles Tillman
Man of the Year Finalist	Thomas Davis
Man of the Year Finalist	Jay Feely

SUPER BOWL XLVIII MOST VALUABLE PLAYER
Pete Rozelle Trophy	Malcolm Smith

2014 PRO BOWL MOST VALUABLE PLAYERS
Pro Bowl Offensive MVP	Nick Foles
Pro Bowl Defensive MVP	Derrick Johnson

FEDEX AIR & GROUND NFL PLAYERS OF THE YEAR
FedEx Air NFL Player of the Year	Peyton Manning
FedEx Ground NFL Player of the Year	LeSean McCoy

PEPSI ROOKIE OF THE YEAR
Rookie of the Year	Keenan Allen

2013 ALL-PRO TEAMS

2013 PFW/PFWA ALL-PRO TEAM
Selected by *Pro Football Weekly* and the Professional Football Writers of America

Offense:
Peyton Manning, Denver	Quarterback
Jamaal Charles, Kansas City	Running Back
LeSean McCoy, Philadelphia	Running Back
Jimmy Graham, New Orleans	Tight End
Calvin Johnson, Detroit	Wide Receiver
Josh Gordon, Cleveland	Wide Receiver
Joe Thomas, Cleveland	Tackle
Joe Staley, San Francisco	Tackle
Evan Mathis, Philadelphia	Guard
Louis Vasquez, Denver	Guard
Ryan Kalil, Carolina	Center

Defense:
J.J. Watt, Houston	End
Robert Quinn, St. Louis	End
Gerald McCoy, Tampa Bay	Tackle
Ndamukong Suh, Detroit	Tackle
Robert Mathis, Indianapolis	Outside Linebacker
Lavonte David, Tampa Bay	Outside Linebacker
Luke Kuechly, Carolina	Inside Linebacker
Richard Sherman, Seattle	Cornerback
Patrick Peterson, Arizona	Cornerback
Earl Thomas, Seattle	Safety
Eric Berry, Kansas City	Safety

Special Teams:
Justin Tucker, Baltimore	Kicker
Johnny Hekker, St. Louis	Punter
Cordarrelle Patterson, Minnesota	Kick Returner
Dexter McCluster, Kansas City	Punt Returner
Justin Bethel, Arizona	Special Teams Player

2012 ASSOCIATED PRESS ALL-PRO TEAM
Selected by the Associated Press

Offense:
Peyton Manning, Denver	Quarterback
LeSean McCoy, Philadelphia	Running Back
Jamaal Charles, Kansas City	Running Back
Mike Tolbert, Carolina	Fullback
Jimmy Graham, New Orleans	Tight End
Calvin Johnson, Detroit	Wide Receiver
Josh Gordon, Cleveland	Wide Receiver
Joe Thomas, Cleveland	Tackle
Jason Peters, Philadelphia	Tackle
Louis Vasquez, Denver	Guard
Evan Mathis, Philadelphia	Guard
Ryan Kalil, Carolina	Center

Defense:
J.J. Watt, Houston	End
Robert Quinn, St. Louis	End
Gerald McCoy, Tampa Bay	Tackle
Ndamukong Suh, Detroit	Tackle
Robert Mathis, Indianapolis	Outside Linebacker
Lavonte David, Tampa Bay	Outside Linebacker
Luke Kuechly, Carolina	Inside Linebacker
NaVorro Bowman, San Francisco	Inside Linebacker
Richard Sherman, Seattle	Cornerback
Patrick Peterson, Arizona	Cornerback
Earl Thomas, Seattle	Safety
Eric Berry, Kansas City	Safety

Special Teams:
Justin Tucker, Baltimore	Kicker
Johnny Hekker, St. Louis	Punter
Cordarrelle Patterson, Minnesota	Kick Returner

2013 ALL-NFL TEAM
Selected by the Associated Press, *Pro Football Weekly,* and the Professional Football Writers of America

Offense:

Peyton Manning, Denver (PFW, AP)	Quarterback
Jamaal Charles, Kansas City (PFW, AP)	Running Back
LeSean McCoy, Philadelphia (PFW, AP)	Running Back
Mike Tolbert, Carolina (AP)	Fullback
Jimmy Graham, New Orleans (PFW, AP)	Tight End
Calvin Johnson, Detroit (PFW, AP)	Wide Receiver
Josh Gordon, Cleveland (PFW, AP)	Wide Receiver
Joe Thomas, Cleveland (PFW, AP)	Tackle
Joe Staley, San Francisco (PFW)	Tackle
Jason Peters, Philadelphia (AP)	Tackle
Evan Mathis, Philadelphia (PFW, AP)	Guard
Louis Vasquez, Denver (PFW, AP)	Guard
Ryan Kalil, Carolina (PFW, AP)	Center

Defense:

J.J. Watt, Houston (PFW, AP)	End
Robert Quinn, St. Louis (PFW, AP)	End
Gerald McCoy, Tampa Bay (PFW, AP)	Tackle
Ndamukong Suh, Detroit (PFW, AP)	Tackle
Robert Mathis, Indianapolis (PFW, AP)	Outside Linebacker
Lavonte David, Tampa Bay (PFW, AP)	Outside Linebacker
Luke Kuechly, Carolina (PFW, AP)	Inside Linebacker
NaVorro Bowman, San Francisco (AP)	Inside Linebacker
Richard Sherman, Seattle (PFW, AP)	Cornerback
Patrick Peterson, Arizona (PFW, AP)	Cornerback
Earl Thomas, Seattle (PFW, AP)	Safety
Eric Berry, Kansas City (PFW, AP)	Safety

Special Teams:

Justin Tucker, Baltimore (PFW, AP)	Kicker
Johnny Hekker, St. Louis (PFW, AP)	Punter
Cordarrelle Patterson, Minnesota (PFW, AP)	Kick Returner
Dexter McCluster, Kansas City (PFW)	Punt Returner
Justin Bethel, Arizona (PFW)	Special Teams Player

2013 PFW/PFWA ALL-ROOKIE TEAM
Selected by *Pro Football Weekly* and the Professional Football Writers of America

Offense:

Mike Glennon, Tampa Bay	Quarterback
Giovani Bernard, Cincinnati	Running Back
Eddie Lacy, Green Bay	Running Back
Jordan Reed, Washington	Tight End
Keenan Allen, San Diego	Wide Receiver
DeAndre Hopkins, Houston	Wide Receiver
D.J. Fluker, San Diego	Tackle
Justin Pugh, New York Giants	Tackle
Kyle Long, Chicago	Guard
Larry Warford, Detroit	Guard
Travis Frederick, Dallas	Center

Defense:

Ziggy Ansah, Detroit	Defensive Lineman
Star Lotulelei, Carolina	Defensive Lineman
Sheldon Richardson, New York Jets	Defensive Lineman
Kawann Short, Carolina	Defensive Lineman
Kiki Alonso, Buffalo	Linebacker
Sio Moore, Oakland	Linebacker
Alec Ogletree, St. Louis	Linebacker
Tyrann Mathieu, Arizona	Cornerback
Desmond Trufant, Atlanta	Cornerback
Eric Reid, San Francisco	Safety
Kenny Vaccaro, New Orleans	Safety

Special Teams:

Caleb Sturgis, Miami	Kicker
Sam Martin, Detroit	Punter
Cordarrelle Patterson, Minnesota	Punt Returner
Tavon Austin, St. Louis	Kick Returner
Don Jones, Miami	Special Teams Player

TEN BEST RUSHING PERFORMANCES, 2013

		Att.	Yards	TD
1.	Knowshon Moreno Denver vs. New England, Nov. 24 (OT)	37	224	1
2.	LeSean McCoy Philadelphia vs. Detroit, Dec. 8	29	217	2
3.	Adrian Peterson Minnesota vs. Chicago, Dec. 1 (OT)	35	211	0
4.	LeGarrette Blount New England vs. Buffalo, Dec. 29	24	189	2
5.	LeSean McCoy Philadelphia vs. Washington, Sept. 9	31	184	1
6.	DeMarco Murray Dallas vs. St. Louis, Sept. 22	26	175	1
7.	Bobby Rainey Tampa Bay vs. Atlanta, Nov. 17	30	163	2
8.	LeSean McCoy Philadelphia vs. Kansas City, Sept. 19	20	158	1
	Mike James Tampa Bay vs. Seattle, Nov. 3 (OT)	28	158	0
10.	LeSean McCoy Philadelphia vs. Green Bay, Nov. 10	25	155	0

There were 97 100-yard rushing performances in 2013.

MOST 100-YARD RUSHING PERFORMANCES, 2013

Player, Team	100-Yd. Games
LeSean McCoy, Philadelphia	7
Ryan Mathews, San Diego	6
Matt Forté, Chicago	5
Adrian Peterson, Minnesota	5
Jamaal Charles, Kansas City	4
Eddie Lacy, Green Bay	4
C.J. Spiller, Buffalo	4
Zac Stacy, St. Louis	4
Reggie Bush, Detroit	3
Frank Gore, San Francisco	3
Chris Ivory, N.Y. Jets	3
Marshawn Lynch, Seattle	3
Alfred Morris, Washington	3
DeMarco Murray, Dallas	3
Andre Brown, N.Y. Giants	2
Arian Foster, Houston	2
Rashad Jennings, Oakland	2
Chris Johnson, Tennessee	2
Terrelle Pryor, Oakland	2
Bobby Rainey, Tampa Bay	2
28 players tied with	1

TEN BEST PASSING PERFORMANCES, 2013

		Att.	Comp.	Yds.	TD
1.	Tony Romo Dallas vs. Denver, Oct. 6	36	25	506	5
2.	Matthew Stafford Detroit vs. Dallas, Oct. 27	48	33	488	1
3.	Aaron Rodgers Green Bay vs. Washington, Sept. 15	42	34	480	4
4.	Peyton Manning Denver vs. Baltimore, Sept. 5	42	27	462	7
5.	Eli Manning N.Y. Giants vs. Dallas, Sept. 8	42	27	450	4
6.	Tom Brady New England vs. Pittsburgh, Nov. 3	33	23	432	4
7.	Michael Vick Philadelphia vs. San Diego, Sept. 15	36	23	428	2
	Nick Foles Philadelphia vs. Minnesota, Dec. 15	48	30	428	3
9.	Matt Ryan Atlanta vs. New England, Sept. 29	54	34	421	2
10.	Philip Rivers San Diego vs. Philadelphia, Sept. 15	47	36	419	3
	Carson Palmer Arizona vs. Jacksonville, Nov. 17	42	30	419	2

There were 118 300-yard passing performances in 2013.

MOST 300-YARD PASSING PERFORMANCES, 2013

Player, Team	300-Yd. Games
Peyton Manning, Denver	12
Drew Brees, New Orleans	11
Matt Ryan, Atlanta	7
Tom Brady, New England	6
Matthew Stafford, Detroit	6
Andy Dalton, Cincinnati	5
Carson Palmer, Arizona	5
Philip Rivers, San Diego	5
Ben Roethlisberger, Pittsburgh	5
Ryan Tannehill, Miami	5
Aaron Rodgers, Green Bay	4
Tony Romo, Dallas	4
Joe Flacco, Baltimore	3
Robert Griffin III, Washington	3
Chad Henne, Jacksonville	3
Andrew Luck, Indianapolis	3
Eli Manning, N.Y. Giants	3
Josh McCown, N.Y. Giants	3
Jay Cutler, Chicago	2
Ryan Fitzpatrick, Tennessee	2
Nick Foles, Philadelphia	2
Colin Kaepernick, San Francisco	2
Matt Schaub, Houston	2
Russell Wilson, Seattle	2
13 players tied with 1	1

TEN BEST RECEIVING PERFORMANCES, 2013

	No.	Yards	TD
1. Calvin Johnson	14	329	1
Detroit vs. Dallas, Oct. 27			
2. Josh Gordon	10	261	2
Cleveland vs. Jacksonville, Dec. 1			
3. Alshon Jeffery	12	249	2
Chicago vs. Minnesota, Dec. 1 (OT)			
4. Josh Gordon	14	237	1
Cleveland vs. Pittsburgh, Nov. 24			
5. Andre Johnson	9	229	3
Houston vs. Indianapolis, Nov. 3			
6. Alshon Jeffery	10	218	1
Chicago vs. New Orleans, Oct. 6			
7. Anquan Boldin	13	208	1
San Francisco vs. Green Bay, Sept. 8			
8. Antonio Brown	9	196	2
Pittsburgh vs. Chicago, Sept. 22			
9. Jamaal Charles	8	195	4
Kansas City vs. Oakland, Dec. 15			
DeSean Jackson	10	195	1
Philadelphia vs. Minnesota, Dec. 15			

There were 208 100-yard receiving performances in 2013.

MOST 100-YARD RECEIVING PERFORMANCES, 2013

Player, Team	100-Yd. Games
Josh Gordon, Cleveland	7
Calvin Johnson, Detroit	7
Jimmy Graham, New Orleans	6
A.J. Green, Cincinnati	6
Andre Johnson, Houston	6
Brandon Marshall, Chicago	6
Demaryius Thomas, Denver	6
Keenan Allen, San Diego	5
Antonio Brown, Pittsburgh	5
Eric Decker, Denver	5
Pierre Garcon, Washington	5
T.Y. Hilton, Indianapolis	5
DeSean Jackson, Philadelphia	5
Alshon Jeffery, Chicago	5
Jordy Nelson, Green Bay	5
Dez Bryant, Dallas	4
Victor Cruz, N.Y. Giants	4
Julian Edelman, New England	4
Vincent Jackson, Tampa Bay	4
Mike Wallace, Miami	4
Danny Amendola, New England	3
Riley Cooper, Philadelphia	3
Harry Douglas, Atlanta	3
Rob Gronkowski, New England	3
Julio Jones, Atlanta	3
Hakeem Nicks, N.Y. Giants	3
Nate Washington, Tennessee	3
Jason Witten, Dallas	3
Justin Blackmon, Jacksonville	2
Anquan Boldin, San Francisco	2
Jarrett Boykin, Green Bay	2
Jordan Cameron, Cleveland	2
Randall Cobb, Green Bay	2
Marques Colston, New Orleans	2
Larry Fitzgerald, Arizona	2
Michael Floyd, Arizona	2
Antonio Gates, San Diego	2
Brian Hartline, Miami	2
Justin Hunter, Tennessee	2
James Jones, Green Bay	2
Jerome Simpson, Minnesota	2
Torrey Smith, Baltimore	2
Golden Tate, Seattle	2
Julius Thomas, Denver	2
Roddy White, Atlanta	2
Kendall Wright, Tennessee	2
35 players tied with	1

TOP QUARTERBACK SACK PERFORMANCES, 2013

	No.
1. Mario Williams	4.5
Buffalo vs. Carolina, Sept. 15	
Justin Houston	4.5
Kansas City vs. Philadelphia, Sept. 19	
3. Justin Tuck	4.0
N.Y. Giants vs. Washington, Dec. 1	
Greg Hardy	4.0
Carolina vs. Atlanta, Dec. 29	
5. Justin Houston	3.0
Kansas City vs. Jacksonville, Sept. 8	
Robert Quinn	3.0
St. Louis vs. Arizona, Sept. 8	
Darnell Dockett	3,0
Arizona vs. New Orleans, Sept. 22	
Greg Hardy	3.0
Carolina vs. N.Y. Giants, Sept. 22	
Robert Mathis	3.0
Indianapolis vs. Jacksonville, Sept. 29	
Terrell Suggs	3.0
Baltimore vs. Miami, Oct. 6	
A.J. Hawk	3.0
Green Bay vs. Baltimore, Oct. 13	
Chris Long	3.0
St. Louis vs. Seattle, Oct. 28	
Robert Quinn	3.0
St. Louis vs. Seattle, Oct. 28	
Cameron Wake	3.0
Miami vs. Cincinnati, Oct. 31 (OT)	
Shea McClellin	3.0
Chicago vs. Green Bay, Nov. 4	
John Abraham	3.0
Arizona vs. Houston, Nov. 10	
Elvis Dumervil	3.0
Baltimore vs. Cincinnati, Nov. 10 (OT)	
Vincent Rey	3.0
Cincinnati vs. Baltimore, Nov. 10 (OT)	
Gerald McCoy	3.0
Tampa Bay vs. Atlanta, Nov. 17	
Olivier Vernon	3.0
Miami vs. N.Y. Jets, Dec. 1	
John Abraham	3.0
Arizona vs. St. Louis, Dec. 8	
Junior Galette	3.0
New Orleans vs. Carolina, Dec. 8	
Trent Cole	3.0
Philadelphia vs. Chicago, Dec. 22	
Greg Hardy	3.0
Carolina vs. New Orleans, Dec. 22	
Robert Quinn	3.0
St. Louis vs. Tampa Bay, Dec. 22	

There were 25 3.0-plus sack performances in 2013.

MOST 3.0-PLUS SACK PERFORMANCES, 2013

Player, Team	3.0-Sack Games
Greg Hardy, Carolina	3
Robert Quinn, St. Louis	3
John Abraham, Arizona	2
Justin Houston, Kansas City	2
15 players tied with	1

For week-by-week listings of top performances from 1970 to the present, please visit www.NFL.com/stats/topperformers.

AMERICAN FOOTBALL CONFERENCE OFFENSE

	Balt.	Buff.	Cin.	Cle.	Den.	Hou.	Ind.	Jax.	KC	Mia.	NE	NYJ	Oak.	Pitt.	SD	Tenn.
First Downs	295	301	330	301	435	307	318	271	323	278	378	280	275	312	373	311
Rushing	68	113	101	77	107	90	88	71	110	61	110	105	90	81	104	103
Passing	189	149	205	200	293	198	191	176	179	205	225	154	168	207	230	172
Penalty	38	39	24	24	35	19	39	24	34	12	43	21	17	24	39	36
Rushes	423	546	481	348	461	414	409	378	442	349	470	493	437	394	486	462
Net Yds. Gained	1328	2307	1755	1383	1873	1743	1743	1260	2056	1440	2065	2158	2000	1383	1965	1894
Avg. Gain	3.1	4.2	3.6	4.0	4.1	4.2	4.3	3.3	4.7	4.1	4.4	4.4	4.6	3.5	4.0	4.1
Avg. Yds. per Game	83.0	144.2	109.7	86.4	117.1	108.9	108.9	78.8	128.5	90.0	129.1	134.9	125.0	86.4	122.8	118.4
Passes Attempted	619	522	587	681	675	633	582	592	546	594	628	480	519	586	544	533
Completed	363	299	364	379	461	371	350	349	333	357	380	266	298	377	378	328
% Completed	58.6	57.3	62.0	55.7	68.3	58.6	60.1	59.0	61.0	60.1	60.5	55.4	57.4	64.3	69.5	61.5
Total Yds. Gained	3914	3373	4318	4372	5572	4183	3952	3751	3561	3966	4343	3270	3629	4306	4478	3710
Times Sacked	48	48	29	49	20	42	32	50	41	58	40	47	44	43	30	37
Yds. Lost	324	270	182	325	128	370	227	310	221	399	256	338	289	289	150	214
Net Yds. Gained	3590	3103	4136	4047	5444	3813	3725	3441	3340	3567	4087	2932	3340	4017	4328	3496
Avg. Yds. per Game	224.4	193.9	258.5	252.9	340.3	238.3	232.8	215.1	208.8	222.9	255.4	183.3	208.8	251.1	270.5	218.5
Net Yds. per Pass Play	5.38	5.44	6.71	5.54	7.83	5.65	6.07	5.36	5.69	5.47	6.12	5.56	5.93	6.39	7.54	6.13
Yds. Gained per Comp.	10.78	11.28	11.86	11.54	12.09	11.27	11.29	10.75	10.69	11.11	11.43	12.29	12.18	11.42	11.85	11.31
Combined Net Yds. Gained	4918	5410	5891	5430	7317	5556	5468	4701	5396	5007	6152	5090	5340	5400	6293	5390
% Total Yds. Rushing	27.0	42.6	29.8	25.5	25.6	31.4	31.9	26.8	38.1	28.8	33.6	42.4	37.5	25.6	31.2	35.1
% Total Yds. Passing	73.0	57.4	70.2	74.5	74.4	68.6	68.1	73.2	61.9	71.2	66.4	57.6	62.5	74.4	68.8	64.9
Avg. Yds. per Game	307.4	338.1	368.2	339.4	457.3	347.3	341.8	293.8	337.3	312.9	384.5	318.1	333.8	337.5	393.3	336.9
Ball Control Plays	1090	1116	1097	1078	1156	1089	1023	1020	1029	1001	1138	1020	1000	1023	1060	1032
Avg. Yds. per Play	4.5	4.8	5.4	5.0	6.3	5.1	5.3	4.6	5.2	5.0	5.4	5.0	5.3	5.3	5.9	5.2
Avg. Time of Poss.	29:51	28:23	31:58	28:41	30:06	31:00	29:41	27:22	30:43	28:27	29:38	29:55	29:54	30:53	32:59	30:00
Third Down Efficiency	36.4	34.0	40.9	35.0	46.3	35.9	37.6	31.1	34.7	35.0	37.6	37.6	39.0	35.0	49.0	41.4
Had Intercepted	23	15	20	20	10	22	10	21	8	19	11	22	20	14	11	16
Yds. Opp Returned	219	298	369	206	131	357	91	355	21	165	56	411	375	170	146	132
Ret. by Opp. for TD	4	2	2	2	2	5	1	3	0	2	1	5	3	1	2	1
Punts	91	96	75	86	66	88	77	95	89	85	77	89	86	76	56	79
Yds. Punted	4138	4124	3330	3713	2893	4189	3499	4338	4034	4150	3523	4018	4107	3125	2417	3386
Avg. Yds. per Punt	45.5	43.0	44.4	43.2	43.8	47.6	45.4	45.7	45.3	48.8	45.8	45.1	47.8	41.1	43.2	42.9
Punt Returns	43	39	47	38	44	42	33	30	59	34	36	25	25	32	22	31
Yds. Returned	609	243	418	418	343	360	326	142	695	264	387	224	206	409	166	240
Avg. Yds. per Return	14.2	6.2	9.0	11.0	7.8	8.6	9.9	4.7	11.8	7.8	10.8	9.0	8.2	12.8	7.5	7.7
Returned for TD	1	0	0	1	1	1	0	0	2	0	0	0	0	1	0	0
Kickoff Returns	44	23	39	40	39	51	43	41	44	42	39	45	54	43	32	44
Yds. Returned	1163	469	980	931	974	1257	1011	1060	1316	893	935	1021	1201	962	707	1096
Avg. Yds. per Return	26.4	20.4	25.1	23.3	25.0	24.6	23.5	25.9	29.9	21.3	24.0	22.7	22.2	22.4	22.1	24.9
Returned for TD	1	0	0	0	1	0	0	0	2	0	0	0	0	0	0	0
Fumbles	15	32	20	17	27	21	14	18	21	16	24	15	27	16	14	27
Lost	6	12	10	9	16	9	4	6	10	7	9	7	11	10	10	9
Out of Bounds	0	3	1	2	3	2	4	1	3	1	0	0	1	0	0	1
Own Rec. for TD	0	0	1	0	0	0	0	0	0	0	0	0	0	0	0	0
Opp. Rec. by	7	6	11	7	9	4	12	10	15	6	12	2	13	10	6	12
Opp. Rec. for TD	0	1	1	1	1	0	0	1	2	0	1	0	2	0	0	2
Penalties	112	110	102	104	117	112	66	96	101	70	69	108	116	80	95	101
Yds. Penalized	942	952	1000	920	1000	1138	576	797	774	598	625	837	912	677	765	900
Total Points Scored	320	339	430	308	606	276	391	247	430	317	444	290	322	379	396	362
Total TDs	29	34	54	35	76	28	40	25	52	34	47	27	37	41	42	41
TDs Rushing	7	15	14	4	16	7	15	7	17	8	19	12	16	9	9	16
TDs Passing	19	16	33	26	55	19	23	16	24	24	25	13	17	28	32	22
TDs on Ret. and Rec.	3	3	7	5	5	2	2	2	11	2	3	2	4	4	1	3
Extra Point Kicks	26	32	52	33	75	26	34	22	52	33	44	27	37	39	42	41
Extra Point Kicks Att.	26	32	53	33	75	26	34	23	52	33	44	27	37	39	42	41
2Pt Conversions	3	2	0	1	0	1	4	0	0	0	2	0	0	1	0	0
2Pt Conversions Att.	3	2	1	2	1	1	6	2	0	1	3	0	0	2	0	0
Safeties	0	0	0	0	0	1	2	3	0	1	0	1	0	1	0	0
Field Goals Made	38	33	18	21	25	26	35	23	22	26	38	33	21	30	34	25
Field Goals Attempted	41	36	22	26	26	35	40	25	28	34	41	36	30	32	37	29
% Successful	92.7	91.7	81.8	80.8	96.2	74.3	87.5	92.0	78.6	76.5	92.7	91.7	70.0	93.8	91.9	86.2

AMERICAN FOOTBALL CONFERENCE DEFENSE

	Balt.	Buff.	Cin.	Cle.	Den.	Hou.	Ind.	Jax.	KC	Mia.	NE	NYJ	Oak.	Pitt.	SD	Tenn.
First Downs	284	308	282	328	339	282	319	353	303	327	338	293	330	303	327	329
Rushing	79	98	72	103	90	88	101	121	88	114	110	68	100	106	98	108
Passing	176	170	178	197	208	158	191	200	189	192	208	198	202	174	208	191
Penalty	29	40	32	28	41	36	27	32	26	21	20	27	28	23	21	30
Rushes	440	471	385	462	420	454	448	507	428	484	481	421	442	433	376	446
Net Yds. Gained	1687	2063	1544	1781	1626	1958	2002	2108	1923	1998	2145	1412	1727	1849	1725	1795
Avg. Gain	3.8	4.4	4.0	3.9	3.9	4.3	4.5	4.2	4.5	4.1	4.5	3.4	3.9	4.3	4.6	4.0
Avg. Yds. per Game	105.4	128.9	96.5	111.3	101.6	122.4	125.1	131.8	120.2	124.9	134.1	88.3	107.9	115.6	107.8	112.2
Passes Attempted	552	561	614	605	613	484	536	551	592	580	589	586	549	569	548	545
Completed	314	310	362	363	357	287	324	354	334	344	336	345	374	329	364	344
% Completed	56.9	55.3	59.0	60.0	58.2	59.3	60.4	64.2	56.4	59.3	57.0	58.9	68.1	57.8	66.4	63.1
Total Yds. Gained	3938	3666	3623	3723	4360	3310	3959	4187	4271	4024	4137	4189	4352	3751	4387	3839
Times Sacked	40	57	43	40	41	32	42	31	47	42	48	41	38	34	35	36
Yds. Lost	257	395	279	185	290	187	248	225	309	272	313	242	260	198	248	227
Net Yds. Gained	3681	3271	3344	3538	4070	3123	3711	3962	3962	3752	3824	3947	4092	3553	4139	3612
Avg. Yds. per Game	230.1	204.4	209.0	221.1	254.4	195.2	231.9	247.6	247.6	234.5	239.0	246.7	255.8	222.1	258.7	225.8
Net Yds. per Pass Play	6.22	5.29	5.09	5.49	6.22	6.05	6.42	6.81	6.20	6.03	6.00	6.30	6.97	5.89	7.10	6.22
Yds. Gained per Comp.	12.54	11.83	10.01	10.26	12.21	11.53	12.22	11.83	12.79	11.70	12.31	12.14	11.64	11.40	12.05	11.16
Combined Net																
Yds. Gained	5368	5334	4888	5319	5696	5081	5713	6070	5885	5750	5969	5359	5819	5402	5864	5407
% Total Yds. Rushing	31.4	38.7	31.6	33.5	28.5	38.5	35.0	34.7	32.7	34.7	35.9	26.3	29.7	34.2	29.4	33.2
% Total Yds. Passing	68.6	61.3	68.4	66.5	71.5	61.5	65.0	65.3	67.3	65.3	64.1	73.7	70.3	65.8	70.6	66.8
Avg. Yds. per Game	335.5	333.4	305.5	332.4	356.0	317.6	357.1	379.4	367.8	359.4	373.1	334.9	363.7	337.6	366.5	337.9
Ball Control Plays	1032	1089	1042	1107	1074	970	1026	1089	1067	1106	1118	1048	1029	1036	959	1027
Avg. Yds. per Play	5.2	4.9	4.7	4.8	5.3	5.2	5.6	5.6	5.5	5.2	5.3	5.1	5.7	5.2	6.1	5.3
Avg. Time of Poss.	30:09	31:37	28:02	31:19	29:54	29:00	30:19	32:38	29:17	31:33	30:22	30:05	30:06	29:07	27:01	30:00
Third Down Efficiency	33.5	37.1	32.9	44.7	38.1	34.6	37.6	42.5	34.1	38.2	42.2	36.8	43.1	39.6	38.9	34.3
Intercepted By	16	23	20	14	17	7	15	11	21	18	17	13	9	10	11	13
Yds. Returned By	160	289	200	274	141	86	186	172	488	204	220	167	83	203	143	113
Returned for TD	1	2	4	3	1	1	1	1	5	2	2	1	1	3	1	1
Punts	98	94	90	88	89	91	75	76	87	78	80	82	77	79	65	76
Yds. Punted	4484	4274	3984	3849	4100	4161	3423	3268	4052	3406	3559	3679	3214	3397	3054	3422
Avg. Yds. per Punt	45.8	45.5	44.3	43.7	46.1	45.7	45.6	43.0	46.6	43.7	44.5	44.9	41.7	43.0	47.0	45.0
Punt Returns	46	45	27	38	28	43	29	47	38	42	29	43	42	35	19	35
Yds. Returned	419	477	254	357	274	530	396	330	246	407	221	488	438	313	158	210
Avg. Yds. per Return	9.1	10.6	9.4	9.4	9.8	12.3	13.7	7.0	6.5	9.7	7.6	11.3	10.4	8.9	8.3	6.0
Returned for TD	0	1	1	0	0	1	1	0	0	0	0	0	1	0	0	0
Kickoff Returns	38	48	52	27	32	39	43	25	43	36	32	42	30	55	73	45
Yds. Returned	873	1122	1219	612	936	1004	1085	509	1048	826	664	938	613	1225	1797	1099
Avg. Yds. per Return	23.0	23.4	23.4	22.7	29.3	25.7	25.2	20.4	24.4	22.9	20.8	22.3	20.4	22.3	24.6	24.4
Returned for TD	0	0	0	0	1	0	0	0	0	0	0	0	0	0	0	0
Fumbles	21	21	16	13	25	15	26	27	22	14	21	18	26	21	15	24
Lost	8	7	11	7	9	4	12	10	15	6	12	2	13	10	6	12
Out of Bounds	3	2	0	0	0	1	3	6	2	0	2	2	3	2	1	1
Own Rec. for TD	0	0	0	0	0	0	0	0	0	0	0	0	0	0	0	0
Opp. Rec. by	6	12	10	9	15	9	4	5	10	7	9	7	11	10	10	9
Opp. Rec. for TD	1	1	1	1	0	2	1	1	0	0	2	1	0	1	1	3
Penalties	126	108	69	95	97	103	112	87	112	95	110	92	87	92	100	95
Yds. Penalized	1196	931	692	745	807	809	990	729	852	748	951	833	686	798	850	779
Total Points Scored	352	388	305	406	399	428	336	449	305	335	338	387	453	370	348	381
Total TDs	37	42	32	46	47	48	38	53	34	33	39	41	54	41	40	40
TDs Rushing	7	10	6	13	15	11	14	20	9	14	11	9	15	18	14	21
TDs Passing	25	28	22	29	29	29	21	29	25	17	25	26	33	21	23	15
TDs on Ret. and Rec.	5	4	4	4	3	8	3	4	0	2	3	6	6	2	3	4
Extra Point Kicks	34	41	31	43	44	46	37	53	33	33	38	40	52	38	39	37
Extra Point Kicks Att.	34	41	31	43	44	46	37	53	33	33	38	40	52	39	39	38
2Pt Conversions	0	1	1	2	1	1	0	0	0	0	0	1	1	1	0	1
2Pt Conversions Att.	3	1	1	3	3	2	1	0	1	0	1	1	2	2	0	1
Safeties	0	0	1	1	1	1	1	0	1	1	0	0	0	0	0	3
Field Goals Made	32	31	26	27	23	30	23	26	22	34	22	33	25	28	23	32
Field Goals Attempted	35	36	31	32	26	35	30	29	28	40	27	37	28	31	30	39
% Successful	91.4	86.1	83.9	84.4	88.5	85.7	76.7	89.7	78.6	85.0	81.5	89.2	89.3	90.3	76.7	82.1

NATIONAL FOOTBALL CONFERENCE OFFENSE

	Ariz.	Atl.	Car.	Chi.	Dall.	Det.	GB	Minn.	NO	NYG	Phil.	StL	SF	Sea.	TB	Wash.
First Downs	329	330	319	344	325	350	351	309	359	280	355	282	286	307	269	329
Rushing	84	64	122	102	80	106	119	106	87	77	133	82	115	116	75	112
Passing	205	227	169	215	213	221	201	173	244	176	197	165	148	160	157	198
Penalty	40	39	28	27	32	23	31	30	28	27	25	35	23	31	37	19
Rushes	422	321	483	404	336	445	459	423	391	381	500	426	505	509	420	453
Net Yds. Gained	1540	1247	2026	1828	1504	1792	2136	2081	1473	1332	2566	1752	2201	2188	1612	2164
Avg. Gain	3.6	3.9	4.2	4.5	4.5	4.0	4.7	4.9	3.8	3.5	5.1	4.1	4.4	4.3	3.8	4.8
Avg. Yds. per Game	96.3	77.9	126.6	114.3	94.0	112.0	133.5	130.1	92.1	83.3	160.4	109.5	137.6	136.8	100.8	135.3
Passes Attempted	574	659	473	579	586	634	570	546	651	567	508	506	417	420	514	611
Completed	363	445	292	373	375	371	366	325	446	325	310	301	244	267	291	355
% Completed	63.2	67.5	61.7	64.4	64.0	58.5	64.2	59.5	68.5	57.3	61.0	59.5	58.5	63.6	56.6	58.1
Total Yds. Gained	4291	4541	3379	4450	4226	4650	4538	3645	5162	3875	4406	3360	3210	3508	3181	4057
Times Sacked	41	44	43	30	35	23	45	44	37	40	46	36	39	44	47	43
Yds. Lost	289	298	336	169	272	168	270	218	244	287	296	235	231	272	361	306
Net Yds. Gained	4002	4243	3043	4281	3954	4482	4268	3427	4918	3588	4110	3125	2979	3236	2820	3751
Avg. Yds. per Game	250.1	265.2	190.2	267.6	247.1	280.1	266.8	214.2	307.4	224.3	256.9	195.3	186.2	202.3	176.3	234.4
Net Yds. per Pass Play	6.51	6.04	5.90	7.03	6.37	6.82	6.94	5.81	7.15	5.91	7.42	5.77	6.53	6.97	5.03	5.74
Yds. Gained per Comp.	11.82	10.20	11.57	11.93	11.27	12.53	12.40	11.22	11.57	11.92	14.21	11.16	13.16	13.14	10.93	11.43
Combined Net																
Yds. Gained	5542	5490	5069	6109	5458	6274	6404	5508	6391	4920	6676	4877	5180	5424	4432	5915
% Total Yds. Rushing	27.8	22.7	40.0	29.9	27.6	28.6	33.4	37.8	23.0	27.1	38.4	35.9	42.5	40.3	36.4	36.6
% Total Yds. Passing	72.2	77.3	60.0	70.1	72.4	71.4	66.6	62.2	77.0	72.9	61.6	64.1	57.5	59.7	63.6	63.4
Avg. Yds. per Game	346.4	343.1	316.8	381.8	341.1	392.1	400.3	344.3	399.4	307.5	417.3	304.8	323.8	339.0	277.0	369.7
Ball Control Plays	1037	1024	999	1013	957	1102	1074	1013	1079	988	1054	968	961	973	981	1107
Avg. Yds. per Play	5.3	5.4	5.1	6.0	5.7	5.7	6.0	5.4	5.9	5.0	6.3	5.0	5.4	5.6	4.5	5.3
Avg. Time of Poss.	30:51	30:15	31:54	30:25	29:02	32:07	30:24	27:39	32:41	29:03	26:24	29:05	30:35	29:57	29:24	30:42
Third Down Efficiency	35.2	43.0	43.8	42.1	35.0	43.0	41.2	36.4	43.9	32.7	39.0	34.4	36.5	37.3	31.2	40.4
Had Intercepted	22	17	13	13	12	19	16	19	12	29	9	11	8	9	12	19
Yds. Opp Returned	399	215	204	225	140	364	279	370	117	377	128	230	117	21	135	214
Ret. by Opp. for TD	1	4	0	3	0	3	3	3	1	3	1	5	0	0	0	2
Punts	78	70	70	69	77	73	64	75	61	91	83	78	79	76	87	85
Yds. Punted	3566	3166	3344	2763	3467	3399	2854	3316	2859	4271	3681	3609	3804	3159	3846	3526
Avg. Yds. per Punt	45.7	45.2	47.8	40.0	45.0	46.6	44.6	44.2	46.9	46.9	44.3	46.3	48.2	41.6	44.2	41.5
Punt Returns	34	30	30	18	31	38	30	22	32	34	26	43	35	52	24	35
Yds. Returned	198	250	316	256	386	392	339	335	194	246	171	378	312	579	268	225
Avg. Yds. per Return	5.8	8.3	10.5	14.2	12.5	10.3	11.3	15.2	6.1	7.2	6.6	8.8	8.9	11.1	11.2	6.4
Returned for TD	0	0	0	1	1	1	1	1	0	0	0	1	0	0	0	0
Kickoff Returns	27	27	28	70	45	34	39	66	22	44	37	37	32	33	34	51
Yds. Returned	540	659	612	1614	1147	816	791	1646	506	933	790	835	726	698	811	1018
Avg. Yds. per Return	20.0	24.4	21.9	23.1	25.5	24.0	20.3	24.9	23.0	21.2	21.4	22.6	22.7	21.2	23.9	20.0
Returned for TD	0	0	0	0	0	1	0	2	0	0	0	0	0	0	0	0
Fumbles	22	17	12	21	18	28	19	23	12	26	19	20	20	26	18	30
Lost	9	11	6	10	8	15	9	13	7	15	10	10	10	10	9	15
Out of Bounds	3	2	1	0	1	2	2	3	2	3	3	3	4	1	0	0
Own Rec. for TD	0	0	0	0	0	1	0	0	0	0	0	0	0	0	0	0
Opp. Rec. by	10	11	10	9	13	7	11	8	7	12	12	15	11	11	10	9
Opp. Rec. for TD	1	1	0	1	3	1	2	1	0	0	1	3	3	1	0	1
Penalties	97	91	80	85	102	110	86	70	95	91	95	123	103	128	121	99
Yds. Penalized	744	788	671	708	867	925	801	695	817	786	846	1009	845	1183	1136	802
Total Points Scored	379	353	366	445	439	395	417	391	414	294	442	348	406	417	288	334
Total TDs	41	40	42	52	51	48	46	45	49	32	53	38	44	45	31	39
TDs Rushing	12	11	14	13	12	15	17	23	10	11	19	10	18	14	6	14
TDs Passing	24	26	24	32	33	29	25	18	39	18	32	22	21	27	22	20
TDs on Ret. and Rec.	5	3	4	7	6	4	4	4	0	3	2	6	5	4	3	5
Extra Point Kicks	37	39	42	45	47	42	42	43	48	31	45	34	44	44	31	33
Extra Point Kicks Att.	37	39	42	46	47	43	42	44	48	31	45	34	44	44	31	33
2Pt Conversions	1	1	0	5	1	2	0	0	0	1	3	3	0	0	0	2
2Pt Conversions Att.	4	1	0	6	4	5	4	1	1	1	8	4	0	1	0	5
Safeties	2	0	0	0	0	2	0	0	0	0	2	1	1	2	1	0
Field Goals Made	30	24	24	26	28	19	33	26	24	23	23	26	32	33	23	21
Field Goals Attempted	36	27	27	29	30	24	37	30	32	26	28	28	36	35	29	26
% Successful	83.3	88.9	88.9	89.7	93.3	79.2	89.2	86.7	75.0	88.5	82.1	92.9	88.9	94.3	79.3	80.8

NATIONAL FOOTBALL CONFERENCE DEFENSE

	Ariz.	Atl.	Car.	Chi.	Dall.	Det.	GB	Minn.	NO	NYG	Phil.	StL	SF	Sea.	TB	Wash.
First Downs	309	326	278	353	388	290	330	368	274	327	368	337	284	282	324	329
Rushing	68	102	70	147	122	62	116	101	82	101	100	87	77	83	95	102
Passing	208	196	178	184	231	197	190	247	168	198	239	203	181	156	190	204
Penalty	33	28	30	22	35	31	24	20	24	28	29	47	26	43	39	23
Rushes	370	455	352	483	437	377	432	443	387	454	443	440	397	422	438	443
Net Yds. Gained	1351	2173	1391	2583	2056	1596	2000	1767	1786	1743	1668	1646	1535	1626	1762	1769
Avg. Gain	3.7	4.8	4.0	5.3	4.7	4.2	4.6	4.0	4.6	3.8	3.8	3.7	3.9	3.9	4.0	4.0
Avg. Yds. per Game	84.4	135.8	86.9	161.4	128.5	99.8	125.0	110.4	111.6	108.9	104.3	102.9	95.9	101.6	110.1	110.6
Passes Attempted	625	516	563	507	623	572	539	648	507	601	670	521	585	524	547	514
Completed	367	341	375	315	403	338	332	419	304	361	408	355	345	309	352	337
% Completed	58.7	66.1	66.6	62.1	64.7	59.1	61.6	64.7	60.0	60.1	60.9	68.1	59.0	59.0	64.4	65.6
Total Yds. Gained	4065	4128	3853	3919	4835	4199	4194	4869	3441	3787	4907	4200	3819	3050	4061	4134
Times Sacked	47	32	60	31	34	33	44	41	49	34	37	53	38	44	35	36
Yds. Lost	337	231	424	189	246	249	238	274	336	214	271	326	283	298	255	238
Net Yds. Gained	3728	3897	3429	3730	4589	3950	3956	4595	3105	3573	4636	3874	3536	2752	3806	3896
Avg. Yds. per Game	233.0	243.6	214.3	233.1	286.8	246.9	247.3	287.2	194.1	223.3	289.8	242.1	221.0	172.0	237.9	243.5
Net Yds. per Pass Play	5.55	7.11	5.50	6.93	6.98	6.53	6.79	6.67	5.58	5.63	6.56	6.75	5.68	4.85	6.54	7.08
Yds. Gained per Comp.	11.08	12.11	10.27	12.44	12.00	12.42	12.63	11.62	11.32	10.49	12.03	11.83	11.07	9.87	11.54	12.27
Combined Net Yds. Gained	5079	6070	4820	6313	6645	5546	5956	6362	4891	5316	6304	5520	5071	4378	5568	5665
% Total Yds. Rushing	26.6	35.8	28.9	40.9	30.9	28.8	33.6	27.8	36.5	32.8	26.5	29.8	30.3	37.1	31.6	31.2
% Total Yds. Passing	73.4	64.2	71.1	59.1	69.1	71.2	66.4	72.2	63.5	67.2	73.5	70.2	69.7	62.9	68.4	68.8
Avg. Yds. per Game	317.4	379.4	301.3	394.6	415.3	346.6	372.3	397.6	305.7	332.3	394.0	345.0	316.9	273.6	348.0	354.1
Ball Control Plays	1042	1003	975	1021	1094	982	1015	1132	943	1089	1150	1014	1020	990	1020	993
Avg. Yds. per Play	4.9	6.1	4.9	6.2	6.1	5.6	5.9	5.6	5.2	4.9	5.5	5.4	5.0	4.4	5.5	5.7
Avg. Time of Poss.	29:09	29:45	28:06	29:35	30:58	27:53	29:36	32:21	27:19	30:57	33:36	30:55	29:26	30:03	30:36	29:18
Third Down Efficiency	35.3	45.9	35.8	41.5	43.3	30.3	38.2	44.2	34.7	40.1	40.3	38.8	34.1	35.2	39.2	34.0
Intercepted By	20	10	20	19	15	15	11	12	12	17	19	14	18	28	21	16
Yds. Returned By	251	176	234	428	257	211	36	78	169	270	294	256	278	385	338	247
Returned for TD	4	2	4	5	2	1	0	0	0	2	1	2	2	3	3	4
Punts	88	62	73	58	61	84	70	77	83	87	74	74	87	82	68	74
Yds. Punted	4084	2898	3321	2581	2880	3733	2994	3325	3853	3774	3146	3597	3884	3779	3002	3437
Avg. Yds. per Punt	46.4	46.7	45.5	44.5	47.2	44.4	42.8	43.2	46.4	43.4	42.5	48.6	44.6	46.1	44.1	46.4
Punt Returns	36	33	36	15	37	32	20	36	24	48	28	30	38	21	35	39
Yds. Returned	321	251	335	111	339	250	261	318	180	655	223	79	330	82	393	655
Avg. Yds. per Return	8.9	7.6	9.3	7.4	9.2	7.8	13.1	8.8	7.5	13.6	8.0	2.6	8.7	3.9	11.2	16.8
Returned for TD	0	0	0	0	0	0	0	1	0	3	1	0	0	0	0	3
Kickoff Returns	54	23	18	47	38	35	61	41	33	33	52	25	54	44	24	47
Yds. Returned	1298	571	407	883	791	924	1577	1113	830	721	1229	544	1104	1056	452	1048
Avg. Yds. per Return	24.0	24.8	22.6	18.8	20.8	26.4	25.9	27.1	25.2	21.8	23.6	21.8	20.4	24.0	18.8	22.3
Returned for TD	0	0	0	1	0	0	1	1	0	0	2	0	0	0	0	1
Fumbles	20	18	17	25	16	19	18	17	15	25	29	27	21	26	18	19
Lost	10	11	10	9	13	7	11	8	7	12	12	15	12	11	10	10
Out of Bounds	1	0	1	2	0	0	0	0	1	2	0	2	3	5	6	3
Own Rec. for TD	0	0	0	1	0	0	1	0	0	0	0	0	0	0	0	0
Opp. Rec. by	9	11	6	10	8	15	8	13	6	15	10	10	10	10	9	15
Opp. Rec. for TD	0	0	0	4	1	1	0	1	1	3	1	0	1	0	2	0
Penalties	111	104	84	69	112	87	99	100	91	105	106	105	96	98	105	83
Yds. Penalized	960	885	753	647	875	681	883	1003	750	904	855	978	878	879	1012	697
Total Points Scored	324	443	241	478	432	376	428	480	304	383	382	364	272	231	389	478
Total TDs	35	49	21	56	51	38	51	57	33	42	43	44	30	22	42	59
TDs Rushing	5	14	4	22	17	10	16	14	11	12	12	18	11	4	10	23
TDs Passing	29	31	17	25	33	24	30	37	20	21	25	21	19	16	30	29
TDs on Ret. and Rec.	1	4	0	9	1	4	5	6	2	9	6	5	0	2	2	7
Extra Point Kicks	33	47	19	54	47	29	48	53	32	40	35	42	28	17	40	59
Extra Point Kicks Att.	33	47	19	54	48	29	49	53	32	40	36	42	28	17	40	59
2Pt Conversions	2	0	1	1	2	4	0	2	1	1	4	1	1	2	1	0
2Pt Conversions Att.	2	2	2	2	3	9	2	4	1	2	7	2	2	5	2	0
Safeties	1	0	2	1	0	0	1	0	0	1	0	1	1	0	1	1
Field Goals Made	25	34	30	28	25	37	24	27	24	29	27	18	20	26	31	21
Field Goals Attempted	32	35	34	30	29	40	30	29	28	30	32	26	25	27	32	25
% Successful	78.1	97.1	88.2	93.3	86.2	92.5	80.0	93.1	85.7	96.7	84.4	69.2	80.0	96.3	96.9	84.0

AFC, NFC, AND NFL SUMMARY

	AFC Offense Total	AFC Offense Average	AFC Defense Total	AFC Defense Average	NFC Offense Total	NFC Offense Average	NFC Defense Total	NFC Defense Average	NFL Total	NFL Average
First Downs	5088	318.0	5045	315.3	5124	320.3	5167	322.9	10212	319.1
Rushing	1479	92.4	1544	96.5	1580	98.8	1515	94.7	3059	95.6
Passing	3141	196.3	3040	190.0	3069	191.8	3170	198.1	6210	194.1
Penalty	468	29.3	461	28.8	475	29.7	482	30.1	943	29.5
Rushes	6993	437.1	7098	443.6	6878	429.9	6773	423.3	13871	433.5
Net Yds. Gained	28353	1772.1	29343	1833.9	29442	1840.1	28452	1778.3	57795	1806.1
Avg. Gain	—	4.1	—	4.1	—	4.3	—	4.2	—	4.2
Avg. Yds. per Game	—	110.8	—	114.6	—	115.0	—	111.1	—	112.9
Passes Attempted	9321	582.6	9074	567.1	8815	550.9	9062	566.4	18136	566.8
Completed	5653	353.3	5441	340.1	5449	340.6	5661	353.8	11102	346.9
% Completed	—	60.6	—	60.0	—	61.8	—	62.5	—	61.2
Total Yds. Gained	64698	4043.6	63716	3982.3	64479	4029.9	65461	4091.3	129177	4036.8
Times Sacked	658	41.1	647	40.4	637	39.8	648	40.5	1295	40.5
Yds. Lost	4292	268.3	4135	258.4	4252	265.8	4409	275.6	8544	267.0
Net Yds. Gained	60406	3775.4	59581	3723.8	60227	3764.2	61052	3815.8	120633	3769.8
Avg. Yds. per Game	—	236.0	—	232.7	—	235.3	—	238.5	—	235.6
Net Yds. per Pass Play	—	6.05	—	6.13	—	6.37	—	6.29	—	6.21
Yds. Gained per Comp.	—	11.44	—	11.71	—	11.83	—	11.56	—	11.64
Combined Net Yds. Gained	88759	5547.4	88924	5557.8	89669	5604.3	89504	5594.0	178428	5575.9
% Total Yds. Rushing	—	31.9	—	33.0	—	32.8	—	31.8	—	32.4
% Total Yds. Passing	—	68.1	—	67.0	—	67.2	—	68.2	—	67.6
Avg. Yds. per Game	—	346.7	—	347.4	—	350.3	—	349.6	—	348.5
Ball Control Plays	16972	1060.8	16819	1051.2	16330	1020.6	16483	1030.2	33302	1040.7
Avg. Yds. per Play	—	5.2	—	5.3	—	5.5	—	5.4	—	5.4
Third Down Efficiency	—	37.8	—	38.0	—	38.5	—	38.2	—	38.1
Interceptions	262	16.4	235	14.7	240	15.0	267	16.7	502	15.7
Yds. Returned	3502	218.9	3129	195.6	3535	220.9	3908	244.3	7037	219.9
Returned for TD	36	2.3	30	1.9	29	1.8	35	2.2	65	2.0
Punts	1311	81.9	1325	82.8	1216	76.0	1202	75.1	2527	79.0
Yds. Punted	58984	3686.5	59326	3707.9	54630	3414.4	54288	3393.0	113614	3550.4
Avg. Yds. per Punt	—	45.0	—	44.8	—	44.9	—	45.2	—	45.0
Punt Returns	580	36.3	586	36.6	514	32.1	508	31.8	1094	34.2
Yds. Returned	5456	341.0	5518	344.9	4845	302.8	4783	298.9	10301	321.9
Avg. Yds. per Return	—	9.4	—	9.4	—	9.4	—	9.4	—	9.4
Returned for TD	7	0.4	5	0.3	6	0.4	8	0.5	13	0.4
Kickoff Returns	663	41.4	660	41.3	626	39.1	629	39.3	1289	40.3
Yds. Returned	15976	998.5	15570	973.1	14142	883.9	14548	909.3	30118	941.2
Avg. Yds. per Return	—	24.1	—	23.6	—	22.6	—	23.1	—	23.4
Returned for TD	4	0.3	1	0.1	3	0.2	6	0.4	7	0.2
Fumbles	324	20.3	325	20.3	331	20.7	330	20.6	655	20.5
Lost	145	9.1	144	9.0	167	10.4	168	10.5	312	9.8
Out of Bounds	22	1.4	28	1.8	32	2.0	26	1.6	54	1.7
Own Rec. for TD	1	0.1	0	0.0	1	0.1	2	0.1	2	0.1
Opp. Rec.	142	8.9	143	8.9	166	10.4	165	10.3	308	9.6
Opp. Rec. for TD	12	0.8	16	1.0	19	1.2	15	0.9	31	1.0
Penalties	1559	97.4	1580	98.8	1576	98.5	1555	97.2	3135	98.0
Yds. Penalized	13413	838.3	13396	837.3	13623	851.4	13640	852.5	27036	844.9
Total Points Scored	5857	366.1	5980	373.8	6128	383.0	6005	375.3	11985	374.5
Total TDs	642	40.1	665	41.6	696	43.5	673	42.1	1338	41.8
TDs Rushing	191	11.9	207	12.9	219	13.7	203	12.7	410	12.8
TDs Passing	392	24.5	397	24.8	412	25.8	407	25.4	804	25.1
TDs on Ret. and Rec.	59	3.7	61	3.8	65	4.1	63	3.9	124	3.9
Extra Point Kicks	615	38.4	639	39.9	647	40.4	623	38.9	1262	39.4
Extra Point Kicks Att.	617	38.6	641	40.1	650	40.6	626	39.1	1267	39.6
2Pt Conversions	14	0.9	10	0.6	19	1.2	23	1.4	33	1.0
2Pt Conversions Att.	24	1.5	22	1.4	45	2.8	47	2.9	69	2.2
Safeties	9	0.6	10	0.6	11	0.7	10	0.6	20	0.6
Field Goals Made	448	28.0	437	27.3	415	25.9	426	26.6	863	27.0
Field Goals Attempted	518	32.4	514	32.1	480	30.0	484	30.3	998	31.2
% Successful	—	86.5	—	85.0	—	86.5	—	88.0	—	86.5

CLUB LEADERS

	Offense	Defense
First Downs	Denver 435	New Orleans 274
Rushing	Philadelphia 133	Detroit 62
Passing	Denver 293	Seattle 156
Penalty	New England 43	Minnesota & New England 20
Rushes	Buffalo 546	Carolina 352
Net Yds. Gained	Philadelphia 2566	Arizona 1351
Avg. Gain	Philadelphia 5.1	N.Y. Jets 3.4
Passes Attempted	Cleveland 681	Houston 484
Completed	Denver 461	Houston 287
% Completed	San Diego 69.5	Buffalo 55.3
Total Yds. Gained	Denver 5572	Seattle 3050
Times Sacked	Denver 20	Carolina 60
Yds. Lost	Denver 128	Carolina 424
Net Yds. Gained	Denver 5444	Seattle 2752
Net Yds. per Pass Play	Denver 7.8	Seattle 4.8
Yds. Gained per Comp.	Philadelphia 14.2	Seattle 9.9
Combined Net Yds. Gained	Denver 7317	Seattle 4378
% Total Yds. Rushing	Buffalo 42.6	N.Y. Jets 26.3
% Total Yds. Passing	Atlanta 77.3	Chicago 59.1
Ball Control Plays	Denver 1156	New Orleans 943
Avg. Yds. per Play	Philadelphia 6.3	Seattle 4.4
Avg. Time of Poss.	San Diego 32:59	
Third Down Efficiency	San Diego 49.0	Detroit 30.3
Interceptions	—	Seattle 28
Yds. Returned	—	Kansas City 488
Returned for TD	—	Chicago & Kansas City 5
Punts	Buffalo 96	—
Yds. Punted	Jacksonville 4338	—
Avg. Yds. per Punt	Miami 48.8	—
Punt Returns	Kansas City 59	Chicago 15
Yds. Returned	Kansas City 695	St. Louis 79
Avg. Yds. per Return	Minnesota 15.2	St. Louis 2.6
Returned for TD	Kansas City 2	—
Kickoff Returns	Chicago 70	Carolina 18
Yds. Returned	Minnesota 1646	Carolina 407
Avg. Yds. per Return	Kansas City 29.9	Chicago 18.8
Returned for TD	Kansas City & Minnesota 2	
Total Points Scored	Denver 606	Seattle 231
Total TDs	Denver 76	Carolina 21
TDs Rushing	Minnesota 23	Carolina & Seattle 4
TDs Passing	Denver 55	Tennessee 15
TDs on Ret. and Rec.	Kansas City 11	Carolina & Kansas City & San Francisco 0
Extra Point Kicks	Denver 75	Seattle 17
2-Point Conversions	Chicago 5	—
Safeties	Jacksonville 3	—
Field Goals Made	Baltimore & New England 38	St. Louis 18
Field Goals Attempted	Baltimore & New England 41	San Francisco & Washington 25
% Successful	Denver 96.2	St. Louis 69.2

NFL CLUB RANKINGS BY YARDS

	Offense			Defense		
	Total	Rush	Pass	Total	Rush	Pass
Arizona	12	23	13	6	*1	14
Atlanta	14	32	7	27T	31	21
Baltimore	29	30	18	12	11	12
Buffalo	19	2	28	10	28	4
Carolina	26	11	29	2	2	6
Chicago	8	16	5	30	32	15
Cincinnati	10	18	8	3	5	5
Cleveland	17	27T	11	9	18	8
Dallas	16	24	14	32	27	30
Denver	*1	15	*1	19	7T	27
Detroit	6	17	3	16	6	23
Green Bay	3	7	6	25	25	24
Houston	11	20T	15	7	23	3
Indianapolis	15	20T	17	20	26	13
Jacksonville	31	31	22	27T	29	25T
Kansas City	21	10	24T	24	22	25T
Miami	27	26	20	21	24	16
Minnesota	13	8	23	31	16	31
New England	7	9	10	26	30	18
New Orleans	4	25	2	4	19	2
New York Giants	28	29	19	8	14	10
New York Jets	25	6	31	11	3	22
Oakland	23	12	24T	22	13	28
Philadelphia	2	*1	9	29	10	32
Pittsburgh	20	27T	12	13	21	9
St. Louis	30	19	27	15	9	19
San Diego	5	13	4	23	12	29
San Francisco	24	3	30	5	4	7
Seattle	18	4	26	*1	7T	*1
Tampa Bay	32	22	32	17	15	17
Tennessee	22	14	21	14	20	11
Washington	9	5	16	18	17	20

T = Tied for position   * = League Leader

AFC TAKEAWAYS/GIVEAWAYS

	Takeaways			Giveaways			Net
	Int	Fum	Total	Int	Fum	Total	Diff.
Kansas City	21	15	36	8	10	18	+18
Indianapolis	15	12	27	10	4	14	+13
New England	17	12	29	11	9	20	+9
Buffalo	23	7	30	15	12	27	+3
Cincinnati	20	11	31	20	10	30	+1
Denver	17	9	26	10	16	26	0
Tennessee	13	12	25	16	9	25	0
Miami	18	6	24	19	7	26	-2
Pittsburgh	10	10	20	14	10	24	-4
San Diego	11	6	17	11	10	21	-4
Baltimore	16	8	24	23	6	29	-5
Jacksonville	11	10	21	21	6	27	-6
Cleveland	14	7	21	20	9	29	-8
Oakland	9	13	22	20	11	31	-9
N.Y. Jets	13	2	15	22	7	29	-14
Houston	7	4	11	22	9	31	-20
Totals	235	144	379	262	145	407	-28

NFC TAKEAWAYS/GIVEAWAYS

	Takeaways			Giveaways			Net
	Int	Fum	Total	Int	Fum	Total	Diff.
Seattle	28	11	39	9	10	19	+20
Philadelphia	19	12	31	9	10	19	+12
San Francisco	18	12	30	8	10	18	+12
Carolina	20	10	30	13	6	19	+11
Tampa Bay	21	10	31	12	9	21	+10
Dallas	15	13	28	12	8	20	+8
St. Louis	14	15	29	11	10	21	+8
Chicago	19	9	28	13	10	23	+5
New Orleans	12	7	19	12	7	19	0
Arizona	20	10	30	22	9	31	-1
Green Bay	11	11	22	16	9	25	-3
Atlanta	10	11	21	17	11	28	-7
Washington	16	10	26	19	15	34	-8
Detroit	15	7	22	19	15	34	-12
Minnesota	12	8	20	19	13	32	-12
N.Y. Giants	17	12	29	29	15	44	-15
Totals	267	168	435	240	167	407	+28

SCORING

POINTS

AFC:	158	Stephen Gostkowski, New England
NFC:	143	Steven Hauschka, Seattle

TOUCHDOWNS

AFC:	19	Jamaal Charles, Kansas City
NFC:	16	Jimmy Graham, New Orleans

EXTRA POINT KICKS

AFC:	75	Matt Prater, Denver
NFC:	47	Dan Bailey, Dallas

TWO-POINT EXTRA POINT PLAYS

AFC:	2	Julian Edelman, New England
	2	Coby Fleener, Indianapolis
NFC:	2	Riley Cooper, Philadelphia
	2	Brandon Marshall, Chicago

FIELD GOALS

AFC:	38	Stephen Gostkowski, New England
	38	Justin Tucker, Baltimore
NFC:	33	Mason Crosby, Green Bay
	33	Steven Hauschka, Seattle

FIELD GOAL ATTEMPTS

AFC:	41	Stephen Gostkowski, New England
	41	Justin Tucker, Baltimore
NFC:	37	Mason Crosby, Green Bay

LONGEST FIELD GOAL

AFC:	64	Matt Prater, Denver vs. Tennessee, December 8
NFC:	58	Robbie Gould, Chicago vs. Cincinnati, September 8

MOST POINTS, GAME

AFC:	30	Jamaal Charles, Kansas City at Oakland, December 15 (5 TD)
NFC:	18	Adrian Peterson, Minnesota at Detroit, September 8 (3 TD)
	18	Victor Cruz, N.Y. Giants at Dallas, September 8 (3 TD)
	18	Marshawn Lynch, Seattle vs. San Francisco, September 15 (3 TD)
	18	Alex Henery, Philadelphia at N.Y. Giants, October 6 (5-5 FG, 3-3 PAT)
	18	* Joseph Fauria, Detroit at Cleveland, October 13 (3 TD)
	18	Matt Forté, Chicago at Washington, October 20 (3 TD)
	18	Roy Helu, Washington vs. Chicago, October 20 (3 TD)
	18	Darrel Young, Washington vs. San Diego, November 3 (3 TD) - (OT)
	18	Riley Cooper, Philadelphia at Oakland, November 3 (3 TD)
	18	* Tavon Austin, St. Louis at Indianapolis, November 10 (3 TD)
	18	Bobby Rainey, Tampa Bay vs. Atlanta, November 17 (3 TD)
	18	Marshawn Lynch, Seattle vs. Minnesota, November 17 (3 TD)
	18	DeMarco Murray, Dallas vs. Oakland, November 28 (3 TD)
	18	Matt Asiata, Minnesota vs. Philadelphia, December 15 (3 TD)
	18	Dan Bailey, Dallas vs. Green Bay, December 15 (5-5 FG, 3-3 PAT)
	18	Matt Forté, Chicago vs. Green Bay, December 29 (3 TD)

TEAM LEADERS, POINTS

AFC   BALTIMORE, 140, Justin Tucker; BUFFALO, 131, Dan Carpenter; CINCINNATI, 106, Mike Nugent; CLEVELAND, 95, Billy Cundiff; DENVER, 150, Matt Prater; HOUSTON, 104, Randy Bullock; INDIANAPOLIS, 139, Adam Vinatieri; JACKSONVILLE, 91, Josh Scobee; KANSAS CITY, 118, Ryan Succop; MIAMI, 111, *Caleb Sturgis; NEW ENGLAND, 158, Stephen Gostkowski; N.Y. JETS, 126, Nick Folk; OAKLAND, 100, Sebastian Janikowski; PITTSBURGH, 129, Shaun Suisham; SAN DIEGO, 144, Nick Novak; TENNESSEE, 116, Rob Bironas

NFC   ARIZONA, 127, Jay Feely; ATLANTA, 111, Matt Bryant; CAROLINA, 114, Graham Gano; CHICAGO, 123, Robbie Gould; DALLAS, 131, Dan Bailey; DETROIT, 99, David Akers; GREEN BAY, 141, Mason Crosby; MINNESOTA, 121, Blair Walsh; NEW ORLEANS, 107, Garrett Hartley; N.Y. GIANTS, 100, Josh Brown; PHILADELPHIA, 114, Alex Henery; ST. LOUIS, 112, Greg Zuerlein; SAN FRANCISCO, 140, Phil Dawson; SEATTLE, 143, Steven Hauschka; TAMPA BAY, 100, Rian Lindell; WASHINGTON, 80, Kai Forbath

TEAM CHAMPION

AFC:	606	Denver
NFC:	445	Chicago

NFL TOP TEN SCORERS—KICKERS

	XP	XPA	FG	FGA	PTS
Stephen Gostkowski, N.E.	44	44	38	41	158
Matt Prater, Den.	75	75	25	26	150
Nick Novak, S.D.	42	42	34	37	144
Steven Hauschka, Sea.	44	44	33	35	143
Mason Crosby, G.B.	42	42	33	37	141
Phil Dawson, S.F.	44	44	32	36	140
Justin Tucker, Bal.	26	26	38	41	140
Adam Vinatieri, Ind.	34	34	35	40	139
Dan Bailey, Dal	47	47	28	30	131
Dan Carpenter, Buf	32	32	33	36	131

NFL TOP TEN SCORERS—NONKICKERS

	TD	TDR	TDP	TDM	2-PT.	PTS
Jamaal Charles, K.C.	19	12	7	0	0	114
Jimmy Graham, N.O.	16	0	16	0	0	96
Marshawn Lynch, Sea.	14	12	2	0	0	84
Demaryius Thomas, Den.	14	0	14	0	0	84
Dez Bryant, Dal.	13	0	13	0	0	78
Vernon Davis, S.F.	13	0	13	0	0	78
Knowshon Moreno, Den.	13	10	3	0	0	78
Brandon Marshall, Chi.	12	0	12	0	2	76
Matt Forté, Chi.	12	9	3	0	1	74
Calvin Johnson, Det	12	0	12	0	0	72
Julius Thomas, Den.	12	0	12	0	0	72

AFC—INDIVIDUAL SCORERS

KICKERS

	XP	XPA	FG	FGA	PTS
Gostkowski, Stephen, N.E.	44	44	38	41	158
Prater, Matt, Den.	75	75	25	26	150
Novak, Nick, S.D.	42	42	34	37	144
Tucker, Justin, Bal.	26	26	38	41	140
Vinatieri, Adam, Ind.	34	34	35	40	139
Carpenter, Dan, Buf.	32	32	33	36	131
Suisham, Shaun, Pit.	39	39	30	32	129
Folk, Nick, NYJ	27	27	33	36	126
Succop, Ryan, K.C.	52	52	22	28	118
Bironas, Rob, Ten.	41	41	25	29	116
* Sturgis, Caleb, Mia.	33	33	26	34	111
Nugent, Mike, Cin.	52	53	18	22	106
Bullock, Randy, Hou.	26	26	26	35	104
Janikowski, Sebastian, Oak.	37	37	21	30	100
Cundiff, Billy, Cle.	32	32	21	26	95
Scobee, Josh, Jac.	22	23	23	25	91
Lanning, Spencer, Cle.	1	1	0	0	1

* Player that was a rookie in 2013

NONKICKERS	TD	TDR	TDP	TDM	2-PT.	PTS
Charles, Jamaal, K.C.	19	12	7	0	0	114
Thomas, Demaryius, Den.	14	0	14	0	0	84
Moreno, Knowshon, Den.	13	10	3	0	0	78
Thomas, Julius, Den.	12	0	12	0	0	72
Decker, Eric, Den.	11	0	11	0	0	66
Green, A.J., Cin.	11	0	11	0	0	66
Cotchery, Jerricho, Pit.	10	0	10	0	0	60
Jackson, Fred, Buf.	10	9	1	0	0	60
Johnson, Chris, Ten.	10	6	4	0	0	60
Jones, Marvin, Cin.	10	0	10	0	0	60
Welker, Wes, Den.	10	0	10	0	0	60
Brown, Antonio, Pit.	9	0	8	1	0	54
Gordon, Josh, Cle.	9	0	9	0	0	54
* Allen, Keenan, S.D.	8	0	8	0	0	48
* Bell, Le'Veon, Pit.	8	8	0	0	0	48
* Bernard, Giovani, Cin.	8	5	3	0	0	48
Brown, Donald, Ind.	8	6	2	0	0	48
Royal, Eddie, S.D.	8	0	8	0	0	48
Woodhead, Danny, S.D.	8	2	6	0	0	48
* Brown, Marlon, Bal.	7	0	7	0	1	44
Blount, LeGarrette, N.E.	7	7	0	0	0	42
Cameron, Jordan, Cle.	7	0	7	0	0	42
Clay, Charles, Mia.	7	1	6	0	0	42
Green-Ellis, BenJarvus, Cin.	7	7	0	0	0	42
Mathews, Ryan, S.D.	7	6	1	0	0	42
Ridley, Stevan, N.E.	7	7	0	0	0	42
Edelman, Julian, N.E.	6	0	6	0	2	40
Sanders, Emmanuel, Pit.	6	0	6	0	1	38
* Smith, Geno, NYJ	6	6	0	0	0	36
Thomas, Daniel, Mia.	6	4	2	0	0	36
Walker, Delanie, Ten.	6	0	6	0	0	36
Bowe, Dwayne, K.C.	5	0	5	0	0	30
* Davis, Knile, K.C.	5	4	0	1	0	30
Graham, Garrett, Hou.	5	0	5	0	0	30
Hilton, T.Y., Ind.	5	0	5	0	0	30
Johnson, Andre, Hou.	5	0	5	0	0	30
Jones-Drew, Maurice, Jac.	5	5	0	0	0	30
McFadden, Darren, Oak.	5	5	0	0	0	30
Moore, Denarius, Oak.	5	0	5	0	0	30
Wallace, Mike, Mia.	5	0	5	0	0	30
Fleener, Coby, Ind.	4	0	4	0	2	28
Rice, Ray, Bal.	4	4	0	0	1	26
Smith, Torrey, Bal.	4	0	4	0	1	26
* Ball, Montee, Den.	4	4	0	0	0	24
Cumberland, Jeff, NYJ	4	0	4	0	0	24
* Dobson, Aaron, N.E.	4	0	4	0	0	24
Gates, Antonio, S.D.	4	0	4	0	0	24
Greene, Shonn, Ten.	4	4	0	0	0	24
Gresham, Jermaine, Cin.	4	0	4	0	0	24
Gronkowski, Rob, N.E.	4	0	4	0	0	24
Hartline, Brian, Mia.	4	0	4	0	0	24
* Hunter, Justin, Ten.	4	0	4	0	0	24
Lewis, Marcedes, Jac.	4	0	4	0	0	24
Luck, Andrew, Ind.	4	4	0	0	0	24
McCluster, Dexter, K.C.	4	0	2	2	0	24
Reece, Marcel, Oak.	4	2	2	0	0	24
Richardson, Trent, Ind.	4	3	1	0	0	24
* Rivera, Mychal, Oak.	4	0	4	0	0	24
Streater, Rod, Oak.	4	0	4	0	0	24
Tate, Ben, Hou.	4	4	0	0	0	24
* Thompkins, Kenbrell, N.E.	4	0	4	0	0	24
Vereen, Shane, N.E.	4	1	3	0	0	24
Johnson, Steve, Buf.	3	0	3	0	1	20
* Woods, Robert, Buf.	3	0	3	0	1	20
Bolden, Brandon, N.E.	3	3	0	0	0	18
Caldwell, Andre, Den.	3	0	3	0	0	18
Clark, Dallas, Bal.	3	0	3	0	0	18
Daniels, Owen, Hou.	3	0	3	0	0	18
Fasano, Anthony, K.C.	3	0	3	0	0	18
Fitzpatrick, Ryan, Ten.	3	3	0	0	0	18
Gibson, Brandon, Mia.	3	0	3	0	0	18
* Goodwin, Marquise, Buf.	3	0	3	0	0	18

	TD	TDR	TDP	TDM	2-PT.	PTS
Green, Ladarius, S.D.	3	0	3	0	0	18
Ivory, Chris, NYJ	3	3	0	0	0	18
Jones, Jacoby, Bal.	3	0	2	1	0	18
Kerley, Jeremy, NYJ	3	0	3	0	0	18
Martin, Keshawn, Hou.	3	0	2	1	0	18
Shorts, Cecil, Jac.	3	0	3	0	0	18
Todman, Jordan, Jac.	3	2	1	0	0	18
Washington, Nate, Ten.	3	0	3	0	0	18
Bess, Davone, Cle.	2	0	2	0	1	14
Foster, Arian, Hou.	2	1	1	0	1	14
Wayne, Reggie, Ind.	2	0	2	0	1	14
Allen, Antonio, NYJ	2	0	0	2	0	12
Amendola, Danny, N.E.	2	0	2	0	0	12
Avery, Donnie, K.C.	2	0	2	0	0	12
Baker, Edwin, Cle.	2	2	0	0	0	12
Barnidge, Gary, Cle.	2	0	2	0	0	12
Berry, Eric, K.C.	2	0	0	2	0	12
Bradshaw, Ahmad, Ind.	2	2	0	0	0	12
Brazill, LaVon, Ind.	2	0	2	0	0	12
Brown, Mike, Jac.	2	0	2	0	0	12
Chandler, Scott, Buf.	2	0	2	0	0	12
Dalton, Andy, Cin.	2	2	0	0	0	12
* Eifert, Tyler, Cin.	2	0	2	0	0	12
Graham, T.J., Buf.	2	0	2	0	0	12
Hali, Tamba, K.C.	2	0	0	2	0	12
Harbor, Clay, Jac.	2	0	2	0	0	12
Hemingway, Junior, K.C.	2	0	2	0	0	12
Holliday, Trindon, Den.	2	0	0	2	0	12
* Hopkins, DeAndre, Hou.	2	0	2	0	0	12
Little, Greg, Cle.	2	0	2	0	0	12
Locker, Jake, Ten.	2	2	0	0	0	12
* Manuel, EJ, Buf.	2	2	0	0	0	12
Matthews, Rishard, Mia.	2	0	2	0	0	12
McGahee, Willis, Cle.	2	2	0	0	0	12
McGrath, Sean, K.C.	2	0	2	0	0	12
Miller, Lamar, Mia.	2	2	0	0	0	12
Nelson, David, NYJ	2	0	2	0	0	12
Ogbonnaya, Chris, Cle.	2	0	2	0	0	12
Pierce, Bernard, Bal.	2	2	0	0	0	12
Preston, Michael, Ten.	2	0	2	0	0	12
Pryor, Terrelle, Oak.	2	2	0	0	0	12
* Richardson, Sheldon, NYJ	2	2	0	0	0	12
* Rogers, Da'Rick, Ind.	2	0	2	0	0	12
Sanu, Mohamed, Cin.	2	0	2	0	0	12
Searcy, Da'Norris, Buf.	2	0	0	2	0	12
Spiller, C.J., Buf.	2	2	0	0	0	12
Stewart, Jeremy, Oak.	2	1	0	1	0	12
Summers, Frank, Buf.	2	1	1	0	0	12
Ward, T.J., Cle.	2	0	0	2	0	12
Whalen, Griff, Ind.	2	0	2	0	0	12
Whittaker, Fozzy, Cle.	2	0	2	0	0	12
Winslow, Kellen, NYJ	2	0	2	0	0	12
Wright, Kendall, Ten.	2	0	2	0	0	12
Heyward-Bey, Darrius, Ind.	1	0	1	0	1	8
Abdullah, Husain, K.C.	1	0	0	1	0	6
Ajirotutu, Seyi, S.D.	1	0	1	0	0	6
Allen, Cortez, Pit.	1	0	0	1	0	6
Allen, Dwayne, Ind.	1	0	1	0	0	6
Battle, Jackie, Ten.	1	1	0	0	0	6
Benjamin, Travis, Cle.	1	0	0	1	0	6
Blackmon, Justin, Jac.	1	0	1	0	0	6
Blackmon, Will, Jac.	1	0	0	1	0	6
Brown, Ronnie, S.D.	1	1	0	0	0	6
Brown, Vincent, S.D.	1	0	1	0	0	6
Burfict, Vontaze, Cin.	1	0	0	1	0	6
Butler, Darius, Ind.	1	0	0	1	0	6
* Cooper, Marcus, K.C.	1	0	0	1	0	6
Crocker, Chris, Cin.	1	0	0	1	0	6
Cushing, Brian, Hou.	1	0	0	1	0	6
Demps, Quintin, K.C.	1	0	0	1	0	6
Develin, James, N.E.	1	1	0	0	0	6
Dickson, Ed, Bal.	1	0	1	0	0	6
Doss, Tandon, Bal.	1	0	0	1	0	6
Dreessen, Joel, Den.	1	0	1	0	0	6

	TD	TDR	TDP	TDM	2-PT.	PTS
Dye, Tony, Cin.	1	0	0	1	0	6
Flacco, Joe, Bal.	1	1	0	0	0	6
Gay, William, Pit.	1	0	0	1	0	6
Gipson, Tashaun, Cle.	1	0	0	1	0	6
* Gragg, Chris, Buf.	1	0	1	0	0	6
* Griffin, Ryan, Hou.	1	0	1	0	0	6
Grimes, Brent, Mia.	1	0	0	1	0	6
Grimes, Jonathan, Hou.	1	1	0	0	0	6
Haden, Joe, Cle.	1	0	0	1	0	6
Havili, Stanley, Ind.	1	0	1	0	0	6
Hill, Stephen, NYJ	1	0	1	0	0	6
Hillman, Ronnie, Den.	1	1	0	0	0	6
Holmes, Andre, Oak.	1	0	1	0	0	6
Holmes, Santonio, NYJ	1	0	1	0	0	6
Hoomanawanui, Michael, N.E.	1	0	1	0	0	6
Howell, Delano, Ind.	1	0	0	1	0	6
* Jenkins, Greg, Oak.	1	0	0	1	0	6
Johnson, Steven, Den.	1	0	0	1	0	6
Johnson, Will, Pit.	1	0	1	0	0	6
Jones, Adam, Cin.	1	0	0	1	0	6
Jones, Chandler, N.E.	1	0	0	1	0	6
Jones, Reshad, Mia.	1	0	0	1	0	6
* Kasa, Nick, Oak.	1	0	1	0	0	6
Keenum, Case, Hou.	1	1	0	0	0	6
Kirkpatrick, Dre, Cin.	1	0	0	1	0	6
Klug, Karl, Ten.	1	0	0	1	0	6
Leach, Vonta, Bal.	1	0	1	0	0	6
Lewis, Thad, Buf.	1	1	0	0	0	6
Lissemore, Sean, S.D.	1	0	0	1	0	6
Manning, Peyton, Den.	1	1	0	0	0	6
McCourty, Jason, Ten.	1	0	0	1	0	6
Miller, Heath, Pit.	1	0	1	0	0	6
Miller, Von, Den.	1	0	0	1	0	6
Moye, Derek, Pit.	1	0	1	0	0	6
Mulligan, Matthew, N.E.	1	0	1	0	0	6
Newman, Terence, Cin.	1	0	0	1	0	6
Noble, Danny, Jac.	1	0	1	0	0	6
Pitta, Dennis, Bal.	1	0	1	0	0	6
Polamalu, Troy, Pit.	1	0	0	1	0	6
Porter, Tracy, Oak.	1	0	0	1	0	6
Posluszny, Paul, Jac.	1	0	0	1	0	6
Powell, Bilal, NYJ	1	1	0	0	0	6
Rey, Vincent, Cin.	1	0	0	1	0	6
* Robey, Nickell, Buf.	1	0	0	1	0	6
Rodgers-Cromartie, Domin, Den.	1	0	0	1	0	6
Roethlisberger, Ben, Pit.	1	1	0	0	0	6
* Ryan, Logan, N.E.	1	0	0	1	0	6
* Sanders, Ace, Jac.	1	0	1	0	0	6
Sherman, Anthony, K.C.	1	0	0	1	0	6
* Sims, Dion, Mia.	1	0	1	0	0	6
Smith, Alex, K.C.	1	1	0	0	0	6
Smith, Daryl, Bal.	1	0	0	1	0	6
Smith, Alex, Cin.	1	0	1	0	0	6
Smith, Sean, K.C.	1	0	0	1	0	6
Spaeth, Matt, Pit.	1	0	1	0	0	6
Tamme, Jacob, Den.	1	0	1	0	0	6
Tannehill, Ryan, Mia.	1	1	0	0	0	6
Taylor, Kerry, Jac.	1	0	1	0	0	6
Thigpen, Marcus, Mia.	1	0	1	0	0	6
Thompson, Taylor, Ten.	1	0	1	0	0	6
Verner, Alterraun, Ten.	1	0	0	1	0	6
Wilson, Tavon, N.E.	1	0	0	1	0	6
Woodson, Charles, Oak.	1	0	0	1	0	6
Mathis, Robert, Ind.	0	0	0	0	0	^2
Mays, Joe, Hou.	0	0	0	0	0	^2
Redding, Cory, Ind.	0	0	0	0	0	^2
Thomas, J.T., Jac.	0	0	0	0	0	^2
Wake, Cameron, Mia.	0	0	0	0	0	^2
Lanning, Spencer, Cle.	0	0	0	0	0	#1

^ Safety
Team safety credited to Jacksonville, N.Y. Jets, and Pittsburgh
Scored kicking extra point

NFC—INDIVIDUAL SCORERS
KICKERS

	XP	XPA	FG	FGA	PTS
Hauschka, Steven, Sea.	44	44	33	35	143
Crosby, Mason, G.B.	42	42	33	37	141
Dawson, Phil, S.F.	44	44	32	36	140
Bailey, Dan, Dal.	47	47	28	30	131
Feely, Jay, Ariz	37	37	30	36	127
Gould, Robbie, Chi.	45	46	26	29	123
Walsh, Blair, Min.	43	44	26	30	121
Gano, Graham, Car.	42	42	24	27	114
Henery, Alex, Phi.	45	45	23	28	114
Zuerlein, Greg, St.L	34	34	26	28	112
Bryant, Matt, Atl.	39	39	24	27	111
Hartley, Garrett, N.O.	41	41	22	30	107
Brown, Josh, NY-G	31	31	23	26	100
Lindell, Rian, T.B.	31	31	23	29	100
Akers, David, Det.	42	43	19	24	99
Forbath, Kai, Was.	26	26	18	22	80
Potter, John, Was.	7	7	3	4	16
Graham, Shayne, N.O.	7	7	2	2	13

NONKICKERS

	TD	TDR	TDP	TDM	X2G	PTS
Graham, Jimmy, N.O.	16	0	16	0	0	96
Lynch, Marshawn, Sea.	14	12	2	0	0	84
Bryant, Dez, Dal.	13	0	13	0	0	78
Davis, Vernon, S.F.	13	0	13	0	0	78
Marshall, Brandon, Chi.	12	0	12	0	2	76
Forté, Matt, Chi.	12	9	3	0	1	74
Johnson, Calvin, Det.	12	0	12	0	0	72
* Lacy, Eddie, G.B.	11	11	0	0	0	66
McCoy, LeSean, Phi.	11	9	2	0	0	66
Peterson, Adrian, Min.	11	10	1	0	0	66
Fitzgerald, Larry, Ariz	10	0	10	0	0	60
Murray, DeMarco, Dal.	10	9	1	0	0	60
Gore, Frank, S.F.	9	9	0	0	0	54
Jackson, DeSean, Phi.	9	0	9	0	0	54
* Patterson, Cordarrelle, Min.	9	3	4	2	0	54
Cooper, Riley, Phi.	8	0	8	0	2	52
Bell, Joique, Det.	8	8	0	0	1	50
Gonzalez, Tony, Atl.	8	0	8	0	1	50
Mendenhall, Rashard, Ariz	8	8	0	0	1	50
Nelson, Jordy, G.B.	8	0	8	0	0	48
* Stacy, Zac, St.L	8	7	1	0	0	48
Witten, Jason, Dal.	8	0	8	0	0	48
* Fauria, Joseph, Det.	7	0	7	0	1	44
Jeffery, Alshon, Chi.	7	0	7	0	1	44
Boldin, Anquan, S.F.	7	0	7	0	0	42
Bush, Reggie, Det.	7	4	3	0	0	42
Jackson, Steven, Atl.	7	6	1	0	0	42
Jackson, Vincent, T.B.	7	0	7	0	0	42
Morris, Alfred, Was.	7	7	0	0	0	42
Tolbert, Mike, Car.	7	5	2	0	0	42
* Austin, Tavon, St.L	6	1	4	1	0	36
Celek, Brent, Phi.	6	0	6	0	0	36
Newton, Cam, Car.	6	6	0	0	0	36
Olsen, Greg, Car.	6	0	6	0	0	36
Rainey, Bobby, T.B.	6	5	1	0	0	36
Randle, Rueben, NY-G	6	0	6	0	0	36
* Williams, Terrance, Dal.	5	0	5	0	1	32
Baldwin, Doug, Sea.	5	0	5	0	0	30
Bennett, Martellus, Chi.	5	0	5	0	0	30
Colston, Marques, N.O.	5	0	5	0	0	30
Cook, Jared, St.L	5	0	5	0	0	30
Floyd, Michael, Ariz	5	0	5	0	0	30
Garcon, Pierre, Was.	5	0	5	0	0	30
Ginn, Ted, Car.	5	0	5	0	0	30
LaFell, Brandon, Car.	5	0	5	0	0	30
Miller, Zach, Sea.	5	0	5	0	0	30
* Stills, Kenny, N.O.	5	0	5	0	0	30
Tate, Golden, Sea.	5	0	5	0	0	30
Thomas, Pierre, N.O.	5	2	3	0	0	30
* Wright, Timothy, T.B.	5	0	5	0	0	30
Bennett, Earl, Chi.	4	0	4	0	1	26

	TD	TDR	TDP	TDM	2-PT	PTS
Kearse, Jermaine, Sea.	4	0	4	0	0	^26
Boykin, Jarrett, G.B.	4	0	3	1	0	24
Bush, Michael, Chi.	4	3	1	0	0	24
Cobb, Randall, G.B.	4	0	4	0	0	24
Cruz, Victor, NY-G	4	0	4	0	0	24
* Ellington, Andre, Ariz	4	3	1	0	0	24
* Ertz, Zach, Phi.	4	0	4	0	0	24
Helu, Roy, Was.	4	4	0	0	0	24
Hunter, Kendall, S.F.	4	3	0	1	0	24
Jacobs, Brandon, NY-G	4	4	0	0	0	24
Jennings, Greg, Min.	4	0	4	0	0	24
Kaepernick, Colin, S.F.	4	4	0	0	0	24
Kendricks, Lance, St.L	4	0	4	0	0	24
Myers, Brandon, NY-G	4	0	4	0	0	24
Pettis, Austin, St.L	4	0	4	0	0	24
Ponder, Christian, Min.	4	4	0	0	0	24
Rodgers, Jacquizz, Atl.	4	2	2	0	0	24
Smith, Steve, Car.	4	0	4	0	0	24
Snelling, Jason, Atl.	4	1	3	0	0	24
Sproles, Darren, N.O.	4	2	2	0	0	24
Starks, James, G.B.	4	3	1	0	0	24
Underwood, Tiquan, T.B.	4	0	4	0	0	24
Williams, DeAngelo, Car.	4	3	1	0	0	24
Young, Darrel, Was.	4	3	1	0	0	24
Brown, Andre, NY-G	3	3	0	0	1	20
Asiata, Matt, Min.	3	3	0	0	0	18
Brees, Drew, N.O.	3	3	0	0	0	18
Finley, Jermichael, G.B.	3	0	3	0	0	18
Foles, Nick, Phi.	3	3	0	0	0	18
Hall, DeAngelo, Was.	3	0	0	3	0	18
Hankerson, Leonard, Was.	3	0	3	0	0	18
Harris, Dwayne, Dal.	3	0	2	1	0	18
Jernigan, Jerrel, NY-G	3	1	2	0	0	18
Jones, James, G.B.	3	0	3	0	0	18
Paulsen, Logan, Was.	3	0	3	0	0	18
Polk, Chris, Phi.	3	3	0	0	0	18
* Reed, Jordan, Was.	3	0	3	0	0	18
Rice, Sidney, Sea.	3	0	3	0	0	18
Ross, Jeremy, Det.	3	0	1	2	0	18
Rudolph, Kyle, Min.	3	0	3	0	0	18
White, Roddy, Atl.	3	0	3	0	0	18
Wright, Jarius, Min.	3	0	3	0	0	18
Brown, Bryce, Phi.	2	2	0	0	1	14
Avant, Jason, Phi.	2	0	2	0	0	12
Ballard, Jake, Ariz	2	0	2	0	0	12
Beasley, Cole, Dal.	2	0	2	0	0	12
Dansby, Karlos, Ariz	2	0	0	2	0	12
Davis, Drew, Atl.	2	0	2	0	0	12
Dixon, Anthony, S.F.	2	2	0	0	0	12
Douglas, Harry, Atl.	2	0	2	0	0	12
Dray, Jim, Ariz	2	0	2	0	0	12
Durham, Kris, Det.	2	0	2	0	0	12
* Escobar, Gavin, Dal.	2	0	2	0	0	12
Foster, Mason, T.B.	2	0	0	2	0	12
Gerhart, Toby, Min.	2	2	0	0	0	12
Harkey, Cory, St.L	2	0	2	0	0	12
Hillis, Peyton, NY-G	2	2	0	0	0	12
Jennings, Tim, Chi.	2	0	0	2	0	12
Jones, Julio, Atl.	2	0	2	0	0	12
Meachem, Robert, N.O.	2	0	2	0	0	12
Moore, Lance, N.O.	2	0	2	0	0	12
Moss, Santana, Was.	2	0	2	0	0	12
Munnerlyn, Captain, Car.	2	0	0	2	0	12
Ogletree, Kevin, T.B.-Det.	2	0	2	0	0	12
Pettigrew, Brandon, Det.	2	0	2	0	0	12
Quarless, Andrew, G.B.	2	0	2	0	0	12
Quick, Brian, St.L	2	0	2	0	0	12
* Randle, Joseph, Dal.	2	2	0	0	0	12
Roberts, Andre, Ariz	2	0	2	0	0	12
Robinson, Aldrick, Was.	2	0	2	0	0	12
Smith, Antone, Atl.	2	2	0	0	0	12
Stafford, Matthew, Det.	2	2	0	0	0	12
* Toilolo, Levine, Atl.	2	0	2	0	0	12
Vick, Michael, Phi.	2	2	0	0	0	12

	TD	TDR	TDP	TDM	2-PT	PTS
Watson, Benjamin, N.O.	2	0	2	0	0	12
Williams, Mike, T.B.	2	0	2	0	0	12
* Cunningham, Benny, St.L	1	1	0	0	1	8
Fairley, Nick, Det.	1	0	0	1	0	^8
* Amerson, David, Was.	1	0	0	1	0	6
* Bailey, Stedman, St.L	1	1	0	0	0	6
* Bass, David, Chi.	1	0	0	1	0	6
* Bates, Daren, St.L	1	0	0	1	0	6
Bennett, Michael, Sea.	1	0	0	1	0	6
Bostick, Brandon, G.B.	1	0	1	0	0	6
Bowman, NaVorro, S.F.	1	0	0	1	0	6
Bowman, Zack, Chi.	1	0	0	1	0	6
Boykin, Brandon, Phi.	1	0	0	1	0	6
Brock, Tramaine, S.F.	1	0	0	1	0	6
* Brown, Jaron, Ariz	1	0	1	0	0	6
Burleson, Nate, Det.	1	0	1	0	0	6
Burnett, Morgan, G.B.	1	0	0	1	0	6
Cadet, Travaris, N.O.	1	0	1	0	0	6
Carlson, John, Min.	1	0	1	0	0	6
Carr, Brandon, Dal.	1	0	0	1	0	6
Cason, Antoine, Ariz	1	0	0	1	0	6
Cassel, Matt, Min.	1	1	0	0	0	6
Church, Barry, Dal.	1	0	0	1	0	6
Coleman, Derrick, Sea.	1	0	1	0	0	6
Collins, Jed, N.O.	1	1	0	0	0	6
Crabtree, Michael, S.F.	1	0	1	0	0	6
Crabtree, Tom, T.B.	1	0	1	0	0	6
Davis, Fred, Was.	1	0	1	0	0	6
Davis, Kellen, Sea.	1	0	1	0	0	6
DeCoud, Thomas, Atl.	1	0	0	1	0	6
Ellison, Rhett, Min.	1	0	1	0	0	6
Florence, Drayton, Car.	1	0	0	1	0	6
* Franklin, Johnathan, G.B.	1	1	0	0	0	6
Giordano, Matt, St.L	1	0	0	1	0	6
Goode, Najee, Phi.	1	0	0	1	0	6
Hayden, Nick, Dal.	1	0	0	1	0	6
* Heath, Jeff, Dal.	1	0	0	1	0	6
Hester, Devin, Chi.	1	0	0	1	0	6
* Hill, Josh, N.O.	1	0	1	0	0	6
Hill, Will, NY-G	1	0	0	1	0	6
Hixon, Domenik, Car.	1	0	1	0	0	6
Housler, Rob, Ariz	1	0	1	0	0	6
* Hyde, Micah, G.B.	1	0	0	1	0	6
Ingram, Mark, N.O.	1	1	0	0	0	6
Jackson, Tarvaris, Sea.	1	1	0	0	0	6
Jennings, M.D., G.B.	1	0	0	1	0	6
* Johnson, Darius, Atl.	1	0	1	0	0	6
Johnson, Leonard, T.B.	1	0	0	1	0	6
Kuhn, John, G.B.	1	1	0	0	0	6
Lee, Sean, Dal.	1	0	0	1	0	6
Levy, DeAndre, Det.	1	0	0	1	0	6
Long, Chris, St.L	1	0	0	1	0	6
Maehl, Jeff, Phi.	1	0	1	0	0	6
Martin, Doug, T.B.	1	1	0	0	0	6
McCown, Josh, Chi.	1	1	0	0	0	6
Murphy, Louis, NY-G	1	0	1	0	0	6
* Ogletree, Alec, St.L	1	0	0	1	0	6
Orakpo, Brian, Was.	1	0	0	1	0	6
Osgood, Kassim, S.F.	1	0	1	0	0	6
Penn, Donald, T.B.	1	0	1	0	0	6
Peppers, Julius, Chi.	1	0	0	1	0	6
Pierre-Paul, Jason, NY-G	1	0	0	1	0	6
Quinn, Robert, St.L	1	0	0	1	0	6
* Riddick, Theo, Det.	1	0	0	1	0	6
* Robinson, Khiry, N.O.	1	1	0	0	0	6
Robison, Brian, Min.	1	0	0	1	0	6
Scott, Da'Rel, NY-G	1	0	1	0	0	6
Shaughnessy, Matt, Ariz	1	0	0	1	0	6
Sherels, Marcus, Min.	1	0	0	1	0	6
Sherman, Richard, Sea.	1	0	0	1	0	6
Simpson, Jerome, Min.	1	0	1	0	0	6
Skuta, Dan, S.F.	1	0	0	1	0	6
Smith, Alfonso, Ariz	1	0	0	1	0	6
Smith, Malcolm, Sea.	1	0	0	1	0	6

	TD	TDR	TDP	TDM	2-PT.	PTS		TD	TDR	TDP	TDM	2-PT.	PTS
Tanner, Phillip, Dal.	1	1	0	0	0	6	Campbell, Calais, Ariz	0	0	0	0	0	^2
* Taylor, Cooper, NY-G	1	0	0	1	0	6	Cole, Trent, Phi.	0	0	0	0	0	^2
Thurmond, Walter, Sea.	1	0	0	1	0	6	David, Lavonte, T.B.	0	0	0	0	0	^2
Tolzien, Scott, G.B.	1	1	0	0	0	6	Griffin III, Robert, Was.	0	0	0	0	1	2
Umenyiora, Osi, Atl.	1	0	0	1	0	6	* Lemonier, Corey, S.F.	0	0	0	0	0	^2
Weatherspoon, Sean, Atl.	1	0	0	1	0	6	Pead, Isaiah, St.L	0	0	0	0	1	2
* White, Melvin, Car.	1	0	0	1	0	6	Sims, Eugene, St.L	0	0	0	0	0	^2
Williams, Dan, Ariz	1	0	0	1	0	6	Suh, Ndamukong, Det.	0	0	0	0	0	^2
* Willson, Luke, Sea.	1	0	1	0	0	6	Thornton, Cedric, Phi.	0	0	0	0	0	^2
Wilson, David, NY-G	1	1	0	0	0	6	* Williams, Nick, Was.	0	0	0	0	1	2
Wilson, Russell, Sea.	1	1	0	0	0	6							
Wright, Major, Chi.	1	0	0	1	0	6	^ Safety						
Abraham, John, Ariz	0	0	0	0	0	^2	Team safety credited to Seattle						
Bradford, Sam, St.L	0	0	0	0	1	2	* Player that was a rookie in 2013						

AMERICAN FOOTBALL CONFERENCE—SCORING

	TD	TDR	TDP	TDM	XKG	XKAtt	X2G	X2Att	FG	FGA	SAF	POINTS
Denver	76	16	55	5	75	75	0	1	25	26	0	606
New England	47	19	25	3	44	44	2	3	38	41	0	444
Cincinnati	54	14	33	7	52	53	0	1	18	22	0	430
Kansas City	52	17	24	11	52	52	0	0	22	28	0	430
San Diego	42	9	32	1	42	42	0	0	34	37	0	396
Indianapolis	40	15	23	2	34	34	4	6	35	40	2	391
Pittsburgh	41	9	28	4	39	39	1	2	30	32	1	379
Tennessee	41	16	22	3	41	41	0	0	25	29	0	362
Buffalo	34	15	16	3	32	32	2	2	33	36	0	339
Oakland	37	16	17	4	37	37	0	0	21	30	0	322
Baltimore	29	7	19	3	26	26	3	3	38	41	0	320
Miami	34	8	24	2	33	33	0	1	26	34	1	317
Cleveland	35	4	26	5	33	33	1	2	21	26	0	308
N.Y. Jets	27	12	13	2	27	27	0	0	33	36	1	290
Houston	28	7	19	2	26	26	1	1	26	35	1	276
Jacksonville	25	7	16	2	22	23	0	2	23	25	3	247
AFC Total	642	191	392	59	615	617	14	24	448	518	9	5857
AFC Average	40.1	11.9	24.5	3.7	38.4	38.6	0.9	1.5	28.0	32.4	0.6	366.1

NATIONAL FOOTBALL CONFERENCE—SCORING

	TD	TDR	TDP	TDM	XKG	XKAtt	X2G	X2Att	FG	FGA	SAF	POINTS
Chicago	52	13	32	7	45	46	5	6	26	29	0	445
Philadelphia	53	19	32	2	45	45	3	8	23	28	2	442
Dallas	51	12	33	6	47	47	1	4	28	30	0	439
Green Bay	46	17	25	4	42	42	0	4	33	37	0	417
Seattle	45	14	27	4	44	44	0	1	33	35	2	417
New Orleans	49	10	39	0	48	48	0	1	24	32	0	414
San Francisco	44	18	21	5	44	44	0	0	32	36	1	406
Detroit	48	15	29	4	42	43	2	5	19	24	2	395
Minnesota	45	23	18	4	43	44	0	1	26	30	0	391
Arizona	41	12	24	5	37	37	1	4	30	36	2	379
Carolina	42	14	24	4	42	42	0	0	24	27	0	366
Atlanta	40	11	26	3	39	39	1	1	24	27	0	353
St. Louis	38	10	22	6	34	34	3	4	26	28	1	348
Washington	39	14	20	5	33	33	2	5	21	26	0	334
N.Y. Giants	32	11	18	3	31	31	1	1	23	26	0	294
Tampa Bay	31	6	22	3	31	31	0	0	23	29	1	288
NFC Total	696	219	412	65	647	650	19	45	415	480	11	6128
NFC Average	43.5	13.7	25.8	4.1	40.4	40.6	1.2	2.8	25.9	30.0	0.7	383.0
NFL Total	1338	410	804	124	1262	1267	33	69	863	998	20	11985
NFL Average	41.8	12.8	25.1	3.9	39.4	39.6	1.0	2.2	27.0	31.2	0.6	374.5

FIELD GOALS

FIELD GOAL PERCENTAGE
AFC: .962 Matt Prater, Denver
NFC: .943 Steven Hauschka, Seattle

FIELD GOALS
AFC: 38 Stephen Gostkowski, New England
38 Justin Tucker, Baltimore
NFC: 33 Steven Hauschka, Seattle
33 Mason Crosby, Green Bay

FIELD GOAL ATTEMPTS
AFC: 41 Stephen Gostkowski, New England
41 Justin Tucker, Baltimore
NFC: 37 Mason Crosby, Green Bay

FIELD GOALS, GAME
AFC: 6 Justin Tucker, Baltimore at Detroit,
December 16 (6 attempts)
NFC: 5 Mason Crosby, Green Bay vs. Detroit,
October 6 (5 attempts)
5 Alex Henery, Philadelphia at N.Y. Giants,
October 6 (5 attempts)
5 Josh Brown, N.Y. Giants at Philadelphia,
October 27 (5 attempts)
5 Dan Bailey, Dallas vs. Green Bay,
December 15 (5 attempts)

LONGEST FIELD GOAL
AFC: 64 Matt Prater, Denver vs. Tennessee,
December 8
NFC: 58 Robbie Gould, Chicago vs. Cincinnati,
September 8

AVERAGE YARDS MADE
AFC: 40.7 Mike Nugent, Cincinnati
NFC: 39.7 Dan Bailey, Dallas

AMERICAN FOOTBALL CONFERENCE—FIELD GOALS

	FG	FGA	Pct	Long
Denver	25	26	.962	64
Pittsburgh	30	32	.938	48
Baltimore	38	41	.927	61
New England	38	41	.927	54
Jacksonville	23	25	.920	55
San Diego	34	37	.919	50
Buffalo	33	36	.917	55
N.Y. Jets	33	36	.917	54
Indianapolis	35	40	.875	52
Tennessee	25	29	.862	55
Cincinnati	18	22	.818	54
Cleveland	21	26	.808	51
Kansas City	22	28	.786	51
Miami	26	34	.765	54
Houston	26	35	.743	51
Oakland	21	30	.700	53
AFC Total	448	518	—	64
AFC Average	28.0	32.4	.865	—

NATIONAL FOOTBALL CONFERENCE—FIELD GOALS

	FG	FGA	Pct	Long
Seattle	33	35	.943	53
Dallas	28	30	.933	53
St. Louis	26	28	.929	54
Chicago	26	29	.897	58
Green Bay	33	37	.892	57
Atlanta	24	27	.889	53
Carolina	24	27	.889	55
San Francisco	32	36	.889	56
N.Y. Giants	23	26	.885	52
Minnesota	26	30	.867	54
Arizona	30	36	.833	52
Philadelphia	23	28	.821	51
Washington	21	26	.808	50
Tampa Bay	23	29	.793	54
Detroit	19	24	.792	53
New Orleans	24	32	.750	55
NFC Total	415	480	—	58
NFC Average	25.9	30.0	.865	—
League Total	863	998	—	64
League Average	27.0	31.2	.865	—

AFC—INDIVIDUAL FIELD GOALS

	1-19 Yards	20-29 Yards	30-39 Yards	40-49 Yards	50 or Longer	Totals	Avg Yds Att	Avg Yds Made	Avg Yds Miss	Long
Prater, Matt, Den.	2-2 1.000	4-4 1.000	5-5 1.000	8-8 1.000	6-7 .857	25-26 .962	40.0	39.5	52.0	64
Suisham, Shaun, Pit.	0-0 —	9-9 1.000	13-15 .867	8-8 1.000	0-0 —	30-32 .938	34.2	34.2	33.0	48
Gostkowski, Stephen, N.E.	1-1 1.000	8-8 1.000	13-13 1.000	11-13 .846	5-6 .833	38-41 .927	37.7	36.9	48.7	54
Tucker, Justin, Bal.	0-0 —	10-10 1.000	12-13 .923	10-11 .909	6-7 .857	38-41 .927	38.0	37.6	43.7	61
Scobee, Josh, Jac.	0-0 —	3-3 1.000	12-12 1.000	4-5 .800	4-5 .800	23-25 .920	39.1	37.8	54.5	55
Novak, Nick, S.D.	1-1 1.000	9-9 1.000	13-16 .813	9-9 1.000	2-2 1.000	34-37 .919	35.2	35.1	37.3	50
Carpenter, Dan, Buf.	0-0 —	13-13 1.000	6-6 1.000	10-11 .909	4-6 .667	33-36 .917	36.2	35.1	48.7	55
Folk, Nick, NYJ	0-0 —	8-8 1.000	10-11 .909	12-14 .857	3-3 1.000	33-36 .917	38.0	37.5	44.0	54
Vinatieri, Adam, Ind.	0-0 —	6-6 1.000	10-11 .909	15-17 .882	4-6 .667	35-40 .875	39.7	39.0	44.6	52
Bironas, Rob, Ten.	0-0 —	10-10 1.000	8-9 .889	5-7 .714	2-3 .667	25-29 .862	35.6	34.4	43.3	55
Nugent, Mike, Cin.	0-0 —	2-2 1.000	6-7 .857	7-9 .778	3-4 .750	18-22 .818	41.3	40.7	43.8	54
Cundiff, Billy, Cle.	0-0 —	7-7 1.000	5-6 .833	7-9 .778	2-4 .500	21-26 .808	38.3	35.9	48.6	51
Succop, Ryan, K.C.	0-0 —	6-6 1.000	9-10 .900	6-8 .750	1-4 .250	22-28 .786	37.4	34.7	47.0	51
* Sturgis, Caleb, Mia.	1-1 1.000	4-4 1.000	10-12 .833	8-10 .800	3-7 .429	26-34 .765	39.5	37.3	46.6	54
Bullock, Randy, Hou.	1-1 1.000	7-7 1.000	5-5 1.000	12-17 .706	1-5 .200	26-35 .743	39.2	36.3	47.7	51
Janikowski, Sebastian, Oak.	0-0 —	6-6 1.000	4-6 .667	8-11 .727	3-7 .429	21-30 .700	40.2	37.7	46.0	53
AFC Totals	6-6 1.000	112-112 1.000	141-157 .898	140-167 .838	49-76 .645	448-518 .865	38.0	36.8	45.8	64
NFL Totals	12-12 1.000	236-242 .975	265-295 .898	254-306 .830	96-143 .671	863-998 .865	37.6	36.4	45.1	64

Leader based on overall percentage, minimum 16 field goals

NFC—INDIVIDUAL FIELD GOALS

	1-19 Yards	20-29 Yards	30-39 Yards	40-49 Yards	50 or Longer	Totals	Avg Yds Att	Avg Yds Made	Avg Yds Miss	Long
Hauschka, Steven, Sea.	0-0 —	10-11 .909	9-9 1.000	11-12 .917	3-3 1.000	33-35 .943	36.5	36.6	36.0	53
Bailey, Dan, Dal.	2-2 1.000	2-2 1.000	8-9 .889	10-10 1.000	6-7 .857	28-30 .933	40.1	39.7	45.5	53
Zuerlein, Greg, St.L	0-0 —	7-7 1.000	10-10 1.000	8-9 .889	1-2 .500	26-28 .929	36.8	36.0	47.0	54
Gould, Robbie, Chi.	0-0 —	11-11 1.000	6-7 .857	6-7 .857	3-4 .750	26-29 .897	36.0	34.5	49.0	58
Crosby, Mason, G.B.	1-1 1.000	13-13 1.000	8-8 1.000	6-8 .750	5-7 .714	33-37 .892	35.5	34.0	47.8	57
Bryant, Matt, Atl.	0-0 —	9-9 1.000	7-8 .875	5-5 1.000	3-5 .600	24-27 .889	36.4	35.2	46.3	53
Dawson, Phil, S.F.	0-0 —	12-13 .923	6-6 1.000	10-11 .909	4-6 .667	32-36 .889	37.9	36.5	49.0	56
Gano, Graham, Car.	0-0 —	9-9 1.000	4-5 .800	5-7 .714	6-6 1.000	24-27 .889	37.6	36.8	44.0	55
Brown, Josh, NY-G	0-0 —	8-8 1.000	7-8 .875	7-8 .875	1-2 .500	23-26 .885	35.4	34.3	44.0	52
Walsh, Blair, Min.	0-0 —	7-7 1.000	12-12 1.000	5-6 .833	2-5 .400	26-30 .867	37.4	35.1	52.3	54
Feely, Jay, Ariz	0-0 —	9-11 .818	7-8 .875	11-12 .917	3-5 .600	30-36 .833	37.2	36.9	38.8	52
Henery, Alex, Phi.	0-0 —	8-8 1.000	7-8 .875	7-10 .700	1-2 .500	23-28 .821	37.4	35.1	47.8	51
Forbath, Kai, Was.	0-0 —	3-4 .750	10-10 1.000	4-6 .667	1-2 .500	18-22 .818	36.9	35.5	43.3	50
Lindell, Rian, T.B.	0-0 —	3-3 1.000	12-14 .857	4-6 .667	4-6 .667	23-29 .793	39.8	38.3	45.5	54
Akers, David, Det.	1-1 1.000	5-5 1.000	6-8 .750	4-7 .571	3-3 1.000	19-24 .792	36.4	35.2	40.8	53
Hartley, Garrett, N.O.	2-2 1.000	5-6 .833	5-8 .625	9-13 .692	1-1 1.000	22-30 .733	36.7	35.8	39.1	55
(Nonqualifiers)										
Potter, John, Was.	0-0 —	2-2 1.000	0-0 —	1-1 1.000	0-1 .000	3-4 .750	34.8	29.7	50.0	43
Graham, Shayne, N.O.	0-0 —	1-1 1.000	0-0 —	1-1 1.000	0-0 —	2-2 1.000	32.0	32.0	—	40
NFC Totals	6-6 1.000	124-130 .954	124-138 .899	114-139 .820	47-67 .701	415-480 .865	37.1	35.9	44.4	58
League Totals	12-12 1.000	236-242 .975	265-295 .898	254-306 .830	96-143 .671	863-998 .865	37.6	36.4	45.1	64

Leader based on overall percentage, minimum 16 field goals
* Player that was a rookie in 2013

RUSHING

YARDS
NFC:	1607	LeSean McCoy, Philadelphia
AFC:	1287	Jamaal Charles, Kansas City

YARDS, GAME
AFC:	224	Knowshon Moreno, Denver at New England, November 24 (37 attempts, 1 TD) - (OT)
NFC:	217	LeSean McCoy, Philadelphia vs. Detroit, December 8 (29 attempts, 2 TD)

LONGEST
AFC:	93	Terrelle Pryor (QB), Oakland vs. Pittsburgh, October 27 - TD
NFC:	80	* Andre Ellington, Arizona vs. Atlanta, October 27 - TD
	80	Bobby Rainey, Tampa Bay vs. Buffalo, December 8 - TD

ATTEMPTS
NFC:	314	LeSean McCoy, Philadelphia
AFC:	285	Ryan Mathews, San Diego

ATTEMPTS, GAME
AFC:	37	Knowshon Moreno, Denver at New England, November 24 (224 yards, 1 TD) - (OT)
NFC:	35	Adrian Peterson, Minnesota vs. Chicago, December 1 (211 yards, 0 TD) - (OT)

YARDS PER ATTEMPT
NFC:	5.5*	Andre Ellington, Arizona
AFC:	5.3	Donald Brown, Indianapolis

TOUCHDOWNS
AFC:	12	Jamaal Charles, Kansas City
NFC:	12	Marshawn Lynch, Seattle

TEAM LEADERS, YARDS
AFC: BALTIMORE, 660, Ray Rice; BUFFALO, 933, C.J. Spiller; CINCINNATI, 756, BenJarvus Green-Ellis; CLEVELAND, 377, Willis McGahee; DENVER, 1038, Knowshon Moreno; HOUSTON, 771, Ben Tate; INDIANAPOLIS, 537, Donald Brown; JACKSONVILLE, 803, Maurice Jones-Drew; KANSAS CITY, 1287, Jamaal Charles; MIAMI, 709, Lamar Miller; NEW ENGLAND, 773, Stevan Ridley; N.Y. JETS, 833, Chris Ivory; OAKLAND, 733, Rashad Jennings; PITTSBURGH, 860, Le'Veon Bell; SAN DIEGO, 1255, Ryan Mathews; TENNESSEE, 1077, Chris Johnson

NFC: ARIZONA, 687, Rashard Mendenhall; ATLANTA, 543, Steven Jackson; CAROLINA, 843, DeAngelo Williams; CHICAGO, 1339, Matt Forté; DALLAS, 1121, DeMarco Murray; DETROIT, 1006, Reggie Bush; GREEN BAY, 1178, Eddie Lacy; MINNESOTA, 1266, Adrian Peterson; NEW ORLEANS, 549, Pierre Thomas; N.Y. GIANTS, 492, Andre Brown; PHILADELPHIA, 1607, LeSean McCoy; ST. LOUIS, 973, Zac Stacy; SAN FRANCISCO, 1128, Frank Gore; SEATTLE, 1257, Marshawn Lynch; TAMPA BAY, 532, Bobby Rainey; WASHINGTON, 1275, Alfred Morris

TEAM CHAMPION
NFC:	2566	Philadelphia
AFC:	2307	Buffalo

Player that was a rookie in 2013

NFL TOP TEN RUSHERS
	Att	Yards	Avg	Long	TD
LeSean McCoy, Phi.	314	1607	5.1	57t	9
Matt Forté, Chi.	289	1339	4.6	55	9
Jamaal Charles, K.C.	259	1287	5.0	46	12
Alfred Morris, Was.	276	1275	4.6	45t	7
Adrian Peterson, Min.	279	1266	4.5	78t	10
Marshawn Lynch, Sea	301	1257	4.2	43	12
Ryan Mathews, S.D.	285	1255	4.4	51	6
* Eddie Lacy, G.B.	284	1178	4.1	60	11
Frank Gore, S.F.	276	1128	4.1	51	9
DeMarco Murray, Dal	217	1121	5.2	43	9

AFC—INDIVIDUAL RUSHERS
	Att	Yards	Avg	Long	TD
Charles, Jamaal, K.C.	259	1287	5.0	46	12
Mathews, Ryan, S.D.	285	1255	4.4	51	6
Johnson, Chris, Ten.	279	1077	3.9	30t	6
Moreno, Knowshon, Den.	241	1038	4.3	31	10
Spiller, C.J., Buf.	202	933	4.6	77	2
Jackson, Fred, Buf.	206	890	4.3	59	9
* Bell, Le'Veon, Pit.	244	860	3.5	43	8
Ivory, Chris, NYJ	182	833	4.6	69	3
Jones-Drew, Maurice, Jac.	234	803	3.4	48	5
Ridley, Stevan, N.E.	178	773	4.3	29	7
Blount, LeGarrette, N.E.	153	772	5.0	47t	7
Tate, Ben, Hou.	181	771	4.3	60	4
Green-Ellis, BenJarvus, Cin.	220	756	3.4	25	7
Jennings, Rashad, Oak.	163	733	4.5	80t	6
Miller, Lamar, Mia.	177	709	4.0	49	2
Powell, Bilal, NYJ	176	697	4.0	39	1
* Bernard, Giovani, Cin.	170	695	4.1	35t	5
Rice, Ray, Bal.	214	660	3.1	47	4
Pryor, Terrelle, Oak.	83	576	6.9	93t	2
Richardson, Trent, Cle.-Ind.	188	563	3.0	22	3
* Ball, Montee, Den.	120	559	4.7	45	4
Foster, Arian, Hou.	121	542	4.5	23	1
Brown, Donald, Ind.	102	537	5.3	51t	6
Pierce, Bernard, Bal.	152	436	2.9	28	2
Smith, Alex, K.C.	76	431	5.7	26	1
Woodhead, Danny, S.D.	106	429	4.0	14	2
Thomas, Daniel, Mia.	109	406	3.7	55	4
McFadden, Darren, Oak.	114	379	3.3	30	5
Luck, Andrew, Ind.	63	377	6.0	29	4
McGahee, Willis, Cle.	138	377	2.7	16	2
* Smith, Geno, NYJ	72	366	5.1	32	6
Greene, Shonn, Ten.	77	295	3.8	29	4
Bolden, Brandon, N.E.	55	271	4.9	46	3
Todman, Jordan, Jac.	76	256	3.4	33	2
* Davis, Knile, K.C.	70	242	3.5	20	4
Ogbonnaya, Chris, Cle.	49	240	4.9	43	0
Tannehill, Ryan, Mia.	40	238	6.0	48	1
Fitzpatrick, Ryan, Ten.	43	225	5.2	26	3
Hillman, Ronnie, Den.	55	218	4.0	19	1
Reece, Marcel, Oak.	46	218	4.7	63t	2
Vereen, Shane, N.E.	44	208	4.7	21	1
Dwyer, Jonathan, Pit.	49	197	4.0	30	0
Bradshaw, Ahmad, Ind.	41	186	4.5	27	2
* Manuel, EJ, Buf.	53	186	3.5	19	2
Jones, Felix, Pit.	48	184	3.8	14	0
Dalton, Andy, Cin.	61	183	3.0	12	2
* Johnson, Dennis, Hou.	49	183	3.7	29	0
Baker, Edwin, Cle.	43	171	4.0	20	2
Choice, Tashard, Buf.-Ind.	46	170	3.7	20	0
Brown, Ronnie, S.D.	45	157	3.5	13	1
Locker, Jake, Ten.	24	155	6.5	39	2
Battle, Jackie, Ten.	36	142	3.9	37	1
Flacco, Joe, Bal.	27	131	4.9	22	1
Campbell, Jason, Cle.	14	107	7.6	21	0
Roethlisberger, Ben, Pit.	27	99	3.7	19	1

	Att	Yards	Avg	Long	TD
Gordon, Josh, Cle.	5	88	17.6	34	0
Whittaker, Fozzy, Cle.	28	79	2.8	11	0
Henne, Chad, Jac.	27	77	2.9	14	0
Grimes, Jonathan, Hou.	21	73	3.5	12	1
Keenum, Case, Hou.	14	72	5.1	22	1
Rivers, Philip, S.D.	28	72	2.6	18	0
* Robinson, Denard, Jac.	20	66	3.3	24	0
Jones, Marvin, Cin.	8	65	8.1	34	0
Taylor, Tyrod, Bal.	8	64	8.0	25	0
Ballard, Vick, Ind.	13	63	4.8	12	0
* Bohanon, Tommy, NYJ	17	62	3.6	8	0
Goodson, Mike, NYJ	7	61	8.7	26	0
Cribbs, Josh, NYJ	13	55	4.2	9	0
Daniel, Chase, K.C.	14	52	3.7	29	0
Lewis, Thad, Buf.	24	52	2.2	8	1
Karim, Deji, Hou.	12	51	4.3	14	0
Summers, Frank, Buf.	12	46	3.8	16	1
Benjamin, Travis, Cle.	1	45	45.0	45	0
Weeden, Brandon, Cle.	12	44	3.7	11	0
* Gray, MarQueis, Cle.	6	43	7.2	18	0
* Anderson, C.J., Den.	7	38	5.4	11	0
Simms, Matt, NYJ	5	37	7.4	22	0
Bruton, David, Den.	1	35	35.0	35	0
Green, Alex, NYJ	11	35	3.2	9	0
* Aubrey, Josh, Cle.	1	34	34.0	34	0
Herron, Dan, Ind.	5	33	6.6	22	0
Wallace, Mike, Mia.	3	33	11.0	13	0
Gabbert, Blaine, Jac.	9	32	3.6	7	0
McClain, Le'Ron, S.D.	11	32	2.9	7	0
Forsett, Justin, Jac.	6	31	5.2	10	0
* McGloin, Matt, Oak.	11	27	2.5	20	0
Heyward-Bey, Darrius, Ind.	3	26	8.7	30	0
Sanders, Emmanuel, Pit.	1	25	25.0	25	0
Gray, Cyrus, K.C.	9	24	2.7	9	0
Schaub, Matt, Hou.	5	24	4.8	7	0
Jones, Taiwan, Oak.	5	23	4.6	19	0
Leach, Vonta, Bal.	11	23	2.1	6	0
* Gillislee, Mike, Mia.	6	21	3.5	6	0
Royal, Eddie, S.D.	3	21	7.0	15	0
Johnson, Josh, Cin.	7	20	2.9	10	0
Stephens-Howling, LaRod, Pit.	6	19	3.2	5	0
Brady, Tom, N.E.	32	18	0.6	11	0
Thigpen, Marcus, Mia.	6	18	3.0	9	0
Peerman, Cedric, Cin.	8	17	2.1	5	0
Streater, Rod, Oak.	2	17	8.5	9	0
* Tuel, Jeff, Buf.	3	17	5.7	14	0
Hoyer, Brian, Cle.	6	16	2.7	11	0
Sanu, Mohamed, Cin.	4	16	4.0	9	0
* Woods, Robert, Buf.	2	16	8.0	13	0
Clay, Charles, Mia.	7	15	2.1	13	1
Ford, Jacoby, Oak.	5	15	3.0	4	0
Graham, T.J., Buf.	4	14	3.5	14	0
Scott, Bernard, Bal.	4	14	3.5	9	0
* Goodwin, Marquise, Buf.	3	13	4.3	17	0
Redman, Isaac, Pit.	10	12	1.2	8	0
Edelman, Julian, N.E.	2	11	5.5	7	0
Kerley, Jeremy, NYJ	4	11	2.8	8	0
Develin, James, N.E.	4	10	2.5	4	1
Johnson, Steve, Buf.	1	10	10.0	10	0
* Wood, Cierre, Hou.	3	9	3.0	5	0
* Graham, Ray, Hou.	4	8	2.0	4	0
Keo, Shiloh, Hou.	1	8	8.0	8	0
Caldwell, Andre, Den.	1	7	7.0	7	0
Havili, Stanley, Ind.	7	7	1.0	4	0
Holliday, Trindon, Den.	1	7	7.0	7	0
Avery, Donnie, K.C.	2	6	3.0	4	0
Hilton, T.Y., Ind.	2	6	3.0	3	0
Jenkins, A.J., K.C.	2	6	3.0	5	0
Olawale, Jamize, Oak.	3	6	2.0	4	0

	Att	Yards	Avg	Long	TD
McCluster, Dexter, K.C.	8	5	0.6	5	0
Wayne, Reggie, Ind.	1	5	5.0	5	0
Brown, Antonio, Pit.	7	4	0.6	10	0
* Richardson, Sheldon, NYJ	4	4	1.0	1t	2
* Sanders, Ace, Jac.	2	4	2.0	4	0
Weddle, Eric, S.D.	2	4	2.0	2	0
* Wingo, Ronnie, Buf.	1	4	4.0	4	0
Hawkins, Andrew, Cin.	2	3	1.5	6	0
Lynch, Corey, Ind.	1	3	3.0	3	0
Sherman, Anthony, K.C.	2	3	1.5	2	0
Draughn, Shaun, Bal.	4	2	0.5	3	0
Jones, Greg, Hou.	2	2	1.0	4	0
Osweiler, Brock, Den.	3	2	0.7	4	0
Stewart, Jeremy, Oak.	2	2	1.0	2t	1
Amendola, Danny, N.E.	1	1	1.0	1	0
Ta'ufo'ou, Will, Jac.	1	1	1.0	1	0
Washington, Leon, N.E.	1	1	1.0	1	0
Anger, Bryan, Jac.	1	0	0.0	0	0
Edwards, Armanti, Cle.	1	0	0.0	0	0
Fields, Brandon, Mia.	1	0	0.0	0	0
Huber, Kevin, Cin.	1	0	0.0	0	0
Jones, Jacoby, Bal.	2	0	0.0	4	0
Kern, Brett, Ten.	2	0	0.0	0	0
Reynaud, Darius, Ten.	1	0	0.0	0	0
* Rogers, Da'Rick, Ind.	1	0	0.0	0	0
Yates, T.J., Hou.	1	0	0.0	0	0
Blackmon, Justin, Jac.	1	-1	-1.0	-1	0
* Brown, Marlon, Bal.	1	-2	-2.0	-2	0
Hasselbeck, Matt, Ind.	2	-2	-1.0	-1	0
Hakim, Saalim, NYJ	2	-3	-1.5	8	0
Cotchery, Jerricho, Pit.	1	-5	-5.0	-5	0
Whitehurst, Charlie, S.D.	6	-5	-0.8	0	0
Burton, Stephen, Jac.	1	-9	-9.0	-9	0
Suisham, Shaun, Pit.	1	-12	-12.0	-12	0
Manning, Peyton, Den.	32	-31	-1.0	1t	1

t = Touchdown
Leader based on most yards gained
* Player that was a rookie in 2013

NFC—INDIVIDUAL RUSHERS

	Att	Yards	Avg	Long	TD
McCoy, LeSean, Phi.	314	1607	5.1	57t	9
Forté, Matt, Chi.	289	1339	4.6	55	9
Morris, Alfred, Was.	276	1275	4.6	45t	7
Peterson, Adrian, Min.	279	1266	4.5	78t	10
Lynch, Marshawn, Sea.	301	1257	4.2	43	12
* Lacy, Eddie, G.B.	284	1178	4.1	60	11
Gore, Frank, S.F.	276	1128	4.1	51	9
Murray, DeMarco, Dal.	217	1121	5.2	43	9
Bush, Reggie, Det.	223	1006	4.5	39	4
* Stacy, Zac, St.L	250	973	3.9	40t	7
Williams, DeAngelo, Car.	201	843	4.2	43t	3
Mendenhall, Rashard, Ariz	217	687	3.2	28	8
* Ellington, Andre, Ariz	118	652	5.5	80t	3
Bell, Joique, Det.	166	650	3.9	20	8
Newton, Cam, Car.	111	585	5.3	56	6
Rainey, Bobby, Cle.-T.B.	150	566	3.8	80t	5
Thomas, Pierre, N.O.	147	549	3.7	18	2
Jackson, Steven, Atl.	157	543	3.5	50	6
Wilson, Russell, Sea.	96	539	5.6	27	1
Kaepernick, Colin, S.F.	92	524	5.7	28	4
Starks, James, G.B.	89	493	5.5	41	3
Brown, Andre, NY-G	139	492	3.5	23t	3
Griffin III, Robert, Was.	86	489	5.7	26	0
Martin, Doug, T.B.	127	456	3.6	28	1
Ingram, Mark, N.O.	78	386	4.9	34	1
Tolbert, Mike, Car.	101	361	3.6	22	5
Hunter, Kendall, S.F.	78	358	4.6	45	3

	Att	Yards	Avg	Long	TD		Att	Yards	Avg	Long	TD
Rodgers, Jacquizz, Atl.	96	332	3.5	19t	2	Garcon, Pierre, Was.	2	19	9.5	10	0
Brown, Bryce, Phi.	75	314	4.2	65t	2	Cooper, Riley, Phi.	0	18	—	18	0
Vick, Michael, Phi.	36	306	8.5	61	2	* Reed, Jordan, Was.	1	18	18.0	18	0
* James, Mike, T.B.	60	295	4.9	24	0	* Dawson, Skye, T.B.	2	15	7.5	14	0
Gerhart, Toby, Min.	36	283	7.9	41t	2	LaFell, Brandon, Car.	2	15	7.5	9	0
Helu, Roy, Was.	62	274	4.4	24	6	Cousins, Kirk, Was.	4	14	3.5	6	0
Turbin, Robert, Sea.	77	264	3.4	15	0	Demps, Jeff, T.B.	1	14	14.0	14	0
* Cunningham, Benny, St.L	47	261	5.6	56	1	Page, Eric, T.B.	2	14	7.0	19	0
Hillis, Peyton, NY-G	73	247	3.4	27	2	Miller, Bruce, S.F.	7	13	1.9	4	0
Jacobs, Brandon, NY-G	58	238	4.1	37	4	Morgan, Josh, Was.	2	13	6.5	9	0
* Robinson, Khiry, N.O.	54	224	4.1	25	1	Tanner, Phillip, Dal.	9	12	1.3	9	1
Foles, Nick, Phi.	57	221	3.9	21	3	Boldin, Anquan, S.F.	2	11	5.5	11	0
Sproles, Darren, N.O.	53	220	4.2	38	2	* Stills, Kenny, N.O.	3	10	3.3	4	0
Richardson, Daryl, St.L	69	215	3.1	14	0	* Ware, Spencer, Sea.	3	10	3.3	5	0
Bush, Michael, Chi.	63	197	3.1	40t	3	Leshoure, Mikel, Det.	2	9	4.5	5	0
Leonard, Brian, T.B.	47	182	3.9	24	0	Moore, Marlon, S.F.	1	9	9.0	9	0
Stewart, Jonathan, Car.	48	180	3.8	16	0	Fitzgerald, Larry, Ariz	2	8	4.0	4	0
Asiata, Matt, Min.	44	166	3.8	39	3	Givens, Chris, St.L	3	8	2.7	16	0
* Randle, Joseph, Dal.	54	164	3.0	19	2	Orton, Kyle, Dal.	1	8	8.0	8	0
Snelling, Jason, Atl.	44	164	3.7	17	1	* Barner, Kenjon, Car.	6	7	1.2	2	0
* Patterson, Cordarrelle, Min.	12	158	13.2	50t	3	Jones, Julio, Atl.	1	7	7.0	7	0
* Austin, Tavon, St.L	9	151	16.8	65t	1	Baldwin, Doug, Sea.	2	6	3.0	3	0
Ponder, Christian, Min.	34	151	4.4	19t	4	Harris, Dwayne, Dal.	1	6	6.0	6	0
Dunbar, Lance, Dal.	30	150	5.0	45	0	Jennings, M.D., G.B.	1	6	6.0	6	0
Wilson, David, NY-G	44	146	3.3	18	1	Smith, Armond, Car.	4	5	1.3	5	0
Smith, Antone, Atl.	5	145	29.0	50t	2	* Williams, Terrance, Dal.	3	4	1.3	5	0
Rodgers, Aaron, G.B.	30	120	4.0	18	0	Coleman, Derrick, Sea.	2	3	1.5	4	0
Cutler, Jay, Chi.	23	118	5.1	18	0	* Martin, Sam, Det.	2	3	1.5	3	0
* Taylor, Stepfan, Ariz	36	115	3.2	15	0	Palmer, Carson, Ariz	27	3	0.1	10	0
* Franklin, Johnathan, G.B.	19	107	5.6	51	1	Jackson, DeSean, Phi.	3	2	0.7	8	0
Jeffery, Alshon, Chi.	16	105	6.6	38	0	Pascoe, Bear, NY-G	1	2	2.0	2	0
Polk, Chris, Phi.	11	98	8.9	38t	3	Smith, Brad, Phi.	2	2	1.0	2	0
* Michael, Christine, Sea.	18	79	4.4	13	0	* Wright, Timothy, T.B.	1	2	2.0	2	0
Cobb, Randall, G.B.	4	78	19.5	67	0	Brockel, Richie, Car.	1	1	1.0	1	0
Scott, Da'Rel, NY-G	20	73	3.7	16	0	Bryant, Dez, Dal.	1	1	1.0	1	0
McCown, Josh, Chi.	13	69	5.3	20	1	Jackson, Tarvaris, Sea.	4	1	0.3	5t	1
Stafford, Matthew, Det.	37	69	1.9	14	2	Vaughan, Josh, Atl.	1	1	1.0	1	0
Flynn, Matt, Oak.-G.B.	20	65	3.3	17	0	Anderson, Derek, Car.	5	0	0.0	2	0
Clemens, Kellen, St.L	23	64	2.8	16	0	Jackson, Vincent, T.B.	1	0	0.0	0	0
James, LaMichael, S.F.	12	59	4.9	21	0	Maragos, Chris, Sea.	1	0	0.0	0	0
Cassel, Matt, Min.	18	57	3.2	13	1	Robinson, Michael, Sea.	1	0	0.0	0	0
Jernigan, Jerrel, NY-G	2	57	28.5	49t	1	Royster, Evan, Was.	2	0	0.0	0	0
Dixon, Anthony, S.F.	28	56	2.0	9	2	Weatherford, Steve, NY-G	1	0	0.0	0	0
Ryan, Matt, Atl.	17	55	3.2	17	0	Meachem, Robert, N.O.	2	-1	-0.5	4	0
Tolzien, Scott, G.B.	5	55	11.0	19	1	* Barkley, Matt, Phi.	2	-2	-1.0	-1	0
Smith, Alfonso, Ariz	18	54	3.0	21	1	Hill, Shaun, Det.	2	-2	-1.0	-1	0
Brees, Drew, N.O.	35	52	1.5	16	3	Lockette, Ricardo, Sea.	1	-2	-2.0	-2	0
Collins, Jed, N.O.	15	45	3.0	12	1	Painter, Curtis, NY-G	3	-2	-0.7	0	0
* Cox, Michael, NY-G	22	43	2.0	9	0	McCown, Luke, N.O.	3	-4	-1.3	-1	0
Young, Darrel, Was.	12	41	3.4	19	3	Robinson, Aldrick, Was.	3	-4	-1.3	9	0
Ross, Jeremy, Det.	2	40	20.0	24	0	Giordano, Matt, St.L	1	-5	-5.0	-5	0
Kuhn, John, G.B.	10	38	3.8	12	1	McCoy, Colt, S.F.	6	-6	-1.0	-1	0
Romo, Tony, Dal.	20	38	1.9	15	0	Burleson, Nate, Det.	2	-8	-4.0	0	0
* Glennon, Mike, T.B.	27	37	1.4	16	0	* Hill, Josh, N.O.	1	-8	-8.0	-8	0
Manning, Eli, NY-G	18	36	2.0	14	0						
* Bailey, Stedman, St.L	2	33	16.5	27t	1	*t = Touchdown*					
Bradford, Sam, St.L	15	31	2.1	23	0	*Leader based on most yards gained*					
Tate, Golden, Sea.	3	31	10.3	20	0	* * Player that was a rookie in 2013*					
Ginn, Ted, Car.	4	29	7.3	14	0						
* Patton, Quinton, S.F.	1	26	26.0	26	0						
Moss, Santana, Was.	3	25	8.3	18	0						
* Riddick, Theo, Det.	9	25	2.8	7	1						
* Hill, Michael, T.B.	9	23	2.6	10	0						
Williams, Kyle, S.F.	2	23	11.5	13	0						
Goldson, Dashon, T.B.	1	22	22.0	22	0						
Pead, Isaiah, St.L	7	21	3.0	11	0						
Peterson, Patrick, Ariz	4	21	5.3	12	0						
Freeman, Josh, T.B.	5	20	4.0	13	0						

AMERICAN FOOTBALL CONFERENCE—RUSHING

	Att	Yards	Avg	Long	TD
Buffalo	546	2307	4.2	77	15
N.Y. Jets	493	2158	4.4	69	12
New England	470	2065	4.4	47t	19
Kansas City	442	2056	4.7	46	17
Oakland	437	2000	4.6	93t	16
San Diego	486	1965	4.0	51	9
Tennessee	462	1894	4.1	39	16
Denver	461	1873	4.1	45	16
Cincinnati	481	1755	3.6	35t	14
Houston	414	1743	4.2	60	7
Indianapolis	409	1743	4.3	51t	15
Miami	349	1440	4.1	55	8
Cleveland	348	1383	4.0	45	4
Pittsburgh	394	1383	3.5	43	9
Baltimore	423	1328	3.1	47	7
Jacksonville	378	1260	3.3	48	7
AFC Total	6993	28353	4.1	93t	191
AFC Average	437.1	1772.1	4.1	—	11.9

NATIONAL FOOTBALL CONFERENCE—RUSHING

	Att	Yards	Avg	Long	TD
Philadelphia	500	2566	5.1	65t	19
San Francisco	505	2201	4.4	51	18
Seattle	509	2188	4.3	43	14
Washington	453	2164	4.8	45t	14
Green Bay	459	2136	4.7	67	17
Minnesota	423	2081	4.9	78t	23
Carolina	483	2026	4.2	56	14
Chicago	404	1828	4.5	55	13
Detroit	445	1792	4.0	39	15
St. Louis	426	1752	4.1	65t	10
Tampa Bay	420	1612	3.8	80t	6
Arizona	422	1540	3.6	80t	12
Dallas	336	1504	4.5	45	12
New Orleans	391	1473	3.8	38	10
N.Y. Giants	381	1332	3.5	49t	11
Atlanta	321	1247	3.9	50t	11
NFC Total	6878	29442	4.3	80t	219
NFC Average	429.9	1840.1	4.3	—	13.7
League Total	13871	57795	—	93t	410
League Average	433.5	1806.1	4.2	—	12.8

PASSING

HIGHEST RATING

NFC:	119.2	Nick Foles, Philadelphia
AFC:	115.1	Peyton Manning, Denver

COMPLETION PERCENTAGE

AFC:	69.5	Philip Rivers, San Diego
NFC:	68.6	Drew Brees, New Orleans

ATTEMPTS

AFC:	659	Peyton Manning, Denver
NFC:	651	Matt Ryan, Atlanta

COMPLETIONS

AFC:	450	Peyton Manning, Denver
NFC:	446	Drew Brees, New Orleans

YARDS

AFC:	5477	Peyton Manning, Denver
NFC:	5162	Drew Brees, New Orleans

YARDS, GAME

NFC:	506	Tony Romo, Dallas vs. Denver, October 6 (25-36, 5 TD)
AFC:	462	Peyton Manning, Denver vs. Baltimore, September 5 (27-42, 7 TD)

LONGEST

AFC:	95	Brandon Weeden (to Josh Gordon), Cleveland vs. Jacksonville, December 1 - TD
NFC:	91	Carson Palmer (to Michael Floyd), Arizona at Jacksonville, November 17 - TD

YARDS PER ATTEMPT

NFC:	9.12	Nick Foles, Philadelphia
AFC:	8.31	Peyton Manning, Denver

TOUCHDOWN PASSES

AFC:	55	Peyton Manning, Denver
NFC:	39	Drew Brees, New Orleans

TOUCHDOWN PASSES, GAME

AFC:	7	Peyton Manning, Denver vs. Baltimore, September 5 (27-42, 462 yards)
NFC:	7	Nick Foles, Philadelphia at Oakland, November 3 (22-28, 406 yards)

LOWEST INTERCEPTION PERCENTAGE

NFC:	0.4	Josh McCown, Chicago
AFC:	1.4	Alex Smith, Kansas City

TEAM CHAMPION (MOST NET YARDS)

AFC:	5444	Denver
NFC:	4918	New Orleans

NFL TOP TEN PASSERS

	Att	Comp	Pct Comp	Yds	Avg Gain	TD	Pct TD	Long	Int	Pct Int	Sack	Yds Lost	Rating Points
Nick Foles, Phi.	317	203	64.0	2891	9.12	27	8.5	63t	2	0.6	28	173	119.2
Peyton Manning, Den.	659	450	68.3	5477	8.31	55	8.3	78t	10	1.5	18	120	115.1
Josh McCown, Chi	224	149	66.5	1829	8.17	13	5.8	80t	1	0.4	11	37	109.0
Philip Rivers, S.D..	544	378	69.5	4478	8.23	32	5.9	60t	11	2.0	30	150	105.5
Aaron Rodgers, G.B.	290	193	66.6	2536	8.74	17	5.9	83t	6	2.1	21	117	104.9
Drew Brees, N.O.	650	446	68.6	5162	7.94	39	6.0	76t	12	1.8	37	244	104.7
Russell Wilson, Sea	407	257	63.1	3357	8.25	26	6.4	80t	9	2.2	44	272	101.2
Tony Romo, Dal.	535	342	63.9	3828	7.16	31	5.8	82t	10	1.9	35	272	96.7
Ben Roethlisberger, Pit..	584	375	64.2	4261	7.30	28	4.8	67	14	2.4	42	282	92.0
Colin Kaepernick, S.F.	416	243	58.4	3197	7.69	21	5.0	64t	8	1.9	39	231	91.6

AMERICAN FOOTBALL CONFERENCE—PASSING

	Att	Comp	Pct Comp	Gross Yards	Sacked	Yds Lost	Net Yards	Yds/ Att	Yards/ Comp	TD	Pct TD	Long	Int	Pct Int
Denver	675	461	68.3	5572	20	128	5444	8.25	12.09	55	8.15	78t	10	1.5
San Diego	544	378	69.5	4478	30	150	4328	8.23	11.85	32	5.88	60t	11	2.0
Cleveland	681	379	55.7	4372	49	325	4047	6.42	11.54	26	3.82	95t	20	2.9
New England	628	380	60.5	4343	40	256	4087	6.92	11.43	25	3.98	81t	11	1.8
Cincinnati	587	364	62.0	4318	29	182	4136	7.36	11.86	33	5.62	82t	20	3.4
Pittsburgh	586	377	64.3	4306	43	289	4017	7.35	11.42	28	4.78	67	14	2.4
Houston	633	371	58.6	4183	42	370	3813	6.61	11.27	19	3.00	66	22	3.5
Miami	594	357	60.1	3966	58	399	3567	6.68	11.11	24	4.04	67	19	3.2
Indianapolis	582	350	60.1	3952	32	227	3725	6.79	11.29	23	3.95	73t	10	1.7
Baltimore	619	363	58.6	3914	48	324	3590	6.32	10.78	19	3.07	74	23	3.7
Jacksonville	592	349	59.0	3751	50	310	3441	6.34	10.75	16	2.70	67t	21	3.5
Tennessee	533	328	61.5	3710	37	214	3496	6.96	11.31	22	4.13	77t	16	3.0
Oakland	519	298	57.4	3629	44	289	3340	6.99	12.18	17	3.28	73t	20	3.9
Kansas City	546	333	61.0	3561	41	221	3340	6.52	10.69	24	4.40	71t	8	1.5
Buffalo	522	299	57.3	3373	48	270	3103	6.46	11.28	16	3.07	59t	15	2.9
N.Y. Jets	480	266	55.4	3270	47	338	2932	6.81	12.29	13	2.71	69t	22	4.6
AFC Total	9321	5653	—	64698	658	4292	60406	—	—	392	—	95t	262	—
AFC Average	582.6	353.3	60.6	4043.6	41.1	268.3	3775.4	6.94	11.44	24.5	4.2	—	16.4	2.8

NATIONAL FOOTBALL CONFERENCE—PASSING

	Att	Comp	Pct Comp	Gross Yards	Sacked	Yds Lost	Net Yards	Yds/ Att	Yards/ Comp	TD	Pct TD	Long	Int	Pct Int
New Orleans	651	446	68.5	5162	37	244	4918	7.93	11.57	39	5.99	76t	12	1.8
Detroit	634	371	58.5	4650	23	168	4482	7.33	12.53	29	4.57	87	19	3.0
Atlanta	659	445	67.5	4541	44	298	4243	6.89	10.20	26	3.95	81t	17	2.6
Green Bay	570	366	64.2	4538	45	270	4268	7.96	12.40	25	4.39	83t	16	2.8
Chicago	579	373	64.4	4450	30	169	4281	7.69	11.93	32	5.53	80t	13	2.2
Philadelphia	508	310	61.0	4406	46	296	4110	8.67	14.21	32	6.30	70	9	1.8
Arizona	574	363	63.2	4291	41	289	4002	7.48	11.82	24	4.18	91t	22	3.8
Dallas	586	375	64.0	4226	35	272	3954	7.21	11.27	33	5.63	82t	12	2.0
Washington	611	355	58.1	4057	43	306	3751	6.64	11.43	20	3.27	62t	19	3.1
N.Y. Giants	567	325	57.3	3875	40	287	3588	6.83	11.92	18	3.17	70t	29	5.1
Minnesota	546	325	59.5	3645	44	218	3427	6.68	11.22	18	3.30	79t	19	3.5
Seattle	420	267	63.6	3508	44	272	3236	8.35	13.14	27	6.43	80t	9	2.1
Carolina	473	292	61.7	3379	43	336	3043	7.14	11.57	24	5.07	79t	13	2.7
St. Louis	506	301	59.5	3360	36	235	3125	6.64	11.16	22	4.35	81t	11	2.2
San Francisco	417	244	58.5	3210	39	231	2979	7.70	13.16	21	5.04	64t	8	1.9
Tampa Bay	514	291	56.6	3181	47	361	2820	6.19	10.93	22	4.28	85t	12	2.3
NFC Total	8815	5449	—	64479	637	4252	60227	—	—	412	—	91t	240	—
NFC Average	550.9	340.6	61.8	4029.9	39.8	265.8	3764.2	7.31	11.83	25.8	4.7	—	15.0	2.7
League Total	18136	11102	—	129177	1295	8544	120633	—	—	804	—	95t	502	—
League Average	566.8	346.9	61.2	4036.8	40.5	267.0	3769.8	7.12	11.64	25.1	4.4	—	15.7	2.8

AFC—INDIVIDUAL PASSERS

	Att	Comp	Pct Comp	Yds	Avg Gain	TD	Pct TD	Long	Int	Pct Int	Sack	Yds Lost	Rating Points
Manning, Peyton, Den.	659	450	68.3	5477	8.31	55	8.3	78t	10	1.5	18	120	115.1
Rivers, Philip, S.D.	544	378	69.5	4478	8.23	32	5.9	60t	11	2.0	30	150	105.5
Roethlisberger, Ben, Pit.	584	375	64.2	4261	7.30	28	4.8	67	14	2.4	42	282	92.0
Smith, Alex, K.C.	508	308	60.6	3313	6.52	23	4.5	71t	7	1.4	39	210	89.1
Dalton, Andy, Cin.	586	363	61.9	4293	7.33	33	5.6	82t	20	3.4	29	182	88.8
Brady, Tom, N.E.	628	380	60.5	4343	6.92	25	4.0	81t	11	1.8	40	256	87.3
Luck, Andrew, Ind.	570	343	60.2	3822	6.71	23	4.0	73t	9	1.6	32	227	87.0
Fitzpatrick, Ryan, Ten.	350	217	62.0	2454	7.01	14	4.0	77t	12	3.4	21	109	82.0
Tannehill, Ryan, Mia.	588	355	60.4	3913	6.65	24	4.1	67	17	2.9	58	399	81.7
Keenum, Case, Hou.	253	137	54.2	1760	6.96	9	3.6	66	6	2.4	19	201	78.2
* Manuel, EJ, Buf.	306	180	58.8	1972	6.44	11	3.6	45	9	2.9	28	159	77.7
Campbell, Jason, Cle.	317	180	56.8	2015	6.36	11	3.5	80t	8	2.5	16	97	76.9
Henne, Chad, Jac.	503	305	60.6	3241	6.44	13	2.6	62t	14	2.8	38	243	76.5
Flacco, Joe, Bal.	614	362	59.0	3912	6.37	19	3.1	74	22	3.6	48	324	73.1
Schaub, Matt, Hou.	358	219	61.2	2310	6.45	10	2.8	46	14	3.9	21	162	73.0
Weeden, Brandon, Cle.	267	141	52.8	1731	6.48	9	3.4	95t	9	3.4	27	180	70.3
Pryor, Terrelle, Oak.	272	156	57.4	1798	6.61	7	2.6	73t	11	4.0	31	203	69.1
* Smith, Geno, NYJ	443	247	55.8	3046	6.88	12	2.7	69t	21	4.7	43	315	66.5
(Nonqualifiers)													
Locker, Jake, Ten.	183	111	60.7	1256	6.86	8	4.4	66t	4	2.2	16	105	86.7
Osweiler, Brock, Den.	16	11	68.8	95	5.94	0	0.0	19	0	0.0	2	8	84.1
Hoyer, Brian, Cle.	96	57	59.4	615	6.41	5	5.2	47t	3	3.1	6	48	82.6
Daniel, Chase, K.C.	38	25	65.8	248	6.53	1	2.6	48	1	2.6	2	11	81.9
Lewis, Thad, Buf.	157	93	59.2	1092	6.96	4	2.5	57	3	1.9	18	100	81.0
* McGloin, Matt, Oak.	211	118	55.9	1547	7.33	8	3.8	52	8	3.8	6	53	76.1
Simms, Matt, NYJ	31	16	51.6	156	5.03	1	3.2	25	1	3.2	4	23	63.4
Hasselbeck, Matt, Ind.	12	7	58.3	130	10.83	0	0.0	57	1	8.3	0	0	61.1
* Tuel, Jeff, Buf.	59	26	44.1	309	5.24	1	1.7	59t	3	5.1	2	11	45.1
Yates, T.J., Hou.	22	15	68.2	113	5.14	0	0.0	20	2	9.1	2	7	42.4
Gabbert, Blaine, Jac.	86	42	48.8	481	5.59	1	1.2	67t	7	8.1	12	67	36.0
(Fewer than Ten Attempts)													
Brown, Antonio, Pit.	1	1	100.0	15	15.00	0	0.0	15	0	0.0	1	7	118.8
Bush, Josh, NYJ	1	0	0.0	0	0.00	0	0.0	—	0	0.0	0	0	39.6
Cribbs, Josh, NYJ	3	2	66.7	38	12.67	0	0.0	25	0	0.0	0	0	109.7
Jones-Drew, Maurice, Jac.	1	1	100.0	8	8.00	1	100.0	8t	0	0.0	0	0	139.6
Kerley, Jeremy, NYJ	1	0	0.0	0	0.00	0	0.0	—	0	0.0	0	0	39.6
Lanning, Spencer, Cle.	1	1	100.0	11	11.00	1	100.0	11t	0	0.0	0	0	152.1
McBriar, Mat, Pit.	1	1	100.0	30	30.00	0	0.0	30	0	0.0	0	0	118.8
McFadden, Darren, Oak.	1	1	100.0	16	16.00	1	100.0	16t	0	0.0	0	0	158.3
Moore, Matt, Mia.	6	2	33.3	53	8.83	0	0.0	50	2	33.3	0	0	27.1
Powell, Bilal, NYJ	1	1	100.0	30	30.00	0	0.0	30	0	0.0	0	0	118.8
Reece, Marcel, Oak.	1	1	100.0	22	22.00	0	0.0	22	0	0.0	0	0	118.8
* Robinson, Denard, Jac.	1	0	0.0	0	0.00	0	0.0	—	0	0.0	0	0	39.6
* Sanders, Ace, Jac.	1	1	100.0	21	21.00	1	100.0	21t	0	0.0	0	0	158.3
Sanu, Mohamed, Cin.	1	1	100.0	25	25.00	0	0.0	25	0	0.0	0	0	118.8
Schillinger, Shann, Atl.	1	1	100.0	-8	-8.00	0	0.0	-8	0	0.0	0	0	79.2
Taylor, Tyrod, Bal.	5	1	20.0	2	0.40	0	0.0	2	1	20.0	0	0	0.0

t = Touchdown
Leader based on rating points, minimum 224 attempts
* Player that was a rookie in 2013

NFC—INDIVIDUAL PASSERS

	Att	Comp	Pct Comp	Yds	Avg Gain	TD	Pct TD	Long	Int	Pct Int	Sack	Yds Lost	Rating Points
Foles, Nick, Phi.	317	203	64.0	2891	9.12	27	8.5	63t	2	0.6	28	173	119.2
McCown, Josh, Chi.	224	149	66.5	1829	8.17	13	5.8	80t	1	0.4	11	37	109.0
Rodgers, Aaron, G.B.	290	193	66.6	2536	8.74	17	5.9	83t	6	2.1	21	117	104.9
Brees, Drew, N.O.	650	446	68.6	5162	7.94	39	6.0	76t	12	1.8	37	244	104.7
Wilson, Russell, Sea.	407	257	63.1	3357	8.25	26	6.4	80t	9	2.2	44	272	101.2
Romo, Tony, Dal.	535	342	63.9	3828	7.16	31	5.8	82t	10	1.9	35	272	96.7
Kaepernick, Colin, S.F.	416	243	58.4	3197	7.69	21	5.0	64t	8	1.9	39	231	91.6
Bradford, Sam, St.L	262	159	60.7	1687	6.44	14	5.3	73	4	1.5	15	97	90.9
Ryan, Matt, Atl.	651	439	67.4	4515	6.94	26	4.0	81t	17	2.6	44	298	89.6
Cutler, Jay, Chi.	355	224	63.1	2621	7.38	19	5.4	67	12	3.4	19	132	89.2
Newton, Cam, Car.	473	292	61.7	3379	7.14	24	5.1	79t	13	2.7	43	336	88.8
Stafford, Matthew, Det.	634	371	58.5	4650	7.33	29	4.6	87	19	3.0	23	168	84.2
Palmer, Carson, Ariz	572	362	63.3	4274	7.47	24	4.2	91t	22	3.8	41	289	83.9
* Glennon, Mike, T.B.	416	247	59.4	2608	6.27	19	4.6	85t	9	2.2	40	314	83.9
Griffin III, Robert, Was.	456	274	60.1	3203	7.02	16	3.5	62t	12	2.6	38	274	82.2
Cassel, Matt, Min.	254	153	60.2	1807	7.11	11	4.3	79t	9	3.5	16	85	81.6
Clemens, Kellen, St.L	242	142	58.7	1673	6.91	8	3.3	81t	7	2.9	21	138	78.8
Ponder, Christian, Min.	239	152	63.6	1648	6.90	7	2.9	47	9	3.8	27	119	77.9
Manning, Eli, NY-G	551	317	57.5	3818	6.93	18	3.3	70t	27	4.9	39	281	69.4
(Nonqualifiers)													
Jackson, Tarvaris, Sea.	13	10	76.9	151	11.62	1	7.7	35t	0	0.0	0	0	140.2
Vick, Michael, Phi.	141	77	54.6	1215	8.62	5	3.5	70	3	2.1	15	99	86.5
Flynn, Matt, Oak.-G.B.	200	124	62.0	1392	6.96	8	4.0	56	5	2.5	24	135	85.7
Orton, Kyle, Dal.	51	33	64.7	398	7.80	2	3.9	39	2	3.9	0	0	85.3
Tolzien, Scott, G.B.	90	55	61.1	717	7.97	1	1.1	52	5	5.6	3	26	66.8
Wallace, Seneca, G.B.	24	16	66.7	139	5.79	0	0.0	17	1	4.2	4	25	64.4
Cousins, Kirk, Was.	155	81	52.3	854	5.51	4	2.6	62	7	4.5	5	32	58.4
Freeman, Josh, T.B.-Min.	147	63	42.9	761	5.18	2	1.4	39	4	2.7	8	61	52.6
* Barkley, Matt, Phi.	49	30	61.2	300	6.12	0	0.0	26	4	8.2	3	24	44.6
Painter, Curtis, NY-G	16	8	50.0	57	3.56	0	0.0	9	2	12.5	1	6	19.0
(Fewer than Ten Attempts)													
* Austin, Tavon, St.L	1	0	0.0	0	0.00	0	0.0	—	0	0.0	0	0	39.6
Davis, Dominique, Atl.	7	5	71.4	34	4.86	0	0.0	14	0	0.0	0	0	81.8
Fitzgerald, Larry, Ariz	1	0	0.0	0	0.00	0	0.0	—	0	0.0	0	0	39.6
Hekker, Johnny, St.L	1	0	0.0	0	0.00	0	0.0	—	0	0.0	0	0	39.6
* James, Mike, T.B.	1	1	100.0	2	2.00	1	100.0	2t	0	0.0	0	0	118.8
Koenen, Michael, T.B.	2	0	0.0	0	0.00	0	0.0	—	0	0.0	0	0	39.6
McCown, Luke, N.O.	1	0	0.0	0	0.00	0	0.0	—	0	0.0	0	0	39.6
McCoy, Colt, S.F.	1	1	100.0	13	13.00	0	0.0	13	0	0.0	0	0	118.8
Peterson, Patrick, Ariz	1	1	100.0	17	17.00	0	0.0	17	0	0.0	0	0	118.8
Rainey, Bobby, T.B.	1	0	0.0	0	0.00	0	0.0	—	0	0.0	0	0	39.6
Schillinger, Shann, Atl.	1	1	100.0	-8	-8.00	0	0.0	-8	0	0.0	0	0	79.2
Smith, Brad, Phi.	1	0	0.0	0	0.00	0	0.0	—	0	0.0	0	0	39.6

t = Touchdown
Leader based on rating points, minimum 224 attempts
* Player that was a rookie in 2013

PASS RECEIVING

RECEPTIONS
NFC: 113 Pierre Garcon, Washington
AFC: 110 Antonio Brown, Pittsburgh

RECEPTIONS, GAME
AFC: 14 Justin Blackmon, Jacksonville at Denver,
          October 13 (190 yards, 0 TD)
      14 Josh Gordon, Cleveland vs. Pittsburgh,
          November 24 (237 yards, 1 TD)
NFC: 14 Calvin Johnson, Detroit vs. Dallas,
          October 27 (329 yards, 1 TD)

YARDS
AFC: 1646 Josh Gordon, Cleveland
NFC: 1492 Calvin Johnson, Detroit

YARDS, GAME
NFC: 329 Calvin Johnson, Detroit vs. Dallas,
           October 27 (14 receptions, 1 TD)
AFC: 261 Josh Gordon, Cleveland vs. Jacksonville,
           December 1 (10 receptions, 2 TD)

LONGEST
AFC: 95 Josh Gordon (from Brandon Weeden),
          Cleveland vs. Jacksonville,
          December 1 - TD
NFC: 91 Michael Floyd (from Carson Palmer),
          Arizona at Jacksonville,
          November 17 - TD

YARDS PER RECEPTION
NFC: 20.0* Kenny Stills, New Orleans
AFC: 18.9   Josh Gordon, Cleveland

TOUCHDOWNS
NFC: 16 Jimmy Graham, New Orleans
AFC: 14 Demaryius Thomas, Denver

TEAM LEADERS, RECEPTIONS
AFC: BALTIMORE, 65, Torrey Smith; BUFFALO, 53, Scott
      Chandler; CINCINNATI, 98, A.J. Green; CLEVELAND,
      87, Josh Gordon; DENVER, 92, Demaryius Thomas;
      HOUSTON, 109, Andre Johnson; INDIANAPOLIS,
      82, T.Y. Hilton; JACKSONVILLE, 66, Cecil Shorts;
      KANSAS CITY, 70, Jamaal Charles; MIAMI, 76, Brian
      Hartline; NEW ENGLAND, 105, Julian Edelman; N.Y.
      JETS, 43, Jeremy Kerley; OAKLAND, 60, Rod
      Streater; PITTSBURGH, 110, Antonio Brown; SAN
      DIEGO, 77, Antonio Gates; TENNESSEE, 94, Kendall
      Wright

NFC   ARIZONA, 82, Larry Fitzgerald; ATLANTA, 85, Harry
      Douglas; CAROLINA, 73, Greg Olsen; CHICAGO,
      100, Brandon Marshall; DALLAS, 93, Dez Bryant;
      DETROIT, 84, Calvin Johnson; GREEN BAY, 85,
      Jordy Nelson; MINNESOTA, 68, Greg Jennings;
      NEW ORLEANS, 86, Jimmy Graham; N.Y. GIANTS,
      73, Victor Cruz; PHILADELPHIA, 82, DeSean Jack-
      son; ST. LOUIS, 51, Jared Cook; SAN FRANCISCO,
      85, Anquan Boldin; SEATTLE, 64, Golden Tate;
      TAMPA BAY, 78, Vincent Jackson; WASHINGTON,
      113, Pierre Garcon

NFL TOP TEN PASS RECEIVERS

	No	Yards	Avg	Long	TD
Pierre Garcon, Was	113	1346	11.9	53t	5
Antonio Brown, Pit	110	1499	13.6	56	8
Andre Johnson, Hou	109	1407	12.9	62t	5
Julian Edelman, N.E.	105	1056	10.1	44	6
Brandon Marshall, Chi.	100	1295	13.0	44	12
A.J. Green, Cin.	98	1426	14.6	82t	11
Kendall Wright, Ten	94	1079	11.5	45	2
Dez Bryant, Dal	93	1233	13.3	79	13
Demaryius Thomas, Den.	92	1430	15.5	78t	14
Alshon Jeffery, Chi	89	1421	16.0	80t	7

NFL TOP TEN RECEIVERS BY YARDS

	Yards	No	Avg	Long	TD
Josh Gordon, Cle.	1646	87	18.9	95t	9
Antonio Brown, Pit	1499	110	13.6	56	8
Calvin Johnson, Det.	1492	84	17.8	87	12
Demaryius Thomas, Den.	1430	92	15.5	78t	14
A.J. Green, Cin	1426	98	14.6	82t	11
Alshon Jeffery, Chi	1421	89	16.0	80t	7
Andre Johnson, Hou.	1407	109	12.9	62t	5
Pierre Garcon, Was	1346	113	11.9	53t	5
DeSean Jackson, Phi	1332	82	16.2	61t	9
Jordy Nelson, G.B..	1314	85	15.5	76t	8

AFC—INDIVIDUAL RECEIVERS

	No	Yards	Avg	Long	TD
Brown, Antonio, Pit.	110	1499	13.6	56	8
Johnson, Andre, Hou.	109	1407	12.9	62t	5
Edelman, Julian, N.E.	105	1056	10.1	44	6
Green, A.J., Cin.	98	1426	14.6	82t	11
Wright, Kendall, Ten.	94	1079	11.5	45	2
Thomas, Demaryius, Den.	92	1430	15.5	78t	14
Gordon, Josh, Cle.	87	1646	18.9	95t	9
Decker, Eric, Den.	87	1288	14.8	61	11
Hilton, T.Y., Ind.	82	1083	13.2	73t	5
Cameron, Jordan, Cle.	80	917	11.5	53	7
Gates, Antonio, S.D.	77	872	11.3	56t	4
Hartline, Brian, Mia.	76	1016	13.4	50	4
Woodhead, Danny, S.D.	76	605	8.0	39	6
Wallace, Mike, Mia.	73	930	12.7	57	5
Welker, Wes, Den.	73	778	10.7	33	10
* Allen, Keenan, S.D.	71	1046	14.7	43t	8
Charles, Jamaal, K.C.	70	693	9.9	71t	7
Clay, Charles, Mia.	69	759	11.0	67	6
Sanders, Emmanuel, Pit.	67	740	11.0	55t	6
Shorts, Cecil, Jac.	66	777	11.8	59	3
Smith, Torrey, Bal.	65	1128	17.4	74	4
Thomas, Julius, Den.	65	788	12.1	74t	12
Streater, Rod, Oak.	60	888	14.8	66	4
Walker, Delanie, Ten.	60	571	9.5	33	6
Moreno, Knowshon, Den.	60	548	9.1	35t	3
Washington, Nate, Ten.	58	919	15.8	77t	3
Miller, Heath, Pit.	58	593	10.2	31	1
Rice, Ray, Bal.	58	321	5.5	22	0
Bowe, Dwayne, K.C.	57	673	11.8	34t	5
* Bernard, Giovani, Cin.	56	514	9.2	41	3
Amendola, Danny, N.E.	54	633	11.7	57	2
Chandler, Scott, Buf.	53	655	12.4	33t	2
McCluster, Dexter, K.C.	53	511	9.6	43	2
* Hopkins, DeAndre, Hou.	52	802	15.4	66	2
Fleener, Coby, Ind.	52	608	11.7	44	4
Johnson, Steve, Buf.	52	597	11.5	45	3
Jones, Marvin, Cin.	51	712	14.0	45	10
* Sanders, Ace, Jac.	51	484	9.5	51	1
Graham, Garrett, Hou.	49	545	11.1	42t	5
* Brown, Marlon, Bal.	49	524	10.7	59	7
Ogbonnaya, Chris, Cle.	48	343	7.1	17	2
Royal, Eddie, S.D.	47	631	13.4	54	8
Sanu, Mohamed, Cin.	47	455	9.7	32	2
Vereen, Shane, N.E.	47	427	9.1	50	3

Player	No	Yards	Avg	Long	TD
Jackson, Fred, Buf.	47	387	8.2	37	1
Moore, Denarius, Oak.	46	695	15.1	73t	5
Cotchery, Jerricho, Pit.	46	602	13.1	36	10
Gresham, Jermaine, Cin.	46	458	10.0	30	4
* Bell, Le'Veon, Pit.	45	399	8.9	43	0
Kerley, Jeremy, NYJ	43	523	12.2	26	3
Jones-Drew, Maurice, Jac.	43	314	7.3	17	0
Bess, Davone, Cle.	42	362	8.6	20t	2
Johnson, Chris, Ten.	42	345	8.2	66t	4
Brown, Vincent, S.D.	41	472	11.5	51	1
Little, Greg, Cle.	41	465	11.3	47	2
Matthews, Rishard, Mia.	41	448	10.9	29	2
Avery, Donnie, K.C.	40	596	14.9	51	2
* Woods, Robert, Buf.	40	587	14.7	57	3
Gronkowski, Rob, N.E.	39	592	15.2	50	4
* Eifert, Tyler, Cin.	39	445	11.4	61	2
Wayne, Reggie, Ind.	38	503	13.2	35	2
* Rivera, Mychal, Oak.	38	407	10.7	37	4
* Dobson, Aaron, N.E.	37	519	14.0	81t	4
Jones, Jacoby, Bal.	37	455	12.3	66t	2
Nelson, David, NYJ	36	423	11.8	31	2
Jennings, Rashad, Oak.	36	292	8.1	24	0
Powell, Bilal, NYJ	36	272	7.6	36	0
Richardson, Trent, Cle.-Ind.	35	316	9.0	24	1
Tate, Ben, Hou.	34	140	4.1	10	0
Spiller, C.J., Buf.	33	185	5.6	27	0
* Thompkins, Kenbrell, N.E.	32	466	14.6	49	4
Brown, Mike, Jac.	32	446	13.9	43	2
Reece, Marcel, Oak.	32	331	10.3	45	2
Winslow, Kellen, NYJ	31	388	12.5	34	2
Clark, Dallas, Bal.	31	343	11.1	45	3
Gibson, Brandon, Mia.	30	326	10.9	46	3
Blackmon, Justin, Jac.	29	415	14.3	67t	1
Heyward-Bey, Darrius, Ind.	29	309	10.7	27	1
Brown, Donald, Ind.	27	214	7.9	33t	2
Cumberland, Jeff, NYJ	26	398	15.3	47	4
McGrath, Sean, K.C.	26	302	11.6	25	2
Mathews, Ryan, S.D.	26	189	7.3	17	1
Miller, Lamar, Mia.	26	170	6.5	22	0
Holmes, Andre, Oak.	25	431	17.2	40	1
Lewis, Marcedes, Jac.	25	359	14.4	41	4
Dickson, Ed, Bal.	25	273	10.9	43	1
Hill, Stephen, NYJ	24	342	14.3	51t	1
Harbor, Clay, Jac.	24	292	12.2	31	2
Whalen, Griff, Ind.	24	259	10.8	25	2
Holmes, Santonio, NYJ	23	456	19.8	69t	1
Graham, T.J., Buf.	23	361	15.7	47	2
Fasano, Anthony, K.C.	23	200	8.7	20	3
Martin, Keshawn, Hou.	22	253	11.5	32	2
Taylor, Kerry, Ariz-Jac.	22	229	10.4	17	1
Foster, Arian, Hou.	22	183	8.3	41	1
Whittaker, Fozzy, Cle.	21	155	7.4	35t	2
Bolden, Brandon, N.E.	21	152	7.2	18	0
Tamme, Jacob, Den.	20	184	9.2	15	1
Pitta, Dennis, Bal.	20	169	8.5	18	1
* Ball, Montee, Den.	20	145	7.3	31	0
Pierce, Bernard, Bal.	20	104	5.2	15	0
Doss, Tandon, Bal.	19	305	16.1	63	0
* Griffin, Ryan, Hou.	19	244	12.8	40	1
* Hunter, Justin, Ten.	18	354	19.7	57	4
Sherman, Anthony, K.C.	18	155	8.6	26	1
Havili, Stanley, Ind.	18	128	7.1	20t	1
Green, Ladarius, S.D.	17	376	22.1	60t	3
* Goodwin, Marquise, Buf.	17	283	16.6	59t	3
McFadden, Darren, Oak.	17	108	6.4	16	0
Caldwell, Andre, Den.	16	200	12.5	36	3
Williams, Damian, Ten.	15	178	11.9	32	0
Posey, DeVier, Hou.	15	155	10.3	42	0
Forsett, Justin, Jac.	15	82	5.5	14	0
Thomas, Daniel, Mia.	15	63	4.2	16	2
* Rogers, Da'Rick, Ind.	14	192	13.7	69t	2
Todman, Jordan, Jac.	14	116	8.3	30	1
Barnidge, Gary, Cle.	13	127	9.8	40t	2
Hemingway, Junior, K.C.	13	125	9.6	24	2
Stokley, Brandon, Bal.	13	115	8.8	18	0
Ford, Jacoby, Oak.	13	99	7.6	22	0
Hawkins, Andrew, Cin.	12	199	16.6	50	0
Brazill, LaVon, Ind.	12	161	13.4	29t	2
Hoomanawanui, Michael, N.E.	12	136	11.3	19	1
Gates, Clyde, NYJ	12	122	10.2	34	0
Hillman, Ronnie, Den.	12	119	9.9	19	0
Britt, Kenny, Ten.	11	96	8.7	15	0
* Davis, Knile, K.C.	11	75	6.8	17	0
* Bohanon, Tommy, NYJ	11	69	6.3	21	0
Leach, Vonta, Bal.	11	47	4.3	12	1
Thompson, Deonte, Bal.	10	96	9.6	33	0
Hogan, Chris, Buf.	10	83	8.3	16	0
Ridley, Stevan, N.E.	10	62	6.2	24	0
Ta'ufo'ou, Will, Jac.	10	40	4.0	11	0
* Boyce, Josh, N.E.	9	121	13.4	30	0
* Butler, Brice, Oak.	9	103	11.4	29	0
Jones, Felix, Pit.	9	63	7.0	15	0
Cooper, Josh, Cle.	9	60	6.7	16	0
Green, Virgil, Den.	9	45	5.0	10	0
Salas, Greg, NYJ	8	143	17.9	44	0
Jenkins, A.J., K.C.	8	130	16.3	48	0
Thigpen, Marcus, Mia.	8	97	12.1	50	1
Burton, Stephen, Jac.	8	76	9.5	22	0
Dwyer, Jonathan, Pit.	8	64	8.0	23	0
Brown, Ronnie, S.D.	8	60	7.5	15	0
Baker, Edwin, Cle.	8	57	7.1	16	0
* Johnson, Dennis, Hou.	8	46	5.8	14	0
Johnson, Will, Pit.	8	41	5.1	9	1
McGahee, Willis, Cle.	8	20	2.5	9	0
Summers, Frank, Buf.	7	79	11.3	34	1
Egnew, Michael, Mia.	7	69	9.9	14	0
Olawale, Jamize, Oak.	7	63	9.0	25	0
Moore, Marlon, S.F.-Mia.	7	62	8.9	13	0
Dreessen, Joel, Den.	7	47	6.7	14	1
Gray, Cyrus, K.C.	7	46	6.6	18	0
Bradshaw, Ahmad, Ind.	7	42	6.0	14	0
Floyd, Malcom, S.D.	6	149	24.8	47	0
Paulson, David, Pit.	6	102	17.0	34	0
Mastrud, Jeron, Oak.	6	88	14.7	41	0
Grimes, Jonathan, Hou.	6	76	12.7	31	0
* Wheaton, Markus, Pit.	6	64	10.7	21	0
Collie, Austin, N.E.	6	63	10.5	19	0
Sanzenbacher, Dane, Cin.	6	61	10.2	23	0
Greene, Shonn, Ten.	6	39	6.5	28	0
Mooney, Collin, Ten.	6	32	5.3	22	0
* Sims, Dion, Mia.	6	32	5.3	8	1
Benjamin, Travis, Cle.	5	105	21.0	39	0
Smith, Lee, Buf.	5	78	15.6	28	0
* Sudfeld, Zach, NYJ	5	63	12.6	25	0
* Gragg, Chris, Buf.	5	53	10.6	28	1
Reisner, Allen, Jac.	5	40	8.0	16	0
Preston, Michael, Ten.	5	37	7.4	10t	2
Jones, Greg, Hou.	5	34	6.8	19	0
* Doyle, Jack, Ind.	5	19	3.8	8	0
Choice, Tashard, Buf.-Ind.	5	15	3.0	5	0
Johnson, David, Pit.	4	70	17.5	32	0
Develin, James, N.E.	4	62	15.5	31	0
Saunders, Weslye, Ind.	4	46	11.5	18	0
Battle, Jackie, Ten.	4	36	9.0	24	0
Jean, Lestar, Hou.	4	35	8.8	11	0
Phillips, John, S.D.	4	30	7.5	13	0
Green-Ellis, BenJarvus, Cin.	4	22	5.5	10	0
Redman, Isaac, Pit.	4	14	3.5	7	0
Ajirotutu, Seyi, S.D.	3	64	21.3	26t	1
Brock, Kevin, K.C.	3	36	12.0	25	0
Criner, Juron, Oak.	3	32	10.7	20	0
Ebert, Jeremy, Jac.	3	18	6.0	8	0

	No	Yards	Avg	Long	TD
Thompson, Taylor, Ten.	3	13	4.3	9t	1
Smith, Alex, Cin.	3	12	4.0	7	1
Noble, Danny, Jac.	2	63	31.5	62t	1
Jones, Taiwan, Oak.	2	55	27.5	52	0
Blount, LeGarrette, N.E.	2	38	19.0	32	0
Jones, Dominique, Ind.	2	34	17.0	21	0
* Thomas, Lamaar, Jac.	2	31	15.5	18	0
Hall, Chad, K.C.	2	20	10.0	11	0
Moye, Derek, Pit.	2	20	10.0	19	1
Goodson, Mike, NYJ	2	19	9.5	10	0
Bajema, Billy, Bal.	2	18	9.0	18	0
Mulligan, Matthew, N.E.	2	16	8.0	15	1
Easley, Marcus, Buf.	2	13	6.5	9	0
Tyms, Brian, Cle.	2	12	6.0	6	0
Stephens-Howling, LaRod, Pit.	2	11	5.5	7	0
Ivory, Chris, NYJ	2	10	5.0	12	0
Scott, Bernard, Bal.	2	10	5.0	8	0
* Gray, MarQueis, Cle.	2	8	4.0	5	0
Green, Alex, NYJ	2	8	4.0	7	0
Cribbs, Josh, NYJ	2	6	3.0	5	0
Stewart, Jeremy, Oak.	2	6	3.0	5	0
Stevens, Craig, Ten.	2	5	2.5	6	0
Shiancoe, Visanthe, Ten.	2	2	1.0	3	0
McClain, Le'Ron, S.D.	2	-7	-3.5	7	0
Herron, Dan, Ind.	1	57	57.0	57	0
Chekwa, Chimdi, Oak.	1	22	22.0	22	0
Allen, Dwayne, Ind.	1	20	20.0	20t	1
Gurley, Tori, Cle.	1	15	15.0	15	0
* Smith, Geno, NYJ	1	13	13.0	13	0
* Graham, Ray, Hou.	1	12	12.0	12	0
Spaeth, Matt, Pit.	1	11	11.0	11t	1
Edwards, Armanti, Cle.	1	10	10.0	10	0
* Kasa, Nick, Oak.	1	9	9.0	9t	1
Meester, Brad, Jac.	1	9	9.0	9	0
Charles, Orson, Cin.	1	8	8.0	8	0
Obomanu, Ben, NYJ	1	8	8.0	8	0
Palmer, Michael, Pit.	1	8	8.0	8	0
Reuland, Konrad, NYJ	1	7	7.0	7	0
Hughes, Robert, Ind.	1	6	6.0	6	0
Tate, Brandon, Cin.	1	6	6.0	6	0
Taylor, Tyrod, Bal.	1	6	6.0	6	0
* Cunningham, Justice, Ind.	1	4	4.0	4	0
Reynaud, Darius, Ten.	1	4	4.0	4	0
Gordon, Richard, K.C.	1	3	3.0	3	0
Reed, David, Ind.	1	2	2.0	2	0
* Wingo, Ronnie, Buf.	1	2	2.0	2	0
Fitzpatrick, Ryan, Ten.	1	0	0.0	0	0
Satele, Samson, Ind.	1	0	0.0	0	0
Karim, Deji, Hou.	1	-1	-1.0	-1	0
Smith, Alex, K.C.	1	-4	-4.0	-4	0
Ballard, Vick, Ind.	1	-5	-5.0	-5	0
Roethlisberger, Ben, Pit.	0	5	—	5	0
Rivers, Philip, S.D.	0	-9	—	-9	0

t = Touchdown; * Player that was a rookie in 2013
Leader based on receptions

NFC—INDIVIDUAL RECEIVERS

	No	Yards	Avg	Long	TD
Garcon, Pierre, Was.	113	1346	11.9	53t	5
Marshall, Brandon, Chi.	100	1295	13.0	44	12
Bryant, Dez, Dal.	93	1233	13.3	79	13
Jeffery, Alshon, Chi.	89	1421	16.0	80t	7
Graham, Jimmy, N.O.	86	1215	14.1	56t	16
Nelson, Jordy, G.B.	85	1314	15.5	76t	8
Boldin, Anquan, S.F.	85	1179	13.9	63	7
Douglas, Harry, Atl.	85	1067	12.6	80t	2
Johnson, Calvin, Det.	84	1492	17.8	87	12
Gonzalez, Tony, Atl.	83	859	10.3	25	8
Jackson, DeSean, Phi.	82	1332	16.2	61t	9
Fitzgerald, Larry, Ariz	82	954	11.6	75t	10

	No	Yards	Avg	Long	TD
Jackson, Vincent, T.B.	78	1224	15.7	60	7
Thomas, Pierre, N.O.	77	513	6.7	29	3
Colston, Marques, N.O.	75	943	12.6	35	5
Forté, Matt, Chi.	74	594	8.0	34	3
Cruz, Victor, NY-G	73	998	13.7	70t	4
Witten, Jason, Dal.	73	851	11.7	34	8
Olsen, Greg, Car.	73	816	11.2	31	6
Sproles, Darren, N.O.	71	604	8.5	48	2
Jennings, Greg, Min.	68	804	11.8	70t	4
Floyd, Michael, Ariz	65	1041	16.0	91t	5
Bennett, Martellus, Chi.	65	759	11.7	43	5
Tate, Golden, Sea.	64	898	14.0	80t	5
Smith, Steve, Car.	64	745	11.6	44	4
White, Roddy, Atl.	63	711	11.3	39t	3
Jones, James, G.B.	59	817	13.8	83t	3
Nicks, Hakeem, NY-G	56	896	16.0	57	0
* Wright, Timothy, T.B.	54	571	10.6	36	5
Bush, Reggie, Det.	54	506	9.4	77t	3
Bell, Joique, Det.	53	547	10.3	37	0
Murray, DeMarco, Dal.	53	350	6.6	22	1
Davis, Vernon, S.F.	52	850	16.3	64t	13
McCoy, LeSean, Phi.	52	539	10.4	70	2
Rodgers, Jacquizz, Atl.	52	341	6.6	22	2
Cook, Jared, St.L	51	671	13.2	47	5
Baldwin, Doug, Sea.	50	778	15.6	52	5
Boykin, Jarrett, G.B.	49	681	13.9	52	3
LaFell, Brandon, Car.	49	627	12.8	79t	5
Simpson, Jerome, Min.	48	726	15.1	51	1
Cooper, Riley, Phi.	47	835	17.8	63t	8
Myers, Brandon, NY-G	47	522	11.1	27t	4
* Reed, Jordan, Was.	45	499	11.1	38	3
* Patterson, Cordarrelle, Min.	45	469	10.4	79t	4
* Williams, Terrance, Dal.	44	736	16.7	82t	5
Roberts, Andre, Ariz	43	471	11.0	34t	2
Moss, Santana, Was.	42	452	10.8	28	2
Randle, Rueben, NY-G	41	611	14.9	37t	6
Jones, Julio, Atl.	41	580	14.1	81t	2
Pettigrew, Brandon, Det.	41	416	10.1	31	2
* Austin, Tavon, St.L	40	418	10.5	81t	4
Burleson, Nate, Det.	39	461	11.8	47	1
Housler, Rob, Ariz	39	454	11.6	31	1
* Ellington, Andre, Ariz	39	371	9.5	38	1
Beasley, Cole, Dal.	39	368	9.4	23	2
Durham, Kris, Det.	38	490	12.9	40	2
Avant, Jason, Phi.	38	447	11.8	31	2
Pettis, Austin, St.L	38	399	10.5	31t	4
Moore, Lance, N.O.	37	457	12.4	44t	2
Ginn, Ted, Car.	36	556	15.4	47t	5
* Ertz, Zach, Phi.	36	469	13.0	38	4
Lynch, Marshawn, Sea.	36	316	8.8	55	2
* Lacy, Eddie, G.B.	35	257	7.3	34	0
Givens, Chris, St.L	34	569	16.7	47	0
Miller, Zach, Sea.	33	387	11.7	60	5
Jackson, Steven, Atl.	33	191	5.8	25	1
* Stills, Kenny, N.O.	32	641	20.0	76t	5
Celek, Brent, Phi.	32	502	15.7	42	6
Carlson, John, Min.	32	344	10.8	30	1
Quarless, Andrew, G.B.	32	312	9.8	22	2
Kendricks, Lance, St.L	32	258	8.1	21	4
Bennett, Earl, Chi.	32	243	7.6	17t	4
Cobb, Randall, G.B.	31	433	14.0	48t	4
Helu, Roy, Was.	31	251	8.1	28	0
Hankerson, Leonard, Was.	30	375	12.5	29	3
Rudolph, Kyle, Min.	30	313	10.4	31t	3
Jernigan, Jerrel, NY-G	29	329	11.3	30	2
Snelling, Jason, Atl.	29	216	7.4	34	3
Leonard, Brian, T.B.	29	179	6.2	19	0
Peterson, Adrian, Min.	29	171	5.9	22	1
Paulsen, Logan, Was.	28	267	9.5	33	3
Tolbert, Mike, Car.	27	184	6.8	18	2
Wright, Jarius, Min.	26	434	16.7	42	3

	No	Yards	Avg	Long	TD		No	Yards	Avg	Long	TD
Williams, DeAngelo, Car.	26	333	12.8	72t	1	Felton, Jerome, Min.	6	37	6.2	11	0
Dray, Jim, Ariz	26	215	8.3	18	2	Murphy, Louis, NY-G	6	37	6.2	8	1
* Stacy, Zac, St.L	26	141	5.4	25	1	Conner, John, NY-G	6	31	5.2	12	0
Finley, Jermichael, G.B.	25	300	12.0	52	3	Taylor, Ryan, G.B.	6	30	5.0	8	0
Miller, Bruce, S.F.	25	243	9.7	43	0	Lockette, Ricardo, Sea.	5	82	16.4	33	0
Underwood, Tiquan, T.B.	24	440	18.3	85t	4	Ellison, Rhett, Min.	5	61	12.2	17	1
Austin, Miles, Dal.	24	244	10.2	20	0	Edwards, Pat, Det.	5	46	9.2	11	0
Kearse, Jermaine, Sea.	22	346	15.7	43t	4	Webb, Joe, Min.	5	33	6.6	15	0
Williams, Mike, T.B.	22	216	9.8	28	2	Asiata, Matt, Min.	5	13	2.6	8	0
* Johnson, Darius, Atl.	22	210	9.5	17	1	Golden, Brittan, Ariz	4	136	34.0	63	0
Ogletree, Kevin, T.B.-Det.	21	269	12.8	43	2	Young, Darrel, Was.	4	71	17.8	62t	1
* Willson, Luke, Sea.	20	272	13.6	39t	1	Page, Eric, T.B.	4	68	17.0	30	0
Morgan, Josh, Was.	20	214	10.7	21	0	Toon, Nick, N.O.	4	68	17.0	35	0
Brown, Andre, NY-G	20	103	5.2	14	0	Maehl, Jeff, Phi.	4	67	16.8	37	1
Crabtree, Michael, S.F.	19	284	14.9	60	1	Polk, Chris, Phi.	4	61	15.3	34	0
Watson, Benjamin, N.O.	19	226	11.9	32	2	Fiammetta, Tony, Chi.	4	57	14.3	30	0
Robinson, Aldrick, Was.	18	365	20.3	62	2	Paul, Niles, Was.	4	51	12.8	25	0
Quick, Brian, St.L	18	302	16.8	73	2	Bush, Michael, Chi.	4	48	12.0	17t	1
* Fauria, Joseph, Det.	18	207	11.5	25	7	* Franklin, Johnathan, G.B.	4	30	7.5	10	0
Mendenhall, Rashard, Ariz	18	134	7.4	24	0	* Riddick, Theo, Det.	4	26	6.5	8	0
* Bailey, Stedman, St.L	17	226	13.3	28	0	Crabtree, Tom, T.B.	4	21	5.3	14	1
Meachem, Robert, N.O.	16	324	20.3	60	2	Byham, Nate, T.B.	3	38	12.7	34	0
Gore, Frank, S.F.	16	141	8.8	29	0	* Patton, Quinton, S.F.	3	34	11.3	29	0
Rice, Sidney, Sea.	15	231	15.4	31t	3	Tanner, Phillip, Dal.	3	33	11.0	17	0
Rainey, Bobby, Cle.-T.B.	15	46	3.1	15	1	Davis, Kellen, Sea.	3	32	10.7	23	1
Richardson, Daryl, St.L	14	121	8.6	19	0	Casey, James, Phi.	3	31	10.3	12	0
Collins, Jed, N.O.	14	54	3.9	8	0	Donnell, Larry, NY-G	3	31	10.3	11	0
Owusu, Chris, T.B.	13	114	8.8	20	0	Dixon, Anthony, S.F.	3	30	10.0	19	0
Harkey, Cory, St.L	13	113	8.7	31t	2	Baldwin, Jon, S.F.	3	28	9.3	15	0
Hillis, Peyton, NY-G	13	96	7.4	16	0	Demps, Jeff, T.B.	3	21	7.0	10	0
Gerhart, Toby, Min.	13	88	6.8	13	0	* Williams, Nick, Was.	3	15	5.0	6	0
Kuhn, John, G.B.	13	81	6.2	20	0	* Cox, Michael, NY-G	3	12	4.0	11	0
Davis, Drew, Atl.	12	216	18.0	59	2	Celek, Garrett, S.F.	2	38	19.0	30	0
Pascoe, Bear, NY-G	12	81	6.8	14	0	Dickerson, Dorin, Det.	2	34	17.0	26	0
Hanna, James, Dal.	12	73	6.1	21	0	Ewing, Bradie, Atl.	2	29	14.5	15	0
Martin, Doug, T.B.	12	66	5.5	13	0	Robinson, Michael, Sea.	2	27	13.5	21	0
Williams, Kyle, S.F.	12	113	9.4	16	0	Smith, Brad, Phi.	2	27	13.5	14	0
* Brown, Jaron, Ariz	11	140	12.7	32	1	* Hill, Michael, T.B.	2	23	11.5	12	0
Ford, Chase, Min.	11	133	12.1	37	0	James, LaMichael, S.F.	2	16	8.0	12	0
Scott, Da'Rel, NY-G	11	102	9.3	23t	1	Johnson, Damaris, Phi.	2	14	7.0	8	0
Pead, Isaiah, St.L	11	78	7.1	14	0	Hunter, Kendall, S.F.	2	13	6.5	9	0
* Toilolo, Levine, Atl.	11	55	5.0	12	2	Jacobs, Brandon, NY-G	2	13	6.5	8	0
Lorig, Erik, T.B.	11	47	4.3	20	0	* Wilson, Marquess, Chi.	2	13	6.5	10	0
Starks, James, G.B.	10	89	8.9	23	1	* Dawson, Skye, T.B.	2	12	6.0	9	0
Smith, Alfonso, Ariz	10	68	6.8	10	0	Smith, Antone, Atl.	2	10	5.0	6	0
* James, Mike, T.B.	10	43	4.3	20	0	Wilson, David, NY-G	2	8	4.0	6	0
* Escobar, Gavin, Dal.	9	134	14.9	25	2	* Barner, Kenjon, Car.	2	7	3.5	5	0
Manningham, Mario, S.F.	9	85	9.4	14	0	Cadet, Travaris, N.O.	2	5	2.5	3t	1
Harris, Dwayne, Dal.	9	80	8.9	24t	2	Williams, Teddy, Ariz	1	51	51.0	51	0
Morris, Alfred, Was.	9	78	8.7	17	0	Harvin, Percy, Sea.	1	17	17.0	17	0
* White, Myles, G.B.	9	66	7.3	15	0	Osgood, Kassim, S.F.	1	17	17.0	17	0
* McDonald, Vance, S.F.	8	119	14.9	25	0	Sperry, Kory, Ariz	1	16	16.0	16	0
Broyles, Ryan, Det.	8	85	10.6	22	0	Staley, Joe, S.F.	1	14	14.0	14	0
Brown, Bryce, Phi.	8	84	10.5	35	0	Rosario, Dante, Chi.	1	13	13.0	13	0
* Taylor, Stepfan, Ariz	8	71	8.9	29	0	Brockel, Richie, Car.	1	12	12.0	12	0
Coleman, Derrick, Sea.	8	62	7.8	12	1	Cone, Kevin, Atl.	1	12	12.0	12	0
* Randle, Joseph, Dal.	8	61	7.6	13	0	Banyard, Joe, Min.	1	11	11.0	11	0
Turbin, Robert, Sea.	8	60	7.5	19	0	* Line, Zach, Min.	1	8	8.0	8	0
DiMarco, Patrick, Atl.	8	49	6.1	12	0	Weems, Eric, Chi.	1	8	8.0	8	0
Bostick, Brandon, G.B.	7	120	17.1	26	1	Hynoski, Henry, NY-G	1	5	5.0	5	0
Scheffler, Tony, Det.	7	82	11.7	22	0	McNeill, Mike, St.L	1	5	5.0	5	0
Ballard, Jake, Ariz	7	75	10.7	29	2	Clutts, Tyler, Dal.	1	4	4.0	4	0
Davis, Fred, Was.	7	70	10.0	23t	1	* Cunningham, Justice, Ind.	1	4	4.0	4	0
Ingram, Mark, N.O.	7	68	9.7	23	0	Royster, Evan, Was.	1	3	3.0	3	0
Dunbar, Lance, Dal.	7	59	8.4	17	0	Penn, Donald, T.B.	1	1	1.0	1t	1
Hixon, Domenik, Car.	7	55	7.9	14t	1	* Long, Kyle, Chi.	1	-1	-1.0	-1	0
Stewart, Jonathan, Car.	7	44	6.3	16	0	Vaughan, Josh, Atl.	1	-5	-5.0	-5	0
Ross, Jeremy, G.B.-Det.	6	67	11.2	19	1	Vick, Michael, Phi.	0	-2	—	-2	0
* Cunningham, Benny, St.L	6	59	9.8	18	0						
Peterson, Patrick, Ariz	6	54	9.0	19	0	*t = Touchdown; * Player that was a rookie in 2013*					
* Hill, Josh, N.O.	6	44	7.3	9	1	*Leader based on receptions*					

INTERCEPTIONS

INTERCEPTIONS

NFC:	8	Richard Sherman, Seattle
AFC:	5	Tashaun Gipson, Cleveland
	5	* Logan Ryan, New England
	5	Alterraun Verner, Tennessee

INTERCEPTIONS, GAME

AFC:
- 2 Dimitri Patterson, Miami at Cleveland, September 8 (2 yards, 0 TD)
- 2 Aqib Talib, New England vs. N.Y. Jets, September 12 (14 yards, 0 TD)
- 2 * Kiko Alonso, Buffalo vs. Baltimore, September 29 (6 yards, 0 TD)
- 2 Aaron Williams, Buffalo vs. Baltimore, September 29 (6 yards, 0 TD)
- 2 Alterraun Verner, Tennessee vs. N.Y. Jets, September 29 (39 yards, 0 TD)
- 2 James Ihedigbo, Baltimore vs. Cincinnati, November 10 (46 yards, 0 TD) - (OT)
- 2 Jairus Byrd, Buffalo vs. N.Y. Jets, November 17 (9 yards, 0 TD)
- 2 Joe Haden, Cleveland at Cincinnati, November 17 (44 yards, 1 TD)
- 2 Corey Graham, Baltimore vs. N.Y. Jets, November 24 (0 yards, 0 TD)
- 2 Cassius Vaughn, Indianapolis vs. Tennessee, December 1 (8 yards, 0 TD)
- 2 Tashaun Gipson, Cleveland vs. Chicago, December 15 (79 yards, 1 TD)
- 2 Darius Butler, Indianapolis vs. Houston, December 15 (38 yards, 0 TD)
- 2 Eric Berry, Kansas City at Oakland, December 15 (96 yards, 1 TD)
- 2 * Logan Ryan, New England at Baltimore, December 22 (1 yard, 0 TD)
- 2 Dre Kirkpatrick, Cincinnati vs. Baltimore, December 29 (21 yards, 1 TD)
- 2 * Dee Milliner, N.Y. Jets at Miami, December 29 (12 yards, 0 TD)

NFC:
- 2 Charles Tillman, Chicago vs. Cincinnati, September 8 (41 yards, 0 TD)
- 2 Louis Delmas, Detroit vs. Chicago, September 29 (2 yards, 0 TD)
- 2 Patrick Peterson, Arizona at Tampa Bay, September 29 (16 yards, 0 TD)
- 2 Tramaine Brock, San Francisco vs. Houston, October 6 (31 yards, 1 TD)
- 2 Tim Jennings, Chicago vs. N.Y. Giants, October 10 (64 yards, 1 TD)
- 2 DeAndre Levy, Detroit at Cleveland, October 13 (0 yards, 0 TD)
- 2 Mike Mitchell, Carolina at Minnesota, October 13 (62 yards, 0 TD)
- 2 Sean Lee, Dallas at Detroit, October 27 (89 yards, 0 TD)
- 2 Rashad Johnson, Arizona vs. Atlanta, October 27 (29 yards, 0 TD)
- 2 DeAngelo Hall, Washington at Denver, October 27 (26 yards, 1 TD)
- 2 Lavonte David, Tampa Bay vs. Buffalo, December 8 (57 yards, 0 TD)
- 2 Zack Bowman, Chicago at Cleveland, December 15 (43 yards, 1 TD)
- 2 Byron Maxwell, Seattle at N.Y. Giants, December 15 (4 yards, 0 TD)
- 2 Richard Sherman, Seattle at N.Y. Giants, December 15 (1 yard, 0 TD)

- 2 Antoine Cason, Arizona at Tennessee, December 15 (36 yards, 1 TD) - (OT)
- 2 Richard Sherman, Seattle vs. Arizona, December 22 (0 yards, 0 TD)
- 2 Trumaine McBride, N.Y. Giants vs. Washington, December 29 (17 yards, 0 TD)

YARDS

NFC:	174	Sean Lee, Dallas
AFC:	143	Tashaun Gipson, Cleveland

LONGEST

AFC:	100	Sean Smith, Kansas City at Buffalo, November 3 - TD
NFC:	98	* Alec Ogletree, St. Louis at Houston, October 13 - TD

TOUCHDOWNS

AFC:	2	Eric Berry, Kansas City
NFC:	2	Karlos Dansby, Arizona
	2	Mason Foster, Tampa Bay
	2	DeAngelo Hall, Washington
	2	Tim Jennings, Chicago
	2	Captain Munnerlyn, Carolina

TEAM LEADERS, INTERCEPTIONS

AFC: BALTIMORE, 4, Corey Graham; BUFFALO, 4, *Kiko Alonso, Jairus Byrd, Jim Leonhard, Aaron Williams; CINCINNATI, 3, Adam Jones, Dre Kirkpatrick; CLEVELAND, 5, Tashaun Gipson; DENVER, 3, Chris Harris, Dominique Rodgers-Cromartie, Danny Trevathan; HOUSTON, 3, Johnathan Joseph; INDIANAPOLIS, 4, Darius Butler; JACKSONVILLE, 2, Alan Ball, *Dwayne Gratz, Geno Hayes, Paul Posluszny; KANSAS CITY, 4, Quintin Demps; MIAMI, 4, Brent Grimes, Dimitri Patterson; NEW ENGLAND, 5, *Logan Ryan; N.Y. JETS, 3, Antonio Cromartie, *Dee Milliner, Ed Reed; OAKLAND, 2, Mike Jenkins, Tracy Porter; PITTSBURGH, 2, Cortez Allen, Ryan Clark, Troy Polamalu, Lawrence Timmons; SAN DIEGO, 2, Marcus Gilchrist, Eric Weddle; TENNESSEE, 5, Alterraun Verner

NFC: ARIZONA, 4, Karlos Dansby; ATLANTA, 3, William Moore; CAROLINA, 4, Luke Kuechly, Mike Mitchell; CHICAGO, 4, Tim Jennings; DALLAS, 4, Sean Lee; DETROIT, 6, DeAndre Levy; GREEN BAY, 4, Sam Shields; MINNESOTA, 3, Chad Greenway; NEW ORLEANS, 4, Keenan Lewis; N.Y. GIANTS, 6, Antrel Rolle; PHILADELPHIA, 6, Brandon Boykin; ST. LOUIS, 3, Trumaine Johnson; SAN FRANCISCO, 5, Tramaine Brock; SEATTLE, 8, Richard Sherman; TAMPA BAY, 5, Lavonte David; WASHINGTON, 4, DeAngelo Hall

TEAM CHAMPION

NFC:	28	Seattle
AFC:	23	Buffalo

NFL TOP TEN INTERCEPTORS

	No	Yards	Avg	Long	TD
Richard Sherman, Sea.	8	125	15.6	58t	1
Brandon Boykin, Phi	6	136	22.7	76	1
DeAndre Levy, Det.	6	76	12.7	66t	1
Antrel Rolle, NY-G	6	23	3.8	25	0
Tashaun Gipson, Cle.	5	143	28.6	44t	1
Lavonte David, T.B.	5	87	17.4	32	0
Tramaine Brock, S.F.	5	82	16.4	41	1
* Logan Ryan, N.E..	5	82	16.4	79t	1
Alterraun Verner, Ten	5	68	13.6	34	1
Earl Thomas, Sea.	5	9	1.8	11	0

AFC—INDIVIDUAL INTERCEPTORS

Player	No	Yards	Avg	Long	TD
Gipson, Tashaun, Cle.	5	143	28.6	44t	1
* Ryan, Logan, N.E.	5	82	16.4	79t	1
Verner, Alterraun, Ten.	5	68	13.6	34	1
Grimes, Brent, Mia.	4	102	25.5	94t	1
Byrd, Jairus, Buf.	4	85	21.3	57	0
Butler, Darius, Ind.	4	79	19.8	41t	1
Leonhard, Jim, Buf.	4	72	18.0	41	0
Demps, Quintin, K.C.	4	61	15.3	35	0
Haden, Joe, Cle.	4	57	14.3	29t	1
Williams, Aaron, Buf.	4	43	10.8	34	0
* Alonso, Kiko, Buf.	4	38	9.5	32	0
Graham, Corey, Bal.	4	28	7.0	28	0
Talib, Aqib, N.E.	4	12	3.0	14	0
Patterson, Dimitri, Mia.	4	7	1.8	3	0
Berry, Eric, K.C.	3	134	44.7	49	2
Rodgers-Cromartie, Domin, Den.	3	75	25.0	75t	1
Joseph, Johnathan, Hou.	3	64	21.3	32	0
Jones, Adam, Cin.	3	60	20.0	60t	1
Ihedigbo, James, Bal.	3	54	18.0	37	0
Reed, Ed, NYJ	3	49	16.3	25	0
Smith, Daryl, Bal.	3	41	13.7	37t	1
Pollard, Bernard, Ten.	3	36	12.0	32	0
* Cooper, Marcus, K.C.	3	32	10.7	20	0
* Milliner, Dee, NYJ	3	31	10.3	19	0
Trevathan, Danny, Den.	3	29	9.7	29	0
Carroll, Nolan, Mia.	3	24	8.0	24	0
Kirkpatrick, Dre, Cin.	3	21	7.0	21t	1
Cromartie, Antonio, NYJ	3	20	6.7	20	0
Vaughn, Cassius, Ind.	3	9	3.0	8	0
Harris, Chris, Den.	3	1	0.3	1	0
Smith, Sean, K.C.	2	96	48.0	100t	1
Posluszny, Paul, Jac.	2	69	34.5	59t	1
Ward, T.J., Cle.	2	57	28.5	44t	1
Clark, Ryan, Pit.	2	50	25.0	37	0
Bethea, Antoine, Ind.	2	48	24.0	46	0
* Harmon, Duron, N.E.	2	44	22.0	42	0
Johnson, Derrick, K.C.	2	44	22.0	41	0
Porter, Tracy, Oak.	2	44	22.0	43t	1
Allen, Cortez, Pit.	2	43	21.5	40t	1
Gilchrist, Marcus, S.D.	2	43	21.5	26	0
Crocker, Chris, Cin.	2	41	20.5	32t	1
Allen, Will, Dal.-Pit.	2	40	20.0	27	0
Hayes, Geno, Jac.	2	39	19.5	28	0
Polamalu, Troy, Pit.	2	36	18.0	19t	1
Parker, Ron, K.C.	2	29	14.5	15	0
Rey, Vincent, Cin.	2	29	14.5	25t	1
Timmons, Lawrence, Pit.	2	26	13.0	23	0
Ellerbe, Dannell, Mia.	2	25	12.5	16	0
Weddle, Eric, S.D.	2	21	10.5	21	0
Wilson, Jimmy, Mia.	2	21	10.5	23	0
* Gratz, Dwayne, Jac.	2	20	10.0	17	0
Webb, Lardarius, Bal.	2	19	9.5	19	0
Freeman, Jerrell, Ind.	2	13	6.5	13	0
Ball, Alan, Jac.	2	8	4.0	8	0
Newman, Terence, Cin.	2	8	4.0	9	0
Gilmore, Stephon, Buf.	2	0	0.0	0	0
Jenkins, Mike, Oak.	2	0	0.0	0	0
Nelson, Reggie, Cin.	2	0	0.0	0	0
Smith, Jimmy, Bal.	2	0	0.0	0	0
Wilson, Tavon, N.E.	1	74	74.0	74t	1
Abdullah, Husain, K.C.	1	44	44.0	44t	1
Wright, Shareece, S.D.	1	41	41.0	41	0
Landry, Dawan, NYJ	1	38	38.0	38	0
Flowers, Brandon, K.C.	1	32	32.0	32	0
Searcy, Da'Norris, Buf.	1	32	32.0	32t	1
Butler, Donald, S.D.	1	30	30.0	30	0
* Cyprien, Johnathan, Jac.	1	27	27.0	27	0
Toler, Greg, Ind.	1	26	26.0	26	0
Young, Usama, Oak.	1	26	26.0	26	0
Jones, Reshad, Mia.	1	25	25.0	25t	1
Allen, Antonio, NYJ	1	23	23.0	23t	1
Gay, William, Pit.	1	21	21.0	21t	1
* Robey, Nickell, Buf.	1	19	19.0	19t	1
Cushing, Brian, Hou.	1	18	18.0	18t	1
* Elam, Matt, Bal.	1	18	18.0	18	0
Maualuga, Rey, Cin.	1	14	14.0	14	0
Woodson, Charles, Oak.	1	13	13.0	13	0
Burfict, Vontaze, Cin.	1	12	12.0	12	0
Robertson, Craig, Cle.	1	12	12.0	12	0
Hali, Tamba, K.C.	1	10	10.0	10t	1
* Webster, Kayvon, Den.	1	10	10.0	10	0
Harrison, James, Cin.	1	9	9.0	9	0
Davis, Ryan, Jac.	1	8	8.0	8	0
Gordy, Josh, Ind.	1	7	7.0	7	0
Johnson, Michael, Cin.	1	7	7.0	7	0
Keiser, Thomas, S.D.	1	6	6.0	6	0
Wilkerson, Muhammad, NYJ	1	6	6.0	6	0
Arrington, Kyle, N.E.	1	5	5.0	5	0
Ayers, Akeem, Ten.	1	5	5.0	5	0
Skrine, Buster, Cle.	1	5	5.0	5	0
Zombo, Frank, K.C.	1	5	5.0	5	0
Angerer, Pat, Ind.	1	4	4.0	4	0
Keo, Shiloh, Hou.	1	4	4.0	4	0
Adams, Mike, Den.	1	3	3.0	3	0
Brown, Zach, Ten.	1	3	3.0	3	0
Phillips, Shaun, Den.	1	3	3.0	3	0
Spikes, Brandon, N.E.	1	3	3.0	3	0
Cox, Derek, S.D.	1	2	2.0	2	0
Knighton, Terrance, Den.	1	2	2.0	2	0
Blackmon, Will, Jac.	1	1	1.0	1	0
Lewis, Kendrick, K.C.	1	1	1.0	1	0
McCarthy, Colin, Ten.	1	1	1.0	1	0
Burnett, Kevin, Oak.	1	0	0.0	0	0
Carter, Tony, Den.	1	0	0.0	0	0
Clemons, Chris, Mia.	1	0	0.0	0	0
Cole, Marquice, N.E.	1	0	0.0	0	0
Davis, DeMario, NYJ	1	0	0.0	0	0
Davis, Vontae, Ind.	1	0	0.0	0	0
Dennard, Alfonzo, N.E.	1	0	0.0	0	0
Griffin, Michael, Ten.	1	0	0.0	0	0
Hall, Leon, Cin.	1	0	0.0	0	0
* Hayden, D.J., Oak.	1	0	0.0	0	0
Jackson, D'Qwell, Cle.	1	0	0.0	0	0
Lawson, Manny, Buf.	1	0	0.0	0	0
Lissemore, Sean, S.D.	1	0	0.0	0t	1
McCain, Brice, Hou.	1	0	0.0	0	0
McCourty, Devin, N.E.	1	0	0.0	0	0
McKelvin, Leodis, Buf.	1	0	0.0	0	0
Patrick, Johnny, S.D.	1	0	0.0	0	0
Roach, Nick, Oak.	1	0	0.0	0	0
Rogers, Justin, Buf.	1	0	0.0	0	0
* Swearinger, D.J., Hou.	1	0	0.0	0	0
Thomas, Cam, S.D.	1	0	0.0	0	0
Thomas, Michael, Mia.	1	0	0.0	0	0
Tyson, DeAngelo, Bal.	1	0	0.0	0	0
Wilson, George, Ten.	1	0	0.0	0	0
Woodyard, Wesley, Den.	1	0	0.0	0	0
Iloka, George, Cin.	1	-1	-1.0	-1	0

t = Touchdown; *Player that was a rookie in 2013
Leader based on interceptions

NFC—INDIVIDUAL INTERCEPTORS

Player	No	Yards	Avg	Long	TD
Sherman, Richard, Sea.	8	125	15.6	58t	1
Boykin, Brandon, Phi.	6	136	22.7	76	1
Levy, DeAndre, Det.	6	76	12.7	66t	1

Player	No	Yards	Avg	Long	TD
Rolle, Antrel, NY-G	6	23	3.8	25	0
David, Lavonte, T.B.	5	87	17.4	32	0
Brock, Tramaine, S.F.	5	82	16.4	41	1
Thomas, Earl, Sea.	5	9	1.8	11	0
Lee, Sean, Dal.	4	174	43.5	74	1
Jennings, Tim, Chi.	4	111	27.8	48t	2
Mitchell, Mike, Car.	4	63	15.8	38	0
* Reid, Eric, S.F.	4	54	13.5	53	0
Hall, DeAngelo, Was.	4	49	12.3	26t	2
Dansby, Karlos, Ariz	4	48	12.0	23t	2
Lewis, Keenan, N.O.	4	34	8.5	20	0
Kuechly, Luke, Car.	4	33	8.3	30	0
Maxwell, Byron, Sea.	4	6	1.5	6	0
Shields, Sam, G.B.	4	3	0.8	7	0
Foster, Mason, T.B.	3	122	40.7	85t	2
Chancellor, Kam, Sea.	3	78	26.0	32	0
Tillman, Charles, Chi.	3	69	23.0	41	0
Bowman, Zack, Chi.	3	67	22.3	43t	1
Peterson, Patrick, Ariz	3	59	19.7	43	0
Quin, Glover, Det.	3	57	19.0	42	0
Carr, Brandon, Dal.	3	49	16.3	49t	1
Conte, Chris, Chi.	3	48	16.0	35	0
Delmas, Louis, Det.	3	44	14.7	42	0
Tandy, Keith, T.B.	3	42	14.0	20	0
Johnson, Trumaine, St.L	3	36	12.0	29	0
Moore, William, Atl.	3	36	12.0	19	0
Johnson, Rashad, Ariz	3	35	11.7	18	0
* Banks, Johnthan, T.B.	3	33	11.0	18	0
Kendricks, Mychal, Phi.	3	25	8.3	18	0
Greenway, Chad, Min.	3	23	7.7	23	0
Williams, Cary, Phi.	3	16	5.3	15	0
Williams, Tramon, G.B.	3	10	3.3	10	0
* Lester, Robert, Car.	3	5	1.7	5	0
Bowman, NaVorro, S.F.	2	93	46.5	89t	1
Munnerlyn, Captain, Car.	2	86	43.0	45t	2
Smith, Malcolm, Sea.	2	69	34.5	37t	1
Meriweather, Brandon, Was.	2	62	31.0	32	0
Washington, Daryl, Ariz	2	49	24.5	41	0
Ryans, DeMeco, Phi.	2	46	23.0	36	0
Wright, Major, Chi.	2	46	23.0	38t	1
* Amerson, David, Was.	2	45	22.5	45t	1
Florence, Drayton, Car.	2	40	20.0	38t	1
Hill, Will, NY-G	2	38	19.0	38t	1
Cason, Antoine, Ariz	2	36	18.0	20t	1
Jenkins, Malcolm, N.O.	2	35	17.5	31	0
Houston, Chris, Det.	2	34	17.0	30	0
Fletcher, Bradley, Phi.	2	30	15.0	25	0
Henderson, Erin, Min.	2	19	9.5	10	0
McBride, Trumaine, NY-G	2	17	8.5	17	0
Rogers, Carlos, S.F.	2	14	7.0	11	0
Laurinaitis, James, St.L	2	9	4.5	9	0
Wagner, Bobby, Sea.	2	9	4.5	9	0
* White, Melvin, Car.	2	9	4.5	8t	1
* Mathieu, Tyrann, Ariz	2	7	3.5	7	0
Whitner, Donte, S.F.	2	7	3.5	7	0
Bell, Yeremiah, Ariz	2	6	3.0	6	0
Smith, Harrison, Min.	2	4	2.0	4	0
Barron, Mark, T.B.	2	3	1.5	3	0
Revis, Darrelle, T.B.	2	3	1.5	3	0
McLeod, Rodney, St.L	2	2	1.0	2	0
* Alford, Robert, Atl.	2	0	0.0	0	0
Scandrick, Orlando, Dal.	2	0	0.0	0	0
* Trufant, Desmond, Atl.	2	0	0.0	0	0
Davis, Thomas, Car.	2	-2	-1.0	0	0
* Ogletree, Alec, St.L	1	98	98.0	98t	1
Mundy, Ryan, NY-G	1	91	91.0	91	0
Giordano, Matt, St.L	1	82	82.0	82t	1
Weatherspoon, Sean, Atl.	1	71	71.0	71t	1
Umenyiora, Osi, Atl.	1	68	68.0	68t	1
Thomas, Terrell, NY-G	1	65	65.0	65	0
Browner, Brandon, Sea.	1	49	49.0	49	0
* Greene, Khaseem, Chi.	1	49	49.0	49	0
Johnson, Leonard, T.B.	1	48	48.0	48t	1
Allen, Nate, Phi.	1	43	43.0	43	0
White, Corey, N.O.	1	43	43.0	43	0
Prater, Shaun, Min.	1	30	30.0	30	0
Orakpo, Brian, Was.	1	29	29.0	29t	1
Thurmond, Walter, Sea.	1	29	29.0	29t	1
* Vaccaro, Kenny, N.O.	1	29	29.0	29	0
Doughty, Reed, Was.	1	25	25.0	25	0
* Bass, David, Chi.	1	24	24.0	24t	1
Pierre-Paul, Jason, NY-G	1	24	24.0	24t	1
Brooks, Ahmad, S.F.	1	22	22.0	22	0
Greer, Jabari, N.O.	1	22	22.0	22	0
Moore, Sterling, Dal.	1	21	21.0	21	0
Witherspoon, Will, St.L	1	20	20.0	20	0
Pugh, Jordan, Was.	1	16	16.0	16	0
Biggers, E.J., Was.	1	15	15.0	15	0
Peppers, Julius, Chi.	1	14	14.0	14	0
House, Davon, G.B.	1	11	11.0	11	0
Beason, Jon, NY-G	1	9	9.0	9	0
Powers, Jerraud, Ariz	1	9	9.0	9	0
Ross, Aaron, NY-G	1	9	9.0	9	0
Irvin, Bruce, Sea.	1	8	8.0	8	0
Hawk, A.J., G.B.	1	7	7.0	7	0
Herring, Will, N.O.	1	6	6.0	6	0
Jerod-Eddie, Tony, S.F.	1	6	6.0	6	0
Hayes, William, St.L	1	5	5.0	5	0
Jenkins, Janoris, St.L	1	5	5.0	5	0
Neal, Mike, G.B.	1	5	5.0	5	0
Jackson, Rob, Was.	1	4	4.0	4	0
McDonald, Clinton, Sea.	1	3	3.0	3	0
Gumbs, Jose, Was.	1	2	2.0	2	0
Williams, Dan, Ariz	1	2	2.0	2t	1
Finnegan, Cortland, St.L	1	1	1.0	1	0
Jefferson, A.J., Min.	1	1	1.0	1	0
Samuel, Asante, Atl.	1	1	1.0	1	0
Sendejo, Andrew, Min.	1	1	1.0	1	0
* Bostic, Jon, Chi.	1	0	0.0	0	0
Bush, Jarrett, G.B.	1	0	0.0	0	0
Carr, Chris, N.O.	1	0	0.0	0	0
Church, Barry, Dal.	1	0	0.0	0	0
Claiborne, Morris, Dal.	1	0	0.0	0	0
Goldson, Dashon, T.B.	1	0	0.0	0	0
Harper, Roman, N.O.	1	0	0.0	0	0
* Heath, Jeff, Dal.	1	0	0.0	0	0
Riley, Perry, Was.	1	0	0.0	0	0
Sherels, Marcus, Min.	1	0	0.0	0	0
Thomas, Josh, Car.	1	0	0.0	0	0
Tulloch, Stephen, Det.	1	0	0.0	0	0
Ware, DeMarcus, Dal.	1	0	0.0	0	0
Watson, Dekoda, T.B.	1	0	0.0	0	0
Williams, Kevin, Min.	1	0	0.0	0	0
Wilson, Josh, Was.	1	0	0.0	0	0
* Wolff, Earl, Phi.	1	0	0.0	0	0
Wright, Eric, S.F.	1	0	0.0	0	0
Barwin, Connor, Phi.	1	-2	-2.0	-2	0
* McDonald, T.J., St.L	1	-2	-2.0	-2	0
Tuck, Justin, NY-G	1	-2	-2.0	-2	0
Amukamara, Prince, NY-G	1	-4	-4.0	-4	0

t = Touchdown; Leader based on interceptions
* Player that was a rookie in 2013

AMERICAN FOOTBALL CONFERENCE—INTERCEPTIONS

	No	Yards	Avg	Long	TD
Buffalo	23	289	12.6	57	2
Kansas City	21	488	23.2	100t	5
Cincinnati	20	200	10.0	60t	4
Miami	18	204	11.3	94t	2
Denver	17	141	8.3	75t	1
New England	17	220	12.9	79t	2
Baltimore	16	160	10.0	37t	1
Indianapolis	15	186	12.4	46	1
Cleveland	14	274	19.6	44t	3
N.Y. Jets	13	167	12.8	38	1
Tennessee	13	113	8.7	34	1
Jacksonville	11	172	15.6	59t	1
San Diego	11	143	13.0	41	1
Pittsburgh	10	203	20.3	40t	3
Oakland	9	83	9.2	43t	1
Houston	7	86	12.3	32	1
AFC Total	235	3129	13.3	100t	30
AFC Average	14.7	195.6	13.3	—	1.9

NATIONAL FOOTBALL CONFERENCE—INTERCEPTIONS

	No	Yards	Avg	Long	TD
Seattle	28	385	13.8	58t	3
Tampa Bay	21	338	16.1	85t	3
Arizona	20	251	12.6	43	4
Carolina	20	234	11.7	45t	4
Chicago	19	428	22.5	49	5
Philadelphia	19	294	15.5	76	1
San Francisco	18	278	15.4	89t	2
N.Y. Giants	17	270	15.9	91	2
Washington	16	247	15.4	45t	4
Dallas	15	257	17.1	74	2
Detroit	15	211	14.1	66t	1
St. Louis	14	256	18.3	98t	2
Minnesota	12	78	6.5	30	0
New Orleans	12	169	14.1	43	0
Green Bay	11	36	3.3	11	0
Atlanta	10	176	17.6	71t	2
NFC Total	267	3908	14.6	98t	35
NFC Average	16.7	244.3	14.6	—	2.2
League Total	502	7037	—	100t	65
League Average	15.7	219.9	14.0	—	2.0

KICKOFF RETURNS

YARDS PER RETURN
NFC: 32.4* Cordarrelle Patterson, Minnesota
AFC: 30.1 Quintin Demps, Kansas City

YARDS
NFC: 1436 Devin Hester, Chicago
AFC: 992 Quintin Demps, Kansas City

YARDS, GAME
NFC: 249 Devin Hester, Chicago vs. Minnesota,
September 15 (5 returns, 0 TD)
AFC: 209 Leon Washington, Tennessee at Denver,
December 8 (5 returns, 0 TD)

LONGEST
NFC: 109 * Cordarrelle Patterson, Minnesota vs. Green
Bay, October 27 - TD
AFC: 108 * Knile Davis, Kansas City vs. Denver,
December 1 - TD

RETURNS
NFC: 52 Devin Hester, Chicago
AFC: 39 Marcus Thigpen, Miami

RETURNS, GAME
AFC: 8 Quintin Demps, Kansas City vs. San Diego,
November 24 (199 yards, 0 TD)
NFC: 8 Niles Paul, Washington vs. Kansas City,
December 8 (179 yards, 0 TD)

TOUCHDOWNS
NFC: 2 * Cordarrelle Patterson, Minnesota
AFC: 1 * Knile Davis, Kansas City
1 Quintin Demps, Kansas City
1 Trindon Holliday, Denver
1 Jacoby Jones, Baltimore

TEAM CHAMPION
AFC: 29.9 Kansas City
NFC: 25.5 Dallas

NFL TOP TEN KICKOFF RETURNERS

	No	Yards	Avg	Long	TD
* Cordarrelle Patterson, Min	43	1393	32.4	109t	2
Dwayne Harris, Dal.	28	857	30.6	90	0
Quintin Demps, K.C.	33	992	30.1	95t	1
Jacoby Jones, Bal	31	892	28.8	77t	1
Trindon Holliday, Den.	28	775	27.7	105t	1
Devin Hester, Chi	52	1436	27.6	80	0
Jordan Todman, Jac.	26	712	27.4	59	0
Keshawn Martin, Hou	36	947	26.3	50	0
Brandon Tate, Cin.	35	914	26.1	71	0
Eric Page, T.B.	f22	548	24.9	44	0

AFC—INDIVIDUAL KICKOFF RETURNERS

	No	Yards	Avg	Long	TD
Demps, Quintin, K.C.	33	992	30.1	95t	1
Jones, Jacoby, Bal.	31	892	28.8	77t	1
Holliday, Trindon, Den.	28	775	27.7	105t	1
Todman, Jordan, Jac.	26	712	27.4	59	0
Martin, Keshawn, Hou.	36	947	26.3	50	0
Tate, Brandon, Cin.	35	914	26.1	71	0
Reed, David, Ind.	24	590	24.6	39	0
Cribbs, Josh, NYJ	20	490	24.5	42	0
Jones, Taiwan, Oak.	26	623	24.0	41	0
Thigpen, Marcus, Mia.	39	870	22.3	50	0
Jones, Felix, Pit.	23	510	22.2	42	0
Whittaker, Fozzy, S.D.-Cle.	29	638	22.0	56	0
(Nonqualifiers)					
Reynaud, Darius, Ten.-NYJ	18	430	23.9	40	0
Washington, Leon, N.E.-Ten.	17	500	29.4	95	0
Blount, LeGarrette, N.E.	17	494	29.1	83	0
* Goodwin, Marquise, Buf.	16	351	21.9	28	0
Woodhead, Danny, S.D.	12	262	21.8	37	0
Ford, Jacoby, Oak.	11	253	23.0	30	0
* Davis, Knile, K.C.	10	321	32.1	108t	1
Sanders, Emmanuel, Pit.	10	268	26.8	46	0
* Jenkins, Greg, Oak.	10	221	22.1	29	0
* Boyce, Josh, N.E.	9	214	23.8	41	0
Gates, Clyde, NYJ	9	209	23.2	36	0
Hawkins, Lavelle, S.D.	8	176	22.0	27	0
Thompson, Deonte, Bal.	7	201	28.7	47	0
Little, Greg, Cle.	7	151	21.6	30	0
Williams, Kyle, S.F.	7	134	19.1	35	0
McCourty, Devin, N.E.	7	132	18.9	27	0
Cromartie, Antonio, NYJ	6	164	27.3	41	0
* Johnson, Dennis, Hou.	6	151	25.2	32	0
Caldwell, Andre, Den.	6	141	23.5	34	0
Rainey, Chris, Ind.	6	131	21.8	27	0
Brown, Ronnie, S.D.	6	113	18.8	28	0
Vaughn, Cassius, Ind.	5	142	28.4	33	0
Williams, Damian, Ten.	5	123	24.6	37	0
Karim, Deji, Hou.	5	104	20.8	31	0
Stewart, Jeremy, Oak.	5	95	19.0	28	0
Burton, Stephen, Jac.	4	99	24.8	32	0
Dwyer, Jonathan, Pit.	4	90	22.5	27	0
* Robinson, Denard, Jac.	4	88	22.0	27	0
Easley, Marcus, Buf.	4	83	20.8	28	0
Peerman, Cedric, Cin.	f4	66	16.5	26	0
Benjamin, Travis, Cle.	3	146	48.7	86	0
* Sanders, Ace, Jac.	3	75	25.0	31	0
Vereen, Shane, N.E.	3	66	22.0	24	0
Brazill, LaVon, Ind.	3	57	19.0	21	0
Taylor, Kerry, Jac.	2	60	30.0	43	0
Draughn, Shaun, Bal.	2	53	26.5	31	0
Bolden, Omar, Den.	2	44	22.0	25	0
* Wheaton, Markus, Pit.	2	37	18.5	25	0
Clay, Charles, Mia.	2	23	11.5	15	0
Douzable, Leger, NYJ	2	20	10.0	10	0
* Juszczyk, Kyle, Bal.	2	17	8.5	9	0
Slater, Matthew, N.E.	2	10	5.0	10	0
Choice, Tashard, Ind.	1	28	28.0	28	0
* Williams, Kerwynn, Ind.	1	28	28.0	28	0
Battle, Jackie, Ten.	1	26	26.0	26	0
Stephens-Howling, LaRod, Pit.	1	25	25.0	25	0
Green, Alex, NYJ	1	22	22.0	22	0
Whalen, Griff, Ind.	1	22	22.0	22	0
Forsett, Justin, Jac.	1	21	21.0	21	0
* Wood, Cierre, Hou.	1	20	20.0	20	0
Graham, T.J., Buf.	1	19	19.0	19	0
Kerley, Jeremy, NYJ	1	19	19.0	19	0
Manning, Danieal, Hou.	1	18	18.0	18	0
Jones, Greg, Hou.	1	17	17.0	17	0
Verner, Alterraun, Ten.	1	17	17.0	17	0
Brown, Antonio, Pit.	1	16	16.0	16	0
* Bohanon, Tommy, NYJ	1	15	15.0	15	0
Herron, Dan, Ind.	1	13	13.0	13	0
Heyward, Cameron, Pit.	1	11	11.0	11	0
* Woods, Robert, Buf.	1	9	9.0	9	0
Unrein, Mitch, Den.	1	8	8.0	8	0
* Davis, Troy, NYJ	1	7	7.0	7	0
Ross, Jay, Buf.	1	7	7.0	7	0
Jackson, Malik, Den.	1	6	6.0	6	0
Olawale, Jamize, Oak.	1	6	6.0	6	0
* McFadden, Leon, Cle.	1	5	5.0	5	0
Palmer, Michael, Pit.	1	5	5.0	5	0
Ta'ufo'ou, Will, Jac.	1	5	5.0	5	0
McCluster, Dexter, K.C.	1	3	3.0	3	0
* Rivera, Mychal, Oak.	1	3	3.0	3	0
* Adongo, Daniel, Ind.	1	0	0.0	0	0
Bailey, Patrick, Ten.	1	0	0.0	0	0
Bellore, Nick, NYJ	1	0	0.0	0	0
Crick, Jared, Hou.	1	0	0.0	0	0
Dickson, Ed, Bal.	1	0	0.0	0	0
Leach, Vonta, Bal.	1	0	0.0	0	0
Spitler, Austin, Mia.	1	0	0.0	0	0
Tamme, Jacob, Den.	1	0	0.0	0	0
Williams, Tourek, S.D.	f0	0	—	0	0

t = Touchdown; f = Fair Catch
Leader based on average return, minimum 20 returns
* Player that was a rookie in 2013

NFC—INDIVIDUAL KICKOFF RETURNERS

	No	Yards	Avg	Long	TD
* Patterson, Cordarrelle, Min.	43	1393	32.4	109t	2
Harris, Dwayne, Dal.	28	857	30.6	90	0
Hester, Devin, Chi.	52	1436	27.6	80	0
Page, Eric, T.B.	f22	548	24.9	44	0
Ross, Jeremy, G.B.-Det.	21	514	24.5	98t	1
* Hyde, Micah, G.B.	22	531	24.1	70	0
Ginn, Ted, Car.	25	595	23.8	38	0
Rodgers, Jacquizz, Atl.	25	575	23.0	34	0
* Cox, Michael, NY-G	20	436	21.8	56	0
Arenas, Javier, Ariz	23	493	21.4	46	0
Paul, Niles, Was.	20	411	20.6	39	0
(Nonqualifiers)					
* Austin, Tavon, St.L	18	398	22.1	32	0
Spurlock, Micheal, Det.-Dal.-Det.	18	389	21.6	36	0
Johnson, Damaris, Phi.	17	441	25.9	33	0
* Cunningham, Benny, St.L	13	299	23.0	32	0
Kearse, Jermaine, Sea.	13	283	21.8	40	0
James, LaMichael, S.F.	12	321	26.8	41	0
Sproles, Darren, N.O.	12	255	21.3	32	0
Morgan, Josh, Was.	12	239	19.9	25	0
Jernigan, Jerrel, NY-G	11	246	22.4	46	0
Cadet, Travaris, N.O.	9	239	26.6	82	0
Wilson, David, NY-G	9	222	24.7	31	0
Boykin, Brandon, Phi.	9	205	22.8	41	0
* Williams, Nick, Was.	9	188	20.9	29	0
Turbin, Robert, Sea.	8	177	22.1	27	0
* Thompson, Chris, Was.	8	160	20.0	28	0
Rainey, Bobby, Cle.-T.B.	7	162	23.1	33	0
Gerhart, Toby, Min.	7	106	15.1	20	0
* Williams, Terrance, Dal.	6	142	23.7	32	0
Pead, Isaiah, St.L	5	138	27.6	31	0
Dixon, Anthony, S.F.	5	101	20.2	47	0
Wylie, Devon, Ten.	5	94	18.8	23	0
Anderson, Joe, Chi.	5	82	16.4	21	0
Weems, Eric, Chi.	5	57	11.4	19	0
* Ford, Michael, Chi.	5	37	7.4	11	0
Smith, Brad, Phi.	4	106	26.5	47	0
Demps, Jeff, T.B.	4	93	23.3	29	0
* Franklin, Johnathan, G.B.	4	82	20.5	26	0
Hunter, Kendall, S.F.	4	81	20.3	30	0

	No	Yards	Avg	Long	TD
Cox, Perrish, S.F.	3	82	27.3	30	0
* Dawson, Skye, T.B.	3	67	22.3	25	0
Tate, Golden, Sea.	3	57	19.0	24	0
Baldwin, Doug, Sea.	2	57	28.5	37	0
Lane, Jeremy, Sea.	2	47	23.5	25	0
Kuhn, John, G.B.	2	40	20.0	21	0
Bosworth, Kyle, Dal.	2	29	14.5	16	0
Asiata, Matt, Min.	2	28	14.0	20	0
Felton, Jerome, Min.	2	22	11.0	13	0
* Barner, Kenjon, Car.	2	17	8.5	17	0
Ford, Chase, Min.	2	17	8.5	15	0
Graham, Brandon, Phi.	2	14	7.0	14	0
Carlson, John, Min.	2	13	6.5	12	0
Rosario, Dante, Chi.	2	10	5.0	6	0
* Floyd, Sharrif, Min.	2	9	4.5	9	0
* Mathieu, Tyrann, Ariz	2	8	4.0	13	0
Harvin, Percy, Sea.	1	58	58.0	58	0
Martin, Doug, T.B.	1	40	40.0	40	0
Dunbar, Lance, Dal.	1	28	28.0	28	0
Ogletree, Kevin, T.B.	1	25	25.0	25	0
Snelling, Jason, Atl.	1	23	23.0	23	0
Bell, Kahlil, G.B.	1	22	22.0	22	0
DiMarco, Patrick, Atl.	1	21	21.0	21	0
* Ellington, Andre, Ariz	1	21	21.0	21	0
Jefferson, A.J., Min.	1	21	21.0	21	0
* Hill, Michael, G.B.	1	19	19.0	19	0
Dickerson, Dorin, Det.	1	18	18.0	18	0
Peterson, Patrick, Ariz	1	18	18.0	18	0
Larsen, Spencer, T.B.	1	17	17.0	17	0
Moss, Santana, Was.	1	15	15.0	15	0
* Willson, Luke, Sea.	1	15	15.0	15	0
Kuhn, Markus, NY-G	1	13	13.0	13	0
* Banjo, Chris, G.B.	1	12	12.0	12	0
Clutts, Tyler, Dal.	1	12	12.0	12	0
* Moore, Damontre, NY-G	1	12	12.0	12	0
* Riddick, Theo, Det.	1	12	12.0	12	0
Thomas, Pierre, N.O.	1	12	12.0	12	0
Beasley, Cole, Dal.	1	11	11.0	11	0
Casey, James, Phi.	1	10	10.0	10	0
Cobb, Randall, G.B.	1	10	10.0	10	0
Jackson, DeSean, Phi.	1	10	10.0	10	0
Smith, Andre, Dal.	1	10	10.0	10	0
Webb, Joe, Min.	1	9	9.0	9	0
Wright, Jarius, Min.	1	9	9.0	9	0
Polk, Chris, Phi.	1	8	8.0	8	0
Ellison, Rhett, Min.	1	7	7.0	7	0
* Patton, Quinton, S.F.	1	7	7.0	7	0
* Randle, Joseph, Dal.	1	7	7.0	7	0
Banyard, Joe, Min.	1	6	6.0	6	0
Lorig, Erik, T.B.	1	6	6.0	6	0
Mitchell, Marvin, Min.	1	6	6.0	6	0
Gandy, Dylan, Det.	1	5	5.0	5	0
Gettis, Adam, Was.	1	5	5.0	5	0
Bell, Joique, Det.	1	4	4.0	4	0
Robinson, Michael, Sea.	1	4	4.0	4	0
Rolle, Antrel, NY-G	1	4	4.0	4	0
Barnes, Tim, St.L	1	0	0.0	0	0
Blackburn, Chase, Car.	1	0	0.0	0	0
Coleman, Derrick, Sea.	1	0	0.0	0	0
Davis, Kellen, Sea.	1	0	0.0	0	0
* Ertz, Zach, Phi.	1	0	0.0	0	0
* Escobar, Gavin, Dal.	1	0	0.0	0	0
Mosley, Brandon, NY-G	1	0	0.0	0	0
* Stoneburner, Jake, G.B.	1	0	0.0	0	0
Cooper, Riley, Phi.	1	-4	-4.0	-4	0
Marshall, Brandon, Chi.	1	-8	-8.0	-8	0
Smith, Antone, Atl.	0	40	—	40	0
Brown, Everette, Dal.	f0	0		0	0

t = Touchdown; f = Fair Catch
Leader based on average return, minimum 20 returns
* Player that was a rookie in 2013

AMERICAN FOOTBALL CONFERENCE—KICKOFF RETURNS

	No	Yards	Avg	Long	TD
Kansas City	44	1316	29.9	108t	2
Baltimore	44	1163	26.4	77t	1
Jacksonville	41	1060	25.9	59	0
Cincinnati	39	980	25.1	71	0
Denver	39	974	25.0	105t	1
Tennessee	44	1096	24.9	95	0
Houston	51	1257	24.6	50	0
New England	39	935	24.0	83	0
Indianapolis	43	1011	23.5	39	0
Cleveland	40	931	23.3	86	0
N.Y. Jets	45	1021	22.7	42	0
Pittsburgh	43	962	22.4	46	0
Oakland	54	1201	22.2	41	0
San Diego	32	707	22.1	42	0
Miami	42	893	21.3	50	0
Buffalo	23	469	20.4	28	0
AFC Total	663	15976	24.1	108t	4
AFC Average	41.4	998.5	24.1	—	0.3

NATIONAL FOOTBALL CONFERENCE—KICKOFF RETURNS

	No	Yards	Avg	Long	TD
Dallas	45	1147	25.5	90	0
Minnesota	66	1646	24.9	109t	2
Atlanta	27	659	24.4	50	0
Detroit	34	816	24.0	98t	1
Tampa Bay	34	811	23.9	44	0
Chicago	70	1614	23.1	80	0
New Orleans	22	506	23.0	82	0
San Francisco	32	726	22.7	47	0
St. Louis	37	835	22.6	32	0
Carolina	28	612	21.9	38	0
Philadelphia	37	790	21.4	47	0
N.Y. Giants	44	933	21.2	56	0
Seattle	33	698	21.2	58	0
Green Bay	39	791	20.3	70	0
Arizona	27	540	20.0	46	0
Washington	51	1018	20.0	39	0
NFC Total	626	14142	22.6	109t	3
NFC Average	39.1	883.9	22.6	—	0.2
League Total	1289	30118	—	109t	7
League Average	40.3	941.2	23.4	—	0.2

2013 INDIVIDUAL STATISTICS—PUNTING

AVERAGE YARDS PER PUNT
AFC: 48.9 Marquette King, Oakland
NFC: 48.2 Andy Lee, San Francisco

NET AVERAGE YARDS PER PUNT
NFC: 44.2 Johnny Hekker, St. Louis
AFC: 42.4 Brandon Fields, Miami

LONGEST
AFC: 84   Robert Malone, N.Y. Jets vs. Tampa Bay,
           September 8
NFC: 72 * Sam Martin, Detroit at Washington,
           September 22
      72   Brad Nortman, Carolina at Miami,
           November 24

PUNTS
AFC: 95 Bryan Anger, Jacksonville
NFC: 91 Steve Weatherford, New York Giants

PUNTS, GAME
AFC: 11 Bryan Anger, Jacksonville vs. Kansas City,
          September 8 (556 yards)
      11 * Ryan Allen, New England vs. N.Y. Jets,
          September 12 (514 yards)
      11 Marquette King, Oakland at Houston,
          November 17 (540 yards)
NFC: 11 Johnny Hekker, St. Louis vs. San Francisco,
          September 26 (490 yards)

TEAM CHAMPION
AFC: 48.8 Miami
NFC: 48.2 San Francisco

AMERICAN FOOTBALL CONFERENCE—PUNTING

	Total Punts	Yards	Long	Avg	TB	Blk	Opp Ret	Return Yards	In 20	Net Avg
Miami	85	4150	74	48.8	7	0	42	407	33	42.4
Oakland	86	4107	66	47.8	11	2	42	438	23	40.1
Houston	88	4189	65	47.6	7	0	43	530	34	40.0
New England	77	3523	65	45.8	12	0	29	221	29	39.8
Jacksonville	95	4338	61	45.7	8	0	47	330	31	40.5
Baltimore	91	4138	69	45.5	9	1	46	419	27	38.9
Indianapolis	77	3499	65	45.4	7	1	29	396	27	38.5
Kansas City	89	4034	65	45.3	12	1	38	246	35	39.9
N.Y. Jets	89	4018	84	45.1	5	1	43	488	24	38.5
Cincinnati	75	3330	75	44.4	4	0	27	254	27	39.9
Denver	66	2893	60	43.8	3	1	28	274	23	38.8
Cleveland	86	3713	59	43.2	6	1	38	357	28	37.6
San Diego	56	2417	61	43.2	1	0	19	158	30	40.0
Buffalo	96	4124	66	43.0	9	0	45	477	26	36.1
Tennessee	79	3386	63	42.9	2	1	35	210	32	39.7
Pittsburgh	76	3125	70	41.1	5	1	35	313	17	35.7
AFC Total	1311	58984	84	—	108	10	586	5518	446	—
AFC Average	81.9	3686.5	—	45.0	6.8	0.6	36.6	344.9	27.9	39.1

NATIONAL FOOTBALL CONFERENCE—PUNTING

	Total Punts	Yards	Long	Avg	TB	Blk	Opp Ret	Return Yards	In 20	Net Avg
San Francisco	79	3804	62	48.2	9	0	38	330	27	41.7
Carolina	70	3344	72	47.8	5	0	36	335	25	41.6
N.Y. Giants	91	4271	68	46.9	7	0	48	655	25	38.2
New Orleans	61	2859	61	46.9	5	0	24	180	25	42.3
Detroit	73	3399	72	46.6	10	1	32	250	22	40.4
St. Louis	78	3609	64	46.3	4	0	30	79	19	44.2
Arizona	78	3566	60	45.7	6	0	36	321	35	40.1
Atlanta	70	3166	63	45.2	2	2	33	251	26	41.1
Dallas	77	3467	62	45.0	6	0	37	339	30	39.1
Green Bay	64	2854	62	44.6	5	0	20	261	22	39.0
Philadelphia	83	3681	70	44.3	5	1	28	223	33	40.5
Minnesota	75	3316	65	44.2	3	0	36	318	23	39.2
Tampa Bay	87	3846	62	44.2	6	0	35	393	19	38.3
Seattle	76	3159	69	41.6	5	2	21	82	28	39.2
Washington	85	3526	63	41.5	0	1	39	655	26	33.8
Chicago	69	2763	65	40.0	2	1	15	111	27	37.9
NFC Total	1216	54630	72	—	80	8	508	4783	412	—
NFC Average	76.0	3414.4	--	44.9	5.0	0.5	31.8	298.9	25.8	39.7
League Total	2527	113614	84	—	188	18	1094	10301	858	—
League Average	79.0	3550.4	—	45.0	5.9	0.6	34.2	321.9	26.8	39.4

NFL TOP TEN PUNTERS

	No	Yards	Long	Avg	Total Punts	TB	Blk	Opp Ret	Return Yards	In 20	Net Avg
Marquette King, Oak.	84	4107	66	48.9	86	11	2	42	438	23	40.1
Brandon Fields, Mia.	85	4150	74	48.8	85	7	0	42	407	33	42.4
Andy Lee, S.F.	79	3804	62	48.2	79	9	0	38	330	27	41.7
Brad Nortman, Car	70	3344	72	47.8	70	5	0	36	335	25	41.6
Shane Lechler, Hou	88	4189	65	47.6	88	7	0	43	530	34	40.0
* Sam Martin, Det.	72	3399	72	47.2	73	10	1	32	250	22	40.4
Steve Weatherford, NY-G.	91	4271	68	46.9	91	7	0	48	655	25	38.2
Thomas Morstead, N.O.	61	2859	61	46.9	61	5	0	24	180	25	42.3
Matt Bosher, Atl.	68	3166	63	46.6	70	2	2	33	251	26	41.1
Johnny Hekker, St. L.	78	3609	64	46.3	78	4	0	30	79	19	44.2

AFC—INDIVIDUAL PUNTERS

	No	Yards	Long	Avg	Total Punts	TB	Blk	Opp Ret	Return Yards	In 20	Net Avg
King, Marquette, Oak.	84	4107	66	48.9	86	11	2	42	438	23	40.1
Fields, Brandon, Mia.	85	4150	74	48.8	85	7	0	42	407	33	42.4
Lechler, Shane, Hou.	88	4189	65	47.6	88	7	0	43	530	34	40.0
McAfee, Pat, Ind.	76	3499	65	46.0	77	7	1	29	396	27	38.5
Colquitt, Dustin, K.C.	87	4005	65	46.0	88	11	1	38	246	35	40.2
Koch, Sam, Bal.	90	4138	69	46.0	91	9	1	46	419	27	38.9
* Allen, Ryan, N.E.	76	3491	65	45.9	76	12	0	29	221	29	39.9
Anger, Bryan, Jac.	95	4338	61	45.7	95	8	0	47	330	31	40.5
Quigley, Ryan, NYJ	72	3278	67	45.5	73	3	1	34	381	21	38.9
Huber, Kevin, Cin.	66	2982	75	45.2	66	4	0	25	229	24	40.5
Powell, Shawn, Buf.-Cin.	42	1881	66	44.8	42	5	0	21	305	13	35.1
Colquitt, Britton, Den.	65	2893	60	44.5	66	3	1	28	274	23	38.8
Lanning, Spencer, Cle.	84	3679	59	43.8	85	5	1	38	357	28	37.9
Kern, Brett, Ten.	78	3386	63	43.4	79	2	1	35	210	32	39.7
Scifres, Mike, S.D.	56	2417	61	43.2	56	1	0	19	158	30	40.0
McBriar, Matt, Pit.	40	1652	70	41.3	41	3	1	18	157	13	35.0
Moorman, Brian, Buf.	61	2511	62	41.2	61	4	0	26	197	16	36.6
(Nonqualifiers)											
Mesko, Zoltan, Pit.	34	1445	65	42.5	34	2	0	17	156	3	36.7
Malone, Robert, NYJ	16	740	84	46.3	16	2	0	9	107	3	37.1
Nugent, Mike, Cin.	2	80	43	40.0	2	0	0	0	0	0	40.0
Cundiff, Billy, Cle.	1	34	34	34.0	1	1	0	0	0	0	14.0
Brady, Tom, N.E.	1	32	32	32.0	1	0	0	0	0	0	32.0
Succop, Ryan, K.C.	1	29	29	29.0	1	1	0	0	0	0	9.0
Roethlisberger, Ben, Pit.	1	28	28	28.0	1	0	0	0	0	1	28.0

Leader based on average, minimum 40 punts

NFC—INDIVIDUAL PUNTERS

	No	Yards	Long	Avg	Total Punts	TB	Blk	Opp Ret	Return Yards	In 20	Net Avg
Lee, Andy, S.F.	79	3804	62	48.2	79	9	0	38	330	27	41.7
Nortman, Brad, Car.	70	3344	72	47.8	70	5	0	36	335	25	41.6
* Martin, Sam, Det.	72	3399	72	47.2	73	10	1	32	250	22	40.4
Weatherford, Steve, NY-G	91	4271	68	46.9	91	7	0	48	655	25	38.2
Morstead, Thomas, N.O.	61	2859	61	46.9	61	5	0	24	180	25	42.3
Bosher, Matt, Atl.	68	3166	63	46.6	70	2	2	33	251	26	41.1
Hekker, Johnny, St.L	78	3609	64	46.3	78	4	0	30	79	19	44.2
Zastudil, Dave, Ariz	78	3566	60	45.7	78	6	0	36	321	35	40.1
Jones, Chris, Dal.	77	3467	62	45.0	77	6	0	37	339	30	39.1
Jones, Donnie, Phi.	82	3681	70	44.9	83	5	1	28	223	33	40.5
Masthay, Tim, G.B.	64	2854	62	44.6	64	5	0	20	261	22	39.0
* Locke, Jeff, Min.	75	3316	65	44.2	75	3	0	36	318	23	39.2
Koenen, Michael, T.B.	87	3846	62	44.2	87	6	0	35	393	19	38.3
Ryan, Jon, Sea.	74	3159	69	42.7	76	5	2	21	82	28	39.2
Rocca, Sav, Was.	84	3526	63	42.0	85	0	1	39	655	26	33.8
Podlesh, Adam, Chi.	68	2763	65	40.6	69	2	1	15	111	27	37.9

Leader based on average, minimum 40 punts
* Player that was a rookie in 2013

PUNT RETURNS

YARDS PER RETURN
AFC: 15.6 Tandon Doss, Baltimore
NFC: 15.2 Marcus Sherels, Minnesota

YARDS
AFC: 686 Dexter McCluster, Kansas City
NFC: 585 Golden Tate, Seattle

YARDS, GAME
AFC: 179 Travis Benjamin, Cleveland vs. Buffalo, October 3 (7 returns, 1 TD)
NFC: 145 * Tavon Austin, St. Louis at Indianapolis, November 10 (4 returns, 1 TD)

LONGEST
NFC: 98 * Tavon Austin, St. Louis at Indianapolis, November 10 - TD
AFC: 89 Dexter McCluster, Kansas City vs. N.Y. Giants, September 29 - TD

RETURNS
AFC: 58 Dexter McCluster, Kansas City
NFC: 51 Golden Tate, Seattle

RETURNS, GAME
AFC: 7 Dexter McCluster, Kansas City at Jacksonville, September 8 (80 yards, 0 TD)
7 Travis Benjamin, Cleveland vs. Buffalo, October 3 (179 yards, 1 TD)
7 Keshawn Martin, Houston vs. Oakland, November 17 (125 yards, 1 TD)
7 Marcus Thigpen, Miami vs. Carolina, November 24 (71 yards, 0 TD)
7 Dexter McCluster, Kansas City at Washington, December 8 (177 yards, 1 TD)
NFC: 7 Golden Tate, Seattle at N.Y. Giants, December 15 (73 yards, 0 TD)

FAIR CATCHES
NFC: 27 Marcus Sherels, Minnesota
AFC: 23 Antonio Brown, Pittsburgh
23 Julian Edelman, New England

TOUCHDOWNS
AFC: 2 Dexter McCluster, Kansas City
NFC: 1 * Tavon Austin, St. Louis
1 Dwayne Harris, Dallas
1 Devin Hester, Chicago
1 * Micah Hyde, Green Bay
1 Jeremy Ross, Green Bay-Detroit
1 Marcus Sherels, Minnesota

TEAM CHAMPION
AFC: 15.2 Minnesota
NFC: 14.2 Baltimore

NFL TOP TEN PUNT RETURNERS

	No	FC	Yards	Avg	Long	TD
Tandon Doss, Bal.	23	7	359	15.6	82t	1
Marcus Sherels, Min	22	27	335	15.2	86t	1
Antonio Brown, Pit	32	23	409	12.8	67t	1
Dwayne Harris, Dal.	20	10	256	12.8	86t	1
* Micah Hyde, G.B.	24	14	296	12.3	93t	1
Ted Ginn, Car	26	26	316	12.2	41	0
Dexter McCluster, K.C.	58	11	686	11.8	89t	2
Travis Benjamin, Cle	22	7	257	11.7	79t	1
Golden Tate, Sea	51	14	585	11.5	71	0
LaMichael James, S.F.	23	12	251	10.9	40	0
Eric Page, T.B.	23	20	251	10.9	52	0

AFC—INDIVIDUAL PUNT RETURNERS

	No	FC	Yards	Avg	Long	TD
Doss, Tandon, Bal.	23	7	359	15.6	82t	1
Brown, Antonio, Pit.	32	23	409	12.8	67t	1
McCluster, Dexter, K.C.	58	11	686	11.8	89t	2
Benjamin, Travis, Cle.	22	7	257	11.7	79t	1
Edelman, Julian, N.E.	35	23	374	10.7	43	0
Tate, Brandon, Cin.	36	16	336	9.3	43	0
Martin, Keshawn, Hou.	39	21	345	8.8	87t	1
Holliday, Trindon, Den.	32	11	271	8.5	81t	1
Thigpen, Marcus, Mia.	34	20	264	7.8	34	0
McKelvin, Leodis, Buf.	32	13	180	5.6	21	0
* Sanders, Ace, Jac.	25	16	140	5.6	17	0
(Nonqualifiers)						
Jones, Jacoby, Bal.	19	2	237	12.5	37	0
Reynaud, Darius, Ten.	18	10	135	7.5	35	0
Hilton, T.Y., Ind.	17	12	159	9.4	34	0
* Allen, Keenan, S.D.	15	13	125	8.3	28	0
Kerley, Jeremy, NYJ	13	5	115	8.8	24	0
Jones, Adam, Cin.	11	0	88	8.0	27	0
Welker, Wes, Den.	10	2	70	7.0	27	0
Ford, Jacoby, Oak.	9	8	77	8.6	14	0
* Poyer, Jordan, Cle.	8	7	114	14.3	38	0
Whalen, Griff, Ind.	8	7	104	13.0	51	0
Cribbs, Josh, NYJ	8	1	96	12.0	21	0
Adams, Phillip, Oak.	8	8	59	7.4	30	0
Leonhard, Jim, Buf.	7	9	63	9.0	25	0
Royal, Eddie, S.D.	7	7	41	5.9	12	0
Washington, Leon, Ten.	6	9	78	13.0	33	0
* Jenkins, Greg, Oak.	6	3	49	8.2	14	0
Blackmon, Will, Jac.	5	5	2	0.4	5	0
Rainey, Chris, Ind.	4	4	29	7.3	18	0
Edwards, Armanti, Cle.	4	0	28	7.0	12	0
Bess, Davone, Cle.	4	14	19	4.8	11	0
Wilson, Kyle, NYJ	4	4	13	3.3	6	0
Williams, Damian, Ten.	4	3	12	3.0	8	0
Brazill, LaVon, Ind.	3	2	25	8.3	17	0
Keo, Shiloh, Hou.	3	0	15	5.0	9	0
Wylie, Devon, Ten.	2	0	4	2.0	4	0
Amendola, Danny, N.E.	1	0	13	13.0	13	0
Webb, Lardarius, Bal.	1	7	13	13.0	13	0
Verner, Alterraun, Ten.	1	0	11	11.0	11	0
Butler, Darius, Ind.	1	0	9	9.0	9	0
Hall, Chad, K.C.	1	0	9	9.0	9	0
Decker, Eric, Den.	1	2	2	2.0	2	0
Carter, Tony, Den.	1	0	0	0.0	0	0
Young, Usama, Oak.	1	0	0	0.0	0	0
Crawford, Jack, Oak.	1	0	-1	-1.0	-1	0
* Hayden, D.J., Oak.	0	0	22	—	22	0

t = Touchdown
Leader based on average return, minimum 20 returns
* Player that was a rookie in 2013

NFC—INDIVIDUAL PUNT RETURNERS

	No	FC	Yards	Avg	Long	TD
Sherels, Marcus, Min.	22	27	335	15.2	86t	1
Harris, Dwayne, Dal.	20	10	256	12.8	86t	1
* Hyde, Micah, G.B.	24	14	296	12.3	93t	1
Ginn, Ted, Car.	26	26	316	12.2	41	0
Tate, Golden, Sea.	51	14	585	11.5	71	0
James, LaMichael, S.F.	23	12	251	10.9	40	0
Page, Eric, T.B.	23	20	251	10.9	52	0
Spurlock, Micheal, Det.-Dal.-Det.	23	12	207	9.0	62	0
* Austin, Tavon, St.L	33	11	280	8.5	98t	1
Randle, Rueben, NY-G	29	24	237	8.2	32	0
Sproles, Darren, N.O.	29	21	194	6.7	28	0
Peterson, Patrick, Ariz	33	22	198	6.0	22	0
(Nonqualifiers)						
McClain, Robert, Atl.	19	9	193	10.2	25	0
Hester, Devin, Chi.	18	11	256	14.2	81t	1
Moss, Santana, Was.	18	8	130	7.2	18	0
Ross, Jeremy, G.B.-Det.	17	17	263	15.5	58t	1
Jackson, DeSean, Phi.	14	8	71	5.1	32	0
Johnson, Damaris, Phi.	12	12	100	8.3	21	0
Williams, Kyle, S.F.	12	20	61	5.1	22	0
Beasley, Cole, Dal.	10	3	68	6.8	14	0
Douglas, Harry, Atl.	10	3	57	5.7	15	0
Morgan, Josh, Was.	8	1	59	7.4	34	0
* Veltung, Justin, St.L	7	0	61	8.7	15	0
* Thompson, Chris, Was.	7	1	36	5.1	11	0
Cobb, Randall, G.B.	3	5	23	7.7	16	0
Hosley, Jayron, NY-G	3	1	9	3.0	8	0
Pettis, Austin, St.L	2	0	37	18.5	32	0
Moore, Lance, N.O.	2	3	0	0.0	0	0
* Dawson, Skye, T.B.	1	0	17	17.0	17	0
Broyles, Ryan, Det.	1	2	4	4.0	4	0
* Alford, Robert, Atl.	1	1	0	0.0	0	0
Arenas, Javier, Ariz	1	0	0	0.0	0	0
Brockel, Richie, Car.	1	0	0	0.0	0	0
Cadet, Travaris, N.O.	1	1	0	0.0	0	0
Florence, Drayton, Car.	1	0	0	0.0	0	0
* James, Charles, NY-G	1	0	0	0.0	0	0
Kuhn, John, G.B.	1	0	0	0.0	0	0
LaFell, Brandon, Car.	1	0	0	0.0	0	0
McBride, Trumaine, NY-G	1	0	0	0.0	0	0
Murphy, Jerome, Was.	1	0	0	0.0	0	0
Reynolds, Chase, St.L	1	0	0	0.0	0	0
Thomas, Josh, Car.	1	0	0	0.0	0	0
* Williams, Nick, Was.	1	1	0	0.0	0	0
Sherman, Richard, Sea.	1	0	-6	-6.0	-6	0
Jernigan, Jerrel, NY-G	0	1	0	—	—	0
* Mathieu, Tyrann, Ariz	0	1	0	—	—	0
* Patterson, Cordarrelle, Min.	0	1	0	—	—	0
Weems, Eric, Chi.	0	1	0	—	—	0

t = Touchdown
Leader based on average return, minimum 20 returns
* Player that was a rookie in 2013

AMERICAN FOOTBALL CONFERENCE—PUNT RETURNS

	No	FC	Yards	Avg	Long	TD
Baltimore	43	16	609	14.2	82t	1
Pittsburgh	32	23	409	12.8	67t	1
Kansas City	59	11	695	11.8	89t	2
Cleveland	38	28	418	11.0	79t	1
New England	36	23	387	10.8	43	0
Indianapolis	33	25	326	9.9	51	0
Cincinnati	47	16	424	9.0	43	0
N.Y. Jets	25	12	224	9.0	24	0
Houston	42	21	360	8.6	87t	1
Oakland	25	19	206	8.2	30	0
Denver	44	15	343	7.8	81t	1
Miami	34	20	264	7.8	34	0
Tennessee	31	20	240	7.7	35	0
San Diego	22	20	166	7.5	28	0
Buffalo	39	22	243	6.2	25	0
Jacksonville	30	21	142	4.7	17	0
AFC Total	580	312	5456	9.4	89t	7
AFC Average	36.3	19.5	341.0	9.4	—	0.4

NATIONAL FOOTBALL CONFERENCE—PUNT RETURNS

	No	FC	Yards	Avg	Long	TD
Minnesota	22	28	335	15.2	86t	1
Chicago	18	12	256	14.2	81t	1
Dallas	31	13	386	12.5	86t	1
Green Bay	30	21	339	11.3	93t	1
Tampa Bay	24	20	268	11.2	52	0
Seattle	52	14	579	11.1	71	0
Carolina	30	26	316	10.5	41	0
Detroit	38	29	392	10.3	58t	1
San Francisco	35	32	312	8.9	40	0
St. Louis	43	11	378	8.8	98t	1
Atlanta	30	13	250	8.3	25	0
N.Y. Giants	34	26	246	7.2	32	0
Philadelphia	26	20	171	6.6	32	0
Washington	35	11	225	6.4	34	0
New Orleans	32	25	194	6.1	28	0
Arizona	34	23	198	5.8	22	0
NFC Total	514	324	4845	9.4	98t	6
NFC Average	32.1	20.3	302.8	9.4	—	0.4
League Total	1094	636	10301	—	98t	13
League Average	34.2	19.9	321.9	9.4	—	0.4

SACKS

MOST SACKS

AFC: 19.5 Robert Mathis, Indianapolis
NFC: 19.0 Robert Quinn, St. Louis

MOST SACKS, GAME

AFC: 4.5 Mario Williams, Buffalo vs. Carolina, September 15
4.5 Justin Houston, Kansas City at Philadelphia, September 19
NFC: 4.0 Justin Tuck, N.Y. Giants at Washington, December 1
4.0 Greg Hardy, Carolina at Atlanta, December 29

TEAM LEADERS, SACKS

AFC: BALTIMORE, 10.0, Terrell Suggs; BUFFALO, 13.0, Mario Williams; CINCINNATI, 7.5, Carlos Dunlap, Wallace Gilberry; CLEVELAND, 5.5, Jabaal Sheard; DENVER, 10.0, Shaun Phillips; HOUSTON, 10.5, J.J. Watt; INDIANAPOLIS, 19.5, Robert Mathis; JACKSONVILLE, 7.5, Jason Babin; KANSAS CITY, 11.0, Tamba Hali, Justin Houston; MIAMI, 11.5, Olivier Vernon; NEW ENGLAND, 11.5, Chandler Jones; N.Y. JETS, 10.5, Muhammad Wilkerson; OAKLAND, 6.0, Lamarr Houston; PITTSBURGH, 8.0, Jason Worilds; SAN DIEGO, 5.5, Corey Liuget; TENNESSEE, 10.5, Jurrell Casey

NFC: ARIZONA, 11.5, John Abraham; ATLANTA, 7.5, Osi Umenyiora; CAROLINA, 15.0, Greg Hardy; CHICAGO, 7.0, Julius Peppers; DALLAS, 11.0, Jason Hatcher; DETROIT, 8.0, *Ezekiel Ansah; GREEN BAY, 7.5, Clay Matthews; MINNESOTA, 11.5, Jared Allen; NEW ORLEANS, 12.5, Cameron Jordan; N.Y. GIANTS, 11.0, Justin Tuck; PHILADELPHIA, 8.0, Trent Cole; ST. LOUIS, 19.0, Robert Quinn; SAN FRANCISCO, 8.5, Ahmad Brooks, Aldon Smith; SEATTLE, 8.5, Michael Bennett; TAMPA BAY, 9.5, Gerald McCoy; WASHINGTON, 10.0, Brian Orakpo

TEAM CHAMPION

NFC: 60 Carolina
AFC: 57 Buffalo

NFL TOP TEN LEADERS—SACKS

	Sacks
Robert Mathis, Ind.	19.5
Robert Quinn, St. L.	19.0
Greg Hardy, Car.	15.0
Mario Williams, Buf.	13.0
Cameron Jordan, N.O.	12.5
Junior Galette, N.O.	12.0
John Abraham, Ariz	11.5
Jared Allen, Min.	11.5
Chandler Jones, N.E.	11.5
Olivier Vernon, Mia.	11.5

AMERICAN FOOTBALL CONFERENCE—SACKS

	Sacks	Yards
Buffalo	57	395
New England	48	313
Kansas City	47	309
Cincinnati	43	279
Indianapolis	42	248
Miami	42	272
Denver	41	290
N.Y. Jets	41	242
Baltimore	40	257
Cleveland	40	185
Oakland	38	260
Tennessee	36	227
San Diego	35	248
Pittsburgh	34	198
Houston	32	187
Jacksonville	31	225
AFC Total	647	4135
AFC Average	40.4	258.4

NATIONAL FOOTBALL CONFERENCE—SACKS

	Sacks	Yards
Carolina	60	424
St. Louis	53	326
New Orleans	49	336
Arizona	47	337
Green Bay	44	238
Seattle	44	298
Minnesota	41	274
San Francisco	38	283
Philadelphia	37	271
Washington	36	238
Tampa Bay	35	255
Dallas	34	246
N.Y. Giants	34	214
Detroit	33	249
Atlanta	32	231
Chicago	31	189
NFC Total	648	4409
NFC Average	40.5	275.6
League Total	1295	8544
League Average	40.5	267.0

AFC—INDIVIDUAL SACKS

Player	Sacks	Player	Sacks	Player	Sacks
Mathis, Robert, Ind.	19.5	Johnson, Jarret, S.D.	3.0	Woodyard, Wesley, Den.	1.5
Williams, Mario, Buf.	13.0	Knighton, Terrance, Den.	3.0	* Addae, Jahleel, S.D.	1.0
Jones, Chandler, N.E.	11.5	Peko, Domata, Cin.	3.0	Allen, Antonio, NYJ	1.0
Vernon, Olivier, Mia.	11.5	Posluszny, Paul, Jac.	3.0	Allen, Russell, Jac.	1.0
Hali, Tamba, K.C.	11.0	Reed, Brooks, Hou.	3.0	Ayers, Akeem, Ten.	1.0
Houston, Justin, K.C.	11.0	Robertson, Craig, Cle.	3.0	Bailey, Allen, K.C.	1.0
Casey, Jurrell, Ten.	10.5	* Robey, Nickell, Buf.	3.0	Bethea, Antoine, Ind.	1.0
Watt, J.J., Hou.	10.5	Siliga, Sealver, N.E.	3.0	Bilukidi, Christo, Oak.	1.0
Wilkerson, Muhammad, NYJ	10.5	Timmons, Lawrence, Pit.	3.0	Blackmon, Will, Jac.	1.0
Williams, Kyle, Buf.	10.5	Walden, Erik, Ind.	3.0	Branch, Tyvon, Oak.	1.0
Hughes, Jerry, Buf.	10.0	Walker, Reggie, S.D.	3.0	Bryant, Corbin, Buf.	1.0
Pace, Calvin, NYJ	10.0	Walker, Vance, Oak.	3.0	Byrd, Jairus, Buf.	1.0
Phillips, Shaun, Den.	10.0	Wimbley, Kamerion, Ten.	3.0	* Catapano, Mike, K.C.	1.0
Suggs, Terrell, Bal.	10.0	Burnett, Kevin, Oak.	2.5	* Charles, Stefan, Buf.	1.0
Dumervil, Elvis, Bal.	9.5	English, Larry, S.D.	2.5	* Cyprien, Johnathan, Jac.	1.0
Wake, Cameron, Mia.	8.5	Jean Francois, Ricky, Ind.	2.5	Davis, DeMario, NYJ	1.0
Ninkovich, Rob, N.E.	8.0	Kelly, Tommy, N.E.	2.5	Davis, Ryan, Jac.	1.0
Worilds, Jason, Pit.	8.0	Owens, Chris, Cle.	2.5	Ellerbe, Dannell, Mia.	1.0
Babin, Jason, Jac.	7.5	Shelby, Derrick, Mia.	2.5	Flowers, Brandon, K.C.	1.0
Dareus, Marcell, Buf.	7.5	* Werner, Bjoern, Ind.	2.5	Fokou, Moise, Ten.	1.0
Dunlap, Carlos, Cin.	7.5	Young, Usama, Oak.	2.5	Gay, William, Pit.	1.0
Gilberry, Wallace, Cin.	7.5	* Alonso, Kiko, Buf.	2.0	Gilchrist, Marcus, S.D.	1.0
Mercilus, Whitney, Hou.	7.0	Arrington, Kyle, N.E.	2.0	Graham, Corey, Bal.	1.0
Atkins, Geno, Cin.	6.0	Barnes, Antwan, NYJ	2.0	Gregory, Steve, N.E.	1.0
Branch, Andre, Jac.	6.0	* Bryant, Armonty, Cle.	2.0	Guy, Winston, Jac.	1.0
Houston, Lamarr, Oak.	6.0	* Buchanan, Michael, N.E.	2.0	Harrison, Damon, NYJ	1.0
Jackson, Malik, Den.	6.0	Canty, Chris, Bal.	2.0	Hayes, Geno, Jac.	1.0
* Jones, Chris, N.E.	6.0	Carroll, Nolan, Mia.	2.0	Hightower, Dont'a, N.E.	1.0
Morgan, Derrick, Ten.	6.0	Carter, Andre, N.E.	2.0	Hughes, John, Cle.	1.0
Ayers, Robert, Den.	5.5	Fletcher, Dane, N.E.	2.0	Ingram, Melvin, S.D.	1.0
Freeman, Jerrell, Ind.	5.5	Groves, Quentin, Cle.	2.0	Irving, Nate, Den.	1.0
Liuget, Corey, S.D.	5.5	Harris, David, NYJ	2.0	Johnson, James-Michael, K.C.	1.0
Roach, Nick, Oak.	5.5	Harrison, James, Cin.	2.0	* Jones, Jarvis, Pit.	1.0
Sheard, Jabaal, Cle.	5.5	* Jordan, Dion, Mia.	2.0	Kirkpatrick, Dre, Cin.	1.0
Heyward, Cameron, Pit.	5.0	Klug, Karl, Ten.	2.0	Landry, Dawan, NYJ	1.0
Miller, Von, Den.	5.0	Lissemore, Sean, S.D.	2.0	Manning, Danieal, Hou.	1.0
* Mingo, Barkevious, Cle.	5.0	McIntyre, Garrett, NYJ	2.0	Martin, Mike, Ten.	1.0
Reyes, Kendall, S.D.	5.0	McPhee, Pernell, Bal.	2.0	Maualuga, Rey, Cin.	1.0
Smith, Antonio, Hou.	5.0	Mincey, Jeremy, Jac.	2.0	Mays, Joe, Hou.	1.0
Smith, Daryl, Bal.	5.0	Misi, Koa, Mia.	2.0	Muir, Daniel, Oak.	1.0
Woodley, LaMarr, Pit.	5.0	Polamalu, Troy, Pit.	2.0	Nelson, Reggie, Cin.	1.0
Coples, Quinton, NYJ	4.5	Ross, Brandian, Oak.	2.0	Parker, Ron, K.C.	1.0
Johnson, Derrick, K.C.	4.5	Rubin, Ahtyba, Cle.	2.0	Patterson, Dimitri, Mia.	1.0
Keiser, Thomas, S.D.	4.5	Sims, Pat, Oak.	2.0	Posey, Julian, Cle.	1.0
Kruger, Paul, Cle.	4.5	Taylor, Phillip, Cle.	2.0	Powe, Jerrell, K.C.	1.0
* Moore, Sio, Oak.	4.5	Trevathan, Danny, Den.	2.0	Sheppard, Kelvin, Ind.	1.0
Odrick, Jared, Mia.	4.5	Tyson, DeAngelo, Bal.	2.0	Skrine, Buster, Cle.	1.0
Poe, Dontari, K.C.	4.5	* Vellano, Joe, N.E.	2.0	Soliai, Paul, Mia.	1.0
Redding, Cory, Ind.	4.5	* Williams, Sylvester, Den.	2.0	Sopoaga, Isaac, N.E.	1.0
Brown, Zach, Ten.	4.0	Winn, Billy, Cle.	2.0	Vickerson, Kevin, Den.	1.0
Jackson, Tyson, K.C.	4.0	Woods, Al, Pit.	2.0	Weddle, Eric, S.D.	1.0
Jones, Arthur, Bal.	4.0	Woodson, Charles, Oak.	2.0	* Williams, Brandon, Bal.	1.0
Keisel, Brett, Pit.	4.0	Zombo, Frank, K.C.	2.0	* Williams, Tourek, S.D.	1.0
Lawson, Manny, Buf.	4.0	Alualu, Tyson, Jac.	1.5	Abdullah, Husain, K.C.	0.5
Marks, Sen'Derrick, Jac.	4.0	Crocker, Chris, Cin.	1.5	Angerer, Pat, Ind.	0.5
Pitoitua, Ropati, Ten.	4.0	Cushing, Brian, Hou.	1.5	* Brown, Arthur, Bal.	0.5
Rey, Vincent, Cin.	4.0	Douzable, Leger, NYJ	1.5	Butler, Donald, S.D.	0.5
Starks, Randy, Mia.	4.0	Jackson, D'Qwell, Cle.	1.5	Deaderick, Brandon, Jac.	0.5
Wolfe, Derek, Den.	4.0	Jones, Reshad, Mia.	1.5	Freeney, Dwight, S.D.	0.5
Berry, Eric, K.C.	3.5	Mayo, Jerod, N.E.	1.5	* Hunt, Margus, Cin.	0.5
Bryant, Desmond, Cle.	3.5	Mitchell, Earl, Hou.	1.5	* Jones, Abry, Jac.	0.5
Johnson, Michael, Cin.	3.5	Moala, Fili, Ind.	1.5	Mathews, Ricardo, Ind.	0.5
* Richardson, Sheldon, NYJ	3.5	Ngata, Haloti, Bal.	1.5	* McGee, Stacy, Oak.	0.5
Searcy, Da'Norris, Buf.	3.5	Patrick, Johnny, S.D.	1.5	Pollard, Bernard, Ten.	0.5
Burfict, Vontaze, Cin.	3.0	Porter, Tracy, Oak.	1.5	Tarpinian, Jeff, Hou.	0.5
Hood, Ziggy, Pit.	3.0	* Ryan, Logan, N.E.	1.5	Westerman, Jamaal, Buf.	0.5
Hunter, Jason, Oak.	3.0	Thompson, Brandon, Cin.	1.5	Wheeler, Philip, Mia.	0.5
Johnson, Antonio, Ten.	3.0	Upshaw, Courtney, Bal.	1.5		
		Ward, T.J., Cle.	1.5	*Player that was a rookie in 2013*	

NFC—INDIVIDUAL SACKS

Player	Sacks	Player	Sacks	Player	Sacks
Quinn, Robert, St.L	19.0	Briggs, Lance, Chi.	3.0	Babineaux, Jonathan, Atl.	1.0
Hardy, Greg, Car.	15.0	Cox, Fletcher, Phi.	3.0	Baker, Chris, Was.	1.0
Jordan, Cameron, N.O.	12.5	Edwards, Dwan, Car.	3.0	* Bass, David, Chi.	1.0
Galette, Junior, N.O.	12.0	* Foster, Glenn, N.O.	3.0	Bell, Yeremiah, Ariz	1.0
Abraham, John, Ariz	11.5	Graham, Brandon, Phi.	3.0	Bowers, Da'Quan, T.B.	1.0
Allen, Jared, Min.	11.5	Greenway, Chad, Min.	3.0	Brown, Everette, Dal.	1.0
Hatcher, Jason, Dal.	11.0	Hawthorne, David, N.O.	3.0	Cole, Audie, Min.	1.0
Johnson, Charles, Car.	11.0	Jones, Brad, G.B.	3.0	Cole, Colin, Car.	1.0
Tuck, Justin, NY-G	11.0	Joseph, Linval, NY-G	3.0	Collins, Nate, Chi.	1.0
Orakpo, Brian, Was.	10.0	* Lotulelei, Star, Car.	3.0	Conrath, Matt, St.L	1.0
McCoy, Gerald, T.B.	9.5	Mikell, Quintin, Car.	3.0	Godfrey, Charles, Car.	1.0
Campbell, Calais, Ariz	9.0	Riley, Perry, Was.	3.0	Goode, Najee, Phi.	1.0
Robison, Brian, Min.	9.0	Shaughnessy, Matt, Ariz	3.0	Guion, Letroy, Min.	1.0
Bennett, Michael, Sea.	8.5	Washington, Daryl, Ariz	3.0	House, Davon, G.B.	1.0
Brooks, Ahmad, S.F.	8.5	Willis, Patrick, S.F.	3.0	* Hyde, Micah, G.B.	1.0
Kerrigan, Ryan, Was.	8.5	Wootton, Corey, Chi.	3.0	Jenkins, Janoris, St.L	1.0
Long, Chris, St.L	8.5	Young, Willie, Det.	3.0	Jennings, M.D., G.B.	1.0
Smith, Aldon, S.F.	8.5	Addison, Mario, Car.	2.5	Jolly, Johnny, G.B.	1.0
* Ansah, Ezekiel, Det.	8.0	Benard, Marcus, Ariz	2.5	Landri, Derek, T.B.	1.0
Avril, Cliff, Sea.	8.0	Cofield, Barry, Was.	2.5	* Lemonier, Corey, S.F.	1.0
Cole, Trent, Phi.	8.0	* Floyd, Sharrif, Min.	2.5	* Mathieu, Tyrann, Ariz	1.0
Matthews, Clay, G.B.	7.5	Jenkins, Malcolm, N.O.	2.5	McClain, Robert, Atl.	1.0
Umenyiora, Osi, Atl.	7.5	* Taylor, Devin, Det.	2.5	* McDonald, T.J., St.L	1.0
David, Lavonte, T.B.	7.0	Williams, Tramon, G.B.	2.5	Meriweather, Brandon, Was.	1.0
Peppers, Julius, Chi.	7.0	Barron, Mark, T.B.	2.0	Moch, Dontay, Ariz	1.0
Selvie, George, Dal.	7.0	* Bostic, Jon, Chi.	2.0	* Mulumba, Andy, G.B.	1.0
Daniels, Mike, G.B.	6.5	Carter, Bruce, Dal.	2.0	Mundy, Ryan, NY-G	1.0
Dansby, Karlos, Ariz	6.5	Delmas, Louis, Det.	2.0	Nicholas, Stephen, Atl.	1.0
Smith, Justin, S.F.	6.5	Dorsey, Glenn, S.F.	2.0	Ozougwu, Cheta, Chi.	1.0
Fairley, Nick, Det.	6.0	Fletcher, London, Was.	2.0	Paysinger, Spencer, NY-G	1.0
Kiwanuka, Mathias, NY-G	6.0	Foster, Mason, T.B.	2.0	* Rambo, Bacarri, Was.	1.0
Ware, DeMarcus, Dal.	6.0	* Gholston, William, T.B.	2.0	Revis, Darrelle, T.B.	1.0
Brockers, Michael, St.L	5.5	* Holloman, DeVonte, Dal.	2.0	Rivers, Keith, NY-G	1.0
Clayborn, Adrian, T.B.	5.5	* Horton, Wes, Car.	2.0	Rucker, Frostee, Ariz	1.0
Griffen, Everson, Min.	5.5	Irvin, Bruce, Sea.	2.0	Schofield, O'Brien, Sea.	1.0
McDonald, Clinton, Sea.	5.5	Jackson, Rob, Was.	2.0	Smith, Malcolm, Sea.	1.0
Suh, Ndamukong, Det.	5.5	Jenkins, Jarvis, Was.	2.0	* Spence, Akeem, T.B.	1.0
Barwin, Connor, Phi.	5.0	Johnson, Tom, N.O.	2.0	Tapp, Darryl, Was.	1.0
Bowman, NaVorro, S.F.	5.0	* Klein, A.J., Car.	2.0	Thomas, Terrell, NY-G	1.0
Hawk, A.J., G.B.	5.0	Kuechly, Luke, Car.	2.0	Thornton, Cedric, Phi.	1.0
Hayes, William, St.L	5.0	Lattimore, Jamari, G.B.	2.0	Thurmond, Walter, Sea.	1.0
Jenkins, Cullen, NY-G	5.0	Lofton, Curtis, N.O.	2.0	* Vaccaro, Kenny, N.O.	1.0
Langford, Kendall, St.L	5.0	* Logan, Bennie, Phi.	2.0	Walker, Tyrunn, N.O.	1.0
Neal, Mike, G.B.	5.0	McDaniel, Tony, Sea.	2.0	Williams, Cary, Phi.	1.0
Peters, Corey, Atl.	5.0	Moore, William, Atl.	2.0	Williams, Dan, Ariz	1.0
Wagner, Bobby, Sea.	5.0	Pierre-Paul, Jason, NY-G	2.0	Wilson, Martez, N.O.	1.0
Clemons, Chris, Sea.	4.5	Quin, Glover, Det.	2.0	Dawson, Keyunta, N.O.	0.5
Dockett, Darnell, Ariz	4.5	Rolle, Antrel, NY-G	2.0	Humber, Ramon, N.O.	0.5
Hicks, Akiem, N.O.	4.5	Scandrick, Orlando, Dal.	2.0	Idonije, Israel, Det.	0.5
Anderson, James, Chi.	4.0	Sims, Eugene, St.L	2.0		
Curry, Vinny, Phi.	4.0	Watson, Dekoda, T.B.	2.0	* Player that was a rookie in 2013	
Davis, Thomas, Car.	4.0	Wilber, Kyle, Dal.	2.0		
Henderson, Erin, Min.	4.0	Williams, D.J., Chi.	2.0		
Kendricks, Mychal, Phi.	4.0	Wilson, Josh, Was.	2.0		
Massaquoi, Jonathan, Atl.	4.0	* Worrilow, Paul, Atl.	2.0		
McClellin, Shea, Chi.	4.0	Wynn, Jarius, S.D.-Dal.	2.0		
Perry, Nick, G.B.	4.0	Bryant, Red, Sea.	1.5		
Ryans, DeMeco, Phi.	4.0	Dent, Akeem, Atl.	1.5		
* Bartu, Joplo, Atl.	3.5	* Hill, Jordan, Sea.	1.5		
Haralson, Parys, N.O.	3.5	* Ogletree, Alec, St.L	1.5		
Jerry, Peria, Atl.	3.5	Paea, Stephen, Chi.	1.5		
* Jones, Datone, G.B.	3.5	Ratliff, Jeremiah, Chi.	1.5		
Laurinaitis, James, St.L	3.5	* Short, Kawann, Car.	1.5		
McDonald, Ray, S.F.	3.5	Wright, K.J., Sea.	1.5		
Mitchell, Mike, Car.	3.5	Acho, Sam, Ariz	1.0		
Munnerlyn, Captain, Car.	3.5	Adams, Michael, T.B.	1.0		
Tulloch, Stephen, Det.	3.5	Alexander, Frank, Car.	1.0		
Williams, Kevin, Min.	3.5	Allen, Nate, Phi.	1.0		
		Arenas, Javier, Ariz	1.0		

FUMBLES

MOST FUMBLES
NFC:	12	Matthew Stafford, Detroit
AFC:	10	Peyton Manning, Denver

MOST FUMBLES, GAME
NFC:	5	Matthew Stafford, Detroit at Philadelphia, December 8
AFC:	3	Ryan Tannehill, Miami at Indianapolis, September 15
	3	Ben Roethlisberger, Pittsburgh vs. Chicago, September 22
	3	Matt Flynn, Oakland vs. Washington, September 29
	3	Thad Lewis, Buffalo at New Orleans, October 27
	3	Alex Smith, Kansas City vs. Indianapolis, December 22

OWN FUMBLES RECOVERED
AFC:	5	Tom Brady, New England
	5	Julian Edelman, New England
NFC:	5	Matthew Stafford, Detroit

OWN FUMBLES RECOVERED, GAME
NFC:	3	Matthew Stafford, Detroit at Philadelphia, December 8 (0 yards, 0 TD)
AFC:	2	Joe Flacco, Baltimore at Chicago, November 17 (0 yards, 0 TD) - (OT)
	2	* Matt McGloin, Oakland at N.Y. Jets, December 8 (0 yards, 0 TD)
	2	Julian Edelman, New England vs. Buffalo, December 29 (0 yards, 0 TD)

OPPONENTS' FUMBLES RECOVERED
NFC:	4	Mychal Kendricks, Philadelphia
AFC:	3	Sen'Derrick Marks, Jacksonville

OPPONENTS' FUMBLES RECOVERED, GAME
AFC:	2	Justin Houston, Kansas City at Philadelphia, September 19 (0 yards, 0 TD)
	2	J.J. Watt, Houston at Arizona, November 10 (0 yards, 0 TD)
NFC:	2	Morgan Burnett, Green Bay at Detroit, November 28 (9 yards, 1 TD)
	2	Jonathan Babineaux, Atlanta vs. Washington, December 15 (8 yards, 0 TD)
	2	William Hayes, St. Louis vs. Tampa Bay, December 22 (0 yards, 0 TD)

YARDS
AFC:	77	Jason McCourty, Tennessee
NFC:	75	DeAngelo Hall, Washington

LONGEST
AFC:	77	Jason McCourty, Tennessee at Seattle, October 13 - TD
NFC:	75	DeAngelo Hall, Washington vs. Philadelphia, September 9 - TD

AFC—TOUCHDOWNS ON FUMBLE RECOVERIES
Will Blackmon, Jac.	1
Vontaze Burfict, Cin.	1
* Marcus Cooper, K.C.	1
Tamba Hali, K.C.	1
* Greg Jenkins, Oak.	1
Chandler Jones, N.E.	1
Karl Klug, Ten.	1
Jason McCourty, Ten.	1
Von Miller, Den.	1
Terence Newman, Cin.	1
Da'Norris Searcy, Buf.	1
T.J. Ward, Cle.	1
Charles Woodson, Oak.	1

NFC—TOUCHDOWNS ON FUMBLE RECOVERIES
* Bates, Daren, St.L	1
Michael Bennett, Sea.	1
Jarrett Boykin, G.B.	1
Morgan Burnett, G.B.	1
Barry Church, Dal.	1
Thomas DeCoud, Atl.	1
Nick Fairley, Det.	1
Najee Goode, Phi.	1
DeAngelo Hall, Was.	1
Nick Hayden, Dal.	1
* Jeff Heath, Dal.	1
Kendall Hunter, S.F.	1
M.D. Jennings, G.B.	1
Chris Long, St.L	1
Kassim Osgood, S.F.	1
Julius Peppers, Chi.	1
Robert Quinn, St.L	1
Brian Robison, Min.	1
Matt Shaughnessy, Ariz	1
Dan Skuta, S.F.	1

AFC FUMBLES—INDIVIDUAL
	Fum	Own Rec	Opp Rec	Yards	Tot Rec
Abdullah, Husain, K.C.	0	0	1	0	1
Adams, Mike, Den.	0	0	1	0	1
Adams, Phillip, Oak.	0	0	1	26	1
* Allen, Keenan, S.D.	2	0	0	0	0
Allen, Russell, Jac.	0	0	2	0	2
Allen, Will, Pit.	0	0	1	49	1
* Alonso, Kiko, Buf.	0	0	2	13	2
* Anderson, C.J., Den.	0	1	0	0	1
Anger, Bryan, Jac.	1	2	0	0	2
Avery, Donnie, K.C.	1	0	0	0	0
Bailey, Patrick, Ten.	1	0	0	0	0
* Ball, Montee, Den.	3	0	0	0	0
* Bell, Le'Veon, Pit.	1	0	0	0	0
Benjamin, Travis, Cle.	2	1	0	0	1
* Bernard, Giovani, Cin.	1	1	0	0	1
Berry, Eric, K.C.	0	0	2	24	2
Bess, Davone, Cle.	1	0	0	0	0
Bethea, Antoine, Ind.	0	0	1	0	1
Blackmon, Will, Jac.	0	0	1	21	1
Blount, LeGarrette, N.E.	3	0	0	0	0
Brady, Tom, N.E.	9	5	0	-10	5
Brazill, LaVon, Ind.	1	0	0	0	0
Brisiel, Mike, Oak.	0	1	0	0	1
Brooks, Brandon, Hou.	0	2	0	0	2
Brown, Antonio, Pit.	1	1	0	0	1
Brown, Donald, Ind.	0	2	0	0	2
Brown, Duane, Hou.	0	1	0	0	1
Brown, Mike, Jac.	2	1	0	0	1
Brown, Sergio, Ind.	0	1	1	6	2
Brown, Zach, Ten.	0	0	1	0	1

	Fum	Own Rec	Opp Rec	Yards	Tot Rec
* Buchanan, Michael, N.E.	0	1	0	0	1
Burfict, Vontaze, Cin.	0	0	2	13	2
Burnett, Kevin, Oak.	0	0	1	3	1
Burris, Miles, Oak.	0	0	1	0	1
* Butler, Brice, Oak.	0	1	0	0	1
Butler, Darius, Ind.	0	0	1	0	1
Butler, Donald, S.D.	0	0	1	0	1
Cameron, Jordan, Cle.	1	0	0	0	0
Campbell, Jason, Cle.	3	0	0	0	0
Carter, Chris, Pit.	0	0	1	0	1
Carter, Tony, Den.	1	0	0	0	0
Casey, Jurrell, Ten.	0	0	1	0	1
Chandler, Scott, Buf.	1	0	0	0	0
Charles, Jamaal, K.C.	4	1	0	0	1
Chekwa, Chimdi, Oak.	0	0	1	0	1
Choice, Tashard, Buf.	0	1	0	0	1
Clark, Ryan, Pit.	0	0	1	0	1
Cole, Marquice, N.E.	0	0	1	0	1
* Collins, Jamie, N.E.	0	0	1	0	1
Conner, Kavell, Ind.	0	0	1	0	1
* Cooper, Marcus, K.C.	0	0	1	0	1
Cox, Morgan, Bal.	0	0	1	0	1
Cumberland, Jeff, NYJ	0	1	0	0	1
Dalton, Andy, Cin.	4	0	0	-14	0
* Davis, Knile, K.C.	3	0	0	0	0
Deaderick, Brandon, Jac.	0	0	1	0	1
Decker, Eric, Den.	2	1	0	0	1
Denney, John, Mia.	0	0	1	0	1
* Dobson, Aaron, N.E.	1	1	0	0	1
Doss, Tandon, Bal.	1	0	0	0	0
Douzable, Leger, NYJ	0	0	1	0	1
Dunlap, Carlos, Cin.	0	0	1	42	1
Ebner, Nate, N.E.	0	0	2	0	2
Edelman, Julian, N.E.	6	5	0	0	5
* Elam, Matt, Bal.	0	0	2	7	2
Ellerbe, Dannell, Mia.	0	0	2	0	2
Fasano, Anthony, K.C.	0	1	0	0	1
Ferguson, D'Brickashaw, NYJ	0	1	0	0	1
Fields, Brandon, Mia.	1	0	0	-7	0
* Fisher, Eric, K.C.	0	1	0	0	1
Fitzpatrick, Ryan, Ten.	9	4	0	-3	4
Flacco, Joe, Bal.	8	2	0	0	2
Fleener, Coby, Ind.	1	0	0	0	0
Fokou, Moise, Ten.	0	0	1	0	1
Ford, Jacoby, Oak.	4	1	0	0	1
Forsett, Justin, Jac.	1	1	0	0	1
Freeman, Jerrell, Ind.	0	0	2	24	2
Gabbert, Blaine, Jac.	2	0	0	0	0
Gates, Antonio, S.D.	2	0	0	0	0
Gilchrist, Marcus, S.D.	0	0	1	0	1
Gilmore, Stephon, Buf.	0	1	0	0	1
* Goodwin, Marquise, Buf.	1	0	0	0	0
Gradkowski, Gino, Bal.	2	1	0	-20	1
Graham, Garrett, Hou.	2	1	0	0	1
Graham, T.J., Buf.	1	0	0	0	0
Gray, Cyrus, K.C.	0	1	1	0	2
Green, A.J., Cin.	1	0	0	0	0
Green, Ladarius, S.D.	0	0	1	0	1
Green-Ellis, BenJarvus, Cin.	2	0	0	0	0
Gresham, Jermaine, Cin.	3	0	0	0	0
Griffin, Michael, Ten.	0	0	1	0	1
* Griffin, Ryan, Hou.	0	1	0	0	1
Grimes, Jonathan, Hou.	1	0	0	0	0
Gurode, Andre, Oak.	0	1	0	0	1
Hali, Tamba, K.C.	0	0	2	11	2
Harbor, Clay, Jac.	2	0	0	0	0
Harris, Mike, Jac.	0	0	1	0	1
Harrison, James, Cin.	0	0	1	0	1
Hawkins, Andrew, Cin.	1	1	0	0	1
Hemingway, Junior, K.C.	2	1	0	0	1
Henne, Chad, Jac.	2	2	0	-1	2
Herron, Dan, Ind.	0	0	1	0	1
Heyward, Cameron, Pit.	0	0	1	8	1
Hill, Sammie Lee, Ten.	0	0	1	0	1
Hill, Stephen, NYJ	1	1	0	0	1
Hillman, Ronnie, Den.	2	0	0	0	0
Hilton, T.Y., Ind.	1	1	0	0	1
Holliday, Trindon, Den.	5	3	0	0	3
Holmes, Andre, Oak.	0	0	1	22	1
Hood, Ziggy, Pit.	0	0	1	0	1
* Hopkins, DeAndre, Hou.	1	0	0	0	0
Houston, Lamarr, Oak.	0	0	1	0	1
Houston, Justin, K.C.	0	0	2	0	2
Huber, Kevin, Cin.	1	1	0	-15	1
Hudson, Rodney, K.C.	1	0	0	0	0
Hughes, John, Cle.	0	0	1	0	1
Hunter, Jason, Oak.	0	0	1	15	1
Ihedigbo, James, Bal.	0	0	2	0	2
Ihenacho, Duke, Den.	0	0	2	0	2
Iloka, George, Cin.	0	0	1	0	1
Ivory, Chris, NYJ	2	1	0	0	1
Jackson, D'Qwell, Cle.	0	0	1	0	1
Jackson, Fred, Buf.	3	1	0	0	1
Jackson, Kareem, Hou.	0	0	1	0	1
Jammer, Quentin, Den.	0	0	1	0	1
* Jenkins, Greg, Oak.	1	0	1	23	1
Jenkins, Mike, Oak.	0	0	1	20	1
Johnson, Andre, Hou.	0	1	0	0	1
Johnson, Chris, Ten.	3	2	0	0	2
Johnson, Derrick, K.C.	0	0	2	11	2
Johnson, Josh, Cin.	1	1	0	0	1
* Johnson, Shelton, Oak.	0	0	1	-1	1
Johnson, Steve, Buf.	1	1	0	0	1
Jones, Adam, Cin.	0	0	2	43	2
Jones, Ben, Hou.	0	1	0	0	1
Jones, Chandler, N.E.	0	0	1	0	1
Jones, Felix, Pit.	1	0	0	0	0
Jones, Greg, Hou.	0	1	0	0	1
Jones, Taiwan, Oak.	0	0	1	0	1
Jones-Drew, Maurice, Jac.	1	1	0	0	1
* Juszczyk, Kyle, Bal.	0	1	0	0	1
Keenum, Case, Hou.	6	0	0	0	0
Keisel, Brett, Pit.	0	0	2	1	2
Kelly, Tommy, N.E.	0	0	1	0	1
Kern, Brett, Ten.	2	2	0	-30	2
Kirkpatrick, Dre, Cin.	0	1	0	9	1
Klug, Karl, Ten.	0	0	1	0	1
Knighton, Terrance, Den.	0	0	1	13	1
Lawson, Manny, Buf.	0	0	1	1	1
Leach, Vonta, Bal.	1	1	0	0	1
Legursky, Doug, Buf.	0	1	0	0	1
Lewis, Marcedes, Jac.	1	0	0	0	0
Lewis, Thad, Buf.	7	1	0	-5	1
Locker, Jake, Ten.	3	1	0	-13	1
Lowery, Dwight, Jac.	0	0	1	0	1
Luck, Andrew, Ind.	6	1	0	0	1
Mack, Alex, Cle.	1	1	0	-14	1
Mangold, Nick, NYJ	2	0	0	-29	0
Manning, Peyton, Den.	10	2	0	-4	2
* Manuel, EJ, Buf.	6	2	0	-5	2
Marks, Sen'Derrick, Jac.	0	0	3	15	3
Marshall, Richard, S.D.	0	0	1	0	1
* Martin, Eric, Cle.	0	0	1	0	1
Martin, Keshawn, Hou.	2	0	0	0	0
Mastrud, Jeron, Oak.	0	1	0	0	1
Mathews, Ryan, S.D.	2	1	0	0	1

	Fum	Own Rec	Opp Rec	Yards	Tot Rec		Fum	Own Rec	Opp Rec	Yards	Tot Rec
Mayo, Jerod, N.E.	0	0	1	2	1	Spikes, Brandon, N.E.	0	0	1	0	1
Mays, Taylor, Cin.	0	0	1	0	1	Spiller, C.J., Buf.	4	2	0	0	2
McClain, Terrell, Hou.	0	0	1	0	1	Starks, Randy, Mia.	0	0	1	0	1
McCluster, Dexter, K.C.	2	1	0	0	1	Streater, Rod, Oak.	1	0	0	0	0
McCourty, Devin, N.E.	0	0	1	44	1	Stuckey, Darrell, S.D.	0	1	0	2	1
McCourty, Jason, Ten.	0	0	1	77	1	Suggs, Terrell, Bal.	0	0	1	0	1
McFadden, Darren, Oak.	1	0	0	0	0	Talib, Aqib, N.E.	0	1	0	0	1
McGahee, Willis, Cle.	1	0	0	0	0	Tannehill, Ryan, Mia.	9	3	0	-7	3
* McGee, Stacy, Oak.	0	0	1	3	1	Tate, Ben, Hou.	5	1	0	0	1
* McGloin, Matt, Oak.	4	3	0	-12	3	Tate, Brandon, Cin.	2	1	0	0	1
McKelvin, Leodis, Buf.	7	4	0	0	4	Thigpen, Marcus, Mia.	3	2	0	0	2
Meester, Brad, Jac.	2	1	0	-9	1	Thomas, Daniel, Mia.	0	1	0	0	1
Miller, Heath, Pit.	1	0	0	0	0	Thomas, Demaryius, Den.	1	0	0	0	0
Miller, Lamar, Mia.	1	0	0	0	0	Thomas, Joe, Cle.	0	2	0	2	2
Miller, Von, Den.	0	0	1	60	1	Timmons, Lawrence, Pit.	0	0	1	29	1
Moala, Fili, Ind.	0	0	1	5	1	* Tinker, Carson, Jac.	1	0	0	-14	0
Moore, Matt, Mia.	1	1	0	0	1	Todman, Jordan, Jac.	0	2	0	0	2
Moorman, Brian, Buf.	1	1	0	0	1	Trevathan, Danny, Den.	1	0	1	0	1
Moreno, Knowshon, Den.	1	2	0	5	2	Urbik, Kraig, Buf.	0	1	0	0	1
Morgan, Derrick, Ten.	0	0	1	0	1	Vaughn, Cassius, Ind.	0	0	1	0	1
Mulligan, Matthew, N.E.	0	1	0	0	1	* Vellano, Joe, N.E.	0	0	1	0	1
Myers, Chris, Hou.	1	0	0	-9	0	Vereen, Shane, N.E.	1	0	0	0	0
Nelson, Reggie, Cin.	2	0	2	12	2	Verner, Alterraun, Ten.	0	0	2	9	2
Newman, Terence, Cin.	0	1	0	58	1	Vollmer, Sebastian, N.E.	0	1	0	0	1
Ninkovich, Rob, N.E.	0	0	2	3	2	* Wagner, Ricky, Bal.	0	1	0	0	1
Noble, Danny, Jac.	0	1	0	0	1	Wake, Cameron, Mia.	0	0	1	0	1
Ogbonnaya, Chris, Cle.	2	0	0	0	0	Walden, Erik, Ind.	1	0	1	10	1
Owens, Chris, Cle.	0	0	1	0	1	Walker, Delanie, Ten.	1	1	0	0	1
Parker, Ron, K.C.	0	1	2	22	3	Ward, T.J., Cle.	0	0	1	51	1
Paulson, David, Pit.	1	0	0	0	0	* Warmack, Chance, Ten.	0	1	0	0	1
Peerman, Cedric, Cin.	0	1	0	0	1	Washington, Leon, Ten.	1	1	0	0	1
Polamalu, Troy, Pit.	0	0	1	0	1	Watt, J.J., Hou.	0	0	2	0	2
Posluszny, Paul, Jac.	0	0	1	0	1	Weddle, Eric, S.D.	0	0	2	27	2
Pouncey, Mike, Mia.	1	0	0	-18	0	Weeden, Brandon, Cle.	6	0	0	0	0
Powell, Bilal, NYJ	1	1	0	0	1	Welker, Wes, Den.	1	0	0	0	0
Pryor, Terrelle, Oak.	7	4	0	-9	4	Wheeler, Philip, Mia.	0	0	1	0	1
Rainey, Chris, Ind.	2	1	0	0	1	Whittaker, Fozzy, S.D.-Cle.	1	1	0	0	1
Redding, Cory, Ind.	0	0	1	0	1	Whitworth, Andrew, Cin.	0	1	0	0	1
Redman, Isaac, Pit.	1	1	0	0	1	* Williams, Brandon, Bal.	0	0	1	0	1
Rey, Vincent, Cin.	0	0	1	0	1	Williams, Damian, Ten.	2	1	0	0	1
Reynaud, Darius, Ten.	1	0	0	0	0	Williams, Kyle, Buf.	0	0	1	0	1
Rice, Ray, Bal.	2	0	0	0	0	* Williams, Sylvester, Den.	0	0	1	0	1
Richardson, Trent, Ind.	2	0	0	0	0	Wisniewski, Stefen, Oak.	3	0	0	-4	0
Ridley, Stevan, N.E.	4	0	0	0	0	Wolfe, Derek, Den.	0	0	1	1	1
* Rivera, Mychal, Oak.	0	1	0	1	1	Woodhead, Danny, S.D.	2	0	0	0	0
Rivers, Philip, S.D.	3	1	0	-6	1	Woodley, LaMarr, Pit.	0	0	1	0	1
Robertson, Craig, Cle.	0	0	1	7	1	Woodson, Charles, Oak.	0	0	2	25	2
* Robey, Nickell, Buf.	0	0	1	0	1	Wright, Kendall, Ten.	2	1	0	0	1
* Robinson, Denard, Jac.	3	1	0	0	1	Wylie, Devon, Ten.	2	1	0	0	1
Robinson, Dunta, K.C.	0	0	1	0	1	Yanda, Marshal, Bal.	0	2	0	0	2
Roethlisberger, Ben, Pit.	9	3	0	0	3	Yates, T.J., Hou.	1	1	0	0	1
Roos, Michael, Ten.	0	1	0	0	1	* Lefeged, Joe, Ind.	0	0	1	0	1
Royal, Eddie, S.D.	1	0	0	0	0	Young, Usama, Oak.	1	1	0	0	1
Sanders, Emmanuel, Pit.	1	1	0	0	1	Zombo, Frank, K.C.	0	0	1	0	1
Sanu, Mohamed, Cin.	1	0	0	0	0						
Sapp, Ricky, NYJ	0	0	1	0	1						
Schaub, Matt, Hou.	2	0	0	-1	0						
* Schwenke, Brian, Ten.	0	1	0	2	1						
Scifres, Mike, S.D.	1	1	0	0	1						
Searcy, Da'Norris, Buf.	0	1	1	74	2						
Sensabaugh, Coty, Ten.	0	0	2	0	2						
Sheard, Jabaal, Cle.	0	0	1	0	1						
Sherman, Anthony, K.C.	1	0	0	0	0						
Simms, Matt, NYJ	1	0	0	-2	0						
Smith, Alex, K.C.	7	1	0	-13	1						
Smith, Alex, Cin.	1	0	0	0	0						
* Smith, Geno, NYJ	8	3	0	-2	3						
Smith, Torrey, Bal.	1	1	0	0	1						

Yards includes aborted plays, own recoveries and opponents' recoveries.

* *Player that was a rookie in 2013*

NFC FUMBLES—INDIVIDUAL

	Fum	Own Rec	Opp Rec	Yards	Tot Rec
Acho, Sam, Ariz	0	1	0	0	1
Addison, Mario, Car.	0	0	1	0	1
Alexander, Frank, Car.	0	0	1	-3	1
* Alford, Robert, Atl.	1	0	1	-5	1
Anderson, James, Chi.	0	0	1	0	1

2013 INDIVIDUAL STATISTICS—FUMBLES

	Fum	Own Rec	Opp Rec	Yards	Tot Rec
Arenas, Javier, Ariz	2	0	0	0	0
* Armstrong, Ray-Ray, St.L	0	0	1	0	1
Asiata, Matt, Min.	1	0	0	0	0
* Austin, Tavon, St.L	4	2	0	0	2
Avant, Jason, Phi.	1	0	0	0	0
Avril, Cliff, Sea.	0	0	1	0	1
Babineaux, Jonathan, Atl.	0	0	2	8	2
Barclay, Don, G.B.	0	1	0	0	1
* Barkley, Matt, Phi.	3	2	0	0	2
* Barner, Kenjon, Car.	1	0	0	0	0
Barron, Mark, T.B.	0	0	1	0	1
Barwin, Connor, Phi.	0	0	1	0	1
* Bates, Daren, St.L	0	0	1	11	1
Beasley, Cole, Dal.	1	0	0	0	0
Bell, Joique, Det.	4	2	0	0	2
Bennett, Martellus, Chi.	1	0	0	0	0
Bennett, Michael, Sea.	0	0	1	22	1
Bethel, Justin, Ariz	0	0	1	-3	1
* Bostic, Jon, Chi.	0	0	1	0	1
* Bowie, Michael, Sea.	0	1	0	0	1
Bowman, NaVorro, S.F.	0	0	2	0	2
Boykin, Jarrett, G.B.	0	2	0	15	2
Bradford, Sam, St.L	3	1	0	0	1
Brees, Drew, N.O.	6	0	0	0	0
Brockel, Richie, Car.	1	0	0	0	0
Brooks, Ahmad, S.F.	1	1	0	0	1
Brown, Andre, NY-G	3	1	0	0	1
Brown, Levi, Ariz	0	1	0	0	1
Brown, Tarell, S.F.	0	0	1	16	2
Bryant, Dez, Dal.	3	0	0	0	0
Burleson, Nate, Det.	1	0	0	0	0
Burnett, Morgan, G.B.	0	0	3	12	3
Bush, Jarrett, G.B.	0	1	0	0	1
Bush, Rafael, N.O.	0	0	1	0	1
Bush, Reggie, Det.	5	1	0	0	1
Bushrod, Jermon, Chi.	0	1	0	0	1
Campbell, Calais, Ariz	0	0	2	2	2
Carlson, John, Min.	1	1	0	0	1
Carr, Brandon, Dal.	0	0	1	21	1
Cason, Antoine, Ariz	0	1	2	59	3
Cassel, Matt, Min.	3	1	0	-3	1
Celek, Brent, Phi.	1	0	0	0	0
Celek, Garrett, S.F.	1	0	0	0	0
Chester, Chris, Was.	0	1	0	0	1
Chung, Patrick, Phi.	0	0	1	0	1
Church, Barry, Dal.	0	0	1	27	1
Claiborne, Morris, Dal.	0	0	1	0	1
Clemens, Kellen, St.L	7	1	0	-3	1
Clutts, Tyler, Mia.-Dal.	1	1	0	0	1
Cofield, Barry, Was.	0	0	1	0	1
Coleman, Derrick, Sea.	1	0	0	0	0
Colledge, Daryn, Ariz	0	1	0	0	1
Collins, Jed, N.O.	0	0	0	0	1
Cook, Jared, St.L	1	0	0	0	0
Costanzo, Blake, Chi.	0	0	1	0	1
Cousins, Kirk, Was.	3	0	0	0	0
Cox, Fletcher, Phi.	0	0	1	3	1
* Cox, Michael, NY-G	0	1	0	0	1
Cox, Perrish, S.F.	1	0	0	0	0
Cruz, Victor, NY-G	1	0	0	0	0
* Cunningham, Benny, St.L	2	1	0	0	1
Cutler, Jay, Chi.	5	1	0	-10	1
Dansby, Karlos, Ariz	0	0	1	0	1
David, Lavonte, T.B.	0	0	1	0	1
Davis, Vernon, S.F.	1	0	0	0	0
* Dawson, Skye, T.B.	1	1	0	0	1
Dean, Larry, Min.	0	0	1	0	1
DeCoud, Thomas, Atl.	0	0	1	30	1

	Fum	Own Rec	Opp Rec	Yards	Tot Rec
DeOssie, Zak, NY-G	1	0	1	-35	1
Diehl, David, NY-G	0	2	0	0	2
Donnell, Larry, NY-G	0	0	1	0	1
Douglas, Harry, Atl.	3	0	0	0	0
Dray, Jim, Ariz	1	0	0	0	0
Dunbar, Lance, Dal.	1	0	0	0	0
Durant, Justin, Dal.	0	0	1	5	1
Durham, Kris, Det.	1	0	0	0	0
Edwards, Dwan, Car.	0	0	2	0	2
* Ellington, Andre, Ariz	1	1	0	0	1
* Escobar, Gavin, Dal.	0	1	0	0	1
Fairley, Nick, Det.	0	0	2	4	2
Fitzgerald, Larry, Ariz	1	0	0	0	0
Fletcher, Bradley, Phi.	0	0	1	0	1
Florence, Drayton, Car.	1	0	0	0	0
* Floyd, Michael, Chi.	1	0	0	0	0
Flynn, Matt, Oak.-G.B.	7	1	0	-5	1
Foles, Nick, Phi.	4	1	0	-10	1
* Ford, Michael, Chi.	0	1	0	0	1
* Forté, Matt, Chi.	2	0	0	0	0
* Franklin, Johnathan, G.B.	2	0	0	0	0
Free, Doug, Dal.	0	0	0	5	0
Freeman, Josh, T.B.	2	0	0	-8	0
Galette, Junior, N.O.	0	0	2	13	2
Garcon, Pierre, Was.	1	1	0	0	1
Garza, Roberto, Chi.	1	0	0	0	0
Gerhart, Toby, Min.	1	0	0	0	0
Ginn, Ted, Car.	0	1	0	0	1
Givens, Chris, St.L	1	0	0	0	0
* Glennon, Mike, T.B.	7	3	0	-16	3
Goldson, Dashon, T.B.	0	0	1	0	1
Goode, Najee, Phi.	0	0	1	2	1
* Goodman, Malliciah, Atl.	0	0	2	13	2
Gore, Frank, S.F.	3	0	0	0	0
Graham, Jimmy, N.O.	0	1	0	-2	1
Griffin III, Robert, Was.	11	2	0	-36	2
Guion, Letroy, Min.	0	0	1	0	1
Hall, DeAngelo, Was.	0	0	1	75	1
Harper, Roman, N.O.	0	0	1	19	1
Harris, Dwayne, Dal.	2	1	1	0	2
Hawk, A.J., G.B.	0	0	1	0	1
Hawley, Joe, Atl.	1	0	0	-16	0
Hayden, Nick, Dal.	0	0	1	0	1
Hayes, William, St.L	0	0	2	0	2
* Heath, Jeff, Dal.	0	0	1	50	1
Helu, Roy, Was.	2	2	0	0	2
Hester, Devin, Chi.	5	2	0	0	2
Hill, Will, NY-G	0	0	1	8	1
Hillis, Peyton, NY-G	2	1	0	0	1
* Holloman, DeVonte, Dal.	0	0	1	0	1
Housler, Rob, Ariz	1	0	0	0	0
Hunter, Kendall, S.F.	1	0	1	2	1
* Hyde, Micah, G.B.	2	1	0	0	1
Jackson, DeSean, Phi.	1	0	0	0	0
Jackson, Vincent, T.B.	1	0	0	0	0
Jacobs, Brandon, NY-G	1	0	0	0	0
* James, Charles, NY-G	1	0	0	0	0
James, LaMichael, S.F.	2	2	0	0	2
* Jefferson, Tony, Ariz	0	1	0	0	1
Jeffery, Alshon, Chi.	3	2	0	0	2
Jenkins, Cullen, NY-G	0	0	2	0	2
Jenkins, Janoris, St.L	0	0	1	0	1
Jennings, M.D., G.B.	0	0	1	24	1
Jennings, Tim, Chi.	0	0	1	0	1
Jernigan, Jerrel, NY-G	1	0	0	0	0
Jerod-Eddie, Tony, S.F.	0	0	1	0	1
Jerry, Peria, Atl.	0	0	1	0	1
Johnson, Calvin, Det.	1	1	0	1	1

	Fum	Own Rec	Opp Rec	Yards	Tot Rec
Johnson, Charles, Car.	0	0	1	0	1
Johnson, Damaris, Phi.	1	0	0	0	0
* Johnson, Darius, Atl.	1	0	0	0	0
Jolly, Johnny, G.B.	0	0	1	0	1
Jones, Brad, G.B.	0	0	1	3	1
Jones, Colin, Car.	0	0	1	0	1
* Jones, Datone, G.B.	0	0	1	20	1
Jones, James, G.B.	2	1	0	0	1
Jones, Julio, Atl.	2	1	0	18	1
Jordan, Cameron, N.O.	0	0	2	11	2
Joseph, Linval, NY-G	0	0	1	0	1
Kaepernick, Colin, S.F.	6	2	0	-2	2
Kearse, Jermaine, Sea.	1	1	0	0	1
Kelce, Jason, Phi.	2	0	0	-1	0
Kendricks, Mychal, Phi.	0	0	4	6	4
Koenen, Michael, T.B.	0	0	1	5	1
Kuhn, John, G.B.	1	0	0	0	0
* Lacy, Eddie, G.B.	1	1	0	0	1
LaFell, Brandon, Car.	1	1	0	0	1
Lane, Jeremy, Sea.	1	0	0	0	0
Larsen, Ted, T.B.	1	2	0	-14	2
Laurinaitis, James, St.L	0	0	2	43	2
Lee, Sean, Dal.	0	0	1	10	1
* Lester, Robert, Car.	0	0	1	0	1
Lichtensteiger, Kory, Was.	0	1	0	0	1
Loeffler, Cullen, Min.	0	0	1	0	1
* Logan, Bennie, Phi.	0	0	1	0	1
Long, Chris, St.L	0	0	2	45	2
* Long, Kyle, Chi.	1	0	0	0	0
Lynch, Marshawn, Sea.	4	0	0	0	0
Manning, Eli, NY-G	7	1	0	-6	1
Maragos, Chris, Sea.	2	1	1	-19	2
Martin, Doug, T.B.	2	1	0	0	1
* Martin, Sam, Det.	2	1	0	-9	1
Matthews, Casey, Phi.	0	0	1	0	1
Maxwell, Byron, Sea.	0	0	1	0	1
McBride, Trumaine, NY-G	1	0	0	0	0
McClain, Robert, Atl.	1	1	1	0	2
McClellin, Shea, Chi.	0	0	1	0	1
McCown, Josh, Chi.	3	2	0	0	2
McCoy, Gerald, T.B.	0	0	1	12	1
McCoy, LeSean, Phi.	1	0	0	0	0
McCray, Kelcie, T.B.	0	0	1	17	1
McDaniel, Tony, Sea.	0	0	1	0	1
McDonald, Clinton, Sea.	0	1	1	0	2
McLeod, Rodney, St.L	0	0	2	9	2
Mebane, Brandon, Sea.	0	0	1	0	1
Melton, Henry, Chi.	0	0	1	-1	1
Mendenhall, Rashard, Ariz	4	0	0	0	0
Meriweather, Brandon, Was.	0	0	1	0	1
Mikell, Quintin, Car.	0	0	1	0	1
Miller, Bruce, S.F.	1	0	0	0	0
* Mills, Jordan, Chi.	0	1	0	0	1
Mitchell, Marvin, Min.	0	0	1	0	1
Moore, Lance, N.O.	1	0	0	0	0
Moore, William, Atl.	0	0	2	0	2
Morgan, Josh, Was.	2	1	0	0	1
Morris, Alfred, Was.	5	1	0	0	1
Mosley, C.J., Det.	0	0	1	0	1
Moss, Santana, Was.	2	0	0	0	0
* Mulumba, Andy, G.B.	0	0	1	0	1
Mundy, Ryan, NY-G	0	0	1	0	1
Munnerlyn, Captain, Car.	0	0	1	0	1
Murphy, Louis, NY-G	1	0	0	0	0
Murray, DeMarco, Dal.	3	1	0	0	1
Nelson, Kyle, Was.	1	0	0	0	0
Newton, Cam, Car.	3	1	0	-8	1
Orakpo, Brian, Was.	0	0	2	0	2
Osgood, Kassim, S.F.	0	0	1	0	1
Page, Eric, T.B.	3	0	0	0	0
Painter, Curtis, NY-G	2	2	0	-6	2
Palmer, Ashlee, Det.	0	0	1	0	1
Palmer, Carson, Ariz	6	1	0	0	1
Paul, Niles, Was.	0	1	0	0	1
Paulsen, Logan, Was.	2	2	0	0	2
Paysinger, Spencer, NY-G	0	0	1	0	1
Peppers, Julius, Chi.	0	0	1	42	1
Peterson, Adrian, Min.	5	1	0	0	1
Peterson, Patrick, Ariz	3	2	0	0	2
Pettigrew, Brandon, Det.	1	0	0	0	0
Pettis, Austin, St.L	1	0	0	0	0
Polumbus, Tyler, Was.	0	1	0	0	1
Ponder, Christian, Min.	7	1	0	-7	1
Quin, Glover, Det.	0	0	1	0	1
Quinn, Robert, St.L	0	0	2	33	2
Rainey, Bobby, Cle.-T.B.	1	1	0	0	1
* Randle, Joseph, Dal.	0	1	0	-7	1
Randle, Rueben, NY-G	3	0	0	0	1
* Reid, Eric, S.F.	0	0	2	0	2
Reiff, Riley, Det.	0	1	0	0	1
Revis, Darrelle, T.B.	0	0	1	0	1
Rice, Sidney, Sea.	1	0	0	0	0
Richardson, Daryl, St.L	0	1	0	0	1
Riley, Perry, Was.	0	0	1	6	1
Rivers, Keith, NY-G	0	0	1	0	1
Robison, Brian, Min.	0	0	1	61	1
Rocca, Sav, Was.	0	1	0	0	1
Rodgers, Aaron, G.B.	4	1	0	-6	1
Rodgers, Jacquizz, Atl.	1	0	0	0	0
Rolle, Antrel, NY-G	0	0	1	10	1
Romo, Tony, Dal.	4	4	0	-6	4
Ross, Jeremy, G.B.-Det.	2	0	0	0	0
Ryan, Matt, Atl.	5	1	0	-2	1
Sanford, Jamarca, Min.	0	0	1	0	1
Selvie, George, Dal.	0	0	1	0	1
Sendlein, Lyle, Ariz	1	1	0	-7	1
Shaughnessy, Matt, Ariz	0	0	3	6	3
Sherels, Marcus, Min.	3	2	0	0	2
Sherman, Richard, Sea.	2	2	0	0	2
Shields, Sam, G.B.	0	0	0	12	0
* Short, Kawann, Car.	0	0	1	0	1
Simpson, Jerome, Min.	1	1	0	1	1
Skuta, Dan, S.F.	0	0	1	47	1
Smith, Alfonso, Ariz	2	0	0	0	0
Smith, Brad, Phi.	1	1	0	-4	1
Smith, Harrison, Min.	0	0	1	0	1
Smith, Tyron, Dal.	0	1	0	0	1
Snelling, Jason, Atl.	0	1	0	0	1
* Spence, Akeem, T.B.	0	0	1	0	1
Sproles, Darren, N.O.	2	0	0	0	0
* Stacy, Zac, St.L	1	1	0	1	1
Stafford, Matthew, Det.	12	5	0	-35	5
Starks, James, G.B.	1	0	0	0	0
Stewart, Darian, St.L	0	0	1	19	1
Stewart, Jonathan, Car.	1	0	0	0	0
Tandy, Keith, T.B.	0	0	1	0	1
Tanner, Phillip, Dal.	1	0	0	0	0
Tate, Golden, Sea.	3	0	0	0	0
Taylor, Ryan, G.B.	1	1	0	0	1
Thomas, Pierre, N.O.	2	1	0	0	1
Thomas, Josh, Car.	1	0	0	0	0
Thurmond, Walter, Sea.	0	0	1	-2	1
Tolbert, Mike, Car.	0	1	0	0	1
* Trufant, Desmond, Atl.	0	0	1	18	1
Turbin, Robert, Sea.	1	0	0	0	0
Unger, Max, Sea.	0	2	0	0	0

	Fum	Own Rec	Opp Rec	Yards	Tot Rec
Ventrone, Raymond, S.F.	0	0	1	0	1
Vick, Michael, Phi.	4	2	0	0	2
Wagner, Bobby, Sea.	0	0	1	0	1
Ware, DeMarcus, Dal.	0	0	1	0	1
Washington, Daryl, Ariz	0	0	1	0	1
Watson, Dekoda, T.B.	0	0	1	0	1
Weems, Eric, Chi.	0	1	0	0	1
White, Corey, N.O.	1	0	1	0	1
White, Roddy, Atl.	2	0	0	0	0
Whitner, Donte, S.F.	1	0	1	-5	1
Wilber, Kyle, Dal.	0	0	2	1	2
Williams, Cary, Phi.	0	0	1	0	1
Williams, DeAngelo, Car.	3	1	0	0	1
Williams, Jacquian, NY-G	0	0	2	5	2
Williams, Kevin, Min.	0	0	1	0	1
Williams, Kyle, S.F.	2	1	0	0	1
* Williams, Nick, Was.	1	1	0	0	1
* Williams, Terrance, Dal.	2	0	0	0	0
Williams, Tramon, G.B.	0	0	2	0	2
Wilson, David, NY-G	2	0	0	0	0
Wilson, Josh, Was.	0	0	3	1	3
Wilson, Russell, Sea.	10	4	1	-4	5
Witherspoon, Will, St.L	0	0	1	0	1
Wootton, Corey, Chi.	0	0	2	1	2
Wright, Jarius, Min.	0	1	0	0	1
Wright, K.J., Sea.	0	0	1	0	1
Young, Willie, Det.	0	0	2	0	2
Zuttah, Jeremy, T.B.	0	1	0	0	1

Yards includes aborted plays, own recoveries and opponents' recoveries.
* *Player that was a rookie in 2013*

AMERICAN FOOTBALL CONFERENCE—FUMBLES

	Fum	Own Rec	Fum OB	TD	Opp Rec	TD	Fum Yards	Tot Rec
Indianapolis	14	6	4	0	12	0	45	18
San Diego	14	4	0	0	6	0	23	10
Baltimore	15	9	0	0	7	0	-13	16
N.Y. Jets	15	8	0	0	2	0	-33	10
Miami	16	8	1	0	6	0	-32	14
Pittsburgh	16	6	0	0	10	0	87	16
Cleveland	17	6	2	0	7	1	46	13
Jacksonville	18	12	1	0	10	1	12	22
Cincinnati	20	9	1	1	11	1	148	20
Houston	21	10	2	0	4	0	-10	14
Kansas City	21	8	3	0	15	2	55	23
New England	24	15	0	0	12	1	39	27
Denver	27	9	3	0	9	1	75	18
Oakland	27	15	1	0	13	2	111	28
Tennessee	27	17	1	0	12	2	42	29
Buffalo	32	17	3	0	6	1	78	23
AFC Total	324	159	22	1	142	12	673	301
AFC Average	20.3	9.9	1.4	0.1	8.9	0.8	42.1	18.8

NATIONAL FOOTBALL CONFERENCE—FUMBLES

	Fum	Own Rec	Fum OB	TD	Opp Rec	TD	Fum Yards	Tot Rec
Atlanta	9	3	2	0	11	1	67	14
New Orleans	13	6	3	0	11	0	2	17
N.Y. Giants	13	7	0	0	14	1	106	21
Green Bay	16	8	0	0	5	1	40	13
Seattle	16	7	1	0	13	1	30	20
Tampa Bay	16	9	1	0	8	0	-7	17
Chicago	20	12	0	0	20	1	20	32
Dallas	20	10	0	0	9	2	44	19
Minnesota	21	8	2	0	12	0	-9	20
Carolina	22	10	2	1	12	0	3	22
Detroit	24	5	3	0	6	0	-7	11
St. Louis	24	12	4	0	4	1	5	16
Arizona	25	10	2	0	11	1	155	21
San Francisco	26	15	3	1	11	1	136	26
Washington	26	17	3	2	9	1	58	26
Philadelphia	37	13	2	0	5	0	-55	18
NFC Total	331	134	32	1	166	19	604	300
NFC Average	20.7	8.4	2.0	0.1	10.4	1.2	37.8	18.8
NFL Total	655	293	54	2	308	31	1277	601
NFL Average	20.5	9.2	1.7	0.1	9.6	1.0	39.9	18.8

Inside the Numbers

GREATEST COMEBACKS IN NFL HISTORY
(Most Points Overcome To Win Game)

REGULAR SEASON GAMES
FROM 28 POINTS BEHIND TO WIN:
December 7, 1980, at San Francisco

New Orleans	14	21	0	0	0	— 35
San Francisco	0	7	14	14	3	— 38

- NO — Harris 33 pass from Manning (Ricardo kick)
- NO — Childs 21 pass from Manning (Ricardo kick)
- NO — Holmes 1 run (Ricardo kick)
- SF — Solomon 57 punt return (Wersching kick)
- NO — Holmes 1 run (Ricardo kick)
- NO — Harris 41 pass from Manning (Ricardo kick)
- SF — Montana 1 run (Wersching kick)
- SF — Clark 71 pass from Montana (Wersching kick)
- SF — Solomon 14 pass from Montana (Wersching kick)
- SF — Elliott 7 run (Wersching kick)
- SF — FG Wersching 36

FROM 26 POINTS BEHIND TO WIN:
September 21, 1997, at Buffalo

Indianapolis	14	12	0	9	— 35
Buffalo	0	10	6	21	— 37

- Ind — Bailey 10 pass from Harbaugh (Blanchard kick)
- Ind — Faulk 10 run (Blanchard kick)
- Ind — FG Blanchard 39
- Ind — FG Blanchard 36
- Ind — FG Blanchard 49
- Ind — FG Blanchard 22
- Buff — Johnson 16 pass from Collins (Christie kick)
- Buff — FG Christie 27
- Buff — A. Smith 15 run (2-pt attempt failed)
- Ind — FG Blanchard 25
- Buff — Early 4 pass from Collins (Christie kick)
- Buff — A. Smith 1 run (Christie kick)
- Buff — A. Smith 54 run (Christie kick)
- Ind — Harrison 2 pass from Justin (2-pt attempt failed)

FROM 25 POINTS BEHIND TO WIN:
November 8, 1987, at St. Louis

Tampa Bay	7	7	14	0	— 28
St. Louis	0	3	0	28	— 31

- TB — Carrier 5 pass from DeBerg (Igwebuike kick)
- TB — Carter 3 pass from DeBerg (Igwebuike kick)
- StL — FG Gallery 31
- TB — Smith 34 pass from DeBerg (Igwebuike kick)
- TB — Smith 3 run (Igwebuike kick)
- StL — Awalt 4 pass from Lomax (Gallery kick)
- StL — Noga 23 fumble recovery (Gallery kick)
- StL — J. Smith 11 pass from Lomax (Gallery kick)
- StL — J. Smith 17 pass from Lomax (Gallery kick)

FROM 24 POINTS BEHIND TO WIN:
October 27, 1946, at Washington

Philadelphia	0	0	14	14	— 28
Washington	10	14	0	0	— 24

- Wash — Rosato 2 run (Poillon kick)
- Wash — FG Poillon 28
- Wash — Rosato 4 run (Poillon kick)
- Wash — Lapka recovered fumble in end zone (Poillon kick)
- Phil — Steele 1 run (Lio kick)
- Phil — Pritchard 45 pass from Thompson (Lio kick)
- Phil — Steinke 7 pass from Thompson (Lio kick)
- Phil — Ferrante 30 pass from Thompson (Lio kick)

FROM 24 POINTS BEHIND TO WIN:
October 20, 1957, at Detroit

Baltimore	7	14	6	0	— 27
Detroit	0	3	7	21	— 31

- Balt — Mutscheller 15 pass from Unitas (Rechichar kick)
- Det — FG Martin 47
- Balt — Moore 72 pass from Unitas (Rechichar kick)
- Balt — Mutscheller 52 pass from Unitas (Rechichar kick)
- Balt — Moore 4 pass from Unitas (kick failed)
- Det — Junker 14 pass from Rote (Layne kick)
- Det — Cassady 26 pass from Layne (Layne kick)
- Det — Johnson 1 run (Layne kick)
- Det — Cassady 29 pass from Layne (Layne kick)

FROM 24 POINTS BEHIND TO WIN:
October 25, 1959, at Minneapolis

Philadelphia	0	0	21	7	— 28
Chicago Cardinals	7	10	7	0	— 24

- Cardinals — Crow 10 pass from Roach (Conrad kick)
- Cardinals — J. Hill 77 blocked field goal return (Conrad kick)
- Cardinals — FG Conrad 15
- Cardinals — Lane 37 interception return (Conrad kick)
- Phil — Barnes 1 run (Walston kick)
- Phil — McDonald 29 pass from Van Brocklin (Walston kick)
- Phil — Barnes 2 run (Walston kick)
- Phil — McDonald 22 pass from Van Brocklin (Walston kick)

FROM 24 POINTS BEHIND TO WIN:
October 23, 1960, at Denver

Boston	10	7	0	7	— 24
Denver	0	0	14	17	— 31

- Bos — FG Cappelletti 12
- Bos — Colclough 10 pass from Songin (Cappelletti kick)
- Bos — Wells 6 pass from Songin (Cappelletti kick)
- Bos — Miller 47 pass from Songin (Cappelletti kick)
- Den — Carmichael 21 pass from Tripucka (Mingo kick)
- Den — Jessup 19 pass from Tripucka (Mingo kick)
- Den — Carmichael 35 lateral from Taylor, pass from Tripucka (Mingo kick)
- Den — Taylor 8 pass from Tripucka (Mingo kick)
- Den — FG Mingo 9

FROM 24 POINTS BEHIND TO WIN:
December 15, 1974, at Miami

New England	21	3	0	3	— 27
Miami	0	17	7	10	— 34

- NE — Hannah recovered fumble in end zone (J. Smith kick)
- NE — Sanders 23 interception return (J. Smith kick)
- NE — Herron 4 pass from Plunkett (J. Smith kick)
- NE — FG J. Smith 46
- Mia — Nottingham 1 run (Yepremian kick)
- Mia — Baker 37 pass from Morrall (Yepremian kick)
- Mia — FG Yepremian 28
- Mia — Baker 46 pass from Morrall (Yepremian kick)
- NE — FG J. Smith 34
- Mia — Nottingham 2 run (Yepremian kick)
- Mia — FG Yepremian 40

FROM 24 POINTS BEHIND TO WIN:
December 4, 1977, at Minnesota

San Francisco	0	10	14	3	— 27
Minnesota	0	0	7	21	— 28

- SF — Delvin Williams 2 run (Wersching kick)
- SF — FG Wersching 31
- SF — Dave Williams 80 kickoff return (Wersching kick)
- SF — Delvin Williams 5 run (Wersching kick)
- Minn — McClanahan 15 pass from Lee (Cox kick)
- Minn — Rashad 8 pass from Kramer (Cox kick)
- Minn — Tucker 9 pass from Kramer (Cox kick)
- SF — FG Wersching 31
- Minn — S. White 69 pass from Kramer (Cox kick)

FROM 24 POINTS BEHIND TO WIN:
September 23, 1979, at Denver

Seattle	10	10	14	0	— 34
Denver	0	10	21	6	— 37

- Sea — FG Herrera 28
- Sea — Doornink 5 run (Herrera kick)
- Den — FG Turner 27
- Sea — Doornink 5 run (Herrera kick)
- Den — Armstrong 2 run (Turner kick)
- Sea — FG Herrera 22
- Sea — McCullum 13 pass from Zorn (Herrera kick)
- Sea — Smith 1 run (Herrera kick)
- Den — Studdard 2 pass from Morton (Turner kick)
- Den — Moses 11 pass from Morton (Turner kick)
- Den — Upchurch 35 pass from Morton (Turner kick)
- Den — Lytle 1 run (kick failed)

FROM 24 POINTS BEHIND TO WIN:
September 23, 1979, at Cincinnati

Houston	0	10	17	3	— 30
Cincinnati	14	10	0	3	— 27

- Cin — Johnson 1 run (Bahr kick)
- Cin — Alexander 2 run (Bahr kick)
- Cin — Johnson 1 run (Bahr kick)
- Cin — FG Bahr 52
- Hou — Burrough 35 pass from Pastorini (Fritsch kick)
- Hou — FG Fritsch 33

Hou — Campbell 8 run
(Fritsch kick)
Hou — Caster 22 pass from Pastorini
(Fritsch kick)
Hou — FG Fritsch 47
Cin — FG Bahr 55
Hou — FG Fritsch 29

FROM 24 POINTS BEHIND TO WIN:
November 22, 1982, at Los Angeles

San Diego	10	14	0	0	—	24
L.A. Raiders	0	7	14	7	—	28

SD — FG Benirschke 19
SD — Scales 29 pass from Fouts
(Benirschke kick)
SD — Muncie 2 run
(Benirschke kick)
SD — Muncie 1 run
(Benirschke kick)
Raiders — Christensen 1 pass from
Plunkett (Bahr kick)
Raiders — Allen 3 run (Bahr kick)
Raiders — Allen 6 run (Bahr kick)
Raiders — Hawkins 1 run (Bahr kick)

FROM 24 POINTS BEHIND TO WIN:
September 26, 1988, at Denver

L.A. Raiders	0	0	14	13	3	— 30
Denver	7	17	0	3	0	— 27

Den — Dorsett 1 run (Karlis kick)
Den — Dorsett 1 run (Karlis kick)
Den — Sewell 7 pass from Elway
(Karlis kick)
Den — FG Karlis 39
Raiders — Smith 40 pass from
Schroeder (Bahr kick)
Raiders — Smith 42 pass from
Schroeder (Bahr kick)
Raiders — FG Bahr 28
Raiders — Allen 4 run (Bahr kick)
Den — FG Karlis 25
Raiders — FG Bahr 44
Raiders — FG Bahr 35

FROM 24 POINTS BEHIND TO WIN:
December 6, 1992, at Tampa

L.A. Rams	0	3	21	7	—	31
Tampa Bay	6	21	0	0	—	27

TB — FG Murray 34
TB — FG Murray 47
TB — Armstrong 81 pass from
Testaverde (Murray kick)
TB — Jones 26 fumble recovery
(Murray kick)
Rams — FG Zendejas 18
TB — Carrier 10 pass from
Testaverde (Murray kick)
Rams — Anderson 40 pass from
Everett (Zendejas kick)
Rams — Chadwick 27 pass from
Everett (Zendejas kick)
Rams — Lang 1 run (Zendejas kick)
Rams — Carter 8 pass from Everett
(Zendejas kick)

FROM 24 POINTS BEHIND TO WIN:
October 2, 2011, at Dallas

Detroit	0	3	14	17	—	34
Dallas	7	13	10	0	—	30

Dall — Bryant 25 pass from Romo
(Bailey kick)
Dall — Bryant 6 pass from Romo
(Bailey kick)
Dall — FG Bailey 41
Det — FG Hanson 33
Dall — FG Bailey 35
Dall — Witten 1 pass from Romo
(Bailey kick)

Det — Carpenter 34 interception
return (Hanson kick)
Det — Houston 56 interception
return (Hanson kick)
Dall — FG Bailey 23
Det — Johnson 23 pass from
Stafford (Hanson kick)
Det — FG Hanson 51
Det — Johnson 2 pass from Stafford
(Hanson kick)

FROM 24 POINTS BEHIND TO WIN:
October 15, 2012, at San Diego

Denver	0	0	14	21	—	35
San Diego	10	14	0	0	—	24

SD — FG Novak
SD — Gates 15 pass from Rivers
(Novak kick)
SD — Jammer 80 interception
return (Novak kick)
SD — Gates 11 pass from Rivers
(Novak kick)
Den — D. Thomas 29 pass from
Manning (Prater kick)
Den — Carter 65 fumble recovery
(Prater kick)
Den — Decker 7 pass from Manning
(Prater kick)
Den — Stokley 21 pass from
Manning (Prater kick)
Den — Harris 46 interception return
(Prater kick)

FROM 24 POINTS BEHIND TO WIN:
November 24, 2013, at New England

Denver	17	7	0	7	0	— 31
New England	0	0	21	10	3	— 34

Den — Miller 60 fumble recovery
(Prater kick)
Den — Moreno 2 run (Prater kick)
Den — FG Prater 27
Den — Tamme 10 pass from
Manning (Prater kick)
NE — Edelman 5 pass from Brady
(Gostkowski kick)
NE — Bolden 1 run (Gostkowski kick)
NE — Gronkowski 6 pass from
Brady (Gostkowski kick)
NE — Edelman 14 pass from
Brady (Gostkowski kick)
NE — FG Gostkowski 31
Den — D. Thomas 11 pass from
Manning (Prater kick)
NE — FG Gostkowski 31

POSTSEASON GAMES
FROM 32 POINTS BEHIND TO WIN:
AFC First-Round Playoff Game
January 3, 1993, at Buffalo

Houston	7	21	7	3	—	38
Buffalo	3	0	28	7	3	— 41

Hou — Jeffires 3 pass from Moon
(Del Greco kick)
Buff — FG Christie 36
Hou — Slaughter 7 pass from Moon
(Del Greco kick)
Hou — Duncan 26 pass from Moon
(Del Greco kick)
Hou — Jeffires 27 pass from Moon
(Del Greco kick)
Hou — McDowell 58 interception
return (Del Greco kick)
Buff — Davis 1 run (Christie kick)
Buff — Beebe 38 pass from Reich
(Christie kick)
Buff — Reed 26 pass from Reich
(Christie kick)
Buff — Reed 18 pass from Reich
(Christie kick)

Buff — Reed 17 pass from Reich
(Christie kick)
Hou — FG Del Greco 26
Buff — FG Christie 32

FROM 28 POINTS BEHIND TO WIN:
AFC First-Round Playoff Game
January 4, 2014, at Indianapolis

Kansas City	10	21	10	3	—	44
Indianapolis	7	3	21	14	—	45

KC — Bowe 6 pass from A. Smith
(Succop kick)
Ind — Hilton 10 pass from Luck
(Vinatieri kick)
KC — FG Succop 19
KC — Avery 79 pass from A. Smith
(Succop kick)
KC — Sherman 5 pass from
A. Smith (Succop kick)
Ind — FG Vinatieri 37
KC — Davis 4 run (Succop kick)
KC — Davis 10 pass from A. Smith
(Succop kick)
Ind — Brown 10 run (Vinatieri kick)
Ind — Brown 3 pass from Luck
(Vinatieri kick)
KC — FG Succop 42
Ind — Fleener 12 pass from Luck
(Vinatieri kick)
KC — FG Succop 43
Ind — Hilton 64 pass from Luck
(Vinatieri kick)

FROM 24 POINTS BEHIND TO WIN:
NFC First-Round Playoff Game
January 5, 2003, at San Francisco

N.Y. Giants	7	21	10	0	—	38
San Francisco	7	7	8	17	—	39

SF — Owens 76 pass from Garcia
(Chandler kick)
NYG — Toomer 12 pass from Collins
(Bryant kick)
NYG — Shockey 2 pass from Collins
(Bryant kick)
SF — Barlow 1 run (Chandler kick)
NYG — Toomer 8 pass from Collins
(Bryant kick)
NYG — Toomer 24 pass from Collins
(Bryant kick)
NYG — Barber 6 run (Bryant kick)
NYG — FG Bryant 21
SF — Owens 26 pass from Garcia
(Owens from Garcia)
SF — Garcia 14 run
(Owens from Garcia)
SF — Garcia 14 run
(Owens from Garcia)
SF — FG Chandler 25
SF — Streets 13 pass from Garcia
(2-pt attempt failed)

FROM 20 POINTS BEHIND TO WIN:
Western Conference Playoff Game
December 22, 1957, at San Francisco

Detroit	0	7	14	10	—	31
San Francisco	14	10	3	0	—	27

SF — Owens 34 pass from Tittle
(Soltau kick)
SF — McElhenny 47 pass from
Tittle (Soltau kick)
Det — Junker 4 pass from Rote
(Martin kick)
SF — Wilson 12 pass from Tittle
(Soltau kick)
SF — FG Soltau 25
SF — FG Soltau 10
Det — Tracy 2 run (Martin kick)
Det — Tracy 58 run (Martin kick)
Det — Gedman 3 run (Martin kick)
Det — FG Martin 14

RECORDS FOR NFL TEAMS FOR MOST POINTS IN A GAME (REGULAR SEASON ONLY)

Note: When the record has been achieved more than once, only the most recent game is shown; summaries are listed in alphabetical order by conference. Bold face indicates team holding record.

BALTIMORE RAVENS
November 11, 2012, at Baltimore

Oakland	0	10	7	3	— 20
Baltimore	10	17	21	7	— 55

TD: Balt—Torrey Smith 2, Joe Flacco, Jacoby Jones, Sam Koch, Dennis Pitta, Ray Rice; Oak—Darrius Heyward-Bey, Denarius Moore. TD Passes: Balt—Joe Flacco 3; Oak—Carson Palmer 2. FG: Balt—Justin Tucker 2; Det—Sebastian Janikowski 2.

BUFFALO BILLS
September 18, 1966, at Buffalo

Miami	3	7	0	14	— 24
Buffalo	21	27	3	7	— 58

TD: Buff—Bobby Burnett 2, Butch Byrd 2, Jack Spikes 2, Bobby Crockett, Jack Kemp; Mia—Dave Kocourek, Bo Roberson, John Roderick. TD Passes: Buff—Jack Kemp, Daryle Lamonica; Mia—George Wilson 3. FG: Buff—Booth Lusteg; Mia—Gene Mingo.

CINCINNATI BENGALS
December 17, 1989, at Cincinnati

Houston	0	0	0	7	— 7
Cincinnati	21	10	21	9	— 61

TD: Cin—Eddie Brown 2, Eric Ball, James Brooks, Ira Hillary, Rodney Holman, Tim McGee, Craig Taylor; Hou—Lorenzo White. TD Passes: Cin—Boomer Esiason 4, Erik Wilhelm. FG: Cin—Jim Breech 2.

CLEVELAND BROWNS
November 7, 1954, at Cleveland

Washington	0	3	0	0	— 3
Cleveland	13	14	21	14	— 62

TD: Cle—Darrell Brewster 2, Mo Bassett, Ken Gorgal, Otto Graham, Dub Jones, Dante Lavelli, Curley Morrison. TD Passes: Cle—George Ratterman 3, Otto Graham. FG: Cle—Lou Groza 2; Wash—Vic Janowicz.

DENVER BRONCOS
September 29, 2013, at Denver

Philadelphia	3	10	0	7	— 20
Denver	14	7	21	10	— 52

TD: Den—Demaryius Thomas 2, Wes Welker 2, Trindon Holliday, Steven Johnson, Knowshon Moreno; Phil—Jeff Maehl, Chris Polk. TD Passes: Den—Peyton Manning 4; Phil—Nick Foles. FG: Den—Matt Prater; Phil—Alex Henery 2.

HOUSTON TEXANS
November 18, 2012 at Houston

Jacksonville	7	10	10	7	3 — 37
Houston	7	10	3	14	9 — 43

TD: Hou—Garrett Graham 2, James Casey, Andre Johnson, Keshawn Martin; Jax—Marcedes Lewis 2, Justin Blackmon, Cecil Shorts. TD Passes: Hou—Matt Schaub 5; Jax—Chad Henne 4. FG: Hou—Shayne Graham 3; Jax—Josh Scobee 3.

INDIANAPOLIS COLTS
December 12, 1976, at Baltimore

Buffalo	3	3	7	7	— 20
Baltimore Colts	7	13	28	10	— 58

TD: Balt—Roger Carr, Raymond Chester, Glenn Doughty, Roosevelt Leaks, Derrel Luce, Lydell Mitchell, Howard Stevens; Buff—Bob Chandler, O.J. Simpson. TD Passes: Balt—Bert Jones 3; Buff—Gary Marangi. FG: Balt—Toni Linhart 3; Buff—George Jakowenko 2.

JACKSONVILLE JAGUARS
December 23, 2007, at Jacksonville

Oakland	0	3	0	8	— 11
Jacksonville	14	14	7	14	— 49

TD: Oak—Zach Miller; Jax—Richard Angulo, David Garrard, Greg Jones, Matt Jones, Maurice Jones-Drew, Fred Taylor, Reggie Williams. TD Passes: Oak—JaMarcus Russell; Jax—David Garrard 2, Quinn Gray 2. FG: Oak—Sebastian Janikowski.

KANSAS CITY CHIEFS
September 7, 1963, at Denver

Kansas City	14	14	21	10	— 59
Denver	0	7	0	0	— 7

TD: KC—Chris Burford 2, Frank Jackson 2, Dave Grayson, Abner Haynes, Sherrill Headrick, Curtis McClinton; Den—Lionel Taylor. TD Passes: KC—Len Dawson 4, Curtis McClinton; Den—Mickey Slaughter. FG: KC—Tommy Brooker.

MIAMI DOLPHINS
November 24, 1977, at St. Louis

Miami	14	14	20	7	— 55
St. Louis Cardinals	7	0	0	7	— 14

TD: Mia—Nat Moore 3, Gary Davis, Duriel Harris, Leroy Harris, Benny Malone, Andre Tillman; StL—Ike Harris, Terry Metcalf. TD Passes: Mia—Bob Griese 6; StL—Jim Hart.

NEW ENGLAND PATRIOTS
November 18, 2012, at New England

Indianapolis	14	3	0	7	— 24
New England	7	17	14	21	— 59

TD: NE—Julian Edelman 2, Rob Gronkowski 2, Alfonzo Dennard, Stevan Ridley, Aqib Talib, Shane Vereen; Ind—T.Y. Hilton 2, Delone Carter. TD Passes: NE—Tom Brady 3; Ind—Andrew Luck 2. FG: NE—Stephen Gostkowski; Ind—Adam Vinatieri.

NEW YORK JETS
November 17, 1985, at New York

Tampa Bay	14	7	7	0	— 28
New York Jets	17	24	14	7	— 62

TD: NYJ—Mickey Shuler 2, Johnny Hector 2, Tony Paige, Al Toon, Wesley Walker; TB—James Wilder 2, Kevin House, Calvin Magee. TD Passes: NYJ—Ken O'Brien 5; TB—Steve DeBerg 2. FG: NYJ—Pat Leahy 2.

OAKLAND RAIDERS
October 24, 2010, at Denver

Oakland	24	14	21	0	— 59
Denver	0	7	7	0	— 14

TD: Oak—Darren McFadden 4, Michael Bush, Chris Johnson, Zach Miller, Marcel Reese; Den—Knowshon Moreno 2. TD Passes: Oak—Jason Campbell 2; Den—Kyle Orton 2. FG: Oak—Sebastian Janikowski.

PITTSBURGH STEELERS
November 30, 1952, at Pittsburgh

New York Giants	0	0	7	0	— 7
Pittsburgh	14	14	7	28	— 63

TD: Pitt—Lynn Chandnois 2, Dick Hensley 2, Jack Butler, George Hays, Ray Mathews, Ed Modzelewski, Elbie Nickel; NYG—Bill Stribling. TD Passes: Pitt—Jim Finks 4, Gary Kerkorian; NYG—Tom Landry.

SAN DIEGO CHARGERS
December 22, 1963, at San Diego

Denver	7	10	3	0	— 20
San Diego	10	16	10	22	— 58

TD: SD—Paul Lowe 2, Chuck Allen, Bobby Jackson, Dave Kocourek, Keith Lincoln, Jacque MacKinnon; Den—Billy Joe, Donnie Stone. TD Passes: SD—John Hadl, Tobin Rote; Den—Don Breaux. FG: SD—George Blair 3; Den—Gene Mingo 2.

TENNESSEE TITANS
December 9, 1990, at Houston

Cleveland	0	7	7	0	— 14
Houston Oilers	14	31	7	6	— 58

TD: Hou—Lorenzo White 4, Ernest Givins, Leonard Harris, Tony Jones, Terry Kinard; Cle—Eric Metcalf 2. TD Passes: Hou—Warren Moon 2, Cody Carlson; Cle—Bernie Kosar. FG: Hou—Teddy Garcia.

ARIZONA CARDINALS
November 13, 1949, at New York

Chicago Cardinals	7	31	14	13	— 65
New York Bulldogs	7	0	6	7	— 20

TD: Chi—Red Cochran 2, Pat Harder 2, Bill Dewell, Mel Kutner, Bob Ravensburg, Vic Schwall, Charlie Trippi; NY—Joe Golding, Frank Muehlheuser, Johnny Rauch. TD Passes: Chi—Paul Christman 3, Jim Hardy 3; NY—Bobby Layne. FG: Chi—Pat Harder.

ATLANTA FALCONS
September 16, 1973, at New Orleans

Atlanta	0	24	21	17	— 62
New Orleans	0	0	7	0	— 7

TD: Atl—Ken Burrow 2, Eddie Ray 2, Wes Chesson, Tom Hayes, Art Malone, Joe Profit; NO—Bill Butler. TD Passes: Atl—Dick Shiner 3, Bob Lee; NO—Archie Manning. FG: Atl—Nick Mike-Mayer 2.

CAROLINA PANTHERS
December 8, 2002, at Carolina

Cincinnati	7	10	14	0	— 31
Carolina	9	7	21	15	— 52

TD: Car—Steve Smith 3, Dee Brown, Muhsin Muhammad, Al Wallace, Wesley Walls; Cin—Peter Warrick 2, Jon Kitna, Takeo Spikes. TD Passes: Car—Rodney Peete 3; Cin—Jon Kitna 2. FG: Cin—Neil Rackers.

CHICAGO BEARS
December 7, 1980, at Chicago

Green Bay	0	7	0	0	— 7
Chicago	0	28	13	20	— 61

TD: Chi—Walter Payton 3, Brian Baschnagel, Robin Earl, Roland Harper, Willie McClendon, Len Walterscheid, Rickey Watts; GB—James Lofton. TD Passes: Chi—Vince Evans 3; GB—Lynn Dickey.

DALLAS COWBOYS
October 12, 1980, at Dallas

San Francisco	0	7	0	7	— 14
Dallas	14	24	14	7	— 59

TD: Dall—Drew Pearson 3, Ron Springs 2, Tony Dorsett, Billy Joe DuPree, Robert Newhouse; SF—Dwight Clark 2. TD Passes: Dall—Danny White 4; SF—Steve DeBerg 2. FG: Dall—Rafael Septien.

DETROIT LIONS
November 27, 1997, at Detroit

Chicago	14	6	0	0	— 20
Detroit	3	14	17	21	— 55

TD: Det—Herman Moore, Johnnie Morton, Ron Rivers, Barry Sanders 3, Tracy Scroggins; Chi—Raymont Harris, Ricky Proehl. TD Passes: Det—Scott Mitchell 2; Chi—Erik Kramer. FG: Det—Jason Hanson 2; Chi—Jeff Jaeger 2.

GREEN BAY PACKERS
October 7, 1945, at Milwaukee

Detroit	0	7	7	7	— 21
Green Bay	0	41	9	7	— 57

TD: GB—Don Hutson 4, Charley Brock, Irv Comp, Ted Fritsch, Clyde Goodnight; Det—Chuck Fenenbock, John Greene, Bob Westfall. TD Passes: GB—Tex McKay 4, Lou Brock, Irv Comp; Det—Dave Ryan.

MINNESOTA VIKINGS
October 18, 1970, at Minnesota

Dallas	3	3	0	7	— 13
Minnesota	14	20	17	3	— 54

TD: Minn—Clint Jones 2, Ed Sharockman 2, John Beasley, Dave Osborn; Dall—Calvin Hill. TD Pass: Minn—Gary Cuozzo. FG: Minn—Fred Cox 4; Dall—Mike Clark 2.

NEW ORLEANS SAINTS
October 23, 2011, at New Orleans

Indianapolis	0	7	0	0	— 7
New Orleans	21	13	14	14	— 62

TD: NO—Marques Colston 2, Jimmy Graham 2, Darren Sproles 2, Jed Collins, Leigh Torrence; IND—Delone Carter. TD Passes: NO—Drew Brees 5. FG: NO—John Kasay 2.

NEW YORK GIANTS
November 26, 1972, at New York

Philadelphia	3	7	0	0	— 10
New York Giants	14	24	10	14	— 62

TD: NYG—Don Herrmann 2, Ron Johnson 2, Bob Tucker 2, Randy Johnson; Phil—Harold Jackson. TD Passes: NYG—Norm Snead 3, Randy Johnson 2; Phil—John Reaves. FG: NYG—Pete Gogolak 2; Phil—Tom Dempsey.

PHILADELPHIA EAGLES
November 6, 1934, at Philadelphia

Cincinnati Reds	0	0	0	0	— 0
Philadelphia	26	6	12	20	— 64

TD: Phil—Joe Carter 3, Swede Hanson 3, Marvin Ellstrom, Roger Kirkman, Ed Matesic, Ed Storm. TD Passes: Phil—Ed Matesic 2, Albert Weiner 2, Marvin Ellstrom.

ST. LOUIS RAMS
October 22, 1950, at Los Angeles

Baltimore	13	0	7	7	— 27
Los Angeles Rams	21	14	14	21	— 70

TD: LA—Bob Boyd 2, Vitamin T. Smith 2, Tom Fears, Elroy (Crazylegs) Hirsch, Dick Hoerner, Ralph Pasquariello, Dan Towler, Bob Waterfield; Balt—Chet Mutryn 2, Adrian Burk, Billy Stone. TD Passes: LA—Norm Van Brocklin 2, Bob Waterfield 2, Glenn Davis; Balt—Adrian Burk 3.

SAN FRANCISCO 49ERS
October 18, 1992, at San Francisco

Atlanta	7	3	0	7	— 17
San Francisco	21	21	14	0	— 56

TD: SF—Jerry Rice 3, Ricky Watters 3, Brent Jones, Tom Rathman; Atl—Michael Haynes, Jason Phillips. TD Passes: SF—Steve Young 3; Atl—Chris Miller, Wade Wilson. FG: Atl—Norm Johnson.

SEATTLE SEAHAWKS
December 9, 2012, at Seattle

Arizona	0	0	0	0	— 0
Seattle	10	28	13	7	— 58

TD: Sea—Marshawn Lynch 3, Zach Miller, Richard Sherman, Malcolm Smith, Leon Washington. TD Passes: Sea—Russell Wilson. FG: Sea—Steven Hauschka 3.

TAMPA BAY BUCCANEERS
December 23, 2001, at Tampa Bay

New Orleans	0	0	7	14	— 21
Tampa Bay	17	13	3	15	— 48

TD: TB—Mike Alstott, Ronde Barber, Warrick Dunn, Dave Moore, Karl Williams; NO—Joe Horn 2, Eddie Williams. TD Passes: TB—Brad Johnson 3; NO—Aaron Brooks 3. FG: TB—Martin Gramatica 4.

WASHINGTON REDSKINS
November 27, 1966, at Washington

New York Giants	0	14	14	13	— 41
Washington	13	21	14	24	— 72

TD: Wash—A.D. Whitfield 3, Brig Owens 2, Charley Taylor 2, Rickie Harris, Joe Don Looney, Bobby Mitchell; NYG—Allen Jacobs, Homer Jones, Dan Lewis, Joe Morrison, Aaron Thomas, Gary Wood. TD Passes: Wash—Sonny Jurgensen 3; NYG—Gary Wood 2, Tom Kennedy. FG: Wash—Charlie Gogolak.

RECORDS OF NFL TEAMS SINCE 1970 AFL-NFL MERGER

AFC	W	L	T	Pct.	Division Titles	Playoff Berths	Postseason Record	Super Bowl Record
Pittsburgh	412	266	2	.607	20	26	33-20	6-2
Miami	400	278	2	.590	13	22	20-20	2-3
Denver	393	281	6	.583	13	20	20-18	2-5
New England	375	305	0	.551	15	20	24-17	3-4
Baltimore***	158	129	1	.550	4	9	14-7	2-0
Oakland	357	317	6	.530	12	18	22-15	3-1
Indianapolis	342	336	2	.504	14	21	16-19	2-1
Kansas City	328	345	7	.487	6	13	3-13	0-0
Tennessee	329	349	2	.485	5	16	12-16	0-1
San Diego	322	353	5	.477	10	13	10-13	0-1
Jacksonville**	144	160	0	.474	2	6	5-6	0-0
Buffalo	311	367	2	.459	7	13	12-13	0-4
Cincinnati	309	370	1	.455	8	12	5-12	0-2
N.Y. Jets	304	374	2	.449	2	12	10-12	0-0
Cleveland+	271	358	3	.431	6	11	4-11	0-0
Houston****	79	113	0	.411	2	2	2-2	0-0

NFC	W	L	T	Pct.	Division Titles	Playoff Berths	Postseason Record	Super Bowl Record
Dallas	397	283	0	.584	17	26	32-21	5-3
San Francisco	387	289	4	.572	19	24	30-19	5-1
Minnesota	379	298	3	.560	16	25	17-25	0-3
Washington	361	317	2	.532	7	17	20-14	3-2
Green Bay	354	317	9	.527	11	18	18-16	2-1
Philadelphia	347	325	8	.516	9	20	15-20	0-2
Chicago	343	336	1	.505	10	14	10-13	1-1
St. Louis	336	339	5	.498	11	19	16-18	1-2
N.Y. Giants	337	340	3	.498	8	15	20-11	4-1
Seattle*	293	303	0	.492	8	13	12-12	1-1
Carolina**	144	160	0	.474	4	5	6-5	0-1
New Orleans	305	371	4	.451	5	10	7-9	1-0
Atlanta	304	371	5	.451	5	12	7-12	0-1
Arizona	279	395	6	.414	4	6	5-6	0-1
Detroit	275	401	4	.407	3	10	1-10	0-0
Tampa Bay*	233	362	1	.392	6	10	6-9	1-0

*Entered NFL in 1976.
**Entered NFL in 1995.
***Entered NFL in 1996.
****Entered NFL in 2002.
+Did not play, 1996-98.
Oakland totals include L.A. Raiders, 1982-1994.
Tennessee totals include Houston, 1970-1996.
Indianapolis totals include Baltimore, 1970-1983.
St. Louis totals include L.A. Rams, 1970-1994.
Arizona totals include St. Louis, 1970-1987, and Phoenix, 1988-1993.
Tie games before 1972 are not calculated in won-lost percentage.

HOME RECORDS OF NFL TEAMS SINCE 1970 AFL-NFL MERGER

AFC	W	L	T	Pct.
Pittsburgh	244	95	1	.719
Baltimore***	100	43	1	.698
Denver	235	102	4	.696
Miami	227	111	1	.671
New England	215	125	0	.632
Oakland	198	140	2	.586
Kansas City	196	140	3	.583
Jacksonville**	85	67	0	.559
Cincinnati	188	151	1	.554
Tennessee	187	152	1	.552
San Diego	184	153	2	.546
Indianapolis	184	154	2	.544
Buffalo	184	156	1	.541
Cleveland+	153	160	2	.489
N.Y. Jets	165	173	1	.488
Houston***	46	50	0	.479

NFC	W	L	T	Pct.
Minnesota	227	113	1	.667
Dallas	226	114	0	.665
Green Bay	211	123	6	.630
San Francisco	212	125	3	.628
Washington	203	134	2	.602
Chicago	202	137	1	.596
Seattle*	177	122	0	.592
Philadelphia	189	149	3	.559
St. Louis	187	151	2	.553
N.Y. Giants	184	156	1	.541
Atlanta	182	158	1	.535
Detroit	177	162	1	.522
Carolina**	79	73	0	.520
Arizona	169	167	3	.503
New Orleans	165	174	1	.487
Tampa Bay*	142	155	1	.478

*Entered NFL in 1976.
**Entered NFL in 1995.
***Entered NFL in 1996.
****Entered NFL in 2002.
+Did not play, 1996-98.
Oakland totals include L.A. Raiders, 1982-1994.
Tennessee totals include Houston, 1970-1996.
Indianapolis totals include Baltimore, 1970-1983.
St. Louis totals include L.A. Rams, 1970-1994.
Arizona totals include St. Louis, 1970-1987, and Phoenix, 1988-1993.
Tie games before 1972 are not calculated in won-lost percentage.

ROAD RECORDS OF NFL TEAMS SINCE 1970 AFL-NFL MERGER

AFC	W	L	T	Pct.
Miami	173	167	1	.509
Pittsburgh	168	171	1	.496
Oakland	159	177	4	.473
New England	160	180	0	.471
Denver	158	179	2	.469
Indianapolis	158	182	0	.465
Tennessee	142	197	1	.419
N.Y. Jets	139	201	1	.409
San Diego	138	200	3	.409
Baltimore***	58	86	0	.403
Kansas City	132	205	4	.393
Jacksonville**	59	93	0	.388
Buffalo	127	211	1	.376
Cleveland+	118	198	1	.374
Cincinnati	121	219	0	.356
Houston***	33	63	0	.344

NFC	W	L	T	Pct.
San Francisco	175	164	1	.516
Dallas	171	169	0	.503
Philadelphia	158	176	5	.473
Washington	158	183	0	.463
N.Y. Giants	153	184	2	.454
Minnesota	152	185	2	.451
St. Louis	149	188	3	.443
Carolina**	65	87	0	.428
Green Bay	143	194	3	.425
New Orleans	140	197	3	.416
Chicago	141	199	0	.415
Seattle*	116	181	0	.391
Atlanta	122	213	4	.365
Arizona	110	228	3	.326
Tampa Bay*	91	207	0	.305
Detroit	98	239	3	.292

*Entered NFL in 1976.
**Entered NFL in 1995.
***Entered NFL in 1996.
****Entered NFL in 2002.
+Did not play, 1996-98.
Oakland totals include L.A. Raiders, 1982-1994.
Tennessee totals include Houston, 1970-1996.
Indianapolis totals include Baltimore, 1970-1983.
St. Louis totals include L.A. Rams, 1970-1994.
Arizona totals include St. Louis, 1970-1987, and Phoenix, 1988-1993.
Tie games before 1972 are not calculated in won-lost percentage.

RECORDS OF TEAMS ON KICKOFF WEEKEND

AFC	W	L	T	Pct.	Longest W Strk.	Longest L Strk.	Current Streak
Denver	34	19	1	.642	4	4	W-2
Houston	7	5	0	.583	4	3	W-4
Jacksonville	11	8	0	.579	6	3	L-2
San Diego	31	23	0	.574	6	6	L-1
New England	30	24	0	.556	10	3	W-10
Pittsburgh	40	35	4	.533	8	3	L-3
Miami	25	22	1	.532	11	5	W-1
Kansas City	28	26	0	.519	7	4	W-1
Tennessee	28	26	0	.519	4	3	W-1
Indianapolis	35	34	1	.507	8	8	W-1
Baltimore	9	9	0	.500	5	4	L-1
Oakland	25	29	0	.463	5	8	L-2
N.Y. Jets	25	29	0	.463	3	5	W-3
Cleveland	27	34	0	.443	5	9	L-9
Cincinnati	20	26	0	.435	4	4	L-2
Buffalo	21	33	0	.389	6	5	L-2

NFC	W	L	T	Pct.	Longest W Strk.	Longest L Strk.	Current Streak
Dallas	36	17	1	.679	17	5	W-2
Chicago	54	35	5	.607	9	6	W-4
N.Y. Giants	49	35	5	.583	4	3	L-3
Green Bay	52	38	3	.578	5	6	L-2
Minnesota	29	23	1	.558	5	3	L-1
Detroit	45	37	2	.549	10	4	W-3
San Francisco	34	29	1	.540	5	3	W-3
Atlanta	25	23	0	.521	5	3	L-1
St. Louis	39	37	0	.513	5	6	W-1
Washington	40	38	4	.513	6	5	L-1
Philadelphia	34	45	1	.430	5	9	W-3
Arizona	38	53	2	.418	6	7	L-1
Tampa Bay	15	23	0	.395	3	5	L-1
Seattle	14	24	0	.368	3	8	W-1
New Orleans	17	30	0	.362	3	6	W-1
Carolina	6	13	0	.316	3	5	L-5

Kansas City totals include Dallas Texans, 1960-62.
Oakland totals include L.A. Raiders, 1982-1994.
San Diego totals include L.A. Chargers, 1960.
Indianapolis totals include Baltimore, 1953-1983.
Tennessee total include Houston, 1960-1996.
New England totals include Boston, 1960-1970.
St. Louis totals include Cleveland, 1937-1942 and 1944-45, and L.A. Rams, 1946-1994.
Detroit totals include Portsmouth, 1930-33.
Arizona totals include Chi. Cardinals, 1920-1959, St. Louis, 1960-1987, and Phoenix, 1988-1993.
Chicago totals include Decatur, 1920.
Washington totals include Boston Braves, 1932 and Boston Redskins, 1933-36.
NOTE: All tied games occurred prior to 1972, when calculation of ties in percentage as half-win.

RECORDS OF NFL TEAMS, 2004-2013

AFC	W	L	T	Pct.	Division Titles	Playoff Berths	Postseason Record	Super Bowl Record
New England	124	36	0	.775	9	9	12-8	1-2
Indianapolis	111	49	0	.694	7	9	8-8	1-1
Pittsburgh	105	55	0	.656	4	6	10-4	2-1
San Diego	100	60	0	.625	5	6	4-6	0-0
Baltimore	95	65	0	.594	3	6	9-5	1-0
Denver	93	67	0	.581	4	5	4-5	0-1
Cincinnati	82	77	1	.516	3	5	0-5	0-0
N.Y. Jets	79	81	0	.494	0	4	5-4	0-0
Tennessee	76	84	0	.475	1	2	0-2	0-0
Jacksonville	71	89	0	.444	0	2	1-2	0-0
Houston	70	90	0	.438	2	2	2-2	0-0
Kansas City	66	94	0	.413	1	3	0-3	0-0
Miami	66	94	0	.413	1	1	0-1	0-0
Buffalo	63	97	0	.394	0	0	0-0	0-0
Cleveland	51	109	0	.319	0	0	0-0	0-0
Oakland	49	111	0	.306	0	0	0-0	0-0

NFC	W	L	T	Pct.	Division Titles	Playoff Berths	Postseason Record	Super Bowl Record
Green Bay	96	63	1	.603	5	7	6-6	1-0
New Orleans	91	69	0	.569	3	5	6-4	1-0
Atlanta	90	70	0	.563	3	5	2-5	0-0
N.Y. Giants	90	70	0	.563	3	5	8-3	2-0
Philadelphia	89	70	1	.559	4	6	5-6	0-1
Chicago	89	71	0	.556	3	3	3-3	0-1
Seattle	88	72	0	.550	6	7	9-6	1-1
Dallas	87	73	0	.544	2	3	1-3	0-0
Carolina	80	80	0	.500	2	3	2-3	0-0
Minnesota	77	82	1	.484	2	4	2-4	0-0
San Francisco	75	84	1	.472	2	3	5-3	0-1
Arizona	71	89	0	.444	2	2	4-2	0-1
Tampa Bay	66	94	0	.413	2	2	0-2	0-0
Washington	66	94	0	.413	1	3	1-3	0-0
St. Louis	51	108	1	.322	0	1	1-1	0-0
Detroit	50	110	0	.313	0	1	0-1	0-0

HOME RECORDS, 2004-2013

AFC	W - L - T	Pct.
New England	68-12-0	.850
Baltimore	62-18-0	.775
Indianapolis	62-18-0	.775
Pittsburgh	59-21-0	.738
San Diego	56-24-0	.700
Denver	51-29-0	.638
Cincinnati	47-32-1	.594
N.Y. Jets	46-34-0	.575
Houston	41-39-0	.513
Tennessee	41-39-0	.513
Jacksonville	40-40-0	.500
Buffalo	38-42-0	.475
Kansas City	37-43-0	.463
Miami	36-44-0	.450
Cleveland	33-47-0	.413
Oakland	27-53-0	.338

NFC	W - L - T	Pct.
Seattle	55-25-0	.688
Green Bay	53-26-1	.669
Atlanta	53-27-0	.663
Chicago	50-30-0	.625
Minnesota	50-30-0	.625
New Orleans	48-32-0	.600
Arizona	47-33-0	.588
Dallas	47-33-0	.588
N.Y. Giants	46-34-0	.575
San Francisco	45-34-1	.569
Philadelphia	44-36-0	.550
Carolina	42-38-0	.525
Tampa Bay	39-41-0	.488
Washington	35-45-0	.438
Detroit	30-50-0	.375
St. Louis	30-50-0	.375

ROAD RECORDS, 2004-2013

AFC	W-L-T	Pct.
New England	56-24-0	.700
Indianapolis	49-31-0	.613
Pittsburgh	46-34-0	.575
San Diego	44-36-0	.550
Denver	42-38-0	.525
Cincinnati	35-45-0	.438
Tennessee	35-45-0	.438
Baltimore	33-47-0	.413
N.Y. Jets	33-47-0	.413
Jacksonville	31-49-0	.388
Miami	30-50-0	.375
Houston	29-51-0	.363
Kansas City	29-51-0	.363
Buffalo	25-55-0	.313
Oakland	22-58-0	.275
Cleveland	18-62-0	.225

NFC	W-L-T	Pct.
Philadelphia	45-34-1	.569
N.Y. Giants	44-36-0	.550
Green Bay	43-37-0	.538
New Orleans	43-37-0	.538
Dallas	40-40-0	.500
Chicago	39-41-0	.488
Carolina	38-42-0	.475
Atlanta	37-43-0	.463
Seattle	33-47-0	.413
Washington	31-49-0	.388
San Francisco	30-50-0	.375
Minnesota	27-52-1	.344
Tampa Bay	27-53-0	.338
Arizona	24-56-0	.300
St. Louis	21-58-1	.269
Detroit	20-60-0	.250

RECORDS BY MONTHS, 2004-2013

AFC	Sept. W-L-T	Oct. W-L-T	Nov. W-L-T	Dec. W-L-T	Total W-L-T	Pct.
New England	23-8-0	33-9-0	26-12-0	42-7-0	124-36-0	.775
Indianapolis	22-10-0	25-12-0	30-12-0	34-15-0	111-49-0	.694
Pittsburgh	18-15-0	27-11-0	26-15-0	34-14-0	105-55-0	.656
San Diego	17-16-0	21-19-0	23-15-0	39-10-0	100-60-0	.625
Baltimore	21-11-0	19-18-0	28-16-0	27-20-0	95-65-0	.594
Denver	22-12-0	22-17-0	24-14-0	25-24-0	93-67-0	.581
Cincinnati	18-15-0	17-24-0	20-17-1	27-21-0	82-77-1	.516
N.Y. Jets	19-14-0	17-23-0	19-19-0	24-25-0	79-81-0	.494
Tennessee	16-17-0	18-22-0	19-19-0	23-26-0	76-84-0	.475
Jacksonville	15-18-0	16-24-0	20-17-0	20-30-0	71-89-0	.444
Houston	14-18-0	20-19-0	14-25-0	22-28-0	70-90-0	.438
Kansas City	13-20-0	22-16-0	12-28-0	19-30-0	66-94-0	.413
Miami	10-23-0	12-26-0	20-20-0	24-25-0	66-94-0	.413
Buffalo	15-18-0	15-24-0	15-24-0	19-30-0	63-97-0	.394
Cleveland	9-25-0	16-22-0	12-27-0	14-35-0	51-109-0	.319
Oakland	11-22-0	16-23-0	11-29-0	11-37-0	49-111-0	.306

December totals include January.

NFC	Sept. W-L-T	Oct. W-L-T	Nov. W-L-T	Dec. W-L-T	Total W-L-T	Pct.
Green Bay	18-15-0	26-13-0	21-19-1	31-16-0	96-63-1	.603
New Orleans	19-14-0	22-18-0	25-14-0	25-23-0	91-69-0	.569
Atlanta	20-14-0	23-13-0	24-18-0	23-25-0	90-70-0	.563
N.Y. Giants	18-15-0	32-8-0	16-22-0	24-25-0	90-70-0	.563
Philadelphia	19-15-0	20-17-0	19-20-1	31-18-0	89-70-1	.559
Chicago	19-14-0	22-15-0	24-17-0	24-25-0	89-71-0	.556
Seattle	22-11-0	16-22-0	22-18-0	28-21-0	88-72-0	.550
Dallas	21-11-0	17-23-0	29-12-0	20-27-0	87-73-0	.544
Carolina	11-21-0	19-21-0	20-19-0	30-19-0	80-80-0	.500
Minnesota	15-19-0	17-21-0	22-16-1	23-26-0	77-82-1	.484
San Francisco	15-19-0	17-22-0	16-21-1	27-22-0	75-84-1	.472
Arizona	15-19-0	13-25-0	18-21-0	25-24-0	71-89-0	.444
Tampa Bay	14-20-0	16-22-0	21-18-0	15-34-0	66-94-0	.413
Washington	16-16-0	16-25-0	12-26-0	22-27-0	66-94-0	.413
St. Louis	9-25-0	16-25-0	11-24-1	15-34-0	51-108-1	.322
Detroit	14-18-0	16-23-0	8-33-0	12-36-0	50-110-0	.313

December totals include January.

TAKEAWAYS/GIVEAWAYS, 2004-2013

AFC	Takeaways Int.	Fum.	Total	Giveaways Int.	Fum.	Total	Net.Diff.
New England	188	124	312	111	88	199	+113
Indianapolis	150	112	262	134	76	210	+52
San Diego	166	101	267	129	97	226	+41
Baltimore	188	103	291	141	113	254	+37
Cincinnati	180	124	304	167	102	269	+35
Pittsburgh	149	108	257	145	108	253	+4
Jacksonville	156	86	242	136	103	239	+3
Kansas City	148	111	259	146	111	257	+2
Tennessee	166	101	267	154	115	269	-2
Buffalo	176	106	282	173	122	295	-13
N.Y. Jets	157	110	267	178	104	282	-15
Denver	138	107	245	137	128	265	-20
Houston	129	98	227	154	104	258	-31
Miami	139	95	234	169	107	276	-42
Cleveland	157	96	253	190	111	301	-48
Oakland	124	97	221	184	126	310	-89

NFC	Takeaways Int.	Fum.	Total	Giveaways Int.	Fum.	Total	Net.Diff.
Carolina	173	127	300	160	99	259	+41
Atlanta	159	114	273	140	93	233	+40
Seattle	173	115	288	150	101	251	+37
Chicago	200	138	338	185	118	303	+35
Green Bay	196	84	280	148	97	245	+35
N.Y. Giants	167	131	298	177	109	286	+12
Tampa Bay	173	107	280	159	115	274	+6
Philadelphia	169	103	272	146	129	275	-3
San Francisco	151	111	262	144	123	267	-5
Minnesota	139	125	264	160	120	280	-16
Dallas	141	109	250	171	103	274	-24
New Orleans	133	108	241	168	101	269	-28
Washington	142	88	230	141	119	260	-30
Arizona	167	122	289	198	132	330	-41
St. Louis	131	110	241	172	110	282	-41
Detroit	136	129	265	194	116	310	-45

BEST TAKEAWAY/GIVEAWAY DIFFERENTIAL, SEASON
+43 Washington, 1983
+28 New England, 2010
   San Francisco, 2011
+26 Kansas City, 1990

HIGH AND LOW SINGLE-GAME YARDAGE TOTALS, 2004-2013
Most Total Yards, Game
653 Houston vs. Jacksonville, Nov. 18, 2012 (ot)
625 New Orleans vs. Dallas, Nov. 10, 2013
623 Detroit vs. Dallas, Oct. 27, 2013
622 New England at Miami, Sept. 12, 2011
621 San Francisco vs. Buffalo, Oct. 7, 2012
Fewest Total Yards, Game
26 Cleveland at Buffalo, Dec. 12, 2004
67 Kansas City at San Diego, Dec. 12, 2010
72 Cincinnati at New York Jets, Jan. 3, 2010
77 Oakland vs. Atlanta, Nov. 2, 2008
86 Tampa Bay vs. New York Giants, Sept. 27, 2009
Most Yards Rushing, Game
378 Minnesota vs. San Diego, Nov. 4, 2007
375 Jacksonville vs. Indianapolis, Dec. 10, 2006
352 Kansas City vs. Indianapolis, Dec. 23, 2012
351 Cleveland at Kansas City, Dec. 20, 2009
332 Tennessee at Kansas City, Oct. 19, 2008
Fewest Yards Rushing, Game
-18 Detroit at Arizona, Nov. 11, 2007
-3 Detroit vs. Minnesota, Dec. 10, 2006
1 Dallas at Washington, Dec. 30, 2007
2 Miami at Tampa Bay, Nov. 11, 2013
4 Seattle at Minnesota, Nov. 22, 2009

Most Yards Passing, Game
516 New England at Miami, Sept. 12, 2011
510 New York Giants vs. Tampa Bay, Sept. 16, 2012
504 New Orleans vs. Cincinnati, Nov. 19, 2006
504 Houston vs. Jacksonville, Nov. 18, 2012 (ot)
502 Detroit at Green Bay, Jan. 1, 2012
Fewest Yards Passing, Game
-7 Tennessee at New England, Oct. 18, 2009
-5 Houston at Oakland, Dec. 3, 2006
-3 Cleveland at Buffalo, Dec. 12, 2004
0 Cincinnati at New York Jets, Jan. 3, 2010
6 Houston vs. Indianapolis, Oct. 23, 2005

NFL INDIVIDUAL LEADERS, 2004-2013

Points		Passing Yards	
David Akers	1,225	Drew Brees	45,468
Jay Feely	1,095	Peyton Manning	40,079
Adam Vinatieri	1,089	Tom Brady	38,916
Sebastian Janikowski	1,044	Eli Manning	35,345
Rob Bironas	1,032	Ben Roethlisberger	34,105

Touchdowns		TD Passes	
LaDainian Tomlinson	120	Drew Brees	334
Adrian Peterson	91	Peyton Manning	324
Larry Fitzgerald	87	Tom Brady	290
Antonio Gates	85	Eli Manning	229
Maurice Jones-Drew	81	Philip Rivers	221

Field Goals		Receptions	
David Akers	274	Reggie Wayne	862
Phil Dawson	253	Andre Johnson	861
Sebastian Janikowski	252	Tony Gonzalez	857
Jay Feely	249	Larry Fitzgerald	846
Rob Bironas	239	Jason Witten	844

Rushes		Reception Yards	
Steven Jackson	2,553	Andre Johnson	11,685
Frank Gore	2,187	Reggie Wayne	11,667
Thomas Jones	2,179	Larry Fitzgerald	11,367
LaDainian Tomlinson	2,150	Steve Smith	10,061
Willis McGahee	2,095	Anquan Boldin	9,967

Rushing Yards		Receiving TDs	
Steven Jackson	10,681	Larry Fitzgerald	87
Adrian Peterson	10,115	Antonio Gates	85
Frank Gore	9,967	Randy Moss	79
LaDainian Tomlinson	9,120	Terrell Owens	72
Thomas Jones	8,700	Reggie Wayne	69

Rushing TDs		Interceptions	
LaDainian Tomlinson	108	Ed Reed	52
Adrian Peterson	86	Asante Samuel	49
Maurice Jones-Drew	68	DeAngelo Hall	43
Michael Turner	66	Charles Woodson	41
Willis McGahee	65	Champ Bailey	34

Pass Attempts		Sacks	
Drew Brees	5,890	Jared Allen	128.5
Peyton Manning	5,069	DeMarcus Ware	117.0
Tom Brady	5,042	Robert Mathis	107.5
Eli Manning	5,008	John Abraham	100.0
Carson Palmer	4,682	Julius Peppers	99.5

Completions	
Drew Brees	3,941
Peyton Manning	3,404
Tom Brady	3,223
Carson Palmer	2,930
Eli Manning	2,929

NFL GAMES IN WHICH A TEAM HAS SCORED 60 OR MORE POINTS

(Home team in capitals)

Regular Season

WASHINGTON 72, New York Giants 41	November 27, 1966
LOS ANGELES RAMS 70, Baltimore 27	October 22, 1950
Chicago Cardinals 65, NEW YORK BULLDOGS 20	November 13, 1949
LOS ANGELES RAMS 65, Detroit 24	October 29, 1950
PHILADELPHIA 64, Cincinnati 0	November 6, 1934
CHICAGO CARDINALS 63, New York Giants 35	October 17, 1948
PITTSBURGH 63, New York Giants 7	November 30, 1952
AKRON 62, Oorang 0	October 29, 1922
CLEVELAND 62, New York Giants 14	December 6, 1953
CLEVELAND 62, Washington 3	November 7, 1954
NEW YORK GIANTS 62, Philadelphia 10	November 26, 1972
Atlanta 62, NEW ORLEANS 7	September 16, 1973
NEW YORK JETS 62, Tampa Bay 28	November 17, 1985
NEW ORLEANS 62, Indianapolis 7	October 23, 2011
CHICAGO 61, San Francisco 20	December 12, 1965
Cincinnati 61, HOUSTON 17	December 17, 1972
CHICAGO 61, Green Bay 7	December 7, 1980
CINCINNATI 61, Houston 7	December 17, 1989
ROCK ISLAND 60, Evansville 0	October 15, 1922
CHICAGO CARDINALS 60, Rochester 0	October 7, 1923

Postseason

Chicago Bears 73, WASHINGTON 0	December 8, 1940
JACKSONVILLE 62, Miami 7	January 15, 2000

YOUNGEST AND OLDEST PLAYERS IN NFL IN 2013

10 Youngest Players

	Birthdate	Games	Starts	Position
Marquess Wilson, Chicago	9/14/1992	10	1	WR
Damontre Moore, N.Y. Giants	9/11/1992	15	0	DE
DeAndre Hopkins, Houston	6/6/1992	16	16	WR
Tyrann Mathieu, Arizona	5/13/1992	13	11	FS
Keenan Allen, San Diego	4/27/1992	15	14	WR
Kenny Stills, New Orleans	4/22/1992	16	10	WR
Robert Woods, Buffalo	4/10/1992	14	14	WR
Johnathan Hankins, N.Y. Giants	3/29/1992	11	0	DT
Jelani Jenkins, Miami	3/13/1992	16	0	LB
Le'Veon Bell, Pittsburgh	2/18/1992	13	13	RB

10 Oldest Players

	Birthdate	Games	Starts	Position
Adam Vinatieri, Indianapolis	12/28/1972	15	0	K
Sav Rocca, Washington	11/20/1973	16	0	P
David Akers, Detroit	12/9/1974	16	0	K
Phil Dawson, San Francisco	1/23/1975	16	0	K
Patrick Mannelly, Chicago	4/18/1975	14	0	LS
London Fletcher, Washington	5/19/1975	16	16	LB
Matt Bryant, Atlanta	5/29/1975	16	0	K
Matt Hasselbeck, Indianapolis	9/25/1975	3	0	QB
Brian Moorman, Buffalo	2/5/1976	11	0	P
Tony Gonzalez, Atlanta	2/27/1976	16	16	TE

YOUNGEST AND OLDEST REGULAR STARTERS BY POSITION IN 2013

Minimum: 8 Games Started

	Youngest		Oldest	
QB	10/10/90	Geno Smith, NYJ	3/24/76	Peyton Manning, Den.
RB	2/18/92	Le'Veon Bell, Pit.	4/25/83	DeAngelo Williams, Car.
WR	6/6/92	DeAndre Hopkins, Hou.	5/12/79	Steve Smith, Car.
TE	9/8/90	Tyler Eifert, Cin.	2/27/76	Tony Gonzalez, Atl
T	9/30/91	David Bakhtiari, G.B.	9/23/79	Bryant McKinnie, Bal.-Mia.
G	9/14/91	Chance Warmack, Ten.	9/15/80	David Diehl, NYG
C	3/22/91	Brian Schwenke, Ten.	3/23/77	Brad Meester, Jac.
DE	12/13/90	Fletcher Cox, Phi.	9/19/78	Brett Keisel, Pit.
DT	11/29/91	Akeem Spence, T.B.	10/8/79	Ryan Pickett, G.B.
LB	9/25/91	Alec Ogletree, StL	5/19/75	London Fletcher, Was.
CB	9/14/91	Dee Milliner, NYJ	9/4/78	Terence Newman, Cin.
S	5/13/92	Tyrann Mathieu, Ari.	10/7/76	Charles Woodson, Oak.

OLDEST INDIVIDUAL SINGLE-SEASON OR SINGLE-GAME RECORDS IN NFL RECORD & FACT BOOK

Most Points, Game—40, Ernie Nevers, Chi. Cardinals vs. Chi. Bears, Nov. 28, 1929 (6-td, 4-pat)

Most Touchdowns Rushing, Game—6, Ernie Nevers, Chi. Cardinals vs. Chi. Bears, Nov. 28, 1929

Highest Rushing Average Gain, Season (Qualifiers)—8.44, Beattie Feathers, Chi. Bears, 1934 (119-1,004)

Highest Punting Average, Season (Qualifiers)—51.40, Sammy Baugh, Washington, 1940 (35-1,799)

Highest Punting Average, Rookie, Season (Qualifiers)—45.92, Frank Sinkwich, Detroit, 1943 (12-551)

Highest Punting Average, Game (minimum: 4 punts)—61.75, Bob Cifers, Detroit vs. Chi. Bears, Nov. 24, 1946 (4-247)

Highest Average Gain, Pass Receptions, Season (minimum: 24 receptions)—32.58, Don Currivan, Boston, 1947 (24-782)

Highest Average Gain, Passing, Game (minimum: 20 passes)—18.58, Sammy Baugh, Washington vs. Boston, Oct. 31, 1948 (24-446)

Most Touchdowns, Fumble Recoveries, Game—2, Fred (Dippy) Evans, Chi. Bears vs. Washington, Nov. 28, 1948

Most Yards Gained, Intercepted Passes, Rookie, Season—301, Don Doll, Detroit, 1949

Most Passes Had Intercepted, Game—8, Jim Hardy, Chi. Cardinals vs. Philadelphia, Sept. 24, 1950

Highest Kickoff Return Average, Game (minimum: 3 returns)—73.50, Wally Triplett, Detroit vs. Los Angeles, Oct. 29, 1950 (4-294)

Highest Punt Return Average, Season (Qualifiers)—23.00, Herb Rich, Baltimore, 1950 (12-276)

Highest Punt Return Average, Rookie, Season (Qualifiers)—23.00, Herb Rich, Baltimore, 1950 (12-276)

Most Yards Passing, Game—554, Norm Van Brocklin, Los Angeles vs. New York Yanks, Sept. 28, 1951

Most Touchdowns, Punt Returns, Rookie, Season—4, Jack Christiansen, Detroit, 1951

Most Interceptions By, Season—14, Dick (Night Train) Lane, Los Angeles, 1952

Most Interceptions By, Rookie, Season—14, Dick (Night Train) Lane, Los Angeles, 1952

Highest Average Gain, Passing, Season (Qualifiers)—11.17, Tommy O'Connell, Cleveland, 1957 (110-1,229)

Most Yards Gained, Pass Receptions, Rookie, Season—1,473, Bill Groman, Houston, 1960

NFL INDIVIDUAL LEADERS OVER RECENT SEASONS

Last 2 Seasons		Last 3 Seasons		Last 4 Seasons	
Points					
311	Stephen Gostkowski	454	Stephen Gostkowski	539	David Akers
283	Matt Prater	396	David Akers	510	Stephen Gostkowski
272	Justin Tucker	394	Mason Crosby	508	Matt Bryant
262	Blair Walsh	390	Dan Bailey	506	Mason Crosby
261	Steven Hauschka	380	Matt Bryant	489	Sebastian Janikowski
Touchdowns					
26	Marshawn Lynch	39	Marshawn Lynch	50	Adrian Peterson
25	Dez Bryant	37	Adrian Peterson	49	Arian Foster
25	Jamaal Charles	36	Jimmy Graham	45	Calvin Johnson
25	Jimmy Graham	36	LeSean McCoy	45	Marshawn Lynch
24	Two tied	34	Dez Bryant	45	LeSean McCoy
Field Goals					
68	Justin Tucker	95	Stephen Gostkowski	124	David Akers
67	Stephen Gostkowski	92	David Akers	116	Sebastian Janikowski
61	Phil Dawson	89	Dan Bailey	114	Dan Carpenter
61	Adam Vinatieri	85	Phil Dawson	112	Matt Bryant
61	Blair Walsh	84	Three tied	110	Adam Vinatieri
Rushes					
627	Adrian Peterson	901	Marshawn Lynch	1,133	Chris Johnson
616	Marshawn Lynch	835	Adrian Peterson	1,118	Adrian Peterson
611	Alfred Morris	817	Chris Johnson	1,103	Marshawn Lynch
555	Chris Johnson	816	Frank Gore	1,077	Arian Foster
544	Jamaal Charles	787	LeSean McCoy	1,069	Ray Rice
Rushing Yards					
3,363	Adrian Peterson	4,333	Adrian Peterson	5,631	Adrian Peterson
2,888	Alfred Morris	4,051	Marshawn Lynch	4,836	LeSean McCoy
2,847	Marshawn Lynch	3,756	LeSean McCoy	4,806	Arian Foster
2,796	Jamaal Charles	3,553	Frank Gore	4,788	Marshawn Lynch
2,447	LeSean McCoy	3,430	Matt Forté	4,731	Chris Johnson
Rushing Touchdowns					
23	Marshawn Lynch	35	Marshawn Lynch	46	Adrian Peterson
22	Adrian Peterson	34	Adrian Peterson	42	Arian Foster
20	Alfred Morris	28	LeSean McCoy	41	Marshawn Lynch
19	Stevan Ridley	28	Cam Newton	37	BenJarvus Green-Ellis
17	Two tied	26	Arian Foster	35	LeSean McCoy
Passes					
1,361	Matthew Stafford	2,024	Matthew Stafford	2,635	Drew Brees
1,320	Drew Brees	1,977	Drew Brees	2,403	Matt Ryan
1,266	Matt Ryan	1,876	Tom Brady	2,368	Tom Brady
1,265	Tom Brady	1,832	Matt Ryan	2,215	Eli Manning
1,242	Peyton Manning	1,705	Tony Romo	2,194	Philip Rivers
Completions					
868	Drew Brees	1,336	Drew Brees	1,784	Drew Brees
861	Matt Ryan	1,227	Matthew Stafford	1,565	Matt Ryan
850	Peyton Manning	1,208	Matt Ryan	1,506	Tom Brady
806	Matthew Stafford	1,182	Tom Brady	1,439	Philip Rivers
781	Tom Brady	1,113	Tony Romo	1,336	Eli Manning
Passing Yards					
10,339	Drew Brees	15,815	Drew Brees	20,435	Drew Brees
10,136	Peyton Manning	14,655	Matthew Stafford	18,305	Tom Brady
9,617	Matthew Stafford	14,405	Tom Brady	17,418	Philip Rivers
9,234	Matt Ryan	13,411	Matt Ryan	17,116	Matt Ryan
9,170	Tom Brady	12,915	Tony Romo	16,701	Eli Manning

Last 2 Seasons	Last 3 Seasons	Last 4 Seasons

Touchdown Passes

92	Peyton Manning	128	Drew Brees	161	Drew Brees
82	Drew Brees	101	Aaron Rodgers	134	Tom Brady
60	Andy Dalton	98	Tom Brady	129	Aaron Rodgers
59	Tom Brady	92	Peyton Manning	125	Peyton Manning
59	Tony Romo	90	Two tied	115	Two tied

Receptions

221	Andre Johnson	313	Wes Welker	399	Wes Welker
218	Brandon Marshall	302	Calvin Johnson	385	Brandon Marshall
206	Calvin Johnson	299	Brandon Marshall	379	Calvin Johnson
195	A.J. Green	270	Jimmy Graham	370	Roddy White
191	Wes Welker	262	Jason Witten	356	Jason Witten

Receiving Yards

3,456	Calvin Johnson	5,137	Calvin Johnson	6,257	Calvin Johnson
3,005	Andre Johnson	4,017	Brandon Marshall	5,031	Brandon Marshall
2,864	Demaryius Thomas	3,833	A.J. Green	4,747	Roddy White
2,803	Brandon Marshall	3,714	Vincent Jackson	4,713	Andre Johnson
2,776	A.J. Green	3,701	Wes Welker	4,549	Wes Welker

Receiving Touchdowns

25	Dez Bryant	36	Jimmy Graham	45	Calvin Johnson
25	Jimmy Graham	34	Dez Bryant	42	Rob Gronkowski
24	Eric Decker	33	Calvin Johnson	41	Jimmy Graham
24	Demaryius Thomas	32	Eric Decker	40	Dez Bryant
23	Brandon Marshall	32	Rob Gronkowski	33	Eric Decker

Interceptions

16	Richard Sherman	20	Richard Sherman	20	Richard Sherman
13	Tim Jennings	15	Tim Jennings	18	Ed Reed
10	Patrick Peterson	12	Jairus Byrd	17	DeAngelo Hall
9	Jairus Byrd	12	Patrick Peterson	16	Tim Jennings
8	Five tied	12	Eric Weddle	16	Asante Samuel

Sacks

31.0	J.J. Watt	45.5	Jared Allen	56.5	Jared Allen
29.5	Robert Quinn	42.0	Aldon Smith	52.5	DeMarcus Ware
28.0	Aldon Smith	37.0	Robert Mathis	48.0	Robert Mathis
27.5	Robert Mathis	37.0	DeMarcus Ware	46.5	Tamba Hali
26.0	Greg Hardy	36.5	J.J. Watt	46.0	Cameron Wake

NFL TEAM LEADERS OVER RECENT SEASONS

Highest Won-Lost Percentage

.813	Denver	.771	New England	.797	New England
.750	New England	.760	San Francisco	.695	Green Bay
.750	Seattle	.719	Green Bay	.664	San Francisco
.734	San Francisco	.708	Denver	.656	Baltimore
.688	Indianapolis	.646	Two tied	.656	New Orleans

Most Points

1,087	Denver	1,514	New England	2,032	New England
1,001	New England	1,422	New Orleans	1,806	New Orleans
875	New Orleans	1,410	Green Bay	1,798	Green Bay
850	Green Bay	1,396	Denver	1,740	Denver
829	Seattle	1,241	Detroit	1,603	Detroit

Most Total Yards

13,683	Denver	20,439	New Orleans	26,399	New Orleans
12,998	New England	19,846	New England	25,666	New England
12,965	New Orleans	19,151	Detroit	24,957	Philadelphia
12,814	Detroit	18,749	Denver	24,574	Detroit
12,341	Philadelphia	18,727	Philadelphia	24,367	Green Bay

INSIDE THE NUMBERS

Last 2 Seasons	Last 3 Seasons	Last 4 Seasons

Most Rushing Yards

Last 2 Seasons	Last 3 Seasons	Last 4 Seasons
4,873 Washington	7,033 Minnesota	9,040 Philadelphia
4,767 Seattle	6,736 San Francisco	8,975 Minnesota
4,715 Minnesota	6,716 Philadelphia	8,971 Kansas City
4,692 San Francisco	6,523 Seattle	8,393 San Francisco
4,524 Buffalo	6,522 Carolina	8,368 Carolina

Most Passing Yards

Last 2 Seasons	Last 3 Seasons	Last 4 Seasons
9,978 Denver	15,262 New Orleans	19,703 New Orleans
9,915 New Orleans	14,223 Detroit	18,033 Detroit
9,409 Detroit	13,833 New England	17,680 New England
8,752 Atlanta	13,241 Green Bay	17,365 Green Bay
8,749 New England	12,944 Atlanta	16,926 Dallas

Fewest Turnovers

Last 2 Seasons	Last 3 Seasons	Last 4 Seasons
34 San Francisco	44 San Francisco	63 New England
36 New England	53 New England	67 San Francisco
37 Seattle	55 Green Bay	77 Green Bay
41 Three tied	60 Seattle	84 Atlanta
	62 New Orleans	86 Houston

Fewest Points Allowed

Last 2 Seasons	Last 3 Seasons	Last 4 Seasons
476 Seattle	774 San Francisco	1,120 San Francisco
545 San Francisco	791 Seattle	1,143 Pittsburgh
604 Carolina	911 Pittsburgh	1,198 Seattle
625 Cincinnati	948 Cincinnati	1,232 Baltimore
652 Miami	962 Baltimore	1,298 Miami

Fewest Total Yards Allowed

Last 2 Seasons	Last 3 Seasons	Last 4 Seasons
9,277 Seattle	14,156 Pittsburgh	18,585 Pittsburgh
9,781 San Francisco	14,592 Seattle	19,956 San Francisco
9,808 Pittsburgh	14,712 San Francisco	20,190 N.Y. Jets
10,003 Cincinnati	14,824 Houston	20,375 Cincinnati
10,149 Carolina	15,063 Cincinnati	20,489 Seattle

Fewest Rushing Yards Allowed

Last 2 Seasons	Last 3 Seasons	Last 4 Seasons
3,042 San Francisco	4,278 San Francisco	5,825 San Francisco
3,082 Tampa Bay	4,896 Pittsburgh	5,900 Pittsburgh
3,084 Denver	4,934 Cincinnati	6,637 Baltimore
3,152 Carolina	5,054 Houston	6,722 San Diego
3,259 Cincinnati	5,072 Seattle	6,777 Cincinnati

Fewest Passing Yards Allowed

Last 2 Seasons	Last 3 Seasons	Last 4 Seasons
6,547 Seattle	9,891 Pittsburgh	13,635 Pittsburgh
6,910 Pittsburgh	10,297 Seattle	14,263 N.Y. Jets
7,191 Houston	10,513 Houston	14,512 Buffalo
7,292 San Francisco	10,809 N.Y. Jets	14,537 Seattle
7,335 Buffalo	11,037 Cleveland	14,694 Cincinnati

Most Opponents' Turnovers

Last 2 Seasons	Last 3 Seasons	Last 4 Seasons
72 Chicago	104 New England	142 New England
70 New England	103 Chicago	138 Chicago
70 Seattle	101 Seattle	134 N.Y. Giants
64 N.Y. Giants	95 N.Y. Giants	123 Seattle
63 Arizona	93 San Francisco	115 Two tied

RETIRED UNIFORM NUMBERS IN NFL

AFC

Team	Player	No.
Baltimore	None	
Buffalo	Jim Kelly	12
Cincinnati	Bob Johnson	54
Cleveland	Otto Graham	14
	Jim Brown	32
	Ernie Davis	45
	Don Fleming	46
	Lou Groza	76
Denver	John Elway	7
	Floyd Little	44
Houston	None	
Indianapolis	Peyton Manning	18
	Johnny Unitas	19
	Buddy Young	22
	Lenny Moore	24
	Art Donovan	70
	Jim Parker	77
	Raymond Berry	82
	Gino Marchetti	89
Jacksonville	None	
Kansas City	Jan Stenerud	3
	Len Dawson	16
	Emmitt Thomas	18
	Abner Haynes	28
	Stone Johnson	33
	Mack Lee Hill	36
	Derrick Thomas	58
	Willie Lanier	63
	Bobby Bell	78
	Buck Buchanan	86
Miami	Bob Griese	12
	Dan Marino	13
	Larry Csonka	39
New England	Gino Cappelletti	20
	Mike Haynes	40
	Steve Nelson	57
	John Hannah	73
	Bruce Armstrong	78
	Jim Lee Hunt	79
	Bob Dee	89
New York Jets	Joe Namath	12
	Don Maynard	13
	Curtis Martin	28
	Joe Klecko	73
	Dennis Byrd	90
Oakland	None	
Pittsburgh	Ernie Stautner	70
San Diego	Dan Fouts	14
	Lance Alworth	19
	Junior Seau	55
Tennessee	Warren Moon	1
	Earl Campbell	34
	Jim Norton	43
	Mike Munchak	63
	Elvin Bethea	65
	Bruce Matthews	74

NFC

Team	Player	No.
Arizona	Larry Wilson	8
	Pat Tillman	40
	Stan Mauldin	77
	J.V. Cain	88
	Marshall Goldberg	99
Atlanta	Steve Bartkowski	10
	William Andrews	31
	Jeff Van Note	57
	Tommy Nobis	60
Carolina	Sam Mills	51
Chicago	Bronko Nagurski	3
	George McAfee	5
	George Halas	7
	Willie Galimore	28
	Walter Payton	34
	Gale Sayers	40
	Brian Piccolo	41
	Sid Luckman	42
	Dick Butkus	51
	Bill Hewitt	56
	Bill George	61
	Bulldog Turner	66
	Red Grange	77
	Mike Ditka	89
Dallas	None	
Detroit	Dutch Clark	7
	Bobby Layne	22
	Doak Walker	37
	Joe Schmidt	56
	Chuck Hughes	85
Green Bay	Tony Canadeo	3
	Don Hutson	14
	Bart Starr	15
	Ray Nitschke	66
	Reggie White	92
Minnesota	Fran Tarkenton	10
	Mick Tingelhoff	53
	Jim Marshall	70
	Korey Stringer	77
	Cris Carter	80
	Alan Page	88
New Orleans	Jim Taylor	31
	Doug Atkins	81
New York Giants	Ray Flaherty	1
	Tuffy Leemans	4
	Mel Hein	7
	Phil Simms	11
	Y.A. Tittle	14
	Frank Gifford	16
	Al Blozis	32
	Joe Morrison	40
	Charlie Conerly	42
	Ken Strong	50
	Lawrence Taylor	56
Philadelphia Eagles	Donovan McNabb	5
	Steve Van Buren	15
	Brian Dawkins	20
	Tom Brookshier	40
	Pete Retzlaff	44
	Chuck Bednarik	60
	Al Wistert	70
	Reggie White	92
	Jerome Brown	99
St. Louis	Bob Waterfield	7
	Marshall Faulk	28
	Eric Dickerson	29
	Merlin Olsen	74
	Deacon Jones	75
	Jackie Slater	78
	Isaac Bruce	80
	Jack Youngblood	85
San Francisco	Steve Young	8
	John Brodie	12
	Joe Montana	16
	Joe Perry	34
	Jimmy Johnson	37
	Hugh McElhenny	39
	Ronnie Lott	42
	Charlie Krueger	70
	Leo Nomellini	73
	Bob St. Clair	79
	Jerry Rice	80
	Dwight Clark	87
Seattle	"Fans/the twelfth man"	12
	Walter Jones	71
	Steve Largent	80
	Cortez Kennedy	96
Tampa Bay	Lee Roy Selmon	6312
	Warren Sapp	99
Washington	Sammy Baugh	33

The NFL rates its passers for statistical purposes against a fixed performance standard based on statistical achievements of all qualified pro passers since 1960. The current system replaced one that rated passers in relation to their position in a total group based on various criteria. The current system, which was adopted in 1973, removes inequities that existed in the former method and, at the same time, provides a means of comparing passing performances from one season to the next.

It is important to remember that the system is used to rate passers, not quarterbacks. Statistics do not reflect leadership, play-calling, and other intangible factors that go into making a successful professional quarterback. Four categories are used as a basis for compiling a rating:

—Percentage of completions per attempt
—Average yards gained per attempt
—Percentage of touchdown passes per attempt
—Percentage of interceptions per attempt

The average standard is 1.000. The bottom is .000. To earn a 2.000 rating, a passer must perform at exceptional levels, i.e., 70 percent in completions, 10 percent in touchdowns, 1.5 percent in interceptions, and 11 yards average gain per pass attempt. The maximum a passer can receive in any category is 2.375.

For example, to gain a 2.375 in completion percentage, a passer would have to complete 77.5 percent of his passes. The NFL record is 71.23 by Drew Brees (New Orleans, 2011). To earn a 2.375 in percentage of touchdowns, a passer would have to achieve a percentage of 11.9. The record is 13.9 by Sid Luckman (Chicago, 1943). To gain 2.375 in percentage of interceptions, a passer would have to go the entire season without an interception. The 2.375 figure in average yards is 12.50, compared with the NFL record of 11.17 by Tommy O'Connell (Cleveland, 1957).

In order to make the rating more understandable, the point rating is then converted into a scale of 100, with 158.3 being the highest rating a passer can achieve. In cases where statistical performance has been superior, it is possible for a passer to sur-

pass a 100 rating. For example, take Aaron Rodgers' record-setting season in 2011 when he completed 343 of 502 passes for 4,643 yards, 45 touchdowns, and 6 interceptions. The four calculations would be:

—Percentage of Completions—343 of 502 is 68.33 percent. Subtract 30 from the completion percentage (38.33) and multiply the result by 0.05. The result is a point rating of 1.916.

Note: If the result is less than zero (Comp. Pct. less than 30.0), award zero points. If the results are greater than 2.375 (Comp. Pct. greater than 77.5), award 2.375.

—Average Yards Gained Per Attempt—4,643 yards divided by 502 attempts is 9.25. Subtract three yards from yards-per-attempt (6.25) and multiply the result by 0.25. The result is 1.562.

Note: If the result is less than zero (yards per attempt less than 3.0), award zero points. If the result is greater than 2.375 (yards per attempt greater than 12.5), award 2.375 points.

—Percentage of Touchdown Passes—45 touchdowns in 502 attempts is 8.96 percent. Multiply the touchdown percentage by 0.2. The result is 1.793.

Note: If the result is greater than 2.375 (touchdown percentage greater than 11.875), award 2.375.

—Percentage of Interceptions—Six interceptions in 502 attempts is 1.20 percent. Multiply the interception percentage by 0.25 (0.299) and subtract the number from 2.375. The result is 2.076.

Note: If the result is less than zero (interception percentage greater than 9.5), award zero points.

The sum of the four steps is (1.916 + 1.562 + 1.793 + 2.076) 7.348. The sum is then divided by six (1.225) and multiplied by 100. In this case, the result is 122.5. This same formula can be used to determine a passer rating for any player who attempts at least one pass.

The following is a list of the Top 25 single-season passer ratings among qualifying players:

TOP 25 NFL SINGLE-SEASON PASSER RATINGS (QUALIFYING PLAYERS)

Player, Team	Season	Rating	Att.	Comp.	Pct.	Yds.	Yds. Avg.	TD	TD Pct.	Int.	Int. Pct.
Aaron Rodgers, Green Bay	2011	*122.5	502	343	68.3	4,643	9.25	45	9.0	6	1.2
Peyton Manning, Indianapolis	2004	121.1	497	336	67.6	4,557	9.17	49	9.9	10	2.0
Nick Foles, Philadelphia	2013	119.2	317	203	64.0	2,891	9.12	27	8.5	2	0.6
Tom Brady, New England	2007	117.2	578	398	68.9	4,806	8.31	50	8.7	8	1.4
Peyton Manning, Denver	2013	115.1	659	450	68.3	*5,477	8.31	*55	8.3	10	1.5
Steve Young, San Francisco	1994	112.8	461	324	70.2	3,969	8.61	35	7.6	10	2.2
Joe Montana, San Francisco	1989	112.4	386	271	70.2	3,521	9.12	26	6.7	8	2.1
Tom Brady, New England	2010	111.0	492	324	65.9	3,900	7.93	36	7.3	4	0.8
Daunte Culpepper, Minnesota	2004	110.9	548	379	69.2	4,717	8.61	39	7.1	11	2.0
Drew Brees, New Orleans	2011	110.6	657	468	*71.2	5,476	8.33	46	7.0	14	2.1
Milt Plum, Cleveland	1960	110.4	250	151	60.4	2,297	9.19	21	8.4	5	2.0
Sammy Baugh, Washington	1945	109.9	182	128	70.3	1,669	9.17	11	6.0	4	2.2
Drew Brees, New Orleans	2009	109.6	514	363	70.6	4,388	8.54	34	6.6	11	2.1
Kurt Warner, St. Louis	1999	109.2	499	325	65.1	4,353	8.72	41	8.2	13	2.6
Josh McCown, Chicago	2013	109.0	224	149	66.5	1,829	8.17	13	5.8	1	0.4
Dan Marino, Miami	1984	108.9	564	362	64.2	5,084	9.01	48	8.5	17	3.0
Aaron Rodgers, Green Bay	2012	108.0	552	371	67.2	4,295	7.78	39	7.1	8	1.4
Sid Luckman, Chicago Bears	1943	107.5	202	110	54.5	2,194	10.86	28	13.9	12	5.9
Brett Favre, Minnesota	2009	107.2	531	363	68.4	4,202	7.91	30	5.6	7	1.3
Steve Young, San Francisco	1992	107.0	402	268	66.7	3,465	8.62	25	6.2	7	1.7
Randall Cunningham, Minnesota	1998	106.0	425	259	60.9	3,704	8.72	34	8.0	10	2.4
Peyton Manning, Denver	2012	105.8	583	400	68.6	4,659	7.99	37	6.3	11	1.9
Tom Brady, New England	2011	105.6	611	401	65.6	5,235	8.57	39	6.4	12	2.0
Philip Rivers, San Diego	2008	105.5	478	312	65.3	4,009	8.39	34	7.1	11	2.3
Philip Rivers, San Diego	2013	105.5	544	378	69.5	4,478	8.23	32	5.9	11	2.0

*NFL Record

HIGHEST NFL POSTSEASON PASSER RATINGS (MINIMUM: 150 ATTEMPTS)

Player	Games	Att.	Comp.	Pct.	Yards	Avg. Gain	TD	Int.	Rating
Bart Starr	10	213	130	61.0	1,753	8.23	15	3	104.8
Aaron Rodgers	10	318	210	66.0	2,489	7.83	19	5	103.1
Kurt Warner	13	462	307	66.5	3,952	8.55	31	14	102.8
Drew Brees	11	464	306	65.9	3,539	7.63	24	6	100.7
Joe Montana	23	734	460	62.7	5,772	7.86	45	21	95.6
Mark Sanchez	6	157	95	60.5	1,155	7.36	9	3	94.3
Ken Anderson	6	166	110	66.3	1,321	7.96	9	6	93.5
Joe Theismann	10	211	128	60.7	1,782	8.45	11	7	91.4
Eli Manning	11	356	219	61.5	2,516	7.07	17	8	89.3
Peyton Manning	23	889	572	64.3	6,589	7.41	37	24	89.2

HIGHEST NFL POSTSEASON PASSER RATINGS, ACTIVE PLAYERS (MINIMUM: 150 ATTEMPTS)

Player	Games	Att.	Comp.	Pct.	Yards	Avg. Gain	TD	Int.	Rating
Aaron Rodgers	10	318	210	66.0	2,489	7.83	19	5	103.1
Drew Brees	11	464	306	65.9	3,539	7.63	24	6	100.7
Mark Sanchez	6	157	95	60.5	1,155	7.36	9	3	94.3
Eli Manning	11	356	219	61.5	2,516	7.07	17	8	89.3
Peyton Manning	23	889	572	64.3	6,589	7.41	37	24	89.2
Tom Brady	26	950	590	62.1	6,424	6.76	43	22	87.5
Colin Kaepernick	6	162	94	58.0	1,374	8.48	7	5	87.3
Joe Flacco	13	373	207	55.5	2,672	7.16	19	8	86.2
Matt Ryan	5	187	124	66.3	1,230	6.58	9	7	85.2
Philip Rivers	9	272	164	60.3	2,165	7.96	11	9	85.2

ALL-TIME RANKINGS OF PLAYERS IN FOUR CATEGORIES THAT DETERMINE NFL PASSER RATING

Minimum: 1,500 Attempts

COMPLETION PERCENTAGE	Pct.	Att.	Comp.
Chad Pennington	66.05	2,471	1,632
Drew Brees	65.91	6,799	4,481
Aaron Rodgers	65.82	2,955	1,945
Kurt Warner	65.50	4,070	2,666
Peyton Manning	65.45	8,452	5,532
Tony Romo	64.61	3,775	2,439
Philip Rivers	64.41	4,108	2,646
Steve Young	64.28	4,149	2,667
Matt Schaub	63.97	3,181	2,035
Matt Ryan	63.66	3,288	2,093

TOUCHDOWN PERCENTAGE	Pct.	Att.	TD
Sid Luckman	7.86	1,744	137
Frank Ryan	6.99	2,133	149
Len Dawson	6.39	3,741	239
Aaron Rodgers	6.36	2,955	188
Daryle Lamonica	6.31	2,601	164
Sammy Baugh	6.24	2,995	187
Charlie Conerly	6.11	2,833	173
Bob Waterfield	6.00	1,617	97
Earl Morrall	5.99	2,689	161
Sonny Jurgensen	5.98	4,262	255

AVERAGE YARDS PER PASS	Avg.	Att.	Yards
Otto Graham	8.63	1,565	13,499
Sid Luckman	8.42	1,744	14,686
Aaron Rodgers	8.19	2,955	24,197
Norm Van Brocklin	8.16	2,895	23,611
Steve Young	7.98	4,149	33,124
Kurt Warner	7.95	4,070	32,344
Philip Rivers	7.88	4,108	32,369
Ed Brown	7.85	1,987	15,600
Ben Roethlisberger	7.85	4,346	34,105
Bart Starr	7.85	3,149	24,718

INTERCEPTION PERCENTAGE	Pct.	Att.	Int.
Aaron Rodgers	1.76	2,955	52
Tom Brady	2.03	6,586	134
Neil O'Donnell	2.11	3,229	68
Sam Bradford	2.16	1,760	38
Donovan McNabb	2.18	5,374	117
Jeff Garcia	2.26	3,676	83
Matt Ryan	2.34	3,288	77
Mark Brunell	2.33	4,640	108
David Garrard	2.37	2,281	54
Jason Campbell	2.40	2,499	60

STARTING RECORDS OF ACTIVE NFL QUARTERBACKS

Minimum: 10 starts

	W - L - T	Pct.
Tom Brady	148-43-0	.775
Russell Wilson	24- 8-0	.750
Colin Kaepernick	17- 6-0	.739
Peyton Manning	167-73-0	.696
Andrew Luck	22-10-0	.688
Ben Roethlisberger	95-47-0	.669
Aaron Rodgers	58-29-0	.667
Joe Flacco	62-34-0	.646
Matt Ryan	60-34-0	.638
Andy Dalton	30-18-0	.625
Philip Rivers	79-49-0	.617
Drew Brees	110-75-0	.595
Tony Romo	63-45-0	.583
Eli Manning	85-66-0	.563
Nick Foles	9- 7-0	.563
Alex Smith	49-40-1	.550
Michael Vick	58-48-1	.547
Jay Cutler	56-48-0	.538
Mark Sanchez	33-29-0	.532
Rex Grossman	25-22-0	.532
Matt Hasselbeck	80-72-0	.526
Cam Newton	25-23-0	.521
Matt Moore	13-12-0	.520
David Garrard	39-37-0	.513
Matt Schaub	46-44-0	.511
Shaun Hill	13-13-0	.500
Tarvaris Jackson	17-17-0	.500
Kyle Orton	35-35-0	.500
Geno Smith	8- 8-0	.500
Matt Cassel	32-36-0	.471
Ryan Tannehill	15-17-0	.469
Carson Palmer	64-73-0	.467
Jake Locker	8-10-0	.444
Robert Griffin III	12-16-0	.429
Kevin Kolb	9-12-0	.429
Josh McCown	16-22-0	.421
Derek Anderson	18-25-0	.419
Christian Ponder	14-20-1	.414
Jason Campbell	32-47-0	.405
Jon Kitna	50-74-0	.403
Josh Freeman	24-36-0	.400
EJ Manuel	4- 6-0	.400
Matthew Stafford	24-37-0	.393
Kellen Clemens	8-13-0	.381
Sam Bradford	18-30-1	.378
Chad Henne	18-32-0	.360
Ryan Fitzpatrick	27-49-1	.357
Mike Glennon	4- 9-0	.308
Bruce Gradkowski	6-14-0	.300
Terrelle Pryor	3- 7-0	.300
Colt McCoy	6-15-0	.286
Seneca Wallace	6-16-0	.273
Brandon Weeden	5-15-0	.250
Brady Quinn	4-16-0	.200
Blaine Gabbert	5-22-0	.185
Dan Orlovsky	2-10-0	.167
Jimmy Clausen	1- 9-0	.100

MOST GAME-WINNING DRIVES IN FOURTH QUARTER OR OVERTIME SINCE 1970

50	Peyton Manning, Indianapolis, 1998-2010; Denver, 2012-13
47	Dan Marino, Miami, 1983-1999
43	Brett Favre, Atlanta, 1991; Green Bay, 1992-2007; New York Jets, 2008; Minnesota, 2009-2010
40	John Elway, Denver, 1983-1998
35	Warren Moon, Houston, 1984-1993; Minnesota, 1994-96; Seattle, 1997-98; Kansas City, 1999-2000
	Tom Brady, New England, 2000-2013

TEAMS THAT FINISHED IN FIRST PLACE IN THEIR DIVISION THE SEASON AFTER FINISHING IN LAST PLACE

Season	Team	Record	Prior Season
1967	Houston	9-4-1	*3-11-0
1968	Minnesota	8-6-0	3-8-3
1970	Cincinnati	8-6-0	4-9-1
1970	San Francisco	10-3-1	4-8-2
1972	Green Bay	10-4-0	4-8-2
1975	Baltimore	10-4-0	2-12-0
1979	Tampa Bay	10-6-0	5-11-0
1981	Cincinnati	12-4-0	6-10-0
1981	Tampa Bay	9-7-0	*5-10-1
1987	Indianapolis	9-6-0	3-13-0
1988	Cincinnati	12-4-0	4-11-0
1990	Cincinnati	9-7-0	8-8-0
1991	Denver	12-4-0	5-11-0
1992	San Diego	11-5-0	4-12-0
1993	Detroit	10-6-0	*5-11-0
1996	Carolina	12-4-0	*7-9-0
1996	Denver	13-3-0	*8-8-0
1997	New York Giants	10-5-1	6-10-0
1999	Indianapolis	13-3-0	3-13-0
1999	St. Louis	13-3-0	*4-12-0
2000	New Orleans	10-6-0	3-13-0
2001	Chicago	13-3-0	5-11-0
2001	New England	11-5-0	5-11-0
2003	Carolina	11-5-0	7-9-0
2003	Kansas City	13-3-0	*8-8-0
2004	Atlanta	11-5-0	5-11-0
2004	San Diego	12-4-0	*4-12-0
2005	Chicago	11-5-0	5-11-0
2005	New York Giants	11-5-0	*6-10-0
2005	Tampa Bay	11-5-0	5-11-0
2006	Baltimore	13-3-0	*6-10-0
2006	New Orleans	10-6-0	3-13-0
2006	Philadelphia	10-6-0	6-10-0
2007	Tampa Bay	9-7-0	4-12-0
2008	Miami	11-5-0	1-15-0
2009	New Orleans	13-3-0	8-8-0
2010	Kansas City	10-6-0	4-12-0
2011	Denver	8-8-0	4-12-0
2011	Houston	10-6-0	*6-10-0
2012	Washington	10-6-0	5-11-0
2013	Philadelphia	10-6-0	4-12-0
2013	Carolina	12-4-0	*7-9-0

*tied for last place

LONGEST WINNING STREAKS SINCE 1970

23	Indianapolis, 2008-09	(9 in 2008; 14 in 2009)
21	New England, 2006-08	(3 in 2006, 16 in 2007, 2 in 2008)
18	New England, 2003-04	(12 in 2003, 6 in 2004)
17	Denver, 2012-13	(11 in 2012; 6 in 2013)
16	Miami, 1971-73	(1 in 1971, 14 in 1972, 1 in 1973)
16	Miami, 1983-84	(5 in 1983, 11 in 1984)
16	Pittsburgh, 2004-05	(14 in 2004, 2 in 2005)
15	San Francisco, 1989-90	(5 in 1989, 10 in 1990)
15	Green Bay, 2010-11	(2 in 2010, 13 in 2011)
14	Oakland, 1976-77	(10 in 1976, 4 in 1977)
14	Denver, 1997-98	(1 in 1997, 13 in 1998)
13	Minnesota, 1974-75	(3 in 1974, 10 in 1975)
13	Chicago, 1984-85	(1 in 1984, 12 in 1985)
13	New York Giants, 1989-90	(3 in 1989, 10 in 1990)
13	Indianapolis, 2005	
13	Tennessee, 2007-08	(3 in 2007, 10 in 2008)
13	New Orleans, 2009	
12	Washington, 1990-91	(1 in 1990, 11 in 1991)
11	Pittsburgh, 1975	
11	Baltimore, 1975-76	(9 in 1975, 2 in 1976)
11	Chicago, 1986-87	(7 in 1986, 4 in 1987)
11	Houston, 1993	
11	San Francisco, 1997	
11	Jacksonville, 1999	
11	Indianapolis, 1999	
11	Seattle, 2005	
11	San Diego, 2006-07	(10 in 2006, 1 in 2007)
11	San Diego, 2009	

NFL PLAYOFF APPEARANCES BY SEASONS

Team	Number of Seasons in Playoffs
New York Giants	31
Dallas	30
Green Bay	29
Minnesota	27
Pittsburgh	27
St. Louis	27
Indianapolis	26
Chicago	25
San Francisco	25
Cleveland	24
Philadelphia	24
Washington	23
Miami	22
New England	21
Oakland	21
Tennessee	21
Denver	20
San Diego	18
Buffalo	17
Kansas City	17
Detroit	15
New York Jets	14
Seattle	13
Atlanta	12
Cincinnati	12
New Orleans	10
Tampa Bay	10
Baltimore	9
Arizona	8
Jacksonville	6
Carolina	5
Houston	2

TEAMS IN SUPER BOWL CONTENTION (1978-2013)

	With 3 Weeks to Play	With 2 Weeks to Play	With 1 Week to Play
1978	20	17	12
1979	19	15	13
1980	20	14	12
1981	21	20	16
1982	*27	25	*22
1983	24	19	15
1984	18	14	13
1985	21	18	13
1986	19	17	14
1987	19	19	15
1988	21	18	15
1989	21	18	17
1990	23	20	15
1991	20	18	13
1992	20	16	14
1993	20	18	16
1994	25	22	15
1995	*27	21	18
1996	23	21	13
1997	22	18	14
1998	22	19	14
1999	23	20	16
2000	19	17	16
2001	23	16	13
2002	21	21	19
2003	22	17	14
2004	*27	*26	17
2005	18	17	14
2006	25	24	20
2007	23	16	15
2008	22	19	18
2009	24	19	17
2010	23	20	16
2011	22	22	16
2012	24	19	15
2013	25	19	18

RECORD OF TEAMS ON THE ROAD (1970-2013)

Year	W	L	T	Pct.
1970	72	101	9	.420
1971	74	100	8	.429
1972	87	90	5	.492
1973	66	109	7	.382
1974	82	99	1	.453
1975	81	101	0	.445
1976	83	112	1	.426
1977	83	113	0	.423
1978	93	130	1	.417
1979	92	132	0	.411
1980	101	122	1	.453
1981	84	139	1	.377
1982	57	68	1	.456
1983	104	119	1	.467
1984	94	129	1	.422
1985	80	144	0	.357
1986	104	118	2	.469
1987	95	114	1	.455
1988	92	131	1	.413
1989	95	128	1	.426
1990	93	131	0	.415
1991	92	132	0	.411
1992	88	136	0	.393
1993	101	123	0	.451
1994	96	128	0	.429
1995	96	144	0	.400
1996	91	149	0	.379
1997	93	145	2	.392
1998	89	151	0	.371
1999	100	148	0	.403
2000	110	138	0	.444
2001	112	136	0	.452
2002	107	148	1	.420
2003	99	157	0	.387
2004	111	145	0	.434
2005	105	151	0	.410
2006	120	136	0	.469
2007	109	147	0	.426
2008	109	146	1	.428
2009	110	146	0	.430
2010	113	143	0	.441
2011	111	145	0	.434
2012	109	146	1	.428
2013	102	153	1	.400

GAMES DECIDED BY 7 POINTS OR FEWER AND 3 POINTS OR FEWER (1970-2013)

	Games Decided by 7 Points or Fewer	Games Decided by 3 Points or Fewer
1970	59 of 182 (32.4%)	34 of 182 (18.7%)
1971	76 of 182 (41.8%)	35 of 182 (19.2%)
1972	71 of 182 (39.0%)	38 of 182 (20.9%)
1973	60 of 182 (32.9%)	28 of 182 (15.4%)
1974	91 of 182 (50.0%)	37 of 182 (20.3%)
1975	62 of 182 (34.1%)	35 of 182 (19.2%)
1976	73 of 196 (37.2%)	38 of 196 (19.4%)
1977	85 of 196 (43.4%)	36 of 196 (18.4%)
1978	108 of 224 (48.2%)	49 of 224 (21.9%)
1979	104 of 224 (46.4%)	51 of 224 (22.8%)
1980	108 of 224 (48.2%)	58 of 224 (25.9%)
1981	91 of 224 (40.6%)	60 of 224 (26.8%)
1982	61 of 126 (48.4%)	33 of 126 (26.2%)
1983	106 of 224 (47.3%)	54 of 224 (24.1%)
1984	95 of 224 (42.4%)	58 of 224 (25.9%)
1985	87 of 224 (38.8%)	38 of 224 (17.0%)
1986	106 of 224 (47.3%)	48 of 224 (21.4%)
1987	99 of 210 (47.1%)	40 of 210 (19.0%)
1988	113 of 224 (50.4%)	62 of 224 (27.7%)
1989	107 of 224 (47.8%)	55 of 224 (24.6%)
1990	97 of 224 (43.3%)	54 of 224 (24.1%)
1991	112 of 224 (50.0%)	57 of 224 (25.4%)
1992	88 of 224 (39.3%)	48 of 224 (21.4%)
1993	*105 of 224 (46.9%)	53 of 224 (23.7%)
1994	115 of 224 (51.3%)	60 of 224 (26.8%)

	Games Decided by 7 Points or Fewer	Games Decided by 3 Points or Fewer
1995	115 of 240 (47.9%)	61 of 240 (25.4%)
1996	109 of 240 (45.4%)	47 of 240 (19.6%)
1997	111 of 240 (46.3%)	67 of 240 (27.9%)
1998	113 of 240 (47.1%)	50 of 240 (20.8%)
1999	115 of 248 (46.4%)	**64 of 248 (25.8%)
2000	109 of 248 (44.0%)	61 of 248 (24.6%)
2001	121 of 248 (48.8%)	62 of 248 (25.0%)
2002	126 of 256 (49.2%)	63 of 256 (24.6%)
2003	124 of 256 (48.4%)	60 of 256 (23.4%)
2004	116 of 256 (45.3%)	61 of 256 (23.8%)
2005	114 of 256 (44.5%)	60 of 256 (23.4%)
2006	117 of 256 (45.7%)	61 of 256 (23.8%)
2007	110 of 256 (43.0%)	55 of 256 (21.5%)
2008	115 of 256 (44.9%)	50 of 256 (19.5%)
2009	110 of 256 (43.0%)	54 of 256 (21.1%)
2010	121 of 256 (47.3%)	65 of 256 (25.4%)
2011	125 of 256 (48.8%)	50 of 256 (19.5%)
2012	120 of 256 (46.9%)	57 of 256 (22.3%)
2013	123 of 256 (48.0%)	65 of 256 (25.4%)

*Week record: Dec. 11-13, 1993 (Week 15), 12 of 14 games (86%) decided by 7 points or fewer.
**Week record: Oct. 10-11, 1999 (Week 5), 10 of 14 games (71%) decided by 3 points or fewer.

GAMES DECIDED BY 8 PTS. OR FEWER (1994-2013)

1994	121 of 224 (54.0%)	2006	126 of 256 (49.2%)
1995	123 of 240 (51.3%)	2007	120 of 256 (46.9%)
1996	115 of 240 (47.9%)	2008	118 of 256 (46.1%)
1997	120 of 240 (50.0%)	2009	120 of 256 (46.9%)
1998	120 of 240 (50.0%)	2010	131 of 256 (51.2%)
1999	124 of 248 (50.0%)	2011	132 of 256 (51.6%)
2000	119 of 248 (48.0%)	2012	131 of 256 (51.2%)
2001	*128 of 248 (51.6%)	2013	131 of 256 (51.2%)
2002	137 of 256 (53.5%)	*Week record: Oct. 14-15,	
2003	132 of 256 (51.6%)	2001 (Week 5), 12 of 14	
2004	121 of 256 (47.3%)	games (86%) decided by 8	
2005	123 of 256 (48.0%)	points or fewer	

TWO-POINT CONVERSION RESULTS (1994-2013)

1994	59 of 116 (50.9%)	2004	37 of 76 (48.7%)
1995	40 of 104 (38.5%)	2005	27 of 53 (50.9%)
1996	44 of 92 (47.8%)	2006	21 of 41 (51.2%)
1997	47 of 109 (43.1%)	2007	30 of 61 (49.2%)
1998	41 of 105 (39.1%)	2008	28 of 68 (41.2%)
1999	31 of 84 (36.9%)	2009	24 of 60 (40.0%)
2000	35 of 85 (41.2%)	2010	26 of 53 (49.1%)
2001	40 of 90 (44.4%)	2011	23 of 50 (46.0%)
2002	47 of 98 (48.0%)	2012	29 of 58 (50.0%)
2003	29 of 66 (43.9%)	2013	33 of 69 (47.8%)

RECORDS AFTER BYE WEEKS (1990-2013)

AFC		NFC	
Baltimore	12-6	Arizona	11-14
Buffalo	15-10	Atlanta	15-10
Cincinnati	7-17-1	Carolina	8-11
Cleveland	7-13	Chicago	17-8
Denver	19-6	Dallas	17-8
Houston	4-8	Detroit	12-13
Indianapolis	15-10	Green Bay	16-9
Jacksonville	10-9	Minnesota	17-8
Kansas City	13-12	New Orleans	13-12
Miami	14-11	New York Giants	10-15
New England	14-11	Philadelphia	20-5
New York Jets	12-13	San Francisco	10-14-1
Oakland	10-15	Seattle	7-18
Pittsburgh	16-9	St. Louis	12-12-1
San Diego	11-13	Tampa Bay	11-14
Tennessee	14-11	Washington	12-13

2013 RECORDS OF TEAMS IN CLOSE GAMES

AFC	Overall Record	Decided by 8 Pts. or Fewer	Decided By 3 Pts. or Fewer
Baltimore	8- 8	6-5	5-4
Buffalo	6-10	4-4	3-3
Cincinnati	11- 5	5-3	2-3
Cleveland	4-12	2-5	0-1
Denver	13- 3	3-3	1-1
Houston	2-14	2-9	1-5
Indianapolis	11- 5	6-1	2-0
Jacksonville	4-12	4-2	1-0
Kansas City	11- 5	3-3	2-2
Miami	8- 8	6-4	1-3
New England	12- 4	7-4	6-1
N.Y. Jets	8- 8	5-1	3-1
Oakland	4-12	2-4	1-0
Pittsburgh	8- 8	2-5	1-2
San Diego	9- 7	4-6	3-2
Tennessee	7- 9	6-6	1-3

NFC	Overall Record	Decided by 8 Pts. or Fewer	Decided By 3 Pts. or Fewer
Arizona	10- 6	5-3	3-3
Atlanta	4-12	4-7	2-3
Carolina	12- 4	5-2	2-1
Chicago	8- 8	6-6	3-2
Dallas	8- 8	5-5	2-5
Detroit	7- 9	4-6	2-5
Green Bay	8- 7-1	4-4-1	3-0-1
Minnesota	5-10-1	4-4-1	2-2-1
New Orleans	11- 5	5-3	2-1
N.Y. Giants	7- 9	4-3	1-1
Philadelphia	10- 6	4-2	2-1
San Francisco	12- 4	3-2	2-2
Seattle	13- 3	5-3	2-1
St. Louis	7- 9	1-3	1-0
Tampa Bay	4-12	2-5	2-4
Washington	3-13	2-7	0-2

SUPER BOWL CHAMPIONS THAT DID NOT MAKE PLAYOFFS THE FOLLOWING YEAR

Baltimore Ravens—Super Bowl XLVII champions did not make playoffs in 2013 season.
New York Giants—Super Bowl XLVI champions did not make playoffs in 2012 season.
Pittsburgh—Super Bowl XLIII champions did not make playoffs in 2009 season.
Pittsburgh—Super Bowl XL champions did not make playoffs in 2006 season.
Tampa Bay—Super Bowl XXXVII champions did not make playoffs in 2003 season.
New England—Super Bowl XXXVI champions did not make playoffs in the 2002 season.
Denver—Super Bowl XXXIII champions did not make playoffs in the 1999 season.
New York Giants—Super Bowl XXV champions did not make playoffs in the 1991 season.
Washington—Super Bowl XXII champions did not make play-offs in the 1988 season.
New York Giants—Super Bowl XXI champions did not make playoffs in the 1987 season.
San Francisco—Super Bowl XVI champions did not make playoffs in the 1982 season.
Oakland—Super Bowl XV champions did not make playoffs in the 1981 season.
Pittsburgh—Super Bowl XIV champions did not make playoffs in the 1980 season.
Kansas City—Super Bowl IV champions did not make playoffs in the 1970 season.
Green Bay—Super Bowl II champions did not make playoffs in the 1968 season.

NON-DIVISION WINNERS THAT PLAYED IN SUPER BOWL

2010	Green Bay Packers ....Super Bowl XLV (Defeated Pittsburgh, 31-25)	
2007	New York Giants ....Super Bowl XLII (Defeated New England, 17-14)	

2005	Pittsburgh Steelers	Super Bowl XL
	(Defeated Seattle, 21-10)	
2000	Baltimore Ravens	Super Bowl XXXV
	(Defeated New York Giants, 34-7)	
1999	Tennessee Titans	Super Bowl XXXIV
	(Lost to St. Louis, 23-16)	
1997	Denver Broncos	Super Bowl XXXII
	(Defeated Green Bay, 31-24)	
1992	Buffalo Bills	Super Bowl XXVII
	(Lost to Dallas, 52-17)	
1985	New England Patriots	Super Bowl XX
	(Lost to Chicago, 46-10)	
1980	Oakland Raiders	Super Bowl XV
	(Defeated Philadelphia, 27-10)	
1975	Dallas Cowboys	Super Bowl X
	(Lost to Pittsburgh, 21-17)	
1969	Kansas City Chiefs	Super Bowl IV
	(Defeated Minnesota, 23-7)	

TEAMS AT OR UNDER .500 IN POSTSEASON PLAY

2011	Denver Broncos	8-8
2010	Seattle Seahawks	7-9
2008	San Diego Chargers	8-8
2006	New York Giants	8-8
2004	Minnesota Vikings	8-8
2004	St. Louis Rams	8-8
1999	Dallas Cowboys	8-8
1999	Detroit Lions	8-8
1991	New York Jets	8-8
1990	New Orleans Saints	8-8
1985	Cleveland Browns	8-8
1982	Cleveland Browns	4-5
1982	Detroit Lions	4-5
1969	Houston Oilers	6-6-2

TEAMS TO BEAT OPPOSING TEAM THREE TIMES IN A SEASON SINCE 1970

Year	Team	Opponent
2009	Dallas Cowboys	Philadelphia Eagles
2008	Pittsburgh Steelers	Baltimore Ravens
2004	St. Louis Rams	Seattle Seahawks
2002	Pittsburgh Steelers	Cleveland Browns
2000	New York Giants	Philadelphia Eagles
1999	Tennessee Titans	Jacksonville Jaguars
1997	Green Bay Packers	Tampa Bay Buccaneers
1997	New England Patriots	Miami Dolphins
1994	Pittsburgh Steelers	Cleveland Browns
1993	Los Angeles Raiders	Denver Broncos
1991	Kansas City Chiefs	Los Angeles Raiders
1986	New York Giants	Washington Redskins
1982	Miami Dolphins	New York Jets

COLDEST NFL GAMES ON RECORD

-13 degrees (-48 degree wind chill)—December 31, 1967, Lambeau Field, Green Bay, Wisconsin, NFL Championship (Green Bay 21, Dallas 17)

-9 degrees (-59 degree wind chill)—January 10, 1982, Riverfront Stadium, Cincinnati, Ohio, AFC Championship (Cincinnati 27, San Diego 7)

-1 degrees (-23 degree wind chill)—January 20, 2008, Lambeau Field, Green Bay, Wisconsin, NFC Championship (New York Giants 23, Green Bay 20 in OT)

TEAM LEADERS

Offense	Most Scored	Fewest Scored
1st Quarter	130 Denver	43 Miami
2nd Quarter	158 Denver	66 Jacksonville
3rd Quarter	135 Denver	33 Tampa Bay
4th Quarter	183 Denver	50 Tampa Bay
Defense	**Fewest Allowed**	**Most Allowed**
1st Quarter	22 Seattle	126 Washington
2nd Quarter	71 Cincinnati	169 Atlanta
3rd Quarter	36 San Francisco	115 Green Bay
4th Quarter	54 Kansas City	145 Cleveland

2013 NFL SCORE BY QUARTERS

AFC Offense	1	2	3	4	OT	PTS
Denver	130	158	135	183	0	606
New England	74	104	85	178	3	444
Cincinnati	87	123	103	114	3	430
Kansas City	124	133	65	108	0	430
San Diego	61	132	85	115	3	396
Indianapolis	70	117	106	98	0	391
Pittsburgh	78	87	106	108	0	379
Tennessee	71	77	65	149	0	362
Buffalo	73	103	75	88	0	339
Oakland	89	98	68	67	0	322
Baltimore	59	79	64	115	3	320
Miami	43	117	88	67	2	317
Cleveland	56	105	71	76	0	308
N.Y. Jets	44	106	63	74	3	290
Houston	64	93	53	60	6	276
Jacksonville	70	66	50	61	0	247

NFC Offense	1	2	3	4	OT	PTS
Chicago	96	124	90	132	3	445
Philadelphia	89	121	110	122	0	442
Dallas	91	125	98	125	0	439
Green Bay	78	105	113	118	3	417
Seattle	69	140	87	115	6	417
New Orleans	86	155	70	103	0	414
San Francisco	97	121	71	117	0	406
Detroit	48	136	90	121	0	395
Minnesota	82	108	85	110	6	391
Arizona	49	122	93	112	3	379
Carolina	64	115	86	101	0	366
Atlanta	79	122	56	93	3	353
St. Louis	67	101	80	100	0	348
Washington	47	114	82	85	6	334
N.Y. Giants	46	90	80	75	3	294
Tampa Bay	80	125	33	50	0	288

AFC Defense	1	2	3	4	OT	PTS
Cincinnati	88	71	83	58	5	305
Kansas City	51	106	91	54	3	305
Miami	67	92	88	88	0	335
Indianapolis	102	102	66	66	0	336
New England	70	74	95	96	3	338
San Diego	68	106	79	89	6	348
Baltimore	63	89	63	134	3	352
Pittsburgh	84	108	57	121	0	370
Tennessee	76	83	88	125	9	381
N.Y. Jets	71	136	89	91	0	387
Buffalo	64	133	82	103	6	388
Denver	64	128	104	100	3	399
Cleveland	67	121	73	145	0	406
Houston	97	113	106	109	3	428
Jacksonville	107	139	102	101	0	449
Oakland	89	150	96	118	0	453

NFC Defense	1	2	3	4	OT	PTS
Seattle	22	108	41	60	0	231
Carolina	31	79	54	77	0	241
San Francisco	31	86	36	119	0	272
New Orleans	87	112	46	59	0	304
Arizona	94	89	41	100	0	324
St. Louis	79	100	85	100	0	364
Detroit	61	120	60	132	3	376
Philadelphia	60	97	100	125	0	382
N.Y. Giants	61	136	87	99	0	383
Tampa Bay	64	140	76	106	3	389
Green Bay	79	103	115	128	3	428
Dallas	67	119	108	138	0	432
Atlanta	54	169	93	127	0	443
Chicago	112	147	97	119	3	478
Washington	126	141	91	120	0	478
Minnesota	105	125	114	133	3	480
NFL TOTALS	**2,361**	**3,622**	**2,606**	**3,340**	**56**	**11,985**

2014 TOP 100 TELEVISION MARKETS
(NFL TEAM MARKETS IN BOLD)

RANK	MARKET	TV HOUSEHOLDS	% of U.S.
1	**New York**	**7,461,030**	**6.442**
2	Los Angeles	5,665,780	4.892
3	**Chicago**	**3,534,080**	**3.052**
4	**Philadelphia**	**2,963,500**	**2.559**
5	**Dallas-Ft. Worth**	**2,655,290**	**2.293**
6	**San Francisco-Oak-San Jose**	**2,518,900**	**2.175**
7	**Boston (Manchester)**	**2,433,040**	**2.101**
8	**Washington, DC (Hagerstown)**	**2,412,250**	**2.083**
9	**Atlanta**	**2,375,050**	**2.051**
10	**Houston**	**2,289,360**	**1.977**
11	**Detroit**	**1,856,400**	**1.603**
12	**Phoenix (Prescott)**	**1,855,310**	**1.602**
13	**Seattle-Tacoma**	**1,847,780**	**1.596**
14	**Tampa-St. Pete (Sarasota)**	**1,827,510**	**1.578**
15	**Minneapolis-St. Paul**	**1,748,070**	**1.509**
16	**Miami-Ft. Lauderdale**	**1,663,290**	**1.436**
17	**Denver**	**1,574,610**	**1.360**
18	Orlando-Daytona Bch-Melbrn	1,490,380	1.287
19	**Cleveland-Akron (Canton)**	**1,484,530**	**1.282**
20	Sacramnto-Stkton-Modesto	1,387,560	1.198
21	**St. Louis**	**1,254,530**	**1.083**
22	Portland, OR	1,185,160	1.023
23	**Pittsburgh**	**1,181,540**	**1.020**
24	Raleigh-Durham (Fayetvlle)	1,165,120	1.006
25	**Charlotte**	**1,157,920**	**1.000**
26	**Indianapolis**	**1,096,650**	**0.947**
27	**Baltimore**	**1,095,240**	**0.946**
28	**San Diego**	**1,080,880**	**0.933**
29	**Nashville**	**1,043,440**	**0.901**
30	Hartford & New Haven	999,990	0.863
31	**Kansas City**	**941,980**	**0.813**
32	Columbus, OH	928,530	0.802
33	Salt Lake City	921,240	0.796
34	Milwaukee	916,590	0.791
35	**Cincinnati**	**908,440**	**0.784**
36	San Antonio	906,210	0.783
37	Greenvll-Spart-Ashevll-And	849,340	0.733
38	West Palm Beach-Ft. Pierce	809,640	0.699
39	Grand Rapids-Kalmzoo-B.Crk	734,480	0.634
40	Austin	733,390	0.633
41	Oklahoma City	730,020	0.630
42	Las Vegas	726,010	0.627
43	Harrisburg-Lncstr-Leb-York	725,340	0.626
44	Birmingham (Ann and Tusc)	719,200	0.621
45	Norfolk-Portsmth-Newpt Nws	718,930	0.621
46	Greensboro-H.Point-W.Salem	705,380	0.609
47	Albuquerque-Santa Fe	690,740	0.596
48	**Jacksonville**	**675,650**	**0.583**
49	Louisville	674,950	0.583
50	Memphis	672,390	0.581

**2014 TOP 100 TELEVISION MARKETS
(NFL TEAM MARKETS IN BOLD)**

RANK	MARKET	TV HOUSEHOLDS	% of U.S.
51	**New Orleans**	**652,180**	**0.563**
52	**Buffalo**	**634,280**	**0.548**
53	Providence-New Bedford	614,880	0.531
54	Wilkes Barre-Scranton-Hztn	584,870	0.505
55	Fresno-Visalia	580,180	0.501
56	Little Rock-Pine Bluff	571,040	0.493
57	Richmond-Petersburg	559,980	0.484
58	Albany-Schenectady-Troy	548,560	0.474
59	Mobile-Pensacola (Ft Walt)	541,060	0.467
60	Tulsa	526,580	0.455
61	Knoxville	525,620	0.454
62	Ft. Myers-Naples	517,920	0.447
63	Lexington	490,920	0.424
64	Dayton	480,430	0.415
65	Charleston-Huntington	457,600	0.395
66	Roanoke-Lynchburg	455,340	0.393
67	Wichita-Hutchinson Plus	454,040	0.392
68	Flint-Saginaw-Bay City	448,960	0.388
69	Honolulu	448,650	0.387
70	**Green Bay-Appleton**	**448,490**	**0.387**
71	Tucson (Sierra Vista)	442,950	0.383
72	Des Moines-Ames	434,500	0.375
73	Spokane	424,790	0.367
74	Omaha	421,960	0.364
75	Springfield, MO	419,450	0.362
76	Toledo	415,000	0.358
77	Columbia, SC	407,140	0.352
78	Rochester, NY	402,300	0.347
79	Huntsville-Decatur (Flor)	397,030	0.343
80	Portland-Auburn	395,010	0.341
81	Paducah-Cape Girard-Harsbg	390,490	0.337
82	Shreveport	388,400	0.335
83	Madison	385,690	0.333
84	Champaign&Sprngfld-Decatur	382,050	0.330
85	Syracuse	380,320	0.328
86	Harlingen-Wslco-Brnsvl-McA	369,240	0.319
87	Chattanooga	360,150	0.311
88	Waco-Temple-Bryan	359,400	0.310
89	Colorado Springs-Pueblo	353,790	0.306
90	Cedar Rapids-Wtrlo-IWC&Dub	349,250	0.302
91	El Paso (Las Cruces)	344,480	0.297
92	Savannah	343,020	0.296
93	Baton Rouge	337,550	0.291
94	Jackson, MS	335,950	0.290
95	Charleston, SC	326,760	0.282
96	South Bend-Elkhart	322,750	0.279
97	Tri-Cities, TN-VA	321,460	0.278
98	Burlington-Plattsburgh	317,960	0.275
99	Greenville-N.Bern-Washngtn	312,470	0.270
100	Davenport-R.Island-Moline	308,220	0.266
	TOTAL NFL MARKETS	**54,671,220**	**47.207**
	TOTAL TOP 100 MARKETS	**99,684,140**	**86.075**
	TOTAL MARKETS	**115,810,740**	**100.00**

ALL-TIME REGULAR-SEASON RECORDS OF CURRENT NFL TEAMS

AFC
BALTIMORE RAVENS

Season	All Games W	L	T	Home Games W	L	T	Road Games W	L	T
1996	4	12		4	4		0	8	
1997	6	9	1	3	4	1	3	5	
1998	6	10		4	4		2	6	
1999	8	8		4	4		4	4	
2000	12	4		6	2		6	2	
2001	10	6		6	2		4	4	
2002	7	9		4	4		3	5	
2003	10	6		7	1		3	5	
2004	9	7		6	2		3	5	
2005	6	10		6	2		0	8	
2006	13	3		7	1		6	2	
2007	5	11		4	4		1	7	
2008	11	5		6	2		5	3	
2009	9	7		6	2		3	5	
2010	12	4		7	1		5	3	
2011	12	4		8	0		4	4	
2012	10	6		6	2		4	4	
2013	8	8		6	2		2	6	
	158	129	1	100	43	1	58	86	

BUFFALO BILLS

Season	All Games W	L	T	Home Games W	L	T	Road Games W	L	T
1960	5	8	1	3	4		2	4	1
1961	6	8		2	5		4	3	
1962	7	6	1	3	3	1	4	3	
1963	7	6	1	4	2	1	3	4	
1964	12	2		6	1		6	1	
1965	10	3	1	5	2		5	1	1
1966	9	4	1	4	2	1	5	2	
1967	4	10		2	5		2	5	
1968	1	12	1	1	6		0	6	1
1969	4	10		4	3		0	7	
1970	3	10	1	1	6		2	4	1
1971	1	13		1	6		0	7	
1972	4	9	1	2	4	1	2	5	
1973	9	5		5	2		4	3	
1974	9	5		5	2		4	3	
1975	8	6		3	4		5	2	
1976	2	12		1	6		1	6	
1977	3	11		1	6		2	5	
1978	5	11		4	4		1	7	
1979	7	9		3	5		4	4	
1980	11	5		6	2		5	3	
1981	10	6		7	1		3	5	
1982	4	5		4	1		0	4	
1983	8	8		3	5		5	3	
1984	2	14		2	6		0	8	
1985	2	14		2	6		0	8	
1986	4	12		3	5		1	7	
1987	7	8		4	4		3	4	
1988	12	4		8	0		4	4	
1989	9	7		6	2		3	5	
1990	13	3		8	0		5	3	
1991	13	3		7	1		6	2	
1992	11	5		6	2		5	3	
1993	12	4		6	2		6	2	
1994	7	9		4	4		3	5	
1995	10	6		6	2		4	4	
1996	10	6		7	1		3	5	
1997	6	10		4	4		2	6	
1998	10	6		6	2		4	4	
1999	11	5		6	2		5	3	
2000	8	8		5	3		3	5	
2001	3	13		1	7		2	6	
2002	8	8		5	3		3	5	
2003	6	10		4	4		2	6	
2004	9	7		5	3		4	4	
2005	5	11		4	4		1	7	
2006	7	9		4	4		3	5	
2007	7	9		4	4		3	5	
2008	7	9		3	5		4	4	
2009	6	10		3	5		3	5	
2010	4	12		2	6		2	6	
2011	6	10		5	3		1	7	
2012	6	10		4	4		2	6	
2013	6	10		4	4		2	6	
	376	436	8	218	189	4	158	247	4

CINCINNATI BENGALS

Season	All Games W	L	T	Home Games W	L	T	Road Games W	L	T
1968	3	11		2	5		1	6	
1969	4	9	1	4	3		0	6	1
1970	8	6		5	2		3	4	
1971	4	10		3	4		1	6	
1972	8	6		4	3		4	3	
1973	10	4		7	0		3	4	
1974	7	7		4	3		3	4	
1975	11	3		6	1		5	2	
1976	10	4		6	1		4	3	
1977	8	6		5	2		3	4	
1978	4	12		3	5		1	7	
1979	4	12		4	4		0	8	
1980	6	10		3	5		3	5	
1981	12	4		6	2		6	2	
1982	7	2		4	0		3	2	
1983	7	9		4	4		3	5	
1984	8	8		5	3		3	5	
1985	7	9		5	3		2	6	
1986	10	6		6	2		4	4	
1987	4	11		1	7		3	4	
1988	12	4		8	0		4	4	
1989	8	8		5	3		3	5	
1990	9	7		5	3		4	4	
1991	3	13		3	5		0	8	
1992	5	11		3	5		2	6	
1993	3	13		3	5		0	8	
1994	3	13		2	6		1	7	
1995	7	9		3	5		4	4	
1996	8	8		6	2		2	6	
1997	7	9		6	2		1	7	
1998	3	13		1	7		2	6	
1999	4	12		2	6		2	6	
2000	4	12		3	5		1	7	
2001	6	10		4	4		2	6	
2002	2	14		1	7		1	7	
2003	8	8		5	3		3	5	
2004	8	8		5	3		3	5	
2005	11	5		5	3		6	2	
2006	8	8		4	4		4	4	
2007	7	9		5	3		2	6	
2008	4	11	1	3	4	1	1	7	
2009	10	6		6	2		4	4	
2010	4	12		3	5		1	7	
2011	9	7		4	4		5	3	
2012	10	6		4	4		6	2	
2013	11	5		8	0		3	5	
	316	390	2	194	159	1	122	231	1

CLEVELAND BROWNS*

Season	All Games W	L	T	Home Games W	L	T	Road Games W	L	T
1950	10	2		5	1		5	1	
1951	11	1		6	0		5	1	
1952	8	4		4	2		4	2	

Season	All Games W	L	T	Home Games W	L	T	Road Games W	L	T
1953	11	1		6	0		5	1	
1954	9	3		5	1		4	2	
1955	9	2	1	5	1		4	1	1
1956	5	7		1	5		4	2	
1957	9	2	1	6	0		3	2	1
1958	9	3		4	2		5	1	
1959	7	5		3	3		4	2	
1960	8	3	1	4	2		4	1	1
1961	8	5	1	4	3		4	2	1
1962	7	6	1	4	2	1	3	4	
1963	10	4		5	2		5	2	
1964	10	3	1	5	1	1	5	2	
1965	11	3		5	2		6	1	
1966	9	5		5	2		4	3	
1967	9	5		6	1		3	4	
1968	10	4		5	2		5	2	
1969	10	3	1	5	1	1	5	2	
1970	7	7		4	3		3	4	
1971	9	5		4	3		5	2	
1972	10	4		4	3		6	1	
1973	7	5	2	5	1	1	2	4	1
1974	4	10		3	4		1	6	
1975	3	11		3	4		0	7	
1976	9	5		6	1		3	4	
1977	6	8		2	5		4	3	
1978	8	8		5	3		3	5	
1979	9	7		5	3		4	4	
1980	11	5		6	2		5	3	
1981	5	11		3	5		2	6	
1982	4	5		2	2		2	3	
1983	9	7		6	2		3	5	
1984	5	11		2	6		3	5	
1985	8	8		5	3		3	5	
1986	12	4		6	2		6	2	
1987	10	5		5	2		5	3	
1988	10	6		6	2		4	4	
1989	9	6	1	5	2	1	4	4	
1990	3	13		2	6		1	7	
1991	6	10		3	5		3	5	
1992	7	9		4	4		3	5	
1993	7	9		4	4		3	5	
1994	11	5		6	2		5	3	
1995	5	11		3	5		2	6	
1999	2	14		0	8		2	6	
2000	3	13		2	6		1	7	
2001	7	9		4	4		3	5	
2002	9	7		3	5		6	2	
2003	5	11		2	6		3	5	
2004	4	12		3	5		1	7	
2005	6	10		4	4		2	6	
2006	4	12		2	6		2	6	
2007	10	6		7	1		3	5	
2008	4	12		1	7		3	5	
2009	5	11		3	5		2	6	
2010	5	11		3	5		2	6	
2011	4	12		3	5		1	7	
2012	5	11		4	4		1	7	
2013	5	11		3	5		1	7	
	451	429	10	246	193	5	205	236	5

*Did not play from 1996-98.

DENVER BRONCOS

Season	All Games W	L	T	Home Games W	L	T	Road Games W	L	T
1960	4	9	1	2	4	1	2	5	
1961	3	11		2	5		1	6	
1962	7	7		3	4		4	3	
1963	2	11	1	2	5		0	6	1
1964	2	11	1	2	4	1	0	7	
1965	4	10		2	5		2	5	

Season	All Games W	L	T	Home Games W	L	T	Road Games W	L	T
1966	4	10		3	4		1	6	
1967	3	11		1	6		2	5	
1968	5	9		3	4		2	5	
1969	5	8	1	4	2	1	1	6	
1970	5	8	1	3	3	1	2	5	
1971	4	9	1	2	4	1	2	5	
1972	5	9		3	4		2	5	
1973	7	5	2	3	3	1	4	2	1
1974	7	6	1	3	3	1	4	3	
1975	6	8		5	2		1	6	
1976	9	5		6	1		3	4	
1977	12	2		6	1		6	1	
1978	10	6		6	2		4	4	
1979	10	6		6	2		4	4	
1980	8	8		4	4		4	4	
1981	10	6		8	0		2	6	
1982	2	7		1	4		1	3	
1983	9	7		6	2		3	5	
1984	13	3		7	1		6	2	
1985	11	5		6	2		5	3	
1986	11	5		7	1		4	4	
1987	10	4	1	7	1		3	3	1
1988	8	8		6	2		2	6	
1989	11	5		6	2		5	3	
1990	5	11		4	4		1	7	
1991	12	4		7	1		5	3	
1992	8	8		7	1		1	7	
1993	9	7		5	3		4	4	
1994	7	9		4	4		3	5	
1995	8	8		6	2		2	6	
1996	13	3		8	0		5	3	
1997	12	4		8	0		4	4	
1998	14	2		8	0		6	2	
1999	6	10		3	5		3	5	
2000	11	5		6	2		5	3	
2001	8	8		6	2		2	6	
2002	9	7		5	3		4	4	
2003	10	6		6	2		4	4	
2004	10	6		6	2		4	4	
2005	13	3		8	0		5	3	
2006	9	7		4	4		5	3	
2007	7	9		5	3		2	6	
2008	8	8		4	4		4	4	
2009	8	8		4	4		4	4	
2010	4	12		3	5		1	7	
2011	8	8		3	5		5	3	
2012	13	3		7	1		6	2	
2013	13	3		7	1		6	2	
	432	378	10	259	145	7	173	233	3

HOUSTON TEXANS

Season	All Games W	L	T	Home Games W	L	T	Road Games W	L	T
2002	4	12		2	6		2	6	
2003	5	11		3	5		2	6	
2004	7	9		3	5		4	4	
2005	2	14		2	6		0	8	
2006	6	10		4	4		2	6	
2007	8	8		6	2		2	6	
2008	8	8		6	2		2	6	
2009	9	7		4	4		5	3	
2010	6	10		4	4		2	6	
2011	10	6		5	3		5	3	
2012	12	4		6	2		6	2	
2013	2	14		1	7		1	7	
	79	113		46	50		33	63	

INDIANAPOLIS COLTS*

Season	All Games W	L	T	Home Games W	L	T	Road Games W	L	T
1953	3	9		2	4		1	5	
1954	3	9		2	4		1	5	
1955	5	6	1	4	1	1	1	5	
1956	5	7		4	2		1	5	
1957	7	5		4	2		3	3	
1958	9	3		6	0		3	3	
1959	9	3		4	2		5	1	
1960	6	6		4	2		2	4	
1961	8	6		5	2		3	4	
1962	7	7		3	4		4	3	
1963	8	6		4	3		4	3	
1964	12	2		7	1		5	1	
1965	10	3	1	5	2		5	1	1
1966	9	5		5	2		4	3	
1967	11	1	2	6	0	1	5	1	1
1968	13	1		6	1		7	0	
1969	8	5	1	4	2	1	4	3	
1970	11	2	1	5	1	1	6	1	
1971	10	4		5	2		5	2	
1972	5	9		2	5		3	4	
1973	4	10		3	4		1	6	
1974	2	12		0	7		2	5	
1975	10	4		5	2		5	2	
1976	11	3		6	1		5	2	
1977	10	4		6	1		4	3	
1978	5	11		2	6		3	5	
1979	5	11		3	5		2	6	
1980	7	9		2	6		5	3	
1981	2	14		1	7		1	7	
1982	0	8	1	0	3	1	0	5	
1983	7	9		3	5		4	4	
1984	4	12		2	6		2	6	
1985	5	11		4	4		1	7	
1986	3	13		1	7		2	6	
1987	9	6		4	4		5	2	
1988	9	7		6	2		3	5	
1989	8	8		6	2		2	6	
1990	7	9		3	5		4	4	
1991	1	15		0	8		1	7	
1992	9	7		4	4		5	3	
1993	4	12		2	6		2	6	
1994	8	8		5	3		3	5	
1995	9	7		5	3		4	4	
1996	9	7		6	2		3	5	
1997	3	13		2	6		1	7	
1998	3	13		3	5		0	8	
1999	13	3		7	1		6	2	
2000	10	6		6	2		4	4	
2001	6	10		3	5		3	5	
2002	10	6		5	3		5	3	
2003	12	4		5	3		7	1	
2004	12	4		7	1		5	3	
2005	14	2		7	1		7	1	
2006	12	4		8	0		4	4	
2007	13	3		6	2		7	1	
2008	12	4		6	2		6	2	
2009	14	2		7	1		7	1	
2010	10	6		6	2		4	4	
2011	2	14		2	6		0	8	
2012	11	5		7	1		4	4	
2013	11	5		6	2		5	3	
	475	420	7	259	188	5	216	232	2

includes Baltimore Colts (1953-1983).

JACKSONVILLE JAGUARS

Season	All Games W	L	T	Home Games W	L	T	Road Games W	L	T
1995	4	12		2	6		2	6	
1996	9	7		7	1		2	6	
1997	11	5		7	1		4	4	
1998	11	5		7	1		4	4	
1999	14	2		7	1		7	1	
2000	7	9		4	4		3	5	
2001	6	10		3	5		3	5	
2002	6	10		3	5		3	5	
2003	5	11		5	3		0	8	
2004	9	7		4	4		5	3	
2005	12	4		6	2		6	2	
2006	8	8		6	2		2	6	
2007	11	5		6	2		5	3	
2008	5	11		2	6		3	5	
2009	7	9		5	3		2	6	
2010	8	8		5	3		3	5	
2011	5	11		4	4		1	7	
2012	2	14		1	7		1	7	
2013	4	12		1	7		3	5	
	144	160		85	67		59	93	

KANSAS CITY CHIEFS*

Season	All Games W	L	T	Home Games W	L	T	Road Games W	L	T
1960	8	6		5	2		3	4	
1961	6	8		4	3		2	5	
1962	11	3		6	1		5	2	
1963	5	7	2	4	3		1	4	2
1964	7	7		4	3		3	4	
1965	7	5	2	5	2		2	3	2
1966	11	2	1	4	2	1	7	0	
1967	9	5		4	3		5	2	
1968	12	2		6	1		6	1	
1969	11	3		6	1		5	2	
1970	7	5	2	4	1	2	3	4	
1971	10	3	1	7	0		3	3	1
1972	8	6		3	4		5	2	
1973	7	5	2	5	1	1	2	4	1
1974	5	9		1	6		4	3	
1975	5	9		3	4		2	5	
1976	5	9		1	6		4	3	
1977	2	12		1	6		1	6	
1978	4	12		3	5		1	7	
1979	7	9		3	5		4	4	
1980	8	8		3	5		5	3	
1981	9	7		5	3		4	4	
1982	3	6		2	2		1	4	
1983	6	10		5	3		1	7	
1984	8	8		5	3		3	5	
1985	6	10		5	3		1	7	
1986	10	6		6	2		4	4	
1987	4	11		3	4		1	7	
1988	4	11	1	4	4		0	7	1
1989	8	7	1	5	3		3	4	1
1990	11	5		6	2		5	3	
1991	10	6		6	2		4	4	
1992	10	6		7	1		3	5	
1993	11	5		7	1		4	4	
1994	9	7		5	3		4	4	
1995	13	3		8	0		5	3	
1996	9	7		5	3		4	4	
1997	13	3		8	0		5	3	
1998	7	9		5	3		2	6	
1999	9	7		6	2		3	5	
2000	7	9		5	3		2	6	
2001	6	10		3	5		3	5	
2002	8	8		6	2		2	6	
2003	13	3		8	0		5	3	
2004	7	9		4	4		3	5	
2005	10	6		7	1		3	5	
2006	9	7		6	2		3	5	
2007	4	12		2	6		2	6	

Season	All Games W	L	T	Home Games W	L	T	Road Games W	L	T
2008	2	14		1	7		1	7	
2009	4	12		1	7		3	5	
2010	10	6		7	1		3	5	
2011	7	9		3	5		4	4	
2012	2	14		1	7		1	7	
2013	11	5		5	3		6	2	
	415	393	12	244	161	4	171	232	8

*includes Dallas Texans (1960-62).

MIAMI DOLPHINS

Season	All Games W	L	T	Home Games W	L	T	Road Games W	L	T
1966	3	11		2	5		1	6	
1967	4	10		4	3		0	7	
1968	5	8	1	1	5	1	4	3	
1969	3	10	1	2	4	1	1	6	
1970	10	4		6	1		4	3	
1971	10	3	1	6	1		4	2	1
1972	14	0		7	0		7	0	
1973	12	2		7	0		5	2	
1974	11	3		7	0		4	3	
1975	10	4		5	2		5	2	
1976	6	8		3	4		3	4	
1977	10	4		6	1		4	3	
1978	11	5		7	1		4	4	
1979	10	6		6	2		4	4	
1980	8	8		5	3		3	5	
1981	11	4	1	6	1	1	5	3	
1982	7	2		4	0		3	2	
1983	12	4		7	1		5	3	
1984	14	2		7	1		7	1	
1985	12	4		8	0		4	4	
1986	8	8		4	4		4	4	
1987	8	7		4	3		4	4	
1988	6	10		4	4		2	6	
1989	8	8		4	4		4	4	
1990	12	4		7	1		5	3	
1991	8	8		5	3		3	5	
1992	11	5		6	2		5	3	
1993	9	7		4	4		5	3	
1994	10	6		6	2		4	4	
1995	9	7		5	3		4	4	
1996	8	8		4	4		4	4	
1997	9	7		6	2		3	5	
1998	10	6		7	1		3	5	
1999	9	7		5	3		4	4	
2000	11	5		5	3		6	2	
2001	11	5		7	1		4	4	
2002	9	7		7	1		2	6	
2003	10	6		4	4		6	2	
2004	4	12		3	5		1	7	
2005	9	7		5	3		4	4	
2006	6	10		4	4		2	6	
2007	1	15		1	7		0	8	
2008	11	5		5	3		6	2	
2009	7	9		4	4		3	5	
2010	7	9		1	7		6	2	
2011	6	10		4	4		2	6	
2012	7	9		5	3		2	6	
2013	8	8		4	4		4	4	
	415	317	4	236	128	3	179	189	1

NEW ENGLAND PATRIOTS*

Season	All Games W	L	T	Home Games W	L	T	Road Games W	L	T
1960	5	9		3	4		2	5	
1961	9	4	1	4	2	1	5	2	
1962	9	4	1	6	1		3	3	1
1963	7	6	1	5	1	1	2	5	
1964	10	3	1	4	2	1	6	1	
1965	4	8	2	1	4	2	3	4	
1966	8	4	2	4	2	1	4	2	1
1967	3	10	1	2	4		1	6	1
1968	4	10		2	5		2	5	
1969	4	10		2	5		2	5	
1970	2	12		1	6		1	6	
1971	6	8		5	2		1	6	
1972	3	11		2	5		1	6	
1973	5	9		3	4		2	5	
1974	7	7		3	4		4	3	
1975	3	11		2	5		1	6	
1976	11	3		6	1		5	2	
1977	9	5		6	1		3	4	
1978	11	5		5	3		6	2	
1979	9	7		6	2		3	5	
1980	10	6		6	2		4	4	
1981	2	14		2	6		0	8	
1982	5	4		3	1		2	3	
1983	8	8		5	3		3	5	
1984	9	7		5	3		4	4	
1985	11	5		7	1		4	4	
1986	11	5		4	4		7	1	
1987	8	7		5	3		3	4	
1988	9	7		7	1		2	6	
1989	5	11		3	5		2	6	
1990	1	15		0	8		1	7	
1991	6	10		4	4		2	6	
1992	2	14		1	7		1	7	
1993	5	11		3	5		2	6	
1994	10	6		5	3		5	3	
1995	6	10		3	5		3	5	
1996	11	5		6	2		5	3	
1997	10	6		6	2		4	4	
1998	9	7		6	2		3	5	
1999	8	8		5	3		3	5	
2000	5	11		3	5		2	6	
2001	11	5		6	2		5	3	
2002	9	7		5	3		4	4	
2003	14	2		8	0		6	2	
2004	14	2		8	0		6	2	
2005	10	6		5	3		5	3	
2006	12	4		5	3		7	1	
2007	16	0		8	0		8	0	
2008	11	5		5	3		6	2	
2009	10	6		8	0		2	6	
2010	14	2		8	0		6	2	
2011	13	3		7	1		6	2	
2012	12	4		6	2		6	2	
2013	12	4		8	0		4	4	
	438	373	9	248	155	6	190	218	3

*includes Boston Patriots (1960-1970).

NEW YORK JETS*

Season	All Games W	L	T	Home Games W	L	T	Road Games W	L	T
1960	7	7		3	4		4	3	
1961	7	7		5	2		2	5	
1962	5	9		2	5		3	4	
1963	5	8	1	4	2	1	1	6	
1964	5	8	1	5	1	1	0	7	
1965	5	8	1	3	3	1	2	5	
1966	6	6	2	4	3		2	3	2
1967	8	5	1	4	2	1	4	3	
1968	11	3		6	1		5	2	
1969	10	4		5	2		5	2	
1970	4	10		2	5		2	5	
1971	6	8		4	3		2	5	
1972	7	7		4	3		3	4	
1973	4	10		2	4		2	6	
1974	7	7		3	4		4	3	

INSIDE THE NUMBERS

Season	All Games W	L	T	Home Games W	L	T	Road Games W	L	T
1975	3	11		1	6		2	5	
1976	3	11		2	5		1	6	
1977	3	11		1	6		2	5	
1978	8	8		4	4		4	4	
1979	8	8		6	2		2	6	
1980	4	12		2	6		2	6	
1981	10	5	1	6	2		4	3	1
1982	6	3		3	1		3	2	
1983	7	9		2	6		5	3	
1984	7	9		3	5		4	4	
1985	11	5		7	1		4	4	
1986	10	6		5	3		5	3	
1987	6	9		4	4		2	5	
1988	8	7	1	5	2	1	3	5	
1989	4	12		1	7		3	5	
1990	6	10		3	5		3	5	
1991	8	8		4	4		4	4	
1992	4	12		3	5		1	7	
1993	8	8		3	5		5	3	
1994	6	10		4	4		2	6	
1995	3	13		2	6		1	7	
1996	1	15		0	8		1	7	
1997	9	7		5	3		4	4	
1998	12	4		7	1		5	3	
1999	8	8		4	4		4	4	
2000	9	7		5	3		4	4	
2001	10	6		3	5		7	1	
2002	9	7		5	3		4	4	
2003	6	10		4	4		2	6	
2004	10	6		6	2		4	4	
2005	4	12		4	4		0	8	
2006	10	6		4	4		6	2	
2007	4	12		3	5		1	7	
2008	9	7		5	3		4	4	
2009	9	7		4	4		5	3	
2010	11	5		5	3		6	2	
2011	8	8		6	2		2	6	
2012	6	10		3	5		3	5	
2013	8	8		6	2		2	6	
	373	439	8	206	198	5	167	241	3

*includes New York Titans (1960-62).

OAKLAND RAIDERS*

Season	All Games W	L	T	Home Games W	L	T	Road Games W	L	T
1960	6	8		3	4		3	4	
1961	2	12		1	6		1	6	
1962	1	13		1	6		0	7	
1963	10	4		6	1		4	3	
1964	5	7	2	5	2		0	5	2
1965	8	5	1	5	2		3	3	1
1966	8	5	1	3	3	1	5	2	
1967	13	1		7	0		6	1	
1968	12	2		6	1		6	1	
1969	12	1	1	7	0		5	1	1
1970	8	4	2	6	1		2	3	2
1971	8	4	2	5	1	1	3	3	1
1972	10	3	1	5	1	1	5	2	
1973	9	4	1	5	2		4	2	1
1974	12	2		6	1		6	1	
1975	11	3		6	1		5	2	
1976	13	1		7	0		6	1	
1977	11	3		6	1		5	2	
1978	9	7		4	4		5	3	
1979	9	7		6	2		3	5	
1980	11	5		6	2		5	3	
1981	7	9		4	4		3	5	
1982	8	1		4	0		4	1	
1983	12	4		6	2		6	2	

Season	All Games W	L	T	Home Games W	L	T	Road Games W	L	T
1984	11	5		6	2		5	3	
1985	12	4		7	1		5	3	
1986	8	8		3	5		5	3	
1987	5	10		3	5		2	5	
1988	7	9		3	5		4	4	
1989	8	8		7	1		1	7	
1990	12	4		6	2		6	2	
1991	9	7		5	3		4	4	
1992	7	9		5	3		2	6	
1993	10	6		5	3		5	3	
1994	9	7		4	4		5	3	
1995	8	8		4	4		4	4	
1996	7	9		4	4		3	5	
1997	4	12		2	6		2	6	
1998	8	8		4	4		4	4	
1999	8	8		5	3		3	5	
2000	12	4		7	1		5	3	
2001	10	6		5	3		5	3	
2002	11	5		6	2		5	3	
2003	4	12		4	4		0	8	
2004	5	11		3	5		2	6	
2005	4	12		2	6		2	6	
2006	2	14		2	6		0	8	
2007	4	12		2	6		2	6	
2008	5	11		2	6		3	5	
2009	5	11		2	6		3	5	
2010	8	8		5	3		3	5	
2011	8	8		3	5		5	3	
2012	4	12		3	5		1	7	
2013	4	12		3	5		1	7	
	434	375	11	242	165	3	192	210	8

*includes Los Angeles Raiders (1982-1994).

PITTSBURGH STEELERS*

Season	All Games W	L	T	Home Games W	L	T	Road Games W	L	T
1933	3	6	2	2	3		1	3	2
1934	2	10		1	5		1	5	
1935	4	8		2	5		2	3	
1936	6	6		4	1		2	5	
1937	4	7		2	4		2	3	
1938	2	9		0	5		2	4	
1939	1	9	1	1	4		0	5	1
1940	2	7	2	1	2	2	1	5	
1941	1	9	1	1	4		0	5	1
1942	7	4		3	2		4	2	
1945	2	8		1	4		1	4	
1946	5	5	1	4	1		1	4	1
1947	8	4		5	1		3	3	
1948	4	8		4	2		0	6	
1949	6	5	1	3	2	1	3	3	
1950	6	6		2	4		4	2	
1951	4	7	1	1	4	1	3	3	
1952	5	7		2	4		3	3	
1953	6	6		3	3		3	3	
1954	5	7		4	2		1	5	
1955	4	8		3	2		1	6	
1956	5	7		3	3		2	4	
1957	6	6		4	2		2	4	
1958	7	4	1	5	1		2	3	1
1959	6	5	1	3	2	1	3	3	
1960	5	6	1	4	2		1	4	1
1961	6	8		4	3		2	5	
1962	9	5		4	3		5	2	
1963	7	4	3	5	0	2	2	4	1
1964	5	9		2	5		3	4	
1965	2	12		1	6		1	6	
1966	5	8	1	3	3	1	2	5	
1967	4	9	1	1	6		3	3	1
1968	2	11	1	1	6		1	5	1

Season	All Games W	L	T	Home Games W	L	T	Road Games W	L	T
1969	1	13		1	6		0	7	
1970	5	9		4	3		1	6	
1971	6	8		5	2		1	6	
1972	11	3		7	0		4	3	
1973	10	4		7	1		3	3	
1974	10	3	1	5	2		5	1	1
1975	12	2		6	1		6	1	
1976	10	4		6	1		4	3	
1977	9	5		6	1		3	4	
1978	14	2		7	1		7	1	
1979	12	4		8	0		4	4	
1980	9	7		6	2		3	5	
1981	8	8		5	3		3	5	
1982	6	3		4	0		2	3	
1983	10	6		4	4		6	2	
1984	9	7		6	2		3	5	
1985	7	9		5	3		2	6	
1986	6	10		4	4		2	6	
1987	8	7		4	3		4	4	
1988	5	11		4	4		1	7	
1989	9	7		4	4		5	3	
1990	9	7		6	2		3	5	
1991	7	9		5	3		2	6	
1992	11	5		7	1		4	4	
1993	9	7		6	2		3	5	
1994	12	4		7	1		5	3	
1995	11	5		6	2		5	3	
1996	10	6		7	1		3	5	
1997	11	5		7	1		4	4	
1998	7	9		5	3		2	6	
1999	6	10		2	6		4	4	
2000	9	7		4	4		5	3	
2001	13	3		7	1		6	2	
2002	10	5	1	5	2	1	5	3	
2003	6	10		4	4		2	6	
2004	15	1		8	0		7	1	
2005	11	5		5	3		6	2	
2006	8	8		5	3		3	5	
2007	10	6		7	1		3	5	
2008	12	4		6	2		6	2	
2009	9	7		6	2		3	5	
2010	12	4		5	3		7	1	
2011	12	4		7	1		5	3	
2012	8	8		5	3		3	5	
2013	8	8		5	3		3	5	
	569	519	20	334	207	9	235	312	11

*includes Pittsburgh Pirates (1933-39).

SAN DIEGO CHARGERS*

Season	All Games W	L	T	Home Games W	L	T	Road Games W	L	T
1960	10	4		5	2		5	2	
1961	12	2		6	1		6	1	
1962	4	10		3	4		1	6	
1963	11	3		6	1		5	2	
1964	8	5	1	4	3		4	2	1
1965	9	2	3	4	1	2	5	1	1
1966	7	6	1	5	2		2	4	1
1967	8	5	1	5	2	1	3	3	
1968	9	5		4	3		5	2	
1969	8	6		5	2		3	4	
1970	5	6	3	2	3	2	3	3	1
1971	6	8		6	1		0	7	
1972	4	9	1	2	5		2	4	1
1973	2	11	1	2	5		0	6	1
1974	5	9		3	4		2	5	
1975	2	12		1	6		1	6	
1976	6	8		3	4		3	4	
1977	7	7		3	4		4	3	
1978	9	7		5	3		4	4	

Season	All Games W	L	T	Home Games W	L	T	Road Games W	L	T
1979	12	4		7	1		5	3	
1980	11	5		6	2		5	3	
1981	10	6		5	3		5	3	
1982	6	3		3	1		3	2	
1983	6	10		4	4		2	6	
1984	7	9		4	4		3	5	
1985	8	8		6	2		2	6	
1986	4	12		2	6		2	6	
1987	8	7		4	3		4	4	
1988	6	10		3	5		3	5	
1989	6	10		4	4		2	6	
1990	6	10		3	5		3	5	
1991	4	12		3	5		1	7	
1992	11	5		6	2		5	3	
1993	8	8		4	4		4	4	
1994	11	5		5	3		6	2	
1995	9	7		5	3		4	4	
1996	8	8		5	3		3	5	
1997	4	12		2	6		2	6	
1998	5	11		4	4		1	7	
1999	8	8		4	4		4	4	
2000	1	15		1	7		0	8	
2001	5	11		4	4		1	7	
2002	8	8		5	3		3	5	
2003	4	12		2	6		2	6	
2004	12	4		7	1		5	3	
2005	9	7		4	4		5	3	
2006	14	2		8	0		6	2	
2007	11	5		7	1		4	4	
2008	8	8		5	3		3	5	
2009	13	3		6	2		7	1	
2010	9	7		6	2		3	5	
2011	8	8		5	3		3	5	
2012	7	9		3	5		4	4	
2013	8	8		5	3		4	4	
	408	401	11	231	174	5	177	227	6

*includes Los Angeles Chargers (1960).

TENNESSEE TITANS*

Season	All Games W	L	T	Home Games W	L	T	Road Games W	L	T
1960	10	4		6	1		4	3	
1961	10	3	1	6	1		4	2	1
1962	11	3		6	1		5	2	
1963	6	8		4	3		2	5	
1964	4	10		3	4		1	6	
1965	4	10		3	4		1	6	
1966	3	11		3	4		0	7	
1967	9	4	1	5	2		4	2	1
1968	7	7		3	4		4	3	
1969	6	6	2	4	2	1	2	4	1
1970	3	10	1	1	6		2	4	1
1971	4	9	1	3	3	1	1	6	
1972	1	13		1	6		0	7	
1973	1	13		0	7		1	6	
1974	7	7		3	4		4	3	
1975	10	4		5	2		5	2	
1976	5	9		3	4		2	5	
1977	8	6		5	2		3	4	
1978	10	6		5	3		5	3	
1979	11	5		6	2		5	3	
1980	11	5		6	2		5	3	
1981	7	9		5	3		2	6	
1982	1	8		1	4		0	4	
1983	2	14		2	6		0	8	
1984	3	13		2	6		1	7	
1985	5	11		4	4		1	7	
1986	5	11		4	4		1	7	
1987	9	6		5	2		4	4	
1988	10	6		7	1		3	5	

Season	All Games W	L	T	Home Games W	L	T	Road Games W	L	T
1989	9	7		6	2		3	5	
1990	9	7		6	2		3	5	
1991	11	5		7	1		4	4	
1992	10	6		5	3		5	3	
1993	12	4		7	1		5	3	
1994	2	14		2	6		0	8	
1995	7	9		3	5		4	4	
1996	8	8		2	6		6	2	
1997	8	8		6	2		2	6	
1998	8	8		3	5		5	3	
1999	13	3		8	0		5	3	
2000	13	3		7	1		6	2	
2001	7	9		3	5		4	4	
2002	11	5		6	2		5	3	
2003	12	4		7	1		5	3	
2004	5	11		2	6		3	5	
2005	4	12		3	5		1	7	
2006	8	8		4	4		4	4	
2007	10	6		5	3		5	3	
2008	13	3		7	1		6	2	
2009	8	8		5	3		3	5	
2010	6	10		3	5		3	5	
2011	9	7		5	3		4	4	
2012	6	10		4	4		2	6	
2013	7	9		3	5		4	4	
	399	415	6	230	178	2	169	237	4

*includes Houston (1960-1996) and Tennessee Oilers (1997-98)

NFC
ARIZONA CARDINALS*

Season	All Games W	L	T	Home Games W	L	T	Road Games W	L	T
1920	6	2	2	5	1	1	1	1	1
1921	3	3	2	3	3	1	0	0	1
1922	8	3		8	3		0	0	
1923	8	4		8	3		0	1	
1924	5	4	1	5	3	1	0	1	
1925	11	2	1	11	2		0	0	1
1926	5	6	1	3	3		2	3	1
1927	3	7	1	2	3	1	1	4	
1928	1	5		1	1		0	4	
1929	6	6	1	3	2		3	4	1
1930	5	6	2	3	2		2	4	2
1931	5	4		3	0		2	4	
1932	2	6	2	1	2	1	1	4	1
1933	1	9	1	0	4	1	1	5	
1934	5	6		2	2		3	4	
1935	6	4	2	2	2		4	2	2
1936	3	8	1	3	1	1	0	7	
1937	5	5	1	1	3		4	2	1
1938	2	9		1	4		1	5	
1939	1	10		0	4		1	6	
1940	2	7	2	2	1	1	0	6	1
1941	3	7	1	0	3	1	3	4	
1942	3	8		2	2		1	6	
1943	0	10		0	3		0	7	
1945	1	9		0	3		1	6	
1946	6	5		2	2		4	3	
1947	9	3		5	0		4	3	
1948	11	1		5	1		6	0	
1949	6	5	1	2	3	1	4	2	
1950	5	7		3	3		2	4	
1951	3	9		1	5		2	4	
1952	4	8		2	4		2	4	
1953	1	10	1	0	5	1	1	5	
1954	2	10		2	4		0	6	
1955	4	7	1	3	2	1	1	5	
1956	7	5		4	2		3	3	
1957	3	9		0	6		3	3	
1958	2	9	1	1	4	1	1	5	

Season	All Games W	L	T	Home Games W	L	T	Road Games W	L	T
1959	2	10		2	4		0	6	
1960	6	5	1	3	2	1	3	3	
1961	7	7		3	4		4	3	
1962	4	9	1	2	4	1	2	5	
1963	9	5		3	4		6	1	
1964	9	3	2	4	1	1	5	2	1
1965	5	9		2	5		3	4	
1966	8	5	1	5	1	1	3	4	
1967	6	7	1	3	3	1	3	4	
1968	9	4	1	4	2	1	5	2	
1969	4	9	1	3	4		1	5	1
1970	8	5	1	6	1		2	4	1
1971	4	9	1	1	5	1	3	4	
1972	4	9	1	2	5		2	4	1
1973	4	9	1	2	4	1	2	5	
1974	10	4		5	2		5	2	
1975	11	3		6	1		5	2	
1976	10	4		6	1		4	3	
1977	7	7		4	3		3	4	
1978	6	10		3	5		3	5	
1979	5	11		3	5		2	6	
1980	5	11		2	6		3	5	
1981	7	9		5	3		2	6	
1982	5	4		1	3		4	1	
1983	8	7	1	4	3	1	4	4	
1984	9	7		5	3		4	4	
1985	5	11		4	4		1	7	
1986	4	11	1	3	5		1	6	1
1987	7	8		4	3		3	5	
1988	7	9		4	4		3	5	
1989	5	11		2	6		3	5	
1990	5	11		3	5		2	6	
1991	4	12		2	6		2	6	
1992	4	12		3	5		1	7	
1993	7	9		4	4		3	5	
1994	8	8		5	3		3	5	
1995	4	12		3	5		1	7	
1996	7	9		5	3		2	6	
1997	4	12		3	5		1	7	
1998	9	7		5	3		4	4	
1999	6	10		4	4		2	6	
2000	3	13		3	5		0	8	
2001	7	9		3	5		4	4	
2002	5	11		3	5		2	6	
2003	4	12		4	4		0	8	
2004	6	10		5	3		1	7	
2005	5	11		3	5		2	6	
2006	5	11		3	5		2	6	
2007	8	8		6	2		2	6	
2008	9	7		6	2		3	5	
2009	10	6		4	4		6	2	
2010	5	11		4	4		1	7	
2011	8	8		6	2		2	6	
2012	5	11		4	4		1	7	
2013	10	6		6	2		4	4	
	511	706	39	302	302	22	209	404	17

*includes Chicago Cardinals (1920-1959), St. Louis Cardinals (1960-1987), and Phoenix Cardinals (1988-1993).

ATLANTA FALCONS

Season	All Games W	L	T	Home Games W	L	T	Road Games W	L	T
1966	3	11		1	6		2	5	
1967	1	12	1	1	5	1	0	7	
1968	2	12		1	6		1	6	
1969	6	8		4	3		2	5	
1970	4	8	2	3	4		1	4	2
1971	7	6	1	4	3		3	3	1
1972	7	7		4	3		3	4	
1973	9	5		4	3		5	2	

Season	All Games W	L	T	Home Games W	L	T	Road Games W	L	T
1974	3	11		2	5		1	6	
1975	4	10		3	4		1	6	
1976	4	10		3	4		1	6	
1977	7	7		4	3		3	4	
1978	9	7		7	1		2	6	
1979	6	10		3	5		3	5	
1980	12	4		6	2		6	2	
1981	7	9		4	4		3	5	
1982	5	4		2	3		3	1	
1983	7	9		4	4		3	5	
1984	4	12		2	6		2	6	
1985	4	12		3	5		1	7	
1986	7	8	1	2	5	1	5	3	
1987	3	12		2	6		1	6	
1988	5	11		2	6		3	5	
1989	3	13		3	5		0	8	
1990	5	11		5	3		0	8	
1991	10	6		6	2		4	4	
1992	6	10		5	3		1	7	
1993	6	10		4	4		2	6	
1994	7	9		5	3		2	6	
1995	9	7		7	1		2	6	
1996	3	13		2	6		1	7	
1997	7	9		3	5		4	4	
1998	14	2		8	0		6	2	
1999	5	11		4	4		1	7	
2000	4	12		3	5		1	7	
2001	7	9		3	5		4	4	
2002	9	6	1	5	3		4	3	1
2003	5	11		2	6		3	5	
2004	11	5		7	1		4	4	
2005	8	8		4	4		4	4	
2006	7	9		3	5		4	4	
2007	4	12		3	5		1	7	
2008	11	5		7	1		4	4	
2009	9	7		6	2		3	5	
2010	13	3		7	1		6	2	
2011	10	6		6	2		4	4	
2012	13	3		7	1		6	2	
2013	4	12		3	5		1	7	
	316	414	6	189	178	2	127	236	4

CAROLINA PANTHERS

Season	All Games W	L	T	Home Games W	L	T	Road Games W	L	T
1995	7	9		5	3		2	6	
1996	12	4		8	0		4	4	
1997	7	9		2	6		5	3	
1998	4	12		2	6		2	6	
1999	8	8		5	3		3	5	
2000	7	9		5	3		2	6	
2001	1	15		0	8		1	7	
2002	7	9		4	4		3	5	
2003	11	5		6	2		5	3	
2004	7	9		3	5		4	4	
2005	11	5		5	3		6	2	
2006	8	8		4	4		4	4	
2007	7	9		2	6		5	3	
2008	12	4		8	0		4	4	
2009	8	8		5	3		3	5	
2010	2	14		2	6		0	8	
2011	6	10		3	5		3	5	
2012	7	9		3	5		4	4	
2013	12	4		7	1		5	3	
	144	160		79	73		65	87	

CHICAGO BEARS*

Season	All Games W	L	T	Home Games W	L	T	Road Games W	L	T
1920	10	1	2	6	0	1	4	1	1
1921	9	1	1	9	1	1	0	0	
1922	9	3		7	1		2	2	
1923	9	2	1	7	1	1	2	1	
1924	6	1	4	5	0	3	1	1	1
1925	9	5	3	7	1	1	2	4	2
1926	12	1	3	10	0	2	2	1	1
1927	9	3	2	7	1	1	2	2	1
1928	7	5	1	6	3		1	2	1
1929	4	9	2	1	5	2	3	4	
1930	9	4	1	5	2	1	4	2	
1931	8	5		6	3		2	2	
1932	7	1	6	6	1	1	1	0	5
1933	10	2	1	6	0		4	2	1
1934	13	0		5	0		8	0	
1935	6	4	2	1	2	2	5	2	
1936	9	3		3	1		6	2	
1937	9	1	1	4	1		5	0	1
1938	6	5		2	3		4	2	
1939	8	3		4	1		4	2	
1940	8	3		5	0		3	3	
1941	10	1		5	1		5	0	
1942	11	0		6	0		5	0	
1943	8	1	1	5	0		3	1	1
1944	6	3	1	4	0	1	2	3	
1945	3	7		2	3		1	4	
1946	8	2	1	4	1	1	4	1	
1947	8	4		4	2		4	2	
1948	10	2		5	1		5	1	
1949	9	3		5	1		4	2	
1950	9	3		6	0		3	3	
1951	7	5		3	3		4	2	
1952	5	7		3	3		2	4	
1953	3	8	1	1	4	1	2	4	
1954	8	4		4	2		4	2	
1955	8	4		5	1		3	3	
1956	9	2	1	6	0		3	2	1
1957	5	7		2	4		3	3	
1958	8	4		5	1		3	3	
1959	8	4		4	2		4	2	
1960	5	6	1	4	2		1	4	1
1961	8	6		5	2		3	4	
1962	9	5		4	3		5	2	
1963	11	1	2	6	0	1	5	1	1
1964	5	9		2	5		3	4	
1965	9	5		5	2		4	3	
1966	5	7	2	4	1	2	1	6	
1967	7	6	1	3	3	1	4	3	
1968	7	7		2	5		5	2	
1969	1	13		1	6		0	7	
1970	6	8		3	4		3	4	
1971	6	8		4	3		2	5	
1972	4	9	1	1	5	1	3	4	
1973	3	11		1	6		2	5	
1974	4	10		4	3		0	7	
1975	4	10		3	4		1	6	
1976	7	7		4	3		3	4	
1977	9	5		5	2		4	3	
1978	7	9		4	4		3	5	
1979	10	6		6	2		4	4	
1980	7	9		5	3		2	6	
1981	6	10		4	4		2	6	
1982	3	6		2	2		1	4	
1983	8	8		5	3		3	5	
1984	10	6		6	2		4	4	
1985	15	1		8	0		7	1	
1986	14	2		7	1		7	1	
1987	11	4		6	2		5	2	
1988	12	4		7	1		5	3	

Season	All Games W	L	T	Home Games W	L	T	Road Games W	L	T
1989	6	10		4	4		2	6	
1990	11	5		7	1		4	4	
1991	11	5		6	2		5	3	
1992	5	11		4	4		1	7	
1993	7	9		3	5		4	4	
1994	9	7		5	3		4	4	
1995	9	7		5	3		4	4	
1996	7	9		6	2		1	7	
1997	4	12		2	6		2	6	
1998	4	12		3	5		1	7	
1999	6	10		3	5		3	5	
2000	5	11		3	5		2	6	
2001	13	3		7	1		6	2	
2002	4	12		3	5		1	7	
2003	7	9		6	2		1	7	
2004	5	11		2	6		3	5	
2005	11	5		7	1		4	4	
2006	13	3		6	2		7	1	
2007	7	9		4	4		3	5	
2008	9	7		6	2		3	5	
2009	7	9		5	3		2	6	
2010	11	5		5	3		6	2	
2011	8	8		5	3		3	5	
2012	10	6		5	3		5	3	
2013	8	8		5	3		3	5	
	730	534	42	429	222	24	301	312	18

includes Decatur Staleys (1920) and Chicago Staleys (1921).

DALLAS COWBOYS

Season	All Games W	L	T	Home Games W	L	T	Road Games W	L	T
1960	0	11	1	0	6		0	5	1
1961	4	9	1	2	4	1	2	5	
1962	5	8	1	2	4	1	3	4	
1963	4	10		3	4		1	6	
1964	5	8	1	2	4	1	3	4	
1965	7	7		5	2		2	5	
1966	10	3	1	6	1		4	2	1
1967	9	5		5	2		4	3	
1968	12	2		5	2		7	0	
1969	11	2	1	6	0	1	5	2	
1970	10	4		6	1		4	3	
1971	11	3		6	1		5	2	
1972	10	4		5	2		5	2	
1973	10	4		6	1		4	3	
1974	8	6		5	2		3	4	
1975	10	4		5	2		5	2	
1976	11	3		6	1		5	2	
1977	12	2		6	1		6	1	
1978	12	4		7	1		5	3	
1979	11	5		6	2		5	3	
1980	12	4		8	0		4	4	
1981	12	4		8	0		4	4	
1982	6	3		3	2		3	1	
1983	12	4		6	2		6	2	
1984	9	7		5	3		4	4	
1985	10	6		7	1		3	5	
1986	7	9		3	5		4	4	
1987	7	8		3	4		4	4	
1988	3	13		1	7		2	6	
1989	1	15		0	8		1	7	
1990	7	9		5	3		2	6	
1991	11	5		6	2		5	3	
1992	13	3		7	1		6	2	
1993	12	4		6	2		6	2	
1994	12	4		6	2		6	2	
1995	12	4		6	2		6	2	
1996	10	6		6	2		4	4	
1997	6	10		5	3		1	7	
1998	10	6		6	2		4	4	

Season	All Games W	L	T	Home Games W	L	T	Road Games W	L	T
1999	8	8		7	1		1	7	
2000	5	11		3	5		2	6	
2001	5	11		4	4		1	7	
2002	5	11		4	4		1	7	
2003	10	6		6	2		4	4	
2004	6	10		4	4		2	6	
2005	9	7		5	3		4	4	
2006	9	7		4	4		5	3	
2007	13	3		6	2		7	1	
2008	9	7		6	2		3	5	
2009	11	5		6	2		5	3	
2010	6	10		2	6		4	4	
2011	8	8		5	3		3	5	
2012	8	8		4	4		4	4	
2013	8	8		5	3		3	5	
	464	348	6	262	143	4	202	205	2

DETROIT LIONS*

Season	All Games W	L	T	Home Games W	L	T	Road Games W	L	T
1930	5	6	3	5	1	2	0	5	1
1931	11	3		8	0		3	3	
1932	6	2	4	3	0	2	3	2	2
1933	6	5		4	1		2	4	
1934	10	3		6	2		4	1	
1935	7	3	2	5	0	1	2	3	1
1936	8	4		5	1		3	3	
1937	7	4		4	2		3	2	
1938	7	4		4	3		3	1	
1939	6	5		4	2		2	3	
1940	5	5	1	3	3		2	2	1
1941	4	6	1	3	2		1	4	1
1942	0	11		0	7		0	4	
1943	3	6	1	2	2	1	1	4	
1944	6	3	1	4	2		2	1	1
1945	7	3		4	1		3	2	
1946	1	10		1	5		0	5	
1947	3	9		2	4		1	5	
1948	2	10		2	4		0	6	
1949	4	8		2	4		2	4	
1950	6	6		4	2		2	4	
1951	7	4	1	3	3	1	4	1	
1952	9	3		6	1		3	2	
1953	10	2		5	1		5	1	
1954	9	2	1	5	0	1	4	2	
1955	3	9		3	4		0	5	
1956	9	3		5	1		4	2	
1957	8	4		5	1		3	3	
1958	4	7	1	2	4		2	3	1
1959	3	8	1	2	4		1	4	1
1960	7	5		5	1		2	4	
1961	8	5	1	2	5		6	0	1
1962	11	3		7	0		4	3	
1963	5	8	1	3	3	1	2	5	
1964	7	5	2	3	3	1	4	2	1
1965	6	7	1	2	4	1	4	3	
1966	4	9	1	3	4		1	5	1
1967	5	7	2	3	4		2	3	2
1968	4	8	2	1	4	2	3	4	
1969	9	4	1	5	2		4	2	1
1970	10	4		6	1		4	3	
1971	7	6	1	3	4		4	2	1
1972	8	5	1	5	2		3	3	1
1973	6	7	1	4	3		2	4	1
1974	7	7		5	2		2	5	
1975	7	7		4	3		3	4	
1976	6	8		5	2		1	6	
1977	6	8		5	2		1	6	
1978	7	9		5	3		2	6	
1979	2	14		2	6		0	8	

Season	All Games W	L	T	Home Games W	L	T	Road Games W	L	T
1980	9	7		6	2		3	5	
1981	8	8		7	1		1	7	
1982	4	5		2	3		2	2	
1983	9	7		6	2		3	5	
1984	4	11	1	2	5	1	2	6	
1985	7	9		6	2		1	7	
1986	5	11		1	7		4	4	
1987	4	11		1	6		3	5	
1988	4	12		2	6		2	6	
1989	7	9		4	4		3	5	
1990	6	10		3	5		3	5	
1991	12	4		8	0		4	4	
1992	5	11		3	5		2	6	
1993	10	6		5	3		5	3	
1994	9	7		6	2		3	5	
1995	10	6		7	1		3	5	
1996	5	11		4	4		1	7	
1997	9	7		6	2		3	5	
1998	5	11		4	4		1	7	
1999	8	8		6	2		2	6	
2000	9	7		4	4		5	3	
2001	2	14		2	6		0	8	
2002	3	13		3	5		0	8	
2003	5	11		5	3		0	8	
2004	6	10		3	5		3	5	
2005	5	11		3	5		2	6	
2006	3	13		2	6		1	7	
2007	7	9		5	3		2	6	
2008	0	16		0	8		0	8	
2009	2	14		2	6		0	8	
2010	6	10		4	4		2	6	
2011	10	6		5	3		5	3	
2012	4	12		2	6		2	6	
2013	7	9		4	4		3	5	
	517	620	32	322	259	14	195	361	18

*includes Portsmouth Spartans (1930-33).

GREEN BAY PACKERS

Season	All Games W	L	T	Home Games W	L	T	Road Games W	L	T
1921	3	2	1	2	1		1	1	
1922	4	3	3	4	1	1	0	2	2
1923	7	2	1	4	2	1	3	0	
1924	7	4		5	0		2	4	
1925	8	5		6	0		2	5	
1926	7	3	3	4	1	2	3	2	1
1927	7	2	1	6	1		1	1	1
1928	6	4	3	2	2	2	4	2	1
1929	12	0	1	5	0		7	0	1
1930	10	3	1	6	0		4	3	1
1931	12	2		8	0		4	2	
1932	10	3	1	5	0	1	5	3	
1933	5	7	1	3	2	1	2	5	
1934	7	6		4	2		3	4	
1935	8	4		5	2		3	2	
1936	10	1	1	5	1		5	0	1
1937	7	4		3	2		4	2	
1938	8	3		4	2		4	1	
1939	9	2		4	1		5	1	
1940	6	4	1	4	2		2	2	1
1941	10	1		4	1		6	0	
1942	8	2	1	4	1		4	1	1
1943	7	2	1	2	1	1	5	1	
1944	8	2		5	0		3	2	
1945	6	4		4	1		2	3	
1946	6	5		2	3		4	2	
1947	6	5	1	4	2		2	3	1
1948	3	9		2	4		1	5	
1949	2	10		1	5		1	5	
1950	3	9		3	3		0	6	
1951	3	9		2	4		1	5	
1952	6	6		3	3		3	3	
1953	2	9	1	1	5		1	4	1
1954	4	8		2	4		2	4	
1955	6	6		5	1		1	5	
1956	4	8		2	4		2	4	
1957	3	9		1	5		2	4	
1958	1	10	1	1	4	1	0	6	
1959	7	5		4	2		3	3	
1960	8	4		4	2		4	2	
1961	11	3		6	1		5	2	
1962	13	1		7	0		6	1	
1963	11	2	1	6	1		5	1	1
1964	8	5	1	4	3		4	2	1
1965	10	3	1	6	1		4	2	1
1966	12	2		6	1		6	1	
1967	9	4	1	4	2	1	5	2	
1968	6	7	1	2	5		4	2	1
1969	8	6		5	2		3	4	
1970	6	8		4	3		2	5	
1971	4	8	2	3	3	1	1	5	1
1972	10	4		4	3		6	1	
1973	5	7	2	3	2	2	2	5	
1974	6	8		4	3		2	5	
1975	4	10		3	4		1	6	
1976	5	9		4	3		1	6	
1977	4	10		2	5		2	5	
1978	8	7	1	5	2	1	3	5	
1979	5	11		4	4		1	7	
1980	5	10	1	4	4		1	6	1
1981	8	8		4	4		4	4	
1982	5	3	1	3	1		2	2	1
1983	8	8		5	3		3	5	
1984	8	8		5	3		3	5	
1985	8	8		5	3		3	5	
1986	4	12		1	7		3	5	
1987	5	9	1	2	5	1	3	4	
1988	4	12		2	6		2	6	
1989	10	6		6	2		4	4	
1990	6	10		3	5		3	5	
1991	4	12		2	6		2	6	
1992	9	7		6	2		3	5	
1993	9	7		6	2		3	5	
1994	9	7		7	1		2	6	
1995	11	5		7	1		4	4	
1996	13	3		8	0		5	3	
1997	13	3		8	0		5	3	
1998	11	5		7	1		4	4	
1999	8	8		5	3		3	5	
2000	9	7		6	2		3	5	
2001	12	4		7	1		5	3	
2002	12	4		8	0		4	4	
2003	10	6		5	3		5	3	
2004	10	6		4	4		6	2	
2005	4	12		3	5		1	7	
2006	8	8		3	5		5	3	
2007	13	3		7	1		6	2	
2008	6	10		4	4		2	6	
2009	11	5		6	2		5	3	
2010	10	6		7	1		3	5	
2011	15	1		8	0		7	1	
2012	11	5		7	1		4	4	
2013	8	7	1	4	3	1	4	4	
	698	537	37	402	216	17	296	321	20

MINNESOTA VIKINGS

Season	All Games W	L	T	Home Games W	L	T	Road Games W	L	T
1961	3	11		3	4		0	7	
1962	2	11	1	1	5	1	1	6	
1963	5	8	1	3	4		2	4	1
1964	8	5	1	4	3		4	2	1
1965	7	7		2	5		5	2	
1966	4	9	1	2	5		2	4	1
1967	3	8	3	1	4	2	2	4	1
1968	8	6		4	3		4	3	
1969	12	2		7	0		5	2	
1970	12	2		7	0		5	2	
1971	11	3		5	2		6	1	
1972	7	7		3	4		4	3	
1973	12	2		7	0		5	2	
1974	10	4		4	3		6	1	
1975	12	2		7	0		5	2	
1976	11	2	1	6	0	1	5	2	
1977	9	5		5	2		4	3	
1978	8	7	1	5	3		3	4	1
1979	7	9		5	3		2	6	
1980	9	7		5	3		4	4	
1981	7	9		5	3		2	6	
1982	5	4		4	1		1	3	
1983	8	8		3	5		5	3	
1984	3	13		2	6		1	7	
1985	7	9		4	4		3	5	
1986	9	7		5	3		4	4	
1987	8	7		5	3		3	4	
1988	11	5		7	1		4	4	
1989	10	6		8	0		2	6	
1990	6	10		4	4		2	6	
1991	8	8		4	4		4	4	
1992	11	5		5	3		6	2	
1993	9	7		4	4		5	3	
1994	10	6		6	2		4	4	
1995	8	8		6	2		2	6	
1996	9	7		5	3		4	4	
1997	9	7		5	3		4	4	
1998	15	1		8	0		7	1	
1999	10	6		6	2		4	4	
2000	11	5		7	1		4	4	
2001	5	11		5	3		0	8	
2002	6	10		4	4		2	6	
2003	9	7		6	2		3	5	
2004	8	8		5	3		3	5	
2005	9	7		6	2		3	5	
2006	6	10		3	5		3	5	
2007	8	8		5	3		3	5	
2008	10	6		6	2		4	4	
2009	12	4		8	0		4	4	
2010	6	10		4	4		2	6	
2011	3	13		1	7		2	6	
2012	10	6		7	1		3	5	
2013	5	10	1	5	3		0	7	1
	431	365	10	254	146	4	177	219	6

NEW ORLEANS SAINTS

Season	All Games W	L	T	Home Games W	L	T	Road Games W	L	T
1967	3	11		2	5		1	6	
1968	4	9	1	3	4		1	5	1
1969	5	9		3	4		2	5	
1970	2	11	1	2	5		0	6	1
1971	4	8	2	2	4	1	2	4	1
1972	2	11	1	2	5		0	6	1
1973	5	9		5	2		0	7	
1974	5	9		4	3		1	6	
1975	2	12		2	5		0	7	
1976	4	10		2	5		2	5	
1977	3	11		2	5		1	6	

(Minnesota Vikings continued — right column)

Season	All Games W	L	T	Home Games W	L	T	Road Games W	L	T
1978	7	9		3	5		4	4	
1979	8	8		3	5		5	3	
1980	1	15		0	8		1	7	
1981	4	12		2	6		2	6	
1982	4	5		2	3		2	2	
1983	8	8		5	3		3	5	
1984	7	9		3	5		4	4	
1985	5	11		3	5		2	6	
1986	7	9		4	4		3	5	
1987	12	3		6	1		6	2	
1988	10	6		5	3		5	3	
1989	9	7		5	3		4	4	
1990	8	8		5	3		3	5	
1991	11	5		6	2		5	3	
1992	12	4		6	2		6	2	
1993	8	8		4	4		4	4	
1994	7	9		3	5		4	4	
1995	7	9		4	4		3	5	
1996	3	13		2	6		1	7	
1997	6	10		3	5		3	5	
1998	6	10		4	4		2	6	
1999	3	13		3	5		0	8	
2000	10	6		3	5		7	1	
2001	7	9		3	5		4	4	
2002	9	7		4	4		5	3	
2003	8	8		5	3		3	5	
2004	8	8		3	5		5	3	
2005	3	13		1	7		2	6	
2006	10	6		4	4		6	2	
2007	7	9		3	5		4	4	
2008	8	8		6	2		2	6	
2009	13	3		6	2		7	1	
2010	11	5		5	3		6	2	
2011	13	3		8	0		5	3	
2012	7	9		4	4		3	5	
2013	11	5		8	0		3	5	
	317	400	5	173	187	1	144	213	4

NEW YORK GIANTS

Season	All Games W	L	T	Home Games W	L	T	Road Games W	L	T
1925	8	4		7	2		1	2	
1926	8	4	1	5	2	1	3	2	
1927	11	1	1	7	1		4	0	1
1928	4	7	2	1	2	2	3	5	
1929	13	1	1	7	1		6	0	1
1930	13	4		6	2		7	2	
1931	7	6	1	4	2	1	3	4	
1932	4	6	2	3	2	1	1	4	1
1933	11	3		7	0		4	3	
1934	8	5		5	1		3	4	
1935	9	3		4	2		5	1	
1936	5	6	1	3	3	1	2	3	
1937	6	3	2	4	2	1	2	1	1
1938	8	2	1	6	1		2	1	1
1939	9	1	1	6	0		3	1	1
1940	6	4	1	4	3		2	1	1
1941	8	3		5	2		3	1	
1942	5	5	1	3	2	1	2	3	
1943	6	3	1	4	2		2	1	1
1944	8	1	1	5	1		3	0	1
1945	3	6	1	2	4		1	2	1
1946	7	3	1	5	1	1	2	2	
1947	2	8	2	2	3	1	0	5	1
1948	4	8		2	4		2	4	
1949	6	6		2	4		4	2	
1950	10	2		5	1		5	1	
1951	9	2	1	5	1		4	1	1
1952	7	5		2	4		5	1	
1953	3	9		2	4		1	5	

Season	All Games W	L	T	Home Games W	L	T	Road Games W	L	T	Season	All Games W	L	T	Home Games W	L	T	Road Games W	L	T
1954	7	5		4	2		3	3		1938	5	6		2	3		3	3	
1955	6	5	1	4	1	1	2	4		1939	1	9	1	1	3	1	0	6	
1956	8	3	1	4	1	1	4	2		1940	1	10		1	4		0	6	
1957	7	5		3	3		4	2		1941	2	8	1	1	4	1	1	4	
1958	9	3		5	1		4	2		1942	2	9		0	5		2	4	
1959	10	2		5	1		5	1		1944	7	1	2	3	1	2	4	0	
1960	6	4	2	1	3	2	5	1		1945	7	3		6	0		1	3	
1961	10	3	1	4	2	1	6	1		1946	6	5		3	2		3	3	
1962	12	2		6	1		6	1		1947	8	4		6	1		2	3	
1963	11	3		5	2		6	1		1948	9	2	1	6	0		3	2	1
1964	2	10	2	2	5		0	5	2	1949	11	1		6	0		5	1	
1965	7	7		3	4		4	3		1950	6	6		2	4		4	2	
1966	1	12	1	1	6		0	6	1	1951	4	8		1	5		3	3	
1967	7	7		5	2		2	5		1952	7	5		4	2		3	3	
1968	7	7		3	4		4	3		1953	7	4	1	5	0	1	2	4	
1969	6	8		5	2		1	6		1954	7	4	1	5	1		2	3	1
1970	9	5		5	2		4	3		1955	4	7	1	4	2		0	5	1
1971	4	10		1	6		3	4		1956	3	8	1	2	3	1	1	5	
1972	8	6		4	3		4	3		1957	4	8		3	3		1	5	
1973	2	11	1	2	4	1	0	7		1958	2	9	1	2	4		0	5	1
1974	2	12		0	7		2	5		1959	7	5		5	1		2	4	
1975	5	9		2	5		3	4		1960	10	2		5	1		5	1	
1976	3	11		3	4		0	7		1961	10	4		5	2		5	2	
1977	5	9		3	4		2	5		1962	3	10	1	2	5		1	5	1
1978	6	10		5	3		1	7		1963	2	10	2	1	5	1	1	5	1
1979	6	10		4	4		2	6		1964	6	8		3	4		3	4	
1980	4	12		2	6		2	6		1965	5	9		2	5		3	4	
1981	9	7		4	4		5	3		1966	9	5		5	2		4	3	
1982	4	5		2	3		2	2		1967	6	7	1	5	2		1	5	1
1983	3	12	1	1	7		2	5	1	1968	2	12		1	6		1	6	
1984	9	7		6	2		3	5		1969	4	9	1	2	5		2	4	1
1985	10	6		6	2		4	4		1970	3	10	1	3	3	1	0	7	
1986	14	2		8	0		6	2		1971	6	7	1	3	4		3	3	1
1987	6	9		5	3		1	6		1972	2	11	1	0	6	1	2	5	
1988	10	6		5	3		5	3		1973	5	8	1	4	3		1	5	1
1989	12	4		7	1		5	3		1974	7	7		5	2		2	5	
1990	13	3		7	1		6	2		1975	4	10		2	5		2	5	
1991	8	8		5	3		3	5		1976	4	10		2	5		2	5	
1992	6	10		4	4		2	6		1977	5	9		4	3		1	6	
1993	11	5		6	2		5	3		1978	9	7		5	3		4	4	
1994	9	7		4	4		5	3		1979	11	5		5	3		6	2	
1995	5	11		3	5		2	6		1980	12	4		7	1		5	3	
1996	6	10		3	5		3	5		1981	10	6		6	2		4	4	
1997	10	5	1	6	2		4	3	1	1982	3	6		1	4		2	2	
1998	8	8		5	3		3	5		1983	5	11		1	7		4	4	
1999	7	9		4	4		3	5		1984	6	9	1	5	3		1	6	1
2000	12	4		5	3		7	1		1985	7	9		4	4		3	5	
2001	7	9		5	3		2	6		1986	5	10	1	2	5	1	3	5	
2002	10	6		5	3		5	3		1987	7	8		4	4		3	4	
2003	4	12		1	7		3	5		1988	10	6		5	3		5	3	
2004	6	10		3	5		3	5		1989	11	5		6	2		5	3	
2005	11	5		7	1		4	4		1990	10	6		6	2		4	4	
2006	8	8		3	5		5	3		1991	10	6		4	4		6	2	
2007	10	6		3	5		7	1		1992	11	5		8	0		3	5	
2008	12	4		7	1		5	3		1993	8	8		3	5		5	3	
2009	8	8		4	4		4	4		1994	7	9		5	3		2	6	
2010	10	6		5	3		5	3		1995	10	6		6	2		4	4	
2011	9	7		4	4		5	3		1996	10	6		5	3		5	3	
2012	9	7		6	2		3	5		1997	6	9	1	6	2		0	7	1
2013	7	9		4	4		3	5		1998	3	13		3	5		0	8	
	661	547	33	367	255	16	294	292	17	1999	5	11		4	4		1	7	
										2000	11	5		5	3		6	2	
										2001	11	5		4	4		7	1	
PHILADELPHIA EAGLES										2002	12	4		7	1		5	3	
Season	All Games W	L	T	Home Games W	L	T	Road Games W	L	T	2003	12	4		5	3		7	1	
1933	3	5	1	2	3	1	1	2		2004	13	3		7	1		6	2	
1934	4	7		2	4		2	3		2005	6	10		4	4		2	6	
1935	2	9		0	5		2	4		2006	10	6		5	3		5	3	
1936	1	11		1	6		0	5		2007	8	8		3	5		5	3	
1937	2	8	1	0	5	1	2	3		2008	9	6	1	6	2		3	4	1

Season	All Games W	L	T	Home Games W	L	T	Road Games W	L	T
2009	11	5		6	2		5	3	
2010	10	6		4	4		6	2	
2011	8	8		3	5		5	3	
2012	4	12		2	6		2	6	
2013	10	6		4	4		6	2	
	526	563	25	293	257	12	233	306	13

ST. LOUIS RAMS*

Season	All Games W	L	T	Home Games W	L	T	Road Games W	L	T
1937	1	10		0	5		1	5	
1938	4	7		2	2		2	5	
1939	5	5	1	3	2	1	2	3	
1940	4	6	1	3	1	1	1	5	
1941	2	9		1	4		1	5	
1942	5	6		3	2		2	4	
1944	4	6		1	2		3	4	
1945	9	1		4	0		5	1	
1946	6	4	1	3	2		3	2	1
1947	6	6		3	3		3	3	
1948	6	5	1	3	2	1	3	3	
1949	8	2	2	5	1		3	1	2
1950	9	3		5	1		4	2	
1951	8	4		5	2		3	2	
1952	9	3		5	1		4	2	
1953	8	3	1	5	1		3	2	1
1954	6	5	1	3	2	1	3	3	
1955	8	3	1	5	1		3	2	1
1956	4	8		4	2		0	6	
1957	6	6		5	1		1	5	
1958	8	4		4	2		4	2	
1959	2	10		0	6		2	4	
1960	4	7	1	2	3	1	2	4	
1961	4	10		4	3		0	7	
1962	1	12	1	0	7		1	5	1
1963	5	9		3	4		2	5	
1964	5	7	2	3	2	2	2	5	
1965	4	10		3	4		1	6	
1966	8	6		5	2		3	4	
1967	11	1	2	5	1	1	6	0	1
1968	10	3	1	5	2		5	1	1
1969	11	3		5	2		6	1	
1970	9	4	1	3	3	1	6	1	
1971	8	5	1	4	2	1	4	3	
1972	6	7	1	4	3		2	4	1
1973	12	2		7	0		5	2	
1974	10	4		6	1		4	3	
1975	12	2		6	1		6	1	
1976	10	3	1	5	2		5	1	1
1977	10	4		7	0		3	4	
1978	12	4		6	2		6	2	
1979	9	7		4	4		5	3	
1980	11	5		6	2		5	3	
1981	6	10		4	4		2	6	
1982	2	7		1	4		1	3	
1983	9	7		5	3		4	4	
1984	10	6		5	3		5	3	
1985	11	5		6	2		5	3	
1986	10	6		6	2		4	4	
1987	6	9		3	4		3	5	
1988	10	6		4	4		6	2	
1989	11	5		6	2		5	3	
1990	5	11		2	6		3	5	
1991	3	13		2	6		1	7	
1992	6	10		4	4		2	6	
1993	5	11		3	5		2	6	
1994	4	12		3	5		1	7	
1995	7	9		4	4		3	5	
1996	6	10		4	4		2	6	
1997	5	11		2	6		3	5	

Season	All Games W	L	T	Home Games W	L	T	Road Games W	L	T
1998	4	12		2	6		2	6	
1999	13	3		8	0		5	3	
2000	10	6		5	3		5	3	
2001	14	2		6	2		8	0	
2002	7	9		6	2		1	7	
2003	12	4		8	0		4	4	
2004	8	8		6	2		2	6	
2005	6	10		3	5		3	5	
2006	8	8		4	4		4	4	
2007	3	13		1	7		2	6	
2008	2	14		1	7		1	7	
2009	1	15		0	8		1	7	
2010	7	9		5	3		2	6	
2011	2	14		1	7		1	7	
2012	7	8	1	4	4		3	4	1
2013	7	9		5	3		2	6	
	527	523	21	294	226	10	233	297	11

*includes Cleveland Rams (1937-1942, 1944-45) and Los Angeles Rams (1946-1994).

SAN FRANCISCO 49ERS

Season	All Games W	L	T	Home Games W	L	T	Road Games W	L	T
1950	3	9		3	3		0	6	
1951	7	4	1	5	1		2	3	1
1952	7	5		3	3		4	2	
1953	9	3		5	1		4	2	
1954	7	4	1	4	2		3	2	1
1955	4	8		2	4		2	4	
1956	5	6	1	3	3		2	3	1
1957	8	4		5	1		3	3	
1958	6	6		4	2		2	4	
1959	7	5		4	2		3	3	
1960	7	5		3	3		4	2	
1961	7	6	1	5	1	1	2	5	
1962	6	8		1	6		5	2	
1963	2	12		2	5		0	7	
1964	4	10		3	4		1	6	
1965	7	6	1	4	2	1	3	4	
1966	6	6	2	4	2	1	2	4	1
1967	7	7		3	4		4	3	
1968	7	6	1	3	3	1	4	3	
1969	4	8	2	3	3	1	1	5	1
1970	10	3	1	5	1	1	5	2	
1971	9	5		4	3		5	2	
1972	8	5	1	4	2	1	4	3	
1973	5	9		3	4		2	5	
1974	6	8		3	4		3	4	
1975	5	9		2	5		3	4	
1976	8	6		4	3		4	3	
1977	5	9		3	4		2	5	
1978	2	14		2	6		0	8	
1979	2	14		2	6		0	8	
1980	6	10		4	4		2	6	
1981	13	3		7	1		6	2	
1982	3	6		0	5		3	1	
1983	10	6		4	4		6	2	
1984	15	1		7	1		8	0	
1985	10	6		5	3		5	3	
1986	10	5	1	6	2		4	3	1
1987	13	2		6	1		7	1	
1988	10	6		4	4		6	2	
1989	14	2		6	2		8	0	
1990	14	2		6	2		8	0	
1991	10	6		7	1		3	5	
1992	14	2		7	1		7	1	
1993	10	6		6	2		4	4	
1994	13	3		7	1		6	2	
1995	11	5		6	2		5	3	
1996	12	4		6	2		6	2	

Season	All Games W	L	T	Home Games W	L	T	Road Games W	L	T
1997	13	3		8	0		5	3	
1998	12	4		8	0		4	4	
1999	4	12		3	5		1	7	
2000	6	10		4	4		2	6	
2001	12	4		7	1		5	3	
2002	10	6		5	3		5	3	
2003	7	9		6	2		1	7	
2004	2	14		1	7		1	7	
2005	4	12		3	5		1	7	
2006	7	9		4	4		3	5	
2007	5	11		3	5		2	6	
2008	7	9		4	4		3	5	
2009	8	8		6	2		2	6	
2010	6	10		5	3		1	7	
2011	13	3		7	1		6	2	
2012	11	4	1	6	1	1	5	3	
2013	12	4		6	2		6	2	
	507	417	14	281	180	8	226	237	6

SEATTLE SEAHAWKS

Season	All Games W	L	T	Home Games W	L	T	Road Games W	L	T
1976	2	12		1	6		1	6	
1977	5	9		3	4		2	5	
1978	9	7		5	3		4	4	
1979	9	7		5	3		4	4	
1980	4	12		0	8		4	4	
1981	6	10		5	3		1	7	
1982	4	5		3	2		1	3	
1983	9	7		5	3		4	4	
1984	12	4		7	1		5	3	
1985	8	8		5	3		3	5	
1986	10	6		7	1		3	5	
1987	9	6		6	2		3	4	
1988	9	7		5	3		4	4	
1989	7	9		3	5		4	4	
1990	9	7		5	3		4	4	
1991	7	9		5	3		2	6	
1992	2	14		1	7		1	7	
1993	6	10		4	4		2	6	
1994	6	10		3	5		3	5	
1995	8	8		5	3		3	5	
1996	7	9		4	4		3	5	
1997	8	8		4	4		4	4	
1998	8	8		6	2		2	6	
1999	9	7		5	3		4	4	
2000	6	10		3	5		3	5	
2001	9	7		6	2		3	5	
2002	7	9		3	5		4	4	
2003	10	6		8	0		2	6	
2004	9	7		5	3		4	4	
2005	13	3		8	0		5	3	
2006	9	7		5	3		4	4	
2007	10	6		7	1		3	5	
2008	4	12		2	6		2	6	
2009	5	11		4	4		1	7	
2010	7	9		5	3		2	6	
2011	7	9		4	4		3	5	
2012	11	5		8	0		3	5	
2013	13	3		7	1		6	2	
	293	303		177	122		116	181	

TAMPA BAY BUCCANEERS

Season	All Games W	L	T	Home Games W	L	T	Road Games W	L	T
1976	0	14		0	7		0	7	
1977	2	12		1	6		1	6	
1978	5	11		3	5		2	6	
1979	10	6		5	3		5	3	
1980	5	10	1	2	5	1	3	5	

Season	All Games W	L	T	Home Games W	L	T	Road Games W	L	T
1981	9	7		6	2		3	5	
1982	5	4		4	1		1	3	
1983	2	14		1	7		1	7	
1984	6	10		6	2		0	8	
1985	2	14		2	6		0	8	
1986	2	14		1	7		1	7	
1987	4	11		2	5		2	6	
1988	5	11		3	5		2	6	
1989	5	11		2	6		3	5	
1990	6	10		4	4		2	6	
1991	3	13		3	5		0	8	
1992	5	11		3	5		2	6	
1993	5	11		3	5		2	6	
1994	6	10		4	4		2	6	
1995	7	9		5	3		2	6	
1996	6	10		5	3		1	7	
1997	10	6		5	3		5	3	
1998	8	8		6	2		2	6	
1999	11	5		7	1		4	4	
2000	10	6		6	2		4	4	
2001	9	7		5	3		4	4	
2002	12	4		6	2		6	2	
2003	7	9		3	5		4	4	
2004	5	11		4	4		1	7	
2005	11	5		6	2		5	3	
2006	4	12		3	5		1	7	
2007	9	7		6	2		3	5	
2008	9	7		6	2		3	5	
2009	3	13		1	7		2	6	
2010	10	6		4	4		6	2	
2011	4	12		3	5		1	7	
2012	7	9		3	5		4	4	
2013	4	12		3	5		1	7	
	233	362	1	142	155	1	91	207	

WASHINGTON REDSKINS*

Season	All Games W	L	T	Home Games W	L	T	Road Games W	L	T
1932	4	4	2	2	3	1	2	1	1
1933	5	5	2	4	2		1	3	2
1934	6	6		4	3		2	3	
1935	2	8	1	2	5		0	3	1
1936	7	5		4	3		3	2	
1937	8	3		4	2		4	1	
1938	6	3	2	3	1	1	3	2	1
1939	8	2	1	5	0	1	3	2	
1940	9	2		6	0		3	2	
1941	6	5		4	2		2	3	
1942	10	1		5	1		5	0	
1943	6	3	1	4	2		2	1	1
1944	6	3	1	4	2		2	1	1
1945	8	2		6	0		2	2	
1946	5	5	1	3	2	1	2	3	
1947	4	8		4	2		0	6	
1948	7	5		4	2		3	3	
1949	4	7	1	3	3		1	4	1
1950	3	9		1	5		2	4	
1951	5	7		2	4		3	3	
1952	4	8		1	5		3	3	
1953	6	5	1	3	3		3	2	1
1954	3	9		3	3		0	6	
1955	8	4		3	3		5	1	
1956	6	6		4	2		2	4	
1957	5	6	1	2	3	1	3	3	
1958	4	7	1	3	2	1	1	5	
1959	3	9		2	4		1	5	
1960	1	9	2	1	4	1	0	5	1
1961	1	12	1	1	6		0	6	1
1962	5	7	2	3	4		2	3	2
1963	3	11		1	6		2	5	

Season	All Games			Home Games			Road Games		
	W	L	T	W	L	T	W	L	T
1964	6	8		4	3		2	5	
1965	6	8		3	4		3	4	
1966	7	7		4	3		3	4	
1967	5	6	3	2	4	1	3	2	2
1968	5	9		3	4		2	5	
1969	7	5	2	4	2	1	3	3	1
1970	6	8		4	3		2	5	
1971	9	4	1	4	2	1	5	2	
1972	11	3		6	1		5	2	
1973	10	4		7	0		3	4	
1974	10	4		6	1		4	3	
1975	8	6		5	2		3	4	
1976	10	4		5	2		5	2	
1977	9	5		5	2		4	3	
1978	8	8		5	3		3	5	
1979	10	6		6	2		4	4	
1980	6	10		4	4		2	6	
1981	8	8		5	3		3	5	
1982	8	1		3	1		5	0	
1983	14	2		7	1		7	1	
1984	11	5		7	1		4	4	
1985	10	6		5	3		5	3	
1986	12	4		7	1		5	3	
1987	11	4		6	1		5	3	
1988	7	9		4	4		3	5	
1989	10	6		4	4		6	2	
1990	10	6		7	1		3	5	
1991	14	2		7	1		7	1	
1992	9	7		6	2		3	5	
1993	4	12		3	5		1	7	
1994	3	13		0	8		3	5	
1995	6	10		4	4		2	6	
1996	9	7		5	3		4	4	
1997	8	7	1	5	2	1	3	5	
1998	6	10		4	4		2	6	
1999	10	6		6	2		4	4	
2000	8	8		4	4		4	4	
2001	8	8		4	4		4	4	
2002	7	9		5	3		2	6	
2003	5	11		3	5		2	6	
2004	6	10		3	5		3	5	
2005	10	6		6	2		4	4	
2006	5	11		3	5		2	6	
2007	9	7		5	3		4	4	
2008	8	8		4	4		4	4	
2009	4	12		3	5		1	7	
2010	6	10		2	6		4	4	
2011	5	11		2	6		3	5	
2012	10	6		5	3		5	3	
2013	3	13		2	6		1	7	
	565	546	27	324	243	11	241	303	16

*includes Boston Braves (1932) and Boston Redskins (1933-36).

ALL-TIME REGULAR-SEASON RECORDS OF NFL TEAMS

AFC	W	L	T	Pct.
Miami	415	317	4	.567
Baltimore	158	129	1	.550
New England	438	373	9	.540
Oakland	434	375	11	.536
Denver	432	378	10	.533
Indianapolis	475	420	7	.531
Pittsburgh	569	519	20	.523
Kansas City	415	393	12	.514
Cleveland	451	429	10	.512
San Diego	408	401	11	.504
Tennessee	399	415	6	.490
Jacksonville	144	160	0	.474
Buffalo	376	436	8	.463
N.Y. Jets	373	439	8	.459
Cincinnati	316	390	2	.448
Houston	79	113	0	.411

NFC	W	L	T	Pct.
Chicago	730	534	42	.577
Dallas	464	348	6	.571
Green Bay	698	537	37	.565
San Francisco	507	417	14	.549
N.Y. Giants	661	547	33	.547
Minnesota	431	365	10	.541
Washington	565	546	27	.509
St. Louis	527	523	21	.502
Seattle	293	303	0	.492
Philadelphia	526	563	25	.483
Carolina	144	160	0	.474
Detroit	517	620	32	.455
New Orleans	317	400	5	.442
Atlanta	316	414	6	.433
Arizona	511	706	39	.420
Tampa Bay	233	362	1	.392

From 1920-1971, tie games were not included in win percentage.

History

The Professional Football Hall of Fame is located in Canton, Ohio, site of the National Football League's organizational meeting on September 17, 1920. The NFL recognized Canton as the Hall of Fame site on April 27, 1961. Canton area individuals, foundations, and companies donated almost $400,000 in cash and services to provide funds for the construction of the original two-building complex, which was dedicated on September 7, 1963. The Mission of the Hall of Fame is to: Honor the Heroes of the Game, Preserve its History, Promote its Values and Celebrate Excellence Everywhere.

The Hall of Fame completed a two-year, $27 million dollar expansion and renovation in 2013. As part of the project, the Ralph Wilson, Jr. Pro Football Research and Preservation Center, a state-of-the-art archive for the world's largest collection of documents and artifacts, opened in August 2012.

The Pro Football Hall of Fame has undergone four expansions (1971, 1978, 1995, and 2012) over the years that have resulted in the museum growing from its original 19,000 square feet to today's 118,000-square foot facility.

Each year fans travel from all 50 states in the U.S. and more than 60 foreign countries to visit the Hall of Fame. The museum welcomed its nine millionth visitor during the summer of 2012. In addition, the Hall of Fame entertains tens of millions of fans through television broadcasts, traveling exhibits, an in-depth website, and numerous outreach events.

New members of the Pro Football Hall of Fame are elected annually by a 46-member Selection Committee, made up of media representatives from every league city, 13 at-large representatives, and a representative of the Pro Football Writers of America. Between four and seven new members are elected each year. An affirmative vote of approximately 80 percent is needed for election.

Any fan may nominate any eligible player or contributor simply by writing to the Pro Football Hall of Fame. Players and coaches must have last played or coached at least five years before he is eligible. Contributors (administrators, owners, et al.) may be elected while they are still active.

The charter class of 17 enshrinees was elected in 1963 and the honor roll now stands at 287 (195 living as of April 25, 2014) with the election of a seven-man class in 2014. That class consists of Derrick Brooks, Ray Guy, Claude Humphrey, Walter Jones, Andre Reed, Michael Strahan, and Aeneas Williams.

ROSTER OF MEMBERS

HERB ADDERLEY
Cornerback. 6-0, 205. Born in Philadelphia, Pennsylvania, June 8, 1939. Michigan State. Inducted in 1980. 1961-69 Green Bay Packers, 1970-72 Dallas Cowboys. **Highlights:** 48 interceptions, 7 touchdowns. Played in four Super Bowls, five Pro Bowls.

TROY AIKMAN
Quarterback. 6-4, 219. Born in West Covina, California, November 21, 1966. Oklahoma, UCLA. Inducted in 2006. 1989-2000 Dallas Cowboys. **Highlights:** His 90 wins in 1990s make him winningest quarterback in that decade. Led Cowboys to three Super Bowl wins. Passed for 32,942 yards, 165 touchdowns. Named to six Pro Bowls.

GEORGE ALLEN
Coach. Born in Detroit, Michigan, April 29, 1918. Died December 31, 1990. Alma College, Eastern Michigan, Marquette, Michigan. Inducted in 2002. 1966-1970 Los Angeles Rams, 1971-77 Washington Redskins. **Highlights:** 118-54-5 overall record. Never suffered a losing season, and ranked tenth in coaching victories at time of retirement.

LARRY ALLEN
Guard-tackle. 6-3, 325. Born in Los Angeles, California, November 27, 1971. Inducted in 2013. 1994-2005 Dallas Cowboys, 2006-07 San Francisco 49ers. **Highlights:** Named first-team All-Pro seven straight seasons. Elected to 11 Pro Bowls. Member of NFL's All-Decade Teams of 1990s and 2000s.

MARCUS ALLEN
Running back. 6-2, 210. Born in San Diego, California, March 26, 1960. Southern California. Inducted in 2003. 1982-1992 Los Angeles Raiders, 1993-1997 Kansas City Chiefs. **Highlights:** First player in NFL history to tally 10,000 rushing yards and 5,000 receiving yards. MVP, Super Bowl XVIII.

LANCE ALWORTH
Wide receiver. 6-0, 184. Born in Houston, Texas, August 3, 1940. Arkansas. Inducted in 1978. 1962-1970 San Diego Chargers, 1971-72 Dallas Cowboys. **Highlights:** 542 receptions for 10,266 yards, 85 touchdowns. All-AFL seven times, seven All-Star games.

DOUG ATKINS
Defensive end. 6-8, 275. Born in Humboldt, Tennessee, May 8, 1930. Tennessee. Inducted in 1982. 1953-54 Cleveland Browns, 1955-1966 Chicago Bears, 1967-69 New Orleans Saints. **Highlights:** Eight Pro Bowls, All-NFL four times. Played for 17 years, 205 games.

MORRIS (RED) BADGRO
End. 6-0, 190. Born in Orillia, Washington, December 1, 1902. Died July 13, 1998. Southern California. Inducted in 1981. 1927-28 New York Yankees, 1930-35 New York Giants, 1936 Brooklyn Dodgers. **Highlights:** First- or second-team All-NFL four times. Scored first touchdown in NFL Championship Game series.

LEM BARNEY
Cornerback. 6-0, 190. Born in Gulfport, Mississippi, September 8, 1945. Jackson State. Inducted in 1992. 1967-1977 Detroit Lions. **Highlights:** 56 interceptions for 1,077 yards, 11 touchdowns (7 defensive, 4 special teams). Seven Pro Bowls, All-NFL/NFC four times.

CLIFF BATTLES
Halfback. 6-1, 195. Born in Akron, Ohio, May 1, 1910. Died April 28, 1981. West Virginia Wesleyan. Inducted in 1968. 1932 Boston Braves, 1933-36 Boston Redskins, 1937 Washington Redskins. **Highlights:** NFL rushing champion 1932, 1937. First to gain more than 200 yards in a game, 1933.

SAMMY BAUGH
Quarterback. 6-2, 180. Born in Temple, Texas, March 17, 1914. Died December 17, 2008. Texas Christian. Inducted in 1963. 1937-1952 Washington Redskins. **Highlights:** Charter enshrinee. Six-time NFL passing leader. NFL passing, punting, interception champ, 1943.

CHUCK BEDNARIK
Center-linebacker. 6-3, 230. Born in Bethlehem, Pennsylvania, May 1, 1925. Pennsylvania. Inducted in 1967. 1949-1962 Philadelphia Eagles. **Highlights:** Eight Pro Bowls. Missed three games in 14 years. Named NFL all-time center, 1969.

BERT BELL
Team owner. Commissioner. Born in Philadelphia, Pennsylvania, February 25, 1895. Died October 11, 1959. Pennsylvania. Inducted in 1963. 1933-1940 Philadelphia Eagles, 1941-42 Pittsburgh Steelers, 1943 Phil-Pitt, 1944 Card-Pitt, 1945-46 Pittsburgh Steelers. Commissioner, 1946-1959. **Highlights:** Charter enshrinee. Built NFL image as commissioner, 1946-1959. Set up long-term television policies.

BOBBY BELL
Linebacker. 6-4, 225. Born in Shelby, North Carolina, June 17, 1940. Minnesota. Inducted in 1983. 1963-1974 Kansas City Chiefs. **Highlights:** 26 interceptions. All-AFL/AFC eight times. Nine career touchdowns, 1 on onside kick return.

RAYMOND BERRY
End. 6-2, 187. Born in Corpus Christi, Texas, February 27, 1933. Southern Methodist. Inducted in 1973. 1955-1967 Baltimore Colts. **Highlights:** 631 receptions for 9,275 yards, 68 touchdowns. Set NFL title game mark with 12 catches for 178 yards, 1958.

ELVIN BETHEA
Defensive end. 6-2, 260. Born in Trenton, New Jersey, March 1, 1946. North Carolina A&T. Inducted in 2003. 1968-1983 Houston Oilers. **Highlights:** Led team in sacks six times. Elected to eight Pro Bowls. Played for 16 years, 210 games.

CHARLES W. BIDWILL SR.
Team owner. Born in Chicago, Illinois, September 16, 1895. Died April 19, 1947. Loyola of Chicago. Inducted in 1967. 1933-1943 Chicago Cardinals, 1944 Card-Pitt, 1945-47 Chicago Cardinals. **Highlights:** Guiding light for NFL during depression years. Built famous "Dream Backfield."

FRED BILETNIKOFF
Wide receiver. 6-1, 190. Born in Erie, Pennsylvania, February 23, 1943. Florida State. Inducted in 1988. 1965-1978 Oakland Raiders. **Highlights:** 589 receptions for 8,974 yards, 76 touchdowns. 40 catches 10 straight years. MVP, Super Bowl XI.

GEORGE BLANDA
Quarterback-kicker. 6-2, 215. Born in Youngwood, Pennsylvania, September 17, 1927. Died September 27, 2010. Kentucky. Inducted in 1981. 1949-1958 Chicago Bears, 1950 Baltimore Colts, 1960-66 Houston Oilers, 1967-1975 Oakland Raiders. **Highlights:** 2,002 career points. 26-season, 340-game career longest in NFL history at retirement.

MEL BLOUNT
Cornerback. 6-3, 205. Born in Vidalia, Georgia, April 10, 1948. Southern University. Inducted in 1989. 1970-1983 Pittsburgh Steelers. **Highlights:** 57 interceptions for 736 yards. NFL defensive MVP, 1975. Started in four Super Bowl victories.

TERRY BRADSHAW
Quarterback. 6-3, 210. Born in Shreveport, Louisiana, September 2, 1948. Louisiana Tech. Inducted in 1989. 1970-1983 Pittsburgh Steelers. **Highlights:** 27,989 yards passing, 212 touchdowns. MVP in Super Bowls XIII, XIV.

DERRICK BROOKS
Linebacker. 6-0, 232. Born in Pensacola, Florida, April 18, 1973. Florida State. Inducted in 2014. 1995-2008 Tampa Bay Buccaneers. **Highlights:** Never missed a game. NFL Defensive Player of the Year in 2002. Named to NFL's All-Decade Team of 2000s.

BOB (BOOMER) BROWN
Tackle. 6-4, 280. Born in Cleveland, Ohio, December 8, 1941. Nebraska. Inducted in 2004. 1964-68 Philadelphia Eagles, 1969-1970 Los Angeles Rams, 1971-73 Oakland Raiders. **Highlights:** All-NFL seven of 10 seasons, six Pro Bowls. Named to 1960s All-Decade Team.

JIM BROWN
Fullback. 6-2, 228. Born in St. Simons, Georgia, February 17, 1936. Syracuse. Inducted in 1971. 1957-1965 Cleveland Browns. **Highlights:** 12,312 yards rushing, 756 points. Led NFL rushers eight years. Nine consecutive Pro Bowls.

PAUL BROWN
Coach. Born in Norwalk, Ohio, September 7, 1908. Died August 5, 1991. Miami (Ohio). Inducted in 1967. 1946-49 Cleveland Browns (AAFC), 1950-1962 Cleveland Browns. **Highlights:** Built Cleveland dynasty with 167-53-8 record, four AAFC titles, three NFL crowns. Returned to coaching with Cincinnati Bengals after induction, 1968-1975.

ROOSEVELT BROWN
Tackle. 6-3, 255. Born in Charlottesville, Virginia, October 20, 1932. Died June 9, 2004. Morgan State. Inducted in 1975. 1953-1965 New York Giants. **Highlights:** All-NFL eight consecutive years, nine Pro Bowls. NFL's lineman of year, 1956.

WILLIE BROWN
Cornerback. 6-1, 210. Born in Yazoo City, Mississippi, December 2, 1940. Grambling. Inducted in 1984. 1963-66 Denver Broncos, 1967-1978 Oakland Raiders. **Highlights:** 54 interceptions for 472 yards. Scored on 75-yard interception in Super Bowl XI.

BUCK BUCHANAN
Defensive tackle. 6-7, 274. Born in Gainesville, Alabama, September 10, 1940. Died July 16, 1992. Grambling. Inducted in 1990. 1963-1975 Kansas City Chiefs. **Highlights:** Led Chiefs defensive efforts in Super Bowl I, IV. Did not miss a game in 13 years.

NICK BUONICONTI
Linebacker. 5-11, 220. Born in Springfield, Massachusetts, December 15, 1940. Notre Dame. Inducted in 2001. 1962-68 Boston Patriots, 1969-1974, 1976 Miami Dolphins. **Highlights:** All-AFL/AFC eight times. Named to AFL's All-Time Team.

DICK BUTKUS
Linebacker. 6-3, 245. Born in Chicago, Illinois, December 9, 1942. Illinois. Inducted in 1979. 1965-1973 Chicago Bears. **Highlights:** All-NFL six years, eight consecutive Pro Bowls. 27 fumble recoveries.

JACK BUTLER
Cornerback. 6-1, 200. Born in Pittsburgh, Pennsylvania, November 12, 1927. Died May 11, 2013. St. Bonaventure. Inducted in 2012. 1951-59 Pittsburgh Steelers. **Highlights:** Retired as NFL's second all-time leading interceptor with 52 career picks returned for 827 yards, 4 TDs. Named to four Pro Bowls and selected to the NFL's All-Decade Team of 1950s.

EARL CAMPBELL
Running back. 5-11, 233. Born in Tyler, Texas, March 29, 1955. Texas. Inducted in 1991. 1978-1984 Houston Oilers, 1984-85 New Orleans Saints. **Highlights:** 9,407 yards rushing, 74 touchdowns. 1,934 yards rushing in 1980, including four games with at least 200 yards.

TONY CANADEO
Halfback. 5-11, 195. Born in Chicago, Illinois, May 5, 1919. Died November 29, 2003. Gonzaga. Inducted in 1974. 1941-44, 1946-1952 Green Bay Packers. **Highlights:** Two-way player. Third player to rush for 1,000 yards in single season, 1949.

JOE CARR
NFL president. Born in Columbus, Ohio, October 23, 1879. Died May 20, 1939. Did not attend college. Inducted in 1963. President, 1921-1939 National Football League. **Highlights:** Charter enshrinee. NFL co-organizer, 1920. Introduced standard player contract.

HARRY CARSON
Linebacker. 6-2, 237. Born in Florence, South Carolina, November 26, 1953. South Carolina State. Inducted in 2006. 1976-1988 New York Giants. **Highlights:** 11 career interceptions. Named to nine Pro Bowls. Named first- or second-team All-NFL six times.

CRIS CARTER
Wide receiver. 6-3, 202. Born in Troy, Ohio, November 25, 1965. Inducted in 2013. 1987-89 Philadelphia Eagles, 1990-2001 Minnesota Vikings, 2002 Miami Dolphins. **Highlights:** Recorded eight straight 1,000-yards seasons. Career statistics include 1,101 receptions for 13,899 yards and 130 TD catches. Elected to eight Pro Bowls. Named to NFL's All-Decade Team of 1990s.

DAVE CASPER
Tight end. 6-4, 240. Born in Bemidji, Minnesota, February 2, 1952. Notre Dame. Inducted in 2002. 1974-1980 Oakland Raiders, 1980-83 Houston Oilers, 1983 Minnesota Vikings, 1984 Los Angeles Raiders. **Highlights:** 378 receptions for 5,216 yards, 52 touchdowns. Five consecutive Pro Bowls.

GUY CHAMBERLIN
End. Coach. 6-2, 196. Born in Blue Springs, Nebraska, January 16, 1894. Died April 4, 1967. Nebraska. Inducted in 1965. 1919 Canton Bulldogs, 1920-21 Decatur Staleys/Chicago Staleys, player-coach 1922-23 Canton Bulldogs, 1924 Cleveland Bulldogs, 1925-26 Frankford Yellowjackets, 1927-28 Chicago Cardinals. **Highlights:** Player-coach of four NFL championship teams. Six-year coaching record of 58-16-7.

JACK CHRISTIANSEN
Safety. 6-1, 185. Born in Sublette, Kansas, December 20, 1928. Died June 29, 1986. Colorado State. Inducted in 1970. 1951-58 Detroit Lions. **Highlights:** 46 interceptions. NFL interception leader, 1953, 1957. Eight punt returns for touchdowns.

EARL (DUTCH) CLARK
Quarterback. 6-0, 185. Born in Fowler, Colorado, October 11, 1906. Died August 5, 1978. Colorado College. Inducted in 1963. 1931-32 Portsmouth Spartans, 1934-38 Detroit Lions. **Highlights:** Charter enshrinee. NFL scoring champion three years. Led Lions to 1935 NFL title.

GEORGE CONNOR
Tackle-linebacker. 6-3, 240. Born in Chicago, Illinois, January 21, 1925. Died March 31, 2003. Holy Cross, Notre Dame. Inducted in 1975. 1948-1955 Chicago Bears. **Highlights:** All-NFL at three positions—T, DT, LB. All-NFL five years. Played in first four Pro Bowls.

JIMMY CONZELMAN
Quarterback. Coach. Team owner. 6-0, 180. Born in St. Louis, Missouri, March 6, 1898. Died July 31, 1970. Washington of St. Louis. Inducted in 1964. 1920 Decatur Staleys, 1921-22 Rock Island Independents, 1922-24 Milwaukee Badgers; owner-coach 1925-26 Detroit Panthers; player-coach 1927-29, coach 1930 Providence Steam Roller; coach 1940-42, 1946-48 Chicago Cardinals. **Highlights:** Player-coach of four NFL teams in 1920s. Coached Cardinals to 1947 NFL crown.

LOU CREEKMUR
Tackle-guard. 6-4, 255. Born in Hopelawn, New Jersey, January 22, 1927. Died July 5, 2009. William & Mary. Inducted in 1996. 1950-59 Detroit Lions. **Highlights:** All-NFL six times, twice at guard and four times at tackle. Selected to eight Pro Bowls and played on three NFL championship teams.

LARRY CSONKA
Running back. 6-3, 235. Born in Stow, Ohio, December 25, 1946. Syracuse. Inducted in 1987. 1968-1974, 1979 Miami Dolphins, 1976-78 New York Giants. **Highlights:** 8,081 yards rushing, 68 touchdowns. MVP Super Bowl VIII. Only 21 fumbles in 1,891 carries and 106 receptions.

CURLEY CULP
Defensive tackle. 6-2, 265. Born in Yuma, Arizona, March 10, 1946. Inducted in 2013. 1968-1974 Kansas City Chiefs, 1974-1980 Houston Oilers, 1980-81 Detroit Lions. **Highlights:** Started in three AFL/AFC championship games and Super Bowl IV. Named to six Pro Bowls. Earned Defensive Player of the Year honors in 1975.

AL DAVIS
Coach-Commissioner-Owner. Born in Brockton, Massachusetts, July 4, 1929. Died October 8, 2011. Wittenberg, Syracuse. Inducted in 1992. 1963-1981, 1995-2011 Oakland Raiders, 1982-1994 Los Angeles Raiders, 1966 American Football League. **Highlights:** Only person to serve in pros as personnel assistant, scout, assistant coach, head coach, general manager, commissioner, team owner/CEO.

WILLIE DAVIS
Defensive end. 6-3, 245. Born in Lisbon, Louisiana, July 24, 1934. Grambling. Inducted in 1981. 1958-59 Cleveland Browns, 1960-69 Green Bay Packers. **Highlights:** All-NFL five seasons, five Pro Bowls. Did not miss game in 12-year career.

DERMONTTI DAWSON
Center. 6-2, 288. Born in Lexington, Kentucky, June 17, 1965. Kentucky. Inducted in 2012. 1988-2000 Pittsburgh Steelers. **Highlights:** Played in 170 straight games. Named first-team All-Pro six consecutive seasons and voted to seven straight Pro Bowls. Is member of the NFL's All-Decade Team of the 1990s.

LEN DAWSON
Quarterback. 6-0, 190. Born in Alliance, Ohio, June 20, 1935. Purdue. Inducted in 1987. 1957-59 Pittsburgh Steelers, 1960-61 Cleveland Browns, 1962 Dallas Texans, 1963-1975 Kansas City Chiefs. **Highlights:** 28,711 yards passing, 239 touchdowns. Four AFL passing crowns. MVP, Super Bowl IV.

FRED DEAN
Defensive end. 6-3, 230. Born in Arcadia, Louisiana, February 24, 1952. Louisiana Tech. Inducted in 2008. 1975-1981 San Diego Chargers, 1981-85 San Francisco 49ers. **Highlights:** Had career-high 17.5 sacks in 1983. Played on two Super Bowl championship teams with 49ers (Super Bowls XVI, XIX).

JOE DeLAMIELLEURE
Guard. 6-3, 254. Born in Detroit, Michigan, March 16, 1951. Michigan State. Inducted in 2003. 1973-1979, 1985 Buffalo Bills, 1980-1984 Cleveland Browns. **Highlights:** Selected All-Pro and All-AFC six consecutive times, 1975-1980. Named to six Pro Bowls. Played 13 years, 185 games.

RICHARD DENT
Defensive end. 6-5, 265. Born in Atlanta, Georgia, December 13, 1960. Tennessee State. Inducted in 2011. 1983-1993, 1995 Chicago Bears, 1994 San Francisco 49ers, 1996 Indianapolis Colts, 1997 Philadelphia Eagles. **Highlights:** Named MVP of Super Bowl XX. Had double-digit sack totals 10 times. Recorded 137.5 career sacks, third most at time of retirement. Named first- or second-team All-NFL four times, voted to four Pro Bowls.

ERIC DICKERSON
Running back. 6-3, 220. Born in Sealy, Texas, September 2, 1960. Southern Methodist. Inducted in 1999. 1983-87 Los Angeles Rams, 1987-1991 Indianapolis Colts, 1992 Los Angeles Raiders, 1993 Atlanta Falcons. **Highlights:** Rushed for 13,259 career yards, including an NFL record 2,105 yards in 1984. All-Pro five times, six Pro Bowls.

DAN DIERDORF
Tackle. 6-3, 290. Born in Canton, Ohio, June 29, 1949. Michigan. Inducted in 1996. 1971-1983 St. Louis Cardinals. **Highlights:** All-Pro five times, played in six Pro Bowls, named NFL's best blocker three times.

MIKE DITKA
Tight end. 6-3, 225. Born in Carnegie, Pennsylvania, October 18, 1939. Pittsburgh. Inducted in 1988. 1961-66 Chicago Bears, 1967-68 Philadelphia Eagles, 1969-1972 Dallas Cowboys. **Highlights:** 427 receptions for 5,812 yards, 43 touchdowns. First tight end selected to Hall of Fame. Five consecutive Pro Bowls.

CHRIS DOLEMAN
Defensive end-linebacker. 6-5, 270. Born in Indianapolis, Indiana, October 16, 1961. Pittsburgh. Inducted in 2012. 1985-1993, 1999 Minnesota Vikings, 1994-95 Atlanta Falcons, 1996-98 San Francisco 49ers. **Highlights:** Career sack total of 150.5 was fourth best all-time at retirement. Recorded 10 or more sacks in a season eight times. Led NFL with 21 sacks, 1989, one short of season record at time. Voted to eight Pro Bowls.

ART DONOVAN
Defensive tackle. 6-3, 265. Born in Bronx, New York, June 5, 1925. Died August 4, 2013. Boston College. Inducted in 1968. 1950 Baltimore Colts, 1951 New York Yanks, 1952 Dallas Texans, 1953-1961 Baltimore Colts. **Highlights:** Five Pro Bowls. Vital part of Baltimore's climb to powerhouse status in 1950s.

TONY DORSETT
Running back. 5-11, 184. Born in Rochester, Pennsylvania, April 7, 1954. Pittsburgh. Inducted in 1994. 1977-1987 Dallas Cowboys, 1988 Denver Broncos. **Highlights:** 12,739 yards rushing, 398 receptions, 91 touchdowns. Ran record 99 yards for touchdown vs. Minnesota, January, 1983.

JOHN (PADDY) DRISCOLL
Quarterback. 5-11, 160. Born in Evanston, Illinois, January 11, 1895. Died June 29, 1968. Northwestern. Inducted in 1965. 1919 Hammond Pros, 1920 Decatur Staleys, 1920-25 Chicago Cardinals, 1926-29 Chicago Bears. **Highlights:** All-NFL seven times. Dropkicked record 4 field goals in one game, 1925.

BILL DUDLEY
Halfback. 5-10, 182. Born in Bluefield, Virginia, December 24, 1921. Died February 4, 2010. Virginia. Inducted in 1966. 1942, 1945-46 Pittsburgh Steelers, 1947-49 Detroit Lions, 1950-51, 1953 Washington Redskins. **Highlights:** Won NFL rushing, interception, punt return titles, 1946. All-NFL 1942, 1946, and 1947.

ALBERT GLEN (TURK) EDWARDS
Tackle. 6-2, 260. Born in Mold, Washington, September 28, 1907. Died January 12, 1973. Washington State. Inducted in 1969. 1932 Boston Braves, 1933-36 Boston Redskins, 1937-1940 Washington Redskins. **Highlights:** All-NFL 1932-34, 1936, 1937. Steamrolling blocker, smothering tackler.

CARL ELLER
Defensive end. 6-6, 247. Born in Winston-Salem, North Carolina, January 25, 1942. Minnesota. Inducted in 2004. 1964-1978 Minnesota Vikings, 1979 Seattle Seahawks. **Highlights:** Fixture on Vikings' "Purple People Eaters" defensive line, All-Pro five time, elected to six Pro Bowls.

JOHN ELWAY
Quarterback. 6-3, 215. Born in Port Angeles, Washington, June 28, 1960. Stanford. Inducted in 2004. 1983-1998 Denver Broncos. **Highlights:** Passed for 51,475 yards, 300 touchdowns. Named to nine Pro Bowls. NFL MVP, 1987; MVP, Super Bowl XXXIII.

WEEB EWBANK
Coach. Born in Richmond, Indiana, May 6, 1907. Died November 17, 1998. Miami (Ohio). Inducted in 1978. 1954-1962 Baltimore Colts, 1963-1973 New York Jets. **Highlights:** Only coach to win championships in both NFL, AFL. Led both Colts (1958 and 1959) and Jets (1968) to championships.

MARSHALL FAULK
Running back. 5-10, 208. Born in New Orleans, Louisiana, February 26, 1973. San Diego State. Inducted in 2011. 1994-98 Indianapolis Colts, 1999-2005 St. Louis Rams. **Highlights:** Became second player to eclipse 1,000 yards in rushing and receiving same season when he set then-record for yards from scrimmage, 1999. NFL's MVP in 2000. Rushed for 1,000 yards in seven of first eight seasons.

TOM FEARS
End. 6-2, 215. Born in Guadalajara, Mexico, December 3, 1922. Died January 4, 2000. Santa Clara, UCLA. Inducted in 1970. 1948-1956 Los Angeles Rams. **Highlights:** 400 receptions for 5,397 yards, 38 touchdowns. Led NFL receivers first three seasons. Had then-record 18 receptions in single game.

JIM FINKS
Administrator. Born in St. Louis, Missouri, August 31, 1927. Died May 8, 1994. Tulsa. Inducted 1995. 1964-1973 Minnesota Vikings, 1974-1982 Chicago Bears, 1986-1993 New Orleans Saints. **Highlights:** Developed Vikings, Bears, Saints—all teams with losing records—into winners.

RAY FLAHERTY
Coach. Born in Spokane, Washington, September 1, 1903. Died July 19, 1994. Gonzaga. Inducted in 1976. 1936-1942 Boston/Washington Redskins, 1946-48 New York Yankees (AAFC), 1949 Chicago Hornets (AAFC). **Highlights:** 82-41-5 coaching record. Introduced screen pass in 1937 title game and platoon system.

LEN FORD
Defensive end. 6-4, 260. Born in Washington, D.C., February 18, 1926. Died March 14, 1972. Morgan State, Michigan. Inducted in 1976. 1948-49 Los Angeles Dons (AAFC), 1950-57 Cleveland Browns, 1958 Green Bay Packers. **Highlights:** All-NFL five times, four Pro Bowls. Recovered 20 opponents' fumbles.

DAN FORTMANN
Guard. 6-0, 210. Born in Pearl River, New York, April 11, 1916. Died May 23, 1995. Colgate. Inducted in 1965. 1936-1943 Chicago Bears. **Highlights:** At 20, became youngest starter in NFL. First- or second-team All-NFL every season of career.

DAN FOUTS
Quarterback. 6-3, 210. Born in San Francisco, California, June 10, 1951. Oregon. Inducted in 1993. 1973-1987 San Diego Chargers. **Highlights:** 43,040 passing yards, 254 touchdowns. Six Pro Bowls, NFL MVP, 1982.

BENNY FRIEDMAN
Quarterback. 5-10, 183. Born in Cleveland, Ohio, March 18, 1905. Died November 23, 1982. Michigan. Inducted in 2005. 1927 Cleveland Bulldogs, 1928 Detroit Wolverines, 1929-1931 New York Giants, 1932-34 Brooklyn Dodgers. **Highlights:** NFL's first great passer. Set league mark for touchdowns with 20 in 1929. Led NFL in touchdown passes each of his first four seasons.

FRANK GATSKI
Center. 6-3, 240. Born in Farmington, West Virginia, March 18, 1919. Marshall, Auburn. Died November 22, 2005. Inducted in 1985. 1946-49 Cleveland Browns (AAFC), 1950-56 Cleveland Browns, 1957 Detroit Lions. **Highlights:** Never missed game in high school, college, or pro football. Played 11 championship games, winning eight.

BILL GEORGE
Linebacker. 6-2, 230. Born in Waynesburg, Pennsylvania, October 27, 1929. Died September 30, 1982. Wake Forest. Inducted in 1974. 1952-1965 Chicago Bears, 1966 Los Angeles Rams. **Highlights:** All-NFL eight years, eight consecutive Pro Bowls. 14 years of service, longest of any Bears player.

JOE GIBBS
Coach. Born in Mocksville, North Carolina, November 25, 1940. Cerritos (Calif.) J.C., San Diego State. Inducted in 1996. 1981-1992 Washington Redskins. **Highlights:** 124-60-0 record in regular season, 16-5 in postseason, including four Super Bowl appearances—winning three. Won 10 or more games eight times.

FRANK GIFFORD
Halfback. 6-1, 195. Born in Santa Monica, California, August 16, 1930. Southern California. Inducted in 1977. 1952-1960, 1962-64 New York Giants. **Highlights:** Starred on both offense and defense. Named to eight Pro Bowls, 1956 NFL player of the year.

SID GILLMAN
Coach. Born in Minneapolis, Minnesota, October 26, 1911. Died January 3, 2003. Ohio State. Inducted in 1983. 1955-59 Los Angeles Rams, 1960-69, 1971 Los Angeles/San Diego Chargers, 1973-74 Houston Oilers. **Highlights:** 123-104-7 coaching record. First to win division titles in both NFL, AFL.

OTTO GRAHAM
Quarterback. 6-1, 195. Born in Waukegan, Illinois, December 6, 1921. Died December 17, 2003. Northwestern. Inducted in 1965. 1946-49 Cleveland Browns (AAFC), 1950-55 Cleveland Browns. **Highlights:** 23,584 passing yards, 174 touchdowns. Guided Browns to 10 division or league crowns in 10 years.

HAROLD (RED) GRANGE
Halfback. 6-0, 185. Born in Forksville, Pennsylvania, June 13, 1903. Died January 28, 1991. Illinois. Inducted in 1963. 1925, 1929-1934 Chicago Bears, 1926 New York Yankees (AFL), 1927 New York Yankees. **Highlights:** Charter enshrinee. Nicknamed "Galloping Ghost." Name produced first huge pro football crowds.

BUD GRANT
Coach. Born in Superior, Wisconsin, May 20, 1927. Minnesota. Inducted in 1994. 1967-1983, 1985 Minnesota Vikings. **Highlights:** 168-108-5 coaching record. Led Vikings to 11 division championships, four Super Bowls.

DARRELL GREEN
Cornerback. . 5-8, 176. Born in Houston, Texas, February 15, 1960. Texas A&I. Inducted in 2008. 1983-2002 Washington Redskins. **Highlights:** 54 interceptions, 621 yards, 6 TDs. Played 20 seasons. Recorded interception in NFL record 19 straight seasons. Selected to seven Pro Bowls.

JOE GREENE
Defensive tackle. 6-4, 260. Born in Temple, Texas, September 24, 1946. North Texas State. Inducted in 1987. 1969-1981 Pittsburgh Steelers. **Highlights:** NFL defensive player of the year, 1972, 1974. Four-time Super Bowl champion, 10 Pro Bowls.

FORREST GREGG
Tackle. 6-4, 250. Born in Birthright, Texas, October 18, 1933. Southern Methodist. Inducted in 1977. 1956, 1958-1970 Green Bay Packers, 1971 Dallas Cowboys. **Highlights:** Played 188 consecutive games. Nine Pro Bowls. Played on six NFL championship teams, three Super Bowl winners.

BOB GRIESE
Quarterback. 6-1, 190. Born in Evansville, Indiana, February 3, 1945. Purdue. Inducted in 1990. 1967-1980 Miami Dolphins. **Highlights:** 25,092 passing yards, 192 touchdowns. Led Miami to three AFC titles, Super Bowl VII, VIII wins.

RUSS GRIMM
Guard. 6-3, 273. Born in Scottdale, Pennsylvania, May 2, 1959. Pittsburgh. Inducted in 2010. 1981-1991 Washington Redskins. **Highlights:** Member of famed "Hogs" offensive line, All-NFL four times, four Pro Bowls. Member of All-Decade Team 1980s.

LOU GROZA
Tackle-kicker. 6-3, 250. Born in Martins Ferry, Ohio, January 25, 1924. Died November 29, 2000. Ohio State. Inducted in 1974. 1946-49 Cleveland Browns (AAFC), 1950-59, 1961-67 Cleveland Browns. **Highlights:** 1,608 points in 21 years. Nine Pro Bowls, All-NFL six years. NFL player of the year, 1954.

RAY GUY
Punter. 6-3, 195. Born in Swainsboro, Georgia, December 22, 1949. Southern Mississippi. Inducted in 2014. 1973-1986 Oakland/Los Angeles Raiders. **Highlights:** Averaged under 40 yards only once. All-Pro six straight years. Played in seven Pro Bowls.

JOE GUYON
Halfback. 6-1, 180. Born on White Earth Indian Reservation, Minnesota, November 26, 1892. Died November 27, 1971. Carlisle, Georgia Tech. Inducted in 1966. 1919-1920 Canton Bulldogs, 1921 Cleveland Indians, 1922-23 Oorang Indians, 1924 Rock Island Independents, 1924-25 Kansas City Cowboys, 1927 New York Giants. **Highlights:** Touchdown pass gave Giants victory over Bears to win 1927 championship.

GEORGE HALAS
End. Coach. Team owner. Born in Chicago, Illinois, February 2, 1895. Died October 31, 1983. Illinois. Inducted in 1963. Player-coach 1920 Decatur Staleys, 1921 Chicago Staleys, 1922-29 Chicago Bears; coach 1933-1942, 1946-1955, 1958-1967 Chicago Bears. **Highlights:** Charter enshrinee. 324 coaching wins. Only person associated with NFL throughout first 50 years. Coached Bears 40 seasons, won six NFL titles.

JACK HAM
Linebacker. 6-1, 225. Born in Johnstown, Pennsylvania, December 23, 1948. Penn State. Inducted in 1988. 1971-1982 Pittsburgh Steelers. **Highlights:** Won four Super Bowls, 21 opponents' fumbles recovered, 32 interceptions. Eight consecutive Pro Bowls.

DAN HAMPTON
Defensive tackle-defensive end. 6-5, 264. Born in Oklahoma City, Oklahoma, September 19, 1957. Arkansas. Inducted in 2002. 1979-1990 Chicago Bears. **Highlights:** A versatile player, he earned all-pro honors at both defensive tackle and defensive end. Named to four Pro Bowls.

CHRIS HANBURGER
Linebacker. 6-2, 218. Born in Fort Bragg, North Carolina, August 13, 1941. North Carolina. Inducted in 2011. 1965-1978 Washington Redskins. **Highlights:** Leader of dominant Redskins defenses. Named first-team All-NFL four times in five-season span. Voted to nine Pro Bowls. Three fumble recoveries for TDs tied for NFL record at time of his retirement.

JOHN HANNAH
Guard. 6-3, 265. Born in Canton, Georgia, April 4, 1951. Alabama. Inducted in 1991. 1973-1985 New England Patriots. **Highlights:** Renowned as premier guard of era. All-Pro 10 years, nine Pro Bowls.

FRANCO HARRIS
Running back. 6-2, 225. Born in Fort Dix, New Jersey, March 7, 1950. Penn State. Inducted in 1990. 1972-1983 Pittsburgh Steelers, 1984 Seattle Seahawks. **Highlights:** 12,120 rushing yards, 100 total touchdowns. 1,556 rushing yards in 19 postseason games. MVP in Super Bowl IX.

BOB HAYES
Wide receiver. 5-11, 185. Born in Jacksonville, Florida, December 20, 1942. Died September 18, 2002. Florida A&M. Inducted in 2009. 1965-1974 Dallas Cowboys, 1975 San Francisco 49ers. **Highlights:** Olympic gold medalist with world class speed led Cowboys in receiving three times. 371 receptions for 7,414 yards, 71 TDs. Three Pro Bowls.

MIKE HAYNES
Cornerback. 6-2, 195. Born in Denison, Texas, July 1, 1953. Arizona State. Inducted in 1997. 1976-1982 New England Patriots, 1983-89 Los Angeles Raiders. **Highlights:** Defensive rookie of the year. Selected to nine Pro Bowls and intercepted 46 passes, plus one pick in Super Bowl XVIII.

ED HEALEY
Tackle. 6-3, 220. Born in Indian Orchard, Massachusetts, December 28, 1894. Died December 9, 1978. Dartmouth. Inducted in 1964. 1920-22 Rock Island Independents, 1922-27 Chicago Bears. **Highlights:** Two-way star. Perennial all-pro with Bears.

MEL HEIN
Center. 6-2, 225. Born in Redding, California, August 22, 1909. Died January 31, 1992. Washington State. Inducted in 1963. 1931-1945 New York Giants. **Highlights:** Charter enshrinee. 60-minute regular for 15 years. All-NFL eight consecutive years.

TED HENDRICKS
Linebacker. 6-7, 235. Born in Guatemala City, Guatemala, November 1, 1947. Miami. Inducted in 1990. 1969-1973 Baltimore Colts, 1974 Green Bay Packers, 1975-1981 Oakland Raiders, 1982-83 Los Angeles Raiders. **Highlights:** 25 blocked field goals, extra points, and punts, 26 interceptions. Played in 215 consecutive games.

WILBUR (PETE) HENRY
Tackle. 6-0, 250. Born in Mansfield, Ohio, October 31, 1897. Died February 7, 1952. Washington & Jefferson. Inducted in 1963. 1920-23, 1925-26 Canton Bulldogs, 1927 New York Giants, 1927-28 Pottsville Maroons. **Highlights:** Charter enshrinee. Largest player of his time at 250 pounds. Bulwark of Canton's championship lines.

ARNIE HERBER
Quarterback. 6-0, 200. Born in Green Bay, Wisconsin, April 2, 1910. Died October 14, 1969. Wisconsin, Regis College. Inducted in 1966. 1930-1940 Green Bay Packers, 1944-45 New York Giants. **Highlights:** NFL passing leader 1932, 1934, 1936. Came out of retirement to lead 1944 Giants to NFL Eastern crown.

BILL HEWITT
End. 5-11, 191. Born in Bay City, Michigan, October 8, 1909. Died January 14, 1947. Michigan. Inducted in 1971. 1932-36 Chicago Bears, 1937-39 Philadelphia Eagles, 1943 Phil-Pitt. **Highlights:** First to be named all-NFL with two teams—1933, 1934, 1936 Bears; 1937 Eagles.

GENE HICKERSON
Guard. 6-3, 248. Born in Trenton, Tennessee, February 15, 1935. Died October 20, 2008. Mississippi. Inducted in 2007. 1958-1973 Cleveland Browns. **Highlights:** Blocked for three Hall of Fame running backs. Voted to six straight Pro Bowls. Named to NFL's All-Decade Team of the 1960s.

CLARKE HINKLE
Fullback. 5-11, 201. Born in Toronto, Ohio, April 10, 1909. Died November 9, 1988. Bucknell. Inducted in 1964. 1932-1941 Green Bay Packers. **Highlights:** 3,860 yards rushing, 379 points. Fullback on offense, linebacker on defense.

ELROY (CRAZYLEGS) HIRSCH
Halfback-end. 6-2, 190. Born in Wausau, Wisconsin, June 17, 1923. Died January 28, 2004. Wisconsin, Michigan. Inducted in 1968. 1946-48 Chicago Rockets (AAFC), 1949-1957 Los Angeles Rams. **Highlights:** 387 receptions for 7,029 yards, 60 touchdowns. Key part of Rams' revolutionary "three end" offense, 1949.

PAUL HORNUNG
Halfback. 6-2, 220. Born in Louisville, Kentucky, December 23, 1935. Notre Dame. Inducted in 1986. 1957-1962, 1964-66 Green Bay Packers. **Highlights:** 760 points. Led NFL scorers three years, including record 176 points, 1960. Record 19 points scored in 1961 NFL title game.

KEN HOUSTON
Safety. 6-3, 198. Born in Lufkin, Texas, November 12, 1944. Prairie View A&M. Inducted in 1986. 1967-1972 Houston Oilers, 1973-1980 Washington Redskins. **Highlights:** 49 interceptions, 898 yards, 9 touchdowns. NFL's premier strong safety of 1970s. 12 Pro Bowls.

ROBERT (CAL) HUBBARD
Tackle. 6-5, 250. Born in Keytesville, Missouri, October 31, 1900. Died October 17, 1977. Centenary, Geneva. Inducted in 1963. 1927-28, 1936 New York Giants, 1929-1933, 1935 Green Bay Packers, 1936 Pittsburgh Pirates. **Highlights:** Charter enshrinee. Most feared lineman of his time. All-NFL six years, 1927-29, 1931-33.

SAM HUFF
Linebacker. 6-1, 230. Born in Morgantown, West Virginia, October 4, 1934. West Virginia. Inducted in 1982. 1956-1963 New York Giants, 1964-67, 1969 Washington Redskins. **Highlights:** 30 interceptions. Played in six NFL title games, five Pro Bowls. Redskins player-coach, 1969.

CLAUDE HUMPHREY
Defensive end. 6-4, 252. Born in Memphis, Tennessee, June 29, 1944. Tennessee State. Inducted in 2014. 1968-1978 Atlanta Falcons, 1979-1981 Philadelphia Eagles. **Highlights:** First team All-Pro five times. Had 122 career sacks, two interceptions, a fumble recovery for a TD, and two safeties.

LAMAR HUNT
Team owner. Born in El Dorado, Arkansas, August 2, 1932. Died December 13, 2006. Southern Methodist. Inducted in 1972. 1960-2006 Dallas Texans/Kansas City Chiefs. **Highlights:** Driving force behind organization of AFL. Spearheaded merger negotiations with NFL, 1966.

DON HUTSON
End. 6-1, 180. Born in Pine Bluff, Arkansas, January 31, 1913. Died June 26, 1997. Alabama. Inducted in 1963. 1935-1945 Green Bay Packers. **Highlights:** Charter enshrinee. 488 receptions for 7,991 yards, 99 touchdowns. NFL receiving champion eight years. NFL MVP, 1941, 1942.

MICHAEL IRVIN
Wide receiver. 6-2, 207. Born in Ft. Lauderdale, Florida, March 5, 1966. Miami. Inducted in 2007. 1988-1999 Dallas Cowboys. **Highlights:** 750 career receptions for 11,904 yards, 65 touchdowns. Had NFL record eleven 100-yard receiving games, 1995.

RICKEY JACKSON
Linebacker. 6-2, 243. Born in Pahokee, Florida, March 20, 1958. Pittsburgh. Inducted in 2010. 1981-1993 New Orleans Saints, 1994-95 San Francisco 49ers. **Highlights:** Recorded double-digit sacks in six seasons. Six Pro Bowls, named All-Pro four times. Finished career as defensive end with 49ers.

JIMMY JOHNSON
Cornerback. 6-2, 187. Born in Dallas, Texas, March 31, 1938. UCLA. Inducted in 1994. 1961-1976 San Francisco 49ers. **Highlights:** 47 interceptions for 615 yards. Five Pro Bowls. Opposing passers avoided throwing in his area.

JOHN HENRY JOHNSON
Fullback. 6-2, 225. Born in Waterproof, Louisiana, November 24, 1929. Died June 3, 2011. St. Mary's, Arizona State. Inducted in 1987. 1954-56 San Francisco 49ers, 1957-59 Detroit Lions, 1960-65 Pittsburgh Steelers, 1966 Houston Oilers. **Highlights:** 6,803 yards rushing, 55 total touchdowns. Member of San Francisco's "Million-Dollar" backfield.

PRO FOOTBALL HALL OF FAME

CHARLIE JOINER
Wide receiver. 5-11, 180. Born in Many, Louisiana, October 14, 1947. Grambling. Inducted in 1996. 1969-1972 Houston Oilers, 1972-75 Cincinnati Bengals, 1976-1986 San Diego Chargers. **Highlights:** 750 receptions for 12,146 yards and 65 touchdowns. Played 18 seasons, 239 games, most ever for wide receiver at time of retirement.

DAVID (DEACON) JONES
Defensive end. 6-5, 260. Born in Eatonville, Florida, December 9, 1938. Died June 3, 2013. South Carolina State, Mississippi Vocational. Inducted in 1980. 1961-1971 Los Angeles Rams, 1972-73 San Diego Chargers, 1974 Washington Redskins. **Highlights:** Specialized in quarterback "sacks," a term he invented. Unanimous all-league five consecutive years.

STAN JONES
Guard-defensive tackle. 6-1, 250. Born in Altoona, Pennsylvania, November 24, 1931. Died May 21, 2010. Maryland. Inducted in 1991. 1954-1965 Chicago Bears, 1966 Washington Redskins. **Highlights:** Seven consecutive Pro Bowls. First to rely on weightlifting for football preparation.

WALTER JONES
Tackle. 6-5, 300. Born in Aliceville, Alabama, January 19, 1974. Holmes Community College, Florida State. Inducted in 2014. 1997-2008 Seattle Seahawks. **Highlights:** First Seahawks lineman to earn a Pro Bowl. Retired with a team-record nine. All-Pro six times and member of NFL's All Decade Team of 2000s.

HENRY JORDAN
Defensive tackle, 6-3, 240. Born in Emporia, Virginia, January 26, 1935. Died February 21, 1977. Virginia. Inducted in 1995. 1957-58 Cleveland Browns, 1959-1969 Green Bay Packers. **Highlights:** Fixture at DT during Packers' dynasty. Played in four Pro Bowls, seven NFL title games, Super Bowls I, II.

SONNY JURGENSEN
Quarterback. 6-0, 203. Born in Wilmington, North Carolina, August 23, 1934. Duke. Inducted in 1983. 1957-1963 Philadelphia Eagles, 1964-1974 Washington Redskins. **Highlights:** 32,224 yards passing, 255 touchdowns, 82.63 passer rating. Surpassed 3,000 yards passing in five seasons.

JIM KELLY
Quarterback. 6-3, 225. Born in Pittsburgh, Pennsylvania, February 14, 1960. Miami. Inducted in 2002. 1986-1996 Buffalo Bills. **Highlights:** Passed for more than 3,000 yards eight times. Mastered the no-huddle offense that propelled Bills to four consecutive Super Bowls.

LEROY KELLY
Running back. 6-0, 205. Born in Philadelphia, Pennsylvania, May 20, 1942. Morgan State. Inducted in 1994. 1964-1973 Cleveland Browns. **Highlights:** 7,274 yards rushing, 90 total touchdowns, 1,000-yard rusher first three years as starter. Punt return champion, 1965.

CORTEZ KENNEDY
Defensive tackle. 6-3, 298. Born in Osceola, Arkansas, August 23, 1968. Northwest Mississippi Community College, Miami. Inducted in 2012. 1990-2000 Seattle Seahawks. **Highlights:** NFL Defensive Player of the Year, 1992. Voted to eight Pro Bowls and selected first-team All-Pro three times. Named to the NFL's All-Decade Team of the 1990s.

WALT KIESLING
Guard. Coach. 6-2, 245. Born in St. Paul, Minnesota, May 27, 1903. Died March 2, 1962. St. Thomas (Minnesota). Inducted in 1966. 1926-27 Duluth Eskimos, 1928 Pottsville Maroons, 1929-1933 Chicago Cardinals, 1934 Chicago Bears, 1935-36 Green Bay Packers, 1937-38 Pittsburgh Pirates; coach, 1939 Pittsburgh Pirates, 1940-42 Pittsburgh Steelers; co-coach, 1943 Phil-Pitt, 1944 Card-Pitt; coach, 1954-56 Pittsburgh Steelers. **Highlights:** 34-year career as pro player, assistant coach, head coach. Led Steelers to first winning season, 1942.

FRANK (BRUISER) KINARD
Tackle. 6-1, 210. Born in Pelahatchie, Mississippi, October 23, 1914. Died September 7, 1985. Mississippi. Inducted in 1971. 1938-1943 Brooklyn Dodgers, 1944 Brooklyn Tigers, 1946-47 New York Yankees (AAFC). **Highlights:** First man to earn both All-NFL, All-AAFC honors. Out because of injury only once.

PAUL KRAUSE
Safety. 6-3, 200. Born in Flint, Michigan, February 19, 1942. Iowa. Inducted in 1998. 1964-67 Washington Redskins, 1968-1979 Minnesota Vikings. **Highlights:** NFL all-time leader with 81 interceptions. Played in eight Pro Bowls. Starting safety in four Super Bowls.

EARL (CURLY) LAMBEAU
Coach. Born in Green Bay, Wisconsin, April 9, 1898. Died June 1, 1965. Notre Dame. Inducted in 1963. 1919-1949 Green Bay Packers, 1950-51 Chicago Cardinals, 1952-53 Washington Redskins. **Highlights:** Charter enshrinee. 229-134-22 coaching record with six NFL championships. Founded pre-NFL Packers, 1919.

JACK LAMBERT
Linebacker. 6-4, 220. Born in Mantua, Ohio, July 8, 1952. Kent State. Inducted in 1990. 1974-1984 Pittsburgh Steelers. **Highlights:** Leader of 'Steel Curtain.' NFL defensive player of year in 1976, nine Pro Bowls.

TOM LANDRY
Coach. Born in Mission, Texas, September 11, 1924. Died February 12, 2000. Texas. Inducted in 1990. 1960-1988 Dallas Cowboys. **Highlights:** 270-178-6 coaching record. 20 consecutive winning seasons. Innovator on offense and defense.

DICK (NIGHT TRAIN) LANE
Cornerback. 6-2, 210. Born in Austin, Texas, April 16, 1928. Died January 29, 2002. Scottsbluff Junior College. Inducted in 1974. 1952-53 Los Angeles Rams, 1954-59 Chicago Cardinals, 1960-65 Detroit Lions. **Highlights:** 68 interceptions for 1,207 yards, 5 touchdowns. Record 14 interceptions as rookie. Seven Pro Bowls.

JIM LANGER
Center. 6-2, 255. Born in Little Falls, Minnesota, May 16, 1948. South Dakota State. Inducted in 1987. 1970-79 Miami Dolphins, 1980-81 Minnesota Vikings. **Highlights:** Played every offensive down in Dolphins' perfect 1972 season. Six Pro Bowls.

WILLIE LANIER
Linebacker. 6-1, 245. Born in Clover, Virginia, August 21, 1945. Morgan State. Inducted in 1986. 1967-1977 Kansas City Chiefs. **Highlights:** 27 interceptions. Defensive star in Super Bowl IV upset. Nicknamed 'Contact' for ferocious tackling.

STEVE LARGENT
Wide receiver. 5-11, 191. Born in Tulsa, Oklahoma, September 28, 1954. Tulsa. Inducted in 1995. 1976-1989 Seattle Seahawks. **Highlights:** 819 receptions for 13,089 yards, 100 touchdowns. Receptions in 177 consecutive games.

YALE LARY
Safety. 5-11, 189. Born in Fort Worth, Texas, November 24, 1930. Texas A&M. Inducted in 1979. 1952-53, 1956-1964 Detroit Lions. **Highlights:** 50 interceptions. Three NFL punting crowns, three touchdowns on punt returns. Nine Pro Bowls.

DANTE LAVELLI
End. 6-0, 199. Born in Hudson, Ohio, February 23, 1923. Died January 20, 2009. Ohio State. Inducted in 1975. 1946-49 Cleveland Browns (AAFC), 1950-56 Cleveland Browns. **Highlights:** 386 receptions for 6,488 yards, 62 touchdowns. 24 catches in six NFL title games.

BOBBY LAYNE
Quarterback. 6-2, 190. Born in Santa Anna, Texas, December 19, 1926. Died December 1, 1986. Texas. Inducted in 1967. 1948 Chicago Bears, 1949 New York Bulldogs, 1950-58 Detroit Lions, 1958-1962 Pittsburgh Steelers. **Highlights:** 26,768 yards passing, 196 touchdowns, 2,451 yards rushing. Late touchdown pass won 1953 NFL title game.

DICK LeBEAU
Cornerback. 6-1, 185. Born in London, Ohio, September 9, 1937. Ohio State. Inducted in 2010. 1959-1972 Detroit Lions. **Highlights:** Recorded 62 career interceptions for 762 yards, 3 TDs, ranked third all-time in interceptions at retirement. Voted to three Pro Bowls.

ALPHONSE (TUFFY) LEEMANS
Fullback. 6-0, 200. Born in Superior, Wisconsin, November 12, 1912. Died January 19, 1979. Oregon, George Washington. Inducted in 1978. 1936-1943 New York Giants. **Highlights:** 3,132 yards rushing, 2,318 yards passing, 422 yards receiving. Led NFL rushers as rookie, 1936.

MARV LEVY
Coach. Born in Chicago, Illinois, August 3, 1925. Wyoming, Coe College, Harvard. Inducted in 2001. 1978-1982 Kansas City Chiefs, 1986-1997 Buffalo Bills. **Highlights:** Led Bills to unprecedented four consecutive Super Bowls. Had 154-120 record. Coaching victories ranked 10th when retired.

BOB LILLY
Defensive tackle. 6-5, 260. Born in Olney, Texas, July 26, 1939. Texas Christian. Inducted in 1980. 1961-1974 Dallas Cowboys. **Highlights:** Eleven Pro Bowls. Played 196 consecutive games. Foundation of great Dallas defensive units.

FLOYD LITTLE
Running back. 5-10, 196. Born in New Haven, Connecticut, July 4, 1942. Syracuse. Inducted in 2010. 1967-1975 Denver Broncos. **Highlights:** Broncos' first 1,000-yard rusher, won NFL rushing title in 1971. Amassed more than 12,000 career all-purpose yards, 54 TDs, five AFL All-Star Games/Pro Bowls.

LARRY LITTLE
Guard. 6-1, 265. Born in Groveland, Georgia, November 2, 1945. Bethune-Cookman. Inducted in 1993. 1967-68 San Diego Chargers, 1969-1980 Miami Dolphins. **Highlights:** Five Pro Bowls, started in three Super Bowls. Epitome of powerful Dolphins rushing game of 1970s.

JAMES LOFTON
Wide receiver. 6-3, 192. Born in Fort Ord, California, July 5, 1956. Stanford. Inducted in 2003. 1978-1986 Green Bay Packers, 1987-88 Los Angeles Raiders, 1989-1992 Buffalo Bills, 1993 Los Angeles Rams, 1993 Philadelphia Eagles. **Highlights:** Played 16 seasons, 233 games. Caught 764 passes for 75 touchdowns and a then-record 14,004 yards. All-Pro four times, eight Pro Bowls.

VINCE LOMBARDI
Coach. Born in Brooklyn, New York, June 11, 1913. Died September 3, 1970. Fordham. Inducted in 1971. 1959-1967 Green Bay Packers, 1969 Washington Redskins. **Highlights:** 105-35-6 coaching record in 10 years, including five NFL titles and victories in Super Bowls I and II.

HOWIE LONG
Defensive end. 6-5, 268. Born in Somerville, Massachusetts, January 6, 1960. Villanova. Inducted in 2000. 1981-1993 Oakland/Los Angeles Raiders. **Highlights:** All-Pro 1983, 1984, 1985. Named All-AFC four times, 1983-1986. Eight Pro Bowls.

RONNIE LOTT
Cornerback-safety. 6-0, 203. Born in Albuquerque, New Mexico, May 8, 1959. Southern California. Inducted in 2000. 1981-1990 San Francisco 49ers, 1991-92 Los Angeles Raiders, 1993-94 New York Jets. **Highlights:** Ten Pro Bowls, 63 career interceptions, and was named to the NFL's 75th Anniversary Team.

SID LUCKMAN
Quarterback. 6-0, 195. Born in Brooklyn, New York, November 21, 1916. Died July 5, 1998. Columbia. Inducted in 1965. 1939-1950 Chicago Bears. **Highlights:** 137 touchdown passes. All-NFL five times. League MVP in 1943.

WILLIAM ROY (LINK) LYMAN
Tackle. 6-2, 252. Born in Table Rock, Nebraska, November 30, 1898. Died December 28, 1972. Nebraska. Inducted in 1964. 1922-23, 1925 Canton Bulldogs, 1924 Cleveland Bulldogs, 1925 Frankford Yellowjackets, 1926-28, 1930-31, 1933-34 Chicago Bears. **Highlights:** Played for four NFL champions. In 16 seasons of college and pro football, played on one losing team.

TOM MACK
Guard. 6-3, 250. Born in Cleveland, Ohio, November 1, 1943. Michigan. Inducted in 1999. 1966-1978 Los Angeles Rams. **Highlights:** Never missed a game in entire 184-game career. Elected to 11 Pro Bowls.

JOHN MACKEY
Tight end. 6-2, 224. Born in New York, New York, September 24, 1941. Died July 6, 2011. Syracuse. Inducted in 1992. 1963-1971 Baltimore Colts, 1972 San Diego Chargers. **Highlights:** 331 receptions for 5,236 yards, 38 touchdowns. Second tight end to enter Hall of Fame.

JOHN MADDEN
Coach. Born in Austin, Minnesota, April 10, 1936. San Mateo Junior College, California Polytechnic College at San Luis Obispo. Inducted in 2006. 1969-1978 Oakland Raiders. **Highlights:** Became one of youngest coaches in history when hired at age 32. 112-39-7 overall record. Owns best regular season winning percentage among coaches with 100 wins.

TIM MARA
Founder-Team Owner. Born in New York, New York, July 29, 1887. Died February 16, 1959. Did not attend college. Inducted in 1963. 1925-1959 New York Giants. **Highlights:** Charter enshrinee. Founder of New York Giants. Built team into powerhouse winning four NFL titles, 10 division titles.

WELLINGTON MARA
Team owner. Born in New York, New York, August 14, 1916. Died October 25, 2005. Fordham. Inducted in 1997. 1937-2005 New York Giants. **Highlights:** Lifetime contributor to NFL and New York Giants. Worked as Giants' ballboy, secretary, vice-president, president and co-CEO. NFC president 1984-present.

GINO MARCHETTI
Defensive end. 6-4, 245. Born in Smithers, West Virginia, January 2, 1927. San Francisco. Inducted in 1972. 1952 Dallas Texans, 1953-1964, 1966 Baltimore Colts. **Highlights:** Named top defensive end of NFL's first 50 years. 10 consecutive Pro Bowls. All-NFL seven times.

DAN MARINO
Quarterback. 6-4, 218. Born in Pittsburgh, Pennsylvania, September 15, 1961. Pittsburgh. Inducted in 2005. 1983-1999 Miami Dolphins. **Highlights:** Held NFL records for career passing yardage (61,361), completions (4,967), attempts (8,358), and touchdowns (420). Voted to nine Pro Bowls.

GEORGE PRESTON MARSHALL
Team owner. Born in Grafton, West Virginia, October 11, 1896. Died August 9, 1969. Randolph-Macon. Inducted in 1963. 1932 Boston Braves, 1933-36 Boston Redskins, 1937-1969 Washington Redskins. **Highlights:** Charter enshrinee. Sponsored progressive rules changes. Organized first team band, pioneered halftime shows.

CURTIS MARTIN
Running back. 5-11, 207. Born in Pittsburgh, Pennsylvania, May 1, 1973. Pittsburgh. Inducted in 2012. 1995-97 New England Patriots, 1998-2005 New York Jets. **Highlights:** Second player in NFL history to start career with 10 straight 1,000-yard rushing seasons. Retired as fourth-leading rusher of all-time with 14,101 yards. Racked up 17,421 combined net yards and 100 career TDs (90 rushing, 10 receiving). NFL rushing title, 2004.

OLLIE MATSON
Halfback. 6-2, 220. Born in Trinity, Texas, May 1, 1930. Died February 19, 2011. San Francisco. Inducted in 1972. 1952, 1954-58 Chicago Cardinals, 1959-1962 Los Angeles Rams, 1963 Detroit Lions, 1964-66 Philadelphia Eagles. **Highlights:** Nine touchdowns on kickoff, punt returns. Traded for nine players in 1959.

BRUCE MATTHEWS
Guard-tackle-center. 6-5, 289. Born in Raleigh, North Carolina, August 8, 1961. Southern California. Inducted in 2007. 1983-2001 Houston Oilers/Tennessee Oilers/Tennessee Titans. **Highlights:** Played in 296 games, most ever by positional player at time of his retirement. Named to a record-tying 14 straight Pro Bowls. All-Pro nine times, All-AFC 12 times.

DON MAYNARD
Wide receiver. 6-1, 185. Born in Crosbyton, Texas. January 25, 1935. Texas Western. Inducted in 1987. 1958 New York Giants, 1960-62 New York Titans, 1963-1972 New York Jets, 1973 St. Louis Cardinals. **Highlights:** 633 receptions for 11,834 yards, 88 touchdowns. At least 50 catches and 1,000 yards in five different seasons.

GEORGE McAFEE
Halfback. 6-0, 177. Born in Corbin, Kentucky, March 13, 1918. Died March 4, 2009. Duke. Inducted in 1966. 1940-41, 1945-1950 Chicago Bears. **Highlights:** Two-way star. 25 interceptions, 234 points. Career punt-return average of 12.78 yards per return.

MIKE McCORMACK
Tackle. 6-4, 250. Born in Chicago, Illinois, June 21, 1930. Died November 15, 2013. Kansas. Inducted in 1984. 1951 New York Yanks, 1954-1962 Cleveland Browns. **Highlights:** Excelled as offensive right tackle for eight years. Six Pro Bowls.

RANDALL McDANIEL
Guard. 6-3, 276. Born in Phoenix, Arizona, December 19, 1964. Arizona State. Inducted in 2009. 1988-1999 Minnesota Vikings, 2000-01 Tampa Bay Buccaneers. **Highlights:** 12 Pro Bowls, All-Pro nine straight times. Blocked for six different 1,000-yard rushers, five 3,000-yard passers.

TOMMY McDONALD
Wide receiver. 5-9, 175. Born in Roy, New Mexico, July 26, 1934. Oklahoma. Inducted in 1998. 1957-1963 Philadelphia Eagles, 1964 Dallas Cowboys, 1965-66 Los Angeles Rams, 1967 Atlanta Falcons, 1968 Cleveland Browns. **Highlights:** Recorded 495 receptions for 8,410 yards, 84 touchdowns.

HUGH McELHENNY
Halfback. 6-1, 198. Born in Los Angeles, California, December 31, 1928. Washington. Inducted in 1970. 1952-1960 San Francisco 49ers, 1961-62 Minnesota Vikings, 1963 New York Giants, 1964 Detroit Lions. **Highlights:** 5,281 rushing yards, 360 points. Totaled 11,369 yards rushing, receiving, and returning kicks.

JOHNNY (BLOOD) McNALLY
Halfback. 6-0, 185. Born in New Richmond, Wisconsin, November 27, 1903. Died November 28, 1985. Notre Dame, St. John's (Minnesota). Inducted in 1963. 1925-26 Milwaukee Badgers, 1926-27 Duluth Eskimos, 1928 Pottsville Maroons, 1929-1933, 1935-36 Green Bay Packers, 1934 Pittsburgh Pirates; player-coach, 1937-38 Pittsburgh Pirates. **Highlights:** Charter enshrinee. 49 touchdowns, 297 points in 14 seasons with five teams.

MIKE MICHALSKE
Guard. 6-0, 209. Born in Cleveland, Ohio, April 24, 1903. Died October 26, 1983. Penn State. Inducted in 1964. 1926 New York Yankees (AFL), 1927-28 New York Yankees, 1929-1935, 1937 Green Bay Packers. **Highlights:** Anchored Packers' championship lines, 1929-1931. First guard enshrined in Canton.

WAYNE MILLNER
End. 6-0, 191. Born in Roxbury, Massachusetts, January 31, 1913. Died November 19, 1976. Notre Dame. Inducted in 1968. 1936 Boston Redskins, 1937-1941, 1945 Washington Redskins. **Highlights:** Redskins' all-time leader with 124 catches when retired. 55- and 78-yard touchdown receptions in 1937 NFL Championship Game.

BOBBY MITCHELL
Running back-wide receiver. 6-0, 195. Born in Hot Springs, Arkansas, June 6, 1935. Illinois. Inducted in 1983. 1958-1961 Cleveland Browns, 1962-68 Washington Redskins. **Highlights:** 91 touchdowns, including 8 on kickoff and punt returns. 14,078 combined yards.

RON MIX
Tackle. 6-4, 255. Born in Los Angeles, California, March 10, 1938. Southern California. Inducted in 1979. 1960 Los Angeles Chargers, 1961-69 San Diego Chargers, 1971 Oakland Raiders. **Highlights:** All-AFL nine times. Only two holding penalties in 10 years with the Chargers.

ART MONK
Wide receiver. 6-3, 210. Born in White Plains, New York, December 5, 1957. Syracuse. Inducted in 2008. 1980-1993 Washington Redskins, 1994 New York Jets, 1995 Philadelphia Eagles. **Highlights:** 940 receptions, 12,721 yards, 68 TDs. Set then-single season record, 106 catches, 1984. Had 50 or more catches in a season nine times.

JOE MONTANA
Quarterback. 6-2, 200. Born in New Eagle, Pennsylvania, June, 11, 1956. Notre Dame. Inducted in 2000. 1979-1990, 1992 San Francisco 49ers, 1993-94 Kansas City Chiefs. **Highlights:** MVP in Super Bowl's XVI, XIX, and XXIV. Eight Pro Bowls and All-NFL three times.

WARREN MOON
Quarterback. 6-3, 212. Born in Los Angeles, California, November 18, 1956. West Los Angeles Junior College, Washington. Inducted in 2006. 1984-1993 Houston Oilers, 1994-1996 Minnesota Vikings, 1997-1998 Seattle Seahawks, 1999-2000 Kansas City Chiefs. **Highlights:** Passed for 49,325 yards and 291 touchdowns in 17 NFL seasons. Elected to nine Pro Bowls including eight straight. Threw for 3,000 yards in nine seasons.

LENNY MOORE
Flanker-running back. 6-1, 198. Born in Reading, Pennsylvania, November 25, 1933. Penn State. Inducted in 1975. 1956-1967 Baltimore Colts. **Highlights:** From 1963-65, scored touchdowns in record 18 consecutive games. 113 career touchdowns, 12,451 combined net yards.

MARION MOTLEY
Fullback. 6-1, 238. Born in Leesburg, Georgia, June 5, 1920. Died June 27, 1999. South Carolina State, Nevada. Inducted in 1968. 1946-49 Cleveland Browns (AAFC), 1950-53 Cleveland Browns, 1955 Pittsburgh Steelers. **Highlights:** AAFC's all-time rushing champion. Led league in rushing in first NFL season.

MIKE MUNCHAK
Guard. 6-3, 281. Born in Scranton, Pennsylvania, March 5, 1960. Penn State. Inducted in 2001. 1982-1993 Houston Oilers. **Highlights:** Devastating blocker, All-AFC seven times, elected to nine Pro Bowls.

ANTHONY MUÑOZ
Tackle. 6-6, 278. Born in Ontario, California, August 19, 1958. Southern California. Inducted in 1998. 1980-1992 Cincinnati Bengals. **Highlights:** All-Pro choice 11 consecutive years, 1981-1991. Selected to 11 straight Pro Bowls.

GEORGE MUSSO
Guard-tackle. 6-2, 270. Born in Collinsville, Illinois. April 8, 1910. Died September 5, 2000. Millikin. Inducted in 1982. 1933-1944 Chicago Bears. **Highlights:** First player to achieve All-NFL status at two positions—tackle in 1935 and guard in 1937.

BRONKO NAGURSKI
Fullback. 6-2, 225. Born in Rainy River, Ontario, Canada, November 3, 1908. Died January 7, 1990. Minnesota. Inducted in 1963. 1930-37, 1943 Chicago Bears. **Highlights:** Charter enshrinee. 2,778 rushing yards in nine seasons. All-NFL five times.

JOE NAMATH
Quarterback. 6-2, 200. Born in Beaver Falls, Pennsylvania, May 31, 1943. Alabama. Inducted in 1985. 1965-1976 New York Jets, 1977 Los Angeles Rams. **Highlights:** First quarterback to pass for more than 4,000 yards in season, 1967. Guaranteed, delivered victory over Colts in Super Bowl III.

EARLE (GREASY) NEALE
Coach. Born in Parkersburg, West Virginia, November 5, 1891. Died November 2, 1973. West Virginia Wesleyan. Inducted in 1969. 1941-42, 1944-1950 Philadelphia Eagles; co-coach, 1943 Phil-Pitt. **Highlights:** Turned Eagles into winners with three consecutive division crowns, NFL championships in 1948 and 1949.

ERNIE NEVERS
Fullback. 6-1, 205. Born in Willow River, Minnesota, June 11, 1903. Died May 3, 1976. Stanford. Inducted in 1963. 1926-27 Duluth Eskimos, 1929-1931 Chicago Cardinals. **Highlights:** Charter enshrinee. Holds NFL's longest-standing record, 40 points in one game in 1929.

OZZIE NEWSOME
Tight end. 6-2, 232. Born in Muscle Shoals, Alabama, March 16, 1956. Alabama. Inducted in 1999. 1978-1990 Cleveland Browns. **Highlights:** Finished career as all-time leader among tight ends with 662 receptions for 7,980 yards.

RAY NITSCHKE
Linebacker. 6-3, 235. Born in Elmwood Park, Illinois, December 29, 1936. Died March 8, 1998. Illinois. Inducted in 1978. 1958-1972 Green Bay Packers. **Highlights:** MVP of 1962 title game. Named NFL's all-time linebacker in 1969.

CHUCK NOLL
Coach. Born in Cleveland, Ohio, January 5, 1932. Dayton. Inducted in 1993. 1969-1991 Pittsburgh Steelers. **Highlights:** Coached for 23 years. Only coach to win four Super Bowl titles (IX, X, XIII, XIV).

LEO NOMELLINI
Defensive tackle. 6-3, 264. Born in Lucca, Italy, June 19, 1924. Died October 17, 2000. Minnesota. Inducted in 1969. 1950-1963 San Francisco 49ers. **Highlights:** Played every 49ers game for 14 seasons. 10 Pro Bowls.

JONATHAN OGDEN
Tackle. 6-9, 345. Born in Washington, D.C., July 31, 1974. Inducted in 2013. 1996-2007 Baltimore Ravens. **Highlights:** First-ever draft pick of the Ravens. Named first-team All-Pro six times. Elected to 11 Pro Bowls. Member of NFL's All-Decade Team of 2000s.

MERLIN OLSEN
Defensive tackle. 6-5, 270. Born in Logan, Utah, September 15, 1940. Died March 11, 2010. Utah State. Inducted in 1982. 1962-1976 Los Angeles Rams. **Highlights:** Member of the Fearsome "Foursome." Named to 14 consecutive Pro Bowls, Rams' all-time team.

JIM OTTO
Center. 6-2, 255. Born in Wausau, Wisconsin, January 5, 1938. Miami. Inducted in 1980. 1960-1974 Oakland Raiders. **Highlights:** Named AFL's all-time center. Played in 210 games, 12 AFL All-Star Games or Pro Bowls, six AFL/AFC title games.

STEVE OWEN
Tackle. Coach. 6-2, 235. Born in Cleo Springs, Oklahoma, April 21, 1898. Died May 17, 1964. Phillips. Inducted in 1966. 1924-25 Kansas City Cowboys, 1925 Cleveland Bulldogs, 1926-1931, 1933 New York Giants; coach, 1930-1953 New York Giants. **Highlights:** Both player and coach. Coached Giants to record of 155-108-17, eight divisional titles, two NFL championships.

ALAN PAGE
Defensive tackle. 6-4, 225. Born in Canton, Ohio, August 7, 1945. Notre Dame. Inducted in 1988. 1967-1978 Minnesota Vikings, 1978-1981 Chicago Bears. **Highlights:** Dominating defensive tackle played in 238 consecutive games, four Super Bowls. Won league MVP honors in 1971.

BILL PARCELLS
Coach. Born in Englewood, New Jersey, August 22, 1941. Inducted in 2013. 1983-1990 New York Giants, 1993-96 New England Patriots, 1997-99 New York Jets, 2003-06 Dallas Cowboys. **Highlights:** Only coach to lead four different teams to the playoffs. Named NFL Coach of the Year twice (1986 and 1994). Led Giants to two Super Bowl titles. Overall record: 183-138-1.

CLARENCE (ACE) PARKER
Quarterback. 5-11, 168. Born in Portsmouth, Virginia, May 17, 1912. Died November 6, 2013. Duke. Inducted in 1972. 1937-1941 Brooklyn Dodgers, 1945 Boston Yanks, 1946 New York Yankees (AAFC). **Highlights:** Two-way threat. Two-time All-NFL performer, league MVP in 1940.

JIM PARKER
Guard-tackle. 6-3, 273. Born in Macon, Georgia, April 3, 1934. Died July 18, 2005. Ohio State. Inducted in 1973. 1957-1967 Baltimore Colts. **Highlights:** First full-time offensive lineman elected to Hall of Fame. All-NFL eight consecutive years, eight Pro Bowls.

WALTER PAYTON
Running back. 5-10, 202. Born in Columbia, Mississippi, July 25, 1954. Died November 1, 1999. Jackson State. Inducted in 1993. 1975-1987 Chicago Bears. **Highlights:** NFL's all-time leading rusher with 16,726 yards and combined net yardage with 21,803 at time of retirement.

PRO FOOTBALL HALL OF FAME

JOE PERRY
Fullback. 6-0, 200. Born in Stevens, Arkansas, January 22, 1927. Died April 25, 2011. Compton Junior College. Inducted in 1969. 1948-49 San Francisco 49ers (AAFC), 1950-1960, 1963 San Francisco 49ers, 1961-62 Baltimore Colts. **Highlights:** First player in NFL history to gain 1,000 yards two consecutive seasons. 12,532 combined yards.

PETE PIHOS
End. 6-1, 210. Born in Orlando, Florida, October 22, 1923. Died August 16, 2011. Indiana. Inducted in 1970. 1947-1955 Philadelphia Eagles. **Highlights:** Three-time NFL receiving champion. Caught winning touchdown in 1949 NFL Championship Game.

FRITZ POLLARD
Halfback-Coach. 5-9, 165. Born in Chicago, Illinois, January 27, 1894. Died May 11, 1986. Brown. Inducted in 2005. 1919-1921, 1925-26 Akron Pros/Indians, 1922 Milwaukee Badgers, 1923, 1925 Hammond Pros, 1925 Providence Steam Roller. **Highlights:** True pioneer as one of two African American players in the NFL in 1920 and helped lead Akron to league title that season. In 1921, became the league's first black head coach.

JOHN RANDLE
Defensive tackle. 6-1, 278. Born in Hearne, Texas, December 12, 1967. Trinity Valley Community College; Texas A&I. Inducted in 2010. 1990-2000 Minnesota Vikings, 2001-03 Seattle Seahawks. **Highlights:** Undrafted free agent rookie, record eight straight seasons with 10 or more sacks, had 137.5 career sacks. Voted to seven Pro Bowls, named All-Pro/NFC six consecutive years, All-AFC once.

HUGH (SHORTY) RAY
Supervisor of officials 1938-1952. Born in Highland Park, Illinois, September 21, 1884. Died September 16, 1956. Illinois. Inducted in 1966. **Highlights:** Supervisor of Officials, 1938-1952. Streamlined rules to improve game tempo, player safety.

ANDRE REED
Wide receiver. 6-2, 190. Born in Allentown, Pennsylvania, January 29, 1964. Kutztown. Inducted in 2014. 1985-1999 Buffalo Bills, 2000 Washington Redskins. **Highlights:** Most prolific receiver in Bill history. His 951 career receptions was third all-time when he retired.

DAN REEVES
Team owner. Born in New York, New York, June 30, 1912. Died April 15, 1971. Georgetown. Inducted in 1967. 1941-45 Cleveland Rams, 1946-1971 Los Angeles Rams. **Highlights:** Moved Rams to Los Angeles in 1946 and opened up West Coast to pro football. First postwar owner to sign African-American player.

MEL RENFRO
Cornerback-safety. 6-0, 192. Born in Houston, Texas, December 30, 1941. Oregon. Inducted in 1996. 1964-1977 Dallas Cowboys. **Highlights:** 52 interceptions for 626 yards and 3 touchdowns. Also added 842 yards on punt returns, 2,246 yards on kickoff returns. Elected to Pro Bowl first 10 seasons.

JERRY RICE
Wide receiver. 6-2, 200. Born in Starksville, Mississippi, October 13, 1962. Mississippi Valley State. Inducted in 2010. 1985-2000 San Francisco 49ers, 2001-04 Oakland Raiders, 2004 Seattle Seahawks. **Highlights:** NFL's all-time reception leader with 1,549 catches for 22,895 yards, 208 total touchdowns. Had 14 seasons with 1,000 yards receiving; 23,546 combined net yards. All-Pro 11 times, Super Bowl XXIII MVP.

LES RICHTER
Linebacker. 6-3, 238. Born in Fresno, California, October 6, 1930. Died June 12, 2010. California. Inducted in 2011. 1954-1962 Los Angeles Rams. **Highlights:** Second overall pick in 1952 by New York Yanks. Rights traded to Rams in exchange for 11 players. Rugged, fierce competitor. Voted to eight straight Pro Bowls. Recorded 16 career interceptions, also handled Rams' placekicking duties early in career.

JOHN RIGGINS
Running back. 6-2, 240. Born in Seneca, Kansas, August 4, 1949. Kansas. Inducted in 1992. 1971-75 New York Jets, 1976-79, 1981-85 Washington Redskins. **Highlights:** 11,352 rushing yards, 116 total touchdowns. MVP of Super Bowl XVII with 166 rushing yards including game-winning 43-yard touchdown.

JIM RINGO
Center. 6-2, 230. Born in Orange, New Jersey, November 21, 1931. Died November 19, 2007. Syracuse. Inducted in 1981. 1953-1963 Green Bay Packers, 1964-67 Philadelphia Eagles. **Highlights:** Ten-time Pro Bowl selection, seven-time All-NFL selection. Started in then-record 182 consecutive games.

WILLIE ROAF
Tackle. 6-5, 300. Born in Pine Bluff, Arkansas, April 18, 1970. Louisiana Tech. Inducted in 2012. 1993-2001 New Orleans Saints, 2002-05 Kansas City Chiefs. **Highlights:** Voted to 11 Pro Bowls, named first-team All-Pro seven times. Member of both the NFL's All-Decade Team of the 1990s and 2000s.

DAVE ROBINSON
Linebacker. 6-3, 245. Born in Mt. Holly, New Jersey, May 3, 1941. Inducted in 2013. 1963-1972 Green Bay Packers, 1973-74 Washington Redskins. **Highlights:** Starting outside linebacker in three NFL championship game and two Super Bowl wins. Recorded 27 career interceptions. Voted to three Pro Bowl Bowls. Named to NFL's All-Decade Team of 1960s.

ANDY ROBUSTELLI
Defensive end. 6-0, 230. Born in Stamford, Connecticut, December 6, 1925. Died May 31, 2011. Arnold College. Inducted in 1971. 1951-55 Los Angeles Rams, 1956-1964 New York Giants. **Highlights:** Anchored defense in eight championship games. Named NFL's top player in 1962.

ART ROONEY
Founder-Team Owner. Born in Coulterville, Pennsylvania, January 27, 1901. Died August 25, 1988. Georgetown, Duquesne. Inducted in 1964. 1933-39 Pittsburgh Pirates, 1940-42, 1945-1988 Pittsburgh Steelers, 1943 Phil-Pitt, 1944 Card-Pitt. **Highlights:** Founded Pittsburgh Pirates in 1933 and renamed them Steelers in 1940. Team won four Super Bowls in 1970s.

DAN ROONEY
Administrator-Team Owner. Born in Pittsburgh, Pennsylvania, July, 20, 1932. Duquesne. Inducted in 2000. 1955-present Pittsburgh Steelers. **Highlights:** Has been on the board of directors for the NFL Trust Fund, NFL Films, and Scheduling Committee. Played a key role in the labor agreement reached in 1993 between the NFL owners and players.

PETE ROZELLE
Commissioner. Born in South Gate, California, March 1, 1926. Died December 6, 1996. Compton Junior College, San Francisco. Inducted in 1985. Commissioner, 1960-1989. **Highlights:** Negotiated first league-wide television contract in 1962. Generally recognized as premiere commissioner in all of sports. Credited with making NFL the nation's most popular sport.

BOB ST. CLAIR
Tackle. 6-9, 265. Born in San Francisco, California, February 18, 1931. San Francisco, Tulsa. Inducted in 1990. 1953-1963 San Francisco 49ers. **Highlights:** Exceptional offensive lineman. Also played goal-line defense and had 10 blocked field goals, 1956.

ED SABOL
Founder-President-Chairman. Born in Atlantic City, New Jersey, September 11, 1916. Ohio State. Inducted in 2011. 1964-1995 NFL Films. **Highlights:** Bid and received rights to film 1962 NFL Championship Game. Two years later, founded NFL Films. During his tenure, NFL Films won 52 Emmys. Vision and innovations changed the way in which sports were presented.

BARRY SANDERS
Running back. 5-8, 203. Born in Wichita, Kansas, July 16, 1968. Oklahoma State. Inducted in 2004. 1989-1998 Detroit Lions. **Highlights:** 15,269 rushing yards, 99 touchdowns. Rushed for 1,000 yards in each of 10 seasons. NFL co-MVP, 1997. Selected to 10 Pro Bowls.

CHARLIE SANDERS
Tight end. 6-4, 230. Born in Richlands, North Carolina, August 25, 1946. Minnesota. Inducted in 2007. 1968-1977 Detroit Lions. **Highlights:** 336 career receptions for 4,817 yards and 31 touchdowns. Selected to seven Pro Bowls. Named to the NFL's All-Decade Team of 1970s.

DEION SANDERS
Cornerback-Kick returner-Punt returner. 6-1, 195. Born in Fort Myers, Florida, August 9, 1967. Florida State. Inducted in 2011. 1989-1993 Atlanta Falcons, 1994 San Francisco 49ers, 1995-99 Dallas Cowboys, 2000 Washington Redskins, 2004-05 Baltimore Ravens. **Highlights:** First-team All-NFL nine times. Voted to the NFL's All-Decade Team of the 1990s at both cornerback and punt returner. 53 career interceptions. Career touchdowns include six on punt returns, three on kickoff returns, nine on interceptions, one fumble recovery, and three receiving.

WARREN SAPP
Defensive tackle. 6-2, 300. Born in Orlando, Florida, December 19, 1972. Inducted in 2013. 1995-2003 Tampa Bay Buccaneers, 2004-07 Oakland Raiders. **Highlights:** Amassed 96.5 career sacks. Named 1999 NFL Defensive Player of the Year. First-team All-Pro four straight seasons. Member of NFL's All-Decade Teams of 1990s and 2000s.

GALE SAYERS
Running back. 6-0, 200. Born in Wichita, Kansas, May 30, 1943. Kansas. Inducted in 1977. 1965-1971 Chicago Bears. **Highlights:** Broke into league by scoring rookie-record 22 touchdowns. Led league in rushing in 1966, 1969. MVP of three Pro Bowls.

JOE SCHMIDT
Linebacker. 6-0, 222. Born in Pittsburgh, Pennsylvania, January 18, 1932. Pittsburgh. Inducted in 1973. 1953-1965 Detroit Lions. **Highlights:** 24 interceptions. Lions' team captain for nine years. Mastered middle linebacker position that evolved in 1950s.

TEX SCHRAMM
Team president-general manager. Born in San Gabriel, California, June 2, 1920. Died July 15, 2003. Texas. Inducted in 1991. 1947-1956 Los Angeles Rams. 1960-1989 Dallas Cowboys. **Highlights:** Played prominent role in AFL-NFL merger. Chairman of Competition Committee from 1966-1988.

LEE ROY SELMON
Defensive end. 6-3, 250. Born in Eufaula, Oklahoma, October 20, 1954. Died September 4, 2011. Oklahoma. Inducted in 1995. 1976-1984 Tampa Bay Buccaneers. **Highlights:** 78½ sacks, 380 quarterback pressures, forced 28 fumbles. Six consecutive Pro Bowl selections.

SHANNON SHARPE
Tight end. 6-2, 230. Born in Chicago, Illinois, June 26, 1968. Savannah State. Inducted in 2011. 1990-99, 2002-03 Denver Broncos, 2000-01 Baltimore Ravens. **Highlights:** Retired as the NFL's all-time leader among tight ends for catches (815), receiving yards (10,060) and TD receptions (62). Selected as first- or second-team All-Pro five times, named to eight Pro Bowls. Played on three Super Bowl championship teams in four seasons.

BILLY SHAW
Guard. 6-2, 258. Born in Natchez, Mississippi, December 15, 1938. Georgia Tech. Inducted in 1999. 1961-69 Buffalo Bills. **Highlights:** First player who played entire career in AFL to be elected to Hall of Fame. Named to AFL's all-time team.

ART SHELL
Tackle. 6-5, 285. Born in Charleston, South Carolina, November 26, 1946. Maryland State-Eastern Shore. Inducted in 1989. 1968-82 Oakland/Los Angeles Raiders. **Highlights:** Cornerstone of Raiders' offensive line in 1970s. 207 regular-season games, 23 postseason games, eight Pro Bowls.

DON SHULA
Coach. Born in Grand River, Ohio, January 4, 1930. John Carroll. Inducted in 1997. 1963-69 Baltimore Colts, 1970-1995 Miami Dolphins. **Highlights:** Won more games (347) than any coach in NFL history. Won two Super Bowl titles, including Super Bowl VII when Dolphins recorded NFL's only perfect season (17-0).

O.J. SIMPSON
Running back. 6-1, 212. Born in San Francisco, California, July 9, 1947. City College (San Francisco), Southern California. Inducted in 1985. 1969-1977 Buffalo Bills, 1978-79 San Francisco 49ers. **Highlights:** In 1973, became first player to rush for 2,000 yards in season. Finished career with four rushing titles, 11,236 yards.

MIKE SINGLETARY
Linebacker. 6-0, 230. Born in Houston, Texas, October 9, 1958. Baylor. Inducted in 1998. 1981-1992 Chicago Bears. **Highlights:** All-Pro choice eight times and All-NFC nine consecutive seasons. Selected to 10 Pro Bowls.

JACKIE SLATER
Tackle. 6-4, 277. Born in Jackson, Mississippi, May 27, 1954. Jackson State. Inducted in 2001. 1976-1995 Los Angeles/St. Louis Rams. **Highlights:** Played 20 seasons, 259 games. Blocked for seven different 1,000-yard rushers. Seven Pro Bowls.

BRUCE SMITH
Defensive end. 6-4, 280. Born in Norfolk, Virginia, June 18, 1963. Virginia Tech. Inducted in 2009. 1985-1999 Buffalo Bills, 2000-03 Washington Redskins. **Highlights:** NFL's all-time leader in sacks with 200. Named All-Pro nine times, 11 Pro Bowls. Selected to NFL's All-Decade Team of 1980s and 1990s.

PRO FOOTBALL HALL OF FAME

EMMITT SMITH
Running back. 5-9, 207. Born in Pensacola, Florida, May 15, 1969. Florida. Inducted in 2010. 1990-2002 Dallas Cowboys, 2003-04 Arizona Cardinals. **Highlights:** Won four rushing titles in five years, recorded record 11 straight 1,000-yard seasons. NFL's all-time leading rusher with 18,355 yards, 164 rushing TDs. Won NFL MVP and Super Bowl XXVIII MVP in 1993.

JACKIE SMITH
Tight end. 6-4, 232. Born in Columbia, Mississippi, February 23, 1940. Northwestern State (Louisiana). Inducted in 1994. 1963-1977 St. Louis Cardinals, 1978 Dallas Cowboys. **Highlights:** 480 receptions for 7,918 yards, 40 touchdowns. Third tight end to be elected to Hall of Fame.

JOHN STALLWORTH
Wide receiver. 6-2, 191. Born in Tuscaloosa, Alabama, July 15, 1952. Alabama A&M. Inducted in 2002. 1974-1987 Pittsburgh Steelers. **Highlights:** 537 receptions for 8,723 yards, 63 touchdowns. Scored go-ahead touchdown in Super Bowl XIV on 73-yard reception.

BART STARR
Quarterback. 6-1, 200. Born in Montgomery, Alabama, January 9, 1934. Alabama. Inducted in 1977. 1956-1971 Green Bay Packers. **Highlights:** Quarterbacked Packers to six division titles, five NFL titles, and first two Super Bowls in which he was MVP.

ROGER STAUBACH
Quarterback. 6-3, 202. Born in Cincinnati, Ohio, February 5, 1942. New Mexico Military Institute, Navy. Inducted in 1985. 1969-1979 Dallas Cowboys. **Highlights:** Led Cowboys to four NFC titles and victories in Super Bowls VI, XII. When retired, 83.4 career passer rating was best of all time.

ERNIE STAUTNER
Defensive tackle. 6-2, 235. Born in Prinzing-by-Cham, Bavaria, April 20, 1925. Died February 16, 2006. Boston College. Inducted in 1969. 1950-1963 Pittsburgh Steelers. **Highlights:** Played in nine Pro Bowls and won the best lineman award in 1957. Recorded 3 safeties.

JAN STENERUD
Kicker. 6-2, 190. Born in Fetsund, Norway, November 26, 1942. Montana State. Inducted in 1991. 1967-1979 Kansas City Chiefs, 1980-83 Green Bay Packers, 1984-85 Minnesota Vikings. **Highlights:** 1,699 points on 580 extra points, 373 field goals. First pure placekicker to enter Hall of Fame.

DWIGHT STEPHENSON
Center. 6-2, 255. Born in Murfreesboro, North Carolina, November 20, 1957. Alabama. Inducted in 1998. 1980-87 Miami Dolphins. **Highlights:** Recognized as premier center of his time. All-Pro, All-AFC five straight years. Selected to five Pro Bowls.

MICHAEL STRAHAN
Defensive end. 6-5, 255. Born in Houston, Texas, November 21, 1971. Texas Southern. Inducted in 2014. 1993-2007 New York Giants. **Highlights:** Recorded 141.5 career sacks. His 22.5 sacks in 2001 is an NFL record. Named to NFL's All-Decade Team of 2000s.

HANK STRAM
Coach. Born in Chicago, Illinois, January 3, 1923. Died July 4, 2005. Purdue. Inducted in 2003. 1960-1974 Dallas Texans/Kansas City Chiefs, 1976-1977 New Orleans Saints. **Highlights:** Overall record of 136-100-10. Recorded most wins in AFL history. Guided teams to titles in 1962, 1966, and 1969. Led Chiefs to AFL win in Super Bowl IV.

KEN STRONG
Halfback. 5-11, 210. Born in West Haven, Connecticut, April 21, 1906. Died October 5, 1979. New York University. Inducted in 1967. 1929-1932 Staten Island Stapletons, 1933-35, 1939, 1944-47 New York Giants, 1936-37 New York Yanks (AFL). **Highlights:** Scored 17 points to lead Giants to victory in 1934 'Sneakers' game, led NFL with 64 points, 1933.

JOE STYDAHAR
Tackle. 6-4, 230. Born in Kaylor, Pennsylvania, March 17, 1912. Died March 23, 1977. West Virginia. Inducted in 1967. 1936-1942, 1945-46 Chicago Bears. **Highlights:** One of stalwarts of Bears' 'Monsters of the Midway.' Played on five divisional, three NFL championship teams.

LYNN SWANN
Wide receiver. 5-11, 180. Born in Alcoa, Tennessee, March 7, 1952. Southern California. Inducted in 2001. 1974-1982 Pittsburgh Steelers. **Highlights:** All-AFC three times. Selected to three Pro Bowls. MVP, Super Bowl X.

FRAN TARKENTON
Quarterback. 6-0, 185. Born in Richmond, Virginia, February 3, 1940. Georgia. Inducted in 1986. 1961-66, 1972-78 Minnesota Vikings, 1967-1971 New York Giants. **Highlights:** At retirement, held NFL records for attempts (6,467), completions (3,686), yards (47,003), and touchdowns (342). Four touchdown passes in first NFL game.

CHARLEY TAYLOR
Running back-wide receiver. 6-3, 210. Born in Grand Prairie, Texas, September 28, 1941. Arizona State. Inducted in 1984. 1964-1975, 1977 Washington Redskins. **Highlights:** Won rookie of year honors as running back. Switched to wide receiver and won receiving titles in 1966, 1967.

JIM TAYLOR
Fullback. 6-0, 216. Born in Baton Rouge, Louisiana, September 20, 1935. Hinds Junior College; Louisiana State. Inducted in 1976. 1958-1966 Green Bay Packers, 1967 New Orleans Saints. **Highlights:** 8,597 rushing yards, 558 points. In 1962, led league in rushing and scoring with 19 touchdowns.

LAWRENCE TAYLOR
Linebacker. 6-3, 237. Born in Williamsburg, Virginia, February 4, 1959. North Carolina. Inducted in 1999. 1981-1993 New York Giants. **Highlights:** Redefined the position of outside linebacker. All-Pro nine times, 10 Pro Bowls. NFL MVP in 1986.

DERRICK THOMAS
Linebacker. 6-3, 243. Born in Miami, Florida, January 1, 1967. Died February 8, 2000. Alabama. Inducted in 2009. 1989-1999 Kansas City Chiefs. **Highlights:** Set NFL record with 7 sacks in one game. Recorded most sacks in NFL during 1990s. Nine Pro Bowls. Named to NFL's All-Decade Team of 1990s.

EMMITT THOMAS
Cornerback. 6-2, 192. Born in Angleton, Texas, June 3, 1943. Bishop. Inducted in 2008. 1966-1978 Kansas City Chiefs. **Highlights:** Undrafted free agent. 58 interceptions, 937 yards, 5 TDs. Ranked fifth all-time in interceptions at retirement. Interception leader —AFL, 1969 and NFL, 1974.

THURMAN THOMAS
Running back. 5-10, 198. Born in Houston, Texas, May 16, 1966. Oklahoma State. Inducted in 2007. 1988-1999 Buffalo Bills, 2000 Miami Dolphins. **Highlights:** Amassed 16,532 total yards including 12,074 yards rushing. Scored 88 touchdowns. Only player in history to lead league in yards from scrimmage four straight seasons.

JIM THORPE
Halfback. 6-1, 190. Born in Prague, Oklahoma, May 28, 1888. Died March 28, 1953. Carlisle. Inducted in 1963. 1915-17, 1919-1920, 1926 Canton Bulldogs, 1921 Cleveland Indians, 1922-23 Oorang Indians, 1924 Rock Island Independents, 1925 New York Giants, 1928 Chicago Cardinals. **Highlights:** Charter enshrinee. First president of American Professional Football Association, 1920. Played for 12 seasons.

ANDRE TIPPETT
Linebacker. 6-3, 240. Born in Birmingham, Alabama, December 27, 1959. Iowa; Ellsworth (IA) Jr. College. Inducted in 2008. 1982-1988, 1990-93 New England Patriots. **Highlights:** Recorded 100 career sacks including personal best 18.5 sacks, 1984. Named to five straight Pro Bowls, 1985-89.

Y.A. TITTLE
Quarterback. 6-0, 200. Born in Marshall, Texas, October 24, 1926. Louisiana State. Inducted in 1971. 1948-49 Baltimore Colts (AAFC), 1950 Baltimore Colts, 1951-1960 San Francisco 49ers, 1961-64 New York Giants. **Highlights:** 33,070 yards, 242 touchdowns. 33 touchdown passes in 1962 and 36 in 1963. Three-time league Player of the Year.

GEORGE TRAFTON
Center. 6-2, 235. Born in Chicago, Illinois, December 6, 1896. Died September 5, 1971. Notre Dame. Inducted in 1964. 1920-1932 Decatur Staleys/Chicago Staleys/Chicago Bears. **Highlights:** First center to snap with one hand. Named top NFL center of 1920s.

CHARLEY TRIPPI
Halfback-quarterback. 6-0, 185. Born in Pittston, Pennsylvania, December 14, 1922. Georgia. Inducted in 1968. 1947-1955 Chicago Cardinals. **Highlights:** One of football's most versatile performers. Played halfback five years, quarterback for two, defense for two.

EMLEN TUNNELL
Safety. 6-1, 200. Born in Bryn Mawr, Pennsylvania, March 29, 1925. Died July 22, 1975. Toledo, Iowa. Inducted in 1967. 1948-1958 New York Giants, 1959-1961 Green Bay Packers. **Highlights:** 79 interceptions. Gained more yards on kickoff, punt, and interception returns (924) in 1952 than that season's NFL rushing leader.

CLYDE (BULLDOG) TURNER
Center. 6-2, 235. Born in Plains, Texas, March 10, 1919. Died October 30, 1998. Hardin-Simmons. Inducted in 1966. 1940-1952 Chicago Bears. Anchored defense for four NFL championship teams, including 4 interceptions in five title games.

JOHNNY UNITAS
Quarterback. 6-1, 195. Born in Pittsburgh, Pennsylvania, May 7, 1933. Died September 11, 2002. Louisville. Inducted in 1979. 1956-1972 Baltimore Colts, 1973 San Diego Chargers. **Highlights:** 40,239 passing yards, 290 touchdowns. Led Colts to two NFL championships. Passed for at least one touchdown in 47 consecutive games.

GENE UPSHAW
Guard. 6-5, 255. Born in Robstown, Texas, August 15, 1945. Died August 20, 2008. Texas A & I. Inducted in 1987. 1967-1981 Oakland Raiders. **Highlights:** Premier guard of his era played in 10 AFL/AFC Championship Games, three Super Bowls, seven Pro Bowls.

NORM VAN BROCKLIN
Quarterback. 6-1, 190. Born in Eagle Butte, South Dakota, March 15, 1926. Died May 2, 1983. Oregon. Inducted in 1971. 1949-1957 Los Angeles Rams, 1958-1960 Philadelphia Eagles. **Highlights:** NFL-record 554 yards passing in 1951 season opener. Guided Eagles to NFL crown as league's Most Outstanding Player in 1960.

STEVE VAN BUREN
Halfback. 6-1, 200. Born in La Ceiba, Honduras, December 28, 1920. Died August 23, 2012. Louisiana State. Inducted in 1965. 1944-1951 Philadelphia Eagles. **Highlights:** Four-time rushing champion. Won 1944 punt-return title and was 1945 kickoff-return champion.

DOAK WALKER
Halfback. 5-11, 173. Born in Dallas, Texas, January 1, 1927. Died September 27, 1998. Southern Methodist. Inducted in 1986. 1950-55 Detroit Lions. **Highlights:** 534 points. Won two NFL scoring titles. Had winning 67-yard scoring run in 1952 title game.

BILL WALSH
Coach. Born in Los Angeles, California, November 30, 1931. Died July 30, 2007. San Jose State. Inducted in 1993. 1979-1988 San Francisco 49ers. **Highlights:** 102-63-1 coaching record. Guided 49ers to three Super Bowl titles (XVI, XIX, XXIII) in 10 years.

PAUL WARFIELD
Wide receiver. 6-0, 188. Born in Warren, Ohio, November 28, 1942. Ohio State. Inducted in 1983. 1964-69, 1976-77 Cleveland Browns, 1970-74 Miami Dolphins. **Highlights:** 8,565 yards receiving, 85 touchdowns. Eight-time Pro Bowl player. Key to both Cleveland and Miami offenses.

BOB WATERFIELD
Quarterback. 6-2, 200. Born in Elmira, New York, July 26, 1920. Died March 25, 1983. UCLA. Inducted in 1965. 1945 Cleveland Rams, 1946-1952 Los Angeles Rams. **Highlights:** NFL MVP as rookie in 1945 and led Rams to NFL title. Grabbed 20 interceptions in limited defensive duties.

MIKE WEBSTER
Center. 6-2, 260. Born in Tomahawk, Wisconsin, March 18, 1952. Died September 24, 2002. Wisconsin. Inducted in 1997. 1974-1988 Pittsburgh Steelers, 1989-1990 Kansas City Chiefs. **Highlights:** Played in 245 games, nine Pro Bowls, and won four Super Bowls during 17-year career.

ROGER WEHRLI
Cornerback. 6-0, 190. Born in New Point, Missouri, November 26, 1947. Missouri. Inducted in 2007. 1969-1982 St. Louis Cardinals. **Highlights:** 40 career interceptions. Named to the NFL's All-Decade Team of 1970s. All-Pro five times, selected to seven Pro Bowls.

ARNIE WEINMEISTER
Defensive tackle. 6-4, 235. Born in Rhein, Saskatchewan, Canada, March 23, 1923. Died June 29, 2000. Washington. Inducted in 1984. 1948-49 New York Yankees (AAFC), 1950-53 New York Giants. **Highlights:** Dominant defensive tackle of his time. Four-time All-NFL selection, four Pro Bowls.

RANDY WHITE
Defensive tackle. 6-4, 265. Born in Pittsburgh, Pennsylvania, January 15, 1953. Maryland. Inducted in 1994. 1975-1988 Dallas Cowboys. **Highlights:** Missed only one game in 14 seasons. Co-MVP of Super Bowl XII. Nine-time Pro Bowl selection.

REGGIE WHITE
Defensive end. 6-5, 291. Born in Chattanooga, Tennessee, December 19, 1961. Died December 26, 2004. Tennessee. Inducted in 2006. 1985-1992 Philadelphia Eagles, 1993-1998 Green Bay Packers, 2000 Carolina Panthers. **Highlights:** Retired as all-time sack leader with 198. Named All-Pro 13 of 15 seasons including 10 as first-team selection. Named to 13 straight Pro Bowls.

DAVE WILCOX
Linebacker. 6-3, 241. Born in Ontario, Oregon, September, 29, 1942. Boise State, Oregon. Inducted in 2000. 1964-1974 San Francisco 49ers. **Highlights:** Seven Pro Bowls, All-NFL five times. Missed only one game because of injury.

AENEAS WILLIAMS
Cornerback-safety. 5-11, 194. Born in New Orleans, Louisiana, January 29, 1968. Southern University. Inducted in 2014. 1991-2000 Phoenix/ Arizona Cardinals, 2001-04 St. Louis Rams. **Highlights:** Named Pro Bowl seven times as a cornerback, once as safety. Recorded 55 interceptions for 807 yards, 9 TDs. Named to NFL's All-Decade Team of 2000s.

BILL WILLIS
Guard. 6-2, 215. Born in Columbus, Ohio, October 5, 1921. Died November 27, 2007. Ohio State. Inducted in 1977. 1946-1953 Cleveland Browns (AAFC/NFL). **Highlights:** Two-way player who excelled on defense. Four-time All-NFL player, played in three Pro Bowls.

LARRY WILSON
Safety. 6-0, 190. Born in Rigby, Idaho, March 24, 1938. Utah. Inducted in 1978. 1960-1972 St. Louis Cardinals. **Highlights:** 52 interceptions. Had interception in seven consecutive games in 1966. Made "safety blitz" famous.

RALPH WILSON, JR.
Owner-founder. Born in Columbus, Ohio, October 17, 1918. Died March 25, 2013. Virginia, Michigan. Inducted in 2009. 1960-present Buffalo Bills. **Highlights:** Founded team. Bills teams captured back-to-back AFL titles in mid-1960s. Unprecedented four straight Super Bowl appearances.

KELLEN WINSLOW
Tight end. 6-5, 250. Born in St. Louis, Missouri, November 5, 1957. Missouri. Inducted in 1995. 1979-1987 San Diego Chargers **Highlights:** 541 receptions for 6,741 yards, 45 touchdowns. 13 catches, blocked field goal in 1981 playoff win over Miami.

ALEX WOJCIECHOWICZ
Center. 6-0, 235. Born in South River, New Jersey, August 12, 1915. Died July 13, 1992. Fordham. Inducted in 1968. 1938-1946 Detroit Lions, 1946-1950 Philadelphia Eagles. **Highlights:** One of league's first iron men. Played both ways for eight years with Lions.

WILLIE WOOD
Safety. 5-10, 190. Born in Washington, D.C., December 23, 1936. Southern California. Inducted in 1989. 1960-1971 Green Bay Packers. **Highlights:** 48 interceptions. Competed in six NFL Championship Games and Super Bowls I and II.

ROD WOODSON
Cornerback-safety. 6-0, 200. Born in Fort Wayne, Indiana, March 10, 1965. Purdue. Inducted in 2009. 1987-1996 Pittsburgh Steelers, 1997 San Francisco 49ers, 1998-2001 Baltimore Ravens, 2002-03 Oakland Raiders. **Highlights:** 71 interceptions returned for 1,483 yards and NFL record 12 TDs. Named NFL Defensive Player of Year, 1993. Member of NFL's 75th Anniversary Team. 11 Pro Bowls.

RAYFIELD WRIGHT
Tackle. 6-6, 255. Born in Griffin, Georgia, August 23, 1945. Fort Valley State. Inducted in 2006. 1967-1979 Dallas Cowboys. **Highlights:** Named first- or second-team All-Pro and voted to Pro Bowl six straight seasons, 1971-76. Played in six NFC championship games and five Super Bowls. Named to NFL's All-Decade Team of 1970s.

RON YARY
Tackle. 6-5, 255. Born in Chicago, Illinois, July 16, 1946. Cerritos (Calif.) J.C., Southern California. Inducted in 2001. 1968-1981 Minnesota Vikings, 1982 Los Angeles Rams. **Highlights:** All-Pro six consecutive seasons, All-NFC eight consecutive years. Named to seven Pro Bowls. Started in four Super Bowls and five NFL/NFC Championship Games.

STEVE YOUNG
Quarterback. 6-2, 205. Born in Salt Lake City, Utah, October 11, 1961. Brigham Young. Inducted in 2005. 1985-86 Tampa Bay Buccaneers, 1987-1999 San Francisco 49ers. **Highlights:** Led the NFL in passing a record-tying six times. Passed for more than 33,000 yards and 232 touchdowns in career. MVP of Super Bowl XXIX. Elected to seven Pro Bowls.

JACK YOUNGBLOOD
Defensive end. 6-4, 247. Born in Jacksonville, Florida, January 26, 1950. Florida. Inducted in 2001. 1971-1984 Los Angeles Rams. **Highlights:** Played in club-record 201 consecutive games. Played in five NFC Championship Games, one Super Bowl. Named All-Pro five times, All-NFC seven times. Elected to seven consecutive Pro Bowls. Lions.

GARY ZIMMERMAN
Tackle. 6-6, 294. Born in Fullerton, California, December 13, 1961. Oregon. Inducted in 2008. 1986-1992 Minnesota Vikings, 1993-97 Denver Broncos. **Highlights:** Named to seven Pro Bowls. One of handful of players to be named to two NFL All-Decade Teams, 1980s and 1990s.

ENSHRINEES BY YEAR OF INDUCTION
Deceased
(Date of enshrinement in parentheses)

1963 CHARTER CLASS
(September 7, 1963)
Sammy Baugh*
Bert Bell*
Joe Carr*
Earl (Dutch) Clark*
Harold (Red) Grange*
George Halas*
Mel Hein*
Wilbur (Pete) Henry*
Robert (Cal) Hubbard*
Don Hutson*
Earl (Curly) Lambeau*
Tim Mara*
George Preston Marshall*
John (Blood) McNally*
Bronko Nagurski*
Ernie Nevers*
Jim Thorpe*

CLASS OF 1964
(September 6, 1964)
Jimmy Conzelman*
Ed Healey*
Clarke Hinkle*
William Roy (Link) Lyman*
Mike Michalske*
Art Rooney*
George Trafton*

CLASS OF 1965
(September 12, 1965)
Guy Chamberlin*
John (Paddy) Driscoll*
Dan Fortmann*
Otto Graham*
Sid Luckman*
Steve Van Buren*
Bob Waterfield*

CLASS OF 1966
(September 17, 1966)
Bill Dudley*
Joe Guyon*
Arnie Herber*
Walt Kiesling*
George McAfee*
Steve Owen*
Hugh (Shorty) Ray*
Clyde (Bulldog) Turner*

CLASS OF 1967
(August 5, 1967)
Chuck Bednarik
Charles W. Bidwill Sr.*
Paul Brown*
Bobby Layne*
Dan Reeves*
Ken Strong*
Joe Stydahar*
Emlen Tunnell*

CLASS OF 1968
(August 3, 1968)
Cliff Battles*
Art Donovan*
Elroy (Crazylegs) Hirsch*
Wayne Millner*
Marion Motley*
Charley Trippi
Alex Wojciechowicz*

CLASS OF 1969
(September 13, 1969)
Albert Glen (Turk) Edwards*
Earle (Greasy) Neale*
Leo Nomellini*
Joe Perry*
Ernie Stautner*

CLASS OF 1970
(August 8, 1970)
Jack Christiansen*
Tom Fears*
Hugh McElhenny
Pete Pihos*

CLASS OF 1971
(July 31, 1971)
Jim Brown
Bill Hewitt*
Frank (Bruiser) Kinard*
Vince Lombardi*
Andy Robustelli*
Y. A. Tittle
Norm Van Brocklin*

CLASS OF 1972
(July 29, 1972)
Lamar Hunt*
Gino Marchetti
Ollie Matson*
Clarence (Ace) Parker*

CLASS OF 1973
(July 28, 1973)
Raymond Berry
Jim Parker*
Joe Schmidt

CLASS OF 1974
(July 27, 1974)
Tony Canadeo*
Bill George*
Lou Groza*
Dick (Night Train) Lane*

CLASS OF 1975
(August 2, 1975)
Roosevelt Brown*
George Connor*
Dante Lavelli*
Lenny Moore

CLASS OF 1976
(July 24, 1976)
Ray Flaherty*
Len Ford*
Jim Taylor

CLASS OF 1977
(July 30, 1977)
Frank Gifford
Forrest Gregg*
Gale Sayers
Bart Starr
Bill Willis*

CLASS OF 1978
(July 29, 1978)
Lance Alworth
Weeb Ewbank*
Alphonse (Tuffy) Leemans*
Ray Nitschke*
Larry Wilson

CLASS OF 1979
(July 28, 1979)
Dick Butkus
Yale Lary
Ron Mix
Johnny Unitas*

CLASS OF 1980
(August 2, 1980)
Herb Adderley
David (Deacon) Jones*
Bob Lilly
Jim Otto

CLASS OF 1981
(August 1, 1981)
Morris (Red) Badgro*
George Blanda*
Willie Davis
Jim Ringo*

CLASS OF 1982
(August 7, 1982)
Doug Atkins
Sam Huff
George Musso*
Merlin Olsen*

CLASS OF 1983
(July 30, 1983)
Bobby Bell
Sid Gillman*
Sonny Jurgensen
Bobby Mitchell
Paul Warfield

CLASS OF 1984
(July 28, 1984)
Willie Brown
Mike McCormack
Charley Taylor
Arnie Weinmeister*

CLASS OF 1985
(August 3, 1985)
Frank Gatski*
Joe Namath
Pete Rozelle*
O. J. Simpson
Roger Staubach

CLASS OF 1986
(August 2, 1986)
Paul Hornung
Ken Houston
Willie Lanier
Fran Tarkenton
Doak Walker*

CLASS OF 1987
(August 8, 1987)
Larry Csonka
Len Dawson
Joe Greene
John Henry Johnson*
Jim Langer
Don Maynard
Gene Upshaw*

CLASS OF 1988
(July 30, 1988)
Fred Biletnikoff
Mike Ditka
Jack Ham
Alan Page

CLASS OF 1989
(August 5, 1989)
Mel Blount
Terry Bradshaw
Art Shell
Willie Wood

CLASS OF 1990
(August 4, 1990)
Buck Buchanan*
Bob Griese
Franco Harris
Ted Hendricks
Jack Lambert
Tom Landry*
Bob St. Clair

CLASS OF 1991
(July 27, 1991)
Earl Campbell
John Hannah
Stan Jones*
Tex Schramm*
Jan Stenerud

CLASS OF 1992
(August 1, 1992)
Lem Barney
Al Davis*
John Mackey*
John Riggins

CLASS OF 1993
(July 31, 1993)
Dan Fouts
Larry Little
Chuck Noll
Walter Payton*
Bill Walsh*

CLASS OF 1994
(July 30, 1994)
Tony Dorsett
Bud Grant
Jimmy Johnson
Leroy Kelly
Jackie Smith
Randy White

CLASS OF 1995
(July 29, 1995)
Jim Finks*
Henry Jordan*
Steve Largent
Lee Roy Selmon*
Kellen Winslow

CLASS OF 1996
(July 27, 1996)
Lou Creekmur*
Dan Dierdorf
Joe Gibbs
Charlie Joiner
Mel Renfro

CLASS OF 1997
(July 26, 1997)
Mike Haynes
Wellington Mara*
Don Shula
Mike Webster*

CLASS OF 1998
(August 1, 1998)
Paul Krause
Tommy McDonald
Anthony Muñoz
Mike Singletary
Dwight Stephenson

CLASS OF 1999
(August 7, 1999)
Eric Dickerson
Tom Mack
Ozzie Newsome
Billy Shaw
Lawrence Taylor

CLASS OF 2000
(July 29, 2000)
Howie Long
Ronnie Lott
Joe Montana
Dan Rooney
Dave Wilcox

CLASS OF 2001
(August 4, 2001)
Nick Buoniconti
Marv Levy
Mike Munchak
Jackie Slater
Lynn Swann
Ron Yary
Jack Youngblood

CLASS OF 2002
(August 3, 2002)
George Allen*
Dave Casper
Dan Hampton
Jim Kelly
John Stallworth

CLASS OF 2003
(August 3, 2003)
Marcus Allen
Elvin Bethea
Joe DeLamielleure
James Lofton
Hank Stram*

PRO FOOTBALL HALL OF FAME

CLASS OF 2004
(August 8, 2004)
Bob (Boomer) Brown
Carl Eller
John Elway
Barry Sanders

CLASS OF 2005
(August 7, 2005)
Benny Friedman*
Dan Marino
Fritz Pollard*
Steve Young

CLASS OF 2006
(August 6, 2006)
Troy Aikman
Harry Carson
John Madden
Warren Moon
Reggie White*
Rayfield Wright

CLASS OF 2007
(August 4, 2007)
Gene Hickerson*
Michael Irvin
Bruce Matthews
Charlie Sanders
Thurman Thomas
Roger Wehrli

CLASS OF 2008
(August 2, 2008)
Fred Dean
Darrell Green
Art Monk
Emmitt Thomas
Andre Tippett
Gary Zimmerman

CLASS OF 2009
(August 8, 2009)
Bob Hayes*
Randall McDaniel
Bruce Smith
Derrick Thomas*
Ralph Wilson, Jr.*
Rod Woodson

CLASS OF 2010
(August 7, 2010)
Russ Grimm
Rickey Jackson
Dick LeBeau
Floyd Little
John Randle
Jerry Rice
Emmitt Smith

CLASS OF 2011
(August 6, 2011)
Richard Dent
Marshall Faulk
Chris Hanburger
Les Richter*
Ed Sabol
Deion Sanders
Shannon Sharpe

CLASS OF 2012
(August 4, 2012)
Jack Butler*
Dermontti Dawson
Chris Doleman
Cortez Kennedy
Curtis Martin
Willie Roaf

CLASS OF 2013
(August 3, 2013)
Larry Allen
Cris Carter
Curley Culp
Jonathan Ogden
Bill Parcells
Dave Robinson
Warren Sapp

CLASS OF 2014
(August 2, 2014)
Derrick Brooks
Ray Guy
Claude Humphrey
Walter Jones
Andre Reed
Michael Strahan
Aeneas Williams

1869

Rutgers and Princeton played a college soccer football game, the first ever, November 6. The game used modified London Football Association rules. During the next seven years, rugby gained favor with the major eastern schools over soccer, and modern football began to develop from rugby.

1876

At the Massasoit convention, the first rules for American football were written. Walter Camp, who would become known as the father of American football, first became involved with the game.

1892

In an era in which football was a major attraction of local athletic clubs, an intense competition between two Pittsburgh-area clubs, the Allegheny Athletic Association (AAA) and the Pittsburgh Athletic Club (PAC), led to the making of the first professional football player. Former Yale All-America guard William (Pudge) Heffelfinger was paid $500 by the AAA to play in a game against the PAC, becoming the first person to be paid to play football, November 12. The AAA won the game 4-0 when Heffelfinger picked up a PAC fumble and ran 35 yards for a touchdown.

1893

The Pittsburgh Athletic Club signed one of its players, probably halfback Grant Dibert, to the first known pro football contract, which covered all of the PAC's games for the year.

1895

John Brallier became the first football player to openly turn pro, accepting $10 and expenses to play for the Latrobe YMCA against the Jeannette Athletic Club.

1896

The Allegheny Athletic Association team fielded the first completely professional team for its abbreviated two-game season.

1897

The Latrobe Athletic Association football team went entirely professional, becoming the first team to play a full season with only professionals.

1898

A touchdown was changed from four points to five.

Chris O'Brien formed a neighborhood team, which played under the name the Morgan Athletic Club, on the south side of Chicago. The team later became known as the Normals, then the Racine (for a street in Chicago) Cardinals, the Chicago Cardinals, the St. Louis Cardinals, the Phoenix Cardinals, and, in 1994, the Arizona Cardinals. The team remains the oldest continuing operation in pro football.

1900

William C. Temple took over the team payments for the Duquesne Country and Athletic Club, becoming the first known individual club owner.

1902

Baseball's Philadelphia Athletics, managed by Connie Mack, and the Philadelphia Phillies formed professional football teams, joining the Pittsburgh Stars in the first attempt at a pro football league, named the National Football League. The Athletics won the first night football game ever played, 39-0 over Kanaweola AC at Elmira, New York, November 21.

All three teams claimed the pro championship for the year, but the league president, Dave Berry, named the Stars the champions. Pitcher Rube Waddell was with the Athletics, and pitcher Christy Mathewson a fullback for Pittsburgh.

The first World Series of pro football, actually a five-team tournament, was played among a team made up of players from both the Athletics and the Phillies, but simply named New York; the New York Knickerbockers; the Syracuse AC; the Warlow AC; and the Orange (New Jersey) AC at New York's original Madison Square Garden. New York and Syracuse played the first indoor football game before 3,000, December 28. Syracuse, with Glen (Pop) Warner at guard, won 6-0 and went on to win the tournament.

1903

The Franklin (Pa.) Athletic Club won the second and last World Series of pro football over the Oreos AC of Asbury Park, New Jersey; the Watertown Red and Blacks; and the Orange AC.

Pro football was popularized in Ohio when the Massillon Tigers, a strong amateur team, hired four Pittsburgh pros to play in the season-ending game against Akron. At the same time, pro football declined in the Pittsburgh area, and the emphasis on the pro game moved west from Pennsylvania to Ohio.

1904

A field goal was changed from five points to four.

Ohio had at least seven pro teams, with Massillon winning the Ohio Independent Championship, that is, the pro title. Talk surfaced about forming a state-wide league to end spiraling salaries brought about by constant bidding for players and to write universal rules for the game. The feeble attempt to start the league failed.

Halfback Charles Follis signed a contract with the Shelby (Ohio) AC, making him the first known black pro football player.

1905

The Canton AC, later to become known as the Bulldogs, became a professional team. Massillon again won the Ohio League championship.

1906

The forward pass was legalized. The first authenticated pass completion in a pro game came on October 25, when George (Peggy) Parratt of Massillon threw a completion to Dan (Bullet) Riley in a victory over a combined Benwood-Moundsville team.

Arch-rivals Canton and Massillon, the two best pro teams in America, played twice, with Canton winning the first game but Massillon winning the second and the Ohio League championship. A betting scandal and the financial disaster wrought upon the two clubs by paying huge salaries caused a temporary decline in interest in pro football in the two cities and, somewhat

1909

A field goal dropped from four points to three.

1912

A touchdown was increased from five points to six.

Jack Cusack revived a strong pro team in Canton.

1913

Jim Thorpe, a former football and track star at the Carlisle Indian School (Pa.) and a double gold medal winner at the 1912 Olympics in Stockholm, played for the Pine Village Pros in Indiana.

1915

Massillon again fielded a major team, reviving the old rivalry with Canton. Cusack signed Thorpe to play for Canton for $250 a game.

1916

With Thorpe and former Carlisle teammate Pete Calac starring, Canton went 9-0-1, won the Ohio League championship, and was acclaimed the pro football champion.

1917

Despite an upset by Massillon, Canton again won the Ohio League championship.

1919

Canton again won the Ohio League championship, despite the team having been turned over from Cusack to Ralph Hay. Thorpe and Calac were joined in the backfield by Joe Guyon.

Earl (Curly) Lambeau and George Calhoun organized the Green Bay Packers. Lambeau's employer at the Indian Packing Company provided $500 for equipment and allowed the team to use the company field for practices. The Packers went 10-1.

1920

Pro football was in a state of confusion due to three major problems: dramatically rising salaries; players continually jumping from one team to another following the highest offer; and the use of college players still enrolled in school. A league in which all the members would follow the same rules seemed the answer. An

throughout Ohio.

organizational meeting, at which the Akron Pros, Canton Bulldogs, Cleveland Indians, and Dayton Triangles were represented, was held at the Jordan and Hupmobile auto showroom in Canton, Ohio, August 20. This meeting resulted in the formation of the American Professional Football Conference.

A second organizational meeting was held in Canton, September 17. The teams were from four states—Akron, Canton, Cleveland, and Dayton from Ohio; the Hammond Pros and Muncie Flyers from Indiana; the Rochester Jeffersons from New York; and the Rock Island Independents, Decatur Staleys, and Racine Cardinals from Illinois. The name of the league was changed to the American Professional Football Association. Hoping to capitalize on his fame, the members elected Thorpe president; Stanley Cofall of Cleveland was elected vice president. A membership fee of $100 per team was charged to give an appearance of respectability, but no team ever paid it. Scheduling was left up to the teams, and there were wide variations, both in the overall number of games played and in the number played against APFA member teams.

Four other teams—the Buffalo All-Americans, Chicago Tigers, Columbus Panhandles, and Detroit Heralds—joined the league sometime during the year. On September 26, the first game featuring an APFA team was played at Rock Island's Douglas Park. A crowd of 800 watched the Independents defeat the St. Paul Ideals 48-0. A week later, October 3, the first game matching two APFA teams was held. At Triangle Park, Dayton defeated Columbus 14-0, with Lou Partlow of Dayton scoring the first touchdown in a game between Association teams. The same day, Rock Island defeated Muncie 45-0.

By the beginning of December, most of the teams in the APFA had abandoned their hopes for a championship, and some of them, including the Chicago Tigers and the Detroit Heralds, had finished their seasons, disbanded, and

had their franchises canceled by the Association. Four teams—Akron, Buffalo, Canton, and Decatur—still had championship aspirations, but a series of late-season games among them left Akron as the only undefeated team in the Association. At one of these games, Akron sold tackle Bob Nash to Buffalo for $300 and five percent of the gate receipts—the first APFA player deal.

1921
At the league meeting in Akron, April 30, the championship of the 1920 season was awarded to the Akron Pros. The APFA was reorganized, with Joe Carr of the Columbus Panhandles named president and Carl Storck of Dayton secretary-treasurer. Carr moved the Association's headquarters to Columbus, drafted a league constitution and by-laws, gave teams territorial rights, restricted player movements, developed membership criteria for the franchises, and issued standings for the first time, so that the APFA would have a clear champion.

The Association's membership increased to 22 teams, including the Green Bay Packers, who were awarded to John Clair of the Acme Packing Company.

Thorpe moved from Canton to the Cleveland Indians, but he was hurt early in the season and played very little.

A.E. Staley turned the Decatur Staleys over to player-coach George Halas, who moved the team to Cubs Park in Chicago. Staley paid Halas $5,000 to keep the name Staleys for one more year. Halas made halfback Ed (Dutch) Sternaman his partner.

Player-coach Fritz Pollard of the Akron Pros became the first black head coach.

The Staleys claimed the APFA championship with a 9-1-1 record, as did Buffalo at 9-1-2. Carr ruled in favor of the Staleys, giving Halas his first championship.

1922
After admitting the use of players who had college eligibility remaining during the 1921 season, Clair and the Green Bay management with-

drew from the APFA, January 28. Curly Lambeau promised to obey league rules and then used $50 of his own money to buy back the franchise. Bad weather and low attendance plagued the Packers, and Lambeau went broke, but local merchants arranged a $2,500 loan for the club. A public nonprofit corporation was set up to operate the team, with Lambeau as head coach and manager.

The American Professional Football Association changed its name to the National Football League, June 24. The Chicago Staleys became the Chicago Bears.

The NFL fielded 18 teams, including the new Oorang Indians of Marion, Ohio, an all-Indian team featuring Thorpe, Joe Guyon, and Pete Calac, and sponsored by the Oorang dog kennels.

Canton, led by player-coach Guy Chamberlin and tackles Link Lyman and Wilbur (Pete) Henry, emerged as the league's first true powerhouse, going 10-0-2.

1923
For the first time, all of the franchises considered to be part of the NFL fielded teams. Thorpe played his second and final season for the Oorang Indians. Against the Bears, Thorpe fumbled, and Halas picked up the ball and returned it 98 yards for a touchdown, a record that would last until 1972.

Canton had its second consecutive undefeated season, going 11-0-1 for the NFL title.

1924
The league had 18 franchises, including new ones in Kansas City, Kenosha, and Frankford, a section of Philadelphia. League champion Canton, successful on the field but not at the box office, was purchased by the owner of the Cleveland franchise, who kept the Canton franchise inactive, while using the best players for his Cleveland team, which he renamed the Bulldogs. Cleveland won the title with a 7-1-1 record.

1925
Five new franchises were admitted to the NFL—the New York Giants, who were award-

ed to Tim Mara and Billy Gibson for $500; the Detroit Panthers, featuring Jimmy Conzelman as owner, coach, and tailback; the Providence Steam Roller; a new Canton Bulldogs team; and the Pottsville Maroons, who had been perhaps the most successful independent pro team. The NFL established its first player limit, at 16 players.

Late in the season, the NFL made its greatest coup in gaining national recognition. Shortly after the University of Illinois season ended in November, All-America halfback Harold (Red) Grange signed a contract to play with the Chicago Bears. On Thanksgiving Day, a crowd of 36,000—the largest in pro football history—watched Grange and the Bears play the Chicago Cardinals to a scoreless tie at Wrigley Field. At the beginning of December, the Bears left on a barnstorming tour that saw them play eight games in 12 days, in St. Louis, Philadelphia, New York City, Washington, Boston, Pittsburgh, Detroit, and Chicago. A crowd of 73,000 watched the game against the Giants at the Polo Grounds, helping assure the future of the troubled NFL franchise in New York. The Bears then played nine more games in the South and West, including a game in Los Angeles, in which 75,000 fans watched them defeat the Los Angeles Tigers in the Los Angeles Memorial Coliseum.

Pottsville and the Chicago Cardinals were the top contenders for the league title, with Pottsville winning a late-season meeting 21-7. Pottsville scheduled a game against a team of former Notre Dame players for Shibe Park in Philadelphia. Frankford lodged a protest not only because the game was in Frankford's protected territory, but because it was being played the same day as a Yellow Jackets home game. Carr gave three different notices forbidding Pottsville to play the game, but Pottsville played anyway, December 12. That day, Carr fined the club, suspended it from all rights and privileges (including the right to play for the NFL championship), and returned its franchise to the league. The Cardinals, who ended the season with the best record in the league, were named the 1925 champions.

1926
Grange's manager, C.C. Pyle, told the Bears that Grange wouldn't play for them unless he was paid a five-figure salary and given one-third ownership of the team. The Bears refused. Pyle leased Yankee Stadium in New York City, then petitioned for an NFL franchise. After he was refused, he started the first American Football League. It lasted one season and included Grange's New York Yankees and eight other teams. The AFL champion Philadelphia Quakers played a December game against the New York Giants, seventh in the NFL, and the Giants won 31-0. At the end of the season, the AFL folded.

Halas pushed through a rule that prohibited any team from signing a player whose college class had not graduated.

The NFL grew to 22 teams, including the Duluth Eskimos, who signed All-America fullback Ernie Nevers of Stanford, giving the league a gate attraction to rival Grange. The 15-member Eskimos, dubbed the Iron Men of the North, played 29 exhibition and league games, 28 on the road, and Nevers played in all but 29 minutes of them.

Frankford edged the Bears for the championship, despite Halas having obtained John (Paddy) Driscoll from the Cardinals. On December 4, the Yellow Jackets scored in the final two minutes to defeat the Bears 7-6 and move ahead of them in the standings.

1927
At a special meeting in Cleveland, April 23, Carr decided to secure the NFL's future by eliminating the financially weaker teams and consolidating the quality players onto a limited number of more successful teams. The new-look NFL dropped to 12 teams, and the center of gravity of the league left the Midwest, where the NFL had started, and began to emerge in the large cities of the East. One of the new teams was Grange's New

York Yankees, but Grange suffered a knee injury and the Yankees finished in the middle of the pack. The NFL championship was won by the cross-town rival New York Giants, who posted 10 shutouts in 13 games.

1928
Grange and Nevers both retired from pro football, and Duluth disbanded, as the NFL was reduced to only 10 teams. The Providence Steam Roller of Jimmy Conzelman and Pearce Johnson won the championship, playing in the Cycledrome, a 10,000-seat oval that had been built for bicycle races.

1929
Chris O'Brien sold the Chicago Cardinals to David Jones, July 27.

The NFL added a fourth official, the field judge, July 28.

Grange and Nevers returned to the NFL. Nevers scored six rushing touchdowns and four extra points as the Cardinals beat Grange's Bears 40-6, November 28. The 40 points set a record that remains the NFL's oldest.

Providence became the first NFL team to host a game at night under floodlights, against the Cardinals, November 6.

The Packers added back Johnny Blood (McNally), tackle Cal Hubbard, and guard Mike Michalske, and won their first NFL championship, edging the Giants, who featured quarterback Benny Friedman.

1930
Dayton, the last of the NFL's original franchises, was purchased by William B. Dwyer and John C. Depler, moved to Brooklyn, and renamed the Dodgers. The Portsmouth, Ohio, Spartans entered the league.

The Packers edged the Giants for the title, but the most improved team was the Bears. Halas retired as a player and replaced himself as coach of the Bears with Ralph Jones, who refined the T-formation by introducing wide ends and a halfback in motion. Jones also introduced rookie All-America fullback-tackle Bronko Nagurski.

The Giants defeated a team of former Notre Dame players coached by Knute Rockne 22-0 before 55,000 at the Polo Grounds, December 14. The proceeds went to the New York Unemployment Fund to help those suffering because of the Great Depression, and the easy victory helped give the NFL credibility with the press and the public.

1931
The NFL decreased to 10 teams, and halfway through the season the Frankford franchise folded. Carr fined the Bears, Packers, and Portsmouth $1,000 each for using players whose college classes had not graduated.

The Packers won an unprecedented third consecutive title, beating out the Spartans, who were led by rookie backs Earl (Dutch) Clark and Glenn Presnell.

1932
George Preston Marshall, Vincent Bendix, Jay O'Brien, and M. Dorland Doyle were awarded a franchise for Boston, July 9. Despite the presence of two rookies—halfback Cliff Battles and tackle Glen (Turk) Edwards—the new team, named the Braves, lost money and Marshall was left as the sole owner at the end of the year.

NFL membership dropped to eight teams, the lowest in history. Official statistics were kept for the first time. The Bears and the Spartans finished the season in the first-ever tie for first place. After the season finale, the league office arranged for an additional regular-season game to determine the league champion. The game was moved indoors to Chicago Stadium because of bitter cold and heavy snow. The arena allowed only an 80-yard field that came right to the walls. The goal posts were moved from the end lines to the goal lines and, for safety, inbounds lines or hashmarks where the ball would be put in play were drawn 10 yards from the walls that butted against the sidelines. The Bears won 9-0, December 18, scoring the winning touchdown on a two-yard pass from Nagurski to Grange. The Spartans claimed Nagurski's pass was thrown

from less than five yards behind the line of scrimmage, violating the existing passing rule, but the play stood.

1933
The NFL, which long had followed the rules of college football, made a number of significant changes from the college game for the first time and began to develop rules serving its needs and the style of play it preferred. The innovations from the 1932 championship game—inbounds line or hashmarks and goal posts on the goal lines—were adopted. Also the forward pass was legalized from anywhere behind the line of scrimmage, February 25.

Marshall and Halas pushed through a proposal that divided the NFL into two divisions, with the winners to meet in an annual championship game, July 8.

Three new franchises joined the league—the Pittsburgh Pirates of Art Rooney, the Philadelphia Eagles of Bert Bell and Lud Wray, and the Cincinnati Reds. The Staten Island Stapletons suspended operations for a year, but never returned to the league. Halas bought out Sternaman, became sole owner of the Bears, and reinstated himself as head coach. Marshall changed the name of the Boston Braves to the Redskins. David Jones sold the Chicago Cardinals to Charles W. Bidwill.

In the first NFL Championship Game scheduled before the season, the Western Division champion Bears defeated the Eastern Division champion Giants 23-21 at Wrigley Field, December 17.

1934
G.A. (Dick) Richards purchased the Portsmouth Spartans, moved them to Detroit, and renamed them the Lions.

Professional football gained new prestige when the Bears were matched against the best college football players in the first Chicago College All-Star Game, August 31. The game ended in a scoreless tie before 79,432 at Soldier Field.

The Cincinnati Reds lost their first eight games, then were suspended from the league for defaulting on payments. The St. Louis Gunners, an independent team, joined the NFL by buying the Cincinnati franchise and went 1-2 the last three weeks.

Rookie Beattie Feathers of the Bears became the NFL's first 1,000-yard rusher, gaining 1,004 on 101 carries. The Thanksgiving Day game between the Bears and the Lions became the first NFL game broadcast nationally, with Graham McNamee the announcer for NBC radio.

In the championship game, on an extremely cold and icy day at the Polo Grounds, the Giants trailed the Bears 13-3 in the third quarter before changing to basketball shoes for better footing. The Giants won 30-13 in what has come to be known as the Sneakers Game, December 9.

The player waiver rule was adopted, December 10.

1935
The NFL adopted Bert Bell's proposal to hold an annual draft of college players, to begin in 1936, with teams selecting in an inverse order of finish, May 19. The inbounds line or hashmarks were moved nearer the center of the field, 15 yards from the sidelines.

All-America end Don Hutson of Alabama joined Green Bay. The Lions defeated the Giants 26-7 in the NFL Championship Game, December 15.

1936
There were no franchise transactions for the first year since the formation of the NFL. It also was the first year in which all member teams played the same number of games.

The Eagles made University of Chicago halfback and Heisman Trophy winner Jay Berwanger the first player ever selected in the NFL draft, February 8. The Eagles traded his rights to the Bears, but Berwanger never played pro football. The first player selected to actually sign was the number-two pick, Riley Smith of Alabama, who was selected by Boston.

A rival league was formed, and it became the second to call itself the American Football League. The Boston Shamrocks were its champions.

Because of poor atten-

dance, Marshall, the owner of the host team, moved the Championship Game from Boston to the Polo Grounds in New York. Green Bay defeated the Redskins 21-6, December 13.

1937
Homer Marshman was granted a Cleveland franchise, named the Rams, February 12. Marshall moved the Redskins to Washington, D.C., February 13. The Redskins signed TCU All-America tailback Sammy Baugh, who led them to a 28-21 victory over the Bears in the NFL Championship Game, December 12.

The Los Angeles Bulldogs had an 8-0 record to win the AFL title, but then the 2-year-old league folded.

1938
At the suggestion of Halas, Hugh (Shorty) Ray became a technical advisor on rules and officiating to the NFL. A new rule called for a 15-yard penalty for roughing the passer.

Rookie Byron (Whizzer) White of the Pittsburgh Pirates led the NFL in rushing. The Giants defeated the Packers 23-17 for the NFL title, December 11.

Marshall, *Los Angeles Times* sports editor Bill Henry, and promoter Tom Gallery established the Pro Bowl game between the NFL champion and a team of pro all-stars.

1939
The New York Giants defeated the Pro All-Stars 13-10 in the first Pro Bowl, at Wrigley Field, Los Angeles, January 15.

Carr, NFL president since 1921, died in Columbus, May 20. Carl Storck was named acting president, May 25.

An NFL game was televised for the first time when NBC broadcast the Brooklyn Dodgers-Philadelphia Eagles game from Ebbets Field to the approximately 1,000 sets then in New York, October 22.

Green Bay defeated New York 27-0 in the NFL Championship Game, December 10 at Milwaukee. NFL attendance exceeded 1 million in a season for the first time, reaching 1,071,200.

1940
A six-team rival league, the third to call itself the American Football League, was formed, and the Columbus Bullies won its championship.

Halas' Bears, with additional coaching by Clark Shaughnessy of Stanford, defeated the Redskins 73-0 in the NFL Championship Game, December 8. The game, which was the most decisive victory in NFL history, popularized the Bears' T-formation with a man-in-motion. It was the first championship carried on network radio, broadcast by Red Barber to 120 stations of the Mutual Broadcasting System, which paid $2,500 for the rights.

Art Rooney sold the Pittsburgh franchise to Alexis Thompson, December 9, then bought part interest in the Philadelphia Eagles.

Bell and Rooney traded the Eagles to Thompson for the Pirates, then re-named their new team the Steelers.

1941
Elmer Layden was named the first Commissioner of the NFL, March 1; Storck, the acting president, resigned, April 5. NFL headquarters were moved to Chicago.

Homer Marshman sold the Rams to Daniel F. Reeves and Fred Levy, Jr.

The league by-laws were revised to provide for playoffs in case there were ties in division races, and sudden-death overtimes in case a playoff game was tied after four quarters. An official *NFL Record Manual* was published for the first time.

Columbus again won the championship of the AFL, but the two-year-old league then folded.

The Bears and the Packers finished in a tie for the Western Division championship, setting up the first divisional playoff game in league history. The Bears won 33-14, then defeated the Giants 37-9 for the NFL championship, December 21.

1942
Players departing for service in World War II depleted the rosters of NFL teams. Halas left the Bears in midseason to join the Navy, and Luke John-

sos and Heartley (Hunk) Anderson served as co-coaches as the Bears went 11-0 in the regular season. The Redskins defeated the Bears 14-6 in the NFL Championship Game, December 13.

1943
The Cleveland Rams, with co-owners Reeves and Levy in the service, were granted permission to suspend operations for one season, April 6. Levy transferred his stock in the team to Reeves, April 16.

The NFL adopted free substitution, April 7. The league also made the wearing of helmets mandatory and approved a 10-game schedule for all teams.

Philadelphia and Pittsburgh were granted permission to merge for one season, June 19. The team, known as Phil-Pitt (and called the Steagles by fans), divided home games between the two cities, and Earle (Greasy) Neale of Philadelphia and Walt Kiesling of Pittsburgh served as co-coaches. The merger automatically dissolved the last day of the season, December 5.

Ted Collins was granted a franchise for Boston, to become active in 1944.

Sammy Baugh led the league in passing, punting, and interceptions. He led the Redskins to a tie with the Giants for the Eastern Division title, and then to a 28-0 victory in a divisional playoff game. The Bears beat the Redskins 41-21 in the NFL Championship Game, December 26.

1944
Collins, who had wanted a franchise in Yankee Stadium in New York, named his new team in Boston the Yanks. Cleveland resumed operations. The Brooklyn Dodgers changed their name to the Tigers.

Coaching from the bench was legalized, April 20.

The Cardinals and the Steelers were granted permission to merge for one year under the name Card-Pitt, April 21. Phil Handler of the Cardinals and Walt Kiesling of the Steelers served as co-coaches. The merger automatically dissolved the last day of the season, December 3.

In the NFL Championship Game, Green Bay defeated the New York Giants 14-7, December 17.

1945

The inbounds lines or hash-marks were moved from 15 yards away from the sidelines to nearer the center of the field—20 yards from the sidelines.

Brooklyn and Boston merged into a team that played home games in both cities and was known simply as The Yanks. The team was coached by former Boston head coach Herb Kopf. In December, the Brooklyn franchise withdrew from the NFL to join the new All-America Football Conference; all the players on its active and reserve lists were assigned to The Yanks, who once again became the Boston Yanks.

Halas rejoined the Bears late in the season after service with the U.S. Navy. Although Halas took over much of the coaching duties, Anderson and Johnsos remained the coaches of record throughout the season.

Steve Van Buren of Philadelphia led the NFL in rushing, kickoff returns, and scoring.

After the Japanese surrendered ending World War II, a count showed that the NFL service roster, limited to men who had played in league games, totaled 638, 21 of whom had died in action.

Rookie quarterback Bob Waterfield led Cleveland to a 15-14 victory over Washington in the NFL Championship Game, December 16.

1946

The contract of Commissioner Layden was not renewed, and Bert Bell, the co-owner of the Steelers, replaced him, January 11. Bell moved the league headquarters from Chicago to the Philadelphia suburb of Bala-Cynwyd.

Free substitution was withdrawn and substitutions were limited to no more than three men at a time. Forward passes were made automatically incomplete upon striking the goal posts, January 11.

The NFL took on a truly national appearance for the first time when Reeves was granted permission by the league to move his NFL champion Rams to Los Angeles.

Halfback Kenny Washington (March 21) and end Woody Strode (May 7) signed with the Los Angeles Rams to become the first African-Americans to play in the NFL in the modern era. Guard Bill Willis (August 6) and running back Marion Motley (August 9) joined the AAFC with the Cleveland Browns.

The rival All-America Football Conference began play with eight teams. The Cleveland Browns, coached by Paul Brown, won the AAFC's first championship, defeating the New York Yankees 14-9.

Bill Dudley of the Steelers led the NFL in rushing, interceptions, and punt returns, and won the league's most valuable player award.

Backs Frank Filchock and Merle Hapes of the Giants were questioned about an attempt by a New York man to fix the championship game with the Bears. Bell suspended Hapes but allowed Filchock to play; he played well, but Chicago won 24-14, December 15.

1947

The NFL added a fifth official, the back judge.

A bonus choice was made for the first time in the NFL draft. One team each year would select the special choice before the first round began. The Chicago Bears won a lottery and the rights to the first choice and drafted back Bob Fenimore of Oklahoma A&M.

The Cleveland Browns again won the AAFC title, defeating the New York Yankees 14-3.

Charles Bidwill, Sr., owner of the Cardinals, died April 19, but his wife and sons retained ownership of the team. On December 28, the Cardinals won the NFL Championship Game 28-21 over the Philadelphia Eagles, who had beaten Pittsburgh 21-0 in a playoff.

1948

Plastic helmets were prohibited. A flexible artificial tee was permitted at the kickoff. Officials other than the referee were equipped with whistles, not horns, January 14.

Fred Mandel sold the Detroit Lions to a syndicate headed by D. Lyle Fife, January 15.

Halfback Fred Gehrke of the Los Angeles Rams painted horns on the Rams' helmets, the first modern helmet emblems in pro football.

The Cleveland Browns won their third straight championship in the AAFC, going 14-0 and then defeating the Buffalo Bills 49-7.

In a blizzard, the Eagles defeated the Cardinals 7-0 in the NFL Championship Game, December 19.

1949

Alexis Thompson sold the champion Eagles to a syndicate headed by James P. Clark, January 15. The Boston Yanks became the New York Bulldogs, sharing the Polo Grounds with the Giants.

Free substitution was adopted for one year, January 20.

The NFL had two 1,000-yard rushers in the same season for the first time—Steve Van Buren of Philadelphia and Tony Canadeo of Green Bay.

The AAFC played its season with a one-division, seven-team format. On December 9, Bell announced a merger agreement in which three AAFC franchises—Cleveland, San Francisco, and Baltimore—would join the NFL in 1950. The Browns won their fourth consecutive AAFC title, defeating the 49ers 21-7, December 11.

In a heavy rain, the Eagles defeated the Rams 14-0 in the NFL Championship Game, December 18.

1950

Unlimited free substitution was restored, opening the way for the era of two platoons and specialization in pro football, January 20.

Curly Lambeau, founder of the franchise and Green Bay's head coach since 1921, resigned under fire, February 1.

The name National Football League was restored after about three months as the National-American Football League. The American and National conferences were created to replace the Eastern and Western divisions, March 3.

The New York Bulldogs became the Yanks and divided the players of the former AAFC Yankees with the Giants. A special allocation draft was held in which the 13 teams drafted the remaining AAFC players, with special consideration for Baltimore, which received 15 choices compared to 10 for other teams.

The Los Angeles Rams became the first NFL team to have all of its games—both home and away—televised. The Washington Redskins followed the Rams in arranging to televise their games; other teams made deals to put selected games on television.

In the first game of the season, former AAFC champion Cleveland defeated NFL champion Philadelphia 35-10. For the first time, deadlocks occurred in both conferences and playoffs were necessary. The Browns defeated the Giants in the American and the Rams defeated the Bears in the National. Cleveland defeated Los Angeles 30-28 in the NFL Championship Game, December 24.

1951

The Pro Bowl game, dormant since 1942, was revived under a new format matching the all-stars of each conference at the Los Angeles Memorial Coliseum. The American Conference defeated the National Conference 28-27, January 14.

Abraham Watner returned the Baltimore franchise and its player contracts back to the NFL for $50,000. Baltimore's former players were made available for drafting at the same time as college players, January 18.

A rule was passed that no tackle, guard, or center would be eligible to catch a forward pass, January 18.

The Rams reversed their television policy and televised only road games.

The NFL Championship Game was televised coast-to-coast for the first time, December 23. The DuMont Network paid $75,000 for the rights to the game, in which the Rams defeated the Browns 24-17.

1952

Ted Collins sold the New York Yanks' franchise back to the NFL, January 19. A new franchise was awarded to a group in Dallas after it purchased the assets of the Yanks, January 24. The new Texans went 1-11, with the owners turning the franchise back to the league in midseason. For the last five games of the season, the commissioner's office operated the Texans as a road team, using Hershey, Pennsylvania, as a home base. At the end of the season the franchise was canceled, the last time an NFL team failed.

The Pittsburgh Steelers abandoned the Single-Wing for the T-formation, the last pro team to do so.

The Detroit Lions won their first NFL championship in 17 years, defeating the Browns 17-7 in the title game, December 28.

1953

A Baltimore group headed by Carroll Rosenbloom was granted a franchise and was awarded the holdings of defunct Dallas organization, January 23. The team, named the Colts, put together the largest trade in league history, acquiring 10 players from Cleveland in exchange for five.

The names of the American and National conferences were changed to the Eastern and Western conferences, January 24.

Jim Thorpe died, March 28.

Mickey McBride, founder of the Cleveland Browns, sold the franchise to a syndicate headed by Dave R. Jones, June 10.

The NFL policy of blacking out home games was upheld by Judge Allan K. Grim of the U.S. District Court in Philadelphia, November 12.

The Lions again defeated the Browns in the NFL Championship Game, winning 17-16, December 27.

1954

The Canadian Football League began a series of raids on NFL teams, signing quarterback Eddie LeBaron and defensive end Gene Brito of Washington and defensive tackle Arnie Weinmeister of the Giants, among others.

Fullback Joe Perry of the 49ers became the first player in league history to gain 1,000 yards rushing in consecutive seasons.

Cleveland defeated Detroit 56-10 in the NFL Championship Game, December 26.

1955

The sudden-death overtime rule was used for the first time in a preseason game between the Rams and Giants at Portland, Oregon, August 28. The Rams won 23-17 three minutes into overtime.

A rule change declared the ball dead immediately if the ball carrier touched the ground with any part of his body except his hands or feet while in the grasp of an opponent.

The Baltimore Colts made an 80-cent phone call to Johnny Unitas and signed him as a free agent. Another quarterback, Otto Graham, played his last game as the Browns defeated the Rams 38-14 in the NFL Championship Game, December 26. Graham had quarterbacked the Browns to 10 championship-game appearances in 10 years.

NBC replaced DuMont as the network for the title game, paying a rights fee of $100,000.

1956

The NFL Players Association was founded.

Grabbing an opponent's facemask (other than the ball carrier) was made illegal. Using radio receivers to communicate with players on the field was prohibited. A natural leather ball with white end stripes replaced the white ball with black stripes for night games.

The Giants moved from the Polo Grounds to Yankee Stadium.

Halas retired as coach of the Bears, and was replaced by Paddy Driscoll.

CBS became the first network to broadcast some NFL regular-season games to selected television markets across the nation.

The Giants routed the Bears 47-7 in the NFL Championship Game, December 30.

1957

Pete Rozelle was named general manager of the Rams. Anthony J. Morabito, founder and co-owner of the 49ers, died of a heart attack during a game against the Bears at Kezar Stadium, October 28.

An NFL-record crowd of 102,368 saw the 49ers-Rams game at the Los Angeles Memorial Coliseum, November 10.

The Lions came from 20 points down to post a 31-27 playoff victory over the 49ers, December 22. Detroit defeated Cleveland 59-14 in the NFL Championship Game, December 29.

1958

The bonus selection in the draft was eliminated, January 29. The last selection was quarterback King Hill of Rice by the Chicago Cardinals.

Halas reinstated himself as coach of the Bears.

Jim Brown of Cleveland gained an NFL-record 1,527 yards rushing. In a divisional playoff game, the Giants held Brown to eight yards and defeated Cleveland 10-0.

Baltimore, coached by Weeb Ewbank, defeated the Giants 23-17 in the first sudden-death overtime in an NFL Championship Game, December 28. The game ended when Colts fullback Alan Ameche scored on a one-yard touchdown run after 8:15 of overtime.

1959

Vince Lombardi was named head coach of the Green Bay Packers, January 28. Tim Mara, the co-founder of the Giants, died, February 17.

Lamar Hunt of Dallas announced his intentions to form a second pro football league. The first meeting was held in Chicago, August 14, and consisted of Dallas; Bob Howsam, Denver; K.S. (Bud) Adams, Houston; Barron Hilton, Los Angeles; Max Winter and Bill Boyer, Minneapolis; and Harry Wismer, New York City. They made plans to begin play in 1960.

The new league was named the American Football League, August 22. Buffalo, owned by Ralph Wilson, became the seventh franchise, October 28. Boston, owned by William H. Sullivan, became the eighth team, November 22. The first AFL draft, lasting 33 rounds, was held, November 22. Joe Foss was named AFL Commissioner, November 30. An additional draft of 20 rounds

was held by the AFL, December 2.

NFL Commissioner Bert Bell died of a heart attack suffered at Franklin Field, Philadelphia, during the last two minutes of a game between the Eagles and the Steelers, October 11. Treasurer Austin Gunsel was named president in the office of the commissioner, October 14.

The Colts again defeated the Giants in the NFL Championship Game, 31-16, December 27.

1960

Pete Rozelle was elected NFL Commissioner as a compromise choice on the twenty-third ballot, January 26. Rozelle moved the league offices to New York City.

Hunt was elected AFL president for 1960, January 26. Minneapolis withdrew from the AFL, January 27, and the same ownership was given an NFL franchise for Minnesota (to start in 1961), January 28. Dallas received an NFL franchise for 1960, January 28. Oakland received an AFL franchise, January 30.

The AFL adopted the two-point option on points after touchdown, January 28. A no-tampering verbal pact, relative to players' contracts, was agreed to between the NFL and AFL, February 9.

The NFL owners voted to allow the transfer of the Chicago Cardinals to St. Louis, March 13.

The AFL signed a five-year television contract with ABC, June 9.

The Boston Patriots defeated the Buffalo Bills 28-7 before 16,000 at Buffalo in the first AFL preseason game, July 30. The Denver Broncos defeated the Patriots 13-10 before 21,597 at Boston in the first AFL regular-season game, September 9.

Philadelphia defeated Green Bay 17-13 in the NFL Championship Game, December 26.

1961

The Houston Oilers defeated the Los Angeles Chargers 24-16 before 32,183 in the first AFL Championship Game, January 1.

Detroit defeated Cleveland 17-16 in the first Playoff Bowl, or Bert Bell Benefit Bowl, between second-place teams in each conference in Miami, January 7.

End Willard Dewveall of the Bears played out his option and joined the Oilers, becoming the first player to play out his contract and jump from the NFL to the AFL, January 14.

Ed McGah, Wayne Valley, and Robert Osborne bought out their partners in the ownership of the Raiders, January 17. The Chargers were transferred to San Diego, February 10. Dave R. Jones sold the Browns to a group headed by Arthur B. Modell, March 22. The Howsam brothers sold the Broncos to a group headed by Calvin Kunz and Gerry Phipps, May 26.

NBC was awarded a two-year contract for radio and television rights to the NFL Championship Game for $615,000 annually, $300,000 of which was to go directly into the NFL Player Benefit Plan, April 5.

Canton, Ohio, where the league that became the NFL was formed in 1920, was chosen as the site of the Pro Football Hall of Fame, April 27.

A bill legalizing single-network television contracts by professional sports leagues was introduced in Congress by Representative Emanuel Celler. It passed the House and Senate and was signed into law by President John F. Kennedy, September 30.

Houston defeated San Diego 10-3 for the AFL championship, December 24. Green Bay won its first NFL championship since 1944, defeating the New York Giants 37-0, December 31.

1962
The Western Division defeated the Eastern Division 47-27 in the first AFL All-Star Game, played before 20,973 in San Diego, January 7.

Both leagues prohibited grabbing any player's facemask. The AFL voted to make the scoreboard clock the official timer of the game.

The NFL entered into a single-network agreement with CBS for telecasting all regular-season games for $4.65 million annually, January 10.

Judge Roszel Thompson of the U.S. District Court in Baltimore ruled against the AFL in

its antitrust suit against the NFL, May 21. The AFL had charged the NFL with monopoly and conspiracy in areas of expansion, television, and player signings. The case lasted two and a half years, the trial two months.

McGah and Valley acquired controlling interest in the Raiders, May 24. The AFL assumed financial responsibility for the New York Titans, November 8. With Commissioner Rozelle as referee, Daniel F. Reeves regained the ownership of the Rams, outbidding his partners in sealed-envelope bidding for the team, November 27.

The Dallas Texans defeated the Oilers 20-17 for the AFL championship at Houston after 17 minutes, 54 seconds of overtime on a 25-yard field goal by Tommy Brooker. The game lasted a then record 77 minutes, 54 seconds, December 23.

Judge Edward Weinfeld of the U.S. District Court in New York City upheld the legality of the NFL's television blackout within a 75-mile radius of home games and denied an injunction that would have forced the championship game between the Giants and the Packers to be televised in the New York City area, December 28. The Packers beat the Giants 16-7 for the NFL title, December 30.

1963
Don Shula, who went on to become the winningest head coach in NFL history, replaced Weeb Ewbank as head coach of the Colts, January 8.

Paul Brown, head coach of the Browns since their inception, was fired on January 9 and replaced the following day by Blanton Collier.

The Dallas Texans transferred to Kansas City, becoming the Chiefs, February 8. The New York Titans were sold to a five-man syndicate headed by David (Sonny) Werblin, March 28. Weeb Ewbank became the Titans' new head coach and the team's name was changed to the Jets, April 15. They began play in the Polo Grounds.

NFL Properties, Inc., was founded to serve as the licensing arm of the NFL.

Rozelle indefinitely sus-

pended Green Bay halfback Paul Hornung and Detroit defensive tackle Alex Karras for placing bets on their own teams and on other NFL games; he also fined five other Detroit players $2,000 each for betting on one game in which they did not participate, and the Detroit Lions Football Company $2,000 on each of two counts for failure to report information promptly and for lack of sideline supervision, April 17.

The AFL allowed the Jets and Raiders to select players from other franchises in hopes of giving the league more competitive balance, May 11.

NBC was awarded exclusive network broadcasting rights for the 1963 NFL Championship Game for $926,000, May 23.

The Pro Football Hall of Fame was dedicated at Canton, Ohio, September 7.

The U.S. Fourth Circuit Court of Appeals reaffirmed the lower court's finding for the NFL in the $10-million suit brought by the AFL, ending three and a half years of litigation, November 21.

Jim Brown of Cleveland rushed for an NFL single-season record 1,863 yards.

Boston defeated Buffalo 26-8 in the first divisional playoff game in AFL history, December 28.

The Bears defeated the Giants 14-10 in the NFL Championship Game, a record sixth and last title for Halas in his thirty-sixth season as the Bears' coach, December 29.

1964
The Chargers defeated the Patriots 51-10 in the AFL Championship Game, January 5.

William Clay Ford, the Lions' president since 1961, purchased the team, January 10. A group representing the late James P. Clark sold the Eagles to a group headed by Jerry Wolman, January 21. Carroll Rosenbloom, the majority owner of the Colts since 1953, acquired complete ownership of the team, January 23.

The AFL signed a five-year, $36-million television contract with NBC to begin with the 1965 season, January 29.

Hornung and Karras were reinstated by Rozelle, March

16.

CBS submitted the winning bid of $14.1 million per year for the NFL regular-season television rights for 1964 and 1965, January 24. CBS acquired the rights to championship games for 1964 and 1965 for $1.8 million per game, April 17.

Pete Gogolak of Cornell signed a contract with Buffalo, becoming the first soccer-style kicker in pro football.

Buffalo defeated San Diego 20-7 in the AFL Championship Game, December 26. Cleveland defeated Baltimore 27-0 in the NFL Championship Game, December 27.

1965
The NFL teams pledged not to sign college seniors until completion of all their games, including bowl games, and empowered the Commissioner to discipline the clubs up to as much as the loss of an entire draft list for a violation of the pledge, February 15.

The NFL added a sixth official, the line judge, February 19. The color of the officials' penalty flags was changed from white to bright gold, April 5.

Commissioner Rozelle negotiated an agreement on behalf of the NFL clubs to purchase Ed Sabol's Blair Motion Pictures, which was renamed NFL Films, April.

Atlanta was awarded an NFL franchise for 1966, with Rankin Smith, Sr., as owner, June 30. Miami was awarded an AFL franchise for 1966, with Joe Robbie and Danny Thomas as owners, August 16.

Field Judge Burl Toler became the first black official in NFL history, September 19.

According to a Harris survey, sports fans chose professional football (41 percent) as their favorite sport, overtaking baseball (38 percent) for the first time, October.

Green Bay defeated Baltimore 13-10 in sudden-death overtime in a Western Conference playoff game. Don Chandler kicked a 25-yard field goal for the Packers after 13 minutes, 39 seconds of overtime, December 26. The Packers then defeated the Browns 23-12 in the NFL Championship Game, January 2.

In the AFL Championship Game, the Bills defeated the

Chargers, 23-0, December 26.

CBS acquired the rights to the NFL regular-season games in 1966 and 1967, with an option for 1968, for $18.8 million per year, December 29.

1966

The AFL-NFL war reached its peak, as the leagues spent a combined $7 million to sign their 1966 draft choices. The NFL signed 75 percent of its 232 draftees, the AFL 46 percent of its 181. Of the 111 common draft choices, 79 signed with the NFL, 28 with the AFL, and 4 went unsigned.

Buddy Young became the first African-American to work in the league office when Commissioner Rozelle named him director of player relations, February 1.

The rights to the 1966 and 1967 NFL Championship Games were sold to CBS for $2 million per game, February 14.

Foss resigned as AFL Commissioner, April 7. Al Davis, the head coach and general manager of the Raiders, was named to replace him, April 8.

Goal posts offset from the goal line, painted bright yellow, and with uprights 20 feet above the cross-bar were made standard in the NFL, May 16.

A series of secret meetings regarding a possible AFL-NFL merger were held in the spring between Hunt of Kansas City and Tex Schramm of Dallas. Rozelle announced the merger, June 8. Under the agreement, the two leagues would combine to form an expanded league with 24 teams, to be increased to 26 in 1968 and to 28 by 1970 or soon thereafter. All existing franchises would be retained, and no franchises would be transferred outside their metropolitan areas. While maintaining separate schedules through 1969, the leagues agreed to play an annual AFL-NFL World Championship Game beginning in January, 1967, and to hold a combined draft, also beginning in 1967. Preseason games would be held between teams of each league starting in 1967. Official regular-season play would start in 1970 when the two leagues would officially merge to form one league with two conferences.

Rozelle was named Commissioner of the expanded league setup.

Davis rejoined the Raiders, and Milt Woodard was named president of the AFL, July 25.

The St. Louis Cardinals moved into newly constructed Busch Memorial Stadium.

Barron Hilton sold the Chargers to a group headed by Eugene Klein and Sam Schulman, August 25.

Congress approved the AFL-NFL merger, passing legislation exempting the agreement itself from antitrust action, October 21.

New Orleans was awarded an NFL franchise to begin play in 1967, November 1. John Mecom, Jr., of Houston was designated majority stockholder and president of the franchise, December 15.

The NFL was realigned for the 1967-69 seasons into the Capitol and Century Divisions in the Eastern Conference and the Central and Coastal Divisions in the Western Conference, December 2. New Orleans and the New York Giants agreed to switch divisions in 1968 and return to the 1967 alignment in 1969.

The rights to the Super Bowl for four years were sold to CBS and NBC for $9.5 million, December 13.

1967

Green Bay earned the right to represent the NFL in the first AFL-NFL World Championship Game by defeating Dallas 34-27, January 1. The same day, Kansas City defeated Buffalo 31-7 to represent the AFL. The Packers defeated the Chiefs 35-10 before 61,946 fans at the Los Angeles Memorial Coliseum in the first game between AFL and NFL teams, January 15. The winning players' share for the Packers was $15,000 each, and the losing players' share for the Chiefs was $7,500 each. The game was televised by both CBS and NBC.

The "sling-shot" goal post and a six-foot-wide border around the field were made standard in the NFL, February 22.

Baltimore made Bubba Smith, a Michigan State defensive lineman, the first choice in the first combined AFL-NFL draft, March 14.

The AFL awarded a franchise to begin play in 1968 to Cincinnati, May 23. A group with Paul Brown as part owner, general manager, and head coach, was awarded the Cincinnati franchise, September 27.

Arthur B. Modell, the president of the Cleveland Browns, was elected president of the NFL, May 28.

Defensive back Emlen Tunnell of the New York Giants became the first black player to enter the Pro Football Hall of Fame, August 5.

An AFL team defeated an NFL team for the first time, when Denver beat Detroit 13-7 in a preseason game, August 5.

Green Bay defeated Dallas 21-17 for the NFL championship on a last-minute 1-yard quarterback sneak by Bart Starr in 13-below-zero temperature at Green Bay, December 31. The same day, Oakland defeated Houston 40-7 for the AFL championship.

1968

Green Bay defeated Oakland 33-14 in Super Bowl II at Miami, January 14. The game had the first $3-million gate in pro football history.

Vince Lombardi resigned as head coach of the Packers, but remained as general manager, January 28.

Werblin sold his shares in the Jets to his partners Don Lillis, Leon Hess, Townsend Martin, and Phil Iselin, May 21. Lillis assumed the presidency of the club, but then died July 23. Iselin was appointed president, August 6.

Halas retired for the fourth and last time as head coach of the Bears, May 27.

The Oilers left Rice Stadium for the Astrodome and became the first NFL team to play its home games in a domed stadium.

The movie *Heidi* became a footnote in sports history when NBC didn't show the last 50 seconds of the Jets-Raiders game in order to permit the children's special to begin on time. The Raiders scored two touchdowns in the last 42 seconds to win 43-32, November 17.

Ewbank became the first coach to win titles in both the NFL and AFL when his Jets

defeated the Raiders 27-23 for the AFL championship, December 29. The same day, Baltimore defeated Cleveland 34-0.

1969

The AFL established a playoff format for the 1969 season, with the winner in one division playing the runner-up in the other, January 11.

An AFL team won the Super Bowl for the first time, as the Jets defeated the Colts 16-7 at Miami, January 12 in Super Bowl III. The title Super Bowl was recognized by the NFL for the first time.

Vince Lombardi became part owner, executive vice-president, and head coach of the Washington Redskins, February 7.

Wolman sold the Eagles to Leonard Tose, May 1.

Baltimore, Cleveland, and Pittsburgh agreed to join the AFL teams to form the 13-team American Football Conference of the NFL in 1970, May 10. The NFL also agreed on a playoff format that would include one "wild-card" team per conference—the second-place team with the best record.

The NFL announced a three-year agreement with ABC to televise *Monday Night Football*. The new series makes the NFL the first league with a regular series of national telecasts in prime time, May 26.

George Preston Marshall, president emeritus of the Redskins, died at 72, August 9.

The NFL marked its fiftieth year by the wearing of a special patch by each of the 16 teams.

1970

Kansas City defeated Minnesota 23-7 in Super Bowl IV at New Orleans, January 11. The gross receipts of approximately $3.8 million were the largest ever for a one-day sports event.

A special league meeting was held to determine the divisional realignment of the National Football Conference. With no consensus, Rozelle ordered the five most viable plans be written down on sheets of paper. Rozelle's assistant, Thelma Elkjer, picked the winning one out of a vase at random, January 17.

Four-year television contracts, under which CBS would televise all NFC games and NBC all AFC games (except Monday night games) and the two would divide televising the Super Bowl and AFC-NFC Pro Bowl games, were announced, January 26.

Art Modell resigned as president of the NFL, March 12. Milt Woodard resigned as president of the AFL, March 13. Lamar Hunt was elected president of the AFC and George Halas was elected president of the NFC, March 19.

The merged 26-team league adopted rules changes putting names on the backs of players' jerseys, making a point after touchdown worth only one point, and making the scoreboard clock the official timing device of the game, March 18.

The Players Negotiating Committee and the NFL Players Association announced a four-year agreement guaranteeing approximately $4,535,000 annually to player pension and insurance benefits, August 3. The owners also agreed to contribute $250,000 annually to improve or implement items such as disability payments, widows' benefits, maternity benefits, and dental benefits. The agreement also provided for increased preseason game and per diem payments, averaging approximately $2.6 million annually.

The Pittsburgh Steelers moved into Three Rivers Stadium. The Cincinnati Bengals moved to Riverfront Stadium.

Vince Lombardi died of cancer at 57, September 3.

The Super Bowl trophy was renamed the Vince Lombardi trophy, September 10.

Tom Dempsey of New Orleans kicked a game-winning NFL-record 63-yard field goal against Detroit, November 8.

1971
Baltimore defeated Dallas 16-13 on Jim O'Brien's 32-yard field goal with five seconds to go in Super Bowl V at Miami, January 17.

The NFC defeated the AFC 27-6 in the first AFC-NFC Pro Bowl at Los Angeles, January 24.

The Boston Patriots changed their name to the New England Patriots, March 25. Their new stadium, Schaefer Stadium, was dedicated in a 20-14 preseason victory over the Giants.

The Philadelphia Eagles left Franklin Field and played their games at the new Veterans Stadium.

The San Francisco 49ers left Kezar Stadium and moved their games to Candlestick Park.

Daniel F. Reeves, the president and general manager of the Rams, died at 58, April 15.

The Dallas Cowboys moved from the Cotton Bowl into their new home, Texas Stadium, October 24.

Miami defeated Kansas City 27-24 in sudden-death overtime in an AFC Divisional Playoff Game, December 25. Garo Yepremian kicked a 37-yard field goal for the Dolphins after 22 minutes, 40 seconds of overtime, as the game lasted 82 minutes, 40 seconds overall, making it the longest game in history.

1972
Dallas defeated Miami 24-3 in Super Bowl VI at New Orleans, January 16.

The inbounds lines or hashmarks were moved nearer the center of the field, 23 yards, 1 foot, 9 inches from the sidelines, March 23. The method of determining won-lost percentage in standings changed. Tie games, previously not counted in the standings, were made equal to a half-game won and a half-game lost, May 24.

Robert Irsay purchased the Los Angeles Rams and transferred ownership of the club to Carroll Rosenbloom in exchange for the Baltimore Colts, July 13.

William V. Bidwill purchased the stock of his brother Charles (Stormy) Bidwill to become the sole owner of the St. Louis Cardinals, September 2.

The National District Attorneys Association endorsed the position of professional leagues in opposing proposed legalization of gambling on professional team sports, September 28.

Franco Harris' "Immaculate Reception" gave the Steelers

their first postseason win ever, 13-7 over the Raiders, December 23.

1973
Rozelle announced that all Super Bowl VII tickets were sold and that the game would be telecast in Los Angeles, the site of the game, on an experimental basis, January 3.

Miami defeated Washington 14-7 in Super Bowl VII at Los Angeles, completing a 17-0 season, the first perfect-record regular-season and postseason mark in NFL history, January 14.

The AFC defeated the NFC 33-28 in the Pro Bowl in Dallas, the first time since 1942 that the game was played outside Los Angeles, January 21.

A jersey numbering system was adopted, April 5: 1-19 for quarterbacks and specialists, 20-49 for running backs and defensive backs, 50-59 for centers and linebackers, 60-79 for defensive linemen and interior offensive linemen other than centers, and 80-89 for wide receivers and tight ends. Players who had been in the NFL in 1972 could continue to use old numbers.

NFL Charities, a nonprofit organization, was created to derive an income from monies generated from NFL Properties' licensing of NFL trademarks and team names, June 26. NFL Charities was set up to support education and charitable activities and to supply economic support to persons formerly associated with professional football who were no longer able to support themselves.

Congress adopted experimental legislation (for three years) requiring any NFL game that had been declared a sellout 72 hours prior to kickoff to be made available for local televising, September 14. The legislation provided for an annual review to be made by the Federal Communications Commission.

The Buffalo Bills moved their home games from War Memorial Stadium to Rich Stadium in nearby Orchard Park. The Giants tied the Eagles 23-23 in the final game in Yankee Stadium, September 23. The Giants played the rest of their home games at the Yale Bowl in New Haven, Connecti-

cut.

A rival league, the World Football League, was formed and was reported in operation, October 2. It had plans to start play in 1974.

O.J. Simpson of Buffalo became the first player to rush for more than 2,000 yards in a season, gaining 2,003.

1974
Miami defeated Minnesota 24-7 in Super Bowl VIII at Houston, the second consecutive Super Bowl championship for the Dolphins, January 13.

Rozelle was given a 10-year contract effective January 1, 1973, February 27.

Tampa Bay was awarded the twenty-seventh franchise to begin operation in 1976, April 24.

Sweeping rules changes were adopted to add action and tempo to games: one sudden-death overtime period was added for preseason and regular-season games; the goal posts were moved from the goal line to the end lines; kickoffs were moved from the 40- to the 35-yard line; after missed field goals from beyond the 20, the ball was to be returned to the line of scrimmage; restrictions were placed on members of the punting team to open up return possibilities; roll-blocking and cutting of wide receivers was eliminated; the extent of downfield contact a defender could have with an eligible receiver was restricted; the penalties for offensive holding, illegal use of the hands, and tripping were reduced from 15 to 10 yards; wide receivers blocking back toward the ball within three yards of the line of scrimmage were prevented from blocking below the waist, April 25.

Seattle was awarded the twenty-eighth NFL franchise to begin play in 1976, June 4. Lloyd W. Nordstrom, president of the Seattle Seahawks, and Hugh Culverhouse, president of the Tampa Bay Buccaneers, signed franchise agreements, December 5.

The Birmingham Americans defeated the Florida Blazers 22-21 in the WFL World Bowl, winning the league championship, December 5.

1975

Pittsburgh defeated Minnesota 16-6 in Super Bowl IX at New Orleans, the Steelers' first championship since entering the NFL in 1933, January 12.

The Memphis Southmen of the WFL signed Larry Csonka, Jim Kiick, and Paul Warfield of Miami, March 31.

The divisional winners with the highest won-loss percentage were made the home team for the divisional playoffs, and the surviving winners with the highest percentage made home teams for the championship games. Previously, the home sites were pre-determined by division on a rotating basis, June 26.

Referees were equipped with wireless microphones for all preseason, regular-season, and playoff games.

The Lions moved to the new Pontiac Silverdome. The Giants played their home games in Shea Stadium. The Saints moved into the Louisiana Superdome.

The World Football League folded, October 22.

1976

Pittsburgh defeated Dallas 21-17 in Super Bowl X in Miami. The Steelers joined Green Bay and Miami as the only teams to win two Super Bowls; the Cowboys became the first wild-card team to play in the Super Bowl, January 18.

Lloyd Nordstrom, the president of the Seahawks, died at 66, January 20. His brother Elmer succeeded him as majority representative of the team.

The owners adopted the use of two 30-second clocks for all games, visible to both players and fans to note the official time between the ready-for-play signal and snap of the ball, March 16.

A veteran player allocation was held to stock the Seattle and Tampa Bay franchises with 39 players each, March 30-31. In the college draft, Seattle and Tampa Bay each received eight extra choices, April 8-9.

The Giants moved into new Giants Stadium in East Rutherford, New Jersey.

The Steelers defeated the College All-Stars in a storm-shortened Chicago College All-Star Game, the last of the series, July 23. St. Louis defeated San Diego 20-10 in a preseason game before 38,000 in Korakuen Stadium, Tokyo, in the first NFL game outside of North America, August 16.

1977

Oakland defeated Minnesota 32-14 in Super Bowl XI at Pasadena, January 9. The paid attendance was a pro record 103,438.

The NFL Players Association and the NFL Management Council ratified a collective bargaining agreement extending until 1982, covering five football seasons while continuing the pension plan—including years 1974, 1975, and 1976—with contributions totaling more than $55 million. The total cost of the agreement was estimated at $107 million. The agreement called for a college draft at least through 1986; contained a no-strike, no-suit clause; established a 43-man active player limit; reduced pension vesting to four years; provided for increases in minimum salaries and preseason and postseason pay; improved insurance, medical, and dental benefits; modified previous practices in player movement and control; and reaffirmed the NFL Commissioner's disciplinary authority. Additionally, the agreement called for the NFL member clubs to make payments totaling $16 million the next 10 years to settle various legal disputes, February 25.

The San Francisco 49ers were sold to Edward J. DeBartolo, Jr., March 28.

A 16-game regular season, 4-game preseason was adopted to begin in 1978. A second wild-card team was adopted for the playoffs beginning in 1978, with the wild-card teams to play each other and the winners advancing to a round of eight postseason series, March 29.

The Seahawks were permanently aligned in the AFC Western Division and the Buccaneers in the NFC Central Division, March 31.

Rules changes were adopted to open up the passing game and to cut down on injuries. Defenders were permitted to make contact with eligible receivers only once; the head slap was outlawed; offensive linemen were prohibited from thrusting their hands to an opponent's neck, face, or head; and wide receivers were prohibited from clipping, even in the legal clipping zone.

Rozelle negotiated contracts with the three television networks to televise all NFL regular-season and postseason games, plus selected preseason games, for four years beginning with the 1978 season. ABC was awarded yearly rights to 16 Monday night games, four primetime games, the AFC-NFC Pro Bowl, and the Hall of Fame games. CBS received the rights to all NFC regular-season and postseason games (except those in the ABC package) and to Super Bowls XIV and XVI. NBC received the rights to all AFC regular-season and postseason games (except those in the ABC package) and to Super Bowls XIII and XV. Industry sources considered it the largest single television package ever negotiated, October 12.

1978

Dallas defeated Denver 27-10 in Super Bowl XII, held indoors for the first time, at the Louisiana Superdome in New Orleans, January 15. Dallas' victory was the first for the NFC in six years.

According to a Louis Harris Sports Survey, 70 percent of the nation's sports fans said they followed football, compared to 54 percent who followed baseball. Football increased its lead as the country's favorite, 26 percent to 16 percent for baseball, January 19.

A seventh official, the side judge, was added to the officiating crew, March 14.

The NFL continued a trend toward opening up the game. Rules changes permitted a defender to maintain contact with a receiver within five yards of the line of scrimmage, but restricted contact beyond that point. The pass-blocking rule was interpreted to permit the extending of arms and open hands, March 17.

A study on the use of instant replay as an officiating aid was made during seven nationally televised preseason games.

The NFL played for the first time in Mexico City, with the Saints defeating the Eagles 14-7 in a preseason game, August 5.

Bolstered by the expansion of the regular-season schedule from 14 to 16 weeks, NFL paid attendance exceeded 12 million (12,771,800) for the first time. The per-game average of 57,017 was the third-highest in league history and the most since 1973.

1979

Pittsburgh defeated Dallas 35-31 in Super Bowl XIII at Miami to become the first team ever to win three Super Bowls, January 21.

NFL rules changes emphasized additional player safety. The changes prohibited players on the receiving team from blocking below the waist during kickoffs, punts, and field-goal attempts; prohibited the wearing of torn or altered equipment and exposed pads that could be hazardous; extended the zone in which there could be no crackback blocks; and instructed officials to quickly whistle a play dead when a quarterback was clearly in the grasp of a tackler, March 16.

Carroll Rosenbloom, the president of the Rams, drowned at 72, April 2. His widow, Georgia, assumed control of the club.

1980

Pittsburgh defeated the Los Angeles Rams 31-19 in Super Bowl XIV at Pasadena to become the first team to win four Super Bowls, January 20.

The AFC-NFC Pro Bowl, won 37-27 by the NFC, was played before 48,060 fans at Aloha Stadium in Honolulu, Hawaii. It was the first time in the 30-year history of the Pro Bowl that the game was played in a non-NFL city.

Rules changes placed greater restrictions on contact in the area of the head, neck, and face. Under the heading of "personal foul," players were prohibited from directly striking, swinging, or clubbing on the head, neck, or face. Starting in 1980, a penalty could be called for such contact whether or not the initial contact was made below the neck area.

CBS, with a record bid of $12 million, won the national radio rights to 26 NFL regular-season games, including Monday Night Football, and all 10 postseason games for the 1980-83 seasons.

The Los Angeles Rams moved their home games to Anaheim Stadium in nearby Orange County, California.

The Oakland Raiders joined the Los Angeles Coliseum Commission's antitrust suit against the NFL. The suit contended the league violated antitrust laws in declining to approve a proposed move by the Raiders from Oakland to Los Angeles.

The NFL Draft is televised for the first time by ESPN, April 29.

Television ratings in 1980 were the second-best in NFL history, trailing only the combined ratings of the 1976 season. All three networks posted gains, and NBC's 15.0 rating was its best ever. CBS and ABC had their best ratings since 1977, with 15.3 and 20.8 ratings, respectively. CBS Radio reported a record audience of 7 million for Monday night and special games.

1981
Oakland defeated Philadelphia 27-10 in Super Bowl XV at the Louisiana Superdome in New Orleans, to become the first wild-card team to win a Super Bowl, January 25.

Edgar F. Kaiser, Jr., purchased the Denver Broncos from Gerald and Allan Phipps, February 26.

The owners adopted a disaster plan for re-stocking a team should the club be involved in a fatal accident, March 20.

A CBS-New York Times poll showed that 48 percent of sports fans preferred football to 31 percent for baseball.

The NFL teams hosted 167 representatives from 44 predominantly black colleges during training camps for a total of 289 days. The program was adopted for renewal during each training camp period.

ABC and CBS set all-time rating highs. ABC finished with a 21.7 rating and CBS with a 17.5 rating. NBC was down slightly to 13.9.

1982
San Francisco defeated Cincinnati 26-21 in Super Bowl XVI at the Pontiac Silverdome, in the first Super Bowl held in the North, January 24. The CBS telecast achieved the highest rating of any televised sports event ever, 49.1 with a 73.0 share.

The NFL signed a five-year contract with the three television networks (ABC, CBS, and NBC) to televise all NFL regular-season and postseason games starting with the 1982 season.

A jury ruled against the NFL in the antitrust trial brought by the Los Angeles Coliseum Commission and the Oakland Raiders, May 7. The verdict cleared the way for the Raiders to move to Los Angeles, where they defeated Green Bay 24-3 in their first preseason game, August 29.

The 1982 season was reduced from a 16-game schedule to nine as the result of a 57-day players' strike. The strike was called by the NFLPA at midnight on Monday, September 20, following the Green Bay at New York Giants game. Play resumed November 21-22 following ratification of the Collective Bargaining Agreement by NFL owners, November 17 in New York.

Under the Collective Bargaining Agreement, which was to run through the 1986 season, the NFL draft was extended through 1992 and the veteran free-agent system was left basically unchanged. A minimum salary schedule for years of experience was established; training camp and postseason pay were increased; players' medical, insurance, and retirement benefits were increased; and a severance-pay system was introduced to aid in career transition, a first in professional sports.

Despite the players' strike, the average paid attendance in 1982 was 58,472, the fifth-highest in league history.

1983
Because of the shortened season, the NFL adopted a format of 16 teams competing in a Super Bowl Tournament for the 1982 playoffs. The NFC's number-one seed, Washing-

ton, defeated the AFC's number-two seed, Miami, 27-17 in Super Bowl XVII at the Rose Bowl in Pasadena, January 30.

Super Bowl XVII was the second-highest rated live television program of all time, giving the NFL a sweep of the top 10 live programs in television history.

George Halas, the owner of the Bears and the last surviving member of the NFL's second organizational meeting, died at 88, October 31.

1984
The Los Angeles Raiders defeated Washington 38-9 in Super Bowl XVIII at Tampa Stadium, January 22.

An 11-man group headed by H.R. (Bum) Bright purchased the Dallas Cowboys from Clint Murchison, Jr., March 20. Club president Tex Schramm was designated as managing general partner.

Wellington Mara was named president of the NFC, March 20.

Patrick Bowlen purchased a majority interest in the Denver Broncos from Edgar Kaiser, Jr., March 21.

The Colts relocated to Indianapolis, March 28. Their new home became the Hoosier Dome.

The New York Jets moved their home games to Giants Stadium in East Rutherford, New Jersey.

Alex G. Spanos purchased a majority interest in the San Diego Chargers from Eugene V. Klein, August 28.

Houston defeated Pittsburgh 23-20 to mark the one-hundredth overtime game in regular-season play since overtime was adopted in 1974, December 2.

On the field, many all-time records were set: Dan Marino of Miami passed for 5,084 yards and 48 touchdowns; Eric Dickerson of the Los Angeles Rams rushed for 2,105 yards; Art Monk of Washington caught 106 passes; and Walter Payton of Chicago broke Jim Brown's career rushing mark, finishing the season with 13,309 yards.

According to a CBS Sports/New York Times survey, 53 percent of the nation's sports fans said they most enjoyed watching football,

compared to 18 percent for baseball, December 2-4.

1985
San Francisco defeated Miami 38-16 in Super Bowl XIX at Stanford Stadium in Stanford, California, January 20. President Ronald Reagan, who took his second oath of office before tossing the coin for the game, was one of 115,936,000 viewers. Super Bowl XIX had a direct economic impact of $113.5 million on the San Francisco Bay area.

NBC Radio and the NFL entered into a two-year agreement granting NBC the radio rights to a 37-game package in each of the 1985-86 seasons, March 6. The package included 27 regular-season games and 10 postseason games.

Norman Braman, in partnership with Edward Leibowitz, bought the Philadelphia Eagles from Leonard Tose, April 29.

A group headed by Tom Benson, Jr., was approved to purchase the New Orleans Saints from John W. Mecom, Jr., June 3.

The NFL owners adopted a resolution calling for a series of overseas preseason games, beginning in 1986, with one game to be played in England/Europe and/or one game in Japan each year. The game would be a fifth preseason game for the clubs involved and all arrangements and selection of the clubs would be under the control of the Commissioner, May 23.

The league-wide conversion to videotape from movie film for coaching study was approved.

A Louis Harris poll in December revealed that pro football remained the sport most followed by Americans. Fifty-nine percent of those surveyed followed pro football, compared with 54 percent who followed baseball.

The Chicago-Miami Monday game had the highest rating, 29.6, and share, 46.0, of any primetime game in NFL history, December 2. The game was viewed in more than 25 million homes.

The NFL showed a ratings increase on all three networks for the season, gaining 4 percent on NBC, 10 on CBS, and

16 on ABC.

1986

Chicago defeated New England 46-10 in Super Bowl XX at the Louisiana Superdome, January 26. The Patriots had earned the right to play the Bears by becoming the first wild-card team to win three consecutive games on the road. The NBC telecast replaced the final episode of *M*A*S*H* as the most-viewed television program in history, with an audience of 127 million viewers, according to A.C. Nielsen figures. In addition to drawing a 48.3 rating and a 70 percent share in the United States, Super Bowl XX was televised to 59 foreign countries and beamed via satellite to the QE II.

The owners adopted limited use of instant replay as an officiating aid, prohibited players from wearing or otherwise displaying equipment, apparel, or other items that carry commercial names, names of organizations, or personal messages of any type, March 11.

After an 11-week trial, a jury in U.S. District Court in New York awarded the United States Football League one dollar in its $1.7 billion antitrust suit against the NFL. The jury rejected all of the USFL's television-related claims, which were the self-proclaimed heart of the USFL's case. The jury deliberated five days, July 29.

Chicago defeated Dallas 17-6 at Wembley Stadium in London in the first American Bowl. The game drew a sellout crowd of 82,699 and the NBC national telecast in this country produced a 12.4 rating and 36 percent share, making it the highest daytime preseason television audience ever with 10.65-million viewers, August 3.

ABC's *NFL Monday Night Football*, in its seventeenth season, became the longest-running primetime series in the history of the network.

1987

The New York Giants defeated Denver 39-20 in Super Bowl XXI and captured their first NFL title since 1956. The game, played in Pasadena's Rose Bowl, drew a sellout crowd of 101,063, January 25.

New three-year TV contracts with ABC, CBS, and NBC were announced for 1987-89 at the NFL annual meeting in Maui, Hawaii, March 15. Commissioner Rozelle and Broadcast Committee Chairman Art Modell also announced a three-year contract with ESPN to televise 13 primetime games each season. The ESPN contract was the first with a cable network. However, NFL games on ESPN also were scheduled for regular television in the city of the visiting team and in the home city if the game was sold out 72 hours in advance.

A special payment program was adopted to benefit nearly 1,000 former NFL players who participated in the League before the current Bert Bell NFL Pension Plan was created and made retroactive to the 1959 season. Players covered by the new program spent at least five years in the League and played all or part of their career prior to 1959. Each vested player would receive $60 per month for each year of service in the League for life.

NFL and CBS Radio jointly announced agreement granting CBS the radio rights to a 40-game package in each of the next three NFL seasons, 1987-89, April 7.

Over 400 former NFL players from the pre-1959 era received first payments from NFL owners, July 1.

The NFL's debut on ESPN produced the two highest-rated and most-watched sports programs in basic cable history. The Chicago at Miami game on August 16 drew an 8.9 rating in 3.81 million homes. Those records fell two weeks later when the Los Angeles Raiders at Dallas game achieved a 10.2 cable rating in 4.36 million homes.

The 1987 season was reduced from a 16-game season to 15 as the result of a 24-day players' strike. The strike was called by the NFLPA on Tuesday, September 22, following the New England at New York Jets game. Games scheduled for the third weekend were canceled but the games of weeks four, five, and six were played with replace-

ment teams. Striking players returned for the seventh week of the season, October 25.

In a three-team deal involving 10 players and/or draft choices, the Los Angeles Rams traded running back Eric Dickerson to the Indianapolis Colts for six draft choices and two players. Buffalo obtained the rights to linebacker Cornelius Bennett from Indianapolis, sending Greg Bell and three draft choices to the Rams. The Colts added Owen Gill and three draft choices of their own to complete the deal with the Rams, October 31.

The Chicago at Minnesota game became the highest-rated and most-watched sports program in basic cable history when it drew a 14.4 cable rating in 6.5 million homes, December 6.

1988

Washington defeated Denver 42-10 in Super Bowl XXII to earn its second victory this decade in the NFL Championship Game. The game, played for the first time in San Diego Jack Murphy Stadium, drew a sellout crowd of 73,302. Doug Williams, the game's MVP, became the first African-American quarterback to play in a Super Bowl, January 31.

In a unanimous 3-0 decision, the 2nd Circuit Court of Appeals in New York upheld the verdict of the jury that in July, 1986, had awarded the United States Football League one dollar in its $1.7 billion antitrust suit against the NFL. In a 91-page opinion, Judge Ralph K. Winter said the USFL sought through court decree the success it failed to gain among football fans, March 10.

By a 23-5 margin, owners voted to continue the instant replay system for the third consecutive season with the Instant Replay Official to be assigned to a regular seven-man, on-the-field crew. At the NFL annual meeting in Phoenix, Arizona, a 45-second clock was also approved to replace the 30-second clock. For a normal sequence of plays, the interval between plays was changed to 45 seconds from the time the ball is signaled dead until it is

snapped on the succeeding play.

NFL owners approved the transfer of the Cardinals' franchise from St. Louis to Phoenix; approved two supplemental drafts each year—one prior to training camp and one prior to the regular season; and voted to initiate an annual series of games in Japan/Asia as early as the 1989 preseason, March 14-18.

The NFL Annual Selection Meeting returned to a separate two-day format and for the first time originated on a Sunday. ESPN drew a 3.6 rating during their seven-hour coverage of the draft, which was viewed in 1.6 million homes, April 24-25.

Art Rooney, founder and owner of the Steelers, died at 87, August 25.

Johnny Grier became the first African-American referee in NFL history, September 4.

Commissioner Rozelle announced that two teams would play a preseason game as part of the American Bowl series on August 6, 1989, in the Korakuen Tokyo Dome in Japan, December 16.

1989

San Francisco defeated Cincinnati 20-16 in Super Bowl XXIII. The game, played for the first time in Joe Robbie Stadium in Miami, was attended by a sellout crowd of 75,129, January 22.

Commissioner Rozelle announced his retirement, pending the naming of a successor, March 22 at the NFL annual meeting in Palm Desert, California.

Following the announcement, AFC president Lamar Hunt and NFC president Wellington Mara announced the formation of a six-man search committee composed of Art Modell, Robert Parins, Dan Rooney, and Ralph Wilson. Hunt and Mara served as co-chairmen.

By a 24-4 margin, owners voted to continue the instant replay system for the fourth straight season. A strengthened policy regarding anabolic steroids and masking agents was announced by Commissioner Rozelle. NFL clubs called for strong disciplinary measures in cases of feigned injuries and adopted a joint proposal by the Long-Range Planning and Finance committees regarding player personnel rules, March 19-23.

Two hundred twenty-nine unconditional free agents signed with new teams under management's Plan B system, April 1.

Jerry Jones purchased a majority interest in the Dallas Cowboys from H.R. (Bum) Bright, April 18.

Tex Schramm was named president of the new World League of American Football to work with a six-man committee of Dan Rooney, chairman; Norman Braman, Lamar Hunt, Victor Kiam, Mike Lynn, and Bill Walsh, April 18.

NFL and CBS Radio jointly announced agreement extending CBS's radio rights to an annual 40-game package through the 1994 season, April 18.

As of opening day, September 10, of the 229 Plan B free agents, 111 were active and 23 others were on teams' reserve lists. Ninety-two others were waived and three retired.

Art Shell was named head coach of the Los Angeles Raiders making him the NFL's first black head coach since Fritz Pollard coached the Akron Pros in 1921, October 3.

The site of the New England Patriots at San Francisco 49ers game scheduled for Candlestick Park on October 22 was switched to Stanford Stadium in the aftermath of the Bay Area Earthquake of October 17. The change was announced on October 19.

Paul Tagliabue became the seventh chief executive of the NFL on October 26 when he was chosen to succeed Commissioner Pete Rozelle on the sixth ballot of a three-day meeting in Cleveland, Ohio.

In all, 12 ballots were required to select Tagliabue. Two were conducted at a meeting in Chicago on July 6, and four at a meeting in Dallas on October 10-11. On the twelfth ballot, with Seattle absent, Tagliabue received more than the 19 affirmative votes required for election from among the 27 clubs present.

The transfer from Commis-

sioner Rozelle to Commissioner Tagliabue took place at 12:01 A.M. on Sunday, November 5.

NFL Charities donated $1 million through United Way to benefit Bay Area earthquake victims, November 6.

1990
San Francisco defeated Denver 55-10 in Super Bowl XXIV at the Louisiana Superdome, January 28. San Francisco joined Pittsburgh as the NFL's only teams to win four Super Bowls.

The NFL announced revisions in its 1990 draft eligibility rules. College juniors became eligible but must renounce their collegiate football eligibility before applying for the NFL Draft, February 16.

Commissioner Tagliabue announced NFL teams will play their 16-game schedule over 17 weeks in 1990-92 and 16 games over 18 weeks in 1993, February 27.

The NFL revised its playoff format to include two additional wild-card teams (one per conference), which raised the total to six wild-card teams.

Commissioner Tagliabue and Broadcast Committee Chairman Art Modell announced a four-year contract with Turner Broadcasting to televise nine Sunday-night games.

New four-year TV agreements were ratified for 1990-93 for ABC, CBS, NBC, ESPN, and TNT at the NFL annual meeting in Orlando, Florida, March 12. The contracts totaled $3.6 billion, the largest in TV history.

The NFL announced plans to expand its American Bowl series of preseason games. In addition to games in London and Tokyo, American Bowl games were scheduled for Berlin, Germany, and Montreal, Canada, in 1990.

For the fifth straight year, NFL owners voted to continue a limited system of Instant Replay. Beginning in 1990, the replay official will have a two-minute time limit to make a decision. The vote was 21-7, March 12.

Commissioner Tagliabue announced the formation of a Committee on Expansion and Realignment, March 13. He also named a Player Advisory

Council, comprised of 12 former NFL players, March 14.

One-hundred eighty-four Plan B unconditional free agents signed with new teams, April 2.

Commissioner Tagliabue appointed Dr. John Lombardo as the League's Drug Advisor for Anabolic Steroids, April 25 and named Dr. Lawrence Brown as the League's Advisor for Drugs of Abuse, May 17.

NFL International Week was celebrated with four preseason games in seven days in Tokyo, London, Berlin, and Montreal. More than 200,000 fans on three continents attended the four games, August 4-11.

Commissioner Tagliabue announced the NFL Teacher of the Month program in which the League furnishes grants and scholarships in recognition of teachers who provided a positive influence upon NFL players in elementary and secondary schools, September 20.

For the first time since 1957, every NFL club won at least one of its first four games, October 1.

The Super Bowl Most Valuable Player trophy was renamed the Pete Rozelle trophy, October 8.

1991
The New York Giants defeated Buffalo 20-19 in Super Bowl XXV to capture their second title in five years. The game was played before a sellout crowd of 73,813 at Tampa Stadium and became the first Super Bowl decided by one point, January 26.

New York businessman Robert Tisch purchased a 50 percent interest in the New York Giants from Mrs. Helen Mara Nugent and her children, Tim Mara and Maura Mara Concannon, February 2.

NFL clubs voted to continue a limited system of Instant Replay for the sixth consecutive year. The vote was 21-7, March 19.

The NFL launched the World League of American Football, the first sports league to operate on a weekly basis on two separate continents, March 23.

NFL Charities presented a $250,000 donation to the

United Service Organization. The donation was the second largest single grant ever by NFL Charities, April 5.

Commissioner Tagliabue named Harold Henderson as Executive Vice President for Labor Relations and Chairman of the NFL Management Council Executive Committee, April 8.

NFL clubs approved a recommendation by the Expansion and Realignment Committee to add two teams for the 1994 season, resulting in six divisions of five teams each, May 22.

"NFL International Week" featured six 1990 playoff teams playing nationally televised games in London, Berlin, and Tokyo on July 28 and August 3-4. The games drew more than 150,000 fans.

Paul Brown, founder of the Cleveland Browns and Cincinnati Bengals, died at age 82, August 5.

NFL clubs approved a resolution establishing an international division. A three-year financial plan for the World League was approved by NFL clubs at a meeting in Dallas, October 23.

1992
The NFL agreed to provide a minimum of $2.5 million in financial support to the NFL Alumni Association and assistance to NFL Alumni-related programs. The agreement included contributions from NFL Charities to the Pre-59ers and Dire Need Programs for former players, January 25.

The Washington Redskins defeated the Buffalo Bills 37-24 in Super Bowl XXVI to capture their third world championship in 10 years, January 26. The game was played before a sellout crowd of 63,130 at the Hubert H. Humphrey Metrodome in Minneapolis.

The use in officiating of a limited system of Instant Replay was not approved. The vote was 17-11 in favor of approval (21 votes were required). Instant Replay had been used for six consecutive years (1986-1991), March 18.

St. Louis businessman James Orthwein purchased controlling interest in the New England Patriots from Victor

Kiam, May 11.

In a Harris Poll taken during the NFL offseason, professional football again was declared the nation's most popular sport. Professional football finished atop similar surveys conducted by Harris in 1985 and 1989, May 23.

NFL clubs accepted the report of the Expansion Committee at a league meeting in Pasadena. The report names five cities as finalists for the two expansion teams—Baltimore, Charlotte, Jacksonville, Memphis, and St. Louis, May 19.

At a league meeting in Dallas, NFL clubs approved a proposal by the World League Board of Directors to restructure the World League and place future emphasis on its international success, September 17.

The Professional and Amateur Sports Protection Act made it unlawful for a government entity to operate a lottery or other betting scheme based on pro or collegiate games. Four states that already had such betting were grandfathered, October 6.

NFL teams played their 16-game regular-season schedule over 18 weeks for the only time in league history.

1993

The NFL and lawyers for the players announced a settlement of various lawsuits and an agreement on the terms of a seven-year deal that included a new player system to be in place through the 1999 season, January 6.

Commissioner Tagliabue announced the establishment of the "NFL World Partnership Program" to develop amateur football internationally through a series of clinics conducted by former NFL players and coaches, January 14.

As part of Super Bowl XXVII, the NFL announced the creation of the first NFL Youth Education Town, a facility located in south central Los Angeles for inner city youth. January 25.

The Dallas Cowboys defeated the Buffalo Bills 52-17 in Super Bowl XXVII to capture their first NFL title since 1978. The game was played before a crowd of 98,374 at the Rose Bowl in Pasadena, California, January 31.

The NFL and the NFL Players Association officially signed a 7-year Collective Bargaining Agreement in Washington, D.C., which guarantees more than $1 billion in pension, health, and post-career benefits for current and retired players—the most extensive benefits plan in pro sports. It was the NFL's first CBA since the 1982 agreement expired in 1987, June 29.

NFL Enterprises, a newly formed division of the NFL responsible for NFL Films, home video, and special domestic and international television programming was announced, August 19.

The NFL celebrated its 75th season by announcing its 75th Anniversary All-Time Team. The team, which was chosen by a selection committee of media and league personnel, was headlined by four Pro Football Hall of Fame quarterbacks – Sammy Baugh, Otto Graham, Joe Montana and Johnny Unitas, August 24.

NFL announced plans to allow fans, for the first time ever, to join players and coaches in selecting the annual AFC and NFC Pro Bowl teams, October 12.

NFL clubs unanimously awarded the league's twenty-ninth franchise to the Carolina Panthers and owner Jerry Richardson at a meeting in Chicago, October 26.

At the same meeting in Chicago, NFL clubs approved a plan to form a European league with joint venture partners, October 27.

Don Shula became the winningest coach in NFL history when Miami beat Philadelphia to give Shula his 325th victory, one more than George Halas, November 14.

NFL clubs awarded the league's thirtieth franchise to the Jacksonville Jaguars and owner Wayne Weaver at a meeting in Chicago, November 30.

The NFL announced new 4-year television agreements with NBC, ABC, ESPN, TNT, and NFL newcomer FOX, which took over the NFC package from CBS, December 18.

The NFL completed its new TV agreements by announcing that NBC would retain the rights to the AFC package, December 20.

1994

The Dallas Cowboys defeated the Buffalo Bills 30-13 in Super Bowl XXVIII to become the fifth team to win back-to-back Super Bowl titles, January 30.

NFL clubs unanimously approved the transfer of the New England Patriots from James Orthwein to Robert Kraft at a meeting in Orlando, February 22.

In a move to increase offensive production, NFL clubs at the league's annual meeting in Orlando adopted a package of changes, including modifications in line play, chucking rules, and the roughing-the-passer rule, plus the adoption of the two-point conversion and moving the spot of the kickoff back to the 30-yard line, March 22.

NFL clubs approved the transfer of the majority interest in the Miami Dolphins from the Robbie family to H. Wayne Huizenga, March 23.

The NFL and FOX announced the formation of a joint venture to create a six-team World League to begin play in Europe in April, 1995, March 23.

The Carolina Panthers earned the right to select first in the 1995 NFL draft by winning a coin toss with the Jacksonville Jaguars. The Jaguars received the second selection in the 1995 draft, April 24.

NFL clubs approved the transfer of the Philadelphia Eagles from Norman Braman to Jeffrey Lurie, May 6.

The NFL launched "NFL Sunday Ticket," a new season subscription service for satellite television dish owners, June 1.

An all-time NFL record crowd of 112,376 attended the American Bowl game between Dallas and Houston in Mexico City. It concluded the biggest American Bowl series in NFL history with four games attracting a record 256,666 fans, August 15.

As part of a celebration of its 75th season, the NFL announced its 75th Anniversary All-Time Team, August 24. Chosen by a selection committee of media and league personnel, the team was headlined by four Pro Football Hall of Fame quarterbacks—Sammy Baugh, Otto Graham, Joe Montana, and Johnny Unitas.

The NFL reached agreement on a new seven-year contract with its game officials, September 22.

The NFL Management Council and the NFL Players Association announced an agreement on the formulation and implementation of the most comprehensive drug and alcohol policy in sports, October 28.

At an NFL meeting in Chicago, Commissioner Tagliabue slotted the two new expansion teams into the AFC Central (Jacksonville Jaguars) and NFC West (Carolina Panthers) for the 1995 season only. He also appointed a special committee on realignment to make recommendations on the 1996 season and beyond, November 2.

1995

The San Francisco 49ers became the first team to win five Super Bowls when they defeated the San Diego Chargers 49-26 in Super Bowl XXIX at Joe Robbie Stadium in Miami, January 29.

Carolina and Jacksonville stocked their expansion rosters with a total of 66 players from other NFL teams in a veteran player allocation draft in New York, February 16.

CBS Radio and the NFL agreed to a new four-year contract for an annual 53-game package of games, continuing a relationship that spanned 15 of the past 17 years, February 22.

NFL clubs approved the transfer of the Tampa Bay Buccaneers from the estate of the late Hugh Culverhouse to South Florida businessman Malcolm Glazer, March 13.

After a two-year hiatus, the World League of American Football returned to action with six teams in Europe, April 8.

The NFL became the first major sports league to establish a site on the Internet system of on-line computer communication, April 10.

The transfer of the Rams from Los Angeles to St. Louis was approved by a vote of the NFL clubs at a meeting in Dallas, April 12.

ABC's *NFL Monday Night Football* finished the 1994-95 television season as the fifth highest-rated show out of 146 with a 17.8 average rating, the highest finish in the 25-year history of the series, April 18.

The Frankfurt Galaxy defeated the Amsterdam Admirals 26-22 to win the 1995 World Bowl before a crowd of 23,847 in Amsterdam's Olympic Stadium, June 23.

The transfer of the Raiders from Los Angeles to Oakland was approved by a vote of the NFL clubs at a meeting in Chicago, July 22.

Jacksonville Municipal Stadium opened in Jacksonville, Florida before a sold-out crowd of more than 70,000 as the St. Louis Rams defeated the Jacksonville Jaguars 27-10 in their first preseason game, August 18.

NFL Charities and 50 NFL players donated $1 million to the United Negro College Fund in honor of the fiftieth anniversary of the UNCF and the integration of the modern NFL, September 15.

The Trans World Dome opened in St. Louis with a sold-out crowd of 65,598 as the Rams defeated the Carolina Panthers 28-17, November 12.

On the field, many significant records and milestones were achieved: Miami's Dan Marino surpassed Pro Football Hall of Famer Fran Tarkenton in four major passing categories—attempts, completions, yards, and touchdowns—to become the NFL's all-time career leader. San Francisco's Jerry Rice became the all-time reception and receiving-yardage leader.

1996
The Dallas Cowboys won their third Super Bowl title in four years when they defeated the Pittsburgh Steelers 27-17 in Super Bowl XXX at Sun Devil Stadium in Tempe, Arizona, January 28.

An agreement between the NFL and the city of Cleveland regarding the Cleveland Browns' relocation was approved by a vote of the NFL clubs, February 9. According to the agreement, the city of Cleveland retained the Browns' heritage and records, including the name, logo, col-

ors, history, playing records, trophies, and memorabilia, and committed to building a new 72,000-seat stadium for a reactivated Browns' franchise to begin play there no later than 1999. Art Modell received approval to move his franchise to Baltimore and rename it.

The transfer of the Oilers from Houston to Nashville for the 1998 season was approved by a vote of the NFL clubs at a meeting in Atlanta, April 30.

The Scottish Claymores defeated the Frankfurt Galaxy 32-27 to win the 1996 World Bowl in front of 38,982 at Murrayfield Stadium in Edinburgh, Scotland, June 23.

The NFL returned to Baltimore when the new Baltimore Ravens defeated the Philadelphia Eagles 17-9 in a preseason game before a crowd of 63,804 at Memorial Stadium, August 3.

Ericsson Stadium opened in Charlotte, North Carolina with a crowd of 65,350 as the Carolina Panthers defeated the Chicago Bears 30-12 in a preseason game, August 3.

Former NFL Commissioner Pete Rozelle died at his home in Rancho Santa Fe, California. Rozelle, regarded as the premier commissioner in sports history, led the NFL for 29 years, from 1960-1989, December 6.

1997
Indianapolis Colts owner Robert Irsay died from complications related to a stroke he suffered in 1995. Irsay acquired the club in 1972 when he traded his Los Angeles Rams to Carrol Rosenbloom for the Colts. He later moved the Colts from Baltimore to Indianapolis in 1984, January 14.

The Green Bay Packers won their first NFL title in 29 years by defeating the New England Patriots 35-21 in Super Bowl XXXI at the Louisiana Superdome in New Orleans, January 26.

The rules governing cross-ownership were modified, permitting NFL club owners to also own teams in other sports in their home market or markets without NFL teams. The vote was 24-5 (one abstention) in favor of approval, March 11.

Washington Redskins owner Jack Kent Cooke died at his home in Washington, D.C. Cooke became majority owner in 1974 and the Redskins won three Super Bowls under his leadership, April 6.

The Barcelona Dragons defeated the Rhein Fire 38-24 to win the 1997 World Bowl in front of 31,100 fans at Estadi Olimpic de Montjuic in Barcelona, Spain, June 22.

NFL clubs approved the transfer of the Seattle Seahawks from Ken Behring to Paul Allen, August 19.

Jack Kent Cooke Stadium opened in Raljon, Maryland with a crowd of 78,270 as the Washington Redskins defeated the Arizona Cardinals 19-13 in overtime, September 14.

The 10,000th regular-season game in NFL history was played when the Seattle Seahawks defeated the Tennessee Oilers 16-13 at the Kingdome in Seattle, October 5.

Atlanta Falcons owner Rankin Smith died of heart failure three days prior to his seventy-third birthday. Smith was the founder of the Falcons and was instrumental in bringing Super Bowls XXVIII and XXXIV to Atlanta, October 26.

1998
The NFL reached agreement on record eight-year television contracts with four networks. ABC (*NFL Monday Night Football*) and FOX (NFC) retained their previous rights, CBS took over the AFC package from NBC, and ESPN won the right to broadcast the entire Sunday night cable package, January 13.

The World League was renamed the NFL Europe League, January 22.

The Denver Broncos won their first Super Bowl by defeating the defending champion Green Bay Packers 31-24 in Super Bowl XXXII at Qualcomm Stadium in San Diego, January 25.

The NFL clubs approved an extension of the Collective Bargaining Agreement through 2003. The extended CBA also created a $100 million fund for youth football, March 22.

The NFL clubs unanimously approved an expansion team for Cleveland to fulfill the commitment to return the Browns to the field in 1999, March 23.

The Rhein Fire defeated the Frankfurt Galaxy 34-10 to win the 1998 World Bowl in front of 47,846 fans in Frankfurt's Waldstadion—the biggest crowd to witness a World Bowl since 1991, June 14.

NFL clubs approved the transfer of the Minnesota Vikings from a 10-man ownership group to Red McCombs, July 28.

The NFL Stadium at Camden Yards opened in Baltimore, Maryland before a crowd of 65,938 as the Baltimore Ravens defeated the Chicago Bears 19-14 in a preseason game, August 8.

Raymond James Stadium opened in Tampa, Florida before a crowd of 62,410 as the Tampa Bay Buccaneers defeated the Chicago Bears 27-15, September 20.

Tennessee Oilers owner Bud Adams announced the team will change its name to the Tennessee Titans following the 1998 season. The NFL announced that the name Oilers will be retired—a first in league history, November 14.

1999
The Denver Broncos won their second consecutive Super Bowl title by defeating the NFC champion Atlanta Falcons 34-19 in Super Bowl XXXIII at Pro Player Stadium in Miami, January 31.

Jim Pyne, a center allocated by the Detroit Lions, was the first selection of the Cleveland Browns in the 1999 NFL Expansion Draft. The Browns eventually selected 37 players, February 9.

CBS Radio/Westwood One agreed to a 3-year extension of their exclusive national radio rights to NFL games, March 11.

By a vote of 28-3, the owners adopted an instant replay system as an officiating aid for the 1999 season, March 17.

New York Jets owner Leon Hess died from complications of a blood disease. Hess had been involved in the ownership of the Jets since 1963 and was sole owner of the club since 1984, May 9.

A group led by Washington area businessman Daniel Snyder is approved by NFL clubs as the new owner of the Washington Redskins at a league meeting in Atlanta, May

25.

The Frankfurt Galaxy became the first team in NFL Europe League history to win a second World Bowl by defeating the Barcelona Dragons 38-24 at Rheinstadion, in Düsseldorf, Germany, June 27.

The Cleveland Browns returned to the field for the first time since 1995 and defeated the Dallas Cowboys 20-17 in overtime in the annual Hall of Fame Game at Canton, Ohio, August 9.

Cleveland Browns Stadium opened in Cleveland, Ohio before a crowd of 71,398 as the Minnesota Vikings defeated the Browns in a preseason game, 24-17, August 21.

Adelphia Coliseum opened in Nashville, Tennessee before a crowd of 65,729 with the Tennessee Titans defeating the Atlanta Falcons 17-3 in a preseason game, August 26.

Houston, Texas and owner Robert McNair were awarded the NFL's thirty-second franchise in a vote of the NFL clubs at a league meeting in Atlanta. The team will begin play in 2002. The NFL clubs also voted to realign into eight divisions of four teams each for the 2002 season, October 6.

Walter Payton, the NFL's all-time leading rusher, died of liver cancer at the age of 45, November 1. The NFL Man of the Year Award, the only NFL award that recognizes a player for his community service activities as well as his excellence on the field, was renamed in his honor shortly after his passing.

Former NFL Commissioner Pete Rozelle, who guided a still-developing league to its position today as America's most popular sport, was named by *The Sporting News* as the most powerful person in sports in the 20th Century, December 15.

2000
New York businessman Robert Wood Johnson IV was approved by NFL clubs as the new owner of the New York Jets at a league meeting, January 18.

The St. Louis Rams won their first Super Bowl by defeating the AFC champion Tennessee Titans 23-16 in

Super Bowl XXXIV at the Georgia Dome in Atlanta, January 30.

For the first time in league history, paid attendance topped 16 million for the regular season and more than 65,000 per game, an increase of 1,300 per game over 1998. Paid attendance for all NFL games increased in 1999 for the third year in a row and was the highest ever in the 80-year history of the league. It marked the first time in league history that the 20-million paid attendance mark was reached for all games in a season, March 27.

The Rhein Fire won their second World Bowl in three years, defeating the Scottish Claymores 13-10 to win World Bowl 2000 in front of 35,680 at Frankfurt's Waldstadion, June 25.

More than 100 of the 136 living members of the Pro Football Hall of Fame gathered to celebrate Pro Football's Greatest Reunion in Canton, Ohio, July 28-31.

Paul Brown Stadium opened in Cincinnati, Ohio with a crowd of 56,180 as the Cincinnati Bengals defeated the Chicago Bears 24-20 in a preseason game, August 19.

Minnesota's Gary Anderson converted a 21-yard field goal against Buffalo to pass George Blanda as the NFL's all-time scoring leader with 2,004 points, October 22.

2001
NFL clubs approved additional league-wide revenue sharing at a special league meeting in Dallas. The teams agreed to pool the visiting team share of gate receipts for all preseason and regular-season games and divide the pool equally starting in 2002, January 17.

The Baltimore Ravens won their first Super Bowl by defeating the NFC champion New York Giants 34-7 in Super Bowl XXXV at Raymond James Stadium in Tampa Bay, January 28.

The *Sports Business Daily* named NFL Commissioner Paul Tagliabue the 2000 Sports Industrialist of the Year, February 28.

NFL owners unanimously approved a realignment plan for the league starting in 2002. With the addition of the

Houston Texans, the league's 32 teams will be divided into eight four-team divisions. Seven clubs change divisions, and the Seattle Seahawks change conferences, moving from the AFC to the NFC. A new scheduling format ensures that every team meets every other team in the league at least once every four years, May 22.

The Berlin Thunder won their first World Bowl, defeating the Barcelona Dragons 24-17 to win World Bowl IX in front of 32,116 at Amsterdam ArenA, June 30.

Heinz Field opened in Pittsburgh, Pennsylvania before a crowd of 57,829 with the Pittsburgh Steelers defeating the Detroit Lions 20-7 in a preseason game; and INVESCO Field at Mile High opened in Denver, Colorado before a crowd of 74,063 with the Denver Broncos defeating the New Orleans Saints 31-24 in a preseason game, August 25.

President George W. Bush became the first United States President to be involved in an NFL regular-season pregame coin toss as he helped kick off the 2001 season from the White House. Via satellite, President Bush tossed the coin for the 10 regular-season games that started at 1:00 P.M. ET, September 9.

In the wake of the September 11 terrorist attacks, Commissioner Paul Tagliabue postponed the games scheduled for September 16-17, September 13.

The league's 16-game regular season was rescheduled when the postponed Week 2 games were rescheduled for the weekend of January 6-7, September 18.

The NFL and its game officials agreed to a new six-year Collective Bargaining Agreement, ending a two-week lockout of the regular officials, who returned to work on September 23, September 19.

The NFL announced that the league's prohibition of anabolic steroids and related substances had been strengthened to include supplements containing ephedrine and other high-risk supplements, September 27.

The NFL announced that the Super Bowl would be rescheduled from January 27 to

February 3 in order to retain the full playoff format for the 2001 season. It will be the first Super Bowl played in February, October 3.

President Bush designated Super Bowl XXXVI as a "National Special Security Event," allowing all security for the game to be coordinated by the Secret Service, November 26.

2002
The NFL and the NFL Players Association agreed to a fourth extension of the 1993 Collective Bargaining Agreement through 2007, January 7.

In an AFC Wild Card matchup, the Oakland Raiders defeated the New York Jets 38-24 in the NFL's first-ever primetime playoff game, January 12.

In a special meeting in New Orleans, NFL owners voted unanimously to approve the purchase of the Atlanta Falcons to Home Depot co-founder Arthur Blank, February 2.

The New England Patriots won their first Super Bowl by defeating the NFC champion St. Louis Rams 20-17 in Super Bowl XXXVI at the Louisiana Superdome in New Orleans. The game marked the first time in Super Bowl history that the winning points came on the final play, a 48-yard field goal by Patriots kicker Adam Vinatieri, February 3.

Tony Boselli, a five-time Pro Bowl tackle allocated by the Jacksonville Jaguars, was the first selection of the Houston Texans in the 2002 NFL Expansion Draft. The Texans selected 19 players, February 18.

The NFL and Westwood One/CBS Radio Sports announced the renewal of a multiyear agreement for Westwood One/CBS Radio Sports to continue as the exclusive network radio home of the NFL, April 9.

NFL Europe kicked off its tenth season with a record 254 players allocated by NFL clubs, April 13-14.

The Berlin Thunder became the first team to win consecutive World Bowls, defeating the Rhein Fire 26-20 to win World Bowl X in front of 53,109 fans at Rheinstadion, June 22.

Seahawks Stadium opened in Seattle, Washington with an attendance of 52,902 fans as the Indianapolis Colts defeated the Seattle Seahawks 28-10 in a preseason game, August 10.

Gillette Stadium opened in Foxboro, Massachusetts with a crowd of 68,436 fans as the New England Patriots defeated the Philadelphia Eagles 16-15 in a preseason game, August 17.

Reliant Stadium opened in Houston, Texas with 69,432 fans in attendance, the largest non-Super Bowl crowd to ever watch an NFL game in Houston as the Miami Dolphins defeated the Houston Texans 24-3 in a preseason game, August 24.

For the first time, the NFL season kicked off on a Thursday night in prime time as the San Francisco 49ers defeated the New York Giants 16-13 at Giants Stadium. The game was preceded by "NFL Kickoff Live From Times Square," presented by New York City and the NFL, a football and music festival honoring the resilient spirit of New York and America, September 5.

Week 1 of the 2002 season produced the highest-scoring and most competitive Kickoff Weekend in NFL history. The 16 games averaged 49.3 points per game. A total of 788 points and 89 touchdowns were scored, the most in league history for an opening weekend. Eleven of the 16 games were decided by one score (eight points or less), a Kickoff Weekend record, September 5-9.

Oakland Raiders wide receiver Jerry Rice became the all-time leader in yards from scrimmage, surpassing Pro Football Hall of Fame running back Walter Payton (21,281 yards), September 29.

Cleveland Browns owner Al Lerner, the NFL Finance Committee Chairman and Chairman and CEO of MBNA Corporation, died at the age of 69, October 23.

Dallas Cowboys running back Emmitt Smith became the NFL's all-time rushing leader, surpassing Pro Football Hall of Fame running back Walter Payton (16,726 yards), October 27.

The NFL and NFLPA announced the creation of USA Football, the first national advocacy organization representing all levels of amateur football, December 5.

NFL clubs implemented an expanded program to promote diversity in their coaching and front office ranks based upon recommendations of the NFL Committee on Workplace Diversity, December 19. The committee, appointed by Commissioner Tagliabue on October 31, comprised 10 owners and team executives with Pittsburgh Steelers owner Dan Rooney serving as chairman.

The 2002 season concluded with 25 overtime games, the most in NFL history, December 30.

2003

The Tampa Bay Buccaneers won their first Super Bowl by defeating the AFC champion Oakland Raiders 48-21 in Super Bowl XXXVII at Qualcomm Stadium in San Diego, January 26.

Chicago Bears chairman emeritus Edward W. McCaskey died at the age of 83, April 8.

The Frankfurt Galaxy became the first team to win three World Bowls, defeating the Rhein Fire 35-16 to win World Bowl XI in front of 28,138 fans at Hampden Park, June 14.

Tex Schramm, the legendary team president and general manager of the Dallas Cowboys and a member of the Pro Football Hall of Fame, died at the age of 83, July 15.

Lincoln Financial Field opened in Philadelphia, Pennsylvania with an attendance of 66,279 fans as the New England Patriots defeated the Philadelphia Eagles 24-12 in a preseason game, August 22.

A renovated Lambeau Field opened in Green Bay, Wisconsin with a crowd of 69,831 fans as the Carolina Panthers defeated the Green Bay Packers 20-7 in a preseason game, August 23.

A renovated Soldier Field opened in Chicago, Illinois with an attendance of 61,500 fans as the Green Bay Packers defeated the Chicago Bears 38-23 in a regular season game on ABC's *NFL Monday Night Football*, September 29.

NFL Network, the first 24-hour, year-round television channel dedicated to the NFL and the sport of football, launched on DirecTV, November 4.

2004

The New England Patriots won their second Super Bowl in three years by defeating the NFC champion Carolina Panthers 32-29 in Super Bowl XXXVIII at Reliant Stadium in Houston, February 1.

By a vote of 29-3, NFL owners extended the instant replay system for another five seasons through 2008, March 30.

Steve Bisciotti took over as the controlling owner of the Baltimore Ravens, succeeding Art Modell, who operated the franchise for 43 years, April 8.

Former Arizona Cardinals safety Pat Tillman was killed in a firefight while on combat patrol with the U.S. Army Rangers in Afghanistan, April 22.

A federal appeals court formally ruled in favor of NFL's draft eligibility rule in Maurice Clarett's lawsuit, citing federal labor policy in permitting the NFL and the Players Association to set rules for when players can enter the league, May 24.

The Berlin Thunder defeated the Frankfurt Galaxy 30-24 to win World Bowl XII in front of 35,413 fans at Arena AufSchalke, June 12.

The New England Patriots defeated the New York Jets 13-7 for their NFL-record 18th consecutive regular-season victory, October 24.

The NFL reached an agreement on six-year contract extensions with two of its network television partners—CBS and FOX—to run through the 2011 season, November 8.

The NFL and DirecTV announced a five-year extension on the NFL Sunday Ticket subscription television package to run through the 2010 season, November 8.

NFL Europe named the Hamburg Sea Devils as the league's newest team, November 24.

2005

Indianapolis Colts quarterback Peyton Manning set the NFL single-season record with 49 touchdown passes, January 2.

The New England Patriots became the second team in NFL history to win three Super Bowls in four seasons by defeating the Philadelphia Eagles 24-21 in Super Bowl XXXIX at ALLTEL Stadium in Jacksonville, February 6.

The Pat Tillman USO Center opened in Afghanistan. The NFL donated $250,000 to the USO to honor the memory of the former Arizona Cardinals player who died in Afghanistan while serving in the U.S. Army, April 1.

The NFL reached long-term agreements for its Sunday and Monday primetime TV packages. NBC returned to the NFL by acquiring the Sunday night package for six years (2006-2011). ESPN agreed on an eight-year deal to televise *Monday Night Football* from 2006-2013, April 18.

The NFL strengthened its steroids program by adopting the Olympic testosterone testing standard, tripling the number of times a player can be randomly tested during the offseason from two to six, adding substances to the list of banned substances, and putting new language in the policy to allow for testing of designer drugs and other substances that may have evaded detection, April 27.

NFL owners voted unanimously to approve the sale of the Minnesota Vikings to real-estate developer Zygi Wilf, May 25.

The Amsterdam Admirals defeated the Berlin Thunder 27-21 to win World Bowl XIII in front of 35,134 fans at LTU Arena in Düsseldorf, Germany, June 11.

The NFL designated September 18-19 as "Hurricane Relief Weekend," which concluded with a telethon in conjunction with a Monday Night Football doubleheader on ABC and ESPN. The New York Giants-New Orleans Saints game, originally scheduled for the Louisiana Superdome, was moved to Giants Stadium following Hurricane Katrina. In total, the NFL, its owners, teams, players, and fans contributed $21 million to aid the Hurricane Katrina rebuilding effort, September 19.

An NFL record 103,467

fans attended the Arizona Cardinals' 31-14 victory over the San Francisco 49ers at Mexico City's Azteca Stadium, the first-ever regular-season NFL game played outside the United States, October 2.

Wellington Mara, the New York Giants' president and co-chief executive officer, died at the age of 89, October 25.

Preston Robert Tisch, the Giants' chairman and co-chief executive officer, died at the age of 79, November 15.

2006

The NFL announced that NFL Network would begin airing a "Road To The Playoffs" package of eight primetime regular season NFL games starting in 2006, January 28.

The Pittsburgh Steelers won their fifth Super Bowl, defeating the Seattle Seahawks 21-10 in Super Bowl XL at Ford Field in Detroit, Michigan, February 5.

The NFL clubs approved an extension of the Collective Bargaining Agreement through 2012, March 8.

Commissioner Tagliabue announced his decision to retire by the end of July. The NFL enjoyed an era of unrivaled prosperity in the Tagliabue Era, including labor peace throughout his 17-year tenure, March 20.

NFL clubs unanimously decided to return the name of the official game ball to "The Duke" in honor of the late New York Giants owner Wellington Mara, March 27.

The Amsterdam Admirals defeated the Berlin Thunder 22-7 to win World Bowl XIV in front of 36,286 fans at LTU Arena in Düsseldorf, Germany, May 27.

Roger Goodell became the eighth chief executive of the NFL on August 8 when he was chosen to succeed Paul Tagliabue as commissioner by a unanimous vote of the clubs at a three-day meeting in Chicago, Illinois. The transfer from Commissioner Tagliabue to Commissioner Goodell took place at 6:00 A.M. on Friday, September 1.

Cardinals Stadium opened in Glendale, Arizona with a crowd of 63,400 fans on August 12 as the Arizona Cardinals defeated the Pittsburgh Steelers 21-13 in a preseason

game. The facility was later renamed University of Phoenix Stadium on September 26.

President George W. Bush signed into law HR 4954, which included the Internet Gambling Prohibition and Enforcement Act. The bill prohibits online gamblers from using credit cards, checks and electronic fund transfers to place and settle bets, strengthening enforcement of federal and state gambling laws that had been evaded by overseas gambling operations using the Internet, October 13.

NFL owners approved a resolution to stage a limited number of international regular-season games—up to two per season—beginning in 2007 and continuing through 2011, October 24.

The NFL Network broadcast its first-ever regular-season game as the Kansas City Chiefs defeated the Denver Broncos 19-10 at Arrowhead Stadium on Thanksgiving night, November 23.

San Diego Chargers running back LaDainian Tomlinson set the NFL single-season record for touchdowns with 29 on December 10. He finished the season with 31 touchdowns and also set a single-season record for points with 186.

Lamar Hunt, founder of the Kansas City Chiefs and the American Football League, died at the age of 74, December 13.

2007

The Indianapolis Colts won their second Super Bowl, defeating the Chicago Bears 29-17 in Super Bowl XLI at Dolphin Stadium in South Florida, February 4. Both teams were coached by African-Americans: Tony Dungy of the Colts and Lovie Smith of the Bears.

NFL clubs approved additional league-wide revenue sharing at a league meeting in Phoenix, Arizona. The teams agreed to redistribute up to $430 million over a four-year span, retroactive to 2006, March 26.

The NFL announced changes to its long-standing personal conduct policy and programs for players, coaches, and other team and league employees. The modifications

focus on expanded educational and support programs in addition to increased levels of discipline for violations of the policy, April 10.

The NFL, NFL Players Association, NFL Retired Players Association, NFL Alumni Association, NFL Charities and Pro Football Hall of Fame formed the first-ever Alliance to coordinate medical support services for former players, May 22.

The Hamburg Sea Devils defeated the Frankfurt Galaxy 37-28 to win World Bowl XV in front of 48,125 fans at Commerzbank-Arena in Frankfurt, Germany, June 23.

The NFL announced it will focus its international business strategy on reaching the widest possible global audience, including the staging of international regular-season games, and discontinued NFL Europa after 15 seasons of operation, June 29.

NFL owners unanimously approved $10 million in additional Alliance funding for retired players to help pay for joint replacement surgeries and other medical assistance, supplementing the initial $7 million committed in July by Alliance members, October 24.

The New York Giants defeated the Miami Dolphins 13-10 at London's in front of 81,176 fans at Wembley Stadium in the first regular-season game played outside of North America, October 28.

On the field in the 2007 season, many significant records and milestones were achieved: Green Bay quarterback Brett Favre surpassed Pro Football Hall of Famer Dan Marino in both passing categories—touchdowns and yards—to become the NFL's all-time career leader. Patriots quarterback Tom Brady set the single-season record with 50 touchdown passes, including 23 to wide receiver Randy Moss—also a record. New England, which became the first team ever to finish 16-0 in the regular season, scored a record 589 points.

2008

The NFL, United States Olympic Committee, United States Anti-Doping Agency and MLB announced a part-

nership to form a clean competition anti-doping research collaborative, January 10.

Georgia Frontiere, majority owner of the St. Louis Rams, died at the age of 80, January 18.

The NFL announced it will stage a regular-season game in the United Kingdom during each of the next three seasons, beginning with the New Orleans Saints hosting the San Diego Chargers on October 26, 2008 at London's Wembley Stadium, February 1.

The New York Giants scored with 35 seconds remaining to win their third Super Bowl, defeating the New England Patriots 17-14 in Super Bowl XLII at University of Phoenix Stadium in Glendale, Arizona, February 3.

The NFL set an all-time paid attendance record in 2007 for the sixth consecutive season. Attendance for all 2007 games was 22,256,502, an increase of 56,790 over the previous mark. The Washington Redskins set an all-time NFL regular-season home paid attendance record of 711,471 for eight games, breaking their own record of 708,852 in 2006.

NFL clubs voted unanimously to exercise their option to shorten by two years the current Collective Bargaining Agreement, which now will run through the 2010 season and 2011 NFL Draft, May 20.

Lucas Oil Stadium opened in Indianapolis, Indiana with a crowd of 65,333 as the Buffalo Bills defeated the Indianapolis Colts by a score of 20-7 in a preseason game, August 24.

The NFL established a new fan code of conduct to help support a positive fan environment at all NFL stadiums, August 5.

NFLPA Executive Director and Pro Football Hall of Famer Gene Upshaw died at the age of 63, August 20.

For the first time, an NFL game was broadcast on NBC and also streamed live in its entirety to fans on the Internet via NFL.com and NBCSports.com as the Giants beat the Redskins 16-7 in the 2009 NFL Kickoff game, September 4.

Owners approved a restructured ownership plan for the Pittsburgh Steelers that will keep the team under the control of chairman Dan Rooney and team president Art Rooney II, December 17.

The NFL announced that the 2010 Pro Bowl will be played a week prior to Super Bowl XLIV on Sunday, January 31, 2010. Both games will be played in South Florida, December 30.

In the 256 regular-season games of 2008, 44.1 points per game were scored—the highest average since 1970.

2009

Stephen M. Ross purchased an additional 45 percent of the Miami Dolphins from Wayne Huizenga and became the team's managing partner. Coupled with his April 1, 2008 purchase of 50 percent of the franchise, the stadium, and the excess developable land, Ross now owns 95 percent of the Dolphins and the stadium while Huizenga retains a five percent share of both and remains a 50 percent partner in that land, January 20.

The NFL re-named its minority coaching internship program the Bill Walsh NFL Minority Coaching Fellowship, honoring the Pro Football Hall of Fame coach who conceived of the program, January 29.

The Pittsburgh Steelers scored a touchdown with 42 seconds remaining to claim their NFL-record sixth Super Bowl title, defeating the Arizona Cardinals 27-23 in Super Bowl XLIII at Raymond James Stadium in Tampa Bay, February 1.

The NFL and Westwood One announced a new two-year agreement for Westwood One to continue as the exclusive network radio partner of the NFL, March 12.

The NFLPA selected Washington-based attorney DeMaurice Smith as its new executive director, March 16.

The NFL and DIRECTV announced an agreement to extend DIRECTV's rights to carry NFL Sunday Ticket through the 2014 season, March 23.

The NFL reached an agreement on two-year contract extensions with two of its network television partners – CBS and FOX – to run through the 2013 season, May 19.

The NFL extended its broadcast partnership with NBC to televise the

Sunday night package through the 2013 season, August 19.

Cowboys Stadium opened in Arlington, Texas with a crowd of 75,720 as the Dallas Cowboys defeated the Tennessee Titans by a score of 30-10 in a preseason game, August 21.

The NFL announced games that were blacked out in home team markets during the 2009 season would be shown on NFL.com in their entirety on a delayed basis, September 10.

The NFL launched a new "Red Zone Channel," offering fans crucial live action cut-ins of all Sunday afternoon games, September 13.

Pro Football Hall of Fame head coach and broadcaster John Madden was appointed special advisor to Commissioner Goodell, September 10.

NFL appointed former head coach Tony Dungy to lead a new NFL Player Advisory Forum and serve as a special advisor to Commissioner Goodell, November 19.

Commissioner Goodell notified NFL teams of new and expanded guidelines on return-to-play for any player who sustains a concussion, December 2.

2010

For the first time, the Pro Bowl was played in the Super Bowl city the week before the Super Bowl, as the AFC All-Stars beat the NFC All-Stars 41-34 in the 2010 Pro Bowl at Sun Life Stadium in South Florida. The game drew 70,697 fans – the highest attendance for a Pro Bowl since 1959, January 31.

The New Orleans Saints won their first Super Bowl title, defeating the Indianapolis Colts 31-17 in Super Bowl XLIV at Sun Life Stadium in South Florida, February 7.

Dr. Hunt Batjer of Northwestern University Feinberg School of Medicine and Dr. Richard G. Ellenbogen of the University of Washington School of Medicine were named the new co-chairs of the NFL Head, Neck and Spine Medical Committee, March 16.

NFL owners voted to amend postseason overtime rules to a modified sudden death format, guaranteeing at least one possession for each club if the receiving team fails to score a

touchdown on its first overtime possession, March 23.

The NFL and NFL Alumni Association announced a new neurological care program for retired players, one of a series of NFL initiatives addressing the quality of life of retired players, March 24.

NFL rules changes emphasized additional player safety. Protection for defenseless players was standardized and expanded, protecting a player who has just completed a catch from blows to the head or neck by an opponent who launches. Additional protection was also given to longsnappers. Play will now stop if a ball carrier's helmet is removed, March 24.

The NFL Draft debuted a new three-day format, with the first two days broadcast in primetime. A record combined total of 45.4 million viewers tuned in to watch the 75th NFL Draft on NFL Network, ESPN and ESPN2, April 22-24.

New Meadowlands Stadium opened in East Rutherford, New Jersey as the New York Giants defeat the New York Jets by a score of 31-16 in a preseason game, August 16.

Stan Kroenke purchased an additional 60 percent of the St. Louis Rams from the Rosenbloom family and became the team's sole owner and chairman, August 25.

A renovated Arrowhead Stadium opened in Kansas City, Missouri as the Philadelphia Eagles defeated the Kansas City Chiefs 20-17 in a preseason game, August 27.

A poster created by the NFL and the Centers for Disease Control and Prevention (CDC) to help educate young athletes on concussions was released to the public. The poster, similar to one on display in NFL locker rooms, stresses the importance of recognizing a concussion, taking time to recover, and not returning to play too soon, October 11.

The NFL, NFL Alumni and Gay Culverhouse Players' Outreach Program announced a partnership to expand services for retired NFL players. The outreach program identifies retired players in need, ensuring they receive comprehensive medical evaluations and assistance in applying for the expanded benefits and ser-

vices created in recent years by the NFL, October 12.

Commissioner Roger Goodell notified NFL teams that more significant discipline, including suspensions, would be imposed on players that strike an opponent in the head or neck area in violation of the rules, October 20.

The NFL and Westwood One Radio announced the renewal of a multi-year agreement for Westwood One to continue as the exclusive network radio home of the NFL, December 22.

2011

The NFL appointed Pro Football Hall of Famers Ronnie Lott and John Madden as co-chairs of a new Player Safety Advisory Panel. The panel provides recommendations on a variety of safety-related football matters, while taking a long-term view towards making the game safer at every level of the sport, January 4.

The Green Bay Packers won their fourth Super Bowl title, defeating the Pittsburgh Steelers 31-25 in Super Bowl XLV at Cowboys Stadium in North Texas, February 6.

The NFL Head, Neck and Spine Committee announced a new standardized sideline concussion assessment protocol for team medical personnel. The new protocol includes a symptom checklist, limited neurologic examination and balance assessment, February 25.

On the steps of the Pro Football Hall of Fame in Canton, Ohio, Commissioner Goodell & NFLPA Executive Director DeMaurice Smith formally announced a comprehensive settlement of litigation and signed a new 10-year Collective Bargaining Agreement, August 4. The agreement included additional funding for player alumni of $1 billion, including a $620 million "Legacy Fund" to increase benefits for pre-1993 retirees.

A record 107.4 million fans tuned into Kickoff Weekend games on CBS, ESPN, FOX and NBC, September 8, 11-12.

The NFL announced an eight-year extension of its contract with ESPN for the broadcast rights to Monday Night Football through the 2021 season, September 8.

NFL teams, players and fans remembered the courage and resilience that followed the events of September 11, 2001 with special tributes in each stadium and on television during all games on Sunday, September 11.

Al Davis, the Oakland Raiders' owner and Pro Football Hall of Famer, died at the age of 82, October 8.

NFL owners approved a resolution to continue playing regular-season games in the United Kingdom through the 2016 season, October 11.

The NFL reached an agreement on nine-year contract extensions of its Sunday broadcast television packages with CBS, FOX and NBC to run through the 2022 season, December 14. The agreements also enabled the NFL to expand its Thursday night package of games on NFL Network, which increased from eight to 13 games for the 2012 season.

NFL clubs unanimously approved the majority ownership transfer of the Jacksonville Jaguars from Wayne Weaver to businessman Shahid Khan at a meeting in Dallas, December 14.

2012

NFL clubs extended Commissioner Goodell's contract through March 31, 2019, January 25.

The New York Giants won their fourth Super Bowl title, defeating the New England Patriots 21-17 in Super Bowl XLVI at Lucas Oil Stadium in Indianapolis, February 5.

The NFL announced a new comprehensive health program, NFL Total Wellness, for former and current players to provide additional resources for physical and mental health issues, July 26.

Art Modell, former owner of the Cleveland Browns-Baltimore Ravens franchise and longtime chairman of the NFL's Broadcast Committee, died at the age of 87, September 6.

NFL Network's *Thursday Night Football* schedule was expanded from eight to 13 regular-season games, debuting with the Green Bay Packers' 23-10 victory against the Chicago Bears, September 13.

The NFL announced an extension of its exclusive radio broadcast agreement with Dial Global through the 2017 season, September 20.

NFL Films President Steve Sabol died at the age of 69, September 18.

The NFL and its game officials agreed to a new eight-year Collective Bargaining Agreement, ending a four-month dispute. The union officials returned to work for Week 4, September 27.

NFL clubs unanimously approved the majority ownership transfer of the Cleveland Browns from Randy Lerner to Jimmy Haslam at a meeting in Chicago, October 16.

The NFL announced the formation of the National Football League Foundation to focus on youth football, health and safety, and community, December 12. The newly created Foundation resulted from the restructuring of the NFL's previous charitable arms – NFL Charities and the NFL Youth Football Fund.

2013

The Baltimore Ravens won their second Super Bowl, defeating the San Francisco 49ers 34-31 in Super Bowl XLVII at the Mercedes-Benz Superdome in New Orleans, February 3.

GE and the NFL announced the Head Health Initiative, a four-year, $60 million collaboration to advance diagnostic tools for treating concussions and the development of new materials for head protection, March 11.

Tennessee Titans owner K.S. "Bud" Adams, Jr. a founding member of the AFL, died at the age of 90, October 21.

On the field, many all-time records were set: 11,985 points were scored, the most of any season in NFL history; games averaged an all-time high 697.0 total net yards per game; and Denver's Peyton Manning passed for 5,477 yards and 55 touchdowns.

2014

The 2014 Pro Bowl introduced a new format for the NFL's All-Star Game, including a draft to determine rosters and major playing rules adjustments. Pro Football Hall of Famers Jerry Rice and Deion Sanders served as team captains. Team Rice defeated Team Sanders 22-21 at Aloha Stadium in Honolulu, Hawaii, January 26.

The Seattle Seahawks won their first Super Bowl, defeating the Denver Broncos 43-8 in Super Bowl XLVIII at MetLife Stadium in the first New York-New Jersey Super Bowl. The game was viewed by an average audience of 112.2 million people, making it the most-watched program in U.S. television history, February 2.

William Clay Ford, Sr., the chairman and owner of the Detroit Lions, died at the age of 88, March 9.

Buffalo Bills owner Ralph Wilson, Jr., a founding member of the AFL, died at the age of 95, March 25.

In addition to its Sunday afternoon package, CBS acquired the rights to broadcast early-season primetime *Thursday Night Football* games, simulcast by NFL Network, for the 2014 season, February 5. NFL Network retained exclusive rights to late-season *TNF* games.

Malcolm Glazer, the owner and president of the Tampa Bay Buccaneers, died at the age of 85, May 28.

NFL COMMISSIONERS AND PRESIDENTS*

1920	Jim Thorpe, President
1921-39	Joe Carr, President
1939-41	Carl Storck, President
1941-46	Elmer Layden, Commissioner
1946-1959	Bert Bell, Commissioner
1960-1989	Pete Rozelle, Commissioner
1989-2006	Paul Tagliabue, Commissioner
2006-present	Roger Goodell, Commissioner

*NFL treasurer Austin Gunsel served as president in the office of the commissioner following the death of Bert Bell (Oct. 11, 1959) until the election of Pete Rozelle (Jan. 26, 1960).

2013

AMERICAN FOOTBALL CONFERENCE

East Division

	W	L	T	Pct.	Pts.	OP
New England	12	4	0	.750	444	338
New York Jets	8	8	0	.500	290	387
Miami	8	8	0	.500	317	335
Buffalo	6	10	0	.375	339	388

North Division

	W	L	T	Pct.	Pts.	OP
Cincinnati	11	5	0	.688	430	305
Pittsburgh	8	8	0	.500	379	370
Baltimore	8	6	0	.500	320	352
Cleveland	4	12	0	.250	308	406

South Division

	W	L	T	Pct.	Pts.	OP
Indianapolis	11	5	0	.688	391	336
Tennessee	7	9	0	.438	362	381
Jacksonville	4	12	0	.250	247	449
Houston	2	14	0	.125	276	428

West Division

	W	L	T	Pct.	Pts.	OP
Denver#	13	3	0	.813	606	399
Kansas City*	11	5	0	.688	430	305
San Diego*	9	7	0	.563	396	348
Oakland	4	12	0	.250	322	453

NATIONAL FOOTBALL CONFERENCE

East Division

	W	L	T	Pct.	Pts.	OP
Philadelphia	10	6	0	.625	442	382
Dallas	8	8	0	.500	439	432
New York Giants	7	9	0	.438	294	383
Washington	3	13	0	.188	334	478

North Division

	W	L	T	Pct.	Pts.	OP
Green Bay	8	7	1	.531	417	428
Chicago	8	8	0	.500	445	478
Detroit	7	9	0	.438	395	376
Minnesota	5	10	1	.344	391	480

South Division

	W	L	T	Pct.	Pts.	OP
Carolina	12	4	0	.750	366	241
New Orleans*	11	5	0	.688	414	304
Atlanta	4	12	0	.250	353	443
Tampa Bay	4	12	0	.250	288	389

West Division

	W	L	T	Pct.	Pts.	OP
Seattle#	13	3	0	.813	417	231
San Francisco*	12	4	0	.750	406	272
Arizona	10	6	0	.625	379	324
St. Louis	7	9	0	.438	348	364

*Wild Card qualifier for playoffs; #Top playoff seed in conference
Cincinnati finished ahead of Indianapolis based on head-to-head victory. New York Jets finished ahead of Miami based on better division record (3-3 to Dolphins' 2-4). Pittsburgh finished ahead of Baltimore based on better division record (4-2 to Ravens' 3-3). Atlanta finished ahead of Tampa Bay based on better conference record (3-9 to Buccaneers' 2-10).
Wild Card Playoff Games: INDIANAPOLIS 45, Kansas City 44; San Diego 27, CINCINNATI 10
Divisional Playoff Games: NEW ENGLAND 43, Indianapolis 22; DENVER 24, San Diego 17
AFC Championship Game: DENVER 26, New England 16
Wild Card Playoff Games: New Orleans 26, PHILADELPHIA 24; San Francisco 23, GREEN BAY 20
Divisional Playoff Games: SEATTLE 23, New Orleans 15; San Francisco 23, CAROLINA 10
NFC Championship Game: SEATTLE 23, San Francisco 17
Super Bowl XLVII: Seattle (NFC) 43, Denver (AFC) 8 at MetLife Stadium, New York-New Jersey

In Past Standings section, home teams in playoff games are indicated by capital letters.

Playoff Seeds

AFC	NFC
1. **Denver**	1. **Seattle**
2. New England	2. Carolina
3. Cincinnati	3. Philadelphia
4. Indianapolis	4. Green Bay
5. Kansas City	5. San Francisco
6. San Diego	6. New Orleans

2012

AMERICAN CONFERENCE

East Division

	W	L	T	Pct.	Pts.	OP
New England	12	4	0	.750	557	331
Miami	7	9	0	.438	288	317
New York Jets	6	10	0	.375	281	375
Buffalo	6	10	0	.375	344	435

North Division

	W	L	T	Pct.	Pts.	OP
Baltimore	10	6	0	.625	398	344
Cincinnati*	10	6	0	.625	391	320
Pittsburgh	8	8	0	.500	336	314
Cleveland	5	11	0	.313	302	368

South Division

	W	L	T	Pct.	Pts.	OP
Houston	12	4	0	.750	416	331
Indianapolis*	11	5	0	.688	357	387
Tennessee	6	10	0	.375	330	471
Jacksonville	2	14	0	.125	255	444

West Division

	W	L	T	Pct.	Pts.	OP
Denver#	13	3	0	.813	481	289
San Diego	7	9	0	.438	350	350
Oakland	4	12	0	.250	290	443
Kansas City	2	14	0	.125	211	425

NATIONAL CONFERENCE

East Division

	W	L	T	Pct.	Pts.	OP
Washington	10	6	0	.625	436	388
New York Giants	9	7	0	.563	429	344
Dallas	8	8	0	.500	376	400
Philadelphia	4	12	0	.250	280	444

North Division

	W	L	T	Pct.	Pts.	OP
Green Bay	11	5	0	.688	433	336
Minnesota*	10	6	0	.625	379	348
Chicago	10	6	0	.625	375	277
Detroit	4	12	0	.250	372	437

South Division

	W	L	T	Pct.	Pts.	OP
Atlanta#	13	3	0	.813	419	299
Carolina	7	9	0	.438	357	363
New Orleans	7	9	0	.438	461	454
Tampa Bay	7	9	0	.438	389	394

West Division

	W	L	T	Pct.	Pts.	OP
San Francisco	11	4	1	.719	397	273
Seattle*	11	5	0	.688	412	245
St. Louis	7	8	1	.469	299	348
Arizona	5	11	0	.313	250	357

*Wild Card qualifier for playoffs; #Top playoff seed in conference
New York Jets finished ahead of Buffalo based on better record in common games (5-7 to Bills' 3-9). Baltimore finished ahead of Cincinnati based on better division record (4-2 to Bengals' 3-3). New England finished ahead of Houston based on head-to-head victory. Minnesota finished ahead of Chicago based on better division record (4-2 to Bears' 3-3). Carolina finished ahead of New Orleans and Tampa Bay based on better record against common opponents than Tampa Bay (6-4 to Buccaneers' 5-5) and head-to-head sweep over the Saints. New Orleans finished ahead of Tampa Bay based on head-to-head sweep.
Wild Card Playoff Games: HOUSTON 19, Cincinnati 13; BALTIMORE 24, Indianapolis 9
Divisional Playoff Games: NEW ENGLAND 41, Houston 28; Baltimore 38, DENVER 35 (2 OT)
AFC Championship Game: Baltimore 28, NEW ENGLAND 13
Wild Card Playoff Games: GREEN BAY 24, Minnesota 10; Seattle 24, WASHINGTON 14
Divisional Playoff Games: ATLANTA 30, Seattle 28; SAN FRANCISCO 45, Green Bay 31
NFC Championship Game: San Francisco 28, ATLANTA 24
Super Bowl XLVII: Baltimore (AFC) 34, San Francisco (NFC) 31 at Mercedes-Benz Superdome, New Orleans, Louisiana

Playoff Seeds

AFC	NFC
1. Denver	1. Atlanta
2. New England	2. **San Francisco**
3. Houston	3. Green Bay
4. **Baltimore**	4. Washington
5. Indianapolis	5. Seattle
6. Cincinnati	6. Minnesota

2011

AMERICAN CONFERENCE

East Division

	W	L	T	Pct.	Pts.	OP
New England#	13	3	0	.813	513	342
New York Jets	8	8	0	.500	377	363
Miami	6	10	0	.375	329	313
Buffalo	6	10	0	.375	372	434

North Division

	W	L	T	Pct.	Pts.	OP
Baltimore	12	4	0	.750	378	266
Pittsburgh*	12	4	0	.750	325	227
Cincinnati*	9	7	0	.563	344	323
Cleveland	4	12	0	.250	218	307

South Division

	W	L	T	Pct.	Pts.	OP
Houston	10	6	0	.625	381	278
Tennessee	9	7	0	.563	325	317
Jacksonville	5	11	0	.313	243	329
Indianapolis	2	14	0	.125	243	430

West Division

	W	L	T	Pct.	Pts.	OP
Denver	8	8	0	.500	309	390
San Diego	8	8	0	.500	406	377
Oakland	8	8	0	.500	359	433
Kansas City	7	9	0	.438	212	338

NATIONAL CONFERENCE

East Division

	W	L	T	Pct.	Pts.	OP
New York Giants	9	7	0	.563	394	400
Philadelphia	8	8	0	.500	396	328
Dallas	8	8	0	.500	369	347
Washington	5	11	0	.313	288	367

North Division

	W	L	T	Pct.	Pts.	OP
Green Bay#	15	1	0	.938	560	359
Detroit*	10	6	0	.625	474	387
Chicago	8	8	0	.500	353	341
Minnesota	3	13	0	.188	340	449

South Division

	W	L	T	Pct.	Pts.	OP
New Orleans	13	3	0	.813	547	339
Atlanta*	10	6	0	.625	402	350
Carolina	6	10	0	.375	406	429
Tampa Bay	4	12	0	.250	287	494

West Division

	W	L	T	Pct.	Pts.	OP
San Francisco	13	3	0	.813	380	229
Arizona	8	8	0	.500	312	348
Seattle	7	9	0	.438	321	315
St. Louis	2	14	0	.125	193	407

*Wild Card qualifier for playoffs; #Top playoff seed in conference
Miami finished ahead of Buffalo based on head-to-head sweep.
Baltimore finished ahead of Pittsburgh based on head-to-head sweep. Denver finished ahead of San Diego and Oakland based on best record in common games (Denver 5-5; Oakland 4-6; San Diego 4-6). San Diego finished ahead of Oakland based on better conference record (7-5 to Raiders' 6-6). Cincinnati finished ahead of Tennessee based on head-to-head victory. Philadelphia finished ahead of Dallas based on head-to-head sweep. Atlanta finished ahead of Detroit based on head-to-head victory. San Francisco finished ahead of New Orleans based on better conference record (10-2 to Saints' 9-3).

Wild Card Playoff Games: HOUSTON 31, Cincinnati 10; DENVER 29, Pittsburgh 23 (OT)
Divisional Playoff Games: NEW ENGLAND 45, Denver 10; BALTIMORE 20, Houston 13
AFC Championship Game: NEW ENGLAND 23, Baltimore 20
Wild Card Playoff Games: NEW ORLEANS 45, Detroit 28; NEW YORK GIANTS 24, Atlanta 2
Divisional Playoff Games: SAN FRANCISCO 36, New Orleans 32; New York Giants 37, GREEN BAY 20
NFC Championship Game: New York Giants 20, SAN FRANCISCO 17 (OT)
Super Bowl XLVI: New York Giants (NFC) 21, New England (AFC) 17 at Lucas Oil Stadium, Indianapolis

Playoff Seeds

AFC	NFC
1. New England	1. Green Bay
2. Baltimore	2. San Francisco
3. Houston	3. New Orleans
4. Denver	**4. New York Giants**
5. Pittsburgh	5. Atlanta
6. Cincinnati	6. Detroit

2010

AMERICAN CONFERENCE

East Division

	W	L	T	Pct.	Pts.	OP
New England#	14	2	0	.875	518	313
New York Jets*	11	5	0	.688	367	304
Miami	7	9	0	.438	273	333
Buffalo	4	12	0	.250	283	425

North Division

	W	L	T	Pct.	Pts.	OP
Pittsburgh	12	4	0	.750	375	232
Baltimore*	12	4	0	.750	357	270
Cleveland	5	11	0	.313	271	332
Cincinnati	4	12	0	.250	322	395

South Division

	W	L	T	Pct.	Pts.	OP
Indianapolis	10	6	0	.625	435	388
Jacksonville	8	8	0	.500	353	419
Houston	6	10	0	.375	390	427
Tennessee	6	10	0	.375	356	339

West Division

	W	L	T	Pct.	Pts.	OP
Kansas City	10	6	0	.625	366	326
San Diego	9	7	0	.563	441	322
Oakland	8	8	0	.500	410	371
Denver	4	12	0	.250	344	471

NATIONAL CONFERENCE

East Division

	W	L	T	Pct.	Pts.	OP
Philadelphia	10	6	0	.625	439	377
New York Giants	10	6	0	.625	394	347
Dallas	6	10	0	.375	394	436
Washington	6	10	0	.375	302	377

North Division

	W	L	T	Pct.	Pts.	OP
Chicago	11	5	0	.688	334	286
Green Bay*	10	6	0	.625	388	240
Detroit	6	10	0	.375	362	369
Minnesota	6	10	0	.375	281	348

South Division

	W	L	T	Pct.	Pts.	OP
Atlanta#	13	3	0	.813	414	288
New Orleans*	11	5	0	.688	384	307
Tampa Bay	10	6	0	.625	341	318
Carolina	2	14	0	.125	196	408

West Division

	W	L	T	Pct.	Pts.	OP
Seattle	7	9	0	.438	310	407
St. Louis	7	9	0	.438	289	328
San Francisco	6	10	0	.375	305	346
Arizona	5	11	0	.313	289	434

*Wild Card qualifier for playoffs; #Top playoff seed in conference
Pittsburgh finished ahead of Baltimore based on better division record (5-1 to 4-2). Indianapolis finished ahead of Kansas City based on head-to-head victory. Houston finished ahead of Tennessee based on better division record (3-3 to 2-4). Philadelphia finished ahead of the Giants based on head-to-head sweep. Dallas finished ahead of Washington based on better division record (3-3 to 2-4). Green Bay finished ahead of the Giants and Tampa Bay based on best strength of victory Green Bay .475; Giants .400; Tampa Bay .344). Detroit finished ahead of Minnesota based on better division record (2-4 to 1-5). Seattle finished ahead of St. Louis based on better division record (4-2 to 3-3).

Wild Card Playoff Games: N.Y. Jets 17, INDIANAPOLIS 16; Baltimore 30, KANSAS CITY 7
Divisional Playoff Games: PITTSBURGH 31, Baltimore 24; N.Y. Jets 28, NEW ENGLAND 21
AFC Championship Game: PITTSBURGH 24, N.Y. Jets 19
Wild Card Playoff Games: SEATTLE 41, New Orleans 36; Green Bay 21, PHILADELPHIA 16
Divisional Playoff Games: Green Bay 48, ATLANTA 21; CHICAGO 35, Seattle 24
NFC Championship Game: Green Bay 21, CHICAGO 14
Super Bowl XLV: Green Bay (NFC) 31, Pittsburgh (AFC) 25 at Cowboys Stadium, North Texas

Playoff Seeds

AFC	NFC
1. New England	1. Atlanta
2. Pittsburgh	2. Chicago
3. Indianapolis	3. Philadelphia
4. Kansas City	4. Seattle
5. Baltimore	5. New Orleans
6. N.Y. Jets	**6. Green Bay**

2009

AMERICAN CONFERENCE
East Division

	W	L	T	Pct.	Pts.	OP
New England	10	6	0	.625	427	285
New York Jets*	9	7	0	.563	348	236
Miami	7	9	0	.438	360	390
Buffalo	6	10	0	.375	258	326

North Division

	W	L	T	Pct.	Pts.	OP
Cincinnati	10	6	0	.625	305	291
Baltimore*	9	7	0	.563	391	261
Pittsburgh	9	7	0	.563	368	324
Cleveland	5	11	0	.313	245	375

South Division

	W	L	T	Pct.	Pts.	OP
Indianapolis#	14	2	0	.875	416	307
Houston	9	7	0	.563	388	333
Tennessee	8	8	0	.500	354	402
Jacksonville	7	9	0	.438	290	380

West Division

	W	L	T	Pct.	Pts.	OP
San Diego	13	3	0	.813	454	320
Denver	8	8	0	.500	326	324
Oakland	5	11	0	.313	197	379
Kansas City	4	12	0	.250	294	424

NATIONAL CONFERENCE
East Division

	W	L	T	Pct.	Pts.	OP
Dallas	11	5	0	.688	361	250
Philadelphia*	11	5	0	.688	429	337
New York Giants	8	8	0	.500	402	427
Washington	4	12	0	.250	266	336

North Division

	W	L	T	Pct.	Pts.	OP
Minnesota	12	4	0	.750	470	312
Green Bay*	11	5	0	.688	461	297
Chicago	7	9	0	.438	327	375
Detroit	2	14	0	.125	262	494

South Division

	W	L	T	Pct.	Pts.	OP
New Orleans#	13	3	0	.813	510	341
Atlanta	9	7	0	.563	363	325
Carolina	8	8	0	.500	315	308
Tampa Bay	3	13	0	.188	244	400

West Division

	W	L	T	Pct.	Pts.	OP
Arizona	10	6	0	.625	375	325
San Francisco	8	8	0	.500	330	281
Seattle	5	11	0	.313	280	390
St. Louis	1	15	0	.063	175	436

*Wild Card qualifier for playoffs; #Top playoff seed in conference
New England finished ahead of Cincinnati based on better strength of victory (.450 to Bengals' .438). Baltimore finished ahead of Pittsburgh based on better division record (3-3 to Steelers' 2-4). New York Jets finished ahead of Baltimore for first Wild Card based on better record vs. common opponents (4-1 to Ravens' 1-4) and ahead of Houston based on better conference record (7-5 to Texans' 6-6). Baltimore was second Wild Card based on better conference record than Houston (7-5 to Texans' 6-6). Dallas finished ahead of Philadelphia based on head-to-head sweep (2-0). Green Bay was first Wild Card ahead of Philadelphia based on better record vs. common opponents (4-1 to Eagles' 3-2).
Wild Card Playoff: New York Jets 24, CINCINNATI 14; Baltimore 33, NEW ENGLAND 14
Divisional Playoff: INDIANAPOLIS 20, Baltimore 3; New York Jets 17, SAN DIEGO 14
AFC Championship: INDIANAPOLIS 30, New York Jets 17
Wild Card Playoff: DALLAS 34, Philadelphia 14; ARIZONA 51, Green Bay 45 (OT)
Divisional Playoff Games: NEW ORLEANS 45, Arizona 14; MINNESOTA 34, Dallas 3
NFC Championship Game: NEW ORLEANS 31, Minnesota 28 (OT)
Super Bowl XLIV: New Orleans (NFC) 31, Indianapolis (AFC) 17 at Sun Life Stadium, South Florida

Playoff Seeds

AFC	NFC
1. Indianapolis	1. New Orleans
2. San Diego	2. Minnesota
3. New England	3. Dallas
4. Cincinnati	4. Arizona
5. New York Jets	5. Green Bay
6. Baltimore	6. Philadelphia

2008

AMERICAN CONFERENCE
East Division

	W	L	T	Pct.	Pts.	OP
Miami	11	5	0	.688	345	317
New England	11	5	0	.688	410	309
New York Jets	9	7	0	.563	405	356
Buffalo	7	9	0	.438	336	342

North Division

	W	L	T	Pct.	Pts.	OP
Pittsburgh	12	4	0	.750	347	223
Baltimore*	11	5	0	.688	385	244
Cincinnati	4	11	1	.281	204	364
Cleveland	4	12	0	.250	232	350

South Division

	W	L	T	Pct.	Pts.	OP
Tennessee#	13	3	0	.813	375	234
Indianapolis*	12	4	0	.750	377	298
Houston	8	8	0	.500	366	394
Jacksonville	5	11	0	.313	302	367

West Division

	W	L	T	Pct.	Pts.	OP
San Diego	8	8	0	.500	439	347
Denver	8	8	0	.500	370	448
Oakland	5	11	0	.313	263	388
Kansas City	2	14	0	.125	291	440

NATIONAL CONFERENCE
East Division

	W	L	T	Pct.	Pts.	OP
New York Giants#	12	4	0	.750	427	294
Philadelphia*	9	6	1	.594	416	289
Dallas	9	7	0	.563	362	365
Washington	8	8	0	.500	265	296

North Division

	W	L	T	Pct.	Pts.	OP
Minnesota	10	6	0	.625	379	333
Chicago	9	7	0	.563	375	350
Green Bay	6	10	0	.375	419	380
Detroit	0	16	0	.000	268	517

South Division

	W	L	T	Pct.	Pts.	OP
Carolina	12	4	0	.750	414	329
Atlanta*	11	5	0	.688	391	325
Tampa Bay	9	7	0	.563	361	323
New Orleans	8	8	0	.500	463	393

West Division

	W	L	T	Pct.	Pts.	OP
Arizona	9	7	0	.563	427	426
San Francisco	7	9	0	.438	339	381
Seattle	4	12	0	.250	294	392
St. Louis	2	14	0	.125	232	465

*Wild Card qualifier for playoffs; #Top playoff seed in conference
Miami finished ahead of New England based on better conference record (8-4 to Patriots' 7-5). Baltimore was second Wild Card ahead of New England based on better conference record (8-4 to Patriots' 7-5). San Diego finished ahead of Denver based on better division record (5-1 to Broncos' 3-3). N.Y. Giants finished ahead of Carolina based on head-to-head victory.
Wild Card Playoff: SAN DIEGO 23, Indianapolis 17; Baltimore 27, MIAMI 9
Divisional Playoff: Baltimore 13, TENNESSEE 10; PITTSBURGH 35, San Diego 24
AFC Championship: PITTSBURGH 23, Baltimore 14
Wild Card Playoff: ARIZONA 30, Atlanta 24; Philadelphia 26, MINNESOTA 14
Divisional Playoff: Arizona 33, CAROLINA 13; Philadelphia 23, N.Y. GIANTS 11
NFC Championship: ARIZONA 32, Philadelphia 25
Super Bowl XLIII: Pittsburgh (AFC) 27, Arizona (NFC) 23 at Raymond James Stadium, Tampa, Florida

Playoff Seeds

AFC	NFC
1. Tennessee	1. N.Y. Giants
2. Pittsburgh	2. Carolina
3. Miami	3. Minnesota
4. San Diego	**4. Arizona**
5. Indianapolis	5. Atlanta
6. Baltimore	6. Philadelphia

2007

AMERICAN CONFERENCE

East Division

	W	L	T	Pct.	Pts.	OP
New England#	16	0	0	1.000	589	274
Buffalo	7	9	0	.438	252	354
New York Jets	4	12	0	.250	268	355
Miami	1	15	0	.063	267	437

North Division

	W	L	T	Pct.	Pts.	OP
Pittsburgh	10	6	0	.625	393	269
Cleveland	10	6	0	.625	402	382
Cincinnati	7	9	0	.438	380	385
Baltimore	5	11	0	.313	275	384

South Division

	W	L	T	Pct.	Pts.	OP
Indianapolis	13	3	0	.813	450	262
Jacksonville*	11	5	0	.688	411	304
Tennessee*	10	6	0	.625	301	297
Houston	8	8	0	.500	379	384

West Division

	W	L	T	Pct.	Pts.	OP
San Diego	11	5	0	.688	412	284
Denver	7	9	0	.438	320	409
Kansas City	4	12	0	.250	226	335
Oakland	4	12	0	.250	283	398

NATIONAL CONFERENCE

East Division

	W	L	T	Pct.	Pts.	OP
Dallas#	13	3	0	.813	455	325
New York Giants*	10	6	0	.625	373	351
Washington*	9	7	0	.563	334	310
Philadelphia	8	8	0	.500	336	300

North Division

	W	L	T	Pct.	Pts.	OP
Green Bay	13	3	0	.813	435	291
Minnesota	8	8	0	.500	365	311
Detroit	7	9	0	.438	346	444
Chicago	7	9	0	.438	334	348

South Division

	W	L	T	Pct.	Pts.	OP
Tampa Bay	9	7	0	.563	334	270
Carolina	7	9	0	.438	267	347
New Orleans	7	9	0	.438	379	388
Atlanta	4	12	0	.250	259	414

West Division

	W	L	T	Pct.	Pts.	OP
Seattle	10	6	0	.625	393	291
Arizona	8	8	0	.500	404	399
San Francisco	5	11	0	.313	219	364
St. Louis	3	13	0	.188	263	438

*Wild Card qualifier for playoffs; #Top playoff seed in conference
Pittsburgh finished ahead of Cleveland based on head-to-head sweep (2-0). Tennessee finished ahead of Cleveland based on better record vs. common opponents (4-1 to Browns' 3-2). Kansas City finished ahead of Oakland based on better record vs. common opponents (2-10 to Raiders' 1-11). Dallas finished ahead of Green Bay based on head-to-head victory. Detroit finished ahead of Chicago based on head-to-head sweep (2-0). Carolina finished ahead of New Orleans based on better conference record (7-5 to Saints' 6-6).
Wild Card Playoff: Jacksonville 31, PITTSBURGH 29; SAN DIEGO 17, Tennessee 6
Divisional Playoff: NEW ENGLAND 31, Jacksonville 20; San Diego 28, INDIANAPOLIS 24
AFC Championship: NEW ENGLAND 21, San Diego 12
Wild Card Playoff: SEATTLE 35, Washington 14; N.Y. Giants 24, TAMPA BAY 14
Divisional Playoff: GREEN BAY 42, Seattle 20; N.Y. Giants 21, DALLAS 17
NFC Championship: N.Y. Giants 23, GREEN BAY 20 (OT)
Super Bowl XLII: N.Y. Giants (NFC) 17, New England (AFC) 14 at University of Phoenix Stadium, Glendale, Arizona

Playoff Seeds

AFC	NFC
1. New England	1. Dallas
2. Indianapolis	2. Green Bay
3. San Diego	3. Seattle
4. Pittsburgh	4. Tampa Bay
5. Jacksonville	5. N.Y. Giants
6. Tennessee	6. Washington

2006

AMERICAN CONFERENCE

East Division

	W	L	T	Pct.	Pts.	OP
New England	12	4	0	.750	385	237
New York Jets*	10	6	0	.625	316	295
Buffalo	7	9	0	.438	300	311
Miami	6	10	0	.375	260	283

North Division

	W	L	T	Pct.	Pts.	OP
Baltimore	13	3	0	.813	353	201
Cincinnati	8	8	0	.500	373	331
Pittsburgh	8	8	0	.500	353	315
Cleveland	4	12	0	.250	238	356

South Division

	W	L	T	Pct.	Pts.	OP
Indianapolis	12	4	0	.750	427	360
Tennessee	8	8	0	.500	324	400
Jacksonville	8	8	0	.500	371	274
Houston	6	10	0	.375	267	366

West Division

	W	L	T	Pct.	Pts.	OP
San Diego#	14	2	0	.875	492	303
Kansas City*	9	7	0	.563	331	315
Denver	9	7	0	.563	319	305
Oakland	2	14	0	.125	168	332

NATIONAL CONFERENCE

East Division

	W	L	T	Pct.	Pts.	OP
Philadelphia	10	6	0	.625	398	328
Dallas*	9	7	0	.563	425	350
New York Giants*	8	8	0	.500	355	362
Washington	5	11	0	.313	307	376

North Division

	W	L	T	Pct.	Pts.	OP
Chicago#	13	3	0	.813	427	255
Green Bay	8	8	0	.500	301	366
Minnesota	6	10	0	.375	282	327
Detroit	3	13	0	.188	305	398

South Division

	W	L	T	Pct.	Pts.	OP
New Orleans	10	6	0	.625	413	322
Carolina	8	8	0	.500	270	305
Atlanta	7	9	0	.438	292	328
Tampa Bay	4	12	0	.250	211	353

West Division

	W	L	T	Pct.	Pts.	OP
Seattle	9	7	0	.563	335	341
St. Louis	8	8	0	.500	367	381
San Francisco	7	9	0	.438	298	412
Arizona	5	11	0	.313	314	389

*Wild Card qualifier for playoffs; #Top playoff seed in conference
Indianapolis finished ahead of New England based on head-to-head victory. Cincinnati finished ahead of Pittsburgh based on better division record (4-2 to Steelers' 3-3). Tennessee finished ahead of Jacksonville based on better division record (4-2 to Jaguars' 2-4). Kansas City finished ahead of Denver based on better division record (4-2 to Broncos' 3-3). New Orleans finished ahead of Philadelphia based on head-to-head victory. N.Y. Giants finished ahead of Carolina and St. Louis based on better conference record (Giants' 7-5 to Panthers' 6-6 and Rams' 6-6) and ahead of Green Bay based on strength of victory (.422 to Packers' .383).
Wild Card Playoff: INDIANAPOLIS 23, Kansas City 8; NEW ENGLAND 37, N.Y. Jets 16
Divisional Playoff: Indianapolis 15, BALTIMORE 6; New England 24, SAN DIEGO 21
AFC Championship: INDIANAPOLIS 38, New England 34
Wild Card Playoff: SEATTLE 21, Dallas 20; PHILADELPHIA 23, N.Y. Giants 20
Divisional Playoff: NEW ORLEANS 27, Philadelphia 24; CHICAGO 27, Seattle 24 (OT)
NFC Championship: CHICAGO 39, New Orleans 14
Super Bowl XLI: Indianapolis (AFC) 29, Chicago (NFC) 17 at Dolphin Stadium, Miami, Florida

Playoff Seeds

AFC	NFC
1. San Diego	1. Chicago
2. Baltimore	2. New Orleans
3. Indianapolis	3. Philadelphia
4. New England	4. Seattle
5. N.Y. Jets	5. Dallas
6. Kansas City	6. N.Y. Giants

2005

AMERICAN CONFERENCE

East Division

	W	L	T	Pct.	Pts.	OP
New England	10	6	0	.625	379	338
Miami	9	7	0	.563	318	317
Buffalo	5	11	0	.313	271	367
N.Y. Jets	4	12	0	.250	240	355

North Division

	W	L	T	Pct.	Pts.	OP
Cincinnati	11	5	0	.688	421	350
Pittsburgh*	11	5	0	.688	389	258
Baltimore	6	10	0	.375	265	299
Cleveland	6	10	0	.375	232	301

South Division

	W	L	T	Pct.	Pts.	OP
Indianapolis#	14	2	0	.875	439	247
Jacksonville*	12	4	0	.750	361	269
Tennessee	4	12	0	.250	299	421
Houston	2	14	0	.125	260	431

West Division

	W	L	T	Pct.	Pts.	OP
Denver	13	3	0	.813	395	258
Kansas City	10	6	0	.625	403	325
San Diego	9	7	0	.563	418	312
Oakland	4	12	0	.250	290	383

NATIONAL CONFERENCE

East Division

	W	L	T	Pct.	Pts.	OP
N.Y. Giants	11	5	0	.688	422	314
Washington*	10	6	0	.625	359	293
Dallas	9	7	0	.563	325	308
Philadelphia	6	10	0	.375	310	388

North Division

	W	L	T	Pct.	Pts.	OP
Chicago	11	5	0	.688	260	202
Minnesota	9	7	0	.563	306	344
Detroit	5	11	0	.313	254	345
Green Bay	4	12	0	.250	298	344

South Division

	W	L	T	Pct.	Pts.	OP
Tampa Bay	11	5	0	.688	300	274
Carolina*	11	5	0	.688	391	259
Atlanta	8	8	0	.500	351	341
New Orleans	3	13	0	.188	235	398

West Division

	W	L	T	Pct.	Pts.	OP
Seattle#	13	3	0	.813	452	271
St. Louis	6	10	0	.375	363	429
Arizona	5	11	0	.313	311	387
San Francisco	4	12	0	.250	239	428

*Wild Card qualifier for playoffs; #Top playoff seed in conference
Cincinnati finished ahead of Pittsburgh based on better division record (5-1 to Steelers' 4-2). Baltimore finished ahead of Cleveland based on better division record (2-4 to Browns' 1-5). Tampa Bay finished ahead of Carolina based on better division record (5-1 to Panthers' 4-2). Chicago finished ahead of Tampa Bay, and Tampa Bay finished ahead of the N.Y. Giants, based on better conference record (Bears' 10-2 to Buccaneers' 9-3 to Giants' 8-4).

Wild Card playoff: NEW ENGLAND 28, Jacksonville 3; Pittsburgh 31, CINCINNATI 17

Divisional playoff: DENVER 27, New England 13; Pittsburgh 21, INDIANAPOLIS 18

AFC Championship: Pittsburgh 34, DENVER 17

Wild Card playoffs: Washington 17, TAMPA BAY 10; Carolina 23, NEW YORK GIANTS 0

Divisional playoff: SEATTLE 20, Washington 10; Carolina 29, CHICAGO 21

NFC Championship: SEATTLE 34, Carolina 14

Super Bowl XL: Pittsburgh (AFC) 21, Seattle (NFC) 10 at Ford Field, Detroit, Michigan

Playoff Seeds

AFC	NFC
1. Indianapolis	**1. Seattle**
2. Denver	2. Chicago
3. Cincinnati	3. Tampa Bay
4. New England	4. New York Giants
5. Jacksonville	5. Carolina
6. Pittsburgh	6. Washington

2004

AMERICAN CONFERENCE

East Division

	W	L	T	Pct.	Pts.	OP
New England	14	2	0	.875	437	260
N.Y. Jets*	10	6	0	.625	333	261
Buffalo	9	7	0	.563	395	284
Miami	4	12	0	.250	275	354

North Division

	W	L	T	Pct.	Pts.	OP
Pittsburgh#	15	1	0	.938	372	251
Baltimore	9	7	0	.563	317	268
Cincinnati	8	8	0	.500	374	372
Cleveland	4	12	0	.250	276	390

South Division

	W	L	T	Pct.	Pts.	OP
Indianapolis	12	4	0	.750	522	351
Jacksonville	9	7	0	.563	261	280
Houston	7	9	0	.438	309	339
Tennessee	5	11	0	.313	344	439

West Division

	W	L	T	Pct.	Pts.	OP
San Diego	12	4	0	.750	446	313
Denver*	10	6	0	.625	381	304
Kansas City	7	9	0	.438	483	435
Oakland	5	11	0	.313	320	442

NATIONAL CONFERENCE

East Division

	W	L	T	Pct.	Pts.	OP
Philadelphia#	13	3	0	.813	386	260
N.Y. Giants	6	10	0	.375	303	347
Dallas	6	10	0	.375	293	405
Washington	6	10	0	.375	240	265

North Division

	W	L	T	Pct.	Pts.	OP
Green Bay	10	6	0	.625	424	380
Minnesota*	8	8	0	.500	405	395
Detroit	6	10	0	.375	296	350
Chicago	5	11	0	.313	231	331

South Division

	W	L	T	Pct.	Pts.	OP
Atlanta	11	5	0	.688	340	337
New Orleans	8	8	0	.500	348	405
Carolina	7	9	0	.438	355	339
Tampa Bay	5	11	0	.313	301	304

West Division

	W	L	T	Pct.	Pts.	OP
Seattle	9	7	0	.563	371	373
St. Louis*	8	8	0	.500	319	392
Arizona	6	10	0	.375	284	322
San Francisco	2	14	0	.125	259	452

*Wild Card qualifier for playoffs; #Top playoff seed in conference
Indianapolis finished ahead of San Diego based on head-to-head victory. N.Y. Jets finished ahead of Denver based on better record vs. common opponents (5-0 to Broncos' 3-2). St. Louis finished ahead of New Orleans and Minnesota based on best conference record (7-5 to Saints' 6-6 to Vikings' 5-7), and Minnesota finished ahead of New Orleans based on head-to-head victory. N.Y. Giants finished ahead of Dallas and Washington based on better head-to-head record (3-1 to Cowboys' 2-2 to Redskins' 1-3), and Dallas finished ahead of Washington based on head-to-head sweep (2-0).

Wild Card playoffs: N.Y. Jets 20, SAN DIEGO 17 (OT); INDIANAPOLIS 49, Denver 24

Divisional playoffs: PITTSBURGH 20, N.Y. Jets 17 (OT); NEW ENGLAND 20, Indianapolis 3

AFC Championship: New England 41, PITTSBURGH 27

Wild Card playoffs: St. Louis 27, SEATTLE 20; Minnesota 31, GREEN BAY 17

Divisional playoffs: ATLANTA 47, St. Louis 17; PHILADELPHIA 27, Minnesota 14

NFC Championship: PHILADELPHIA 27, Atlanta 10

Super Bowl XXXIX: New England (AFC) 24, Philadelphia (NFC) 21 at Alltel Stadium, Jacksonville, Florida

Playoff Seeds

AFC	NFC
1. Pittsburgh	**1. Philadelphia**
2. New England	2. Atlanta
3. Indianapolis	3. Green Bay
4. San Diego	4. Seattle
5. N.Y. Jets	5. St. Louis
6. Denver	6. Minnesota

2003

AMERICAN CONFERENCE

East Division

	W	L	T	Pct.	Pts.	OP
New England#	14	2	0	.875	348	238
Miami	10	6	0	.625	311	261
Buffalo	6	10	0	.375	243	279
N.Y. Jets	6	10	0	.375	283	299

North Division

	W	L	T	Pct.	Pts.	OP
Baltimore	10	6	0	.625	391	281
Cincinnati	8	8	0	.500	346	384
Pittsburgh	6	10	0	.375	300	327
Cleveland	5	11	0	.313	254	322

South Division

	W	L	T	Pct.	Pts.	OP
Indianapolis	12	4	0	.750	447	336
Tennessee*	12	4	0	.750	435	324
Jacksonville	5	11	0	.313	276	331
Houston	5	11	0	.313	255	380

West Division

	W	L	T	Pct.	Pts.	OP
Kansas City	13	3	0	.813	484	332
Denver*	10	6	0	.625	381	301
Oakland	4	12	0	.250	270	379
San Diego	4	12	0	.250	313	441

NATIONAL CONFERENCE

East Division

	W	L	T	Pct.	Pts.	OP
Philadelphia#	12	4	0	.750	374	287
Dallas*	10	6	0	.625	289	260
Washington	5	11	0	.313	287	372
N.Y. Giants	4	12	0	.250	243	387

North Division

	W	L	T	Pct.	Pts.	OP
Green Bay	10	6	0	.625	442	307
Minnesota	9	7	0	.563	416	353
Chicago	7	9	0	.438	283	346
Detroit	5	11	0	.313	270	379

South Division

	W	L	T	Pct.	Pts.	OP
Carolina	11	5	0	.688	325	304
New Orleans	8	8	0	.500	340	326
Tampa Bay	7	9	0	.438	301	264
Atlanta	5	11	0	.313	299	422

West Division

	W	L	T	Pct.	Pts.	OP
St. Louis	12	4	0	.750	447	328
Seattle*	10	6	0	.625	404	327
San Francisco	7	9	0	.438	384	337
Arizona	4	12	0	.250	225	452

*Wild Card qualifier for playoffs; #Top playoff seed in conference
Buffalo finished ahead of N.Y. Jets based on better division record (2-4 to Jets' 1-5). Indianapolis finished ahead of Tennessee based on head-to-head sweep (2-0). Jacksonville finished ahead of Houston based on better division record (2-4 to Texans' 1-5). Denver finished ahead of Miami based on better conference record (9-3 to Dolphins' 7-5). Oakland finished ahead of San Diego based on better conference record (3-9 to Chargers' 2-10). Philadelphia finished ahead of St. Louis based on better conference record (9-3 to Rams' 8-4). Seattle finished ahead of Dallas based on better strength of victory (65-95 to Cowboys' 62-98).

Wild Card playoffs: Tennessee 20, BALTIMORE 17; INDIANAPOLIS 41, Denver 10
Divisional playoffs: NEW ENGLAND 17, Tennessee 14; Indianapolis 38, KANSAS CITY 31
AFC Championship: NEW ENGLAND 24, Indianapolis 14
Wild Card playoffs: CAROLINA 29, Dallas 10; GREEN BAY 33, Seattle 27 (OT)
Divisional playoffs: Carolina 29, ST. LOUIS 23 (2OT); PHILADELPHIA 20, Green Bay 17 (OT)
NFC Championship: Carolina 14, PHILADELPHIA 3
Super Bowl XXXVIII: New England (AFC) 32, Carolina (NFC) 29 at Reliant Stadium, Houston, Texas

Playoff Seeds

AFC	NFC
1. New England	1. Philadelphia
2. Kansas City	2. St. Louis
3. Indianapolis	3. Carolina
4. Baltimore	4. Green Bay
5. Tennessee	5. Seattle
6. Denver	6. Dallas

2002

AMERICAN CONFERENCE

East Division

	W	L	T	Pct.	Pts.	OP
N.Y. Jets	9	7	0	.563	359	336
New England	9	7	0	.563	381	346
Miami	9	7	0	.563	378	301
Buffalo	8	8	0	.500	379	397

North Division

	W	L	T	Pct.	Pts.	OP
Pittsburgh	10	5	1	.656	390	345
Cleveland*	9	7	0	.563	344	320
Baltimore	7	9	0	.438	316	354
Cincinnati	2	14	0	.125	279	456

South Division

	W	L	T	Pct.	Pts.	OP
Tennessee	11	5	0	.688	367	324
Indianapolis*	10	6	0	.625	349	313
Jacksonville	6	10	0	.375	328	315
Houston	4	12	0	.250	213	356

West Division

	W	L	T	Pct.	Pts.	OP
Oakland#	11	5	0	.688	450	304
Denver	9	7	0	.563	392	344
San Diego	8	8	0	.500	333	367
Kansas City	8	8	0	.500	467	399

NATIONAL CONFERENCE

East Division

	W	L	T	Pct.	Pts.	OP
Philadelphia#	12	4	0	.750	415	241
N.Y. Giants*	10	6	0	.625	320	279
Washington	7	9	0	.438	307	365
Dallas	5	11	0	.313	217	329

North Division

	W	L	T	Pct.	Pts.	OP
Green Bay	12	4	0	.750	398	328
Minnesota	6	10	0	.375	390	442
Chicago	4	12	0	.250	281	379
Detroit	3	13	0	.188	306	451

South Division

	W	L	T	Pct.	Pts.	OP
Tampa Bay	12	4	0	.750	346	196
Atlanta*	9	6	1	.594	402	314
New Orleans	9	7	0	.563	432	388
Carolina	7	9	0	.438	258	302

West Division

	W	L	T	Pct.	Pts.	OP
San Francisco	10	6	0	.625	367	351
St. Louis	7	9	0	.438	316	369
Seattle	7	9	0	.438	355	369
Arizona	5	11	0	.313	262	417

*Wild Card qualifier for playoffs; #Top playoff seed in conference
New York Jets finished ahead of New England based on better record in common games (8-4 to Patriots' 7-5) and Miami based on better division record (4-2 to Dolphins' 2-4). New England finished ahead of Miami based on better division record (4-2 to Dolphins' 2-4). Cleveland finished ahead of Denver and New England based on better conference record (7-5 to Broncos' 5-7 and Patriots' 6-6). Oakland finished ahead of Tennessee based on better head-to-head record (1-0). San Diego finished ahead of Kansas City based on better division record (3-3 to Chiefs' 2-4). Philadelphia finished ahead of Green Bay and Tampa Bay based on better conference record (11-1 to Packers' 9-3 and Buccaneers' 9-3). Tampa Bay finished ahead of Green Bay based on better head-to-head record (1-0). St. Louis finished ahead of Seattle based on better division record (4-2 to Seahawks' 2-4).

Wild Card playoffs: N.Y. JETS 41, Indianapolis 0; PITTSBURGH 36, Cleveland 33
Divisional playoffs: TENNESSEE 34, Pittsburgh 31 (OT); OAKLAND 30, N.Y. Jets 10
AFC Championship: OAKLAND 41, Tennessee 24
Wild Card playoffs: Atlanta 27, GREEN BAY 7; SAN FRANCISCO 39, N.Y. Giants 38
Divisional playoffs: PHILADELPHIA 20, Atlanta 6; TAMPA BAY 31, San Francisco 6
NFC Championship: Tampa Bay 27, PHILADELPHIA 10
Super Bowl XXXVII: Tampa Bay (NFC) 48, Oakland (AFC) 21 at Qualcomm Stadium, San Diego, California

Playoff Seeds

AFC	NFC
1. Oakland	1. Philadelphia
2. Tennessee	2. Tampa Bay
3. Pittsburgh	3. Green Bay
4. N.Y. Jets	4. San Francisco
5. Indianapolis	5. N.Y. Giants
6. Cleveland	6. Atlanta

2001

AMERICAN CONFERENCE

Eastern Division

	W	L	T	Pct.	Pts.	OP
New England	11	5	0	.688	371	272
Miami*	11	5	0	.688	344	290
N.Y. Jets*	10	6	0	.625	308	295
Indianapolis	6	10	0	.375	413	486
Buffalo	3	13	0	.188	265	420

Central Division

	W	L	T	Pct.	Pts.	OP
Pittsburgh#	13	3	0	.813	352	212
Baltimore*	10	6	0	.625	303	265
Cleveland	7	9	0	.438	285	319
Tennessee	7	9	0	.438	336	388
Jacksonville	6	10	0	.375	294	286
Cincinnati	6	10	0	.375	226	309

Western Division

	W	L	T	Pct.	Pts.	OP
Oakland	10	6	0	.625	399	327
Seattle	9	7	0	.563	301	324
Denver	8	8	0	.500	340	339
Kansas City	6	10	0	.375	320	344
San Diego	5	11	0	.313	332	321

NATIONAL CONFERENCE

Eastern Division

	W	L	T	Pct.	Pts.	OP
Philadelphia	11	5	0	.688	343	208
Washington	8	8	0	.500	256	303
N.Y. Giants	7	9	0	.438	294	321
Arizona	7	9	0	.438	295	343
Dallas	5	11	0	.313	246	338

Central Division

	W	L	T	Pct.	Pts.	OP
Chicago	13	3	0	.813	338	203
Green Bay*	12	4	0	.750	390	266
Tampa Bay*	9	7	0	.563	324	280
Minnesota	5	11	0	.313	290	390
Detroit	2	14	0	.125	270	424

Western Division

	W	L	T	Pct.	Pts.	OP
St. Louis#	14	2	0	.875	503	273
San Francisco*	12	4	0	.750	409	282
New Orleans	7	9	0	.438	333	409
Atlanta	7	9	0	.438	291	377
Carolina	1	15	0	.063	253	410

*Wild Card qualifier for playoffs; #Top playoff seed in conference
New England finished ahead of Miami based on better division record (6-2 to Dolphins' 5-3). Baltimore was second Wild Card ahead of N.Y. Jets based on better record against common opponents (3-2 to Jets' 2-2). Cleveland finished ahead of Tennessee based on better division record (5-5 to Titans' 3-7). Jacksonville finished ahead of Cincinnati based on head-to-head record (2-0). N.Y. Giants finished ahead of Arizona based on head-to-head record (2-0). Green Bay was first Wild Card ahead of San Francisco based on better conference record (9-3 to 49ers' 8-4). New Orleans finished ahead of Atlanta based on better division record (4-4 to Falcons' 3-5).
Wild Card playoffs: OAKLAND 38, N.Y. Jets 24; Baltimore 20, MIAMI 3
Divisional playoffs: NEW ENGLAND 16, Oakland 13 (OT); PITTSBURGH 27, Baltimore 10
AFC Championship: New England 24, PITTSBURGH 17
Wild Card playoffs: PHILADELPHIA 31, Tampa Bay 9; GREEN BAY 25, San Francisco 15
Divisional playoffs: Philadelphia 33, CHICAGO 19; ST. LOUIS 45, Green Bay 17
NFC Championship: ST. LOUIS 29, Philadelphia 24
Super Bowl XXXVI: New England (AFC) 20, St. Louis (NFC) 17 at Louisiana Superdome, New Orleans, Louisiana

Playoff Seeds

AFC	NFC
1. Pittsburgh	**1. St. Louis**
2. New England	2. Chicago
3. Oakland	3. Philadelphia
4. Miami	4. Green Bay
5. Baltimore	5. San Francisco
6. N.Y. Jets	6. Tampa Bay

2000

AMERICAN CONFERENCE

Eastern Division

	W	L	T	Pct.	Pts.	OP
Miami	11	5	0	.688	323	226
Indianapolis*	10	6	0	.625	429	326
N.Y. Jets	9	7	0	.563	321	321
Buffalo	8	8	0	.500	315	350
New England	5	11	0	.313	276	338

Central Division

	W	L	T	Pct.	Pts.	OP
Tennessee#	13	3	0	.813	346	191
Baltimore*	12	4	0	.750	333	165
Pittsburgh	9	7	0	.563	321	255
Jacksonville	7	9	0	.438	367	327
Cincinnati	4	12	0	.250	185	359
Cleveland	3	13	0	.188	161	419

Western Division

	W	L	T	Pct.	Pts.	OP
Oakland	12	4	0	.750	479	299
Denver*	11	5	0	.688	485	369
Kansas City	7	9	0	.438	355	354
Seattle	6	10	0	.375	320	405
San Diego	1	15	0	.063	269	440

NATIONAL CONFERENCE

Eastern Division

	W	L	T	Pct.	Pts.	OP
N.Y. Giants#	12	4	0	.750	328	246
Philadelphia*	11	5	0	.688	351	245
Washington	8	8	0	.500	281	269
Dallas	5	11	0	.313	294	361
Arizona	3	13	0	.188	210	443

Central Division

	W	L	T	Pct.	Pts.	OP
Minnesota	11	5	0	.688	397	371
Tampa Bay*	10	6	0	.625	388	269
Green Bay	9	7	0	.563	353	323
Detroit	9	7	0	.563	307	307
Chicago	5	11	0	.313	216	355

Western Division

	W	L	T	Pct.	Pts.	OP
New Orleans	10	6	0	.625	354	305
St. Louis*	10	6	0	.625	540	471
Carolina	7	9	0	.438	310	310
San Francisco	6	10	0	.375	388	422
Atlanta	4	12	0	.250	252	413

*Wild Card qualifier for playoffs; #Top playoff seed in conference
Green Bay finished ahead of Detroit based on better division record (5-3 to Lions' 3-5). New Orleans finished ahead of St. Louis based on better division record (7-1 to Rams' 5-3). Tampa Bay was second Wild Card based on head-to-head victory over St. Louis (1-0).
Wild Card playoffs: MIAMI 23, Indianapolis 17 (OT); BALTIMORE 21, Denver 3
Divisional playoffs: OAKLAND 27, Miami 0; Baltimore 24, TENNESSEE 10
AFC Championship: Baltimore 16, OAKLAND 3
Wild Card playoffs: NEW ORLEANS 31, St. Louis 28; PHILADELPHIA 21, Tampa Bay 3
Divisional playoffs: MINNESOTA 34, New Orleans 16; N.Y. GIANTS 20, Philadelphia 10
NFC Championship: N.Y. GIANTS 41, Minnesota 0
Super Bowl XXXV: Baltimore (AFC) 34, N.Y. Giants (NFC) 7 at Raymond James Stadium, Tampa, Florida

Playoff Seeds

AFC	NFC
1. Tennessee	**1. N.Y. Giants**
2. Oakland	2. Minnesota
3. Miami	3. New Orleans
4. Baltimore	4. Philadelphia
5. Denver	5. Tampa Bay
6. Indianapolis	6. St. Louis

1999

AMERICAN CONFERENCE

Eastern Division

	W	L	T	Pct.	Pts.	OP
Indianapolis	13	3	0	.813	423	333
Buffalo*	11	5	0	.688	320	229
Miami*	9	7	0	.563	326	336
N.Y. Jets	8	8	0	.500	308	309
New England	8	8	0	.500	299	284

Central Division

	W	L	T	Pct.	Pts.	OP
Jacksonville#	14	2	0	.875	396	217
Tennessee*	13	3	0	.813	392	324
Baltimore	8	8	0	.500	324	277
Pittsburgh	6	10	0	.375	317	320
Cincinnati	4	12	0	.250	283	460
Cleveland	2	14	0	.125	217	437

Western Division

	W	L	T	Pct.	Pts.	OP
Seattle	9	7	0	.563	338	298
Kansas City	9	7	0	.563	390	322
San Diego	8	8	0	.500	269	316
Oakland	8	8	0	.500	390	329
Denver	6	10	0	.375	314	318

NATIONAL CONFERENCE

Eastern Division

	W	L	T	Pct.	Pts.	OP
Washington	10	6	0	.625	443	377
Dallas*	8	8	0	.500	352	276
N.Y. Giants	7	9	0	.438	299	358
Arizona	6	10	0	.375	245	382
Philadelphia	5	11	0	.313	272	357

Central Division

	W	L	T	Pct.	Pts.	OP
Tampa Bay	11	5	0	.688	270	235
Minnesota*	10	6	0	.625	399	335
Detroit*	8	8	0	.500	322	323
Green Bay	8	8	0	.500	357	341
Chicago	6	10	0	.375	272	341

Western Division

	W	L	T	Pct.	Pts.	OP
St. Louis#	13	3	0	.813	526	242
Carolina	8	8	0	.500	421	381
Atlanta	5	11	0	.313	285	380
San Francisco	4	12	0	.250	295	453
New Orleans	3	13	0	.188	260	434

*Wild Card qualifier for playoffs; #Top playoff seed in conference
Miami was third Wild Card ahead of Kansas City based on better record against common opponents (6-1 to Chiefs' 5-3). N.Y. Jets finished ahead of New England based on better division record (4-4 to Patriots' 2-6). Seattle finished ahead of Kansas City based on head-to-head sweep (2-0). San Diego finished ahead of Oakland based on better division record (5-3 to Raiders' 3-5). Dallas was second Wild Card based on better record against common opponents (4-2 to Lions' 3-3) and better conference record than Carolina (7-5 to Panthers' 6-6). Detroit was third Wild Card based on better conference record than Green Bay (7-5 to Packers' 6-6) and head-to-head victory over Carolina.
Wild Card playoffs: TENNESSEE 22, Buffalo 16; Miami 20, SEATTLE 17
Divisional playoffs: JACKSONVILLE 62, Miami 7; Tennessee 19, INDIANAPOLIS 16
AFC Championship: Tennessee 33, JACKSONVILLE 14
Wild Card playoffs: WASHINGTON 27, Detroit 13; MINNESOTA 27, Dallas 10
Divisional playoffs: TAMPA BAY 14, Washington 13; ST. LOUIS 49, Minnesota 37
NFC Championship: ST. LOUIS 11, Tampa Bay 6
Super Bowl XXXIV: St. Louis (NFC) 23, Tennessee (AFC) 16 at Georgia Dome, Atlanta, Georgia

Playoff Seeds

AFC	NFC
1. Jacksonville	1. St. Louis
2. Indianapolis	2. Tampa Bay
3. Seattle	3. Washington
4. Tennessee	4. Minnesota
5. Buffalo	5. Dallas
6. Miami	6. Detroit

1998

AMERICAN CONFERENCE

Eastern Division

	W	L	T	Pct.	Pts.	OP
N.Y. Jets	12	4	0	.750	416	266
Miami*	10	6	0	.625	321	265
Buffalo*	10	6	0	.625	400	333
New England*	9	7	0	.563	337	329
Indianapolis	3	13	0	.188	310	444

Central Division

	W	L	T	Pct.	Pts.	OP
Jacksonville	11	5	0	.688	392	338
Tennessee	8	8	0	.500	330	320
Pittsburgh	7	9	0	.438	263	303
Baltimore	6	10	0	.375	269	335
Cincinnati	3	13	0	.188	268	452

Western Division

	W	L	T	Pct.	Pts.	OP
Denver#	14	2	0	.875	501	309
Oakland	8	8	0	.500	288	356
Seattle	8	8	0	.500	372	310
Kansas City	7	9	0	.438	327	363
San Diego	5	11	0	.313	241	342

NATIONAL CONFERENCE

Eastern Division

	W	L	T	Pct.	Pts.	OP
Dallas	10	6	0	.625	381	275
Arizona*	9	7	0	.563	325	378
N.Y. Giants	8	8	0	.500	287	309
Washington	6	10	0	.375	319	421
Philadelphia	3	13	0	.188	161	344

Central Division

	W	L	T	Pct.	Pts.	OP
Minnesota#	15	1	0	.938	556	296
Green Bay*	11	5	0	.688	408	319
Tampa Bay	8	8	0	.500	314	295
Detroit	5	11	0	.313	306	378
Chicago	4	12	0	.250	276	368

Western Division

	W	L	T	Pct.	Pts.	OP
Atlanta	14	2	0	.875	442	289
San Francisco*	12	4	0	.750	479	328
New Orleans	6	10	0	.375	305	359
Carolina	4	12	0	.250	336	413
St. Louis	4	12	0	.250	285	378

*Wild Card qualifier for playoffs; #Top playoff seed in conference
Miami finished ahead of Buffalo based on better net division points (6 to Bills' 0). Oakland finished ahead of Seattle based on head-to-head sweep (2-0). Carolina finished ahead of St. Louis based on head-to-head sweep (2-0).
Wild Card playoffs: MIAMI 24, Buffalo 17; JACKSONVILLE 25, New England 10
Divisional playoffs: DENVER 38, Miami 3; N.Y. JETS 34, Jacksonville 24
AFC Championship: DENVER 23, N.Y. Jets 10
Wild Card playoffs: Arizona 20, DALLAS 7; SAN FRANCISCO 30, Green Bay 27
Divisional playoffs: ATLANTA 20, San Francisco 18; MINNESOTA 41, Arizona 21
NFC Championship: Atlanta 30, MINNESOTA 27 (OT)
Super Bowl XXXIII: Denver (AFC) 34, Atlanta (NFC) 19, at Pro Player Stadium, Miami, Florida

Playoff Seeds

AFC	NFC
1. Denver	1. Minnesota
2. N.Y. Jets	2. Atlanta
3. Jacksonville	3. Dallas
4. Miami	4. San Francisco
5. Buffalo	5. Green Bay
6. New England	6. Arizona

1997

AMERICAN CONFERENCE

Eastern Division

	W	L	T	Pct.	Pts.	OP
New England	10	6	0	.625	369	289
Miami*	9	7	0	.563	339	327
N.Y. Jets	9	7	0	.563	348	287
Buffalo	6	10	0	.375	255	367
Indianapolis	3	13	0	.188	313	401

Central Division

	W	L	T	Pct.	Pts.	OP
Pittsburgh	11	5	0	.688	372	307
Jacksonville*	11	5	0	.688	394	318
Tennessee	8	8	0	.500	333	310
Cincinnati	7	9	0	.438	355	405
Baltimore	6	9	1	.406	326	345

Western Division

	W	L	T	Pct.	Pts.	OP
Kansas City#	13	3	0	.813	375	232
Denver*	12	4	0	.750	472	287
Seattle	8	8	0	.500	365	362
Oakland	4	12	0	.250	324	419
San Diego	4	12	0	.250	266	425

NATIONAL CONFERENCE

Eastern Division

	W	L	T	Pct.	Pts.	OP
N.Y. Giants	10	5	1	.656	307	265
Washington	8	7	1	.531	327	289
Philadelphia	6	9	1	.406	317	372
Dallas	6	10	0	.375	304	314
Arizona	4	12	0	.250	283	379

Central Division

	W	L	T	Pct.	Pts.	OP
Green Bay	13	3	0	.813	422	282
Tampa Bay*	10	6	0	.625	299	263
Detroit*	9	7	0	.563	379	306
Minnesota*	9	7	0	.563	354	359
Chicago	4	12	0	.250	263	421

Western Division

	W	L	T	Pct.	Pts.	OP
San Francisco#	13	3	0	.813	375	265
Carolina	7	9	0	.438	265	314
Atlanta	7	9	0	.438	320	361
New Orleans	6	10	0	.375	237	327
St. Louis	5	11	0	.313	299	359

*Wild Card qualifier for playoffs; #Top playoff seed in conference
Miami finished ahead of N.Y. Jets based on head-to-head sweep (2-0). Pittsburgh finished ahead of Jacksonville based on better net division points (78 to Jaguars' 23). Oakland finished ahead of San Diego based on better division record (2-6 to Chargers' 1-7). San Francisco was top playoff seed based on better conference record than Green Bay (11-1 to Packers' 10-2). Detroit finished ahead of Minnesota based on head-to-head sweep (2-0). Carolina finished ahead of Atlanta based on head-to-head sweep (2-0).
Wild Card playoffs: DENVER 42, Jacksonville 17; NEW ENGLAND 17, Miami 3
Divisional playoffs: PITTSBURGH 7, New England 6; Denver 14, KANSAS CITY 10
AFC Championship: Denver 24, PITTSBURGH 21
Wild Card playoffs: Minnesota 23, N.Y. GIANTS 22; TAMPA BAY 20, Detroit 10
Divisional playoffs: SAN FRANCISCO 38, Minnesota 22; GREEN BAY 21, Tampa Bay 7
NFC Championship: Green Bay 23, SAN FRANCISCO 10
Super Bowl XXXII: Denver (AFC) 31, Green Bay (NFC) 24, at Qualcomm Stadium, San Diego, California

Playoff Seeds

AFC	NFC
1. Kansas City	1. San Francisco
2. Pittsburgh	**2. Green Bay**
3. New England	3. N.Y. Giants
4. Denver	4. Tampa Bay
5. Jacksonville	5. Detroit
6. Miami	6. Minnesota

1996

AMERICAN CONFERENCE

Eastern Division

	W	L	T	Pct.	Pts.	OP
New England	11	5	0	.688	418	313
Buffalo*	10	6	0	.625	319	266
Indianapolis*	9	7	0	.563	317	334
Miami	8	8	0	.500	339	325
N.Y. Jets	1	15	0	.063	279	454

Central Division

	W	L	T	Pct.	Pts.	OP
Pittsburgh	10	6	0	.625	344	257
Jacksonville*	9	7	0	.563	325	335
Cincinnati	8	8	0	.500	372	369
Houston	8	8	0	.500	345	319
Baltimore	4	12	0	.250	371	441

Western Division

	W	L	T	Pct.	Pts.	OP
Denver#	13	3	0	.813	391	275
Kansas City	9	7	0	.563	297	300
San Diego	8	8	0	.500	310	376
Oakland	7	9	0	.438	340	293
Seattle	7	9	0	.438	317	376

NATIONAL CONFERENCE

Eastern Division

	W	L	T	Pct.	Pts.	OP
Dallas	10	6	0	.625	286	250
Philadelphia*	10	6	0	.625	363	341
Washington	9	7	0	.563	364	312
Arizona	7	9	0	.438	300	397
N.Y. Giants	6	10	0	.375	242	297

Central Division

	W	L	T	Pct.	Pts.	OP
Green Bay#	13	3	0	.813	456	210
Minnesota*	9	7	0	.563	298	315
Chicago	7	9	0	.438	283	305
Tampa Bay	6	10	0	.375	221	293
Detroit	5	11	0	.313	302	368

Western Division

	W	L	T	Pct.	Pts.	OP
Carolina	12	4	0	.750	367	218
San Francisco*	12	4	0	.750	398	257
St. Louis	6	10	0	.375	303	409
Atlanta	3	13	0	.188	309	461
New Orleans	3	13	0	.188	229	339

*Wild Card qualifier for playoffs; #Top playoff seed in conference
Jacksonville was second Wild Card ahead of Indianapolis and Kansas City based on better conference record (7-5 to Colts' 6-6 and Chiefs' 5-7). Indianapolis was third Wild Card based on head-to-head victory over Kansas City (1-0). Cincinnati finished ahead of Houston based on better net division points (19 to Oilers' 11). Oakland finished ahead of Seattle based on better division record (3-5 to Seahawks' 2-6). Dallas finished ahead of Philadelphia based on better record against common opponents (7-4 to Eagles' 6-5). Minnesota was third Wild Card based on better conference record than Washington (8-4 to Redskins' 6-6). Carolina finished ahead of San Francisco based on head-to-head sweep (2-0). Atlanta finished ahead of New Orleans based on head-to-head sweep (2-0).
Wild Card playoffs: Jacksonville 30, BUFFALO 27; PITTSBURGH 42, Indianapolis 14
Divisional playoffs: Jacksonville 30, DENVER 27; NEW ENGLAND 28, Pittsburgh 3
AFC Championship: NEW ENGLAND 20, Jacksonville 6
Wild Card playoffs: DALLAS 40, Minnesota 15; SAN FRANCISCO 14, Philadelphia 0
Divisional playoffs: GREEN BAY 35, San Francisco 14; CAROLINA 26, Dallas 17
NFC Championship: GREEN BAY 30, Carolina 13
Super Bowl XXXI: Green Bay (NFC) 35, New England (AFC) 21, at Louisiana Superdome, New Orleans, Louisiana

Playoff Seeds

AFC	NFC
1. Denver	**1. Green Bay**
2. New England	2. Carolina
3. Pittsburgh	3. Dallas
4. Buffalo	4. San Francisco
5. Jacksonville	5. Philadelphia
6. Indianapolis	6. Minnesota

1995

AMERICAN CONFERENCE
Eastern Division

	W	L	T	Pct.	Pts.	OP
Buffalo	10	6	0	.625	350	335
Indianapolis*	9	7	0	.563	331	316
Miami*	9	7	0	.563	398	332
New England	6	10	0	.375	294	377
N.Y. Jets	3	13	0	.188	233	384

Central Division

	W	L	T	Pct.	Pts.	OP
Pittsburgh	11	5	0	.688	407	327
Cincinnati	7	9	0	.438	349	374
Houston	7	9	0	.438	348	324
Cleveland	5	11	0	.313	289	356
Jacksonville	4	12	0	.250	275	404

Western Division

	W	L	T	Pct.	Pts.	OP
Kansas City#	13	3	0	.813	358	241
San Diego*	9	7	0	.563	321	323
Seattle	8	8	0	.500	363	366
Denver	8	8	0	.500	388	345
Oakland	8	8	0	.500	348	332

NATIONAL CONFERENCE
Eastern Division

	W	L	T	Pct.	Pts.	OP
Dallas#	12	4	0	.750	435	291
Philadelphia*	10	6	0	.625	318	338
Washington	6	10	0	.375	326	359
N.Y. Giants	5	11	0	.313	290	340
Arizona	4	12	0	.250	275	422

Central Division

	W	L	T	Pct.	Pts.	OP
Green Bay	11	5	0	.688	404	314
Detroit*	10	6	0	.625	436	336
Chicago	9	7	0	.563	392	360
Minnesota	8	8	0	.500	412	385
Tampa Bay	7	9	0	.438	238	335

Western Division

	W	L	T	Pct.	Pts.	OP
San Francisco	11	5	0	.688	457	258
Atlanta*	9	7	0	.563	362	349
St. Louis	7	9	0	.438	309	418
Carolina	7	9	0	.438	289	325
New Orleans	7	9	0	.438	319	348

*Wild Card qualifier for playoffs; #Top playoff seed in conference
Indianapolis finished ahead of Miami based on head-to-head sweep (2-0). San Diego was first Wild Card based on head-to-head victory over Indianapolis (1-0). Cincinnati finished ahead of Houston based on better division record (4-4 to Oilers' 3-5). Seattle finished ahead of Denver and Oakland based on best head-to-head record (3-1 to Broncos' 2-2 and Raiders' 1-3). Denver finished ahead of Oakland based on head-to-head sweep (2-0). Philadelphia was first Wild Card ahead of Detroit based on better conference record (9-3 to Lions' 7-5). San Francisco was second playoff seed ahead of Green Bay based on better conference record (8-4 to Packers' 7-5). Atlanta was third Wild Card ahead of Chicago based on better record against common opponents (4-2 to Bears' 3-3). St. Louis finished ahead of Carolina and New Orleans based on best head-to-head record (3-1 to Panthers' 1-3 and Saints' 2-2). Carolina finished ahead of New Orleans based on better conference record (4-8 to 3-9).
Wild Card playoffs: BUFFALO 37, Miami 22; Indianapolis 35, SAN DIEGO 20
Divisional playoffs: PITTSBURGH 40, Buffalo 21; Indianapolis 10, KANSAS CITY 7
AFC Championship: PITTSBURGH 20, Indianapolis 16
Wild Card playoffs: PHILADELPHIA 58, Detroit 37; GREEN BAY 37, Atlanta 20
Divisional playoffs: Green Bay 27, SAN FRANCISCO 17; DALLAS 30, Philadelphia 11
NFC Championship: DALLAS 38, Green Bay 27
Super Bowl XXX: Dallas (NFC) 27, Pittsburgh (AFC) 17, at Sun Devil Stadium, Tempe, Arizona

Playoff Seeds

AFC	NFC
1. Kansas City	1. Dallas
2. Pittsburgh	2. San Francisco
3. Buffalo	3. Green Bay
4. San Diego	4. Philadelphia
5. Indianapolis	5. Detroit
6. Miami	6. Atlanta

1994

AMERICAN CONFERENCE
Eastern Division

	W	L	T	Pct.	Pts.	OP
Miami	10	6	0	.625	389	327
New England*	10	6	0	.625	351	312
Indianapolis	8	8	0	.500	307	320
Buffalo	7	9	0	.438	340	356
N.Y. Jets	6	10	0	.375	264	320

Central Division

	W	L	T	Pct.	Pts.	OP
Pittsburgh#	12	4	0	.750	316	234
Cleveland*	11	5	0	.688	340	204
Cincinnati	3	13	0	.188	276	406
Houston	2	14	0	.125	226	352

Western Division

	W	L	T	Pct.	Pts.	OP
San Diego	11	5	0	.688	381	306
Kansas City*	9	7	0	.563	319	298
L.A. Raiders	9	7	0	.563	303	327
Denver	7	9	0	.438	347	396
Seattle	6	10	0	.375	287	323

NATIONAL CONFERENCE
Eastern Division

	W	L	T	Pct.	Pts.	OP
Dallas	12	4	0	.750	414	248
N.Y. Giants	9	7	0	.563	279	305
Arizona	8	8	0	.500	235	267
Philadelphia	7	9	0	.438	308	308
Washington	3	13	0	.188	320	412

Central Division

	W	L	T	Pct.	Pts.	OP
Minnesota	10	6	0	.625	356	314
Green Bay*	9	7	0	.563	382	287
Detroit*	9	7	0	.563	357	342
Chicago*	9	7	0	.563	271	307
Tampa Bay	6	10	0	.375	251	351

Western Division

	W	L	T	Pct.	Pts.	OP
San Francisco#	13	3	0	.813	505	296
New Orleans	7	9	0	.438	348	407
Atlanta	7	9	0	.438	317	385
L.A. Rams	4	12	0	.250	286	365

*Wild Card qualifier for playoffs; #Top playoff seed in conference
Miami finished ahead of New England based on head-to-head sweep (2-0). Kansas City finished ahead of L.A. Raiders based on head-to-head sweep (2-0). Green Bay was first Wild Card based on best head-to-head record (3-1) vs. Detroit (2-2) and Chicago (1-3) and better conference record (8-4) than N.Y. Giants (6-6). Detroit was second Wild Card based on better division record (4-4) than Chicago (3-5) and head-to-head victory over N.Y. Giants (1-0). Chicago was third Wild Card based on better record against common opponents (4-4) than N.Y. Giants (3-5). New Orleans finished ahead of Atlanta based on head-to-head sweep (2-0).
Wild Card playoffs: MIAMI 27, Kansas City 17; CLEVELAND 20, New England 13
Divisional playoffs: PITTSBURGH 29, Cleveland 9; SAN DIEGO 22, Miami 21
AFC Championship: San Diego 17, PITTSBURGH 13
Wild Card playoffs: GREEN BAY 16, Detroit 12; Chicago 35, MINNESOTA 18
Divisional playoffs: SAN FRANCISCO 44, Chicago 15; DALLAS 35, Green Bay 9
NFC Championship: SAN FRANCISCO 38, Dallas 28
Super Bowl XXIX: San Francisco (NFC) 49, San Diego (AFC) 26, at Joe Robbie Stadium, Miami, Florida

Playoff Seeds

AFC	NFC
1. Pittsburgh	1. San Francisco
2. San Diego	2. Dallas
3. Miami	3. Minnesota
4. Cleveland	4. Green Bay
5. New England	5. Detroit
6. Kansas City	6. Chicago

1993

AMERICAN CONFERENCE

Eastern Division

	W	L	T	Pct.	Pts.	OP
Buffalo#	12	4	0	.750	329	242
Miami	9	7	0	.563	349	351
N.Y. Jets	8	8	0	.500	270	247
New England	5	11	0	.313	238	286
Indianapolis	4	12	0	.250	189	378

Central Division

	W	L	T	Pct.	Pts.	OP
Houston	12	4	0	.750	368	238
Pittsburgh*	9	7	0	.563	308	281
Cleveland	7	9	0	.438	304	307
Cincinnati	3	13	0	.188	187	319

Western Division

	W	L	T	Pct.	Pts.	OP
Kansas City	11	5	0	.688	328	291
L.A. Raiders*	10	6	0	.625	306	326
Denver*	9	7	0	.563	373	284
San Diego	8	8	0	.500	322	290
Seattle	6	10	0	.375	280	314

NATIONAL CONFERENCE

Eastern Division

	W	L	T	Pct.	Pts.	OP
Dallas#	12	4	0	.750	376	229
N.Y. Giants*	11	5	0	.688	288	205
Philadelphia	8	8	0	.500	293	315
Phoenix	7	9	0	.438	326	269
Washington	4	12	0	.250	230	345

Central Division

	W	L	T	Pct.	Pts.	OP
Detroit	10	6	0	.625	298	292
Minnesota*	9	7	0	.563	277	290
Green Bay*	9	7	0	.563	340	282
Chicago	7	9	0	.438	234	230
Tampa Bay	5	11	0	.313	237	376

Western Division

	W	L	T	Pct.	Pts.	OP
San Francisco	10	6	0	.625	473	295
New Orleans	8	8	0	.500	317	343
Atlanta	6	10	0	.375	316	385
L.A. Rams	5	11	0	.313	221	367

*Wild Card qualifier for playoffs; #Top playoff seed in conference
Buffalo was top playoff seed based on head-to-head victory over
Houston (1-0). Denver was second Wild Card ahead of Pittsburgh
and Miami based on better conference record (8-4 to Steelers'
7-5 to Dolphins' 6-6). Pittsburgh was third Wild Card ahead of
Miami based on head-to-head victory. San Francisco was second
playoff seed based on head-to-head victory over Detroit (1-0).
Minnesota finished ahead of Green Bay based on head-to-head
sweep (2-0).
Wild Card playoffs: KANSAS CITY 27, Pittsburgh 24 (OT);
    L.A. RAIDERS 42, Denver 24
Divisional playoffs: BUFFALO 29, L.A. Raiders 23;
    Kansas City 28, HOUSTON 20
AFC Championship: BUFFALO 30, Kansas City 13
Wild Card playoffs: Green Bay 28, DETROIT 24;
    N.Y. GIANTS 17, Minnesota 10
Divisional playoffs: SAN FRANCISCO 44, N.Y. Giants 3;
    DALLAS 27, Green Bay 17
NFC Championship: DALLAS 38, San Francisco 21
Super Bowl XXVIII: Dallas (NFC) 30, Buffalo (AFC) 13,
    at Georgia Dome, Atlanta, Georgia

Playoff Seeds

AFC	NFC
1. Buffalo	**1. Dallas**
2. Houston	2. San Francisco
3. Kansas City	3. Detroit
4. L.A. Raiders	4. N.Y. Giants
5. Denver	5. Minnesota
6. Pittsburgh	6. Green Bay

1992

AMERICAN CONFERENCE

Eastern Division

	W	L	T	Pct.	Pts.	OP
Miami	11	5	0	.688	340	281
Buffalo*	11	5	0	.688	381	283
Indianapolis	9	7	0	.563	216	302
N.Y. Jets	4	12	0	.250	220	315
New England	2	14	0	.125	205	363

Central Division

	W	L	T	Pct.	Pts.	OP
Pittsburgh#	11	5	0	.688	299	225
Houston*	10	6	0	.625	352	258
Cleveland	7	9	0	.438	272	275
Cincinnati	5	11	0	.313	274	364

Western Division

	W	L	T	Pct.	Pts.	OP
San Diego	11	5	0	.688	335	241
Kansas City*	10	6	0	.625	348	282
Denver	8	8	0	.500	262	329
L.A. Raiders	7	9	0	.438	249	281
Seattle	2	14	0	.125	140	312

NATIONAL CONFERENCE

Eastern Division

	W	L	T	Pct.	Pts.	OP
Dallas	13	3	0	.813	409	243
Philadelphia*	11	5	0	.688	354	245
Washington*	9	7	0	.563	300	255
N.Y. Giants	6	10	0	.375	306	367
Phoenix	4	12	0	.250	243	332

Central Division

	W	L	T	Pct.	Pts.	OP
Minnesota	11	5	0	.688	374	249
Green Bay	9	7	0	.563	276	296
Tampa Bay	5	11	0	.313	267	365
Chicago	5	11	0	.313	295	361
Detroit	5	11	0	.313	273	332

Western Division

	W	L	T	Pct.	Pts.	OP
San Francisco#	14	2	0	.875	431	236
New Orleans*	12	4	0	.750	330	202
Atlanta	6	10	0	.375	327	414
L.A. Rams	6	10	0	.375	313	383

*Wild Card qualifier for playoffs; #Top playoff seed in conference
Pittsburgh was top playoff seed, and Miami was second playoff seed
ahead of San Diego, based on conference record (10-2 to Dolphins' 9-3 to Chargers' 9-5). Miami finished ahead of Buffalo
based on better conference record (9-3 to Bills' 7-5). Houston
was second Wild Card based on head-to-head victory over
Kansas City (1-0). Washington was third Wild Card based on
better conference record than Green Bay (7-5 to Packers' 6-6).
Tampa Bay finished ahead of Chicago and Chicago finished ahead
of Detroit based on better conference record (5-9 to Bears' 4-8
and Lions' 3-9). Atlanta finished ahead of L.A. Rams based on
better record against common opponents (5-7 to Rams' 4-8).
Wild Card playoffs: SAN DIEGO 17, Kansas City 0;
    BUFFALO 41, Houston 38 (OT)
Divisional playoffs: Buffalo 24, PITTSBURGH 3;
    MIAMI 31, San Diego 0
AFC Championship: Buffalo 29, MIAMI 10
Wild Card playoffs: Washington 24, MINNESOTA 7;
    Philadelphia 36, NEW ORLEANS 20
Divisional playoffs: SAN FRANCISCO 20, Washington 13;
    DALLAS 34, Philadelphia 10
NFC Championship: Dallas 30, SAN FRANCISCO 20
Super Bowl XXVII: Dallas (NFC) 52, Buffalo (AFC) 17,
    at Rose Bowl, Pasadena, California

Playoff Seeds

AFC	NFC
1. Pittsburgh	1. San Francisco
2. Miami	**2. Dallas**
3. San Diego	3. Minnesota
4. Buffalo	4. New Orleans
5. Houston	5. Philadelphia
6. Kansas City	6. Washington

1991

AMERICAN CONFERENCE

Eastern Division

	W	L	T	Pct.	Pts.	OP
Buffalo#	13	3	0	.813	458	318
N.Y. Jets*	8	8	0	.500	314	293
Miami	8	8	0	.500	343	349
New England	6	10	0	.375	211	305
Indianapolis	1	15	0	.063	143	381

Central Division

	W	L	T	Pct.	Pts.	OP
Houston	11	5	0	.688	386	251
Pittsburgh	7	9	0	.438	292	344
Cleveland	6	10	0	.375	293	298
Cincinnati	3	13	0	.188	263	435

Western Division

	W	L	T	Pct.	Pts.	OP
Denver	12	4	0	.750	304	235
Kansas City*	10	6	0	.625	322	252
L.A. Raiders*	9	7	0	.563	298	297
Seattle	7	9	0	.438	276	261
San Diego	4	12	0	.250	274	342

NATIONAL CONFERENCE

Eastern Division

	W	L	T	Pct.	Pts.	OP
Washington#	14	2	0	.875	485	224
Dallas*	11	5	0	.688	342	310
Philadelphia	10	6	0	.625	285	244
N.Y. Giants	8	8	0	.500	281	297
Phoenix	4	12	0	.250	196	344

Central Division

	W	L	T	Pct.	Pts.	OP
Detroit	12	4	0	.750	339	295
Chicago*	11	5	0	.688	299	269
Minnesota	8	8	0	.500	301	306
Green Bay	4	12	0	.250	273	313
Tampa Bay	3	13	0	.188	199	365

Western Division

	W	L	T	Pct.	Pts.	OP
New Orleans	11	5	0	.688	341	211
Atlanta*	10	6	0	.625	361	338
San Francisco	10	6	0	.625	393	239
L.A. Rams	3	13	0	.188	234	390

*Wild Card qualifier for playoffs; #Top playoff seed in conference
N.Y. Jets finished ahead of Miami based on head-to-head sweep (2-0). Chicago was first Wild Card based on better conference record than Dallas (9-3 to Cowboys' 8-4). Atlanta finished ahead of San Francisco based on head-to-head sweep (2-0), and was third Wild Card ahead of Philadelphia based on better conference record (7-5 to Eagles' 6-6).
Wild Card playoffs: KANSAS CITY 10, L.A. Raiders 6; HOUSTON 17, N.Y. Jets 10
Divisional playoffs: DENVER 26, Houston 24; BUFFALO 37, Kansas City 14
AFC Championship: BUFFALO 10, Denver 7
Wild Card playoffs: Atlanta 27, NEW ORLEANS 20; Dallas 17, CHICAGO 13
Divisional playoffs: WASHINGTON 24, Atlanta 7; DETROIT 38, Dallas 6
NFC Championship: WASHINGTON 41, Detroit 10
Super Bowl XXVI: Washington (NFC) 37, Buffalo (AFC) 24, at Hubert H. Humphrey Metrodome, Minneapolis, Minnesota

Playoff Seeds

AFC	NFC
1. Buffalo	1. Washington
2. Denver	2. Detroit
3. Houston	3. New Orleans
4. Kansas City	4. Chicago
5. L.A. Raiders	5. Dallas
6. N.Y. Jets	6. Atlanta

1990

AMERICAN CONFERENCE

Eastern Division

	W	L	T	Pct.	Pts.	OP
Buffalo#	13	3	0	.813	428	263
Miami*	12	4	0	.750	336	242
Indianapolis	7	9	0	.438	281	353
N.Y. Jets	6	10	0	.375	295	345
New England	1	15	0	.063	181	446

Central Division

	W	L	T	Pct.	Pts.	OP
Cincinnati	9	7	0	.563	360	352
Houston*	9	7	0	.563	405	307
Pittsburgh	9	7	0	.563	292	240
Cleveland	3	13	0	.188	228	462

Western Division

	W	L	T	Pct.	Pts.	OP
L.A. Raiders	12	4	0	.750	337	268
Kansas City*	11	5	0	.688	369	257
Seattle	9	7	0	.563	306	286
San Diego	6	10	0	.375	315	281
Denver	5	11	0	.313	331	374

NATIONAL CONFERENCE

Eastern Division

	W	L	T	Pct.	Pts.	OP
N.Y. Giants	13	3	0	.813	335	211
Philadelphia*	10	6	0	.625	396	299
Washington*	10	6	0	.625	381	301
Dallas	7	9	0	.438	244	308
Phoenix	5	11	0	.313	268	396

Central Division

	W	L	T	Pct.	Pts.	OP
Chicago	11	5	0	.688	348	280
Tampa Bay	6	10	0	.375	264	367
Detroit	6	10	0	.375	373	413
Green Bay	6	10	0	.375	271	347
Minnesota	6	10	0	.375	351	326

Western Division

	W	L	T	Pct.	Pts.	OP
San Francisco#	14	2	0	.875	353	239
New Orleans*	8	8	0	.500	274	275
L.A. Rams	5	11	0	.313	345	412
Atlanta	5	11	0	.313	348	365

*Wild Card qualifier for playoffs; #Top playoff seed in conference
Cincinnati finished ahead of Houston and Pittsburgh based on best head-to-head record (3-1 to Oilers' 2-2 to Steelers' 1-3). Houston was Wild Card based on better conference record (8-4) than Seattle (7-5) and Pittsburgh (6-6). Philadelphia finished ahead of Washington based on better division record (5-3 to Redskins' 4-4). Tampa Bay was second in NFC Central based on best head-to-head record (5-1) against Detroit (2-4), Green Bay (3-3), and Minnesota (2-4). Detroit finished third based on best net division points (minus 8) against Green Bay (minus 40). Green Bay finished ahead of Minnesota based on better conference record (5-7 to Vikings' 4-8). The L.A. Rams finished ahead of Atlanta based on net points in division (plus 1 to Falcons' minus 31).
Wild Card playoffs: MIAMI 17, Kansas City 16; CINCINNATI 41, Houston 14
Divisional playoffs: BUFFALO 44, Miami 34; L.A. RAIDERS 20, Cincinnati 10
AFC Championship: BUFFALO 51, L.A. Raiders 3
Wild Card playoffs: Washington 20, PHILADELPHIA 6; CHICAGO 16, New Orleans 6
Divisional playoffs: SAN FRANCISCO 28, Washington 10; N.Y. GIANTS 31, Chicago 3
NFC Championship: N.Y. Giants 15, SAN FRANCISCO 13
Super Bowl XXV: N.Y. Giants (NFC) 20, Buffalo (AFC) 19, at Tampa Stadium, Tampa, Florida

Playoff Seeds

AFC	NFC
1. Buffalo	1. San Francisco
2. L.A. Raiders	2. N.Y. Giants
3. Cincinnati	3. Chicago
4. Miami	4. Philadelphia
5. Kansas City	5. Washington
6. Houston	6. New Orleans

1989

AMERICAN CONFERENCE

Eastern Division

	W	L	T	Pct.	Pts.	OP
Buffalo	9	7	0	.563	409	317
Indianapolis	8	8	0	.500	298	301
Miami	8	8	0	.500	331	379
New England	5	11	0	.313	297	391
N.Y. Jets	4	12	0	.250	253	411

Central Division

	W	L	T	Pct.	Pts.	OP
Cleveland	9	6	1	.594	334	254
Houston*	9	7	0	.563	365	412
Pittsburgh*	9	7	0	.563	265	326
Cincinnati	8	8	0	.500	404	285

Western Division

	W	L	T	Pct.	Pts.	OP
Denver#	11	5	0	.688	362	226
Kansas City	8	7	1	.531	318	286
L.A. Raiders	8	8	0	.500	315	297
Seattle	7	9	0	.438	241	327
San Diego	6	10	0	.375	266	290

NATIONAL CONFERENCE

Eastern Division

	W	L	T	Pct.	Pts.	OP
N.Y. Giants	12	4	0	.750	348	252
Philadelphia*	11	5	0	.688	342	274
Washington	10	6	0	.625	386	308
Phoenix	5	11	0	.313	258	377
Dallas	1	15	0	.063	204	393

Central Division

	W	L	T	Pct.	Pts.	OP
Minnesota	10	6	0	.625	351	275
Green Bay	10	6	0	.625	362	356
Detroit	7	9	0	.438	312	364
Chicago	6	10	0	.375	358	377
Tampa Bay	5	11	0	.313	320	419

Western Division

	W	L	T	Pct.	Pts.	OP
San Francisco#	14	2	0	.875	442	253
L.A. Rams*	11	5	0	.688	426	344
New Orleans	9	7	0	.563	386	301
Atlanta	3	13	0	.188	279	437

*Wild Card qualifier for playoffs; #Top playoff seed in conference Indianapolis finished ahead of Miami based on better conference record (7-5 vs. Dolphins' 6-8). Houston finished ahead of Pittsburgh based on head-to-head sweep (2-0). The L.A. Rams did not play San Francisco in the divisional playoffs because, from 1970-1989, two teams from the same division could not meet prior to the conference championship game. Philadelphia was first Wild Card ahead of L.A. Rams based on better record against common opponents (7-3 to Rams' 5-4). Minnesota finished ahead of Green Bay based on better division record (6-2 vs. Packers' 5-3).

Wild Card playoff: Pittsburgh 26, HOUSTON 23 (OT)
Divisional playoffs: CLEVELAND 34, Buffalo 30;
    DENVER 24, Pittsburgh 23
AFC Championship: DENVER 37, Cleveland 21
Wild Card playoff: L.A. Rams 21, PHILADELPHIA 7
Divisional playoffs: L.A. Rams 19, N.Y. GIANTS 13 (OT);
    SAN FRANCISCO 41, Minnesota 13
NFC Championship: SAN FRANCISCO 30, L.A. Rams 3
Super Bowl XXIV: San Francisco (NFC) 55, Denver (AFC) 10,
    at Louisiana Superdome, New Orleans, Louisiana

1988

AMERICAN CONFERENCE

Eastern Division

	W	L	T	Pct.	Pts.	OP
Buffalo	12	4	0	.750	329	237
Indianapolis	9	7	0	.563	354	315
New England	9	7	0	.563	250	284
N.Y. Jets	8	7	1	.531	372	354
Miami	6	10	0	.375	319	380

Central Division

	W	L	T	Pct.	Pts.	OP
Cincinnati#	12	4	0	.750	448	329
Cleveland*	10	6	0	.625	304	288
Houston*	10	6	0	.625	424	365
Pittsburgh	5	11	0	.313	336	421

Western Division

	W	L	T	Pct.	Pts.	OP
Seattle	9	7	0	.563	339	329
Denver	8	8	0	.500	327	352
L.A. Raiders	7	9	0	.438	325	369
San Diego	6	10	0	.375	231	332
Kansas City	4	11	1	.281	254	320

NATIONAL CONFERENCE

Eastern Division

	W	L	T	Pct.	Pts.	OP
Philadelphia	10	6	0	.625	379	319
N.Y. Giants	10	6	0	.625	359	304
Washington	7	9	0	.438	345	387
Phoenix	7	9	0	.438	344	398
Dallas	3	13	0	.188	265	381

Central Division

	W	L	T	Pct.	Pts.	OP
Chicago#	12	4	0	.750	312	215
Minnesota*	11	5	0	.688	406	233
Tampa Bay	5	11	0	.313	261	350
Detroit	4	12	0	.250	220	313
Green Bay	4	12	0	.250	240	315

Western Division

	W	L	T	Pct.	Pts.	OP
San Francisco	10	6	0	.625	369	294
L.A. Rams*	10	6	0	.625	407	293
New Orleans	10	6	0	.625	312	283
Atlanta	5	11	0	.313	244	315

*Wild Card qualifier for playoffs; #Top playoff seed in conference Cincinnati was top playoff seed ahead of Buffalo based on head-to-head victory (1-0). Indianapolis finished ahead of New England based on better record against common opponents (7-5 to Patriots' 6-6). Cleveland finished ahead of Houston based on better division record (4-2 to Oilers' 3-3). Houston did not play Cincinnati, and Minnesota did not play Chicago in the divisional playoffs because, from 1970-1989, two teams from the same division could not meet prior to the conference championship game. Philadelphia finished first in NFC East based on head-to-head sweep of N.Y. Giants (2-0). Washington finished third in NFC East based on better division record (4-4) than Phoenix (3-5). Detroit finished fourth in NFC Central based on head-to-head sweep of Green Bay (2-0). San Francisco finished first in NFC West based on better head-to-head record (3-1) against L.A. Rams (2-2) and New Orleans (1-3). San Francisco finished with second playoff seed ahead of Philadelphia based on better record against common opponents (5-3 to Eagles' 5-4). L.A. Rams finished second in NFC West based on better division record (4-2) than New Orleans (3-3) and earned Wild-Card position based on better conference record (8-4) than N.Y. Giants (9-5) and New Orleans (6-6).

Wild Card playoff: Houston 24, CLEVELAND 23
Divisional playoffs: CINCINNATI 21, Seattle 13;
    BUFFALO 17, Houston 10
AFC Championship: CINCINNATI 21, Buffalo 10
Wild Card playoff: MINNESOTA 28, L.A. Rams 17
Divisional playoffs: CHICAGO 20, Philadelphia 12;
    SAN FRANCISCO 34, Minnesota 9
NFC Championship: San Francisco 28, CHICAGO 3
Super Bowl XXIII: San Francisco (NFC) 20, Cincinnati (AFC) 16,
    at Joe Robbie Stadium, Miami, Florida

1987

AMERICAN CONFERENCE

Eastern Division

	W	L	T	Pct.	Pts.	OP
Indianapolis	9	6	0	.600	300	238
New England	8	7	0	.533	320	293
Miami	8	7	0	.533	362	335
Buffalo	7	8	0	.467	270	305
N.Y. Jets	6	9	0	.400	334	360

Central Division

	W	L	T	Pct.	Pts.	OP
Cleveland	10	5	0	.667	390	239
Houston*	9	6	0	.600	345	349
Pittsburgh	8	7	0	.533	285	299
Cincinnati	4	11	0	.267	285	370

Western Division

	W	L	T	Pct.	Pts.	OP
Denver#	10	4	1	.700	379	288
Seattle*	9	6	0	.600	371	314
San Diego	8	7	0	.533	253	317
L.A. Raiders	5	10	0	.333	301	289
Kansas City	4	11	0	.267	273	388

NATIONAL CONFERENCE

Eastern Division

	W	L	T	Pct.	Pts.	OP
Washington	11	4	0	.733	379	285
Dallas	7	8	0	.467	340	348
St. Louis	7	8	0	.467	362	368
Philadelphia	7	8	0	.467	337	380
N.Y. Giants	6	9	0	.400	280	312

Central Division

	W	L	T	Pct.	Pts.	OP
Chicago	11	4	0	.733	356	282
Minnesota*	8	7	0	.533	336	335
Green Bay	5	9	1	.367	255	300
Tampa Bay	4	11	0	.267	286	360
Detroit	4	11	0	.267	269	384

Western Division

	W	L	T	Pct.	Pts.	OP
San Francisco#	13	2	0	.867	459	253
New Orleans*	12	3	0	.800	422	283
L.A. Rams	6	9	0	.400	317	361
Atlanta	3	12	0	.200	205	436

*Wild Card qualifier for playoffs; #Top playoff seed in conference
New England finished ahead of Miami based on head-to-head sweep (2-0). Houston was first Wild Card ahead of Seattle based on better conference record (7-4 to Seahawks' 5-6). Chicago was second playoff seed ahead of Washington based on better conference record (9-2 to Redskins' 9-3). Dallas finished ahead of St. Louis and Philadelphia based on better division record (4-4 to Cardinals' 3-5 and Eagles' 3-5). St. Louis finished ahead of Philadelphia based on better conference record (7-7 to Eagles' 4-7). Tampa Bay finished ahead of Detroit based on better division record (3-4 to Lions' 2-5).
Wild Card playoff: HOUSTON 23, Seattle 20 (OT)
Divisional playoffs: CLEVELAND 38, Indianapolis 21; DENVER 34, Houston 10
AFC Championship: DENVER 38, Cleveland 33
Wild Card playoff: Minnesota 44, NEW ORLEANS 10
Divisional playoffs: Minnesota 36, SAN FRANCISCO 24; Washington 21, CHICAGO 17
NFC Championship: WASHINGTON 17, Minnesota 10
Super Bowl XXII: Washington (NFC) 42, Denver (AFC) 10, at San Diego Jack Murphy Stadium, San Diego, California
Note: 1987 regular season was reduced from 16 to 15 games for each team due to players' strike.

1986

AMERICAN CONFERENCE

Eastern Division

	W	L	T	Pct.	Pts.	OP
New England	11	5	0	.688	412	307
N.Y. Jets*	10	6	0	.625	364	386
Miami	8	8	0	.500	430	405
Buffalo	4	12	0	.250	287	348
Indianapolis	3	13	0	.188	229	400

Central Division

	W	L	T	Pct.	Pts.	OP
Cleveland#	12	4	0	.750	391	310
Cincinnati	10	6	0	.625	409	394
Pittsburgh	6	10	0	.375	307	336
Houston	5	11	0	.313	274	329

Western Division

	W	L	T	Pct.	Pts.	OP
Denver	11	5	0	.688	378	327
Kansas City*	10	6	0	.625	358	326
Seattle	10	6	0	.625	366	293
L.A. Raiders	8	8	0	.500	323	346
San Diego	4	12	0	.250	335	396

NATIONAL CONFERENCE

Eastern Division

	W	L	T	Pct.	Pts.	OP
N.Y. Giants#	14	2	0	.875	371	236
Washington*	12	4	0	.750	368	296
Dallas	7	9	0	.438	346	337
Philadelphia	5	10	1	.344	256	312
St. Louis	4	11	1	.281	218	351

Central Division

	W	L	T	Pct.	Pts.	OP
Chicago	14	2	0	.875	352	187
Minnesota	9	7	0	.563	398	273
Detroit	5	11	0	.313	277	326
Green Bay	4	12	0	.250	254	418
Tampa Bay	2	14	0	.125	239	473

Western Division

	W	L	T	Pct.	Pts.	OP
San Francisco	10	5	1	.656	374	247
L.A. Rams*	10	6	0	.625	309	267
Atlanta	7	8	1	.469	280	280
New Orleans	7	9	0	.438	288	287

*Wild Card qualifier for playoffs; #Top playoff seed in conference
Denver was second playoff seed ahead of New England based on head-to-head victory (1-0). N.Y. Jets were first Wild Card based on better conference record (8-4) than Kansas City (9-5), Seattle (7-5), and Cincinnati (7-5). Kansas City was second Wild Card based on better conference record (9-5) than Seattle (7-5) and Cincinnati (7-5). N.Y. Giants were top playoff seed based on better conference record than Chicago (11-1 to Bears' 10-2). Washington did not play the N.Y. Giants in the divisional playoffs because, from 1970-1989, two teams from the same division could not meet prior to the conference championship game.
Wild Card playoff: N.Y. JETS 35, Kansas City 15
Divisional playoffs: CLEVELAND 23, N.Y. Jets 20 (OT); DENVER 22, New England 17
AFC Championship: Denver 23, CLEVELAND 20 (OT)
Wild Card playoff: WASHINGTON 19, L.A. Rams 7
Divisional playoffs: Washington 27, CHICAGO 13
N.Y. GIANTS 49, San Francisco 3
NFC Championship: N.Y. GIANTS 17, Washington 0
Super Bowl XXI: N.Y. Giants (NFC) 39, Denver (AFC) 20, at Rose Bowl, Pasadena, California

1985

AMERICAN CONFERENCE

Eastern Division

	W	L	T	Pct.	Pts.	OP
Miami	12	4	0	.750	428	320
N.Y. Jets*	11	5	0	.688	393	264
New England*	11	5	0	.688	362	290
Indianapolis	5	11	0	.313	320	386
Buffalo	2	14	0	.125	200	381

Central Division

	W	L	T	Pct.	Pts.	OP
Cleveland	8	8	0	.500	287	294
Cincinnati	7	9	0	.438	441	437
Pittsburgh	7	9	0	.438	379	355
Houston	5	11	0	.313	284	412

Western Division

	W	L	T	Pct.	Pts.	OP
L.A. Raiders#	12	4	0	.750	354	308
Denver	11	5	0	.688	380	329
Seattle	8	8	0	.500	349	303
San Diego	8	8	0	.500	467	435
Kansas City	6	10	0	.375	317	360

NATIONAL CONFERENCE

Eastern Division

	W	L	T	Pct.	Pts.	OP
Dallas	10	6	0	.625	357	333
N.Y. Giants*	10	6	0	.625	399	283
Washington	10	6	0	.625	297	312
Philadelphia	7	9	0	.438	286	310
St. Louis	5	11	0	.313	278	414

Central Division

	W	L	T	Pct.	Pts.	OP
Chicago#	15	1	0	.938	456	198
Green Bay	8	8	0	.500	337	355
Minnesota	7	9	0	.438	346	359
Detroit	7	9	0	.438	307	366
Tampa Bay	2	14	0	.125	294	448

Western Division

	W	L	T	Pct.	Pts.	OP
L.A. Rams	11	5	0	.688	340	277
San Francisco*	10	6	0	.625	411	263
New Orleans	5	11	0	.313	294	401
Atlanta	4	12	0	.250	282	452

*Wild Card qualifier for playoffs; #Top playoff seed in conference
L.A. Raiders were top playoff seed ahead of Miami based on better record against common opponents (5-1 to 4-2). N.Y. Jets were first Wild Card based on better conference record (9-3) than New England (8-4) and Denver (8-4). New England was second Wild Card ahead of Denver based on better record against common opponents (4-2 to Broncos' 3-3). Cincinnati finished ahead of Pittsburgh based on head-to-head sweep (2-0). Seattle finished ahead of San Diego based on head-to-head sweep (2-0). Dallas finished ahead of N.Y. Giants and Washington based on head-to-head record (4-0 to Giants' 1-3 and Redskins' 1-3). N.Y. Giants were first Wild Card based on better conference record (8-4) than San Francisco (7-5) and Washington (6-6). San Francisco was second Wild Card based on head-to-head victory over Washington (1-0). Minnesota finished ahead of Detroit based on better division record (3-5 to Lions' 2-6).
Wild Card playoff: New England 26, N.Y. JETS 14
Divisional playoffs: MIAMI 24, Cleveland 21;
    New England 27, L.A. RAIDERS 20
AFC Championship: New England 31, MIAMI 14
Wild Card playoff: N.Y. GIANTS 17, San Francisco 3
Divisional playoffs: L.A. RAMS 20, Dallas 0;
    CHICAGO 21, N.Y. Giants 0
NFC Championship: CHICAGO 24, L.A. Rams 0
Super Bowl XX: Chicago (NFC) 46, New England (AFC) 10,
    at Louisiana Superdome, New Orleans, Louisiana

1984

AMERICAN CONFERENCE

Eastern Division

	W	L	T	Pct.	Pts.	OP
Miami#	14	2	0	.875	513	298
New England	9	7	0	.563	362	352
N.Y. Jets	7	9	0	.438	332	364
Indianapolis	4	12	0	.250	239	414
Buffalo	2	14	0	.125	250	454

Central Division

	W	L	T	Pct.	Pts.	OP
Pittsburgh	9	7	0	.563	387	310
Cincinnati	8	8	0	.500	339	339
Cleveland	5	11	0	.313	250	297
Houston	3	13	0	.188	240	437

Western Division

	W	L	T	Pct.	Pts.	OP
Denver	13	3	0	.813	353	241
Seattle*	12	4	0	.750	418	282
L.A. Raiders*	11	5	0	.688	368	278
Kansas City	8	8	0	.500	314	324
San Diego	7	9	0	.438	394	413

NATIONAL CONFERENCE

Eastern Division

	W	L	T	Pct.	Pts.	OP
Washington	11	5	0	.688	426	310
N.Y. Giants*	9	7	0	.563	299	301
St. Louis	9	7	0	.563	423	345
Dallas	9	7	0	.563	308	308
Philadelphia	6	9	1	.406	278	320

Central Division

	W	L	T	Pct.	Pts.	OP
Chicago	10	6	0	.625	325	248
Green Bay	8	8	0	.500	390	309
Tampa Bay	6	10	0	.375	335	380
Detroit	4	11	1	.281	283	408
Minnesota	3	13	0	.188	276	484

Western Division

	W	L	T	Pct.	Pts.	OP
San Francisco#	15	1	0	.938	475	227
L.A. Rams*	10	6	0	.625	346	316
New Orleans	7	9	0	.438	298	361
Atlanta	4	12	0	.250	281	382

*Wild Card qualifier for playoffs; #Top playoff seed in conference
N.Y. Giants finished ahead of St. Louis and Dallas based on best head-to-head record (3-1 to Cardinals' 2-2 and Cowboys' 1-3). St. Louis finished ahead of Dallas based on better division record (5-3 to Cowboys' 3-5).
Wild Card playoff: SEATTLE 13, L.A. Raiders 7
Divisional playoffs: MIAMI 31, Seattle 10;
    Pittsburgh 24, DENVER 17
AFC Championship: MIAMI 45, Pittsburgh 28
Wild Card playoff: N.Y. Giants 16, L.A. RAMS 13
Divisional playoffs: SAN FRANCISCO 21, N.Y. Giants 10;
    Chicago 23, WASHINGTON 19
NFC Championship: SAN FRANCISCO 23, Chicago 0
Super Bowl XIX: San Francisco (NFC) 38, Miami (AFC) 16,
    at Stanford Stadium, Stanford, California

1983

AMERICAN CONFERENCE

Eastern Division

	W	L	T	Pct.	Pts.	OP
Miami	12	4	0	.750	389	250
New England	8	8	0	.500	274	289
Buffalo	8	8	0	.500	283	351
Baltimore	7	9	0	.438	264	354
N.Y. Jets	7	9	0	.438	313	331

Central Division

	W	L	T	Pct.	Pts.	OP
Pittsburgh	10	6	0	.625	355	303
Cleveland	9	7	0	.563	356	342
Cincinnati	7	9	0	.438	346	302
Houston	2	14	0	.125	288	460

Western Division

	W	L	T	Pct.	Pts.	OP
L.A. Raiders#	12	4	0	.750	442	338
Seattle*	9	7	0	.563	403	397
Denver*	9	7	0	.563	302	327
San Diego	6	10	0	.375	358	462
Kansas City	6	10	0	.375	386	367

NATIONAL CONFERENCE

Eastern Division

	W	L	T	Pct.	Pts.	OP
Washington#	14	2	0	.875	541	332
Dallas*	12	4	0	.750	479	360
St. Louis	8	7	1	.531	374	428
Philadelphia	5	11	0	.313	233	322
N.Y. Giants	3	12	1	.219	267	347

Central Division

	W	L	T	Pct.	Pts.	OP
Detroit	9	7	0	.563	347	286
Green Bay	8	8	0	.500	429	439
Chicago	8	8	0	.500	311	301
Minnesota	8	8	0	.500	316	348
Tampa Bay	2	14	0	.125	241	380

Western Division

	W	L	T	Pct.	Pts.	OP
San Francisco	10	6	0	.625	432	293
L.A. Rams*	9	7	0	.563	361	344
New Orleans	8	8	0	.500	319	337
Atlanta	7	9	0	.438	370	389

*Wild Card qualifier for playoffs; #Top playoff seed in conference

L.A. Raiders were top playoff seed ahead of Miami based on head-to-head victory (1-0). Seattle was first Wild Card ahead of Denver based on better division record (5-3 to Broncos' 3-5) after Cleveland was eliminated from three-way tie based on losing head-to-head to both Seattle and Denver. Seattle did not play the L.A. Raiders in the divisional playoffs because, from 1970-1989, two teams from the same division could not meet prior to the conference championship game. New England finished ahead of Buffalo based on head-to-head sweep (2-0). Baltimore finished ahead of N.Y. Jets based on better conference record (5-9 to Jets' 4-8). San Diego finished ahead of Kansas City based on head-to-head sweep (2-0). Green Bay finished ahead of Chicago based on better record against common opponents (4-4 to Bears' 3-5) after Minnesota was eliminated from three-way tie based on conference record (Chicago 7-7 and Green Bay 6-6 to Vikings' 4-8).

Wild Card playoff: SEATTLE 31, Denver 7
Divisional playoffs: Seattle 27, MIAMI 20;
  L.A. RAIDERS 38, Pittsburgh 10
AFC Championship: L.A. RAIDERS 30, Seattle 14
Wild Card playoff: L.A. Rams 24, DALLAS 17
Divisional playoffs: SAN FRANCISCO 24, Detroit 23;
  WASHINGTON 51, L.A. Rams 7
NFC Championship: WASHINGTON 24, San Francisco 21
Super Bowl XVIII: L.A. Raiders (AFC) 38, Washington (NFC) 9,
  at Tampa Stadium, Tampa, Florida

1982

AMERICAN CONFERENCE

	W	L	T	Pct.	Pts.	OP
L.A. Raiders#	8	1	0	.889	260	200
Miami	7	2	0	.778	198	131
Cincinnati	7	2	0	.778	232	177
Pittsburgh	6	3	0	.667	204	146
San Diego	6	3	0	.667	288	221
N.Y. Jets	6	3	0	.667	245	166
New England	5	4	0	.556	143	157
Cleveland	4	5	0	.444	140	182
Buffalo	4	5	0	.444	150	154
Seattle	4	5	0	.444	127	147
Kansas City	3	6	0	.333	176	184
Denver	2	7	0	.222	148	226
Houston	1	8	0	.111	136	245
Baltimore	0	8	1	.056	113	236

NATIONAL CONFERENCE

	W	L	T	Pct.	Pts.	OP
Washington#	8	1	0	.889	190	128
Dallas	6	3	0	.667	226	145
Green Bay	5	3	1	.611	226	169
Minnesota	5	4	0	.556	187	198
Atlanta	5	4	0	.556	183	199
St. Louis	5	4	0	.556	135	170
Tampa Bay	5	4	0	.556	158	178
Detroit	4	5	0	.444	181	176
New Orleans	4	5	0	.444	129	160
N.Y. Giants	4	5	0	.444	164	160
San Francisco	3	6	0	.333	209	206
Chicago	3	6	0	.333	141	174
Philadelphia	3	6	0	.333	191	195
L.A. Rams	2	7	0	.222	200	250

As the result of a 57-day players' strike, the 1982 NFL regular season schedule was reduced from 16 weeks to 9. At the conclusion of the regular season, the NFL conducted a 16-team postseason Super Bowl Tournament. Eight teams from each conference were seeded 1-8 based on their records during the season.

#Top playoff seed in conference

Miami finished ahead of Cincinnati based on better conference record (6-1 to Bengals' 6-2). Pittsburgh finished ahead of San Diego based on better record against common opponents (3-1 to Chargers' 2-1) after N.Y. Jets were eliminated from three-way tie based on conference record (Pittsburgh and San Diego 5-3 to Jets' 2-3). Cleveland finished ahead of Buffalo and Seattle based on better conference record (4-3 to Bills' 3-3 to Seahawks' 3-5). Buffalo finished ahead of Seattle based on better conference record (3-3 to Seahawks' 3-5). Minnesota (4-1), Atlanta (4-3), St. Louis (5-4), Tampa Bay (3-3) seeds were determined by best won-lost record in conference games. Detroit finished ahead of New Orleans and the N.Y. Giants based on best conference record (4-4 to Saints' 3-5 to Giants' 3-5). New Orleans finished ahead of N.Y. Giants based on better record against common opponents (1-3 to Giants' 0-4). San Francisco finished ahead of Chicago, and Chicago finished ahead of Philadelphia, based on conference record (49ers' 2-3 to Bears' 2-5 to Eagles' 1-5).

First round playoff: MIAMI 28, New England 13;
  L.A. RAIDERS 27, Cleveland 10;
  N.Y. Jets 44, CINCINNATI 17;
  San Diego 31, PITTSBURGH 28
Second round playoff: N.Y. Jets 17, L.A. RAIDERS 14;
  MIAMI 34, San Diego 13
AFC Championship: MIAMI 14, N.Y. Jets 0
First round playoff: WASHINGTON 31, Detroit 7;
  GREEN BAY 41, St. Louis 16;
  MINNESOTA 30, Atlanta 24;
  DALLAS 30, Tampa Bay 17
Second round playoff: WASHINGTON 21, Minnesota 7;
  DALLAS 37, Green Bay 26
NFC Championship: WASHINGTON 31, Dallas 17
Super Bowl XVII: Washington (NFC) 27, Miami (AFC) 17,
  at Rose Bowl, Pasadena, California

1981

AMERICAN CONFERENCE

Eastern Division

	W	L	T	Pct.	Pts.	OP
Miami	11	4	1	.719	345	275
N.Y. Jets*	10	5	1	.656	355	287
Buffalo*	10	6	0	.625	311	276
Baltimore	2	14	0	.125	259	533
New England	2	14	0	.125	322	370

Central Division

	W	L	T	Pct.	Pts.	OP
Cincinnati#	12	4	0	.750	421	304
Pittsburgh	8	8	0	.500	356	297
Houston	7	9	0	.438	281	355
Cleveland	5	11	0	.313	276	375

Western Division

	W	L	T	Pct.	Pts.	OP
San Diego	10	6	0	.625	478	390
Denver	10	6	0	.625	321	289
Kansas City	9	7	0	.563	343	290
Oakland	7	9	0	.438	273	343
Seattle	6	10	0	.375	322	388

NATIONAL CONFERENCE

Eastern Division

	W	L	T	Pct.	Pts.	OP
Dallas	12	4	0	.750	367	277
Philadelphia*	10	6	0	.625	368	221
N.Y. Giants*	9	7	0	.563	295	257
Washington	8	8	0	.500	347	349
St. Louis	7	9	0	.438	315	408

Central Division

	W	L	T	Pct.	Pts.	OP
Tampa Bay	9	7	0	.563	315	268
Detroit	8	8	0	.500	397	322
Green Bay	8	8	0	.500	324	361
Minnesota	7	9	0	.438	325	369
Chicago	6	10	0	.375	253	324

Western Division

	W	L	T	Pct.	Pts.	OP
San Francisco#	13	3	0	.813	357	250
Atlanta	7	9	0	.438	426	355
Los Angeles	6	10	0	.375	303	351
New Orleans	4	12	0	.250	207	378

*Wild Card qualifier for playoffs; #Top playoff seed in conference
Baltimore finished ahead of New England based on head-to-head sweep (2-0). San Diego finished ahead of Denver based on better division record (6-2 to Broncos' 5-3). Buffalo was second Wild Card based on head-to-head victory over Denver (1-0). Detroit finished ahead of Green Bay based on better record against common opponents (4-4 to Packers' 3-5).
Wild Card playoff: Buffalo 31, N.Y. JETS 27
Divisional playoffs: San Diego 41, MIAMI 38 (OT);
   CINCINNATI 28, Buffalo 21
AFC Championship: CINCINNATI 27, San Diego 7
Wild Card playoff: N.Y. Giants 27, PHILADELPHIA 21
Divisional playoffs: DALLAS 38, Tampa Bay 0;
   SAN FRANCISCO 38, N.Y. Giants 24
NFC Championship: SAN FRANCISCO 28, Dallas 27
Super Bowl XVI: San Francisco (NFC) 26, Cincinnati (AFC) 21,
   at Silverdome, Pontiac, Michigan

1980

AMERICAN CONFERENCE

Eastern Division

	W	L	T	Pct.	Pts.	OP
Buffalo	11	5	0	.688	320	260
New England	10	6	0	.625	441	325
Miami	8	8	0	.500	266	305
Baltimore	7	9	0	.438	355	387
N.Y. Jets	4	12	0	.250	302	395

Central Division

	W	L	T	Pct.	Pts.	OP
Cleveland	11	5	0	.688	357	310
Houston*	11	5	0	.688	295	251
Pittsburgh	9	7	0	.563	352	313
Cincinnati	6	10	0	.375	244	312

Western Division

	W	L	T	Pct.	Pts.	OP
San Diego#	11	5	0	.688	418	327
Oakland*	11	5	0	.688	364	306
Kansas City	8	8	0	.500	319	336
Denver	8	8	0	.500	310	323
Seattle	4	12	0	.250	291	408

NATIONAL CONFERENCE

Eastern Division

	W	L	T	Pct.	Pts.	OP
Philadelphia	12	4	0	.750	384	222
Dallas*	12	4	0	.750	454	311
Washington	6	10	0	.375	261	293
St. Louis	5	11	0	.313	299	350
N.Y. Giants	4	12	0	.250	249	425

Central Division

	W	L	T	Pct.	Pts.	OP
Minnesota	9	7	0	.563	317	308
Detroit	9	7	0	.563	334	272
Chicago	7	9	0	.438	304	264
Tampa Bay	5	10	1	.344	271	341
Green Bay	5	10	1	.344	231	371

Western Division

	W	L	T	Pct.	Pts.	OP
Atlanta#	12	4	0	.750	405	272
Los Angeles*	11	5	0	.688	424	289
San Francisco	6	10	0	.375	320	415
New Orleans	1	15	0	.063	291	487

*Wild Card qualifier for playoffs; #Top playoff seed in conference
San Diego was top playoff seed based on better conference record than Cleveland and Buffalo (9-3 to Browns' 8-4 and Bills' 8-4). Cleveland was second playoff seed based on better record against common opponents (5-2 to Bills' 5-3). Cleveland finished ahead of Houston based on better conference record (8-4 to Oilers' 7-5). Oakland was first Wild Card based on better conference record than Houston (9-3 to Oilers' 7-5). San Diego finished ahead of Oakland based on better net points in division games (plus 60 net points to Raiders' plus 37). Oakland did not play San Diego in the divisional playoffs because, from 1970-1989, two teams from the same division could not meet prior to the conference championship game. Kansas City finished ahead of Denver based on head-to-head sweep (2-0). Atlanta was top playoff seed based on head-to-head victory over Philadelphia (1-0). Philadelphia finished ahead of Dallas based on better net points in division games (plus 84 net points to Cowboys' plus 50). Minnesota finished ahead of Detroit based on better conference record (8-4 to Lions' 9-5). Tampa Bay finished ahead of Green Bay based on better head-to-head record (1-0-1 to Packers' 0-1-1).
Wild Card playoff: OAKLAND 27, Houston 7
Divisional playoffs: SAN DIEGO 20, Buffalo 14;
   Oakland 14, CLEVELAND 12
AFC Championship: Oakland 34, SAN DIEGO 27
Wild Card playoff: DALLAS 34, Los Angeles 13
Divisional playoffs: PHILADELPHIA 31, Minnesota 16;
   Dallas 30, ATLANTA 27
NFC Championship: PHILADELPHIA 20, Dallas 7
Super Bowl XV: Oakland (AFC) 27, Philadelphia (NFC) 10,
   at Louisiana Superdome, New Orleans, Louisiana

1979

AMERICAN CONFERENCE

Eastern Division

	W	L	T	Pct.	Pts.	OP
Miami	10	6	0	.625	341	257
New England	9	7	0	.563	411	326
N.Y. Jets	8	8	0	.500	337	383
Buffalo	7	9	0	.438	268	279
Baltimore	5	11	0	.313	271	351

Central Division

	W	L	T	Pct.	Pts.	OP
Pittsburgh	12	4	0	.750	416	262
Houston*	11	5	0	.688	362	331
Cleveland	9	7	0	.563	359	352
Cincinnati	4	12	0	.250	337	421

Western Division

	W	L	T	Pct.	Pts.	OP
San Diego#	12	4	0	.750	411	246
Denver*	10	6	0	.625	289	262
Seattle	9	7	0	.563	378	372
Oakland	9	7	0	.563	365	337
Kansas City	7	9	0	.438	238	262

NATIONAL CONFERENCE

Eastern Division

	W	L	T	Pct.	Pts.	OP
Dallas#	11	5	0	.688	371	313
Philadelphia*	11	5	0	.688	339	282
Washington	10	6	0	.625	348	295
N.Y. Giants	6	10	0	.375	237	323
St. Louis	5	11	0	.313	307	358

Central Division

	W	L	T	Pct.	Pts.	OP
Tampa Bay	10	6	0	.625	273	237
Chicago*	10	6	0	.625	306	249
Minnesota	7	9	0	.438	259	337
Green Bay	5	11	0	.313	246	316
Detroit	2	14	0	.125	219	365

Western Division

	W	L	T	Pct.	Pts.	OP
Los Angeles	9	7	0	.563	323	309
New Orleans	8	8	0	.500	370	360
Atlanta	6	10	0	.375	300	388
San Francisco	2	14	0	.125	308	416

*Wild Card qualifier for playoffs; #Top playoff seed in conference
San Diego was top playoff seed based on head-to-head victory over Pittsburgh (1-0). Seattle finished ahead of Oakland based on head-to-head sweep (2-0). Dallas finished ahead of Philadelphia based on better conference record (10-2 to Eagles' 9-3). Philadelphia did not play Dallas in the divisional playoffs because, from 1970-1989, two teams from the same division could not meet prior to the conference championship game. Tampa Bay finished ahead of Chicago based on a better division record (6-2 to Bears' 5-3). Chicago was second Wild Card ahead of Washington based on better net points in all games (57 to Redskins' 53).
Wild Card playoff: HOUSTON 13, Denver 7
Divisional playoffs: Houston 17, SAN DIEGO 14;
    PITTSBURGH 34, Miami 14
AFC Championship: PITTSBURGH 27, Houston 13
Wild Card playoff: PHILADELPHIA 27, Chicago 17
Divisional playoffs: TAMPA BAY 24, Philadelphia 17;
    Los Angeles 21, DALLAS 19
NFC Championship: Los Angeles 9, TAMPA BAY 0
Super Bowl XIV: Pittsburgh (AFC) 31, Los Angeles (NFC) 19,
    at Rose Bowl, Pasadena, California

1978

AMERICAN CONFERENCE

Eastern Division

	W	L	T	Pct.	Pts.	OP
New England	11	5	0	.688	358	286
Miami*	11	5	0	.688	372	254
N.Y. Jets	8	8	0	.500	359	364
Buffalo	5	11	0	.313	302	354
Baltimore	5	11	0	.313	239	421

Central Division

	W	L	T	Pct.	Pts.	OP
Pittsburgh#	14	2	0	.875	356	195
Houston*	10	6	0	.625	283	298
Cleveland	8	8	0	.500	334	356
Cincinnati	4	12	0	.250	252	284

Western Division

	W	L	T	Pct.	Pts.	OP
Denver	10	6	0	.625	282	198
Oakland	9	7	0	.563	311	283
Seattle	9	7	0	.563	345	358
San Diego	9	7	0	.563	355	309
Kansas City	4	12	0	.250	243	327

NATIONAL CONFERENCE

Eastern Division

	W	L	T	Pct.	Pts.	OP
Dallas	12	4	0	.750	384	208
Philadelphia*	9	7	0	.563	270	250
Washington	8	8	0	.500	273	283
St. Louis	6	10	0	.375	248	296
N.Y. Giants	6	10	0	.375	264	298

Central Division

	W	L	T	Pct.	Pts.	OP
Minnesota	8	7	1	.531	294	306
Green Bay	8	7	1	.531	249	269
Detroit	7	9	0	.438	290	300
Chicago	7	9	0	.438	253	274
Tampa Bay	5	11	0	.313	241	259

Western Division

	W	L	T	Pct.	Pts.	OP
Los Angeles#	12	4	0	.750	316	245
Atlanta*	9	7	0	.563	240	290
New Orleans	7	9	0	.438	281	298
San Francisco	2	14	0	.125	219	350

*Wild Card qualifier for playoffs; #Top playoff seed in conference
New England finished ahead of Miami based on better division record (6-2 to Dolphins' 5-3). Buffalo finished ahead of Baltimore based on head-to-head sweep (2-0). Oakland finished ahead of Seattle and San Diego based on better record against common opponents (6-2 to Seahawks' 5-3 and Chargers' 4-4). Atlanta was first Wild Card ahead of Philadelphia based on better record against common opponents (5-2 to Eagles' 5-3). Houston did not play Pittsburgh, and Atlanta did not play Los Angeles in the divisional playoffs because, from 1970-1989, two teams from the same division could not meet prior to the conference championship game. Los Angeles was top playoff seed based on head-to-head victory over Dallas (1-0). St. Louis finished ahead of N.Y. Giants based on better division record (3-5 to Giants' 2-6). Minnesota finished ahead of Green Bay based on better head-to-head record (1-0-1). Detroit finished ahead of Chicago based on better division record (4-4 to Bears' 3-5).
Wild Card playoff: Houston 17, MIAMI 9
Divisional playoffs: Houston 31, NEW ENGLAND 14;
    PITTSBURGH 33, Denver 10
AFC Championship: PITTSBURGH 34, Houston 5
Wild Card playoff: ATLANTA 14, Philadelphia 13
Divisional playoffs: DALLAS 27, Atlanta 20;
    LOS ANGELES 34, Minnesota 10
NFC Championship: Dallas 28, LOS ANGELES 0
Super Bowl XIII: Pittsburgh (AFC) 35, Dallas (NFC) 31,
    at Orange Bowl, Miami, Florida

1977

AMERICAN CONFERENCE

Eastern Division

	W	L	T	Pct.	Pts.	OP
Baltimore	10	4	0	.714	295	221
Miami	10	4	0	.714	313	197
New England	9	5	0	.643	278	217
N.Y. Jets	3	11	0	.214	191	300
Buffalo	3	11	0	.214	160	313

Central Division

	W	L	T	Pct.	Pts.	OP
Pittsburgh	9	5	0	.643	283	243
Houston	8	6	0	.571	299	230
Cincinnati	8	6	0	.571	238	235
Cleveland	6	8	0	.429	269	267

Western Division

	W	L	T	Pct.	Pts.	OP
Denver#	12	2	0	.857	274	148
Oakland*	11	3	0	.786	351	230
San Diego	7	7	0	.500	222	205
Seattle	5	9	0	.357	282	373
Kansas City	2	12	0	.143	225	349

NATIONAL CONFERENCE

Eastern Division

	W	L	T	Pct.	Pts.	OP
Dallas#	12	2	0	.857	345	212
Washington	9	5	0	.643	196	189
St. Louis	7	7	0	.500	272	287
Philadelphia	5	9	0	.357	220	207
N.Y. Giants	5	9	0	.357	181	265

Central Division

	W	L	T	Pct.	Pts.	OP
Minnesota	9	5	0	.643	231	227
Chicago*	9	5	0	.643	255	253
Detroit	6	8	0	.429	183	252
Green Bay	4	10	0	.286	134	219
Tampa Bay	2	12	0	.143	103	223

Western Division

	W	L	T	Pct.	Pts.	OP
Los Angeles	10	4	0	.714	302	146
Atlanta	7	7	0	.500	179	129
San Francisco	5	9	0	.357	220	260
New Orleans	3	11	0	.214	232	336

*Wild Card qualifier for playoffs; #Top playoff seed in conference
Baltimore finished ahead of Miami based on better conference record (9-3 to Dolphins' 8-4). N.Y. Jets finished ahead of Buffalo based on better point-differential in head-to-head competition (1 point). Houston finished ahead of Cincinnati based on better point-differential in head-to-head competition (2 points). Oakland did not play Denver in the divisional playoffs because, from 1970-1989, two teams from the same division could not meet prior to the conference championship game. Minnesota finished ahead of Chicago based on better point-differential in head-to-head competition (3 points). Chicago won Wild Card ahead of Washington based on better net points in conference games (48 to Redskins' 4). Philadelphia finished ahead of N.Y. Giants based on head-to-head sweep (2-0).
Divisional playoffs: DENVER 34, Pittsburgh 21;
  Oakland 37, BALTIMORE 31 (OT)
AFC Championship: DENVER 20, Oakland 17
Divisional playoffs: DALLAS 37, Chicago 7;
  Minnesota 14, LOS ANGELES 7
NFC Championship: DALLAS 23, Minnesota 6
Super Bowl XII: Dallas (NFC) 27, Denver (AFC) 10,
  at Louisiana Superdome, New Orleans, Louisiana

1976

AMERICAN CONFERENCE

Eastern Division

	W	L	T	Pct.	Pts.	OP
Baltimore	11	3	0	.786	417	246
New England*	11	3	0	.786	376	236
Miami	6	8	0	.429	263	264
N.Y. Jets	3	11	0	.214	169	383
Buffalo	2	12	0	.143	245	363

Central Division

	W	L	T	Pct.	Pts.	OP
Pittsburgh	10	4	0	.714	342	138
Cincinnati	10	4	0	.714	335	210
Cleveland	9	5	0	.643	267	287
Houston	5	9	0	.357	222	273

Western Division

	W	L	T	Pct.	Pts.	OP
Oakland#	13	1	0	.929	350	237
Denver	9	5	0	.643	315	206
San Diego	6	8	0	.429	248	285
Kansas City	5	9	0	.357	290	376
Tampa Bay	0	14	0	.000	125	412

NATIONAL CONFERENCE

Eastern Division

	W	L	T	Pct.	Pts.	OP
Dallas	11	3	0	.786	296	194
Washington*	10	4	0	.714	291	217
St. Louis	10	4	0	.714	309	267
Philadelphia	4	10	0	.286	165	286
N.Y. Giants	3	11	0	.214	170	250

Central Division

	W	L	T	Pct.	Pts.	OP
Minnesota#	11	2	1	.821	305	176
Chicago	7	7	0	.500	253	216
Detroit	6	8	0	.429	262	220
Green Bay	5	9	0	.357	218	299

Western Division

	W	L	T	Pct.	Pts.	OP
Los Angeles	10	3	1	.750	351	190
San Francisco	8	6	0	.571	270	190
New Orleans	4	10	0	.286	253	346
Atlanta	4	10	0	.286	172	312
Seattle	2	12	0	.143	229	429

*Wild Card qualifier for playoffs; #Top playoff seed in conference
Baltimore finished ahead of New England based on better division record (7-1 to Patriots' 6-2). Pittsburgh finished ahead of Cincinnati based on head-to-head sweep (2-0). Washington finished ahead of St. Louis based on head-to-head sweep (2-0). New Orleans finished ahead of Atlanta based on better point-differential in head-to-head competition (27 points).
Divisional playoffs: OAKLAND 24, New England 21;
  Pittsburgh 40, BALTIMORE 14
AFC Championship: OAKLAND 24, Pittsburgh 7
Divisional playoffs: MINNESOTA 35, Washington 20;
  Los Angeles 14, DALLAS 12
NFC Championship: MINNESOTA 24, Los Angeles 13
Super Bowl XI: Oakland (AFC) 32, Minnesota (NFC) 14,
  at Rose Bowl, Pasadena, California

1975

AMERICAN CONFERENCE

Eastern Division

	W	L	T	Pct.	Pts.	OP
Baltimore	10	4	0	.714	395	269
Miami	10	4	0	.714	357	222
Buffalo	8	6	0	.571	420	355
N.Y. Jets	3	11	0	.214	258	433
New England	3	11	0	.214	258	358

Central Division

	W	L	T	Pct.	Pts.	OP
Pittsburgh#	12	2	0	.857	373	162
Cincinnati*	11	3	0	.786	340	246
Houston	10	4	0	.714	293	226
Cleveland	3	11	0	.214	218	372

Western Division

	W	L	T	Pct.	Pts.	OP
Oakland	11	3	0	.786	375	255
Denver	6	8	0	.429	254	307
Kansas City	5	9	0	.357	282	341
San Diego	2	12	0	.143	189	345

NATIONAL CONFERENCE

Eastern Division

	W	L	T	Pct.	Pts.	OP
St. Louis	11	3	0	.786	356	276
Dallas*	10	4	0	.714	350	268
Washington	8	6	0	.571	325	276
N.Y. Giants	5	9	0	.357	216	306
Philadelphia	4	10	0	.286	225	302

Central Division

	W	L	T	Pct.	Pts.	OP
Minnesota#	12	2	0	.857	377	180
Detroit	7	7	0	.500	245	262
Chicago	4	10	0	.286	191	379
Green Bay	4	10	0	.286	226	285

Western Division

	W	L	T	Pct.	Pts.	OP
Los Angeles	12	2	0	.857	312	135
San Francisco	5	9	0	.357	255	286
Atlanta	4	10	0	.286	240	289
New Orleans	2	12	0	.143	165	360

*Wild Card qualifier for playoffs; #Top playoff seed in conference
Baltimore finished ahead of Miami based on head-to-head sweep (2-0). Cincinnati did not play Pittsburgh in the divisional playoffs because, from 1970-1989, two teams from the same division could not meet prior to the conference championship game. N.Y. Jets finished ahead of New England based on head-to-head sweep (2-0). Minnesota was top playoff seed based on better Point Rating system than Los Angeles (3 to 6). Chicago finished ahead of Green Bay based on better division record (2-4 to Bears' 1-5).
Divisional playoffs: PITTSBURGH 28, Baltimore 10; OAKLAND 31, Cincinnati 28
AFC Championship: PITTSBURGH 16, Oakland 10
Divisional playoffs: LOS ANGELES 35, St. Louis 23; Dallas 17, MINNESOTA 14
NFC Championship: Dallas 37, LOS ANGELES 7
Super Bowl X: Pittsburgh (AFC) 21, Dallas (NFC) 17, at Orange Bowl, Miami, Florida

1974

AMERICAN CONFERENCE

Eastern Division

	W	L	T	Pct.	Pts.	OP
Miami	11	3	0	.786	327	216
Buffalo*	9	5	0	.643	264	244
N.Y. Jets	7	7	0	.500	279	300
New England	7	7	0	.500	348	289
Baltimore	2	12	0	.143	190	329

Central Division

	W	L	T	Pct.	Pts.	OP
Pittsburgh	10	3	1	.750	305	189
Houston	7	7	0	.500	236	282
Cincinnati	7	7	0	.500	283	259
Cleveland	4	10	0	.286	251	344

Western Division

	W	L	T	Pct.	Pts.	OP
Oakland	12	2	0	.857	355	228
Denver	7	6	1	.536	302	294
Kansas City	5	9	0	.357	233	293
San Diego	5	9	0	.357	212	285

NATIONAL CONFERENCE

Eastern Division

	W	L	T	Pct.	Pts.	OP
St. Louis	10	4	0	.714	285	218
Washington*	10	4	0	.714	320	196
Dallas	8	6	0	.571	297	235
Philadelphia	7	7	0	.500	242	217
N.Y. Giants	2	12	0	.143	195	299

Central Division

	W	L	T	Pct.	Pts.	OP
Minnesota	10	4	0	.714	310	195
Detroit	7	7	0	.500	256	270
Green Bay	6	8	0	.429	210	206
Chicago	4	10	0	.286	152	279

Western Division

	W	L	T	Pct.	Pts.	OP
Los Angeles	10	4	0	.714	263	181
San Francisco	6	8	0	.429	226	236
New Orleans	5	9	0	.357	166	263
Atlanta	3	11	0	.214	111	271

*Wild Card qualifier for playoffs
N.Y. Jets finished ahead of New England based on better conference record (5-6 to Patriots' 4-7). Houston finished ahead of Cincinnati based on head-to-head sweep (2-0). Kansas City finished ahead of San Diego based on better point-differential in head-to-head competition (3 points). St. Louis finished ahead of Washington based on head-to-head sweep (2-0).
Divisional playoffs: OAKLAND 28, Miami 26; PITTSBURGH 32, Buffalo 14
AFC Championship: Pittsburgh 24, OAKLAND 13
Divisional playoffs: MINNESOTA 30, St. Louis 14; LOS ANGELES 19, Washington 10
NFC Championship: MINNESOTA 14, Los Angeles 10
Super Bowl IX: Pittsburgh (AFC) 16, Minnesota (NFC) 6, at Tulane Stadium, New Orleans, Louisiana

From 1933-1974, sites for league/conference championship games alternated by division.

1973

AMERICAN CONFERENCE

Eastern Division

	W	L	T	Pct.	Pts.	OP
Miami	12	2	0	.857	343	150
Buffalo	9	5	0	.643	259	230
New England	5	9	0	.357	258	300
N.Y. Jets	4	10	0	.286	240	306
Baltimore	4	10	0	.286	226	341

Central Division

	W	L	T	Pct.	Pts.	OP
Cincinnati	10	4	0	.714	286	231
Pittsburgh*	10	4	0	.714	347	210
Cleveland	7	5	2	.571	234	255
Houston	1	13	0	.071	199	447

Western Division

	W	L	T	Pct.	Pts.	OP
Oakland	9	4	1	.679	292	175
Kansas City	7	5	2	.571	231	192
Denver	7	5	2	.571	354	296
San Diego	2	11	1	.179	188	386

NATIONAL CONFERENCE

Eastern Division

	W	L	T	Pct.	Pts.	OP
Dallas	10	4	0	.714	382	203
Washington*	10	4	0	.714	325	198
Philadelphia	5	8	1	.393	310	393
St. Louis	4	9	1	.321	286	365
N.Y. Giants	2	11	1	.179	226	362

Central Division

	W	L	T	Pct.	Pts.	OP
Minnesota	12	2	0	.857	296	168
Detroit	6	7	1	.464	271	247
Green Bay	5	7	2	.429	202	259
Chicago	3	11	0	.214	195	334

Western Division

	W	L	T	Pct.	Pts.	OP
Los Angeles	12	2	0	.857	388	178
Atlanta	9	5	0	.643	318	224
San Francisco	5	9	0	.357	262	319
New Orleans	5	9	0	.357	163	312

Wild Card qualifier for playoffs

Cincinnati finished ahead of Pittsburgh based on better conference record (8-3 to Steelers' 7-4). N.Y. Jets finished ahead of Baltimore based on head-to-head sweep (2-0). Kansas City finished ahead of Denver based on better division record (4-2 to Broncos' 3-2-1). Dallas finished ahead of Washington based on better point differential in head-to-head games (13 points). San Francisco finished ahead of New Orleans based on better division record (2-4 to Saints' 1-5).

Divisional playoffs: OAKLAND 33, Pittsburgh 14; MIAMI 34, Cincinnati 16

AFC Championship: MIAMI 27, Oakland 10

Divisional playoffs: MINNESOTA 27, Washington 20; DALLAS 27, Los Angeles 16

NFC Championship: Minnesota 27, DALLAS 10

Super Bowl VIII: Miami (AFC) 24, Minnesota (NFC) 7, at Rice Stadium, Houston, Texas

1972

AMERICAN CONFERENCE

Eastern Division

	W	L	T	Pct.	Pts.	OP
Miami	14	0	0	1.000	385	171
N.Y. Jets	7	7	0	.500	367	324
Baltimore	5	9	0	.357	235	252
Buffalo	4	9	1	.321	257	377
New England	3	11	0	.214	192	446

Central Division

	W	L	T	Pct.	Pts.	OP
Pittsburgh	11	3	0	.786	343	175
Cleveland*	10	4	0	.714	268	249
Cincinnati	8	6	0	.571	299	229
Houston	1	13	0	.071	164	380

Western Division

	W	L	T	Pct.	Pts.	OP
Oakland	10	3	1	.750	365	248
Kansas City	8	6	0	.571	287	254
Denver	5	9	0	.357	325	350
San Diego	4	9	1	.321	264	344

NATIONAL CONFERENCE

Eastern Division

	W	L	T	Pct.	Pts.	OP
Washington	11	3	0	.786	336	218
Dallas*	10	4	0	.714	319	240
N.Y. Giants	8	6	0	.571	331	247
St. Louis	4	9	1	.321	193	303
Philadelphia	2	11	1	.179	145	352

Central Division

	W	L	T	Pct.	Pts.	OP
Green Bay	10	4	0	.714	304	226
Detroit	8	5	1	.607	339	290
Minnesota	7	7	0	.500	301	252
Chicago	4	9	1	.321	225	275

Western Division

	W	L	T	Pct.	Pts.	OP
San Francisco	8	5	1	.607	353	249
Atlanta	7	7	0	.500	269	274
Los Angeles	6	7	1	.464	291	286
New Orleans	2	11	1	.179	215	361

Wild Card qualifier for playoffs

Dallas did not play Washington in the divisional playoffs because, from 1970-1989, two teams from the same division could not meet prior to the conference championship game.

Divisional playoffs: PITTSBURGH 13, Oakland 7; MIAMI 20, Cleveland 14

AFC Championship: Miami 21, PITTSBURGH 17

Divisional playoffs: Dallas 30, SAN FRANCISCO 28; WASHINGTON 16, Green Bay 3

NFC Championship: WASHINGTON 26, Dallas 3

Super Bowl VII: Miami (AFC) 14, Washington (NFC) 7, at Memorial Coliseum, Los Angeles, California

1971

AMERICAN CONFERENCE

Eastern Division

	W	L	T	Pct.	Pts.	OP
Miami	10	3	1	.769	315	174
Baltimore*	10	4	0	.714	313	140
New England	6	8	0	.429	238	325
N.Y. Jets	6	8	0	.429	212	299
Buffalo	1	13	0	.071	184	394

Central Division

	W	L	T	Pct.	Pts.	OP
Cleveland	9	5	0	.643	285	273
Pittsburgh	6	8	0	.429	246	292
Houston	4	9	1	.308	251	330
Cincinnati	4	10	0	.286	284	265

Western Division

	W	L	T	Pct.	Pts.	OP
Kansas City	10	3	1	.769	302	208
Oakland	8	4	2	.667	344	278
San Diego	6	8	0	.429	311	341
Denver	4	9	1	.308	203	275

NATIONAL CONFERENCE

Eastern Division

	W	L	T	Pct.	Pts.	OP
Dallas	11	3	0	.786	406	222
Washington*	9	4	1	.692	276	190
Philadelphia	6	7	1	.462	221	302
St. Louis	4	9	1	.308	231	279
N.Y. Giants	4	10	0	.286	228	362

Central Division

	W	L	T	Pct.	Pts.	OP
Minnesota	11	3	0	.786	245	139
Detroit	7	6	1	.538	341	286
Chicago	6	8	0	.429	185	276
Green Bay	4	8	2	.333	274	298

Western Division

	W	L	T	Pct.	Pts.	OP
San Francisco	9	5	0	.643	300	216
Los Angeles	8	5	1	.615	313	260
Atlanta	7	6	1	.538	274	277
New Orleans	4	8	2	.333	266	347

*Wild Card qualifier for playoffs
New England finished ahead of N.Y. Jets based on better point-differential in head-to-head competition (13 points).
Divisional playoffs: Miami 27, KANSAS CITY 24 (OT);
   Baltimore 20, CLEVELAND 3
AFC Championship: MIAMI 21, Baltimore 0
Divisional playoffs: Dallas 20, MINNESOTA 12;
   SAN FRANCISCO 24, Washington 20
NFC Championship: DALLAS 14, San Francisco 3
Super Bowl VI: Dallas (NFC) 24, Miami (AFC) 3,
   at Tulane Stadium, New Orleans, Louisiana

From 1920-1971, tie games were not included in winning percentage.

1970

AMERICAN CONFERENCE

Eastern Division

	W	L	T	Pct.	Pts.	OP
Baltimore	11	2	1	.846	321	234
Miami*	10	4	0	.714	297	228
N.Y. Jets	4	10	0	.286	255	286
Buffalo	3	10	1	.231	204	337
Boston Patriots	2	12	0	.143	149	361

Central Division

	W	L	T	Pct.	Pts.	OP
Cincinnati	8	6	0	.571	312	255
Cleveland	7	7	0	.500	286	265
Pittsburgh	5	9	0	.357	210	272
Houston	3	10	1	.231	217	352

Western Division

	W	L	T	Pct.	Pts.	OP
Oakland	8	4	2	.667	300	293
Kansas City	7	5	2	.583	272	244
San Diego	5	6	3	.455	282	278
Denver	5	8	1	.385	253	264

NATIONAL CONFERENCE

Eastern Division

	W	L	T	Pct.	Pts.	OP
Dallas	10	4	0	.714	299	221
N.Y. Giants	9	5	0	.643	301	270
St. Louis	8	5	1	.615	325	228
Washington	6	8	0	.429	297	314
Philadelphia	3	10	1	.231	241	332

Central Division

	W	L	T	Pct.	Pts.	OP
Minnesota	12	2	0	.857	335	143
Detroit*	10	4	0	.714	347	202
Green Bay	6	8	0	.429	196	293
Chicago	6	8	0	.429	256	261

Western Division

	W	L	T	Pct.	Pts.	OP
San Francisco	10	3	1	.769	352	267
Los Angeles	9	4	1	.692	325	202
Atlanta	4	8	2	.333	206	261
New Orleans	2	11	1	.154	172	347

*Wild Card qualifier for playoffs
Miami did not play Baltimore, and Detroit did not play Minnesota, in the divisional playoffs because, from 1970-1989, two teams from the same division could not meet prior to the conference championship game. Green Bay finished ahead of Chicago based on better division record (2-4 to Bears' 1-5).
Divisional playoffs: BALTIMORE 17, Cincinnati 0;
   OAKLAND 21, Miami 14
AFC Championship: BALTIMORE 27, Oakland 17
Divisional playoffs: DALLAS 5, Detroit 0;
   San Francisco 17, MINNESOTA 14
NFC Championship: Dallas 17, SAN FRANCISCO 10
Super Bowl V: Baltimore (AFC) 16, Dallas (NFC) 13,
   at Orange Bowl, Miami, Florida

1969 NFL

EASTERN CONFERENCE
Capitol Division

	W	L	T	Pct.	Pts.	OP
Dallas	11	2	1	.846	369	223
Washington	7	5	2	.583	307	319
New Orleans	5	9	0	.357	311	393
Philadelphia	4	9	1	.308	279	377

Century Division

	W	L	T	Pct.	Pts.	OP
Cleveland	10	3	1	.769	351	300
N.Y. Giants	6	8	0	.429	264	298
St. Louis	4	9	1	.308	314	389
Pittsburgh	1	13	0	.071	218	404

WESTERN CONFERENCE
Coastal Division

	W	L	T	Pct.	Pts.	OP
Los Angeles	11	3	0	.786	320	243
Baltimore	8	5	1	.615	279	268
Atlanta	6	8	0	.429	276	268
San Francisco	4	8	2	.333	277	319

Central Division

	W	L	T	Pct.	Pts.	OP
Minnesota	12	2	0	.857	379	133
Detroit	9	4	1	.692	259	188
Green Bay	8	6	0	.571	269	221
Chicago	1	13	0	.071	210	339

Conference championships: Cleveland 38, DALLAS 14;
MINNESOTA 23, Los Angeles 20
NFL championship: MINNESOTA 27, Cleveland 7
Super Bowl IV: Kansas City (AFL) 23, Minnesota (NFL) 7,
at Tulane Stadium, New Orleans, Louisiana

1969 AFL

EASTERN DIVISION

	W	L	T	Pct.	Pts.	OP
N.Y. Jets	10	4	0	.714	353	269
Houston	6	6	2	.500	278	279
Boston Patriots	4	10	0	.286	266	316
Buffalo	4	10	0	.286	230	359
Miami	3	10	1	.231	233	332

WESTERN DIVISION

	W	L	T	Pct.	Pts.	OP
Oakland	12	1	1	.923	377	242
Kansas City	11	3	0	.786	359	177
San Diego	8	6	0	.571	288	276
Denver	5	8	1	.385	297	344
Cincinnati	4	9	1	.308	280	367

Divisional playoffs: Kansas City 13, N.Y. JETS 6;
OAKLAND 56, Houston 7
AFL championship: Kansas City 17, OAKLAND 7

1968 NFL

EASTERN CONFERENCE
Capitol Division

	W	L	T	Pct.	Pts.	OP
Dallas	12	2	0	.857	431	186
N.Y. Giants	7	7	0	.500	294	325
Washington	5	9	0	.357	249	358
Philadelphia	2	12	0	.143	202	351

Century Division

	W	L	T	Pct.	Pts.	OP
Cleveland	10	4	0	.714	394	273
St. Louis	9	4	1	.692	325	289
New Orleans	4	9	1	.308	246	327
Pittsburgh	2	11	1	.154	244	397

WESTERN CONFERENCE
Coastal Division

	W	L	T	Pct.	Pts.	OP
Baltimore	13	1	0	.929	402	144
Los Angeles	10	3	1	.769	312	200
San Francisco	7	6	1	.538	303	310
Atlanta	2	12	0	.143	170	389

Central Division

	W	L	T	Pct.	Pts.	OP
Minnesota	8	6	0	.571	282	242
Chicago	7	7	0	.500	250	333
Green Bay	6	7	1	.462	281	227
Detroit	4	8	2	.333	207	241

Conference championships: CLEVELAND 31, Dallas 20;
BALTIMORE 24, Minnesota 14
NFL championship: Baltimore 34, CLEVELAND 0
Super Bowl III: N.Y. Jets (AFL) 16, Baltimore (NFL) 7,
at Orange Bowl, Miami, Florida

1968 AFL

EASTERN DIVISION

	W	L	T	Pct.	Pts.	OP
N.Y. Jets	11	3	0	.786	419	280
Houston	7	7	0	.500	303	248
Miami	5	8	1	.385	276	355
Boston Patriots	4	10	0	.286	229	406
Buffalo	1	12	1	.077	199	367

WESTERN DIVISION

	W	L	T	Pct.	Pts.	OP
Oakland	12	2	0	.857	453	233
Kansas City	12	2	0	.857	371	170
San Diego	9	5	0	.643	382	310
Denver	5	9	0	.357	255	404
Cincinnati	3	11	0	.214	215	329

Western Division playoff: OAKLAND 41, Kansas City 6
AFL championship: N.Y. JETS 27, Oakland 23

1967 NFL

EASTERN CONFERENCE
Capitol Division

	W	L	T	Pct.	Pts.	OP
Dallas	9	5	0	.643	342	268
Philadelphia	6	7	1	.462	351	409
Washington	5	6	3	.455	347	353
New Orleans	3	11	0	.214	233	379

Century Division

	W	L	T	Pct.	Pts.	OP
Cleveland	9	5	0	.643	334	297
N.Y. Giants	7	7	0	.500	369	379
St. Louis	6	7	1	.462	333	356
Pittsburgh	4	9	1	.308	281	320

WESTERN CONFERENCE
Coastal Division

	W	L	T	Pct.	Pts.	OP
Los Angeles	11	1	2	.917	398	196
Baltimore	11	1	2	.917	394	198
San Francisco	7	7	0	.500	273	337
Atlanta	1	12	1	.077	175	422

Central Division

	W	L	T	Pct.	Pts.	OP
Green Bay	9	4	1	.692	332	209
Chicago	7	6	1	.538	239	218
Detroit	5	7	2	.417	260	259
Minnesota	3	8	3	.273	233	294

Los Angeles finished ahead of Baltimore based on better point differential in head-to-head games (net 24 points).
Conference championships: DALLAS 52, Cleveland 14;
GREEN BAY 28, Los Angeles 7
NFL championship: GREEN BAY 21, Dallas 17
Super Bowl II: Green Bay (NFL) 33, Oakland (AFL) 14,
at Orange Bowl, Miami, Florida

1967 AFL

EASTERN DIVISION

	W	L	T	Pct.	Pts.	OP
Houston	9	4	1	.692	258	199
N.Y. Jets	8	5	1	.615	371	329
Buffalo	4	10	0	.286	237	285
Miami	4	10	0	.286	219	407
Boston Patriots	3	10	1	.231	280	389

WESTERN DIVISION

	W	L	T	Pct.	Pts.	OP
Oakland	13	1	0	.929	468	233
Kansas City	9	5	0	.643	408	254
San Diego	8	5	1	.615	360	352
Denver	3	11	0	.214	256	409

AFL championship: OAKLAND 40, Houston 7

1966 NFL

EASTERN CONFERENCE

	W	L	T	Pct.	Pts.	OP
Dallas	10	3	1	.769	445	239
Cleveland	9	5	0	.643	403	259
Philadelphia	9	5	0	.643	326	340
St. Louis	8	5	1	.615	264	265
Washington	7	7	0	.500	351	355
Pittsburgh	5	8	1	.385	316	347
Atlanta	3	11	0	.214	204	437
N.Y. Giants	1	12	1	.077	263	501

WESTERN CONFERENCE

	W	L	T	Pct.	Pts.	OP
Green Bay	12	2	0	.857	335	163
Baltimore	9	5	0	.643	314	226
Los Angeles	8	6	0	.571	289	212
San Francisco	6	6	2	.500	320	325
Chicago	5	7	2	.417	234	272
Detroit	4	9	1	.308	206	317
Minnesota	4	9	1	.308	292	304

NFL championship: Green Bay 34, DALLAS 27
Super Bowl I: Green Bay (NFL) 35, Kansas City (AFL) 10,
at Memorial Coliseum, Los Angeles, California

1966 AFL

EASTERN DIVISION

	W	L	T	Pct.	Pts.	OP
Buffalo	9	4	1	.692	358	255
Boston Patriots	8	4	2	.677	315	283
N.Y. Jets	6	6	2	.500	322	312
Houston	3	11	0	.214	335	396
Miami	3	11	0	.214	213	362

WESTERN DIVISION

	W	L	T	Pct.	Pts.	OP
Kansas City	11	2	1	.846	448	276
Oakland	8	5	1	.615	315	288
San Diego	7	6	1	.538	335	284
Denver	4	10	0	.286	196	381

AFL championship: Kansas City 31, BUFFALO 7

1965 NFL

EASTERN CONFERENCE	W	L	T	Pct.	Pts.	OP	WESTERN CONFERENCE	W	L	T	Pct.	Pts.	OP
Cleveland	11	3	0	.786	363	325	Green Bay	10	3	1	.769	316	224
Dallas	7	7	0	.500	325	280	Baltimore	10	3	1	.769	389	284
N.Y. Giants	7	7	0	.500	270	338	Chicago	9	5	0	.643	409	275
Washington	6	8	0	.429	257	301	San Francisco	7	6	1	.538	421	402
Philadelphia	5	9	0	.357	363	359	Minnesota	7	7	0	.500	383	403
St. Louis	5	9	0	.357	296	309	Detroit	6	7	1	.462	257	295
Pittsburgh	2	12	0	.143	202	397	Los Angeles	4	10	0	.286	269	328

Western Conference playoff: GREEN BAY 13, Baltimore 10 (OT)
NFL championship: GREEN BAY 23, Cleveland 12

1965 AFL

EASTERN DIVISION	W	L	T	Pct.	Pts.	OP	WESTERN DIVISION	W	L	T	Pct.	Pts.	OP
Buffalo	10	3	1	.769	313	226	San Diego	9	2	3	.818	340	227
N.Y. Jets	5	8	1	.385	285	303	Oakland	8	5	1	.615	298	239
Boston Patriots	4	8	2	.333	244	302	Kansas City	7	5	2	.583	322	285
Houston	4	10	0	.286	298	429	Denver	4	10	0	.286	303	392

AFL championship: Buffalo 23, SAN DIEGO 0

1964 NFL

EASTERN CONFERENCE	W	L	T	Pct.	Pts.	OP	WESTERN CONFERENCE	W	L	T	Pct.	Pts.	OP
Cleveland	10	3	1	.769	415	293	Baltimore	12	2	0	.857	428	225
St. Louis	9	3	2	.750	357	331	Green Bay	8	5	1	.615	342	245
Philadelphia	6	8	0	.429	312	313	Minnesota	8	5	1	.615	355	296
Washington	6	8	0	.429	307	305	Detroit	7	5	2	.583	280	260
Dallas	5	8	1	.385	250	289	Los Angeles	5	7	2	.417	283	339
Pittsburgh	5	9	0	.357	253	315	Chicago	5	9	0	.357	260	379
N.Y. Giants	2	10	2	.167	241	399	San Francisco	4	10	0	.286	236	330

NFL championship: CLEVELAND 27, Baltimore 0

1964 AFL

EASTERN DIVISION	W	L	T	Pct.	Pts.	OP	WESTERN DIVISION	W	L	T	Pct.	Pts.	OP
Buffalo	12	2	0	.857	400	242	San Diego	8	5	1	.615	341	300
Boston Patriots	10	3	1	.769	365	297	Kansas City	7	7	0	.500	366	306
N.Y. Jets	5	8	1	.385	278	315	Oakland	5	7	2	.417	303	350
Houston	4	10	0	.286	310	355	Denver	2	11	1	.154	240	438

AFL championship: BUFFALO 20, San Diego 7

1963 NFL

EASTERN CONFERENCE	W	L	T	Pct.	Pts.	OP	WESTERN CONFERENCE	W	L	T	Pct.	Pts.	OP
N.Y. Giants	11	3	0	.786	448	280	Chicago	11	1	2	.917	301	144
Cleveland	10	4	0	.714	343	262	Green Bay	11	2	1	.846	369	206
St. Louis	9	5	0	.643	341	283	Baltimore	8	6	0	.571	316	285
Pittsburgh	7	4	3	.636	321	295	Detroit	5	8	1	.385	326	265
Dallas	4	10	0	.286	305	378	Minnesota	5	8	1	.385	309	390
Washington	3	11	0	.214	279	398	Los Angeles	5	9	0	.357	210	350
Philadelphia	2	10	2	.167	242	381	San Francisco	2	12	0	.143	198	391

NFL championship: CHICAGO 14, N.Y. Giants 10

1963 AFL

EASTERN DIVISION	W	L	T	Pct.	Pts.	OP	WESTERN DIVISION	W	L	T	Pct.	Pts.	OP
Boston Patriots	7	6	1	.538	327	257	San Diego	11	3	0	.786	399	255
Buffalo	7	6	1	.538	304	291	Oakland	10	4	0	.714	363	282
Houston	6	8	0	.429	302	372	Kansas City	5	7	2	.417	347	263
N.Y. Jets	5	8	1	.385	249	399	Denver	2	11	1	.154	301	473

Eastern Division playoff: Boston 26, BUFFALO 8
AFL championship: SAN DIEGO 51, Boston 10

1962 NFL

EASTERN CONFERENCE	W	L	T	Pct.	Pts.	OP	WESTERN CONFERENCE	W	L	T	Pct.	Pts.	OP
N.Y. Giants	12	2	0	.857	398	283	Green Bay	13	1	0	.929	415	148
Pittsburgh	9	5	0	.643	312	363	Detroit	11	3	0	.786	315	177
Cleveland	7	6	1	.538	291	257	Chicago	9	5	0	.643	321	287
Washington	5	7	2	.417	305	376	Baltimore	7	7	0	.500	293	288
Dallas Cowboys	5	8	1	.385	398	402	San Francisco	6	8	0	.429	282	331
St. Louis	4	9	1	.308	287	361	Minnesota	2	11	1	.154	254	410
Philadelphia	3	10	1	.231	282	356	Los Angeles	1	12	1	.077	220	334

NFL championship: Green Bay 16, N.Y. GIANTS 7

1962 AFL

EASTERN DIVISION	W	L	T	Pct.	Pts.	OP	WESTERN DIVISION	W	L	T	Pct.	Pts.	OP
Houston	11	3	0	.786	387	270	Dallas Texans	11	3	0	.786	389	233
Boston Patriots	9	4	1	.692	346	295	Denver	7	7	0	.500	353	334
Buffalo	7	6	1	.538	309	272	San Diego	4	10	0	.286	314	392
N.Y. Titans	5	9	0	.357	278	423	Oakland	1	13	0	.071	213	370

AFL championship: Dallas Texans 20, HOUSTON 17 (OT)

1961 NFL

EASTERN CONFERENCE	W	L	T	Pct.	Pts.	OP	WESTERN CONFERENCE	W	L	T	Pct.	Pts.	OP
N.Y. Giants	10	3	1	.769	368	220	Green Bay	11	3	0	.786	391	223
Philadelphia	10	4	0	.714	361	297	Detroit	8	5	1	.615	270	258
Cleveland	8	5	1	.615	319	270	Baltimore	8	6	0	.571	302	307
St. Louis	7	7	0	.500	279	267	Chicago	8	6	0	.571	326	302
Pittsburgh	6	8	0	.429	295	287	San Francisco	7	6	1	.538	346	272
Dallas Cowboys	4	9	1	.308	236	380	Los Angeles	4	10	0	.286	263	333
Washington	1	12	1	.077	174	392	Minnesota	3	11	0	.214	285	407

NFL championship: GREEN BAY 37, N.Y. Giants 0

1961 AFL

EASTERN DIVISION	W	L	T	Pct.	Pts.	OP	WESTERN DIVISION	W	L	T	Pct.	Pts.	OP
Houston	10	3	1	.769	513	242	San Diego	12	2	0	.857	396	219
Boston Patriots	9	4	1	.692	413	313	Dallas Texans	6	8	0	.429	334	343
N.Y. Titans	7	7	0	.500	301	390	Denver	3	11	0	.214	251	432
Buffalo	6	8	0	.429	294	342	Oakland	2	12	0	.143	237	458

AFL championship: Houston 10, SAN DIEGO 3

1960 NFL

EASTERN CONFERENCE	W	L	T	Pct.	Pts.	OP	WESTERN CONFERENCE	W	L	T	Pct.	Pts.	OP
Philadelphia	10	2	0	.833	321	246	Green Bay	8	4	0	.667	332	209
Cleveland	8	3	1	.727	362	217	Detroit	7	5	0	.583	239	212
N.Y. Giants	6	4	2	.600	271	261	San Francisco	7	5	0	.583	208	205
St. Louis	6	5	1	.545	288	230	Baltimore	6	6	0	.500	288	234
Pittsburgh	5	6	1	.455	240	275	Chicago	5	6	1	.455	194	299
Washington	1	9	2	.100	178	309	L.A. Rams	4	7	1	.364	265	297
							Dallas Cowboys	0	11	1	.000	177	369

NFL championship: PHILADELPHIA 17, Green Bay 13

1960 AFL

EASTERN CONFERENCE	W	L	T	Pct.	Pts.	OP	WESTERN CONFERENCE	W	L	T	Pct.	Pts.	OP
Houston	10	4	0	.714	379	285	L.A. Chargers	10	4	0	.714	373	336
N.Y. Titans	7	7	0	.500	382	399	Dallas Texans	8	6	0	.571	362	253
Buffalo	5	8	1	.385	296	303	Oakland	6	8	0	.429	319	388
Boston Patriots	5	9	0	.357	286	349	Denver	4	9	1	.308	309	393

AFL championship: HOUSTON 24, L.A. Chargers 16

1959

EASTERN CONFERENCE	W	L	T	Pct.	Pts.	OP	WESTERN CONFERENCE	W	L	T	Pct.	Pts.	OP
N.Y. Giants	10	2	0	.833	284	170	Baltimore	9	3	0	.750	374	251
Cleveland	7	5	0	.583	270	214	Chi. Bears	8	4	0	.667	252	196
Philadelphia	7	5	0	.583	268	278	Green Bay	7	5	0	.583	248	246
Pittsburgh	6	5	1	.545	257	216	San Francisco	7	5	0	.583	255	237
Washington	3	9	0	.250	185	350	Detroit	3	8	1	.273	203	275
Chi. Cardinals	2	10	0	.167	234	324	Los Angeles	2	10	0	.167	242	315

NFL championship: BALTIMORE 31, N.Y. Giants 16

1958

EASTERN CONFERENCE	W	L	T	Pct.	Pts.	OP	WESTERN CONFERENCE	W	L	T	Pct.	Pts.	OP
N.Y. Giants	9	3	0	.750	246	183	Baltimore	9	3	0	.750	381	203
Cleveland	9	3	0	.750	302	217	Chi. Bears	8	4	0	.667	298	230
Pittsburgh	7	4	1	.636	261	230	Los Angeles	8	4	0	.667	344	278
Washington	4	7	1	.364	214	268	San Francisco	6	6	0	.500	257	324
Chi. Cardinals	2	9	1	.182	261	356	Detroit	4	7	1	.364	261	276
Philadelphia	2	9	1	.182	235	306	Green Bay	1	10	1	.091	193	382

Eastern Conference playoff: N.Y. GIANTS 10, Cleveland 0
NFL championship: Baltimore 23, N.Y. GIANTS 17 (OT)

1957

EASTERN CONFERENCE	W	L	T	Pct.	Pts.	OP	WESTERN CONFERENCE	W	L	T	Pct.	Pts.	OP
Cleveland	9	2	1	.818	269	172	Detroit	8	4	0	.667	251	231
N.Y. Giants	7	5	0	.583	254	211	San Francisco	8	4	0	.667	260	264
Pittsburgh	6	6	0	.500	161	178	Baltimore	7	5	0	.583	303	235
Washington	5	6	1	.455	251	230	Los Angeles	6	6	0	.500	307	278
Philadelphia	4	8	0	.333	173	230	Chi. Bears	5	7	0	.417	203	211
Chi. Cardinals	3	9	0	.250	200	299	Green Bay	3	9	0	.250	218	311

Western Conference playoff: Detroit 31, SAN FRANCISCO 27
NFL championship: DETROIT 59, Cleveland 14

1956

EASTERN CONFERENCE	W	L	T	Pct.	Pts.	OP	WESTERN CONFERENCE	W	L	T	Pct.	Pts.	OP
N.Y. Giants	8	3	1	.727	264	197	Chi. Bears	9	2	1	.818	363	246
Chi. Cardinals	7	5	0	.583	240	182	Detroit	9	3	0	.750	300	188
Washington	6	6	0	.500	183	225	San Francisco	5	6	1	.455	233	284
Cleveland	5	7	0	.417	167	177	Baltimore	5	7	0	.417	270	322
Pittsburgh	5	7	0	.417	217	250	Green Bay	4	8	0	.333	264	342
Philadelphia	3	8	1	.273	143	215	Los Angeles	4	8	0	.333	291	307

NFL championship: N.Y. GIANTS 47, Chi. Bears 7

1955

EASTERN CONFERENCE	W	L	T	Pct.	Pts.	OP	WESTERN CONFERENCE	W	L	T	Pct.	Pts.	OP
Cleveland	9	2	1	.818	349	218	Los Angeles	8	3	1	.727	260	231
Washington	8	4	0	.667	246	222	Chi. Bears	8	4	0	.667	294	251
N.Y. Giants	6	5	1	.545	267	223	Green Bay	6	6	0	.500	258	276
Chi. Cardinals	4	7	1	.364	224	252	Baltimore	5	6	1	.455	214	239
Philadelphia	4	7	1	.364	248	231	San Francisco	4	8	0	.333	216	298
Pittsburgh	4	8	0	.333	195	285	Detroit	3	9	0	.250	230	275

NFL championship: Cleveland 38, LOS ANGELES 14

1954

EASTERN CONFERENCE	W	L	T	Pct.	Pts.	OP	WESTERN CONFERENCE	W	L	T	Pct.	Pts.	OP
Cleveland	9	3	0	.750	336	162	Detroit	9	2	1	.818	337	189
Philadelphia	7	4	1	.636	284	230	Chi. Bears	8	4	0	.667	301	279
N.Y. Giants	7	5	0	.583	293	184	San Francisco	7	4	1	.636	313	251
Pittsburgh	5	7	0	.417	219	263	Los Angeles	6	5	1	.545	314	285
Washington	3	9	0	.250	207	432	Green Bay	4	8	0	.333	234	251
Chi. Cardinals	2	10	0	.167	183	347	Baltimore	3	9	0	.250	131	279

NFL championship: CLEVELAND 56, Detroit 10

1953

EASTERN CONFERENCE	W	L	T	Pct.	Pts.	OP	WESTERN CONFERENCE	W	L	T	Pct.	Pts.	OP
Cleveland	11	1	0	.917	348	162	Detroit	10	2	0	.833	271	205
Philadelphia	7	4	1	.636	352	215	San Francisco	9	3	0	.750	372	237
Washington	6	5	1	.545	208	215	Los Angeles	8	3	1	.727	366	236
Pittsburgh	6	6	0	.500	211	263	Chi. Bears	3	8	1	.273	218	262
N.Y. Giants	3	9	0	.250	179	277	Baltimore	3	9	0	.250	182	350
Chi. Cardinals	1	10	1	.091	190	337	Green Bay	2	9	1	.182	200	338

NFL championship: DETROIT 17, Cleveland 16

1952

AMERICAN CONFERENCE	W	L	T	Pct.	Pts.	OP	NATIONAL CONFERENCE	W	L	T	Pct.	Pts.	OP
Cleveland	8	4	0	.667	310	213	Detroit	9	3	0	.750	344	192
N.Y. Giants	7	5	0	.583	234	231	Los Angeles	9	3	0	.750	349	234
Philadelphia	7	5	0	.583	252	271	San Francisco	7	5	0	.583	285	221
Pittsburgh	5	7	0	.417	300	273	Green Bay	6	6	0	.500	295	312
Chi. Cardinals	4	8	0	.333	172	221	Chi. Bears	5	7	0	.417	245	326
Washington	4	8	0	.333	240	287	Dallas Texans	1	11	0	.083	182	427

National Conference playoff: DETROIT 31, Los Angeles 21
NFL championship: Detroit 17, CLEVELAND 7

1951

AMERICAN CONFERENCE	W	L	T	Pct.	Pts.	OP	NATIONAL CONFERENCE	W	L	T	Pct.	Pts.	OP
Cleveland	11	1	0	.917	331	152	Los Angeles	8	4	0	.667	392	261
N.Y. Giants	9	2	1	.818	254	161	Detroit	7	4	1	.636	336	259
Washington	5	7	0	.417	183	296	San Francisco	7	4	1	.636	255	205
Pittsburgh	4	7	1	.364	183	235	Chi. Bears	7	5	0	.583	286	282
Philadelphia	4	8	0	.333	234	264	Green Bay	3	9	0	.250	254	375
Chi. Cardinals	3	9	0	.250	210	287	N.Y. Yanks	1	9	2	.100	241	382

NFL championship: LOS ANGELES 24, Cleveland 17

1950

AMERICAN CONFERENCE	W	L	T	Pct.	Pts.	OP	NATIONAL CONFERENCE	W	L	T	Pct.	Pts.	OP
Cleveland	10	2	0	.833	310	144	Los Angeles	9	3	0	.750	466	309
N.Y. Giants	10	2	0	.833	268	150	Chi. Bears	9	3	0	.750	279	207
Philadelphia	6	6	0	.500	254	141	N.Y. Yanks	7	5	0	.583	366	367
Pittsburgh	6	6	0	.500	180	195	Detroit	6	6	0	.500	321	285
Chi. Cardinals	5	7	0	.417	233	287	Green Bay	3	9	0	.250	244	406
Washington	3	9	0	.250	232	326	San Francisco	3	9	0	.250	213	300
							Baltimore	1	11	0	.083	213	462

American Conference playoff: CLEVELAND 8, N.Y. Giants 3
National Conference playoff: LOS ANGELES 24, Chi. Bears 14
NFL championship: CLEVELAND 30, Los Angeles 28

1949

EASTERN DIVISION

	W	L	T	Pct.	Pts.	OP
Philadelphia	11	1	0	.917	364	134
Pittsburgh	6	5	1	.545	224	214
N.Y. Giants	6	6	0	.500	287	298
Washington	4	7	1	.364	268	339
N.Y. Bulldogs	1	10	1	.091	153	368

WESTERN DIVISION

	W	L	T	Pct.	Pts.	OP
Los Angeles	8	2	2	.800	360	239
Chi. Bears	9	3	0	.750	332	218
Chi. Cardinals	6	5	1	.545	360	301
Detroit	4	8	0	.333	237	259
Green Bay	2	10	0	.167	114	329

NFL championship: Philadelphia 14, LOS ANGELES 0

1948

EASTERN DIVISION

	W	L	T	Pct.	Pts.	OP
Philadelphia	9	2	1	.818	376	156
Washington	7	5	0	.583	291	287
N.Y. Giants	4	8	0	.333	297	388
Pittsburgh	4	8	0	.333	200	243
Boston	3	9	0	.250	174	372

WESTERN DIVISION

	W	L	T	Pct.	Pts.	OP
Chi. Cardinals	11	1	0	.917	395	226
Chi. Bears	10	2	0	.833	375	151
Los Angeles	6	5	1	.545	327	269
Green Bay	3	9	0	.250	154	290
Detroit	2	10	0	.167	200	407

NFL championship: PHILADELPHIA 7, Chi. Cardinals 0

1947

EASTERN DIVISION

	W	L	T	Pct.	Pts.	OP
Philadelphia	8	4	0	.667	308	242
Pittsburgh	8	4	0	.667	240	259
Boston	4	7	1	.364	168	256
Washington	4	8	0	.333	295	367
N.Y. Giants	2	8	2	.200	190	309

WESTERN DIVISION

	W	L	T	Pct.	Pts.	OP
Chi. Cardinals	9	3	0	.750	306	231
Chi. Bears	8	4	0	.667	363	241
Green Bay	6	5	1	.545	274	210
Los Angeles	6	6	0	.500	259	214
Detroit	3	9	0	.250	231	305

Eastern Division playoff: Philadelphia 21, PITTSBURGH 0
NFL championship: CHI. CARDINALS 28, Philadelphia 21

1946

EASTERN DIVISION

	W	L	T	Pct.	Pts.	OP
N.Y. Giants	7	3	1	.700	236	162
Philadelphia	6	5	0	.545	231	220
Washington	5	5	1	.500	171	191
Pittsburgh	5	5	1	.500	136	117
Boston	2	8	1	.200	189	273

WESTERN DIVISION

	W	L	T	Pct.	Pts.	OP
Chi. Bears	8	2	1	.800	289	193
Los Angeles	6	4	1	.600	277	257
Green Bay	6	5	0	.545	148	158
Chi. Cardinals	6	5	0	.545	260	198
Detroit	1	10	0	.091	142	310

NFL championship: Chi. Bears 24, N.Y. GIANTS 14

1945

EASTERN DIVISION

	W	L	T	Pct.	Pts.	OP
Washington	8	2	0	.800	209	121
Philadelphia	7	3	0	.700	272	133
N.Y. Giants	3	6	1	.333	179	198
Boston	3	6	1	.333	123	211
Pittsburgh	2	8	0	.200	79	220

WESTERN DIVISION

	W	L	T	Pct.	Pts.	OP
Cleveland	9	1	0	.900	244	136
Detroit	7	3	0	.700	195	194
Green Bay	6	4	0	.600	258	173
Chi. Bears	3	7	0	.300	192	235
Chi. Cardinals	1	9	0	.100	98	228

NFL championship: CLEVELAND 15, Washington 14

1944

EASTERN DIVISION

	W	L	T	Pct.	Pts.	OP
N.Y. Giants	8	1	1	.889	206	75
Philadelphia	7	1	2	.875	267	131
Washington	6	3	1	.667	169	180
Boston	2	8	0	.200	82	233
Brooklyn	0	10	0	.000	69	166

WESTERN DIVISION

	W	L	T	Pct.	Pts.	OP
Green Bay	8	2	0	.800	238	141
Chi. Bears	6	3	1	.667	258	172
Detroit	6	3	1	.667	216	151
Cleveland	4	6	0	.400	188	224
Card-Pitt	0	10	0	.000	108	328

NFL championship: Green Bay 14, N.Y. GIANTS 7

1943

EASTERN DIVISION

	W	L	T	Pct.	Pts.	OP
Washington	6	3	1	.667	229	137
N.Y. Giants	6	3	1	.667	197	170
Phil-Pitt	5	4	1	.556	225	230
Brooklyn	2	8	0	.200	65	234

WESTERN DIVISION

	W	L	T	Pct.	Pts.	OP
Chi. Bears	8	1	1	.889	303	157
Green Bay	7	2	1	.778	264	172
Detroit	3	6	1	.333	178	218
Chi. Cardinals	0	10	0	.000	95	238

Eastern Division playoff: Washington 28, N.Y. GIANTS 0
NFL championship: CHI. BEARS 41, Washington 21

1942

EASTERN DIVISION

	W	L	T	Pct.	Pts.	OP
Washington	10	1	0	.909	227	102
Pittsburgh	7	4	0	.636	167	119
N.Y. Giants	5	5	1	.500	155	139
Brooklyn	3	8	0	.273	100	168
Philadelphia	2	9	0	.182	134	239

WESTERN DIVISION

	W	L	T	Pct.	Pts.	OP
Chi. Bears	11	0	0	1.000	376	84
Green Bay	8	2	1	.800	300	215
Cleveland	5	6	0	.455	150	207
Chi. Cardinals	3	8	0	.273	98	209
Detroit	0	11	0	.000	38	263

NFL championship: WASHINGTON 14, Chi. Bears 6

1941

EASTERN DIVISION

	W	L	T	Pct.	Pts.	OP
N.Y. Giants	8	3	0	.727	238	114
Brooklyn	7	4	0	.636	158	127
Washington	6	5	0	.545	176	174
Philadelphia	2	8	1	.200	119	218
Pittsburgh	1	9	1	.100	103	276

WESTERN DIVISION

	W	L	T	Pct.	Pts.	OP
Chi. Bears	10	1	0	.909	396	147
Green Bay	10	1	0	.909	258	120
Detroit	4	6	1	.400	121	195
Chi. Cardinals	3	7	1	.300	127	197
Cleveland	2	9	0	.182	116	244

Western Division playoff: CHI. BEARS 33, Green Bay 14
NFL championship: CHI. BEARS 37, N.Y. Giants 9

1940

EASTERN DIVISION

	W	L	T	Pct.	Pts.	OP
Washington	9	2	0	.818	245	142
Brooklyn	8	3	0	.727	186	120
N.Y. Giants	6	4	1	.600	131	133
Pittsburgh	2	7	2	.222	60	178
Philadelphia	1	10	0	.091	111	211

WESTERN DIVISION

	W	L	T	Pct.	Pts.	OP
Chi. Bears	8	3	0	.727	238	152
Green Bay	6	4	1	.600	238	155
Detroit	5	5	1	.500	138	153
Cleveland	4	6	1	.400	171	191
Chi. Cardinals	2	7	2	.222	139	222

NFL championship: Chi. Bears 73, WASHINGTON 0

1939

EASTERN DIVISION

	W	L	T	Pct.	Pts.	OP
N.Y. Giants	9	1	1	.900	168	85
Washington	8	2	1	.800	242	94
Brooklyn	4	6	1	.400	108	219
Philadelphia	1	9	1	.100	105	200
Pittsburgh	1	9	1	.100	114	216

WESTERN DIVISION

	W	L	T	Pct.	Pts.	OP
Green Bay	9	2	0	.818	233	153
Chi. Bears	8	3	0	.727	298	157
Detroit	6	5	0	.545	145	150
Cleveland	5	5	1	.500	195	164
Chi. Cardinals	1	10	0	.091	84	254

NFL championship: GREEN BAY 27, N.Y. Giants 0

1938

EASTERN DIVISION

	W	L	T	Pct.	Pts.	OP
N.Y. Giants	8	2	1	.800	194	79
Washington	6	3	2	.667	148	154
Brooklyn	4	4	3	.500	131	161
Philadelphia	5	6	0	.455	154	164
Pittsburgh	2	9	0	.182	79	169

WESTERN DIVISION

	W	L	T	Pct.	Pts.	OP
Green Bay	8	3	0	.727	223	118
Detroit	7	4	0	.636	119	108
Chi. Bears	6	5	0	.545	194	148
Cleveland	4	7	0	.364	131	215
Chi. Cardinals	2	9	0	.182	111	168

NFL championship: N.Y. GIANTS 23, Green Bay 17

1937

EASTERN DIVISION

	W	L	T	Pct.	Pts.	OP
Washington	8	3	0	.727	195	120
N.Y. Giants	6	3	2	.667	128	109
Pittsburgh	4	7	0	.364	122	145
Brooklyn	3	7	1	.300	82	174
Philadelphia	2	8	1	.200	86	177

WESTERN DIVISION

	W	L	T	Pct.	Pts.	OP
Chi. Bears	9	1	1	.900	201	100
Green Bay	7	4	0	.636	220	122
Detroit	7	4	0	.636	180	105
Chi. Cardinals	5	5	1	.500	135	165
Cleveland	1	10	0	.091	75	207

NFL championship: Washington 28, CHI. BEARS 21

1936

EASTERN DIVISION

	W	L	T	Pct.	Pts.	OP
Boston	7	5	0	.583	149	110
Pittsburgh	6	6	0	.500	98	187
N.Y. Giants	5	6	1	.455	115	163
Brooklyn	3	8	1	.273	92	161
Philadelphia	1	11	0	.083	51	206

WESTERN DIVISION

	W	L	T	Pct.	Pts.	OP
Green Bay	10	1	1	.909	248	118
Chi. Bears	9	3	0	.750	222	94
Detroit	8	4	0	.667	235	102
Chi. Cardinals	3	8	1	.273	74	143

NFL championship: Green Bay 21, Boston 6, at Polo Grounds, N.Y.

1935

EASTERN DIVISION

	W	L	T	Pct.	Pts.	OP
N.Y. Giants	9	3	0	.750	180	96
Brooklyn	5	6	1	.455	90	141
Pittsburgh	4	8	0	.333	100	209
Boston	2	8	1	.200	65	123
Philadelphia	2	9	0	.182	60	179

WESTERN DIVISION

	W	L	T	Pct.	Pts.	OP
Detroit	7	3	2	.700	191	111
Green Bay	8	4	0	.667	181	96
Chi. Bears	6	4	2	.600	192	106
Chi. Cardinals	6	4	2	.600	99	97

NFL championship: DETROIT 26, N.Y. Giants 7
One game between Boston and Philadelphia was canceled.

1934

EASTERN DIVISION

	W	L	T	Pct.	Pts.	OP
N.Y. Giants	8	5	0	.615	147	107
Boston	6	6	0	.500	107	94
Brooklyn	4	7	0	.364	61	153
Philadelphia	4	7	0	.364	127	85
Pittsburgh	2	10	0	.167	51	206

WESTERN DIVISION

	W	L	T	Pct.	Pts.	OP
Chi. Bears	13	0	0	1.000	286	86
Detroit	10	3	0	.769	238	59
Green Bay	7	6	0	.538	156	112
Chi. Cardinals	5	6	0	.455	80	84
St. Louis	1	2	0	.333	27	61
Cincinnati	0	8	0	.000	10	243

NFL championship: N.Y. GIANTS 30, Chi. Bears 13

1933

EASTERN DIVISION

	W	L	T	Pct.	Pts.	OP
N.Y. Giants	11	3	0	.786	244	101
Brooklyn	5	4	1	.556	93	54
Boston	5	5	2	.500	103	97
Philadelphia	3	5	1	.375	77	158
Pittsburgh	3	6	2	.333	67	208

WESTERN DIVISION

	W	L	T	Pct.	Pts.	OP
Chi. Bears	10	2	1	.833	133	82
Portsmouth	6	5	0	.545	128	87
Green Bay	5	7	1	.417	170	107
Cincinnati	3	6	1	.333	38	110
Chi. Cardinals	1	9	1	.100	52	101

NFL championship: CHI. BEARS 23, N.Y. Giants 21

1932

	W	L	T	Pct.
Chicago Bears	7	1	6	.875
Green Bay Packers	10	3	1	.769
Portsmouth Spartans	6	2	4	.750
Boston Braves	4	4	2	.500
New York Giants	4	6	2	.400
Brooklyn Dodgers	3	9	0	.250
Chicago Cardinals	2	6	2	.250
Staten Island Stapletons	2	7	3	.222

Chicago Bears and Portsmouth finished regularly scheduled games tied for first place. Bears won playoff game, which counted in standings, 9-0.

1931

	W	L	T	Pct.
Green Bay Packers	12	2	0	.857
Portsmouth Spartans	11	3	0	.786
Chicago Bears	8	5	0	.615
Chicago Cardinals	5	4	0	.556
New York Giants	7	6	1	.538
Providence Steam Roller	4	4	3	.500
Staten Island Stapletons	4	6	1	.400
Cleveland Indians	2	8	0	.200
Brooklyn Dodgers	2	12	0	.143
Frankford Yellow Jackets	1	6	1	.143

1930

	W	L	T	Pct.
Green Bay Packers	10	3	1	.769
New York Giants	13	4	0	.765
Chicago Bears	9	4	1	.692
Brooklyn Dodgers	7	4	1	.636
Providence Steam Roller	6	4	1	.600
Staten Island Stapletons	5	5	2	.500
Chicago Cardinals	5	6	2	.455
Portsmouth Spartans	5	6	3	.455
Frankford Yellow Jackets	4	13	1	.222
Minneapolis Red Jackets	1	7	1	.125
Newark Tornadoes	1	10	1	.091

1929

	W	L	T	Pct.
Green Bay Packers	12	0	1	1.000
New York Giants	13	1	1	.929
Frankford Yellow Jackets	10	4	5	.714
Chicago Cardinals	6	6	1	.500
Boston Bulldogs	4	4	0	.500
Staten Island Stapletons	3	4	3	.429
Providence Steam Roller	4	6	2	.400
Orange Tornadoes	3	5	4	.375
Chicago Bears	4	9	2	.308
Buffalo Bisons	1	7	1	.125
Minneapolis Red Jackets	1	9	0	.100
Dayton Triangles	0	6	0	.000

1928

	W	L	T	Pct.
Providence Steam Roller	8	1	2	.889
Frankford Yellow Jackets	11	3	2	.786
Detroit Wolverines	7	2	1	.778
Green Bay Packers	6	4	3	.600
Chicago Bears	7	5	1	.583
New York Giants	4	7	2	.364
New York Yankees	4	8	1	.333
Pottsville Maroons	2	8	0	.200
Chicago Cardinals	1	5	0	.167
Dayton Triangles	0	7	0	.000

1927

	W	L	T	Pct.
New York Giants	11	1	1	.917
Green Bay Packers	7	2	1	.778
Chicago Bears	9	3	2	.750
Cleveland Bulldogs	8	4	1	.667
Providence Steam Roller	8	5	1	.615
New York Yankees	7	8	1	.467
Frankford Yellow Jackets	6	9	3	.400
Pottsville Maroons	5	8	0	.385
Chicago Cardinals	3	7	1	.300
Dayton Triangles	1	6	1	.143
Duluth Eskimos	1	8	0	.111
Buffalo Bisons	0	5	0	.000

1926

	W	L	T	Pct.
Frankford Yellow Jackets	14	1	2	.933
Chicago Bears	12	1	3	.923
Pottsville Maroons	10	2	2	.833
Kansas City Cowboys	8	3	0	.727
Green Bay Packers	7	3	3	.700
Los Angeles Buccaneers	6	3	1	.667
New York Giants	8	4	1	.667
Duluth Eskimos	6	5	3	.545
Buffalo Rangers	4	4	2	.500
Chicago Cardinals	5	6	1	.455
Providence Steam Roller	5	7	1	.417
Detroit Panthers	4	6	2	.400
Hartford Blues	3	7	0	.300
Brooklyn Lions	3	8	0	.273
Milwaukee Badgers	2	7	0	.222
Akron Indians	1	4	3	.200
Dayton Triangles	1	4	1	.200
Racine Tornadoes	1	4	0	.200
Columbus Tigers	1	6	0	.143
Canton Bulldogs	1	9	3	.100
Hammond Pros	0	4	0	.000
Louisville Colonels	0	4	0	.000

1925

	W	L	T	Pct.
Chicago Cardinals	11	2	1	.846
Pottsville Maroons	10	2	0	.833
Detroit Panthers	8	2	2	.800
New York Giants	8	4	0	.667
Akron Indians	4	2	2	.667
Frankford Yellow Jackets	13	7	0	.650
Chicago Bears	9	5	3	.643
Rock Island Independents	5	3	3	.625
Green Bay Packers	8	5	0	.615
Providence Steam Roller	6	5	1	.545
Canton Bulldogs	4	4	0	.500
Cleveland Bulldogs	5	8	1	.385
Kansas City Cowboys	2	5	1	.286
Hammond Pros	1	4	0	.200
Buffalo Bisons	1	6	2	.143
Duluth Kelleys	0	3	0	.000
Rochester Jeffersons	0	6	1	.000
Milwaukee Badgers	0	6	0	.000
Dayton Triangles	0	7	1	.000
Columbus Tigers	0	9	0	.000

PAST STANDINGS

1924

	W	L	T	Pct.
Cleveland Bulldogs	7	1	1	.875
Chicago Bears	6	1	4	.857
Frankford Yellow Jackets	11	2	1	.846
Duluth Kelleys	5	1	0	.833
Rock Island Independents	5	2	2	.714
Green Bay Packers	7	4	0	.636
Racine Legion	4	3	3	.571
Chicago Cardinals	5	4	1	.556
Buffalo Bisons	6	5	0	.545
Columbus Tigers	4	4	0	.500
Hammond Pros	2	2	1	.500
Milwaukee Badgers	5	8	0	.385
Akron Indians	2	6	0	.250
Dayton Triangles	2	6	0	.250
Kansas City Blues	2	7	0	.222
Kenosha Maroons	0	4	1	.000
Minneapolis Marines	0	6	0	.000
Rochester Jeffersons	0	7	0	.000

1923

	W	L	T	Pct.
Canton Bulldogs	11	0	1	1.000
Chicago Bears	9	2	1	.818
Green Bay Packers	7	2	1	.778
Milwaukee Badgers	7	2	3	.778
Cleveland Indians	3	1	3	.750
Chicago Cardinals	8	4	0	.667
Duluth Kelleys	4	3	0	.571
Buffalo All-Americans	5	4	3	.556
Columbus Tigers	5	4	1	.556
Racine Legion	4	4	2	.500
Toledo Maroons	3	3	2	.500
Rock Island Independents	2	3	3	.400
Minneapolis Marines	2	5	2	.286
St. Louis All-Stars	1	4	2	.200
Hammond Pros	1	5	1	.167
Dayton Triangles	1	6	1	.143
Akron Indians	1	6	0	.143
Oorang Indians	1	10	0	.091
Louisville Brecks	0	3	0	.000
Rochester Jeffersons	0	4	0	.000

1922

	W	L	T	Pct.
Canton Bulldogs	10	0	2	1.000
Chicago Bears	9	3	0	.750
Chicago Cardinals	8	3	0	.727
Toledo Maroons	5	2	2	.714
Rock Island Independents	4	2	1	.667
Racine Legion	6	4	1	.600
Dayton Triangles	4	3	1	.571
Green Bay Packers	4	3	3	.571
Buffalo All-Americans	5	4	1	.556
Akron Pros	3	5	2	.375
Milwaukee Badgers	2	4	3	.333
Oorang Indians	3	6	0	.333
Minneapolis Marines	1	3	0	.250
Louisville Brecks	1	3	0	.250
Evansville Crimson Giants	0	3	0	.000
Rochester Jeffersons	0	4	1	.000
Hammond Pros	0	5	1	.000
Columbus Panhandles	0	8	0	.000

1921

	W	L	T	Pct.
Chicago Staleys	9	1	1	.900
Buffalo All-Americans	9	1	2	.900
Akron Pros	8	3	1	.727
Canton Bulldogs	5	2	3	.714
Rock Island Independents	4	2	1	.667
Evansville Crimson Giants	3	2	0	.600
Green Bay Packers	3	2	1	.600
Dayton Triangles	4	4	1	.500
Chicago Cardinals	3	3	2	.500
Rochester Jeffersons	2	3	0	.400
Cleveland Indians	3	5	0	.375
Washington Senators	1	2	0	.333
Cincinnati Celts	1	3	0	.250
Hammond Pros	1	3	1	.250
Minneapolis Marines	1	3	0	.250
Detroit Tigers	1	5	1	.167
Columbus Panhandles	1	8	0	.111
Tonawanda Kardex	0	1	0	.000
Muncie Flyers	0	2	0	.000
Louisville Brecks	0	2	0	.000
New York Giants	0	2	0	.000

1920*

	W	L	T	Pct.
Akron Pros	8	0	3	1.000
Decatur Staleys	10	1	2	.909
Buffalo All-Americans	9	1	1	.900
Chicago Cardinals	6	2	2	.750
Rock Island Independents	6	2	2	.750
Dayton Triangles	5	2	2	.714
Rochester Jeffersons	6	3	2	.667
Canton Bulldogs	7	4	2	.636
Detroit Heralds	2	3	3	.400
Cleveland Tigers	2	4	2	.333
Chicago Tigers	2	5	1	.286
Hammond Pros	2	5	0	.286
Columbus Panhandles	2	6	2	.250
Muncie Flyers	0	1	0	.000

*No official standings were maintained for the 1920 season, and the championship was awarded to the Akron Pros in a League meeting on April 30, 1921. Clubs played schedules that included games against nonleague opponents.

2014 NFL Record & Fact Book

RS=REGULAR SEASON
PS=POSTSEASON
*ARIZONA vs. ATLANTA
RS: Cardinals lead series, 15-12
PS: Cardinals lead series, 1-0
1966—Falcons, 16-10 (Atl)
1968—Cardinals, 17-12 (StL)
1971—Cardinals, 26-9 (Atl)
1973—Cardinals, 32-10 (Atl)
1975—Cardinals, 23-20 (StL)
1978—Cardinals, 42-21 (StL)
1980—Falcons, 33-27 (StL) OT
1981—Falcons, 41-20 (Atl)
1982—Cardinals, 23-20 (Atl)
1986—Falcons, 33-13 (Atl)
1987—Cardinals, 34-21 (Atl)
1989—Cardinals, 34-20 (P)
1990—Cardinals, 24-13 (Atl)
1991—Cardinals, 16-10 (P)
1992—Falcons, 20-17 (Atl)
1993—Cardinals, 27-10 (Atl)
1994—Falcons, 10-6 (Atl)
1995—Cardinals, 40-37 (Ariz) OT
1997—Cardinals, 29-26 (Ariz)
1999—Falcons, 37-14 (Atl)
2001—Falcons, 34-14 (Ariz)
2004—Falcons, 6-3 (Atl)
2006—Falcons, 32-10 (Atl)
2007—Cardinals, 30-27 (Ariz) OT
2008—**Cardinals, 30-24 (Ariz)
2010—Falcons, 41-7 (Atl)
2012—Falcons, 23-19 (Atl)
2013—Cardinals, 27-13 (Ariz)
(RS Pts.—Falcons 595, Cardinals 584)
(PS Pts.—Cardinals 30, Falcons 24)
*Franchise known as Phoenix prior to
1994 and in St. Louis prior to 1988*
**NFC First-Round Playoff
*ARIZONA vs. BALTIMORE
RS: Ravens lead series, 4-1
1997—Cardinals, 16-13 (B)
2000—Ravens, 13-7 (A)
2003—Ravens, 26-18 (A)
2007—Ravens, 26-23 (B)
2011—Ravens, 30-27 (B)
(RS Pts.—Ravens 108, Cardinals 91)
*ARIZONA vs. BUFFALO
RS: Bills lead series, 6-4
1971—Cardinals, 28-23 (B)
1975—Bills, 32-14 (StL)
1981—Cardinals, 24-0 (StL)
1984—Cardinals, 37-7 (StL)
1986—Bills, 17-10 (B)
1990—Bills, 45-14 (B)
1999—Bills, 31-21 (A)
2004—Bills, 38-14 (B)
2008—Cardinals, 41-17 (A)
2012—Bills, 19-16 (A) OT
(RS Pts.—Bills 229, Cardinals 219)
*Franchise known as Phoenix prior to
1994 and in St. Louis prior to 1988*
ARIZONA vs. CAROLINA
RS: Panthers lead series, 8-4
PS: Cardinals lead series, 1-0
1995—Panthers, 27-7 (C)
2001—Cardinals, 30-7 (C)
2002—Cardinals, 16-13 (C)
2003—Panthers, 20-17 (A)
2004—Panthers, 35-10 (C)
2005—Panthers, 24-20 (A)
2007—Panthers, 25-10 (A)
2008—Panthers, 27-23 (C)
    *Cardinals, 33-13 (C)

2009—Panthers, 34-21 (A)
2010—Panthers, 19-12 (C)
2011—Cardinals, 28-21 (A)
2013—Cardinals, 22-6 (A)
(RS Pts.—Panthers 258, Cardinals 216)
(PS Pts.—Cardinals 33, Panthers 13)
*NFC Divisional Playoff
*ARIZONA vs. **CHICAGO
RS: Bears lead series, 56-27-6
(NP denotes Normal Park;
Wr denotes Wrigley Field;
Co denotes Comiskey Park;
So denotes Soldier Field;
all Chicago)
1920—Cardinals, 7-6 (NP)
    Staleys, 10-0 (Wr)
1921—Tie, 0-0 (Wr)
1922—Cardinals, 6-0 (Co)
    Cardinals, 9-0 (Co)
1923—Bears, 3-0 (Wr)
1924—Bears, 6-0 (Wr)
    Bears, 21-0 (Co)
1925—Cardinals, 9-0 (Co)
    Tie, 0-0 (Wr)
1926—Bears, 16-0 (Wr)
    Bears, 10-0 (So)
    Tie, 0-0 (Wr)
1927—Bears, 9-0 (NP)
    Cardinals, 3-0 (Wr)
1928—Bears, 15-0 (NP)
    Bears, 34-0 (Wr)
1929—Tie, 0-0 (Wr)
    Cardinals, 40-6 (Co)
1930—Bears, 32-6 (Co)
    Bears, 6-0 (Wr)
1931—Bears, 26-13 (Wr)
    Bears, 18-7 (Wr)
1932—Tie, 0-0 (Wr)
    Bears, 34-0 (Wr)
1933—Bears, 12-9 (Wr)
    Bears, 22-6 (Wr)
1934—Bears, 20-0 (Wr)
    Bears, 17-6 (Wr)
1935—Tie, 7-7 (Wr)
    Bears, 13-0 (Wr)
1936—Bears, 7-3 (Wr)
    Cardinals, 14-7 (Wr)
1937—Bears, 16-7 (Wr)
    Bears, 42-28 (Wr)
1938—Bears, 16-13 (So)
    Bears, 34-28 (Wr)
1939—Bears, 44-7 (Wr)
    Bears, 48-7 (Co)
1940—Cardinals, 21-7 (Co)
    Bears, 31-23 (Wr)
1941—Bears, 53-7 (Wr)
    Bears, 34-24 (Co)
1942—Bears, 41-14 (Wr)
    Bears, 21-7 (Co)
1943—Bears, 20-0 (Wr)
    Bears, 35-24 (Co)
1945—Cardinals, 16-7 (Wr)
    Bears, 28-20 (Co)
1946—Bears, 34-17 (Co)
    Cardinals, 35-28 (Wr)
1947—Cardinals, 31-7 (Co)
    Cardinals, 30-21 (Wr)
1948—Bears, 28-17 (Co)
    Cardinals, 24-21 (Wr)
1949—Bears, 17-7 (Co)
    Bears, 52-21 (Wr)
1950—Bears, 27-6 (Wr)
    Cardinals, 20-10 (Co)

1951—Cardinals, 28-14 (Co)
    Cardinals, 24-14 (Wr)
1952—Cardinals, 21-10 (Co)
    Bears, 10-7 (Wr)
1953—Cardinals, 24-17 (Wr)
1954—Bears, 29-7 (Co)
1955—Bears, 53-14 (Co)
1956—Bears, 10-3 (Wr)
1957—Bears, 14-6 (Co)
1958—Bears, 30-14 (Wr)
1959—Bears, 31-7 (So)
1965—Bears, 34-13 (Wr)
1966—Cardinals, 24-17 (StL)
1967—Bears, 30-3 (Wr)
1969—Cardinals, 20-17 (StL)
1972—Bears, 27-10 (StL)
1975—Cardinals, 34-20 (So)
1977—Cardinals, 16-13 (StL)
1978—Bears, 17-10 (So)
1979—Bears, 42-6 (So)
1982—Cardinals, 10-7 (So)
1984—Bears, 38-21 (StL)
1990—Bears, 31-21 (P)
1994—Bears, 19-16 (A) OT
1998—Cardinals, 20-7 (A)
2001—Bears, 20-13 (C)
2003—Bears, 28-3 (C)
2006—Bears, 24-23 (A)
2009—Cardinals, 41-21 (C)
2012—Bears, 28-13 (A)
(RS Pts.—Bears 1,695, Cardinals 1,127)
*Franchise known as Phoenix prior to
1994, in St. Louis prior to 1988, and in
Chicago prior to 1960*
***Franchise in Decatur prior to 1921 and
known as Staleys prior to 1922*
*ARIZONA vs. CINCINNATI
RS: Bengals lead series, 6-4
1973—Bengals, 42-24 (C)
1979—Bengals, 34-28 (C)
1985—Cardinals, 41-27 (StL)
1988—Bengals, 21-14 (C)
1994—Cardinals, 28-7 (A)
1997—Bengals, 24-21 (C)
2000—Bengals, 24-13 (C)
2003—Cardinals, 17-14 (A)
2007—Cardinals, 35-27 (C)
2011—Bengals, 23-16 (C)
(RS Pts.—Bengals 243, Cardinals 237)
*Franchise known as Phoenix prior to
1994 and in St. Louis prior to 1988*
*ARIZONA vs. CLEVELAND
RS: Browns lead series, 33-13-3
1950—Browns, 34-24 (Cle)
    Browns, 10-7 (Chi)
1951—Browns, 34-17 (Chi)
    Browns, 49-28 (Cle)
1952—Browns, 28-13 (Chi)
    Browns, 10-0 (Chi)
1953—Browns, 27-7 (Chi)
    Browns, 27-16 (Cle)
1954—Browns, 31-7 (Cle)
    Browns, 35-3 (Chi)
1955—Browns, 26-20 (Chi)
    Browns, 35-24 (Cle)
1956—Cardinals, 9-7 (Chi)
    Cardinals, 24-7 (Cle)
1957—Browns, 17-7 (Chi)
    Browns, 31-0 (Cle)
1958—Browns, 35-28 (Chi)
    Browns, 38-24 (Chi)
1959—Browns, 34-7 (Chi)
    Browns, 17-7 (Cle)

1960—Browns, 28-27 (Cle)
Tie, 17-17 (StL)
1961—Browns, 20-17 (Cle)
Browns, 21-10 (StL)
1962—Browns, 34-7 (StL)
Browns, 38-14 (Cle)
1963—Cardinals, 20-14 (Cle)
Browns, 24-10 (StL)
1964—Tie, 33-33 (Cle)
Cardinals, 28-19 (StL)
1965—Cardinals, 49-13 (Cle)
Browns, 27-24 (StL)
1966—Cardinals, 34-28 (Cle)
Browns, 38-10 (StL)
1967—Browns, 20-16 (Cle)
Browns, 20-16 (StL)
1968—Cardinals, 27-21 (Cle)
Cardinals, 27-16 (StL)
1969—Tie, 21-21 (Cle)
Browns, 27-21 (StL)
1974—Cardinals, 29-7 (StL)
1979—Browns, 38-20 (StL)
1985—Cardinals, 27-24 (Cle) OT
1988—Browns, 29-21 (P)
1994—Browns, 32-0 (Cle)
2000—Cardinals, 29-21 (A)
2003—Browns, 44-6 (Cle)
2007—Cardinals, 27-21 (A)
2011—Cardinals, 20-17 (A) OT
(RS Pts.—Browns 1,244, Cardinals 879)
*Franchise known as Phoenix prior to
1994, in St. Louis prior to 1988,
and in Chicago prior to 1960
ARIZONA vs. DALLAS
RS: Cowboys lead series, 55-30-1
PS: Cardinals lead series, 1-0
1960—Cardinals, 12-10 (StL)
1961—Cardinals, 31-17 (D)
Cardinals, 31-13 (StL)
1962—Cardinals, 28-24 (D)
Cardinals, 52-20 (StL)
1963—Cardinals, 34-7 (D)
Cowboys, 28-24 (StL)
1964—Cardinals, 16-6 (D)
Cowboys, 31-13 (StL)
1965—Cardinals, 20-13 (StL)
Cowboys, 27-13 (D)
1966—Tie, 10-10 (StL)
Cowboys, 31-17 (D)
1967—Cowboys, 46-21 (D)
1968—Cowboys, 27-10 (StL)
1969—Cowboys, 24-3 (D)
1970—Cardinals, 20-7 (StL)
Cardinals, 38-0 (D)
1971—Cowboys, 16-13 (StL)
Cowboys, 31-12 (D)
1972—Cowboys, 33-24 (D)
Cowboys, 27-6 (StL)
1973—Cowboys, 45-10 (D)
Cowboys, 30-3 (StL)
1974—Cardinals, 31-28 (StL)
Cowboys, 17-14 (D)
1975—Cowboys, 37-31 (D) OT
Cardinals, 31-17 (StL)
1976—Cardinals, 21-17 (StL)
Cowboys, 19-14 (D)
1977—Cowboys, 30-24 (StL)
Cardinals, 24-17 (D)
1978—Cowboys, 21-12 (D)
Cowboys, 24-21 (StL) OT
1979—Cowboys, 22-21 (D)
Cowboys, 22-13 (D)
1980—Cowboys, 27-24 (StL)

Cowboys, 31-21 (D)
1981—Cowboys, 30-17 (D)
Cardinals, 20-17 (StL)
1982—Cowboys, 24-7 (StL)
1983—Cowboys, 34-17 (StL)
Cowboys, 35-17 (D)
1984—Cardinals, 31-20 (D)
Cowboys, 24-17 (StL)
1985—Cardinals, 21-10 (StL)
Cowboys, 35-17 (D)
1986—Cowboys, 31-7 (StL)
Cowboys, 37-6 (D)
1987—Cardinals, 24-13 (StL)
Cowboys, 21-16 (D)
1988—Cowboys, 17-14 (P)
Cardinals, 16-10 (D)
1989—Cardinals, 19-10 (D)
Cardinals, 24-20 (P)
1990—Cardinals, 20-3 (P)
Cowboys, 41-10 (D)
1991—Cowboys, 17-9 (P)
Cowboys, 27-7 (D)
1992—Cowboys, 31-20 (D)
Cowboys, 16-10 (D)
1993—Cowboys, 17-10 (P)
Cowboys, 20-15 (D)
1994—Cowboys, 38-3 (D)
Cowboys, 28-21 (A)
1995—Cowboys, 34-20 (D)
Cowboys, 37-13 (A)
1996—Cowboys, 17-3 (D)
Cowboys, 10-6 (A)
1997—Cardinals, 25-22 (A) OT
Cowboys, 24-6 (D)
1998—Cowboys, 38-10 (A)
Cowboys, 35-28 (A)
**Cardinals, 20-7 (D)
1999—Cowboys, 35-7 (D)
Cardinals, 13-9 (A)
2000—Cardinals, 32-31 (A)
Cowboys, 48-7 (D)
2001—Cowboys, 17-3 (D)
Cardinals, 17-10 (A)
2002—Cardinals, 9-6 (A) OT
2003—Cowboys, 24-7 (D)
2005—Cowboys, 34-13 (D)
2006—Cowboys, 27-10 (A)
2008—Cardinals, 30-24 (A) OT
2010—Cardinals, 27-26 (A)
2011—Cardinals, 19-13 (A) OT
(RS Pts.—Cowboys 1,999, Cardinals 1,483)
(PS Pts.—Cardinals 20, Cowboys 7)
*Franchise known as Phoenix prior to
1994 and in St. Louis prior to 1988
**NFC First-Round Playoff
ARIZONA vs. DENVER
RS: Broncos lead series, 7-1-1
1973—Tie, 17-17 (StL)
1977—Broncos, 7-0 (D)
1989—Broncos, 37-0 (P)
1991—Broncos, 24-19 (D)
1995—Broncos, 38-6 (D)
2001—Broncos, 38-17 (A)
2002—Broncos, 37-7 (D)
2006—Broncos, 37-20 (A)
2010—Cardinals, 43-13 (A)
(RS Pts.—Broncos 248, Cardinals 129)
*Franchise known as Phoenix prior to
1994 and in St. Louis prior to 1988
ARIZONA vs. **DETROIT
RS: Lions lead series, 31-26-5
1930—Tie, 0-0 (Port)
Cardinals, 23-0 (C)

1931—Spartans, 13-3 (Port)
Cardinals, 20-19 (C)
1932—Tie, 7-7 (Port)
1933—Spartans, 7-6 (Port)
1934—Lions, 6-0 (D)
Lions, 17-13 (C)
1935—Tie, 10-10 (D)
Lions, 7-6 (C)
1936—Lions, 39-0 (D)
Lions, 14-7 (C)
1937—Lions, 16-7 (C)
Lions, 16-7 (D)
1938—Lions, 10-0 (D)
Lions, 7-3 (C)
1939—Lions, 21-3 (D)
Lions, 17-3 (C)
1940—Tie, 0-0 (Buffalo)
Lions, 43-14 (C)
1941—Tie, 14-14 (C)
Lions, 21-3 (D)
1942—Cardinals, 13-0 (C)
Cardinals, 7-0 (D)
1943—Lions, 35-17 (D)
Lions, 7-0 (Buffalo)
1945—Lions, 10-0 (Milwaukee)
Lions, 26-0 (D)
1946—Lions, 34-14 (C)
Cardinals, 36-14 (D)
1947—Cardinals, 45-21 (C)
Cardinals, 17-7 (D)
1948—Cardinals, 56-20 (C)
Cardinals, 28-14 (D)
1949—Lions, 24-7 (C)
Cardinals, 42-19 (D)
1959—Lions, 45-21 (D)
1961—Lions, 45-14 (StL)
1967—Cardinals, 38-28 (StL)
1969—Lions, 20-0 (D)
1970—Lions, 16-3 (D)
1973—Lions, 20-16 (StL)
1975—Cardinals, 24-13 (D)
1978—Cardinals, 21-14 (StL)
1980—Lions, 20-7 (D)
Cardinals, 24-23 (StL)
1989—Cardinals, 16-13 (D)
1993—Lions, 26-20 (D)
Lions, 21-14 (Phx)
1995—Cardinals, 20-17 (D)
1998—Cardinals, 17-15 (D)
1999—Cardinals, 23-19 (A)
2001—Cardinals, 45-38 (A)
2002—Cardinals, 23-20 (A) OT
2003—Lions, 42-24 (D)
2004—Lions, 26-12 (D)
2005—Lions, 29-21 (D)
2006—Cardinals, 17-10 (A)
2007—Cardinals, 31-21 (A)
2009—Cardinals, 31-24 (A)
2012—Cardinals, 38-10 (A)
2013—Cardinals, 25-21 (A)
(RS Pts.—Lions 1,124, Cardinals 1,006)
*Franchise known as Phoenix prior to
1994, in St. Louis prior to 1988,
and in Chicago prior to 1960
**Franchise in Portsmouth prior to 1934
and known as the Spartans
ARIZONA vs. GREEN BAY
RS: Packers lead series, 44-22-4
PS: Series tied, 1-1
1921—Tie, 3-3 (C)
1922—Cardinals, 16-3 (C)
1924—Cardinals, 3-0 (C)
1925—Cardinals, 9-6 (C)

1926—Cardinals, 13-7 (GB)
    Packers, 3-0 (C)
1927—Packers, 13-0 (GB)
    Tie, 6-6 (C)
1928—Packers, 20-0 (GB)
1929—Packers, 9-2 (GB)
    Packers, 7-6 (C)
    Packers, 12-0 (C)
1930—Packers, 14-0 (GB)
    Cardinals, 13-6 (C)
1931—Packers, 26-7 (GB)
    Cardinals, 21-13 (C)
1932—Packers, 15-7 (GB)
    Packers, 19-9 (C)
1933—Packers, 14-6 (C)
1934—Packers, 15-0 (GB)
    Cardinals, 9-0 (Mil)
    Cardinals, 6-0 (C)
1935—Cardinals, 7-6 (GB)
    Cardinals, 3-0 (Mil)
    Cardinals, 9-7 (C)
1936—Packers, 10-7 (GB)
    Packers, 24-0 (Mil)
    Tie, 0-0 (C)
1937—Cardinals, 14-7 (GB)
    Packers, 34-13 (Mil)
1938—Packers, 28-7 (Mil)
    Packers, 24-22 (Buffalo)
1939—Packers, 14-10 (GB)
    Packers, 27-20 (Mil)
1940—Packers, 31-6 (Mil)
    Packers, 28-7 (C)
1941—Packers, 14-13 (Mil)
    Packers, 17-9 (GB)
1942—Packers, 17-13 (C)
    Packers, 55-24 (GB)
1943—Packers, 28-7 (C)
    Packers, 35-14 (Mil)
1945—Packers, 33-14 (GB)
1946—Packers, 19-7 (C)
    Cardinals, 24-6 (GB)
1947—Cardinals, 14-10 (GB)
    Cardinals, 21-20 (C)
1948—Cardinals, 17-7 (Mil)
    Cardinals, 42-7 (C)
1949—Cardinals, 39-17 (Mil)
    Cardinals, 41-21 (C)
1955—Packers, 31-14 (GB)
1956—Packers, 24-21 (C)
1962—Packers, 17-0 (Mil)
1963—Packers, 30-7 (StL)
1967—Packers, 31-23 (StL)
1969—Packers, 45-28 (GB)
1971—Tie, 16-16 (StL)
1973—Packers, 25-21 (GB)
1976—Cardinals, 29-0 (StL)
1982—**Packers, 41-16 (GB)
1984—Packers, 24-23 (GB)
1985—Cardinals, 43-28 (StL)
1988—Packers, 26-17 (P)
1990—Packers, 24-21 (P)
1999—Packers, 49-24 (GB)
2000—Packers, 29-3 (A)
2003—Cardinals, 20-13 (A)
2006—Packers, 31-14 (GB)
2009—Packers, 33-7 (A)
    **Cardinals, 51-45 (A) OT
2012—Packers, 31-17 (GB)
(RS Pts.—Packers 1,264, Cardinals 908)
(PS Pts.—Packers 86, Cardinals 67)
*Franchise known as Phoenix prior to
1994, in St. Louis prior to 1988,
and in Chicago prior to 1960

**NFC First-Round Playoff
ARIZONA vs. HOUSTON
RS: Cardinals lead series, 2-1
2005—Texans, 30-19 (H)
2009—Cardinals, 28-21 (A)
2013—Cardinals, 27-24 (A)
(RS Pts.—Texans 75, Cardinals 74)
*ARIZONA vs. **INDIANAPOLIS
RS: Colts lead series, 8-7
1961—Colts, 16-0 (B)
1964—Colts, 47-27 (B)
1968—Colts, 27-0 (B)
1972—Cardinals, 10-3 (B)
1976—Cardinals, 24-17 (StL)
1978—Colts, 30-17 (StL)
1980—Cardinals, 17-10 (B)
1981—Cardinals, 35-24 (B)
1984—Cardinals, 34-33 (I)
1990—Cardinals, 20-17 (P)
1992—Colts, 16-13 (I)
1996—Colts, 20-13 (I)
2005—Colts, 17-13 (I)
2009—Colts, 31-10 (A)
2013—Cardinals, 40-11 (A)
(RS Pts.—Colts 319, Cardinals 273)
*Franchise known as Phoenix prior to
1994 and in St. Louis prior to 1988
**Franchise in Baltimore prior to 1984
ARIZONA vs. JACKSONVILLE
RS: Series tied, 2-2
2000—Jaguars, 44-10 (J)
2005—Jaguars, 24-17 (A)
2009—Cardinals, 31-17 (J)
2013—Cardinals, 27-14 (A)
(RS Pts.—Jaguars 99, Cardinals 85)
*ARIZONA vs. KANSAS CITY
RS: Chiefs lead series, 8-2-1
1970—Tie, 6-6 (KC)
1974—Chiefs, 17-13 (StL)
1980—Chiefs, 21-13 (StL)
1983—Chiefs, 38-14 (KC)
1986—Cardinals, 23-14 (StL)
1995—Chiefs, 24-3 (A)
1998—Chiefs, 34-24 (KC)
2001—Cardinals, 24-16 (A)
2002—Chiefs, 49-0 (KC)
2006—Chiefs, 23-20 (A)
2010—Chiefs, 31-13 (KC)
(RS Pts.—Chiefs 273, Cardinals 153)
*Franchise known as Phoenix prior to
1994 and in St. Louis prior to 1988
*ARIZONA vs. MIAMI
RS: Dolphins lead series, 8-3
1972—Dolphins, 31-10 (M)
1977—Dolphins, 55-14 (StL)
1978—Dolphins, 24-10 (M)
1981—Dolphins, 20-7 (StL)
1984—Dolphins, 36-28 (StL)
1990—Dolphins, 23-3 (M)
1996—Dolphins, 38-10 (A)
1999—Dolphins, 19-16 (M)
2004—Cardinals, 24-23 (M)
2008—Cardinals, 31-10 (A)
2012—Cardinals, 24-21 (A) OT
(RS Pts.—Dolphins 300, Cardinals 177)
*Franchise known as Phoenix prior to
1994 and in St. Louis prior to 1988
*ARIZONA vs. MINNESOTA
RS: Vikings lead series, 13-10
PS: Vikings lead series, 2-0
1963—Cardinals, 56-14 (M)
1967—Cardinals, 34-24 (M)
1969—Vikings, 27-10 (StL)

1972—Cardinals, 19-17 (M)
1974—Vikings, 28-24 (StL)
    **Vikings, 30-14 (M)
1977—Cardinals, 27-7 (M)
1979—Cardinals, 37-7 (StL)
1981—Cardinals, 30-17 (StL)
1983—Cardinals, 41-31 (StL)
1991—Vikings, 34-7 (M)
    Vikings, 28-0 (P)
1994—Cardinals, 17-7 (A)
1995—Vikings, 30-24 (A) OT
1996—Vikings, 41-17 (M)
1997—Vikings, 20-19 (A)
1998—**Vikings, 41-21 (M)
2000—Vikings, 31-14 (M)
2003—Cardinals, 18-17 (A)
2006—Vikings, 31-26 (A)
2008—Vikings, 35-14 (A)
2009—Cardinals, 30-17 (A)
2010—Vikings, 27-24 (M) OT
2011—Vikings, 34-10 (A)
2012—Vikings, 21-14 (M)
(RS Pts.—Vikings 545, Cardinals 512)
(PS Pts.—Vikings 71, Cardinals 35)
*Franchise known as Phoenix prior to
1994 and in St. Louis prior to 1988
**NFC Divisional Playoff
*ARIZONA vs. **NEW ENGLAND
RS: Cardinals lead series, 7-6
1970—Cardinals, 31-0 (StL)
1975—Cardinals, 24-17 (StL)
1978—Patriots, 16-6 (StL)
1981—Cardinals, 27-20 (NE)
1984—Cardinals, 33-10 (NE)
1990—Cardinals, 34-14 (P)
1991—Cardinals, 24-10 (P)
1993—Patriots, 23-21 (P)
1996—Patriots, 31-0 (NE)
1999—Patriots, 27-3 (A)
2004—Patriots, 23-12 (A)
2008—Patriots, 47-7 (NE)
2012—Cardinals, 20-18 (NE)
(RS Pts.—Patriots 256, Cardinals 242)
*Franchise known as Phoenix prior to
1994 and in St. Louis prior to 1988
**Franchise in Boston prior to 1971
*ARIZONA vs. NEW ORLEANS
RS: Cardinals lead series, 14-13
PS: Saints lead series, 1-0
1967—Cardinals, 31-20 (StL)
1968—Cardinals, 21-20 (NO)
    Cardinals, 31-17 (StL)
1969—Saints, 51-42 (StL)
1970—Cardinals, 24-17 (StL)
1974—Saints, 14-0 (NO)
1977—Cardinals, 49-31 (NO)
1980—Cardinals, 40-7 (NO)
1981—Cardinals, 30-3 (StL)
1982—Cardinals, 21-7 (NO)
1983—Saints, 28-17 (NO)
1984—Saints, 34-24 (NO)
1985—Cardinals, 28-16 (StL)
1986—Saints, 16-7 (StL)
1987—Cardinals, 24-19 (StL)
1990—Saints, 28-7 (NO)
1991—Saints, 27-3 (P)
1992—Saints, 30-21 (P)
1993—Saints, 20-17 (P)
1996—Cardinals, 28-14 (NO)
1997—Saints, 27-10 (NO)
1998—Cardinals, 19-17 (A)
2000—Saints, 21-10 (A)
2004—Cardinals, 34-10 (A)

2007—Saints, 31-24 (NO)
2009—**Saints, 45-14 (NO)
2010—Cardinals, 30-20 (A)
2013—Saints, 31-7 (NO)
(RS Pts.—Cardinals 599, Saints 576)
(PS Pts.—Saints 45, Cardinals 14)
*Franchise known as Phoenix prior to
1994 and in St. Louis prior to 1988
**NFC Divisional Playoff
ARIZONA vs. N.Y. GIANTS
RS: Giants lead series, 80-42-2
1926—Giants, 20-0 (NY)
1927—Giants, 28-7 (NY)
1929—Giants, 24-21 (NY)
1930—Giants, 25-12 (NY)
          Giants, 13-7 (C)
1935—Cardinals, 14-13 (NY)
1936—Giants, 14-6 (NY)
1938—Giants, 6-0 (NY)
1939—Giants, 17-7 (NY)
1941—Cardinals, 10-7 (NY)
1942—Giants, 21-7 (NY)
1943—Giants, 24-13 (NY)
1946—Giants, 28-24 (NY)
1947—Giants, 35-31 (NY)
1948—Cardinals, 63-35 (NY)
1949—Giants, 41-38 (C)
1950—Cardinals, 17-3 (C)
          Giants, 51-21 (NY)
1951—Giants, 28-17 (NY)
          Giants, 10-0 (C)
1952—Cardinals, 24-23 (NY)
          Giants, 28-6 (C)
1953—Giants, 21-7 (NY)
          Giants, 23-20 (C)
1954—Giants, 41-10 (C)
          Giants, 31-17 (NY)
1955—Cardinals, 28-17 (C)
          Giants, 10-0 (NY)
1956—Cardinals, 35-27 (C)
          Giants, 23-10 (NY)
1957—Giants, 27-14 (NY)
          Giants, 28-21 (C)
1958—Giants, 37-7 (Buffalo)
          Cardinals, 23-6 (NY)
1959—Giants, 9-3 (NY)
          Giants, 30-20 (Minn)
1960—Giants, 35-14 (StL)
          Cardinals, 20-13 (NY)
1961—Cardinals, 21-10 (NY)
          Giants, 24-9 (StL)
1962—Giants, 31-14 (StL)
          Giants, 31-28 (NY)
1963—Giants, 38-21 (StL)
          Cardinals, 24-17 (NY)
1964—Giants, 34-17 (NY)
          Tie, 10-10 (StL)
1965—Giants, 14-10 (NY)
          Giants, 28-15 (StL)
1966—Cardinals, 24-19 (StL)
          Cardinals, 20-17 (NY)
1967—Giants, 37-20 (StL)
          Giants, 37-14 (NY)
1968—Cardinals, 28-21 (NY)
1969—Cardinals, 42-17 (StL)
          Giants, 49-6 (NY)
1970—Giants, 35-17 (NY)
          Giants, 34-17 (StL)
1971—Giants, 21-20 (StL)
          Cardinals, 24-7 (NY)
1972—Giants, 27-21 (NY)
          Giants, 13-7 (StL)
1973—Cardinals, 35-27 (StL)

Giants, 24-13 (New Haven)
1974—Cardinals, 23-21 (New Haven)
          Cardinals, 26-14 (StL)
1975—Cardinals, 26-14 (StL)
          Cardinals, 20-13 (NY)
1976—Cardinals, 27-21 (StL)
          Cardinals, 17-14 (NY)
1977—Cardinals, 28-0 (StL)
          Giants, 27-7 (NY)
1978—Cardinals, 20-10 (StL)
          Giants, 17-0 (NY)
1979—Cardinals, 27-14 (NY)
          Cardinals, 29-20 (StL)
1980—Giants, 41-35 (StL)
          Cardinals, 23-7 (NY)
1981—Giants, 34-14 (NY)
          Giants, 20-10 (StL)
1982—Cardinals, 24-21 (StL)
1983—Tie, 20-20 (StL) OT
          Cardinals, 10-6 (NY)
1984—Giants, 16-10 (NY)
          Cardinals, 31-21 (StL)
1985—Giants, 27-17 (NY)
          Giants, 34-3 (StL)
1986—Giants, 13-6 (StL)
          Giants, 27-7 (NY)
1987—Giants, 30-7 (NY)
          Cardinals, 27-24 (StL)
1988—Cardinals, 24-17 (P)
          Giants, 44-7 (NY)
1989—Giants, 35-7 (NY)
          Giants, 20-13 (P)
1990—Giants, 20-19 (NY)
          Giants, 24-21 (P)
1991—Giants, 20-9 (NY)
          Giants, 21-14 (P)
1992—Giants, 31-21 (NY)
          Cardinals, 19-0 (P)
1993—Giants, 19-17 (NY)
          Cardinals, 17-6 (P)
1994—Giants, 20-17 (A)
          Cardinals, 10-9 (NY)
1995—Giants, 27-21 (NY) OT
          Giants, 10-6 (A)
1996—Giants, 16-8 (NY)
          Cardinals, 31-23 (A)
1997—Giants, 27-13 (A)
          Giants, 19-10 (NY)
1998—Giants, 34-7 (NY)
          Giants, 23-19 (A)
1999—Cardinals, 14-3 (A)
          Cardinals, 34-24 (NY)
2000—Giants, 21-16 (NY)
          Giants, 31-7 (A)
2001—Giants, 17-10 (A)
          Giants, 17-13 (NY)
2002—Cardinals, 21-7 (A)
2004—Cardinals, 17-14 (A)
2005—Giants, 42-19 (NY)
2008—Giants, 37-29 (A)
2009—Cardinals, 24-17 (NY)
2011—Giants, 31-27 (A)
(RS Pts.—Giants 2,746, Cardinals 2,126)
*Franchise known as Phoenix prior to
1994, in St. Louis prior to 1988,
and in Chicago prior to 1960
ARIZONA vs. N.Y. JETS
RS: Jets lead series, 6-2
1971—Cardinals, 17-10 (StL)
1975—Cardinals, 37-6 (NY)
1978—Jets, 23-10 (NY)
1996—Jets, 31-21 (A)
1999—Jets, 12-7 (NY)

2004—Jets, 13-3 (A)
2008—Jets, 56-35 (NY)
2012—Jets, 7-6 (NY)
(RS Pts.—Jets 158, Cardinals 136)
*Franchise known as Phoenix prior to
1994 and in St. Louis prior to 1988
ARIZONA vs. **OAKLAND
RS: Raiders lead series, 5-3
1973—Raiders, 17-10 (StL)
1983—Cardinals, 34-24 (LA)
1989—Raiders, 16-14 (LA)
1998—Raiders, 23-20 (A)
2001—Cardinals, 34-31 (O) OT
2002—Raiders, 41-20 (A)
2006—Raiders, 22-9 (O)
2010—Cardinals, 24-23 (A)
(RS Pts.— Raiders 197, Cardinals 165)
*Franchise known as Phoenix prior to
1994 and in St. Louis prior to 1988
**Franchise in Los Angeles from
1982-1994
ARIZONA vs. PHILADELPHIA
RS: Cardinals lead series, 55-54-5
PS: Cardinals lead series, 2-1
1935—Cardinals, 12-3 (C)
1936—Cardinals, 13-0 (C)
1937—Tie, 6-6 (P)
1938—Eagles, 7-0 (Erie, Pa.)
1941—Eagles, 21-14 (P)
1945—Eagles, 21-6 (P)
1947—Cardinals, 45-21 (P)
          **Cardinals, 28-21 (C)
1948—Cardinals, 21-14 (C)
          **Eagles, 7-0 (P)
1949—Eagles, 28-3 (P)
1950—Eagles, 45-7 (C)
          Cardinals, 14-10 (P)
1951—Eagles, 17-14 (C)
1952—Eagles, 10-7 (P)
          Cardinals, 28-22 (C)
1953—Eagles, 56-17 (C)
          Eagles, 38-0 (P)
1954—Eagles, 35-16 (C)
          Eagles, 30-14 (P)
1955—Tie, 24-24 (C)
          Eagles, 27-3 (P)
1956—Cardinals, 20-6 (P)
          Cardinals, 28-17 (C)
1957—Eagles, 38-21 (C)
          Cardinals, 31-27 (P)
1958—Tie, 21-21 (C)
          Eagles, 49-21 (P)
1959—Eagles, 28-24 (Minn)
          Eagles, 27-17 (P)
1960—Eagles, 31-27 (P)
          Eagles, 20-6 (StL)
1961—Cardinals, 30-27 (P)
          Eagles, 20-7 (StL)
1962—Cardinals, 27-21 (P)
          Cardinals, 45-35 (StL)
1963—Cardinals, 28-24 (P)
          Cardinals, 38-14 (StL)
1964—Cardinals, 38-13 (P)
          Cardinals, 36-34 (StL)
1965—Eagles, 34-27 (P)
          Eagles, 28-24 (StL)
1966—Cardinals, 16-13 (StL)
          Cardinals, 41-10 (P)
1967—Cardinals, 48-14 (StL)
1968—Cardinals, 45-17 (P)
1969—Eagles, 34-30 (StL)
1970—Cardinals, 35-20 (P)
          Cardinals, 23-14 (StL)

1971—Eagles, 37-20 (StL)
Eagles, 19-7 (P)
1972—Tie, 6-6 (P)
Cardinals, 24-23 (StL)
1973—Cardinals, 34-23 (P)
Eagles, 27-24 (StL)
1974—Cardinals, 7-3 (StL)
Cardinals, 13-3 (P)
1975—Cardinals, 31-20 (StL)
Cardinals, 24-23 (P)
1976—Cardinals, 33-14 (StL)
Cardinals, 17-14 (P)
1977—Cardinals, 21-17 (P)
Cardinals, 21-16 (StL)
1978—Cardinals, 16-10 (P)
Eagles, 14-10 (StL)
1979—Eagles, 24-20 (StL)
Eagles, 16-13 (P)
1980—Cardinals, 24-14 (StL)
Eagles, 17-3 (P)
1981—Eagles, 52-10 (StL)
Eagles, 38-0 (P)
1982—Cardinals, 23-20 (P)
1983—Cardinals, 14-11 (P)
Cardinals, 31-7 (StL)
1984—Cardinals, 34-14 (P)
Cardinals, 17-16 (StL)
1985—Eagles, 30-7 (P)
Eagles, 24-14 (StL)
1986—Cardinals, 13-10 (StL)
Tie, 10-10 (P) OT
1987—Eagles, 28-23 (P)
Cardinals, 31-19 (P)
1988—Eagles, 31-21 (P)
Eagles, 23-17 (Phx)
1989—Eagles, 17-5 (Phx)
Eagles, 31-14 (P)
1990—Cardinals, 23-21 (P)
Eagles, 23-21 (Phx)
1991—Cardinals, 26-10 (P)
Eagles, 34-14 (Phx)
1992—Cardinals, 31-14 (Phx)
Eagles, 7-3 (P)
1993—Eagles, 23-17 (P)
Cardinals, 16-3 (Phx)
1994—Eagles, 17-7 (P)
Cardinals, 12-6 (A)
1995—Eagles, 31-19 (A)
Eagles, 21-20 (P)
1996—Cardinals, 36-30 (A)
Eagles, 29-19 (P)
1997—Eagles, 13-10 (P) OT
Cardinals, 31-21 (A)
1998—Cardinals, 17-3 (A)
Cardinals, 20-17 (P) OT
1999—Cardinals, 25-24 (P)
Cardinals, 21-17 (A)
2000—Eagles, 33-14 (A)
Eagles, 34-9 (P)
2001—Cardinals, 21-20 (P)
Eagles, 21-7 (A)
2002—Eagles, 38-14 (P)
2005—Cardinals, 27-21 (A)
2008—Eagles, 48-20 (P)
***Cardinals, 32-25 (A)
2011—Cardinals, 21-17 (P)
2012—Cardinals, 27-6 (A)
2013—Eagles, 24-21 (P)
(RS Pts.—Eagles 2,435, Cardinals 2,222)
(PS Pts.—Cardinals 60, Eagles 53)
*Franchise known as Phoenix prior to
1994, in St. Louis prior to 1988,
and in Chicago prior to 1960

**NFL Championship
***NFC Championship
**ARIZONA vs. **PITTSBURGH
RS: Steelers lead series, 32-23-3
PS: Steelers lead series, 1-0
1933—Pirates, 14-13 (P)
1935—Pirates, 17-13 (P)
1936—Cardinals, 14-6 (C)
1937—Cardinals, 13-7 (P)
1939—Cardinals, 10-0 (P)
1940—Tie, 7-7 (P)
1942—Steelers, 19-3 (P)
1945—Steelers, 23-0 (P)
1946—Steelers, 14-7 (P)
1948—Cardinals, 24-7 (P)
1950—Steelers, 28-17 (C)
Steelers, 28-7 (P)
1951—Steelers, 28-14 (C)
1952—Steelers, 34-28 (C)
Steelers, 17-14 (P)
1953—Steelers, 31-28 (P)
Steelers, 21-17 (C)
1954—Cardinals, 17-14 (C)
Steelers, 20-17 (P)
1955—Steelers, 14-7 (P)
Cardinals, 27-13 (C)
1956—Steelers, 14-7 (P)
Cardinals, 38-27 (C)
1957—Steelers, 29-20 (P)
Steelers, 27-2 (C)
1958—Steelers, 27-20 (C)
Steelers, 38-21 (P)
1959—Cardinals, 45-24 (C)
Steelers, 35-20 (P)
1960—Steelers, 27-14 (P)
Cardinals, 38-7 (StL)
1961—Steelers, 30-27 (P)
Cardinals, 20-0 (StL)
1962—Steelers, 26-17 (StL)
Steelers, 19-7 (P)
1963—Steelers, 23-10 (P)
Cardinals, 24-23 (StL)
1964—Cardinals, 34-30 (StL)
Cardinals, 21-20 (P)
1965—Cardinals, 20-7 (P)
Cardinals, 21-17 (StL)
1966—Steelers, 30-9 (P)
Cardinals, 6-3 (StL)
1967—Cardinals, 28-14 (P)
Tie, 14-14 (StL)
1968—Tie, 28-28 (StL)
Cardinals, 20-10 (P)
1969—Cardinals, 27-14 (P)
Cardinals, 47-10 (StL)
1972—Steelers, 25-19 (StL)
1979—Steelers, 24-21 (StL)
1985—Steelers, 23-10 (P)
1988—Cardinals, 31-14 (Phx)
1994—Cardinals, 20-17 (A) OT
1997—Steelers, 26-20 (A) OT
2003—Steelers, 28-15 (P)
2007—Cardinals, 21-14 (A)
2008—***Steelers, 27-23 (Tampa Bay)
2011—Steelers, 32-20 (A)
(RS Pts.—Steelers 1,138, Cardinals 1,079)
(PS Pts.—Steelers 27, Cardinals 23)
*Franchise known as Phoenix prior to
1994, in St. Louis prior to 1988,
and in Chicago prior to 1960
**Steelers known as Pirates prior to 1940
***Super Bowl XLIII
**ARIZONA vs. **ST. LOUIS
RS: Series tied, 34-34-2

PS: Rams lead series, 1-0
1937—Cardinals, 6-0 (Cle)
Cardinals, 13-7 (Chi)
1938—Cardinals, 7-6 (Cle)
Cardinals, 31-17 (Chi)
1939—Rams, 24-0 (Chi)
Rams, 14-0 (Cle)
1940—Rams, 26-14 (Cle)
Cardinals, 17-7 (Chi)
1941—Rams, 10-6 (Cle)
Cardinals, 7-0 (Chi)
1942—Cardinals, 7-0 (Buffalo)
Rams, 7-3 (Cle)
1945—Rams, 21-0 (Cle)
Rams, 35-21 (Chi)
1946—Cardinals, 34-10 (Chi)
Rams, 17-14 (LA)
1947—Rams, 27-7 (LA)
Cardinals, 17-10 (Chi)
1948—Cardinals, 27-22 (LA)
Cardinals, 27-24 (Chi)
1949—Tie, 28-28 (Chi)
Cardinals, 31-27 (LA)
1951—Rams, 45-21 (LA)
1953—Tie, 24-24 (Chi)
1954—Rams, 28-17 (LA)
1958—Rams, 20-14 (Chi)
1960—Cardinals, 43-21 (LA)
1965—Rams, 27-3 (StL)
1968—Rams, 24-13 (LA)
1970—Rams, 34-13 (LA)
1972—Cardinals, 24-14 (StL)
1975—***Rams, 35-23 (LA)
1976—Cardinals, 30-28 (LA)
1979—Rams, 21-0 (LA)
1980—Rams, 21-13 (StL)
1984—Rams, 16-13 (StL)
1985—Rams, 46-14 (LA)
1986—Rams, 16-10 (StL)
1987—Rams, 27-24 (StL)
1988—Cardinals, 41-27 (LA)
1989—Rams, 37-14 (LA)
1991—Cardinals, 24-14 (LA)
1992—Cardinals, 20-14 (LA)
1993—Cardinals, 38-10 (P)
1994—Rams, 14-12 (LA)
1996—Cardinals, 31-28 (A) OT
1998—Cardinals, 20-17 (StL)
2002—Rams, 27-14 (A)
Rams, 30-28 (StL)
2003—Rams, 37-13 (StL)
Rams, 30-27 (A) OT
2004—Rams, 17-10 (StL)
Cardinals, 31-7 (A)
2005—Rams, 17-12 (A)
Cardinals, 38-28 (StL)
2006—Rams, 16-14 (A)
Cardinals, 34-20 (A)
2007—Cardinals, 34-31 (StL)
Cardinals, 48-19 (A)
2008—Cardinals, 34-13 (A)
Cardinals, 34-10 (A)
2009—Cardinals, 21-13 (StL)
Cardinals, 31-10 (A)
2010—Cardinals, 17-13 (StL)
Rams, 19-6 (A)
2011—Cardinals, 19-13 (A) OT
Cardinals, 23-20 (StL)
2012—Rams, 17-3 (StL)
Rams, 31-17 (A)
2013—Rams, 27-24 (StL)
Cardinals, 30-10 (A)
(RS Pts.—Rams 1,387, Cardinals 1,355)

(PS Pts.—Rams 35, Cardinals 23)
*Franchise known as Phoenix prior to
1994, in St. Louis prior to 1988,
and in Chicago prior to 1960
**Franchise in Los Angeles prior to 1995
and in Cleveland prior to 1946
***NFC Divisional Playoff
ARIZONA vs. SAN DIEGO
RS: Chargers lead series, 9-3
1971—Chargers, 20-17 (SD)
1976—Chargers, 43-24 (SD)
1983—Cardinals, 44-14 (StL)
1987—Chargers, 28-24 (SD)
1989—Chargers, 24-13 (P)
1992—Chargers, 27-21 (P)
1995—Chargers, 28-25 (SD)
1998—Cardinals, 16-13 (A)
2001—Cardinals, 20-17 (SD)
2002—Chargers, 23-15 (A)
2006—Chargers, 27-20 (SD)
2010—Chargers, 41-10 (SD)
(RS Pts.—Chargers 305, Cardinals 249)
*Franchise known as Phoenix prior to
1994, in St. Louis prior to 1988,
ARIZONA vs. SAN FRANCISCO
RS: 49ers lead series, 28-17
1951—Cardinals, 27-21 (SF)
1957—Cardinals, 20-10 (SF)
1962—49ers, 24-17 (StL)
1964—Cardinals, 23-13 (SF)
1968—49ers, 35-17 (SF)
1971—49ers, 26-14 (StL)
1974—Cardinals, 34-9 (SF)
1976—Cardinals, 23-20 (StL) OT
1978—Cardinals, 16-10 (StL)
1979—Cardinals, 13-10 (StL)
1980—49ers, 24-21 (SF) OT
1982—49ers, 31-20 (StL)
1983—49ers, 42-27 (StL)
1986—49ers, 43-17 (SF)
1987—49ers, 34-28 (SF)
1988—Cardinals, 24-23 (P)
1991—49ers, 14-10 (SF)
1992—Cardinals, 24-14 (P)
1993—49ers, 28-14 (SF)
1999—49ers, 24-10 (A)
2000—49ers, 27-20 (SF)
2002—49ers, 38-28 (SF)
    49ers, 17-14 (A)
2003—Cardinals, 16-13 (A) OT
    49ers, 50-14 (SF)
2004—49ers, 31-28 (SF) OT
    49ers, 31-28 (A) OT
2005—Cardinals, 31-14 (Mex. City)
    Cardinals, 17-10 (SF)
2006—Cardinals, 34-27 (A)
    Cardinals, 26-20 (SF)
2007—49ers, 20-17 (SF)
    49ers, 37-31 (A) OT
2008—Cardinals, 23-13 (SF)
    Cardinals, 29-24 (A)
2009—49ers, 20-16 (A)
    49ers, 24-9 (SF)
2010—49ers, 27-6 (A)
    49ers, 38-7 (SF)
2011—49ers, 23-7 (SF)
    Cardinals, 21-19 (A)
2012—49ers, 24-3 (A)
    49ers, 27-13 (SF)
2013—49ers, 32-20 (SF)
    49ers, 23-20 (A)
(RS Pts.—49ers 1,084, Cardinals 877)
*Franchise known as Phoenix prior to

1994, in St. Louis prior to 1988,
and in Chicago prior to 1960
ARIZONA vs. SEATTLE
RS: Cardinals lead series, 16-14
1976—Cardinals, 30-24 (S)
1983—Cardinals, 33-28 (StL)
1989—Cardinals, 34-24 (S)
1993—Cardinals, 30-27 (S) OT
1995—Cardinals, 20-14 (A) OT
1998—Seahawks, 33-14 (S)
2002—Cardinals, 24-13 (S)
    Seahawks, 27-6 (A)
2003—Seahawks, 38-0 (A)
    Seahawks, 28-10 (S)
2004—Cardinals, 25-17 (A)
    Seahawks, 24-21 (S)
2005—Seahawks, 37-12 (S)
    Seahawks, 33-19 (A)
2006—Seahawks, 21-10 (S)
    Cardinals, 27-21 (A)
2007—Cardinals, 23-20 (A)
    Seahawks, 42-21 (S)
2008—Cardinals, 26-20 (S)
    Cardinals, 34-21 (A)
2009—Cardinals, 27-3 (S)
    Cardinals, 31-20 (A)
2010—Seahawks, 22-10 (S)
    Seahawks, 36-18 (A)
2011—Seahawks, 13-10 (S)
    Cardinals, 23-20 (A) OT
2012—Cardinals, 20-16 (A)
    Seahawks, 58-0 (S)
2013—Seahawks, 34-22 (A)
    Cardinals, 17-10 (S)
(RS Pts.—Seahawks 744, Cardinals 597)
*Franchise known as Phoenix prior to
1994 and in St. Louis prior to 1988
ARIZONA vs. TAMPA BAY
RS: Series tied, 9-9
1977—Buccaneers, 17-7 (TB)
1981—Buccaneers, 20-10 (TB)
1983—Cardinals, 34-27 (TB)
1985—Buccaneers, 16-0 (TB)
1986—Buccaneers, 30-19 (TB)
    Cardinals, 21-17 (StL)
1987—Cardinals, 31-28 (StL)
    Cardinals, 31-14 (TB)
1988—Cardinals, 30-24 (TB)
1989—Buccaneers, 14-13 (P)
1992—Buccaneers, 23-7 (TB)
    Buccaneers, 7-3 (P)
1996—Cardinals, 13-9 (A)
1997—Buccaneers, 19-18 (TB)
2004—Cardinals, 12-7 (A)
2007—Buccaneers, 17-10 (TB)
2010—Buccaneers, 38-35 (A)
2013—Cardinals, 13-10 (TB)
(RS Pts.—Buccaneers 326, Cardinals 318)
*Franchise known as Phoenix prior to
1994 and in St. Louis prior to 1988
ARIZONA vs. **TENNESSEE
RS: Cardinals lead series, 6-4
1970—Cardinals, 44-0 (StL)
1974—Cardinals, 31-27 (H)
1979—Cardinals, 24-17 (H)
1985—Oilers, 20-10 (StL)
1988—Oilers, 38-20 (H)
1994—Cardinals, 30-12 (H)
1997—Oilers, 41-14 (A)
2005—Cardinals, 20-10 (A)
2009—Titans, 20-17 (T)
2013—Cardinals, 37-34 (T) OT
(RS Pts.—Cardinals 247, Titans 219)

*Franchise known as Phoenix prior to
1994 and in St. Louis prior to 1988
**Franchise in Houston prior to 1997;
known as Oilers prior to 1999
ARIZONA vs. **WASHINGTON
RS: Redskins lead series, 74-44-2
1932—Cardinals, 9-0 (B)
    Braves, 8-6 (C)
1933—Redskins, 10-0 (C)
    Tie, 0-0 (B)
1934—Redskins, 9-0 (B)
1935—Cardinals, 6-0 (B)
1936—Redskins, 13-10 (B)
1937—Cardinals, 21-14 (W)
1939—Redskins, 28-7 (W)
1940—Redskins, 28-21 (W)
1942—Redskins, 28-0 (W)
1943—Redskins, 13-7 (W)
1945—Redskins, 24-21 (W)
1947—Redskins, 45-21 (W)
1949—Cardinals, 38-7 (C)
1950—Cardinals, 38-28 (W)
1951—Redskins, 7-3 (C)
    Redskins, 20-17 (W)
1952—Redskins, 23-7 (C)
    Cardinals, 17-6 (W)
1953—Cardinals, 24-13 (C)
    Redskins, 28-17 (W)
1954—Cardinals, 38-16 (C)
    Redskins, 37-20 (W)
1955—Cardinals, 24-10 (W)
    Redskins, 31-0 (C)
1956—Cardinals, 31-3 (W)
    Redskins, 17-14 (C)
1957—Redskins, 37-14 (C)
    Cardinals, 44-14 (W)
1958—Cardinals, 37-10 (C)
    Redskins, 45-31 (W)
1959—Cardinals, 49-21 (C)
    Redskins, 23-14 (W)
1960—Cardinals, 44-7 (StL)
    Cardinals, 26-14 (W)
1961—Cardinals, 24-0 (W)
    Cardinals, 38-24 (StL)
1962—Redskins, 24-14 (W)
    Tie, 17-17 (StL)
1963—Cardinals, 21-7 (W)
    Cardinals, 24-20 (StL)
1964—Cardinals, 23-17 (W)
    Cardinals, 38-24 (StL)
1965—Cardinals, 37-16 (W)
    Redskins, 24-20 (StL)
1966—Cardinals, 23-7 (StL)
    Redskins, 26-20 (W)
1967—Cardinals, 27-21 (W)
1968—Cardinals, 41-14 (StL)
1969—Redskins, 33-17 (W)
1970—Cardinals, 27-17 (StL)
    Redskins, 28-27 (W)
1971—Redskins, 24-17 (StL)
    Redskins, 20-0 (W)
1972—Redskins, 24-10 (W)
    Redskins, 33-3 (StL)
1973—Cardinals, 34-27 (StL)
    Redskins, 31-13 (W)
1974—Cardinals, 17-10 (W)
    Cardinals, 23-20 (StL)
1975—Redskins, 27-17 (W)
    Cardinals, 20-17 (StL) OT
1976—Redskins, 20-10 (W)
    Redskins, 16-10 (StL)
1977—Redskins, 24-14 (W)
    Redskins, 26-20 (StL)

1978—Redskins, 28-10 (StL)
    Cardinals, 27-17 (W)
1979—Redskins, 17-7 (StL)
    Redskins, 30-28 (W)
1980—Redskins, 23-0 (W)
    Redskins, 31-7 (StL)
1981—Cardinals, 40-30 (StL)
    Redskins, 42-21 (W)
1982—Redskins, 12-7 (StL)
    Redskins, 28-0 (W)
1983—Redskins, 38-14 (StL)
    Redskins, 45-7 (W)
1984—Cardinals, 26-24 (StL)
    Redskins, 29-27 (W)
1985—Redskins, 27-10 (W)
    Redskins, 27-16 (StL)
1986—Redskins, 28-21 (W)
    Redskins, 20-17 (StL)
1987—Redskins, 28-21 (W)
    Redskins, 34-17 (StL)
1988—Cardinals, 30-21 (P)
    Redskins, 33-17 (W)
1989—Redskins, 30-28 (W)
    Redskins, 29-10 (P)
1990—Redskins, 31-0 (W)
    Redskins, 38-10 (P)
1991—Redskins, 34-0 (W)
    Redskins, 20-14 (P)
1992—Cardinals, 27-24 (P)
    Redskins, 41-3 (W)
1993—Cardinals, 17-10 (W)
    Cardinals, 36-6 (P)
1994—Cardinals, 19-16 (W) OT
    Cardinals, 17-15 (A)
1995—Redskins, 27-7 (W)
    Cardinals, 24-20 (A)
1996—Cardinals, 37-34 (W) OT
    Cardinals, 27-26 (A)
1997—Redskins, 19-13 (W) OT
    Redskins, 38-28 (A)
1998—Cardinals, 29-27 (A)
    Cardinals, 45-42 (W)
1999—Cardinals, 24-10 (A)
    Redskins, 28-3 (W)
2000—Cardinals, 16-15 (A)
    Redskins, 20-3 (W)
2001—Redskins, 20-10 (A)
    Redskins, 20-17 (W)
2002—Redskins, 31-23 (W)
2005—Redskins, 17-13 (A)
2007—Redskins, 21-19 (W)
2008—Redskins, 24-17 (W)
2011—Redskins, 22-21 (W)
(RS Pts.—Redskins 2,667, Cardinals 2,224)
*Franchise known as Phoenix prior to
1994, in St. Louis prior to 1988,
and in Chicago prior to 1960
**Franchise in Boston prior to 1937 and
known as Braves prior to 1933

ATLANTA vs. ARIZONA
RS: Cardinals lead series, 15-12
PS: Cardinals lead series, 1-0;
See Arizona vs. Atlanta
ATLANTA vs. BALTIMORE
RS: Series tied, 2-2
1999—Ravens, 19-13 (A) OT
2002—Falcons, 20-17 (A)
2006—Ravens, 24-10 (B)
2010—Falcons, 26-21 (A)
(RS Pts.—Ravens 81, Falcons 69)
ATLANTA vs. BUFFALO
RS: Falcons lead series, 7-4

1973—Bills, 17-6 (A)
1977—Bills, 3-0 (B)
1980—Falcons, 30-14 (B)
1983—Falcons, 31-14 (A)
1989—Falcons, 30-28 (A)
1992—Bills, 41-14 (B)
1995—Bills, 23-17 (B)
2001—Falcons, 33-30 (A)
2005—Falcons, 24-16 (B)
2009—Falcons, 31-3 (A)
2013—Falcons, 34-31 (Toronto) OT
(RS Pts.—Falcons 250, Bills 220)
ATLANTA vs. CAROLINA
RS: Falcons lead series, 23-15
1995—Falcons, 23-20 (A) OT
    Panthers, 21-17 (C)
1996—Panthers, 29-6 (C)
    Falcons, 20-17 (A)
1997—Panthers, 9-6 (A)
    Panthers, 21-12 (C)
1998—Falcons, 19-14 (C)
    Falcons, 51-23 (A)
1999—Falcons, 27-20 (A)
    Panthers, 34-28 (C)
2000—Falcons, 15-10 (C)
    Falcons, 13-12 (A)
2001—Falcons, 24-16 (A)
    Falcons, 10-7 (C)
2002—Falcons, 30-0 (A)
    Falcons, 41-0 (C)
2003—Panthers, 23-3 (C)
    Falcons, 20-14 (A) OT
2004—Falcons, 27-10 (C)
    Falcons, 34-31 (A) OT
2005—Falcons, 24-6 (C)
    Panthers, 44-11 (A)
2006—Falcons, 20-6 (A)
    Panthers, 10-3 (A)
2007—Falcons, 27-20 (A)
    Falcons, 20-13 (C)
2008—Panthers, 24-9 (C)
    Falcons, 45-28 (A)
2009—Falcons, 28-20 (A)
    Panthers, 28-19 (C)
2010—Falcons, 31-10 (C)
    Falcons, 31-10 (A)
2011—Falcons, 31-17 (A)
    Falcons, 31-23 (C)
2012—Falcons, 30-28 (A)
    Panthers, 30-20 (C)
2013—Panthers, 34-10 (C)
    Panthers, 21-20 (A)
(RS Pts.—Falcons 811, Panthers 728)
ATLANTA vs. CHICAGO
RS: Bears lead series, 13-12
1966—Bears, 23-6 (C)
1967—Bears, 23-14 (A)
1968—Falcons, 16-13 (C)
1969—Falcons, 48-31 (A)
1970—Bears, 23-14 (A)
1972—Falcons, 37-21 (C)
1973—Falcons, 46-6 (A)
1974—Falcons, 13-10 (A)
1976—Falcons, 10-0 (C)
1977—Falcons, 16-10 (C)
1978—Bears, 13-7 (C)
1980—Falcons, 28-17 (A)
1983—Falcons, 20-17 (C)
1985—Bears, 36-0 (C)
1986—Bears, 13-10 (A)
1990—Bears, 30-24 (C)
1992—Bears, 41-31 (C)
1993—Bears, 6-0 (C)

1998—Falcons, 20-13 (A)
2001—Bears, 31-3 (A)
2002—Bears, 14-13 (A)
2005—Bears, 16-3 (C)
2008—Falcons, 22-20 (A)
2009—Falcons, 21-14 (A)
2011—Bears, 30-12 (C)
(RS Pts.—Bears 471, Falcons 434)
ATLANTA vs. CINCINNATI
RS: Bengals lead series, 7-5
1971—Falcons, 9-6 (C)
1975—Bengals, 21-14 (A)
1978—Bengals, 37-7 (C)
1981—Bengals, 30-28 (A)
1984—Bengals, 35-14 (C)
1987—Bengals, 16-10 (A)
1990—Falcons, 38-17 (A)
1993—Bengals, 21-17 (C)
1996—Bengals, 41-31 (C)
2002—Falcons, 30-3 (A)
2006—Falcons, 29-27 (C)
2010—Falcons, 39-32 (A)
(RS Pts.—Bengals 286, Falcons 266)
ATLANTA vs. CLEVELAND
RS: Browns lead series, 10-3
1966—Browns, 49-17 (A)
1968—Browns, 30-7 (C)
1971—Falcons, 31-14 (A)
1976—Browns, 20-17 (A)
1978—Browns, 24-16 (A)
1981—Browns, 28-17 (C)
1984—Browns, 23-7 (A)
1987—Browns, 38-3 (C)
1990—Browns, 13-10 (C)
1993—Falcons, 17-14 (A)
2002—Browns, 24-16 (C)
2006—Browns, 17-13 (A)
2010—Falcons, 20-10 (C)
(RS Pts.—Browns 304, Falcons 191)
ATLANTA vs. DALLAS
RS: Cowboys lead series, 14-9
PS: Cowboys lead series, 2-0
1966—Cowboys, 47-14 (A)
1967—Cowboys, 37-7 (D)
1969—Cowboys, 24-17 (A)
1970—Cowboys, 13-0 (D)
1974—Cowboys, 24-0 (A)
1976—Falcons, 17-10 (A)
1978—*Cowboys, 27-20 (D)
1980—*Cowboys, 30-27 (A)
1985—Cowboys, 24-10 (D)
1986—Falcons, 37-35 (D)
1987—Falcons, 21-10 (D)
1988—Cowboys, 26-20 (D)
1989—Falcons 27-21 (A)
1990—Falcons, 26-7 (A)
1991—Cowboys, 31-27 (D)
1992—Cowboys, 41-17 (A)
1993—Falcons, 27-14 (A)
1995—Cowboys, 28-13 (A)
1996—Cowboys, 32-28 (D)
1999—Cowboys, 24-7 (D)
2001—Falcons, 20-13 (A)
2003—Cowboys, 27-13 (D)
2006—Cowboys, 38-28 (A)
2009—Cowboys, 37-21 (D)
2012—Falcons, 19-13 (A)
(RS Pts.—Cowboys 562, Falcons 430)
(PS Pts.—Cowboys 57, Falcons 47)
*NFC Divisional Playoff
ATLANTA vs. DENVER
RS: Broncos lead series, 8-5
PS: Broncos lead series, 1-0

1970—Broncos, 24-10 (D)
1972—Falcons, 23-20 (A)
1975—Falcons, 35-21 (A)
1979—Broncos, 20-17 (A) OT
1982—Falcons, 34-27 (D)
1985—Broncos, 44-28 (A)
1988—Broncos, 30-14 (D)
1994—Broncos, 32-28 (D)
1997—Broncos, 29-21 (A)
1998—*Broncos, 34-19 (South Florida)
2000—Broncos, 42-14 (D)
2004—Falcons, 41-28 (D)
2008—Broncos, 24-20 (A)
2012—Falcons, 27-21 (A)
(RS Pts.—Broncos 362, Falcons 312)
(PS Pts.—Broncos 34, Falcons 19)
*Super Bowl XXXIII
ATLANTA vs. DETROIT
RS: Lions lead series, 23-12
1966—Lions, 28-10 (D)
1967—Lions, 24-3 (D)
1968—Lions, 24-7 (A)
1969—Lions, 27-21 (D)
1971—Lions, 41-38 (D)
1972—Lions, 26-23 (A)
1973—Lions, 31-6 (D)
1975—Lions, 17-14 (A)
1976—Lions, 24-10 (D)
1977—Falcons, 17-6 (A)
1978—Falcons, 14-0 (A)
1979—Lions, 24-23 (D)
1980—Falcons, 43-28 (A)
1983—Falcons, 30-14 (D)
1984—Lions, 27-24 (A) OT
1985—Lions, 28-27 (A)
1986—Falcons, 20-6 (D)
1987—Lions, 30-13 (A)
1988—Lions, 31-17 (D)
1989—Lions, 31-24 (A)
1990—Lions, 21-14 (D)
1993—Lions, 30-13 (D)
1994—Lions, 31-28 (D) OT
1995—Falcons, 34-22 (A)
1996—Lions, 28-24 (D)
1997—Lions, 28-17 (D)
1998—Lions, 24-17 (D)
2000—Lions, 13-10 (D)
2002—Falcons, 36-15 (A)
2004—Lions, 17-10 (A)
2005—Falcons, 27-7 (D)
2006—Lions, 30-14 (D)
2008—Falcons, 34-21 (A)
2011—Falcons, 23-16 (D)
2012—Falcons, 31-18 (D)
(RS Pts.—Lions 781, Falcons 723)
ATLANTA vs. GREEN BAY
RS: Packers lead series, 14-12
PS: Packers lead series, 2-1
1966—Packers, 56-3 (Mil)
1967—Packers, 23-0 (Mil)
1968—Packers, 38-7 (A)
1969—Packers, 28-10 (GB)
1970—Packers, 27-24 (GB)
1971—Falcons, 28-21 (A)
1972—Falcons, 10-9 (Mil)
1974—Falcons, 10-3 (A)
1975—Packers, 22-13 (GB)
1976—Falcons, 24-20 (A)
1979—Falcons, 25-7 (A)
1981—Falcons, 31-17 (GB)
1982—Packers, 38-7 (A)
1983—Falcons, 47-41 (A) OT
1988—Falcons, 20-0 (A)

1989—Packers, 23-21 (Mil)
1991—Falcons, 35-31 (A)
1992—Falcons, 24-10 (A)
1994—Packers, 21-17 (Mil)
1995—*Packers, 37-20 (GB)
2001—Falcons, 23-20 (GB)
2002—Packers, 37-34 (GB) OT
       *Falcons, 27-7 (GB)
2005—Packers, 33-25 (A)
2008—Falcons, 27-24 (GB)
2010—Falcons, 20-17 (A)
       **Packers, 48-21 (A)
2011—Packers, 25-14 (A)
2013—Packers, 22-21 (GB)
(RS Pts.—Packers 617, Falcons 516)
(PS Pts.—Packers 92, Falcons 68)
*NFC First-Round Playoff
**NFC Divisional Playoff
ATLANTA vs. HOUSTON
RS: Texans lead series, 2-1
2003—Texans, 17-13 (H)
2007—Falcons, 26-16 (A)
2011—Texans, 17-10 (H)
(RS Pts.—Texans 50, Falcons 49)
ATLANTA vs. *INDIANAPOLIS
RS: Colts lead series, 13-2
1966—Colts, 19-7 (A)
1967—Colts, 38-31 (B)
       Colts, 49-7 (A)
1968—Colts, 28-20 (A)
       Colts, 44-0 (B)
1969—Colts, 21-14 (A)
       Colts, 13-6 (B)
1974—Colts, 17-7 (A)
1986—Colts, 28-23 (A)
1989—Colts, 13-9 (I)
1998—Falcons, 28-21 (A)
2001—Colts, 41-27 (I)
2003—Colts, 38-7 (I)
2007—Colts, 31-13 (A)
2011—Falcons, 31-7 (I)
(RS Pts.—Colts 408, Falcons 230)
*Franchise in Baltimore prior to 1984
ATLANTA vs. JACKSONVILLE
RS: Jaguars lead series, 3-2
1996—Jaguars, 19-17 (J)
1999—Jaguars, 30-7 (A)
2003—Falcons, 21-14 (A)
2007—Jaguars, 13-7 (J)
2011—Falcons, 41-14 (A)
(RS Pts.—Falcons 93, Jaguars 90)
ATLANTA vs. KANSAS CITY
RS: Chiefs lead series, 5-3
1972—Chiefs, 17-14 (A)
1985—Chiefs, 38-10 (KC)
1991—Chiefs, 14-3 (KC)
1994—Chiefs, 30-10 (A)
2000—Falcons, 29-13 (A)
2004—Chiefs, 56-10 (KC)
2008—Falcons, 38-14 (A)
2012—Falcons, 40-24 (KC)
(RS Pts.—Chiefs 206, Falcons 154)
ATLANTA vs. MIAMI
RS: Dolphins lead series, 8-4
1970—Dolphins, 20-7 (A)
1974—Dolphins, 42-7 (M)
1980—Dolphins, 20-17 (A)
1983—Dolphins, 31-24 (M)
1986—Falcons, 20-14 (M)
1992—Dolphins, 21-17 (M)
1995—Dolphins, 21-20 (M)
1998—Falcons, 38-16 (A)
2001—Dolphins, 21-14 (M)

2005—Falcons, 17-10 (M)
2009—Falcons, 19-7 (A)
2013—Dolphins, 27-23 (M)
(RS Pts.—Dolphins 250, Falcons 223)
ATLANTA vs. MINNESOTA
RS: Vikings lead series, 15-10
PS: Series tied, 1-1
1966—Falcons, 20-13 (M)
1967—Falcons, 21-20 (A)
1968—Vikings, 47-7 (M)
1969—Falcons, 10-3 (A)
1970—Vikings, 37-7 (A)
1971—Vikings, 24-7 (M)
1973—Falcons, 20-14 (A)
1974—Vikings, 23-10 (M)
1975—Vikings, 38-0 (A)
1977—Vikings, 14-7 (A)
1980—Falcons, 24-23 (M)
1981—Falcons, 31-30 (A)
1982—*Vikings, 30-24 (M)
1984—Vikings, 27-20 (M)
1985—Falcons, 14-13 (A)
1987—Vikings, 24-13 (M)
1989—Vikings, 43-17 (M)
1991—Falcons, 20-19 (A)
1996—Vikings, 23-17 (A)
1998—**Falcons, 30-27 (M) OT
1999—Vikings, 17-14 (A)
2002—Falcons, 30-24 (M) OT
2003—Vikings, 39-26 (A)
2005—Falcons, 30-10 (A)
2007—Vikings, 24-3 (M)
2008—Falcons, 24-17 (M)
2011—Falcons, 24-14 (A)
(RS Pts.—Vikings 582, Falcons 414)
(PS Pts.—Vikings 57, Falcons 54)
*NFC First-Round Playoff
**NFC Championship
ATLANTA vs. NEW ENGLAND
RS: Patriots lead series, 7-6
1972—Patriots, 21-20 (NE)
1977—Patriots, 16-10 (A)
1980—Falcons, 37-21 (NE)
1983—Falcons, 24-13 (A)
1986—Patriots, 25-17 (NE)
1989—Falcons, 16-15 (A)
1992—Falcons, 34-0 (A)
1995—Falcons, 30-17 (A)
1998—Falcons, 41-10 (NE)
2001—Patriots, 24-10 (A)
2005—Patriots, 31-28 (A)
2009—Patriots, 26-10 (NE)
2013—Patriots, 30-23 (A)
(RS Pts.—Patriots 300, Patriots 249)
ATLANTA vs. NEW ORLEANS
RS: Falcons lead series, 46-43
PS: Falcons lead series, 1-0
1967—Saints, 27-24 (NO)
1969—Falcons, 45-17 (A)
1970—Falcons, 14-3 (NO)
       Falcons, 32-14 (A)
1971—Falcons, 28-6 (A)
       Falcons, 24-20 (NO)
1972—Falcons, 21-14 (NO)
       Falcons, 36-20 (A)
1973—Falcons, 62-7 (NO)
       Falcons, 14-10 (A)
1974—Saints, 14-13 (NO)
       Saints, 13-3 (A)
1975—Falcons, 14-7 (A)
       Saints, 23-7 (NO)
1976—Saints, 30-0 (NO)
       Falcons, 23-20 (A)

1977—Saints, 21-20 (NO)
    Falcons, 35-7 (A)
1978—Falcons, 20-17 (NO)
    Falcons, 20-17 (A)
1979—Falcons, 40-34 (NO) OT
    Saints, 37-6 (A)
1980—Falcons, 41-14 (NO)
    Falcons, 31-13 (A)
1981—Falcons, 27-0 (A)
    Falcons, 41-10 (NO)
1982—Falcons, 35-0 (A)
    Saints, 35-6 (NO)
1983—Saints, 19-17 (A)
    Falcons, 27-10 (NO)
1984—Falcons, 36-28 (NO)
    Saints, 17-13 (A)
1985—Falcons, 31-24 (A)
    Falcons, 16-10 (NO)
1986—Falcons, 31-10 (NO)
    Saints, 14-9 (A)
1987—Saints, 38-0 (A)
1988—Saints, 29-21 (A)
    Saints, 10-9 (NO)
1989—Saints, 20-13 (NO)
    Saints, 26-17 (A)
1990—Falcons, 28-27 (A)
    Saints, 10-7 (NO)
1991—Saints, 27-6 (A)
    Falcons, 23-20 (NO) OT
    *Falcons, 27-20 (NO)
1992—Falcons, 10-7 (A)
    Saints, 22-14 (NO)
1993—Saints, 34-31 (A)
    Falcons, 26-15 (NO)
1994—Saints, 33-32 (NO)
    Saints, 29-20 (A)
1995—Falcons, 27-24 (NO) OT
    Falcons, 19-14 (A)
1996—Falcons, 17-15 (A)
    Falcons, 31-15 (NO)
1997—Falcons, 23-17 (NO)
    Falcons, 20-3 (A)
1998—Falcons, 31-23 (A)
    Falcons, 27-17 (NO)
1999—Falcons, 20-17 (NO)
    Falcons, 35-12 (A)
2000—Saints, 21-19 (A)
    Saints, 23-7 (NO)
2001—Falcons, 20-13 (NO)
    Saints, 28-10 (A)
2002—Falcons, 37-35 (NO)
    Falcons, 24-17 (A)
2003—Saints, 45-17 (A)
    Saints, 23-20 (NO) OT
2004—Falcons, 24-21 (A)
    Saints, 26-13 (NO)
2005—Falcons, 34-31 (San Antonio)
    Falcons, 36-17 (A)
2006—Saints, 23-3 (NO)
    Saints, 31-13 (A)
2007—Saints, 22-16 (NO)
    Saints, 34-14 (A)
2008—Falcons, 34-20 (A)
    Saints, 29-25 (NO)
2009—Saints, 35-27 (NO)
    Saints, 26-23 (A)
2010—Falcons, 27-24 (NO) OT
    Saints, 17-14 (A)
2011—Saints, 26-23 (A) OT
    Saints, 45-16 (NO)
2012—Saints, 31-27 (NO)
    Falcons, 23-13 (A)
2013—Saints, 23-17 (NO)

Saints, 17-13 (A)
(RS Pts.—Falcons 1,925, Saints 1,822)
(PS Pts.—Falcons 27, Saints 20)
*NFC First-Round Playoff

ATLANTA vs. N.Y. GIANTS
RS: Falcons lead series, 11-10
PS: Giants lead series, 1-0
1966—Falcons, 27-16 (NY)
1968—Falcons, 24-21 (A)
1971—Giants, 21-17 (A)
1974—Falcons, 14-7 (New Haven)
1977—Falcons, 17-3 (A)
1978—Falcons, 23-20 (A)
1979—Giants, 24-3 (NY)
1981—Giants, 27-24 (A) OT
1982—Falcons, 16-14 (NY)
1983—Giants, 16-13 (A) OT
1984—Falcons, 19-7 (A)
1988—Giants, 23-16 (A)
1998—Falcons, 34-20 (NY)
2000—Giants, 13-6 (A)
2002—Falcons, 17-10 (NY)
2003—Falcons, 27-7 (NY)
2004—Falcons, 14-10 (NY)
2006—Giants, 27-14 (A)
2007—Giants, 31-10 (A)
2009—Giants, 34-31 (NY) OT
2011—*Giants, 24-2 (NY)
2012—Falcons, 34-0 (A)
(RS Pts.—Falcons 388, Giants 363)
(PS Pts.—Giants 24, Falcons 2)
*NFC First-Round Playoff

ATLANTA vs. N.Y. JETS
RS: Falcons lead series, 6-5
1973—Falcons, 28-20 (NY)
1980—Jets, 14-7 (A)
1983—Falcons, 27-21 (NY)
1986—Jets, 28-14 (A)
1989—Jets, 27-7 (NY)
1992—Falcons, 20-17 (A)
1995—Falcons, 13-3 (A)
1998—Jets, 28-3 (NY)
2005—Falcons, 27-14 (A)
2009—Falcons, 10-7 (NY)
2013—Jets, 30-28 (A)
(RS Pts.—Jets 209, Falcons 184)

ATLANTA vs. *OAKLAND
RS: Raiders lead series, 7-6
1971—Falcons, 24-13 (A)
1975—Raiders, 37-34 (O) OT
1979—Raiders, 50-19 (O)
1982—Raiders, 38-14 (A)
1985—Raiders, 34-24 (A)
1988—Falcons, 12-6 (LA)
1991—Falcons, 21-17 (A)
1994—Raiders, 30-17 (LA)
1997—Raiders, 36-31 (A)
2000—Raiders, 41-14 (O)
2004—Falcons, 35-10 (A)
2008—Falcons, 24-0 (O)
2012—Falcons, 23-20 (A)
(RS Pts.—Raiders 332, Falcons 292)
*Franchise in Los Angeles from 1982-1994

ATLANTA vs. PHILADELPHIA
RS: Eagles lead series, 15-12-1
PS: Eagles lead series, 2-1
1966—Eagles, 23-10 (P)
1967—Eagles, 38-7 (A)
1969—Falcons, 27-3 (P)
1970—Tie, 13-13 (P)
1973—Falcons, 44-27 (P)
1976—Eagles, 14-13 (A)
1978—*Falcons, 14-13 (A)

1979—Falcons, 14-10 (P)
1980—Falcons, 20-17 (P)
1981—Eagles, 16-13 (P)
1983—Eagles, 28-24 (A)
1984—Falcons, 26-10 (A)
1985—Eagles, 23-17 (P) OT
1986—Eagles, 16-0 (A)
1988—Falcons, 27-24 (P)
1990—Eagles, 24-23 (A)
1994—Falcons, 28-21 (A)
1996—Eagles, 33-18 (A)
1997—Falcons, 20-17 (A)
1998—Falcons, 17-12 (A)
2000—Eagles, 38-10 (P)
2002—**Eagles, 20-6 (P)
2003—Eagles, 23-16 (A)
2004—***Eagles, 27-10 (P)
2005—Falcons, 14-10 (A)
2006—Eagles, 24-17 (P)
2008—Eagles, 27-14 (P)
2009—Eagles, 34-7 (A)
2010—Eagles, 31-17 (P)
2011—Falcons, 35-31 (A)
2012—Falcons, 30-17 (P)
(RS Pts.—Eagles 604, Falcons 521)
(PS Pts.—Eagles 60, Falcons 30)
*NFC First-Round Playoff
**NFC Divisional Playoff
***NFC Championship

ATLANTA vs. PITTSBURGH
RS: Steelers lead series, 12-2-1
1966—Steelers, 57-33 (A)
1968—Steelers, 41-21 (A)
1970—Falcons, 27-16 (A)
1974—Steelers, 24-17 (P)
1978—Steelers, 31-7 (P)
1981—Steelers, 34-20 (A)
1984—Steelers, 35-10 (P)
1987—Steelers, 28-12 (A)
1990—Steelers, 21-9 (P)
1993—Steelers, 45-17 (A)
1996—Steelers, 20-17 (A)
1999—Steelers, 13-9 (P)
2002—Tie, 34-34 (P) OT
2006—Falcons, 41-38 (A) OT
2010—Steelers, 15-9 (P) OT
(RS Pts.—Steelers 452, Falcons 283)

ATLANTA vs. *ST. LOUIS
RS: Rams lead series, 47-27-2
PS: Falcons lead series, 1-0
1966—Rams, 19-14 (A)
1967—Rams, 31-3 (A)
    Rams, 20-3 (LA)
1968—Rams, 27-14 (LA)
    Rams, 17-10 (A)
1969—Rams, 17-7 (LA)
    Rams, 38-6 (A)
1970—Tie, 10-10 (LA)
    Rams, 17-7 (A)
1971—Tie, 20-20 (LA)
    Rams, 24-16 (A)
1972—Falcons, 31-3 (A)
    Rams, 20-7 (LA)
1973—Rams, 31-0 (LA)
    Falcons, 15-13 (A)
1974—Rams, 21-0 (LA)
    Rams, 30-7 (A)
1975—Rams, 22-7 (LA)
    Rams, 16-7 (A)
1976—Rams, 30-14 (A)
    Rams, 59-0 (LA)
1977—Falcons, 17-6 (A)
    Rams, 23-7 (LA)

1978—Rams, 10-0 (LA)
    Falcons, 15-7 (A)
1979—Rams, 20-14 (LA)
    Rams, 34-13 (A)
1980—Falcons, 13-10 (A)
    Rams, 20-17 (LA) OT
1981—Rams, 37-35 (A)
    Rams, 21-16 (LA)
1982—Falcons, 34-17 (A)
1983—Rams, 27-21 (LA)
    Rams, 36-13 (A)
1984—Falcons, 30-28 (LA)
    Rams, 24-10 (A)
1985—Rams, 17-6 (LA)
    Falcons, 30-14 (A)
1986—Falcons, 26-14 (A)
    Rams, 14-7 (LA)
1987—Falcons, 24-20 (A)
    Rams, 33-0 (LA)
1988—Rams, 33-0 (A)
    Rams, 22-7 (LA)
1989—Rams, 31-21 (A)
    Rams, 26-14 (LA)
1990—Rams, 44-24 (LA)
    Falcons, 20-13 (A)
1991—Falcons, 31-14 (A)
    Falcons, 31-14 (LA)
1992—Falcons, 30-28 (A)
    Rams, 38-27 (LA)
1993—Falcons, 30-24 (A)
    Falcons, 13-0 (LA)
1994—Falcons, 31-13 (A)
    Falcons, 8-5 (LA)
1995—Rams, 21-19 (StL)
    Falcons, 31-6 (A)
1996—Rams, 59-16 (StL)
    Rams, 34-27 (A)
1997—Falcons, 34-31 (A)
    Falcons, 27-21 (StL)
1998—Falcons, 37-15 (A)
    Falcons, 21-10 (StL)
1999—Rams, 35-7 (StL)
    Rams, 41-13 (A)
2000—Rams, 41-20 (A)
    Rams, 45-29 (StL)
2001—Rams, 35-6 (A)
    Rams, 31-13 (StL)
2003—Rams, 36-0 (StL)
2004—Falcons, 34-17 (A)
    **Falcons, 47-17 (A)
2007—Rams, 28-16 (StL)
2008—Falcons, 31-27 (A)
2010—Falcons, 34-17 (StL)
2013—Falcons, 31-24 (A)
(RS Pts.—Rams 1,796, Falcons 1,279)
(PS Pts.—Falcons 47, Rams 17)
*Franchise in Los Angeles prior to 1995
**NFC Divisional Playoff
ATLANTA vs. SAN DIEGO
RS: Falcons lead series, 8-1
1973—Falcons, 41-0 (SD)
1979—Falcons, 28-26 (SD)
1988—Chargers, 10-7 (A)
1991—Falcons, 13-10 (SD)
1994—Falcons, 10-9 (A)
1997—Falcons, 14-3 (SD)
2004—Falcons, 21-20 (A)
2008—Falcons, 22-16 (SD)
2012—Falcons, 27-3 (SD)
(RS Pts.—Falcons 183, Chargers 97)
ATLANTA vs. SAN FRANCISCO
RS: 49ers lead series, 45-29-1
PS: Series tied, 1-1

1966—49ers, 44-7 (A)
1967—49ers, 38-7 (SF)
    49ers, 34-28 (A)
1968—49ers, 28-13 (SF)
    49ers, 14-12 (A)
1969—Falcons, 24-12 (A)
    Falcons, 21-7 (SF)
1970—Falcons, 21-20 (A)
    49ers, 24-20 (SF)
1971—Falcons, 20-17 (A)
    49ers, 24-3 (SF)
1972—49ers, 49-14 (A)
    49ers, 20-0 (SF)
1973—49ers, 13-9 (A)
    Falcons, 17-3 (SF)
1974—49ers, 16-10 (A)
    49ers, 27-0 (SF)
1975—Falcons, 17-3 (SF)
    Falcons, 31-9 (A)
1976—49ers, 15-0 (SF)
    Falcons, 21-16 (A)
1977—49ers, 7-0 (SF)
    49ers, 10-3 (A)
1978—Falcons, 20-17 (SF)
    Falcons, 21-10 (A)
1979—49ers, 20-15 (SF)
    Falcons, 31-21 (A)
1980—Falcons, 20-17 (SF)
    Falcons, 35-10 (A)
1981—Falcons, 34-17 (A)
    49ers, 17-14 (SF)
1982—Falcons, 17-7 (SF)
1983—49ers, 24-20 (SF)
    Falcons, 28-24 (A)
1984—49ers, 14-5 (SF)
    49ers, 35-17 (A)
1985—49ers, 35-16 (SF)
    49ers, 38-17 (A)
1986—Tie, 10-10 (A) OT
    49ers, 20-0 (SF)
1987—49ers, 25-17 (A)
    49ers, 35-7 (SF)
1988—Falcons, 34-17 (SF)
    49ers, 13-3 (A)
1989—49ers, 45-3 (SF)
    49ers, 23-10 (A)
1990—49ers, 19-13 (SF)
    49ers, 45-35 (A)
1991—Falcons, 39-34 (SF)
    Falcons, 17-14 (A)
1992—49ers, 56-17 (SF)
    49ers, 41-3 (A)
1993—49ers, 37-30 (SF)
    Falcons, 27-24 (A)
1994—49ers, 42-3 (A)
    49ers, 50-14 (SF)
1995—49ers, 41-10 (SF)
    Falcons, 28-27 (A)
1996—49ers, 39-17 (SF)
    49ers, 34-10 (A)
1997—49ers, 34-7 (SF)
    49ers, 35-28 (A)
1998—49ers, 31-20 (A)
    Falcons, 31-19 (A)
    *Falcons, 20-18 (A)
1999—49ers, 26-7 (SF)
    Falcons, 34-29 (A)
2000—Falcons, 36-28 (A)
    49ers, 16-6 (SF)
2001—49ers, 16-13 (SF) OT
    49ers, 37-31 (A) OT
2004—Falcons, 21-19 (SF)
2007—Falcons, 20-16 (A)

2009—Falcons, 45-10 (SF)
2010—Falcons, 16-14 (A)
2012—**49ers, 28-24 (A)
2013—49ers, 34-24 (SF)
(RS Pts.—49ers 1,804, Falcons 1,301)
(PS Pts.—49ers 46, Falcons 44)
*NFC Divisional Playoff
**NFC Championship
ATLANTA vs. SEATTLE
RS: Seahawks lead series, 9-5
PS: Falcons lead series, 1-0
1976—Seahawks, 30-13 (S)
1979—Seahawks, 31-28 (A)
1985—Seahawks, 30-26 (S)
1988—Seahawks, 31-20 (A)
1991—Falcons, 26-13 (A)
1997—Falcons, 24-17 (S)
2000—Seahawks, 30-10 (A)
2002—Seahawks, 30-24 (A) OT
2004—Seahawks, 28-26 (A)
2005—Falcons, 21-18 (S)
2007—Falcons, 44-41 (A)
2010—Seahawks, 34-18 (S)
2011—Falcons, 30-28 (S)
2012—*Falcons, 30-28 (A)
2013—Seahawks, 33-10 (A)
(RS Pts.—Seahawks 381, Falcons 333)
(PS Pts.—Falcons 30, Seahawks 28)
*NFC Divisional Playoff
ATLANTA vs. TAMPA BAY
RS: Buccaneers lead series, 21-20
1977—Falcons, 17-0 (TB)
1978—Buccaneers, 14-9 (TB)
1979—Falcons, 17-14 (A)
1981—Buccaneers, 24-23 (TB)
1984—Buccaneers, 23-6 (TB)
1986—Falcons, 23-20 (TB) OT
1987—Buccaneers, 48-10 (TB)
1988—Falcons, 17-10 (A)
1990—Buccaneers, 23-17 (TB)
1991—Falcons, 43-7 (A)
1992—Falcons, 35-7 (TB)
1993—Buccaneers, 31-24 (A)
1994—Falcons, 34-13 (A)
1995—Falcons, 24-21 (TB)
1997—Buccaneers, 31-10 (A)
1999—Buccaneers, 19-10 (TB)
2000—Buccaneers, 27-14 (A)
2002—Buccaneers, 20-6 (A)
    Buccaneers, 34-10 (TB)
2003—Buccaneers, 31-10 (A)
    Falcons, 30-28 (TB)
2004—Falcons, 24-14 (A)
    Buccaneers, 27-0 (TB)
2005—Buccaneers, 30-27 (A)
    Buccaneers, 27-24 (TB) OT
2006—Falcons, 14-3 (A)
    Falcons, 17-6 (TB)
2007—Buccaneers, 31-7 (A)
    Buccaneers, 37-3 (TB)
2008—Buccaneers, 24-9 (TB)
    Falcons, 13-10 (A) OT
2009—Falcons, 20-17 (A)
    Falcons, 20-10 (TB)
2010—Falcons, 27-21 (A)
    Falcons, 28-24 (TB)
2011—Buccaneers, 16-13 (TB)
    Falcons, 45-24 (A)
2012—Falcons, 24-23 (TB)
    Buccaneers, 22-17 (A)
2013—Falcons, 31-23 (A)
    Buccaneers, 41-28 (TB)
(RS Pts.—Buccaneers 875, Falcons 780)

ATLANTA vs. *TENNESSEE
RS: Titans lead series, 7-6
1972—Falcons, 20-10 (A)
1976—Oilers, 20-14 (H)
1978—Falcons, 20-14 (A)
1981—Falcons, 31-27 (H)
1984—Falcons, 42-10 (A)
1987—Oilers, 37-33 (H)
1990—Falcons, 47-27 (A)
1993—Oilers, 33-17 (H)
1996—Oilers, 23-13 (A)
1999—Titans, 30-17 (T)
2003—Titans, 38-31 (A)
2007—Titans, 20-13 (T)
2011—Falcons, 23-17 (A)
(RS Pts.—Falcons 321, Titans 306)
*Franchise in Houston prior to 1997;
known as Oilers prior to 1999
ATLANTA vs. WASHINGTON
RS: Redskins lead series, 14-8-1
PS: Redskins lead series, 1-0
1966—Redskins, 33-20 (W)
1967—Tie, 20-20 (A)
1969—Redskins, 27-20 (W)
1972—Redskins, 24-13 (W)
1975—Redskins, 30-27 (A)
1977—Redskins, 10-6 (W)
1978—Falcons, 20-17 (A)
1979—Redskins, 16-7 (A)
1980—Falcons, 10-6 (A)
1983—Redskins, 37-21 (W)
1984—Redskins, 27-14 (W)
1985—Redskins, 44-10 (A)
1987—Falcons, 21-20 (A)
1989—Redskins, 31-30 (A)
1991—Redskins, 56-17 (W)
    *Redskins, 24-7 (W)
1992—Redskins, 24-17 (W)
1993—Redskins, 30-17 (W)
1994—Falcons, 27-20 (W)
2003—Redskins, 33-31 (A)
2006—Falcons, 24-14 (A)
2009—Falcons, 31-17 (A)
2012—Falcons, 24-17 (W)
2013—Falcons, 27-26 (A)
(RS Pts.—Redskins 579, Falcons 454)
(PS Pts.—Redskins 24, Falcons 7)
*NFC Divisional Playoff

BALTIMORE vs. ARIZONA
RS: Ravens lead series, 4-1;
See Arizona vs. Baltimore
BALTIMORE vs. ATLANTA
RS: Series tied, 2-2;
See Atlanta vs. Baltimore
BALTIMORE vs. BUFFALO
RS: Series tied, 3-3
1999—Bills, 13-10 (Balt)
2004—Ravens, 20-6 (Balt)
2006—Ravens, 19-7 (Balt)
2007—Bills, 19-14 (Buf)
2010—Ravens, 37-34 (Balt) OT
2013—Bills, 23-20 (Buf)
(RS Pts.—Ravens 120, Bills 102)
BALTIMORE vs. CAROLINA
RS: Panthers lead series, 3-1
1996—Panthers, 27-16 (C)
2002—Panthers, 10-7 (C)
2006—Panthers, 23-21 (B)
2010—Ravens, 37-13 (C)
(RS Pts.—Ravens 81, Panthers 73)
BALTIMORE vs. CHICAGO
RS: Bears lead series, 3-2

1998—Bears, 24-3 (C)
2001—Ravens, 17-6 (B)
2005—Bears, 10-6 (C)
2009—Ravens, 31-7 (C)
2013—Bears, 23-20 (C) OT
(RS Pts.—Ravens 77, Bears 70)
BALTIMORE vs. CINCINNATI
RS: Ravens lead series, 20-16
1996—Bengals, 24-21 (B)
    Bengals, 21-14 (C)
1997—Ravens, 23-10 (B)
    Bengals, 16-14 (C)
1998—Ravens, 31-24 (B)
    Ravens, 20-13 (C)
1999—Ravens, 34-31 (C)
    Ravens, 22-0 (B)
2000—Ravens, 37-0 (B)
    Ravens, 27-7 (C)
2001—Bengals, 21-10 (C)
    Ravens, 16-0 (B)
2002—Ravens, 38-27 (B)
    Ravens, 27-23 (C)
2003—Bengals, 34-26 (B)
    Ravens, 31-13 (B)
2004—Ravens, 23-9 (C)
    Bengals, 27-26 (B)
2005—Bengals, 21-9 (B)
    Bengals, 42-29 (C)
2006—Ravens, 26-20 (B)
    Bengals, 13-7 (C)
2007—Bengals, 27-20 (C)
    Bengals, 21-7 (B)
2008—Ravens, 17-10 (B)
    Ravens, 34-3 (C)
2009—Bengals, 17-14 (B)
    Bengals, 17-7 (C)
2010—Ravens, 15-10 (C)
    Ravens, 13-7 (B)
2011—Ravens, 31-24 (B)
    Ravens, 24-16 (C)
2012—Ravens, 44-13 (B)
    Bengals, 23-17 (C)
2013—Ravens, 20-17 (B) OT
    Bengals, 34-17 (C)
(RS Pts.—Ravens 786, Bengals 640)
BALTIMORE vs. CLEVELAND
RS: Ravens lead series, 22-8
1999—Ravens, 17-10 (B)
    Ravens, 41-9 (C)
2000—Ravens, 12-0 (C)
    Ravens, 44-7 (B)
2001—Browns, 24-14 (C)
    Browns, 27-17 (B)
2002—Ravens, 26-21 (C)
    Browns, 14-13 (B)
2003—Ravens, 33-13 (B)
    Ravens, 35-0 (C)
2004—Browns, 20-3 (C)
    Ravens, 27-13 (B)
2005—Ravens, 16-3 (B)
    Browns, 20-16 (C)
2006—Ravens, 15-14 (C)
    Ravens, 27-17 (B)
2007—Browns, 27-13 (C)
    Browns, 33-30 (B) OT
2008—Ravens, 28-10 (B)
    Ravens, 37-27 (C)
2009—Ravens, 34-3 (B)
    Ravens, 16-0 (C)
2010—Ravens, 24-17 (B)
    Ravens, 20-10 (C)
2011—Ravens, 24-10 (C)
    Ravens, 20-14 (B)

2012—Ravens, 23-16 (B)
    Ravens, 25-15 (C)
2013—Ravens, 14-6 (B)
    Browns, 24-18 (C)
(RS Pts.—Ravens 682, Browns 424)
BALTIMORE vs. DALLAS
RS: Ravens lead series, 4-0
2000—Ravens, 27-0 (B)
2004—Ravens, 30-10 (D)
2008—Ravens, 33-24 (D)
2012—Ravens, 31-29 (B)
(RS Pts.—Ravens 121, Cowboys 63)
BALTIMORE vs. DENVER
RS: Series tied, 5-5
PS: Ravens lead series, 2-0
1996—Broncos, 45-34 (D)
2000—*Ravens, 21-3 (B)
2001—Ravens, 20-13 (D)
2002—Ravens, 34-23 (B)
2003—Ravens, 26-6 (B)
2005—Broncos, 12-10 (D)
2006—Broncos, 13-3 (D)
2009—Ravens, 30-7 (B)
2010—Ravens, 31-17 (D)
2012—Broncos, 34-17 (D)
    **Ravens, 38-35 (D) 2 OT
2013—Broncos, 49-27 (D)
(RS Pts.—Ravens 232, Broncos 219)
(PS Pts.—Ravens 59, Broncos 38)
*AFC First-Round Playoff
**AFC Divisional Playoff
BALTIMORE vs. DETROIT
RS: Ravens lead series, 3-1
1998—Ravens, 19-10 (D)
2005—Lions, 35-17 (D)
2009—Ravens, 48-3 (B)
2013—Ravens, 18-16 (D)
(RS Pts.—Ravens 102, Lions 64)
BALTIMORE vs. GREEN BAY
RS: Packers lead series, 4-1
1998—Packers, 28-10 (GB)
2001—Packers, 31-23 (GB)
2005—Ravens, 48-3 (B)
2009—Packers, 27-14 (GB)
2013—Packers, 19-17 (B)
(RS Pts.—Ravens 112, Packers 108)
BALTIMORE vs. HOUSTON
RS: Ravens lead series, 6-1
PS: Ravens lead series, 1-0
2002—Ravens, 23-19 (H)
2005—Ravens, 16-15 (H)
2008—Ravens, 41-13 (H)
2010—Ravens, 34-28 (H) OT
2011—Ravens, 29-14 (B)
    *Ravens, 20-13 (B)
2012—Texans, 43-13 (H)
2013—Ravens, 30-9 (B)
(RS Pts.—Ravens 186, Texans 141)
(PS Pts.—Ravens 20, Texans 13)
*AFC Divisional Playoff
BALTIMORE vs. INDIANAPOLIS
RS: Colts lead series, 7-3
PS: Colts lead series, 2-1
1996—Colts, 26-21 (I)
1998—Ravens, 38-31 (B)
2001—Ravens, 39-27 (B)
2002—Colts, 22-20 (I)
2004—Colts, 20-10 (I)
2005—Colts, 24-7 (B)
2006—*Colts, 15-6 (B)
2007—Colts, 44-20 (B)
2008—Colts, 31-3 (I)

2009—Colts, 17-15 (B)
   *Colts, 20-3 (I)
2011—Ravens, 24-10 (B)
2012—**Ravens, 24-9 (B)
(RS Pts.—Colts 252, Ravens 197)
(PS Pts.—Colts 44, Ravens 33)
*AFC Divisional Playoff
**AFC First-Round Playoff
BALTIMORE vs. JACKSONVILLE
RS: Jaguars lead series, 10-7
1996—Jaguars, 30-27 (J)
   Jaguars, 28-25 (B) OT
1997—Jaguars, 28-27 (B)
   Jaguars, 29-27 (J)
1998—Jaguars, 24-10 (J)
   Jaguars, 45-19 (J)
1999—Jaguars, 6-3 (J)
   Jaguars, 30-23 (B)
2000—Ravens, 39-36 (B)
   Ravens, 15-10 (J)
2001—Ravens, 18-17 (B)
   Ravens, 24-21 (J)
2002—Ravens, 17-10 (B)
2003—Ravens, 24-17 (B)
2005—Jaguars, 30-3 (J)
2008—Ravens, 27-7 (B)
2011—Jaguars, 12-7 (J)
(RS Pts.—Jaguars 380, Ravens 335)
BALTIMORE vs. KANSAS CITY
RS: Series tied, 3-3
PS: Ravens lead series, 1-0
1999—Chiefs, 35-8 (B)
2003—Chiefs, 17-10 (B)
2004—Chiefs, 27-24 (B)
2006—Ravens, 20-10 (KC)
2009—Ravens, 38-24 (B)
2010—*Ravens, 30-7 (KC)
2012—Ravens, 9-6 (KC)
(RS Pts.—Chiefs 119, Ravens 109)
(PS Pts.—Ravens 30, Chiefs 7)
*AFC First-Round Playoff
BALTIMORE vs. MIAMI
RS: Dolphins lead series, 5-4
PS: Ravens lead series, 2-0
1997—Dolphins, 24-13 (B)
2000—Dolphins, 19-6 (M)
2001—*Ravens, 20-3 (M)
2002—Dolphins, 26-7 (M)
2003—Dolphins, 9-6 (M) OT
2004—Ravens, 30-23 (B)
2007—Dolphins, 22-16 (M) OT
2008—Ravens, 27-13 (M)
   *Ravens, 27-9 (M)
2010—Ravens, 26-10 (B)
2013—Ravens, 26-23 (M)
(RS Pts.—Dolphins 169, Ravens 157)
(PS Pts.—Ravens 47, Dolphins 12)
*AFC First-Round Playoff
BALTIMORE vs. MINNESOTA
RS: Ravens lead series, 3-2
1998—Vikings, 38-28 (B)
2001—Ravens, 19-3 (B)
2005—Ravens, 30-23 (B)
2009—Vikings, 33-31 (M)
2013—Ravens, 29-26 (B)
(RS Pts.—Ravens 137, Vikings 123)
BALTIMORE vs. NEW ENGLAND
RS: Patriots lead series, 7-1
PS: Ravens lead series, 2-1
1996—Patriots, 46-38 (B)
1999—Patriots, 20-3 (NE)
2004—Patriots, 24-3 (NE)
2007—Patriots, 27-24 (B)

2009—Patriots, 27-21 (NE)
   *Ravens, 33-14 (NE)
2010—Patriots, 23-20 (NE) OT
2011—**Patriots, 23-20 (NE)
2012—Ravens, 31-30 (B)
   **Ravens, 28-13 (NE)
2013—Patriots, 41-7 (B)
(RS Pts.—Patriots 238, Ravens 147)
(PS Pts.—Ravens 81, Patriots 50)
*AFC First-Round Playoff
**AFC Championship
BALTIMORE vs. NEW ORLEANS
RS: Ravens lead series, 4-1
1996—Ravens, 17-10 (B)
1999—Ravens, 31-8 (B)
2002—Saints, 37-25 (B)
2006—Ravens, 35-22 (NO)
2010—Ravens, 30-24 (B)
(RS Pts.—Ravens 138, Saints 101)
BALTIMORE vs. N.Y. GIANTS
RS: Ravens lead series, 3-1
PS: Ravens lead series, 1-0
1997—Ravens, 24-23 (NY)
2000—*Ravens, 34-7 (Tampa)
2004—Ravens, 37-14 (B)
2008—Giants, 30-10 (NY)
2012—Ravens, 33-14 (B)
(RS Pts.—Ravens 104, Giants 81)
(PS Pts.—Ravens 34, Giants 7)
*Super Bowl XXXV
BALTIMORE vs. N.Y. JETS
RS: Ravens lead series, 8-1
1997—Jets, 19-16 (NY) OT
1998—Ravens, 24-10 (NY)
2000—Ravens, 34-20 (B)
2004—Ravens, 20-17 (NY) OT
2005—Ravens, 13-3 (B)
2007—Ravens, 20-13 (B)
2010—Ravens, 10-9 (NY)
2011—Ravens, 34-17 (B)
2013—Ravens, 19-3 (B)
(RS Pts.—Ravens 190, Jets 111)
BALTIMORE vs. OAKLAND
RS: Ravens lead series, 6-1
PS: Ravens lead series, 1-0
1996—Ravens, 19-14 (B)
1998—Ravens, 13-10 (B)
2000—*Ravens, 16-3 (O)
2003—Raiders, 20-12 (B)
2006—Ravens, 28-6 (B)
2008—Ravens, 29-10 (B)
2009—Ravens, 21-13 (O)
2012—Ravens, 55-20 (B)
(RS Pts.—Ravens 177, Raiders 93)
(PS Pts.—Ravens 16, Raiders 3)
*AFC Championship
BALTIMORE vs. PHILADELPHIA
RS: Eagles lead series, 2-1-1
1997—Tie, 10-10 (B) OT
2004—Eagles, 15-10 (P)
2008—Ravens, 36-7 (B)
2012—Eagles, 24-23 (P)
(RS Pts.—Ravens 79, Eagles 56)
BALTIMORE vs. PITTSBURGH
RS: Steelers lead series, 20-16
PS: Steelers lead series, 3-0
1996—Steelers, 31-17 (P)
   Ravens, 31-17 (B)
1997—Steelers, 42-34 (B)
   Steelers, 37-0 (P)
1998—Steelers, 20-13 (B)
   Steelers, 16-6 (P)
1999—Steelers, 23-20 (B)

   Ravens, 31-24 (P)
2000—Ravens, 16-0 (P)
   Steelers, 9-6 (B)
2001—Ravens, 13-10 (P)
   Steelers, 26-21 (B)
   *Steelers, 27-10 (P)
2002—Steelers, 31-18 (B)
   Steelers, 34-31 (P)
2003—Steelers, 34-15 (P)
   Ravens, 13-10 (B) OT
2004—Ravens, 30-13 (B)
   Steelers, 20-7 (P)
2005—Steelers, 20-19 (P)
   Ravens, 16-13 (B) OT
2006—Ravens, 27-0 (B)
   Ravens, 31-7 (P)
2007—Steelers, 38-7 (P)
   Ravens, 27-21 (B)
2008—Steelers, 23-20 (P) OT
   Steelers, 13-9 (B)
   **Steelers, 23-14 (P)
2009—Ravens, 20-17 (B) OT
   Steelers, 23-20 (P)
2010—Ravens, 17-14 (P)
   Steelers, 13-10 (B)
   *Steelers, 31-24 (P)
2011—Ravens, 35-7 (B)
   Ravens, 23-20 (P)
2012—Ravens, 13-10 (P)
   Steelers, 23-20 (B)
2013—Steelers, 19-16 (P)
   Ravens, 22-20 (B)
(RS Pts.—Steelers 698, Ravens 674)
(PS Pts.—Steelers 81, Ravens 48)
*AFC Divisional Playoff
**AFC Championship
BALTIMORE vs. ST. LOUIS
RS: Ravens lead series, 3-2
1996—Ravens, 37-31 (B) OT
1999—Rams, 27-10 (StL)
2003—Rams, 33-22 (StL)
2007—Ravens, 22-3 (B)
2011—Ravens, 37-7 (StL)
(RS Pts.—Ravens 128, Rams 101)
BALTIMORE vs. SAN DIEGO
RS: Ravens lead series, 5-4
1997—Chargers, 21-17 (SD)
1998—Chargers, 14-13 (SD)
2000—Ravens, 24-3 (B)
2003—Ravens, 24-10 (SD)
2006—Ravens, 16-13 (B)
2007—Chargers, 32-14 (SD)
2009—Ravens, 31-26 (SD)
2011—Chargers, 34-14 (SD)
2012—Ravens, 16-13 (SD) OT
(RS Pts.—Ravens 169, Chargers 166)
BALTIMORE vs. SAN FRANCISCO
RS: Ravens lead series, 3-1
PS: Ravens lead series, 1-0
1996—49ers, 38-20 (SF)
2003—Ravens, 44-6 (B)
2007—Ravens, 9-7 (SF)
2011—Ravens, 16-6 (B)
2012—*Ravens, 34-31 (New Orleans)
(RS Pts.—Ravens 89, 49ers 57)
(PS Pts.—Ravens 34, 49ers 31)
*Super Bowl XLVII
BALTIMORE vs. SEATTLE
RS: Series tied, 2-2
1997—Ravens, 31-24 (B)
2003—Ravens, 44-41 (B) OT
2007—Seahawks, 27-6 (S)
2011—Seahawks, 22-17 (S)

(RS Pts.—Seahawks 114, Ravens 98)
BALTIMORE vs. TAMPA BAY
RS: Series tied, 2-2
2001—Buccaneers, 22-10 (TB)
2002—Buccaneers, 25-0 (B)
2006—Ravens, 27-0 (TB)
2010—Ravens, 17-10 (B)
(RS Pts.—Buccaneers 57, Ravens 54)
BALTIMORE vs. *TENNESSEE
RS: Titans lead series, 9-8
PS: Ravens lead series, 2-1
1996—Oilers, 29-13 (H)
    Oilers, 24-21 (B)
1997—Ravens, 36-10 (T)
    Ravens, 21-19 (B)
1998—Oilers, 12-8 (B)
    Oilers, 16-14 (T)
1999—Titans, 14-11 (T)
    Ravens, 41-14 (B)
2000—Titans, 14-6 (B)
    Ravens, 24-23 (T)
    **Ravens, 24-10 (T)
2001—Ravens, 26-7 (B)
    Ravens, 16-10 (T)
2002—Ravens, 13-12 (B)
2003—***Titans, 20-17 (B)
2005—Titans, 25-10 (T)
2006—Ravens, 27-26 (T)
2008—Titans, 13-10 (B)
    **Ravens, 13-10 (T)
2011—Titans, 26-13 (T)
(RS Pts.—Ravens 310, Titans 294)
(PS Pts.—Ravens 54, Titans 40)
*Franchise in Houston prior to 1997;
known as Oilers prior to 1999
**AFC Divisional Playoff
***AFC First-Round Playoff
BALTIMORE vs. WASHINGTON
RS: Ravens lead series, 3-2
1997—Ravens, 20-17 (W)
2000—Redskins, 10-3 (W)
2004—Ravens, 17-10 (W)
2008—Ravens, 24-10 (B)
2012—Redskins, 31-28 (W) OT
(RS Pts.—Ravens 92, Redskins 78)

BUFFALO vs. ARIZONA
RS: Bills lead series, 6-4;
See Arizona vs. Buffalo
BUFFALO vs. ATLANTA
RS: Falcons lead series, 7-4;
See Atlanta vs. Buffalo
BUFFALO vs. BALTIMORE
RS: Series tied, 3-3;
See Baltimore vs. Buffalo
BUFFALO vs. CAROLINA
RS: Bills lead series, 5-1
1995—Bills, 31-9 (B)
1998—Bills, 30-14 (B)
2001—Bills, 25-24 (B)
2005—Panthers, 13-9 (B)
2009—Bills, 20-9 (C)
2013—Bills, 24-23 (B)
(RS Pts.—Bills 139, Panthers 92)
BUFFALO vs. CHICAGO
RS: Bears lead series, 7-4
1970—Bears, 31-13 (C)
1974—Bills, 16-6 (B)
1979—Bears, 7-0 (B)
1988—Bears, 24-3 (C)
1991—Bills, 35-20 (B)
1994—Bears, 20-13 (C)
1997—Bears, 20-3 (C)

2000—Bills, 20-3 (B)
2002—Bills, 33-27 (B) OT
2006—Bears, 40-7 (C)
2010—Bears, 22-19 (Toronto)
(RS Pts.—Bears 220, Bills 162)
BUFFALO vs. CINCINNATI
RS: Bills lead series, 15-11
PS: Bengals lead series, 2-0
1968—Bengals, 34-23 (C)
1969—Bills, 16-13 (B)
1970—Bengals, 43-14 (B)
1973—Bengals, 16-13 (B)
1975—Bengals, 33-24 (C)
1978—Bills, 5-0 (B)
1979—Bills, 51-24 (B)
1980—Bills, 14-0 (C)
1981—Bengals, 27-24 (C) OT
    *Bengals, 28-21 (C)
1983—Bills, 10-6 (C)
1984—Bengals, 52-21 (C)
1985—Bengals, 23-17 (B)
1986—Bengals, 36-33 (C) OT
1988—Bengals, 35-21 (C)
    **Bengals, 21-10 (C)
1989—Bills, 24-7 (B)
1991—Bills, 35-16 (B)
1996—Bills, 31-17 (B)
1998—Bills, 33-20 (C)
2002—Bills, 27-9 (B)
2003—Bills, 22-16 (B) OT
2004—Bills, 33-17 (C)
2005—Bills, 37-27 (C)
2007—Bills, 33-21 (B)
2010—Bills, 49-31 (C)
2011—Bengals, 23-20 (C)
2013—Bengals, 27-24 (B) OT
(RS Pts.—Bills 654, Bengals 573)
(PS Pts.—Bengals 49, Bills 31)
*AFC Divisional Playoff
**AFC Championship
BUFFALO vs. CLEVELAND
RS: Browns lead series, 11-7
PS: Browns lead series, 1-0
1972—Browns, 27-10 (C)
1974—Bills, 15-10 (C)
1977—Browns, 27-16 (B)
1978—Browns, 41-20 (C)
1981—Bills, 22-13 (B)
1984—Browns, 13-10 (B)
1985—Browns, 17-7 (C)
1986—Browns, 21-17 (B)
1987—Browns, 27-21 (C)
1989—*Browns, 34-30 (C)
1990—Bills, 42-0 (C)
1995—Bills, 22-19 (C)
2004—Bills, 37-7 (B)
2007—Browns, 8-0 (C)
2008—Browns, 29-27 (B)
2009—Browns, 6-3 (B)
2010—Bills, 13-6 (B)
2012—Bills, 24-14 (C)
2013—Browns, 37-24 (C)
(RS Pts.—Bills 330, Browns 322)
(PS Pts.—Browns 34, Bills 30)
*AFC Divisional Playoff
BUFFALO vs. DALLAS
RS: Cowboys lead series, 6-3
PS: Cowboys lead series, 2-0
1971—Cowboys, 49-37 (B)
1976—Cowboys, 17-10 (D)
1981—Cowboys, 27-14 (D)
1984—Bills, 14-3 (B)
1992—*Cowboys, 52-17 (Pasadena)

1993—Bills, 13-10 (D)
    **Cowboys, 30-13 (Atlanta)
1996—Bills, 10-7 (B)
2003—Cowboys, 10-6 (D)
2007—Cowboys, 25-24 (B)
2011—Cowboys, 44-7 (D)
(RS Pts.—Cowboys 192, Bills 135)
(PS Pts.—Cowboys 82, Bills 30)
*Super Bowl XXVII
**Super Bowl XXVIII
BUFFALO vs. DENVER
RS: Bills lead series, 19-15-1
PS: Bills lead series, 1-0
1960—Broncos, 27-21 (B)
    Tie, 38-38 (D)
1961—Broncos, 22-10 (B)
    Bills, 23-10 (D)
1962—Broncos, 23-20 (B)
    Bills, 45-38 (D)
1963—Bills, 30-28 (B)
    Bills, 27-17 (B)
1964—Bills, 30-19 (D)
    Bills, 30-19 (D)
1965—Bills, 30-15 (B)
    Bills, 31-13 (D)
1966—Bills, 38-21 (B)
1967—Bills, 17-16 (B)
    Broncos, 21-20 (B)
1968—Broncos, 34-32 (D)
1969—Bills, 41-28 (B)
1970—Broncos, 25-10 (B)
1975—Bills, 38-14 (B)
1977—Broncos, 26-6 (D)
1979—Broncos, 19-16 (B)
1981—Bills, 9-7 (B)
1984—Broncos, 37-7 (B)
1987—Bills, 21-14 (B)
1989—Broncos, 28-14 (B)
1990—Bills, 29-28 (B)
1991—*Bills, 10-7 (B)
1992—Bills, 27-17 (B)
1994—Bills, 27-20 (B)
1995—Broncos, 22-7 (D)
1997—Broncos, 23-20 (B) OT
2002—Broncos, 28-23 (B)
2005—Broncos, 28-17 (B)
2007—Broncos, 15-14 (B)
2008—Bills, 30-23 (D)
2011—Bills, 40-14 (B)
(RS Pts.—Bills 838, Broncos 771)
(PS Pts.—Bills 10, Broncos 7)
*AFC Championship
BUFFALO vs. DETROIT
RS: Series tied, 4-4-1
1972—Tie, 21-21 (B)
1976—Lions, 27-14 (D)
1979—Bills, 20-17 (D)
1991—Lions, 17-14 (B) OT
1994—Lions, 35-21 (D)
1997—Bills, 22-13 (B)
2002—Bills, 24-17 (B)
2006—Lions, 20-17 (D)
2010—Bills, 14-12 (B)
(RS Pts.—Lions 179, Bills 167)
BUFFALO vs. GREEN BAY
RS: Bills lead series, 7-4
1974—Bills, 27-7 (GB)
1979—Bills, 19-12 (B)
1982—Packers, 33-21 (Mil)
1988—Bills, 28-0 (B)
1991—Bills, 34-24 (Mil)
1994—Bills 29-20 (B)
1997—Packers, 31-21 (GB)

2000—Bills 27-18 (B)
2002—Packers, 10-0 (GB)
2006—Bills, 24-10 (B)
2010—Packers, 34-7 (GB)
(RS Pts.—Bills 237, Packers 199)
BUFFALO vs. HOUSTON
RS: Series tied, 3-3
2002—Bills, 31-24 (H)
2003—Texans, 12-10 (B)
2005—Bills, 22-7 (B)
2006—Bills, 24-21 (H)
2009—Texans, 31-10 (B)
2012—Texans, 21-9 (H)
(RS Pts.—Texans 116, Bills 106)
BUFFALO vs. *INDIANAPOLIS
RS: Bills lead series, 35-31-1
1970—Tie, 17-17 (Balt)
        Colts, 20-14 (Buff)
1971—Colts, 43-0 (Buff)
        Colts, 24-0 (Balt)
1972—Colts, 17-0 (Buff)
        Colts, 35-7 (Balt)
1973—Bills, 31-13 (Buff)
        Bills, 24-17 (Balt)
1974—Bills, 27-14 (Balt)
        Bills, 6-0 (Buff)
1975—Bills, 38-31 (Balt)
        Colts, 42-35 (Buff)
1976—Colts, 31-13 (Buff)
        Colts, 58-20 (Balt)
1977—Colts, 17-14 (Balt)
        Colts, 31-13 (Buff)
1978—Bills, 24-17 (Balt)
        Bills, 21-14 (Buff)
1979—Bills, 31-13 (Balt)
        Colts, 14-13 (Buff)
1980—Colts, 17-12 (Buff)
        Colts, 28-24 (Balt)
1981—Bills, 35-3 (Balt)
        Bills, 23-17 (Buff)
1982—Bills, 20-0 (Buff)
1983—Bills, 28-23 (Buff)
        Bills, 30-7 (Balt)
1984—Colts, 31-17 (I)
        Bills, 21-15 (Buff)
1985—Colts, 49-17 (I)
        Bills, 21-9 (Buff)
1986—Bills, 24-13 (Buff)
        Colts, 24-14 (I)
1987—Colts, 47-6 (Buff)
        Bills, 27-3 (I)
1988—Bills, 34-23 (Buff)
        Colts, 17-14 (I)
1989—Colts, 37-14 (I)
        Bills, 30-7 (Buff)
1990—Bills, 26-10 (Buff)
        Bills, 31-7 (I)
1991—Bills, 42-6 (Buff)
        Bills, 35-7 (I)
1992—Bills, 38-0 (Buff)
        Colts, 16-13 (I) OT
1993—Bills, 23-9 (Buff)
        Bills, 30-10 (I)
1994—Colts, 27-17 (Buff)
        Colts, 10-9 (I)
1995—Bills, 20-14 (Buff)
        Bills, 16-10 (I)
1996—Bills, 16-13 (Buff) OT
        Colts, 13-10 (I) OT
1997—Bills, 37-35 (B)
        Bills, 9-6 (I)
1998—Bills, 31-24 (I)
        Bills, 34-11 (B)

1999—Colts, 31-14 (I)
        Bills, 31-6 (B)
2000—Colts, 18-16 (B)
        Colts, 44-20 (I)
2001—Colts, 42-26 (I)
        Colts, 30-14 (B)
2003—Colts, 17-14 (B)
2006—Colts, 17-16 (I)
2009—Bills, 30-7 (B)
2012—Colts, 20-13 (I)
(RS Pts.—Bills 1,390, Colts 1,298)
*Franchise in Baltimore prior to 1984
BUFFALO vs. JACKSONVILLE
RS: Bills lead series, 7-5
PS: Jaguars lead series, 1-0
1996—*Jaguars, 30-27 (B)
1997—Jaguars, 20-14 (B)
1998—Bills, 17-16 (B)
2001—Bills, 13-10 (J)
2003—Bills, 38-17 (J)
2004—Jaguars, 13-10 (B)
2006—Bills, 27-24 (B)
2007—Jaguars, 36-14 (J)
2008—Bills, 20-16 (J)
2009—Jaguars, 18-15 (J)
2010—Jaguars, 36-26 (B)
2012—Bills, 34-18 (B)
2013—Bills, 27-20 (J)
(RS Pts.—Bills 255, Jaguars 244)
(PS Pts.—Jaguars 30, Bills 27)
*AFC First-Round Playoff
BUFFALO vs. *KANSAS CITY
RS: Bills lead series, 23-18-1
PS: Bills lead series, 2-1
1960—Texans, 45-28 (B)
        Texans, 24-7 (D)
1961—Bills, 27-24 (B)
        Bills, 30-20 (D)
1962—Texans, 41-21 (D)
        Bills, 23-14 (B)
1963—Tie, 27-27 (B)
        Bills, 35-26 (KC)
1964—Bills, 34-17 (B)
        Bills, 35-22 (KC)
1965—Bills, 23-7 (KC)
        Bills, 34-25 (B)
1966—Chiefs, 42-20 (B)
        Bills, 29-14 (KC)
        **Chiefs, 31-7 (B)
1967—Chiefs, 23-13 (KC)
1968—Chiefs, 18-7 (B)
1969—Bills, 29-7 (B)
        Chiefs, 22-19 (KC)
1971—Chiefs, 22-9 (KC)
1973—Bills, 23-14 (B)
1976—Bills, 50-17 (B)
1978—Bills, 28-13 (B)
        Chiefs, 14-10 (KC)
1982—Bills, 14-9 (B)
1983—Bills, 14-9 (KC)
1986—Chiefs, 20-17 (B)
        Bills, 17-14 (KC)
1991—Chiefs, 33-6 (KC)
        ***Bills, 37-14 (B)
1993—Chiefs, 23-7 (KC)
        ****Bills, 30-13 (B)
1994—Bills, 44-10 (B)
1996—Bills, 20-9 (B)
1997—Chiefs, 22-16 (KC)
2000—Bills, 21-17 (KC)
2002—Chiefs, 17-16 (KC)
2003—Chiefs, 38-5 (KC)
2005—Bills, 14-3 (B)

2008—Bills, 54-31 (KC)
2009—Bills, 16-10 (KC)
2010—Chiefs, 13-10 (KC) OT
2011—Bills, 41-7 (KC)
2012—Bills, 35-17 (B)
2013—Chiefs, 23-13 (B)
(RS Pts.—Bills 919, Chiefs 845)
(PS Pts.—Bills 74, Chiefs 58)
*Franchise in Dallas prior to 1963 and
known as Texans
**AFL Championship
***AFC Divisional Playoff
****AFC Championship
BUFFALO vs. MIAMI
RS: Dolphins lead series, 56-39-1
PS: Bills lead series, 3-1
1966—Bills, 58-24 (B)
        Bills, 29-0 (M)
1967—Bills, 35-13 (B)
        Dolphins, 17-14 (M)
1968—Tie, 14-14 (M)
        Dolphins, 21-17 (B)
1969—Dolphins, 24-6 (M)
        Bills, 28-3 (B)
1970—Dolphins, 33-14 (B)
        Dolphins, 45-7 (M)
1971—Dolphins, 29-14 (B)
        Dolphins, 34-0 (M)
1972—Dolphins, 24-23 (M)
        Dolphins, 30-16 (B)
1973—Dolphins, 27-6 (M)
        Dolphins, 17-0 (B)
1974—Dolphins, 24-16 (M)
        Dolphins, 35-28 (M)
1975—Dolphins, 35-30 (B)
        Dolphins, 31-21 (M)
1976—Dolphins, 30-21 (B)
        Dolphins, 45-27 (M)
1977—Dolphins, 13-0 (B)
        Dolphins, 31-14 (M)
1978—Dolphins, 31-24 (M)
        Dolphins, 25-24 (B)
1979—Dolphins, 9-7 (B)
        Dolphins, 17-7 (M)
1980—Bills, 17-7 (B)
        Dolphins, 17-14 (M)
1981—Bills, 31-21 (B)
        Dolphins, 16-6 (M)
1982—Dolphins, 9-7 (B)
        Dolphins, 27-10 (M)
1983—Dolphins, 12-0 (B)
        Bills, 38-35 (M) OT
1984—Dolphins, 21-17 (B)
        Dolphins, 38-7 (M)
1985—Dolphins, 23-14 (B)
        Dolphins, 28-0 (M)
1986—Dolphins, 27-14 (M)
        Dolphins, 34-24 (B)
1987—Dolphins, 34-31 (M) OT
        Bills, 27-0 (B)
1988—Bills, 9-6 (B)
        Bills, 31-6 (M)
1989—Bills, 27-24 (M)
        Bills, 31-17 (B)
1990—Dolphins, 30-7 (M)
        Bills, 24-14 (B)
        *Bills, 44-34 (B)
1991—Bills, 35-31 (B)
        Bills, 41-27 (M)
1992—Dolphins, 37-10 (B)
        Bills, 26-20 (M)
        **Bills, 29-10 (M)

1993—Dolphins, 22-13 (B)
    Bills, 47-34 (M)
1994—Bills, 21-11 (B)
    Bills, 42-31 (M)
1995—Dolphins, 23-6 (M)
    Bills, 23-20 (B)
    ***Bills, 37-22 (B)
1996—Dolphins, 21-7 (B)
    Dolphins, 16-14 (M)
1997—Bills, 9-6 (B)
    Dolphins, 30-13 (M)
1998—Dolphins, 13-7 (M)
    Bills, 30-24 (B)
    ***Dolphins, 24-17 (M)
1999—Bills, 23-18 (M)
    Bills, 23-3 (B)
2000—Dolphins, 22-13 (M)
    Dolphins, 33-6 (B)
2001—Dolphins, 34-27 (B)
    Dolphins, 34-7 (M)
2002—Bills, 23-10 (M)
    Bills, 38-21 (B)
2003—Dolphins, 17-7 (M)
    Dolphins, 20-3 (B)
2004—Bills, 20-13 (B)
    Bills, 42-32 (M)
2005—Bills, 20-14 (B)
    Dolphins, 24-23 (M)
2006—Bills, 16-6 (M)
    Bills, 21-0 (B)
2007—Bills, 13-10 (M)
    Bills, 38-17 (B)
2008—Dolphins, 25-16 (M)
    Dolphins, 16-3 (Toronto)
2009—Dolphins, 38-10 (M)
    Bills, 31-14 (B)
2010—Dolphins, 15-10 (B)
    Bills, 17-14 (M)
2011—Dolphins, 35-8 (M)
    Dolphins, 30-23 (B)
2012—Bills, 19-14 (B)
    Dolphins, 24-10 (M)
2013—Bills, 23-21 (M)
    Bills, 19-0 (B)
(RS Pts.—Dolphins 2,064, Bills 1,785)
(PS Pts.—Bills 127, Dolphins 90)
*AFC Divisional Playoff
**AFC Championship
***AFC First-Round Playoff
BUFFALO vs. MINNESOTA
RS: Vikings lead series, 8-4
1971—Vikings, 19-0 (M)
1975—Vikings, 35-13 (B)
1979—Vikings, 10-3 (M)
1982—Bills, 23-22 (B)
1985—Vikings, 27-20 (B)
1988—Bills, 13-10 (B)
1994—Vikings, 21-17 (B)
1997—Bills, 34-13 (B)
2000—Vikings, 31-27 (M)
2002—Bills, 45-39 (M) OT
2006—Bills, 17-12 (B)
2010—Vikings, 38-14 (M)
(RS Pts.—Vikings 298, Bills 205)
BUFFALO vs. *NEW ENGLAND
RS: Patriots lead series, 65-41-1
PS: Patriots lead series, 1-0
1960—Bills, 13-0 (Bos)
    Bills, 38-14 (Buff)
1961—Patriots, 23-21 (Buff)
    Patriots, 52-21 (Bos)
1962—Tie, 28-28 (Buff)
    Patriots, 21-10 (Bos)

1963—Bills, 28-21 (Buff)
    Patriots, 17-7 (Bos)
    **Patriots, 26-8 (Buff)
1964—Patriots, 36-28 (Buff)
    Bills, 24-14 (Bos)
1965—Bills, 24-7 (Buff)
    Bills, 23-7 (Bos)
1966—Patriots, 20-10 (Buff)
    Patriots, 14-3 (Bos)
1967—Patriots, 23-0 (Buff)
    Bills, 44-16 (Bos)
1968—Patriots, 16-7 (Buff)
    Patriots, 23-6 (Bos)
1969—Bills, 23-16 (Buff)
    Patriots, 35-21 (Bos)
1970—Bills, 45-10 (Bos)
    Patriots, 14-10 (Buff)
1971—Patriots, 38-33 (NE)
    Bills, 27-20 (Buff)
1972—Bills, 38-14 (Buff)
    Bills, 27-24 (NE)
1973—Bills, 31-13 (NE)
    Bills, 37-13 (Buff)
1974—Bills, 30-28 (Buff)
    Bills, 29-28 (NE)
1975—Bills, 45-31 (Buff)
    Bills, 34-14 (NE)
1976—Patriots, 26-22 (Buff)
    Patriots, 20-10 (NE)
1977—Bills, 24-14 (NE)
    Patriots, 20-7 (Buff)
1978—Patriots, 14-10 (Buff)
    Patriots, 26-24 (NE)
1979—Patriots, 26-6 (Buff)
    Bills, 16-13 (NE) OT
1980—Bills, 31-13 (Buff)
    Patriots, 24-2 (NE)
1981—Bills, 20-17 (Buff)
    Bills, 19-10 (NE)
1982—Patriots, 30-19 (NE)
1983—Patriots, 31-0 (NE)
    Patriots, 21-7 (NE)
1984—Patriots, 21-17 (Buff)
    Patriots, 38-10 (NE)
1985—Patriots, 17-14 (Buff)
    Patriots, 14-3 (NE)
1986—Patriots, 23-3 (Buff)
    Patriots, 22-19 (NE)
1987—Patriots, 14-7 (NE)
    Patriots, 13-7 (Buff)
1988—Bills, 16-14 (NE)
    Bills, 23-20 (Buff)
1989—Bills, 31-10 (Buff)
    Patriots, 33-24 (NE)
1990—Patriots, 27-10 (NE)
    Bills, 14-0 (Buff)
1991—Bills, 22-17 (Buff)
    Patriots, 16-13 (NE)
1992—Bills, 41-7 (NE)
    Bills, 16-7 (Buff)
1993—Bills, 38-14 (Buff)
    Bills, 13-10 (NE) OT
1994—Bills, 38-35 (NE)
    Patriots, 41-17 (Buff)
1995—Patriots, 27-14 (NE)
    Patriots, 35-25 (Buff)
1996—Bills, 17-10 (Buff)
    Patriots, 28-25 (NE)
1997—Patriots, 33-6 (NE)
    Patriots, 31-10 (Buff)
1998—Bills, 13-10 (NE)
    Patriots, 25-21 (NE)
1999—Bills, 17-7 (Buff)

    Bills, 13-10 (NE) OT
2000—Bills, 16-13 (NE) OT
    Patriots, 13-10 (Buff) OT
2001—Patriots, 21-11 (NE)
    Patriots, 12-9 (Buff) OT
2002—Patriots, 38-7 (Buff)
    Patriots, 27-17 (NE)
2003—Bills, 31-0 (Buff)
    Patriots, 31-0 (NE)
2004—Patriots, 31-17 (Buff)
    Patriots, 29-6 (NE)
2005—Patriots, 21-16 (NE)
    Patriots, 35-7 (Buff)
2006—Patriots, 19-17 (NE)
    Patriots, 28-6 (Buff)
2007—Patriots, 38-7 (NE)
    Patriots, 56-10 (Buff)
2008—Patriots, 20-10 (NE)
    Patriots, 13-0 (Buff)
2009—Patriots, 25-24 (NE)
    Patriots, 17-10 (Buff)
2010—Patriots, 38-30 (NE)
    Patriots, 34-3 (Buff)
2011—Bills, 34-31 (Buff)
    Patriots, 49-21 (NE)
2012—Patriots, 52-28 (B)
    Patriots, 37-31 (NE)
2013—Patriots, 23-21 (B)
    Patriots, 34-20 (NE)
(RS Pts.—Patriots 2,352, Bills 1,975)
(PS Pts.—Patriots 26, Bills 8)
*Franchise in Boston prior to 1971
**Division Playoff
BUFFALO vs. NEW ORLEANS
RS: Saints lead series, 6-4
1973—Saints, 13-0 (NO)
1980—Bills, 35-26 (NO)
1983—Bills, 27-21 (B)
1989—Saints, 22-19 (B)
1992—Bills, 20-16 (NO)
1998—Bills, 45-33 (NO)
2001—Saints, 24-6 (B)
2005—Saints, 19-7 (San Antonio)
2009—Saints, 27-7 (B)
2013—Saints, 35-17 (NO)
(RS Pts.—Saints 236, Bills 183)
BUFFALO vs. N.Y. GIANTS
RS: Bills lead series, 6-5
PS: Giants lead series, 1-0
1970—Giants, 20-6 (NY)
1975—Giants, 17-14 (B)
1978—Bills, 41-17 (B)
1987—Bills, 6-3 (B) OT
1990—Bills, 17-13 (NY)
    *Giants, 20-19 (Tampa)
1993—Bills, 17-14 (B)
1996—Bills, 23-20 (NY) OT
1999—Giants, 19-17 (B)
2003—Bills, 24-7 (NY)
2007—Giants, 38-21 (B)
2011—Giants, 27-24 (NY)
(RS Pts.—Bills 210, Giants 195)
(PS Pts.—Giants 20, Bills 19)
*Super Bowl XXV
BUFFALO vs. *N.Y. JETS
RS: Bills lead series, 55-51
PS: Bills lead series, 1-0
1960—Titans, 27-3 (NY)
    Titans, 17-13 (B)
1961—Bills, 41-31 (B)
    Titans, 21-14 (NY)
1962—Titans, 17-6 (B)
    Bills, 20-3 (NY)

1963—Bills, 45-14 (B)
    Bills, 19-10 (NY)
1964—Bills, 34-24 (B)
    Bills, 20-7 (NY)
1965—Bills, 33-21 (B)
    Jets, 14-12 (NY)
1966—Bills, 33-23 (NY)
    Bills, 14-3 (B)
1967—Bills, 20-17 (B)
    Jets, 20-10 (NY)
1968—Bills, 37-35 (B)
    Jets, 25-21 (NY)
1969—Jets, 33-19 (B)
    Jets, 16-6 (NY)
1970—Bills, 34-31 (B)
    Bills, 10-6 (NY)
1971—Jets, 28-17 (NY)
    Jets, 20-7 (B)
1972—Jets, 41-24 (B)
    Jets, 41-3 (NY)
1973—Bills, 9-7 (B)
    Bills, 34-14 (NY)
1974—Bills, 16-12 (B)
    Jets, 20-10 (NY)
1975—Jets, 42-14 (B)
    Bills, 24-23 (NY)
1976—Jets, 17-14 (NY)
    Jets, 19-14 (B)
1977—Jets, 24-19 (B)
    Bills, 14-10 (NY)
1978—Jets, 21-20 (B)
    Jets, 45-14 (NY)
1979—Bills, 46-31 (B)
    Bills, 14-12 (NY)
1980—Bills, 20-10 (B)
    Bills, 31-24 (NY)
1981—Bills, 31-0 (B)
    Jets, 33-14 (NY)
    **Bills, 31-27 (NY)
1983—Jets, 34-10 (B)
    Bills, 24-17 (NY)
1984—Jets, 28-26 (B)
    Jets, 21-17 (NY)
1985—Jets, 42-3 (NY)
    Jets, 27-7 (B)
1986—Jets, 28-24 (B)
    Jets, 14-13 (NY)
1987—Jets, 31-28 (B)
    Bills, 17-14 (NY)
1988—Bills, 37-14 (NY)
    Bills, 9-6 (B) OT
1989—Bills, 34-3 (B)
    Bills, 37-0 (NY)
1990—Bills, 30-7 (NY)
    Bills, 30-27 (B)
1991—Bills, 23-20 (NY)
    Bills, 24-13 (B)
1992—Bills, 24-20 (NY)
    Jets, 24-17 (B)
1993—Bills, 19-10 (NY)
    Bills, 16-14 (B)
1994—Jets, 23-3 (B)
    Jets, 22-17 (NY)
1995—Bills, 29-10 (B)
    Bills, 28-26 (NY)
1996—Bills, 25-22 (NY)
    Bills, 35-10 (B)
1997—Bills, 28-22 (NY)
    Bills, 20-10 (B)
1998—Jets, 34-12 (NY)
    Jets, 17-10 (B)
1999—Bills, 17-3 (B)
    Jets, 17-7 (NY)

2000—Jets, 27-14 (NY)
    Bills, 23-20 (B)
2001—Jets, 42-36 (B)
    Bills, 14-9 (NY)
2002—Jets, 37-31 (B) OT
    Jets, 31-13 (NY)
2003—Jets, 30-3 (NY)
    Bills, 17-6 (B)
2004—Jets, 16-14 (NY)
    Bills, 22-17 (B)
2005—Bills, 27-17 (B)
    Jets, 30-26 (NY)
2006—Jets, 28-20 (B)
    Bills, 31-13 (NY)
2007—Bills, 17-14 (B)
    Bills, 13-3 (NY)
2008—Jets, 26-17 (B)
    Jets, 31-27 (NY)
2009—Bills, 16-13 (NY) OT
    Jets, 19-13 (Toronto)
2010—Jets, 38-14 (B)
    Jets, 38-7 (NY)
2011—Jets, 27-11 (B)
    Jets, 28-24 (NY)
2012—Jets, 48-28 (NY)
    Bills, 28-9 (B)
2013—Jets, 27-20 (NY)
    Bills, 37-14 (B)
(RS Pts.—Jets 2,169, Bills 2,164)
(PS Pts.—Bills 31, Jets 27)
*Jets known as Titans prior to 1963
**AFC First-Round Playoff
BUFFALO vs. *OAKLAND
RS: Raiders lead series, 19-17
PS: Bills lead series, 2-0
1960—Bills, 38-9 (B)
    Raiders, 20-7 (O)
1961—Raiders, 31-22 (B)
    Bills, 26-21 (O)
1962—Bills, 14-6 (B)
    Bills, 10-6 (O)
1963—Raiders, 35-17 (B)
    Bills, 12-0 (B)
1964—Bills, 23-20 (B)
    Raiders, 16-13 (O)
1965—Bills, 17-12 (B)
    Bills, 17-14 (O)
1966—Bills, 31-10 (O)
1967—Raiders, 24-20 (B)
    Raiders, 28-21 (O)
1968—Raiders, 48-6 (B)
    Raiders, 13-10 (O)
1969—Raiders, 50-21 (O)
1972—Raiders, 28-16 (O)
1974—Bills, 21-20 (B)
1977—Raiders, 34-13 (O)
1980—Bills, 24-7 (B)
1983—Raiders, 27-24 (B)
1987—Raiders, 34-21 (LA)
1988—Bills, 37-21 (B)
1990—Bills, 38-24 (B)
    **Bills, 51-3 (B)
1991—Bills, 30-27 (LA) OT
1992—Bills, 20-3 (LA)
1993—Raiders, 25-24 (B)
    ***Bills, 29-23 (B)
1998—Bills, 44-21 (B)
1999—Raiders, 20-14 (B)
2002—Raiders, 49-31 (B)
2004—Raiders, 13-10 (O)
2005—Raiders, 38-17 (O)
2008—Bills, 24-23 (B)
2011—Bills, 38-35 (B)

(RS Pts.—Raiders 829, Bills 754)
(PS Pts.—Bills 80, Raiders 26)
*Franchise in Los Angeles from 1982-1994
**AFC Championship
***AFC Divisional Playoff
BUFFALO vs. PHILADELPHIA
RS: Series tied, 6-6
1973—Bills, 27-26 (B)
1981—Eagles, 20-14 (B)
1984—Eagles, 27-17 (B)
1985—Eagles, 21-17 (P)
1987—Eagles, 17-7 (P)
1990—Bills, 30-23 (B)
1993—Bills, 10-7 (P)
1996—Bills, 24-17 (P)
1999—Bills, 26-0 (B)
2003—Eagles, 23-13 (B)
2007—Eagles, 17-9 (P)
2011—Bills, 31-24 (B)
(RS Pts.—Bills 225, Eagles 222)
BUFFALO vs. PITTSBURGH
RS: Steelers lead series, 13-8
PS: Steelers lead series, 2-1
1970—Steelers, 23-10 (P)
1972—Steelers, 38-21 (B)
1974—*Steelers, 32-14 (P)
1975—Bills, 30-21 (P)
1978—Steelers, 28-17 (B)
1979—Steelers, 28-0 (P)
1980—Bills, 28-13 (B)
1982—Bills, 13-0 (B)
1985—Steelers, 30-24 (P)
1986—Bills, 16-12 (B)
1988—Bills, 36-28 (B)
1991—Bills, 52-34 (B)
1992—Bills, 28-20 (B)
    *Bills, 24-3 (P)
1993—Steelers, 23-0 (P)
1994—Steelers, 23-10 (P)
1995—*Steelers, 40-21 (P)
1996—Steelers, 24-6 (P)
1999—Bills, 24-21 (B)
2001—Steelers, 20-3 (B)
2004—Steelers, 29-24 (B)
2007—Steelers, 26-3 (P)
2010—Steelers, 19-16 (B) OT
2013—Steelers, 23-10 (P)
(RS Pts.—Steelers 483, Bills 371)
(PS Pts.—Steelers 75, Bills 59)
*AFC Divisional Playoff
BUFFALO vs. *ST. LOUIS
RS: Bills lead series, 6-5
1970—Rams, 19-0 (B)
1974—Rams, 19-14 (LA)
1980—Bills, 10-7 (B) OT
1983—Rams, 41-17 (LA)
1989—Bills, 23-20 (B)
1992—Bills, 40-7 (B)
1995—Bills, 45-27 (StL)
1998—Rams, 34-33 (B)
2004—Bills, 37-17 (B)
2008—Bills, 31-14 (StL)
2012—Rams, 15-12 (B)
(RS Pts.—Bills 262, Rams 220)
*Franchise in Los Angeles prior to 1995
BUFFALO vs. *SAN DIEGO
RS: Chargers lead series, 21-10-2
PS: Bills lead series, 2-1
1960—Chargers, 24-10 (B)
    Bills, 32-3 (LA)
1961—Chargers, 19-11 (B)
    Chargers, 28-10 (SD)

1962—Bills, 35-10 (B)
　　　Bills, 40-20 (SD)
1963—Chargers, 14-10 (SD)
　　　Chargers, 23-13 (B)
1964—Bills, 30-3 (B)
　　　Bills, 27-24 (SD)
　　　**Bills, 20-7 (B)
1965—Chargers, 34-3 (B)
　　　Tie, 20-20 (SD)
　　　**Bills, 23-0 (SD)
1966—Chargers, 27-7 (SD)
　　　Tie, 17-17 (B)
1967—Chargers, 37-17 (B)
1968—Chargers, 21-6 (B)
1969—Chargers, 45-6 (SD)
1971—Chargers, 20-3 (SD)
1973—Chargers, 34-7 (SD)
1976—Chargers, 34-13 (B)
1979—Chargers, 27-19 (SD)
1980—Bills, 26-24 (SD)
　　　***Chargers, 20-14 (SD)
1981—Bills, 28-27 (SD)
1985—Chargers, 14-9 (B)
　　　Chargers, 40-7 (SD)
1998—Chargers, 16-14 (SD)
2000—Bills, 27-24 (B) OT
2001—Chargers, 27-24 (SD)
2002—Bills, 20-13 (B)
2005—Chargers, 48-10 (SD)
2006—Chargers, 24-21 (B)
2008—Bills, 23-14 (B)
2011—Chargers, 37-10 (SD)
(RS Pts.—Chargers 792, Bills 555)
(PS Pts.—Bills 57, Chargers 27)
*Franchise in Los Angeles prior to 1961
**AFL Championship
***AFC Divisional Playoff
BUFFALO vs. SAN FRANCISCO
RS: 49ers lead series, 6-5
1972—Bills, 27-20 (B)
1980—Bills, 18-13 (SF)
1983—49ers, 23-10 (B)
1989—49ers, 21-10 (SF)
1992—Bills, 34-31 (B)
1995—49ers, 27-17 (SF)
1998—Bills, 26-21 (B)
2001—49ers, 35-0 (SF)
2004—Bills, 41-7 (SF)
2008—49ers, 10-3 (B)
2012—49ers, 45-3 (SF)
(RS Pts.—49ers 253, Bills 189)
BUFFALO vs. SEATTLE
RS: Seahawks lead series, 7-5
1977—Seahawks, 56-17 (S)
1984—Seahawks, 31-28 (S)
1988—Bills, 13-3 (S)
1989—Seahawks, 17-16 (S)
1995—Bills, 27-21 (B)
1996—Seahawks, 26-18 (S)
1999—Seahawks, 26-16 (S)
2000—Bills, 42-23 (S)
2001—Seahawks, 23-20 (B)
2004—Bills, 38-9 (S)
2008—Bills, 34-10 (B)
2012—Seahawks, 50-17 (Toronto)
(RS Pts.—Seahawks 295, Bills 286)
BUFFALO vs. TAMPA BAY
RS: Buccaneers lead series, 7-3
1976—Bills, 14-9 (TB)
1978—Buccaneers, 31-10 (TB)
1982—Buccaneers, 24-23 (TB)
1986—Buccaneers, 34-28 (TB)
1988—Buccaneers, 10-5 (TB)

1991—Bills, 17-10 (TB)
2000—Buccaneers, 31-17 (TB)
2005—Buccaneers, 19-3 (TB)
2009—Bills, 33-20 (B)
2013—Buccaneers, 27-6 (TB)
(RS Pts.—Buccaneers 215, Bills 156)
BUFFALO vs. *TENNESSEE
RS: Titans lead series, 27-14
PS: Bills lead series, 2-1
1960—Bills, 25-24 (B)
　　　Oilers, 31-23 (H)
1961—Oilers, 22-12 (H)
　　　Oilers, 28-16 (B)
1962—Oilers, 28-23 (B)
　　　Oilers, 17-14 (H)
1963—Oilers, 31-20 (B)
　　　Oilers, 28-14 (H)
1964—Oilers, 48-17 (H)
　　　Bills, 24-10 (B)
1965—Oilers, 19-17 (B)
　　　Bills, 29-18 (H)
1966—Bills, 27-20 (B)
　　　Bills, 42-20 (H)
1967—Oilers, 20-3 (B)
　　　Oilers, 10-3 (H)
1968—Oilers, 30-7 (B)
　　　Oilers, 35-6 (H)
1969—Oilers, 17-3 (B)
　　　Oilers, 28-14 (H)
1971—Oilers, 20-14 (B)
1974—Bills, 21-9 (B)
1976—Oilers, 13-3 (B)
1978—Oilers, 17-10 (H)
1983—Bills, 30-13 (B)
1985—Bills, 20-0 (B)
1986—Oilers, 16-7 (H)
1987—Oilers, 34-30 (B)
1988—**Bills, 17-10 (B)
1989—Bills, 47-41 (H) OT
1990—Oilers, 27-24 (H)
1992—Oilers, 27-3 (H)
　　　***Bills, 41-38 (B) OT
1993—Bills, 35-7 (B)
1994—Bills, 15-7 (H)
1995—Oilers, 28-17 (B)
1997—Oilers, 31-14 (T)
1999—***Titans, 22-16 (T)
2000—Bills, 16-13 (B)
2003—Titans, 28-26 (T)
2006—Titans, 30-29 (B)
2009—Titans, 41-17 (T)
2011—Bills, 23-17 (B)
2012—Titans, 35-34 (B)
(RS Pts.—Titans 911, Bills 801)
(PS Pts.—Bills 74, Titans 70)
*Franchise in Houston prior to 1997;
known as Oilers prior to 1999
**AFC Divisional Playoff
***AFC First-Round Playoff
BUFFALO vs. WASHINGTON
RS: Bills lead series, 8-4
PS: Redskins lead series, 1-0
1972—Bills, 24-17 (W)
1977—Redskins, 10-0 (S)
1981—Bills, 21-14 (B)
1984—Redskins, 41-14 (W)
1987—Redskins, 27-7 (B)
1990—Redskins, 29-14 (W)
1991—*Redskins, 37-24 (Minneapolis)
1993—Bills, 24-10 (B)
1996—Bills, 38-13 (B)
1999—Bills, 34-17 (W)
2003—Bills, 24-7 (B)

2007—Bills, 17-16 (W)
2011—Bills, 23-0 (Toronto)
(RS Pts.—Bills 240, Redskins 201)
(PS Pts.—Redskins 37, Bills 24)
*Super Bowl XXVI

CAROLINA vs. ARIZONA
RS: Panthers lead series, 8-4
PS: Cardinals lead series, 1-0;
See Arizona vs. Carolina
CAROLINA vs. ATLANTA
RS: Falcons lead series, 23-15;
See Atlanta vs. Carolina
CAROLINA vs. BALTIMORE
RS: Panthers lead series, 3-1;
See Baltimore vs. Carolina
CAROLINA vs. BUFFALO
RS: Bills lead series, 5-1;
See Buffalo vs. Carolina
CAROLINA vs. CHICAGO
RS: Bears lead series, 5-2
PS: Panthers lead series, 1-0
1995—Bears, 31-27 (Chi)
2002—Panthers, 24-14 (Car)
2005—Bears, 13-3 (Chi)
　　　*Panthers, 29-21 (Chi)
2008—Panthers, 20-17 (Car)
2010—Bears, 23-6 (Car)
2011—Bears, 34-29 (Chi)
2012—Bears, 23-22 (Chi)
(RS Pts.—Bears 155, Panthers 131)
(PS Pts.—Panthers 29, Bears 21)
*NFC Divisional Playoff
CAROLINA vs. CINCINNATI
RS: Series tied, 2-2
1999—Panthers, 27-3 (Car)
2002—Panthers, 52-31 (Car)
2006—Bengals, 17-14 (Cin)
2010—Bengals, 20-7 (Car)
(RS Pts.—Panthers 100, Bengals 71)
CAROLINA vs. CLEVELAND
RS: Panthers lead series, 3-1
1999—Panthers, 31-17 (Cle)
2002—Panthers, 13-6 (Cle)
2006—Panthers, 20-12 (Cle)
2010—Browns, 24-23 (Cle)
(RS Pts.—Panthers 87, Browns 59)
CAROLINA vs. DALLAS
RS: Cowboys lead series, 9-1
PS: Panthers lead series, 2-0
1996—*Panthers, 26-17 (C)
1997—Panthers, 23-13 (D)
1998—Cowboys, 27-20 (D)
2000—Cowboys, 16-13 (C) OT
2002—Cowboys, 14-13 (D)
2003—Cowboys, 24-20 (D)
　　　**Panthers, 29-10 (C)
2005—Cowboys, 24-20 (C)
2006—Cowboys, 35-14 (C)
2007—Cowboys, 20-13 (C)
2009—Cowboys, 21-7 (D)
2012—Cowboys, 19-14 (C)
(RS Pts.—Cowboys 213, Panthers 157)
(PS Pts.—Panthers 55, Cowboys 27)
*NFC Divisional Playoff
*NFC First-Round Playoff
CAROLINA vs. DENVER
RS: Broncos lead series, 3-1
1997—Broncos, 34-0 (D)
2004—Broncos, 20-17 (D)
2008—Panthers, 30-10 (C)
2012—Broncos, 36-14 (C)
(RS Pts.—Broncos 100, Panthers 61)

ALL-TIME TEAM VS. TEAM RESULTS

CAROLINA vs. DETROIT
RS: Panthers lead series, 4-2
1999—Lions, 24-9 (C)
2002—Panthers, 31-7 (C)
2003—Panthers, 20-14 (C)
2005—Panthers, 21-20 (D)
2008—Panthers, 31-22 (C)
2011—Lions, 49-35 (D)
(RS Pts.—Panthers 147, Lions 136)

CAROLINA vs. GREEN BAY
RS: Packers lead series, 7-4
PS: Packers lead series, 1-0
1996—*Packers, 30-13 (GB)
1997—Packers, 31-10 (C)
1998—Packers, 37-30 (C)
1999—Panthers, 33-31 (GB)
2000—Panthers, 31-14 (C)
2001—Packers, 28-7 (C)
2002—Packers, 17-14 (GB)
2004—Packers, 24-14 (C)
2005—Panthers, 32-29 (C)
2007—Packers, 31-17 (GB)
2008—Packers, 35-31 (GB)
2011—Packers, 30-23 (C)
(RS Pts.—Packers 303, Panthers 246)
(PS Pts.—Packers 30, Panthers 13)
*NFC Championship

CAROLINA vs. HOUSTON
RS: Texans lead series, 2-1
2003—Texans, 14-10 (H)
2007—Texans, 34-21 (C)
2011—Panthers, 28-13 (H)
(RS Pts.—Texans 61, Panthers 59)

CAROLINA vs. INDIANAPOLIS
RS: Panthers lead series, 4-1
1995—Panthers, 13-10 (C)
1998—Panthers, 27-19 (I)
2003—Panthers, 23-20 (I) OT
2007—Colts, 31-7 (C)
2011—Panthers, 27-19 (I)
(RS Pts.—Colts 99, Panthers 97)

CAROLINA vs. JACKSONVILLE
RS: Jaguars lead series, 3-2
1996—Jaguars, 24-14 (J)
1999—Jaguars, 22-20 (C)
2003—Panthers, 24-23 (C)
2007—Jaguars, 37-6 (J)
2011—Panthers, 16-10 (C)
(RS Pts.—Jaguars 116, Panthers 80)

CAROLINA vs. KANSAS CITY
RS: Chiefs lead series, 3-2
1997—Chiefs, 35-14 (C)
2000—Chiefs, 15-14 (KC)
2004—Panthers, 28-17 (KC)
2008—Panthers, 34-0 (C)
2012—Chiefs, 27-21 (KC)
(RS Pts.—Panthers 111, Chiefs 94)

CAROLINA vs. MIAMI
RS: Dolphins lead series, 4-1
1998—Dolphins, 13-9 (C)
2001—Dolphins, 23-6 (M)
2005—Dolphins, 27-24 (M)
2009—Dolphins, 24-17 (C)
2013—Panthers, 20-16 (M)
(RS Pts.—Dolphins 103, Panthers 76)

CAROLINA vs. MINNESOTA
RS: Vikings lead series, 6-5
1996—Vikings, 14-12 (M)
1997—Vikings, 21-14 (M)
2000—Vikings, 31-17 (M)
2001—Panthers, 24-13 (M)
2002—Panthers, 21-14 (M)
2005—Panthers, 38-13 (C)

2006—Vikings, 16-13 (M) OT
2008—Vikings, 20-10 (M)
2009—Panthers, 26-7 (C)
2011—Vikings, 24-21 (C)
2013—Panthers, 35-10 (M)
(RS Pts.—Panthers 231, Vikings 183)

CAROLINA vs. NEW ENGLAND
RS: Panthers lead series, 3-2
PS: Patriots lead series, 1-0
1995—Panthers, 20-17 (NE) OT
2001—Patriots, 38-6 (C)
2003—*Patriots, 32-29 (Houston)
2005—Panthers, 27-17 (C)
2009—Patriots, 20-10 (NE)
2013—Panthers, 24-20 (C)
(RS Pts.—Patriots 112, Panthers 87)
(PS Pts.—Patriots 32, Panthers 29)
*Super Bowl XXXVIII

CAROLINA vs. NEW ORLEANS
RS: Panthers lead series, 20-18
1995—Panthers, 20-3 (C)
    Saints, 34-26 (NO)
1996—Panthers, 22-20 (NO)
    Panthers, 19-7 (C)
1997—Panthers, 13-0 (NO)
    Saints, 16-13 (C)
1998—Panthers, 19-14 (NO)
    Panthers, 31-17 (C)
1999—Saints, 19-10 (NO)
    Panthers, 45-13 (C)
2000—Saints, 24-6 (NO)
    Saints, 20-10 (C)
2001—Saints, 27-25 (C)
    Saints, 27-23 (NO)
2002—Saints, 34-24 (C)
    Panthers, 10-6 (NO)
2003—Panthers, 19-13 (C)
    Panthers, 23-20 (NO) OT
2004—Panthers, 32-21 (NO)
    Saints, 21-18 (C)
2005—Saints, 23-20 (C)
    Panthers, 27-10 (Baton Rouge)
2006—Panthers, 21-18 (C)
    Panthers, 31-21 (NO)
2007—Panthers, 16-13 (NO)
    Saints, 31-6 (C)
2008—Panthers, 30-7 (C)
    Panthers, 33-31 (NO)
2009—Saints, 30-20 (NO)
    Panthers, 23-10 (C)
2010—Saints, 16-14 (NO)
    Saints, 34-3 (C)
2011—Saints, 30-27 (C)
    Saints, 45-17 (NO)
2012—Panthers, 35-27 (C)
    Panthers, 44-38 (NO)
2013—Saints, 31-13 (NO)
    Panthers, 17-13 (C)
(RS Pts.—Panthers 800, Saints 789)

CAROLINA vs. N.Y. GIANTS
RS: Series tied, 4-4
PS: Panthers lead series, 1-0
1996—Panthers, 27-17 (C)
2003—Panthers, 37-24 (NY)
2005—*Panthers, 23-0 (NY)
2006—Giants, 27-13 (C)
2008—Giants, 34-28 (NY) OT
2009—Panthers, 41-9 (NY)
2010—Giants, 31-18 (NY)
2012—Giants, 36-7 (C)
2013—Panthers, 38-0 (C)
(RS Pts.—Panthers 209, Giants 178)
(PS Pts.—Panthers 23, Giants 0)

*NFC First-Round Playoff

CAROLINA vs. N.Y. JETS
RS: Series tied, 3-3
1995—Panthers, 26-15 (C)
1998—Jets, 48-21 (NY)
2001—Jets, 13-12 (C)
2005—Panthers, 30-3 (C)
2009—Jets, 17-6 (NY)
2013—Panthers, 30-20 (C)
(RS Pts.—Panthers 125, Jets 116)

CAROLINA vs. OAKLAND
RS: Panthers lead series, 3-2
1997—Panthers, 38-14 (C)
2000—Raiders, 52-9 (O)
2004—Raiders, 27-24 (C)
2008—Panthers, 17-6 (O)
2012—Panthers, 17-6 (C)
(RS Pts.— Panthers 105, Raiders 105)

CAROLINA vs. PHILADELPHIA
RS: Eagles lead series, 5-2
PS: Panthers lead series, 1-0
1996—Eagles, 20-9 (P)
1999—Panthers, 33-7 (C)
2003—Eagles, 25-16 (P)
    *Panthers, 14-3 (P)
2004—Eagles, 30-8 (P)
2006—Eagles, 27-24 (P)
2009—Eagles, 38-10 (C)
2012—Panthers, 30-22 (P)
(RS Pts.—Eagles 169, Panthers 130)
(PS Pts.—Panthers 14, Eagles 3)
*NFC Championship

CAROLINA vs. PITTSBURGH
RS: Steelers lead series, 4-1
1996—Panthers, 18-14 (C)
1999—Steelers, 30-20 (P)
2002—Steelers, 30-14 (P)
2006—Steelers, 37-3 (C)
2010—Steelers, 27-3 (P)
(RS Pts.—Steelers 138, Panthers 58)

CAROLINA vs. ST. LOUIS
RS: Panthers lead series, 11-8
PS: Panthers lead series, 1-0
1995—Rams, 31-10 (C)
    Rams, 28-17 (StL)
1996—Panthers, 45-13 (C)
    Panthers, 20-10 (StL)
1997—Panthers, 16-10 (StL)
    Rams, 30-18 (C)
1998—Panthers, 24-20 (StL)
    Panthers, 20-13 (C)
1999—Rams, 35-10 (StL)
    Rams, 34-21 (C)
2000—Panthers, 27-24 (StL)
    Panthers, 16-3 (C)
2001—Rams, 48-14 (StL)
    Rams, 38-32 (C)
2003—*Panthers, 29-23 (StL) 2OT
2004—Panthers, 20-7 (C)
2006—Panthers, 15-0 (C)
2007—Panthers, 27-13 (StL)
2010—Rams, 20-10 (StL)
2013—Panthers, 30-15 (C)
(RS Pts.—Panthers 392, Rams 392)
(PS Pts.—Panthers 29, Rams 23)
*NFC Divisional Playoff

CAROLINA vs. SAN DIEGO
RS: Panthers lead series, 4-1
1997—Panthers, 26-7 (SD)
2000—Panthers, 30-22 (C)
2004—Chargers, 17-6 (C)
2008—Panthers, 26-24 (SD)
2012—Panthers, 31-7 (SD)

(RS Pts.—Panthers 119, Chargers 77)
CAROLINA vs. SAN FRANCISCO
RS: Panthers lead series, 11-7
PS: 49ers lead series, 1-0
1995—Panthers, 13-7 (SF)
     49ers, 31-10 (C)
1996—Panthers, 23-7 (C)
     Panthers, 30-24 (SF)
1997—49ers, 34-21 (C)
     49ers, 27-19 (SF)
1998—49ers, 25-23 (SF)
     49ers, 31-28 (C) OT
1999—Panthers, 31-29 (SF)
     Panthers, 41-24 (C)
2000—Panthers, 38-22 (SF)
     Panthers, 34-16 (C)
2001—49ers, 24-14 (SF)
     49ers, 25-22 (C) OT
2004—Panthers, 37-27 (SF)
2007—Panthers, 31-14 (C)
2010—Panthers, 23-20 (C)
2013—Panthers, 10-9 (SF)
     *49ers, 23-10 (C)
(RS Pts.—Panthers 448, 49ers 396)
(PS Pts.—49ers 23, Panthers 10)
*NFC Divisional Playoff
CAROLINA vs. SEATTLE
RS: Seahawks lead series, 4-2
PS: Seahawks lead series, 1-0
2000—Panthers, 26-3 (C)
2004—Seahawks, 23-17 (S)
2005—*Seahawks, 34-14 (S)
2007—Panthers, 13-10 (C)
2010—Seahawks, 31-14 (S)
2012—Seahawks, 16-12 (C)
2013—Seahawks, 12-7 (C)
(RS Pts.—Seahawks 95, Panthers 89)
(PS Pts.—Seahawks 34, Panthers 14)
*NFC Championship
CAROLINA vs. TAMPA BAY
RS: Panthers lead series, 16-11
1995—Buccaneers, 20-13 (C)
1996—Panthers, 24-0 (C)
1998—Buccaneers, 16-13 (TB)
2002—Buccaneers, 12-9 (C)
     Buccaneers, 23-10 (TB)
2003—Panthers, 12-9 (TB) OT
     Panthers, 27-24 (C)
2004—Panthers, 21-14 (C)
     Panthers, 37-20 (TB)
2005—Panthers, 34-14 (TB)
     Buccaneers, 20-10 (C)
2006—Panthers, 26-24 (TB)
     Panthers, 24-10 (C)
2007—Buccaneers, 20-7 (C)
     Panthers, 31-23 (TB)
2008—Buccaneers, 27-3 (TB)
     Panthers, 38-23 (C)
2009—Panthers, 28-21 (TB)
     Panthers, 16-6 (C)
2010—Buccaneers, 20-7 (C)
     Buccaneers, 31-16 (TB)
2011—Panthers, 38-19 (TB)
     Panthers, 48-16 (C)
2012—Buccaneers, 16-10 (TB)
     Buccaneers, 27-21 (C) OT
2013—Panthers, 31-13 (TB)
     Panthers, 27-6 (C)
(RS Pts.—Panthers 581, Buccaneers 474)
CAROLINA vs. *TENNESSEE
RS: Titans lead series, 3-1
1996—Panthers, 31-6 (H)
2003—Titans, 37-17 (C)

2007—Titans, 20-7 (T)
2011—Titans, 30-3 (C)
(RS Pts.—Titans 93, Panthers 58)
*Franchise in Houston prior to 1997;
known as Oilers prior to 1999
CAROLINA vs. WASHINGTON
RS: Redskins lead series, 7-4
1995—Redskins, 20-17 (W)
1997—Redskins, 24-10 (C)
1998—Redskins, 28-25 (C)
1999—Redskins, 38-36 (W)
2000—Redskins, 20-17 (W)
2001—Redskins, 17-14 (W) OT
2003—Panthers, 20-17 (C)
2006—Redskins, 17-13 (W)
2009—Panthers, 20-17 (C)
2011—Panthers, 33-20 (C)
2012—Panthers, 21-13 (W)
(RS Pts.—Redskins 231, Panthers 226)

CHICAGO vs. ARIZONA
RS: Bears lead series, 56-27-6;
See Arizona vs. Chicago
CHICAGO vs. ATLANTA
RS: Bears lead series, 13-12;
See Atlanta vs. Chicago
CHICAGO vs. BALTIMORE
RS: Bears lead series, 3-2;
See Baltimore vs. Chicago
CHICAGO vs. BUFFALO
RS: Bears lead series, 7-4;
See Buffalo vs. Chicago
CHICAGO vs. CAROLINA
RS: Bears lead series, 5-2
PS: Panthers lead series, 1-0;
See Carolina vs. Chicago
CHICAGO vs. CINCINNATI
RS: Bengals lead series, 6-4
1972—Bengals, 13-3 (Chi)
1980—Bengals, 17-14 (Chi) OT
1986—Bears, 44-7 (Cin)
1989—Bears, 17-14 (Chi)
1992—Bengals, 31-28 (Chi) OT
1995—Bengals, 16-10 (Cin)
2001—Bears, 24-0 (Cin)
2005—Bengals, 24-7 (Chi)
2009—Bengals, 45-10 (Cin)
2013—Bears, 24-21 (Chi)
(RS Pts.—Bengals 188, Bears 181)
CHICAGO vs. CLEVELAND
RS: Browns lead series, 9-6
1951—Browns, 42-21 (Cle)
1954—Browns, 39-10 (Chi)
1960—Browns, 42-0 (Cle)
1961—Bears, 17-14 (Chi)
1967—Browns, 24-0 (Cle)
1969—Browns, 28-24 (Chi)
1972—Bears, 17-0 (Cle)
1980—Browns, 27-21 (Cle)
1986—Bears, 41-31 (Chi)
1989—Bears, 27-7 (Cle)
1992—Browns, 27-14 (Cle)
2001—Bears, 27-21 (Chi) OT
2005—Browns, 20-10 (Cle)
2009—Bears, 30-6 (Chi)
2013—Bears, 38-31 (Cle)
(RS Pts.—Browns 379, Bears 277)
CHICAGO vs. DALLAS
RS: Series tied, 11-11
PS: Cowboys lead series, 2-0
1960—Bears, 17-7 (C)
1962—Bears, 34-33 (D)
1964—Cowboys, 24-10 (C)

1968—Cowboys, 34-3 (C)
1971—Bears, 23-19 (C)
1973—Cowboys, 20-17 (C)
1976—Cowboys, 31-21 (D)
1977—*Cowboys, 37-7 (D)
1979—Cowboys, 24-20 (D)
1981—Cowboys, 10-9 (D)
1984—Cowboys, 23-14 (C)
1985—Bears, 44-0 (C)
1986—Bears, 24-10 (D)
1988—Bears, 17-7 (C)
1991—**Cowboys, 17-13 (C)
1992—Cowboys, 27-14 (D)
1996—Bears, 22-6 (C)
1997—Cowboys, 27-3 (D)
1998—Bears, 13-12 (C)
2004—Cowboys, 21-7 (D)
2007—Cowboys, 34-10 (C)
2010—Bears, 27-20 (D)
2012—Bears, 34-18 (D)
2013—Bears, 45-28 (C)
(RS Pts.—Cowboys 435, Bears 428)
(PS Pts.—Cowboys 54, Bears 20)
*NFC Divisional Playoff
**NFC First-Round Playoff
CHICAGO vs. DENVER
RS: Series tied, 7-7
1971—Broncos, 6-3 (D)
1973—Bears, 33-14 (D)
1976—Broncos, 28-14 (C)
1978—Broncos, 16-7 (D)
1981—Bears, 35-24 (D)
1983—Bears, 31-14 (C)
1984—Bears, 27-0 (C)
1987—Broncos, 31-29 (D)
1990—Bears, 16-13 (D) OT
1993—Broncos, 13-3 (C)
1996—Broncos, 17-12 (D)
2003—Bears, 19-10 (D)
2007—Bears, 37-34 (C) OT
2011—Broncos, 13-10 (D) OT
(RS Pts.—Bears 276, Broncos 233)
CHICAGO vs. *DETROIT
RS: Bears lead series, 96-67-5
1930—Spartans, 7-6 (P)
     Bears, 14-6 (C)
1931—Bears, 9-6 (C)
     Spartans, 3-0 (P)
1932—Tie, 13-13 (C)
     Tie, 7-7 (P)
     Bears, 9-0 (C)
1933—Bears, 17-14 (C)
     Bears, 17-7 (P)
1934—Bears, 19-16 (D)
     Bears, 10-7 (C)
1935—Tie, 20-20 (C)
     Lions, 14-2 (D)
1936—Bears, 12-10 (C)
     Lions, 13-7 (D)
1937—Bears, 28-20 (C)
     Bears, 13-0 (D)
1938—Lions, 13-7 (C)
     Lions, 14-7 (D)
1939—Lions, 10-0 (C)
     Bears, 23-13 (D)
1940—Bears, 7-0 (C)
     Lions, 17-14 (D)
1941—Bears, 49-0 (C)
     Bears, 24-7 (D)
1942—Bears, 16-0 (C)
     Bears, 42-0 (D)
1943—Bears, 27-21 (D)
     Bears, 35-14 (C)

1944—Tie, 21-21 (C)
    Lions, 41-21 (D)
1945—Lions, 16-10 (D)
    Lions, 35-28 (C)
1946—Bears, 42-6 (C)
    Bears, 45-24 (D)
1947—Bears, 33-24 (C)
    Bears, 34-14 (D)
1948—Bears, 28-0 (C)
    Bears, 42-14 (D)
1949—Bears, 27-24 (C)
    Bears, 28-7 (D)
1950—Bears, 35-21 (D)
    Bears, 6-3 (C)
1951—Bears, 28-23 (C)
    Lions, 41-28 (C)
1952—Bears, 24-23 (C)
    Lions, 45-21 (D)
1953—Lions, 20-16 (C)
    Lions, 13-7 (D)
1954—Lions, 48-23 (D)
    Bears, 28-24 (C)
1955—Bears, 24-14 (D)
    Bears, 21-20 (C)
1956—Lions, 42-10 (D)
    Bears, 38-21 (C)
1957—Bears, 27-7 (D)
    Lions, 21-13 (C)
1958—Bears, 20-7 (D)
    Bears, 21-16 (C)
1959—Bears, 24-14 (D)
    Bears, 25-14 (C)
1960—Bears, 28-7 (C)
    Lions, 36-0 (D)
1961—Bears, 31-17 (D)
    Lions, 16-15 (C)
1962—Lions, 11-3 (D)
    Bears, 3-0 (C)
1963—Bears, 37-21 (D)
    Bears, 24-14 (C)
1964—Lions, 10-0 (C)
    Bears, 27-24 (D)
1965—Bears, 38-10 (C)
    Bears, 17-10 (D)
1966—Bears, 14-3 (D)
    Tie, 10-10 (C)
1967—Bears, 14-3 (C)
    Bears, 27-13 (D)
1968—Lions, 42-0 (D)
    Lions, 28-10 (C)
1969—Lions, 13-7 (D)
    Lions, 20-3 (C)
1970—Lions, 28-14 (D)
    Lions, 16-10 (C)
1971—Bears, 28-23 (D)
    Lions, 28-3 (C)
1972—Lions, 38-24 (C)
    Lions, 14-0 (D)
1973—Lions, 30-7 (C)
    Lions, 40-7 (D)
1974—Bears, 17-9 (C)
    Lions, 34-17 (D)
1975—Lions, 27-7 (D)
    Bears, 25-21 (C)
1976—Bears, 10-3 (C)
    Lions, 14-10 (D)
1977—Bears, 30-20 (C)
    Bears, 31-14 (D)
1978—Bears, 19-0 (D)
    Lions, 21-17 (C)
1979—Bears, 35-7 (C)
    Lions, 20-0 (D)
1980—Bears, 24-7 (C)

    Bears, 23-17 (D) OT
1981—Lions, 48-17 (D)
    Lions, 23-7 (C)
1982—Lions, 17-10 (D)
    Bears, 20-17 (C)
1983—Lions, 31-17 (D)
    Lions, 38-17 (C)
1984—Bears, 16-14 (C)
    Bears, 30-13 (D)
1985—Bears, 24-3 (C)
    Bears, 37-17 (D)
1986—Bears, 13-7 (C)
    Bears, 16-13 (D)
1987—Bears, 30-10 (C)
1988—Bears, 24-7 (D)
    Bears, 13-12 (C)
1989—Bears, 47-27 (D)
    Lions, 27-17 (C)
1990—Bears, 23-17 (C) OT
    Lions, 38-21 (D)
1991—Bears, 20-10 (C)
    Lions, 16-6 (D)
1992—Bears, 27-24 (C)
    Lions, 16-3 (D)
1993—Bears, 10-6 (D)
    Lions, 20-14 (C)
1994—Lions, 21-16 (D)
    Bears, 20-10 (C)
1995—Lions, 24-17 (C)
    Lions, 27-7 (D)
1996—Lions, 35-16 (D)
    Bears, 31-14 (C)
1997—Lions, 32-7 (C)
    Lions, 55-20 (D)
1998—Bears, 31-27 (C)
    Lions, 26-3 (D)
1999—Lions, 21-17 (D)
    Bears, 28-10 (C)
2000—Lions, 21-14 (C)
    Bears, 23-20 (D)
2001—Bears, 13-10 (C)
    Bears, 24-0 (D)
2002—Lions, 23-20 (D) OT
    Bears, 20-17 (C) OT
2003—Bears, 24-16 (C)
    Lions, 12-10 (D)
2004—Lions, 20-16 (C)
    Lions, 19-13 (D)
2005—Bears, 38-6 (C)
    Bears, 19-13 (D) OT
2006—Bears, 34-7 (C)
    Bears, 26-21 (D)
2007—Lions, 37-27 (D)
    Lions, 16-7 (C)
2008—Bears, 34-7 (D)
    Bears, 27-23 (C)
2009—Bears, 48-24 (C)
    Bears, 37-23 (D)
2010—Bears, 19-14 (C)
    Bears, 24-20 (D)
2011—Lions, 24-13 (D)
    Bears, 37-13 (C)
2012—Bears, 13-7 (C)
    Bears, 26-24 (D)
2013—Lions, 40-32 (D)
    Lions, 21-19 (D)
(RS Pts.—Bears 3,256, Lions 2,956)
*Franchise in Portsmouth prior to 1934
and known as the Spartans
CHICAGO vs. GREEN BAY
RS: Bears lead series, 92-88-6
PS: Series tied, 1-1
1921—Staleys, 20-0 (C)

1923—Bears, 3-0 (GB)
1924—Bears, 3-0 (C)
1925—Packers, 14-10 (GB)
    Bears, 21-0 (C)
1926—Tie, 6-6 (GB)
    Bears, 19-13 (C)
    Tie, 3-3 (C)
1927—Bears, 7-6 (GB)
    Bears, 14-6 (C)
1928—Tie, 12-12 (GB)
    Packers, 16-6 (C)
    Packers, 6-0 (C)
1929—Packers, 23-0 (GB)
    Packers, 14-0 (C)
    Packers, 25-0 (C)
1930—Packers, 7-0 (GB)
    Packers, 13-12 (C)
    Bears, 21-0 (C)
1931—Packers, 7-0 (GB)
    Packers, 6-2 (C)
    Bears, 7-6 (C)
1932—Tie, 0-0 (GB)
    Packers, 2-0 (C)
    Bears, 9-0 (C)
1933—Bears, 14-7 (GB)
    Bears, 10-7 (C)
    Bears, 7-6 (C)
1934—Bears, 24-10 (GB)
    Bears, 27-14 (C)
1935—Bears, 7-0 (GB)
    Packers, 17-14 (C)
1936—Bears, 30-3 (GB)
    Packers, 21-10 (C)
1937—Bears, 14-2 (GB)
    Packers, 24-14 (C)
1938—Bears, 2-0 (GB)
    Packers, 24-17 (C)
1939—Packers, 21-16 (GB)
    Bears, 30-27 (C)
1940—Bears, 41-10 (GB)
    Bears, 14-7 (C)
1941—Bears, 25-17 (GB)
    Packers, 16-14 (C)
    **Bears, 33-14 (C)
1942—Bears, 44-28 (GB)
    Bears, 38-7 (C)
1943—Tie, 21-21 (GB)
    Bears, 21-7 (C)
1944—Packers, 42-28 (GB)
    Bears, 21-0 (C)
1945—Packers, 31-21 (GB)
    Bears, 28-24 (C)
1946—Bears, 30-7 (GB)
    Bears, 10-7 (C)
1947—Packers, 29-20 (GB)
    Bears, 20-17 (C)
1948—Bears, 45-7 (GB)
    Bears, 7-6 (C)
1949—Bears, 17-0 (GB)
    Bears, 24-3 (C)
1950—Packers, 31-21 (GB)
    Bears, 28-14 (C)
1951—Bears, 31-20 (GB)
    Bears, 24-13 (C)
1952—Bears, 24-14 (GB)
    Packers, 41-28 (C)
1953—Bears, 17-13 (GB)
    Tie, 21-21 (C)
1954—Bears, 10-3 (GB)
    Bears, 28-23 (C)
1955—Packers, 24-3 (GB)
    Bears, 52-31 (C)

1956—Bears, 37-21 (GB)
    Bears, 38-14 (C)
1957—Packers, 21-17 (GB)
    Bears, 21-14 (C)
1958—Bears, 34-20 (GB)
    Bears, 24-10 (C)
1959—Packers, 9-6 (GB)
    Bears, 28-17 (C)
1960—Bears, 17-14 (GB)
    Packers, 41-13 (C)
1961—Packers, 24-0 (GB)
    Packers, 31-28 (C)
1962—Packers, 49-0 (GB)
    Packers, 38-7 (C)
1963—Bears, 10-3 (GB)
    Bears, 26-7 (C)
1964—Packers, 23-12 (GB)
    Packers, 17-3 (C)
1965—Packers, 23-14 (GB)
    Bears, 31-10 (C)
1966—Bears, 17-0 (C)
    Packers, 13-6 (GB)
1967—Packers, 13-10 (GB)
    Packers, 17-13 (C)
1968—Bears, 13-10 (GB)
    Packers, 28-27 (C)
1969—Packers, 17-0 (GB)
    Packers, 21-3 (C)
1970—Packers, 20-19 (GB)
    Bears, 35-17 (C)
1971—Packers, 17-14 (C)
    Packers, 31-10 (GB)
1972—Packers, 20-17 (GB)
    Packers, 23-17 (C)
1973—Bears, 31-17 (GB)
    Packers, 21-0 (C)
1974—Bears, 10-9 (C)
    Packers, 20-3 (Mil)
1975—Bears, 27-14 (C)
    Packers, 28-7 (GB)
1976—Bears, 24-13 (C)
    Bears, 16-10 (GB)
1977—Bears, 26-0 (GB)
    Bears, 21-10 (C)
1978—Packers, 24-14 (GB)
    Bears, 14-0 (C)
1979—Bears, 6-3 (C)
    Bears, 15-14 (GB)
1980—Packers, 12-6 (GB) OT
    Bears, 61-7 (C)
1981—Packers, 16-9 (C)
    Packers, 21-17 (GB)
1983—Packers, 31-28 (GB)
    Bears, 23-21 (C)
1984—Bears, 9-7 (GB)
    Packers, 20-14 (C)
1985—Bears, 23-7 (C)
    Bears, 16-10 (GB)
1986—Bears, 25-12 (GB)
    Bears, 12-10 (C)
1987—Bears, 26-24 (GB)
    Bears, 23-10 (C)
1988—Bears, 24-6 (GB)
    Bears, 16-0 (C)
1989—Packers, 14-13 (GB)
    Packers, 40-28 (C)
1990—Bears, 31-13 (GB)
    Bears, 27-13 (C)
1991—Bears, 10-0 (GB)
    Bears, 27-13 (C)
1992—Bears, 30-10 (GB)
    Packers, 17-3 (C)
1993—Packers, 17-3 (GB)

Bears, 30-17 (C)
1994—Packers, 33-6 (C)
    Packers, 40-3 (GB)
1995—Packers, 27-24 (C)
    Packers, 35-28 (GB)
1996—Packers, 37-6 (C)
    Packers, 28-17 (GB)
1997—Packers, 38-24 (GB)
    Packers, 24-23 (C)
1998—Packers, 26-20 (GB)
    Packers, 16-13 (C)
1999—Bears, 14-13 (GB)
    Packers, 35-19 (C)
2000—Bears, 27-24 (GB)
    Packers, 28-6 (C)
2001—Packers, 20-12 (C)
    Packers, 17-7 (GB)
2002—Packers, 34-21 (C)
    Packers, 30-20 (GB)
2003—Packers, 38-23 (C)
    Packers, 34-21 (GB)
2004—Bears, 21-10 (GB)
    Packers, 31-14 (C)
2005—Bears, 19-7 (C)
    Bears, 24-17 (GB)
2006—Bears, 26-0 (GB)
    Packers, 26-7 (C)
2007—Packers, 27-20 (GB)
    Bears, 35-7 (C)
2008—Packers, 37-3 (GB)
    Bears, 20-17 (C) OT
2009—Packers, 21-15 (GB)
    Packers, 21-14 (C)
2010—Packers, 20-17 (C)
    Packers, 10-3 (GB)
    ***Packers, 21-14 (C)
2011—Packers, 27-17 (C)
    Packers, 35-21 (GB)
2012—Packers, 23-10 (GB)
    Packers, 21-13 (C)
2013—Bears, 27-20 (GB)
    Packers, 33-28 (C)
(RS Pts.—Bears 3,176, Packers 3,107)
(PS Pts.—Bears 47, Packers 35)
*Bears known as Staleys prior to 1922
**Division Playoff
***NFC Championship
CHICAGO vs. HOUSTON
RS: Texans lead series, 3-0
2004—Texans, 24-5 (C)
2008—Texans, 31-24 (H)
2012—Texans, 13-6 (C)
(RS Pts.—Texans 68, Bears 35)
CHICAGO vs. *INDIANAPOLIS
RS: Colts lead series, 22-19
PS: Colts lead series, 1-0
1953—Colts, 13-9 (B)
    Colts, 16-14 (C)
1954—Bears, 28-9 (C)
    Bears, 28-13 (B)
1955—Colts, 23-17 (B)
    Colts, 38-10 (C)
1956—Colts, 28-21 (B)
    Bears, 58-27 (C)
1957—Bears, 21-10 (B)
    Colts, 29-14 (C)
1958—Colts, 51-38 (B)
    Colts, 17-0 (C)
1959—Bears, 26-21 (B)
    Colts, 21-7 (C)
1960—Colts, 42-7 (B)
    Colts, 24-20 (C)
1961—Bears, 24-10 (C)

    Bears, 21-20 (B)
1962—Bears, 35-15 (C)
    Bears, 57-0 (B)
1963—Bears, 10-3 (C)
    Bears, 17-7 (B)
1964—Colts, 52-0 (B)
    Colts, 40-24 (C)
1965—Colts, 26-21 (C)
    Bears, 13-0 (B)
1966—Bears, 27-17 (C)
    Colts, 21-16 (B)
1967—Colts, 24-3 (C)
1968—Colts, 28-7 (B)
1969—Colts, 24-21 (C)
1970—Colts, 21-20 (B)
1975—Colts, 35-7 (C)
1983—Colts, 22-19 (B) OT
1985—Bears, 17-10 (C)
1988—Bears, 17-13 (I)
1991—Bears, 31-17 (I)
2000—Bears, 27-24 (C)
2004—Colts, 41-10 (C)
2006—**Colts, 29-17 (South Florida)
2008—Bears, 29-13 (I)
2012—Bears, 41-21 (C)
(RS Pts.—Colts 869, Bears 849)
(PS: Pts.—Colts 29, Bears 17)
*Franchise in Baltimore prior to 1984
**Super Bowl XLI
CHICAGO vs. JACKSONVILLE
RS: Bears lead series, 4-2
1995—Bears, 30-27 (J)
1998—Jaguars, 24-23 (C)
2001—Bears, 33-13 (C)
2004—Jaguars, 22-3 (J)
2008—Bears, 23-10 (C)
2012—Bears, 41-3 (J)
(RS Pts.—Bears 153, Jaguars 99)
CHICAGO vs. KANSAS CITY
RS: Bears lead series, 6-5
1973—Chiefs, 19-7 (KC)
1977—Bears, 28-27 (C)
1981—Bears, 16-13 (KC) OT
1987—Bears, 31-28 (C)
1990—Chiefs, 21-10 (C)
1993—Bears, 19-17 (KC)
1996—Chiefs, 14-10 (KC)
1999—Bears, 20-17 (C)
2003—Chiefs, 31-3 (KC)
2007—Bears, 20-10 (C)
2011—Chiefs, 10-3 (C)
(RS Pts.—Chiefs 207, Bears 167)
CHICAGO vs. MIAMI
RS: Dolphins lead series, 7-4
1971—Dolphins, 34-3 (M)
1975—Dolphins, 46-13 (C)
1979—Dolphins, 31-16 (M)
1985—Dolphins, 38-24 (M)
1988—Bears, 34-7 (C)
1991—Dolphins, 16-13 (C) OT
1994—Bears, 17-14 (M)
1997—Bears, 36-33 (M) OT
2002—Dolphins, 27-9 (M)
2006—Dolphins, 31-13 (C)
2010—Bears, 16-0 (M)
(RS Pts.—Dolphins 277, Bears 194)
CHICAGO vs. MINNESOTA
RS: Vikings lead series, 54-49-2
PS: Bears lead series, 1-0
1961—Vikings, 37-13 (M)
    Bears, 52-35 (C)
1962—Bears, 13-0 (M)
    Bears, 31-30 (C)

1963—Bears, 28-7 (M)
    Tie, 17-17 (C)
1964—Bears, 34-28 (M)
    Vikings, 41-14 (C)
1965—Bears, 45-37 (M)
    Vikings, 24-17 (C)
1966—Bears, 13-10 (M)
    Bears, 41-28 (C)
1967—Bears, 17-7 (M)
    Tie, 10-10 (C)
1968—Bears, 27-17 (M)
    Bears, 26-24 (C)
1969—Vikings, 31-0 (C)
    Vikings, 31-14 (M)
1970—Vikings, 24-0 (C)
    Vikings, 16-13 (M)
1971—Bears, 20-17 (M)
    Vikings, 27-10 (C)
1972—Bears, 13-10 (C)
    Vikings, 23-10 (M)
1973—Vikings, 22-13 (C)
    Vikings, 31-13 (M)
1974—Vikings, 11-7 (M)
    Vikings, 17-0 (C)
1975—Vikings, 28-3 (M)
    Vikings, 13-9 (C)
1976—Vikings, 20-19 (M)
    Bears, 14-13 (C)
1977—Vikings, 22-16 (M) OT
    Bears, 10-7 (C)
1978—Vikings, 24-20 (C)
    Vikings, 17-14 (M)
1979—Bears, 26-7 (C)
    Vikings, 30-27 (M)
1980—Vikings, 34-14 (C)
    Vikings, 13-7 (M)
1981—Vikings, 24-21 (M)
    Bears, 10-9 (C)
1982—Vikings, 35-7 (M)
1983—Vikings, 23-14 (C)
    Bears, 19-13 (M)
1984—Bears, 16-7 (C)
    Bears, 34-3 (M)
1985—Bears, 33-24 (M)
    Bears, 27-9 (C)
1986—Bears, 23-0 (C)
    Vikings, 23-7 (M)
1987—Bears, 27-7 (C)
    Bears, 30-24 (M)
1988—Vikings, 31-7 (C)
    Vikings, 28-27 (M)
1989—Bears, 38-7 (C)
    Vikings, 27-16 (M)
1990—Bears, 19-16 (C)
    Vikings, 41-13 (M)
1991—Bears, 10-6 (C)
    Bears, 34-17 (M)
1992—Vikings, 21-20 (M)
    Vikings, 38-10 (C)
1993—Vikings, 10-7 (M)
    Vikings, 19-12 (C)
1994—Vikings, 42-14 (C)
    Vikings, 33-27 (M) OT
    *Bears, 35-18 (M)
1995—Bears, 31-14 (C)
    Bears, 14-6 (M)
1996—Vikings, 20-14 (C)
    Bears, 15-13 (M)
1997—Vikings, 27-24 (C)
    Vikings, 29-22 (M)
1998—Vikings, 31-28 (C)
    Vikings, 48-22 (M)
1999—Bears, 24-22 (M)

    Vikings, 27-24 (C) OT
2000—Vikings, 30-27 (M)
    Vikings, 28-16 (C)
2001—Bears, 17-10 (C)
    Bears, 13-6 (M)
2002—Bears, 27-23 (C)
    Vikings, 25-7 (M)
2003—Vikings, 24-13 (M)
    Bears, 13-10 (C)
2004—Vikings, 27-22 (M)
    Bears, 24-14 (C)
2005—Bears, 28-3 (C)
    Vikings, 34-10 (M)
2006—Bears, 19-16 (M)
    Bears, 23-13 (C)
2007—Vikings, 34-31 (C)
    Vikings, 20-13 (M)
2008—Bears, 48-41 (C)
    Vikings, 34-14 (M)
2009—Vikings, 36-10 (M)
    Bears, 36-30 (C) OT
2010—Bears, 27-13 (C)
    Bears, 40-14 (M)
2011—Bears, 39-10 (C)
    Bears, 17-13 (M)
2012—Bears, 28-10 (C)
    Vikings, 21-14 (M)
2013—Bears, 31-30 (C)
    Vikings, 23-20 (M) OT
RS Pts.—Vikings 2,206, Bears 2,057)
(PS Pts.—Bears 35, Vikings 18)
*NFC First-Round Playoff
CHICAGO vs. NEW ENGLAND
RS: Patriots lead series, 8-3
PS: Bears lead series, 1-0
1973—Patriots, 13-10 (C)
1979—Patriots, 27-7 (C)
1982—Bears, 26-13 (C)
1985—Bears, 20-7 (C)
    *Bears, 46-10 (New Orleans)
1988—Patriots, 30-7 (NE)
1994—Patriots, 13-3 (C)
1997—Patriots, 31-3 (NE)
2000—Bears, 24-17 (C)
2002—Patriots, 33-30 (C)
2006—Patriots, 17-13 (NE)
2010—Patriots, 36-7 (C)
(RS Pts.—Patriots 237, Bears 150)
(PS Pts.—Bears 46, Patriots 10)
*Super Bowl XX
CHICAGO vs. NEW ORLEANS
RS: Series tied, 13-13
PS: Bears lead series, 2-0
1968—Bears, 23-17 (NO)
1970—Bears, 24-3 (NO)
1971—Bears, 35-14 (C)
1973—Saints, 21-16 (NO)
1974—Bears, 24-10 (C)
1975—Bears, 42-17 (NO)
1977—Saints, 42-24 (C)
1980—Bears, 22-3 (C)
1982—Saints, 10-0 (C)
1983—Saints, 34-31 (NO) OT
1984—Bears, 20-7 (C)
1987—Saints, 19-17 (C)
1990—*Bears, 16-6 (C)
1991—Bears, 20-17 (NO)
1992—Saints, 28-6 (NO)
1994—Bears, 17-7 (C)
1996—Saints, 27-24 (NO)
1997—Saints, 20-17 (C)
1999—Bears, 14-10 (C)
2000—Saints, 31-10 (C)

2002—Saints, 29-23 (C)
2003—Saints, 20-13 (NO)
2005—Bears, 20-17 (Baton Rouge)
2006—**Bears, 39-14 (C)
2007—Bears, 33-25 (C)
2008—Bears, 27-24 (C) OT
2011—Saints, 30-13 (NO)
2013—Saints, 26-18 (C)
(RS Pts.—Bears 533, Saints 508)
(PS Pts.—Bears 55, Saints 20)
*NFC First-Round Playoff
**NFC Championship
CHICAGO vs. N.Y. GIANTS
RS: Bears lead series, 28-19-2
PS: Bears lead series, 5-3
1925—Bears, 19-7 (NY)
    Giants, 9-0 (C)
1926—Bears, 7-0 (C)
1927—Giants, 13-7 (NY)
1928—Bears, 13-0 (C)
1929—Giants, 26-14 (C)
    Giants, 34-0 (NY)
    Giants, 14-9 (C)
1930—Giants, 12-0 (C)
    Bears, 12-0 (NY)
1931—Bears, 6-0 (C)
    Bears, 12-6 (NY)
    Giants, 25-6 (C)
1932—Bears, 28-8 (NY)
    Bears, 6-0 (C)
1933—Bears, 14-10 (C)
    Giants, 3-0 (NY)
    *Bears, 23-21 (C)
1934—Bears, 27-7 (C)
    Bears, 10-9 (NY)
    *Giants, 30-13 (NY)
1935—Bears, 20-3 (NY)
    Giants, 3-0 (C)
1936—Bears, 25-7 (NY)
1937—Tie, 3-3 (NY)
1939—Giants, 16-13 (NY)
1940—Bears, 37-21 (NY)
1941—*Bears, 37-9 (C)
1942—Bears, 26-7 (NY)
1943—Bears, 56-7 (NY)
1946—Giants, 14-0 (NY)
    *Bears, 24-14 (NY)
1948—Bears, 35-14 (C)
1949—Bears, 35-28 (NY)
1956—Tie, 17-17 (NY)
    *Giants, 47-7 (NY)
1962—Giants, 26-24 (C)
1963—*Bears, 14-10 (C)
1965—Bears, 35-14 (NY)
1967—Bears, 34-7 (C)
1969—Giants, 28-24 (NY)
1970—Bears, 24-16 (NY)
1974—Bears, 16-13 (C)
1977—Bears, 12-9 (NY) OT
1985—**Bears, 21-0 (C)
1987—Bears, 34-19 (C)
1990—**Giants, 31-3 (NY)
1991—Bears, 20-17 (C)
1992—Giants, 27-14 (C)
1993—Giants, 26-20 (C)
1995—Bears, 27-24 (NY)
2000—Giants, 14-7 (C)
2004—Bears, 28-21 (NY)
2006—Bears, 38-20 (NY)
2007—Giants, 21-16 (C)
2010—Giants, 17-3 (NY)
2013—Bears, 27-21 (C)
(RS Pts.—Bears 853, Giants 670)

(PS Pts.—Giants 162, Bears 142)
*NFL Championship
**NFC Divisional Playoff
CHICAGO vs. N.Y. JETS
RS: Bears lead series, 7-3
1974—Jets, 23-21 (C)
1979—Bears, 23-13 (C)
1985—Bears, 19-6 (NY)
1991—Bears, 19-13 (C) OT
1994—Bears, 19-7 (NY)
1997—Jets, 23-15 (C)
2000—Jets, 17-10 (NY)
2002—Bears, 20-13 (C)
2006—Bears, 10-0 (NY)
2010—Bears, 38-34 (C)
(RS Pts.—Bears 194, Jets 149)
CHICAGO vs. *OAKLAND
RS: Raiders lead series, 7-6
1972—Raiders, 28-21 (O)
1976—Raiders, 28-27 (C)
1978—Raiders, 25-19 (C) OT
1981—Bears, 23-6 (O)
1984—Bears, 17-6 (C)
1987—Bears, 6-3 (LA)
1990—Raiders, 24-10 (LA)
1993—Raiders, 16-14 (C)
1996—Bears, 19-17 (C)
1999—Raiders, 24-17 (O)
2003—Bears, 24-21 (C)
2007—Bears, 17-6 (O)
2011—Raiders, 25-20 (O)
(RS Pts.—Bears 234, Raiders 229)
*Franchise in Los Angeles from 1982-1994
CHICAGO vs. PHILADELPHIA
RS: Bears lead series, 28-10-1
PS: Eagles lead series, 2-1
1933—Tie, 3-3 (P)
1935—Bears, 39-0 (P)
1936—Bears, 17-0 (P)
          Bears, 28-7 (P)
1938—Bears, 28-6 (P)
1939—Bears, 27-14 (C)
1941—Bears, 49-14 (C)
1942—Bears, 45-14 (C)
1944—Bears, 28-7 (P)
1946—Bears, 21-14 (C)
1947—Bears, 40-7 (C)
1948—Eagles, 12-7 (P)
1949—Bears, 38-21 (C)
1955—Bears, 17-10 (C)
1961—Eagles, 16-14 (P)
1963—Bears, 16-7 (C)
1968—Bears, 29-16 (P)
1970—Bears, 20-16 (C)
1972—Bears, 21-12 (P)
1975—Bears, 15-13 (C)
1979—*Eagles, 27-17 (P)
1980—Eagles, 17-14 (P)
1983—Bears, 7-6 (P)
          Bears, 17-14 (C)
1986—Bears, 13-10 (C) OT
1987—Bears, 35-3 (P)
1988—**Bears, 20-12 (C)
1989—Bears, 27-13 (C)
1993—Bears, 17-6 (P)
1994—Eagles, 30-22 (P)
1995—Bears, 20-14 (C)
1999—Eagles, 20-16 (C)
2000—Eagles, 13-9 (P)
2001—**Eagles, 33-19 (C)
2002—Eagles, 19-13 (C)
2004—Eagles, 19-9 (C)
2007—Bears, 19-16 (P)

2008—Bears, 24-20 (C)
2009—Eagles, 24-20 (C)
2010—Bears, 31-26 (C)
2011—Bears, 30-24 (P)
2013—Eagles, 54-11 (P)
(RS Pts.—Bears 856, Eagles 557)
(PS Pts.—Eagles 72, Bears 56)
*NFC First-Round Playoff
**NFC Divisional Playoff
CHICAGO vs. *PITTSBURGH
RS: Bears lead series, 18-7-1
1934—Bears, 28-0 (P)
1935—Bears, 23-7 (P)
1936—Bears, 27-9 (P)
          Bears, 26-7 (C)
1937—Bears, 7-0 (P)
1939—Bears, 32-0 (P)
1941—Bears, 34-7 (C)
1945—Bears, 28-7 (C)
1947—Bears, 49-7 (C)
1949—Bears, 30-21 (C)
1958—Steelers, 24-10 (P)
1959—Bears, 27-21 (C)
1963—Tie, 17-17 (P)
1967—Steelers, 41-13 (P)
1969—Bears, 38-7 (C)
1971—Bears, 17-15 (C)
1975—Steelers, 34-3 (P)
1980—Steelers, 38-3 (P)
1986—Bears, 13-10 (C) OT
1989—Bears, 20-0 (P)
1992—Bears, 30-6 (C)
1995—Steelers, 37-34 (C) OT
1998—Steelers, 17-12 (P)
2005—Steelers, 21-9 (P)
2009—Bears, 17-14 (C)
2013—Bears, 40-23 (P)
(RS Pts.—Bears 587, Steelers 390)
*Steelers known as Pirates prior to 1940
CHICAGO vs. *ST. LOUIS
RS: Bears lead series, 51-35-3
PS: Series tied, 1-1
1937—Bears, 20-2 (Cle)
          Bears, 15-7 (C)
1938—Rams, 14-7 (C)
          Rams, 23-21 (Cle)
1939—Bears, 30-21 (Cle)
          Bears, 35-21 (C)
1940—Bears, 21-14 (Cle)
          Bears, 47-25 (C)
1941—Bears, 48-21 (Cle)
          Bears, 31-13 (C)
1942—Bears, 21-7 (Cle)
          Bears, 47-0 (C)
1944—Rams, 19-7 (Cle)
          Bears, 28-21 (C)
1945—Rams, 17-0 (Cle)
          Rams, 41-21 (C)
1946—Tie, 28-28 (C)
          Bears, 27-21 (LA)
1947—Bears, 41-21 (LA)
          Rams, 17-14 (C)
1948—Bears, 42-21 (C)
          Bears, 21-6 (LA)
1949—Rams, 31-16 (C)
          Rams, 27-24 (LA)
1950—Bears, 24-20 (LA)
          Bears, 24-14 (C)
          **Rams, 24-14 (LA)
1951—Rams, 42-17 (C)
1952—Rams, 31-7 (LA)
          Rams, 40-24 (C)
1953—Rams, 38-24 (LA)

          Bears, 24-21 (C)
1954—Rams, 42-38 (LA)
          Bears, 24-13 (C)
1955—Bears, 31-20 (LA)
          Bears, 24-3 (C)
1956—Bears, 35-24 (LA)
          Bears, 30-21 (C)
1957—Bears, 34-26 (C)
          Bears, 16-10 (LA)
1958—Bears, 31-10 (C)
          Rams, 41-35 (LA)
1959—Rams, 28-21 (C)
          Bears, 26-21 (LA)
1960—Bears, 34-27 (C)
          Tie, 24-24 (LA)
1961—Bears, 21-17 (LA)
          Bears, 28-24 (C)
1962—Bears, 27-23 (C)
          Bears, 30-14 (C)
1963—Bears, 52-14 (LA)
          Bears, 6-0 (C)
1964—Bears, 38-17 (C)
          Bears, 34-24 (LA)
1965—Rams, 30-28 (LA)
          Bears, 31-6 (C)
1966—Rams, 31-17 (LA)
          Bears, 17-10 (C)
1967—Rams, 28-17 (C)
1968—Bears, 17-16 (LA)
1969—Rams, 9-7 (C)
1971—Rams, 17-3 (LA)
1972—Tie, 13-13 (C)
1973—Rams, 26-0 (C)
1975—Bears, 38-10 (LA)
1976—Rams, 20-12 (LA)
1977—Bears, 24-23 (C)
1979—Bears, 27-23 (C)
1981—Bears, 24-7 (C)
1982—Bears, 34-26 (LA)
1983—Rams, 21-14 (LA)
1984—Rams, 29-13 (LA)
1985—***Bears, 24-0 (C)
1986—Bears, 20-17 (C)
1988—Rams, 23-3 (LA)
1989—Bears, 20-10 (C)
1990—Rams, 38-9 (C)
1993—Rams, 20-6 (LA)
1994—Bears, 27-13 (C)
1995—Rams, 34-28 (StL)
1996—Bears, 35-9 (C)
1997—Bears, 13-10 (StL)
1998—Rams, 20-12 (C)
1999—Rams, 34-12 (StL)
2002—Rams, 21-16 (StL)
2003—Rams, 23-21 (C)
2006—Bears, 42-27 (StL)
2008—Bears, 27-3 (StL)
2009—Bears, 17-9 (C)
2012—Bears, 23-6 (C)
2013—Rams, 42-21 (StL)
(RS Pts.—Bears 2,064, Rams 1,810)
(PS Pts.—Bears 38, Rams 24)
*Franchise in Los Angeles prior to 1995
and in Cleveland prior to 1946
**Conference Playoff
***NFC Championship
CHICAGO vs. SAN DIEGO
RS: Bears lead series, 6-5
1970—Chargers, 20-7 (C)
1974—Chargers, 28-21 (SD)
1978—Chargers, 40-7 (SD)
1981—Bears, 20-17 (C) OT
1984—Chargers, 20-7 (SD)

1993—Bears, 16-13 (SD)
1996—Bears, 27-14 (C)
1999—Bears, 23-20 (SD) OT
2003—Bears, 20-7 (C)
2007—Chargers, 14-3 (SD)
2011—Bears, 31-20 (C)
(RS Pts.—Chargers 213, Bears 182)
CHICAGO vs. SAN FRANCISCO
RS: Series tied, 29-29-1
PS: 49ers lead series, 3-0
1950—Bears, 32-20 (SF)
    Bears, 17-0 (C)
1951—Bears, 13-7 (C)
1952—49ers, 40-16 (C)
    Bears, 20-17 (SF)
1953—49ers, 35-28 (C)
    49ers, 24-14 (SF)
1954—49ers, 31-24 (C)
    Bears, 31-27 (SF)
1955—49ers, 20-19 (C)
    Bears, 34-23 (SF)
1956—Bears, 31-7 (C)
    Bears, 38-21 (SF)
1957—49ers, 21-17 (C)
    49ers, 21-17 (SF)
1958—Bears, 28-6 (C)
    Bears, 27-14 (SF)
1959—49ers, 20-17 (SF)
    Bears, 14-3 (C)
1960—Bears, 27-10 (C)
    49ers, 25-7 (SF)
1961—Bears, 31-0 (C)
    49ers, 41-31 (SF)
1962—Bears, 30-14 (SF)
    49ers, 34-27 (C)
1963—49ers, 20-14 (SF)
    Bears, 27-7 (C)
1964—49ers, 31-21 (SF)
    Bears, 23-21 (C)
1965—49ers, 52-24 (SF)
    Bears, 61-20 (C)
1966—Tie, 30-30 (C)
    49ers, 41-14 (SF)
1967—Bears, 28-14 (SF)
1968—Bears, 27-19 (C)
1969—49ers, 42-21 (C)
1970—49ers, 37-16 (C)
1971—49ers, 13-0 (SF)
1972—49ers, 34-21 (C)
1974—49ers, 34-0 (C)
1975—49ers, 31-3 (SF)
1976—Bears, 19-12 (SF)
1978—Bears, 16-13 (SF)
1979—Bears, 28-27 (SF)
1981—49ers, 28-17 (SF)
1983—Bears, 13-3 (C)
1984—*49ers, 23-0 (SF)
1985—Bears, 26-10 (SF)
1987—49ers, 41-0 (SF)
1988—Bears, 10-9 (C)
    *49ers, 28-3 (C)
1989—49ers, 26-0 (SF)
1991—49ers, 52-14 (SF)
1994—**49ers, 44-15 (SF)
2000—49ers, 17-0 (SF)
2001—Bears, 37-31 (C) OT
2003—49ers, 49-7 (SF)
2004—Bears, 23-13 (C)
2005—Bears, 17-9 (C)
2006—Bears, 41-10 (C)
2009—Bears, 10-6 (SF)
2012—49ers, 32-7 (SF)
(RS Pts.—49ers 1,319, Bears 1,201)

(PS Pts.—49ers 95, Bears 18)
*NFC Championship
**NFC Divisional Playoff
CHICAGO vs. SEATTLE
RS: Seahawks lead series, 10-4
PS: Bears lead series, 2-0
1976—Bears, 34-7 (S)
1978—Seahawks, 31-29 (C)
1982—Seahawks, 20-14 (S)
1984—Seahawks, 38-9 (S)
1987—Seahawks, 34-21 (C)
1990—Bears, 17-0 (C)
1999—Seahawks, 14-13 (C)
2003—Seahawks, 24-17 (S)
2006—Bears, 37-6 (C)
    *Bears, 27-24 (C) OT
2007—Seahawks, 30-23 (S)
2009—Bears, 25-19 (S)
2010—Seahawks, 23-20 (C)
    *Bears, 35-24 (C)
2011—Seahawks, 38-14 (C)
2012—Seahawks, 23-17 (C) OT
(RS Pts.—Seahawks 307, Bears 290)
(PS Pts.—Bears 62, Seahawks 48)
*NFC Divisional Playoff
CHICAGO vs. TAMPA BAY
RS: Bears lead series, 36-18
1977—Bears, 10-0 (TB)
1978—Buccaneers, 33-19 (TB)
    Bears, 14-3 (C)
1979—Buccaneers, 17-13 (C)
    Bears, 14-0 (TB)
1980—Bears, 23-0 (C)
    Bears, 14-13 (TB)
1981—Bears, 28-17 (C)
    Buccaneers, 20-10 (TB)
1982—Buccaneers, 26-23 (TB) OT
1983—Bears, 17-10 (C)
    Bears, 27-0 (TB)
1984—Bears, 34-14 (C)
    Bears, 44-9 (TB)
1985—Bears, 38-28 (C)
    Bears, 27-19 (TB)
1986—Bears, 23-3 (TB)
    Bears, 48-14 (C)
1987—Bears, 20-3 (C)
    Bears, 27-26 (TB)
1988—Bears, 28-10 (C)
    Bears, 27-15 (TB)
1989—Buccaneers, 42-35 (TB)
    Buccaneers, 32-31 (C)
1990—Bears, 26-6 (TB)
    Bears, 27-14 (C)
1991—Bears, 21-20 (TB)
    Bears, 27-0 (C)
1992—Bears, 31-14 (C)
    Buccaneers, 20-17 (TB)
1993—Bears, 47-17 (C)
    Buccaneers, 13-10 (TB)
1994—Bears, 21-9 (C)
    Bears, 20-6 (TB)
1995—Bears, 25-6 (TB)
    Bears, 31-10 (C)
1996—Bears, 13-10 (C)
    Buccaneers, 34-19 (TB)
1997—Bears, 13-7 (C)
    Buccaneers, 31-15 (TB)
1998—Buccaneers, 27-15 (TB)
    Buccaneers, 31-17 (C)
1999—Buccaneers, 6-3 (TB)
    Buccaneers, 20-6 (C)
2000—Buccaneers, 41-0 (TB)
    Bears, 13-10 (C)

2001—Bears, 27-24 (TB)
    Bears, 27-3 (C)
2002—Buccaneers, 15-0 (C)
2004—Buccaneers, 19-7 (TB)
2005—Bears, 13-10 (TB)
2006—Bears, 34-31 (C) OT
2008—Buccaneers, 27-24 (C) OT
2011—Bears, 24-18 (London)
(RS Pts.—Bears 1,167, Buccaneers 853)
CHICAGO vs. *TENNESSEE
RS: Bears lead series, 6-5
1973—Bears, 35-14 (C)
1977—Oilers, 47-0 (H)
1980—Oilers, 10-6 (H)
1986—Bears, 20-7 (H)
1989—Oilers, 33-28 (C)
1992—Oilers, 24-7 (H)
1995—Bears, 35-32 (C)
1998—Bears, 23-20 (T)
2004—Bears, 19-17 (T) OT
2008—Titans, 21-14 (C)
2012—Bears, 51-20 (T)
(RS Pts.—Titans 245, Bears 238)
*Franchise in Houston prior to 1997;
known as Oilers prior to 1999
CHICAGO vs. *WASHINGTON
RS: Bears lead series, 20-20-1
PS: Redskins lead series, 4-3
1932—Tie, 7-7 (B)
1933—Bears, 7-0 (C)
    Redskins, 10-0 (B)
1934—Bears, 21-0 (B)
1935—Bears, 30-14 (B)
1936—Bears, 26-0 (B)
1937—**Redskins, 28-21 (C)
1938—Bears, 31-7 (C)
1940—Redskins, 7-3 (W)
    **Bears, 73-0 (W)
1941—Bears, 35-21 (C)
1942—**Redskins, 14-6 (W)
1943—Redskins, 21-7 (W)
    **Bears, 41-21 (C)
1945—Redskins, 28-21 (C)
1946—Bears, 24-20 (C)
1947—Bears, 56-20 (W)
1948—Bears, 48-13 (C)
1949—Bears, 31-21 (W)
1951—Bears, 27-0 (W)
1953—Bears, 27-24 (W)
1957—Redskins, 14-3 (C)
1964—Redskins, 27-20 (W)
1968—Redskins, 38-28 (C)
1971—Bears, 16-15 (C)
1974—Redskins, 42-0 (W)
1976—Bears, 33-7 (C)
1978—Bears, 14-10 (W)
1980—Bears, 35-21 (C)
1981—Redskins, 24-7 (C)
1984—***Bears, 23-19 (W)
1985—Bears, 45-10 (C)
1986—***Redskins, 27-13 (C)
1987—***Redskins, 21-17 (C)
1988—Bears, 34-14 (W)
1989—Redskins, 38-14 (W)
1990—Redskins, 10-9 (W)
1991—Bears, 20-7 (C)
1996—Redskins, 10-3 (C)
1997—Redskins, 31-8 (C)
1999—Redskins, 48-22 (W)
2001—Bears, 20-15 (W)
2003—Bears, 27-24 (C)
2004—Redskins, 13-10 (C)
2005—Redskins, 9-7 (W)

2007—Redskins, 24-16 (W)
2010—Redskins, 17-14 (C)
2013—Redskins, 45-41 (W)
(RS Pts.—Bears 834, Redskins 739)
(PS Pts.—Bears 194, Redskins 130)
*Franchise in Boston prior to 1937 and
known as Braves prior to 1933
**NFL Championship
***NFC Divisional Playoff

CINCINNATI vs. ARIZONA
RS: Bengals lead series, 6-4;
See Arizona vs. Cincinnati
CINCINNATI vs. ATLANTA
RS: Bengals lead series, 7-5;
See Atlanta vs. Cincinnati
CINCINNATI vs. BALTIMORE
RS: Ravens lead series, 20-16;
See Baltimore vs. Cincinnati
CINCINNATI vs. BUFFALO
RS: Bills lead series, 15-11
PS: Bengals lead series, 2-0;
See Buffalo vs. Cincinnati
CINCINNATI vs. CAROLINA
RS: Series tied, 2-2;
See Carolina vs. Cincinnati
CINCINNATI vs. CHICAGO
RS: Bengals lead series, 6-4;
See Chicago vs. Cincinnati
CINCINNATI vs. CLEVELAND
RS: Bengals lead series, 43-38
1970—Browns, 30-27 (Cle)
　　　　Bengals, 14-10 (Cin)
1971—Browns, 27-24 (Cin)
　　　　Browns, 31-27 (Cle)
1972—Browns, 27-6 (Cle)
　　　　Browns, 27-24 (Cin)
1973—Browns, 17-10 (Cle)
　　　　Bengals, 34-17 (Cin)
1974—Bengals, 33-7 (Cin)
　　　　Bengals, 34-24 (Cle)
1975—Bengals, 24-17 (Cin)
　　　　Browns, 35-23 (Cle)
1976—Bengals, 45-24 (Cle)
　　　　Bengals, 21-6 (Cin)
1977—Browns, 13-3 (Cin)
　　　　Bengals, 10-7 (Cle)
1978—Browns, 13-10 (Cle) OT
　　　　Bengals, 48-16 (Cin)
1979—Browns, 28-27 (Cle)
　　　　Bengals, 16-12 (Cin)
1980—Browns, 31-7 (Cle)
　　　　Browns, 27-24 (Cin)
1981—Browns, 20-17 (Cin)
　　　　Bengals, 41-21 (Cle)
1982—Bengals, 23-10 (Cin)
1983—Browns, 17-7 (Cle)
　　　　Bengals, 28-21 (Cin)
1984—Bengals, 12-9 (Cin)
　　　　Bengals, 20-17 (Cle) OT
1985—Bengals, 27-10 (Cle)
　　　　Browns, 24-6 (Cle)
1986—Bengals, 30-13 (Cle)
　　　　Browns, 34-3 (Cin)
1987—Browns, 34-0 (Cin)
　　　　Browns, 38-24 (Cle)
1988—Bengals, 24-17 (Cin)
　　　　Browns, 23-16 (Cle)
1989—Bengals, 21-14 (Cin)
　　　　Bengals, 21-0 (Cle)
1990—Bengals, 34-13 (Cin)
　　　　Bengals, 21-14 (Cin)
1991—Browns, 14-13 (Cle)

Bengals, 23-21 (Cin)
1992—Bengals, 30-10 (Cin)
　　　　Browns, 37-21 (Cle)
1993—Browns, 27-14 (Cle)
　　　　Browns, 28-17 (Cin)
1994—Browns, 28-20 (Cin)
　　　　Browns, 37-13 (Cle)
1995—Browns, 29-26 (Cin) OT
　　　　Browns, 26-10 (Cle)
1999—Bengals, 18-17 (Cle)
　　　　Bengals, 44-28 (Cin)
2000—Browns, 24-7 (Cin)
　　　　Bengals, 12-3 (Cle)
2001—Bengals, 24-14 (Cin)
　　　　Browns, 18-0 (Cle)
2002—Bengals, 20-7 (Cin)
　　　　Browns, 27-20 (Cin)
2003—Bengals, 21-14 (Cle)
　　　　Browns, 22-14 (Cin)
2004—Browns, 34-17 (Cle)
　　　　Bengals, 58-48 (Cin)
2005—Bengals, 27-13 (Cle)
　　　　Bengals, 23-20 (Cin)
2006—Bengals, 34-17 (Cin)
　　　　Bengals, 30-0 (Cle)
2007—Browns, 51-45 (Cle)
　　　　Bengals, 19-14 (Cin)
2008—Browns, 20-12 (Cin)
　　　　Bengals, 14-0 (Cle)
2009—Bengals, 23-20 (Cle) OT
　　　　Bengals, 16-7 (Cin)
2010—Bengals, 23-20 (Cle)
　　　　Bengals, 19-17 (Cin)
2011—Bengals, 27-17 (Cin)
　　　　Bengals, 23-20 (Cin)
2012—Bengals, 34-27 (Cin)
　　　　Browns, 34-24 (Cle)
2013—Bengals, 17-6 (Cle)
　　　　Bengals, 41-20 (Cin)
(RS Pts.—Bengals 1,732, Browns 1,658)
CINCINNATI vs. DALLAS
RS: Cowboys lead series, 7-4
1973—Cowboys, 38-10 (D)
1979—Cowboys, 38-13 (D)
1985—Cowboys, 50-24 (C)
1988—Bengals, 38-24 (D)
1991—Cowboys, 35-23 (D)
1994—Cowboys, 23-20 (C)
1997—Bengals, 31-24 (C)
2000—Cowboys, 23-6 (D)
2004—Bengals, 26-3 (C)
2008—Cowboys, 31-22 (D)
2012—Cowboys, 20-19 (C)
(RS Pts.—Cowboys 283, Bengals 258)
CINCINNATI vs. DENVER
RS: Broncos lead series, 19-8
1968—Bengals, 24-10 (C)
　　　　Broncos, 10-7 (D)
1969—Bengals, 30-23 (C)
　　　　Broncos, 27-16 (D)
1971—Bengals, 24-10 (C)
1972—Bengals, 21-10 (C)
1973—Bengals, 28-10 (D)
1975—Bengals, 17-16 (D)
1976—Bengals, 17-7 (C)
1977—Broncos, 24-13 (C)
1979—Broncos, 10-0 (D)
1981—Bengals, 38-21 (C)
1983—Broncos, 24-17 (D)
1984—Broncos, 20-17 (D)
1986—Broncos, 34-28 (D)
1991—Broncos, 45-14 (D)
1994—Broncos, 15-13 (D)

1996—Broncos, 14-10 (C)
1997—Broncos, 38-20 (D)
1998—Broncos, 33-26 (C)
2000—Bengals, 31-21 (C)
2003—Broncos, 30-10 (C)
2004—Bengals, 23-10 (C)
2006—Broncos, 24-23 (D)
2009—Bengals, 12-7 (C)
2011—Broncos, 24-22 (D)
2012—Broncos, 31-23 (C)
(RS Pts.—Broncos 578, Bengals 494)
CINCINNATI vs. DETROIT
RS: Bengals lead series, 8-3
1970—Lions, 38-3 (D)
1974—Lions, 23-19 (C)
1983—Bengals, 17-9 (C)
1986—Bengals, 24-17 (D)
1989—Bengals, 42-7 (C)
1992—Lions, 19-13 (C)
1998—Bengals, 34-28 (D) OT
2001—Bengals, 31-27 (D)
2005—Bengals, 41-17 (D)
2009—Bengals, 23-13 (C)
2013—Bengals, 27-24 (D)
(RS Pts.—Bengals 274, Lions 222)
CINCINNATI vs. GREEN BAY
RS: Bengals lead series, 7-5
1971—Packers, 20-17 (GB)
1976—Bengals, 28-7 (C)
1977—Bengals, 17-7 (Mil)
1980—Packers, 14-9 (GB)
1983—Bengals, 34-14 (C)
1986—Bengals, 34-28 (Mil)
1992—Packers, 24-23 (GB)
1995—Packers, 24-10 (GB)
1998—Packers, 13-6 (C)
2005—Bengals, 21-14 (C)
2009—Bengals, 31-24 (GB)
2013—Bengals, 34-30 (C)
(RS Pts.—Bengals 264, Packers 219)
CINCINNATI vs. HOUSTON
RS: Series tied, 3-3
PS: Texans lead series, 2-0
2002—Bengals, 38-3 (H)
2003—Bengals, 34-27 (C)
2005—Bengals, 16-10 (C)
2008—Texans, 35-6 (H)
2009—Texans, 28-17 (C)
2011—Texans, 20-19 (C)
　　　　*Texans, 31-10 (H)
2012—*Texans, 19-13 (H)
(RS Pts.—Bengals 130, Texans 123)
(PS Pts.—Texans 50, Bengals 23)
*AFC First-Round Playoff
CINCINNATI vs. *INDIANAPOLIS
RS: Colts lead series, 16-10
PS: Colts lead series, 1-0
1970—**Colts, 17-0 (B)
1972—Colts, 20-19 (C)
1974—Bengals, 24-14 (B)
1976—Colts, 28-27 (B)
1979—Colts, 38-28 (B)
1980—Bengals, 34-33 (C)
1981—Bengals, 41-19 (B)
1982—Bengals, 20-17 (B)
1983—Colts, 34-31 (C)
1987—Bengals, 23-21 (I)
1989—Colts, 23-12 (C)
1990—Colts, 34-20 (C)
1992—Colts, 21-17 (C)
1993—Colts, 9-6 (C)
1994—Colts, 17-13 (C)
1995—Bengals, 24-21 (I) OT

1996—Bengals, 31-24 (C)
1997—Bengals, 28-13 (I)
1998—Colts, 39-26 (I)
1999—Colts, 31-10 (I)
2002—Colts, 28-21 (I)
2005—Colts, 45-37 (C)
2006—Colts, 34-16 (I)
2008—Colts, 35-3 (I)
2010—Colts, 23-17 (I)
2011—Bengals, 27-17 (C)
2013—Bengals, 42-28 (C)
(RS Pts.—Colts 666, Bengals 597)
(PS Pts.—Colts 17, Bengals 0)
*Franchise in Baltimore prior to 1984
**AFC Divisional Playoff
CINCINNATI vs. JACKSONVILLE
RS: Jaguars lead series, 11-8
1995—Bengals, 24-17 (C)
    Bengals, 17-13 (J)
1996—Bengals, 28-21 (C)
    Jaguars, 30-27 (J)
1997—Jaguars, 21-13 (J)
    Bengals, 31-26 (C)
1998—Jaguars, 24-11 (J)
    Jaguars, 34-17 (C)
1999—Jaguars, 41-10 (C)
    Jaguars, 24-7 (J)
2000—Jaguars, 13-0 (J)
    Bengals, 17-14 (C)
2001—Jaguars, 30-13 (J)
    Jaguars, 14-10 (C)
2002—Jaguars, 29-15 (C)
2005—Jaguars, 23-20 (J)
2008—Bengals, 21-19 (C)
2011—Bengals, 30-20 (J)
2012—Bengals, 27-10 (J)
(RS Pts.—Jaguars 423, Bengals 338)
CINCINNATI vs. KANSAS CITY
RS: Bengals lead series, 14-13
1968—Chiefs, 13-3 (KC)
    Chiefs, 16-9 (C)
1969—Bengals, 24-19 (C)
    Chiefs, 42-22 (KC)
1970—Chiefs, 27-19 (C)
1972—Bengals, 23-16 (KC)
1973—Bengals, 14-6 (C)
1974—Bengals, 33-6 (C)
1976—Bengals, 27-24 (KC)
1977—Bengals, 27-7 (KC)
1978—Chiefs, 24-23 (C)
1979—Chiefs, 10-7 (C)
1980—Bengals, 20-6 (KC)
1983—Chiefs, 20-15 (KC)
1984—Chiefs, 27-22 (C)
1986—Chiefs, 24-14 (KC)
1987—Bengals, 30-27 (C) OT
1988—Chiefs, 31-28 (KC)
1989—Bengals, 21-17 (KC)
1993—Chiefs, 17-15 (KC)
2003—Bengals, 24-19 (C)
2005—Chiefs, 37-3 (KC)
2006—Bengals, 23-10 (KC)
2007—Chiefs, 27-20 (KC)
2008—Bengals, 16-6 (C)
2009—Bengals, 17-10 (C)
2012—Bengals, 28-6 (KC)
(RS Pts.—Bengals 527, Chiefs 494)
CINCINNATI vs. MIAMI
RS: Dolphins lead series, 15-5
PS: Dolphins lead series, 1-0
1968—Dolphins, 24-22 (C)
    Bengals, 38-21 (M)
1969—Bengals, 27-21 (C)

1971—Dolphins, 23-13 (C)
1973—*Dolphins, 34-16 (M)
1974—Dolphins, 24-3 (M)
1977—Bengals, 23-17 (C)
1978—Bengals, 21-0 (M)
1980—Dolphins, 17-16 (M)
1983—Dolphins, 38-14 (M)
1987—Dolphins, 20-14 (C)
1989—Dolphins, 20-13 (C)
1991—Dolphins, 37-13 (M)
1994—Dolphins, 23-7 (C)
1995—Dolphins, 26-23 (C)
2000—Dolphins, 31-16 (C)
2004—Bengals, 16-13 (C)
2007—Bengals, 38-25 (M)
2010—Dolphins, 22-14 (C)
2012—Dolphins, 17-13 (C)
2013—Dolphins, 22-20 (M) OT
(RS Pts.—Dolphins 462, Bengals 343)
(PS Pts.—Dolphins 34, Bengals 16)
*AFC Divisional Playoff
CINCINNATI vs. MINNESOTA
RS: Series tied, 6-6
1973—Bengals, 27-0 (C)
1977—Vikings, 42-10 (M)
1980—Bengals, 14-0 (C)
1983—Vikings, 20-14 (M)
1986—Bengals, 24-20 (C)
1989—Vikings, 29-21 (M)
1992—Vikings, 42-7 (C)
1995—Bengals, 27-24 (C)
1998—Vikings, 24-3 (M)
2005—Bengals, 37-8 (C)
2009—Vikings, 30-10 (M)
2013—Bengals, 42-14 (C)
(RS Pts.—Vikings 253, Bengals 236)
CINCINNATI vs. *NEW ENGLAND
RS: Patriots lead series, 14-9
1968—Patriots, 33-14 (B)
1969—Patriots, 25-14 (C)
1970—Bengals, 45-7 (C)
1972—Bengals, 31-7 (NE)
1975—Bengals, 27-10 (C)
1978—Patriots, 10-3 (C)
1979—Patriots, 20-14 (C)
1984—Patriots, 20-14 (NE)
1985—Patriots, 34-23 (NE)
1986—Bengals, 31-7 (NE)
1988—Bengals, 27-21 (NE)
1990—Bengals, 41-7 (C)
1991—Bengals, 29-7 (C)
1992—Bengals, 20-10 (C)
1993—Patriots, 7-2 (NE)
1994—Patriots, 31-28 (C)
2000—Patriots, 16-13 (NE)
2001—Bengals, 23-17 (C)
2004—Patriots, 35-28 (NE)
2006—Patriots, 38-13 (C)
2007—Patriots, 34-13 (C)
2010—Patriots, 38-24 (NE)
2013—Bengals, 13-6 (C)
(RS Pts.—Bengals 484, Patriots 446)
*Franchise in Boston prior to 1971
CINCINNATI vs. NEW ORLEANS
RS: Series tied, 6-6
1970—Bengals, 26-6 (C)
1975—Bengals, 21-0 (NO)
1978—Saints, 20-18 (C)
1981—Saints, 17-7 (NO)
1984—Bengals, 24-21 (NO)
1987—Saints, 41-24 (C)
1990—Saints, 21-7 (C)
1993—Saints, 20-13 (NO)

1996—Bengals, 30-15 (C)
2002—Bengals, 20-13 (C)
2006—Bengals, 31-16 (NO)
2010—Saints, 34-30 (C)
(RS Pts.—Bengals 251, Saints 224)
CINCINNATI vs. N.Y. GIANTS
RS: Bengals lead series, 6-3
1972—Bengals, 13-10 (C)
1977—Bengals, 30-13 (C)
1985—Bengals, 35-30 (C)
1991—Bengals, 27-24 (C)
1994—Bengals, 27-20 (NY)
1997—Giants, 29-27 (NY)
2004—Bengals, 23-22 (C)
2008—Giants, 26-23 (NY) OT
2012—Bengals, 31-13 (C)
(RS Pts.—Bengals 229, Giants 194)
CINCINNATI vs. N.Y. JETS
RS: Jets lead series, 15-8
PS: Jets lead series, 2-0
1968—Jets, 27-14 (NY)
1969—Jets, 21-7 (C)
    Jets, 40-7 (NY)
1971—Jets, 35-21 (NY)
1973—Bengals, 20-14 (C)
1976—Bengals, 42-3 (NY)
1981—Bengals, 31-30 (NY)
1982—*Jets, 44-17 (C)
1984—Jets, 43-23 (NY)
1985—Jets, 29-20 (C)
1986—Bengals, 52-21 (NY)
1987—Jets, 27-20 (NY)
1988—Bengals, 36-19 (C)
1990—Bengals, 25-20 (C)
1992—Jets, 17-14 (NY)
1993—Jets, 17-12 (NY)
1997—Jets, 31-14 (C)
2001—Jets, 15-14 (NY)
2004—Jets, 31-24 (NY)
2007—Bengals, 38-31 (NY)
2008—Jets, 26-14 (NY)
2009—Jets, 37-0 (NY)
    *Jets, 24-14 (C)
2010—Jets, 26-10 (NY)
2013—Bengals, 49-9 (C)
(RS Pts.—Jets 569, Bengals 507)
(PS Pts.—Jets 68, Bengals 31)
*AFC First-Round Playoff
CINCINNATI vs. *OAKLAND
RS: Raiders lead series, 18-9
PS: Raiders lead series, 2-0
1968—Raiders, 31-10 (O)
    Raiders, 34-0 (C)
1969—Bengals, 31-17 (C)
    Raiders, 37-17 (O)
1970—Bengals, 31-21 (C)
1971—Raiders, 31-27 (O)
1972—Raiders, 20-14 (C)
1974—Raiders, 30-27 (O)
1975—Bengals, 14-10 (C)
    **Raiders, 31-28 (O)
1976—Raiders, 35-20 (O)
1978—Raiders, 34-21 (C)
1980—Raiders, 28-17 (O)
1982—Bengals, 31-17 (C)
1983—Raiders, 20-10 (C)
1985—Raiders, 13-6 (LA)
1988—Bengals, 45-21 (LA)
1989—Raiders, 28-7 (LA)
1990—Raiders, 24-7 (LA)
    **Raiders, 20-10 (LA)
1991—Raiders, 38-14 (C)
1992—Bengals, 24-21 (C) OT

1993—Bengals, 16-10 (C)
1995—Raiders, 20-17 (C)
1998—Raiders, 27-10 (O)
2003—Raiders, 23-20 (O)
2006—Bengals, 27-10 (C)
2009—Raiders, 20-17 (O)
2012—Bengals, 34-10 (C)
(RS Pts.—Raiders 630, Bengals 514)
(PS Pts.—Raiders 51, Bengals 38)
*Franchise in Los Angeles from 1982-1994
**AFC Divisional Playoff
CINCINNATI vs. PHILADELPHIA
RS: Bengals lead series, 8-3-1
1971—Bengals, 37-14 (C)
1975—Bengals, 31-0 (P)
1979—Bengals, 37-13 (C)
1982—Bengals, 18-14 (P)
1988—Bengals, 28-24 (P)
1991—Eagles, 17-10 (P)
1994—Bengals, 33-30 (P)
1997—Eagles, 44-42 (P)
2000—Eagles, 16-7 (P)
2004—Bengals, 38-10 (P)
2008—Tie, 13-13 (C) OT
2012—Bengals, 34-13 (P)
(RS Pts.—Bengals 328, Eagles 208)
CINCINNATI vs. PITTSBURGH
RS: Steelers lead series, 53-34
PS: Steelers lead series, 1-0
1970—Steelers, 21-10 (P)
Bengals, 34-7 (C)
1971—Steelers, 21-10 (P)
Steelers, 21-13 (C)
1972—Bengals, 15-10 (C)
Steelers, 40-17 (P)
1973—Bengals, 19-7 (C)
Steelers, 20-13 (P)
1974—Bengals, 17-10 (C)
Steelers, 27-3 (P)
1975—Steelers, 30-24 (C)
Steelers, 35-14 (P)
1976—Steelers, 23-6 (P)
Steelers, 7-3 (C)
1977—Steelers, 20-14 (P)
Bengals, 17-10 (C)
1978—Steelers, 28-3 (C)
Steelers, 7-6 (P)
1979—Bengals, 34-10 (C)
Steelers, 37-17 (P)
1980—Bengals, 30-28 (C)
Bengals, 17-16 (P)
1981—Bengals, 34-7 (C)
Bengals, 17-10 (P)
1982—Steelers, 26-20 (P) OT
1983—Steelers, 24-14 (C)
Bengals, 23-10 (P)
1984—Steelers, 38-17 (P)
Bengals, 22-20 (C)
1985—Bengals, 37-24 (P)
Bengals, 26-21 (C)
1986—Bengals, 24-22 (C)
Steelers, 30-9 (P)
1987—Steelers, 23-20 (P)
Steelers, 30-16 (C)
1988—Bengals, 17-12 (P)
Bengals, 42-7 (C)
1989—Bengals, 41-10 (C)
Bengals, 26-16 (P)
1990—Bengals, 27-3 (C)
Bengals, 16-12 (P)
1991—Steelers, 33-27 (C) OT
Steelers, 17-10 (P)
1992—Steelers, 20-0 (P)

Steelers, 21-9 (C)
1993—Steelers, 34-7 (P)
Steelers, 24-16 (C)
1994—Steelers, 14-10 (P)
Steelers, 38-15 (C)
1995—Bengals, 27-9 (P)
Steelers, 49-31 (C)
1996—Steelers, 20-10 (P)
Bengals, 34-24 (C)
1997—Steelers, 26-10 (C)
Steelers, 20-3 (P)
1998—Bengals, 25-20 (C)
Bengals, 25-24 (P)
1999—Steelers, 17-3 (C)
Bengals, 27-20 (P)
2000—Steelers, 15-0 (P)
Steelers, 48-28 (C)
2001—Steelers, 16-7 (P)
Bengals, 26-23 (C) OT
2002—Steelers, 34-7 (C)
Steelers, 29-21 (P)
2003—Steelers, 17-10 (C)
Bengals, 24-20 (P)
2004—Steelers, 28-17 (P)
Steelers, 19-14 (C)
2005—Steelers, 27-13 (C)
Bengals, 38-31 (P)
*Steelers, 31-17 (C)
2006—Bengals, 28-20 (P)
Steelers, 23-17 (C) OT
2007—Steelers, 24-13 (C)
Steelers, 24-10 (P)
2008—Steelers, 38-10 (C)
Steelers, 27-10 (P)
2009—Bengals, 23-20 (C)
Bengals, 18-12 (P)
2010—Steelers, 27-21 (C)
Steelers, 23-7 (P)
2011—Steelers, 24-17 (C)
Steelers, 35-7 (P)
2012—Steelers, 24-17 (C)
Bengals, 13-10 (P)
2013—Bengals, 20-10 (C)
Steelers, 30-20 (P)
(RS Pts.—Steelers 1,888, Bengals 1,529)
(PS Pts.—Steelers 31, Bengals 17)
*AFC First-Round Playoff
CINCINNATI vs. *ST. LOUIS
RS: Bengals lead series, 7-5
1972—Rams, 15-12 (LA)
1976—Bengals, 20-12 (C)
1978—Bengals, 20-19 (LA)
1981—Bengals, 24-10 (C)
1984—Rams, 24-14 (C)
1990—Bengals, 34-31 (LA) OT
1993—Bengals, 15-3 (C)
1996—Rams, 26-16 (StL)
1999—Rams, 38-10 (C)
2003—Rams, 27-10 (StL)
2007—Bengals, 19-10 (C)
2011—Bengals, 20-13 (StL)
(RS Pts.—Rams 228, Bengals 214)
*Franchise in Los Angeles prior to 1995
CINCINNATI vs. SAN DIEGO
RS: Chargers lead series, 19-13
PS: Series tied, 1-1
1968—Chargers, 29-13 (SD)
Chargers, 31-10 (C)
1969—Bengals, 34-20 (C)
Chargers, 21-14 (SD)
1970—Bengals, 17-14 (SD)
1971—Bengals, 31-0 (C)
1973—Bengals, 20-13 (SD)

1974—Chargers, 20-17 (C)
1975—Bengals, 47-17 (C)
1977—Chargers, 24-3 (SD)
1978—Chargers, 22-13 (SD)
1979—Chargers, 26-24 (C)
1980—Chargers, 31-14 (C)
1981—Bengals, 40-17 (SD)
*Bengals, 27-7 (C)
1982—Chargers, 50-34 (SD)
1985—Chargers, 44-41 (C)
1987—Chargers, 10-9 (C)
1988—Bengals, 27-10 (C)
1990—Bengals, 21-16 (SD)
1992—Chargers, 27-10 (SD)
1994—Chargers, 27-10 (SD)
1996—Chargers, 27-14 (SD)
1997—Bengals, 38-31 (C)
1999—Chargers, 34-7 (C)
2001—Chargers, 28-14 (SD)
2002—Chargers, 34-6 (C)
2003—Bengals, 34-27 (SD)
2006—Chargers, 49-41 (C)
2009—Chargers, 27-24 (SD)
2010—Bengals, 34-20 (C)
2012—Bengals, 20-13 (SD)
2013—Bengals, 17-10 (SD)
**Chargers, 27-10 (C)
(RS Pts.—Chargers 769, Bengals 698)
(PS Pts.—Bengals 37, Chargers 34)
*AFC Championship
**AFC First-Round Playoff
CINCINNATI vs. SAN FRANCISCO
RS: 49ers lead series, 9-3
PS: 49ers lead series, 2-0
1974—Bengals, 21-3 (SF)
1978—49ers, 28-12 (SF)
1981—Bengals, 21-3 (C)
*49ers, 26-21 (Detroit)
1984—49ers, 23-17 (SF)
1987—49ers, 27-26 (C)
1988—**49ers, 20-16 (South Florida) OT
1990—49ers, 20-17 (C) OT
1993—49ers, 21-8 (SF)
1996—49ers, 28-21 (SF)
1999—Bengals, 44-30 (C)
2003—Bengals, 41-38 (C)
2007—49ers, 20-13 (SF)
2011—49ers, 13-8 (C)
(RS Pts.—49ers 272, Bengals 231)
(PS Pts.—49ers 46, Bengals 37)
*Super Bowl XVI
**Super Bowl XXIII
CINCINNATI vs. SEATTLE
RS: Series tied, 9-9
PS: Bengals lead series, 1-0
1977—Bengals, 42-20 (C)
1981—Bengals, 27-21 (C)
1982—Bengals, 24-10 (C)
1984—Seahawks, 26-6 (C)
1985—Seahawks, 28-24 (C)
1986—Bengals, 34-7 (C)
1987—Bengals, 17-10 (S)
1988—*Bengals, 21-13 (C)
1989—Seahawks, 24-17 (C)
1990—Seahawks, 31-16 (S)
1991—Seahawks, 13-7 (C)
1992—Bengals, 21-3 (S)
1993—Seahawks, 19-10 (C)
1994—Bengals, 20-17 (S) OT
1995—Seahawks, 24-21 (S)
1999—Seahawks, 37-20 (S)
2003—Bengals, 27-24 (C)
2007—Seahawks, 24-21 (S)

2011—Bengals, 34-12 (S)
(RS Pts.—Bengals 388, Seahawks 350)
(PS Pts.—Bengals 21, Seahawks 13)
*AFC Divisional Playoff
CINCINNATI vs. TAMPA BAY
RS: Buccaneers lead series, 7-3
1976—Bengals, 21-0 (C)
1980—Buccaneers, 17-12 (C)
1983—Bengals, 23-17 (TB)
1989—Bengals, 56-23 (C)
1995—Buccaneers, 19-16 (TB)
1998—Buccaneers, 35-0 (C)
2001—Buccaneers, 16-13 (C) OT
2002—Buccaneers, 35-7 (C)
2006—Buccaneers, 14-13 (TB)
2010—Buccaneers, 24-21 (C)
(RS Pts.— Buccaneers 200, Bengals 182)
CINCINNATI vs. *TENNESSEE
RS: Titans lead series, 39-32-1
PS: Bengals lead series, 1-0
1968—Oilers, 27-17 (C)
1969—Tie, 31-31 (H)
1970—Oilers, 20-13 (C)
    Bengals, 30-20 (H)
1971—Oilers, 10-6 (H)
    Bengals, 28-13 (C)
1972—Bengals, 30-7 (C)
    Bengals, 61-17 (H)
1973—Bengals, 24-10 (C)
    Bengals, 27-24 (H)
1974—Oilers, 34-21 (C)
    Oilers, 20-3 (H)
1975—Bengals, 21-19 (H)
    Bengals, 23-19 (C)
1976—Bengals, 27-7 (H)
    Bengals, 31-27 (C)
1977—Bengals, 13-10 (C) OT
    Oilers, 21-16 (H)
1978—Bengals, 28-13 (C)
    Oilers, 17-10 (H)
1979—Oilers, 30-27 (C) OT
    Oilers, 42-21 (H)
1980—Oilers, 13-10 (C)
    Oilers, 23-3 (H)
1981—Oilers, 17-10 (H)
    Bengals, 34-21 (C)
1982—Bengals, 27-6 (C)
    Bengals, 35-27 (H)
1983—Bengals, 55-14 (H)
    Bengals, 38-10 (C)
1984—Bengals, 13-3 (C)
    Bengals, 31-13 (H)
1985—Oilers, 44-27 (H)
    Bengals, 45-27 (C)
1986—Bengals, 31-28 (C)
    Oilers, 32-28 (H)
1987—Oilers, 31-29 (H)
    Oilers, 21-17 (H)
1988—Bengals, 44-21 (C)
    Oilers, 41-6 (H)
1989—Oilers, 26-24 (H)
    Bengals, 61-7 (C)
1990—Oilers, 48-17 (H)
    Bengals, 40-20 (C)
    **Bengals, 41-14 (C)
1991—Oilers, 30-7 (C)
    Oilers, 35-3 (H)
1992—Oilers, 38-24 (C)
    Oilers, 26-10 (H)
1993—Oilers, 28-12 (H)
    Oilers, 38-3 (C)
1994—Oilers, 20-13 (H)
    Bengals, 34-31 (C)

1995—Oilers, 38-28 (C)
    Bengals, 32-25 (H)
1996—Oilers, 30-27 (C) OT
    Bengals, 21-13 (H)
1997—Oilers, 30-7 (T)
    Bengals, 41-14 (C)
1998—Oilers, 23-14 (C)
    Oilers, 44-14 (T)
1999—Titans, 36-35 (T)
    Titans, 24-14 (C)
2000—Titans, 23-14 (C)
    Titans, 35-3 (T)
2001—Titans, 20-7 (C)
    Bengals, 23-21 (T)
2002—Titans, 30-24 (C)
2004—Titans, 27-20 (C)
2005—Bengals, 31-23 (T)
2007—Bengals, 35-6 (C)
2008—Titans, 24-7 (C)
2011—Bengals, 24-17 (T)
(RS Pts.—Titans 1,680, Bengals 1,660)
(PS Pts.—Bengals 41, Titans 14)
*Franchise in Houston prior to 1997;
known as Oilers prior to 1999
**AFC First-Round Playoff
CINCINNATI vs. WASHINGTON
RS: Bengals lead series, 5-4
1970—Redskins, 20-0 (W)
1974—Bengals, 28-17 (C)
1979—Redskins, 28-14 (W)
1985—Redskins, 27-24 (W)
1988—Bengals, 20-17 (C) OT
1991—Redskins, 34-27 (C)
2004—Bengals, 17-10 (W)
2008—Bengals, 20-13 (C)
2012—Bengals, 38-31 (W)
(RS Pts.—Redskins 197, Bengals 188)

CLEVELAND vs. ARIZONA
RS: Browns lead series, 33-13-3;
See Arizona vs. Cleveland
CLEVELAND vs. ATLANTA
RS: Browns lead series, 10-3;
See Atlanta vs. Cleveland
CLEVELAND vs. BALTIMORE
RS: Ravens lead series, 22-8;
See Baltimore vs. Cleveland
CLEVELAND vs. BUFFALO
RS: Browns lead series, 11-7
PS: Browns lead series, 1-0;
See Buffalo vs. Cleveland
CLEVELAND vs. CAROLINA
RS: Panthers lead series, 3-1;
See Carolina vs. Cleveland
CLEVELAND vs. CHICAGO
RS: Browns lead series, 9-6;
See Chicago vs. Cleveland
CLEVELAND vs. CINCINNATI
RS: Bengals lead series, 43-38;
See Cincinnati vs. Cleveland
CLEVELAND vs. DALLAS
RS: Browns lead series, 15-12
PS: Browns lead series, 2-1
1960—Browns, 48-7 (D)
1961—Browns, 25-7 (C)
    Browns, 38-17 (D)
1962—Browns, 19-10 (C)
    Cowboys, 45-21 (D)
1963—Browns, 41-24 (D)
    Browns, 27-17 (C)
1964—Browns, 27-6 (C)
    Browns, 20-16 (D)
1965—Browns, 23-17 (C)

    Browns, 24-17 (D)
1966—Browns, 30-21 (C)
    Cowboys, 26-14 (D)
1967—Cowboys, 21-14 (C)
    *Cowboys, 52-14 (D)
1968—Cowboys, 28-7 (D)
    *Browns, 31-20 (C)
1969—Browns, 42-10 (C)
    *Browns, 38-14 (D)
1970—Cowboys, 6-2 (C)
1974—Cowboys, 41-17 (D)
1979—Browns, 26-7 (C)
1982—Cowboys, 31-14 (D)
1985—Cowboys, 20-7 (D)
1988—Browns, 24-21 (C)
1991—Cowboys, 26-14 (C)
1994—Browns, 19-14 (D)
2004—Cowboys, 19-12 (C)
2008—Cowboys, 28-10 (C)
2012—Cowboys, 23-20 (D) OT
(RS Pts.—Browns 585, Cowboys 525)
(PS Pts.—Cowboys 86, Browns 83)
*Conference Championship
CLEVELAND vs. DENVER
RS: Broncos lead series, 19-5
PS: Broncos lead series, 3-0
1970—Browns, 27-13 (D)
1971—Broncos, 27-0 (C)
1972—Broncos, 27-20 (D)
1974—Browns, 23-21 (C)
1975—Broncos, 16-15 (D)
1976—Broncos, 44-13 (D)
1978—Broncos, 19-7 (C)
1980—Broncos, 19-16 (C)
1981—Broncos, 23-20 (D) OT
1983—Broncos, 27-6 (D)
1984—Broncos, 24-14 (C)
1986—*Broncos, 23-20 (C) OT
1987—*Broncos, 38-33 (D)
1988—Broncos, 30-7 (D)
1989—Browns, 16-13 (C)
    *Broncos, 37-21 (D)
1990—Browns, 30-29 (D)
1991—Broncos, 17-7 (C)
1992—Broncos, 12-0 (C)
1993—Broncos, 29-14 (C)
1994—Broncos, 26-14 (D)
2000—Broncos, 44-10 (D)
2003—Broncos, 23-20 (D) OT
2006—Broncos, 17-7 (C)
2008—Broncos, 34-30 (C)
2009—Broncos, 27-6 (D)
2012—Broncos, 34-12 (D)
(RS Pts.—Broncos 588, Browns 341)
(PS Pts.—Broncos 98, Browns 74)
*AFC Championship
CLEVELAND vs. DETROIT
RS: Lions lead series, 15-4
PS: Lions lead series, 3-1
1952—Lions, 17-6 (D)
    *Lions, 17-7 (C)
1953—*Lions, 17-16 (D)
1954—Lions, 14-10 (C)
    *Browns, 56-10 (C)
1957—Lions, 20-7 (D)
    *Lions, 59-14 (D)
1958—Lions, 30-10 (C)
1963—Lions, 38-10 (C)
1964—Browns, 37-21 (C)
1967—Lions, 31-14 (C)
1969—Lions, 28-21 (C)
1970—Lions, 41-24 (D)
1975—Lions, 21-10 (D)

1983—Browns, 31-26 (D)
1986—Browns, 24-21 (C)
1989—Lions, 13-10 (D)
1992—Lions, 24-14 (B)
1995—Lions, 38-20 (D)
2001—Browns, 24-14 (C)
2005—Lions, 13-10 (C)
2009—Lions, 38-37 (D)
2013—Lions, 31-17 (C)
(RS Pts.—Lions 479, Browns 336)
(PS Pts.—Lions 103, Browns 93)
*NFL Championship

CLEVELAND vs. GREEN BAY
RS: Packers lead series, 11-7
PS: Packers lead series, 1-0
1953—Browns, 27-0 (Mil)
1955—Browns, 41-10 (C)
1956—Browns, 24-7 (Mil)
1961—Packers, 49-17 (C)
1964—Packers, 28-21 (Mil)
1965—*Packers, 23-12 (GB)
1966—Packers, 21-20 (C)
1967—Packers, 55-7 (Mil)
1969—Browns, 20-7 (C)
1972—Packers, 26-10 (C)
1980—Browns, 26-21 (C)
1983—Packers, 35-21 (Mil)
1986—Browns, 17-14 (C)
1992—Browns, 17-6 (C)
1995—Packers, 31-20 (C)
2001—Packers, 30-7 (GB)
2005—Browns, 26-24 (GB)
2009—Packers, 31-3 (C)
2013—Packers, 31-13 (GB)
(RS Pts.—Packers 429, Browns 334)
(PS Pts.—Packers 23, Browns 12)
*NFL Championship

CLEVELAND vs. HOUSTON
RS: Texans lead series, 4-3
2002—Browns, 34-17 (C)
2004—Browns, 22-14 (H)
2005—Texans, 19-16 (H)
2006—Texans, 14-6 (H)
2007—Browns, 27-17 (C)
2008—Texans, 16-6 (C)
2011—Texans, 30-12 (H)
(RS Pts.—Texans 127, Browns 123)

CLEVELAND vs. *INDIANAPOLIS
RS: Browns lead series, 14-13
PS: Series tied, 2-2
1956—Colts, 21-7 (C)
1959—Browns, 38-31 (B)
1962—Colts, 36-14 (C)
1964—**Browns, 27-0 (C)
1968—Browns, 30-20 (B)
      **Colts, 34-0 (C)
1971—Browns, 14-13 (B)
      ***Colts, 20-3 (C)
1973—Browns, 24-14 (C)
1975—Colts, 21-7 (B)
1978—Browns, 45-24 (B)
1979—Browns, 13-10 (C)
1980—Browns, 28-27 (B)
1981—Browns, 42-28 (C)
1983—Browns, 41-23 (C)
1986—Browns, 24-9 (I)
1987—Colts, 9-7 (C)
      ***Browns, 38-21 (C)
1988—Browns, 23-17 (C)
1989—Colts, 23-17 (I) OT
1991—Browns, 31-0 (I)
1992—Colts, 14-3 (I)
1993—Colts, 23-10 (I)

1994—Browns, 21-14 (I)
1999—Colts, 29-28 (C)
2002—Colts, 28-23 (C)
2003—Colts, 9-6 (C)
2005—Colts, 13-6 (I)
2008—Colts, 10-6 (C)
2011—Browns, 27-19 (I)
2012—Colts, 17-13 (I)
(RS Pts.—Browns 548, Colts 502)
(PS Pts.—Colts 75, Browns 68)
*Franchise in Baltimore prior to 1984
**NFL Championship
***AFC Divisional Playoff

CLEVELAND vs. JACKSONVILLE
RS: Jaguars lead series, 10-5
1995—Jaguars, 23-15 (C)
      Jaguars, 24-21 (J)
1999—Jaguars, 24-7 (J)
      Jaguars, 24-14 (C)
2000—Jaguars, 27-7 (C)
      Jaguars, 48-0 (J)
2001—Jaguars, 23-14 (J)
      Jaguars, 15-10 (C)
2002—Browns, 21-20 (J)
2005—Jaguars, 20-14 (C)
2008—Browns, 23-17 (J)
2009—Browns, 23-17 (C)
2010—Jaguars, 24-20 (J)
2011—Browns, 14-10 (C)
2013—Jaguars, 32-28 (C)
(RS Pts.—Jaguars 339, Browns 240)

CLEVELAND vs. KANSAS CITY
RS: Series, 11-11-2
1971—Chiefs, 13-7 (KC)
1972—Chiefs, 31-7 (C)
1973—Tie, 20-20 (KC)
1975—Browns, 40-14 (C)
1976—Chiefs, 39-14 (KC)
1977—Browns, 44-7 (C)
1978—Chiefs, 17-3 (KC)
1979—Browns, 27-24 (KC)
1980—Browns, 20-13 (C)
1984—Chiefs, 10-6 (KC)
1986—Browns, 20-7 (C)
1988—Browns, 6-3 (KC)
1989—Tie, 10-10 (C) OT
1990—Chiefs, 34-0 (KC)
1991—Browns, 20-15 (C)
1994—Chiefs, 20-13 (KC)
1995—Browns, 35-17 (C)
2002—Chiefs, 40-39 (C)
2003—Chiefs, 41-20 (KC)
2006—Browns, 31-28 (C) OT
2009—Browns, 41-34 (KC)
2010—Chiefs, 16-14 (C)
2012—Browns, 30-7 (C)
2013—Chiefs, 23-17 (KC)
(RS Pts.—Browns 484, Chiefs 483)

CLEVELAND vs. MIAMI
RS: Series tied, 8-8
PS: Dolphins lead series, 2-0
1970—Browns, 28-0 (M)
1972—*Dolphins, 20-14 (M)
1973—Dolphins, 17-9 (C)
1976—Browns, 17-13 (C)
1979—Browns, 30-24 (C) OT
1985—*Dolphins, 24-21 (M)
1986—Browns, 26-16 (C)
1988—Dolphins, 38-31 (M)
1989—Dolphins, 13-10 (M) OT
1990—Dolphins, 30-13 (C)
1992—Dolphins, 27-23 (C)
1993—Dolphins, 24-14 (C)

2004—Dolphins, 10-7 (M)
2005—Browns, 22-0 (C)
2007—Browns, 41-31 (C)
2010—Browns, 13-10 (M)
2011—Browns, 17-16 (C)
2013—Dolphins, 23-10 (C)
(RS Pts.—Browns 311, Dolphins 292)
(PS Pts.—Dolphins 44, Browns 35)
*AFC Divisional Playoff

CLEVELAND vs. MINNESOTA
RS: Vikings lead series, 10-4
PS: Vikings lead series, 1-0
1965—Vikings, 27-17 (C)
1967—Browns, 14-10 (C)
1969—Vikings, 51-3 (M)
      *Vikings, 27-7 (C)
1973—Vikings, 26-3 (M)
1975—Vikings, 42-10 (C)
1980—Vikings, 28-23 (M)
1983—Vikings, 27-21 (C)
1986—Browns, 23-20 (M)
1989—Browns, 23-17 (C) OT
1992—Vikings, 17-13 (M)
1995—Vikings, 27-11 (M)
2005—Vikings, 24-12 (M)
2009—Vikings, 34-20 (C)
2013—Browns, 31-27 (M)
(RS Pts.—Vikings 377, Browns 224)
(PS Pts.—Vikings 27, Browns 7)
*NFL Championship

CLEVELAND vs. NEW ENGLAND
RS: Browns lead series, 12-10
PS: Browns lead series, 1-0
1971—Browns, 27-7 (C)
1974—Browns, 21-14 (NE)
1977—Browns, 30-27 (C) OT
1980—Patriots, 34-17 (NE)
1982—Browns, 10-7 (C)
1983—Browns, 30-0 (NE)
1984—Patriots, 17-16 (C)
1985—Browns, 24-20 (C)
1987—Browns, 20-10 (NE)
1991—Browns, 20-0 (NE)
1992—Browns, 19-17 (NE)
1993—Patriots, 20-17 (C)
1994—Browns, 13-6 (C)
      *Browns, 20-13 (C)
1995—Patriots, 17-14 (NE)
1999—Patriots, 19-7 (C)
2000—Browns, 19-11 (C)
2001—Patriots, 27-16 (NE)
2003—Patriots, 9-3 (NE)
2004—Patriots, 42-15 (C)
2007—Patriots, 34-17 (NE)
2010—Browns, 34-14 (C)
2013—Patriots, 27-26 (NE)
(RS Pts.—Browns 415, Patriots 379)
(PS Pts.—Browns 20, Patriots 13)
*AFC First-Round Playoff

CLEVELAND vs. NEW ORLEANS
RS: Browns lead series, 12-4
1967—Browns, 42-7 (NO)
1968—Browns, 24-10 (NO)
      Browns, 35-17 (C)
1969—Browns, 27-17 (NO)
1971—Browns, 21-17 (NO)
1975—Browns, 17-16 (C)
1978—Browns, 24-16 (NO)
1981—Browns, 20-17 (C)
1984—Saints, 16-14 (C)
1987—Saints, 28-21 (C)
1990—Saints, 25-20 (NO)
1993—Browns, 17-13 (C)

1999—Browns, 21-16 (NO)
2002—Browns, 24-15 (NO)
2006—Saints, 19-14 (C)
2010—Browns, 30-17 (NO)
(RS Pts.—Browns 371, Saints 266)
CLEVELAND vs. N.Y. GIANTS
RS: Browns lead series, 26-20-2
PS: Series tied, 1-1
1950—Giants, 6-0 (C)
    Giants, 17-13 (NY)
    *Browns, 8-3 (C)
1951—Browns, 14-13 (C)
    Browns, 10-0 (NY)
1952—Giants, 17-9 (C)
    Giants, 37-34 (NY)
1953—Browns, 7-0 (NY)
    Browns, 62-14 (C)
1954—Browns, 24-14 (C)
    Browns, 16-7 (NY)
1955—Browns, 24-14 (C)
    Tie, 35-35 (NY)
1956—Giants, 21-9 (C)
    Browns, 24-7 (NY)
1957—Browns, 6-3 (C)
    Browns, 34-28 (NY)
1958—Giants, 21-17 (C)
    Giants, 13-10 (NY)
    *Giants, 10-0 (NY)
1959—Giants, 10-6 (C)
    Giants, 48-7 (NY)
1960—Giants, 17-13 (C)
    Browns, 48-34 (NY)
1961—Giants, 37-21 (C)
    Tie, 7-7 (NY)
1962—Browns, 17-7 (C)
    Giants, 17-13 (NY)
1963—Browns, 35-24 (NY)
    Giants, 33-6 (C)
1964—Browns, 42-20 (C)
    Browns, 52-20 (NY)
1965—Browns, 38-14 (NY)
    Browns, 34-21 (C)
1966—Browns, 28-7 (NY)
    Browns, 49-40 (C)
1967—Giants, 38-34 (NY)
    Browns, 24-14 (C)
1968—Browns, 45-10 (C)
1969—Browns, 28-17 (C)
    Giants, 27-14 (NY)
1973—Browns, 12-10 (C)
1977—Browns, 21-7 (NY)
1985—Giants, 35-33 (NY)
1991—Giants, 13-10 (C)
1994—Giants, 16-13 (C)
2000—Giants, 24-3 (C)
2004—Giants, 27-10 (NY)
2008—Browns, 35-14 (C)
2012—Giants, 41-27 (NY)
(RS Pts.—Browns 1,075, Giants 914)
(PS Pts.—Giants 13, Browns 8)
*Conference Playoff
CLEVELAND vs. N.Y. JETS
RS: Browns lead series, 12-9
PS: Browns lead series, 1-0
1970—Browns, 31-21 (C)
1972—Browns, 26-10 (NY)
1976—Browns, 38-17 (C)
1978—Browns, 37-34 (C) OT
1979—Browns, 25-22 (NY) OT
1980—Browns, 17-14 (C)
1981—Jets, 14-13 (C)
1983—Browns, 10-7 (C)
1984—Jets, 24-20 (C)

1985—Jets, 37-10 (NY)
1986—*Browns, 23-20 (C) OT
1988—Jets, 23-3 (C)
1989—Browns, 38-24 (C)
1990—Jets, 24-21 (NY)
1991—Jets, 17-14 (C)
1994—Browns, 27-7 (C)
2002—Browns, 24-21 (NY)
2004—Jets, 10-7 (C)
2006—Browns, 20-13 (C)
2007—Browns, 24-18 (NY)
2010—Jets, 26-20 (NY) OT
2013—Jets, 24-13 (NY)
(RS Pts.—Browns 438, Jets 407)
(PS Pts.—Browns 23, Jets 20)
*AFC Divisional Playoff
CLEVELAND vs. *OAKLAND
RS: Raiders lead series, 11-9
PS: Raiders lead series, 2-0
1970—Raiders, 23-20 (O)
1971—Raiders, 34-20 (C)
1973—Browns, 7-3 (O)
1974—Raiders, 40-24 (C)
1975—Raiders, 38-17 (O)
1977—Raiders, 26-10 (C)
1979—Raiders, 19-14 (O)
1980—**Raiders, 14-12 (C)
1982—***Raiders, 27-10 (LA)
1985—Raiders, 21-20 (C)
1986—Raiders, 27-14 (LA)
1987—Browns, 24-17 (LA)
1992—Browns, 28-16 (LA)
1993—Browns, 19-16 (LA)
2000—Raiders, 36-10 (O)
2003—Browns, 13-7 (C)
2005—Browns, 9-7 (O)
2006—Browns, 24-21 (O)
2007—Raiders, 26-24 (O)
2009—Browns, 23-9 (C)
2011—Raiders, 24-17 (O)
2012—Browns, 20-17 (O)
(RS Pts.—Raiders 427, Browns 357)
(PS Pts.—Raiders 41, Browns 22)
*Franchise in Los Angeles from 1982-1994
**AFC Divisional Playoff
***AFC First-Round Playoff
CLEVELAND vs. PHILADELPHIA
RS: Browns lead series, 31-16-1
1950—Browns, 35-10 (P)
    Browns, 13-7 (C)
1951—Browns, 20-17 (C)
    Browns, 24-9 (P)
1952—Browns, 49-7 (P)
    Eagles, 28-20 (C)
1953—Browns, 37-13 (C)
    Eagles, 42-27 (P)
1954—Eagles, 28-10 (P)
    Browns, 6-0 (C)
1955—Browns, 21-17 (C)
    Eagles, 33-17 (P)
1956—Browns, 16-0 (C)
    Browns, 17-14 (C)
1957—Browns, 24-7 (C)
    Eagles, 17-7 (P)
1958—Browns, 28-14 (C)
    Browns, 21-14 (P)
1959—Browns, 28-7 (C)
    Browns, 28-21 (P)
1960—Browns, 41-24 (P)
    Eagles, 31-29 (C)
1961—Eagles, 27-20 (P)
    Browns, 45-24 (C)
1962—Eagles, 35-7 (P)

    Tie, 14-14 (C)
1963—Browns, 37-7 (C)
    Browns, 23-17 (P)
1964—Browns, 28-20 (P)
    Browns, 38-24 (C)
1965—Browns, 35-17 (P)
    Browns, 38-34 (C)
1966—Browns, 27-7 (C)
    Eagles, 33-21 (P)
1967—Eagles, 28-24 (P)
1968—Browns, 47-13 (C)
1969—Browns, 27-20 (P)
1972—Browns, 27-17 (C)
1976—Browns, 24-3 (C)
1979—Browns, 24-19 (P)
1982—Eagles, 24-21 (C)
1988—Browns, 19-3 (C)
1991—Eagles, 32-30 (C)
1994—Browns, 26-7 (P)
2000—Eagles, 35-24 (C)
2004—Eagles, 34-31 (C) OT
2008—Eagles, 30-10 (P)
2012—Eagles, 17-16 (C)
(RS Pts.—Browns 1,201, Eagles 901)
CLEVELAND vs. PITTSBURGH
RS: Steelers lead series, 65-57
PS: Steelers lead series, 2-0
1950—Browns, 30-17 (P)
    Browns, 45-7 (C)
1951—Browns, 17-0 (C)
    Browns, 28-0 (P)
1952—Browns, 21-20 (P)
    Browns, 29-28 (C)
1953—Browns, 34-16 (C)
    Browns, 20-16 (P)
1954—Steelers, 55-27 (P)
    Browns, 42-7 (C)
1955—Browns, 41-14 (C)
    Browns, 30-7 (P)
1956—Browns, 14-10 (P)
    Steelers, 24-16 (C)
1957—Browns, 23-12 (P)
    Browns, 24-0 (C)
1958—Browns, 45-12 (P)
    Browns, 27-10 (C)
1959—Steelers, 17-7 (P)
    Steelers, 21-20 (C)
1960—Browns, 28-20 (C)
    Steelers, 14-10 (P)
1961—Browns, 30-28 (C)
    Steelers, 17-13 (C)
1962—Browns, 41-14 (P)
    Browns, 35-14 (C)
1963—Browns, 35-23 (C)
    Steelers, 9-7 (P)
1964—Steelers, 23-7 (C)
    Browns, 30-17 (P)
1965—Browns, 24-19 (C)
    Browns, 42-21 (P)
1966—Browns, 41-10 (C)
    Steelers, 16-6 (P)
1967—Browns, 21-10 (C)
    Browns, 34-14 (P)
1968—Browns, 31-24 (C)
    Browns, 45-24 (P)
1969—Browns, 42-31 (C)
    Browns, 24-3 (P)
1970—Browns, 15-7 (C)
    Steelers, 28-9 (P)
1971—Browns, 27-17 (C)
    Steelers, 26-9 (P)
1972—Browns, 26-24 (C)
    Steelers, 30-0 (P)

1973—Steelers, 33-6 (P)
    Browns, 21-16 (C)
1974—Steelers, 20-16 (P)
    Steelers, 26-16 (C)
1975—Steelers, 42-6 (C)
    Steelers, 31-17 (P)
1976—Steelers, 31-14 (P)
    Browns, 18-16 (C)
1977—Steelers, 28-14 (C)
    Steelers, 35-31 (P)
1978—Steelers, 15-9 (P) OT
    Steelers, 34-14 (C)
1979—Steelers, 51-35 (C)
    Steelers, 33-30 (P) OT
1980—Browns, 27-26 (C)
    Steelers, 16-13 (P)
1981—Steelers, 13-7 (P)
    Steelers, 32-10 (C)
1982—Browns, 10-9 (C)
    Steelers, 37-21 (P)
1983—Steelers, 44-17 (P)
    Browns, 30-17 (C)
1984—Browns, 20-10 (C)
    Steelers, 23-20 (P)
1985—Browns, 17-7 (C)
    Steelers, 10-9 (P)
1986—Browns, 27-24 (P)
    Browns, 37-31 (C) OT
1987—Browns, 34-10 (C)
    Browns, 19-13 (P)
1988—Browns, 23-9 (P)
    Browns, 27-7 (C)
1989—Browns, 51-0 (P)
    Steelers, 17-7 (C)
1990—Browns, 13-3 (C)
    Steelers, 35-0 (P)
1991—Browns, 17-14 (C)
    Steelers, 17-10 (P)
1992—Browns, 17-9 (C)
    Steelers, 23-13 (P)
1993—Browns, 28-23 (C)
    Steelers, 16-9 (P)
1994—Steelers, 17-10 (C)
    Steelers, 17-7 (P)
    *Steelers, 29-9 (P)
1995—Steelers, 20-3 (P)
    Steelers, 20-17 (C)
1999—Steelers, 43-0 (C)
    Browns, 16-15 (P)
2000—Browns, 23-20 (C)
    Steelers, 22-0 (P)
2001—Steelers, 15-12 (C) OT
    Steelers, 28-7 (P)
2002—Steelers, 16-13 (P) OT
    Steelers, 23-20 (C)
    **Steelers, 36-33 (P)
2003—Browns, 33-13 (P)
    Steelers, 13-6 (C)
2004—Steelers, 34-23 (P)
    Steelers, 24-10 (C)
2005—Steelers, 34-21 (P)
    Steelers, 41-0 (C)
2006—Steelers, 24-20 (C)
    Steelers, 27-7 (P)
2007—Steelers, 34-7 (C)
    Steelers, 31-28 (P)
2008—Steelers, 10-6 (C)
    Steelers, 31-0 (P)
2009—Steelers, 27-14 (P)
    Browns, 13-6 (C)
2010—Steelers, 28-10 (P)
    Steelers, 41-9 (C)
2011—Steelers, 14-3 (P)

    Steelers, 13-9 (C)
2012—Browns, 20-14 (C)
    Steelers, 24-10 (P)
2013—Steelers, 27-11 (C)
    Steelers, 20-7 (P)
(RS Pts.—Steelers 2,468, Browns 2,347)
(PS Pts.—Steelers 65, Browns 42)
*AFC Divisional Playoff
**AFC First-Round Playoff
CLEVELAND vs. *ST. LOUIS
RS: Rams lead series, 10-9
PS: Browns lead series, 2-1
1950—**Browns, 30-28 (C)
1951—Browns, 38-23 (LA)
    **Rams, 24-17 (LA)
1952—Browns, 37-7 (C)
1955—**Browns, 38-14 (LA)
1957—Browns, 45-31 (C)
1958—Browns, 30-27 (LA)
1963—Browns, 20-6 (C)
1965—Rams, 42-7 (LA)
1968—Rams, 24-6 (C)
1973—Rams, 30-17 (LA)
1977—Rams, 9-0 (C)
1978—Browns, 30-19 (C)
1981—Rams, 27-16 (LA)
1984—Rams, 20-17 (LA)
1987—Browns, 30-17 (C)
1990—Rams, 38-23 (C)
1993—Browns, 42-14 (LA)
1999—Rams, 34-3 (StL)
2003—Rams, 26-20 (C)
2007—Browns, 27-20 (StL)
2011—Rams, 13-12 (C)
(RS Pts.—Rams 427, Browns 420)
(PS Pts.—Browns 85, Rams 66)
*Franchise in Los Angeles prior to 1995
**NFL Championship
CLEVELAND vs. SAN DIEGO
RS: Chargers lead series, 14-8-1
1970—Chargers, 27-10 (C)
1972—Browns, 21-17 (SD)
1973—Tie, 16-16 (C)
1974—Chargers, 36-35 (SD)
1976—Browns, 21-17 (C)
1977—Chargers, 37-14 (SD)
1981—Chargers, 44-14 (C)
1982—Chargers, 30-13 (C)
1983—Browns, 30-24 (SD) OT
1985—Browns, 21-7 (SD)
1986—Browns, 47-17 (C)
1987—Chargers, 27-24 (SD) OT
1990—Chargers, 24-14 (C)
1991—Browns, 30-24 (SD) OT
1992—Chargers, 14-13 (C)
1995—Chargers, 31-13 (SD)
1999—Chargers, 23-10 (SD)
2001—Browns, 20-16 (C)
2003—Chargers, 26-20 (C)
2004—Chargers, 21-0 (C)
2006—Chargers, 32-25 (SD)
2009—Chargers, 30-23 (C)
2012—Browns, 7-6 (C)
(RS Pts.—Chargers 546, Browns 441)
CLEVELAND vs. SAN FRANCISCO
RS: Browns lead series, 11-7
1950—Browns, 34-14 (C)
1951—49ers, 24-10 (SF)
1953—Browns, 23-21 (C)
1955—Browns, 38-3 (SF)
1959—49ers, 21-20 (C)
1962—Browns, 13-10 (SF)
1968—Browns, 33-21 (SF)

1970—49ers, 34-31 (SF)
1974—Browns, 7-0 (C)
1978—Browns, 24-7 (C)
1981—Browns, 15-12 (SF)
1984—49ers, 41-7 (C)
1987—49ers, 38-24 (SF)
1990—49ers, 20-17 (SF)
1993—Browns, 23-13 (C)
2003—Browns, 13-12 (SF)
2007—Browns, 20-7 (C)
2011—49ers, 20-10 (SF)
(RS Pts.—Browns 362, 49ers 318)
CLEVELAND vs. SEATTLE
RS: Seahawks lead series, 11-6
1977—Seahawks, 20-19 (S)
1978—Seahawks, 47-24 (S)
1979—Seahawks, 29-24 (C)
1980—Browns, 27-3 (S)
1981—Seahawks, 42-21 (S)
1982—Browns, 21-7 (S)
1983—Seahawks, 24-9 (C)
1984—Seahawks, 33-0 (S)
1985—Seahawks, 31-13 (S)
1988—Seahawks, 16-10 (C)
1989—Browns, 17-7 (S)
1993—Seahawks, 22-5 (S)
1994—Browns, 35-9 (C)
2001—Seahawks, 9-6 (C)
2003—Seahawks, 34-7 (S)
2007—Browns, 33-30 (C) OT
2011—Browns, 6-3 (C)
(RS Pts.—Seahawks 366, Browns 277)
CLEVELAND vs. TAMPA BAY
RS: Browns lead series, 5-3
1976—Browns, 24-7 (TB)
1980—Browns, 34-27 (TB)
1983—Browns, 20-0 (C)
1989—Browns, 42-31 (TB)
1995—Browns, 22-6 (C)
2002—Buccaneers 17-3 (TB)
2006—Buccaneers, 22-7 (C)
2010—Buccaneers, 17-14 (TB)
(RS Pts.—Browns 166, Buccaneers 127)
CLEVELAND vs. *TENNESSEE
RS: Browns lead series, 33-28
PS: Titans lead series, 1-0
1970—Browns, 28-14 (C)
    Browns, 21-10 (H)
1971—Browns, 31-0 (C)
    Browns, 37-24 (H)
1972—Browns, 23-17 (H)
    Browns, 20-0 (C)
1973—Browns, 42-13 (H)
    Browns, 23-13 (H)
1974—Browns, 20-7 (C)
    Oilers, 28-24 (H)
1975—Oilers, 40-10 (H)
    Oilers, 21-10 (H)
1976—Browns, 21-7 (H)
    Browns, 13-10 (C)
1977—Browns, 24-23 (H)
    Oilers, 19-15 (C)
1978—Oilers, 16-13 (C)
    Oilers, 14-10 (H)
1979—Oilers, 31-10 (H)
    Browns, 14-7 (C)
1980—Oilers, 16-7 (C)
    Browns, 17-14 (H)
1981—Oilers, 9-3 (C)
    Oilers, 17-13 (H)
1982—Browns, 20-14 (H)
1983—Browns, 25-19 (C) OT
    Oilers, 34-27 (H)

1984—Browns, 27-10 (C)
    Browns, 27-20 (H)
1985—Browns, 21-6 (H)
    Browns, 28-21 (C)
1986—Browns, 23-20 (H)
    Browns, 13-10 (C) OT
1987—Oilers, 15-10 (C)
    Browns, 40-7 (H)
1988—Oilers, 24-17 (H)
    Browns, 28-23 (C)
    **Oilers, 24-23 (C)
1989—Browns, 28-17 (C)
    Browns, 24-20 (H)
1990—Oilers, 35-23 (C)
    Oilers, 58-14 (H)
1991—Oilers, 28-24 (H)
    Oilers, 17-14 (C)
1992—Browns, 24-14 (H)
    Oilers, 17-14 (C)
1993—Oilers, 27-20 (C)
    Oilers, 19-17 (H)
1994—Browns, 11-8 (H)
    Browns, 34-10 (C)
1995—Browns, 14-7 (H)
    Oilers, 37-10 (C)
1999—Titans, 26-9 (T)
    Titans, 33-21 (C)
2000—Titans, 24-10 (T)
    Titans, 24-0 (C)
2001—Titans, 31-15 (C)
    Browns, 41-38 (T)
2002—Browns, 31-28 (T) OT
2005—Browns, 20-14 (C)
2008—Titans, 28-9 (T)
2011—Titans, 31-13 (C)
(RS Pts.—Browns 1,195, Titans 1,184)
(PS Pts.—Titans 24, Browns 23)
*Franchise in Houston prior to 1997;
known as Oilers prior to 1999
**AFC First-Round Playoff
CLEVELAND vs. WASHINGTON
RS: Browns lead series, 33-11-1
1950—Browns, 20-14 (C)
    Browns, 45-21 (W)
1951—Browns, 45-0 (C)
1952—Browns, 19-15 (C)
    Browns, 48-24 (W)
1953—Browns, 30-14 (W)
    Browns, 27-3 (C)
1954—Browns, 62-3 (C)
    Browns, 34-14 (W)
1955—Redskins, 27-17 (C)
    Browns, 24-14 (W)
1956—Redskins, 20-9 (W)
    Redskins, 20-17 (C)
1957—Browns, 21-17 (C)
    Tie, 30-30 (W)
1958—Browns, 20-10 (W)
    Browns, 21-14 (C)
1959—Browns, 34-7 (C)
    Browns, 31-17 (W)
1960—Browns, 31-10 (W)
    Browns, 27-16 (C)
1961—Browns, 31-7 (C)
    Browns, 17-6 (W)
1962—Redskins, 17-16 (C)
    Redskins, 17-9 (W)
1963—Browns, 37-14 (C)
    Browns, 27-20 (W)
1964—Browns, 27-13 (W)
    Browns, 34-24 (C)
1965—Browns, 17-7 (W)
    Browns, 24-16 (C)

1966—Browns, 38-14 (W)
    Browns, 14-3 (C)
1967—Browns, 42-37 (C)
1968—Browns, 24-21 (W)
1969—Browns, 27-23 (C)
1971—Browns, 20-13 (W)
1975—Redskins, 23-7 (C)
1979—Redskins, 13-9 (C)
1985—Redskins, 14-7 (C)
1988—Browns, 17-13 (W)
1991—Redskins, 42-17 (W)
2004—Browns, 17-13 (C)
2008—Redskins, 14-11 (W)
2012—Redskins, 38-21 (C)
(RS Pts.—Browns 1,122, Redskins 732)

DALLAS vs. ARIZONA
RS: Cowboys lead series, 55-30-1
PS: Cardinals lead series, 1-0;
See Arizona vs. Dallas
DALLAS vs. ATLANTA
RS: Cowboys lead series, 14-9
PS: Cowboys lead series, 2-0;
See Atlanta vs. Dallas
DALLAS vs. BALTIMORE
RS: Ravens lead series, 4-0;
See Baltimore vs. Dallas
DALLAS vs. BUFFALO
RS: Cowboys lead series, 6-3
PS: Cowboys lead series, 2-0;
See Buffalo vs. Dallas
DALLAS vs. CAROLINA
RS: Cowboys lead series, 9-1
PS: Panthers lead series, 2-0;
See Carolina vs. Dallas
DALLAS vs. CHICAGO
RS: Series tied, 11-11
PS: Cowboys lead series, 2-0;
See Chicago vs. Dallas
DALLAS vs. CINCINNATI
RS: Cowboys lead series, 7-4;
See Cincinnati vs. Dallas
DALLAS vs. CLEVELAND
RS: Browns lead series, 15-12
PS: Browns lead series, 2-1;
See Cleveland vs. Dallas
DALLAS vs. DENVER
RS: Broncos lead series, 7-4
PS: Cowboys lead series, 1-0
1973—Cowboys, 22-10 (Den)
1977—Cowboys, 14-6 (Dal)
    *Cowboys, 27-10 (New Orleans)
1980—Broncos, 41-20 (Den)
1986—Broncos, 29-14 (Den)
1992—Cowboys, 31-27 (Den)
1995—Cowboys, 31-21 (Dal)
1998—Broncos, 42-23 (Den)
2001—Broncos, 26-24 (Dal)
2005—Broncos, 24-21 (Dal) OT
2009—Broncos, 17-10 (Den)
2013—Broncos, 51-48 (Dal)
(RS Pts.—Broncos 294, Cowboys 258)
(PS Pts.—Cowboys 27, Broncos 10)
*Super Bowl XII
DALLAS vs. DETROIT
RS: Cowboys lead series, 12-11
PS: Series tied, 1-1
1960—Lions, 23-14 (Det)
1963—Cowboys, 17-14 (Dal)
1968—Cowboys, 59-13 (Dal)
1970—*Cowboys, 5-0 (Dal)
1972—Cowboys, 28-24 (Dal)
1975—Cowboys, 36-10 (Det)

1977—Cowboys, 37-0 (Dal)
1981—Lions, 27-24 (Det)
1985—Lions, 26-21 (Det)
1986—Cowboys, 31-7 (Det)
1987—Lions, 27-17 (Det)
1991—Lions, 34-10 (Det)
    *Lions, 38-6 (Det)
1992—Cowboys, 37-3 (Det)
1994—Lions, 20-17 (Dal) OT
2001—Lions, 15-10 (Det)
2002—Lions, 9-7 (Det)
2003—Cowboys, 38-7 (Det)
2004—Cowboys, 31-21 (Dal)
2005—Cowboys, 20-7 (Dal)
2006—Lions, 39-31 (Dal)
2007—Cowboys, 28-27 (Det)
2010—Cowboys, 35-19 (Dal)
2011—Lions, 34-30 (Dal)
2013—Lions, 31-30 (Det)
(RS Pts.—Cowboys 608, Lions 437)
(PS Pts.—Lions 38, Cowboys 11)
*NFC Divisional Playoff
DALLAS vs. GREEN BAY
RS: Packers lead series, 13-12
PS: Cowboys lead series, 4-2
1960—Packers, 41-7 (GB)
1964—Packers, 45-21 (D)
1965—Packers, 13-3 (Mil)
1966—*Packers, 34-27 (D)
1967—*Packers, 21-17 (GB)
1968—Packers, 28-17 (D)
1970—Cowboys, 16-3 (D)
1972—Packers, 16-13 (Mil)
1975—Packers, 19-17 (D)
1978—Cowboys, 42-14 (Mil)
1980—Cowboys, 28-7 (Mil)
1982—**Cowboys, 37-26 (D)
1984—Cowboys, 20-6 (D)
1989—Packers, 31-13 (GB)
    Packers, 20-10 (D)
1991—Cowboys, 20-17 (Mil)
1993—Cowboys, 36-14 (D)
    ***Cowboys, 27-17 (D)
1994—Cowboys, 42-31 (D)
    ***Cowboys, 35-9 (D)
1995—Cowboys, 34-24 (D)
    ****Cowboys, 38-27 (D)
1996—Cowboys, 21-6 (D)
1997—Packers, 45-17 (GB)
1999—Cowboys, 27-13 (D)
2004—Packers, 41-20 (GB)
2007—Cowboys, 37-27 (D)
2008—Cowboys, 27-16 (GB)
2009—Packers, 17-7 (GB)
2010—Packers, 45-7 (GB)
2013—Packers, 37-36 (D)
(RS Pts.—Packers 576, Cowboys 538)
(PS Pts.—Cowboys 181, Packers 134)
*NFL Championship
**NFC Second-Round Playoff
***NFC Divisional Playoff
****NFC Championship
DALLAS vs. HOUSTON
RS: Cowboys lead series, 2-1
2002—Texans, 19-10 (H)
2006—Cowboys, 34-6 (D)
2010—Cowboys, 27-13 (H)
(RS Pts.—Cowboys 71, Texans 38)
DALLAS vs. *INDIANAPOLIS
RS: Cowboys lead series, 9-5
PS: Colts lead series, 1-0
1960—Colts, 45-7 (D)
1967—Colts, 23-17 (B)

1969—Cowboys, 27-10 (D)
1970—**Colts, 16-13 (Miami)
1972—Cowboys, 21-0 (B)
1976—Cowboys, 30-27 (D)
1978—Cowboys, 38-0 (D)
1981—Cowboys, 37-13 (B)
1984—Cowboys, 22-3 (D)
1993—Cowboys, 27-3 (I)
1996—Colts, 25-24 (D)
1999—Colts, 34-24 (I)
2002—Colts, 20-3 (I)
2006—Cowboys, 21-14 (D)
2010—Cowboys, 38-35 (I) OT
(RS Pts.—Cowboys 336, Colts 252)
(PS Pts.—Colts 16, Cowboys 13)
*Franchise in Baltimore prior to 1984
**Super Bowl V

DALLAS vs. JACKSONVILLE
RS: Jaguars lead series, 3-2
1997—Cowboys, 26-22 (D)
2000—Jaguars, 23-17 (D) OT
2002—Cowboys, 21-19 (D)
2006—Jaguars, 24-17 (J)
2010—Jaguars, 35-17 (D)
(RS Pts.—Jaguars 123, Cowboys 98)

DALLAS vs. KANSAS CITY
RS: Cowboys lead series, 6-4
1970—Cowboys, 27-16 (KC)
1975—Chiefs, 34-31 (D)
1983—Cowboys, 41-21 (D)
1989—Chiefs, 36-28 (KC)
1992—Cowboys, 17-10 (D)
1995—Cowboys, 24-12 (D)
1998—Chiefs, 20-17 (KC)
2005—Cowboys, 31-28 (D)
2009—Cowboys, 26-20 (KC) OT
2013—Chiefs, 17-16 (KC)
(RS Pts.—Cowboys 258, Chiefs 214)

DALLAS vs. MIAMI
RS: Dolphins lead series, 7-5
PS: Cowboys lead series, 1-0
1971—*Cowboys, 24-3 (New Orleans)
1973—Dolphins, 14-7 (D)
1978—Dolphins, 23-16 (M)
1981—Cowboys, 28-27 (D)
1984—Dolphins, 28-21 (M)
1987—Dolphins, 20-14 (D)
1989—Dolphins, 17-14 (D)
1993—Dolphins, 16-14 (D)
1996—Cowboys, 29-10 (M)
1999—Cowboys, 20-0 (D)
2003—Dolphins, 40-21 (D)
2007—Cowboys, 37-20 (M)
2011—Cowboys, 20-19 (D)
(RS Pts.—Cowboys 241, Dolphins 234)
(PS Pts.—Cowboys 24, Dolphins 3)
*Super Bowl VI

DALLAS vs. MINNESOTA
RS: Series tied, 11-11
PS: Cowboys lead series, 4-3
1961—Cowboys, 21-7 (D)
        Cowboys, 28-0 (M)
1966—Cowboys, 28-17 (D)
1968—Cowboys, 20-7 (M)
1970—Vikings, 54-13 (M)
1971—*Cowboys, 20-12 (M)
1973—**Vikings, 27-10 (D)
1974—Vikings, 23-21 (D)
1975—*Cowboys, 17-14 (M)
1977—Cowboys, 16-10 (M) OT
        **Cowboys, 23-6 (D)
1978—Vikings, 21-10 (D)
1979—Cowboys, 36-20 (M)

1982—Vikings, 31-27 (M)
1983—Cowboys, 37-24 (M)
1987—Vikings, 44-38 (D) OT
1988—Vikings, 43-3 (D)
1993—Cowboys, 37-20 (M)
1995—Cowboys, 23-17 (M) OT
1996—***Cowboys, 40-15 (D)
1998—Vikings, 46-36 (D)
1999—Vikings, 27-17 (M)
        ***Vikings, 27-10 (M)
2000—Vikings, 27-15 (D)
2004—Vikings, 35-17 (M)
2007—Cowboys, 24-14 (D)
2009—*Vikings, 34-3 (M)
2010—Vikings, 24-21 (M)
2013—Cowboys, 27-23 (D)
(RS Pts.—Vikings 534, Cowboys 515)
(PS Pts.—Vikings 135, Cowboys 123)
*NFC Divisional Playoff
**NFC Championship
***NFC First-Round Playoff

DALLAS vs. NEW ENGLAND
RS: Cowboys lead series, 7-4
1971—Cowboys, 44-21 (D)
1975—Cowboys, 34-31 (NE)
1978—Cowboys, 17-10 (D)
1981—Cowboys, 35-21 (NE)
1984—Cowboys, 20-17 (D)
1987—Cowboys, 23-17 (NE) OT
1996—Cowboys, 12-6 (D)
1999—Patriots, 13-6 (NE)
2003—Patriots, 12-0 (NE)
2007—Patriots, 48-27 (D)
2011—Patriots, 20-16 (NE)
(RS Pts.—Cowboys 234, Patriots 216)

DALLAS vs. NEW ORLEANS
RS: Cowboys lead series, 15-11
1967—Cowboys, 14-10 (D)
        Cowboys, 27-10 (NO)
1968—Cowboys, 17-3 (NO)
1969—Cowboys, 21-17 (NO)
        Cowboys, 33-17 (D)
1971—Saints, 24-14 (NO)
1973—Cowboys, 40-3 (D)
1976—Cowboys, 24-6 (NO)
1978—Cowboys, 27-7 (D)
1982—Cowboys, 21-7 (D)
1983—Cowboys, 21-20 (D)
1984—Cowboys, 30-27 (D) OT
1988—Saints, 20-17 (NO)
1989—Saints, 28-0 (NO)
1990—Cowboys, 17-13 (D)
1991—Cowboys, 23-14 (D)
1994—Cowboys, 24-16 (NO)
1998—Saints, 22-3 (NO)
1999—Saints, 31-24 (NO)
2003—Saints, 13-7 (NO)
2004—Saints, 27-13 (D)
2006—Saints, 42-17 (D)
2009—Cowboys, 24-17 (NO)
2010—Saints, 30-27 (D)
2012—Saints, 34-31 (D) OT
2013—Saints, 49-17 (NO)
(RS Pts.—Cowboys 533, Saints 507)

DALLAS vs. N.Y. GIANTS
RS: Cowboys lead series, 59-42-2
PS: Giants lead series, 1-0
1960—Tie, 31-31 (NY)
1961—Giants, 31-10 (D)
        Cowboys, 17-16 (NY)
1962—Giants, 41-10 (D)
        Giants, 41-31 (NY)
1963—Giants, 37-21 (NY)

        Giants, 34-27 (D)
1964—Tie, 13-13 (D)
        Cowboys, 31-21 (NY)
1965—Cowboys, 31-2 (D)
        Cowboys, 38-20 (NY)
1966—Cowboys, 52-7 (D)
        Cowboys, 17-7 (NY)
1967—Cowboys, 38-24 (D)
1968—Giants, 27-21 (D)
        Cowboys, 28-10 (NY)
1969—Cowboys, 25-3 (D)
1970—Cowboys, 28-10 (D)
        Giants, 23-20 (NY)
1971—Cowboys, 20-13 (D)
        Cowboys, 42-14 (NY)
1972—Cowboys, 23-14 (NY)
        Giants, 23-3 (D)
1973—Cowboys, 45-28 (D)
        Cowboys, 23-10 (New Haven)
1974—Giants, 14-6 (D)
        Cowboys, 21-7 (New Haven)
1975—Cowboys, 13-7 (NY)
        Cowboys, 14-3 (D)
1976—Cowboys, 24-14 (D)
        Cowboys, 9-3 (D)
1977—Cowboys, 41-21 (D)
        Cowboys, 24-10 (NY)
1978—Cowboys, 34-24 (NY)
        Cowboys, 24-3 (D)
1979—Cowboys, 16-14 (NY)
        Cowboys, 28-7 (D)
1980—Cowboys, 24-3 (D)
        Giants, 38-35 (NY)
1981—Cowboys, 18-10 (D)
        Giants, 13-10 (NY) OT
1983—Cowboys, 28-13 (D)
        Cowboys, 38-20 (NY)
1984—Giants, 28-7 (D)
        Giants, 19-7 (D)
1985—Cowboys, 30-29 (NY)
        Cowboys, 28-21 (D)
1986—Cowboys, 31-28 (D)
        Giants, 17-14 (NY)
1987—Cowboys, 16-14 (NY)
        Cowboys, 33-24 (D)
1988—Giants, 12-10 (D)
        Giants, 29-21 (NY)
1989—Giants, 30-13 (D)
        Giants, 15-0 (NY)
1990—Giants, 28-7 (D)
        Giants, 31-17 (NY)
1991—Cowboys, 21-16 (D)
        Giants, 22-9 (NY)
1992—Cowboys, 34-28 (NY)
        Cowboys, 30-3 (D)
1993—Cowboys, 31-9 (D)
        Cowboys, 16-13 (NY) OT
1994—Cowboys, 38-10 (D)
        Giants, 15-10 (NY)
1995—Cowboys, 35-0 (NY)
        Cowboys, 21-20 (D)
1996—Cowboys, 27-0 (D)
        Giants, 20-6 (NY)
1997—Giants, 20-17 (NY)
        Giants, 20-7 (D)
1998—Cowboys, 31-7 (NY)
        Cowboys, 16-6 (D)
1999—Giants, 13-10 (NY)
        Cowboys, 26-18 (D)
2000—Giants, 19-14 (NY)
        Giants, 17-13 (D)
2001—Giants, 27-24 (NY) OT
        Cowboys, 20-13 (D)

2002—Giants, 21-17 (D)
    Giants, 37-7 (NY)
2003—Cowboys, 35-32 (NY) OT
    Cowboys, 19-3 (D)
2004—Giants, 26-10 (D)
    Giants, 28-24 (NY)
2005—Cowboys, 16-13 (D) OT
    Giants, 17-10 (NY)
2006—Giants, 36-22 (D)
    Cowboys, 23-20 (NY)
2007—Cowboys, 45-35 (D)
    Cowboys, 31-20 (NY)
    *Giants, 21-17 (D)
2008—Giants, 35-14 (NY)
    Cowboys, 20-8 (D)
2009—Giants, 33-31 (D)
    Giants, 31-24 (NY)
2010—Giants, 41-35 (D)
    Cowboys, 33-20 (NY)
2011—Giants, 37-34 (D)
    Giants, 31-14 (NY)
2012—Cowboys, 24-17 (NY)
    Giants, 29-24 (D)
2013—Cowboys, 36-31 (D)
    Cowboys, 24-21 (NY)
(RS Pts.—Cowboys 2,314, Giants 1,987)
(PS Pts.—Giants 21, Cowboys 17)
*NFC Divisional Playoff
DALLAS vs. N.Y. JETS
RS: Cowboys lead series, 7-3
1971—Cowboys, 52-10 (D)
1975—Cowboys, 31-21 (NY)
1978—Cowboys, 30-7 (NY)
1987—Cowboys, 38-24 (NY)
1990—Jets, 24-9 (NY)
1993—Cowboys, 28-7 (NY)
1999—Jets, 22-21 (D)
2003—Cowboys, 17-6 (NY)
2007—Cowboys, 34-3 (D)
2011—Jets, 27-24 (NY)
(RS Pts.—Cowboys 284, Jets 151)
DALLAS vs. *OAKLAND
RS: Raiders lead series, 6-5
1974—Raiders, 27-23 (O)
1980—Cowboys, 19-13 (O)
1983—Raiders, 40-38 (D)
1986—Raiders, 17-13 (D)
1992—Cowboys, 28-13 (LA)
1995—Cowboys, 34-21 (O)
1998—Raiders, 13-12 (D)
2001—Raiders, 28-21 (O)
2005—Raiders, 19-13 (O)
2009—Cowboys, 24-7 (D)
2013—Cowboys, 31-24 (D)
(RS Pts.—Cowboys 256, Raiders 222)
*Franchise in Los Angeles from 1982-1994
DALLAS vs. PHILADELPHIA
RS: Cowboys lead series, 59-47
PS: Cowboys lead series, 3-1
1960—Eagles, 27-25 (D)
1961—Eagles, 43-7 (D)
    Eagles, 35-13 (P)
1962—Cowboys, 41-19 (D)
    Eagles, 28-14 (P)
1963—Eagles, 24-21 (P)
    Cowboys, 27-20 (D)
1964—Eagles, 17-14 (D)
    Eagles, 24-14 (P)
1965—Eagles, 35-24 (D)
    Cowboys, 21-19 (P)
1966—Cowboys, 56-7 (D)
    Eagles, 24-23 (P)
1967—Eagles, 21-14 (P)

Cowboys, 38-17 (D)
1968—Cowboys, 45-13 (P)
    Cowboys, 34-14 (D)
1969—Cowboys, 38-7 (P)
    Cowboys, 49-14 (D)
1970—Cowboys, 17-7 (P)
    Cowboys, 21-17 (D)
1971—Cowboys, 42-7 (P)
    Cowboys, 20-7 (D)
1972—Cowboys, 28-6 (D)
    Cowboys, 28-7 (P)
1973—Eagles, 30-16 (P)
    Cowboys, 31-10 (D)
1974—Eagles, 13-10 (P)
    Cowboys, 31-24 (D)
1975—Cowboys, 20-17 (P)
    Cowboys, 27-17 (D)
1976—Cowboys, 27-7 (D)
    Cowboys, 26-7 (P)
1977—Cowboys, 16-10 (P)
    Cowboys, 24-14 (D)
1978—Cowboys, 14-7 (D)
    Cowboys, 31-13 (P)
1979—Eagles, 31-21 (D)
    Cowboys, 24-17 (P)
1980—Eagles, 17-10 (P)
    Cowboys, 35-27 (D)
    *Eagles, 20-7 (P)
1981—Cowboys, 17-14 (P)
    Cowboys, 21-10 (D)
1982—Eagles, 24-20 (P)
1983—Cowboys, 37-7 (D)
    Cowboys, 27-20 (P)
1984—Cowboys, 23-17 (D)
    Cowboys, 26-10 (P)
1985—Eagles, 16-14 (P)
    Cowboys, 34-17 (D)
1986—Cowboys, 17-14 (P)
    Eagles, 23-21 (D)
1987—Cowboys, 41-22 (D)
    Eagles, 37-20 (P)
1988—Eagles, 24-23 (P)
    Eagles, 23-7 (D)
1989—Eagles, 27-0 (D)
    Eagles, 20-10 (P)
1990—Eagles, 21-20 (P)
    Eagles, 17-3 (D)
1991—Eagles, 24-0 (D)
    Cowboys, 25-13 (P)
1992—Eagles, 31-7 (D)
    Cowboys, 20-10 (D)
    **Cowboys, 34-10 (D)
1993—Cowboys, 23-10 (P)
    Cowboys, 23-17 (D)
1994—Cowboys, 24-13 (D)
    Cowboys, 31-19 (P)
1995—Cowboys, 34-12 (D)
    Eagles, 20-17 (P)
    **Cowboys, 30-11 (D)
1996—Cowboys, 23-19 (P)
    Eagles, 31-21 (D)
1997—Cowboys, 21-20 (D)
    Eagles, 13-12 (P)
1998—Cowboys, 34-0 (P)
    Cowboys, 13-9 (D)
1999—Eagles, 13-10 (P)
    Cowboys, 20-10 (D)
2000—Eagles, 41-14 (D)
    Eagles, 16-13 (P) OT
2001—Eagles, 40-18 (P)
    Eagles, 36-3 (D)
2002—Eagles, 44-13 (D)
    Eagles, 27-3 (D)

2003—Cowboys, 23-21 (D)
    Eagles, 36-10 (P)
2004—Eagles, 49-21 (D)
    Eagles, 12-7 (P)
2005—Cowboys, 33-10 (D)
    Cowboys, 21-20 (P)
2006—Eagles, 38-24 (P)
    Eagles, 23-7 (D)
2007—Cowboys, 38-17 (P)
    Eagles, 10-6 (D)
2008—Cowboys, 41-37 (D)
    Eagles, 44-6 (P)
2009—Cowboys, 20-16 (D)
    Cowboys, 24-0 (D)
    ***Cowboys, 34-14 (D)
2010—Eagles, 30-27 (D)
    Cowboys, 14-13 (P)
2011—Eagles, 34-7 (P)
    Eagles, 20-7 (D)
2012—Cowboys, 38-23 (P)
    Cowboys, 38-33 (D)
2013—Cowboys, 17-3 (P)
    Eagles, 24-22 (D)
(RS Pts.—Cowboys 2,291, Eagles 2,084)
(PS Pts.—Cowboys 105, Eagles 55)
*NFC Championship
**NFC Divisional Playoff
***NFC First-Round Playoff
DALLAS vs. PITTSBURGH
RS: Cowboys lead series, 15-13
PS: Steelers lead series, 2-1
1960—Steelers, 35-28 (D)
1961—Cowboys, 27-24 (D)
    Steelers, 37-7 (P)
1962—Steelers, 30-28 (D)
    Cowboys, 42-27 (P)
1963—Steelers, 27-21 (P)
    Steelers, 24-19 (D)
1964—Steelers, 23-17 (P)
    Cowboys, 17-14 (D)
1965—Steelers, 22-13 (P)
    Cowboys, 24-17 (D)
1966—Cowboys, 52-21 (D)
    Cowboys, 20-7 (P)
1967—Cowboys, 24-21 (P)
1968—Cowboys, 28-7 (D)
1969—Cowboys, 10-7 (P)
1972—Cowboys, 17-13 (D)
1975—*Steelers, 21-17 (Miami)
1977—Steelers, 28-13 (P)
1978—**Steelers, 35-31 (Miami)
1979—Steelers, 14-3 (P)
1982—Steelers, 36-28 (D)
1985—Cowboys, 27-13 (D)
1988—Steelers, 24-21 (P)
1991—Cowboys, 20-10 (P)
1994—Cowboys, 26-9 (D)
1995—***Cowboys, 27-17 (Tempe)
1997—Cowboys, 37-7 (P)
2004—Steelers, 24-20 (D)
2008—Steelers, 20-13 (P)
2012—Cowboys, 27-24 (D)
(RS Pts.—Cowboys 629, Steelers 565)
(PS Pts.—Cowboys 75, Steelers 73)
*Super Bowl X
**Super Bowl XIII
***Super Bowl XXX
DALLAS vs. *ST. LOUIS
RS: Cowboys lead series, 12-11
PS: Series tied, 4-4
1960—Rams, 38-13 (D)
1962—Cowboys, 27-17 (LA)
1967—Rams, 35-13 (D)

1969—Rams, 24-23 (LA)
1971—Cowboys, 28-21 (D)
1973—Rams, 37-31 (LA)
   **Cowboys, 27-16 (D)
1975—Cowboys, 18-7 (D)
   ***Cowboys, 37-7 (LA)
1976—**Rams, 14-12 (D)
1978—Rams, 27-14 (LA)
   ***Cowboys, 28-0 (LA)
1979—Cowboys, 30-6 (D)
   **Rams, 21-19 (D)
1980—Rams, 38-14 (LA)
   ****Cowboys, 34-13 (D)
1981—Cowboys, 29-17 (D)
1983—****Rams, 24-17 (D)
1984—Cowboys, 20-13 (LA)
1985—**Rams, 20-0 (LA)
1986—Rams, 29-10 (LA)
1987—Cowboys, 29-21 (LA)
1989—Rams, 35-31 (D)
1990—Cowboys, 24-21 (LA)
1992—Rams, 27-23 (D)
2002—Cowboys, 13-10 (StL)
2005—Rams, 20-10 (D)
2007—Cowboys, 35-7 (D)
2008—Rams, 34-14 (StL)
2011—Cowboys, 34-7 (D)
2013—Cowboys, 31-7 (D)
(RS Pts.—Cowboys 514, Rams 498)
(PS Pts.—Cowboys 174, Rams 115)
*Franchise in Los Angeles prior to 1995
**NFC Divisional Playoff
***NFC Championship
****NFC First-Round Playoff
DALLAS vs. SAN DIEGO
RS: Cowboys lead series, 6-4
1972—Cowboys, 34-28 (SD)
1980—Cowboys, 42-31 (D)
1983—Chargers, 24-23 (SD)
1986—Cowboys, 24-21 (SD)
1990—Cowboys, 17-14 (D)
1995—Cowboys, 23-9 (SD)
2001—Chargers, 32-21 (D)
2005—Cowboys, 28-24 (SD)
2009—Chargers, 20-17 (D)
2013—Chargers, 30-21 (SD)
(RS Pts.—Cowboys 250, Chargers 233)
DALLAS vs. SAN FRANCISCO
RS: 49ers lead series, 14-11-1
PS: Cowboys lead series, 5-2
1960—49ers, 26-14 (D)
1963—49ers, 31-24 (SF)
1965—49ers, 39-31 (D)
1967—49ers, 24-16 (SF)
1969—Tie, 24-24 (D)
1970—*Cowboys, 17-10 (SF)
1971—*Cowboys, 14-3 (D)
1972—49ers, 31-10 (D)
   **Cowboys, 30-28 (SF)
1974—Cowboys, 20-14 (D)
1977—Cowboys, 42-35 (SF)
1979—Cowboys, 21-13 (SF)
1980—Cowboys, 59-14 (D)
1981—49ers, 45-14 (SF)
   *49ers, 28-27 (SF)
1983—49ers, 42-17 (SF)
1985—49ers, 31-16 (SF)
1989—49ers, 31-14 (D)
1990—49ers, 24-6 (D)
1992—*Cowboys, 30-20 (SF)
1993—Cowboys, 26-17 (D)
   *Cowboys, 38-21 (D)
1994—49ers, 21-14 (SF)

   *49ers, 38-28 (SF)
1995—49ers, 38-20 (D)
1996—Cowboys, 20-17 (SF) OT
1997—49ers, 17-10 (SF)
2000—49ers, 41-24 (D)
2001—Cowboys, 27-21 (D)
2002—49ers, 31-27 (D)
2005—Cowboys, 34-31 (SF)
2008—Cowboys, 35-22 (D)
2011—Cowboys, 27-24 (SF) OT
(RS Pts.—49ers 696, Cowboys 600)
(PS Pts.—Cowboys 184, 49ers 148)
*NFC Championship
**NFC Divisional Playoff
DALLAS vs. SEATTLE
RS: Cowboys lead series, 9-5
PS: Seahawks lead series, 1-0
1976—Cowboys, 28-13 (S)
1980—Cowboys, 51-7 (D)
1983—Cowboys, 35-10 (S)
1986—Seahawks, 31-14 (D)
1992—Cowboys, 27-0 (D)
1998—Cowboys, 30-22 (D)
2001—Seahawks, 29-3 (S)
2002—Seahawks, 17-14 (D)
2004—Cowboys, 43-39 (S)
2005—Seahawks, 13-10 (S)
2006—*Seahawks, 21-20 (S)
2008—Cowboys, 34-9 (D)
2009—Cowboys, 38-17 (D)
2011—Cowboys, 23-13 (D)
2012—Seahawks, 27-7 (S)
(RS Pts.—Cowboys 357, Seahawks 247)
(PS Pts.—Seahawks 21, Cowboys 20)
*NFC First-Round Playoff
DALLAS vs. TAMPA BAY
RS: Cowboys lead series, 11-3
PS: Cowboys lead series, 2-0
1977—Cowboys, 23-7 (D)
1980—Cowboys, 28-17 (D)
1981—*Cowboys, 38-0 (D)
1982—Cowboys, 14-9 (D)
   **Cowboys, 30-17 (D)
1983—Cowboys, 27-24 (D) OT
1990—Cowboys, 14-10 (D)
   Cowboys, 17-13 (TB)
2000—Buccaneers, 27-7 (TB)
2001—Buccaneers, 10-6 (D)
2003—Buccaneers, 16-0 (TB)
2006—Cowboys, 38-10 (D)
2008—Cowboys, 13-9 (D)
2009—Cowboys, 34-21 (TB)
2011—Cowboys, 31-15 (TB)
2012—Cowboys, 16-10 (D)
(RS Pts.—Cowboys 268, Buccaneers 198)
(PS Pts.—Cowboys 68, Buccaneers 17)
*NFC Divisional Playoff
**NFC First-Round Playoff
DALLAS vs. *TENNESSEE
RS: Cowboys lead series, 7-6
1970—Cowboys, 52-10 (H)
1974—Cowboys, 10-0 (H)
1979—Oilers, 30-24 (D)
1982—Cowboys, 37-7 (H)
1985—Cowboys, 17-10 (H)
1988—Oilers, 25-17 (D)
1991—Oilers, 26-23 (H) OT
1994—Cowboys, 20-17 (D)
1997—Oilers, 27-14 (D)
2000—Titans, 31-0 (T)
2002—Cowboys, 21-13 (D)
2006—Cowboys, 45-14 (T)
2010—Titans, 34-27 (D)

(RS Pts.—Cowboys 307, Titans 244)
*Franchise in Houston prior to 1997;
known as Oilers prior to 1999
DALLAS vs. WASHINGTON
RS: Cowboys lead series, 64-40-2
PS: Redskins lead series, 2-0
1960—Redskins, 26-14 (W)
1961—Tie, 28-28 (D)
   Redskins, 34-24 (W)
1962—Tie, 35-35 (D)
   Cowboys, 38-10 (W)
1963—Redskins, 21-17 (W)
   Cowboys, 35-20 (D)
1964—Cowboys, 24-18 (D)
   Redskins, 28-16 (W)
1965—Cowboys, 27-7 (D)
   Redskins, 34-31 (W)
1966—Cowboys, 31-30 (W)
   Redskins, 34-31 (D)
1967—Cowboys, 17-14 (W)
   Redskins, 27-20 (D)
1968—Cowboys, 44-24 (W)
   Cowboys, 29-20 (D)
1969—Cowboys, 41-28 (W)
   Cowboys, 20-10 (D)
1970—Cowboys, 45-21 (W)
   Cowboys, 34-0 (D)
1971—Redskins, 20-16 (D)
   Cowboys, 13-0 (W)
1972—Cowboys, 24-20 (D)
   Cowboys, 34-24 (D)
   *Redskins, 26-3 (W)
1973—Redskins, 14-7 (W)
   Cowboys, 27-7 (D)
1974—Redskins, 28-21 (W)
   Cowboys, 24-23 (D)
1975—Redskins, 30-24 (W) OT
   Cowboys, 31-10 (D)
1976—Cowboys, 20-7 (W)
   Redskins, 27-14 (D)
1977—Cowboys, 34-16 (D)
   Cowboys, 14-7 (W)
1978—Redskins, 9-5 (W)
   Cowboys, 37-10 (D)
1979—Redskins, 34-20 (W)
   Cowboys, 35-34 (D)
1980—Cowboys, 17-3 (W)
   Cowboys, 14-10 (D)
1981—Cowboys, 26-10 (W)
   Cowboys, 24-10 (D)
1982—Cowboys, 24-10 (W)
   *Redskins, 31-17 (W)
1983—Cowboys, 31-30 (W)
   Redskins, 31-10 (D)
1984—Redskins, 34-14 (W)
   Redskins, 30-28 (D)
1985—Cowboys, 44-14 (W)
   Cowboys, 13-7 (W)
1986—Cowboys, 30-6 (D)
   Redskins, 41-14 (W)
1987—Redskins, 13-7 (D)
   Redskins, 24-20 (W)
1988—Redskins, 35-17 (D)
   Cowboys, 24-17 (W)
1989—Redskins, 30-7 (D)
   Cowboys, 13-3 (W)
1990—Redskins, 19-15 (W)
   Cowboys, 27-17 (D)
1991—Redskins, 33-31 (D)
   Cowboys, 24-21 (W)
1992—Cowboys, 23-10 (D)
   Redskins, 20-17 (W)

1993—Redskins, 35-16 (W)
    Cowboys, 38-3 (D)
1994—Cowboys, 34-7 (W)
    Cowboys, 31-7 (D)
1995—Redskins, 27-23 (W)
    Redskins, 24-17 (D)
1996—Cowboys, 21-10 (D)
    Redskins, 37-10 (D)
1997—Redskins, 21-16 (W)
    Cowboys, 17-14 (D)
1998—Cowboys, 31-10 (W)
    Cowboys, 23-7 (D)
1999—Cowboys, 41-35 (W) OT
    Cowboys, 38-20 (D)
2000—Cowboys, 27-21 (W)
    Cowboys, 32-13 (D)
2001—Cowboys, 9-7 (D)
    Cowboys, 20-14 (W)
2002—Cowboys, 27-20 (D)
    Redskins, 20-14 (W)
2003—Cowboys, 21-14 (D)
    Cowboys, 27-0 (W)
2004—Cowboys, 21-18 (W)
    Cowboys, 13-10 (D)
2005—Redskins, 14-13 (D)
    Redskins, 35-7 (W)
2006—Cowboys, 27-10 (D)
    Redskins, 22-19 (W)
2007—Cowboys, 28-23 (D)
    Redskins, 27-6 (W)
2008—Redskins, 26-24 (D)
    Cowboys, 14-10 (W)
2009—Cowboys, 7-6 (D)
    Cowboys, 17-0 (W)
2010—Redskins, 13-7 (W)
    Cowboys, 33-30 (D)
2011—Cowboys, 18-16 (D)
    Cowboys, 27-24 (W) OT
2012—Redskins, 38-31 (D)
    Redskins, 28-18 (W)
2013—Cowboys, 31-16 (D)
    Cowboys, 24-23 (W)
(RS Pts.—Cowboys 2,429, Redskins 2,026)
(PS Pts.—Redskins 57, Cowboys 20)
*NFC Championship

DENVER vs. ARIZONA
RS: Broncos lead series, 7-1-1;
See Arizona vs. Denver
DENVER vs. ATLANTA
RS: Broncos lead series, 8-5
PS: Broncos lead series, 1-0;
See Atlanta vs. Denver
DENVER vs. BALTIMORE
RS: Series tied, 5-5
PS: Ravens lead series, 2-0;
See Baltimore vs. Denver
DENVER vs. BUFFALO
RS: Bills lead series, 19-15-1
PS: Bills lead series, 1-0;
See Buffalo vs. Denver
DENVER vs. CAROLINA
RS: Broncos lead series, 3-1;
See Carolina vs. Denver
DENVER vs. CHICAGO
RS: Series tied, 7-7;
See Chicago vs. Denver
DENVER vs. CINCINNATI
RS: Broncos lead series, 19-8;
See Cincinnati vs. Denver
DENVER vs. CLEVELAND
RS: Broncos lead series, 19-5
PS: Broncos lead series, 3-0;

See Cleveland vs. Denver
DENVER vs. DALLAS
RS: Broncos lead series, 7-4
PS: Cowboys lead series, 1-0;
See Dallas vs. Denver
DENVER vs. DETROIT
RS: Broncos lead series, 6-5
1971—Lions, 24-20 (Den)
1974—Broncos, 31-27 (Det)
1978—Lions, 17-14 (Det)
1981—Broncos, 27-21 (Den)
1984—Broncos, 28-7 (Det)
1987—Broncos, 34-0 (Den)
1990—Lions, 40-27 (Det)
1999—Broncos, 17-7 (Den)
2003—Broncos, 20-16 (Den)
2007—Lions, 44-7 (Det)
2011—Lions, 45-10 (Den)
(RS Pts.—Lions 248, Broncos 235)
DENVER vs. GREEN BAY
RS: Packers lead series, 6-5-1
PS: Broncos lead series, 1-0
1971—Packers, 34-13 (Mil)
1975—Broncos, 23-13 (D)
1978—Broncos, 16-3 (D)
1984—Broncos, 17-14 (D)
1987—Tie, 17-17 (Mil) OT
1990—Broncos, 22-13 (D)
1993—Packers, 30-27 (GB)
1996—Packers, 41-6 (GB)
1997—*Broncos, 31-24 (San Diego)
1999—Broncos, 31-10 (D)
2003—Packers, 31-3 (GB)
2007—Packers, 19-13 (D) OT
2011—Packers, 49-23 (GB)
(RS Pts.—Packers 274, Broncos 211)
(PS Pts.—Broncos 31, Packers 24)
*Super Bowl XXXII
DENVER vs. HOUSTON
RS: Broncos lead series, 3-2
2004—Broncos, 31-13 (D)
2007—Texans, 31-13 (H)
2010—Broncos, 24-23 (D)
2012—Texans, 31-25 (D)
2013—Broncos, 37-13 (H)
(RS Pts.—Broncos 130, Texans 111)
DENVER vs. *INDIANAPOLIS
RS: Broncos lead series, 11-9
PS: Colts lead series, 2-0
1974—Broncos, 17-6 (B)
1977—Broncos, 27-13 (D)
1978—Colts, 7-6 (B)
1981—Broncos, 28-10 (D)
1983—Broncos, 17-10 (B)
    Broncos, 21-19 (D)
1985—Broncos, 15-10 (I)
1988—Colts, 55-23 (I)
1989—Broncos, 14-3 (D)
1990—Broncos, 27-17 (I)
1993—Broncos, 35-13 (D)
2001—Colts, 29-10 (I)
2002—Colts, 23-20 (D) OT
2003—Broncos, 31-17 (I)
    **Colts, 41-10 (I)
2004—Broncos, 33-14 (D)
    **Colts, 49-24 (I)
2006—Colts, 34-31 (D)
2007—Colts, 38-20 (I)
2009—Colts, 28-16 (I)
2010—Colts, 27-13 (D)
2013—Colts, 39-33 (I)
(RS Pts.—Broncos 437, Colts 412)
(PS Pts.—Colts 90, Broncos 34)

*Franchise in Baltimore prior to 1984
**AFC First-Round Playoff
DENVER vs. JACKSONVILLE
RS: Jaguars lead series, 5-4
PS: Series tied, 1-1
1995—Broncos, 31-23 (D)
1996—*Jaguars, 30-27 (D)
1997—**Broncos, 42-17 (D)
1998—Broncos, 37-24 (D)
1999—Jaguars, 27-24 (J)
2004—Jaguars, 7-6 (J)
2005—Broncos, 20-7 (J)
2007—Jaguars, 23-14 (D)
2008—Jaguars, 24-17 (D)
2010—Jaguars, 24-17 (J)
2013—Broncos, 35-19 (D)
(RS Pts.—Broncos 201, Jaguars 178)
(PS Pts.—Broncos 69, Jaguars 47)
*AFC Divisional Playoff
**AFC First-Round Playoff
DENVER vs. *KANSAS CITY
RS: Chiefs lead series, 56-51
PS: Broncos lead series, 1-0
1960—Texans, 17-14 (D)
    Texans, 34-7 (Dal)
1961—Texans, 19-12 (D)
    Texans, 49-21 (Dal)
1962—Texans, 24-3 (D)
    Texans, 17-10 (Dal)
1963—Chiefs, 59-7 (D)
    Chiefs, 52-21 (KC)
1964—Broncos, 33-27 (D)
    Chiefs, 49-39 (KC)
1965—Chiefs, 31-23 (D)
    Chiefs, 45-35 (KC)
1966—Chiefs, 37-10 (KC)
    Chiefs, 56-10 (D)
1967—Chiefs, 52-9 (D)
    Chiefs, 38-24 (D)
1968—Chiefs, 34-2 (KC)
    Chiefs, 30-7 (D)
1969—Chiefs, 26-13 (D)
    Chiefs, 31-17 (KC)
1970—Broncos, 26-13 (D)
    Chiefs, 16-0 (KC)
1971—Chiefs, 16-3 (D)
    Chiefs, 28-10 (KC)
1972—Chiefs, 45-24 (D)
    Chiefs, 24-21 (KC)
1973—Chiefs, 16-14 (KC)
    Broncos, 14-10 (D)
1974—Broncos, 17-14 (KC)
    Chiefs, 42-34 (D)
1975—Broncos, 37-33 (D)
    Chiefs, 26-13 (KC)
1976—Broncos, 35-26 (KC)
    Broncos, 17-16 (D)
1977—Broncos, 23-7 (D)
    Broncos, 14-7 (KC)
1978—Broncos, 23-17 (KC) OT
    Broncos, 24-3 (D)
1979—Broncos, 24-10 (KC)
    Broncos, 20-3 (D)
1980—Chiefs, 23-17 (D)
    Chiefs, 31-14 (KC)
1981—Chiefs, 28-14 (D)
    Broncos, 16-13 (D)
1982—Chiefs, 37-16 (D)
1983—Broncos, 27-24 (D)
    Chiefs, 48-17 (KC)
1984—Broncos, 21-0 (D)
    Chiefs, 16-13 (KC)
1985—Broncos, 30-10 (KC)

Broncos, 14-13 (D)
1986—Broncos, 38-17 (D)
Chiefs, 37-10 (KC)
1987—Broncos, 26-17 (KC)
Broncos, 20-17 (D)
1988—Chiefs, 20-13 (KC)
Broncos, 17-11 (D)
1989—Broncos, 34-20 (D)
Broncos, 16-13 (KC)
1990—Broncos, 24-23 (D)
Chiefs, 31-20 (KC)
1991—Broncos, 19-16 (D)
Broncos, 24-20 (KC)
1992—Broncos, 20-19 (D)
Chiefs, 42-20 (KC)
1993—Chiefs, 15-7 (KC)
Broncos, 27-21 (D)
1994—Chiefs, 31-28 (D)
Broncos, 20-17 (KC) OT
1995—Chiefs, 21-7 (D)
Chiefs, 20-17 (KC)
1996—Chiefs, 17-14 (KC)
Broncos, 34-7 (D)
1997—Broncos, 19-3 (D)
Chiefs, 24-22 (KC)
**Broncos, 14-10 (KC)
1998—Broncos, 30-7 (KC)
Broncos, 35-31 (D)
1999—Chiefs, 26-10 (KC)
Chiefs, 16-10 (D)
2000—Chiefs, 23-22 (D)
Chiefs, 20-7 (KC)
2001—Broncos, 20-6 (D)
Chiefs, 26-23 (KC) OT
2002—Broncos, 37-34 (KC) OT
Broncos, 31-24 (D)
2003—Chiefs, 24-23 (KC)
Broncos, 45-27 (D)
2004—Broncos, 34-24 (D)
Chiefs, 45-17 (KC)
2005—Broncos, 30-10 (D)
Chiefs, 31-27 (KC)
2006—Broncos, 9-6 (D) OT
Chiefs, 19-10 (KC)
2007—Broncos, 27-11 (KC)
Broncos, 41-7 (D)
2008—Chiefs, 33-19 (KC)
Broncos, 24-17 (D)
2009—Broncos, 44-13 (KC)
Chiefs, 44-24 (D)
2010—Broncos, 49-29 (D)
Chiefs, 10-6 (KC)
2011—Broncos, 17-10 (KC)
Chiefs, 7-3 (D)
2012—Broncos, 17-9 (KC)
Broncos, 38-3 (D)
2013—Broncos, 27-17 (D)
Broncos, 35-28 (KC)
(RS Pts.—Chiefs 2,458, Broncos 2,196)
(PS Pts.—Broncos 14, Chiefs 10)
*Franchise in Dallas prior to 1963 and
known as Texans
**AFC Divisional Playoff
DENVER vs. MIAMI
RS: Dolphins lead series, 11-4-1
PS: Broncos lead series, 1-0
1966—Dolphins, 24-7 (M)
Broncos, 17-7 (D)
1967—Dolphins, 35-21 (M)
1968—Broncos, 21-14 (D)
1969—Dolphins, 27-24 (M)
1971—Tie, 10-10 (D)
1975—Dolphins, 14-13 (M)

1985—Dolphins, 30-26 (D)
1998—Dolphins, 31-21 (M)
*Broncos, 38-3 (D)
1999—Dolphins, 38-21 (D)
2001—Dolphins, 21-10 (M)
2002—Dolphins, 24-22 (D)
2004—Broncos, 20-17 (D)
2005—Dolphins, 34-10 (M)
2008—Dolphins, 26-17 (D)
2011—Broncos, 18-15 (M) OT
(RS Pts.—Dolphins 367, Broncos 278)
(PS Pts.—Broncos 38, Dolphins 3)
*AFC Divisional Playoff
DENVER vs. MINNESOTA
RS: Vikings lead series, 7-6
1972—Vikings, 23-20 (D)
1978—Vikings, 12-9 (M) OT
1981—Broncos, 19-17 (D)
1984—Broncos, 42-21 (D)
1987—Vikings, 34-27 (M)
1990—Vikings, 27-22 (M)
1991—Broncos, 13-6 (M)
1993—Vikings, 26-23 (D)
1996—Broncos, 21-17 (M)
1999—Vikings, 23-20 (D)
2003—Vikings, 28-20 (M)
2007—Broncos, 22-19 (D) OT
2011—Broncos, 35-32 (M)
(RS Pts.—Broncos 293, Vikings 285)
DENVER vs. *NEW ENGLAND
RS: Broncos lead series, 25-19
PS: Broncos lead series, 3-1
1960—Broncos, 13-10 (B)
Broncos, 31-24 (D)
1961—Patriots, 45-17 (B)
Patriots, 28-24 (D)
1962—Patriots, 41-16 (B)
Patriots, 33-29 (D)
1963—Broncos, 14-10 (D)
Patriots, 40-21 (B)
1964—Patriots, 39-10 (D)
Patriots, 12-7 (B)
1965—Broncos, 27-10 (B)
Patriots, 28-20 (D)
1966—Patriots, 24-10 (D)
Broncos, 17-10 (B)
1967—Broncos, 26-21 (D)
1968—Patriots, 20-17 (D)
Broncos, 35-14 (B)
1969—Broncos, 35-7 (D)
1972—Broncos, 45-21 (D)
1976—Patriots, 38-14 (NE)
1979—Broncos, 45-10 (D)
1980—Patriots, 23-14 (NE)
1984—Broncos, 26-19 (D)
1986—Broncos, 27-20 (D)
**Broncos, 22-17 (D)
1987—Broncos, 31-20 (D)
1988—Broncos, 21-10 (D)
1991—Broncos, 9-6 (NE)
Broncos, 20-3 (D)
1995—Broncos, 37-3 (NE)
1996—Broncos, 34-8 (NE)
1997—Broncos, 34-13 (D)
1998—Broncos, 27-21 (D)
1999—Patriots, 24-23 (NE)
2000—Broncos, 28-19 (D)
2001—Broncos, 31-20 (D)
2002—Broncos, 24-16 (NE)
2003—Patriots, 30-26 (D)
2005—Broncos, 28-20 (D)
**Broncos, 27-13 (D)
2006—Broncos, 17-7 (NE)

2008—Patriots, 41-7 (NE)
2009—Broncos, 20-17 (D) OT
2011—Patriots, 41-23 (D)
**Patriots, 45-10 (NE)
2012—Patriots, 31-21 (NE)
2013—Patriots, 34-31 (NE) OT
***Broncos, 26-16 (D)
(RS Pts.—Broncos 1,023, Patriots 940)
(PS Pts.—Patriots 91, Broncos 85)
*Franchise in Boston prior to 1971
**AFC Divisional Playoff
***AFC Championship
DENVER vs. NEW ORLEANS
RS: Broncos lead series, 8-2
1970—Broncos, 31-6 (NO)
1974—Broncos, 33-17 (D)
1979—Broncos, 10-3 (D)
1985—Broncos, 34-23 (D)
1988—Saints, 42-0 (NO)
1994—Saints, 30-28 (D)
2000—Broncos, 38-23 (NO)
2004—Broncos, 34-13 (NO)
2008—Broncos, 34-32 (D)
2012—Broncos, 34-14 (D)
(RS Pts.—Broncos 276, Saints 203)
DENVER vs. N.Y. GIANTS
RS: Broncos lead series, 6-5
PS: Giants lead series, 1-0
1972—Giants, 29-17 (NY)
1976—Broncos, 14-13 (D)
1980—Broncos, 14-9 (NY)
1986—Giants, 19-16 (NY)
*Giants, 39-20 (Pasadena)
1989—Giants, 14-7 (D)
1992—Broncos, 27-13 (D)
1998—Broncos, 20-16 (NY)
2001—Broncos, 31-20 (D)
2005—Giants, 24-23 (NY)
2009—Broncos, 26-6 (D)
2013—Broncos, 41-23 (NY)
(RS Pts.—Broncos 232, Giants 190)
(PS Pts.—Giants 39, Broncos 20)
*Super Bowl XXI
DENVER vs. *N.Y. JETS
RS: Broncos lead series, 17-15-1
PS: Broncos lead series, 1-0
1960—Titans, 28-24 (NY)
Titans, 30-27 (D)
1961—Titans, 35-28 (NY)
Broncos, 27-10 (D)
1962—Broncos, 32-10 (NY)
Titans, 46-45 (D)
1963—Tie, 35-35 (NY)
Jets, 14-9 (D)
1964—Jets, 30-6 (NY)
Broncos, 20-16 (D)
1965—Broncos, 16-13 (D)
Jets, 45-10 (NY)
1966—Jets, 16-7 (D)
1967—Jets, 38-24 (D)
Broncos, 33-24 (NY)
1968—Broncos, 21-13 (NY)
1969—Broncos, 21-19 (D)
1973—Broncos, 40-28 (NY)
1976—Broncos, 46-3 (D)
1978—Jets, 31-28 (D)
1980—Broncos, 31-24 (D)
1986—Jets, 22-10 (NY)
1992—Broncos, 27-16 (D)
1993—Broncos, 26-20 (NY)
1994—Jets, 25-22 (NY) OT
1996—Broncos, 31-6 (D)
1998—**Broncos, 23-10 (D)

1999—Jets, 21-13 (D)
2000—Broncos, 30-23 (NY)
2002—Jets, 19-13 (NY)
2005—Broncos, 27-0 (D)
2008—Broncos, 34-17 (NY)
2010—Jets, 24-20 (D)
2011—Broncos, 17-13 (D)
(RS Pts.—Broncos 800, Jets 714)
(PS Pts.—Broncos 23, Jets 10)
*Jets known as Titans prior to 1963
**AFC Championship
DENVER vs. *OAKLAND
RS: Raiders lead series, 59-46-2
PS: Series tied, 1-1
1960—Broncos, 31-14 (D)
        Raiders, 48-10 (O)
1961—Raiders, 33-19 (O)
        Broncos, 27-24 (D)
1962—Broncos, 44-7 (D)
        Broncos, 23-6 (O)
1963—Raiders, 26-10 (D)
        Raiders, 35-31 (O)
1964—Raiders, 40-7 (O)
        Tie, 20-20 (D)
1965—Raiders, 28-20 (D)
        Raiders, 24-13 (O)
1966—Raiders, 17-3 (D)
        Raiders, 28-10 (O)
1967—Raiders, 51-0 (O)
        Raiders, 21-17 (D)
1968—Raiders, 43-7 (D)
        Raiders, 33-27 (O)
1969—Raiders, 24-14 (D)
        Raiders, 41-10 (O)
1970—Raiders, 35-23 (D)
        Raiders, 24-19 (D)
1971—Raiders, 27-16 (D)
        Raiders, 21-13 (O)
1972—Broncos, 30-23 (O)
        Raiders, 37-20 (D)
1973—Tie, 23-23 (D)
        Raiders, 21-17 (O)
1974—Raiders, 28-17 (D)
        Broncos, 20-17 (O)
1975—Raiders, 42-17 (D)
        Raiders, 17-10 (O)
1976—Raiders, 17-10 (D)
        Raiders, 19-6 (O)
1977—Broncos, 30-7 (O)
        Raiders, 24-14 (D)
        **Broncos, 20-17 (D)
1978—Broncos, 14-6 (D)
        Broncos, 21-6 (O)
1979—Raiders, 27-3 (O)
        Raiders, 14-10 (D)
1980—Raiders, 9-3 (O)
        Raiders, 24-21 (D)
1981—Broncos, 9-7 (D)
        Broncos, 17-0 (O)
1982—Raiders, 27-10 (LA)
1983—Raiders, 22-7 (D)
        Raiders, 22-20 (LA)
1984—Broncos, 16-13 (D)
        Broncos, 22-19 (LA) OT
1985—Raiders, 31-28 (LA) OT
        Raiders, 17-14 (D) OT
1986—Broncos, 38-36 (D)
        Broncos, 21-10 (LA)
1987—Broncos, 30-14 (D)
        Broncos, 23-17 (LA)
1988—Raiders, 30-27 (D) OT
        Raiders, 21-20 (LA)
1989—Broncos, 31-21 (D)

Raiders, 16-13 (LA) OT
1990—Raiders, 14-9 (LA)
        Raiders, 23-20 (D)
1991—Raiders, 16-13 (LA)
        Raiders, 17-16 (D)
1992—Broncos, 17-13 (D)
        Raiders, 24-0 (LA)
1993—Raiders, 23-20 (D)
        Raiders, 33-30 (LA) OT
        ***Raiders, 42-24 (LA)
1994—Raiders, 48-16 (D)
        Raiders, 23-13 (LA)
1995—Broncos, 27-0 (D)
        Broncos, 31-28 (O)
1996—Broncos, 22-21 (O)
        Broncos, 24-19 (D)
1997—Raiders, 28-25 (O)
        Broncos, 31-3 (D)
1998—Broncos, 34-17 (O)
        Broncos, 40-14 (D)
1999—Broncos, 16-13 (O)
        Broncos, 27-21 (D) OT
2000—Broncos, 33-24 (O)
        Broncos, 27-24 (D)
2001—Raiders, 38-28 (O)
        Broncos, 23-17 (D)
2002—Raiders, 34-10 (D)
        Raiders, 28-16 (O)
2003—Broncos, 31-10 (D)
        Broncos, 22-8 (O)
2004—Broncos, 31-3 (O)
        Raiders, 25-24 (D)
2005—Broncos, 31-17 (O)
        Broncos, 22-3 (D)
2006—Broncos, 13-3 (D)
        Broncos, 17-13 (O)
2007—Broncos, 23-20 (D) OT
        Raiders, 34-20 (O)
2008—Broncos, 41-14 (O)
        Raiders, 31-10 (D)
2009—Broncos, 23-3 (O)
        Raiders, 20-19 (D)
2010—Raiders, 59-14 (O)
        Raiders, 39-23 (O)
2011—Raiders, 23-20 (O)
        Broncos, 38-24 (O)
2012—Broncos, 37-6 (D)
        Broncos, 26-13 (O)
2013—Broncos, 37-21 (D)
        Broncos, 34-14 (O)
(RS Pts.—Raiders 2,320, Broncos 2,170)
(PS Pts.—Raiders 59, Broncos 44)
*Franchise in Los Angeles from 1982-1994
**AFC Championship
***AFC First-Round Playoff
DENVER vs. PHILADELPHIA
RS: Eagles lead series, 7-5
1971—Eagles, 17-16 (P)
1975—Broncos, 25-10 (D)
1980—Eagles, 27-6 (P)
1983—Eagles, 13-10 (D)
1986—Broncos, 33-7 (P)
1989—Eagles, 28-24 (P)
1992—Eagles, 30-0 (P)
1995—Eagles, 31-13 (P)
1998—Broncos, 41-16 (D)
2005—Broncos, 49-21 (D)
2009—Eagles, 30-27 (P)
2013—Broncos, 52-20 (D)
(RS Pts.—Broncos 296, Eagles 250)
DENVER vs. PITTSBURGH
RS: Broncos lead series, 14-7-1
PS: Broncos lead series, 4-3

1970—Broncos, 16-13 (D)
1971—Broncos, 22-10 (P)
1973—Broncos, 23-13 (P)
1974—Tie, 35-35 (D) OT
1975—Steelers, 20-9 (P)
1977—Broncos, 21-7 (D)
        *Broncos, 34-21 (D)
1978—Steelers, 21-17 (D)
        *Steelers, 33-10 (P)
1979—Steelers, 42-7 (P)
1983—Broncos, 14-10 (P)
1984—*Steelers, 24-17 (D)
1985—Broncos, 31-23 (P)
1986—Broncos, 21-10 (P)
1988—Steelers, 39-21 (P)
1989—Broncos, 34-7 (D)
        *Broncos, 24-23 (D)
1990—Steelers, 34-17 (D)
1991—Broncos, 20-13 (D)
1993—Broncos, 37-13 (D)
1997—Steelers, 35-24 (P)
        **Broncos, 24-21 (P)
2003—Broncos, 17-14 (D)
2005—**Steelers, 34-17 (D)
2006—Broncos, 31-20 (P)
2007—Broncos, 31-28 (D)
2009—Steelers, 28-10 (D)
2011—***Broncos, 29-23 (D) OT
2012—Broncos, 31-19 (D)
(RS Pts.—Broncos 489, Steelers 454)
(PS Pts.—Steelers 179, Broncos 155)
*AFC Divisional Playoff
**AFC Championship
***AFC First-Round Playoff
DENVER vs. *ST. LOUIS
RS: Rams lead series, 7-5
1972—Broncos, 16-10 (LA)
1974—Rams, 17-10 (D)
1979—Rams, 13-9 (D)
1982—Broncos, 27-24 (LA)
1985—Rams, 20-16 (LA)
1988—Broncos, 35-24 (D)
1994—Rams, 27-21 (LA)
1997—Broncos, 35-14 (D)
2000—Rams, 41-36 (StL)
2002—Rams, 23-16 (D)
2006—Rams, 18-10 (StL)
2010—Rams, 36-33 (D)
(RS Pts.—Broncos 271, Rams 260)
*Franchise in Los Angeles prior to 1995
DENVER vs. *SAN DIEGO
RS: Broncos lead series, 58-49-1
PS: Broncos lead series, 1-0
1960—Chargers, 23-19 (D)
        Chargers, 41-33 (LA)
1961—Chargers, 37-0 (SD)
        Chargers, 19-16 (D)
1962—Broncos, 30-21 (D)
        Broncos, 23-20 (SD)
1963—Broncos, 50-34 (D)
        Chargers, 58-20 (SD)
1964—Chargers, 42-14 (SD)
        Chargers, 31-20 (D)
1965—Chargers, 34-31 (SD)
        Chargers, 33-21 (D)
1966—Chargers, 24-17 (SD)
        Broncos, 20-17 (D)
1967—Chargers, 38-21 (D)
        Chargers, 24-20 (SD)
1968—Chargers, 55-24 (SD)
        Chargers, 47-23 (D)
1969—Broncos, 13-0 (D)
        Chargers, 45-24 (SD)

1970—Chargers, 24-21 (SD)
  Tie, 17-17 (D)
1971—Broncos, 20-16 (D)
  Chargers, 45-17 (SD)
1972—Chargers, 37-14 (SD)
  Broncos, 38-13 (D)
1973—Broncos, 30-19 (D)
  Broncos, 42-28 (SD)
1974—Broncos, 27-7 (D)
  Chargers, 17-0 (SD)
1975—Broncos, 27-17 (SD)
  Broncos, 13-10 (D) OT
1976—Broncos, 26-0 (D)
  Broncos, 17-0 (SD)
1977—Broncos, 17-14 (SD)
  Broncos, 17-9 (D)
1978—Broncos, 27-14 (D)
  Chargers, 23-0 (SD)
1979—Broncos, 7-0 (D)
  Chargers, 17-7 (SD)
1980—Chargers, 30-13 (D)
  Broncos, 20-13 (SD)
1981—Broncos, 42-24 (D)
  Chargers, 34-17 (SD)
1982—Chargers, 23-3 (D)
  Chargers, 30-20 (SD)
1983—Broncos, 14-6 (D)
  Chargers, 31-7 (SD)
1984—Broncos, 16-13 (SD)
  Broncos, 16-13 (D)
1985—Chargers, 30-10 (SD)
  Broncos, 30-24 (D) OT
1986—Broncos, 31-14 (SD)
  Chargers, 9-3 (D)
1987—Broncos, 31-17 (SD)
  Broncos, 24-0 (D)
1988—Broncos, 34-3 (D)
  Broncos, 12-0 (SD)
1989—Broncos, 16-10 (D)
  Chargers, 19-16 (SD)
1990—Chargers, 19-7 (SD)
  Broncos, 20-10 (D)
1991—Broncos, 27-19 (D)
  Broncos, 17-14 (SD)
1992—Broncos, 21-13 (D)
  Chargers, 24-21 (SD)
1993—Broncos, 34-17 (D)
  Chargers, 13-10 (SD)
1994—Chargers, 37-34 (D)
  Broncos, 20-15 (SD)
1995—Chargers, 17-6 (SD)
  Broncos, 30-27 (D)
1996—Broncos, 28-17 (D)
  Chargers, 16-10 (SD)
1997—Broncos, 38-28 (SD)
  Broncos, 38-3 (D)
1998—Broncos, 27-10 (D)
  Broncos, 31-16 (SD)
1999—Broncos, 33-17 (SD)
  Chargers, 12-6 (D)
2000—Broncos, 21-7 (SD)
  Broncos, 38-37 (D)
2001—Chargers, 27-10 (SD)
  Broncos, 26-16 (D)
2002—Broncos, 26-9 (D)
  Chargers, 30-27 (SD) OT
2003—Broncos, 37-13 (SD)
  Broncos, 37-8 (D)
2004—Broncos, 23-13 (D)
  Chargers, 20-17 (SD)
2005—Broncos, 20-17 (D)
  Broncos, 23-7 (SD)

2006—Chargers, 35-27 (D)
  Chargers, 48-20 (SD)
2007—Chargers, 41-3 (D)
  Chargers, 23-3 (SD)
2008—Broncos, 39-38 (D)
  Chargers, 52-21 (SD)
2009—Broncos, 34-23 (SD)
  Chargers, 32-3 (D)
2010—Chargers, 35-14 (SD)
  Chargers, 33-28 (D)
2011—Chargers, 29-24 (D)
  Broncos, 16-13 (SD) OT
2012—Broncos, 35-24 (SD)
  Broncos, 30-23 (D)
2013—Broncos, 28-20 (SD)
  Chargers, 27-20 (D)
  **Broncos, 24-17 (D)
(RS Pts.—Chargers 2,359, Broncos 2,306)
(PS Pts.—Broncos 24, Chargers 17)
*Franchise in Los Angeles prior to 1961
**AFC Divisional Playoff
DENVER vs. SAN FRANCISCO
RS: Series tied, 6-6
PS: 49ers lead series, 1-0
1970—49ers, 19-14 (SF)
1973—49ers, 36-34 (D)
1979—Broncos, 38-28 (SF)
1982—Broncos, 24-21 (D)
1985—Broncos, 17-16 (D)
1988—Broncos, 16-13 (SF) OT
1989—*49ers, 55-10 (New Orleans)
1994—49ers, 42-19 (SF)
1997—49ers, 34-17 (SF)
2000—Broncos, 38-9 (D)
2002—Broncos, 24-14 (SF)
2006—49ers, 26-23 (D) OT
2010—49ers, 24-16 (London)
(RS Pts.—49ers 282, Broncos 280)
(PS Pts.—49ers 55, Broncos 10)
*Super Bowl XXIV
DENVER vs. SEATTLE
RS: Broncos lead series, 34-18
PS: Seahawks lead series, 2-0
1977—Broncos, 24-13 (S)
1978—Broncos, 28-7 (D)
  Broncos, 20-17 (S) OT
1979—Broncos, 37-34 (D)
  Seahawks, 28-23 (S)
1980—Broncos, 36-20 (D)
  Broncos, 25-17 (S)
1981—Seahawks, 13-10 (S)
  Broncos, 23-13 (D)
1982—Broncos, 17-10 (D)
  Seahawks, 13-11 (S)
1983—Seahawks, 27-19 (S)
  Broncos, 38-27 (D)
  *Seahawks, 31-7 (S)
1984—Seahawks, 27-24 (D)
  Broncos, 31-14 (S)
1985—Broncos, 13-10 (D) OT
  Broncos, 27-24 (S)
1986—Broncos, 20-13 (D)
  Seahawks, 41-16 (S)
1987—Broncos, 40-17 (D)
  Seahawks, 28-21 (S)
1988—Seahawks, 21-14 (D)
  Seahawks, 42-14 (S)
1989—Broncos, 24-21 (S) OT
  Broncos, 41-14 (D)
1990—Broncos, 34-31 (D) OT
  Seahawks, 17-12 (S)
1991—Broncos, 16-10 (D)
  Seahawks, 13-10 (S)

1992—Seahawks, 16-13 (S) OT
  Broncos, 10-6 (D)
1993—Broncos, 28-17 (D)
  Broncos, 17-9 (S)
1994—Broncos, 16-9 (S)
  Broncos, 17-10 (D)
1995—Seahawks, 27-10 (S)
  Seahawks, 31-27 (D)
1996—Broncos, 30-20 (S)
  Broncos, 34-7 (D)
1997—Broncos, 35-14 (S)
  Broncos, 30-27 (D)
1998—Broncos, 21-16 (D)
  Broncos, 28-21 (D)
1999—Seahawks, 20-17 (S)
  Broncos, 36-30 (D) OT
2000—Broncos, 38-31 (S)
  Broncos, 31-24 (D)
2001—Seahawks, 34-21 (S)
  Broncos, 20-7 (D)
2002—Broncos, 31-9 (S)
2006—Seahawks, 23-20 (D)
2010—Broncos, 31-14 (D)
2013—**Seahawks, 43-8 (New Jersey)
(RS Pts.—Broncos 1,222, Seahawks 1,011)
(PS Pts.—Seahawks 74, Broncos 15)
*AFC First-Round Playoff
**Super Bowl XLVIII
DENVER vs. TAMPA BAY
RS: Broncos lead series, 6-2
1976—Broncos, 48-13 (D)
1981—Broncos, 24-7 (TB)
1993—Buccaneers, 17-10 (D)
1996—Broncos, 27-23 (D)
1999—Buccaneers, 13-10 (TB)
2004—Broncos, 16-13 (TB)
2008—Broncos, 16-13 (D)
2012—Broncos, 31-23 (D)
(RS Pts.—Broncos 182, Buccaneers 122)
DENVER vs. *TENNESSEE
RS: Titans lead series, 21-15-1
PS: Broncos lead series, 2-1
1960—Oilers, 45-25 (D)
  Oilers, 20-10 (H)
1961—Oilers, 55-14 (D)
  Oilers, 45-14 (H)
1962—Broncos, 20-10 (D)
  Oilers, 34-17 (H)
1963—Oilers, 20-14 (H)
  Oilers, 33-24 (D)
1964—Oilers, 38-17 (D)
  Oilers, 34-15 (H)
1965—Broncos, 28-17 (D)
  Broncos, 31-21 (H)
1966—Oilers, 45-7 (H)
  Broncos, 40-38 (D)
1967—Oilers, 10-6 (H)
  Oilers, 20-18 (D)
1968—Oilers, 38-17 (H)
1969—Oilers, 24-21 (H)
  Tie, 20-20 (D)
1970—Oilers, 31-21 (H)
1972—Broncos, 30-17 (D)
1973—Broncos, 48-20 (D)
1974—Broncos, 37-14 (D)
1976—Oilers, 17-3 (H)
1977—Broncos, 24-14 (H)
1979—**Oilers, 13-7 (H)
1980—Oilers, 20-16 (D)
1983—Broncos, 26-14 (H)
1985—Broncos, 31-20 (D)
1987—Oilers, 40-10 (D)
  ***Broncos, 34-10 (D)

1991—Oilers, 42-14 (H)
***Broncos, 26-24 (D)
1992—Broncos, 27-21 (D)
1995—Oilers, 42-33 (H)
2004—Broncos, 37-16 (T)
2007—Broncos, 34-20 (D)
2010—Broncos, 26-20 (T)
2011—Titans, 17-14 (T)
2013—Broncos, 51-28 (D)
(RS Pts.—Titans 980, Broncos 840)
(PS Pts.—Broncos 67, Titans 47)
*Franchise in Houston prior to 1997;
known as the Oilers prior to 1999
**AFC First-Round Playoff
***AFC Divisional Playoff
DENVER vs. WASHINGTON
RS: Broncos lead series, 7-5
PS: Redskins lead series, 1-0
1970—Redskins, 19-3 (D)
1974—Redskins, 30-3 (W)
1980—Broncos, 20-17 (D)
1986—Broncos, 31-30 (D)
1987—*Redskins, 42-10 (San Diego)
1989—Broncos, 14-10 (W)
1992—Redskins, 34-3 (W)
1995—Broncos, 38-31 (D)
1998—Broncos, 38-16 (W)
2001—Redskins, 17-10 (D)
2005—Broncos, 21-19 (D)
2009—Redskins, 27-17 (W)
2013—Broncos, 45-21 (D)
(RS Pts.—Redskins 271, Broncos 243)
(PS Pts.—Redskins 42, Broncos 10)
*Super Bowl XXII

DETROIT vs. ARIZONA
RS: Lions lead series, 31-26-5;
See Arizona vs. Detroit
DETROIT vs. ATLANTA
RS: Lions lead series, 23-12;
See Atlanta vs. Detroit
DETROIT vs. BALTIMORE
RS: Ravens lead series, 3-1;
See Baltimore vs. Detroit
DETROIT vs. BUFFALO
RS: Series tied, 4-4-1;
See Buffalo vs. Detroit
DETROIT vs. CAROLINA
RS: Panthers lead series, 4-2;
See Carolina vs. Detroit
DETROIT vs. CHICAGO
RS: Bears lead series, 96-67-5;
See Chicago vs. Detroit
DETROIT vs. CINCINNATI
RS: Bengals lead series, 8-3;
See Cincinnati vs. Detroit
DETROIT vs. CLEVELAND
RS: Lions lead series, 15-4
PS: Lions lead series, 3-1;
See Cleveland vs. Detroit
DETROIT vs. DALLAS
RS: Cowboys lead series, 12-11
PS: Series tied, 1-1;
See Dallas vs. Detroit
DETROIT vs. DENVER
RS: Broncos lead series, 6-5;
See Denver vs. Detroit
*DETROIT vs. GREEN BAY
RS: Packers lead series, 94-66-7
PS: Packers lead series, 2-0
1930—Packers, 47-13 (GB)
Tie, 6-6 (P)
1932—Packers, 15-10 (GB)

Spartans, 19-0 (P)
1933—Packers, 17-0 (GB)
Spartans, 7-0 (P)
1934—Lions, 3-0 (GB)
Packers, 3-0 (D)
1935—Packers, 13-9 (Mil)
Packers, 31-7 (GB)
Lions, 20-10 (D)
1936—Packers, 20-18 (GB)
Packers, 26-17 (D)
1937—Packers, 26-6 (GB)
Packers, 14-13 (D)
1938—Lions, 17-7 (GB)
Packers, 28-7 (D)
1939—Packers, 26-7 (GB)
Packers, 12-7 (D)
1940—Lions, 23-14 (GB)
Packers, 50-7 (D)
1941—Packers, 23-0 (GB)
Packers, 24-7 (D)
1942—Packers, 38-7 (Mil)
Packers, 28-7 (D)
1943—Packers, 35-14 (GB)
Packers, 27-6 (D)
1944—Packers, 27-6 (Mil)
Packers, 14-0 (D)
1945—Packers, 57-21 (Mil)
Lions, 14-3 (D)
1946—Packers, 10-7 (Mil)
Packers, 9-0 (D)
1947—Packers, 34-17 (GB)
Packers, 35-14 (D)
1948—Packers, 33-21 (GB)
Lions, 24-20 (D)
1949—Packers, 16-14 (Mil)
Lions, 21-7 (D)
1950—Lions, 45-7 (GB)
Lions, 24-21 (D)
1951—Lions, 24-17 (GB)
Lions, 52-35 (D)
1952—Lions, 52-17 (GB)
Lions, 48-24 (D)
1953—Lions, 14-7 (GB)
Lions, 34-15 (D)
1954—Lions, 21-17 (GB)
Lions, 28-24 (D)
1955—Packers, 20-17 (GB)
Lions, 24-10 (D)
1956—Lions, 20-16 (GB)
Packers, 24-20 (D)
1957—Lions, 24-14 (GB)
Lions, 18-6 (D)
1958—Tie, 13-13 (GB)
Lions, 24-14 (D)
1959—Packers, 28-10 (GB)
Packers, 24-17 (D)
1960—Packers, 28-9 (GB)
Lions, 23-10 (D)
1961—Lions, 17-13 (Mil)
Packers, 17-9 (D)
1962—Packers, 9-7 (GB)
Lions, 26-14 (D)
1963—Packers, 31-10 (Mil)
Tie, 13-13 (D)
1964—Packers, 14-10 (D)
Packers, 30-7 (GB)
1965—Packers, 31-21 (D)
Lions, 12-7 (GB)
1966—Packers, 23-14 (GB)
Packers, 31-7 (D)
1967—Tie, 17-17 (GB)
Packers, 27-17 (D)
1968—Lions, 23-17 (GB)

Tie, 14-14 (D)
1969—Packers, 28-17 (D)
Lions, 16-10 (GB)
1970—Lions, 40-0 (GB)
Lions, 20-0 (D)
1971—Lions, 31-28 (D)
Tie, 14-14 (Mil)
1972—Packers, 24-23 (D)
Packers, 33-7 (GB)
1973—Tie, 13-13 (GB)
Lions, 34-0 (D)
1974—Packers, 21-19 (Mil)
Lions, 19-17 (D)
1975—Lions, 30-16 (Mil)
Lions, 13-10 (D)
1976—Packers, 24-14 (GB)
Lions, 27-6 (D)
1977—Lions, 10-6 (D)
Packers, 10-9 (GB)
1978—Packers, 13-7 (D)
Packers, 35-14 (Mil)
1979—Packers, 24-16 (Mil)
Packers, 18-13 (D)
1980—Lions, 29-7 (Mil)
Lions, 24-3 (D)
1981—Lions, 31-27 (D)
Packers, 31-17 (GB)
1982—Lions, 30-10 (GB)
Lions, 27-24 (D)
1983—Lions, 38-14 (D)
Lions, 23-20 (Mil) OT
1984—Packers, 41-9 (GB)
Lions, 31-28 (D)
1985—Packers, 43-10 (GB)
Packers, 26-23 (D)
1986—Lions, 21-14 (GB)
Packers, 44-40 (D)
1987—Lions, 19-16 (GB) OT
Packers, 34-33 (D)
1988—Lions, 19-9 (Mil)
Lions, 30-14 (D)
1989—Packers, 23-20 (Mil) OT
Lions, 31-22 (D)
1990—Packers, 24-21 (D)
Lions, 24-17 (GB)
1991—Lions, 23-14 (D)
Lions, 21-17 (GB)
1992—Packers, 27-13 (D)
Packers, 38-10 (Mil)
1993—Packers, 26-17 (Mil)
Lions, 30-20 (D)
**Packers, 28-24 (D)
1994—Packers, 38-30 (Mil)
Lions, 34-31 (D)
**Packers, 16-12 (GB)
1995—Packers, 30-21 (GB)
Lions, 24-16 (D)
1996—Packers, 28-18 (GB)
Packers, 31-3 (D)
1997—Lions, 26-15 (D)
Packers, 20-10 (GB)
1998—Packers, 38-19 (GB)
Lions, 27-20 (D)
1999—Lions, 23-15 (D)
Packers, 26-17 (GB)
2000—Lions, 31-24 (D)
Packers, 26-13 (GB)
2001—Packers, 28-6 (GB)
Packers, 29-27 (D)
2002—Packers, 37-31 (D)
Packers, 40-14 (GB)
2003—Packers, 31-6 (GB)
Lions, 22-14 (D)

2004—Packers, 38-10 (D)
 Packers, 16-13 (GB)
2005—Lions, 17-3 (D)
 Packers, 16-13 (GB) OT
2006—Packers, 31-24 (D)
 Packers, 17-9 (GB)
2007—Packers, 37-26 (D)
 Packers, 34-13 (GB)
2008—Packers, 48-25 (D)
 Packers, 31-21 (GB)
2009—Packers, 26-0 (GB)
 Packers, 34-12 (D)
2010—Packers, 28-26 (GB)
 Lions, 7-3 (D)
2011—Packers, 27-15 (D)
 Packers, 45-41 (GB)
2012—Packers, 24-20 (D)
 Packers, 27-20 (GB)
2013—Packers, 22-9 (GB)
 Lions, 40-10 (D)
(RS Pts.—Packers 3,541, Lions 3,034)
(PS Pts.—Packers 44, Lions 36)
*Franchise in Portsmouth prior to 1934
and known as the Spartans
**NFC First-Round Playoff
DETROIT vs. HOUSTON
RS: Texans lead series, 2-1
2004—Lions, 28-16 (D)
2008—Texans, 28-21 (H)
2012—Texans, 34-31 (D) OT
(RS Pts.—Lions 80, Texans 78)
DETROIT vs. *INDIANAPOLIS
RS: Colts lead series, 21-18-2
1953—Lions, 27-17 (B)
 Lions, 17-7 (D)
1954—Lions, 35-0 (D)
 Lions, 27-3 (B)
1955—Colts, 28-13 (B)
 Lions, 24-14 (D)
1956—Lions, 31-14 (B)
 Lions, 27-3 (D)
1957—Colts, 34-14 (B)
 Lions, 31-27 (D)
1958—Colts, 28-15 (B)
 Colts, 40-14 (D)
1959—Colts, 21-9 (B)
 Colts, 31-24 (D)
1960—Lions, 30-17 (D)
 Lions, 20-15 (B)
1961—Lions, 16-15 (B)
 Colts, 17-14 (D)
1962—Lions, 29-20 (B)
 Lions, 21-14 (D)
1963—Colts, 25-21 (D)
 Colts, 24-21 (B)
1964—Colts, 34-0 (D)
 Lions, 31-14 (B)
1965—Colts, 31-7 (B)
 Tie, 24-24 (D)
1966—Colts, 45-14 (B)
 Lions, 20-14 (D)
1967—Colts, 41-7 (B)
1968—Colts, 27-10 (D)
1969—Tie, 17-17 (B)
1973—Colts, 29-27 (D)
1977—Lions, 13-10 (B)
1980—Colts, 10-9 (D)
1985—Colts, 14-6 (I)
1991—Lions, 33-24 (I)
1997—Lions, 32-10 (D)
2000—Colts, 30-18 (I)
2004—Colts, 41-9 (D)
2008—Colts, 31-21 (I)

2012—Colts, 35-33 (D)
(RS Pts.—Colts 895, Lions 811)
*Franchise in Baltimore prior to 1984
DETROIT vs. JACKSONVILLE
RS: Jaguars lead series, 3-2
1995—Lions, 44-0 (D)
1998—Jaguars, 37-22 (J)
2004—Jaguars, 23-17 (J) OT
2008—Jaguars, 38-14 (D)
2012—Lions, 31-14 (J)
(RS Pts.—Lions 128, Jaguars 112)
DETROIT vs. KANSAS CITY
RS: Chiefs lead series, 7-5
1971—Lions, 32-21 (D)
1975—Chiefs, 24-21 (KC) OT
1980—Chiefs, 20-17 (KC)
1981—Lions, 27-10 (D)
1987—Chiefs, 27-20 (D)
1988—Lions, 7-6 (KC)
1990—Chiefs, 43-24 (KC)
1996—Chiefs, 28-24 (D)
1999—Chiefs, 31-21 (KC)
2003—Chiefs, 45-17 (KC)
2007—Lions, 25-20 (D)
2011—Lions, 48-3 (D)
(RS Pts.—Lions 283, Chiefs 278)
DETROIT vs. MIAMI
RS: Dolphins lead series, 7-3
1973—Dolphins, 34-7 (M)
1979—Dolphins, 28-10 (D)
1985—Lions, 31-21 (D)
1991—Lions, 17-13 (D)
1994—Dolphins, 27-20 (M)
1997—Dolphins, 33-30 (M)
2000—Dolphins, 23-8 (D)
2002—Dolphins, 49-21 (M)
2006—Dolphins, 27-10 (D)
2010—Lions, 34-27 (M)
(RS Pts.—Dolphins 282, Lions 188)
DETROIT vs. MINNESOTA
RS: Vikings lead series, 69-34-2
1961—Lions, 37-10 (M)
 Lions, 13-7 (D)
1962—Lions, 17-6 (M)
 Lions, 37-23 (D)
1963—Lions, 28-10 (D)
 Vikings, 34-31 (M)
1964—Lions, 24-20 (M)
 Tie, 23-23 (D)
1965—Lions, 31-29 (M)
 Vikings, 29-7 (D)
1966—Lions, 32-31 (M)
 Vikings, 28-16 (D)
1967—Tie, 10-10 (M)
 Lions, 14-3 (D)
1968—Vikings, 24-10 (M)
 Vikings, 13-6 (D)
1969—Vikings, 24-10 (M)
 Vikings, 27-0 (D)
1970—Vikings, 30-17 (D)
 Vikings, 24-20 (M)
1971—Vikings, 16-13 (D)
 Vikings, 29-10 (M)
1972—Vikings, 34-10 (D)
 Vikings, 16-14 (M)
1973—Vikings, 23-9 (D)
 Vikings, 28-7 (M)
1974—Vikings, 7-6 (D)
 Lions, 20-16 (M)
1975—Vikings, 25-19 (M)
 Lions, 17-10 (D)
1976—Vikings, 10-9 (D)
 Vikings, 31-23 (M)

1977—Vikings, 14-7 (M)
 Vikings, 30-21 (D)
1978—Vikings, 17-7 (M)
 Lions, 45-14 (D)
1979—Vikings, 13-10 (D)
 Vikings, 14-7 (M)
1980—Lions, 27-7 (D)
 Vikings, 34-0 (M)
1981—Vikings, 26-24 (M)
 Lions, 45-7 (D)
1982—Vikings, 34-31 (D)
1983—Vikings, 20-17 (M)
 Lions, 13-2 (D)
1984—Vikings, 29-28 (D)
 Lions, 16-14 (M)
1985—Vikings, 16-13 (M)
 Lions, 41-21 (D)
1986—Lions, 13-10 (D)
 Vikings, 24-10 (D)
1987—Vikings, 34-19 (M)
 Vikings, 17-14 (D)
1988—Vikings, 44-17 (M)
 Vikings, 23-0 (D)
1989—Vikings, 24-17 (M)
 Vikings, 20-7 (D)
1990—Lions, 34-27 (M)
 Vikings, 17-7 (D)
1991—Lions, 24-20 (D)
 Lions, 34-14 (M)
1992—Lions, 31-17 (D)
 Vikings, 31-14 (M)
1993—Lions, 30-27 (M)
 Vikings, 13-0 (D)
1994—Vikings, 10-3 (M)
 Lions, 41-19 (D)
1995—Vikings, 20-10 (M)
 Lions, 44-38 (D)
1996—Vikings, 17-13 (M)
 Vikings, 24-22 (D)
1997—Lions, 38-15 (D)
 Lions, 14-13 (M)
1998—Vikings, 29-6 (M)
 Vikings, 34-13 (D)
1999—Lions, 25-23 (D)
 Vikings, 24-17 (M)
2000—Vikings, 31-24 (D)
 Vikings, 24-17 (M)
2001—Vikings, 31-26 (M)
 Lions, 27-24 (D)
2002—Vikings, 31-24 (M)
 Vikings, 38-36 (D)
2003—Vikings, 23-13 (D)
 Vikings, 24-14 (M)
2004—Vikings, 22-19 (M)
 Vikings, 28-27 (D)
2005—Vikings, 27-14 (M)
 Vikings, 21-16 (D)
2006—Vikings, 26-17 (M)
 Vikings, 30-20 (D)
2007—Lions, 20-17 (D) OT
 Vikings, 42-10 (M)
2008—Vikings, 12-10 (M)
 Vikings, 20-16 (D)
2009—Vikings, 27-13 (D)
 Vikings, 27-10 (M)
2010—Vikings, 24-10 (M)
 Lions, 20-13 (D)
2011—Vikings, 26-23 (M) OT
 Lions, 34-28 (D)
2012—Vikings, 20-13 (D)
 Vikings, 34-24 (M)
2013—Lions, 34-24 (D)
 Vikings, 14-13 (M)

(RS Pts.—Vikings 2,295, Lions 1,956)

DETROIT vs. NEW ENGLAND
RS: Patriots lead series, 6-4
1971—Lions, 34-7 (NE)
1976—Lions, 30-10 (D)
1979—Patriots, 24-17 (NE)
1985—Patriots, 23-6 (NE)
1993—Lions, 19-16 (NE) OT
1994—Patriots, 23-17 (D)
2000—Lions, 34-9 (D)
2002—Patriots, 20-12 (D)
2006—Patriots, 28-21 (NE)
2010—Patriots, 45-24 (D)
(RS Pts.—Lions 214, Patriots 205)

DETROIT vs. NEW ORLEANS
RS: Saints lead series, 11-9-1
PS: Saints lead series, 1-0
1968—Tie, 20-20 (D)
1970—Saints, 19-17 (NO)
1972—Lions, 27-14 (D)
1973—Saints, 20-13 (NO)
1974—Lions, 19-14 (D)
1976—Saints, 17-16 (NO)
1977—Lions, 23-19 (D)
1979—Saints, 17-7 (NO)
1980—Lions, 24-13 (D)
1988—Lions, 22-14 (D)
1989—Lions, 21-14 (D)
1990—Lions, 27-10 (NO)
1992—Lions, 13-7 (D)
1993—Saints, 14-3 (NO)
1997—Saints, 35-17 (NO)
2000—Lions, 14-10 (NO)
2002—Lions, 26-21 (D)
2005—Lions, 13-12 (San Antonio)
2008—Saints, 42-7 (D)
2009—Saints, 45-27 (NO)
2011—Saints, 31-17 (NO)
          *Saints, 45-28 (NO)
(RS Pts.—Saints 422, Lions 359)
(PS Pts.—Saints 45, Lions 28)
*NFC First-Round Playoff

*DETROIT vs. N.Y. GIANTS
RS: Series tied, 20-20-1
PS: Lions lead series, 1-0
1930—Giants, 19-6 (P)
1931—Spartans, 14-6 (P)
          Giants, 14-0 (NY)
1932—Spartans, 7-0 (P)
          Spartans, 6-0 (NY)
1933—Spartans, 17-7 (P)
          Giants, 13-10 (NY)
1934—Lions, 9-0 (D)
1935—**Lions, 26-7 (D)
1936—Giants, 14-7 (NY)
          Lions, 38-0 (D)
1937—Lions, 17-0 (NY)
1939—Lions, 18-14 (D)
1941—Giants, 20-13 (NY)
1943—Tie, 0-0 (D)
1945—Lions, 35-14 (NY)
1947—Lions, 35-7 (D)
1949—Lions, 45-21 (NY)
1953—Lions, 27-16 (NY)
1955—Giants, 24-19 (D)
1958—Giants, 19-17 (D)
1962—Giants, 17-14 (NY)
1964—Lions, 26-3 (D)
1967—Lions, 30-7 (NY)
1969—Lions, 24-0 (D)
1972—Lions, 30-16 (D)
1974—Lions, 20-19 (D)
1976—Giants, 24-10 (NY)

1982—Giants, 13-6 (D)
1983—Lions, 15-9 (D)
1988—Giants, 30-10 (NY)
          Giants, 13-10 (D) OT
1989—Giants, 24-14 (NY)
1990—Giants, 20-0 (NY)
1994—Lions, 28-25 (NY) OT
1996—Giants, 35-7 (D)
1997—Giants, 26-20 (D) OT
2000—Lions, 31-21 (NY)
2004—Lions, 28-13 (NY)
2007—Giants, 16-10 (D)
2010—Lions, 28-20 (NY)
2013—Giants, 23-20 (D) OT
(RS Pts.—Lions 692, Giants 611)
(PS Pts.—Lions 26, Giants 7)
*Franchise in Portsmouth prior to 1934
and known as the Spartans
**NFL Championship

DETROIT vs. N.Y. JETS
RS: Series tied, 6-6
1972—Lions, 37-20 (D)
1979—Jets, 31-10 (NY)
1982—Jets, 28-13 (D)
1985—Lions, 31-20 (D)
1988—Jets, 17-10 (D)
1991—Lions, 34-20 (D)
1994—Lions, 18-7 (NY)
1997—Lions, 13-10 (D)
2000—Lions, 10-7 (NY)
2002—Jets, 31-14 (D)
2006—Jets, 31-24 (NY)
2010—Jets, 23-20 (D) OT
(RS Pts.—Jets 245, Lions 234)

DETROIT vs. *OAKLAND
RS: Raiders lead series, 6-5
1970—Lions, 28-14 (D)
1974—Raiders, 35-13 (O)
1978—Raiders, 29-17 (O)
1981—Lions, 16-0 (D)
1984—Raiders, 24-3 (D)
1987—Raiders, 27-7 (LA)
1990—Raiders, 38-31 (D)
1996—Raiders, 37-21 (O)
2003—Lions, 23-13 (D)
2007—Lions, 36-21 (O)
2011—Lions, 28-27 (O)
(RS Pts.—Raiders 265, Lions 223)
*Franchise in Los Angeles from 1982-1994

*DETROIT vs. PHILADELPHIA
RS: Eagles lead series, 15-13-2
PS: Eagles lead series, 1-0
1933—Spartans, 25-0 (P)
1934—Lions, 10-0 (D)
1935—Lions, 35-0 (D)
1936—Lions, 23-0 (P)
1938—Eagles, 21-7 (D)
1940—Lions, 21-0 (P)
1941—Lions, 21-17 (D)
1945—Lions, 28-24 (D)
1948—Eagles, 45-21 (P)
1949—Eagles, 22-14 (D)
1951—Lions, 28-10 (P)
1954—Tie, 13-13 (D)
1957—Lions, 27-16 (P)
1960—Eagles, 28-10 (P)
1961—Eagles, 27-24 (D)
1965—Lions, 35-28 (P)
1968—Eagles, 12-0 (D)
1971—Eagles, 23-20 (D)
1974—Eagles, 28-17 (P)
1977—Lions, 17-13 (D)
1979—Eagles, 44-7 (P)

1984—Tie, 23-23 (D) OT
1986—Lions, 13-11 (P)
1995—**Eagles, 58-37 (P)
1996—Eagles, 24-17 (D)
1998—Eagles, 10-9 (P)
2004—Eagles, 30-13 (D)
2007—Eagles, 56-21 (P)
2010—Eagles, 35-32 (D)
2012—Eagles, 26-23 (P) OT
2013—Eagles, 34-20 (D)
(RS Pts.—Eagles 617, Lions 577)
(PS Pts.—Eagles 58, Lions 37)
*Franchise in Portsmouth prior to 1934
and known as the Spartans
**NFC First-Round Playoff

DETROIT vs. *PITTSBURGH
RS: Steelers lead series, 16-14-1
1934—Lions, 40-7 (D)
1936—Lions, 28-3 (D)
1937—Lions, 7-3 (D)
1938—Lions, 16-7 (D)
1940—Steelers, 10-7 (D)
1942—Steelers, 35-7 (D)
1946—Lions, 17-7 (D)
1947—Steelers, 17-10 (P)
1948—Lions, 17-14 (D)
1949—Steelers, 14-7 (P)
1950—Lions, 10-7 (D)
1952—Lions, 31-6 (P)
1953—Lions, 38-21 (D)
1955—Lions, 31-28 (D)
1956—Lions, 45-7 (D)
1959—Tie, 10-10 (P)
1962—Lions, 45-7 (D)
1966—Steelers, 17-3 (P)
1967—Steelers, 24-14 (D)
1969—Steelers, 16-13 (P)
1973—Steelers, 24-10 (P)
1983—Lions, 45-3 (D)
1986—Steelers, 27-17 (P)
1989—Steelers, 23-3 (D)
1992—Steelers, 17-14 (P)
1995—Steelers, 23-20 (P)
1998—Lions, 19-16 (D) OT
2001—Steelers, 47-14 (P)
2005—Steelers, 35-21 (P)
2009—Steelers, 28-20 (D)
2013—Steelers, 37-27 (P)
(RS Pts.—Lions 606, Steelers 540)
*Steelers known as Pirates prior to 1940

DETROIT vs. *ST. LOUIS
RS: Rams lead series, 42-39-1
PS: Lions lead series, 1-0
1937—Lions, 28-0 (C)
          Lions, 27-7 (D)
1938—Rams, 21-17 (C)
          Lions, 6-0 (D)
1939—Lions, 15-7 (D)
          Rams, 14-3 (C)
1940—Lions, 6-0 (D)
          Rams, 24-0 (C)
1941—Lions, 17-7 (D)
          Lions, 14-0 (C)
1942—Lions, 14-0 (D)
          Rams, 27-7 (C)
1944—Rams, 20-17 (D)
          Lions, 26-14 (C)
1945—Rams, 28-21 (D)
1946—Rams, 35-14 (LA)
          Rams, 41-20 (D)
1947—Rams, 27-13 (D)
          Rams, 28-17 (LA)

1948—Rams, 44-7 (LA)
    Rams, 34-27 (D)
1949—Rams, 27-24 (LA)
    Rams, 21-10 (D)
1950—Rams, 30-28 (D)
    Rams, 65-24 (LA)
1951—Rams, 27-21 (D)
    Lions, 24-22 (LA)
1952—Lions, 17-14 (LA)
    Lions, 24-16 (D)
    **Lions, 31-21 (D)
1953—Lions, 31-19 (D)
    Rams, 37-24 (LA)
1954—Lions, 21-3 (D)
    Lions, 27-24 (LA)
1955—Rams, 17-10 (D)
    Rams, 24-13 (LA)
1956—Lions, 24-21 (D)
    Lions, 16-7 (LA)
1957—Lions, 10-7 (D)
    Rams, 35-17 (LA)
1958—Rams, 42-28 (D)
    Lions, 41-24 (LA)
1959—Lions, 17-7 (LA)
    Lions, 23-17 (D)
1960—Rams, 48-35 (LA)
    Lions, 12-10 (D)
1961—Lions, 14-13 (D)
    Lions, 28-10 (LA)
1962—Lions, 13-10 (D)
    Lions, 12-3 (LA)
1963—Lions, 23-2 (LA)
    Rams, 28-21 (D)
1964—Tie, 17-17 (LA)
    Lions, 37-17 (D)
1965—Lions, 20-0 (D)
    Lions, 31-7 (LA)
1966—Rams, 14-7 (D)
    Rams, 23-3 (LA)
1967—Rams, 31-7 (D)
1968—Rams, 10-7 (LA)
1969—Lions, 28-0 (D)
1970—Lions, 28-23 (LA)
1971—Rams, 21-13 (D)
1972—Lions, 34-17 (LA)
1974—Rams, 16-13 (LA)
1975—Rams, 20-0 (D)
1976—Rams, 20-17 (D)
1980—Lions, 41-20 (D)
1981—Rams, 20-13 (LA)
1982—Lions, 19-14 (LA)
1983—Rams, 21-10 (LA)
1986—Rams, 14-10 (LA)
1987—Rams, 37-16 (D)
1988—Rams, 17-10 (LA)
1991—Lions, 21-10 (D)
1993—Lions, 16-13 (LA)
1999—Lions, 31-27 (D)
2001—Rams, 35-0 (D)
2003—Lions, 30-20 (D)
2006—Rams, 41-34 (StL)
2009—Rams, 17-10 (D)
2010—Lions, 44-6 (D)
2012—Lions, 27-23 (D)
(RS Pts.—Rams 1,605, Lions 1,516)
(PS Pts.—Lions 31, Rams 21)
*Franchise in Los Angeles prior to 1995
and in Cleveland prior to 1946
**Conference Playoff
DETROIT vs. SAN DIEGO
RS: Chargers lead series, 6-4
1972—Lions, 34-20 (D)
1977—Lions, 20-0 (D)

1978—Lions, 31-14 (D)
1981—Chargers, 28-23 (SD)
1984—Chargers, 27-24 (SD)
1996—Chargers, 27-21 (SD)
1999—Chargers, 20-10 (D)
2003—Chargers, 14-7 (D)
2007—Chargers, 51-14 (SD)
2011—Lions, 38-10 (D)
(RS Pts.—Lions 222, Chargers 211)
DETROIT vs. SAN FRANCISCO
RS: 49ers lead series, 36-26-1
PS: Series tied, 1-1
1950—Lions, 24-7 (D)
    49ers, 28-27 (SF)
1951—49ers, 20-10 (D)
    49ers, 21-17 (SF)
1952—49ers, 17-3 (SF)
    49ers, 28-0 (D)
1953—Lions, 24-21 (D)
    Lions, 14-10 (SF)
1954—49ers, 37-31 (SF)
    Lions, 48-7 (D)
1955—49ers, 27-24 (D)
    49ers, 38-21 (SF)
1956—Lions, 20-17 (D)
    Lions, 17-13 (SF)
1957—49ers, 35-31 (D)
    Lions, 31-10 (D)
    *Lions, 31-27 (SF)
1958—49ers, 24-21 (SF)
    Lions, 35-21 (D)
1959—49ers, 34-13 (D)
    49ers, 33-7 (SF)
1960—49ers, 14-10 (D)
    Lions, 24-0 (SF)
1961—49ers, 49-0 (D)
    Tie, 20-20 (SF)
1962—Lions, 45-24 (D)
    Lions, 38-24 (SF)
1963—Lions, 26-3 (D)
    Lions, 45-7 (SF)
1964—Lions, 26-17 (SF)
    Lions, 24-7 (D)
1965—49ers, 27-21 (D)
    49ers, 17-14 (SF)
1966—49ers, 27-24 (SF)
    49ers, 41-14 (D)
1967—Lions, 45-3 (SF)
1968—49ers, 14-7 (D)
1969—Lions, 26-14 (SF)
1970—Lions, 28-7 (D)
1971—49ers, 31-27 (SF)
1973—Lions, 30-20 (D)
1974—Lions, 17-13 (D)
1975—Lions, 28-17 (SF)
1977—49ers, 28-7 (SF)
1978—Lions, 33-14 (D)
1980—Lions, 17-13 (D)
1981—Lions, 24-17 (D)
1983—**49ers, 24-23 (SF)
1984—Lions, 30-27 (D)
1985—Lions, 23-21 (D)
1988—49ers, 20-13 (SF)
1991—49ers, 35-3 (D)
1992—49ers, 24-6 (SF)
1993—49ers, 55-17 (D)
1994—49ers, 27-21 (D)
1995—Lions, 27-24 (D)
1996—49ers, 24-14 (SF)
1998—49ers, 35-13 (SF)
2001—49ers, 21-13 (SF)
2003—49ers, 24-17 (SF)
2006—49ers, 19-13 (D)

2008—49ers, 31-13 (SF)
2009—49ers, 20-6 (SF)
2011—49ers, 25-19 (D)
2012—49ers, 27-19 (SF)
(RS Pts.—49ers 1,378, Lions 1,302)
(PS Pts.—Lions 54, 49ers 51)
*Conference Playoff
**NFC Divisional Playoff
DETROIT vs. SEATTLE
RS: Seahawks lead series, 7-5
1976—Lions, 41-14 (S)
1978—Seahawks, 28-16 (S)
1984—Seahawks, 38-17 (S)
1987—Seahawks, 37-14 (D)
1990—Seahawks, 30-10 (S)
1993—Lions, 30-10 (D)
1996—Lions, 17-16 (D)
1999—Lions, 28-20 (S)
2003—Seahawks, 35-14 (S)
2006—Seahawks, 9-6 (D)
2009—Seahawks, 32-20 (S)
2012—Lions, 28-24 (D)
(RS Pts.—Seahawks 293, Lions 241)
DETROIT vs. TAMPA BAY
RS: Lions lead series, 29-26
PS: Buccaneers lead series, 1-0
1977—Lions, 16-7 (D)
1978—Lions, 15-7 (TB)
    Lions, 34-23 (D)
1979—Buccaneers, 31-16 (TB)
    Buccaneers, 16-14 (D)
1980—Lions, 24-10 (TB)
    Lions, 27-14 (D)
1981—Buccaneers, 28-10 (TB)
    Buccaneers, 20-17 (D)
1982—Buccaneers, 23-21 (TB)
1983—Lions, 11-0 (TB)
    Lions, 23-20 (D)
1984—Buccaneers, 21-17 (TB)
    Lions, 13-7 (D) OT
1985—Lions, 30-9 (D)
    Buccaneers, 19-16 (TB) OT
1986—Buccaneers, 24-20 (D)
    Lions, 38-17 (TB)
1987—Buccaneers, 31-27 (D)
    Lions, 20-10 (TB)
1988—Buccaneers, 23-20 (D)
    Buccaneers, 21-10 (TB)
1989—Lions, 17-16 (TB)
    Lions, 33-7 (D)
1990—Buccaneers, 38-21 (D)
    Buccaneers, 23-20 (TB)
1991—Lions, 31-3 (D)
    Buccaneers, 30-21 (TB)
1992—Buccaneers, 27-23 (D)
    Lions, 38-7 (TB)
1993—Buccaneers, 27-10 (TB)
    Lions, 23-0 (D)
1994—Buccaneers, 24-14 (TB)
    Lions, 14-9 (D)
1995—Lions, 27-24 (D)
    Lions, 37-10 (TB)
1996—Lions, 21-6 (D)
    Lions, 27-0 (TB)
1997—Buccaneers, 24-17 (D)
    Lions, 27-9 (TB)
    *Buccaneers, 20-10 (TB)
1998—Lions, 27-6 (D)
    Lions, 28-25 (TB)
1999—Lions, 20-3 (D)
    Buccaneers, 23-16 (TB)
2000—Buccaneers, 31-10 (D)
    Lions, 28-14 (TB)

2001—Buccaneers, 20-17 (D)
    Buccaneers, 15-12 (TB)
2002—Buccaneers, 23-20 (D)
2005—Buccaneers, 17-13 (TB)
2007—Lions, 23-16 (D)
2008—Buccaneers, 38-20 (D)
2010—Lions, 23-20 (TB) OT
2011—Lions, 27-20 (TB)
2013—Buccaneers, 24-21 (D)
(RS Pts.—Lions 1,165, Buccaneers 960)
(PS Pts.—Buccaneers 20, Lions 10)
*NFC First-Round Playoff
DETROIT vs. *TENNESSEE
RS: Titans lead series, 8-3
1971—Lions, 31-7 (H)
1975—Oilers, 24-8 (H)
1983—Oilers, 27-17 (H)
1986—Lions, 24-13 (D)
1989—Oilers, 35-31 (H)
1992—Oilers, 24-21 (H)
1995—Lions, 24-17 (H)
2001—Titans, 27-24 (D)
2004—Titans, 24-19 (T)
2008—Titans, 47-10 (D)
2012—Titans, 44-41 (T) OT
(RS Pts.—Titans 289, Lions 250)
*Franchise in Houston prior to 1997;
known as Oilers prior to 1999
DETROIT vs. **WASHINGTON
RS: Redskins lead series, 27-13
PS: Redskins lead series, 3-0
1932—Spartans, 10-0 (P)
1933—Spartans, 13-0 (B)
1934—Lions, 24-0 (D)
1935—Lions, 17-7 (B)
    Lions, 14-0 (D)
1938—Redskins, 7-5 (D)
1939—Redskins, 31-7 (W)
1940—Redskins, 20-14 (D)
1942—Redskins, 15-3 (D)
1943—Redskins, 42-20 (W)
1946—Redskins, 17-16 (W)
1947—Lions, 38-21 (D)
1948—Redskins, 46-21 (W)
1951—Lions, 35-17 (D)
1956—Redskins, 18-17 (W)
1965—Lions, 14-10 (D)
1968—Redskins, 14-3 (W)
1970—Redskins, 31-10 (W)
1973—Redskins, 20-0 (D)
1976—Redskins, 20-7 (W)
1978—Redskins, 21-19 (D)
1979—Redskins, 27-24 (D)
1981—Redskins, 33-31 (W)
1982—***Redskins, 31-7 (W)
1983—Redskins, 38-17 (W)
1984—Redskins, 28-14 (D)
1985—Redskins, 24-3 (W)
1987—Redskins, 20-13 (W)
1990—Redskins, 41-38 (D) OT
1991—Redskins, 45-0 (W)
    ****Redskins, 41-10 (W)
1992—Redskins, 13-10 (W)
1995—Redskins, 36-30 (W) OT
1997—Redskins, 30-7 (W)
1999—Lions, 33-17 (D)
    ***Redskins, 27-13 (W)
2000—Lions, 15-10 (D)
2004—Redskins, 17-10 (D)
2007—Redskins, 34-3 (W)
2008—Redskins, 25-17 (D)
2009—Lions, 19-14 (D)
2010—Lions, 37-25 (D)

2013—Lions, 27-20 (W)
(RS Pts.—Redskins 854, Lions 655)
(PS Pts.—Redskins 99, Lions 30)
*Franchise in Portsmouth prior to 1934
and known as the Spartans.
**Franchise in Boston prior to 1937
***NFC First-Round Playoff
****NFC Championship

GREEN BAY vs. ARIZONA
RS: Packers lead series, 44-22-4
PS: Series tied, 1-1;
See Arizona vs. Green Bay
GREEN BAY vs. ATLANTA
RS: Packers lead series, 14-12
PS: Packers lead series, 2-1;
See Atlanta vs. Green Bay
GREEN BAY vs. BALTIMORE
RS: Packers lead series, 4-1;
See Baltimore vs. Green Bay
GREEN BAY vs. BUFFALO
RS: Bills lead series, 7-4;
See Buffalo vs. Green Bay
GREEN BAY vs. CAROLINA
RS: Packers lead series, 7-4
PS: Packers lead series, 1-0;
See Carolina vs. Green Bay
GREEN BAY vs. CHICAGO
RS: Bears lead series, 92-88-6
PS: Series tied, 1-1;
See Chicago vs. Green Bay
GREEN BAY vs. CINCINNATI
RS: Bengals lead series, 7-5;
See Cincinnati vs. Green Bay
GREEN BAY vs. CLEVELAND
RS: Packers lead series, 11-7
PS: Packers lead series, 1-0;
See Cleveland vs. Green Bay
GREEN BAY vs. DALLAS
RS: Packers lead series, 13-12
PS: Cowboys lead series, 4-2;
See Dallas vs. Green Bay
GREEN BAY vs. DENVER
RS: Packers lead series, 6-5-1
PS: Broncos lead series, 1-0;
See Denver vs. Green Bay
GREEN BAY vs. DETROIT
RS: Packers lead series, 94-66-7
PS: Packers lead series, 2-0;
See Detroit vs. Green Bay
GREEN BAY vs. HOUSTON
RS: Packers lead series, 2-1
2004—Packers, 16-13 (H)
2008—Texans, 24-21 (GB)
2012—Packers, 42-24 (H)
(RS Pts.—Packers 79, Texans 61)
GREEN BAY vs. *INDIANAPOLIS
RS: Colts lead series, 21-20-1
PS: Packers lead series, 1-0
1953—Packers, 37-14 (GB)
    Packers, 35-24 (B)
1954—Packers, 7-6 (B)
    Packers, 24-13 (Mil)
1955—Colts, 24-20 (Mil)
    Colts, 14-10 (B)
1956—Packers, 38-33 (Mil)
    Colts, 28-21 (B)
1957—Colts, 45-17 (Mil)
    Packers, 24-21 (B)
1958—Colts, 24-17 (Mil)
    Colts, 56-0 (B)
1959—Colts, 38-21 (B)
    Colts, 28-24 (Mil)

1960—Packers, 35-21 (GB)
    Colts, 38-24 (B)
1961—Packers, 45-7 (GB)
    Colts, 45-21 (B)
1962—Packers, 17-6 (B)
    Packers, 17-13 (GB)
1963—Packers, 31-20 (GB)
    Packers, 34-20 (B)
1964—Colts, 21-20 (GB)
    Colts, 24-21 (B)
1965—Packers, 20-17 (Mil)
    Packers, 42-27 (B)
    **Packers, 13-10 (GB) OT
1966—Packers, 24-3 (Mil)
    Packers, 14-10 (B)
1967—Colts, 13-10 (B)
1968—Colts, 16-3 (GB)
1969—Colts, 14-6 (B)
1970—Colts, 13-10 (Mil)
1974—Packers, 20-13 (B)
1982—Tie, 20-20 (B) OT
1985—Colts, 37-10 (I)
1988—Colts, 20-13 (GB)
1991—Packers, 14-10 (Mil)
1997—Colts, 41-38 (I)
2000—Packers, 26-24 (GB)
2004—Colts, 45-31 (I)
2008—Packers, 34-14 (GB)
2012—Colts, 30-27 (I)
(RS Pts.—Colts 950, Packers 922)
(PS Pts.—Packers 13, Colts 10)
*Franchise in Baltimore prior to 1984
**Conference Playoff
GREEN BAY vs. JACKSONVILLE
RS: Packers lead series, 3-2
1995—Packers, 24-14 (J)
2001—Packers, 28-21 (J)
2004—Jaguars, 28-25 (GB)
2008—Jaguars, 20-16 (J)
2012—Packers, 24-15 (GB)
(RS Pts.—Packers 117, Jaguars 98)
GREEN BAY vs. KANSAS CITY
RS: Chiefs lead series, 7-2-1
PS: Packers lead series, 1-0
1966—*Packers, 35-10 (Los Angeles)
1973—Tie, 10-10 (Mil)
1977—Chiefs, 20-10 (KC)
1987—Packers, 23-3 (KC)
1989—Chiefs, 21-3 (GB)
1990—Chiefs, 17-3 (GB)
1993—Chiefs, 23-16 (KC)
1996—Packers, 27-20 (KC)
2003—Chiefs, 40-34 (GB) OT
2007—Packers, 33-22 (KC)
2011—Chiefs, 19-14 (KC)
(RS Pts.—Chiefs 202, Packers 166)
(PS Pts.—Packers 35, Chiefs 10)
*Super Bowl I
GREEN BAY vs. MIAMI
RS: Dolphins lead series, 10-3
1971—Dolphins, 27-6 (Mia)
1975—Dolphins, 31-7 (GB)
1979—Dolphins, 27-7 (Mia)
1985—Dolphins, 34-24 (GB)
1988—Dolphins, 24-17 (Mia)
1989—Dolphins, 23-20 (Mia)
1991—Dolphins, 16-13 (Mia)
1994—Dolphins, 24-14 (Mil)
1997—Packers, 23-18 (GB)
2000—Dolphins, 28-20 (Mia)
2002—Packers, 24-10 (GB)
2006—Packers, 34-24 (M)
2010—Dolphins, 23-20 (GB) OT

(RS Pts.—Dolphins 309, Packers 229)
GREEN BAY vs. MINNESOTA
RS: Packers lead series, 55-48-2
PS: Series tied, 1-1
1961—Packers, 33-7 (Minn)
　　　Packers, 28-10 (Mil)
1962—Packers, 34-7 (GB)
　　　Packers, 48-21 (Min)
1963—Packers, 37-28 (Minn)
　　　Packers, 28-7 (GB)
1964—Vikings, 24-23 (GB)
　　　Packers, 42-13 (Minn)
1965—Packers, 38-13 (GB)
　　　Packers, 24-19 (GB)
1966—Vikings, 20-17 (GB)
　　　Packers, 28-16 (Minn)
1967—Vikings, 10-7 (Mil)
　　　Packers, 30-27 (Minn)
1968—Vikings, 26-13 (Mil)
　　　Vikings, 14-10 (Minn)
1969—Vikings, 19-7 (Minn)
　　　Vikings, 9-7 (Mil)
1970—Packers, 13-10 (Mil)
　　　Vikings, 10-3 (Minn)
1971—Vikings, 24-13 (GB)
　　　Vikings, 3-0 (Minn)
1972—Vikings, 27-13 (GB)
　　　Packers, 23-7 (Minn)
1973—Vikings, 11-3 (Minn)
　　　Vikings, 31-7 (GB)
1974—Vikings, 32-17 (GB)
　　　Packers, 19-7 (Minn)
1975—Vikings, 28-17 (GB)
　　　Vikings, 24-3 (Minn)
1976—Vikings, 17-10 (Mil)
　　　Vikings, 20-9 (Minn)
1977—Vikings, 19-7 (Minn)
　　　Vikings, 13-6 (GB)
1978—Vikings, 21-7 (Minn)
　　　Tie, 10-10 (GB) OT
1979—Vikings, 27-21 (Minn) OT
　　　Packers, 19-7 (Mil)
1980—Packers, 16-3 (GB)
　　　Packers, 25-13 (Minn)
1981—Vikings, 30-13 (Mil)
　　　Packers, 35-23 (Minn)
1982—Packers, 26-7 (Mil)
1983—Vikings, 20-17 (GB) OT
　　　Packers, 29-21 (Minn)
1984—Packers, 45-17 (Mil)
　　　Packers, 38-14 (Min)
1985—Packers, 20-17 (Mil)
　　　Packers, 27-17 (Minn)
1986—Vikings, 42-7 (Minn)
　　　Vikings, 32-6 (GB)
1987—Packers, 23-16 (Minn)
　　　Packers, 16-10 (Mil)
1988—Packers, 34-14 (Minn)
　　　Packers, 18-6 (GB)
1989—Vikings, 26-14 (Min)
　　　Packers, 20-19 (Mil)
1990—Packers, 24-10 (Mil)
　　　Vikings, 23-7 (Minn)
1991—Vikings, 35-21 (GB)
　　　Packers, 27-7 (Minn)
1992—Vikings, 23-20 (GB) OT
　　　Vikings, 27-7 (Minn)
1993—Vikings, 15-13 (Minn)
　　　Vikings, 21-17 (Mil)
1994—Packers, 16-10 (GB)
　　　Vikings, 13-10 (Minn) OT
1995—Packers, 38-21 (GB)
　　　Vikings, 27-24 (Minn)

1996—Vikings, 30-21 (Minn)
　　　Packers, 38-10 (GB)
1997—Packers, 38-32 (GB)
　　　Packers, 27-11 (Minn)
1998—Vikings, 37-24 (GB)
　　　Vikings, 28-14 (Minn)
1999—Packers, 23-20 (GB)
　　　Vikings, 24-20 (Minn)
2000—Packers, 26-20 (GB) OT
　　　Packers, 33-28 (Minn)
2001—Vikings, 35-13 (Minn)
　　　Packers, 24-13 (GB)
2002—Vikings, 31-21 (Minn)
　　　Packers, 26-22 (GB)
2003—Vikings, 30-25 (GB)
　　　Packers, 30-27 (Minn)
2004—Packers, 34-31 (GB)
　　　Packers, 34-31 (Minn)
　　　*Vikings, 31-17 (GB)
2005—Packers, 23-20 (Minn)
　　　Vikings, 20-17 (GB)
2006—Packers, 23-17 (Minn)
　　　Packers, 9-7 (GB)
2007—Packers, 23-16 (Minn)
　　　Packers, 34-0 (GB)
2008—Packers, 24-19 (GB)
　　　Vikings, 28-27 (Minn)
2009—Vikings, 30-23 (Minn)
　　　Vikings, 38-26 (GB)
2010—Packers, 28-24 (GB)
　　　Packers, 31-3 (Minn)
2011—Packers, 33-27 (Minn)
　　　Packers, 45-7 (GB)
2012—Packers, 23-14 (GB)
　　　Vikings, 37-34 (Minn)
　　　*Packers, 24-10 (GB)
2013—Packers, 44-31 (Minn)
　　　Tie, 26-26 (GB) OT
(RS Pts.—Packers 2,228, Vikings 2,044)
(PS Pts.—Packers 41, Vikings 41)
*NFC First-Round Playoff
GREEN BAY vs. NEW ENGLAND
RS: Patriots lead series, 5-4
PS: Packers lead series, 1-0
1973—Patriots, 33-24 (NE)
1979—Packers, 27-14 (GB)
1985—Patriots, 26-20 (NE)
1988—Packers, 45-3 (Mil)
1994—Patriots, 17-16 (NE)
1996—*Packers, 35-21 (New Orleans)
1997—Packers, 28-10 (NE)
2002—Packers, 28-10 (NE)
2006—Patriots, 35-0 (GB)
2010—Patriots, 31-27 (NE)
(RS Pts.—Packers 215, Patriots 179)
(PS Pts.—Packers 35, Patriots 21)
*Super Bowl XXXI
GREEN BAY vs. NEW ORLEANS
RS: Packers lead series, 16-7
1968—Packers, 29-7 (Mil)
1971—Saints, 29-21 (Mil)
1972—Packers, 30-20 (NO)
1973—Packers, 30-10 (Mil)
1975—Saints, 20-19 (NO)
1976—Packers, 32-27 (Mil)
1977—Packers, 24-20 (NO)
1978—Packers, 28-17 (Mil)
1979—Packers, 28-19 (Mil)
1981—Packers, 35-7 (NO)
1984—Packers, 23-13 (NO)
1985—Packers, 38-14 (Mil)
1986—Saints, 24-10 (NO)
1987—Saints, 33-24 (NO)

1989—Packers, 35-34 (GB)
1993—Packers, 19-17 (NO)
1995—Packers, 34-23 (NO)
2002—Saints, 35-20 (NO)
2005—Packers, 52-3 (GB)
2006—Saints, 34-27 (GB)
2008—Saints, 51-29 (NO)
2011—Packers, 42-34 (GB)
2012—Packers, 28-27 (GB)
(RS Pts.—Packers 657, Saints 518)
GREEN BAY vs. N.Y. GIANTS
RS: Packers lead series, 27-23-2
PS: Packers lead series, 4-3
1928—Giants, 6-0 (GB)
　　　Packers, 7-0 (NY)
1929—Packers, 20-6 (NY)
1930—Packers, 14-7 (GB)
　　　Giants, 13-6 (NY)
1931—Packers, 27-7 (GB)
　　　Packers, 14-10 (NY)
1932—Packers, 13-0 (GB)
　　　Giants, 6-0 (NY)
1933—Packers, 10-7 (Mil)
　　　Giants, 17-6 (NY)
1934—Packers, 20-6 (Mil)
　　　Giants, 17-3 (NY)
1935—Packers, 16-7 (GB)
1936—Packers, 26-14 (NY)
1937—Giants, 10-0 (NY)
1938—Giants, 15-3 (NY)
　　　*Giants, 23-17 (NY)
1939—*Packers, 27-0 (Mil)
1940—Giants, 7-3 (NY)
1942—Tie, 21-21 (NY)
1943—Packers, 35-21 (NY)
1944—Giants, 24-0 (NY)
　　　*Packers, 14-7 (NY)
1945—Packers, 23-14 (NY)
1947—Tie, 24-24 (NY)
1948—Giants, 49-3 (Mil)
1949—Giants, 30-10 (GB)
1952—Packers, 17-3 (NY)
1957—Giants, 31-17 (GB)
1959—Giants, 20-3 (NY)
1961—Packers, 20-17 (NY)
　　　*Packers, 37-0 (GB)
1962—*Packers, 16-7 (NY)
1967—Packers, 48-21 (NY)
1969—Packers, 20-10 (Mil)
1971—Giants, 42-40 (NY)
1973—Packers, 16-14 (New Haven)
1975—Packers, 40-14 (Mil)
1980—Giants, 27-21 (NY)
1981—Packers, 27-14 (NY)
　　　Packers, 26-24 (Mil)
1982—Packers, 27-19 (NY)
1983—Giants, 27-3 (NY)
1985—Packers, 23-20 (GB)
1986—Giants, 55-24 (NY)
1987—Giants, 20-10 (NY)
1992—Giants, 27-7 (NY)
1995—Packers, 14-6 (NY)
1998—Packers, 37-3 (NY)
2001—Packers, 34-25 (NY)
2004—Giants, 14-7 (GB)
2007—Packers, 35-13 (NY)
　　　**Giants, 23-20 (GB) OT
2010—Packers, 45-17 (GB)
2011—Packers, 38-35 (NY)
　　　***Giants, 37-20 (GB)
2012—Giants, 38-10 (NY)
2013—Giants, 27-13 (NY)
(RS Pts.—Giants 924, Packers 923)

(PS Pts.—Packers 151, Giants 97)
*NFL Championship
**NFC Championship Game
***NFC Divisional Playoff
GREEN BAY vs. N.Y. JETS
RS: Jets lead series, 8-3
1973—Packers, 23-7 (Mil)
1979—Jets, 27-22 (GB)
1981—Jets, 28-3 (NY)
1982—Jets, 15-13 (NY)
1985—Jets, 24-3 (Mil)
1991—Jets, 19-16 (NY) OT
1994—Packers, 17-10 (GB)
2000—Jets, 20-16 (GB)
2002—Jets, 42-17 (NY)
2006—Jets, 38-10 (GB)
2010—Packers, 9-0 (NY)
(RS Pts.—Jets 230, Packers 149)
GREEN BAY vs. *OAKLAND
RS: Packers lead series, 6-5
PS: Packers lead series, 1-0
1967—**Packers, 33-14 (Miami)
1972—Raiders, 20-14 (GB)
1976—Raiders, 18-14 (O)
1978—Raiders, 28-3 (GB)
1984—Raiders, 28-7 (LA)
1987—Packers, 20-0 (GB)
1990—Packers, 29-16 (LA)
1993—Packers, 28-0 (GB)
1999—Packers, 28-24 (GB)
2003—Packers, 41-7 (O)
2007—Packers, 38-7 (GB)
2011—Packers, 46-16 (GB)
(RS Pts.—Packers 248, Raiders 184)
(PS Pts.—Packers 33, Raiders 14)
*Franchise in Los Angeles from 1982-1994
**Super Bowl II
GREEN BAY vs. PHILADELPHIA
RS: Packers lead series, 24-14
PS: Eagles lead series, 2-1
1933—Packers, 35-9 (GB)
        Packers, 10-0 (P)
1934—Packers, 19-6 (GB)
1935—Packers, 13-6 (P)
1937—Packers, 37-7 (Mil)
1939—Packers, 23-16 (P)
1940—Packers, 27-20 (GB)
1942—Packers, 7-0 (P)
1946—Packers, 19-7 (P)
1947—Eagles, 28-14 (P)
1951—Packers, 37-24 (GB)
1952—Packers, 12-10 (Mil)
1954—Packers, 37-14 (P)
1958—Packers, 38-35 (GB)
1960—*Eagles, 17-13 (P)
1962—Packers, 49-0 (P)
1968—Packers, 30-13 (GB)
1970—Packers, 30-17 (Mil)
1974—Eagles, 36-14 (P)
1976—Packers, 28-13 (GB)
1978—Eagles, 10-3 (P)
1979—Eagles, 21-10 (GB)
1987—Packers, 16-10 (GB) OT
1990—Eagles, 31-0 (P)
1991—Eagles, 20-3 (GB)
1992—Packers, 27-24 (Mil)
1993—Eagles, 20-17 (GB)
1994—Eagles, 13-7 (P)
1996—Packers, 39-13 (GB)
1997—Eagles, 10-9 (P)
1998—Packers, 24-16 (GB)
2000—Packers, 6-3 (GB)

2003—Eagles, 17-14 (GB)
        **Eagles, 20-17 (P) OT
2004—Eagles, 47-17 (P)
2005—Eagles, 19-14 (P)
2006—Eagles, 31-9 (P)
2007—Packers, 16-13 (GB)
2010—Packers, 27-20 (P)
        ***Packers, 21-16 (P)
2013—Packers, 27-13 (GB)
(RS Pts.—Packers 750, Eagles 626)
(PS Pts.—Eagles 53, Packers 51)
*NFL Championship
**NFC Divisional Playoff
***NFC First-Round Playoff
GREEN BAY vs. *PITTSBURGH
RS: Packers lead series, 18-15
PS: Packers lead series, 1-0
1933—Packers, 47-0 (GB)
1935—Packers, 27-0 (GB)
        Packers, 34-14 (P)
1936—Packers, 42-10 (Mil)
1938—Packers, 20-0 (GB)
1940—Packers, 24-3 (Mil)
1941—Packers, 54-7 (P)
1942—Packers, 24-21 (Mil)
1946—Packers, 17-7 (GB)
1947—Steelers, 18-17 (Mil)
1948—Steelers, 38-7 (P)
1949—Steelers, 30-7 (Mil)
1951—Packers, 35-33 (Mil)
        Steelers, 28-7 (P)
1953—Steelers, 31-14 (P)
1954—Steelers, 21-20 (GB)
1957—Packers, 27-10 (P)
1960—Packers, 19-13 (P)
1963—Packers, 33-14 (Mil)
1965—Packers, 41-9 (P)
1967—Steelers, 24-17 (Mil)
1969—Packers, 38-34 (P)
1970—Packers, 20-12 (P)
1975—Steelers, 16-13 (Mil)
1980—Steelers, 22-20 (P)
1983—Packers, 25-21 (GB)
1986—Steelers, 27-3 (P)
1992—Packers, 17-3 (GB)
1995—Packers, 24-19 (GB)
1998—Steelers, 27-20 (P)
2005—Steelers, 20-10 (GB)
2009—Steelers, 37-36 (P)
2010—**Packers, 31-25 (North Texas)
2013—Steelers, 38-31 (GB)
(RS Pts.—Packers 786, Steelers 611)
(PS Pts.—Packers 31, Steelers 25)
*Steelers known as Pirates prior to 1940
**Super Bowl XLV
GREEN BAY vs. *ST. LOUIS
RS: Rams lead series, 45-44-2
PS: Series tied, 1-1
1937—Packers, 35-10 (C)
        Packers, 35-7 (GB)
1938—Packers, 26-17 (GB)
        Packers, 28-7 (C)
1939—Rams, 27-24 (GB)
        Packers, 7-6 (C)
1940—Packers, 31-14 (GB)
        Tie, 13-13 (C)
1941—Packers, 24-7 (Mil)
        Packers, 17-14 (C)
1942—Packers, 45-28 (GB)
        Packers, 30-12 (C)
1944—Packers, 30-21 (GB)
        Packers, 42-7 (C)
1945—Rams, 27-14 (GB)

        Rams, 20-7 (C)
1946—Rams, 21-17 (Mil)
        Rams, 38-17 (LA)
1947—Packers, 17-14 (Mil)
        Packers, 30-10 (LA)
1948—Packers, 16-0 (GB)
        Rams, 24-10 (LA)
1949—Rams, 48-7 (GB)
        Rams, 35-7 (LA)
1950—Rams, 45-14 (Mil)
        Rams, 51-14 (LA)
1951—Rams, 28-0 (Mil)
        Rams, 42-14 (LA)
1952—Rams, 30-28 (Mil)
        Rams, 45-27 (LA)
1953—Rams, 38-20 (Mil)
        Rams, 33-17 (LA)
1954—Packers, 35-17 (Mil)
        Rams, 35-27 (LA)
1955—Packers, 30-28 (Mil)
        Rams, 31-17 (LA)
1956—Packers, 42-17 (Mil)
        Rams, 49-21 (LA)
1957—Rams, 31-27 (Mil)
        Rams, 42-17 (LA)
1958—Rams, 20-7 (GB)
        Rams, 34-20 (LA)
1959—Rams, 45-6 (Mil)
        Packers, 38-20 (LA)
1960—Rams, 33-31 (Mil)
        Packers, 35-21 (LA)
1961—Packers, 35-17 (GB)
        Packers, 24-17 (LA)
1962—Packers, 41-10 (Mil)
        Packers, 20-17 (LA)
1963—Packers, 42-10 (GB)
        Packers, 31-14 (LA)
1964—Packers, 27-17 (Mil)
        Tie, 24-24 (LA)
1965—Packers, 6-3 (Mil)
        Rams, 21-10 (LA)
1966—Packers, 24-13 (GB)
        Packers, 27-23 (LA)
1967—Rams, 27-24 (LA)
        **Packers, 28-7 (Mil)
1968—Rams, 16-14 (Mil)
1969—Rams, 34-21 (LA)
1970—Rams, 31-21 (GB)
1971—Rams, 30-13 (LA)
1973—Rams, 24-7 (LA)
1974—Packers, 17-6 (Mil)
1975—Rams, 22-5 (LA)
1977—Rams, 24-6 (Mil)
1978—Rams, 31-14 (LA)
1980—Rams, 51-21 (LA)
1981—Rams, 35-23 (LA)
1982—Packers, 35-23 (Mil)
1983—Packers, 27-24 (Mil)
1984—Packers, 31-6 (Mil)
1985—Rams, 34-17 (LA)
1988—Packers, 34-7 (GB)
1989—Packers, 41-38 (LA)
1990—Packers, 36-24 (GB)
1991—Rams, 23-21 (LA)
1992—Packers, 28-13 (GB)
1993—Packers, 36-6 (Mil)
1994—Packers, 24-17 (GB)
1995—Rams, 17-14 (GB)
1996—Packers, 24-9 (StL)
1997—Packers, 17-7 (GB)
2001—***Rams, 45-17 (StL)
2003—Packers, 34-24 (StL)
2004—Packers, 45-17 (GB)

2006—Rams, 23-20 (GB)
2007—Packers, 33-14 (StL)
2009—Packers, 36-17 (StL)
2011—Packers, 24-3 (GB)
2012—Packers, 30-20 (StL)
(RS Pts.—Rams 2,095, Packers 2,070)
(PS Pts.—Rams 52, Packers 45)
*Franchise in Los Angeles prior to 1995
and in Cleveland prior to 1946
**Conference Championship
***NFC Divisional Playoff
GREEN BAY vs. SAN DIEGO
RS: Packers lead series, 9-1
1970—Packers, 22-20 (SD)
1974—Packers, 34-0 (GB)
1978—Packers, 24-3 (SD)
1984—Chargers, 34-28 (GB)
1993—Packers, 20-13 (SD)
1996—Packers, 42-10 (GB)
1999—Packers, 31-3 (SD)
2003—Packers, 38-21 (SD)
2007—Packers, 31-24 (GB)
2011—Packers, 45-38 (SD)
(RS Pts.—Packers 315, Chargers 166)
GREEN BAY vs. SAN FRANCISCO
RS: Packers lead series, 30-27-1
PS: Packers lead series, 4-3
1950—Packers, 25-21 (GB)
        49ers, 30-14 (SF)
1951—Packers, 31-19 (GB)
1952—49ers, 24-14 (SF)
1953—49ers, 37-7 (Mil)
        49ers, 48-14 (SF)
1954—49ers, 23-17 (Mil)
        49ers, 35-0 (SF)
1955—Packers, 27-21 (Mil)
        Packers, 28-7 (SF)
1956—49ers, 17-16 (GB)
        49ers, 38-20 (SF)
1957—49ers, 24-14 (Mil)
        49ers, 27-20 (SF)
1958—49ers, 33-12 (Mil)
        49ers, 48-21 (SF)
1959—Packers, 21-20 (GB)
        Packers, 36-14 (SF)
1960—Packers, 41-14 (Mil)
        Packers, 13-0 (SF)
1961—Packers, 30-10 (GB)
        49ers, 22-21 (SF)
1962—Packers, 31-13 (Mil)
        Packers, 31-21 (SF)
1963—Packers, 28-10 (Mil)
        Packers, 21-17 (SF)
1964—Packers, 24-14 (Mil)
        49ers, 24-14 (SF)
1965—Packers, 27-10 (GB)
        Tie, 24-24 (SF)
1966—49ers, 21-20 (SF)
        Packers, 20-7 (Mil)
1967—Packers, 13-0 (SF)
1968—49ers, 27-20 (SF)
1969—Packers, 14-7 (Mil)
1970—Packers, 26-10 (SF)
1972—Packers, 34-24 (Mil)
1973—49ers, 20-6 (SF)
1974—49ers, 7-6 (SF)
1976—49ers, 26-14 (GB)
1977—Packers, 16-14 (Mil)
1980—Packers, 23-16 (Mil)
1981—49ers, 13-3 (Mil)
1986—49ers, 31-17 (Mil)
1987—49ers, 23-12 (GB)
1989—Packers, 21-17 (SF)

1990—49ers, 24-20 (GB)
1995—*Packers, 27-17 (SF)
1996—Packers, 23-20 (GB) OT
        *Packers, 35-14 (GB)
1997—**Packers, 23-10 (SF)
1998—Packers, 36-22 (GB)
        ***49ers, 30-27 (SF)
1999—Packers, 20-3 (SF)
2000—Packers, 31-28 (GB)
2001—***Packers, 25-15 (GB)
2002—Packers, 20-14 (SF)
2003—Packers, 20-10 (GB)
2006—Packers, 30-19 (GB)
2009—Packers, 30-24 (GB)
2010—Packers, 34-16 (GB)
2012—49ers, 30-22 (GB)
        *49ers, 45-31 (SF)
2013—49ers, 34-28 (SF)
        ***49ers, 23-20 (GB)
(RS Pts.—49ers 1,200, Packers 1,193)
(PS Pts.—Packers 188, 49ers 154)
*NFC Divisional Playoff
**NFC Championship
***NFC First-Round Playoff
GREEN BAY vs. SEATTLE
RS: Packers lead series, 8-6
PS: Packers lead series, 2-0
1976—Packers, 27-20 (Mil)
1978—Packers, 45-28 (Mil)
1981—Packers, 34-24 (GB)
1984—Seahawks, 30-24 (Mil)
1987—Seahawks, 24-13 (S)
1990—Seahawks, 20-14 (Mil)
1996—Packers, 31-10 (S)
1999—Seahawks, 27-7 (GB)
2003—Packers, 35-13 (GB)
        *Packers, 33-27 (GB) OT
2005—Packers, 23-17 (GB)
2006—Seahawks, 34-24 (S)
2007—**Packers, 42-20 (GB)
2008—Packers, 27-17 (S)
2009—Packers, 48-10 (GB)
2012—Seahawks, 14-12 (S)
(RS Pts.—Packers 364, Seahawks 288)
(PS Pts.—Packers 75, Seahawks 47)
*NFC First-Round Playoff
**NFC Divisional Playoff
GREEN BAY vs. TAMPA BAY
RS: Packers lead series, 30-31-1
PS: Packers lead series, 1-0
1977—Packers, 13-0 (TB)
1978—Packers, 9-7 (GB)
        Packers, 17-7 (TB)
1979—Buccaneers, 21-10 (GB)
        Buccaneers, 21-3 (TB)
1980—Tie, 14-14 (TB) OT
        Buccaneers, 20-17 (Mil)
1981—Buccaneers, 21-10 (GB)
        Buccaneers, 37-3 (TB)
1983—Packers, 55-14 (GB)
        Packers, 12-9 (TB) OT
1984—Buccaneers, 30-27 (TB) OT
        Packers, 27-14 (GB)
1985—Packers, 21-0 (GB)
        Packers, 20-17 (TB)
1986—Packers, 31-7 (Mil)
        Packers, 21-7 (TB)
1987—Buccaneers, 23-17 (Mil)
1988—Buccaneers, 13-10 (GB)
        Buccaneers, 27-24 (TB)
1989—Buccaneers, 23-21 (GB)
        Packers, 17-16 (TB)
1990—Buccaneers, 26-14 (TB)

        Packers, 20-10 (Mil)
1991—Packers, 15-13 (GB)
        Packers, 27-0 (TB)
1992—Buccaneers, 31-3 (TB)
        Packers, 19-14 (Mil)
1993—Packers, 37-14 (TB)
        Packers, 13-10 (GB)
1994—Packers, 30-3 (GB)
        Packers, 34-19 (TB)
1995—Packers, 35-13 (GB)
        Buccaneers, 13-10 (TB) OT
1996—Packers, 34-3 (TB)
        Packers, 13-7 (GB)
1997—Packers, 21-16 (GB)
        Packers, 17-6 (TB)
        *Packers, 21-7 (GB)
1998—Packers, 23-15 (GB)
        Buccaneers, 24-22 (TB)
1999—Packers, 26-23 (GB)
        Buccaneers, 29-10 (TB)
2000—Buccaneers, 20-15 (TB)
        Packers, 17-14 (GB) OT
2001—Buccaneers, 14-10 (TB)
        Packers, 21-20 (GB)
2002—Buccaneers, 21-7 (TB)
2003—Packers, 20-13 (TB)
2005—Buccaneers, 17-16 (GB)
2008—Buccaneers, 30-21 (TB)
2009—Buccaneers, 38-28 (TB)
2011—Packers, 35-26 (GB)
(RS Pts.—Packers 1,012, Buccaneers 850)
(PS Pts.—Packers 21, Buccaneers 7)
*NFC Divisional Playoff
GREEN BAY vs. *TENNESSEE
RS: Titans lead series, 6-5
1972—Packers, 23-10 (H)
1977—Oilers, 16-10 (GB)
1980—Oilers, 22-3 (GB)
1983—Packers, 41-38 (H) OT
1986—Oilers, 31-3 (GB)
1992—Packers, 16-14 (H)
1998—Packers, 30-22 (GB)
2001—Titans, 26-20 (T)
2004—Titans, 48-27 (GB)
2008—Titans, 19-16 (T) OT
2012—Packers, 55-7 (GB)
(RS Pts.—Titans 253, Packers 244)
*Franchise in Houston prior to 1997;
known as Oilers prior to 1999
GREEN BAY vs. *WASHINGTON
RS: Packers lead series, 18-13-1
PS: Series tied, 1-1
1932—Packers, 21-0 (B)
1933—Tie, 7-7 (GB)
        Redskins, 20-7 (B)
1934—Packers, 10-0 (B)
1936—Packers, 31-2 (GB)
        Packers, 7-3 (B)
        **Packers, 21-6 (New York)
1937—Redskins, 14-6 (W)
1939—Packers, 24-14 (Mil)
1941—Packers, 22-17 (W)
1943—Redskins, 33-7 (Mil)
1946—Packers, 20-7 (W)
1947—Packers, 27-10 (Mil)
1948—Redskins, 23-7 (Mil)
1949—Redskins, 30-0 (W)
1950—Packers, 35-21 (Mil)
1952—Packers, 35-20 (Mil)
1958—Redskins, 37-21 (W)
1959—Packers, 21-0 (GB)
1968—Packers, 27-7 (W)
1972—Redskins, 21-16 (W)

***Redskins, 16-3 (W)
1974—Redskins, 17-6 (GB)
1977—Redskins, 10-9 (W)
1979—Redskins, 38-21 (W)
1983—Packers, 48-47 (GB)
1986—Redskins, 16-7 (GB)
1988—Redskins, 20-17 (Mil)
2001—Packers, 37-0 (GB)
2002—Packers, 30-9 (GB)
2004—Packers, 28-14 (W)
2007—Packers, 17-14 (GB)
2010—Redskins, 16-13 (W) OT
2013—Packers, 38-20 (GB)
(RS Pts.—Packers 622, Redskins 507)
(PS Pts.—Packers 24, Redskins 22)
*Franchise in Boston prior to 1937 and
known as Braves prior to 1933
**NFL Championship
***NFC Divisional Playoff

HOUSTON vs. ARIZONA
RS: Cardinals lead series, 2-1;
See Arizona vs. Houston
HOUSTON vs. ATLANTA
RS: Texans lead series, 2-1;
See Atlanta vs. Houston
HOUSTON vs. BALTIMORE
RS: Ravens lead series, 6-1
PS: Ravens lead series, 1-0;
See Baltimore vs. Houston
HOUSTON vs. BUFFALO
RS: Series tied, 3-3;
See Buffalo vs. Houston
HOUSTON vs. CAROLINA
RS: Texans lead series, 2-1;
See Carolina vs. Houston
HOUSTON vs. CHICAGO
RS: Texans lead series, 3-0;
See Chicago vs. Houston
HOUSTON vs. CINCINNATI
RS: Series tied, 3-3
PS: Texans lead series, 2-0;
See Cincinnati vs. Houston
HOUSTON vs. CLEVELAND
RS: Texans lead series, 4-3;
See Cleveland vs. Houston
HOUSTON vs. DALLAS
RS: Cowboys lead series, 2-1;
See Dallas vs. Houston
HOUSTON vs. DENVER
RS: Broncos lead series, 3-2;
See Denver vs. Houston
HOUSTON vs. DETROIT
RS: Texans lead series, 2-1;
See Detroit vs. Houston
HOUSTON vs. GREEN BAY
RS: Packers lead series, 2-1;
See Green Bay vs. Houston
HOUSTON vs. INDIANAPOLIS
RS: Colts lead series, 20-4
2002—Colts, 23-3 (H)
        Colts, 19-3 (I)
2003—Colts, 30-21 (I)
        Colts, 20-17 (H)
2004—Colts, 49-14 (I)
        Colts, 23-14 (H)
2005—Colts, 38-20 (H)
        Colts, 31-17 (I)
2006—Colts, 43-24 (I)
        Texans, 27-24 (H)
2007—Colts, 30-24 (H)
        Colts, 38-15 (I)
2008—Colts, 31-27 (H)

Colts, 33-27 (I)
2009—Colts, 20-17 (I)
        Colts, 35-27 (H)
2010—Texans, 34-24 (H)
        Colts, 30-17 (I)
2011—Texans, 34-7 (H)
        Colts, 19-16 (I)
2012—Texans, 29-17 (H)
        Colts, 28-16 (I)
2013—Colts, 27-24 (H)
        Colts, 25-3 (I)
(RS Pts.—Colts 664, Texans 470)
HOUSTON vs. JACKSONVILLE
RS: Texans lead series, 13-11
2002—Texans, 21-19 (J)
        Jaguars, 24-21 (H)
2003—Texans, 24-20 (H)
        Jaguars, 27-0 (J)
2004—Texans, 20-6 (H)
        Texans, 21-0 (J)
2005—Jaguars, 21-14 (J)
        Jaguars, 38-20 (H)
2006—Texans, 27-7 (H)
        Texans, 13-10 (J)
2007—Jaguars, 37-17 (J)
        Texans, 42-28 (H)
2008—Jaguars, 30-27 (J) OT
        Texans, 30-17 (H)
2009—Jaguars, 31-24 (H)
        Jaguars, 23-18 (J)
2010—Jaguars, 31-24 (J)
        Texans, 34-17 (H)
2011—Texans, 24-14 (H)
        Texans, 20-13 (J)
2012—Texans, 27-7 (J)
        Texans, 43-37 (H) OT
2013—Jaguars, 13-6 (H)
        Jaguars, 27-20 (J)
(RS Pts.—Texans 537, Jaguars 497)
HOUSTON vs. KANSAS CITY
RS: Series tied, 3-3
2003—Chiefs, 42-14 (H)
2004—Texans, 24-21 (KC)
2005—Chiefs, 45-17 (H)
2007—Texans, 20-3 (H)
2010—Texans, 35-31 (H)
2013—Chiefs, 17-16 (KC)
(RS Pts.—Chiefs 159, Texans 126)
HOUSTON vs. MIAMI
RS: Texans lead series, 7-0
2003—Texans, 21-20 (M)
2006—Texans, 17-15 (H)
2007—Texans, 22-19 (H)
2008—Texans, 29-28 (H)
2009—Texans, 27-20 (M)
2011—Texans, 23-13 (M)
2012—Texans, 30-10 (H)
(RS Pts.—Texans 169, Dolphins 125)
HOUSTON vs. MINNESOTA
RS: Vikings lead series, 3-0
2004—Vikings, 34-28 (H) OT
2008—Vikings, 28-21 (M)
2012—Vikings, 23-6 (H)
(RS Pts.—Vikings 85, Texans 55)
HOUSTON vs. NEW ENGLAND
RS: Patriots lead series, 4-1
PS: Patriots lead series, 1-0
2003—Patriots, 23-20 (H) OT
2006—Patriots, 40-7 (NE)
2009—Texans, 34-27 (H)
2012—Patriots, 42-14 (NE)
        *Patriots, 41-28 (NE)
2013—Patriots, 34-31

(RS Pts.—Patriots 166, Texans 106)
(PS Pts.—Patriots 41, Texans 28)
*AFC Divisional Playoff
HOUSTON vs. NEW ORLEANS
RS: Saints lead series, 2-1
2003—Saints, 31-10 (NO)
2007—Texans, 23-10 (H)
2011—Saints, 40-33 (NO)
(RS Pts.—Saints 81, Texans 66)
HOUSTON vs. N.Y. GIANTS
RS: Giants lead series, 2-1
2002—Texans, 16-14 (H)
2006—Giants, 14-10 (NY)
2010—Giants, 34-10 (H)
(RS Pts.—Giants 62, Texans 36)
HOUSTON vs. N.Y. JETS
RS: Jets lead series, 5-1
2003—Jets, 19-14 (H)
2004—Jets, 29-7 (NY)
2006—Texans, 26-11 (NY)
2009—Jets, 24-7 (H)
2010—Jets, 30-27 (NY)
2012—Texans, 23-17 (NY)
(RS Pts.—Jets 145, Texans 89)
HOUSTON vs. OAKLAND
RS: Texans lead series, 5-3
2004—Texans, 30-17 (H)
2006—Texans, 23-14 (O)
2007—Texans, 24-17 (O)
2008—Raiders, 27-16 (O)
2009—Texans, 29-6 (H)
2010—Texans, 31-24 (O)
2011—Raiders, 25-20 (H)
2013—Raiders, 28-23 (H)
(RS Pts.—Texans 196, Raiders 158)
HOUSTON vs. PHILADELPHIA
RS: Eagles lead series, 3-0
2002—Eagles, 35-17 (P)
2006—Eagles, 24-10 (H)
2010—Eagles, 34-24 (P)
(RS Pts.—Eagles 93, Texans 51)
HOUSTON vs. PITTSBURGH
RS: Series tied, 2-2
2002—Texans, 24-6 (P)
2005—Steelers, 27-7 (H)
2008—Steelers, 38-17 (P)
2011—Texans, 17-10 (H)
(RS Pts.—Steelers 81, Texans 65)
HOUSTON vs. ST. LOUIS
RS: Rams lead series, 2-1
2005—Rams, 33-27 (H) OT
2009—Texans, 16-13 (StL)
2013—Rams, 38-13 (H)
(RS Pts.—Rams 84, Texans 56)
HOUSTON vs. SAN DIEGO
RS: Chargers lead series, 4-1
2002—Chargers, 24-3 (SD)
2004—Chargers, 27-20 (H)
2007—Chargers, 35-10 (SD)
2010—Chargers, 29-23 (H)
2013—Texans, 31-28 (SD)
(RS Pts.—Chargers 143, Texans 87)
HOUSTON vs. SAN FRANCISCO
RS: 49ers lead series, 2-1
2005—49ers, 20-17 (SF) OT
2009—Texans, 24-21 (H)
2013—49ers, 34-3 (SF)
(RS Pts.—49ers 75, Texans 44)
HOUSTON vs. SEATTLE
RS: Seahawks lead series, 2-1
2005—Seahawks, 42-10 (S)
2009—Texans, 34-7 (H)
2013—Seahawks, 23-20 (H) OT

(RS Pts.—Seahawks 72, Texans 64)

HOUSTON vs. TAMPA BAY
RS: Texans lead series, 2-1
2003—Buccaneers, 16-3 (TB)
2007—Texans, 28-14 (H)
2011—Texans, 37-9 (TB)
(RS Pts.—Texans 68, Buccaneers 39)

HOUSTON vs. TENNESSEE
RS: Titans lead series, 15-9
2002—Titans, 17-10 (T)
    Titans, 13-3 (H)
2003—Titans, 38-17 (T)
    Titans, 27-24 (H)
2004—Texans, 20-10 (T)
    Texans, 31-21 (H)
2005—Titans, 34-20 (H)
    Titans, 13-10 (T)
2006—Titans, 28-22 (T)
    Titans, 26-20 (H) OT
2007—Titans, 38-36 (H)
    Titans, 28-20 (T)
2008—Titans, 31-12 (T)
    Texans, 13-12 (H)
2009—Texans, 34-31 (T)
    Titans, 20-17 (H)
2010—Texans, 20-0 (H)
    Titans, 31-17 (T)
2011—Texans, 41-7 (T)
    Titans, 23-22 (H)
2012—Texans, 38-14 (H)
    Texans, 24-10 (T)
2013—Texans, 30-24 (H) OT
    Titans, 16-10 (T)
(RS Pts.—Titans 512, Texans 511)

HOUSTON vs. WASHINGTON
RS: Redskins lead series, 2-1
2002—Redskins, 26-10 (W)
2006—Redskins, 31-15 (H)
2010—Texans, 30-27 (W) OT
(RS Pts.—Redskins 84, Texans 55)

INDIANAPOLIS vs. ARIZONA
RS: Colts lead series, 8-7;
See Arizona vs. Indianapolis

INDIANAPOLIS vs. ATLANTA
RS: Colts lead series, 13-2;
See Atlanta vs. Indianapolis

INDIANAPOLIS vs. BALTIMORE
RS: Colts lead series, 7-3
PS: Colts lead series, 2-1;
See Baltimore vs. Indianapolis

INDIANAPOLIS vs. BUFFALO
RS: Bills lead series, 35-31-1;
See Buffalo vs. Indianapolis

INDIANAPOLIS vs. CAROLINA
RS: Panthers lead series, 4-1;
See Carolina vs. Indianapolis

INDIANAPOLIS vs. CHICAGO
RS: Colts lead series, 22-19
PS: Colts lead series, 1-0;
See Chicago vs. Indianapolis

INDIANAPOLIS vs. CINCINNATI
RS: Colts lead series, 16-10
PS: Colts lead series, 1-0;
See Cincinnati vs. Indianapolis

INDIANAPOLIS vs. CLEVELAND
RS: Browns lead series, 14-13
PS: Series tied, 2-2;
See Cleveland vs. Indianapolis

INDIANAPOLIS vs. DALLAS
RS: Cowboys lead series, 9-5
PS: Colts lead series, 1-0;
See Dallas vs. Indianapolis

INDIANAPOLIS vs. DENVER
RS: Broncos lead series, 11-9
PS: Colts lead series, 2-0;
See Denver vs. Indianapolis

INDIANAPOLIS vs. DETROIT
RS: Colts lead series, 21-18-2;
See Detroit vs. Indianapolis

INDIANAPOLIS vs. GREEN BAY
RS: Colts lead series, 21-20-1
PS: Packers lead series, 1-0;
See Green Bay vs. Indianapolis

INDIANAPOLIS vs. HOUSTON
RS: Colts lead series, 20-4;
See Houston vs. Indianapolis

INDIANAPOLIS vs. JACKSONVILLE
RS: Colts lead series, 18-8
1995—Colts, 41-31 (J)
2000—Colts, 43-14 (I)
2002—Colts, 28-25 (J)
    Colts, 20-13 (I)
2003—Colts, 23-13 (I)
    Jaguars, 28-23 (J)
2004—Colts, 24-17 (J)
    Jaguars, 27-24 (I)
2005—Colts, 10-3 (I)
    Colts, 26-18 (J)
2006—Colts, 21-14 (I)
    Jaguars, 44-17 (J)
2007—Colts, 29-7 (J)
    Colts, 28-25 (I)
2008—Jaguars, 23-21 (I)
    Colts, 31-24 (J)
2009—Colts, 14-12 (I)
    Colts, 35-31 (J)
2010—Jaguars, 31-28 (J)
    Colts, 34-24 (I)
2011—Jaguars, 17-3 (I)
    Jaguars, 19-13 (J)
2012—Jaguars, 22-17 (I)
    Colts, 27-10 (J)
2013—Colts, 37-3 (J)
    Colts, 30-10 (I)
(RS Pts.—Colts 647, Jaguars 505)

***INDIANAPOLIS vs. KANSAS CITY**
RS: Colts lead series, 12-8
PS: Colts lead series, 4-0
1970—Chiefs, 44-24 (B)
1972—Chiefs, 24-10 (KC)
1975—Colts, 28-14 (B)
1977—Colts, 17-6 (KC)
1979—Chiefs, 14-0 (KC)
    Chiefs, 10-7 (B)
1980—Colts, 31-24 (KC)
    Chiefs, 38-28 (B)
1985—Chiefs, 20-7 (KC)
1990—Colts, 23-19 (I)
1995—**Colts, 10-7 (KC)
1996—Colts, 24-19 (KC)
1999—Colts, 25-17 (I)
2000—Colts, 27-14 (KC)
2001—Colts, 35-28 (KC)
2003—**Colts, 38-31 (KC)
2004—Chiefs, 45-35 (KC)
2006—***Colts, 23-8 (I)
2007—Colts, 13-10 (I)
2010—Colts, 19-9 (I)
2011—Chiefs, 28-24 (I)
2012—Colts, 20-13 (KC)
2013—Colts, 23-7 (KC)
    ***Colts, 45-44 (I)
(RS Pts.—Colts 420, Chiefs 403)
(PS Pts.—Colts 116, Chiefs 90)
Franchise in Baltimore prior to 1984

**AFC Divisional Playoff*
***AFC First-Round Playoff*
***INDIANAPOLIS vs. MIAMI**
RS: Dolphins lead series, 45-25
PS: Dolphins lead series, 2-0
1970—Colts, 35-0 (B)
    Dolphins, 34-17 (M)
1971—Dolphins, 17-14 (M)
    Colts, 14-3 (B)
    **Dolphins, 21-0 (M)
1972—Dolphins, 23-0 (B)
    Dolphins, 16-0 (M)
1973—Dolphins, 44-0 (M)
    Colts, 16-3 (B)
1974—Dolphins, 17-7 (M)
    Dolphins, 17-16 (B)
1975—Colts, 33-17 (M)
    Colts, 10-7 (B) OT
1976—Colts, 28-14 (B)
    Colts, 17-16 (M)
1977—Colts, 45-28 (B)
    Dolphins, 17-6 (M)
1978—Dolphins, 42-0 (B)
    Dolphins, 26-8 (M)
1979—Dolphins, 19-0 (M)
    Dolphins, 28-24 (B)
1980—Colts, 30-17 (M)
    Dolphins, 24-14 (B)
1981—Dolphins, 31-28 (B)
    Dolphins, 27-10 (M)
1982—Dolphins, 24-20 (M)
    Dolphins, 34-7 (B)
1983—Dolphins, 21-7 (B)
    Dolphins, 37-0 (M)
1984—Dolphins, 44-7 (M)
    Dolphins, 35-17 (I)
1985—Dolphins, 30-13 (M)
    Dolphins, 34-20 (I)
1986—Dolphins, 30-10 (M)
    Dolphins, 17-13 (I)
1987—Dolphins, 23-10 (I)
    Colts, 40-21 (M)
1988—Colts, 15-13 (I)
    Colts, 31-28 (M)
1989—Dolphins, 19-13 (M)
    Colts, 42-13 (I)
1990—Dolphins, 27-7 (I)
    Dolphins, 23-17 (M)
1991—Dolphins, 17-6 (M)
    Dolphins, 10-6 (I)
1992—Colts, 31-20 (M)
    Dolphins, 28-0 (I)
1993—Dolphins, 24-20 (I)
    Dolphins, 41-27 (M)
1994—Dolphins, 22-21 (M)
    Colts, 10-6 (I)
1995—Colts, 27-24 (M) OT
    Colts, 36-28 (I)
1996—Colts, 10-6 (I)
    Dolphins, 37-13 (M)
1997—Dolphins, 16-10 (M)
    Colts, 41-0 (I)
1998—Dolphins, 24-15 (I)
    Dolphins, 27-14 (M)
1999—Dolphins, 34-31 (I)
    Colts, 37-34 (M)
2000—Dolphins, 17-14 (I)
    Colts, 20-13 (M)
    ***Dolphins 23-17 (M) OT
2001—Dolphins, 27-24 (I)
    Dolphins, 41-6 (M)
2002—Dolphins, 21-13 (I)
2003—Colts, 23-17 (M)

2006—Colts, 27-22 (I)
2009—Colts, 27-23 (M)
2012—Colts, 23-20 (I)
2013—Dolphins, 24-20 (I)
(RS Pts.—Dolphins 1,583, Colts 1,213)
(PS Pts.—Dolphins 44, Colts 17)
*Franchise in Baltimore prior to 1984
**AFC Championship
***AFC First-Round Playoff
INDIANAPOLIS vs. MINNESOTA
RS: Colts lead series, 15-7-1
PS: Colts lead series, 1-0
1961—Colts, 34-33 (B)
       Vikings, 28-20 (M)
1962—Colts, 34-7 (M)
       Colts, 42-17 (B)
1963—Colts, 37-34 (M)
       Colts, 41-10 (B)
1964—Vikings, 34-24 (M)
       Colts, 17-14 (B)
1965—Colts, 35-16 (B)
       Colts, 41-21 (M)
1966—Colts, 38-23 (M)
       Colts, 20-17 (B)
1967—Tie, 20-20 (M)
1968—Colts, 21-9 (B)
       **Colts, 24-14 (B)
1969—Vikings, 52-14 (M)
1971—Vikings, 10-3 (M)
1982—Vikings, 13-10 (M)
1988—Vikings, 12-3 (M)
1997—Vikings, 39-28 (M)
2000—Colts, 31-10 (I)
2004—Colts, 31-28 (I)
2008—Colts, 18-15 (M)
2012—Colts, 23-20 (I)
(RS Pts.—Colts 585, Vikings 482)
(PS Pts.—Colts 24, Vikings 14)
*Franchise in Baltimore prior to 1984
**Conference Championship
INDIANAPOLIS vs. **NEW ENGLAND
RS: Patriots lead series, 45-28
PS: Patriots lead series, 3-1
1970—Colts, 14-6 (Bos)
       Colts, 27-3 (Balt)
1971—Colts, 23-3 (NE)
       Patriots, 21-17 (Balt)
1972—Colts, 24-17 (NE)
       Colts, 31-0 (Balt)
1973—Patriots, 24-16 (NE)
       Colts, 18-13 (Balt)
1974—Patriots, 42-3 (NE)
       Patriots, 27-17 (Balt)
1975—Patriots, 21-10 (NE)
       Colts, 34-21 (Balt)
1976—Colts, 27-13 (NE)
       Patriots, 21-14 (Balt)
1977—Patriots, 17-3 (NE)
       Colts, 30-24 (Balt)
1978—Colts, 34-27 (NE)
       Patriots, 35-14 (Balt)
1979—Colts, 31-26 (Balt)
       Patriots, 50-21 (NE)
1980—Patriots, 37-21 (Balt)
       Patriots, 47-21 (NE)
1981—Colts, 29-28 (NE)
       Colts, 23-21 (Balt)
1982—Patriots, 24-13 (Balt)
1983—Colts, 29-23 (NE) OT
       Colts, 12-7 (Balt)
1984—Patriots, 50-17 (I)
       Patriots, 16-10 (NE)
1985—Patriots, 34-15 (NE)

Patriots, 38-31 (I)
1986—Patriots, 33-3 (NE)
       Patriots, 30-21 (I)
1987—Colts, 30-16 (I)
       Patriots, 24-0 (NE)
1988—Patriots, 21-17 (NE)
       Colts, 24-21 (I)
1989—Patriots, 23-20 (I) OT
       Patriots, 22-16 (NE)
1990—Patriots, 16-14 (I)
       Colts, 13-10 (NE)
1991—Patriots, 16-7 (I)
       Patriots, 23-17 (NE) OT
1992—Patriots, 37-34 (I) OT
       Colts, 6-0 (NE)
1993—Colts, 9-6 (I)
       Patriots, 38-0 (NE)
1994—Patriots, 12-10 (I)
       Patriots, 28-13 (NE)
1995—Colts, 24-10 (NE)
       Colts, 10-7 (I)
1996—Patriots, 27-9 (I)
       Patriots, 27-13 (NE)
1997—Patriots, 31-6 (I)
       Patriots, 20-17 (NE)
1998—Patriots, 29-6 (NE)
       Patriots, 21-16 (I)
1999—Patriots, 31-28 (NE)
       Colts, 20-15 (I)
2000—Patriots, 24-16 (NE)
       Colts, 30-23 (I)
2001—Patriots, 44-13 (NE)
       Patriots, 38-17 (I)
2003—Patriots, 38-34 (I)
       ***Patriots, 24-14 (NE)
2004—Patriots, 27-24 (NE)
       ****Patriots, 20-3 (NE)
2005—Colts, 40-21 (NE)
2006—Colts, 27-20 (NE)
       ***Colts, 38-34 (I)
2007—Patriots, 24-20 (I)
2008—Colts, 18-15 (I)
2009—Colts, 35-34 (I)
2010—Patriots, 31-28 (NE)
2011—Patriots, 31-24 (NE)
2012—Patriots, 59-24 (NE)
2013—****Patriots, 43-22 (NE)
(RS Pts.—Patriots 1,759, Colts 1,382)
(PS Pts.—Patriots 121, Colts 77)
*Franchise in Baltimore prior to 1984
**Franchise in Boston prior to 1971
***AFC Championship
****AFC Divisional Playoff
INDIANAPOLIS vs. NEW ORLEANS
RS: Saints lead series, 6-5
PS: Saints lead series, 1-0
1967—Colts, 30-10 (B)
1969—Colts, 30-10 (NO)
1973—Colts, 14-10 (B)
1986—Saints, 17-14 (I)
1989—Saints, 41-6 (NO)
1995—Saints, 17-14 (NO)
1998—Saints, 19-13 (I) OT
2001—Saints, 34-20 (NO)
2003—Colts, 55-21 (NO)
2007—Colts, 41-10 (I)
2009—**Saints 31-17 (South Florida)
2011—Saints, 62-7 (NO)
(RS Pts.—Saints 251, Colts 244)
(PS Pts.—Saints 31, Colts 17)
*Franchise in Baltimore prior to 1984
**Super Bowl XLIV
INDIANAPOLIS vs. N.Y. GIANTS

RS: Colts lead series, 8-6
PS: Colts lead series, 2-0
1954—Colts, 20-14 (B)
1955—Giants, 17-7 (NY)
1958—Giants, 24-21 (NY)
       **Colts, 23-17 (NY) OT
1959—**Colts, 31-16 (B)
1963—Giants, 37-28 (B)
1968—Colts, 26-0 (NY)
1971—Colts, 31-7 (NY)
1975—Colts, 21-0 (NY)
1979—Colts, 31-7 (NY)
1990—Giants, 24-7 (I)
1993—Giants, 20-6 (NY)
1999—Colts, 27-19 (NY)
2002—Giants, 44-27 (I)
2006—Colts, 26-21 (NY)
2010—Colts, 38-14 (I)
(RS Pts.—Colts 316, Giants 248)
(PS Pts.—Colts 54, Giants 33)
*Franchise in Baltimore prior to 1984
**NFL Championship
INDIANAPOLIS vs. N.Y. JETS
RS: Colts lead series, 40-27
PS: Jets lead series, 3-1
1968—**Jets 16-7 (Miami)
1970—Colts, 29-22 (NY)
       Colts, 35-20 (B)
1971—Colts, 22-0 (B)
       Colts, 14-13 (NY)
1972—Jets, 44-34 (B)
       Jets, 24-20 (NY)
1973—Jets, 34-10 (B)
       Jets, 20-17 (NY)
1974—Colts, 35-20 (NY)
       Jets, 45-38 (B)
1975—Colts, 45-28 (NY)
       Colts, 52-19 (B)
1976—Colts, 20-0 (NY)
       Colts, 33-16 (B)
1977—Colts, 20-12 (NY)
       Colts, 33-12 (B)
1978—Jets, 33-10 (NY)
       Jets, 24-16 (NY)
1979—Colts, 10-8 (B)
       Jets, 30-17 (NY)
1980—Colts, 17-14 (NY)
       Colts, 35-21 (B)
1981—Jets, 41-14 (B)
       Jets, 25-0 (NY)
1982—Jets, 37-0 (NY)
1983—Colts, 17-14 (NY)
       Jets, 10-6 (B)
1984—Jets, 23-14 (I)
       Colts, 9-5 (NY)
1985—Jets, 25-20 (NY)
       Jets, 35-17 (I)
1986—Jets, 26-7 (I)
       Jets, 31-16 (NY)
1987—Colts, 6-0 (I)
       Colts, 19-14 (NY)
1988—Colts, 38-14 (I)
       Jets, 34-16 (NY)
1989—Colts, 17-10 (NY)
       Colts, 27-10 (I)
1990—Colts, 17-14 (I)
       Colts, 29-21 (NY)
1991—Jets, 17-6 (I)
       Colts, 28-27 (NY)
1992—Jets, 6-3 (I) OT
       Colts, 10-6 (NY)
1993—Jets, 31-17 (I)
       Colts, 9-6 (NY)

1994—Jets, 16-6 (NY)
    Colts, 28-25 (I)
1995—Colts, 27-24 (NY) OT
    Colts, 17-10 (I)
1996—Colts, 21-7 (NY)
    Colts, 34-29 (I)
1997—Jets, 16-12 (I)
    Colts, 22-14 (NY)
1998—Jets, 44-6 (NY)
    Colts, 24-23 (I)
1999—Colts, 16-13 (NY)
    Colts, 13-6 (I)
2000—Colts, 23-15 (I)
    Jets, 27-17 (NY)
2001—Colts, 45-24 (NY)
    Jets, 29-28 (I)
2002—***Jets, 41-0 (NY)
2003—Colts, 38-31 (NY)
2006—Colts, 31-28 (NY)
2009—Jets, 29-15 (I)
    ****Colts, 30-17 (I)
2010—***Jets, 17-16 (I)
2012—Jets, 35-9 (NY)
(RS Pts.—Jets 1,383, Colts 1,359)
(PS Pts.—Jets 91, Colts 53)
*Franchise in Baltimore prior to 1984
**Super Bowl III
***AFC First-Round Playoff
****AFC Championship
INDIANAPOLIS vs. **OAKLAND
RS: Raiders lead series, 7-6
PS: Series tied, 1-1
1970—***Colts, 27-17 (B)
1971—Colts, 37-14 (O)
1973—Raiders, 34-21 (B)
1975—Raiders, 31-20 (B)
1977—****Raiders, 37-31 (B) OT
1984—Raiders, 21-7 (LA)
1986—Colts, 30-24 (LA)
1991—Raiders, 16-0 (LA)
1995—Raiders, 30-17 (O)
2000—Raiders, 38-31 (I)
2001—Raiders, 23-18 (I)
2004—Colts, 35-14 (I)
2007—Colts, 21-14 (O)
2010—Colts, 31-26 (O)
2013—Colts, 21-17 (I)
(RS Pts.—Raiders 302, Colts 289)
(PS Pts.—Colts 58, Raiders 54)
*Franchise in Baltimore prior to 1984
**Franchise in Los Angeles from 1982-1994
***AFC Championship
****AFC Divisional Playoff
INDIANAPOLIS vs. PHILADELPHIA
RS: Colts lead series, 10-7
1953—Eagles, 45-14 (P)
1965—Colts, 34-24 (B)
1967—Colts, 38-6 (P)
1969—Colts, 24-20 (B)
1970—Colts, 29-10 (B)
1974—Eagles, 30-10 (P)
1978—Eagles, 17-14 (B)
1981—Eagles, 38-13 (P)
1983—Colts, 22-21 (P)
1984—Eagles, 16-7 (P)
1990—Colts, 24-23 (I)
1993—Eagles, 20-10 (I)
1996—Colts, 37-10 (I)
1999—Colts, 44-17 (P)
2002—Colts, 35-13 (P)
2006—Colts, 45-21 (I)
2010—Eagles, 26-24 (P)

(RS Pts.—Colts 424, Eagles 357)
*Franchise in Baltimore prior to 1984
INDIANAPOLIS vs. PITTSBURGH
RS: Steelers lead series, 14-6
PS: Steelers lead series, 5-0
1957—Steelers, 19-13 (B)
1968—Colts, 41-7 (P)
1971—Colts, 34-21 (B)
1974—Steelers, 30-0 (P)
1975—**Steelers, 28-10 (P)
1976—**Steelers, 40-14 (B)
1977—Colts, 31-21 (B)
1978—Steelers, 35-13 (P)
1979—Steelers, 17-13 (P)
1980—Steelers, 20-17 (B)
1983—Steelers, 24-13 (B)
1984—Colts, 17-16 (I)
1985—Steelers, 45-3 (P)
1987—Steelers, 21-7 (P)
1991—Colts, 21-3 (I)
1992—Steelers, 30-14 (P)
1994—Steelers, 31-21 (P)
1995—***Steelers, 20-16 (P)
1996—****Steelers, 42-14 (P)
1997—Steelers, 24-22 (P)
2002—Steelers, 28-10 (P)
2005—Colts, 26-7 (I)
    **Steelers, 21-18 (I)
2008—Colts, 24-20 (P)
2011—Steelers, 23-20 (I)
(RS Pts.—Steelers 460, Colts 342)
(PS Pts.—Steelers 151, Colts 72)
*Franchise in Baltimore prior to 1984
**AFC Divisional Playoff
***AFC Championship
****AFC First-Round Playoff
INDIANAPOLIS vs. **ST. LOUIS
RS: Colts lead series, 23-18-2
1953—Rams, 21-13 (B)
    Rams, 45-2 (LA)
1954—Rams, 48-0 (B)
    Colts, 22-21 (LA)
1955—Tie, 17-17 (B)
    Rams, 20-14 (LA)
1956—Colts, 56-21 (B)
    Rams, 31-7 (LA)
1957—Colts, 31-14 (B)
    Rams, 37-21 (LA)
1958—Colts, 34-7 (B)
    Rams, 30-28 (LA)
1959—Colts, 35-21 (B)
    Colts, 45-26 (LA)
1960—Colts, 31-17 (B)
    Rams, 10-3 (LA)
1961—Colts, 27-24 (B)
    Rams, 34-17 (LA)
1962—Colts, 30-27 (B)
    Colts, 14-2 (LA)
1963—Rams, 17-16 (LA)
    Colts, 19-16 (B)
1964—Colts, 35-20 (B)
    Colts, 24-7 (LA)
1965—Colts, 35-20 (B)
    Colts, 20-17 (LA)
1966—Colts, 17-3 (LA)
    Rams, 23-7 (B)
1967—Tie, 24-24 (B)
    Rams, 34-10 (LA)
1968—Colts, 27-10 (B)
    Colts, 28-24 (LA)
1969—Rams, 27-20 (B)
    Colts, 13-7 (LA)
1971—Colts, 24-17 (B)

1975—Rams, 24-13 (LA)
1986—Rams, 24-7 (I)
1989—Rams, 31-17 (LA)
1995—Colts, 21-18 (I)
2001—Rams, 42-17 (StL)
2005—Colts, 45-28 (I)
2009—Colts, 42-6 (StL)
2013—Rams, 38-8 (I)
(RS Pts.—Rams 950, Colts 936)
*Franchise in Baltimore prior to 1984
**Franchise in Los Angeles prior to 1995
INDIANAPOLIS vs. SAN DIEGO
RS: Chargers lead series, 16-9
PS: Chargers lead series, 2-1
1970—Colts, 16-14 (SD)
1972—Chargers, 23-20 (B)
1976—Colts, 37-21 (SD)
1981—Chargers, 43-14 (B)
1982—Chargers, 44-26 (SD)
1984—Chargers, 38-10 (I)
1986—Chargers, 17-3 (I)
1987—Chargers, 16-13 (I)
    Colts, 20-7 (SD)
1988—Colts, 16-0 (SD)
1989—Colts, 10-6 (I)
1992—Chargers, 34-14 (I)
    Chargers, 26-0 (SD)
1993—Chargers, 31-0 (I)
1995—Chargers, 27-24 (I)
    **Colts, 35-20 (SD)
1996—Chargers, 26-19 (I)
1997—Chargers, 35-19 (SD)
1998—Colts, 17-12 (I)
1999—Colts, 27-19 (SD)
2004—Colts, 34-31 (I) OT
2005—Chargers, 26-17 (I)
2007—Chargers, 23-21 (SD)
    ***Chargers, 28-24 (I)
2008—Colts, 23-20 (SD)
    **Chargers, 23-17 (SD) OT
2010—Chargers, 36-14 (I)
2013—Chargers, 19-9 (SD)
(RS Pts.—Chargers 594, Colts 423)
(PS Pts.—Colts 76, Chargers 71)
*Franchise in Baltimore prior to 1984
**AFC First-Round Playoff
***AFC Divisional Playoff
INDIANAPOLIS vs. SAN FRANCISCO
RS: Colts lead series, 25-18
1953—49ers, 38-21 (B)
    49ers, 45-14 (SF)
1954—Colts, 17-13 (B)
    49ers, 10-7 (SF)
1955—Colts, 26-14 (B)
    49ers, 35-24 (SF)
1956—49ers, 20-17 (B)
    49ers, 30-17 (SF)
1957—Colts, 27-21 (B)
    49ers, 17-13 (SF)
1958—Colts, 35-27 (B)
    49ers, 21-12 (SF)
1959—Colts, 45-14 (B)
    Colts, 34-14 (SF)
1960—49ers, 30-22 (B)
    49ers, 34-10 (SF)
1961—Colts, 20-17 (B)
    Colts, 27-24 (SF)
1962—49ers, 21-13 (B)
    Colts, 22-3 (SF)
1963—Colts, 20-14 (SF)
    Colts, 20-3 (B)
1964—Colts, 37-7 (B)
    Colts, 14-3 (SF)

1965—Colts, 27-24 (B)
    Colts, 34-28 (SF)
1966—Colts, 36-14 (B)
    Colts, 30-14 (SF)
1967—Colts, 41-7 (B)
    Colts, 26-9 (SF)
1968—Colts, 27-10 (B)
    Colts, 42-14 (SF)
1969—49ers, 24-21 (B)
    49ers, 20-17 (SF)
1972—49ers, 24-21 (SF)
1986—49ers, 35-14 (SF)
1989—Colts, 30-24 (I)
1995—Colts, 18-17 (I)
1998—49ers, 34-31 (SF)
2001—49ers, 40-21 (I)
2005—Colts, 28-3 (SF)
2009—Colts, 18-14 (I)
2013—Colts, 27-7 (SF)
(RS Pts.—Colts 1,017, 49ers 843)
Franchise in Baltimore prior to 1984
*INDIANAPOLIS vs. SEATTLE
RS: Colts lead series, 7-4
1977—Colts, 29-14 (S)
1978—Colts, 17-14 (S)
1991—Seahawks, 31-3 (S)
1994—Colts, 17-15 (I)
    Colts, 31-19 (S)
1997—Seahawks, 31-3 (S)
1998—Seahawks, 27-23 (S)
2000—Colts, 37-24 (S)
2005—Seahawks, 28-13 (S)
2009—Colts, 34-17 (I)
2013—Colts, 34-28 (I)
(RS Pts.—Seahawks 248, Colts 241)
Franchise in Baltimore prior to 1984
*INDIANAPOLIS vs. TAMPA BAY
RS: Colts lead series, 7-5
1976—Colts, 42-17 (B)
1979—Buccaneers, 29-26 (B) OT
1985—Colts, 31-23 (TB)
1987—Colts, 24-6 (I)
1988—Colts, 35-31 (I)
1991—Buccaneers, 17-3 (TB)
1992—Colts, 24-14 (TB)
1994—Buccaneers, 24-10 (TB)
1997—Buccaneers, 31-28 (I)
2003—Colts, 38-35 (TB) OT
2007—Colts, 33-14 (I)
2011—Buccaneers, 24-17 (TB)
(RS Pts.—Colts 311, Buccaneers 265)
Franchise in Baltimore prior to 1984
*INDIANAPOLIS vs. **TENNESSEE
RS: Colts lead series, 25-13
PS: Titans lead series, 1-0
1970—Colts, 24-20 (H)
1973—Oilers, 31-27 (B)
1976—Colts, 38-14 (B)
1979—Oilers, 28-16 (B)
1980—Oilers, 21-16 (H)
1983—Colts, 20-10 (B)
1984—Colts, 35-21 (H)
1985—Colts, 34-16 (I)
1986—Oilers, 31-17 (H)
1987—Colts, 51-27 (I)
1988—Oilers, 17-14 (I) OT
1990—Oilers, 24-10 (H)
1992—Oilers, 20-10 (I)
1994—Colts, 45-21 (I)
1999—***Titans, 19-16 (I)
2002—Titans, 23-15 (I)
    Titans, 27-17 (T)
2003—Colts, 33-7 (I)

    Colts, 29-27 (T)
2004—Colts, 31-17 (T)
    Colts, 51-24 (I)
2005—Colts, 31-10 (T)
    Colts, 35-3 (I)
2006—Colts, 14-13 (I)
    Titans, 20-17 (T)
2007—Colts, 22-20 (T)
    Titans, 16-10 (I)
2008—Titans, 31-21 (T)
    Colts, 23-0 (I)
2009—Colts, 31-9 (T)
    Colts, 27-17 (I)
2010—Colts, 30-28 (T)
    Colts, 23-20 (I)
2011—Titans, 27-10 (T)
    Colts, 27-13 (I)
2012—Colts, 19-13 (T) OT
    Colts, 27-23 (I)
2013—Colts, 30-27 (T)
    Colts, 22-14 (I)
(RS Pts.—Colts 952, Titans 730)
(PS Pts.—Titans 19, Colts 16)
Franchise in Baltimore prior to 1984
**Franchise in Houston prior to 1997;
known as Oilers prior to 1999*
***AFC Divisional Playoff*
*INDIANAPOLIS vs. WASHINGTON
RS: Colts lead series, 19-10
1953—Colts, 27-17 (B)
1954—Redskins, 24-21 (W)
1955—Redskins, 14-13 (B)
1956—Colts, 19-17 (B)
1957—Colts, 21-17 (W)
1958—Colts, 35-10 (B)
1959—Redskins, 27-24 (W)
1960—Colts, 20-0 (B)
1961—Colts, 27-6 (W)
1962—Colts, 34-21 (B)
1963—Colts, 36-20 (W)
1964—Colts, 45-17 (B)
1965—Colts, 38-7 (W)
1966—Colts, 37-10 (B)
1967—Colts, 17-13 (W)
1969—Colts, 41-17 (B)
1973—Redskins, 22-14 (W)
1977—Colts, 10-3 (B)
1978—Colts, 21-17 (B)
1981—Redskins, 38-14 (W)
1984—Redskins, 35-7 (I)
1990—Colts, 35-28 (I)
1993—Redskins, 30-24 (W)
1994—Redskins, 41-27 (I)
1996—Redskins, 31-16 (W)
1999—Colts, 24-21 (I)
2002—Redskins, 26-21 (W)
2006—Colts, 36-22 (I)
2010—Colts, 27-24 (W)
(RS Pts.—Colts 731, Redskins 575)
Franchise in Baltimore prior to 1984

JACKSONVILLE vs. ARIZONA
RS: Series tied, 2-2;
See Arizona vs. Jacksonville
JACKSONVILLE vs. ATLANTA
RS: Jaguars lead series, 3-2;
See Atlanta vs. Jacksonville
JACKSONVILLE vs. BALTIMORE
RS: Jaguars lead series, 10-7;
See Baltimore vs. Jacksonville
JACKSONVILLE vs. BUFFALO
RS: Bills lead series, 7-5
PS: Jaguars lead series, 1-0;

See Buffalo vs. Jacksonville
JACKSONVILLE vs. CAROLINA
RS: Jaguars lead series, 3-2;
See Carolina vs. Jacksonville
JACKSONVILLE vs. CHICAGO
RS: Bears lead series, 4-2;
See Chicago vs. Jacksonville
JACKSONVILLE vs. CINCINNATI
RS: Jaguars lead series, 11-8;
See Cincinnati vs. Jacksonville
JACKSONVILLE vs. CLEVELAND
RS: Jaguars lead series, 10-5;
See Cleveland vs. Jacksonville
JACKSONVILLE vs. DALLAS
RS: Jaguars lead series, 3-2;
See Dallas vs. Jacksonville
JACKSONVILLE vs. DENVER
RS: Jaguars lead series, 5-4
PS: Series tied, 1-1;
See Denver vs. Jacksonville
JACKSONVILLE vs. DETROIT
RS: Jaguars lead series, 3-2;
See Detroit vs. Jacksonville
JACKSONVILLE vs. GREEN BAY
RS: Packers lead series, 3-2;
See Green Bay vs. Jacksonville
JACKSONVILLE vs. HOUSTON
RS: Texans lead series, 13-11;
See Houston vs. Jacksonville
JACKSONVILLE vs. INDIANAPOLIS
RS: Colts lead series, 18-8;
See Indianapolis vs. Jacksonville
JACKSONVILLE vs. KANSAS CITY
RS: Jaguars lead series, 6-4
1997—Jaguars, 24-10 (J)
1998—Jaguars, 21-16 (J)
2001—Chiefs, 30-26 (J)
2002—Jaguars, 23-16 (KC)
2004—Jaguars, 22-16 (J)
2006—Chiefs, 35-30 (KC)
2007—Jaguars, 17-7 (KC)
2009—Jaguars, 24-21 (J)
2010—Chiefs, 42-20 (KC)
2013—Chiefs, 28-2 (J)
(RS Pts.—Chiefs 221, Jaguars 209)
JACKSONVILLE vs. MIAMI
RS: Dolphins lead series, 3-2
PS: Jaguars lead series, 1-0
1998—Jaguars, 28-21 (J)
1999—*Jaguars, 62-7 (J)
2003—Dolphins, 24-10 (J)
2006—Jaguars, 24-10 (M)
2009—Dolphins, 14-10 (J)
2012—Dolphins, 24-3 (M)
(RS Pts.—Dolphins, 93, Jaguars 75)
(PS Pts.—Jaguars 62, Dolphins 7)
AFC Divisional Playoff
JACKSONVILLE vs. MINNESOTA
RS: Vikings lead series, 4-1
1998—Vikings, 50-10 (M)
2001—Jaguars, 33-3 (M)
2004—Vikings, 27-16 (M)
2008—Vikings, 30-12 (J)
2012—Vikings, 26-23 (M) OT
(RS Pts.—Vikings 136, Jaguars 94)
JACKSONVILLE vs. NEW ENGLAND
RS: Patriots lead series, 6-0
PS: Patriots lead series, 3-1
1996—Patriots, 28-25 (NE) OT
    *Patriots, 20-6 (NE)
1997—Patriots, 26-20 (J)
1998—**Jaguars, 25-10 (J)
2003—Patriots, 27-13 (NE)

2005—**Patriots, 28-3 (NE)
2006—Patriots, 24-21 (J)
2007—***Patriots, 31-20 (NE)
2009—Patriots, 35-7 (NE)
2012—Patriots, 23-16 (J)
(RS Pts.—Patriots 163, Jaguars 102)
(PS Pts.—Patriots 89, Jaguars 54)
*AFC Championship
**AFC First-Round Playoff
***AFC Divisional Playoff
JACKSONVILLE vs. NEW ORLEANS
RS: Saints lead series, 3-2
1996—Saints, 17-13 (NO)
1999—Jaguars, 41-23 (J)
2003—Jaguars, 20-19 (J)
2007—Saints, 41-24 (NO)
2011—Saints, 23-10 (J)
(RS Pts.—Saints 123, Jaguars 108)
JACKSONVILLE vs. N.Y. GIANTS
RS: Giants lead series, 3-2
1997—Jaguars, 40-13 (J)
2000—Giants, 28-25 (NY)
2002—Giants, 24-17 (NY)
2006—Jaguars, 26-10 (J)
2010—Giants, 24-20 (NY)
(RS Pts.—Jaguars 128, Giants 99)
JACKSONVILLE vs. N.Y. JETS
RS: Jaguars lead series, 6-4
PS: Jets lead series, 1-0
1995—Jets, 27-10 (NY)
1996—Jaguars, 21-17 (J)
1998—*Jets, 34-24 (NY)
1999—Jaguars, 16-6 (NY)
2002—Jaguars, 28-3 (J)
2003—Jets, 13-10 (NY)
2005—Jaguars, 26-20 (NY) OT
2006—Jaguars, 41-0 (J)
2009—Jaguars, 24-22 (NY)
2011—Jets, 32-3 (NY)
2012—Jets, 17-10 (J)
(RS Pts.—Jaguars 189, Jets 157)
(PS Pts.—Jets 34, Jaguars 24)
*AFC Divisional Playoff
JACKSONVILLE vs. OAKLAND
RS: Jaguars lead series, 4-3
1996—Raiders, 17-3 (O)
1997—Jaguars, 20-9 (O)
2004—Jaguars, 13-6 (O)
2007—Jaguars, 49-11 (J)
2010—Jaguars, 38-31 (J)
2012—Raiders, 26-23 (O) OT
2013—Jaguars, 19-9 (O)
(RS Pts.—Jaguars 155, Raiders 119)
JACKSONVILLE vs. PHILADELPHIA
RS: Jaguars lead series, 3-1
1997—Jaguars, 38-21 (J)
2002—Jaguars, 28-25 (J)
2006—Jaguars, 13-6 (P)
2010—Eagles, 28-3 (J)
(RS Pts.—Jaguars 82, Eagles 80)
JACKSONVILLE vs. PITTSBURGH
RS: Jaguars lead series, 11-10
PS: Jaguars lead series, 1-0
1995—Jaguars, 20-16 (J)
         Steelers, 24-7 (P)
1996—Jaguars, 24-9 (J)
         Steelers, 28-3 (P)
1997—Jaguars, 30-21 (J)
         Steelers, 23-17 (P) OT
1998—Steelers, 30-15 (P)
         Jaguars, 21-3 (J)
1999—Jaguars, 17-3 (P)
         Jaguars, 20-6 (J)

2000—Steelers, 24-13 (J)
         Jaguars, 34-24 (P)
2001—Jaguars, 21-3 (J)
         Steelers, 20-7 (P)
2002—Steelers, 25-23 (J)
2004—Steelers, 17-16 (J)
2005—Jaguars, 23-17 (P) OT
2006—Jaguars, 9-0 (J)
2007—Jaguars, 29-22 (P)
         *Jaguars, 31-29 (P)
2008—Steelers, 26-21 (J)
2011—Steelers, 17-13 (P)
(RS Pts.—Jaguars 383, Steelers 358)
(PS Pts.—Jaguars 31, Steelers 29)
*AFC First-Round Playoff
JACKSONVILLE vs. ST. LOUIS
RS: Rams lead series, 3-1
1996—Rams, 17-14 (StL)
2005—Rams, 24-21 (StL)
2009—Jaguars, 23-20 (J) OT
2013—Rams, 34-20 (StL)
(RS Pts.—Rams 95, Jaguars 78)
JACKSONVILLE vs. SAN DIEGO
RS: Chargers lead series, 4-2
2003—Jaguars, 27-21 (J)
2004—Chargers, 34-21 (SD)
2007—Jaguars, 24-17 (J)
2010—Chargers, 38-13 (SD)
2011—Chargers, 38-14 (J)
2013—Chargers, 24-6 (J)
(RS Pts.—Chargers 172, Jaguars 105)
JACKSONVILLE vs. SAN FRANCISCO
RS: Series tied, 2-2
1999—Jaguars, 41-3 (J)
2005—Jaguars, 10-9 (J)
2009—49ers, 20-3 (SF)
2013—49ers, 42-10 (London)
(RS Pts.—49ers 74, Jaguars 64)
JACKSONVILLE vs. SEATTLE
RS: Seahawks lead series, 5-2
1995—Seahawks, 47-30 (J)
1996—Jaguars, 20-13 (J)
2000—Seahawks, 28-21 (J)
2001—Seahawks, 24-15 (S)
2005—Jaguars, 26-14 (J)
2009—Seahawks, 41-0 (S)
2013—Seahawks, 45-17 (S)
(RS Pts.—Seahawks 212, Jaguars 129)
JACKSONVILLE vs. TAMPA BAY
RS: Jaguars lead series, 4-1
1995—Buccaneers, 17-16 (TB)
1998—Jaguars, 29-24 (J)
2003—Jaguars, 17-10 (J)
2007—Jaguars, 24-23 (TB)
2011—Jaguars, 41-14 (J)
(RS Pts.—Jaguars 127, Buccaneers 88)
JACKSONVILLE vs. *TENNESSEE
RS: Titans lead series, 21-17
PS: Titans lead, 1-0
1995—Oilers, 10-3 (J)
         Jaguars, 17-16 (H)
1996—Oilers, 34-27 (J)
         Jaguars, 23-17 (H)
1997—Jaguars, 30-24 (T)
         Jaguars, 17-9 (J)
1998—Jaguars, 27-22 (T)
         Oilers, 16-13 (J)
1999—Titans, 20-19 (J)
         Titans, 41-14 (T)
         **Titans, 33-14 (J)
2000—Titans, 27-13 (T)
         Jaguars, 16-13 (J)
2001—Jaguars, 13-6 (J)

Titans, 28-24 (T)
2002—Titans, 23-14 (T)
         Titans, 28-10 (J)
2003—Titans, 30-17 (J)
         Titans, 10-3 (T)
2004—Jaguars, 15-12 (T)
         Titans, 18-15 (J)
2005—Jaguars, 31-28 (T)
         Jaguars, 40-13 (J)
2006—Jaguars, 37-7 (J)
         Titans, 24-17 (T)
2007—Titans, 13-10 (J)
         Jaguars, 28-13 (T)
2008—Titans, 17-10 (T)
         Titans, 24-14 (J)
2009—Jaguars, 37-17 (J)
         Titans, 30-13 (T)
2010—Titans, 30-3 (J)
         Jaguars, 17-6 (T)
2011—Jaguars, 16-14 (J)
         Titans, 23-17 (T)
2012—Jaguars, 24-19 (J)
         Titans, 38-20 (T)
2013—Jaguars, 29-27 (T)
         Titans, 20-16 (J)
(RS Pts.—Titans 767, Jaguars 709)
(PS Pts.—Titans 33, Jaguars 14)
*Franchise in Houston prior to 1997;
known as Oilers prior to 1999
**AFC Championship
JACKSONVILLE vs. WASHINGTON
RS: Redskins lead series, 4-1
1997—Redskins, 24-12 (W)
2000—Redskins, 35-16 (J)
2002—Jaguars, 26-7 (J)
2006—Redskins, 36-30 (W) OT
2010—Redskins, 20-17 (J) OT
(RS Pts.—Redskins 122, Jaguars 101)

KANSAS CITY vs. ARIZONA
RS: Chiefs lead series, 8-2-1;
See Arizona vs. Kansas City
KANSAS CITY vs. ATLANTA
RS: Chiefs lead series, 5-3;
See Atlanta vs. Kansas City
KANSAS CITY vs. BALTIMORE
RS: Series tied, 3-3
PS: Ravens lead series, 1-0;
See Baltimore vs. Kansas City
KANSAS CITY vs. BUFFALO
RS: Bills lead series, 23-18-1
PS: Bills lead series, 2-1;
See Buffalo vs. Kansas City
KANSAS CITY vs. CAROLINA
RS: Chiefs lead series, 3-2;
See Carolina vs. Kansas City
KANSAS CITY vs. CHICAGO
RS: Bears lead series, 6-5;
See Chicago vs. Kansas City
KANSAS CITY vs. CINCINNATI
RS: Bengals lead series, 14-13;
See Cincinnati vs. Kansas City
KANSAS CITY vs. CLEVELAND
RS: Series tied, 11-11-2;
See Cleveland vs. Kansas City
KANSAS CITY vs. DALLAS
RS: Cowboys lead series, 6-4;
See Dallas vs. Kansas City
KANSAS CITY vs. DENVER
RS: Chiefs lead series, 56-51
PS: Broncos lead series, 1-0;
See Denver vs. Kansas City
KANSAS CITY vs. DETROIT

RS: Chiefs lead series, 7-5;
See Detroit vs. Kansas City
KANSAS CITY vs. GREEN BAY
RS: Chiefs lead series, 7-2-1
PS: Packers lead series, 1-0;
See Green Bay vs. Kansas City
KANSAS CITY vs. HOUSTON
RS: Series tied, 3-3;
See Houston vs. Kansas City
KANSAS CITY vs. INDIANAPOLIS
RS: Colts lead series, 12-8
PS: Colts lead series, 4-0;
See Indianapolis vs. Kansas City
KANSAS CITY vs. JACKSONVILLE
RS: Jaguars lead series, 6-4;
See Jacksonville vs. Kansas City
KANSAS CITY vs. MIAMI
RS: Dolphins lead series, 13-12
PS: Dolphins lead series, 3-0
1966—Chiefs, 34-16 (KC)
    Chiefs, 19-18 (M)
1967—Chiefs, 24-0 (M)
    Chiefs, 41-0 (KC)
1968—Chiefs, 48-3 (M)
1969—Chiefs, 17-10 (KC)
1971—*Dolphins, 27-24 (KC) OT
1972—Dolphins, 20-10 (KC)
1974—Dolphins, 9-3 (M)
1976—Chiefs, 20-17 (M) OT
1981—Dolphins, 17-7 (KC)
1983—Dolphins, 14-6 (M)
1985—Dolphins, 31-0 (M)
1987—Dolphins, 42-0 (M)
1989—Chiefs, 26-21 (KC)
    Chiefs, 27-24 (M)
1990—**Dolphins, 17-16 (M)
1991—Chiefs, 42-7 (KC)
1993—Dolphins, 30-10 (M)
1994—Dolphins, 45-28 (M)
    **Dolphins, 27-17 (M)
1995—Dolphins, 13-6 (M)
1997—Dolphins, 17-14 (M)
2002—Chiefs, 48-30 (KC)
2005—Chiefs, 30-20 (M)
2006—Dolphins, 13-10 (M)
2008—Dolphins, 38-31 (KC)
2011—Dolphins, 31-3 (KC)
(RS Pts.—Chiefs 504, Dolphins 486)
(PS Pts.—Dolphins 71, Chiefs 57)
*AFC Divisional Playoff
**AFC First-Round Playoff
KANSAS CITY vs. MINNESOTA
RS: Chiefs lead series, 6-4
PS: Chiefs lead series, 1-0
1969—*Chiefs, 23-7 (New Orleans)
1970—Vikings, 27-10 (M)
1974—Vikings, 35-15 (KC)
1981—Chiefs, 10-6 (M)
1990—Chiefs, 24-21 (KC)
1993—Vikings, 30-10 (M)
1996—Chiefs, 21-6 (M)
1999—Chiefs, 31-28 (KC)
2003—Vikings, 45-20 (M)
2007—Chiefs, 13-10 (KC)
2011—Chiefs, 22-17 (KC)
(RS Pts.—Vikings 225, Chiefs 176)
(PS Pts.—Chiefs 23, Vikings 7)
*Super Bowl IV
KANSAS CITY vs. **NEW ENGLAND
RS: Chiefs lead series, 16-13-3
1960—Patriots, 42-14 (B)
    Texans, 34-0 (D)
1961—Patriots, 18-17 (D)

Patriots, 28-21 (B)
1962—Texans, 42-28 (D)
    Texans, 27-7 (B)
1963—Tie, 24-24 (B)
    Chiefs, 35-3 (KC)
1964—Patriots, 24-7 (B)
    Patriots, 31-24 (KC)
1965—Chiefs, 27-17 (KC)
    Tie, 10-10 (B)
1966—Chiefs, 43-24 (B)
    Tie, 27-27 (KC)
1967—Chiefs, 33-10 (B)
1968—Chiefs, 31-17 (KC)
1969—Chiefs, 31-0 (B)
1970—Chiefs, 23-10 (KC)
1973—Chiefs, 10-7 (NE)
1977—Patriots, 21-17 (NE)
1981—Patriots, 33-17 (NE)
1990—Chiefs, 37-7 (KC)
1992—Chiefs, 27-20 (KC)
1995—Chiefs, 31-26 (KC)
1998—Patriots, 40-10 (NE)
1999—Chiefs, 16-14 (KC)
2000—Patriots, 30-24 (NE)
2002—Patriots, 41-38 (NE) OT
2004—Patriots, 27-19 (KC)
2005—Chiefs, 26-16 (KC)
2008—Patriots, 17-10 (NE)
2011—Patriots, 34-3 (NE)
(RS Pts.—Chiefs 755, Patriots 653)
*Franchise located in Dallas prior to 1963
and known as Texans
**Franchise in Boston prior to 1971
KANSAS CITY vs. NEW ORLEANS
RS: Series tied, 5-5
1972—Chiefs, 20-17 (NO)
1976—Saints, 27-17 (KC)
1982—Saints, 27-17 (NO)
1985—Chiefs, 47-27 (NO)
1991—Saints, 17-10 (KC)
1994—Chiefs, 30-17 (NO)
1997—Saints, 25-13 (KC)
2004—Saints, 27-20 (NO)
2008—Saints, 30-20 (KC)
2012—Chiefs, 27-24 (NO)
(RS Pts.—Chiefs 233, Saints 226)
KANSAS CITY vs. N.Y. GIANTS
RS: Giants lead series, 10-3
1974—Giants, 33-27 (KC)
1978—Giants, 26-10 (NY)
1979—Giants, 21-17 (KC)
1983—Chiefs, 38-17 (KC)
1984—Giants, 28-27 (NY)
1988—Giants, 28-12 (NY)
1992—Giants, 35-21 (NY)
1995—Chiefs, 20-17 (KC) OT
1998—Giants, 28-7 (NY)
2001—Giants, 13-3 (KC)
2005—Giants, 27-17 (NY)
2009—Giants, 27-16 (KC)
2013—Chiefs, 31-7 (KC)
(RS Pts.—Giants 307, Chiefs 246)
***KANSAS CITY vs. **N.Y. JETS**
RS: Jets lead series, 17-16-1
PS: Series tied, 1-1
1960—Titans, 37-35 (D)
    Titans, 41-35 (NY)
1961—Titans, 28-7 (NY)
    Texans, 35-24 (D)
1962—Texans, 20-17 (D)
    Texans, 52-31 (NY)
1963—Jets, 17-0 (NY)
    Chiefs, 48-0 (KC)

1964—Jets, 27-14 (NY)
    Chiefs, 24-7 (KC)
1965—Chiefs, 14-10 (NY)
    Jets, 13-10 (KC)
1966—Chiefs, 32-24 (NY)
1967—Chiefs, 42-18 (KC)
    Chiefs, 21-7 (NY)
1968—Jets, 20-19 (KC)
1969—Chiefs, 34-16 (NY)
    ***Chiefs, 13-6 (NY)
1971—Jets, 13-10 (NY)
1974—Chiefs, 24-16 (KC)
1975—Jets, 30-24 (KC)
1982—Chiefs, 37-13 (KC)
1984—Jets, 17-16 (KC)
    Jets, 28-7 (NY)
1986—****Jets, 35-15 (NY)
1987—Jets, 16-9 (KC)
1988—Tie, 17-17 (NY)
    Chiefs, 38-34 (KC)
1992—Chiefs, 23-7 (NY)
1998—Jets, 20-17 (KC)
2001—Jets, 27-7 (NY)
2002—Chiefs, 29-25 (NY)
2005—Chiefs, 27-7 (KC)
2007—Jets, 13-10 (NY) OT
2008—Jets, 28-24 (NY)
2011—Jets, 37-10 (NY)
(RS Pts.—Chiefs 771, Jets 685)
(PS Pts.—Jets 41, Chiefs 28)
*Franchise in Dallas prior to 1963 and
known as Texans
**Jets known as Titans prior to 1963
***Inter-Divisional Playoff
****AFC First-Round Playoff
***KANSAS CITY vs. **OAKLAND**
RS: Chiefs lead series, 55-50-2
PS: Chiefs lead series, 2-1
1960—Texans, 34-16 (O)
    Raiders, 20-19 (D)
1961—Texans, 42-35 (O)
    Texans, 43-11 (D)
1962—Texans, 26-16 (O)
    Texans, 35-7 (D)
1963—Chiefs, 10-7 (O)
    Raiders, 22-7 (KC)
1964—Chiefs, 21-9 (O)
    Chiefs, 42-7 (KC)
1965—Raiders, 37-10 (O)
    Chiefs, 14-7 (KC)
1966—Chiefs, 32-10 (KC)
    Raiders, 34-13 (O)
1967—Raiders, 23-21 (O)
    Raiders, 44-22 (KC)
1968—Chiefs, 24-10 (KC)
    Raiders, 38-21 (O)
    ***Raiders, 41-6 (O)
1969—Raiders, 27-24 (KC)
    Raiders, 10-6 (O)
    ****Chiefs, 17-7 (O)
1970—Tie, 17-17 (KC)
    Raiders, 20-6 (O)
1971—Tie, 20-20 (O)
    Chiefs, 16-14 (KC)
1972—Chiefs, 27-14 (KC)
    Raiders, 26-3 (O)
1973—Chiefs, 16-3 (KC)
    Raiders, 37-7 (O)
1974—Raiders, 27-7 (O)
    Raiders, 7-6 (KC)
1975—Chiefs, 42-10 (KC)
    Raiders, 28-20 (O)
1976—Raiders, 24-21 (KC)

Raiders, 21-10 (O)
1977—Raiders, 37-28 (KC)
Raiders, 21-20 (O)
1978—Raiders, 28-6 (O)
Raiders, 20-10 (KC)
1979—Chiefs, 35-7 (KC)
Chiefs, 24-21 (O)
1980—Raiders, 27-14 (KC)
Chiefs, 31-17 (O)
1981—Chiefs, 27-0 (KC)
Chiefs, 28-17 (O)
1982—Raiders, 21-16 (KC)
1983—Raiders, 21-20 (LA)
Raiders, 28-20 (KC)
1984—Raiders, 22-20 (KC)
Raiders, 17-7 (LA)
1985—Chiefs, 36-20 (KC)
Raiders, 19-10 (LA)
1986—Raiders, 24-17 (KC)
Chiefs, 20-17 (LA)
1987—Raiders, 35-17 (LA)
Chiefs, 16-10 (KC)
1988—Raiders, 27-17 (KC)
Raiders, 17-10 (LA)
1989—Chiefs, 24-19 (KC)
Raiders, 20-14 (LA)
1990—Chiefs, 9-7 (KC)
Chiefs, 27-24 (LA)
1991—Chiefs, 24-21 (KC)
Chiefs, 27-21 (LA)
*****Chiefs, 10-6 (KC)
1992—Chiefs, 27-7 (KC)
Raiders, 28-7 (LA)
1993—Chiefs, 24-9 (KC)
Chiefs, 31-20 (LA)
1994—Chiefs, 13-3 (KC)
Chiefs, 19-9 (LA)
1995—Chiefs, 23-17 (KC) OT
Chiefs, 29-23 (O)
1996—Chiefs, 19-3 (KC)
Raiders, 26-7 (O)
1997—Chiefs, 28-27 (O)
Chiefs, 30-0 (KC)
1998—Chiefs, 28-8 (KC)
Chiefs, 31-24 (O)
1999—Chiefs, 37-34 (O)
Raiders, 41-38 (KC) OT
2000—Raiders, 20-17 (KC)
Raiders, 49-31 (O)
2001—Raiders, 27-24 (KC)
Raiders, 28-26 (O)
2002—Chiefs, 20-10 (KC)
Raiders, 24-0 (O)
2003—Chiefs, 17-10 (O)
Chiefs, 27-24 (KC)
2004—Chiefs, 34-27 (O)
Chiefs, 31-30 (KC)
2005—Chiefs, 23-17 (O)
Chiefs, 27-23 (KC)
2006—Chiefs, 17-13 (KC)
Chiefs, 20-9 (O)
2007—Chiefs, 12-10 (O)
Raiders, 20-17 (KC)
2008—Raiders, 23-8 (KC)
Chiefs, 20-13 (O)
2009—Raiders, 13-10 (KC)
Chiefs, 16-10 (O)
2010—Raiders, 23-20 (O) OT
Raiders, 31-10 (KC)
2011—Chiefs, 28-0 (O)
Raiders, 16-13 (KC) OT
2012—Raiders, 26-16 (KC)
Raiders, 15-0 (O)

2013—Chiefs, 24-7 (KC)
Chiefs, 56-31 (O)
(RS Pts.—Chiefs 2,210, Raiders 2,074)
(PS Pts.—Raiders 54, Chiefs 33)
*Franchise in Dallas prior to 1963 and known as Texans
**Franchise in Los Angeles from 1982-1994
***Division Playoff
****AFL Championship
*****AFC First-Round Playoff
KANSAS CITY vs. PHILADELPHIA
RS: Eagles lead series, 4-3
1972—Eagles, 21-20 (KC)
1992—Chiefs, 24-17 (KC)
1998—Chiefs, 24-21 (P)
2001—Eagles, 23-10 (KC)
2005—Eagles, 37-31 (KC)
2009—Eagles, 34-14 (P)
2013—Chiefs, 26-16 (P)
(RS Pts.—Eagles 169, Chiefs 149)
KANSAS CITY vs. PITTSBURGH
RS: Steelers lead series, 19-9
PS: Chiefs lead series, 1-0
1970—Chiefs, 31-14 (P)
1971—Chiefs, 38-16 (KC)
1972—Steelers, 16-7 (P)
1974—Steelers, 34-24 (KC)
1975—Steelers, 28-3 (P)
1976—Steelers, 45-0 (KC)
1978—Steelers, 27-24 (P)
1979—Steelers, 30-3 (KC)
1980—Steelers, 21-16 (P)
1981—Chiefs, 37-33 (P)
1982—Steelers, 35-14 (P)
1984—Steelers, 37-27 (P)
1985—Steelers, 36-28 (KC)
1986—Chiefs, 24-19 (P)
1987—Steelers, 17-16 (KC)
1988—Steelers, 16-10 (P)
1989—Steelers, 23-17 (P)
1992—Steelers, 27-3 (KC)
1993—*Chiefs, 27-24 (KC) OT
1996—Steelers, 17-7 (KC)
1997—Chiefs, 13-10 (KC)
1998—Steelers, 20-13 (KC)
1999—Chiefs, 35-19 (KC)
2001—Steelers, 20-17 (KC)
2003—Chiefs, 41-20 (KC)
2006—Steelers, 45-7 (P)
2009—Chiefs, 27-24 (KC) OT
2011—Steelers, 13-9 (KC)
2012—Steelers, 16-13 (P) OT
(RS Pts.—Steelers 668, Chiefs 514)
(PS Pts.—Chiefs 27, Steelers 24)
*AFC First-Round Playoff
KANSAS CITY vs. *ST. LOUIS
RS: Chiefs lead series, 6-4
1973—Rams, 23-13 (KC)
1982—Rams, 20-14 (LA)
1985—Rams, 16-0 (KC)
1991—Chiefs, 27-20 (LA)
1994—Rams, 16-0 (KC)
1997—Chiefs, 28-20 (StL)
2000—Chiefs, 54-34 (KC)
2002—Chiefs, 49-10 (KC)
2006—Chiefs, 31-17 (StL)
2010—Chiefs, 27-13 (StL)
(RS Pts.—Chiefs 243, Rams 189)
*Franchise in Los Angeles prior to 1995
*KANSAS CITY vs. **SAN DIEGO
RS: Chargers lead series, 54-52-1
PS: Chargers lead series, 1-0

1960—Chargers, 21-20 (LA)
Texans, 17-0 (D)
1961—Chargers, 26-10 (D)
Chargers, 24-14 (SD)
1962—Chargers, 32-28 (SD)
Texans, 26-17 (D)
1963—Chargers, 24-10 (SD)
Chargers, 38-17 (KC)
1964—Chargers, 28-14 (KC)
Chiefs, 49-6 (SD)
1965—Tie, 10-10 (SD)
Chiefs, 31-7 (KC)
1966—Chiefs, 24-14 (KC)
Chiefs, 27-17 (SD)
1967—Chargers, 45-31 (SD)
Chargers, 17-16 (KC)
1968—Chiefs, 27-20 (KC)
Chiefs, 40-3 (SD)
1969—Chiefs, 27-9 (SD)
Chiefs, 27-3 (KC)
1970—Chiefs, 26-14 (KC)
Chargers, 31-13 (SD)
1971—Chargers, 21-14 (SD)
Chiefs, 31-10 (KC)
1972—Chiefs, 26-14 (SD)
Chargers, 27-17 (KC)
1973—Chiefs, 19-0 (SD)
Chiefs, 33-6 (KC)
1974—Chiefs, 24-14 (SD)
Chargers, 14-7 (KC)
1975—Chiefs, 12-10 (SD)
Chargers, 28-20 (KC)
1976—Chargers, 30-16 (KC)
Chiefs, 23-20 (SD)
1977—Chargers, 23-7 (KC)
Chiefs, 21-16 (SD)
1978—Chargers, 29-23 (SD) OT
Chiefs, 23-0 (KC)
1979—Chargers, 20-14 (KC)
Chargers, 28-7 (SD)
1980—Chargers, 24-7 (KC)
Chargers, 20-7 (SD)
1981—Chargers, 42-31 (KC)
Chargers, 22-20 (SD)
1982—Chiefs, 19-12 (KC)
1983—Chargers, 17-14 (KC)
Chargers, 41-38 (SD)
1984—Chiefs, 31-13 (KC)
Chiefs, 42-21 (SD)
1985—Chargers, 31-20 (SD)
Chiefs, 38-34 (KC)
1986—Chiefs, 42-41 (KC)
Chiefs, 24-23 (SD)
1987—Chiefs, 20-13 (KC)
Chargers, 42-21 (SD)
1988—Chargers, 24-23 (KC)
Chargers, 24-13 (SD)
1989—Chargers, 21-6 (SD)
Chargers, 20-13 (KC)
1990—Chiefs, 27-10 (KC)
Chiefs, 24-21 (SD)
1991—Chiefs, 14-13 (SD)
Chiefs, 20-17 (KC) OT
1992—Chiefs, 24-10 (SD)
Chiefs, 16-14 (KC)
***Chargers, 17-0 (SD)
1993—Chiefs, 17-14 (SD)
Chiefs, 28-24 (KC)
1994—Chargers, 20-6 (SD)
Chargers, 14-13 (KC)
1995—Chargers, 29-23 (KC) OT
Chiefs, 22-7 (SD)
1996—Chargers, 22-19 (SD)

Chargers, 28-14 (KC)
1997—Chiefs, 31-3 (KC)
Chiefs, 29-7 (SD)
1998—Chiefs, 23-7 (KC)
Chargers, 38-37 (SD)
1999—Chargers, 21-14 (SD)
Chiefs, 34-0 (SD)
2000—Chiefs, 42-10 (KC)
Chargers, 17-16 (SD)
2001—Chiefs, 25-20 (SD)
Chiefs, 20-17 (KC)
2002—Chargers, 35-34 (SD)
Chiefs, 24-22 (KC)
2003—Chiefs, 27-14 (KC)
Chiefs, 28-24 (SD)
2004—Chargers, 34-31 (KC)
Chargers, 24-17 (SD)
2005—Chargers, 28-20 (SD)
Chiefs, 20-7 (KC)
2006—Chiefs, 30-27 (KC)
Chargers, 20-9 (SD)
2007—Chiefs, 30-16 (SD)
Chargers, 24-10 (KC)
2008—Chargers, 20-19 (SD)
Chargers, 22-21 (KC)
2009—Chargers, 37-7 (KC)
Chargers, 43-14 (SD)
2010—Chiefs, 21-14 (KC)
Chargers, 31-0 (SD)
2011—Chargers, 20-17 (SD)
Chiefs, 23-20 (KC) OT
2012—Chargers, 37-20 (KC)
Chiefs, 31-13 (SD)
2013—Chargers, 41-38 (KC)
Chargers, 27-24 (SD) OT
(RS Pts.—Chiefs 2,311, Chargers 2,196)
(PS Pts.—Chargers 17, Chiefs 0)
*Franchise in Dallas prior to 1963 and
known as Texans
**Franchise in Los Angeles prior to 1961
***AFC First-Round Playoff
KANSAS CITY vs. SAN FRANCISCO
RS: 49ers lead series, 6-5
1971—Chiefs, 26-17 (SF)
1975—49ers, 20-3 (KC)
1982—49ers, 26-13 (KC)
1985—49ers, 31-3 (SF)
1991—49ers, 28-14 (SF)
1994—Chiefs, 24-17 (KC)
1997—Chiefs, 44-9 (KC)
2000—49ers, 21-7 (SF)
2002—49ers, 17-13 (SF)
2006—Chiefs, 41-10 (KC)
2010—Chiefs, 31-10 (KC)
(PS Pts.—Chiefs 219, 49ers 196)
KANSAS CITY vs. SEATTLE
RS: Chiefs lead series, 32-18
1977—Seahawks, 34-31 (KC)
1978—Seahawks, 13-10 (KC)
Seahawks, 23-19 (S)
1979—Chiefs, 24-6 (S)
Chiefs, 37-21 (KC)
1980—Seahawks, 17-16 (KC)
Chiefs, 31-30 (S)
1981—Chiefs, 20-14 (S)
Chiefs, 40-13 (KC)
1983—Chiefs, 17-13 (KC)
Seahawks, 51-48 (S) OT
1984—Seahawks, 45-0 (S)
Chiefs, 34-7 (KC)
1985—Chiefs, 28-7 (KC)
Seahawks, 24-6 (S)
1986—Seahawks, 23-17 (S)

Chiefs, 27-7 (KC)
1987—Seahawks, 43-14 (S)
Chiefs, 41-20 (KC)
1988—Seahawks, 31-10 (S)
Chiefs, 27-24 (KC)
1989—Chiefs, 20-16 (S)
Chiefs, 20-10 (KC)
1990—Seahawks, 19-7 (S)
Seahawks, 17-16 (KC)
1991—Chiefs, 20-13 (KC)
Chiefs, 19-6 (S)
1992—Chiefs, 26-7 (KC)
Chiefs, 24-14 (S)
1993—Chiefs, 31-16 (S)
Chiefs, 34-24 (KC)
1994—Chiefs, 38-23 (KC)
Seahawks, 10-9 (S)
1995—Chiefs, 34-10 (S)
Chiefs, 26-3 (KC)
1996—Chiefs, 35-17 (S)
Chiefs, 34-16 (KC)
1997—Chiefs, 20-17 (KC) OT
Chiefs, 19-14 (S)
1998—Chiefs, 17-6 (KC)
Seahawks, 24-12 (S)
1999—Seahawks, 31-19 (KC)
Seahawks, 23-14 (S)
2000—Chiefs, 24-17 (KC)
Chiefs, 24-19 (S)
2001—Chiefs, 19-7 (KC)
Seahawks, 21-18 (S)
2002—Seahawks, 39-32 (S)
2006—Chiefs, 35-28 (KC)
2010—Chiefs, 42-24 (S)
(RS Pts.—Chiefs 1,185, Seahawks 957)
KANSAS CITY vs. TAMPA BAY
RS: Buccaneers lead series, 6-5
1976—Chiefs, 28-19 (TB)
1978—Buccaneers, 30-13 (KC)
1979—Buccaneers, 3-0 (TB)
1981—Chiefs, 19-10 (KC)
1984—Chiefs, 24-20 (KC)
1986—Chiefs, 27-20 (KC)
1993—Chiefs, 27-3 (TB)
1999—Buccaneers, 17-10 (TB)
2004—Buccaneers, 34-31 (TB)
2008—Buccaneers, 30-27 (KC) OT
2012—Buccaneers, 38-10 (TB)
(RS Pts.—Buccaneers 224, Chiefs 216)
***KANSAS CITY vs. **TENNESSEE**
RS: Chiefs lead series, 27-20
PS: Chiefs lead series, 2-0
1960—Oilers, 20-10 (H)
Texans, 24-0 (D)
1961—Texans, 26-21 (D)
Oilers, 38-7 (H)
1962—Texans, 31-7 (H)
Oilers, 14-6 (D)
***Texans, 20-17 (H) OT
1963—Chiefs, 28-7 (KC)
Oilers, 28-7 (H)
1964—Chiefs, 28-7 (KC)
Chiefs, 28-19 (H)
1965—Chiefs, 52-21 (KC)
Oilers, 38-36 (H)
1966—Chiefs, 48-23 (KC)
1967—Chiefs, 25-20 (H)
Oilers, 24-19 (KC)
1968—Chiefs, 26-21 (H)
Chiefs, 24-10 (KC)
1969—Chiefs, 24-0 (KC)
1970—Chiefs, 24-9 (KC)
1971—Chiefs, 20-16 (H)

1973—Chiefs, 38-14 (KC)
1974—Chiefs, 17-7 (H)
1975—Oilers, 17-13 (KC)
1977—Oilers, 34-20 (H)
1978—Oilers, 20-17 (KC)
1979—Oilers, 20-6 (H)
1980—Chiefs, 21-20 (KC)
1981—Chiefs, 23-10 (KC)
1983—Chiefs, 13-10 (H) OT
1984—Oilers, 17-16 (KC)
1985—Oilers, 23-20 (H)
1986—Chiefs, 27-13 (KC)
1988—Oilers, 7-6 (H)
1989—Chiefs, 34-0 (KC)
1990—Oilers, 27-10 (KC)
1991—Oilers, 17-7 (H)
1992—Oilers, 23-20 (H) OT
1993—Oilers, 30-0 (H)
****Chiefs, 28-20 (H)
1994—Chiefs, 31-9 (KC)
1995—Chiefs, 20-13 (KC)
1996—Chiefs, 20-19 (H)
2000—Titans, 17-14 (T) OT
2004—Chiefs, 49-38 (T)
2007—Titans, 26-17 (KC)
2008—Titans, 34-10 (KC)
2010—Chiefs, 34-14 (KC)
2013—Chiefs, 26-17 (T)
(RS Pts.—Chiefs 1,022, Titans 839)
(PS Pts.—Chiefs 48, Titans 37)
*Franchise in Dallas prior to 1963 and
known as Texans
**Franchise in Houston prior to 1997;
known as Oilers prior to 1999
***AFL Championship
****AFC Divisional Playoff
KANSAS CITY vs. WASHINGTON
RS: Chiefs lead series, 8-1
1971—Chiefs, 27-20 (KC)
1976—Chiefs, 33-30 (W)
1983—Redskins, 27-12 (W)
1992—Chiefs, 35-16 (KC)
1995—Chiefs, 24-3 (KC)
2001—Chiefs, 45-13 (W)
2005—Chiefs, 28-21, (KC)
2009—Chiefs, 14-6 (W)
2013—Chiefs, 45-10 (W)
(RS Pts.—Chiefs 263, Redskins 146)

MIAMI vs. ARIZONA
RS: Dolphins lead series, 8-3;
See Arizona vs. Miami
MIAMI vs. ATLANTA
RS: Dolphins lead series, 8-4;
See Atlanta vs. Miami
MIAMI vs. BALTIMORE
RS: Dolphins lead series, 5-4
PS: Ravens lead series, 2-0;
See Baltimore vs. Miami
MIAMI vs. BUFFALO
RS: Dolphins lead series, 56-39-1
PS: Bills lead series, 3-1;
See Buffalo vs. Miami
MIAMI vs. CAROLINA
RS: Dolphins lead series, 4-1;
See Carolina vs. Miami
MIAMI vs. CHICAGO
RS: Dolphins lead series, 7-4;
See Chicago vs. Miami
MIAMI vs. CINCINNATI
RS: Dolphins lead series, 15-5
PS: Dolphins lead series, 1-0;
See Cincinnati vs. Miami

MIAMI vs. CLEVELAND
RS: Series tied, 8-8
PS: Dolphins lead series, 2-0;
See Cleveland vs. Miami
MIAMI vs. DALLAS
RS: Dolphins lead series, 7-5
PS: Cowboys lead series, 1-0;
See Dallas vs. Miami
MIAMI vs. DENVER
RS: Dolphins lead series, 11-4-1
PS: Broncos lead series, 1-0;
See Denver vs. Miami
MIAMI vs. DETROIT
RS: Dolphins lead series, 7-3;
See Detroit vs. Miami
MIAMI vs. GREEN BAY
RS: Dolphins lead series, 10-3;
See Green Bay vs. Miami
MIAMI vs. HOUSTON
RS: Texans lead series, 7-0;
See Houston vs. Miami
MIAMI vs. INDIANAPOLIS
RS: Dolphins lead series, 45-25
PS: Dolphins lead series, 2-0;
See Indianapolis vs. Miami
MIAMI vs. JACKSONVILLE
RS: Dolphins lead series, 3-2
PS: Jaguars lead series, 1-0;
See Jacksonville vs. Miami
MIAMI vs. KANSAS CITY
RS: Dolphins lead series, 13-12
PS: Dolphins lead series, 3-0;
See Kansas City vs. Miami
MIAMI vs. MINNESOTA
RS: Dolphins lead series, 6-4
PS: Dolphins lead series, 1-0
1972—Dolphins, 16-14 (Minn)
1973—*Dolphins, 24-7 (Houston)
1976—Vikings, 29-7 (Mia)
1979—Dolphins, 27-12 (Minn)
1982—Dolphins, 22-14 (Mia)
1988—Dolphins, 24-7 (Mia)
1994—Vikings, 38-35 (Minn)
2000—Vikings, 13-7 (Minn)
2002—Vikings, 20-17 (Minn)
2006—Dolphins, 24-20 (Mia)
2010—Dolphins, 14-10 (Minn)
(RS Pts.—Dolphins 193, Vikings 177)
(PS Pts.—Dolphins 24, Vikings 7)
*Super Bowl VIII
MIAMI vs. *NEW ENGLAND
RS: Dolphins lead series, 50-44
PS: Patriots lead series, 2-1
1966—Patriots, 20-14 (M)
1967—Patriots, 41-10 (B)
       Dolphins, 41-32 (M)
1968—Dolphins, 34-10 (B)
       Dolphins, 38-7 (M)
1969—Dolphins, 17-16 (B)
       Patriots, 38-23 (Tampa)
1970—Patriots, 27-14 (B)
       Dolphins, 37-20 (M)
1971—Dolphins, 41-3 (M)
       Patriots, 34-13 (NE)
1972—Dolphins, 52-0 (M)
       Dolphins, 37-21 (NE)
1973—Dolphins, 44-23 (M)
       Dolphins, 30-14 (NE)
1974—Patriots, 34-24 (NE)
       Dolphins, 34-27 (M)
1975—Dolphins, 22-14 (NE)
       Dolphins, 20-7 (M)
1976—Patriots, 30-14 (NE)

       Dolphins, 10-3 (M)
1977—Dolphins, 17-5 (M)
       Patriots, 14-10 (NE)
1978—Patriots, 33-24 (NE)
       Dolphins, 23-3 (M)
1979—Patriots, 28-13 (NE)
       Dolphins, 39-24 (M)
1980—Patriots, 34-0 (NE)
       Dolphins, 16-13 (M) OT
1981—Dolphins, 30-27 (NE) OT
       Dolphins, 24-14 (M)
1982—Patriots, 3-0 (NE)
       **Dolphins, 28-13 (M)
1983—Dolphins, 34-24 (M)
       Patriots, 17-6 (NE)
1984—Dolphins, 28-7 (M)
       Dolphins, 44-24 (NE)
1985—Patriots, 17-13 (NE)
       Dolphins, 30-27 (M)
       ***Patriots, 31-14 (M)
1986—Dolphins, 34-7 (NE)
       Patriots, 34-27 (M)
1987—Patriots, 28-21 (NE)
       Patriots, 24-10 (M)
1988—Patriots, 21-10 (NE)
       Patriots, 6-3 (M)
1989—Dolphins, 24-10 (NE)
       Dolphins, 31-10 (M)
1990—Dolphins, 27-24 (NE)
       Dolphins, 17-10 (M)
1991—Dolphins, 20-10 (NE)
       Dolphins, 30-20 (M)
1992—Dolphins, 38-17 (M)
       Dolphins, 16-13 (NE) OT
1993—Dolphins, 17-13 (M)
       Patriots, 33-27 (NE) OT
1994—Dolphins, 39-35 (M)
       Dolphins, 23-3 (NE)
1995—Dolphins, 20-3 (M)
       Patriots, 34-17 (M)
1996—Dolphins, 24-10 (M)
       Patriots, 42-23 (NE)
1997—Patriots, 27-24 (NE)
       Patriots, 14-12 (M)
       **Patriots, 17-3 (NE)
1998—Dolphins, 12-9 (M) OT
       Patriots, 26-23 (NE)
1999—Dolphins, 31-30 (NE)
       Dolphins, 27-17 (M)
2000—Dolphins, 10-3 (M)
       Dolphins, 27-24 (NE)
2001—Dolphins, 30-10 (M)
       Patriots, 20-13 (NE)
2002—Dolphins, 26-13 (M)
       Patriots, 27-24 (NE) OT
2003—Patriots, 19-13 (M) OT
       Patriots, 12-0 (NE)
2004—Patriots, 24-10 (NE)
       Dolphins, 29-28 (M)
2005—Patriots, 23-16 (M)
       Dolphins, 28-26 (NE)
2006—Patriots, 20-10 (NE)
       Dolphins, 21-0 (M)
2007—Patriots, 49-28 (M)
       Patriots, 28-7 (NE)
2008—Dolphins, 38-13 (NE)
       Patriots, 48-28 (M)
2009—Patriots, 27-17 (NE)
       Dolphins, 22-21 (M)
2010—Patriots, 41-14 (M)
       Patriots, 38-7 (NE)
2011—Patriots, 38-24 (M)
       Patriots, 27-24 (NE)

2012—Patriots, 23-16 (M)
       Patriots, 28-0 (NE)
2013—Patriots, 27-17 (NE)
       Dolphins, 24-20 (M)
(RS Pts.—Dolphins 2,043, Patriots 1,969)
(PS Pts.—Patriots 61, Dolphins 45)
*Franchise in Boston prior to 1971
**AFC First-Round Playoff
***AFC Championship
MIAMI vs. NEW ORLEANS
RS: Dolphins lead series, 6-5
1970—Dolphins, 21-10 (M)
1974—Dolphins, 21-0 (NO)
1980—Dolphins, 21-16 (M)
1983—Saints, 17-7 (NO)
1986—Dolphins, 31-27 (NO)
1992—Saints, 24-13 (NO)
1995—Saints, 33-30 (NO)
1998—Dolphins, 30-10 (M)
2005—Dolphins, 21-6 (Baton Rouge)
2009—Saints, 46-34 (M)
2013—Saints, 38-17 (NO)
(RS Pts.—Dolphins 246, Saints 227)
MIAMI vs. N.Y. GIANTS
RS: Giants lead series, 5-2
1972—Dolphins, 23-13 (NY)
1990—Giants, 20-3 (NY)
1993—Giants, 19-14 (M)
1996—Dolphins, 17-7 (M)
2003—Dolphins, 23-10 (NY)
2007—Giants, 13-10 (London)
2011—Giants, 20-17 (NY)
(RS Pts.—Giants 112, Dolphins 97)
MIAMI vs. N.Y. JETS
RS: Jets lead series, 50-45-1
PS: Dolphins lead series, 1-0
1966—Jets, 19-14 (M)
       Jets, 30-13 (NY)
1967—Jets, 29-7 (NY)
       Jets, 33-14 (M)
1968—Jets, 35-17 (NY)
       Jets, 31-7 (M)
1969—Jets, 34-31 (NY)
       Jets, 27-9 (M)
1970—Dolphins, 20-6 (NY)
       Dolphins, 16-10 (M)
1971—Jets, 14-10 (M)
       Dolphins, 30-14 (NY)
1972—Dolphins, 27-17 (NY)
       Dolphins, 28-24 (M)
1973—Dolphins, 31-3 (M)
       Dolphins, 24-14 (NY)
1974—Dolphins, 21-17 (M)
       Jets, 17-14 (NY)
1975—Dolphins, 43-0 (NY)
       Dolphins, 27-7 (M)
1976—Dolphins, 16-0 (M)
       Dolphins, 27-7 (NY)
1977—Dolphins, 21-17 (M)
       Dolphins, 14-10 (NY)
1978—Jets, 33-20 (NY)
       Jets, 24-13 (M)
1979—Jets, 33-27 (NY)
       Jets, 27-24 (M)
1980—Jets, 17-14 (NY)
       Jets, 24-17 (M)
1981—Tie, 28-28 (M) OT
       Jets, 16-15 (NY)
1982—Dolphins, 45-28 (NY)
       Dolphins, 20-19 (M)
       *Dolphins, 14-0 (M)
1983—Jets, 32-14 (NY)
       Dolphins, 34-14 (M)

1984—Dolphins, 31-17 (NY)
    Dolphins, 28-17 (M)
1985—Jets, 23-7 (NY)
    Dolphins, 21-17 (M)
1986—Jets, 51-45 (NY) OT
    Dolphins, 45-3 (M)
1987—Jets, 37-31 (NY) OT
    Dolphins, 37-28 (M)
1988—Jets, 44-30 (M)
    Jets, 38-34 (NY)
1989—Jets, 40-33 (M)
    Dolphins, 31-23 (NY)
1990—Dolphins, 20-16 (M)
    Dolphins, 17-3 (NY)
1991—Jets, 41-23 (NY)
    Jets, 23-20 (M) OT
1992—Jets, 26-14 (NY)
    Dolphins, 19-17 (M)
1993—Jets, 24-14 (M)
    Jets, 27-10 (NY)
1994—Dolphins, 28-14 (M)
    Dolphins, 28-24 (NY)
1995—Dolphins, 52-14 (M)
    Jets, 17-16 (NY)
1996—Dolphins, 36-27 (M)
    Dolphins, 31-28 (NY)
1997—Dolphins, 31-20 (NY)
    Dolphins, 24-17 (M)
1998—Jets, 20-9 (NY)
    Jets, 21-16 (M)
1999—Jets, 28-20 (NY)
    Jets, 38-31 (M)
2000—Jets, 40-37 (NY) OT
    Jets, 20-3 (M)
2001—Jets, 21-17 (NY)
    Jets, 24-0 (M)
2002—Dolphins, 30-3 (M)
    Jets, 13-10 (NY)
2003—Dolphins, 21-10 (NY)
    Dolphins, 23-21 (M)
2004—Jets, 17-9 (M)
    Jets, 41-14 (NY)
2005—Jets, 17-7 (NY)
    Dolphins, 24-20 (M)
2006—Jets, 20-17 (NY)
    Jets, 13-10 (M)
2007—Jets, 31-28 (NY)
    Jets, 40-13 (M)
2008—Jets, 20-14 (M)
    Dolphins, 24-17 (NY)
2009—Dolphins, 31-27 (M)
    Dolphins, 30-25 (NY)
2010—Jets, 31-23 (M)
    Dolphins, 10-6 (NY)
2011—Jets, 24-6 (NY)
    Dolphins, 19-17 (M)
2012—Jets, 23-20 (M) OT
    Dolphins, 30-9 (NY)
2013—Jets, 23-3 (NY)
    Jets, 20-7 (M)
(RS Pts.—Dolphins 2,102, Jets 2,048)
(PS Pts.—Dolphins 14, Jets 0)
*AFC Championship
MIAMI vs. *OAKLAND
RS: Raiders lead series, 16-15-1
PS: Raiders lead series, 3-1
1966—Raiders, 23-14 (M)
    Raiders, 21-10 (O)
1967—Raiders, 31-17 (O)
1968—Raiders, 47-21 (M)
1969—Raiders, 20-17 (O)
    Tie, 20-20 (M)
1970—Dolphins, 20-13 (M)

**Raiders, 21-14 (O)
1973—Raiders, 12-7 (O)
    ***Dolphins, 27-10 (M)
1974—**Raiders, 28-26 (O)
1975—Raiders, 31-21 (M)
1978—Dolphins, 23-6 (M)
1979—Raiders, 13-3 (O)
1980—Raiders, 16-10 (O)
1981—Raiders, 33-17 (M)
1983—Raiders, 27-14 (LA)
1984—Raiders, 45-34 (M)
1986—Raiders, 30-28 (M)
1988—Dolphins, 24-14 (LA)
1990—Raiders, 13-10 (M)
1992—Dolphins, 20-7 (M)
1994—Dolphins, 20-17 (M) OT
1996—Raiders, 17-7 (O)
1997—Dolphins, 34-16 (O)
1998—Dolphins, 27-17 (O)
1999—Dolphins, 16-9 (O)
2000—**Raiders, 27-0 (O)
2001—Dolphins, 18-15 (M)
2002—Dolphins, 23-17 (M)
2005—Dolphins, 33-21 (O)
2007—Raiders, 35-17 (M)
2008—Dolphins, 17-15 (M)
2010—Dolphins, 33-17 (O)
2011—Dolphins, 34-14 (M)
2012—Dolphins, 35-13 (M)
(RS Pts.—Raiders 645, Dolphins 644)
(PS Pts.—Raiders 86, Dolphins 67)
*Franchise in Los Angeles from 1982-1994
**AFC Divisional Playoff
***AFC Championship
MIAMI vs. PHILADELPHIA
RS: Dolphins lead series, 7-6
1970—Eagles, 24-17 (P)
1975—Dolphins, 24-16 (M)
1978—Eagles, 17-3 (P)
1981—Dolphins, 13-10 (M)
1984—Dolphins, 24-23 (M)
1987—Dolphins, 28-10 (P)
1990—Dolphins, 23-20 (M) OT
1993—Dolphins, 19-14 (P)
1996—Eagles, 35-28 (P)
1999—Dolphins, 16-13 (M)
2003—Eagles, 34-27 (M)
2007—Eagles, 17-7 (P)
2011—Eagles, 26-10 (M)
(RS Pts.—Eagles 259, Dolphins 239)
MIAMI vs. PITTSBURGH
RS: Steelers lead series, 12-10
PS: Dolphins lead series, 2-1
1971—Dolphins, 24-21 (M)
1972—*Dolphins, 21-17 (P)
1973—Dolphins, 30-26 (M)
1976—Steelers, 14-3 (P)
1979—**Steelers, 34-14 (P)
1980—Steelers, 23-10 (P)
1981—Dolphins, 30-10 (M)
1984—Dolphins, 31-7 (P)
    *Dolphins, 45-28 (M)
1985—Dolphins, 24-20 (M)
1987—Dolphins, 35-24 (M)
1988—Steelers, 40-24 (P)
1989—Steelers, 34-14 (M)
1990—Dolphins, 28-6 (P)
1993—Steelers, 21-20 (M)
1994—Steelers, 16-13 (P) OT
1995—Dolphins, 23-10 (M)
1996—Dolphins, 24-17 (M)
1998—Dolphins, 21-0 (M)
2004—Steelers, 13-3 (M)

2006—Steelers, 28-17 (P)
2007—Steelers, 3-0 (P)
2009—Steelers, 30-24 (M)
2010—Steelers, 23-22 (M)
2013—Dolphins, 34-28 (P)
(RS Pts.—Dolphins 447, Steelers 421)
(PS Pts.—Dolphins 80, Steelers 79)
*AFC Championship
**AFC Divisional Playoff
MIAMI vs. *ST. LOUIS
RS: Dolphins lead series, 10-2
1971—Dolphins, 20-14 (LA)
1976—Rams, 31-28 (M)
1980—Dolphins, 35-14 (LA)
1983—Dolphins, 30-14 (M)
1986—Dolphins, 37-31 (LA) OT
1992—Dolphins, 26-10 (M)
1995—Dolphins, 41-22 (StL)
1998—Dolphins, 14-0 (M)
2001—Rams, 42-10 (StL)
2004—Dolphins, 31-14 (M)
2008—Dolphins, 16-12 (StL)
2012—Dolphins, 17-14 (M)
(RS Pts.—Dolphins 305, Rams 218)
*Franchise in Los Angeles prior to 1995
MIAMI vs. SAN DIEGO
RS: Dolphins lead series, 13-12
PS: Series tied, 2-2
1966—Chargers, 44-10 (SD)
1967—Chargers, 24-0 (SD)
    Dolphins, 41-24 (M)
1968—Chargers, 34-28 (SD)
1969—Chargers, 21-14 (M)
1972—Dolphins, 24-10 (M)
1974—Dolphins, 28-21 (SD)
1977—Chargers, 14-13 (M)
1978—Dolphins, 28-21 (SD)
1980—Chargers, 27-24 (M) OT
1981—*Chargers, 41-38 (M) OT
1982—**Dolphins, 34-13 (M)
1984—Chargers, 34-28 (SD) OT
1986—Chargers, 50-28 (SD)
1988—Dolphins, 31-28 (SD)
1991—Chargers, 38-30 (SD)
1992—*Dolphins, 31-0 (M)
1993—Chargers, 45-20 (SD)
1994—*Chargers, 22-21 (SD)
1995—Dolphins, 24-14 (SD)
1999—Dolphins, 12-9 (M)
2000—Dolphins, 17-7 (SD)
2002—Dolphins, 30-3 (M)
2003—Dolphins, 26-10 (Ariz)
2005—Dolphins, 23-21 (SD)
2008—Dolphins, 17-10 (M)
2009—Chargers, 23-13 (SD)
2011—Chargers, 26-16 (SD)
2013—Dolphins, 20-16 (M)
(RS Pts.—Chargers 574, Dolphins 545)
(PS Pts.—Dolphins 124, Chargers 76)
*AFC Divisional Playoff
**AFC Second-Round Playoff
MIAMI vs. SAN FRANCISCO
RS: Dolphins lead series, 6-5
PS: 49ers lead series, 1-0
1973—Dolphins, 21-13 (M)
1977—Dolphins, 19-15 (SF)
1980—Dolphins, 17-13 (M)
1983—Dolphins, 20-17 (SF)
1984—*49ers, 38-16 (Stanford)
1986—49ers, 31-16 (M)
1992—49ers, 27-3 (SF)
1995—49ers, 44-20 (M)
2001—49ers, 21-0 (SF)

2004—Dolphins, 24-17 (SF)
2008—Dolphins, 14-9 (M)
2012—49ers, 27-13 (SF)
(RS Pts.—49ers 237, Dolphins 167)
(PS Pts.—49ers 38, Dolphins 16)
*Super Bowl XIX
MIAMI vs. SEATTLE
RS: Dolphins lead series, 8-3
PS: Dolphins lead series, 2-1
1977—Dolphins, 31-13 (M)
1979—Dolphins, 19-10 (M)
1983—*Seahawks, 27-20 (M)
1984—*Dolphins, 31-10 (M)
1987—Seahawks, 24-20 (S)
1990—Dolphins, 24-17 (M)
1992—Dolphins, 19-17 (S)
1996—Seahawks, 22-15 (M)
1999—**Dolphins, 20-17 (S)
2000—Dolphins, 23-0 (M)
2001—Dolphins, 24-20 (S)
2004—Seahawks, 24-17 (S)
2008—Dolphins, 21-19 (M)
2012—Dolphins, 24-21 (M)
(RS Pts.—Dolphins 237, Seahawks 187)
(PS Pts.—Dolphins 71, Seahawks 54)
*AFC Divisional Playoff
**AFC First-Round Playoff
MIAMI vs. TAMPA BAY
RS: Series tied, 5-5
1976—Dolphins, 23-20 (TB)
1982—Buccaneers, 23-17 (TB)
1985—Dolphins, 41-38 (M)
1988—Dolphins, 17-14 (TB)
1991—Dolphins, 33-14 (M)
1997—Buccaneers, 31-21 (M)
2000—Dolphins, 16-13 (M)
2005—Buccaneers, 27-13 (TB)
2009—Dolphins, 25-23 (M)
2013—Buccaneers, 22-19 (TB)
(RS Pts.—Buccaneers 228, Dolphins 222)
MIAMI vs. *TENNESSEE
RS: Dolphins lead series, 18-15
PS: Titans lead series, 1-0
1966—Dolphins, 20-13 (H)
       Dolphins, 29-28 (M)
1967—Oilers, 17-14 (H)
       Oilers, 41-10 (M)
1968—Oilers, 24-10 (M)
       Dolphins, 24-7 (H)
1969—Oilers, 22-10 (H)
       Oilers, 32-7 (M)
1970—Dolphins, 20-10 (H)
1972—Dolphins, 34-13 (M)
1975—Oilers, 20-19 (H)
1977—Dolphins, 27-7 (M)
1978—Oilers, 35-30 (H)
       **Oilers, 17-9 (M)
1979—Oilers, 9-6 (H)
1981—Dolphins, 16-10 (H)
1983—Dolphins, 24-17 (M)
1984—Dolphins, 28-10 (M)
1985—Oilers, 26-23 (H)
1986—Dolphins, 28-7 (M)
1989—Oilers, 39-7 (H)
1991—Dolphins, 17-13 (M)
1992—Dolphins, 19-16 (M)
1996—Dolphins, 23-20 (H)
1997—Dolphins, 16-13 (M) OT
1999—Dolphins, 17-0 (M)
2001—Dolphins, 31-23 (T)
2003—Titans, 31-7 (T)
2004—Titans, 17-7 (M)
2005—Dolphins, 24-10 (M)

2006—Dolphins, 13-10 (M)
2009—Titans, 27-24 (T) OT
2010—Dolphins, 29-17 (M)
2012—Titans, 37-3 (M)
(RS Pts.—Titans 625, Dolphins 612)
(PS Pts.—Titans 17, Dolphins 9)
*Franchise in Houston prior to 1997;
known as Oilers prior to 1999
**AFC First-Round Playoff
MIAMI vs. WASHINGTON
RS: Dolphins lead series, 7-4
PS: Series tied, 1-1
1972—*Dolphins, 14-7 (Los Angeles)
1974—Redskins, 20-17 (W)
1978—Dolphins, 16-0 (W)
1981—Dolphins, 13-10 (M)
1982—**Redskins, 27-17 (Pasadena)
1984—Dolphins, 35-17 (W)
1987—Dolphins, 23-21 (M)
1990—Redskins, 42-20 (W)
1993—Dolphins, 17-10 (M)
1999—Redskins, 21-10 (M)
2003—Dolphins, 24-23 (M)
2007—Redskins, 16-13 (W) OT
2011—Dolphins, 20-9 (M)
(RS Pts.—Dolphins 208, Redskins 189)
(PS Pts.—Redskins 34, Dolphins 31)
*Super Bowl VII
**Super Bowl XVII

MINNESOTA vs. ARIZONA
RS: Vikings lead series, 13-10
PS: Vikings lead series, 2-0;
See Arizona vs. Minnesota
MINNESOTA vs. ATLANTA
RS: Vikings lead series, 15-10
PS: Series tied, 1-1;
See Atlanta vs. Minnesota
MINNESOTA vs. BALTIMORE
RS: Ravens lead series, 3-2;
See Baltimore vs. Minnesota
MINNESOTA vs. BUFFALO
RS: Vikings lead series, 8-4;
See Buffalo vs. Minnesota
MINNESOTA vs. CAROLINA
RS: Vikings lead series, 6-5;
See Carolina vs. Minnesota
MINNESOTA vs. CHICAGO
RS: Vikings lead series, 54-49-2
PS: Bears lead series, 1-0;
See Chicago vs. Minnesota
MINNESOTA vs. CINCINNATI
RS: Series tied, 6-6;
See Cincinnati vs. Minnesota
MINNESOTA vs. CLEVELAND
RS: Vikings lead series, 10-4
PS: Vikings lead series, 1-0;
See Cleveland vs. Minnesota
MINNESOTA vs. DALLAS
RS: Series tied, 11-11
PS: Cowboys lead series, 4-3;
See Dallas vs. Minnesota
MINNESOTA vs. DENVER
RS: Vikings lead series, 7-6;
See Denver vs. Minnesota
MINNESOTA vs. DETROIT
RS: Vikings lead series, 69-34-2;
See Detroit vs. Minnesota
MINNESOTA vs. GREEN BAY
RS: Packers lead series, 55-48-2
PS: Series tied, 1-1;
See Green Bay vs. Minnesota
MINNESOTA vs. HOUSTON

RS: Vikings lead series, 3-0;
See Houston vs. Minnesota
MINNESOTA vs. INDIANAPOLIS
RS: Colts lead series, 15-7-1
PS: Colts lead series, 1-0;
See Indianapolis vs. Minnesota
MINNESOTA vs. JACKSONVILLE
RS: Vikings lead series, 4-1;
See Jacksonville vs. Minnesota
MINNESOTA vs. KANSAS CITY
RS: Chiefs lead series, 6-4
PS: Chiefs lead series, 1-0;
See Kansas City vs. Minnesota
MINNESOTA vs. MIAMI
RS: Dolphins lead series, 6-4
PS: Dolphins lead series, 1-0;
See Miami vs. Minnesota
MINNESOTA vs. *NEW ENGLAND
RS: Patriots lead series, 7-4
1970—Vikings, 35-14 (B)
1974—Patriots, 17-14 (NE)
1979—Patriots, 27-23 (NE)
1988—Vikings, 36-6 (M)
1991—Patriots, 26-23 (NE) OT
1994—Patriots, 26-20 (NE) OT
1997—Vikings, 23-18 (M)
2000—Vikings, 21-13 (NE)
2002—Patriots, 24-17 (NE)
2006—Patriots, 31-7 (M)
2010—Patriots, 28-18 (NE)
(RS Pts.—Vikings 237, Patriots 230)
*Franchise in Boston prior to 1971
MINNESOTA vs. NEW ORLEANS
RS: Vikings lead series, 18-9
PS: Vikings lead series, 2-1
1968—Saints, 20-17 (NO)
1970—Vikings, 26-0 (M)
1971—Vikings, 23-10 (NO)
1972—Vikings, 37-6 (M)
1974—Vikings, 29-9 (M)
1975—Vikings, 20-7 (NO)
1976—Vikings, 40-9 (NO)
1978—Saints, 31-24 (NO)
1980—Vikings, 23-20 (NO)
1981—Vikings, 20-10 (M)
1983—Saints, 17-16 (M)
1985—Saints, 30-23 (M)
1986—Vikings, 33-17 (M)
1987—*Vikings, 44-10 (NO)
1988—Vikings, 45-3 (M)
1990—Vikings, 32-3 (M)
1991—Saints, 26-0 (NO)
1993—Saints, 17-14 (M)
1994—Vikings, 21-20 (M)
1995—Vikings, 43-24 (M)
1998—Vikings, 31-24 (M)
2000—**Vikings, 34-16 (M)
2001—Saints, 28-15 (NO)
2002—Vikings, 32-31 (NO)
2004—Vikings, 38-31 (NO)
2005—Vikings, 33-16 (M)
2008—Vikings, 30-27 (NO)
2009—***Saints, 31-28 (NO) OT
2010—Saints, 14-9 (NO)
2011—Saints, 42-20 (M)
(RS Pts.—Vikings 694, Saints 492)
(PS Pts.—Vikings 106, Saints 57)
*NFC First-Round Playoff
**NFC Divisional Playoff
***NFC Championship
MINNESOTA vs. N.Y. GIANTS
RS: Vikings lead series, 13-10
PS: Giants lead series, 2-1

1964—Vikings, 30-21 (NY)
1965—Vikings, 40-14 (M)
1967—Vikings, 27-24 (M)
1969—Giants, 24-23 (NY)
1971—Vikings, 17-10 (NY)
1973—Vikings, 31-7 (New Haven)
1976—Vikings, 24-7 (M)
1986—Giants, 22-20 (M)
1989—Giants, 24-14 (NY)
1990—Giants, 23-15 (NY)
1993—*Giants, 17-10 (NY)
1994—Vikings, 27-10 (NY)
1996—Giants, 15-10 (NY)
1997—*Vikings, 23-22 (NY)
1999—Vikings, 34-17 (NY)
2000—**Giants, 41-0 (NY)
2001—Vikings, 28-16 (M)
2002—Giants, 27-20 (M)
2003—Giants, 29-17 (M)
2004—Giants, 34-13 (M)
2005—Vikings, 24-21 (NY)
2007—Vikings, 41-17 (NY)
2008—Vikings, 20-19 (M)
2009—Vikings, 44-7 (M)
2010—Giants, 21-3 (Detroit)
2013—Giants, 23-7 (NY)
(RS Pts.—Vikings 529, Giants 432)
(PS Pts.—Giants 80, Vikings 33)
*NFC First-Round Playoff
**NFC Championship
MINNESOTA vs. N.Y. JETS
RS: Jets lead series, 8-1
1970—Jets, 20-10 (NY)
1975—Vikings, 29-21 (M)
1979—Jets, 14-7 (NY)
1982—Jets, 42-14 (M)
1994—Jets, 31-21 (M)
1997—Jets, 23-21 (NY)
2002—Jets, 20-7 (NY)
2006—Jets, 26-13 (M)
2010—Jets, 29-20 (NY)
(RS Pts.—Jets 226, Vikings 142)
MINNESOTA vs. *OAKLAND
RS: Raiders lead series, 9-4
PS: Raiders lead series, 1-0
1973—Vikings, 24-16 (M)
1976—**Raiders, 32-14 (Pasadena)
1977—Raiders, 35-13 (O)
1978—Raiders, 27-20 (O)
1981—Raiders, 36-10 (M)
1984—Raiders, 23-20 (LA)
1987—Vikings, 31-20 (M)
1990—Raiders, 28-24 (M)
1993—Raiders, 24-7 (LA)
1996—Vikings, 16-13 (O) OT
1999—Vikings, 22-17 (M)
2003—Raiders, 28-18 (O)
2007—Vikings, 29-22 (M)
2011—Raiders, 27-21 (M)
(RS Pts.—Raiders 321, Vikings 250)
(PS Pts.—Raiders 32, Vikings 14)
*Franchise in Los Angeles from 1982-1994
**Super Bowl XI
MINNESOTA vs. PHILADELPHIA
RS: Vikings lead series, 13-9
PS: Eagles lead series, 3-0
1962—Vikings, 31-21 (M)
1963—Vikings, 34-13 (P)
1968—Vikings, 24-17 (P)
1971—Vikings, 13-0 (P)
1973—Vikings, 28-21 (M)
1976—Vikings, 31-12 (M)
1978—Vikings, 28-27 (M)

1980—Eagles, 42-7 (M)
*Eagles, 31-16 (P)
1981—Vikings, 35-23 (M)
1984—Eagles, 19-17 (P)
1985—Vikings, 28-23 (P)
Eagles, 37-35 (M)
1988—Vikings, 23-21 (M)
1989—Eagles, 10-9 (P)
1990—Vikings, 32-24 (P)
1992—Eagles, 28-17 (P)
1997—Vikings, 28-19 (M)
2001—Eagles, 48-17 (P)
2004—Eagles, 27-16 (P)
*Eagles, 27-14 (P)
2007—Eagles, 23-16 (M)
2008—**Eagles, 26-14 (M)
2010—Vikings, 24-14 (P)
2013—Vikings, 48-30 (M)
(RS Pts.—Vikings 533, Eagles 507)
(PS Pts.—Eagles 84, Vikings 44)
*NFC Divisional Playoff
**NFC First-Round Playoff
MINNESOTA vs. PITTSBURGH
RS: Vikings lead series, 9-7
PS: Steelers lead series, 1-0
1962—Steelers, 39-31 (P)
1964—Vikings, 30-10 (M)
1967—Vikings, 41-27 (M)
1969—Vikings, 52-14 (M)
1972—Steelers, 23-10 (P)
1974—*Steelers, 16-6 (New Orleans)
1976—Vikings, 17-6 (M)
1980—Steelers, 23-17 (M)
1983—Vikings, 17-14 (P)
1986—Vikings, 31-7 (M)
1989—Steelers, 27-14 (P)
1992—Vikings, 6-3 (P)
1995—Vikings, 44-24 (P)
2001—Steelers, 21-16 (P)
2005—Vikings, 18-3 (M)
2009—Steelers, 27-17 (P)
2013—Vikings, 34-27 (London)
(RS Pts.—Vikings 380, Steelers 310)
(PS Pts.—Steelers 16, Vikings 6)
*Super Bowl IX
MINNESOTA vs. *ST. LOUIS
RS: Vikings lead series, 19-14-2
PS: Vikings lead series, 5-2
1961—Rams, 31-17 (LA)
Vikings, 42-21 (M)
1962—Vikings, 38-14 (LA)
Tie, 24-24 (M)
1963—Rams, 27-24 (LA)
Vikings, 21-13 (M)
1964—Rams, 22-13 (LA)
Vikings, 34-13 (M)
1965—Vikings, 38-35 (LA)
Vikings, 24-13 (M)
1966—Vikings, 35-7 (M)
Rams, 21-6 (LA)
1967—Rams, 39-3 (LA)
1968—Rams, 31-3 (M)
1969—Vikings, 20-13 (LA)
**Vikings, 23-20 (M)
1970—Vikings, 13-3 (M)
1972—Vikings, 45-41 (LA)
1973—Vikings, 10-9 (M)
1974—Rams, 20-17 (LA)
***Vikings, 14-10 (M)
1976—Tie, 10-10 (M) OT
***Vikings, 24-13 (M)
1977—Rams, 35-3 (LA)
****Vikings, 14-7 (LA)

1978—Rams, 34-17 (M)
****Rams, 34-10 (LA)
1979—Rams, 27-21 (LA) OT
1985—Rams, 13-10 (LA)
1987—Vikings, 21-16 (LA)
1988—*****Vikings, 28-17 (M)
1989—Vikings, 23-21 (M) OT
1991—Vikings, 20-14 (M)
1992—Vikings, 31-17 (LA)
1998—Vikings, 38-31 (StL)
1999—****Rams, 49-37 (StL)
2000—Rams, 40-29 (StL)
2003—Rams, 48-17 (StL)
2005—Vikings, 27-13 (M)
2006—Rams, 41-21 (M)
2009—Rams, 38-10 (StL)
2012—Vikings, 36-22 (StL)
(RS Pts.—Rams 789, Vikings 789)
(PS Pts.—Rams 150, Vikings 150)
*Franchise in Los Angeles prior to 1995
**Conference Championship
***NFC Championship
****NFC Divisional Playoff
*****NFC First-Round Playoff
MINNESOTA vs. SAN DIEGO
RS: Chargers lead series, 6-5
1971—Chargers, 30-14 (SD)
1975—Vikings, 28-13 (M)
1978—Chargers, 13-7 (M)
1981—Vikings, 33-31 (SD)
1984—Chargers, 42-13 (M)
1985—Vikings, 21-17 (M)
1993—Chargers, 30-17 (M)
1999—Vikings, 35-27 (M)
2003—Chargers, 42-28 (SD)
2007—Vikings, 35-17 (M)
2011—Chargers, 24-17 (SD)
(RS Pts.—Chargers 286, Vikings 248)
MINNESOTA vs. SAN FRANCISCO
RS: Vikings lead series, 21-18-1
PS: 49ers lead series, 4-1
1961—49ers, 38-24 (M)
49ers, 38-28 (SF)
1962—49ers, 21-7 (SF)
49ers, 35-12 (M)
1963—Vikings, 24-20 (SF)
Vikings, 45-14 (M)
1964—Vikings, 27-22 (SF)
Vikings, 24-7 (M)
1965—Vikings, 42-41 (SF)
49ers, 45-24 (M)
1966—Tie, 20-20 (SF)
Vikings, 28-3 (M)
1967—49ers, 27-21 (M)
1968—Vikings, 30-20 (SF)
1969—Vikings, 10-7 (M)
1970—*49ers, 17-14 (M)
1971—49ers, 13-9 (M)
1972—49ers, 20-17 (SF)
1973—Vikings, 17-13 (SF)
1975—Vikings, 27-17 (M)
1976—49ers, 20-16 (SF)
1977—Vikings, 28-27 (M)
1979—Vikings, 28-22 (M)
1983—49ers, 48-17 (M)
1984—49ers, 51-7 (SF)
1985—Vikings, 28-21 (M)
1986—*49ers, 27-24 (SF) OT
1987—*Vikings, 36-24 (SF)
1988—49ers, 24-21 (SF)
*49ers, 34-9 (SF)
1989—*49ers, 41-13 (SF)
1990—49ers, 20-17 (M)

1991—Vikings, 17-14 (M)
1992—49ers, 20-17 (M)
1993—49ers, 38-19 (SF)
1994—Vikings, 21-14 (M)
1995—49ers, 37-30 (SF)
1997—49ers, 28-17 (SF)
  *49ers, 38-22 (SF)
1999—Vikings, 40-16 (M)
2003—Vikings, 35-7 (M)
2006—49ers, 9-3 (SF)
2007—Vikings, 27-7 (SF)
2009—Vikings, 27-24 (M)
2012—Vikings, 24-13 (M)
(RS Pts.—49ers 905, Vikings 902)
(PS Pts.—49ers 154, Vikings 94)
*NFC Divisional Playoff

MINNESOTA vs. SEATTLE
RS: Seahawks lead series, 8-5
1976—Vikings, 27-21 (M)
1978—Seahawks, 29-28 (S)
1984—Seahawks, 20-12 (M)
1987—Seahawks, 28-17 (S)
1990—Vikings, 24-21 (S)
1996—Seahawks, 42-23 (S)
2002—Seahawks, 48-23 (S)
2003—Vikings, 34-7 (M)
2004—Seahawks, 27-23 (M)
2006—Vikings, 31-13 (S)
2009—Vikings, 35-9 (M)
2012—Seahawks, 30-20 (S)
2013—Seahawks, 41-20 (S)
(RS Pts.—Seahawks 336, Vikings 317)

MINNESOTA vs. TAMPA BAY
RS: Vikings lead series, 31-22
1977—Vikings, 9-3 (TB)
1978—Buccaneers, 16-10 (M)
  Vikings, 24-7 (TB)
1979—Buccaneers, 12-10 (M)
  Vikings, 23-22 (TB)
1980—Vikings, 38-30 (M)
  Vikings, 21-10 (TB)
1981—Buccaneers, 21-13 (TB)
  Vikings, 25-10 (M)
1982—Vikings, 17-10 (M)
1983—Vikings, 19-16 (TB) OT
  Buccaneers, 17-12 (M)
1984—Buccaneers, 35-31 (TB)
  Vikings, 27-24 (M)
1985—Vikings, 31-16 (TB)
  Vikings, 26-7 (M)
1986—Vikings, 23-10 (TB)
  Vikings, 45-13 (M)
1987—Buccaneers, 20-10 (TB)
  Vikings, 23-17 (M)
1988—Vikings, 14-13 (M)
  Vikings, 49-20 (TB)
1989—Vikings, 17-3 (M)
  Vikings, 24-10 (TB)
1990—Buccaneers, 23-20 (M) OT
  Buccaneers, 26-13 (TB)
1991—Vikings, 28-13 (M)
  Vikings, 26-24 (TB)
1992—Vikings, 26-20 (M)
  Vikings, 35-7 (TB)
1993—Vikings, 15-0 (M)
  Buccaneers, 23-10 (TB)
1994—Vikings, 36-13 (TB)
  Buccaneers, 20-17 (M) OT
1995—Buccaneers, 20-17 (TB) OT
  Vikings, 31-17 (M)
1996—Buccaneers, 24-13 (TB)
  Vikings, 21-10 (M)
1997—Buccaneers, 28-14 (M)

Vikings, 10-6 (TB)
1998—Vikings, 31-7 (M)
  Buccaneers, 27-24 (TB)
1999—Vikings, 21-14 (M)
  Buccaneers, 24-17 (TB)
2000—Vikings, 30-23 (M)
  Buccaneers, 41-13 (TB)
2001—Vikings, 20-16 (M)
  Buccaneers, 41-14 (TB)
2002—Buccaneers, 38-24 (TB)
2005—Buccaneers, 24-13 (M)
2008—Buccaneers, 19-13 (TB)
2011—Buccaneers, 24-20 (M)
2012—Buccaneers, 36-17 (M)
(RS Pts.—Vikings 1,130, Buccaneers 970)

MINNESOTA vs. *TENNESSEE
RS: Vikings lead series, 8-4
1974—Vikings, 51-10 (M)
1980—Oilers, 20-16 (H)
1983—Vikings, 34-14 (M)
1986—Oilers, 23-10 (H)
1989—Vikings, 38-7 (M)
1992—Oilers, 17-13 (M)
1995—Vikings, 23-17 (M) OT
1998—Vikings, 26-16 (T)
2001—Vikings, 42-24 (M)
2004—Vikings, 20-3 (M)
2008—Titans, 30-17 (T)
2012—Vikings, 30-7 (M)
(RS Pts.—Vikings 320, Titans 188)
*Franchise in Houston prior to 1997;
known as Oilers prior to 1999

MINNESOTA vs. WASHINGTON
RS: Series tied, 9-9
PS: Redskins lead series, 3-2
1968—Vikings, 27-14 (M)
1970—Vikings, 19-10 (W)
1972—Redskins, 24-21 (M)
1973—*Vikings, 27-20 (M)
1975—Redskins, 31-30 (W)
1976—*Vikings, 35-20 (M)
1980—Vikings, 39-14 (M)
1982—**Redskins, 21-7 (W)
1984—Redskins, 31-17 (M)
1986—Redskins, 44-38 (W) OT
1987—Redskins, 27-24 (M) OT
  ***Redskins, 17-10 (W)
1992—Redskins, 15-13 (M)
  ****Redskins, 24-7 (M)
1993—Vikings, 14-9 (W)
1998—Vikings, 41-7 (M)
2004—Vikings, 21-18 (W)
2006—Vikings, 19-16 (W)
2007—Redskins, 32-21 (M)
2010—Vikings, 17-13 (W)
2011—Vikings, 33-26 (W)
2012—Redskins, 38-26 (W)
2013—Vikings, 34-27 (M)
(RS Pts.—Vikings 451, Redskins 399)
(PS Pts.—Redskins 102, Vikings 86)
*NFC Divisional Playoff
**NFC Second-Round Playoff
***NFC Championship
****NFC First-Round Playoff

NEW ENGLAND vs. ARIZONA
RS: Cardinals lead series, 7-6;
See Arizona vs. New England
NEW ENGLAND vs. ATLANTA
RS: Patriots lead series, 7-6;
See Atlanta vs. New England
NEW ENGLAND vs. BALTIMORE
RS: Patriots lead series, 7-1

PS: Ravens lead series, 2-1;
See Baltimore vs. New England
NEW ENGLAND vs. BUFFALO
RS: Patriots lead series, 65-41-1
PS: Patriots lead series, 1-0;
See Buffalo vs. New England
NEW ENGLAND vs. CAROLINA
RS: Panthers lead series, 3-2
PS: Patriots lead series, 1-0;
See Carolina vs. New England
NEW ENGLAND vs. CHICAGO
RS: Patriots lead series, 8-3
PS: Bears lead series, 1-0;
See Chicago vs. New England
NEW ENGLAND vs. CINCINNATI
RS: Patriots lead series, 14-9;
See Cincinnati vs. New England
NEW ENGLAND vs. CLEVELAND
RS: Browns lead series, 12-10
PS: Browns lead series, 1-0;
See Cleveland vs. New England
NEW ENGLAND vs. DALLAS
RS: Cowboys lead series, 7-4;
See Dallas vs. New England
NEW ENGLAND vs. DENVER
RS: Broncos lead series, 25-19
PS: Broncos lead series, 3-1;
See Denver vs. New England
NEW ENGLAND vs. DETROIT
RS: Patriots lead series, 6-4;
See Detroit vs. New England
NEW ENGLAND vs. GREEN BAY
RS: Patriots lead series, 5-4
PS: Packers lead series, 1-0;
See Green Bay vs. New England
NEW ENGLAND vs. HOUSTON
RS: Patriots lead series, 4-1
PS: Patriots lead series, 1-0;
See Houston vs. New England
NEW ENGLAND vs. INDIANAPOLIS
RS: Patriots lead series, 45-28
PS: Patriots lead series, 3-1;
See Indianapolis vs. New England
NEW ENGLAND vs. JACKSONVILLE
RS: Patriots lead series, 6-0
PS: Patriots lead series, 3-1;
See Jacksonville vs. New England
NEW ENGLAND vs. KANSAS CITY
RS: Chiefs lead series, 16-13-3;
See Kansas City vs. New England
NEW ENGLAND vs. MIAMI
RS: Dolphins lead series, 50-44
PS: Patriots lead series, 2-1;
See Miami vs. New England
NEW ENGLAND vs. MINNESOTA
RS: Patriots lead series, 7-4;
See Minnesota vs. New England
NEW ENGLAND vs. NEW ORLEANS
RS: Patriots lead series, 9-4
1972—Patriots, 17-10 (NO)
1976—Patriots, 27-6 (NE)
1980—Patriots, 38-27 (NO)
1983—Patriots, 7-0 (NE)
1986—Patriots, 21-20 (NE)
1989—Saints, 28-24 (NE)
1992—Saints, 31-14 (NE)
1995—Saints, 31-17 (NE)
1998—Patriots, 30-27 (NO)
2001—Patriots, 34-17 (NE)
2005—Patriots, 24-17 (NE)
2009—Saints, 38-17 (NO)
2013—Patriots, 30-27 (NE)
(RS Pts.—Patriots 300, Saints 279)

*NEW ENGLAND vs. N.Y. GIANTS
RS: Patriots lead series, 5-4
PS: Giants lead series, 2-0;
1970—Giants, 16-0 (B)
1974—Patriots, 28-20 (New Haven)
1987—Giants, 17-10 (NY)
1990—Giants, 13-10 (NE)
1996—Patriots, 23-22 (NY)
1999—Patriots, 16-14 (NE)
2003—Patriots, 17-6 (NE)
2007—Patriots, 38-35 (NY)
    **Giants, 17-14 (Arizona)
2011—Giants, 24-20 (NE)
      ***Giants, 21-17 (Indianapolis)
(RS Pts.—Giants 167, Patriots 162)
(PS Pts.—Giants 38, Patriots 31)
Franchise in Boston prior to 1971
**Super Bowl XLII
***Super Bowl XLVI
*NEW ENGLAND vs. **N.Y. JETS
RS: Patriots lead series, 54-52-1
PS: Patriots lead series, 2-1
1960—Patriots, 28-24 (NY)
    Patriots, 38-21 (B)
1961—Titans, 21-20 (B)
    Titans, 37-30 (NY)
1962—Patriots, 43-14 (NY)
    Patriots, 24-17 (B)
1963—Patriots, 38-14 (B)
    Jets, 31-24 (NY)
1964—Patriots, 26-10 (B)
    Jets, 35-14 (NY)
1965—Jets, 30-20 (B)
    Patriots, 27-23 (NY)
1966—Tie, 24-24 (B)
    Jets, 38-28 (NY)
1967—Jets, 30-23 (NY)
    Jets, 29-24 (B)
1968—Jets, 47-31 (Birmingham)
    Jets, 48-14 (NY)
1969—Jets, 23-14 (B)
    Jets, 23-17 (NY)
1970—Jets, 31-21 (B)
    Jets, 17-3 (NY)
1971—Patriots, 20-0 (NE)
    Jets, 13-6 (NY)
1972—Jets, 41-13 (NE)
    Jets, 34-10 (NY)
1973—Jets, 9-7 (NE)
    Jets, 33-13 (NY)
1974—Patriots, 24-0 (NY)
    Jets, 21-16 (NE)
1975—Jets, 36-7 (NY)
    Jets, 30-28 (NE)
1976—Patriots, 41-7 (NE)
    Patriots, 38-24 (NY)
1977—Jets, 30-27 (NY)
    Patriots, 24-13 (NE)
1978—Patriots, 55-21 (NE)
    Patriots, 19-17 (NY)
1979—Patriots, 56-3 (NE)
    Jets, 27-26 (NY)
1980—Patriots, 21-11 (NY)
    Patriots, 34-21 (NE)
1981—Jets, 28-24 (NY)
    Jets, 17-6 (NE)
1982—Jets, 31-7 (NY)
1983—Patriots, 23-13 (NE)
    Jets, 26-3 (NY)
1984—Patriots, 28-21 (NY)
    Patriots, 30-20 (NE)
1985—Patriots, 20-13 (NE)
    Jets, 16-13 (NY) OT

      ***Patriots, 26-14 (NY)
1986—Patriots, 20-6 (NY)
    Jets, 31-24 (NE)
1987—Jets, 43-24 (NY)
    Patriots, 42-20 (NE)
1988—Patriots, 28-3 (NE)
    Patriots, 14-13 (NY)
1989—Patriots, 27-24 (NY)
    Jets, 27-26 (NY)
1990—Jets, 37-13 (NE)
    Jets, 42-7 (NY)
1991—Jets, 28-21 (NE)
    Patriots, 6-3 (NY)
1992—Jets, 30-21 (NY)
    Patriots, 24-3 (NE)
1993—Jets, 45-7 (NY)
    Jets, 6-0 (NE)
1994—Jets, 24-17 (NY)
    Patriots, 24-13 (NE)
1995—Patriots, 20-7 (NY)
    Patriots, 31-28 (NE)
1996—Patriots, 31-27 (NY)
    Patriots, 34-10 (NE)
1997—Patriots, 27-24 (NE) OT
    Jets, 24-19 (NY)
1998—Jets, 24-14 (NE)
    Jets, 31-10 (NY)
1999—Patriots, 30-28 (NY)
    Jets, 24-17 (NE)
2000—Jets, 20-19 (NY)
    Jets, 34-17 (NE)
2001—Jets, 10-3 (NE)
    Patriots, 17-16 (NY)
2002—Patriots, 44-7 (NY)
    Jets, 30-17 (NE)
2003—Patriots, 23-16 (NE)
    Patriots, 21-16 (NY)
2004—Patriots, 13-7 (NE)
    Patriots, 23-7 (NY)
2005—Patriots, 16-3 (NE)
    Patriots, 31-21 (NY)
2006—Patriots, 24-17 (NE)
    Jets, 17-14 (NE)
      ***Patriots, 37-16 (NE)
2007—Patriots, 38-14 (NY)
    Patriots, 20-10 (NE)
2008—Patriots, 19-10 (NY)
    Jets, 34-31 (NE) OT
2009—Jets, 16-9 (NY)
    Patriots, 31-14 (NE)
2010—Jets, 28-14 (NY)
    Patriots, 45-3 (NE)
      ****Jets, 28-21 (NE)
2011—Patriots, 30-21 (NE)
    Patriots, 37-16 (NY)
2012—Patriots, 29-26 (NE) OT
    Patriots, 49-19 (NY)
2013—Patriots, 13-10 (NE)
    Jets, 30-27 (NY) OT
(RS Pts.—Patriots 2,422, Jets 2,260)
(PS Pts.—Patriots 84, Jets 58)
Franchise in Boston prior to 1971
**Jets known as Titans prior to 1963
***AFC First-Round Playoff
****AFC Divisional Playoff
*NEW ENGLAND vs. **OAKLAND
RS: Patriots lead series, 15-14-1
PS: Patriots lead series, 2-1
1960—Raiders, 27-14 (O)
    Patriots, 34-28 (B)
1961—Patriots, 20-17 (B)
    Patriots, 35-21 (O)
1962—Patriots, 26-16 (B)

    Raiders, 20-0 (O)
1963—Patriots, 20-14 (O)
    Patriots, 20-14 (B)
1964—Patriots, 17-14 (O)
    Tie, 43-43 (B)
1965—Raiders, 24-10 (B)
    Raiders, 30-21 (O)
1966—Patriots, 24-21 (B)
1967—Patriots, 35-7 (O)
    Raiders, 48-14 (B)
1968—Raiders, 41-10 (O)
1969—Raiders, 38-23 (B)
1971—Patriots, 20-6 (NE)
1974—Raiders, 41-26 (O)
1976—Patriots, 48-17 (NE)
      ***Raiders, 24-21 (O)
1978—Patriots, 21-14 (O)
1981—Raiders, 27-17 (O)
1985—Raiders, 35-20 (NE)
      ***Patriots, 27-20 (LA)
1987—Patriots, 26-23 (NE)
1989—Raiders, 24-21 (LA)
1994—Raiders, 21-17 (NE)
2001—***Patriots, 16-13 (NE) OT
2002—Raiders, 27-20 (O)
2005—Patriots, 30-20 (NE)
2008—Patriots, 49-26 (O)
2011—Patriots, 31-19 (O)
(RS Pts.—Raiders 751, Patriots 684)
(PS Pts.—Patriots 64, Raiders 57)
Franchise in Boston prior to 1971
**Franchise in Los Angeles from
1982-1994
***AFC Divisional Playoff
NEW ENGLAND vs. PHILADELPHIA
RS: Eagles lead series, 6-5
PS: Patriots lead series, 1-0
1973—Eagles, 24-23 (P)
1977—Patriots, 14-6 (NE)
1978—Patriots, 24-14 (NE)
1981—Eagles, 13-3 (P)
1984—Eagles, 27-17 (P)
1987—Eagles, 34-31 (NE) OT
1990—Eagles, 48-20 (P)
1999—Eagles, 24-9 (P)
2003—Patriots, 31-10 (P)
2004—*Patriots, 24-21 (Jacksonville)
2007—Patriots, 31-28 (NE)
2011—Patriots, 38-20 (P)
(RS Pts.—Eagles 248, Patriots 241)
(PS Pts.—Patriots 24, Eagles 21)
*Super Bowl XXXIX
NEW ENGLAND vs. PITTSBURGH
RS: Steelers lead series, 14-9
PS: Patriots lead series, 3-1
1972—Steelers, 33-3 (P)
1974—Steelers, 21-17 (NE)
1976—Patriots, 30-27 (P)
1979—Steelers, 16-13 (NE) OT
1981—Steelers, 27-21 (P) OT
1982—Steelers, 37-14 (P)
1983—Patriots, 28-23 (P)
1986—Patriots, 34-0 (P)
1989—Steelers, 28-10 (P)
1990—Steelers, 24-3 (P)
1991—Steelers, 20-6 (P)
1993—Steelers, 17-14 (P)
1995—Steelers, 41-27 (P)
1996—*Patriots, 28-3 (NE)
1997—Steelers, 24-21 (NE) OT
      *Steelers, 7-6 (P)
1998—Patriots, 23-9 (P)
2001—**Patriots, 24-17 (P)

2002—Patriots, 30-14 (NE)
2004—Steelers, 34-20 (P)
   **Patriots, 41-27 (P)
2005—Patriots, 23-20 (P)
2007—Patriots, 34-13 (NE)
2008—Steelers, 33-10 (NE)
2010—Patriots, 39-26 (P)
2011—Steelers, 25-17 (P)
2013—Patriots, 55-31 (NE)
(RS Pts.—Steelers 543, Patriots 492)
(PS Pts.—Patriots 99, Steelers 54)
*AFC Divisional Playoff
**AFC Championship
NEW ENGLAND vs. *ST. LOUIS
RS: Patriots lead series, 6-5
PS: Patriots lead series, 1-0
1974—Patriots, 20-14 (NE)
1980—Rams, 17-14 (NE)
1983—Patriots, 21-7 (LA)
1986—Patriots, 30-28 (LA)
1989—Rams, 24-20 (NE)
1992—Rams, 14-0 (LA)
1998—Patriots, 32-18 (StL)
2001—Rams, 24-17 (NE)
   **Patriots, 20-17 (New Orleans)
2004—Patriots, 40-22 (StL)
2008—Patriots, 23-16 (NE)
2012—Patriots, 45-7 (London)
(RS Pts.—Patriots 248, Rams 205)
(PS Pts.—Patriots 20, Rams 17)
*Franchise in Los Angeles prior to 1995
**Super Bowl XXXVI
NEW ENGLAND vs. **SAN DIEGO
RS: Patriots lead series, 20-14-2
PS: Patriots lead series, 2-1
1960—Patriots, 35-0 (LA)
   Chargers, 45-16 (B)
1961—Chargers, 38-27 (B)
   Patriots, 41-0 (SD)
1962—Patriots, 24-20 (B)
   Patriots, 20-14 (SD)
1963—Patriots, 17-13 (SD)
   Chargers, 7-6 (B)
   ***Chargers, 51-10 (SD)
1964—Patriots, 33-28 (SD)
   Chargers, 26-17 (B)
1965—Tie, 10-10 (B)
   Patriots, 22-6 (SD)
1966—Chargers, 24-0 (B)
   Patriots, 35-17 (B)
1967—Chargers, 28-14 (SD)
   Tie, 31-31 (SD)
1968—Chargers, 27-17 (B)
1969—Chargers, 13-10 (B)
   Chargers, 28-18 (SD)
1970—Chargers, 16-14 (B)
1973—Patriots, 30-14 (NE)
1975—Patriots, 33-19 (SD)
1977—Patriots, 24-20 (SD)
1978—Patriots, 28-23 (NE)
1979—Patriots, 27-21 (NE)
1983—Patriots, 37-21 (NE)
1994—Patriots, 23-17 (NE)
1996—Patriots, 45-7 (SD)
1997—Patriots, 41-7 (NE)
2001—Patriots, 29-26 (NE) OT
2002—Chargers, 21-14 (SD)
2005—Chargers, 41-17 (NE)
2006—****Patriots, 24-21 (SD)
2007—Patriots, 38-14 (NE)
   *****Patriots, 21-12 (NE)
2008—Chargers, 30-10 (SD)
2010—Patriots, 23-20 (SD)

2011—Patriots, 35-21 (NE)
(RS Pts.—Patriots 860, Chargers 720)
(PS Pts.—Chargers 84, Patriots 55)
*Franchise in Boston prior to 1971
**Franchise in Los Angeles prior to 1961
***AFL Championship
****AFC Divisional Playoff
*****AFC Championship
NEW ENGLAND vs. SAN FRANCISCO
RS: 49ers lead series, 8-4
1971—49ers, 27-10 (SF)
1975—49ers, 24-16 (NE)
1980—49ers, 21-17 (SF)
1983—49ers, 33-13 (NE)
1986—49ers, 29-24 (NE)
1989—49ers, 37-20 (SF)
1992—49ers, 24-12 (NE)
1995—49ers, 28-3 (SF)
1998—Patriots, 24-21 (NE)
2004—Patriots, 21-7 (NE)
2008—Patriots, 30-21 (SF)
2012—49ers, 41-34 (NE)
(RS Pts.—49ers 305, Patriots 232)
NEW ENGLAND vs. SEATTLE
RS: Series tied, 8-8
1977—Patriots, 31-0 (NE)
1980—Patriots, 37-31 (S)
1982—Patriots, 16-0 (S)
1983—Seahawks, 24-6 (S)
1984—Patriots, 38-23 (NE)
1985—Patriots, 20-13 (S)
1986—Seahawks, 38-31 (NE)
1988—Patriots, 13-7 (NE)
1989—Seahawks, 24-3 (NE)
1990—Seahawks, 33-20 (NE)
1992—Seahawks, 10-6 (NE)
1993—Seahawks, 17-14 (NE)
   Seahawks, 10-9 (S)
2004—Patriots, 30-20 (NE)
2008—Patriots, 24-21 (S)
2012—Seahawks, 24-23 (S)
(RS Pts.—Patriots 321, Seahawks 295)
NEW ENGLAND vs. TAMPA BAY
RS: Patriots lead series, 6-2
1976—Patriots, 31-14 (TB)
1985—Patriots, 32-14 (TB)
1988—Patriots, 10-7 (NE) OT
1997—Buccaneers, 27-7 (TB)
2000—Buccaneers, 21-16 (NE)
2005—Patriots, 28-0 (NE)
2009—Patriots, 35-7 (London)
2013—Patriots, 23-3 (NE)
(RS Pts.—Patriots 182, Buccaneers 93)
NEW ENGLAND vs. **TENNESSEE
RS: Patriots lead series, 22-15-1
PS: Series tied, 1-1
1960—Oilers, 24-10 (B)
   Oilers, 37-21 (H)
1961—Tie, 31-31 (B)
   Oilers, 27-15 (H)
1962—Patriots, 34-21 (B)
   Oilers, 21-17 (H)
1963—Patriots, 45-3 (B)
   Patriots, 46-28 (H)
1964—Patriots, 25-24 (B)
   Patriots, 34-17 (H)
1965—Oilers, 31-10 (H)
   Patriots, 42-14 (B)
1966—Patriots, 27-21 (B)
   Patriots, 38-14 (H)
1967—Patriots, 18-7 (B)
   Oilers, 27-6 (H)
1968—Oilers, 16-0 (B)

   Oilers, 45-17 (H)
1969—Patriots, 24-0 (B)
   Oilers, 27-23 (H)
1971—Patriots, 28-20 (NE)
1973—Patriots, 32-0 (H)
1975—Oilers, 7-0 (NE)
1978—Oilers, 26-23 (NE)
   ***Oilers, 31-14 (NE)
1980—Oilers, 38-34 (NE)
1981—Patriots, 38-10 (NE)
1982—Patriots, 29-21 (NE)
1987—Patriots, 21-7 (H)
1988—Oilers, 31-6 (H)
1989—Patriots, 23-13 (NE)
1991—Patriots, 24-20 (NE)
1993—Oilers, 28-14 (NE)
1998—Patriots, 27-16 (NE)
2002—Titans, 24-7 (T)
2003—Patriots, 38-30 (NE)
   ***Patriots, 17-14 (NE)
2006—Patriots, 40-23 (T)
2009—Patriots, 59-0 (NE)
2012—Patriots, 34-13 (T)
(RS Pts.—Patriots 960, Titans 762)
(PS Pts.—Titans 45, Patriots 31)
*Franchise in Boston prior to 1971
**Franchise in Houston prior to 1997; known as Oilers prior to 1999
***AFC Divisional Playoff
NEW ENGLAND vs. WASHINGTON
RS: Redskins lead series, 6-3
1972—Patriots, 24-23 (NE)
1978—Redskins, 16-14 (NE)
1981—Redskins, 24-22 (W)
1984—Redskins, 26-10 (NE)
1990—Redskins, 25-10 (NE)
1996—Redskins, 27-22 (NE)
2003—Redskins, 20-17 (W)
2007—Patriots, 52-7 (NE)
2011—Patriots, 34-27 (W)
(RS Pts.—Patriots 205, Redskins 195)

NEW ORLEANS vs. ARIZONA
RS: Cardinals lead series, 14-13
PS: Saints lead series, 1-0;
See Arizona vs. New Orleans
NEW ORLEANS vs. ATLANTA
RS: Falcons lead series, 46-43
PS: Falcons lead series, 1-0;
See Atlanta vs. New Orleans
NEW ORLEANS vs. BALTIMORE
RS: Ravens lead series, 4-1;
See Baltimore vs. New Orleans
NEW ORLEANS vs. BUFFALO
RS: Saints lead series, 6-4;
See Buffalo vs. New Orleans
NEW ORLEANS vs. CAROLINA
RS: Panthers lead series, 20-18;
See Carolina vs. New Orleans
NEW ORLEANS vs. CHICAGO
RS: Series tied, 13-13
PS: Bears lead series, 2-0;
See Chicago vs. New Orleans
NEW ORLEANS vs. CINCINNATI
RS: Series tied, 6-6;
See Cincinnati vs. New Orleans
NEW ORLEANS vs. CLEVELAND
RS: Browns lead series, 12-4;
See Cleveland vs. New Orleans
NEW ORLEANS vs. DALLAS
RS: Cowboys lead series, 15-11;
See Dallas vs. New Orleans
NEW ORLEANS vs. DENVER

RS: Broncos lead series, 8-2;
See Denver vs. New Orleans
NEW ORLEANS vs. DETROIT
RS: Saints lead series, 11-9-1
PS: Saints lead series, 1-0;
See Detroit vs. New Orleans
NEW ORLEANS vs. GREEN BAY
RS: Packers lead series, 16-7;
See Green Bay vs. New Orleans
NEW ORLEANS vs. HOUSTON
RS: Saints lead series, 2-1;
See Houston vs. New Orleans
NEW ORLEANS vs. INDIANAPOLIS
RS: Saints lead series, 6-5
PS: Saints lead series, 1-0;
See Indianapolis vs. New Orleans
NEW ORLEANS vs. JACKSONVILLE
RS: Saints lead series, 3-2;
See Jacksonville vs. New Orleans
NEW ORLEANS vs. KANSAS CITY
RS: Series tied, 5-5;
See Kansas City vs. New Orleans
NEW ORLEANS vs. MIAMI
RS: Dolphins lead series, 6-5;
See Miami vs. New Orleans
NEW ORLEANS vs. MINNESOTA
RS: Vikings lead series, 18-9
PS: Vikings lead series, 2-1;
See Minnesota vs. New Orleans
NEW ORLEANS vs. NEW ENGLAND
RS: Patriots lead series, 9-4;
See New England vs. New Orleans
NEW ORLEANS vs. N.Y. GIANTS
RS: Giants lead series, 15-12
1967—Giants, 27-21 (NY)
1968—Giants, 38-21 (NY)
1969—Saints, 25-24 (NY)
1970—Saints, 14-10 (NO)
1972—Giants, 45-21 (NY)
1975—Saints, 28-14 (NY)
1978—Saints, 28-17 (NY)
1979—Saints, 24-14 (NO)
1981—Giants, 20-7 (NY)
1984—Saints, 10-3 (NY)
1985—Giants, 21-13 (NO)
1986—Giants, 20-17 (NY)
1987—Saints, 23-14 (NO)
1988—Giants, 13-12 (NO)
1993—Saints, 24-14 (NO)
1994—Saints, 27-22 (NO)
1995—Giants, 45-29 (NY)
1996—Saints, 17-3 (NY)
1997—Giants, 14-9 (NY)
1999—Giants, 31-3 (NY)
2001—Giants, 21-13 (NY)
2003—Saints, 45-7 (NO)
2005—Giants, 27-10 (NY*)
2006—Saints, 30-7 (NY)
2009—Saints, 48-27 (NO)
2011—Saints, 49-24 (NO)
2012—Giants, 52-27 (NY)
(RS Pts.—Giants 598, Saints 571)
*Saints home game
NEW ORLEANS vs. N.Y. JETS
RS: Series tied, 6-6
1972—Jets, 18-17 (NY)
1977—Jets, 16-13 (NO)
1980—Saints, 21-20 (NY)
1983—Jets, 31-28 (NO)
1986—Jets, 28-23 (NY)
1989—Saints, 29-14 (NO)
1992—Saints, 20-0 (NY)
1995—Saints, 12-0 (NY)

2001—Jets, 16-9 (NO)
2005—Saints, 21-19 (NY)
2009—Saints, 24-10 (NO)
2013—Jets, 26-20 (NY)
(RS Pts.—Saints 237, Jets 198)
NEW ORLEANS vs. *OAKLAND
RS: Saints lead series, 6-5-1
1971—Tie, 21-21 (NO)
1975—Raiders, 48-10 (O)
1979—Raiders, 42-35 (NO)
1985—Raiders, 23-13 (LA)
1988—Saints, 20-6 (NO)
1991—Saints, 27-0 (NO)
1994—Raiders, 24-19 (LA)
1997—Saints, 13-10 (O)
2000—Raiders, 31-22 (NO)
2004—Saints, 31-26 (O)
2008—Saints, 34-3 (NO)
2012—Saints, 38-17 (O)
(RS Pts.—Saints 283, Raiders 251)
*Franchise in Los Angeles from 1982-1994
NEW ORLEANS vs. PHILADELPHIA
RS: Eagles lead series, 15-11
PS: Saints lead series, 2-1
1967—Saints, 31-24 (NO)
    Eagles, 48-21 (P)
1968—Eagles, 29-17 (P)
1969—Eagles, 13-10 (P)
    Saints, 26-17 (NO)
1972—Saints, 21-3 (NO)
1974—Saints, 14-10 (NO)
1977—Eagles, 28-7 (P)
1978—Eagles, 24-17 (NO)
1979—Eagles, 26-14 (NO)
1980—Eagles, 34-21 (NO)
1981—Eagles, 31-14 (NO)
1983—Saints, 20-17 (P) OT
1985—Saints, 23-21 (NO)
1987—Eagles, 27-17 (P)
1989—Saints, 30-20 (NO)
1991—Saints, 13-6 (P)
1992—Eagles, 15-13 (P)
    *Eagles, 36-20 (NO)
1993—Eagles, 37-26 (P)
1995—Eagles, 15-10 (NO)
2000—Saints, 21-7 (NO)
2003—Eagles, 33-20 (P)
2006—Saints, 27-24 (NO)
    **Saints, 27-24 (NO)
2007—Eagles, 38-23 (NO)
2009—Saints, 48-22 (P)
2012—Saints, 28-13 (NO)
2013—*Saints, 26-24 (P)
(RS Pts.—Eagles 596, Saints 518)
(PS Pts.—Eagles 84, Saints 73)
*NFC First-Round Playoff
**NFC Divisional Playoff
NEW ORLEANS vs. PITTSBURGH
RS: Series tied, 7-7
1967—Steelers, 14-10 (NO)
1968—Saints, 16-12 (P)
    Saints, 24-14 (NO)
1969—Saints, 27-24 (NO)
1974—Steelers, 28-7 (NO)
1978—Steelers, 20-14 (P)
1981—Steelers, 20-6 (NO)
1984—Saints, 27-24 (NO)
1987—Saints, 20-16 (P)
1990—Steelers, 9-6 (NO)
1993—Steelers, 37-14 (P)
2002—Saints, 32-29 (NO)
2006—Steelers, 38-31 (P)
2010—Saints, 20-10 (NO)

(RS Pts.—Steelers 295, Saints 254)
NEW ORLEANS vs. *ST. LOUIS
RS: Rams lead series, 40-31
PS: Saints lead series, 1-0
1967—Rams, 27-13 (NO)
1969—Rams, 36-17 (LA)
1970—Rams, 30-17 (NO)
    Rams, 34-16 (LA)
1971—Saints, 24-20 (NO)
    Rams, 45-28 (LA)
1972—Rams, 34-14 (LA)
    Saints, 19-16 (NO)
1973—Rams, 29-7 (LA)
    Rams, 24-13 (NO)
1974—Rams, 24-0 (LA)
    Saints, 20-7 (NO)
1975—Rams, 38-14 (LA)
    Rams, 14-7 (NO)
1976—Rams, 16-10 (NO)
    Rams, 33-14 (LA)
1977—Rams, 14-7 (LA)
    Saints, 27-26 (NO)
1978—Rams, 26-20 (NO)
    Saints, 10-3 (LA)
1979—Rams, 35-17 (NO)
    Saints, 29-14 (LA)
1980—Rams, 45-31 (LA)
    Rams, 27-7 (NO)
1981—Rams, 23-17 (LA)
    Saints, 21-13 (LA)
1983—Rams, 30-27 (LA)
    Rams, 26-24 (NO)
1984—Rams, 28-10 (NO)
    Rams, 34-21 (LA)
1985—Rams, 28-10 (LA)
    Saints, 29-3 (NO)
1986—Saints, 6-0 (NO)
    Rams, 26-13 (LA)
1987—Rams, 37-10 (NO)
    Saints, 31-14 (LA)
1988—Rams, 12-10 (NO)
    Saints, 14-10 (LA)
1989—Saints, 40-21 (LA)
    Rams, 20-17 (NO) OT
1990—Saints, 24-20 (LA)
    Saints, 20-17 (NO)
1991—Saints, 24-7 (NO)
    Saints, 24-17 (LA)
1992—Saints, 13-10 (NO)
    Saints, 37-14 (LA)
1993—Saints, 37-6 (LA)
    Rams, 23-20 (NO)
1994—Saints, 37-34 (NO)
    Saints, 31-15 (LA)
1995—Rams, 17-13 (StL)
    Saints, 19-10 (NO)
1996—Rams, 26-10 (NO)
    Rams, 14-13 (StL)
1997—Rams, 38-24 (StL)
    Rams, 34-27 (NO)
1998—Saints, 24-17 (StL)
    Saints, 24-3 (NO)
1999—Rams, 43-12 (StL)
    Rams, 30-14 (NO)
2000—Saints, 31-24 (NO)
    Rams, 26-21 (NO)
    **Saints, 31-28 (NO)
2001—Saints, 34-31 (StL)
    Rams, 34-21 (NO)
2004—Saints, 28-25 (StL) OT
2005—Rams, 28-17 (StL)
2007—Rams, 37-29 (NO)
2009—Saints, 28-23 (StL)

2010—Saints, 31-13 (NO)
2011—Rams, 31-21 (StL)
2013—Rams, 27-16 (StL)
(RS Pts.—Rams 1,603, Saints 1,438)
(PS Pts.—Saints 31, Rams 28)
*Franchise in Los Angeles prior to 1995
**NFC First-Round Playoff
NEW ORLEANS vs. SAN DIEGO
RS: Chargers lead series, 7-4
1973—Chargers, 17-14 (SD)
1977—Chargers, 14-0 (NO)
1979—Chargers, 35-0 (NO)
1988—Saints, 23-17 (SD)
1991—Chargers, 24-21 (SD)
1994—Chargers, 36-22 (NO)
1997—Chargers, 20-6 (NO)
2000—Saints, 28-27 (SD)
2004—Chargers, 43-17 (SD)
2008—Saints, 37-32 (London)
2012—Saints, 31-24 (NO)
(RS Pts.—Chargers 289, Saints 199)
NEW ORLEANS vs. SAN FRANCISCO
RS: 49ers lead series, 46-25-2
PS: 49ers lead series, 1-0
1967—49ers, 27-13 (SF)
1969—Saints, 43-38 (NO)
1970—Tie, 20-20 (SF)
　　　49ers, 38-27 (NO)
1971—49ers, 38-20 (NO)
　　　Saints, 26-20 (SF)
1972—49ers, 37-2 (NO)
　　　Tie, 20-20 (SF)
1973—49ers, 40-0 (SF)
　　　Saints, 16-10 (NO)
1974—49ers, 17-13 (NO)
　　　49ers, 35-21 (SF)
1975—49ers, 35-21 (SF)
　　　49ers, 16-6 (NO)
1976—49ers, 33-3 (SF)
　　　49ers, 27-7 (NO)
1977—49ers, 10-7 (NO) OT
　　　49ers, 20-17 (SF)
1978—Saints, 14-7 (SF)
　　　Saints, 24-13 (NO)
1979—Saints, 30-21 (SF)
　　　Saints, 31-20 (NO)
1980—49ers, 26-23 (NO)
　　　49ers, 38-35 (SF) OT
1981—49ers, 21-14 (SF)
　　　Saints, 21-17 (NO)
1982—Saints, 23-20 (SF)
1983—49ers, 32-13 (NO)
　　　49ers, 27-0 (SF)
1984—49ers, 30-20 (SF)
　　　49ers, 35-3 (NO)
1985—Saints, 20-17 (SF)
　　　49ers, 31-19 (NO)
1986—49ers, 26-17 (SF)
　　　Saints, 23-10 (NO)
1987—49ers, 24-22 (NO)
　　　Saints, 26-24 (SF)
1988—49ers, 34-33 (NO)
　　　49ers, 30-17 (SF)
1989—49ers, 24-20 (NO)
　　　49ers, 31-13 (SF)
1990—49ers, 13-12 (NO)
　　　Saints, 13-10 (SF)
1991—Saints, 10-3 (NO)
　　　49ers, 38-24 (SF)
1992—49ers, 16-10 (NO)
　　　49ers, 21-20 (SF)
1993—Saints, 16-13 (NO)
　　　49ers, 42-7 (SF)

1994—49ers, 24-13 (SF)
　　　49ers, 35-14 (NO)
1995—49ers, 24-22 (NO)
　　　Saints, 11-7 (SF)
1996—49ers, 27-11 (SF)
　　　49ers, 24-17 (NO)
1997—49ers, 33-7 (SF)
　　　49ers, 23-0 (NO)
1998—49ers, 31-0 (NO)
　　　49ers, 31-20 (SF)
1999—49ers, 28-21 (SF)
　　　Saints, 24-6 (NO)
2000—Saints, 31-15 (NO)
　　　Saints, 31-27 (SF)
2001—49ers, 28-27 (SF)
　　　49ers, 38-0 (NO)
2002—Saints, 35-27 (NO)
2004—Saints, 30-27 (NO)
2006—Saints, 34-10 (NO)
2007—Saints, 31-10 (NO)
2008—Saints, 31-17 (NO)
2010—Saints, 25-22 (SF)
2011—*49ers, 36-32 (SF)
2012—49ers, 31-21 (NO)
2013—Saints, 23-20 (NO)
(RS Pts.—49ers 1,764, Saints 1,330)
(PS Pts.—49ers 36, Saints 32)
*NFC Divisional Playoff
NEW ORLEANS vs. SEATTLE
RS: Series tied, 6-6
PS: Seahawks lead series, 2-0
1976—Saints, 51-27 (S)
1979—Seahawks, 38-24 (S)
1985—Seahawks, 27-3 (NO)
1988—Saints, 20-19 (S)
1991—Saints, 27-24 (NO)
1997—Saints, 20-17 (NO) OT
2000—Seahawks, 20-10 (S)
2003—Seahawks, 27-10 (S)
2004—Seahawks, 21-7 (NO)
2007—Saints, 28-17 (S)
2010—Saints, 34-19 (NO)
　　　*Seahawks, 41-36 (S)
2013—Seahawks, 34-7 (S)
　　　**Seahawks, 23-15 (S)
(RS Pts.—Seahawks 290, Saints 241)
(PS Pts.—Seahawks 64, Saints 51)
*NFC First-Round Playoff
**NFC Divisional Playoff
NEW ORLEANS vs. TAMPA BAY
RS: Saints lead series, 27-17
1977—Buccaneers, 33-14 (NO)
1978—Saints, 17-10 (TB)
1979—Saints, 42-14 (TB)
1981—Buccaneers, 31-14 (NO)
1982—Buccaneers, 13-10 (NO)
1983—Saints, 24-21 (TB)
1984—Saints, 17-13 (NO)
1985—Saints, 20-13 (NO)
1986—Saints, 38-7 (NO)
1987—Saints, 44-34 (NO)
1988—Saints, 13-9 (NO)
1989—Buccaneers, 20-10 (TB)
1990—Saints, 35-7 (NO)
1991—Saints, 23-7 (NO)
1992—Saints, 23-21 (NO)
1994—Saints, 9-7 (NO)
1996—Buccaneers, 13-7 (TB)
1998—Saints, 9-3 (NO)
1999—Buccaneers, 31-16 (NO)
2001—Buccaneers, 48-21 (TB)
2002—Saints, 26-20 (TB) OT
　　　Saints, 23-20 (NO)

2003—Saints, 17-14 (TB)
　　　Buccaneers, 14-7 (NO)
2004—Buccaneers, 20-17 (NO)
　　　Saints, 21-17 (TB)
2005—Buccaneers, 10-3 (Baton Rouge)
　　　Buccaneers, 27-13 (TB)
2006—Saints, 24-21 (NO)
　　　Saints, 31-14 (TB)
2007—Buccaneers, 31-14 (TB)
　　　Buccaneers, 27-23 (NO)
2008—Saints, 24-20 (NO)
　　　Buccaneers, 23-20 (TB)
2009—Saints, 38-7 (TB)
　　　Buccaneers, 20-17 (NO) OT
2010—Saints, 31-6 (TB)
　　　Buccaneers, 23-13 (NO)
2011—Buccaneers, 26-20 (TB)
　　　Saints, 27-16 (NO)
2012—Saints, 35-28 (TB)
　　　Saints, 41-0 (NO)
2013—Saints, 16-14 (TB)
　　　Saints, 42-17 (NO)
(RS Pts.—Saints 949, Buccaneers 790)
NEW ORLEANS vs. *TENNESSEE
RS: Titans lead series, 7-5-1
1971—Tie, 13-13 (H)
1976—Oilers, 31-26 (NO)
1978—Oilers, 17-12 (NO)
1981—Saints, 27-24 (H)
1984—Saints, 27-10 (H)
1987—Saints, 24-10 (NO)
1990—Oilers, 23-10 (H)
1993—Saints, 33-21 (NO)
1996—Oilers, 31-14 (NO)
1999—Titans, 24-21 (NO)
2003—Titans, 27-12 (T)
2007—Titans, 31-14 (NO)
2011—Saints, 22-17 (T)
(RS Pts.—Titans 279, Saints 255)
*Franchise in Houston prior to 1997;
known as Oilers prior to 1999
NEW ORLEANS vs. WASHINGTON
RS: Redskins lead series, 16-8
1967—Redskins, 30-10 (NO)
　　　Saints, 30-14 (W)
1968—Saints, 37-17 (NO)
1969—Redskins, 26-20 (NO)
　　　Redskins, 17-14 (W)
1971—Redskins, 24-14 (W)
1973—Saints, 19-3 (NO)
1975—Redskins, 41-3 (W)
1979—Saints, 14-10 (W)
1980—Redskins, 22-14 (W)
1982—Redskins, 27-10 (NO)
1986—Redskins, 14-6 (NO)
1988—Redskins, 27-24 (W)
1989—Redskins, 16-14 (W)
1990—Redskins, 31-17 (W)
1992—Saints, 20-3 (NO)
1994—Redskins, 38-24 (NO)
2001—Redskins, 40-10 (NO)
2002—Saints, 43-27 (W)
2003—Saints, 24-20 (W)
2006—Redskins, 16-10 (NO)
2008—Redskins, 29-24 (W)
2009—Saints, 33-30 (W) OT
2012—Redskins, 40-32 (NO)
(RS Pts.—Redskins 562, Saints 466)

N.Y. GIANTS vs. ARIZONA
RS: Giants lead series, 80-42-2;
See Arizona vs. N.Y. Giants
N.Y. GIANTS vs. ATLANTA

RS: Falcons lead series, 11-10
PS: Giants lead series, 1-0;
See Atlanta vs. N.Y. Giants
N.Y. GIANTS vs. BALTIMORE
RS: Ravens lead series, 3-1
PS: Ravens lead series, 1-0;
See Baltimore vs. N.Y. Giants
N.Y. GIANTS vs. BUFFALO
RS: Bills lead series, 6-5
PS: Giants lead series, 1-0;
See Buffalo vs. N.Y. Giants
N.Y. GIANTS vs. CAROLINA
RS: Series tied, 4-4
PS: Panthers lead series, 1-0;
See Carolina vs. N.Y. Giants
N.Y. GIANTS vs. CHICAGO
RS: Bears lead series, 28-19-2
PS: Bears lead series, 5-3;
See Chicago vs. N.Y. Giants
N.Y. GIANTS vs. CINCINNATI
RS: Bengals lead series, 6-3;
See Cincinnati vs. N.Y. Giants
N.Y. GIANTS vs. CLEVELAND
RS: Browns lead series, 26-20-2
PS: Series tied, 1-1;
See Cleveland vs. N.Y. Giants
N.Y. GIANTS vs. DALLAS
RS: Cowboys lead series, 59-42-2
PS: Giants lead series, 1-0;
See Dallas vs. N.Y. Giants
N.Y. GIANTS vs. DENVER
RS: Broncos lead series, 6-5
PS: Giants lead series, 1-0;
See Denver vs. N.Y. Giants
N.Y. GIANTS vs. DETROIT
RS: Series tied, 20-20-1
PS: Lions lead series, 1-0;
See Detroit vs. N.Y. Giants
N.Y. GIANTS vs. GREEN BAY
RS: Packers lead series, 27-23-2
PS: Packers lead series, 4-3;
See Green Bay vs. N.Y. Giants
N.Y. GIANTS vs. HOUSTON
RS: Giants lead series, 2-1;
See Houston vs. N.Y. Giants
N.Y. GIANTS vs. INDIANAPOLIS
RS: Colts lead series, 8-6
PS: Colts lead series, 2-0;
See Indianapolis vs. N.Y. Giants
N.Y. GIANTS vs. JACKSONVILLE
RS: Giants lead series, 3-2;
See Jacksonville vs. N.Y. Giants
N.Y. GIANTS vs. KANSAS CITY
RS: Giants lead series, 10-3;
See Kansas City vs. N.Y. Giants
N.Y. GIANTS vs. MIAMI
RS: Giants lead series, 5-2;
See Miami vs. N.Y. Giants
N.Y. GIANTS vs. MINNESOTA
RS: Vikings lead series, 13-10
PS: Giants lead series, 2-1;
See Minnesota vs. N.Y. Giants
N.Y. GIANTS vs. NEW ENGLAND
RS: Patriots lead series, 5-4
PS: Giants lead series, 2-0;
See New England vs. N.Y. Giants
N.Y. GIANTS vs. NEW ORLEANS
RS: Giants lead series, 15-12;
See New Orleans vs. N.Y. Giants
N.Y. GIANTS vs. N.Y. JETS
RS: Giants lead series, 8-4
1970—Giants, 22-10 (NYJ)
1974—Jets, 26-20 (New Haven) OT

1981—Jets, 26-7 (NYG)
1984—Giants, 20-10 (NYJ)
1987—Giants, 20-7 (NYG)
1988—Jets, 27-21 (NYJ)
1993—Jets, 10-6 (NYG)
1996—Giants, 13-6 (NYJ)
1999—Giants, 41-28 (NYG)
2003—Giants, 31-28 (NYJ) OT
2007—Giants, 35-24 (NYG)
2011—Giants, 29-14 (NYJ)
(RS Pts.—Giants 265, Jets 216)
N.Y. GIANTS vs. *OAKLAND
RS: Raiders lead series, 7-5
1973—Raiders, 42-0 (O)
1980—Raiders, 33-17 (NY)
1983—Raiders, 27-12 (LA)
1986—Giants, 14-9 (LA)
1989—Giants, 34-17 (NY)
1992—Raiders, 13-10 (LA)
1995—Raiders, 17-13 (NY)
1998—Raiders, 20-17 (O)
2001—Raiders, 28-10 (NY)
2005—Giants, 30-21 (O)
2009—Giants, 44-7 (NY)
2013—Giants, 24-20 (NY)
(RS Pts.—Raiders 254, Giants 225)
Franchise in Los Angeles from 1982-1994
N.Y. GIANTS vs. PHILADELPHIA
RS: Giants lead series, 82-74-2
PS: Series tied, 2-2
1933—Giants, 56-0 (NY)
        Giants, 20-14 (P)
1934—Giants, 17-0 (NY)
        Eagles, 6-0 (P)
1935—Giants, 10-0 (NY)
        Giants, 21-14 (P)
1936—Eagles, 10-7 (P)
        Giants, 21-17 (NY)
1937—Giants, 16-7 (P)
        Giants, 21-0 (NY)
1938—Eagles, 14-10 (P)
        Giants, 17-7 (NY)
1939—Giants, 13-3 (P)
        Giants, 27-10 (NY)
1940—Giants, 20-14 (P)
        Giants, 17-7 (NY)
1941—Giants, 24-0 (NY)
        Giants, 16-0 (P)
1942—Giants, 35-17 (NY)
        Giants, 14-0 (P)
1944—Eagles, 24-17 (NY)
        Tie, 21-21 (P)
1945—Eagles, 38-17 (P)
        Giants, 28-21 (NY)
1946—Eagles, 24-14 (P)
        Giants, 45-17 (NY)
1947—Eagles, 23-0 (P)
        Eagles, 41-24 (NY)
1948—Eagles, 45-0 (P)
        Eagles, 35-14 (NY)
1949—Eagles, 24-3 (NY)
        Eagles, 17-3 (P)
1950—Giants, 7-3 (NY)
        Giants, 9-7 (P)
1951—Giants, 26-24 (NY)
        Giants, 23-7 (P)
1952—Giants, 31-7 (P)
        Eagles, 14-10 (NY)
1953—Eagles, 30-7 (P)
        Giants, 37-28 (NY)
1954—Giants, 27-14 (NY)
        Eagles, 29-14 (P)
1955—Eagles, 27-17 (P)

        Giants, 31-7 (NY)
1956—Giants, 20-3 (NY)
        Giants, 21-7 (P)
1957—Giants, 24-20 (P)
        Giants, 13-0 (NY)
1958—Eagles, 27-24 (P)
        Giants, 24-10 (NY)
1959—Eagles, 49-21 (P)
        Giants, 24-7 (NY)
1960—Eagles, 17-10 (NY)
        Eagles, 31-23 (P)
1961—Giants, 38-21 (NY)
        Giants, 28-24 (P)
1962—Giants, 29-13 (P)
        Giants, 19-14 (NY)
1963—Giants, 37-14 (P)
        Giants, 42-14 (NY)
1964—Eagles, 38-7 (P)
        Eagles, 23-17 (NY)
1965—Giants, 16-14 (P)
        Giants, 35-27 (NY)
1966—Eagles, 35-17 (P)
        Eagles, 31-3 (NY)
1967—Giants, 44-7 (NY)
1968—Giants, 34-25 (P)
        Giants, 7-6 (NY)
1969—Eagles, 23-20 (NY)
1970—Giants, 30-23 (NY)
        Eagles, 23-20 (P)
1971—Eagles, 23-7 (P)
        Eagles, 41-28 (NY)
1972—Giants, 27-12 (P)
        Giants, 62-10 (NY)
1973—Tie, 23-23 (NY)
        Giants, 20-16 (P)
1974—Eagles, 35-7 (P)
        Eagles, 20-7 (New Haven)
1975—Giants, 23-14 (P)
        Eagles, 13-10 (NY)
1976—Eagles, 20-7 (P)
        Giants, 10-0 (NY)
1977—Eagles, 28-10 (NY)
        Eagles, 17-14 (P)
1978—Eagles, 19-17 (NY)
        Eagles, 20-3 (P)
1979—Eagles, 23-17 (P)
        Eagles, 17-13 (NY)
1980—Eagles, 35-3 (P)
        Eagles, 31-16 (NY)
1981—Eagles, 24-10 (NY)
        Giants, 20-10 (P)
        *Giants, 27-21 (P)
1982—Giants, 23-7 (NY)
        Giants, 26-24 (P)
1983—Eagles, 17-13 (NY)
        Giants, 23-0 (P)
1984—Giants, 28-27 (NY)
        Eagles, 24-10 (P)
1985—Giants, 21-0 (NY)
        Giants, 16-10 (P) OT
1986—Giants, 35-3 (P)
        Giants, 17-14 (P)
1987—Giants, 20-17 (P)
        Giants, 23-20 (NY) OT
1988—Eagles, 24-13 (P)
        Eagles, 23-17 (NY) OT
1989—Eagles, 21-19 (P)
        Eagles, 24-17 (NY)
1990—Giants, 27-20 (NY)
        Eagles, 31-13 (P)
1991—Eagles, 30-7 (P)
        Eagles, 19-14 (NY)
1992—Eagles, 47-34 (NY)

Eagles, 20-10 (P)
1993—Giants, 21-10 (NY)
Giants, 7-3 (P)
1994—Giants, 28-23 (NY)
Giants, 16-13 (P)
1995—Eagles, 17-14 (NY)
Eagles, 28-19 (P)
1996—Eagles, 19-10 (NY)
Eagles, 24-0 (P)
1997—Giants, 31-17 (NY)
Giants, 31-21 (P)
1998—Giants, 20-0 (NY)
Giants, 20-10 (P)
1999—Giants, 16-15 (NY)
Giants, 23-17 (P) OT
2000—Giants, 33-18 (P)
Giants, 24-7 (NY)
**Giants, 20-10 (NY)
2001—Eagles, 10-9 (NY)
Eagles, 24-21 (P)
2002—Eagles, 17-3 (P)
Giants, 10-7 (NY) OT
2003—Eagles, 14-10 (NY)
Eagles, 28-10 (P)
2004—Eagles, 31-17 (P)
Eagles, 27-6 (NY)
2005—Giants, 27-17 (NY)
Giants, 26-23 (P) OT
2006—Giants, 30-24 (P) OT
Eagles, 36-22 (NY)
*Eagles, 23-20 (P)
2007—Giants, 16-3 (NY)
Giants, 16-13 (P)
2008—Giants, 36-31 (P)
Eagles, 20-14 (NY)
**Eagles, 23-11 (NY)
2009—Eagles, 40-17 (P)
Eagles, 45-38 (NY)
2010—Eagles, 27-17 (NY)
Eagles, 38-31 (NY)
2011—Giants, 29-16 (P)
Eagles, 17-10 (NY)
2012—Eagles, 19-17 (P)
Giants, 42-7 (NY)
2013—Eagles, 36-21 (NY)
Giants, 15-7 (P)
(RS Pts.—Giants 3,043, Eagles 2,919)
(PS Pts.—Giants 78, Eagles 77)
*NFC First-Round Playoff
**NFC Divisional Playoff
N.Y. GIANTS vs. *PITTSBURGH
RS: Giants lead series, 44-29-3
1933—Giants, 23-2 (P)
Giants, 27-3 (NY)
1934—Giants, 14-12 (P)
Giants, 17-7 (NY)
1935—Giants, 42-7 (P)
Giants, 13-0 (NY)
1936—Pirates, 10-7 (P)
1937—Giants, 10-7 (P)
Giants, 17-0 (NY)
1938—Giants, 27-14 (P)
Pirates, 13-10 (NY)
1939—Giants, 14-7 (P)
Giants, 23-7 (NY)
1940—Tie, 10-10 (P)
Giants, 12-0 (NY)
1941—Giants, 37-10 (P)
Giants, 28-7 (NY)
1942—Steelers, 13-10 (P)
Steelers, 17-9 (NY)
1945—Giants, 34-6 (P)
Steelers, 21-7 (NY)

1946—Giants, 17-14 (P)
Giants, 7-0 (NY)
1947—Steelers, 38-21 (NY)
Steelers, 24-7 (P)
1948—Giants, 34-27 (NY)
Steelers, 38-28 (P)
1949—Steelers, 28-7 (P)
Steelers, 21-17 (NY)
1950—Giants, 18-7 (P)
Steelers, 17-6 (NY)
1951—Tie, 13-13 (P)
Giants, 14-0 (NY)
1952—Steelers, 63-7 (P)
1953—Steelers, 24-14 (P)
Steelers, 14-10 (NY)
1954—Giants, 30-6 (P)
Giants, 24-3 (NY)
1955—Steelers, 30-23 (P)
Steelers, 19-17 (NY)
1956—Giants, 38-10 (NY)
Giants, 17-14 (P)
1957—Giants, 35-0 (NY)
Steelers, 21-10 (P)
1958—Giants, 17-6 (NY)
Steelers, 31-10 (P)
1959—Giants, 21-16 (P)
Steelers, 14-9 (NY)
1960—Giants, 19-17 (P)
Giants, 27-24 (NY)
1961—Giants, 17-14 (P)
Giants, 42-21 (NY)
1962—Giants, 31-27 (P)
Steelers, 20-17 (NY)
1963—Steelers, 31-0 (P)
Giants, 33-17 (NY)
1964—Steelers, 27-24 (P)
Steelers, 44-17 (NY)
1965—Giants, 23-13 (P)
Giants, 35-10 (NY)
1966—Tie, 34-34 (P)
Steelers, 47-28 (NY)
1967—Giants, 27-24 (P)
Giants, 28-20 (NY)
1968—Giants, 34-20 (P)
1969—Giants, 10-7 (NY)
Giants, 21-17 (P)
1971—Steelers, 17-13 (P)
1976—Steelers, 27-0 (NY)
1985—Giants, 28-10 (NY)
1991—Giants, 23-20 (P)
1994—Steelers, 10-6 (NY)
2000—Giants, 30-10 (NY)
2004—Steelers, 33-30 (NY)
2008—Giants, 21-14 (P)
2012—Steelers, 24-20 (NY)
(RS Pts.—Giants 1,500, Steelers 1,270)
*Steelers known as Pirates prior to 1940
N.Y. GIANTS vs. *ST. LOUIS
RS: Rams lead series, 25-14
PS: Series tied, 1-1
1938—Giants, 28-0 (NY)
1940—Rams, 13-0 (NY)
1941—Giants, 49-14 (NY)
1945—Rams, 21-17 (NY)
1946—Rams, 31-21 (NY)
1947—Rams, 34-10 (LA)
1948—Rams, 52-37 (NY)
1953—Rams, 21-7 (LA)
1954—Rams, 17-16 (NY)
1959—Giants, 23-21 (LA)
1961—Giants, 24-14 (LA)
1966—Rams, 55-14 (LA)
1968—Rams, 24-21 (LA)

1970—Rams, 31-3 (NY)
1973—Rams, 40-6 (LA)
1976—Rams, 24-10 (LA)
1978—Rams, 20-17 (NY)
1979—Giants, 20-14 (LA)
1980—Rams, 28-7 (NY)
1981—Giants, 10-7 (NY)
1983—Rams, 16-6 (NY)
1984—Rams, 33-12 (LA)
**Giants, 16-13 (LA)
1985—Giants, 24-19 (NY)
1988—Rams, 45-31 (NY)
1989—Rams, 31-10 (LA)
***Rams, 19-13 (NY) OT
1990—Giants, 31-7 (LA)
1991—Rams, 19-13 (LA)
1992—Rams, 38-17 (LA)
1993—Giants, 20-10 (NY)
1994—Rams, 17-10 (LA)
1997—Rams, 13-3 (StL)
1999—Rams, 31-10 (NY)
2000—Rams, 38-24 (NY)
2001—Rams, 15-14 (StL)
2002—Rams, 26-21 (StL)
2003—Giants, 23-13 (NY)
2005—Giants, 44-24 (NY)
2008—Giants, 41-13 (StL)
2011—Giants, 28-16 (NY)
(RS Pts.—Rams 900, Giants 727)
(PS Pts.—Rams 32, Giants 29)
*Franchise in Los Angeles prior to 1995
and in Cleveland prior to 1946
**NFC First-Round Playoff
***NFC Divisional Playoff
N.Y. GIANTS vs. SAN DIEGO
RS: Chargers lead series, 6-5
1971—Giants, 35-17 (NY)
1975—Giants, 35-24 (NY)
1980—Chargers, 44-7 (SD)
1983—Chargers, 41-34 (NY)
1986—Giants, 20-7 (NY)
1989—Giants, 20-13 (SD)
1995—Chargers, 27-17 (NY)
1998—Giants, 34-16 (SD)
2005—Chargers, 45-23 (SD)
2009—Chargers, 21-20 (NY)
2013—Chargers, 37-14 (SD)
(RS Pts.—Chargers 292, Giants 259)
N.Y. GIANTS vs. SAN FRANCISCO
RS: Giants lead series, 15-14
PS: Series tied, 4-4
1952—Giants, 23-14 (NY)
1956—Giants, 38-21 (SF)
1957—49ers, 27-17 (NY)
1960—Giants, 21-19 (SF)
1963—Giants, 48-14 (NY)
1968—49ers, 26-10 (NY)
1972—Giants, 23-17 (SF)
1975—Giants, 26-23 (SF)
1977—Giants, 20-17 (NY)
1978—Giants, 27-10 (NY)
1979—Giants, 32-16 (NY)
1980—49ers, 12-0 (SF)
1981—49ers, 17-10 (NY)
*49ers, 38-24 (SF)
1984—49ers, 31-10 (NY)
*49ers, 21-10 (SF)
1985—**Giants, 17-3 (NY)
1986—Giants, 21-17 (SF)
*Giants, 49-3 (NY)
1987—49ers, 41-21 (NY)
1988—49ers, 20-17 (NY)
1989—49ers, 34-24 (SF)

1990—49ers, 7-3 (SF)
***Giants, 15-13 (SF)
1991—Giants, 16-14 (NY)
1992—49ers, 31-14 (NY)
1993—*49ers, 44-3 (SF)
1995—49ers, 20-6 (SF)
1998—49ers, 31-7 (SF)
2002—Giants, 16-13 (NY)
**49ers, 39-38 (SF)
2005—Giants, 24-6 (SF)
2007—Giants, 33-15 (NY)
2008—Giants, 29-17 (NY)
2011—49ers, 27-20 (SF)
***Giants, 20-17 (SF) OT
2012—Giants, 26-3 (SF)
(RS Pts.—Giants 579, 49ers 563)
(PS Pts.—49ers 178, Giants 176)
*NFC Divisional Playoff
**NFC First-Round Playoff
***NFC Championship

N.Y. GIANTS vs. SEATTLE
RS: Giants lead series, 9-7
1976—Giants, 28-16 (NY)
1980—Giants, 27-21 (S)
1981—Giants, 32-0 (S)
1983—Seahawks, 17-12 (NY)
1986—Seahawks, 17-12 (S)
1989—Giants, 15-3 (NY)
1992—Giants, 23-10 (NY)
1995—Seahawks, 30-28 (S)
2001—Giants, 27-24 (NY)
2002—Giants, 9-6 (NY)
2005—Seahawks, 24-21 (S) OT
2006—Seahawks, 42-30 (S)
2008—Giants, 44-6 (NY)
2010—Giants, 41-7 (S)
2011—Seahawks, 36-25 (NY)
2013—Seahawks, 23-0 (NY)
(RS Pts.—Giants 374, Seahawks 282)

N.Y. GIANTS vs. TAMPA BAY
RS: Giants lead series, 12-6
PS: Giants lead series, 1-0
1977—Giants, 10-0 (TB)
1978—Giants, 19-13 (TB)
Giants, 17-14 (NY)
1979—Giants, 17-14 (NY)
Buccaneers, 31-3 (TB)
1980—Buccaneers, 30-13 (TB)
1984—Giants, 17-14 (NY)
Buccaneers, 20-17 (TB)
1985—Giants, 22-20 (NY)
1991—Giants, 21-14 (TB)
1993—Giants, 23-7 (NY)
1997—Buccaneers, 20-8 (NY)
1998—Buccaneers, 20-3 (TB)
1999—Giants, 17-13 (NY)
2003—Buccaneers, 19-13 (TB)
2006—Giants, 17-3 (NY)
2007—*Giants, 24-14 (TB)
2009—Giants, 24-0 (TB)
2012—Giants, 41-34 (NY)
(RS Pts.—Giants 302, Buccaneers 286)
(PS Pts.—Giants 24, Buccaneers 14)
*NFC First-Round Playoff

N.Y. GIANTS vs. *TENNESSEE
RS: Series tied, 5-5
1973—Giants, 34-14 (NY)
1982—Giants, 17-14 (NY)
1985—Giants, 35-14 (H)
1991—Giants, 24-20 (NY)
1994—Giants, 13-10 (H)
1997—Oilers, 10-6 (T)
2000—Titans, 28-14 (T)

2002—Titans, 32-29 (NY) OT
2006—Titans, 24-21 (T)
2010—Titans, 29-10 (NY)
(RS Pts.—Giants 203, Titans 195)
*Franchise in Houston prior to 1997;
known as Oilers prior to 1999

N.Y. GIANTS vs. *WASHINGTON
RS: Giants lead series, 94-64-4
PS: Series tied, 1-1
1932—Braves, 14-6 (B)
Tie, 0-0 (NY)
1933—Redskins, 21-20 (B)
Giants, 7-0 (NY)
1934—Giants, 16-13 (B)
Giants, 3-0 (NY)
1935—Giants, 20-12 (B)
Giants, 17-6 (NY)
1936—Giants, 7-0 (B)
Redskins, 14-0 (NY)
1937—Redskins, 13-3 (W)
Redskins, 49-14 (NY)
1938—Giants, 10-7 (W)
Giants, 36-0 (NY)
1939—Tie, 0-0 (W)
Giants, 9-7 (NY)
1940—Redskins, 21-7 (W)
Giants, 21-7 (NY)
1941—Giants, 17-10 (W)
Giants, 20-13 (NY)
1942—Giants, 14-7 (W)
Redskins, 14-7 (NY)
1943—Giants, 14-10 (NY)
Giants, 31-7 (W)
**Redskins, 28-0 (NY)
1944—Giants, 16-13 (NY)
Giants, 31-0 (W)
1945—Redskins, 24-14 (NY)
Redskins, 17-0 (W)
1946—Redskins, 24-14 (W)
Giants, 31-0 (NY)
1947—Redskins, 28-20 (W)
Giants, 35-10 (NY)
1948—Redskins, 41-10 (W)
Redskins, 28-21 (NY)
1949—Giants, 45-35 (W)
Giants, 23-7 (NY)
1950—Giants, 21-17 (W)
Giants, 24-21 (NY)
1951—Giants, 35-14 (W)
Giants, 28-14 (NY)
1952—Giants, 14-10 (W)
Redskins, 27-17 (NY)
1953—Redskins, 13-9 (W)
Redskins, 24-21 (NY)
1954—Giants, 51-21 (W)
Giants, 24-7 (NY)
1955—Giants, 35-7 (W)
Giants, 27-20 (W)
1956—Redskins, 33-7 (W)
Giants, 28-14 (NY)
1957—Giants, 24-20 (W)
Redskins, 31-14 (NY)
1958—Giants, 21-14 (W)
Giants, 30-0 (NY)
1959—Giants, 45-14 (NY)
Giants, 24-10 (W)
1960—Tie, 24-24 (NY)
Giants, 17-3 (W)
1961—Giants, 24-21 (W)
Giants, 53-0 (NY)
1962—Giants, 49-34 (NY)
Giants, 42-24 (W)
1963—Giants, 24-14 (W)

Giants, 44-14 (NY)
1964—Giants, 13-10 (NY)
Redskins, 36-21 (W)
1965—Redskins, 23-7 (NY)
Giants, 27-10 (W)
1966—Giants, 13-10 (NY)
Redskins, 72-41 (W)
1967—Redskins, 38-34 (W)
Giants, 13-10 (NY)
1968—Giants, 48-21 (NY)
Giants, 13-10 (W)
1969—Redskins, 20-14 (W)
1970—Giants, 35-33 (NY)
Giants, 27-24 (W)
1971—Redskins, 30-3 (NY)
Redskins, 23-7 (W)
1972—Redskins, 23-16 (NY)
Redskins, 27-13 (W)
1973—Redskins, 21-3 (New Haven)
Redskins, 27-24 (W)
1974—Redskins, 13-10 (New Haven)
Redskins, 24-3 (W)
1975—Redskins, 49-13 (W)
Redskins, 21-13 (NY)
1976—Redskins, 19-17 (W)
Giants, 12-9 (NY)
1977—Giants, 20-17 (NY)
Giants, 17-6 (W)
1978—Giants, 17-6 (NY)
Redskins, 16-13 (W) OT
1979—Redskins, 27-0 (W)
Giants, 14-6 (NY)
1980—Redskins, 23-21 (NY)
Redskins, 16-13 (W)
1981—Giants, 17-7 (W)
Redskins, 30-27 (NY) OT
1982—Redskins, 27-17 (NY)
Redskins, 15-14 (W)
1983—Redskins, 33-17 (NY)
Redskins, 31-22 (W)
1984—Redskins, 30-14 (W)
Giants, 37-13 (NY)
1985—Giants, 17-3 (NY)
Redskins, 23-21 (W)
1986—Giants, 27-20 (NY)
Giants, 24-14 (W)
***Giants, 17-0 (NY)
1987—Giants, 38-12 (NY)
Redskins, 23-19 (W)
1988—Giants, 27-20 (NY)
Giants, 24-23 (W)
1989—Giants, 27-24 (NY)
Giants, 20-17 (W)
1990—Giants, 24-20 (W)
Giants, 21-10 (NY)
1991—Redskins, 17-13 (NY)
Redskins, 34-17 (W)
1992—Giants, 24-7 (W)
Redskins, 28-10 (NY)
1993—Giants, 41-7 (W)
Giants, 20-6 (NY)
1994—Giants, 31-23 (NY)
Giants, 21-19 (W)
1995—Giants, 24-15 (NY)
Giants, 20-13 (W)
1996—Redskins, 31-10 (NY)
Redskins, 31-21 (W)
1997—Tie, 7-7 (W) OT
Giants, 30-10 (NY)
1998—Giants, 31-24 (NY)
Redskins, 21-14 (W)
1999—Redskins, 50-21 (NY)
Redskins, 23-13 (W)
2000—Redskins, 16-6 (NY)

Giants, 9-7 (W)
2001—Giants, 23-9 (NY)
Redskins, 35-21 (W)
2002—Giants, 19-17 (NY)
Giants, 27-21 (W)
2003—Giants, 24-21 (W) OT
Redskins, 20-7 (NY)
2004—Giants, 20-14 (NY)
Redskins, 31-7 (W)
2005—Giants, 36-0 (NY)
Redskins, 35-20 (W)
2006—Giants, 19-3 (NY)
Giants, 34-28 (W)
2007—Giants, 24-17 (W)
Redskins, 22-10 (NY)
2008—Giants, 16-7 (NY)
Giants, 23-7 (W)
2009—Giants, 23-17 (NY)
Giants, 45-12 (W)
2010—Giants, 31-7 (NY)
Giants, 17-14 (W)
2011—Redskins, 28-14 (W)
Redskins, 23-10 (NY)
2012—Giants, 27-23 (NY)
Redskins, 17-16 (W)
2013—Giants, 24-17 (W)
Giants, 20-6 (NY)
(RS Pts.—Giants 3,245, Redskins 2,908)
(PS Pts.—Redskins 28, Giants 17)
*Franchise in Boston prior to 1937 and
known as Braves prior to 1933
**Division Playoff
***NFC Championship

N.Y. JETS vs. ARIZONA
RS: Jets lead series, 6-2;
See Arizona vs. N.Y. Jets
N.Y. JETS vs. ATLANTA
RS: Falcons lead series, 6-5;
See Atlanta vs. N.Y. Jets
N.Y. JETS vs. BALTIMORE
RS: Ravens lead series, 8-1;
See Baltimore vs. N.Y. Jets
N.Y. JETS vs. BUFFALO
RS: Bills lead series, 55-51
PS: Bills lead series, 1-0;
See Buffalo vs. N.Y. Jets
N.Y. JETS vs. CAROLINA
RS: Series tied, 3-3;
See Carolina vs. N.Y. Jets
N.Y. JETS vs. CHICAGO
RS: Bears lead series, 7-3;
See Chicago vs. N.Y. Jets
N.Y. JETS vs. CINCINNATI
RS: Jets lead series, 15-8
PS: Jets lead series, 2-0;
See Cincinnati vs. N.Y. Jets
N.Y. JETS vs. CLEVELAND
RS: Browns lead series, 12-9
PS: Browns lead series, 1-0;
See Cleveland vs. N.Y. Jets
N.Y. JETS vs. DALLAS
RS: Cowboys lead series, 7-3;
See Dallas vs. N.Y. Jets
N.Y. JETS vs. DENVER
RS: Broncos lead series, 17-15-1
PS: Broncos lead series, 1-0;
See Denver vs. N.Y. Jets
N.Y. JETS vs. DETROIT
RS: Series tied, 6-6;
See Detroit vs. N.Y. Jets
N.Y. JETS vs. GREEN BAY
RS: Jets lead series, 8-3;

See Green Bay vs. N.Y. Jets
N.Y. JETS vs. HOUSTON
RS: Jets lead series, 5-1;
See Houston vs. N.Y. Jets
N.Y. JETS vs. INDIANAPOLIS
RS: Colts lead series, 40-27
PS: Jets lead series, 3-1;
See Indianapolis vs. N.Y. Jets
N.Y. JETS vs. JACKSONVILLE
RS: Jaguars lead series, 6-4
PS: Jets lead series, 1-0;
See Jacksonville vs. N.Y. Jets
N.Y. JETS vs. KANSAS CITY
RS: Jets lead series, 17-16-1
PS: Series tied, 1-1;
See Kansas City vs. N.Y. Jets
N.Y. JETS vs. MIAMI
RS: Jets lead series, 50-45-1
PS: Dolphins lead series, 1-0;
See Miami vs. N.Y. Jets
N.Y. JETS vs. MINNESOTA
RS: Jets lead series, 8-1;
See Minnesota vs. N.Y. Jets
N.Y. JETS vs. NEW ENGLAND
RS: Patriots lead series, 54-52-1
PS: Patriots lead series, 2-1;
See New England vs. N.Y. Jets
N.Y. JETS vs. NEW ORLEANS
RS: Series tied, 6-6;
See New Orleans vs. N.Y. Jets
N.Y. JETS vs. N.Y. GIANTS
RS: Giants lead series, 8-4;
See N.Y. Giants vs. N.Y. Jets
*N.Y. JETS vs. **OAKLAND
RS: Raiders lead series, 21-16-2
PS: Series tied, 2-2
1960—Raiders, 28-27 (NY)
Titans, 31-28 (NY)
1961—Titans, 14-6 (O)
Titans, 23-12 (NY)
1962—Titans, 28-17 (O)
Titans, 31-21 (NY)
1963—Jets, 10-7 (NY)
Raiders, 49-26 (O)
1964—Jets, 35-13 (NY)
Raiders, 35-26 (O)
1965—Tie, 24-24 (NY)
Raiders, 24-14 (O)
1966—Raiders, 24-21 (NY)
Tie, 28-28 (O)
1967—Jets, 27-14 (NY)
Raiders, 38-29 (O)
1968—Raiders, 43-32 (O)
***Jets, 27-23 (NY)
1969—Raiders, 27-14 (NY)
1970—Raiders, 14-13 (NY)
1972—Raiders, 24-16 (O)
1977—Raiders, 28-27 (NY)
1979—Jets, 28-19 (NY)
1982—*****Jets, 17-14 (LA)
1985—Raiders, 31-0 (LA)
1989—Raiders, 14-7 (NY)
1993—Raiders, 24-20 (LA)
1995—Raiders, 47-10 (NY)
1996—Raiders, 34-13 (NY)
1997—Jets 23-22 (NY)
1999—Raiders, 24-23 (O)
2000—Raiders, 31-7 (O)
2001—Jets, 24-22 (O)
*****Raiders, 38-24 (O)
2002—Raiders, 26-20 (O)
2003—Jets, 27-24 (O) OT

2005—Jets, 26-10 (NY)
2006—Jets, 23-3 (NY)
2008—Raiders, 16-13 (O) OT
2009—Jets, 38-0 (O)
2011—Raiders, 34-24 (O)
2013—Jets, 37-27 (NY)
(RS Pts.—Raiders 912, Jets 859)
(PS Pts.—Raiders 105, Jets 78)
*Jets known as Titans prior to 1963
**Franchise in Los Angeles from
1982-1994
***AFL Championship
****AFC Second-Round Playoff
*****AFC First-Round Playoff
N.Y. JETS vs. PHILADELPHIA
RS: Eagles lead series, 9-0
1973—Eagles, 24-23 (P)
1977—Eagles, 27-0 (P)
1978—Eagles, 17-9 (P)
1987—Eagles, 38-27 (NY)
1993—Eagles, 35-30 (NY)
1996—Eagles, 21-20 (NY)
2003—Eagles, 24-17 (P)
2007—Eagles, 16-9 (NY)
2011—Eagles, 45-19 (P)
(RS Pts.—Eagles 247, Jets 154)
N.Y. JETS vs. PITTSBURGH
RS: Steelers lead series, 17-4
PS: Steelers lead series, 2-0
1970—Steelers, 21-17 (P)
1973—Steelers, 26-14 (P)
1975—Steelers, 20-7 (NY)
1977—Steelers, 23-20 (NY)
1978—Steelers, 28-17 (NY)
1981—Steelers, 38-10 (P)
1983—Steelers, 34-7 (NY)
1984—Steelers, 23-17 (NY)
1986—Steelers, 45-24 (NY)
1988—Jets, 24-20 (NY)
1989—Steelers, 13-0 (NY)
1990—Steelers, 24-7 (NY)
1992—Steelers, 27-10 (P)
2000—Steelers, 20-3 (NY)
2001—Steelers, 18-7 (P)
2003—Jets, 6-0 (NY)
2004—Steelers, 17-6 (P)
*Steelers, 20-17 (P) OT
2007—Jets, 19-16 (NY) OT
2010—Jets, 22-17 (P)
**Steelers, 24-19 (P)
2012—Steelers, 27-10 (P)
2013—Jets, 19-6 (NY)
(RS Pts.—Steelers 476, Jets 253)
(PS Pts.—Steelers 44, Jets 36)
*AFC Divisional Playoff
**AFC Championship
N.Y. JETS vs. *ST. LOUIS
RS: Rams lead series, 9-4
1970—Jets, 31-20 (LA)
1974—Rams, 20-13 (NY)
1980—Rams, 38-13 (LA)
1983—Jets, 27-24 (NY) OT
1986—Rams, 17-3 (NY)
1989—Rams, 38-14 (LA)
1992—Rams, 18-10 (LA)
1995—Rams, 23-20 (NY)
1998—Rams, 30-10 (StL)
2001—Rams, 34-14 (NY)
2004—Rams, 32-29 (StL) OT
2008—Jets, 47-3 (NY)
2012—Jets, 27-13 (StL)
(RS Pts.—Rams 310, Jets 258)
*Franchise in Los Angeles prior to 1995

*N.Y. JETS vs. **SAN DIEGO
RS: Chargers lead series, 20-12-1
PS: Jets lead series, 2-0
1960—Chargers, 21-7 (NY)
   Chargers, 50-43 (LA)
1961—Chargers, 25-10 (NY)
   Chargers, 48-13 (SD)
1962—Chargers, 40-14 (SD)
   Titans, 23-3 (NY)
1963—Chargers, 24-20 (SD)
   Chargers, 53-7 (NY)
1964—Tie, 17-17 (NY)
   Chargers, 38-3 (SD)
1965—Chargers, 34-9 (NY)
   Chargers, 38-7 (SD)
1966—Jets, 17-16 (NY)
   Chargers, 42-27 (SD)
1967—Jets, 42-31 (SD)
1968—Jets, 23-20 (NY)
   Jets, 37-15 (SD)
1969—Chargers, 34-27 (SD)
1971—Chargers, 49-21 (SD)
1974—Jets, 27-14 (NY)
1975—Chargers, 24-16 (SD)
1983—Jets, 41-29 (SD)
1989—Jets, 20-17 (SD)
1990—Chargers, 39-3 (NY)
   Chargers, 38-17 (SD)
1991—Jets, 24-3 (NY)
1994—Jets, 21-6 (NY)
2002—Jets, 44-13 (SD)
2004—Jets, 34-28 (SD)
   ***Jets, 20-17 (SD) OT
2005—Chargers, 31-26 (NY)
2008—Chargers, 48-29 (SD)
2009—****Jets, 17-14 (SD)
2011—Jets, 27-21 (NY)
2012—Chargers, 27-17 (NY)
(RS Pts.—Chargers 951, Jets 698)
(PS Pts.—Jets 37, Chargers 31)
*Jets known as Titans prior to 1963
**Franchise in Los Angeles prior to 1961
***AFC First-Round Playoff
****AFC Divisional Playoff
N.Y. JETS vs. SAN FRANCISCO
RS: 49ers lead series, 10-2
1971—49ers, 24-21 (NY)
1976—49ers, 17-6 (SF)
1980—49ers, 37-27 (NY)
1983—Jets, 27-13 (SF)
1986—49ers, 24-10 (SF)
1989—49ers, 23-10 (NY)
1992—49ers, 31-14 (NY)
1998—49ers, 36-30 (SF) OT
2001—49ers, 19-17 (NY)
2004—Jets, 22-14 (NY)
2008—49ers, 24-14 (SF)
2012—49ers, 34-0 (NY)
(RS Pts.—49ers 296, Jets 198)
N.Y. JETS vs. SEATTLE
RS: Seahawks lead series, 10-8
1977—Seahawks, 17-0 (NY)
1978—Seahawks, 24-17 (NY)
1979—Seahawks, 30-7 (S)
1980—Seahawks, 27-17 (NY)
1981—Seahawks, 19-3 (NY)
   Seahawks, 27-23 (S)
1983—Seahawks, 17-10 (NY)
1985—Jets, 17-14 (NY)
1986—Jets, 38-7 (S)
1987—Jets, 30-14 (NY)
1991—Seahawks, 20-13 (S)
1995—Jets, 16-10 (S)

1997—Jets, 41-3 (S)
1998—Jets, 32-31 (NY)
1999—Jets, 19-9 (NY)
2004—Jets, 37-14 (NY)
2008—Seahawks, 13-3 (S)
2012—Seahawks, 28-7 (S)
(RS Pts.—Jets 330, Seahawks 324)
N.Y. JETS vs. TAMPA BAY
RS: Jets lead series, 10-1
1976—Jets, 34-0 (NY)
1982—Jets, 32-17 (NY)
1984—Buccaneers, 41-21 (TB)
1985—Jets, 62-28 (NY)
1990—Jets, 16-14 (TB)
1991—Jets, 16-13 (NY)
1997—Jets, 31-0 (NY)
2000—Jets, 21-17 (TB)
2005—Jets, 14-12 (NY)
2009—Jets, 26-3 (TB)
2013—Jets, 18-17 (NY)
(RS Pts.—Jets 291, Buccaneers 162)
*N.Y. JETS vs. **TENNESSEE
RS: Titans lead series, 23-17-1
PS: Titans lead series, 1-0
1960—Oilers, 27-21 (H)
   Oilers, 42-28 (NY)
1961—Oilers, 49-13 (H)
   Oilers, 48-21 (NY)
1962—Oilers, 56-17 (H)
   Oilers, 44-10 (NY)
1963—Jets, 24-17 (NY)
   Oilers, 31-27 (H)
1964—Jets, 24-21 (NY)
   Oilers, 33-17 (H)
1965—Oilers, 27-21 (H)
   Jets, 41-14 (NY)
1966—Jets, 52-13 (NY)
   Oilers, 24-0 (H)
1967—Tie, 28-28 (NY)
1968—Jets, 20-14 (H)
   Jets, 26-7 (NY)
1969—Jets, 26-17 (NY)
   Jets, 34-26 (H)
1972—Oilers, 26-20 (H)
1974—Oilers, 27-22 (NY)
1977—Oilers, 20-0 (H)
1979—Oilers, 27-24 (H) OT
1980—Jets, 31-28 (NY) OT
1981—Jets, 33-17 (NY)
1984—Oilers, 31-20 (H)
1988—Jets, 45-3 (NY)
1990—Jets, 17-12 (H)
1991—Jets, 23-20 (NY)
   ***Oilers, 17-10 (H)
1993—Oilers, 24-0 (H)
1994—Oilers, 24-10 (H)
1995—Oilers, 23-6 (H)
1996—Oilers, 35-10 (NY)
1998—Jets, 24-3 (T)
2003—Jets, 24-17 (NY)
2006—Jets, 23-16 (T)
2007—Titans, 10-6 (T)
2008—Jets, 34-13 (T)
2009—Jets, 24-17 (NY)
2012—Titans, 14-10 (T)
2013—Titans, 38-13 (T)
(RS Pts.—Titans 986, Jets 866)
(PS Pts.—Titans 17, Jets 10)
*Jets known as Titans prior to 1963
**Franchise in Houston prior to 1997;
known as Oilers prior to 1999
***AFC First-Round Playoff
N.Y. JETS vs. WASHINGTON

RS: Redskins lead series, 8-2
1972—Redskins, 35-17 (NY)
1976—Redskins, 37-16 (NY)
1978—Redskins, 23-3 (W)
1987—Redskins, 17-16 (W)
1993—Jets, 3-0 (W)
1996—Redskins, 31-16 (W)
1999—Redskins, 27-20 (NY)
2003—Redskins, 16-13 (W)
2007—Redskins 23-20 (NY) OT
2011—Jets, 34-19 (W)
(RS Pts.—Redskins 228, Jets 158)

OAKLAND vs. ARIZONA
RS: Raiders lead series, 5-3;
See Arizona vs. Oakland
OAKLAND vs. ATLANTA
RS: Raiders lead series, 7-6;
See Atlanta vs. Oakland
OAKLAND vs. BALTIMORE
RS: Ravens lead series, 6-1
PS: Ravens lead series, 1-0;
See Baltimore vs. Oakland
OAKLAND vs. BUFFALO
RS: Raiders lead series, 19-17
PS: Bills lead series, 2-0;
See Buffalo vs. Oakland
OAKLAND vs. CAROLINA
RS: Panthers lead series, 3-2;
See Carolina vs. Oakland
OAKLAND vs. CHICAGO
RS: Raiders lead series, 7-6;
See Chicago vs. Oakland
OAKLAND vs. CINCINNATI
RS: Raiders lead series, 18-9
PS: Raiders lead series, 2-0;
See Cincinnati vs. Oakland
OAKLAND vs. CLEVELAND
RS: Raiders lead series, 11-9
PS: Raiders lead series, 2-0;
See Cleveland vs. Oakland
OAKLAND vs. DALLAS
RS: Raiders lead series, 6-5;
See Dallas vs. Oakland
OAKLAND vs. DENVER
RS: Raiders lead series, 59-46-2
PS: Series tied, 1-1;
See Denver vs. Oakland
OAKLAND vs. DETROIT
RS: Raiders lead series, 6-5;
See Detroit vs. Oakland
OAKLAND vs. GREEN BAY
RS: Packers lead series, 6-5
PS: Packers lead series, 1-0;
See Green Bay vs. Oakland
OAKLAND vs. HOUSTON
RS: Texans lead series, 5-3;
See Houston vs. Oakland
OAKLAND vs. INDIANAPOLIS
RS: Raiders lead series, 7-6
PS: Series tied, 1-1;
See Indianapolis vs. Oakland
OAKLAND vs. JACKSONVILLE
RS: Jaguars lead series, 4-3;
See Jacksonville vs. Oakland
OAKLAND vs. KANSAS CITY
RS: Chiefs lead series, 55-50-2
PS: Chiefs lead series, 2-1;
See Kansas City vs. Oakland
OAKLAND vs. MIAMI
RS: Raiders lead series, 16-15-1
PS: Raiders lead series, 3-1;
See Miami vs. Oakland

OAKLAND vs. MINNESOTA
RS: Raiders lead series, 9-4
PS: Raiders lead series, 1-0;
See Minnesota vs. Oakland
OAKLAND vs. NEW ENGLAND
RS: Patriots lead series, 15-14-1
PS: Patriots lead series, 2-1;
See New England vs. Oakland
OAKLAND vs. NEW ORLEANS
RS: Saints lead series, 6-5-1;
See New Orleans vs. Oakland
OAKLAND vs. N.Y. GIANTS
RS: Raiders lead series, 7-5;
See N.Y. Giants vs. Oakland
OAKLAND vs. N.Y. JETS
RS: Raiders lead series, 21-16-2
PS: Series tied, 2-2;
See N.Y. Jets vs. Oakland
*OAKLAND vs. PHILADELPHIA
RS: Eagles lead series, 6-5
PS: Raiders lead series, 1-0
1971—Raiders, 34-10 (O)
1976—Raiders, 26-7 (P)
1980—Eagles, 10-7 (P)
　　　**Raiders, 27-10 (New Orleans)
1986—Eagles, 33-27 (LA) OT
1989—Eagles, 10-7 (P)
1992—Eagles, 31-10 (P)
1995—Raiders, 48-17 (O)
2001—Raiders, 20-10 (P)
2005—Eagles, 23-20 (P)
2009—Raiders, 13-9 (O)
2013—Eagles, 49-20 (O)
(RS Pts.—Raiders 232, Eagles 209)
(PS Pts.—Raiders 27, Eagles 10)
*Franchise in Los Angeles from 1982-1994
**Super Bowl XV
*OAKLAND vs. PITTSBURGH
RS: Raiders lead series, 12-9
PS: Series tied, 3-3
1970—Raiders, 31-14 (O)
1972—Steelers, 34-28 (P)
　　　**Steelers, 13-7 (P)
1973—Steelers, 17-9 (O)
　　　**Raiders, 33-14 (O)
1974—Raiders, 17-0 (P)
　　　***Steelers, 24-13 (O)
1975—***Steelers, 16-10 (P)
1976—Raiders, 31-28 (O)
　　　***Raiders, 24-7 (O)
1977—Raiders, 16-7 (P)
1980—Raiders, 45-34 (P)
1981—Raiders, 30-27 (O)
1983—**Raiders, 38-10 (LA)
1984—Steelers, 13-7 (LA)
1990—Raiders, 20-3 (LA)
1994—Steelers, 21-3 (LA)
1995—Steelers, 29-10 (LA)
2000—Steelers, 21-20 (P)
2002—Raiders, 30-17 (P)
2003—Steelers, 27-7 (P)
2004—Raiders, 24-21 (P)
2006—Raiders, 20-13 (O)
2009—Raiders, 27-24 (P)
2010—Steelers, 35-3 (P)
2012—Raiders, 34-31 (O)
2013—Raiders, 21-18 (O)
(RS Pts.—Steelers 437, Raiders 430)
(PS Pts.—Raiders 125, Steelers 84)
*Franchise in Los Angeles from 1982-1994
**AFC Divisional Playoff
***AFC Championship
*OAKLAND vs. **ST. LOUIS

RS: Raiders lead series, 8-4
1972—Raiders, 45-17 (O)
1977—Rams, 20-14 (LA)
1979—Raiders, 24-17 (LA)
1982—Raiders, 37-31 (LA Raiders)
1985—Raiders, 16-6 (LA Rams)
1988—Rams, 22-17 (LA Raiders)
1991—Raiders, 20-17 (LA Raiders)
1994—Raiders, 20-17 (LA Rams)
1997—Raiders, 35-17 (O)
2002—Rams, 28-13 (StL)
2006—Rams, 20-0 (O)
2010—Raiders, 16-14 (O)
(RS Pts.—Raiders 257, Rams 226)
*Franchise in Los Angeles from 1982-1994
**Franchise in Los Angeles prior to 1995
*OAKLAND vs. **SAN DIEGO
RS: Raiders lead series, 58-48-2
PS: Raiders lead series, 1-0
1960—Chargers, 52-28 (LA)
　　　Chargers, 41-17 (O)
1961—Chargers, 44-0 (SD)
　　　Chargers, 41-10 (O)
1962—Chargers, 42-33 (O)
　　　Chargers, 31-21 (SD)
1963—Raiders, 34-33 (SD)
　　　Raiders, 41-27 (O)
1964—Chargers, 31-17 (SD)
　　　Raiders, 21-20 (O)
1965—Chargers, 17-6 (O)
　　　Chargers, 24-14 (SD)
1966—Chargers, 29-20 (O)
　　　Raiders, 41-19 (SD)
1967—Raiders, 51-10 (O)
　　　Raiders, 41-21 (SD)
1968—Chargers, 23-14 (O)
　　　Raiders, 34-27 (SD)
1969—Raiders, 24-12 (SD)
　　　Raiders, 21-16 (O)
1970—Tie, 27-27 (SD)
　　　Raiders, 20-17 (O)
1971—Raiders, 34-0 (SD)
　　　Raiders, 34-33 (O)
1972—Tie, 17-17 (O)
　　　Raiders, 21-19 (SD)
1973—Raiders, 27-17 (SD)
　　　Raiders, 31-3 (O)
1974—Raiders, 14-10 (SD)
　　　Raiders, 17-10 (O)
1975—Raiders, 6-0 (SD)
　　　Raiders, 25-0 (O)
1976—Raiders, 27-17 (SD)
　　　Raiders, 24-0 (O)
1977—Raiders, 24-0 (O)
　　　Chargers, 12-7 (SD)
1978—Raiders, 21-20 (SD)
　　　Chargers, 27-23 (O)
1979—Chargers, 30-10 (SD)
　　　Raiders, 45-22 (O)
1980—Chargers, 30-24 (SD) OT
　　　Raiders, 38-24 (O)
　　　***Raiders, 34-27 (SD)
1981—Chargers, 55-21 (O)
　　　Chargers, 23-10 (SD)
1982—Raiders, 28-24 (LA)
　　　Raiders, 41-34 (SD)
1983—Raiders, 42-10 (SD)
　　　Raiders, 30-14 (LA)
1984—Raiders, 33-30 (LA)
　　　Raiders, 44-37 (SD)
1985—Raiders, 34-21 (LA)
　　　Chargers, 40-34 (SD) OT
1986—Raiders, 17-13 (LA)

　　　Raiders, 37-31 (SD) OT
1987—Chargers, 23-17 (LA)
　　　Chargers, 16-14 (SD)
1988—Raiders, 24-13 (LA)
　　　Raiders, 13-3 (SD)
1989—Raiders, 40-14 (LA)
　　　Chargers, 14-12 (SD)
1990—Raiders, 24-9 (SD)
　　　Raiders, 17-12 (LA)
1991—Chargers, 21-13 (LA)
　　　Raiders, 9-7 (SD)
1992—Chargers, 27-3 (SD)
　　　Chargers, 36-14 (LA)
1993—Chargers, 30-23 (LA)
　　　Raiders, 12-7 (SD)
1994—Chargers, 26-24 (LA)
　　　Raiders, 24-17 (SD)
1995—Raiders, 17-7 (O)
　　　Chargers, 12-6 (SD)
1996—Chargers, 40-34 (O)
　　　Raiders, 23-14 (SD)
1997—Chargers, 25-10 (O)
　　　Raiders, 38-13 (SD)
1998—Raiders, 7-6 (O)
　　　Raiders, 17-10 (SD)
1999—Raiders, 28-9 (O)
　　　Chargers, 23-20 (SD)
2000—Raiders, 9-6 (O)
　　　Raiders, 15-13 (SD)
2001—Raiders, 34-24 (O)
　　　Raiders, 13-6 (SD)
2002—Chargers, 27-21 (O) OT
　　　Raiders, 27-7 (SD)
2003—Raiders, 34-31 (O) OT
　　　Chargers, 21-14 (SD)
2004—Chargers, 42-14 (SD)
　　　Chargers, 23-17 (O)
2005—Chargers, 27-14 (O)
　　　Chargers, 34-10 (SD)
2006—Chargers, 27-0 (O)
　　　Chargers, 21-14 (SD)
2007—Chargers, 28-14 (SD)
　　　Chargers, 30-17 (O)
2008—Chargers, 28-18 (O)
　　　Chargers, 34-7 (SD)
2009—Chargers, 24-20 (O)
　　　Chargers, 24-16 (SD)
2010—Raiders, 35-27 (O)
　　　Raiders, 28-13 (SD)
2011—Raiders, 24-17 (SD)
　　　Chargers, 38-26 (O)
2012—Chargers, 22-14 (O)
　　　Chargers, 24-21 (SD)
2013—Raiders, 27-17 (O)
　　　Chargers, 26-13 (SD)
(RS Pts.—Raiders 2,374, Chargers 2,322)
(PS Pts.—Raiders 34, Chargers 27)
*Franchise in Los Angeles from 1982-1994
**Franchise in Los Angeles prior to 1961
***AFC Championship
*OAKLAND vs. SAN FRANCISCO
RS: Series tied, 6-6
1970—49ers, 38-7 (O)
1974—Raiders, 35-24 (SF)
1979—Raiders, 23-10 (O)
1982—Raiders, 23-17 (SF)
1985—49ers, 34-10 (LA)
1988—Raiders, 9-3 (SF)
1991—Raiders, 12-6 (LA)
1994—49ers, 44-14 (SF)
2000—Raiders, 34-28 (SF) OT
2002—49ers, 23-20 (O) OT
2006—49ers, 34-20 (SF)

2010—49ers, 17-9 (SF)
(RS Pts.—49ers 278, Raiders 216)
Franchise in Los Angeles from 1982-1994
*OAKLAND vs. SEATTLE
RS: Raiders lead series, 28-23
PS: Series tied, 1-1
1977—Raiders, 44-7 (O)
1978—Seahawks, 27-7 (S)
　　　Seahawks, 17-16 (O)
1979—Seahawks, 27-10 (S)
　　　Seahawks, 29-24 (O)
1980—Raiders, 33-14 (O)
　　　Raiders, 19-17 (S)
1981—Raiders, 20-10 (O)
　　　Raiders, 32-31 (S)
1982—Raiders, 28-23 (LA)
1983—Seahawks, 38-36 (S)
　　　Seahawks, 34-21 (LA)
　　　**Raiders, 30-14 (LA)
1984—Raiders, 28-14 (LA)
　　　Seahawks, 17-14 (S)
　　　***Seahawks, 13-7 (S)
1985—Seahawks, 33-3 (S)
　　　Raiders, 13-3 (LA)
1986—Raiders, 14-10 (LA)
　　　Seahawks, 37-0 (S)
1987—Seahawks, 35-13 (LA)
　　　Raiders, 37-14 (S)
1988—Seahawks, 35-27 (S)
　　　Seahawks, 43-37 (LA)
1989—Seahawks, 24-20 (LA)
　　　Seahawks, 23-17 (S)
1990—Raiders, 17-13 (S)
　　　Raiders, 24-17 (LA)
1991—Raiders, 23-20 (S) OT
　　　Raiders, 31-7 (LA)
1992—Raiders, 19-0 (S)
　　　Raiders, 20-3 (LA)
1993—Raiders, 17-13 (S)
　　　Raiders, 27-23 (LA)
1994—Seahawks, 38-9 (LA)
　　　Raiders, 17-16 (S)
1995—Raiders, 34-14 (O)
　　　Seahawks, 44-10 (S)
1996—Raiders, 27-21 (O)
　　　Seahawks, 28-21 (O)
1997—Seahawks, 45-34 (S)
　　　Seahawks, 22-21 (O)
1998—Raiders, 31-18 (S)
　　　Raiders, 20-17 (O)
1999—Seahawks, 22-21 (S)
　　　Raiders, 30-21 (O)
2000—Raiders, 31-3 (O)
　　　Seahawks, 27-24 (S)
2001—Raiders, 38-14 (O)
　　　Seahawks, 34-27 (S)
2002—Raiders, 31-17 (O)
2006—Seahawks, 16-0 (S)
2010—Raiders, 33-3 (O)
(RS Pts.—Raiders 1,150, Seahawks 1,078)
(PS Pts.—Raiders 37, Seahawks 27)
Franchise in Los Angeles from 1982-1994
**AFC Championship*
*****AFC First-Round Playoff*
*OAKLAND vs. TAMPA BAY
RS: Raiders lead series, 6-2
PS: Buccaneers lead series, 1-0
1976—Raiders, 49-16 (O)
1981—Raiders, 18-16 (O)
1993—Raiders, 27-20 (LA)
1996—Buccaneers, 20-17 (TB) OT
1999—Raiders, 45-0 (O)
2002—**Buccaneers, 48-21 (San Diego)

2004—Raiders, 30-20 (O)
2008—Raiders, 31-24 (TB)
2012—Buccaneers, 42-32 (O)
(RS Pts.—Raiders 249, Buccaneers 158)
(PS Pts.—Buccaneers 48, Raiders 21)
Franchise in Los Angeles from 1982-1994
****Super Bowl XXXVII*
*OAKLAND vs. **TENNESSEE
RS: Raiders lead series, 23-20
PS: Raiders lead series, 4-0
1960—Oilers, 37-22 (O)
　　　Raiders, 14-13 (H)
1961—Oilers, 55-0 (H)
　　　Oilers, 47-16 (O)
1962—Oilers, 28-20 (O)
　　　Oilers, 32-17 (H)
1963—Raiders, 24-13 (H)
　　　Raiders, 52-49 (O)
1964—Oilers, 42-28 (H)
　　　Raiders, 20-10 (O)
1965—Raiders, 21-17 (O)
　　　Raiders, 33-21 (H)
1966—Oilers, 31-0 (H)
　　　Raiders, 38-23 (O)
1967—Raiders, 19-7 (H)
　　　***Raiders, 40-7 (O)
1968—Raiders, 24-15 (H)
1969—Raiders, 21-17 (O)
　　　****Raiders, 56-7 (O)
1971—Raiders, 41-21 (O)
1972—Raiders, 34-0 (H)
1973—Raiders, 17-6 (H)
1975—Oilers, 27-26 (O)
1976—Raiders, 14-13 (H)
1977—Raiders, 34-29 (O)
1978—Raiders, 21-17 (O)
1979—Oilers, 31-17 (H)
1980—*****Raiders, 27-7 (O)
1981—Oilers, 17-16 (H)
1983—Raiders, 20-6 (LA)
1984—Raiders, 24-14 (H)
1986—Raiders, 28-17 (H)
1988—Oilers, 38-35 (H)
1989—Oilers, 23-7 (H)
1991—Oilers, 47-17 (H)
1994—Raiders, 17-14 (LA)
1997—Oilers, 24-21 (T) OT
1999—Titans, 21-14 (T)
2001—Titans, 13-10 (O)
2002—Raiders, 52-25 (O)
　　　******Raiders, 41-24 (O)
2003—Titans, 25-20 (T)
2004—Raiders, 40-35 (O)
2005—Raiders, 34-25 (T)
2007—Titans, 13-9 (T)
2010—Titans, 38-13 (T)
2013—Titans, 23-19 (O)
(RS Pts.—Titans 1,019, Raiders 969)
(PS Pts.—Raiders 164, Titans 45)
Franchise in Los Angeles from 1982-1994
****Franchise in Houston prior to 1997;*
known as Oilers prior to 1999
*****AFL Championship*
******Inter-Divisional Playoff*
*******AFC First-Round Playoff*
********AFC Championship*
*OAKLAND vs. WASHINGTON
RS: Raiders lead series, 7-5
PS: Raiders lead series, 1-0
1970—Raiders, 34-20 (O)
1975—Raiders, 26-23 (W) OT
1980—Raiders, 24-21 (O)
1983—Redskins, 37-35 (W)

　　　**Raiders, 38-9 (Tampa)
1986—Redskins, 10-6 (W)
1989—Raiders, 37-24 (LA)
1992—Raiders, 21-20 (W)
1995—Raiders, 20-8 (W)
1998—Redskins, 29-19 (O)
2005—Raiders, 16-13 (W)
2009—Redskins, 34-13 (O)
2013—Redskins, 24-14 (O)
(RS Pts.—Raiders 265, Redskins 263)
(PS Pts.—Raiders 38, Redskins 9)
Franchise in Los Angeles from 1982-1994
****Super Bowl XVIII*

PHILADELPHIA vs. ARIZONA
RS: Cardinals lead series, 55-54-5
PS: Cardinals lead series, 2-1;
See Arizona vs. Philadelphia
PHILADELPHIA vs. ATLANTA
RS: Eagles lead series, 15-12-1
PS: Eagles lead series, 2-1;
See Atlanta vs. Philadelphia
PHILADELPHIA vs. BALTIMORE
RS: Eagles lead series, 2-1-1;
See Baltimore vs. Philadelphia
PHILADELPHIA vs. BUFFALO
RS: Series tied, 6-6;
See Buffalo vs. Philadelphia
PHILADELPHIA vs. CAROLINA
RS: Eagles lead series, 5-2
PS: Panthers lead series, 1-0;
See Carolina vs. Philadelphia
PHILADELPHIA vs. CHICAGO
RS: Bears lead series, 28-10-1
PS: Eagles lead series, 2-1;
See Chicago vs. Philadelphia
PHILADELPHIA vs. CINCINNATI
RS: Bengals lead series, 8-3-1;
See Cincinnati vs. Philadelphia
PHILADELPHIA vs. CLEVELAND
RS: Browns lead series, 31-16-1;
See Cleveland vs. Philadelphia
PHILADELPHIA vs. DALLAS
RS: Cowboys lead series, 59-47
PS: Cowboys lead series, 3-1;
See Dallas vs. Philadelphia
PHILADELPHIA vs. DENVER
RS: Eagles lead series, 7-5;
See Denver vs. Philadelphia
PHILADELPHIA vs. DETROIT
RS: Eagles lead series, 15-13-2
PS: Eagles lead series, 1-0;
See Detroit vs. Philadelphia
PHILADELPHIA vs. GREEN BAY
RS: Packers lead series, 24-14
PS: Eagles lead series, 2-1;
See Green Bay vs. Philadelphia
PHILADELPHIA vs. HOUSTON
RS: Eagles lead series, 3-0;
See Houston vs. Philadelphia
PHILADELPHIA vs. INDIANAPOLIS
RS: Colts lead series, 10-7;
See Indianapolis vs. Philadelphia
PHILADELPHIA vs. JACKSONVILLE
RS: Jaguars lead series, 3-1;
See Jacksonville vs. Philadelphia
PHILADELPHIA vs. KANSAS CITY
RS: Eagles lead series, 4-3;
See Kansas City vs. Philadelphia
PHILADELPHIA vs. MIAMI
RS: Dolphins lead series, 7-6;
See Miami vs. Philadelphia

PHILADELPHIA vs. MINNESOTA
RS: Vikings lead series, 13-9
PS: Eagles lead series, 3-0;
See Minnesota vs. Philadelphia
PHILADELPHIA vs. NEW ENGLAND
RS: Eagles lead series, 6-5
PS: Patriots lead series, 1-0;
See New England vs. Philadelphia
PHILADELPHIA vs. NEW ORLEANS
RS: Eagles lead series, 15-11
PS: Saints lead series, 2-1;
See New Orleans vs. Philadelphia
PHILADELPHIA vs. N.Y. GIANTS
RS: Giants lead series, 82-74-2
PS: Series tied, 2-2;
See N.Y. Giants vs. Philadelphia
PHILADELPHIA vs. N.Y. JETS
RS: Eagles lead series, 9-0;
See N.Y. Jets vs. Philadelphia
PHILADELPHIA vs. OAKLAND
RS: Eagles lead series, 6-5
PS: Raiders lead series, 1-0;
See Oakland vs. Philadelphia
PHILADELPHIA vs. *PITTSBURGH
RS: Eagles lead series, 46-28-3
PS: Eagles lead series, 1-0
1933—Eagles, 25-6 (Phila)
1934—Eagles, 17-0 (Pitt)
    Pirates, 9-7 (Phila)
1935—Pirates, 17-7 (Phila)
    Eagles, 17-6 (Pitt)
1936—Pirates, 17-0 (Pitt)
    Pirates, 6-0 (Johnstown, Pa.)
1937—Pirates, 27-14 (Pitt)
    Pirates, 16-7 (Pitt)
1938—Eagles, 27-7 (Buffalo)
    Eagles, 14-7 (Charleston, W. Va.)
1939—Eagles, 17-14 (Phila)
    Pirates, 24-12 (Pitt)
1940—Steelers, 7-3 (Pitt)
    Eagles, 7-0 (Phila)
1941—Eagles, 10-7 (Pitt)
    Tie, 7-7 (Phila)
1942—Eagles, 24-14 (Pitt)
    Steelers, 14-0 (Phila)
1945—Eagles, 45-3 (Pitt)
    Eagles, 30-6 (Phila)
1946—Steelers, 10-7 (Pitt)
    Eagles, 10-7 (Phila)
1947—Steelers, 35-24 (Pitt)
    Eagles, 21-0 (Phila)
    **Eagles, 21-0 (Pitt)
1948—Eagles, 34-7 (Pitt)
    Eagles, 17-0 (Phila)
1949—Eagles, 38-7 (Pitt)
    Eagles, 34-17 (Phila)
1950—Eagles, 17-10 (Pitt)
    Steelers, 9-7 (Phila)
1951—Eagles, 34-13 (Pitt)
    Steelers, 17-13 (Phila)
1952—Eagles, 31-25 (Pitt)
    Eagles, 26-21 (Phila)
1953—Eagles, 23-17 (Phila)
    Eagles, 35-7 (Pitt)
1954—Eagles, 24-22 (Phila)
    Steelers, 17-7 (Pitt)
1955—Steelers, 13-7 (Pitt)
    Eagles, 24-0 (Phila)
1956—Eagles, 35-21 (Pitt)
    Eagles, 14-7 (Phila)
1957—Steelers, 6-0 (Pitt)
    Eagles, 7-6 (Phila)
1958—Steelers, 24-3 (Pitt)

    Steelers, 31-24 (Phila)
1959—Eagles, 28-24 (Phila)
    Steelers, 31-0 (Pitt)
1960—Eagles, 34-7 (Phila)
    Steelers, 27-21 (Pitt)
1961—Eagles, 21-16 (Phila)
    Eagles, 35-24 (Pitt)
1962—Steelers, 13-7 (Pitt)
    Steelers, 26-17 (Phila)
1963—Tie, 21-21 (Phila)
    Tie, 20-20 (Pitt)
1964—Eagles, 21-7 (Phila)
    Eagles, 34-10 (Pitt)
1965—Steelers, 20-14 (Phila)
    Eagles, 47-13 (Pitt)
1966—Eagles, 31-14 (Pitt)
    Eagles, 27-23 (Phila)
1967—Eagles, 34-24 (Phila)
1968—Steelers, 6-3 (Pitt)
1969—Eagles, 41-27 (Phila)
1970—Eagles, 30-20 (Phila)
1974—Steelers, 27-0 (Pitt)
1979—Eagles, 17-14 (Phila)
1988—Eagles, 27-26 (Phila)
1991—Eagles, 23-14 (Phila)
1994—Steelers, 14-3 (Pitt)
1997—Eagles, 23-20 (Phila)
2000—Eagles, 26-23 (Pitt) OT
2004—Steelers, 27-3 (Phila)
2008—Eagles, 15-6 (Phila)
2012—Steelers, 16-14 (Pitt)
(RS Pts.—Eagles 1,443, Steelers 1,113)
(PS Pts.—Eagles 21, Steelers 0)
*Steelers known as Pirates prior to 1940
**Division Playoff
PHILADELPHIA vs. *ST. LOUIS
RS: Eagles lead series, 18-17-1
PS: Rams lead series, 2-1
1937—Rams, 21-3 (P)
1939—Rams, 35-13 (Colorado Springs)
1940—Rams, 21-13 (C)
1942—Rams, 24-14 (Akron)
1944—Eagles, 26-13 (P)
1945—Eagles, 28-14 (P)
1946—Eagles, 25-14 (LA)
1947—Eagles, 14-7 (P)
1948—Tie, 28-28 (LA)
1949—Eagles, 38-14 (P)
    **Eagles, 14-0 (LA)
1950—Eagles, 56-20 (P)
1955—Rams, 23-21 (P)
1956—Rams, 27-7 (LA)
1957—Rams, 17-13 (LA)
1959—Eagles, 23-20 (P)
1964—Rams, 20-10 (LA)
1967—Rams, 33-17 (LA)
1969—Rams, 23-17 (P)
1972—Rams, 34-3 (P)
1975—Rams, 42-3 (P)
1977—Rams, 20-0 (LA)
1978—Rams, 16-14 (P)
1983—Eagles, 13-9 (P)
1985—Rams, 17-6 (P)
1986—Eagles, 34-20 (P)
1988—Eagles, 30-24 (P)
1989—***Rams, 21-7 (P)
1990—Eagles, 27-21 (LA)
1995—Eagles, 20-9 (P)
1998—Eagles, 17-14 (P)
1999—Eagles, 38-31 (P)
2001—Rams, 20-17 (P) OT
    ****Rams, 29-24 (StL)
2002—Eagles, 10-3 (P)

2004—Rams, 20-7 (StL)
2005—Eagles, 17-16 (StL)
2008—Eagles, 38-3 (P)
2011—Eagles, 31-13 (StL)
(RS Pts.—Rams 706, Eagles 691)
(PS Pts.—Rams 50, Eagles 45)
*Franchise in Los Angeles prior to 1995
and in Cleveland prior to 1946
**NFL Championship
***NFC First-Round Playoff
****NFC Championship
PHILADELPHIA vs. SAN DIEGO
RS: Chargers lead series, 7-4
1974—Eagles, 13-7 (SD)
1980—Chargers, 22-21 (SD)
1985—Chargers, 20-14 (SD)
1986—Eagles, 23-7 (P)
1989—Chargers, 20-17 (SD)
1995—Chargers, 27-21 (P)
1998—Chargers, 13-10 (SD)
2001—Eagles, 24-14 (P)
2005—Eagles, 20-17 (P)
2009—Chargers, 31-23 (SD)
2013—Chargers, 33-30 (P)
(RS Pts.—Eagles 216, Chargers 211)
PHILADELPHIA vs. SAN FRANCISCO
RS: 49ers lead series, 17-12-1
PS: 49ers lead series, 1-0
1951—Eagles, 21-14 (P)
1953—49ers, 31-21 (SF)
1956—Tie, 10-10 (P)
1958—49ers, 30-24 (P)
1959—49ers, 24-14 (SF)
1964—49ers, 28-24 (P)
1966—Eagles, 35-34 (SF)
1967—49ers, 28-27 (P)
1969—49ers, 14-13 (SF)
1971—49ers, 31-3 (P)
1973—49ers, 38-28 (SF)
1975—Eagles, 27-17 (P)
1983—Eagles, 22-17 (SF)
1984—49ers, 21-9 (P)
1985—Eagles, 24-13 (SF)
1989—49ers, 38-28 (P)
1991—49ers, 23-7 (P)
1992—Eagles, 20-14 (SF)
1993—Eagles, 37-34 (SF) OT
1994—Eagles, 40-8 (SF)
1996—*49ers, 14-0 (SF)
1997—Eagles, 24-12 (P)
2001—49ers, 13-3 (SF)
2002—Eagles, 38-17 (SF)
2003—49ers, 31-28 (P) OT
2005—Eagles, 42-3 (P)
2006—Eagles, 38-24 (SF)
2008—Eagles, 40-26 (SF)
2009—Eagles, 27-13 (P)
2010—Eagles, 27-24 (SF)
2011—49ers, 24-23 (P)
(RS Pts.—Eagles 695, 49ers 683)
(PS Pts.—49ers 14, Eagles 0)
*NFC First-Round Playoff
PHILADELPHIA vs. SEATTLE
RS: Eagles lead series, 7-6
1976—Eagles, 27-10 (P)
1980—Eagles, 27-20 (S)
1986—Seahawks, 24-20 (S)
1989—Eagles, 31-7 (P)
1992—Eagles, 20-17 (S) OT
1995—Seahawks, 26-14 (S)
1998—Eagles, 38-0 (P)
2001—Eagles, 27-3 (S)
2002—Eagles, 27-20 (S)

2005—Seahawks, 42-0 (P)
2007—Seahawks, 28-24 (P)
2008—Eagles, 26-7 (S)
2011—Seahawks, 31-14 (S)
(RS Pts.—Seahawks 273, Eagles 257)

PHILADELPHIA vs. TAMPA BAY
RS: Eagles lead series, 8-5
PS: Series tied, 2-2
1977—Eagles, 13-3 (P)
1979—*Buccaneers, 24-17 (TB)
1981—Eagles, 20-10 (P)
1988—Eagles, 41-14 (TB)
1991—Buccaneers, 14-13 (TB)
1995—Buccaneers, 21-6 (P)
1999—Buccaneers, 19-5 (P)
2000—**Eagles, 21-3 (P)
2001—Eagles, 17-13 (TB)
     **Eagles, 31-9 (P)
2002—Eagles, 20-10 (P)
     ***Buccaneers, 27-10 (P)
2003—Buccaneers, 17-0 (P)
2006—Buccaneers, 23-21 (TB)
2009—Eagles, 33-14 (P)
2012—Eagles, 23-21 (TB)
2013—Eagles, 31-20 (TB)
(RS Pts.—Eagles 243, Buccaneers 199)
(PS Pts.—Eagles 79, Buccaneers 63)
*NFC Divisional Playoff
**NFC First-Round Playoff
***NFC Championship

PHILADELPHIA vs. *TENNESSEE
RS: Eagles lead series, 6-4
1972—Eagles, 18-17 (H)
1979—Eagles, 26-20 (H)
1982—Eagles, 35-14 (P)
1988—Eagles, 32-23 (P)
1991—Eagles, 13-6 (H)
1994—Eagles, 21-6 (P)
2000—Titans, 15-13 (P)
2002—Titans, 27-24 (T)
2006—Titans, 31-13 (P)
2010—Titans, 37-19 (T)
(RS Pts.—Eagles 214, Titans 196)
*Franchise in Houston prior to 1997;
known as Oilers prior to 1999

PHILADELPHIA vs. *WASHINGTON
RS: Redskins lead series, 80-72-5
PS: Redskins lead series, 1-0
1934—Redskins, 6-0 (B)
     Redskins, 14-7 (P)
1935—Eagles, 7-6 (B)
1936—Redskins, 26-3 (P)
     Redskins, 17-7 (B)
1937—Eagles, 14-0 (W)
     Redskins, 10-7 (P)
1938—Redskins, 26-23 (P)
     Redskins, 20-14 (W)
1939—Redskins, 7-0 (P)
     Redskins, 7-6 (W)
1940—Redskins, 34-17 (P)
     Redskins, 13-6 (W)
1941—Redskins, 21-17 (P)
     Redskins, 20-14 (W)
1942—Redskins, 14-10 (P)
     Redskins, 30-27 (W)
1944—Tie, 31-31 (P)
     Eagles, 37-7 (W)
1945—Redskins, 24-14 (W)
     Eagles, 16-0 (P)
1946—Eagles, 28-24 (W)
     Redskins, 27-10 (P)
1947—Eagles, 45-42 (P)
     Eagles, 38-14 (W)

1948—Eagles, 45-0 (W)
     Eagles, 42-21 (P)
1949—Eagles, 49-14 (P)
     Eagles, 44-21 (W)
1950—Eagles, 35-3 (P)
     Eagles, 33-0 (W)
1951—Redskins, 27-23 (P)
     Eagles, 35-21 (W)
1952—Eagles, 38-20 (P)
     Redskins, 27-21 (W)
1953—Tie, 21-21 (P)
     Redskins, 10-0 (W)
1954—Eagles, 49-21 (W)
     Eagles, 41-33 (P)
1955—Redskins, 31-30 (P)
     Redskins, 34-21 (W)
1956—Eagles, 13-9 (P)
     Redskins, 19-17 (W)
1957—Eagles, 21-12 (P)
     Redskins, 42-7 (W)
1958—Redskins, 24-14 (P)
     Redskins, 20-0 (W)
1959—Eagles, 30-23 (P)
     Eagles, 34-14 (W)
1960—Eagles, 19-13 (P)
     Eagles, 38-28 (W)
1961—Eagles, 14-7 (P)
     Eagles, 27-24 (W)
1962—Redskins, 27-21 (P)
     Eagles, 37-14 (W)
1963—Eagles, 37-24 (W)
     Redskins, 13-10 (P)
1964—Redskins, 35-20 (W)
     Redskins, 21-10 (P)
1965—Redskins, 23-21 (W)
     Eagles, 21-14 (P)
1966—Redskins, 27-13 (P)
     Eagles, 37-28 (W)
1967—Eagles, 35-24 (P)
     Tie, 35-35 (W)
1968—Redskins, 17-14 (W)
     Redskins, 16-10 (P)
1969—Tie, 28-28 (W)
     Redskins, 34-29 (P)
1970—Redskins, 33-21 (P)
     Redskins, 24-6 (W)
1971—Tie, 7-7 (W)
     Redskins, 20-13 (P)
1972—Redskins, 14-0 (W)
     Redskins, 23-7 (P)
1973—Redskins, 28-7 (P)
     Redskins, 38-20 (W)
1974—Redskins, 27-20 (P)
     Redskins, 26-7 (W)
1975—Eagles, 26-10 (P)
     Eagles, 26-3 (W)
1976—Redskins, 20-17 (P) OT
     Redskins, 24-0 (W)
1977—Redskins, 23-17 (W)
     Redskins, 17-14 (P)
1978—Redskins, 35-30 (W)
     Eagles, 17-10 (P)
1979—Eagles, 28-17 (P)
     Redskins, 17-7 (W)
1980—Eagles, 24-14 (P)
     Eagles, 24-0 (W)
1981—Eagles, 36-13 (P)
     Redskins, 15-13 (W)
1982—Redskins, 37-34 (P) OT
     Redskins, 13-9 (W)
1983—Redskins, 23-13 (P)
     Redskins, 28-24 (W)
1984—Redskins, 20-0 (W)

     Eagles, 16-10 (P)
1985—Eagles, 19-6 (W)
     Redskins, 17-12 (P)
1986—Redskins, 41-14 (W)
     Redskins, 21-14 (P)
1987—Redskins, 34-24 (W)
     Eagles, 31-27 (P)
1988—Redskins, 17-10 (W)
     Redskins, 20-19 (P)
1989—Eagles, 42-37 (W)
     Redskins, 10-3 (P)
1990—Redskins, 13-7 (W)
     Eagles, 28-14 (P)
     **Redskins, 20-6 (P)
1991—Redskins, 23-0 (W)
     Eagles, 24-22 (P)
1992—Redskins, 16-12 (W)
     Eagles, 17-13 (P)
1993—Eagles, 34-31 (P)
     Eagles, 17-14 (W)
1994—Eagles, 21-17 (P)
     Eagles, 31-29 (W)
1995—Eagles, 37-34 (P) OT
     Eagles, 14-7 (W)
1996—Eagles, 17-14 (W)
     Redskins, 26-21 (P)
1997—Eagles, 24-10 (P)
     Redskins, 35-32 (W)
1998—Eagles, 17-12 (P)
     Redskins, 28-3 (W)
1999—Eagles, 35-28 (P)
     Redskins, 20-17 (W) OT
2000—Redskins, 17-14 (P)
     Eagles, 23-20 (W)
2001—Redskins, 13-3 (P)
     Eagles, 20-6 (W)
2002—Eagles, 37-7 (W)
     Eagles, 34-21 (P)
2003—Eagles, 27-25 (P)
     Eagles, 31-7 (W)
2004—Eagles, 28-6 (P)
     Eagles, 17-14 (W)
2005—Redskins, 17-10 (W)
     Redskins, 31-20 (P)
2006—Eagles, 27-3 (P)
     Eagles, 21-19 (W)
2007—Redskins, 20-12 (P)
     Eagles, 33-25 (W)
2008—Redskins, 23-17 (P)
     Redskins, 10-3 (W)
2009—Eagles, 27-17 (W)
     Eagles, 27-24 (P)
2010—Redskins, 17-12 (P)
     Eagles, 59-28 (W)
2011—Eagles, 20-13 (W)
     Eagles, 34-10 (P)
2012—Redskins, 31-6 (W)
     Redskins, 27-20 (P)
2013—Eagles, 33-27 (W)
     Eagles, 24-16 (P)
(RS Pts.—Eagles 3,255, Redskins 3,078)
(PS Pts.—Redskins 20, Eagles 6)
*Franchise in Boston prior to 1937
**NFC First-Round Playoff

PITTSBURGH vs. ARIZONA
RS: Steelers lead series, 32-23-3
PS: Steelers lead series, 1-0;
See Arizona vs. Pittsburgh
PITTSBURGH vs. ATLANTA
RS: Steelers lead series, 12-2-1;
See Atlanta vs. Pittsburgh

PITTSBURGH vs. BALTIMORE
RS: Steelers lead series, 20-16
PS: Steelers lead series, 3-0;
See Baltimore vs. Pittsburgh
PITTSBURGH vs. BUFFALO
RS: Steelers lead series, 13-8
PS: Steelers lead series, 2-1;
See Buffalo vs. Pittsburgh
PITTSBURGH vs. CAROLINA
RS: Steelers lead series, 4-1;
See Carolina vs. Pittsburgh
PITTSBURGH vs. CHICAGO
RS: Bears lead series, 18-7-1;
See Chicago vs. Pittsburgh
PITTSBURGH vs. CINCINNATI
RS: Steelers lead series, 53-34
PS: Steelers lead series, 1-0;
See Cincinnati vs. Pittsburgh
PITTSBURGH vs. CLEVELAND
RS: Steelers lead series, 65-57
PS: Steelers lead series, 2-0;
See Cleveland vs. Pittsburgh
PITTSBURGH vs. DALLAS
RS: Cowboys lead series, 15-13
PS: Steelers lead series, 2-1;
See Dallas vs. Pittsburgh
PITTSBURGH vs. DENVER
RS: Broncos lead series, 14-7-1
PS: Broncos lead series, 4-3;
See Denver vs. Pittsburgh
PITTSBURGH vs. DETROIT
RS: Steelers lead series, 16-14-1;
See Detroit vs. Pittsburgh
PITTSBURGH vs. GREEN BAY
RS: Packers lead series, 18-15
PS: Packers lead series, 1-0;
See Green Bay vs. Pittsburgh
PITTSBURGH vs. HOUSTON
RS: Series tied, 2-2;
See Houston vs. Pittsburgh
PITTSBURGH vs. INDIANAPOLIS
RS: Steelers lead series, 14-6
PS: Steelers lead series, 5-0;
See Indianapolis vs. Pittsburgh
PITTSBURGH vs. JACKSONVILLE
RS: Jaguars lead series, 11-10
PS: Jaguars lead series, 1-0;
See Jacksonville vs. Pittsburgh
PITTSBURGH vs. KANSAS CITY
RS: Steelers lead series, 19-9
PS: Chiefs lead series, 1-0;
See Kansas City vs. Pittsburgh
PITTSBURGH vs. MIAMI
RS: Steelers lead series, 12-10
PS: Dolphins lead series, 2-1;
See Miami vs. Pittsburgh
PITTSBURGH vs. MINNESOTA
RS: Vikings lead series, 9-7
PS: Steelers lead series, 1-0;
See Minnesota vs. Pittsburgh
PITTSBURGH vs. NEW ENGLAND
RS: Steelers lead series, 14-9
PS: Patriots lead series, 3-1;
See New England vs. Pittsburgh
PITTSBURGH vs. NEW ORLEANS
RS: Series tied, 7-7;
See New Orleans vs. Pittsburgh
PITTSBURGH vs. N.Y. GIANTS
RS: Giants lead series, 44-29-3;
See N.Y. Giants vs. Pittsburgh
PITTSBURGH vs. N.Y. JETS
RS: Steelers lead series, 17-4
PS: Steelers lead series, 2-0;

See N.Y. Jets vs. Pittsburgh
PITTSBURGH vs. OAKLAND
RS: Raiders lead series, 12-9
PS: Series tied, 3-3;
See Oakland vs. Pittsburgh
PITTSBURGH vs. PHILADELPHIA
RS: Eagles lead series, 46-28-3
PS: Eagles lead series, 1-0;
See Philadelphia vs. Pittsburgh
*PITTSBURGH vs. **ST. LOUIS
RS: Rams lead series, 15-7-2
PS: Steelers lead series, 1-0
1938—Rams, 13-7 (New Orleans)
1939—Tie, 14-14 (C)
1941—Rams, 17-14 (Akron)
1947—Rams, 48-7 (P)
1948—Rams, 31-14 (LA)
1949—Tie, 7-7 (P)
1952—Rams, 28-14 (LA)
1955—Rams, 27-26 (LA)
1956—Steelers, 30-13 (P)
1961—Rams, 24-14 (LA)
1964—Rams, 26-14 (P)
1968—Rams, 45-10 (LA)
1971—Rams, 23-14 (P)
1975—Rams, 10-3 (LA)
1978—Rams, 10-7 (LA)
1979—***Steelers, 31-19 (Pasadena)
1981—Steelers, 24-0 (P)
1984—Steelers, 24-14 (P)
1987—Rams, 31-21 (LA)
1990—Steelers, 41-10 (P)
1993—Rams, 27-0 (LA)
1996—Steelers, 42-6 (P)
2003—Rams, 33-21 (P)
2007—Steelers, 41-24 (StL)
2011—Steelers, 27-0 (P)
(RS Pts.—Rams 481, Steelers 436)
(PS Pts.—Steelers 31, Rams 19)
*Steelers known as Pirates prior to 1940
**Franchise in Los Angeles prior to 1995
and in Cleveland prior to 1946
***Super Bowl XIV
PITTSBURGH vs. SAN DIEGO
RS: Steelers lead series, 21-7
PS: Chargers lead series, 2-1
1971—Steelers, 21-17 (P)
1972—Steelers, 24-2 (SD)
1973—Steelers, 38-21 (P)
1975—Steelers, 37-0 (SD)
1976—Steelers, 23-0 (P)
1977—Steelers, 10-9 (SD)
1979—Chargers, 35-7 (SD)
1980—Chargers, 26-17 (SD)
1982—*Chargers, 31-28 (P)
1983—Steelers, 26-3 (P)
1984—Steelers, 52-24 (SD)
1985—Chargers, 54-44 (SD)
1987—Steelers, 20-16 (SD)
1988—Chargers, 20-14 (SD)
1989—Steelers, 20-17 (P)
1990—Steelers, 36-14 (P)
1991—Steelers, 26-20 (P)
1992—Steelers, 23-6 (SD)
1993—Steelers, 16-3 (P)
1994—Chargers, 37-34 (SD)
  **Chargers, 17-13 (SD)
1995—Steelers, 31-16 (P)
1996—Steelers, 16-3 (P)
2000—Steelers, 34-21 (SD)
2003—Steelers, 40-24 (P)
2005—Steelers, 24-22 (SD)
2006—Chargers, 23-13 (SD)

2008—Steelers, 11-10 (P)
  ***Steelers, 35-24 (P)
2009—Steelers, 38-28 (P)
2012—Chargers, 34-24 (P)
(RS Pts.—Steelers 719, Chargers 505)
(PS Pts.—Steelers 76, Chargers 72)
*AFC First-Round Playoff
**AFC Championship
***AFC Divisional Playoff
PITTSBURGH vs. SAN FRANCISCO
RS: 49ers lead series, 11-9
1951—49ers, 28-24 (P)
1952—Steelers, 24-7 (SF)
1954—49ers, 31-3 (SF)
1958—49ers, 23-20 (SF)
1961—Steelers, 20-10 (P)
1965—49ers, 27-17 (SF)
1968—49ers, 45-28 (P)
1973—Steelers, 37-14 (SF)
1977—Steelers, 27-0 (P)
1978—Steelers, 24-7 (SF)
1981—49ers, 17-14 (P)
1984—Steelers, 20-17 (SF)
1987—Steelers, 30-17 (P)
1990—49ers, 27-7 (SF)
1993—49ers, 24-13 (P)
1996—49ers, 25-15 (P)
1999—Steelers, 27-6 (SF)
2003—49ers, 30-14 (SF)
2007—Steelers, 37-16 (P)
2011—49ers, 20-3 (SF)
(RS Pts.—Steelers 404, 49ers 391)
PITTSBURGH vs. SEATTLE
RS: Series tied, 8-8
PS: Steelers lead series, 1-0
1977—Steelers, 30-20 (P)
1978—Steelers, 21-10 (P)
1981—Seahawks, 24-21 (S)
1982—Seahawks, 16-0 (S)
1983—Steelers, 27-21 (S)
1986—Seahawks, 30-0 (S)
1987—Steelers, 13-9 (P)
1991—Seahawks, 27-7 (P)
1992—Steelers, 20-14 (P)
1993—Seahawks, 16-6 (S)
1994—Seahawks, 30-13 (S)
1998—Steelers, 13-10 (P)
1999—Seahawks, 29-10 (P)
2003—Seahawks, 23-16 (S)
2005—*Steelers, 21-10 (Detroit)
2007—Steelers, 21-0 (P)
2011—Steelers, 24-0 (P)
(RS Pts.—Seahawks 279, Steelers 242)
(PS Pts.—Steelers 21, Seahawks 10)
*Super Bowl XL
PITTSBURGH vs. TAMPA BAY
RS: Steelers lead series, 8-1
1976—Steelers, 42-0 (P)
1980—Steelers, 24-21 (TB)
1983—Steelers, 17-12 (P)
1989—Steelers, 31-22 (TB)
1998—Buccaneers, 16-3 (TB)
2001—Steelers, 17-10 (TB)
2002—Steelers, 17-7 (TB)
2006—Steelers, 20-3 (TB)
2010—Steelers, 38-13 (TB)
(RS Pts.—Steelers 209, Buccaneers 104)
PITTSBURGH vs. *TENNESSEE
RS: Steelers lead series, 41-31
PS: Steelers lead series, 3-1
1970—Oilers, 19-7 (P)
  Steelers, 7-3 (H)
1971—Steelers, 23-16 (P)

Oilers, 29-3 (H)
1972—Steelers, 24-7 (P)
Steelers, 9-3 (H)
1973—Steelers, 36-7 (H)
Steelers, 33-7 (P)
1974—Steelers, 13-7 (H)
Oilers, 13-10 (P)
1975—Steelers, 24-17 (P)
Steelers, 32-9 (H)
1976—Steelers, 32-16 (P)
Steelers, 21-0 (H)
1977—Oilers, 27-10 (H)
Steelers, 27-10 (P)
1978—Oilers, 24-17 (P)
Steelers, 13-3 (H)
**Steelers, 34-5 (P)
1979—Steelers, 38-7 (P)
Oilers, 20-17 (H)
**Steelers, 27-13 (P)
1980—Steelers, 31-17 (P)
Oilers, 6-0 (H)
1981—Steelers, 26-13 (P)
Oilers, 21-20 (H)
1982—Steelers, 24-10 (H)
1983—Steelers, 40-28 (H)
Steelers, 17-10 (P)
1984—Steelers, 35-7 (P)
Oilers, 23-20 (H) OT
1985—Steelers, 20-0 (P)
Steelers, 30-7 (H)
1986—Steelers, 22-16 (H) OT
Steelers, 21-10 (P)
1987—Oilers, 23-3 (P)
Oilers, 24-16 (H)
1988—Oilers, 34-14 (P)
Steelers, 37-34 (H)
1989—Oilers, 27-0 (H)
Oilers, 23-16 (P)
***Steelers, 26-23 (H) OT
1990—Steelers, 20-9 (P)
Oilers, 34-14 (H)
1991—Steelers, 26-14 (P)
Oilers, 31-6 (H)
1992—Steelers, 29-24 (H)
Steelers, 21-20 (P)
1993—Oilers, 23-3 (H)
Oilers, 26-17 (P)
1994—Steelers, 30-14 (P)
Steelers, 12-9 (H) OT
1995—Steelers, 34-17 (H)
Steelers, 21-7 (P)
1996—Steelers, 30-16 (P)
Oilers, 23-13 (H)
1997—Steelers, 37-24 (P)
Oilers, 16-6 (T)
1998—Oilers, 41-31 (P)
Oilers, 23-14 (T)
1999—Titans, 16-10 (T)
Titans, 47-36 (P)
2000—Titans, 23-20 (P)
Titans, 9-7 (T)
2001—Steelers, 34-7 (P)
Steelers, 34-24 (T)
2002—Titans, 31-23 (P)
****Titans, 34-31 (T) OT
2003—Titans, 30-13 (P)
2005—Steelers, 34-7 (P)
2008—Titans, 31-14 (T)
2009—Steelers, 13-10 (P) OT
2010—Steelers, 19-11 (T)
2011—Steelers, 38-17 (P)
2012—Titans, 26-23 (P)
2013—Titans, 16-9 (P)

(RS Pts.—Steelers 1,479, Titans 1,253)
(PS Pts.—Steelers 118, Titans 75)
*Franchise in Houston prior to 1997;
known as Oilers prior to 1999
**AFC Championship
***AFC First-Round Playoff
****AFC Divisional Playoff
**PITTSBURGH vs. **WASHINGTON
RS: Redskins lead series, 42-32-3
1933—Redskins, 21-6 (P)
Pirates, 16-14 (B)
1934—Redskins, 7-0 (P)
Redskins, 39-0 (B)
1935—Pirates, 6-0 (P)
Redskins, 13-3 (B)
1936—Pirates, 10-0 (P)
Redskins, 30-0 (B)
1937—Redskins, 34-20 (W)
Pirates, 21-13 (P)
1938—Redskins, 7-0 (P)
Redskins, 15-0 (W)
1939—Redskins, 44-14 (W)
Redskins, 21-14 (P)
1940—Redskins, 40-10 (P)
Redskins, 37-10 (W)
1941—Redskins, 24-20 (P)
Redskins, 23-3 (W)
1942—Redskins, 28-14 (W)
Redskins, 14-0 (P)
1945—Redskins, 14-0 (P)
Redskins, 24-0 (W)
1946—Tie, 14-14 (W)
Steelers, 14-7 (P)
1947—Redskins, 27-26 (W)
Steelers, 21-14 (P)
1948—Redskins, 17-14 (W)
Steelers, 10-7 (P)
1949—Redskins, 27-14 (P)
Redskins, 27-14 (W)
1950—Steelers, 26-7 (W)
Redskins, 24-7 (P)
1951—Redskins, 22-7 (P)
Steelers, 20-10 (W)
1952—Redskins, 28-24 (P)
Steelers, 24-23 (W)
1953—Redskins, 17-9 (P)
Steelers, 14-13 (W)
1954—Steelers, 37-7 (P)
Redskins, 17-14 (W)
1955—Redskins, 23-14 (P)
Redskins, 28-17 (W)
1956—Steelers, 30-13 (P)
Steelers, 23-0 (W)
1957—Steelers, 28-7 (P)
Redskins, 10-3 (W)
1958—Redskins, 24-16 (P)
Tie, 14-14 (W)
1959—Redskins, 23-17 (P)
Steelers, 27-6 (W)
1960—Tie, 27-27 (W)
Steelers, 22-10 (P)
1961—Steelers, 20-0 (P)
Steelers, 30-14 (W)
1962—Steelers, 23-21 (P)
Steelers, 27-24 (W)
1963—Steelers, 38-27 (P)
Steelers, 34-28 (W)
1964—Redskins, 30-0 (P)
Steelers, 14-7 (W)
1965—Steelers, 31-3 (P)
Redskins, 35-14 (W)
1966—Redskins, 33-27 (P)
Redskins, 24-10 (W)

1967—Redskins, 15-10 (P)
1968—Redskins, 16-13 (W)
1969—Redskins, 14-7 (P)
1973—Steelers, 21-16 (P)
1979—Steelers, 38-7 (P)
1985—Redskins, 30-23 (P)
1988—Redskins, 30-29 (W)
1991—Redskins, 41-14 (P)
1997—Steelers, 14-13 (P)
2000—Steelers, 24-3 (P)
2004—Steelers, 16-7 (P)
2008—Steelers, 23-6 (W)
2012—Steelers, 27-12 (P)
(RS Pts.—Redskins 1,431, Steelers 1,221)
*Steelers known as Pirates prior to 1940
**Franchise in Boston prior to 1937

ST. LOUIS vs. ARIZONA
RS: Series tied, 34-34-2
PS: Rams lead series, 1-0;
See Arizona vs. St. Louis
ST. LOUIS vs. ATLANTA
RS: Rams lead series, 47-27-2
PS: Falcons lead series, 1-0;
See Atlanta vs. St. Louis
ST. LOUIS vs. BALTIMORE
RS: Ravens lead series, 3-2;
See Baltimore vs. St. Louis
ST. LOUIS vs. BUFFALO
RS: Bills lead series, 6-5;
See Buffalo vs. St. Louis
ST. LOUIS vs. CAROLINA
RS: Panthers lead series, 11-8
PS: Panthers lead series, 1-0;
See Carolina vs. St. Louis
ST. LOUIS vs. CHICAGO
RS: Bears lead series, 51-35-3
PS: Series tied, 1-1;
See Chicago vs. St. Louis
ST. LOUIS vs. CINCINNATI
RS: Bengals lead series, 7-5;
See Cincinnati vs. St. Louis
ST. LOUIS vs. CLEVELAND
RS: Rams lead series, 10-9
PS: Browns lead series, 2-1;
See Cleveland vs. St. Louis
ST. LOUIS vs. DALLAS
RS: Cowboys lead series, 12-11
PS: Series tied, 4-4;
See Dallas vs. St. Louis
ST. LOUIS vs. DENVER
RS: Rams lead series, 7-5;
See Denver vs. St. Louis
ST. LOUIS vs. DETROIT
RS: Rams lead series, 42-39-1
PS: Lions lead series, 1-0;
See Detroit vs. St. Louis
ST. LOUIS vs. GREEN BAY
RS: Rams lead series, 45-44-2
PS: Series tied, 1-1;
See Green Bay vs. St. Louis
ST. LOUIS vs. HOUSTON
RS: Rams lead series, 2-1;
See Houston vs. St. Louis
ST. LOUIS vs. INDIANAPOLIS
RS: Colts lead series, 23-18-2;
See Indianapolis vs. St. Louis
ST. LOUIS vs. JACKSONVILLE
RS: Rams lead series, 3-1;
See Jacksonville vs. St. Louis
ST. LOUIS vs. KANSAS CITY
RS: Chiefs lead series; 6-4;
See Kansas City vs. St. Louis

ST. LOUIS vs. MIAMI
RS: Dolphins lead series, 10-2;
See Miami vs. St. Louis
ST. LOUIS vs. MINNESOTA
RS: Vikings lead series, 19-14-2
PS: Vikings lead series, 5-2;
See Minnesota vs. St. Louis
ST. LOUIS vs. NEW ENGLAND
RS: Patriots lead series, 6-5
PS: Patriots lead series, 1-0;
See New England vs. St. Louis
ST. LOUIS vs. NEW ORLEANS
RS: Rams lead series, 40-31
PS: Saints lead series, 1-0;
See New Orleans vs. St. Louis
ST. LOUIS vs. N.Y. GIANTS
RS: Rams lead series, 25-14
PS: Series tied, 1-1;
See N.Y. Giants vs. St. Louis
ST. LOUIS vs. N.Y. JETS
RS: Rams lead series, 9-4;
See N.Y. Jets vs. St. Louis
ST. LOUIS vs. OAKLAND
RS: Raiders lead series, 8-4;
See Oakland vs. St. Louis
ST. LOUIS vs. PHILADELPHIA
RS: Eagles lead series, 18-17-1
PS: Rams lead series, 2-1;
See Philadelphia vs. St. Louis
ST. LOUIS vs. PITTSBURGH
RS: Rams lead series, 15-7-2
PS: Steelers lead series, 1-0;
See Pittsburgh vs. St. Louis
*ST. LOUIS vs. SAN DIEGO
RS: Rams lead series, 6-4
1970—Rams, 37-10 (LA)
1975—Rams, 13-10 (SD) OT
1979—Chargers, 40-16 (LA)
1988—Chargers, 38-24 (LA)
1991—Rams, 30-24 (LA)
1994—Chargers, 31-17 (SD)
2000—Rams, 57-31 (StL)
2002—Rams, 28-24 (StL)
2006—Chargers, 38-24 (SD)
2010—Rams, 20-17 (StL)
(RS Pts.—Rams 266, Chargers 263)
Franchise in Los Angeles prior to 1995
*ST. LOUIS vs. SAN FRANCISCO
RS: Rams lead series, 63-62-3
PS: 49ers lead series, 1-0
1950—Rams, 35-14 (SF)
　　　 Rams, 28-21 (LA)
1951—49ers, 44-17 (SF)
　　　 Rams, 23-16 (LA)
1952—Rams, 35-9 (LA)
　　　 Rams, 34-21 (SF)
1953—49ers, 31-30 (SF)
　　　 49ers, 31-27 (LA)
1954—Tie, 24-24 (LA)
　　　 Rams, 42-34 (SF)
1955—Rams, 23-14 (SF)
　　　 Rams, 27-14 (LA)
1956—49ers, 33-30 (SF)
　　　 Rams, 30-6 (LA)
1957—49ers, 23-20 (SF)
　　　 Rams, 37-24 (LA)
1958—Rams, 33-3 (SF)
　　　 Rams, 56-7 (LA)
1959—49ers, 34-0 (SF)
　　　 49ers, 24-16 (LA)
1960—49ers, 13-9 (SF)
　　　 49ers, 23-7 (LA)
1961—49ers, 35-0 (SF)

Rams, 17-7 (LA)
1962—Rams, 28-14 (SF)
　　　 49ers, 24-17 (LA)
1963—Rams, 28-21 (LA)
　　　 Rams, 21-17 (SF)
1964—Rams, 42-14 (LA)
　　　 49ers, 28-7 (SF)
1965—49ers, 45-21 (LA)
　　　 49ers, 30-27 (SF)
1966—Rams, 34-3 (LA)
　　　 49ers, 21-13 (SF)
1967—49ers, 27-24 (LA)
　　　 Rams, 17-7 (SF)
1968—Rams, 24-10 (LA)
　　　 Tie, 20-20 (SF)
1969—Rams, 27-21 (SF)
　　　 Rams, 41-30 (LA)
1970—49ers, 20-6 (LA)
　　　 Rams, 30-13 (SF)
1971—Rams, 20-13 (SF)
　　　 Rams, 17-6 (LA)
1972—Rams, 31-7 (LA)
　　　 Rams, 26-16 (SF)
1973—Rams, 40-20 (SF)
　　　 Rams, 31-13 (LA)
1974—Rams, 37-14 (LA)
　　　 Rams, 15-13 (SF)
1975—Rams, 23-14 (SF)
　　　 49ers, 24-23 (LA)
1976—49ers, 16-0 (LA)
　　　 Rams, 23-3 (SF)
1977—Rams, 34-14 (LA)
　　　 Rams, 23-10 (SF)
1978—Rams, 27-10 (LA)
　　　 Rams, 31-28 (SF)
1979—Rams, 27-24 (LA)
　　　 Rams, 26-20 (SF)
1980—Rams, 48-26 (LA)
　　　 Rams, 31-17 (SF)
1981—49ers, 20-17 (SF)
　　　 49ers, 33-31 (LA)
1982—49ers, 30-24 (LA)
　　　 Rams, 21-20 (SF)
1983—Rams, 10-7 (SF)
　　　 49ers, 45-35 (LA)
1984—49ers, 33-0 (LA)
　　　 49ers, 19-16 (SF)
1985—49ers, 28-14 (LA)
　　　 Rams, 27-20 (SF)
1986—Rams, 16-13 (LA)
　　　 49ers, 24-14 (SF)
1987—49ers, 31-10 (LA)
　　　 49ers, 48-0 (SF)
1988—49ers, 24-21 (LA)
　　　 Rams, 38-16 (SF)
1989—Rams, 13-12 (SF)
　　　 49ers, 30-27 (LA)
　　　 **49ers, 30-3 (SF)
1990—Rams, 28-17 (SF)
　　　 49ers, 26-10 (LA)
1991—49ers, 27-10 (SF)
　　　 49ers, 33-10 (LA)
1992—49ers, 27-24 (SF)
　　　 49ers, 27-10 (LA)
1993—49ers, 40-17 (SF)
　　　 49ers, 35-10 (LA)
1994—49ers, 34-19 (LA)
　　　 49ers, 31-27 (SF)
1995—49ers, 44-10 (StL)
　　　 49ers, 41-13 (SF)
1996—49ers, 34-0 (SF)
　　　 49ers, 28-11 (StL)
1997—49ers, 15-12 (StL)

　　　 49ers, 30-10 (SF)
1998—49ers, 28-10 (StL)
　　　 49ers, 38-19 (SF)
1999—Rams, 42-20 (StL)
　　　 Rams, 23-7 (SF)
2000—Rams, 41-24 (StL)
　　　 Rams, 34-24 (SF)
2001—Rams, 30-26 (SF)
　　　 Rams, 27-14 (StL)
2002—49ers, 37-13 (SF)
　　　 Rams, 31-20 (StL)
2003—Rams, 27-24 (StL) OT
　　　 49ers, 30-10 (SF)
2004—Rams, 24-14 (SF)
　　　 Rams, 16-6 (StL)
2005—49ers, 28-25 (StL)
　　　 49ers, 24-20 (StL)
2006—49ers, 20-13 (StL)
　　　 Rams, 20-17 (StL)
2007—49ers, 17-16 (StL)
　　　 Rams, 13-9 (SF)
2008—49ers, 35-16 (SF)
　　　 49ers, 17-16 (StL)
2009—49ers, 35-0 (SF)
　　　 49ers, 28-6 (StL)
2010—49ers, 23-20 (SF) OT
　　　 Rams, 25-17 (StL)
2011—49ers, 26-0 (SF)
　　　 49ers, 34-27 (StL)
2012—Tie, 24-24 (SF) OT
　　　 Rams, 16-13 (StL) OT
2013—49ers, 35-11 (StL)
　　　 49ers, 23-13 (SF)
(RS Pts.—49ers 2,857, Rams 2,743)
(PS Pts.—49ers 30, Rams 3)
Franchise in Los Angeles prior to 1995
**NFC Championship
*ST. LOUIS vs. SEATTLE
RS: Seahawks lead series, 20-11
PS: Rams lead series, 1-0
1976—Rams, 45-6 (LA)
1979—Rams, 24-0 (Sea)
1985—Rams, 35-24 (Sea)
1988—Rams, 31-10 (LA)
1991—Seahawks, 23-9 (Sea)
1997—Seahawks, 17-9 (StL)
2000—Rams, 37-34 (Sea)
2002—Rams, 37-20 (StL)
　　　 Seahawks, 30-10 (Sea)
2003—Seahawks, 24-23 (Sea)
　　　 Rams, 27-22 (StL)
2004—Seahawks, 33-27 (Sea) OT
　　　 Rams, 23-12 (StL)
　　　 **Rams, 27-20 (Sea)
2005—Seahawks, 37-31 (StL)
　　　 Seahawks, 31-16 (Sea)
2006—Seahawks, 30-28 (StL)
　　　 Seahawks, 24-22 (Sea)
2007—Seahawks, 33-6 (Sea)
　　　 Seahawks, 24-19 (StL)
2008—Seahawks, 37-13 (Sea)
　　　 Seahawks, 23-20 (StL)
2009—Seahawks, 28-0 (Sea)
　　　 Seahawks, 27-17 (StL)
2010—Rams, 20-3 (StL)
　　　 Seahawks, 16-6 (Sea)
2011—Seahawks, 24-7 (StL)
　　　 Seahawks, 30-13 (Sea)
2012—Rams, 19-13 (StL)
　　　 Seahawks, 20-13 (Sea)
2013—Seahawks, 14-9 (StL)
　　　 Seahawks, 27-9 (Sea)
(RS Pts.—Seahawks 690, Rams 611)

(PS Pts.—Rams 27, Seahawks 20)
Franchise in Los Angeles prior to 1995
**NFC First-Round Playoff*
ST. LOUIS vs. TAMPA BAY
RS: Rams lead series, 11-8
PS: Rams lead series, 2-0
1977—Rams, 31-0 (LA)
1978—Rams, 26-23 (LA)
1979—Buccaneers, 21-6 (TB)
    **Rams, 9-0 (TB)
1980—Buccaneers, 10-9 (TB)
1984—Rams, 34-33 (TB)
1985—Rams, 31-27 (TB)
1986—Rams, 26-20 (LA) OT
1987—Rams, 35-3 (LA)
1990—Rams, 35-14 (TB)
1992—Rams, 31-27 (TB)
1994—Buccaneers, 24-14 (TB)
1999—**Rams, 11-6 (StL)
2000—Buccaneers, 38-35 (TB)
2001—Buccaneers, 24-17 (StL)
2002—Buccaneers, 26-14 (TB)
2004—Rams, 28-21 (StL)
2007—Buccaneers, 24-3 (TB)
2010—Buccaneers, 18-17 (TB)
2012—Rams, 28-13 (TB)
2013—Rams, 23-13 (StL)
(RS Pts.—Rams 443, Buccaneers 379)
(PS Pts.—Rams 20, Buccaneers 6)
Franchise in Los Angeles prior to 1995
**NFC Championship*
ST. LOUIS vs. **TENNESSEE
RS: Rams lead series, 6-5
PS: Rams lead series, 1-0
1973—Rams, 31-26 (H)
1978—Rams, 10-6 (H)
1981—Oilers, 27-20 (LA)
1984—Rams, 27-16 (LA)
1987—Oilers, 20-16 (H)
1990—Rams, 17-13 (LA)
1993—Rams, 28-13 (H)
1999—Titans, 24-21 (T)
    ***Rams, 23-16 (Atlanta)
2005—Rams, 31-27 (StL)
2009—Titans, 47-7 (T)
2013—Titans, 28-21 (StL)
(RS Pts.—Titans 247, Rams 229)
(PS Pts.—Rams 23, Titans 16)
Franchise in Los Angeles prior to 1995
**Franchise in Houston prior to 1997;*
known as Oilers prior to 1999
***Super Bowl XXXIV*
ST. LOUIS vs. WASHINGTON
RS: Redskins lead series, 22-10-1
PS: Series tied, 2-2
1937—Redskins, 16-7 (C)
1938—Redskins, 37-13 (W)
1941—Redskins, 17-13 (W)
1942—Redskins, 33-14 (W)
1944—Redskins, 14-10 (W)
1945—**Rams, 15-14 (C)
1948—Rams, 41-13 (W)
1949—Rams, 53-27 (LA)
1951—Redskins, 31-21 (W)
1962—Redskins, 20-14 (W)
1963—Redskins, 37-14 (LA)
1967—Tie, 28-28 (LA)
1969—Rams, 24-13 (W)
1971—Redskins, 38-24 (LA)
1974—Redskins, 23-17 (LA)
    ***Rams, 19-10 (LA)
1977—Redskins, 17-14 (W)
1981—Redskins, 30-7 (LA)

1983—Redskins, 42-20 (LA)
    ***Redskins, 51-7 (W)
1986—****Redskins, 19-7 (W)
1987—Rams, 30-26 (W)
1991—Redskins, 27-6 (LA)
1993—Rams, 10-6 (LA)
1994—Redskins, 24-21 (LA)
1995—Redskins, 35-23 (StL)
1996—Redskins, 17-10 (StL)
1997—Rams, 23-20 (W)
2000—Redskins, 33-20 (StL)
2002—Redskins, 20-17 (W)
2005—Redskins, 24-9 (StL)
2006—Rams, 37-31 (StL) OT
2008—Rams, 19-17 (W)
2009—Redskins, 9-7 (W)
2010—Rams, 30-16 (StL)
2011—Redskins, 17-10 (StL)
2012—Rams, 31-28 (StL)
(RS Pts.—Redskins 786, Rams 637)
(PS Pts.—Redskins 94, Rams 48)
Franchise in Los Angeles prior to 1995
and in Cleveland prior to 1946
**NFL Championship*
***NFC Divisional Playoff*
****NFC First-Round Playoff*

SAN DIEGO vs. ARIZONA
RS: Chargers lead series, 9-3;
See Arizona vs. San Diego
SAN DIEGO vs. ATLANTA
RS: Falcons lead series, 8-1;
See Atlanta vs. San Diego
SAN DIEGO vs. BALTIMORE
RS: Ravens lead series, 5-4;
See Baltimore vs. San Diego
SAN DIEGO vs. BUFFALO
RS: Chargers lead series, 21-10-2
PS: Bills lead series, 2-1;
See Buffalo vs. San Diego
SAN DIEGO vs. CAROLINA
RS: Panthers lead series, 4-1;
See Carolina vs. San Diego
SAN DIEGO vs. CHICAGO
RS: Bears lead series, 6-5;
See Chicago vs. San Diego
SAN DIEGO vs. CINCINNATI
RS: Chargers lead series, 19-13
PS: Series tied, 1-1;
See Cincinnati vs. San Diego
SAN DIEGO vs. CLEVELAND
RS: Chargers lead series, 14-8-1;
See Cleveland vs. San Diego
SAN DIEGO vs. DALLAS
RS: Cowboys lead series, 6-4;
See Dallas vs. San Diego
SAN DIEGO vs. DENVER
RS: Broncos lead series, 58-49-1
PS: Broncos lead series, 1-0;
See Denver vs. San Diego
SAN DIEGO vs. DETROIT
RS: Chargers lead series, 6-4;
See Detroit vs. San Diego
SAN DIEGO vs. GREEN BAY
RS: Packers lead series, 9-1;
See Green Bay vs. San Diego
SAN DIEGO vs. HOUSTON
RS: Chargers lead series, 4-1;
See Houston vs. San Diego
SAN DIEGO vs. INDIANAPOLIS
RS: Chargers lead series, 16-9
PS: Chargers lead series, 2-1;
See Indianapolis vs. San Diego

SAN DIEGO vs. JACKSONVILLE
RS: Chargers lead series, 4-2;
See Jacksonville vs. San Diego
SAN DIEGO vs. KANSAS CITY
RS: Chargers lead series, 54-52-1
PS: Chargers lead series, 1-0;
See Kansas City vs. San Diego
SAN DIEGO vs. MIAMI
RS: Dolphins lead series, 13-12
PS: Series tied, 2-2;
See Miami vs. San Diego
SAN DIEGO vs. MINNESOTA
RS: Chargers lead series, 6-5;
See Minnesota vs. San Diego
SAN DIEGO vs. NEW ENGLAND
RS: Patriots lead series, 20-14-2
PS: Patriots lead series, 2-1;
See New England vs. San Diego
SAN DIEGO vs. NEW ORLEANS
RS: Chargers lead series, 7-4;
See New Orleans vs. San Diego
SAN DIEGO vs. N.Y. GIANTS
RS: Chargers lead series, 6-5;
See N.Y. Giants vs. San Diego
SAN DIEGO vs. N.Y. JETS
RS: Chargers lead series, 20-12-1
PS: Jets lead series, 2-0;
See N.Y. Jets vs. San Diego
SAN DIEGO vs. OAKLAND
RS: Raiders lead series, 58-48-2
PS: Raiders lead series, 1-0;
See Oakland vs. San Diego
SAN DIEGO vs. PHILADELPHIA
RS: Chargers lead series, 7-4;
See Philadelphia vs. San Diego
SAN DIEGO vs. PITTSBURGH
RS: Steelers lead series, 21-7
PS: Chargers lead series, 2-1;
See Pittsburgh vs. San Diego
SAN DIEGO vs. ST. LOUIS
RS: Rams lead series, 6-4;
See St. Louis vs. San Diego
SAN DIEGO vs. SAN FRANCISCO
RS: Series tied, 6-6
PS: 49ers lead series, 1-0
1972—49ers, 34-3 (SF)
1976—Chargers, 13-7 (SD) OT
1979—Chargers, 31-9 (SD)
1982—Chargers, 41-37 (SF)
1988—49ers, 48-10 (SD)
1991—49ers, 34-14 (SF)
1994—49ers, 38-15 (SD)
    *49ers, 49-26 (South Florida)
1997—49ers, 17-10 (SF)
2000—49ers, 45-17 (SD)
2002—Chargers, 20-17 (SD) OT
2006—Chargers, 48-19 (SF)
2010—Chargers, 34-7 (SD)
(RS Pts.—49ers 312, Chargers 256)
(PS Pts.—49ers 49, Chargers 26)
Super Bowl XXIX
SAN DIEGO vs. SEATTLE
RS: Seahawks lead series, 26-23
1977—Chargers, 30-28 (Sea)
1978—Chargers, 24-20 (Sea)
    Chargers, 37-10 (SD)
1979—Chargers, 33-16 (Sea)
    Chargers, 20-10 (SD)
1980—Chargers, 34-13 (Sea)
    Chargers, 21-14 (SD)
1981—Chargers, 24-10 (SD)
    Seahawks, 44-23 (Sea)
1983—Seahawks, 34-31 (Sea)

Chargers, 28-21 (SD)
1984—Seahawks, 31-17 (Sea)
Seahawks, 24-0 (SD)
1985—Seahawks, 49-35 (SD)
Seahawks, 26-21 (Sea)
1986—Seahawks, 33-7 (Sea)
Seahawks, 34-24 (SD)
1987—Seahawks, 34-3 (Sea)
1988—Chargers, 17-6 (SD)
Seahawks, 17-14 (Sea)
1989—Seahawks, 17-16 (SD)
Seahawks, 10-7 (Sea)
1990—Chargers, 31-14 (Sea)
Seahawks, 13-10 (SD) OT
1991—Seahawks, 20-9 (Sea)
Chargers, 17-14 (SD)
1992—Chargers, 17-6 (SD)
Chargers, 31-14 (Sea)
1993—Chargers, 18-12 (SD)
Seahawks, 31-14 (Sea)
1994—Chargers, 24-10 (Sea)
Chargers, 35-15 (SD)
1995—Chargers, 14-10 (SD)
Chargers, 35-25 (Sea)
1996—Chargers, 29-7 (SD)
Seahawks, 32-13 (Sea)
1997—Seahawks, 26-22 (Sea)
Seahawks, 37-31 (SD)
1998—Chargers, 27-20 (SD)
Seahawks, 38-17 (Sea)
1999—Chargers, 13-10 (SD)
Chargers, 19-16 (Sea)
2000—Seahawks, 20-12 (SD)
Seahawks, 17-15 (Sea)
2001—Seahawks, 13-10 (Sea) OT
Seahawks, 25-22 (SD)
2002—Seahawks, 31-28 (SD) OT
2006—Chargers, 20-17 (Sea)
2010—Seahawks, 27-20 (Sea)
(RS Pts.—Seahawks 1,028, Chargers 1,012)
SAN DIEGO vs. TAMPA BAY
RS: Chargers lead series, 8-2
1976—Chargers, 23-0 (TB)
1981—Chargers, 24-23 (TB)
1987—Chargers, 17-13 (TB)
1990—Chargers, 41-10 (SD)
1992—Chargers, 29-14 (SD)
1993—Chargers, 32-17 (TB)
1996—Buccaneers, 25-17 (SD)
2004—Chargers, 31-24 (SD)
2008—Chargers, 41-24 (TB)
2012—Buccaneers, 34-24 (TB)
(RS Pts.—Chargers 279, Buccaneers 184)
*SAN DIEGO vs. **TENNESSEE
RS: Chargers lead series, 25-14-1
PS: Titans lead series, 3-1
1960—Oilers, 38-28 (H)
Chargers, 24-21 (LA)
***Oilers, 24-16 (H)
1961—Chargers, 34-24 (SD)
Oilers, 33-13 (H)
***Oilers, 10-3 (SD)
1962—Oilers, 42-17 (SD)
Oilers, 33-27 (H)
1963—Chargers, 27-0 (SD)
Chargers 20-14 (H)
1964—Chargers, 27-21 (SD)
Chargers, 20-17 (H)
1965—Chargers, 31-14 (SD)
Chargers, 37-26 (H)
1966—Chargers, 28-22 (H)
1967—Chargers, 13-3 (SD)
Oilers, 24-17 (H)

1968—Chargers, 30-14 (SD)
1969—Chargers, 21-17 (H)
1970—Tie, 31-31 (SD)
1971—Oilers, 49-33 (H)
1972—Chargers, 34-20 (SD)
1974—Oilers, 21-14 (H)
1975—Oilers, 33-17 (H)
1976—Chargers, 30-27 (SD)
1978—Chargers, 45-24 (H)
1979—****Oilers, 17-14 (SD)
1984—Chargers, 31-14 (SD)
1985—Oilers, 37-35 (H)
1986—Chargers, 27-0 (SD)
1987—Oilers, 33-18 (H)
1989—Oilers, 34-27 (SD)
1990—Oilers, 17-7 (SD)
1992—Oilers, 27-0 (H)
1993—Chargers, 18-17 (SD)
1998—Chargers, 13-7 (T)
2004—Chargers, 38-17 (SD)
2006—Chargers, 40-7 (SD)
2007—Chargers, 23-17 (T) OT
*****Chargers, 17-6 (SD)
2009—Chargers, 42-17 (T)
2010—Chargers, 33-25 (SD)
2012—Chargers, 38-10 (SD)
2013—Titans, 20-17 (T)
(RS Pts.—Chargers 1,025, Titans 867)
(PS Pts.—Titans 57, Chargers 50)
Franchise in Los Angeles prior to 1961
**Franchise in Houston prior to 1997;
known as Oilers prior to 1999
***AFL Championship
****AFC Divisional Playoff
*****AFC First-Round Playoff
SAN DIEGO vs. WASHINGTON
RS: Redskins lead series, 7-3
1973—Redskins, 38-0 (W)
1980—Redskins, 40-17 (W)
1983—Redskins, 27-24 (SD)
1986—Redskins, 30-27 (SD)
1989—Redskins, 26-21 (W)
1998—Redskins, 24-20 (W)
2001—Chargers, 30-3 (SD)
2005—Chargers, 23-17 (W) OT
2009—Chargers, 23-20 (SD)
2013—Redskins, 30-24 (W) OT
(RS Pts.—Redskins 255, Chargers 209)

SAN FRANCISCO vs. ARIZONA
RS: 49ers lead series, 28-17;
See Arizona vs. San Francisco
SAN FRANCISCO vs. ATLANTA
RS: 49ers lead series, 45-29-1
PS: Series tied, 1-1;
See Atlanta vs. San Francisco
SAN FRANCISCO vs. BALTIMORE
RS: Ravens lead series, 3-1
PS: Ravens lead series, 1-0;
See Baltimore vs. San Francisco
SAN FRANCISCO vs. BUFFALO
RS: 49ers lead series, 6-5;
See Buffalo vs. San Francisco
SAN FRANCISCO vs. CAROLINA
RS: Panthers lead series, 11-7
PS: 49ers lead series, 1-0;
See Carolina vs. San Francisco
SAN FRANCISCO vs. CHICAGO
RS: Series tied, 29-29-1
PS: 49ers lead series, 3-0;
See Chicago vs. San Francisco
SAN FRANCISCO vs. CINCINNATI
RS: 49ers lead series, 9-3

PS: 49ers lead series, 2-0;
See Cincinnati vs. San Francisco
SAN FRANCISCO vs. CLEVELAND
RS: Browns lead series, 11-7;
See Cleveland vs. San Francisco
SAN FRANCISCO vs. DALLAS
RS: 49ers lead series, 14-11-1
PS: Cowboys lead series, 5-2;
See Dallas vs. San Francisco
SAN FRANCISCO vs. DENVER
RS: Series tied, 6-6
PS: 49ers lead series, 1-0;
See Denver vs. San Francisco
SAN FRANCISCO vs. DETROIT
RS: 49ers lead series, 36-26-1
PS: Series tied, 1-1;
See Detroit vs. San Francisco
SAN FRANCISCO vs. GREEN BAY
RS: Packers lead series, 30-27-1
PS: Packers lead series, 4-3;
See Green Bay vs. San Francisco
SAN FRANCISCO vs. HOUSTON
RS: 49ers lead series, 2-1;
See Houston vs. San Francisco
SAN FRANCISCO vs. INDIANAPOLIS
RS: Colts lead series, 25-18;
See Indianapolis vs. San Francisco
SAN FRANCISCO vs. JACKSONVILLE
RS: Series tied, 2-2;
See Jacksonville vs. San Francisco
SAN FRANCISCO vs. KANSAS CITY
RS: 49ers lead series, 6-5;
See Kansas City vs. San Francisco
SAN FRANCISCO vs. MIAMI
RS: Dolphins lead series, 6-5
PS: 49ers lead series, 1-0;
See Miami vs. San Francisco
SAN FRANCISCO vs. MINNESOTA
RS: Vikings lead series, 21-18-1
PS: 49ers lead series, 4-1;
See Minnesota vs. San Francisco
SAN FRANCISCO vs. NEW ENGLAND
RS: 49ers lead series, 8-4;
See New England vs. San Francisco
SAN FRANCISCO vs. NEW ORLEANS
RS: 49ers lead series, 46-25-2
PS: 49ers lead series, 1-0;
See New Orleans vs. San Francisco
SAN FRANCISCO vs. N.Y. GIANTS
RS: Giants lead series, 15-14
PS: Series tied, 4-4;
See N.Y. Giants vs. San Francisco
SAN FRANCISCO vs. N.Y. JETS
RS: 49ers lead series, 10-2;
See N.Y. Jets vs. San Francisco
SAN FRANCISCO vs. OAKLAND
RS: Series tied, 6-6;
See Oakland vs. San Francisco
SAN FRANCISCO vs. PHILADELPHIA
RS: 49ers lead series, 17-12-1
PS: 49ers lead series, 1-0;
See Philadelphia vs. San Francisco
SAN FRANCISCO vs. PITTSBURGH
RS: 49ers lead series, 11-9;
See Pittsburgh vs. San Francisco
SAN FRANCISCO vs. ST. LOUIS
RS: 49ers lead series, 63-62-3
PS: 49ers lead series, 1-0;
See St. Louis vs. San Francisco
SAN FRANCISCO vs. SAN DIEGO
RS: Series tied, 6-6
PS: 49ers lead series, 1-0;
See San Diego vs. San Francisco

SAN FRANCISCO vs. SEATTLE
RS: Series tied, 15-15
PS: Seahawks lead series, 1-0
1976—49ers, 37-21 (Sea)
1979—Seahawks, 35-24 (SF)
1985—49ers, 19-6 (SF)
1988—49ers, 38-7 (Sea)
1991—49ers, 24-22 (Sea)
1997—Seahawks, 38-9 (Sea)
2002—49ers, 28-21 (Sea)
    49ers, 31-24 (SF)
2003—Seahawks, 20-19 (Sea)
    Seahawks, 24-17 (SF)
2004—Seahawks, 34-0 (Sea)
    Seahawks, 42-27 (SF)
2005—Seahawks, 27-25 (SF)
    Seahawks, 41-3 (Sea)
2006—49ers, 20-14 (SF)
    49ers, 24-14 (Sea)
2007—Seahawks, 23-3 (SF)
    Seahawks, 24-0 (Sea)
2008—49ers, 33-30 (Sea) OT
    Seahawks, 34-13 (SF)
2009—49ers, 23-10 (SF)
    Seahawks, 20-17 (Sea)
2010—Seahawks, 31-6 (Sea)
    49ers, 40-21 (SF)
2011—49ers, 33-17 (SF)
    49ers, 19-17 (Sea)
2012—49ers, 13-6 (SF)
    Seahawks, 42-13 (Sea)
2013—Seahawks, 29-3 (Sea)
    49ers, 19-17 (SF)
    *Seahawks, 23-17 (Sea)
(RS Pts.—Seahawks 711, 49ers 580)
(PS Pts.—Seahawks 23, 49ers 17)
*NFC Championship

SAN FRANCISCO vs. TAMPA BAY
RS: 49ers lead series, 17-4
PS: Buccaneers lead series, 1-0
1977—49ers, 20-10 (SF)
1978—49ers, 6-3 (SF)
1979—49ers, 23-7 (SF)
1980—Buccaneers, 24-23 (SF)
1983—49ers, 35-21 (SF)
1984—49ers, 24-17 (SF)
1986—49ers, 31-7 (TB)
1987—49ers, 24-10 (TB)
1989—49ers, 20-16 (TB)
1990—49ers, 31-7 (SF)
1992—49ers, 21-14 (SF)
1993—49ers, 45-21 (TB)
1994—49ers, 41-16 (SF)
1997—Buccaneers, 13-6 (TB)
2002—*Buccaneers, 31-6 (TB)
2003—49ers, 24-7 (SF)
2004—Buccaneers, 35-3 (TB)
2005—49ers, 15-10 (SF)
2007—49ers, 21-19 (SF)
2010—Buccaneers, 21-0 (SF)
2011—49ers, 48-3 (SF)
2013—49ers, 33-14 (TB)
(RS Pts.—49ers 494, Buccaneers 295)
(PS Pts.—Buccaneers 31, 49ers 6)
*NFC Divisional Playoff

SAN FRANCISCO vs. *TENNESSEE
RS: 49ers lead series, 8-5
1970—49ers, 30-20 (H)
1975—Oilers, 27-13 (SF)
1978—Oilers, 20-19 (H)
1981—49ers, 28-6 (H)
1984—49ers, 34-21 (H)
1987—49ers, 27-20 (SF)

1990—49ers, 24-21 (H)
1993—Oilers, 10-7 (SF)
1996—49ers, 10-9 (H)
1999—49ers, 24-22 (SF)
2005—Titans, 33-22 (T)
2009—Titans, 34-27 (SF)
2013—49ers, 31-17 (T)
(RS Pts.—49ers 296, Titans 260)
*Franchise in Houston prior to 1997;
known as Oilers prior to 1999

SAN FRANCISCO vs. WASHINGTON
RS: 49ers lead series, 16-9-1
PS: 49ers lead series, 3-1
1952—49ers, 23-17 (W)
1954—49ers, 41-7 (SF)
1955—Redskins, 7-0 (W)
1961—49ers, 35-3 (SF)
1967—Redskins, 31-28 (W)
1969—Tie, 17-17 (SF)
1970—49ers, 26-17 (SF)
1971—*49ers, 24-20 (SF)
1973—Redskins, 33-9 (W)
1976—Redskins, 24-21 (SF)
1978—Redskins, 38-20 (W)
1981—49ers, 30-17 (W)
1983—**Redskins, 24-21 (W)
1984—49ers, 37-31 (SF)
1985—49ers, 35-8 (W)
1986—Redskins, 14-6 (W)
1988—49ers, 37-21 (SF)
1990—49ers, 26-13 (SF)
    *49ers, 28-10 (SF)
1992—*49ers, 20-13 (SF)
1994—49ers, 37-22 (W)
1996—49ers, 19-16 (W) OT
1998—49ers, 45-10 (W)
1999—Redskins, 26-20 (SF) OT
2002—49ers, 20-10 (SF)
2004—Redskins, 26-16 (SF)
2005—Redskins, 52-17 (W)
2008—49ers, 27-24 (SF)
2011—49ers, 19-11 (W)
2013—49ers, 27-6 (W)
(RS Pts.—49ers 638, Redskins 501)
(PS Pts.—49ers 93, Redskins 67)
*NFC Divisional Playoff
**NFC Championship

SEATTLE vs. ARIZONA
RS: Cardinals lead series, 16-14;
See Arizona vs. Seattle
SEATTLE vs. ATLANTA
RS: Seahawks lead series, 9-5
PS: Falcons lead series 1-0;
See Atlanta vs. Seattle
SEATTLE vs. BALTIMORE
RS: Series tied, 2-2;
See Baltimore vs. Seattle
SEATTLE vs. BUFFALO
RS: Seahawks lead series, 7-5;
See Buffalo vs. Seattle
SEATTLE vs. CAROLINA
RS: Seahawks lead series, 4-2
PS: Seahawks lead series, 1-0;
See Carolina vs. Seattle
SEATTLE vs. CHICAGO
RS: Seahawks lead series, 10-4
PS: Bears lead series, 2-0;
See Chicago vs. Seattle
SEATTLE vs. CINCINNATI
RS: Series tied, 9-9
PS: Bengals lead series, 1-0;
See Cincinnati vs. Seattle

SEATTLE vs. CLEVELAND
RS: Seahawks lead series, 11-6;
See Cleveland vs. Seattle
SEATTLE vs. DALLAS
RS: Cowboys lead series, 9-5
PS: Seahawks lead series, 1-0;
See Dallas vs. Seattle
SEATTLE vs. DENVER
RS: Broncos lead series, 34-18
PS: Seahawks lead series, 2-0;
See Denver vs. Seattle
SEATTLE vs. DETROIT
RS: Seahawks lead series, 7-5;
See Detroit vs. Seattle
SEATTLE vs. GREEN BAY
RS: Packers lead series, 8-6
PS: Packers lead series, 2-0;
See Green Bay vs. Seattle
SEATTLE vs. HOUSTON
RS: Seahawks lead series, 2-1;
See Houston vs. Seattle
SEATTLE vs. INDIANAPOLIS
RS: Colts lead series, 7-4;
See Indianapolis vs. Seattle
SEATTLE vs. JACKSONVILLE
RS: Seahawks lead series, 5-2;
See Jacksonville vs. Seattle
SEATTLE vs. KANSAS CITY
RS: Chiefs lead series, 32-18;
See Kansas City vs. Seattle
SEATTLE vs. MIAMI
RS: Dolphins lead series, 8-3
PS: Dolphins lead series, 2-1;
See Miami vs. Seattle
SEATTLE vs. MINNESOTA
RS: Seahawks lead series, 8-5;
See Minnesota vs. Seattle
SEATTLE vs. NEW ENGLAND
RS: Series tied, 8-8;
See New England vs. Seattle
SEATTLE vs. NEW ORLEANS
RS: Series tied, 6-6
PS: Seahawks lead series, 2-0;
See New Orleans vs. Seattle
SEATTLE vs. N.Y. GIANTS
RS: Giants lead series, 9-7;
See N.Y. Giants vs. Seattle
SEATTLE vs. N.Y. JETS
RS: Seahawks lead series, 10-8;
See N.Y. Jets vs. Seattle
SEATTLE vs. OAKLAND
RS: Raiders lead series, 28-23
PS: Series tied, 1-1;
See Oakland vs. Seattle
SEATTLE vs. PHILADELPHIA
RS: Eagles lead series, 7-6;
See Philadelphia vs. Seattle
SEATTLE vs. PITTSBURGH
RS: Series tied, 8-8
PS: Steelers lead series, 1-0;
See Pittsburgh vs. Seattle
SEATTLE vs. ST. LOUIS
RS: Seahawks lead series, 20-11
PS: Rams lead series, 1-0;
See St. Louis vs. Seattle
SEATTLE vs. SAN DIEGO
RS: Seahawks lead series, 26-23;
See San Diego vs. Seattle
SEATTLE vs. SAN FRANCISCO
RS: Series tied, 15-15
PS: Seahawks lead series, 1-0;
See San Francisco vs. Seattle

SEATTLE vs. TAMPA BAY
RS: Seahawks lead series, 8-4
1976—Seahawks, 13-10 (TB)
1977—Seahawks, 30-23 (S)
1994—Seahawks, 22-21 (S)
1996—Seahawks, 17-13 (TB)
1999—Buccaneers, 16-3 (S)
2004—Seahawks, 10-6 (TB)
2006—Seahawks, 23-7 (TB)
2007—Seahawks, 20-6 (S)
2008—Buccaneers, 20-10 (TB)
2009—Buccaneers, 24-7 (S)
2010—Buccaneers, 38-15 (TB)
2013—Seahawks, 27-24 (S) OT
(RS Pts.—Buccaneers 208, Seahawks 197)
SEATTLE vs. *TENNESSEE
RS: Seahawks lead series, 10-5
PS: Titans lead series, 1-0
1977—Oilers, 22-10 (S)
1979—Seahawks, 34-14 (S)
1980—Seahawks, 26-7 (H)
1981—Oilers, 35-17 (H)
1982—Oilers, 23-21 (H)
1987—**Oilers, 23-20 (H) OT
1988—Seahawks, 27-24 (S)
1990—Seahawks, 13-10 (S) OT
1993—Oilers, 24-14 (H)
1994—Seahawks, 16-14 (H)
1996—Seahawks, 23-16 (S)
1997—Seahawks, 16-13 (S)
1998—Seahawks, 20-18 (S)
2005—Seahawks, 28-24 (T)
2009—Titans, 17-13 (S)
2013—Seahawks, 20-13 (S)
(RS Pts.—Seahawks 298, Titans 274)
(PS Pts.—Titans 23, Seahawks 20)
*Franchise in Houston prior to 1997;
known as Oilers prior to 1999
**AFC First-Round Playoff
SEATTLE vs. WASHINGTON
RS: Redskins lead series, 11-4
PS: Seahawks lead series, 3-0
1976—Redskins, 31-7 (W)
1980—Seahawks, 14-0 (W)
1983—Redskins, 27-17 (S)
1986—Seahawks, 19-14 (W)
1989—Redskins, 29-0 (S)
1992—Redskins, 16-3 (S)
1994—Seahawks, 28-7 (W)
1995—Seahawks, 27-20 (W)
1998—Seahawks, 24-14 (S)
2001—Redskins, 27-14 (W)
2002—Redskins, 14-3 (S)
2003—Redskins, 27-20 (W)
2005—Redskins, 20-17 (W) OT
*Seahawks, 20-10 (S)
2007—**Seahawks, 35-14 (S)
2008—Redskins, 20-17 (S)
2011—Redskins, 23-17 (S)
2012—**Seahawks, 24-14 (W)
(RS Pts.—Redskins 294, Seahawks 222)
(PS Pts.—Seahawks 79, Redskins 38)
*NFC Divisional Playoff
**NFC First-Round Playoff

TAMPA BAY vs. ARIZONA
RS: Series tied, 9-9;
See Arizona vs. Tampa Bay
TAMPA BAY vs. ATLANTA
RS: Buccaneers lead series, 21-20;
See Atlanta vs. Tampa Bay
TAMPA BAY vs. BALTIMORE
RS: Series tied, 2-2;

See Baltimore vs. Tampa Bay
TAMPA BAY vs. BUFFALO
RS: Buccaneers lead series, 7-3;
See Buffalo vs. Tampa Bay
TAMPA BAY vs. CAROLINA
RS: Panthers lead series, 16-11;
See Carolina vs. Tampa Bay
TAMPA BAY vs. CHICAGO
RS: Bears lead series, 36-18;
See Chicago vs. Tampa Bay
TAMPA BAY vs. CINCINNATI
RS: Buccaneers lead series, 7-3;
See Cincinnati vs. Tampa Bay
TAMPA BAY vs. CLEVELAND
RS: Browns lead series, 5-3;
See Cleveland vs. Tampa Bay
TAMPA BAY vs. DALLAS
RS: Cowboys lead series, 11-3
PS: Cowboys lead series, 2-0;
See Dallas vs. Tampa Bay
TAMPA BAY vs. DENVER
RS: Broncos lead series, 6-2;
See Denver vs. Tampa Bay
TAMPA BAY vs. DETROIT
RS: Lions lead series, 29-26
PS: Buccaneers lead series, 1-0;
See Detroit vs. Tampa Bay
TAMPA BAY vs. GREEN BAY
RS: Packers lead series, 30-21-1
PS: Packers lead series, 1-0;
See Green Bay vs. Tampa Bay
TAMPA BAY vs. HOUSTON
RS: Texans lead series, 2-1;
See Houston vs. Tampa Bay
TAMPA BAY vs. INDIANAPOLIS
RS: Colts lead series, 7-5;
See Indianapolis vs. Tampa Bay
TAMPA BAY vs. JACKSONVILLE
RS: Jaguars lead series, 4-1;
See Jacksonville vs. Tampa Bay
TAMPA BAY vs. KANSAS CITY
RS: Buccaneers lead series, 6-5;
See Kansas City vs. Tampa Bay
TAMPA BAY vs. MIAMI
RS: Series tied, 5-5;
See Miami vs. Tampa Bay
TAMPA BAY vs. MINNESOTA
RS: Vikings lead series, 31-22;
See Minnesota vs. Tampa Bay
TAMPA BAY vs. NEW ENGLAND
RS: Patriots lead series, 6-2;
See New England vs. Tampa Bay
TAMPA BAY vs. NEW ORLEANS
RS: Saints lead series, 27-17;
See New Orleans vs. Tampa Bay
TAMPA BAY vs. N.Y. GIANTS
RS: Giants lead series, 12-6
PS: Giants lead series, 1-0;
See N.Y. Giants vs. Tampa Bay
TAMPA BAY vs. N.Y. JETS
RS: Jets lead series, 10-1;
See N.Y. Jets vs. Tampa Bay
TAMPA BAY vs. OAKLAND
RS: Raiders lead series, 6-2
PS: Buccaneers lead series, 1-0;
See Oakland vs. Tampa Bay
TAMPA BAY vs. PHILADELPHIA
RS: Eagles lead series, 8-5
PS: Series tied, 2-2;
See Philadelphia vs. Tampa Bay
TAMPA BAY vs. PITTSBURGH
RS: Steelers lead series, 8-1;
See Pittsburgh vs. Tampa Bay

TAMPA BAY vs. ST. LOUIS
RS: Rams lead series, 11-8
PS: Rams lead series, 2-0;
See St. Louis vs. Tampa Bay
TAMPA BAY vs. SAN DIEGO
RS: Chargers lead series, 8-2;
See San Diego vs. Tampa Bay
TAMPA BAY vs. SAN FRANCISCO
RS: 49ers lead series, 17-4
PS: Buccaneers lead series, 1-0;
See San Francisco vs. Tampa Bay
TAMPA BAY vs. SEATTLE
RS: Seahawks lead series, 8-4;
See Seattle vs. Tampa Bay
TAMPA BAY vs. *TENNESSEE
RS: Titans lead series, 8-2
1976—Oilers, 20-0 (H)
1980—Oilers, 20-14 (H)
1983—Buccaneers, 33-24 (TB)
1989—Oilers, 20-17 (H)
1995—Oilers, 19-7 (H)
1998—Oilers, 31-22 (TB)
2001—Titans, 31-28 (Tenn) OT
2003—Titans, 33-13 (Tenn)
2007—Buccaneers, 13-10 (TB)
2011—Titans, 23-17 (Tenn)
(RS Pts.—Titans 231, Buccaneers 164)
*Franchise in Houston prior to 1997;
known as Oilers prior to 1999
TAMPA BAY vs. WASHINGTON
RS: Series tied, 9-9
PS: Series tied, 1-1
1977—Redskins, 10-0 (TB)
1982—Redskins, 21-13 (TB)
1989—Redskins, 32-28 (W)
1993—Redskins, 23-17 (TB)
1994—Buccaneers, 26-21 (TB)
Buccaneers, 17-14 (W)
1995—Buccaneers, 14-6 (TB)
1996—Buccaneers, 24-10 (TB)
1998—Redskins, 20-16 (W)
1999—*Buccaneers, 14-13 (TB)
2000—Redskins, 20-17 (W) OT
2003—Buccaneers, 35-13 (W)
2004—Redskins, 16-10 (W)
2005—Buccaneers, 36-35 (TB)
**Redskins, 17-10 (TB)
2006—Buccaneers, 20-17 (TB)
2007—Buccaneers, 19-13 (TB)
2009—Redskins, 16-13 (W)
2010—Buccaneers, 17-16 (W)
2012—Redskins, 24-22 (TB)
(RS Pts.—Buccaneers 344, Redskins 327)
(PS Pts.—Redskins 30, Buccaneers 24)
*NFC Divisional Playoff
**NFC First-Round Playoff

TENNESSEE vs. ARIZONA
RS: Cardinals lead series, 6-4;
See Arizona vs. Tennessee
TENNESSEE vs. ATLANTA
RS: Titans lead series, 7-6;
See Atlanta vs. Tennessee
TENNESSEE vs. BALTIMORE
RS: Titans lead series, 9-8
PS: Ravens lead series, 2-1;
See Baltimore vs. Tennessee
TENNESSEE vs. BUFFALO
RS: Titans lead series, 27-14
PS: Bills lead series, 2-1;
See Buffalo vs. Tennessee
TENNESSEE vs. CAROLINA
RS: Titans lead series, 3-1;

See Carolina vs. Tennessee
TENNESSEE vs. CHICAGO
RS: Bears lead series, 6-5;
See Chicago vs. Tennessee
TENNESSEE vs. CINCINNATI
RS: Titans lead series, 39-32-1
PS: Bengals lead series, 1-0;
See Cincinnati vs. Tennessee
TENNESSEE vs. CLEVELAND
RS: Browns lead series, 33-28
PS: Titans lead series, 1-0;
See Cleveland vs. Tennessee
TENNESSEE vs. DALLAS
RS: Cowboys lead series, 7-6;
See Dallas vs. Tennessee
TENNESSEE vs. DENVER
RS: Titans lead series, 21-15-1
PS: Broncos lead series, 2-1;
See Denver vs. Tennessee
TENNESSEE vs. DETROIT
RS: Titans lead series, 8-3;
See Detroit vs. Tennessee
TENNESSEE vs. GREEN BAY
RS: Titans lead series, 6-5;
See Green Bay vs. Tennessee
TENNESSEE vs. HOUSTON
RS: Titans lead series, 15-9;
See Houston vs. Tennessee
TENNESSEE vs. INDIANAPOLIS
RS: Colts lead series, 25-19
PS: Titans lead series, 1-0;
See Indianapolis vs. Tennessee
TENNESSEE vs. JACKSONVILLE
RS: Titans lead series, 21-17
PS: Titans lead series, 1-0;
See Jacksonville vs. Tennessee
TENNESSEE vs. KANSAS CITY
RS: Chiefs lead series, 27-20
PS: Chiefs lead series, 2-0;
See Kansas City vs. Tennessee
TENNESSEE vs. MIAMI
RS: Dolphins lead series, 18-15
PS: Titans lead series, 1-0;
See Miami vs. Tennessee
TENNESSEE vs. MINNESOTA
RS: Vikings lead series, 8-4;
See Minnesota vs. Tennessee
TENNESSEE vs. NEW ENGLAND
RS: Patriots lead series, 22-15-1
PS: Series tied, 1-1;
See New England vs. Tennessee
TENNESSEE vs. NEW ORLEANS
RS: Titans lead series, 7-5-1;
See New Orleans vs. Tennessee
TENNESSEE vs. N.Y. GIANTS
RS: Series tied, 5-5;
See N.Y. Giants vs. Tennessee
TENNESSEE vs. N.Y. JETS
RS: Titans lead series, 23-17-1
PS: Titans lead series, 1-0;
See N.Y. Jets vs. Tennessee
TENNESSEE vs. OAKLAND
RS: Raiders lead series, 23-20
PS: Raiders lead series, 4-0;
See Oakland vs. Tennessee
TENNESSEE vs. PHILADELPHIA
RS: Eagles lead series, 6-4;
See Philadelphia vs. Tennessee
TENNESSEE vs. PITTSBURGH
RS: Steelers lead series, 41-31
PS: Steelers lead series, 3-1;
See Pittsburgh vs. Tennessee
TENNESSEE vs. ST. LOUIS

RS: Rams lead series, 6-5
PS: Rams lead series, 1-0;
See St. Louis vs. Tennessee
TENNESSEE vs. SAN DIEGO
RS: Chargers lead series, 25-14-1
PS: Titans lead series, 3-1;
See San Diego vs. Tennessee
TENNESSEE vs. SAN FRANCISCO
RS: 49ers lead series, 8-5;
See San Francisco vs. Tennessee
TENNESSEE vs. SEATTLE
RS: Seahawks lead series, 10-5
PS: Titans lead series, 1-0;
See Seattle vs. Tennessee
TENNESSEE vs. TAMPA BAY
RS: Titans lead series, 8-2;
See Tampa Bay vs. Tennessee
*TENNESSEE vs. WASHINGTON
RS: Titans lead series, 6-5
1971—Redskins, 22-13 (W)
1975—Oilers, 13-10 (H)
1979—Oilers, 29-27 (W)
1985—Redskins, 16-13 (W)
1988—Oilers, 41-17 (H)
1991—Redskins, 16-13 (W) OT
1997—Oilers, 28-14 (T)
2000—Titans, 27-21 (W)
2002—Redskins, 31-14 (T)
2006—Titans, 25-22 (W)
2010—Redskins, 19-16 (T) OT
(RS—Titans 232, Redskins 215)
*Franchise in Houston prior to 1997;
known as Oilers prior to 1999*

WASHINGTON vs. ARIZONA
RS: Redskins lead series, 74-44-2;
See Arizona vs. Washington
WASHINGTON vs. ATLANTA
RS: Redskins lead series, 14-8-1
PS: Redskins lead series, 1-0;
See Atlanta vs. Washington
WASHINGTON vs. BALTIMORE
RS: Ravens lead series, 3-2;
See Baltimore vs. Washington
WASHINGTON vs. BUFFALO
RS: Bills lead series, 8-4
PS: Redskins lead series, 1-0;
See Buffalo vs. Washington
WASHINGTON vs. CAROLINA
RS: Redskins lead series, 7-4;
See Carolina vs. Washington
WASHINGTON vs. CHICAGO
RS: Series tied, 20-20-1
PS: Redskins lead series, 4-3;
See Chicago vs. Washington
WASHINGTON vs. CINCINNATI
RS: Bengals lead series, 5-4;
See Cincinnati vs. Washington
WASHINGTON vs. CLEVELAND
RS: Browns lead series, 33-11-1;
See Cleveland vs. Washington
WASHINGTON vs. DALLAS
RS: Cowboys lead series, 64-40-2
PS: Redskins lead series, 2-0;
See Dallas vs. Washington
WASHINGTON vs. DENVER
RS: Broncos lead series, 7-5
PS: Redskins lead series, 1-0;
See Denver vs. Washington
WASHINGTON vs. DETROIT
RS: Redskins lead series, 27-13
PS: Redskins lead series, 3-0;
See Detroit vs. Washington

WASHINGTON vs. GREEN BAY
RS: Packers lead series, 18-13-1
PS: Series tied, 1-1;
See Green Bay vs. Washington
WASHINGTON vs. HOUSTON
RS: Redskins lead series, 2-1;
See Houston vs. Washington
WASHINGTON vs. INDIANAPOLIS
RS: Colts lead series, 19-10;
See Indianapolis vs. Washington
WASHINGTON vs. JACKSONVILLE
RS: Redskins lead series, 4-1;
See Jacksonville vs. Washington
WASHINGTON vs. KANSAS CITY
RS: Chiefs lead series, 8-1;
See Kansas City vs. Washington
WASHINGTON vs. MIAMI
RS: Dolphins lead series, 7-4
PS: Series tied, 1-1;
See Miami vs. Washington
WASHINGTON vs. MINNESOTA
RS: Series tied, 9-9
PS: Redskins lead series, 3-2;
See Minnesota vs. Washington
WASHINGTON vs. NEW ENGLAND
RS: Redskins lead series, 6-3;
See New England vs. Washington
WASHINGTON vs. NEW ORLEANS
RS: Redskins lead series, 16-8;
See New Orleans vs. Washington
WASHINGTON vs. N.Y. GIANTS
RS: Giants lead series, 94-64-4
PS: Series tied, 1-1;
See N.Y. Giants vs. Washington
WASHINGTON vs. N.Y. JETS
RS: Redskins lead series, 8-2;
See N.Y. Jets vs. Washington
WASHINGTON vs. OAKLAND
RS: Raiders lead series, 7-5
PS: Raiders lead series, 1-0;
See Oakland vs. Washington
WASHINGTON vs. PHILADELPHIA
RS: Redskins lead series, 80-72-5
PS: Redskins lead series, 1-0;
See Philadelphia vs. Washington
WASHINGTON vs. PITTSBURGH
RS: Redskins lead series, 42-32-3;
See Pittsburgh vs. Washington
WASHINGTON vs. ST. LOUIS
RS: Redskins lead series, 22-10-1
PS: Series tied, 2-2;
See St. Louis vs. Washington
WASHINGTON vs. SAN DIEGO
RS: Redskins lead series, 7-3;
See San Diego vs. Washington
WASHINGTON vs. SAN FRANCISCO
RS: 49ers lead series, 16-9-1
PS: 49ers lead series, 3-1;
See San Francisco vs. Washington
WASHINGTON vs. SEATTLE
RS: Redskins lead series, 11-4
PS: Seahawks lead series, 3-0;
See Seattle vs. Washington
WASHINGTON vs. TAMPA BAY
RS: Series tied, 9-9
PS: Series tied, 1-1;
See Tampa Bay vs. Washington
WASHINGTON vs. TENNESSEE
RS: Titans lead series, 6-5;
See Tennessee vs. Washington

SUPER BOWL COMPOSITE STANDINGS

	W	L	Pct.	Pts.	OP
Baltimore Ravens	2	0	1.000	68	38
New Orleans Saints	1	0	1.000	31	17
New York Jets	1	0	1.000	16	7
Tampa Bay Buccaneers	1	0	1.000	48	21
San Francisco 49ers	5	1	.833	219	123
Green Bay Packers	4	1	.800	158	101
New York Giants	4	1	.800	104	104
Pittsburgh Steelers	6	2	.750	193	164
Dallas Cowboys	5	3	.625	221	132
Oakland/L.A. Raiders	3	2	.600	132	114
Washington Redskins	3	2	.600	122	103
Indianapolis/Baltimore Colts	2	2	.500	69	77
Chicago Bears	1	1	.500	63	39
Kansas City Chiefs	1	1	.500	33	42
Seattle Seahawks	1	1	.500	53	29
New England Patriots	3	4	.429	138	186
Miami Dolphins	2	3	.400	74	103
St. Louis/L.A. Rams	1	2	.333	59	67
Denver Broncos	2	5	.286	123	249
Arizona Cardinals	0	1	.000	23	27
Atlanta Falcons	0	1	.000	19	34
Carolina Panthers	0	1	.000	29	32
San Diego Chargers	0	1	.000	26	49
Tennessee Titans	0	1	.000	16	23
Cincinnati Bengals	0	2	.000	37	46
Philadelphia Eagles	0	2	.000	31	51
Buffalo Bills	0	4	.000	73	139
Minnesota Vikings	0	4	.000	34	95

SUPER BOWL HOST CITIES

New Orleans	10	
South Florida	10	
Los Angeles	7	(LA Coliseum 2, Rose Bowl 5)
Tampa Bay	4	
San Diego	3	
Arizona	2	
Atlanta	2	
Detroit	2	
Houston	2	
New York-New Jersey	1	
Indianapolis	1	
Jacksonville	1	
Minneapolis	1	
North Texas	1	
Stanford	1	

FUTURE SUPER BOWL SITES

Super Bowl XLIX Feb. 1, 2015 University of Phoenix Stadium
(awarded October 11, 2011) Arizona

Super Bowl L Feb. 7, 2016 Levi's Stadium
(awarded May 21, 2013) San Francisco

Super Bowl LI Feb. 5, 2017 Reliant Stadium
(awarded May 21, 2013) Houston

Super Bowl LII Feb. 4, 2018* New Vikings Stadium
(awarded May 20, 2014) Minnesota

*Tentative date

PETE ROZELLE TROPHY/SUPER BOWL MVPs*

Super Bowl I	— QB Bart Starr, Green Bay
Super Bowl II	— QB Bart Starr, Green Bay
Super Bowl III	— QB Joe Namath, N.Y. Jets
Super Bowl IV	— QB Len Dawson, Kansas City
Super Bowl V	— LB Chuck Howley, Dallas
Super Bowl VI	— QB Roger Staubach, Dallas
Super Bowl VII	— S Jake Scott, Miami
Super Bowl VIII	— RB Larry Csonka, Miami
Super Bowl IX	— RB Franco Harris, Pittsburgh
Super Bowl X	— WR Lynn Swann, Pittsburgh
Super Bowl XI	— WR Fred Biletnikoff, Oakland
Super Bowl XII	— DT Randy White and DE Harvey Martin, Dallas
Super Bowl XIII	— QB Terry Bradshaw, Pittsburgh
Super Bowl XIV	— QB Terry Bradshaw, Pittsburgh
Super Bowl XV	— QB Jim Plunkett, Oakland
Super Bowl XVI	— QB Joe Montana, San Francisco
Super Bowl XVII	— RB John Riggins, Washington
Super Bowl XVIII	— RB Marcus Allen, L.A. Raiders
Super Bowl XIX	— QB Joe Montana, San Francisco
Super Bowl XX	— DE Richard Dent, Chicago
Super Bowl XXI	— QB Phil Simms, N.Y. Giants
Super Bowl XXII	— QB Doug Williams, Washington
Super Bowl XXIII	— WR Jerry Rice, San Francisco
Super Bowl XXIV	— QB Joe Montana, San Francisco
Super Bowl XXV	— RB Ottis Anderson, N.Y. Giants
Super Bowl XXVI	— QB Mark Rypien, Washington
Super Bowl XXVII	— QB Troy Aikman, Dallas
Super Bowl XXVIII	— RB Emmitt Smith, Dallas
Super Bowl XXIX	— QB Steve Young, San Francisco
Super Bowl XXX	— CB Larry Brown, Dallas
Super Bowl XXXI	— KR-PR Desmond Howard, Green Bay
Super Bowl XXXII	— RB Terrell Davis, Denver
Super Bowl XXXIII	— QB John Elway, Denver
Super Bowl XXXIV	— QB Kurt Warner, St. Louis
Super Bowl XXXV	— LB Ray Lewis, Baltimore
Super Bowl XXXVI	— QB Tom Brady, New England
Super Bowl XXXVII	— S Dexter Jackson, Tampa Bay
Super Bowl XXXVIII	— QB Tom Brady, New England
Super Bowl XXXIX	— WR Deion Branch, New England
Super Bowl XL	— WR Hines Ward, Pittsburgh
Super Bowl XLI	— QB Peyton Manning, Indianapolis
Super Bowl XLII	— QB Eli Manning, N.Y. Giants
Super Bowl XLIII	— WR Santonio Holmes, Pittsburgh
Super Bowl XLIV	— QB Drew Brees, New Orleans
Super Bowl XLV	— QB Aaron Rodgers, Green Bay
Super Bowl XLVI	— QB Eli Manning, N.Y. Giants
Super Bowl XLVII	— QB Joe Flacco, Baltimore
Super Bowl XLVIII	— LB Malcolm Smith, Seattle

* Award named Pete Rozelle Trophy since Super Bowl XXV.

SUPER BOWL MVP BY POSITION

Quarterback	26
Running Back	7
Wide Receiver	6
Linebacker	3
Defensive End	2
Safety	2
Cornerback	1
Defensive Tackle	1
Kick Returner-Punt Returner	1

A defensive end and defensive tackle shared the Super Bowl XII MVP award.

RESULTS

NFC leads AFC, 26-22

Super Bowl	Date	Winner (Share)	Loser (Share)	Score	Site	Attendance
XLVIII	2-2-14	Seattle ($92,000)	Denver ($46,000)	43-8	New York-New Jersey	82,529
XLVII	2-3-13	Baltimore ($88,000)	San Francisco ($44,000)	34-31	New Orleans	71,024
XLVI	2-5-12	N.Y. Giants ($88,000)	New England ($44,000)	21-17	Indianapolis	68,658
XLV	2-6-11	Green Bay ($83,000)	Pittsburgh ($42,000)	31-25	North Texas	91,060
XLIV	2-7-10	New Orleans ($83,000)	Indianapolis ($42,000)	31-17	South Florida	74,059
XLIII	2-1-09	Pittsburgh ($78,000)	Arizona ($40,000)	27-23	Tampa Bay	70,774
XLII	2-3-08	N.Y. Giants ($78,000)	New England ($40,000)	17-14	Arizona	71,101
XLI	2-4-07	Indianapolis ($73,000)	Chicago ($38,000)	29-17	South Florida	74,512
XL	2-5-06	Pittsburgh ($73,000)	Seattle ($38,000)	21-10	Detroit	68,206
XXXIX	2-6-05	New England ($68,000)	Philadelphia ($36,500)	24-21	Jacksonville	78,125
XXXVIII	2-1-04	New England ($68,000)	Carolina ($36,500)	32-29	Houston	71,525
* XXXVII	1-26-03	Tampa Bay ($63,000)	Oakland ($35,000)	48-21	San Diego	67,603
* XXXVI	2-3-02	New England ($63,000)	St. Louis ($34,500)	20-17	New Orleans	72,922
XXXV	1-28-01	Baltimore ($58,000)	N.Y. Giants ($34,500)	34-7	Tampa Bay	71,921
* XXXIV	1-30-00	St. Louis ($58,000)	Tennessee ($33,000)	23-16	Atlanta	72,625
XXXIII	1-31-99	Denver ($53,000)	Atlanta ($32,500)	34-19	South Florida	74,803
XXXII	1-25-98	Denver ($48,000)	Green Bay ($29,000)	31-24	San Diego	68,912
XXXI	1-26-97	Green Bay ($48,000)	New England ($29,000)	35-21	New Orleans	72,301
XXX	1-28-96	Dallas ($42,000)	Pittsburgh ($27,000)	27-17	Arizona	76,347
XXIX	1-29-95	San Francisco ($42,000)	San Diego ($26,000)	49-26	South Florida	74,107
* XXVIII	1-30-94	Dallas ($38,000)	Buffalo ($23,500)	30-13	Atlanta	72,817
XXVII	1-31-93	Dallas ($36,000)	Buffalo ($18,000)	52-17	Pasadena	98,374
XXVI	1-26-92	Washington ($36,000)	Buffalo ($18,000)	37-24	Minneapolis	63,130
* XXV	1-27-91	N.Y. Giants ($36,000)	Buffalo ($18,000)	20-19	Tampa Bay	73,813
XXIV	1-28-90	San Francisco ($36,000)	Denver ($18,000)	55-10	New Orleans	72,919
XXIII	1-22-89	San Francisco ($36,000)	Cincinnati ($18,000)	20-16	South Florida	75,129
XXII	1-31-88	Washington ($36,000)	Denver ($18,000)	42-10	San Diego	73,302
XXI	1-25-87	N.Y. Giants ($36,000)	Denver ($18,000)	39-20	Pasadena	101,063
XX	1-26-86	Chicago ($36,000)	New England ($18,000)	46-10	New Orleans	73,818
XIX	1-20-85	San Francisco ($36,000)	Miami ($18,000)	38-16	Stanford	84,059
XVIII	1-22-84	L.A. Raiders ($36,000)	Washington ($18,000)	38-9	Tampa Bay	72,920
* XVII	1-30-83	Washington ($36,000)	Miami ($18,000)	27-17	Pasadena	103,667
XVI	1-24-82	San Francisco ($18,000)	Cincinnati ($9,000)	26-21	Pontiac	81,270
XV	1-25-81	Oakland ($18,000)	Philadelphia ($9,000)	27-10	New Orleans	76,135
XIV	1-20-80	Pittsburgh ($18,000)	Los Angeles ($9,000)	31-19	Pasadena	103,985
XIII	1-21-79	Pittsburgh ($18,000)	Dallas ($9,000)	35-31	South Florida	79,484
XII	1-15-78	Dallas ($18,000)	Denver ($9,000)	27-10	New Orleans	75,583
XI	1-9-77	Oakland ($15,000)	Minnesota ($7,500)	32-14	Pasadena	103,438
X	1-18-76	Pittsburgh ($15,000)	Dallas ($7,500)	21-17	South Florida	80,187
IX	1-12-75	Pittsburgh ($15,000)	Minnesota ($7,500)	16-6	New Orleans	80,997
VIII	1-13-74	Miami ($15,000)	Minnesota ($7,500)	24-7	Houston	71,882
VII	1-14-73	Miami ($15,000)	Washington ($7,500)	14-7	Los Angeles	90,182
VI	1-16-72	Dallas ($15,000)	Miami ($7,500)	24-3	New Orleans	81,023
V	1-17-71	Baltimore ($15,000)	Dallas ($7,500)	16-13	South Florida	79,204
* IV	1-11-70	Kansas City ($15,000)	Minnesota ($7,500)	23-7	New Orleans	80,562
III	1-12-69	N.Y. Jets ($15,000)	Baltimore ($7,500)	16-7	South Florida	75,389
II	1-14-68	Green Bay ($15,000)	Oakland ($7,500)	33-14	South Florida	75,546
I	1-15-67	Green Bay ($15,000)	Kansas City ($7,500)	35-10	Los Angeles	61,946

* One week between conference championship games and Super Bowl; all others had two weeks between conference championship games and Super Bowl.

For historical Super Bowl game recaps, box scores, and video highlights, please visit www.NFL.com/SuperBowl.

SUPER BOWL XLVIII

MetLife Stadium,
East Rutherford, New Jersey
February 2, 2014, Attendance: 82,529

SEATTLE 43, DENVER 8—En route to winning their first NFL title, the Seahawks' defense forced four turnovers and Percy Harvin returned a kickoff 87 yards for a touchdown as Seattle posted the largest margin of victory in a Super Bowl in 21 years. The game, the first Super Bowl played in an outdoor cold-weather stadium with a 49-degree temperature at kick-off, featured the NFL's number-one defense against the highest-scoring team in NFL history. On the first play from scrimmage, Manny Ramirez' shotgun snap from the 14-yard-line sailed past Peyton Manning. Knowshon Moreno recovered the loose ball in the end zone for a safety just 12 seconds into the game, the quickest score in Super Bowl history. The Seahawks took the ensuing free kick and drove 51 yards for a 5-0 lead. The defense then forced a three-and-out, and Russell Wilson completed 3 third-down passes on a 13-play drive that resulted in Steven Hauschka's second field goal and a 8-0 lead. Kam Chancellor intercepted Manning three plays later to set up Marshawn Lynch's 1-yard touch-down run for a 15-0 lead with 12:00 left in the second quarter. At that moment the Seahawks had run 29 plays compared to seven for the Broncos. Denver responded with a 15-play drive, with three third-down conversions. Faced with third-and-13 from the Seahawks' 35, Cliff Avril pressured Manning. His pass intended for Moreno was underthrown and Malcolm Smith intercepted the pass and returned it untouched 69 yards for a touchdown and 22-0 lead. The Broncos drove to the Seahawks' 19, but on fourth-and-2 Chris Clemons tipped Manning's pass and it fell incomplete. Harvin began the second half by taking the kickoff and weaving his way 87 yards for a touchdown and 29-0 lead. Later in the quarter Byron Maxwell forced Demaryius Thomas to fumble and Smith recovered at the Seahawks' 20. Wilson completed a third-down pass to Luke Willson and a few plays later connected with Jermaine Kearse on a 23-yard scoring pass for a 36-0 lead with 2:58 left in the third quarter. Manning completed the last four passes on the next drive, including 12- and 22-yard passes to Wes Welker, and capped by his 14-yard scoring pass to Thomas on a crossing pattern to end the third quarter. Welker caught a 2-point conversion pass to cut the deficit to 36-8. Zach Miller recovered the onside kick and Wilson completed five consecutive passes culminated by a 10-yard touchdown pass to Doug Baldwin for a 43-8 advantage with 11:45 to play. Wilson was 18 of 25 for 206 yards and 2 touchdowns. Manning had a Super Bowl-record 34 completions, out of 49 attempts, for 280 yards and 1 touchdown, with 2 interceptions. Thomas had 13 catches for 118 yards.

Seattle (43)   Denver (8)
Offense

Doug Baldwin	WR	Demaryius Thomas
Russell Okung	LT	Chris Clark
James Carpenter	LG	Zane Beadles
Max Unger	C	Manny Ramirez
J.R. Sweezy	RG	Louis Vazquez
Breno Giacomini	RT	Orlando Franklin
Alvin Bailey	T/TE	Julius Thomas
Zach Miller	TE/WR	Eric Decker
Russell Wilson	QB	Peyton Manning
Golden Tate	WR	Wes Welker
Marshawn Lynch	RB	Knowshon Moreno

Defense

Cliff Avril	DE	Malik Jackson
Michael Bennett	DT	Sylvester Williams
Clinton McDonald	DT/NT	Terrance Knighton
Chris Clemons	RE	Shaun Phillips
K.J. Wright	OLB/SLB	Nate Irving
Bobby Wagner	MLB	Paris Lenon
Walter Thurmond	CB/WLB	Danny Trevathan
Richard Sherman	LCB	Champ Bailey
Byron Maxwell	RCB	D. Rodgers-Cromartie
Kam Chancellor	SS	Duke Ihenacho
Earl Thomas	FS	Mike Adams

SUBSTITUTIONS

SEATTLE—Specialists: K—Steven Hauschka. P—Jon Ryan. LS—Clint Gresham. Offense: QB—Tarvaris Jackson. RB—Rorbert Turbin. FB—Derrick Coleman, Michael Robinson. WR—Percy Harvin, Jermaine Kearse, Ricardo Lockette. TE—Luke Willson. C—Lemuel Jeanpierre.

G—Paul McQuistan. Defense: DT—Brandon Mebane, Tony McDaniel. DE—Red Bryant, O'Brien Schofield. LB—Heath Farwell, Bruce Irvin, Mike Morgan, Malcolm Smith. CB—Jeremy Lane, DeShawn Shead. S—Chris Maragos. Not Active: RB—Christine Michael. WR—Bryan Walters. TE—Kellen Davis. T—Michael Bowie, Caylin Hauptmann. DT—Jordan Hill. DE—Benson Mayowa.

DENVER—Specialists: K—Matt Prater. P—Britton Colquitt. LS—Aaron Brewer. Offense: RB—C.J. Anderson, Montee Ball. WR—Andre Caldwell, Trindon Holliday. TE—Virgil Green, Jacob Tamme. C—Steve Vallos. Defense: DE—Robert Ayers, Jeremy Mincey. DT—Mitch Unrein. LB—Steven Johnson, Brandon Marshall, Wesley Woodyard. CB—Tony Carter, Marquice Cole, Kayvon Webster. S—Omar Bolden, David Bruton. DNP: QB—Brock Osweiler. T—Winston Justice. S—Michael Huff. Not Active: QB—Zac Dysert. RB—Ronnie Hillman. TE—Joel Dreessen. G—Chris Kuper. T—Vinston Painter. DT—Sione Fua. CB—Quentin Jammer.

OFFICIALS

Referee—Terry McAulay. Umpire—Carl Paganelli. Head Linesman—Jim Mello. Line Judge—Thomas Symonette. Side Judge—David Wyant. Field Judge—Scott Steenson. Back Judge—Steve Freeman. Replay Official—Earnie Frantz.

SCORING

Seattle (NFC)		8 14 14 7 — 43
Denver (AFC)		0 0 8 0 — 8

Sea — Safety, Avril tackled Moreno in end zone (14:48)
Sea — FG Hauschka 31 (10:21)
Sea — FG Hauschka 33 (2:16)
Sea — Lynch 1 run (Hauschka kick) (12:00)
Sea — Smith 69 interception return (Hauschka kick) (3:21)
Sea — Harvin 87 kickoff return (Hauschka kick) (14:48)
Sea — Kearse 23 pass from Wilson (Hauschka kick) (2:58)
Den — D. Thomas 14 pass from Manning (Welker pass from Manning) (0:00)
Sea — Baldwin 10 pass from Wilson (Hauschka kick) (11:45)

TEAM STATISTICS

	SEA	DEN
Total First Downs	17	18
Rushing	6	2
Passing	10	13
Penalty	1	3
Total Net Yardage	341	306
Total Offensive Plays	55	64
Avg. Gain Per Offensive Play	6.2	4.8
Rushes	29	14
Yards Gained Rushing (Net)	135	27
Avg. Yards per Rush	4.7	1.9
Passes Attempted	26	49
Passes Completed	18	34
Had Intercepted	0	2
Tackled Attempting to Pass	0	1
Yards Lost Attempting to Pass	0	1
Yards Gained Passing (Net)	206	279
Punts	1	2
Avg. Distance	45.0	30.0
Punt Returns	0	1
Punt Return Yardage	0	9
Kickoff Returns	2	5
Kickoff Return Yardage	107	105
Interception Return Yardage	71	0
Total Return Yardage (excl. Kickoff)	71	9
Fumbles	0	4
Fumbles Lost	0	2
Own Fumbles Recovered	0	2
Opponent Fumbles Recovered	2	2
Penalties	10	5
Yards Penalized	104	44
Field Goals	2	0
Field Goals Attempted	2	0
Third-Down Efficiency	7/12	6/13
Fourth-Down Efficiency	0/2	0/3
Time of Possession	31:53	28:07

INDIVIDUAL STATISTICS

RUSHING: Sea: Harvin 2-45-0, Lynch 15-39-1, Wilson 3-26-0, Turbin 9-25-0. Den: Moreno 5-17-0, Anderson 2-9-0, Ball 6-1-0, Manning 1-0-0.

PASSING: Sea: Wilson 25-18-206-2-0, Jackson 1-0-0-0-0. Den: Manning 49-34-280-1-2.

RECEIVING: Sea: Baldwin 5-66-1, Kearse 4-65-1, Tate 3-17-0, Willson 2-17-0, Lockette 1-19-0, Miller 1-10-0, Robinson 1-7-0, Harvin 1-5-0. Den: D. Thomas 13-118-1, Welker 8-84-0, J. Thomas 4-27-0, Moreno 3-20-0, Tamme 2-9-0, Ball 2-2-0, Anderson 1-14-0, Decker 1-6-0.

KICKOFF RETURNS: Sea: Harvin 1-87-1, Tate 1-20-0. Den: Holliday 5-105-0.

PUNT RETURNS: Sea: Tate 0-0-0. Den: Decker 1-9-0.

PUNTING: Sea: Ryan 1-45-45.0. Den: Colquitt 2-60-30.0.

INTERCEPTIONS: Sea: Smith 1-69-1, Chancellor 1-2-0. Den: None.

SACKS: Sea: Clemons 1. Den: None.

AFC CHAMPIONSHIP GAME RESULTS
Includes AFL Championship Games (1960-69)

Season	Date	Winner (Share)	Loser (Share)	Score	Site	Attendance
2013	Jan. 19	Denver ($42,000)	New England ($42,000)	26-16	Denver	77,110
2012	Jan. 20	Baltimore ($40,000)	New England ($40,000)	28-13	Foxborough	68,756
2011	Jan. 22	New England ($40,000)	Baltimore ($40,000)	23-20	Foxborough	68,756
2010	Jan. 23	Pittsburgh ($38,000)	N.Y. Jets ($38,000)	24-19	Pittsburgh	66,662
2009	Jan. 24	Indianapolis ($38,000)	N.Y. Jets ($38,000)	30-17	Indianapolis	67,650
2008	Jan. 18	Pittsburgh ($37,500)	Baltimore ($37,500)	23-14	Pittsburgh	65,350
2007	Jan. 20	New England ($37,500)	San Diego ($37,500)	21-12	Foxborough	68,756
2006	Jan. 21	Indianapolis ($37,000)	New England ($37,000)	38-34	Indianapolis	57,433
2005	Jan. 22	Pittsburgh ($37,000)	Denver ($37,000)	34-17	Denver	76,775
2004	Jan. 23	New England ($36,500)	Pittsburgh ($36,500)	41-27	Pittsburgh	65,242
2003	Jan. 18	New England ($36,500)	Indianapolis ($36,500)	24-14	Foxborough	68,436
2002	Jan. 19	Oakland ($35,000)	Tennessee ($35,000)	41-24	Oakland	62,544
2001	Jan. 27	New England ($34,500)	Pittsburgh ($34,500)	24-17	Pittsburgh	64,704
2000	Jan. 14	Baltimore ($34,500)	Oakland ($34,500)	16-3	Oakland	62,784
1999	Jan. 23	Tennessee ($33,000)	Jacksonville ($33,000)	33-14	Jacksonville	75,206
1998	Jan. 17	Denver ($32,500)	N.Y. Jets ($32,500)	23-10	Denver	75,482
1997	Jan. 11	Denver ($30,000)	Pittsburgh ($30,000)	24-21	Pittsburgh	61,382
1996	Jan. 12	New England ($29,000)	Jacksonville ($29,000)	20-6	Foxborough	60,190
1995	Jan. 14	Pittsburgh ($27,000)	Indianapolis ($27,000)	20-16	Pittsburgh	61,062
1994	Jan. 15	San Diego ($26,000)	Pittsburgh ($26,000)	17-13	Pittsburgh	61,545
1993	Jan. 23	Buffalo ($23,500)	Kansas City ($23,500)	30-13	Buffalo	76,642
1992	Jan. 17	Buffalo ($18,000)	Miami ($18,000)	29-10	Miami	72,703
1991	Jan. 12	Buffalo ($18,000)	Denver ($18,000)	10-7	Buffalo	80,272
1990	Jan. 20	Buffalo ($18,000)	L.A. Raiders ($18,000)	51-3	Buffalo	80,325
1989	Jan. 14	Denver ($18,000)	Cleveland ($18,000)	37-21	Denver	76,046
1988	Jan. 8	Cincinnati ($18,000)	Buffalo ($18,000)	21-10	Cincinnati	59,747
1987	Jan. 17	Denver ($18,000)	Cleveland ($18,000)	38-33	Denver	76,197
1986	Jan. 11	Denver ($18,000)	Cleveland ($18,000)	23-20*	Cleveland	79,973
1985	Jan. 12	New England ($18,000)	Miami ($18,000)	31-14	Miami	75,662
1984	Jan. 6	Miami ($18,000)	Pittsburgh ($18,000)	45-28	Miami	76,029
1983	Jan. 8	L.A. Raiders ($18,000)	Seattle ($18,000)	30-14	Los Angeles	91,445
1982	Jan. 23	Miami ($18,000)	N.Y. Jets ($18,000)	14-0	Miami	67,396
1981	Jan. 10	Cincinnati ($9,000)	San Diego ($9,000)	27-7	Cincinnati	46,302
1980	Jan. 11	Oakland ($9,000)	San Diego ($9,000)	34-27	San Diego	52,675
1979	Jan. 6	Pittsburgh ($9,000)	Houston ($9,000)	27-13	Pittsburgh	50,475
1978	Jan. 7	Pittsburgh ($9,000)	Houston ($9,000)	34-5	Pittsburgh	50,725
1977	Jan. 1	Denver ($9,000)	Oakland ($9,000)	20-17	Denver	75,044
1976	Dec. 26	Oakland ($8,500)	Pittsburgh ($5,500)	24-7	Oakland	53,821
1975	Jan. 4	Pittsburgh ($8,500)	Oakland ($5,500)	16-10	Pittsburgh	50,609
1974	Dec. 29	Pittsburgh ($8,500)	Oakland ($5,500)	24-13	Oakland	53,800
1973	Dec. 30	Miami ($8,500)	Oakland ($5,500)	27-10	Miami	79,325
1972	Dec. 31	Miami ($8,500)	Pittsburgh ($5,500)	21-17	Pittsburgh	50,845
1971	Jan. 2	Miami ($8,500)	Baltimore ($5,500)	21-0	Miami	76,622
1970	Jan. 3	Baltimore ($8,500)	Oakland ($5,500)	27-17	Baltimore	54,799
1969	Jan. 4	Kansas City ($7,755)	Oakland ($6,252)	17-7	Oakland	53,564
1968	Dec. 29	N.Y. Jets ($7,007)	Oakland ($5,349)	27-23	New York	62,627
1967	Dec. 31	Oakland ($6,321)	Houston ($4,996)	40-7	Oakland	53,330
1966	Jan. 1	Kansas City ($5,309)	Buffalo ($3,799)	31-7	Buffalo	42,080
1965	Dec. 26	Buffalo ($5,189)	San Diego ($3,447)	23-0	San Diego	30,361
1964	Dec. 26	Buffalo ($2,668)	San Diego ($1,738)	20-7	Buffalo	40,242
1963	Jan. 5	San Diego ($2,498)	Boston ($1,596)	51-10	San Diego	30,127
1962	Dec. 23	Dallas ($2,206)	Houston ($1,471)	20-17*	Houston	37,981
1961	Dec. 24	Houston ($1,792)	San Diego ($1,111)	10-3	San Diego	29,556
1960	Jan. 1	Houston ($1,025)	L.A. Chargers ($718)	24-16	Houston	32,183

*Overtime

AFC CHAMPIONSHIP GAME COMPOSITE STANDINGS

	W	L	Pct.	Pts.	OP
Cincinnati Bengals	2	0	1.000	48	17
Denver Broncos	7	2	.778	215	182
Buffalo Bills	6	2	.750	180	92
Kansas City Chiefs*	3	1	.750	81	61
Miami Dolphins	5	2	.714	152	115
New England Patriots**	7	4	.636	257	253
Pittsburgh Steelers	8	7	.533	332	303
Indianapolis Colts#	3	3	.500	125	133
Baltimore Ravens	2	2	.500	78	62
Tennessee Titans##	3	5	.375	133	195
Oakland Raiders###	5	9	.357	272	304
New York Jets	1	4	.200	73	114
San Diego Chargers***	2	7	.222	140	182
Seattle Seahawks	0	1	.000	14	30
Jacksonville Jaguars	0	2	.000	20	53
Cleveland Browns	0	3	.000	74	98

* One game played when franchise was in Dallas (Texans) (Won 20-17)
** One game played when franchise was in Boston (Lost 51-10)
*** One game played when franchise was in Los Angeles (Lost 24-16)
\# Two games played when franchise was in Baltimore (Won 27-17, lost 21-0)
\## Six games played when franchise was in Houston and known as Oilers (Won 2, lost 4)
\### Two games played when franchise was in Los Angeles (Won 30-14, lost 51-3)

2013 AFC CHAMPIONSHIP GAME

Sports Authority Field at Mile High Stadium, Denver, Colorado
January 19, 2014, Attendance: 77,110

DENVER 26, NEW ENGLAND 16—Peyton Manning passed for 400 yards and 2 touchdowns to send the Denver Broncos to its first Super Bowl appearance in 15 years. Denver outgained the New England Patriots by almost 200 yards (507-320) and maintained possession for 35 minutes, 44 seconds of the game's 60 minutes. Leading 3-0 early in the second quarter, the Broncos' defense forced a punt for the third consecutive possession. The offense then drove 93 yards in 15 plays, consuming 7:01 off the clock, with four third-down conversions, and capped by Manning's 1-yard touchdown pass to Jacob Tamme. The Patriots answered with a field goal, but Denver responded with a 63-yard drive and Matt Prater's second field goal just before halftime for a 13-3 lead. Denver began the second half with a 13-play, 80-yard drive that lasted more than seven minutes, with Demaryius Thomas' 3-yard touchdown catch staking Denver to a 20-3 lead. The Patriots drove to the Broncos' 29, but on fourth-and-3 Terrance Knighton sacked Tom Brady. The Broncos drove 60 yards and Prater's third field goal gave Denver a 23-3 lead with 12:02 remaining. Brady engineered an 80-yard touchdown drive to cut the deficit to 23-10 with 9:26 left, but Prater's fourth field goal gave Denver a 26-10 advantage with 7:00 left. Brady needed less than four minutes to drive another 80 yards, and his 5-yard scramble pulled New England to within 26-16 with 3:07 to play. The Patriots went for the 2-point conversion, but Shane Vereen was stopped on his run up the middle. New England then attempted an onside kick but Eric Decker recovered. Tamme caught a 23-yard pass for one first down and Montee Ball gained 5 yards on fourth-and-2 with 1:19 remaining to clinch the victory. Manning completed 32 of 43 passes for 400 yards and 2 touchdowns. Demaryius Thomas had 7 catches for 134 yards. Brady was 24 of 38 for 277 yards and 1 touchdown. Julian Edelman had 10 receptions for 89 yards.

New England (16)	Offense	Denver (26)
Danny Amendola	WR	Demaryius Thomas
Nate Solder	LT	Chris Clark
Logan Mankins	LG	Zane Beadles
Ryan Wendell	C	Manny Ramirez
Dan Connolly	RG	Luis Vazquez
Marcus Cannon	RT	Orlando Franklin
Michael Hoomanawanui	TE	Julius Thomas
Julian Edelman	WR	Eric Decker
Tom Brady	QB	Peyton Manning
James Develin	RB/WR	Wes Welker
Shane Vereen	RB	Knowshon Moreno
	Defense	
Rob Ninkovich	DE	Malik Jackson
Sealver Siliga	DT	Sylvester Williams
Chris Jones	DT/NT	Terrance Knighton
Chandler Jones	RE	Shaun Phillips
Jamie Collins	LB/SLB	Nate Irving
Dont'a Hightower	LB/MLB	Paris Lenon
Kyle Arrington	CB/WLB	Danny Trevathan
Aqib Talib	LCB	Champ Bailey
Alfonzo Dennard	RCB	Dominique Rodgers-Cromartie
Steve Gregory	S/SS	Duke Ihenacho
Devin McCourty	S/FS	Mike Adams

SUBSTITUTIONS

NEW ENGLAND—Specialists: K—Stephen Gostkowski. P—Ryan Allen. LS—Danny Aiken. Offense: RB—LeGarrette Blount, Brandon Bolden, Stevan Ridley. WR—Austin Collie, Aaron Dobson, Matthew Slater. TE—Matthew Mulligan. OL—Will Svitek. Defense: DE—Andre Carter. DL—Michael Buchanan. DT—Joe Vellano. LB—Ja'Gared Davis, Dane Fletcher, Chris White. CB—Logan Ryan. DB—Nate Ebner, Duron Harmon, Tavon Wilson. DNP: QB—Ryan Mallett. OL—Josh Kline. Not Active: WR—Kenbrell Thompkins. TE—D.J. Williams. OL—Chris Barker. DE—Jake Bequette. DT—Isaac Sopoaga. LB—Steve Beauharnais.

DB—Justin Green.

DENVER—Specialists: K—Matt Prater. P—Britton Colquitt. LS—Aaron Brewer. Offense: RB—Montee Ball. WR—Andre Caldwell, Trindon Holliday. TE—Virgil Green, Jacob Tamme. C—Steve Vallos. T—Winston Justice. Defense: DE—Robert Ayers, Jeremy Mincey. DT—Mitch Unrein LB—Steven Johnson, Brandon Marshall, Wesley Woodyard. CB—Tony Carter, Quentin Jammer, Kayvon Webster. S—Omar Bolden, David Bruton, Michael Huff. DNP: QB—Brock Osweiler. RB—C.J. Anderson. Not Active: QB—Zac Dysert. RB—Ronnie Hillman. TE—Joel Dreessen. G—Chris Kuper. T—Vinston Painter. DT—Sione Fua. CB—Marquice Cole.

OFFICIALS

Referee—Tony Corrente. Umpire—Paul King. Head Linesman—Kent Payne. Line Judge—John Hussey. Side Judge—Tom Hill. Field Judge—Craig Wrolstad. Back Judge—Gregory Wilson. Replay Official—Carl Madsen.

SCORING

New England	0	3	0	13	—	16
Denver	3	10	7	6	—	26

Den	—	FG Prater 27
Den	—	Tamme 1 pass from Manning (Prater kick)
NE	—	FG Gostkowski 47
Den	—	FG Prater 35
Den	—	D. Thomas 3 pass from Manning (Prater kick)
Den	—	FG Prater 19
NE	—	Edelman 7 pass from Brady (Gostkowski kick)
Den	—	FG Prater 54
NE	—	Brady 5 run (run failed)

TEAM STATISTICS	NE	DEN
Total First Downs	19	27
Rushing	4	5
Passing	15	21
Penalty	0	1
Total Net Yardage	320	507
Total Offensive Plays	56	71
Average Gain Per Offensive Play	5.7	7.1
Rushes	16	28
Yards Gained Rushing (Net)	64	107
Average Yards per Rush	4.0	3.8
Passes Attempted	38	43
Passes Completed	24	32
Had Intercepted	0	0
Tackled Attempting to Pass	2	0
Yards Lost Attempting to Pass	21	0
Yards Gained Passing (Net)	256	400
Punts	3	1
Average Distance	49.0	48.0
Punt Returns	0	0
Punt Return Yardage	0	0
Kickoff Returns	0	1
Kickoff Return Yardage	0	4
Interception Return Yardage	0	0
Total Return Yardage (not incl. kickoffs)	0	0
Fumbles	0	0
Fumbles Lost	0	0
Own Fumbles Recovered	0	0
Opponent Fumbles Recovered	0	0
Penalties	2	4
Yards Penalized	15	34
Field Goals	1	4
Field Goals Attempted	1	4
Third-Down Efficiency	6/12	7/13
Fourth-Down Efficiency	1/2	1/1
Time of Possession	24:16	35:44

INDIVIDUAL STATISTICS

RUSHING: NE: Vereen 4-34-0, Ridley 5-17-0, Brady 2-7-1, Blount 5-6-0. DEN: Moreno 14-59-0, Ball 12-43-0, Green 1-6-0, Manning 1-(-1)-0.
PASSING: NE: Brady 38-24-277-1-0.

DEN: Manning 43-32-400-2-0.
RECEIVING: NE: Edelman 10-89-1, Vereen 5-59-0, Collie 4-57-0, Dobson 2-33-0, Hoomanawanui 2-33-0, Mulligan 1-6-0. DEN: J. Thomas 8-85-0, D. Thomas 7-134-1, Decker 5-73-0, Welker 4-38-0, Ball 3-13-0, Tamme 2-24-1, Moreno 2-22-0, Caldwell 1-11-0.

KICKOFF RETURNS: NE: None. DEN: Holliday 1-4-0.
PUNT RETURNS: NE: None. DEN: None.
PUNTING: NE: Allen 3-147-49.0. DEN: Colquitt 1-48-48.0.
INTERCEPTIONS: NE: None. DEN: None.
SACKS: NE: None. DEN: Ayers, Knighton.

NFC CHAMPIONSHIP GAME RESULTS
Includes NFL Championship Games (1933-1969)

Season	Date	Winner (Share)	Loser (Share)	Score	Site	Attendance
2013	Jan. 19	Seattle ($42,000)	San Francisco ($42,000)	23-17	Seattle	68,454
2012	Jan. 20	San Francisco ($40,000)	Atlanta ($40,000)	28-24	Atlanta	70,863
2011	Jan. 22	N.Y. Giants ($40,000)	San Francisco ($40,000)	20-17*	San Francisco	69,732
2010	Jan. 23	Green Bay ($38,000)	Chicago ($38,000)	21-14	Chicago	62,377
2009	Jan. 24	New Orleans ($38,000)	Minnesota ($38,000)	31-28*	New Orleans	71,276
2008	Jan. 18	Arizona ($37,500)	Philadelphia ($37,500)	32-25	Glendale	70,650
2007	Jan. 20	N.Y. Giants ($37,500)	Green Bay ($37,500)	23-20*	Green Bay	72,740
2006	Jan. 21	Chicago ($37,000)	New Orleans ($37,000)	39-14	Chicago	61,817
2005	Jan. 22	Seattle ($37,000)	Carolina ($37,000)	34-14	Seattle	67,837
2004	Jan. 23	Philadelphia ($36,500)	Atlanta ($36,500)	27-10	Philadelphia	67,717
2003	Jan. 18	Carolina ($36,500)	Philadelphia ($36,500)	14-3	Philadelphia	67,862
2002	Jan. 19	Tampa Bay ($35,000)	Philadelphia ($35,000)	27-10	Philadelphia	66,713
2001	Jan. 27	St. Louis ($34,500)	Philadelphia ($34,500)	29-24	St. Louis	66,502
2000	Jan. 14	N.Y. Giants ($34,500)	Minnesota ($34,500)	41-0	East Rutherford	79,310
1999	Jan. 23	St. Louis ($33,000)	Tampa Bay ($33,000)	11-6	St. Louis	66,396
1998	Jan. 17	Atlanta ($32,500)	Minnesota ($32,500)	30-27*	Minneapolis	64,060
1997	Jan. 11	Green Bay ($30,000)	San Francisco ($30,000)	23-10	San Francisco	68,987
1996	Jan. 12	Green Bay ($29,000)	Carolina ($29,000)	30-13	Green Bay	60,216
1995	Jan. 14	Dallas ($27,000)	Green Bay ($27,000)	38-27	Dallas	65,135
1994	Jan. 15	San Francisco ($26,000)	Dallas ($26,000)	38-28	San Francisco	69,125
1993	Jan. 23	Dallas ($23,500)	San Francisco ($23,500)	38-21	Dallas	64,902
1992	Jan. 17	Dallas ($18,000)	San Francisco ($18,000)	30-20	San Francisco	64,920
1991	Jan. 12	Washington ($18,000)	Detroit ($18,000)	41-10	Washington	55,585
1990	Jan. 20	N.Y. Giants ($18,000)	San Francisco ($18,000)	15-13	San Francisco	65,750
1989	Jan. 14	San Francisco ($18,000)	L.A. Rams ($18,000)	30-3	San Francisco	65,634
1988	Jan. 8	San Francisco ($18,000)	Chicago ($18,000)	28-3	Chicago	66,946
1987	Jan. 17	Washington ($18,000)	Minnesota ($18,000)	17-10	Washington	55,212
1986	Jan. 11	New York Giants ($18,000)	Washington ($18,000)	17-0	East Rutherford	76,891
1985	Jan. 12	Chicago ($18,000)	L.A. Rams ($18,000)	24-0	Chicago	66,030
1984	Jan. 6	San Francisco ($18,000)	Chicago ($18,000)	23-0	San Francisco	61,336
1983	Jan. 8	Washington ($18,000)	San Francisco ($18,000)	24-21	Washington	55,363
1982	Jan. 22	Washington ($18,000)	Dallas ($18,000)	31-17	Washington	55,045
1981	Jan. 10	San Francisco ($9,000)	Dallas ($9,000)	28-27	San Francisco	60,525
1980	Jan. 11	Philadelphia ($9,000)	Dallas ($9,000)	20-7	Philadelphia	71,522
1979	Jan. 6	Los Angeles ($9,000)	Tampa Bay ($9,000)	9-0	Tampa	72,033
1978	Jan. 7	Dallas ($9,000)	Los Angeles ($9,000)	28-0	Los Angeles	71,086
1977	Jan. 1	Dallas ($9,000)	Minnesota ($9,000)	23-6	Dallas	64,293
1976	Dec. 26	Minnesota ($8,500)	Los Angeles ($5,500)	24-13	Minneapolis	48,379
1975	Jan. 4	Dallas ($8,500)	Los Angeles ($5,500)	37-7	Los Angeles	88,919
1974	Dec. 29	Minnesota ($8,500)	Los Angeles ($5,500)	14-10	Minneapolis	48,444
1973	Dec. 30	Minnesota ($8,500)	Dallas ($5,500)	27-10	Dallas	64,422
1972	Dec. 31	Washington ($8,500)	Dallas ($5,500)	26-3	Washington	53,129
1971	Jan. 2	Dallas ($8,500)	San Francisco ($5,500)	14-3	Dallas	63,409
1970	Jan. 3	Dallas ($8,500)	San Francisco ($5,500)	17-10	San Francisco	59,364
1969	Jan. 4	Minnesota ($7,930)	Cleveland ($5,118)	27-7	Minneapolis	46,503
1968	Dec. 29	Baltimore ($9,306)	Cleveland ($5,963)	34-0	Cleveland	78,410
1967	Dec. 31	Green Bay ($7,950)	Dallas ($5,299)	21-17	Green Bay	50,861
1966	Jan. 1	Green Bay ($9,813)	Dallas ($6,527)	34-27	Dallas	74,152
1965	Jan. 2	Green Bay ($7,819)	Cleveland ($5,288)	23-12	Green Bay	50,777
1964	Dec. 27	Cleveland ($8,052)	Baltimore ($5,571)	27-0	Cleveland	79,544
1963	Dec. 29	Chicago ($5,899)	New York ($4,218)	14-10	Chicago	45,801
1962	Dec. 30	Green Bay ($5,888)	New York ($4,166)	16-7	New York	64,892
1961	Dec. 31	Green Bay ($5,195)	New York ($3,339)	37-0	Green Bay	39,029
1960	Dec. 26	Philadelphia ($5,116)	Green Bay ($3,105)	17-13	Philadelphia	67,325
1959	Dec. 27	Baltimore ($4,674)	New York ($3,083)	31-16	Baltimore	57,545
1958	Dec. 28	Baltimore ($4,718)	New York ($3,111)	23-17*	New York	64,185
1957	Dec. 29	Detroit ($4,295)	Cleveland ($2,750)	59-14	Detroit	55,263
1956	Dec. 30	New York ($3,779)	Chi. Bears ($2,485)	47-7	New York	56,836
1955	Dec. 26	Cleveland ($3,508)	Los Angeles ($2,316)	38-14	Los Angeles	85,693
1954	Dec. 26	Cleveland ($2,478)	Detroit ($1,585)	56-10	Cleveland	43,827
1953	Dec. 27	Detroit ($2,424)	Cleveland ($1,654)	17-16	Detroit	54,577
1952	Dec. 28	Detroit ($2,274)	Cleveland ($1,712)	17-7	Cleveland	50,934

Season	Date	Winner (Share)	Loser (Share)	Score	Site	Attendance
1951	Dec. 23	Los Angeles ($2,108)	Cleveland ($1,483)	24-17	Los Angeles	57,522
1950	Dec. 24	Cleveland ($1,113)	Los Angeles ($686)	30-28	Cleveland	29,751
1949	Dec. 18	Philadelphia ($1,094)	Los Angeles ($739)	14-0	Los Angeles	27,980
1948	Dec. 19	Philadelphia ($1,540)	Chi. Cardinals ($874)	7-0	Philadelphia	36,309
1947	Dec. 28	Chi. Cardinals ($1,132)	Philadelphia ($754)	28-21	Chicago	30,759
1946	Dec. 15	Chi. Bears ($1,975)	New York ($1,295)	24-14	New York	58,346
1945	Dec. 16	Cleveland ($1,469)	Washington ($902)	15-14	Cleveland	32,178
1944	Dec. 17	Green Bay ($1,449)	New York ($814)	14-7	New York	46,016
1943	Dec. 26	Chi. Bears ($1,146)	Washington ($765)	41-21	Chicago	34,320
1942	Dec. 13	Washington ($965)	Chi. Bears ($637)	14-6	Washington	36,006
1941	Dec. 21	Chi. Bears ($430)	New York ($288)	37-9	Chicago	13,341
1940	Dec. 8	Chi. Bears ($873)	Washington ($606)	73-0	Washington	36,034
1939	Dec. 10	Green Bay ($703.97)	New York ($455.57)	27-0	Milwaukee	32,279
1938	Dec. 11	New York ($504.45)	Green Bay ($368.81)	23-17	New York	48,120
1937	Dec. 12	Washington ($225.90)	Chi. Bears ($127.78)	28-21	Chicago	15,870
1936	Dec. 13	Green Bay ($250)	Boston ($180)	21-6	New York	29,545
1935	Dec. 15	Detroit ($313.35)	New York ($200.20)	26-7	Detroit	15,000
1934	Dec. 9	New York ($621)	Chi. Bears ($414.02)	30-13	New York	35,059
1933	Dec. 17	Chi. Bears ($210.34)	New York ($140.22)	23-21	Chicago	26,000

*Overtime

NFC CHAMPIONSHIP GAME COMPOSITE STANDINGS

	W	L	0	Pct.	Pts.	OP
Seattle Seahawks	2	0		1.000	57	31
Baltimore Colts	3	1		.750	88	60
Green Bay Packers	11	4		.733	344	214
Detroit Lions	4	2		.667	139	141
Arizona Cardinals**	2	1		.667	60	53
Washington Redskins*	7	5		.583	222	255
Chicago Bears	8	7		.533	339	280
Dallas Cowboys	8	8		.500	361	319
Philadelphia Eagles	5	5		.500	168	160
Atlanta Falcons	1	2		.333	64	82
New Orleans Saints	1	1		.500	45	67
Minnesota Vikings	4	5		.444	163	182
New York Giants	8	11		.421	324	359
San Francisco 49ers	6	9		.400	307	289
Cleveland Browns	4	7		.364	224	253
St. Louis Rams***	5	9		.357	163	300
Carolina Panthers	1	2		.333	41	67
Tampa Bay Buccaneers	1	2		.333	33	30

*One game played when franchise was in Boston (Lost 21-6)
**Both games played when franchise was in Chicago (Won 28-21, lost 7-0)
***One game played when franchise was in Cleveland (Won 15-14), and 11 games when franchise was in Los Angeles (Won 2, lost 9, scored 108 points, allowed 256 points).

2013 NFC CHAMPIONSHIP GAME

CenturyLink Field, Seattle, Washington
January 19, 2014, Attendance: 68,454

SEATTLE 23, SAN FRANCISCO 17—Richard Sherman tipped a pass and Malcolm Smith intercepted the ball in the end zone with 22 seconds remaining to propel the Seattle Seahawks to their second Super Bowl appearance. The San Francisco 49ers, playing in their third consecutive NFC Championship Game, began quickly. Aldon Smith sacked Russell Wilson on the game's first play, forcing him to fumble and recovering the ball at the Seahawks' 15. Seattle's defense limited the damage by allowing a 25-yard field goal to Phil Dawson. Early in the second quarter, Colin Kaepernick scrambled for 58 yards to help the 49ers reach the Seahawks' 1-yard line. On fourth-and-goal, Anthony Dixon scored on a 1-yard plunge for a 10-0 lead. Wilson responded with a 51-yard pass to Doug Baldwin to set up Steven Hauschka's 32-yard field goal. The 49ers began the third quarter with the ball but were forced to punt. Four plays later, on third-and-1, Marshawn Lynch rumbled 40 yards for a game-tying touchdown. On the 49ers' next possession, Michael Bennett forced Kaepernick to fumble but center Jonathan Goodwin recovered and advanced the ball 6 yards to the Seahawks' 26. On the following play, Kaepernick completed a 26-yard touchdown pass to Anquan Boldin to give the 49ers a 17-10 lead with 6:29 left in the third quarter. Baldwin returned the ensuing kickoff 69 yards to set up Hauschka's second field goal, and the Seahawks' defense forced a three-and-out. Seattle drove to the 49ers' 35 and, on fourth-and-7, San Francisco jumped offside. Knowing he had a free play, Wilson launched a pass into coverage in the end zone where Jermaine Kearse made a leaping catch to give Seattle's first lead, 20-17, with 13:44 to play. A few plays later, Cliff Avril sacked Kaepernick and forced him to fumble. Bennett recovered the ball and returned it to the 49ers' 6. The 49ers' defense held as, on fourth-and-goal from the 1-yard line, Wilson and Lynch fumbled the handoff exchange. Two plays later, Kam Chancellor intercepted a pass at the 49ers' 40, setting up Hauschka's 47-yard field goal for a 23-17 lead with 3:37 remaining. The 49ers began their final drive on their own 22. On fourth-and-2 from the 30-yard-line Kaepernick completed a 17-yard pass to Frank Gore. A 16-yard pass to Crabtree on third-and-2 and an 11-yard pass to Vernon Davis put the 49ers at the Seahawks' 18 with 30 seconds left and two timeouts. Kaepernick dropped back and lofted a pass to the back corner of the right end zone. Crabtree was a step behind Sherman, but Sherman leaped and with one hand tipped the ball slightly back toward the field. Smith was trailing the play and cradled the ball in his hands in the end zone for a touchback with 22 seconds left. Wilson was 16 of 25 for 215 yards and 1 touchdown. Lynch carried 22 times for 109 yards. Baldwin had 6 receptions for 109 yards. Kaepernick was 14 of 24 for 153 yards and 1 touchdown, with 2 interceptions, along with his game-high 130 rushing yards on 11 carries.

San Francisco (17)	Offense	Seattle (23)
Vance McDonald	TE	Kellen Davis
Joe Staley	LT	Russell Okung
Mike Iupati	LG	James Carpenter
Jonathan Goodwin	C	Max Unger
Alex Boone	RG	J.R. Sweezy
Anthony Davis	RT	Breno Giacomini
Vernon Davis	TE	Zach Miller
Anquan Boldin	WR	Jermaine Kearse
Colin Kaepernick	QB	Russell Wilson
Anthony Dixon	FB	Michael Robinson
Frank Gore	RB	Marshawn Lynch
	Defense	
Ray McDonald	LDT/LDE	Red Bryant
Glenn Dorsey	NT/LDT	Tony McDaniel
Justin Smith	RDT/RDT	Brandon Mebane
Ahmad Brooks	OLB/RDE	Chris Clemons
NaVorro Bowman	ILB/OLB	Bruce Irvin
Patrick Willis	ILB/MLB	Bobby Wagner

Aldon Smith	OLB	Malcolm Smith	
Tramaine Brock	LCB	Richard Sherman	
Tarell Brown	RCB	Byron Maxwell	
Donte Whitner	SS	Kam Chancellor	
Eric Reid	FS	Earl Thomas	

SUBSTITUTIONS

SAN FRANCISCO—Specialists: K—Phil Dawson. P—Andy Lee. LS—Kevin McDermott. TE/DT—Demarcus Dobbs. Offense: RB—Kendall Hunter, LaMichael James. FB—Will Tukuafu. WR—Michael Crabtree, Kassim Osgood, Quinton Patton. TE—Garrett Celek. G—Adam Snyder. G/C—Daniel Kilgore. Defense: DT—Tony Jerod-Eddie. LB—Corey Lemonier, Dan Skuta, Michael Wilhoite. CB—Perrish Cox, Darryl Morris, Carlos Rogers. S—Craig Dahl, C.J. Spillman, Bubba Ventrone. Did Not Play: QB—Colt McCoy. Not Active: WR—Jon Baldwin. TE—Derek Carrier. G—Joe Looney, Ryan Seymour. DT—Quinton Dial. LB—Nick Moody. CB—Eric Wright.

SEATTLE—Specialists: K—Steven Hauschka. P—Jon Ryan. LS—Clint Gresham. Offense: RB—Robert Turbin. FB—Derrick Coleman. WR—Doug Baldwin, Ricardo Lockette, Golden Tate, Bryan Walters. TE—Luke Willson. C—Lemuel Jeanpierre. G—Paul McQuistan. T—Alvin Bailey. Defense: DT—Clinton McDonald. DE—Cliff Avril, Michael Bennett. LB—Heath Farwell, Mike Morgan, K.J. Wright. CB—Jeremy Lane, DeShawn Shead, Walter Thurmond. S—Chris Maragos. Did Not Play: QB—Tarvaris Jackson. Not Active: RB—Christine Michael. WR—Percy Harvin. T—Michael Bowie, Caylin Hauptmann. DT—Jordan Hill. DE—Benson Mayowa, O'Brien Schofield.

OFFICIALS

Referee—Gene Steratore. Umpire—Bill Schuster. Head Linesman—Dana McKenzie. Line Judge—Byron Boston. Side Judge—Greg Meyer. Field Judge—Scott Edwards. Back Judge—Perry Paganelli. Reply Official—Paul Weidner.

SCORING

San Francisco	3	7	7	0	—	17	
Seattle	0	3	10	10	—	23	

SF	—	FG Dawson 25
SF	—	Dixon 1 run (Dawson kick)
Sea	—	FG Hauschka 32
Sea	—	Lynch 40 run (Hauschka kick)
SF	—	Boldin 26 pass from Kaepernick (Dawson kick)
Sea	—	FG Hauschka 40
Sea	—	Kearse 35 pass from Wilson (Hauschka kick)
Sea	—	FG Hauschka 47

TEAM STATISTICS

	SF	SEA
Total First Downs	16	14
Rushing	7	5
Passing	8	8
Penalty	1	1
Total Net Yardage	308	308
Total Offensive Plays	54	58
Average Gain Per Offensive Play	5.7	5.3
Rushes	28	29
Yards Gained Rushing (Net)	161	115
Average Yards per Rush	5.8	4.0
Passes Attempted	24	25
Passes Completed	14	16
Had Intercepted	2	0
Tackled Attempting to Pass	2	4
Yards Lost Attempting to Pass	6	22
Yards Gained Passing (Net)	147	193
Punts	4	2
Average Distance	42.0	45.5
Punt Returns	1	3
Punt Return Yardage	0	10
Kickoff Returns	4	3
Kickoff Return Yardage	92	109
Interception Return Yardage	0	0
Total Return Yardage (excluding Kickoffs)	0	10
Fumbles	3	3
Fumbles Lost	1	1
Own Fumbles Recovered	2	2
Opponent Fumbles Recovered	1	1
Penalties	7	8
Yards Penalized	65	66
Field Goals	1	3
Field Goals Attempted	1	3
Third-Down Efficiency	3/11	5/14
Fourth-Down Efficiency	2/2	1/3
Time of Possession	28:32	31:28

INDIVIDUAL STATISTICS

RUSHING: SF: Kaepernick 11-130-0, Hunter 3-16-0, Gore 11-14-0, Dixon 2-1-1, James 1-0-0. SEA: Lynch 22-109-1, Turbin 2-6-0, Wilson 5-0-0.

PASSING: SF: Kaepernick 24-14-153-1-2. SEA: Wilson 25-16-215-1-0.

RECEIVING: SF: Boldin 5-53-1, Crabtree 4-52-0, Davis 2-16-0, Gore 1-17-0, McDonald 1-13-0, Patton 1-2-0. SEA: Baldwin 6-106-0, Tate 4-31-0, Miller 3-25-0, Kearse 2-44-1, Turbin 1-9-0.

KICKOFF RETURNS: SF: James 3-64-0. SEA: Baldwin 3-109-0.

PUNT RETURNS: SF: James 1-0-0. SEA: Tate 3-10-0.

PUNTING: SF: Lee 4-168-42.0. SEA: Ryan 2-91-45.5.

INTERCEPTIONS: SF: None. SEA: Chancellor 1-0-0, Smith 1-0-0.

SACKS: SF: A. Smith 2, Bowman 1, Skuta 1. SEA: Avril 1, Bennett 1.

AFC DIVISIONAL PLAYOFF GAMES RESULTS

Includes Second-Round Playoff Games (1982), AFC Inter-Divisional Games (1969), and special playoff games to break ties for AFL Division Championships (1963, 1968)

Season	Date	Winner (Share)	Loser (Share)	Score	Site	Attendance
2013	Jan. 12	Denver ($23,000)	San Diego ($23,000)	24-17	Denver	76,969
	Jan. 11	New England ($23,000)	Indianapolis ($23,000)	43-22	Foxborough	68,756
2012	Jan. 13	New England ($22,000)	Houston ($22,000)	41-28	Foxborough	68,756
	Jan. 12	Baltimore ($22,000)	Denver ($22,000)	38-35*	Denver	76,732
2011	Jan. 15	Baltimore ($22,000)	Houston ($22,000)	20-13	Baltimore	71,547
	Jan. 14	New England ($22,000)	Denver ($22,000)	45-10	Foxborough	68,756
2010	Jan. 16	N.Y. Jets ($21,000)	New England ($21,000)	28-21	Foxborough	68,756
	Jan. 15	Pittsburgh ($21,000)	Baltimore ($21,000)	31-24	Pittsburgh	64,879
2009	Jan. 17	N.Y. Jets ($21,000)	San Diego ($21,000)	17-14	San Diego	69,498
	Jan. 16	Indianapolis ($21,000)	Baltimore ($21,000)	20-3	Indianapolis	67,535
2008	Jan. 11	Pittsburgh ($20,000)	San Diego ($20,000)	35-24	Pittsburgh	63,899
	Jan. 10	Baltimore ($20,000)	Tennessee ($20,000)	13-10	Nashville	69,143
2007	Jan. 13	San Diego ($20,000)	Indianapolis ($20,000)	28-24	Indianapolis	56,950
	Jan. 12	New England ($20,000)	Jacksonville ($20,000)	31-20	Foxborough	68,756
2006	Jan. 14	New England ($19,000)	San Diego ($19,000)	24-21	San Diego	68,810
	Jan. 13	Indianapolis ($19,000)	Baltimore ($19,000)	15-6	Baltimore	71,162
2005	Jan. 15	Pittsburgh ($19,000)	Indianapolis ($19,000)	21-18	Indianapolis	57,449
	Jan. 14	Denver ($19,000)	New England ($19,000)	27-13	Denver	76,238

Season	Date	Winner (Share)	Loser (Share)	Score	Site	Attendance
2004	Jan. 16	New England ($18,000)	Indianapolis ($18,000)	20-3	Foxborough	68,756
	Jan. 15	Pittsburgh ($18,000)	N.Y. Jets ($18,000)	20-17*	Pittsburgh	64,915
2003	Jan. 11	Indianapolis ($18,000)	Kansas City ($18,000)	38-31	Kansas City	79,159
	Jan. 10	New England ($18,000)	Tennessee ($18,000)	17-14	Foxborough	68,436
2002	Jan. 12	Oakland ($17,000)	N.Y. Jets ($17,000)	30-10	Oakland	62,207
	Jan. 11	Tennessee ($17,000)	Pittsburgh ($17,000)	34-31*	Nashville	68,809
2001	Jan. 20	Pittsburgh ($17,000)	Baltimore ($17,000)	27-10	Pittsburgh	63,976
	Jan. 19	New England ($17,000)	Oakland ($17,000)	16-13*	Foxborough	60,292
2000	Jan. 7	Baltimore ($16,000)	Tennessee ($16,000)	24-10	Nashville	68,527
	Jan. 6	Oakland ($16,000)	Miami ($16,000)	27-0	Oakland	61,998
1999	Jan. 16	Tennessee ($16,000)	Indianapolis ($16,000)	19-16	Indianapolis	57,097
	Jan. 15	Jacksonville ($16,000)	Miami ($16,000)	62-7	Jacksonville	75,173
1998	Jan. 10	N.Y. Jets ($15,000)	Jacksonville ($15,000)	34-24	East Rutherford	78,817
	Jan. 9	Denver ($15,000)	Miami ($15,000)	38-3	Denver	75,729
1997	Jan. 4	Denver ($15,000)	Kansas City ($15,000)	14-10	Kansas City	76,965
	Jan. 3	Pittsburgh ($15,000)	New England ($15,000)	7-6	Pittsburgh	61,228
1996	Jan. 5	New England ($14,000)	Pittsburgh ($14,000)	28-3	Foxborough	60,188
	Jan. 4	Jacksonville ($14,000)	Denver ($14,000)	30-27	Denver	75,678
1995	Jan. 7	Indianapolis ($13,000)	Kansas City ($13,000)	10-7	Kansas City	77,594
	Jan. 6	Pittsburgh ($13,000)	Buffalo ($13,000)	40-21	Pittsburgh	59,072
1994	Jan. 8	San Diego ($12,000)	Miami ($12,000)	22-21	San Diego	63,381
	Jan. 7	Pittsburgh ($12,000)	Cleveland ($12,000)	29-9	Pittsburgh	58,185
1993	Jan. 16	Kansas City ($12,000)	Houston ($12,000)	28-20	Houston	64,011
	Jan. 15	Buffalo ($12,000)	L.A. Raiders ($12,000)	29-23	Buffalo	61,923
1992	Jan. 10	Miami ($10,000)	San Diego ($10,000)	31-0	Miami	71,224
	Jan. 9	Buffalo ($10,000)	Pittsburgh ($10,000)	24-3	Pittsburgh	60,407
1991	Jan. 5	Buffalo ($10,000)	Kansas City ($10,000)	37-14	Buffalo	80,182
	Jan. 4	Denver ($10,000)	Houston ($10,000)	26-24	Denver	75,301
1990	Jan. 13	L.A. Raiders ($10,000)	Cincinnati ($10,000)	20-10	Los Angeles	92,045
	Jan. 12	Buffalo ($10,000)	Miami ($10,000)	44-34	Buffalo	77,087
1989	Jan. 7	Denver ($10,000)	Pittsburgh ($10,000)	24-23	Denver	75,477
	Jan. 6	Cleveland ($10,000)	Buffalo ($10,000)	34-30	Cleveland	78,921
1988	Jan. 1	Buffalo ($10,000)	Houston ($10,000)	17-10	Buffalo	79,532
	Dec. 31	Cincinnati ($10,000)	Seattle ($10,000)	21-13	Cincinnati	58,560
1987	Jan. 10	Denver ($10,000)	Houston ($10,000)	34-10	Denver	75,440
	Jan. 9	Cleveland ($10,000)	Indianapolis ($10,000)	38-21	Cleveland	79,372
1986	Jan. 4	Denver ($10,000)	New England ($10,000)	22-17	Denver	75,262
	Jan. 3	Cleveland ($10,000)	N.Y. Jets ($10,000)	23-20*	Cleveland	79,720
1985	Jan. 5	New England ($10,000)	L.A. Raiders ($10,000)	27-20	Los Angeles	87,163
	Jan. 4	Miami ($10,000)	Cleveland ($10,000)	24-21	Miami	74,667
1984	Dec. 30	Pittsburgh ($10,000)	Denver ($10,000)	24-17	Denver	74,981
	Dec. 29	Miami ($10,000)	Seattle ($10,000)	31-10	Miami	73,469
1983	Jan. 1	L.A. Raiders ($10,000)	Pittsburgh ($10,000)	38-10	Los Angeles	90,380
	Dec. 31	Seattle ($10,000)	Miami ($10,000)	27-20	Miami	74,136
1982	Jan. 16	Miami ($10,000)	San Diego ($10,000)	34-13	Miami	71,383
	Jan. 15	N.Y. Jets ($10,000)	L.A. Raiders ($10,000)	17-14	Los Angeles	90,038
1981	Jan. 3	Cincinnati ($5,000)	Buffalo ($5,000)	28-21	Cincinnati	55,420
	Jan. 2	San Diego ($5,000)	Miami ($5,000)	41-38*	Miami	73,735
1980	Jan. 4	Oakland ($5,000)	Cleveland ($5,000)	14-12	Cleveland	78,245
	Jan. 3	San Diego ($5,000)	Buffalo ($5,000)	20-14	San Diego	52,253
1979	Dec. 30	Pittsburgh ($5,000)	Miami ($5,000)	34-14	Pittsburgh	50,214
	Dec. 29	Houston ($5,000)	San Diego ($5,000)	17-14	San Diego	51,192
1978	Dec. 31	Houston ($5,000)	New England ($5,000)	31-14	Foxborough	60,735
	Dec. 30	Pittsburgh ($5,000)	Denver ($5,000)	33-10	Pittsburgh	50,230
1977	Dec. 24	Oakland ($5,000)	Baltimore ($5,000)	37-31*	Baltimore	59,925
	Dec. 24	Denver ($5,000)	Pittsburgh ($5,000)	34-21	Denver	75,059
1976	Dec. 19	Pittsburgh ($5,000)	Baltimore ($5,000)	40-14	Baltimore	59,296
	Dec. 18	Oakland [$]	New England [$]	24-21	Oakland	53,050
1975	Dec. 28	Oakland [$]	Cincinnati [$]	31-28	Oakland	53,030
	Dec. 27	Pittsburgh [$]	Baltimore [$]	28-10	Pittsburgh	49,557
1974	Dec. 22	Pittsburgh [$]	Buffalo [$]	32-14	Pittsburgh	49,841
	Dec. 21	Oakland [$]	Miami [$]	28-26	Oakland	53,023
1973	Dec. 23	Miami [$]	Cincinnati [$]	34-16	Miami	78,928
	Dec. 22	Oakland [$]	Pittsburgh [$]	33-14	Oakland	52,646
1972	Dec. 24	Miami [$]	Cleveland [$]	20-14	Miami	78,916
	Dec. 23	Pittsburgh [$]	Oakland [$]	13-7	Pittsburgh	50,327
1971	Dec. 26	Baltimore [$]	Cleveland [$]	20-3	Cleveland	70,734
	Dec. 25	Miami [$]	Kansas City [$]	27-24*	Kansas City	50,374
1970	Dec. 27	Oakland [$]	Miami [$]	21-14	Oakland	52,594
	Dec. 26	Baltimore [$]	Cincinnati [$]	17-0	Baltimore	49,694
1969	Dec. 21	Oakland [$]	Houston [$]	56-7	Oakland	53,539
	Dec. 20	Kansas City [$]	N.Y. Jets [$]	13-6	New York	62,977
1968	Dec. 22	Oakland [$]	Kansas City [$]	41-6	Oakland	53,605
1963	Dec. 28	Boston [$]	Buffalo [$]	26-8	Buffalo	33,044

*Overtime
$ Players received 1/14 of annual salary for playoff appearances.

2013 AFC DIVISIONAL PLAYOFF GAMES

Sports Authority Field at Mile High, Denver, Colorado
January 12, 2014, Attendance: 76,969

DENVER 24, SAN DIEGO 17—Peyton Manning passed for 2 touchdowns and the Denver Broncos' defense allowed just 69 total yards in the first three quarters en route to victory. The Broncos scored a pair of touchdowns in the first half, on drives covering seven minutes, one second and five minutes, 13 seconds. On their other two possessions, the Broncos were stopped by turnovers, including Donald Butler's interception in the end zone for a touchback with 30 seconds left in the half to keep the score at 14-0. The Broncos began the second half with a five minute, 25 second drive that resulted in Matt Prater's 45-yard field goal for a 17-0 lead. On Denver's next possession Prater missed from 47 yards, and the San Diego Chargers responded with a 63-yard drive, keyed by Eddie Royal's 30-yard catch on third-and-3, and capped by Philip Rivers' 16-yard touchdown pass to Keenan Allen, also on third down, to pull within 17-7 with 12:59 remaining. The Broncos answered with another time-consuming drive, this one four minutes, 47 seconds, including a 17-yard pass to Julius Thomas on third down, and capped by Knowshon Moreno's 3-yard run with 8:12 left for a 24-7 lead. On the next possession, Allen caught a 49-yard pass on fourth-and-5 to set up his second 16-yard touchdown catch. The Chargers' Richard Marshall then recovered the ensuing onside kick and Rivers completed passes of 17 and 25 yards to Allen to set up Nick Novak's 30-yard field goal with 3:53 to play to cut the deficit to 24-17. The Chargers eschewed the onside kick and instead attempted a pop fly kick, but Trindon Holliday caught it at the Broncos' 27. On third-and-17 with 3:06 to play, Manning completed a 21-yard pass to Thomas along the sideline. Three plays later, on third-and-6, Manning and Thomas connected for 9 yards. Moreno secured the victory with a 6-yard run on third-and-1 with 1:12 remaining. Manning was 25 of 36 for 230 yards and 2 touchdowns, with 1 interception. Rivers was 18 of 27 for 217 yards and 2 touchdowns. Allen had 6 catches for 142 yards.

San Diego	0	0	0	17	—	17
Denver	7	7	3	7	—	24

Den	—	D. Thomas 2 pass from Manning (Prater kick)
Den	—	Welker 3 pass from Manning (Prater kick)
Den	—	FG Prater 45
SD	—	Allen 16 pass from Rivers (Novak kick)
Den	—	Moreno 3 run (Prater kick)
SD	—	Allen 16 pass from Rivers (Novak kick)
SD	—	FG Novak 30

Gillette Stadium, Foxborough, Massachusetts
January 11, 2014, Attendance: 68,756

NEW ENGLAND 43, INDIANAPOLIS 22—LeGarrette Blount rushed for 166 yards and 4 touchdowns as New England won an AFC Divisional Playoff home game for the third consecutive year. On the game's third play, Alfonzo Dennard intercepted a pass and returned it 27 yards to the Colts' 2-yard line, setting up Blount's first touchdown just 1:19 into the game. The Patriots' defense forced a three-and-out and the offense drove 74 yards and took a 14-0 lead on Blount with 7:19 left in the first quarter. The Patriots led 21-10 in the second quarter when, on fourth-and-7 from the Patriots' 44, Danny Aiken's snap sailed over punter Ryan Allen's head. Allen picked it up near the goal line and then fumbled the ball out of the end zone for a safety to pull within 21-12 with 2:18 left in the half. The Colts drove to the Patriots' 39, but Dont'a Hightower intercepted a pass from Andrew Luck to allow New England to maintain a 9-point halftime lead. The Colts' defense forced a three-and-out to begin the second half and drove 60 yards to Adam Vinatieri's second field goal to cut the deficit to 21-15. New England responded with a 9-play, 88-yard touchdown drive, capped by Stevan Ridley's 3-yard touchdown run, and 2-point conversion rush, for a 29-15 lead. Indianapolis needed just three plays to pull within seven points on LaVon Brazill's 35-yard touchdown pass from Luck. After each team punted twice, Blount gave the Patriots a 2-touchdown lead with 12:55 remaining with Blount's 73-yard scoring run over right guard. He became the first Patriots' player to rush for 4 touchdowns in a game, regular season or postseason. Two plays later Jamie Collins intercepted a pass and returned it 20 yards to the Colts' 18, setting up Ridley's 1-yard touchdown run with 11:12 left to finish the scoring. Tom Brady was 13 of 25 for 198 yards. Blount had 24 carries for 166 yards with 4 touchdowns. Luck was 20 of 41 for 331 yards and 2 touchdowns, 4 interceptions.

Indianapolis	7	5	10	0	—	22
New England	14	7	8	14	—	43

NE	—	Blount 2 run (Gostkowski kick)
NE	—	Blount 2 run (Gostkowski kick)
Ind	—	Brazill 38 pass from Luck (Vinatieri kick)
NE	—	Blount 2 run (Gostkowski kick)
Ind	—	FG Vinatieri 36
Ind	—	Safety, Allen fumbled ball out of end zone
Ind	—	FG Vinatieri 21
NE	—	Ridley 3 run (Ridley run)
Ind	—	Brazill 35 pass from Luck (Vinatieri kick)
NE	—	Blount 73 run (Gostkowski kick)
NE	—	Ridley 1 run (Gostkowski kick)

NFC DIVISIONAL PLAYOFF GAMES RESULTS

Includes Second-Round Playoff Games (1982), NFL Conference Championship Games (1967-69), and special playoff games to break ties for NFL Division or Conference Championships (1941, 1943, 1947, 1950, 1952, 1957, 1958, 1965)

Season	Date	Winner (Share)	Loser (Share)	Score	Site	Attendance
2013	Jan. 12	San Francisco ($23,000)	Carolina ($23,000)	23-10	Charlotte	73,784
	Jan. 11	Seattle ($23,000)	New Orleans ($23,000)	23-15	Seattle	68,388
2012	Jan. 13	Atlanta ($22,000)	Seattle ($22,000)	30-28	Atlanta	70,366
	Jan. 12	San Francisco ($22,000)	Green Bay ($22,000)	45-31	San Francisco	69,732
2011	Jan. 15	N.Y. Giants ($22,000)	Green Bay ($22,000)	37-20	Green Bay	72,080
	Jan. 14	San Francisco ($22,000)	New Orleans ($22,000)	36-32	San Francisco	69,732
2010	Jan. 16	Chicago ($21,000)	Seattle ($21,000)	35-24	Chicago	62,265
	Jan. 15	Green Bay ($21,000)	Atlanta ($21,000)	48-21	Atlanta	69,210
2009	Jan. 17	Minnesota ($21,000)	Dallas ($21,000)	34-3	Minneapolis	63,547
	Jan. 16	New Orleans ($21,000)	Arizona ($21,000)	45-14	New Orleans	70,149
2008	Jan. 11	Philadelphia ($20,000)	N.Y. Giants ($20,000)	23-11	East Rutherford	79,193
	Jan. 10	Arizona ($20,000)	Carolina ($20,000)	33-13	Charlotte	73,695
2007	Jan. 13	N.Y. Giants ($20,000)	Dallas ($20,000)	21-17	Dallas	63,660
	Jan. 12	Green Bay ($20,000)	Seattle ($20,000)	42-20	Green Bay	72,168
2006	Jan. 14	Chicago ($19,000)	Seattle ($19,000)	27-24*	Chicago	62,184
	Jan. 13	New Orleans ($19,000)	Philadelphia ($19,000)	27-24	New Orleans	70,001
2005	Jan. 15	Carolina ($19,000)	Chicago ($19,000)	29-21	Chicago	62,209
	Jan. 14	Seattle ($19,000)	Washington ($19,000)	20-10	Seattle	67,551
2004	Jan. 16	Philadelphia ($18,000)	Minnesota ($18,000)	27-14	Philadelphia	67,722
	Jan. 15	Atlanta ($18,000)	St. Louis ($18,000)	47-17	Atlanta	70,709

Season	Date	Winner (Share)	Loser (Share)	Score	Site	Attendance
2003	Jan. 11	Philadelphia ($18,000)	Green Bay ($18,000)	20-17*	Philadelphia	67,707
	Jan. 10	Carolina ($18,000)	St. Louis ($18,000)	29-23*	St. Louis	66,165
2002	Jan. 12	Tampa Bay ($17,000)	San Francisco ($17,000)	31-6	Tampa	65,599
	Jan. 11	Philadelphia ($17,000)	Atlanta ($17,000)	20-6	Philadelphia	66,452
2001	Jan. 20	St. Louis ($17,000)	Green Bay ($17,000)	45-17	St. Louis	66,338
	Jan. 19	Philadelphia ($17,000)	Chicago ($17,000)	33-19	Chicago	66,944
2000	Jan. 7	N.Y. Giants ($16,000)	Philadelphia ($16,000)	20-10	East Rutherford	78,765
	Jan. 6	Minnesota ($16,000)	New Orleans ($16,000)	34-16	Minneapolis	63,881
1999	Jan. 16	St. Louis ($16,000)	Minnesota ($16,000)	49-37	St. Louis	66,194
	Jan. 15	Tampa Bay ($16,000)	Washington ($16,000)	14-13	Tampa	65,835
1998	Jan. 10	Minnesota ($15,000)	Arizona ($15,000)	41-21	Minneapolis	63,760
	Jan. 9	Atlanta ($15,000)	San Francisco ($15,000)	20-18	Atlanta	70,262
1997	Jan. 4	Green Bay ($15,000)	Tampa Bay ($15,000)	21-7	Green Bay	60,327
	Jan. 3	San Francisco ($15,000)	Minnesota ($15,000)	38-22	San Francisco	65,018
1996	Jan. 5	Carolina ($14,000)	Dallas ($14,000)	26-17	Charlotte	72,808
	Jan. 4	Green Bay ($14,000)	San Francisco ($14,000)	35-14	Green Bay	60,787
1995	Jan. 7	Dallas ($13,000)	Philadelphia ($13,000)	30-11	Dallas	64,371
	Jan. 6	Green Bay ($13,000)	San Francisco ($13,000)	27-17	San Francisco	69,311
1994	Jan. 8	Dallas ($12,000)	Green Bay ($12,000)	35-9	Dallas	64,745
	Jan. 7	San Francisco ($12,000)	Chicago ($12,000)	44-15	San Francisco	64,644
1993	Jan. 16	Dallas ($12,000)	Green Bay ($12,000)	27-17	Dallas	64,790
	Jan. 15	San Francisco ($12,000)	N.Y. Giants ($12,000)	44-3	San Francisco	67,143
1992	Jan. 10	Dallas ($10,000)	Philadelphia ($10,000)	34-10	Dallas	63,721
	Jan. 9	San Francisco ($10,000)	Washington ($10,000)	20-13	San Francisco	64,991
1991	Jan. 5	Detroit ($10,000)	Dallas ($10,000)	38-6	Detroit	78,290
	Jan. 4	Washington ($10,000)	Atlanta ($10,000)	24-7	Washington	55,181
1990	Jan. 13	N.Y. Giants ($10,000)	Chicago ($10,000)	31-3	East Rutherford	77,025
	Jan. 12	San Francisco ($10,000)	Washington ($10,000)	28-10	San Francisco	65,292
1989	Jan. 7	L.A. Rams ($10,000)	N.Y. Giants ($10,000)	19-13*	East Rutherford	76,526
	Jan. 6	San Francisco ($10,000)	Minnesota ($10,000)	41-13	San Francisco	64,918
1988	Jan. 1	San Francisco ($10,000)	Minnesota ($10,000)	34-9	San Francisco	61,848
	Dec. 31	Chicago ($10,000)	Philadelphia ($10,000)	20-12	Chicago	65,534
1987	Jan. 10	Washington ($10,000)	Chicago ($10,000)	21-17	Chicago	65,268
	Jan. 9	Minnesota ($10,000)	San Francisco ($10,000)	36-24	San Francisco	63,008
1986	Jan. 4	N.Y. Giants ($10,000)	San Francisco ($10,000)	49-3	East Rutherford	75,691
	Jan. 3	Washington ($10,000)	Chicago ($10,000)	27-13	Chicago	65,524
1985	Jan. 5	Chicago ($10,000)	N.Y. Giants ($10,000)	21-0	Chicago	65,670
	Jan. 4	L.A. Rams ($10,000)	Dallas ($10,000)	20-0	Anaheim	66,581
1984	Dec. 30	Chicago ($10,000)	Washington ($10,000)	23-19	Washington	55,431
	Dec. 29	San Francisco ($10,000)	N.Y. Giants ($10,000)	21-10	San Francisco	60,303
1983	Jan. 1	Washington ($10,000)	L.A. Rams ($10,000)	51-7	Washington	54,440
	Dec. 31	San Francisco ($10,000)	Detroit ($10,000)	24-23	San Francisco	59,979
1982	Jan. 16	Dallas ($10,000)	Green Bay ($10,000)	37-26	Dallas	63,972
	Jan. 15	Washington ($10,000)	Minnesota ($10,000)	21-7	Washington	54,593
1981	Jan. 3	San Francisco ($5,000)	N.Y. Giants ($5,000)	38-24	San Francisco	58,360
	Jan. 2	Dallas ($5,000)	Tampa Bay ($5,000)	38-0	Dallas	64,848
1980	Jan. 4	Dallas ($5,000)	Atlanta ($5,000)	30-27	Atlanta	59,793
	Jan. 3	Philadelphia ($5,000)	Minnesota ($5,000)	31-16	Philadelphia	70,178
1979	Dec. 30	Los Angeles ($5,000)	Dallas ($5,000)	21-19	Dallas	64,792
	Dec. 29	Tampa Bay ($5,000)	Philadelphia ($5,000)	24-17	Tampa	71,402
1978	Dec. 31	Los Angeles ($5,000)	Minnesota ($5,000)	34-10	Los Angeles	70,436
	Dec. 30	Dallas ($5,000)	Atlanta ($5,000)	27-20	Dallas	63,406
1977	Dec. 26	Dallas ($5,000)	Chicago ($5,000)	37-7	Dallas	63,260
	Dec. 26	Minnesota ($5,000)	Los Angeles ($5,000)	14-7	Los Angeles	70,203
1976	Dec. 19	Los Angeles [$]	Dallas [$]	14-12	Dallas	63,283
	Dec. 18	Minnesota [$]	Washington [$]	35-20	Minneapolis	47,466
1975	Dec. 28	Dallas [$]	Minnesota [$]	17-14	Minneapolis	48,050
	Dec. 27	Los Angeles [$]	St. Louis [$]	35-23	Los Angeles	73,459
1974	Dec. 22	Los Angeles [$]	Washington [$]	19-10	Los Angeles	77,925
	Dec. 21	Minnesota [$]	St. Louis [$]	30-14	Minneapolis	48,150
1973	Dec. 23	Dallas [$]	Los Angeles [$]	27-16	Dallas	63,272
	Dec. 22	Minnesota [$]	Washington [$]	27-20	Minneapolis	48,040
1972	Dec. 24	Washington [$]	Green Bay [$]	16-3	Washington	52,321
	Dec. 23	Dallas [$]	San Francisco [$]	30-28	San Francisco	59,746
1971	Dec. 26	San Francisco [$]	Washington [$]	24-20	San Francisco	45,327
	Dec. 25	Dallas [$]	Minnesota [$]	20-12	Minneapolis	47,307
1970	Dec. 27	San Francisco [$]	Minnesota [$]	17-14	Minneapolis	45,103
	Dec. 26	Dallas [$]	Detroit [$]	5-0	Dallas	69,613
1969	Dec. 28	Cleveland [$]	Dallas [$]	38-14	Dallas	69,321
	Dec. 27	Minnesota [$]	Los Angeles [$]	23-20	Minneapolis	47,900
1968	Dec. 22	Baltimore [$]	Minnesota [$]	24-14	Baltimore	60,238
	Dec. 21	Cleveland [$]	Dallas [$]	31-20	Cleveland	81,497
1967	Dec. 24	Dallas [$]	Cleveland [$]	52-14	Dallas	70,786
	Dec. 23	Green Bay [$]	Los Angeles [$]	28-7	Milwaukee	49,861
1965	Dec. 26	Green Bay [$]	Baltimore [$]	13-10*	Green Bay	50,484
1958	Dec. 21	N.Y. Giants (#)	Cleveland (#)	10-0	New York	61,274

PLAYOFF GAME SUMMARIES

Season	Date	Winner (Share)	Loser (Share)	Score	Site	Attendance
1957	Dec. 22	Detroit (#)	San Francisco (#)	31-27	San Francisco	60,118
1952	Dec. 21	Detroit (#)	Los Angeles (#)	31-21	Detroit	47,645
1950	Dec. 17	Los Angeles (#)	Chicago Bears (#)	24-14	Los Angeles	83,501
	Dec. 17	Cleveland (#)	N.Y. Giants (#)	8-3	Cleveland	33,054
1947	Dec. 21	Philadelphia (#)	Pittsburgh (#)	21-0	Pittsburgh	35,729
1943	Dec. 19	Washington (¢)	N.Y. Giants (¢)	28-0	New York	42,800
1941	Dec. 14	Chicago Bears (¢)	Green Bay (¢)	33-14	Chicago	43,425

*Overtime
$ Players received 1/14 of annual salary for playoff appearances.
# Players received 1/12 of annual salary for playoff appearances.
¢ Players received 1/10 of annual salary for playoff appearances.

2013 NFC DIVISIONAL PLAYOFF GAMES

Bank of America Stadium, Charlotte, North Carolina
January 12, 2014, Attendance: 73,784
SAN FRANCISCO 23, CAROLINA 10—San Francisco's defense forced 2 turnovers and had 3 goal-line stands to help propel Jim Harbaugh's club to the NFC Championship Game for the third time in his three years as the 49ers' head coach. Phil Dawson kicked 2 first-quarter field goals, the second set up by Patrick Willis' interception, for a 6-0 lead. Late in the first quarter the Panthers drove to the 49ers' 1-yard-line, but Mike Tolbert was stopped on third-and-goal and Cam Newton was held to no gain on fourth-and-goal. The Panthers' defensed forced a three-and-out and Ted Ginn Jr. returned the punt 24 yards to set up Newton's 31-yard touchdown pass to Steve Smith for a 7-6 lead. Later in the quarter Carolina had second-and-goal from the 49ers' 1, but Newton was sacked for no gain and Tolbert lost a yard. Carolina settled for a field goal and 10-6 lead, and the 49ers' offense responded with a 12-play, 80-yard drive capped by Colin Kaepernick's 1-yard touchdown pass to Vernon Davis, who toe-tapped both feet in the back right corner of the end zone, for a 13-10 halftime lead. The 49ers' defense began the second half by forcing a three-and-out, and Kaepernick completed a 45-yard pass to Anquan Boldin to set up his own 4-yard run for a 20-10 advantage. The Panthers held the ball for more than eight minutes on its next possession, but back-to-back sacks by NaVorro Bowman and Ahmad Brooks took Carolina out of field-goal range and forced a punt. The 49ers then held the ball for seven minutes, 58 seconds and extended the lead on Dawson's 34-yard field goal with 7:35 to play. Carolina drove to the 49ers' 28, but Donte Whitner intercepted a pass and the 49ers ran out all but the final 12 seconds to secure the victory. Kaepernick completed 15 of 28 passes for 196 yards and 1 touchdown. Boldin had 8 receptions for 136 yards. Newton was 16 of 25 for 267 yards and 1 touchdown, with 2 interceptions. Ginn had 4 catches for 104 yards.

San Francisco	6	7	7	3	—	23
Carolina	0	10	0	0	—	10

SF — FG Dawson 49
SF — FG Dawson 33
Car — Smith 31 pass from Newton (Gano kick)
Car — FG Gano 24
SF — Davis 1 pass from Kaepernick (Dawson kick)
SF — Kaepernick 4 run (Dawson kick)
SF — FG Dawson 34

CenturyLink Field, Seattle, Washington
January 11, 2014, Attendance: 68,388
SEATTLE 23, NEW ORLEANS 15—Marshawn Lynch rushed for 140 yards and 2 touchdowns as the number-one seeded Seattle Seahawks advanced to the NFC Championship Game. The New Orleans Saints outgained the Seahawks in total yards (409-277), but were able to convert just 3 of 12 third-down situations while the Seahawks' defense forced 2 turnovers and the offense converted 5 of 14 third-down plays. Seattle scored on its first two possessions, the second set up by a missed 45-yard field goal to take a 6-0 lead. On the first play of the second quarter, Michael Bennett forced and recovered Mark Ingram's fumble at the Saints' 24. Two plays later, Lynch scored on a 15-yard run and Seattle had a 13-0 lead to the delight of the raucous 12th Man crowd. Seattle led 16-0 entering the fourth quarter before Khiry Robinson finished a 74-yard drive with a 1-yard run. Ingram scored on the 2-point conversion to cut the deficit to 16-8 with 13:11 to play. The Saints' defense forced two punts, the second of which generated a 42-yard drive. Faced with fourth-and-15 from the Seahawks' 30 with 3:56 to play, the Saints opted for a field goal but Shayne Graham's 48-yard kick sailed wide left. With 2:57 remaining, on third-and-3, Russell Wilson lofted a 24-yard pass to Doug Baldwin for a first down. Lynch ran around left end for a 31-yard touchdown on the next play for a 23-8 lead with 2:40 to play. Marques Colston's 9-yard touchdown catch on fourth-and-6 pulled the Saints to within 23-15 with 26 seconds left. Colston then recovered the onside kick. Three plays later, with 11 seconds left from the Saints' 49, Colston caught a 13-yard pass near the sideline, but instead of stepping out of bounds attempted a lateral across field which landed as a forward pass. The penalty had a 10-second runoff, ending the game. Wilson was 9 of 18 for 103 yards. Lynch carried 28 times for 140 yards. Brees completed 24 of 43 passes for 309 yards and 1 touchdown. Colston had 11 receptions for 144 yards.

New Orleans	0	0	0	15	—	15
Seattle	6	10	0	7	—	23

Sea — FG Hauschka 38
Sea — FG Hauschka 49
Sea — Lynch 15 run (Hauschka kick)
Sea — FG Hauschka 26
NO — Robinson 1 run (Ingram run)
Sea — Lynch 31 run (Hauschka kick)
NO — Colston 9 pass from Brees (S. Graham kick)

AFC WILD CARD PLAYOFF GAMES RESULTS

Season	Date	Winner (Share)	Loser (Share)	Score	Site	Attendance
2013	Jan. 5	San Diego ($21,000)	Cincinnati ($23,000)	27-10	Cincinnati	62,277
	Jan. 4	Indianapolis ($23,000)	Kansas City ($21,000)	45-44	Indianapolis	63,551
2012	Jan. 6	Baltimore ($22,000)	Indianapolis ($20,000)	24-9	Baltimore	71,379
	Jan. 5	Houston ($22,000)	Cincinnati ($20,000)	19-13	Houston	71,738
2011	Jan. 8	Denver ($22,000)	Pittsburgh ($20,000)	29-23*	Denver	75,970
	Jan. 7	Houston ($22,000)	Cincinnati ($20,000)	31-10	Houston	71,725
2010	Jan. 9	Baltimore ($19,000)	Kansas City ($21,000)	30-7	Kansas City	72,190
	Jan. 8	N.Y. Jets ($19,000)	Indianapolis ($21,000)	17-16	Indianapolis	65,332
2009	Jan. 10	Baltimore ($19,000)	New England ($21,000)	33-14	Foxborough	68,756
	Jan. 9	N.Y. Jets ($19,000)	Cincinnati ($21,000)	24-14	Cincinnati	63,686
2008	Jan. 4	Baltimore ($18,000)	Miami ($20,000)	27-9	Miami	74,240
	Jan. 3	San Diego ($20,000)	Indianapolis ($18,000)	23-17*	San Diego	68,082
2007	Jan. 6	San Diego ($20,000)	Tennessee ($18,000)	17-6	San Diego	65,640
	Jan. 5	Jacksonville ($18,000)	Pittsburgh ($20,000)	31-29	Pittsburgh	63,629

Season	Date	Winner (Share)	Loser (Share)	Score	Site	Attendance
2006	Jan. 7	New England ($19,000)	N.Y. Jets ($17,000)	37-16	Foxborough	68,756
	Jan. 6	Indianapolis ($19,000)	Kansas City ($17,000)	23-8	Indianapolis	57,215
2005	Jan. 8	Pittsburgh ($17,000)	Cincinnati ($19,000)	31-17	Cincinnati	65,870
	Jan. 7	New England ($19,000)	Jacksonville ($17,000)	28-3	Foxborough	68,756
2004	Jan. 9	Indianapolis ($18,000)	Denver ($15,000)	49-24	Indianapolis	56,609
	Jan. 8	N.Y. Jets ($15,000)	San Diego ($18,000)	20-17*	San Diego	67,536
2003	Jan. 4	Indianapolis ($18,000)	Denver ($15,000)	41-10	Indianapolis	56,586
	Jan. 3	Tennessee ($15,000)	Baltimore ($18,000)	20-17	Baltimore	69,452
2002	Jan. 5	Pittsburgh ($17,000)	Cleveland ($12,500)	36-33	Pittsburgh	62,595
	Jan. 4	N.Y. Jets ($17,000)	Indianapolis ($12,500)	41-0	East Rutherford	78,524
2001	Jan. 13	Baltimore ($12,500)	Miami ($12,500)	20-3	Miami	72,251
	Jan. 12	Oakland ($17,000)	N.Y. Jets ($12,500)	38-24	Oakland	61,503
2000	Dec. 31	Baltimore (12,500)	Denver ($12,500)	21-3	Baltimore	69,638
	Dec. 30	Miami ($16,000)	Indianapolis ($12,500)	23-17*	Miami	73,193
1999	Jan. 9	Miami ($10,000)	Seattle ($16,000)	20-17	Seattle	66,170
	Jan. 8	Tennessee ($10,000)	Buffalo ($10,000)	22-16	Nashville	66,672
1998	Jan. 3	Jacksonville ($15,000)	New England ($10,000)	25-10	Jacksonville	71,139
	Jan. 2	Miami ($10,000)	Buffalo ($10,000)	24-17	Miami	72,698
1997	Dec. 28	New England ($15,000)	Miami ($10,000)	17-3	Foxborough	60,041
	Dec. 27	Denver ($10,000)	Jacksonville ($10,000)	42-17	Denver	74,481
1996	Dec. 29	Pittsburgh ($14,000)	Indianapolis ($10,000)	42-14	Pittsburgh	58,078
	Dec. 28	Jacksonville ($10,000)	Buffalo ($10,000)	30-27	Buffalo	70,213
1995	Dec. 31	Indianapolis ($7,500)	San Diego ($7,500)	35-20	San Diego	61,182
	Dec. 30	Buffalo ($13,000)	Miami ($7,500)	37-22	Buffalo	73,103
1994	Jan. 1	Cleveland ($7,500)	New England ($7,500)	20-13	Cleveland	77,452
	Dec. 31	Miami ($12,000)	Kansas City ($7,500)	27-17	Miami	67,487
1993	Jan. 9	L.A. Raiders ($7,500)	Denver ($7,500)	42-24	Los Angeles	65,314
	Jan. 8	Kansas City ($12,000)	Pittsburgh ($7,500)	27-24*	Kansas City	74,515
1992	Jan. 3	Buffalo ($6,000)	Houston ($6,000)	41-38*	Buffalo	75,141
	Jan. 2	San Diego ($10,000)	Kansas City ($6,000)	17-0	San Diego	58,278
1991	Dec. 29	Houston ($10,000)	N.Y. Jets ($6,000)	17-10	Houston	61,485
	Dec. 28	Kansas City ($6,000)	L.A. Raiders ($6,000)	10-6	Kansas City	75,827
1990	Jan. 6	Cincinnati ($10,000)	Houston ($6,000)	41-14	Cincinnati	60,012
	Jan. 5	Miami ($6,000)	Kansas City ($6,000)	17-16	Miami	67,276
1989	Dec. 31	Pittsburgh ($6,000)	Houston ($6,000)	26-23*	Houston	59,406
1988	Dec. 26	Houston ($6,000)	Cleveland ($6,000)	24-23	Cleveland	75,896
1987	Jan. 3	Houston ($6,000)	Seattle ($6,000)	23-20*	Houston	50,519
1986	Dec. 28	N.Y. Jets ($6,000)	Kansas City ($6,000)	35-15	East Rutherford	75,210
1985	Dec. 28	New England ($6,000)	N.Y. Jets ($6,000)	26-14	East Rutherford	75,945
1984	Dec. 22	Seattle ($6,000)	L.A. Raiders ($6,000)	13-7	Seattle	62,049
1983	Dec. 24	Seattle ($6,000)	Denver ($6,000)	31-7	Seattle	64,275
1982	Jan. 9	N.Y. Jets ($6,000)	Cincinnati ($6,000)	44-17	Cincinnati	57,560
	Jan. 9	San Diego ($6,000)	Pittsburgh ($6,000)	31-28	Pittsburgh	53,546
	Jan. 8	L.A. Raiders ($6,000)	Cleveland ($6,000)	27-10	Los Angeles	56,555
	Jan. 8	Miami ($6,000)	New England ($6,000)	28-13	Miami	68,842
1981	Dec. 27	Buffalo ($3,000)	N.Y. Jets ($3,000)	31-27	New York	57,050
1980	Dec. 28	Oakland ($3,000)	Houston ($3,000)	27-7	Oakland	53,333
1979	Dec. 23	Houston ($3,000)	Denver ($3,000)	13-7	Houston	48,776
1978	Dec. 24	Houston ($3,000)	Miami ($3,000)	17-9	Miami	72,445

*Overtime

2013 AFC WILD CARD PLAYOFF GAMES
Paul Brown Stadium, Cincinnati, Ohio
January 5, 2014, Attendance: 62,277

SAN DIEGO 27, CINCINNATI 10—The Chargers' defense forced 4 turnovers and the offense rushed for 196 yards as San Diego won its first postseason game since 2007. In the first half the Bengals outgained the Chargers 226-122 yards, with 86 of the Chargers' yards coming on one touchdown drive. The Bengals had a chance to take the lead late in the first half, but Donald Butler tackled Giovanni Bernard from behind at the Chargers' 4-yard-line and Richard Marshall recovered the fumble. The Bengals did force a punt and Mike Nugent kicked a 46-yard field goal as the half expired for a 10-7 lead. The Chargers' defense forced a punt to begin the second half, and Philip Rivers completed all 6 pass attempts on a 10-play, 80-yard drive capped by Ladarius Green's 4-yard leaping touchdown catch, for a 14-10 lead. Andy Dalton fumbled three plays later and Jamie Addae recovered at the Bengals' 46, setting up a Nick Novak field goal. Three plays later, Shareece Wright intercepted a pass to set up another Novak field goal for a 20-10 lead early in the fourth quarter. Melvin Ingram intercepted a pass to thwart Cincinnati's ensuing possession. The Bengals twice drove to the Chargers' 40, but Dalton's fourth down passes fell incomplete. Ronnie Brown scored from 58 yards out with 2:17 remaining to finish the scoring. Rivers was 12 of 16 for 128 yards and 1 touchdown. Dalton completed 29 of 51 pass attempts for 334 yards and 1 touchdown, with 2 interceptions. Marvin Jones had 8 receptions for 130 yards.

San Diego	7	0	10	10	—	27
Cincinnati	0	10	0	0	—	10

SD	— Woodhead 5 run (Novak kick)
Cin	— Gresham 4 pass from Dalton (Nugent kick)
Cin	— FG Nugent 46
SD	— Green 4 pass from Rivers (Novak kick)
SD	— FG Novak 25
SD	— FG Novak 23
SD	— Brown 58 run (Novak kick)

Lucas Oil Stadium, Indianapolis, Indiana
January 4, 2014, Attendance: 63,551
INDIANAPOLIS 45, KANSAS CITY 44—The Indianapolis Colts rallied from a 28-point second-half deficit to post second greatest comeback in postseason history. The Colts trailed 38-10 with 13:39 left in the third quarter before the offense scored touchdowns on five of its next six possessions and the defense allowed just 2 field goals. The teams combined for 1,049 yards but the Colts won despite committing 4 turnovers and only forcing one. The Kansas City Chiefs scored on their first five possessions, with four of the five drives covering at least 73 yards and two of which consumed more than 6 minutes, 45 seconds off the clock, en route to a 31-10 halftime lead. Kansas City did this despite losing the AFC's leading rusher, Jamaal Charles, to injury in the first series. Husain Abdullah then intercepted Andrew Luck's first pass of the second half to set up Knile Davis' 4-yard touchdown run for a 38-10 lead with 13:39 remaining in the third quarter. Indianapolis answered quickly with Luck's 46-yard pass to Da'Rick Rogers leading to Donald Brown's 10-yard touchdown run. Robert Mathis then forced Kansas City's lone turnover, stripping Alex Smith of the ball and Khiry Sheppard recovering at the Chiefs' 41. Brown scored five plays later to cut the deficit to 38-24 with 7:32 left in the third quarter. The Colts' defense forced a three-and-out, but Abdullah's second interception of the half set up Ryan Succop's 42-yard field goal for a 41-24 Kansas City lead with 4:12 left in the third quarter. Undaunted, Luck completed passes of 25 yards to Brown and 30 yards to LaVon Brazill to setup Coby Fleener's 12-yard touchdown catch to pull the Colts to within 10 points with 2:31 remaining in the third quarter. Davis suffered an injury on the Chiefs' next possession, and Smith barely overthrew third-string running back Cyrus Gray early in the fourth quarter, leading to a punt. The Colts began at their own 10-yard line and drove to the Chiefs' 2. On second-

and-goal Eric Berry forced Brown to fumble. The ball bounced to Luck, who vaulted over the pile into the end zone for a 5-yard touchdown to cut the lead to 41-38 with 10:38 to play. The Chiefs drove and Succop kicked a 43-yard field goal with 5:36 remaining, but four plays later Luck completed a 64-yard touchdown pass to Hilton deep down the middle for a 45-44 lead with 4:21 to play. The Colts scored 35 points in 22 minutes, 26 seconds. The Chiefs drove to the Colts' 43, where Smith's fourth-and-11 pass for Dwayne Bowe was caught just out of bounds with 1:55 left, completing the comeback for the Colts. Luck was 29 of 45 for 443 yards and 4 touchdowns, with 3 interceptions. Hilton had 13 catches for 224 yards, the third-most in NFL postseason history. Smith was 30 of 46 for 378 yards and 4 touchdowns. Bowe had 8 receptions for 150 yards.

| Kansas City | 10 | 21 | 10 | 3 | — | 44 |
| Indianapolis | 7 | 3 | 21 | 14 | — | 45 |

KC — Bowe 6 pass from Smith (Succop kick)
Ind — Hilton 10 pass from Luck (Vinatieri kick)
KC — FG Succop 19
KC — Avery 79 pass from Smith (Succop kick)
KC — Sherman 5 pass from Smith (Succop kick)
Ind — FG Vinatieri 37
KC — Davis 4 run (Succop kick)
KC — Davis 10 pass from Smith (Succop kick)
Ind — Brown 10 run (Vinatieri kick)
Ind — Brown 3 pass from Luck (Vinatieri kick)
KC — FG Succop 42
Ind — Fleener 12 pass from Luck (Vinatieri kick)
Ind — Luck 2 fumble recovery (Vinatieri kick)
KC — FG Succop 43
Ind — Hilton 64 pass from Luck (Vinatieri kick)

NFC WILD CARD PLAYOFF GAMES RESULTS

Season	Date	Winner (Share)	Loser (Share)	Score	Site	Attendance
2013	Jan. 5	San Francisco ($21,000)	Green Bay ($23,000)	23-20	Green Bay	77,525
	Jan. 4	New Orleans ($21,000)	Philadelphia ($23,000)	26-24	Philadelphia	69,144
2012	Jan. 6	Seattle ($20,000)	Washington ($22,000)	24-14	Washington	84,325
	Jan. 5	Green Bay ($22,000)	Minnesota ($20,000)	24-10	Green Bay	71,548
2011	Jan. 8	N.Y. Giants ($22,000)	Atlanta ($20,000)	24-2	East Rutherford	79,909
	Jan. 7	New Orleans ($22,000)	Detroit ($20,000)	45-28	New Orleans	73,038
2010	Jan. 9	Green Bay ($19,000)	Philadelphia ($21,000)	21-16	Philadelphia	69,144
	Jan. 8	Seattle ($21,000)	New Orleans ($19,000)	41-36	Seattle	66,336
2009	Jan. 10	Arizona ($21,000)	Green Bay ($19,000)	51-45*	Glendale	61,926
	Jan. 9	Dallas ($21,000)	Philadelphia ($19,000)	34-14	Dallas	92,951
2008	Jan. 4	Philadelphia ($18,000)	Minnesota ($20,000)	26-14	Minneapolis	61,746
	Jan. 3	Arizona ($20,000)	Atlanta ($18,000)	30-24	Glendale	62,848
2007	Jan. 6	N.Y. Giants ($18,000)	Tampa Bay ($20,000)	24-14	Tampa	65,621
	Jan. 5	Seattle ($20,000)	Washington ($18,000)	35-14	Seattle	68,297
2006	Jan. 7	Philadelphia ($19,000)	N.Y. Giants ($17,000)	23-20	Philadelphia	69,094
	Jan. 6	Seattle ($19,000)	Dallas ($17,000)	21-20	Seattle	68,058
2005	Jan. 8	Carolina ($17,000)	N.Y. Giants ($19,000)	23-0	East Rutherford	79,378
	Jan. 7	Washington ($17,000)	Tampa Bay ($19,000)	17-10	Tampa	65,514
2004	Jan. 9	Minnesota ($15,000)	Green Bay ($18,000)	31-17	Green Bay	71,075
	Jan. 8	St. Louis ($15,000)	Seattle ($18,000)	27-20	Seattle	65,397
2003	Jan. 4	Green Bay ($18,000)	Seattle ($15,000)	33-27*	Green Bay	71,457
	Jan. 3	Carolina ($18,000)	Dallas ($15,000)	29-10	Charlotte	73,014
2002	Jan. 5	San Francisco ($17,000)	N.Y. Giants ($12,500)	39-38	San Francisco	66,318
	Jan. 4	Atlanta ($12,500)	Green Bay ($17,000)	27-7	Green Bay	65,358
2001	Jan. 13	Green Bay ($12,500)	San Francisco ($12,500)	25-15	Green Bay	59,825
	Jan. 12	Philadelphia ($17,000)	Tampa Bay ($12,500)	31-9	Philadelphia	65,847
2000	Dec. 31	Philadelphia ($12,500)	Tampa Bay ($12,500)	21-3	Philadelphia	65,813
	Dec. 30	New Orleans ($16,000)	St. Louis ($12,500)	31-28	New Orleans	64,900
1999	Jan. 9	Minnesota ($10,000)	Dallas ($10,000)	27-10	Minneapolis	64,056
	Jan. 8	Washington ($16,000)	Detroit ($10,000)	27-13	Washington	79,411
1998	Jan. 3	San Francisco ($10,000)	Green Bay ($10,000)	30-27	San Francisco	66,506
	Jan. 2	Arizona ($10,000)	Dallas ($15,000)	20-7	Dallas	62,969
1997	Dec. 28	Tampa Bay ($10,000)	Detroit ($10,000)	20-10	Tampa	73,361
	Dec. 27	Minnesota ($10,000)	N.Y. Giants ($15,000)	23-22	East Rutherford	77,497
1996	Dec. 29	San Francisco ($10,000)	Philadelphia ($10,000)	14-0	San Francisco	56,460
	Dec. 28	Dallas ($14,000)	Minnesota ($10,000)	40-15	Dallas	64,682
1995	Dec. 31	Green Bay ($13,000)	Atlanta ($7,500)	37-20	Green Bay	60,453
	Dec. 30	Philadelphia ($7,500)	Detroit ($7,500)	58-37	Philadelphia	66,099

Season	Date	Winner (Share)	Loser (Share)	Score	Site	Attendance
1994	Jan. 1	Chicago ($7,500)	Minnesota ($12,000)	35-18	Minnesota	60,347
	Dec. 31	Green Bay ($7,500)	Detroit ($7,500)	16-12	Green Bay	58,125
1993	Jan. 9	N.Y. Giants ($7,500)	Minnesota ($7,500)	17-10	East Rutherford	75,089
	Jan. 8	Green Bay ($7,500)	Detroit ($12,000)	28-24	Detroit	68,479
1992	Jan. 3	Philadelphia ($6,000)	New Orleans ($6,000)	36-20	New Orleans	68,893
	Jan. 2	Washington ($6,000)	Minnesota ($10,000)	24-7	Minnesota	57,353
1991	Dec. 29	Dallas ($6,000)	Chicago ($6,000)	17-13	Chicago	62,594
	Dec. 28	Atlanta ($6,000)	New Orleans ($10,000)	27-20	New Orleans	68,794
1990	Jan. 6	Chicago ($10,000)	New Orleans ($6,000)	16-6	Chicago	60,767
	Jan. 5	Washington ($6,000)	Philadelphia ($6,000)	20-6	Philadelphia	65,287
1989	Dec. 31	L.A. Rams ($6,000)	Philadelphia ($6,000)	21-7	Philadelphia	65,479
1988	Dec. 26	Minnesota ($6,000)	L.A. Rams ($6,000)	28-17	Minnesota	61,204
1987	Jan. 3	Minnesota ($6,000)	New Orleans ($6,000)	44-10	New Orleans	68,546
1986	Dec. 28	Washington ($6,000)	L.A. Rams ($6,000)	19-7	Washington	54,567
1985	Dec. 29	N.Y. Giants ($6,000)	San Francisco ($6,000)	17-3	East Rutherford	75,131
1984	Dec. 23	N.Y. Giants ($6,000)	L.A. Rams ($6,000)	16-13	Anaheim	67,037
1983	Dec. 26	L.A. Rams ($6,000)	Dallas ($6,000)	24-17	Dallas	62,118
1982	Jan. 9	Dallas ($6,000)	Tampa Bay ($6,000)	30-17	Dallas	65,042
	Jan. 9	Minnesota ($6,000)	Atlanta ($6,000)	30-24	Minnesota	60,560
	Jan. 8	Green Bay ($6,000)	St. Louis ($6,000)	41-16	Green Bay	54,282
	Jan. 8	Washington ($6,000)	Detroit ($6,000)	31-7	Washington	55,045
1981	Dec. 27	N.Y. Giants ($3,000)	Philadelphia ($3,000)	27-21	Philadelphia	71,611
1980	Dec. 28	Dallas ($3,000)	Los Angeles ($3,000)	34-13	Dallas	63,052
1979	Dec. 23	Philadelphia ($3,000)	Chicago ($3,000)	27-17	Philadelphia	69,397
1978	Dec. 24	Atlanta ($3,000)	Philadelphia ($3,000)	14-13	Atlanta	59,403

*Overtime

2013 NFC WILD CARD PLAYOFF GAMES

Lambeau Field, Green Bay, Wisconsin
January 5, 2014, Attendance: 77,525

SAN FRANCISCO 23, GREEN BAY 20—Phil Dawson kicked a 33-yard field goal as time expired as the 12-4 San Francisco 49ers knocked the Green Bay Packers out of the postseason for the second consecutive year. The 49ers drove inside the Packers' 30 on each of their first three first-half possessions,, but Green Bay's defense forced two short field goals and an interception by Tramon Williams thwarted the third drive. Aaron Rodgers engineered a 14-play, 70-yard touchdown drive following the interception to stake the Packers to a 7-6 lead. A 42-yard run by Colin Kaepernick on the ensuing possession led to Frank Gore's 10-yard touchdown run for a 13-7 49ers' lead with 1:48 left in the half. With the score 13-10, the Packers drove 12 plays in 80 yards, highlighted by Randall Cobb's 26-yard reception on fourth-and-2 to the 49ers' 4, and capped by John Kuhn's 1-yard scoring run with 12:06 to play, for a 17-13 Green Bay lead. The 49ers needed less than two minutes to retake the lead, as LaMichael James returned the ensuing kickoff 37 yards, Kaepernick scrambled for 24 yards and then completed a 28-yard touchdown pass to Vernon Davis deep down the middle for a 20-17 lead with 10:31 remaining. Cobb's 25-yard catch to the 49ers' 9-yard line put the Packers within striking distance, but the 49ers' defense stiffened in the red zone and Crosby's 24-yard field goal tied the game with 5:06 left. With 4:09 remaining, Kaepernick completed a 17-yard pass to Michael Crabtree on third-and-10, and with 1:13 left his 11-yard scramble on third-and-8 to the Packers' 27 set up Dawson's game-winning 33-yard field goal as time expired. Kaepernick completed 16 of 30 passes for 227 yards and 1 touchdown, with 1 interception. In addition, he had seven carries for a game-high 98 rushing yards. Crabtree had eight receptions for 125 yards and 1 touchdown. Rodgers was 17 of 26 for 177 yards and 1 touchdown.

San Francisco	6	7	0	10	—	23
Green Bay	0	10	0	10	—	20

SF — FG Dawson 22
SF — FG Dawson 25
GB — Nelson 5 pass from Rodgers (Crosby kick)
SF — Gore 10 run (Dawson kick)
GB — FG Crosby 34
GB — Kuhn 1 run (Crosby kick)
SF — Davis 28 pass from Kaepernick (Dawson kick)
GB — FG Crosby 34
SF — FG Dawson 33

Lincoln Financial Field, Philadelphia, Pennsylvania
January 4, 2014, Attendance: 69,144

NEW ORLEANS 26, PHILADELPHIA 24—Shayne Graham kicked a 32-yard field goal as time expired to lift the New Orleans Saints to the first postseason road victory in franchise history. The Saints outgained the Philadelphia Eagles 434-256 total yards and controlled the ball for nearly 35 of the games' 60 minutes. DeMeco Ryans' interception and 23-yard return in the second quarter set up Nick Foles' 10-yard touchdown pass to Riley Cooper to give the Eagles a 7-3 lead. The Saints responded by driving for a field goal just before halftime, and then driving 57 and 66 yards on their first two second-half possessions for touchdowns to take a 20-7 lead with 3:54 left in the third quarter. Brad Smith returned the ensuing kickoff 35 yards and connected on a 40-yard pass to DeSean Jackson. On fourth-and-goal, LeSean McCoy scored on a 1-yard run to cut the deficit to 20-14. Graham's third field goal gave New Orleans a 23-17 lead with 8:04 to play, but the Eagles with a 77-yard drive, capped by Foles' 3-yard touchdown pass to Jake Ertz for a 24-23 lead with 4:54 to play. Darren Sproles responded with a 39-yard kickoff return, with a 15-yard horse-collar tackle penalty added at the end, to put the ball on the Eagles' 48. Drew Brees twice converted quarterback sneaks on third-and-1 to set up Graham's winning kick. Brees was 20 of 30 for 250 yards and 1 touchdown, with 2 interceptions. Foles was 23 of 33 for 195 yards and 2 touchdowns.

New Orleans	0	6	14	6	—	26
Philadelphia	0	7	7	10	—	24

NO — FG S. Graham 36
Phil — Cooper 10 pass from Foles (Henery kick)
NO — FG S. Graham 46
NO — Moore 24 pass from Brees (S. Graham kick)
NO — Ingram 4 run (S. Graham kick)
Phil — McCoy 1 run (Henery kick)
Phil — FG Henery 31
NO — FG S. Graham 35
Phil — Ertz 3 pass from Foles (Henery kick)
NO — FG S. Graham 32

Includes AFL All-Star Game played after the 1961-69 seasons.

Date	Result/Honored players	Site (attendance)
Jan. 15, 1939	New York Giants 13, Pro All-Stars 10	Wrigley Field, Los Angeles (20,000)
Jan. 14, 1940	Green Bay 16, NFL All-Stars 7	Gilmore Stadium, Los Angeles (18,000)
Dec. 29, 1940	Chicago Bears 28, NFL All-Stars 14	Gilmore Stadium, Los Angeles (21,624)
Jan. 4, 1942	Chicago Bears 35, NFL All-Stars 24	Polo Grounds, New York (17,725)
Dec. 27, 1942	NFL All-Stars 17, Washington 14	Shibe Park, Philadelphia (18,671)
Jan. 14, 1951	American Conf. 28, National Conf. 27	Los Angeles Memorial Coliseum (53,676)
	Otto Graham, Cleveland, player of the game	
Jan. 12, 1952	National Conf. 30, American Conf. 13	Los Angeles Memorial Coliseum (19,400)
	Dan Towler, Los Angeles, player of the game	
Jan. 10, 1953	National Conf. 27, American Conf. 7	Los Angeles Memorial Coliseum (34,208)
	Don Doll, Detroit, player of the game	
Jan. 17, 1954	East 20, West 9	Los Angeles Memorial Coliseum (44,214)
	Chuck Bednarik, Philadelphia, player of the game	
Jan. 16, 1955	West 26, East 19	Los Angeles Memorial Coliseum (43,972)
	Billy Wilson, San Francisco, player of the game	
Jan. 15, 1956	East 31, West 30	Los Angeles Memorial Coliseum (37,867)
	Ollie Matson, Chi. Cardinals, player of the game	
Jan. 13, 1957	West 19, East 10	Los Angeles Memorial Coliseum (44,177)
	Bert Rechichar, Baltimore, outstanding back	
	Ernie Stautner, Pittsburgh, outstanding lineman	
Jan. 12, 1958	West 26, East 7	Los Angeles Memorial Coliseum (66,634)
	Hugh McElhenny, San Francisco, outstanding back	
	Gene Brito, Washington, outstanding lineman	
Jan. 11, 1959	East 28, West 21	Los Angeles Memorial Coliseum (72,250)
	Frank Gifford, N.Y. Giants, outstanding back	
	Doug Atkins, Chi. Bears, outstanding lineman	
Jan. 17, 1960	West 38, East 21	Los Angeles Memorial Coliseum (56,876)
	Johnny Unitas, Baltimore, outstanding back	
	Gene (Big Daddy) Lipscomb, Baltimore, outstanding lineman	
Jan. 15, 1961	West 35, East 31	Los Angeles Memorial Coliseum (62,971)
	Johnny Unitas, Baltimore, outstanding back	
	Sam Huff, N.Y. Giants, outstanding lineman	
Jan. 7, 1962	AFL West 47, East 27	Balboa Stadium, San Diego (20,973)
	Cotton Davidson, Dallas Texans, player of the game	
Jan. 14, 1962	NFL West 31, East 30	Los Angeles Memorial Coliseum (57,409)
	Jim Brown, Cleveland, outstanding back	
	Henry Jordan, Green Bay, outstanding lineman	
Jan. 13, 1963	AFL West 21, East 14	Balboa Stadium, San Diego (27,641)
	Curtis McClinton, Dallas Texans, outstanding offensive player	
	Earl Faison, San Diego, outstanding defensive player	
Jan. 13, 1963	NFL East 30, West 20	Los Angeles Memorial Coliseum (61,374)
	Jim Brown, Cleveland, outstanding back	
	Gene (Big Daddy) Lipscomb, Pittsburgh, outstanding lineman	
Jan. 12, 1964	NFL West 31, East 17	Los Angeles Memorial Coliseum (67,242)
	Johnny Unitas, Baltimore, player of the game	
	Gino Marchetti, Baltimore, outstanding lineman	
Jan. 19, 1964	AFL West 27, East 24	Balboa Stadium, San Diego (20,016)
	Keith Lincoln, San Diego, outstanding offensive player	
	Archie Matsos, Oakland, outstanding defensive player	
Jan. 10, 1965	NFL West 34, East 14	Los Angeles Memorial Coliseum (60,598)
	Fran Tarkenton, Minnesota, outstanding back	
	Terry Barr, Detroit, outstanding lineman	
Jan. 16, 1965	AFL West 38, East 14	Jeppesen Stadium, Houston (15,446)
	Keith Lincoln, San Diego, outstanding offensive player	
	Willie Brown, Denver, outstanding defensive player	
Jan. 15, 1966	AFL All-Stars 30, Buffalo 19	Rice Stadium, Houston (35,572)
	Joe Namath, N.Y. Jets, most valuable player, offense	
	Frank Buncom, San Diego, most valuable player, defense	
Jan. 15, 1966	NFL East 36, West 7	Los Angeles Memorial Coliseum (60,124)
	Jim Brown, Cleveland, outstanding back	
	Dale Meinert, St. Louis, outstanding lineman	
Jan. 21, 1967	AFL East 30, West 23	Oakland-Alameda County Coliseum (18,876)
	Babe Parilli, Boston, outstanding offensive player	
	Verlon Biggs, N.Y. Jets, outstanding defensive player	
Jan. 22, 1967	NFL East 20, West 10	Los Angeles Memorial Coliseum (15,062)
	Gale Sayers, Chicago, outstanding back	
	Floyd Peters, Philadelphia, outstanding lineman	

PRO BOWL ALL-TIME RESULTS

Date	Result	Venue
Jan. 21, 1968	AFL East 25, West 24	Gator Bowl, Jacksonville, Fla. (40,103)
	Joe Namath and Don Maynard, N.Y. Jets, out. off. players	
	Leslie (Speedy) Duncan, San Diego, out. def. player	
Jan. 21, 1968	NFL West 38, East 20	Los Angeles Memorial Coliseum (53,289)
	Gale Sayers, Chicago, outstanding back	
	Dave Robinson, Green Bay, outstanding lineman	
Jan. 19, 1969	AFL West 38, East 25	Gator Bowl, Jacksonville, Fla. (41,058)
	Len Dawson, Kansas City, outstanding offensive player	
	George Webster, Houston, outstanding defensive player	
Jan. 19, 1969	NFL West 10, East 7	Los Angeles Memorial Coliseum (32,050)
	Roman Gabriel, Los Angeles, outstanding back	
	Merlin Olsen, Los Angeles, outstanding lineman	
Jan. 17, 1970	AFL West 26, East 3	Astrodome, Houston (30,170)
	John Hadl, San Diego, player of the game	
Jan. 18, 1970	NFL West 16, East 13	Los Angeles Memorial Coliseum (57,786)
	Gale Sayers, Chicago, outstanding back	
	George Andrie, Dallas, outstanding lineman	
Jan. 24, 1971	NFC 27, AFC 6	Los Angeles Memorial Coliseum (48,222)
	Mel Renfro, Dallas, outstanding back	
	Fred Carr, Green Bay, outstanding lineman	
Jan. 23, 1972	AFC 26, NFC 13	Los Angeles Memorial Coliseum (53,647)
	Jan Stenerud, Kansas City, outstanding offensive player	
	Willie Lanier, Kansas City, outstanding defensive player	
Jan. 21, 1973	AFC 33, NFC 28	Texas Stadium, Irving (37,091)
	O.J. Simpson, Buffalo, player of the game	
Jan. 20, 1974	AFC 15, NFC 13	Arrowhead Stadium, Kansas City (66,918)
	Garo Yepremian, Miami, player of the game	
Jan. 20, 1975	NFC 17, AFC 10	Orange Bowl, Miami (26,484)
	James Harris, Los Angeles, player of the game	
Jan. 26, 1976	NFC 23, AFC 20	Louisiana Superdome, New Orleans (30,546)
	Billy Johnson, Houston, player of the game	
Jan. 17, 1977	AFC 24, NFC 14	Kingdome, Seattle (64,752)
	Mel Blount, Pittsburgh, player of the game	
Jan. 23, 1978	NFC 14, AFC 13	Tampa Stadium (51,337)
	Walter Payton, Chicago, player of the game	
Jan. 29, 1979	NFC 13, AFC 7	Los Angeles Memorial Coliseum (46,281)
	Ahmad Rashad, Minnesota, player of the game	
Jan. 27, 1980	NFC 37, AFC 27	Aloha Stadium, Honolulu (49,800)
	Chuck Muncie, New Orleans, player of the game	
Feb. 1, 1981	NFC 21, AFC 7	Aloha Stadium, Honolulu (50,360)
	Eddie Murray, Detroit, player of the game	
Jan. 31, 1982	AFC 16, NFC 13	Aloha Stadium, Honolulu (50,402)
	Kellen Winslow, San Diego, and Lee Roy Selmon, Tampa Bay, players of the game	
Feb. 6, 1983	NFC 20, AFC 19	Aloha Stadium, Honolulu (49,883)
	Dan Fouts, San Diego, and John Jefferson, Green Bay, players of the game	
Jan. 29, 1984	NFC 45, AFC 3	Aloha Stadium, Honolulu (50,445)
	Joe Theismann, Washington, player of the game	
Jan. 27, 1985	AFC 22, NFC 14	Aloha Stadium, Honolulu (50,385)
	Mark Gastineau, N.Y. Jets, player of the game	
Feb. 2, 1986	NFC 28, AFC 24	Aloha Stadium, Honolulu (50,101)
	Phil Simms, N.Y. Giants, player of the game	
Feb. 1, 1987	AFC 10, NFC 6	Aloha Stadium, Honolulu (50,101)
	Reggie White, Philadelphia, player of the game	
Feb. 7, 1988	AFC 15, NFC 6	Aloha Stadium, Honolulu (50,113)
	Bruce Smith, Buffalo, player of the game	
Jan. 29, 1989	NFC 34, AFC 3	Aloha Stadium, Honolulu (50,113)
	Randall Cunningham, Philadelphia, player of the game	
Feb. 4, 1990	NFC 27, AFC 21	Aloha Stadium, Honolulu (50,445)
	Jerry Gray, L.A. Rams, player of the game	
Feb. 3, 1991	AFC 23, NFC 21	Aloha Stadium, Honolulu (50,345)
	Jim Kelly, Buffalo, player of the game	
Feb. 2, 1992	NFC 21, AFC 15	Aloha Stadium, Honolulu (50,209)
	Michael Irvin, Dallas, player of the game	
Feb. 7, 1993	AFC 23, NFC 20 (OT)	Aloha Stadium, Honolulu (50,007)
	Steve Tasker, Buffalo, player of the game	
Feb. 6, 1994	NFC 17, AFC 3	Aloha Stadium, Honolulu (50,026)
	Andre Rison, Atlanta, player of the game	
Feb. 5, 1995	AFC 41, NFC 13	Aloha Stadium, Honolulu (50,529)
	Marshall Faulk, Indianapolis, player of the game	

Feb. 4, 1996   NFC 20, AFC 13...Aloha Stadium, Honolulu (50,034)
       Jerry Rice, San Francisco, player of the game

Feb. 2, 1997   AFC 26, NFC 23 (OT)...Aloha Stadium, Honolulu (50,031)
       Mark Brunell, Jacksonville, player of the game

Feb. 1, 1998   AFC 29, NFC 24...Aloha Stadium, Honolulu (49,995)
       Warren Moon, Seattle, player of the game

Feb. 7, 1999   AFC 23, NFC 10...Aloha Stadium, Honolulu (50,075)
       Keyshawn Johnson, N.Y. Jets and Ty Law, New England, co-players of the game

Feb. 6, 2000   NFC 51, AFC 31...Aloha Stadium, Honolulu (50,112)
       Randy Moss, Minnesota, player of the game

Feb. 4, 2001   AFC 38, NFC 17...Aloha Stadium, Honolulu (50,128)
       Rich Gannon, Oakland, player of the game

Feb. 9, 2002   AFC 38, NFC 30...Aloha Stadium, Honolulu (50,301)
       Rich Gannon, Oakland, player of the game

Feb. 2, 2003   AFC 45, NFC 20...Aloha Stadium, Honolulu (50,125)
       Ricky Williams, Miami, player of the game

Feb. 8, 2004   NFC 55, AFC 52...Aloha Stadium, Honolulu (50,127)
       Marc Bulger, St. Louis, player of the game

Feb. 13, 2005   AFC 38, NFC 27...Aloha Stadium, Honolulu (50,225)
       Peyton Manning, Indianapolis, player of the game

Feb. 12, 2006   NFC 23, AFC 17...Aloha Stadium, Honolulu (50,190)
       Derrick Brooks, Tampa Bay, player of the game

Feb. 10, 2007   AFC 31, NFC 28...Aloha Stadium, Honolulu (50,410)
       Carson Palmer, Cincinnati, player of the game

Feb. 10, 2008   NFC 42, AFC 30...Aloha Stadium, Honolulu (50,044)
       Adrian Peterson, Minnesota, most valuable player

Feb. 8, 2009   NFC 30, AFC 21...Aloha Stadium, Honolulu (49,958)
       Larry Fitzgerald, Arizona, most valuable player

Jan. 31, 2010   AFC 41, NFC 34...Sun Life Stadium, South Florida (70,697)
       Matt Schaub, Houston, most valuable player

Jan. 30, 2011   NFC 55, AFC 41...Aloha Stadium, Honolulu (49,331)
       DeAngelo Hall, Washington, most valuable player

Jan. 29, 2012   AFC 59, NFC 41...Aloha Stadium, Honolulu (48,423)
       Brandon Marshall, Miami, most valuable playerr

Jan. 27, 2013   NFC 62, AFC 35...Aloha Stadium, Honolulu (47,134)
       Kyle Rudolph, Minnesota, most valuable player

Jan. 26, 2014   Team Rice 22, Team Sanders 21 ....Aloha Stadium, Honolulu (47,270)
       Nick Foles (Team Sanders), Philadelphia, Offensive MVP
       Derrick Johnson (Team Rice), Kansas City, Defensive MVP

NFL/HALL OF FAME GAME (50)

Date	Winner	Loser	Attendance
August 11, 1962	New York Giants 21 (tie)	St. Louis Cardinals 21 (tie)	14,000
September 8, 1963	Pittsburgh Steelers 16	Cleveland Browns 7	18,462
September 6, 1964	Baltimore Colts 48	Pittsburgh Steelers 17	11,479
September 12, 1965	Washington Redskins 20	Detroit Lions 3	14,416
1966	No game was played		
August 5, 1967	Philadelphia Eagles 28	Cleveland Browns 13	17,304
August 3, 1968	Chicago Bears 30	Dallas Cowboys 24	14,578
September 13, 1969	Green Bay Packers 38	Atlanta Falcons 24	17,411
August 8, 1970	New Orleans Saints 14	Minnesota Vikings 13	17,932
July 31, 1971	Los Angeles Rams (NFC) 17	Houston Oilers (AFC) 6	19,384
July 29, 1972	Kansas City Chiefs (AFC) 23	New York Giants (NFC) 17	19,304
July 28, 1973	San Francisco 49ers (NFC) 20	New England Patriots (AFC) 7	19,685
July 27, 1974	St. Louis Cardinals (NFC) 21	Buffalo Bills (AFC) 13	17,286
August 2, 1975	Washington Redskins (NFC) 17	Cincinnati Bengals (AFC) 9	19,360
July 24, 1976	Denver Broncos (AFC) 10	Detroit Lions (NFC) 7	17,639
July 30, 1977	Chicago Bears (NFC) 20	New York Jets (AFC) 6	19,057
July 29, 1978	Philadelphia Eagles (NFC) 17	Miami Dolphins (AFC) 3	19,255
July 28, 1979	Oakland Raiders (AFC) 20	Dallas Cowboys (NFC) 13	20,648
August 2, 1980*	San Diego Chargers (AFC) 0	Green Bay Packers (NFC) 0	19,972
August 1, 1981	Cleveland Browns (AFC) 24	Atlanta Falcons (NFC) 10	23,921
August 7, 1982	Minnesota Vikings (NFC) 30	Baltimore Colts (AFC) 14	23,379
July 30, 1983	Pittsburgh Steelers (AFC) 27	New Orleans Saints (NFC) 14	23,909
July 28, 1984	Seattle Seahawks (AFC) 38	Tampa Bay Buccaneers (NFC) 0	22,250
August 3, 1985	New York Giants (NFC) 21	Houston Oilers (AFC) 20	23,940
August 2, 1986	New England Patriots (AFC) 21	St. Louis Cardinals (NFC) 16	22,739
August 8, 1987	San Francisco 49ers (NFC) 20	Kansas City Chiefs (AFC) 7	23,826
July 30, 1988	Cincinnati Bengals (AFC) 14	Los Angeles Rams (NFC) 7	23,801
August 5, 1989	Washington Redskins (NFC) 31	Buffalo Bills (AFC) 6	23,948
August 4, 1990	Chicago Bears (NFC) 13	Cleveland Browns (AFC) 0	23,952
July 27, 1991	Detroit Lions (NFC) 14	Denver Broncos (AFC) 3	23,815
August 1, 1992	New York Jets (AFC) 41	Philadelphia Eagles (NFC) 14	23,853
July 31, 1993	Los Angeles Raiders (AFC) 19	Green Bay Packers (NFC) 3	23,863
July 30, 1994	Atlanta Falcons (NFC) 21	San Diego Chargers (AFC) 17	23,185
July 29, 1995	Carolina Panthers (NFC) 20	Jacksonville Jaguars (AFC) 14	24,625
July 27, 1996	Indianapolis Colts (AFC) 10	New Orleans Saints (NFC) 3	23,376
July 26, 1997	Minnesota Vikings (NFC) 28	Seattle Seahawks (AFC) 26	23,846
August 1, 1998	Tampa Bay Buccaneers (NFC) 30	Pittsburgh Steelers (AFC) 6	23,875
August 9, 1999	Cleveland Browns (AFC) 20	Dallas Cowboys (NFC) 17 (OT)	25,156
July 31, 2000	New England Patriots (AFC) 20	San Francisco 49ers (NFC) 0	22,840
August 6, 2001	St. Louis Rams (NFC) 17	Miami Dolphins (AFC) 10	22,736
August 5, 2002	New York Giants (NFC) 34	Houston Texans (AFC) 17	22,461
August 4, 2003**	Kansas City Chiefs (AFC) 9	Green Bay Packers (NFC) 0	22,385
August 9, 2004	Washington Redskins (NFC) 20	Denver Broncos (AFC) 17	22,177
August 8, 2005	Chicago Bears (NFC) 27	Miami Dolphins (AFC) 24	22,292
August 6, 2006	Oakland Raiders (AFC) 16	Philadelphia Eagles (NFC) 10	22,200
August 5, 2007	Pittsburgh Steelers (AFC) 20	New Orleans Saints (NFC) 7	22,302
August 3, 2008	Washington Redskins (NFC) 30	Indianapolis Colts (AFC) 16	22,216
August 9, 2009	Tennessee Titans (AFC) 21	Buffalo Bills (AFC) 18	22,153
August 8, 2010	Dallas Cowboys (NFC) 16	Cincinnati Bengals (AFC) 7	22,364
2011	No game was played		
August 5, 2012	New Orleans Saints (NFC) 17	Arizona Cardinals (NFC) 10	18,100
August 4, 2013	Dallas Cowboys (NFC) 24	Miami Dolphins (AFC) 20	22,364

*Game called with 5:29 remaining in the fourth quarter because of severe thunder and lightning.
**Game called with 5:49 remaining in the third quarter because of lightning and torrential rain.

SUNDAY NIGHT WON-LOST RECORDS, 1978-2013
AMERICAN FOOTBALL CONFERENCE

	Balt.	Buff.	Cin.	Clev.	Den.	Hou.	Ind.	Jax.	K.C.	Mia.	N.E.	N.Y.J.	Oak.	Pitt.	S.D.	Tenn.
Total	13-10	10-10	3-12	1-9	22-17	2-6	20-19	5-6	10-7	19-8	20-16	10-13	17-18	20-20	16-17	11-9
2013		0-1	2-2	0-2	2-0				0-2		2-0		1-0	1-1	0-1	
2012	2-0	0-1	2-0	1-1							0-2			1-2	0-1	
2011	2-1						0-2		0-1		1-0	1-2		2-1	1-0	
2010	0-1						2-1	0-1			2-0	1-0		1-2	1-0	
2009	1-0	0-1					3-0				0-1	1-0		1-1	0-1	0-1
2008	1-0		0-1	0-1			2-1	0-1			0-2			2-0	2-1	
2007	0-1	0-1	0-1	1-0	1-2						3-0			1-1	1-1	1-0
2006				2-2	3-0				0-1		0-2		0-1	0-1	3-0	
2005	1-1	0-1	0-1	0-1		0-2	1-0	1-0	2-0		1-0	0-1	0-2	1-0	2-0	
2004	2-1	0-1	1-0	0-2	1-1	0-1	1-0	0-1	0-1	1-2	1-0		2-0	2-0		
2003	1-1	0-2		1-0	1-0		1-1	1-0	1-0	2-0	1-0		0-1	0-2		1-0
2002	1-0		0-1	0-1	0-2	1-0	1-1	0-1	1-1	0-2	2-0	2-0	0-1			
2001	0-1	0-1		2-0	0-2				1-0	0-1	2-0	1-1	1-0			0-1
2000	1-1	1-0					1-0	1-1	1-0			0-2	2-0	0-1	0-1	0-1
1999		2-0	0-1	0-1			1-0	1-0	1-0	2-0	0-1	0-1	1-0			0-1
1998	1-0	1-0	0-1	1-0			0-1	0-1	2-0	0-1	1-0	1-0	1-1		0-1	1-0
1997	0-1			1-0	0-1				1-1	1-0	0-1	1-0		2-0	0-2	
1996	0-1	1-1	0-1	1-1	1-0				1-0	2-0	0-1	0-1		1-1		1-0
1995		0-2		2-1				0-1	1-0	1-0	0-1	0-1	1-1		0-1	0-1
1994		1-0	0-1	0-1	0-1				2-0	2-1	1-0	0-1	1-1	0-1	1-0	
1993		1-0	0-1	0-1	0-3		0-1		1-0	0-1	1-1	1-0	0-1	0-2		2-1
1992		1-1	1-0	2-0	0-1		1-1		1-0	0-1	1-1	0-2	1-0	1-0		1-1
1991		1-0	0-1	0-1	2-0	0-2			1-0	0-1			2-0	1-1	0-1	2-0
1990		1-0	1-1	0-2					1-0				0-1	1-2	0-1	1-1
1989					1-0						0-1	0-1	0-2	1-0		
1988		0-1							0-1	1-0			1-0	1-0	0-1	1-1
1987			0-1	0-1							2-0	0-1	0-1		1-0	
1986																
1985														0-1	1-0	
1984			0-1	1-0												
1983											1-0					
1982																
1981																
1980															0-1	
1979																
1978					1-0					1-0			0-2	0-1		

SUNDAY NIGHT FOOTBALL ALL-TIME STANDINGS
AMERICAN FOOTBALL CONFERENCE

East	W	L	T	Pct.	South	W	L	T	Pct.
Miami	19	8	0	.704	Tennessee	11	9	0	.550
New England	20	16	0	.556	Indianapolis	20	19	0	.513
Buffalo	10	10	0	.500	Jacksonville	5	6	0	.455
New York Jets	10	13	0	.435	Houston	2	6	0	.250

North	W	L	T	Pct.	West	W	L	T	Pct.
Baltimore	13	10	0	.565	Kansas City	10	7	0	.588
Pittsburgh	20	20	0	.500	Denver	22	17	0	.564
Cincinnati	3	12	0	.200	Oakland	17	18	0	.486
Cleveland	1	9	0	.100	San Diego	16	17	0	.485

SUNDAY NIGHT WON-LOST RECORDS, 1978-2013
NATIONAL FOOTBALL CONFERENCE

	Ariz.	Atl.	Car.	Chi.	Dall.	Det.	G.B.	Minn.	N.O.	N.Y.G.	Phil.	St. L.	S.F.	Sea.	T.B.	Wash.
Total	7-13	9-9	5-8	15-20	23-27	5-10	21-6	15-17	17-13	18-23-1	20-14	10-12	14-11	18-11	6-11	16-16-1
2013		0-1	0-1	1-1	2-2		1-0	0-1	2-0	0-1	2-0		1-1	1-0		0-1
2012		1-0	0-1	1-2	0-2	2-1			1-1	1-1	1-1	2-1	1-0			1-0
2011		1-1	1-1	0-4	0-1	2-0		0-1	2-0	2-1	2-1					
2010			0-1	0-3		2-1	0-1	1-0	1-2	3-0		0-1	0-1	1-0		1-1
2009	2-1	1-0	1-0	0-3	2-1		1-0	0-2	1-2	2-1						0-1
2008		0-1		2-1	3-0		1-0		2-1	0-2				0-1	1-0	0-2
2007			1-1	3-0			0-1	0-1	1-0	1-2	0-3			0-1		2-0
2006			0-1	2-1	2-1		1-0		1-0	0-2	0-1			1-1		0-1
2005	1-0	0-1		1-0	0-1	0-1	1-0	0-1	1-0	0-1	0-1	1-0	0-1	1-0		1-0
2004		1-0		0-1			1-0	1-0	0-1	1-0	1-0	0-2			0-1	0-2
2003		1-0	0-1	0-1	0-1		1-0	1-1	1-1	0-1		1-0	0-1	1-0	0-1	0-1
2002	0-1	1-0		0-1	0-1		1-0	0-2	1-0	1-0		1-0		1-0	1-1	1-0
2001	0-1		0-1	1-0	0-1		0-1	0-2			2-0	1-0	2-0	1-1	0-1	1-0
2000	1-1	0-1	1-0	0-2	0-2		1-0	1-0		2-1	1-0	0-1				1-0
1999	0-2	0-1	1-0	0-1	1-0	1-0	0-1	0-1	0-1			0-1	2-0	0-2		2-0
1998	1-0	1-0	0-1	0-2	1-0	1-0		2-0	0-1	0-1	0-1	1-0	0-2	0-1		0-1
1997	1-0	0-1	1-1	1-1	0-1	0-2	1-0	1-0	1-0	0-0-1	0-1	0-1	0-1	1-0	1-0	1-0-1
1996	0-1	0-1	1-0			0-1	1-0	2-0	0-1	0-2	1-0	0-1	1-0	0-1	0-1	1-0
1995	0-1	0-2	0-1		1-0		1-1	0-1	1-0	1-0	2-0		1-0	1-0	1-0	0-1
1994	1-1		1-0		1-1		1-0		1-0	1-0		0-1	1-0	0-1	0-1	1-0
1993	0-1		1-0	1-0	1-0	2-0	1-2	1-0	0-1	1-0		1-0	0-1	1-0		1-0
1992	0-1		0-1			1-0			1-1	1-1	1-0	1-1	1-0	0-1	0-1	0-1
1991	0-1	1-0		1-0	0-1		1-1	1-1	0-1		0-2			1-1	0-1	2-0
1990	0-1	1-0	1-1	0-1	1-1	0-1	2-0		1-0	0-2	0-1	1-0	2-0	1-0		1-0
1989			0-1	1-0			1-0		0-1			1-0		1-0		0-1
1988				0-1			1-0		0-1			1-0	0-1	1-0		0-1
1987			1-0	0-1					1-0			0-1	2-0	1-0		0-1
1986				0-1								1-0				
1985				1-0						0-1						
1984				1-0					0-1							
1983				0-1												
1982		1-0												0-1		
1981				1-0								0-1				
1980				1-0												
1979				1-0								0-1				
1978												1-0				

SUNDAY NIGHT FOOTBALL ALL-TIME STANDINGS
NATIONAL FOOTBALL CONFERENCE

East	W	L	T	Pct.
Philadelphia	20	14	0	.588
Washington	16	16	1	.500
Dallas	23	27	0	.460
New York Giants	18	23	1	.440

North	W	L	T	Pct.
Green Bay	21	6	0	.778
Minnesota	15	17	0	.469
Chicago	15	20	0	.429
Detroit	5	10	0	.333

South	W	L	T	Pct.
New Orleans	17	13	0	.567
Atlanta	9	9	0	.500
Carolina	5	8	0	.385
Tampa Bay	6	11	0	.353

West	W	L	T	Pct.
Seattle	18	11	0	.621
San Francisco	14	11	0	.560
St. Louis	10	12	0	.455
Arizona	7	13	0	.350

MONDAY NIGHT WON-LOST RECORDS, 1970-2013

AMERICAN FOOTBALL CONFERENCE

	Balt.	Buff.	Cin.	Cle.	Den.	Hou.	Ind.	Jax.	K.C.	Mia.	N.E.	N.Y.J.	Oak.	Pitt.	S.D.	Tenn.
Total	9-9	17-23	10-20	15-14	29-36-1	3-4	21-13	8-7	22-17	40-40	22-23	20-27	37-27-1	40-24	22-19	21-16
2013	1-0		1-0		1-0	1-0	0-1		0-2		0-1	1-0		0-1	0-1	1-1
2012	1-0	0-1	1-1			1-1	0-1				1-0	0-2	0-1	1-0	1-1	1-0
2011	0-1			0-1		0-1	1-1	1-1	0-2		2-0	1-0	1-0	0-1	1-1	
2010	2-0		0-1		0-1	0-2	1-0	0-1	1-0	0-1	2-0	1-2		1-0	1-1	1-0
2009	1-1	0-1		0-1	1-1	0-1	1-0			1-1	1-1	0-1	0-1	1-0	1-1	1-0
2008	0-1	0-1		2-1	1-1	1-0	0-1	0-1			1-0	0-1		2-0	1-0	1-0
2007	0-3	0-1	1-1		1-2	1-0	0-1		0-1		2-0			2-0	1-0	1-1
2006	0-1	0-1	1-0			1-0	2-0	0-1	0-1	1-0	1-0		0-2	0-1	1-0	
2005	1-1		1-0		3-0		0-1				1-1	0-2		2-1	0-1	
2004	0-1	1-0	0-1		1-0		2-1		1-1	1-1	1-0					1-1
2003			0-1		1-1		1-0		0-1		1-1		0-3	0-1		0-1
2002	1-0		0-2		0-1					1-1	1-1	0-1	2-0	2-1	1-0	
2001	2-0		1-1		0-1	0-1			1-0			0-1		1-0	1-0	0-2
2000		0-1	1-1		2-0	0-2	1-1	0-1	1-1	2-0		0-1				3-0
1999		1-0	1-2				2-0		1-2	0-1		2-1	0-1	1-0		
1998			2-1				2-0	0-2	1-2	1-2	1-0			2-1		
1997		1-1	2-1			0-1	1-0	2-0	1-2	1-2			0-2	0-2		
1996		0-2	1-0			1-0			0-2	1-2			2-1	3-0	1-1	
1995		1-1	0-2		1-0					1-1	2-1	1-0	0-2	1-1	1-1	
1994		1-1			0-2					1-1	1-0		1-1	2-0	0-1	0-3
1993		2-1	1-0		0-2	0-1			2-0	1-2			1-0	3-0	2-0	0-1
1992		2-0	0-1	0-1	0-2				1-0	2-1		0-1	0-2	1-0		1-0
1991		2-1	0-2							2-1	1-1	0-1	0-2	0-1		1-1
1990		1-1	1-1	1-1	1-1	0-1				0-1		0-1	2-0	1-0		1-0
1989		1-2	1-2	1-1	2-0							0-1	1-0			1-0
1988		2-0	1-2	0-2		1-1					1-1	0-1	1-1			1-0
1987		1-0	2-1								1-1	1-1	2-1	1-1		
1986		1-0	1-0	1-1							1-2	1-0	1-1	0-1	0-2	0-1
1985		1-0	1-0	1-0							2-1	0-1	1-0	2-0	0-2	0-1
1984	0-1	0-1			1-0					3-0		0-1		2-1	1-1	1-2
1983	0-1	0-2							0-1	1-1		2-0	1-0	1-0		1-1
1982	0-1	0-1								1-1		1-0	1-0	1-0	1-1	0-1
1981	1-1		0-1		1-0					1-1	0-1		2-1	1-1	2-1	0-1
1980		1-1			1-2				1-1	1-2	1-0		3-0	0-2	1-0	2-0
1979		1-0			0-2				0-2	0-2	1-1		2-0	2-1	1-0	2-0
1978		1-2			1-1	2-1			2-1	0-2	1-0		1-1	1-0		2-0
1977	0-1	0-1	1-0				1-1		0-1	1-0	0-1		2-0	2-0		
1976		0-2	1-1				2-0		0-1	1-1	1-0	0-1	2-0	0-1		0-1
1975		0-2	1-0		1-1				1-0	1-1	0-1	0-1	2-0	1-0	1-0	0-1
1974	1-0	0-1			0-2		1-0		2-0			0-1	0-1	2-0		
1973	1-0		0-1	0-0-1						1-1	2-0	0-1	0-0-1	1-1		
1972		1-0			1-0		1-0		0-1	0-1		2-0			0-1	0-1
1971		0-1					1-1		2-0	1-0		0-1	1-0	0-1	1-0	
1970		0-1	2-0		1-1		1-0		1-0			0-1	1-0	1-0	0-1	0-1

MONDAY NIGHT FOOTBALL ALL-TIME STANDINGS

AMERICAN FOOTBALL CONFERENCE

East	W	L	T	Pct.		South	W	L	T	Pct.
Miami	40	40	0	.500		Indianapolis	21	13	0	.618
New England	22	23	0	.489		Tennessee	21	16	0	.568
New York Jets	20	27	0	.426		Jacksonville	8	7	0	.533
Buffalo	17	23	0	.425		Houston	3	4	0	.429

North	W	L	T	Pct.		West	W	L	T	Pct.
Pittsburgh	40	24	0	.625		Oakland	37	27	1	.577
Cleveland	15	14	0	.517		Kansas City	22	17	0	.564
Baltimore	9	9	0	.500		San Diego	22	19	0	.537
Cincinnati	10	20	0	.333		Denver	29	36	1	.447

From 1970-71, tie games were not included in winning percentage.

MONDAY NIGHT WON-LOST RECORDS, 1970-2013
NATIONAL FOOTBALL CONFERENCE

	Ariz.	Atl.	Car.	Chi.	Dall.	Det.	G.B.	Minn.	N.O.	N.Y.G.	Phil.	St.L.	S.F.	Sea.	T.B.	Wash.
Total	6-15-1	10-26	7-4	27-35	43-32	12-15-1	28-31-1	26-29	17-18	22-33-1	28-25	26-30	45-25	20-8	10-9	27-36
2013		0-2	1-0	2-0	0-1	0-1	0-1	0-1	1-1	1-0	1-0	0-1	2-0	2-0	1-0	0-2
2012	0-1	1-0	1-0	2-1	0-1	0-1	0-1		1-0	0-1	0-2		2-0	1-0		1-0
2011		0-1	1-1	1-0	1-0	1-0	0-1	2-0	1-1	0-1	0-1	0-2	1-0	1-0	1-0	0-1
2010	0-1	0-1		2-0	0-1		0-1	0-2	2-0	1-0	1-0		1-1			0-1
2009	0-1	0-1	0-1	1-0	1-0		1-1	1-1	2-0	1-0	1-0		1-0			0-2
2008	1-0		1-0	1-0	1-0		1-2	1-1	1-1	0-1	1-1		0-1		0-1	0-1
2007	0-1	0-2		0-1	1-0		1-0	1-0	1-1	1-0	0-1		1-1	1-0		1-0
2006	0-1	0-1	1-1	2-0	0-1		0-2	1-1	1-0	1-1	2-0	0-1		2-0	0-1	0-1
2005		3-0	1-0		1-1		0-3	1-0	0-2	1-0	0-3	0-1		1-0		1-0
2004		0-1		2-1	2-1	0-2					2-1	2-1		0-1	0-1	0-1
2003	0-1		0-1	1-0			2-1			0-2	2-1	2-0	1-0		2-1	
2002		0-3					2-0			0-1	3-0	2-1	1-2	0-1	1-1	0-1
2001				1-0	0-1		2-0	1-1	0-1	0-3	1-0	2-1	1-0		1-0	0-2
2000		1-0		1-1			1-1	1-1				1-2		0-1	1-1	1-2
1999	0-1	1-2		1-2			1-2	2-1	1-0				1-2	1-0	1-0	
1998				2-0	1-1		0-3	1-0	0-2		0-1		3-0		1-1	0-1
1997			1-1	1-1	1-2		3-0	0-1			0-2		3-0			1-0
1996		0-1	2-0	2-1	0-2	2-1	0-1				0-2		2-1			
1995	0-1		1-2	3-0	2-0	1-0	0-2		0-1		0-1		2-1			
1994				0-2	2-1	1-0	1-0	2-0	0-2	1-2	2-0		2-1			
1993		0-1		0-1	1-1	0-1	1-0	0-2	1-0	1-1			1-2			1-2
1992		0-2		0-3	2-1	0-1	1-0	1-0	1-0				2-0	1-0		1-2
1991				2-1	0-1				0-1	1-0	2-1	2-1	2-1			2-0
1990					0-1		1-1	1-1	1-1	2-0	0-3		3-0	1-0		0-1
1989		1-1					1-1	1-1	2-1	0-2	0-2		3-0	1-0		0-2
1988	0-1			1-2	1-1		1-0	1-0	1-1	1-0	1-0	1-1	1-0			0-2
1987		1-2		2-1			1-0			0-3		1-2	2-0	0-2		1-1
1986	0-1			2-1	2-0	0-1			2-1			1-0	0-2	2-0		1-1
1985	1-1			1-1	1-0		0-1					2-1	1-2	0-2		2-1
1984		0-2		0-1	1-1	0-1	0-1		1-0	0-1		1-1	2-0	2-0		1-1
1983	0-0-1	0-1		1-1	2-0	2-1	0-1		0-1	1-1-1		1-0	1-0		0-1	1-2
1982		1-2		0-1	1-0	1-0				0-1					1-0	
1981		1-2		0-2	2-0	1-0	0-3				1-1	2-0	1-0			
1980		1-1		1-1					0-1	0-1	1-0	2-0		0-1	0-1	0-2
1979	1-2			0-2		1-0	0-1	0-1	1-0	1-1				2-0		1-0
1978	1-0	0-3		1-1			2-0					0-2	0-1			1-1
1977	2-0			1-0	1-1		0-1		0-1			1-1	0-2			1-1
1976	0-1			1-0			1-1				0-1	0-2	2-0			2-0
1975	0-1			0-1	1-1	0-1	0-1	1-0	1-0			0-1	1-0			1-0
1974	0-1	0-1		1-0	0-1	1-0	0-1	1-0	0-1		1-0	1-1	0-2			2-0
1973				1-1	0-1	1-1	1-0	1-1	0-1	0-1		1-0	1-0			1-1
1972	0-1	0-1		1-0	1-0	0-2	1-0	0-2	0-1	1-0	0-1	1-0	0-1			2-0
1971	1-1	1-0		1-0	0-1-1	0-1-1	2-0		0-1			0-2	0-1			1-0
1970	1-0	0-1		0-1	2-0	1-1	1-0		0-1	1-0	0-2					0-1

MONDAY NIGHT FOOTBALL ALL-TIME STANDINGS
NATIONAL FOOTBALL CONFERENCE

East	W	L	T	Pct.
Dallas	43	32	0	.573
Philadelphia	28	25	0	.528
Washington	27	36	0	.429
New York Giants	22	33	1	.402

North	W	L	T	Pct.
Green Bay	28	31	1	.475
Minnesota	26	29	0	.473
Detroit	12	15	1	.444
Chicago	27	35	0	.435

South	W	L	T	Pct.
Carolina	7	4	0	.636
Tampa Bay	10	9	0	.526
New Orleans	17	18	0	.486
Atlanta	10	26	0	.278

West	W	L	T	Pct.
Seattle	20	8	0	.714
San Francisco	45	25	0	.643
St. Louis	26	30	0	.464
Arizona	6	15	1	.295

From 1970-71, tie games were not included in winning percentage.

Compiled by Elias Sports Bureau
*NFL record.

MONDAY NIGHT RECORDS

SCORING
TOUCHDOWNS
Most Touchdowns, Career
- 36 Jerry Rice, San Francisco, 1985-2000; Oakland, 2001-04; Seattle 2004
- 24 Emmitt Smith, Dallas, 1990-2002; Arizona 2003-04
- 20 Terrell Owens, San Francisco, 1996-2003; Philadelphia, 2004-05; Dallas, 2006-08; Buffalo, 2009; Cincinnati, 2010

Most Touchdowns, Game
- 4 Ron Johnson, N.Y. Giants at Philadelphia, Oct. 2, 1972
  Earl Campbell, Houston vs. Miami, Nov. 20, 1978
  Marcus Allen, L.A. Raiders vs. San Diego, Sept. 24, 1984
  Eric Dickerson, Indianapolis vs. Denver, Oct. 31, 1988
  Emmitt Smith, Dallas at N.Y. Giants, Sept. 4, 1995
  Marshall Faulk, St. Louis at Tampa Bay, Dec. 18, 2000

FIELD GOALS
Most Field Goals, Career
- 51 Gary Anderson, Pittsburgh, 1982-1994; Philadelphia, 1995-96; San Francisco, 1997; Minnesota, 1998-2002; Tennessee, 2003-04
- 50 Jason Elam, Denver, 1993-2007; Atlanta, 2008-09
- 42 Ryan Longwell, Green Bay, 1997-2005; Minnesota, 2006-2011; Seattle, 2012

Most Field Goals, Game
- 7 Chris Boniol, Dallas vs. Green Bay, Nov. 18, 1996*
  Billy Cundiff, Dallas at N.Y. Giants, Sept. 15, 2003 (OT)*
- 6 Dan Bailey, Dallas vs. Washington, Sept. 26, 2011
  Justin Tucker, Baltimore at Detroit, December 16, 2013
- 5 Tim Mazzetti, Atlanta vs. Los Angeles, Oct. 30, 1978
  Roger Ruzek, Dallas at L.A. Rams, Dec. 21, 1987
  Rich Karlis, Minnesota vs. Cincinnati, Dec. 25, 1989
  Nick Lowery, Kansas City vs. Denver, Sept. 20, 1993
  Chris Jacke, Green Bay vs. San Francisco, Oct. 14, 1996 (OT)
  Richie Cunningham, Dallas vs. Philadelphia, Sept. 15, 1997
  Phil Dawson, Cleveland vs. Buffalo, Nov. 17, 2008
  Nick Folk, N.Y. Jets vs. Minnesota, Oct. 11, 2010
  Nate Kaeding, San Diego at Oakland, Sept. 10, 2012

RUSHING
YARDS GAINED
Most Yards Gained, Career
- 2,434 Emmitt Smith, Dallas, 1990-2002; Arizona, 2003-04
- 1,897 Tony Dorsett, Dallas, 1977-1987; Denver, 1988
- 1,769 Thurman Thomas, Buffalo, 1988-1999; Miami, 2000

Most Yards Gained, Game
- 221 Bo Jackson, L.A. Raiders at Seattle, Nov. 30, 1987
- 216 Ricky Williams, Miami vs. Chicago, Dec. 9, 2002
- 214 Thurman Thomas, Buffalo at N.Y. Jets, Sept. 24, 1990

Longest Run From Scrimmage, Game
- 99 Tony Dorsett, Dallas at Minnesota, Jan. 3, 1983 (TD)*
- 94 Chris Johnson, Tennessee vs. N.Y. Jets, Dec. 17, 2012 (TD)
- 91 Bo Jackson, L.A. Raiders at Seattle, Nov. 30, 1987 (TD)

TOUCHDOWNS
Most Rushing Touchdowns, Career
- 23 Emmitt Smith, Dallas, 1990-2002; Arizona, 2003-04
- 17 Marcus Allen, L.A. Raiders, 1982-1992; Kansas City, 1993-97
- 14 Eric Dickerson, L.A. Rams, 1983-87; Indianapolis, 1987-1991; L.A. Raiders, 1992; Atlanta, 1993

Most Rushing Touchdowns, Game
- 4 Earl Campbell, Houston vs. Miami, Nov. 20, 1978
  Eric Dickerson, Indianapolis vs. Denver, Oct. 31, 1988
  Emmitt Smith, Dallas at N.Y. Giants, Sept. 4, 1995

PASSING
YARDS GAINED
Most Yards Gained, Career
- 9,654 Dan Marino, Miami, 1983-1999
- 9,068 Brett Favre, Atlanta, 1991; Green Bay, 1992-2007; N.Y. Jets, 2008; Minnesota, 2009-2010
- 5,148 Joe Montana, San Francisco, 1979-1992; Kansas City, 1993-94

Most Yards Gained, Game
- 517 Tom Brady, New England vs. Miami, Sept. 12, 2011
- 458 Joe Montana, San Francisco at L.A. Rams, Dec. 11, 1989
- 448 Marc Bulger, St. Louis at Green Bay, Nov. 29, 2004

Longest Pass Play
- 99 Brett Favre to Robert Brooks, Green Bay at Chicago, Sept. 11, 1995 (TD)*
  Tom Brady to Wes Welker, New England vs. Miami, Sept. 12, 2011*
- 97 Bernie Kosar to Webster Slaughter, Cleveland vs. Chicago, Oct. 23, 1989 (TD)
- 95 Joe Montana to John Taylor, San Francisco at L.A. Rams, Dec. 11, 1989 (TD)

TOUCHDOWNS
Most Touchdown Passes, Career
- 74 Dan Marino, Miami, 1983-1999
- 69 Brett Favre, Atlanta, 1991; Green Bay, 1992-2007; N.Y. Jets, 2008; Minnesota, 2009-2010
- 42 Steve Young, Tampa Bay, 1985-86; San Francisco, 1987-1999
  Tom Brady, New England, 2000-2013

Most Touchdown Passes, Game
- 5 Dave Krieg, Seattle vs. L.A. Raiders, Nov. 28, 1988
  Jim Kelly, Buffalo vs. Cincinnati, Oct. 21, 1991
  Vinny Testaverde, N.Y. Jets vs. Miami, Oct. 23, 2000 (OT)
  Ben Roethlisberger, Pittsburgh vs. Baltimore, Nov. 5, 2007
  Drew Brees, New Orleans vs. New England, Nov. 30, 2009

RECEIVING
PASS RECEPTIONS
Most Pass Receptions, Career
- 254 Jerry Rice, San Francisco, 1985-2000; Oakland, 2001-04; Seattle, 2004
- 124 Andre Reed, Buffalo, 1985-1999; Washington, 2000
- 123 Cris Carter, Philadelphia, 1987-89; Minnesota, 1990-2001; Miami, 2002

Most Pass Receptions, Game
- 14 Herman Moore, Detroit vs. Chicago, Dec. 4, 1995
  Jerry Rice, San Francisco vs. Minnesota, Dec. 18, 1995
- 13 Andre Reed, Buffalo vs. Denver, Sept. 18, 1989
  Terrell Owens, San Francisco vs. Philadelphia, Nov. 25, 2002
  Darren McFadden, Oakland vs. San Diego, Sept. 10, 2012
  Jason Witten, Dallas vs. Chicago, Oct. 1, 2012

YARDS GAINED
Most Yards Gained, Career
- 4,029 Jerry Rice, San Francisco, 1985-2000;
  Oakland, 2001-04; Seattle, 2004
- 1,783 Andre Reed, Buffalo, 1985-1999; Washington, 2000
- 1,697 Terrell Owens, San Francisco, 1996-2003;
  Philadelphia, 2004-05; Dallas, 2006-08;
  Buffalo, 2009; Cincinnati, 2010

Most Yards Gained, Game
- 289 Jerry Rice, San Francisco vs. Minnesota,
  Dec. 18, 1995
- 286 John Taylor, San Francisco at L.A. Rams,
  Dec. 11, 1989
- 260 Wes Chandler, San Diego vs. Cincinnati,
  Dec. 20, 1982

TOUCHDOWN
Most Receiving Touchdowns, Career
- 34 Jerry Rice, San Francisco, 1985-2000;
  Oakland, 2001-04; Seattle, 2004
- 20 Terrell Owens, San Francisco, 1996-2003;
  Philadelphia, 2004-05; Dallas, 2006-08;
  Buffalo, 2009; Cincinnati, 2010
- 18 Randy Moss, Minnesota, 1998-2004;
  Oakland, 2005-06; New England, 2007-2010;
  Minnesota, 2010; Tennessee, 2010;
  San Francisco, 2012

Most Receiving Touchdowns, Game
- 3 Ron Johnson, N.Y. Giants at Philadelphia,
  Oct. 2, 1972
  Wesley Walker, N.Y. Jets at Detroit, Dec. 6, 1982
  Steve Largent, Seattle at San Diego, Oct. 29, 1984
  Mark Clayton, Miami vs. Dallas, Dec. 17, 1984
  Jerry Rice, San Francisco vs. Chicago,
  Dec. 14, 1987
  Jerry Rice, San Francisco vs. Minnesota,
  Dec. 18, 1995
  Lamar Thomas, Miami vs. Denver, Dec. 21, 1998
  Ed McCaffrey, Denver vs. Miami, Sept. 13, 1999
  Randy Moss, Minnesota vs. N.Y. Giants,
  Nov. 19, 2001
  Isaac Bruce, St. Louis at New Orleans,
  Dec. 17, 2001
  Terrell Owens, Philadelphia at Dallas, Nov. 15, 2004
  Drew Bennett, Tennessee vs. Kansas City,
  Dec. 13, 2004
  Marvin Harrison, Indianapolis vs. Cincinnati,
  Dec. 18, 2006

YARDS FROM SCRIMMAGE
Most Scrimmage Yards, Career
- 4,116 Jerry Rice, San Francisco, 1985-2000;
  Oakland, 2001-04; Seattle, 2004
- 2,836 Emmitt Smith, Dallas, 1990-2002; Arizona, 2003-04
- 2,567 Tony Dorsett, Dallas, 1977-1987; Denver, 1988

INTERCEPTIONS BY
Most Interceptions, Career
- 11 Everson Walls, Dallas, 1981-89; N.Y. Giants,
  1990-92; Cleveland, 1992-93
- 9 Merton Hanks, San Francisco, 1991-98;
  Seattle, 1999
- 8 Emmitt Thomas, Kansas City, 1966-1978
  Darren Sharper, Green Bay, 1997-2004; Minnesota,
  2005-08; New Orleans, 2009-2010

Most Interceptions, Game
- 4 Dick Anderson, Miami vs. Pittsburgh, Dec. 3, 1973*
- 3 Johnny Robinson, Kansas City at Baltimore,
  Sept. 28, 1970
  Charlie Babb, Miami vs. Oakland, Sept. 22, 1975
  Charles Phillips, Oakland vs. Denver, Dec. 8, 1975
  Mark Murphy, Washington at San Diego,

Oct. 31, 1983
  Ken Easley, Seattle at San Diego, Oct. 29, 1984
  Dwayne Harper, San Diego vs. Oakland,
  Nov. 27, 1995
  Marcus Coleman, N.Y. Jets vs. Miami,
  Oct. 23, 2000 (OT)
  Keith Bulluck, Tennessee vs. New Orleans,
  Sept. 24, 2007

Longest Interception Return
- 102 Eddie Anderson, L.A. Raiders at Miami,
  Dec. 14, 1992 (TD)
- 101 Lito Sheppard, Philadelphia at Dallas,
  Nov. 15, 2004 (TD)
- 100 Darrelle Revis, N.Y. Jets vs. Miami,
  Oct. 17, 2011 (TD)

SACKS
Most Sacks, Career
- 24.5 Bruce Smith, Buffalo, 1985-1999; Washington,
  2000-03
- 20.0 Richard Dent, Chicago, 1983-1993, 1995;
  San Francisco, 1994; Indianapolis, 1996;
  Philadelphia, 1997
- 18.0 Kevin Greene, L.A. Rams, 1985-1992; Pittsburgh,
  1993-95; Carolina, 1996, 1998-99;
  San Francisco, 1997

PUNTING
Highest Punt Average, Career (Minimum: 25 Punts)
- 48.38 Shane Lechler, Oakland, 2000-2012; Houston, 2013
- 47.81 Mike Scifres, San Diego, 2003-2013
- 47.73 Andy Lee, San Francisco, 2004-2013

Longest Punt
- 90 Rodney Williams, N.Y. Giants at Denver,
  Sept. 10, 2001
- 83 Bryan Barker, Jacksonville vs. N.Y. Jets,
  Oct. 11, 1999
- 77 Shane Lechler, Oakland vs. Denver, Sept. 12, 2011

PUNT RETURNS
Longest Punt Return
- 95 John Taylor, San Francisco vs. Washington,
  Nov. 21, 1988 (TD)
- 94 Dennis McKinnon, Chicago vs. N.Y. Giants,
  Sept. 14, 1987 (TD)
  Dexter McCluster, Kansas City vs. San Diego,
  Sept. 13, 2010 (TD)
- 93 Dez Bryant, Dallas vs. N.Y. Giants,
  Oct. 25, 2010 (TD)

KICKOFF RETURNS
Longest Kickoff Return
- 105 Terry Fair, Detroit vs. Tampa Bay,
  Sept. 28, 1998 (TD)
- 104 Allen Rossum, San Francisco vs. Arizona,
  Nov. 10, 2008 (TD)
- 103 Terrence McGee, Buffalo vs. Dallas,
  Oct. 8, 2007 (TD)
  Brandon Tate, New England at Miami,
  Oct. 4, 2010 (TD)
  David Reed, Baltimore at Houston,
  Dec. 13, 2010 (TD)

FUMBLES
Longest Fumble Return
- 99 Don Griffin, San Francisco vs. Chicago,
  Dec. 23, 1991 (TD)
- 96 Joe Lavender, Philadelphia vs. Dallas,
  Sept. 23, 1974 (TD)
- 93 Adam Archuleta, St. Louis vs. Tampa Bay,
  Oct. 18, 2004 (TD)

INTERNATIONAL GAMES

NFL INTERNATIONAL GAMES (72)

REGULAR SEASON GAMES (15)
(Home Team in capitals)

Date	Site	Teams
October 2, 2005	Mexico City, Mexico	ARIZONA 31, San Francisco 14
October 28, 2007	London, England	N.Y. Giants 13, MIAMI 10
October 26, 2008	London, England	NEW ORLEANS 37, San Diego 32
December 7, 2008	Toronto, Canada	Miami 16, BUFFALO 3
October 25, 2009	London, England	New England 35, TAMPA BAY 7
December 3, 2009	Toronto, Canada	N.Y. Jets 19, BUFFALO 13
October 31, 2010	London, England	SAN FRANCISCO 24, Denver 16
November 7, 2010	Toronto, Canada	Chicago 22, BUFFALO 19
October 23, 2011	London, England	Chicago 24, TAMPA BAY 18
October 30, 2011	Toronto, Canada	BUFFALO 23, Washington 0
October 28, 2012	London, England	New England 45, ST. LOUIS 7
December 16, 2012	Toronto, Canada	Seattle 50, BUFFALO 17
September 29, 2013	London, England	MINNESOTA 34, Pittsburgh 27
October 27, 2013	London, England	San Francisco 42, JACKSONVILLE 10
December 1, 2013	Toronto, Canada	Atlanta 34, BUFFALO 31 (OT)

PRESEASON GAMES (57)

Date	Site	Teams
August 12, 1950	Ottawa, Canada	N.Y. Giants 27, Ottawa Rough Riders 6
August 11, 1951	Ottawa, Canada	N.Y. Giants 41, Ottawa Rough Riders 18
August 5, 1959	Toronto, Canada	Chi. Cardinals 55, Tor. Argonauts 26
August 3, 1960	Toronto, Canada	Pittsburgh 43, Toronto Argonauts 16
August 15, 1960	Toronto, Canada	Chicago 16, N.Y. Giants 7
August 2, 1961	Toronto, Canada	St. Louis 36, Toronto Argonauts 7
August 5, 1961	Montreal, Canada	Chicago 34, Montreal Alouettes 16
August 8, 1961	Hamilton, Canada	Hamilton Tiger-Cats 38, Buffalo 21
August 25, 1969	Montreal, Canada	Detroit 22, Boston 9
September 11, 1969	Montreal, Canada	Pittsburgh 17, N.Y. Giants 13
August 16, 1976	Tokyo, Japan	St. Louis 20, San Diego 10
August 5, 1978	Mexico City, Mexico	New Orleans 14, Philadelphia 7
August 6, 1983	London, England	Minnesota 28, St. Louis 10
* August 3, 1986	London, England	Chicago 17, Dallas 6
* August 9, 1987	London, England	L.A. Rams 28, Denver 27
* July 31, 1988	London, England	Miami 27, San Francisco 21
August 14, 1988	Goteborg, Sweden	Minnesota 28, Chicago 21
August 18, 1988	Montreal, Canada	N.Y. Jets 11, Cleveland 7
* August 5, 1989	Tokyo, Japan	L.A. Rams 16, San Francisco 13 (OT)
* August 6, 1989	London, England	Philadelphia 17, Cleveland 13
* August 4, 1990	Tokyo, Japan	Denver 10, Seattle 7
* August 5, 1990	London, England	New Orleans 17, L.A. Raiders 10
* August 9, 1990	Montreal, Canada	Pittsburgh 30, New England 14
* August 11, 1990	Berlin, Germany	L.A. Rams 19, Kansas City 3
* July 28, 1991	London, England	Buffalo 17, Philadelphia 13
* August 3, 1991	Berlin, Germany	San Francisco 21, Chicago 7
* August 3, 1991	Tokyo, Japan	Miami 19, L.A. Raiders 17
* August 1, 1992	Tokyo, Japan	Houston 34, Dallas 23
* August 15, 1992	Berlin, Germany	Miami 31, Denver 27
* August 16, 1992	London, England	San Francisco 17, Washington 15
* July 31, 1993	Tokyo, Japan	New Orleans 28, Philadelphia 16
* August 1, 1993	Barcelona, Spain	San Francisco 21, Pittsburgh 14
* August 7, 1993	Berlin, Germany	Minnesota 20, Buffalo 6
* August 8, 1993	London, England	Dallas 13, Detroit 13 (OT)
August 14, 1993	Toronto, Canada	Cleveland 12, New England 9
* July 31, 1994	Barcelona, Spain	L.A. Raiders 25, Denver 22
* August 6, 1994	Tokyo, Japan	Minnesota 17, Kansas City 9
* August 13, 1994	Berlin, Germany	N.Y. Giants 28, San Diego 20
* August 15, 1994	Mexico City, Mexico	Houston 6, Dallas 0
* August 5, 1995	Tokyo, Japan	Denver 24, San Francisco 10
* August 12, 1995	Toronto, Canada	Buffalo 9, Dallas 7
* July 27, 1996	Tokyo, Japan	San Diego 20, Pittsburgh 10
* August 5, 1996	Monterrey, Mexico	Kansas City 32, Dallas 6
* July 27, 1997	Dublin, Ireland	Pittsburgh 30, Chicago 17
* August 4, 1997	Mexico City, Mexico	Miami 38, Denver 19
* August 16, 1997	Toronto, Canada	Green Bay 35, Buffalo 3
* August 1, 1998	Tokyo, Japan	Green Bay 27, Kansas City 24 (OT)
* August 15, 1998	Vancouver, Canada	San Francisco 24, Seattle 21

Date	Site	Teams
* August 17, 1998	Mexico City, Mexico	New England 21, Dallas 3
* August 7, 1999	Sydney, Australia	Denver 20, San Diego 17
* August 5, 2000	Tokyo, Japan	Atlanta 20, Dallas 9
* August 19, 2000	Mexico City, Mexico	Indianapolis 24, Pittsburgh 23
* August 27, 2001	Mexico City, Mexico	Dallas 21, Oakland 6
* August 3, 2002	Osaka, Japan	Washington 38, San Francisco 7
* August 2, 2003	Tokyo, Japan	Tampa Bay 30, N.Y. Jets 14
* August 6, 2005	Tokyo, Japan	Atlanta 27, Indianapolis 21
August 14, 2008	Toronto, Canada	Buffalo 24, Pittsburgh 21
August 19, 2010	Toronto, Canada	Buffalo 34, Indianapolis 21

* American Bowl Game

NFL OPENING KICKOFF GAMES (12)
(Home Team in capitals)
The first site listed each year designates location of Thursday Night NFL Kickoff Weekend game; subsequent locations indicate site(s) of NFL Kickoff Weekend concert.

Date	Sites	Teams
Sept. 5, 2002	Giants Stadium (East Rutherford, New Jersey) Times Square (New York, New York)	San Francisco 16, N.Y. GIANTS 13
Sept. 4, 2003	FedExField (Landover, Maryland) National Mall (Washington, D.C.)	WASHINGTON 16, N.Y. Jets 13
Sept. 9, 2004	Gillette Stadium (Foxboro, Massachusetts) Metropolitan Park (Jacksonville, Florida)	NEW ENGLAND 27, Indianapolis 24
Sept. 8, 2005	Gillette Stadium (Foxboro, Massachusetts) Detroit, Michigan Los Angeles Coliseum (Los Angeles, California)	NEW ENGLAND 30, Oakland 20
Sept. 7, 2006	Heinz Field (Pittsburgh, Pennsylvania) Miami, Florida	PITTSBURGH 28, Miami 17
Sept. 6, 2007	RCA Dome (Indianapolis, Indianapolis)	INDIANAPOLIS 41, New Orleans 10
Sept. 4, 2008	Giants Stadium (East Rutherford, New Jersey) Columbus Circle (New York, New York)	N.Y. GIANTS 16, Washington 7
Sept. 10, 2009	Heinz Field (Pittsburgh, Pennsylvania) Point State Park (Pittsburgh, Pennsylvania)	PITTSBURGH 13, Tennessee 10 (OT)
Sept. 9, 2010	Louisiana Superdome (New Orleans, Louisiana) Jackson Square (New Orleans, Louisiana)	NEW ORLEANS 14, Minnesota 9
Sept. 8, 2011	Lambeau Field (Green Bay, Wisconsin)	GREEN BAY 42, New Orleans 34
Sept. 5, 2012*	MetLife Stadium (East Rutherford, New Jersey) Rockefeller Center (New York, New York)	Dallas 24, N.Y. GIANTS 17
Sept. 5, 2013	Sports Authority Field at Mile High (Denver, Colorado) Baltimore's Inner Harbor (Baltimore, Maryland)	DENVER 49, Baltimore 27

*Wednesday night

OVERTIME PROCEDURES

MODIFIED SUDDEN DEATH OVERTIME

For the 2010 postseason, the NFL installed a modified sudden death system to determine the winner when the score is tied at the end of regulation. In 2012, the system was expanded to cover all NFL games, including regular-season and preseason games.

Modified sudden death guarantees each team a possession or the opportunity to possess, unless the team that receives the opening kickoff scores a touchdown on its initial possession.

Key Definitions:

Possession: Actual possession of the ball with complete control. The defense gains possession when it catches, intercepts, or recovers a loose ball.

Opportunity to possess: The opportunity to possess occurs only during kicking plays. A kickoff is an opportunity to possess for the receiving team. If the kicking team legally recovers the kick, the receiving team is considered to have had its opportunity. A punt or a field goal that crosses the line of scrimmage and is muffed by the receiving team is considered to be an opportunity to possess for the receivers. Normal touching rules by the kicking team apply.

REGULAR SEASON

At the end of regulation time, the Referee will immediately toss coin at center of field in accordance with rules pertaining to the usual pregame toss. The captain of the visiting team will call the toss prior to the coin being flipped.

Following a three-minute intermission after the end of the regulation game, there shall be a maximum of one 15-minute period. Each team must possess or have the opportunity to possess the ball unless the team that has the ball first scores a touchdown on its initial possession. Play continues in sudden death until a winner is determined, and the game automatically ends upon any score (by safety, field goal, or touchdown) or when a score is awarded by Referee for a palpably unfair act. Each team shall be entitled to two timeouts, and if there is an excess timeout, the usual rules shall apply. Try is not attempted if touchdown scored. Disqualified players are not allowed to return.

If the score is tied at the end of a 15-minute overtime period, the game shall result in a tie.

Instant Replay: No challenges. Reviews to be initiated by the replay official.

POSTSEASON
At the end of regulation time, the Referee will immediately toss coin at center of field in accordance with rules pertaining to the usual pregame toss. The captain of the visiting team will call the toss prior to the coin being flipped.

Following a three-minute intermission after the end of the regulation game, play will be continued in 15-minute periods until a winner is declared. Each team must possess or have the opportunity to possess the ball unless the team that has the ball first scores a touchdown on its initial possession. Play continues in sudden death until a winner is determined, and the game automatically ends upon any score (by safety, field goal, or touchdown) or when a score is awarded by Referee for a palpably unfair act. Each team has three time outs per half and all general timing provisions apply as during a regular game. Try is not attempted if touchdown scored. Disqualified players are not allowed to return.

Instant Replay: No challenges. Reviews to be initiated by the replay official.

For overtime game capsules dating back to 1974, please visit www.NFL.com.

* indicates Monday-night game
 # indicates Thursday/Saturday/Sunday-night game
+ indicates Thanksgiving Day game

REGULAR SEASON

Sept. 15, 2013—Houston 30, Tennessee 24, at Houston; Texans win toss. K. Martin returns kickoff 26 yards. Drive begins on Houston 22. Schaub completes 3-yard touchdown to D. Hopkins at 10:32.

Sept. 29, 2013—Seattle 23, Houston 20, at Houston; Texans win toss. Touchback. Drive begins on Houston 20. Drive ends on Houston 40. Lechler punts 60 yards. Touchback. Drive begins on Seattle 20. Drive ends on Houston 47. Ryan punts 34 yards and Martin makes fair catch at Houston 13. Drive begins on Houston 13. Drive ends on Houston 40. Lechler punts 61 yards to and Tate returns 32 yards. Drive begins on Seattle 31. Hauschka kicks 45-yard field goal at 3:23.

Oct. 13, 2013—Cincinnati 27, Buffalo 24, at Buffalo; Bengals win toss. Tate returns kickoff 27 yards. Drive begins on Cincinnati 23. Drive ends on Buffalo 37. Huber punts 30 yards and McKelvin makes fair catch at Buffalo 7. Drive begins on Buffalo 7. Drive ends on Buffalo 11. Moorman punts 51 yards to Cincinnati 38 and Tate returns 29 yards. Drive begins on Buffalo 33. Nugent kicks 43-yard field goal at 6:49.

Oct. 20, 2013—New York Jets 30, New England 27, at New York; Patriots win toss. Blount returns kickoff 22 yards. Drive begins on New England 22. Drive ends on New England 38. Allen punts 62 yards. Touchback. Drive begins on New York 20. Folk kicks 42-yard field goal at 5:12.

Oct. 31, 2013—Miami 22, Cincinnati 20, at Miami; Dolphins win toss. Touchback. Drive begins on Miami 20. Drive ends on Miami 29. Fields punts 48 yards and Tate returns 2 yards. Drive begins on Cincinnati 25. Drive ends on Miami 39. Huber punts 25 yards and Thigpen makes fair catch at Miami 14. Drive begins on Miami 14. Drive ends on Cincinnati 40. Fields punts 32 yards to Cincinnati 8. Drive begins on Cincinnati 8. Dalton sacked in end zone by Wake for safety at 6:38.

Nov. 3, 2013—Washington 30, San Diego 24, at Washington; Redskins win toss. Morgan returns kickoff 24 yards. Drive begins on Washington 22. Young rushes for 4-yard touchdown at 8:59.

Nov. 3, 2013—Seattle 27, Tampa Bay 24, at Seattle; Buccaneers win toss. Touchback. Drive begins on Tampa Bay 20. Drive ends on Tampa Bay 16. Koenen punts 52 yards and Tate returns 8 yards. Drive begins on Seattle 40. Hauschka kicks 27-yard field goal at 8:16.

Nov. 10, 2013—Baltimore 20, Cincinnati 17, at Baltimore; Bengals win toss. Touchback. Drive begins on Cincinnati 20. Dalton completes pass to RB G. Bernard for -11 yards on 4th-and-2. Drive ends on Baltimore 44. Drive begins on Baltimore 44. Tucker kicks 46-yard field goal at 5:34.

Nov. 17, 2013—Chicago 23, Baltimore 20, at Chicago; Ravens win toss. Touchback. Drive begins on Baltimore 20. Drive ends on Chicago 46. Koch punts 26 yards. Drive begins on Chicago 20. Gould kicks 38-yard field goal at 8:46.

Nov. 24, 2013—Minnesota 26, Green Bay 26, at Green Bay; Packers win toss. Hyde returns kickoff 21 yards. Drive begins on Green Bay 21. Crosby kicks 20-yard field goal at 10:28. Patterson returns kickoff 25 yards. Drive begins on Minnesota 20. Walsh kicks 35-yard field goal. Touchback. Drive begins on Green Bay 20. Drive ends on Green Bay 21. Masthay punts 40 yards. Drive begins on Minnesota 39. Drive ends on Minnesota 44. Locke punts 46 yards. Drive begins on Green Bay 10. Drive ends on Green Bay 27. Masthay punts 39

yards. Ponder completes pass to Patterson for 21 yards to Green Bay 45 as time expires.

Nov. 24, 2013—New England 34, Denver 31, at New England; Patriots win toss and elect to defend north goal. Touchback. Drive begins on Denver 20. Drive ends on Denver 42. Colquitt punts 40 yards. Drive begins on New England 18. Drive ends on New England 37. Allen punts 51 yards and Welker returns 1 yard. Drive begins on Denver 13. Drive ends on New England 42. Colquitt punts 22 yards. Drive begins on New England 20. Drive ends on New England 43. Allen punts 42 yards. Carter muffs punt and Edner recovers for New England. Drive begins on Denver 13. Gostkowski kicks 31-yard field goal at 2:00.

Dec. 1, 2013—Minnesota 23, Chicago 20, at Minnesota; Bears win toss. Ford returns kickoff 9 yards. Drive begins on Chicago 29. Drive ends on Chicago 46. Podlesh punts 32 yards. Drive begins on Minnesota 20. Walsh misses 57-yard field goal. Drive begins on Chicago 47. Gould misses 47-yard field goal. Drive begins on Minnesota 37. Walsh kicks 34-yard field goal at 1:47.

Dec. 1, 2013—Atlanta 34, Buffalo 31, at Buffalo in Toronto; Bills win toss. Touchback. Drive begins on Buffalo 20. Manuel throws 22 yard pass to Chandler and W. Moore forces fumble, which is recovered by Alford. Drive begins on Buffalo 47. Bryant kicks 36-yard field goal at 12:04.

Dec. 15, 2013—Arizona 37, Tennessee 34, at Tennessee; Titans win toss. Washington returns kickoff 24 yards. Drive begins on Tennessee 24. Fitzpatrick's pass intercepted by Cason, who returns it 16 yards. Drive begins on Arizona 46. Feely kicks 41-yard field goal at 10:22.

Dec. 22, 2013—New York Giants 23, Detroit Lions 20, at Detroit; Giants win toss. Cox returns kickoff 56 yards. Drive begins on New York 49. Brown rushes for 7 yards and Fairley forces fumble, which is recovered by Young. Drive begins on Detroit 28. Martin punts 53 yards. Drive begins on New York 28. Brown kicks 45-yard field goal at 7:37.

Dec. 29, 2013—San Diego 27, Kansas City 24, at San Diego; Chargers win toss. Touchback. Drive begins on San Diego 20. Novak kicks 36-yard field goal. Demps returns kickoff 30 yards. Drive begins on Kansas City 26. Daniel pass incomplete to A. Jenkins on fourth-and-15 at 3:25.

For capsules of all 30 postseason overtime game capsules dating back to 1958, please visit www.NFL.com.

NFL POSTSEASON OVERTIME GAMES
(BY LENGTH OF GAME)

Dec. 25, 1971	Miami 27, KANSAS CITY 24	82:40
Dec. 23, 1962	Dallas Texans 20, HOUSTON 17	77:54
Jan. 3, 1987	CLEVELAND 23, N.Y. Jets 20	77:02
Jan. 12, 2013	Baltimore 38, DENVER 35	76:42
Dec. 24, 1977	Oakland 37, BALTIMORE 31	75:43
Jan. 10, 2004	Carolina 29, ST. LOUIS 23	75:10
Jan. 8, 2005	N.Y. Jets 20, SAN DIEGO 17	74:55
Jan 2, 1982	San Diego 41, MIAMI 38	73:52
Dec. 26, 1965	GREEN BAY 13, Baltimore 10	73:39
Jan. 17, 1999	Atlanta 30, MINNESOTA 27	71:52
Dec. 30, 2000	MIAMI 23, Indianapolis 17	71:16
Jan. 15, 2005	PITTSBURGH 20, N.Y. Jets 17	71:04
Jan. 8, 1994	KANSAS CITY 27, Pittsburgh 24	71:03
Jan. 19, 2002	NEW ENGLAND 16, Oakland 13	68:29
Dec. 28, 1958	Baltimore 23, N.Y. GIANTS 17	68:15
Jan. 3, 1988	HOUSTON 23, Seattle 20	68:05
Jan. 22, 2012	N.Y. Giants 20, SAN FRANCISCO 17	67:54
Jan. 3, 2009	SAN DIEGO 23, Indianapolis 17	66:12
Jan. 11, 1987	Denver 23, CLEVELAND 20	65:38
Jan. 14, 2007	CHICAGO 27, Seattle 24	64:53
Jan. 11, 2004	PHILADELPHIA 20, Green Bay 17	64:48
Jan. 24, 2010	NEW ORLEANS 31, Minnesota 28	64:45
Jan. 4, 2004	GREEN BAY 33, Seattle 27	64:25
Dec. 31, 1989	Pittsburgh 26, HOUSTON 23	63:26
Jan. 3, 1993	BUFFALO 41, Houston 38	63:06
Jan. 20, 2008	N.Y. Giants 23, GREEN BAY 20	62:26
Jan. 11, 2003	TENNESSEE 34, Pittsburgh 31	62:15
Jan. 10, 2010	ARIZONA 51, Green Bay 45	61:18
Jan. 7, 1990	L.A. Rams 19, N.Y. GIANTS 13	61:06
Jan. 8, 2012	DENVER 29, Pittsburgh 23	60:11

Home team in CAPS

OVERTIME GAMES BY YEAR
(REGULAR SEASON)

2013-16	2002-25*	1992-10	1982- 4
2012-22	2001-17	1991-15	1981-10
2011-13	2000-17	1990-10	1980-13
2010-19	1999-11	1989-11	1979-12
2009-13	1998-7	1988- 9	1978-11
2008-15	1997-17	1987-13	1977-6
2007-15	1996-14	1986-16	1976-5
2006-11	1995-21	1985-10	1975-9
2005-14	1994-16	1984- 9	1974-2
2004-12	1993-7	1983-19	
2003-23			

*Record

OVERTIME WON-LOST RECORDS, 1974-2013
(REGULAR SEASON)

Team	Win	Loss	Tie	Pct.
AFC				
Baltimore	11	9	1	.548
Buffalo	19	14	0	.576
Cincinnati	16	13	1	.550
Cleveland	16	17	1	.485
Denver	25	16	2	.605
Houston	4	8	0	.333
Indianapolis	13	10	1	.563
Jacksonville	7	7	0	.500
Kansas City	14	20	2	.417
Miami	14	22	1	.392
New England	19	21	0	.475
N.Y. Jets	20	17	2	.538
Oakland	17	17	0	.500
Pittsburgh	21	15	2	.579
San Diego	13	21	0	.382
Tennessee	15	21	0	.417
NFC				
Arizona	24	16	2	.595
Atlanta	14	20	2	.417
Carolina	4	10	0	.286
Chicago	23	18	0	.561
Dallas	19	14	0	.576
Detroit	15	19	1	.443
Green Bay	11	15	5	.435
Minnesota	20	18	3	.524
New Orleans	10	12	0	.455
N.Y. Giants	19	14	2	.571
Philadelphia	11	17	4	.406
St. Louis	13	11	2	.538
San Francisco	19	15	2	.556
Seattle	11	18	0	.379
Tampa Bay	15	17	1	.470
Washington	24	14	1	.628

OVERTIME GAME SUMMARY—1974-2013

There have been 515 overtime games in regular season play since the rule was adopted in 1974 (16 in 2013 season). Breakdown follows:

RESULTS

272 (7) times the team which won the toss won the game (52.8%)

224 (8) times the team which lost the toss won the game (43.5%)

19(1) games ended tied (3.7%). Last time: Nov. 24, 2013, Minnesota 26 at Green Bay 26.

POSSESSIONS

370 (14) times both teams had at least one possession (71.8%)

145 (2) times the team which won the toss drove for winning score (104 FG, 41 TD) (28.2%)

Of the 515 overtime games, there were 13 miscellaneous situations in which non-standard possessions took place:

9 (0) times the defense or special teams won without registering an official possession (5 INT, 2 blocked punts, 1 FR, 1 blocked FG) (1.8%)

1 (0) times the special teams forced a fumble on the opening kickoff and drove for winning score (0.2%)

1 (0) times the punting team recovered a muffed punt and drove for winning score with team muffing punt having no official possessions (0.2%)

2 (0) times the team that won the toss elected to kick and the team receiving the ball drove for winning score (0.4%)

SCORING
368 (12) games were decided by a field goal (71.5%)
125 (2) games were decided by a touchdown (24.2%)
3 (1) games were decided by a safety (0.6%)
19 (1) games ended tied (3.7%). Last time: Nov. 24, 2013, Minnesota 26 at Green Bay 26.

COIN TOSS
505 (15) times the team which won the toss elected to receive (98.1%)
10 (1) times the team which won the toss elected to kick off (5 wins) (1.9%)

Note: The number in parentheses is the 2013 Season Total.

MOST OVERTIME GAMES, SEASON
5 Green Bay Packers, 1983
4 Denver Broncos, 1985, 2007
Cleveland Browns, 1989
Minnesota Vikings, 1994, 1995
Arizona Cardinals, 1995, 1997
San Francisco 49ers, 2001
Atlanta Falcons, 2002
San Diego Chargers, 2002
Carolina Panthers, 2003
Washington Redskins, 2010
Arizona Cardinals, 2011

LONGEST CONSECUTIVE GAME STREAKS
WITHOUT OVERTIME (Current)
26 Philadelphia Eagles (Last OT Game, 10/14/2012 vs. Detroit Lions)
Oakland Raiders (Last OT Game, 10/21/2012 vs. Jacksonville Jaguars)
(Record: 110, St. Louis/Phoenix Cardinals, 12/7/86-12/19/93)

There have been 30 overtime postseason games dating back to 1958. In 24 cases, both teams had at least one possession. Last time: 1/12/13, Baltimore 38, DENVER 35.

SHORTEST OVERTIME GAMES
0:11 *DENVER 29, Pittsburgh 23; 1/8/12
0:14 New York Jets 37, BUFFALO 31; 9/8/02
0:16 CHICAGO 37, San Francisco 31; 10/28/01
0:16 Green Bay 19, DENVER 13; 10/29/07
0:17 NEW ORLEANS 20, Seattle 17; 11/16/97
0:21 Chicago 23, DETROIT 17; 11/27/80
0:30 Baltimore 29, NEW ENGLAND 23; 9/4/83
0:34 San Diego 23, WASHINGTON 17; 11/27/05
0:55 New York Giants 16, PHILADELPHIA 10; 9/29/85
0:55 PITTSBURGH 16, Kansas City 13; 11/12/12
*Postseason game

LONGEST OVERTIME GAMES
(ALL POSTSEASON GAMES)
22:40 Miami 27, KANSAS CITY 24; 12/25/71
17:54 Dallas Texans 20, HOUSTON 17; 12/23/62
17:02 CLEVELAND 23, New York Jets 20; 1/3/87
16:42 Baltimore 38, DENVER 35; 1/12/13
15:43 Oakland 37, BALTIMORE 31; 12/24/77
15:10 Carolina 29, ST. LOUIS 23; 1/10/04

OVERTIME SCORING SUMMARY
368 were decided by a field goal
60 were decided by a touchdown pass
33 were decided by a touchdown run
18 were decided by an interception (Atlanta 40, New Orleans 34, 9/2/79; Atlanta 47, Green Bay 41, 11/27/83; New York Giants 16, Philadelphia 10, 9/29/85; Indianapolis 23, Cleveland 17, 12/10/89; Cleveland 30, San Diego 24, 10/20/91; Kansas City 23, Oakland 17, 9/17/95; New York Giants 27, Ari-

zona 21, 10/8/95; Washington 36, Detroit 30, 10/22/95; Arizona 20, Seattle 14, 10/29/95; Cincinnati 34, Detroit 28, 9/13/98; New York Giants 23, Philadelphia 17, 10/31/99; Chicago 37, San Francisco 31, 10/28/01; Chicago 27, Cleveland 21, 11/4/01; New Orleans 26, Tampa Bay 20, 9/8/02; Atlanta 20, Carolina 14, 12/7/03; Jacksonville 23, Pittsburgh 17, 10/16/05; Chicago 19, Detroit 13, 10/30/05; Baltimore 29, Houston 28, 12/13/10)

3 were decided by a fumble recovery (Baltimore 29, New England 23, 9/4/83; Denver 36, Seattle 30, 12/19/99; San Francisco 37, Arizona 31, 11/24/07)

3 were decided by a safety (Minnesota 23, Los Angeles Rams 21, 11/5/89; Chicago 19, Tennessee 17, 11/14/04; Miami 22, Cincinnati 20, 10/31/13)

2 were decided on a fake field goal/touchdown pass (Minnesota 22, Chicago 16, 10/16/77; Cleveland 23, Minnesota 17, 12/17/89)

2 were decided by a kickoff return (Chicago 23, Detroit 17, 11/27/80; New York Jets 37, Buffalo 31, 9/8/02)

2 was decided by a punt return (Kansas City 29, San Diego 23, 10/9/95; Arizona 19, St. Louis 13, 11/6/11)

1 was decided on a fake field goal/touchdown run (Los Angeles Rams 27, Minnesota 21, 12/2/79)

1 was decided on a blocked field goal (Denver 30, San Diego 24, 11/17/85)

1 was decided on a blocked field goal/recovery by kicker (Green Bay 12, Chicago 6, 9/7/80)

1 was decided on a blocked field goal/recovery by kicking team (Philadelphia 23, New York Giants 17, 11/20/88)

1 was decided by a blocked punt (Arizona 30, Dallas 24, 10/12/08)

19 ended tied

OVERTIME RECORDS (REGULAR SEASON)
Longest Touchdown Pass
99 Yards — Ron Jaworski to Mike Quick, Philadelphia 23, Atlanta 17 (11/10/85)
82 Yards — Tom Brady to Troy Brown, New England 19, Miami 13 (10/19/03); Brett Favre to Greg Jennings, Green Bay 19, Denver 13 (10/29/07)
76 Yards — Troy Aikman to Raghib Ismail, Dallas 41, Washington 35 (9/12/99)

Longest Touchdown Run
96 Yards — Garrison Hearst, San Francisco 36, New York Jets 30 (9/6/98)
60 Yards — Herschel Walker, Dallas 23, New England 17 (11/15/87)
50 Yards — Rashard Mendenhall, Pittsburgh 15, Atlanta 9 (9/12/10)

Longest Field Goal
57 Yards — Sebastian Janikowski, Oakland 16, New York Jets 13 (10/19/08)
54 Yards — Greg Zuerlein, St. Louis 16, San Francisco 13 (12/2/12)
53 Yards — Chris Jacke, Green Bay 23, San Francisco 20 (10/4/96)

Longest Touchdown Plays
99 Yards — (Pass) Ron Jaworski to Mike Quick, Philadelphia 23, Atlanta 17 (11/10/85)
99 Yards — (Punt return) Patrick Peterson, Arizona 19, St. Louis 13 (11/6/11)
96 Yards — (Run) Garrison Hearst, San Francisco 36, New York Jets 30 (9/6/98)
96 Yards — (Kickoff return) Chad Morton, New York Jets 37, Buffalo 31 (9/8/02)
95 Yards — (Kickoff return) Dave Williams, Chicago 23, Detroit 17 (11/27/80)

THANKSGIVING DAY FOOTBALL, 1920-2013
(Home Team in capitals, games listed in chronological order.)
(AFL)-American Football League, 1960-69.

Nov. 25, 1920
AKRON PROS 7, Canton Bulldogs 0
Decatur Staleys 6, CHICAGO TIGERS 0
ELYRIA (OH) ATHLETICS* 0, Columbus Panhandles 0
DAYTON TRIANGLES 28, Detroit Heralds 0
CHICAGO BOOSTERS* 27, Hammond Pros 0
All-Tonawanda (NY) 14, ROCHESTER JEFFERSONS 3
* Non league team. Games between league teams and non league teams counted in standings in 1920.

Nov. 24, 1921
Canton Bulldogs 14, AKRON PROS 0
Buffalo All-Americans 7, CHICAGO STALEYS 6

Nov. 30, 1922
Buffalo All-Americans 21, ROCHESTER JEFFERSONS 0
CHICAGO CARDINALS 6, Chicago Bears 0
RACINE LEGION 3, Milwaukee Badgers 0
Oorang Indians 18, COLUMBUS PANHANDLES 6
CANTON BULLDOGS 14, Akron Pros 0

Nov. 29, 1923
CANTON BULLDOGS 28, Toledo Maroons 0
CHICAGO BEARS 3, Chicago Cardinals 0
GREEN BAY PACKERS 19, Hammond Pros 0
Milwaukee Badgers 16, RACINE LEGION 0
AKRON PROS 2, Buffalo All-Americans 0

Nov. 27, 1924
AKRON PROS 22, Buffalo Bisons 0
Chicago Bears 21, CHICAGO CARDINALS 0
FRANKFORD YELLOWJACKETS 32, Dayton Triangles 7
CLEVELAND BULLDOGS 53, Milwaukee Badgers 10 (at Canton, Ohio)
Green Bay Packers 17, KANSAS CITY BLUES 6

Nov. 26, 1925
CHICAGO BEARS 0, Chicago Cardinals 0
Kansas City Cowboys 17, CLEVELAND BULLDOGS 0 (at Hartford, Connecticut)
Rock Island Independents 6, DETROIT PANTHERS 3
POTTSVILLE MAROONS 31, Green Bay Packers 0

Nov. 25, 1926
New York Giants 17, BROOKLYN LIONS 0
Los Angeles Buccaneers 9, DETROIT PANTHERS 6
CHICAGO BEARS 0, Chicago Cardinals 0
FRANKFORD YELLOWJACKETS 20, Green Bay Packers 14
POTTSVILLE MAROONS 8, Providence Steam Roller 0
CANTON BULLDOGS 0, Akron Pros 0

Nov. 24, 1927
Chicago Cardinals 3, CHICAGO BEARS 0
POTTSVILLE MAROONS 6, Providence Steam Roller 0
Green Bay Packers 17, FRANKFORD YELLOWJACKETS 9
Cleveland Bulldogs 30, NEW YORK YANKEES 19

Nov. 29, 1928
Providence Steam Roller 7, POTTSVILLE MAROONS 0
DETROIT WOLVERINES 33, Dayton Triangles 0
FRANKFORD YELLOWJACKETS 2, Green Bay Packers 0
CHICAGO BEARS 34, Chicago Cardinals 0

Nov. 28, 1929
New York Giants 21, STATEN ISLAND STAPLETONS 7
FRANKFORD YELLOWJACKETS 0, Green Bay Packers 0
Chicago Cardinals 40, CHICAGO BEARS 6

Nov. 27, 1930
STATEN ISLAND STAPLETONS 7, New York Giants 6
BROOKLYN DODGERS 33, Providence Steam Roller 12
Green Bay Packers 25, FRANKFORD YELLOWJACKETS 7
CHICAGO BEARS 6, Chicago Cardinals 0

Nov. 26, 1931
Green Bay Packers 38, PROVIDENCE STEAM ROLLER 7
STATEN ISLAND STAPLETONS 9, New York Giants 6
CHICAGO BEARS 18, Chicago Cardinals 7

Nov. 24, 1932
CHICAGO BEARS 34, Chicago Cardinals 0
Green Bay Packers 7, BROOKLYN DODGERS 0
STATEN ISLAND STAPLETONS 13, New York Giants 13

Nov. 30, 1933
Chicago Bears 22, CHICAGO CARDINALS 6
New York Giants 10, BROOKLYN DODGERS 0

Nov. 29, 1934
CHICAGO CARDINALS 6, Green Bay Packers 0
Chicago Bears 19, DETROIT LIONS 16
New York Giants 27, BROOKLYN DODGERS 0

Nov. 28, 1935
New York Giants 21, BROOKLYN DODGERS 0
CHICAGO CARDINALS 9, Green Bay Packers 7
DETROIT LIONS 14, Chicago Bears 2

| Nov. 26, 1936 | DETROIT LIONS 13, Chicago Bears 7 |
| | New York Giants 14, BROOKLYN DODGERS 0 |

| Nov. 25, 1937 | Chicago Bears 13, DETROIT LIONS 0 |
| | BROOKLYN DODGERS 13, New York Giants 13 |

| Nov. 24, 1938 | DETROIT LIONS 14, Chicago Bears 7 |
| | BROOKLYN DODGERS 7, New York Giants 7 |

Nov. 23, 1939#   PHILADELPHIA EAGLES 17, Pittsburgh Steelers 14

Nov. 28, 1940#   PHILADELPHIA EAGLES 7, Pittsburgh Steelers 0

In 1939 and 1940, President Roosevelt moved Thanksgiving one week earlier. Various states celebrated on the date declared by the President, while other states recognized the traditional fourth Thursday of the month. In 1941, Thanksgiving was sanctioned by Congress to be celebrated on the fourth Thursday of November, which it has been ever since.

Nov. 22, 1945   Cleveland Rams 28, DETROIT LIONS 21

Nov. 28, 1946   Boston Yanks 34, DETROIT LIONS 10

Nov. 27, 1947   Chicago Bears 34, DETROIT LIONS 14

Nov. 25, 1948   Chicago Cardinals 28, DETROIT LIONS 14

Nov. 24, 1949   Chicago Bears 28, DETROIT LIONS 7

| Nov. 23, 1950 | DETROIT LIONS 49, New York Yanks 14 |
| | Pittsburgh Steelers 28, CHICAGO CARDINALS 17 |

Nov. 22, 1951   DETROIT LIONS 52, Green Bay Packers 35

| Nov. 27, 1952 | DETROIT LIONS 48, Green Bay Packers 24 |
| | DALLAS TEXANS 27, Chicago Bears 23 (at Akron, Ohio) |

Nov. 26, 1953   DETROIT LIONS 34, Green Bay Packers 15

Nov. 25, 1954   DETROIT LIONS 28, Green Bay Packers 24

Nov. 24, 1955   DETROIT LIONS 24, Green Bay Packers 10

Nov. 22, 1956   Green Bay Packers 24, DETROIT LIONS 20

Nov. 28, 1957   DETROIT LIONS 18, Green Bay Packers 6

Nov. 27, 1958   DETROIT LIONS 24, Green Bay Packers 14

Nov. 26, 1959   Green Bay Packers 24, DETROIT LIONS 17

| Nov. 24, 1960 | DETROIT LIONS 23, Green Bay Packers 10 |
| | (AFL) - NEW YORK TITANS 41, Dallas Texans 35 |

| Nov. 23, 1961 | Green Bay Packers 17, DETROIT LIONS 9 |
| | (AFL) - NEW YORK TITANS 21, Buffalo Bills 14 |

| Nov. 22, 1962 | DETROIT LIONS 26, Green Bay Packers 14 |
| | (AFL) - New York Titans 46, DENVER BRONCOS 45 |

| Nov. 28, 1963 | DETROIT LIONS 13, Green Bay Packers 13 |
| | (AFL) - Oakland Raiders 26, DENVER BRONCOS 10 |

| Nov. 26, 1964 | Chicago Bears 27, DETROIT LIONS 24 |
| | (AFL) - Buffalo Bills 27, SAN DIEGO CHARGERS 24 |

| Nov. 25, 1965 | DETROIT LIONS 24, Baltimore Colts 24 |
| | (AFL) - SAN DIEGO CHARGERS 20, Buffalo Bills 20 |

Nov. 24, 1966	San Francisco 49ers 41, DETROIT LIONS 14
	DALLAS COWBOYS 26, Cleveland Browns 14
	(AFL) - Buffalo Bills 31, OAKLAND RAIDERS 10

Nov. 23, 1967	Los Angeles Rams 31, DETROIT LIONS 7
	DALLAS COWBOYS 46, St. Louis Cardinals 21
	(AFL) - Oakland Raiders 44, KANSAS CITY CHIEFS 22
	(AFL) - SAN DIEGO CHARGERS 24, Denver Broncos 20

Nov. 28, 1968	Philadelphia Eagles 12, DETROIT LIONS 0
	DALLAS COWBOYS 29, Washington Redskins 20
	(AFL) - OAKLAND RAIDERS 13, Buffalo Bills 10
	(AFL) - KANSAS CITY CHIEFS 24, Houston Oilers 10

THANKSGIVING DAY FOOTBALL

Nov. 27, 1969	Minnesota Vikings 27, DETROIT LIONS 0 DALLAS COWBOYS 24, San Francisco 49ers 24 (AFL) - KANSAS CITY CHIEFS 31, Denver Broncos 17 (AFL) - San Diego Chargers 21, HOUSTON OILERS 17
Nov. 26, 1970	DETROIT LIONS 28, Oakland Raiders 14 DALLAS COWBOYS 16, Green Bay Packers 3
Nov. 25, 1971	DETROIT LIONS 32, Kansas City Chiefs 21 DALLAS COWBOYS 28, Los Angeles Rams 21
Nov. 23, 1972	DETROIT LIONS 37, New York Jets 20 San Francisco 49ers 31, DALLAS COWBOYS 10
Nov. 22, 1973	Washington Redskins 20, DETROIT LIONS 0 Miami Dolphins 14, DALLAS COWBOYS 7
Nov. 28, 1974	Denver Broncos 31, DETROIT LIONS 27 DALLAS COWBOYS 24, Washington Redskins 23
Nov. 27, 1975	Los Angeles Rams 20, DETROIT LIONS 0 Buffalo Bills 32, ST. LOUIS CARDINALS 14
Nov. 25, 1976	DETROIT LIONS 27, Buffalo Bills 14 DALLAS COWBOYS 19, St. Louis Cardinals 14
Nov. 24, 1977	Chicago Bears 31, DETROIT LIONS 14 Miami Dolphins 55, ST. LOUIS CARDINALS 14
Nov. 23, 1978	DETROIT LIONS 17, Denver Broncos 14 DALLAS COWBOYS 37, Washington Redskins 10
Nov. 22, 1979	DETROIT LIONS 20, Chicago Bears 0 Houston Oilers 30, DALLAS COWBOYS 24
Nov. 27, 1980	Chicago Bears 23, DETROIT LIONS 17 (OT) DALLAS COWBOYS 51, Seattle Seahawks 7
Nov. 26, 1981	DETROIT LIONS 27, Kansas City Chiefs 10 DALLAS COWBOYS 10, Chicago Bears 9
Nov. 25, 1982	New York Giants 13, DETROIT LIONS 6 DALLAS COWBOYS 31, Cleveland Browns 14
Nov. 24, 1983	DETROIT LIONS 45, Pittsburgh Steelers 3 DALLAS COWBOYS 35, St. Louis Cardinals 17
Nov. 22, 1984	DETROIT LIONS 31, Green Bay Packers 28 DALLAS COWBOYS 20, New England Patriots 17
Nov. 28, 1985	DETROIT LIONS 31, New York Jets 20 DALLAS COWBOYS 35, St. Louis Cardinals 17
Nov. 27, 1986	Green Bay Packers 44, DETROIT LIONS 40 Seattle Seahawks 31, DALLAS COWBOYS 14
Nov. 26, 1987	Kansas City Chiefs 27, DETROIT LIONS 20 Minnesota Vikings 44, DALLAS COWBOYS 38 (OT)
Nov. 24, 1988	Minnesota Vikings 23, DETROIT LIONS 0 Houston Oilers 25, DALLAS COWBOYS 17
Nov. 23, 1989	DETROIT LIONS 13, Cleveland Browns 10 Philadelphia Eagles 27, DALLAS COWBOYS 0
Nov. 22, 1990	DETROIT LIONS 40, Denver Broncos 27 DALLAS COWBOYS 27, Washington Redskins 17
Nov. 28, 1991	DETROIT LIONS 16, Chicago Bears 6 DALLAS COWBOYS 20, Pittsburgh Steelers 10
Nov. 26, 1992	Houston Oilers 24, DETROIT LIONS 21 DALLAS COWBOYS 30, New York Giants 3
Nov. 25, 1993	Chicago Bears 10, DETROIT LIONS 6 Miami Dolphins 16, DALLAS COWBOYS 14
Nov. 24, 1994	DETROIT LIONS 35, Buffalo Bills 21 DALLAS COWBOYS 42, Green Bay Packers 31
Nov. 23, 1995	DETROIT LIONS 44, Minnesota Vikings 38 DALLAS COWBOYS 24, Kansas City Chiefs 12

Nov. 28, 1996	Kansas City Chiefs 28, DETROIT LIONS 24 DALLAS COWBOYS 21, Washington Redskins 10
Nov. 27, 1997	DETROIT LIONS 55, Chicago Bears 20 Tennessee Titans 27, DALLAS COWBOYS 14
Nov. 26, 1998	DETROIT LIONS 19, Pittsburgh Steelers 16 (OT) Minnesota Vikings 46, DALLAS COWBOYS 36
Nov. 25, 1999	DETROIT LIONS 21, Chicago Bears 17 DALLAS COWBOYS 20, Miami Dolphins 0
Nov. 23, 2000	DETROIT LIONS 34, New England Patriots 9 Minnesota Vikings 27, DALLAS COWBOYS 15
Nov. 22, 2001	Green Bay Packers 29, DETROIT LIONS 27 Denver Broncos 26, DALLAS COWBOYS 24
Nov. 28, 2002	New England Patriots 20, DETROIT LIONS 12 DALLAS COWBOYS 27, Washington Redskins 20
Nov. 27, 2003	DETROIT LIONS 22, Green Bay Packers 14 Miami Dolphins 40, DALLAS COWBOYS 21
Nov. 25, 2004	Indianapolis Colts 41, DETROIT LIONS 9 DALLAS COWBOYS 21, Chicago Bears 7
Nov. 24, 2005	Atlanta Falcons 27, DETROIT LIONS 7 Denver Broncos 24, DALLAS COWBOYS 21 (OT)
Nov. 23, 2006	Miami Dolphins 27, DETROIT LIONS 10 DALLAS COWBOYS 38, Tampa Bay Buccaneers 10 KANSAS CITY CHIEFS 19, Denver Broncos 10
Nov. 22, 2007	Green Bay Packers 37, DETROIT LIONS 26 DALLAS COWBOYS 34, New York Jets 3 Indianapolis Colts 31, ATLANTA FALCONS 13
Nov. 27, 2008	Tennessee Titans 47, DETROIT LIONS 10 DALLAS COWBOYS 34, Seattle Seahawks 9 PHILADELPHIA EAGLES 48, Arizona Cardinals 20
Nov. 26, 2009	Green Bay Packers 34, DETROIT LIONS 12 DALLAS COWBOYS 24, Oakland Raiders 7 DENVER BRONCOS 26, New York Giants 6
Nov. 25, 2010	New England Patriots 45, DETROIT LIONS 24 New Orleans Saints 30, DALLAS COWBOYS 27 NEW YORK JETS 26, Cincinnati Bengals 10
Nov. 24, 2011	Green Bay Packers 27, DETROIT LIONS 15 DALLAS COWBOYS 20, Miami Dolphins 19 BALTIMORE RAVENS 16, San Francisco 49ers 6
Nov. 22, 2012	Houston Texans 34, DETROIT LIONS 31 (OT) Washington Redskins 38, DALLAS COWBOYS 31 New England Patriots 49, NEW YORK JETS 19
Nov. 28, 2013	DETROIT LIONS 40, Green Bay Packers 10 DALLAS COWBOYS 31, Oakland Raiders 24 BALTIMORE RAVENS 22, Pittsburgh Steelers 20

THANKSGIVING DAY RECORDS
*NFL record; stats compiled by Elias Sports Bureau.

SCORING / Most Touchdowns, Game
6   Ernie Nevers, Chi. Cardinals vs. Chi. Bears, Nov. 28, 1929*
4   Doc Elliott, Cleveland vs. Milwaukee, Nov. 27, 1924
     Sterling Sharpe, Green Bay at Dallas, Nov. 24, 1994
     Brian Westbrook, Philadelphia vs. Arizona, Nov. 27, 2008
3   By many players

RUSHING / Most Yards Rushing, Game
273   O.J. Simpson, Buffalo at Detroit, Nov. 25, 1976
198   Bob Hoernschemeyer, Detroit vs. N.Y. Yankees, Nov. 23, 1950
195   Earl Campbell, Houston at Dallas, Nov. 22, 1979

PASSING / Most Yards Passing, Game
455   Troy Aikman, Dallas vs. Minnesota, Nov. 26, 1998
441   Matthew Stafford, Detroit vs. Houston, Nov. 22, 2012 (OT)
     Tony Romo, Dallas vs. Washington, Nov. 22, 2012
410   Scott Mitchell, Detroit vs. Minnesota, Nov. 23, 1995

PASS RECEIVING
RECEPTIONS / Most Pass Receptions, Game
12   Brett Perriman, Detroit vs. Minnesota, Nov. 23, 1995
     Marvin Harrison, Indianapolis at Detroit, Nov. 25, 2004
11   Daryl Johnston, Dallas vs. Miami, Nov. 25, 1993
     Michael Irvin, Dallas vs. Kansas City, Nov. 23, 1995

YARDS GAINED / Most Yards on Pass Receptions, Game
303   Jim Benton, Cleveland at Detroit, Nov. 22, 1945
188   Andre Johnson, Houston at Detroit, Nov. 22, 2012 (OT)
185   Lance Alworth, San Diego vs. Buffalo, Nov. 26, 1964

AFC VS. NFC (REGULAR SEASON), 1970-2013

	Balt	Buff	Cin	Cle	Den	Hou	Ind	Jax	KC	Mia
1970		0-3	1-2	0-3	2-2		3-0		0-2-1	2-1
1971		0-3	1-2	2-1	1-3		2-1		2-1	3-0
1972		2-0-1	2-1	1-2	1-3		0-3		2-1	3-0
1973		2-1	2-1	1-2	0-3-1		2-1		1-1-1	3-0
1974		2-1	2-1	1-2	2-2		1-2		1-2	2-1
1975		1-2	3-0	1-3	2-1		2-1		2-1	3-0
1976		0-2	2-0	2-0	2-0		0-2		1-1	0-2
1977		1-1	2-1	1-1	1-1		1-1		1-1	2-0
1978		1-1	2-2	4-0	2-2		2-2		0-2	3-1
1979		2-2	2-2	3-1	3-1		1-1		0-2	4-0
1980		3-1	2-2	3-1	3-1		1-1		2-0	4-0
1981		1-3	2-2	3-1	3-1		0-4		2-2	3-1
1982		1-2	1-0	0-2	2-1		0-1-1		0-3	1-1
1983		1-3	3-1	2-2	0-2		2-0		2-2	3-1
1984		1-3	2-2	1-3	3-1		0-4		1-1	4-0
1985		0-2	2-2	1-3	3-1		3-1		2-2	3-1
1986		1-1	3-1	2-2	3-1		1-3		1-1	2-2
1987		1-2	1-2	2-2	2-1-1		1-0		1-2	3-0
1988		2-2	4-0	4-0	3-1		2-2		0-2	3-1
1989		1-3	2-2	3-1	2-2		1-3		2-0	2-0
1990		3-1	1-3	1-3	1-3		2-2		4-0	2-2
1991		3-1	1-3	0-4	2-0		0-4		2-2	3-1
1992		4-0	1-3	2-2	1-3		2-0		2-2	2-2
1993		4-0	2-2	3-1	1-3		0-4		2-2	3-1
1994		1-3	1-3	3-1	1-3		0-2		3-1	2-2
1995		3-1	2-2	1-3	2-2		2-2	0-4	3-1	2-2
1996	2-2	4-0	2-2		3-1		3-1	2-2	4-0	1-3
1997	2-1-1	1-3	2-2		3-1		1-3	2-2	4-0	1-3
1998	1-3	3-1	1-3		3-1		0-4	3-1	3-1	3-1
1999	2-1	3-1	1-2	1-2	2-2		4-0	4-0	2-2	2-2
2000	2-1	2-2	1-2	0-3	3-1		2-2	2-2	2-2	2-2
2001	2-2	1-3	1-2	1-2	3-1		1-3	1-2	1-3	2-2
2002	0-4	1-3	1-3	2-2	4-0	2-2	2-2	2-2	2-2	2-2
2003	3-1	2-2	2-2	2-2	1-3	2-2	3-1	2-2	3-1	3-1
2004	3-1	4-0	4-0	1-3	3-1	1-3	4-0	3-1	1-3	2-2
2005	2-2	0-4	4-0	2-2	3-1	1-3	3-1	3-1	1-3	2-2
2006	3-1	2-2	2-2	1-3	1-3	0-4	3-1	3-1	4-0	3-1
2007	3-1	1-3	1-3	3-1	1-3	3-1	4-0	3-1	1-3	0-4
2008	3-1	2-2	1-2-1	1-3	3-1	3-1	2-2	2-2	0-4	3-1
2009	2-2	2-2	3-1	0-4	2-2	3-1	4-0	1-3	1-3	2-2
2010	3-1	1-3	1-3	2-2	1-3	1-3	2-2	1-3	4-0	2-2
2011	3-1	2-2	3-1	1-3	2-2	2-2	0-4	1-3	3-1	1-3
2012	2-2	1-3	3-1	0-4	3-1	2-2	3-1	0-4	2-2	2-2
2013	2-2	1-3	3-1	1-3	4-0	0-4	2-2	0-4	4-0	1-3
Total	40-29-1	76-81-1	85-74-1	65-85	93-71-2	20-28	74-76-1	35-40	81-67-2	101-60

AFC VS. NFC (REGULAR SEASON), 1970-2013

	NE	NYJ	Oak	Pitt	SD	Sea	TB	Ten	TOTALS
1970	0-3	2-1	1-2	0-3	1-2			0-3	12-27-1
1971	0-3	0-3	1-1-1	1-2	2-1			0-2-1	15-23-2
1972	3-0	1-2	3-0	2-1	0-3			0-3	20-19-1
1973	2-1	0-3	2-1	3-0	1-2			0-3	19-19-2
1974	3-0	2-1	3-0	3-0	1-2			0-3	23-17
1975	1-2	0-3	3-0	2-1	0-3			3-0	23-17
1976	1-1	0-2	3-0	1-1	2-0		0-1	2-0	16-12
1977	2-0	1-1	1-1	2-0	1-1	1-0		2-0	19-9
1978	2-2	1-3	4-0	3-1	2-2	3-1		2-2	31-21
1979	3-1	3-1	4-0	3-1	3-1	3-1		2-2	36-16
1980	1-3	1-3	2-2	4-0	2-2	1-3		4-0	33-19
1981	0-4	2-0	2-2	3-1	2-2	0-2		1-3	24-28
1982	0-1	4-0	3-0	1-0	1-0	1-0		0-3	15-14-1
1983	2-2	3-1	2-2	2-2	2-2	1-3		1-3	26-26
1984	0-4	0-2	3-1	3-1	4-0	4-0		0-4	26-26
1985	3-1	2-2	3-1	1-3	1-1	2-2		1-3	27-25
1986	3-1	2-2	1-3	2-2	0-4	3-1		2-2	26-26
1987	0-3	0-4	2-2	2-2	2-0	4-0		2-2	23-22-1
1988	2-2	2-0	1-3	1-3	2-2	1-3		3-1	30-22
1989	0-4	1-3	2-2	3-1	2-2	0-4		3-1	24-28
1990	0-4	2-0	3-1	3-1	1-1	2-2		1-3	26-26
1991	1-1	2-2	2-2	0-4	1-3	1-3		1-3	19-33
1992	0-4	0-4	2-2	1-3	2-0	0-4		3-1	22-30
1993	1-1	2-2	3-1	2-2	2-2	0-2		2-2	27-25
1994	4-0	1-3	3-1	2-2	2-2	2-0		0-4	25-27
1995	0-4	0-4	3-1	2-2	3-1	3-1		1-3	27-33
1996	2-2	1-3	1-3	2-2	1-3	2-2		2-2	32-28
1997	1-3	3-1	2-2	2-2	1-3	2-2		4-0	31-28-1
1998	2-2	2-2	3-1	2-2	1-3	3-1		1-3	31-29
1999	3-1	2-2	3-1	3-0	1-3	2-2		3-1	38-22
2000	0-4	3-1	4-0	1-2	0-4	2-2		4-0	30-30
2001	3-1	2-2	3-1	3-0	2-2	1-3		3-1	30-30
2002	3-1	3-1	2-2	2-1-1	2-2			2-2	34-29-1
2003	3-1	0-4	1-3	1-3	2-2			4-0	34-30
2004	4-0	3-1	2-2	4-0	3-1			2-2	44-20
2005	3-1	1-3	2-2	4-0	2-2			1-3	34-30
2006	4-0	3-1	1-3	3-1	4-0			3-1	40-24
2007	4-0	0-4	0-4	3-1	2-2			3-1	32-32
2008	4-0	2-2	1-3	2-2	1-3			4-0	34-29-1
2009	3-1	2-2	1-3	3-1	4-0			4-0	37-27
2010	4-0	2-2	2-2	3-1	2-2			3-1	34-30
2011	3-1	2-2	2-2	3-1	1-3			2-2	31-33
2012	1-3	2-2	0-4	3-1	0-4			1-3	25-39
2013	3-1	3-1	0-4	2-2	3-1			1-3	30-34
Total	**84-74**	**70-88**	**92-73-1**	**98-61-1**	**74-81**	**44-44**	**0-1**	**83-81-1**	**1,215-1,114-11**

INTERCONFERENCE GAMES

NFC VS. AFC (REGULAR SEASON), 1970-2013

	Ariz	Atl	Car	Chi	Dall	Det	GB	Minn	NO
1970	2-0-1	1-2		1-2	3-0	3-0	2-1	2-1	0-3
1971	2-1	3-0		1-2	3-0	4-0	2-1	2-1	0-1-2
1972	1-2	2-2		1-2	3-0	2-0-1	2-1	1-2	0-3
1973	0-2-1	2-1		2-2	2-1	0-3	1-1-1	2-1	1-2
1974	2-1	0-3		0-3	2-1	1-2	2-1	2-1	0-3
1975	2-1	1-2		0-3	2-1	1-2	0-3	4-0	0-3
1976	1-1	0-2		0-2	2-0	2-0	0-2	2-0	1-2
1977	0-2	0-2		1-1	1-1	2-0	0-3	1-1	0-2
1978	0-4	1-3		0-4	3-1	2-2	2-2	1-3	1-3
1979	1-3	1-3		2-2	1-3	0-4	1-3	1-3	0-4
1980	1-1	2-2		0-4	3-1	0-2	1-3	1-3	1-3
1981	3-1	1-3		4-0	4-0	2-2	1-1	1-3	2-2
1982		1-1		1-1	2-1	0-1	1-1-1	1-3	1-0
1983	3-1	3-1		1-1	2-2	1-3	2-2	4-0	1-3
1984	3-1	1-3		2-2	2-2	0-4	0-4	0-4	3-1
1985	2-2	0-4		3-1	3-1	2-2	0-4	2-0	0-4
1986	1-1	1-3		4-0	1-3	1-3	1-3	1-3	1-3
1987	0-1	0-4		2-2	2-1	0-4	1-2-1	2-1	4-0
1988	1-3	1-3		3-1	0-4	1-1	1-3	2-2	4-0
1989	1-3	2-2		2-2	0-2	1-3	0-2	2-2	4-0
1990	2-2	2-2		2-2	1-1	1-3	1-3	2-2	2-2
1991	1-1	3-1		2-2	3-1	4-0	1-3	0-2	3-1
1992	0-2	2-2		1-3	4-0	2-2	3-1	3-1	3-1
1993	1-1	1-3		2-2	2-2	2-0	3-1	2-2	2-2
1994	3-1	1-3		3-1	3-1	2-2	1-3	2-2	1-3
1995	1-3	2-2	3-1	2-2	4-0	3-1	4-0	3-1	4-0
1996	0-4	0-4	3-1	2-2	2-2	1-3	3-1	1-3	1-3
1997	1-3	2-2	2-2	2-2	2-2	2-2	3-1	3-1	2-2
1998	1-3	3-1	1-3	2-2	1-3	1-3	3-1	4-0	1-3
1999	0-4	0-4	2-2	2-2	1-3	1-3	2-2	2-2	0-4
2000	1-3	1-3	2-2	2-2	1-3	2-2	1-3	3-1	1-3
2001	3-1	1-3	0-4	3-1	0-4	0-4	3-1	1-3	2-2
2002	0-4	2-1-1	3-1	1-3	2-2	0-4	3-1	1-3	2-2
2003	1-3	1-3	2-2	3-1	2-2	1-3	3-1	2-2	1-3
2004	1-3	3-1	1-3	1-3	1-3	1-3	1-3	3-1	2-2
2005	1-3	3-1	3-1	1-3	2-2	2-2	0-4	1-3	2-2
2006	0-4	2-2	2-2	2-2	3-1	1-3	1-3	0-4	1-3
2007	3-1	1-3	0-4	3-1	3-1	3-1	4-0	2-2	1-3
2008	2-2	3-1	4-0	2-2	2-2	0-4	1-3	2-2	3-1
2009	2-2	3-1	0-4	2-2	2-2	1-3	2-2	3-1	4-0
2010	2-2	3-1	0-4	3-1	2-2	1-3	2-2	1-3	2-2
2011	1-3	3-1	3-1	1-3	2-2	4-0	3-1	0-4	4-0
2012	2-2	4-0	2-2	3-1	3-1	1-3	3-1	3-1	2-2
2013	4-0	1-3	3-1	4-0	1-3	1-3	2-2	1-3	2-2
Total	**59-88-2**	**70-94-1**	**36-40**	**81-82**	**90-70**	**62-95-1**	**73-86-3**	**79-83**	**72-90-2**

NFC VS. AFC (REGULAR SEASON), 1970-2013

	NYG	Phil	StL	SF	Sea	TB	Wash	TOTALS
1970	3-0	2-1	2-1	4-0			2-1	27-12-1
1971	1-2	1-2	1-2	2-1			1-2	23-15-2
1972	1-2	2-1	1-2	2-1			1-2	19-20-1
1973	1-2	2-1	3-0	1-2			2-1	19-19-2
1974	1-2	2-1	3-1	0-3			2-1	17-23
1975	2-1	0-3	3-0	1-2			1-2	17-23
1976	0-2	0-2	1-1	1-1	1-0		1-1	12-16
1977	0-2	1-1	2-0	0-2		0-1	1-1	9-19
1978	1-1	3-1	2-2	1-3		2-0	2-2	21-31
1979	1-1	2-2	2-2	0-4		2-0	2-2	16-36
1980	1-3	3-1	2-2	2-2		1-3	1-3	19-33
1981	1-1	3-1	1-3	3-1		0-4	2-2	28-24
1982	1-0	2-1	1-2	1-3		2-1		14-15-1
1983	0-4	1-1	1-3	2-2		1-3	4-0	26-26
1984	2-0	3-1	3-1	3-1		1-1	3-1	26-26
1985	2-2	1-1	3-1	3-1		0-4	4-0	25-27
1986	3-1	2-2	2-2	4-0		1-1	3-1	26-26
1987	2-1	3-1	1-2	3-1		0-2	2-1	22-23-1
1988	1-1	2-2	2-2	2-2		1-3	1-3	22-30
1989	4-0	3-1	3-1	4-0		0-4	2-2	28-24
1990	3-1	1-3	2-2	4-0		0-2	3-1	26-26
1991	3-1	4-0	1-3	3-1		1-3	4-0	33-19
1992	2-2	3-1	2-2	3-1		0-2	2-2	30-22
1993	2-2	2-2	2-2	2-2		1-3	1-3	25-27
1994	3-1	1-3	2-2	3-1		1-1	1-1	27-25
1995	0-4	1-3	1-3	3-1		2-2	0-4	33-27
1996	2-2	2-2	2-2	4-0		2-2	3-1	28-32
1997	1-3	2-1-1	0-4	2-2		3-1	1-3	28-31-1
1998	3-1	0-4	3-1	2-2		2-2	2-2	29-31
1999	2-2	1-3	3-1	1-3		3-1	2-2	22-38
2000	3-1	3-1	3-1	2-2		3-1	2-2	30-30
2001	2-2	3-1	4-0	4-0		2-2	2-2	30-30
2002	2-2	1-3	2-2	2-2	2-2	3-1	3-1	29-34-1
2003	1-3	3-1	4-0	1-3	2-2	1-3	2-2	30-34
2004	1-3	2-2	1-3	0-4	1-3	1-3	0-4	20-44
2005	3-1	3-1	3-1	1-3	3-1	2-2	0-4	30-34
2006	1-3	1-3	2-2	2-2	2-2	2-2	2-2	24-40
2007	3-1	3-1	0-4	1-3	2-2	1-3	2-2	32-32
2008	3-1	2-1-1	0-4	2-2	1-3	1-3	1-3	29-34-1
2009	2-2	2-2	0-4	1-3	1-3	0-4	2-2	27-37
2010	2-2	3-1	2-2	2-2	1-3	2-2	2-2	30-34
2011	4-0	2-2	1-3	3-1	1-3	1-3	0-4	33-31
2012	1-3	2-2	1-3	4-0	3-1	3-1	2-2	39-25
2013	1-3	1-3	3-1	3-1	3-1	2-2	2-2	34-30
Total	78-74	86-73-2	83-82	94-73	23-26	50-78	78-81	1,114-1,215-11

INTERCONFERENCE GAMES

INTERCONFERENCE VICTORIES, 1970-2013

	AFC	NFC	Tie
1970	12	27	1
1971	15	23	2
1972	20	19	1
1973	19	19	2
1974	23	17	0
1975	23	17	0
1976	16	12	0
1977	19	9	0
1978	31	21	0
1979	36	16	0
1980	33	19	0
1981	24	28	0
1982	15	14	1
1983	26	26	0
1984	26	26	0
1985	27	25	0
1986	26	26	0
1987	23	22	1
1988	30	22	0
1989	24	28	0
1990	26	26	0
1991	19	33	0
1992	22	30	0
1993	27	25	0
1994	25	27	0
1995	27	33	0
1996	32	28	0
1997	31	28	1
1998	31	29	0
1999	38	22	0
2000	30	30	0
2001	30	30	0
2002	34	29	1
2003	34	30	0
2004	44	20	0
2005	34	30	0
2006	40	24	0
2007	32	32	0
2008	34	29	1
2009	37	27	0
2010	34	30	0
2011	31	33	0
2012	25	39	0
2013	30	34	0
Total	1,215	1,114	11

REGULAR SEASON INTERCONFERENCE RECORDS, 1970-2013

AMERICAN FOOTBALL CONFERENCE

East	W	L	T	Pct.
Miami	101	60	0	.627
New England	84	74	0	.532
Buffalo	76	81	1	.484
New York Jets	70	88	0	.443
North	**W**	**L**	**T**	**Pct.**
Pittsburgh	98	61	1	.616
Baltimore	40	29	1	.579
Cincinnati	85	74	1	.534
Cleveland	65	85	0	.433
South	**W**	**L**	**T**	**Pct.**
Tennessee	83	81	1	.506
Indianapolis	74	76	1	.493
Jacksonville	35	40	0	.467
Houston	20	28	0	.417
West	**W**	**L**	**T**	**Pct.**
Denver	93	71	2	.566
Oakland	92	73	1	.558
Kansas City	81	67	2	.547
San Diego	74	81	0	.477

NATIONAL FOOTBALL CONFERENCE

East	W	L	T	Pct.
Dallas	90	70	0	.563
Philadelphia	86	73	2	.540
New York Giants	78	74	0	.513
Washington	78	81	0	.491
North	**W**	**L**	**T**	**Pct.**
Chicago	81	82	0	.497
Minnesota	79	83	0	.488
Green Bay	73	86	3	.460
Detroit	62	95	1	.396
South	**W**	**L**	**T**	**Pct.**
Carolina	36	40	0	.474
New Orleans	72	90	2	.444
Atlanta	70	94	1	.427
Tampa Bay*	50	79	0	.388
West	**W**	**L**	**T**	**Pct.**
San Francisco	94	73	0	.563
St. Louis	83	82	0	.503
Seattle* #	67	70	0	.489
Arizona	59	88	2	.402

* Records include one game played between Seattle and Tampa Bay, won by the Seahawks 13-10, in their inaugural season (1976) when Seattle competed in the NFC and Tampa Bay in the AFC.

\# Seattle was a member of the AFC from 1977-2001.
From 1970-71, tie games were not included in winning percentage.

WALTER PAYTON NFL MAN OF THE YEAR

The Walter Payton NFL Man of the Year Award is the only NFL award that recognizes a player for his community service activities as well as his excellence on the field. Renamed in 1999 for the legendary Chicago Bears Pro Football Hall of Fame running back, the Walter Payton NFL Man of the Year Award has been given annually since 1970.

YEAR	PLAYER	POS.	TEAM
1970	Johnny Unitas	QB	Baltimore Colts
1971	John Hadl	QB	San Diego Chargers
1972	Willie Lanier	LB	Kansas City Chiefs
1973	Len Dawson	QB	Kansas City Chiefs
1974	George Blanda	QB	Oakland Raiders
1975	Ken Anderson	QB	Cincinnati Bengals
1976	Franco Harris	RB	Pittsburgh Steelers
1977	Walter Payton	RB	Chicago Bears
1978	Roger Staubach	QB	Dallas Cowboys
1979	Joe Greene	DT	Pittsburgh Steelers
1980	Harold Carmichael	WR	Philadelphia Eagles
1981	Lynn Swann	WR	Pittsburgh Steelers
1982	Joe Theismann	QB	Washington Redskins
1983	Rolf Benirschke	K	San Diego Chargers
1984	Marty Lyons	T	New York Jets
1985	Dwight Stephenson	C	Miami Dolphins
1986	Reggie Williams	LB	Cincinnati Bengals
1987	Dave Duerson	S	Chicago Bears
1988	Steve Largent	WR	Seattle Seahawks
1989	Warren Moon	QB	Houston Oilers
1990	Mike Singletary	LB	Chicago Bears
1991	Anthony Muñoz	T	Cincinnati Bengals
1992	John Elway	QB	Denver Broncos
1993	Derrick Thomas	LB	Kansas City Chiefs
1994	Junior Seau	LB	San Diego Chargers
1995	Boomer Esiason	QB	New York Jets
1996	Darrell Green	CB	Washington Redskins
1997	Troy Aikman	QB	Dallas Cowboys
1998	Dan Marino	QB	Miami Dolphins
1999	Cris Carter	WR	Minnesota Vikings
2000*	Derrick Brooks	LB	Tampa Bay Buccaneers
	Jim Flanigan	DT	Chicago Bears
2001	Jerome Bettis	RB	Pittsburgh Steelers
2002	Troy Vincent	CB	Philadelphia Eagles
2003	Will Shields	G	Kansas City Chiefs
2004	Warrick Dunn	RB	Atlanta Falcons
2005	Peyton Manning	QB	Indianapolis Colts
2006*	Drew Brees	QB	New Orleans Saints
	LaDainian Tomlinson	RB	San Diego Chargers
2007	Jason Taylor	DE	Miami Dolphins
2008	Kurt Warner	QB	Arizona Cardinals
2009	Brian Waters	G	Kansas City Chiefs
2010	Madieu Williams	S	Minnesota Vikings
2011	Matt Birk	C	Baltimore Ravens
2012	Jason Witten	TE	Dallas Cowboys
2013	Charles Tillman	CB	Chicago Bears

* The award was shared in 2000 and 2006.

ASSOCIATED PRESS NFL MOST OUTSTANDING/VALUABLE PLAYERS

THE FOLLOWING AWARDS WERE NAMED BY ASSOCIATED PRESS IN BALLOTING BY A NATIONWIDE PANEL OF MEDIA.

NFL MOST OUTSTANDING PLAYER AWARD

YEAR	PLAYER	POS.	TEAM	ACCOMPLISHMENTS
1957	Jim Brown	RB	Cleveland Browns	Rushed for league-leading 942 yards and added 9 touchdowns as a rookie.
1958	Jim Brown	RB	Cleveland Browns	Rushed for NFL-record 1,527 yards and added 17 touchdowns. Led Browns to 9-3 record.
1959	Charley Conerly	QB	New York Giants	Passed for 14 touchdowns and only 4 interceptions. Led offense to division-leading 284 points.
1960	Norm Van Brocklin	QB	Philadelphia Eagles	Guided Eagles to first division title since 1949. Passed for 2,471 yards and 24 touchdowns.

NFL MOST VALUABLE PLAYER AWARD

YEAR	PLAYER	POS.	TEAM	ACCOMPLISHMENTS
1961	Paul Hornung	RB	Green Bay Packers	Led league in scoring for second straight season with 146 points (10 TD, 15 FG, 41 PAT).
1962	Jim Taylor	RB	Green Bay Packers	League rushing champion with 1,474 yards. Scored all-time record 19 touchdowns.
1963	Y.A. Tittle	QB	New York Giants	Set all-time season record with 36 touchdown passes. Guided league's top offense (5,024 yards).
1964	Johnny Unitas	QB	Baltimore Colts	Guided Colts to NFL's best record (12-2) and league's top offensive attack (4,779 yards).
1965	Jim Brown	RB	Cleveland Browns	Leader of NFL's top rushing attack. Led league with 1,544 yards, added 21 total touchdowns.
1966	Bart Starr	QB	Green Bay Packers	Passed for 14 touchdowns and only 3 interceptions. Led Packers to league-best 12-2 record.
1967	Johnny Unitas	QB	Baltimore Colts	Passed for 3,428 yards and 20 touchdowns. Led Colts to 11-1-2 record.
1968	Earl Morrall	QB	Baltimore Colts	Guided Colts to NFL-best 13-1 record. Led league with 26 touchdown passes.
1969	Roman Gabriel	QB	Los Angeles Rams	Led NFL with 24 touchdown passes. Guided Rams to 11-3 record.
1970	John Brodie	QB	San Francisco 49ers	Took 49ers to first division title. Threw NFL-best 24 touchdown passes.
1971	Alan Page	DT	Minnesota Vikings	Led defense that allowed NFL-low 139 points. Vikings won fourth straight NFC Central title.
1972	Larry Brown	RB	Washington Redskins	Led conference with 1,216 rushing yards. Redskins had NFC-best 11-3 record.
1973	O.J. Simpson	RB	Buffalo Bills	Rushed for all-time record 2,003 yards, including three 200-yard performances.
1974	Ken Stabler	QB	Oakland Raiders	Led league with 26 touchdown passes and only 12 interceptions. Raiders had NFL-best 12-2 record.
1975	Fran Tarkenton	QB	Minnesota Vikings	Tied for league-best 12-2 record. Led NFC with 91.7 passer rating.
1976	Bert Jones	QB	Baltimore Colts	Threw 24 touchdowns and only 9 interceptions for 102.5 passer rating.
1977	Walter Payton	RB	Chicago Bears	Rushed for league-leading 1,852 yards and 16 total touchdowns.
1978	Terry Bradshaw	QB	Pittsburgh Steelers	Led Steelers to league-leading 14-2 mark. Set club record with 28 touchdown passes.
1979	Earl Campbell	RB	Houston Oilers	Led league with 1,697 rushing yards and 19 touchdowns.
1980	Brian Sipe	QB	Cleveland Browns	NFL-best 91.4 passer rating. Set Browns' records with 30 touchdown passes and 4,132 yards.
1981	Ken Anderson	QB	Cincinnati Bengals	Led Bengals to first division title since 1973. NFL-high 98.5 passer rating.
1982	Mark Moseley	K	Washington Redskins	Converted 20 of 21 FGs. Set consecutive field-goal record at 23 (including last three in '81).
1983	Joe Theismann	QB	Washington Redskins	Leader of offense that scored NFL record 541 points. Redskins had NFL-best 14-2 record.
1984	Dan Marino	QB	Miami Dolphins	Set NFL records with 5,084 yards and 48 touchdown passes. Led Dolphins to AFC-best 14-2 mark.
1985	Marcus Allen	RB	Los Angeles Raiders	Rushed for league-leading 1,759 yards. Tied for AFC lead with 11 rushing touchdowns.
1986	Lawrence Taylor	LB	New York Giants	Recorded league-high 20.5 sacks, and led Giants' second-ranked defense (297.3).
1987	John Elway	QB	Denver Broncos	In 12 games, passed for 19 touchdowns and 3,198 yards, including four 300-yard games.
1988	Boomer Esiason	QB	Cincinnati Bengals	Led NFL with 97.4 passer rating. Tied for AFC lead with 28 TD passes.
1989	Joe Montana	QB	San Francisco 49ers	Set NFL record with 112.4 passer rating, including 70.2 completion percentage.
1990	Joe Montana	QB	San Francisco 49ers	Led 49ers to league-best 14-2 record. Completed NFC-high 61.7 percent of passes.
1991	Thurman Thomas	RB	Buffalo Bills	Recorded league-high 2,038 yards from scrimmage (1,407 rushing, 631 receiving).
1992	Steve Young	QB	San Francisco 49ers	NFL's top passer with 107.0 rating. Led 49ers to NFL-best 14-2 record.

1993	Emmitt Smith	RB	Dallas Cowboys	Led league in rushing (1,486 yards) for third straight year despite missing first two games.
1994	Steve Young	QB	San Francisco 49ers	Compiled NFL all-time best 112.8 passer rating. Completed more than 70 percent of his passes.
1995	Brett Favre	QB	Green Bay Packers	Led league with 38 touchdown passes and NFC with 99.5 passer rating.
1996	Brett Favre	QB	Green Bay Packers	Led Packers to top conference record (13-3). Threw NFL-best 39 touchdown passes.
1997*	Brett Favre	QB	Green Bay Packers	Led league with 35 touchdown passes. Led NFC with 3,867 passing yards.
	Barry Sanders	RB	Detroit Lions	Rushed for all-time second-best 2,053 yards, including record 14 straight 100-yard games.
1998	Terrell Davis	RB	Denver Broncos	Rushed for 2,008 yards and scored league-best 23 total touchdowns.
1999	Kurt Warner	QB	St. Louis Rams	Became the second QB in history to have 40 touchdown passes in a season (41).
2000	Marshall Faulk	RB	St. Louis Rams	Set NFL record with 26 touchdowns and led NFC with 2,189 yards from scrimmage.
2001	Kurt Warner	QB	St. Louis Rams	Led NFL with 4,830 passing yards, 36 touchdowns, 68.7 completion percentage, and 101.4 passer rating.
2002	Rich Gannon	QB	Oakland Raiders	Set single-season records with 10 300-yard passing games and 418 completions, and led NFL with 4,689 passing yards.
2003*	Peyton Manning	QB	Indianapolis Colts	Led NFL with 4,267 passing yards, had AFC-best 29 touchdown passes, and posted 99.0 passer rating.
	Steve McNair	QB	Tennessee Titans	Posted NFL-best 100.4 passer rating, passing for 3,215 yards with 24 touchdowns against 7 interceptions.
2004	Peyton Manning	QB	Indianapolis Colts	Set NFL records with 49 touchdown passes and 121.1 passer rating while passing for 4,557 yards.
2005	Shaun Alexander	RB	Seattle Seahawks	Set NFL record with 28 touchdowns and led league with 1,880 rushing yards.
2006	LaDainian Tomlinson	RB	San Diego Chargers	Set NFL record for touchdowns (31) and points scored (186). Rushed for team-record 1,815 yards.
2007	Tom Brady	QB	New England Patriots	Set NFL record with 50 passing touchdowns. Led New England to first 16-0 regular-season record in league history.
2008	Peyton Manning	QB	Indianapolis Colts	Threw for 4,002 yards and 27 touchdowns and 95.0 passer rating. Led Indianapolis to 12-4 record.
2009	Peyton Manning	QB	Indianapolis Colts	Threw for 4,500 yards with 33 touchdowns for 99.9 passer rating while leading Colts to NFL-best 14-2 record.
2010	Tom Brady	QB	New England Patriots	Led league with 111.0 passer rating, throwing for 3,900 yards and 36 touchdowns while guiding Patriots to NFL-best 14-2 record.
2011	Aaron Rodgers	QB	Green Bay Packers	Set NFL record with 122.5 passer rating. Guided Green Bay to NFL-best 15-1 record.
2012	Adrian Peterson	RB	Minnesota Vikings	Rushed for league-leading 2,096 yards and scored 13 total touchdowns.
2013	Peyton Manning	QB	Denver Broncos	Set NFL records with 5,477 passing yards and 55 touchdown passes.

Total Associated Press NFL MVPs: 55
Five-time Winner: Peyton Manning
Three-time Winner: Brett Favre
Two-time Winners: Tom Brady, Joe Montana, Johnny Unitas, Kurt Warner, Steve Young
* The award was shared in 1997 and 2003.

ASSOCIATED PRESS MVPs WHO WON SUPER BOWL/ NFL CHAMPIONSHIP IN SAME SEASON: 13

1961	Paul Hornung	Green Bay Packers
1962	Jim Taylor	Green Bay Packers
1966	Bart Starr	Green Bay Packers
1968	Earl Morrall	Baltimore Colts
1978	Terry Bradshaw	Pittsburgh Steelers
1982	Mark Moseley	Washington Redskins
1986	Lawrence Taylor	New York Giants
1989	Joe Montana	San Francisco 49ers
1993	Emmitt Smith	Dallas Cowboys
1994	Steve Young	San Francisco 49ers
1996	Brett Favre	Green Bay Packers
1998	Terrell Davis	Denver Broncos
1999	Kurt Warner	St. Louis Rams

ASSOCIATED PRESS NFL MVP BY POSITION

Quarterback:	36	Kicker:	1
Running Back:	16	Linebacker:	1
Defensive Tackle:	1		

ASSOCIATED PRESS MVPs BY TEAM

8	Indianapolis/Baltimore Colts	2	Buffalo Bills
			Cincinnati Bengals
7	Green Bay Packers		Cleveland Browns
			Houston Oilers/
5	San Francisco 49ers		Tennessee Titans
			New England Patriots
4	St. Louis/Los Angeles Rams		New York Giants
3	Denver Broncos	1	Chicago Bears
	Minnesota Vikings		Dallas Cowboys
	Oakland/Los Angeles Raiders		Detroit Lions
	Washington Redskins		Miami Dolphins
			Pittsburgh Steelers
			San Diego Chargers
			Seattle Seahawks

AP OFFENSIVE PLAYER OF THE YEAR

1973	O.J. Simpson	RB	Buffalo Bills
1974	Ken Stabler	QB	Oakland Raiders
1975	Fran Tarkenton	QB	Minnesota Vikings
1976	Bert Jones	QB	Baltimore Colts
1977	Walter Payton	RB	Chicago Bears
1978	Earl Campbell	RB	Houston Oilers
1979	Earl Campbell	RB	Houston Oilers
1980	Earl Campbell	RB	Houston Oilers
1981	Ken Anderson	QB	Cincinnati Bengals
1982	Dan Fouts	QB	San Diego Chargers
1983	Joe Theismann	QB	Washington Redskins
1984	Dan Marino	QB	Miami Dolphins
1985	Marcus Allen	RB	Los Angeles Raiders
1986	Eric Dickerson	RB	Los Angeles Rams
1987	Jerry Rice	WR	San Francisco 49ers
1988	Roger Craig	RB	San Francisco 49ers
1989	Joe Montana	QB	San Francisco 49ers
1990	Warren Moon	QB	Houston Oilers
1991	Thurman Thomas	RB	Buffalo Bills
1992	Steve Young	QB	San Francisco 49ers
1993	Jerry Rice	WR	San Francisco 49ers
1994	Barry Sanders	RB	Detroit Lions
1995	Brett Favre	QB	Green Bay Packers
1996	Terrell Davis	RB	Denver Broncos
1997	Barry Sanders	RB	Detroit Lions
1998	Terrell Davis	RB	Denver Broncos
1999	Marshall Faulk	RB	St. Louis Rams
2000	Marshall Faulk	RB	St. Louis Rams
2001	Marshall Faulk	RB	St. Louis Rams
2002	Priest Holmes	RB	Kansas City Chiefs
2003	Jamal Lewis	RB	Baltimore Ravens
2004	Peyton Manning	QB	Indianapolis Colts
2005	Shaun Alexander	RB	Seattle Seahawks
2006	LaDainian Tomlinson	RB	San Diego Chargers
2007	Tom Brady	QB	New England Patriots
2008	Drew Brees	QB	New Orleans Saints
2009	Chris Johnson	RB	Tennessee Titans
2010	Tom Brady	QB	New England Patriots
2011	Drew Brees	QB	New Orleans Saints
2012	Adrian Peterson	RB	Minnesota Vikings
2013	Peyton Manning	QB	Denver Broncos

AP OFFENSIVE ROOKIE OF THE YEAR

1957	Jim Brown	RB	Cleveland Browns
1958	Jimmy Orr	WR	Pittsburgh Steelers
1959	Nick Pietrosante	RB	Detroit Lions
1960	Gail Cogdill	WR	Detroit Lions
1961	Mike Ditka	TE	Chicago Bears
1962	Ron Bull	RB	Chicago Bears
1963	Paul Flatley	WR	Minnesota Vikings
1964	Charley Taylor	WR	Washington Redskins
1965	Gale Sayers	RB	Chicago Bears
1966	Johnny Roland	RB	St. Louis Cardinals
1967	Mel Farr	RB	Detroit Lions
1968	Earl McCullouch	WR	Detroit Lions
1969	Calvin Hill	RB	Dallas Cowboys
1970	Duane Thomas	RB	Dallas Cowboys
1971	John Brockington	RB	Green Bay Packers
1972	Franco Harris	RB	Pittsburgh Steelers
1973	Chuck Foreman	RB	Minnesota Vikings
1974	Don Woods	RB	San Diego Chargers
1975	Mike Thomas	RB	Washington Redskins
1976	Sammy White	WR	Minnesota Vikings
1977	Tony Dorsett	RB	Dallas Cowboys
1978	Earl Campbell	RB	Houston Oilers
1979	Ottis Anderson	RB	St. Louis Cardinals
1980	Billy Sims	RB	Detroit Lions
1981	George Rogers	RB	New Orleans Saints

1982	Marcus Allen	RB	Los Angeles Raiders
1983	Eric Dickerson	RB	Los Angeles Rams
1984	Louis Lipps	WR	Pittsburgh Steelers
1985	Eddie Brown	WR	Cincinnati Bengals
1986	Rueben Mayes	RB	New Orleans Saints
1987	Troy Stradford	RB	Miami Dolphins
1988	John Stephens	RB	New England Patriots
1989	Barry Sanders	RB	Detroit Lions
1990	Emmitt Smith	RB	Dallas Cowboys
1991	Leonard Russell	RB	New England Patriots
1992	Carl Pickens	WR	Cincinnati Bengals
1993	Jerome Bettis	RB	Los Angeles Rams
1994	Marshall Faulk	RB	Indianapolis Colts
1995	Curtis Martin	RB	New England Patriots
1996	Eddie George	RB	Houston Oilers
1997	Warrick Dunn	RB	Tampa Bay Buccaneers
1998	Randy Moss	WR	Minnesota Vikings
1999	Edgerrin James	RB	Indianapolis Colts
2000	Mike Anderson	RB	Denver Broncos
2001	Anthony Thomas	RB	Chicago Bears
2002	Clinton Portis	RB	Denver Broncos
2003	Anquan Boldin	WR	Arizona Cardinals
2004	Ben Roethlisberger	QB	Pittsburgh Steelers
2005	Carnell Williams	RB	Tampa Bay Buccaneers
2006	Vince Young	QB	Tennessee Titans
2007	Adrian Peterson	RB	Minnesota Vikings
2008	Matt Ryan	QB	Atlanta Falcons
2009	Percy Harvin	WR	Minnesota Vikings
2010	Sam Bradford	QB	St. Louis Rams
2011	Cam Newton	QB	Carolina Panthers
2012	Robert Griffin III	QB	Washington Redskins
2013	Eddie Lacy	RB	Green Bay Packers

AP DEFENSIVE PLAYER OF THE YEAR

1971	Alan Page	DT	Minnesota Vikings
1972	Joe Greene	DT	Pittsburgh Steelers
1973	Dick Anderson	S	Miami Dolphins
1974	Joe Greene	DT	Pittsburgh Steelers
1975	Mel Blount	CB	Pittsburgh Steelers
1976	Jack Lambert	LB	Pittsburgh Steelers
1977	Harvey Martin	DE	Dallas Cowboys
1978	Randy Gradishar	LB	Denver Broncos
1979	Lee Roy Selmon	DE	Tampa Bay Buccaneers
1980	Lester Hayes	CB	Oakland Raiders
1981	Lawrence Taylor	LB	New York Giants
1982	Lawrence Taylor	LB	New York Giants
1983	Doug Betters	DE	Miami Dolphins
1984	Kenny Easley	S	Seattle Seahawks
1985	Mike Singletary	LB	Chicago Bears
1986	Lawrence Taylor	LB	New York Giants
1987	Reggie White	DT	Philadelphia Eagles
1988	Mike Singletary	LB	Chicago Bears
1989	Keith Millard	DT	Minnesota Vikings
1990	Bruce Smith	DE	Buffalo Bills
1991	Pat Swilling	LB	New Orleans Saints
1992	Cortez Kennedy	DT	Seattle Seahawks
1993	Rod Woodson	CB	Pittsburgh Steelers
1994	Deion Sanders	CB	San Francisco 49ers
1995	Bryce Paup	LB	Buffalo Bills
1996	Bruce Smith	DE	Buffalo Bills
1997	Dana Stubblefield	DT	San Francisco 49ers
1998	Reggie White	DE	Green Bay Packers
1999	Warren Sapp	DT	Tampa Bay Buccaneers
2000	Ray Lewis	LB	Baltimore Ravens
2001	Michael Strahan	DE	New York Giants
2002	Derrick Brooks	LB	Tampa Bay Buccaneers
2003	Ray Lewis	LB	Baltimore Ravens
2004	Ed Reed	S	Baltimore Ravens
2005	Brian Urlacher	LB	Chicago Bears
2006	Jason Taylor	DE	Miami Dolphins

2007	Bob Sanders	S	Indianapolis Colts
2008	James Harrison	LB	Pittsburgh Steelers
2009	Charles Woodson	CB	Green Bay Packers
2010	Troy Polamalu	S	Pittsburgh Steelers
2011	Terrell Suggs	LB	Baltimore Ravens
2012	J.J. Watt	DE	Houston Texans
2013	Luke Kuechly	LB	Carolina Panthers

AP DEFENSIVE ROOKIE OF THE YEAR

1967	Lem Barney	CB	Detroit Lions
1968	Claude Humphrey	DE	Atlanta Falcons
1969	Joe Greene	DT	Pittsburgh Steelers
1970	Bruce Taylor	CB	San Francisco 49ers
1971	Isiah Robertson	LB	Los Angeles Rams
1972	Willie Buchanon	CB	Green Bay Packers
1973	Wally Chambers	DT	Chicago Bears
1974	Jack Lambert	LB	Pittsburgh Steelers
1975	Robert Brazile	LB	Houston Oilers
1976	Mike Haynes	S	New England Patriots
1977	A.J. Duhe	DT	Miami Dolphins
1978	Al Baker	DE	Detroit Lions
1979	Jim Haslett	LB	Buffalo Bills
1980*	Buddy Curry	LB	Atlanta Falcons
	Al Richardson	LB	Atlanta Falcons
1981	Lawrence Taylor	LB	New York Giants
1982	Chip Banks	LB	Cleveland Browns
1983	Vernon Maxwell	LB	Baltimore Colts
1984	Bill Maas	NT	Kansas City Chiefs
1985	Duane Bickett	LB	Indianapolis Colts
1986	John Offerdahl	LB	Miami Dolphins
1987	Shane Conlan	LB	Buffalo Bills
1988	Erik McMillan	S	New York Jets
1989	Derrick Thomas	LB	Kansas City Chiefs
1990	Mark Carrier	S	Chicago Bears
1991	Mike Croel	LB	Denver Broncos
1992	Dale Carter	CB	Kansas City Chiefs
1993	Dana Stubblefield	DT	San Francisco 49ers
1994	Tim Bowens	DT	Miami Dolphins
1995	Hugh Douglas	DE	New York Jets
1996	Simeon Rice	DE	Arizona Cardinals
1997	Peter Boulware	LB	Baltimore Ravens
1998	Charles Woodson	CB	Oakland Raiders
1999	Jevon Kearse	DE	Tennessee Titans
2000	Brian Urlacher	LB	Chicago Bears
2001	Kendrell Bell	LB	Pittsburgh Steelers
2002	Julius Peppers	DE	Carolina Panthers
2003	Terrell Suggs	LB	Baltimore Ravens
2004	Jonathan Vilma	LB	New York Jets
2005	Shawne Merriman	LB	San Diego Chargers
2006	DeMeco Ryans	LB	Houston Texans
2007	Patrick Willis	LB	San Francisco 49ers
2008	Jerod Mayo	LB	New England Patriots
2009	Brian Cushing	LB	Houston Texans
2010	Ndamukong Suh	DT	Detroit Lions
2011	Von Miller	LB	Denver Broncos
2012	Luke Kuechly	LB	Carolina Panthers
2013	Sheldon Richardson	DL	New York Jets

*The award was shared in 1980.

AP COMEBACK PLAYER OF THE YEAR

1998	Doug Flutie	QB	Buffalo Bills
1999	Bryant Young	DT	San Francisco 49ers
2000	Joe Johnson	DE	New Orleans Saints
2001	Garrison Hearst	RB	San Francisco 49ers
2002	Tommy Maddox	QB	Pittsburgh Steelers
2003	Jon Kitna	QB	Cincinnati Bengals
2004	Drew Brees	QB	San Diego Chargers
2005*	Steve Smith	WR	Carolina Panthers
	Tedy Bruschi	LB	New England Patriots

2006	Chad Pennington	QB	New York Jets
2007	Greg Ellis	DE	Dallas Cowboys
2008	Chad Pennington	QB	Miami Dolphins
2009	Tom Brady	QB	New England Patriots
2010	Michael Vick	QB	Philadelphia Eagles
2011	Matthew Stafford	QB	Detroit Lions
2012	Peyton Manning	QB	Denver Broncos
2013	Philip Rivers	QB	San Diego Chargers

*The award was shared in 2005.

AP COACH OF THE YEAR

1957	George Wilson	Detroit Lions
1958	Weeb Ewbank	Baltimore Colts
1959	Vince Lombardi	Green Bay Packers
1960	Buck Shaw	Philadelphia Eagles
1961	Allie Sherman	New York Giants
1962	Allie Sherman	New York Giants
1963	George Halas	Chicago Bears
1964	Don Shula	Baltimore Colts
1965	George Halas	Chicago Bears
1966	Tom Landry	Dallas Cowboys
1967*	George Allen	Los Angeles Rams
	Don Shula	Baltimore Colts
1968	Don Shula	Baltimore Colts
1969	Bud Grant	Minnesota Vikings
1970	Paul Brown	Cincinnati Bengals
1971	George Allen	Washington Redskins
1972	Don Shula	Miami Dolphins
1973	Chuck Knox	Los Angeles Rams
1974	Don Coryell	St. Louis Cardinals
1975	Ted Marchibroda	Baltimore Colts
1976	Forrest Gregg	Cleveland Browns
1977	Red Miller	Denver Broncos
1978	Jack Patera	Seattle Seahawks
1979	Jack Pardee	Washington Redskins
1980	Chuck Knox	Buffalo Bills
1981	Bill Walsh	San Francisco 49ers
1982	Joe Gibbs	Washington Redskins
1983	Joe Gibbs	Washington Redskins
1984	Chuck Knox	Seattle Seahawks
1985	Mike Ditka	Chicago Bears
1986	Bill Parcells	New York Giants
1987	Jim Mora	New Orleans Saints
1988	Mike Ditka	Chicago Bears
1989	Lindy Infante	Green Bay Packers
1990	Jimmy Johnson	Dallas Cowboys
1991	Wayne Fontes	Detroit Lions
1992	Bill Cowher	Pittsburgh Steelers
1993	Dan Reeves	New York Giants
1994	Bill Parcells	New England Patriots
1995	Ray Rhodes	Philadelphia Eagles
1996	Dom Capers	Carolina Panthers
1997	Jim Fassel	New York Giants
1998	Dan Reeves	Atlanta Falcons
1999	Dick Vermeil	St. Louis Rams
2000	Jim Haslett	New Orleans Saints
2001	Dick Jauron	Chicago Bears
2002	Andy Reid	Philadelphia Eagles
2003	Bill Belichick	New England Patriots
2004	Marty Schottenheimer	San Diego Chargers
2005	Lovie Smith	Chicago Bears
2006	Sean Payton	New Orleans Saints
2007	Bill Belichick	New England Patriots
2008	Mike Smith	Atlanta Falcons
2009	Marvin Lewis	Cincinnati Bengals
2010	Bill Belichick	New England Patriots
2011	Jim Harbaugh	San Francisco 49ers
2012	Bruce Arians	Indianapolis Colts
2013	Ron Rivera	Carolina Panthers

*The award was shared in 1967.

NUMBER-ONE DRAFT CHOICES

NUMBER-ONE DRAFT CHOICES

Season	Date	Team	Player	Position	College
2014	May 8-10	Houston	Jadeveon Clowney	DE	South Carolina
2013	April 25-27	Kansas City	Eric Fisher	T	Central Michigan
2012	April 26-28	Indianapolis	Andrew Luck	QB	Stanford
2011	April 28-30	Carolina	Cam Newton	QB	Auburn
2010	April 22-24	St. Louis	Sam Bradford	QB	Oklahoma
2009	April 25-26	Detroit	Matthew Stafford	QB	Georgia
2008	April 26-27	Miami	Jake Long	T	Michigan
2007	April 28-29	Oakland	JaMarcus Russell	QB	Louisiana State
2006	April 29-30	Houston	Mario Williams	DE	North Carolina State
2005	April 23-24	San Francisco	Alex Smith	QB	Utah
2004	April 24-25	San Diego	Eli Manning	QB	Mississippi
2003	April 26-27	Cincinnati	Carson Palmer	QB	Southern California
2002	April 20-21	Houston	David Carr	QB	Fresno State
2001	April 21-22	Atlanta	Michael Vick	QB	Virginia Tech
2000	April 15-16	Cleveland	Courtney Brown	DE	Penn State
1999	April 17-18	Cleveland	Tim Couch	QB	Kentucky
1998	April 18-19	Indianapolis	Peyton Manning	QB	Tennessee
1997	April 19-20	St. Louis	Orlando Pace	T	Ohio State
1996	April 20-21	New York Jets	Keyshawn Johnson	WR	Southern California
1995	April 22-23	Cincinnati	Ki-Jana Carter	RB	Penn State
1994	April 24-25	Cincinnati	Dan Wilkinson	DT	Ohio State
1993	April 25-26	New England	Drew Bledsoe	QB	Washington State
1992	April 26-27	Indianapolis	Steve Emtman	DT	Washington
1991	April 21-22	Dallas	Russell Maryland	DT	Miami
1990	April 22-23	Indianapolis	Jeff George	QB	Illinois
1989	April 23-24	Dallas	Troy Aikman	QB	UCLA
1988	April 24-25	Atlanta	Aundray Bruce	LB	Auburn
1987	April 28-29	Tampa Bay	Vinny Testaverde	QB	Miami
1986	April 29-30	Tampa Bay	Bo Jackson	RB	Auburn
1985	April 30-May 1	Buffalo	Bruce Smith	DE	Virginia Tech
1984	May 1-2	New England	Irving Fryar	WR	Nebraska
1983	April 26-27	Baltimore	John Elway	QB	Stanford
1982	April 27-28	New England	Kenneth Sims	DT	Texas
1981	April 28-29	New Orleans	George Rogers	RB	South Carolina
1980	April 29-30	Detroit	Billy Sims	RB	Oklahoma
1979	May 3-4	Buffalo	Tom Cousineau	LB	Ohio State
1978	May 2-3	Houston	Earl Campbell	RB	Texas
1977	May 3-4	Tampa Bay	Ricky Bell	RB	Southern California
1976	April 8-9	Tampa Bay	Lee Roy Selmon	DE	Oklahoma
1975	January 28-29	Atlanta	Steve Bartkowski	QB	California
1974	January 29-30	Dallas	Ed Jones	DE	Tennessee State
1973	January 30-31	Houston	John Matuszak	DE	Tampa
1972	February 1-2	Buffalo	Walt Patulski	DE	Notre Dame
1971	January 28-29	New England	Jim Plunkett	QB	Stanford
1970	January 27-28	Pittsburgh	Terry Bradshaw	QB	Louisiana Tech
1969	January 28-29	Buffalo (AFL)	O.J. Simpson	RB	Southern California
1968	January 30-31	Minnesota	Ron Yary	T	Southern California
1967	March 14	Baltimore	Bubba Smith	DT	Michigan State
1966	November 27, 1965	Atlanta	Tommy Nobis	LB	Texas
	November 28, 1965	Miami (AFL)	Jim Grabowski	RB	Illinois
1965	November 28, 1964	New York Giants	Tucker Frederickson	RB	Auburn
	November 28, 1964	Houston (AFL)	Lawrence Elkins	E	Baylor
1964	December 2, 1963	San Francisco	Dave Parks	E	Texas Tech
	November 30, 1963	Boston (AFL)	Jack Concannon	QB	Boston College
1963	December 3, 1962	Los Angeles	Terry Baker	QB	Oregon State
	December 1, 1962	Kansas City (AFL)	Buck Buchanan	DT	Grambling
1962	December 4, 1961	Washington	Ernie Davis	RB	Syracuse
	December 2, 1961	Oakland (AFL)	Roman Gabriel	QB	North Carolina State
1961	December 27-28, 1960	Minnesota	Tommy Mason	RB	Tulane
	November 23, 1960	Buffalo (AFL)	Ken Rice	G	Auburn

Season	Date	Team	Player	Position	College
1960	Secret Draft	Los Angeles	Billy Cannon	RB	Louisiana State
	November 22, December 2, 1959	(AFL had no formal first pick)			
1959	December 2, 1958	Green Bay	Randy Duncan	QB	Iowa
1958	December 2, 1957	Chicago Cardinals	King Hill	QB	Rice
1957	November 27, 1956	Green Bay	Paul Hornung	HB	Notre Dame
1956	November 29, 1955	Pittsburgh	Gary Glick	DB	Colorado A&M
1955	January 27-28	Baltimore	George Shaw	QB	Oregon
1954	January 28	Cleveland	Bobby Garrett	QB	Stanford
1953	January 22	San Francisco	Harry Babcock	E	Georgia
1952	January 17	Los Angeles	Bill Wade	QB	Vanderbilt
1951	January 18-19	New York Giants	Kyle Rote	HB	Southern Methodist
1950	January 21-22	Detroit	Leon Hart	E	Notre Dame
1949	December 21, 1948	Philadelphia	Chuck Bednarik	C	Pennsylvania
1948	December 19, 1947	Washington	Harry Gilmer	QB	Alabama
1947	December 16, 1946	Chicago Bears	Bob Fenimore	HB	Oklahoma A&M
1946	January 14	Boston	Frank Dancewicz	QB	Notre Dame
1945	April 6	Chicago Cardinals	Charley Trippi	HB	Georgia
1944	April 19	Boston	Angelo Bertelli	QB	Notre Dame
1943	April 8	Detroit	Frank Sinkwich	HB	Georgia
1942	December 22, 1941	Pittsburgh	Bill Dudley	HB	Virginia
1941	December 10, 1940	Chicago Bears	Tom Harmon	HB	Michigan
1940	December 9, 1939	Chicago Cardinals	George Cafego	HB	Tennessee
1939	December 8, 1938	Chicago Cardinals	Ki Aldrich	C	Texas Christian
1938	December 12, 1937	Cleveland	Corbett Davis	FB	Indiana
1937	December 12, 1936	Philadelphia	Sam Francis	FB	Nebraska
1936	February 8	Philadelphia	Jay Berwanger	HB	Chicago

Note: From 1947 through 1958, the first selection in the draft was a Bonus pick, awarded to the winner of a random draw. That club, in turn, forfeited its last-round draft choice. The winner of the Bonus choice was eliminated from future draws. The system was abolished after 1958, by which time all clubs had received a Bonus choice.

NUMBER-ONE DRAFT CHOICES BY POSITION

Quarterbacks:	31
Running Backs:	23
Defensive Linemen:	14
Offensive Linemen:	7
Wide Receivers:	6
Linebackers:	3
Defensive Backs:	1

NFL DRAFT, NUMBER OF ROUNDS

1936:	9
1937:	10
1938-1942:	22
1943-1948:	32
1949:	25
1950-59:	30
1960-66:	20
1967-1976:	17
1977-1992:	12
1993:	8
1994-2014:	7

FIRST-ROUND SELECTIONS

If club had no first-round selection, first player drafted is listed with round in parentheses.

ARIZONA CARDINALS
Year Player, College, Position
1936 Jim Lawrence, Texas Christian, B
1937 Ray Buivid, Marquette, B
1938 Jack Robbins, Arkansas, B
1939 Charles (Ki) Aldrich, TCU, C
1940 George Cafego, Tennessee, B
1941 John Kimbrough, Texas A&M, B
1942 Steve Lach, Duke, B
1943 Glenn Dobbs, Tulsa, B
1944 Pat Harder, Wisconsin, B
1945 Charley Trippi, Georgia, B
1946 Dub Jones, Louisiana State, B
1947 DeWitt (Tex) Coulter, Army, T
1948 Jim Spavital, Oklahoma A&M, B
1949 Bill Fischer, Notre Dame, G
1950 Jack Jennings, Ohio State, T (2)
1951 Jerry Groom, Notre Dame, C
1952 Ollie Matson, San Francisco, B
1953 Johnny Olszewski, California, B
1954 Lamar McHan, Arkansas, B
1955 Max Boydston, Oklahoma, E
1956 Joe Childress, Auburn, B
1957 Jerry Tubbs, Oklahoma, C
1958 King Hill, Rice, B
        John David Crow, Texas A&M, B
1959 Bill Stacy, Mississippi State, B
1960 George Izo, Notre Dame, QB
1961 Ken Rice, Auburn, T
1962 Fate Echols, Northwestern, DT
        Irv Goode, Kentucky, C
1963 Jerry Stovall, Louisiana State, S
        Don Brumm, Purdue, DE
1964 Ken Kortas, Louisville, DT
1965 Joe Namath, Alabama, QB
1966 Carl McAdams, Oklahoma, LB
1967 Dave Williams, Washington, WR
1968 MacArthur Lane, Utah State, RB
1969 Roger Wehrli, Missouri, DB
1970 Larry Stegent, Texas A&M, RB
1971 Norm Thompson, Utah, CB
1972 Ahmad Rashad, Oregon, RB-WR
1973 Dave Butz, Purdue, DT
1974 J.V. Cain, Colorado, TE
1975 Tim Gray, Texas A&M, DB
1976 Mike Dawson, Arizona, DT
1977 Steve Pisarkiewicz, Missouri, QB
1978 Steve Little, Arkansas, K
        Ken Greene, Washington State, DB
1979 Ottis Anderson, Miami, RB
1980 Curtis Greer, Michigan, DE
1981 E.J. Junior, Alabama, LB
1982 Luis Sharpe, UCLA, T
1983 Leonard Smith, McNeese St., DB
1984 Clyde Duncan, Tennessee, WR
1985 Freddie Joe Nunn, Mississippi, LB
1986 Anthony Bell, Michigan State, LB
1987 Kelly Stouffer, Colorado State, QB
1988 Ken Harvey, California, LB
1989 Eric Hill, Louisiana State, LB
        Joe Wolf, Boston College, G
1990 Anthony Thompson, Indiana, RB (2)
1991 Eric Swann, No College, DE
1992 Tony Sacca, Penn State, QB (2)
1993 Garrison Hearst, Georgia, RB
        Ernest Dye, South Carolina, T
1994 Jamir Miller, UCLA, LB

1995 Frank Sanders, Auburn, WR (2)
1996 Simeon Rice, Illinois, DE
1997 Tom Knight, Iowa, DB
1998 Andre Wadsworth, Florida St., DE
1999 David Boston, Ohio State, WR
        L.J. Shelton, Eastern Michigan, T
2000 Thomas Jones, Virginia, RB
2001 Leonard Davis, Texas, T
2002 Wendell Bryant, Wisconsin, DT
2003 Bryant Johnson, Penn State, WR
        Calvin Pace, Wake Forest, DE
2004 Larry Fitzgerald, Pittsburgh, WR
2005 Antrel Rolle, Miami, DB
2006 Matt Leinart, So. California, QB
2007 Levi Brown, Penn State, T
2008 Dominique Rodgers-Cromartie, Tenn. St., DB
2009 Beanie Wells, Ohio State, RB
2010 Dan Williams, Tennessee, DT
2011 Patrick Peterson, Louisiana St., DB
2012 Michael Floyd, Notre Dame, WR
2013 Jonathan Cooper, North Carolina, G
2014 Deone Bucannon, Washington St., DB

ATLANTA FALCONS
Year Player, College, Position
1966 Tommy Nobis, Texas, LB
        Randy Johnson, Texas A&I, QB
1967 Leo Carroll, San Diego St., DE (2)
1968 Claude Humphrey, Tennessee St., DE
1969 George Kunz, Notre Dame, T
1970 John Small, Citadel, LB
1971 Joe Profit, Northeast Louisiana, RB
1972 Clarence Ellis, Notre Dame, DB
1973 Greg Marx, Notre Dame, DT (2)
1974 Gerald Tinker, Kent State, WR (2)
1975 Steve Bartkowski, California, QB
1976 Bubba Bean, Texas A&M, RB
1977 Warren Bryant, Kentucky, T
        Wilson Faumuina, San Jose St., DT
1978 Mike Kenn, Michigan, T
1979 Don Smith, Miami, DE
1980 Junior Miller, Nebraska, TE
1981 Bobby Butler, Florida State, DB
1982 Gerald Riggs, Arizona State, RB
1983 Mike Pitts, Alabama, DE
1984 Rick Bryan, Oklahoma, DT
1985 Bill Fralic, Pittsburgh, T
1986 Tony Casillas, Oklahoma, NT
        Tim Green, Syracuse, LB
1987 Chris Miller, Oregon, QB
1988 Aundray Bruce, Auburn, LB
1989 Deion Sanders, Florida State, DB
        Shawn Collins, No. Arizona, WR
1990 Steve Broussard, Washington St., RB
1991 Bruce Pickens, Nebraska, DB
        Mike Pritchard, Colorado, WR
1992 Bob Whitfield, Stanford, T
        Tony Smith, So. Mississippi, RB
1993 Lincoln Kennedy, Washington, T
1994 Bert Emanuel, Rice, WR (2)
1995 Devin Bush, Florida State, DB
1996 Shannon Brown, Alabama, DT (3)
1997 Michael Booker, Nebraska, DB
1998 Keith Brooking, Georgia Tech, LB
1999 Patrick Kerney, Virginia, DE
2000 Travis Claridge, So. California, T (2)
2001 Michael Vick, Virginia Tech, QB
2002 T.J. Duckett, Michigan State, RB
2003 Bryan Scott, Penn State, DB (2)
2004 DeAngelo Hall, Virginia Tech, DB
        Michael Jenkins, Ohio State, WR
2005 Roddy White, Ala.-Birmingham, WR

2006 Jimmy Williams, Virginia Tech, DB (2)
2007 Jamaal Anderson, Arkansas, DE
2008 Matt Ryan, Boston College, QB
        Sam Baker, So. California, T
2009 Peria Jerry, Mississippi, DT
2010 Sean Weatherspoon, Missouri, LB
2011 Julio Jones, Alabama, WR
2012 Peter Konz, Wisconsin, G (2)
2013 Desmond Trufant, Washington, DB
2014 Jake Matthews, Texas A&M, T

BALTIMORE RAVENS
Year Player, College, Position
1996 Jonathan Ogden, UCLA, T
        Ray Lewis, Miami, LB
1997 Peter Boulware, Florida State, DE
1998 Duane Starks, Miami, DB
1999 Chris McAlister, Arizona, DB
2000 Jamal Lewis, Tennessee, RB
        Travis Taylor, Florida, WR
2001 Todd Heap, Arizona State, TE
2002 Ed Reed, Miami, DB
2003 Terrell Suggs, Arizona State, DE
        Kyle Boller, California, QB
2004 Dwan Edwards, Oregon St., DT (2)
2005 Mark Clayton, Oklahoma, WR
2006 Haloti Ngata, Oregon, DT
2007 Ben Grubbs, Auburn, G
2008 Joe Flacco, Delaware, QB
2009 Michael Oher, Mississippi, T
2010 Sergio Kindle, Texas, LB (2)
2011 Jimmy Smith, Colorado, DB
2012 Courtney Upshaw, Alabama, LB (2)
2013 Matt Elam, Florida, DB
2014 C.J. Mosley, Alabama, LB

BUFFALO BILLS
Year Player, College, Position
1960 Richie Lucas, Penn State, QB
1961 Ken Rice, Auburn, T
1962 Ernie Davis, Syracuse, RB
1963 Dave Behrman, Michigan State, C
1964 Carl Eller, Minnesota, DE
1965 Jim Davidson, Ohio State, T
1966 Mike Dennis, Mississippi, RB
1967 John Pitts, Arizona State, S
1968 Haven Moses, San Diego St., WR
1969 O.J. Simpson, So. California, RB
1970 Al Cowlings, So. California, DE
1971 J.D. Hill, Arizona State, WR
1972 Walt Patulski, Notre Dame, DE
1973 Paul Seymour, Michigan, TE
        Joe DeLamielleure, Michigan St., G
1974 Reuben Gant, Oklahoma State, TE
1975 Tom Ruud, Nebraska, LB
1976 Mario Clark, Oregon, DB
1977 Phil Dokes, Oklahoma State, DT
1978 Terry Miller, Oklahoma State, RB
1979 Tom Cousineau, Ohio State, LB
        Jerry Butler, Clemson, WR
1980 Jim Ritcher, North Carolina St., C
1981 Booker Moore, Penn State, RB
1982 Perry Tuttle, Clemson, WR
1983 Tony Hunter, Notre Dame, TE
        Jim Kelly, Miami, QB
1984 Greg Bell, Notre Dame, RB
1985 Bruce Smith, Virginia Tech, DE
        Derrick Burroughs, Memphis St., DB
1986 Ronnie Harmon, Iowa, RB
        Will Wolford, Vanderbilt, T
1987 Shane Conlan, Penn State, LB
1988 Thurman Thomas, Oklahoma St., RB (2)

1989 Don Beebe, Chadron, Neb., WR (3)	1947 Bob Fenimore, Oklahoma State, B	2005 Cedric Benson, Texas, RB
1990 James Williams, Fresno State, DB	Don Kindt, Wisconsin, B	2006 Danieal Manning, Abilene Christian, DB (2)
1991 Henry Jones, Illinois, DB	1948 Bobby Layne, Texas, QB	2007 Greg Olsen, Miami, TE
1992 John Fina, Arizona, T	Max Bumgardner, Texas, E	2008 Chris Williams, Vanderbilt, T
1993 Thomas Smith, North Carolina, DB	1949 Dick Harris, Texas, C	2009 Jarron Gilbert, San Jose State, DT (3)
1994 Jeff Burris, Notre Dame, DB	1950 Chuck Hunsinger, Florida, B	2010 Major Wright, Florida, DB (3)
1995 Ruben Brown, Pittsburgh, G	Fred Morrison, Ohio State, B	2011 Gabe Carimi, Wisconsin, T
1996 Eric Moulds, Mississippi St., WR	1951 Bob Williams, Notre Dame, B	2012 Shea McClellin, Boise State, DE
1997 Antowain Smith, Houston, RB	Billy Stone, Bradley, B	2013 Kyle Long, Oregon, G
1998 Sam Cowart, Florida State, LB (2)	Gene Schroeder, Virginia, E	2014 Kyle Fuller, Virginia Tech, DB
1999 Antoine Winfield, Ohio State, DB	1952 Jim Dooley, Miami, B	
2000 Erik Flowers, Arizona State, DE	1953 Billy Anderson, Compton (Calif.) J.C., B	**CINCINNATI BENGALS**
2001 Nate Clements, Ohio State, DB	1954 Stan Wallace, Illinois, B	**Year Player, College, Position**
2002 Mike Williams, Texas, T	1955 Ron Drzewiecki, Marquette, B	1968 Bob Johnson, Tennessee, C
2003 Willis McGahee, Miami, RB	1956 Menan (Tex) Schriewer, Texas, E	1969 Greg Cook, Cincinnati, QB
2004 Lee Evans, Wisconsin, WR	1957 Earl Leggett, Louisiana State, T	1970 Mike Reid, Penn State, DT
J.P. Losman, Tulane, QB	1958 Chuck Howley, West Virginia, G	1971 Vernon Holland, Tennessee St., T
2005 Roscoe Parrish, Miami, WR (2)	1959 Don Clark, Ohio State, B	1972 Sherman White, California, DE
2006 Donte' Whitner, Ohio State, DB	1960 Roger Davis, Syracuse, G	1973 Isaac Curtis, San Diego State, WR
John McCargo, North Carolina St., DT	1961 Mike Ditka, Pittsburgh, E	1974 Bill Kollar, Montana State, DT
2007 Marshawn Lynch, California, RB	1962 Ronnie Bull, Baylor, RB	1975 Glenn Cameron, Florida, LB
2008 Leodis McKelvin, Troy, DB	1963 Dave Behrman, Michigan State, C	1976 Billy Brooks, Oklahoma, WR
2009 Aaron Maybin, Penn State, DE	1964 Dick Evey, Tennessee, DT	Archie Griffin, Ohio State, RB
Eric Wood, Louisville, C	1965 Dick Butkus, Illinois, LB	1977 Eddie Edwards, Miami, DT
2010 C.J. Spiller, Clemson, RB	Gale Sayers, Kansas, RB	Wilson Whitley, Houston, DT
2011 Marcell Dareus, Alabama, DT	Steve DeLong, Tennessee, T	Mike Cobb, Michigan State, TE
2012 Stephon Gilmore, South Carolina, DB	1966 George Rice, Louisiana State, DT	1978 Ross Browner, Notre Dame, DT
2013 E.J. Manuel, Florida State, QB	1967 Loyd Phillips, Arkansas, DE	Blair Bush, Washington, C
2014 Sammy Watkins, Clemson, WR	1968 Mike Hull, Southern California, RB	1979 Jack Thompson, Washington St., QB
	1969 Rufus Mayes, Ohio State, T	Charles Alexander, Louisiana St., RB
CAROLINA PANTHERS	1970 George Farmer, UCLA, WR (3)	1980 Anthony Muñoz, So. California, T
Year Player, College, Position	1971 Joe Moore, Missouri, RB	1981 David Verser, Kansas, WR
1995 Kerry Collins, Penn State, QB	1972 Lionel Antoine, Southern Illinois, T	1982 Glen Collins, Mississippi State, DE
Tyrone Poole, Ft. Valley State, DB	Craig Clemons, Iowa, DB	1983 Dave Rimington, Nebraska, C
Blake Brockermeyer, Texas, T	1973 Wally Chambers, Eastern Kentucky, DE	1984 Ricky Hunley, Arizona, LB
1996 Tim Biakabutuka, Michigan, RB	1974 Waymond Bryant, Tennessee St., LB	Pete Koch, Maryland, DE
1997 Rae Carruth, Colorado, WR	Dave Gallagher, Michigan, DT	Brian Blados, North Carolina, T
1998 Jason Peter, Nebraska, DT	1975 Walter Payton, Jackson State, RB	1985 Eddie Brown, Miami, WR
1999 Chris Terry, Georgia, T (2)	1976 Dennis Lick, Wisconsin, T	Emanuel King, Alabama, LB
2000 Rashard Anderson, Jackson St., DB	1977 Ted Albrecht, California, T	1986 Joe Kelly, Washington, LB
2001 Dan Morgan, Miami, LB	1978 Brad Shearer, Texas, DT (3)	Tim McGee, Tennessee, WR
2002 Julius Peppers, North Carolina, DE	1979 Dan Hampton, Arkansas, DT	1987 Jason Buck, Brigham Young, DE
2003 Jordan Gross, Utah, T	Al Harris, Arizona State, DE	1988 Rickey Dixon, Oklahoma, DB
2004 Chris Gamble, Ohio State, DB	1980 Otis Wilson, Louisville, LB	1989 Eric Ball, UCLA, RB (2)
2005 Thomas Davis, Georgia, DB	1981 Keith Van Horne, So. California, T	1990 James Francis, Baylor, LB
2006 DeAngelo Williams, Memphis, RB	1982 Jim McMahon, Brigham Young, QB	1991 Alfred Williams, Colorado, LB
2007 Jon Beason, Miami, LB	1983 Jim Covert, Pittsburgh, T	1992 David Klingler, Houston, QB
2008 Jonathan Stewart, Oregon, RB	Willie Gault, Tennessee, WR	Darryl Williams, Miami, DB
Jeff Otah, Pittsburgh, T	1984 Wilber Marshall, Florida, LB	1993 John Copeland, Alabama, DE
2009 Everette Brown, Florida St., DE (2)	1985 William Perry, Clemson, DT	1994 Dan Wilkinson, Ohio State, DT
2010 Jimmy Clausen, Notre Dame, QB (2)	1986 Neal Anderson, Florida, RB	1995 Ki-Jana Carter, Penn State, RB
2011 Cam Newton, Auburn, QB	1987 Jim Harbaugh, Michigan, QB	1996 Willie Anderson, Auburn, T
2012 Luke Kuechly, Boston College, LB	1988 Brad Muster, Stanford, RB	1997 Reinard Wilson, Florida State, LB
2013 Star Lotulelei, Utah, DT	Wendell Davis, Louisiana St., WR	1998 Takeo Spikes, Auburn, LB
2014 Kelvin Benjamin, Florida State, WR	1989 Donnell Woolford, Clemson, DB	Brian Simmons, North Carolina, LB
	Trace Armstrong, Florida, DE	1999 Akili Smith, Oregon, QB
CHICAGO BEARS	1990 Mark Carrier, So. California, DB	2000 Peter Warrick, Florida State, WR
Year Player, College, Position	1991 Stan Thomas, Texas, T	2001 Justin Smith, Missouri, DE
1936 Joe Stydahar, West Virginia, T	1992 Alonzo Spellman, Ohio State, DE	2002 Levi Jones, Arizona State, T
1937 Les McDonald, Nebraska, E	1993 Curtis Conway, So. California, WR	2003 Carson Palmer, Southern California, QB
1938 Joe Gray, Oregon State, B	1994 John Thierry, Alcorn State, DE	2004 Chris Perry, Michigan, RB
1939 Sid Luckman, Columbia, QB	1995 Rashaan Salaam, Colorado, RB	2005 David Pollack, Georgia, LB
Bill Osmanski, Holy Cross, B	1996 Walt Harris, Mississippi State, DB	2006 Johnathan Joseph, South Carolina, DB
1940 Clyde (Bulldog) Turner, Hardin-Simmons, C	1997 John Allred, So. California, TE (2)	2007 Leon Hall, Michigan, DB
1941 Tom Harmon, Michigan, B	1998 Curtis Enis, Penn State, RB	2008 Keith Rivers, So. California, LB
Norm Standlee, Stanford, B	1999 Cade McNown, UCLA, QB	2009 Andre Smith, Alabama, T
Don Scott, Ohio State, B	2000 Brian Urlacher, New Mexico, LB	2010 Jermaine Gresham, Oklahoma, TE
1942 Frankie Albert, Stanford, B	2001 David Terrell, Michigan, WR	2011 A.J. Green, Georgia, WR
1943 Bob Steber, Missouri, B	2002 Marc Colombo, Boston College, T	2012 Dre Kirkpatrick, Alabama, DB
1944 Ray Evans, Kansas, B	2003 Michael Haynes, Penn State, DE	Kevin Zeitler, Wisconsin, G
1945 Don Lund, Michigan, B	Rex Grossman, Florida, QB	2013 Tyler Eifert, Notre Dame, TE
1946 Johnny Lujack, Notre Dame, QB	2004 Tommie Harris, Oklahoma, DT	2014 Darqueze Dennard, Michigan St., DB

FIRST-ROUND SELECTIONS

CLEVELAND BROWNS

Year	Player, College, Position
1950	Ken Carpenter, Oregon State, B
1951	Ken Konz, Louisiana State, B
1952	Bert Rechichar, Tennessee, DB
	Harry Agganis, Boston U., QB
1953	Doug Atkins, Tennessee, DE
1954	Bobby Garrett, Stanford, QB
	John Bauer, Illinois, G
1955	Kurt Burris, Oklahoma, C
1956	Preston Carpenter, Arkansas, B
1957	Jim Brown, Syracuse, RB
1958	Jim Shofner, Texas Christian, DB
1959	Rich Kreitling, Illinois, DE
1960	Jim Houston, Ohio State, DE
1961	Bobby Crespino, Mississippi, TE
1962	Gary Collins, Maryland, WR
	Leroy Jackson, Western Illinois, RB
1963	Tom Hutchinson, Kentucky, WR
1964	Paul Warfield, Ohio State, WR
1965	James Garcia, Purdue, T (2)
1966	Milt Morin, Massachusetts, TE
1967	Bob Matheson, Duke, LB
1968	Marvin Upshaw, Trinity, Tex., DT-DE
1969	Ron Johnson, Michigan, RB
1970	Mike Phipps, Purdue, QB
	Bob McKay, Texas, T
1971	Clarence Scott, Kansas State, CB
1972	Thom Darden, Michigan, DB
1973	Steve Holden, Arizona State, WR
	Pete Adams, Southern California, T
1974	Billy Corbett, Johnson C. Smith, T (2)
1975	Mack Mitchell, Houston, DE
1976	Mike Pruitt, Purdue, RB
1977	Robert Jackson, Texas A&M, LB
1978	Clay Matthews, So. California, LB
	Ozzie Newsome, Alabama, TE
1979	Willis Adams, Houston, WR
1980	Charles White, So. California, RB
1981	Hanford Dixon, So. Mississippi, DB
1982	Chip Banks, So. California, LB
1983	Ron Brown, Arizona State, WR (2)
1984	Don Rogers, UCLA, DB
1985	Greg Allen, Florida State, RB (2)
1986	Webster Slaughter, San Diego St., WR (2)
1987	Mike Junkin, Duke, LB
1988	Clifford Charlton, Florida, LB
1989	Eric Metcalf, Texas, RB
1990	Leroy Hoard, Michigan, RB (2)
1991	Eric Turner, UCLA, DB
1992	Tommy Vardell, Stanford, RB
1993	Steve Everitt, Michigan, C
1994	Antonio Langham, Alabama, DB
	Derrick Alexander, Michigan, WR
1995	Craig Powell, Ohio State, LB
1999	Tim Couch, Kentucky, QB
2000	Courtney Brown, Penn State, DE
2001	Gerard Warren, Florida, DT
2002	William Green, Boston College, RB
2003	Jeff Faine, Norte Dame, C
2004	Kellen Winslow, Miami, TE
2005	Braylon Edwards, Michigan, WR
2006	Kamerion Wimbley, Florida St., DE
2007	Joe Thomas, Wisconsin, T
	Brady Quinn, Notre Dame, QB
2008	Beau Bell, Nevada-Las Vegas, LB (4)
2009	Alex Mack, California, C
2010	Joe Haden, Florida, DB
2011	Phil Taylor, Baylor, DT
2012	Trent Richardson, Alabama, RB
	Brandon Weeden, Oklahoma St., QB
2013	Barkevious Mingo, Louisiana St., DE

2014	Justin Gilbert, Oklahoma St., DB
	Johnny Manziel, Texas A&M, QB

DALLAS COWBOYS

Year	Player, College, Position
1960	None
1961	Bob Lilly, Texas Christian, DT
1962	Sonny Gibbs, TCU, QB (2)
1963	Lee Roy Jordan, Alabama, LB
1964	Scott Appleton, Texas, DT
1965	Craig Morton, California, QB
1966	John Niland, Iowa, G
1967	Phil Clark, Northwestern, DB (3)
1968	Dennis Homan, Alabama, WR
1969	Calvin Hill, Yale, RB
1970	Duane Thomas, West Texas St., RB
1971	Tody Smith, So. California, DE
1972	Bill Thomas, Boston College, RB
1973	Billy Joe DuPree, Michigan St., TE
1974	Ed (Too Tall) Jones, Tennessee St., DE
	Charley Young, North Carolina St., RB
1975	Randy White, Maryland, LB
	Thomas Henderson, Langston, LB
1976	Aaron Kyle, Wyoming, DB
1977	Tony Dorsett, Pittsburgh, RB
1978	Larry Bethea, Michigan State, DE
1979	Robert Shaw, Tennessee, C
1980	Bill Roe, Colorado, LB (3)
1981	Howard Richards, Missouri, T
1982	Rod Hill, Kentucky State, DB
1983	Jim Jeffcoat, Arizona State, DE
1984	Billy Cannon, Jr., Texas A&M, LB
1985	Kevin Brooks, Michigan, DE
1986	Mike Sherrard, UCLA, WR
1987	Danny Noonan, Nebraska, DT
1988	Michael Irvin, Miami, WR
1989	Troy Aikman, UCLA, QB
1990	Emmitt Smith, Florida, RB
1991	Russell Maryland, Miami, DT
	Alvin Harper, Tennessee, WR
	Kelvin Pritchett, Mississippi, DT
1992	Kevin Smith, Texas A&M, DB
	Robert Jones, East Carolina, LB
1993	Kevin Williams, Miami, WR (2)
1994	Shante Carver, Arizona State, DE
1995	Sherman Williams, Alabama, RB (2)
1996	Kavika Pittman, McNeese St., DE (2)
1997	David LaFleur, Louisiana State, TE
1998	Greg Ellis, North Carolina, DE
1999	Ebenezer Ekuban, North Carolina, DE
2000	Dwayne Goodrich, Tennessee, DB (2)
2001	Quincy Carter, Georgia, QB (2)
2002	Roy Williams, Oklahoma, DB
2003	Terence Newman, Kansas State, DB
2004	Julius Jones, Notre Dame, RB (2)
2005	DeMarcus Ware, Troy, DE
	Marcus Spears, Louisiana St., DE
2006	Bobby Carpenter, Ohio State, LB
2007	Anthony Spencer, Purdue, LB
2008	Felix Jones, Arkansas, RB
	Mike Jenkins, South Florida, DB
2009	Jason Williams, Western Illinois, LB (3)
2010	Dez Bryant, Oklahoma State, WR
2011	Tyron Smith, Southern California, T
2012	Morris Claiborne, Louisiana St., DB
2013	Travis Frederick, Wisconsin, C
2014	Zack Martin, Notre Dame, G

DENVER BRONCOS

Year	Player, College, Position
1960	Roger LeClerc, Trinity, Conn., C
1961	Bob Gaiters, New Mexico St., RB

1962	Merlin Olsen, Utah State, DT
1963	Kermit Alexander, UCLA, CB
1964	Bob Brown, Nebraska, T
1965	Dick Butkus, Illinois, LB (2)
1966	Jerry Shay, Purdue, DT
1967	Floyd Little, Syracuse, RB
1968	Curley Culp, Arizona State, DE (2)
1969	Grady Cavness, Texas-El Paso, DB (2)
1970	Bob Anderson, Colorado, RB
1971	Marv Montgomery, So. California, T
1972	Riley Odoms, Houston, TE
1973	Otis Armstrong, Purdue, RB
1974	Randy Gradishar, Ohio State, LB
1975	Louis Wright, San Jose State, DB
1976	Tom Glassic, Virginia, G
1977	Steve Schindler, Boston College, G
1978	Don Latimer, Miami, DT
1979	Kelvin Clark, Nebraska, T
1980	Rulon Jones, Utah State, DE (2)
1981	Dennis Smith, So. California, DB
1982	Gerald Willhite, San Jose St., RB
1983	Chris Hinton, Northwestern, G
1984	Andre Townsend, Mississippi, DE (2)
1985	Steve Sewell, Oklahoma, RB
1986	Jim Juriga, Illinois, T (4)
1987	Ricky Nattiel, Florida, WR
1988	Ted Gregory, Syracuse, NT
1989	Steve Atwater, Arkansas, DB
1990	Alton Montgomery, Houston, DB (2)
1991	Mike Croel, Nebraska, LB
1992	Tommy Maddox, UCLA, QB
1993	Dan Williams, Toledo, DE
1994	Allen Aldridge, Houston, LB (2)
1995	Jamie Brown, Florida A&M, T (4)
1996	John Mobley, Kutztown, LB
1997	Trevor Pryce, Clemson, DT
1998	Marcus Nash, Tennessee, WR
1999	Al Wilson, Tennessee, LB
2000	Deltha O'Neal, California, DB
2001	Willie Middlebrooks, Minnesota, DB
2002	Ashley Lelie, Hawaii, WR
2003	George Foster, Georgia, T
2004	D.J. Williams, Miami, LB
2005	Darrent Williams, Oklahoma St., DB (2)
2006	Jay Cutler, Vanderbilt, QB
2007	Jarvis Moss, Florida, DE
2008	Ryan Clady, Boise State, T
2009	Knowshon Moreno, Georgia, RB
	Robert Ayers, Tennessee, DE
2010	Demaryius Thomas, Georgia Tech, WR
	Tim Tebow, Florida, QB
2011	Von Miller, Texas A&M, LB
2012	Derek Wolfe, Cincinnati, DT (2)
2013	Sylvester Williams, North Carolina, DT
2014	Bradley Roby, Ohio State, DB

DETROIT LIONS

Year	Player, College, Position
1936	Sid Wagner, Michigan State, G
1937	Lloyd Cardwell, Nebraska, B
1938	Alex Wojciechowicz, Fordham, C
1939	John Pingel, Michigan State, B
1940	Doyle Nave, Southern California, B
1941	Jim Thomason, Texas A&M, B
1942	Bob Westfall, Michigan, B
1943	Frank Sinkwich, Georgia, B
1944	Otto Graham, Northwestern, B
1945	Frank Szymanski, Notre Dame, C
1946	Bill Dellastatious, Missouri, B
1947	Glenn Davis, Army, B
1948	Y.A. Tittle, Louisiana State, B
1949	John Rauch, Georgia, B

1950 Leon Hart, Notre Dame, E
     Joe Watson, Rice, C
1951 Dick Stanfel, San Francisco, G (2)
1952 Yale Lary, Texas A&M, B (3)
1953 Harley Sewell, Texas, G
1954 Dick Chapman, Rice, T
1955 Dave Middleton, Auburn, B
1956 Hopalong Cassady, Ohio State, B
1957 Bill Glass, Baylor, G
1958 Alex Karras, Iowa, T
1959 Nick Pietrosante, Notre Dame, B
1960 John Robinson, Louisiana State, S
1961 Danny LaRose, Missouri, T (2)
1962 John Hadl, Kansas, QB
1963 Daryl Sanders, Ohio State, T
1964 Pete Beathard, So. California, QB
1965 Tom Nowatzke, Indiana, RB
1966 Nick Eddy, Notre Dame, RB (2)
1967 Mel Farr, UCLA, RB
1968 Greg Landry, Massachusetts, QB
     Earl McCullouch, So. California, WR
1969 Altie Taylor, Utah State, RB (2)
1970 Steve Owens, Oklahoma, RB
1971 Bob Bell, Cincinnati, DT
1972 Herb Orvis, Colorado, DE
1973 Ernie Price, Texas A&I, DE
1974 Ed O'Neil, Penn State, LB
1975 Lynn Boden, South Dakota St., G
1976 James Hunter, Grambling, DB
     Lawrence Gaines, Wyoming, RB
1977 Walt Williams, New Mexico St., DB (2)
1978 Luther Bradley, Notre Dame, DB
1979 Keith Dorney, Penn State, T
1980 Billy Sims, Oklahoma, RB
1981 Mark Nichols, San Jose State, WR
1982 Jimmy Williams, Nebraska, LB
1983 James Jones, Florida, RB
1984 David Lewis, California, TE
1985 Lomas Brown, Florida, T
1986 Chuck Long, Iowa, QB
1987 Reggie Rogers, Washington, DE
1988 Bennie Blades, Miami, DB
1989 Barry Sanders, Oklahoma St., RB
1990 Andre Ware, Houston, QB
1991 Herman Moore, Virginia, WR
1992 Robert Porcher, South Carolina St., DE
1993 Ryan McNeil, Miami, DB (2)
1994 Johnnie Morton, So. California, WR
1995 Luther Elliss, Utah, DT
1996 Reggie Brown, Texas A&M, LB
     Jeff Hartings, Penn State, G
1997 Bryant Westbrook, Texas, DB
1998 Terry Fair, Tennessee, DB
1999 Chris Claiborne, So. California, LB
     Aaron Gibson, Wisconsin, T
2000 Stockar McDougle, Oklahoma, T
2001 Jeff Backus, Michigan, T
2002 Joey Harrington, Oregon, QB
2003 Charles Rogers, Michigan State, WR
2004 Roy Williams, Texas, WR
     Kevin Jones, Virginia Tech, RB
2005 Mike Williams, So. California, WR
2006 Ernie Sims, Florida State, LB
2007 Calvin Johnson, Georgia Tech, WR
2008 Gosder Cherilus, Boson College, T
2009 Matthew Stafford, Georgia, QB
     Brandon Pettigrew, Oklahoma St., TE
2010 Ndamukong Suh, Nebraska, DT
     Jahvid Best, California, RB
2011 Nick Fairley, Auburn, DT
2012 Riley Reiff, Iowa, T
2013 Ezekiel Ansah, Brigham Young, DE

2014 Eric Ebron, North Carolina, TE

GREEN BAY PACKERS
Year Player, College, Position
1936 Russ Letlow, San Francisco, G
1937 Eddie Jankowski, Wisconsin, B
1938 Cecil Isbell, Purdue, B
1939 Larry Buhler, Minnesota, B
1940 Harold Van Every, Minnesota, B
1941 George Paskvan, Wisconsin, B
1942 Urban Odson, Minnesota, T
1943 Dick Wildung, Minnesota, T
1944 Merv Pregulman, Michigan, G
1945 Walt Schlinkman, Texas Tech, B
1946 Johnny Strzykalski, Marquette, B
1947 Ernie Case, UCLA, B
1948 Earl (Jug) Girard, Wisconsin, B
1949 Stan Heath, Nevada, B
1950 Clayton Tonnemaker, Minnesota, C
1951 Bob Gain, Kentucky, T
1952 Babe Parilli, Kentucky, QB
1953 Al Carmichael, So. California, B
1954 Art Hunter, Notre Dame, T
     Veryl Switzer, Kansas State, B
1955 Tom Bettis, Purdue, G
1956 Jack Losch, Miami, B
1957 Paul Hornung, Notre Dame, B
     Ron Kramer, Michigan, E
1958 Dan Currie, Michigan State, C
1959 Randy Duncan, Iowa, B
1960 Tom Moore, Vanderbilt, RB
1961 Herb Adderley, Michigan State, CB
1962 Earl Gros, Louisiana State, RB
1963 Dave Robinson, Penn State, LB
1964 Lloyd Voss, Nebraska, DT
1965 Donny Anderson, Texas Tech, RB
     Lawrence Elkins, Baylor, E
1966 Jim Grabowski, Illinois, RB
     Gale Gillingham, Minnesota, T
1967 Bob Hyland, Boston College, C
     Don Horn, San Diego State, QB
1968 Fred Carr, Texas-El Paso, LB
     Bill Lueck, Arizona, G
1969 Rich Moore, Villanova, DT
1970 Mike McCoy, Notre Dame, DT
     Rich McGeorge, Elon, TE
1971 John Brockington, Ohio State, RB
1972 Willie Buchanon, San Diego St., DB
     Jerry Tagge, Nebraska, QB
1973 Barry Smith, Florida State, WR
1974 Barty Smith, Richmond, RB
1975 Bill Bain, So. California, G (2)
1976 Mark Koncar, Colorado, T
1977 Mike Butler, Kansas, DE
     Ezra Johnson, Morris Brown, DE
1978 James Lofton, Stanford, WR
     John Anderson, Michigan, LB
1979 Eddie Lee Ivery, Georgia Tech, RB
1980 Bruce Clark, Penn State, DE
     George Cumby, Oklahoma, LB
1981 Rich Campbell, California, QB
1982 Ron Hallstrom, Iowa, G
1983 Tim Lewis, Pittsburgh, DB
1984 Alphonso Carreker, Florida St., DE
1985 Ken Ruettgers, So. California, T
1986 Kenneth Davis, TCU, RB (2)
1987 Brent Fullwood, Auburn, RB
1988 Sterling Sharpe, South Carolina, WR
1989 Tony Mandarich, Michigan State, T
1990 Tony Bennett, Mississippi, LB
     Darrell Thompson, Minnesota, RB
1991 Vinnie Clark, Ohio State, DB

1992 Terrell Buckley, Florida State, DB
1993 Wayne Simmons, Clemson, LB
     George Teague, Alabama, DB
1994 Aaron Taylor, Notre Dame, T
1995 Craig Newsome, Arizona State, DB
1996 John Michels, Southern California, T
1997 Ross Verba, Iowa, T
1998 Vonnie Holliday, North Carolina, DT
1999 Antuan Edwards, Clemson, DB
2000 Bubba Franks, Miami, TE
2001 Jamal Reynolds, Florida State, DE
2002 Javon Walker, Florida State, WR
2003 Nick Barnett, Oregon State, LB
2004 Ahmad Carroll, Arkansas, DB
2005 Aaron Rodgers, California, QB
2006 A.J. Hawk, Ohio State, LB
2007 Justin Harrell, Tennessee, DT
2008 Jordy Nelson, Kansas State, WR (2)
2009 B.J. Raji, Boston College, DT
     Clay Matthews, So. California, LB
2010 Bryan Bulaga, Iowa, T
2011 Derek Sherrod, Mississippi State, T
2012 Nick Perry, Southern California, LB
2013 Datone Jones, UCLA, DE
2014 Ha Ha Clinton-Dix, Alabama, DB

HOUSTON TEXANS
Year Player, College, Position
2002 David Carr, Fresno State, QB
2003 Andre Johnson, Miami, WR
2004 Dunta Robinson, South Carolina, DB
     Jason Babin, Western Michigan, LB
2005 Travis Johnson, Florida State, DE
2006 Mario Williams, North Carolina St., DE
2007 Amobi Okoye, Louisville, DT
2008 Duane Brown, Virginia Tech, T
2009 Brian Cushing, So. California, LB
2010 Kareem Jackson, Alabama, DB
2011 J.J. Watt, Wisconsin, DE
2012 Whitney Mercilus, Illinois, LB
2013 DeAndre Hopkins, Clemson, WR
2014 Jadeveon Clowney, South Carolina, DE

INDIANAPOLIS COLTS
Year Player, College, Position
1953 Billy Vessels, Oklahoma, B
1954 Cotton Davidson, Baylor, B
1955 George Shaw, Oregon, B
     Alan Ameche, Wisconsin, FB
1956 Lenny Moore, Penn State, B
1957 Jim Parker, Ohio State, G
1958 Lenny Lyles, Louisville, B
1959 Jackie Burkett, Auburn, C
1960 Ron Mix, Southern California, T
1961 Tom Matte, Ohio State, RB
1962 Wendell Harris, Louisiana State, S
1963 Bob Vogel, Ohio State, T
1964 Marv Woodson, Indiana, CB
1965 Mike Curtis, Duke, LB
1966 Sam Ball, Kentucky, T
1967 Bubba Smith, Michigan State, DT
     Jim Detwiler, Michigan, RB
1968 John Williams, Minnesota, G
1969 Eddie Hinton, Oklahoma, WR
1970 Norman Bulaich, Texas Christian, RB
1971 Don McCauley, North Carolina, RB
     Leonard Dunlap, North Texas St., DB
1972 Tom Drougas, Oregon, T
1973 Bert Jones, Louisiana State, QB
     Joe Ehrmann, Syracuse, DT
1974 John Dutton, Nebraska, DE
     Roger Carr, Louisiana Tech, WR

1975 Ken Huff, North Carolina, G
1976 Ken Novak, Purdue, DT
1977 Randy Burke, Kentucky, WR
1978 Reese McCall, Auburn, TE
1979 Barry Krauss, Alabama, LB
1980 Curtis Dickey, Texas A&M, RB
     Derrick Hatchett, Texas, DB
1981 Randy McMillan, Pittsburgh, RB
     Donnell Thompson, North Carolina, DT
1982 Johnie Cooks, Mississippi St., LB
     Art Schlichter, Ohio State, QB
1983 John Elway, Stanford, QB
1984 Leonard Coleman, Vanderbilt, DB
     Ron Solt, Maryland, G
1985 Duane Bickett, So. California, LB
1986 Jon Hand, Alabama, DE
1987 Cornelius Bennett, Alabama, LB
1988 Chris Chandler, Washington, QB (3)
1989 Andre Rison, Michigan State, WR
1990 Jeff George, Illinois, QB
1991 Shane Curry, Miami, DE (2)
1992 Steve Emtman, Washington, DT
     Quentin Coryatt, Texas A&M, LB
1993 Sean Dawkins, California, WR
1994 Marshall Faulk, San Diego St., RB
     Trev Alberts, Nebraska, LB
1995 Ellis Johnson, Florida, DT
1996 Marvin Harrison, Syracuse, WR
1997 Tarik Glenn, California, T
1998 Peyton Manning, Tennessee, QB
1999 Edgerrin James, Miami, RB
2000 Rob Morris, Brigham Young, LB
2001 Reggie Wayne, Miami, WR
2002 Dwight Freeney, Syracuse, DE
2003 Dallas Clark, Iowa, TE
2004 Bob Sanders, Iowa, DB (2)
2005 Marlin Jackson, Michigan, DB
2006 Joseph Addai, Louisiana State, RB
2007 Anthony Gonzalez, Ohio State, WR
2008 Mike Pollak, Arizona State, G (2)
2009 Donald Brown, Connecticut, RB
2010 Jerry Hughes, Texas Christian, DE
2011 Anthony Castonzo, Boston College, T
2012 Andrew Luck, Stanford, QB
2013 Bjoern Werner, Florida State, DE
2014 Jack Mewhort, Ohio State, G (2)

JACKSONVILLE JAGUARS
Year Player, College, Position
1995 Tony Boselli, Southern California, T
     James Stewart, Tennessee, RB
1996 Kevin Hardy, Illinois, LB
1997 Renaldo Wynn, Notre Dame, DT
1998 Fred Taylor, Florida, RB
     Donovin Darius, Syracuse, DB
1999 Fernando Bryant, Alabama, DB
2000 R. Jay Soward, So. California, WR
2001 Marcus Stroud, Georgia, DT
2002 John Henderson, Tennessee, DT
2003 Byron Leftwich, Marshall, QB
2004 Reggie Williams, Washington, WR
2005 Matt Jones, Arkansas, WR
2006 Marcedes Lewis, UCLA, TE
2007 Reggie Nelson, Florida, DB
2008 Derrick Harvey, Florida, DE
2009 Eugene Monroe, Virginia, T
2010 Tyson Alualu, California, DT
2011 Blaine Gabbert, Missouri, QB
2012 Justin Blackmon, Oklahoma St., WR
2013 Luke Joeckel, Texas A&M, T
2014 Blake Bortles, Central Florida, QB

KANSAS CITY CHIEFS
Year Player, College, Position
1960 Don Meredith, So. Methodist, QB
1961 E.J. Holub, Texas Tech, C
1962 Ronnie Bull, Baylor, RB
1963 Buck Buchanan, Grambling, DT
     Ed Budde, Michigan State, G
1964 Pete Beathard, So. California, QB
1965 Gale Sayers, Kansas, RB
1966 Aaron Brown, Minnesota, DE
1967 Gene Trosch, Miami, DE-DT
1968 Mo Moorman, Texas A&M, G
     George Daney, Texas-El Paso, G
1969 Jim Marsalis, Tennessee State, CB
1970 Sid Smith, Southern California, T
1971 Elmo Wright, Houston, WR
1972 Jeff Kinney, Nebraska, RB
1973 Gary Butler, Rice, TE (2)
1974 Woody Green, Arizona State, RB
1975 Elmore Stephens, Kentucky, TE (2)
1976 Rod Walters, Iowa, G
1977 Gary Green, Baylor, DB
1978 Art Still, Kentucky, DE
1979 Mike Bell, Colorado State, DE
     Steve Fuller, Clemson, QB
1980 Brad Budde, Southern California, G
1981 Willie Scott, South Carolina, TE
1982 Anthony Hancock, Tennessee, WR
1983 Todd Blackledge, Penn State, QB
1984 Bill Maas, Pittsburgh, DT
     John Alt, Iowa, T
1985 Ethan Horton, North Carolina, RB
1986 Brian Jozwiak, West Virginia, T
1987 Paul Palmer, Temple, RB
1988 Neil Smith, Nebraska, DE
1989 Derrick Thomas, Alabama, LB
1990 Percy Snow, Michigan State, LB
1991 Harvey Williams, Louisiana St., RB
1992 Dale Carter, Tennessee, DB
1993 Will Shields, Nebraska, G (3)
1994 Greg Hill, Texas A&M, RB
1995 Trezelle Jenkins, Michigan, T
1996 Jerome Woods, Memphis, DB
1997 Tony Gonzalez, California, TE
1998 Victor Riley, Auburn, T
1999 John Tait, Brigham Young, T
2000 Sylvester Morris, Jackson St., WR
2001 Eric Downing, Syracuse, DT (3)
2002 Ryan Sims, North Carolina, DT
2003 Larry Johnson, Penn State, RB
2004 Junior Siavii, Oregon, DT (2)
2005 Derrick Johnson, Texas, LB
2006 Tamba Hali, Penn State, DE
2007 Dwayne Bowe, Louisiana State, WR
2008 Glenn Dorsey, Louisiana State, DT
     Branden Albert, Virginia, T
2009 Tyson Jackson, Louisiana State, DE
2010 Eric Berry, Tennessee, DB
2011 Jonathan Baldwin, Pittsburgh, WR
2012 Dontari Poe, Memphis, NT
2013 Eric Fisher, Central Michigan, T
2014 Dee Ford, Auburn, DE

MIAMI DOLPHINS
Year Player, College, Position
1966 Jim Grabowski, Illinois, RB
     Rick Norton, Kentucky, QB
1967 Bob Griese, Purdue, QB
1968 Larry Csonka, Syracuse, RB
     Doug Crusan, Indiana, T
1969 Bill Stanfill, Georgia, DE
1970 Jim Mandich, Michigan, TE (2)

1971 Otto Stowe, Iowa State, WR (2)
1972 Mike Kadish, Notre Dame, DT
1973 Chuck Bradley, Oregon, C (2)
1974 Donald Reese, Jackson State, DE
1975 Darryl Carlton, Tampa, T
1976 Larry Gordon, Arizona State, LB
     Kim Bokamper, San Jose State, LB
1977 A.J. Duhe, Louisiana State, DT
1978 Guy Benjamin, Stanford, QB (2)
1979 Jon Giesler, Michigan, T
1980 Don McNeal, Alabama, DB
1981 David Overstreet, Oklahoma, RB
1982 Roy Foster, Southern California, G
1983 Dan Marino, Pittsburgh, QB
1984 Jackie Shipp, Oklahoma, LB
1985 Lorenzo Hampton, Florida, RB
1986 John Offerdahl, Western Michigan, LB (2)
1987 John Bosa, Boston College, DE
1988 Eric Kumerow, Ohio State, DE
1989 Sammie Smith, Florida State, RB
     Louis Oliver, Florida, DB
1990 Richmond Webb, Texas A&M, T
1991 Randal Hill, Miami, WR
1992 Troy Vincent, Wisconsin, DB
     Marco Coleman, Georgia Tech, LB
1993 O.J. McDuffie, Penn State, WR
1994 Tim Bowens, Mississippi, DT
1995 Billy Milner, Houston, T
1996 Daryl Gardener, Baylor, DT
1997 Yatil Green, Miami, WR
1998 John Avery, Mississippi, RB
1999 J.J. Johnson, Mississippi St., RB (2)
2000 Todd Wade, Mississippi, T (2)
2001 Jamar Fletcher, Wisconsin, DB
2002 Seth McKinney, Texas A&M, C (3)
2003 Eddie Moore, Tennessee, LB (2)
2004 Vernon Carey, Miami, T
2005 Ronnie Brown, Auburn, RB
2006 Jason Allen, Tennessee, DB
2007 Ted Ginn, Ohio State, WR
2008 Jake Long, Michigan, T
2009 Vontae Davis, Illinois, DB
2010 Jared Odrick, Penn State, DT
2011 Mike Pouncey, Florida, C
2012 Ryan Tannehill, Texas A&M, QB
2013 Dion Jordan, Oregon, DE
2014 Ja'Wuan James, Tennessee, T

MINNESOTA VIKINGS
Year Player, College, Position
1961 Tommy Mason, Tulane, RB
1962 Bill Miller, Miami, WR (3)
1963 Jim Dunaway, Mississippi, T
1964 Carl Eller, Minnesota, DE
1965 Jack Snow, Notre Dame, WR
1966 Jerry Shay, Purdue, DT
1967 Clint Jones, Michigan State, RB
     Gene Washington, Michigan St., WR
     Alan Page, Notre Dame, DT
1968 Ron Yary, Southern California, T
1969 Ed White, California, G (2)
1970 John Ward, Oklahoma State, T
1971 Leo Hayden, Ohio State, RB
1972 Jeff Siemon, Stanford, LB
1973 Chuck Foreman, Miami, RB
1974 Fred McNeill, UCLA, LB
     Steve Riley, Southern California, T
1975 Mark Mullaney, Colorado State, DE
1976 James White, Oklahoma State, DT
1977 Tommy Kramer, Rice, QB
1978 Randy Holloway, Pittsburgh, DE
1979 Ted Brown, North Carolina St., RB

1980	Doug Martin, Washington, DT
1981	Mardye McDole, Mississippi St., WR (2)
1982	Darrin Nelson, Stanford, RB
1983	Joey Browner, So. California, DB
1984	Keith Millard, Washington St., DE
1985	Chris Doleman, Pittsburgh, LB
1986	Gerald Robinson, Auburn, DE
1987	D.J. Dozier, Penn State, RB
1988	Randall McDaniel, Arizona State, G
1989	David Braxton, Wake Forest, LB (2)
1990	Mike Jones, Texas A&M, TE (3)
1991	Carlos Jenkins, Michigan St., LB (3)
1992	Robert Harris, Southern Univ., DE (2)
1993	Robert Smith, Ohio State, RB
1994	DeWayne Washington, N. Carolina St., DB
	Todd Steussie, California, T
1995	Derrick Alexander, Florida St., DE
	Korey Stringer, Ohio State, T
1996	Duane Clemons, California, DE
1997	Dwayne Rudd, Alabama, LB
1998	Randy Moss, Marshall, WR
1999	Daunte Culpepper, Central Florida, QB
	Dimitrius Underwood, Michigan St., DE
2000	Chris Hovan, Boston College, DT
2001	Michael Bennett, Wisconsin, RB
2002	Bryant McKinnie, Miami, T
2003	Kevin Williams, Oklahoma State, DT
2004	Kenechi Udeze, Southern California, DE
2005	Troy Williamson, South Carolina, WR
	Erasmus James, Wisconsin, DE
2006	Chad Greenway, Iowa, LB
2007	Adrian Peterson, Oklahoma, RB
2008	Tyrell Johnson, Arkansas State, DB (2)
2009	Percy Harvin, Florida, WR
2010	Chris Cook, Virginia, DB (2)
2011	Christian Ponder, Florida State, QB
2012	Matt Kalil, Southern California, T
	Harrison Smith, Notre Dame, DB
2013	Shariff Floyd, Florida, DT
	Xavier Rhodes, Florida State, DB
	Cordarrelle Patterson, Tennessee, WR
2014	Anthony Barr, UCLA, LB
	Teddy Bridgewater, Louisville, QB

NEW ENGLAND PATRIOTS
Year Player, College, Position

1960	Ron Burton, Northwestern, RB
1961	Tommy Mason, Tulane, RB
1962	Gary Collins, Maryland, WR
1963	Art Graham, Boston College, WR
1964	Jack Concannon, Boston College, QB
1965	Jerry Rush, Michigan State, DE
1966	Karl Singer, Purdue, T
1967	John Charles, Purdue, S
1968	Dennis Byrd, North Carolina St., DE
1969	Ron Sellers, Florida State, WR
1970	Phil Olsen, Utah State, DE
1971	Jim Plunkett, Stanford, QB
1972	Tom Reynolds, San Diego St., WR (2)
1973	John Hannah, Alabama, G
	Sam Cunningham, So. California, RB
	Darryl Stingley, Purdue, WR
1974	Steve Corbett, Boston College, G (2)
1975	Russ Francis, Oregon, TE
1976	Mike Haynes, Arizona State, DB
	Pete Brock, Colorado, C
	Tim Fox, Ohio State, DB
1977	Raymond Clayborn, Texas, DB
	Stanley Morgan, Tennessee, WR
1978	Bob Cryder, Alabama, G
1979	Rick Sanford, South Carolina, DB

1980	Roland James, Tennessee, DB
	Vagas Ferguson, Notre Dame, RB
1981	Brian Holloway, Stanford, T
1982	Kenneth Sims, Texas, DT
	Lester Williams, Miami, DT
1983	Tony Eason, Illinois, QB
1984	Irving Fryar, Nebraska, WR
1985	Trevor Matich, Brigham Young, C
1986	Reggie Dupard, So. Methodist, RB
1987	Bruce Armstrong, Louisville, T
1988	John Stephens, Northwestern St., La., RB
1989	Hart Lee Dykes, Oklahoma St., WR
1990	Chris Singleton, Arizona, LB
	Ray Agnew, North Carolina St., DE
1991	Pat Harlow, Southern California, T
	Leonard Russell, Arizona St., RB
1992	Eugene Chung, Virginia Tech, T
1993	Drew Bledsoe, Washington St., QB
1994	Willie McGinest, So. California, DE
1995	Ty Law, Michigan, DB
1996	Terry Glenn, Ohio State, WR
1997	Chris Canty, Kansas State, DB
1998	Robert Edwards, Georgia, RB
	Tebucky Jones, Syracuse, DB
1999	Damien Woody, Boston College, C
	Andy Katzenmoyer, Ohio State, LB
2000	Adrian Klemm, Hawaii, T (2)
2001	Richard Seymour, Georgia, DT
2002	Daniel Graham, Colorado, TE
2003	Ty Warren, Texas A&M, DT
2004	Vince Wilfork, Miami, DT
	Ben Watson, Georgia, TE
2005	Logan Mankins, Fresno State, G
2006	Laurence Maroney, Minnesota, RB
2007	Brandon Meriweather, Miami, DB
2008	Jerod Mayo, Tennessee, LB
2009	Patrick Chung, Oregon, DB (2)
2010	Devin McCourty, Rutgers, DB
2011	Nate Solder, Colorado, T
2012	Chandler Jones, Syracuse, DE
	Dont'a Hightower, Alabama, LB
2013	Jamie Collins, So. Mississippi, LB (2)
2014	Dominique Easley, Florida, DE

NEW ORLEANS SAINTS
Year Player, College, Position

1967	Les Kelley, Alabama, RB
1968	Kevin Hardy, Notre Dame, DE
1969	John Shinners, Xavier, G
1970	Ken Burrough, Texas Southern, WR
1971	Archie Manning, Mississippi, QB
1972	Royce Smith, Georgia, G
1973	Derland Moore, Oklahoma, DE (2)
1974	Rick Middleton, Ohio State, LB
1975	Larry Burton, Purdue, WR
	Kurt Schumacher, Ohio State, T
1976	Chuck Muncie, California, RB
1977	Joe Campbell, Maryland, DE
1978	Wes Chandler, Florida, WR
1979	Russell Erxleben, Texas, P-K
1980	Stan Brock, Colorado, T
1981	George Rogers, South Carolina, RB
1982	Lindsay Scott, Georgia, WR
1983	Steve Korte, Arkansas, G (2)
1984	James Geathers, Wichita State, DE
1985	Alvin Toles, Tennessee, LB
1986	Jim Dombrowski, Virginia, T
1987	Shawn Knight, Brigham Young, DT
1988	Craig Heyward, Pittsburgh, RB
1989	Wayne Martin, Arkansas, DE
1990	Renaldo Turnbull, West Virginia, DE
1991	Wesley Carroll, Miami, WR (2)

1992	Vaughn Dunbar, Indiana, RB
1993	Willie Roaf, Louisiana Tech, T
	Irv Smith, Notre Dame, TE
1994	Joe Johnson, Louisville, DE
1995	Mark Fields, Washington State, LB
1996	Alex Molden, Oregon, DB
1997	Chris Naeole, Colorado, G
1998	Kyle Turley, San Diego State, T
1999	Ricky Williams, Texas, RB
2000	Darren Howard, Kansas St., DE (2)
2001	Deuce McAllister, Mississippi, RB
2002	Donte' Stallworth, Tennessee, WR
	Charles Grant, Georgia, DE
2003	Johnathan Sullivan, Georgia, DT
2004	Will Smith, Ohio State, DE
2005	Jammal Brown, Oklahoma, T
2006	Reggie Bush, So. California, RB
2007	Robert Meachem, Tennessee, WR
2008	Sedrick Ellis, So. California, DT
2009	Malcolm Jenkins, Ohio State, DB
2010	Patrick Robinson, Florida State, DB
2011	Cameron Jordan, California, DE
	Mark Ingram, Alabama, RB
2012	Akiem Hicks, Regina, DT (3)
2013	Kenny Vaccaro, Texas, DB
2014	Brandin Cooks, Oregon State, WR

NEW YORK GIANTS
Year Player, College, Position

1936	Art Lewis, Ohio U., T
1937	Ed Widseth, Minnesota, T
1938	George Karamatic, Gonzaga, B
1939	Walt Neilson, Arizona, B
1940	Grenville Lansdell, So. California, B
1941	George Franck, Minnesota, B
1942	Merle Hapes, Mississippi, B
1943	Steve Filipowicz, Fordham, B
1944	Billy Hillenbrand, Indiana, B
1945	Elmer Barbour, Wake Forest, B
1946	George Connor, Notre Dame, T
1947	Vic Schwall, Northwestern, B
1948	Tony Minisi, Pennsylvania, B
1949	Paul Page, Southern Methodist, B
1950	Travis Tidwell, Auburn, B
1951	Kyle Rote, Southern Methodist, B
	Jim Spavital, Oklahoma A&M, B
1952	Frank Gifford, Southern California, B
1953	Bobby Marlow, Alabama, B
1954	Ken Buck, Pacific, C (2)
1955	Joe Heap, Notre Dame, B
1956	Henry Moore, Arkansas, B (2)
1957	Sam DeLuca, South Carolina, T (2)
1958	Phil King, Vanderbilt, B
1959	Lee Grosscup, Utah, B
1960	Lou Cordileone, Clemson, G
1961	Bruce Tarbox, Syracuse, G (2)
1962	Jerry Hillebrand, Colorado, LB
1963	Frank Lasky, Florida, T (2)
1964	Joe Don Looney, Oklahoma, RB
1965	Tucker Frederickson, Auburn, RB
1966	Francis Peay, Missouri, T
1967	Louis Thompson, Alabama, DT (4)
1968	Dick Buzin, Penn State, T (2)
1969	Fred Dryer, San Diego State, DE
1970	Jim Files, Oklahoma, LB
1971	Rocky Thompson, West Texas St., WR
1972	Eldridge Small, Texas A&I, DB
	Larry Jacobson, Nebraska, DE
1973	Brad Van Pelt, Michigan St., LB (2)
1974	John Hicks, Ohio State, G
1975	Al Simpson, Colorado State, T (2)
1976	Troy Archer, Colorado, DE

1977	Gary Jeter, Southern California, DT
1978	Gordon King, Stanford, T
1979	Phil Simms, Morehead State, QB
1980	Mark Haynes, Colorado, DB
1981	Lawrence Taylor, North Carolina, LB
1982	Butch Woolfolk, Michigan, RB
1983	Terry Kinard, Clemson, DB
1984	Carl Banks, Michigan State, LB
	William Roberts, Ohio State, T
1985	George Adams, Kentucky, RB
1986	Eric Dorsey, Notre Dame, DE
1987	Mark Ingram, Michigan State, WR
1988	Eric Moore, Indiana, T
1989	Brian Williams, Minnesota, C-G
1990	Rodney Hampton, Georgia, RB
1991	Jarrod Bunch, Michigan, RB
1992	Derek Brown, Notre Dame, TE
1993	Michael Strahan, Texas Southern, DE (2)
1994	Thomas Lewis, Indiana, WR
1995	Tyrone Wheatley, Michigan, RB
1996	Cedric Jones, Oklahoma, DE
1997	Ike Hilliard, Florida, WR
1998	Shaun Williams, UCLA, DB
1999	Luke Petitgout, Notre Dame, T
2000	Ron Dayne, Wisconsin, RB
2001	Will Allen, Syracuse, DB
2002	Jeremy Shockey, Miami, TE
2003	William Joseph, Miami, DT
2004	Philip Rivers, North Carolina St., QB
2005	Corey Webster, Louisiana St., DB (2)
2006	Mathias Kiwanuka, Boston College, DE
2007	Aaron Ross, Texas, DB
2008	Kenny Phillips, Miami, DB
2009	Hakeem Nicks, North Carolina, WR
2010	Jason Pierre-Paul, South Florida, DE
2011	Prince Amukamara, Nebraska, DB
2012	David Wilson, Virginia Tech, RB
2013	Justin Pugh, Syracuse, T
2014	Odell Beckham, Louisiana St., WR

NEW YORK JETS
Year Player, College, Position

1960	George Izo, Notre Dame, QB
1961	Tom Brown, Minnesota, G
1962	Sandy Stephens, Minnesota, QB
1963	Jerry Stovall, Louisiana State, S
1964	Matt Snell, Ohio State, RB
1965	Joe Namath, Alabama, QB
	Tom Nowatzke, Indiana, RB
1966	Bill Yearby, Michigan, DT
1967	Paul Seiler, Notre Dame, T
1968	Lee White, Weber State, RB
1969	Dave Foley, Ohio State, T
1970	Steve Tannen, Florida, CB
1971	John Riggins, Kansas, RB
1972	Jerome Barkum, Jackson St., WR
	Mike Taylor, Michigan, LB
1973	Burgess Owens, Miami, DB
1974	Carl Barzilauskas, Indiana, DT
1975	Anthony Davis, So. California, RB (2)
1976	Richard Todd, Alabama, QB
1977	Marvin Powell, So. California, T
1978	Chris Ward, Ohio State, T
1979	Marty Lyons, Alabama, DE
1980	Johnny (Lam) Jones, Texas, WR
1981	Freeman McNeil, UCLA, RB
1982	Bob Crable, Notre Dame, LB
1983	Ken O'Brien, Cal-Davis, QB
1984	Russell Carter, So. Methodist, DB
	Ron Faurot, Arkansas, DE
1985	Al Toon, Wisconsin, WR
1986	Mike Haight, Iowa, T

1987	Roger Vick, Texas A&M, RB
1988	Dave Cadigan, So. California, T
1989	Jeff Lageman, Virginia, LB
1990	Blair Thomas, Penn State, RB
1991	Browning Nagle, Louisville, QB (2)
1992	Johnny Mitchell, Nebraska, TE
1993	Marvin Jones, Florida State, LB
1994	Aaron Glenn, Texas A&M, DB
1995	Kyle Brady, Penn State, TE
	Hugh Douglas, Central St., Ohio, DE
1996	Keyshawn Johnson, So. California, WR
1997	James Farrior, Virginia, LB
1998	Dorian Boose, Washington St., DE (2)
1999	Randy Thomas, Mississippi St., G (2)
2000	Shaun Ellis, Tennessee, DE
	John Abraham, South Carolina, LB
	Chad Pennington, Marshall, QB
	Anthony Becht, West Virginia, TE
2001	Santana Moss, Miami, WR
2002	Bryan Thomas, Ala.-Birmingham, DE
2003	Dewayne Robertson, Kentucky, DT
2004	Jonathan Vilma, Miami, LB
2005	Mike Nugent, Ohio State, K (2)
2006	D'Brickashaw Ferguson, Virginia, T
	Nick Mangold, Ohio State, C
2007	Darrelle Revis, Pittsburgh, DB
2008	Vernon Gholston, Ohio State, LB
	Dustin Keller, Purdue, TE
2009	Mark Sanchez, So. California, QB
2010	Kyle Wilson, Boise State, DB
2011	Muhammad Wilkerson, Temple, DT
2012	Quinton Coples, North Carolina, DE
2013	Dee Milliner, Alabama, DB
	Sheldon Richardson, Missouri, DT
2014	Calvin Pryor, Louisville, DB

OAKLAND RAIDERS
Year Player, College, Position

1960	Dale Hackbart, Wisconsin, CB
1961	Joe Rutgens, Illinois, D
1962	Roman Gabriel, North Carolina St., QB
1963	George Wilson, Alabama, RB (6)
1964	Tony Lorick, Arizona State, RB
1965	Harry Schuh, Memphis State, T
1966	Rodger Bird, Kentucky, S
1967	Gene Upshaw, Texas A&I, G
1968	Eldridge Dickey, Tennessee St., QB
1969	Art Thoms, Syracuse, DT
1970	Raymond Chester, Morgan St., TE
1971	Jack Tatum, Ohio State, S
1972	Mike Siani, Villanova, WR
1973	Ray Guy, Southern Mississippi, P
1974	Henry Lawrence, Florida A&M, T
1975	Neal Colzie, Ohio State, DB
1976	Charles Philyaw, Texas Southern, DT (2)
1977	Mike Davis, Colorado, DB (2)
1978	Dave Browning, Washington, DE (2)
1979	Willie Jones, Florida State, DE (2)
1980	Marc Wilson, Brigham Young, QB
1981	Ted Watts, Texas Tech, DB
	Curt Marsh, Washington, T
1982	Marcus Allen, So. California, RB
1983	Don Mosebar, So. California, T
1984	Sean Jones, Northeastern, DE (2)
1985	Jessie Hester, Florida State, WR
1986	Bob Buczkowski, Pittsburgh, DE
1987	John Clay, Missouri, T
1988	Tim Brown, Notre Dame, WR
	Terry McDaniel, Tennessee, DB
	Scott Davis, Illinois, DE
1989	Jeff Francis, Tennessee, QB (6)
1990	Anthony Smith, Arizona, DE

1991	Todd Marinovich, So. California, QB
1992	Chester McGlockton, Clemson, DE
1993	Patrick Bates, Texas A&M, DB
1994	Rob Fredrickson, Michigan St., LB
1995	Napoleon Kaufman, Washington, RB
1996	Rickey Dudley, Ohio State, TE
1997	Darrell Russell, Southern California, DT
1998	Charles Woodson, Michigan, DB
	Mo Collins, Florida, T
1999	Matt Stinchcomb, Georgia, T
2000	Sebastian Janikowski, Florida St., K
2001	Derrick Gibson, Florida State, DB
2002	Phillip Buchanon, Miami, DB
	Napoleon Harris, Northwestern, LB
2003	Nnamdi Asomugha, California, DB
	Tyler Brayton, Colorado, DE
2004	Robert Gallery, Iowa, T
2005	Fabian Washington, Nebraska, DB
2006	Michael Huff, Texas, DB
2007	JaMarcus Russell, Louisiana State, QB
2008	Darren McFadden, Arkansas, RB
2009	Darrius Heyward-Bey, Maryland, WR
2010	Rolando McClain, Alabama, LB
2011	Stefan Wisniewski, Penn State, C (2)
2012	Tony Bergstrom, Utah, G (3)
2013	D.J. Hayden, Houston, DB
2014	Khalil Mack, Buffalo, LB

PHILADELPHIA EAGLES
Year Player, College, Position

1936	Jay Berwanger, Chicago, B
1937	Sam Francis, Nebraska, B
1938	Jim McDonald, Ohio State, B
1939	Davey O'Brien, Texas Christian, B
1940	George McAfee, Duke, B
1941	Art Jones, Richmond, B (2)
1942	Pete Kmetovic, Stanford, B
1943	Joe Muha, Virginia Military, B
1944	Steve Van Buren, Louisiana St., B
1945	John Yonaker, Notre Dame, E
1946	Leo Riggs, Southern California, B
1947	Neill Armstrong, Oklahoma A&M, E
1948	Clyde (Smackover) Scott, Arkansas, B
1949	Chuck Bednarik, Pennsylvania, C
	Frank Tripucka, Notre Dame, B
1950	Harry (Bud) Grant, Minnesota, E
1951	Ebert Van Buren, Louisiana St., B
	Chet Mutryn, Xavier, B
1952	Johnny Bright, Drake, B
1953	Al Conway, Army, B (2)
1954	Neil Worden, Notre Dame, B
1955	Dick Bielski, Maryland, B
1956	Bob Pellegrini, Maryland, C
1957	Clarence Peaks, Michigan State, B
1958	Walt Kowalczyk, Michigan State, B
1959	J.D. Smith, Rice, T (2)
1960	Ron Burton, Northwestern, RB
1961	Art Baker, Syracuse, RB
1962	Pete Case, Georgia, G (2)
1963	Ed Budde, Michigan State, G
1964	Bob Brown, Nebraska, T
1965	Ray Rissmiller, Georgia, T (2)
1966	Randy Beisler, Indiana, DE
1967	Harry Jones, Arkansas, RB
1968	Tim Rossovich, So. California, DE
1969	Leroy Keyes, Purdue, RB
1970	Steve Zabel, Oklahoma, TE
1971	Richard Harris, Grambling, DE
1972	John Reaves, Florida, QB
1973	Jerry Sisemore, Texas, T
	Charle Young, So. California, TE
1974	Mitch Sutton, Kansas, DT (3)

1975 Bill Capraun, Miami, T (7)
1976 Mike Smith, Florida, DE (4)
1977 Skip Sharp, Kansas, DB (5)
1978 Reggie Wilkes, Georgia Tech, LB (3)
1979 Jerry Robinson, UCLA, LB
1980 Roynell Young, Alcorn State, DB
1981 Leonard Mitchell, Houston, DE
1982 Mike Quick, North Carolina St., WR
1983 Michael Haddix, Mississippi St., RB
1984 Kenny Jackson, Penn State, WR
1985 Kevin Allen, Indiana, T
1986 Keith Byars, Ohio State, RB
1987 Jerome Brown, Miami, DT
1988 Keith Jackson, Oklahoma, TE
1989 Jessie Small, Eastern Kentucky, LB (2)
1990 Ben Smith, Georgia, DB
1991 Antone Davis, Tennessee, T
1992 Siran Stacy, Alabama, RB (2)
1993 Lester Holmes, Jackson State, T
      Leonard Renfro, Colorado, DT
1994 Bernard Williams, Georgia, T
1995 Mike Mamula, Boston College, DE
1996 Jermane Mayberry, Texas A&M-Kingsville, T
1997 Jon Harris, Virginia, DE
1998 Tra Thomas, Florida State, T
1999 Donovan McNabb, Syracuse, QB
2000 Corey Simon, Florida State, DT
2001 Freddie Mitchell, UCLA, WR
2002 Lito Sheppard, Florida, DB
2003 Jerome McDougle, Miami, DE
2004 Shawn Andrews, Arkansas, T
2005 Mike Patterson, So. California, DT
2006 Brodrick Bunkley, Florida State, DT
2007 Kevin Kolb, Houston, QB (2)
2008 Trevor Laws, Notre Dame, DT (2)
2009 Jeremy Maclin, Missouri, WR
2010 Brandon Graham, Michigan, DE
2011 Danny Watkins, Baylor, G
2012 Fletcher Cox, Mississippi St., DT
2013 Lane Johnson, Oklahoma, T
2014 Marcus Smith, Louisville, LB

PITTSBURGH STEELERS
Year   Player, College, Position
1936 Bill Shakespeare, Notre Dame, B
1937 Mike Basrak, Duquesne, C
1938 Byron (Whizzer) White, Colorado, B
1939 Bill Patterson, Baylor, B (3)
1940 Kay Eakin, Arkansas, B
1941 Chet Gladchuk, Boston College, C (2)
1942 Bill Dudley, Virginia, B
1943 Bill Daley, Minnesota, B
1944 Johnny Podesto, St. Mary's, Calif., B
1945 Paul Duhart, Florida, B
1946 Felix (Doc) Blanchard, Army, B
1947 Hub Bechtol, Texas, E
1948 Dan Edwards, Georgia, E
1949 Bobby Gage, Clemson, B
1950 Lynn Chandnois, Michigan St., B
1951 Butch Avinger, Alabama, B
1952 Ed Modzelewski, Maryland, B
1953 Ted Marchibroda, St. Bonaventure, B
1954 Johnny Lattner, Notre Dame, B
1955 Frank Varrichione, Notre Dame, T
1956 Gary Glick, Colorado A&M, B
      Art Davis, Mississippi State, B
1957 Len Dawson, Purdue, B
1958 Larry Krutko, West Virginia, B (2)
1959 Tom Barnett, Purdue, B (8)
1960 Jack Spikes, Texas Christian, RB
1961 Myron Pottios, Notre Dame, LB (2)
1962 Bob Ferguson, Ohio State, RB

1963 Frank Atkinson, Stanford, T (8)
1964 Paul Martha, Pittsburgh, S
1965 Roy Jefferson, Utah, WR (2)
1966 Dick Leftridge, West Virginia, RB
1967 Don Shy, San Diego State, RB (2)
1968 Mike Taylor, Southern California, T
1969 Joe Greene, North Texas State, DT
1970 Terry Bradshaw, Louisiana Tech, QB
1971 Frank Lewis, Grambling, WR
1972 Franco Harris, Penn State, RB
1973 J.T. Thomas, Florida State, DB
1974 Lynn Swann, So. California, WR
1975 Dave Brown, Michigan, DB
1976 Bennie Cunningham, Clemson, TE
1977 Robin Cole, New Mexico, LB
1978 Ron Johnson, Eastern Michigan, DB
1979 Greg Hawthorne, Baylor, RB
1980 Mark Malone, Arizona State, QB
1981 Keith Gary, Oklahoma, DE
1982 Walter Abercrombie, Baylor, RB
1983 Gabriel Rivera, Texas Tech, DT
1984 Louis Lipps, So. Mississippi, WR
1985 Darryl Sims, Wisconsin, DE
1986 John Rienstra, Temple, G
1987 Rod Woodson, Purdue, DB
1988 Aaron Jones, Eastern Kentucky, DE
1989 Tim Worley, Georgia, RB
      Tom Ricketts, Pittsburgh, T
1990 Eric Green, Liberty, TE
1991 Huey Richardson, Florida, DE
1992 Leon Searcy, Miami, T
1993 Deon Figures, Colorado, DB
1994 Charles Johnson, Colorado, WR
1995 Mark Bruener, Washington, TE
1996 Jamain Stephens, North Carolina A&T, T
1997 Chad Scott, Maryland, DB
1998 Alan Faneca, Louisiana State, G
1999 Troy Edwards, Louisiana Tech, WR
2000 Plaxico Burress, Michigan St., WR
2001 Casey Hampton, Texas, DT
2002 Kendall Simmons, Auburn, G
2003 Troy Polamalu, Southern California, DB
2004 Ben Roethlisberger, Miami (OH), QB
2005 Heath Miller, Virginia, TE
2006 Santonio Holmes, Ohio State, WR
2007 Lawrence Timmons, Florida State, LB
2008 Rashard Mendenhall, Illinois, RB
2009 Evander Hood, Missouri, DE
2010 Maurkice Pouncey, Florida, C
2011 Cameron Heyward, Ohio State, DE
2012 David DeCastro, Stanford, G
2013 Jarvis Jones, Georgia, LB
2014 Ryan Shazier, Ohio State, LB

ST. LOUIS RAMS
Year   Player, College, Position
1937 Johnny Drake, Purdue, B
1938 Corbett Davis, Indiana, B
1939 Parker Hall, Mississippi, B
1940 Ollie Cordill, Rice, B
1941 Rudy Mucha, Washington, C
1942 Jack Wilson, Baylor, B
1943 Mike Holovak, Boston College, B
1944 Tony Butkovich, Illinois, B
1945 Elroy (Crazylegs) Hirsch, Wisconsin, B
1946 Emil Sitko, Notre Dame, B
1947 Herman Wedemeyer, St. Mary's, Calif., B
1948 Tom Keane, West Virginia, B (2)
1949 Bobby Thomason, Virginia Military, B
1950 Ralph Pasquariello, Villanova, B
      Stan West, Oklahoma, G
1951 Bud McFadin, Texas, G

1952 Bill Wade, Vanderbilt, QB
      Bob Carey, Michigan State, E
1953 Donn Moomaw, UCLA, C
      Ed Barker, Washington State, E
1954 Ed Beatty, Cincinnati, C
1955 Larry Morris, Georgia Tech, C
1956 Joe Marconi, West Virginia, B
      Charles Horton, Vanderbilt, B
1957 Jon Arnett, Southern California, B
      Del Shofner, Baylor, E
1958 Lou Michaels, Kentucky, T
      Jim Phillips, Auburn, E
1959 Dick Bass, Pacific, B
      Paul Dickson, Baylor, T
1960 Billy Cannon, Louisiana State, RB
1961 Marlin McKeever, So. California, E-LB
1962 Roman Gabriel, North Carolina St., QB
      Merlin Olsen, Utah State, DT
1963 Terry Baker, Oregon State, QB
      Rufus Guthrie, Georgia Tech, G
1964 Bill Munson, Utah State, QB
1965 Clancy Williams, Washington St., CB
1966 Tom Mack, Michigan, G
1967 Willie Ellison, Texas Southern, RB (2)
1968 Gary Beban, UCLA, QB (2)
1969 Larry Smith, Florida, RB
      Jim Seymour, Notre Dame, WR
      Bob Klein, Southern California, TE
1970 Jack Reynolds, Tennessee, LB
1971 Isiah Robertson, Southern, LB
      Jack Youngblood, Florida, DE
1972 Jim Bertelsen, Texas, RB (2)
1973 Cullen Bryant, Colorado, DB (2)
1974 John Cappelletti, Penn State, RB
1975 Mike Fanning, Notre Dame, DT
      Dennis Harrah, Miami, T
      Doug France, Ohio State, T
1976 Kevin McLain, Colorado State, LB
1977 Bob Brudzinski, Ohio State, LB
1978 Elvis Peacock, Oklahoma, RB
1979 George Andrews, Nebraska, LB
      Kent Hill, Georgia Tech, T
1980 Johnnie Johnson, Texas, DB
1981 Mel Owens, Michigan, LB
1982 Barry Redden, Richmond, RB
1983 Eric Dickerson, So. Methodist, RB
1984 Hal Stephens, East Carolina, DE (5)
1985 Jerry Gray, Texas, DB
1986 Mike Schad, Queen's Univ., Canada, T
1987 Donald Evans, Winston-Salem, DE (2)
1988 Gaston Green, UCLA, RB
      Aaron Cox, Arizona State, WR
1989 Bill Hawkins, Miami, DE
      Cleveland Gary, Miami, RB
1990 Bern Brostek, Washington, C
1991 Todd Lyght, Notre Dame, DB
1992 Sean Gilbert, Pittsburgh, DE
1993 Jerome Bettis, Notre Dame, RB
1994 Wayne Gandy, Auburn, T
1995 Kevin Carter, Florida, DE
1996 Lawrence Phillips, Nebraska, RB
      Eddie Kennison, Louisiana St., WR
1997 Orlando Pace, Ohio State, T
1998 Grant Wistrom, Nebraska, DE
1999 Torry Holt, North Carolina St., WR
2000 Trung Canidate, Arizona, RB
2001 Damione Lewis, Miami, DT
      Adam Archuleta, Arizona State, DB
      Ryan Pickett, Ohio State, DT
2002 Robert Thomas, UCLA, LB
2003 Jimmy Kennedy, Penn State, DT
2004 Steven Jackson, Oregon State, RB

2005 Alex Barron, Florida State, T
2006 Tye Hill, Clemson, DB
2007 Adam Carriker, Nebraska, DE
2008 Chris Long, Virginia, DE
2009 Jason Smith, Baylor, T
2010 Sam Bradford, Oklahoma, QB
2011 Robert Quinn, North Carolina, DE
2012 Michael Brockers, Louisiana St., DT
2013 Tavon Austin, West Virginia, WR
　　　 Alec Ogletree, Georgia, LB
2014 Greg Robinson, Auburn, T
　　　 Aaron Donald, Pittsburgh, DT

SAN DIEGO CHARGERS
Year Player, College, Position
1960 Monty Stickles, Notre Dame, E
1961 Earl Faison, Indiana, DE
1962 Bob Ferguson, Ohio State, RB
1963 Walt Sweeney, Syracuse, G
1964 Ted Davis, Georgia Tech, LB
1965 Steve DeLong, Tennessee, DE
1966 Don Davis, Cal St.-Los Angeles, DT
1967 Ron Billingsley, Wyoming, DE
1968 Russ Washington, Missouri, DT
　　　 Jimmy Hill, Texas A&I, DB
1969 Marty Domres, Columbia, QB
　　　 Bob Babich, Miami, Ohio, LB
1970 Walker Gillette, Richmond, WR
1971 Leon Burns, Long Beach State, RB
1972 Pete Lazetich, Stanford, DE (2)
1973 Johnny Rodgers, Nebraska, WR
1974 Bo Matthews, Colorado, RB
　　　 Don Goode, Kansas, LB
1975 Gary Johnson, Grambling, DT
　　　 Mike Williams, Louisiana State, DB
1976 Joe Washington, Oklahoma, RB
1977 Bob Rush, Memphis State, C
1978 John Jefferson, Arizona State, WR
1979 Kellen Winslow, Missouri, TE
1980 Ed Luther, San Jose State, QB (4)
1981 James Brooks, Auburn, RB
1982 Hollis Hall, Clemson, DB (7)
1983 Billy Ray Smith, Arkansas, LB
　　　 Gary Anderson, Arkansas, WR
　　　 Gill Byrd, San Jose State, DB
1984 Mossy Cade, Texas, DB
1985 Jim Lachey, Ohio State, G
1986 Leslie O'Neal, Oklahoma State, DE
　　　 James FitzPatrick, So. California, T
1987 Rod Bernstine, Texas A&M, TE
1988 Anthony Miller, Tennessee, WR
1989 Burt Grossman, Pittsburgh, DE
1990 Junior Seau, So. California, LB
1991 Stanley Richard, Texas, DB
1992 Chris Mims, Tennessee, DE
1993 Darrien Gordon, Stanford, DB
1994 Isaac Davis, Arkansas, G (2)
1995 Terrance Shaw, Stephen F. Austin, DB (2)
1996 Bryan Still, Virginia Tech, WR (2)
1997 Freddie Jones, North Carolina, TE (2)
1998 Ryan Leaf, Washington State, QB
1999 Jermaine Fazande, Arkansas, RB (2)
2000 Rogers Beckett, Marshall, DB (2)
2001 LaDainian Tomlinson, TCU, RB
2002 Quentin Jammer, Texas, DB
2003 Sammy Davis, Texas A&M, DB
2004 Eli Manning, Mississippi, QB
2005 Shawne Merriman, Maryland, LB
　　　 Luis Castillo, Northwestern, DT
2006 Antonio Cromartie, Florida State, DB
2007 Craig Davis, Louisiana State, WR
2008 Antoine Cason, Arizona, DB

2009 Larry English, Northern Illinois, LB
2010 Ryan Mathews, Fresno State, RB
2011 Corey Liuget, Illinois, DE
2012 Melvin Ingram, South Carolina, LB
2013 D.J. Fluker, Alabama, T
2014 Jason Verrett, Texas Christian, DB

SAN FRANCISCO 49ERS
Year Player, College, Position
1950 Leo Nomellini, Minnesota, T
1951 Y.A. Tittle, Louisiana State, B
1952 Hugh McElhenny, Washington, B
1953 Harry Babcock, Georgia, E
　　　 Tom Stolhandske, Texas, E
1954 Bernie Faloney, Maryland, B
1955 Dickie Moegle, Rice, B
1956 Earl Morrall, Michigan State, B
1957 John Brodie, Stanford, B
1958 Jim Pace, Michigan, B
　　　 Charlie Krueger, Texas A&M, T
1959 Dave Baker, Oklahoma, B
　　　 Dan James, Ohio State, C
1960 Monty Stickles, Notre Dame, E
1961 Jimmy Johnson, UCLA, CB
　　　 Bernie Casey, Bowling Green, WR
　　　 Bill Kilmer, UCLA, QB
1962 Lance Alworth, Arkansas, WR
1963 Kermit Alexander, UCLA, CB
1964 Dave Parks, Texas Tech, WR
1965 Ken Willard, North Carolina, RB
　　　 George Donnelly, Illinois, DB
1966 Stan Hindman, Mississippi, DE
1967 Steve Spurrier, Florida, QB
　　　 Cas Banaszek, Northwestern, T
1968 Forrest Blue, Auburn, C
1969 Ted Kwalick, Penn State, TE
　　　 Gene Washington, Stanford, WR
1970 Cedrick Hardman, North Texas St., DE
　　　 Bruce Taylor, Boston U., DB
1971 Tim Anderson, Ohio State, DB
1972 Terry Beasley, Auburn, WR
1973 Mike Holmes, Texas Southern, DB
1974 Wilbur Jackson, Alabama, RB
　　　 Bill Sandifer, UCLA, DT
1975 Jimmy Webb, Mississippi St., DT
1976 Randy Cross, UCLA, C (2)
1977 Elmo Boyd, Eastern Kentucky, WR (3)
1978 Ken MacAfee, Notre Dame, TE
　　　 Dan Bunz, Cal St.-Long Beach, LB
1979 James Owens, UCLA, WR (2)
1980 Earl Cooper, Rice, RB
　　　 Jim Stuckey, Clemson, DT
1981 Ronnie Lott, So. California, DB
1982 Bubba Paris, Michigan, T (2)
1983 Roger Craig, Nebraska, RB (2)
1984 Todd Shell, Brigham Young, LB
1985 Jerry Rice, Mississippi Valley St., WR
1986 Larry Roberts, Alabama, DE (2)
1987 Harris Barton, North Carolina, T
　　　 Terrence Flagler, Clemson, RB
1988 Danny Stubbs, Miami, DE (2)
1989 Keith DeLong, Tennessee, LB
1990 Dexter Carter, Florida State, RB
1991 Ted Washington, Louisville, DT
1992 Dana Hall, Washington, DB
1993 Dana Stubblefield, Kansas, DT
　　　 Todd Kelly, Tennessee, DE
1994 Bryant Young, Notre Dame, DT
　　　 William Floyd, Florida State, RB
1995 J.J. Stokes, UCLA, WR
1996 Israel Ifeanyi, So.California, DE (2)
1997 Jim Druckenmiller, Virginia Tech, QB

1998 R.W. McQuarters, Oklahoma St., DB
1999 Reggie McGrew, Florida, DT
2000 Julian Peterson, Michigan St., LB
　　　 Ahmed Plummer, Ohio State, DB
2001 Andre Carter, California, DE
2002 Mike Rumph, Miami, DB
2003 Kwame Harris, Stanford, T
2004 Rashaun Woods, Oklahoma St., WR
2005 Alex Smith, Utah, QB
2006 Vernon Davis, Maryland, TE
　　　 Manny Lawson, North Carolina St., DE
2007 Patrick Willis, Mississippi, LB
　　　 Joe Staley, Central Michigan, T
2008 Kentwan Balmer, North Carolina, DE
2009 Michael Crabtree, Texas Tech, WR
2010 Anthony Davis, Rutgers, T
　　　 Mike Iupati, Idaho, G
2011 Aldon Smith, Missouri, LB
2012 A.J. Jenkins, Illinois, WR
2013 Eric Reid, Louisiana State, DB
2014 Jimmie Ward, Northern Illinois, DB

SEATTLE SEAHAWKS
Year Player, College, Position
1976 Steve Niehaus, Notre Dame, DT
1977 Steve August, Tulsa, G
1978 Keith Simpson, Memphis St., DB
1979 Manu Tuiasosopo, UCLA, DT
1980 Jacob Green, Texas A&M, DE
1981 Ken Easley, UCLA, DB
1982 Jeff Bryant, Clemson, DE
1983 Curt Warner, Penn State, RB
1984 Terry Taylor, Southern Illinois, DB
1985 Owen Gill, Iowa, RB (2)
1986 John L. Williams, Florida, RB
1987 Tony Woods, Pittsburgh, LB
1988 Brian Blades, Miami, WR (2)
1989 Andy Heck, Notre Dame, T
1990 Cortez Kennedy, Miami, DT
1991 Dan McGwire, San Diego St., QB
1992 Ray Roberts, Virginia, T
1993 Rick Mirer, Notre Dame, QB
1994 Sam Adams, Texas A&M, DT
1995 Joey Galloway, Ohio State, WR
1996 Pete Kendall, Boston College, T
1997 Shawn Springs, Ohio State, DB
　　　 Walter Jones, Florida State, T
1998 Anthony Simmons, Clemson, LB
1999 Lamar King, Saginaw Valley St., DE
2000 Shaun Alexander, Alabama, RB
　　　 Chris McIntosh, Wisconsin, T
2001 Koren Robinson, North Carolina St., WR
　　　 Steve Hutchinson, Michigan, G
2002 Jerramy Stevens, Washington, TE
2003 Marcus Trufant, Washington State, DB
2004 Marcus Tubbs, Texas, DT
2005 Chris Spencer, Mississippi, C
2006 Kelly Jennings, Miami, DB
2007 Josh Wilson, Maryland, DB (2)
2008 Lawrence Jackson, So. California, DE
2009 Aaron Curry, Wake Forest, LB
2010 Russell Okung, Oklahoma State, T
　　　 Earl Thomas, Texas, DB
2011 James Carpenter, Alabama, T
2012 Bruce Irvin, West Virginia, DE
2013 Christine Michael, Texas A&M, RB (2)
2014 Paul Richardson, Colorado, WR (2)

TAMPA BAY BUCCANEERS
Year Player, College, Position
1976 Lee Roy Selmon, Oklahoma, DT
1977 Ricky Bell, Southern California, RB

1978 Doug Williams, Grambling, QB
1979 Greg Roberts, Oklahoma, G (2)
1980 Ray Snell, Wisconsin, G
1981 Hugh Green, Pittsburgh, LB
1982 Sean Farrell, Penn State, G
1983 Randy Grimes, Baylor, C (2)
1984 Keith Browner, So. California, LB (2)
1985 Ron Holmes, Washington, DE
1986 Bo Jackson, Auburn, RB
     Roderick Jones, So. Methodist, DB
1987 Vinny Testaverde, Miami, QB
1988 Paul Gruber, Wisconsin, T
1989 Broderick Thomas, Nebraska, LB
1990 Keith McCants, Alabama, LB
1991 Charles McRae, Tennessee, T
1992 Courtney Hawkins, Michigan St., WR (2)
1993 Eric Curry, Alabama, DE
1994 Trent Dilfer, Fresno State, QB
1995 Warren Sapp, Miami, DT
     Derrick Brooks, Florida State, LB
1996 Regan Upshaw, California, DE
     Marcus Jones, North Carolina, DT
1997 Warrick Dunn, Florida State, RB
     Reidel Anthony, Florida, WR
1998 Jacquez Green, Florida, WR (2)
1999 Anthony McFarland, Louisiana St., DT
2000 Cosey Coleman, Tennessee, G (2)
2001 Kenyatta Walker, Florida, T
2002 Marquise Walker, Michigan, WR (3)
2003 Dewayne White, Louisville, DE (2)
2004 Michael Clayton, Louisiana St., WR
2005 Carnell Williams, Auburn, RB
2006 Davin Joseph, Oklahoma, G
2007 Gaines Adams, Clemson, DE
2008 Aqib Talib, Kansas, DB
2009 Josh Freeman, Kansas State, QB
2010 Gerald McCoy, Oklahoma, DT
2011 Adrian Clayborn, Iowa, DE
2012 Mark Barron, Alabama, DB
     Doug Martin, Boise State, RB
2013 Johnthan Banks, Mississippi St., DB (2)
2014 Mike Evans, Texas A&M, WR

TENNESSEE TITANS
Year Player, College, Position
1960 Billy Cannon, Louisiana State, RB
1961 Mike Ditka, Pittsburgh, E
1962 Ray Jacobs, Howard Payne, DT
1963 Danny Brabham, Arkansas, LB
1964 Scott Appleton, Texas, DT
1965 Lawrence Elkins, Baylor, WR
1966 Tommy Nobis, Texas, LB
1967 George Webster, Michigan St., LB
     Tom Regner, Notre Dame, G
1968 Mac Haik, Mississippi, WR (2)
1969 Ron Pritchard, Arizona State, LB
1970 Doug Wilkerson, N. Carolina Central, G
1971 Dan Pastorini, Santa Clara, QB
1972 Greg Sampson, Stanford, DE
1973 John Matuszak, Tampa, DE
     George Amundson, Iowa State, RB
1974 Steve Manstedt, Nebraska, LB (4)
1975 Robert Brazile, Jackson State, LB
     Don Hardeman, Texas A&I, RB
1976 Mike Barber, Louisiana Tech, TE (2)
1977 Morris Towns, Missouri, T
1978 Earl Campbell, Texas, RB
1979 Mike Stensrud, Iowa State, DE (2)
1980 Angelo Fields, Michigan St., T (2)
1981 Michael Holston, Morgan St., WR (3)
1982 Mike Munchak, Penn State, G
1983 Bruce Matthews, So. California, T

1984 Dean Steinkuhler, Nebraska, T
1985 Ray Childress, Texas A&M, DE
     Richard Johnson, Wisconsin, DB
1986 Jim Everett, Purdue, QB
1987 Alonzo Highsmith, Miami, RB
     Haywood Jeffires, North Carolina St., WR
1988 Lorenzo White, Michigan State, RB
1989 David Williams, Florida, T
1990 Lamar Lathon, Houston, LB
1991 Mike Dumas, Indiana, DB (2)
1992 Eddie Robinson, Alabama St., LB (2)
1993 Brad Hopkins, Illinois, T
1994 Henry Ford, Arkansas, DE
1995 Steve McNair, Alcorn State, QB
1996 Eddie George, Ohio State, RB
1997 Kenny Holmes, Miami, DE
1998 Kevin Dyson, Utah, WR
1999 Jevon Kearse, Florida, DE
2000 Keith Bulluck, Syracuse, LB
2001 Andre Dyson, Utah, DB (2)
2002 Albert Haynesworth, Tennessee, DT
2003 Andre Woolfolk, Oklahoma, DB
2004 Ben Troupe, Florida, TE (2)
2005 Adam Jones, West Virginia, DB
2006 Vince Young, Texas, QB
2007 Michael Griffin, Texas, DB
2008 Chris Johnson, East Carolina, RB
2009 Kenny Britt, Rutgers, WR
2010 Derrick Morgan, Georgia Tech, DE
2011 Jake Locker, Washington, QB
2012 Kendall Wright, Baylor, WR
2013 Chance Warmack, Alabama, G
2014 Taylor Lewan, Michigan, T

WASHINGTON REDSKINS
Year Player, College, Position
1936 Riley Smith, Alabama, B
1937 Sammy Baugh, Texas Christian, B
1938 Andy Farkas, Detroit, B
1939 I.B. Hale, Texas Christian, T
1940 Ed Boell, New York U., B
1941 Forest Evashevski, Michigan, B
1942 Orban (Spec) Sanders, Texas, B
1943 Jack Jenkins, Missouri, B
1944 Mike Micka, Colgate, B
1945 Jim Hardy, Southern California, B
1946 Cal Rossi, UCLA, B*
1947 Cal Rossi, UCLA, B
1948 Harry Gilmer, Alabama, B
     Lowell Tew, Alabama, B
1949 Rob Goode, Texas A&M, B
1950 George Thomas, Oklahoma, B
1951 Leon Heath, Oklahoma, B
1952 Larry Isbell, Baylor, B
1953 Jack Scarbath, Maryland, B
1954 Steve Meilinger, Kentucky, E
1955 Ralph Guglielmi, Notre Dame, B
1956 Ed Vereb, Maryland, B
1957 Don Bosseler, Miami, B
1958 Mike Sommer, George
     Washington, B (2)
1959 Don Allard, Boston College, B
1960 Richie Lucas, Penn State, QB
1961 Norman Snead, Wake Forest, QB
     Joe Rutgens, Illinois, DT
1962 Ernie Davis, Syracuse, RB
1963 Pat Richter, Wisconsin, TE
1964 Charley Taylor, Arizona St., RB-WR
1965 Bob Breitenstein, Tulsa, T (2)
1966 Charlie Gogolak, Princeton, K
1967 Ray McDonald, Idaho, RB
1968 Jim Smith, Oregon, DB

1969 Eugene Epps, Texas-El Paso, DB (2)
1970 Bill Bundige, Colorado, DT (2)
1971 Cotton Speyrer, Texas, WR (2)
1972 Moses Denson, Maryland St., RB (8)
1973 Charles Cantrell, Lamar, G (5)
1974 Jon Keyworth, Colorado, TE (6)
1975 Mike Thomas, Nevada-Las Vegas, RB (6)
1976 Mike Hughes, Baylor, G (5)
1977 Duncan McColl, Stanford, DE (4)
1978 Tony Green, Florida, RB (6)
1979 Don Warren, San Diego St., TE (4)
1980 Art Monk, Syracuse, WR
1981 Mark May, Pittsburgh, T
1982 Vernon Dean, San Diego St., DB (2)
1983 Darrell Green, Texas A&I, DB
1984 Bob Slater, Oklahoma, DT (2)
1985 Tory Nixon, San Diego St., DB (2)
1986 Markus Koch, Boise State, DE (2)
1987 Brian Davis, Nebraska, DB (2)
1988 Chip Lohmiller, Minnesota, K (2)
1989 Tracy Rocker, Auburn, DT (3)
1990 Andre Collins, Penn State, LB (2)
1991 Bobby Wilson, Michigan State, DT
1992 Desmond Howard, Michigan, WR
1993 Tom Carter, Notre Dame, DB
1994 Heath Shuler, Tennessee, QB
1995 Michael Westbrook, Colorado, WR
1996 Andre Johnson, Penn State, T
1997 Kenard Lang, Miami, DE
1998 Stephen Alexander, Oklahoma, TE (2)
1999 Champ Bailey, Georgia, DB
2000 LaVar Arrington, Penn State, LB
     Chris Samuels, Alabama, T
2001 Rod Gardner, Clemson, WR
2002 Patrick Ramsey, Tulane, QB
2003 Taylor Jacobs, Florida, WR (2)
2004 Sean Taylor, Miami, DB
2005 Carlos Rogers, Auburn, DB
     Jason Campbell, Auburn, QB
2006 Rocky McIntosh, Miami, LB (2)
2007 LaRon Landry, Louisiana State, DB
2008 Devin Thomas, Michigan State, WR (2)
2009 Brian Orakpo, Texas, DE
2010 Trent Williams, Oklahoma, T
2011 Ryan Kerrigan, Purdue, LB
2012 Robert Griffin III, Baylor, QB
2013 David Amerson, North Carolina St., DB (2)
2014 Trent Murphy, Stanford, LB (2)
Choice lost because of ineligibility

ATTENDANCE/TV RATINGS

NFL'S 10 HIGHEST SCORING WEEKENDS

Point Total	Date	Weekend
859	December 5, 8-9, 2013	14th
844	December 12, 15-16, 2013	15th
837	November 20-24, 2008	12th
791	September 5, 9-10, 2012	1st
788	December 29-30, 2007	17th
788	December 5-6, 2004	13th
788	September 5, 8-9, 2002	1st
779	December 16, 19-20, 2010	15th
765	September 13, 16-17, 2012	2nd
762	November 10-11, 1996	11th

TOP 10 TELEVISED SPORTS EVENTS OF ALL-TIME
(Based on Nielsen Company Figures)

Program	Date	Network	Share	Rating
Super Bowl XVI	1/24/82	CBS	73%	49.1
Super Bowl XVII	1/30/83	NBC	69%	48.6
Winter Olympics	2/23/94	CBS	64%	48.5
Super Bowl XX	1/26/86	NBC	70%	48.3
Super Bowl XII	1/15/78	CBS	67%	47.2
Super Bowl XIII	1/21/79	NBC	74%	47.1
Super Bowl XLVI	2/5/12	NBC	71%	47.0
Super Bowl XLVIII	2/2/14	FOX	69%	46.7
Super Bowl XVIII	1/22/84	CBS	71%	46.4
Super Bowl XIX	1/20/85	ABC	63%	46.4
Super Bowl XLVII	2/3/13	CBS	69%	46.4

TEN MOST WATCHED TV PROGRAMS & ESTIMATED TOTAL NUMBER OF VIEWERS
(Based on Nielsen Company Figures)

Program	Date	Network	*Total Viewers
Super Bowl XLVII	Feb. 3, 2013	CBS	164,100,000
Super Bowl XLV	Feb. 6, 2011	FOX	162,900,000
Super Bowl XLVIII	Feb. 2, 2014	FOX	161,100,000
Super Bowl XLVI	Feb. 5, 2012	NBC	159,200,000
Super Bowl XLIV	Feb. 7, 2010	CBS	153,400,000
Super Bowl XLIII	Feb. 1, 2009	NBC	151,600,000
Super Bowl XLII	Feb. 3, 2008	FOX	148,300,000
Super Bowl XXXVIII	Feb. 1, 2004	CBS	144,400,000
Super Bowl XL	Feb. 5, 2006	ABC	141,400,000
Super Bowl XLI	Feb. 4, 2007	CBS	139,800,000

NFL'S TOP FIVE PAID ATTENDANCE TOTALS FOR ALL GAMES

Year	Preseason	Regular Season	Postseason	All Games
2007	4,119,278	17,345,205	792,019	22,256,502
2006	4,083,282	17,340,879	775,551	22,199,712
2008	3,995,942	17,055,982	806,840	21,858,764
2005	3,977,388	17,012,453	802,255	21,792,096
2004	3,918,848	17,000,811	788,965	21,708,624

TEN HIGHEST-RATED *NFL MONDAY NIGHT FOOTBALL* GAMES OF ALL-TIME
(Based on Nielsen Company Figures)

Game	Date	Share	Rating
Chicago at Miami	12/2/85	46%	29.6
N.Y. Giants at San Francisco	12/3/90	42%	26.9
Dallas at Washington	10/2/78	43%	26.8
Pittsburgh at San Diego	12/22/80	40%	25.3
Philadelphia at Miami	11/30/81	40%	25.3
Pittsburgh at Houston	12/10/79	40%	25.1
Dallas at Miami	12/17/84	40%	25.1
Pittsburgh at Dallas	9/13/82	42%	24.9
Cincinnati at Oakland	12/6/76	40%	24.7
Dallas at Washington	10/8/73	40%	24.6
Minnesota at Atlanta	11/19/73	40%	24.6

NFL'S 10 BIGGEST SINGLE-GAME ATTENDANCE TOTALS

Date	Site	Game	Teams	Attendance
August 15, 1994	Azteca Stadium	American Bowl (Mexico City)	Cowboys vs. Oilers	112,376
August 17, 1998	Azteca Stadium	American Bowl (Mexico City)	Cowboys vs. Patriots	106,424
August 22, 1947	Soldier Field	College All-Star	Bears vs. All-Stars	105,840
September 20, 2009	Cowboys Stadium	Regular Season	Cowboys vs. Giants	105,121
August 4, 1997	Estadio Guillermo Canedo	American Bowl (Mexico City)	Broncos vs. Dolphins	104,629
January 20, 1980	Rose Bowl	Super Bowl XIV	Steelers vs. Rams	103,985
January 30, 1983	Rose Bowl	Super Bowl XVII	Redskins vs. Dolphins	103,667
October 2, 2005	Azteca Stadium	Regular Season	49ers at Cardinals	103,467
January 9, 1977	Rose Bowl	Super Bowl XI	Raiders vs. Vikings	103,438
November 10, 1957	L.A. Coliseum	Regular Season	49ers at Rams	102,368

NFL'S TOP 10 PAID ATTENDANCE WEEKENDS

Weekend	Games	Attendance
September 8, 11-12, 2005	16	1,115,018
December 6, 9-10, 2007	16	1,113,376
November 20-21, 2005	16	1,112,555
December 27-28, 2003	16	1,106,818
November 19-20, 2006	16	1,106,739
September 23-24, 2007	16	1,103,570
December 24-26, 2005	16	1,102,701
September 7, 10-11, 2006	16	1,102,102
September 9, 12-13, 2004	16	1,101,332
December 7, 10-11, 2006	16	1,099,794

NFL'S TOP 10 TEAM SINGLE-SEASON HOME PAID ATTENDANCE TOTALS

Year	Club	Games	Attendance
2007	Washington Redskins	8	711,471
2008	Washington Redskins	8	710,049
2006	Washington Redskins	8	708,952
2004	Washington Redskins	8	707,920
2005	Washington Redskins	8	707,614
2009	Washington Redskins	8	681,703
2010	Washington Redskins	8	680,966
2003	Washington Redskins	8	667,033
2002	Washington Redskins	8	663,536
2001	Washington Redskins	8	661,970

NFL PAID ATTENDANCE

For detailed 2013 attendance, see page 246.

Year	Regular Season		Average	Postseason	Total
2013	16,837,676	(256 games)	65,772	822,651 (12)	17,660,327
2012	16,658,950	(256 games)	65,074	821,433 (12)	17,480,383
2011	16,562,706	(256 games)	64,698	828,457 (12)	17,391,163
2010	16,569,514	(255 games****)	64,978	800,426 (12)	17,369,940
2009	16,651,126	(256 games)	65,043	823,882 (12)	17,475,008
2008	17,055,982	(256 games)	66,625	806,840 (12)	17,862,822
2007	17,345,205	(256 games)	#67,755	792,019 (12)	#18,137,224
2006	17,340,879	(256 games)	67,738	775,551 (12)	18,116,430
2005	17,012,453	(256 games)	66,455	802,255 (12)	17,814,708
2004	17,000,811	(256 games)	66,409	788,965 (12)	17,789,776
2003	16,913,584	(255 games***)	66,328	805,546 (12)	17,719,130
2002	16,833,310	(256 games)	65,755	781,944 (12)	17,615,254
2001	16,166,258	(248 games)	65,187	766,905 (12)	16,933,163
2000	16,387,289	(248 games)	66,078	809,132 (12)	17,196,421
1999	16,206,640	(248 games)	65,349	793,759 (12)	17,000,399
1998	15,364,873	(240 games)	64,020	822,885 (12)	16,187,758
1997	14,967,314	(240 games)	62,364	801,879 (12)	15,769,193
1996	14,612,417	(240 games)	60,885	769,310 (12)	15,381,727
1995	15,043,562	(240 games)	62,682	790,906 (12)	15,834,468
1994	14,030,435	(224 games)	62,636	779,738 (12)	14,810,173
1993	13,966,843	(224 games)	62,352	814,607 (12)	14,781,450
1992	13,828,887	(224 games)	61,736	815,910 (12)	14,644,797
1991	13,841,459	(224 games)	61,792	813,247 (12)	14,654,706
1990	13,959,896	(224 games)	62,321	847,543 (12)	14,807,439
1989	13,625,662	(224 games)	60,829	685,771 (10)	14,311,433
1988	13,539,848	(224 games)	60,446	658,317 (10)	14,198,165
1987	11,406,166	(210 games**)	54,315	656,977 (10)	12,063,143
1986	13,588,551	(224 games)	60,663	734,002 (10)	14,322,553
1985	13,345,047	(224 games)	59,567	710,768 (10)	14,055,815
1984	13,398,112	(224 games)	59,813	665,194 (10)	14,063,306
1983	13,277,222	(224 games)	59,273	675,513 (10)	13,952,735
1982	7,367,438	(126 games*)	58,472	#1,033,153 (16)	8,400,591
1981	13,606,990	(224 games)	60,745	637,763 (10)	14,244,753
1980	13,392,230	(224 games)	59,787	624,430 (10)	14,016,660
1979	13,182,039	(224 games)	58,848	630,326 (10)	13,812,365
1978	12,771,800	(224 games)	57,017	624,388 (10)	13,396,188
1977	11,018,632	(196 games)	56,218	534,925 (8)	11,553,557
1976	11,070,543	(196 games)	56,482	492,884 (8)	11,563,427
1975	10,213,193	(182 games)	56,116	475,919 (8)	10,689,112
1974	10,236,322	(182 games)	56,244	438,664 (8)	10,674,986
1973	10,730,933	(182 games)	58,961	525,433 (8)	11,256,366
1972	10,445,827	(182 games)	57,395	483,345 (8)	10,929,172
1971	10,076,035	(182 games)	55,363	483,891 (8)	10,559,926
1970	9,533,333	(182 games)	52,381	458,493 (8)	9,991,826
1969	6,096,127	(112 games) NFL	54,430	162,279 (3)	6,258,406
	2,843,373	(70 games) AFL	40,620	167,088 (3)	3,010,461
1968	5,882,313	(112 games) NFL	52,521	215,902 (3)	6,098,215
	2,635,004	(70 games) AFL	37,643	114,438 (2)	2,749,442
1967	5,938,924	(112 games) NFL	53,026	166,208 (3)	6,105,132
	2,295,697	(63 games) AFL	36,439	53,330 (1)	2,349,027
1966	5,337,044	(105 games) NFL	50,829	74,152 (1)	5,411,196
	2,160,369	(63 games) AFL	34,291	42,080 (1)	2,202,449

PAID ATTENDANCE

Year	Regular Season			Average	Postseason	Total
1965	4,634,021	(98 games)	NFL	47,286	100,304 (2)	4,734,325
	1,782,384	(56 games)	AFL	31,828	30,361 (1)	1,812,745
1964	4,563,049	(98 games)	NFL	46,562	79,544 (1)	4,642,593
	1,447,875	(56 games)	AFL	25,855	40,242 (1)	1,488,117
1963	4,163,643	(98 games)	NFL	42,486	45,801 (1)	4,209,444
	1,208,697	(56 games)	AFL	21,584	63,171 (2)	1,271,868
1962	4,003,421	(98 games)	NFL	40,851	64,892 (1)	4,068,313
	1,147,302	(56 games)	AFL	20,487	37,981 (1)	1,185,283
1961	3,986,159	(98 games)	NFL	40,675	39,029 (1)	4,025,188
	1,002,657	(56 games)	AFL	17,904	29,556 (1)	1,032,213
1960	3,128,296	(78 games)	NFL	40,106	67,325 (1)	3,195,621
	926,156	(56 games)	AFL	16,538	32,183 (1)	958,339
1959	3,140,000	(72 games)		43,617	57,545 (1)	3,197,545
1958	3,006,124	(72 games)		41,752	123,659 (2)	3,129,783
1957	2,836,318	(72 games)		39,393	119,579 (2)	2,955,897
1956	2,551,263	(72 games)		35,434	56,836 (1)	2,608,099
1955	2,521,836	(72 games)		35,026	85,693 (1)	2,607,529
1954	2,190,571	(72 games)		30,425	43,827 (1)	2,234,398
1953	2,164,585	(72 games)		30,064	54,577 (1)	2,219,162
1952	2,052,126	(72 games)		28,502	97,507 (2)	2,149,633
1951	1,913,019	(72 games)		26,570	57,522 (1)	1,970,541
1950	1,977,753	(78 games)		25,356	136,647 (3)	2,114,400
1949	1,391,735	(60 games)		23,196	27,980 (1)	1,419,715
1948	1,525,243	(60 games)		25,421	36,309 (1)	1,561,552
1947	1,837,437	(60 games)		30,624	66,268 (2)	1,903,705
1946	1,732,135	(55 games)		31,493	58,346 (1)	1,790,481
1945	1,270,401	(50 games)		25,408	32,178 (1)	1,302,579
1944	1,019,649	(50 games)		20,393	46,016 (1)	1,065,665
1943	969,128	(40 games)		24,228	71,315 (2)	1,040,443
1942	887,920	(55 games)		16,144	36,006 (1)	923,926
1941	1,108,615	(55 games)		20,157	55,870 (2)	1,164,485
1940	1,063,025	(55 games)		19,328	36,034 (1)	1,099,059
1939	1,071,200	(55 games)		19,476	32,279 (1)	1,103,479
1938	937,197	(55 games)		17,040	48,120 (1)	985,317
1937	963,039	(55 games)		17,510	15,878 (1)	978,917
1936	816,007	(54 games)		15,111	29,545 (1)	845,552
1935	638,178	(53 games)		12,041	15,000 (1)	653,178
1934	492,684	(60 games)		8,211	35,059 (1)	527,743

Record

*Players' 57-day strike reduced 224-game schedule to 126 games.
**Players' 24-day strike reduced 224-game schedule to 210 games.
***The Week 8 Miami at San Diego game is not included. The game was moved to Arizona due to the San Diego wildfires and tickets were distributed at no charge.
****The Week 14 N.Y. Giants at Minnesota game is not included. The game was moved to Detroit due to the Minneapolis blizzard. Original game tickets were cross-honored at Ford Field. Remaining tickets were distributed at no charge.

Records

Compiled by Elias Sports Bureau.

The following records reflect all available official information on the National Football League from its formation in 1920 to date. Also included are all applicable records from the American Football League, 1960-69.

Individuals eligible for Rookie records are players who were in their first season of professional football and had not been on the roster or practice squad of another professional football team, including teams in other leagues, for any regular-season or post-season games in a previous season. Eligible players, therefore, include those who were under contract to a National Football League club for a previous season but were terminated prior to their club's first regular-season game and not re-signed, or who were placed on Reserve/Injured (or another category of the Reserve List) prior to their club's first regular-season game and were not activated during the rest of the regular season or post-season.

INDIVIDUAL RECORDS

SERVICE
Most Seasons
26 George Blanda, Chi. Bears, 1949, 1950-58; Baltimore, 1950; Houston, 1960-66; Oakland, 1967-1975
25 Morten Andersen, New Orleans, 1982-1994; Atlanta, 1995-2000; N.Y. Giants, 2001; Kansas City, 2002-03; Minnesota, 2004; Atlanta, 2006-07
23 Gary Anderson, Pittsburgh, 1982-1994; Philadelphia, 1995-96; San Francisco, 1997; Minnesota, 1998-2002; Tennessee, 2003-04
   John Carney, Tampa Bay, 1988-89; L.A. Rams, 1990: San Diego, 1990-2000; New Orleans, 2001-06; Jacksonville, 2007; Kansas City, 2007; N.Y. Giants, 2008; New Orleans, 2009-2010

Most Seasons, One Club
21 Jason Hanson, Detroit, 1992-2012
20 Jackie Slater, L.A. Rams, 1976-1994; St. Louis, 1995
   Darrell Green, Washington, 1983-2002
19 Jim Marshall, Minnesota, 1961-1979
   Bruce Matthews, Houston, 1983-1996; Tennessee, 1997-2001

Most Games Played, Career
382 Morten Andersen, New Orleans, 1982-1994; Atlanta, 1995-2000; N.Y. Giants, 2001; Kansas City, 2002-03; Minnesota, 2004; Atlanta, 2006-07
353 Gary Anderson, Pittsburgh, 1982-1994; Philadelphia, 1995-96; San Francisco, 1997; Minnesota, 1998-2002; Tennessee, 2003-04
352 Jeff Feagles, New England, 1988-89; Philadelphia, 1990-93; Arizona, 1994-97; Seattle, 1998-2002; N.Y. Giants, 2003-09

Most Consecutive Games Played, Career
352 Jeff Feagles, New England, 1988-89; Philadelphia, 1990-93; Arizona, 1994-97; Seattle, 1998-2002; N.Y. Giants, 2003-09
299 Brett Favre, Green Bay, 1992-2007; N.Y. Jets, 2008; Minnesota, 2009-2010
282 Jim Marshall, Cleveland, 1960; Minnesota, 1961-1979

SCORING
Most Seasons Leading League
5 Don Hutson, Green Bay, 1940-44
   Gino Cappelletti, Boston, 1961, 1963-66
3 Earl (Dutch) Clark, Portsmouth, 1932; Detroit, 1935-36
   Pat Harder, Chi. Cardinals, 1947-49
   Paul Hornung, Green Bay, 1959-1961
   Stephen Gostkowski, New England, 2008, 2012-13

2 By 10 players
Most Consecutive Seasons Leading League
5 Don Hutson, Green Bay, 1940-44
4 Gino Cappelletti, Boston, 1963-66
3 Pat Harder, Chi. Cardinals, 1947-49
   Paul Hornung, Green Bay, 1959-1961

POINTS
Most Points, Career
2,544 Morten Andersen, New Orleans, 1982-1994; Atlanta, 1995-2000; N.Y. Giants, 2001; Kansas City, 2002-03; Minnesota, 2004; Atlanta, 2006-07 (849-pat, 565-fg)
2,434 Gary Anderson, Pittsburgh, 1982-1994; Philadelphia 1995-96; San Francisco, 1997; Minnesota, 1998-2002; Tennessee, 2003-04 (820-pat, 538-fg)
2,150 Jason Hanson, Detroit, 1992-2012 (665-pat, 495-fg)

Most Points, Season
186 LaDainian Tomlinson, San Diego, 2006 (31-td)
176 Paul Hornung, Green Bay, 1960 (15-td, 41-pat, 15-fg)
168 Shaun Alexander, Seattle, 2005 (28-td)

Most Points, No Touchdowns, Season
166 David Akers, San Francisco, 2011 (34-pat, 44-fg)
164 Gary Anderson, Minnesota, 1998 (59-pat, 35-fg)
163 Jeff Wilkins, St. Louis, 2003 (46-pat, 39-fg)

Most Seasons, 100 or More Points
16 Jason Elam, Denver, 1993-2007; Atlanta, 2008
   Adam Vinatieri, New England, 1996-2005; Indianapolis, 2006-08, 2010, 2012-13
14 Gary Anderson, Pittsburgh, 1983-85, 1988, 1991-94; Philadelphia 1996; San Francisco, 1997; Minnesota, 1998-2000; Tennessee, 2003
   Morten Andersen, New Orleans, 1985-89, 1991-94; Atlanta, 1995, 1997-98; Kansas City, 2002-03
12 Matt Stover, Cleveland, 1994-95; Baltimore, 1997, 1999-2001, 2003-08
   David Akers, Philadelphia, 2000-04, 2006-2010; San Francisco 2011-12
   Jason Hanson, Detroit, 1993, 1995, 1997-2000, 2002, 2004, 2006-07, 2011-12

Most Points, Rookie Season
144 Kevin Butler, Chicago, 1985 (51-pat, 31-fg)
141 Mason Crosby, Green Bay, 2007 (48-pat, 31-fg)
   Blair Walsh, Minnesota, 2012 (36-pat, 35-fg)
135 Dan Bailey, Dallas, 2011 (39-pat, 32-fg)

Most Points, Game
40 Ernie Nevers, Chi. Cardinals vs. Chi. Bears, Nov. 28, 1929 (6-td, 4-pat)
36 Dub Jones, Cleveland vs. Chi. Bears, Nov. 25, 1951 (6-td)
   Gale Sayers, Chicago vs. San Francisco, Dec. 12, 1965 (6-td)
33 Paul Hornung, Green Bay vs. Baltimore, Oct. 8, 1961 (4-td, 6-pat, 1-fg)

Most Consecutive Games Scoring
360 Morten Andersen, New Orleans, 1983-1994; Atlanta, 1995-2000; N.Y. Giants, 2001; Kansas City, 2002-03; Minnesota, 2004; Atlanta, 2006-07
263 Jason Elam, Denver, 1993-2007; Atlanta, 2008-09
186 Jim Breech, Oakland, 1979; Cincinnati, 1980-1992

TOUCHDOWNS
Most Seasons Leading League
8 Don Hutson, Green Bay, 1935-38, 1941-44
3 Jim Brown, Cleveland, 1958-59, 1963
   Lance Alworth, San Diego, 1964-66
   Emmitt Smith, Dallas, 1992, 1994-95
2 By many players

Most Consecutive Seasons Leading League
  4   Don Hutson, Green Bay, 1935-38, 1941-44
  3   Lance Alworth, San Diego, 1964-66
  2   By many players
Most Touchdowns, Career
  208   Jerry Rice, San Francisco, 1985-2000;
          Oakland, 2001-04;
          Seattle, 2004 (10-r, 197-p, 1-ret)
  175   Emmitt Smith, Dallas, 1990-2002; Arizona, 2003-04
          (164-r, 11-p)
  162   LaDainian Tomlinson, San Diego, 2001-09;
          N.Y. Jets, 2010-11 (145-r, 17-p)
Most Touchdowns, Season
  31   LaDainian Tomlinson, San Diego, 2006 (28-r, 3-p)
  28   Shaun Alexander, Seattle, 2005 (27-r, 1-p)
  27   Priest Holmes, Kansas City, 2003 (27-r)
Most Touchdowns, Rookie, Season
  22   Gale Sayers. Chicago, 1965 (14-r, 6-p)
  20   Eric Dickerson, Rams, 1983 (18-r, 2-p)
  17   Fred Taylor, Jacksonville, 1998 (14-r, 3-p)
          Randy Moss, Minnesota, 1998 (17-p)
          Edgerrin James, Indianapolis, 1999 (13-r, 4-p)
          Clinton Portis, Denver, 2002 (15-r, 2-p)
Most Touchdowns, Game
  6   Ernie Nevers, Chi. Cardinals vs. Chi. Bears,
          Nov. 28, 1929 (6-r)
          Dub Jones, Cleveland vs. Chi. Bears, Nov. 25, 1951
          (4-r, 2-p)
          Gale Sayers, Chicago vs. San Francisco, Dec. 12, 1965
          (4-r, 1-p, 1-ret)
  5   Jimmy Conzelman, Rock Island vs. Evansville,
          Oct. 15, 1922 (5-r)
          Bob Shaw, Chi. Cardinals vs. Baltimore, Oct. 2, 1950
          (5-p)
          Jim Brown, Cleveland vs. Baltimore, Nov. 1, 1959 (5-r)
          Abner Haynes, Dall. Texans vs. Oakland,
          Nov. 26, 1961 (4-r, 1-p)
          Billy Cannon, Houston vs. N.Y. Titans, Dec. 10, 1961
          (3-r, 2-p)
          Cookie Gilchrist, Buffalo vs. N.Y. Jets, Dec. 8, 1963 (5-r)
          Paul Hornung, Green Bay vs. Baltimore,
          Dec. 12, 1965 (3-r, 2-p)
          Kellen Winslow, San Diego vs. Oakland,
          Nov. 22, 1981 (5-p)
          Jerry Rice, San Francisco vs. Atlanta, Oct. 14, 1990
          (5-p)
          James Stewart, Jacksonville vs. Philadelphia,
          Oct. 12, 1997 (5-r)
          Shaun Alexander, Seattle vs. Minnesota,
          Sept. 29, 2002 (4-r, 1-p)
          Clinton Portis, Denver vs. Kansas City, Dec. 7, 2003
          (5-r)
          Jamaal Charles, Kansas City vs. Oakland,
          Dec. 15, 2013 (4-p, 1-r)
  4   By many players. Last time:
          Eric Decker, Denver vs. Kansas City, Dec. 1, 2013
          (4-p)
Most Consecutive Games Scoring Touchdowns
  18   Lenny Moore, Baltimore, 1963-65
          LaDainian Tomlinson, San Diego, 2004-05
  14   O.J. Simpson, Buffalo, 1975
  13   John Riggins, Washington, 1982-83
          George Rogers, Washington, 1985-86
          Jerry Rice, San Francisco, 1986-87

POINTS AFTER TOUCHDOWN
Most Seasons Leading League
  8   George Blanda, Chi. Bears, 1956; Houston,
          1961-62; Oakland, 1967-69, 1972, 1974

  4   Bob Waterfield, Cleveland, 1945; Los Angeles, 1946,
          1950, 1952
  3   Earl (Dutch) Clark, Portsmouth, 1932; Detroit,
          1935-36 Jack Manders, Chi. Bears, 1933-35
          Don Hutson, Green Bay, 1941-42, 1945
Most (Kicking) Points After Touchdown Attempted, Career
  959   George Blanda, Chi. Bears, 1949, 1950-58; Baltimore,
          1950; Houston, 1960-66; Oakland, 1967-1975
  859   Morten Andersen, New Orleans, 1982-1994;
          Atlanta, 1995-2000; N.Y. Giants, 2001;
          Kansas City, 2002-03; Minnesota, 2004;
          Atlanta, 2006-07
  827   Gary Anderson, Pittsburgh, 1982-1994; Philadelphia
          1995-96; San Francisco, 1997; Minnesota,
          1998-2002; Tennessee, 2003-04
Most (Kicking) Points After Touchdown Attempted, Season
  75   Matt Prater, Denver, 2013
  74   Stephen Gostkowski, New England, 2007
  70   Uwe von Schamann, Miami, 1984
Most (Kicking) Points After Touchdown Attempted, Game
  10   Charlie Gogolak, Washington vs. N.Y. Giants,
          Nov. 27, 1966
  9   Pat Harder, Chi. Cardinals vs. N.Y. Giants,
          Oct. 17, 1948; vs. N.Y. Bulldogs, Nov. 13, 1949
          Bob Waterfield, Los Angeles vs. Baltimore,
          Oct. 22, 1950
          Bob Thomas, Chicago vs. Green Bay, Dec. 7, 1980
  8   By many players
Most (One-Point) Points After Touchdown, Career
  943   George Blanda, Chi. Bears, 1949, 1950-58; Baltimore,
          1950; Houston, 1960-66; Oakland, 1967-1975
  849   Morten Andersen, New Orleans, 1982-1994;
          Atlanta, 1995-2000; N.Y. Giants, 2001;
          Kansas City, 2002-03; Minnesota, 2004,
          Atlanta, 2006-07
  820   Gary Anderson, Pittsburgh, 1982-1994; Philadelphia
          1995-96; San Francisco, 1997; Minnesota,
          1998-2002; Tennessee, 2003-04
Most (One-Point) Points After Touchdown, Season
  75   Matt Prater, Denver, 2013
  74   Stephen Gostkowski, New England, 2007
  68   Mason Crosby, Green Bay, 2011
Most (One-Point) Points After Touchdown, Game
  9   Pat Harder, Chi. Cardinals vs. N.Y. Giants,
          Oct. 17, 1948
          Bob Waterfield, Los Angeles vs. Baltimore,
          Oct. 22, 1950
          Charlie Gogolak, Washington vs. N.Y. Giants,
          Nov. 27, 1966
  8   By many players
Most Consecutive (Kicking) Points After Touchdown
  422   Matt Stover, Baltimore, 1996-2008; Indianapolis,
          2009
  371   Jason Elam, Denver, 1993-2002
          Jeff Wilkins, St. Louis, 1999-2007
  360   Stephen Gostkowski, New England, 2006-2013
          (current)
Highest (Kicking) Points After Touchdown Percentage, Career
(200 points after touchdown)
  100.00   Nick Folk, Dallas, 2007-09; N.Y. Jets, 2010-13
          (269-269)
  99.77   Rian Lindell, Seattle, 2000-02; Buffalo, 2003-2012;
          Tampa Bay, 2013 (432-433)
  99.75   Stephen Gostkowski, New England, 2006-2013
          (399-400)
Most (Kicking) Points After Touchdown, No Misses, Season
  75   Matt Prater, Denver, 2013
  74   Stephen Gostkowski, New England, 2007
  66   Stephen Gostkowski, New England, 2012

Most (Kicking) Points After Touchdown, No Misses, Game
9   Pat Harder, Chi. Cardinals vs. N.Y. Giants,
      Oct. 17, 1948
      Bob Waterfield, Los Angeles vs. Baltimore,
      Oct. 22, 1950
8   By many players

Most Two-Point Conversions, Career
Two-point conversions include AFL (1960-69) and NFL (since 1994).
7   Marshall Faulk, Indianapolis, 1994-98; St. Louis,
      1999-2005
6   Terance Mathis, Atlanta, 1994-2001; Pittsburgh, 2002
5   Cris Carter, Minnesota, 1994-2001; Miami, 2002
      Rob Moore, N.Y. Jets, 1994; Arizona, 1995-99
      Willie Jackson, Jacksonville, 1995-97; Cincinnati,
      1998-99; New Orleans, 2000-01; Washington,
      2002
      Keenan McCardell, Cleveland, 1994-95; Jacksonville,
      1996-2001; Tampa Bay, 2002-03; San Diego,
      2004-06, Washington, 2007
      Marvin Harrison, Indianapolis, 1996-2008
      Marcus Pollard, Indianapolis, 1995-2004; Detroit,
      2005-06; Seattle, 2007; Atlanta, 2008
      Todd Heap, Baltimore, 2001-2010; Arizona, 2011-12
      Hines Ward, Pittsburgh, 1998-2011
      Edgerrin James, Indianapolis, 1999-2005;
      Arizona, 2006-08; Seattle, 2009

Most Two-Point Conversions, Season
4   Todd Heap, Baltimore, 2003
3   Gino Cappelletti, Boston, 1960
      Richie Lucas, Buffalo, 1961
      Ronnie Harmon, San Diego, 1994
      Haywood Jeffires, Houston, 1994
      Tom Tupa, Cleveland, 1994
      Terance Mathis, Atlanta, 1995
      Lamar Smith, Seattle, 1996
      Cris Carter, Minnesota, 1997
      Terrell Davis, Denver, 1997
      James Stewart, Detroit, 2000
      Hines Ward, Pittsburgh, 2002
      Brian Finneran, Atlanta, 2005
      Reggie Bush, New Orleans, 2007
2   By many players

Most Two-Point Conversions, Game
2   Brett Perriman, Detroit vs. Green Bay, Nov. 6, 1994
      Michael Jackson, Baltimore vs. New England,
      Oct. 6, 1996
      Terrell Davis, Denver vs. Atlanta, Sept. 28, 1997
      Charles Johnson, Pittsburgh vs. Tennessee,
      Nov. 1, 1998
      Marshall Faulk, St. Louis vs. Atlanta, Oct. 15, 2000
      Todd Heap, Baltimore vs. Cincinnati, Oct. 19, 2003
      Reggie Bush, New Orleans vs. St. Louis,
      Nov. 11, 2007
      Tarvaris Jackson, Minnesota vs. Denver,
      Dec. 30, 2007 (ot)
      Mewelde Moore, Pittsburgh vs. New England,
      Nov. 14, 2010
      Lance Moore, New Orleans vs. Houston,
      Sept. 25, 2011

FIELD GOALS
Most Seasons Leading League
5   Lou Groza, Cleveland, 1950, 1952-54, 1957
4   Jack Manders, Chi. Bears, 1933-34, 1936-37
      Ward Cuff, N.Y. Giants, 1938-39, 1943; Green Bay,
      1947
      Mark Moseley, Washington, 1976-77, 1979, 1982
3   Bob Waterfield, Los Angeles, 1947, 1949, 1951
      Gino Cappelletti, Boston, 1961, 1963-64
      Fred Cox, Minnesota, 1965, 1969-1970

      Jan Stenerud, Kansas City, 1967, 1970, 1975

Most Consecutive Seasons Leading League
3   Lou Groza, Cleveland, 1952-54
2   Jack Manders, Chi. Bears, 1933-34
      Armand Niccolai, Pittsburgh, 1935-36
      Jack Manders, Chi. Bears, 1936-37
      Ward Cuff, N.Y. Giants, 1938-39
      Clark Hinkle, Green Bay, 1940-41
      Cliff Patton, Philadelphia, 1948-49
      Gino Cappelletti, Boston, 1963-64
      Jim Turner, N.Y. Jets, 1968-69
      Fred Cox, Minnesota, 1969-1970
      Mark Moseley, Washington, 1976-77
      Chip Lohmiller, Washington, 1991-92
      Pete Stoyanovich, Miami, 1991-92

Most Field Goals Attempted, Career
709   Morten Andersen, New Orleans, 1982-1994; Atlanta,
      1995-2000; N.Y. Giants, 2001; Kansas City,
      2002-03; Minnesota, 2004; Atlanta, 2006-07
672   Gary Anderson, Pittsburgh, 1982-1994; Philadelphia,
      1995-96; San Francisco, 1997; Minnesota,
      1998-2002; Tennessee, 2003-04
641   George Blanda, Chi. Bears, 1949, 1950-58;
      Baltimore, 1950; Houston, 1960-66; Oakland,
      1967-1975

Most Field Goals Attempted, Season
52   David Akers, San Francisco, 2011
49   Bruce Gossett, Los Angeles, 1966
      Curt Knight, Washington, 1971
48   Chester Marcol, Green Bay, 1972

Most Field Goals Attempted, Game
9   Jim Bakken, St. Louis vs. Pittsburgh, Sept. 24, 1967
8   Lou Michaels, Pittsburgh vs. St. Louis, Dec. 2, 1962
      Garo Yepremian, Detroit vs. Minnesota, Nov. 13, 1966
      Jim Turner, N.Y. Jets vs. Buffalo, Nov. 3, 1968
      Billy Cundiff, Dallas vs. N.Y. Giants, Sept. 15, 2003 (ot)
      Rob Bironas, Tennessee vs. Houston, Oct. 21, 2007
7   By many players

Most Field Goals, Career
565   Morten Andersen, New Orleans, 1982-1994; Atlanta,
      1995-2000; N.Y. Giants, 2001; Kansas City,
      2002-03; Minnesota, 2004; Atlanta, 2006-07
538   Gary Anderson, Pittsburgh, 1982-1994; Philadelphia,
      1995-96; San Francisco, 1997; Minnesota,
      1998-2002; Tennessee, 2003-04
495   Jason Hanson, Detroit, 1992-2012

Most Field Goals, Season
44   David Akers, San Francisco, 2011
40   Neil Rackers, Arizona, 2005
39   Olindo Mare, Miami, 1999
      Jeff Wilkins, St. Louis, 2003

Most Field Goals, Rookie, Season
35   Ali Haji-Sheikh, N.Y. Giants, 1983
      Blair Walsh, Minnesota, 2012
34   Richie Cunningham, Dallas, 1997
33   Chester Marcol, Green Bay, 1972

Most Field Goals, Game
8   Rob Bironas, Tennessee vs. Houston, Oct. 21, 2007
7   Jim Bakken, St. Louis vs. Pittsburgh, Sept. 24, 1967
      Rich Karlis, Minnesota vs. L.A. Rams,
      Nov. 5, 1989 (ot)
      Chris Boniol, Dallas vs. Green Bay, Nov. 18, 1996
      Billy Cundiff, Dallas vs. N.Y. Giants, Sept. 15, 2003 (ot)
      Shayne Graham, Cincinnati vs. Baltimore, Nov. 11, 2007
6   By many players

Most Field Goals, One Quarter
4   Garo Yepremian, Detroit vs. Minnesota, Nov. 13, 1966
      (second quarter)
      Curt Knight, Washington vs. N.Y. Giants, Nov. 15, 1970
      (second quarter)

Roger Ruzek, Dallas vs. N.Y. Giants, Nov. 2, 1987
(fourth quarter)
Cary Blanchard, Indianapolis vs. Buffalo,
Sept. 21 1997 (second quarter)
Sebastian Janikowski, Oakland vs. Chicago,
Oct. 5, 2003 (second quarter)
Jeff Wilkins, St. Louis vs. Baltimore, Nov. 9, 2003
(fourth quarter)
Lawrence Tynes, Kansas City vs. New England,
Nov. 27, 2005 (second quarter)
Shayne Graham, Cincinnati vs. Baltimore,
Nov. 11, 2007 (fourth quarter)
3   By many players

Most Consecutive Games Scoring Field Goals
38   Matt Stover, Baltimore, 1999-2001
34   David Akers, Philadelphia, 2010;
San Francisco, 2011-12; Detroit, 2013
31   Fred Cox, Minnesota, 1968-1970

Most Consecutive Field Goals
42   Mike Vanderjagt, Indianapolis, 2002-04
40   Gary Anderson, San Francisco, 1997;
Minnesota, 1998
36   Matt Stover, Baltimore, 2005-06

Longest Field Goal
64   Matt Prater, Denver vs. Tennessee, Dec. 8, 2013
63   Tom Dempsey, New Orleans vs. Detroit, Nov. 8, 1970
Jason Elam, Denver vs. Jacksonville, Oct. 25, 1998
Sebastian Janikowski, Oakland vs. Denver,
Sept. 12, 2011
David Akers, San Francisco vs. Green Bay,
Sept. 9, 2012
62   Matt Bryant, Tampa Bay vs. Philadelphia,
Oct. 22, 2006

Highest Field Goal Pct., Career (100 field goals)
86.47   Mike Vanderjagt, Indianapolis, 1998-2005; Dallas,
2006 (230-266)
86.19   Nate Kaeding, San Diego, 2004-2011; Miami, 2012
(181-210)
86.03   Robbie Gould, Chicago, 2005-2013 (234-272)

Highest Field Goal Pct., Season (Qualifiers)
100.00   Tony Zendejas, L.A. Rams, 1991 (17-17)
Gary Anderson, Minnesota, 1998 (35-35)
Jeff Wilkins, St. Louis, 2000 (17-17)
Mike Vanderjagt, Indianapolis, 2003 (37-37)
96.43   Chris Boniol, Dallas, 1995 (28-27)
96.30   Norm Johnson, Atlanta, 1993 (27-26)
Pete Stoyanovich, Kansas City, 1997 (27-26)

Most Field Goals, No Misses, Game
8   Rob Bironas, Tennessee vs. Houston, Oct. 21, 2007
7   Rich Karlis, Minnesota vs. L.A. Rams, Nov. 5, 1989
(ot)
Chris Boniol, Dallas vs. Green Bay, Nov. 18, 1996
Shayne Graham, Cincinnati vs. Baltimore,
Nov. 11, 2007
6   By many players

Most Field Goals, 50 or More Yards, Career
52   Jason Hanson, Detroit, 1992-2012
45   Sebastian Janikowski, Oakland, 2000-2013
42   John Kasay, Seattle, 1991-94; Carolina, 1995-99,
2001-2010; New Orleans, 2011

Most Field Goals, 50 or More Yards, Season
10   Blair Walsh, Minnesota, 2012
8   Morten Andersen, Atlanta, 1995
Jason Hanson, Detroit, 2008
7   David Akers, San Francisco, 2011
Phil Dawson, Cleveland, 2011
Sebastian Janikowski, Oakland, 2011
Phil Dawson, Cleveland, 2012
Greg Zuerlein, St. Louis, 2012

Most Field Goals, 50 or More Yards, Game
3   Morten Andersen, Atlanta vs. New Orleans,
Dec. 10, 1995
Neil Rackers, Arizona vs. Seattle, Oct. 24, 2004
Kris Brown, Houston vs. Miami, Oct. 7, 2007
Conner Barth, Tampa Bay vs. Miami, Nov. 15, 2009
Sebastian Janikowski, Oakland vs. Houston,
Oct. 9, 2011
Josh Scobee, Jacksonville vs. Baltimore,
Oct. 24, 2011
Phil Dawson, Cleveland vs. Baltimore,
Sept. 27, 2012
Blair Walsh, Minnesota vs. St. Louis, Dec. 16, 2012
2   By many players. Last time:
Justin Tucker, Baltimore vs. Detroit, Dec. 16, 2013

SAFETIES
Most Safeties, Career
4   Ted Hendricks, Baltimore, 1969-1973; Green Bay,
1974; Oakland, 1975-1981; L.A. Raiders, 1982-83
Doug English, Detroit, 1975-79, 1981-85
Jared Allen, Kansas City, 2004-07;
Minnesota, 2008-2013
3   Bill McPeak, Pittsburgh, 1949-1957
Charlie Krueger, San Francisco, 1959-1973
Ernie Stautner, Pittsburgh, 1950-1963
Jim Katcavage, N.Y. Giants, 1956-1968
Roger Brown, Detroit, 1960-66; Los Angeles,
1967-69
Bruce Maher, Detroit, 1960-67; N.Y. Giants, 1968-69
Ron McDole, St. Louis, 1961; Houston, 1962;
Buffalo, 1963-1970; Washington, 1971-78
Alan Page, Minnesota, 1967-1978; Chicago,
1979-1981
Lyle Alzado, Denver, 1971-78; Cleveland,
1979-1981; L.A. Raiders, 1982-85
Rulon Jones, Denver, 1980-88
Steve McMichael, New England, 1980; Chicago,
1981-1993; Green Bay, 1994
Kevin Greene, L.A. Rams, 1985-1992; Pittsburgh,
1993-95; Carolina, 1996, 1998-99;
San Francisco, 1997
Burt Grossman, San Diego, 1989-1993;
Philadelphia, 1994
Eric Swann, Phoenix, 1991-93; Arizona, 1994-99;
Carolina, 2000
Dan Saleaumua, Detroit, 1987-88; Kansas City,
1989-1996; Seattle, 1997-98
Derrick Thomas, Kansas City, 1989-1999
Bryant Young, San Francisco, 1994-2007
Jason Taylor, Miami, 1997-2007; Washington, 2008;
Miami, 2009; N.Y. Jets, 2010; Miami, 2011
2   By many players

Most Safeties, Season
2   Tom Nash, Green Bay, 1932
Willie Wilkin, Washington, 1942
Roger Brown, Detroit, 1962
Ron McDole, Buffalo, 1964
Alan Page, Minnesota, 1971
Fred Dryer, Los Angeles, 1973
Benny Barnes, Dallas, 1973
James Young, Houston, 1977
Doug English, Detroit, 1983
Don Blackmon, New England, 1985
Tim Harris, Green Bay, 1988
Brian Jordan, Atlanta, 1991
Burt Grossman, San Diego, 1992
Rod Stephens, Seattle, 1993
Bryant Young, San Francisco, 1996
Jared Allen, Minnesota, 2008

    Jameel McClain, Baltimore, 2008

Most Safeties, Game
- 2 Fred Dryer, Los Angeles vs. Green Bay,
    Oct. 21, 1973

RUSHING

Most Seasons Leading League
- 8 Jim Brown, Cleveland, 1957-1961, 1963-65
- 4 Steve Van Buren, Philadelphia, 1945, 1947-49
    O.J. Simpson, Buffalo, 1972-73, 1975-76
    Eric Dickerson, L.A. Rams, 1983-84, 1986;
      Indianapolis, 1988
    Emmitt Smith, Dallas, 1991-93, 1995
    Barry Sanders, Detroit, 1990, 1994, 1996-97
- 3 Earl Campbell, Houston, 1978-1980

Most Consecutive Seasons Leading League
- 5 Jim Brown, Cleveland, 1957-1961
- 3 Steve Van Buren, Philadelphia, 1947-49
    Jim Brown, Cleveland, 1963-65
    Earl Campbell, Houston, 1978-1980
    Emmitt Smith, Dallas, 1991-93
- 2 By many players

ATTEMPTS

Most Seasons Leading League
- 6 Jim Brown, Cleveland, 1958-59, 1961, 1963-65
- 4 Steve Van Buren, Philadelphia, 1947-1950
    Walter Payton, Chicago, 1976-79
- 3 Cookie Gilchrist, Buffalo, 1963-64; Denver, 1965
    Jim Nance, Boston, 1966-67, 1969
    O.J. Simpson, Buffalo, 1973-75
    Eric Dickerson, L.A. Rams, 1983, 1986;
      Indianapolis, 1988
    Emmitt Smith, Dallas, 1991, 1994-95

Most Consecutive Seasons Leading League
- 4 Steve Van Buren, Philadelphia, 1947-1950
    Walter Payton, Chicago, 1976-79
- 3 Jim Brown, Cleveland, 1963-65
    Cookie Gilchrist, Buffalo, 1963-64; Denver, 1965
    O.J. Simpson, Buffalo, 1973-75
- 2 By many players

Most Attempts, Career
- 4,409 Emmitt Smith, Dallas, 1990-2002; Arizona, 2003-04
- 3,838 Walter Payton, Chicago, 1975-1987
- 3,518 Curtis Martin, New England, 1995-97;
        N.Y. Jets, 1998-2005

Most Attempts, Season
- 416 Larry Johnson, Kansas City, 2006
- 410 Jamal Anderson, Atlanta, 1998
- 407 James Wilder, Tampa Bay, 1984

Most Attempts, Rookie, Season
- 390 Eric Dickerson, L.A. Rams, 1983
- 378 George Rogers, New Orleans, 1981
- 369 Edgerrin James, Indianapolis, 1999

Most Attempts, Game
- 45 Jamie Morris, Washington vs. Cincinnati,
      Dec. 17, 1988 (ot)
- 43 Butch Woolfolk, N.Y. Giants vs. Philadelphia,
      Nov. 20, 1983
    James Wilder, Tampa Bay vs. Green Bay,
      Sept. 30, 1984 (ot)
    Rudi Johnson, Cincinnati vs. Houston, Nov. 9, 2003
- 42 James Wilder, Tampa Bay vs. Pittsburgh,
      Oct. 30, 1983
    Terrell Davis, Denver vs. Buffalo, Oct. 26, 1997 (ot)
    Ricky Williams, Miami vs. Buffalo, Sept. 21, 2003

YARDS GAINED

Most Yards Gained, Career
- 18,355 Emmitt Smith, Dallas, 1990-2002; Arizona, 2003-04

- 16,726 Walter Payton, Chicago, 1975-1987
- 15,269 Barry Sanders, Detroit, 1989-1998

Most Seasons, 1,000 or More Yards Rushing
- 11 Emmitt Smith, Dallas, 1991-2001
- 10 Walter Payton, Chicago, 1976-1981, 1983-86
    Barry Sanders, Detroit, 1989-1998
    Curtis Martin, New England, 1995-97; N.Y. Jets,
      1998-2004
- 8 Franco Harris, Pittsburgh, 1972, 1974-79, 1983
    Tony Dorsett, Dallas, 1977-1981, 1983-85
    Thurman Thomas, Buffalo, 1989-1996
    Jerome Bettis, L.A. Rams, 1993-94; Pittsburgh,
      1996-2001
    LaDainian Tomlinson, San Diego, 2001-08
    Steven Jackson, St. Louis, 2005-2012

Most Consecutive Seasons, 1,000 or More Yards Rushing
- 11 Emmitt Smith, Dallas, 1991-2001
- 10 Barry Sanders, Detroit, 1989-1998
    Curtis Martin, New England, 1995-97; N.Y. Jets,
      1998-2004
- 8 Thurman Thomas, Buffalo, 1989-1996
    LaDainian Tomlinson, San Diego, 2001-08
    Steven Jackson, St. Louis, 2005-2012

Most Yards Gained, Season
- 2,105 Eric Dickerson, L.A. Rams, 1984
- 2,097 Adrian Peterson, Minnesota, 2012
- 2,066 Jamal Lewis, Baltimore, 2003

Most Yards Gained, Rookie, Season
- 1,808 Eric Dickerson, L.A. Rams, 1983
- 1,674 George Rogers, New Orleans, 1981
- 1,613 Alfred Morris, Washington, 2012

Most Yards Gained, Game
- 296 Adrian Peterson, Minnesota vs. San Diego,
      Nov. 4, 2007
- 295 Jamal Lewis, Baltimore vs. Cleveland,
      Sept. 14, 2003
- 286 Jerome Harrison, Cleveland vs. Kansas City,
      Dec. 20, 2009

Most Games, 200 or More Yards Rushing, Career
- 6 O.J. Simpson, Buffalo, 1969-1977; San Francisco,
    1978-79
- 5 Tiki Barber, N.Y. Giants, 1997-2006
    Adrian Peterson, Minnesota, 2007-2013
- 4 Jim Brown, Cleveland, 1957-1965
    Earl Campbell, Houston, 1978-1984; New Orleans,
    1984-85
    Barry Sanders, Detroit, 1989-1998
    LaDainian Tomlinson, San Diego, 2001-09;
      N.Y. Jets, 2010-11

Most Games, 200 or More Yards Rushing, Season
- 4 Earl Campbell, Houston, 1980
- 3 O.J. Simpson, Buffalo, 1973
    Tiki Barber, N.Y. Giants, 2005
- 2 Jim Brown, Cleveland, 1963
    O.J. Simpson, Buffalo, 1976
    Walter Payton, Chicago, 1977
    Eric Dickerson, L.A. Rams, 1984
    Greg Bell, L.A. Rams, 1989
    Terrell Davis, Denver, 1997
    Barry Sanders, Detroit, 1997
    Corey Dillon, Cincinnati, 2000
    Marshall Faulk, St. Louis, 2000
    LaDainian Tomlinson, San Diego, 2002
    Ricky Williams, Miami, 2002
    Jamal Lewis, Baltimore, 2003
    LaDainian Tomlinson, San Diego, 2003
    Larry Johnson, Kansas City, 2005
    Willie Parker, Pittsburgh, 2006
    Adrian Peterson, Minnesota, 2007
    Michael Turner, Atlanta, 2008

Jamaal Charles, Kansas City, 2012
Adrian Peterson, Minnesota, 2012

Most Consecutive Games, 200 or More Yards Rushing
2 O.J. Simpson, Buffalo, 1973, 1976
   Earl Campbell, Houston, 1980
   Ricky Williams, Miami, 2002

Most Games, 100 or more Yards Rushing, Career
78 Emmitt Smith, Dallas, 1990-2002; Arizona, 2003-04
77 Walter Payton, Chicago, 1975-1987
76 Barry Sanders, Detroit, 1989-1998

Most Games, 100 or More Yards Rushing, Season
14 Barry Sanders, Detroit, 1997
12 Eric Dickerson, L.A. Rams, 1984
   Barry Foster, Pittsburgh, 1992
   Jamal Anderson, Atlanta, 1998
   Jamal Lewis, Baltimore, 2003
   Chris Johnson, Tennessee, 2009
11 O.J. Simpson, Buffalo, 1973
   Earl Campbell, Houston, 1979
   Marcus Allen, L.A. Raiders, 1985
   Eric Dickerson, L.A. Rams, 1986
   Emmitt Smith, Dallas, 1995
   Terrell Davis, Denver, 1998
   Shaun Alexander, Seattle, 2005
   Larry Johnson, Kansas City, 2006

Most Consecutive Games, 100 or More Yards Rushing
14 Barry Sanders, Detroit, 1997
12 Chris Johnson, Tennessee, 2009-2010
11 Marcus Allen, L.A. Raiders, 1985-86

Longest Run from Scrimmage
99 Tony Dorsett, Dallas vs. Minnesota, Jan. 3, 1983
   (TD)
98 Ahman Green, Green Bay vs. Denver, Dec. 28, 2003
   (TD)
97 Andy Uram, Green Bay vs. Chi. Cardinals,
   Oct. 8, 1939 (TD)
   Bob Gage, Pittsburgh vs. Chi. Bears, Dec. 4, 1949
   (TD)

AVERAGE GAIN

Highest Average Gain, Career (750 attempts)
7.08 Michael Vick, Atlanta, 2001-06; Philadelphia,
     2009-2013 (827-5,857)
6.36 Randall Cunningham, Philadelphia, 1985-1995;
     Minnesota, 1997-99; Dallas, 2000; Baltimore,
     2001 (775-4,928)
5.58 Jamaal Charles, Kansas City, 2008-2013
     (1,043-5,823)

Highest Average Gain, Season (Qualifiers)
8.45 Michael Vick, Atlanta, 2006 (123-1,039)
8.44 Beattie Feathers, Chi. Bears, 1934 (119-1,004)
7.98 Randall Cunningham, Philadelphia, 1990 (118-942)

Highest Average Gain, Game (10 attempts)
17.30 Michael Vick, Atlanta vs. Minnesota, Dec. 1, 2002
      (10-173)
17.09 Marion Motley, Cleveland vs. Pittsburgh,
      Oct. 29, 1950 (11-188)
16.70 Billy Grimes, Green Bay vs. N.Y. Yanks, Oct. 8, 1950
      (10-167)

TOUCHDOWNS

Most Seasons Leading League
5 Jim Brown, Cleveland, 1957-59, 1963, 1965
4 Steve Van Buren, Philadelphia, 1945, 1947-49
3 Abner Haynes, Dall. Texans, 1960-62
   Cookie Gilchrist, Buffalo, 1962-64
   Paul Lowe, L.A. Chargers, 1960; San Diego, 1961,
   1965
   Leroy Kelly, Cleveland, 1966-68
   Emmitt Smith, Dallas, 1992, 1994-95

LaDainian Tomlinson, San Diego, 2004, 2006-07

Most Consecutive Seasons Leading League
3 Steve Van Buren, Philadelphia, 1947-49
   Jim Brown, Cleveland, 1957-59
   Abner Haynes, Dall. Texans, 1960-62
   Cookie Gilchrist, Buffalo, 1962-64
   Leroy Kelly, Cleveland, 1966-68

Most Touchdowns, Career
164 Emmitt Smith, Dallas, 1990-2002; Arizona, 2003-04
145 LaDainian Tomlinson, San Diego, 2001-09;
     N.Y. Jets, 2010-11
123 Marcus Allen, L.A. Raiders, 1982-1992; Kansas City,
     1993-97

Most Rushing Touchdowns, Season
28 LaDainian Tomlinson, San Diego, 2006
27 Priest Holmes, Kansas City, 2003
   Shaun Alexander, Seattle, 2005
25 Emmitt Smith, Dallas, 1995

Most Touchdowns, Rookie, Season
18 Eric Dickerson, L.A. Rams, 1983
15 Ickey Woods, Cincinnati, 1988
   Mike Anderson, Denver, 2000
   Clinton Portis, Denver, 2002
14 Gale Sayers, Chicago, 1965
   Barry Sanders, Detroit, 1989
   Curtis Martin, New England, 1995
   Fred Taylor, Jacksonville, 1998
   Cam Newton, Carolina, 2011

Most Touchdowns, Game
6 Ernie Nevers, Chi. Cardinals vs. Chi. Bears,
   Nov. 28, 1929
5 Jimmy Conzelman, Rhode Island vs. Evansville,
   Oct. 15, 1922
   Jim Brown, Cleveland vs. Baltimore, Nov. 1, 1959
   Cookie Gilchrist, Buffalo vs. N.Y. Jets, Dec. 8, 1963
   James Stewart, Jacksonville vs. Philadelphia,
   Oct. 12, 1997
   Clinton Portis, Denver vs. Kansas City, Dec. 7, 2003
4 By many players

Most Consecutive Games Rushing for Touchdowns
18 LaDainian Tomlinson, San Diego, 2004-05
13 John Riggins, Washington, 1982-83
   George Rogers, Washington, 1985-86
11 Lenny Moore, Baltimore, 1963-64
   Emmitt Smith, Dallas, 1994-95
   Emmitt Smith, Dallas, 1995
   Priest Holmes, Kansas City, 2002

PASSING

Most Seasons Leading League (Passer Rating)
6 Sammy Baugh, Washington, 1937, 1940, 1943,
   1945, 1947, 1949
   Steve Young San Francisco, 1991-94, 1996-97
4 Len Dawson, Dall. Texans; 1962; Kansas City, 1964,
   1966, 1968
   Roger Staubach, Dallas, 1971, 1973, 1978-79
   Ken Anderson, Cincinnati, 1974-75, 1981-82
3 Arnie Herber, Green Bay, 1932, 1934, 1936
   Norm Van Brocklin, Los Angeles, 1950, 1952, 1954
   Bart Starr, Green Bay, 1962, 1964, 1966
   Peyton Manning, Indianapolis, 2004-06

Most Consecutive Seasons Leading League (Passer Rating)
4 Steve Young, San Francisco, 1991-94
3 Peyton Manning, Indianapolis, 2004-06
2 Cecil Isbell, Green Bay, 1941-42
   Milt Plum, Cleveland, 1960-61
   Ken Anderson, Cincinnati, 1974-75, 1981-82
   Roger Staubach, Dallas, 1978-79
   Steve Young, San Francisco, 1996-97
   Aaron Rodgers, Green Bay, 2011-12

PASSER RATING

Highest Passer Rating, Career (1,500 attempts)
- 104.9   Aaron Rodgers, Green Bay, 2005-2013
- 97.2   Peyton Manning, Indianapolis, 1998-2010; Denver, 2012-13
- 96.8   Steve Young, Tampa Bay, 1985-86; San Francisco, 1987-1999

Highest Passer Rating, Season (Qualifiers)
- 122.5   Aaron Rodgers, Green Bay, 2011
- 121.1   Peyton Manning, Indianapolis, 2004
- 119.2   Nick Foles, Philadelphia, 2013

Highest Passer Rating, Rookie, Season (Qualifiers)
- 102.4   Robert Griffin III, Washington, 2012
- 100.0   Russell Wilson, Seattle, 2012
- 98.1   Ben Roethlisberger, Pittsburgh, 2004

ATTEMPTS

Most Seasons Leading League
- 5   Dan Marino, Miami, 1984, 1986, 1988, 1992, 1997
- 4   Sammy Baugh, Washington, 1937, 1943, 1947-48
-    Johnny Unitas, Baltimore, 1957, 1959-1961
-    George Blanda, Chi. Bears, 1953; Houston, 1963-65
- 3   Arnie Herber, Green Bay, 1932, 1934, 1936
-    Sonny Jurgensen, Washington, 1966-67, 1969
-    Drew Bledsoe, New England, 1994-96
-    Brett Favre, Green Bay, 1999, 2005-06
-    Peyton Manning, Indianapolis, 1998, 2010; Denver, 2013

Most Consecutive Seasons Leading League
- 3   Johnny Unitas, Baltimore, 1959-1961
-    George Blanda, Houston, 1963-65
-    Drew Bledsoe, New England, 1994-96
- 2   By many players

Most Passes Attempted, Career
- 10,169   Brett Favre, Atlanta, 1991; Green Bay, 1992-2007; N.Y. Jets, 2008; Minnesota, 2009-2010
- 8,452   Peyton Manning, Indianapolis, 1998-2010; Denver, 2012-13
- 8,358   Dan Marino, Miami, 1983-1999

Most Passes Attempted, Season
- 727   Matthew Stafford, Detroit, 2012
- 691   Drew Bledsoe, New England, 1994
- 679   Peyton Manning, Indianapolis, 2010

Most Passes Attempted, Rookie, Season
- 627   Andrew Luck, Indianapolis, 2012
- 590   Sam Bradford, St. Louis, 2010
- 575   Peyton Manning, Indianapolis, 1998

Most Passes Attempted, Game
- 70   Drew Bledsoe, New England vs. Minnesota, Nov. 13, 1994
- 69   Vinny Testaverde, N.Y. Jets vs. Baltimore, Dec. 24, 2000
- 68   George Blanda, Houston vs. Buffalo, Nov. 1, 1964
-    Jon Kitna, Cincinnati vs. Pittsburgh, Dec. 30, 2001

COMPLETIONS

Most Seasons Leading League
- 6   Dan Marino, Miami, 1984-86, 1988, 1992, 1997
- 5   Sammy Baugh, Washington, 1937, 1943, 1945, 1947-48
- 4   George Blanda, Chi. Bears, 1953; Houston, 1963-65
-    Sonny Jurgensen, Philadelphia, 1961; Washington, 1966-67, 1969
-    Peyton Manning, Indianapolis, 2000, 2003, 2010; Denver, 2013

Most Consecutive Seasons Leading League
- 3   George Blanda, Houston, 1963-65
-    Dan Marino, Miami, 1984-86
- 2   By many players

Most Passes Completed, Career
- 6,300   Brett Favre, Atlanta, 1991; Green Bay, 1992-2007; N.Y. Jets, 2008, Minnesota, 2009-2010
- 5,532   Peyton Manning, Indianapolis, 1998-2010; Denver, 2012-13
- 4,967   Dan Marino, Miami, 1983-1999

Most Passes Completed, Season
- 468   Drew Brees, New Orleans, 2011
- 450   Peyton Manning, Indianapolis, 2010
-    Peyton Manning, Denver, 2013
- 448   Drew Brees, New Orleans, 2010

Most Passes Completed, Rookie, Season
- 354   Sam Bradford, St. Louis, 2010
- 339   Andrew Luck, Indianapolis, 2012
- 326   Peyton Manning, Indianapolis, 1998

Most Passes Completed, Game
- 45   Drew Bledsoe, New England vs. Minnesota, Nov. 13, 1994 (ot)
- 43   Rich Gannon, Oakland vs. Pittsburgh, Sept. 15, 2002
-    Matt Schaub, Houston vs. Jacksonville, Nov. 18, 2012 (ot)
- 42   Richard Todd, N.Y. Jets vs. San Francisco, Sept. 21, 1980
-    Vinny Testaverde, N.Y. Jets vs. Seattle, Dec. 6, 1998

Most Consecutive Passes Completed
- 24   Donovan McNabb, Philadelphia vs. N.Y. Giants (10), Nov. 28, 2004; vs. Green Bay (14), Dec. 5, 2004
- 23   Peyton Manning, Indianapolis vs. Detroit (6), Dec. 14, 2008; vs. Jacksonville (17), Dec. 18, 2008
- 22   Joe Montana, San Francisco vs. Cleveland (5), Nov. 29, 1987; vs. Green Bay (17), Dec. 6, 1987
-    Mark Brunell, Washington vs. Houston, Sept. 24, 2006
-    David Carr, Houston vs. Buffalo, Nov. 19, 2006
-    Matt Ryan, Atlanta vs. N.Y. Giants (10), Dec. 16, 2012; vs. Detroit (12), Dec. 22, 2012

COMPLETION PERCENTAGE

Most Seasons Leading League
- 8   Len Dawson, Dall. Texans, 1962; Kansas City, 1964-69, 1975
- 7   Sammy Baugh, Washington, 1940, 1942-43, 1945, 1947-49
- 5   Joe Montana, San Francisco, 1980-81, 1985, 1987, 1989
-    Steve Young, San Francisco, 1992, 1994-97

Most Consecutive Seasons Leading League
- 6   Len Dawson, Kansas City, 1964-69
- 4   Steve Young, San Francisco, 1994-97
- 3   Sammy Baugh, Washington, 1947-49
-    Otto Graham, Cleveland, 1953-55
-    Milt Plum, Cleveland, 1959-1961
-    Kurt Warner, St. Louis, 1999-2001
-    Drew Brees, New Orleans, 2009-2011

Highest Completion Percentage, Career (1,500 attempts)
- 66.05   Chad Pennington, N.Y. Jets, 2000-07; Miami, 2008-2010 (2,471-1,632)
- 65.91   Drew Brees, San Diego, 2001-05; New Orleans, 2006-2013 (6,799-4,481)
- 65.82   Aaron Rodgers, Green Bay, 2005-2013 (2,955-1,945)

Highest Completion Percentage, Season (Qualifiers)
- 71.23   Drew Brees, New Orleans, 2011 (657-468)
- 70.62   Drew Brees, New Orleans, 2009 (514-363)
- 70.55   Ken Anderson, Cincinnati, 1982 (309-218)

Highest Completion Percentage, Rookie, Season (Qualifiers)
- 66.44   Ben Roethlisberger, Pittsburgh, 2004 (295-196)
- 65.65   Robert Griffin III, Washington, 2012 (393-258)

64.12   Russell Wilson, Seattle, 2012 (393-252)

Highest Completion Percentage, Game (20 attempts)
92.31   Kurt Warner, Arizona vs. Jacksonville, Sept. 20,
          2009 (26-24)
91.30   Vinny Testaverde, Cleveland vs. L.A. Rams, Dec. 26,
          1993 (23-21)
90.91   Ken Anderson, Cincinnati vs. Pittsburgh, Nov. 10,
          1974 (22-20))

YARDS GAINED
Most Seasons Leading League
5   Sonny Jurgensen, Philadelphia, 1961-62;
      Washington, 1966-67, 1969
      Dan Marino, Miami, 1984-86, 1988, 1992
4   Sammy Baugh, Washington, 1937, 1940, 1947-48
      Johnny Unitas, Baltimore, 1957, 1959-1960, 1963
      Dan Fouts, San Diego, 1979-1982
      Drew Brees, New Orleans, 2006, 2008, 2011-12
3   Arnie Herber, Green Bay, 1932, 1934, 1936
      Sid Luckman, Chi. Bears, 1943, 1945-46
      John Brodie, San Francisco, 1965, 1968, 1970
      John Hadl, San Diego, 1965, 1968, 1971
      Joe Namath, N.Y. Jets, 1966-67, 1972
      Peyton Manning, Indianapolis, 2000, 2003;
      Denver, 2013

Most Consecutive Seasons Leading League
4   Dan Fouts, San Diego, 1979-1982
3   Dan Marino, Miami, 1984-86
2   By many players

Most Yards Gained, Career
71,838   Brett Favre, Atlanta, 1991; Green Bay, 1992-2007;
            N.Y. Jets, 2008, Minnesota, 2009-2010
64,964   Peyton Manning, Indianapolis, 1998-2010;
            Denver, 2012-13
61,361   Dan Marino, Miami, 1983-1999

Most Seasons, 3,000 or More Yards Passing
18   Brett Favre, Green Bay, 1992-2007; N.Y. Jets, 2008;
       Minnesota, 2009
15   Peyton Manning, Indianapolis, 1998-2010;
       Denver, 2012-13
13   Dan Marino, Miami, 1984-1992, 1994-95, 1997-98

Most Yards Gained, Season
5,477   Peyton Manning, Denver, 2013
5,476   Drew Brees, New Orleans, 2011
5,235   Tom Brady, New England, 2011

Most Yards Gained, Rookie, Season
4,374   Andrew Luck, Indianapolis, 2012
4,051   Cam Newton, Carolina, 2011
3,739   Peyton Manning, Indianapolis, 1998

Most Yards Gained, Game
554   Norm Van Brocklin, Los Angeles vs. N.Y. Yanks,
         Sept. 28, 1951
527   Warren Moon, Houston vs. Kansas City,
         Dec. 16, 1990
         Matt Schaub, Houston vs. Jacksonville,
         Nov. 18, 2012 (ot)
522   Boomer Esiason, Arizona vs. Washington,
         Nov. 10, 1996 (ot)

Most Games, 400 or More Yards Passing, Career
13   Dan Marino, Miami, 1983-1999
12   Peyton Manning, Indianapolis, 1998-2010;
       Denver, 2012-13
10   Drew Brees, San Diego, 2001-05; New Orleans,
       2006-2013

Most Games, 400 or More Yards Passing, Season
4   Dan Marino, Miami, 1984
      Peyton Manning, Denver, 2013
3   Dan Marino, Miami, 1986
      Eli Manning, N.Y. Giants, 2011
      Tony Romo, Dallas, 2012

Philip Rivers, San Diego, 2013
2   By many players

Most Consecutive Games, 400 or More Yards Passing
2   Dan Fouts, San Diego, 1982
      Dan Marino, Miami, 1984
      Phil Simms, N.Y. Giants, 1985
      Billy Volek, Tennessee, 2004
      Matt Cassel, New England, 2008
      Tom Brady, New England, 2011
      Cam Newton, Carolina, 2011
      Philip Rivers, San Diego, 2013

Most Games, 300 or More Yards Passing, Career
84   Peyton Manning, Indianapolis, 1998-2010;
       Denver, 2012-13
78   Drew Brees, San Diego, 2001-05; New Orleans,
       2006-2013
63   Dan Marino, Miami, 1983-1999

Most Games, 300 or More Yards Passing, Season
13   Drew Brees, New Orleans, 2011
12   Peyton Manning, Denver, 2013
11   Tom Brady, New England, 2011
       Drew Brees, New Orleans, 2013

Most Consecutive Games, 300 or More Yards Passing
9   Drew Brees, New Orleans, 2011-12
      Drew Brees, New Orleans, 2013
7   Peyton Manning, Denver, 2012-13
6   Steve Young, San Francisco, 1998
      Kurt Warner, St. Louis, 2000
      Rich Gannon, Oakland, 2002

Longest Pass Completion (All TDs except as noted)
99   Frank Filchock (to Farkas), Washington vs.
       Pittsburgh, Oct. 15, 1939
       George Izo (to Mitchell), Washington vs. Cleveland,
       Sept. 15, 1963
       Karl Sweetan (to Studstill), Detroit vs. Baltimore,
       Oct. 16, 1966
       Sonny Jurgensen (to Allen), Washington vs.
       Chicago, Sept. 15, 1968
       Jim Plunkett (to Branch), L.A. Raiders vs.
       Washington, Oct. 2, 1983
       Ron Jaworski (to Quick), Philadelphia vs. Atlanta,
       Nov. 10, 1985
       Stan Humphries (to Martin), San Diego vs. Seattle,
       Sept. 18, 1994
       Brett Favre (to Brooks), Green Bay vs. Chicago,
       Sept. 11, 1995
       Trent Green (to Boerigter), Kansas City vs.
       San Diego, Dec. 22, 2002
       Jeff Garcia (to Davis), Cleveland vs. Cincinnati,
       Oct. 17, 2004
       Gus Frerotte (to Berrian), Minnesota vs. Chicago,
       Nov. 30, 2008
       Tom Brady (to Welker), New England vs. Miami,
       Sept. 12, 2011
       Eli Manning (to Cruz), N.Y. Giants vs. N.Y. Jets,
       Dec. 24, 2011
98   Doug Russell (to Tinsley), Chi. Cardinals vs.
       Cleveland, Nov. 27, 1938
       Ogden Compton (to Lane), Chi. Cardinals vs.
       Green Bay, Nov. 13, 1955
       Bill Wade (to Farrington), Chicago Bears vs. Detroit,
       Oct. 8, 1961
       Jacky Lee (to Dewveall), Houston vs. San Diego,
       Nov. 25, 1962
       Earl Morrall (to Jones), N.Y. Giants vs. Pittsburgh,
       Sept. 11, 1966
       Jim Hart (to Rashad), St. Louis vs. Los Angeles,
       Dec. 10, 1972 (no TD)
       Bobby Hebert (to Haynes), Atlanta vs. New Orleans,
       Sept. 12, 1993

Charlie Batch (to Morton), Detroit vs. Chicago,
   Oct. 4, 1998
Ryan Fitzpatrick (to Owens), Buffalo vs. Jacksonville,
   Nov. 22, 2009
97 Pat Coffee (to Tinsley), Chi. Cardinals vs. Chi. Bears,
   Dec. 5, 1937
Bobby Layne (to Box), Detroit vs. Green Bay,
   Nov. 26, 1953
George Shaw (to Tarr), Denver vs. Boston,
   Sept. 21, 1962
Bernie Kosar (to Slaughter), Cleveland vs. Chicago,
   Oct. 23, 1989
Steve Young (to Taylor), San Francisco vs. Atlanta,
   Nov. 3, 1991

AVERAGE GAIN
Most Seasons Leading League
7 Sid Luckman, Chi. Bears, 1939-1943, 1946-47
5 Steve Young, San Francisco, 1991-94, 1997
3 Arnie Herber, Green Bay, 1932, 1934, 1936
   Norm Van Brocklin, Los Angeles, 1950, 1952, 1954
   Len Dawson, Dall. Texans, 1962; Kansas City, 1966,
   1968
   Bart Starr, Green Bay, 1966-68
   Kurt Warner, St. Louis, 1999-2001
   Philip Rivers, San Diego, 2008-2010
Most Consecutive Seasons Leading League
5 Sid Luckman, Chi. Bears, 1939-1943
4 Steve Young, San Francisco, 1991-94
3 Bart Starr, Green Bay, 1966-68
   Kurt Warner, St. Louis, 1999-2001
   Philip Rivers, San Diego, 2008-2010
Highest Average Gain, Career (1,500 Attempts)
8.63 Otto Graham, Cleveland, 1950-55 (1,565-13,499)
8.42 Sid Luckman, Chi. Bears, 1939-1950 (1,744-14,686)
8.19 Aaron Rodgers, Green Bay, 2005-2012
   (2,955-24,197)
Highest Average Gain, Season (Qualifiers)
11.17 Tommy O'Connell, Cleveland, 1957 (110-1,229)
10.86 Sid Luckman, Chi. Bears, 1943 (202-2,194)
10.55 Otto Graham, Cleveland, 1953 (258-2,722)
Highest Average Gain, Rookie, Season (Qualifiers)
9.411 Greg Cook, Cincinnati, 1969 (197-1,854)
9.409 Bob Waterfield, Cleveland, 1945 (171-1,609)
8.88 Ben Roethlisberger, Pittsburgh, 2004 (295-2,621)
Highest Average Gain, Game (20 attempts)
18.58 Sammy Baugh, Washington vs. Boston,
   Oct. 31, 1948 (24-446)
18.50 Johnny Unitas, Baltimore vs. Atlanta, Nov. 12, 1967
   (20-370)
17.71 Joe Namath, N.Y. Jets vs. Baltimore, Sept. 24, 1972
   (28-496)

TOUCHDOWNS
Most Seasons Leading League
4 Johnny Unitas, Baltimore, 1957-1960
   Len Dawson, Dall. Texans, 1962; Kansas City, 1963,
   1965-66
   Steve Young, San Francisco, 1992-94, 1998
   Brett Favre, Green Bay, 1995-97, 2003
   Drew Brees, New Orleans, 2008-09, 2011-12
   Peyton Manning, Indianapolis, 2000, 2004, 2006;
   Denver, 2013
3 Arnie Herber, Green Bay, 1932, 1934, 1936
   Sid Luckman, Chi. Bears, 1943, 1945-46
   Y.A. Tittle, San Francisco, 1955; N.Y. Giants, 1962-63
   Dan Marino, Miami, 1984-86
   Tom Brady, New England, 2002, 2007, 2010
2 By many players

Most Consecutive Seasons Leading League
4 Johnny Unitas, Baltimore, 1957-1960
3 Dan Marino, Miami, 1984-86
   Steve Young, San Francisco, 1992-94
   Brett Favre, Green Bay, 1995-97
2 By many players
Most Touchdown Passes, Career
508 Brett Favre, Atlanta, 1991; Green Bay, 1992-2007;
   N.Y. Jets, 2008, Minnesota, 2009-2010
491 Peyton Manning, Indianapolis, 1998-2010;
   Denver, 2012-13
420 Dan Marino, Miami, 1983-1999
Most Touchdown Passes, Season
55 Peyton Manning, Denver, 2013
50 Tom Brady, New England, 2007
49 Peyton Manning, Indianapolis, 2004
Most Touchdown Passes, Rookie, Season
26 Peyton Manning, Indianapolis, 1998
   Russell Wilson, Seattle, 2012
23 Andrew Luck, Indianapolis, 2012
22 Charlie Conerly, N.Y. Giants, 1948
Most Touchdown Passes, Game
7 Sid Luckman, Chi. Bears vs. N.Y. Giants,
   Nov. 14, 1943
   Adrian Burk, Philadelphia vs. Washington,
   Oct. 17, 1954
   George Blanda, Houston vs. N.Y. Titans,
   Nov. 19, 1961
   Y.A. Tittle, N.Y. Giants vs. Washington, Oct. 28, 1962
   Joe Kapp, Minnesota vs. Baltimore, Sept. 28, 1969
   Peyton Manning, Denver vs. Baltimore,
   Sept. 5, 2013
   Nick Foles, Philadelphia vs. Oakland, Nov. 3, 2013
6 By many players. Last time:
   Aaron Rodgers, Green Bay vs. Houston,
   Oct. 14, 2012
Most Games, Four or More Touchdown Passes, Career
31 Peyton Manning, Indianapolis, 1998-2010;
   Denver, 2012
25 Drew Brees, San Diego, 1001-05;
   New Orleans, 2006-13
23 Brett Favre, Atlanta, 1991; Green Bay, 1992-2007;
   N.Y. Jets, 2008; Minnesota, 2009-2010
Most Games, Four or More Touchdown Passes, Season
9 Peyton Manning, Denver, 2013
6 Dan Marino, Miami, 1984
   Peyton Manning, Indianapolis, 2004
5 Dan Marino, Miami, 1986
   Brett Favre, Green Bay, 1996
   Donovan McNabb, Philadelphia, 2004
   Tom Brady, New England, 2007
   Drew Brees, New Orleans, 2011
   Aaron Rodgers, Green Bay, 2011
   Drew Brees, New Orleans, 2013
Most Consecutive Games, Four or More Touchdown Passes
5 Peyton Manning, Indianapolis, 2004
4 Dan Marino, Miami, 1984
3 Drew Brees, 2011
Most Consecutive Games, Touchdown Passes
54 Drew Brees, New Orleans, 2009-2012
52 Tom Brady, New England, 2010-13
47 Johnny Unitas, Baltimore, 1956-1960

HAD INTERCEPTED
Most Consecutive Passes Attempted, None Intercepted
358 Tom Brady, New England, 2010-11
308 Bernie Kosar, Cleveland, 1990-91
294 Bart Starr, Green Bay, 1964-65

Most Passes Had Intercepted, Career
- 336   Brett Favre, Atlanta, 1991; Green Bay, 1992-2007; N.Y. Jets, 2008; Minnesota, 2009-2010
- 277   George Blanda, Chi. Bears, 1949, 1950-58; Baltimore, 1950; Houston, 1960-66; Oakland, 1967-1975
- 268   John Hadl, San Diego, 1962-1972; Los Angeles, 1973-74; Green Bay, 1974-75; Houston, 1976-77

Most Passes Had Intercepted, Season
- 42   George Blanda, Houston, 1962
- 35   Vinny Testaverde, Tampa Bay, 1988
- 34   Frank Tripucka, Denver, 1960

Most Passes Had Intercepted, Game
- 8   Jim Hardy, Chi. Cardinals vs. Philadelphia, Sept. 24, 1950
- 7   Parker Hall, Cleveland vs. Green Bay, Nov. 8, 1942
-    Frank Sinkwich, Detroit vs. Green Bay, Oct. 24, 1943
-    Bob Waterfield, Los Angeles vs. Green Bay, Oct. 17, 1948
-    Zeke Bratkowski, Chicago vs. Baltimore, Oct. 2, 1960
-    Tommy Wade, Pittsburgh vs. Philadelphia, Dec. 12, 1965
-    Ken Stabler, Oakland vs. Denver, Oct. 16, 1977
-    Steve DeBerg, Tampa Bay vs. San Francisco, Sept. 7, 1986
-    Ty Detmer, Detroit vs. Cleveland, Sept. 23, 2001
- 6   By many players

Most Attempts, No Interceptions, Game
- 70   Drew Bledsoe, New England vs. Minnesota, Nov. 13, 1994 (ot)
- 63   Rich Gannon, Minnesota vs. New England, Oct. 20, 1991 (ot)
- 61   Matthew Stafford, Detroit vs. Houston, Nov. 22, 2012 (ot)

LOWEST PERCENTAGE, PASSES HAD INTERCEPTED

Most Seasons Leading League, Lowest Percentage, Passes Had Intercepted
- 5   Sammy Baugh, Washington, 1940, 1942, 1944-45, 1947
- 3   Charlie Conerly, N.Y. Giants, 1950, 1956, 1959
-    Bart Starr, Green Bay, 1962, 1964, 1966
-    Roger Staubach, Dallas, 1971, 1977, 1979
-    Ken Anderson, Cincinnati, 1972, 1981-82
-    Ken O'Brien, N.Y. Jets, 1985, 1987-88
- 2   By many players

Lowest Pct., Passes Had Intercepted, Career (1,500 attempts)
- 1.76   Aaron Rodgers, Green Bay, 2005-2013 (2,955-52)
- 2.03   Tom Brady, New England, 2000-2013 (6,586-134)
- 2.11   Neil O'Donnell, Pittsburgh, 1991-95; N.Y. Jets, 1996-97; Cincinnati, 1998; Tennessee, 1999-2003 (3,229-68)

Lowest Pct., Passes Had Intercepted, Season (Qualifiers)
- 0.41   Damon Huard, Kansas City, 2006 (244-1)
- 0.45   Josh McCown, Chicago, 2013 (224-1)
- 0.63   Nick Foles, Philadelphia, (317-2)

Lowest Pct., Passes Had Intercepted, Rookie, Season (Qualifiers)
- 1.27   Robert Griffin III, Washington, 2012 (393-5)
- 1.89   Nick Foles, Philadelphia, 2012 (265-5)
- 1.98   Charlie Batch, Detroit, 1998 (303-6)

TIMES SACKED

Times Sacked has been compiled since 1963.

Most Times Sacked, Career
- 525   Brett Favre, Atlanta, 1991; Green Bay, 1992-2007; N.Y. Jets, 2008; Minnesota, 2009-2010
- 516   John Elway, Denver, 1983-1998

- 494   Dave Krieg, Seattle, 1980-1991; Kansas City, 1992-93; Detroit, 1994; Arizona, 1995; Chicago, 1996; Tennessee, 1997-98

Most Times Sacked, Season
- 76   David Carr, Houston, 2002
- 72   Randall Cunningham, Philadelphia, 1986
- 68   David Carr, Houston, 2005

Most Times Sacked, Game
- 12   Bert Jones, Baltimore vs. St. Louis, Oct. 26, 1980
-    Warren Moon, Houston vs. Dallas, Sept. 29, 1985
-    Donovan McNabb, Philadelphia vs. N.Y. Giants, Sept. 30, 2007
- 11   Charley Johnson, St. Louis vs. N.Y. Giants, Nov. 1, 1964
-    Bart Starr, Green Bay vs. Detroit, Nov. 7, 1965
-    Jack Kemp, Buffalo vs. Oakland, Oct. 15, 1967
-    Bob Berry, Atlanta vs. St. Louis, Nov. 24, 1968
-    Greg Landry, Detroit vs. Dallas, Oct. 6, 1975
-    Ron Jaworski, Philadelphia vs. St. Louis, Dec. 18, 1983
-    Paul McDonald, Cleveland vs. Kansas City, Sept. 30, 1984
-    Archie Manning, Minnesota vs. Chicago, Oct. 28, 1984
-    Steve Pelluer, Dallas vs. San Diego, Nov. 16, 1986
-    Randall Cunningham, Philadelphia vs. L.A. Raiders, Nov. 30, 1986 (ot)
-    David Norrie, N.Y. Jets vs. Dallas, Oct. 4, 1987
-    Troy Aikman, Dallas vs. Philadelphia, Sept. 15, 1991
-    Bernie Kosar, Cleveland vs. Indianapolis, Sept. 6, 1992
-    Greg McElroy, N.Y. Jets vs. San Diego, Dec. 23, 2012
- 10   By many players

RECEIVING

Most Seasons Leading League
- 8   Don Hutson, Green Bay, 1936-37, 1939, 1941-45
- 5   Lionel Taylor, Denver, 1960-63, 1965
- 3   Tom Fears, Los Angeles, 1948-1950
-    Pete Pihos, Philadelphia, 1953-55
-    Billy Wilson, San Francisco, 1954, 1956-57
-    Raymond Berry, Baltimore, 1958-1960
-    Lance Alworth, San Diego, 1966, 1968-69
-    Sterling Sharpe, Green Bay, 1989, 1992-93
-    Wes Welker, New England, 2007, 2009, 2011

Most Consecutive Seasons Leading League
- 5   Don Hutson, Green Bay, 1941-45
- 4   Lionel Taylor, Denver, 1960-63
- 3   Tom Fears, Los Angeles, 1948-1950
-    Pete Pihos, Philadelphia, 1953-55
-    Raymond Berry, Baltimore, 1958-1960

Most Pass Receptions, Career
- 1,549   Jerry Rice, San Francisco, 1985-2000; Oakland, 2001-04; Seattle, 2004
- 1,325   Tony Gonzalez, Kansas City, 1997-2008; Atlanta, 2009-2013
- 1,102   Marvin Harrison, Indianapolis, 1996-2008

Most Seasons, 50 or More Pass Receptions
- 17   Jerry Rice, San Francisco, 1986-1996, 1998-2000; Oakland, 2001-03
- 16   Tony Gonzalez, Kansas City, 1998-2008; Atlanta, 2009-2013
- 13   Andre Reed, Buffalo, 1986-1994, 1996-99
-    Terrell Owens, San Francisco, 1997-2003; Philadelphia, 2004; Dallas, 2006-08; Buffalo, 2009; Cincinnati, 2010

Most Pass Receptions, Season
- 143   Marvin Harrison, Indianapolis, 2002
- 123   Herman Moore, Detroit, 1995

     Wes Welker, New England, 2009
122 Cris Carter, Minnesota, 1994
     Jerry Rice, San Francisco, 1995
     Cris Carter, Minnesota, 1995
     Wes Welker, New England, 2011
     Calvin Johnson, Detroit, 2012

Most Pass Receptions, Rookie, Season
101 Anquan Boldin, Arizona, 2003
 91 Eddie Royal, Denver, 2008
 90 Terry Glenn, New England, 1996

Most Pass Receptions, Game
 21 Brandon Marshall, Denver vs. Indianapolis,
     Dec. 13, 2009
 20 Terrell Owens, San Francisco vs. Chicago,
     Dec. 17, 2000
 18 Tom Fears, Los Angeles vs. Green Bay, Dec. 3, 1950
     Brandon Marshall, Denver vs. San Diego,
     Sept. 14, 2008
     Jason Witten, Dallas vs. N.Y. Giants, Oct. 28, 2012

Most Consecutive Games, Pass Receptions
274 Jerry Rice, San Francisco, 1985-2000; Oakland,
     2001-04
211 Tony Gonzalez, Kansas City, 2000-08; Atlanta,
     2009-2013 (current)
190 Marvin Harrison, Indianapolis, 1996-2008

YARDS GAINED

Most Seasons Leading League
  7 Don Hutson, Green Bay, 1936, 1938-39, 1941-44
  6 Jerry Rice, San Francisco, 1986, 1989-1990,
     1993-95
  3 Raymond Berry, Baltimore, 1957, 1959-1960
     Lance Alworth, San Diego, 1965-66, 1968

Most Consecutive Seasons Leading League
  4 Don Hutson, Green Bay, 1941-44
  3 Jerry Rice, San Francisco, 1993-95
  2 By many players

Most Yards Gained, Career
22,895 Jerry Rice, San Francisco, 1985-2000; Oakland,
     2001-04; Seattle, 2004
15,934 Terrell Owens, San Francisco, 1996-2003;
     Philadelphia, 2004-05; Dallas, 2006-08;
     Buffalo, 2009; Cincinnati, 2010
15,292 Randy Moss, Minnesota, 1998-2004, 2010;
     Oakland, 2005-06; New England, 2007-2010;
     Tennessee, 2010; San Francisco, 2012

Most Seasons, 1,000 or More Yards, Pass Receiving
 14 Jerry Rice, San Francisco, 1986-1996, 1998;
     Oakland, 2001-02
 10 Randy Moss, Minnesota, 1998-2003; Oakland,
     2005; New England, 2007-09
  9 Tim Brown, L.A. Raiders, 1993-94; Oakland,
     1995-2001
     Jimmy Smith, Jacksonville, 1996-2002, 2004-05
     Terrell Owens, San Francisco, 1998, 2000-03;
     Philadelphia, 2004; Dallas, 2006-08

Most Yards Gained, Season
1,964 Calvin Johnson, Detroit, 2012
1,848 Jerry Rice, San Francisco, 1995
1,781 Isaac Bruce, St. Louis, 1995

Most Yards Gained, Rookie, Season
1,473 Bill Groman, Houston, 1960
1,377 Anquan Boldin, Arizona, 2003
1,313 Randy Moss, Minnesota, 1998

Most Yards Gained, Game
336 Flipper Anderson, L.A. Rams vs. New Orleans,
     Nov. 26, 1989
329 Calvin Johnson, Detroit vs. Dallas, Oct. 27, 2013
309 Stephone Paige, Kansas City vs. San Diego,
     Dec. 22, 1985

Most Games, 200 or More Yards Pass Receiving, Career
  5 Lance Alworth, San Diego, 1962-1970; Dallas,
     1971-72
     Calvin Johnson, Detroit, 2007-2013
  4 Don Hutson, Green Bay, 1935-45
     Charley Hennigan, Houston, 1960-66
     Jerry Rice, San Francisco, 1985-2000; Oakland,
     2001-04; Seattle, 2004
  3 Don Maynard, N.Y. Giants, 1958; N.Y. Jets,
     1960-1972; St. Louis, 1973
     Wes Chandler, New Orleans, 1978-1981; San Diego,
     1981-87; San Francisco, 1988
     Isaac Bruce, L.A. Rams, 1994; St. Louis, 1995-2007;
     San Francisco, 2008
     Terrell Owens, San Francisco, 1996-2003;
     Philadelphia, 2004-05; Dallas, 2006-08; Buffalo,
     2009; Cincinnati, 2010
     Andre Johnson, Houston, 2003-2013

Most Games, 200 or More Yards Pass Receiving, Season
  3 Charley Hennigan, Houston, 1961
  2 Don Hutson, Green Bay, 1942
     Gene Roberts, N.Y. Giants, 1949
     Lance Alworth, San Diego, 1963
     Don Maynard, N.Y. Jets, 1968
     Calvin Johnson, Detroit, 2011
     Calvin Johnson, Detroit, 2012
     Josh Gordon, Cleveland, 2013
     Alshon Jeffery, Chicago, 2013

Most Games, 100 or More Yards Pass Receiving, Career
 76 Jerry Rice, San Francisco, 1985-2000; Oakland,
     2001-04; Seattle, 2004
 64 Randy Moss, Minnesota, 1998-2004, 2010;
     Oakland, 2005-06; New England, 2007-2010;
     Tennessee, 2010; San Francisco, 2012
 59 Marvin Harrison, Indianapolis, 1996-2008

Most Games, 100 or More Yards Pass Receiving, Season
 11 Michael Irvin, Dallas, 1995
     Calvin Johnson, Detroit, 2012
 10 Charley Hennigan, Houston, 1961
     Herman Moore, Detroit, 1995
     Marvin Harrison, Indianapolis, 2002
     Torry Holt, St. Louis, 2003
  9 Elroy (Crazylegs) Hirsch, Los Angeles, 1951
     Bill Groman, Houston, 1960
     Lance Alworth, San Diego, 1965
     Don Maynard, N.Y. Jets, 1967
     Stanley Morgan, New England, 1986
     Mark Carrier, Tampa Bay, 1989
     Robert Brooks, Green Bay, 1995
     Isaac Bruce, St. Louis, 1995
     Jerry Rice, San Francisco, 1995
     Marvin Harrison, Indianapolis, 1999
     Jimmy Smith, Jacksonville, 1999
     David Boston, Arizona, 2001
     Steve Smith, Carolina, 2005
     Randy Moss, New England, 2007

Most Consecutive Games, 100 or More Yards Pass Receiving
  8 Calvin Johnson, Detroit, 2012
  7 Charley Hennigan, Houston, 1961
     Michael Irvin, Dallas, 1995
  6 Raymond Berry, Baltimore, 1960
     Bill Groman, Houston, 1961
     Pat Studstill, Detroit, 1966
     Isaac Bruce, St. Louis, 1995
     Mike Wallace, Pittsburgh, 2010-11

Longest Pass Reception (All TDs except as noted)
 99 Andy Farkas (from Filchock), Washington vs.
     Pittsburgh, Oct. 15, 1939
     Bobby Mitchell (from Izo), Washington vs. Cleveland,
     Sept. 15, 1963

Pat Studstill (from Sweetan), Detroit vs. Baltimore, Oct. 16, 1966

Gerry Allen (from Jurgensen), Washington vs. Chicago, Sept. 15, 1968

Cliff Branch (from Plunkett), L.A. Raiders vs. Washington, Oct. 2, 1983

Mike Quick (from Jaworski), Philadelphia vs. Atlanta, Nov. 10, 1985

Tony Martin (from Humphries), San Diego vs. Seattle, Sept. 18, 1994

Robert Brooks (from Favre), Green Bay vs. Chicago, Sept. 11, 1995

Marc Boerigter (from Green), Kansas City vs. San Diego, Dec. 22, 2002

Andre Davis (from Garcia), Cleveland vs. Cincinnati, Oct. 17, 2004

Bernard Berrian (from Frerotte), Minnesota vs. Chicago, Nov. 30, 2008

Wes Welker (from Brady), New England vs. Miami, Sept. 12, 2011

Victor Cruz (from Manning), N.Y. Giants vs. N.Y. Jets, Dec. 24, 2011

98 Gaynell Tinsley (from Russell), Chi. Cardinals vs. Cleveland, Nov. 17, 1938

Dick (Night Train) Lane (from Compton), Chi. Cardinals vs. Green Bay, Nov. 13, 1955

John Farrington (from Wade), Chicago vs. Detroit, Oct. 8, 1961

Willard Dewveall (from Lee), Houston vs. San Diego, Nov. 25, 1962

Homer Jones (from Morrall), N.Y. Giants vs. Pittsburgh, Sept. 11, 1966

Ahmad Rashad (from Hart), St. Louis vs. Los Angeles, Dec. 10, 1972 (no TD)

Michael Haynes (from Hebert), Atlanta vs. New Orleans, Sept. 12, 1993

Johnnie Morton (from Batch), Detroit vs. Chicago, Oct. 4, 1998

Terrell Owens (from Fitzpatrick), Buffalo vs. Jacksonville, Nov. 22, 2009

97 Gaynell Tinsley (from Coffee), Chi. Cardinals vs. Chi. Bears, Dec. 5, 1937

Cloyce Box (from Layne), Detroit vs. Green Bay, Nov. 26, 1953

Jerry Tarr (from Shaw), Denver vs. Boston, Sept. 21, 1962

Webster Slaughter (from Kosar), Cleveland vs. Chicago, Oct. 23, 1989

John Taylor (from Young), San Francisco vs. Atlanta, Nov. 3, 1991

AVERAGE GAIN

Highest Avg. Gain, Career (200 receptions)

22.26   Homer Jones, N.Y. Giants, 1964-69; Cleveland, 1970 (224-4,986)

20.83   Buddy Dial, Pittsburgh, 1959-1963; Dallas, 1964-66 (261-5,436)

20.24   Harlon Hill, Chi. Bears, 1954-1961; Pittsburgh, 1962; Detroit, 1962 (233-4,717)

Highest Avg. Gain, Season (24 receptions)

32.58   Don Currivan, Boston, 1947 (24-782)

31.44   Bucky Pope, Los Angeles, 1964 (25-786)

28.60   Bobby Duckworth, San Diego, 1984 (25-715)

Highest Average Gain, Game (3 receptions)

63.00   Torry Holt, St. Louis vs. Atlanta, Sept. 24, 2000 (3-189)

60.67   Bill Groman, Houston vs. Denver, Nov. 20, 1960 (3-182)

Homer Jones, N.Y. Giants vs. Washington, Dec. 12, 1965 (3-182)

60.33   Don Currivan, Boston vs. Washington, Nov. 30, 1947 (3-181)

TOUCHDOWNS

Most Seasons Leading League

9   Don Hutson, Green Bay, 1935-38, 1940-44

6   Jerry Rice, San Francisco, 1986-87, 1989-1991, 1993

5   Randy Moss, Minnesota, 1998, 2000, 2003; New England, 2007, 2009

Most Consecutive Seasons Leading League

5   Don Hutson, Green Bay, 1940-44

4   Don Hutson, Green Bay, 1935-38

3   Lance Alworth, San Diego, 1964-66

    Jerry Rice, San Francisco, 1989-1991

Most Touchdowns, Career

197   Jerry Rice, San Francisco, 1985-2000; Oakland, 2001-04; Seattle, 2004

156   Randy Moss, Minnesota, 1998-2004, 2010; Oakland, 2005-06; New England, 2007-2010; Tennessee, 2010; San Francisco, 2012

153   Terrell Owens, San Francisco, 1996-2003; Philadelphia, 2004-05; Dallas, 2006-08; Buffalo, 2009; Cincinnati, 2010

Most Touchdowns, Season

23   Randy Moss, New England, 2007

22   Jerry Rice, San Francisco, 1987

18   Mark Clayton, Miami, 1984

    Sterling Sharpe, Green Bay, 1994

Most Touchdowns, Rookie, Season

17   Randy Moss, Minnesota, 1998

13   Bill Howton, Green Bay, 1952

    John Jefferson, San Diego, 1978

12   Harlon Hill, Chi. Bears, 1954

    Bill Groman, Houston, 1960

    Mike Ditka, Chicago, 1961

    Bob Hayes, Dallas, 1965

Most Touchdowns, Game

5   Bob Shaw, Chi. Cardinals vs. Baltimore, Oct. 2, 1950

    Kellen Winslow, San Diego vs. Oakland, Nov. 22, 1981

    Jerry Rice, San Francisco vs. Atlanta, Oct. 14, 1990

4   By many players. Last time: Jamaal Charles, Kansas City vs. Oakland, Dec. 15, 2013

Most Consecutive Games, Touchdowns

13   Jerry Rice, San Francisco, 1986-87

11   Elroy (Crazylegs) Hirsch, Los Angeles, 1950-51

    Buddy Dial, Pittsburgh, 1959-1960

10   Carl Pickens, Cincinnati, 1994-95

    Randy Moss, Minnesota, 2003-04

YARDS FROM SCRIMMAGE

Most Scrimmage Yards, Career

23,540   Jerry Rice, San Francisco 1985-2000; Oakland, 2001-04; Seattle, 2004

21,579   Emmitt Smith, Dallas, 1990-2002; Arizona, 2003-04

21,264   Walter Payton, Chicago, 1975-1987

Most Scrimmage Yards, Season

2,509   Chris Johnson, Tennessee, 2009

2,429   Marshall Faulk, St. Louis, 1999

2,390   Tiki Barber, N.Y. Giants, 2005

Most Scrimmage Yards, Rookie, Season

2,212   Eric Dickerson, L.A. Rams, 1983

2,139   Edgerrin James, Indianapolis, 1999

1,926   Doug Martin, Tampa Bay, 2012

Most Scrimmage Yards, Game

336   Flipper Anderson, L.A. Rams vs. New Orleans, Nov. 26, 1989 (ot)

330   Billy Cannon, Houston vs. N.Y. Titans, Dec. 10, 1961

329   Calvin Johnson, Detroit vs. Dallas, Oct. 27, 2013

INTERCEPTIONS BY

Most Seasons Leading League
- 3　Everson Walls, Dallas, 1981-82, 1985
- Ed Reed, Baltimore, 2004, 2008, 2010
- 2　Dick (Night Train) Lane, Los Angeles, 1952;
- Chi. Cardinals, 1954
- Jack Christiansen, Detroit, 1953, 1957
- Milt Davis, Baltimore, 1957, 1959
- Dick Lynch, N.Y. Giants, 1961, 1963
- Johnny Robinson, Kansas City, 1966, 1970
- Bill Bradley, Philadelphia, 1971-72
- Emmitt Thomas, Kansas City, 1969, 1974
- Ronnie Lott, San Francisco, 1986; L.A. Raiders, 1991
- Rod Woodson, Baltimore, 1999; Oakland, 2002
- Ty Law, New England, 1998; N.Y. Jets, 2005
- Darren Sharper, Green Bay, 2000; New Orleans, 2009
- Asante Samuel, New England, 2006;
- Philadelphia, 2009
- Charles Woodson, Green Bay, 2009, 2011

Most Interceptions By, Career
- 81　Paul Krause, Washington, 1964-67; Minnesota, 1968-1979
- 79　Emlen Tunnell, N.Y. Giants, 1948-1958; Green Bay, 1959-1961
- 71　Rod Woodson, Pittsburgh, 1987-1996; San Francisco, 1997; Baltimore, 1998-2001; Oakland, 2002-03

Most Interceptions By, Season
- 14　Dick (Night Train) Lane, Los Angeles, 1952
- 13　Dan Sandifer, Washington, 1948
- Orban (Spec) Sanders, N.Y. Yanks, 1950
- Lester Hayes, Oakland, 1980
- 12　By nine players

Most Interceptions By, Rookie, Season
- 14　Dick (Night Train) Lane, Los Angeles, 1952
- 13　Dan Sandifer, Washington, 1948
- 12　Woodley Lewis, Los Angeles, 1950
- Paul Krause, Washington, 1964

Most Interceptions By, Game
- 4　Sammy Baugh, Washington vs. Detroit, Nov. 14, 1943
- Dan Sandifer, Washington vs. Boston, Oct. 31, 1948
- Don Doll, Detroit vs. Chi. Cardinals, Oct. 23, 1949
- Bob Nussbaumer, Chi. Cardinals vs. N.Y. Bulldogs, Nov. 13, 1949
- Russ Craft, Philadelphia vs. Chi. Cardinals, Sept. 24, 1950
- Bobby Dillon, Green Bay vs. Detroit, Nov. 26, 1953
- Jack Butler, Pittsburgh vs. Washington, Dec. 13, 1953
- Austin (Goose) Gonsoulin, Denver vs. Buffalo, Sept. 18, 1960
- Jerry Norton, St. Louis vs. Washington, Nov. 20, 1960; vs. Pittsburgh, Nov. 26, 1961
- Dave Baker, San Francisco vs. L.A. Rams, Dec. 4, 1960
- Bobby Ply, Dall. Texans vs. San Diego, Dec. 16, 1962
- Bobby Hunt, Kansas City vs. Houston, Oct. 4, 1964
- Willie Brown, Denver vs. N.Y. Jets, Nov. 15, 1964
- Dick Anderson, Miami vs. Pittsburgh, Dec. 3, 1973
- Willie Buchanon, Green Bay vs. San Diego, Sept. 24, 1978
- Deron Cherry, Kansas City vs. Seattle, Sept. 29, 1985
- Kwamie Lassiter, Arizona vs. San Diego, Dec. 27, 1998
- Deltha O'Neal, Denver vs. Kansas City, Oct. 7, 2001
- DeAngelo Hall, Washington vs. Chicago, Oct. 24, 2010

Most Consecutive Games, Passes Intercepted By
- 8　Tom Morrow, Oakland, 1962-63
- 7　Tom Landry, N.Y. Giants, 1950-51
- Paul Krause, Washington, 1964
- Larry Wilson, St. Louis, 1966

Ben Davis, Cleveland, 1968
- 6　By many players.
- Last time: Brian Russell, Minnesota, 2003

YARDS GAINED

Most Seasons Leading League
- 3　Darren Sharper, Green Bay, 2002; Minnesota, 2005; New Orleans, 2009
- 2　Dick (Night Train) Lane, Los Angeles, 1952; Chi. Cardinals, 1954
- Herb Adderley, Green Bay, 1965, 1969
- Dick Anderson, Miami, 1968, 1970
- Ed Reed, Baltimore, 2004, 2010

Most Yards Gained, Career
- 1,590　Ed Reed, Baltimore, 2002-2012; Houston, 2013; N.Y. Jets, 2013
- 1,483　Rod Woodson, Pittsburgh, 1987-1996; San Francisco, 1997; Baltimore, 1998-2001; Oakland, 2002-03
- 1,412　Darren Sharper, Green Bay, 1997-2004; Minnesota, 2005-08; New Orleans, 2009-2010

Most Yards Gained, Season
- 376　Darren Sharper, New Orleans, 2009
- 358　Ed Reed, Baltimore, 2004
- 349　Charlie McNeil, San Diego, 1961

Most Yards Gained, Rookie, Season
- 301　Don Doll, Detroit, 1949
- 298　Dick (Night Train) Lane, Los Angeles, 1952
- 275　Woodley Lewis, Los Angeles, 1950

Most Yards Gained, Game
- 177　Charlie McNeil, San Diego vs. Houston, Sept. 24, 1961
- 170　Louis Oliver, Miami vs. Buffalo, Oct. 4, 1992
- 167　Dick Jauron, Detroit vs. Chicago, Nov. 18, 1973

Longest Return (All TDs)
- 107　Ed Reed, Baltimore vs. Philadelphia, Nov. 23, 2008
- 106　Ed Reed, Baltimore vs. Cleveland, Nov. 7, 2004
- 103　Vencie Glenn, San Diego vs. Denver, Nov. 29, 1987
- Louis Oliver, Miami vs. Buffalo, Oct. 4, 1992

TOUCHDOWNS

Most Touchdowns, Career
- 12　Rod Woodson, Pittsburgh, 1987-1996; San Francisco, 1997; Baltimore, 1998-2001; Oakland, 2002-03
- 11　Darren Sharper, Green Bay, 1997-2004; Minnesota, 2005-08; New Orleans, 2009-2010
- Charles Woodson, Oakland, 1998-2005; Green Bay, 2006-2012; Oakland, 2013
- 9　Ken Houston, Houston, 1967-1972; Washington, 1973-1980
- Aeneas Williams, Phoenix, 1991-93; Arizona, 1994-2000; St. Louis, 2001-04
- Deion Sanders, Atlanta, 1989-1993; San Francisco, 1994; Dallas, 1995-99; Washington, 2000; Baltimore, 2004-05

Most Touchdowns, Season
- 4　Ken Houston, Houston, 1971
- Jim Kearney, Kansas City, 1972
- Eric Allen, Philadelphia, 1993
- 3　Dick Harris, San Diego, 1961
- Dick Lynch, N.Y. Giants, 1963
- Herb Adderley, Green Bay, 1965
- Lem Barney, Detroit, 1967
- Miller Farr, Houston, 1967
- Monte Jackson, Los Angeles, 1976
- Rod Perry, Los Angeles, 1978
- Ronnie Lott, San Francisco, 1981
- Lloyd Burruss, Kansas City, 1986
- Wayne Haddix, Tampa Bay, 1990
- Robert Massey, Phoenix, 1992

Ray Buchanan, Indianapolis, 1994
Deion Sanders, San Francisco, 1994
Mark McMillian, Kansas City, 1997
Otis Smith, N.Y. Jets, 1997
Jimmy Hitchcock, Minnesota, 1998
Eric Allen, Oakland, 2000
Derrick Brooks, Tampa Bay, 2002
Antrel Rolle, Arizona, 2007
Nick Collins, Green Bay, 2008
Darren Sharper, New Orleans, 2009
Charles Woodson, Green Bay, 2009
Janoris Jenkins, St. Louis, 2012
Charles Tillman, Chicago, 2012
2   By many players

Most Touchdowns, Rookie, Season
3   Lem Barney, Detroit, 1967
Ronnie Lott, San Francisco, 1981
Janoris Jenkins, St. Louis, 2012
2   By many players

Most Touchdowns, Game
2   Guy Chamberlain, Canton vs. Chi. Cardinals,
Nov. 26, 1922
Hoot Flanagan, Pottsville vs. Frankford,
Nov. 29, 1925
Tom Leary, Newark vs. Frankford, Oct. 4, 1930
Bill Blackburn, Chi. Cardinals vs. Boston,
Oct. 24, 1948
Dan Sandifer, Washington vs. Boston, Oct. 31, 1948
Bob Franklin, Cleveland vs. Chicago, Dec. 11, 1960
Bill Stacy, St. Louis vs. Dall. Cowboys, Nov. 5, 1961
Jerry Norton, St. Louis vs. Pittsburgh, Nov. 26, 1961
Miller Farr, Houston vs. Buffalo, Dec. 7, 1968
Ken Houston, Houston vs. San Diego, Dec. 19, 1971
Jim Kearney, Kansas City vs. Denver, Oct. 1, 1972
Lemar Parrish, Cincinnati vs. Houston, Dec. 17, 1972
Dick Anderson, Miami vs. Pittsburgh, Dec. 3, 1973
Prentice McCray, New England vs. N.Y. Jets,
Nov. 21, 1976
Kenny Johnson, Atlanta vs. Green Bay,
Nov. 27, 1983 (ot)
Mike Kozlowski, Miami vs. N.Y. Jets, Dec. 16, 1983
Dave Brown, Seattle vs. Kansas City, Nov. 4, 1984
Lloyd Burruss, Kansas City vs. San Diego,
Oct. 19, 1986
Henry Jones, Buffalo vs. Indianapolis, Sept. 20, 1992
Robert Massey, Phoenix vs. Washington, Oct. 4, 1992
Eric Allen, Philadelphia vs. New Orleans,
Dec. 26, 1993
Ken Norton, San Francisco vs. St. Louis,
Oct. 22, 1995
Otis Smith, N.Y. Jets vs. Tampa Bay, Dec. 14, 1997
Dewayne Washington, Pittsburgh vs. Jacksonville,
Nov. 22, 1998
Aaron Glenn, Houston vs. Pittsburgh, Dec. 8, 2002
Ronde Barber, Tampa Bay vs. Philadelphia,
Oct. 22, 2006
Antrel Rolle, Arizona vs. Cincinnati, Nov. 18, 2007
Derrick Johnson, Kansas City vs. Denver,
Jan. 3, 2010
David Bowens, Cleveland vs. New Orleans,
Oct. 24, 2010
Janoris Jenkins, St. Louis vs. Arizona, Nov. 25, 2012
Zach Brown, Tennessee vs. Jacksonville,
Dec. 30, 2012

PUNTING
Most Punts, Career
1,713 Jeff Feagles, New England, 1988-89; Philadelphia,
1990-93; Arizona, 1994-97; Seattle, 1998-
2002; N.Y. Giants, 2003-09

1,401 Sean Landeta, N.Y. Giants, 1985-1993; L.A. Rams,
1993-94; St. Louis, 1995-96; Tampa Bay, 1997;
Green Bay, 1998; Philadelphia, 1999-2002;
St. Louis, 2003-04; Philadelphia, 2005
1,339 Brad Maynard, N.Y. Giants, 1997-2000; Chicago,
2001-2010; Cleveland, 2011

Most Punts, Season
114 Bob Parsons, Chicago, 1981
Chad Stanley, Houston, 2002
112 Dave Zastudil, Arizona, 2012
111 Brad Maynard, N.Y. Giants, 1997

Most Punts, Rookie, Season
111 Brad Maynard, N.Y. Giants, 1997
108 John Teltschik, Philadelphia, 1986
101 Daniel Pope, Kansas City, 1999

Most Punts, Game
16 Leo Araguz, Oakland vs. San Diego, Oct. 11, 1998
15 John Teltschik, Philadelphia vs. N.Y. Giants,
Dec. 6, 1987 (ot)
14 Dick Nesbitt, Chi. Cardinals vs. Chi. Bears,
Nov. 30, 1933
Keith Molesworth, Chi. Bears vs. Green Bay,
Dec. 10, 1933
Sammy Baugh, Washington vs. Philadelphia,
Nov. 5, 1939
Carl Kinscherf, N.Y. Giants vs. Detroit, Nov. 7, 1943
George Taliaferro, N.Y. Yanks vs. Los Angeles,
Sept. 28, 1951

Longest Punt
98 Steve O'Neal, N.Y. Jets vs. Denver, Sept. 21, 1969
94 Joe Lintzenich, Chi. Bears vs. N.Y. Giants, Nov. 16, 1931
93 Shawn McCarthy, New England vs. Buffalo,
Nov. 3, 1991

AVERAGE YARDAGE
Highest Average, Punting, Career (250 punts)
47.55 Shane Lechler, Oakland, 2000-2012; Houston, 2013
(1,102-52,404)
47.08 Thomas Morstead, New Orleans, 2009-2013
(296-13,936)
46.81 Brandon Fields, Miami, 2007-2013 (536-25,092)

Highest Avg. Punting, Season (Qualifiers)
51.40 Sammy Baugh, Washington, 1940 (35-1,799)
51.14 Shane Lechler, Oakland, 2009 (96-4,909)
50.90 Andy Lee, San Francisco, 2011 (78-3,970)

Highest Avg. Punting, Rookie, Season
47.84 Bryan Anger, Jacksonville, 2012 (91-4,353)
47.21 Sam Martin, Detroit, 2013 (72-3,399)
46.74 Brett Kern, Denver, 2008 (46-2,150)

Highest Avg. Punting, Game (4 punts)
61.75 Bob Cifers, Detroit vs. Chi. Bears, Nov. 24, 1946
(4-247)
61.60 Roy McKay, Green Bay vs. Chi. Cardinals,
Oct. 28, 1945 (5-308)
60.00 Jon Ryan, Seattle vs. New England, Oct. 14, 2012
(4-240)

NET AVERAGE
Net average has been compiled since 1976.
Highest Net Average, Punting, Career (250 punts)
40.67 Thomas Morstead, New Orleans, 2009-2013
(297-12,079)
39.45 Andy Lee, San Francisco, 2004-2013 (872-34,403)
39.33 Britton Colquitt, Kansas City, 2010-2013
(320-12,584)

Highest Net Average, Punting, Season (Qualifiers)
44.23 Johnny Hekker, St. Louis, 2013 (78-3,609)
43.99 Andy Lee, San Francisco, 2011 (79-3,475)
43.85 Shane Lechler, Oakland, 2009 (96-4,210)

Highest Net Average, Punting, Rookie, Season (Qualifiers)
- 40.85 Bryan Anger, Jacksonville, 2012 (92-3,758)
- 40.40 Sam Martin, Detroit, 2013 (73-2,949)
- 39.93 Johnny Hekker, St. Louis, 2012 (82-3,274)

Highest Net Average, Punting, Game (4 punts)
- 59.50 Rohn Stark, Indianapolis vs. Houston, Sept. 13, 1992 (4-238)
- 55.50 Kevin Huber, Cincinnati vs. San Diego, Dec. 1, 2013 (4-222)
- 54.20 Andy Lee, San Francisco vs. Seattle, Sept. 11, 2011 (5-271)

PUNTS HAD BLOCKED

Most Consecutive Punts, None Blocked
- 1,177 Chris Gardocki, Chicago, 1992-94; Indianapolis, 1995-98; Cleveland, 1999-2003; Pittsburgh, 2004-06
- 878 Bryan Barker, Kansas City, 1993; Philadelphia, 1994; Jacksonville, 1995-2000; Washington, 2001-03; Green Bay, 2004; St. Louis, 2005
- 735 Brian Moorman, Buffalo, 2002-2011

Most Punts Had Blocked, Career
- 14 Herman Weaver, Detroit, 1970-76; Seattle, 1977-1980 Harry Newsome, Pittsburgh, 1985-89; Minnesota, 1990-93
- 12 Jerrel Wilson, Kansas City, 1963-1977; New England, 1978 Tom Blanchard, N.Y. Giants, 1971-73; New Orleans, 1974-78; Tampa Bay, 1979-1981 Jeff Feagles, New England, 1988-89; Philadelphia, 1990-93; Arizona, 1994-97; Seattle, 1998-2002; N.Y. Giants, 2003-09
- 11 David Lee, Baltimore, 1966-1978

Most Punts Had Blocked, Season
- 6 Harry Newsome, Pittsburgh, 1988
- 4 Bryan Wagner, Cleveland, 1990 Mike Scifres, San Diego, 2010
- 3 By many players

PUNTS INSIDE THE 20

Punts Inside the 20 have been compiled since 1976.

Most Punts Inside the 20, Career
- 554 Jeff Feagles, New England, 1988-89; Philadelphia, 1990-93; Arizona, 1994-97; Seattle, 1998-2002; N.Y. Giants, 2003-09
- 439 Brad Maynard, N.Y. Giants, 1997-2000; Chicago, 2001-2010; Cleveland, 2011
- 399 Craig Hentrich, Green Bay, 1994-97; Tennessee, 1998-2009

Most Punts Inside the 20, Season
- 46 Dave Zastudil, Arizona, 2012
- 45 Dustin Colquitt, Kansas City, 2012
- 42 Andy Lee, San Francisco, 2007 Ben Graham, Arizona, 2009 Steve Weatherford, N.Y. Jets, 2010

Most Punts Inside the 20, Game
- 8 Mark Royals, Pittsburgh vs. Houston, Nov. 6, 1994 (ot) Bryan Barker, Jacksonville vs. Baltimore, Nov. 14, 1999
- 7 Josh Miller, Pittsburgh vs. Cincinnati, Dec. 20, 1998 David Zastudil. Cleveland vs. Buffalo, Oct. 11, 2009 Thomas Morstead, New Orleans vs. Carolina, Jan. 3, 2010 Donnie Jones, Philadelphia vs. Arizona, Dec. 1, 2013
- 6 By many players

PUNT RETURNS

Most Seasons Leading League
- 3 Les (Speedy) Duncan, San Diego, 1965-66; Washington, 1971

- Rick Upchurch, Denver, 1976, 1978, 1982
- 2 Dick Christy, N.Y. Titans, 1961-62 Claude Gibson, Oakland, 1963-64 Billy (White Shoes) Johnson, Houston, 1975, 1977 Mel Gray, New Orleans, 1987; Detroit, 1991 Jermaine Lewis, Baltimore, 1997, 2000 Roscoe Parrish, Buffalo, 2007-08 Devin Hester, Chicago, 2010-11

PUNT RETURNS

Most Punt Returns, Career
- 463 Brian Mitchell, Washington, 1990-99; Philadelphia, 2000-02; N.Y. Giants, 2003
- 351 Eric Metcalf, Cleveland, 1989-1994; Atlanta, 1995-96; San Diego, 1997; Arizona, 1998; Carolina, 1999; Washington, 2001; Green Bay, 2002
- 349 David Meggett, N.Y. Giants, 1989-1994; New England, 1995-97; N.Y. Jets, 1998

Most Punt Returns, Season
- 70 Danny Reece, Tampa Bay, 1979
- 62 Fulton Walker, Miami-L.A. Raiders, 1985
- 58 J.T. Smith, Kansas City, 1979 Greg Pruitt, L.A. Raiders, 1983 Leo Lewis, Minnesota, 1988 Desmond Howard, Green Bay, 1996 Nate Burleson, Seattle, 2007 Dexter McCluster, Kansas City, 2013

Most Punt Returns, Rookie, Season
- 57 Lew Barnes, Chicago, 1986
- 55 B.J. Sams, Baltimore, 2004
- 54 James Jones, Dallas, 1980

Most Punt Returns, Game
- 11 Eddie Brown, Washington vs. Tampa Bay, Oct. 9, 1977
- 10 Theo Bell, Pittsburgh vs. Buffalo, Dec. 16, 1979 Mike Nelms, Washington vs. New Orleans, Dec. 26, 1982 Ronnie Harris, New England vs. Pittsburgh, Dec. 5, 1993
- 9 Rodger Bird, Oakland vs. Denver, Sept. 10, 1967 Ralph McGill, San Francisco vs. Atlanta, Oct. 29, 1972 Ed Podolak, Kansas City vs. San Diego, Nov. 10, 1974 Anthony Leonard, San Francisco vs. New Orleans, Oct. 17, 1976 Butch Johnson, Dallas vs. Buffalo, Nov. 15, 1976 Larry Marshall, Philadelphia vs. Tampa Bay, Sept. 18, 1977 Nesby Glasgow, Baltimore vs. Kansas City, Sept. 2, 1979 Mike Nelms, Washington vs. St. Louis, Dec. 21, 1980 Leon Bright, N.Y. Giants vs. Philadelphia, Dec. 11, 1982 Pete Shaw, N.Y. Giants vs. Philadelphia, Nov. 20, 1983 Cleotha Montgomery, L.A. Raiders vs. Detroit, Dec. 10, 1984 Phil McConkey, N.Y. Giants vs. Philadelphia, Dec. 6, 1987 (ot) Andre Hastings, Pittsburgh vs. Cleveland, Nov. 13, 1995 Steve Smith, Carolina vs. Detroit, Sept. 15, 2002 Reggie Swinton, Arizona vs. Philadelphia, Dec. 24, 2005

FAIR CATCHES

Most Fair Catches, Career
- 231 Brian Mitchell, Washington, 1990-99; Philadelphia, 2000-02; N.Y. Giants, 2003

162   Tim Brown, L.A. Raiders, 1988-1994; Oakland, 1995-2003; Tampa Bay, 2004
144   Glyn Milburn, Denver, 1993-95; Detroit, 1996-97; Chicago, 1998-2001; San Diego, 2001

Most Fair Catches, Season
36   Jeremy Kerley, N.Y. Jets, 2012
33   Brian Mitchell, Philadelphia, 2000
29   Wes Welker, Miami, 2006

Most Fair Catches, Game
7   Bake Turner, N.Y. Jets vs. Miami, Nov. 20, 1966
    Lem Barney, Detroit vs. Chicago, Nov. 21, 1976
    Bobby Morse, Philadelphia vs. Buffalo, Dec. 27, 1987
    Chris Carr, Tennessee vs. Jacksonville, Nov. 16, 2008
6   Jake Scott, Miami vs. Buffalo, Dec. 20, 1970
    Greg Pruitt, L.A. Raiders vs. Seattle, Oct. 7, 1984
    Phil McConkey, San Diego vs. Kansas City, Dec. 17, 1989
    Gerald McNeil, Houston vs. Pittsburgh, Sept. 16, 1990
    Bobby Engram, Chicago vs. Minnesota, Sept. 15, 1996
    Eddie Kennison, New Orleans vs. Baltimore, Dec. 19, 1999
    R.W. McQuarters, N.Y. Giants vs. Atlanta, Oct. 15, 2007
    Emanuel Sanders, Pittsburgh vs. Cleveland, Nov. 25, 2012
    Jeremy Kerley, N.Y. Jets vs. Arizona, Dec. 2, 2012
    Jeremy Kerley, N.Y. Jets vs. Tennessee, Dec. 17, 2012
    Patrick Peterson, Arizona vs. Seattle, Dec. 22, 2013
5   By many players

YARDS GAINED
Most Seasons Leading League
3   Alvin Haymond, Baltimore, 1965-66; Los Angeles, 1969
2   Bill Dudley, Pittsburgh, 1942, 1946
    Emlen Tunnell, N.Y. Giants, 1951-52
    Dick Christy, N.Y. Titans, 1961-62
    Claude Gibson, Oakland, 1963-64
    Rodger Bird, Oakland, 1966-67
    J.T. Smith, Kansas City, 1979-1980
    Vai Sikahema, St. Louis, 1986-87
    David Meggett, N.Y. Giants, 1989-1990
    Tamarick Vanover, Kansas City, 1995, 1999
    Devin Hester, Chicago, 2006, 2010

Most Yards Gained, Career
4,999   Brian Mitchell, Washington, 1990-99; Philadelphia, 2000-02; N.Y. Giants, 2003
3,708   Dave Meggett, N.Y. Giants, 1989-1994; New England, 1995-97; N.Y. Jets, 1998
3,601   Darrien Gordon, San Diego, 1993-94, 1996; Denver, 1997-98; Oakland, 1999-2000; Atlanta, 2001; Green Bay, 2002

Most Yards Gained, Season
875   Desmond Howard, Green Bay, 1996
699   Patrick Peterson, Arizona, 2011
692   Fulton Walker, Miami-L.A. Raiders, 1985

Most Yards Gained, Rookie, Season
699   Patrick Peterson, Arizona, 2011
656   Louis Lipps, Pittsburgh, 1984
655   Neal Colzie, Oakland, 1975

Most Yards Gained, Game
207   LeRoy Irvin, Los Angeles vs. Atlanta, Oct. 11, 1981
205   George Atkinson, Oakland vs. Buffalo, Sept. 15, 1968
199   Eddie Drummond, Detroit vs. Jacksonville, Nov. 14, 2004 (ot)

Longest Punt Return (All TDs)
103   Robert Bailey, L.A. Rams vs. New Orleans, Oct. 23, 1994
99   Patrick Peterson, Arizona vs. St. Louis, Nov. 6, 2011
98   Gil LeFebvre, Cincinnati vs. Brooklyn, Dec. 3, 1933
    Charlie West, Minnesota vs. Washington, Nov. 3, 1968
    Dennis Morgan, Dallas vs. St. Louis, Oct. 13, 1974
    Terance Mathis, N.Y. Jets vs. Dallas, Nov. 4, 1990
    Damaris Johnson, Philadelphia vs. Dallas, Dec. 2, 2012
    Tavon Austin, St. Louis vs. Indianapolis, Nov. 10, 2013

AVERAGE YARDAGE
Highest Average, Career (75 returns)
12.78   George McAfee, Chi. Bears, 1940-41; 1945-1950 (112-1,431)
12.75   Jack Christiansen, Detroit, 1951-58 (85-1,084)
12.55   Claude Gibson, San Diego, 1961-62; Oakland, 1963-65 (110-1,381)

Highest Average, Season (Qualifiers)
23.00   Herb Rich, Baltimore, 1950 (12-276)
21.47   Jack Christiansen, Detroit, 1952 (15-322)
21.28   Dick Christy, N.Y. Titans, 1961 (18-383)

Highest Average, Rookie, Season (Qualifiers)
23.00   Herb Rich, Baltimore, 1950 (12-276)
20.88   Jerry Davis, Chi. Cardinals, 1948 (16-334)
20.73   Frankie Sinkwich, Detroit, 1943 (11-228)

Highest Average, Game
53.33   Darius Reynaud, Tennessee vs. Jacksonville, Dec. 30, 2012 (3-160)
51.00   Steve Smith, Carolina vs. Cincinnati, Dec. 8, 2002 (3-153)
47.67   Chuck Latourette, St. Louis vs. New Orleans, Sept. 29, 1968 (3-143)

TOUCHDOWNS
Most Touchdowns, Career
13   Devin Hester, Chicago, 2006-2013
10   Eric Metcalf, Cleveland, 1989-1994; Atlanta, 1995-96; San Diego, 1997; Arizona, 1998; Carolina, 1999; Washington, 2001; Green Bay, 2002
9   Brian Mitchell, Washington, 1990-99; Philadelphia 2000-02; N.Y. Giants, 2003

Most Touchdowns, Season
4   Jack Christiansen, Detroit, 1951
    Rick Upchurch, Denver, 1976
    Devin Hester, Chicago, 2007
    Patrick Peterson, Arizona, 2011
3   Emlen Tunnell, N.Y. Giants, 1951
    Billy (White Shoes) Johnson, Houston, 1975
    LeRoy Irvin, Los Angeles, 1981
    Desmond Howard, Green Bay, 1996
    Darrien Gordon, Denver, 1997
    Eric Metcalf, San Diego, 1997
    Devin Hester, Chicago, 2006
    Adam Jones, Tennessee, 2006
    Reggie Bush, New Orleans, 2008
    Johnnie Lee Higgins, Oakland, 2008
    Devin Hester, Chicago, 2010
2   By many players

Most Touchdowns, Rookie, Season
4   Jack Christiansen, Detroit, 1951
    Patrick Peterson, Arizona, 2011
3   Devin Hester, Chicago, 2006
2   By many players

Most Touchdowns, Game
2   Jack Christiansen, Detroit vs. Los Angeles, Oct. 14, 1951; vs. Green Bay, Nov. 22, 1951

Dick Christy, N.Y. Titans vs. Denver, Sept. 24, 1961
Rick Upchurch, Denver vs. Cleveland, Sept. 26, 1976
LeRoy Irvin, Los Angeles vs. Atlanta, Oct. 11, 1981
Vai Sikahema, St. Louis vs. Tampa Bay,
   Dec. 21, 1986
Todd Kinchen, L.A. Rams vs. Atlanta, Dec. 27, 1992
Eric Metcalf, Cleveland vs. Pittsburgh, Oct. 24, 1993;
   San Diego vs. Cincinnati, Nov. 2, 1997
Darrien Gordon, Denver vs. Carolina, Nov. 9, 1997
Jermaine Lewis, Baltimore vs. Seattle, Dec. 7, 1997
   Baltimore vs. N.Y. Jets, Dec. 24, 2000
Steve Smith, Carolina vs. Cincinnati, Dec. 8, 2002
Eddie Drummond, Detroit vs. Jacksonville,
   Nov. 14, 2004 (ot)
Reggie Bush, New Orleans vs. Minnesota,
   Oct. 6, 2008
Darius Reynaud, Tennessee vs. Jacksonville,
   Dec. 30, 2012

KICKOFF RETURNS
Most Seasons Leading League
3   Abe Woodson, San Francisco, 1959, 1962-63
2   Lynn Chandnois, Pittsburgh, 1951-52
    Bobby Jancik, Houston, 1962-63
    Travis Williams, Green Bay, 1967; Los Angeles, 1971
    Mel Gray, Detroit, 1991, 1994
    Michael Bates, Carolina, 1996-97

KICKOFF RETURNS
Most Kickoff Returns, Career
607   Brian Mitchell, Washington, 1990-99; Philadelphia,
      2000-02; N.Y. Giants, 2003
514   Allen Rossum, Philadelphia, 1998-99; Green Bay,
      2000-01; Atlanta, 2002-06; Pittsburgh, 2007;
      San Francisco, 2008-09; Dallas, 2009
426   Dante Hall, Kansas City, 2000-06; St. Louis,
      2007-08
Most Kickoff Returns, Season
82   MarTay Jenkins, Arizona, 2000
73   Josh Scobey, Arizona, 2003
    Chris Carr, Oakland, 2005
70   Tyrone Hughes, New Orleans, 1996
    Michael Lewis, New Orleans, 2002
Most Kickoff Returns, Rookie, Season
73   Josh Scobey, Arizona, 2003
    Chris Carr, Oakland, 2005
67   Ronney Jenkins, San Diego, 2000
64   Tab Perry, Cincinnati, 2005
Most Kickoff Returns, Game
10   Desmond Howard, Oakland vs. Seattle, Oct. 26, 1997
    Richard Alston, Cleveland vs. Cincinnati,
      Nov. 28, 2004
9   Noland Smith, Kansas City vs. Oakland, Nov. 23, 1967
    Dino Hall, Cleveland vs. Pittsburgh, Oct. 7, 1979
    Paul Palmer, Kansas City vs. Seattle, Sept. 20, 1987
    Eric Metcalf, Atlanta vs. San Francisco,
      Sept. 29, 1996; vs. St. Louis, Nov. 10, 1996
    Michael Bates, Carolina vs. Atlanta, Oct. 4, 1998
    Nate Jacquet, Minnesota vs. Philadelphia,
      Nov. 11, 2001
    Ahmad Merritt, Chicago vs. San Francisco,
      Sept. 7, 2003
    Josh Scobey, Arizona vs. Cleveland, Nov. 16, 2003
    Maurice Hicks, San Francisco vs. San Diego,
      Oct. 15, 2006
    Aveion Cason, Detroit vs. San Diego, Dec. 16, 2007
    Allen Rossum, San Francisco vs. Philadelphia,
      Oct. 12, 2008
    Steve Breaston, Arizona vs. New England,
      Dec. 21, 2008

Danny Amendola, St. Louis vs. Tennessee,
   Dec. 13, 2009
Brandon James, Indianapolis vs. San Diego,
   Nov. 28, 2010
8   By many players

YARDS GAINED
Most Seasons Leading League
3   Bruce Harper, N.Y. Jets, 1977-79
    Tyrone Hughes, New Orleans, 1994-96
2   Marshall Goldberg, Chi. Cardinals, 1941-42
    Woodley Lewis, Los Angeles, 1953-54
    Al Carmichael, Green Bay, 1956-57
    Timmy Brown, Philadelphia, 1961, 1963
    Bobby Jancik, Houston, 1963, 1966
    Ron Smith, Atlanta, 1966-67
    Chris Carr, Oakland, 2005-06
Most Yards Gained, Career
14,014   Brian Mitchell, Washington, 1990-99; Philadelphia,
        2000-02; N.Y. Giants, 2006
11,947   Allen Rossum, Philadelphia, 1998-99; Green Bay,
        2000-01; Atlanta, 2002-06; Pittsburgh, 2007; San
        Francisco, 2008-09; Dallas, 2009
10,505   Josh Cribbs, Cleveland, 2005-2012; N.Y. Jets, 2013
Most Yards Gained, Season
2,186   MarTay Jenkins, Arizona, 2000
1,809   Josh Cribbs, Cleveland, 2007
1,807   Michael Lewis, New Orleans, 2002
Most Yards Gained, Rookie, Season
1,752   Chris Carr, Oakland, 2005
1,684   Josh Scobey, Arizona, 2003
1,577   Justin Miller, N.Y. Jets, 2005
Most Yards Gained, Game
304   Tyrone Hughes, New Orleans vs. L.A. Rams,
     Oct. 23, 1994
299   Ted Ginn, Jr., Miami vs. N.Y. Jets, Nov. 1, 2009
294   Wally Triplett, Detroit vs. Los Angeles, Oct. 29, 1950
Longest Kickoff Return (All TDs)
109   Cordarrelle Patterson, Minnesota vs. Green Bay,
     Oct. 27, 2013
108   Ellis Hobbs, New England, vs. N.Y. Jets, Sept. 9, 2007
     Randall Cobb, Green Bay vs. New Orleans,
      Sept. 8, 2011
     Jacoby Jones, Baltimore vs. Dallas, Oct. 14, 2012
     Knile Davis, Kansas City vs. Denver, Dec. 1, 2013
107   Joe McKnight, N.Y. Jets vs. Baltimore, Oct. 2, 2011

AVERAGE YARDAGE
Highest Average, Career (75 returns)
30.56   Gale Sayers, Chicago, 1965-1971 (91-2,781)
29.57   Lynn Chandnois, Pittsburgh, 1950-56 (92-2,720)
29.01   Joe McKnight, N.Y. Jets, 2010-12 (76-2,205)
Highest Average, Season (Qualifiers)
41.06   Travis Williams, Green Bay, 1967 (18-739)
37.69   Gale Sayers, Chicago, 1967 (16-603)
35.50   Ollie Matson, Chi. Cardinals, 1958 (14-497)
Highest Average, Rookie, Season (Qualifiers)
41.06   Travis Williams, Green Bay, 1967 (18-739)
33.08   Tom Moore, Green Bay, 1960 (12-397)
32.88   Duriel Harris, Miami, 1976 (17-559)
Highest Average, Game (3 returns)
73.50   Wally Triplett, Detroit vs. Los Angeles, Oct. 29, 1950
      (4-294)
67.33   Lenny Lyles, San Francisco vs. Baltimore,
      Dec. 18, 1960 (3-202)
65.33   Ken Hall, Houston vs. N.Y. Titans, Oct. 23, 1960
      (3-196)

TOUCHDOWNS

Most Touchdowns, Career

8 Josh Cribbs, Cleveland, 2005-2012; N.Y. Jets, 2013
Leon Washington, N.Y. Jets, 2006-09;
Seattle, 2010-12; New England, 2013;
Tennessee, 2013

6 Ollie Matson, Chi. Cardinals, 1952, 1954-58;
L.A. Rams, 1959-1962; Detroit, 1963;
Philadelphia, 1964
Gale Sayers, Chicago, 1965-1971
Travis Williams, Green Bay, 1967-1970;
Los Angeles, 1971
Mel Gray, New Orleans, 1986-88; Detroit,
1989-1994; Houston, 1995-96; Tennessee,
1997; Philadelphia, 1997
Dante Hall, Kansas City, 2000-06; St. Louis, 2007-08

5 By many players

Most Touchdowns, Season

4 Travis Williams, Green Bay, 1967
Cecil Turner, Chicago, 1970

3 Verda (Vitamin T) Smith, Los Angeles, 1950
Abe Woodson, San Francisco, 1963
Gale Sayers, Chicago, 1967
Raymond Clayborn, New England, 1977
Ron Brown, L.A. Rams, 1985
Mel Gray, Detroit, 1994
Darrick Vaughn, Atlanta, 2000
Terrence McGee, Buffalo, 2004
André Davis, Houston, 2007
Leon Washington, N.Y. Jets, 2007
Josh Cribbs, Cleveland, 2009
Jacoby Ford, Oakland, 2010
Leon Washington, Seattle, 2010

2 By many players

Most Touchdowns, Rookie, Season

4 Travis Williams, Green Bay, 1967

3 Raymond Clayborn, New England, 1977
Darrick Vaughn, Atlanta, 2000
Jacoby Ford, Oakland, 2010

2 By many players

Most Touchdowns, Game

2 Timmy Brown, Philadelphia vs. Dallas, Nov. 6, 1966
Travis Williams, Green Bay vs. Cleveland,
Nov. 12, 1967
Ron Brown, L.A. Rams vs. Green Bay, Nov. 24, 1985
Tyrone Hughes, New Orleans vs. L.A. Rams,
Oct. 23, 1994
Chad Morton, N.Y. Jets vs. Buffalo, Sept. 8, 2002 (ot)
Devin Hester, Chicago vs. St. Louis, Dec. 11, 2006
André Davis, Houston vs. Jacksonville, Dec. 30, 2007
Ted Ginn, Jr., Miami vs. N.Y. Jets, Nov. 1, 2009
Josh Cribbs, Cleveland vs. Kansas City, Dec. 20, 2009
Leon Washington, Seattle vs. San Diego,
Sept. 26, 2010

COMBINED KICK RETURNS

Most Combined Kick Returns, Career

1,070 Brian Mitchell, Washington, 1990-99; Philadelphia,
2000-02; N.Y. Giants, 2003 (p-463, k-607)

821 Allen Rossum, Philadelphia, 1998-99; Green Bay,
2000-01; Atlanta, 2002-06; Pittsburgh, 2007;
San Francisco, 2008-09; Dallas, 2009
(p-307, k-514)

711 Glyn Milburn, Denver, 1993-95; Detroit, 1996-97;
Chicago, 1998-2001; San Diego, 2001 (p-304,
k-407)

Most Combined Kick Returns, Season

114 Michael Lewis, New Orleans, 2002 (p-44, k-70)
B.J. Sams, Baltimore, 2004 (p-55, k-59)

107 Chris Carr, Oakland, 2005 (p-34, k-73)

Dante Hall, Kansas City, 2005 (p-42, k-65)

105 Reggie Swinton, Arizona, 2005 (p-42, k-63)

Most Combined Kick Returns, Game

13 Stump Mitchell, St. Louis vs. Atlanta, Oct. 18, 1981
(p-6, k-7)
Ronnie Harris, New England vs. Pittsburgh,
Dec. 5, 1993 (p-10, k-3)

12 Mel Renfro, Dallas vs. Green Bay, Nov. 29, 1964
(p-4, k-8)
Larry Jones, Washington vs. Dallas, Dec. 13, 1975
(p-6, k-6)
Eddie Brown, Washington vs. Tampa Bay,
Oct. 9, 1977 (p-11, k-1)
Nesby Glasgow, Baltimore vs. Denver, Sept. 2, 1979
(p-9, k-3)
Tim Dwight, Atlanta vs. Detroit, Nov. 12, 2000
(p-8, k-4)
Wes Welker, Miami vs. Buffalo, Dec. 5, 2004
(p-6, k-6)
Reggie Swinton, Arizona vs. Philadelphia,
Dec. 24, 2005 (p-9, k-3)
Devin Hester, Chicago vs. Detroit, Sept. 30, 2007
(p-5, k-7)
Brandon James, Indianapolis vs. San Diego,
Nov. 28, 2010 (p-3, k-9)

11 By many players

YARDS GAINED

Most Yards Returned, Career

19,013 Brian Mitchell, Washington, 1990-99; Philadelphia,
2000-02; N.Y. Giants, 2003 (p-4,999; k-14,014)

15,003 Allen Rossum, Philadelphia, 1998-99; Green Bay,
2000-01; Atlanta, 2002-06; Pittsburgh, 2007;
San Francisco, 2008-09; Dallas, 2009
(p-3,056; k-11,947)

13,003 Mel Gray, New Orleans, 1986-88; Detroit, 1989-
1994; Houston, 1995-96; Tennessee, 1997;
Philadelphia, 1997 (p-2,753; k-10,250)

Most Yards Returned, Season

2,432 Michael Lewis, New Orleans, 2002 (p-625; k-1,807)
2,214 Josh Cribbs, Cleveland, 2007 (p-405; k-1,809)
2,187 MarTay Jenkins, Arizona, 2000 (pr-1; k-2,186)

Most Yards Returned, Game

347 Tyrone Hughes, New Orleans vs. L.A. Rams,
Oct. 23, 1994 (p-43; k-304)

314 Devin Hester, Chicago vs. Detroit, Sept. 30, 2007
(p-95; k-219)

306 Josh Cribbs, Cleveland vs. Baltimore, Nov. 18, 2007
(p-61; k-245) (ot)

TOUCHDOWNS

Most Touchdowns, Career

18 Devin Hester, Chicago, 2006-2013 (p-13, k-5)

13 Brian Mitchell, Washington, 1990-99; Philadelphia,
2000-02; N.Y. Giants, 2003 (p-9, k-4)

12 Eric Metcalf, Cleveland, 1989-1994; Atlanta,
1995-96; San Diego, 1997; Arizona, 1998;
Carolina, 1999; Washington, 2001; Green Bay,
2002 (p-10, k-2)
Dante Hall, Kansas City, 2000-06;
St. Louis, 2007-08 (p-6, k-6)

Most Touchdowns, Season

6 Devin Hester, Chicago, 2007 (p-4, k-2)

5 Devin Hester, Chicago, 2006 (p-3, k-2)

4 Jack Christiansen, Detroit, 1951 (p-4)
Emlen Tunnell, N.Y. Giants, 1951 (p-3, k-1)
Gale Sayers, Chicago, 1967 (p-1, k-3)
Travis Williams, Green Bay, 1967 (k-4)
Cecil Turner, Chicago, 1970 (k-4)
Billy Johnson, Houston, 1975 (p-3, k-1)

Rick Upchurch, Denver, 1976 (p-4)
Dante Hall, Kansas City, 2003 (p-2, r-2)
Eddie Drummond, Detroit, 2004 (p-2, k-2)
Josh Cribbs, Cleveland, 2009 (p-1, k-3)
Patrick Peterson, Arizona, 2011 (p-4)

Most Touchdowns, Game

2   Jack Christiansen, Detroit vs. Los Angeles,
Oct. 14, 1951 (p-2); vs. Green Bay,
Nov. 22, 1951 (p-2)
Jim Patton, N.Y. Giants vs. Washington,
Oct. 30, 1955 (p-1, k-1)
Bobby Mitchell, Cleveland vs. Philadelphia,
Nov. 23, 1958 (p-1, k-1)
Dick Christy, N.Y. Titans vs. Denver, Sept. 24, 1961
(p-2)
Al Frazier, Denver vs. Boston, Dec. 3, 1961 (p-1, k-1)
Timmy Brown, Philadelphia vs. Dallas, Nov. 6, 1966
(k-2)
Travis Williams, Green Bay vs. Cleveland,
Nov. 12, 1967 (k-2); vs. Pittsburgh,
Nov. 2, 1969 (p-1, k-1)
Gale Sayers, Chicago vs. San Francisco,
Dec. 3, 1967 (p-1, k-1)
Rick Upchurch, Denver vs. Cleveland,
Sept. 26, 1976 (p-2)
Eddie Payton, Detroit vs. Minnesota, Dec. 17, 1977
(p-1, k-1)
LeRoy Irvin, Los Angeles vs. Atlanta, Oct. 11, 1981
(p-2)
Ron Brown, L.A. Rams vs. Green Bay,
Nov. 24, 1985 (k-2)
Vai Sikahema, St. Louis vs. Tampa Bay,
Dec. 21, 1986 (p-2)
Todd Kinchen, L.A. Rams vs. Atlanta, Dec. 27, 1992
(p-2)
Eric Metcalf, Cleveland vs. Pittsburgh, Oct. 24, 1993
(p-2); San Diego vs. Cincinnati, Nov. 2, 1997
(p-2)
Tyrone Hughes, New Orleans vs. L.A. Rams,
Oct. 23, 1994 (k-2)
Darrien Gordon, Denver vs. Carolina, Nov. 9, 1997
(p-2)
Jermaine Lewis, Baltimore vs. Seattle, Dec. 7, 1997
(p-2); Baltimore vs. N.Y. Jets, Dec. 24, 2000
(p-2)
Chad Morton, N.Y. Jets vs. Buffalo, Sept. 8, 2002
(ot) (k-2)
Michael Lewis, New Orleans vs. Washington,
Oct. 13, 2002 (p-1, k-1)
Dante Hall, Kansas City vs. St. Louis, Dec. 8, 2002
(p-1, k-1)
Steve Smith, Carolina vs. Cincinnati, Dec. 8, 2002
(p-2)
Eddie Drummond, Detroit vs. Jacksonville,
Nov. 14, 2004 (ot) (p-2)
Devin Hester, Chicago vs. St. Louis, Dec. 11, 2006
(k-2)
Darren Sproles, San Diego vs. Indianapolis,
Nov. 11, 2007 (p-1, k-1)
Devin Hester, Chicago vs. Denver, Nov. 25, 2007
(p-1, k-1)
André Davis, Houston vs. Jacksonville,
Dec. 30, 2007 (k-2)
Reggie Bush, New Orleans vs. Minnesota,
Oct. 6, 2008
Eddie Royal, Denver vs. San Diego, Oct. 19, 2009
(p-1, k-1)
Ted Ginn, Jr., Miami vs. N.Y. Jets, Nov. 1, 2009
(k-2); San Francisco vs. Seattle, Sept. 11, 2011
(p-1, k-1)

Josh Cribbs, Cleveland vs. Kansas City,
Dec. 20, 2009 (k-2)
Leon Washington, Seattle vs. San Diego,
Sept. 26, 2010 (k-2)
Darius Reynaud, Tennessee vs. Jacksonville,
Dec. 30, 2012 (p-2)
Jeremy Ross, Detroit vs. Philadelphia, Dec. 8. 2013

FUMBLES

Most Fumbles, Career

166   Brett Favre, Atlanta, 1991; Green Bay, 1992-2007;
N.Y. Jets, 2008; Minnesota, 2009-2010
161   Warren Moon, Houston, 1984-1993; Minnesota,
1994-96; Seattle, 1997-98; Kansas City,
1999-2000
153   Dave Krieg, Seattle, 1980-1991; Kansas City,
1992-93; Detroit, 1994; Arizona, 1995;
Chicago, 1996; Tennessee, 1997-98

Most Fumbles, Season

23   Kerry Collins, N.Y. Giants, 2001
Daunte Culpepper, Minnesota, 2002
21   Tony Banks, St. Louis, 1996
David Carr, Houston, 2002
18   Dave Krieg, Seattle, 1989
Warren Moon, Houston, 1990

Most Fumbles, Game

7   Len Dawson, Kansas City vs. San Diego,
Nov. 15, 1964
6   Sam Etcheverry, St. Louis vs. N.Y. Giants,
Sept. 17, 1961
Dave Krieg, Seattle vs. Kansas City, Nov. 5, 1989
Brett Favre, Green Bay vs. Tampa Bay, Dec. 7, 1998
Kurt Warner, St. Louis vs. N.Y. Giants, Sept. 7, 2003
Chad Pennington, N.Y. Jets vs. Kansas City,
Sept. 11, 2005
5   Paul Christman, Chi. Cardinals vs. Green Bay,
Nov. 10, 1946
Joe Perry, San Francisco vs. Cleveland,
Nov. 12, 1950
Charlie Conerly, N.Y. Giants vs. San Francisco,
Dec. 1, 1957
Tom Yewcic, Boston vs. Oakland, Dec. 16, 1962
Jack Kemp, Buffalo vs. Houston, Oct. 29, 1967
Roman Gabriel, Philadelphia vs. Oakland,
Nov. 21, 1976
Randall Cunningham, Philadelphia vs. L.A. Raiders,
Nov. 30, 1986 (ot)
Willie Totten, Buffalo vs. Indianapolis, Oct. 4, 1987
Dave Walter, Cincinnati vs. Seattle, Oct. 11, 1987
Dave Krieg, Seattle vs. San Diego, Nov. 25, 1990 (ot)
Andre Ware, Detroit vs. Green Bay, Dec. 6, 1992
Steve Beuerlein, Carolina vs. San Francisco,
Nov. 8, 1998
Patrick Ramsey, Washington vs. Green Bay,
Oct. 20, 2002
Eli Manning, N.Y. Giants vs. Buffalo, Dec. 23, 2007
Josh Johnson, Tampa Bay vs. Carolina,
Oct. 18, 2009
Matthew Stafford, Detroit vs. Philadelphia,
Dec. 8, 2013

FUMBLES RECOVERED

Most Fumbles Recovered, Career, Own and Opponents'

56   Warren Moon, Houston, 1984-1993; Minnesota,
1994-96; Seattle, 1997-98; Kansas City,
1999-2000 (56 own)
47   Dave Krieg, Seattle, 1980-1991; Kansas City,
1992-93; Detroit, 1994; Arizona, 1995; Chicago, 1996; Tennessee, 1997-98 (47 own)

45   Boomer Esiason, Cincinnati, 1984-1992, 1997;
      N.Y. Jets, 1993-95; Arizona, 1996 (45 own)

Most Fumbles Recovered, Season, Own and Opponents'
12   David Carr, Houston, 2002 (12 own)
 9   Don Hultz, Minnesota, 1963 (9 opp)
      Dave Krieg, Seattle, 1989 (9 own)
      Brian Griese, Denver, 1999 (9 own)
      Jon Kitna, Seattle, 2000 (9 own)
 8   Paul Christman, Chi. Cardinals, 1945 (8 own)
      Joe Schmidt, Detroit, 1955 (8 opp)
      Bill Butler, Minnesota, 1963 (8 own)
      Kermit Alexander, San Francisco, 1965
      (4 own, 4 opp)
      Jack Lambert, Pittsburgh, 1976 (1 own, 7 opp)
      Danny White, Dallas, 1981 (8 own)
      Dan Marino, Miami, 1988 (7 own, 1 opp)
      Tony Banks, St. Louis, 1998 (8 own)
      Ryan Fitzpatrick, Cincinnati, 2008 (8 own)
      Donovan McNabb, Washington, 2010 (8 own)

Most Fumbles Recovered, Game, Own and Opponents'
 4   Otto Graham, Cleveland vs. N.Y. Giants,
      Oct. 25, 1953 (4 own)
      Sam Etcheverry, St. Louis vs. N.Y. Giants,
      Sept. 17, 1961 (4 own)
      Roman Gabriel, Los Angeles vs. San Francisco,
      Oct. 12, 1969 (4 own)
      Randall Cunningham, Philadelphia vs. L.A. Raiders,
      Nov. 30, 1986 (ot) (4 own)
      Joe Ferguson, Buffalo vs. Miami, Sept. 18, 1977
      (4 own)
      Tony Romo, Dallas vs. Washington, Sept. 26, 2011
      (4-own)
      Patrick Peterson, Arizona vs. Miami,
      Sept. 30, 2012 (ot) (3 own, 1 opp)
 3   By many players

OWN FUMBLES RECOVERED
Most Own Fumbles Recovered, Career
56   Warren Moon, Houston, 1984-1993; Minnesota,
      1994-96; Seattle, 1997-98; Kansas City,
      1999-2000
47   Dave Krieg, Seattle, 1980-1991; Kansas City,
      1992-93; Detroit, 1994; Arizona, 1995;
      Chicago, 1996; Tennessee, 1997-98
45   Boomer Esiason, Cincinnati, 1984-1992, 1997;
      N.Y. Jets, 1993-95; Arizona, 1996

Most Own Fumbles Recovered, Season
12   David Carr, Houston, 2002
 9   Dave Krieg, Seattle, 1989
      Brian Griese, Denver, 1999
      Jon Kitna, Seattle, 2000
 8   Paul Christman, Chi. Cardinals, 1945
      Bill Butler, Minnesota, 1963
      Danny White, Dallas, 1981
      Tony Banks, St. Louis, 1998
      Ryan Fitzpatrick, Cincinnati, 2008
      Donovan McNabb, Washington, 2010

Most Own Fumbles Recovered, Game
 4   Otto Graham, Cleveland vs. N.Y. Giants, Oct. 25, 1953
      Sam Etcheverry, St. Louis vs. N.Y. Giants,
      Sept. 17, 1961
      Roman Gabriel, Los Angeles vs. San Francisco,
      Oct. 12, 1969
      Joe Ferguson, Buffalo vs. Miami, Sept. 18, 1977

      Randall Cunningham, Philadelphia vs. L.A. Raiders,
      Nov. 30, 1986 (ot)
      Tony Romo, Dallas vs. Washington, Sept. 26, 2011
 3   By many players

OPPONENTS' FUMBLES RECOVERED
Most Opponents' Fumbles Recovered, Career
29   Jim Marshall, Cleveland, 1960; Minnesota, 1961-1979
      Jason Taylor, Miami, 1997-2007; Washington, 2008;
      Miami, 2009; N.Y. Jets, 2010; Miami, 2011
28   Rickey Jackson, New Orleans, 1981-1993;
      San Francisco, 1994-95
26   Kevin Greene, L.A. Rams, 1985-1992; Pittsburgh,
      1993-95; Carolina, 1996; San Francisco, 1997;
      Carolina, 1998-99
      Cornelius Bennett, Buffalo, 1987-1995; Atlanta,
      1996-98; Indianapolis, 1999-2000

Most Opponents' Fumbles Recovered, Season
 9   Don Hultz, Minnesota, 1963
 8   Joe Schmidt, Detroit, 1955
 7   Alan Page, Minnesota, 1970
      Jack Lambert, Pittsburgh, 1976
      Ray Childress, Houston, 1988
      Rickey Jackson, New Orleans, 1990

Most Opponents' Fumbles Recovered, Game
 3   Corwin Clatt, Chi. Cardinals vs. Detroit, Nov. 6, 1949
      Vic Sears, Philadelphia vs. Green Bay, Nov. 2, 1952
      Ed Beatty, San Francisco vs. Los Angeles,
      Oct. 7, 1956
      Ron Carroll, Houston vs. Cincinnati, Oct. 27, 1974
      Maurice Spencer, New Orleans vs. Atlanta,
      Oct. 10, 1976
      Steve Nelson, New England vs. Philadelphia,
      Oct. 8, 1978
      Charles Jackson, Kansas City vs. Pittsburgh,
      Sept. 6, 1981
      Willie Buchanon, San Diego vs. Denver,
      Sept. 27, 1981
      Joey Browner, Minnesota vs. San Francisco,
      Sept. 8, 1985
      Ray Childress, Houston vs. Washington, Oct. 30, 1988
      John Thierry, Chicago vs. Houston, Oct. 22, 1995
      Stephen Boyd, Detroit vs. Chicago, Oct. 4, 1998
      Darryl Williams, Seattle vs. Kansas City, Oct. 4, 1998
      Rod Woodson, Oakland vs. Pittsburgh, Sept. 15, 2002
      Brian Young, St. Louis vs. Baltimore, Nov. 9, 2003
 2   By many players

YARDS RETURNING FUMBLES
Longest Fumble Run (All TDs)
104 Jack Tatum, Oakland vs. Green Bay, Sept. 24, 1972
      Aeneas Williams, Arizona vs. Washington,
      Nov. 5, 2000
102 Travis Davis, Pittsburgh vs. Carolina, Dec. 26, 1999
100 Chris Martin, Kansas City vs. Miami, Oct. 13, 1991

TOUCHDOWNS
Most Touchdowns, Career (Total)
 6   Jason Taylor, Miami, 1997-2007; Washington, 2008;
      Miami, 2009; N.Y. Jets, 2010; Miami, 2011
 5   Jessie Tuggle, Atlanta, 1987-2000
 4   Bill Thompson, Denver, 1969-1981
      Derrick Thomas, Kansas City, 1989-1999
      Keith Bulluck, Tennessee, 2000-09;
      N.Y. Giants, 2010
      Ronde Barber, Tampa Bay, 1997-2012
      DeAngelo Hall, Atlanta, 2004-07; Oakland, 2008;
      Washington, 2008-2013

Most Touchdowns, Season (Total)
 2   Harold McPhail, Boston, 1934
      Harry Ebding, Detroit, 1937
      John Morelli, Boston, 1944
      Frank Maznicki, Boston, 1947
      Fred (Dippy) Evans, Chi. Bears, 1948
      Ralph Heywood, Boston, 1948

Art Tait, N.Y. Yanks, 1951
John Dwyer, Los Angeles, 1952
Leo Sugar, Chi. Cardinals, 1957
Doug Cline, Houston, 1961
Jim Bradshaw, Pittsburgh, 1964
Royce Berry, Cincinnati, 1970
Ahmad Rashad, Buffalo, 1974
Tim Gray, Kansas City, 1977
Charles Phillips, Oakland, 1978
Kenny Johnson, Atlanta, 1981
George Martin, N.Y. Giants, 1981
Del Rodgers, Green Bay, 1982
Mike Douglass, Green Bay, 1983
Shelton Robinson, Seattle, 1983
Erik McMillan, N.Y. Jets, 1989
Les Miller, San Diego, 1990
Seth Joyner, Philadelphia, 1991
Robert Goff, New Orleans, 1992
Willie Clay, Detroit, 1993
Tyrone Hughes, New Orleans, 1994
Chad Brown, Seattle, 1997
Marcus Robertson, Tennessee, 1997
Dwayne Rudd, Minnesota, 1998
Keith McKenzie, Green Bay, 1999
Ronde Barber, Tampa Bay, 2004
Leonard Little, St. Louis, 2004
Antwan Odom, Tennessee, 2005
Adalius Thomas, Baltimore, 2005
Kevin Curtis, Philadelphia, 2007
Kerry Rhodes, Arizona, 2010
Juqua Parker, Philadelphia, 2011

Most Touchdowns, Career (Own recovered)
2 Ken Kavanaugh, Chi. Bears, 1940-41, 1945-1950
    Mike Ditka, Chicago, 1961-66; Philadelphia,
      1967-68; Dallas, 1969-1972
    Gail Cogdill, Detroit, 1960-68; Baltimore, 1968;
      Atlanta, 1969-1970
    Ahmad Rashad, St. Louis, 1972-73; Buffalo, 1974;
      Minnesota, 1976-1982
    Jim Mitchell, Atlanta, 1969-1979
    Drew Pearson, Dallas, 1973-1983
    Del Rodgers, Green Bay, 1982, 1984; San Francisco,
      1987-88
    Alan Ricard, Baltimore, 2001-05
    Kevin Curtis, St. Louis, 2003-06; Philadelphia,
      2007-09; Miami, 2010

Most Touchdowns, Season (Own recovered)
2 Ahmad Rashad, Buffalo, 1974
    Del Rodgers, Green Bay, 1982
    Kevin Curtis, Philadelphia, 2007
1 By many players

Most Touchdowns, Career (Opponents' recovered)
6 Jason Taylor, Miami, 1997-2007; Washington, 2008;
    Miami, 2009; N.Y. Jets, 2010; Miami, 2011
5 Jessie Tuggle, Atlanta, 1987-2000
4 Derrick Thomas, Kansas City, 1989-1999
    Keith Bulluck, Tennessee, 2000-09;
      N.Y. Giants, 2010
    Ronde Barber, Tampa Bay, 1997-2012
    DeAngelo Hall, Atlanta, 2004-07; Oakland, 2008;
      Washington, 2008-2013

Most Touchdowns, Season (Opponents' recovered)
2 Harold McPhail, Boston, 1934
    Harry Ebding, Detroit, 1937
    John Morelli, Boston, 1944
    Frank Maznicki, Boston, 1947
    Fred (Dippy) Evans, Chi. Bears, 1948
    Ralph Heywood, Boston, 1948
    Art Tait, N.Y. Yanks, 1951
    John Dwyer, Los Angeles, 1952

Leo Sugar, Chi. Cardinals, 1957
Doug Cline, Houston, 1961
Jim Bradshaw, Pittsburgh, 1964
Royce Berry, Cincinnati, 1970
Tim Gray, Kansas City, 1977
Charles Phillips, Oakland, 1978
Kenny Johnson, Atlanta, 1981
George Martin, N.Y. Giants, 1981
Mike Douglass, Green Bay, 1983
Shelton Robinson, Seattle, 1983
Erik McMillan, N.Y. Jets, 1989
Les Miller, San Diego, 1990
Seth Joyner, Philadelphia, 1991
Robert Goff, New Orleans, 1992
Willie Clay, Detroit, 1993
Tyrone Hughes, New Orleans, 1994
Chad Brown, Seattle, 1997
Marcus Robertson, Tennessee, 1997
Dwayne Rudd, Minnesota, 1998
Keith McKenzie, Green Bay, 1999
Ronde Barber, Tampa Bay, 2004
Leonard Little, St. Louis, 2004
Antwan Odom, Tennessee, 2005
Adalius Thomas, Baltimore, 2005
Kerry Rhodes, Arizona, 2010
Juqua Parker, Philadelphia, 2011

Most Touchdowns, Game (Opponents' recovered)
2 Fred (Dippy) Evans, Chi. Bears vs. Washington,
    Nov. 28, 1948

COMBINED NET YARDS GAINED
Rushing, receiving, interception returns, punt returns, kickoff
returns, and fumble returns

Most Seasons Leading League
5 Jim Brown, Cleveland, 1958-1961, 1964
4 Brian Mitchell, Washington, 1994-96, 1998
3 Cliff Battles, Boston, 1932-33; Washington, 1937
    Gale Sayers, Chicago, 1965-67
    Eric Dickerson, L.A. Rams, 1983-84, 1986
    Thurman Thomas, Buffalo, 1989, 1991-92

Most Consecutive Seasons Leading League
4 Jim Brown, Cleveland, 1958-1961
3 Gale Sayers, Chicago, 1965-67
    Brian Mitchell, Washington, 1994-96
2 Cliff Battles, Boston, 1932-33
    Charley Trippi, Chi. Cardinals, 1948-49
    Timmy Brown, Philadelphia, 1962-63
    Floyd Little, Denver, 1967-68
    James Brooks, San Diego, 1981-82
    Eric Dickerson, L.A. Rams, 1983-84
    Thurman Thomas, Buffalo, 1991-92
    Dante Hall, Kansas City, 2003-04

ATTEMPTS
Most Attempts, Career
4,939 Emmitt Smith. Dallas, 1990-2002; Arizona, 2003-04
4,368 Walter Payton, Chicago, 1975-1987
4,016 Curtis Martin, New England, 1995-97; N.Y. Jets,
        1998-2005

Most Attempts, Season
496 James Wilder, Tamp Bay, 1984
458 Larry Johnson, Kansas City, 2006
455 Eddie George, Tennessee, 2000

Most Attempts, Rookie, Season
442 Eric Dickerson, L.A. Rams, 1983
433 Edgerrin James, Indianapolis, 1999
401 Curtis Martin, New England, 1995

Most Attempts, Game
48 James Wilder, Tampa Bay vs. Pittsburgh, Oct. 30, 1983

    LaDainian Tomlinson, San Diego vs. Denver, Dec. 1, 2002 (ot)
47   James Wilder, Tampa Bay vs. Green Bay, Sept. 30, 1984 (ot)
    Terrell Davis, Denver vs. Buffalo, Oct. 26, 1997 (ot)
46   Gerald Riggs, Atlanta vs. L.A. Rams, Nov. 17, 1985

YARDS GAINED
Most Yards Gained, Career
23,546   Jerry Rice, San Francisco, 1985-2000; Oakland, 2001-04; Seattle, 2004
23,330   Brian Mitchell, Washington, 1990-99; Philadelphia, 2000-02; N.Y. Giants, 2003
21,803   Walter Payton, Chicago, 1975-1987
Most Yards Gained, Season
2,696   Darren Sproles, New Orleans, 2011
2,690   Derrick Mason, Tennessee, 2000
2,647   Michael Lewis, New Orleans, 2002
Most Yards Gained, Rookie, Season
2,317   Tim Brown, L.A. Raiders, 1988
2,272   Gale Sayers, Chicago, 1965
2,250   Maurice Jones-Drew, Jacksonville, 2006
Most Yards Gained, Game
  404   Glyn Milburn, Denver vs. Seattle, Dec. 10, 1995
  373   Billy Cannon, Houston vs. N.Y. Titans, Dec. 10. 1961
  361   Adrian Peterson, Minnesota vs. Chicago, Oct. 14, 2007

SACKS
Sacks have been compiled since 1982.
Most Seasons Leading League
2   Mark Gastineau, N.Y. Jets, 1983-84
    Reggie White, Philadelphia, 1987-88
    Kevin Greene, Pittsburgh, 1994; Carolina, 1996
    Michael Strahan, N.Y. Giants, 2001, 2003
    DeMarcus Ware, Dallas, 2008, 2010
    Jared Allen, Kansas City, 2007; Minnesota, 2011
Most Sacks, Career
200.0   Bruce Smith, Buffalo, 1985-1999; Washington, 2000-03
198.0   Reggie White, Philadelphia, 1985-1992; Green Bay, 1993-98; Carolina, 2000
160.0   Kevin Greene, L.A. Rams, 1985-1992; Pittsburgh, 1993-95; Carolina, 1996, 1998-99; San Francisco, 1997
Most Sacks, Season
22.5   Michael Strahan, N.Y. Giants, 2001
22.0   Mark Gastineau, N.Y. Jets, 1984
    Jared Allen, Minnesota, 2011
21.0   Reggie White, Philadelphia, 1987
    Chris Doleman, Minnesota, 1989
Most Sacks, Rookie, Season
14.5   Jevon Kearse, Tennessee, 1999
14.0   Aldon Smith, San Francisco, 2011
13.0   Dwight Freeney, Indianapolis, 2002
Most Sacks, Game
7.0   Derrick Thomas, Kansas City vs. Seattle, Nov. 11, 1990
6.0   Fred Dean, San Francisco vs. New Orleans, Nov. 13, 1983
    Derrick Thomas, Kansas City vs. Oakland, Sept. 6, 1998
    Osi Umenyiora, N.Y. Giants vs. Philadelphia, Sept. 30, 2007
5.5   William Gay, Detroit vs. Tampa Bay, Sept. 4, 1983
    Aldon Smith, San Francisco vs. Chicago, Nov. 19, 2012
Most Seasons, 10 or More Sacks
13   Bruce Smith, Buffalo, 1986-1990, 1992-98; Washington, 2000

12   Reggie White, Philadelphia, 1985-1992; Green Bay, 1993, 1995, 1997-98
10   Kevin Greene, L.A. Rams, 1988-1990, 1992; Pittsburgh, 1993-94; Carolina, 1996, 1998-99; San Francisco, 1997
Most Consecutive Seasons, 10 or More Sacks
9   Reggie White, Philadelphia, 1985-1992; Green Bay, 1993
8   John Randle, Minnesota, 1992-99
7   Lawrence Taylor, N.Y. Giants, 1984-1990
    Bruce Smith, Buffalo, 1992-98
    DeMarcus Ware, Dallas, 2006-2012
    Jared Allen, Kansas City, 2007; Minnesota, 2008-2013 (current)
Most Consecutive Games, Sack
10   Simon Fletcher, Denver, Nov. 15, 1992-Sept. 20, 1993
    DeMarcus Ware, Dallas, Dec. 16, 2007-Oct. 19, 2008
9   Bruce Smith, Buffalo, Nov. 16, 1986-Oct. 25, 1987
    Kevin Greene, San Francisco-Carolina, Dec. 7, 1997-Oct. 18, 1998
    Dwight Freeney, Indianapolis, Dec. 18, 2008-Nov. 8, 2009
8   By many players

MISCELLANEOUS
Longest Return of Missed Field Goal (All TDs)
109   Antonio Cromartie, San Diego vs. Minnesota, Nov. 4, 2007
108   Nathan Vasher, Chicago vs. San Francisco, Nov. 13, 2005
    Devin Hester, Chicago vs. N.Y. Giants, Nov. 12, 2006
107   Chris McAlister, Baltimore vs. Denver, Sept. 30, 2002

TEAM RECORDS

CHAMPIONSHIPS
Most Seasons League Champion
13   Green Bay, 1929-1931, 1936, 1939, 1944, 1961-62, 1965-67, 1996, 2010
9   Chi. Bears, 1921, 1932-33, 1940-41, 1943, 1946, 1963, 1985
8   N.Y. Giants, 1927, 1934, 1938, 1956, 1986, 1990, 2007, 2011
Most Consecutive Seasons League Champion
3   Green Bay, 1929-1931
    Green Bay, 1965-67
2   Canton, 1922-23
    Chi. Bears, 1932-33
    Chi. Bears, 1940-41
    Philadelphia, 1948-49
    Detroit, 1952-53
    Cleveland, 1954-55
    Baltimore, 1958-59
    Houston, 1960-61
    Green Bay, 1961-62
    Buffalo, 1964-65
    Miami, 1972-73
    Pittsburgh, 1974-75
    Pittsburgh, 1978-79
    San Francisco, 1988-89
    Dallas, 1992-93
    Denver, 1997-98
    New England, 2003-04
Most Times Finishing First, Regular Season
24   Green Bay, 1929-1931, 1936, 1938-39, 1944, 1960-62, 1965-67, 1972, 1995-97, 2002-04, 2007, 2011-13
23   N.Y. Giants, 1927, 1933-35, 1938-39, 1941, 1944, 1946, 1956, 1958-59, 1961-63, 1986, 1989-1990, 1997, 2000, 2005, 2008, 2011

22   Chi. Bears, 1921, 1932-34, 1937, 1940-43, 1946, 1956, 1963, 1984-88, 1990, 2001, 2005-06, 2010

Most Consecutive Times Finishing First, Regular Season
7   Los Angeles, 1973-79
6   Cleveland, 1950-55
    Dallas, 1966-1971
    Minnesota, 1973-78
    Pittsburgh, 1974-79
5   Oakland, 1972-76
    Chicago, 1984-88
    San Francisco, 1986-1990
    Dallas, 1992-96
    Indianapolis, 2003-07
    New England, 2003-07
    New England, 2009-2013 (current)

GAMES WON

Most Consecutive Games Won
23   Indianapolis, 2008-09
21   New England, 2006-08
18   New England, 2003-04

Most Consecutive Games Without Defeat
25   Canton, 1921-23 (won 22, tied 3)
24   Chi. Bears, 1941-43 (won 23, tied 1)
23   Green Bay, 1928-1930 (won 21, tied 2)
    Indianapolis, 2008-09 (won 23)

Most Games Won, Season
16   New England, 2007
15   San Francisco, 1984
    Chicago, 1985
    Minnesota, 1998
    Pittsburgh, 2004
    Green Bay, 2011
14   By many teams

Most Consecutive Games Won, Season
16   New England, 2007, entire season
14   Miami, 1972, entire season
    Pittsburgh, 2004
    Indianapolis, 2009
13   Chi. Bears, 1934, entire season
    Denver, 1998
    Indianapolis, 2005
    New Orleans, 2009
    Green Bay, 2011

Most Consecutive Games Won, Start of Season
16   New England, 2007, entire season
14   Miami, 1972, entire season
    Indianapolis, 2009
13   Chi. Bears, 1934, entire season
    Denver, 1998
    Indianapolis, 2005
    New Orleans, 2009
    Green Bay, 2011

Most Consecutive Games Won, End of Season
16   New England, 2007, entire season
14   Miami, 1972, entire season
    Pittsburgh, 2004
13   Chi. Bears, 1934, entire season

Most Consecutive Games Without Defeat, Season
16   New England, 2007 (won 16), entire season
14   Miami, 1972 (won 14), entire season
    Pittsburgh, 2004 (won 14)
    Indianapolis, 2009 (won 14)
13   Chi. Bears, 1926 (won 11, tied 2)
    Green Bay, 1929 (won 12, tied 1)
    Chi. Bears, 1934 (won 13), entire season
    Baltimore, 1967 (won 11, tied 2)
    Denver, 1998 (won 13)
    Indianapolis, 2005 (won 13)

    New Orleans, 2009 (won 13)
    Green Bay, 2011 (won 13)

Most Consecutive Games Without Defeat, Start of Season
16   New England, 2007 (won 16), entire season
14   Miami, 1972 (won 14), entire season
    Indianapolis, 2009 (won 14)
13   Chi. Bears, 1926 (won 11, tied 2)
    Green Bay, 1929 (won 12, tied 1), entire season
    Chi. Bears, 1934 (won 13), entire season
    Baltimore, 1967 (won 11, tied 2)
    Denver, 1998 (won 13)
    Indianapolis, 2005 (won 13)
    New Orleans, 2009 (won 13)
    Green Bay, 2011 (won 13)

Most Consecutive Games Without Defeat, End of Season
16   New England, 2007 (won 16), entire season
14   Miami, 1972 (won 14), entire season
    Pittsburgh, 2004 (won 14)
13   Green Bay, 1929 (won 12, tied 1), entire season
    Chi. Bears, 1934 (won 13), entire season

Most Consecutive Home Games Won
27   Miami, 1971-74
25   Green Bay, 1995-98
24   Denver, 1996-98

Most Consecutive Home Games Without Defeat
29   Green Bay, 1928-1933 (won 26, tied 3)
27   Miami, 1971-74 (won 27)
25   Green Bay, 1995-98 (won 25)

Most Consecutive Road Games Won
18   San Francisco, 1988-1990
12   New England, 2006-08
11   L.A. Chargers/San Diego, 1960-61
    San Francisco, 1987-88
    Pittsburgh, 2004-05
    Indianapolis, 2008-09

Most Consecutive Road Games Without Defeat
18   San Francisco, 1988-1990 (won 18)
13   Chi. Bears, 1941-43 (won 12, tied 1)
12   Green Bay, 1928-1930 (won 10, tied 2)
    New England, 2006-08 (won 12)

Most Shutout Games Won or Tied, Season
10   Pottsville, 1926 (won 9, tied 1)
    N.Y. Giants, 1927 (won 9, tied 1)
9   Akron, 1921 (won 8, tied 1)
    Canton, 1922 (won 7, tied 2)
    Frankford, 1926 (won 9)
    Frankford, 1929 (won 6, tied 3)
8   By many teams

Most Consecutive Shutout Games Won or Tied
13   Akron, 1920-21 (won 10, tied 3)
7   Pottsville, 1926 (won 6, tied 1)
    Detroit, 1934 (won 7)
6   Buffalo, 1920-21 (won 5, tied 1)
    Frankford, 1926 (won 6)
    Detroit, 1926 (won 4, tied 2)
    N.Y. Giants, 1926-27 (won 5, tied 1)

GAMES LOST

Most Consecutive Games Lost
26   Tampa Bay, 1976-1977
19   Chi. Cardinals, 1942-43, 1945
    Oakland, 1961-62
    Detroit, 2007-09
18   Houston, 1972-73

Most Consecutive Games Without Victory
26   Tampa Bay, 1976-77 (lost 26)
23   Rochester, 1922-25 (lost 21, tied 2)
    Washington, 1960-61 (lost 20, tied 3)
19   Dayton, 1927-29 (lost 18, tied 1)
    Chi. Cardinals, 1942-43, 1945 (lost 19)

New Orleans, 2009 (won 13)
Green Bay, 2011 (won 13)

Oakland, 1961-62 (lost 19)
Detroit, 2007-09 (lost 19)

Most Games Lost, Season
16 Detroit, 2008
15 New Orleans, 1980
Dallas, 1989
New England, 1990
Indianapolis, 1991
N.Y. Jets, 1996
San Diego, 2000
Carolina, 2001
Miami, 2007
St. Louis, 2009
14 By many teams

Most Consecutive Games Lost, Season
16 Detroit, 2008, entire season
15 Carolina, 2001
14 Tampa Bay, 1976
New Orleans, 1980
Baltimore, 1981
New England, 1990
Houston, 2013

Most Consecutive Games Lost, Start of Season
16 Detroit, 2008, entire season
14 Tampa Bay, 1976, entire season
New Orleans, 1980
13 Oakland, 1962
Indianapolis, 1986
Miami, 2007
Indianapolis, 2011

Most Consecutive Games Lost, End of Season
16 Detroit, 2008, entire season
15 Carolina, 2001
14 Tampa Bay, 1976, entire season
New England, 1990
Houston, 2013

Most Consecutive Games Without Victory, Season
16 Detroit, 2008 (lost 16), entire season
15 Carolina, 2001 (lost 15)
14 Tampa Bay, 1976 (lost 14), entire season
New Orleans, 1980 (lost 14)
Baltimore, 1981 (lost 14)
New England, 1990 (lost 14)
Houston, 2013 (lost 14)

Most Consecutive Games Without Victory, Start of Season
16 Detroit, 2008 (lost 16), entire season
14 Tampa Bay, 1976 (lost 14), entire season
New Orleans, 1980 (lost 14)
13 Washington, 1961 (lost 12, tied 1)
Oakland, 1962 (lost 13)
Indianapolis, 1986 (lost 13)
Miami, 2007 (lost 13)
Indianapolis, 2011 (lost 13)

Most Consecutive Games Without Victory, End of Season
16 Detroit, 2008 (lost 16), entire season
15 Carolina, 2001
14 Tampa Bay, 1976, (lost 14), entire season
New England, 1990 (lost 14)
Houston, 2013 (lost 14)

Most Consecutive Home Games Lost
14 Dallas, 1988-89
St. Louis, 2008-2010
13 Houston, 1972-73
Tampa Bay, 1976-77
N.Y. Jets, 1995-97
11 Oakland, 1961-62
Los Angeles, 1961-63
Cincinnati, 1998-99

Most Consecutive Home Games Without Victory
14 Dallas, 1988-89 (lost 14)

St. Louis, 2008-2010 (lost 14)
13 Houston, 1972-73 (lost 13)
Tampa Bay, 1976-77 (lost 13)
N.Y. Jets, 1995-97 (lost 13)
Philadelphia, 1936-38 (lost 12, tied 1)

Most Consecutive Road Games Lost
26 Detroit, 2007-2010
24 Detroit, 2001-03
23 Houston, 1981-84

Most Consecutive Road Games Without Victory
26 Detroit, 2007-2010 (lost 26)
24 Detroit, 2001-03 (lost 24)
23 Houston, 1981-84 (lost 23)

Most Shutout Games Lost or Tied, Season
8 Frankford, 1927 (lost 6, tied 2)
Brooklyn, 1931 (lost 8)
7 Dayton, 1925 (lost 6, tied 1)
Orange, 1929 (lost 4, tied 3)
Frankford, 1931 (lost 6, tied 1)
6 By many teams

Most Consecutive Shutout Games Lost or Tied
8 Rochester, 1922-24 (lost 8)
7 Hammond, 1922-23 (lost 6, tied 1)
6 Providence, 1926-27 (lost 5, tied 1)
Brooklyn, 1942-43 (lost 6)

TIE GAMES
Most Tie Games, Season
6 Chi. Bears, 1932
5 Frankford, 1929
4 Chi. Bears, 1924
Orange, 1929
Portsmouth, 1932

Most Consecutive Tie Games
3 Chi. Bears, 1932
2 By many teams

SCORING
Most Seasons Leading League
10 Chi. Bears, 1932, 1934-35, 1939, 1941-43,
1946-47, 1956
9 San Francisco, 1953, 1965, 1970, 1987, 1989,
1992-95
L.A./St. Louis Rams, 1950-52, 1957, 1967, 1973,
1999-2001
8 Green Bay, 1931, 1936-38, 1961-62, 1996, 2011

Most Consecutive Seasons Leading League
4 San Francisco, 1992-1995
3 Green Bay, 1936-38
Chi. Bears, 1941-43
Los Angeles, 1950-52
Oakland, 1967-69
St. Louis, 1999-2001
2 By many teams

POINTS
Most Points, Season
606 Denver, 2013
589 New England, 2007
560 Green Bay, 2011

Fewest Points, Season (Since 1932)
37 Cincinnati/St. Louis, 1934
38 Cincinnati, 1933
Detroit, 1942
51 Pittsburgh, 1934
Philadelphia, 1936

Most Points, Game
72 Washington vs. N.Y. Giants, Nov. 27, 1966
70 Los Angeles vs. Baltimore, Oct. 22, 1950
66 Rochester vs. *Fort Porter, Oct. 10, 1920

**Not a member of the American Professional
   Football Association*
  65 Chi. Cardinals vs. N.Y. Bulldogs, Nov. 13, 1949
      Los Angeles vs. Detroit, Oct. 29, 1950

Most Points, Both Teams, Game
 113 Washington (72) vs. N.Y. Giants (41), Nov. 27, 1966
 106 Cincinnati (58) vs. Cleveland (48), Nov. 28, 2004
 101 Oakland (52) vs. Houston (49), Dec. 22, 1963

Fewest Points, Both Teams, Game
   0 In many games. Last time: N.Y. Giants vs. Detroit,
      Nov. 7, 1943

Most Points, Shutout Victory Game
  66 Rochester vs. *Fort Porter, Oct. 10, 1920
      *Not a member of the American Professional
      Football Association
  64 Philadelphia vs. Cincinnati, Nov. 6, 1934
  62 Akron vs. Oorang, Oct. 29, 1922

Most Consecutive Games Scoring
 420 San Francisco, 1977-2004
 341 Denver, 1992-2013 (current)
 321 Indianapolis, 1994-2013 (current)

Fewest Points, Shutout Victory, Game
   2 Akron vs. Buffalo, Nov. 29, 1923
      Kansas City vs. Buffalo, Nov. 21, 1926
      Frankford vs. Green Bay, Nov. 29, 1928
      Green Bay vs. Chi. Bears, Oct. 16, 1932
      Chi. Bears vs. Green Bay, Sept. 18, 1938

Most Points Overcome to Win Game
  28 San Francisco vs. New Orleans, Dec. 7, 1980 (ot)
      (trailed 7-35, won 38-35)
  26 Buffalo vs. Indianapolis, Sept., 21, 1997
      (trailed 0-26, won 37-35)
  25 St. Louis vs. Tampa Bay, Nov. 8, 1987
      (trailed 3-28, won 31-28)

Most Points Overcome to Tie Game
  31 Denver vs. Buffalo, Nov. 27, 1960
      (trailed 7-38, tied 38-38)
  28 Los Angeles vs. Philadelphia, Oct. 3, 1948
      (trailed 0-28, tied 28-28)

Most Points, Each Half
1st: 49 Green Bay vs. Tampa Bay, Oct. 2, 1983
     48 Buffalo vs. Miami, Sept. 18, 1966
     45 Green Bay vs. Cleveland, Nov. 12, 1967
         Indianapolis vs. Denver, Oct. 31, 1988
         Houston vs. Cleveland, Dec. 9, 1990
         Seattle vs. Minnesota, Sept. 29, 2002
         New England vs. Tennessee, Oct. 18, 2009
         Philadelphia vs. Washington, Nov. 15, 2010
2nd: 49 Chi. Bears vs. Philadelphia, Nov. 30, 1941
     48 Chi. Cardinals vs. Baltimore, Oct. 2, 1950
         N.Y. Giants vs. Baltimore, Nov. 19, 1950
     45 Cincinnati vs. Houston, Dec. 17, 1972
         New England vs. Buffalo, Sept. 30, 2012

Most Points, Both Teams, Each Half
1st: 70 Houston (35) vs. Oakland (35), Dec. 22, 1963
     63 Philadelphia (42) vs. Detroit (21), Sept. 23, 2007
     62 N.Y. Jets (41) vs. Tampa Bay (21), Nov. 17, 1985
         Indianapolis (35) vs. Cincinnati (27), Nov. 20, 2005
2nd: 66 Cleveland (35) vs. Cincinnati (31), Nov. 28, 2004
     65 Washington (38) vs. N.Y. Giants (27), Nov. 27, 1966
     62 L.A. Raiders (31) vs. San Diego (31), Jan. 2, 1983
         Baltimore (38) vs. Seattle (24), Nov. 23, 2003

Most Points, One Quarter
  41 Green Bay vs. Detroit, Oct. 7, 1945 (second quarter)
      Los Angeles vs. Detroit, Oct. 29, 1950
      (third quarter)
  37 Los Angeles vs. Green Bay, Sept. 21, 1980
      (second quarter)
  35 Chi. Cardinals vs. Boston, Oct. 24, 1948
      (third quarter)

      Green Bay vs. Cleveland, Nov. 12, 1967 (first quarter)
      Green Bay vs. Tampa Bay, Oct. 2, 1983
      (second quarter)
      New England vs. Tennessee, Oct. 18, 2009
      (second quarter)
      New England vs. N.Y. Jets, Nov. 22, 2012
      (second quarter)

Most Points, Both Teams, One Quarter
  49 Oakland (28) vs. Houston (21), Dec. 22, 1963
      (second quarter)
  48 Green Bay (41) vs. Detroit (7), Oct. 7, 1945
      (second quarter)
      Los Angeles (41) vs. Detroit (7), Oct. 29, 1950
      (third quarter)
      Detroit (34) vs. Chicago (14), Sept. 30, 2007
      (fourth quarter)
  47 St. Louis (27) vs. Philadelphia (20), Dec. 13, 1964
      (second quarter)

Most Points, Each Quarter
1st: 35 Green Bay vs. Cleveland, Nov. 12, 1967
     31 Buffalo vs. Kansas City, Sept. 13, 1964
     28 By 11 teams
2nd: 41 Green Bay vs. Detroit, Oct. 7, 1945
     37 Los Angeles vs. Green Bay, Sept. 21, 1980
     35 Green Bay vs. Tampa Bay, Oct. 2, 1983
         New England vs. Tennessee, Oct. 18, 2009
         New England vs. N.Y. Jets, Nov. 22, 2012
3rd: 41 Los Angeles vs. Detroit, Oct. 29, 1950
     35 Chi. Cardinals vs. Boston, Oct. 24, 1948
     28 By 10 teams
4th: 34 Detroit vs. Chicago, Sept. 30, 2007
     31 Oakland vs. Denver, Dec. 17, 1960
         Oakland vs. San Diego, Dec. 8, 1963
         Atlanta vs. Green Bay, Sept. 13, 1981
         New England vs. Buffalo, Sept. 30, 2012
         Denver vs. Washington, Oct. 27, 2013
     30 N.Y. Jets vs. Miami, Oct. 23, 2000

Most Points, Both Teams, Each Quarter
1st: 42 Green Bay (35) vs. Cleveland (7), Nov. 12, 1967
     41 Tennessee (24) vs. Indianapolis (17), Dec. 5, 2004
     35 Dall. Texans (21) vs. N.Y. Titans (14), Nov. 11, 1962
         Dallas (28) vs. Philadelphia (7), Oct. 19, 1969
         Kansas City (21) vs. Seattle (14), Dec. 11, 1977
         Detroit (21) vs. L.A. Raiders (14), Dec. 10, 1990
         Dallas (21) vs. Atlanta (14), Dec. 22, 1991
         Indianapolis (21) vs. Green Bay (14), Sept 26, 2004
         Miami (21) vs. Buffalo (14), Dec. 5, 2004
         Philadelphia (21) vs. New Orleans (14), Dec. 23, 2007
2nd: 49 Oakland (28) vs. Houston (21), Dec. 22, 1963
     48 Green Bay (41) vs. Detroit (7), Oct. 7, 1945
     47 St. Louis (27) vs. Philadelphia (20), Dec. 13, 1964
3rd: 48 Los Angeles (41) vs. Detroit (7), Oct. 29, 1950
     42 Washington (28) vs. Philadelphia (14), Oct. 1, 1955
     41 Green Bay (21) vs. N.Y. Yanks (20), Oct. 8, 1950
4th: 48 Detroit (34) vs. Chicago (14), Sept. 30, 2007
     46 Detroit (25) vs. Tennessee (21), Sept. 23, 2012
     43 Atlanta (28) vs. Carolina (15), Nov. 23, 2008

TOUCHDOWNS

Most Seasons Leading League, Touchdowns
  13 Chi. Bears, 1932, 1934-35, 1939, 1941-44,
      1946-48, 1956, 1965
   7 Dallas, 1966, 1968, 1971, 1973, 1977-78, 1980
      San Francisco, 1953, 1970, 1987, 1992-95
      L.A./St. Louis Rams, 1949-1952, 1999-2001
      San Diego, 1963, 1965, 1979, 1981-82, 1985,
      2006
      Green Bay, 1932, 1937-38, 1961-62, 1996, 2011
   6 Oakland, 1967-69, 1972, 1974, 1977

Baltimore/Indianapolis Colts, 1957-59, 1964, 1976, 2004

Most Consecutive Seasons Leading League, Touchdowns
- 4 Chi. Bears, 1941-44
  - Los Angeles, 1949-1952
  - San Francisco, 1992-95
- 3 Chi. Bears, 1946-48
  - Baltimore, 1957-59
  - Oakland, 1967-69
  - St. Louis, 1999-2001
- 2 By many teams

Most Touchdowns, Season
- 76 Denver, 2013
- 75 New England, 2007
- 70 Miami, 1984
  - Green Bay, 2011

Fewest Touchdowns, Season (Since 1932)
- 3 Cincinnati, 1933
- 4 Cincinnati/St. Louis, 1934
- 5 Detroit, 1942

Most Touchdowns, Game
- 10 Rochester vs. *Fort Porter, Oct. 10, 1920
  - *Not a member of the American Professional Football Association
  - Philadelphia vs. Cincinnati, Nov. 6, 1934
  - Los Angeles vs. Baltimore, Oct. 22, 1950
  - Washington vs. N.Y. Giants, Nov. 27, 1966
- 9 Rock Island vs. Evansville, Oct. 15, 1922
  - Akron vs. Oorang, Oct. 29, 1922
  - Racine vs. Louisville, Nov. 5, 1922
  - Chi. Cardinals vs. Rochester, Oct. 7, 1923
  - Chi. Cardinals vs. Milwaukee, Dec. 10, 1925
  - Chi. Cardinals vs. N.Y. Giants, Oct. 17, 1948
  - Chi. Cardinals vs. N.Y. Bulldogs, Nov. 13, 1949
  - Los Angeles vs. Detroit, Oct. 29, 1950
  - Pittsburgh vs. N.Y. Giants, Nov. 30, 1952
  - Chicago vs. San Francisco, Dec. 12, 1965
  - Chicago vs. Green Bay, Dec. 7, 1980
- 8 By many teams

Most Touchdowns, Both Teams, Game
- 16 Washington (10) vs. N.Y. Giants (6), Nov. 27, 1966
- 14 Chi. Cardinals (9) vs. N.Y. Giants (5), Oct. 17, 1948
  - Los Angeles (10) vs. Baltimore (4), Oct. 22, 1950
  - Houston (7) vs. Oakland (7), Dec. 22, 1963
- 13 New Orleans (7) vs. St. Louis (6), Nov. 2, 1969
  - Kansas City (7) vs. Seattle (6), Nov. 27, 1983 (ot)
  - San Diego (8) vs. Pittsburgh (5), Dec. 8, 1985
  - N.Y. Jets (7) vs. Miami (6), Sept. 21, 1986 (ot)
  - Cincinnati (7) vs. Cleveland (6), Nov. 28, 2004

Most Consecutive Games Scoring Touchdowns
- 166 Cleveland, 1957-1969
- 151 San Diego, 2002-2012
- 136 Indianapolis, 2003-2011

POINTS AFTER TOUCHDOWN
Most (One-Point) Points After Touchdown, Season
- 75 Denver, 2013
- 74 New England, 2007
- 68 Green Bay, 2011

Fewest (One-Point) Points After Touchdown, Season
- 2 Chi. Cardinals, 1933
- 3 Cincinnati, 1933
  - Pittsburgh, 1934
- 4 Cincinnati/St. Louis, 1934

Most (One-Point) Points After Touchdown, Game
- 10 Los Angeles vs. Baltimore, Oct. 22, 1950
- 9 Chi. Cardinals vs. N.Y. Giants, Oct. 17, 1948
  - Pittsburgh vs. N.Y. Giants, Nov. 30, 1952
  - Washington vs. N.Y. Giants, Nov. 27, 1966
- 8 By many teams

Most (One-Point) Points After Touchdown, Both Teams, Game
- 14 Chi. Cardinals (9) vs. N.Y. Giants (5), Oct. 17, 1948
  - Houston (7) vs. Oakland (7), Dec. 22, 1963
  - Washington (9) vs. N.Y. Giants (5), Nov. 27, 1966
- 13 Los Angeles (10) vs. Baltimore (3), Oct. 22, 1950
  - Cincinnati (7) vs. Cleveland (6), Nov. 28, 2004
- 12 In many games

Most Two-Point Conversions, Season
- 6 Miami, 1994
  - Minnesota, 1997
- 5 Arizona, 1995
  - Baltimore, 1996
  - Jacksonville, 1996
  - Chicago, 1997
  - San Francisco, 1998
  - Pittsburgh, 2002
  - St. Louis, 2012
  - Chicago, 2013
- 4 By many teams

Most Two-Point Conversions, Game
- 4 St. Louis vs. Atlanta, Oct. 15, 2000
- 3 Baltimore vs. New England, Oct. 6, 1996
  - Pittsburgh vs. Tennessee, Nov. 1, 1998
- 2 By many teams

Most Two-Point Conversions, Both Teams, Game
- 5 Baltimore (3) vs. New England (2), Oct. 6, 1996
  - St. Louis (4) vs. Atlanta (1), Oct. 15, 2000
- 3 Seattle (2) vs. Kansas City (1), Oct. 23, 1994
  - Minnesota (2) vs. Seattle (1), Nov. 10, 1996
  - Pittsburgh (3) vs. Tennessee (0), Nov. 1, 1998
  - Philadelphia (2) vs. Detroit (1), Dec. 8, 2013
- 2 In many games

FIELD GOALS
Most Seasons Leading League, Field Goals
- 11 Green Bay, 1935-36, 1940-43, 1946-47, 1955, 1972, 1974
- 9 L.A./St. Louis Rams, 1949, 1951, 1958, 1966, 1973, 1978, 2003, 2006, 2010
- 8 Washington, 1945, 1956, 1971, 1976-77, 1979, 1982, 1992
  - N.Y. Giants, 1933, 1937, 1939, 1941, 1944, 1959, 1983, 2008

Most Consecutive Seasons Leading League, Field Goals
- 4 Green Bay, 1940-43
- 3 Cleveland, 1952-54
- 2 By many teams

Most Field Goals Attempted, Season
- 52 San Francisco, 2011
- 49 Los Angeles, 1966
  - Washington, 1971
- 48 Green Bay, 1972

Fewest Field Goals Attempted, Season (Since 1938)
- 0 Chi. Bears, 1944
- 2 Cleveland, 1939
  - Card-Pitt, 1944
  - Boston, 1946
  - Chi. Bears, 1947
- 3 Chi. Bears, 1945
  - Cleveland, 1945

Most Field Goals Attempted, Game
- 9 St. Louis vs. Pittsburgh, Sept. 24, 1967
- 8 Pittsburgh vs. St. Louis, Dec. 2, 1962
  - Detroit vs. Minnesota, Nov. 13, 1966
  - N.Y. Jets vs. Buffalo, Nov. 3, 1968
  - Dallas vs. N.Y. Giants, Sept. 15, 2003 (ot)
  - Tennessee vs. Houston, Oct. 21, 2007
- 7 By many teams

Most Field Goals Attempted, Both Teams, Game
- 11 St. Louis (6) vs. Pittsburgh (5), Nov. 13, 1966

Washington (6) vs. Chicago (5), Nov. 14, 1971
Green Bay (6) vs. Detroit (5), Sept. 29, 1974
Washington (6) vs. N.Y. Giants (5), Nov. 14, 1976
10 In many games

Most Field Goals, Season
44 San Francisco, 2011
43 Arizona, 2005
39 Miami, 1999
    St. Louis, 2003

Fewest Field Goals, Season (Since 1932)
0 Boston, 1932, 1935
   Chi. Cardinals, 1932, 1945
   Green Bay, 1932, 1944
   N.Y. Giants, 1932
   Brooklyn, 1944
   Card-Pitt, 1944
   Chi. Bears, 1944, 1947
   Boston, 1946
   Baltimore, 1950
   Dallas, 1952

Most Field Goals, Game
8 Tennessee vs. Houston, Oct. 21, 2007
7 St. Louis vs. Pittsburgh, Sept. 24, 1967
   Minnesota vs. L.A. Rams, Nov. 5, 1989 (ot)
   Dallas vs. Green Bay, Nov. 18, 1996
   Dallas vs. N.Y. Giants, Sept. 15, 2003 (ot)
   Cincinnati vs. Baltimore, Nov. 11, 2007
6 By many teams

Most Field Goals, Both Teams, Game
9 San Diego (5) vs. Kansas City (4), Sept. 29, 1996
   Miami (6) vs. New England (3), Oct. 17, 1999
   Houston (5) vs. Miami (4), Oct. 7, 2007
   Dallas (6) vs. Washington (3), Sept. 26, 2011
8 Cleveland (4) vs. St. Louis (4), Sept. 20, 1964
   Chicago (5) vs. Philadelphia (3), Oct. 20, 1968
   Washington (5) vs. Chicago (3), Nov. 14, 1971
   Kansas City (5) vs. Buffalo (3), Dec. 19, 1971
   Detroit (4) vs. Green Bay (4), Sept. 29, 1974
   Cleveland (5) vs. Denver (3), Oct. 19, 1975
   New England (4) vs. San Diego (4), Nov. 9, 1975
   San Francisco (6) vs. New Orleans (2), Oct. 16, 1983
   Seattle (5) vs. L.A. Raiders (3), Dec. 18, 1988
   Atlanta (6) vs. New Orleans (2), Nov. 13, 1994
   Indianapolis (4) vs. San Diego (4), Nov. 3, 1996
   Dallas (7) vs. N.Y. Giants (1), Sept. 15, 2003 (ot)
   Oakland (5) vs. Chicago (3), Oct. 5, 2003
   Buffalo (5) vs. Tennessee (3), Dec. 24, 2006
   Tennessee (8) vs. Houston (0), Oct. 21, 2007
   Buffalo (5) vs. Washington (3), Dec. 2, 2007
   Kansas City (4) vs. Denver (4), Sept. 28, 2008
   San Francisco (4) vs. Philadelphia (4), Oct. 12, 2008
   Pittsburgh (4) vs. Cincinnati (4), Nov. 15, 2009
   Miami (5) vs. Pittsburgh (3), Oct. 24, 2010
   Oakland (6) vs. Chicago (2), Nov. 27, 2011
7 In many games

Most Consecutive Games Scoring Field Goals
38 Baltimore, 1999-2001
36 San Francisco, 2010-13
34 New England, 2010-12

SAFETIES
Most Safeties, Season
4 Cleveland, 1927
   Detroit, 1962
   Seattle, 1993
   San Francisco, 1996
   Tennessee, 1999
3 By many teams

Most Safeties, Game
3 L.A. Rams vs. N.Y. Giants, Sept. 30, 1984

2 N.Y. Giants vs. Pottsville, Oct. 30, 1927
   Chi. Bears vs. Pottsville, Nov. 13, 1927
   Detroit vs. Brooklyn, Dec. 1, 1935
   N.Y. Giants vs. Pittsburgh, Sept. 17, 1950
   N.Y. Giants vs. Washington, Nov. 5, 1961
   Chicago vs. Pittsburgh, Nov. 9, 1969
   Dallas vs. Philadelphia, Nov. 19, 1972
   Los Angeles vs. Green Bay, Oct. 21, 1973
   Oakland vs. San Diego, Oct. 26, 1975
   Denver vs. Seattle, Jan. 2, 1983
   New Orleans vs. Cleveland, Sept. 13, 1987
   Buffalo vs. Denver, Nov. 8, 1987
   San Francisco vs. St. Louis, Sept. 8, 1996
   Jacksonville vs. Pittsburgh, Oct. 3, 1999
   Minnesota vs. Atlanta, Oct. 5, 2003
   Dallas vs. Arizona, Oct. 5, 2003
   Buffalo vs. Houston, Nov. 16, 2003
   Minnesota vs. Green Bay, Nov. 9, 2008
   St. Louis vs. Arizona, Nov. 6, 2011 (ot)

Most Safeties, Both Teams, Game
3 L.A. Rams (3) vs. N.Y. Giants (0), Sept. 30, 1984
2 Chi. Cardinals (1) vs. Frankford (1), Nov. 19, 1927
   Chi. Cardinals (1) vs. Cincinnati (1), Nov. 12, 1933
   Chi. Bears (1) vs. San Francisco (1), Oct. 19, 1952
   Cincinnati (1) vs. Los Angeles (1), Oct. 22, 1972
   Chi. Bears (1) vs. San Francisco (1), Sept. 19, 1976
   Baltimore (1) vs. Miami (1), Oct. 29, 1978
   Atlanta (1) vs. Detroit (1), Oct. 5, 1980
   Houston (1) vs. Philadelphia (1), Oct. 2, 1988
   Cleveland (1) vs. Seattle (1), Nov. 14, 1993
   Arizona (1) vs. Houston (1), Dec. 4, 1994
   (Also see previous record)

FIRST DOWNS
Most Seasons Leading League
9 Chi. Bears, 1935, 1939, 1941, 1943, 1945,
      1947-49, 1955
7 San Diego, 1965, 1969, 1980-83, 1985
   L.A./St. Louis Rams, 1946, 1950-51, 1954, 1957,
      1973, 2001
   Baltimore/Indianapolis Colts, 1958-59, 1967, 2003,
      2005-06, 2010
6 San Francisco, 1965, 1987, 1989, 1993-94, 1998

Most Consecutive Seasons Leading League
4 San Diego, 1980-83
3 Chi. Bears, 1947-49
   New England, 2007-09
2 By many teams

Most First Downs, Season
444 New England, 2012
435 Denver, 2013
416 New Orleans, 2011

Fewest First Downs, Season
51 Cincinnati, 1933
64 Pittsburgh, 1935
67 Philadelphia, 1937

Most First Downs, Game
40 New Orleans vs. Dallas, Nov. 10, 2013
39 N.Y. Jets vs. Miami, Nov. 27, 1988
    Washington vs. Detroit, Nov. 4, 1990 (ot)
    Houston vs. Jacksonville, Nov. 18, 2012 (ot)
    Denver vs. Tennessee, Dec. 8, 2013
38 Los Angeles vs. N.Y. Giants, Nov. 13, 1966

Fewest First Downs, Game
0 N.Y. Giants vs. Green Bay, Oct. 1, 1933
   Pittsburgh vs. Boston, Oct. 29, 1933
   Philadelphia vs. Detroit, Sept. 20, 1935
   N.Y. Giants vs. Washington, Sept. 27, 1942
   Denver vs. Houston, Sept. 3, 1966

Most First Downs, Both Teams, Game
- 64 Seattle (32) vs. Kansas City (32), Nov. 24, 2002
- 62 San Diego (32) vs. Seattle (30), Sept. 15, 1985
  - Oakland (31) vs. Kansas City (31), Nov. 5, 2000
  - Buffalo (35) vs. New England (27), Nov. 11, 2012
- 61 New England (33) vs. Baltimore (28), Sept. 23, 2012

Fewest First Downs, Both Teams, Game
- 7 Chi. Cardinals (2) vs. Detroit (5), Sept. 15, 1940
- 9 Pittsburgh (1) vs. Boston (8), Oct. 27, 1935
  - Boston (4) vs. Brooklyn (5), Nov. 24, 1935
  - N.Y. Giants (3) vs. Detroit (6), Nov. 7, 1943
  - Pittsburgh (4) vs. Chi. Cardinals (5), Nov. 11, 1945
  - N.Y. Bulldogs (1) vs. Philadelphia (8), Sept. 22, 1949
- 10 Philadelphia (4) vs. Brooklyn (6), Nov. 5, 1944
  - N.Y. Giants (4) vs. Washington (6), Dec. 11, 1960

Most First Downs, Rushing, Season
- 181 New England, 1978
- 177 Los Angeles, 1973
- 176 Chicago, 1985

Fewest First Downs, Rushing, Season
- 36 Cleveland, 1942
  - Boston, 1944
- 39 Brooklyn, 1943
- 40 Philadelphia, 1940
  - Detroit, 1945

Most First Downs, Rushing, Game
- 25 Philadelphia vs. Washington, Dec. 2, 1951
- 23 St. Louis vs. New Orleans, Oct. 5, 1980
- 21 Cleveland vs. Philadelphia, Dec. 13, 1959
  - Green Bay vs. Philadelphia, Nov. 11, 1962
  - Los Angeles vs. New Orleans, Nov. 25, 1973
  - Pittsburgh vs. Kansas City, Nov. 7, 1976
  - New England vs. Denver, Nov. 28, 1976
  - Oakland vs. Green Bay, Sept. 17, 1978
  - Buffalo vs. Washington, Nov. 3, 1996
  - San Francisco vs. Detroit, Dec. 14, 1998
  - Kansas City vs. Atlanta, Oct. 24, 2004

Fewest First Downs, Rushing, Game
- 0 By many teams. Last time:
  - Green Bay vs. Detroit, Nov. 28, 2013

Most First Downs, Rushing, Both Teams, Game
- 36 Philadelphia (25) vs. Washington (11), Dec. 2, 1951
- 31 Detroit (18) vs. Washington (13), Sept. 30, 1951
- 30 Los Angeles (17) vs. Minnesota (13), Nov. 5, 1961
  - New Orleans (17) vs. Green Bay (13), Sept. 9, 1979
  - New Orleans (16) vs. San Francisco (14), Nov. 11, 1979
  - New England (16) vs. Kansas City (14), Oct. 4, 1981
  - Indianapolis (18) vs. Denver (12), Sept. 30, 2007

Fewest First Downs, Rushing, Both Teams, Game
- 1 Oakland (0) vs. Tennessee (1), Sept. 7, 2003
  - Carolina (0) vs. Detroit (1), Oct. 16, 2005
- 2 Houston (0) vs. Denver (2), Dec. 2, 1962
  - N.Y. Jets, (1) vs. St. Louis (1), Dec. 3, 1995
  - Miami (1) vs. San Diego (1), Dec. 19, 1999
  - New Orleans (0) vs. Baltimore (2), Dec. 19, 1999
  - Baltimore (0) vs. Tennessee (2), Sept. 18, 2005
  - Pittsburgh (1) vs. Baltimore (1), Nov. 5, 2007
  - Arizona (1) vs. San Francisco (1), Sept. 13, 2009
- 3 In many games

Most First Downs, Passing, Season
- 293 Denver, 2013
- 280 New Orleans, 2011
- 272 Detroit, 2012

Fewest First Downs, Passing, Season
- 18 Pittsburgh, 1941
- 23 Brooklyn, 1942
  - N.Y. Giants, 1944
- 24 N.Y. Giants, 1943

Most First Downs, Passing, Game
- 29 N.Y. Giants vs. Cincinnati, Oct. 13, 1985

- 28 Tennessee vs. Oakland, Dec. 19, 2004
- 27 San Diego vs. Seattle, Sept. 15, 1985
  - Detroit vs. Green Bay, Jan. 1, 2012

Fewest First Downs, Passing, Game
- 0 By many teams. Last time:
  - Pittsburgh vs. Tennessee, Sept. 19, 2010

Most First Downs, Passing, Both Teams, Game
- 47 Detroit (27) vs. Green Bay (20), Jan. 1, 2012
- 44 New Orleans (23) vs. Green Bay (21),
  - Sept. 30, 2012
- 43 San Diego (23) vs. Cincinnati (20), Dec. 20, 1982
  - Miami (24) vs. N.Y. Jets (19), Sept. 21, 1986 (ot)
  - Tennessee (28) vs. Oakland (15), Dec. 19, 2004
  - New England (23) vs. San Diego (20),
  - Sept. 18, 2011

Fewest First Downs, Passing, Both Teams, Game
- 0 Brooklyn vs. Pittsburgh, Nov. 29, 1942
- 1 Green Bay (0) vs. Cleveland (1), Sept. 21, 1941
  - Pittsburgh (0) vs. Brooklyn (1), Oct. 11, 1942
  - N.Y. Giants (0) vs. Detroit (1), Nov. 7, 1943
  - Pittsburgh (0) vs. Chi. Cardinals (1), Nov. 11, 1945
  - N.Y. Bulldogs (0) vs. Philadelphia (1), Sept. 22, 1949
  - Chicago (0) vs. Buffalo (1), Oct. 7, 1979
- 2 In many games

Most First Downs, Penalty, Season
- 47 Buffalo, 2002
  - Indianapolis, 2004
- 44 Dallas, 2005
- 43 Denver, 1994
  - Green Bay, 2012
  - New England, 2013

Fewest First Downs, Penalty, Season
- 2 Brooklyn, 1940
- 4 Chi. Cardinals, 1940
  - N.Y. Giants, 1942, 1944
  - Washington, 1944
  - Cleveland, 1952
  - Kansas City, 1969
- 5 Brooklyn, 1939
  - Chi. Bears, 1939
  - Detroit, 1953
  - Los Angeles, 1953
  - Houston, 1982

Most First Downs, Penalty, Game
- 11 Denver vs. Houston, Oct. 6, 1985
- 10 Dallas vs. Cleveland, Nov. 18, 2012 (ot)
  - N.Y. Giants vs. Denver, Sept. 15, 2013
- 9 Chi. Bears vs. Cleveland, Nov. 25, 1951
  - Baltimore vs. Pittsburgh, Oct. 30, 1977
  - N.Y. Jets vs. Houston, Sept. 18, 1988
  - Dallas vs. Detroit, Nov. 20, 2005

Most First Downs, Penalty, Both Teams, Game
- 13 New England (8) vs. Baltimore (5), Sept. 23, 2012
- 12 Buffalo (7) vs. San Francisco (5), Oct. 4, 1998
  - Detroit (8) vs. Baltimore (4), Oct. 9, 2005
  - Dallas (10) vs. Cleveland (2), Nov. 18, 2012 (ot)
- 11 Chi. Bears (9) vs. Cleveland (2), Nov. 25, 1951
  - Cincinnati (8) vs. N.Y. Jets (3), Oct. 6, 1985
  - Denver (11) vs. Houston (0), Oct. 6, 1985
  - Detroit (6) vs. Dallas (5), Nov. 8, 1987
  - N.Y. Jets (9) vs. Houston (2), Sept. 18, 1988
  - Kansas City (8) vs. L.A. Raiders (3), Oct. 3, 1993
  - Detroit (6) vs. San Diego (5), Nov. 11, 1996
  - Philadelphia (8) vs. Chicago (3), Nov. 3, 2002
  - Arizona (6) vs. St. Louis (5), Dec. 3, 2006
  - Indianapolis (6) vs. Green Bay (5), Oct. 19, 2008
  - Buffalo (8) vs. N.Y. Jets (3), Sept. 22, 2013

NET YARDS GAINED RUSHING AND PASSING

Most Seasons Leading League
- 12 Chi. Bears, 1932, 1934-35, 1939, 1941-44, 1947, 1949, 1955-56
- 9 L.A./St. Louis Rams, 1946, 1950-51, 1954, 1957, 1973, 1999-2001
- 8 San Diego, 1963, 1965, 1980-83, 1985, 2010

Most Consecutive Seasons Leading League
- 4 Chi. Bears, 1941-44
  San Diego, 1980-83
- 3 Baltimore, 1958-1960
  Houston, 1960-62
  Oakland, 1968-1970
  St. Louis, 1999-2001
- 2 By many teams

Most Yards Gained, Season
- 7,474 New Orleans, 2011
- 7,317 Denver, 2013
- 7,075 St. Louis, 2000

Fewest Yards Gained, Season
- 1,150 Cincinnati, 1933
- 1,443 Chi. Cardinals, 1934
- 1,486 Chi. Cardinals, 1933

Most Yards Gained, Game
- 735 Los Angeles vs. N.Y. Yanks, Sept. 28, 1951
- 683 Pittsburgh vs. Chi. Cardinals, Dec. 13, 1958
- 682 Chi. Bears vs. N.Y. Giants, Nov. 14, 1943

Fewest Yards Gained, Game
- −7 Seattle vs. Los Angeles, Nov. 4, 1979
- −5 Denver vs. Oakland, Sept. 10, 1967
- 14 Chi. Cardinals vs. Detroit, Sept. 15, 1940

Most Yards Gained, Both Teams, Game
- 1,133 Los Angeles (636) vs. N.Y. Yanks (497), Nov. 19, 1950
- 1,125 Detroit (575) vs. Green Bay (550), Jan. 1, 2012
- 1,111 Houston (653) vs. Jacksonville (458), Nov. 18, 2012 (ot)

Fewest Yards Gained, Both Teams, Game
- 30 Chi. Cardinals (14) vs. Detroit (16), Sept. 15, 1940
- 136 Chi. Cardinals (50) vs. Green Bay (86), Nov. 18, 1934
- 154 N.Y. Giants (51) vs. Washington (103), Dec. 11, 1960

Most Consecutive Games, 400 or More Yards Gained
- 11 San Diego, 1982-83
- 10 Denver, 2012-13
- 9 New England, 2006-07

Most Consecutive Games, 300 or More Yards Gained
- 36 Minnesota, 2002-04
- 30 Minnesota, 1999-2000
  St. Louis, 2000-02
- 29 Los Angeles, 1949-1951
  New Orleans, 2008-09
  Denver, 2012-13

RUSHING

Most Seasons Leading League
- 16 Chi. Bears, 1932, 1934-35, 1939-1942, 1951, 1955-56, 1968, 1977, 1983-86
- 7 Buffalo, 1962, 1964, 1973, 1975, 1982, 1991-92
- 6 Cleveland, 1958-59, 1963, 1965-67
  San Francisco, 1952-54, 1987, 1998-99
  Dall. Texans/K.C. Chiefs, 1961, 1966, 1968-69, 1995, 2010

Most Consecutive Seasons Leading League
- 4 Chi. Bears, 1939-1942
  Chi. Bears, 1983-86
- 3 Detroit, 1936-38
  San Francisco, 1952-54
  Cleveland, 1965-67
  Atlanta, 2004-06

2 By many teams

ATTEMPTS

Most Rushing Attempts, Season
- 681 Oakland, 1977
- 674 Chicago, 1984
- 671 New England, 1978

Fewest Rushing Attempts, Season
- 211 Philadelphia, 1982
- 219 San Francisco, 1982
- 225 Houston, 1982

Most Rushing Attempts, Game
- 72 Chi. Bears vs. Brooklyn, Oct. 20, 1935
- 70 Chi. Cardinals vs. Green Bay, Dec. 5, 1948
- 69 Chi. Cardinals vs. Green Bay, Dec. 6, 1936
  Kansas City vs. Cincinnati, Sept. 3, 1978

Fewest Rushing Attempts, Game
- 6 Chi. Cardinals vs. Boston, Oct. 22, 1933
  New England vs. Pittsburgh, Oct. 31, 2004
  Arizona vs. Minnesota, Nov. 26, 2006
- 7 Oakland vs. Buffalo, Oct. 5, 1963
  Houston vs. N.Y. Giants, Dec. 8, 1985
  Seattle vs. L.A. Raiders, Nov. 17, 1991
  Green Bay vs. Miami, Sept. 11, 1994
  Detroit vs. Minnesota, Dec. 2, 2007
  Arizona vs. Minnesota, Dec. 14, 2008
- 8 Denver vs. Oakland, Dec. 17, 1960
  Buffalo vs. St. Louis, Sept. 9, 1984
  Detroit vs. San Francisco, Oct. 20, 1991
  Atlanta vs. Detroit, Sept. 5, 1993
  St. Louis vs. San Francisco, Nov. 2, 2003
  N.Y. Jets vs. Denver, Nov. 20, 2005
  St. Louis vs. Carolina, Nov. 19, 2006
  Detroit vs. Arizona, Nov. 11, 2007
  San Diego vs. Pittsburgh, Oct. 4, 2009
  San Diego vs. Oakland, Dec. 5, 2010

Most Rushing Attempts, Both Teams, Game
- 108 Chi. Bears (70) vs. Green Bay (38), Dec. 5, 1948
- 105 Oakland (62) vs. Atlanta (43), Nov. 30, 1975 (ot)
- 104 Chi. Bears (64) vs. Pittsburgh (40), Oct. 18, 1936

Fewest Rushing Attempts, Both Teams, Game
- 16 Chi. Cardinals (6) vs. Boston (10), Oct. 22, 1933
- 30 Minnesota (15) vs. New England (15), Oct. 30, 2006
- 31 Green Bay (12) vs. Pittsburgh (19), Dec. 20, 2009

YARDS GAINED

Most Yards Gained Rushing, Season
- 3,165 New England, 1978
- 3,088 Buffalo, 1973
- 2,986 Kansas City, 1978

Fewest Yards Gained Rushing, Season
- 298 Philadelphia, 1940
- 467 Detroit, 1946
- 471 Boston, 1944

Most Yards Gained Rushing, Game
- 426 Detroit vs. Pittsburgh, Nov. 4, 1934
- 423 N.Y. Giants vs. Baltimore, Nov. 19, 1950
- 420 Boston vs. N.Y. Giants, Oct. 8, 1933

Fewest Yards Gained Rushing, Game
- −53 Detroit vs. Chi. Cardinals, Oct. 17, 1943
- −36 Philadelphia vs. Chi. Bears, Nov. 19, 1939
- −33 Brooklyn vs. Phil-Pitt, Oct. 2, 1943

Most Yards Gained Rushing, Both Teams, Game
- 595 Los Angeles (371) vs. N.Y. Yankees (224), Nov. 18, 1951
- 574 Chi. Bears (396) vs. Pittsburgh (178), Oct. 10, 1934
- 558 Boston (420) vs. N.Y. Giants (138), Oct. 8, 1933

Fewest Yards Gained Rushing, Both Teams, Game
- −15 Detroit (−53) vs. Chi. Cardinals (38), Oct. 17, 1943
- 4 Detroit (−10) vs. Chi. Cardinals (14), Sept. 15, 1940

45　San Diego (21) vs. Philadelphia (24), Oct. 23, 2005

AVERAGE GAIN
Highest Average Gain, Rushing, Season
　5.74　Cleveland, 1963
　5.65　San Francisco, 1954
　5.56　San Diego, 1963
Lowest Average Gain, Rushing, Season
　0.94　Philadelphia, 1940
　1.45　Boston, 1944
　1.55　Pittsburgh, 1935

TOUCHDOWNS
Most Touchdowns, Rushing, Season
　36　Green Bay, 1962
　33　Pittsburgh, 1976
　32　Kansas City, 2003
　　　San Diego, 2006
Fewest Touchdowns, Rushing, Season
　1　Brooklyn, 1934
　2　Chi. Cardinals, 1933
　　　Cincinnati, 1933
　　　Pittsburgh, 1934
　　　Philadelphia, 1935
　　　Philadelphia, 1936
　　　Philadelphia, 1937
　　　Philadelphia, 1938
　　　Pittsburgh, 1940
　　　Philadelphia, 1972
　　　N.Y. Jets, 1995
　　　Arizona, 2005
　3　By many teams
Most Touchdowns, Rushing, Game
　9　Rock Island vs. Evansville, Oct. 15, 1922
　　　Racine vs. Louisville, Nov. 5, 1922
　8　Chi. Cardinals vs. Rochester, Oct. 7, 1923
　　　Kansas City vs. Atlanta, Oct. 24, 2004
　7　By many teams
Most Touchdowns, Rushing, Both Teams, Game
　9　Rock Island (9) vs. Evansville (0), Oct. 15, 1922
　　　Racine (9) vs. Louisville (0), Nov. 5, 1922
　8　Chi. Cardinals (8) vs. Rochester (0), Oct. 7, 1923
　　　Canton (7) vs. Cleveland (1), Nov. 25, 1923
　　　Los Angeles (6) vs. N.Y. Yanks (2), Nov. 18, 1951
　　　Chi. Bears (5) vs. Green Bay (3), Nov. 6, 1955
　　　Denver (5) vs. Kansas City (3), Dec. 7, 2003
　　　Kansas City (8) vs. Atlanta (0), Oct. 24, 2004
　7　In many games

PASSING

ATTEMPTS
Most Passes Attempted, Season
　740　Detroit, 2012
　709　Minnesota, 1981
　699　New England, 1994
Fewest Passes Attempted, Season
　102　Cincinnati, 1933
　106　Boston, 1933
　120　Detroit, 1937
Most Passes Attempted, Game
　70　New England vs. Minnesota, Nov. 13, 1994 (ot)
　69　N.Y. Jets vs. Baltimore, Dec. 24, 2000
　68　Houston vs. Buffalo, Nov 1, 1964
　　　Cincinnati vs. Pittsburgh, Dec. 30, 2001 (ot)
Fewest Passes Attempted, Game
　0　Green Bay vs. Portsmouth, Oct. 8, 1933
　　　Detroit vs. Cleveland, Sept. 10, 1937
　　　Pittsburgh vs. Brooklyn, Nov. 16, 1941
　　　Pittsburgh vs. Los Angeles, Nov. 13, 1949

Cleveland vs. Philadelphia, Dec. 3, 1950
Most Passes Attempted, Both Teams, Game
　112　New England (70) vs. Minnesota (42),
　　　Nov. 13, 1994 (ot)
　109　Detroit (61) vs. Houston (48), Nov. 22, 2012 (ot)
　104　Miami (55) vs. N.Y. Jets (49), Oct. 18. 1987 (ot)
　　　N.Y. Jets (58) vs. San Francisco (46),
　　　Sept. 6, 1998 (ot)
　　　Baltimore (62) vs. Denver (42), Sept. 5, 2013
Fewest Passes Attempted, Both Teams, Game
　4　Chi. Cardinals (1) vs. Detroit (3), Nov. 3, 1935
　　　Detroit (0) vs. Cleveland (4), Sept. 10, 1937
　6　Chi. Cardinals (2) vs. Detroit (4), Sept. 15, 1940
　8　Brooklyn (2) vs. Philadelphia (6), Oct. 1, 1939

COMPLETIONS
Most Passes Completed, Season
　472　New Orleans, 2011
　461　Denver, 2013
　450　Indianapolis, 2010
　　　New Orleans, 2010
Fewest Passes Completed, Season
　25　Cincinnati, 1933
　33　Boston, 1933
　34　Chi. Cardinals, 1934
Most Passes Completed, Game
　45　New England vs. Minnesota, Nov. 13, 1994 (ot)
　43　Washington vs. Detroit, Nov. 4, 1990 (ot)
　　　Oakland vs. Pittsburgh, Sept. 15, 2002
　　　Detroit vs. Tennessee, Sept. 23, 2012 (ot)
　　　Houston vs. Jacksonville, Nov. 18, 2012 (ot)
　42　N.Y. Jets vs. San Francisco, Sept. 21, 1980
　　　N.Y. Jets vs. Seattle, Dec. 6, 1998
Fewest Passes Completed, Game
　0　By many teams. Last time: Buffalo vs. N.Y. Jets,
　　　Sept. 29, 1974
Most Passes Completed, Both Teams, Game
　72　Detroit (43) vs. Tennessee (29), Sept. 23, 2012 (ot)
　71　New England (45) vs. Minnesota (26),
　　　Nov. 13, 1994 (ot)
　68　San Francisco (37) vs. Atlanta (31), Oct. 6, 1985
　　　Denver (34) vs. Oakland (34), Nov. 11, 2002
Fewest Passes Completed, Both Teams, Game
　1　Chi. Cardinals (0) vs. Philadelphia (1), Nov. 8, 1936
　　　Detroit (0) vs. Cleveland (1), Sept. 10, 1937
　　　Chi. Cardinals (0) vs. Detroit (1), Sept. 15, 1940
　　　Brooklyn (0) vs. Pittsburgh (1), Nov. 29, 1942
　2　Chi. Cardinals (0) vs. Detroit (2), Nov. 3, 1935
　　　Buffalo (0) vs. N.Y. Jets (2), Sept. 29, 1974
　　　Chi. Cardinals (0) vs. Green Bay (2), Nov. 18, 1934
　3　In seven games

YARDS GAINED
Most Seasons Leading League, Passing Yardage
　10　San Diego, 1965, 1968, 1971, 1978-1983, 1985
　8　Chi. Bears, 1932, 1939, 1941, 1943, 1945, 1949,
　　　1954, 1964
　　　Washington, 1938, 1940, 1944, 1947-48, 1967,
　　　1974, 1989
　　　Balt./Indianapolis, 1957, 1959, 1960, 1963, 1976,
　　　2003-04, 2010
　7　Houston, 1960-61, 1963-64, 1990-92
　　　L.A./St. Louis Rams, 1946, 1950-51, 1956,
　　　1999-2001
Most Consecutive Seasons Leading League, Passing Yardage
　6　San Diego, 1978-1983
　4　Green Bay, 1934-37
　3　Miami, 1986-88
　　　Houston, 1990-92
　　　St. Louis, 1999-2001

Most Yards Gained, Passing, Season
5,444 Denver, 2013
5,347 New Orleans, 2011
5,232 St. Louis, 2000

Fewest Yards Gained, Passing, Season
302 Chi. Cardinals, 1934
357 Cincinnati, 1933
459 Boston, 1934

Most Yards Gained Passing, Game
554 Los Angeles vs. N.Y. Yankees, Sept. 28, 1951
530 Minnesota vs. Baltimore, Sept. 28, 1969
521 Miami vs. N.Y. Jets, Oct. 23, 1988

Fewest Yards Gained, Passing, Game
−53 Denver vs. Oakland, Sept. 10, 1967
−52 Cincinnati vs. Houston, Oct. 31, 1971
−39 Atlanta vs. San Francisco, Oct. 23, 1976

Most Yards Gained, Passing, Both Teams, Game
971 Detroit (502) vs. Green Bay (469), Jan. 1, 2012
906 New England (516) vs. Miami (390), Sept. 12, 2011
884 N.Y. Jets (449) vs. Miami (435), Sept. 21, 1986 (ot)
Dallas (470) vs. Denver (414), Oct. 6, 2013

Fewest Yards Gained, Passing, Both Teams, Game
−11 Green Bay (−10) vs. Dallas (−1), Oct. 24, 1965
1 Chi. Cardinals (0) vs. Philadelphia (1), Nov. 8, 1936
7 Brooklyn (0) vs. Pittsburgh (7), Nov. 29, 1942

TIMES SACKED

Most Seasons Leading League, Fewest Times Sacked
10 Miami, 1973, 1982-1990
7 Indianapolis, 1999-2000, 2004-06, 2009, 2012
5 N.Y. Jets, 1965-66, 1968, 1993, 2000

Most Consecutive Seasons Leading League, Fewest Times Sacked
9 Miami, 1982-1990
3 St. Louis, 1974-76
Indianapolis, 2004-06
2 By many teams

Most Times Sacked, Season
104 Philadelphia, 1986
78 Arizona, 1997
76 Houston, 2002

Fewest Times Sacked, Season
7 Miami, 1988
8 San Francisco, 1970
St. Louis, 1975
9 N.Y. Jets, 1966
Washington, 1991

Most Times Sacked, Game
12 Pittsburgh vs. Dallas, Nov. 20, 1966
Baltimore vs. St. Louis, Oct. 26, 1980
Detroit vs. Chicago, Dec. 16, 1984
Houston vs. Dallas, Sept. 29, 1985
Philadelphia vs. N.Y. Giants, Sept. 30, 2007
11 St. Louis vs. N.Y. Giants, Nov. 1, 1964
Los Angeles vs. Baltimore, Nov. 22, 1964
Denver vs. Buffalo, Dec. 13, 1964
Green Bay vs. Detroit, Nov. 7, 1965
Buffalo vs. Oakland, Oct. 15, 1967
Denver vs. Oakland, Nov. 5, 1967
Atlanta vs. St. Louis, Nov. 24, 1968
Detroit vs. Dallas, Oct. 6, 1975
Philadelphia vs. St. Louis, Dec. 18, 1983
Cleveland vs. Kansas City, Sept. 30, 1984
Minnesota vs. Chicago, Oct. 28, 1984
Atlanta vs. Cleveland, Nov. 18, 1984
Dallas vs. San Diego, Nov. 16, 1986
Philadelphia vs. Detroit, Nov. 16, 1986
Philadelphia vs. L.A. Raiders, Nov. 30, 1986 (ot)
L.A. Raiders vs. Seattle, Dec. 8, 1986
N.Y. Jets vs. Dallas, Oct. 4, 1987
Philadelphia vs. Chicago, Oct. 4, 1987

Dallas vs. Philadelphia, Sept. 15, 1991
Cleveland vs. Indianapolis, Sept. 6, 1992
N.Y. Jets vs. San Diego, Dec. 23, 2012
10 By many teams

Most Times Sacked, Both Teams, Game
18 Green Bay (10) vs. San Diego (8), Sept. 24, 1978
17 Buffalo (10) vs. N.Y. Titans (7), Nov. 23, 1961
Pittsburgh (12) vs. Dallas (5), Nov. 20, 1966
Atlanta (9) vs. Philadelphia (8), Dec. 16, 1984
Philadelphia (11) vs. L.A. Raiders (6), Nov. 30, 1986 (ot)
16 Los Angeles (11) vs. Baltimore (5), Nov. 22, 1964
Buffalo (11) vs. Oakland (5), Oct. 15, 1967

COMPLETION PERCENTAGE

Most Seasons Leading League, Completion Percentage
14 San Francisco, 1952, 1957-58, 1965, 1981, 1983, 1987, 1989, 1992-97
11 Washington, 1937, 1939-1940, 1942-45, 1947-48, 1969-1970
8 Green Bay, 1936, 1941, 1961-62, 1964, 1966, 1968, 1998

Most Consecutive Seasons Leading League, Completion Percentage
6 San Francisco, 1992-97
4 Washington, 1942-45
Kansas City, 1966-69
3 Cleveland, 1953-55
St. Louis, 1999-2001
New Orleans, 2009-2011

Highest Completion Percentage, Season
71.30 New Orleans, 2011 (662-472)
70.65 Cincinnati, 1982 (310-219)
70.25 San Francisco, 1994 (511-359)

Lowest Completion Percentage, Season
22.9 Philadelphia, 1936 (170-39)
24.5 Cincinnati, 1933 (102-25)
25.0 Pittsburgh, 1941 (168-42)

TOUCHDOWNS

Most Touchdowns, Passing, Season
55 Denver, 2013
51 Indianapolis, 2004
Green Bay, 2011
50 New England, 2007

Fewest Touchdowns, Passing, Season
0 Cincinnati, 1933
Pittsburgh, 1945
1 Boston, 1932
Boston, 1933
Chi. Cardinals, 1934
Cincinnati/St. Louis, 1934
Detroit, 1942
2 Chi. Cardinals, 1932
Stapleton, 1932
Chi. Cardinals, 1935
Brooklyn, 1936
Pittsburgh, 1942

Most Touchdowns, Passing, Game
7 Chi. Bears vs. N.Y. Giants, Nov. 14, 1943
Philadelphia vs. Washington, Oct. 17, 1954
Houston vs. N.Y. Titans, Nov. 19, 1961
Houston vs. N.Y. Titans, Oct. 14, 1962
N.Y. Giants vs. Washington, Oct. 28, 1962
Minnesota vs. Baltimore, Sept. 28, 1969
San Diego vs. Oakland, Nov. 22, 1981
Denver vs. Baltimore, Sept. 5, 2013
Philadelphia vs. Oakland, Nov. 3, 2013
6 By many teams

Most Touchdowns, Passing, Both Teams, Game
12 New Orleans (6) vs. St. Louis (6), Nov. 2, 1969

11 N.Y. Giants (7) vs. Washington (4), Oct. 28, 1962
   Oakland (6) vs. Houston (5), Dec. 22, 1963
   Cincinnati (6) vs. Cleveland, (5), Sept. 16, 2007
   Green Bay (6) vs. Detroit (5), Jan. 1, 2012
10 San Diego (5) vs. Seattle (5), Sept. 15, 1985
   Miami (6) vs. N.Y. Jets (4), Sept. 21, 1986 (ot)
   San Francisco (6) vs. Atlanta (4), Oct. 14, 1990

PASSES HAD INTERCEPTED
Most Passes Had Intercepted, Season
48 Houston, 1962
45 Denver, 1961
41 Card-Pitt, 1944
Fewest Passes Had Intercepted, Season
5 Cleveland, 1960
   Green Bay, 1966
   Kansas City, 1990
   N.Y. Giants, 1990
   New England, 2010
   San Francisco, 2011
6 Green Bay, 1964
   St. Louis, 1982
   Dallas, 1993
   Jacksonville, 2005
   Washington, 2008
   Tampa Bay, 2010
7 Los Angeles, 1969
   Denver, 2005
   Miami, 2008
   Minnesota, 2009
Most Passes Had Intercepted, Game
9 Detroit vs. Green Bay, Oct. 24, 1943
   Pittsburgh vs. Philadelphia, Dec. 12, 1965
8 Green Bay vs. N.Y. Giants, Nov. 21, 1948
   Chi. Cardinals vs. Philadelphia, Sept. 24, 1950
   N.Y. Yanks vs. N.Y. Giants, Dec. 16, 1951
   Denver vs. Houston, Dec. 2, 1962
   Chi. Bears vs. Detroit, Sept. 22, 1968
   Baltimore vs. N.Y. Jets, Sept. 23, 1973
7 By many teams. Last time: Detroit vs. Cleveland,
   Sept. 23, 2001
Most Passes Had Intercepted, Both Teams, Game
13 Denver (8) vs. Houston (5), Dec. 2, 1962
11 Philadelphia (7) vs. Boston (4), Nov. 3, 1935
   Boston (6) vs. Pittsburgh (5), Dec. 1, 1935
   Cleveland (7) vs. Green Bay (4), Oct. 30, 1938
   Green Bay (7) vs. Detroit (4), Oct. 20, 1940
   Detroit (7) vs. Chi. Bears (4), Nov. 22, 1942
   Detroit (7) vs. Cleveland (4), Nov. 26, 1944
   Chi. Cardinals (8) vs. Philadelphia (3), Sept. 24, 1950
   Washington (7) vs. N.Y. Giants (4), Dec. 8, 1963
   Pittsburgh (9) vs. Philadelphia (2), Dec 12, 1965
10 In many games

PUNTING
Most Seasons Leading League (Average Distance)
9 Oakland, 1974-75, 1977-78, 2003-04, 2007, 2009,
   2013
7 Denver 1962-64, 1966-67, 1982, 1999
6 Washington, 1940-43, 1945, 1958
   Kansas City, 1968, 1971-73, 1979, 1984
   L.A. Rams, 1946, 1949, 1955-56, 1994, 2008
Most Consecutive Seasons Leading League
(Average Distance)
4 Washington, 1940-43
3 Cleveland, 1950-52
   Denver, 1962-64
   Kansas City, 1971-73
Most Punts, Season
116 Houston, 2002

114 Chicago, 1981
113 Boston, 1934
    Brooklyn, 1934
    Dallas, 2002
Fewest Punts, Season
23 San Diego, 1982
31 Cincinnati, 1982
32 Chi. Bears, 1941
Most Punts, Game
17 Chi. Bears vs. Green Bay, Oct. 22, 1933
   Cincinnati vs. Pittsburgh, Oct. 22, 1933
16 Cincinnati vs. Portsmouth, Sept. 17, 1933
   Chi. Cardinals vs. Chi. Bears, Nov. 30, 1933
   Chi. Cardinals vs. Detroit, Sept. 15, 1940
   Oakland vs. San Diego, Oct. 11, 1998
15 Chi. Cardinals vs. Cincinnati, Nov. 12, 1933
   N.Y. Giants vs. Chi. Bears, Nov. 17, 1935
   Philadelphia vs. N.Y. Giants, Dec. 6, 1987 (ot)
Fewest Punts, Game
0 By many teams. Last time:
   Chicago vs. Dallas, Dec. 9, 2013
Most Punts, Both Teams, Game
31 Chi. Bears (17) vs. Green Bay (14), Oct. 22, 1933
   Cincinnati (17), vs. Pittsburgh (14), Oct. 22, 1933
29 Chi. Cardinals (15) vs. Cincinnati (14), Nov. 12, 1933
   Chi. Cardinals (16) vs. Chi. Bears (13), Nov. 30, 1933
   Chi. Cardinals (16) vs. Detroit (13), Sept. 15, 1940
28 Philadelphia (14) vs. Washington (14), Nov. 5, 1939
Fewest Punts, Both Teams, Game
0 Buffalo vs. San Francisco, Sept. 13, 1992
1 Baltimore (0) vs. Cleveland (1), Nov. 1, 1959
   Dall. Cowboys (0) vs. Cleveland (1), Dec. 3, 1961
   Chicago (0) vs. Detroit (1), Oct. 1, 1972
   San Francisco (0) vs. N.Y. Giants (1), Oct. 15, 1972
   Green Bay (0) vs. Buffalo (1), Dec. 5, 1982
   Miami (0) vs. Buffalo (1), Oct. 12, 1986
   Green Bay (0) vs. Chicago (1), Dec. 17, 1989
   Oakland (0) vs. Seattle (1), Dec. 5, 1999
   Tampa Bay (0) vs. Minnesota (1), Oct. 29, 2000
   New Orleans (0) vs. San Francisco (1), Oct. 20, 2002
   San Diego (0) vs. Oakland (1), Jan. 1, 2012
   Denver (0) vs. Dallas (1), Oct. 6, 2013
2 In many games

AVERAGE YARDAGE
Highest Avg. Distance, Punting, Season
51.1 Oakland, 2009
50.9 San Francisco, 2011
50.8 Oakland, 2011
Lowest Average Distance, Punting, Season
32.7 Card-Pitt, 1944 (60-1,964)
33.8 Cincinnati, 1986 (59-1,996)
33.9 Detroit, 1969 (74-2,510)

PUNT RETURNS
Most Seasons Leading League (Average Return)
9 Detroit, 1943-45, 1951-52, 1962, 1966, 1969, 1991
7 Chi. Cardinals/St. Louis, 1948-49, 1955-56, 1959,
   1986-87
6 Green Bay, 1950, 1953-54, 1961, 1972, 1996
   Dallas/Kansas City, 1960, 1968, 1970, 1979-1980,
   2003
Most Consecutive Seasons Leading League (Average Return)
3 Detroit, 1943-45
2 By many teams
Most Punt Returns, Season
71 Pittsburgh, 1976
   Tampa Bay, 1979
   L.A. Raiders, 1985
67 Pittsburgh, 1974

Los Angeles, 1978
L.A. Raiders, 1984
65 San Francisco, 1976
Fewest Punt Returns, Season
12 Baltimore, 1981
San Diego, 1982
14 Los Angeles, 1961
Philadelphia, 1962
Baltimore, 1982
15 Houston, 1960
Washington, 1960
Oakland, 1961
N.Y. Giants, 1969
Philadelphia, 1973
Kansas City, 1982
Most Punt Returns, Game
12 Philadelphia vs. Cleveland, Dec. 3, 1950
11 Chi. Bears vs. Chi. Cardinals, Oct. 8, 1950
Washington vs. Tampa Bay, Oct. 9, 1977
10 Philadelphia vs. N.Y. Giants, Nov. 26, 1950
Philadelphia vs. Tampa Bay, Sept. 18, 1977
Pittsburgh vs. Buffalo, Dec. 16, 1979
Washington vs. New Orleans, Dec. 26, 1982
Philadelphia vs. Seattle, Dec. 13, 1992 (ot)
New England vs. Pittsburgh, Dec. 5, 1993
Most Punt Returns, Both Teams, Game
17 Philadelphia (12) vs. Cleveland (5), Dec. 3, 1950
16 N.Y. Giants (9) vs. Philadelphia (7), Dec. 12, 1954
Washington (11) vs. Tampa Bay (5), Oct. 9, 1977
Oakland (8) vs. San Diego (8), Oct. 11, 1998
15 Detroit (8) vs. Cleveland (7), Sept. 27, 1942
Los Angeles (8) vs. Baltimore (7), Nov. 27, 1966
Pittsburgh (8) vs. Houston (7), Dec. 1, 1974
Philadelphia (10) vs. Tampa Bay (5), Sept. 18, 1977
Baltimore (9) vs. Kansas City (6), Sept. 2, 1979
Washington (10) vs. New Orleans (5), Dec. 26, 1982
L.A. Raiders (8) vs. Cleveland (7), Nov. 16, 1986

FAIR CATCHES
Most Fair Catches, Season
38 N.Y. Jets, 2012
34 Baltimore, 1971
33 Philadelphia, 2000
Fewest Fair Catches, Season
0 San Diego, 1975
New England, 1976
Tampa Bay, 1976
Pittsburgh, 1977
Dallas, 1982
1 Cleveland, 1974
San Francisco, 1975
Kansas City, 1976
St. Louis, 1976
San Diego, 1976
L.A. Rams, 1982
St. Louis, 1982
Tampa Bay, 1982
Arizona, 2001
2 By many teams
Most Fair Catches, Game
7 Minnesota vs. Dallas, Sept. 25, 1966
N.Y. Jets vs. Miami, Nov. 20, 1966
Detroit vs. Chicago, Nov. 21, 1976
Philadelphia vs. Buffalo, Dec. 27, 1987
Tennessee vs. Jacksonville, Nov. 16, 2008
6 By many teams

YARDS GAINED
Most Yards, Punt Returns, Season
875 Green Bay, 1996

785 L.A. Raiders, 1985
781 Chi. Bears, 1948
Fewest Yards, Punt Returns, Season
27 St. Louis, 1965
35 N.Y. Giants, 1965
37 New England, 1972
Most Yards, Punt Returns, Game
231 Detroit vs. San Francisco, Oct. 6, 1963
225 Oakland vs. Buffalo, Sept. 15, 1968
219 L.A. Rams vs. Atlanta, Oct. 11, 1981
Fewest Yards, Punt Returns, Game
-28 Washington vs. Dallas, Dec. 11, 1966
-23 N.Y. Giants vs. Buffalo, Oct. 20, 1975
Pittsburgh vs. Houston, Sept. 20, 1970
-20 New Orleans vs. Pittsburgh, Oct. 20, 1968
Most Yards, Punt Returns, Both Teams, Game
282 L.A. Rams (219) vs. Atlanta (63), Oct. 11, 1981
245 Detroit (231) vs. San Francisco (14), Oct. 6, 1963
244 Oakland (225) vs. Buffalo (19), Sept. 15, 1968
Fewest Yards, Punt Returns, Both Teams, Game
-18 Buffalo (-18) vs. Pittsburgh (0), Oct. 29, 1972
-14 Miami (-14) vs. Boston (0), Nov. 30, 1969
Tennessee (-14) vs. New Orleans (0),
Sept. 21, 2003
-13 N.Y. Giants (-13) vs. Cleveland (0), Nov. 14, 1965

AVERAGE YARDS RETURNING PUNTS
Highest Average, Punt Returns, Season
20.2 Chi. Bears, 1941
19.1 Chi. Cardinals, 1948
18.2 Chi. Cardinals, 1949
Lowest Average, Punt Returns, Season
1.2 St. Louis, 1965 (23-27)
1.5 N.Y. Giants, 1965 (24-35)
1.7 Washington, 1970 (27-45)

TOUCHDOWNS RETURNING PUNTS
Most Touchdowns, Punt Returns, Season
5 Chi. Cardinals, 1959
4 Chi. Cardinals, 1948
Detroit, 1951
N.Y. Giants, 1951
Denver, 1976
Chicago, 2007
Arizona, 2011
3 Washington, 1941
Detroit, 1952
Pittsburgh, 1952
Houston, 1975
Los Angeles, 1981
Cleveland, 1993
Green Bay, 1996
Denver, 1997
San Diego, 1997
Chicago, 2006
Tennessee, 2006
New Orleans, 2008
Oakland, 2008
Chicago, 2010
Dallas, 2010
Tennessee, 2012
Most Touchdowns, Punt Returns, Game
2 Detroit vs. Los Angeles, Oct. 14, 1951
Detroit vs. Green Bay, Nov. 22, 1951
Chi. Cardinals vs. Pittsburgh, Nov. 1, 1959
Chi. Cardinals vs. N.Y. Giants, Nov. 22, 1959
N.Y. Titans vs. Denver, Sept. 24, 1961
Denver vs. Cleveland, Sept. 26, 1976
Los Angeles vs. Atlanta, Oct. 11, 1981
St. Louis vs. Tampa Bay, Dec. 21, 1986

L.A. Rams vs. Atlanta, Dec. 27, 1992
Cleveland vs. Pittsburgh, Oct. 24, 1993
San Diego vs. Cincinnati, Nov. 2, 1997
Denver vs. Carolina, Nov. 9, 1997
Baltimore vs. Seattle, Dec. 7, 1997
Baltimore vs. N.Y. Jets, Dec. 24, 2000
Oakland vs. Tennessee, Sept. 29, 2002
Carolina vs. Cincinnati, Dec. 8, 2002
Detroit at Jacksonville, Nov. 14, 2004 (ot)
New Orleans vs. Minnesota, Oct. 6, 2008
Tennessee vs. Jacksonville, Dec. 30, 2012

Most Touchdowns, Punt Returns, Both Teams, Game
2　Philadelphia (1) vs. Washington (1), Nov. 9, 1952
　Kansas City (1) vs. Buffalo (1), Sept. 11, 1966
　Baltimore (1) vs. New England (1), Nov. 18, 1979
　L.A. Raiders (1) vs. Philadelphia (1),
　　Nov. 30, 1986 (ot)
　Cincinnati (1) vs. Green Bay (1), Sept. 20, 1992
　Oakland (1) vs. Seattle (1), Nov. 15, 1998
　Atlanta (1) vs. Tennessee (1), Nov. 23, 2003
　San Diego (1) vs. Denver (1), Oct. 19, 2009
　St. Louis (1) vs. Arizona (1), Nov. 27, 2011
(Also see previous record)

KICKOFF RETURNS
Most Seasons Leading League (Average Return)
8　Washington, 1942, 1947, 1962-63, 1973-74, 1981,
　　1995
6　Chicago Bears, 1943, 1948, 1958, 1966, 1972, 1985
　N.Y. Giants, 1944, 1946, 1949, 1951, 1953, 2004
5　Green Bay, 1954, 1964, 1967, 1993, 1998
　New England, 1977, 1980, 1982, 1997, 2006
　Hou. Oilers/ Tenn. Titans, 1960, 1962-63, 1968, 2008
　Dallas/Kansas City, 1961, 1969, 1978, 2003, 2013

Most Consecutive Seasons Leading League (Average Return)
3　Denver, 1965-67
2　By many teams

Most Kickoff Returns, Season
96　Detroit, 2009
89　Cleveland, 1999
88　New Orleans, 1980

Fewest Kickoff Returns, Season
17　N.Y. Giants, 1944
20　N.Y. Giants, 1941, 1943
　Chi. Bears, 1942
22　New Orleans, 2013

Most Kickoff Returns, Game
12　N.Y. Giants vs. Washington, Nov. 27, 1966
11　Kansas City vs. Buffalo, Nov. 23, 2008
10　By many teams

Most Kickoff Returns, Both Teams, Game
19　N.Y. Giants (12) vs. Washington (7), Nov. 27, 1966
　Cleveland (10) vs. Cincinnati (9), Nov. 28, 2004
18　Houston (10) vs. Oakland (8), Dec. 22, 1963
17　Washington (9) vs. Green Bay (8), Oct. 17, 1983
　San Diego (9) vs. Pittsburgh (8), Dec. 8, 1985
　Detroit (9) vs. Green Bay (8), Nov. 27, 1986
　L.A. Raiders (9) vs. Seattle (8), Dec. 18, 1988
　Oakland (10) vs. Seattle (7), Oct. 26, 1997
　Buffalo (9) vs. Minnesota (8), Sept. 15, 2002 (ot)
　Cincinnati (10) vs. Cleveland (7), Sept. 16, 2007
　Kansas City (11) vs. Buffalo (6), Nov. 23, 2008

YARDS GAINED
Most Yards, Kickoff Returns, Season
2,296　Arizona, 2000
2,173　Houston, 2005
2,084　Arizona, 2010

Fewest Yards, Kickoff Returns, Season
282　N.Y. Giants, 1940

381　Green Bay, 1940
424　Chicago, 1963

Most Yards, Kickoff Returns, Game
367　Baltimore vs. Minnesota, Dec. 13, 1998
362　Detroit vs. Los Angeles, Oct. 29, 1950
304　Chi. Bears vs. Green Bay, Nov. 9, 1952
　New Orleans vs. L.A. Rams, Oct. 23, 1994

Most Yards, Kickoff Returns, Both Teams, Game
560　Detroit (362) vs. L.A. Rams (198), Oct. 29, 1950
511　Baltimore (367) vs. Minnesota (144), Dec. 13, 1998
501　New Orleans (304) vs. L.A. Rams (197), Oct. 23,
　　1994

AVERAGE YARDAGE
Highest Average, Kickoff Returns, Season
29.9　Kansas City, 2013
29.4　Chicago, 1972
28.9　Pittsburgh, 1952

Lowest Average, Kickoff Returns, Season
14.7　N.Y. Jets, 1993 (46-675)
15.8　N.Y. Giants, 1993 (32-507)
15.9　Tampa Bay, 1993 (58-922)

TOUCHDOWNS
Most Touchdowns, Kickoff Returns, Season
4　Green Bay, 1967
　Chicago, 1970
　Detroit, 1994
　Houston, 2007
3　Los Angeles, 1950
　Chi. Cardinals, 1954
　San Francisco, 1963
　Denver, 1966
　Chicago, 1967
　New England, 1977
　L.A. Rams, 1985
　Atlanta, 2000
　Buffalo, 2004
　N.Y. Jets, 2007
　Cleveland, 2009
　Oakland, 2010
　Seattle, 2010
2　By many teams

Most Touchdowns, Kickoff Returns, Game
2　Chi. Bears vs. Green Bay, Sept. 22, 1940
　Chi. Bears vs. Green Bay, Nov. 9, 1952
　Philadelphia vs. Dallas, Nov. 6, 1966
　Green Bay vs. Cleveland, Nov. 12, 1967
　L.A. Rams vs. Green Bay, Nov. 24, 1985
　New Orleans vs. L.A. Rams, Oct. 23, 1994
　Baltimore vs. Minnesota, Dec. 13, 1998
　N.Y. Jets vs. Buffalo, Sept. 8, 2002 (ot)
　Chicago vs. St. Louis, Dec. 11, 2006
　Houston vs. Jacksonville, Dec. 30, 2007
　Miami vs. N.Y. Jets, Nov. 1, 2009
　Cleveland vs. Kansas City, Dec. 20, 2009
　Seattle vs. San Diego, Sept. 26, 2010

Most Touchdowns, Kickoff Returns, Both Teams, Game
3　Baltimore (2) vs. Minnesota (1), Dec. 13, 1998
2　In many games

FUMBLES
Most Fumbles, Season
56　Chi. Bears, 1938
　San Francisco, 1978
54　Philadelphia, 1946
51　New England, 1973

Fewest Fumbles, Season
6　New Orleans, 2011
7　Kansas City, 2002

   8 Cleveland, 1959

Most Fumbles, Game
- 10 Phil-Pitt vs. N.Y. Giants, Oct. 9, 1943
  - Detroit vs. Minnesota, Nov. 12, 1967
  - Kansas City vs. Houston, Oct. 12, 1969
  - San Francisco vs. Detroit, Dec. 17, 1978
- 9 Philadelphia vs. Green Bay, Oct. 13, 1946
  - Boston at Oakland, Dec. 16, 1962
  - Kansas City vs. San Diego, Nov. 15, 1964
  - N.Y. Giants vs. Buffalo, Oct. 20, 1975
  - St. Louis vs. Washington, Oct. 25, 1976
  - San Diego vs. Green Bay, Sept. 24, 1978
  - Pittsburgh vs. Cincinnati, Oct. 14, 1979
  - Cleveland vs. Seattle, Dec. 20, 1981
  - Cleveland vs. Pittsburgh, Dec. 23, 1990
  - Oakland vs. Seattle, Dec. 22, 1996
- 8 By many teams

Most Fumbles, Both Teams, Game
- 14 Chi. Bears (7) vs. Cleveland (7), Nov. 24, 1940
  - St. Louis (8) vs. N.Y. Giants (6), Sept. 17, 1961
  - Kansas City (10) vs. Houston (4), Oct. 12, 1969
- 13 Washington (8) vs. Pittsburgh (5), Nov. 14, 1937
  - Philadelphia (7) vs. Boston (6), Dec. 8, 1946
  - N.Y. Giants (7) vs. Washington (6), Nov. 5, 1950
  - Kansas City (9) vs. San Diego (4), Nov. 15, 1964
  - Buffalo (7) vs. Denver (6), Dec. 13, 1964
  - N.Y. Jets (7) vs. Houston (6), Sept. 12, 1965
  - Cleveland (7) vs. New Orleans (6), Dec. 12, 1971
  - Houston (8) vs. Pittsburgh (5), Dec. 9, 1973
  - St. Louis (9) vs. Washington (4), Oct. 25, 1976
  - Cleveland (9) vs. Seattle (4), Dec. 20, 1981
  - Green Bay (7) vs. Detroit (6), Oct. 6, 1985
- 12 In many games

FUMBLES LOST

Most Fumbles Lost, Season
- 36 Chi. Cardinals, 1959
- 31 Green Bay, 1952
- 29 Chi. Cardinals, 1946
  - Pittsburgh, 1950
  - Cleveland, 1978

Fewest Fumbles Lost, Season
- 2 Kansas City, 2002
- 3 Philadelphia, 1938
  - Minnesota, 1980
  - N.Y. Giants, 2008
- 4 San Francisco, 1960
  - Kansas City, 1982
  - Minnesota, 1998
  - Detroit, 2003
  - Atlanta, 2012
  - Houston, 2012
  - Indianapolis, 2013

Most Fumbles Lost, Game
- 8 St. Louis vs. Washington, Oct. 25, 1976
  - Cleveland vs. Pittsburgh, Dec. 23, 1990
- 7 Cincinnati vs. Buffalo, Nov. 30, 1969
  - Pittsburgh vs. Cincinnati, Oct. 14, 1979
  - Cleveland vs. Seattle, Dec. 20, 1981
- 6 By many teams

FUMBLES RECOVERED

Most Fumbles Recovered, Season, Own and Opponents'
- 58 Minnesota, 1963 (27 own, 31 opp)
- 51 Chi. Bears, 1938 (37 own, 14 opp)
  - San Francisco, 1978 (24 own, 27 opp)
- 50 Philadelphia, 1987 (23 own, 27 opp)

Fewest Fumbles Recovered, Season, Own and Opponents'
- 7 New Orleans, 2011 (0 own, 7 opp)
  - Pittsburgh, 2011 (3 own, 4 opp)

   9 San Francisco, 1982 (5 own, 4 opp)
- 10 Jacksonville, 2006 (6 own, 4 opp)
  - N.Y. Jets, 2013 (8 own, 2 opp)
  - San Diego, 2013 (4 own, 6 opp)

Most Fumbles Recovered, Game, Own and Opponents'
- 10 Denver vs. Buffalo, Dec. 13, 1964 (5 own, 5 opp)
  - Pittsburgh vs. Houston, Dec. 9, 1973 (5 own, 5 opp)
  - Washington vs. St. Louis, Oct. 25, 1976 (2 own, 8 opp)
- 9 St. Louis vs. N.Y. Giants, Sept. 17, 1961 (6 own, 3 opp)
  - Houston vs. Cincinnati, Oct. 27, 1974 (4 own, 5 opp)
  - Kansas City vs. Dallas, Nov. 10, 1975 (4 own, 5 opp)
  - Green Bay vs. Detroit, Oct. 6, 1985 (5 own, 4 opp)
  - Pittsburgh vs. Cleveland, Dec. 23, 1990 (1 own, 8 opp)
- 8 By many teams

Most Own Fumbles Recovered, Season
- 37 Chi. Bears, 1938
- 28 Pittsburgh, 1987
- 27 Philadelphia, 1946
  - Minnesota, 1963

Fewest Own Fumbles Recovered, Season
- 0 New Orleans, 2011
- 1 Indianapolis, 2006
  - Philadelphia, 2008
- 2 Washington, 1958
  - Miami, 2000
  - Atlanta, 2011

Most Opponents' Fumbles Recovered, Season
- 31 Minnesota, 1963
- 29 Cleveland, 1951
- 28 Green Bay, 1946
  - Houston, 1977
  - Seattle, 1983

Fewest Opponents' Fumbles Recovered, Season
- 2 N.Y. Jets, 2013
- 3 Los Angeles, 1974
  - Green Bay, 1995
  - Miami, 2011
  - Indianapolis, 2012
- 4 Philadelphia, 1944
  - San Francisco, 1982
  - Jacksonville, 2006
  - Jacksonville, 2008
  - Pittsburgh, 2011
  - San Diego, 2011
  - St. Louis, 2012
  - Houston, 2013

Most Opponents' Fumbles Recovered, Game
- 8 Washington vs. St. Louis, Oct. 25, 1976
  - Pittsburgh vs. Cleveland, Dec. 23, 1990
- 7 Buffalo vs. Cincinnati, Nov. 30, 1969
  - Cincinnati vs. Pittsburgh, Oct. 14, 1979
  - Seattle vs. Cleveland, Dec. 20, 1981
- 6 By many teams

TOUCHDOWNS

Most Touchdowns, Fumbles Recovered, Season, Own and Opponents'
- 7 Arizona, 2010 (3 own, 4 opp)
- 5 Chi. Bears, 1942 (1 own, 4 opp)
  - Los Angeles, 1952 (1 own, 4 opp)
  - San Francisco, 1965 (1 own, 4 opp)
  - Oakland, 1978 (2 own, 3 opp)
- 4 Chi. Bears, 1948 (1 own, 3 opp)
  - Boston, 1948 (4 opp)
  - Denver, 1979 (1 own, 3 opp)
  - Atlanta, 1981 (1 own, 3 opp)
  - Denver, 1984 (4 opp)

St. Louis, 1987 (4 opp)
Minnesota, 1989 (4 opp)
Atlanta, 1991 (4 opp)
Philadelphia, 1995 (4 opp)
Atlanta, 1998 (4 opp)
New Orleans, 1998 (4 opp)
Kansas City, 1999 (4 opp)
New England, 2012 (1 own, 3 opp)

Most Touchdowns, Own Fumbles Recovered, Season
3 Arizona, 2010
2 Chi. Bears, 1953
   New England, 1973
   Buffalo, 1974
   Denver, 1975
   Oakland, 1978
   Green Bay, 1982
   New Orleans, 1983
   Cleveland, 1986
   Green Bay, 1989
   Miami, 1996
   Buffalo, 2000
   Philadelphia, 2007
   Washington, 2012

Most Touchdowns, Opponents' Fumbles Recovered, Season
4 Detroit, 1937
   Chi. Bears, 1942
   Boston, 1948
   Los Angeles, 1952
   San Francisco, 1965
   Denver, 1984
   St. Louis, 1987
   Minnesota, 1989
   Atlanta, 1991
   Philadelphia, 1995
   Atlanta, 1998
   New Orleans, 1998
   Kansas City, 1999
   Arizona, 2010
3 By many teams

Most Touchdowns, Fumbles Recovered, Game, Own and Opponents'
2 By many teams

Most Touchdowns, Fumbles Recovered, Game, Both Teams, Own and Opponents'
3 Detroit (2) vs. Minnesota (1), Dec. 9, 1962 (2 own, 1 opp)
   Green Bay (2) vs. Dallas (1), Nov. 29, 1964 (3 opp)
   Oakland (2) vs. Buffalo (1), Dec. 24, 1967 (3 opp)
   Oakland (2) vs. Philadelphia (1), Sept. 24, 1995 (3 opp)
   Tennessee (2) vs. Pittsburgh (1), Jan. 2, 2000 (3 opp)

Most Touchdowns, Own Fumbles Recovered, Game
2 Miami vs. New England, Sept.1, 1996

Most Touchdowns, Opponents' Fumbles Recovered, Game
2 Many times. Last time:
     New England vs. N.Y. Jets, Nov. 22, 2012

Most Touchdowns, Opponents' Fumbles Recovered, Game, Both Teams
3 Green Bay (2) vs. Dallas (1), Nov. 29, 1964
   Oakland (2) vs. Buffalo (1), Dec. 24, 1967
   Oakland (2) vs. Philadelphia (1), Sept. 24, 1995
   Tennessee (2) vs. Pittsburgh (1), Jan. 2, 2000

TURNOVERS
(Number of times losing the ball on interceptions and fumbles.)

Most Turnovers, Season
65 Denver, 1961
63 San Francisco, 1978
58 Chi. Bears, 1947
    Pittsburgh, 1950
    N.Y. Giants, 1983

Fewest Turnovers, Season
10 New England, 2010
    San Francisco, 2011
12 Kansas City, 1982
13 Miami, 2008
    N.Y. Giants, 2008

Most Turnovers, Game
12 Detroit vs. Chi. Bears, Nov. 22, 1942
    Chi. Cardinals vs. Philadelphia, Sept. 24, 1950
    Pittsburgh vs. Philadelphia, Dec. 12, 1965
11 San Diego vs. Green Bay, Sept. 24, 1978
10 Washington vs. N.Y. Giants, Dec. 4, 1938
    Pittsburgh vs. Green Bay, Nov. 23, 1941
    Detroit vs. Green Bay, Oct. 24, 1943
    Chi. Cardinals vs. Green Bay, Nov. 10, 1946
    Chi. Cardinals vs. N.Y. Giants, Nov. 2, 1952
    Minnesota vs. Detroit, Dec. 9, 1962
    Houston vs. Oakland, Sept. 7, 1963
    Washington vs. N.Y. Giants, Dec. 8, 1963
    Chicago vs. Detroit, Sept. 22, 1968
    St. Louis vs. Washington, Oct. 25, 1976
    N.Y. Jets vs. New England, Nov. 21, 1976
    San Francisco vs. Dallas, Oct. 12, 1980
    Cleveland vs. Seattle, Dec. 20, 1981
    Detroit vs. Denver, Oct. 7, 1984

Most Turnovers, Both Teams, Game
17 Detroit (12) vs. Chi. Bears (5), Nov. 22, 1942
    Boston (9) vs. Philadelphia (8), Dec. 8, 1946
16 Chi. Cardinals (12) vs. Philadelphia (4), Sept. 24, 1950
    Chi. Cardinals (8) vs. Chi. Bears (8), Dec. 7, 1958
    Minnesota (10) vs. Detroit (6), Dec. 9, 1962
    Houston (9) vs. Kansas City (7), Oct. 12, 1969
15 Philadelphia (8) vs. Chi. Cardinals (7), Oct. 3, 1954
    Denver (9) vs. Houston (6), Dec. 2, 1962
    Washington (10) vs. N.Y. Giants (5), Dec. 8, 1963
    St. Louis (9) vs. Kansas City (6), Oct. 2, 1983

PENALTIES
Most Seasons Leading League, Fewest Penalties
13 Miami, 1968, 1976-1984, 1986, 1990-91
9 Pittsburgh, 1946-47, 1950-52, 1954, 1963, 1965, 1968
8 Boston/New England, 1962, 1964-65, 1973, 1987, 1989, 1993, 2008

Most Consecutive Seasons Leading League, Fewest Penalties
9 Miami, 1976-1984
3 Pittsburgh, 1950-52
2 By many teams

Most Seasons Leading League, Most Penalties
17 Oakland/L.A. Raiders, 1963, 1966, 1968-69, 1975, 1982, 1984, 1991, 1993-96, 2003-05, 2010-11
16 Chi. Bears, 1941-44, 1946-49, 1951, 1959-1961, 1963, 1965, 1968, 1976
8 L.A./St. Louis Rams, 1950, 1952, 1962, 1969, 1978, 1980, 1997, 2012

Most Consecutive Seasons Leading League, Most Penalties
4 Chi. Bears, 1941-44, 1946-49
   Oakland/L.A. Raiders, 1993-96
3 Chi. Cardinals, 1954-56
   Chi. Bears, 1959-1961

Oakland, 2003-05

Fewest Penalties, Season
19　Detroit, 1937
21　Boston, 1935
24　Philadelphia, 1936

Most Penalties, Season
163　Oakland, 2011
158　Kansas City, 1998
156　L.A. Raiders, 1994
　　　Oakland, 1996

Fewest Penalties, Game
0　By many teams. Last time:
　　　New England vs. Houston, Dec. 1, 2013

Most Penalties, Game
22　Brooklyn vs. Green Bay, Sept. 17, 1944
　　　Chi. Bears vs. Philadelphia, Nov. 26, 1944
　　　San Francisco vs. Buffalo, Oct. 4, 1998
21　Cleveland vs. Chi. Bears, Nov. 25, 1951
　　　Baltimore vs. Detroit, Oct. 9, 2005
20　Tampa Bay vs. Seattle, Oct. 17, 1976
　　　Oakland vs. Denver, Dec. 15, 1996
　　　N.Y. Jets vs. Buffalo, Sept. 22, 2013

Fewest Penalties, Both Teams, Game
0　Brooklyn vs. Pittsburgh, Oct. 28, 1934
　　　Brooklyn vs. Boston, Sept. 27, 1936
　　　Cleveland vs. Chi. Bears, Oct. 9, 1938
　　　Pittsburgh vs. Philadelphia, Nov. 10, 1940

Most Penalties, Both Teams, Game
37　Cleveland (21) vs. Chi. Bears (16), Nov. 25, 1951
35　Tampa Bay (20) vs. Seattle (15), Oct. 17, 1976
34　San Francisco (22) vs. Buffalo (12), Oct. 4, 1998

YARDS PENALIZED

Most Seasons Leading League, Fewest Yards Penalized
14　Miami, 1967-68, 1973, 1977-1984, 1990-91, 2010
10　Boston/Washington, 1935, 1953-54, 1956-58,
　　　1970, 1985, 1995, 1997
8　Boston/New England, 1962, 1964-66, 1987, 1989,
　　　1993, 2008

Most Consecutive Seasons Leading League, Fewest Yards Penalized
8　Miami, 1977-1984
3　Washington, 1956-58
　　　Boston, 1964-66
2　By many teams

Most Seasons Leading League, Most Yards Penalized
15　Chi. Bears, 1935, 1937, 1939-1944, 1946-47,
　　　1949, 1951, 1961-62, 1968
14　Oakland/L.A. Raiders, 1963-64, 1968-69, 1975,
　　　1982, 1984, 1991, 1993-94, 1996, 2003,
　　　2010-11
6　Buffalo, 1962, 1967, 1970, 1972, 1981, 1983
　　　Houston, 1961, 1985-86, 1988-1990

Most Consecutive Seasons Leading League, Most Yards Penalized
6　Chi. Bears, 1939-1944
3　Houston, 1988-1990
2　By many teams

Fewest Yards Penalized, Season
139　Detroit, 1937
146　Philadelphia, 1937
159　Philadelphia, 1936

Most Yards Penalized, Season
1,358　Oakland, 2011
1,304　Kansas City, 1998
1,276　Oakland, 2010

Fewest Yards Penalized, Game
0　By many teams. Last time:
　　　New England vs. Houston, Dec. 1, 2013

Most Yards Penalized, Game
212　Tennessee vs. Baltimore, Oct. 10, 1999
209　Cleveland vs. Chi. Bears, Nov. 25, 1951
191　Philadelphia vs. Seattle, Dec. 13, 1992 (ot)

Fewest Yards Penalized, Both Teams, Game
0　Brooklyn vs. Pittsburgh, Oct. 28, 1934
　　　Brooklyn vs. Boston, Sept. 27, 1936
　　　Cleveland vs. Chi. Bears, Oct. 9, 1938
　　　Pittsburgh vs. Philadelphia, Nov. 10, 1940

Most Yards Penalized, Both Teams, Game
374　Cleveland (209) vs. Chi. Bears (165), Nov. 25, 1951
310　Tampa Bay (190) vs. Seattle (120), Oct. 17, 1976
　　　Green Bay (175) vs. Baltimore (135), Dec. 7, 2009
309　Green Bay (184) vs. Boston (125), Oct. 21, 1945

DEFENSE

SCORING

Most Seasons Leading League, Fewest Points Allowed
11　N.Y. Giants, 1927, 1935, 1938-39, 1941, 1944,
　　　1958-59, 1961, 1990, 1993
　　　Chi. Bears, 1932, 1936-37, 1942, 1948, 1963,
　　　1985-86, 1988, 2001, 2005
7　Cleveland, 1951, 1953-57, 1994
　　　Green Bay, 1929, 1935, 1947, 1962, 1965-66, 1996
　　　Pittsburgh, 1946, 1976, 1978, 2004, 2008, 2010-11
6　Dallas/Kansas City, 1960, 1962, 1968-69, 1995,
　　　1997

Most Consecutive Seasons Leading League, Fewest Points Allowed
5　Cleveland, 1953-57
3　Buffalo, 1964-66
　　　Minnesota, 1969-1971
2　By many teams

Fewest Points Allowed, Season (Since 1932)
44　Chi. Bears, 1932
54　Brooklyn, 1933
59　Detroit, 1934

Most Points Allowed, Season
533　Baltimore, 1981
517　Detroit, 2008
501　N.Y. Giants, 1966

Fewest TDs Allowed, Season (Since 1932)
6　Chi. Bears, 1932
　　　Brooklyn, 1933
7　Detroit, 1934
8　Green Bay, 1932

Most Touchdowns Allowed, Season
68　Baltimore, 1981
66　N.Y. Giants, 1966
63　Baltimore, 1950
　　　Detroit, 2008

FIRST DOWNS

Fewest First Downs Allowed, Season
77　Detroit, 1935
79　Boston, 1935
82　Washington, 1937

Most First Downs Allowed, Season
406　Baltimore, 1981
388　Dallas, 2013
380　New Orleans, 2012

Fewest First Downs Allowed, Rushing, Season
35　Chi. Bears, 1942
40　Green Bay, 1939
41　Brooklyn, 1944

Most First Downs Allowed, Rushing, Season
179　Detroit, 1985
178　New Orleans, 1980
175　Seattle, 1981

Fewest First Downs Allowed, Passing, Season
- 33 Chi. Bears, 1943
- 34 Pittsburgh, 1941
  - Washington, 1943
- 35 Detroit, 1940
  - Philadelphia, 1940
  - Philadelphia, 1944

Most First Downs Allowed, Passing, Season
- 247 Minnesota, 2013
- 246 Green Bay, 2011
- 245 New England, 2011

Fewest First Downs Allowed, Penalty, Season
- 1 Boston, 1944
- 3 Philadelphia, 1940
  - Pittsburgh, 1945
  - Washington, 1957
- 4 Cleveland, 1940
  - Green Bay, 1943
  - N.Y. Giants, 1943

Most First Downs Allowed, Penalty, Season
- 58 Oakland, 2011
- 56 Kansas City, 1998
- 48 Houston, 1985

NET YARDS ALLOWED RUSHING AND PASSING
Most Seasons Leading League, Fewest Yards Allowed
- 10 Pittsburgh, 1957, 1974, 1976, 1990, 2001, 2004, 2007-08, 2011-12
- 8 Chi. Bears, 1942-43, 1948, 1958, 1963, 1984-86
- 6 N.Y. Giants, 1938, 1940-41, 1951, 1956, 1959
  - Philadelphia, 1944-45, 1949, 1953, 1981, 1991
  - Minnesota, 1969-1970, 1975, 1988-89, 1993

Most Consecutive Seasons Leading League, Fewest Yards Allowed
- 3 Boston/Washington, 1935-37
  - Chicago, 1984-86
- 2 By many teams

Fewest Yards Allowed, Season
- 1,539 Chi. Cardinals, 1934
- 1,703 Chi. Bears, 1942
- 1,789 Brooklyn, 1933

Most Yards Allowed, Season
- 7,042 New Orleans, 2012
- 6,793 Baltimore, 1981
- 6,645 Dallas, 2013

RUSHING
Most Seasons Leading League, Fewest Yards Allowed
- 10 Chi. Bears, 1937, 1939, 1942, 1946, 1949, 1963, 1984-85, 1987-88
- 8 Pittsburgh, 1961, 1976, 1982, 1997, 2001-02, 2004, 2010
- 7 Detroit, 1938, 1950, 1952, 1962, 1970, 1980-81
  - Philadelphia, 1944-45, 1947-48, 1953, 1990-91
  - Dallas, 1966-69, 1972, 1978, 1992

Most Consecutive Seasons Leading League, Fewest Yards Allowed
- 4 Dallas, 1966-69
- 3 Minnesota, 2006-08
- 2 By many teams

Fewest Yards Allowed, Rushing, Season
- 519 Chi. Bears, 1942
- 558 Philadelphia, 1944
- 762 Pittsburgh, 1982

Most Yards Allowed, Rushing, Season
- 3,228 Buffalo, 1978
- 3,106 New Orleans, 1980
- 3,010 Baltimore, 1978

Fewest Touchdowns Allowed, Rushing, Season
- 2 Detroit, 1934
  - N.Y. Giants, 1944

Dallas, 1968
Minnesota, 1971
- 3 By many teams

Most Touchdowns Allowed, Rushing, Season
- 36 Oakland, 1961
- 31 N.Y. Giants, 1980
  - Tampa Bay, 1986
  - Detroit, 2008
- 30 Baltimore, 1981

PASSING
Most Seasons Leading League, Fewest Yards Allowed
- 10 Green Bay, 1947-48, 1962, 1964-68, 1996, 2005
- 9 Pittsburgh, 1941, 1946, 1951, 1955, 1974, 1990, 2008, 2011-12
- 7 Washington, 1939, 1942, 1945, 1952-53, 1980, 1985
  - Philadelphia 1934, 1936, 1940, 1949, 1981, 1991, 1998

Most Consecutive Seasons Leading League, Fewest Yards Allowed
- 5 Green Bay, 1964-68
- 2 By many teams

Fewest Yards Allowed Passing, Season
- 545 Philadelphia, 1934
- 558 Portsmouth, 1933
- 585 Chi. Cardinals, 1934

Most Yards Allowed, Passing, Season
- 4,796 Green Bay, 2011
- 4,758 Tampa Bay, 2012
- 4,703 New England, 2011

Fewest Touchdowns Allowed, Passing, Season
- 1 Portsmouth, 1932
  - Philadelphia, 1934
- 2 Brooklyn, 1933
  - Chi. Bears, 1934
- 3 Chi. Bears, 1932
  - Green Bay, 1932
  - Green Bay, 1934
  - Chi. Bears, 1936
  - New York, 1939
  - New York, 1944

Most Touchdowns Allowed, Passing, Season
- 40 Denver, 1963
- 38 St. Louis, 1969
- 37 Washington, 1961
  - Baltimore, 1981
  - Minnesota, 2013

SACKS
Most Seasons Leading League
- 5 Oakland/L.A. Raiders, 1966-68, 1982, 1986
  - Dallas, 1966, 1968-69, 1978, 2008
  - L.A./St. Louis Rams, 1968, 1970, 1988, 1999, 2012
- 4 New England/Boston, 1961, 1963, 1977, 1979
  - Dallas/Kansas City, 1960, 1965, 1969, 1990
  - N.Y. Giants, 1963, 1985, 1998, 2007
  - Pittsburgh, 1974, 1994, 2001, 2010
- 3 San Francisco, 1967, 1972, 1976
  - N.Y. Giants, 1963, 1985, 1998
  - New Orleans, 1992, 1997, 2000
  - San Diego, 1962, 1980, 2006
  - Philadelphia, 1991, 2002, 2011

Most Consecutive Seasons Leading League
- 3 Oakland, 1966-68
- 2 Dallas, 1968-69

Most Sacks, Season
- 72 Chicago, 1984
- 71 Minnesota, 1989
- 70 Chicago, 1987

Fewest Sacks, Season
- 10 Kansas City, 2008
- 11 Baltimore, 1982
- 12 Buffalo, 1982

Most Sacks, Game
- 12 Dallas vs. Pittsburgh, Nov. 20, 1966
- St. Louis vs. Baltimore, Oct. 26, 1980
- Chicago vs. Detroit, Dec. 16, 1984
- Dallas vs. Houston, Sept. 29, 1985
- N.Y. Giants vs. Philadelphia, Sept. 30, 2007
- 11 N.Y. Giants vs. St. Louis, Nov. 1, 1964
- Baltimore vs. Los Angeles, Nov. 22, 1964
- Buffalo vs. Denver, Dec. 13, 1964
- Detroit vs. Green Bay, Nov. 7, 1965
- Oakland vs. Buffalo, Oct. 15, 1967
- Oakland vs. Denver, Nov. 5, 1967
- St. Louis vs. Atlanta, Nov. 24, 1968
- Dallas vs. Detroit, Oct. 6, 1975
- St. Louis vs. Philadelphia, Dec. 18, 1983
- Kansas City vs. Cleveland, Sept. 30, 1984
- Chicago vs. Minnesota, Oct. 28, 1984
- Cleveland vs. Atlanta, Nov. 18, 1984
- Detroit vs. Philadelphia, Nov. 16, 1986
- San Diego vs. Dallas, Nov. 16, 1986
- L.A. Raiders vs. Philadelphia, Nov. 30, 1986 (ot)
- Seattle vs. L.A. Raiders, Dec. 8, 1986
- Chicago vs. Philadelphia, Oct. 4, 1987
- Dallas vs. N.Y. Jets, Oct. 4, 1987
- Philadelphia vs. Dallas, Sept. 15, 1991
- Indianapolis vs. Cleveland, Sept. 6, 1992
- San Diego vs. N.Y. Jets, Dec. 23, 2012
- 10 By many teams

Most Opponents Yards Lost Attempting to Pass, Season
- 666 Oakland, 1967
- 583 Chicago, 1984
- 573 San Francisco, 1976

Fewest Opponents Yards Lost Attempting to Pass, Season
- 62 Kansas City, 2008
- 72 Jacksonville, 1995
- 75 Green Bay, 1956

INTERCEPTIONS BY

Most Seasons Leading League
- 10 N.Y. Giants, 1933, 1937-39, 1944, 1948, 1951, 1954, 1961, 1997
- Green Bay, 1940, 1942-43, 1947, 1955, 1957, 1962, 1965, 2009, 2011
- 9 Chi. Bears, 1935-36, 1941-42, 1946, 1963, 1985, 1990, 2012
- 6 Kansas City, 1966-1970, 1974

Most Consecutive Seasons Leading League
- 5 Kansas City, 1966-1970
- 3 N.Y. Giants, 1937-39
- 2 By many teams

Most Passes Intercepted, Season
- 49 San Diego, 1961
- 42 Green Bay, 1943
- 41 N.Y. Giants, 1951

Fewest Passes Intercepted By, Season
- 3 Houston, 1982
- 4 Detroit, 2008
- 5 Baltimore, 1982
- Oakland, 2005

Most Passes Intercepted By, Game
- 9 Green Bay vs. Detroit, Oct. 24, 1943
- Philadelphia vs. Pittsburgh, Dec. 12, 1965
- 8 N.Y. Giants vs. Green Bay, Nov. 21, 1948
- Philadelphia vs. Chi. Cardinals, Sept. 24, 1950
- N.Y. Giants vs. N.Y. Yanks, Dec. 16, 1951
- Houston vs. Denver, Dec. 2, 1962

- Detroit vs. Chicago, Sept. 22, 1968
- N.Y. Jets vs. Baltimore, Sept. 23, 1973
- 7 By many teams. Last time:
- Cleveland vs. Detroit, Sept. 23, 2001

Most Consecutive Games, One or More Interceptions By
- 46 L.A. Chargers/San Diego, 1960-63
- 37 Detroit, 1960-63
- 36 Boston, 1944-47

Most Yards Returning Interception, Season
- 929 San Diego, 1961
- 712 Los Angeles, 1952
- 700 Baltimore, 2004

Fewest Yards Returning Interceptions, Season
- 5 Los Angeles, 1959
- 16 Detroit, 2008
- 25 Washington, 2006

Most Yards Returning Interceptions, Game
- 325 Seattle vs. Kansas City, Nov. 4, 1984
- 314 Los Angeles vs. San Francisco, Oct. 18, 1964
- 245 Houston vs. N.Y. Jets, Oct. 15, 1967

Most Yards Returning Interceptions, Both Teams, Game
- 356 Seattle (325) vs. Kansas City (31), Nov. 4, 1984
- 338 Los Angeles (314) vs. San Francisco (24), Oct. 18, 1964
- 308 Dallas (182) vs. Los Angeles (126), Nov. 2, 1952

Most Touchdowns, Returning Interceptions, Season
- 9 San Diego, 1961
- 8 Seattle, 1998
- Chicago, 2012
- 7 Seattle, 1984
- St. Louis, 1999

Most Touchdowns Returning Interceptions, Game
- 4 Seattle vs. Kansas City, Nov. 4, 1984
- 3 Baltimore vs. Green Bay, Nov. 5, 1950
- Cleveland vs. Chicago, Dec. 11, 1960
- Philadelphia vs. Pittsburgh, Dec. 12, 1965
- Baltimore vs. Pittsburgh, Sept. 29, 1968
- Buffalo vs. N.Y. Jets, Sept. 29, 1968
- Houston vs. San Diego, Dec. 19, 1971
- Cincinnati vs. Houston, Dec. 17, 1972
- Tampa Bay vs. New Orleans, Dec. 11, 1977
- Minnesota vs. N.Y. Giants, Nov. 25, 2007
- 2 By many teams

Most Touchdown Returning Interceptions, Both Teams, Game
- 4 Philadelphia (3) vs. Pittsburgh (1), Dec. 12, 1965
- Seattle (4) vs. Kansas City (0), Nov. 4, 1984
- 3 Los Angeles (2) vs. Detroit (1), Nov. 1, 1953
- Cleveland (2) vs. N.Y. Giants (1), Dec. 18, 1960
- Pittsburgh (2) vs. Cincinnati (1), Oct. 10, 1983
- Kansas City (2) vs. San Diego (1), Oct. 19, 1986
- Arizona (2) vs. St. Louis (1), Dec. 30, 2007
- (Also see previous record)

PUNT RETURNS

Fewest Opponents Punt Returns, Season
- 7 Washington, 1962
- San Diego, 1982
- 10 Buffalo, 1982
- 11 Boston, 1962
- New England, 2008

Most Opponents Punt Returns, Season
- 71 Tampa Bay, 1976, 1977
- 69 N.Y. Giants, 1953
- Cleveland, 2000
- 68 Cleveland, 1974
- Cleveland, 1999

Fewest Yards Allowed, Punt Returns, Season
- 22 Green Bay, 1967
- 30 Buffalo, 1982
- 34 Washington, 1962

Most Yards Allowed, Punt Returns, Season
- 932   Green Bay, 1949
- 913   Boston, 1947
- 906   New Orleans, 1974

Lowest Avg. Allowed, Punt Returns, Season
- 1.20   Chi. Cardinals, 1954
- 1.22   Cleveland, 1959
- 1.55   Chi. Cardinals, 1953

Highest Average Allowed, Punt Returns, Season
- 18.9   San Diego, 2010 (28-528)
- 18.6   Green Bay, 1949 (50-932)
- 18.0   Cleveland, 1977 (31-558)

Most Touchdowns Allowed, Punt Returns, Season
- 4   Los Angeles, 1951
-    N.Y. Giants, 1959
-    Atlanta, 1992
-    Minnesota, 2008
- 3   Green Bay, 1949
-    Chi. Cardinals, 1951
-    L.A. Rams, 1951, 1994
-    Washington, 1952
-    Dallas, 1952
-    Pittsburgh, 1959, 1993
-    N.Y. Jets, 1968
-    Cleveland, 1977
-    Atlanta, 1986
-    Tampa Bay, 1986
-    Arizona, 2002
-    Cincinnati, 2002
-    Tennessee, 2002
-    Carolina, 2011
-    N.Y. Giants, 2013
-    Washington, 2013
- 2   By many teams

KICKOFF RETURNS

Fewest Opponents Kickoff Returns, Season
- 10   Brooklyn, 1943
- 13   Denver, 1992
- 15   Detroit, 1942
-    Brooklyn, 1944

Most Opponents Kickoff Returns, Season
- 93   Indianapolis, 2003
- 92   Indianapolis, 2004
-    New England, 2007
- 91   Washington, 1983
-    Minnesota, 2009

Fewest Yards Allowed, Kickoff Returns, Season
- 225   Brooklyn, 1943
- 254   Denver, 1992
- 293   Brooklyn, 1944

Most Yards Allowed, Kickoff Returns, Season
- 2,194   St. Louis, 2001
- 2,115   St. Louis, 1999
- 2,060   Minnesota, 2009

Lowest Average Allowed, Kickoff Returns, Season
- 14.3   Cleveland, 1980
- 14.9   Indianapolis, 1993
- 15.0   Seattle, 1982

Highest Average Allowed, Kickoff Returns, Season
- 30.7   Indianapolis, 2011 (19-584)
- 29.5   N.Y. Jets, 1972 (47-1,386)
- 29.4   Los Angeles, 1950 (48-1,411)

Most Touchdowns Allowed, Kickoff Returns, Season
- 4   Minnesota, 1998
-    Pittsburgh, 2009
- 3   Minnesota, 1963, 1970
-    Dallas, 1966
-    Detroit, 1980
-    Pittsburgh, 1986

-    Buffalo, 1997
-    Atlanta, 2000
-    Arizona, 2005
-    Indianapolis, 2007
-    San Diego, 2010
- 2   By many teams

FUMBLES

Fewest Opponents Fumbles, Season
- 11   Cleveland, 1956
-    Baltimore, 1982
-    Tennessee, 1998
-    San Diego, 2011
-    Indianapolis, 2012
- 12   Green Bay, 1995
-    Cincinnati, 1998
-    Jacksonville, 2006
-    Baltimore, 2007
-    Jacksonville, 2010
- 13   Los Angeles, 1956
-    Chicago, 1960
-    Cleveland, 1963
-    Cleveland, 1965
-    Detroit, 1967
-    San Diego, 1969
-    New England, 2005
-    Cleveland, 2006
-    San Diego, 2010
-    Oakland, 2011
-    Pittsburgh, 2011
-    Cleveland, 2013

Most Opponents Fumbles, Season
- 50   Minnesota, 1963
-    San Francisco, 1978
- 48   N.Y. Giants, 1980
-    N.Y. Jets, 1986
- 47   N.Y. Giants, 1977
-    Seattle, 1984

TURNOVERS

(Number of times losing the ball on interceptions and fumbles.)

Fewest Opponents Turnovers, Season
- 11   Baltimore, 1982
-    Houston, 2013
- 12   Washington, 2006
- 13   San Francisco, 1982
-    Denver, 2008
-    Kansas City, 2012
-    Philadelphia 2012

Most Opponent Turnovers, Season
- 66   San Diego, 1961
- 63   Seattle, 1984
- 61   Washington, 1983

Most Opponent Turnovers, Game
- 12   Chi. Bears vs. Detroit, Nov. 22, 1942
-    Philadelphia vs. Chi. Cardinals, Sept. 24, 1950
-    Philadelphia vs. Pittsburgh, Dec. 12, 1965
- 11   Green Bay vs. San Diego, Sept. 24, 1978
- 10   By 14 teams

1,000 YARDS RUSHING IN A SEASON

Year	Player, Team	Att.	Yards	Avg.	Long	TD
2013	LeSean McCoy, Philadelphia[3]	314	1,607	5.1	57	9
	Matt Forté, Chicago[4]	289	1,339	4.6	55	9
	Jamaal Charles, Kansas City[4]	259	1,287	5.0	46	12
	Alfred Morris, Washington[2]	276	1,275	4.6	45	7
	Adrian Peterson, Minnesota[6]	279	1,266	4.5	78	10
	Marshawn Lynch, Seattle[5]	301	1,257	4.2	43	12
	Ryan Mathews, San Diego[2]	285	1,255	4.4	51	6
	*Eddie Lacy, Green Bay	284	1,178	4.1	60	11
	Frank Gore, San Francisco[7]	276	1,128	4.1	51	9
	DeMarco Murray, Dallas	217	1,121	5.2	43	9
	Chris Johnson, Tennessee[6]	279	1,077	3.9	30	6
	Knowshon Moreno, Denver	241	1,038	4.3	31	10
	Reggie Bush, Detroit[2]	223	1,006	4.5	39	4
2012	Adrian Peterson, Minnesota[5]	348	2,097	6.0	82	12
	*Alfred Morris, Washington	335	1,613	4.8	39	13
	Marshawn Lynch, Seattle[4]	315	1,590	5.0	77	11
	Jamaal Charles, Kansas City[3]	285	1,509	5.3	91	5
	*Doug Martin, Tampa Bay	319	1,454	4.6	70	11
	Arian Foster, Houston[3]	351	1,424	4.1	46	15
	Stevan Ridley, New England	290	1,263	4.4	41	12
	C.J. Spiller, Buffalo	207	1,244	6.0	62	6
	Chris Johnson, Tennessee[5]	276	1,243	4.5	94	6
	Frank Gore, San Francisco[6]	258	1,214	4.7	37	8
	Ray Rice, Baltimore[4]	257	1,143	4.4	46	9
	Matt Forté, Chicago[3]	248	1,094	4.4	46	5
	BenJarvus Green-Ellis, Cincinnati[2]	278	1,094	3.9	48	6
	Shonn Greene, N.Y. Jets[2]	276	1,063	3.9	36	8
	Steven Jackson, St. Louis[8]	257	1,042	4.1	46	4
	Ahmad Bradshaw, N.Y. Giants[2]	221	1,015	4.6	37	6
2011	Maurice Jones-Drew, Jacksonville[3]	343	1,606	4.7	56	8
	Ray Rice, Baltimore[3]	291	1,364	4.7	70	12
	Michael Turner, Atlanta[3]	301	1,340	4.5	81	11
	LeSean McCoy, Philadelphia[2]	273	1,309	4.8	60	17
	Arian Foster, Houston[2]	278	1,224	4.4	43	10
	Frank Gore, San Francisco[5]	282	1,211	4.3	55	8
	Marshawn Lynch, Seattle[3]	285	1,204	4.2	47	12
	Willis McGahee, Denver[4]	249	1,199	4.8	60	4
	Steven Jackson, St. Louis[7]	260	1,145	4.4	47	5
	Ryan Mathews, San Diego	222	1,091	4.9	39	6
	Reggie Bush, Miami	216	1,086	5.0	76	6
	Cedric Benson, Cincinnati[3]	273	1,067	3.9	42	6
	Shonn Greene, N.Y. Jets	253	1,054	4.2	31	6
	Chris Johnson, Tennessee[4]	262	1,047	4.0	48	4
	Beanie Wells, Arizona	245	1,047	4.3	71	10
2010	Arian Foster, Houston	327	1,616	4.9	74	16
	Jamaal Charles, Kansas City[2]	230	1,467	6.4	80	5
	Michael Turner, Atlanta[2]	334	1,371	4.1	55	12
	Chris Johnson, Tennessee[3]	316	1,364	4.3	76	11
	Maurice Jones-Drew, Jacksonville[2]	299	1,324	4.4	37	5
	Adrian Peterson, Minnesota[4]	283	1,298	4.6	80	12
	Rashard Mendenhall, Pittsburgh[2]	324	1,273	3.9	50	13
	Steven Jackson, St. Louis[6]	330	1,241	3.8	42	6
	Ahmad Bradshaw, N.Y. Giants	276	1,235	4.5	48	8
	Ray Rice, Baltimore[2]	307	1,220	4.0	50	5
	Peyton Hillis, Cleveland	270	1,177	4.4	48	11
	Darren McFadden, Oakland	223	1,157	5.2	57	7
	Cedric Benson, Cincinnati[2]	321	1,111	3.5	26	7
	LeSean McCoy, Philadelphia	207	1,080	5.2	62	7
	Matt Forté, Chicago[2]	237	1,069	4.5	68	6
	BenJarvus Green-Ellis, New England	229	1,008	4.4	33	13
	*LeGarrette Blount, Tampa Bay	201	1,007	5.0	53	6
2009	Chris Johnson, Tennessee[2]	358	2,006	5.6	91	14
	Steven Jackson, St. Louis[5]	324	1,416	4.8	58	4
	Thomas Jones, N.Y. Jets[5]	331	1,402	4.2	71	14
	Maurice Jones-Drew, Jacksonville	312	1,391	4.5	80	15
	Adrian Peterson, Minnesota[3]	314	1,383	4.4	64	18
	Ray Rice, Baltimore	254	1,339	5.3	59	7
	Ryan Grant, Green Bay[2]	282	1,253	4.4	62	11

Year	Player, Team	Att.	Yards	Avg.	Long	TD
	Cedric Benson, Cincinnati	301	1,251	4.2	42	6
	Jonathan Stewart, Carolina	221	1,133	5.1	67	10
	Ricky Williams, Miami[5]	241	1,121	4.6	68	11
	Jamaal Charles, Kansas City	190	1,120	5.9	76	7
	Frank Gore, San Francisco[4]	229	1,120	4.9	80	10
	DeAngelo Williams, Carolina[2]	216	1,117	5.2	77	7
	Rashard Mendenhall, Pittsburgh	242	1,108	4.6	60	7
	Fred Jackson, Buffalo	237	1,062	4.5	43	2
2008	Adrian Peterson, Minnesota[2]	363	1,760	4.9	67	10
	Michael Turner, Atlanta	376	1,699	4.5	70	17
	DeAngelo Williams, Carolina	273	1,515	5.6	69	18
	Clinton Portis, Washington[6]	342	1,487	4.4	31	9
	Thomas Jones, N.Y. Jets[4]	290	1,312	4.5	59	13
	*Steve Slaton, Houston	268	1,282	4.8	71	9
	*Matt Forté, Chicago	316	1,238	3.9	50	8
	*Chris Johnson, Tennessee	251	1,228	4.9	66	9
	Ryan Grant, Green Bay	312	1,203	3.9	57	4
	LaDainian Tomlinson, San Diego[8]	292	1,110	3.8	45	11
	Brandon Jacobs, N.Y. Giants[2]	219	1,089	5.0	44	15
	Steven Jackson, St. Louis[4]	253	1,042	4.1	56	7
	Frank Gore, San Francisco[3]	240	1,036	4.3	41	6
	Marshawn Lynch, Buffalo[2]	250	1,036	4.1	50	8
	Derrick Ward, N.Y. Giants	182	1,025	5.6	51	2
	Jamal Lewis, Cleveland[7]	279	1,002	3.6	29	4
2007	LaDainian Tomlinson, San Diego[7]	315	1,474	4.7	49	15
	*Adrian Peterson, Minnesota	238	1,341	5.6	73	12
	Brian Westbrook, Philadelphia[2]	278	1,333	4.8	36	7
	Willie Parker, Pittsburgh[3]	321	1,316	4.1	32	2
	Jamal Lewis, Cleveland[6]	298	1,304	4.4	66	9
	Clinton Portis, Washington[5]	325	1,262	3.9	32	11
	Edgerrin James, Arizona[7]	324	1,222	3.8	27	7
	Willis McGahee, Baltimore[3]	294	1,207	4.1	46	7
	Fred Taylor, Jacksonville[7]	223	1,202	5.4	80	5
	Thomas Jones, N.Y. Jets[3]	310	1,119	3.6	36	1
	*Marshawn Lynch, Buffalo	280	1,115	4.0	56	7
	LenDale White, Tennessee	303	1,110	3.7	28	7
	Frank Gore, San Francisco[2]	260	1,102	4.2	43	5
	Joseph Addai, Indianapolis[2]	261	1,072	4.1	23	12
	Justin Fargas, Oakland	222	1,009	4.6	48	4
	Brandon Jacobs, N.Y. Giants	202	1,009	5.0	43	4
	Steven Jackson, St. Louis[3]	237	1,002	4.2	54	5
2006	LaDainian Tomlinson, San Diego[6]	348	1,815	5.2	85	28
	Larry Johnson, Kansas City[2]	416	1,789	4.3	47	17
	Frank Gore, San Francisco	312	1,695	5.4	72	8
	Tiki Barber, N.Y. Giants[6]	327	1,662	5.1	55	5
	Steven Jackson, St. Louis[2]	346	1,528	4.4	59	13
	Willie Parker, Pittsburgh[2]	337	1,494	4.4	76	13
	Rudi Johnson, Cincinnati[3]	341	1,309	3.8	22	12
	Brian Westbrook, Philadelphia	240	1,217	5.1	71	7
	Chester Taylor, Minnesota	303	1,216	4.0	95	6
	Travis Henry, Tennessee[3]	270	1,211	4.5	70	7
	Thomas Jones, Chicago[2]	296	1,210	4.1	30	6
	Edgerrin James, Arizona[6]	337	1,159	3.4	18	6
	Ladell Betts, Washington	245	1,154	4.7	26	4
	Fred Taylor, Jacksonville[6]	231	1,146	5.0	76	5
	Warrick Dunn, Atlanta[5]	286	1,140	4.0	90	4
	Jamal Lewis, Baltimore[5]	314	1,132	3.6	52	9
	Julius Jones, Dallas	267	1,084	4.1	77	4
	*Joseph Addai, Indianapolis	226	1,081	4.8	41	7
	Ahman Green, Green Bay[6]	266	1,059	4.0	70	5
	Deuce McAllister, New Orleans[4]	244	1,057	4.3	57	10
	Michael Vick, Atlanta	123	1,039	8.5	51	2
	Tatum Bell, Denver	233	1,025	4.4	51	2
	Ronnie Brown, Miami	241	1,008	4.2	47	5
2005	Shaun Alexander, Seattle[5]	370	1,880	5.1	88	27
	Tiki Barber, N.Y. Giants[5]	357	1,860	5.2	95	9
	Larry Johnson, Kansas City	336	1,750	5.2	49	20
	Clinton Portis, Washington[4]	352	1,516	4.3	47	11
	Edgerrin James, Indianapolis[5]	360	1,506	4.2	33	13

Year	Player, Team	Att.	Yards	Avg.	Long	TD
	LaDainian Tomlinson, San Diego[5]	339	1,462	4.3	62	18
	Rudi Johnson, Cincinnati[2]	337	1,458	4.3	33	12
	Warrick Dunn, Atlanta[4]	280	1,416	5.1	65	3
	Thomas Jones, Chicago	314	1,335	4.3	42	9
	Willis McGahee, Buffalo[2]	325	1,247	3.8	27	5
	Reuben Droughns, Cleveland[2]	309	1,232	4.0	75	2
	Willie Parker, Pittsburgh	255	1,202	4.7	80	4
	*Carnell Williams, Tampa Bay	290	1,178	4.1	71	6
	Steven Jackson, St. Louis	254	1,046	4.1	51	8
	LaMont Jordan, Oakland	272	1,025	3.8	26	9
	Mike Anderson, Denver[2]	239	1,014	4.2	44	12
2004	Curtis Martin, N.Y. Jets[10]	371	1,697	4.6	25	12
	Shaun Alexander, Seattle[4]	353	1,696	4.8	44	16
	Corey Dillon, New England[7]	345	1,635	4.7	44	12
	Edgerrin James, Indianapolis[4]	334	1,548	4.6	40	9
	Tiki Barber, N.Y. Giants[4]	322	1,518	4.7	72	13
	Rudi Johnson, Cincinnati	361	1,454	4.0	52	12
	LaDainian Tomlinson, San Diego[4]	339	1,335	3.9	42	17
	Clinton Portis, Washington[3]	343	1,315	3.8	64	5
	Reuben Droughns, Denver	275	1,240	4.5	51	6
	Fred Taylor, Jacksonville[5]	260	1,224	4.7	46	2
	Domanick Davis, Houston[2]	302	1,188	3.9	44	13
	Ahman Green, Green Bay[6]	259	1,163	4.5	90	7
	*Kevin Jones, Detroit	241	1,133	4.7	74	5
	Willis McGahee, Buffalo	284	1,128	4.0	41	13
	Warrick Dunn, Atlanta[3]	265	1,106	4.2	60	9
	Deuce McAllister, New Orleans[3]	269	1,074	4.0	71	9
	Chris Brown, Tennessee	220	1,067	4.9	52	6
	Jamal Lewis, Baltimore[4]	235	1,006	4.3	75	7
2003	Jamal Lewis, Baltimore[3]	387	2,066	5.3	82	14
	Ahman Green, Green Bay[4]	355	1,883	5.3	98	15
	LaDainian Tomlinson, San Diego[3]	313	1,645	5.3	73	13
	Deuce McAllister, New Orleans[2]	351	1,641	4.7	76	8
	Clinton Portis, Denver[2]	290	1,591	5.5	65	14
	Fred Taylor, Jacksonville[4]	345	1,572	4.6	62	6
	Stephen Davis, Carolina[4]	318	1,444	4.5	40	8
	Shaun Alexander, Seattle[3]	326	1,435	4.4	55	14
	Priest Holmes, Kansas City[4]	320	1,420	4.4	31	27
	Ricky Williams, Miami[4]	392	1,372	3.5	45	9
	Travis Henry, Buffalo[2]	331	1,356	4.1	64	10
	Curtis Martin, N.Y. Jets[9]	323	1,308	4.1	56	2
	Edgerrin James, Indianapolis[3]	310	1,259	4.1	43	11
	Tiki Barber, N.Y. Giants[3]	278	1,216	4.4	27	2
	*Domanick Davis, Houston	238	1,031	4.3	51	8
	Eddie George, Tennessee[7]	312	1,031	3.3	27	5
	Kevan Barlow, San Francisco	201	1,024	5.1	78	6
	Anthony Thomas, Chicago[2]	244	1,024	4.2	67	6
2002	Ricky Williams, Miami[3]	383	1,853	4.8	63	16
	LaDainian Tomlinson, San Diego[2]	372	1,683	4.5	76	14
	Priest Holmes, Kansas City[3]	313	1,615	5.2	56	21
	*Clinton Portis, Denver	273	1,508	5.5	59	15
	Travis Henry, Buffalo	325	1,438	4.4	34	13
	Deuce McAllister, New Orleans	325	1,388	4.3	62	13
	Tiki Barber, N.Y. Giants[2]	304	1,387	4.6	70	11
	Jamal Lewis, Baltimore[2]	308	1,327	4.3	75	6
	Fred Taylor, Jacksonville[3]	287	1,314	4.6	63	8
	Corey Dillon, Cincinnati[6]	314	1,311	4.2	67	7
	Michael Bennett, Minnesota	255	1,296	5.1	85	5
	Ahman Green, Green Bay[3]	286	1,240	4.3	43	7
	Shaun Alexander, Seattle[2]	295	1,175	4.0	58	16
	Eddie George, Tennessee[6]	343	1,165	3.4	35	12
	Curtis Martin, N.Y. Jets[8]	261	1,094	4.2	35	7
	Duce Staley, Philadelphia[3]	269	1,029	3.8	57	5
	James Stewart, Detroit[2]	231	1,021	4.4	56	4
2001	Priest Holmes, Kansas City[2]	327	1,555	4.8	41	8
	Curtis Martin, N.Y. Jets[7]	333	1,513	4.5	47	10
	Stephen Davis, Washington[3]	356	1,432	4.0	32	5
	Ahman Green, Green Bay[2]	304	1,387	4.6	83	9
	Marshall Faulk, St. Louis[7]	260	1,382	5.3	71	12

Year	Player, Team	Att.	Yards	Avg.	Long	TD
	Shaun Alexander, Seattle	309	1,318	4.3	88	14
	Corey Dillon, Cincinnati[5]	340	1,315	3.9	96	10
	Ricky Williams, New Orleans[2]	313	1,245	4.0	46	6
	*LaDainian Tomlinson, San Diego	339	1,236	3.6	54	10
	Garrison Hearst, San Francisco[4]	252	1,206	4.8	43	4
	*Anthony Thomas, Chicago	278	1,183	4.3	46	7
	Antowain Smith, New England[2]	287	1,157	4.0	44	12
	*Dominic Rhodes, Indianapolis	233	1,104	4.7	77	9
	Jerome Bettis, Pittsburgh[8]	225	1,072	4.8	48	4
	Emmitt Smith, Dallas[11]	261	1,021	3.9	44	3
2000	Edgerrin James, Indianapolis[2]	387	1,709	4.4	30	13
	Robert Smith, Minnesota[4]	295	1,521	5.2	72	7
	Eddie George, Tennessee[5]	403	1,509	3.7	35	14
	*Mike Anderson, Denver	297	1,487	5.0	80	15
	Corey Dillon, Cincinnati[4]	315	1,435	4.6	80	7
	Fred Taylor, Jacksonville[2]	292	1,399	4.8	71	12
	*Jamal Lewis, Baltimore	309	1,364	4.4	45	6
	Marshall Faulk, St. Louis[6]	253	1,359	5.4	36	18
	Jerome Bettis, Pittsburgh[7]	355	1,341	3.8	30	8
	Stephen Davis, Washington[2]	332	1,318	4.0	50	11
	Ricky Watters, Seattle[7]	278	1,242	4.5	55	7
	Curtis Martin, N.Y. Jets[6]	316	1,204	3.8	55	9
	Emmitt Smith, Dallas[10]	294	1,203	4.1	52	9
	James Stewart, Detroit	339	1,184	3.5	34	10
	Ahman Green, Green Bay	263	1,175	4.5	39	10
	Charlie Garner, San Francisco[2]	258	1,142	4.4	42	7
	Lamar Smith, Miami	309	1,139	3.7	68	14
	Warrick Dunn, Tampa Bay[2]	248	1,133	4.6	70	8
	James Allen, Chicago	290	1,120	3.9	29	2
	Tyrone Wheatley, Oakland	232	1,046	4.5	80	9
	Jamal Anderson, Atlanta[4]	282	1,024	3.6	42	6
	Tiki Barber, N.Y. Giants	213	1,006	4.7	78	8
	Ricky Williams, New Orleans	248	1,000	4.0	26	8
1999	*Edgerrin James, Indianapolis	369	1,553	4.2	72	13
	Curtis Martin, N.Y. Jets[5]	367	1,464	4.0	50	5
	Stephen Davis, Washington	290	1,405	4.8	76	17
	Emmitt Smith, Dallas[9]	329	1,397	4.3	63	11
	Marshall Faulk, St. Louis[5]	253	1,381	5.5	58	7
	Eddie George, Tennessee[4]	320	1,304	4.1	40	9
	Duce Staley, Philadelphia[2]	325	1,273	3.9	29	4
	Charlie Garner, San Francisco	241	1,229	5.1	53	4
	Ricky Watters, Seattle[6]	325	1,210	3.7	45	5
	Corey Dillon, Cincinnati[3]	263	1,200	4.6	50	5
	*Olandis Gary, Denver	276	1,159	4.2	71	7
	Jerome Bettis, Pittsburgh[6]	299	1,091	3.7	35	7
	Dorsey Levens, Green Bay[2]	279	1,034	3.7	36	9
	Robert Smith, Minnesota[3]	221	1,015	4.6	70	2
1998	Terrell Davis, Denver[4]	392	2,008	5.1	70	21
	Jamal Anderson, Atlanta[3]	410	1,846	4.5	48	14
	Garrison Hearst, San Francisco[3]	310	1,570	5.1	96	7
	Barry Sanders, Detroit[10]	343	1,491	4.3	73	4
	Emmitt Smith, Dallas[8]	319	1,332	4.2	32	13
	Marshall Faulk, Indianapolis[4]	324	1,319	4.1	68	6
	Eddie George, Tennessee[3]	348	1,294	3.7	37	5
	Curtis Martin, N.Y. Jets[4]	369	1,287	3.5	60	8
	Ricky Watters, Seattle[5]	319	1,239	3.9	39	9
	*Fred Taylor, Jacksonville	264	1,223	4.6	77	14
	Robert Smith, Minnesota[2]	249	1,187	4.8	74	6
	Jerome Bettis, Pittsburgh[5]	316	1,185	3.8	42	3
	Corey Dillon, Cincinnati[2]	262	1,130	4.3	66	4
	Antowain Smith, Buffalo	300	1,124	3.7	30	8
	*Robert Edwards, New England	291	1,115	3.8	53	9
	Duce Staley, Philadelphia	258	1,065	4.1	64	5
	Gary Brown, N.Y. Giants[2]	247	1,063	4.3	45	5
	Adrian Murrell, Arizona[3]	274	1,042	3.8	32	8
	Warrick Dunn, Tampa Bay	245	1,026	4.2	50	2
	Priest Holmes, Baltimore	233	1,008	4.3	56	7
1997	Barry Sanders, Detroit[9]	335	2,053	6.1	82	11
	Terrell Davis, Denver[3]	369	1,750	4.7	50	15

Year	Player, Team	Att.	Yards	Avg.	Long	TD
	Jerome Bettis, Pittsburgh[4]	375	1,665	4.4	34	7
	Dorsey Levens, Green Bay	329	1,435	4.4	52	7
	Eddie George, Tennessee[2]	357	1,399	3.9	30	6
	Napoleon Kaufman, Oakland	272	1,294	4.8	83	6
	Robert Smith, Minnesota	232	1,266	5.5	78	6
	Curtis Martin, New England[3]	274	1,160	4.2	70	4
	*Corey Dillon, Cincinnati	233	1,129	4.8	71	10
	Ricky Watters, Philadelphia[4]	285	1,110	3.9	28	7
	Adrian Murrell, N.Y. Jets[2]	300	1,086	3.6	43	7
	Emmitt Smith, Dallas[7]	261	1,074	4.1	44	4
	Marshall Faulk, Indianapolis[3]	264	1,054	4.0	45	7
	Raymont Harris, Chicago	275	1,033	3.8	68	10
	Garrison Hearst, San Francisco[2]	234	1,019	4.4	51	4
	Jamal Anderson, Atlanta[2]	290	1,002	3.5	39	7
1996	Barry Sanders, Detroit[8]	307	1,553	5.1	54	11
	Terrell Davis, Denver[2]	345	1,538	4.5	71	13
	Jerome Bettis, Pittsburgh[3]	320	1,431	4.5	50	11
	Ricky Watters, Philadelphia[3]	353	1,411	4.0	56	13
	*Eddie George, Houston	335	1,368	4.1	76	8
	Terry Allen, Washington[4]	347	1,353	3.9	49	21
	Adrian Murrell, N.Y. Jets	301	1,249	4.1	78	6
	Emmitt Smith, Dallas[6]	327	1,204	3.7	42	12
	Curtis Martin, New England[2]	316	1,152	3.6	57	14
	Anthony Johnson, Carolina	300	1,120	3.7	29	6
	*Karim Abdul-Jabbar, Miami	307	1,116	3.6	29	11
	Jamal Anderson, Atlanta	232	1,055	4.5	32	5
	Thurman Thomas, Buffalo[8]	281	1,033	3.7	36	8
1995	Emmitt Smith, Dallas[5]	377	1,773	4.7	60	25
	Barry Sanders, Detroit[7]	314	1,500	4.8	75	11
	*Curtis Martin, New England	368	1,487	4.0	49	14
	Chris Warren, Seattle[4]	310	1,346	4.3	52	15
	Terry Allen, Washington[3]	338	1,309	3.9	28	10
	Ricky Watters, Philadelphia[2]	337	1,273	3.8	57	11
	Errict Rhett, Tampa Bay[2]	332	1,207	3.6	21	11
	Rodney Hampton, N.Y. Giants[5]	306	1,182	3.9	32	10
	*Terrell Davis, Denver	237	1,117	4.7	60	7
	Harvey Williams, Oakland	255	1,114	4.4	60	9
	Craig Heyward, Atlanta	236	1,083	4.6	31	6
	Marshall Faulk, Indianapolis[2]	289	1,078	3.7	40	11
	*Rashaan Salaam, Chicago	296	1,074	3.6	42	10
	Garrison Hearst, Arizona	284	1,070	3.8	38	1
	Edgar Bennett, Green Bay	316	1,067	3.4	23	3
	Thurman Thomas, Buffalo[7]	267	1,005	3.8	49	6
1994	Barry Sanders, Detroit[6]	331	1,883	5.7	85	7
	Chris Warren, Seattle[3]	333	1,545	4.6	41	9
	Emmitt Smith, Dallas[4]	368	1,484	4.0	46	21
	Natrone Means, San Diego	343	1,350	3.9	25	12
	*Marshall Faulk, Indianapolis	314	1,282	4.1	52	11
	Thurman Thomas, Buffalo[6]	287	1,093	3.8	29	7
	Rodney Hampton, N.Y. Giants[4]	327	1,075	3.3	27	6
	Terry Allen, Minnesota[2]	255	1,031	4.0	45	8
	Jerome Bettis, L.A. Rams[2]	319	1,025	3.2	19	3
	*Errict Rhett, Tampa Bay	284	1,011	3.6	27	7
1993	Emmitt Smith, Dallas[3]	283	1,486	5.3	62	9
	*Jerome Bettis, L.A. Rams	294	1,429	4.9	71	7
	Thurman Thomas, Buffalo[5]	355	1,315	3.7	27	6
	Erric Pegram, Atlanta	292	1,185	4.1	29	3
	Barry Sanders, Detroit[5]	243	1,115	4.6	42	3
	Leonard Russell, New England	300	1,088	3.6	21	7
	Rodney Hampton, N.Y. Giants[3]	292	1,077	3.7	20	5
	Chris Warren, Seattle[2]	273	1,072	3.9	45	7
	*Reggie Brooks, Washington	223	1,063	4.8	85	3
	*Ron Moore, Phoenix	263	1,018	3.9	20	9
	Gary Brown, Houston	195	1,002	5.1	26	6
1992	Emmitt Smith, Dallas[2]	373	1,713	4.6	68	18
	Barry Foster, Pittsburgh	390	1,690	4.3	69	11
	Thurman Thomas, Buffalo[4]	312	1,487	4.8	44	9
	Barry Sanders, Detroit[4]	312	1,352	4.3	55	9
	Lorenzo White, Houston	265	1,226	4.6	44	7

Year	Player, Team	Att.	Yards	Avg.	Long	TD
	Terry Allen, Minnesota	266	1,201	4.5	51	13
	Reggie Cobb, Tampa Bay	310	1,171	3.8	25	9
	Harold Green, Cincinnati	265	1,170	4.4	53	2
	Rodney Hampton, N.Y. Giants[2]	257	1,141	4.4	63	14
	Cleveland Gary, L.A. Rams	279	1,125	4.0	63	7
	Herschel Walker, Philadelphia[2]	267	1,070	4.0	38	8
	Chris Warren, Seattle	223	1,017	4.6	52	3
	Ricky Watters, San Francisco	206	1,013	4.9	43	9
1991	Emmitt Smith, Dallas	365	1,563	4.3	75	12
	Barry Sanders, Detroit[3]	342	1,548	4.5	69	16
	Thurman Thomas, Buffalo[3]	288	1,407	4.9	33	7
	Rodney Hampton, N.Y. Giants	256	1,059	4.1	44	10
	Earnest Byner, Washington[3]	274	1,048	3.8	32	5
	Gaston Green, Denver	261	1,037	4.0	63	4
	Christian Okoye, Kansas City[2]	225	1,031	4.6	48	9
1990	Barry Sanders, Detroit[2]	255	1,304	5.1	45	13
	Thurman Thomas, Buffalo[2]	271	1,297	4.8	80	11
	Marion Butts, San Diego	265	1,225	4.6	52	8
	Earnest Byner, Washington[2]	297	1,219	4.1	22	6
	Bobby Humphrey, Denver[2]	288	1,202	4.2	37	7
	Neal Anderson, Chicago[3]	260	1,078	4.1	52	10
	Barry Word, Kansas City	204	1,015	5.0	53	4
	James Brooks, Cincinnati[3]	195	1,004	5.1	56	5
1989	Christian Okoye, Kansas City	370	1,480	4.0	59	12
	*Barry Sanders, Detroit	280	1,470	5.3	34	14
	Eric Dickerson, Indianapolis[7]	314	1,311	4.2	21	7
	Neal Anderson, Chicago[2]	274	1,275	4.7	73	11
	Dalton Hilliard, New Orleans	344	1,262	3.7	40	13
	Thurman Thomas, Buffalo	298	1,244	4.2	38	6
	James Brooks, Cincinnati[2]	221	1,239	5.6	65	7
	*Bobby Humphrey, Denver	294	1,151	3.9	40	7
	Greg Bell, L.A. Rams[3]	272	1,137	4.2	47	15
	Roger Craig, San Francisco[3]	271	1,054	3.9	27	6
	Ottis Anderson, N.Y. Giants[6]	325	1,023	3.1	36	14
1988	Eric Dickerson, Indianapolis[6]	388	1,659	4.3	41	14
	Herschel Walker, Dallas	361	1,514	4.2	38	5
	Roger Craig, San Francisco[2]	310	1,502	4.8	46	9
	Greg Bell, L.A. Rams[2]	288	1,212	4.2	44	16
	*John Stephens, New England	297	1,168	3.9	52	4
	Gary Anderson, San Diego	225	1,119	5.0	36	3
	Neal Anderson, Chicago	249	1,106	4.4	80	12
	Joe Morris, N.Y. Giants[3]	307	1,083	3.5	27	5
	*Ickey Woods, Cincinnati	203	1,066	5.3	56	15
	Curt Warner, Seattle[4]	266	1,025	3.9	29	10
	John Settle, Atlanta	232	1,024	4.4	62	7
	Mike Rozier, Houston	251	1,002	4.0	28	10
1987	Charles White, L.A. Rams	324	1,374	4.2	58	11
	Eric Dickerson, L.A. Rams-Indianapolis[5]	283	1,288	4.6	57	6
1986	Eric Dickerson, L.A. Rams[4]	404	1,821	4.5	42	11
	Joe Morris, N.Y. Giants[2]	341	1,516	4.4	54	14
	Curt Warner, Seattle[3]	319	1,481	4.6	60	13
	*Rueben Mayes, New Orleans	286	1,353	4.7	50	8
	Walter Payton, Chicago[10]	321	1,333	4.2	41	8
	Gerald Riggs, Atlanta[3]	343	1,327	3.9	31	9
	George Rogers, Washington[4]	303	1,203	4.0	42	18
	James Brooks, Cincinnati	205	1,087	5.3	56	5
1985	Marcus Allen, L.A. Raiders[3]	390	1,759	4.6	61	11
	Gerald Riggs, Atlanta[2]	397	1,719	4.3	50	10
	Walter Payton, Chicago[9]	324	1,551	4.8	40	9
	Joe Morris, N.Y. Giants	294	1,336	4.5	65	21
	Freeman McNeil, N.Y. Jets[2]	294	1,331	4.5	69	3
	Tony Dorsett, Dallas[8]	305	1,307	4.3	60	7
	James Wilder, Tampa Bay[2]	365	1,300	3.6	28	10
	Eric Dickerson, L.A. Rams[3]	292	1,234	4.2	43	12
	Craig James, New England	263	1,227	4.7	65	5
	Kevin Mack, Cleveland	222	1,104	5.0	61	7
	Curt Warner, Seattle[2]	291	1,094	3.8	38	8
	George Rogers, Washington[3]	231	1,093	4.7	35	7
	Roger Craig, San Francisco	214	1,050	4.9	62	9

Year	Player, Team	Att.	Yards	Avg.	Long	TD
	Earnest Jackson, Philadelphia[2]	282	1,028	3.6	59	5
	Stump Mitchell, St. Louis	183	1,006	5.5	64	7
	Earnest Byner, Cleveland	244	1,002	4.1	36	8
1984	Eric Dickerson, L.A. Rams[2]	379	2,105	5.6	66	14
	Walter Payton, Chicago[8]	381	1,684	4.4	72	11
	James Wilder, Tampa Bay	407	1,544	3.8	37	13
	Gerald Riggs, Atlanta	353	1,486	4.2	57	13
	Wendell Tyler, San Francisco[3]	246	1,262	5.1	40	7
	John Riggins, Washington[5]	327	1,239	3.8	24	14
	Tony Dorsett, Dallas[7]	302	1,189	3.9	31	6
	Earnest Jackson, San Diego	296	1,179	4.0	32	8
	Ottis Anderson, St. Louis[5]	289	1,174	4.1	24	6
	Marcus Allen, L.A. Raiders[2]	275	1,168	4.2	52	13
	Sammy Winder, Denver	296	1,153	3.9	24	4
	*Greg Bell, Buffalo	262	1,100	4.2	85	7
	Freeman McNeil, N.Y. Jets	229	1,070	4.7	53	5
1983	*Eric Dickerson, L.A. Rams	390	1,808	4.6	85	18
	William Andrews, Atlanta[4]	331	1,567	4.7	27	7
	*Curt Warner, Seattle	335	1,449	4.3	60	13
	Walter Payton, Chicago[7]	314	1,421	4.5	49	6
	John Riggins, Washington[4]	375	1,347	3.6	44	24
	Tony Dorsett, Dallas[6]	289	1,321	4.6	77	8
	Earl Campbell, Houston[5]	322	1,301	4.0	42	12
	Ottis Anderson, St. Louis[4]	296	1,270	4.3	43	5
	Mike Pruitt, Cleveland[4]	293	1,184	4.0	27	10
	George Rogers, New Orleans[2]	256	1,144	4.5	76	5
	Joe Cribbs, Buffalo[3]	263	1,131	4.3	45	3
	Curtis Dickey, Baltimore	254	1,122	4.4	56	4
	Tony Collins, New England	219	1,049	4.8	50	10
	Billy Sims, Detroit[3]	220	1,040	4.7	41	7
	Marcus Allen, L.A. Raiders	266	1,014	3.8	19	9
	Franco Harris, Pittsburgh[8]	279	1,007	3.6	19	5
1981	*George Rogers, New Orleans	378	1,674	4.4	79	13
	Tony Dorsett, Dallas[5]	342	1,646	4.8	75	4
	Billy Sims, Detroit[2]	296	1,437	4.9	51	13
	Wilbert Montgomery, Philadelphia[3]	286	1,402	4.9	41	8
	Ottis Anderson, St. Louis[3]	328	1,376	4.2	28	9
	Earl Campbell, Houston[4]	361	1,376	3.8	43	10
	William Andrews, Atlanta[3]	289	1,301	4.5	29	10
	Walter Payton, Chicago[6]	339	1,222	3.6	39	6
	Chuck Muncie, San Diego[2]	251	1,144	4.6	73	19
	*Joe Delaney, Kansas City	234	1,121	4.8	82	3
	Mike Pruitt, Cleveland[3]	247	1,103	4.5	21	7
	Joe Cribbs, Buffalo[2]	257	1,097	4.3	35	3
	Pete Johnson, Cincinnati	274	1,077	3.9	39	12
	Wendell Tyler, Los Angeles[2]	260	1,074	4.1	69	12
	Ted Brown, Minnesota	274	1,063	3.9	34	6
1980	Earl Campbell, Houston[3]	373	1,934	5.2	55	13
	Walter Payton, Chicago[5]	317	1,460	4.6	69	6
	Ottis Anderson, St. Louis[2]	301	1,352	4.5	52	9
	William Andrews, Atlanta[2]	265	1,308	4.9	33	4
	*Billy Sims, Detroit	313	1,303	4.2	52	13
	Tony Dorsett, Dallas[4]	278	1,185	4.3	56	11
	*Joe Cribbs, Buffalo	306	1,185	3.9	48	11
	Mike Pruitt, Cleveland[2]	249	1,034	4.2	56	6
1979	Earl Campbell, Houston[2]	368	1,697	4.6	61	19
	Walter Payton, Chicago[4]	369	1,610	4.4	43	14
	*Ottis Anderson, St. Louis	331	1,605	4.8	76	8
	Wilbert Montgomery, Philadelphia[2]	338	1,512	4.5	62	9
	Mike Pruitt, Cleveland	264	1,294	4.9	77	9
	Ricky Bell, Tampa Bay	283	1,263	4.5	49	7
	Chuck Muncie, New Orleans	238	1,198	5.0	69	11
	Franco Harris, Pittsburgh[7]	267	1,186	4.4	71	11
	John Riggins, Washington[3]	260	1,153	4.4	66	9
	Wendell Tyler, Los Angeles	218	1,109	5.1	63	9
	Tony Dorsett, Dallas[3]	250	1,107	4.4	41	6
	*William Andrews, Atlanta	239	1,023	4.3	23	3
1978	*Earl Campbell, Houston	302	1,450	4.8	81	13
	Walter Payton, Chicago[3]	333	1,395	4.2	76	11

Year	Player, Team	Att.	Yards	Avg.	Long	TD
	Tony Dorsett, Dallas[2]	290	1,325	4.6	63	7
	Delvin Williams, Miami[2]	272	1,258	4.6	58	8
	Wilbert Montgomery, Philadelphia	259	1,220	4.7	47	9
	Terdell Middleton, Green Bay	284	1,116	3.9	76	11
	Franco Harris, Pittsburgh[6]	310	1,082	3.5	37	8
	Mark van Eeghen, Oakland[3]	270	1,080	4.0	34	9
	*Terry Miller, Buffalo	238	1,060	4.5	60	7
	Tony Reed, Kansas City	206	1,053	5.1	62	5
	John Riggins, Washington[2]	248	1,014	4.1	31	5
1977	Walter Payton, Chicago[2]	339	1,852	5.5	73	14
	Mark van Eeghen, Oakland[2]	324	1,273	3.9	27	7
	Lawrence McCutcheon, Los Angeles[4]	294	1,238	4.2	48	7
	Franco Harris, Pittsburgh[5]	300	1,162	3.9	61	11
	Lydell Mitchell, Baltimore[3]	301	1,159	3.9	64	3
	Chuck Foreman, Minnesota[3]	270	1,112	4.1	51	6
	Greg Pruitt, Cleveland[3]	236	1,086	4.6	78	3
	Sam Cunningham, New England	270	1,015	3.8	31	4
	*Tony Dorsett, Dallas	208	1,007	4.8	84	12
1976	O.J. Simpson, Buffalo[5]	290	1,503	5.2	75	8
	Walter Payton, Chicago	311	1,390	4.5	60	13
	Delvin Williams, San Francisco	248	1,203	4.9	80	7
	Lydell Mitchell, Baltimore[2]	289	1,200	4.2	43	5
	Lawrence McCutcheon, Los Angeles[3]	291	1,168	4.0	40	9
	Chuck Foreman, Minnesota[2]	278	1,155	4.2	46	13
	Franco Harris, Pittsburgh[4]	289	1,128	3.9	30	14
	Mike Thomas, Washington	254	1,101	4.3	28	5
	Rocky Bleier, Pittsburgh	220	1,036	4.7	28	5
	Mark van Eeghen, Oakland	233	1,012	4.3	21	3
	Otis Armstrong, Denver[2]	247	1,008	4.1	31	5
	Greg Pruitt, Cleveland[2]	209	1,000	4.8	64	4
1975	O.J. Simpson, Buffalo[4]	329	1,817	5.5	88	16
	Franco Harris, Pittsburgh[3]	262	1,246	4.8	36	10
	Lydell Mitchell, Baltimore	289	1,193	4.1	70	11
	Jim Otis, St. Louis	269	1,076	4.0	30	5
	Chuck Foreman, Minnesota	280	1,070	3.8	31	13
	Greg Pruitt, Cleveland	217	1,067	4.9	50	8
	John Riggins, N.Y. Jets	238	1,005	4.2	42	8
	Dave Hampton, Atlanta	250	1,002	4.0	22	5
1974	Otis Armstrong, Denver	263	1,407	5.3	43	9
	*Don Woods, San Diego	227	1,162	5.1	56	7
	O.J. Simpson, Buffalo[3]	270	1,125	4.2	41	3
	Lawrence McCutcheon, Los Angeles[2]	236	1,109	4.7	23	3
	Franco Harris, Pittsburgh[2]	208	1,006	4.8	54	5
1973	O.J. Simpson, Buffalo[2]	332	2,003	6.0	80	12
	John Brockington, Green Bay[3]	265	1,144	4.3	53	3
	Calvin Hill, Dallas[2]	273	1,142	4.2	21	6
	Lawrence McCutcheon, Los Angeles	210	1,097	5.2	37	2
	Larry Csonka, Miami[3]	219	1,003	4.6	25	5
1972	O.J. Simpson, Buffalo	292	1,251	4.3	94	6
	Larry Brown, Washington[2]	285	1,216	4.3	38	8
	Ron Johnson, N.Y. Giants[2]	298	1,182	4.0	35	9
	Larry Csonka, Miami[2]	213	1,117	5.2	45	6
	Marv Hubbard, Oakland	219	1,100	5.0	39	4
	*Franco Harris, Pittsburgh	188	1,055	5.6	75	10
	Calvin Hill, Dallas	245	1,036	4.2	26	6
	Mike Garrett, San Diego[2]	272	1,031	3.8	41	6
	John Brockington, Green Bay[2]	274	1,027	3.7	30	8
	Eugene (Mercury) Morris, Miami	190	1,000	5.3	33	12
1971	Floyd Little, Denver	284	1,133	4.0	40	6
	*John Brockington, Green Bay	216	1,105	5.1	52	4
	Larry Csonka, Miami	195	1,051	5.4	28	7
	Steve Owens, Detroit	246	1,035	4.2	23	8
	Willie Ellison, Los Angeles	211	1,000	4.7	80	4
1970	Larry Brown, Washington	237	1,125	4.7	75	5
	Ron Johnson, N.Y. Giants	263	1,027	3.9	68	8
1969	Gale Sayers, Chicago[2]	236	1,032	4.4	28	8
1968	Leroy Kelly, Cleveland[3]	248	1,239	5.0	65	16
	*Paul Robinson, Cincinnati	238	1,023	4.3	87	8
1967	Jim Nance, Boston[2]	269	1,216	4.5	53	7

Year	Player, Team	Att.	Yards	Avg.	Long	TD
	Leroy Kelly, Cleveland[2]	235	1,205	5.1	42	11
	Hoyle Granger, Houston	236	1,194	5.1	67	6
	Mike Garrett, Kansas City	236	1,087	4.6	58	9
1966	Jim Nance, Boston	299	1,458	4.9	65	11
	Gale Sayers, Chicago	229	1,231	5.4	58	8
	Leroy Kelly, Cleveland	209	1,141	5.5	70	15
	Dick Bass, Los Angeles[2]	248	1,090	4.4	50	8
1965	Jim Brown, Cleveland[7]	289	1,544	5.3	67	17
	Paul Lowe, San Diego[2]	222	1,121	5.0	59	7
1964	Jim Brown, Cleveland[6]	280	1,446	5.2	71	7
	Jim Taylor, Green Bay[5]	235	1,169	5.0	84	12
	John Henry Johnson, Pittsburgh[2]	235	1,048	4.5	45	7
1963	Jim Brown, Cleveland[5]	291	1,863	6.4	80	12
	Clem Daniels, Oakland	215	1,099	5.1	74	3
	Jim Taylor, Green Bay[4]	248	1,018	4.1	40	9
	Paul Lowe, San Diego	177	1,010	5.7	66	8
1962	Jim Taylor, Green Bay[3]	272	1,474	5.4	51	19
	John Henry Johnson, Pittsburgh	251	1,141	4.5	40	7
	Cookie Gilchrist, Buffalo	214	1,096	5.1	44	13
	Abner Haynes, Dall. Texans	221	1,049	4.7	71	13
	Dick Bass, Los Angeles	196	1,033	5.3	57	6
	Charlie Tolar, Houston	244	1,012	4.1	25	7
1961	Jim Brown, Cleveland[4]	305	1,408	4.6	38	8
	Jim Taylor, Green Bay[2]	243	1,307	5.4	53	15
1960	Jim Brown, Cleveland[3]	215	1,257	5.8	71	9
	Jim Taylor, Green Bay	230	1,101	4.8	32	11
	John David Crow, St. Louis	183	1,071	5.9	57	6
1959	Jim Brown, Cleveland[2]	290	1,329	4.6	70	14
	J.D. Smith, San Francisco	207	1,036	5.0	73	10
1958	Jim Brown, Cleveland	257	1,527	5.9	65	17
1956	Rick Casares, Chi. Bears	234	1,126	4.8	68	12
1954	Joe Perry, San Francisco[2]	173	1,049	6.1	58	8
1953	Joe Perry, San Francisco	192	1,018	5.3	51	10
1949	Steve Van Buren, Philadelphia[2]	263	1,146	4.4	41	11
	Tony Canadeo, Green Bay	208	1,052	5.1	54	4
1947	Steve Van Buren, Philadelphia	217	1,008	4.6	45	13
1934	*Beattie Feathers, Chi. Bears	119	1,004	8.4	82	8

*First season of professional football.

200 YARDS RUSHING IN A GAME

Date	Player, Team, Opponent	Att.	Yards	TD
Dec. 8, 2013	LeSean McCoy, Philadelphia vs. Detroit	29	217	2
Dec. 1, 2013	Adrian Peterson, Minnesota vs. Chicago (OT)	35	211	0
Nov. 24, 2013	Knowshon Moreno, Denver vs. New England (OT)	37	224	1
Dec. 30, 2012	DeAngelo Williams, Carolina vs. New Orleans	21	210	2
Dec. 30, 2012	*Alfred Morris, Washington vs. Dallas	33	200	3
Dec. 23, 2012	Jamaal Charles, Kansas City vs. Indianapolis	22	226	1
Dec. 16, 2012	Adrian Peterson, Minnesota vs. St. Louis	24	212	1
Dec. 2, 2012	Adrian Peterson, Minnesota vs. Green Bay	21	210	1
Nov. 4, 2012	*Doug Martin, Tampa Bay vs. Oakland	25	251	4
Oct. 7, 2012	Ahmad Bradshaw, N.Y. Giants vs. Cleveland	30	200	1
Sept. 23, 2012	Jamaal Charles, Kansas City vs. New Orleans (OT)	33	233	1
Dec. 18, 2011	Reggie Bush, Miami vs. Buffalo	25	203	1
Dec. 4, 2011	Ray Rice, Baltimore vs. Cleveland	29	204	1
Nov. 27, 2011	Beanie Wells, Arizona vs. St. Louis	27	228	1
Oct. 23, 2011	*DeMarco Murray, Dallas vs. St. Louis	25	253	1
Oct. 2, 2011	Matt Forté, Chicago vs. Carolina	25	205	1
Sept. 12, 2010	Arian Foster, Houston vs. Indianapolis	33	231	3
Jan. 3, 2010	Jamaal Charles, Kansas City vs. Denver	25	259	2
Jan. 3, 2010	Fred Jackson, Buffalo vs. Indianapolis	33	212	0
Dec. 27, 2009	Jonathan Stewart, Carolina vs. N.Y. Giants	28	206	1
Dec. 20, 2009	Jerome Harrison, Cleveland vs. Kansas City	34	286	3
Nov. 1, 2009	Chris Johnson, Tennessee vs. Jacksonville	24	228	1
Oct. 18, 2009	Thomas Jones, N.Y. Jets vs. Buffalo (OT)	22	210	1
Sept. 20, 2009	Frank Gore, San Francisco vs. Seattle	16	207	2
Dec. 28, 2008	Michael Turner, Atlanta vs. St. Louis	25	208	1
Dec. 21, 2008	Derrick Ward, N.Y. Giants vs. Carolina (OT)	15	215	0
Sept. 7, 2008	Michael Turner, Atlanta vs. Detroit	22	220	2
Nov. 4, 2007	*Adrian Peterson, Minnesota vs. San Diego	30	296	3

Date	Player, Team, Opponent	Att.	Yards	TD
Oct. 14, 2007	*Adrian Peterson, Minnesota vs. Chicago	20	224	3
Sept. 16, 2007	Jamal Lewis, Cleveland vs. Cincinnati	27	216	1
Dec. 30, 2006	Tiki Barber, N.Y. Giants vs. Washington	23	234	3
Dec. 7, 2006	Willie Parker, Pittsburgh vs. Cleveland	32	223	1
Nov. 27, 2006	Shaun Alexander, Seattle vs. Green Bay	40	201	0
Nov. 19, 2006	Frank Gore, San Francisco vs. Seattle	24	212	0
Nov. 12, 2006	Willie Parker, Pittsburgh vs. New Orleans	22	213	2
Jan. 1, 2006	Larry Johnson, Kansas City vs. Cincinnati	26	201	3
Dec. 31, 2005	Tiki Barber, N.Y. Giants vs. Oakland	28	203	1
Dec. 17, 2005	Tiki Barber, N.Y. Giants vs. Kansas City	29	220	2
Nov. 20, 2005	Larry Johnson, Kansas City vs. Houston	36	211	2
Oct. 30, 2005	Tiki Barber, N.Y. Giants vs. Washington	24	206	1
Nov. 28, 2004	Rudi Johnson, Cincinnati vs. Cleveland	26	202	2
Nov. 21, 2004	Edgerrin James, Indianapolis vs. Chicago	23	204	1
Dec. 28, 2003	Ahman Green, Green Bay vs. Denver	20	218	2
Dec. 28, 2003	LaDainian Tomlinson, San Diego vs. Oakland	31	243	2
Dec. 21, 2003	Jamal Lewis, Baltimore vs. Cleveland	22	205	2
Dec. 7, 2003	Clinton Portis, Denver vs. Kansas City	22	218	5
Oct. 19, 2003	LaDainian Tomlinson, San Diego vs. Cleveland	26	200	1
Sept. 14, 2003	Jamal Lewis, Baltimore vs. Cleveland	30	295	2
Dec. 29, 2002	*Clinton Portis, Denver vs. Arizona	24	228	2
Dec. 28, 2002	Tiki Barber, N.Y. Giants vs. Philadelphia	32	203	0
Dec. 9, 2002	Ricky Williams, Miami vs. Chicago	31	216	2
Dec. 1, 2002	LaDainian Tomlinson, San Diego vs. Denver	37	220	3
Dec. 1, 2002	Ricky Williams, Miami vs. Buffalo	27	228	2
Sept. 29, 2002	LaDainian Tomlinson, San Diego vs. New England	27	217	2
Dec. 23, 2001	Marshall Faulk, St. Louis vs. Carolina	30	202	2
Nov. 11, 2001	Shaun Alexander, Seattle vs. Oakland	35	266	3
Dec. 24, 2000	Marshall Faulk, St. Louis vs. New Orleans	32	220	2
Dec. 3, 2000	Corey Dillon, Cincinnati vs. Arizona	35	216	1
Dec. 3, 2000	Warrick Dunn, Tampa Bay vs. Dallas	22	210	2
Dec. 3, 2000	*Mike Anderson, Denver vs. New Orleans	37	251	4
Dec. 3, 2000	Curtis Martin, N.Y. Jets vs. Indianapolis	30	203	1
Nov. 19, 2000	Fred Taylor, Jacksonville vs. Pittsburgh	30	234	3
Oct. 22, 2000	Corey Dillon, Cincinnati vs. Denver	22	278	2
Oct. 15, 2000	Marshall Faulk, St. Louis vs. Atlanta	25	208	1
Oct. 15, 2000	Edgerrin James, Indianapolis vs. Seattle	38	219	3
Sept. 24, 2000	Charlie Garner, San Francisco vs. Dallas	36	201	1
Sept. 3, 2000	Duce Staley, Philadelphia vs. Dallas	26	201	1
Nov. 22, 1998	Priest Holmes, Baltimore vs. Cincinnati	36	227	1
Oct. 11, 1998	Terrell Davis, Denver vs. Seattle	30	208	1
Dec. 4, 1997	*Corey Dillon, Cincinnati vs. Tennessee	39	246	4
Nov. 23, 1997	Barry Sanders, Detroit vs. Indianapolis	24	216	2
Oct. 26, 1997	Terrell Davis, Denver vs. Buffalo (OT)	42	207	1
Oct. 19, 1997	Napoleon Kaufman, Oakland vs. Denver	28	227	1
Oct. 12, 1997	Barry Sanders, Detroit vs. Tampa Bay	24	215	2
Sept. 21, 1997	Terrell Davis, Denver vs. Cincinnati	27	215	1
Aug. 31, 1997	Eddie George, Tennessee vs. Oakland (OT)	35	216	1
Sept. 22, 1996	LeShon Johnson, Arizona vs. New Orleans	21	214	2
Nov. 13, 1994	Barry Sanders, Detroit vs. Tampa Bay	26	237	0
Dec. 12, 1993	*Jerome Bettis, L.A. Rams vs. New Orleans	28	212	1
Oct. 31, 1993	Emmitt Smith, Dallas vs. Philadelphia	30	237	1
Nov. 24, 1991	Barry Sanders, Detroit vs. Minnesota	23	220	4
Dec. 23, 1990	James Brooks, Cincinnati vs. Houston	20	201	1
Oct. 14, 1990	Barry Word, Kansas City vs. Detroit	18	200	2
Sept. 24, 1990	Thurman Thomas, Buffalo vs. N.Y. Jets	18	214	0
Dec. 24, 1989	Greg Bell, L.A. Rams vs. New England	26	210	1
Sept. 24, 1989	Greg Bell, L.A. Rams vs. Green Bay	28	221	2
Sept. 17, 1989	Gerald Riggs, Washington vs. Philadelphia	29	221	1
Dec. 18, 1988	Gary Anderson, San Diego vs. Kansas City	34	217	1
Nov. 30, 1987	*Bo Jackson, L.A. Raiders vs. Seattle	18	221	2
Nov. 15, 1987	Charles White, L.A. Rams vs. St. Louis	34	213	2
Dec. 7, 1986	Rueben Mayes, New Orleans vs. Miami	28	203	2
Oct. 5, 1986	Eric Dickerson, L.A. Rams vs. Tampa Bay (OT)	30	207	2
Dec. 21, 1985	George Rogers, Washington vs. St. Louis	34	206	1
Dec. 21, 1985	Joe Morris, N.Y. Giants vs. Pittsburgh	36	202	3
Dec. 9, 1984	Eric Dickerson, L.A. Rams vs. Houston	27	215	2
Nov. 18, 1984	*Greg Bell, Buffalo vs. Dallas	27	206	1
Nov. 4, 1984	Eric Dickerson, L.A. Rams vs. St. Louis	21	208	0
Sept. 2, 1984	Gerald Riggs, Atlanta vs. New Orleans	35	202	2
Nov. 27, 1983	*Curt Warner, Seattle vs. Kansas City (OT)	32	207	3

Date	Player, Team, Opponent	Att.	Yards	TD
Nov. 6, 1983	James Wilder, Tampa Bay vs. Minnesota	31	219	1
Sept. 18, 1983	Tony Collins, New England vs. N.Y. Jets	23	212	3
Sept. 4, 1983	George Rogers, New Orleans vs. St. Louis	24	206	2
Dec. 21, 1980	Earl Campbell, Houston vs. Minnesota	29	203	1
Nov. 16, 1980	Earl Campbell, Houston vs. Chicago	31	206	0
Oct. 26, 1980	Earl Campbell, Houston vs. Cincinnati	27	202	2
Oct. 19, 1980	Earl Campbell, Houston vs. Tampa Bay	33	203	0
Nov. 26, 1978	*Terry Miller, Buffalo vs. N.Y. Giants	21	208	2
Dec. 4, 1977	*Tony Dorsett, Dallas vs. Philadelphia	23	206	2
Nov. 20, 1977	Walter Payton, Chicago vs. Minnesota	40	275	1
Oct. 30, 1977	Walter Payton, Chicago vs. Green Bay	23	205	2
Dec. 5, 1976	O.J. Simpson, Buffalo vs. Miami	24	203	1
Nov. 25, 1976	O.J. Simpson, Buffalo vs. Detroit	29	273	2
Oct. 24, 1976	Chuck Foreman, Minnesota vs. Philadelphia	28	200	2
Dec. 14, 1975	Greg Pruitt, Cleveland vs. Kansas City	26	214	3
Sept. 28, 1975	O.J. Simpson, Buffalo vs. Pittsburgh	28	227	1
Dec. 16, 1973	O.J. Simpson, Buffalo vs. N.Y. Jets	34	200	1
Dec. 9, 1973	O.J. Simpson, Buffalo vs. New England	22	219	1
Sept. 16, 1973	O.J. Simpson, Buffalo vs. New England	29	250	2
Dec. 5, 1971	Willie Ellison, Los Angeles vs. New Orleans	26	247	1
Dec. 20, 1970	John (Frenchy) Fuqua, Pittsburgh vs. Philadelphia	20	218	2
Nov. 3, 1968	Gale Sayers, Chicago vs. Green Bay	24	205	0
Oct. 30, 1966	Jim Nance, Boston vs. Oakland	38	208	2
Oct. 10, 1964	John Henry Johnson, Pittsburgh vs. Cleveland	30	200	3
Dec. 8, 1963	Cookie Gilchrist, Buffalo vs. N.Y. Jets	36	243	5
Nov. 3, 1963	Jim Brown, Cleveland vs. Philadelphia	28	223	1
Oct. 20, 1963	Clem Daniels, Oakland vs. N.Y. Jets	27	200	2
Sept. 22, 1963	Jim Brown, Cleveland vs. Dallas	20	232	2
Dec. 10, 1961	Billy Cannon, Houston vs. N.Y. Titans	25	216	3
Nov. 19, 1961	Jim Brown, Cleveland vs. Philadelphia	34	237	4
Dec. 18, 1960	John David Crow, St. Louis vs. Pittsburgh	24	203	0
Nov. 15, 1959	Bobby Mitchell, Cleveland vs. Washington	14	232	3
Nov. 24, 1957	*Jim Brown, Cleveland vs. Los Angeles	31	237	4
Dec. 16, 1956	*Tom Wilson, Los Angeles vs. Green Bay	23	223	0
Nov. 22, 1953	Dan Towler, Los Angeles vs. Baltimore	14	205	1
Nov. 12, 1950	Gene Roberts, N.Y. Giants vs. Chi. Cardinals	26	218	2
Nov. 27, 1949	Steve Van Buren, Philadelphia vs. Pittsburgh	27	205	0
Oct. 8, 1933	Cliff Battles, Boston vs. N.Y. Giants	16	215	1

*First season of professional football.

TIMES 200 OR MORE

137 times by 87 players...Simpson 6; Barber, Peterson 5; Brown, Campbell, Sanders, Tomlinson 4; Bell, Charles, Davis, Dickerson, Dillon, Faulk, Lewis 3; Alexander, Gore, James, L. Johnson, Parker, Payton, Portis, Riggs, Rogers, Turner, Williams 2.

4,000 YARDS PASSING IN A SEASON

Year	Player, Team	Att.	Comp.	Pct.	Yards	TD	Int.
2013	Peyton Manning, Denver[13]	659	450	68.3	5,477	55	10
	Drew Brees, New Orleans[8]	650	446	68.6	5,162	39	12
	Matthew Stafford, Detroit[3]	634	371	58.5	4,650	29	19
	Matt Ryan, Atlanta[3]	651	439	67.4	4,515	26	17
	Philip Rivers, San Diego[5]	544	378	69.5	4,478	32	11
	Tom Brady, New England[6]	628	380	60.5	4,343	25	11
	Andy Dalton, Cincinnati	586	363	61.9	4,293	33	20
	Carson Palmer, Arizona[4]	572	362	63.3	4,274	24	22
	Ben Roethlisberger, Pittsburgh[3]	584	375	64.2	4,261	28	14
2012	Drew Brees, New Orleans[7]	670	422	63.0	5,177	43	19
	Matthew Stafford, Detroit[2]	727	435	59.8	4,967	20	17
	Tony Romo, Dallas[4]	648	425	65.6	4,903	28	19
	Tom Brady, New England[5]	637	401	63.0	4,827	34	8
	Matt Ryan, Atlanta[2]	615	422	68.6	4,719	32	14
	Peyton Manning, Denver[12]	583	400	68.6	4,659	37	11
	*Andrew Luck, Indianapolis	627	339	54.1	4,374	23	18
	Aaron Rodgers, Green Bay[4]	552	371	67.2	4,295	39	8
	Josh Freeman, Tampa Bay	558	306	54.8	4,065	27	17
	Carson Palmer, Oakland[3]	565	345	61.1	4,018	22	14
	Matt Schaub, Houston[3]	544	350	64.3	4,008	22	12
2011	Drew Brees, New Orleans[6]	657	468	71.2	5,476	46	14

Year	Player, Team	Att.	Comp.	Pct.	Yards	TD	Int.
	Tom Brady, New England[4]	611	401	65.6	5,235	39	12
	Matthew Stafford, Detroit	663	421	63.5	5,038	41	16
	Eli Manning, N.Y. Giants[3]	589	359	61.0	4,933	29	16
	Aaron Rodgers, Green Bay[3]	502	343	68.3	4,643	45	6
	Philip Rivers, San Diego[4]	582	366	62.9	4,624	27	20
	Tony Romo, Dallas[3]	522	346	66.3	4,184	31	10
	Matt Ryan, Atlanta	566	347	61.3	4,177	29	12
	Ben Roethlisberger, Pittsburgh[2]	513	324	63.2	4,077	21	14
	*Cam Newton, Carolina	517	310	60.0	4,051	21	17
2010	Philip Rivers, San Diego[3]	541	357	66.0	4,710	30	13
	Peyton Manning, Indianapolis[11]	679	450	66.3	4,700	33	17
	Drew Brees, New Orleans[5]	658	448	68.1	4,620	33	22
	Matt Schaub, Houston[2]	574	365	63.6	4,370	24	12
	Eli Manning, N.Y. Giants[2]	539	339	62.9	4,002	31	25
2009	Matt Schaub, Houston	583	396	67.9	4,770	29	15
	Peyton Manning, Indianapolis[10]	571	393	68.8	4,500	33	16
	Tony Romo, Dallas[2]	550	347	63.1	4,483	26	9
	Aaron Rodgers, Green Bay[2]	541	350	64.7	4,434	30	7
	Tom Brady, New England[3]	565	371	65.7	4,398	28	13
	Drew Brees, New Orleans[4]	514	363	70.6	4,388	34	11
	Ben Roethlisberger, Pittsburgh	506	337	66.6	4,328	26	12
	Philip Rivers, San Diego[2]	486	317	65.2	4,254	28	9
	Brett Favre, Minnesota[6]	531	363	68.4	4,202	33	7
	Eli Manning, N.Y. Giants	509	317	62.3	4,021	27	14
2008	Drew Brees, New Orleans[3]	635	413	65.0	5,069	34	17
	Kurt Warner, Arizona[3]	598	401	67.1	4,583	30	14
	Jay Cutler, Denver	616	384	62.3	4,526	25	18
	Aaron Rodgers, Green Bay	536	341	63.6	4,038	28	13
	Philip Rivers, San Diego	478	312	65.3	4,009	34	11
	Peyton Manning, Indianapolis[9]	555	371	66.8	4,002	27	12
2007	Tom Brady, New England[2]	578	398	68.9	4,806	50	8
	Drew Brees, New Orleans[2]	652	440	67.5	4,423	28	18
	Tony Romo, Dallas	520	335	64.4	4,211	36	19
	Brett Favre, Green Bay[5]	535	356	66.5	4,155	28	15
	Carson Palmer, Cincinnati[2]	575	373	64.9	4,131	26	20
	Jon Kitna, Detroit[2]	561	355	63.3	4,068	18	20
	Peyton Manning, Indianapolis[8]	515	337	65.4	4,040	31	14
2006	Drew Brees, New Orleans	554	356	64.3	4,418	26	11
	Peyton Manning, Indianapolis[7]	557	362	65.0	4,397	31	9
	Marc Bulger, St. Louis	588	370	62.9	4,301	24	8
	Jon Kitna, Detroit	596	372	62.4	4,208	21	22
	Carson Palmer, Cincinnati	520	324	62.3	4,035	28	13
2005	Tom Brady, New England	530	334	63.0	4,110	26	14
	Trent Green, Kansas City[3]	507	317	62.5	4,014	17	10
2004	Daunte Culpepper, Minnesota	548	379	69.2	4,717	39	11
	Trent Green, Kansas City[2]	556	369	66.4	4,591	27	17
	Peyton Manning, Indianapolis[6]	497	336	67.6	4,557	49	10
	Jake Plummer, Denver	521	303	58.2	4,089	27	20
	Brett Favre, Green Bay[4]	540	346	64.1	4,088	30	17
2003	Peyton Manning, Indianapolis[5]	566	379	67.0	4,267	29	10
	Trent Green, Kansas City	523	330	63.1	4,039	24	12
2002	Rich Gannon, Oakland	618	418	67.6	4,689	26	10
	Drew Bledsoe, Buffalo[3]	610	375	61.5	4,359	24	15
	Peyton Manning, Indianapolis[4]	591	392	66.3	4,200	27	19
	Kerry Collins, N.Y. Giants	545	335	61.5	4,073	19	14
2001	Kurt Warner, St. Louis[2]	546	375	68.7	4,830	36	22
	Peyton Manning, Indianapolis[3]	547	343	62.7	4,131	26	23
2000	Peyton Manning, Indianapolis[2]	571	357	62.5	4,413	33	15
	Jeff Garcia, San Francisco	561	355	63.3	4,278	31	10
	Elvis Grbac, Kansas City	547	326	59.6	4,169	28	14
1999	Steve Beuerlein, Carolina	571	343	60.1	4,436	36	15
	Kurt Warner, St. Louis	499	325	65.1	4,353	41	13
	Peyton Manning, Indianapolis	533	331	62.1	4,135	26	15
	Brett Favre, Green Bay[3]	595	341	57.3	4,091	22	23
	Brad Johnson, Washington	519	316	60.9	4,005	24	13
1998	Brett Favre, Green Bay[2]	551	347	63.0	4,212	31	23
	Steve Young, San Francisco[2]	517	322	62.3	4,170	36	12
1996	Mark Brunell, Jacksonville	557	353	63.4	4,367	19	20

Year	Player, Team	Att.	Comp.	Pct.	Yards	TD	Int.
	Vinny Testaverde, Baltimore	549	325	59.2	4,177	33	19
	Drew Bledsoe, New England[2]	623	373	59.9	4,086	27	15
1995	Brett Favre, Green Bay	570	359	63.0	4,413	38	13
	Scott Mitchell, Detroit	583	346	59.3	4,338	32	12
	Warren Moon, Minnesota[4]	606	377	62.2	4,228	33	14
	Jeff George, Atlanta	557	336	60.3	4,143	24	11
1994	Drew Bledsoe, New England	691	400	57.9	4,555	25	27
	Dan Marino, Miami[6]	615	385	62.6	4,453	30	17
	Warren Moon, Minnesota[3]	601	371	61.7	4,264	18	19
1993	John Elway, Denver	551	348	63.2	4,030	25	10
	Steve Young, San Francisco	462	314	68.0	4,023	29	16
1992	Dan Marino, Miami[5]	554	330	59.6	4,116	24	16
1991	Warren Moon, Houston[2]	655	404	61.7	4,690	23	21
1990	Warren Moon, Houston	584	362	62.0	4,689	33	13
1989	Don Majkowski, Green Bay	599	353	58.9	4,318	27	20
	Jim Everett, L.A. Rams	518	304	58.7	4,310	29	17
1988	Dan Marino, Miami[4]	606	354	58.4	4,434	28	23
1986	Dan Marino, Miami[3]	623	378	60.7	4,746	44	23
	Jay Schroeder, Washington	541	276	51.0	4,109	22	22
1985	Dan Marino, Miami[2]	567	336	59.3	4,137	30	21
1984	Dan Marino, Miami	564	362	64.2	5,084	48	17
	Neil Lomax, St. Louis	560	345	61.6	4,614	28	16
	Phil Simms, N.Y. Giants	533	286	53.7	4,044	22	18
1983	Lynn Dickey, Green Bay	484	289	59.7	4,458	32	29
	Bill Kenney, Kansas City	603	346	57.4	4,348	24	18
1981	Dan Fouts, San Diego[3]	609	360	59.1	4,802	33	17
1980	Dan Fouts, San Diego[2]	589	348	59.1	4,715	30	24
	Brian Sipe, Cleveland	554	337	60.8	4,132	30	14
1979	Dan Fouts, San Diego	530	332	62.6	4,082	24	24
1967	Joe Namath, N.Y. Jets	491	258	52.5	4,007	26	28

First season of professional football.

400 YARDS PASSING IN A GAME

Date	Player, Team, Opponent	Att.	Comp.	Yards	TD
Dec. 29, 2013	Carson Palmer, Arizona vs. San Francisco	49	28	407	2
Dec. 22, 2013	Peyton Manning, Denver vs. Houston	51	32	400	4
Dec. 15, 2013	Ryan Fitzpatrick, Tennessee vs. Arizona (OT)	58	36	402	4
Dec. 15, 2013	Nick Foles, Philadelphia vs. Minnesota	48	30	428	3
Dec. 8, 2013	Tom Brady, New England vs. Cleveland	52	32	418	2
Dec. 1, 2013	Peyton Manning, Denver vs. Kansas City	35	22	403	5
Nov. 17, 2013	Carson Palmer, Arizona vs. Jacksonville	42	30	419	2
Nov. 3, 2013	Nick Foles, Philadelphia vs. Oakland	28	22	406	7
Nov. 3, 2013	Ben Roethlisberger, Pittsburgh vs. New England	48	28	400	4
Nov. 3, 2013	Tom Brady, New England vs. Pittsburgh	33	23	432	4
Oct. 27, 2013	Matthew Stafford, Detroit vs. Dallas	48	33	488	1
Oct. 6, 2013	Tony Romo, Dallas vs. Denver	36	25	506	5
Oct. 6, 2013	Peyton Manning, Denver vs. Dallas	42	33	414	4
Oct. 6, 2013	Philip Rivers, San Diego vs. Oakland	48	35	411	2
Sept. 30, 2013	Drew Brees, New Orleans vs. Miami	39	30	413	4
Sept. 29, 2013	Philip Rivers, San Diego vs. Dallas	42	35	401	3
Sept. 29, 2013	Matt Ryan, Atlanta vs. New England	54	34	421	2
Sept. 22, 2013	Ben Roethlisberger, Pittsburgh vs. Chicago	41	26	406	2
Sept. 15, 2013	Aaron Rodgers, Green Bay vs. Washington	42	34	480	4
Sept. 15, 2013	Philip Rivers, San Diego vs. Philadelphia	47	36	419	3
Sept. 15, 2013	Michael Vick, Philadelphia vs. San Diego	36	23	428	2
Sept. 8, 2013	Eli Manning, N.Y. Giants vs. Dallas	42	27	450	4
Sept. 8, 2013	Colin Kaepernick, San Francisco vs. Green Bay	39	27	412	3
Sept. 5, 2013	Peyton Manning, Denver vs. Baltimore	42	27	462	7
Dec. 23, 2012	Drew Brees, New Orleans vs. Dallas (OT)	53	37	446	3
Dec. 23, 2012	Tony Romo, Dallas vs. New Orleans (OT)	43	26	416	4
Dec. 22, 2012	Matthew Stafford, Detroit vs. Atlanta	56	37	443	0
Dec. 16, 2012	Tom Brady, New England vs. San Francisco	65	36	443	1
Nov. 22, 2012	Tony Romo, Dallas vs. Washington	62	37	441	3
Nov. 22, 2012	Matthew Stafford, Detroit vs. Houston (OT)	61	31	441	2
Nov. 18, 2012	Matt Schaub, Houston vs. Jacksonville (OT)	55	43	527	5
Nov. 11, 2012	Matt Ryan, Atlanta vs. New Orleans	52	34	411	3
Nov. 4, 2012	*Andrew Luck, Indianapolis vs. Miami	48	30	433	2
Nov. 4, 2012	Carson Palmer, Oakland vs. Tampa Bay	61	39	414	4

Date	Player, Team, Opponent	Att.	Comp.	Yards	TD
Oct. 28, 2012	Tony Romo, Dallas vs. N.Y. Giants	62	36	437	1
Oct. 21, 2012	Josh Freeman, Tampa Bay vs. New Orleans	42	24	420	3
Sept. 30, 2012	Drew Brees, New Orleans vs. Green Bay	54	35	446	3
Sept. 30, 2012	*Ryan Tannehill, Miami vs. Arizona (OT)	41	26	431	1
Sept. 16, 2012	Eli Manning, N.Y. Giants vs. Tampa Bay	51	31	510	3
Jan. 1, 2012	Carson Palmer, Oakland vs. San Diego	43	28	417	2
Jan. 1, 2012	Matthew Stafford, Detroit vs. Green Bay	59	36	520	5
Jan. 1, 2012	Matt Flynn, Green Bay vs. Detroit	44	31	480	6
Dec. 18, 2011	Drew Brees, New Orleans vs. Minnesota	40	32	412	5
Dec. 11, 2011	Eli Manning, N.Y. Giants vs. Dallas	47	27	400	2
Dec. 4, 2011	Matthew Stafford, Detroit vs. New Orleans	44	31	408	1
Nov. 28, 2011	Eli Manning, N.Y. Giants vs. New Orleans	47	33	406	2
Nov. 27, 2011	Vince Young, Philadelphia vs. New England	48	26	400	1
Oct. 9, 2011	Eli Manning, N.Y. Giants vs. Seattle	39	24	420	3
Oct. 9, 2011	Matt Schaub, Houston vs. Oakland	51	24	416	2
Oct. 2, 2011	Aaron Rodgers, Green Bay vs. Denver	38	29	408	4
Oct. 2, 2011	Michael Vick, Philadelphia vs. San Francisco	46	30	416	2
Sept. 18, 2011	Tom Brady, New England vs. San Diego	40	31	423	3
Sept. 18, 2011	*Cam Newton, Carolina vs. Green Bay	46	28	432	1
Sept. 12, 2011	Chad Henne, Miami vs. New England	49	30	416	2
Sept. 12, 2011	Tom Brady, New England vs. Miami	48	32	517	4
Sept. 11, 2011	*Cam Newton, Carolina vs. Arizona	37	24	422	2
Sept. 8, 2011	Drew Brees, New Orleans vs. Green Bay	49	32	419	3
Dec. 26, 2010	Aaron Rodgers, Green Bay vs. N.Y. Giants	37	25	404	4
Nov. 14, 2010	Matt Cassel, Kansas City vs. Denver	53	33	469	4
Nov. 7, 2010	Brett Favre, Minnesota vs. Arizona (OT)	47	36	446	2
Oct. 24, 2010	Carson Palmer, Cincinnati vs. Atlanta	50	36	412	3
Oct. 10, 2010	Tony Romo, Dallas vs. Tennessee	46	31	406	3
Oct. 10, 2010	Philip Rivers, San Diego vs. Oakland	42	27	431	2
Sept. 26, 2010	Kyle Orton, Denver vs. Indianapolis	57	37	476	1
Sept. 26, 2010	Philip Rivers, San Diego vs. Seattle	53	29	455	2
Sept. 19, 2010	Matt Schaub, Houston vs. Washington	52	38	497	3
Sept. 19, 2010	Donovan McNabb, Washington vs. Houston	38	28	426	1
Sept. 12, 2010	Peyton Manning, Indianapolis vs. Houston	57	40	433	3
Jan. 3, 2010	Kyle Orton, Denver vs. Kansas City	56	32	431	1
Dec. 20, 2009	Ben Roethlisberger, Pittsburgh vs. Green Bay	46	29	503	3
Dec. 6, 2009	Drew Brees, New Orleans vs. Washington (OT)	49	35	419	2
Nov. 22, 2009	Matthew Stafford, Detroit vs. Cleveland	43	26	422	5
Nov. 15, 2009	Donovan McNabb, Philadelphia vs. San Diego	55	35	450	2
Oct. 18, 2009	Ben Roethlisberger, Pittsburgh vs. Cleveland	35	23	417	2
Sept. 20, 2009	Philip Rivers, San Diego vs. Baltimore	45	25	436	2
Dec. 7, 2008	Matt Schaub, Houston vs. Green Bay	42	28	414	2
Nov. 23, 2008	Matt Cassel, New England vs. Miami	43	30	415	3
Nov. 13, 2008	Matt Cassel, New England vs. N.Y. Jets (OT)	51	30	400	3
Nov. 9, 2008	Drew Brees, New Orleans vs. Atlanta	58	31	422	2
Nov. 6, 2008	Jay Cutler, Denver vs. Cleveland	42	24	447	3
Sept. 28, 2008	Kurt Warner, Arizona vs. N.Y. Jets	57	40	472	2
Sept. 21, 2008	Drew Brees, New Orleans vs. Denver	48	39	421	1
Sept. 21, 2008	Brian Griese, Tampa Bay vs. Chicago (OT)	67	38	407	2
Nov. 25, 2007	Kurt Warner, Arizona vs. San Francisco (OT)	48	34	484	2
Nov. 4, 2007	Drew Brees, New Orleans vs. Jacksonville	49	35	445	3
Sept. 23, 2007	Jon Kitna, Detroit vs. Philadelphia	46	29	446	2
Sept. 16, 2007	Carson Palmer, Cincinnati vs. Cleveland	50	33	401	6
Dec. 10, 2006	Chris Weinke, Carolina vs. N.Y. Giants	61	34	423	1
Nov. 26, 2006	Matt Leinart, Arizona vs. Minnesota	51	31	405	1
Nov. 19, 2006	Drew Brees, New Orleans vs. Cincinnati	52	37	510	2
Nov. 12, 2006	Carson Palmer, Cincinnati vs. San Diego	42	31	440	3
Nov. 5, 2006	Ben Roethlisberger, Pittsburgh vs. Denver	54	38	433	1
Oct. 22, 2006	Joey Harrington, Miami vs. Green Bay	62	33	414	2
Sept. 17, 2006	Peyton Manning, Indianapolis vs. Houston	38	26	400	3
Oct. 2, 2005	Marc Bulger, St. Louis vs. N.Y. Giants	62	40	442	2
Jan. 2, 2005	Marc Bulger, St. Louis vs. N.Y. Jets (OT)	39	29	450	3
Dec. 19, 2004	Daunte Culpepper, Minnesota vs. Detroit	35	25	404	3
Dec. 19, 2004	Billy Volek, Tennessee vs. Oakland	60	40	492	4
Dec. 13, 2004	Billy Volek, Tennessee vs. Kansas City	43	29	426	4
Dec. 6, 2004	Matt Hasselbeck, Seattle vs. Dallas	40	28	414	3
Dec. 5, 2004	Peyton Manning, Indianapolis vs. Tennessee	33	25	425	3
Dec. 5, 2004	Donovan McNabb, Philadelphia vs. Green Bay	43	32	464	5

Date	Player, Team, Opponent	Att.	Comp.	Yards	TD
Nov. 29, 2004	Marc Bulger, St. Louis vs. Green Bay	53	35	448	2
Nov. 28, 2004	Kelly Holcomb, Cleveland vs. Cincinnati	39	30	413	5
Oct. 31, 2004	Peyton Manning, Indianapolis vs. Kansas City	44	25	472	5
Oct. 31, 2004	Jake Plummer, Denver vs. Atlanta	55	31	499	4
Oct. 17, 2004	Daunte Culpepper, Minnesota vs. New Orleans	37	26	425	5
Oct. 10, 2004	Tim Rattay, San Francisco vs. Arizona (OT)	57	38	417	2
Nov. 16, 2003	Peyton Manning, Indianapolis vs. N.Y. Jets	36	27	401	1
Oct. 12, 2003	Trent Green, Kansas City vs. Green Bay (OT)	45	27	400	3
Oct. 12, 2003	Steve McNair, Tennessee vs. Houston	27	18	421	3
Dec. 29, 2002	Matt Hasselbeck, Seattle vs. San Diego (OT)	53	36	449	2
Dec. 1, 2002	Matt Hasselbeck, Seattle vs. San Francisco	55	30	427	3
Nov. 10, 2002	Marc Bulger, St. Louis vs. San Diego	48	36	453	4
Nov. 10, 2002	Tommy Maddox, Pittsburgh vs. Atlanta (OT)	41	28	473	4
Oct. 6, 2002	Drew Bledsoe, Buffalo vs. Oakland	53	32	417	2
Sept. 22, 2002	Tom Brady, New England vs. Kansas City (OT)	54	39	410	4
Sept. 15, 2002	Drew Bledsoe, Buffalo vs. Minnesota (OT)	49	35	463	3
Sept. 15, 2002	Rich Gannon, Oakland vs. Pittsburgh	64	43	403	1
Dec. 30, 2001	Jon Kitna, Cincinnati vs. Pittsburgh	68	35	411	2
Dec. 23, 2001	Chris Chandler, Atlanta vs. Buffalo	40	28	431	2
Nov. 18, 2001	Charlie Batch, Detroit vs. Arizona	62	36	436	3
Nov. 18, 2001	Kurt Warner, St. Louis vs. New England	42	30	401	3
Sept. 23, 2001	Peyton Manning, Indianapolis vs. Buffalo	29	23	421	4
Dec. 24, 2000	Vinny Testaverde, N.Y. Jets vs. Baltimore	69	36	481	2
Dec. 17, 2000	Jeff Garcia, San Francisco vs. Chicago	44	36	402	2
Dec. 3, 2000	Aaron Brooks, New Orleans vs. Denver	48	30	441	2
Nov. 19, 2000	Gus Frerotte, Denver vs. San Diego	58	36	462	5
Nov. 5, 2000	Elvis Grbac, Kansas City vs. Oakland	53	39	504	2
Nov. 5, 2000	Trent Green, St. Louis vs. Carolina	42	29	431	2
Sept. 25, 2000	Peyton Manning, Indianapolis vs. Jacksonville	36	23	440	4
Sept. 4, 2000	Kurt Warner, St. Louis vs. Denver	35	25	441	3
Dec. 26, 1999	Brad Johnson, Washington vs. San Francisco (OT)	47	32	471	2
Dec. 5, 1999	Jeff Garcia, San Francisco vs. Cincinnati	49	33	437	3
Nov. 28, 1999	Jim Harbaugh, San Diego vs. Minnesota	39	25	404	1
Nov. 14, 1999	Jim Miller, Chicago vs. Minnesota (OT)	48	34	422	3
Sept. 26, 1999	Peyton Manning, Indianapolis vs. San Diego	54	29	404	2
Dec. 6, 1998	Vinny Testaverde, N.Y. Jets vs. Seattle	63	42	418	2
Dec. 6, 1998	John Elway, Denver vs. Kansas City	32	22	400	2
Nov. 26, 1998	Troy Aikman, Dallas vs. Minnesota	57	34	455	1
Nov. 23, 1998	Drew Bledsoe, New England vs. Miami	54	28	423	2
Nov. 15, 1998	Jake Plummer, Arizona vs. Dallas	56	31	465	3
Oct. 5, 1998	Randall Cunningham, Minnesota vs. Green Bay	32	20	442	4
Sept. 6, 1998	Glenn Foley, N.Y. Jets vs. San Francisco (OT)	58	30	415	3
Nov. 2, 1997	Tony Banks, St. Louis vs. Atlanta	34	23	401	2
Oct. 26, 1997	Warren Moon, Seattle vs. Oakland	44	28	409	5
Nov. 10, 1996	Boomer Esiason, Arizona vs. Washington (OT)	59	35	522	3
Nov. 3, 1996	Drew Bledsoe, New England vs. Miami	41	30	419	3
Oct. 27, 1996	Vinny Testaverde, Baltimore vs. St. Louis (OT)	51	31	429	3
Oct. 20, 1996	Mark Brunell, Jacksonville vs. St. Louis	52	37	421	0
Sept. 22, 1996	Mark Brunell, Jacksonville vs. New England (OT)	39	23	432	3
Dec. 18, 1995	Steve Young, San Francisco vs. Minnesota	49	30	425	3
Nov. 26, 1995	Dave Krieg, Arizona vs. Atlanta (OT)	43	27	413	4
Nov. 23, 1995	Scott Mitchell, Detroit vs. Minnesota	45	30	410	4
Oct. 1, 1995	Dan Marino, Miami vs. Cincinnati	48	33	450	2
Nov. 20, 1994	Warren Moon, Minnesota vs. N.Y. Jets	50	33	400	2
Nov. 13, 1994	Drew Bledsoe, New England vs. Minnesota (OT)	70	45	426	3
Nov. 6, 1994	Warren Moon, Minnesota vs. New Orleans	57	33	420	3
Sept. 25, 1994	Dan Marino, Miami vs. Minnesota	54	29	431	3
Sept. 4, 1994	Dan Marino, Miami vs. New England (OT)	42	23	473	5
Sept. 4, 1994	Drew Bledsoe, New England vs. Miami (OT)	51	32	421	4
Dec. 19, 1993	Steve Beuerlein, Phoenix vs. Seattle	53	34	431	3
Dec. 5, 1993	Brett Favre, Green Bay vs. Chicago	54	36	402	2
Nov. 28, 1993	Steve Young, San Francisco vs. L.A. Rams	32	26	462	4
Oct. 31, 1993	Jeff Hostetler, L.A. Raiders vs. San Diego	32	20	424	2
Sept. 13, 1992	Steve Young, San Francisco vs. Buffalo	37	26	449	3
Sept. 13, 1992	Jim Kelly, Buffalo vs. San Francisco	33	22	403	3
Nov. 10, 1991	Warren Moon, Houston vs. Dallas (OT)	56	41	432	0
Nov. 10, 1991	Mark Rypien, Washington vs. Atlanta	31	16	442	6
Oct. 13, 1991	Warren Moon, Houston vs. N.Y. Jets	50	35	423	2

Date	Player, Team, Opponent	Att.	Comp.	Yards	TD
Dec. 16, 1990	Warren Moon, Houston vs. Kansas City	45	27	527	3
Nov. 4, 1990	Joe Montana, San Francisco vs. Green Bay	40	25	411	3
Oct. 14, 1990	Joe Montana, San Francisco vs. Atlanta	49	32	476	6
Oct. 7, 1990	Boomer Esiason, Cincinnati vs. L.A. Rams (OT)	45	31	490	3
Dec. 23, 1989	Warren Moon, Houston vs. Cleveland	51	32	414	2
Dec. 11, 1989	Joe Montana, San Francisco vs. L.A. Rams	42	30	458	3
Nov. 26, 1989	Jim Everett, L.A. Rams vs. New Orleans (OT)	51	29	454	1
Nov. 26, 1989	Mark Rypien, Washington vs. Chicago	47	30	401	4
Oct. 2, 1989	Randall Cunningham, Philadelphia vs. Chicago	62	32	401	1
Sept. 24, 1989	Joe Montana, San Francisco vs. Philadelphia	34	25	428	5
Sept. 24, 1989	Dan Marino, Miami vs. N.Y. Jets	55	33	427	3
Sept. 17, 1989	Randall Cunningham, Philadelphia vs. Washington	46	34	447	5
Dec. 18, 1988	Dave Krieg, Seattle vs. L.A. Raiders	32	19	410	4
Dec. 12, 1988	Dan Marino, Miami vs. Cleveland	50	30	404	4
Oct. 23, 1988	Dan Marino, Miami vs. N.Y. Jets	60	35	521	3
Oct. 16, 1988	Vinny Testaverde, Tampa Bay vs. Indianapolis	42	25	469	2
Sept. 11, 1988	Doug Williams, Washington vs. Pittsburgh	52	30	430	2
Nov. 29, 1987	Tom Ramsey, New England vs. Philadelphia	53	34	402	3
Nov. 22, 1987	Boomer Esiason, Cincinnati vs. Pittsburgh	53	30	409	0
Sept. 20, 1987	Neil Lomax, St. Louis vs. San Diego	61	32	457	3
Dec. 21, 1986	Boomer Esiason, Cincinnati vs. N.Y. Jets	30	23	425	5
Dec. 14, 1986	Dan Marino, Miami vs. L.A. Rams (OT)	46	29	403	5
Nov. 23, 1986	Bernie Kosar, Cleveland vs. Pittsburgh (OT)	46	28	414	2
Nov. 17, 1986	Joe Montana, San Francisco vs. Washington	60	33	441	0
Nov. 16, 1986	Dan Marino, Miami vs. Buffalo	54	39	404	4
Nov. 10, 1986	Bernie Kosar, Cleveland vs. Miami	50	32	401	0
Nov. 2, 1986	Tommy Kramer, Minnesota vs. Washington (OT)	35	20	490	4
Nov. 2, 1986	Ken O'Brien, N.Y. Jets vs. Seattle	32	26	431	4
Oct. 27, 1986	Jay Schroeder, Washington vs. N.Y. Giants	40	22	420	1
Oct. 12, 1986	Steve Grogan, New England vs. N.Y. Jets	42	23	401	4
Sept. 21, 1986	Ken O'Brien, N.Y. Jets vs. Miami (OT)	43	29	479	4
Sept. 21, 1986	Dan Marino, Miami vs. N.Y. Jets (OT)	50	30	448	6
Sept. 21, 1986	Tony Eason, New England vs. Seattle	45	26	414	3
Dec. 20, 1985	John Elway, Denver vs. Seattle	42	24	432	1
Nov. 10, 1985	Dan Fouts, San Diego vs. L.A. Raiders (OT)	41	26	436	4
Oct. 13, 1985	Phil Simms, N.Y. Giants vs. Cincinnati	62	40	513	1
Oct. 13, 1985	Dave Krieg, Seattle vs. Atlanta	51	33	405	4
Oct. 6, 1985	Phil Simms, N.Y. Giants vs. Dallas	36	18	432	3
Oct. 6, 1985	Joe Montana, San Francisco vs. Atlanta	57	37	429	5
Sept. 19, 1985	Tommy Kramer, Minnesota vs. Chicago	55	28	436	3
Sept. 15, 1985	Dan Fouts, San Diego vs. Seattle	43	29	440	4
Dec. 16, 1984	Neil Lomax, St. Louis vs. Washington	46	37	468	2
Dec. 9, 1984	Dan Marino, Miami vs. Indianapolis	41	29	404	4
Dec. 2, 1984	Dan Marino, Miami vs. L.A. Raiders	57	35	470	4
Nov. 25, 1984	Dave Krieg, Seattle vs. Denver	44	30	406	3
Nov. 4, 1984	Dan Marino, Miami vs. N.Y. Jets	42	23	422	2
Oct. 21, 1984	Dan Fouts, San Diego vs. L.A. Raiders	45	24	410	3
Sept. 30, 1984	Dan Marino, Miami vs. St. Louis	36	24	429	3
Sept. 2, 1984	Phil Simms, N.Y. Giants vs. Philadelphia	30	23	409	4
Dec. 11, 1983	Bill Kenney, Kansas City vs. San Diego	41	31	411	4
Nov. 20, 1983	Dave Krieg, Seattle vs. Denver	42	31	418	3
Oct. 9, 1983	Joe Ferguson, Buffalo vs. Miami (OT)	55	38	419	5
Oct. 2, 1983	Joe Theismann, Washington vs. L.A. Raiders	39	23	417	3
Sept. 25, 1983	Richard Todd, N.Y. Jets vs. L.A. Rams (OT)	50	37	446	2
Dec. 26, 1982	Vince Ferragamo, L.A. Rams vs. Chicago	46	30	509	3
Dec. 20, 1982	Dan Fouts, San Diego vs. Cincinnati	40	25	435	1
Dec. 20, 1982	Ken Anderson, Cincinnati vs. San Diego	56	40	416	2
Dec. 11, 1982	Dan Fouts, San Diego vs. San Francisco	48	33	444	5
Nov. 21, 1982	Joe Montana, San Francisco vs. St. Louis	39	26	408	3
Nov. 15, 1981	Steve Bartkowski, Atlanta vs. Pittsburgh	50	33	416	2
Oct. 25, 1981	Brian Sipe, Cleveland vs. Baltimore	41	30	444	4
Oct. 25, 1981	David Woodley, Miami vs. Dallas	37	21	408	3
Oct. 11, 1981	Tommy Kramer, Minnesota vs. San Diego	43	27	444	4
Dec. 14, 1980	Tommy Kramer, Minnesota vs. Cleveland	49	38	456	4
Nov. 16, 1980	Doug Williams, Tampa Bay vs. Minnesota	55	30	486	4
Oct. 19, 1980	Dan Fouts, San Diego vs. N.Y. Giants	41	26	444	3
Oct. 12, 1980	Lynn Dickey, Green Bay vs. Tampa Bay (OT)	51	35	418	1
Sept. 21, 1980	Richard Todd, N.Y. Jets vs. San Francisco	60	42	447	3

OUTSTANDING PERFORMERS

Date	Player, Team, Opponent	Att.	Comp.	Yards	TD
Oct. 3, 1976	James Harris, Los Angeles vs. Miami	29	17	436	2
Nov. 17, 1975	Ken Anderson, Cincinnati vs. Buffalo	46	30	447	2
Nov. 18, 1974	Charley Johnson, Denver vs. Kansas City	42	28	445	2
Dec. 11, 1972	Joe Namath, N.Y. Jets vs. Oakland	46	25	403	1
Sept. 24, 1972	Joe Namath, N.Y. Jets vs. Baltimore	28	15	496	6
Dec. 21, 1969	Don Horn, Green Bay vs. St. Louis	31	22	410	5
Sept. 28, 1969	Joe Kapp, Minnesota vs. Baltimore	43	28	449	7
Sept. 9, 1968	Pete Beathard, Houston vs. Kansas City	48	23	413	2
Nov. 26, 1967	Sonny Jurgensen, Washington vs. Cleveland	50	32	418	3
Oct. 1, 1967	Joe Namath, N.Y. Jets vs. Miami	39	23	415	3
Sept. 17, 1967	Johnny Unitas, Baltimore vs. Atlanta	32	22	401	2
Nov. 13, 1966	Don Meredith, Dallas vs. Washington	29	21	406	2
Nov. 28, 1965	Sonny Jurgensen, Washington vs. Dallas	43	26	411	3
Oct. 24, 1965	Fran Tarkenton, Minnesota vs. San Francisco	35	21	407	3
Nov. 1, 1964	Len Dawson, Kansas City vs. Denver	38	23	435	6
Oct. 25, 1964	Cotton Davidson, Oakland vs. Denver	36	23	427	5
Oct. 16, 1964	Babe Parilli, Boston vs. Oakland	47	25	422	4
Dec. 22, 1963	Tom Flores, Oakland vs. Houston	29	17	407	6
Nov. 17, 1963	Norm Snead, Washington vs. Pittsburgh	40	23	424	2
Nov. 10, 1963	Don Meredith, Dallas vs. San Francisco	48	30	460	3
Oct. 13, 1963	Charley Johnson, St. Louis vs. Pittsburgh	41	20	428	2
Dec. 16, 1962	Sonny Jurgensen, Philadelphia vs. St. Louis	34	15	419	5
Nov. 18, 1962	Bill Wade, Chicago vs. Dall. Cowboys	46	28	466	2
Oct. 28, 1962	Y.A. Tittle, N.Y. Giants vs. Washington	39	27	505	7
Sept. 15, 1962	Frank Tripucka, Denver vs. Buffalo	56	29	447	2
Dec. 17, 1961	Sonny Jurgensen, Philadelphia vs. Detroit	42	27	403	3
Nov. 19, 1961	George Blanda, Houston vs. N.Y. Titans	32	20	418	7
Oct. 29, 1961	George Blanda, Houston vs. Buffalo	32	18	464	4
Oct. 29, 1961	Sonny Jurgensen, Philadelphia vs. Washington	41	27	436	3
Oct. 13, 1961	Jacky Lee, Houston vs. Boston	41	27	457	2
Dec. 13, 1958	Bobby Layne, Pittsburgh vs. Chi. Cardinals	49	23	409	2
Nov. 8, 1953	Bobby Thomason, Philadelphia vs. N.Y. Giants	44	22	437	4
Oct. 4, 1952	Otto Graham, Cleveland vs. Pittsburgh	49	21	401	3
Sept. 28, 1951	Norm Van Brocklin, Los Angeles vs. N.Y. Yanks	41	27	554	5
Dec. 11, 1949	Johnny Lujack, Chi. Bears vs. Chi. Cardinals	39	24	468	6
Oct. 31, 1948	Sammy Baugh, Washington vs. Boston	24	17	446	4
Oct. 31, 1948	Jim Hardy, Los Angeles vs. Chi. Cardinals	53	28	406	3
Nov. 14, 1943	Sid Luckman, Chi. Bears vs. N.Y. Giants	32	21	433	7

*First season of professional football.

TIMES 400 OR MORE

276 times by 123 players...Marino 13; P. Manning 12; Brees 10; Montana, Moon, Palmer 7; Bledsoe, Brady, Fouts, Rivers, Stafford 6; Jurgensen, Krieg, E. Manning, Roethlisberger, Romo 5; Bulger, Esiason, Kramer, Schaub, Testaverde, Warner 4; Cassel, Cunningham, Hasselbeck, McNabb, Namath, Rodgers, Simms, Young 3; Anderson, Blanda, Brunell, Culpepper, Elway, Favre, Foles, Garcia, Green, C. Johnson, Kitna, Kosar, Lomax, Meredith, Newton, O'Brien, Orton, Plummer, Rypien, Todd, Vick, Volek, D. Williams 2.

100 PASS RECEPTIONS IN A SEASON

Year	Player, Team	No.	Yards	Avg.	Long	TD
2013	Pierre Garcon, Washington	113	1,346	11.9	53	5
	Antonio Brown, Pittsburgh	110	1,499	13.6	56	8
	Andre Johnson, Houston[5]	109	1,407	12.9	62	5
	Julian Edelman, New England	105	1,056	10.1	44	6
	Brandon Marshall, Chicago[5]	100	1,295	13.0	44	12
2012	Calvin Johnson, Detroit	122	1,964	16.1	53	5
	Brandon Marshall, Chicago[4]	118	1,508	12.8	56	11
	Wes Welker, New England[5]	118	1,354	11.5	59	6
	Andre Johnson, Houston[4]	112	1,598	14.3	60	4
	Jason Witten, Dallas	110	1,039	9.4	36	3
	Reggie Wayne, Indianapolis[4]	106	1,355	12.8	33	5
2011	Wes Welker, New England[4]	122	1,569	12.9	99	9
	Roddy White, Atlanta[2]	100	1,296	13.0	43	8
2010	Roddy White, Atlanta	115	1,389	12.1	46	10
	Reggie Wayne, Indianapolis[3]	111	1,355	12.2	50	6
2009	Wes Welker, New England[3]	123	1,348	11.0	58	4
	Steve Smith, N.Y. Giants	107	1,220	11.4	51	7
	Andre Johnson, Houston[3]	101	1,569	15.5	72	9
	Brandon Marshall, Denver[3]	101	1,120	11.1	75	10

Year	Player, Team	No.	Yards	Avg.	Long	TD
	Dallas Clark, Indianapolis	100	1,106	11.1	80	10
	Reggie Wayne, Indianapolis[2]	100	1,264	12.6	65	10
2008	Andre Johnson, Houston[2]	115	1,575	13.7	65	8
	Wes Welker, New England[2]	111	1,165	10.5	64	3
	Brandon Marshall, Denver[2]	104	1,265	12.2	47	6
2007	T.J. Houshmandzadeh, Cincinnati	112	1,143	10.2	42	12
	Wes Welker, New England	112	1,175	10.5	42	8
	Reggie Wayne, Indianapolis	104	1,510	14.5	64	10
	Derrick Mason, Baltimore	103	1,087	10.6	79	5
	Brandon Marshall, Denver	102	1,325	13.0	68	7
	Larry Fitzgerald, Arizona[2]	100	1,409	14.1	48	10
2006	Andre Johnson, Houston	103	1,147	11.1	53	5
2005	Larry Fitzgerald, Arizona	103	1,409	13.7	47	10
	Steve Smith, Carolina	103	1,563	15.2	80	12
	Anquan Boldin, Arizona[2]	102	1,402	13.7	54	7
	Torry Holt, St. Louis[2]	102	1,331	13.0	44	9
2004	Tony Gonzalez, Kansas City	102	1,258	12.3	32	7
2003	Torry Holt, St. Louis	117	1,696	14.5	48	12
	Randy Moss, Minnesota[2]	111	1,632	14.7	72	17
	*Anquan Boldin, Arizona	101	1,377	13.6	71	8
	LaDainian Tomlinson, San Diego	100	725	7.3	73	4
2002	Marvin Harrison, Indianapolis[4]	143	1,722	12.0	69	11
	Hines Ward, Pittsburgh	112	1,329	11.9	72	12
	Randy Moss, Minnesota	106	1,347	12.7	60	7
	Eric Moulds, Buffalo	100	1,292	12.9	70	10
	Terrell Owens, San Francisco	100	1,300	13.0	76	13
2001	Rod Smith, Denver[2]	113	1,343	11.9	65	11
	Jimmy Smith, Jacksonville[2]	112	1,373	12.3	35	8
	Marvin Harrison, Indianapolis[3]	109	1,524	14.0	68	15
	Keyshawn Johnson, Tampa Bay	106	1,266	11.9	47	1
	Troy Brown, New England	101	1,199	11.9	60	5
	Marty Booker, Chicago	100	1,071	10.7	66	8
2000	Marvin Harrison, Indianapolis[2]	102	1,413	13.9	78	14
	Muhsin Muhammad, Carolina	102	1,183	11.6	36	6
	Ed McCaffrey, Denver	101	1,317	13.0	61	9
	Rod Smith, Denver	100	1,602	16.0	49	8
1999	Jimmy Smith, Jacksonville	116	1,636	14.1	62	6
	Marvin Harrison, Indianapolis	115	1,663	14.5	57	12
1997	Tim Brown, Oakland	104	1,408	13.5	59	5
	Herman Moore, Detroit[3]	104	1,293	12.4	79	8
1996	Jerry Rice, San Francisco[4]	108	1,254	11.6	39	8
	Herman Moore, Detroit[2]	106	1,296	12.2	50	9
	Carl Pickens, Cincinnati	100	1,180	11.8	61	12
1995	Herman Moore, Detroit	123	1,686	13.7	69	14
	Jerry Rice, San Francisco[3]	122	1,848	15.1	81	15
	Cris Carter, Minnesota[2]	122	1,371	11.2	60	17
	Isaac Bruce, St. Louis	119	1,781	15.0	72	13
	Michael Irvin, Dallas	111	1,603	14.4	50	10
	Brett Perriman, Detroit	108	1,488	13.8	91	9
	Eric Metcalf, Atlanta	104	1,189	11.4	62	8
	Robert Brooks, Green Bay	102	1,497	14.7	99	13
	Larry Centers, Arizona	101	962	9.5	32	2
1994	Cris Carter, Minnesota	122	1,256	10.3	65	7
	Jerry Rice, San Francisco[2]	112	1,499	13.4	69	13
	Terance Mathis, Atlanta	111	1,342	12.1	81	11
1993	Sterling Sharpe, Green Bay[2]	112	1,274	11.4	54	11
1992	Sterling Sharpe, Green Bay	108	1,461	13.5	76	13
1991	Haywood Jeffires, Houston	100	1,181	11.8	44	7
1990	Jerry Rice, San Francisco	100	1,502	15.0	64	13
1984	Art Monk, Washington	106	1,372	12.9	72	7
1964	Charley Hennigan, Houston	101	1,546	15.3	53	8
1961	Lionel Taylor, Denver	100	1,176	11.8	52	4

First season of professional football.

1,000 YARDS PASS RECEIVING IN A SEASON

Year	Player, Team	No.	Yards	Avg.	Long	TD
2013	Josh Gordon, Cleveland	87	1,646	18.9	95	9
	Antonio Brown, Pittsburgh[2]	110	1,499	13.6	56	8
	Calvin Johnson, Detroit[5]	84	1,492	17.8	87	12

Year	Player, Team	No.	Yards	Avg.	Long	TD
	Demaryius Thomas, Denver[2]	92	1,430	15.5	78	14
	A.J. Green, Cincinnati[3]	98	1,426	14.6	82	11
	Alshon Jeffery, Chicago	89	1,421	16.0	80	7
	Andre Johnson, Houston[7]	109	1,407	12.9	62	5
	Pierre Garcon, Washington	113	1,346	11.9	53	5
	DeSean Jackson, Philadelphia[3]	82	1,332	16.2	61	9
	Jordy Nelson, Green Bay[2]	85	1,314	15.5	76	8
	Brandon Marshall, Chicago[7]	100	1,295	13.0	44	12
	Eric Decker, Denver[2]	87	1,288	14.8	61	11
	Dez Bryant, Dallas[2]	93	1,233	13.3	79	13
	Vincent Jackson, Tampa Bay[5]	78	1,224	15.7	60	7
	Jimmy Graham, New Orleans[2]	86	1,215	14.1	56	16
	Anquan Boldin, San Francisco[6]	85	1,179	13.9	63	7
	Torrey Smith, Baltimore	65	1,128	17.4	74	4
	T.Y. Hilton, Indianapolis	82	1,083	13.2	73	5
	Kendall Wright, Tennessee	94	1,079	11.5	45	2
	Harry Douglas, Atlanta	85	1,067	12.6	80	2
	Julian Edelman, New England	105	1,056	10.1	44	6
	*Keenan Allen, San Diego	71	1,046	14.7	43	8
	Michael Floyd, Arizona	65	1,041	16.0	91	5
	Brian Hartline, Miami[2]	76	1,016	13.4	50	4
2012	Calvin Johnson, Detroit[4]	122	1,964	16.1	53	5
	Andre Johnson, Houston[6]	112	1,598	14.3	60	4
	Brandon Marshall, Chicago[6]	118	1,508	12.8	56	11
	Demaryius Thomas, Denver	94	1,434	15.3	71	10
	Vincent Jackson, Tampa Bay[4]	72	1,384	19.2	95	8
	Dez Bryant, Dallas	92	1,382	15.0	85	12
	Reggie Wayne, Indianapolis[8]	106	1,355	12.8	33	5
	Wes Welker, New England[5]	118	1,354	11.5	59	6
	Roddy White, Atlanta[6]	92	1,351	14.7	59	7
	A.J. Green, Cincinnati[2]	97	1,350	13.9	73	11
	Julio Jones, Atlanta	79	1,198	15.2	80	10
	Steve Smith, Carolina[7]	73	1,174	16.1	66	4
	Marques Colston, New Orleans[6]	83	1,154	13.9	60	10
	Michael Crabtree, San Francisco	85	1,105	13.0	49	9
	Victor Cruz, N.Y. Giants[2]	86	1,092	12.7	80	10
	Brian Hartline, Miami	74	1,083	14.6	80	1
	Eric Decker, Denver	85	1,064	12.5	55	13
	Steve Johnson, Buffalo[3]	79	1,046	13.2	63	6
	Lance Moore, New Orleans	65	1,041	16.0	51	6
	Jason Witten, Dallas[4]	110	1,039	9.4	36	3
2011	Calvin Johnson, Detroit[3]	96	1,681	17.5	73	16
	Wes Welker, New England[4]	122	1,569	12.9	99	9
	Victor Cruz, N.Y. Giants	82	1,536	18.7	99	9
	Larry Fitzgerald, Arizona[6]	80	1,411	17.6	73	8
	Steve Smith, Carolina[6]	79	1,394	17.6	77	7
	Rob Gronkowski, New England	90	1,327	14.7	52	17
	Jimmy Graham, New Orleans	99	1,310	13.2	59	11
	Roddy White, Atlanta[5]	100	1,296	13.0	43	8
	Jordy Nelson, Green Bay	68	1,263	18.6	93	15
	Brandon Marshall, Miami[5]	81	1,214	15.0	65	6
	Mike Wallace, Pittsburgh[2]	72	1,193	16.6	95	8
	Hakeem Nicks, N.Y. Giants[2]	76	1,192	15.7	68	7
	Dwayne Bowe, Kansas City[3]	81	1,159	14.3	52	5
	Marques Colston, New Orleans[5]	80	1,143	14.3	50	8
	Antonio Brown, Pittsburgh	69	1,108	16.1	79	2
	Vincent Jackson, San Diego[3]	60	1,106	18.4	58	9
	*A.J. Green, Cincinnati	65	1,057	16.3	58	7
	Nate Washington, Tennessee	74	1,023	13.8	57	7
	Steve Johnson, Buffalo[2]	76	1,004	13.2	55	7
2010	Brandon Lloyd, Denver	77	1,448	18.8	71	11
	Roddy White, Atlanta[4]	115	1,389	12.1	46	10
	Reggie Wayne, Indianapolis[7]	111	1,355	12.2	50	6
	Greg Jennings, Green Bay[3]	76	1,265	16.6	86	12
	Mike Wallace, Pittsburgh	60	1,257	20.9	56	10
	Andre Johnson, Houston[5]	86	1,216	14.1	60	8
	Dwayne Bowe, Kansas City[2]	72	1,162	16.1	75	15
	Larry Fitzgerald, Arizona[5]	90	1,137	12.6	41	6
	Calvin Johnson, Detroit[2]	77	1,120	14.6	87	12

Year	Player, Team	No.	Yards	Avg.	Long	TD
	Santana Moss, Washington[4]	93	1,115	12.0	56	6
	Steve Johnson, Buffalo	82	1,073	13.1	45	10
	DeSean Jackson, Philadelphia[2]	47	1,056	22.5	91	6
	Hakeem Nicks, N.Y. Giants	79	1,052	13.3	46	11
	Miles Austin, Dallas[2]	69	1,041	15.1	69	7
	Marques Colston, New Orleans[4]	84	1,023	12.2	43	7
	Brandon Marshall, Miami[4]	86	1,014	11.8	46	3
	Jason Witten, Dallas[3]	94	1,002	10.7	33	9
2009	Andre Johnson, Houston[4]	101	1,569	15.5	72	9
	Wes Welker, New England[3]	123	1,348	11.0	58	4
	Miles Austin, Dallas	81	1,320	16.3	60	11
	Sidney Rice, Minnesota	83	1,321	15.8	63	8
	Randy Moss, New England[10]	83	1,264	15.2	71	13
	Reggie Wayne, Indianapolis[6]	100	1,264	12.6	65	10
	Santonio Holmes, Pittsburgh	79	1,248	15.8	57	5
	Steve Smith, N.Y. Giants	107	1,220	11.4	51	7
	Vincent Jackson, San Diego[2]	68	1,167	17.2	55	9
	Hines Ward, Pittsburgh[6]	95	1,167	12.3	54	6
	Antonio Gates, San Diego[2]	79	1,157	14.6	56	8
	DeSean Jackson, Philadelphia	62	1,156	18.6	71	9
	Roddy White, Atlanta[3]	85	1,153	13.6	90	11
	Brandon Marshall, Denver[3]	101	1,120	11.1	75	10
	Greg Jennings, Green Bay[2]	68	1,113	16.4	83	4
	Dallas Clark, Indianapolis	100	1,106	11.1	80	10
	Larry Fitzgerald, Arizona[4]	97	1,092	11.3	34	13
	Marques Colston, New Orleans[3]	70	1,074	15.3	68	9
	Donald Driver, Green Bay[7]	70	1,061	15.2	71	6
	Chad Johnson, Cincinnati[7]	72	1,047	14.5	50	9
	Jason Witten, Dallas[2]	94	1,030	11.0	69	2
	Derrick Mason, Baltimore[8]	73	1,028	14.1	72	7
	Anquan Boldin, Arizona[5]	84	1,024	12.2	44	4
2008	Andre Johnson, Houston[3]	115	1,575	13.7	65	8
	Larry Fitzgerald, Arizona[3]	96	1,431	14.9	78	12
	Steve Smith, Carolina[5]	78	1,421	18.2	65	6
	Roddy White, Atlanta[2]	88	1,382	15.7	70	7
	Calvin Johnson, Detroit	78	1,331	17.1	96	12
	Greg Jennings, Green Bay	80	1,292	16.1	63	9
	Brandon Marshall, Denver[2]	104	1,265	12.2	47	6
	Antonio Bryant, Tampa Bay[2]	83	1,248	15.0	71	7
	Wes Welker, New England[2]	111	1,165	10.5	64	3
	Reggie Wayne, Indianapolis[5]	82	1,145	14.0	65	6
	Vincent Jackson, San Diego	59	1,098	18.6	60	7
	Tony Gonzalez, Kansas City[4]	96	1,058	11.0	35	10
	Terrell Owens, Dallas[9]	69	1,052	15.2	75	10
	Santana Moss, Washington[3]	79	1,044	13.2	67	6
	Hines Ward, Pittsburgh[5]	81	1,043	12.9	49	7
	Anquan Boldin, Arizona[4]	89	1,038	11.7	79	11
	Derrick Mason, Baltimore[7]	80	1,037	13.0	54	5
	Dwayne Bowe, Kansas City	86	1,022	11.9	36	7
	Lee Evans, Buffalo[2]	63	1,017	16.1	87	3
	Donald Driver, Green Bay[6]	74	1,012	13.7	71	5
	Randy Moss, New England[9]	69	1,008	14.6	76	11
	Steve Breaston, Arizona	77	1,006	13.1	58	3
2007	Reggie Wayne, Indianapolis[4]	104	1,510	14.5	64	10
	Randy Moss, New England[8]	98	1,493	15.2	65	23
	Chad Johnson, Cincinnati[6]	93	1,440	15.5	70	8
	Larry Fitzgerald, Arizona[2]	100	1,409	14.1	48	10
	Terrell Owens, Dallas[9]	81	1,355	16.7	52	15
	Brandon Marshall, Denver	102	1,325	13.0	68	7
	Braylon Edwards, Cleveland	80	1,289	16.1	78	16
	Marques Colston, New Orleans[2]	98	1,202	12.3	45	11
	Roddy White, Atlanta	83	1,202	14.5	69	6
	Torry Holt, St. Louis[8]	93	1,189	12.8	40	7
	Wes Welker, New England	112	1,175	10.5	42	8
	Tony Gonzalez, Kansas City[3]	99	1,172	11.8	31	5
	Bobby Engram, Seattle	94	1,147	12.2	49	6
	Jason Witten, Dallas	96	1,145	11.9	53	7
	T.J. Houshmandzadeh, Cincinnati[2]	112	1,143	10.2	42	12
	Jerricho Cotchery, N.Y. Jets	82	1,130	13.8	50	2

Year	Player, Team	No.	Yards	Avg.	Long	TD
	Kevin Curtis, Philadelphia	77	1,110	14.4	75	6
	Kellen Winslow, Cleveland	82	1,106	13.5	49	5
	Derrick Mason, Baltimore[6]	103	1,087	10.6	79	5
	Donald Driver, Green Bay[5]	82	1,048	12.8	47	2
	Plaxico Burress, N.Y. Giants[4]	70	1,025	14.6	60	12
	Joey Galloway, Tampa Bay[6]	57	1,014	17.8	69	6
	Steve Smith, Carolina[4]	87	1,002	11.5	74	7
2006	Chad Johnson, Cincinnati[5]	87	1,369	15.7	74	7
	Marvin Harrison, Indianapolis[8]	95	1,366	14.4	68	12
	Reggie Wayne, Indianapolis[3]	86	1,310	15.2	51	9
	Roy Williams, Detroit	82	1,310	16.0	60	7
	Donald Driver, Green Bay[4]	92	1,295	14.1	82	8
	Lee Evans, Buffalo	82	1,292	15.8	83	8
	Anquan Boldin, Arizona[3]	83	1,203	14.5	64	4
	Torry Holt, St. Louis[7]	93	1,188	12.8	67	10
	Terrell Owens, Dallas[7]	85	1,180	13.9	56	13
	Steve Smith, Carolina[3]	83	1,166	14.1	72	8
	Andre Johnson, Houston[2]	103	1,147	11.1	53	5
	Isaac Bruce, St. Louis[8]	74	1,098	14.8	45	3
	Laveranues Coles, N.Y. Jets[2]	91	1,098	12.1	58	6
	Mike Furrey, Detroit	98	1,086	11.1	31	6
	Javon Walker, Denver[2]	69	1,084	15.7	83	8
	T.J. Houshmandzadeh, Cincinnati	90	1,081	12.0	40	9
	Joey Galloway, Tampa Bay[5]	62	1,057	17.1	64	7
	Terry Glenn, Dallas[4]	70	1,047	15.0	54	6
	*Marques Colston, New Orleans	70	1,038	14.8	86	8
2005	Steve Smith, Carolina[2]	103	1,563	15.2	80	12
	Santana Moss, Washington[2]	84	1,483	17.7	78	9
	Chad Johnson, Cincinnati[4]	97	1,432	14.8	70	9
	Larry Fitzgerald, Arizona	103	1,409	13.7	47	10
	Anquan Boldin, Arizona[2]	102	1,402	13.7	54	7
	Torry Holt, St. Louis[6]	102	1,331	13.0	44	9
	Joey Galloway, Tampa Bay[4]	83	1,287	15.5	80	10
	Donald Driver, Green Bay[3]	86	1,221	14.2	59	5
	Plaxico Burress, N.Y. Giants[3]	76	1,214	16.0	78	7
	Marvin Harrison, Indianapolis[7]	82	1,146	14.0	80	12
	Terry Glenn, Dallas[3]	62	1,136	18.3	71	7
	Chris Chambers, Miami	82	1,118	13.6	77	11
	Rod Smith, Denver[8]	85	1,105	13.0	72	6
	Eddie Kennison, Kansas City[2]	68	1,102	16.2	55	5
	Antonio Gates, San Diego	89	1,101	12.4	38	10
	Derrick Mason, Baltimore[5]	86	1,073	12.5	39	3
	Reggie Wayne, Indianapolis[2]	83	1,055	12.7	66	5
	Jimmy Smith, Jacksonville[9]	70	1,023	14.6	45	6
	Antonio Bryant, Cleveland	69	1,009	14.6	54	4
	Randy Moss, Oakland[7]	60	1,005	16.8	79	8
2004	Muhsin Muhammad, Carolina[3]	93	1,405	15.1	51	16
	Joe Horn, New Orleans[4]	94	1,399	14.9	57	11
	Javon Walker, Green Bay	89	1,382	15.5	79	12
	Torry Holt, St. Louis[5]	94	1,372	14.6	75	10
	Isaac Bruce, St. Louis[7]	89	1,292	14.5	56	6
	Chad Johnson, Cincinnati[3]	95	1,274	13.4	53	9
	Tony Gonzalez, Kansas City[2]	102	1,258	12.3	32	7
	Drew Bennett, Tennessee	80	1,247	15.6	48	11
	Reggie Wayne, Indianapolis	77	1,210	15.7	71	12
	Donald Driver, Green Bay[2]	84	1,208	14.4	50	9
	Terrell Owens, Philadelphia[6]	77	1,200	15.6	59	14
	Darrell Jackson, Seattle[3]	87	1,199	13.8	56	7
	*Michael Clayton, Tampa Bay	80	1,193	14.9	75	7
	Jimmy Smith, Jacksonville[8]	74	1,172	15.8	65	6
	Derrick Mason, Tennessee[4]	96	1,168	12.2	37	7
	Rod Smith, Denver[7]	79	1,144	14.5	85	7
	Andre Johnson, Houston	79	1,142	14.5	54	6
	Marvin Harrison, Indianapolis[6]	86	1,113	12.9	59	15
	Eddie Kennison, Kansas City	62	1,086	17.5	70	8
	Ashley Lelie, Denver	54	1,084	20.1	58	7
	Brandon Stokley, Indianapolis	68	1,077	15.8	69	10
	Eric Moulds, Buffalo[4]	88	1,043	11.9	49	5
	Nate Burleson, Minnesota	68	1,006	14.8	68	9

Year	Player, Team	No.	Yards	Avg.	Long	TD
	Hines Ward, Pittsburgh[4]	80	1,004	12.6	58	4
2003	Torry Holt, St. Louis[4]	117	1,696	14.5	48	12
	Randy Moss, Minnesota[6]	111	1,632	14.7	72	17
	*Anquan Boldin, Arizona	101	1,377	13.6	71	8
	Chad Johnson, Cincinnati[2]	90	1,355	15.1	82	10
	Derrick Mason, Tennessee[3]	95	1,303	13.7	50	8
	Marvin Harrison, Indianapolis[5]	94	1,272	13.5	79	10
	Laveranues Coles, Washington[2]	82	1,204	14.7	64	6
	Keenan McCardell, Tampa Bay[5]	84	1,174	14.0	76	8
	Hines Ward, Pittsburgh[3]	95	1,163	12.2	50	10
	Darrell Jackson, Seattle[2]	68	1,137	16.7	80	9
	Steve Smith, Carolina	88	1,110	12.6	67	7
	Santana Moss, N.Y. Jets	74	1,105	14.9	65	10
	Terrell Owens, San Francisco[5]	80	1,102	13.8	75	9
	Amani Toomer, N.Y. Giants[5]	63	1,057	16.8	77	5
2002	Marvin Harrison, Indianapolis[4]	143	1,722	12.0	69	11
	Randy Moss, Minnesota[5]	106	1,347	12.7	60	7
	Amani Toomer, N.Y. Giants[4]	82	1,343	16.4	82	8
	Hines Ward, Pittsburgh[2]	112	1,329	11.9	72	12
	Plaxico Burress, Pittsburgh[2]	78	1,325	17.0	62	7
	Joe Horn, New Orleans[3]	88	1,312	14.9	63	7
	Torry Holt, St. Louis[3]	91	1,302	14.3	58	4
	Terrell Owens, San Francisco[4]	100	1,300	13.0	76	13
	Eric Moulds, Buffalo[3]	100	1,292	12.9	70	10
	Laveranues Coles, N.Y. Jets	89	1,264	14.2	43	5
	Peerless Price, Buffalo	94	1,252	13.3	73	9
	Koren Robinson, Seattle	78	1,240	15.9	83	5
	Jerry Rice, Oakland[14]	92	1,211	13.2	75	7
	Marty Booker, Chicago[2]	97	1,189	12.3	54	6
	Chad Johnson, Cincinnati	69	1,166	16.9	72	5
	Keyshawn Johnson, Tampa Bay[4]	76	1,088	14.3	76	5
	Isaac Bruce, St. Louis[6]	79	1,075	13.6	34	7
	Donald Driver, Green Bay	70	1,064	15.2	85	9
	Jimmy Smith, Jacksonville[7]	80	1,027	12.8	47	7
	Rod Smith, Denver[6]	89	1,027	11.5	46	5
	Derrick Mason, Tennessee[2]	79	1,012	12.8	40	5
	Rod Gardner, Washington	71	1,006	14.2	43	8
2001	David Boston, Arizona[2]	98	1,598	16.3	61	8
	Marvin Harrison, Indianapolis[3]	109	1,524	14.0	68	15
	Terrell Owens, San Francisco[3]	93	1,412	15.2	60	16
	Jimmy Smith, Jacksonville[6]	112	1,373	12.3	35	8
	Torry Holt, St. Louis[2]	81	1,363	16.8	51	7
	Rod Smith, Denver[5]	113	1,343	11.9	65	11
	Keyshawn Johnson, Tampa Bay[3]	106	1,266	11.9	47	1
	Joe Horn, New Orleans[2]	83	1,265	15.2	56	9
	Randy Moss, Minnesota[4]	82	1,233	15.0	73	10
	Troy Brown, New England	101	1,199	11.9	60	5
	Tim Brown, Oakland[9]	91	1,165	12.8	46	9
	Johnnie Morton, Detroit[4]	77	1,154	15.0	76	4
	Jerry Rice, Oakland[13]	83	1,139	13.7	40	9
	Derrick Mason, Tennessee	73	1,128	15.5	71	9
	Curtis Conway, San Diego[3]	71	1,125	15.8	72	6
	Keenan McCardell, Jacksonville[4]	93	1,110	11.9	45	6
	Isaac Bruce, St. Louis[5]	64	1,106	17.3	51	6
	Kevin Johnson, Cleveland	84	1,097	13.1	55	9
	Darrell Jackson, Seattle	70	1,081	15.4	64	8
	Marty Booker, Chicago	100	1,071	10.7	66	8
	Qadry Ismail, Baltimore[2]	74	1,059	14.3	77	7
	Amani Toomer, N.Y. Giants[3]	72	1,054	14.6	60	5
	Willie Jackson, New Orleans	81	1,046	12.9	63	5
	Plaxico Burress, Pittsburgh	66	1,008	15.3	43	6
	Hines Ward, Pittsburgh	94	1,003	10.7	34	4
2000	Torry Holt, St. Louis	82	1,635	19.9	85	6
	Rod Smith, Denver[4]	100	1,602	16.0	49	8
	Isaac Bruce, St. Louis[4]	87	1,471	16.9	78	9
	Terrell Owens, San Francisco[2]	97	1,451	15.0	69	13
	Randy Moss, Minnesota[3]	77	1,437	18.7	78	15
	Marvin Harrison, Indianapolis[2]	102	1,413	13.9	78	14
	Derrick Alexander, Kansas City[3]	78	1,391	17.8	81	10

Year	Player, Team	No.	Yards	Avg.	Long	TD
	Joe Horn, New Orleans	94	1,340	14.3	52	8
	Eric Moulds, Buffalo[2]	94	1,326	14.1	52	5
	Ed McCaffrey, Denver[3]	101	1,317	13.0	61	9
	Cris Carter, Minnesota[8]	96	1,274	13.3	53	9
	Jimmy Smith, Jacksonville[5]	91	1,213	13.3	65	8
	Keenan McCardell, Jacksonville[3]	94	1,207	12.8	67	5
	Tony Gonzalez, Kansas City	93	1,203	12.9	39	9
	Muhsin Muhammad, Carolina[2]	102	1,183	11.6	36	6
	David Boston, Arizona	71	1,156	16.3	70	7
	Tim Brown, Oakland[8]	76	1,128	14.8	45	11
	Amani Toomer, N.Y. Giants[2]	78	1,094	14.0	54	7
1999	Marvin Harrison, Indianapolis	115	1,663	14.5	57	12
	Jimmy Smith, Jacksonville[4]	116	1,636	14.1	62	6
	Randy Moss, Minnesota[2]	80	1,413	17.7	67	11
	Marcus Robinson, Chicago	84	1,400	16.7	80	9
	Tim Brown, Oakland[7]	90	1,344	14.9	47	6
	Germane Crowell, Detroit	81	1,338	16.5	77	7
	Muhsin Muhammad, Carolina	96	1,253	13.1	60	8
	Cris Carter, Minnesota[7]	90	1,241	13.8	68	13
	Michael Westbrook, Washington	65	1,191	18.3	65	9
	Amani Toomer, N.Y. Giants	79	1,183	15.0	80	6
	Keyshawn Johnson, N.Y. Jets[2]	89	1,170	13.2	65	8
	Isaac Bruce, St. Louis[3]	77	1,165	15.1	60	12
	Terry Glenn, New England[2]	69	1,147	16.6	67	4
	Albert Connell, Washington	62	1,132	18.3	62	7
	Johnnie Morton, Detroit[3]	80	1,129	14.1	48	5
	Qadry Ismail, Baltimore	68	1,105	16.3	76	6
	Raghib Ismail, Dallas[2]	80	1,097	13.7	76	6
	Patrick Jeffers, Carolina	63	1,082	17.2	88	12
	Antonio Freeman, Green Bay[3]	74	1,074	14.5	51	6
	Bill Schroeder, Green Bay	74	1,051	14.2	51	5
	Marshall Faulk, St. Louis	87	1,048	12.1	57	5
	Tony Martin, Miami[4]	67	1,037	15.5	69	5
	Darnay Scott, Cincinnati	68	1,022	15.0	76	7
	Rod Smith, Denver[3]	79	1,020	12.9	71	4
	Ed McCaffrey, Denver[2]	71	1,018	14.3	78	7
	Terance Mathis, Atlanta[4]	81	1,016	12.5	52	6
1998	Antonio Freeman, Green Bay[2]	84	1,424	17.0	84	14
	Eric Moulds, Buffalo	67	1,368	20.4	84	9
	*Randy Moss, Minnesota	69	1,313	19.0	61	17
	Rod Smith, Denver[2]	86	1,222	14.2	58	6
	Jimmy Smith, Jacksonville[3]	78	1,182	15.2	72	8
	Tony Martin, Atlanta[3]	66	1,181	17.9	62	6
	Jerry Rice, San Francisco[12]	82	1,157	14.1	75	9
	Frank Sanders, Arizona[2]	89	1,145	12.9	42	3
	Terance Mathis, Atlanta[3]	64	1,136	17.8	78	11
	Keyshawn Johnson, N.Y. Jets	83	1,131	13.6	41	10
	Terrell Owens, San Francisco	67	1,097	16.4	79	14
	Wayne Chrebet, N.Y. Jets	75	1,083	14.4	63	8
	Michael Irvin, Dallas[7]	74	1,057	14.3	51	1
	Ed McCaffrey, Denver	64	1,053	16.5	48	10
	O.J. McDuffie, Miami	90	1,050	11.7	61	7
	Joey Galloway, Seattle[3]	65	1,047	16.1	81	10
	Johnnie Morton, Detroit[2]	69	1,028	14.9	98	2
	Raghib Ismail, Carolina	69	1,024	14.8	62	8
	Carl Pickens, Cincinnati[4]	82	1,023	12.5	67	5
	Tim Brown, Oakland[6]	81	1,012	12.5	49	9
	Cris Carter, Minnesota[6]	78	1,011	13.0	54	12
1997	Rob Moore, Arizona[3]	97	1,584	16.3	47	8
	Tim Brown, Oakland[5]	104	1,408	13.5	59	5
	Yancey Thigpen, Pittsburgh[2]	79	1,398	17.7	69	7
	Jimmy Smith, Jacksonville[2]	82	1,324	16.1	75	4
	Irving Fryar, Philadelphia[5]	86	1,316	15.3	72	6
	Herman Moore, Detroit[4]	104	1,293	12.4	79	8
	Antonio Freeman, Green Bay	81	1,243	15.3	58	12
	Michael Irvin, Dallas[6]	75	1,180	15.7	55	9
	Rod Smith, Denver	70	1,180	16.9	78	12
	Keenan McCardell, Jacksonville[2]	85	1,164	13.7	60	5
	Jake Reed, Minnesota[4]	68	1,138	16.7	56	6

Year	Player, Team	No.	Yards	Avg.	Long	TD
	Shannon Sharpe, Denver[3]	72	1,107	15.4	68	3
	Andre Rison, Kansas City[5]	72	1,092	15.2	45	7
	Cris Carter, Minnesota[5]	89	1,069	12.0	43	13
	Johnnie Morton, Detroit	80	1,057	13.2	73	6
	Joey Galloway, Seattle[2]	72	1,049	14.6	53	12
	Frank Sanders, Arizona	75	1,017	13.6	70	4
	Robert Brooks, Green Bay[2]	60	1,010	16.8	48	7
	Derrick Alexander, Baltimore[2]	65	1,009	15.5	92	9
1996	Isaac Bruce, St. Louis[2]	84	1,338	15.9	70	7
	Jake Reed, Minnesota[3]	72	1,320	18.3	82	7
	Herman Moore, Detroit[3]	106	1,296	12.2	50	9
	Jerry Rice, San Francisco[11]	108	1,254	11.6	39	8
	Jimmy Smith, Jacksonville	83	1,244	15.0	62	7
	Michael Jackson, Baltimore	76	1,201	15.8	86	14
	Irving Fryar, Philadelphia[4]	88	1,195	13.6	42	11
	Carl Pickens, Cincinnati[3]	100	1,180	11.8	61	12
	Tony Martin, San Diego[2]	85	1,171	13.8	55	14
	Cris Carter, Minnesota[4]	96	1,163	12.1	43	10
	*Terry Glenn, New England	90	1,132	12.6	37	6
	Keenan McCardell, Jacksonville	85	1,129	13.3	52	3
	Tim Brown, Oakland[4]	90	1,104	12.3	42	9
	Derrick Alexander, Baltimore	62	1,099	17.7	64	9
	Shannon Sharpe, Denver[2]	80	1,062	13.3	51	10
	Curtis Conway, Chicago[2]	81	1,049	13.0	58	7
	Andre Reed, Buffalo[4]	66	1,036	15.7	67	6
	Brett Perriman, Detroit[2]	94	1,021	10.9	44	5
	Rob Moore, Arizona[2]	58	1,016	17.5	69	4
	Henry Ellard, Washington[7]	52	1,014	19.5	51	2
	Charles Johnson, Pittsburgh	60	1,008	16.8	70	3
1995	Jerry Rice, San Francisco[10]	122	1,848	15.1	81	15
	Isaac Bruce, St. Louis	119	1,781	15.0	72	13
	Herman Moore, Detroit[2]	123	1,686	13.7	69	14
	Michael Irvin, Dallas[5]	111	1,603	14.4	50	10
	Robert Brooks, Green Bay	102	1,497	14.7	99	13
	Brett Perriman, Detroit	108	1,488	13.8	91	9
	Cris Carter, Minnesota[3]	122	1,371	11.2	60	17
	Tim Brown, Oakland[3]	89	1,342	15.1	80	10
	Yancey Thigpen, Pittsburgh	85	1,307	15.4	43	5
	Jeff Graham, Chicago	82	1,301	15.9	51	4
	Carl Pickens, Cincinnati[2]	99	1,234	12.5	68	17
	Tony Martin, San Diego	90	1,224	13.6	51	6
	Eric Metcalf, Atlanta	104	1,189	11.4	62	8
	Jake Reed, Minnesota[2]	72	1,167	16.2	55	9
	Quinn Early, New Orleans	81	1,087	13.4	70	8
	Anthony Miller, Denver[5]	59	1,079	18.3	62	14
	Bert Emanuel, Atlanta	74	1,039	14.0	52	5
	*Joey Galloway, Seattle	67	1,039	15.5	59	7
	Terance Mathis, Atlanta[2]	78	1,039	13.3	54	9
	Curtis Conway, Chicago	62	1,037	16.7	76	12
	Henry Ellard, Washington[6]	56	1,005	17.9	59	5
	Mark Carrier, Carolina[2]	66	1,002	15.2	66	3
	Brian Blades, Seattle[4]	77	1,001	13.0	49	4
1994	Jerry Rice, San Francisco[9]	112	1,499	13.4	69	13
	Henry Ellard, Washington[5]	74	1,397	18.9	73	6
	Terance Mathis, Atlanta	111	1,342	12.1	81	11
	Tim Brown, L.A. Raiders[2]	89	1,309	14.7	77	9
	Andre Reed, Buffalo[2]	90	1,303	14.5	83	8
	Irving Fryar, Miami[3]	73	1,270	17.4	54	7
	Cris Carter, Minnesota[2]	122	1,256	10.3	65	7
	Michael Irvin, Dallas[4]	79	1,241	15.7	65	6
	Jake Reed, Minnesota	85	1,175	13.8	59	4
	Ben Coates, New England	96	1,174	12.2	62	7
	Herman Moore, Detroit	72	1,173	16.3	51	11
	Fred Barnett, Philadelphia[2]	78	1,127	14.4	54	5
	Carl Pickens, Cincinnati	71	1,127	15.9	70	11
	Sterling Sharpe, Green Bay[4]	94	1,119	11.9	49	18
	Anthony Miller, Denver[4]	60	1,107	18.5	76	5
	Andre Rison, Atlanta[3]	81	1,088	13.4	69	8

Year	Player, Team	No.	Yards	Avg.	Long	TD
	Brian Blades, Seattle[3]	81	1,088	13.4	45	4
	Rob Moore, N.Y. Jets	78	1,010	12.9	41	6
	Shannon Sharpe, Denver	87	1,010	11.6	44	4
1993	Jerry Rice, San Francisco[8]	98	1,503	15.3	80	15
	Michael Irvin, Dallas[3]	88	1,330	15.1	61	7
	Sterling Sharpe, Green Bay[4]	112	1,274	11.4	54	11
	Andre Rison, Atlanta[3]	86	1,242	14.4	53	15
	Tim Brown, L.A. Raiders	80	1,180	14.8	71	7
	Anthony Miller, San Diego[3]	84	1,162	13.8	66	7
	Cris Carter, Minnesota	86	1,071	12.5	58	9
	Reggie Langhorne, Indianapolis	85	1,038	12.2	72	3
	Irving Fryar, Miami[2]	64	1,010	15.8	65	5
1992	Sterling Sharpe, Green Bay[3]	108	1,461	13.5	76	13
	Michael Irvin, Dallas[2]	78	1,396	17.9	87	7
	Jerry Rice, San Francisco[7]	84	1,201	14.3	80	10
	Andre Rison, Atlanta[2]	93	1,119	12.0	71	11
	Fred Barnett, Philadelphia	67	1,083	16.2	71	6
	Anthony Miller, San Diego[2]	72	1,060	14.7	67	7
	Eric Martin, New Orleans[3]	68	1,041	15.3	52	5
1991	Michael Irvin, Dallas	93	1,523	16.4	66	8
	Gary Clark, Washington[5]	70	1,340	19.1	82	10
	Jerry Rice, San Francisco[6]	80	1,206	15.1	73	14
	Haywood Jeffires, Houston[2]	100	1,181	11.8	44	7
	Michael Haynes, Atlanta	50	1,122	22.4	80	11
	Andre Reed, Buffalo[2]	81	1,113	13.7	55	10
	Drew Hill, Houston[5]	90	1,109	12.3	61	4
	Mark Duper, Miami[4]	70	1,085	15.5	43	5
	James Lofton, Buffalo[6]	57	1,072	18.8	77	8
	Mark Clayton, Miami[5]	70	1,053	15.0	43	12
	Henry Ellard, L.A. Rams[4]	64	1,052	16.4	38	3
	Art Monk, Washington[5]	71	1,049	14.8	64	8
	Irving Fryar, New England	68	1,014	14.9	56	3
	John Taylor, San Francisco[2]	64	1,011	15.8	97	9
	Brian Blades, Seattle[2]	70	1,003	14.3	52	2
1990	Jerry Rice, San Francisco[5]	100	1,502	15.0	64	13
	Henry Ellard, L.A. Rams[3]	76	1,294	17.0	50	4
	Andre Rison, Atlanta	82	1,208	14.7	75	10
	Gary Clark, Washington[4]	75	1,112	14.8	53	8
	Sterling Sharpe, Green Bay[2]	67	1,105	16.5	76	6
	Flipper Anderson, L.A. Rams[2]	51	1,097	21.5	55	4
	Haywood Jeffires, Houston	74	1,048	14.2	87	8
	Stephone Paige, Kansas City	65	1,021	15.7	86	5
	Drew Hill, Houston[4]	74	1,019	13.8	57	5
	Anthony Carter, Minnesota[3]	70	1,008	14.4	56	8
1989	Jerry Rice, San Francisco[4]	82	1,483	18.1	68	17
	Sterling Sharpe, Green Bay	90	1,423	15.8	79	12
	Mark Carrier, Tampa Bay	86	1,422	16.5	78	9
	Henry Ellard, L.A. Rams[2]	70	1,382	19.7	53	8
	Andre Reed, Buffalo	88	1,312	14.9	78	9
	Anthony Miller, San Diego	75	1,252	16.7	69	10
	Webster Slaughter, Cleveland	65	1,236	19.0	97	6
	Gary Clark, Washington[3]	79	1,229	15.6	80	9
	Tim McGee, Cincinnati	65	1,211	18.6	74	8
	Art Monk, Washington[4]	86	1,186	13.8	60	8
	Flipper Anderson, L.A. Rams	44	1,146	26.0	78	5
	Ricky Sanders, Washington[2]	80	1,138	14.2	68	4
	Vance Johnson, Denver	76	1,095	14.4	69	7
	Richard Johnson, Detroit	70	1,091	15.6	75	8
	Eric Martin, New Orleans[2]	68	1,090	16.0	53	8
	John Taylor, San Francisco	60	1,077	18.0	95	10
	Mervyn Fernandez, L.A. Raiders	57	1,069	18.8	75	9
	Anthony Carter, Minnesota[2]	65	1,066	16.4	50	4
	Brian Blades, Seattle	77	1,063	13.8	60	5
	Mark Clayton, Miami[4]	64	1,011	15.8	78	9
1988	Henry Ellard, L.A. Rams	86	1,414	16.4	68	10
	Jerry Rice, San Francisco[3]	64	1,306	20.4	96	9
	Eddie Brown, Cincinnati	53	1,273	24.0	86	9
	Anthony Carter, Minnesota	72	1,225	17.0	67	6

Year	Player, Team	No.	Yards	Avg.	Long	TD
	Ricky Sanders, Washington	73	1,148	15.7	55	12
	Drew Hill, Houston[3]	72	1,141	15.8	57	10
	Mark Clayton, Miami[3]	86	1,129	13.1	45	14
	Roy Green, Phoenix[3]	68	1,097	16.1	52	7
	Eric Martin, New Orleans	85	1,083	12.7	40	7
	Al Toon, N.Y. Jets[2]	93	1,067	11.5	42	5
	Bruce Hill, Tampa Bay	58	1,040	17.9	42	9
	Lionel Manuel, N.Y. Giants	65	1,029	15.8	46	4
1987	J.T. Smith, St. Louis[2]	91	1,117	12.3	38	8
	Jerry Rice, San Francisco[2]	65	1,078	16.6	57	22
	Gary Clark, Washington[2]	56	1,066	19.0	84	7
	Carlos Carson, Kansas City[3]	55	1,044	19.0	81	7
1986	Jerry Rice, San Francisco	86	1,570	18.3	66	15
	Stanley Morgan, New England[3]	84	1,491	17.8	44	10
	Mark Duper, Miami[3]	67	1,313	19.6	85	11
	Gary Clark, Washington	74	1,265	17.1	55	7
	Al Toon, N.Y. Jets	85	1,176	13.8	62	8
	Todd Christensen, L.A. Raiders[3]	95	1,153	12.1	35	8
	Mark Clayton, Miami[2]	60	1,150	19.2	68	10
	*Bill Brooks, Indianapolis	65	1,131	17.4	84	8
	Drew Hill, Houston[2]	65	1,112	17.1	81	5
	Steve Largent, Seattle[8]	70	1,070	15.3	38	9
	Art Monk, Washington[3]	73	1,068	14.6	69	4
	*Ernest Givins, Houston	61	1,062	17.4	60	3
	Cris Collinsworth, Cincinnati[4]	62	1,024	16.5	46	10
	Wesley Walker, N.Y. Jets[2]	49	1,016	20.7	83	12
	J.T. Smith, St. Louis	80	1,014	12.7	45	6
	Mark Bavaro, N.Y. Giants	66	1,001	15.2	41	4
1985	Steve Largent, Seattle[7]	79	1,287	16.3	43	6
	Mike Quick, Philadelphia[3]	73	1,247	17.1	99	11
	Art Monk, Washington[2]	91	1,226	13.5	53	2
	Wes Chandler, San Diego[4]	67	1,199	17.9	75	10
	Drew Hill, Houston	64	1,169	18.3	57	9
	James Lofton, Green Bay[5]	69	1,153	16.7	56	4
	Louis Lipps, Pittsburgh	59	1,134	19.2	51	12
	Cris Collinsworth, Cincinnati[3]	65	1,125	17.3	71	5
	Tony Hill, Dallas[3]	74	1,113	15.0	53	7
	Lionel James, San Diego	86	1,027	11.9	67	6
	Roger Craig, San Francisco	92	1,016	11.0	73	6
1984	Roy Green, St. Louis[2]	78	1,555	19.9	83	12
	John Stallworth, Pittsburgh[3]	80	1,395	17.4	51	11
	Mark Clayton, Miami	73	1,389	19.0	65	18
	Art Monk, Washington	106	1,372	12.9	72	7
	James Lofton, Green Bay[4]	62	1,361	22.0	79	7
	Mark Duper, Miami[2]	71	1,306	18.4	80	8
	Steve Watson, Denver[3]	69	1,170	17.0	73	7
	Steve Largent, Seattle[6]	74	1,164	15.7	65	12
	Tim Smith, Houston[2]	69	1,141	16.5	75	4
	Stacey Bailey, Atlanta	67	1,138	17.0	61	6
	Carlos Carson, Kansas City[2]	57	1,078	18.9	57	4
	Mike Quick, Philadelphia[2]	61	1,052	17.2	90	9
	Todd Christensen, L.A. Raiders[2]	80	1,007	12.6	38	7
	Kevin House, Tampa Bay[2]	76	1,005	13.2	55	5
	Ozzie Newsome, Cleveland[2]	89	1,001	11.2	52	5
1983	Mike Quick, Philadelphia	69	1,409	20.4	83	13
	Carlos Carson, Kansas City	80	1,351	16.9	50	7
	James Lofton, Green Bay[3]	58	1,300	22.4	74	8
	Todd Christensen, L.A. Raiders	92	1,247	13.6	45	12
	Roy Green, St. Louis	78	1,227	15.7	71	14
	Charlie Brown, Washington	78	1,225	15.7	75	8
	Tim Smith, Houston	83	1,176	14.2	47	6
	Kellen Winslow, San Diego[3]	88	1,172	13.3	46	8
	Earnest Gray, N.Y. Giants	78	1,139	14.6	62	5
	Steve Watson, Denver[2]	59	1,133	19.2	78	5
	Cris Collinsworth, Cincinnati[2]	66	1,130	17.1	63	5
	Steve Largent, Seattle[5]	72	1,074	14.9	46	11
	Mark Duper, Miami	51	1,003	19.7	85	10
1982	Wes Chandler, San Diego[3]	49	1,032	21.1	66	9

Year	Player, Team	No.	Yards	Avg.	Long	TD
1981	Alfred Jenkins, Atlanta[2]	70	1,358	19.4	67	13
	James Lofton, Green Bay[2]	71	1,294	18.2	75	8
	Steve Watson, Denver	60	1,244	20.7	95	13
	Frank Lewis, Buffalo[2]	70	1,244	17.8	33	4
	Steve Largent, Seattle[4]	75	1,224	16.3	57	9
	Charlie Joiner, San Diego[4]	70	1,188	17.0	57	7
	Kevin House, Tampa Bay	56	1,176	21.0	84	9
	Wes Chandler, New Orleans/San Diego[2]	69	1,142	16.6	51	6
	Dwight Clark, San Francisco	85	1,105	13.0	78	4
	John Stallworth, Pittsburgh[2]	63	1,098	17.4	55	5
	Kellen Winslow, San Diego[2]	88	1,075	12.2	67	10
	Pat Tilley, St. Louis	66	1,040	15.8	75	3
	Stanley Morgan, New England[2]	44	1,029	23.4	76	6
	Harold Carmichael, Philadelphia[3]	61	1,028	16.9	85	6
	Freddie Scott, Detroit	53	1,022	19.3	48	5
	*Cris Collinsworth, Cincinnati	67	1,009	15.1	74	8
	Joe Senser, Minnesota	79	1,004	12.7	53	8
	Ozzie Newsome, Cleveland	69	1,002	14.5	62	6
	Sammy White, Minnesota	66	1,001	15.2	53	3
1980	John Jefferson, San Diego[3]	82	1,340	16.3	58	13
	Kellen Winslow, San Diego	89	1,290	14.5	65	9
	James Lofton, Green Bay	71	1,226	17.3	47	4
	Charlie Joiner, San Diego[3]	71	1,132	15.9	51	4
	Ahmad Rashad, Minnesota[2]	69	1,095	15.9	76	5
	Steve Largent, Seattle[3]	66	1,064	16.1	67	6
	Tony Hill, Dallas[2]	60	1,055	17.6	58	8
	Alfred Jenkins, Atlanta	57	1,026	18.0	57	6
1979	Steve Largent, Seattle[2]	66	1,237	18.7	55	9
	John Stallworth, Pittsburgh	70	1,183	16.9	65	8
	Ahmad Rashad, Minnesota	80	1,156	14.5	52	9
	John Jefferson, San Diego[2]	61	1,090	17.9	65	10
	Frank Lewis, Buffalo	54	1,082	20.0	55	2
	Wes Chandler, New Orleans	65	1,069	16.4	85	6
	Tony Hill, Dallas	60	1,062	17.7	75	10
	Drew Pearson, Dallas[2]	55	1,026	18.7	56	8
	Wallace Francis, Atlanta	74	1,013	13.7	42	8
	Harold Jackson, New England[3]	45	1,013	22.5	59	7
	Charlie Joiner, San Diego[2]	72	1,008	14.0	39	4
	Stanley Morgan, New England	44	1,002	22.8	63	12
1978	Wesley Walker, N.Y. Jets	48	1,169	24.4	77	8
	Steve Largent, Seattle	71	1,168	16.5	57	8
	Harold Carmichael, Philadelphia[2]	55	1,072	19.5	56	8
	*John Jefferson, San Diego	56	1,001	17.9	46	13
1976	Roger Carr, Baltimore	43	1,112	25.9	79	11
	Cliff Branch, Oakland[2]	46	1,111	24.2	88	12
	Charlie Joiner, San Diego	50	1,056	21.1	81	7
1975	Ken Burrough, Houston	53	1,063	20.1	77	8
1974	Cliff Branch, Oakland	60	1,092	18.2	67	13
	Drew Pearson, Dallas	62	1,087	17.5	50	2
1973	Harold Carmichael, Philadelphia	67	1,116	16.7	73	9
1972	Harold Jackson, Philadelphia[2]	62	1,048	16.9	77	4
	John Gilliam, Minnesota	47	1,035	22.0	66	7
1971	Otis Taylor, Kansas City[2]	57	1,110	19.5	82	7
1970	Gene Washington, San Francisco	53	1,100	20.8	79	12
	Marlin Briscoe, Buffalo	57	1,036	18.2	48	8
	Dick Gordon, Chicago	71	1,026	14.5	69	13
	Gary Garrison, San Diego[2]	44	1,006	22.9	67	12
1969	Warren Wells, Oakland[2]	47	1,260	26.8	80	14
	Harold Jackson, Philadelphia	65	1,116	17.2	65	9
	Roy Jefferson, Pittsburgh[2]	67	1,079	16.1	63	9
	Dan Abramowicz, New Orleans	73	1,015	13.9	49	7
	Lance Alworth, San Diego[7]	64	1,003	15.7	76	4
1968	Lance Alworth, San Diego[6]	68	1,312	19.3	80	10
	Don Maynard, N.Y. Jets[5]	57	1,297	22.8	87	10
	George Sauer, N.Y. Jets[3]	66	1,141	17.3	43	3
	Warren Wells, Oakland	53	1,137	21.5	94	11
	Gary Garrison, San Diego	52	1,103	21.2	84	10
	Roy Jefferson, Pittsburgh	58	1,074	18.5	62	11
	Paul Warfield, Cleveland	50	1,067	21.3	65	12

Year	Player, Team	No.	Yards	Avg.	Long	TD
	Homer Jones, N.Y. Giants[3]	45	1,057	23.5	84	7
	Fred Biletnikoff, Oakland	61	1,037	17.0	82	6
	Lance Rentzel, Dallas	54	1,009	18.7	65	6
1967	Don Maynard, N.Y. Jets[4]	71	1,434	20.2	75	10
	Ben Hawkins, Philadelphia	59	1,265	21.4	87	10
	Homer Jones, N.Y. Giants[2]	49	1,209	24.7	70	13
	Jackie Smith, St. Louis	56	1,205	21.5	76	9
	George Sauer, N.Y. Jets[2]	75	1,189	15.9	61	6
	Lance Alworth, San Diego[5]	52	1,010	19.4	71	9
1966	Lance Alworth, San Diego[4]	73	1,383	18.9	78	13
	Otis Taylor, Kansas City	58	1,297	22.4	89	8
	Pat Studstill, Detroit	67	1,266	18.9	99	5
	Bob Hayes, Dallas[2]	64	1,232	19.3	95	13
	Charlie Frazier, Houston	57	1,129	19.8	79	12
	Charley Taylor, Washington	72	1,119	15.5	86	12
	George Sauer, N.Y. Jets	63	1,081	17.2	77	5
	Homer Jones, N.Y. Giants	48	1,044	21.8	98	8
	Art Powell, Oakland[5]	53	1,026	19.4	46	11
1965	Lance Alworth, San Diego[3]	69	1,602	23.2	85	14
	Dave Parks, San Francisco	80	1,344	16.8	53	12
	Don Maynard, N.Y. Jets[3]	68	1,218	17.9	56	14
	Pete Retzlaff, Philadelphia	66	1,190	18.0	78	10
	Lionel Taylor, Denver[4]	85	1,131	13.3	63	6
	Tommy McDonald, Los Angeles[3]	67	1,036	15.5	51	9
	*Bob Hayes, Dallas	46	1,003	21.8	82	12
1964	Charley Hennigan, Houston[3]	101	1,546	15.3	53	8
	Art Powell, Oakland[4]	76	1,361	17.9	77	11
	Lance Alworth, San Diego[2]	61	1,235	20.2	82	13
	Johnny Morris, Chicago	93	1,200	12.9	63	10
	Elbert Dubenion, Buffalo	42	1,139	27.1	72	10
	Terry Barr, Detroit[2]	57	1,030	18.1	58	9
1963	Bobby Mitchell, Washington[2]	69	1,436	20.8	99	7
	Art Powell, Oakland[3]	73	1,304	17.9	85	16
	Buddy Dial, Pittsburgh[2]	60	1,295	21.6	83	9
	Lance Alworth, San Diego	61	1,205	19.8	85	11
	Del Shofner, N.Y. Giants[4]	64	1,181	18.5	70	9
	Lionel Taylor, Denver[3]	78	1,101	14.1	72	10
	Terry Barr, Detroit	66	1,086	16.5	75	13
	Charley Hennigan, Houston[2]	61	1,051	17.2	83	10
	Sonny Randle, St. Louis[2]	51	1,014	19.9	68	12
	Bake Turner, N.Y. Jets	71	1,009	14.2	53	6
1962	Bobby Mitchell, Washington	72	1,384	19.2	81	11
	Sonny Randle, St. Louis	63	1,158	18.4	86	7
	Tommy McDonald, Philadelphia[2]	58	1,146	19.8	60	10
	Del Shofner, N.Y. Giants[3]	53	1,133	21.4	69	12
	Art Powell, N.Y. Titans[2]	64	1,130	17.7	80	8
	Frank Clarke, Dall. Cowboys	47	1,043	22.2	66	14
	Don Maynard, N.Y. Titans[2]	56	1,041	18.6	86	8
1961	Charley Hennigan, Houston	82	1,746	21.3	80	12
	Lionel Taylor, Denver[2]	100	1,176	11.8	52	4
	Bill Groman, Houston[2]	50	1,175	23.5	80	17
	Tommy McDonald, Philadelphia	64	1,144	17.9	66	13
	Del Shofner, N.Y. Giants[2]	68	1,125	16.5	46	11
	Jim Phillips, Los Angeles	78	1,092	14.0	69	5
	*Mike Ditka, Chicago	56	1,076	19.2	76	12
	Dave Kocourek, San Diego	55	1,055	19.2	76	4
	Buddy Dial, Pittsburgh	53	1,047	19.8	88	12
	R.C. Owens, San Francisco	55	1,032	18.8	54	5
1960	*Bill Groman, Houston	72	1,473	20.5	92	12
	Raymond Berry, Baltimore	74	1,298	17.5	70	10
	Don Maynard, N.Y. Titans	72	1,265	17.6	65	6
	Lionel Taylor, Denver	92	1,235	13.4	80	12
	Art Powell, N.Y. Titans	69	1,167	16.9	76	14
1958	Del Shofner, Los Angeles	51	1,097	21.5	92	8
1956	Bill Howton, Green Bay[2]	55	1,188	21.6	66	12
	Harlon Hill, Chi. Bears[2]	47	1,128	24.0	79	11
1954	Bob Boyd, Los Angeles	53	1,212	22.9	80	6
	*Harlon Hill, Chi. Bears	45	1,124	25.0	76	12
1953	Pete Pihos, Philadelphia	63	1,049	16.7	59	10

OUTSTANDING PERFORMERS

Year	Player, Team	No.	Yards	Avg.	Long	TD
1952	*Bill Howton, Green Bay	53	1,231	23.2	90	13
1951	Elroy (Crazylegs) Hirsch, Los Angeles	66	1,495	22.7	91	17
1950	Tom Fears, Los Angeles[2]	84	1,116	13.3	53	7
	Cloyce Box, Detroit	50	1,009	20.2	82	11
1949	Bob Mann, Detroit	66	1,014	15.4	64	4
	Tom Fears, Los Angeles	77	1,013	13.2	51	9
1945	Jim Benton, Cleveland	45	1,067	23.7	84	8
1942	Don Hutson, Green Bay	74	1,211	16.4	73	17

*First season of professional football.

250 YARDS PASS RECEIVING IN A GAME

Date	Player, Team, Opponent	No.	Yards	TD
Dec. 1, 2013	Josh Gordon, Cleveland vs. Jacksonville	10	261	2
Oct. 27, 2013	Calvin Johnson, Detroit vs. Dallas	14	329	1
Nov. 18, 2012	Andre Johnson, Houston vs. Jacksonville (OT)	14	273	1
Sept. 30, 2012	Brian Hartline, Miami vs. Arizona (OT)	12	253	1
Oct. 11, 2009	Miles Austin, Dallas vs. Kansas City	10	250	2
Nov. 19, 2006	Lee Evans, Buffalo vs. Houston	11	265	2
Nov. 12, 2006	Chad Johnson, Cincinnati vs. San Diego	11	260	2
Nov. 10, 2002	Plaxico Burress, Pittsburgh vs. Atlanta (OT)	9	253	2
Dec. 17, 2000	Terrell Owens, San Francisco vs. Chicago	20	283	1
Sept. 10, 2000	Jimmy Smith, Jacksonville vs. Baltimore	15	291	3
Dec. 12, 1999	Qadry Ismail, Baltimore vs. Pittsburgh	6	258	3
Dec. 18, 1995	Jerry Rice, San Francisco vs. Minnesota	14	289	3
Dec. 11, 1989	John Taylor, San Francisco vs. L.A. Rams	11	286	2
Nov. 26, 1989	Flipper Anderson, L.A. Rams vs. New Orleans (OT)	15	336	1
Oct. 18, 1987	Steve Largent, Seattle vs. Detroit	15	261	3
Oct. 4, 1987	Anthony Allen, Washington vs. St. Louis	7	255	3
Dec. 22, 1985	Stephone Paige, Kansas City vs. San Diego	8	309	2
Dec. 20, 1982	Wes Chandler, San Diego vs. Cincinnati	10	260	2
Sept. 23, 1979	*Jerry Butler, Buffalo vs. N.Y. Jets	10	255	4
Nov. 4, 1962	Sonny Randle, St. Louis vs. N.Y. Giants	16	256	1
Oct. 28, 1962	Del Shofner, N.Y. Giants vs. Washington	11	269	1
Oct. 13, 1961	Charley Hennigan, Houston vs. Boston	13	272	1
Oct. 21, 1956	Billy Howton, Green Bay vs. Los Angeles	7	257	2
Dec. 3, 1950	Cloyce Box, Detroit vs. Baltimore	12	302	4
Nov. 22, 1945	Jim Benton, Cleveland vs. Detroit	10	303	1

*First season of professional football.

2,000 COMBINED NET YARDS GAINED IN A SEASON

Year	Player, Team	Rushing Att.-Yds.	Pass Rec.	Punt Ret.	Kickoff Ret.	Fum. Ret.	Total Yds.
2013	LeSean McCoy, Philadelphia	314-1,607	52-539	0-0	0-0	0-0	366-2,146
	*Cordarrelle Patterson, Minnesota	12-158	45-469	0-0	43-1,393	0-0	100-2,020
2012	Randall Cobb, Green Bay	10-132	80-954	31-292	38-964	3-0	162-2,342
	Adrian Peterson, Minnesota[2]	348-2,097	40-217	0-0	0-0	0-0	388-2,314
2011	Darren Sproles, New Orleans[4]	87-603	86-710	29-294	40-1,089	0-0	242-2,696
	Antonio Brown, Pittsburgh	7-41	69-1,108	30-325	27-737	0-0	133-2,211
	Ray Rice, Baltimore[2]	291-1,364	76-704	0-0	0-0	0-0	367-2,068
2010	Danny Amendola, St. Louis[2]	7-81	85-689	40-452	50-1,142	0-0	182-2,364
	Arian Foster, Houston	327-1,616	66-604	0-0	0-0	1-0	394-2,221
	Darren Sproles, San Diego[3]	50-267	59-520	24-166	51-1,257	0-0	184-2,210
2009	Fred Jackson, Buffalo	237-1,062	46-371	6-69	41-1,014	0-0	330-2,516
	Josh Cribbs, Cleveland[2]	55-381	20-135	38-452	56-1,542	2-0	171-2,510
	Chris Johnson, Tennessee	358-2,006	50-503	0-0	0-0	1-0	409-2,509
	Jamaal Charles, Kansas City	190-1,120	40-297	0-0	36-925	3-0	269-2,342
	Darren Sproles, San Diego[2]	93-343	45-497	26-183	54-1,300	1-0	219-2,323
	Danny Amendola, St. Louis	3-2	43-326	31-360	66-1,618	1-0	144-2,302
	*Percy Harvin, Minnesota	15-135	60-790	0-0	42-1,156	0-0	117-2,081
	Ray Rice, Baltimore	254-1,339	78-702	0-0	0-0	1-2	333-2,043
2008	Leon Washington, N.Y. Jets[2]	76-448	47-355	29-303	48-1,231	4-(-5)	204-2,332
	Darren Sproles, San Diego	61-330	29-342	22-249	53-1,376	1-(-2)	166-2,295
	Jerious Norwood, Atlanta[2]	95-489	36-338	0-0	51-1,311	0-0	182-2,138
2007	Josh Cribbs, Cleveland	9-61	3-37	30-405	59-1,809	2-0	103-2,312
	Jerious Norwood, Atlanta	103-613	28-277	0-0	52-1,317	0-0	183-2,207
	Brian Westbrook, Philadelphia	278-1,333	90-771	4-79	0-0	0-0	372-2,183
	*Ted Ginn Jr., Miami	4-3	34-420	24-230	63-1,433	2-(-9)	127-2,077
	Leon Washington, N.Y. Jets	71-353	36-213	20-183	47-1,291	1-0	175-2,040
	*Adrian Peterson, Minnesota	238-1,341	19-268	0-0	16-412	3-0	276-2,014

Year	Player, Team	Rushing Att.-Yds.	Pass Rec.	Punt Ret.	Kickoff Ret.	Fum. Ret.	Total Yds.
	Maurice Jones-Drew, Jacksonville[2]	167-768	40-407	3-28	31-811	0-0	241-2,014
2006	Steven Jackson, St. Louis	346-1,528	90,806	0-0	0-0	2-0	438-2,334
	LaDainian Tomlinson, San Diego[3]	348-1,815	56-508	0-0	0-0	1-0	405-2,323
	*Maurice Jones-Drew, Jacksonville	166-941	46-436	1-13	31-860	0-0	244-2,250
	Larry Johnson, Kansas City[2]	416-1,789	41-410	0-0	0-0	1-0	458-2,199
	Frank Gore, San Francisco	312-1,695	61-485	0-0	0-0	0-0	373-2,180
	Wes Welker, Miami[2]	0-0	67-687	41-378	48-1,064	1-0	157-2,129
	Tiki Barber, N.Y. Giants[4]	327-1,662	58-465	0-0	0-0	1-0	386-2,127
	Chris Carr, Oakland	0-0	0-0	35-216	69-1,762	1-0	106-2,078
2005	Tiki Barber, N.Y. Giants[3]	357-1,860	54-530	0-0	0-0	1-0	412-2,390
	Dante Hall, Kansas City[4]	7-11	34-436	42-276	65-1,560	2-0	150-2,283
	Wes Welker, Miami	1-5	29-434	43-390	61-1,379	4-0	138-2,208
	Larry Johnson, Kansas City	336-1,750	33-343	0-0	0-0	3-0	372-2,093
2004	Dante Hall, Kansas City[3]	8-56	25-230	23-232	68-1,718	0-0	124-2,236
	Tiki Barber, N.Y. Giants[2]	322-1,518	52-578	0-0	0-0	2-0	376-2,096
	Edgerrin James, Indianapolis[3]	334-1,548	51-483	0-0	0-0	1-0	386-2,031
2003	Dante Hall, Kansas City[2]	16-73	40-423	29-472	57-1,478	0-0	142-2,446
	LaDainian Tomlinson, San Diego[2]	313-1,645	100-725	0-0	0-0	2-0	415-2,370
	Jamal Lewis, Baltimore	387-2,066	26-205	0-0	0-0	1-0	414-2,271
	Ahman Green, Green Bay	355-1,883	50-367	0-0	0-0	2-0	407-2,250
	Deuce McAllister, New Orleans	351-1,641	69-516	0-0	0-0	3-(-3)	423-2,154
	Priest Holmes, Kansas City[3]	320-1,420	74-690	0-0	0-0	0-0	394-2,110
2002	Michael Lewis, New Orleans	1-15	8-200	44-625	70-1,807	2-0	125-2,647
	Priest Holmes, Kansas City[2]	313-1,615	70-672	0-0	0-0	0-0	383-2,287
	Ricky Williams, Miami	383-1,853	47-363	0-0	0-0	1-0	431-2,216
	LaDainian Tomlinson, San Diego	372-1,683	79-489	0-0	0-0	0-0	451-2,172
	Dante Hall, Kansas City	11-54	20-322	29-390	57-1,354	1-0	118-2,120
2001	Priest Holmes, Kansas City	327-1,555	62-614	0-0	0-0	0-0	389-2,169
	Marshall Faulk, St. Louis[4]	260-1,382	83-765	0-0	0-0	2-0	345-2,147
	Derrick Mason, Tennessee[2]	0-0	73-1,128	20-128	34-748	1-0	128-2,004
2000	Derrick Mason, Tennessee	1-1	63-895	51-662	42-1,132	1-0	158-2,690
	MarTay Jenkins, Arizona	1-(-4)	17-219	1-1	82-2,186	0-0	101-2,402
	Edgerrin James, Indianapolis[2]	387-1,709	63-594	0-0	0-0	0-0	450-2,303
	Marshall Faulk, St. Louis[3]	253-1,359	81-830	0-0	1-18	2-0	337-2,207
	Tiki Barber, N.Y. Giants	213-1,006	70-719	39-332	1-28	5-0	328-2,085
1999	Marshall Faulk, St. Louis[2]	253-1,381	87-1,048	0-0	0-0	0-0	340-2,429
	*Edgerrin James, Indianapolis	369-1,553	62-586	0-0	0-0	2-0	433-2,139
	*Terrence Wilkins, Indianapolis	1-2	42-565	41-388	51-1,134	1-0	136-2,089
	Glyn Milburn, Chicago[2]	16-102	20-151	30-346	61-1,426	2-0	129-2,025
1998	Brian Mitchell, Washington[4]	39-208	44-306	44-506	59-1,337	0-0	186-2,357
	Marshall Faulk, Indianapolis	324-1,319	86-908	0-0	0-0	2-13	412-2,240
	Terrell Davis, Denver[2]	392-2,008	25-217	0-0	0-0	1-0	418-2,225
	Jamal Anderson, Atlanta	410-1,846	27-319	0-0	0-0	1-0	438-2,165
	Garrison Hearst, San Francisco	310-1,570	39-535	0-0	0-0	1-0	350-2,105
1997	Barry Sanders, Detroit[2]	335-2,053	33-305	0-0	0-0	1-0	369-2,358
	Kevin Williams, Arizona	1-(-2)	20-273	40-462	59-1,458	1-0	121-2,191
	Brian Mitchell, Washington[3]	23-107	36-438	38-442	47-1,094	0-0	144-2,081
	Terrell Davis, Denver	369-1,750	42-287	0-0	0-0	2-(-7)	413-2,030
	Jermaine Lewis, Baltimore	3-35	42-648	28-437	41-905	2-0	116-2,025
1995	Brian Mitchell, Washington[2]	46-301	38-324	25-315	55-1,408	0-0	164-2,348
	Emmitt Smith, Dallas[2]	377-1,773	62-375	0-0	0-0	0-0	439-2,148
	Glyn Milburn, Denver	49-266	22-191	31-354	47-1,269	0-0	149-2,080
	Ernie Mills, Pittsburgh	5-39	39-679	0-0	54-1,306	0-0	98-2,024
1994	Brian Mitchell, Washington	78-311	26-236	32-452	58-1,478	0-0	194-2,477
	Barry Sanders, Detroit	331-1,883	44-283	0-0	0-0	0-0	375-2,166
1992	Thurman Thomas, Buffalo[2]	312-1,487	58-626	0-0	0-0	1-0	371-2,113
	Emmitt Smith, Dallas	373-1,713	59-335	0-0	0-0	1-0	433-2,048
	Barry Foster, Pittsburgh	390-1,690	36-344	0-0	0-0	2-(-20)	428-2,014
1991	Thurman Thomas, Buffalo	288-1,407	62-631	0-0	0-0	0-0	350-2,038
1990	Herschel Walker, Minnesota[2]	184-770	35-315	0-0	44-966	4-0	267-2,051
1988	*Tim Brown, L.A. Raiders	14-50	43-725	49-444	41-1,098	7-0	154-2,317
	Roger Craig, San Francisco[2]	310-1,502	76-534	0-0	2-32	2-0	390-2,068
	Eric Dickerson, Indianapolis[4]	388-1,659	36-377	0-0	0-0	1-0	425-2,036
	Herschel Walker, Dallas	361-1,514	53-505	0-0	0-0	3-0	417-2,019
1986	Eric Dickerson, L.A. Rams[3]	404-1,821	26-205	0-0	0-0	2-0	432-2,026
	Gary Anderson, San Diego	127-442	80-871	25-227	24-482	2-0	258-2,022
1985	Lionel James, San Diego	105-516	86-1,027	25-213	36-779	1-0	253-2,535
	Marcus Allen, L.A. Raiders	380-1,759	67-555	0-0	0-0	2-(-6)	449-2,308

Year	Player, Team	Rushing Att.-Yds.	Pass Rec.	Punt Ret.	Kickoff Ret.	Fum. Ret.	Total Yds.
	Roger Craig, San Francisco	214-1,050	92-1,016	0-0	0-0	0-0	306-2,066
	Walter Payton, Chicago[4]	324-1,551	49-483	0-0	0-0	1-0	374-2,034
1984	Eric Dickerson, L.A. Rams[2]	379-2,105	21-139	0-0	0-0	4-15	404-2,259
	James Wilder, Tampa Bay	407-1,544	85-685	0-0	0-0	4-0	496-2,229
	Walter Payton, Chicago[3]	381-1,684	45-368	0-0	0-0	1-0	427-2,052
1983	*Eric Dickerson, L.A. Rams	390-1,808	51-404	0-0	0-0	1-0	442-2,212
	William Andrews, Atlanta[2]	331-1,567	59-609	0-0	0-0	2-0	392-2,176
	Walter Payton, Chicago[2]	314-1,421	53-607	0-0	0-0	2-0	369-2,028
1981	*James Brooks, San Diego	109-525	46-329	22-290	40-949	2-0	219-2,093
	William Andrews, Atlanta	289-1,301	81-735	0-0	0-0	0-0	370-2,036
1980	Bruce Harper, N.Y. Jets[2]	45-126	50-634	28-242	49-1,070	3-0	175-2,072
1979	Wilbert Montgomery, Philadelphia	338-1,512	41-494	0-0	1-6	2-0	382-2,012
1978	Bruce Harper, N.Y. Jets	58-303	13-196	30-378	55-1,280	1-0	157-2,157
1977	Walter Payton, Chicago	339-1,852	27-269	0-0	2-95	5-0	373-2,216
	Terry Metcalf, St. Louis[3]	149-739	34-403	14-108	32-772	1-0	230-2,022
1975	Terry Metcalf, St. Louis[2]	165-816	43-378	23-285	35-960	2-23	268-2,462
	O.J. Simpson, Buffalo[2]	329-1,817	28-426	0-0	0-0	1-0	358-2,243
1974	Mack Herron, New England	231-824	38-474	35-517	28-629	3-0	335-2,444
	Otis Armstrong, Denver	263-1,407	38-405	0-0	16-386	1-0	318-2,198
	Terry Metcalf, St. Louis	152-718	50-377	26-340	20-623	7-0	255-2,058
1973	O.J. Simpson, Buffalo	332-2,003	6-70	0-0	0-0	0-0	338-2,073
1966	Gale Sayers, Chicago[2]	229-1,231	34-447	6-44	23-718	3-0	295-2,440
	Leroy Kelly, Cleveland	209-1,141	32-366	13-104	19-403	0-0	273-2,014
1965	*Gale Sayers, Chicago	166-867	29-507	16-238	21-660	4-0	236-2,272
1963	Timmy Brown, Philadelphia[2]	192-841	36-487	16-152	33-945	2-3	279-2,428
	Jim Brown, Cleveland	291-1,863	24-268	0-0	0-0	0-0	315-2,131
1962	Timmy Brown, Philadelphia	137-545	52-849	6-81	30-831	4-0	229-2,306
	Dick Christy, N.Y. Titans	114-535	62-538	15-250	38-824	2-0	231-2,147
1961	Billy Cannon, Houston	200-948	43-586	9-70	18-439	2-0	272-2,043
1960	*Abner Haynes, Dallas Texans	156-875	55-576	14-215	19-434	4-0	248-2,100

*First season of professional football.

300 COMBINED NET YARDS GAINED IN A GAME

Date	Player, Team, Opponent	No.	Yards	TD
Dec. 29, 2013	LeGarrette Blount, New England vs. Buffalo	26	334	2
Nov. 10, 2013	*Tavon Austin, St. Louis vs. Indianapolis	9	314	3
Oct. 27, 2013	Calvin Johnson, Detroit vs. Dallas	14	329	1
Dec. 9, 2012	*David Wilson, N.Y. Giants vs. New Orleans	17	327	3
Nov. 28, 2010	*Jacoby Ford, Oakland vs. Miami	12	329	2
Nov. 7, 2010	*Jacoby Ford, Oakland vs. Kansas City (OT)	10	306	1
Dec. 20, 2009	Josh Cribbs, Cleveland vs. Kansas City	14	316	2
Oct. 18, 2009	Domenik Hixon, N.Y. Giants vs. New Orleans	12	303	0
Sept. 28, 2008	Steve Breaston, Arizona vs. N.Y. Jets	19	324	0
Sept. 14, 2008	Darren Sproles, San Diego vs. Denver	14	317	2
Nov. 18, 2007	Josh Cribbs, Cleveland vs. Baltimore (OT)	12	309	0
Nov. 4, 2007	*Adrian Peterson, Minnesota vs. San Diego	31	315	3
Oct. 14, 2007	*Adrian Peterson, Minnesota vs. Chicago	25	361	3
Sept. 30, 2007	Devin Hester, Chicago vs. Detroit	13	317	1
Dec. 10, 2006	*Maurice Jones-Drew, Jacksonville vs. Indianapolis	19	303	3
Dec. 14, 2003	Derrick Mason, Tennessee vs. Buffalo	21	302	0
Nov. 16, 2003	Jonathan Carter, N.Y. Jets vs. Indianapolis	7	304	2
Dec. 8, 2002	Steve Smith, Carolina vs. Cincinnati	9	313	3
Nov. 24, 2002	Priest Holmes, Kansas City vs. Seattle	30	307	3
Oct. 13, 2002	Michael Lewis, New Orleans vs. Washington	8	356	2
Dec. 22, 1999	Jason Tucker, Dallas vs. New Orleans	13	331	1
Dec. 7, 1997	Jermaine Lewis, Baltimore vs. Seattle	10	308	3
Dec. 25, 1995	Kevin Williams, Dallas vs. Arizona	16	307	2
Dec. 10, 1995	Glyn Milburn, Denver vs. Seattle	33	404	0
Oct. 23, 1994	Tyrone Hughes, New Orleans vs. L.A. Rams	11	347	2
Dec. 11, 1989	John Taylor, San Francisco vs. L.A. Rams	14	321	2
Nov. 26, 1989	Flipper Anderson, L.A. Rams vs. New Orleans (OT)	15	336	1
Nov. 28, 1988	*Tim Brown, L.A. Raiders vs. Seattle	12	306	1
Dec. 22, 1985	Stephone Paige, Kansas City vs. San Diego	8	309	2
Nov. 10, 1985	Lionel James, San Diego vs. L.A. Raiders (OT)	23	345	0
Sept. 22, 1985	Lionel James, San Diego vs. Cincinnati	20	316	2
Dec. 21, 1975	*Walter Payton, Chicago vs. New Orleans	32	300	1
Nov. 23, 1975	Greg Pruitt, Cleveland vs. Cincinnati	28	304	2
Nov. 1, 1970	Eugene (Mercury) Morris, Miami vs. Baltimore	17	302	0
Oct. 4, 1970	O.J. Simpson, Buffalo vs. N.Y. Jets	26	303	2

Date	Player, Team, Opponent	No.	Yards	TD
Dec. 6, 1969	Jerry LeVias, Houston vs. N.Y. Jets	18	329	1
Nov. 2, 1969	Travis Williams, Green Bay vs. Pittsburgh	11	314	3
Dec. 18, 1966	Gale Sayers, Chicago vs. Minnesota	20	339	2
Dec. 12, 1965	*Gale Sayers, Chicago vs. San Francisco	17	336	6
Nov. 17, 1963	Gary Ballman, Pittsburgh vs. Washington	12	320	2
Dec. 16, 1962	Timmy Brown, Philadelphia vs. St. Louis	19	341	2
Dec. 10, 1961	Billy Cannon, Houston vs. N.Y. Titans	32	373	5
Nov. 19, 1961	Jim Brown, Cleveland vs. Philadelphia	38	313	4
Dec. 3, 1950	Cloyce Box, Detroit vs. Baltimore	13	302	4
Oct. 29, 1950	Wally Triplett, Detroit vs. Los Angeles	11	331	1
Nov. 22, 1945	Jim Benton, Cleveland vs. Detroit	10	303	1

*First season of professional football.

2,000 SCRIMMAGE YARDS GAINED IN A SEASON

Year	Player, Team	Att.	Rushing Yards	Receptions	Receiving Yards	Scrimm. Yards
2013	LeSean McCoy, Philadelphia	314	1,607	52	539	2,146
2012	Adrian Peterson, Minnesota	348	2,097	40	217	2,314
2011	Ray Rice, Baltimore[2]	291	1,364	76	704	2,068
2010	Arian Foster, Houston	327	1,616	66	604	2,220
2009	Chris Johnson, Tennessee	358	2,006	50	503	2,509
	Ray Rice, Baltimore	254	1,339	78	702	2,041
2007	Brian Westbrook, Philadelphia	278	1,333	90	771	2,104
2006	Steven Jackson, St. Louis	346	1,528	90	806	2,334
	LaDainian Tomlinson, San Diego[3]	348	1,815	56	508	2,323
	Larry Johnson, Kansas City[2]	416	1,789	41	410	2,199
	Frank Gore, San Francisco	312	1,695	61	485	2,180
	Tiki Barber, N.Y. Giants[3]	327	1,662	58	465	2,127[3]
2005	Tiki Barber, N.Y. Giants[2]	357	1,860	54	530	2,390
	Larry Johnson, Kansas City	336	1,750	33	343	2,093
2004	Tiki Barber, N.Y. Giants	322	1.518	52	578	2,096
	Edgerrin James, Indianapolis[3]	334	1,548	51	483	2,031
2003	LaDainian Tomlinson, San Diego[2]	313	1,645	100	725	2,370
	Jamal Lewis, Baltimore	387	2,066	26	205	2,271
	Ahman Green, Green Bay	355	1,883	50	367	2,250
	Deuce McAllister, New Orleans	351	1,641	69	516	2,157
	Priest Holmes, Kansas City[3]	320	1,420	74	690	2,110
2002	Priest Holmes, Kansas City[2]	313	1,615	70	672	2,287
	Ricky Williams, Miami	383	1,853	47	363	2,216
	LaDainian Tomlinson, San Diego	372	1,683	79	489	2,172
2001	Priest Holmes, Kansas City	327	1,555	62	614	2,169
	Marshall Faulk, St. Louis[4]	260	1,382	83	765	2,147
2000	Edgerrin James, Indianapolis[2]	387	1,709	63	594	2,303
	Marshall Faulk, St. Louis[3]	253	1,359	81	830	2,189
1999	Marshall Faulk, St. Louis[2]	253	1,381	87	1,048	2,429
	*Edgerrin James, Indianapolis	369	1,553	62	586	2,139
1998	Marshall Faulk, Indianapolis	324	1,319	86	908	2,227
	Terrell Davis, Denver[2]	392	2,008	25	217	2,225
	Jamal Anderson, Atlanta	410	1,846	27	319	2,165
	Garrison Hearst, San Francisco	310	1,570	39	535	2,105
1997	Barry Sanders, Detroit[2]	335	2,053	33	305	2,358
	Terrell Davis, Denver	369	1,750	42	287	2,037
1995	Emmitt Smith, Dallas[2]	377	1,773	62	375	2,148
1994	Barry Sanders, Detroit	331	1,883	44	283	2,166
1992	Thurman Thomas, Buffalo[2]	312	1,487	58	626	2,113
	Emmitt Smith, Dallas	373	1,713	59	335	2,048
	Barry Foster, Pittsburgh	390	1,690	36	344	2,034
1991	Thurman Thomas, Buffalo	288	1,407	62	631	2,038
1988	Roger Craig, San Francisco[2]	310	1,502	76	534	2,036
	Eric Dickerson, Indianapolis[4]	388	1,659	36	377	2,036
	Herschel Walker, Dallas	361	1,514	53	505	2,019
1986	Eric Dickerson, L.A. Rams[3]	404	1,821	26	205	2,026
1985	Marcus Allen, L.A. Raiders	380	1,759	67	555	2,314
	Roger Craig, San Francisco	214	1,050	92	1,016	2,066
	Walter Payton, Chicago[4]	324	1,551	49	483	2,034
1984	Eric Dickerson, L. A. Rams[2]	379	2,105	21	139	2,244
	James Wilder, Tampa Bay	407	1,544	85	685	2,229
	Walter Payton, Chicago[3]	381	1,684	45	368	2,052
1983	*Eric Dickerson, L.A. Rams	390	1,808	51	404	2,212
	William Andrews, Atlanta[2]	331	1,567	59	609	2,176

Year	Player, Team	Att.	Rushing Yards	Receptions	Receiving Yards	Scrimm. Yards
	Walter Payton, Chicago[2]	314	1,421	53	607	2,028
1981	William Andrews, Atlanta	289	1,301	81	735	2,036
1979	Wilbert Montgomery, Philadelphia	338	1,512	41	494	2,006
1977	Walter Payton, Chicago	339	1,852	27	269	2,121
1975	O.J. Simpson, Buffalo[2]	329	1,817	28	426	2,243
1973	O.J. Simpson, Buffalo	332	2,003	6	70	2,073
1963	Jim Brown, Cleveland	291	1,863	24	268	2,131

*First season of professional football.

300 SCRIMMAGE YARDS GAINED IN A GAME

Date	Player, Team, Opponent	Att.	Yards	TD
Oct. 27, 2013	Calvin Johnson, Detroit vs. Dallas	14	329	1
Nov. 4, 2007	*Adrian Peterson, Minnesota vs. San Diego	31	315	3
Nov. 24, 2002	Priest Holmes, Kansas City vs. Seattle	30	307	3
Nov. 26, 1989	Flipper Anderson, L.A. Rams vs. New Orleans (OT)	15	336	1
Dec. 22, 1985	Stephone Paige, Kansas City vs. San Diego	8	309	2
Dec. 10, 1961	Billy Cannon, Houston vs. N.Y. Titans	30	330	5
Dec. 3, 1950	Cloyce Box, Detroit vs. Baltimore	12	302	4
Nov. 22, 1945	Jim Benton, Cleveland vs. Detroit	10	303	1

*First season of professional football.

TOP 20 SCORERS

Player		Years	TD	FG	PA.	
1.	Morten Andersen	25	0	565	849	
2.	Gary Anderson	23	0	538	820	2,4▸
3.	Jason Hanson	21	0	495	665	2,150
4.	John Carney	23	0	478	628	2,062
5.	Adam Vinatieri	18	0	448	660	2,006
6.	Matt Stover	19	0	471	591	2,004
7.	George Blanda	26	9	335	943	2,002
8.	Jason Elam	17	0	436	675	1,983
9.	John Kasay	20	0	461	587	1,970
10.	Norm Johnson	18	0	366	638	1,736
11.	David Akers	16	0	386	563	1,721
12.	Nick Lowery	18	0	383	562	1,711
13.	Jan Stenerud	19	0	373	580	1,699
14.	Ryan Longwell	15	0	361	604	1,687
15.	Eddie Murray	19	0	352	538	1,594
16.	Al Del Greco	17	0	347	543	1,584
17.	Olindo Mare	16	0	356	487	1,555
18.	Sebastian Janikowski	14	0	345	454	1,489
19.	Steve Christie	15	0	336	468	1,476
20.	Pat Leahy	18	0	304	558	1,470

TOP 20 TOUCHDOWN SCORERS

Player		Years	Rush	Rec.	Total Returns	TD
1.	Jerry Rice	20	10	197	1	208
2.	Emmitt Smith	15	164	11	0	175
3.	LaDainian Tomlinson	11	145	17	0	162
4.	Randy Moss	14	0	156	1	157
5.	Terrell Owens	15	3	153	0	156
6.	Marcus Allen	16	123	21	1	145
7.	Marshall Faulk	12	100	36	0	136
8.	Cris Carter	16	0	130	1	131
9.	Marvin Harrison	13	0	128	0	128
10.	Jim Brown	9	106	20	0	126
11.	Walter Payton	13	110	15	0	125
12.	John Riggins	14	104	12	0	116
13.	Lenny Moore	12	63	48	2	113
14.	Shaun Alexander	9	100	12	0	112
15.	Tony Gonzalez	17	0	111	0	111
16.	Barry Sanders	10	99	10	0	109
17.	Tim Brown	17	1	100	4	105
	Don Hutson	11	3	99	3	105
19.	Steve Largent	14	1	100	0	101
20.	Franco Harris	13	91	9	0	100
	Curtis Martin	11	90	10	0	100

TOP 20 RUSHERS

Player		Years	Att.	Yards	Avg.	Long	TD
1.	Emmitt Smith	15	4,409	18,355	4.2	75	164
2.	Walter Payton	13	3,838	16,726	4.4	76	110
3.	Barry Sanders	10	3,062	15,269	5.0	85	99
4.	Curtis Martin	11	3,518	14,101	4.0	70	90
5.	LaDainian Tomlinson	11	3,174	13,684	4.3	85	145
6.	Jerome Bettis	13	3,479	13,662	3.9	71	91
7.	Eric Dickerson	11	2,996	13,259	4.4	85	90
8.	Tony Dorsett	12	2,936	12,739	4.3	99	77
9.	Jim Brown	9	2,359	12,312	5.2	80	106
10.	Marshall Faulk	12	2,836	12,279	4.3	71	100
11.	Edgerrin James	11	3,028	12,246	4.0	72	80
12.	Marcus Allen	16	3,022	12,243	4.1	61	123
13.	Franco Harris	13	2,949	12,120	4.1	75	91
14.	Thurman Thomas	13	2,877	12,074	4.2	80	65
15.	Fred Taylor	13	2,534	11,695	4.6	80	66
16.	John Riggins	14	2,916	11,352	3.9	66	104
17.	Corey Dillon	10	2,618	11,241	4.3	96	82
18.	O.J. Simpson	11	2,404	11,236	4.7	94	61
19.	Warrick Dunn	12	2,669	10,967	4.1	90	49
20.	Steven Jackson	10	2,553	10,681	4.2	59	62

TOP 20 PASS RECEIVERS

Player	Years	No.	Yards	Avg.	Long	TD
1. Jerry Rice	20	1,549	22,895	14.8	96	197
2. Tony Gonzalez	17	1,325	15,127	11.4	73	111
3. Marvin Harrison	13	1,102	14,580	13.2	80	128
4. Cris Carter	16	1,101	13,899	12.6	80	130
5. Tim Brown	17	1,094	14,934	13.7	80	100
6. Terrell Owens	15	1,078	15,934	14.8	98	153
7. Isaac Bruce	16	1,024	15,208	14.9	80	91
8. Reggie Wayne	13	1,006	13,566	13.5	71	80
9. Hines Ward	14	1,000	12,083	12.1	85	85
10. Randy Moss	14	982	15,292	15.6	82	156
11. Andre Reed	16	951	13,198	13.9	83	87
12. Derrick Mason	15	943	12,061	12.8	79	66
13. Art Monk	16	940	12,721	13.5	79	68
14. Andre Johnson	11	927	12,661	13.7	77	61
15. Torry Holt	11	920	13,382	14.5	85	74
16. Keenan McCardell	16	883	11,373	12.9	76	63
17. Jason Witten	11	879	9,799	11.1	69	52
18. Jimmy Smith	12	862	12,287	14.3	75	67
19. Muhsin Muhammad	14	860	11,438	13.3	72	62
20. Anquan Boldin	11	857	11,344	13.2	79	65

TOP 20 INTERCEPTORS

Player	Years	No.	Yards	Avg.	Long	TD
1. Paul Krause	16	81	1,185	14.6	81	3
2. Emlen Tunnell	14	79	1,282	16.2	55	4
3. Rod Woodson	17	71	1,483	20.9	98	12
4. Dick (Night Train) Lane	14	68	1,207	17.8	80	5
5. Ken Riley	15	65	596	9.2	66	5
6. Ed Reed	12	64	1,590	24.8	107	7
7. Ronnie Lott	14	63	730	11.6	83	5
Darren Sharper	14	63	1,412	22.4	99	11
9. Dave Brown	15	62	698	11.3	90	5
Dick LeBeau	14	62	762	12.3	70	3
11. Emmitt Thomas	13	58	937	16.2	73	5
12. Mel Blount	14	57	736	12.9	52	2
Bobby Boyd	9	57	994	17.4	74	4
Eugene Robinson	16	57	762	13.4	49	1
Johnny Robinson	12	57	741	13.0	57	1
Everson Walls	13	57	504	8.8	40	1
17. Lem Barney	11	56	1,077	19.2	71	7
Pat Fischer	17	56	941	16.8	69	4
Charles Woodson	16	56	909	16.2	62	11
20. Aeneas Williams	14	55	807	14.7	65	9

TOP 20 PUNTERS (MINIMUM 250 PUNTS)

Player	Years	No.	Yards	Avg.	Long	Blk.
1. Shane Lechler	14	1,102	52,404	47.6	80	4
2. Thomas Morstead	5	296	13,936	47.1	70	1
3. Brandon Fields	7	536	25,092	46.8	74	2
4. Andy Lee	10	869	40,099	46.1	82	3
5. Britton Colquitt	4	319	14,616	45.8	67	1
6. Pat McAfee	5	366	16,685	45.6	66	3
7. Donnie Jones	10	818	37,210	45.5	80	4
8. Mat McBriar	10	589	26,581	45.1	75	5
9. Mike Scifres	11	629	28,375	45.1	71	8
10. Sammy Baugh	16	338	15,245	45.1	85	9
11. Dustin Colquitt	9	744	33,386	44.9	81	4
12. Sam Koch	8	648	29,029	44.8	74	3
13. Brett Kern	6	432	19,350	44.8	71	3
14. Jon Ryan	8	622	27,835	44.8	77	5
15. Tommy Davis	11	511	22,833	44.7	82	2
16. Chris Kluwe	8	623	27,683	44.4	70	1
17. Steve Weatherford	8	594	26,358	44.4	68	0
18. Tim Masthay	4	260	11,517	44.3	71	1
19. Yale Lary	11	503	22,279	44.3	74	4
20. Kevin Huber	5	390	17,250	44.2	75	1

TOP 20 COMBINED YARDS GAINED

Player	Years	Tot.	Rush.	Rec.	Int. Ret.	Punt Ret.	Kickoff Ret.	Fumble Ret.
1. Jerry Rice	20	23,546	645	22,895	0	0	6	0
2. Brian Mitchell	14	23,330	1,967	2,336	0	4,999	14,014	14
3. Walter Payton	13	21,803	16,726	4,538	0	0	539	0
4. Emmitt Smith	15	21,583	18,355	3,224	0	0	0	4
5. Tim Brown	17	19,682	190	14,934	0	3,320	1,235	3
6. Marshall Faulk	12	19,190	12,279	6,875	0	0	18	18
7. LaDainian Tomlinson	11	18,456	13,684	4,772	0	0	0	0
8. Barry Sanders	10	18,308	15,269	2,921	0	0	118	0
9. Herschel Walker	12	18,168	8,225	4,859	0	0	5,084	0
10. Marcus Allen	16	17,648	12,243	5,411	0	0	0	-6
11. Curtis Martin	11	17,430	14,101	3,329	0	0	0	0
12. Tiki Barber	10	17,359	10,449	5,183	0	1,181	544	2
13. Eric Metcalf	13	17,230	2,392	5,572	0	3,453	5,813	0
14. Derrick Mason	15	17,150	3	12,061	0	1,590	3,496	0
15. Steve Smith	13	16,614	387	12,197	0	1,652	2,371	7
16. Thurman Thomas	13	16,532	12,074	4,458	0	0	0	0
17. Tony Dorsett	12	16,347	12,739	3,554	0	0	0	54
18. Terrell Owens	15	16,276	251	15,934	0	0	78	13
19. Wes Welker	10	16,134	151	9,358	0	2,487	4,138	0
20. Henry Ellard	16	15,718	50	13,777	0	1,527	364	0

TOP 20 YARDS FROM SCRIMMAGE

Player	Years	Scrimmage Yards	Rushing Yards	Receiving Yards
1. Jerry Rice	20	23,540	645	22,895
2. Emmitt Smith	15	21,579	18,355	3,224
3. Walter Payton	13	21,264	16,726	4,538
4. Marshall Faulk	12	19,154	12,279	6,875
5. LaDainian Tomlinson	11	18,456	13,684	4,772
6. Barry Sanders	10	18,190	15,269	2,921
7. Marcus Allen	16	17,654	12,243	5,411
8. Curtis Martin	11	17,430	14,101	3,329
9. Thurman Thomas	13	16,532	12,074	4,458
10. Tony Dorsett	12	16,293	12,739	3,554
11. Terrell Owens	15	16,185	251	15,934
12. Tiki Barber	10	15,632	10,449	5,183
13. Edgerrin James	11	15,610	12,246	3,364
14. Randy Moss	16	15,451	159	15,292
15. Eric Dickerson	11	15,396	13,259	2,137
16. Isaac Bruce	16	15,347	139	15,208
17. Warrick Dunn	12	15,306	10,967	4,339
18. Tony Gonzalez	17	15,141	14	15,127
19. Tim Brown	17	15,124	190	14,934
20. Jerome Bettis	13	15,111	13,662	1,449

TOP 20 PASSERS

Player	Years	Att.	Comp.	Pct. Comp.	Yards	Avg. Gain	TD	Pct. TD	Int.	Pct. Int.	Rating
1. Aaron Rodgers	9	2,955	1,945	65.8	24,197	8.19	188	6.4	52	1.8	104.9
2. Peyton Manning	15	8,452	5,532	65.5	64,964	7.69	491	5.8	219	2.6	97.2
3. Steve Young	15	4,149	2,667	64.3	33,124	7.98	232	5.6	107	2.6	96.8
4. Philip Rivers	10	4,108	2,646	64.4	32,369	7.88	221	5.4	104	2.5	96.0
5. Tony Romo	10	3,775	2,439	64.6	29,565	7.83	208	5.5	101	2.7	95.8
6. Tom Brady	14	6,586	4,178	63.4	49,149	7.46	359	5.5	134	2.0	95.7
7. Drew Brees	13	6,799	4,481	65.9	51,081	7.51	363	5.3	177	2.6	95.3
8. Kurt Warner	12	4,070	2,666	65.5	32,344	7.95	208	5.1	128	3.1	93.7
9. Ben Roethlisberger	10	4,346	2,749	63.3	34,105	7.85	219	5.0	122	2.8	92.6
10. Joe Montana	15	5,391	3,409	63.2	40,551	7.52	273	5.1	139	2.6	92.3
11. Matt Ryan	6	3,288	2,093	63.7	23,472	7.14	153	4.7	77	2.3	90.6
12. Chad Pennington	11	2,471	1,632	66.0	17,823	7.21	102	4.1	64	2.6	90.1
13. Matt Schaub	10	3,181	2,035	64.0	24,254	7.62	130	4.1	84	2.6	89.8
14. Daunte Culpepper	11	3,199	2,016	63.0	24,153	7.55	149	4.7	106	3.3	87.8
15. Jeff Garcia	11	3,676	2,264	61.6	25,537	6.95	161	4.4	83	2.3	87.5
16. Dan Marino	17	8,358	4,967	59.4	61,361	7.34	420	5.0	252	3.0	86.4
17. Trent Green	11	3,740	2,266	60.6	28,475	7.61	162	4.3	114	3.0	86.0
18. Brett Favre	20	10,169	6,300	62.0	71,838	7.06	508	5.0	336	3.3	86.0
19. Carson Palmer	11	4,682	2,930	62.6	33,739	7.21	213	4.5	152	3.2	85.9
20. David Garrard	9	2,281	1,406	61.6	16,003	7.02	89	3.9	54	2.4	85.8

1,500 or more attempts. The passing ratings are based on performance standards established for completion percentage, interception percentage, touchdown percentage, and average gain. Please consult page 312 for more information.

TOP 20 LEADERS IN PASSES COMPLETED

1.	Brett Favre	6,300
2.	Peyton Manning	5,532
3.	Dan Marino	4,967
4.	Drew Brees	4,481
5.	Tom Brady	4,178
6.	John Elway	4,123
7.	Warren Moon	3,988
8.	Drew Bledsoe	3,839
9.	Vinny Testaverde	3,787
10.	Fran Tarkenton	3,686
11.	Kerry Collins	3,487
12.	Joe Montana	3,409
13.	Dan Fouts	3,297
14.	Donovan McNabb	3,170
15.	Dave Krieg	3,105
16.	Matt Hasselbeck	3,036
17.	Boomer Esiason	2,969
18.	Carson Palmer	2,930
19.	Eli Manning	2,929
20.	Troy Aikman	2,898

TOP 20 LEADERS IN TOUCHDOWN PASSES

1.	Brett Favre	508
2.	Peyton Manning	491
3.	Dan Marino	420
4.	Drew Brees	363
5.	Tom Brady	359
6.	Fran Tarkenton	342
7.	John Elway	300
8.	Warren Moon	291
9.	Johnny Unitas	290
10.	Vinny Testaverde	275
11.	Joe Montana	273
12.	Dave Krieg	261
13.	Sonny Jurgensen	255
14.	Dan Fouts	254
15.	Drew Bledsoe	251
16.	Boomer Esiason	247
17.	John Hadl	244
18.	Len Dawson	239
19.	Jim Kelly	237
20.	George Blanda	236

TOP 20 LEADERS IN PASSING YARDS

1.	Brett Favre	71,838
2.	Peyton Manning	64,964
3.	Dan Marino	61,361
4.	John Elway	51,475
5.	Drew Brees	51,081
6.	Warren Moon	49,325
7.	Tom Brady	49,149
8.	Fran Tarkenton	47,003
9.	Vinny Testaverde	46,233
10.	Drew Bledsoe	44,611
11.	Dan Fouts	43,040
12.	Kerry Collins	40,922
13.	Joe Montana	40,551
14.	Johnny Unitas	40,239
15.	Dave Krieg	38,147
16.	Boomer Esiason	37,920
17.	Donovan McNabb	37,276
18.	Jim Kelly	35,467
19.	Eli Manning	35,345
20.	Jim Everett	34,837

TOP 20 LEADERS IN RECEPTION YARDS

1.	Jerry Rice	22,895
2.	Terrell Owens	15,934
3.	Randy Moss	15,292
4.	Isaac Bruce	15,208
5.	Tony Gonzalez	15,127
6.	Tim Brown	14,934
7.	Marvin Harrison	14,580
8.	James Lofton	14,004
9.	Cris Carter	13,899
10.	Henry Ellard	13,777
11.	Reggie Wayne	13,566
12.	Torry Holt	13,382
13.	Andre Reed	13,198
14.	Steve Largent	13,089
15.	Irving Fryar	12,785
16.	Art Monk	12,721
17.	Andre Johnson	12,661
18.	Jimmy Smith	12,287
19.	Steve Smith	12,197
20.	Charlie Joiner	12,146

TOP 20 KICKOFF RETURNERS (MINIMUM 75 RETURNS)

Player	Years	No.	Yards	Avg.	Long	TD
1. Gale Sayers	7	91	2,781	30.6	103	6
2. Lynn Chandnois	7	92	2,720	29.6	93	3
3. Joe McKnight	3	76	2,205	29.0	107	2
4. Abe Woodson	9	193	5,538	28.7	105	5
5. Percy Harvin	5	115	3,241	28.2	105	5
6. Buddy Young	6	90	2,514	27.9	104	2
7. Travis Williams	5	102	2,801	27.5	105	6
8. Quintin Demps	6	96	2,630	27.4	100	2
9. Joe Arenas	7	139	3,798	27.3	96	1
10. Clifton Smith	3	75	2,038	27.2	97	1
11. Clarence Davis	8	79	2,140	27.1	76	0
12. Danieal Manning	8	116	3,102	26.8	83	1
13. Steve Van Buren	8	76	2,030	26.7	98	3
14. Jacoby Jones	7	133	3,549	26.7	108	4
15. Lenny Lyles	12	81	2,161	26.7	103	3
16. Mercury Morris	8	111	2,947	26.5	105	3
17. Ellis Hobbs	6	141	3,739	26.5	108	3
18. Bobby Jancik	6	158	4,185	26.5	61	0
19. Leodis McKelvin	6	91	2,407	26.5	98	1
20. Mel Renfro	14	85	2,246	26.4	100	2

TOP 20 PUNT RETURNERS (MINIMUM 75 RETURNS)

Player	Years	No.	Yards	Avg.	Long	TD
1. George McAfee	8	112	1,431	12.8	74	2
2. Jack Christiansen	8	85	1,084	12.8	89	8
3. Claude Gibson	5	110	1,381	12.6	85	3
4. Julian Edelman	5	107	1,317	12.3	94	3
5. Devin Hester	8	264	3,241	12.3	89	13
6. Bill Dudley	9	124	1,515	12.2	96	3
7. Rick Upchurch	9	248	3,008	12.1	92	8
8. Dexter McCluster	4	79	959	12.1	94	3
9. Desmond Howard	11	244	2,895	11.9	95	8
10. Billy Johnson	14	282	3,317	11.8	87	6
11. Mack Herron	3	84	982	11.7	66	0
12. Roscoe Parrish	8	165	1,920	11.6	82	3
13. Billy Thompson	13	157	1,814	11.6	60	0
14. Darrien Gordon	9	314	3,601	11.5	94	6
15. Henry Ellard	16	135	1,527	11.3	83	4
16. Rodger Bird	3	94	1,063	11.3	78	0
17. Bosh Pritchard	6	95	1,072	11.3	81	2
18. Ted Ginn Jr.	7	156	1,741	11.2	87	3
19. Terry Metcalf	6	84	936	11.1	69	1
20. Bob Hayes	11	104	1,158	11.1	90	3

TOP 20 LEADERS IN SACKS

Player	*Years	No.
1. Bruce Smith	19	200.0
2. Reggie White	15	198.0
3. Kevin Greene	15	160.0
4. Chris Doleman	15	150.5
5. Michael Strahan	15	141.5
6. Jason Taylor	15	139.5
7. Richard Dent	15	137.5
John Randle	14	137.5
9. John Abraham	14	133.5
10. Leslie O'Neal	13	132.5
Lawrence Taylor	12	132.5
12. Jared Allen	10	128.5
13. Rickey Jackson	14	128.0
14. Derrick Thomas	11	126.5
15. Simeon Rice	12	122.0
16. Clyde Simmons	15	121.5
17. Julius Peppers	12	118.5
18. DeMarcus Ware	9	117.0
19. Sean Jones	13	113.0
20. Robert Mathis	11	111.0

*Years played since 1982 when sacks became an official statistic.

POSTSEASON LEADERS

TOP 10 POSTSEASON RUSHERS

Player	Att.	Yards	Avg.	Long	TD
1. Emmitt Smith	349	1,586	4.5	65	19
2. Franco Harris	400	1,556	3.9	50	16
3. Thurman Thomas	339	1,442	4.3	40	16
4. Tony Dorsett	302	1,383	4.6	53	9
5. Marcus Allen	267	1,347	5.0	74	11
6. Terrell Davis	204	1,140	5.6	62	12
7. John Riggins	251	996	4.0	43	12
8. Larry Csonka	225	891	4.0	49	9
9. Chuck Foreman	229	860	3.8	62	7
10. Edgerrin James	218	852	3.9	34	6

TOP 10 POSTSEASON PASSERS

Player	Att.	Comp.	Pct. Comp.	Yards	Avg. Gain	TD	Pct. TD	Int.	Pct. Int.	Rating
1. Bart Starr	213	130	61.0	1,753	8.23	15	7.0	3	1.4	104.8
2. Aaron Rodgers	318	210	66.0	2,489	7.83	19	6.0	5	1.6	103.1
3. Kurt Warner	462	307	66.5	3,952	8.55	31	6.7	14	3.0	102.8
4. Drew Brees	464	306	65.9	3,539	7.63	24	5.2	6	1.3	100.7
5. Joe Montana	734	460	62.7	5,772	7.86	45	6.1	21	2.9	95.6
6. Mark Sanchez	157	95	60.5	1,155	7.36	9	5.7	3	1.9	94.3
7. Ken Anderson	166	110	66.3	1,321	7.96	9	5.4	6	3.6	93.5
8. Joe Theismann	211	128	60.7	1,782	8.45	11	5.2	7	3.3	91.4
9. Eli Manning	356	219	61.5	2,516	7.07	17	4.8	8	2.2	89.3
10. Peyton Manning	889	572	64.3	6,589	7.41	37	4.2	24	2.7	89.2

TOP 10 POSTSEASON PASS RECEIVERS

Player	No.	Yards	Avg.	Long	TD
1. Jerry Rice	151	2,245	14.9	72	22
2. Reggie Wayne	92	1,242	13.5	72	9
3. Hines Ward	88	1,181	13.4	45	10
4. Michael Irvin	87	1,315	15.1	53	8
Wes Welker	87	846	9.7	47	5
6. Andre Reed	85	1,229	14.5	72	9
7. Thurman Thomas	76	672	8.8	27	5
8. Cliff Branch	73	1,289	17.7	72	5
9. Fred Biletnikoff	70	1,167	16.7	57	10
10. Art Monk	69	1,062	15.4	48	7

TOP 10 POSTSEASON INTERCEPTION LEADERS

Player	Interceptions
1. Ronnie Lott	9
Ed Reed	9
Bill Simpson	9
Charlie Waters	9
5. Lester Hayes	8
6. Willie Brown	7
Rodney Harrison	7
Asante Samuel	7
Dennis Thurman	7
10. Bobby Bryant	6
Eric Davis	6
Glen Edwards	6
Darrell Green	6
Cliff Harris	6
Ty Law	6
Vernon Perry	6
Aeneas Williams	6

TOP 10 POSTSEASON SACK LEADERS

Player	Sacks
1. Willie McGinest	16.0
2. Bruce Smith	14.5
3. Reggie White	12.0
Terrell Suggs	12.0
5. Charles Haley	11.0
LaMarr Woodley	11.0
7. Richard Dent	10.5
8. Trace Armstrong	10.0
Charles Mann	10.0
Tony Tolbert	10.0

*Sacks became an official statistic in 1982.

ANNUAL SCORING LEADERS

Year	Player, Team	TD	FG	PAT	TP
2013	Stephen Gostkowski, New England, AFC	0	38	44	158
	Steven Hauschka, Seattle, NFC	0	33	44	143
2012	Stephen Gostkowski, New England, AFC	0	29	66	153
	Lawrence Tynes, N.Y. Giants, NFC	0	33	46	145
2011	David Akers, San Francisco, NFC	0	44	34	166
	Stephen Gostkowski, New England, AFC	0	28	59	143
2010	David Akers, Philadelphia, NFC	0	32	47	143
	Sebastian Janikowski, Oakland, AFC	0	33	43	142
2009	Nate Kaeding, San Diego, AFC	0	32	50	146
	David Akers, Philadelphia, NFC	0	32	43	139
2008	Stephen Gostkowski, New England, AFC	0	36	40	148
	David Akers, Philadelphia, NFC	0	33	45	144
2007	*Mason Crosby, Green Bay, NFC	0	31	48	141
	Randy Moss, New England, AFC	23	0	0	138
2006	LaDainian Tomlinson, AFC	31	0	0	186
	Robbie Gould, Chicago, NFC	0	32	47	143
2005	Shaun Alexander, Seattle, NFC	28	0	0	168
	Shayne Graham, Cincinnati, AFC	0	28	47	131
2004	Adam Vinatieri, New England, AFC	0	31	48	141
	David Akers, Philadelphia, NFC	0	27	41	122
2003	Jeff Wilkins, St. Louis, NFC	0	39	46	163
	Priest Holmes, Kansas City, AFC	27	0	0	162
2002	Priest Holmes, Kansas City, AFC	24	0	0	144
	Jay Feely, Atlanta, NFC	0	32	42	138
2001	Marshall Faulk, St. Louis, NFC	21	0	0	#128
	Mike Vanderjagt, Indianapolis, AFC	0	28	41	125
2000	Marshall Faulk, St. Louis, NFC	26	0	0	##160
	Matt Stover, Baltimore, AFC	0	35	30	135
1999	Mike Vanderjagt, Indianapolis, AFC	0	34	43	145
	Jeff Wilkins, St. Louis, NFC	0	20	64	124
1998	Gary Anderson, Minnesota, NFC	0	35	59	164
	Steve Christie, Buffalo, AFC	0	33	41	140
1997	Mike Hollis, Jacksonville, AFC	0	31	41	134
	Richie Cunningham, Dallas, NFC	0	34	24	126
1996	John Kasay, Carolina, NFC	0	37	34	145
	Cary Blanchard, Indianapolis, AFC	0	36	27	135
1995	Emmitt Smith, Dallas, NFC	25	0	0	150
	Norm Johnson, Pittsburgh, AFC	0	34	39	141
1994	John Carney, San Diego, AFC	0	34	33	135
	Fuad Reveiz, Minnesota, NFC	0	34	30	132
1993	Jeff Jaeger, L.A. Raiders, AFC	0	35	27	132
	Jason Hanson, Detroit, NFC	0	34	28	130
1992	Pete Stoyanovich, Miami, AFC	0	30	34	124
	Morten Andersen, New Orleans, NFC	0	29	33	120
	Chip Lohmiller, Washington, NFC	0	30	30	120
1991	Chip Lohmiller, Washington, NFC	0	31	56	149
	Pete Stoyanovich, Miami, AFC	0	31	28	121
1990	Nick Lowery, Kansas City, AFC	0	34	37	139
	Chip Lohmiller, Washington, NFC	0	30	41	131
1989	Mike Cofer, San Francisco, NFC	0	29	49	136
	*David Treadwell, Denver, AFC	0	27	39	120
1988	Scott Norwood, Buffalo, AFC	0	32	33	129
	Mike Cofer, San Francisco, NFC	0	27	40	121
1987	Jerry Rice, San Francisco, NFC	23	0	0	138
	Jim Breech, Cincinnati, AFC	0	24	25	97
1986	Tony Franklin, New England, AFC	0	32	44	140
	Kevin Butler, Chicago, NFC	0	28	36	120
1985	*Kevin Butler, Chicago, NFC	0	31	51	144
	Gary Anderson, Pittsburgh, AFC	0	33	40	139
1984	Ray Wersching, San Francisco, NFC	0	25	56	131
	Gary Anderson, Pittsburgh, AFC	0	24	45	117
1983	Mark Moseley, Washington, NFC	0	33	62	161
	Gary Anderson, Pittsburgh, AFC	0	27	38	119
1982	*Marcus Allen, L.A. Raiders, AFC	14	0	0	84
	Wendell Tyler, L.A. Rams, NFC	13	0	0	78
1981	Ed Murray, Detroit, NFC	0	25	46	121
	Rafael Septien, Dallas, NFC	0	27	40	121
	Jim Breech, Cincinnati, AFC	0	22	49	115
	Nick Lowery, Kansas City, AFC	0	26	37	115

Year	Player, Team	TD	FG	PAT	TP
1980	John Smith, New England, AFC	0	26	51	129
	*Ed Murray, Detroit, NFC	0	27	35	116
1979	John Smith, New England, AFC	0	23	46	115
	Mark Moseley, Washington, NFC	0	25	39	114
1978	*Frank Corral, Los Angeles, NFC	0	29	31	118
	Pat Leahy, N.Y. Jets, AFC	0	22	41	107
1977	Errol Mann, Oakland, AFC	0	20	39	99
	Walter Payton, Chicago, NFC	16	0	0	96
1976	Toni Linhart, Baltimore, AFC	0	20	49	109
	Mark Moseley, Washington, NFC	0	22	31	97
1975	O.J. Simpson, Buffalo, AFC	23	0	0	138
	Chuck Foreman, Minnesota, NFC	22	0	0	132
1974	Chester Marcol, Green Bay, NFC	0	25	19	94
	Roy Gerela, Pittsburgh, AFC	0	20	33	93
1973	David Ray, Los Angeles, NFC	0	30	40	130
	Roy Gerela, Pittsburgh, AFC	0	29	36	123
1972	*Chester Marcol, Green Bay, NFC	0	33	29	128
	Bobby Howfield, N.Y. Jets, AFC	0	27	40	121
1971	Garo Yepremian, Miami, AFC	0	28	33	117
	Curt Knight, Washington, NFC	0	29	27	114
1970	Fred Cox, Minnesota, NFC	0	30	35	125
	Jan Stenerud, Kansas City, AFC	0	30	26	116
1969	Jim Turner, N.Y. Jets, AFL	0	32	33	129
	Fred Cox, Minnesota, NFL	0	26	43	121
1968	Jim Turner, N.Y. Jets, AFL	0	34	43	145
	Leroy Kelly, Cleveland, NFL	20	0	0	120
1967	Jim Bakken, St. Louis, NFL	0	27	36	117
	George Blanda, Oakland, AFL	0	20	56	116
1966	Gino Cappelletti, Boston, AFL	6	16	35	119
	Bruce Gossett, Los Angeles, NFL	0	28	29	113
1965	*Gale Sayers, Chicago, NFL	22	0	0	132
	Gino Cappelletti, Boston, AFL	9	17	27	132
1964	Gino Cappelletti, Boston, AFL	7	25	36	#155
	Lenny Moore, Baltimore, NFL	20	0	0	120
1963	Gino Cappelletti, Boston, AFL	2	22	35	113
	Don Chandler, N.Y. Giants, NFL	0	18	52	106
1962	Gene Mingo, Denver, AFL	4	27	32	137
	Jim Taylor, Green Bay, NFL	19	0	0	114
1961	Gino Cappelletti, Boston, AFL	8	17	48	147
	Paul Hornung, Green Bay, NFL	10	15	41	146
1960	Paul Hornung, Green Bay, NFL	15	15	41	176
	*Gene Mingo, Denver, AFL	6	18	33	123
1959	Paul Hornung, Green Bay	7	7	31	94
1958	Jim Brown, Cleveland	18	0	0	108
1957	Sam Baker, Washington	1	14	29	77
	Lou Groza, Cleveland	0	15	32	77
1956	Bobby Layne, Detroit	5	12	33	99
1955	Doak Walker, Detroit	7	9	27	96
1954	Bobby Walston, Philadelphia	11	4	36	114
1953	Gordy Soltau, San Francisco	6	10	48	114
1952	Gordy Soltau, San Francisco	7	6	34	94
1951	Elroy (Crazylegs) Hirsch, Los Angeles	17	0	0	102
1950	*Doak Walker, Detroit	11	8	38	128
1949	Pat Harder, Chi. Cardinals	8	3	45	102
	Gene Roberts, N.Y. Giants	17	0	0	102
1948	Pat Harder, Chi. Cardinals	6	7	53	110
1947	Pat Harder, Chi. Cardinals	7	7	39	102
1946	Ted Fritsch, Green Bay	10	9	13	100
1945	Steve Van Buren, Philadelphia	18	0	2	110
1944	Don Hutson, Green Bay	9	0	31	85
1943	Don Hutson, Green Bay	12	3	36	117
1942	Don Hutson, Green Bay	17	1	33	138
1941	Don Hutson, Green Bay	12	1	20	95
1940	Don Hutson, Green Bay	7	0	15	57
1939	Andy Farkas, Washington	11	0	2	68
1938	Clarke Hinkle, Green Bay	7	3	7	58
1937	Jack Manders, Chi. Bears	5	8	15	69
1936	Earl (Dutch) Clark, Detroit	7	4	19	73
1935	Earl (Dutch) Clark, Detroit	6	1	16	55
1934	Jack Manders, Chi. Bears	3	10	31	79

Year	Player, Team	TD	FG	PAT	TP
1933	Ken Strong, N.Y. Giants	6	5	13	64
	Glenn Presnell, Portsmouth	6	6	10	64
1932	Earl (Dutch) Clark, Portsmouth	6	3	10	55

First season of professional football.
#Cappelletti's total and Faulk's total in 2001 include a two-point conversion.
##Faulk's total in 2000 includes 2 two-point conversions.

ANNUAL TOUCHDOWN LEADERS

Year	Player, Team	TD	Rush	Pass	Ret.
2013	Jamaal Charles, Kansas City, AFC	19	12	7	0
	Jimmy Graham, New Orleans, NFC	16	0	16	0
2012	Arian Foster, Houston, AFC	17	15	2	0
	James Jones, Green Bay, NFC	14	0	14	0
2011	LeSean McCoy, Philadelphia, NFC	20	17	3	0
	Rob Gronkowski, New England, AFC	18	1	17	0
2010	Arian Foster, Houston, AFC	18	16	2	0
	Adrian Peterson, Minnesota, NFC	13	12	1	0
2009	Adrian Peterson, Minnesota, NFC	18	18	0	0
	Chris Johnson, Tennessee, AFC	16	14	2	0
	Maurice Jones-Drew, Jacksonville, AFC	16	15	1	0
2008	DeAngelo Williams, Carolina, NFC	20	18	2	0
	Thomas Jones, N.Y. Jets, AFC	15	13	2	0
	LenDale White, Tennessee, AFC	15	15	0	0
2007	Randy Moss, New England, AFC	23	0	23	0
	Terrell Owens, Dallas, NFC	15	0	15	0
2006	LaDainian Tomlinson, San Diego, AFC	31	28	3	0
	Marion Barber, Dallas, NFC	16	14	2	0
	Steven Jackson, St. Louis, NFC	16	13	3	0
2005	Shaun Alexander, Seattle, NFC	28	27	1	0
	Larry Johnson, Kansas City, AFC	21	20	1	0
2004	Shaun Alexander, Seattle, NFC	20	16	4	0
	LaDainian Tomlinson, San Diego, AFC	18	17	1	0
2003	Priest Holmes, Kansas City, AFC	27	27	0	0
	Ahman Green, Green Bay, NFC	20	15	5	0
2002	Priest Holmes, Kansas City, AFC	24	21	3	0
	Shaun Alexander, Seattle, NFC	18	16	2	0
2001	Marshall Faulk, St. Louis, NFC	21	12	9	0
	Shaun Alexander, Seattle, AFC	16	14	2	0
2000	Marshall Faulk, St. Louis, NFC	26	18	8	0
	Edgerrin James, Indianapolis, AFC	18	13	5	0
1999	Stephen Davis, Washington, NFC	17	17	0	0
	*Edgerrin James, Indianapolis, AFC	17	13	4	0
1998	Terrell Davis, Denver, AFC	23	21	2	0
	*Randy Moss, Minnesota, NFC	17	0	17	0
1997	Karim Abdul-Jabbar, Miami, AFC	16	15	1	0
	Barry Sanders, Detroit, NFC	14	11	3	0
1996	Terry Allen, Washington, NFC	21	21	0	0
	Curtis Martin, New England, AFC	17	14	3	0
1995	Emmitt Smith, Dallas, NFC	25	25	0	0
	Carl Pickens, Cincinnati, AFC	17	0	17	0
1994	Emmitt Smith, Dallas, NFC	22	21	1	0
	*Marshall Faulk, Indianapolis, AFC	12	11	1	0
	Natrone Means, San Diego, AFC	12	12	0	0
1993	Jerry Rice, San Francisco, NFC	16	1	15	0
	Marcus Allen, Kansas City, AFC	15	12	3	0
1992	Emmitt Smith, Dallas, NFC	19	18	1	0
	Thurman Thomas, Buffalo, AFC	12	9	3	0
1991	Barry Sanders, Detroit, NFC	17	16	1	0
	Mark Clayton, Miami, AFC	12	0	12	0
	Thurman Thomas, Buffalo, AFC	12	7	5	0
1990	Barry Sanders, Detroit, NFC	16	13	3	0
	Derrick Fenner, Seattle, AFC	15	14	1	0
1989	Dalton Hilliard, New Orleans, NFC	18	13	5	0
	Christian Okoye, Kansas City, AFC	12	12	0	0
	Thurman Thomas, Buffalo, AFC	12	6	6	0
1988	Greg Bell, L.A. Rams, NFC	18	16	2	0
	Eric Dickerson, Indianapolis, AFC	15	14	1	0
	*Ickey Woods, Cincinnati, AFC	15	15	0	0
1987	Jerry Rice, San Francisco, NFC	23	1	22	0
	Johnny Hector, N.Y. Jets, AFC	11	11	0	0

Year	Player, Team	TD	Rush	Pass	Ret.
1986	George Rogers, Washington, NFC	18	18	0	0
	Sammy Winder, Denver, AFC	14	9	5	0
1985	Joe Morris, N.Y. Giants, NFC	21	21	0	0
	Louis Lipps, Pittsburgh, AFC	15	1	12	2
1984	Marcus Allen, L.A. Raiders, AFC	18	13	5	0
	Mark Clayton, Miami, AFC	18	0	18	0
	Eric Dickerson, L.A. Rams, NFC	14	14	0	0
	John Riggins, Washington, NFC	14	14	0	0
1983	John Riggins, Washington, NFC	24	24	0	0
	Pete Johnson, Cincinnati, AFC	14	14	0	0
	*Curt Warner, Seattle, AFC	14	13	1	0
1982	*Marcus Allen, L.A. Raiders, AFC	14	11	3	0
	Wendell Tyler, L.A. Rams, NFC	13	9	4	0
1981	Chuck Muncie, San Diego, AFC	19	19	0	0
	Wendell Tyler, Los Angeles, NFC	17	12	5	0
1980	*Billy Sims, Detroit, NFC	16	13	3	0
	Earl Campbell, Houston, AFC	13	13	0	0
	*Curtis Dickey, Baltimore, AFC	13	11	2	0
	John Jefferson, San Diego, AFC	13	0	13	0
1979	Earl Campbell, Houston, AFC	19	19	0	0
	Walter Payton, Chicago, NFC	16	14	2	0
1978	David Sims, Seattle, AFC	15	14	1	0
	Terdell Middleton, Green Bay, NFC	12	11	1	0
1977	Walter Payton, Chicago, NFC	16	14	2	0
	Nat Moore, Miami, AFC	13	1	12	0
1976	Chuck Foreman, Minnesota, NFC	14	13	1	0
	Franco Harris, Pittsburgh, AFC	14	14	0	0
1975	O.J. Simpson, Buffalo, AFC	23	16	7	0
	Chuck Foreman, Minnesota, NFC	22	13	9	0
1974	Chuck Foreman, Minnesota, NFC	15	9	6	0
	Cliff Branch, Oakland, AFC	13	0	13	0
1973	Larry Brown, Washington, NFC	14	8	6	0
	Floyd Little, Denver, AFC	13	12	1	0
1972	Emerson Boozer, N.Y. Jets, AFC	14	11	3	0
	Ron Johnson, N.Y. Giants, NFC	14	9	5	0
1971	Duane Thomas, Dallas, NFC	13	11	2	0
	Leroy Kelly, Cleveland, AFC	12	10	2	0
1970	Dick Gordon, Chicago, NFC	13	0	13	0
	MacArthur Lane, St. Louis, NFC	13	11	2	0
	Gary Garrison, San Diego, AFC	12	0	12	0
1969	Warren Wells, Oakland, AFL	14	0	14	0
	Tom Matte, Baltimore, NFL	13	11	2	0
	Lance Rentzel, Dallas, NFL	13	0	12	1
1968	Leroy Kelly, Cleveland, NFL	20	16	4	0
	Warren Wells, Oakland, AFL	12	1	11	0
1967	Homer Jones, N.Y. Giants, NFL	14	1	13	0
	Emerson Boozer, N.Y. Jets, AFL	13	10	3	0
1966	Leroy Kelly, Cleveland, NFL	16	15	1	0
	Dan Reeves, Dallas, NFL	16	8	8	0
	Lance Alworth, San Diego, AFL	13	0	13	0
1965	*Gale Sayers, Chicago, NFL	22	14	6	2
	Lance Alworth, San Diego, AFL	14	0	14	0
	Don Maynard, N.Y. Jets, AFL	14	0	14	0
1964	Lenny Moore, Baltimore, NFL	20	16	3	1
	Lance Alworth, San Diego, AFL	15	2	13	0
1963	Art Powell, Oakland, AFL	16	0	16	0
	Jim Brown, Cleveland, NFL	15	12	3	0
1962	Abner Haynes, Dallas, AFL	19	13	6	0
	Jim Taylor, Green Bay, NFL	19	19	0	0
1961	Bill Groman, Houston, AFL	18	1	17	0
	Jim Taylor, Green Bay, NFL	16	15	1	0
1960	Paul Hornung, Green Bay, NFL	15	13	2	0
	Sonny Randle, St. Louis, NFL	15	0	15	0
	Art Powell, N.Y. Titans, AFL	14	0	14	0
1959	Raymond Berry, Baltimore	14	0	14	0
	Jim Brown, Cleveland	14	14	0	0
1958	Jim Brown, Cleveland	18	17	1	0
1957	Lenny Moore, Baltimore	11	3	7	1
1956	Rick Casares, Chi. Bears	14	12	2	0

Year	Player, Team	TD	Rush	Pass	Ret.
1955	*Alan Ameche, Baltimore	9	9	0	0
	Harlon Hill, Chi. Bears	9	0	9	0
1954	*Harlon Hill, Chi. Bears	12	0	12	0
1953	Joseph Perry, San Francisco	13	10	3	0
1952	Cloyce Box, Detroit	15	0	15	0
1951	Elroy (Crazylegs) Hirsch, Los Angeles	17	0	17	0
1950	Bob Shaw, Chi. Cardinals	12	0	12	0
1949	Gene Roberts, N.Y. Giants	17	9	8	0
1948	Mal Kutner, Chi. Cardinals	15	1	14	0
1947	Steve Van Buren, Philadelphia	14	13	0	1
1946	Ted Fritsch, Green Bay	10	9	1	0
1945	Steve Van Buren, Philadelphia	18	15	2	1
1944	Don Hutson, Green Bay	9	0	9	0
	Bill Paschal, N.Y. Giants	9	9	0	0
1943	Don Hutson, Green Bay	12	0	11	1
	*Bill Paschal, N.Y. Giants	12	10	2	0
1942	Don Hutson, Green Bay	17	0	17	0
1941	Don Hutson, Green Bay	12	2	10	0
	George McAfee, Chi. Bears	12	6	3	3
1940	John Drake, Cleveland	9	9	0	0
	Richard Todd, Washington	9	4	4	1
1939	Andrew Farkas, Washington	11	5	5	1
1938	Don Hutson, Green Bay	9	0	9	0
1937	Cliff Battles, Washington	7	5	1	1
	Clarke Hinkle, Green Bay	7	5	2	0
	Don Hutson, Green Bay	7	0	7	0
1936	Don Hutson, Green Bay	9	0	8	1
1935	*Don Hutson, Green Bay	7	0	6	1
1934	*Beattie Feathers, Chi. Bears	9	8	1	0
1933	*Charlie (Buckets) Goldenberg, Green Bay	7	4	1	2
	John (Shipwreck) Kelly, Brooklyn	7	2	3	2
	*Elvin (Kink) Richards, N.Y. Giants	7	4	3	0
1932	Earl (Dutch) Clark, Portsmouth	6	3	3	0
	Red Grange, Chi. Bears	6	3	3	0

*First season of professional football.

ANNUAL LEADERS—MOST FIELD GOALS MADE

Year	Player, Team	Att.	Made	Pct.
2013	Stephen Gostkowski, New England, AFC	41	38	92.7
	Justin Tucker, Baltimore, AFC	41	38	92.7
	Steven Hauschka, Seattle, NFC	35	33	94.3
	Mason Crosby, Green Bay, NFC	37	33	89.2
2012	*Blair Walsh, Minnesota, NFC	38	35	92.1
	Sebastian Janikowski, Oakland, AFC	34	31	91.2
	Shayne Graham, Houston, AFC	38	31	81.6
2011	David Akers, San Francisco, NFC	52	44	84.6
	Mike Nugent, Cincinnati, AFC	38	33	86.8
2010	Josh Brown, St. Louis, NFC	39	33	84.6
	Sebastian Janikowski, Oakland, AFC	41	33	80.5
2009	Nate Kaeding, San Diego, AFC	35	32	91.4
	David Akers, Philadelphia, NFC	37	32	86.5
2008	Stephen Gostkowski, New England, AFC	40	36	90.0
	John Carney, N.Y. Giants, NFC	38	35	92.1
2007	Rob Bironas, Tennessee, AFC	39	35	89.7
	*Mason Crosby, Green Bay, NFC	39	31	79.5
	Robbie Gould, Chicago, NFC	36	31	86.1
2006	Robbie Gould, Chicago, NFC	36	32	88.9
	Jeff Wilkins, St. Louis, NFC	37	32	86.5
	Matt Stover, Baltimore, AFC	30	28	93.3
2005	Neil Rackers, Arizona, NFC	42	40	95.2
	Matt Stover, Baltimore, AFC	34	30	88.2
2004	Adam Vinatieri, New England, AFC	33	31	93.9
	David Akers, Philadelphia, NFC	32	27	84.4
2003	Jeff Wilkins, St. Louis, NFC	42	39	92.9
	Mike Vanderjagt, Indianapolis, AFC	37	37	100.0
2002	Jay Feely, Atlanta, NFC	40	32	80.0
	Martín Gramatica, Tampa Bay, NFC	39	32	82.1
	Adam Vinatieri, New England, AFC	30	27	90.0
2001	Jason Elam, Denver, AFC	36	31	86.1
	*Jay Feely, Atlanta, NFC	37	29	78.4

Year	Player, Team	Att.	Made	Pct.
2000	Matt Stover, Baltimore, AFC	39	35	89.7
	Ryan Longwell, Green Bay, NFC	38	33	86.8
1999	Olindo Mare, Miami, AFC	46	39	84.8
	*Martin Gramatica, Tampa Bay, NFC	32	27	84.4
1998	Al Del Greco, Tennessee, AFC	39	36	92.3
	Gary Anderson, Minnesota, NFC	35	35	100.0
1997	Richie Cunningham, Dallas, NFC	37	34	91.9
	Cary Blanchard, Indianapolis, AFC	41	32	78.1
1996	John Kasay, Carolina, NFC	45	37	82.2
	Cary Blanchard, Indianapolis, AFC	40	36	90.0
1995	Norm Johnson, Pittsburgh, AFC	41	34	82.9
	Morten Andersen, Atlanta, NFC	37	31	83.8
1994	John Carney, San Diego, AFC	38	34	89.5
	Fuad Reveiz, Minnesota, NFC	39	34	87.2
1993	Jeff Jaeger, L.A. Raiders, AFC	44	35	79.5
	Jason Hanson, Detroit, NFC	43	34	79.1
1992	Pete Stoyanovich, Miami, AFC	37	30	81.1
	Chip Lohmiller, Washington, NFC	40	30	75.0
1991	Pete Stoyanovich, Miami, AFC	37	31	83.8
	Chip Lohmiller, Washington, NFC	43	31	72.1
1990	Nick Lowery, Kansas City, AFC	37	34	91.9
	Chip Lohmiller, Washington, NFC	40	30	75.0
1989	Rich Karlis, Minnesota, NFC	39	31	79.5
	*David Treadwell, Denver, AFC	33	27	81.8
1988	Scott Norwood, Buffalo, AFC	37	32	86.5
	Mike Cofer, San Francisco, NFC	38	27	71.1
1987	Morten Andersen, New Orleans, NFC	36	28	77.8
	Dean Biasucci, Indianapolis, AFC	27	24	88.9
	Jim Breech, Cincinnati, AFC	30	24	80.0
1986	Tony Franklin, New England, AFC	41	32	78.0
	Kevin Butler, Chicago, NFC	41	28	68.3
1985	Gary Anderson, Pittsburgh, AFC	42	33	78.6
	Morten Andersen, New Orleans, NFC	35	31	88.6
	*Kevin Butler, Chicago, NFC	37	31	83.8
1984	*Paul McFadden, Philadelphia, NFC	37	30	81.1
	Gary Anderson, Pittsburgh, AFC	32	24	75.0
	Matt Bahr, Cleveland, AFC	32	24	75.0
1983	*Ali-Haji-Sheikh, N.Y. Giants, NFC	42	35	83.3
	*Raul Allegre, Baltimore, AFC	35	30	85.7
1982	Mark Moseley, Washington, NFC	21	20	95.2
	Nick Lowery, Kansas City, AFC	24	19	79.2
1981	Rafael Septien, Dallas, NFC	35	27	77.1
	Nick Lowery, Kansas City, AFC	36	26	72.2
1980	*Ed Murray, Detroit, NFC	42	27	64.3
	John Smith, New England, AFC	34	26	76.5
	Fred Steinfort, Denver, AFC	34	26	76.5
1979	Mark Moseley, Washington, NFC	33	25	75.8
	John Smith, New England, AFC	33	23	69.7
1978	*Frank Corral, Los Angeles, NFC	43	29	67.4
	Pat Leahy, N.Y. Jets, AFC	30	22	73.3
1977	Mark Moseley, Washington, NFC	37	21	56.8
	Errol Mann, Oakland, AFC	28	20	71.4
1976	Mark Moseley, Washington, NFC	34	22	64.7
	Jan Stenerud, Kansas City, AFC	38	21	55.3
1975	Jan Stenerud, Kansas City, AFC	32	22	68.8
	Toni Fritsch, Dallas, NFC	35	22	62.9
1974	Chester Marcol, Green Bay, NFC	39	25	64.1
	Roy Gerela, Pittsburgh, AFC	29	20	69.0
1973	David Ray, Los Angeles, NFC	47	30	63.8
	Roy Gerela, Pittsburgh, AFC	43	29	67.4
1972	*Chester Marcol, Green Bay, NFC	48	33	68.8
	Roy Gerela, Pittsburgh, AFC	41	28	68.3
1971	Curt Knight, Washington, NFC	49	29	59.2
	Garo Yepremian, Miami, AFC	40	28	70.0
1970	Jan Stenerud, Kansas City, AFC	42	30	71.4
	Fred Cox, Minnesota, NFC	46	30	65.2
1969	Jim Turner, N.Y. Jets, AFL	47	32	68.1
	Fred Cox, Minnesota, NFL	37	26	70.3
1968	Jim Turner, N.Y. Jets, AFL	46	34	73.9
	Mac Percival, Chicago, NFL	36	25	69.4

Year	Player, Team	Att.	Made	Pct.
1967	Jim Bakken, St. Louis, NFL	39	27	69.2
	Jan Stenerud, Kansas City, AFL	36	21	58.3
1966	Bruce Gossett, Los Angeles, NFL	49	28	57.1
	Mike Mercer, Oakland-Kansas City, AFL	30	21	70.0
1965	Pete Gogolak, Buffalo, AFL	46	28	60.9
	Fred Cox, Minnesota, NFL	35	23	65.7
1964	Jim Bakken, St. Louis, NFL	38	25	65.8
	Gino Cappelletti, Boston, AFL	39	25	64.1
1963	Jim Martin, Baltimore, NFL	39	24	61.5
	Gino Cappelletti, Boston, AFL	38	22	57.9
1962	Gene Mingo, Denver, AFL	39	27	69.2
	Lou Michaels, Pittsburgh, NFL	42	26	61.9
1961	Steve Myhra, Baltimore, NFL	39	21	53.8
	Gino Cappelletti, Boston, AFL	32	17	53.1
1960	Tommy Davis, San Francisco, NFL	32	19	59.4
	*Gene Mingo, Denver, AFL	28	18	64.3
1959	Pat Summerall, N.Y. Giants	29	20	69.0
1958	Paige Cothren, Los Angeles	25	14	56.0
	*Tom Miner, Pittsburgh	28	14	50.0
1957	Lou Groza, Cleveland	22	15	68.2
1956	Sam Baker, Washington	25	17	68.0
1955	Fred Cone, Green Bay	24	16	66.7
1954	Lou Groza, Cleveland	24	16	66.7
1953	Lou Groza, Cleveland	26	23	88.5
1952	Lou Groza, Cleveland	33	19	57.6
1951	Bob Waterfield, Los Angeles	23	13	56.5
1950	Lou Groza, Cleveland	19	13	68.4
1949	Cliff Patton, Philadelphia	18	9	50.0
	Bob Waterfield, Los Angeles	16	9	56.3
1948	Cliff Patton, Philadelphia	12	8	66.7
1947	Ward Cuff, Green Bay	16	7	43.8
	Pat Harder, Chi. Cardinals	10	7	70.0
	Bob Waterfield, Los Angeles	16	7	43.8
1946	Ted Fritsch, Green Bay	17	9	52.9
1945	Joe Aguirre, Washington	13	7	53.8
1944	Ken Strong, N.Y. Giants	12	6	50.0
1943	Ward Cuff, N.Y. Giants	9	3	33.3
	Don Hutson, Green Bay	5	3	60.0
1942	Bill Daddio, Chi. Cardinals	10	5	50.0
1941	Clarke Hinkle, Green Bay	14	6	42.9
1940	Clarke Hinkle, Green Bay	14	9	64.3
1939	Ward Cuff, N.Y. Giants	16	7	43.8
1938	Ward Cuff, N.Y. Giants	9	5	55.6
	Ralph Kercheval, Brooklyn	13	5	38.5
1937	Jack Manders, Chi. Bears		8	
1936	Jack Manders, Chi. Bears		7	
	Armand Niccolai, Pittsburgh		7	
1935	Armand Niccolai, Pittsburgh		6	
	Bill Smith, Chi. Cardinals		6	
1934	Jack Manders, Chi. Bears		10	
1933	*Jack Manders, Chi. Bears		6	
	Glenn Presnell, Portsmouth		6	
1932	Earl (Dutch) Clark, Portsmouth		3	

*First season of professional football.

ANNUAL RUSHING LEADERS

Year	Player, Team	Att.	Yards	Avg.	TD
2013	LeSean McCoy, Philadelphia, NFC	314	1,607	5.1	9
	Jamaal Charles, Kansas City, AFC	259	1,287	5.0	12
2012	Adrian Peterson, Minnesota, NFC	348	2,097	6.0	12
	Jamaal Charles, Kansas City, AFC	285	1,509	5.3	5
2011	Maurice Jones-Drew, Jacksonville, AFC	343	1,606	4.7	8
	Michael Turner, Atlanta, NFC	301	1,340	4.5	11
2010	Arian Foster, Houston, AFC	327	1,616	4.9	16
	Michael Turner, Atlanta, NFC	334	1,371	4.1	12
2009	Chris Johnson, Tennessee, AFC	358	2,006	5.6	14
	Steven Jackson, St. Louis, NFC	324	1,416	4.4	4
2008	Adrian Peterson, Minnesota, NFC	363	1,760	4.9	10
	Thomas Jones, N.Y. Jets, AFC	290	1,312	4.5	13

Year	Player, Team	Att.	Yards	Avg.	TD
2007	LaDainian Tomlinson, San Diego, AFC	315	1,474	4.7	15
	*Adrian Peterson, Minnesota, NFC	238	1,341	5.6	12
2006	LaDainian Tomlinson, San Diego, AFC	348	1,815	5.2	28
	Frank Gore, San Francisco, NFC	312	1,695	5.4	8
2005	Shaun Alexander, Seattle, NFC	370	1,880	5.1	27
	Larry Johnson, Kansas City, AFC	336	1,750	5.2	20
2004	Curtis Martin, N.Y. Jets, AFC	371	1,697	4.6	12
	Shaun Alexander, Seattle, NFC	353	1,696	4.8	16
2003	Jamal Lewis, Baltimore, AFC	387	2,066	5.3	14
	Ahman Green, Green Bay, NFC	355	1,883	5.3	15
2002	Ricky Williams, Miami, AFC	383	1,853	4.8	16
	Deuce McAllister, New Orleans, NFC	325	1,388	4.3	13
2001	Priest Holmes, Kansas City, AFC	327	1,555	4.8	8
	Stephen Davis, Washington, NFC	356	1,432	4.0	5
2000	Edgerrin James, Indianapolis, AFC	387	1,709	4.4	13
	Robert Smith, Minnesota, NFC	295	1,521	5.2	7
1999	*Edgerrin James, Indianapolis, AFC	369	1,553	4.2	13
	Stephen Davis, Washington, NFC	290	1,405	4.8	17
1998	Terrell Davis, Denver, AFC	392	2,008	5.1	21
	Jamal Anderson, Atlanta, NFC	410	1,846	4.5	14
1997	Barry Sanders, Detroit, NFC	335	2,053	6.1	11
	Terrell Davis, Denver, AFC	369	1,750	4.7	15
1996	Barry Sanders, Detroit, NFC	307	1,553	5.1	11
	Terrell Davis, Denver, AFC	345	1,538	4.5	13
1995	Emmitt Smith, Dallas, NFC	377	1,773	4.7	25
	*Curtis Martin, New England, AFC	368	1,487	4.0	14
1994	Barry Sanders, Detroit, NFC	331	1,883	5.7	7
	Chris Warren, Seattle, AFC	333	1,545	4.6	9
1993	Emmitt Smith, Dallas, NFC	283	1,486	5.3	9
	Thurman Thomas, Buffalo, AFC	355	1,315	3.7	6
1992	Emmitt Smith, Dallas, NFC	373	1,713	4.6	18
	Barry Foster, Pittsburgh, AFC	390	1,690	4.3	11
1991	Emmitt Smith, Dallas, NFC	365	1,563	4.3	12
	Thurman Thomas, Buffalo, AFC	288	1,407	4.9	7
1990	Barry Sanders, Detroit, NFC	255	1,304	5.1	13
	Thurman Thomas, Buffalo, AFC	271	1,297	4.8	11
1989	Christian Okoye, Kansas City, AFC	370	1,480	4.0	12
	*Barry Sanders, Detroit, NFC	280	1,470	5.3	14
1988	Eric Dickerson, Indianapolis, AFC	388	1,659	4.3	14
	Herschel Walker, Dallas, NFC	361	1,514	4.2	5
1987	Charles White, L.A. Rams, NFC	324	1,374	4.2	11
	Eric Dickerson, Indianapolis, AFC	223	1,011	4.5	5
1986	Eric Dickerson, L.A. Rams, NFC	404	1,821	4.5	11
	Curt Warner, Seattle, AFC	319	1,481	4.6	13
1985	Marcus Allen, L.A. Raiders, AFC	380	1,759	4.6	11
	Gerald Riggs, Atlanta, NFC	397	1,719	4.3	10
1984	Eric Dickerson, L.A. Rams, NFC	379	2,105	5.6	14
	Earnest Jackson, San Diego, AFC	296	1,179	4.0	8
1983	*Eric Dickerson, L.A. Rams, NFC	390	1,808	4.6	18
	*Curt Warner, Seattle, AFC	335	1,449	4.3	13
1982	Freeman McNeil, N.Y. Jets, AFC	151	786	5.2	6
	Tony Dorsett, Dallas, NFC	177	745	4.2	5
1981	*George Rogers, New Orleans, NFC	378	1,674	4.4	13
	Earl Campbell, Houston, AFC	361	1,376	3.8	10
1980	Earl Campbell, Houston, AFC	373	1,934	5.2	13
	Walter Payton, Chicago, NFC	317	1,460	4.6	6
1979	Earl Campbell, Houston, AFC	368	1,697	4.6	19
	Walter Payton, Chicago, NFC	369	1,610	4.4	14
1978	*Earl Campbell, Houston, AFC	302	1,450	4.8	13
	Walter Payton, Chicago, NFC	333	1,395	4.2	11
1977	Walter Payton, Chicago, NFC	339	1,852	5.5	14
	Mark van Eeghen, Oakland, AFC	324	1,273	3.9	7
1976	O.J. Simpson, Buffalo, AFC	290	1,503	5.2	8
	Walter Payton, Chicago, NFC	311	1,390	4.5	13
1975	O.J. Simpson, Buffalo, AFC	329	1,817	5.5	16
	Jim Otis, St. Louis, NFC	269	1,076	4.0	5
1974	Otis Armstrong, Denver, AFC	263	1,407	5.3	9
	Lawrence McCutcheon, Los Angeles, NFC	236	1,109	4.7	3
1973	O.J. Simpson, Buffalo, AFC	332	2,003	6.0	12
	John Brockington, Green Bay, NFC	265	1,144	4.3	3

Year	Player, Team	Att.	Yards	Avg.	TD
1972	O.J. Simpson, Buffalo, AFC	292	1,251	4.3	6
	Larry Brown, Washington, NFC	285	1,216	4.3	8
1971	Floyd Little, Denver, AFC	284	1,133	4.0	6
	*John Brockington, Green Bay, NFC	216	1,105	5.1	4
1970	Larry Brown, Washington, NFC	237	1,125	4.7	5
	Floyd Little, Denver, AFC	209	901	4.3	3
1969	Gale Sayers, Chicago, NFL	236	1,032	4.4	8
	Dickie Post, San Diego, AFL	182	873	4.8	6
1968	Leroy Kelly, Cleveland, NFL	248	1,239	5.0	16
	*Paul Robinson, Cincinnati, AFL	238	1,023	4.3	8
1967	Jim Nance, Boston, AFL	269	1,216	4.5	7
	Leroy Kelly, Cleveland, NFL	235	1,205	5.1	11
1966	Jim Nance, Boston, AFL	299	1,458	4.9	11
	Gale Sayers, Chicago, NFL	229	1,231	5.4	8
1965	Jim Brown, Cleveland, NFL	289	1,544	5.3	17
	Paul Lowe, San Diego, AFL	222	1,121	5.0	7
1964	Jim Brown, Cleveland, NFL	280	1,446	5.2	7
	Cookie Gilchrist, Buffalo, AFL	230	981	4.3	6
1963	Jim Brown, Cleveland, NFL	291	1,863	6.4	12
	Clem Daniels, Oakland, AFL	215	1,099	5.1	3
1962	Jim Taylor, Green Bay, NFL	272	1,474	5.4	19
	Cookie Gilchrist, Buffalo, AFL	214	1,096	5.1	13
1961	Jim Brown, Cleveland, NFL	305	1,408	4.6	8
	Billy Cannon, Houston, AFL	200	948	4.7	6
1960	Jim Brown, Cleveland, NFL	215	1,257	5.8	9
	*Abner Haynes, Dall. Texans, AFL	156	875	5.6	9
1959	Jim Brown, Cleveland	290	1,329	4.6	14
1958	Jim Brown, Cleveland	257	1,527	5.9	17
1957	*Jim Brown, Cleveland	202	942	4.7	9
1956	Rick Casares, Chi. Bears	234	1,126	4.8	12
1955	*Alan Ameche, Baltimore	213	961	4.5	9
1954	Joe Perry, San Francisco	173	1,049	6.1	8
1953	Joe Perry, San Francisco	192	1,018	5.3	10
1952	Dan Towler, Los Angeles	156	894	5.7	10
1951	Eddie Price, N.Y. Giants	271	971	3.6	7
1950	Marion Motley, Cleveland	140	810	5.8	3
1949	Steve Van Buren, Philadelphia	263	1,146	4.4	11
1948	Steve Van Buren, Philadelphia	201	945	4.7	10
1947	Steve Van Buren, Philadelphia	217	1,008	4.6	13
1946	Bill Dudley, Pittsburgh	146	604	4.1	3
1945	Steve Van Buren, Philadelphia	143	832	5.8	15
1944	Bill Paschal, N.Y. Giants	196	737	3.8	9
1943	*Bill Paschal, N.Y. Giants	147	572	3.9	10
1942	*Bill Dudley, Pittsburgh	162	696	4.3	5
1941	Clarence (Pug) Manders, Brooklyn	111	486	4.4	5
1940	Byron (Whizzer) White, Detroit	146	514	3.5	5
1939	*Bill Osmanski, Chicago	121	699	5.8	7
1938	*Byron (Whizzer) White, Pittsburgh	152	567	3.7	4
1937	Cliff Battles, Washington	216	874	4.0	5
1936	*Alphonse (Tuffy) Leemans, N.Y. Giants	206	830	4.0	2
1935	Doug Russell, Chi. Cardinals	140	499	3.6	0
1934	*Beattie Feathers, Chi. Bears	119	1,004	8.4	8
1933	Jim Musick, Boston	173	809	4.7	5
1932	*Cliff Battles, Boston	148	576	3.9	3

*First season of professional football.

ANNUAL PASSING LEADERS

(Current rating system implemented in 1973)

Year	Player, Team	Att.	Comp.	Yards	TD	Int.	Rating
2013	Nick Foles, Philadelphia, NFC	317	203	2,891	27	2	119.2
	Peyton Manning, Denver, AFC	659	450	5,477	55	10	115.1
2012	Aaron Rodgers, Green Bay, NFC	552	371	4,295	39	8	108.0
	Peyton Manning, Denver, AFC	583	400	4,659	37	11	105.8
2011	Aaron Rodgers, Green Bay, NFC	502	343	4,643	45	6	122.5
	Tom Brady, New England, AFC	611	401	5,235	39	12	105.6
2010	Tom Brady, New England, AFC	492	324	3,900	36	4	111.0
	Aaron Rodgers, Green Bay, NFC	475	312	3,922	28	11	101.2
2009	Drew Brees, New Orleans, NFC	514	363	4,388	34	11	109.6
	Philip Rivers, San Diego, AFC	486	317	4,254	28	9	104.4

Year	Player, Team	Att.	Comp.	Yards	TD	Int.	Rating
2008	Philip Rivers, San Diego, AFC	478	312	4,009	34	11	105.5
	Kurt Warner, Arizona, NFC	598	401	4,583	30	14	96.9
2007	Tom Brady, New England, AFC	578	398	4,806	50	8	117.2
	Tony Romo, Dallas, NFC	520	335	4,211	36	19	97.4
2006	Peyton Manning, Indianapolis, AFC	557	362	4,397	31	9	101.0
	Drew Brees, New Orleans, NFC	554	356	4,418	26	11	96.2
2005	Peyton Manning, Indianapolis, AFC	453	305	3,747	28	10	104.1
	Matt Hasselbeck, Seattle, NFC	449	294	3,459	24	9	98.2
2004	Peyton Manning, Indianapolis, AFC	497	336	4,557	49	10	121.1
	Daunte Culpepper, Minnesota, NFC	548	379	4,717	39	11	110.9
2003	Steve McNair, Tennessee, AFC	400	250	3,215	24	7	100.4
	Daunte Culpepper, Minnesota, NFC	454	295	3,479	25	11	96.4
2002	Chad Pennington, N.Y. Jets, AFC	399	275	3,120	22	6	104.2
	Brad Johnson, Tampa Bay, NFC	451	281	3,049	22	6	92.9
2001	Kurt Warner, St. Louis, NFC	546	375	4,830	36	22	101.4
	Rich Gannon, Oakland, AFC	549	361	3,828	27	9	95.5
2000	Brian Griese, Denver, AFC	336	216	2,688	19	4	102.9
	Trent Green, St. Louis, NFC	240	145	2,063	16	5	101.8
1999	Kurt Warner, St. Louis, NFC	499	325	4,353	41	13	109.2
	Peyton Manning, Indianapolis, AFC	533	331	4,135	26	15	90.7
1998	Randall Cunningham, Minnesota, NFC	425	259	3,704	34	10	106.0
	Vinny Testaverde, N.Y. Jets, AFC	421	259	3,256	29	7	101.6
1997	Steve Young, San Francisco, NFC	356	241	3,029	19	6	104.7
	Mark Brunell, Jacksonville, AFC	435	264	3,281	18	7	91.2
1996	Steve Young, San Francisco NFC	316	214	2,410	14	6	97.2
	John Elway, Denver, AFC	466	287	3,328	26	14	89.2
1995	Jim Harbaugh, Indianapolis, AFC	314	200	2,575	17	5	100.7
	Brett Favre, Green Bay, NFC	570	359	4,413	38	13	99.5
1994	Steve Young, San Francisco, NFC	461	324	3,969	35	10	112.8
	Dan Marino, Miami, AFC	615	385	4,453	30	17	89.2
1993	Steve Young, San Francisco, NFC	462	314	4,023	29	16	101.5
	John Elway, Denver, AFC	551	348	4,030	25	10	92.8
1992	Steve Young, San Francisco, NFC	402	268	3,465	25	7	107.0
	Warren Moon, Houston, AFC	346	224	2,521	18	12	89.3
1991	Steve Young, San Francisco, NFC	279	180	2,517	17	8	101.8
	Jim Kelly, Buffalo, AFC	474	304	3,844	33	17	97.6
1990	Jim Kelly, Buffalo, AFC	346	219	2,829	24	9	101.2
	Phil Simms, N.Y. Giants, NFC	311	184	2,284	15	4	92.7
1989	Joe Montana, San Francisco, NFC	386	271	3,521	26	8	112.4
	Boomer Esiason, Cincinnati, AFC	455	258	3,525	28	11	92.1
1988	Boomer Esiason, Cincinnati, AFC	388	223	3,572	28	14	97.4
	Wade Wilson, Minnesota, NFC	332	204	2,746	15	9	91.5
1987	Joe Montana, San Francisco, NFC	398	266	3,054	31	13	102.1
	Bernie Kosar, Cleveland, AFC	389	241	3,033	22	9	95.4
1986	Tommy Kramer, Minnesota, NFC	372	208	3,000	24	10	92.6
	Dan Marino, Miami, AFC	623	378	4,746	44	23	92.5
1985	Ken O'Brien, N.Y. Jets, AFC	488	297	3,888	25	8	96.2
	Joe Montana, San Francisco, NFC	494	303	3,653	27	13	91.3
1984	Dan Marino, Miami, AFC	564	362	5,084	48	17	108.9
	Joe Montana, San Francisco, NFC	432	279	3,630	28	10	102.9
1983	Steve Bartkowski, Atlanta, NFC	432	274	3,167	22	5	97.6
	*Dan Marino, Miami, AFC	296	173	2,210	20	6	96.0
1982	Ken Anderson, Cincinnati, AFC	309	218	2,495	12	9	95.3
	Joe Theismann, Washington, NFC	252	161	2,033	13	9	91.3
1981	Ken Anderson, Cincinnati, AFC	479	300	3,754	29	10	98.4
	Joe Montana, San Francisco, NFC	488	311	3,565	19	12	88.4
1980	Brian Sipe, Cleveland, AFC	554	337	4,132	30	14	91.4
	Ron Jaworski, Philadelphia, NFC	451	257	3,529	27	12	91.0
1979	Roger Staubach, Dallas, NFC	461	267	3,586	27	11	92.3
	Dan Fouts, San Diego, AFC	530	332	4,082	24	24	82.6
1978	Roger Staubach, Dallas, NFC	413	231	3,190	25	16	84.9
	Terry Bradshaw, Pittsburgh, AFC	368	207	2,915	28	20	84.7
1977	Bob Griese, Miami, AFC	307	180	2,252	22	13	87.8
	Roger Staubach, Dallas, NFC	361	210	2,620	18	9	87.0
1976	Ken Stabler, Oakland, AFC	291	194	2,737	27	17	103.4
	James Harris, Los Angeles, NFC	158	91	1,460	8	6	89.6
1975	Ken Anderson, Cincinnati, AFC	377	228	3,169	21	11	93.9
	Fran Tarkenton, Minnesota, NFC	425	273	2,994	25	13	91.8
1974	Ken Anderson, Cincinnati, AFC	328	213	2,667	18	10	95.7
	Sonny Jurgensen, Washington, NFC	167	107	1,185	11	5	94.5

Year	Player, Team	Att.	Comp.	Yards	TD	Int.	Rating
1973	Roger Staubach, Dallas, NFC	286	179	2,428	23	15	94.6
	Ken Stabler, Oakland, AFC	260	163	1,997	14	10	88.3
1972	Norm Snead, N.Y. Giants, NFC	325	196	2,307	17	12	
	Earl Morrall, Miami, AFC	150	83	1,360	11	7	
1971	Roger Staubach, Dallas, NFC	211	126	1,882	15	4	
	Bob Griese, Miami, AFC	263	145	2,089	19	9	
1970	John Brodie, San Francisco, NFC	378	223	2,941	24	10	
	Daryle Lamonica, Oakland, AFC	356	179	2,516	22	15	
1969	Sonny Jurgensen, Washington, NFL	442	274	3,102	22	15	
	*Greg Cook, Cincinnati, AFL	197	106	1,854	15	11	
1968	Len Dawson, Kansas City, AFL	224	131	2,109	17	9	
	Earl Morrall, Baltimore, NFL	317	182	2,909	26	17	
1967	Sonny Jurgensen, Washington, NFL	508	288	3,747	31	16	
	Daryle Lamonica, Oakland, AFL	425	220	3,228	30	20	
1966	Bart Starr, Green Bay, NFL	251	156	2,257	14	3	
	Len Dawson, Kansas City, AFL	284	159	2,527	26	10	
1965	Rudy Bukich, Chicago, NFL	312	176	2,641	20	9	
	John Hadl, San Diego, AFL	348	174	2,798	20	21	
1964	Len Dawson, Kansas City, AFL	354	199	2,879	30	18	
	Bart Starr, Green Bay, NFL	272	163	2,144	15	4	
1963	Y.A. Tittle, N.Y. Giants, NFL	367	221	3,145	36	14	
	Tobin Rote, San Diego, AFL	286	170	2,510	20	17	
1962	Len Dawson, Dallas Texans, AFL	310	189	2,759	29	17	
	Bart Starr, Green Bay, NFL	285	178	2,438	12	9	
1961	George Blanda, Houston, AFL	362	187	3,330	36	22	
	Milt Plum, Cleveland, NFL	302	177	2,416	18	10	
1960	Milt Plum, Cleveland, NFL	250	151	2,297	21	5	
	Jack Kemp, L.A. Chargers, AFL	406	211	3,018	20	25	
1959	Charlie Conerly, N.Y. Giants	194	113	1,706	14	4	
1958	Eddie LeBaron, Washington	145	79	1,365	11	10	
1957	Tommy O'Connell, Cleveland	110	63	1,229	9	8	
1956	Ed Brown, Chicago Bears	168	96	1,667	11	12	
1955	Otto Graham, Cleveland	185	98	1,721	15	8	
1954	Norm Van Brocklin, Los Angeles	260	139	2,637	13	21	
1953	Otto Graham, Cleveland	258	167	2,722	11	9	
1952	Norm Van Brocklin, Los Angeles	205	113	1,736	14	17	
1951	Bob Waterfield, Los Angeles	176	88	1,566	13	10	
1950	Norm Van Brocklin, Los Angeles	233	127	2,061	18	14	
1949	Sammy Baugh, Washington	255	145	1,903	18	14	
1948	Tommy Thompson, Philadelphia	246	141	1,965	25	11	
1947	Sammy Baugh, Washington	354	210	2,938	25	15	
1946	Bob Waterfield, Los Angeles	251	127	1,747	18	17	
1945	Sammy Baugh, Washington	182	128	1,669	11	4	
	Sid Luckman, Chicago Bears	217	117	1,725	14	10	
1944	Frank Filchock, Washington	147	84	1,139	13	9	
1943	Sammy Baugh, Washington	239	133	1,754	23	19	
1942	Cecil Isbell, Green Bay	268	146	2,021	24	14	
1941	Cecil Isbell, Green Bay	206	117	1,479	15	11	
1940	Sammy Baugh, Washington	177	111	1,367	12	10	
1939	*Parker Hall, Cleveland	208	106	1,227	9	13	
1938	Ed Danowski, N.Y. Giants	129	70	848	7	8	
1937	*Sammy Baugh, Washington	171	81	1,127	8	14	
1936	Arnie Herber, Green Bay	173	77	1,239	11	13	
1935	Ed Danowski, N.Y. Giants	113	57	794	10	9	
1934	Arnie Herber, Green Bay	115	42	799	8	12	
1933	*Harry Newman, N.Y. Giants	136	53	973	11	17	
1932	Arnie Herber, Green Bay	101	37	639	9	9	

*First season of professional football.

ANNUAL PASSING TOUCHDOWN LEADERS

Year	Player, Team	TD
2013	Peyton Manning, Denver, AFC	55
	Drew Brees, New Orleans, NFC	39
2012	Drew Brees, New Orleans, NFC	43
	Peyton Manning, Denver, AFC	37
2011	Drew Brees, New Orleans, NFC	46
	Tom Brady, New England, AFC	39
2010	Tom Brady, New England, AFC	36
	Drew Brees, New Orleans, NFC	33

Year	Player, Team	TD
2009	Drew Brees, New Orleans, NFC	34
	Peyton Manning, Indianapolis, AFC	33
2008	Drew Brees, New Orleans, NFC	34
	Philip Rivers, San Diego, AFC	34
2007	Tom Brady, New England, AFC	50
	Tony Romo, Dallas, NFC	36
2006	Peyton Manning, Indianapolis, AFC	31
	Drew Brees, New Orleans, NFC	26

Year	Player, Team	TD
2005	Carson Palmer, Cincinnati, AFC	32
	Jake Delhomme, Carolina, NFC	24
	Matt Hasselbeck, Seattle, NFC	24
	Eli Manning, N.Y. Giants, NFC	24
2004	Peyton Manning, Indianapolis, AFC	49
	Daunte Culpepper, Minnesota, NFC	39
2003	Brett Favre, Green Bay, NFC	32
	Peyton Manning, Indianapolis, AFC	29
2002	Tom Brady, New England, AFC	28
	Aaron Brooks, New Orleans, NFC	27
	Brett Favre, Green Bay, NFC	27
2001	Kurt Warner, St. Louis, NFC	36
	Rich Gannon, Oakland, AFC	27
2000	Daunte Culpepper, Minnesota, NFC	33
	Peyton Manning, Indianapolis, AFC	33
1999	Kurt Warner, St. Louis, NFC	41
	Peyton Manning, Indianapolis, AFC	26
1998	Steve Young, San Francisco, NFC	36
	Vinny Testaverde, N.Y. Jets, AFC	29
1997	Brett Favre, Green Bay, NFC	35
	Jeff George, Oakland, AFC	29
1996	Brett Favre, Green Bay, NFC	39
	Vinny Testaverde, Baltimore, AFC	33
1995	Brett Favre, Green Bay, NFC	38
	Jeff Blake, Cincinnati, AFC	28
1994	Steve Young, San Francisco, NFC	35
	Dan Marino, Miami, AFC	30
1993	Steve Young, San Francisco, NFC	29
	John Elway, Denver, AFC	25
1992	Steve Young, San Francisco, NFC	25
	Dan Marino, Miami, AFC	24
1991	Jim Kelly, Buffalo, AFC	33
	Mark Rypien, Washington, NFC	28
1990	Warren Moon, Houston, AFC	33
	Randall Cunningham, Philadelphia, NFC	30
1989	Jim Everett, L.A. Rams, NFC	29
	Boomer Esiason, Cincinnati, AFC	28
1988	Jim Everett, L.A. Rams, NFC	31
	Boomer Esiason, Cincinnati, AFC	28
	Dan Marino, Miami, AFC	28
1987	Joe Montana, San Francisco, NFC	31
	Dan Marino, Miami, AFC	26
1986	Dan Marino, Miami, AFC	44
	Tommy Kramer, Minnesota, NFC	24
1985	Dan Marino, Miami, AFC	30
	Joe Montana, San Francisco, NFC	27
1984	Dan Marino, Miami, AFC	48
	Neil Lomax, St. Louis, NFC	28
	Joe Montana, San Francisco, NFC	28
1983	Lynn Dickey, Green Bay, NFC	32
	Joe Ferguson, Buffalo, AFC	26
	Brian Sipe, Cleveland, AFC	26
1982	Terry Bradshaw, Pittsburgh, AFC	17
	Dan Fouts, San Diego, AFC	17
	Joe Montana, San Francisco, NFC	17
1981	Dan Fouts, San Diego, AFC	33
	Steve Bartkowski, Atlanta, NFC	30
1980	Steve Bartkowski, Atlanta, NFC	31
	Dan Fouts, San Diego, AFC	30
	Brian Sipe, Cleveland, AFC	30
1979	Steve Grogan, New England, AFC	28
	Brian Sipe, Cleveland, AFC	28
	Roger Staubach, Dallas, NFC	27
1978	Terry Bradshaw, Pittsburgh, AFC	28
	Roger Staubach, Dallas, NFC	25
	Fran Tarkenton, Minnesota, NFC	25
1977	Bob Griese, Miami, AFC	22
	Ron Jaworski, Philadelphia, NFC	18
	Roger Staubach, Dallas, NFC	18

Year	Player, Team	TD
1976	Ken Stabler, Oakland, AFC	27
	Jim Hart, St. Louis, NFC	18
1975	Joe Ferguson, Buffalo, AFC	25
	Fran Tarkenton, Minnesota, NFC	25
1974	Ken Stabler, Oakland, AFC	26
	Jim Hart, St. Louis, NFC	20
1973	Roman Gabriel, Philadelphia, NFC	23
	Roger Staubach, Dallas, NFC	23
	Charley Johnson, Denver, AFC	20
1972	Billy Kilmer, Washington, NFC	19
	Joe Namath, N.Y. Jets, AFC	19
1971	John Hadl, San Diego, AFC	21
	John Brodie, San Francisco, NFC	18
1970	John Brodie, San Francisco, NFC	24
	John Hadl, San Diego, AFC	22
	Daryle Lamonica, Oakland, AFC	22
1969	Daryle Lamonica, Oakland, AFL	34
	Roman Gabriel, Los Angeles, NFL	24
1968	John Hadl, San Diego, AFL	27
	Earl Morrall, Baltimore, NFL	26
1967	Sonny Jurgensen, Washington, NFL	31
	Daryle Lamonica, Oakland, AFL	30
1966	Frank Ryan, Cleveland, NFL	29
	Len Dawson, Kansas City, AFL	26
1965	John Brodie, San Francisco, NFL	30
	Len Dawson, Kansas City, AFL	21
1964	Babe Parilli, Boston, AFL	31
	Frank Ryan, Cleveland, NFL	25
1963	Y.A. Tittle, N.Y. Giants, NFL	36
	Len Dawson, Kansas City, AFL	26
1962	Y.A. Tittle, N.Y. Giants, NFL	33
	Len Dawson, Dallas, AFL	29
1961	George Blanda, Houston, AFL	36
	Sonny Jurgensen, Philadelphia, NFL	32
1960	Al Dorow, N.Y. Titans, AFL	26
	Johnny Unitas, Baltimore, NFL	25
1959	Johnny Unitas, Baltimore	32
1958	Johnny Unitas, Baltimore	19
1957	Johnny Unitas, Baltimore	24
1956	Tobin Rote, Green Bay	18
1955	Tobin Rote, Green Bay	17
	Y.A. Tittle, San Francisco	17
1954	Adrian Burk, Philadelphia	23
1953	Robert Thomason, Philadelphia	21
1952	Jim Finks, Pittsburgh	20
	Otto Graham, Cleveland	20
1951	Bobby Layne, Detroit	26
1950	George Ratterman, N.Y. Yanks	22
1949	Johnny Lujack, Chi. Bears	23
1948	Tommy Thompson, Philadelphia	25
1947	Sammy Baugh, Washington	25
1946	Sid Luckman, Chi. Bears	17
	Bob Waterfield, Los Angeles	17
1945	Sid Luckman, Chi. Bears	14
	*Bob Waterfield, Cleveland	14
1944	Frank Filchock, Washington	13
1943	Sid Luckman, Chi. Bears	28
1942	Cecil Isbell, Green Bay	24
1941	Cecil Isbell, Green Bay	15
1940	Sammy Baugh, Washington	12
1939	Frank Filchock, Washington	11
1938	Bob Monnett, Green Bay	9
1937	Bernie Masterson, Chi. Bears	9
1936	Arnie Herber, Green Bay	11
1935	Ed Danowski, N.Y. Giants	10
1934	Arnie Herber, Green Bay	8
1933	*Harry Newman, N.Y. Giants	11
1932	Arnie Herber, Green Bay	9

First season of professional football.

ANNUAL PASS RECEIVING LEADERS

Year	Player, Team	No.	Yards	Avg.	TD
2013	Pierre Garcon, Washington, NFC	113	1,346	11.9	5
	Antonio Brown, Pittsburgh, AFC	110	1,499	13.6	8
2012	Calvin Johnson, Detroit, NFC	122	1,964	16.1	5
	Wes Welker, New England, AFC	118	1,354	11.5	6
2011	Wes Welker, New England, AFC	122	1,569	12.9	9
	Roddy White, Atlanta, NFC	100	1,296	13.0	8
2010	Roddy White, Atlanta, NFC	115	1,389	12.1	10
	Reggie Wayne, Indianapolis, AFC	111	1,355	12.2	6
2009	Wes Welker, New England, AFC	123	1,348	11.0	4
	Steve Smith, N.Y. Giants, NFC	107	1,220	11.4	7
2008	Andre Johnson, Houston, AFC	115	1,575	13.7	8
	Larry Fitzgerald, Arizona, NFC	96	1,431	14.9	12
2007	T.J. Houshmandzadeh, Cincinnati, AFC	112	1,143	10.2	12
	Wes Welker, New England, AFC	112	1,175	10.5	8
	Larry Fitzgerald, Arizona, NFC	100	1,409	14.1	10
2006	Andre Johnson, Houston, AFC	103	1,147	11.1	5
	Mike Furrey, Detroit, NFC	98	1,086	11.1	6
2005	Steve Smith, Carolina, NFC	103	1,563	15.2	12
	Larry Fitzgerald, Arizona, NFC	103	1,409	13.7	10
	Chad Johnson, Cincinnati, AFC	97	1,432	14.8	9
2004	Tony Gonzalez, Kansas City, AFC	102	1,258	12.3	7
	Joe Horn, New Orleans, NFC	94	1,399	14.9	11
	Torry Holt, St. Louis, NFC	94	1,372	14.6	10
2003	Torry Holt, St. Louis, NFC	117	1,696	14.5	12
	LaDainian Tomlinson, San Diego, AFC	100	725	7.3	4
2002	Marvin Harrison, Indianapolis, AFC	143	1,722	12.0	11
	Randy Moss, Minnesota, NFC	106	1,347	12.7	7
2001	Rod Smith, Denver, AFC	113	1,343	11.9	11
	Keyshawn Johnson, Tampa Bay, NFC	106	1,266	11.9	1
2000	Marvin Harrison, Indianapolis, AFC	102	1,413	13.9	14
	Muhsin Muhammad, Carolina, NFC	102	1,183	11.6	6
1999	Jimmy Smith, Jacksonville, AFC	116	1,636	14.1	6
	Muhsin Muhammad, Carolina, NFC	96	1,253	13.1	8
1998	O.J. McDuffie, Miami, AFC	90	1,050	11.7	7
	Frank Sanders, Arizona, NFC	89	1,145	12.9	3
1997	Tim Brown, Oakland, AFC	104	1,408	13.5	5
	Herman Moore, Detroit, NFC	104	1,293	12.4	8
1996	Jerry Rice, San Francisco, NFC	108	1,254	11.6	8
	Carl Pickens, Cincinnati, AFC	100	1,180	11.8	12
1995	Herman Moore, Detroit, NFC	123	1,686	13.7	14
	Carl Pickens, Cincinnati, AFC	99	1,234	12.5	17
1994	Cris Carter, Minnesota, NFC	122	1,256	10.3	7
	Ben Coates, New England, AFC	96	1,174	12.2	7
1993	Sterling Sharpe, Green Bay, NFC	112	1,274	11.4	11
	Reggie Langhorne, Indianapolis, AFC	85	1,038	12.2	3
1992	Sterling Sharpe, Green Bay, NFC	108	1,461	13.5	13
	Haywood Jeffires, Houston, AFC	90	913	10.1	9
1991	Haywood Jeffires, Houston, AFC	100	1,181	11.8	7
	Michael Irvin, Dallas, NFC	93	1,523	16.4	8
1990	Jerry Rice, San Francisco, NFC	100	1,502	15.0	13
	Haywood Jeffires, Houston, AFC	74	1,048	14.2	8
	Drew Hill, Houston, AFC	74	1,019	13.8	5
1989	Sterling Sharpe, Green Bay, NFC	90	1,423	15.8	12
	Andre Reed, Buffalo, AFC	88	1,312	14.9	9
1988	Al Toon, N.Y. Jets, AFC	93	1,067	11.5	5
	Henry Ellard, L.A. Rams, NFC	86	1,414	16.4	10
1987	J.T. Smith, St. Louis, NFC	91	1,117	12.3	8
	Al Toon, N.Y. Jets, AFC	68	976	14.4	5
1986	Todd Christensen, L.A. Raiders, AFC	95	1,153	12.1	8
	Jerry Rice, San Francisco, NFC	86	1,570	18.3	15
1985	Roger Craig, San Francisco, NFC	92	1,016	11.0	6
	Lionel James, San Diego, AFC	86	1,027	11.9	6
1984	Art Monk, Washington, NFC	106	1,372	12.9	7
	Ozzie Newsome, Cleveland, AFC	89	1,001	11.2	5
1983	Todd Christensen, L.A. Raiders, AFC	92	1,247	13.6	12
	Roy Green, St. Louis, NFC	78	1,227	15.7	14
	Charlie Brown, Washington, NFC	78	1,225	15.7	8
	Earnest Gray, N.Y. Giants, NFC	78	1,139	14.6	5

Year	Player, Team	No.	Yards	Avg.	TD
1982	Dwight Clark, San Francisco, NFC	60	913	15.2	5
	Kellen Winslow, San Diego, AFC	54	721	13.4	6
1981	Kellen Winslow, San Diego, AFC	88	1,075	12.2	10
	Dwight Clark, San Francisco, NFC	85	1,105	13.0	4
1980	Kellen Winslow, San Diego, AFC	89	1,290	14.5	9
	*Earl Cooper, San Francisco, NFC	83	567	6.8	4
1979	Joe Washington, Baltimore, AFC	82	750	9.1	3
	Ahmad Rashad, Minnesota, NFC	80	1,156	14.5	9
1978	Rickey Young, Minnesota, NFC	88	704	8.0	5
	Steve Largent, Seattle, AFC	71	1,168	16.5	8
1977	Lydell Mitchell, Baltimore, AFC	71	620	8.7	4
	Ahmad Rashad, Minnesota, NFC	51	681	13.4	2
1976	MacArthur Lane, Kansas City, AFC	66	686	10.4	1
	Drew Pearson, Dallas, NFC	58	806	13.9	6
1975	Chuck Foreman, Minnesota, NFC	73	691	9.5	9
	Reggie Rucker, Cleveland, AFC	60	770	12.8	3
	Lydell Mitchell, Baltimore, AFC	60	544	9.1	4
1974	Lydell Mitchell, Baltimore, AFC	72	544	7.6	2
	Charles Young, Philadelphia, NFC	63	696	11.0	3
1973	Harold Carmichael, Philadelphia, NFC	67	1,116	16.7	9
	Fred Willis, Houston, AFC	57	371	6.5	1
1972	Harold Jackson, Philadelphia, NFC	62	1,048	16.9	4
	Fred Biletnikoff, Oakland, AFC	58	802	13.8	7
1971	Fred Biletnikoff, Oakland, AFC	61	929	15.2	9
	Bob Tucker, N.Y. Giants, NFC	59	791	13.4	4
1970	Dick Gordon, Chicago, NFC	71	1,026	14.5	13
	Marlin Briscoe, Buffalo, AFC	57	1,036	18.2	8
1969	Dan Abramowicz, New Orleans, NFL	73	1,015	13.9	7
	Lance Alworth, San Diego, AFL	64	1,003	15.7	4
1968	Clifton McNeil, San Francisco, NFL	71	994	14.0	7
	Lance Alworth, San Diego, AFL	68	1,312	19.3	10
1967	George Sauer, N.Y. Jets, AFL	75	1,189	15.9	6
	Charley Taylor, Washington, NFL	70	990	14.1	9
1966	Lance Alworth, San Diego, AFL	73	1,383	18.9	13
	Charley Taylor, Washington, NFL	72	1,119	15.5	12
1965	Lionel Taylor, Denver, AFL	85	1,131	13.3	6
	Dave Parks, San Francisco, NFL	80	1,344	16.8	12
1964	Charley Hennigan, Houston, AFL	101	1,546	15.3	8
	Johnny Morris, Chicago, NFL	93	1,200	12.9	10
1963	Lionel Taylor, Denver, AFL	78	1,101	14.1	10
	Bobby Joe Conrad, St. Louis, NFL	73	967	13.2	10
1962	Lionel Taylor, Denver, AFL	77	908	11.8	4
	Bobby Mitchell, Washington, NFL	72	1,384	19.2	11
1961	Lionel Taylor, Denver, AFL	100	1,176	11.8	4
	Jim (Red) Phillips, Los Angeles, NFL	78	1,092	14.0	5
1960	Lionel Taylor, Denver, AFL	92	1,235	13.4	12
	Raymond Berry, Baltimore, NFL	74	1,298	17.5	10
1959	Raymond Berry, Baltimore	66	959	14.5	14
1958	Raymond Berry, Baltimore	56	794	14.2	9
	Pete Retzlaff, Philadelphia	56	766	13.7	2
1957	Billy Wilson, San Francisco	52	757	14.6	6
1956	Billy Wilson, San Francisco	60	889	14.8	5
1955	Pete Pihos, Philadelphia	62	864	13.9	7
1954	Pete Pihos, Philadelphia	60	872	14.5	10
	Billy Wilson, San Francisco	60	830	13.8	5
1953	Pete Pihos, Philadelphia	63	1,049	16.7	10
1952	Mac Speedie, Cleveland	62	911	14.7	5
1951	Elroy (Crazylegs) Hirsch, Los Angeles	66	1,495	22.7	17
1950	Tom Fears, Los Angeles	84	1,116	13.3	7
1949	Tom Fears, Los Angeles	77	1,013	13.2	9
1948	*Tom Fears, Los Angeles	51	698	13.7	4
1947	Jim Keane, Chi. Bears	64	910	14.2	10
1946	Jim Benton, Los Angeles	63	981	15.6	6
1945	Don Hutson, Green Bay	47	834	17.7	9
1944	Don Hutson, Green Bay	58	866	14.9	9
1943	Don Hutson, Green Bay	47	776	16.5	11
1942	Don Hutson, Green Bay	74	1,211	16.4	17
1941	Don Hutson, Green Bay	58	738	12.7	10
1940	*Don Looney, Philadelphia	58	707	12.2	4
1939	Don Hutson, Green Bay	34	846	24.9	6

Year	Player, Team	No.	Yards	Avg.	TD
1938	Gaynell Tinsley, Chi. Cardinals	41	516	12.6	1
1937	Don Hutson, Green Bay	41	552	13.5	7
1936	Don Hutson, Green Bay	34	536	15.8	8
1935	*Tod Goodwin, N.Y. Giants	26	432	16.6	4
1934	Joe Carter, Philadelphia	16	238	14.9	4
	Morris (Red) Badgro, N.Y. Giants	16	206	12.9	1
1933	John (Shipwreck) Kelly, Brooklyn	22	246	11.2	3
1932	Ray Flaherty, N.Y. Giants	21	350	16.7	3

First season of professional football.

ANNUAL PASS RECEIVING LEADERS (YARDS)

Year	Player, Team	No.	Yards	Avg.	TD
2013	Josh Gordon, Cleveland, AFC	87	1,646	18.9	9
	Calvin Johnson, Detroit, NFC	84	1,492	17.8	12
2012	Calvin Johnson, Detroit, NFC	122	1,964	16.1	5
	Andre Johnson, Houston, AFC	112	1,598	14.3	4
2011	Calvin Johnson, Detroit, NFC	96	1,681	17.5	16
	Wes Welker, New England, AFC	122	1,569	12.9	9
2010	Brandon Lloyd, Denver, AFC	77	1,448	18.8	11
	Roddy White, Atlanta, NFC	115	1,389	12.1	10
2009	Andre Johnson, Houston, AFC	101	1,569	15.5	9
	Miles Austin, Dallas, NFC	81	1,320	16.3	11
2008	Andre Johnson, Houston, AFC	115	1,575	13.7	8
	Larry Fitzgerald, Arizona, NFC	96	1,431	14.9	12
2007	Reggie Wayne, Indianapolis, AFC	104	1,510	14.5	10
	Larry Fitzgerald, Arizona, NFC	100	1,409	14.1	10
2006	Chad Johnson, Cincinnati, AFC	87	1,369	15.7	7
	Roy Williams, Detroit, NFC	82	1,310	16.0	7
2005	Steve Smith, Carolina, NFC	103	1,563	15.2	12
	Chad Johnson, Cincinnati, AFC	97	1,432	14.8	9
2004	Muhsin Muhammad, Carolina, NFC	93	1,405	15.1	16
	Chad Johnson, Cincinnati, AFC	95	1,274	13.4	9
2003	Torry Holt, St. Louis, NFC	117	1,696	14.5	12
	Chad Johnson, Cincinnati, AFC	90	1,355	15.1	10
2002	Marvin Harrison, Indianapolis, AFC	143	1,722	12.0	11
	Randy Moss, Minnesota, NFC	106	1,347	12.7	7
2001	David Boston, Arizona, NFC	98	1,598	16.3	8
	Marvin Harrison, Indianapolis, AFC	109	1,524	14.0	15
2000	Torry Holt, St. Louis, NFC	82	1,635	19.9	6
	Rod Smith, Denver, AFC	100	1,602	16.0	8
1999	Marvin Harrison, Indianapolis, AFC	115	1,663	14.5	12
	Randy Moss, Minnesota, NFC	80	1,413	17.7	11
1998	Antonio Freeman, Green Bay, NFC	84	1,424	17.0	14
	Eric Moulds, Buffalo, AFC	67	1,368	20.4	9
1997	Rob Moore, Arizona, NFC	97	1,584	16.3	8
	Tim Brown, Oakland, AFC	104	1,408	13.5	5
1996	Isaac Bruce, St. Louis, NFC	84	1,338	15.9	7
	Jimmy Smith, Jacksonville, AFC	83	1,244	15.0	7
1995	Jerry Rice, San Francisco, NFC	122	1,848	15.1	15
	Tim Brown, Oakland, AFC	89	1,342	15.1	10
1994	Jerry Rice, San Francisco, NFC	112	1,499	13.4	13
	Tim Brown, L.A. Raiders, AFC	89	1,309	14.7	9
1993	Jerry Rice, San Francisco, NFC	98	1,503	15.3	15
	Tim Brown, L.A. Raiders, AFC	80	1,180	14.8	7
1992	Sterling Sharpe, Green Bay, NFC	108	1,461	13.5	13
	Anthony Miller, San Diego, AFC	72	1,060	14.7	7
1991	Michael Irvin, Dallas, NFC	93	1,523	16.4	8
	Haywood Jeffires, Houston, AFC	100	1,181	11.8	7
1990	Jerry Rice, San Francisco, NFC	100	1,502	15.0	13
	Haywood Jeffires, Houston, AFC	74	1,048	14.2	8
1989	Jerry Rice, San Francisco, NFC	82	1,483	18.1	17
	Andre Reed, Buffalo, AFC	88	1,312	14.9	9
1988	Henry Ellard, L.A. Rams, NFC	86	1,414	16.4	10
	Eddie Brown, Cincinnati, AFC	53	1,273	24.0	9
1987	J.T. Smith, St. Louis, NFC	91	1,117	12.3	8
	Carlos Carson, Kansas City, AFC	55	1,044	19.0	7
1986	Jerry Rice, San Francisco, NFC	86	1,570	18.3	15
	Stanley Morgan, New England, AFC	84	1,491	17.8	10
1985	Steve Largent, Seattle, AFC	79	1,287	16.3	6
	Mike Quick, Philadelphia, NFC	73	1,247	17.1	11

Year	Player, Team	No.	Yards	Avg.	TD
1984	Roy Green, St. Louis, NFC	78	1,555	19.9	12
	John Stallworth, Pittsburgh, AFC	80	1,395	17.4	11
1983	Mike Quick, Philadelphia, NFC	69	1,409	20.4	13
	Carlos Carson, Kansas City, AFC	80	1,351	16.9	7
1982	Wes Chandler, San Diego, AFC	49	1,032	21.1	9
	Dwight Clark, San Francisco, NFC	60	913	15.2	5
1981	Alfred Jenkins, Atlanta, NFC	70	1,358	19.4	13
	Frank Lewis, Buffalo, AFC	70	1,244	17.8	4
	Steve Watson, Denver, AFC	60	1,244	20.7	13
1980	John Jefferson, San Diego, AFC	82	1,340	16.3	13
	James Lofton, Green Bay, NFC	71	1,226	17.3	4
1979	Steve Largent, Seattle, AFC	66	1,237	18.7	9
	Ahmad Rashad, Minnesota, NFC	80	1,156	14.5	9
1978	Wesley Walker, N.Y. Jets, AFC	48	1,169	24.4	8
	Harold Carmichael, Philadelphia, NFC	55	1,072	19.5	8
1977	Drew Pearson, Dallas, NFC	48	870	18.1	2
	Ken Burrough, Houston, AFC	43	816	19.0	8
1976	Roger Carr, Baltimore, AFC	43	1,112	25.9	11
	*Sammy White, Minnesota, NFC	51	906	17.8	10
1975	Ken Burrough, Houston, AFC	53	1,063	20.1	8
	Mel Gray, St. Louis, NFC	48	926	19.3	11
1974	Cliff Branch, Oakland, AFC	60	1,092	18.2	13
	Drew Pearson, Dallas, NFC	62	1,087	17.5	2
1973	Harold Carmichael, Philadelphia, NFC	67	1,116	16.7	9
	*Isaac Curtis, Cincinnati, AFC	45	843	18.7	9
1972	Harold Jackson, Philadelphia, NFC	62	1,048	16.9	4
	Rich Caster, N.Y. Jets, AFC	39	833	21.4	10
1971	Otis Taylor, Kansas City, AFC	57	1,110	19.5	7
	Gene Washington, San Francisco, NFC	46	884	19.2	4
1970	Gene Washington, San Francisco, NFC	53	1,100	20.8	12
	Marlin Briscoe, Buffalo, AFC	57	1,036	18.2	8
1969	Warren Wells, Oakland, AFL	47	1,260	26.8	14
	Harold Jackson, Philadelphia, NFL	65	1,116	17.2	9
1968	Lance Alworth, San Diego, AFL	68	1,312	19.3	10
	Roy Jefferson, Pittsburgh, NFL	58	1,074	18.5	11
1967	Don Maynard, N.Y. Jets, AFL	71	1,434	20.3	10
	Ben Hawkins, Philadelphia, NFL	59	1,265	21.4	10
1966	Lance Alworth, San Diego, AFL	73	1,383	18.9	13
	Pat Studstill, Detroit, NFL	67	1,266	18.9	5
1965	Lance Alworth, San Diego, AFL	69	1,602	23.2	14
	Dave Parks, San Francisco, NFL	80	1,344	16.8	12
1964	Charley Hennigan, Houston, AFL	101	1,546	15.3	8
	Johnny Morris, Chicago, NFL	93	1,200	12.9	10
1963	Bobby Mitchell, Washington, NFL	69	1,436	20.8	7
	Art Powell, Oakland, AFL	73	1,304	17.8	16
1962	Bobby Mitchell, Washington, NFL	72	1,384	19.2	11
	Art Powell, N.Y. Titans, AFL	64	1,130	17.6	8
1961	Charley Hennigan, Houston, AFL	82	1,746	21.3	12
	Tommy McDonald, Philadelphia, NFL	64	1,144	17.9	13
1960	*Bill Groman, Houston, AFL	72	1,473	20.5	12
	Raymond Berry, Baltimore, NFL	74	1,298	17.5	10
1959	Raymond Berry, Baltimore	66	959	14.5	14
1958	Del Shofner, Los Angeles	51	1,097	21.5	8
1957	Raymond Berry, Baltimore	47	800	17.0	6
1956	Billy Howton, Green Bay	55	1,188	21.6	12
1955	Pete Pihos, Philadelphia	62	864	13.9	7
1954	Bob Boyd, Los Angeles	53	1,212	22.9	6
1953	Pete Pihos, Philadelphia	63	1,049	16.7	10
1952	*Billy Howton, Green Bay	53	1,231	23.2	13
1951	Elroy (Crazylegs) Hirsch, Los Angeles	66	1,495	22.7	17
1950	Tom Fears, Los Angeles	84	1,116	13.3	7
1949	Bob Mann, Detroit	66	1,014	15.4	4
1948	Mal Kutner, Chi. Cardinals	41	943	23.0	14
1947	Mal Kutner, Chi. Cardinals	43	944	21.9	7
1946	Jim Benton, Los Angeles	63	981	15.5	6
1945	Jim Benton, Cleveland	45	1,067	23.7	8
1944	Don Hutson, Green Bay	58	866	14.6	9
1943	Don Hutson, Green Bay	47	776	16.5	11
1942	Don Hutson, Green Bay	74	1,211	16.4	17
1941	Don Hutson, Green Bay	58	738	12.7	10

Year	Player, Team	No.	Yards	Avg.		TD
1940	*Don Looney, Philadelphia	58	707	12.2		4
1939	Don Hutson, Green Bay	34	846	24.9		6
1938	Don Hutson, Green Bay	32	548	17.1		9
1937	*Gaynell Tinsley, Chi. Cardinals	36	675	18.8		5
1936	Don Hutson, Green Bay	34	526	15.5		8
1935	Charley Malone, Boston	22	433	19.7		2
1934	Harry Ebding, Detroit	9	257	28.6		2
1933	*Paul Moss, Pittsburgh	13	283	21.8		2
1932	Johnny (Blood) McNally, Green Bay	19	326	17.2		3

*First season of professional football.

ANNUAL PUNT RETURN LEADERS

Year	Player, Team	No.	Yards	Avg.	Long	TD
2013	Tandon Doss, Baltimore, AFC	23	359	15.6	82	1
	Marcus Sherels, Minnesota, NFC	22	335	15.2	86	1
2012	Leodis McKelvin, Buffalo, AFC	23	431	18.7	88	2
	Dwayne Harris, Dallas, NFC	22	354	16.1	78	1
2011	Devin Hester, Chicago, NFC	28	454	16.2	82	2
	Javier Arenas, Kansas City, AFC	32	410	12.8	37	0
2010	Devin Hester, Chicago, NFC	33	564	17.1	89	3
	Julian Edelman, New England, AFC	21	321	15.3	94	1
2009	DeSean Jackson, Philadelphia, NFC	29	441	15.2	85	2
	Wes Welker, New England, AFC	27	338	12.5	69	0
2008	Roscoe Parrish, Buffalo, AFC	21	322	15.3	63	1
	*Clifton Smith, Tampa Bay, NFC	23	324	14.1	70	1
2007	Roscoe Parrish, Buffalo, AFC	27	440	16.3	74	1
	Devin Hester, Chicago, NFC	42	651	15.5	89	4
2006	Adam Jones, Tennessee, AFC	34	440	12.9	90	3
	*Devin Hester, Chicago, NFC	47	600	12.8	84	3
2005	Reno Mahe, Philadelphia, NFC	21	269	12.8	44	0
	B.J. Sams, Baltimore, AFC	33	401	12.2	51	0
2004	Eddie Drummond, Detroit, NFC	24	316	13.2	83	2
	Dennis Northcutt, Cleveland, AFC	36	432	12.0	44	0
2003	Dante Hall, Kansas City, AFC	29	472	16.3	93	2
	Brian Westbrook, Philadelphia, NFC	20	306	15.3	84	2
2002	Jimmy Williams, San Francisco, NFC	20	336	16.8	89	1
	Santana Moss, N.Y. Jets, AFC	25	413	16.5	63	2
2001	Troy Brown, New England, AFC	29	413	14.2	85	2
	Darrien Gordon, Atlanta, NFC	31	437	14.1	74	0
2000	Jermaine Lewis, Baltimore, AFC	36	578	16.1	89	2
	Az-Zahir Hakim, St. Louis, NFC	32	489	15.3	86	1
1999	*Charlie Rogers, Seattle, AFC	22	318	14.5	94	1
	*Mac Cody, Arizona, NFC	32	373	11.7	31	0
1998	Deion Sanders, Dallas, NFC	24	375	15.6	69	1
	Reggie Barlow, Jacksonville, AFC	43	555	12.9	85	1
1997	Jermaine Lewis, Baltimore, AFC	28	437	15.6	89	2
	David Palmer, Minnesota, NFC	34	444	13.1	57	0
1996	Desmond Howard, Green Bay, NFC	58	875	15.1	92	3
	Darrien Gordon, San Diego, AFC	36	537	14.9	81	1
1995	David Palmer, Minnesota, NFC	26	342	13.2	74	1
	Andre Coleman, San Diego, AFC	28	326	11.6	88	1
1994	Brian Mitchell, Washington, NFC	32	452	14.1	78	2
	Darrien Gordon, San Diego, AFC	36	475	13.2	90	2
1993	*Tyrone Hughes, New Orleans, NFC	37	503	13.6	83	2
	Eric Metcalf, Cleveland, AFC	36	464	12.9	91	2
1992	Johnny Bailey, Phoenix, NFC	20	263	13.2	65	0
	Rod Woodson, Pittsburgh, AFC	32	364	11.4	80	1
1991	Mel Gray, Detroit, NFC	25	385	15.4	78	1
	Rod Woodson, Pittsburgh, AFC	28	320	11.4	40	0
1990	Clarence Verdin, Indianapolis, AFC	31	396	12.8	36	0
	*Johnny Bailey, Chicago, NFC	36	399	11.1	95	1
1989	Walter Stanley, Detroit, NFC	36	496	13.8	74	0
	Clarence Verdin, Indianapolis, AFC	23	296	12.9	49	1
1988	John Taylor, San Francisco, NFC	44	556	12.6	95	2
	JoJo Townsell, N.Y. Jets, AFC	35	409	11.7	59	1
1987	Mel Gray, New Orleans, NFC	24	352	14.7	80	0
	Bobby Joe Edmonds, Seattle, AFC	20	251	12.6	40	0
1986	*Bobby Joe Edmonds, Seattle, AFC	34	419	12.3	75	1
	*Vai Sikahema, St. Louis, NFC	43	522	12.1	71	2

Year	Player, Team	No.	Yards	Avg.	Long	TD
1985	Irving Fryar, New England, AFC	37	520	14.1	85	2
	Henry Ellard, L.A. Rams, NFC	37	501	13.5	80	1
1984	Mike Martin, Cincinnati, AFC	24	376	15.7	55	0
	Henry Ellard, L.A. Rams, NFC	30	403	13.4	83	2
1983	*Henry Ellard, L.A. Rams, NFC	16	217	13.6	72	1
	Kirk Springs, N.Y. Jets, AFC	23	287	12.5	76	1
1982	Rick Upchurch, Denver, AFC	15	242	16.1	78	2
	Billy Johnson, Atlanta, NFC	24	273	11.4	71	0
1981	LeRoy Irvin, Los Angeles, NFC	46	615	13.4	84	3
	*James Brooks, San Diego, AFC	22	290	13.2	42	0
1980	J.T. Smith, Kansas City, AFC	40	581	14.5	75	2
	*Kenny Johnson, Atlanta, NFC	23	281	12.2	56	0
1979	John Sciarra, Philadelphia, NFC	16	182	11.4	38	0
	*Tony Nathan, Miami, AFC	28	306	10.9	86	1
1978	Rick Upchurch, Denver, AFC	36	493	13.7	75	1
	Jackie Wallace, Los Angeles, NFC	52	618	11.9	58	0
1977	Billy Johnson, Houston, AFC	35	539	15.4	87	2
	Larry Marshall, Philadelphia, NFC	46	489	10.6	48	0
1976	Rick Upchurch, Denver, AFC	39	536	13.7	92	4
	Eddie Brown, Washington, NFC	48	646	13.5	71	1
1975	Billy Johnson, Houston, AFC	40	612	15.3	83	3
	Terry Metcalf, St. Louis, NFC	23	285	12.4	69	1
1974	Lemar Parrish, Cincinnati, AFC	18	338	18.8	90	2
	Dick Jauron, Detroit, NFC	17	286	16.8	58	0
1973	Bruce Taylor, San Francisco, NFC	15	207	13.8	61	0
	Ron Smith, San Diego, AFC	27	352	13.0	84	2
1972	Ken Ellis, Green Bay, NFC	14	215	15.4	80	1
	Chris Farasopoulos, N.Y. Jets, AFC	17	179	10.5	65	1
1971	Les (Speedy) Duncan, Washington, NFC	22	233	10.6	33	0
	Leroy Kelly, Cleveland, AFC	30	292	9.7	74	0
1970	Ed Podolak, Kansas City, AFC	23	311	13.5	60	0
	*Bruce Taylor, San Francisco, NFC	43	516	12.0	76	0
1969	Alvin Haymond, Los Angeles, NFL	33	435	13.2	52	0
	*Bill Thompson, Denver, AFL	25	288	11.5	40	0
1968	Bob Hayes, Dallas, NFL	15	312	20.8	90	2
	Noland Smith, Kansas City, AFL	18	270	15.0	80	1
1967	Floyd Little, Denver, AFL	16	270	16.9	72	1
	Ben Davis, Cleveland, NFL	18	229	12.7	52	1
1966	Les (Speedy) Duncan, San Diego, AFL	18	238	13.2	81	1
	Johnny Roland, St. Louis, NFL	20	221	11.1	86	1
1965	Leroy Kelly, Cleveland, NFL	17	265	15.6	67	2
	Les (Speedy) Duncan, San Diego, AFL	30	464	15.5	66	2
1964	Bobby Jancik, Houston, AFL	12	220	18.3	82	1
	Tommy Watkins, Detroit, NFL	16	238	14.9	68	2
1963	Dick James, Washington, NFL	16	214	13.4	39	0
	Claude (Hoot) Gibson, Oakland, AFL	26	307	11.8	85	2
1962	Dick Christy, N.Y. Titans, AFL	15	250	16.7	73	2
	Pat Studstill, Detroit, NFL	29	457	15.8	44	0
1961	Dick Christy, N.Y. Titans, AFL	18	383	21.3	70	2
	Willie Wood, Green Bay, NFL	14	225	16.1	72	2
1960	*Abner Haynes, Dall. Texans, AFL	14	215	15.4	46	1
	Abe Woodson, San Francisco, NFL	13	174	13.4	48	0
1959	Johnny Morris, Chi. Bears	14	171	12.2	78	1
1958	Jon Arnett, Los Angeles	18	223	12.4	58	0
1957	Bert Zagers, Washington	14	217	15.5	76	2
1956	Ken Konz, Cleveland	13	187	14.4	65	1
1955	Ollie Matson, Chi. Cardinals	13	245	18.8	78	2
1954	*Veryl Switzer, Green Bay	24	306	12.8	93	1
1953	Charley Trippi, Chi. Cardinals	21	239	11.4	38	0
1952	Jack Christiansen, Detroit	15	322	21.5	79	2
1951	Claude (Buddy) Young, N.Y. Yanks	12	231	19.3	79	1
1950	*Herb Rich, Baltimore	12	276	23.0	86	1
1949	Verda (Vitamin T) Smith, Los Angeles	27	427	15.8	85	1
1948	George McAfee, Chi. Bears	30	417	13.9	60	1
1947	*Walt Slater, Pittsburgh	28	435	15.5	33	0
1946	Bill Dudley, Pittsburgh	27	385	14.3	52	0
1945	*Dave Ryan, Detroit	15	220	14.7	56	0
1944	*Steve Van Buren, Philadelphia	15	230	15.3	55	1
1943	Andy Farkas, Washington	15	168	11.2	33	0
1942	Merlyn Condit, Brooklyn	21	210	10.0	23	0

Year	Player, Team	No.	Yards	Avg.	Long	TD
1941	Byron (Whizzer) White, Detroit	19	262	13.8	64	0

First season of professional football.

ANNUAL KICKOFF RETURN LEADERS

Year	Player, Team	No.	Yards	Avg.	Long	TD
2013	*Cordarrelle Patterson, Minnesota, NFC	43	1,393	32.4	109	2
	Quintin Demps, Kansas City, AFC	33	992	30.1	95	1
2012	Jacoby Jones, Baltimore, AFC	38	1,167	30.7	108	2
	Leon Washington, Seattle, NFC	27	784	29.0	98	1
2011	Joe McKnight, N.Y. Jets, AFC	34	1,073	31.6	107	1
	*Randall Cobb, Green Bay, NFC	34	941	27.7	108	1
2010	*David Reed, Baltimore, AFC	21	616	29.3	103	1
	Eric Weems, Atlanta, NFC	40	1,100	27.5	102	1
2009	Clifton Smith, Tampa Bay, NFC	31	902	29.1	83	0
	Josh Cribbs, Cleveland, AFC	56	1,542	27.5	103	3
2008	Danieal Manning, Chicago, NFC	36	1,070	29.7	83	1
	Ellis Hobbs, New England, AFC	45	1,281	28.5	95	1
2007	Josh Cribbs, Cleveland, AFC	59	1,809	30.7	100	2
	*Aundrae Allison, Minnesota, NFC	20	574	28.7	104	1
2006	Justin Miller, N.Y. Jets, AFC	46	1,304	28.3	103	2
	*Devin Hester, Chicago, NFC	20	528	26.4	96	2
2005	Terrence McGee, Buffalo, AFC	46	1,391	30.2	99	1
	Koren Robinson, Minnesota, NFC	47	1,221	26.0	86	1
2004	Willie Ponder, N.Y. Giants, NFC	36	967	26.9	91	1
	Terrence McGee, Buffalo, AFC	52	1,370	26.3	104	3
2003	Jerry Azumah, Chicago, NFC	41	1,191	29.0	89	2
	*Bethel Johnson, New England, AFC	30	847	28.2	92	1
2002	MarTay Jenkins, Arizona, NFC	20	559	28.0	95	1
	Kevin Faulk, New England, AFC	26	725	27.9	87	2
2001	Ronney Jenkins, San Diego, AFC	58	1,541	26.6	93	2
	*Steve Smith, Carolina, NFC	56	1,431	25.6	99	2
2000	*Darrick Vaughn, Atlanta, NFC	39	1,082	27.7	100	3
	Derrick Mason, Tennessee, AFC	42	1,132	27.0	66	0
1999	Tony Horne, St. Louis, NFC	30	892	29.7	101	2
	Tremain Mack, Cincinnati, AFC	51	1,382	27.1	99	1
1998	*Terry Fair, Detroit, NFC	51	1,428	28.0	105	2
	Corey Harris, Baltimore, AFC	35	965	27.6	95	1
1997	Michael Bates, Carolina, NFC	47	1,281	27.3	56	0
	Aaron Glenn, N.Y. Jets, AFC	28	741	26.5	96	1
1996	Michael Bates, Carolina, NFC	33	998	30.2	93	1
	Tamarick Vanover, Kansas City, AFC	33	854	25.9	97	1
1995	Ron Carpenter, N.Y. Jets, AFC	20	553	27.7	58	0
	Brian Mitchell, Washington, NFC	55	1,408	25.6	59	0
1994	Mel Gray, Detroit, NFC	45	1,276	28.4	102	3
	Randy Baldwin, Cleveland, AFC	28	753	26.9	85	1
1993	Robert Brooks, Green Bay, NFC	23	611	26.6	95	1
	*Raghib Ismail, L.A. Raiders, AFC	25	605	24.2	66	0
1992	Jon Vaughn, New England, AFC	20	564	28.2	100	1
	Deion Sanders, Atlanta, NFC	40	1,067	26.7	99	2
1991	Mel Gray, Detroit, NFC	36	929	25.8	71	0
	Nate Lewis, San Diego, AFC	23	578	25.1	95	1
1990	Kevin Clark, Denver, AFC	20	505	25.3	75	0
	David Meggett, N.Y. Giants, NFC	21	492	23.4	58	0
1989	Rod Woodson, Pittsburgh, AFC	36	982	27.3	84	1
	Mel Gray, Detroit, NFC	24	640	26.7	57	0
1988	*Tim Brown, L.A. Raiders, AFC	41	1,098	26.8	97	1
	Donnie Elder, Tampa Bay, NFC	34	772	22.7	51	0
1987	Sylvester Stamps, Atlanta, NFC	24	660	27.5	97	1
	Paul Palmer, Kansas City, AFC	38	923	24.3	95	2
1986	Dennis Gentry, Chicago, NFC	20	576	28.8	91	1
	Lupe Sanchez, Pittsburgh, AFC	25	591	23.6	64	0
1985	Ron Brown, L.A. Rams, NFC	28	918	32.8	98	3
	Glen Young, Cleveland, AFC	35	898	25.7	63	0
1984	*Bobby Humphery, N.Y. Jets, AFC	22	675	30.7	97	1
	Barry Redden, L.A. Rams, NFC	23	530	23.0	40	0
1983	Fulton Walker, Miami, AFC	36	962	26.7	78	0
	Darrin Nelson, Minnesota, NFC	18	445	24.7	50	0
1982	*Mike Mosley, Buffalo, AFC	18	487	27.1	66	0
	Alvin Hall, Detroit, NFC	16	426	26.6	96	1

Year	Player, Team	No.	Yards	Avg.	Long	TD
1981	Mike Nelms, Washington, NFC	37	1,099	29.7	84	0
	Carl Roaches, Houston, AFC	28	769	27.5	96	1
1980	Horace Ivory, New England, AFC	36	992	27.6	98	1
	Rich Mauti, New Orleans, NFC	31	798	25.7	52	0
1979	Larry Brunson, Oakland, AFC	17	441	25.9	89	0
	Jimmy Edwards, Minnesota, NFC	44	1,103	25.1	83	0
1978	Steve Odom, Green Bay, NFC	25	677	27.1	95	1
	*Keith Wright, Cleveland, AFC	30	789	26.3	86	0
1977	*Raymond Clayborn, New England, AFC	28	869	31.0	101	3
	*Wilbert Montgomery, Philadelphia, NFC	23	619	26.9	99	1
1976	*Duriel Harris, Miami, AFC	17	559	32.9	69	0
	Cullen Bryant, Los Angeles, NFC	16	459	28.7	90	1
1975	*Walter Payton, Chicago, NFC	14	444	31.7	70	0
	Harold Hart, Oakland, AFC	17	518	30.5	102	1
1974	Terry Metcalf, St. Louis, NFC	20	623	31.2	94	1
	Greg Pruitt, Cleveland, AFC	22	606	27.5	88	1
1973	Carl Garrett, Chicago, NFC	16	486	30.4	67	0
	*Wallace Francis, Buffalo, AFC	23	687	29.9	101	2
1972	Ron Smith, Chicago, NFC	30	924	30.8	94	1
	*Bruce Laird, Baltimore, AFC	29	843	29.1	73	0
1971	Travis Williams, Los Angeles, NFC	25	743	29.7	105	1
	Eugene (Mercury) Morris, Miami, AFC	15	423	28.2	94	1
1970	Jim Duncan, Baltimore, AFC	20	707	35.4	99	1
	Cecil Turner, Chicago, NFC	23	752	32.7	96	4
1969	Bobby Williams, Detroit, NFL	17	563	33.1	96	1
	*Bill Thompson, Denver, AFL	18	513	28.5	63	0
1968	Preston Pearson, Baltimore, NFL	15	527	35.1	102	2
	*George Atkinson, Oakland, AFL	32	802	25.1	60	0
1967	*Travis Williams, Green Bay, NFL	18	739	41.1	104	4
	*Zeke Moore, Houston, AFL	14	405	28.9	92	1
1966	Gale Sayers, Chicago, NFL	23	718	31.2	93	2
	*Goldie Sellers, Denver, AFL	19	541	28.5	100	2
1965	Tommy Watkins, Detroit, NFL	17	584	34.4	94	0
	Abner Haynes, Denver, AFL	34	901	26.5	60	0
1964	*Clarence Childs, N.Y. Giants, NFL	34	987	29.0	100	1
	Bo Roberson, Oakland, AFL	36	975	27.1	59	0
1963	Abe Woodson, San Francisco, NFL	29	935	32.2	103	3
	Bobby Jancik, Houston, AFL	45	1,317	29.3	53	0
1962	Abe Woodson, San Francisco, NFL	37	1,157	31.3	79	0
	*Bobby Jancik, Houston, AFL	24	826	30.3	61	0
1961	Dick Bass, Los Angeles, NFL	23	698	30.3	64	0
	*Dave Grayson, Dall. Texans, AFL	16	453	28.3	73	0
1960	*Tom Moore, Green Bay, NFL	12	397	33.1	84	0
	Ken Hall, Houston, AFL	19	594	31.3	104	1
1959	Abe Woodson, San Francisco	13	382	29.4	105	1
1958	Ollie Matson, Chi. Cardinals	14	497	35.5	101	2
1957	*Jon Arnett, Los Angeles	18	504	28.0	98	1
1956	*Tom Wilson, Los Angeles	15	477	31.8	103	1
1955	Al Carmichael, Green Bay	14	418	29.9	100	1
1954	Billy Reynolds, Cleveland	14	413	29.5	51	0
1953	Joe Arenas, San Francisco	16	551	34.4	82	0
1952	Lynn Chandnois, Pittsburgh	17	599	35.2	93	2
1951	Lynn Chandnois, Pittsburgh	12	390	32.5	55	0
1950	Verda (Vitamin T) Smith, Los Angeles	22	742	33.7	97	3
1949	*Don Doll, Detroit	21	536	25.5	56	0
1948	*Joe Scott, N.Y. Giants	20	569	28.5	99	1
1947	Eddie Saenz, Washington	29	797	27.5	94	2
1946	Abe Karnofsky, Boston	21	599	28.5	97	1
1945	Steve Van Buren, Philadelphia	13	373	28.7	98	1
1944	Bob Thurbon, Card.-Pitt.	12	291	24.3	55	0
1943	Ken Heineman, Brooklyn	16	444	27.8	69	0
1942	Marshall Goldberg, Chi. Cardinals	15	393	26.2	95	1
1941	Marshall Goldberg, Chi. Cardinals	12	290	24.2	41	0

*First season of professional football.

ANNUAL INTERCEPTION LEADERS

Year	Player, Team	No.	Yards	TD
2013	Richard Sherman, Seattle, NFC	8	125	1
	Tashaun Gipson, Cleveland, AFC	5	143	1
	*Logan Ryan, New England, AFC	5	82	1
	Alterraun Verner, Tennessee, AFC	5	68	1
2012	Tim Jennings, Chicago, NFC	9	105	1
	Jairus Byrd, Buffalo, AFC	5	81	0
	Devin McCourty, New England, AFC	5	53	0
2011	Kyle Arrington, New England, AFC	7	92	0
	Eric Weddle, San Diego, AFC	7	89	0
	Charles Woodson, Green Bay, NFC	7	63	1
2010	Ed Reed, Baltimore, AFC	8	183	0
	Asante Samuel, Philadelphia, NFC	7	70	0
2009	*Jairus Byrd, Buffalo, AFC	9	118	0
	Asante Samuel, Philadelphia, NFC	9	117	0
	Darren Sharper, New Orleans, NFC	9	376	3
	Charles Woodson, Green Bay, NFC	9	179	3
2008	Ed Reed, Baltimore, AFC	9	264	2
	Nick Collins, Green Bay, NFC	7	295	3
	Charles Woodson, Green Bay, NFC	7	169	2
2007	Antonio Cromartie, San Diego, AFC	10	144	1
	O.J. Atogwe, St. Louis, NFC	8	125	1
2006	Champ Bailey, Denver, AFC	10	162	1
	Asante Samuel, New England, AFC	10	120	0
	Walt Harris, San Francisco, NFC	8	84	1
	Charles Woodson, Green Bay, NFC	8	61	1
2005	Ty Law, N.Y. Jets, AFC	10	195	1
	Deltha O'Neal, Cincinnati, AFC	10	103	1
	Darren Sharper, Minnesota, NFC	9	276	2
2004	Ed Reed, Baltimore, AFC	9	358	1
	Ken Lucas, Seattle, NFC	6	46	1
	*Chris Gamble, Carolina, NFC	6	15	0
2003	Tony Parrish, San Francisco, NFC	9	202	0
	Brian Russell, Minnesota, NFC	9	185	0
	Ed Reed, Baltimore, AFC	7	132	1
	Marcus Coleman, Houston, AFC	7	95	0
	Patrick Surtain, Miami, AFC	7	59	0
2002	Rod Woodson, Oakland, AFC	8	225	2
	Brian Kelly, Tampa Bay, NFC	8	68	0
2001	*Anthony Henry, Cleveland, AFC	10	177	1
	Ronde Barber, Tampa Bay, NFC	10	86	1
2000	Darren Sharper, Green Bay, NFC	9	109	0
	Samari Rolle, Tennessee, AFC	7	140	1
	Brian Walker, Miami, AFC	7	80	0
1999	Rod Woodson, Baltimore, AFC	7	195	2
	Sam Madison, Miami, AFC	7	164	1
	James Hasty, Kansas City, AFC	7	98	2
	Donnie Abraham, Tampa Bay, NFC	7	115	2
	Troy Vincent, Philadelphia, NFC	7	91	0
1998	Ty Law, New England, AFC	9	133	1
	Kwamie Lassiter, Arizona, NFC	8	80	1
1997	Ryan McNeil, St. Louis, NFC	9	127	1
	Mark McMillian, Kansas City, AFC	8	274	3
	Darryl Williams, Seattle, AFC	8	172	1
1996	Tyrone Braxton, Denver, AFC	9	128	1
	Keith Lyle, St. Louis, NFC	9	152	0
1995	*Orlando Thomas, Minnesota, NFC	9	108	1
	Willie Williams, Pittsburgh, AFC	7	122	1
1994	Eric Turner, Cleveland, AFC	9	199	1
	Aeneas Williams, Arizona, NFC	9	89	0
1993	Eugene Robinson, Seattle, AFC	9	80	1
	Nate Odomes, Buffalo, AFC	9	65	0
	Deion Sanders, Atlanta, NFC	7	91	0
1992	Henry Jones, Buffalo, AFC	8	263	2
	Audray McMillian, Minnesota, NFC	8	157	2
1991	Ronnie Lott, L.A. Raiders, AFC	8	52	0
	Ray Crockett, Detroit, NFC	6	141	1
	Deion Sanders, Atlanta, NFC	6	119	1
	*Aeneas Williams, Phoenix, NFC	6	60	0
	Tim McKyer, Atlanta, NFC	6	24	0
1990	*Mark Carrier, Chicago, NFC	10	39	0
	Richard Johnson, Houston, AFC	8	100	1
1989	Felix Wright, Cleveland, AFC	9	91	1
	Eric Allen, Philadelphia, NFC	8	38	0
1988	Scott Case, Atlanta, NFC	10	47	0
	Erik McMillan, N.Y. Jets, AFC	8	168	2
1987	Barry Wilburn, Washington, NFC	9	135	1
	Mike Prior, Indianapolis, AFC	6	57	0
	Mark Kelso, Buffalo, AFC	6	25	0
	Keith Bostic, Houston, AFC	6	-14	0
1986	Ronnie Lott, San Francisco, NFC	10	134	1
	Deron Cherry, Kansas City, AFC	9	150	0
1985	Everson Walls, Dallas, NFC	9	31	0
	Albert Lewis, Kansas City, AFC	8	59	0
	Eugene Daniel, Indianapolis, AFC	8	53	0
1984	Ken Easley, Seattle, AFC	10	126	2
	*Tom Flynn, Green Bay, NFC	9	106	0
1983	Mark Murphy, Washington, NFC	9	127	0
	Ken Riley, Cincinnati, AFC	8	89	2
	Vann McElroy, L.A. Raiders, AFC	8	68	0
1982	Everson Walls, Dallas, NFC	7	61	0
	Ken Riley, Cincinnati, AFC	5	88	1
	Bobby Jackson, N.Y. Jets, AFC	5	84	1
	Dwayne Woodruff, Pittsburgh, AFC	5	53	0
	Donnie Shell, Pittsburgh, AFC	5	27	0
1981	*Everson Walls, Dallas, NFC	11	133	0
	John Harris, Seattle, AFC	10	155	2
1980	Lester Hayes, Oakland, AFC	13	273	1
	Nolan Cromwell, Los Angeles, NFC	8	140	1
1979	Mike Reinfeldt, Houston, AFC	12	205	0
	Lemar Parrish, Washington, NFC	9	65	0
1978	Thom Darden, Cleveland, AFC	10	200	0
	Ken Stone, St. Louis, NFC	9	139	0
	Willie Buchanon, Green Bay, NFC	9	93	1
1977	Lyle Blackwood, Baltimore, AFC	10	163	0
	Rolland Lawrence, Atlanta, NFC	7	138	0
1976	Monte Jackson, Los Angeles, NFC	10	173	3
	Ken Riley, Cincinnati, AFC	9	141	1
1975	Mel Blount, Pittsburgh, AFC	11	121	0
	Paul Krause, Minnesota, NFC	10	201	0
1974	Emmitt Thomas, Kansas City, AFC	12	214	2
	Ray Brown, Atlanta, NFC	8	164	1
1973	Dick Anderson, Miami, AFC	8	163	2
	Mike Wagner, Pittsburgh, AFC	8	134	0
	Bobby Bryant, Minnesota, NFC	7	105	1
1972	Bill Bradley, Philadelphia, NFC	9	73	0
	Mike Sensibaugh, Kansas City, AFC	8	65	0
1971	Bill Bradley, Philadelphia, NFC	11	248	0
	Ken Houston, Houston, AFC	9	220	4
1970	Johnny Robinson, Kansas City, AFC	10	155	0
	Dick LeBeau, Detroit, NFC	9	96	0
1969	Mel Renfro, Dallas, NFL	10	118	0
	Emmitt Thomas, Kansas City, AFL	9	146	1
1968	Dave Grayson, Oakland, AFL	10	195	1
	Willie Williams, N.Y. Giants, NFL	10	103	0
1967	Miller Farr, Houston, AFL	10	264	3
	*Lem Barney, Detroit, NFL	10	232	3
	Tom Janik, Buffalo, AFL	10	222	2
	Dave Whitsell, New Orleans, NFL	10	178	2
	Dick Westmoreland, Miami, AFL	10	127	1
1966	Larry Wilson, St. Louis, NFL	10	180	2
	Johnny Robinson, Kansas City, AFL	10	136	1
	Bobby Hunt, Kansas City, AFL	10	113	0
1965	W.K. Hicks, Houston, AFL	9	156	0
	Bobby Boyd, Baltimore, NFL	9	78	1
1964	Dainard Paulson, N.Y. Jets, AFL	12	157	1
	*Paul Krause, Washington, NFL	12	140	1
1963	Fred Glick, Houston, AFL	12	180	1
	Dick Lynch, N.Y. Giants, NFL	9	251	3
	Roosevelt Taylor, Chicago, NFL	9	172	1

Year	Player, Team	No.	Yards	TD
1962	Lee Riley, N.Y. Titans, AFL	11	122	0
	Willie Wood, Green Bay, NFL	9	132	0
1961	Billy Atkins, Buffalo, AFL	10	158	0
	Dick Lynch, N.Y. Giants, NFL	9	60	
1960	*Austin (Goose) Gonsoulin, Denver, AFL	11	98	0
	Dave Baker, San Francisco, NFL	10	96	0
	Jerry Norton, St. Louis, NFL	10	96	0
1959	Dean Derby, Pittsburgh	7	127	0
	Milt Davis, Baltimore	7	119	1
	Don Shinnick, Baltimore	7	70	0
1958	Jim Patton, N.Y. Giants	11	183	0
1957	Milt Davis, Baltimore	10	219	2
	Jack Christiansen, Detroit	10	137	1
	Jack Butler, Pittsburgh	10	85	0
1956	Linden Crow, Chi. Cardinals	11	170	0
1955	Will Sherman, Los Angeles	11	101	0
1954	Dick (Night Train) Lane, Chi. Cardinals	10	181	0
1953	Jack Christiansen, Detroit	12	238	1
1952	*Dick (Night Train) Lane, Los Angeles	14	298	2
1951	Otto Schnellbacher, N.Y. Giants	11	194	2
1950	Orban (Spec) Sanders, N.Y. Yanks	13	199	0
1949	Bob Nussbaumer, Chi. Cardinals	12	157	0
1948	*Dan Sandifer, Washington	13	258	2
1947	Frank Reagan, N.Y. Giants	10	203	0
	Frank Seno, Boston	10	100	0
1946	Bill Dudley, Pittsburgh	10	242	1
1945	Roy Zimmerman, Philadelphia	7	90	0
1944	*Howard Livingston, N.Y. Giants	9	172	1
1943	Sammy Baugh, Washington	11	112	0
1942	Clyde (Bulldog) Turner, Chi. Bears	8	96	1
1941	Marshall Goldberg, Chi. Cardinals	7	54	0
	*Art Jones, Pittsburgh	7	35	0
1940	Clarence (Ace) Parker, Brooklyn	6	146	1
	Kent Ryan, Detroit	6	65	0
	Don Hutson, Green Bay	6	24	0

*First season of professional football.

ANNUAL PUNTING LEADERS

Year	Player, Team	No.	Avg.	Long
2013	Marquette King, Oakland, AFC	84	48.9	66
	Andy Lee, San Francisco, NFC	79	48.2	62
2012	Brandon Fields, Miami, AFC	74	50.2	67
	Thomas Morstead, New Orleans, NFC	74	50.1	70
2011	Andy Lee, San Francisco, NFC	78	50.9	68
	Shane Lechler, Oakland, AFC	78	50.8	80
2010	Mat McBriar, Dallas, NFC	65	47.9	65
	Shane Lechler, Oakland, AFC	77	47.0	68
2009	Shane Lechler, Oakland, AFC	96	51.1	70
	Andy Lee, San Francisco, NFC	99	47.6	64
2008	Donnie Jones, St. Louis, NFC	82	50.0	68
	Shane Lechler, Oakland, AFC	90	48.8	70
2007	Shane Lechler, Oakland, AFC	73	49.1	70
	Andy Lee, San Francisco, NFC	105	47.3	74
2006	Mat McBriar, Dallas, NFC	56	48.2	75
	Shane Lechler, Oakland, AFC	77	47.5	67
2005	Brian Moorman, Buffalo, AFC	71	45.7	68
	Josh Bidwell, Tampa Bay, NFC	90	45.6	61
2004	Shane Lechler, Oakland, AFC	73	46.7	67
	Tom Tupa, Washington, NFC	103	44.1	61
2003	Shane Lechler, Oakland, AFC	96	46.9	73
	Todd Sauerbrun, Carolina, NFC	77	44.6	64
2002	Todd Sauerbrun, Carolina, NFC	104	45.5	67
	Chris Hanson, Jacksonville, AFC	81	44.2	64
2001	Todd Sauerbrun, Carolina, NFC	93	47.5	73
	Shane Lechler, Oakland, AFC	73	46.2	65
2000	Darren Bennett, San Diego, AFC	92	46.2	66
	Mitch Berger, Minnesota, NFC	62	44.7	60
1999	Tom Rouen, Denver, AFC	84	46.5	65
	Mitch Berger, Minnesota, NFC	61	45.4	75

Year	Player, Team	No.	Avg.	Long
1998	Craig Hentrich, Tennessee, AFC	69	47.2	71
	Mark Royals, New Orleans, NFC	88	45.6	64
1997	Mark Royals, New Orleans, NFC	88	45.9	66
	Tom Tupa, New England, AFC	78	45.8	73
1996	John Kidd, Miami, AFC	78	46.3	63
	Matt Turk, Washington, NFC	75	45.1	63
1995	Rick Tuten, Seattle, AFC	83	45.0	73
	Sean Landeta, St. Louis, NFC	83	44.3	63
1994	Sean Landeta, L.A. Rams, NFC	78	44.8	62
	Jeff Gossett, L.A. Raiders, AFC	77	43.9	65
1993	Greg Montgomery, Houston, AFC	54	45.6	77
	Jim Arnold, Detroit, NFC	72	44.5	68
1992	Greg Montgomery, Houston, AFC	53	46.9	66
	Harry Newsome, Minnesota, NFC	72	45.0	84
1991	Reggie Roby, Miami, AFC	54	45.7	64
	Harry Newsome, Minnesota, AFC	68	45.5	65
1990	Mike Horan, Denver, AFC	58	44.4	67
	Sean Landeta, N.Y. Giants, NFC	75	44.1	67
1989	Rich Camarillo, Phoenix, NFC	76	43.4	58
	Greg Montgomery, Houston, AFC	56	43.3	63
1988	Harry Newsome, Pittsburgh, AFC	65	45.4	62
	Jim Arnold, Detroit, NFC	97	42.4	69
1987	Rick Donnelly, Atlanta, NFC	61	44.0	62
	Ralf Mojsiejenko, San Diego, AFC	67	42.9	57
1986	Rohn Stark, Indianapolis, AFC	76	45.2	63
	Sean Landeta, N.Y. Giants, NFC	79	44.8	61
1985	Rohn Stark, Indianapolis, AFC	78	45.9	68
	*Rick Donnelly, Atlanta, NFC	59	43.6	68
1984	Jim Arnold, Kansas City, AFC	98	44.9	63
	*Brian Hansen, New Orleans, NFC	69	43.8	66
1983	Rohn Stark, Baltimore, AFC	91	45.3	68
	Frank Garcia, Tampa Bay, NFC	95	42.2	64
1982	Luke Prestridge, Denver, AFC	45	45.0	63
	Carl Birdsong, St. Louis, NFC	54	43.8	65
1981	Pat McInally, Cincinnati, AFC	72	45.4	62
	Tom Skladany, Detroit, NFC	64	43.5	74
1980	Dave Jennings, N.Y. Giants, NFC	94	44.8	63
	Luke Prestridge, Denver, AFC	70	43.9	57
1979	*Bob Grupp, Kansas City, AFC	89	43.6	74
	Dave Jennings, N.Y. Giants, NFC	104	42.7	72
1978	Pat McInally, Cincinnati, AFC	91	43.1	65
	*Tom Skladany, Detroit, NFC	86	42.5	63
1977	Ray Guy, Oakland, AFC	59	43.3	74
	Tom Blanchard, New Orleans, NFC	82	42.4	66
1976	Marv Bateman, Buffalo, AFC	86	42.8	78
	John James, Atlanta, NFC	101	42.1	67
1975	Ray Guy, Oakland, AFC	68	43.8	64
	Herman Weaver, Detroit, NFC	80	42.0	61
1974	Ray Guy, Oakland, AFC	74	42.2	66
	Tom Blanchard, New Orleans, NFC	88	42.1	71
1973	Jerrel Wilson, Kansas City, AFC	80	45.5	68
	*Tom Wittum, San Francisco, NFC	79	43.7	62
1972	Jerrel Wilson, Kansas City, AFC	66	44.8	69
	Dave Chapple, Los Angeles, NFC	53	44.2	70
1971	Dave Lewis, Cincinnati, AFC	72	44.8	56
	Tom McNeill, Philadelphia, NFC	73	42.0	64
1970	Dave Lewis, Cincinnati, AFC	79	46.2	63
	*Julian Fagan, New Orleans, NFC	77	42.5	64
1969	David Lee, Baltimore, NFL	57	45.3	66
	Dennis Partee, San Diego, AFL	71	44.6	62
1968	Jerrel Wilson, Kansas City, AFL	63	45.1	70
	Billy Lothridge, Atlanta, NFL	75	44.3	70
1967	Bob Scarpitto, Denver, AFL	105	44.9	73
	Billy Lothridge, Atlanta, NFL	87	43.7	62
1966	Bob Scarpitto, Denver, AFL	76	45.8	70
	*David Lee, Baltimore, NFL	49	45.6	64
1965	Gary Collins, Cleveland, NFL	65	46.7	71
	Jerrel Wilson, Kansas City, AFL	69	45.4	64
1964	Bobby Walden, Minnesota, NFL	72	46.4	73
	Jim Fraser, Denver, AFL	73	44.2	67

Year	Player, Team	No.	Avg.	Long
1963	Yale Lary, Detroit, NFL	35	48.9	73
	Jim Fraser, Denver, AFL	81	44.4	66
1962	Tommy Davis, San Francisco, NFL	48	45.6	82
	Jim Fraser, Denver, AFL	55	43.6	75
1961	Yale Lary, Detroit, NFL	52	48.4	71
	Billy Atkins, Buffalo, AFL	85	44.5	70
1960	Jerry Norton, St. Louis, NFL	39	45.6	62
	*Paul Maguire, L.A. Chargers, AFL	43	40.5	61
1959	Yale Lary, Detroit	45	47.1	67
1958	Sam Baker, Washington	48	45.4	64
1957	Don Chandler, N.Y. Giants	60	44.6	61
1956	Norm Van Brocklin, Los Angeles	48	43.1	72
1955	Norm Van Brocklin, Los Angeles	60	44.6	61
1954	Pat Brady, Pittsburgh	66	43.2	72
1953	Pat Brady, Pittsburgh	80	46.9	64
1952	Horace Gillom, Cleveland	61	45.7	73
1951	Horace Gillom, Cleveland	73	45.5	66
1950	*Fred (Curly) Morrison, Chi. Bears	57	43.3	65
1949	*Mike Boyda, N.Y. Bulldogs	56	44.2	61
1948	Joe Muha, Philadelphia	57	47.3	82
1947	Jack Jacobs, Green Bay	57	43.5	74
1946	Roy McKay, Green Bay	64	42.7	64
1945	Roy McKay, Green Bay	44	41.2	73
1944	Frank Sinkwich, Detroit	45	41.0	73
1943	Sammy Baugh, Washington	50	45.9	81
1942	Sammy Baugh, Washington	37	48.2	74
1941	Sammy Baugh, Washington	30	48.7	75
1940	Sammy Baugh, Washington	35	51.4	85
1939	*Parker Hall, Cleveland	58	40.8	80

First season of professional football.

ANNUAL LEADERS IN SACKS (SINCE 1982)

Year	Player, Team	Sacks
2013	Robert Mathis, Indianapolis, AFC	19.5
	Robert Quinn, St. Louis, NFC	19.0
2012	J.J. Watt, Houston, AFC	20.5
	Aldon Smith, San Francisco, NFC	19.5
2011	Jared Allen, Minnesota, NFC.	22.0
	Terrell Suggs, Baltimore, AFC	14.0
2010	DeMarcus Ware, Dallas, NFC	15.5
	Tamba Hali, Kansas City, AFC	14.5
2009	Elvis Dumervil, Denver, AFC	17.0
	Jared Allen, Minnesota, NFC	14.5
2008	DeMarcus Ware, Dallas, NFC	20.0
	Joey Porter, Miami, AFC	17.5
2007	Jared Allen, Kansas City, AFC	15.5
	Patrick Kerney, Seattle, NFC	14.5
2006	Shawne Merriman, San Diego, AFC	17.0
	Aaron Kampman, Green Bay, NFC	15.5
2005	Derrick Burgess, Oakland, AFC	16.0
	Osi Umenyiora, N.Y. Giants, NFC	14.5
2004	Dwight Freeney, Indianapolis, AFC	16.0
	Bertrand Berry, Arizona, NFC	14.5
2003	Michael Strahan, N.Y. Giants, NFC	18.5
	Adewale Ogunleye, Miami, AFC	15.0
2002	Jason Taylor, Miami, AFC	18.5
	Simeon Rice, Tampa Bay, NFC	15.5
2001	Michael Strahan, N.Y. Giants, NFC	22.5
	Peter Boulware, Baltimore, AFC	15.0
2000	La'Roi Glover, New Orleans, NFC	17.0
	Trace Armstrong, Miami, AFC	16.5
1999	Kevin Carter, St. Louis, NFC	17.0
	*Jevon Kearse, Tennessee, AFC	14.5
1998	Michael Sinclair, Seattle, AFC	16.5
	Reggie White, Green Bay, NFC	16.0
1997	John Randle, Minnesota, NFC	15.5
	Bruce Smith, Buffalo, AFC	14.0
1996	Kevin Greene, Carolina, NFC	14.5
	Michael McCrary, Seattle, AFC	13.5
	Bruce Smith, Buffalo, AFC	13.5

Year	Player, Team	Sacks
1995	Bryce Paup, Buffalo, AFC	17.5
	William Fuller, Philadelphia, NFC	13.0
	Wayne Martin, New Orleans, NFC	13.0
1994	Kevin Greene, Pittsburgh, AFC	14.0
	Ken Harvey, Washington, NFC	13.5
	John Randle, Minnesota, NFC	13.5
1993	Neil Smith, Kansas City, AFC	15.0
	Renaldo Turnbull, New Orleans, NFC	13.0
	Reggie White, Green Bay, NFC	13.0
1992	Clyde Simmons, Philadelphia, NFC	19.0
	Leslie O'Neal, San Diego, AFC	17.0
1991	Pat Swilling, New Orleans, NFC	17.0
	William Fuller, Houston, AFC	15.0
1990	Derrick Thomas, Kansas City, AFC	20.0
	Charles Haley, San Francisco, NFC	16.0
1989	Chris Doleman, Minnesota, NFC	21.0
	Lee Williams, San Diego, AFC	14.0
1988	Reggie White, Philadelphia, NFC	18.0
	Greg Townsend, L.A. Raiders, AFC	11.5
1987	Reggie White, Philadelphia, NFC	21.0
	Andre Tippett, New England, AFC	12.5
1986	Lawrence Taylor, N.Y. Giants, NFC	20.5
	Sean Jones, L.A. Raiders, AFC	15.5
1985	Richard Dent, Chicago, NFC	17.0
	Andre Tippett, New England, AFC	16.5
1984	Mark Gastineau, N.Y. Jets, AFC	22.0
	Richard Dent, Chicago, NFC	17.5
1983	Mark Gastineau, N.Y. Jets, AFC	19.0
	Fred Dean, San Francisco, NFC	17.5
1982	Doug Martin, Minnesota, NFC	11.5
	Jesse Baker, Houston, AFC	7.5

First season of professional football.

POINTS SCORED

Year	Team	Points
2013	Denver, AFC	606
	Chicago, NFC	445
2012	New England, AFC	557
	New Orleans, NFC	461
2011	Green Bay, NFC	560
	New England, AFC	513
2010	New England, AFC	518
	Philadelphia, NFC	439
2009	New Orleans, NFC	510
	San Diego, AFC	454
2008	New Orleans, NFC	463
	San Diego, AFC	439
2007	New England, AFC	589
	Dallas, NFC	455
2006	San Diego, AFC	492
	Chicago, NFC	427
2005	Seattle, NFC	452
	Indianapolis, AFC	439
2004	Indianapolis, AFC	522
	Green Bay, NFC	424
2003	Kansas City, AFC	484
	St. Louis, NFC	447
2002	Kansas City, AFC	467
	New Orleans, NFC	432
2001	St. Louis, NFC	503
	Indianapolis, AFC	413
2000	St. Louis, NFC	540
	Denver, AFC	485
1999	St. Louis, NFC	526
	Indianapolis, AFC	423
1998	Minnesota, NFC	556
	Denver, AFC	501
1997	Denver, AFC	472
	Green Bay, NFC	422

Year	Team	Points
1996	Green Bay, NFC	456
	New England, AFC	418
1995	San Francisco, NFC	457
	Pittsburgh, AFC	407
1994	San Francisco, NFC	505
	Miami, AFC	389
1993	San Francisco, NFC	473
	Denver, AFC	373
1992	San Francisco, NFC	431
	Buffalo, AFC	381
1991	Washington, NFC	485
	Buffalo, AFC	458
1990	Buffalo, AFC	428
	Philadelphia, NFC	396
1989	San Francisco, NFC	442
	Buffalo, AFC	409
1988	Cincinnati, AFC	448
	L.A. Rams, NFC	407
1987	San Francisco, NFC	459
	Cleveland, AFC	390
1986	Miami, AFC	430
	Minnesota, NFC	398
1985	San Diego, AFC	467
	Chicago, NFC	456
1984	Miami, AFC	513
	San Francisco, NFC	475
1983	Washington, NFC	541
	L.A. Raiders, AFC	442
1982	San Diego, AFC	288
	Dallas, NFC	226
	Green Bay, NFC	226
1981	San Diego, AFC	478
	Atlanta, NFC	426
1980	Dallas, NFC	454
	New England, AFC	441
1979	Pittsburgh, AFC	416
	Dallas, NFC	371
1978	Dallas, NFC	384
	Miami, AFC	372
1977	Oakland, AFC	351
	Dallas, NFC	345
1976	Baltimore, AFC	417
	Los Angeles, NFC	351
1975	Buffalo, AFC	420
	Minnesota, NFC	377
1974	Oakland, AFC	355
	Washington, NFC	320
1973	Los Angeles, NFC	388
	Denver, AFC	354
1972	Miami, AFC	385
	San Francisco, NFC	353
1971	Dallas, NFC	406
	Oakland, AFC	344
1970	San Francisco, NFC	352
	Baltimore, AFC	321
1969	Minnesota, NFL	379
	Oakland, AFL	377
1968	Oakland, AFL	453
	Dallas, NFL	431
1967	Oakland, AFL	468
	Los Angeles, NFL	398
1966	Kansas City, AFL	448
	Dallas, NFL	445
1965	San Francisco, NFL	421
	San Diego, AFL	340
1964	Baltimore, NFL	428
	Buffalo, AFL	400
1963	N.Y. Giants, NFL	448
	San Diego, AFL	399

Year	Team	Points
1962	Green Bay, NFL	415
	Dall. Texans, AFL	389
1961	Houston, AFL	513
	Green Bay, NFL	391
1960	N.Y. Titans, AFL	382
	Cleveland, NFL	362
1959	Baltimore	374
1958	Baltimore	381
1957	Los Angeles	307
1956	Chi. Bears	363
1955	Cleveland	349
1954	Detroit	337
1953	San Francisco	372
1952	Los Angeles	349
1951	Los Angeles	392
1950	Los Angeles	466
1949	Philadelphia	364
1948	Chi. Cardinals	395
1947	Chi. Bears	363
1946	Chi. Bears	289
1945	Philadelphia	272
1944	Philadelphia	267
1943	Chi. Bears	303
1942	Chi. Bears	376
1941	Chi. Bears	396
1940	Washington	245
1939	Chi. Bears	298
1938	Green Bay	223
1937	Green Bay	220
1936	Green Bay	248
1935	Chi. Bears	192
1934	Chi. Bears	286
1933	N.Y. Giants	244
1932	Chi. Bears	160

TOTAL YARDS GAINED

Year	Team	Yards
2013	Denver, AFC	7,317
	Philadelphia, NFC	6,676
2012	New England, AFC	6,846
	New Orleans, NFC	6,574
2011	New Orleans, NFC	7,474
	New England, AFC	6,848
2010	San Diego, AFC	6,329
	Philadelphia, NFC	6,230
2009	New Orleans, NFC	6,461
	New England, AFC	6,357
2008	New Orleans, NFC	6,571
	Denver, AFC	6,333
2007	New England, AFC	6,580
	Green Bay, NFC	5,931
2006	New Orleans, NFC	6,264
	Indianapolis, AFC	6,070
2005	Kansas City, AFC	6,192
	Seattle, NFC	5,915
2004	Kansas City, AFC	6,695
	Green Bay, NFC	6,357
2003	Minnesota, NFC	6,294
	Kansas City, AFC	5,910
2002	Oakland, AFC	6,237
	Minnesota, NFC	6,192
2001	St. Louis, NFC	6,690
	Indianapolis, AFC	5,955
2000	St. Louis, NFC	7,075
	Denver, AFC	6,554
1999	St. Louis, NFC	6,412
	Indianapolis, AFC	5,726
1998	San Francisco, NFC	6,800
	Denver, AFC	6,092

Year	Team	Yards	Year	Team	Yards
1997	Denver, AFC	5,872	1962	N.Y. Giants, NFL	5,005
	Detroit, NFC	5,798		Houston, AFL	4,971
1996	Denver, AFC	5,791	1961	Houston, AFL	6,288
	Philadelphia, NFC	5,627		Philadelphia, NFL	5,112
1995	Detroit, NFC	6,113	1960	Houston, AFL	4,936
	Denver, AFC	6,040		Baltimore, NFL	4,245
1994	Miami, AFC	6,078	1959	Baltimore	4,458
	San Francisco, NFC	6,060	1958	Baltimore	4,539
1993	San Francisco, NFC	6,435	1957	Los Angeles	4,143
	Miami, AFC	5,812	1956	Chi. Bears	4,537
1992	San Francisco, NFC	6,195	1955	Chi. Bears	4,316
	Buffalo, AFC	5,893	1954	Los Angeles	5,187
1991	Buffalo, AFC	6,252	1953	Philadelphia	4,811
	San Francisco, NFC	5,858	1952	Cleveland	4,352
1990	Houston, AFC	6,222	1951	Los Angeles	5,506
	San Francisco, NFC	5,895	1950	Los Angeles	5,420
1989	San Francisco, NFC	6,268	1949	Chi. Bears	4,873
	Cincinnati, AFC	6,101	1948	Chi. Cardinals	4,705
1988	Cincinnati, AFC	6,057	1947	Chi. Bears	5,053
	San Francisco, NFC	5,900	1946	Los Angeles	3,793
1987	San Francisco, NFC	5,987	1945	Washington	3,549
	Denver, AFC	5,624	1944	Chi. Bears	3,239
1986	Cincinnati, AFC	6,490	1943	Chi. Bears	4,045
	San Francisco, NFC	6,082	1942	Chi. Bears	3,900
1985	San Diego, AFC	6,535	1941	Chi. Bears	4,265
	San Francisco, NFC	5,920	1940	Green Bay	3,400
1984	Miami, AFC	6,936	1939	Chi. Bears	3,988
	San Francisco, NFC	6,366	1938	Green Bay	3,037
1983	San Diego, AFC	6,197	1937	Green Bay	3,201
	Green Bay, NFC	6,172	1936	Detroit	3,703
1982	San Diego, AFC	4,048	1935	Chi. Bears	3,454
	San Francisco, NFC	3,242	1934	Chi. Bears	3,900
1981	San Diego, AFC	6,744	1933	N.Y. Giants	2,973
	Detroit, NFC	5,933	1932	Chi. Bears	2,755
1980	San Diego, AFC	6,410			
	Los Angeles, NFC	6,006	**YARDS RUSHING**		
1979	Pittsburgh, AFC	6,258	Year	Team	Yards
	Dallas, NFC	5,968	2013	Philadelphia, NFC	2,566
1978	New England, AFC	5,965		Buffalo, AFC	2,307
	Dallas, NFC	5,959	2012	Washington, NFC	2,709
1977	Dallas, NFC	4,812		Kansas City, AFC	2,395
	Oakland, AFC	4,736	2011	Denver, AFC	2,632
1976	Baltimore, AFC	5,236		Carolina, NFC	2,408
	St. Louis, NFC	5,136	2010	Kansas City, AFC	2,627
1975	Buffalo, AFC	5,467		Philadelphia, NFC	2,324
	Dallas, NFC	5,025	2009	N.Y. Jets, AFC	2,756
1974	Dallas, NFC	4,983		Carolina, NFC	2,498
	Oakland, AFC	4,718	2008	N.Y. Giants, NFC	2,518
1973	Los Angeles, NFC	4,906		Baltimore, AFC	2,376
	Oakland, AFC	4,773	2007	Minnesota, NFC	2,634
1972	Miami, AFC	5,036		Jacksonville, AFC	2,391
	N.Y. Giants, NFC	4,483	2006	Atlanta, NFC	2,939
1971	Dallas, NFC	5,035		San Diego, AFC	2,578
	San Diego, AFC	4,738	2005	Atlanta, NFC	2,546
1970	Oakland, AFC	4,829		Denver, AFC	2,539
	San Francisco, NFC	4,503	2004	Atlanta, NFC	2,672
1969	Dallas, NFL	5,122		Pittsburgh, AFC	2,464
	Oakland, AFL	5,036	2003	Baltimore, AFC	2,674
1968	Oakland, AFL	5,696		Green Bay, NFC	2,558
	Dallas, NFL	5,117	2002	Minnesota, NFC	2,507
1967	N.Y. Jets, AFL	5,152		Miami, AFC	2,502
	Baltimore, NFL	5,008	2001	Pittsburgh, AFC	2,774
1966	Dallas, NFL	5,145		San Francisco, NFC	2,244
	Kansas City, AFL	5,114	2000	Oakland, AFC	2,470
1965	San Francisco, NFL	5,270		Minnesota, NFC	2,129
	San Diego, AFL	5,188	1999	San Francisco, NFC	2,095
1964	Buffalo, AFL	5,206		Jacksonville, AFC	2,091
	Baltimore, NFL	4,779	1998	San Francisco, NFC	2,544
1963	San Diego, AFL	5,153		Denver, AFC	2,468
	N.Y. Giants, NFL	5,024			

Year	Team	Yards	Year	Team	Yards
1997	Pittsburgh, AFC	2,479	1962	Buffalo, AFL	2,480
	Detroit, NFC	2,464		Green Bay, NFL	2,460
1996	Denver, AFC	2,362	1961	Green Bay, NFL	2,350
	Washington, NFC	1,910		Dall. Texans, AFL	2,189
1995	Kansas City, AFC	2,222	1960	St. Louis, NFL	2,356
	Dallas, NFC	2,201		Oakland, AFL	2,056
1994	Pittsburgh, AFC	2,180	1959	Cleveland	2,149
	Detroit, NFC	2,080	1958	Cleveland	2,526
1993	N.Y. Giants, NFC	2,210	1957	Los Angeles	2,142
	Seattle, AFC	2,015	1956	Chi. Bears	2,468
1992	Buffalo, AFC	2,436	1955	Chi. Bears	2,388
	Philadelphia, NFC	2,388	1954	San Francisco	2,498
1991	Buffalo, AFC	2,381	1953	San Francisco	2,230
	Minnesota, NFC	2,201	1952	San Francisco	1,905
1990	Philadelphia, NFC	2,556	1951	Chi. Bears	2,408
	San Diego, AFC	2,257	1950	N.Y. Giants	2,336
1989	Cincinnati, AFC	2,483	1949	Philadelphia	2,607
	Chicago, NFC	2,287	1948	Chi. Cardinals	2,560
1988	Cincinnati, AFC	2,710	1947	Los Angeles	2,171
	San Francisco, NFC	2,523	1946	Green Bay	1,765
1987	San Francisco, NFC	2,237	1945	Cleveland	1,714
	L.A. Raiders, AFC	2,197	1944	Philadelphia	1,661
1986	Chicago, NFC	2,700	1943	Phil-Pitt	1,730
	Cincinnati, AFC	2,533	1942	Chi. Bears	1,881
1985	Chicago, NFC	2,761	1941	Chi. Bears	2,263
	Indianapolis, AFC	2,439	1940	Chi. Bears	1,818
1984	Chicago, NFC	2,974	1939	Chi. Bears	2,043
	N.Y. Jets, AFC	2,189	1938	Detroit	1,893
1983	Chicago, NFC	2,727	1937	Detroit	2,074
	Baltimore, AFC	2,695	1936	Detroit	2,885
1982	Buffalo, AFC	1,371	1935	Chi. Bears	2,096
	Dallas, NFC	1,313	1934	Chi. Bears	2,847
1981	Detroit, NFC	2,795	1933	Boston	2,260
	Kansas City, AFC	2,633	1932	Chi. Bears	1,770
1980	Los Angeles, NFC	2,799			
	Houston, AFC	2,635			

YARDS PASSING

Leadership in this category has been based on net yards since 1952.

Year	Team	Yards
1979	N.Y. Jets, AFC	2,646
	St. Louis, NFC	2,582
1978	New England, AFC	3,165
	Dallas, NFC	2,783
1977	Chicago, NFC	2,811
	Oakland, AFC	2,627
1976	Pittsburgh, AFC	2,971
	Los Angeles, NFC	2,528
1975	Buffalo, AFC	2,974
	Dallas, NFC	2,432
1974	Dallas, NFC	2,454
	Pittsburgh, AFC	2,417
1973	Buffalo, AFC	3,088
	Los Angeles, NFC,	2,925
1972	Miami, AFC	2,960
	Chicago, NFC	2,360
1971	Miami, AFC	2,429
	Detroit, NFC	2,376
1970	Dallas, NFC	2,300
	Miami, AFC	2,082
1969	Dallas, NFL	2,276
	Kansas City, AFL	2,220
1968	Chicago, NFL	2,377
	Kansas City, AFL	2,227
1967	Cleveland, NFL	2,139
	Houston, AFL	2,122
1966	Kansas City, AFL	2,274
	Cleveland, NFL	2,166
1965	Cleveland, NFL	2,331
	San Diego, AFL	2,085
1964	Green Bay, NFL	2,276
	Buffalo, AFL	2,040
1963	Cleveland, NFL	2,639
	San Diego, AFL	2,203

YARDS PASSING

Leadership in this category has been based on net yards since 1952.

Year	Team	Yards
2013	Denver, AFC	5,444
	New Orleans, NFC	4,918
2012	New Orleans, NFC	4,997
	New England, AFC	4,662
2011	New Orleans, NFC	5,347
	New England, AFC	5,084
2010	Indianapolis, AFC	4,609
	New Orleans, NFC	4,441
2009	Houston, AFC	4,654
	New Orleans, NFC	4,355
2008	New Orleans, NFC	4,977
	Denver, AFC	4,471
2007	New England, AFC	4,731
	Green Bay, NFC	4,334
2006	New Orleans, NFC	4,503
	Indianapolis, AFC	4,308
2005	Arizona, NFC	4,437
	New England, AFC	4,120
2004	Indianapolis, AFC	4,623
	Minnesota, NFC	4,516
2003	Indianapolis, AFC	4,179
	St. Louis, NFC	3,961
2002	Oakland, AFC	4,475
	St. Louis, NFC	4,154
2001	St. Louis, NFC	4,663
	Indianapolis, AFC	3,989
2000	St. Louis, NFC	5,232
	Indianapolis, AFC	4,282
1999	St. Louis, NFC	4,353
	Indianapolis, AFC	4,066

Year	Team	Yards
1998	Minnesota, NFC	4,328
	N.Y. Jets, AFC	3,836
1997	Seattle, AFC	3,959
	Green Bay, NFC	3,705
1996	Jacksonville, AFC	4,110
	Philadelphia, NFC	3,745
1995	San Francisco, NFC	4,608
	Miami, AFC	4,210
1994	New England, AFC	4,444
	Minnesota, NFC	4,324
1993	Miami, AFC	4,353
	San Francisco, NFC	4,302
1992	Houston, AFC	4,029
	San Francisco, NFC	3,880
1991	Houston, AFC	4,621
	San Francisco, NFC	3,997
1990	Houston, AFC	4,805
	San Francisco, NFC	4,177
1989	Washington, NFC	4,349
	Miami, AFC	4,216
1988	Miami, AFC	4,516
	Washington, NFC	4,136
1987	Miami, AFC	3,876
	San Francisco, NFC	3,750
1986	Miami, AFC	4,779
	San Francisco, NFC	4,096
1985	San Diego, AFC	4,870
	Dallas, NFC	3,861
1984	Miami, AFC	5,018
	St. Louis, NFC	4,257
1983	San Diego, AFC	4,661
	Green Bay, NFC	4,365
1982	San Diego, AFC	2,927
	San Francisco, NFC	2,502
1981	San Diego, AFC	4,739
	Minnesota, NFC	4,333
1980	San Diego, AFC	4,531
	Minnesota, NFC	3,688
1979	San Diego, AFC	3,915
	San Francisco, NFC	3,641
1978	San Diego, AFC	3,375
	Minnesota, NFC	3,243
1977	Buffalo, AFC	2,530
	St. Louis, NFC	2,499
1976	Baltimore, AFC	2,933
	Minnesota, NFC	2,855
1975	Cincinnati, AFC	3,241
	Washington, NFC	2,917
1974	Washington, NFC	2,978
	Cincinnati, AFC	2,804
1973	Philadelphia, NFC	2,998
	Denver, AFC	2,519
1972	N.Y. Jets, AFC	2,777
	San Francisco, NFC	2,735
1971	San Diego, AFC	3,134
	Dallas, NFC	2,786
1970	San Francisco, NFC	2,923
	Oakland, AFC	2,865
1969	Oakland, AFL	3,271
	San Francisco, NFL	3,158
1968	San Diego, AFL	3,623
	Dallas, NFL	3,026
1967	N.Y. Jets, AFL	3,845
	Washington, NFL	3,730
1966	N.Y. Jets, AFL	3,464
	Dallas, NFL	3,023
1965	San Francisco, NFL	3,487
	San Diego, AFL	3,103
1964	Houston, AFL	3,527
	Chicago, NFL	2,841

Year	Team	Yards
1963	Baltimore, NFL	3,296
	Houston, AFL	3,222
1962	Denver, AFL	3,404
	Philadelphia, NFL	3,385
1961	Houston, AFL	4,392
	Philadelphia, NFL	3,605
1960	Houston, AFL	3,203
	Baltimore, NFL	2,956
1959	Baltimore	2,753
1958	Pittsburgh	2,752
1957	Baltimore	2,388
1956	Los Angeles	2,419
1955	Philadelphia	2,472
1954	Chi. Bears	3,104
1953	Philadelphia	3,089
1952	Cleveland	2,566
1951	Los Angeles	3,296
1950	Los Angeles	3,709
1949	Chi. Bears	3,055
1948	Washington	2,861
1947	Washington	3,336
1946	Los Angeles	2,080
1945	Chi. Bears	1,857
1944	Washington	2,021
1943	Chi. Bears	2,310
1942	Green Bay	2,407
1941	Chi. Bears	2,002
1940	Washington	1,887
1939	Chi. Bears	1,965
1938	Washington	1,536
1937	Green Bay	1,398
1936	Green Bay	1,629
1935	Green Bay	1,449
1934	Green Bay	1,165
1933	N.Y. Giants	1,348
1932	Chi. Bears	1,013

FEWEST POINTS ALLOWED

Year	Team	Points
2013	Seattle, NFC	231
	Cincinnati, AFC	305
	Kansas City, AFC	305
2012	Seattle, NFC	245
	Denver, AFC	289
2011	Pittsburgh, AFC	227
	San Francisco, NFC	229
2010	Pittsburgh, AFC	232
	Green Bay, NFC	240
2009	N.Y. Jets, AFC	236
	Dallas, NFC	250
2008	Pittsburgh, AFC	223
	Philadelphia, NFC	289
2007	Indianapolis, AFC	262
	Tampa Bay, NFC	270
2006	Baltimore, AFC	201
	Chicago, NFC	255
2005	Chicago, NFC	202
	Indianapolis, AFC	247
2004	Pittsburgh, AFC	251
	Philadelphia, NFC	260
2003	New England, AFC	238
	Dallas, NFC	260
2002	Tampa Bay, NFC	196
	Miami, AFC	301
2001	Chicago, NFC	203
	Pittsburgh, AFC	212
2000	Baltimore, AFC	165
	Philadelphia, NFC	245
1999	Jacksonville, AFC	217
	Tampa Bay, NFC	235

Year	Team	Points
1998	Miami, AFC	265
	Dallas, NFC	275
1997	Kansas City, AFC	232
	Tampa Bay, NFC	263
1996	Green Bay, NFC	210
	Pittsburgh, AFC	257
1995	Kansas City, AFC	241
	San Francisco, NFC	258
1994	Cleveland, AFC	204
	Dallas, NFC	248
1993	N.Y. Giants, NFC	205
	Houston, AFC	238
1992	New Orleans, NFC	202
	Pittsburgh, AFC	225
1991	New Orleans, NFC	211
	Denver, AFC	235
1990	N.Y. Giants, NFC	211
	Pittsburgh, AFC	240
1989	Denver, AFC	226
	N.Y. Giants, NFC	252
1988	Chicago, NFC	215
	Buffalo, AFC	237
1987	Indianapolis, AFC	238
	San Francisco, NFC	253
1986	Chicago, NFC	187
	Seattle, AFC	293
1985	Chicago, NFC	198
	N.Y. Jets, AFC	264
1984	San Francisco, NFC	227
	Denver, AFC	241
1983	Miami, AFC	250
	Detroit, NFC	286
1982	Washington, NFC	128
	Miami, AFC	131
1981	Philadelphia, NFC	221
	Miami, AFC	275
1980	Philadelphia, NFC	222
	Houston, AFC	251
1979	Tampa Bay, NFC	237
	San Diego, AFC	246
1978	Pittsburgh, AFC	195
	Dallas, NFC	208
1977	Atlanta, NFC	129
	Denver, AFC	148
1976	Pittsburgh, AFC	138
	Minnesota, NFC	176
1975	Los Angeles, NFC	135
	Pittsburgh, AFC	162
1974	Los Angeles, NFC	181
	Pittsburgh, AFC	189
1973	Miami, AFC	150
	Minnesota, NFC	168
1972	Miami, AFC	171
	Washington, NFC	218
1971	Minnesota, NFC	139
	Baltimore, AFC	140
1970	Minnesota, NFC	143
	Miami, AFC	228
1969	Minnesota, NFL	133
	Kansas City, AFL	177
1968	Baltimore, NFL	144
	Kansas City, AFL	170
1967	Los Angeles, NFL	196
	Houston, AFL	199
1966	Green Bay, NFL	163
	Buffalo, AFL	255
1965	Green Bay, NFL	224
	Buffalo, AFL	226
1964	Baltimore, NFL	225
	Buffalo, AFL	242

Year	Team	Points
1963	Chicago, NFL	144
	San Diego, AFL	255
1962	Green Bay, NFL	148
	Dall. Texans, AFL	233
1961	San Diego, AFL	219
	N.Y. Giants, NFL	220
1960	San Francisco, NFL	205
	Dall. Texans, AFL	253
1959	N.Y. Giants	170
1958	N.Y. Giants	183
1957	Cleveland	172
1956	Cleveland	177
1955	Cleveland	218
1954	Cleveland	162
1953	Cleveland	162
1952	Detroit	192
1951	Cleveland	152
1950	Philadelphia	141
1949	Philadelphia	134
1948	Chi. Bears	151
1947	Green Bay	210
1946	Pittsburgh	117
1945	Washington	121
1944	N.Y. Giants	75
1943	Washington	137
1942	Chi. Bears	84
1941	N.Y. Giants	114
1940	Brooklyn	120
1939	N.Y. Giants	85
1938	N.Y. Giants	79
1937	Chi. Bears	100
1936	Chi. Bears	94
1935	Green Bay	96
	N.Y. Giants	96
1934	Detroit	59
1933	Brooklyn	54
1932	Chi. Bears	44

FEWEST TOTAL YARDS ALLOWED

Year	Team	Yards
2013	Seattle, NFC	4,378
	Cincinnati, AFC	4,888
2012	Pittsburgh, AFC	4,413
	San Francisco, NFC	4,710
2011	Pittsburgh, AFC	4,348
	San Francisco, NFC	4,931
2010	San Diego, AFC	4,345
	New Orleans, NFC	4,900
2009	N.Y. Jets, AFC	4,037
	Green Bay, NFC	4,551
2008	Pittsburgh, AFC	3,795
	Philadelphia, NFC	4,389
2007	Pittsburgh, AFC	4,262
	Tampa Bay, NFC	4,454
2006	Baltimore, AFC	4,225
	Chicago, NFC	4,706
2005	Tampa Bay, NFC	4,444
	Pittsburgh, AFC	4,544
2004	Pittsburgh, AFC	4,134
	Washington, NFC	4,281
2003	Dallas, NFC	4,056
	Buffalo, AFC	4,313
2002	Tampa Bay, NFC	4,044
	Miami, AFC	4,656
2001	Pittsburgh, AFC	4,137
	St. Louis, NFC	4,471
2000	Tennessee, AFC	3,813
	Washington, NFC	4,474
1999	Buffalo, AFC	4,045
	Tampa Bay, NFC	4,280

Year	Team	Yards
1998	San Diego, AFC	4,208
	Tampa Bay, NFC	4,345
1997	San Francisco, NFC	4,013
	Denver, AFC	4,671
1996	Green Bay, NFC	4,156
	Pittsburgh, AFC	4,362
1995	San Francisco, NFC	4,398
	Kansas City, AFC	4,549
1994	Dallas, NFC	4,313
	Pittsburgh, AFC	4,326
1993	Minnesota, NFC	4,406
	Pittsburgh, AFC	4,531
1992	Dallas, NFC	3,931
	Houston, AFC	4,211
1991	Philadelphia, NFC	3,549
	Denver, AFC	4,549
1990	Pittsburgh, AFC	4,115
	N.Y. Giants, NFC	4,206
1989	Minnesota, NFC	4,184
	Kansas City, AFC	4,293
1988	Minnesota, NFC	4,091
	Buffalo, AFC	4,578
1987	San Francisco, NFC	4,095
	Cleveland, AFC	4,264
1986	Chicago, NFC	4,130
	L.A. Raiders, AFC	4,804
1985	Chicago, NFC	4,135
	L.A. Raiders, AFC	4,603
1984	Chicago, NFC	3,863
	Cleveland, AFC	4,641
1983	Cincinnati, AFC	4,327
	New Orleans, NFC	4,691
1982	Miami, AFC	2,312
	Tampa Bay, NFC	2,442
1981	Philadelphia, NFC	4,447
	N.Y. Jets, AFC	4,871
1980	Buffalo, AFC	4,101
	Philadelphia, NFC	4,443
1979	Tampa Bay, NFC	3,949
	Pittsburgh, AFC	4,270
1978	Los Angeles, NFC	3,893
	Pittsburgh, AFC	4,168
1977	Dallas, NFC	3,213
	New England, AFC	3,638
1976	Pittsburgh, AFC	3,323
	San Francisco, NFC	3,562
1975	Minnesota, NFC	3,153
	Oakland, AFC	3,629
1974	Pittsburgh, AFC	3,074
	Washington, NFC	3,285
1973	Los Angeles, NFC	2,951
	Oakland, AFC	3,160
1972	Miami, AFC	3,297
	Green Bay, NFC	3,474
1971	Baltimore, AFC	2,852
	Minnesota, NFC	3,406
1970	Minnesota, NFC	2,803
	N.Y. Jets, AFC	3,655
1969	Minnesota, NFL	2,720
	Kansas City, AFL	3,163
1968	Los Angeles, NFL	3,118
	N.Y. Jets, AFL	3,363
1967	Oakland, AFL	3,294
	Green Bay, NFL	3,300
1966	St. Louis, NFL	3,492
	Oakland, AFL	3,910
1965	San Diego, AFL	3,262
	Detroit, NFL	3,557
1964	Green Bay, NFL	3,179
	Buffalo, AFL	3,878

Year	Team	Yards
1963	Chicago, NFL	3,176
	Boston, AFL	3,834
1962	Detroit, NFL	3,217
	Dall. Texans, AFL	3,951
1961	San Diego, AFL	3,726
	Baltimore, NFL	3,782
1960	St. Louis, NFL	3,029
	Buffalo, AFL	3,866
1959	N.Y. Giants	2,843
1958	Chi. Bears	3,066
1957	Pittsburgh	2,791
1956	N.Y. Giants	3,081
1955	Cleveland	2,841
1954	Cleveland	2,658
1953	Philadelphia	2,998
1952	Cleveland	3,075
1951	N.Y. Giants	3,250
1950	Cleveland	3,154
1949	Philadelphia	2,831
1948	Chi. Bears	2,931
1947	Green Bay	3,396
1946	Washington	2,451
1945	Philadelphia	2,073
1944	Philadelphia	1,943
1943	Chi. Bears	2,262
1942	Chi. Bears	1,703
1941	N.Y. Giants	2,368
1940	N.Y. Giants	2,219
1939	Washington	2,116
1938	N.Y. Giants	2,029
1937	Washington	2,123
1936	Boston	2,181
1935	Boston	1,996
1934	Chi. Cardinals	1,539
1933	Brooklyn	1,789

FEWEST RUSHING YARDS ALLOWED

Year	Team	Yards
2013	Arizona, NFC	1,351
	N.Y. Jets, AFC	1,412
2012	Tampa Bay, NFC	1,320
	Pittsburgh, AFC	1,450
2011	San Francisco, NFC	1,236
	Baltimore, AFC	1,482
2010	Pittsburgh, AFC	1,004
	Chicago, NFC	1,441
2009	Green Bay, NFC	1,333
	Pittsburgh, AFC	1,438
2008	Minnesota, NFC	1,230
	Pittsburgh, AFC	1,284
2007	Minnesota, NFC	1,185
	Baltimore, AFC	1,268
2006	Minnesota, NFC	985
	Baltimore, AFC	1,214
2005	San Diego, AFC	1,349
	Carolina, NFC	1,465
2004	Pittsburgh, AFC	1,299
	Washington, NFC	1,304
2003	Tennessee, AFC	1,295
	Dallas, NFC	1,425
2002	Pittsburgh, AFC	1,375
	Tampa Bay, NFC	1,554
2001	Pittsburgh, AFC	1,195
	Chicago, NFC	1,313
2000	Baltimore, AFC	970
	N.Y. Giants, NFC	1,156
1999	St. Louis, NFC	1,189
	Baltimore, AFC	1,231
1998	San Diego, AFC	1,140
	Atlanta, NFC	1,203

Year	Team	Yards	Year	Team	Yards
1997	Pittsburgh, AFC	1,318	1963	Boston, AFL	1,107
	San Francisco, NFC	1,366		Chicago, NFL	1,442
1996	Denver, AFC	1,331	1962	Detroit, NFL	1,231
	Green Bay, NFC	1,416		Dall. Texans, AFL	1,250
1995	San Francisco, NFC	1,061	1961	Boston, AFL	1,041
	Pittsburgh, AFC	1,321		Pittsburgh, NFL	1,463
1994	Minnesota, NFC	1,090	1960	St. Louis, NFL	1,212
	San Diego, AFC	1,404		Dall. Texans, AFL	1,338
1993	Houston, AFC	1,273	1959	N.Y. Giants	1,261
	Minnesota, NFC	1,536	1958	Baltimore	1,291
1992	Dallas, NFC	1,244	1957	Baltimore	1,174
	Buffalo, AFC	1,395	1956	N.Y. Giants	1,443
	San Diego, AFC	1,395	1955	Cleveland	1,189
1991	Philadelphia, NFC	1,136	1954	Cleveland	1,050
	N.Y. Jets, AFC	1,442	1953	Philadelphia	1,117
1990	Philadelphia, NFC	1,169	1952	Detroit	1,145
	San Diego, AFC	1,515	1951	N.Y. Giants	913
1989	New Orleans, NFC	1,326	1950	Detroit	1,367
	Denver, AFC	1,580	1949	Chi. Bears	1,196
1988	Chicago, NFC	1,326	1948	Philadelphia	1,209
	Houston, AFC	1,592	1947	Philadelphia	1,329
1987	Chicago, NFC	1,413	1946	Chi. Bears	1,060
	Cleveland, AFC	1,433	1945	Philadelphia	817
1986	N.Y. Giants, NFC	1,284	1944	Philadelphia	558
	Denver, AFC	1,651	1943	Phil-Pitt	793
1985	Chicago, NFC	1,319	1942	Chi. Bears	519
	N.Y. Jets, AFC	1,516	1941	Washington	1,042
1984	Chicago, NFC	1,377	1940	N.Y. Giants	977
	Pittsburgh, AFC	1,617	1939	Chi. Bears	812
1983	Washington, NFC	1,289	1938	Detroit	1,081
	Cincinnati, AFC	1,499	1937	Chi. Bears	933
1982	Pittsburgh, AFC	762	1936	Boston	1,148
	Detroit, NFC	854	1935	Boston	998
1981	Detroit, NFC	1,623	1934	Chi. Cardinals	954
	Kansas City, AFC	1,747	1933	Brooklyn	964
1980	Detroit, NFC	1,599			
	Cincinnati, AFC	1,680			
1979	Denver, AFC	1,693			
	Tampa Bay, NFC	1,873			
1978	Dallas, NFC	1,721			
	Pittsburgh, AFC	1,774			
1977	Denver, AFC	1,531			
	Dallas, NFC	1,651			
1976	Pittsburgh, AFC	1,457			
	Los Angeles, NFC	1,564			
1975	Minnesota, NFC	1,532			
	Houston, AFC	1,680			
1974	Los Angeles, NFC	1,302			
	New England, AFC	1,587			
1973	Los Angeles, NFC	1,270			
	Oakland, AFC	1,470			
1972	Dallas, NFC	1,515			
	Miami, AFC	1,548			
1971	Baltimore, AFC	1,113			
	Dallas, NFC	1,144			
1970	Detroit, NFC	1,152			
	N.Y. Jets, AFC	1,283			
1969	Dallas, NFL	1,050			
	Kansas City, AFL	1,091			
1968	Dallas, NFL	1,195			
	N.Y. Jets, AFL	1,195			
1967	Dallas, NFL	1,081			
	Oakland, AFL	1,129			
1966	Buffalo, AFL	1,051			
	Dallas, NFL	1,176			
1965	San Diego, AFL	1,094			
	Los Angeles, NFL	1,409			
1964	Buffalo, AFL	913			
	Los Angeles, NFL	1,501			

FEWEST PASSING YARDS ALLOWED

Leadership in this category has been based on net yards since 1952.

Year	Team	Yards
2013	Seattle, NFC	2,752
	Houston, AFC	3,123
2012	Pittsburgh, AFC	2,963
	San Francisco, NFC	3,203
2011	Pittsburgh, AFC	2,751
	St. Louis, NFC	3,301
2010	San Diego, AFC	2,845
	New Orleans, NFC	3,103
2009	N.Y. Jets, AFC	2,459
	Carolina, NFC	3,056
2008	Pittsburgh, AFC	2,511
	Philadelphia, NFC	2,913
2007	Tampa Bay, NFC	2,728
	Indianapolis, AFC	2,764
2006	Oakland, AFC	2,413
	New Orleans, NFC	2,854
2005	Green Bay, NFC	2,680
	N.Y. Jets, AFC	2,755
2004	Tampa Bay, NFC	2,579
	Miami, AFC	2,592
2003	Dallas, NFC	2,631
	Buffalo, AFC	2,707
2002	Tampa Bay, NFC	2,490
	Indianapolis, AFC	2,917
2001	Miami, AFC	2,829
	Philadelphia, NFC	2,864
2000	Tennessee, AFC	2,423
	Washington, NFC	2,621
1999	Buffalo, AFC	2,675
	Tampa Bay, NFC	2,873

Year	Team	Yards	Year	Team	Yards
1998	Philadelphia, NFC	2,720	1963	Chicago, NFL	1,734
	Oakland, AFC	2,876		Oakland, AFL	2,589
1997	Dallas, NFC	2,522	1962	Green Bay, NFL	1,746
	Indianapolis, AFC	2,820		Oakland, AFL	2,306
1996	Green Bay, NFC	2,740	1961	Baltimore, NFL	1,913
	Pittsburgh, AFC	2,947		San Diego, AFL	2,363
1995	N.Y. Jets, AFC	2,740	1960	Chicago, NFL	1,388
	Philadelphia, NFC	2,816		Buffalo, AFL	2,124
1994	Dallas, NFC	2,752	1959	N.Y. Giants	1,582
	Houston, AFC	2,795	1958	Chi. Bears	1,769
1993	New Orleans, NFC	2,606	1957	Cleveland	1,300
	Cincinnati, AFC	2,798	1956	Cleveland	1,103
1992	New Orleans, NFC	2,470	1955	Pittsburgh	1,295
	Kansas City, AFC	2,537	1954	Cleveland	1,608
1991	Philadelphia, NFC	2,413	1953	Washington	1,751
	Denver, AFC	2,755	1952	Washington	1,580
1990	Pittsburgh, AFC	2,500	1951	Pittsburgh	1,687
	Dallas, NFC	2,639	1950	Cleveland	1,581
1989	Minnesota, NFC	2,501	1949	Philadelphia	1,607
	Kansas City, AFC	2,527	1948	Green Bay	1,626
1988	Kansas City, AFC	2,434	1947	Green Bay	1,790
	Minnesota, NFC	2,489	1946	Pittsburgh	939
1987	San Francisco, NFC	2,484	1945	Washington	1,121
	L.A. Raiders, AFC	2,727	1944	Chi. Bears	1,052
1986	St. Louis, NFC	2,637	1943	Chi. Bears	980
	New England, AFC	2,978	1942	Washington	1,093
1985	Washington, NFC	2,746	1941	Pittsburgh	1,168
	Pittsburgh, AFC	2,783	1940	Philadelphia	1,012
1984	New Orleans, NFC	2,453	1939	Washington	1,116
	Cleveland, AFC	2,696	1938	Chi. Bears	897
1983	New Orleans, NFC	2,691	1937	Detroit	804
	Cincinnati, AFC	2,828	1936	Philadelphia	853
1982	Miami, AFC	1,027	1935	Chi. Cardinals	793
	Tampa Bay, NFC	1,384	1934	Philadelphia	545
1981	Philadelphia, NFC	2,696	1933	Portsmouth	558
	Buffalo, AFC	2,870			
1980	Washington, NFC	2,171			
	Buffalo, AFC	2,282			
1979	Tampa Bay, NFC	2,076			
	Buffalo, AFC	2,530			
1978	Buffalo, AFC	1,960			
	Los Angeles, NFC	2,048			
1977	Atlanta, NFC	1,384			
	San Diego, AFC	1,725			
1976	Minnesota, NFC	1,575			
	Cincinnati, AFC	1,758			
1975	Minnesota, NFC	1,621			
	Cincinnati, AFC	1,729			
1974	Pittsburgh, AFC	1,466			
	Atlanta, NFC	1,572			
1973	Miami, AFC	1,290			
	Atlanta, NFC	1,430			
1972	Minnesota, NFC	1,699			
	Cleveland, AFC	1,736			
1971	Atlanta, NFC	1,638			
	Baltimore, AFC	1,739			
1970	Minnesota, NFC	1,438			
	Kansas City, AFC	2,010			
1969	Minnesota, NFL	1,631			
	Kansas City, AFL	2,072			
1968	Houston, AFL	1,671			
	Green Bay, NFL	1,796			
1967	Green Bay, NFL	1,377			
	Buffalo, AFL	1,825			
1966	Green Bay, NFL	1,959			
	Oakland, AFL	2,118			
1965	Green Bay, NFL	1,981			
	San Diego, AFL	2,168			
1964	Green Bay, NFL	1,647			
	San Diego, AFL	2,518			

SUPER BOWL RECORDS

Compiled by Elias Sports Bureau

Super Bowl I, 1/15/67	Super Bowl XXV, 1/27/91
Super Bowl II, 1/14/68	Super Bowl XXVI, 1/26/92
Super Bowl III, 1/12/69	Super Bowl XXVII, 1/31/93
Super Bowl IV, 1/11/70	Super Bowl XXVIII, 1/30/94
Super Bowl V, 1/17/71	Super Bowl XXIX, 1/29/95
Super Bowl VI, 1/16/72	Super Bowl XXX, 1/28/96
Super Bowl VII, 1/14/73	Super Bowl XXXI, 1/26/97
Super Bowl VIII, 1/13/74	Super Bowl XXXII, 1/25/98
Super Bowl IX, 1/12/75	Super Bowl XXXIII, 1/31/99
Super Bowl X, 1/18/76	Super Bowl XXXIV, 1/30/00
Super Bowl XI, 1/9/77	Super Bowl XXXV, 1/28/01
Super Bowl XII, 1/15/78	Super Bowl XXXVI, 2/3/02
Super Bowl XIII, 1/21/79	Super Bowl XXXVII, 1/26/03
Super Bowl XIV, 1/20/80	Super Bowl XXXVIII, 2/1/04
Super Bowl XV, 1/25/81	Super Bowl XXXIX, 2/6/05
Super Bowl XVI, 1/24/82	Super Bowl XL, 2/5/06
Super Bowl XVII, 1/30/83	Super Bowl XLI, 2/4/07
Super Bowl XVIII, 1/22/84	Super Bowl XLII, 2/3/08
Super Bowl XIX, 1/20/85	Super Bowl XLIII, 2/1/09
Super Bowl XX, 1/26/86	Super Bowl XLIV, 2/7/10
Super Bowl XXI, 1/25/87	Super Bowl XLV, 2/6/11
Super Bowl XXII, 1/31/88	Super Bowl XLVI, 2/5/12
Super Bowl XXIII, 1/22/89	Super Bowl XLVII, 2/3/13
Super Bowl XXIV, 1/28/90	Super Bowl XLVIII, 2/2/14

INDIVIDUAL RECORDS

SERVICE
Most Games
- 6 Mike Lodish, Buffalo, XXV-XXVIII; Denver, XXXII-XXXIII
- 5 Marv Fleming, Green Bay, I-II; Miami, VI-VIII
  Larry Cole, Dallas, V-VI, X, XII-XIII
  Cliff Harris, Dallas, V-VI, X, XII-XIII
  Charles Haley, San Francisco, XXIII-XXIV; Dallas, XXVII-XXVIII, XXX
  D.D. Lewis, Dallas, V-VI, X, XII-XIII
  Preston Pearson, Baltimore, III; Pittsburgh, IX; Dallas, X, XII-XIII
  Charlie Waters, Dallas, V-VI, X, XII-XIII
  Rayfield Wright, Dallas, V-VI, X, XII-XIII
  Cornelius Bennett, Buffalo, XXV-XXVIII; Atlanta, XXXIII
  John Elway, Denver, XXI-XXII, XXIV, XXXII-XXXIII
  Glenn Parker, Buffalo, XXV-XXVIII; N.Y. Giants, XXXV
  Bill Romanowski, San Francisco, XXIII-XXIV; Denver, XXXII-XXXIII; Oakland, XXXVII
  Adam Vinatieri, New England, XXXI, XXXVI, XXXVIII, XXXIX; Indianapolis, XLI
  Tedy Bruschi, New England, XXXI, XXXVI, XXXVIII-XXXIX, XLII
  Tom Brady, New England, XXXVI, XXXVIII-XXXIX, XLII, XLVI
  Matt Light, New England, XXXVI, XXXVIII-XXXIX, XLII, XLVI
- 4 By many players

Most Games, Winning Team
- 5 Charles Haley, San Francisco, XXIII-XXIV; Dallas, XXVII-XXVIII, XXX
- 4 By many players

Most Games, Coach
- 6 Don Shula, Baltimore, III; Miami, VI-VIII, XVII, XIX
- 5 Tom Landry, Dallas, V-VI, X, XII-XIII
  Bill Belichick, New England, XXXVI, XXXVIII-XXXIX, XLII, XLVI
- 4 Bud Grant, Minnesota, IV, VIII-IX, XI
  Chuck Noll, Pittsburgh, IX-X, XIII-XIV
  Joe Gibbs, Washington, XVII-XVIII, XXII, XXVI
  Marv Levy, Buffalo, XXV-XXVIII
  Dan Reeves, Denver, XXI-XXII, XXIV; Atlanta, XXXIII

Most Games, Winning Team, Coach
- 4 Chuck Noll, Pittsburgh, IX-X, XIII-XIV
- 3 Bill Walsh, San Francisco, XVI, XIX, XXIII

Joe Gibbs, Washington, XVII, XXII, XXVI
Bill Belichick, New England, XXXVI, XXXVIII-XXXIX
- 2 Vince Lombardi, Green Bay, I-II
  Tom Landry, Dallas, VI, XII
  Don Shula, Miami, VII-VIII
  Tom Flores, Oakland, XV; L.A. Raiders, XVIII
  Bill Parcells, N.Y. Giants, XXI, XXV
  Jimmy Johnson, Dallas, XXVII-XXVIII
  George Seifert, San Francisco, XXIV, XXIX
  Mike Shanahan, Denver, XXXII-XXXIII
  Tom Coughlin, N.Y. Giants, XLII, XLVI

Most Games, Losing Team, Coach
- 4 Bud Grant, Minnesota, IV, VIII-IX, XI
  Don Shula, Baltimore, III; Miami, VI, XVII, XIX
  Marv Levy, Buffalo, XXV-XXVIII
  Dan Reeves, Denver, XXI-XXII, XXIV; Atlanta, XXXIII
- 3 Tom Landry, Dallas, V, X, XIII

SCORING
POINTS
Most Points, Career
- 48 Jerry Rice, San Francisco-Oakland, 4 games (8-td)
- 34 Adam Vinatieri, New England-Indianapolis, 5 games (7-fg, 13-xp)
- 30 Emmitt Smith, Dallas, 3 games (5-td)

Most Points, Game
- 18 Roger Craig, San Francisco vs. Miami, XIX (3-td)
  Jerry Rice, San Francisco vs. Denver, XXIV (3-td); vs. San Diego, XXIX (3-td)
  Ricky Watters, San Francisco vs. San Diego, XXIX (3-td)
  Terrell Davis, Denver vs. Green Bay, XXXII (3-td)
- 15 Don Chandler, Green Bay vs. Oakland, II (3-pat, 4-fg)
- 14 Ray Wersching, San Francisco vs. Cincinnati, XVI (2-pat, 4-fg)
  Kevin Butler, Chicago vs. New England, XX (5-pat, 3-fg)

TOUCHDOWNS
Most Touchdowns, Career
- 8 Jerry Rice, San Francisco-Oakland, 4 games (8-p)
- 5 Emmitt Smith, Dallas, 3 games (5-r)
- 4 Franco Harris, Pittsburgh, 4 games (4-r)
  Roger Craig, San Francisco, 3 games (2-r, 2-p)
  Thurman Thomas, Buffalo, 4 games (4-r)
  John Elway, Denver, 5 games (4-r)

Most Touchdowns, Game
- 3 Roger Craig, San Francisco vs. Miami, XIX (1-r, 2-p)
  Jerry Rice, San Francisco. vs. Denver, XXIV (3-p); vs. San Diego, XXIX (3-p)
  Ricky Watters, San Francisco vs. San Diego, XXIX (1-r, 2-p)
  Terrell Davis, Denver vs. Green Bay, XXXII (3-r)
- 2 Max McGee, Green Bay vs. Kansas City, I (2-p)
  Elijah Pitts, Green Bay vs. Kansas City, I (2-r)
  Bill Miller, Oakland vs. Green Bay, II (2-p)
  Larry Csonka, Miami vs. Minnesota, VIII (2-r)
  Pete Banaszak, Oakland vs. Minnesota, XI (2-r)
  John Stallworth, Pittsburgh vs. Dallas, XIII (2-p)
  Franco Harris, Pittsburgh vs. Los Angeles, XIV (2-r)
  Cliff Branch, Oakland vs. Philadelphia, XV (2-p)
  Dan Ross, Cincinnati vs. San Francisco, XVI (2-p)
  Marcus Allen, L.A. Raiders vs. Washington, XVIII (2-r)
  Jim McMahon, Chicago vs. New England, XX (2-r)
  Ricky Sanders, Washington vs. Denver, XXII (2-p)
  Timmy Smith, Washington vs. Denver, XXII (2-r)
  Tom Rathman, San Francisco vs. Denver, XXIV (2-r)
  Gerald Riggs, Washington vs. Buffalo, XXVI (2-r)
  Michael Irvin, Dallas vs. Buffalo, XXVII (2-p)
  Emmitt Smith, Dallas vs. Buffalo, XXVIII (2-r)
  Emmitt Smith, Dallas vs. Pittsburgh, XXX (2-r)
  Antonio Freeman, Green Bay vs. Denver, XXXII (2-p)
  Howard Griffith, Denver vs. Atlanta, XXXIII (2-r)

Eddie George, Tennessee vs. St. Louis, XXXIV (2-r)
Keenan McCardell, Tampa Bay vs. Oakland, XXXVII (2-r)
Dwight Smith, Tampa Bay vs. Oakland, XXXVII (2-ret)
Larry Fitzgerald, Arizona vs. Pittsburgh, XLIII (2-p)
Greg Jennings, Green Bay vs. Pittsburgh, XLV (2-p)
Jacoby Jones, Baltimore vs. San Francisco, XLVII (1-r, 1-ret)

POINTS AFTER TOUCHDOWN

Most (One-Point) Points After Touchdown, Career

13	Adam Vinatieri, New England-Indianapolis, 5 games (13 att)	
9	Mike Cofer, San Francisco, 2 games (10 att)	
8	Don Chandler, Green Bay, 2 games (8 att)	
	Roy Gerela, Pittsburgh, 3 games (9 att)	
	Chris Bahr, Oakland-L.A. Raiders, 2 games (8 att)	
	Jason Elam, Denver, 2 games (8 att)	

Most (One-Point) Points After Touchdown, Game

7 Mike Cofer, San Francisco vs. Denver, XXIV (8 att)
   Lin Elliott, Dallas vs. Buffalo, XXVII (7 att)
   Doug Brien, San Francisco vs. San Diego, XXIX (7 att)
6 Ali Haji-Sheikh, Washington vs. Denver, XXII (6 att)
   Martín Gramatica, Tampa Bay vs. Oakland, XXXVII (6 att)
5 Don Chandler, Green Bay vs. Kansas City, I (5 att)
   Roy Gerela, Pittsburgh vs. Dallas, XIII (5 att)
   Chris Bahr, L.A. Raiders vs. Washington, XVIII (5 att)
   Ray Wersching, San Francisco vs. Miami, XIX (5 att)
   Kevin Butler, Chicago vs. New England, XX (5 att)
   Steven Hauschka, Seattle vs. Denver, XLVIII (5 att)

Most Two-Point Conversions, Game

1 Mark Seay, San Diego vs. San Francisco, XXIX
   Alfred Pupunu, San Diego vs. San Francisco, XXIX
   Mark Chmura, Green Bay vs. New England, XXXI
   Kevin Faulk, New England vs. Carolina, XXXVIII
   Lance Moore, New Orleans vs. Indianapolis, XLIV
   Antwaan Randle El, Pittsburgh vs. Green Bay, XLV
   Wes Welker, Denver vs. Seattle, XLVIII

FIELD GOALS

Field Goals Attempted, Career

10 Adam Vinatieri, New England-Indianapolis, 5 games
6 Jim Turner, N.Y. Jets-Denver, 2 games
   Roy Gerela, Pittsburgh, 3 games
   Rich Karlis, Denver, 2 games
   Jeff Wilkins, St. Louis, 2 games
5 Efren Herrera, Dallas, 1 game
   Ray Wersching, San Francisco, 2 games
   Jason Elam, Denver, 2 games
   Matt Stover, Baltimore-Indianapolis, 2 games

Most Field Goals Attempted, Game

5 Jim Turner, N.Y. Jets vs. Baltimore, III
   Efren Herrera, Dallas vs. Denver, XII
4 Don Chandler, Green Bay vs. Oakland, II
   Roy Gerela, Pittsburgh vs. Dallas, X
   Ray Wersching, San Francisco vs. Cincinnati, XVI
   Rich Karlis, Denver vs. N.Y. Giants, XXI
   Mike Cofer, San Francisco vs. Cincinnati, XXIII
   Jason Elam, Denver vs. Atlanta, XXXIII
   Jeff Wilkins, St. Louis vs. Tennessee, XXXIV
   Adam Vinatieri, Indianapolis vs. Chicago, XLI

Most Field Goals, Career

7 Adam Vinatieri, New England-Indianapolis, 5 games (10 att)
5 Ray Wersching, San Francisco, 2 games (5 att)
4 Don Chandler, Green Bay, 2 games (4 att)
   Jim Turner, N.Y. Jets-Denver, 2 games (6 att)
   Uwe von Schamann, Miami, 2 games (4 att)
   Jeff Wilkins, St. Louis, 2 games (6 att)

Most Field Goals, Game

4 Don Chandler, Green Bay vs. Oakland, II
   Ray Wersching, San Francisco vs. Cincinnati, XVI

3 Jim Turner, N.Y. Jets vs. Baltimore, III
   Jan Stenerud, Kansas City vs. Minnesota, IV
   Uwe von Schamann, Miami vs. San Francisco, XIX
   Kevin Butler, Chicago vs. New England, XX
   Jim Breech, Cincinnati vs. San Francisco, XXIII
   Chip Lohmiller, Washington vs. Buffalo, XXVI
   Eddie Murray, Dallas vs. Buffalo, XXVIII
   Jeff Wilkins, St. Louis vs. Tennessee, XXXIV
   Adam Vinatieri, Indianapolis vs. Chicago, XLI
   Garrett Hartley, New Orleans vs. Indianapolis, XLIV
   David Akers, San Francisco vs. Baltimore, XLVII

Longest Field Goal

54 Steve Christie, Buffalo vs. Dallas, XXVIII
51 Jason Elam, Denver vs. Green Bay, XXXII
50 Jeff Wilkins, St. Louis vs. New England, XXXVI
   John Kasay, Carolina vs. New England, XXXVIII

SAFETIES

Most Safeties, Game

1 Dwight White, Pittsburgh vs. Minnesota, IX
   Reggie Harrison, Pittsburgh vs. Dallas, X
   Henry Waechter, Chicago vs. New England, XX
   George Martin, N.Y. Giants vs. Denver, XXI
   Bruce Smith, Buffalo vs. N.Y. Giants, XXV
   Chris Culliver, San Francisco vs. Baltimore, XLVII
   Cliff Avril, Seattle vs. Denver, XLVIII

RUSHING

ATTEMPTS

Most Attempts, Career

101 Franco Harris, Pittsburgh, 4 games
 70 Emmitt Smith, Dallas, 3 games
 64 John Riggins, Washington, 2 games

Most Attempts, Game

38 John Riggins, Washington vs. Miami, XVII
34 Franco Harris, Pittsburgh vs. Minnesota, IX
33 Larry Csonka, Miami vs. Minnesota, VIII

YARDS GAINED

Most Yards Gained, Career

354 Franco Harris, Pittsburgh, 4 games
297 Larry Csonka, Miami, 3 games
289 Emmitt Smith, Dallas, 3 games

Most Yards Gained, Game

204 Timmy Smith, Washington vs. Denver, XXII
191 Marcus Allen, L.A. Raiders vs. Washington, XVIII
166 John Riggins, Washington vs. Miami, XVII

Longest Run From Scrimmage

75 Willie Parker, Pittsburgh vs. Seattle, XL (TD)
74 Marcus Allen, L.A. Raiders vs. Washington, XVIII (TD)
58 Tom Matte, Baltimore vs. N.Y. Jets, III
   Timmy Smith, Washington vs. Denver, XXII (TD)

AVERAGE GAIN

Highest Average Gain, Career (20 attempts)

9.6 Marcus Allen, L.A. Raiders, 1 game (20-191)
9.3 Timmy Smith, Washington, 1 game (22-204)
5.4 Dominic Rhodes, Indianapolis, 1 game (21-113)

Highest Average Gain, Game (10 attempts)

10.5 Tom Matte, Baltimore vs. N.Y. Jets, III (11-116)
9.6 Marcus Allen, L.A. Raiders vs. Washington, XVIII (20-191)
9.3 Willie Parker, Pittsburgh vs. Seattle, XL (10-93)

TOUCHDOWNS

Most Touchdowns, Career

5 Emmitt Smith, Dallas, 3 games
4 Franco Harris, Pittsburgh, 4 games
   Thurman Thomas, Buffalo, 4 games
   John Elway, Denver, 5 games
3 Terrell Davis, Denver, 2 games

Most Touchdowns, Game
- 3   Terrell Davis, Denver vs. Green Bay, XXXII
- 2   Elijah Pitts, Green Bay vs. Kansas City, I
-     Larry Csonka, Miami vs. Minnesota, VIII
-     Pete Banaszak, Oakland vs. Minnesota, XI
-     Franco Harris, Pittsburgh vs. Los Angeles, XIV
-     Marcus Allen, L.A. Raiders vs. Washington, XVIII
-     Jim McMahon, Chicago vs. New England, XX
-     Timmy Smith, Washington vs. Denver, XXII
-     Tom Rathman, San Francisco vs. Denver, XXIV
-     Gerald Riggs, Washington vs. Buffalo, XXVI
-     Emmitt Smith, Dallas vs. Buffalo, XXVIII
-     Emmitt Smith, Dallas vs. Pittsburgh, XXX
-     Howard Griffith, Denver vs. Atlanta, XXXIII
-     Eddie George, Tennessee vs. St. Louis, XXXIV

PASSING
PASSER RATING
Highest Passer Rating, Career (40 attempts)
- 127.8   Joe Montana, San Francisco, 4 games
- 122.8   Jim Plunkett, Oakland-L.A. Raiders, 2 games
- 112.8   Terry Bradshaw, Pittsburgh, 4 games

ATTEMPTS
Most Passes Attempted, Career
- 197   Tom Brady, New England, 5 games
- 152   John Elway, Denver, 5 games
- 145   Jim Kelly, Buffalo, 4 games

Most Passes Attempted, Game
- 58   Jim Kelly, Buffalo vs. Washington, XXVI
- 51   Donovan McNabb, Philadelphia vs. New England, XXXIX
- 50   Dan Marino, Miami vs. San Francisco, XIX
-     Jim Kelly, Buffalo vs. Dallas, XXVIII

COMPLETIONS
Most Passes Completed, Career
- 127   Tom Brady, New England, 5 games
- 90   Peyton Manning, Indianapolis-Denver, 3 games
- 83   Joe Montana, San Francisco, 4 games
-     Kurt Warner, St. Louis-Arizona, 3 games

Most Passes Completed, Game
- 34   Peyton Manning, Denver vs. Seattle, XLVIII
- 32   Tom Brady, New England vs. Carolina, XXXVIII
-     Drew Brees, New Orleans vs. Indianapolis, XLIV
- 31   Jim Kelly, Buffalo vs. Dallas, XXVIII
-     Kurt Warner, Arizona vs. Pittsburgh, XLIII
-     Peyton Manning, Indianapolis vs. New Orleans, XLIV

Most Consecutive Completions, Game
- 16   Tom Brady, New England vs. N.Y. Giants, XLVI
- 13   Joe Montana, San Francisco vs. Denver, XXIV
- 10   Phil Simms, N.Y. Giants vs. Denver, XXI
-     Troy Aikman, Dallas vs. Pittsburgh, XXX
-     Kurt Warner, Arizona vs. Pittsburgh, XLIII
-     Drew Brees, New Orleans vs. Indianapolis, XLIV

COMPLETION PERCENTAGE
Highest Completion Percentage, Career (40 attempts)
- 70.0   Troy Aikman, Dallas, 3 games, (80-56)
- 68.2   Peyton Manning, Indianapolis-Denver, 3 games (132-90)
- 68.0   Joe Montana, San Francisco, 4 games (122-83)

Highest Completion Percentage, Game (20 attempts)
- 88.0   Phil Simms, N.Y. Giants vs. Denver, XXI (25-22)
- 82.1   Drew Brees, New Orleans vs. Indianapolis, XLIV (39-32)
- 75.9   Joe Montana, San Francisco vs. Denver, XXIV (29-22)

YARDS GAINED
Most Yards Gained, Career
- 1,277   Tom Brady, New England, 5 games
- 1,156   Kurt Warner, St. Louis-Arizona, 3 games

- 1,142   Joe Montana, San Francisco, 4 games

Most Yards Gained, Game
- 414   Kurt Warner, St. Louis vs. Tennessee, XXXIV
- 377   Kurt Warner, Arizona vs. Pittsburgh, XLIII
- 365   Kurt Warner, St. Louis vs. New England, XXXVI

Longest Pass Completion
- 85   Jake Delhomme (to Muhammad), Carolina vs. New England, XXXVIII (TD)
- 81   Brett Favre (to Freeman), Green Bay vs. New England, XXXI (TD)
- 80   Jim Plunkett (to King), Oakland vs. Philadelphia, XV (TD)
-     Doug Williams (to Sanders), Washington vs. Denver, XXII (TD)
-     John Elway (to R. Smith), Denver vs. Atlanta, XXXIII (TD)

AVERAGE GAIN
Highest Average Gain, Career (40 attempts)
- 11.10   Terry Bradshaw, Pittsburgh, 4 games (84-932)
- 9.62   Bart Starr, Green Bay, 2 games (47-452)
- 9.41   Jim Plunkett, Oakland-L.A. Raiders, 2 games (46-433)

Highest Average Gain, Game (20 attempts)
- 14.71   Terry Bradshaw, Pittsburgh vs. Los Angeles, XIV (21-309)
- 12.80   Jim McMahon, Chicago vs. New England, XX (20-256)
- 12.43   Jim Plunkett, Oakland vs. Philadelphia, XV (21-261)

TOUCHDOWNS
Most Touchdown Passes, Career
- 11   Joe Montana, San Francisco, 4 games
- 9   Terry Bradshaw, Pittsburgh, 4 games
-    Tom Brady, New England, 5 games
- 8   Roger Staubach, Dallas, 4 games

Most Touchdown Passes, Game
- 6   Steve Young, San Francisco vs. San Diego, XXIX
- 5   Joe Montana, San Francisco vs. Denver, XXIV
- 4   Terry Bradshaw, Pittsburgh vs. Dallas, XIII
-    Doug Williams, Washington vs. Denver, XXII
-    Troy Aikman, Dallas vs. Buffalo, XXVII

HAD INTERCEPTED
Lowest Percentage, Passes Had Intercepted, Career (40 attempts)
- 0.00   Jim Plunkett, Oakland-L.A. Raiders, 2 games (46-0)
-      Joe Montana, San Francisco, 4 games (122-0)
- 1.02   Tom Brady, New England, 5 games (197-2)
- 1.25   Troy Aikman, Dallas, 3 games (80-1)

Most Attempts, Without Interception, Game
- 48   Tom Brady, New England vs. N.Y. Giants, XLII
- 45   Kurt Warner, St. Louis vs. Tennessee, XXXIV
- 40   Eli Manning, N.Y. Giants vs. New England, XLVI

Most Passes Had Intercepted, Career
- 8   John Elway, Denver, 5 games
- 7   Craig Morton, Dallas-Denver, 2 games
-    Jim Kelly, Buffalo, 4 games
- 6   Fran Tarkenton, Minnesota, 3 games

Most Passes Had Intercepted, Game
- 5   Rich Gannon, Oakland vs. Tampa Bay, XXXVII
- 4   Craig Morton, Denver vs. Dallas, XII
-    Jim Kelly, Buffalo vs. Washington, XXVI
-    Drew Bledsoe, New England vs. Green Bay, XXXI
-    Kerry Collins, N.Y. Giants vs. Baltimore, XXXV
- 3   By 11 players

PASS RECEIVING
RECEPTIONS
Most Receptions, Career
- 33   Jerry Rice, San Francisco-Oakland, 4 games
- 27   Andre Reed, Buffalo, 4 games
- 26   Wes Welker, New England-Denver, 3 games

Most Receptions, Game
- 13   Demaryius Thomas, Denver vs. Seattle, XLVIII

11   Dan Ross, Cincinnati vs. San Francisco, XVI
       Jerry Rice, San Francisco vs. Cincinnati, XXIII
       Deion Branch, New England vs. Philadelphia, XXXIX
       Wes Welker, New England vs. N.Y. Giants, XLII
10   Tony Nathan, Miami vs. San Francisco, XIX
       Jerry Rice, San Francisco vs. San Diego, XXIX
       Andre Hastings, Pittsburgh vs. Dallas, XXX
       Deion Branch, New England vs. Carolina, XXXVIII
       Joseph Addai, Indianapolis vs. Chicago, XLI
       Hakeem Nicks, N.Y. Giants vs. New England, XLVI

YARDS GAINED
Most Yards Gained, Career
  589   Jerry Rice, San Francisco-Oakland, 4 games
  364   Lynn Swann, Pittsburgh, 4 games
  323   Andre Reed, Buffalo, 4 games
Most Yards Gained, Game
  215   Jerry Rice, San Francisco vs. Cincinnati, XXIII
  193   Ricky Sanders, Washington vs. Denver, XXII
  162   Isaac Bruce, St. Louis vs. Tennessee, XXXIV
Longest Reception
   85   Muhsin Muhammad (from Delhomme), Carolina vs.
        New England, XXXVIII
   81   Antonio Freeman (from Favre), Green Bay vs.
        New England, XXXI (TD)
   80   Kenny King (from Plunkett), Oakland vs.
        Philadelphia, XV (TD)
       Ricky Sanders (from Williams), Washington vs.
        Denver, XXII (TD)
       Rod Smith (from Elway), Denver vs. Atlanta, XXXIII

AVERAGE GAIN
Highest Average Gain, Career (8 receptions)
  24.4   John Stallworth, Pittsburgh, 4 games (11-268)
  23.4   Ricky Sanders, Washington, 2 games (10-234)
  22.8   Lynn Swann, Pittsburgh, 4 games (16-364)
Highest Average Gain, Game (3 receptions)
  40.33 John Stallworth, Pittsburgh vs. Los Angeles, XIV
        (3-121)
  40.25 Lynn Swann, Pittsburgh vs. Dallas, X (4-161)
  38.33 John Stallworth, Pittsburgh vs. Dallas, XIII (3-115)

TOUCHDOWNS
Most Touchdowns, Career
   8   Jerry Rice, San Francisco-Oakland, 4 games
   3   John Stallworth, Pittsburgh, 4 games
      Lynn Swann, Pittsburgh, 4 games
      Cliff Branch, Oakland-L.A. Raiders, 3 games
      Antonio Freeman, Green Bay, 2 games
   2   Max McGee, Green Bay, 2 games
      Bill Miller, Oakland, 1 game
      Butch Johnson, Dallas, 2 games
      Dan Ross, Cincinnati, 1 game
      Roger Craig, San Francisco, 3 games
      Ricky Sanders, Washington, 2 games
      John Taylor, San Francisco, 3 games
      Gary Clark, Washington, 2 games
      Don Beebe, Buffalo-Green Bay, 4 games
      Michael Irvin, Dallas, 3 games
      Ricky Watters, San Francisco, 1 game
      Jay Novacek, Dallas, 3 games
      Keenan McCardell, Tampa Bay, 1 game
      Ricky Proehl, St. Louis-Carolina, 3 games
      David Givens, New England, 2 games
      Mike Vrabel, New England, 4 games
      Muhsin Muhammad, Carolina-Chicago, 2 games
      Larry Fitzgerald, Arizona, 1 game
      Greg Jennings, Green Bay, 1 game
      Hines Ward, Pittsburgh, 3 games
Most Touchdowns, Game
   3   Jerry Rice, San Francisco vs. Denver, XXIV; vs.
        San Diego, XXIX
   2   Max McGee, Green Bay vs. Kansas City, I

Bill Miller, Oakland vs. Green Bay, II
John Stallworth, Pittsburgh vs. Dallas, XIII
Cliff Branch, Oakland vs. Philadelphia, XV
Dan Ross, Cincinnati vs. San Francisco, XVI
Roger Craig, San Francisco vs. Miami, XIX
Ricky Sanders, Washington vs. Denver, XXII
Michael Irvin, Dallas vs. Buffalo, XXVII
Ricky Watters, San Francisco vs. San Diego, XXIX
Antonio Freeman, Green Bay vs. Denver, XXXII
Keenan McCardell, Tampa Bay vs. Oakland, XXXVII
Larry Fitzgerald, Arizona vs. Pittsburgh, XLIII
Greg Jennings, Green Bay vs. Pittsburgh, XLV

INTERCEPTIONS BY
Most Interceptions By, Career
   3   Chuck Howley, Dallas, 2 games
      Rod Martin, Oakland-L.A. Raiders, 2 games
      Larry Brown, Dallas, 3 games
   2   Randy Beverly, N.Y. Jets, 1 game
      Jake Scott, Miami, 3 games
      Mike Wagner, Pittsburgh, 3 games
      Mel Blount, Pittsburgh, 4 games
      Eric Wright, San Francisco, 4 games
      Barry Wilburn, Washington, 1 game
      Brad Edwards, Washington, 1 game
      Thomas Everett, Dallas, 2 games
      James Washington, Dallas, 2 games
      Darrien Gordon, San Diego-Denver-Oakland,
        4 games
      Dexter Jackson, Tampa Bay, 1 game
      Dwight Smith, Tampa Bay, 1 game
      Rodney Harrison, San Diego-New England, 4 games
Most Interceptions By, Game
   3   Rod Martin, Oakland vs. Philadelphia, XV
   2   Randy Beverly, N.Y. Jets vs. Baltimore, III
      Chuck Howley, Dallas vs. Baltimore, V
      Jake Scott, Miami vs. Washington, VII
      Barry Wilburn, Washington vs. Denver, XXII
      Brad Edwards, Washington vs. Buffalo, XXVI
      Thomas Everett, Dallas vs. Buffalo, XXVII
      Larry Brown, Dallas vs. Pittsburgh, XXX
      Darrien Gordon, Denver vs. Atlanta, XXXIII
      Dexter Jackson, Tampa Bay vs. Oakland, XXXVII
      Dwight Smith, Tampa Bay vs. Oakland, XXXVII
      Rodney Harrison, New England vs. Philadelphia,
        XXXIX

YARDS GAINED
Most Yards Gained, Career
  108   Darrien Gordon, San Diego-Denver-Oakland,
        4 games
  100   James Harrison, Pittsburgh, 2 games
   94   Dwight Smith, Tampa Bay, 1 game
Most Yards Gained, Game
  108   Darrien Gordon, Denver vs. Atlanta, XXXIII
  100   James Harrison, Pittsburgh vs. Arizona, XLIII
   94   Dwight Smith, Tampa Bay vs. Oakland, XXXVII
Longest Return
  100   James Harrison, Pittsburgh vs. Arizona, XLIII (TD)
   76   Kelly Herndon, Seattle vs. Pittsburgh, XL
   75   Willie Brown, Oakland vs. Minnesota, XI (TD)

TOUCHDOWNS
Most Touchdowns, Game
   2   Dwight Smith, Tampa Bay vs. Oakland, XXXVII
   1   Herb Adderley, Green Bay vs. Oakland, II
      Willie Brown, Oakland vs. Minnesota, XI
      Jack Squirek, L.A. Raiders vs. Washington, XVIII
      Reggie Phillips, Chicago vs. New England, XX
      Duane Starks, Baltimore vs. N.Y. Giants, XXXV
      Ty Law, New England vs. St. Louis, XXXVI
      Derrick Brooks, Tampa Bay vs. Oakland, XXXVII
      Kelvin Hayden, Indianapolis vs. Chicago, XLI

James Harrison, Pittsburgh vs. Arizona, XLIII
Tracy Porter, New Orleans vs. Indianapolis, XLIV
Nick Collins, Green Bay vs. Pittsburgh, XLV
Malcolm Smith, Seattle vs. Denver, XLVIII

PUNTING
Most Punts, Career
17 Mike Eischeid, Oakland-Minnesota, 3 games
Mike Horan, Denver-St. Louis, 4 games
16 Brad Maynard, N.Y. Giants-Chicago, 2 games
15 Larry Seiple, Miami, 3 games
Most Punts, Game
11 Brad Maynard, N.Y. Giants vs. Baltimore, XXXV
10 Kyle Richardson, Baltimore vs. N.Y. Giants, XXXV
9 Ron Widby, Dallas vs. Baltimore, V
Longest Punt
63 Lee Johnson, Cincinnati vs. San Francisco, XXIII
62 Rich Camarillo, New England vs. Chicago, XX
61 Jerrel Wilson, Kansas City vs. Green Bay, I

AVERAGE YARDAGE
Highest Average, Punting, Career (10 punts)
46.5 Jerrel Wilson, Kansas City, 2 games (11-511)
43.8 Tom Rouen, Denver-Seattle, 3 games (11-482)
43.0 Kyle Richardson, Baltimore, 1 game (10-430)
Tom Tupa, New England-Tampa Bay, 2 games
(12-516)
Highest Average, Punting, Game (4 punts)
50.2 Tom Rouen, Seattle vs. Pittsburgh, XL (6-301)
48.8 Bryan Wagner, San Diego vs. San Francisco, XXIX
(4-195)
48.7 Chris Gardocki, Pittsburgh vs. Seattle, XL (6-292)

PUNT RETURNS
Most Punt Returns, Career
8 Troy Brown, New England, 3 games
6 Willie Wood, Green Bay, 2 games
Jake Scott, Miami, 3 games
Theo Bell, Pittsburgh, 2 games
Mike Nelms, Washington, 1 game
John Taylor, San Francisco, 3 games
Desmond Howard, Green Bay, 1 game
David Meggett, N.Y. Giants-New England, 2 games
Darrien Gordon, San Diego-Denver-Oakland,
4 games
5 Dana McLemore, San Francisco, 1 game
Most Punt Returns, Game
6 Mike Nelms, Washington vs. Miami, XVII
Desmond Howard, Green Bay vs. New England, XXXI
5 Willie Wood, Green Bay vs. Oakland, II
Dana McLemore, San Francisco vs. Miami, XIX
4 By 10 players
Most Fair Catches, Game
4 Jermaine Lewis, Baltimore vs. N.Y. Giants, XXXV
Karl Williams, Tampa Bay vs. Oakland, XXXVII
3 Ron Gardin, Baltimore vs. Dallas, V
Golden Richards, Dallas vs. Pittsburgh, X
Greg Pruitt, L.A. Raiders vs. Washington, XVIII
Al Edwards, Buffalo vs. N.Y. Giants, XXV
David Meggett, N.Y. Giants vs. Buffalo, XXV

YARDS GAINED
Most Yards Gained, Career
94 John Taylor, San Francisco, 3 games
90 Desmond Howard, Green Bay, 1 game
67 David Meggett, N.Y. Giants-New England, 2 games
Most Yards Gained, Game
90 Desmond Howard, Green Bay vs. New England, XXXI
56 John Taylor, San Francisco vs. Cincinnati, XXIII
52 Mike Nelms, Washington vs. Miami, XXII
Longest Return
45 John Taylor, San Francisco vs. Cincinnati, XXIII
34 Darrell Green, Washington vs. L.A. Raiders, XVIII

Desmond Howard, Green Bay vs. New England, XXXI
Jermaine Lewis, Baltimore vs. N.Y. Giants, XXXV
Steve Breaston, Arizona vs. Pittsburgh, XLIII
32 Desmond Howard, Green Bay vs. New England, XXXI
Ted Ginn, San Francisco vs. Baltimore, XLVII

AVERAGE YARDAGE
Highest Average, Career (4 returns)
15.7 John Taylor, San Francisco, 3 games (6-94)
15.0 Desmond Howard, Green Bay, 1 game (6-90)
11.2 David Meggett, N.Y. Giants-New England, 2 games
(6-67)
Highest Average, Game (3 returns)
18.7 John Taylor, San Francisco vs. Cincinnati, XXIII (3-56)
15.0 Desmond Howard, Green Bay vs. New England, XXXI
(6-90)
14.0 Terrence Wilkins, Indianapolis vs. Chicago, XLI
(3-42)

TOUCHDOWNS
Most Touchdowns, Game
None

KICKOFF RETURNS
Most Kickoff Returns, Career
10 Ken Bell, Denver, 3 games
8 Larry Anderson, Pittsburgh, 2 games
Fulton Walker, Miami, 2 games
Andre Coleman, San Diego, 1 game
Marcus Knight, Oakland, 1 game
7 Preston Pearson, Baltimore-Pittsburgh-Dallas, 5 games
Stephen Starring, New England, 1 game
David Meggett, N.Y. Giants-New England, 2 games
Most Kickoff Returns, Game
8 Andre Coleman, San Diego vs. San Francisco, XXIX
Marcus Knight, Oakland vs. Tampa Bay, XXXVII
7 Stephen Starring, New England vs. Chicago, XX
6 Darren Carrington, Denver vs. San Francisco, XXIV
Antonio Freeman, Green Bay vs. Denver, XXXII
Ron Dixon, N.Y. Giants vs. Baltimore, XXXV

YARDS GAINED
Most Yards Gained, Career
283 Fulton Walker, Miami, 2 games
244 Andre Coleman, San Diego, 1 game
210 Tim Dwight, Atlanta, 1 game
Most Yards Gained, Game
244 Andre Coleman, San Diego vs. San Francisco, XXIX
210 Tim Dwight, Atlanta vs. Denver, XXXIII
206 Jacoby Jones, Baltimore vs. San Francisco, XLVII
Longest Return
108 Jacoby Jones, Baltimore vs. San Francisco, XLVII
(TD)
99 Desmond Howard, Green Bay vs. New England, XXXI
(TD)
98 Fulton Walker, Miami vs. Washington, XVII (TD)
Andre Coleman, San Diego vs. San Francisco, XXIX
(TD)

AVERAGE YARDAGE
Highest Average, Career (4 returns)
42.0 Tim Dwight, Atlanta, 1 game (5-210)
41.2 Jacoby Jones, Baltimore, 1 game (5-206)
38.5 Desmond Howard, Green Bay, 1 game (4-154)
Highest Average, Game (3 returns)
47.5 Fulton Walker, Miami vs. Washington, XVII (4-190)
42.0 Tim Dwight, Atlanta vs. Denver, XXXIII (5-210)
41.2 Jacoby Jones, Baltimore vs. San Francisco, XLVII
(5-206)

TOUCHDOWNS
Most Touchdowns, Game
- 1 Fulton Walker, Miami vs. Washington, XVII
     Stanford Jennings, Cincinnati vs. San Francisco, XXIII
     Andre Coleman, San Diego vs. San Francisco, XXIX
     Desmond Howard, Green Bay vs. New England, XXXI
     Tim Dwight, Atlanta vs. Denver, XXXIII
     Ron Dixon, N.Y. Giants vs. Baltimore, XXXV
     Jermaine Lewis, Baltimore vs. N.Y. Giants, XXXV
     Devin Hester, Chicago vs. Indianapolis, XLI
     Jacoby Jones, Baltimore vs. San Francisco, XLVII
     Percy Harvin, Seattle vs. Denver, XLVIII

FUMBLES
Most Fumbles, Career
- 5 Roger Staubach, Dallas, 4 games
- 4 Jim Kelly, Buffalo, 4 games
     Kurt Warner, St. Louis-Arizona, 3 games
- 3 Franco Harris, Pittsburgh, 4 games
     Terry Bradshaw, Pittsburgh, 4 games
     John Elway, Denver, 5 games
     Frank Reich, Buffalo, 4 games
     Thurman Thomas, Buffalo, 4 games

Most Fumbles, Game
- 3 Roger Staubach, Dallas vs. Pittsburgh, X
     Jim Kelly, Buffalo vs. Washington, XXVI
     Frank Reich, Buffalo vs. Dallas, XXVII
- 2 Franco Harris, Pittsburgh vs. Minnesota, IX
     Butch Johnson, Dallas vs. Denver, XII
     Terry Bradshaw, Pittsburgh vs. Dallas, XIII
     Joe Montana, San Francisco vs. Cincinnati, XXIII
     John Elway, Denver vs. San Francisco, XXIV
     Thurman Thomas, Buffalo vs. Dallas, XXVIII
     Rex Grossman, Chicago vs. Indianapolis, XLI
     Eli Manning, N.Y. Giants vs. New England, XLII
     Kurt Warner, Arizona vs. Pittsburgh, XLIII

RECOVERIES
Most Fumbles Recovered, Career
- 2 Jake Scott, Miami, 3 games (1 own, 1 opp)
     Fran Tarkenton, Minnesota, 3 games (2 own)
     Franco Harris, Pittsburgh, 4 games (2 own)
     Roger Staubach, Dallas, 4 games (2 own)
     Bobby Walden, Pittsburgh, 2 games (2 own)
     John Fitzgerald, Dallas, 4 games (2 own)
     Randy Hughes, Dallas, 3 games (2 own)
     Butch Johnson, Dallas, 2 games (2 own)
     Mike Singletary, Chicago, 1 game (2 opp)
     John Elway, Denver, 5 games (2 own)
     Jimmie Jones, Dallas, 2 games (2 opp)
     Kenneth Davis, Buffalo, 4 games (2 own)
     Kurt Warner, St. Louis-Arizona, 3 games (2 own)

Most Fumbles Recovered, Game
- 2 Jake Scott, Miami vs. Minnesota, VIII (1 own, 1 opp)
     Roger Staubach, Dallas vs. Pittsburgh, X (2 own)
     Randy Hughes, Dallas vs. Denver, XII (2 own)
     Butch Johnson, Dallas vs. Denver, XII (2 own)
     Mike Singletary, Chicago vs. New England, XX (2 opp)
     Jimmie Jones, Dallas vs. Buffalo, XXVII (2 opp)

YARDS GAINED
Most Yards Gained, Game
- 64 Leon Lett, Dallas vs. Buffalo, XXVII (opp)
- 49 Mike Bass, Washington vs. Miami, VII (opp)
- 46 James Washington, Dallas vs. Buffalo, XXVIII (opp)

Longest Return
- 64 Leon Lett, Dallas vs. Buffalo, XXVII
- 49 Mike Bass, Washington vs. Miami, VII (TD)
- 46 James Washington, Dallas vs. Buffalo, XXVIII (TD)

TOUCHDOWNS
Most Touchdowns, Game
- 1 Mike Bass, Washington vs. Miami, VII (opp 49 yds)
     Mike Hegman, Dallas vs. Pittsburgh, XIII (opp 37 yds)
     Jimmie Jones, Dallas vs. Buffalo, XXVII (opp 2 yds)
     Ken Norton, Dallas vs. Buffalo, XXVII (opp 9 yds)
     James Washington, Dallas vs. Buffalo, XXVIII
       (opp 46 yds)

COMBINED NET YARDS GAINED
(Rushing, receiving, interception returns, punt returns, kickoff returns, and fumble returns)
ATTEMPTS
Most Attempts, Career
- 108 Franco Harris, Pittsburgh, 4 games
- 81 Emmitt Smith, Dallas, 3 games
- 72 Roger Craig, San Francisco, 3 games
     Thurman Thomas, Buffalo, 4 games

Most Attempts, Game
- 39 John Riggins, Washington vs. Miami, XVII
- 35 Franco Harris, Pittsburgh vs. Minnesota, IX
- 34 Matt Snell, N.Y. Jets vs. Baltimore, III
     Emmitt Smith, Dallas vs. Buffalo, XXVIII

YARDS GAINED
Most Yards Gained, Career
- 604 Jerry Rice, San Francisco-Oakland, 4 games
- 468 Franco Harris, Pittsburgh, 4 games
- 410 Roger Craig, San Francisco, 3 games

Most Yards Gained, Game
- 290 Jacoby Jones, Baltimore vs. San Francisco, XLVII
- 244 Andre Coleman, San Diego vs. San Francisco, XXIX
     Desmond Howard, Green Bay vs. New England, XXXI
- 235 Ricky Sanders, Washington vs. Denver, XXII

SACKS
Sacks have been compiled since XVII.
Most Sacks, Career
- 4.5 Charles Haley, San Francisco-Dallas, 5 games
- 4.0 Justin Tuck, N.Y. Giants, 2 games
- 3.0 Danny Stubbs, San Francisco, 2 games
     Leonard Marshall, N.Y. Giants, 2 games
     Jeff Wright, Buffalo, 4 games
     Reggie White, Green Bay, 2 games
     Willie McGinest, New England, 4 games
     Tedy Bruschi, New England, 5 games
     Mike Vrabel, New England, 4 games
     Darnell Dockett, Arizona, 1 game
     LaMarr Woodley, Pittsburgh, 2 games

Most Sacks, Game
- 3.0 Reggie White, Green Bay vs. New England, XXXI
     Darnell Dockett, Arizona vs. Pittsburgh, XLIII
- 2.0 Dwaine Board, San Francisco vs. Miami, XIX
     Dennis Owens, New England vs. Chicago, XX
     Otis Wilson, Chicago vs. New England, XX
     Leonard Marshall, N.Y. Giants vs. Denver, XXI
     Alvin Walton, Washington vs. Denver, XXII
     Charles Haley, San Francisco vs. Cincinnati, XXIII
     Danny Stubbs, San Francisco vs. Denver, XXIV
     Jeff Wright, Buffalo vs. Dallas, XXVIII
     Raylee Johnson, San Diego vs. San Francisco, XXIX
     Chad Hennings, Dallas vs. Pittsburgh, XXX
     Tedy Bruschi, New England vs. Green Bay, XXXI
     Michael McCrary, Baltimore vs. N.Y. Giants, XXXV
     Simeon Rice, Tampa Bay vs. Oakland, XXXVII
     Mike Vrabel, New England vs. Carolina, XXXVIII
     Adalius Thomas, New England vs. N.Y. Giants, XLII
     Justin Tuck, N.Y. Giants vs. New England, XLII;
       vs. New England, XLVI
     LaMarr Woodley, Pittsburgh vs. Arizona, XLIII
     Paul Kruger, Baltimore vs. San Francisco, XLVII

TEAM RECORDS

GAMES, VICTORIES, DEFEATS
Most Games
8   Dallas, V-VI, X, XII-XIII, XXVII-XXVIII, XXX
    Pittsburgh, IX-X, XIII-XIV, XXX, XL, XLIII, XLV
7   New England, XX, XXXI, XXXVI, XXXVIII-XXXIX, XLII, XLVI
    Denver, XII, XXI-XXII, XXIV, XXXII-XXXIII, XLVIII
6   San Francisco, XVI, XIX, XXIII-XXIV, XXIX, XLVII

Most Consecutive Games
4   Buffalo, XXV-XXVIII
3   Miami, VI-VIII
2   Green Bay, I-II; XXXI-XXXII
    Dallas, V-VI; XII-XIII; XXVII-XXVIII
    Minnesota, VIII-IX
    Pittsburgh, IX-X; XIII-XIV
    Washington, XVII-XVIII
    Denver, XXI-XXII; XXXII-XXXIII
    San Francisco, XXIII-XXIV
    New England, XXXVIII-XXXIX

Most Games Won
6   Pittsburgh, IX-X, XIII-XIV, XL, XLIII
5   San Francisco, XVI, XIX, XXIII-XXIV, XXIX
    Dallas, VI, XII, XXVII-XXVIII, XXX
4   Green Bay, I-II, XXXI, XLV
    N.Y. Giants, XXI, XXV, XLII, XLVI

Most Consecutive Games Won
2   Green Bay, I-II
    Miami, VII-VIII
    Pittsburgh, IX-X, XIII-XIV
    San Francisco, XXIII-XXIV
    Dallas, XXVII-XXVIII
    Denver, XXXII-XXXIII
    New England, XXXVIII-XXXIX

Most Games Lost
5   Denver, XII, XXI-XXII, XXIV, XLVIII
4   Minnesota, IV, VIII-IX, XI
    Buffalo, XXV-XXVIII
    New England, XX, XXXI, XLII, XLVI
3   Dallas, V, X, XIII
    Miami, VI, XVII, XIX

Most Consecutive Games Lost
4   Buffalo, XXV-XXVIII
2   Minnesota, VIII-IX
    Denver, XXI-XXII

SCORING
Most Points, Game
55   San Francisco vs. Denver, XXIV
52   Dallas vs. Buffalo, XXVII
49   San Francisco vs. San Diego, XXIX
Fewest Points, Game
3   Miami vs. Dallas, VI
6   Minnesota vs. Pittsburgh, IX
7   By five teams
Most Points, Both Teams, Game
75   San Francisco (49) vs. San Diego (26), XXIX
69   Dallas (52) vs. Buffalo (17), XXVII
     Tampa Bay (48) vs. Oakland (21), XXXVII
66   Pittsburgh (35) vs. Dallas (31), XIII
Fewest Points, Both Teams, Game
21   Washington (7) vs. Miami (14), VII
22   Minnesota (6) vs. Pittsburgh (16), IX
23   Baltimore (7) vs. N.Y. Jets (16), III
Largest Margin of Victory, Game
45   San Francisco vs. Denver, XXIV (55-10)
36   Chicago vs. New England, XX (46-10)
35   Dallas vs. Buffalo, XXVII (52-17)
     Seattle vs. Denver, XLVIII (43-8)
Most Points, Each Half
1st: 35   Washington vs. Denver, XXII

2nd: 30   N.Y. Giants vs. Denver, XXI
Most Points, Each Quarter
1st: 14   Miami vs. Minnesota, VIII
          Oakland vs. Philadelphia, XV
          Dallas vs. Buffalo, XXVII
          San Francisco vs. San Diego, XXIX
          New England vs. Green Bay, XXXI
          Chicago vs. Indianapolis, XLI
          Green Bay vs. Pittsburgh, XLV
2nd: 35   Washington vs. Denver, XXII
3rd: 21   Chicago vs. New England, XX
4th: 21   Dallas vs. Buffalo, XXVII
Most Points, Both Teams, Each Half
1st: 45   Washington (35) vs. Denver (10), XXII
2nd: 46   Tampa Bay (28) vs. Oakland (18), XXXVII
Fewest Points, Both Teams, Each Half
1st: 2   Minnesota (0) vs. Pittsburgh (2), IX
2nd: 7   Miami (0) vs. Washington (7), VII
          Denver (0) vs. Washington (7), XXII
Most Points, Both Teams, Each Quarter
1st: 24   New England (14) vs. Green Bay (10), XXXI
2nd: 35   Washington (35) vs. Denver (0), XXII
3rd: 24   Washington (14) vs. Buffalo (10), XXVI
          San Francisco (17) vs. Baltimore (7), XLVII
4th: 37   Carolina (19) vs. New England (18), XXXVIII

TOUCHDOWNS
Most Touchdowns, Game
8   San Francisco vs. Denver, XXIV
7   Dallas vs. Buffalo, XXVII
    San Francisco vs. San Diego, XXIX
6   Washington vs. Denver, XXII
    Tampa Bay vs. Oakland, XXXVII
Fewest Touchdowns, Game
0   Miami vs. Dallas, VI
1   By 20 teams
Most Touchdowns, Both Teams, Game
10   San Francisco (7) vs. San Diego (3), XXIX
9   Pittsburgh (5) vs. Dallas (4), XIII
     San Francisco (8) vs. Denver (1), XXIV
     Dallas (7) vs. Buffalo (2), XXVII
     Tampa Bay (6) vs. Oakland (3), XXXVII
8   Carolina (4) vs. New England (4), XXXVIII
Fewest Touchdowns, Both Teams, Game
2   Baltimore (1) vs. N.Y. Jets (1), III
3   In six games

POINTS AFTER TOUCHDOWN
Most (One-Point) Points After Touchdown, Game
7   San Francisco vs. Denver, XXIV
    Dallas vs. Buffalo, XXVII
    San Francisco vs. San Diego, XXIX
6   Washington vs. Denver, XXII
    Tampa Bay vs. Oakland, XXXVII
5   Green Bay vs. Kansas City, I
    Pittsburgh vs. Dallas, XIII
    L.A. Raiders vs. Washington, XVIII
    San Francisco vs. Miami, XIX
    Chicago vs. New England, XX
    Seattle vs. Denver, XLVIII
Most (One-Point) Points After Touchdown, Both Teams, Game
9   Pittsburgh (5) vs. Dallas (4), XIII
    Dallas (7) vs. Buffalo (2), XXVII
8   San Francisco (7) vs. Denver (1), XXIV
    San Francisco (7) vs. San Diego (1), XXIX
7   Washington (6) vs. Denver (1), XXII
    Washington (4) vs. Buffalo (3), XXVI
    Denver (4) vs. Green Bay (3), XXXII
Fewest (One-Point) Points After Touchdown, Both Teams, Game
2   Baltimore (1) vs. N.Y. Jets (1), III
    Baltimore (1) vs. Dallas (1), V
    Minnesota (0) vs. Pittsburgh (2), IX

Most Two-Point Conversions, Game
2 San Diego vs. San Francisco, XXIX
Most Two-Point Conversions, Both Teams, Game
2 San Diego (2) vs. San Francisco (0), XXIX

FIELD GOALS
Most Field Goals Attempted, Game
5 N.Y. Jets vs. Baltimore, III
    Dallas vs. Denver, XII
4 Green Bay vs. Oakland, II
    Pittsburgh vs. Dallas, XX
    San Francisco vs. Cincinnati, XVI; XXIII
    Denver vs. N.Y. Giants, XXI
    Denver vs. Atlanta, XXXIII
    St. Louis vs. Tennessee, XXXIV
    Indianapolis vs. Chicago, XLI
Most Field Goals Attempted, Both Teams, Game
7 N.Y. Jets (5) vs. Baltimore (2), III
    San Francisco (4) vs. Cincinnati (3), XXIII
    St. Louis (4) vs. Tennessee (3), XXXIV
    Denver (4) vs. Atlanta (3), XXXIII
6 Dallas (5) vs. Denver (1), XII
5 Green Bay (4) vs. Oakland (1), II
    Pittsburgh (4) vs. Dallas (1), X
    Oakland (3) vs. Philadelphia (2), XV
    Denver (4) vs. N.Y. Giants (1), XXI
    Dallas (3) vs. Buffalo (2), XXVIII
    Indianapolis (4) vs. Chicago (1), XLI
    New Orleans (3) vs. Indianapolis (2), XLIV
    San Francisco (3) vs. Baltimore (2), XLVII
Fewest Field Goals Attempted, Both Teams, Game
1 Minnesota (0) vs. Miami (1), VIII
    San Francisco (0) vs. Denver (1), XXIV
    Philadelphia (0) vs. New England (1), XXXIX
    New England (0) vs. N.Y. Giants (1), XLII
2 Green Bay (0) vs. Kansas City (2), I
    Miami (1) vs. Washington (1), VII
    Minnesota (1) vs. Pittsburgh (1), IX
    Dallas (1) vs. Pittsburgh (1), XIII
    Dallas (1) vs. Buffalo (1), XXVII
    San Diego (1) vs. San Francisco (1), XXIX
    Denver (1) vs. Green Bay (1), XXXII
    Arizona (0) vs. Pittsburgh (2), XLIII
    Denver (0) vs. Seattle (2), XLVIII
Most Field Goals, Game
4 Green Bay vs. Oakland, II
    San Francisco vs. Cincinnati, XVI
3 N.Y. Jets vs. Baltimore, III
    Kansas City vs. Minnesota, IV
    Miami vs. San Francisco, XIX
    Chicago vs. New England, XX
    Cincinnati vs. San Francisco, XXIII
    Washington vs. Buffalo, XXVI
    Dallas vs. Buffalo, XXVIII
    St. Louis vs. Tennessee, XXXIV
    Indianapolis vs. Chicago, XLI
    New Orleans vs. Indianapolis, XLIV
    San Francisco vs. Baltimore, XLVII
Most Field Goals, Both Teams, Game
5 Cincinnati (3) vs. San Francisco (2), XXIII
    Dallas (3) vs. Buffalo (2), XXVIII
    San Francisco (3) vs. Baltimore (2), XLVII
4 Green Bay (4) vs. Oakland (0), II
    San Francisco (4) vs. Cincinnati (0), XVI
    Miami (3) vs. San Francisco (1), XIX
    Chicago (3) vs. New England (1), XX
    Washington (3) vs. Buffalo (1), XXVI
    Atlanta (2) vs. Denver (2), XXXIII
    St. Louis (3) vs. Tennessee (1), XXXIV
    Indianapolis (3) vs. Chicago (1), XLI
    New Orleans (3) vs. Indianapolis (1), XLIV
3 In 14 games

Fewest Field Goals, Both Teams, Game
0 Miami vs. Washington, VII
    Pittsburgh vs. Minnesota, IX
1 Green Bay (0) vs. Kansas City (1), I
    Minnesota (0) vs. Miami (1), VIII
    Pittsburgh (0) vs. Dallas (1), XIII
    Washington (0) vs. Denver (1), XXII
    San Francisco (0) vs. Denver (1), XXIV
    San Francisco (0) vs. San Diego (1), XXIX
    Philadelphia (0) vs. New England (1), XXXIX
    Pittsburgh (0) vs. Seattle (1), XLI
    New England (0) vs. N.Y. Giants (1), XLII

SAFETIES
Most Safeties, Game
1 Pittsburgh vs. Minnesota, IX; vs. Dallas, X
    Chicago vs. New England, XX
    N.Y. Giants vs. Denver, XXI; vs. New England, XLVI
    Buffalo vs. N.Y. Giants, XXV
    Arizona vs. Pittsburgh, XLIII
    San Francisco vs. Baltimore, XLVII
    Seattle vs. Denver, XLVIII

FIRST DOWNS
Most First Downs, Game
31 San Francisco vs. Miami, XIX
29 New England vs. Carolina, XXXVIII
28 San Francisco vs. Denver, XXIV
    San Francisco vs. San Diego, XXIX
Fewest First Downs, Game
9 Minnesota vs. Pittsburgh, IX
    Miami vs. Washington, XVII
10 Dallas vs. Baltimore, V
    Miami vs. Dallas, VI
11 Denver vs. Dallas, XII
    N.Y. Giants vs. Baltimore, XXXV
    Oakland vs. Tampa Bay, XXXVII
    Chicago vs. Indianapolis, XLI
Most First Downs, Both Teams, Game
50 San Francisco (31) vs. Miami (19), XIX
    Tennessee (27) vs. St. Louis (23), XXXIV
49 Buffalo (25) vs. Washington (24), XXVI
48 San Francisco (28) vs. San Diego (20), XXIX
Fewest First Downs, Both Teams, Game
24 Dallas (10) vs. Baltimore (14), V
    N.Y. Giants (11) vs. Baltimore (13), XXXV
26 Minnesota (9) vs. Pittsburgh (17), IX
27 Pittsburgh (13) vs. Dallas (14), X

RUSHING
Most First Downs, Rushing, Game
16 San Francisco vs. Miami, XIX
15 Dallas vs. Miami, VI
14 Washington vs. Miami, XVII
    San Francisco vs. Denver, XXIV
    Denver vs. Green Bay, XXXII
Fewest First Downs, Rushing, Game
1 New England vs. Chicago, XX
    St. Louis vs. Tennessee, XXXIV
    Oakland vs. Tampa Bay, XXXVII
2 Minnesota vs. Kansas City, IV; vs. Pittsburgh, IX;
    vs. Oakland, XI
    Pittsburgh vs. Dallas, XIII
    Miami vs. San Francisco, XIX
    N.Y. Giants vs. Baltimore, XXXV
    Arizona vs. Pittsburgh, XLIII
    Denver vs. Seattle, XLVIII
3 Miami vs. Dallas, VI
    Philadelphia vs. Oakland, XV
    New England vs. Green Bay, XXXI
    Carolina vs. New England, XXXVIII
    Chicago vs. Indianapolis, XLI
    New England vs. N.Y. Giants, XLII

New Orleans vs. Indianapolis, XLIV

Most First Downs, Rushing, Both Teams, Game
21   Washington (14) vs. Miami (7), XVII
19   Washington (13) vs. Denver (6), XXII
     San Francisco (14) vs. Denver (5), XXIV
18   Dallas (15) vs. Miami (3), VI
     Miami (13) vs. Minnesota (5), VIII
     San Francisco (16) vs. Miami (2), XIX
     N.Y. Giants (10) vs. Buffalo (8), XXV
     Denver (14) vs. Green Bay (4), XXXII

Fewest First Downs, Rushing, Both Teams, Game
6   Arizona (2) vs. Pittsburgh (4), XLIII
7   Oakland (1) vs. Tampa Bay (6), XXXVIII
   New England (3) vs. N.Y. Giants (4), XLII
8   Baltimore (4) vs. Dallas (4), V
   Pittsburgh (2) vs. Dallas (6), XIII
   N.Y. Giants (2) vs. Baltimore (6), XXXV
   Denver (2) vs. Seattle (6), XLVIII

PASSING
Most First Downs, Passing, Game
20   Arizona vs. Pittsburgh, XLIII
19   New England vs. Carolina, XXXVIII
18   Buffalo vs. Washington, XXVI
     St. Louis vs. Tennessee, XXXIV
     Philadelphia vs. New England, XXXIX
     N.Y. Giants vs. New England, XLVI

Fewest First Downs, Passing, Game
1   Denver vs. Dallas, XII
2   Miami vs. Washington, XVII
4   Miami vs. Minnesota, VIII

Most First Downs, Passing, Both Teams, Game
33   N.Y. Giants (18) vs. New England (15), XLVI
32   Miami (17) vs. San Francisco (15), XIX
     Philadelphia (18) vs. New England (14), XXXIX
     Arizona (20) vs. Pittsburgh (12), XLIII
     Indianapolis (16) vs. New Orleans (16), XLIV
31   San Francisco (17) vs. San Diego (14), XXIX
     St. Louis (18) vs. Tennessee (13), XXXIV
     New England (19) vs. Carolina (12), XXXVIII

Fewest First Downs, Passing, Both Teams, Game
9   Denver (1) vs. Dallas (8), XII
10   Minnesota (5) vs. Pittsburgh (5), IX
11   Dallas (5) vs. Baltimore (6), V
     Miami (2) vs. Washington (9), XVII

PENALTY
Most First Downs, Penalty, Game
4   Baltimore vs. Dallas, V
   Miami vs. Minnesota, VIII
   Cincinnati vs. San Francisco, XVI
   Buffalo vs. Dallas, XXVII
   St. Louis vs. Tennessee, XXXIV
   Pittsburgh vs. Arizona, XLIII
3   Kansas City vs. Minnesota, IV
   Minnesota vs. Oakland, XI
   Buffalo vs. Washington, XXVI
   Green Bay vs. Denver, XXXII
   N.Y. Giants vs. Baltimore, XXXV
   St. Louis vs. New England, XXXVI
   Tampa Bay vs. Oakland, XXXVII
   New England vs. Carolina, XXXVIII
   Denver vs. Seattle, XLVIII

Most First Downs, Penalty, Both Teams, Game
6   Cincinnati (4) vs. San Francisco (2), XVI
   St. Louis (4) vs. Tennessee (2), XXXIV
5   Baltimore (4) vs. Dallas (1), V
   Miami (4) vs. Minnesota (1), VIII
   Buffalo (3) vs. Washington (2), XXVI
   Green Bay (3) vs. Denver (2), XXXII
   New England (3) vs. Carolina (2), XXXVIII
   Pittsburgh (4) vs. Arizona (1), XLIII
4   Kansas City (3) vs. Minnesota (1), IV

Buffalo (4) vs. Dallas (0), XXVII
N.Y. Giants (3) vs. Baltimore (1), XXXV
St. Louis (3) vs. New England (1), XXXVI
Tampa Bay (3) vs. Oakland (1), XXXVII
Denver (3) vs. Seattle (1), XLVIII

Fewest First Downs, Penalty, Both Teams, Game
0   Dallas vs. Miami, VI
   Miami vs. Washington, VII
   Dallas vs. Pittsburgh, X
   Miami vs. San Francisco, XIX
   Pittsburgh vs. Seattle, XL
   Green Bay vs. Pittsburgh, XLV
1   Green Bay (0) vs. Kansas City (1), I
   Miami (0) vs. Washington (1), XVII
   Cincinnati (0) vs. San Francisco (1), XXIII
   San Francisco (0) vs. Denver (1), XXIV
   Dallas (0) vs. Buffalo (1), XXVIII
   Dallas (0) vs. Pittsburgh (1), XXX
   Denver (0) vs. Atlanta (1), XXXIII
   Chicago (0) vs. Indianapolis (1), XLI
   New England (0) vs. N.Y. Giants (1), XLVI

NET YARDS GAINED RUSHING AND PASSING
Most Yards Gained, Game
602   Washington vs. Denver, XXII
537   San Francisco vs. Miami, XIX
481   New England vs. Carolina, XXXVIII

Fewest Yards Gained, Game
119   Minnesota vs. Pittsburgh, IX
123   New England vs. Chicago, XX
152   N.Y. Giants vs. Baltimore, XXXV

Most Yards Gained, Both Teams, Game
929   Washington (602) vs. Denver (327), XXII
868   New England (481) vs. Carolina (387), XXXVIII
851   San Francisco (537) vs. Miami (314), XIX

Fewest Yards Gained, Both Teams, Game
396   N.Y. Giants (152) vs. Baltimore (244), XXXV
452   Minnesota (119) vs. Pittsburgh (333), IX
481   Washington (228) vs. Miami (253), VII
     Denver (156) vs. Dallas (325), XII

RUSHING
ATTEMPTS
Most Attempts, Game
57   Pittsburgh vs. Minnesota, IX
53   Miami vs. Minnesota, VIII
52   Oakland vs. Minnesota, XI
     Washington vs. Miami, XVII

Fewest Attempts, Game
9   Miami vs. San Francisco, XIX
11   New England vs. Chicago, XX
     Oakland vs. Tampa Bay, XXXVII
12   Arizona vs. Pittsburgh, XLIII

Most Attempts, Both Teams, Game
81   Washington (52) vs. Miami (29), XVII
78   Pittsburgh (57) vs. Minnesota (21), IX
     Oakland (52) vs. Minnesota (26), XI
77   Miami (53) vs. Minnesota (24), VIII
     Pittsburgh (46) vs. Dallas (31), X

Fewest Attempts, Both Teams, Game
36   Green Bay (13) vs. Pittsburgh (23), XLV
37   Arizona (12) vs. Pittsburgh (25), XLIII
     New Orleans (18) vs. Indianapolis (19), XLIV
42   New England (16) vs. N.Y. Giants (26), XLII

YARDS GAINED
Most Yards Gained, Game
280   Washington vs. Denver, XXII
276   Washington vs. Miami, XVII
266   Oakland vs. Minnesota, XI

Fewest Yards Gained, Game
7   New England vs. Chicago, XX
17   Minnesota vs. Pittsburgh, IX

19 Oakland vs. Tampa Bay, XXXVII
Most Yards Gained, Both Teams, Game
377 Washington (280) vs. Denver (97), XXII
372 Washington (276) vs. Miami (96), XVII
338 N.Y. Giants (172) vs. Buffalo (166), XXV
Fewest Yards Gained, Both Teams, Game
91 Arizona (33) vs. Pittsburgh (58), XLIII
136 New England (45) vs. N.Y. Giants (91), XLII
150 New Orleans (51) vs. Indianapolis (99), XLIV

AVERAGE GAIN
Highest Average Gain, Game
7.00 L.A. Raiders vs. Washington, XVIII (33-231)
Washington vs. Denver, XXII (40-280)
6.64 Buffalo vs. N.Y. Giants, XXV (25-166)
6.28 San Francisco vs. Baltimore, XLVII (29-182)
Lowest Average Gain, Game
0.64 New England vs. Chicago, XX (11-7)
0.81 Minnesota vs. Pittsburgh, IX (21-17)
1.73 Oakland vs. Tampa Bay, XXXVII (11-19)

TOUCHDOWNS
Most Touchdowns, Game
4 Chicago vs. New England, XX
Denver vs. Green Bay, XXXII
3 Green Bay vs. Kansas City, I
Miami vs. Minnesota, VIII
San Francisco vs. Denver, XXIV
Denver vs. Atlanta, XXXIII
2 Oakland vs. Minnesota, XI
Pittsburgh vs. Los Angeles, XIV
L.A. Raiders vs. Washington, XVIII
San Francisco vs. Miami, XIX
N.Y. Giants vs. Denver, XXI
Washington vs. Denver, XXII; vs. Buffalo, XXVI
Buffalo vs. N.Y. Giants, XXV
Dallas vs. Buffalo, XXVIII; vs. Pittsburgh, XXX
Tennessee vs. St. Louis, XXXIV
Pittsburgh vs. Seattle, XL
San Francisco vs. Baltimore, XLVII
Fewest Touchdowns, Game
0 By 34 teams
Most Touchdowns, Both Teams, Game
4 Miami (3) vs. Minnesota (1), VIII
Chicago (4) vs. New England (0), XX
San Francisco (3) vs. Denver (1), XXIV
Denver (4) vs. Green Bay (0), XXXII
3 In nine games
Fewest Touchdowns, Both Teams, Game
0 Pittsburgh vs. Dallas, X
Oakland vs. Philadelphia, XV
Cincinnati vs. San Francisco, XXIII
1 In 18 games

PASSING
ATTEMPTS
Most Passes Attempted, Game
59 Buffalo vs. Washington, XXVI
55 San Diego vs. San Francisco, XXIX
51 Philadelphia vs. New England, XXXIX
Fewest Passes Attempted, Game
7 Miami vs. Minnesota, VIII
11 Miami vs. Washington, VII
14 Pittsburgh vs. Minnesota, IX
Most Passes Attempted, Both Teams, Game
93 San Diego (55) vs. San Francisco (38), XXIX
92 Buffalo (59) vs. Washington (33), XXVI
85 Miami (50) vs. San Francisco (35), XIX
Fewest Passes Attempted, Both Teams, Game
35 Miami (7) vs. Minnesota (28), VIII
39 Miami (11) vs. Washington (28), VII
40 Pittsburgh (14) vs. Minnesota (26), IX
Miami (17) vs. Washington (23), XVII

COMPLETIONS
Most Passes Completed, Game
34 Denver vs. Seattle, XLVIII
32 New England vs. Carolina, XXXVIII
New Orleans vs. Indianapolis, XLIV
31 Buffalo vs. Dallas, XXVIII
Arizona vs. Pittsburgh, XLIII
Indianapolis vs. New Orleans, XLIV
Fewest Passes Completed, Game
4 Miami vs. Washington, XVII
6 Miami vs. Minnesota, VIII
8 Miami vs. Washington, VII
Denver vs. Dallas, XII
Most Passes Completed, Both Teams, Game
63 New Orleans (32) vs. Indianapolis (31), XLIV
57 N.Y. Giants (30) vs. New England (27), XLVI
53 Miami (29) vs. San Francisco (24), XIX
Philadelphia (30) vs. New England (23), XXXIX
Fewest Passes Completed, Both Teams, Game
19 Miami (4) vs. Washington (15), XVII
20 Pittsburgh (9) vs. Minnesota (11), IX
22 Miami (8) vs. Washington (14), VII

COMPLETION PERCENTAGE
Highest Completion Percentage, Game (20 attempts)
88.0 N.Y. Giants vs. Denver, XXI (25-22)
82.1 New Orleans vs. Indianapolis, XLIV (39-32)
75.0 San Francisco vs. Denver, XXIV (32-24)
N.Y. Giants vs. New England, XLVI (40-30)
Lowest Completion Percentage, Game (20 attempts)
32.0 Denver vs. Dallas, XII (25-8)
37.9 Denver vs. San Francisco, XXIV (29-11)
38.5 Denver vs. Washington, XXII (39-15)
N.Y. Giants vs. Baltimore, XXXV (39-15)

YARDS GAINED
Most Yards Gained, Game
407 St. Louis vs. Tennessee, XXXIV
374 Arizona vs. Pittsburgh, XLIII
354 New England vs. Carolina, XXXVIII
Fewest Yards Gained, Game
35 Denver vs. Dallas, XII
63 Miami vs. Minnesota, VIII
69 Miami vs. Washington, VII
Most Yards Gained, Both Teams, Game
649 New England (354) vs. Carolina (295), XXXVIII
615 San Francisco (326) vs. Miami (289), XIX
St. Louis (407) vs. Tennessee (208), XXXIV
614 Indianapolis (333) vs. New Orleans (281), XLIV
Fewest Yards Gained, Both Teams, Game
156 Miami (69) vs. Washington (87), VII
186 Pittsburgh (84) vs. Minnesota (102), IX
204 Miami (80) vs. Washington (124), XVII

TIMES SACKED
Most Times Sacked, Game
7 Dallas vs. Pittsburgh, X
New England vs. Chicago, XX
6 Kansas City vs. Green Bay, I
Washington vs. L.A. Raiders, XVIII
Denver vs. San Francisco, XXIV
5 Dallas vs. Denver, XII; vs. Pittsburgh, XIII
Cincinnati vs. San Francisco, XVI; XXIII
Denver vs. Washington, XXII
Buffalo vs. Washington, XXVI
Green Bay vs. New England, XXXI
New England vs. Green Bay, XXXI
Oakland vs. Tampa Bay, XXXVIII
New England vs. N.Y. Giants, XLII
Fewest Times Sacked, Game
0 Baltimore vs. N.Y. Jets, III; vs. Dallas, V
Minnesota vs. Pittsburgh, IX

Pittsburgh vs. Los Angeles, XIV
Philadelphia vs. Oakland, XV
Washington vs. Buffalo, XXVI
Denver vs. Green Bay, XXXII; vs. Atlanta, XXXIII
Tampa Bay vs. Oakland, XXXVII
New England vs. Carolina, XXXVIII
Indianapolis vs. New Orleans, XLIV
Seattle vs. Denver, XLVIII
1 By 19 teams

Most Times Sacked, Both Teams, Game
10 New England (7) vs. Chicago (3), XX
    Green Bay (5) vs. New England (5), XXXI
9 Kansas City (6) vs. Green Bay (3), I
    Dallas (7) vs. Pittsburgh (2), X
    Dallas (5) vs. Denver (4), XII
    Dallas (5) vs. Pittsburgh (4), XIII
    Cincinnati (5) vs. San Francisco (4), XXIII
8 Washington (6) vs. L.A. Raiders (2), XVIII
    New England (5) vs. N.Y. Giants (3), XLII

Fewest Times Sacked, Both Teams, Game
1 Philadelphia (0) vs. Oakland (1), XV
    Denver (0) vs. Green Bay (1), XXXII
    Indianapolis (0) vs. New Orleans (1), XLIV
    Seattle (0) vs. Denver (1), XLVIII
2 Baltimore (0) vs. N.Y. Jets (2), III
    Baltimore (0) vs. Dallas (2), V
    Minnesota (0) vs. Pittsburgh (2), IX
    Denver (0) vs. Atlanta (2), XXXIII
    Chicago (1) vs. Indianapolis (1), XLI
3 In five games

TOUCHDOWNS

Most Touchdowns, Game
6 San Francisco vs. San Diego, XXIX
5 San Francisco vs. Denver, XXIV
4 Pittsburgh vs. Dallas, XIII
    Washington vs. Denver, XXII
    Dallas vs. Buffalo, XXVII

Fewest Touchdowns, Game
0 By 19 teams

Most Touchdowns, Both Teams, Game
7 Pittsburgh (4) vs. Dallas (3), XIII
    San Francisco (6) vs. San Diego (1), XXIX
6 Carolina (3) vs. New England (3), XXXVIII
5 Washington (4) vs. Denver (1), XXII
    San Francisco (5) vs. Denver (0), XXIV
    Dallas (4) vs. Buffalo (1), XXVII
    Philadelphia (3) vs. New England (2), XXXIX
    Green Bay (3) vs. Pittsburgh (2), XLV

Fewest Touchdowns, Both Teams, Game
0 N.Y. Jets vs. Baltimore, III
    Miami vs. Minnesota, VIII
    Buffalo vs. Dallas, XXVIII
1 In seven games

INTERCEPTIONS BY

Most Interceptions By, Game
5 Tampa Bay vs. Oakland, XXXVII
4 N.Y. Jets vs. Baltimore, III
    Dallas vs. Denver, XII
    Washington vs. Buffalo, XXVI
    Dallas vs. Buffalo, XXVII
    Green Bay vs. New England, XXXI
    Baltimore vs. N.Y. Giants, XXXV
3 By 13 teams

Most Interceptions By, Both Teams, Game
6 Baltimore (3) vs. Dallas (3), V
    Tampa Bay (5) vs. Oakland (1), XXXVII
5 Washington (4) vs. Buffalo (1), XXVI
4 In 10 games

Fewest Interceptions By, Both Teams, Game
0 Buffalo vs. N.Y. Giants, XXV
    St. Louis vs. Tennessee, XXXIV

1 Oakland (0) vs. Green Bay (1), II
    Miami (0) vs. Dallas (1), VI
    Minnesota (0) vs. Miami (1), VIII
    N.Y. Giants (0) vs. Denver (1), XXI
    Cincinnati (0) vs. San Francisco (1), XXIII
    New England (0) vs. Carolina (1), XXXVIII
    N.Y. Giants (0) vs. New England (1), XLII
    Indianapolis (0) vs. New Orleans (1), XLIV
    New England (0) vs. N.Y. Giants (1), XLVI
    San Francisco (0) vs. Baltimore (1), XLVII

YARDS GAINED

Most Yards Gained, Game
172 Tampa Bay vs. Oakland, XXXVII
136 Denver vs. Atlanta, XXXIII
100 Pittsburgh vs. Arizona, XLIII

Most Yards Gained, Both Teams, Game
184 Tampa Bay (172) vs. Oakland (12), XXXVII
137 Denver (136) vs. Atlanta (1), XXXIII
100 Seattle (76) vs. Pittsburgh (24), XL
     Indianapolis (94) vs. Chicago (6), XLI

TOUCHDOWNS

Most Touchdowns, Game
3 Tampa Bay vs. Oakland, XXXVII
1 Green Bay vs. Oakland, II
    Oakland vs. Minnesota, XI
    L.A. Raiders vs. Washington, XVIII
    Chicago vs. New England, XX
    Baltimore vs. N.Y. Giants, XXXV
    New England vs. St. Louis, XXXVI
    Indianapolis vs. Chicago, XLI
    Pittsburgh vs. Arizona, XLIII
    New Orleans vs. Indianapolis, XLIV
    Green Bay vs. Pittsburgh, XLV
    Seattle vs. Denver, XLVIII

PUNTING

Most Punts, Game
11 N.Y. Giants vs. Baltimore, XXXV
10 Baltimore vs. N.Y. Giants, XXXV
9 Dallas vs. Baltimore, V

Fewest Punts, Game
1 Atlanta vs. Denver, XXXIII
    Denver vs. Atlanta, XXXIII
    Seattle vs. Denver, XLVIII
2 Pittsburgh vs. Los Angeles, XIV
    Denver vs. N.Y. Giants, XXI; vs. Seattle, XLVIII
    St. Louis vs. Tennessee, XXXIV
    Indianapolis vs. New Orleans, XLIV
    New Orleans vs. Indianapolis, XLIV
3 By 16 teams

Most Punts, Both Teams, Game
21 N.Y. Giants (11) vs. Baltimore (10), XXXV
15 Washington (8) vs. L.A. Raiders (7), XVIII
    New England (8) vs. Green Bay (7), XXXI
13 Dallas (9) vs. Baltimore (4), V
    Pittsburgh (7) vs. Minnesota (6), IX

Fewest Punts, Both Teams, Game
2 Atlanta (1) vs. Denver (1), XXXIII
3 Seattle (1) vs. Denver (2), XLVIII
4 Indianapolis (2) vs. New Orleans (2), XLIV

AVERAGE YARDAGE

Highest Average, Game (4 punts)
50.17 Seattle vs. Pittsburgh, XL (6-301)
48.75 San Diego vs. San Francisco, XXIX (4-195)
48.67 Pittsburgh vs. Seattle, XL (6-292)

Lowest Average, Game (4 punts)
31.00 Tampa Bay vs. Oakland, XXXVII (5-155)
31.20 Washington vs. Miami, VII (5-156)
32.38 Washington vs. L.A. Raiders, XVIII (8-259)

PUNT RETURNS

Most Punt Returns, Game
6   Washington vs. Miami, XVII
    Green Bay vs. New England, XXXI
5   By seven teams

Fewest Punt Returns, Game
0   Minnesota vs. Miami, VIII
    Buffalo vs. N.Y. Giants, XXV
    Washington vs. Buffalo, XXVI
    Denver vs. Green Bay, XXXII
    Green Bay vs. Denver, XXXII
    Atlanta vs. Denver, XXXIII
    Denver vs. Atlanta, XXXIII
    New England vs. N.Y. Giants, XLVI
    Seattle vs. Denver, XLVIII
1   By 27 teams

Most Punt Returns, Both Teams, Game
10 Green Bay (6) vs. New England (4), XXXI
9   Pittsburgh (5) vs. Minnesota (4), IX
8   Green Bay (5) vs. Oakland (3), II
    Baltimore (5) vs. Dallas (3), V
    Washington (6) vs. Miami (2), XVII
    N.Y. Giants (5) vs. Baltimore (3), XXXV

Fewest Punt Returns, Both Teams, Game
0   Denver vs. Green Bay, XXXII
    Atlanta vs. Denver, XXXIII
1   New England (0) vs. N.Y. Giants (1), XLVI
    Seattle (0) vs. Denver (1), XLVIII
2   Dallas (1) vs. Miami (1), VI
    Denver (1) vs. N.Y. Giants (1), XXI
    Buffalo (0) vs. N.Y. Giants (2), XXV
    Buffalo (1) vs. Dallas (1), XXVIII
    Indianapolis (1) vs. New Orleans (1), XLIV

YARDS GAINED

Most Yards Gained, Game
90 Green Bay vs. New England, XXXI
56 San Francisco vs. Cincinnati, XXIII
52 Washington vs. Miami, XVII

Fewest Yards Gained, Game
−1 Dallas vs. Miami, VI
    Tennessee vs. St. Louis, XXXIV
0   By 16 teams

Most Yards Gained, Both Teams, Game
120 Green Bay (90) vs. New England (30), XXXI
80 N.Y. Giants (46) vs. Baltimore (34), XXXV
74 Washington (52) vs. Miami (22), XVII

Fewest Yards Gained, Both Teams, Game
0   Denver vs. Green Bay, XXXII
    Atlanta vs. Denver, XXXIII
4   Indianapolis (0) vs. New Orleans (4), XLIV
5   Green Bay (0) vs. Pittsburgh (5), XLV

AVERAGE RETURN

Highest Average, Game (3 returns)
18.7 San Francisco vs. Cincinnati, XXIII (3-56)
15.0 Green Bay vs. New England, XXXI (6-90)
14.0 Indianapolis vs. Chicago, XLI (3-42)

TOUCHDOWNS

Most Touchdowns, Game
None

KICKOFF RETURNS

Most Kickoff Returns, Game
9   Denver vs. San Francisco, XXIV
    Oakland vs. Tampa Bay, XXXVII
8   San Diego vs. San Francisco, XXIX
7   By eight teams

Fewest Kickoff Returns, Game
1   N.Y. Jets vs. Baltimore, III
    L.A. Raiders vs. Washington, XVIII

Washington vs. Buffalo, XXVI
2   By 11 teams

Most Kickoff Returns, Both Teams, Game
13 Oakland (9) vs. Tampa Bay (4), XXXVII
12 Denver (9) vs. San Francisco (3), XXIV
    San Diego (8) vs. San Francisco (4), XXIX
11 Los Angeles (6) vs. Pittsburgh (5), XIV
    Miami (7) vs. San Francisco (4), XIX
    New England (7) vs. Chicago (4), XX
    Green Bay (6) vs. Denver (5), XXXII

Fewest Kickoff Returns, Both Teams, Game
5   N.Y. Jets (1) vs. Baltimore (4), III
    Miami (2) vs. Washington (3), VII
    Washington (1) vs. Buffalo (4), XXVI
6   In five games

YARDS GAINED

Most Yards Gained, Game
244 San Diego vs. San Francisco, XXIX
227 Atlanta vs. Denver, XXXIII
222 Miami vs. Washington, XVII

Fewest Yards Gained, Game
16 Washington vs. Buffalo, XXVI
17 L.A. Raiders vs. Washington, XVIII
25 N.Y. Jets vs. Baltimore, III

Most Yards Gained, Both Teams, Game
312 Baltimore (206) vs. San Francisco (106), XLVII
292 San Diego (244) vs. San Francisco (48), XXIX
289 Green Bay (154) vs. New England (135), XXXI

Fewest Yards Gained, Both Teams, Game
78 Miami (33) vs. Washington (45), VII
82 Pittsburgh (32) vs. Minnesota (50), IX
92 San Francisco (40) vs. Cincinnati (52), XVI

AVERAGE GAIN

Highest Average, Game (3 returns)
44.0 Cincinnati vs. San Francisco, XXIII (3-132)
41.2 Baltimore vs. San Francisco, XLVII (5-206)
38.5 Green Bay vs. New England, XXXI (4-154)

TOUCHDOWNS

Most Touchdowns, Game
1   Miami vs. Washington, XVII
    Cincinnati vs. San Francisco, XXIII
    San Diego vs. San Francisco, XXIX
    Green Bay vs. New England, XXXI
    Atlanta vs. Denver, XXXIII
    Baltimore vs. N.Y. Giants, XXXV
    N.Y. Giants vs. Baltimore, XXXV
    Chicago vs. Indianapolis, XLI
    Baltimore vs. San Francisco, XLVII
    Seattle vs. Denver, XLVIII

Most Touchdowns, Both Teams, Game
2   Baltimore (1) vs. N.Y. Giants (1), XXXV

PENALTIES

Most Penalties, Game
12 Dallas vs. Denver, XII
    Carolina vs. New England, XXXVIII
11 Arizona vs. Pittsburgh, XLIII
10 Dallas vs. Baltimore, V
    Seattle vs. Denver, XLVIII

Fewest Penalties, Game
0   Miami vs. Dallas, VI
    Pittsburgh vs. Dallas, X
    Denver vs. San Francisco, XXIV
    Atlanta vs. Denver, XXXIII
1   Green Bay vs. Oakland, II
    Miami vs. Minnesota, VIII; vs. San Francisco, XIX
    Buffalo vs. Dallas, XXVIII
2   By seven teams

Most Penalties, Both Teams, Game
20 Dallas (12) vs. Denver (8), XII
Carolina (12) vs. New England (8), XXXVIII
18 Arizona (11) vs. Pittsburgh (7), XLIII
16 Cincinnati (8) vs. San Francisco (8), XVI
Green Bay (9) vs. Denver (7), XXXII

Fewest Penalties, Both Teams, Game
2 Pittsburgh (0) vs. Dallas (2), X
3 Miami (0) vs. Dallas (3), VI
Miami (1) vs. San Francisco (2), XIX
4 Denver (0) vs. San Francisco (4), XXIV
Atlanta (0) vs. Denver (4), XXXIII

YARDS PENALIZED

Most Yards Penalized, Game
133 Dallas vs. Baltimore, X
122 Pittsburgh vs. Minnesota, IX
106 Arizona vs. Pittsburgh, XLIII

Fewest Yards Penalized, Game
0 Miami vs. Dallas, VI
Pittsburgh vs. Dallas, X
Denver vs. San Francisco, XXIV
Atlanta vs. Denver, XXXIII
4 Miami vs. Minnesota, VIII
10 Miami vs. San Francisco, XIX
San Francisco vs. Miami, XIX
Buffalo vs. Dallas, XXVIII

Most Yards Penalized, Both Teams, Game
164 Dallas (133) vs. Baltimore (31), V
162 Arizona (106) vs. Pittsburgh (56), XLIII
154 Dallas (94) vs. Denver (60), XII

Fewest Yards Penalized, Both Teams, Game
15 Miami (0) vs. Dallas (15), VI
20 Pittsburgh (0) vs. Dallas (20), X
Miami (10) vs. San Francisco (10), XIX
38 Denver (0) vs. San Francisco (38), XXIV

FUMBLES

Most Fumbles, Game
8 Buffalo vs. Dallas, XXVII
6 Dallas vs. Denver, XII
Buffalo vs. Washington, XXVI
5 Baltimore vs. Dallas, V

Fewest Fumbles, Game
0 By 24 teams

Most Fumbles, Both Teams, Game
12 Buffalo (8) vs. Dallas (4), XXVII
10 Dallas (6) vs. Denver (4), XII
8 Dallas (4) vs. Pittsburgh (4), X

Fewest Fumbles, Both Teams, Game
0 Los Angeles vs. Pittsburgh, XIV
Green Bay vs. New England, XXXI
Pittsburgh vs. Seattle, XL
Indianapolis vs. New Orleans, XLIV
1 Oakland (0) vs. Minnesota (1), XI
Oakland (0) vs. Philadelphia (1), XV
Denver (0) vs. Washington (1), XXII
N.Y. Giants (0) vs. Buffalo (1), XXV
Denver (0) vs. Atlanta (1), XXXIII
2 In 11 games

Most Fumbles Lost, Game
5 Buffalo vs. Dallas, XXVII
4 Baltimore vs. Dallas, V
Denver vs. Dallas, XII
New England vs. Chicago, XX
3 Chicago vs. Indianapolis, XLI

Most Fumbles Lost, Both Teams, Game
7 Buffalo (5) vs. Dallas (2), XXVII
6 Denver (4) vs. Dallas (2), XII
New England (4) vs. Chicago (2), XX
5 Baltimore (4) vs. Dallas (1), V
Chicago (3) vs. Indianapolis (2), XLI

Fewest Fumbles Lost, Both Teams, Game
0 Green Bay vs. Kansas City, I
Dallas vs. Pittsburgh, X
Los Angeles vs. Pittsburgh, XIV
Denver vs. N.Y. Giants, XXI; vs. Washington, XXII
Buffalo vs. N.Y. Giants, XXV
San Diego vs. San Francisco, XXIX
Dallas vs. Pittsburgh, XXX
Green Bay vs. New England, XXXI
St. Louis vs. Tennessee, XXXIV
Oakland vs. Tampa Bay, XXXVII
Pittsburgh vs. Seattle, XL
Indianapolis vs. New Orleans, XLIV
New England vs. N.Y. Giants, XLVI

Most Fumbles Recovered, Game
8 Dallas vs. Denver, XII (4 own, 4 opp.)
6 Dallas vs. Buffalo, XXVII (1 own, 5 opp.)
5 Chicago vs. New England, XX (1 own, 4 opp.)

TURNOVERS

(Number of times losing the ball on interceptions and fumbles.)

Most Turnovers, Game
9 Buffalo vs. Dallas, XXVII
8 Denver vs. Dallas, XII
7 Baltimore vs. Dallas, V

Fewest Turnovers, Game
0 Green Bay vs. Oakland, II
Miami vs. Minnesota, VIII
Pittsburgh vs. Dallas, X
Oakland vs. Minnesota, XI; vs. Philadelphia, XV
N.Y. Giants vs. Denver, XXI; vs. Buffalo, XXV
San Francisco vs. Denver, XXIV; vs. San Diego, XXIX
Buffalo vs. N.Y. Giants, XXV
Dallas vs. Pittsburgh, XXX
Green Bay vs. New England, XXXI
St. Louis vs. Tennessee, XXXIV
Tennessee vs. St. Louis, XXXIV
Baltimore vs. N.Y. Giants, XXXV
New England vs. St. Louis, XXXVI
New Orleans vs. Indianapolis, XLIV
Green Bay vs. Pittsburgh, XLV
N.Y. Giants vs. New England, XLVI
Seattle vs. Denver, XLVIII
1 By many teams

Most Turnovers, Both Teams, Game
11 Baltimore (7) vs. Dallas (4), V
Buffalo (9) vs. Dallas (2), XXVII
10 Denver (8) vs. Dallas (2), XII
8 New England (6) vs. Chicago (2), XX
Chicago (5) vs. Indianapolis (3), XLI

Fewest Turnovers, Both Teams, Game
0 Buffalo vs. N.Y. Giants, XXV
St. Louis vs. Tennessee, XXXIV
1 N.Y. Giants (0) vs. Denver (1), XXI
New Orleans (0) vs. Indianapolis (1), XLIV
N.Y. Giants (0) vs. New England (1), XLVI
2 Green Bay (1) vs. Kansas City, I
Miami (0) vs. Minnesota (2), VIII
Cincinnati (1) vs. San Francisco (1), XXIII
Carolina (1) vs. New England (1), XXXVIII
New England (1) vs. N.Y. Giants (1), XLII

Compiled by Elias Sports Bureau

Throughout this all-time postseason record section, the following abbreviations are used to indicate various levels of postseason games:

SB — Super Bowl (1966 to date)

AFC — AFC Championship Game (1970 to date) or AFL Championship Game (1960-69)

NFC — NFC Championship Game (1970 to date) or NFL Championship Game (1933-69)

AFC-D — AFC Divisional Playoff Game (1970 to date), AFC Second-Round Playoff Game (1982), AFL Inter-Divisional Playoff Game (1969), or special playoff game to break tie for AFL Division Championship (1963, 1968)

NFC-D — NFC Divisional Playoff Game (1970 to date), NFC Second-Round Playoff Game (1982), NFL Conference Championship Game (1967-69), or special playoff game to break tie for NFL Division or Conference Championship (1941, 1943, 1947, 1950, 1952, 1957, 1958, 1965)

AFC-FR — AFC First-Round Playoff Game (1978 to date)

NFC-FR — NFC First-Round Playoff Game (1978 to date)

Year indicates season in which game took place and does not necessarily reflect calendar year.

POSTSEASON GAME COMPOSITE STANDINGS

	W	L	PCT.	PTS.	OP
Baltimore Ravens	14	7	.667	456	326
Green Bay Packers	30	19	.612	1,211	1,008
Pittsburgh Steelers	33	21	.611	1,283	1,123
San Francisco 49ers	30	20	.600	1,264	1,047
New England Patriots*	25	18	.581	963	882
Oakland Raiders**	25	18	.581	1,028	797
Dallas Cowboys	33	25	.569	1,355	1,098
Washington Redskins***	23	18	.561	833	731
Carolina Panthers	6	5	.545	229	226
Denver Broncos	20	18	.526	826	976
New York Giants	24	24	.500	865	889
Miami Dolphins	20	20	.500	789	875
Seattle Seahawks	12	12	.500	562	522
Houston Texans	2	2	.500	91	84
Chicago Bears	17	18	.486	751	726
Buffalo Bills	14	15	.483	681	658
New York Jets	12	13	.480	510	508
Indianapolis Colts****	20	22	.476	861	897
Philadelphia Eagles	19	21	.475	781	746
Arizona Cardinals†	6	7	.462	305	361
Jacksonville Jaguars	5	6	.455	262	288
St. Louis Rams††	19	24	.442	770	944
New Orleans Saints	7	9	.438	405	459
Tennessee Titans†††	14	19	.424	579	762
Minnesota Vikings	19	27	.413	910	1,041
Tampa Bay Buccaneers	6	9	.400	230	279
San Diego Chargers††††	11	17	.393	532	626
Detroit Lions	7	11	.389	393	449
Atlanta Falcons	7	12	.368	399	489
Cleveland Browns	11	20	.355	629	728
Kansas City Chiefs#	8	15	.348	391	520
Cincinnati Bengals	5	12	.294	310	389

* Two games played when franchise was in Boston (won 26-8, lost 51-10).

** 12 games played when franchise was in Los Angeles (won 6, lost 6, 268 points scored, 224 points allowed).

*** One game played when franchise was in Boston (lost 21-6).

**** 15 games played when franchise was in Baltimore (won 8, lost 7, 264 points scored, 262 points allowed).

† Two games played when franchise was in Chicago (won 28-21, lost 7-0), three games played when franchise was in St. Louis (lost 30-14, lost 35-23, lost 41-16).

†† One game played when franchise was in Cleveland (won 15-14), 32 games played when franchise was in Los Angeles (won 12, lost 20, 486 points scored, 683 points allowed).

††† 22 games played when franchise was in Houston and known as the Oilers (won 9, lost 13, 371 points scored, 533 points allowed).

†††† One game played when franchise was in Los Angeles (lost 24-16).

One game played when franchise was Dallas Texans (won 20-17).

INDIVIDUAL RECORDS

SERVICE

Most Games, Career

29 Jerry Rice, San Francisco-Oakland-Seattle (SB 4, NFC 6, AFC 1, NFC-D 11, AFC-D 2, NFC-FR 4, AFC-FR 1)

27 D.D. Lewis, Dallas (SB 5, NFC 9, NFC-D 12, NFC-FR 1)
   Adam Vinatieri, New England-Indianapolis (SB 5, AFC 5, AFC-D 9, AFC-FR 8)

26 Larry Cole, Dallas (SB 5, NFC 8, NFC-D 12, NFC-FR 1)
   Bill Romanowski, San Francisco-Philadelphia-Denver-Oakland (SB 5, NFC 3, NFC-D 6, AFC-D 4, NFC-FR 1, AFC-FR 2)
   Tom Brady, New England (SB 5, AFC 8, AFC-D 10, AFC-FR 3)

Most Games, Head Coach

36 Tom Landry, Dallas
   Don Shula, Baltimore-Miami

28 Bill Belichick, Cleveland-New England

24 Chuck Noll, Pittsburgh
   Mike Holmgren, Green Bay-Seattle
   Joe Gibbs, Washington

Most Championships Won, Head Coach

6 George Halas, Chicago
   Curly Lambeau, Green Bay

5 Vince Lombardi, Green Bay

4 Guy Chamberlin, Canton Bulldogs-Cleveland Bulldogs-Frankford Yellow Jackets
   Chuck Noll, Pittsburgh

Most Games Won, Head Coach

20 Tom Landry, Dallas

19 Don Shula, Baltimore-Miami
   Bill Belichick, Cleveland-New England

17 Joe Gibbs, Washington

Most Games Lost, Head Coach

17 Don Shula, Baltimore-Miami

16 Tom Landry, Dallas

13 Marty Schottenheimer, Cleveland-Kansas City-San Diego

SCORING

POINTS

Most Points, Career

213 Adam Vinatieri, New England-Indianapolis, 27 games (60-pat, 51-fg)

175 David Akers, Philadelphia-San Francisco, 24 games (58-pat, 39-fg)

153 Gary Anderson, Pittsburgh-Philadelphia-San Francisco-Minnesota-Tennessee, 22 games (57-pat, 32-fg)

Most Points, Game

30 Ricky Watters, NFC-D: San Francisco vs. N.Y. Giants, 1993 (5-td)

24 LeGarrette Blount, AFC-D: New England vs. Indianapolis, 2013 (4-td)

19 Pat Harder, NFC-D: Detroit vs. Los Angeles, 1952 (2-td, 4-pat, 1-fg)
   Paul Hornung, NFC: Green Bay vs. N.Y. Giants, 1961 (1-td, 4-pat, 3-fg)

Most Consecutive Games Scoring

27 Adam Vinatieri, New England-Indianapolis, 1996-98, 2001, 2003-08, 2010, 2012-13 (current)

24 David Akers, Philadelphia-San Francisco, 2000-06, 2008-2012 (current)

19 George Blanda, Chi. Bears-Houston-Oakland, 1956-1975

TOUCHDOWNS

Most Touchdowns, Career
- 22 Jerry Rice, San Francisco-Oakland-Seattle, 29 games (22-p)
- 21 Thurman Thomas, Buffalo, 21 games (16-r, 5-p)
  Emmitt Smith, Dallas, 17 games (19-r, 2-p)
- 17 Franco Harris, Pittsburgh, 19 games (16-r, 1-p)

Most Touchdowns, Game
- 5 Ricky Watters, NFC-D: San Francisco vs. N.Y. Giants, 1993 (5-r)
- 4 LeGarrette Blount, AFC-D: New England vs. Indianapolis, 2013 (4-r)
- 3 By many players. Most recent:
  Shane Vereen, AFC-D: New England vs. Houston, 2012 (1-r, 2-p)

Most Consecutive Games Scoring Touchdowns
- 9 Thurman Thomas, Buffalo, 1992-98
- 8 John Stallworth, Pittsburgh, 1978-1983
  Emmitt Smith, Dallas, 1993-96
- 7 John Riggins, Washington, 1982-84
  Marcus Allen, L.A. Raiders, 1982-85
  Terrell Davis, Denver, 1996-98
  David Givens, New England, 2003-05

POINTS AFTER TOUCHDOWN

Most (One-Point) Points After Touchdown, Career
- 60 Adam Vinatieri, New England-Indianapolis, 27 games (60 att)
- 58 David Akers, Philadelphia-San Francisco, 24 games (59 att)
- 57 Gary Anderson, Pittsburgh-Philadelphia-San Francisco-Minnesota-Tennessee, 22 games (57 att)

Most (One-Point) Points After Touchdown, Game
- 8 Lou Groza, NFC: Cleveland vs. Detroit, 1954 (8 att)
  Jim Martin, NFC: Detroit vs. Cleveland, 1957 (8 att)
  George Blanda, AFC-D: Oakland vs. Houston, 1969 (8 att)
  Mike Hollis, AFC-D: Jacksonville vs. Miami, 1999 (8 att)
- 7 Danny Villanueva, NFC-D: Dallas vs. Cleveland, 1967 (7 att)
  Raul Allegre, NFC-D: N.Y. Giants vs. San Francisco, 1986 (7 att)
  Mike Cofer, SB: San Francisco vs. Denver, 1989 (8 att)
  Lin Elliott, SB: Dallas vs. Buffalo, 1992 (7 att)
  Doug Brien, SB: San Francisco vs. San Diego, 1994 (7 att)
  Gary Anderson, NFC-FR: Philadelphia vs. Detroit, 1995 (7 att)
  Jeff Wilkins, NFC-D: St. Louis vs. Minnesota, 1999 (7 att)
  Mike Vanderjagt, AFC-FR: Indianapolis vs. Denver, 2004 (7 att)
- 6 George Blair, AFC: San Diego vs. Boston, 1963 (6 att)
  Mark Moseley, NFC-D: Washington vs. L.A. Rams, 1983 (6 att)
  Uwe von Schamann, AFC: Miami vs. Pittsburgh, 1984 (6 att)
  Ali Haji-Sheikh, SB: Washington vs. Denver, 1987 (6 att)
  Scott Norwood, AFC: Buffalo vs. L.A. Raiders, 1990 (7 att)
  Jeff Jaeger, AFC-D: L.A. Raiders vs. Denver, 1993 (6 att)
  Jason Elam, AFC-FR: Denver vs. Jacksonville, 1997 (6 att)
  Jeff Wilkins, NFC-D: St. Louis vs. Green Bay, 2001 (6 att)
  Martin Gramatica, SB: Tampa Bay vs. Oakland, 2002 (6 att)
  Jay Feely, NFC-D: Atlanta vs. St. Louis, 2004 (6 att)
  Mason Crosby, NFC-D: Green Bay vs. Seattle, 2007 (6 att)
  Neil Rackers, NFC-FR: Arizona vs. Green Bay, 2009 (ot) (6 att)
  Mason Crosby, NFC-FR: Green Bay vs. Arizona, 2009 (ot) (6 att)
  Garrett Hartley, NFC-D: New Orleans vs. Arizona, 2009 (6 att)
  Mason Crosby, NFC-D: Green Bay vs. Atlanta, 2010 (6 att)
  John Kasay, NFC-FR: New Orleans vs. Detroit, 2011 (6 att)
  Stephen Gostkowski, AFC-D: New England vs. Denver, 2011 (6 att)
  David Akers, NFC-D: San Francisco vs. Green Bay, 2012 (6 att),
  Adam Vinatieri, AFC-FR: Indianapolis vs. Kansas City, 2013 (6 att)

Most (Kicking) Points After Touchdown, No Misses, Career
- 60 Adam Vinatieri, New England-Indianapolis, 27 games
- 57 Gary Anderson, Pittsburgh-Philadelphia-San Francisco-Minnesota-Tennessee, 22 games
- 49 George Blanda, Chi. Bears-Houston-Oakland, 19 games

Most Two-Point Conversions, Career
- 2 Terrell Owens, San Francisco-Philadelphia-Dallas, 12 games
  Kevin Faulk, New England, 19 games

Most Two-Point Conversions, Game
- 2 Terrell Owens, NFC-FR: San Francisco vs. N.Y. Giants, 2002

FIELD GOALS

Most Field Goals Attempted, Career
- 61 Adam Vinatieri, New England-Indianapolis, 27 games
- 47 David Akers, Philadelphia-San Francisco, 24 games
- 40 Gary Anderson, Pittsburgh-Philadelphia-San Francisco-Minnesota-Tennessee, 22 games

Most Field Goals Attempted, Game
- 6 George Blanda, AFC: Oakland vs. Houston, 1967
  David Ray, NFC-D: Los Angeles vs. Dallas, 1973
  Mark Moseley, AFC-D: Cleveland vs. N.Y. Jets, 1986 (ot)
  Matt Bahr, NFC: N.Y. Giants vs. San Francisco, 1990
  Steve Christie, AFC: Buffalo vs. Miami, 1992
  Jeff Wilkins, NFC-D: St. Louis vs. Carolina, 2003 (2 ot)
- 5 By many players

Most Field Goals, Career
- 51 Adam Vinatieri, New England-Indianapolis, 27 games
- 39 David Akers, Philadelphia-San Francisco, 24 games
- 32 Gary Anderson, Pittsburgh-Philadelphia-San Francisco-Minnesota-Tennessee, 22 games

Most Field Goals, Game
- 5 Chuck Nelson, NFC-D: Minnesota vs. San Francisco, 1987
  Matt Bahr, NFC: N.Y. Giants vs. San Francisco, 1990
  Steve Christie, AFC: Buffalo vs. Miami, 1992
  Brad Daluiso, NFC-FR: N.Y. Giants vs. Minnesota, 1997
  John Kasay, NFC-FR: Carolina vs. Dallas, 2003
  Jeff Wilkins, NFC-D: St. Louis vs. Carolina, 2003 (2 ot)
  Adam Vinatieri, AFC: New England vs. Indianapolis, 2003
  Adam Vinatieri, AFC-D: Indianapolis vs. Baltimore, 2006
- 4 Gino Cappelletti, AFC-D: Boston vs. Buffalo, 1963
  George Blanda, AFC: Oakland vs. Houston, 1967
  Don Chandler, SB: Green Bay vs. Oakland, 1967
  Curt Knight, NFC: Washington vs. Dallas, 1972
  George Blanda, AFC-D: Oakland vs. Pittsburgh, 1973
  Ray Wersching, SB: San Francisco vs. Cincinnati, 1981
  Tony Franklin, AFC-FR: New England vs. N.Y. Jets, 1985
  Jess Atkinson, NFC-FR: Washington vs. L.A. Rams, 1986
  Luis Zendejas, NFC-D: Philadelphia vs. Chicago, 1988
  Gary Anderson, NFC-D: Pittsburgh vs. Houston, 1989 (ot)
  Norm Johnson, AFC-D: Pittsburgh vs. Buffalo, 1995
  Chris Boniol, NFC-FR: Dallas vs. Minnesota, 1996
  John Kasay, NFC-D: Carolina vs. Dallas, 1996
  Mike Hollis, AFC-D: Jacksonville vs. New England, 1998
  Al Del Greco, AFC-D: Tennessee vs. Indianapolis, 1999
  David Akers, NFC-D: Philadelphia vs. Chicago, 2001
  Nate Kaeding, AFC-D: San Diego vs. New England, 2007
  David Akers, NFC-FR: Philadelphia vs. Minnesota, 2008
  Neil Rackers, NFC-D: Arizona vs. Carolina, 2008
  Shayne Graham, AFC-FR: Houston vs. Cincinnati, 2012
  Shayne Graham, NFC-FR: New Orleans vs. Philadelphia, 2013
  Matt Prater, AFC: Denver vs. New England, 2013
- 3 By many players

Most Consecutive Games Scoring Field Goals
- 13 Toni Fritsch, Dallas-Houston, 1972-79
- 12 Adam Vinatieri, New England, 1997-2004
- 11 Jason Elam, Denver-Atlanta, 1997-2000, 2003-05, 2008
  Adam Vinatieri, New England-Indianapolis, 2005-08, 2010, 2012-13 (current)

Most Consecutive Field Goals
- 19 David Akers, Philadelphia, 2000-04, 2006, 2008
- 16 Gary Anderson, Pittsburgh-Philadelphia, 1989-1995
  Matt Stover, Baltimore, 2001, 2003, 2006, 2008;
  Indianapolis, 2009
- 15 Rafael Septien, Dallas, 1978-1982

Longest Field Goal
- 58 Pete Stoyanovich, AFC-FR: Miami vs. Kansas City, 1990
- 55 Jeff Wilkins, NFC-D: St. Louis vs. Atlanta, 2004
  Shayne Graham, AFC-D: Houston vs. New England, 2012
- 54 Ed Murray, NFC-D: Detroit vs. San Francisco, 1983
  Steve Christie, SB: Buffalo vs. Dallas, 1993
  John Carney, AFC-FR: San Diego vs. Indianapolis, 1995
  Matt Prater, AFC: Denver vs. New England, 2013

Highest Field Goal Percentage, Career (10 field goals)
- 100.0 Steven Hauschka, Seattle, 7 games (11-11)
- 92.9 Martin Gramatica, Tampa Bay-Indianapolis-Dallas,
  9 games (14-13)
- 92.0 John Kasay, Carolina-New Orleans, 12 games (25-23)

SAFETIES
Most Safeties, Game
- 1 Bill Willis, NFC-D: Cleveland vs. N.Y. Giants, 1950
  Carl Eller, NFC-D: Minnesota vs. Los Angeles, 1969
  George Andrie, NFC-D: Dallas vs. Detroit, 1970
  Alan Page, NFC-D: Minnesota vs. Dallas, 1971
  Dwight White, SB: Pittsburgh vs. Minnesota, 1974
  Reggie Harrison, SB: Pittsburgh vs. Dallas, 1975
  Jim Jensen, NFC-D: Dallas vs. Los Angeles, 1976
  Ted Washington, AFC: Houston vs. Pittsburgh, 1978
  Randy White, NFC-D: Dallas vs. Los Angeles, 1979
  Henry Waechter, SB: Chicago vs. New England, 1985
  Rulon Jones, AFC-FR: Denver vs. New England, 1986
  George Martin, SB: N.Y. Giants vs. Denver, 1986
  D.D. Hoggard, AFC: Cleveland vs. Denver, 1987
  Bruce Smith, SB: Buffalo vs. N.Y. Giants, 1990
  Reggie White, NFC-FR: Philadelphia vs. New Orleans, 1992
  Willie Clay, NFC-FR: Detroit vs. Green Bay, 1994
  Carnell Lake, AFC-D: Pittsburgh vs. Cleveland, 1994
  Reuben Davis, AFC-D: San Diego vs. Miami, 1994
  Jevon Kearse, AFC-FR: Tennessee vs. Buffalo, 1999
  Brady Smith, NFC-D: Atlanta vs. St. Louis, 2004
  Antonio Smith, NFC-FR: Arizona vs. Atlanta, 2008
  Mike DeVito, AFC: N.Y. Jets vs. Pittsburgh, 2010
  Chris Culliver, SB: San Francisco vs. Baltimore, 2012
  Cliff Avril, SB: Seattle vs. Denver, 2013

RUSHING
ATTEMPTS
Most Attempts, Career
- 400 Franco Harris, Pittsburgh, 19 games
- 349 Emmitt Smith, Dallas, 17 games
- 339 Thurman Thomas, Buffalo, 21 games

Most Attempts, Game
- 40 Lamar Smith, AFC-FR: Miami vs. Indianapolis, 2000 (ot)
- 38 Ricky Bell, NFC-D: Tampa Bay vs. Philadelphia, 1979
  John Riggins, SB: Washington vs. Miami, 1982
- 37 Lawrence McCutcheon, NFC-D: Los Angeles vs. St. Louis,
  1975
  John Riggins, NFC-D: Washington vs. Minnesota, 1982

YARDS GAINED
Most Yards Gained, Career
- 1,586 Emmitt Smith, Dallas, 17 games
- 1,556 Franco Harris, Pittsburgh, 19 games
- 1,442 Thurman Thomas, Buffalo, 21 games

Most Yards Gained, Game
- 248 Eric Dickerson, NFC-D: L.A. Rams vs. Dallas, 1985
- 209 Lamar Smith, AFC-FR: Miami vs. Indianapolis, 2000 (ot)
- 206 Keith Lincoln, AFC: San Diego vs. Boston, 1963

Most Games, 100 or More Yards Rushing, Career
- 7 Emmitt Smith, Dallas, 17 games

Terrell Davis, Denver, 8 games
- 6 John Riggins, Washington, 9 games
  Thurman Thomas, Buffalo, 21 games
- 5 Franco Harris, Pittsburgh, 19 games
  Marcus Allen, L.A. Raiders-Kansas City, 16 games

Most Consecutive Games, 100 or More Yards Rushing
- 7 Terrell Davis, Denver, 1997-98
- 6 John Riggins, Washington, 1982-83
- 4 Thurman Thomas, Buffalo, 1990-91

Longest Run From Scrimmage
- 90 Fred Taylor, AFC-D: Jacksonville vs. Miami, 1999 (TD)
- 83 Ray Rice, AFC-FR: Baltimore vs. New England, 2009 (TD)
- 80 Roger Craig, NFC-D: San Francisco vs. Minnesota, 1988 (TD)
  Charlie Garner, AFC-FR: Oakland vs. N.Y. Jets, 2001 (TD)

AVERAGE GAIN
Highest Average Gain, Career (100 attempts)
- 5.59 Terrell Davis, Denver, 8 games (204-1,140)
- 5.04 Marcus Allen, L.A. Raiders-Kansas City, 16 games
  (267-1,347)
- 4.90 Arian Foster, Houston, 4 games (105-515)

Highest Average Gain, Game (10 attempts)
- 15.90 Elmer Angsman, NFC: Chi. Cardinals vs. Philadelphia,
  1947 (10-159)
- 15.85 Keith Lincoln, AFC: San Diego vs. Boston, 1963 (13-206)
- 11.82 Colin Kaepernick, NFC: San Francisco vs. Seattle,
  2013 (11-130)

TOUCHDOWNS
Most Touchdowns, Career
- 19 Emmitt Smith, Dallas, 17 games
- 16 Franco Harris, Pittsburgh, 19 games
  Thurman Thomas, Buffalo, 21 games
- 12 John Riggins, Washington, 9 games
  Terrell Davis, Denver, 8 games

Most Touchdowns, Game
- 5 Ricky Watters, NFC-D: San Francisco vs. N.Y. Giants, 1993
- 4 LeGarrette Blount, AFC-D: New England vs. Indianapolis, 2013
- 3 Andy Farkas, NFC-D: Washington vs. N.Y. Giants, 1943
  Otto Graham, NFC: Cleveland vs. Detroit, 1954
  Tom Matte, NFC: Baltimore vs. Cleveland, 1968
  Larry Schreiber, NFC-D: San Francisco vs. Dallas, 1972
  Larry Csonka, AFC: Miami vs. Oakland, 1973
  Franco Harris, AFC-D: Pittsburgh vs. Buffalo, 1974
  John Riggins, NFC-D: Washington vs. L.A. Rams, 1983
  Kenneth Davis, AFC: Buffalo vs. L.A. Raiders, 1990
  Napoleon McCallum, AFC-FR: L.A. Raiders vs. Denver, 1993
  Thurman Thomas, AFC: Buffalo vs. Kansas City, 1993
  William Floyd, NFC-D: San Francisco vs. Chicago, 1994
  Emmitt Smith, NFC-D: Dallas vs. Green Bay, 1995
  Curtis Martin, AFC-D: New England vs. Pittsburgh, 1996
  Terrell Davis, SB: Denver vs. Green Bay, 1997
  Mario Bates, NFC-D: Arizona vs. Minnesota, 1998
  Shaun Alexander, NFC-FR: Seattle vs. Green Bay, 2003 (ot)
  Ryan Grant, NFC-D: Green Bay vs. Seattle, 2007
  Adrian Peterson, NFC: Minnesota vs. New Orleans, 2009 (ot)

Most Consecutive Games Rushing for Touchdowns
- 8 Emmitt Smith, Dallas, 1993-96
  Thurman Thomas, Buffalo, 1992-98
- 7 John Riggins, Washington, 1982-84
  Terrell Davis, Denver, 1996-98
- 5 Franco Harris, Pittsburgh, 1974-75
  Franco Harris, Pittsburgh, 1977-79
  Curtis Martin, New England-N.Y. Jets, 1996-98
  Jerome Bettis, Pittsburgh, 2004-05
  Marshawn Lynch, Seattle, 2012-13 (current)

PASSING
PASSER RATING
Highest Passer Rating, Career (150 attempts)
- 104.8 Bart Starr, Green Bay, 10 games
- 103.1 Aaron Rodgers, Green Bay, 10 games

102.8   Kurt Warner, St. Louis-Arizona, 13 games

ATTEMPTS
Most Passes Attempted, Career
- 950   Tom Brady, New England, 26 games
- 889   Peyton Manning, Indianapolis-Denver, 23 games
- 791   Brett Favre, Green Bay-Minnesota, 24 games

Most Passes Attempted, Game
- 65   Steve Young, NFC-D: San Francisco vs. Green Bay, 1995
- 64   Bernie Kosar, AFC-D: Cleveland vs. N.Y. Jets, 1986 (ot)
- Dan Marino, AFC-FR: Miami vs. Buffalo, 1995
- 63   Drew Brees, NFC-D: New Orleans vs. San Francisco, 2011

COMPLETIONS
Most Passes Completed, Career
- 590   Tom Brady, New England, 26 games
- 572   Peyton Manning, Indianapolis-Denver, 23 games
- 481   Brett Favre, Green Bay-Minnesota, 24 games

Most Passes Completed, Game
- 40   Drew Brees, NFC-D: New Orleans vs. San Francisco, 2011
- 39   Drew Brees, NFC-FR: New Orleans vs. Seattle, 2010
- 36   Warren Moon, AFC-FR: Houston vs. Buffalo, 1992 (ot)

COMPLETION PERCENTAGE
Highest Completion Percentage, Career (150 attempts)
- 66.50   Kurt Warner, St. Louis-Arizona, 13 games (462-307)
- 66.31   Matt Ryan, Atlanta, 5 games, (187-124)
- 66.27   Ken Anderson, Cincinnati, 6 games (166-110)

Highest Completion Percentage, Game (15 completions)
- 92.9   Tom Brady, AFC-D: New England vs. Jacksonville, 2007 (28-26)
- 88.0   Phil Simms, SB: N.Y. Giants vs. Denver, 1986 (25-22)
- 87.9   Kurt Warner, NFC-FR: Arizona vs. Green Bay, 2009 (ot) (33-29)

YARDS GAINED
Most Yards Gained, Career
- 6,589   Peyton Manning, Indianapolis-Denver, 23 games
- 6,424   Tom Brady, New England, 26 games
- 5,855   Brett Favre, Green Bay-Minnesota, 24 games

Most Yards Gained, Game
- 489   Bernie Kosar, AFC-D: Cleveland vs. N.Y. Jets, 1986 (ot)
- 466   Drew Brees, NFC-FR: New Orleans vs. Detroit, 2011
- 462   Drew Brees, NFC-D: New Orleans vs. San Francisco, 2011

Most Games, 300 or More Yards Passing, Career
- 9   Peyton Manning, Indianapolis-Denver, 23 games
- 6   Joe Montana, San Francisco-Kansas City, 23 games
- Kurt Warner, St. Louis-Arizona, 13 games
- Tom Brady, New England, 26 games
- Drew Brees, San Diego-New Orleans, 11 games
- 5   Dan Fouts, San Diego, 7 games

Most Consecutive Games, 300 or More Yards Passing
- 4   Dan Fouts, San Diego, 1979-1981
- 3   Jim Kelly, Buffalo, 1989-1990
- Warren Moon, Houston, 1991-93
- Drew Brees, New Orleans, 2010-11
- 2   Daryle Lamonica, Oakland, 1968
- Ken Anderson, Cincinnati, 1981-82
- Terry Bradshaw, Pittsburgh, 1979-1982
- Joe Montana, San Francisco, 1983-84
- Dan Marino, Miami, 1984
- Troy Aikman, Dallas, 1994
- Steve Young, San Francisco, 1994-95
- Kurt Warner, St. Louis, 1999-2000
- Peyton Manning, Indianapolis, 2003
- Marc Bulger, St. Louis, 2003-04
- Matt Hasselbeck, Seattle, 2003-04
- Peyton Manning, Indianapolis, 2007-08
- Donovan McNabb, Philadelphia, 2004, 2008
- Kurt Warner, Arizona, 2008-09
- Peyton Manning, Indianapolis, 2009
- Eli Manning, N.Y. Giants, 2011

Tom Brady, New England, 2012
Andrew Luck, Indianapolis, 2013 (current)

Longest Pass Completion
- 96   Trent Dilfer (to Sharpe), AFC: Baltimore vs. Oakland, 2000 (TD)
- 94   Troy Aikman (to Harper), NFC-D: Dallas vs. Green Bay, 1994 (TD)
- 93   Daryle Lamonica (to Dubenion), AFC-D: Buffalo vs. Boston, 1963 (TD)

AVERAGE GAIN
Highest Average Gain, Career (150 attempts)
- 8.55   Kurt Warner, St. Louis-Arizona, 13 games (462-3,952)
- 8.48   Colin Kaepernick, San Francisco, 6 games (162-1,374)
- 8.45   Joe Theismann, Washington, 10 games (211-1,782)

Highest Average Gain, Game (20 attempts)
- 15.05   Tim Tebow, AFC-FR: Denver vs. Pittsburgh, 2011 (21-316)
- 14.71   Terry Bradshaw, SB: Pittsburgh vs. Los Angeles, 1979 (21-309)
- 14.50   Peyton Manning, AFC-FR: Indianapolis vs. Denver, 2003 (26-377)

TOUCHDOWNS
Most Touchdown Passes, Career
- 45   Joe Montana, San Francisco-Kansas City, 23 games
- 44   Brett Favre, Green Bay-Minnesota, 24 games
- 43   Tom Brady, New England, 26 games

Most Touchdown Passes, Game
- 6   Daryle Lamonica, AFC-D: Oakland vs. Houston, 1969
- Steve Young, SB: San Francisco vs. San Diego, 1994
- Tom Brady, AFC-D: New England vs. Denver, 2011
- 5   Sid Luckman, NFC: Chi. Bears vs. Washington, 1943
- Daryle Lamonica, AFC-D: Oakland vs. Kansas City, 1968
- Joe Montana, SB: San Francisco vs. Denver, 1989
- Kurt Warner, NFC-D: St. Louis vs. Minnesota, 1999
- Kerry Collins, NFC: N.Y. Giants vs. Minnesota, 2000
- Peyton Manning, AFC-FR: Indianapolis vs. Denver, 2003
- Kurt Warner, NFC-FR: Arizona vs. Green Bay, 2009 (ot)
- 4   By many players. Last time:
- Alex Smith, AFC-FR: Kansas City vs. Indianapolis, 2013
- Andrew Luck, AFC-FR: Indianapolis vs. Kansas City, 2013

Most Consecutive Games, Touchdown Passes
- 20   Brett Favre, Green Bay-Minnesota, 1995-2009
- 18   Tom Brady, New England, 2001-2011
- 13   Dan Marino, Miami, 1983-1995

HAD INTERCEPTED
Lowest Percentage, Passes Had Intercepted, Career (150 attempts)
- 1.29   Drew Brees, San Diego-New Orleans, 11 games (464-4)
- 1.41   Bart Starr, Green Bay, 10 games (213-3)
- 1.57   Aaron Rodgers, Green Bay, 10 games (318-5)

Most Attempts Without Interception, Game
- 60   Drew Brees, NFC-FR: New Orleans vs. Seattle, 2010
- 58   Eli Manning, NFC: N.Y. Giants vs. San Francisco, 2011 (ot)
- 54   Neil O'Donnell, AFC: Pittsburgh vs. San Diego, 1994

Most Passes Had Intercepted, Career
- 30   Brett Favre, Green Bay-Minnesota, 24 games
- 28   Jim Kelly, Buffalo, 17 games
- 26   Terry Bradshaw, Pittsburgh, 19 games

Most Passes Had Intercepted, Game
- 6   Frank Filchock, NFC: N.Y. Giants vs. Chi. Bears, 1946
- Bobby Layne, NFC: Detroit vs. Cleveland, 1954
- Norm Van Brocklin, NFC: Los Angeles vs. Cleveland, 1955
- Brett Favre, NFC-D: Green Bay vs. St. Louis, 2001
- 5   Frank Filchock, NFC: Washington vs. Chi. Bears, 1940
- George Blanda, AFC: Houston vs. San Diego, 1961
- George Blanda, AFC: Houston vs. Dall. Texans, 1962 (ot)
- Y.A. Tittle, NFC: N.Y. Giants vs. Chicago, 1963
- Mike Phipps, AFC-D: Cleveland vs. Miami, 1972
- Dan Pastorini, AFC: Houston vs. Pittsburgh, 1978
- Dan Fouts, AFC-D: San Diego vs. Houston, 1979
- Tommy Kramer, NFC-D: Minnesota vs. Philadelphia, 1980

Dan Fouts, AFC-D: San Diego vs. Miami, 1982
Richard Todd, AFC: N.Y. Jets vs. Miami, 1982
Gary Danielson, NFC-D: Detroit vs. San Francisco, 1983
Jay Schroeder, AFC: L.A. Raiders vs. Buffalo, 1990
Rich Gannon, SB: Oakland vs. Tampa Bay, 2002
Jake Delhomme, NFC-D: Carolina vs. Arizona, 2008
4   By many players

PASS RECEIVING

RECEPTIONS

Most Receptions, Career
151   Jerry Rice, San Francisco-Oakland-Seattle, 29 games
92   Reggie Wayne, Indianapolis, 18 games
88   Hines Ward, Pittsburgh, 18 games

Most Receptions, Game
15   Darren Sproles, NFC-D: New Orleans vs. San Francisco, 2011
13   Kellen Winslow, AFC-D: San Diego vs. Miami, 1981 (ot)
      Thurman Thomas, AFC-D: Buffalo vs. Cleveland, 1989
      Shannon Sharpe, AFC-FR: Denver vs. L.A. Raiders, 1993
      Chad Morton, NFC-D: New Orleans vs. Minnesota, 2000
      T.Y. Hilton, AFC-FR: Indianapolis vs. Kansas City, 2013
      Demaryius Thomas, SB: Denver vs. Seattle, 2013
12   Raymond Berry, NFC: Baltimore vs. N.Y. Giants, 1958
      Michael Irvin, NFC: Dallas vs. San Francisco, 1994
      Darrell Jackson, NFC-FR: Seattle vs. St. Louis, 2004
      Steve Smith, NFC-D: Carolina vs. Chicago, 2005
      Calvin Johnson, NFC-FR: Detroit vs. New Orleans, 2011

Most Consecutive Games, Pass Receptions
28   Jerry Rice, San Francisco-Oakland, 1985-2002
22   Drew Pearson, Dallas, 1973-1983
18   Paul Warfield, Cleveland-Miami, 1964-1974
      Cliff Branch, Oakland/L.A. Raiders, 1974-1983
      Thurman Thomas, Buffalo, 1989-1998
      Shannon Sharpe, Denver-Baltimore-Denver, 1991-2003
      Reggie Wayne, Indianapolis, 2002-2012 (current)

YARDS GAINED

Most Yards Gained, Career
2,245   Jerry Rice, San Francisco-Oakland-Seattle, 29 games
1,315   Michael Irvin, Dallas, 16 games
1,289   Cliff Branch, Oakland/L.A. Raiders, 22 games

Most Yards Gained, Game
240   Eric Moulds, AFC-FR: Buffalo vs. Miami, 1998
227   Anthony Carter, NFC-D: Minnesota vs. San Francisco, 1987
224   T.Y. Hilton, AFC-FR: Indianapolis vs. Kansas City, 2013

Most Games, 100 or More Yards Receiving, Career
8   Jerry Rice, San Francisco-Oakland-Seattle, 29 games
6   Michael Irvin, Dallas, 16 games
5   John Stallworth, Pittsburgh, 18 games
    Andre Reed, Buffalo, 21 games
    Hines Ward, Pittsburgh, 18 games

Most Consecutive Games, 100 or More Yards Receiving, Career
4   Larry Fitzgerald, Arizona, 2008
3   Tom Fears, Los Angeles, 1950-51
    Jerry Rice, San Francisco, 1988-89
    Randy Moss, Minnesota, 1999-2000
2   By many players

Longest Reception
96   Shannon Sharpe (from Dilfer), AFC: Baltimore vs. Oakland, 2000 (TD)
94   Alvin Harper (from Aikman), NFC-D: Dallas vs. Green Bay, 1994 (TD)
93   Elbert Dubenion (from Lamonica), AFC-D: Buffalo vs. Boston, 1963 (TD)

AVERAGE GAIN

Highest Average Gain, Career (20 receptions)
27.3   Alvin Harper, Dallas, 10 games (24-655)
23.7   Willie Gault, Chicago-L.A. Raiders, 12 games (21-497)
22.8   Harold Jackson, Los Angeles-New England-Minnesota-Seattle, 14 games (24-548)

Highest Average Gain, Game (3 receptions)
51.0   Demaryius Thomas, AFC-FR: Denver vs. Pittsburgh, 2011 (4-204)
46.3   Harold Jackson, NFC: Los Angeles vs. Minnesota, 1974 (3-139)
42.7   Billy Cannon, AFC: Houston vs. L.A. Chargers, 1960 (3-128)

TOUCHDOWNS

Most Touchdowns, Career
22   Jerry Rice, San Francisco-Oakland-Seattle, 29 games
12   John Stallworth, Pittsburgh, 18 games
10   Fred Biletnikoff, Oakland, 19 games
     Antonio Freeman, Green Bay-Philadelphia-Green Bay, 16 games
     Randy Moss, Minnesota-New England-San Francisco, 15 games
     Hines Ward, Pittsburgh, 18 games

Most Touchdowns, Game
3   Tom Fears, NFC-D: Los Angeles vs. Chi. Bears, 1950
     Gary Collins, NFC: Cleveland vs. Baltimore, 1964
     Fred Biletnikoff, AFC-D: Oakland vs. Kansas City, 1968
     Preston Pearson, NFC: Dallas vs. Los Angeles, 1975
     Dave Casper, AFC-D: Oakland vs. Baltimore, 1977 (ot)
     Alvin Garrett, NFC-FR: Washington vs. Detroit, 1982
     Jerry Rice, NFC-D: San Francisco vs. Minnesota, 1988
     Jerry Rice, SB: San Francisco vs. Denver, 1989
     Andre Reed, AFC-FR: Buffalo vs. Houston, 1992 (ot)
     Sterling Sharpe, NFC-FR: Green Bay vs. Detroit, 1993
     Jerry Rice, SB: San Francisco vs. San Diego, 1994
     Willie Jackson, NFC-FR: New Orleans vs. St. Louis, 2000
     Amani Toomer, NFC-FR: N.Y. Giants vs. San Francisco, 2002
     Larry Fitzgerald, NFC: Arizona vs. Philadelphia, 2008
     Sidney Rice, NFC-D: Minnesota vs. Dallas, 2009
     Rob Gronkowski, AFC-D: New England vs. Denver, 2011

Most Consecutive Games, Touchdown Passes Caught
8   John Stallworth, Pittsburgh, 1978-1983
7   David Givens, New England, 2003-05)
5   James Lofton, Green Bay-Buffalo, 1982-1990
     Randy Moss, Minnesota, 1998-2000
     Antonio Freeman, Green Bay, 1997-2001
     Hines Ward, Pittsburgh, 2002-05
     Larry Fitzgerald, Arizona, 2008-09

INTERCEPTIONS BY

Most Interceptions, Career
9   Charlie Waters, Dallas, 25 games
     Bill Simpson, Los Angeles-Buffalo, 11 games
     Ronnie Lott, San Francisco-L.A. Raiders, 20 games
     Ed Reed, Baltimore, 15 games
8   Lester Hayes, Oakland/L.A. Raiders, 13 games
7   Willie Brown, Oakland, 17 games
     Dennis Thurman, Dallas, 14 games
     Rodney Harrison, San Diego-New England, 13 games
     Asante Samuel, New England-Philadelphia-Atlanta, 21 games

Most Interceptions, Game
4   Vernon Perry, AFC-D: Houston vs. San Diego, 1979
3   Joe Laws, NFC: Green Bay vs. N.Y. Giants, 1944
     Charlie Waters, NFC-D: Dallas vs. Chicago, 1977
     Rod Martin, SB: Oakland vs. Philadelphia, 1980
     Dennis Thurman, NFC-D: Dallas vs. Green Bay, 1982
     A.J. Duhe, AFC: Miami vs. N.Y. Jets, 1982
     Ty Law, AFC: New England vs. Indianapolis, 2003
     Ricky Manning Jr., NFC: Carolina vs. Philadelphia, 2003
2   By many players

Most Consecutive Games, Interceptions
4   Aeneas Williams, Arizona-St. Louis, 1998-2001
     Rodney Harrison, New England, 2004, 2007
3   By many players. Last time:
     Ed Reed, Baltimore, 2006, 2008

YARDS GAINED

Most Yards Gained, Career
- 227 Asante Samuel, New England-Philadelphia-Atlanta, 21 games
- 196 Willie Brown, Oakland, 17 games
- 187 Ronnie Lott, San Francisco-L.A.-Raiders, 20 games

Most Yards Gained, Game
- 108 Darrien Gordon, SB: Denver vs. Atlanta, 1998
- 101 George Teague, NFC-FR: Green Bay vs. Detroit, 1993
- 100 Champ Bailey, AFC-D: Denver vs. New England, 2005
- James Harrison, SB: Pittsburgh vs. Arizona, 2008

Longest Return
- 101 George Teague, NFC-FR: Green Bay vs. Detroit, 1993 (TD)
- 100 Champ Bailey, AFC-D: Denver vs. New England, 2005
- James Harrison, SB: Pittsburgh vs. Arizona, 2008 (TD)
- 98 Darrol Ray, AFC-FR: N.Y. Jets vs. Cincinnati, 1982 (TD)

TOUCHDOWNS

Most Touchdowns, Career
- 4 Asante Samuel, New England-Philadelphia-Atlanta, 21 games
- 3 Willie Brown, Oakland, 17 games
- 2 Lester Hayes, Oakland/L.A. Raiders, 13 games
- Ronnie Lott, San Francisco-L.A. Raiders, 20 games
- Darrell Green, Washington, 18 games
- Melvin Jenkins, Seattle-Detroit, 5 games
- George Teague, Green Bay-Dallas-Miami-Dallas, 12 games
- Aeneas Williams, Arizona-St. Louis, 6 games
- Dwight Smith, Tampa Bay, 4 games

Most Touchdowns, Game
- 2 Aeneas Williams, NFC-D: St. Louis vs. Green Bay, 2001
- Dwight Smith, SB: Tampa Bay vs. Oakland, 2002
- 1 By many players

PUNTING

Most Punts, Career
- 111 Ray Guy, Oakland/L.A. Raiders, 22 games
- 101 Craig Hentrich, Green Bay-Tennessee, 22 games
- 84 Danny White, Dallas, 18 games
- Sean Landeta, N.Y. Giants-Tampa Bay-Green Bay-Philadelphia-St. Louis, 18 games

Most Punts, Game
- 14 Dave Jennings, AFC-D: N.Y. Jets vs. Cleveland, 1986 (ot)
- 12 David Lee, AFC-D: Baltimore vs. Oakland, 1977 (ot)
- Steve Weatherford, NFC: N.Y. Giants vs. San Francisco, 2011 (ot)
- 11 Ken Strong, NFC: N.Y. Giants vs. Chi. Bears, 1933
- Jim Norton, AFC: Houston vs. Oakland, 1967
- Ode Burrell, AFC-D: Houston vs. Oakland, 1969
- Dale Hatcher, NFC: L.A. Rams vs. Chicago, 1985
- Brad Maynard, SB: N.Y. Giants vs. Baltimore, 2000

Longest Punt
- 76 Ed Danowski, NFC: N.Y. Giants vs. Detroit, 1935
- Mike Horan, AFC: Denver vs. Buffalo, 1991
- 72 Charlie Conerly, NFC-D: N.Y. Giants vs. Cleveland, 1950
- Yale Lary, NFC: Detroit vs. Cleveland, 1953
- 71 Ray Guy, AFC: Oakland vs. San Diego, 1980

AVERAGE YARDAGE

Highest Average, Career (25 punts)
- 46.4 Pat McAfee, Indianapolis, 7 games (26-1,207)
- 46.3 Andy Lee, San Francisco, 8 games (36-1,667)
- 44.8 Mike Scifres, San Diego, 10 games (52-2,330)

Highest Average, Game (4 punts)
- 56.0 Ray Guy, AFC: Oakland vs. San Diego, 1980 (4-224)
- 53.8 Sam Koch, AFC-D: Baltimore vs. Pittsburgh, 2010 (4-215)
- 53.3 Craig Hentrich, AFC-D: Tennessee vs. Baltimore, 2008 (4-213)

PUNT RETURNS

Most Punt Returns, Career
- 34 David Meggett, N.Y. Giants-New England-N.Y. Jets, 13 games
- Brian Mitchell, Washington-Philadelphia, 16 games
- 33 Troy Brown, New England, 20 games
- 26 Antwaan Randle El, Pittsburgh-Washington, 12 games

Most Punt Returns, Game
- 8 Kyle Williams, NFC: San Francisco vs. N.Y. Giants, 2011 (ot)
- 7 Ron Gardin, AFC-D: Baltimore vs. Cincinnati, 1970
- Carl Roaches, AFC-FR: Houston vs. Oakland, 1980
- Gerald McNeil, AFC-D: Cleveland vs. N.Y. Jets, 1986 (ot)
- Phil McConkey, NFC-D: N.Y. Giants vs. San Francisco, 1986
- David Meggett, AFC-D: New England vs. Pittsburgh, 1996
- Reggie Barlow, AFC-FR: Jacksonville vs. New England, 1998
- 6 By many players

YARDS GAINED

Most Yards Gained, Career
- 339 Brian Mitchell, Washington-Philadelphia, 16 games
- 315 Troy Brown, New England, 20 games
- 312 David Meggett, N.Y. Giants-New England-N.Y. Jets, 13 games

Most Yards Gained, Game
- 152 Allen Rossum, NFC-D: Atlanta vs. St. Louis, 2004
- 143 Anthony Carter, NFC-FR: Minnesota vs. New Orleans, 1987
- 141 Bob Hayes, NFC-D: Dallas vs. Cleveland, 1967

Longest Return
- 90 Trindon Holliday, AFC-D: Denver vs. Baltimore, 2012 (2 ot) (TD)
- 88 Jermaine Lewis, AFC-D: Baltimore vs. Pittsburgh, 2001 (TD)
- 84 Anthony Carter, NFC-FR: Minnesota vs. New Orleans, 1987 (TD)

AVERAGE YARDAGE

Highest Average, Career (10 returns)
- 23.9 Allen Rossum, Green Bay-Atlanta, 6 games (10-239)
- 15.8 DeSean Jackson, Philadelphia, 6 games (11-174)
- 15.3 Robert Brooks, Green Bay, 11 games (14-214)

Highest Average Gain, Game (3 returns)
- 50.7 Allen Rossum, NFC-D: Atlanta vs. St. Louis, 2004 (3-152)
- 47.0 Bob Hayes, NFC-D: Dallas vs. Cleveland, 1967 (3-141)
- 36.3 Reggie Bush, NFC-D: New Orleans vs. Arizona, 2009 (3-109)

TOUCHDOWNS

Most Touchdowns
- 1 Hugh Gallarneau, NFC-D: Chicago Bears vs. Green Bay, 1941
- Bosh Pritchard, NFC-D: Philadelphia vs. Pittsburgh, 1947
- Charley Trippi, NFC: Chicago Cardinals vs. Philadelphia, 1947
- Verda (Vitamin T) Smith, NFC-D: Los Angeles vs. Detroit, 1952
- George (Butch) Byrd, AFC: Buffalo vs. San Diego, 1965
- Golden Richards, NFC: Dallas vs. Minnesota, 1973
- Wes Chandler, AFC-D: San Diego vs. Miami, 1981 (ot)
- Shaun Gayle, NFC: Chicago vs. N.Y. Giants, 1985
- Anthony Carter, NFC-FR: Minnesota vs. New Orleans, 1987
- Darrell Green, NFC-D: Washington vs. Chicago, 1987
- Antonio Freeman, NFC-FR: Green Bay vs. Atlanta, 1995
- Desmond Howard, NFC-D: Green Bay vs. San Francisco, 1996
- Jermaine Lewis, AFC-D: Baltimore vs. Pittsburgh, 2001
- Troy Brown, AFC: New England vs. Pittsburgh, 2001
- Antwaan Randle El, AFC-FR: Pittsburgh vs. Cleveland, 2002
- Santana Moss, AFC-D: N.Y. Jets vs. Pittsburgh, 2004 (ot)

Allen Rossum, NFC-D: Atlanta vs. St. Louis, 2004
Steve Smith, NFC: Carolina vs. Seattle, 2005
Santonio Holmes, AFC: Pittsburgh vs. San Diego, 2008
Reggie Bush, NFC-D: New Orleans vs. Arizona, 2009
Trindon Holliday, AFC-D: Denver vs. Baltimore, 2012 (2 ot)

KICKOFF RETURNS
Most Kickoff Returns, Career
36   Brian Mitchell, Washington-Philadelphia, 16 games
31   Kevin Williams, Dallas-Buffalo, 12 games
     Darren Sproles, San Diego-New Orleans, 10 games
29   Fulton Walker, Miami-L.A. Raiders, 10 games
Most Kickoff Returns, Game
8   Marc Logan, AFC-D: Miami vs. Buffalo, 1990
     Andre Coleman, SB: San Diego vs. San Francisco, 1994
     Marcus Knight, SB: Oakland vs. Tampa Bay, 2002
7   Don Bingham, NFC: Chi. Bears vs. N.Y. Giants, 1956
     Reggie Brown, NFC-FR: Atlanta vs. Minnesota, 1982
     David Verser, AFC-FR: Cincinnati vs. N.Y. Jets, 1982
     Del Rodgers, NFC-D: Green Bay vs. Dallas, 1982
     Henry Ellard, NFC-D: L.A. Rams vs. Washington, 1983
     Stephen Starring, SB: New England vs. Chicago, 1985
     Darick Holmes, AFC-D: Buffalo vs. Pittsburgh, 1995
     Antonio Freeman, NFC: Green Bay vs. Dallas, 1995
     Roell Preston, NFC-FR: Green Bay vs. San Francisco, 1998
     Robert Tate, NFC-D: Minnesota vs. St. Louis, 1999
     Fred McAfee, NFC-D: New Orleans vs. Minnesota, 2000
     Michael Bates, NFC-FR: Dallas vs. Carolina, 2003
     Dante Hall, AFC-D: Kansas City vs. Indianapolis, 2003
     Michael Lewis, NFC: New Orleans vs. Chicago, 2006
     Quintin Demps, AFC-FR: Kansas City vs. Indianapolis, 2013
6   By many players

YARDS GAINED
Most Yards Gained, Career
875 Brian Mitchell, Washington-Philadelphia, 16 games
770 Darren Sproles, San Diego-New Orleans, 10 games
677 Fulton Walker, Miami-L.A. Raiders, 10 games
Most Yards Gained, Game
244 Andre Coleman, SB: San Diego vs. San Francisco, 1994
220 Ellis Hobbs, AFC: New England vs. Indianapolis, 2006
216 Danieal Manning, AFC-D: Houston vs. New England, 2012
Longest Return
108 Jacoby Jones, SB: Baltimore vs. San Francisco, 2012 (TD)
104 Trindon Holliday, AFC-D: Denver vs. Baltimore, 2012 (2 ot) (TD)
102 Eric Weems, NFC-D: Atlanta vs. Green Bay, 2010 (TD)

AVERAGE YARDAGE
Highest Average, Career (10 returns)
35.8 Danieal Manning, Chicago-Houston, 9 games (12-429)
30.1 Carl Garrett, Oakland, 5 games (16-481)
30.0 Reggie Barlow, Jacksonville, 8 games (12-360)
Highest Average, Game (3 returns)
56.7 Les (Speedy) Duncan, NFC-D: Washington vs. San Francisco, 1971 (3-170)
54.0 Danieal Manning, AFC-D: Houston vs. New England, 2012 (4-216)
52.7 Trindon Holliday, AFC-D: Denver vs. Baltimore, 2012 (2 ot) (3-158)

TOUCHDOWNS
Most Touchdowns, Career
2   Ron Dixon, N.Y. Giants, 4 games
1   By many players
Most Touchdowns, Game
1   Vic Washington, NFC-D: San Francisco vs. Dallas, 1972
     Nat Moore, AFC-D: Miami vs. Oakland, 1974
     Marshall Johnson, AFC-D: Baltimore vs. Oakland, 1977 (ot)
     Fulton Walker, SB: Miami vs. Washington, 1982

Stanford Jennings, SB: Cincinnati vs. San Francisco, 1988
Eric Metcalf, AFC-D: Cleveland vs. Buffalo, 1989
Andre Coleman, SB: San Diego vs. San Francisco, 1994
Desmond Howard, SB: Green Bay vs. New England, 1996
Chuck Levy, NFC: San Francisco vs. Green Bay, 1997
Tim Dwight, SB: Atlanta vs. Denver, 1998
Kevin Dyson, AFC-FR: Tennessee vs. Buffalo, 1999
Charlie Rogers, AFC-FR: Seattle vs. Miami, 1999
Brian Mitchell, NFC-D: Washington vs. Tampa Bay, 1999
Tony Horne, NFC-D: St. Louis vs. Minnesota, 1999
Derrick Mason, AFC: Tennessee vs. Jacksonville, 1999
Ron Dixon, NFC-D: N.Y. Giants vs. Philadelphia, 2000;
     SB: N.Y. Giants vs. Baltimore, 2000
Jermaine Lewis, SB: Baltimore vs. N.Y. Giants, 2000
Dante Hall, AFC-D: Kansas City vs. Indianapolis, 2003
Miles Austin, NFC-FR: Dallas vs. Seattle, 2006
Devin Hester, SB: Chicago vs. Indianapolis, 2006
Eric Weems, NFC-D: Atlanta vs. Green Bay, 2010
Trindon Holliday, AFC-D: Denver vs. Baltimore, 2012 (2 ot)
Jacoby Jones, SB: Baltimore vs. San Francisco, 2012
Percy Harvin, SB: Seattle vs. Denver, 2013

FUMBLES
Most Fumbles, Career
16   Warren Moon, Houston-Minnesota, 10 games
14   John Elway, Denver, 22 games
     Donovan McNabb, Philadelphia, 16 games
13   Tony Dorsett, Dallas, 17 games
Most Fumbles, Game
5   Warren Moon, AFC-D: Houston vs. Kansas City, 1993
4   Brian Sipe, AFC-D: Cleveland vs. Oakland, 1980
     Randall Cunningham, NFC-FR: Minnesota vs. N.Y. Giants, 1997
3   By many players

RECOVERIES
Most Own Fumbles Recovered, Career
8   Warren Moon, Houston-Minnesota, 10 games
7   John Elway, Denver, 22 games
6   Jim Kelly, Buffalo, 17 games
Most Opponents' Fumbles Recovered, Career
4   Cliff Harris, Dallas, 21 games
     Harvey Martin, Dallas, 22 games
     Ted Hendricks, Baltimore-Oakland/L.A. Raiders, 21 games
     Alvin Walton, Washington, 9 games
     Monte Coleman, Washington, 21 games
     Dave Thomas, Dallas-Jacksonville-N.Y. Giants, 13 games
3   Paul Krause, Minnesota, 19 games
     Jack Lambert, Pittsburgh, 18 games
     Fred Dryer, Los Angeles, 14 games
     Charlie Waters, Dallas, 25 games
     Jack Ham, Pittsburgh, 16 games
     Mike Hegman, Dallas, 16 games
     Tom Jackson, Denver, 10 games
     Rich Milot, Washington, 13 games
     Mike Singletary, Chicago, 12 games
     Darryl Grant, Washington, 16 games
     Wes Hopkins, Philadelphia, 3 games
     Wilber Marshall, Chicago-Washington, 15 games
     Tyrone Braxton, Denver-Miami-Denver, 19 games
     Neil Smith, Kansas City-Denver, 16 games
     Tony Brackens, Jacksonville, 7 games
     Phil Hansen, Buffalo, 14 games
     Carnell Lake, Pittsburgh-Jacksonville-Baltimore, 17 games
     Jason Gildon, Pittsburgh, 13 games
     Tedy Bruschi, New England, 22 games
     Jim Leonhard, Baltimore-N.Y. Jets-Denver, 7 games
     Clay Matthews, Green Bay, 8 games
2   By many players
Most Fumbles Recovered, Game, Own and Opponents'
3   Jack Lambert, AFC: Pittsburgh vs. Oakland, 1975 (3 opp)

Ron Jaworski, NFC-FR: Philadelphia vs. N.Y. Giants, 1981 (3 own)
Devin Hester, NFC-D: Chicago vs. Seattle, 2006 (3-own)
2 By many players

YARDS GAINED
Longest Return
93 Andy Russell, AFC-D: Pittsburgh vs. Baltimore, 1975 (opp, TD)
79 Neil Smith, AFC-D: Denver vs. Miami, 1998 (opp, TD)
64 Leon Lett, SB: Dallas vs. Buffalo, 1992 (opp)

TOUCHDOWNS
Most Touchdowns
1 By many players

COMBINED NET YARDS GAINED
Rushing, receiving, interception returns, punt returns, kickoff returns, and fumble returns.
ATTEMPTS
Most Attempts, Career
454 Franco Harris, Pittsburgh, 19 games
417 Thurman Thomas, Buffalo, 21 games
397 Emmitt Smith, Dallas, 17 games
Most Attempts, Game
43 Lamar Smith, AFC-FR: Miami vs. Indianapolis, 2000 (ot)
42 Curtis Martin, AFC-D: N.Y. Jets vs. Jacksonville, 1998
40 Lawrence McCutcheon, NFC-D: Los Angeles vs. St. Louis, 1975
Arian Foster, AFC-FR: Houston vs. Cincinnati, 2012

YARDS GAINED
Most Yards Gained, Career
2,289 Jerry Rice, San Francisco-Oakland-Seattle, 29 games
2,124 Thurman Thomas, Buffalo, 21 games
2,060 Franco Harris, Pittsburgh, 19 games
Most Yards Gained, Game
350 Ed Podolak, AFC-D: Kansas City vs. Miami, 1971 (ot)
329 Keith Lincoln, AFC: San Diego vs. Boston, 1963
328 Darren Sproles, AFC-FR: San Diego vs. Indianapolis, 2008 (ot)

SACKS
Sacks have been compiled since 1982.
Most Sacks, Career
16.0 Willie McGinest, New England, 18 games
14.5 Bruce Smith, Buffalo, 20 games
12.0 Reggie White, Philadelphia-Green Bay, 19 games
Terrell Suggs, Baltimore, 15 games
Most Sacks, Game
4.5 Willie McGinest, AFC-FR: New England vs. Jacksonville, 2005
3.5 Rich Milot, NFC-D: Washington vs. Chicago, 1984
Richard Dent, NFC-D: Chicago vs. N.Y. Giants, 1985
3.0 Richard Dent, NFC-D: Chicago vs. Washington, 1984
Garin Veris, AFC-FR: New England vs. N.Y. Jets, 1985
Gary Jeter, NFC-D: L.A. Rams vs. Dallas, 1985
Carl Hairston, AFC-D: Cleveland vs. N.Y. Jets, 1986 (ot)
Charles Mann, NFC-D: Washington vs. Chicago, 1987
Kevin Greene, NFC-FR: L.A. Rams vs. Minnesota, 1988
Greg Townsend, AFC-D: L.A. Raiders vs. Cincinnati, 1990
Wilber Marshall, NFC: Washington vs. Detroit, 1991
Fred Stokes, NFC-FR: Washington vs. Minnesota, 1992
Pierce Holt, NFC-D: San Francisco vs. Washington, 1992
Tony Casillas, NFC: Dallas vs. San Francisco, 1992
Gerald Williams, AFC-FR: Pittsburgh vs. Kansas City, 1993
Chad Brown, AFC-FR: Pittsburgh vs. Indianapolis, 1996
Reggie White, SB: Green Bay vs. New England, 1996
Warren Sapp, NFC-D: Tampa Bay vs. Green Bay, 1997
Trace Armstrong, AFC-FR: Miami vs. Seattle, 1999
Michael McCrary, AFC-FR: Baltimore vs. Denver, 2000

Willie McGinest, AFC-D: New England vs. Tennessee, 2003
Darnell Dockett, SB: Arizona vs. Pittsburgh, 2008
Ray Edwards, NFC-D: Minnesota vs. Dallas, 2009
James Harrison, AFC-D: Pittsburgh vs. Baltimore, 2010
Terrell Suggs, AFC-D: Baltimore vs. Pittsburgh, 2010

TEAM RECORDS

CHAMPIONSHIPS
Most Seasons League Champion
13 Green Bay, 1929-1931, 1936, 1939, 1944, 1961-62, 1965-67, 1996, 2010
9 Chi. Bears, 1921, 1932-33, 1940-41, 1943, 1946, 1963, 1985
8 N.Y. Giants, 1927, 1934, 1938, 1956, 1986, 1990, 2007, 2011
Most Consecutive Seasons League Champion
3 Green Bay, 1929-1931
Green Bay, 1965-67
2 Canton, 1922-23
Chi. Bears, 1932-33
Chi. Bears, 1940-41
Philadelphia, 1948-49
Detroit, 1952-53
Cleveland, 1954-55
Baltimore, 1958-59
Houston, 1960-61
Green Bay, 1961-62
Buffalo, 1964-65
Miami, 1972-73
Pittsburgh, 1974-75
Pittsburgh, 1978-79
San Francisco, 1988-89
Dallas, 1992-93
Denver, 1997-98
New England, 2003-04

GAMES, VICTORIES, DEFEATS
Most Seasons Participating in Postseason Games
31 N.Y. Giants, 1933-35, 1938-39, 1941, 1943-44, 1946, 1950, 1956, 1958-59, 1961-63, 1981, 1984-86, 1989-1990, 1993, 1997, 2000, 2002, 2005-08, 2011
30 Dallas, 1966-1973, 1975-1983, 1985, 1991-96, 1998-99, 2003, 2006-07, 2009
29 Green Bay, 1936, 1938-39, 1941, 1944, 1960-62, 1965-67, 1972, 1982, 1993-98, 2001-04, 2007, 2009-2013
Most Consecutive Seasons Participating in Postseason Games
9 Dallas, 1975-1983
Indianapolis, 2002-2010
8 Dallas, 1966-1973
Pittsburgh, 1972-79
Los Angeles, 1973-1980
San Francisco, 1983-1990
7 Houston, 1987-1993
San Francisco, 1992-98
Most Games
58 Dallas, 1966-1973, 1975-1983, 1985, 1991-96, 1998-99, 2003, 2006-07, 2009
54 Pittsburgh, 1947, 1972-79, 1982-84, 1989, 1992-97, 2001-02, 2004-05, 2007-08, 2010-11
50 San Francisco, 1957, 1970-72, 1981, 1983-1990, 1992-98, 2001-02, 2011-13
Most Games Won
33 Dallas, 1967, 1970-73, 1975, 1977-78, 1980-82, 1991-96, 2009
Pittsburgh, 1972, 1974-76, 1978-79, 1984, 1989, 1994-97, 2001-02, 2004-05, 2008, 2010
30 Green Bay, 1936, 1939, 1944, 1961-62, 1965-67, 1982, 1993-97, 2001, 2003, 2007, 2010, 2012

San Francisco, 1970-71, 1981, 1983-84, 1988-1990, 1992-94, 1996-98, 2002, 2011-13
25 Oakland/L.A. Raiders, 1967-1970, 1973-77, 1980, 1982-83, 1990, 1993, 2000-02
Boston/New England, 1963, 1985, 1996-97, 2001, 2003-07, 2011-13

Most Consecutive Games Won
10 New England, 2001, 2003-05
9 Green Bay, 1961-62, 1965-67
7 Pittsburgh, 1974-76
San Francisco, 1988-1990
Dallas, 1992-94
Denver, 1997-98

Most Games Lost
27 Minnesota, 1968-1971, 1973-78, 1980, 1982, 1987-89, 1992-94, 1996-2000, 2004, 2008-09, 2012
25 Dallas, 1966-1970, 1972-73, 1975-76, 1978-1983, 1985, 1991, 1994, 1996, 1998-99, 2003, 2006-07, 2009
24 L.A./St. Louis Rams, 1949-1950, 1952, 1955, 1967, 1969, 1973-1980, 1983-86, 1988-89, 2000-01, 2003-04
N.Y. Giants, 1933, 1935, 1939, 1941, 1943-44, 1946, 1950, 1958-59, 1961-63, 1981, 1984-85, 1989, 1993, 1997, 2000, 2002, 2005-06, 2008

Most Consecutive Games Lost
8 Kansas City, 1993-95, 1997, 2003, 2006, 2010, 2013 (current)
7 Detroit, 1991, 1993-95, 1997, 1999, 2011 (current)
6 N.Y. Giants, 1939, 1941, 1943-44, 1946, 1950
Cleveland, 1969, 1971-72, 1980, 1982, 1985
Minnesota, 1988-89, 1992-94, 1996
Seattle, 1984, 1987-88, 1999, 2003-04
Dallas, 1996, 1998-99, 2003, 2006-07
Cincinnati, 1990, 2005, 2009, 2011-13 (current)

SCORING
Most Points, Game
73 NFC: Chi. Bears vs. Washington, 1940
62 AFC-D: Jacksonville vs. Miami, 1999
59 NFC: Detroit vs. Cleveland, 1957

Most Points, Both Teams, Game
96 NFC-FR: Arizona (51) vs. Green Bay (45), 2009
95 NFC-FR: Philadelphia (58) vs. Detroit (37), 1995
89 AFC-FR: Indianapolis (45) vs. Kansas City (44), 2013

Fewest Points, Both Teams, Game
5 NFC-D: Detroit (0) vs. Dallas (5), 1970
7 NFC: Chi. Cardinals (0) vs. Philadelphia (7), 1948
9 NFC: Tampa Bay (0) vs. Los Angeles (9), 1979

Largest Margin of Victory, Game
73 NFC: Chi. Bears vs. Washington, 1940 (73-0)
55 AFC-D: Jacksonville vs. Miami, 1999 (62-7)
49 AFC-D: Oakland vs. Houston, 1969 (56-7)

Most Points, Shutout Victory, Game
73 NFC: Chi. Bears vs. Washington, 1940
41 NFC: N.Y. Giants vs. Minnesota, 2000
AFC-FR: N.Y. Jets vs. Indianapolis, 2002
38 NFC-D: Dallas vs. Tampa Bay, 1981

Most Points Overcome to Win Game
32 AFC-FR: Buffalo vs. Houston, 1992 (trailed 3-35, won 41-38) (ot)
28 AFC-FR: Indianapolis vs. Kansas City, 2013 (trailed 10-38, won 45-44)
24 NFC-FR: San Francisco vs. N.Y. Giants, 2002 (trailed 14-38, won 39-38)

Most Points, Each Half
1st: 41 AFC: Buffalo vs. L.A. Raiders, 1990
AFC-D: Jacksonville vs. Miami, 1999
38 NFC-D: Washington vs. L.A. Rams, 1983
NFC-FR: Philadelphia vs. Detroit, 1995
35 NFC: Cleveland vs. Detroit, 1954
AFC-D: Oakland vs. Houston, 1969
SB: Washington vs. Denver, 1987

AFC-FR: Indianapolis vs. Denver, 2004
NFC-D: New Orleans vs. Arizona, 2009
AFC-D: New England vs. Denver, 2011
2nd: 45 NFC: Chi. Bears vs. Washington, 1940
35 AFC-FR: Buffalo vs. Houston, 1992
NFC-D: St. Louis vs. Minnesota, 1999
NFC-FR: Green Bay vs. Arizona, 2009
NFC-FR: New Orleans vs. Detroit, 2011
AFC-FR: Indianapolis vs. Kansas City, 2013
32 AFC: Indianapolis vs. New England, 2006

Most Points, Each Quarter
1st: 28 AFC-D: Oakland vs. Houston, 1969
24 AFC-D: San Diego vs. Miami, 1981
AFC-D: Jacksonville vs. Miami, 1999
AFC-D: Baltimore vs. New England, 2009
21 NFC: Chi. Bears vs. Washington, 1940
AFC: San Diego vs. Boston, 1963
AFC-D: Oakland vs. Kansas City, 1968
AFC: Oakland vs. San Diego, 1980
AFC: Buffalo vs. L.A. Raiders, 1990
NFC: San Francisco vs. Dallas, 1994
NFC-D: New Orleans vs. Arizona, 2009
2nd: 35 SB: Washington vs. Denver, 1987
31 NFC-FR: Philadelphia vs. Detroit, 1995
28 NFC-D: Green Bay vs. Atlanta, 2010
3rd: 28 AFC-FR: Buffalo vs. Houston, 1992
26 NFC: Chi. Bears vs. Washington, 1940
21 NFC-D: Dallas vs. Cleveland, 1967
NFC-D: Dallas vs. Tampa Bay, 1981
AFC-D: L.A. Raiders vs. Pittsburgh, 1983
SB: Chicago vs. New England, 1985
NFC-D: N.Y. Giants vs. San Francisco, 1986
AFC: Cleveland vs. Denver, 1987
AFC: Cleveland vs. Denver, 1989
NFC-D: St. Louis vs. Minnesota, 1999
AFC-FR: Indianapolis vs. Kansas City, 2013
4th: 27 NFC: N.Y. Giants vs. Chi. Bears, 1934
26 NFC-FR: Philadelphia vs. New Orleans, 1992
24 NFC: Baltimore vs. N.Y. Giants, 1959
OT: 6 NFC: Baltimore vs. N.Y. Giants, 1958
AFC-D: Oakland vs. Baltimore, 1977
NFC-D: L.A. Rams vs. N.Y. Giants, 1989
AFC-FR: Miami vs. Indianapolis, 2000
NFC-FR: Green Bay vs. Seattle, 2003
NFC-D: Carolina vs. St. Louis, 2003
AFC-FR: San Diego vs. Indianapolis, 2008
NFC-FR: Arizona vs. Green Bay, 2009
AFC-FR: Denver vs. Pittsburgh, 2011

TOUCHDOWNS
Most Touchdowns, Game
11 NFC: Chi. Bears vs. Washington, 1940
8 NFC: Cleveland vs. Detroit, 1954
NFC: Detroit vs. Cleveland, 1957
AFC-D: Oakland vs. Houston, 1969
SB: San Francisco vs. Denver, 1989
AFC-D: Jacksonville vs. Miami, 1999
7 AFC: San Diego vs. Boston, 1963
NFC-D: Dallas vs. Cleveland, 1967
NFC-D: N.Y. Giants vs. San Francisco, 1986
AFC: Buffalo vs. L.A. Raiders, 1990
SB: Dallas vs. Buffalo, 1992
SB: San Francisco vs. San Diego, 1994
NFC-FR: Philadelphia vs. Detroit, 1995
NFC-D: St. Louis vs. Minnesota, 1999
AFC-FR: Indianapolis vs. Denver, 2004
NFC-FR: Arizona vs. Green Bay, 2009 (ot)

Most Touchdowns, Both Teams, Game
13 NFC-FR: Arizona (7) vs. Green Bay (6), 2009 (ot)
12 NFC-FR: Philadelphia (7) vs. Detroit (5), 1995
NFC-D: St. Louis (7) vs. Minnesota (5), 1999
11 NFC: Chi. Bears (11) vs. Washington (0), 1940

AFC-FR: Indianapolis (6) vs. Kansas City (5), 2013

Fewest Touchdowns, Both Teams, Game
- 0 NFC-D: N.Y. Giants vs. Cleveland, 1950
  - NFC-D: Dallas vs. Detroit, 1970
  - NFC: Los Angeles vs. Tampa Bay, 1979
  - AFC-D: Baltimore vs. Indianapolis, 2006
- 1 NFC: Chi. Cardinals (0) vs. Philadelphia (1), 1948
  - NFC-D: Cleveland (0) vs. N.Y. Giants (1), 1958
  - AFC: San Diego (0) vs. Houston (1), 1961
  - AFC-D: N.Y. Jets (0) vs. Kansas City (1), 1969
  - NFC-D: Green Bay (0) vs. Washington (1), 1972
  - NFC-FR: New Orleans (0) vs. Chicago (1), 1990
  - NFC: N.Y. Giants (0) vs. San Francisco (1), 1990
  - AFC-FR: L.A. Raiders (0) vs. Kansas City (1), 1991
  - AFC-D: New England (0) vs. Pittsburgh (1), 1997
  - NFC: Tampa Bay (0) vs. St. Louis (1), 1999
  - AFC: Oakland (0) vs. Baltimore (1), 2000
- 2 In many games

POINTS AFTER TOUCHDOWN
Most (One-Point) Points After Touchdown, Game
- 8 NFC: Cleveland vs. Detroit, 1954
  - NFC: Detroit vs. Cleveland, 1957
  - AFC-D: Oakland vs. Houston, 1969
  - AFC-D: Jacksonville vs. Miami, 1999
- 7 NFC: Chi. Bears vs. Washington, 1940
  - NFC-D: Dallas vs. Cleveland, 1967
  - NFC-D: N.Y. Giants vs. San Francisco, 1986
  - SB: San Francisco vs. Denver, 1989
  - SB: Dallas vs. Buffalo, 1992
  - SB: San Francisco vs. San Diego, 1994
  - NFC-FR: Philadelphia vs. Detroit, 1995
  - NFC-D: St. Louis vs. Minnesota, 1999
  - AFC-FR: Indianapolis vs. Denver, 2004
- 6 AFC: San Diego vs. Boston, 1963
  - NFC-D: Washington vs. L.A. Rams, 1983
  - AFC: Miami vs. Pittsburgh, 1984
  - SB: Washington vs. Denver, 1987
  - AFC: Buffalo vs. L.A. Raiders, 1990
  - AFC-FR: L.A. Raiders vs. Denver, 1993
  - AFC-FR: Denver vs. Jacksonville, 1997
  - NFC-D: St. Louis vs. Green Bay, 2001
  - SB: Tampa Bay vs. Oakland, 2002
  - NFC-D: Atlanta vs. St. Louis, 2004)
  - NFC-FR: Green Bay vs. Seattle, 2007
  - NFC-FR: Arizona vs. Green Bay, 2009 (ot)
  - NFC-FR: Green Bay vs. Arizona, 2009 (ot)
  - NFC-D: New Orleans vs. Arizona, 2009
  - NFC-D: Green Bay vs. Atlanta, 2010
  - NFC-FR: New Orleans vs. Detroit, 2011
  - AFC-D: New England vs. Denver, 2011
  - NFC-D: San Francisco vs. Green Bay, 2012
  - AFC-FR: Indianapolis vs. Kansas City, 2013

Most (One-Point) Points After Touchdown, Both Teams, Game
- 12 NFC-FR: Arizona (6) vs. Green Bay (6), 2009
- 11 AFC-FR: Indianapolis (6) vs. Kansas City (5), 2013
- 10 NFC: Detroit (8) vs. Cleveland (2), 1957
  - AFC-D: Miami (5) vs. San Diego (5), 1981 (ot)
  - AFC: Miami (6) vs. Pittsburgh (4), 1984
  - AFC-FR: Buffalo (5) vs. Houston (5), 1992 (ot)
  - NFC-FR: Philadelphia (7) vs. Detroit (3), 1995
  - AFC-FR: Indianapolis (7) vs. Denver (3), 2004
  - NFC-FR: New Orleans (6) vs. Detroit (4), 2011
  - AFC-D: Baltimore (5) vs. Denver (5), 2012
  - NFC-D: San Francisco (6) vs. Green Bay (4), 2012

Fewest (One-Point) Points After Touchdown, Both Teams, Game
- 0 NFC-D: N.Y. Giants vs. Cleveland, 1950
  - NFC-D: Dallas vs. Detroit, 1970
  - NFC: Los Angeles vs. Tampa Bay, 1979
  - NFC: St. Louis vs. Tampa Bay, 1999
  - AFC-D: Baltimore vs. Indianapolis, 2006

Most Two-Point Conversions, Game
- 2 SB: San Diego vs. San Francisco, 1994
  - NFC-FR: Detroit vs. Philadelphia, 1995
  - NFC-FR: San Francisco vs.. N.Y. Giants, 2002
- 1 By many teams

FIELD GOALS
Most Field Goals, Game
- 5 NFC-D: Minnesota vs. San Francisco, 1987
  - NFC: N.Y. Giants vs. San Francisco, 1990
  - AFC: Buffalo vs. Miami, 1992
  - NFC-FR: N.Y. Giants vs. Minnesota, 1997
  - NFC-FR: Carolina vs. Dallas, 2003
  - NFC-D: St. Louis vs. Carolina, 2003 (2 ot)
  - AFC: New England vs. Indianapolis, 2003
  - AFC-D: Indianapolis vs. Baltimore, 2006
- 4 AFC-D: Boston vs. Buffalo, 1963
  - AFC: Oakland vs. Houston, 1967
  - SB: Green Bay vs. Oakland, 1967
  - NFC: Washington vs. Dallas, 1972
  - AFC-D: Oakland vs. Pittsburgh, 1973
  - SB: San Francisco vs. Cincinnati, 1981
  - AFC-FR: New England vs. N.Y. Jets, 1985
  - NFC-FR: Washington vs. L.A. Rams, 1986
  - NFC-D: Philadelphia vs. Chicago, 1988
  - AFC-FR: Pittsburgh vs. Houston, 1989 (ot)
  - AFC-D: Pittsburgh vs. Buffalo, 1995
  - NFC-FR: Dallas vs. Minnesota, 1996
  - NFC-D: Carolina vs. Dallas, 1996
  - AFC-FR: Jacksonville vs. New England, 1998
  - AFC-D: Tennessee vs. Indianapolis, 1999
  - NFC-D: Philadelphia vs. Chicago, 2001
  - AFC: San Diego vs. New England, 2007
  - NFC-FR: Philadelphia vs. Minnesota, 2008
  - NFC-D: Arizona vs. Carolina, 2008
  - AFC-FR: Houston vs. Cincinnati, 2012
  - NFC-FR: New Orleans vs. Philadelphia, 2013
  - AFC: Denver vs. New England, 2013
- 3 By many teams

Most Field Goals, Both Teams, Game
- 8 NFC-FR: N.Y. Giants (5) vs. Minnesota (3), 1997
  - NFC-D: St. Louis (5) vs. Carolina (3), 2003 (2 ot)
- 7 AFC-FR: Pittsburgh (4) vs. Houston (3), 1989 (ot)
  - NFC: N.Y. Giants (5) vs. San Francisco (2), 1990
  - NFC-D: Carolina (4) vs. Dallas (3), 1996
  - AFC-D: Tennessee (4) vs. Indianapolis (3), 1999
  - AFC-D: Indianapolis (5) vs. Baltimore (2), 2006
- 6 NFC-D: Minnesota (5) vs. San Francisco (1), 1987
  - NFC-D: Philadelphia (4) vs. Chicago (2), 1988
  - AFC: Buffalo (5) vs. Miami (1), 1992
  - NFC-FR: Carolina (5) vs. Dallas (1), 2003
  - AFC-FR: New England (3) vs. N.Y. Jets (3), 2006
  - NFC-D: N.Y. Giants (3) vs. Philadelphia (3), 2008
  - AFC-FR: Denver (3) vs. Pittsburgh (3), 2011 (ot)
  - AFC-FR: Houston (4) vs. Cincinnati (2), 2012

Most Field Goals Attempted, Game
- 6 AFC: Oakland vs. Houston, 1967
  - NFC-D: Los Angeles vs. Dallas, 1973
  - AFC-D: Cleveland vs. N.Y. Jets, 1986 (2 ot)
  - NFC: N.Y. Giants vs. San Francisco, 1990
  - AFC: Buffalo vs. Miami, 1992
  - NFC-D: St. Louis vs. Carolina, 2003 (2 ot)
- 5 By many teams

Most Field Goals Attempted, Both Teams, Game
- 11 NFC-D: St. Louis (6) vs. Carolina (5), 2003 (2 ot)
- 9 NFC-D: Philadelphia (5) vs. Chicago (4), 1988
  - NFC-FR: N.Y. Giants (5) vs. Minnesota (4), 1997
- 8 NFC-D: Los Angeles (6) vs. Dallas (2), 1973
  - NFC-D: Detroit (5) vs. San Francisco (3), 1983
  - AFC-D: Cleveland (6) vs. N.Y. Jets (2), 1986 (ot)
  - NFC-D: Minnesota (5) vs. San Francisco (3), 1987
  - AFC-FR: Houston (4) vs. Pittsburgh (4), 1989 (ot)

NFC-FR: Chicago (4) vs. New Orleans (4), 1990
NFC: N.Y. Giants (6) vs. San Francisco (2), 1990
NFC-D: N.Y. Giants (5) vs. Philadelphia (3), 2008

SAFETIES
Most Safeties, Game
  1 By many teams
Most Safeties, Both Teams, Game
  1 In many games

FIRST DOWNS
Most First Downs, Game
  34 AFC-D: San Diego vs. Miami, 1981 (ot)
      NFC-FR: New Orleans vs. Detroit, 2011
  33 AFC-D: Cleveland vs. N.Y. Jets, 1986 (ot)
  32 AFC: Indianapolis vs. New England, 2006
      NFC-FR: Green Bay vs. Arizona, 2009 (ot)
      NFC-FR: New Orleans vs. Seattle, 2010
Fewest First Downs, Game
  6 NFC: N.Y. Giants vs. Green Bay, 1961
     AFC-D: Baltimore vs. Tennessee, 2000
  7 NFC: Green Bay vs. Boston, 1936
     NFC-D: Pittsburgh vs. Philadelphia, 1947
     NFC: Chi. Cardinals vs. Philadelphia, 1948
     NFC: Los Angeles vs. Philadelphia, 1949
     NFC-D: Cleveland vs. N.Y. Giants, 1958
     AFC-D: Cincinnati vs. Baltimore, 1970
     NFC-D: Detroit vs. Dallas, 1970
     NFC: Tampa Bay vs. Los Angeles, 1979
     AFC-D: Baltimore vs. Pittsburgh, 2001
     AFC-FR: Kansas City vs. Indianapolis, 2006
  8 By many teams
Most First Downs, Both Teams, Game
  62 NFC-FR: Green Bay (32) vs. Arizona (30), 2009 (ot)
  59 AFC-D: San Diego (34) vs. Miami (25), 1981 (ot)
  58 AFC-FR: Kansas City (30) vs. Indianapolis (28), 2013
Fewest First Downs, Both Teams, Game
  15 NFC: Green Bay (7) vs. Boston (8), 1936
  19 NFC: N.Y. Giants (9) vs. Green Bay (10), 1939
     NFC: Washington (9) vs. Chi. Bears (10), 1942
  20 NFC-D: Cleveland (9) vs. N.Y. Giants (11), 1950

RUSHING
Most First Downs, Rushing, Game
  19 NFC-FR: Dallas vs. Los Angeles, 1980
  18 AFC-D: Miami vs. Cincinnati, 1973
     AFC: Miami vs. Oakland, 1973
     AFC-D: Pittsburgh vs. Buffalo, 1974
     AFC-FR: Buffalo vs. Miami, 1995
     AFC-FR: Denver vs. Jacksonville, 1997
  17 AFC-D: Cincinnati vs. Seattle, 1988
     AFC: Buffalo vs. Kansas City, 1993
Fewest First Downs, Rushing, Game
  0 NFC: Los Angeles vs. Philadelphia, 1949
     AFC-D: Buffalo vs. Boston, 1963
     AFC: Oakland vs. Pittsburgh, 1974
     NFC-FR: New Orleans vs. Minnesota, 1987
     NFC: L.A. Rams vs. San Francisco, 1989
     NFC-D: Chicago vs. N.Y. Giants, 1990
     AFC-FR: Indianapolis vs. Pittsburgh, 1996
     AFC-FR: Seattle vs. Miami, 1999
     AFC-D: Miami vs. Jacksonville, 1999
     AFC-D: Miami vs. Oakland, 2000
     AFC-D: Baltimore vs. Pittsburgh, 2001
     AFC-D: Indianapolis vs. New England, 2004
     NFC-FR: Philadelphia vs. Dallas, 2009
  1 By many teams
Most First Downs, Rushing, Both Teams, Game
  26 AFC: Buffalo (14) vs. L.A. Raiders (12), 1990
  25 NFC-FR: Dallas (19) vs. Los Angeles (6), 1980
  23 NFC: Cleveland (15) vs. Detroit (8), 1952
     AFC-D: Miami (18) vs. Cincinnati (5), 1973

AFC-D: Pittsburgh (18) vs. Buffalo (5), 1974
AFC-FR: Buffalo (18) vs. Miami (5), 1995
Fewest First Downs, Rushing, Both Teams, Game
  2 NFC-FR: New Orleans (1) vs. St. Louis (1), 2000
  5 AFC-D: Buffalo (0) vs. Boston (5), 1963
     NFC-D: Washington (1) vs. Tampa Bay (4), 1999
     AFC-FR: Cleveland (2) vs. Pittsburgh (3), 2002
     AFC-D: Baltimore (2) vs. Indianapolis (3), 2009
  6 NFC: Green Bay (2) vs. Boston (4), 1936
     NFC-D: Baltimore (2) vs. Minnesota (4), 1968
     AFC-D: Houston (1) vs. Oakland (5), 1969
     AFC-FR: N.Y. Jets (1) vs. Houston (5), 1991
     AFC-FR: Denver (1) vs. Baltimore (5), 2000
     AFC: Pittsburgh (1) vs. Baltimore (5), 2008
     SB: Arizona (2) vs. Pittsburgh (4), 2008

PASSING
Most First Downs, Passing, Game
  24 AFC-FR: Pittsburgh vs. Cleveland, 2002
  23 NFC-D: New Orleans vs. San Francisco, 2011
     AFC-FR: Indianapolis vs. Kansas City, 2013
  22 NFC-FR: New Orleans vs. Seattle, 2010
Fewest First Downs, Passing, Game
  0 NFC: Philadelphia vs. Chi. Cardinals, 1948
  1 NFC-D: N.Y. Giants vs. Washington, 1943
     NFC: Cleveland vs. Detroit, 1953
     SB: Denver vs. Dallas, 1977
  2 By many teams
Most First Downs, Passing, Both Teams, Game
  42 AFC-D: Miami (21) vs. San Diego (21), 1981 (ot)
     AFC-FR: Pittsburgh (24) vs. Cleveland (18), 2002
  40 NFC-FR: New Orleans (20) vs. Detroit (20), 2011
  39 AFC-FR: Indianapolis (23) vs. Kansas City (16), 2013
Fewest First Downs, Passing, Both Teams, Game
  2 NFC: Philadelphia (0) vs. Chi. Cardinals (2), 1948
  4 NFC-D: Cleveland (2) vs. N.Y. Giants (2), 1950
  5 NFC: Detroit (2) vs. N.Y. Giants (3), 1935
     NFC: Green Bay (2) vs. N.Y. Giants (3), 1939

PENALTY
Most First Downs, Penalty, Game
  7 AFC-D: New England vs. Oakland, 1976
     AFC: Tennessee vs. Oakland, 2002
  6 AFC-D: Cleveland vs. N.Y. Jets, 1986 (ot)
     NFC-D: Chicago vs. Carolina, 2005
     NFC-FR: Green Bay vs. Arizona, 2009 (ot)
     AFC-D: Denver vs. Baltimore, 2012 (2 ot)
  5 AFC-FR: Cleveland vs. L. A. Raiders, 1982
     NFC-D: San Francisco vs. Minnesota, 1997
     AFC-FR: Miami vs. Buffalo, 1998
     NFC-D: Arizona vs. Minnesota, 1998
     AFC: Pittsburgh vs. New England, 2001
     AFC-D: Pittsburgh vs. Tennessee, 2002 (ot)
     AFC-FR: Cincinnati vs. N.Y. Jets, 2009
     NFC-D: San Francisco vs. Carolina, 2013
Most First Downs, Penalty, Both Teams, Game
  10 AFC: Tennessee (7) vs. Oakland (3), 2002
  9 AFC-D: New England (7) vs. Oakland (2), 1976
     AFC-D: Denver (6) vs. Baltimore (3), 2012 (2 ot)
  8 NFC-FR: Atlanta (4) vs. Minnesota (4), 1982
     AFC-FR: Miami (5) vs. Buffalo (3), 1998
     NFC-FR: Dallas (4) vs. Philadelphia (4), 2009
     NFC-FR: Green Bay (6) vs. Arizona (2), 2009 (ot)

NET YARDS GAINED RUSHING AND PASSING
Most Yards Gained, Game
  626 NFC-FR: New Orleans vs. Detroit, 2011
  610 AFC: San Diego vs. Boston, 1963
  602 SB: Washington vs. Denver, 1987
Fewest Yards Gained, Game
  86 NFC-D: Cleveland vs. N.Y. Giants, 1958
  99 NFC: Chi. Cardinals vs. Philadelphia, 1948

112 NFC-D: N.Y. Giants vs. Washington, 1943

Most Yards Gained, Both Teams, Game
1,049 AFC-FR: Indianapolis (536) vs. Kansas City (513), 2013
1,038 AFC-FR: Buffalo (536) vs. Miami (502), 1995
NFC-FR: New Orleans (626) vs. Detroit (412), 2011
1,036 AFC-D: San Diego (564) vs. Miami (472), 1981 (ot)

Fewest Yards Gained, Both Teams, Game
331 NFC: Chi. Cardinals (99) vs. Philadelphia (232), 1948
332 NFC-D: N.Y. Giants (150) vs. Cleveland (182), 1950
336 NFC: Boston (116) vs. Green Bay (220), 1936

RUSHING
ATTEMPTS
Most Attempts, Game
65 NFC: Detroit vs. N.Y. Giants, 1935
61 NFC: Philadelphia vs. Los Angeles, 1949
59 AFC: New England vs. Miami, 1985

Fewest Attempts, Game
8 AFC-D: Miami vs. San Diego, 1994
9 SB: Miami vs. San Francisco, 1984
NFC: Minnesota vs. N.Y. Giants, 2000
10 NFC: L.A. Rams vs. San Francisco, 1989
NFC-FR: Atlanta vs. Green Bay, 1995
NFC-FR: Detroit vs. Washington, 1999
NFC-FR: Detroit vs. New Orleans, 2011

Most Attempts, Both Teams, Game
109 NFC: Detroit (65) vs. N.Y. Giants (44), 1935
97 AFC-D: Baltimore (50) vs. Oakland (47), 1977 (ot)
91 NFC: Philadelphia (57) vs. Chi. Cardinals (34), 1948

Fewest Attempts, Both Teams, Game
32 AFC-D: Houston (14) vs. Kansas City (18), 1993
36 SB: Green Bay (13) vs. Pittsburgh (23), 2010
NFC-D: New Orleans (14) vs. San Francisco (22), 2011
37 SB: Arizona (12) vs. Pittsburgh (25), 2008
SB: New Orleans (18) vs. Indianapolis (19), 2009

YARDS GAINED
Most Yards Gained, Game
382 NFC: Chi. Bears vs. Washington, 1940
341 AFC-FR: Buffalo vs. Miami, 1995
338 NFC-FR: Dallas vs. Los Angeles, 1980

Fewest Yards Gained, Game
– 4 NFC-FR: Detroit vs. Green Bay, 1994
7 AFC-D: Buffalo vs. Boston, 1963
SB: New England vs. Chicago, 1985
14 AFC: Miami vs. Denver, 1998
AFC: N.Y. Jets vs. Denver, 1998

Most Yards Gained, Both Teams, Game
430 NFC-FR: Dallas (338) vs. Los Angeles (92), 1980
427 NFC-D: San Francisco (323) vs. Green Bay (104), 2012
426 NFC: Cleveland (227) vs. Detroit (199), 1952

Fewest Yards Gained, Both Teams, Game
77 NFC-FR: Detroit (–4) vs. Green Bay (81), 1994
84 NFC-FR: St. Louis (34) vs. New Orleans (50), 2000
90 AFC-D: Buffalo (7) vs. Boston (83), 1963
NFC-D: Tampa Bay (44) vs. Washington (46), 1999

AVERAGE GAIN
Highest Average Gain, Game
9.94 AFC: San Diego vs. Boston, 1963 (32-318)
9.29 NFC-D: Green Bay vs. Dallas, 1982 (17-158)
8.18 NFC-D: Atlanta vs. St. Louis, 2004 (40-327)

Lowest Average Gain, Game
– 0.27 NFC-FR: Detroit vs. Green Bay, 1994 (15-(– 4))
0.58 AFC-D: Buffalo vs. Boston, 1963 (12-7)
0.64 SB: New England vs. Chicago, 1985 (11-7)

TOUCHDOWNS
Most Touchdowns, Game
7 NFC: Chi. Bears vs. Washington, 1940
6 NFC-D: San Francisco vs. N.Y. Giants, 1993
AFC-D: New England vs. Indianapolis, 2013

5 NFC: Cleveland vs. Detroit, 1954
NFC-D: San Francisco vs. Chicago, 1994
AFC-FR: Pittsburgh vs. Indianapolis, 1996
AFC-FR: Denver vs. Jacksonville, 1997

Most Touchdowns, Both Teams, Game
7 NFC: Chi. Bears (7) vs. Washington (0), 1940
6 NFC: Cleveland (5) vs. Detroit (1), 1954
NFC-D: San Francisco (6) vs. N.Y. Giants (0), 1993
NFC-D: San Francisco (5) vs. Chicago (1), 1994
AFC-FR: Denver (5) vs. Jacksonville (1), 1997
AFC-D: New England (6) vs. Indianapolis (0), 2013
5 NFC: Chi. Cardinals (3) vs. Philadelphia (2), 1947
AFC: San Diego (4) vs. Boston (1), 1963
AFC-D: Cincinnati (3) vs. Buffalo (2), 1981
AFC-FR: Pittsburgh (5) vs. Indianapolis (0), 1996
NFC-D: Arizona (3) vs. Minnesota (2), 1998
NFC-FR: Seattle (3) vs. Green Bay (2), 2003 (ot)
NFC-D: San Francisco (4) vs. Green Bay (1), 2012

PASSING
ATTEMPTS
Most Attempts, Game
66 AFC-FR: Miami vs. Buffalo, 1995
65 AFC-D: Cleveland vs. N.Y. Jets, 1986 (ot)
NFC-D: San Francisco vs. Green Bay, 1995
63 NFC-D: New Orleans vs. San Francisco, 2011

Fewest Attempts, Game
5 NFC: Detroit vs. N.Y. Giants, 1935
6 AFC: Miami vs. Oakland, 1973
7 SB: Miami vs. Minnesota, 1973

Most Attempts, Both Teams, Game
105 NFC-D: New Orleans (63) vs. San Francisco (42), 2011
102 AFC-D: San Diego (54) vs. Miami (48), 1981 (ot)
96 AFC: N.Y. Jets (49) vs. Oakland (47), 1968

Fewest Attempts, Both Teams, Game
18 NFC: Detroit (5) vs. N.Y. Giants (13), 1935
23 NFC: Chi. Cardinals (11) vs. Philadelphia (12), 1948
24 NFC-D: Cleveland (9) vs. N.Y. Giants (15), 1950

COMPLETIONS
Most Completions, Game
40 NFC-D: New Orleans vs. San Francisco, 2011
39 NFC-FR: New Orleans vs. Seattle, 2010
36 AFC-FR: Houston vs. Buffalo, 1992 (ot)

Fewest Completions, Game
2 NFC: Detroit vs. N.Y. Giants, 1935
NFC: Philadelphia vs. Chi. Cardinals, 1948
3 NFC: N.Y. Giants vs. Chi. Bears, 1941
NFC: Green Bay vs. N.Y. Giants, 1944
NFC: Chi. Cardinals vs. Philadelphia, 1947
NFC: Chi. Cardinals vs. Philadelphia, 1948
NFC-D: Cleveland vs. N.Y. Giants, 1950
NFC-D: N.Y. Giants vs. Cleveland, 1950
NFC: Cleveland vs. Detroit, 1953
AFC: Miami vs. Oakland, 1973
4 NFC: N.Y. Giants vs. Detroit, 1935
NFC-D: N.Y. Giants vs. Washington, 1943
NFC-D: Pittsburgh vs. Philadelphia, 1947
NFC-D: Dallas vs. Detroit, 1970
AFC: Miami vs. Baltimore, 1971
SB: Miami vs. Washington, 1982
AFC-FR: Seattle vs. L.A. Raiders, 1984
AFC-FR: Baltimore vs. New England, 2009

Most Completions, Both Teams, Game
64 AFC-D: San Diego (33) vs. Miami (31), 1981 (ot)
NFC-D: New Orleans (40) vs. San Francisco (24), 2011
63 SB: New Orleans (32) vs. Indianapolis (31), 2009
61 NFC-FR: New Orleans (39) vs. Seattle (22), 2010
NFC-FR: New Orleans (33) vs. Detroit (28), 2011

Fewest Completions, Both Teams, Game
5 NFC: Philadelphia (2) vs. Chi. Cardinals (3), 1948

6   NFC: Detroit (2) vs. N.Y. Giants (4), 1935
    NFC-D: Cleveland (3) vs. N.Y. Giants (3), 1950
11 NFC: Green Bay (3) vs. N.Y. Giants (8), 1944
    NFC-D: Dallas (4) vs. Detroit (7), 1970

COMPLETION PERCENTAGE
Highest Completion Percentage, Game (20 attempts)
92.9 AFC-D: New England vs. Jacksonville, 2007 (28-26)
88.0 SB: N.Y. Giants vs. Denver, 1986 (25-22)
87.9 NFC-FR: Arizona vs. Green Bay, 2009 (33-29) (ot)
Lowest Completion Percentage, Game (20 attempts)
18.5 NFC: Tampa Bay vs. Los Angeles, 1979 (27-5)
20.0 NFC-D: N.Y. Giants vs. Washington, 1943 (20-4)
25.8 NFC: Chi. Bears vs. Washington, 1937 (31-8)

YARDS GAINED
Most Yards Gained, Game
483 AFC-D: Cleveland vs. N.Y. Jets, 1986 (ot)
459 NFC-FR: New Orleans vs. Detroit, 2011
454 AFC-FR: Indianapolis vs. Denver, 2004
Fewest Yards Gained, Game
3   NFC: Chi. Cardinals vs. Philadelphia, 1948
7   NFC: Philadelphia vs. Chi. Cardinals, 1948
9   NFC-D: N.Y. Giants vs. Cleveland, 1950
    NFC: Cleveland vs. Detroit, 1953
Most Yards Gained, Both Teams, Game
839 New Orleans (459) vs. Detroit (380), 2011
809 AFC-D: San Diego (415) vs. Miami (394), 1981 (ot)
799 AFC-FR: Indianapolis (436) vs. Kansas City (363), 2013
Fewest Yards Gained, Both Teams, Game
10 NFC: Chi. Cardinals (3) vs. Philadelphia (7), 1948
38 NFC-D: N.Y. Giants (9) vs. Cleveland (29), 1950
102 NFC-D: Dallas (22) vs. Detroit (80), 1970

TIMES SACKED
Most Times Sacked, Game
9   AFC: Kansas City vs. Buffalo, 1966
    NFC: Chicago vs. San Francisco, 1984
    AFC-D: N.Y. Jets vs. Cleveland, 1986 (ot)
    AFC-D: Houston vs. Kansas City, 1993
8   NFC: Green Bay vs. Dallas, 1967
    NFC: Minnesota vs. Washington, 1987
    NFC-D: Philadelphia vs. Green Bay, 2003 (ot)
7   NFC-D: Dallas vs. Los Angeles, 1973
    SB: Dallas vs. Pittsburgh, 1975
    AFC-FR: Houston vs. Oakland, 1980
    NFC-D: Washington vs. Chicago, 1984
    SB: New England vs. Chicago, 1985
    AFC-FR: Kansas City vs. San Diego, 1992
    AFC-D: Pittsburgh vs. Buffalo, 1992
Most Times Sacked, Both Teams, Game
13 AFC: Kansas City (9) vs. Buffalo (4), 1966
    AFC-D: N.Y. Jets (9) vs. Cleveland (4), 1986 (ot)
12 NFC-D: Dallas (7) vs. Los Angeles (5), 1973
    NFC-D: Washington (7) vs. Chicago (5), 1984
    NFC: Chicago (9) vs. San Francisco (3), 1984
    AFC-FR: Kansas City (7) vs. San Diego (5), 1992
11 AFC-D: Houston (9) vs. Kansas City (2), 1993
    AFC-D: Pittsburgh (6) vs. Baltimore (5), 2010
Fewest Times Sacked, Both Teams, Game
0   AFC-D: Buffalo vs. Pittsburgh, 1974
    AFC-FR: Pittsburgh vs. San Diego, 1982
    AFC: Miami vs. Pittsburgh, 1984
    AFC-D: Buffalo vs. Miami, 1990
    AFC-D: Denver vs. Houston, 1991
    AFC-FR: Buffalo vs. Miami, 1995
    AFC-D: Indianapolis vs. Tennessee, 1999
    AFC-D: Indianapolis vs. San Diego, 2007
    NFC-D: N.Y. Giants vs. Philadelphia, 2008
1   In many games

TOUCHDOWNS
Most Touchdowns, Game
6   AFC-D: Oakland vs. Houston, 1969
    SB: San Francisco vs. San Diego, 1994
    AFC-D: New England vs. Denver, 2011
5   NFC: Chi. Bears vs. Washington, 1943
    NFC: Detroit vs. Cleveland, 1957
    AFC-D: Oakland vs. Kansas City, 1968
    SB: San Francisco vs. Denver, 1989
    NFC-D: St. Louis vs. Minnesota, 1999
    NFC: N.Y. Giants vs. Minnesota, 2000
    AFC-FR: Indianapolis vs. Denver, 2003
    NFC-FR: Arizona vs. Green Bay, 2009 (ot)
4   By many teams
Most Touchdowns, Both Teams, Game
9   NFC-D: St. Louis (5) vs. Minnesota (4), 1999
    NFC-FR: Arizona (5) vs. Green Bay (4), 2009 (ot)
8   AFC-FR: Buffalo (4) vs. Houston (4), 1992 (ot)
    AFC-FR: Indianapolis (4) vs. Kansas City (4), 2013
7   NFC: Chi. Bears (5) vs. Washington (2), 1943
    AFC-D: Oakland (6) vs. Houston (1), 1969
    SB: Pittsburgh (4) vs. Dallas (3), 1978
    AFC-D: Miami (4) vs. San Diego (3), 1981 (ot)
    AFC: Miami (4) vs. Pittsburgh (3), 1984
    AFC-D: Buffalo (4) vs. Cleveland (3), 1989
    SB: San Francisco (6) vs. San Diego (1), 1994
    NFC-FR: Detroit (4) vs. Philadelphia (3), 1995
    NFC-FR: New Orleans (4) vs. St. Louis (3), 2000
    NFC-FR: N.Y. Giants (4) vs. San Francisco (3), 2002
    NFC: Arizona (4) vs. Philadelphia (3), 2008
    NFC-D: New Orleans (4) vs. San Francisco (3), 2011

INTERCEPTIONS BY
Most Interceptions By, Game
8   NFC: Chi. Bears vs. Washington, 1940
7   NFC: Cleveland vs. Los Angeles, 1955
6   NFC: Green Bay vs. N.Y. Giants, 1939
    NFC: Chi. Bears vs. N.Y. Giants, 1946
    NFC: Cleveland vs. Detroit, 1954
    AFC: San Diego vs. Houston, 1961
    AFC: Buffalo vs. L.A. Raiders, 1990
    NFC-FR: Philadelphia vs. Detroit, 1995
    NFC-D: St. Louis vs. Green Bay, 2001
Most Interceptions By, Both Teams, Game
10 NFC: Cleveland (7) vs. Los Angeles (3), 1955
    AFC: San Diego (6) vs. Houston (4), 1961
9   NFC: Green Bay (6) vs. N.Y. Giants (3), 1939
8   NFC: Chi. Bears (8) vs. Washington (0), 1940
    NFC: Chi. Bears (6) vs. N.Y. Giants (2), 1946
    NFC: Cleveland (6) vs. Detroit (2), 1954
    AFC-FR: Buffalo (4) vs. N.Y. Jets (4), 1981
    AFC: Miami (5) vs. N.Y. Jets (3), 1982

YARDS GAINED
Most Yards Gained, Game
172 SB: Tampa Bay vs. Oakland, 2002
161 NFC-D: St. Louis vs. Green Bay, 2001
138 AFC-FR: N.Y. Jets vs. Cincinnati, 1982
Most Yards Gained, Both Teams, Game
184 SB: Tampa Bay (172) vs. Oakland (12), 2002
161 NFC-D: St. Louis (161) vs. Green Bay (0), 2001
149 NFC: Cleveland (103) vs. Los Angeles (46), 1955

TOUCHDOWNS
Most Touchdowns, Game
3   NFC: Chi. Bears vs. Washington, 1940
    NFC-D: St. Louis vs. Green Bay, 2001
    SB: Tampa Bay vs. Oakland, 2002
2   NFC-D: Los Angeles vs. St. Louis, 1975
    NFC-FR: Philadelphia vs. Detroit, 1995)
    NFC-FR: Seattle vs. Washington, 2007
1   In many games

Most Touchdowns, Both Teams, Game
- 3 NFC: Chi. Bears (3) vs. Washington (0), 1940
  NFC-D: St. Louis (3) vs. Green Bay (0), 2001
  SB: Tampa Bay (3) vs. Oakland (0), 2002
- 2 NFC-D: Los Angeles (2) vs. St. Louis (0), 1975
  NFC-D: Dallas (1) vs. Green Bay (1), 1982
  NFC-D: Minnesota (1) vs. San Francisco (1), 1987
  NFC-FR: Detroit (1) vs. Green Bay (1), 1993
  NFC-FR: Philadelphia (2) vs. Detroit (0), 1995
  AFC-FR: Buffalo (1) vs. Jacksonville (1), 1996)
  NFC-FR: Seattle (2) vs. Washington (0), 2007
- 1 In many games

PUNTING
Most Punts, Game
- 14 AFC-D: N.Y. Jets vs. Cleveland, 1986 (ot)
- 13 NFC: N.Y. Giants vs. Chi. Bears, 1933
  AFC-D: Baltimore vs. Oakland, 1977 (ot)
- 12 NFC: N.Y. Giants vs. San Francisco, 2011 (ot)

Fewest Punts, Game
- 0 NFC-FR: St. Louis vs. Green Bay, 1982
  AFC-FR: N.Y. Jets vs. Cincinnati, 1982
  AFC: Indianapolis vs. Denver, 2003
  AFC-D: Kansas City vs. Indianapolis, 2003
  AFC-D: Indianapolis vs. Kansas City, 2003
  NFC-D: Green Bay vs. Atlanta, 2010
  NFC-FR: New Orleans vs. Detroit, 2011
  AFC-D: Denver vs. San Diego, 2013
- 1 By many teams

Most Punts, Both Teams, Game
- 23 NFC: N.Y. Giants (13) vs. Chi. Bears (10), 1933
- 22 AFC-D: N.Y. Jets (14) vs. Cleveland (8), 1986 (ot)
- 21 AFC-D: Baltimore (13) vs. Oakland (8), 1977 (ot)
  NFC: L.A. Rams (11) vs. Chicago (10), 1985
  SB: N.Y. Giants (11) vs. Baltimore (10), 2000

Fewest Punts, Both Teams, Game
- 0 AFC-D: Kansas City vs. Indianapolis, 2003
- 1 NFC-FR: St. Louis (0) vs. Green Bay (1), 1982
- 2 AFC-FR: N.Y. Jets (0) vs. Cincinnati (2), 1982
  SB: Atlanta (1) vs. Denver (1), 1998
  AFC-FR: Indianapolis (0) vs. Denver (2), 2003)
  AFC-D: New England (1) vs. Jacksonville (1), 2007
  NFC-D: Arizona (1) vs. Green Bay (1), 2009 (ot)

AVERAGE YARDAGE
Highest Average, Punting, Game (4 punts)
- 56.0 AFC: Oakland vs. San Diego, 1980
- 53.8 AFC-D: Baltimore vs. Pittsburgh, 2010
- 53.3 AFC-D: Tennessee vs. Baltimore, 2008

Lowest Average, Punting, Game (4 punts)
- 24.9 NFC: Washington vs. Chi. Bears, 1937
- 25.3 AFC-FR: Pittsburgh vs. Houston, 1989
- 25.5 NFC: Green Bay vs. N.Y. Giants, 1962

PUNT RETURNS
Most Punt Returns, Game
- 8 NFC: Green Bay vs. N.Y. Giants, 1944
  NFC: San Francisco vs. N.Y. Giants, 2011 (ot)
- 7 By many teams

Most Punt Returns, Both Teams, Game
- 14 NFC: San Francisco (8) vs. N.Y. Giants (6), 2011 (ot)
- 13 AFC-FR: Houston (7) vs. Oakland (6), 1980
- 12 AFC-D: New England (7) vs. Pittsburgh (5), 1996

Fewest Punt Returns, Both Teams, Game
- 0 NFC: Chi. Bears vs. N.Y. Giants, 1941
  AFC: Boston vs. San Diego, 1963
  NFC-FR: Green Bay vs. St. Louis, 1982
  AFC-FR: Houston vs. N.Y. Jets, 1991
  AFC-D: Denver vs. Houston, 1991
  NFC-D: San Francisco vs. Washington, 1992
  SB: Denver vs. Green Bay, 1997

SB: Atlanta vs. Denver, 1998
AFC-FR: Oakland vs. N.Y. Jets, 2001
AFC-D: N.Y. Jets vs. Oakland, 2002
AFC-FR: Denver vs. Indianapolis, 2003
NFC-D: Carolina vs. St. Louis, 2003
AFC-D: Indianapolis vs. Kansas City, 2003
AFC-FR: Kansas City vs. Baltimore, 2010
NFC-D: Atlanta vs. Green Bay, 2010
AFC: Denver vs. New England, 2013
- 1 In many games

YARDS GAINED
Most Yards Gained, Game
- 155 NFC-D: Dallas vs. Cleveland, 1967
- 152 NFC-D: Atlanta vs. St. Louis, 2004
- 150 NFC: Chi. Cardinals vs. Philadelphia, 1947

Fewest Yards Gained, Game
- −10 NFC: Green Bay vs. Cleveland, 1965
- −9 NFC: Dallas vs. Green Bay, 1966
  AFC: Kansas City vs. Oakland, 1968
- −7 NFC-D: San Francisco vs. Atlanta, 1998

Most Yards Gained, Both Teams, Game
- 166 NFC-D: Dallas (155) vs. Cleveland (11), 1967
  AFC-D: Baltimore (99) vs. Pittsburgh (67), 2001
- 160 NFC: Chi. Cardinals (150) vs. Philadelphia (10), 1947
- 152 NFC-D: Atlanta (152) vs. St. Louis (0), 2004

Fewest Yards Gained, Both Teams, Game
- −9 NFC: Dallas (−9) vs. Green Bay (0), 1966
- −6 AFC-D: Miami (−5) vs. Oakland (−1), 1970
- −3 NFC-D: San Francisco (−5) vs. Dallas (2), 1972

TOUCHDOWNS
Most Touchdowns, Game
- 1 By 21 teams

KICKOFF RETURNS
Most Kickoff Returns, Game
- 10 NFC-D: L.A. Rams vs. Washington, 1983
  NFC-FR: Detroit vs. Philadelphia, 1995
- 9 NFC: Chi. Bears vs. N.Y. Giants, 1956
  AFC: Boston vs. San Diego, 1963
  AFC: Houston vs. Oakland, 1967
  SB: Denver vs. San Francisco, 1989
  AFC-D: Miami vs. Buffalo, 1990
  AFC: L.A. Raiders vs. Buffalo, 1990
  AFC-D: Miami vs. Jacksonville, 1999
  SB: Oakland vs. Tampa Bay, 2002
- 8 By many teams

Most Kickoff Returns, Both Teams, Game
- 15 AFC-D: Miami (9) vs. Buffalo (6), 1990
- 14 NFC-FR: Detroit (10) vs. Philadelphia (4), 1995
- 13 NFC-D: Green Bay (7) vs. Dallas (6), 1982
  NFC-FR: Green Bay (7) vs. San Francisco (6), 1998
  AFC-FR: N.Y. Jets (8) vs. Oakland (5), 2001
  NFC-FR: San Francisco (7) vs. N.Y. Giants (6), 2002
  AFC-D: Tennessee (7) vs. Pittsburgh (6), 2002
  SB: Oakland (9) vs. Tampa Bay (4), 2002
  NFC-FR: Seattle (7) vs. Green Bay (6), 2003 (ot)
  AFC-D: Kansas City (7) vs. Indianapolis (6), 2003
  AFC: Pittsburgh (8) vs. New England (5), 2004
  AFC: New England (8) vs. Indianapolis (5), 2006

Fewest Kickoff Returns, Both Teams, Game
- 1 NFC: Green Bay (0) vs. Boston (1), 1936
  AFC-FR: San Diego (0) vs. Kansas City (1), 1992
  AFC-FR: Houston (0) vs. Cincinnati (1), 2011
  AFC-FR: Pittsburgh (0) vs. Denver (1), 2011 (ot)
  AFC: New England (0) vs. Denver (1), 2013
- 2 NFC-D: Los Angeles (0) vs. Chi. Bears (2), 1950
  AFC: Houston (0) vs. San Diego (2), 1961
  AFC-D: Oakland (1) vs. Pittsburgh (1), 1972
  AFC: N.Y. Jets (0) vs. L.A. Raiders (2), 1982
  AFC: Miami (1) vs. N.Y. Jets (1), 1982

NFC: N.Y. Giants (0) vs. Washington (2), 1986
AFC-FR: Indianapolis (0) vs. Baltimore (2), 2012
  3 In many games

YARDS GAINED
Most Yards Gained, Game
  244 SB: San Diego vs. San Francisco, 1994
  232 NFC-D: Atlanta vs. Green Bay, 2010
  231 AFC: New England vs. Indianapolis, 2006
Most Yards Gained, Both Teams, Game
  379 AFC-D: Baltimore (193) vs. Oakland (186), 1977 (ot)
  348 NFC-D: Minnesota (174) vs. St. Louis (174), 1999
  323 AFC-D: New England (231) vs. Indianapolis (92), 2006
Fewest Yards Gained, Both Teams, Game
    4 AFC: New England (0) vs. Denver (4), 2013
    5 AFC-FR: San Diego (0) vs. Kansas City (5), 1992
   15 NFC: N.Y. Giants (0) vs. Washington (15), 1986

TOUCHDOWNS
Most Touchdowns, Game
    1 NFC-D: San Francisco vs. Dallas, 1972
       AFC: Miami vs. Oakland, 1974
       AFC-D: Baltimore vs. Oakland, 1977 (ot)
       SB: Miami vs. Washington, 1982
       SB: Cincinnati vs. San Francisco, 1988
       AFC-D: Cleveland vs. Buffalo, 1989
       SB: San Diego vs. San Francisco, 1994
       SB: Green Bay vs. New England, 1996
       NFC: San Francisco vs. Green Bay, 1997
       SB: Atlanta vs. Denver, 1998
       AFC-FR: Tennessee vs. Buffalo, 1999
       AFC-FR: Seattle vs. Miami, 1999
       NFC-D: Washington vs. Tampa Bay, 1999
       NFC-D: St. Louis vs. Minnesota, 1999
       AFC: Tennessee vs. Jacksonville, 1999
       NFC-D: N.Y. Giants vs. Philadelphia, 2000
       SB: Baltimore vs. N.Y. Giants, 2000
       SB: N.Y. Giants vs. Baltimore, 2000
       AFC-D: Kansas City vs. Indianapolis, 2003
       NFC-FR: Dallas vs. Seattle, 2006
       SB: Chicago vs. Indianapolis, 2006
       NFC-D: Atlanta vs. Green Bay, 2010
       AFC-D: Denver vs. Baltimore, 2012 (2 ot)
       SB: Baltimore vs. San Francisco, 2012
       SB: Seattle vs. Denver, 2013
Most Touchdowns, Both Teams, Game
    2 SB: Baltimore (1) vs. N.Y. Giants (1), 2000

PENALTIES
Most Penalties, Game
   17 AFC-FR: L.A. Raiders vs. Denver, 1993
   14 AFC-FR: Oakland vs. Houston, 1980
       NFC-D: San Francisco vs. N.Y. Giants, 1981
       AFC: Oakland vs. Tennessee, 2002
       NFC-FR: Dallas vs. Philadelphia, 2009
   13 AFC-FR: Houston vs. Cleveland, 1988
       AFC-D: Houston vs. Denver, 1991
       NFC-D: Arizona vs. Minnesota, 1998
       NFC-D: Carolina vs. St. Louis, 2003 (2 ot)
Fewest Penalties, Game
    0 NFC: Philadelphia vs. Green Bay, 1960
       NFC-D: Detroit vs. Dallas, 1970
       AFC-D: Miami vs. Oakland, 1970
       SB: Miami vs. Dallas, 1971
       NFC-D: Washington vs. Minnesota, 1973
       SB: Pittsburgh vs. Dallas, 1975
       NFC: San Francisco vs. Chicago, 1988
       SB: Denver vs. San Francisco, 1989
       AFC-D: L.A. Raiders vs. Cincinnati, 1990
       AFC-D: Miami vs. San Diego, 1992
       SB: Atlanta vs. Denver, 1998
       AFC-FR: N.Y. Jets vs. Oakland, 2001

NFC-FR: Carolina vs. Dallas, 2003
NFC-D: New Orleans vs. San Francisco, 2011
AFC-D: Baltimore vs. Houston, 2011
  1 By many teams
Most Penalties, Both Teams, Game
  27 AFC-FR: L.A. Raiders (17) vs. Denver (10), 1993
  23 NFC-FR: Dallas (14) vs. Philadelphia (9), 2009
  22 AFC-FR: Oakland (14) vs. Houston (8), 1980
      NFC-D: San Francisco (14) vs. N.Y. Giants (8), 1981
      AFC-FR: Houston (13) vs. Cleveland (9), 1988
      NFC-D: Arizona (13) vs. Minnesota (9), 1998
Fewest Penalties, Both Teams, Game
    1 AFC-D: L.A. Raiders (0) vs. Cincinnati (1), 1990
    2 NFC: Washington (1) vs. Chi. Bears (1), 1937
      NFC-D: Washington (0) vs. Minnesota (2), 1973
      SB: Pittsburgh (0) vs. Dallas (2), 1975
      NFC-FR: Carolina (0) vs. Dallas (2), 2003
    3 AFC: Miami (1) vs. Baltimore (2), 1971
      NFC: San Francisco (1) vs. Dallas (2), 1971
      SB: Miami (0) vs. Dallas (3), 1971
      AFC-D: Pittsburgh (1) vs. Oakland (2), 1972
      AFC-D: Miami (1) vs. Cincinnati (2), 1973
      SB: Miami (1) vs. San Francisco (2), 1984
      NFC: San Francisco (0) vs. Chicago (3), 1988
      AFC: New England (1) vs. Pittsburgh (2), 2004
      AFC: San Diego (1) vs. New England (2), 2007
      NFC-D: New Orleans (0) vs. San Francisco (3), 2011
      AFC-D: Baltimore (0) vs. Houston (3), 2011

YARDS PENALIZED
Most Yards Penalized, Game
  145 NFC-D: San Francisco vs. N.Y. Giants, 1981
  133 SB: Dallas vs. Baltimore, 1970
  130 AFC-FR: L.A. Raiders vs. Denver, 1993
Fewest Yards Penalized, Game
    0 By many teams
Most Yards Penalized, Both Teams, Game
  228 NFC-FR: Philadelphia (116) vs. Dallas (112), 2009
  227 AFC-FR: L.A. Raiders (130) vs. Denver (97), 1993
  206 NFC-D: San Francisco (145) vs. N.Y. Giants (61), 1981
Fewest Yards Penalized, Both Teams, Game
    5 AFC-D: L.A. Raiders (0) vs. Cincinnati (5), 1990
    9 NFC-D: Washington (0) vs. Minnesota (9), 1973
   11 NFC-FR: Carolina (0) vs. Dallas (11), 2003

FUMBLES
Most Fumbles, Game
    8 SB: Buffalo vs. Dallas, 1992
    7 AFC-D: Houston vs. Kansas City, 1993
    6 By 13 teams
Most Fumbles, Both Teams, Game
   12 AFC: Houston (6) vs. Pittsburgh (6), 1978
      SB: Buffalo (8) vs. Dallas (4), 1992
   10 NFC: Chi. Bears (5) vs. N.Y. Giants (5), 1934
      SB: Dallas (6) vs. Denver (4), 1977
      AFC: Jacksonville (5) vs. Tennessee (5), 1999
    9 NFC-D: San Francisco (6) vs. Detroit (3), 1957
      NFC-D: San Francisco (5) vs. Dallas (4), 1972
      NFC: Dallas (5) vs. Philadelphia (4), 1980
      NFC: Minnesota (6) vs. New Orleans (3), 2009 (OT)
Most Fumbles Lost, Game
    5 SB: Buffalo vs. Dallas, 1992
      AFC-D: Miami vs. Jacksonville, 1999
    4 NFC: N.Y. Giants vs. Baltimore, 1958 (ot)
      AFC: Kansas City vs. Oakland, 1969
      SB: Baltimore vs. Dallas, 1970
      AFC: Pittsburgh vs. Oakland, 1975
      SB: Denver vs. Dallas, 1977
      AFC: Houston vs. Pittsburgh, 1978
      AFC: Miami vs. New England, 1985
      SB: New England vs. Chicago, 1985
      NFC-FR: L.A. Rams vs. Washington, 1986

NFC-FR: Minnesota vs. Dallas, 1996
AFC-FR: Buffalo vs. Miami, 1998
AFC: N.Y. Jets vs. Denver, 1998
AFC: Jacksonville vs. Tennessee, 1999
3 By many teams

Fewest Fumbles, Both Teams, Game
0 NFC: Green Bay vs. Cleveland, 1965
   AFC-D: Houston vs. San Diego, 1979
   NFC-D: Dallas vs. Los Angeles, 1979
   SB: Los Angeles vs. Pittsburgh, 1979
   AFC-D: Buffalo vs. Cincinnati, 1981
   NFC: Minnesota vs. Washington, 1987
   NFC-D: San Francisco vs. Washington, 1990
   NFC: Dallas vs. Green Bay, 1995
   AFC-D: New England vs. Pittsburgh, 1996
   SB: Green Bay vs. New England, 1996
   AFC-FR: Miami vs. Seattle, 1999
   AFC-FR: Miami vs. Indianapolis, 2000 (ot)
   AFC-D: Baltimore vs. Tennessee, 2000
   SB: Pittsburgh vs. Seattle, 2005
   SB: Indianapolis vs. New Orleans, 2009
   NFC-FR: N.Y. Giants vs. Atlanta, 2011
   NFC-FR: Philadelphia vs. New Orleans, 2013
   AFC: Denver vs. New England, 2013
1 In many games

RECOVERIES
Most Total Fumbles Recovered, Game
8 SB: Dallas vs. Denver, 1977 (4 own, 4 opp)
7 NFC: Chi. Bears vs. N.Y. Giants, 1934 (5 own, 2 opp)
   NFC-D: San Francisco vs. Detroit, 1957 (4 own, 3 opp)
   NFC-D: San Francisco vs. Dallas, 1972 (4 own, 3 opp)
   AFC: Pittsburgh vs. Houston, 1978 (3 own, 4 opp)
6 AFC: Houston vs. San Diego, 1961 (4 own, 2 opp)
   AFC-D: Cleveland vs. Baltimore, 1971 (4 own, 2 opp)
   AFC-D: Cleveland vs. Oakland, 1980 (5 own, 1 opp)
   NFC: Philadelphia vs. Dallas, 1980 (3 own, 3 opp)
   SB: Dallas vs. Buffalo, 1992 (1 own, 5 opp)
   NFC-D: Green Bay vs. San Francisco, 1996 (4 own, 2 opp)
   AFC: Denver vs. N.Y. Jets, 1998 (2 own, 4 opp)
   AFC: Tennessee vs. Jacksonville, 1999 (2 own, 4 opp)

Most Own Fumbles Recovered, Game
5 NFC: Chi. Bears vs. N.Y. Giants, 1934
   AFC-D: Cleveland vs. Oakland, 1980
4 By many teams

TOUCHDOWNS
Most Touchdowns, Game
2 SB: Dallas vs. Buffalo, 1992

TURNOVERS
Numbers of times losing the ball on interceptions and fumbles.
Most Turnovers, Game
9 NFC: Washington vs. Chi. Bears, 1940
   NFC: Detroit vs. Cleveland, 1954
   AFC: Houston vs. Pittsburgh, 1978
   SB: Buffalo vs. Dallas, 1992
8 NFC: N.Y. Giants vs. Chi. Bears, 1946
   NFC: Los Angeles vs. Cleveland, 1955
   NFC: Cleveland vs. Detroit, 1957
   SB: Denver vs. Dallas, 1977
   NFC-D: Minnesota vs. Philadelphia, 1980
   NFC-D: Green Bay vs. St. Louis, 2001
7 In many games

Fewest Turnovers, Game
0 By many teams

Most Turnovers, Both Teams, Game
14 AFC: Houston (9) vs. Pittsburgh (5), 1978
13 NFC: Detroit (9) vs. Cleveland (4), 1954
   AFC: Houston (7) vs. San Diego (6), 1961
12 AFC: Pittsburgh (7) vs. Oakland (5), 1975

Fewest Turnovers, Both Teams, Game
0 SB: Buffalo vs. N.Y. Giants, 1990
   AFC-FR: Kansas City vs. Pittsburgh, 1993 (ot)
   NFC-FR: Detroit vs. Green Bay, 1994
   AFC-FR: Denver vs. Jacksonville, 1996
   SB: St. Louis vs. Tennessee, 1999
   NFC-FR: N.Y. Giants vs. Atlanta, 2011
   AFC: Denver vs. New England, 2013
1 In many games. Most recent:
     NFC-D: Seattle (0) vs. New Orleans (1), 2013

Staff

2014 NFL ROSTER OF OFFICIALS AS OF MAY 2014
Dean Blandino, Vice President of Officiating
Alberto Riveron, Senior Director of Officiating
David Coleman, Director of Officiating
Garth DeFelice, Supervisor of Officials

Neely Dunn, Supervisor of Officials
Johnny Grier, Supervisor of Officials
Gary Slaughter, Supervisor of Officials

No.	Name	Position	College	No.	Name	Position	College
122	Allen, Brad	Umpire	Pembroke State	107	Marinucci, Ron	Line Judge	Glassboro State
20	Anderson, Barry	Field Judge	North Carolina State	39	Martinez, Rich	Back Judge	Canisius
66	Anderson, Walt	Referee	Texas	77	McAulay, Terry	Referee	Louisiana State
108	Arthur, Gary	Line Judge	Wright State	5	McGrath, John	Head Linesman	Kentucky
72	Banks, Michael	Side Judge	Illinois State	8	McKenzie, Dana	Head Linesman	Toledo
56	Baynes, Allen	Side Judge	Auburn	110	McKinnely, Phil	Head Linesman	UCLA
59	Baynes, Rusty	Line Judge	Auburn-Montgomery	48	Mello, Jim	Head Linesman	Northeastern
32	Bergman, Jeff	Line Judge	Robert Morris	118	Meslow, David	Field Judge	Augsburg College
91	Bergman, Jerry	Head Linesman	Robert Morris	78	Meyer, Greg	Side Judge	Texas Christian
34	Blakeman, Clete	Referee	Nebraska	115	Michalek, Tony	Umpire	Indiana
23	Boger, Jerome	Referee	Morehouse College	111	Miles, Terrence	Back Judge	Arizona State
18	Boston, Byron	Line Judge	Austin	135	Morelli, Pete	Referee	St. Mary's
74	Bowers, Derick	Head Linesman	East Central	92	Neale, Bryan	Umpire	Indiana
98	Bradley, Greg	Head Linesman	Tennessee	1	Novak, Scott	Side Judge	Phoenix
31	Brown, Chad	Umpire	East Texas State	124	Paganelli, Carl	Umpire	Michigan State
43	Brown, Terry	Field Judge	Tennessee-Knoxville	105	Paganelli, Dino	Back Judge	Aquinas College
11	Bryan, Fred	Umpire	Northern Iowa	46	Paganelli, Perry	Back Judge	Hope College
86	Buchanan, Jimmy	Field Judge	South Carolina State	132	Parry, John	Referee	Purdue
134	Camp, Ed	Head Linesman	William Paterson	17	Patrick, Steve	Back Judge	Jacksonville State
94	Carey, Mike	Referee	Santa Clara	15	Patterson, Rick	Side Judge	Wofford
60	Cavaletto, Gary	Field Judge	Hancock	79	Payne, Kent	Head Linesman	Nebraska Wesleyan
41	Cheek, Boris	Field Judge	Morgan State	9	Perlman, Mark	Line Judge	Salem
51	Cheffers, Carl	Referee	California-Irvine	47	Podraza, Tim	Line Judge	Nebraska
95	Coleman, James	Side Judge	Arkansas	109	Prioleau, Dyrol	Field Judge	Johnson C. Smith
65	Coleman, Walt	Referee	Arkansas	30	Prukop, Todd	Back Judge	Cal State-Fullerton
99	Corrente, Tony	Referee	Cal State-Fullerton	63	Quirk, Jim	Back Judge	Middlebury
58	DeBell, Jimmy	Side Judge	SUNY-Brockport	44	Rice, Jeff	Umpire	Northwestern
6	Dornan, Kirk	Back Judge	Central Washington	67	Rosenbaum, Doug	Field Judge	Illinois Wesleyan
27	Dyer, Lee	Back Judge	Tennessee-Chattanooga	129	Schuster, Bill	Umpire	Alfred
3	Edwards, Scott	Field Judge	Alabama	45	Seeman, Jeff	Line Judge	Minnesota
81	Ellison, Roy	Umpire	Savannah State	104	Shaw, Dale	Back Judge	Allegheny
61	Ferguson, Keith	Back Judge	San Jose State	90	Spanier, Mike	Line Judge	St. Cloud State
64	Ferrell, Dan	Umpire	Cal State-Fullerton	24	Stabile, Tom	Head Linesman	Slippery Rock
71	Fowler, Ruben	Umpire	Huston-Tillotson	12	Steed, Greg	Back Judge	Howard
88	Freeman, Brad	Field Judge	Mississippi State	84	Steinkerchner, Mark	Line Judge	Akron
133	Freeman, Steve	Back Judge	Mississippi State	22	Stelljes, Steve	Head Linesman	Friends
80	Gautreaux, Greg	Field Judge	S.W. Louisiana	68	Stephan, Tom	Line Judge	Pittsburg State
103	Hall, Eugene	Field Judge	North Texas	114	Steratore, Gene	Referee	Kent State
49	Hall, Rich	Umpire	Arizona	112	Steratore, Tony	Back Judge	California
40	Hannah, Butch	Umpire	Middle Tennessee State	102	Stritesky, Bruce	Umpire	Embry Riddle
125	Hayes, Laird	Side Judge	Princeton	100	Symonette, Tom	Line Judge	Florida
54	Hayward, George	Head Linesman	Missouri Western	62	Torbert, Ronald	Referee	Michigan State
93	Helverson, Scott	Back Judge	Iowa	42	Triplette, Jeff	Referee	Wake Forest
29	Hill, Adrian	Field Judge	Buffalo	13	Turner, Patrick	Head Linesman	Cal State-Long Beach
97	Hill, Tom	Side Judge	Carson Newman	75	Vernatchi, Rob	Side Judge	California-Riverside
28	Hittner, Mark	Head Linesman	Pittsburg State	36	Veteri, Tony	Head Linesman	Manhattan College
85	Hochuli, Ed	Referee	Texas-El Paso	52	Vinovich, Bill	Referee	San Diego
83	Hochuli, Shawn	Side Judge	Claremont	25	Waggoner, Bob	Field Judge	Juniata College
82	Horton, Buddy	Field Judge	Oregon State	123	Walker, Ed	Line Judge	San Jose State
37	Howey, Jim	Field Judge	Erskine College	96	Wash, Undrey	Umpire	Texas-Arlington
35	Hussey, John	Line Judge	Idaho State	7	Washington, Keith	Side Judge	Virginia Military Institute
76	Jenkins, Darrell	Umpire	San Jose State	116	Weatherford, Mike	Side Judge	Oklahoma State
117	Jenkins, John	Field Judge	St. Mary's	50	Weir, Mike	Field Judge	Missouri
101	Johnson, Carl	Line Judge	Nicholls State	119	Wilson, Greg	Back Judge	USC
55	Kemp, Alex	Side Judge	Central Michigan	4	Wrolstad, Craig	Referee	Washington
121	King, Paul	Umpire	Nicholls State	38	Yette, Greg	Back Judge	Howard
21	Lamberth, Jeff	Side Judge	Texas A&M	33	Zimmer, Steve	Field Judge	Hofstra
73	Larrew, Joe	Side Judge	St. Louis				
127	Leavy, Bill	Referee	San Jose State		*Roster as of May 2014*		
130	Lewis, Darryll	Line Judge	Dartmouth				
89	Lucivansky, Jon	Field Judge	Minnesota				
106	Mackie, Wayne	Head Linesman	Colgate				
10	Mapp, Julian	Head Linesman	Grambling State				

NUMERICAL ROSTER

No.	Name	Position
1	Scott Novak	SJ
3	Scott Edwards	FJ
4	Craig Wrolstad	R
5	John McGrath	HL
6	Kirk Dornan	BJ
7	Keith Washington	SJ
8	Dana McKenzie	HL
9	Mark Perlman	LJ
10	Julian Mapp	HL
11	Fred Bryan	U
12	Greg Steed	BJ
13	Patrick Turner	BJ
15	Rick Patterson	SJ
17	Steve Patrick	BJ
18	Byron Boston	LJ
20	Barry Anderson	FJ
21	Jeff Lamberth	SJ
22	Steve Stelljes	HL
23	Jerome Boger	R
24	Tom Stabile	HL
25	Bob Waggoner	FJ
27	Lee Dyer	BJ
28	Mark Hittner	HL
29	Adrian Hill	FJ
30	Todd Prukop	BJ
31	Chad Brown	U
32	Jeff Bergman	LJ
33	Steve Zimmer	FJ
34	Clete Blakeman	R
35	John Hussey	LJ
36	Tony Veteri	HL
37	Jim Howey	FJ
38	Greg Yette	BJ
39	Rich Martinez	BJ
40	Butch Hannah	U
41	Boris Cheek	FJ
42	Jeff Triplette	R
43	Terry Brown	FJ
44	Jeff Rice	U
45	Jeff Seeman	LJ
46	Perry Paganelli	BJ
47	Tim Podraza	LJ
48	Jim Mello	HL
49	Rich Hall	U
50	Mike Weir	FJ
51	Carl Cheffers	R
52	Bill Vinovich	R
54	George Hayward	HL
55	Alex Kemp	SJ
56	Allen Baynes	SJ
58	Jimmy DeBell	SJ
59	Rusty Baynes	LJ
60	Gary Cavaletto	FJ
61	Keith Ferguson	BJ
62	Ronald Torbert	R
63	Jim Quirk	BJ
64	Dan Ferrell	U
65	Walt Coleman	R
66	Walt Anderson	R
67	Doug Rosenbaum	FJ
68	Tom Stephan	LJ
71	Ruben Fowler	U
72	Michael Banks	SJ
73	Joe Larrew	SJ
74	Derick Bowers	HL
75	Rob Vernatchi	SJ
76	Darrell Jenkins	U
77	Terry McAulay	R

No.	Name	Position
78	Greg Meyer	SJ
79	Kent Payne	HL
80	Greg Gautreaux	FJ
81	Roy Ellison	U
82	Buddy Horton	FJ
83	Shawn Hochuli	SJ
84	Mark Steinkerchner	LJ
85	Ed Hochuli	R
86	Jimmy Buchanan	FJ
88	Brad Freeman	FJ
89	Jon Lucivansky	FJ
90	Mike Spanier	LJ
91	Jerry Bergman	HL
92	Bryan Neale	U
93	Scott Helverson	BJ
94	Mike Carey	R
95	James Coleman	SJ
96	Undrey Wash	U
97	Tom Hill	SJ
98	Greg Bradley	HL
99	Tony Corrente	R
100	Tom Symonette	LJ
101	Carl Johnson	LJ
102	Bruce Stritesky	U
103	Eugene Hall	FJ
104	Dale Shaw	BJ
105	Dino Paganelli	BJ
106	Wayne Mackie	HL
107	Ron Marinucci	LJ
108	Gary Arthur	LJ
109	Dyrol Prioleau	FJ
110	Phil McKinnely	HL
111	Terrence Miles	BJ
112	Tony Steratore	BJ
114	Gene Steratore	R
115	Tony Michalek	U
116	Mike Weatherford	SJ
117	John Jenkins	FJ
118	David Meslow	FJ
119	Greg Wilson	BJ
121	Paul King	U
122	Brad Allen	U
123	Ed Walker	LJ
124	Carl Paganelli	U
125	Laird Hayes	SJ
126	Don Carey	BJ
127	Bill Leavy	R
129	Bill Schuster	U
130	Darryll Lewis	LJ
132	John Parry	R
133	Steve Freeman	BJ
134	Ed Camp	HL
135	Pete Morelli	R

Roster as of May 2014

OFFICIALS

2014 OFFICIALS AT A GLANCE

REFEREES
Walt Anderson, No. **66,** Texas, college officiating coordinator, retired dentist, 19th year.
Clete Blakeman, No. **34,** Nebraska, attorney, 7th year.
Jerome Boger, No. **23,** Morehouse College, commercial insurance underwriter, 11th year.
Mike Carey, No. **94,** Santa Clara, owner, skiing accessories, 25th year.
Carl Cheffers, No. **51,** California-Irvine, sales manager, 15th year.
Walt Coleman, No. **65,** Arkansas, manager dairy processor, 26th year.
Tony Corrente, No. **99,** Cal State-Fullerton, educator, 20th year.
Ed Hochuli, No. **85,** Texas-El Paso, attorney, 25th year.
Bill Leavy, No. **127,** San Jose State, retired firefighter, 20th year.
Terry McAulay, No. **77,** Louisiana State, college officiating coordinator, 17th year.
Pete Morelli, No. **135,** St. Mary's, high school principal, 18th year.
John Parry, No. **132,** Purdue, financial advisor, 15th year.
Gene Steratore, No. **114,** Kent State, co-owner, supply company, 12th year.
Ronald Torbert, No. **62,** Michigan State, attorney, 5th year.
Jeff Triplette, No. **42,** Wake Forest, restructuring consultant, 19th year.
Bill Vinovich, No. **52,** San Diego, certified public accountant, 9th year.
Craig Wrolstad, No. **4,** Washington, athletic director, 12th year.

UMPIRES
Brad Allen, No. **122,** Pembroke State, non-profit CEO, 1st year.
Chad Brown, No. **31,** East Texas State, executive manager of facilities/student affairs administration, 23rd year.
Fred Bryan, No. **11,** Northern Iowa, superintendent, juvenile correctional facility, 6th year.
Roy Ellison, No. **81,** Savannah State, technical staff member, 12th year.
Dan Ferrell, No. **64,** Cal State-Fullerton, director, parts logistics, 12th year.
Ruben Fowler, No. **71,** Huston-Tillotson, retired firefighter, 9th year.
Rich Hall, No. **49,** Arizona, custom cabinetry, 11th year.
Butch Hannah, No. **40,** Middle Tennessee State, retired federal probation officer, 16th year.
Darrell Jenkins, No. **76,** San Jose State, retired, 13th year.
Paul King, No. **121,** Nicholls State, teacher, 6th year.
Tony Michalek, No. **115,** Indiana, USA Football officiating director, 13th year.
Bryan Neale, No. **92,** Indiana, sales consultant, 1st year.
Carl Paganelli, No. **124,** Michigan State, federal probation officer, 16th year.
Jeff Rice, No. **44,** Northwestern, attorney, 20th year.
Bill Schuster, No. **129,** Alfred, insurance broker, 15th year.
Bruce Stritesky, No. **102,** Embry Riddle, airline pilot, 9th year.
Undrey Wash, No. **96,** Texas-Arlington, claims controller, 15th year.

HEAD LINESMEN
Jerry Bergman, No. **91,** Robert Morris, sales executive, 13th year.
Derick Bowers, No. **74,** East Central, sales representative, 12th year.
Greg Bradley, No. **98,** Tennessee, chemical engineer, 6th year.
Ed Camp, No. **134,** William Paterson, physical education teacher, 15th year.
George Hayward, No. **54,** Missouri Western, vice-president and manager, warehouse company, 24th year.
Mark Hittner, No. **28,** Pittsburg State, investment broker, 18th year.
Wayne Mackie, No. **106,** Colgate, director of housing, 8th year.
Julian Mapp, No. **10,** Grambling State, project leader, 6th year.
John McGrath, No. **5,** Kentucky, vice president of sales, 13th year.
Dana McKenzie, No. **8,** Toledo, claims adjuster, 7th year.
Phil McKinnely, No. **110,** UCLA, inventory control, 12th year.
Jim Mello, No. **48,** Northeastern, facilities manager, 11th year.
Kent Payne, No. **79,** Nebraska Wesleyan, teacher, 11th year.
Tom Stabile, No. **24,** Slippery Rock, secondary educational administrator, 20th year.
Steve Stelljes, No. **22,** Friends, business planning manager, 13th year.
Patrick Turner, No. **13,** Cal State-Long Beach, plant manager, 1st year.
Tony Veteri, No. **36,** Manhattan College, physical education teacher, 23nd year.

LINE JUDGES
Gary Arthur, No. **108,** Wright State, president, commercial printing company, 18th year.
Rusty Baynes, No. **59,** Auburn-Montgomery, general manager, safety services, 5th year.
Jeff Bergman, No. **32,** Robert Morris, president and chief executive officer, medical services, 23rd year.
Byron Boston, No. **18,** Austin, tax consultant, 20th year.
John Hussey, No. **35,** Idaho State, sales representative, retail logistics group, 13th year.
Carl Johnson, No. **101,** Nicholls State, full-time official, 11th year.
Darryll Lewis, No. **130,** Dartmouth, associate professor, 16th year.
Ron Marinucci, No. **107,** Glassboro State, vice president, novelty cone company, 18th year.
Mark Perlman, No. **9,** Salem, teacher, 14th year.
Tim Podraza, No. **47,** Nebraska, banker, 7th year.
Jeff Seeman, No. **45,** Minnesota, brokerage sales, 13th year.
Mike Spanier, No. **90,** St. Cloud State, middle school principal, 16th year.
Mark Steinkerchner, No. **84,** Akron, vice-president, 21st year.
Tom Stephan, No. **68,** Pittsburg State, president and CEO, 16th year.
Tom Symonette, No. **100,** Florida, certified public accountant, 11th year.
Ed Walker, No. **123,** San Jose State, real estate management, 1st year.

Roster as of May 2014

FIELD JUDGES

Barry Anderson, No. **20,** North Carolina State, builder/developer, 8th year.
Terry Brown, No. **43,** Tennessee, probation supervisor, 9th year.
Jimmy Buchanan, No. **86,** South Carolina State, insurance agent, 6th year.
Gary Cavaletto, No. **60,** Hancock, general manager, agricultural operations, 12th year.
Boris Cheek, No. **41,** Morgan State, director of operations and management, 19th year.
Scott Edwards, No. **3,** Alabama, environmental engineer, 16th year.
Brad Freeman, No. **88,** Mississippi State, sports park director, 1st year.
Greg Gautreaux, No. **80,** S.W. Louisiana, athletic programs manager, 13th year.
Eugene Hall, No. **103,** North Texas, federal agent, 1st year.
Adrian Hill, No. **29,** Buffalo, software engineer, 5th year.
Buddy Horton, No. **82,** Oregon State, water service worker, 16th year.
Jim Howey, No. **37,** Erskine College, director of adult education, 16th year.
John Jenkins, No. **117,** St. Mary's, sales executive, 1st year.
Jon Lucivansky, No. **89,** Minnesota, college educator, 6th year.
David Meslow, No. **118,** Augsburg College, marketing manager, 4th year.
Dyrol Prioleau, No. **109,** Johnson C. Smith, manager, law firm, 8th year.
Doug Rosenbaum, No. **67,** Illinois Wesleyan, financial consultant, 14th year.
Bob Waggoner, No. **25,** Juniata College, probation officer, 18th year.
Mike Weir, No. **50,** Missouri, owner, sporting goods store, 13th year.
Steve Zimmer, No. **33,** Hofstra, attorney, 18th year.

SIDE JUDGES

Michael Banks, No. **72,** Illinois State, carpenter foreman, 13th year.
Allen Baynes, No. **56,** Auburn, realtor, 7th year.
James Coleman, No. **95,** Arkansas, electrical engineer, 10th year.
Jimmy DeBell, No. **58,** SUNY-Brockport, high school teacher, 6th year.
Laird Hayes, No. **125,** Princeton, professor, physical education & athletics, 20th year.
Tom Hill, No. **97,** Carson Newman, teacher, 16th year.
Shawn Hochuli, No. **83,** Claremont, financial advisor, 1st year.
Alex Kemp, No. **55,** Central Michigan, insurance agent, 1st year.
Jeff Lamberth, No. **21,** Texas A&M, attorney, 13th year.
Joe Larrew, No. **73,** St. Louis, attorney, 13th year.
Greg Meyer, No. **78,** Texas Christian, banker, 13th year.
Scott Novak, No. **1,** Phoenix, sales manager, 1st year.
Rick Patterson, No. **15,** Wofford, banker, 19th year.
Rob Vernatchi, No. **75,** California-Riverside, enforcement investigator, 11th year.
Keith Washington, No. **7,** Virginia Military Institute, program financial analyst, 7th year.
Mike Weatherford, No. **116,** Oklahoma State, energy trader, 13th year.

BACK JUDGES

Kirk Dornan, No. **6,** Central Washington, purchasing manager, 21st year.
Lee Dyer, No. **27,** Tennessee-Chattanooga, sales manager, 12th year.
Keith Ferguson, No. **61,** San Jose State, sales, 15th year.
Steve Freeman, No. **133,** Mississippi State, custom home builder, 14th year.
Scott Helverson, No. **93,** Iowa, sales, printing and promotions, 12th year.
Rich Martinez, No. **39,** Canisius, sales manager, 1st year.
Terrence Miles, No. **111,** Arizona State, quality control manager, 7th year.
Dino Paganelli, No. **105,** Aquinas College, educator, 9th year.
Perry Paganelli, No. **46,** Hope College, retired high school administrator, 17th year.
Steve Patrick, No. **17,** Jacksonville State, owner, supply company, 1st year.
Todd Prukop, No. **30,** Cal State-Fullerton, medical sales representative, 6th year.
Jim Quirk, No. **63,** Middlebury, financial advisor, 5th year.
Dale Shaw, No. **104,** Allegheny, pharmaceutical sales, 2nd year.
Greg Steed, No. **12,** Howard, computer systems analyst, 12th year.
Tony Steratore, No. **112,** California, PA., co-owner, supply company, 15th year.
Greg Wilson, No. **119,** USC, law enforcement, 7th year.
Greg Yette, No. **38,** Howard, defense contractor, 5th year.

Roster as of May 2014

345 Park Avenue, New York, New York 10154 (212) 450-2000

www.NFL.com

Commissioner: Roger Goodell

Executive Vice President of NFL Ventures and Business Operations: Eric Grubman

Executive Vice President of Human Resources/Chief Diversity Officer: Robert Gulliver

Executive Vice President of Communications and Public Affairs: Paul Hicks

Executive Vice President/General Counsel: Jeff Pash

Executive Vice President of Media/
  President and Chief Executive Officer of NFL Network: Brian Rolapp

Executive Vice President/Chief Financial Officer: Joe Siclare

Executive Vice President/Football Operations: Troy Vincent